# VOX
# SPANISH
## and
# ENGLISH
## School Dictionary

**Second Edition**

D0037240

# VOX

# SPANISH
## and
# ENGLISH
## School Dictionary

### Second Edition

New York   Chicago   San Francisco   Athens   London   Madrid
Mexico City   Milan   New Delhi   Singapore   Sydney   Toronto

5  6  7  8  9  10  11  12  13    QLM/QLM    1  0  9  8  7  6

ISBN   978-0-07-181665-6   (hardcover)
MHID        0-07-181665-8

ISBN   978-0-07-181664-9   (paperback)
MHID        0-07-181664-X

**Library of Congress Cataloging-in-Publication Data**

Vox Spanish and English school dictionary / Larousse Editorial. — Second Edition.
      pages cm. — (VOX Dictionaries)
   ISBN 0-07-181665-8 (hard cover) — ISBN 0-07-181664-X (pbk.)
1.  Spanish language—Dictionaries—English.    2.  English language—Dictionaries—Spanish.    I. Larousse (Firm)    II. Title: Spanish and English school dictionary.
   PC4640.V6966    2014
   463'.21—dc23

                                                                2013033383

*Dirección editorial:* Jordi Induráin Pons

*Coordinación editorial:* Ma José Simón Aragón, Jordi Tebé Soriano

*Asesoría pedagógica:* Lluís Figueras Havidich, Ma Rosa Raméntol Estela

*Realización:* dos més dos edicions, s.l.

*Ilustraciones:* Juanjo Barco (Alins ilustración), Estudi Farrés

*Cartografía:* Santi Maicas

*Diseño de cubierta:* Francesc Sala

# Table of Contents

# INTRODUCTION

Maybe you are already in the habit of using a dictionary, or maybe this is the first time you've looked at one. Whatever the case, it will be useful for you to read these pages to discover all that you can learn from it. First some figures: you'll find 30,000 words or entries (17,000 of them English) and 70,000 translations. Of course, there are bigger dictionaries, but, unlike this one, they are not specially designed for your grade or language level. Let time take its course and the day will come when you'll be ready for them; for the moment, you're better off with the words our experts and panel of teachers have selected to meet your specific needs. That way, you'll learn gradually and solidly, improving your knowledge day by day.

Almost without realizing it, you learn new vocabulary every day: in class, watching a film, listening to a song, or surfing the Internet. Sometimes you can deduce the meaning of a new word because it belongs to the same family as another one you have already studied, but sometimes it isn't so easy. This is when you should reach for your dictionary: you'll find the meaning of the new word, examples of how to use it, and other information that, with your teacher's help, will allow you to improve your Spanish.

Maybe you've wondered what it would be like to speak only Spanish to your teachers and classmates. In these pages, you'll find a selection of phrases organized by subject that you can practice. No doubt you'll enjoy learning expressions that you'd like to be able to use in Spanish, but which you can't find in your books! Your teachers will help you to get the most out of these words and phrases.

And now that you know your dictionary better, get as much out of it as you can. *¿Estás preparado?*

# How to Use
# This Dictionary

Perhaps you think that a dictionary does nothing
more than show you the translation of a word.
Well, we're going to show you all that you can do with it,
because some of it's bound to be new to you:

▶ Have you seen a word that was spelled differently from the way
you thought? Every day we use lots of words, but sometimes
we don't know how to spell them or we feel lazy about looking
them up. Remember every word that you look up, it will help you
to build up a solid vocabulary base.

**appearance** [ə'pɪərəns] n **1** (becoming
visible) aparición f. **2** (before a court, etc)
comparecencia. **3** (look) apariencia.

**aparcamiento** nm **1** (acción) parking. **2**
(en la calle) place to park, parking
place…

**arithmetic** [(n) ə'rɪθmətɪk; (adj) ærɪθ-
'metɪk] n aritmética.
▶ adj aritmético,-a.

**aproximación** nf **1** (gen) approximation. **2** (acercamiento) bringing together; (de países) rapprochement.

▶ Do you see the square brackets [ ] immediately after the English
headword? Here you will find the exact pronunciation of the
English headword. Maybe there are some symbols that you don't
understand, but we'll explain what they mean in another section.

**achievement** [ə'tʃiːvmənt] n **1** (completion) realización f. **2** (attainment)
logro. **3** (feat) hazaña, proeza.

▶ Have you seen the abbreviation that comes right after the Spanish headword? This tells you the part of speech of the headword: if it's a feminine or masculine noun, a transitive or intransitive verb, and so on. Your language teachers will have taught you what these words mean. Here you can put into practice what they have explained to you: sometimes a word can be a noun and an adjective and have different meanings. You should pay attention to a word's part of speech so that you don't make mistakes when you are translating.

---

**behind** [bɪˈhaɪnd] *prep* detrás de.
▶ *adv* **1** detrás, atrás. **2** *(late)* atrasado,-a.
▶ *n fam (buttocks)* trasero.

**alemán,-ana** *adj* German.
▶ *nm & nf (persona)* German.
▶ *nm* **alemán** *(idioma)* German.

---

▶ Have you noticed that in some entries there are numbers? These show you the different meanings of the word. The number **1** indicates the commonest meaning, but the others are important too; all of them can help you to find the translation you're looking for.

---

**capital** [ˈkæpɪtəl] *n* **1** *(of country, etc)* capital *f.* **2** FIN capital *m: starting capital* capital inicial. **3** *(letter)* mayúscula: *write it in capitals* escríbelo con mayúsculas.

**ampliar** *vt* **1** to enlarge, extend. **2** ARQUIT to build an extension onto. **3** *(fotografía)* to enlarge. **4** *(capital)* to increase. **5** *(estudios)* to further. **6** *(tema, idea)* to develop, expand on.

---

▶ There are some words that are used only in a certain expression, or which require a certain preposition. Others have some peculiarity, such as an irregular plural. Because of this, you must be sure to read everything in the entry. You're bound to learn something new that will help you to understand what the word means and how it's used.

---

**capability** [keɪpəˈbɪlɪtɪ] *n* capacidad *f* **(to, para/de)**.
① *pl* **capabilities.**

**absorto,-a** *adj* **1** *(pasmado)* amazed, bewildered. **2** *(ensimismado)* absorbed **(en, in)**.

▶ Have you seen a box with the letters COMP? This means that the word is often used with another word and that together they have a different meaning. Have you see the letters LOC too? Now you can learn phrases and expressions with this word and see what verbs normally go with it.

---

**elementary** [elɪ'mentərɪ] *adj* **1** *(basic)* elemental, básico,-a. **2** *(easy)* fácil, sencillo,-a. COMP **elementary education** enseñanza primaria.
**faithfully** ['feɪθfʊlɪ] *adv* fielmente. LOC **yours faithfully** *(in letter)* atentamente.

**accidente** *nm* **1** accident: *sufrir un accidente* to have an accident. **2** *(terreno)* unevenness. LOC **por accidente** by chance. COMP **accidente de trabajo** industrial accident. ❙ **accidente de tráfico** road accident. ❙ **accidentes geográficos** geographical features.

---

▶ Have you seen some letters (for example, GB) after one of the numbers that indicate the different meanings? They tell you whether the word is used only in British English, in the United States, Canada, or Australia. If there are other letters after these, these tell you the field the word is used in, for example cookery or medicine.

---

**dresser** ['dresə'] *n* **1** GB *(in kitchen)* aparador *m*. **2** US *(chest of drawers)* tocador *m*.
**fail** [feɪl] *n* EDUC suspenso.
▶ *vt* **1** *(let down)* fallar, decepcionar; *(desert)* fallar, faltar. **2** EDUC suspender.

**ADN** *abrev* MED *(ácido desoxirribonucleico)* desoxyribonucleic acid; *(abreviatura)* DNA.
**adobar** *vt* **1** CULIN to marinate, marinade. **2** *(pieles)* to tan.

---

▶ If you see a box with this symbol ☒, read it carefully; this information is very interesting. Some Spanish words look very similar to English words, but they do not always mean the same thing and you can make a mistake.

---

**fabric** ['fæbrɪk] *n* **1** *(material)* tela, tejido. **2** *(structure)* fábrica, estructura.
☒ Fabric no significa 'fábrica', que se traduce por **factory**.

▶ Sometimes a dictionary is like a mini-encyclopedia. If you see a text with a shaded background and a globe symbol, here you will find information about customs and culture.

> **GCSE** [ˈdʒiːˈsiːˈesˈiː] *abbr* GB (General Certificate of Secondary Education) ≈ Enseñanza Secundaria Obligatoria; *(abbreviation)* ESO *f*.
>
> 🌐 GSCE es el examen que se hace en Gran Bretaña al final de la enseñanza secundaria, a los 16 años aproximadamente.

▶ Have you looked up a word you didn't know and found an arrow and another word you didn't know? Well, you're in luck! You're going to learn two new words. The arrow means that to find the meaning of the word, you have to go to another more important word which it comes from or is related to. You will find what you're looking for at the second word.

> **got** [gɒt] *pt & pp* → **get**.

> **adecuado,-a** *pp* → adecuar.
> ▶ *adj* adequate, suitable.

▶ You will also find a lot of other information about words: their plural, if they are irregular or not, or explanations about how to use them. So that you can find this information quickly, it is marked with an ① or a ✎.

> **enseguida** *adv* at once, straight away, immediately.
> ✎ También se escribe en seguida.

We hope that this explanation has been helpful to you and that you will use it. Now you are ready and can start to use your dictionary.

# ABBREVIATIONS USED IN THIS DICTIONARY

| | | | |
|---|---|---|---|
| *abr* | abreviatura, abbreviation | *fam* | familiar use, uso familiar |
| *adj* | adjective, adjetivo | *fig* | figurative use, uso figurado |
| *abbr* | abbreviation, abreviatura | FIN | finance, finanzas |
| *adv* | adverb, adverbio | FÍS | física, physics |
| AER | aeronautics, aeronáutica | *fml* | formal use, uso formal |
| AGR | agriculture, agricultura | *fut* | future, futuro |
| AM | American Spanish, español americano | GB | British English, inglés británico |
| ANAT | anatomy, anatomía | *gen* | in general, en general |
| ARCH | architecture, arquitectura | GEOG | geography, geografía |
| *arg* | argot, slang | GEOL | geology, geología |
| ARQ | arquitectura, architecture | *ger* | gerund, gerundio |
| ART | art, arte | GRAM | grammar, gramática |
| *art* | article, artículo | HIST | history, historia |
| *art def* | artículo definido, definite article | *imperat* | imperative, imperativo |
| | | *imperf* | imperfect, imperfecto |
| *art indef* | artículo indefinido, indefinite article | *indef art* | indefinite article, artículo indefinido |
| AUTO | automobiles, automóvil | *indic* | indicative, indicativo |
| AV | aviation, aviación | *inf* | infinitive, infinitivo |
| BIOL | biology, biología | INFORM | informática, computing |
| BOT | botany, botánica | *interj* | interjection, interjección |
| CHEM | chemistry, química | *iron* | ironic, irónico |
| CINEM | cinema, cinematografía | *irón* | irónico, ironic |
| COM | comercio, commerce | JUR | law, derecho |
| COMM | commerce, comercio | LING | linguistics, lingüística |
| *comp* | comparative, comparativo | LIT | literature, literatura |
| COMPUT | computing, informática | *loc* | locución, phrase |
| *conj* | conjunction, conjunción | MAR | maritime, marítimo |
| *contr* | contraction, contracción | MAT | matemáticas, mathematics |
| COST | costura, sewing | MATH | mathematics, matemáticas |
| CULIN | cookery, cocina | MED | medicine, medicina |
| *def art* | definite article, artículo definido | METEOR | meteorology, meteorología |
| DEP | deporte, sport | MIL | military, militar |
| EDUC | education, educación | MUS | music, música |
| ELEC | electricity, electricidad | MÚS | música, music |
| *etc* | etcetera, etcétera | *n* | noun, nombre |
| *euf* | uso eufemístico, euphemistic use | *neut* | neuter, neutro |
| *euph* | euphemistic use, uso eufemístico | *nf* | feminine noun, nombre femenino |

| | | | |
|---|---|---|---|
| *nf pl* | plural feminine noun, nombre femenino plural | *v aux* | auxiliary verb, verbo auxiliar |
| *nm* | masculine noun, nombre masculino | *vi* | intransitive verb, verbo intransitivo |
| *nm o nf* | masculine or feminine noun, nombre de género ambiguo | *vpr* | pronominal verb, verbo pronominal |
| *nm & nf* | masculine and feminine noun, nombre de género común | *vt* | transitive verb, verbo transitivo |
| *nm pl* | masculine plural noun, nombre masculino plural | *vt insep* | inseparable transitive phrasal verb, verbo preposicional transitivo inseparable |
| *npl* | plural noun, nombre plural | *vt sep* | separable transitive phrasal verb, verbo preposicional transitivo separable |
| *pej* | pejorative, peyorativo | | |
| *pers* | person, persona | | |
| *pey* | peyorativo, pejorative | | |
| *phr* | phrase, locución | ZOOL | zoology, zoología |
| PHYS | physics, física | ≈ | approximately equivalent to, aproximadamente equivalente a |
| POL | politics, política | | |
| *pp* | past participle, participio pasado | → | see, véase |
| *pref* | prefix, prefijo | ► | different part of speech, cambio de categoría gramatical |
| *prep* | preposition, preposición | | |
| *pres* | present, presente | | |
| *pron* | pronoun, pronombre | ◆ | phrasal verb |
| *pt* | past, pasado | LOC | block of idioms and phrases, bloque de frases y locuciones |
| QUÍM | química, chemistry | | |
| RAD | radio | | |
| REL | religion, religión | COMP | block of compound nouns, bloque de compuestos |
| SEW | sewing, costura | | |
| *sím* | símbolo, symbol | | |
| *sing* | singular | ⓘ | note about some type of irregularity, nota sobre algún tipo de irregularidad morfológica |
| *sl* | slang, argot | | |
| SP | sport, deporte | | |
| *subj* | subjunctive, subjuntivo | ✎ | note about a peculiarity of the headword, nota sobre alguna particularidad de la palabra |
| *superl* | superlative, superlativo | | |
| *symb* | symbol, símbolo | | |
| TEAT | teatro, theatre | | |
| TÉC | técnica, technical | 🗷 | note about a false friend, nota sobre un «falso amigo» |
| TECH | technical, técnica | | |
| THEAT | theatre, teatro | | |
| TV | television, televisión | ⊕ | cultural note, nota de tipo cultural |
| US | American English, inglés norteamericano | | |

ENGLISH
SPANISH

**A, a** [eɪ] *n* **1** *(the letter)* A, a. **2** MUS la. COMP **A road** carretera principal.

**a** [eɪ, *unstressed* ə] *indef art* **1** un, una: *a man and a woman* un hombre y una mujer. **2** *(not translated)*: *I'm a history teacher* soy profesor de historia; *two and a half litres* dos litros y medio. **3** *(per)* por: *three times a week* tres veces por semana; *£3 a kilo* tres libras el kilo. **4** *(a certain)* un tal, una tal: *a Mr Fletcher would like to see you* un tal Sr. Fletcher quiere verle.

✎ Se usa delante de las palabras que empiezan con sonido no vocálico. Consulta también an.

**aback** [əˈbæk] *adv* hacia atrás. LOC **to be taken aback** asombrarse.

**abacus** [ˈæbəkəs] *n* ábaco.

**abandon** [əˈbændən] *vt* abandonar.

**abate** [əˈbeɪt] *vi* *(gen)* reducirse; *(storm, anger)* amainar; *(wind)* cesar.
▶ *vt (reduce)* reducir; *(stop)* acabar con.

**abattoir** [ˈæbətwɑːˈ] *n* matadero.

**abbey** [ˈæbɪ] *n* abadía.

**abbot** [ˈæbət] *n* abad *m*.

**abbreviate** [əˈbriːvɪeɪt] *vt* abreviar.

**abbreviation** [əbriːvɪˈeɪʃən] *n* **1** *(shortening)* abreviación *f*. **2** *(shortened form)* abreviatura.

**abdicate** [ˈæbdɪkeɪt] *vi* abdicar.

**abdomen** [ˈæbdəmən] *n* abdomen *m*.

**abdominal** [æbˈdɒmɪnəl] *adj* abdominal. COMP **abdominal muscles** músculos abdominales.

**abduct** [æbˈdʌkt] *vt* raptar, secuestrar.

**abhor** [əbˈhɔːˈ] *vt* aborrecer, detestar.
ⓘ *pt & pp* **abhorred**, *ger* **abhorring**.

**abide** [əˈbaɪd] *vt (bear, stand)* soportar, aguantar: *I can't abide that woman* no aguanto a esa mujer.
◆ **to abide by** *vt insep (promise)* cumplir con; *(rules, decision)* acatar.

**ability** [əˈbɪlɪtɪ] *n* **1** *(capability)* capacidad *f*, aptitud *f*. **2** *(talent)* talento.
ⓘ *pl* abilities.

**ablation** [əˈbleɪʃən] *n* ablación *f*.

**ablaze** [əˈbleɪz] *adj* ardiendo, en llamas.

**able** [ˈeɪbəl] *adj* **1** que puede: *those able to escape did so* aquéllos que podían se escaparon. **2** *(capable)* hábil, capaz, competente: *he's a very able administrator* es un gestor muy competente. LOC **to be able to** poder.

✎ En pasado, to be able to se emplea en vez de could para expresar una capacidad relacionada con un acontecimiento concreto: we weren't able to go no pudimos ir.

**abnormal** [æbˈnɔːməl] *adj* **1** *(not normal)* anormal. **2** *(unusual)* inusual.

**aboard** [əˈbɔːd] *adv (ship, plane)* a bordo; *(train)* en el tren; *(bus)* en el autobús.
▶ *prep (ship, plane)* a bordo de; *(train, bus)* en. LOC **to go aboard 1** *(ship, plane)* embarcar, subir a bordo. **2** *(train, bus)* subir.

**abode** [əˈbəʊd] *n* LOC **of no fixed abode** sin domicilio fijo.

**abolish** [əˈbɒlɪʃ] *vt* **1** abolir, suprimir. **2** JUR derogar.

**abominable** [əˈbɒmɪnəbəl] *adj* abominable; *(terrible)* terrible, horrible. COMP **the Abominable Snowman** el Yeti.

**aborigine** [æbəˈrɪdʒɪnɪ] *n* aborigen *mf*.

**abort** [əˈbɔːt] *vi* abortar.
▶ *vt* **1** *(foetus)* abortar. **2** *(mission, program, etc)* abortar.

**abortion** [əˈbɔːʃən] *n* **1** *(of foetus)* aborto. **2** *(of mission, etc)* interrupción *f*.

**abound** [əˈbaʊnd] *vi* abundar.

**about** [əˈbaʊt] *prep* **1** *(concerning)* sobre, acerca de: *to speak about...* hablar de...; *what is the book about?* ¿de qué trata el libro? **2** *(showing where)* por, en; *(around)* alrededor de: *he's somewhere about the house* está por algún rincón de la casa.
▸ *adv* **1** *(approximately)* alrededor de: *at about three o'clock* a eso de las tres; *it cost about £500* costó unas quinientas libras. **2** *fam (almost)* casi: *she's about finished* está a punto de acabar. **3** *(near)* por aquí, por ahí: *there was nobody about* no había nadie. ⌐LOC⌐ **to be about to ...** estar a punto de... ▮ **how/what about + noun** ¿qué te parece + *sustantivo*?: *how about a pizza?* ¿qué te parece si tomamos una pizza? ▮ **how/what about + -ing** ¿y si + *subj*?: *how about going to Paris?* ¿y si fuéramos a París?

**above** [əˈbʌv] *prep* **1** *(higher than)* por encima de: *above our heads* por encima de nuestras cabezas. **2** *(more than)* más de, más que: *above 5,000 people* más de 5.000 personas.
▸ *adv* **1** arriba, en lo alto: *the palace, seen from above* el palacio, visto desde arriba. **2** *(in writing)* arriba: *see above* véase arriba. ⌐LOC⌐ **above all** sobre todo.

**above-board** [əbʌvˈbɔːd] *adj* legítimo,-a, legal.

**abreast** [əˈbrest] *adv* ⌐LOC⌐ **to walk abreast** caminar uno al lado de otro; **to keep abreast of things** estar al tanto de las cosas.

**abridge** [əˈbrɪdʒ] *vt* resumir, abreviar.

**abroad** [əˈbrɔːd] *adv* *(position)* en el extranjero; *(movement)* al extranjero.

**abrupt** [əˈbrʌpt] *adj* **1** *(sudden)* repentino,-a. **2** *(rude)* brusco,-a, arisco,-a. **3** *(slope)* empinado,-a.

**ABS** [ˈeɪbiːˈes] *abbr* **(anti-lock braking system)** sistema *m* de antibloqueo; *(abbreviation)* ABS.

**abscess** [ˈæbses] *n* *(gen)* absceso; *(on gum)* flemón *m*.

**abscond** [əbˈskɒnd] *vi* fugarse.

**abseil** [ˈæbseɪl] *vi* hacer rappel.

**absence** [ˈæbsəns] *n* **1** *(of person)* ausencia. **2** *(of thing)* falta, carencia.

**absent** [*(adj)* ˈæbsənt; *(vb)* æbˈsent] *adj* **1** ausente. **2** *(expression)* distraído,-a.

**absentee** [æbsənˈtiː] *n* ausente *mf*.

**absenteeism** [æbsənˈtiːɪzəm] *n* absentismo.

**absent-minded** [æbsəntˈmaɪndɪd] *adj* distraído,-a, despistado,-a.

**absolute** [ˈæbsəluːt] *adj* **1** *(gen)* absoluto,-a. **2** *(total)* total: *there was absolute silence* hubo silencio total. ⌐COMP⌐ **absolute zero** cero absoluto.

**absolutely** [æbsəˈluːtlɪ] *adv* completamente, totalmente.
▸ *interj (agreement)* ¡por supuesto!, ¡desde luego!: *I think we should sell. What about you John? – Oh, absolutely!* creo que deberíamos vender. ¿Y tú John? –Oh, ¡por supuesto!

**absolution** [æbsəˈluːʃən] *n* absolución *f*.

**absolutism** [ˈæbsəluːtɪzəm] *n* absolutismo.

**absolve** [əbˈzɒlv] *vt* absolver (of/from, de).

**absorb** [əbˈzɔːb] *vt* **1** *(liquids, etc)* absorber; *(shock)* amortiguar. **2** *(time)* ocupar.

**absorption** [əbˈzɔːpʃən] *n* absorción *f*.

**abstain** [əbˈsteɪn] *vi* abstenerse (from, de).

**abstemious** [æbˈstiːmɪəs] *adj* abstemio,-a, sobrio,-a.

**abstention** [æbˈstenʃən] *n* abstención *f*.

**abstinence** [ˈæbstɪnəns] *n* abstinencia.

**abstract** [*(adj-n)* ˈæbstrækt; *(vb)* æbˈstrækt] *adj (not concrete)* abstracto,-a.
▸ *n (summary)* resumen *m*.

**absurd** [əbˈsɜːd] *adj* absurdo,-a.

**abundance** [əˈbʌndəns] *n* abundancia.

**abundant** [əˈbʌndənt] *adj* abundante.

**abuse** [*(n)* əˈbjuːs; *(vb)* əˈbjuːz] *n* **1** *(verbal)* insultos *mpl*; *(physical)* malos tratos *mpl*. **2** *(misuse)* abuso.
▸ *vt* **1** *(verbally)* insultar; *(physically)* maltratar. **2** *(misuse)* abusar de.

**abyss** [əˈbɪs] *n* abismo.

**abysmal** [əˈbɪzməl] *adj* pésimo,-a.

**AC** [ˈeɪˈsiː] *abbr* ELEC **(alternating current)** corriente *f* alterna; *(abbreviation)* CA *f*.

**academic** [ækəˈdemɪk] *adj* **1** *(gen)* académico,-a. **2** *(theoretical)* teórico: *it's a*

*purely academic question* es una cuestión puramente teórica.
▶ *n (scholar)* académico,-a; *(lecturer)* profesor,-ra universitario,-a. COMP **academic year** año académico.

**academy** [ə'kædəmɪ] *n* **1** academia. **2** *(in Scotland)* instituto de enseñanza media.
ⓘ *pl* **academies**.

**accelerate** [æk'seləreɪt] *vt* acelerar.
▶ *vi* acelerarse.

**acceleration** [ækselə'reɪʃ°n] *n* aceleración *f*.

**accelerator** [ək'seləreɪtə'] *n* acelerador *m*.

**accent** [*(n)* 'æksənt; *(vb)* æk'sent] *n* acento.
▶ *vt* acentuar.

**accentuate** [æk'sentʃʊeɪt] *vt* acentuar.

**accentuation** [æksentʃʊ'eɪʃ°n] *n* acentuación *f*.

**accept** [ək'sept] *vt* aceptar, admitir.

**acceptable** [ək'septəb°l] *adj* aceptable, admisible.

**acceptance** [ək'septəns] *n* **1** *(act of accepting)* aceptación *f*. **2** *(approval)* acogida.

**access** ['ækses] *n* acceso.
▶ *vt* COMPUT acceder a, entrar en. COMP **access code** código de acceso. **access road** carretera de acceso.

**accessibility** [æksesɪ'bɪlɪtɪ] *n* accesibilidad *f*.

**accessible** [æk'sesɪb°l] *adj* **1** accesible. **2** *(person)* asequible, tratable.

**accessory** [æk'sesərɪ] *n* **1** *(gadget)* accesorio. **2** JUR *(accomplice)* cómplice *mf*.
▶ *n pl* **accessories** *(bag, gloves, etc)* complementos *mpl*.
ⓘ *pl* **accessories**.

**accident** ['æksɪdənt] *n* accidente *m*.
LOC **by accident** por casualidad.

**accidental** [æksɪ'dent°l] *adj* fortuito,-a.

**acclaim** [ə'kleɪm] *n* **1** *(welcome)* aclamación *f*. **2** *(praise)* elogios *mpl*, alabanza.
▶ *vt* **1** *(welcome)* aclamar. **2** *(praise)* elogiar, alabar.

**acclimatize** [ə'klaɪmətaɪz] *vt* aclimatar.
▶ *vi* aclimatarse.

**accommodate** [ə'kɒmədeɪt] *vt* alojar.

**accommodation** [əkɒmə'deɪʃ°n] *n* alojamiento.

**accomplice** [ə'kɒmplɪs] *n* cómplice *mf*.

**accomplish** [ə'kɒmplɪʃ] *vt* lograr.

**accomplishment** [ə'kɒmplɪʃmənt] *n* **1** *(act of achieving)* realización *f*. **2** *(achievement)* logro.
▶ *n pl* **accomplishments** *(skills)* aptitudes *fpl*, dotes *fpl*, habilidades *fpl*.

**accord** [ə'kɔːd] *n* *(agreement)* acuerdo: *the Oslo accords* los acuerdos de Oslo. LOC **of one's own accord** espontáneamente, por propia voluntad.
▶ *vt (award)* conceder, otorgar.

🗙 To accord no significa 'acordar', que se traduce por to agree.

**accordance** [ə'kɔːd°ns] LOC **in accordance with** de acuerdo con.

**according** [ə'kɔːdɪŋ] *prep* **according to** **1** según: *according to Philip/the paper/my watch* según Philip/el periódico/mi reloj. **2** *(consistent with)* de acuerdo con: *it went according to plan* salió tal como se había previsto.

**accordion** [ə'kɔːdɪən] *n* acordeón *m*.

**account** [ə'kaʊnt] *n* **1** *(in bank)* cuenta. **2** *(report)* relación *f*, relato, informe *m*: *he gave us an account of his experiences* nos contó sus experiencias. **on account of** por, a causa de: *don't leave on my account* no te vayas por mí. **on no account** bajo ningún concepto. **to keep the accounts** llevar las cuentas. **to take into account** tener en cuenta. COMP **accounts department** sección *f* de contabilidad.
◆ **to account for** *vi* explicar.

**accountable** [ə'kaʊntəb°l] *adj* LOC **to be accountable to SB for STH** ser responsable ante ALGN de ALGO.

**accountant** [ə'kaʊntənt] *n* contable *mf*.

**accumulate** [ə'kjuːmjʊleɪt] *vt* acumular.
▶ *vi* acumularse.

**accumulation** [əkjuːmjʊ'leɪʃ°n] *n* acumulación *f*.

**accumulator** [ə'kjuːmjʊleɪtə'] *n* acumulador *m*.

**accuracy** ['ækjʊrəsɪ] *n* **1** *(of numbers, instrument, information)* exactitud *f*, precisión *f*. **2** *(of shot)* certeza.

**accurate** [ˈækjʊrət] *adj* **1** *(numbers, etc)* exacto,-a, preciso,-a. **2** *(instrument)* de precisión. **3** *(shot)* certero,-a.

**accusation** [ækjuːˈzeɪʃⁿn] *n* acusación *f*.

**accuse** [əˈkjuːz] *vt* acusar (of, de).

**accused** [əˈkjuːzd] *n* the accused *(man)* el acusado; *(woman)* la acusada.

**accustom** [əˈkʌstəm] *vt* acostumbrar (to, a).

**accustomed** [əˈkʌstəmᵈd] *adj* LOC to be accustomed to esar acostumbrado a.

**ace** [eɪs] *n* **1** *(gen)* as *m*. **2** *(tennis)* ace *m*.

**acetic** [əˈsiːtɪk] *adj* acético,-a. COMP acetic acid ácido acético.

**acetone** [ˈæsɪtəʊn] *n* acetona.

**acetylene** [əˈsetɪliːn] *n* acetileno.

**ache** [eɪk] *n* dolor *m*.
▶ *vi* doler: *my head aches* me duele la cabeza, tengo dolor de cabeza.

✎ Ache se usa para formar palabras compuestas como headache *(dolor de cabeza)*, toothache *(dolor de muelas)*, earache *(dolor de oídos)* o stomach-ache *(dolor de estómago)*.

**achieve** [əˈtʃiːv] *vt* **1** *(finish)* realizar, llevar a cabo. **2** *(attain)* lograr, conseguir.

**achievement** [əˈtʃiːvmənt] *n* **1** *(completion)* realización *f*. **2** *(attainment)* logro. **3** *(feat)* hazaña, proeza.

**Achilles** [əˈkɪliːz] *n* Aquiles. COMP Achilles' heel *fig* talón *m* de Aquiles. ‖ Achilles' tendon ANAT tendón *m* de Aquiles.

**acid** [ˈæsɪd] *adj* **1** CHEM ácido,-a. **2** *(taste)* agrio,-a. COMP acid rain lluvia ácida.
▶ *n* CHEM ácido,-a.

**acknowledge** [əkˈnɒlɪdʒ] *vt* **1** *(admit)* admitir, reconocer. **2** *(be thankful)* agradecer, expresar agradecimiento por. LOC to acknowledge receipt of acusar recibo de.

**acknowledgement** [əkˈnɒlɪdʒmənt] *n* **1** *(recognition)* reconocimiento. **2** *(thanks)* muestra de agradecimiento. COMP acknowledgement of receipt acuse *m* de recibo.

**acknowledgment** [əkˈnɒlɪdʒmənt] *n* → acknowledgement.

**acne** [ˈækni] *n* acné *f*.

**acorn** [ˈeɪkɔːn] *n* bellota.

**acoustic** [əˈkuːstɪk] *adj* acústico,-a.

**acoustics** [əˈkuːstɪks] *n (science)* acústica.
▶ *n pl (sound conditions)* acústica *f sing*.

**acquaint** [əˈkweɪnt] *vt* informar (with, de). LOC to acquaint os with STH familiarizarse con ALGO. ‖ to be acquainted with SB conocer a ALGN, tener trato con ALGN.

**acquaintance** [əˈkweɪntəns] *n (person)* conocido,-a: *an acquaintance of mine* un conocido mío. LOC to make SB's acquaintance conocer a ALGN.

**acquiesce** [ækwɪˈes] *vi* consentir (in, en), conformarse (in, con).

**acquire** [əˈkwaɪəʳ] *vt* adquirir.

**acquisition** [ækwɪˈzɪʃⁿn] *n* adquisición *f*.

**acquit** [əˈkwɪt] *vt* absolver, declarar inocente.
ⓘ *pt & pp* acquitted, *ger* acquitting.

**acquittal** [əˈkwɪtᵊl] *n* absolución *f*.

**acre** [ˈeɪkəʳ] *n* acre *m*.

✎ Un acre equivale a 40,47 hectáreas.

**acrobat** [ˈækrəbæt] *n* acróbata *mf*.

**acrobatic** [ækrəˈbætɪk] *adj* acrobático,-a.

**acronym** [ˈækrənɪm] *n* sigla.

**acropolis** [əˈkrɒpəlɪs] *n* acrópolis *f*.

**across** [əˈkrɒs] *prep* **1** *(movement)* a través de, de un lado a otro de: *to swim across a river* cruzar un río nadando/a nado. **2** *(position)* al otro lado de: *they live across the road* viven enfrente.
▶ *adv* de un lado a otro: *it's 4 metres across* mide 4 metros de lado a lado.

✎ Con verbos como walk, run, swim, etc, se suele traducir por 'cruzar' o 'atravesar'.

**acrylic** [əˈkrɪlɪk] *adj* acrílico,-a.

**act** [ækt] *n* **1** acto, acción *f*. **2** THEAT acto. **3** *(of parliament)* ley *f*. COMP act of God fuerza mayor.
▶ *vi* **1** *(do something)* actuar. **2** *(behave)* portarse, comportarse: *she acts like a little girl* se comporta como una niña. **3** *(in theatre)* actuar, hacer teatro; *(in cinema)* actuar, hacer cine.

► *vt* hacer el papel de: *she's acting (the part of) Portia* ella hace el papel de Portia.
◆ **to act as** *vt insep* hacer de: *I had to act as interpreter* tuve que hacer de intérprete.

**acting** ['æktɪŋ] *adj* en funciones.
► *n* **1** THEAT *(profession)* teatro. **2** *(performance)* interpretación *f*, actuación *f*.

**actinium** [æk'tɪnɪəm] *n* actinio.

**action** ['æk∫(ə)n] *n* **1** *(gen)* acción *f*. **2** JUR demanda. COMP **action replay** repetición *f* de la jugada. ‖ **action stations** zafarrancho de combate.

☒ Action no significa 'acción' (de una empresa), que se traduce por share.

**activate** ['æktɪveɪt] *vt (mechanism, bomb)* activar.

**activation** [æktɪ'veɪ∫(ə)n] *n (of mechanism, bomb)* activación *f*.

**active** ['æktɪv] *adj* activo,-a. COMP **the active voice** la voz activa.

**activism** ['æktɪvɪz(ə)m] *n* activismo.

**activist** ['æktɪvɪst] *n* activista *mf*.

**activity** [æk'tɪvɪtɪ] *n* actividad *f*.
① *pl* activities.

**actor** ['æktə<sup>r</sup>] *n* actor *m*.

**actress** ['æktrəs] *n* actriz *f*.

**actual** ['æktʃʊəl] *adj* real, verdadero,-a.

☒ Actual no significa 'actual', que se traduce por present, current o up-to-date.

**actually** ['æktjʊəlɪ] *adv* **1** en realidad, realmente, de hecho: *I haven't actually decided what to do yet* en realidad, todavía no he decidido qué hacer. **2** *(indicating surprise)* incluso, hasta: *she actually accused me of stealing her bag* hasta me acusó de robarle el bolso.

☒ Actually no significa 'actualmente', que se traduce por nowadays, at present.

**acupuncture** ['ækjʊpʌnktʃə] *n* acupuntura.

**acupuncturist** ['ækjʊpʌnktʃərɪst] *n* acupunturista *mf*.

**acute** [ə'kjuːt] *adj* **1** *(gen)* agudo,-a. **2** *(angle)* agudo,-a. **3** *(hearing, etc)* muy fino,-a, muy desarrollado,-a. COMP **acute accent** acento agudo. ‖ **acute triangle** triángulo acutángulo.

**AD** ['eɪ'diː] *abbr* **(Anno Domini)** después de Cristo; *(abbreviation)* d.J.C.

**ad** [æd] *n fam* anuncio.

**Adam** ['ædəm] *n* Adán *m*. COMP **Adam's apple** nuez *f* (de la garganta).

**adamant** ['ædəmənt] *adj* firme, inflexible. LOC **to be adamant about** STH mantenerse firme en ALGO.

**adapt** [ə'dæpt] *vt* adaptar.
► *vi* adaptarse.

**adaptable** [ə'dæptəb(ə)l] *adj (person)* capaz de adaptarse.

**adaptation** [ædəp'teɪ∫(ə)n] *n* adaptación *f*.

**adapter** [ə'dæptə<sup>r</sup>] *n* ELEC → adaptor.

**adaptor** [ə'dæptə<sup>r</sup>] *n* ELEC ladrón *m*.

**add** [æd] *vt* **1** *(gen)* añadir, agregar. **2** *(numbers)* sumar.
◆ **to add to** *vt insep* aumentar.
◆ **to add up** *vt sep (numbers)* sumar.
► *vi fig* cuadrar: *there's something funny going on; it doesn't add up* pasa algo raro; es que no cuadra.

**addend** ['ædənd] *n* MAT sumando.

**adder** ['ædə<sup>r</sup>] *n* ZOOL víbora.

**addict** ['ædɪkt] *n* **1** adicto,-a. **2** *fam (fanatic)* fanático,-a.

**addicted** [ə'dɪktɪd] *adj* adicto,-a.

**addiction** [ə'dɪk∫(ə)n] *n* adicción *f*.

**addictive** [ə'dɪktɪv] *adj* que crea adicción: *nicotine is addictive* la nicotina crea adicción.

**addition** [ə'dɪ∫(ə)n] *n* **1** adición *f*, añadidura. **2** MATH adición *f*, suma. LOC **in addition to** además de.

**additional** [ə'dɪ∫(ə)n(ə)l] *adj* adicional.

**additive** ['ædɪtɪv] *n* aditivo.

**additive-free** ['ædɪtɪv'friː] *adj* sin aditivos.

**address** [ə'dres] *n* **1** *(on letter)* dirección *f*, señas *fpl*. **2** *(speech)* discurso, alocución *f*.
► *vt* **1** *(problem)* abordar. **2** *(person)* dirigirse a. COMP **address book** libro de direcciones. ‖ **form of address** tratamiento.

**adductor** [ə'dʌktəʳ] *n* ANAT aductor,-ra.

**adenoids** ['ædənɔɪdz] *n pl* adenoides *mpl*, vegetaciones *fpl*.

**adept** [ə'dept] *adj* experto,-a, diestro,-a.

⊠ Adept no significa 'adepto, seguidor', que se traducen por **follower, supporter**.

**adequate** ['ædɪkwət] *adj* **1** *(enough)* suficiente. **2** *(satisfactory)* satisfactorio,-a.

**adhere** [əd'hɪəʳ] *vi (stick)* adherirse, pegarse.

**adherent** [əd'hɪərənt] *adj* adherente.

**adhesive** [əd'hi:sɪv] *adj* adhesivo,-a.
▶ *n* adhesivo.

**adipose** ['ædɪpəuz] *adj* adiposo,-a.

**adjacent** [ə'dʒeɪsənt] *adj* adyacente.
COMP **adjacent angles** ángulos adyacentes.

**adjective** ['ædʒɪktɪv] *n* adjetivo.

**adjoin** [ə'dʒɔɪn] *vt* lindar con.
▶ *vi* colindar.

**adjoining** [ə'dʒɔɪnɪŋ] *adj* **1** *(building)* contiguo,-a. **2** *(land)* colindante.

**adjourn** [ə'dʒɜ:n] *vt* aplazar, suspender.
▶ *vi* suspenderse.

**adjournment** [ə'dʒɜ:nmənt] *n* aplazamiento, suspensión *f*.

**adjust** [ə'dʒʌst] *vt* ajustar, arreglar.
▶ *vi (person)* adaptarse.

**adjustable** [ə'dʒʌstəbəl] *adj* regulable.
COMP **adjustable spanner** llave *f* inglesa.

**adjustment** [ə'dʒʌstmənt] *n* **1** ajuste *m*, arreglo. **2** *(person)* adaptación *f*. **3** *(change)* cambio.

**administer** [əd'mɪnɪstəʳ] *vt* **1** *(control)* administrar. **2** *(give)* administrar, dar; *(laws, punishment)* aplicar.

**administration** [ədmɪnɪs'treɪʃən] *n* **1** administración *f*. **2** *(of law, etc)* aplicación *f*.

**administrator** [əd'mɪnɪstreɪtəʳ] *n* administrador,-ra.

**admirable** ['ædmɪrəbəl] *adj* admirable.

**admiral** ['ædmərəl] *n* almirante *m*.

**admiration** [ædmɪ'reɪʃən] *n* admiración *f*.

**admire** [əd'maɪəʳ] *vt* admirar.

**admirer** [əd'maɪərəʳ] *n (gen)* admirador,-ra; *(suitor)* pretendiente *mf*.

**admissible** [əd'mɪsɪbəl] *adj* admisible.

**admission** [əd'mɪʃən] *n* **1** *(gen)* admisión *f*; *(to hospital)* ingreso. **2** *(price)* entrada. **3** *(acknowledgement)* reconocimiento.

**admit** [əd'mɪt] *vt* **1** *(allow in)* admitir; *(to hospital)* ingresar. **2** *(acknowledge)* reconocer.
ⓘ *pt & pp* admitted, *ger* admitting.

**admittance** [əd'mɪtəns] *n* entrada. LOC «No admittance» «Prohibida la entrada».

**admittedly** [əd'mɪtɪdlɪ] *adv* es verdad que, lo cierto es que.

**admonish** [əd'mɒnɪʃ] *vt* amonestar.

**ado** [ə'du:] *n* LOC **without further ado** sin más preámbulos.

**adobe** [ə'dəubɪ] *n* adobe *m*.

**adolescence** [ædə'lesəns] *n* adolescencia.

**adolescent** [ædə'lesənt] *adj* adolescente.
▶ *n* adolescente *mf*.

**adopt** [ə'dɒpt] *vt* adoptar.

**adoption** [ə'dɒpʃən] *n* adopción *f*.

**adoptive** [ə'dɒptɪv] *adj* adoptivo,-a.

**adore** [ə'dɔ:ʳ] *vt* adorar.

**adorn** [ə'dɔ:n] *vt* adornar.

**adrenalin** [ə'drenəlɪn] *n* adrenalina.

**Adriatic** [eɪdrɪ'ætɪk] *adj* adriático,-a. COMP **the Adriatic (Sea)** el (mar) Adriático.

**adrift** [ə'drɪft] *adj* a la deriva.

**adulate** ['ædjuleɪt] *vt* adular.

**adult** ['ædʌlt] *adj* **1** *(gen)* adulto,-a. **2** *(film, etc)* para adultos.
▶ *n* adulto,-a.

**adulterate** [ə'dʌltəreɪt] *vt* adulterar.

**adultery** [ə'dʌltərɪ] *n* adulterio.

**advance** [əd'vɑ:ns] *n* **1** *(gen)* avance *m*. **2** *(payment)* anticipo. LOC **in advance 1** *(gen)* antes. **2** *(rent, etc)* por adelantado.
▶ *vt* **1** *(gen)* avanzar. **2** *(money, date)* adelantar.

**advantage** [əd'vɑ:ntɪdʒ] *n* **1** ventaja. **2** *(benefit)* provecho. LOC **to take advantage of 1** *(thing)* aprovechar. **2** *(person)* aprovecharse de.

**advantageous** [ædvən'teɪdʒəs] *adj* ventajoso,-a, provechoso,-a.

**adventure** [əd'ventʃə<sup>r</sup>] *n* aventura. COMP **adventure playground** parque *m* infantil.

**adverb** ['ædvɜːb] *n* adverbio.

**adversary** ['ædvəsərɪ] *n* adversario,-a.
① *pl* adversaries.

**adversative** [æd'vɜːsətɪv] *adj* adversativo,-a.

**adverse** ['ædvɜːs] *adj* desfavorable.

**adversity** [əd'vɜːsɪtɪ] *n* adversidad *f*.
① *pl* adversities.

**advert** ['ædvɜːt] *n* fam anuncio.

**advertise** ['ædvətaɪz] *vt* anunciar.
▶ *vi* hacer publicidad.

**advertisement** [əd'vɜːtɪsmənt] *n* anuncio.
▶ *n pl* **advertisements** *(on television)* publicidad *f*, anuncios *mpl*.

☒ Advertisement no significa 'advertencia', que se traduce por **warning**.

**advertiser** ['ædvətaɪzə<sup>r</sup>] *n* anunciante *mf*.

**advertising** ['ædvətaɪzɪŋ] *n* publicidad *f*. COMP **advertising agency** agencia de publicidad. ‖ **advertising campaign** campaña publicitaria.

**advice** [əd'vaɪs] *n* consejos *mpl*. COMP **a piece of advice** un consejo.

**advise** [əd'vaɪz] *vt* aconsejar.

☒ To advise no significa 'avisar', que se traduce por **to warn**.

**adviser** [əd'vaɪzə<sup>r</sup>] *n* consejero,-a.

**advocate** [*(n)* 'ædvəkət; *(vb)* 'ædvəkeɪt] *n* **1** *(supporter)* partidario,-a. **2** *(lawyer)* abogado,-a defensor,-ra.
▶ *vt* abogar por, propugnar.

**Aegean** [ɪ'dʒiːən] *adj* egeo,-a. COMP **the Aegean (Sea)** el (mar) Egeo.

**aerial** ['eərɪəl] *adj* aéreo,-a.
▶ *n* antena.

**aerobe** ['eərəub] *n* aerobio.

**aerobics** [eə'rəubɪks] *n* aerobic *m*, aeróbic *m*.

**aerodrome** ['eərədrəum] *n* aeródromo.

**aerodynamics** [eərəudaɪ'næmɪks] *n* aerodinámica.

**aeronautics** [eərə'nɔːtɪks] *n* aeronáutica.

**aeroplane** ['eərəpleɪn] *n* aeroplano, avión *m*.

**aerosol** ['eərəsɒl] *n* aerosol *m*.

**aerostatic** [eərə'stætɪk] *adj* aerostático,-a.

**aesthetic** [iːs'θetɪk] *adj* estético,-a.

**aesthetics** [iːs'θetɪks] *n* estética.

**affair** [ə'feə<sup>r</sup>] *n* **1** *(matter)* asunto: *that's your affair* eso es asunto tuyo. **2** *(case)* caso: *the Watergate affair* el caso Watergate. COMP **current affairs** actualidad *f sing*.

**affect** [ə'fekt] *vt* **1** *(gen)* afectar. **2** *(feign)* fingir, afectar: *he affected indifference* fingió indiferencia.

**affection** [ə'fekʃ<sup>ə</sup>n] *n* afecto, cariño.

**affectionate** [ə'fekʃ<sup>ə</sup>nət] *adj* afectuoso,-a, cariñoso,-a.

**affiliate** [ə'fɪlɪət] *n* afiliado,-a.
▶ *vt* afiliar.
▶ *vi* afiliar.

**affinity** [ə'fɪnɪtɪ] *n* afinidad *f*.
① *pl* affinities.

**affirm** [ə'fɜːm] *vt* afirmar, asegurar.

**affirmation** [æfə'meɪʃ<sup>ə</sup>n] *n* afirmación *f*.

**affirmative** [ə'fɜːmətɪv] *adj* afirmativo,-a.

**affix** [ə'fɪks] *vt (stamp)* poner; *(poster)* fijar.

**afflict** [ə'flɪkt] *vt* afligir.

**affluence** ['æflʊəns] *n* riqueza, prosperidad *f*.

**affluent** ['æflʊənt] *adj* rico,-a.

**afford** [ə'fɔːd] *vt* permitirse, costear: *I can't afford to pay £750 for a coat* no puedo (permitirme) pagar 750 libras por un abrigo.

**afforestation** [əfɒrɪ'steɪʃ<sup>ə</sup>n] *n* repoblación *f* forestal.

**affricate** ['æfrɪkət] *n* africada.

**Afghan** ['æfgæn] *adj* afgano,-a.
▶ *n* **1** *(person)* afgano,-a. **2** *(language)* afgano.

**Afghanistan** [æfgænɪ'stæn] *n* Afganistán *m*.

**afield** [ə'fiːld] *adv* LOC **far afield** lejos: *they went as far afield as Canada* llegaron hasta Canadá.

**afloat** [əˈfləʊt] *adj* a flote.

**afoot** [əˈfʊt] *adv* en marcha, en proceso.

**afraid** [əˈfreɪd] *adj* temeroso,-a. LOC to be afraid 1 *(frightened)* tener miedo. 2 *(sorry)* temer, sentir, lamentar: *I'm afraid so/not* me temo que sí/no. ‖ to be afraid of STH/SB tener miedo de ALGO/ALGN.

**afresh** [əˈfreʃ] *adv* de nuevo: *he had to start afresh* tuvo que volver a empezar.

**África** [ˈæfrɪkə] *n* África. COMP South Africa Sudáfrica.

**African** [ˈæfrɪkən] *adj* africano,-a.
▶ *n* africano,-a. COMP South African sudafricano,-a.

**Afro** [ˈæfrəʊ] *adj & n (hairstyle)* afro.

**Afro-American** [æfrəʊəˈmerɪkən] *adj* afroamericano,-a.
▶ *n* afroamericano,-a.

⊕ Afro-American es el término más adecuado para referirse a los estadounidenses cuyos antepasados eran originarios del África subsahariana y que, en su mayoría, fueron llevados como esclavos a América entre los siglos XVI y XIX.

**after** [ˈɑːftər] *prep* 1 *(time)* después de: *after class* después de la clase. 2 *(following)* detrás de: *the police are after us* la policía nos está persiguiendo. 3 US *(past)* y: *it's a quarter after four* son las cuatro y cuarto.
▶ *adv* después: *the day after* el día después.
▶ *conj* después que, después de que: *after he left, I went to bed* después de que se marchara, me acosté.
▶ *n pl* afters GB *fam* postre *m*.

**afterbirth** [ˈɑːftəbɜːθ] *n* placenta.

**after-effect** [ˈɑːftərɪfekt] *n* efecto secundario, secuela.

**afterlife** [ˈɑːftəlaɪf] *n* más allá *m*.

**afternoon** [ɑːftəˈnuːn] *n* tarde *f*: *in the afternoon* por la tarde.

**after-sales service** [ɑːftəˈseɪlzsɜːvɪs] *n* servicio posventa.

**aftershave** [ˈɑːftəʃeɪv] *n* loción *f* para después del afeitado.

**aftertaste** [ˈɑːftəteɪst] *n* regusto.

**afterwards** [ˈɑːftəwədz] *adv* después, luego.

**again** [əˈgen, əˈgeɪn] *adv* 1 *(once more)* otra vez, de nuevo: *play me that song again* tócame esa canción otra vez. 2 *(in questions)*: *where do you live again?* ¿dónde has dicho que vives? LOC again and again repetidamente. ‖ now and again de vez en cuando.

**against** [əˈgenst, əˈgeɪnst] *prep* 1 *(gen)* contra: *against the wall* contra la pared; *Leeds played against Liverpool* Leeds jugó contra Liverpool. 2 *(opposed to)* en contra de: *I voted against the proposal* voté en contra de la propuesta.

**age** [eɪdʒ] *n* edad *f*. LOC of age mayor de edad. ‖ under age menor de edad.
▶ *vt & vi* envejecer.

**aged** [eɪdʒd] *adj* de (tantos años de) edad: *a boy aged ten* un muchacho de diez años. COMP the aged los ancianos *mpl*.

**agency** [ˈeɪdʒənsi] *n* 1 *(commercial)* agencia: *a travel/advertising/employment agency* una agencia de viajes/publicidad/empleo. 2 *(governmental, etc)* organismo. ⓘ *pl* agencies.

**agenda** [əˈdʒendə] *n* orden *m* del día.

❌ Agenda no significa 'agenda', que se traduce por diary.

**agent** [ˈeɪdʒənt] *n* agente *mf*.

**aggravate** [ˈægrəveɪt] *vt* 1 *(make worse)* agravar. 2 *fam (annoy)* irritar, molestar.

**aggression** [əˈgreʃn] *n* 1 *(act)* agresión *f*. 2 *(feeling)* agresividad *f*.

**aggressive** [əˈgresɪv] *adj* 1 *(gen)* agresivo,-a. 2 *(dynamic)* emprendedor,-ra.

**aggressor** [əˈgresər] *n* agresor,-ra.

**aghast** [əˈgɑːst] *adj* horrorizado,-a.

**agile** [ˈædʒaɪl] *adj* ágil.

**agility** [əˈdʒɪlɪti] *n* agilidad *f*.

**agitate** [ˈædʒɪteɪt] *vt* agitar.

**agnostic** [ægˈnɒstɪk] *adj* agnóstico,-a.
▶ *n* agnóstico,-a.

**ago** [əˈgəʊ] *adv* hace: *ten days ago* hace diez días; *it happened a long time ago* ocurrió hace mucho tiempo.

✎ Ago se usa siempre con el verbo en pasado. Consulta también for, since.

**agonise** [ˈægənaɪz] *vi* → agonize.

**agonize** ['ægənaɪz] *vi* agonizar.

**agony** ['ægəni] *n* **1** *(pain)* dolor *m* muy agudo. **2** *(anguish)* angustia.
ⓘ *pl* agonies.

❌ Agony no significa 'agonía (antes de morir)', que se traduce por dying breath.

**agora** ['ægərə] *n* ágora.
ⓘ *pl* agoras o agorae ['ægəraɪ, 'ægəri:].

**agree** [ə'gri:] *vi* **1** *(be in agreement)* estar de acuerdo (with, con): *do you agree with me?* ¿estás de acuerdo conmigo? **2** *(reach an agreement)* ponerse de acuerdo (on, en): *they can't agree on a name for the baby* no se ponen de acuerdo en el nombre del bebé. **4** *(food, climate, etc)* sentar bien (with, -): *the prawns didn't agree with me* las gambas no me sentaron bien.
▶ *vt (grammatically)* concordar (with, con).

**agreeable** [ə'gri:əbəl] *adj* **1** *(pleasant)* agradable. **2** *(in agreement)* conforme.

**agreement** [ə'gri:mənt] *n* **1** acuerdo: *the two men reached an agreement* los dos hombres llegaron a un acuerdo. **2** *(grammatical)* concordancia.

**agricultural** [ægrɪkʌltʃərəl] *adj* agrícola.

**agriculture** ['ægrɪkʌltʃəʳ] *n* agricultura.

**agronomy** [ə'grɒnəmi] *n* agronomía.

**aground** [ə'graʊnd] *adj* encallado,-a.
[LOC] **to run aground** encallar.

**ahead** [ə'hed] *adv (in front)* delante: *there's a police checkpoint ahead* hay un control de policía aquí delante; *we finished ahead of schedule* acabamos antes de lo previsto. [LOC] **go ahead!** ¡adelante!

**aid** [eɪd] *n (help)* ayuda; *(rescue)* auxilio. [COMP] **humanitarian aid** ayuda humanitaria.
▶ *vt* ayudar, auxiliar.

**AIDS** [eɪdz] *n* (Acquired Immune Deficiency Syndrome) sida *m*.

**aileron** ['eɪlərɒn] *n* alerón *m*.

**ailing** ['eɪlɪŋ] *adj* enfermo,-a.

**ailment** ['eɪlmənt] *n* dolencia, achaque *m*.

**aim** [eɪm] *n* **1** *(marksmanship)* puntería: *his aim is good* tiene buena puntería. **2** *(objective)* meta, objetivo: *what's your aim in life?* ¿qué objetivo tienes en la vida?

▶ *vt* **1** *(gun)* apuntar (at, a). **2** *(attack)* dirigir (at, a).

**ain't** [eɪnt] *contr fam* → am not, is not, are not, has not, have not.

**air** [eəʳ] *n* aire *m*. [LOC] **by air 1** *(send letter)* por avión. **2** *(travel)* en avión. [COMP] **air hostess** azafata. **air lane** ruta aérea. **air pressure** presión *f* atmosférica. **air rifle** escopeta de aire comprimido. **air terminal** terminal *f* aérea. **air traffic controller** controlador,-ra aéreo,-a.
▶ *vt* **1** *(gen)* airear. **2** *(room)* ventilar.

**airbag** ['eəbæg] *n* airbag *m*.

**airbase** ['eəbeɪs] *n* base *f* aérea.

**air-bed** ['eəbed] *n* GB colchón *m* de aire.

**air-conditioned** [eəkən'dɪʃənd] *adj* con aire acondicionado, refrigerado,-a.

**air-conditioning** [eəkən'dɪʃ°nɪŋ] *n* aire *m* acondicionado.

**aircraft** ['eəkrɑ:ft] *n (gen)* aeronave *f*; *(plane)* avión *m*.
ⓘ *pl* aircraft.

**aircraft-carrier** ['eəkrɑ:ftkæriəʳ] *n* portaaviones *m inv*.

**airfield** ['eəfi:ld] *n* campo de aviación.

**airforce** ['eəfɔ:s] *n* fuerza aérea, fuerzas *fpl* aéreas.

**airline** ['eəlaɪn] *n* línea aérea.

**airliner** ['eəlaɪnəʳ] *n* avión *m* de pasajeros *(grande)*.

**airmail** ['eəmeɪl] *n* correo aéreo.

**airplane** ['eəpleɪn] *n* US aeroplano, avión *m*.

**airport** ['eəpɔ:t] *n* aeropuerto.

**airship** ['eəʃɪp] *n* dirigible *m*.

**airsick** ['eəsɪk] *adj* mareado,-a. [LOC] **to be airsick** marearse.

**airspace** ['eəspeɪs] *n* espacio aéreo.

**airstrip** ['eəstrɪp] *n* pista de aterrizaje.

**airtight** ['eətaɪt] *adj* hermético,-a.

**airway** ['eəweɪ] *n* **1** *(route)* ruta aérea, vía aérea. **2** *(airline)* línea aérea.

**airy** ['eəri] *adj* **1** *(ventilated)* bien ventilado,-a. **2** *(light)* ligero,-a.
ⓘ *comp* airier, *superl* airiest.

**aisle** [aɪl] *n* **1** *(between seats, shelves, etc)* pasillo. **2** *(section of church)* nave *f* lateral.

**aitch** [eɪtʃ] *n* hache *f*.

**ajar** [ə'dʒɑːʳ] *adj* entreabierto,-a.

**akimbo** [ə'kɪmbəʊ] *adv* en jarras.

**akin** [ə'kɪn] *adj* parecido,-a (**to**, a).

**alabaster** ['æləbɑːstəʳ] *n* alabastro.

**alarm** [ə'lɑːm] *n* **1** *(device)* alarma. **2** *(fear)* temor *m*, alarma. COMP **alarm clock** despertador *m*.
  ▶ *vt* alarmar, asustar.

**alarmism** [ə'lɑːmɪzᵉm] *n* alarmismo.

**Albanian** [æl'beɪnɪən] *adj* albanés,-esa.
  ▶ *n* **1** *(person)* albanés,-esa. **2** *(language)* albanés *m*.

**albatross** ['ælbətrɒs] *n* albatros *m*.

**albino** [æl'biːnəʊ] *adj* albino,-a.
  ▶ *n* albino,-a.
  ⓘ *pl* albinos.

**album** ['ælbəm] *n* álbum *m*.

**albumen** ['ælbjuːmɪn, US æl'bjuːmən] *n* **1** *(white of egg)* clara de huevo. **2** *(in plants)* albumen *m*.

**albumin** ['ælbjumɪn, US æl'bjuːmən] *n* albúmina.

**alcohol** ['ælkəhɒl] *n* alcohol *m*.

**alcohol-free** ['ælkəhɒlfriː] *adj* sin alcohol.

**alcoholism** ['ælkəhɒlɪzᵉm] *n* alcoholismo.

**aldehyde** ['ældɪhaɪd] *n* aldehído.

**ale** [eɪl] *n* cerveza.

**alert** [ə'lɜːt] *adj* **1** *(quick to act)* alerta, vigilante. **2** *(lively)* vivo,-a.
  ▶ *n* alarma.
  ▶ *vt* alertar, avisar.

**A-level** ['eɪlevᵉl] *abbr* GB (Advanced level) ≈ segundo curso de bachillerato.

**alfalfa** [æl'fælfə] *n* alfalfa.

**algae** ['ældʒiː] *n pl* algas *fpl*.
  ⓘ *sing* alga ['ælgə].

**algebra** ['ældʒɪbrə] *n* álgebra.

**algebraic** [ældʒɪ'breɪɪk] *adj* algebraico,-a.

**Algeria** [æl'dʒɪərɪə] *n* Argelia.

**Algerian** [æl'dʒɪərɪən] *adj* argelino,-a.
  ▶ *n* argelino,-a.

**algorithm** ['ælgərɪðᵉm] *n* algoritmo.

**alias** ['eɪlɪəs] *adv* alias.
  ▶ *n* alias *m*.

**alibi** ['ælɪbaɪ] *n* coartada.

**alien** ['eɪlɪən] *adj* **1** *(foreign)* extranjero,-a. **2** *(extraterrestrial)* extraterrestre. **3** *(strange)* extraño,-a, ajeno,-a: *his ideas are alien to me* sus ideas me son ajenas.
  ▶ *n* **1** *(foreigner)* extranjero,-a. **2** *(extraterrestrial)* extraterrestre *mf*.

**alight** [ə'laɪt] *adj* encendido,-a, ardiendo.

**align** [ə'laɪn] *vt* alinear (**with**, con).

**alike** [ə'laɪk] *adj (the same)* iguales; *(similar)* parecidos,-as: *they are alike in all respects* son iguales en todo.
  ▶ *adv* igual: *they dress alike* visten igual.

**alimentary** [ælɪ'mentᵉrɪ] *adj* alimenticio,-a. COMP **alimentary canal** tubo digestivo.

**alimony** ['ælɪmənɪ] *n* pensión *f* alimenticia.

**alive** [ə'laɪv] *adj* vivo,-a.

**alkaline** ['ælkəlaɪn] *adj* alcalino,-a.

**all** [ɔːl] *adj (singular)* todo,-a; *(plural)* todos,-as: *all the chairs* todas las sillas; *all day/month/year* todo el día/mes/año.
  ▶ *pron* **1** *(everything)* todo, la totalidad *f*: *all was lost in the fire* se perdió todo en el incendio. **2** *(everybody)* todos *mpl*, todo el mundo: *all of them helped/they all helped* ayudaron todos.
  ▶ *adv* completamente, totalmente: *she was dressed all in leather* iba vestida toda de cuero. LOC **after all 1** *(despite everything)* después de todo. **2** *(it must be remembered)* no hay que olvidarlo. ▌**all over** en todas partes. ▌**to be all over** acabar: *in ten minutes it was all over* en diez minutos todo había acabado. ▌**all right 1** *(acceptable)* bien, bueno,-a: *the film's all right, but I've seen better ones* la película no está mal, pero las he visto mejores. **2** *(well, safe)* bien: *are you all right? ¿*estás bien? **3** *(accepting suggestion)* vale, bueno: *are you coming? –all right ¿*te vienes? –vale. ▌**all that** tan: *he's not all that fast* no es tan rápido. ▌**all the + comp** tanto + *adj/adv*, más + *adj/adv*: *all the better* tanto mejor. ▌**all the time** todo el rato, siempre. ▌**at all** en absoluto. ▌**in all** en total. ▌**not at all** no hay de qué.

**Allah** ['ælə] *n* Alá *m*.

**alleged** [ə'ledʒd] *adj* presunto,-a.

**allegory** ['ælɪgərɪ] *n* alegoría.
  ⓘ *pl* allegories.

**allergic** [əˈlɜːdʒɪk] *adj* alérgico,-a (**to**, a).

**allergy** [ˈælədʒɪ] *n* alergia.
ⓘ *pl* allergies.

**alleviate** [əˈliːvɪeɪt] *vt* aliviar, mitigar.

**alley** [ˈælɪ] *n* callejuela, callejón *m*.

**alliance** [əˈlaɪəns] *n* alianza.

**allied** [ˈælaɪd] *adj* **1** POL aliado,-a. **2** *(related)* relacionado,-a, afín.

**alligator** [ˈælɪgeɪtəʳ] *n* caimán *m*.

**alliteration** [əlɪtəˈreɪʃ°n] *n* aliteración *f*.

**allocate** [ˈæləkeɪt] *vt (money)* destinar; *(time, space, job, etc)* asignar.

**allocation** [æləˈkeɪʃ°n] *n* **1** *(distribution)* asignación *f*; *(of money)* distribución *f*. **2** *(money given)* cuota.

**allot** [əˈlɒt] *vt* asignar.
ⓘ *pt & pp* allotted, *ger* allotting.

**all-out** [ɔːlˈaʊt] *adj* total.

**allow** [əˈlaʊ] *vt* **1** *(permit)* permitir, dejar. **2** *(set aside)* conceder, dar, dejar. **3** *(admit)* admitir, reconocer.
◆ **to allow for** *vt insep* tener en cuenta.

**allowance** [əˈlaʊəns] *n* **1** *(from government)* subsidio, prestación *f*. **2** *(from employer)* dietas *fpl*, asignación *f*. **3** US *(pocket money)* paga semanal. LOC **to make allowances for 1** *(take into account)* tener en cuenta. **2** *(be permissive)* tener paciencia con.

**alloy** [ˈælɔɪ] *n* aleación *f*.

**all-purpose** [ɔːlˈpɜːpəs] *adj* multiuso.

**all-star** [ˈɔːlstɑːʳ] *adj* estelar: *an all-star cast* un reparto estelar.

**all-terrain** [ɔːltəˈreɪn] *adj* todo terreno.

**allude** [əˈluːd] *vi* aludir (**to**, a).

**allure** [əˈljʊəʳ] *n* atractivo, encanto.
▶ *vt* atraer, seducir.

**alluring** [əˈljʊərɪŋ] *adj* seductor,-ra.

**allusion** [əˈluːʒ°n] *n* alusión *f*.

**alluvial** [əˈluːvɪəl] *adj* aluvial.

**ally** [ˈælaɪ] *n* aliado,-a.
ⓘ *pl* allies.
▶ *vt* aliar (**with**, con).
▶ *vi* aliarse (**with**, con).
ⓘ *pt & pp* allied, *ger* allying.

**almighty** [ɔːlˈmaɪtɪ] *adj* todopoderoso,-a.
▶ *n* the Almighty el Todopoderoso.

**almond** [ˈɑːmənd] *n* almendra. COMP almond tree almendro.

**almost** [ˈɔːlməʊst] *adv* casi.

**alone** [əˈləʊn] *adj (unaccompanied)* solo,-a.
▶ *adv (only)* solo, solamente. LOC **to leave STH alone** no tocar ALGO. ‖ **to leave SB alone** dejar a ALGN en paz.

**along** [əˈlɒŋ] *prep* **1** por, a lo largo de: *we walked along the riverbank* caminamos por la orilla del río. **2** *(in)*: *his office is along this corridor* su despacho está en este pasillo.
▶ *adv* adelante, hacia adelante: *move along, please* circulen, por favor. LOC **along with** junto con. ‖ **come along 1** *(sing)* ven. **2** *(plural)* venid.

**alongside** [əlɒŋˈsaɪd] *prep* al lado de.
▶ *adv* al costado, al lado.

**aloof** [əˈluːf] *adj* distante.
▶ *adv* a distancia.

**alopecia** [æləˈpiːʃə] *n* alopecia.

**aloud** [əˈlaʊd] *adv* en voz alta.

**alpha** [ˈælfə] *n* alfa. COMP alpha ray rayo alfa.

**alphabet** [ˈælfəbet] *n* alfabeto, abecedario.

**alphabetical** [ælfəˈbetɪk°l] *adj* alfabético,-a. LOC **in alphabetical order** por orden alfabético.

**alphanumeric** [ælfənjuˈmerɪk] *adj* alfanumérico,-a.

**alpine** [ˈælpaɪn] *adj* alpino,-a.

**Alps** [ælps] *n pl* the Alps los Alpes *mpl*.

**already** [ɔːlˈredɪ] *adv* ya: *they've already left* ya se han ido.

**also** [ˈɔːlsəʊ] *adv* también.

**altar** [ˈɔːltəʳ] *n* altar *m*.

**altarpiece** [ˈɔːltəpiːs] *n* retablo.

**alter** [ˈɔːltəʳ] *vt (gen)* cambiar; *(clothes)* arreglar.
▶ *vi* cambiar, cambiarse.

**alteration** [ɔːltəˈreɪʃ°n] *n* modificación *f*.
▶ *n pl* alterations reformas *fpl*.

**alternate** [*(adj)* ɔːlˈtɜːnət; *(vb)* ˈɔːltɜːneɪt] *adj* alterno,-a.
▶ *vt* alternar.
▶ *vi* alternarse.

**alternating** [ˈɔːltɜːneɪtɪŋ] COMP alternating current corriente *f* alterna.

**alternative** [ɔːlˈtɜːnətɪv] *adj* alternativo,-a.
▶ *n (option)* opción *f*, alternativa.

**alternator** [ˈɔːltəneɪtəʳ] *n* alternador *m*.

**although** [ɔːlˈðəʊ] *conj* aunque.

**altimeter** [ˈæltɪmiːtəʳ] *n* altímetro.

**altitude** [ˈæltɪtjuːd] *n* altitud *f*, altura.

**altogether** [ɔːltəˈgeðəʳ] *adv* **1** *(completely)* del todo. **2** *(on the whole)* en conjunto. **3** *(in total)* en total.

**altruism** [ˈæltruɪzᵊm] *n* altruismo.

**aluminium** [æljuˈmɪnɪəm] *n* aluminio. COMP aluminium foil papel *m* de aluminio, papel *m* de plata.

**aluminum** [əˈluːmɪnəm] *n* US aluminio.

**alveolar** [ælvɪˈəʊləʳ] *adj* alveolar. COMP alveolar sacs ANAT sacos alveolares.

**alveolus** [ælˈvɪələs] *n* alveolo, alvéolo.
ⓘ *pl* alveoli [ælˈvɪəlaɪ].

**always** [ˈɔːlweɪz] *adv* siempre.

**am** [æm] *pres* → be.

**a.m.** [ˈeɪˈem] *abbr* (ante meridiem) de la mañana.

**amass** [əˈmæs] *vt* acumular.

**amateur** [ˈæmətəʳ] *adj* aficionado,-a.
▶ *n* aficionado,-a.

**amateurism** [ˈæmətʃərɪzᵊm] *n* amateurismo.

**amaze** [əˈmeɪz] *vt* asombrar, pasmar.

**amazement** [əˈmeɪzmənt] *n* asombro, pasmo.

**amazing** [əˈmeɪzɪŋ] *adj* asombroso,-a, pasmoso,-a.

**Amazon** [ˈæməzᵊn] *n* the Amazon **1** *(river)* el Amazonas *m*. **2** *(basin)* Amazonia.

**ambassador** [æmˈbæsədəʳ] *n* embajador,-ra.

**amber** [ˈæmbəʳ] *n* ámbar *m*.
▶ *adj* ámbar.

**ambience** [ˈæmbɪəns] *n* ambiente *m*.

**ambiguity** [æmbɪˈgjuːɪtɪ] *n* ambigüedad *f*.
ⓘ *pl* ambiguities.

**ambiguous** [æmˈbɪgjʊəs] *adj* ambiguo,-a.

**ambition** [æmˈbɪʃᵊn] *n* ambición *f*.

**ambitious** [æmˈbɪʃəs] *adj* ambicioso,-a.

**ambulance** [ˈæmbjʊləns] *n* ambulancia.

**ambush** [ˈæmbʊʃ] *n* emboscada.
▶ *vt* poner una emboscada a.

**ameba** [əˈmiːbə] *n* US → amoeba.

**ameliorate** [əˈmiːlɪəreɪt] *vt* mejorarse.
▶ *vi* mejorar.

**amelioration** [əmiːlɪəˈreɪʃᵊn] *n* mejora.

**amen** [ɑːˈmen] *interj* amén.

**amenable** [əˈmiːnəbᵊl] *adj* tratable, bien dispuesto,-a.

**amend** [əˈmend] *vt (law)* enmendar; *(error)* corregir.

**amendment** [əˈmendmənt] *n* enmienda.

**amenities** [əˈmiːnɪtɪz] *n pl* servicios *mpl*, prestaciones *fpl*.

**America** [əˈmerɪkə] *n* América. COMP Central America América Central, Centroamérica. ‖ Latin America América Latina, Latinoamérica. ‖ North America América del Norte, Norteamérica. ‖ South America América del Sur, Sudamérica.

✎ Los estadounidenses suelen referirse a su propio país (Estados Unidos), como America y a ellos, como Americans.

**American** [əˈmerɪkən] *adj* **1** *(gen)* americano,-a. **2** *(from USA)* estadounidense. COMP American football fútbol *m* americano.
▶ *n* **1** *(gen)* americano,-a. **2** *(from USA)* estadounidense *mf*.

⊕ En Estados Unidos, llaman football al fútbol americano (más parecido al rugby que al fútbol europeo) y denominan soccer a lo que nosotros llamamos «fútbol».

**americium** [æməˈrɪsɪəm] *n* americio.

**amethyst** [ˈæməθɪst] *n* amatista.

**amiable** [ˈeɪmɪəbᵊl] *adj* afable, amable.

**amicable** [ˈæmɪkəbᵊl] *adj* amistoso,-a, amigable.

**amid** [əˈmɪd] *prep* en medio de, entre.

**amidst** [əˈmɪdst] *prep* → amid.

**amine** [əˈmiːn] *n* amina.

**amino acid** [æmi:nəʊˈæsɪd] *n* aminoácido.

**amiss** [əˈmɪs] *adv* mal. LOC **to take amiss** tomar a mal.

**ammonia** [əˈməʊnɪ] *n* amoníaco.

**ammunition** [æmjʊˈnɪʃ⁰n] *n* municiones *fpl*.

**amnesia** [æmˈni:zɪə] *n* amnesia.

**amnesty** [ˈæmnəstɪ] *n* amnistía.
ⓘ *pl* amnesties.

**amniotic** [æmnɪˈɒtɪk] *adj* amniótico,-a.

**amoeba** [æˈmi:bə] *n* ameba.
ⓘ *pl* amoebae [əˈmi:bi:].

**amok** [əˈmɒk] LOC **to run amok** volverse loco,-a y causar destrozos.

**among** [əˈmʌŋ] *prep* entre.

**amongst** [əˈmʌŋst] *prep* → among.

**amorphous** [əˈmɔ:fəs] *adj* amorfo,-a.

**amount** [əˈmaʊnt] *n* cantidad *f*.
◆ **to amount to** *vt insep* **1** ascender a. **2** *fig* equivaler a.

**amp** [æmp] *n* (*abbr of* ampere) amperio, ampere *m*.

**ampere** [ˈæmpeə<sup>r</sup>] *n* amperio.

**amphetamine** [æmˈfetəmi:n] *n* anfetamina.

**amphibian** [æmˈfɪbɪən] *n* anfibio.

**amphibious** [æmˈfɪbɪəs] *adj* anfibio,-a.

**amphitheater** [ˈæmfɪθɪətə<sup>r</sup>] *n* US anfiteatro.

**amphitheatre** [ˈæmfɪθɪətə<sup>r</sup>] *n* anfiteatro.

**amphora** [ˈæmfərə] *n* ánfora.
ⓘ *pl* amphoras o amphorae [ˈæmfəri:].

**ample** [ˈæmp⁰l] *adj* **1** (*enough*) bastante. **2** (*plenty*) más que suficiente. **3** (*large, generous*) amplio,-a.

**amplification** [æmplɪfɪˈkeɪʃ⁰n] *n* amplificación *f*.

**amplifier** [ˈæmplɪfaɪə<sup>r</sup>] *n* amplificador *m*.

**amplify** [ˈæmplɪfaɪ] *vt* **1** (*sound*) amplificar. **2** (*statement*) ampliar.
ⓘ *pt & pp* amplified, *ger* amplifying.

**amplitude** [ˈæmplɪtju:d] *n* amplitud *f*.

**amputate** [ˈæmpjuteɪt] *vt* amputar.

**amputation** [æmpjuˈteɪʃ⁰n] *n* amputación *f*.

**amuck** [əˈmʌk] *adv* → amok.

**amulet** [ˈæmjʊlət] *n* amuleto.

**amuse** [əˈmju:z] *vt* entretener, divertir.

**amusement** [əˈmju:zmənt] *n* **1** (*enjoyment*) diversión *f*, entretenimiento. **2** (*pastime*) pasatiempo. COMP **amusement arcade** salón *m* de juegos. ▌ **amusement park** parque *m* de atracciones.

**amusing** [əˈmju:zɪŋ] *adj* entretenido,-a, divertido,-a.

**an** [ən, æn] *indef art* **1** un, una. **2** (*per*) por.

✎ Se usa delante de las palabras que empiezan con sonido vocálico. Consulta también **a**.

**anabolism** [əˈnæbəlɪz⁰m] *n* anabolismo.

**anachronistic** [ænəˈkrɒnɪk] *adj* anacrónico,-a.

**anaconda** [ænəˈkɒndə] *n* anaconda.

**anaemia** [əˈni:mɪə] *n* anemia.

**anaemic** [əˈni:mɪk] *adj* anémico,-a.

**anaerobic** [æneəˈrəʊbɪk] *adj* anaerobio,-a.

**anaesthesia** [ænəsˈθi:zɪə] *n* anestesia.

**anaesthetic** [ænəsˈθetɪk] *adj* anestésico,-a.
▶ *n* anestésico.

**anaesthetise** [əˈni:sθətaɪz] *vt* → anaesthetize.

**anaesthetize** [əˈni:sθətaɪz] *vt* anestesiar.

**anagram** [ˈænəgræm] *n* anagrama *m*.

**anal** [ˈeɪn⁰l] *adj* anal.

**analgesic** [ænəlˈdʒi:zɪk] *adj* analgésico,-a.
▶ *n* analgésico.

**analog** [ˈænəlɒg] *adj-n* US → analogue.

**analogue** [ˈænəlɒg] *adj* analógico,-a.
▶ *n* análogo.

**analogy** [əˈnælədʒɪ] *n* analogía, semejanza.
ⓘ *pl* analogies.

**analyse** [ˈænəlaɪz] *vt* analizar.

**analysis** [əˈnælɪsɪs] *n* análisis *m*.
ⓘ *pl* analyses [əˈnælɪsi:z].

**analyst** [ˈænəlɪst] *n* analista *mf*.

**anarchism** [ˈænəkɪz⁰m] *n* anarquismo.

**anarchist** [ˈænəkɪst] *n* anarquista *mf*.

**anarchy** [ˈænəkɪ] *n* anarquía.
ⓘ *pl* anarchies.

**anatomy** [ə'nætəmɪ] *n* anatomía.
ⓘ *pl* anatomies.

**ancestor** ['ænsəstə'] *n* antepasado.

**anchor** ['æŋkə'] *n* ancla.
▶ *vt* **1** *(ship)* anclar. **2** *(make secure)* sujetar.

**anchovy** ['æntʃəvɪ] *n* *(salted)* anchoa; *(fresh)* boquerón *m*.
ⓘ *pl* anchovies.

**ancient** ['eɪnʃ°nt] *adj* **1** antiguo,-a; *(monument)* histórico,-a. **2** *fam* viejísimo,-a. COMP **ancient history** historia antigua.

✎ Ancient no se emplea en el sentido de 'anterior' con el que a menudo se usa «antiguo» en español *(mi antiguo jefe)*. La palabra inglesa para este sentido de «antiguo» es *former (my former boss)*.

**and** [ænd, *unstressed* ənd] *conj* **1** y; *(before i- and* hi-) e: *black and white* blanco y negro; *opinions and ideas* opiniones e ideas. **2** *(with infinitives)*: *go and look for it* ve a buscarlo; *wait and see what happens* espera a ver lo que pasa. **3** *(expressing repetition, increase)*: *it rained and rained* no paró de llover. **4** *(with numbers)*: *a hundred and twenty* ciento veinte; *two thousand and eighty four* dos mil ochenta y cuatro. **5** *(in sums)* más: *four and six are ten* cuatro más seis son diez.

**Andes** ['ændiːz] *n pl* **the Andes** los Andes *mpl*.

**Andorra** [æn'dɔːrə] *n* Andorra.

**Andorran** [æn'dɔːrən] *adj* andorrano,-a.
▶ *n* andorrano,-a.

**android** ['ændrɔɪd] *n* androide *m*.

**anecdote** ['ænɪkdəʊt] *n* anécdota.

**anemia** [ə'niːmɪə] *n US* → **anaemia**.

**anemic** [ə'niːmɪk] *adj US* → **anaemic**.

**anemometer** [ænɪ'mɒmɪtə'] *n* anemómetro.

**anemone** [ə'nemənɪ] *n BOT* anémona.

**anesthesia** [ænəs'θiːzɪə] *n* → **anaesthesia**.

**anesthetic** [ænəs'θetɪk] *adj-n* → **anaesthetic**.

**anesthetize** [ə'niːsθətaɪz] *vt* → **anaesthetize**.

**angel** ['eɪndʒ°l] *n* ángel *m*.

**anger** ['æŋgə'] *n* cólera, ira, furia.
▶ *vt* encolerizar, enojar, enfurecer.

**angina** [æn'dʒaɪnə] [also angina pectoris ] *n* angina de pecho.

✖ Angina no significa 'anginas', que se traduce por sore throat.

**angiosperm** ['ændʒɪəspɜːm] *n* angiosperma.

**angle¹** ['æŋg°l] *n* ángulo.

**angle²** ['æŋg°l] *vi* pescar con caña.

**anglepoise lamp** ['æŋg°lpɔɪzlæmp] *n* flexo.

**angler** ['ændlə'] *n* pescador,-a.

**Anglican** ['æŋglɪkən] *adj* anglicano,-a.
▶ *n* anglicano,-a.

**angling** ['æŋglɪŋ] *n* pesca con caña.

**Anglo-Saxon** [æŋgləʊ'sæks°n] *adj* anglosajón,-ona.
▶ *n* **1** *(person)* anglosajón,-ona. **2** *(language)* anglosajón *m*.

**Angola** [æn'gəʊlə] *n* Angola.

**Angolan** [æn'gəʊlən] *adj* angoleño,-a.
▶ *n* angoleño,-a.

**angry** ['æŋgrɪ] *adj* enojado,-a, enfadado,-a.
ⓘ *comp* angrier, *superl* angriest.

**angstrom** ['æŋgstrəm] *n* ángstrom *m*.

**anguish** ['æŋgwɪʃ] *n* angustia.

**angular** ['æŋgjʊlə'] *adj* angular.

**anhydride** [æn'haɪdraɪd] *n* anhídrido.

**animal** ['ænɪm°l] *adj* animal.
▶ *n* animal *m*.

**animate** [ *(adj)* 'ænɪmət; *(vb)* 'ænɪmeɪt]] *adj* animado,-a, vivo,-a.
▶ *vt* **1** animar. **2** *fig* estimular.

**animation** [ænɪ'meɪʃ°n] *n* **1** animación *f*. **2** *(life)* vida, marcha.

**animator** ['ænɪmeɪtə'] *n* animador,-ra.

**animism** ['ænɪmɪz°m] *n* animismo.

**anion** ['ænaɪən] *n* anión *m*.

**anise** ['ænɪs] *n* *(plant)* anís *m*.

**ankle** ['æŋk°l] *n* tobillo.

**annelid** ['ænəlɪd] *n* anélido.

**annexe** ['ænəks] *n* anexo, anejo.

**annihilate** [ə'naɪəleɪt] *vt* aniquilar.

**anniversary** [ænɪ'vɜːsərɪ] *n* aniversario.
ⓘ *pl* anniversaries.

**announce** [əˈnauns] *vt* anunciar.

**announcement** [əˈnaunsmənt] *n* anuncio.

**announcer** [əˈnaunsəʳ] *n (on TV, radio)* presentador,-ra, locutor,-ra.

**annoy** [əˈnɔɪ] *vt* molestar, fastidiar.

**annoying** [əˈnɔɪɪŋ] *adj* molesto,-a.

**annual** [ˈænjuəl] *adj* anual.

**annul** [əˈnʌl] *vt* anular.
ⓘ *pt & pp* annulled, *ger* annulling.

**annular** [ˈænjʊləʳ] *adj* anular.

**anode** [ˈænəʊd] *n* ánodo.

**anomaly** [əˈnɒməlɪ] *n* anomalía.
ⓘ *pl* anomalies.

**anonymous** [əˈnɒnɪməs] *adj* anónimo,-a.

**anopheles** [əˈnɒfəliːz] *n* anofeles *m*.

**anorak** [ˈænəræk] *n* anorak *m*.

**anorexia** [ænəˈreksɪə] *n* anorexia.

**another** [əˈnʌðəʳ] *adj* otro,-a.
▶ *pron* otro,-a.

**answer** [ˈɑːnsəʳ] *n* respuesta, contestación *f*.
▶ *vt & vi* responder, contestar.
◆ **to answer back** *vt sep & vi* replicar.
◆ **to answer for** *vt insep* **1** *(guarantee)* responder por, garantizar. **2** *(accept responsibility)* responder de.

**answering machine** [ˈɑːnsərɪŋməʃiːn] *n* contestador *m* automático.

**answerphone** [ˈɑːnsəfəʊn] *n* contestador *m* automático.

**ant** [ænt] *n* hormiga. COMP **ant hill** hormiguero.

**Antarctic** [æntˈɑːktɪk] *adj* antártico,-a.
▶ *n* **the Antarctic** la Antártida. COMP **Antarctic Circle** Círculo polar antártico.

**Antarctica** [æntˈɑːktɪkə] *n* Antártida.

**anteater** [ˈæntiːtəʳ] *n* oso hormiguero.

**antecedent** [æntɪˈsiːdⁿt] *n* antecedente *n*.

**antediluvian** [æntɪdɪˈluːvɪən] *adj* antediluviano,-a.

**antenatal** [æntɪˈneɪtⁿl] *adj* prenatal.

**antenna** [ænˈtenə] *n* **1** [*pl* antennae [ænˈteniː]] *(of insect)* antena. **2** [*pl* antennas] *(aerial)* antena.

**anterior** [ænˈtɪərɪəʳ] *adj* anterior.

**anthem** [ˈænθəm] *n* motete *m*.

**anther** [ˈænθəʳ] *n* antera.

**anthology** [ænˈθɒlədʒɪ] *n* antología.
ⓘ *pl* anthologies.

**anthracite** [ˈænθrəsaɪt] *n* antracita.

**anthropology** [ænθrəˈpɒlədʒɪ] *n* antropología.

**antibiotic** [æntɪbaɪˈɒtɪk] *adj* antibiótico,-a.
▶ *n* antibiótico.

**antibody** [ˈæntɪbɒdɪ] *n* anticuerpo.
ⓘ *pl* antibodies.

**anticipate** [ænˈtɪsɪpeɪt] *vt* **1** *(expect)* esperar. **2** *(get ahead of)* adelantarse a. **3** *(foresee)* anticiparse a, prever.

**anticipation** [æntɪsɪˈpeɪⁿn] *n* **1** *(expectation)* expectación *f*. **2** *(foresight)* previsión *f*.

**anticline** [ˈæntɪklaɪn] *n* anticlinal *m*.

**anticlockwise** [æntɪˈklɒkwaɪz] *adj* en el sentido contrario a las agujas del reloj.

**anticyclone** [æntɪˈsaɪkləun] *n* anticiclón *m*.

**antidote** [ˈæntɪdəut] *n* antídoto.

**antifreeze** [ˈæntɪfriːz] *n* anticongelante *m*.

**antigen** [ˈæntɪdʒen] *n* antígeno.

**Antilles** [ænˈtɪliːz] *n pl* Antillas *fpl*.

**antimony** [ˈæntɪmənɪ] *n* antimonio.

**antipodes** [ænˈtɪpədiːz] *n pl* antípodas *fpl*.

**antipyretic** [æntɪpaɪˈretɪk] *n* antipirético.

**antique** [ænˈtiːk] *adj* antiguo,-a. COMP **antique shop** tienda de antigüedades.
▶ *n* antigüedad *f*.

**antiquity** [ænˈtɪkwɪtɪ] *n* antigüedad *f*.
ⓘ *pl* antiquities.

**antiseptic** [æntɪˈseptɪk] *adj* antiséptico,-a.
▶ *n* antiséptico.

**antiviral** [æntɪˈvaɪrⁿl] *adj* MED antivirus.

**antivirus** [æntɪˈvaɪrəs] *adj* INFORM antivirus.

**antlers** [ˈæntləʳ] *n pl* cornamenta *f sing*.

**antonym** [ˈæntənɪm] *n* antónimo.

**anus** [ˈeɪnəs] *n* ano.

**anvil** [ˈænvɪl] *n* yunque *m*.

**anxiety** [ænˈzaɪətɪ] *n* ansiedad *f*.
ⓘ *pl* anxieties.

**anxious** [ˈæŋkʃəs] *adj* **1** *(worried)* preo-cupado,-a (**about**, por). **2** *(desirous)* ansioso,-a.

**any** [ˈenɪ] *adj* **1** *(in questions)* algún,-una: *are there any biscuits left?* ¿queda alguna galleta? **2** *(negative)* ningún,-una: *he hasn't bought any milk/biscuits* no ha com-prado leche/galletas; *without any difficul-ty* sin ninguna dificultad. **3** *(no matter which)* cualquier,-ra: *any old rag will do* cualquier trapo sirve.

▶ *pron* **1** *(in questions)* alguno,-a: *there are foxes round here, have you seen any?* hay zorros por aquí, ¿has visto alguno? **2** *(negative)* ninguno,-a: *they're very cheap, but I haven't sold any* son muy baratos, pero no he vendido ninguno. **3** *(no mat-ter which)* cualquiera: *any of these books will do* cualquiera de estos libros sirve.

▶ *adv no suele traducirse*: *I don't work there any more* ya no trabajo allí; *do you want any more?* ¿quieres más?.

✎ En preguntas y frases negativas, con los sustantivos contables en singular no se usa *any* sino *a* o *an*.

**anybody** [ˈenɪbɒdɪ] *pron* **1** *(in questions)* alguien: *has anybody seen my car?* ¿ha visto alguien mi coche? **2** *(negative)* na-die: *there isn't anybody in the room* no hay nadie en la sala. **3** *(no matter who)* cual-quiera: *anybody would tell you the same* cualquiera te diría lo mismo.

**anyhow** [ˈenɪhaʊ] *adv* **1** → **anyway**. **2** *(carelessly)* de cualquier forma, de cualquier manera.

**anyone** [ˈenɪwʌn] *pron* → **anybody**.

**anyplace** [ˈenɪpleɪs] *adv* US → **anywhere**.

**anything** [ˈenɪθɪŋ] *pron* **1** *(in questions)* algo, alguna cosa: *is there anything left?* ¿queda algo? **2** *(negative)* nada: *there isn't anything left* no queda nada. **3** *(no matter what)* cualquier cosa: *anything will do* cualquier cosa sirve; *they can cost anything from £5 to £5,000* el precio va desde cinco libras a cinco mil.

**anyway** [ˈenɪweɪ] *adv* **1** *(in any case)* de todas formas, de todos modos. **2** *(in conversation)* bueno, bueno pues, to-tal, en cualquier caso: *anyway, as I was saying, …* bueno pues, como te decía, …

**anywhere** [ˈenɪweəʳ] *adv* **1** *(in questions - situation)* en algún sitio, en alguna parte; *(- direction)* a algún sitio, a algu-na parte: *have you seen my keys anywhere?* ¿has visto mis llaves en alguna parte?; *are you going anywhere this weekend?* ¿vas a algún sitio el fin de semana? **2** *(negative - situation)* en ningún sitio, en ningu-na parte; *(- direction)* a ningún sitio, a ninguna parte: *I can't find him anywhere* no lo encuentro en ninguna parte; *we're not going anywhere* no vamos a ningún sitio. **3** *(no matter where - situation)* donde sea, en cualquier sitio; *(- direction)* a donde sea, a cualquier sitio: *I'd live anywhere as long as it's with you* viviría en cualquier sitio mientras sea contigo; *she'd travel anywhere to see Bruce* viajaría a cualquier sitio para ver a Bruce.

**aorta** [erˈɔːtə] *n* aorta.

**apart** [əˈpɑːt] *adv* **1** *(not together)* separado,-a; *(distant)* alejado,-a. **2** *(in pieces)* en piezas. ⎣LOC⎦ **apart from** apar-te de. ‖ **to fall apart** deshacerse. ‖ **to tell apart** distinguir.

**apartheid** [əˈpɑːthaɪt] *n* apartheid *m*.

**apartment** [əˈpɑːtmənt] *n* piso, aparta-mento. ⎣COMP⎦ **apartment block / apart-ment building** bloque *m* de pisos.

**apathetic** [æpəˈθetɪk] *adj* apático,-a.

**apathy** [ˈæpəθɪ] *n* apatía.

**ape** [eɪp] *n* simio.

▶ *vt* imitar.

**Apennines** [ˈæpənaɪnz] *n* **the Apen-nines** los (montes) Apeninos *mpl*.

**aperitif** [əperɪˈtiːf] *n* aperitivo.

**aperture** [ˈæpətjəʳ] *n* abertura.

✘ Aperture no significa 'apertura (de una tienda)', que se traduce por opening.

**apex** [ˈeɪpeks] *n* ápice *m*; *(of triangle)* vér-tice *m*.

ⓘ *pl* apexes o apices.

**apiculture** [ˈeɪpɪkʌltʃəʳ] *n* apicultura.

**apiece** [əˈpiːs] *adv* cada uno,-a: *she gave us three apiece* nos dio tres a cada uno.

**apocalypse** [əˈpɒkəlɪps] *n* apocalipsis *m*.

**apogee** [ˈæpədʒiː] *n* apogeo.

**apologise** [əˈpɒlədʒaɪz] *vi* → apologize.

**apologize** [əˈpɒlədʒaɪz] *vi* disculparse, pedir perdón.

**apology** [əˈpɒlədʒɪ] *n* **1** *(for mistake)* disculpa. **2** *fml (of beliefs)* apología.
ⓘ *pl* apologies.

**apoplexy** [ˈæpəpleksɪ] *n* apoplejía.
ⓘ *pl* apoplexies.

**apophthegm** [ˈæpəθem] *n* apotema.

**apostle** [əˈpɒsl] *n* apóstol *m*.

**apostrophe** [əˈpɒstrəfɪ] *n* apóstrofo.

**apothegm** [ˈæpəθem] *vt* → apophthegm.

**appal** [əˈpɔːl] *vt* horrorizar.
ⓘ *pt & pp* appalled, *ger* appalling.

**Appalachians** [æpəˈleɪ⁽ə⁾ns] *n* the Appalachians los (montes) Apalaches *mpl*.

**appall** [əˈpɔːl] *vt* US → appal.

**appalling** [əˈpɔːlɪŋ] *adj* **1** *(horrific)* horroroso,-a. **2** *(bad)* malísimo,-a.

**apparatus** [æpəˈreɪtəs] *n* **1** *(equipment)* aparatos *mpl*; *(piece of equipment)* aparato. **2** *(structure)* aparato.

**apparent** [əˈpærənt] *adj* **1** *(obvious)* evidente. **2** *(seeming)* aparente.

**apparently** [əˈpærəntlɪ] *adv* **1** *(obviously)* evidentemente. **2** *(seemingly)* aparentemente.

**appeal** [əˈpiːl] *n* **1** *(request)* ruego, llamamiento; *(plea)* súplica. **2** *(attraction)* atractivo. **3** JUR apelación *f*.
▶ *vi* **1** *(request)* pedir, solicitar; *(plead)* suplicar. **2** *(attract)* atraer: *it doesn't appeal to me* no me atrae. **3** JUR apelar (against, -), recurrir (against, -).

**appealing** [əˈpiːlɪŋ] *adj* **1** *(moving)* suplicante. **2** *(attractive)* atractivo,-a.

**appear** [əˈpɪər] *vi* **1** *(become visible)* aparecer. **2** *(before a court, etc)* comparecer (before, ante). **3** *(seem)* parecer.

**appearance** [əˈpɪərəns] *n* **1** *(becoming visible)* aparición *f*. **2** *(before a court, etc)* comparecencia. **3** *(look)* apariencia.

**appendices** [əˈpendɪsiːz] *n pl* → appendix.

**appendicitis** [əpendɪˈsaɪtɪs] *n* apendicitis *f*.

**appendix** [əˈpendɪks] *n* **1** [*pl* appendices] *(in book)* apéndice *m*. **2** [*pl* appendixes] MED apéndice *m*.

**appetite** [ˈæpɪtaɪt] *n* apetito.

**appetizer** [ˈæpɪtaɪzəʳ] *n* aperitivo.

**appetizing** [ˈæpɪtaɪzɪŋ] *adj* apetitoso,-a.

**applaud** [əˈplɔːd] *vi* *(clap)* aplaudir.
▶ *vt* **1** *(clap)* aplaudir. **2** *(praise)* alabar.

**applause** [əˈplɔːz] *n* aplauso.

**apple** [ˈæpl] *n* manzana. COMP **apple pie** tarta de manzana. ‖ **apple tree** manzano. ‖ **the Big Apple** Nueva York.

**applet** [ˈæplət] *n* COMPUT applet *m*.

**appliance** [əˈplaɪəns] *n* **1** *(device)* aparato. **2** *(fire engine)* coche *m* de bomberos.

**applicable** [ˈæplɪkəbᵊl] *adj* aplicable.

**applicant** [ˈæplɪkənt] *n* *(for job)* candidato,-a, solicitante *mf*.

**application** [æplɪˈkeɪʃᵊn] *n* **1** *(for job)* solicitud *f*. **2** *(of ointment, theory, etc)* aplicación *f*. **3** *(effort)* diligencia.

**apply** [əˈplaɪ] *vt* aplicar.
▶ *vi* **1** *(be true)* aplicarse, ser aplicable. **2** *(for job)* solicitar.
ⓘ *pt & pp* applied, *ger* applying.

**appoint** [əˈpɔɪnt] *vt* **1** *(person for job)* nombrar. **2** *(day, date, etc)* fijar, señalar.

**appointment** [əˈpɔɪntmənt] *n* **1** *(meeting - with lawyer, etc)* cita; *(- with hairdresser, dentist, doctor)* hora. **2** *(person for job)* nombramiento.

**apposition** [æpəˈzɪʃᵊn] *n* aposición *f*.

**appraisal** [əˈpreɪzᵊl] *n* valoración *f*, evaluación *f*.

**appraise** [əˈpreɪz] *vt* valorar, evaluar.

**appreciate** [əˈpriːʃɪeɪt] *vt* **1** *(be thankful for)* agradecer. **2** *(understand)* entender, comprender. **3** *(value)* valorar, apreciar.
▶ *vi* revalorizarse, valorizarse.

**appreciation** [əpriːʃɪˈeɪʃᵊn] *n* **1** *(thanks)* agradecimiento, gratitud *f*. **2** *(understanding)* comprensión *f*. **3** *(appraisal)* evaluación *f*. **4** *(increase in value)* apreciación *f*, aumento en valor.

**apprehend** [æprɪˈhend] *vt* **1** *(arrest)* detener, capturar. **2** *(understand)* comprender.

**apprehension** [æprɪˈhenʃᵊn] *n* **1** *(arrest)* detención *f*, captura. **2** *(fear)* aprensión *f*, temor *m*, recelo.

**apprehensive** [æprɪˈhensɪv] *adj* *(fearful)* aprensivo,-a.

**apprentice** [ə'prentɪs] *n* aprendiz,-za.

**approach** [ə'prəutʃ] *n* **1** *(coming near)* aproximación *f*, acercamiento; *(arrival)* llegada. **2** *(way in)* acceso, entrada. **3** *(to problem)* enfoque *m*.
▶ *vi* *(come near)* acercarse, aproximarse.
▶ *vt* **1** *(come near)* acercarse a, aproximarse a. **2** *(tackle - problem)* enfocar, abordar; *(- person)* dirigirse a. COMP **approach road** vía de acceso.

**appropriate** [ə'prəuprɪət] *adj* apropiado,-a, adecuado,-a, indicado,-a.

**approval** [ə'pruːvəl] *n* aprobación *f*.
LOC **on approval** a prueba.

**approve** [ə'pruːv] *vt* aprobar.

> ❌ To approve no significa 'aprobar (un examen)', que se traduce por to pass.

**approximate** [*(adj)* ə'prɒksɪmət; *(vb)* ə'prɒksɪmeɪt] *adj* aproximado,-a.
▶ *vi* aproximarse (**to**, a).

**apricot** ['eɪprɪkɒt] *n* *(fruit)* albaricoque *m*. COMP **apricot tree** albaricoquero.

**April** ['eɪprɪl] *n* abril *m*. COMP **April Fool's Day** el día 1 de abril (≈ día de los Santos Inocentes).

> ✎ Para ejemplos de uso, consulta May.

**apron** ['eɪprən] *n* **1** *(garment - domestic)* delantal *m*; *(- workman's)* mandil *m*. **2** *(at airport)* pista de estacionamiento.

**apse** [æps] *n* ábside *m*.

**apt** [æpt] *adj* **1** *(suitable)* apropiado,-a; *(remark)* acertado,-a. **2** *(liable to)* propenso,-a.

**APT** ['eɪ'piː'tiː] *abbr* GB (Advanced Passenger Train) ≈ AVE *m*.

**aptitude** ['æptɪtjuːd] *n* aptitud *f*.

**aquarium** [ə'kweərɪəm] *n* acuario.
ⓘ *pl* aquaria o aquariums.

**Aquarius** [ə'kweərɪəs] *n* Acuario.

**aquatic** [ə'kwætɪk] *adj* acuático,-a.

**aqueduct** ['ækwɪdʌkt] *n* acueducto.

**aquifer** ['ækwɪfər] *n* acuífero.

**Arab** ['ærəb] *adj* árabe.
▶ *n* *(person)* árabe *mf*.

**Arabia** [ə'reɪbɪə] *n* Arabia.

**Arabian** [ə'reɪbɪən] *adj* árabe, arábigo,-a.
▶ *n* árabe *mf*. COMP **Arabian Peninsula** Península Arábiga. ▎**Arabian Sea** Mar *m* Arábigo.

**Arabic** ['ærəbɪk] *adj* Árabe.
▶ *n* *(language)* Árabe *m*. COMP **arabic numerals** números *mpl* arábigos.

**arachnid** [ə'ræknɪd] *n* arácnido.

**aragonite** [ə'rægənaɪt] *n* aragonito.

**arbitrary** ['ɑːbɪtrərɪ] *adj* arbitrario,-a.

**arbitrate** ['ɑːbɪtreɪt] *vt & vi* arbitrar.

**arc** [ɑːk] *n* arco.

**arcade** [ɑː'keɪd] *n* pasaje *m*. COMP **shopping arcade** galerías *fpl* comerciales.

**arch** [ɑːtʃ] *n* **1** *(gen)* arco; *(vault)* bóveda. **2** *(of foot)* empeine *m*.
▶ *vt* **1** *(back, eyebrows)* arquear, enarcar. **2** *(vault)* abovedar.

**archaeological** [ɑːkɪə'lɒdʒɪkəl] *adj* arqueológico,-a.

**archaeologist** [ɑːkɪ'ɒlədʒɪst] *n* arqueólogo,-a.

**archaeology** [ɑːkɪ'ɒlədʒɪ] *n* arqueología.

**archaic** [ɑː'keɪɪk] *adj* arcaico,-a.

**archaism** ['ɑːkeɪɪzəm] *n* arcaísmo.

**archangel** [ɑː'keɪndʒəl] *n* arcángel *m*.

**archbishop** [ɑːtʃ'bɪʃəp] *n* arzobispo.

**archeological** [ɑːkɪə'lɒdʒɪkəl] *adj* US → archaeological.

**archeologist** [ɑːkɪ'ɒlədʒɪst] *n* US → archaeologist.

**archeology** [ɑːkɪ'ɒlədʒɪ] *n* US → archaeology.

**archer** ['ɑːtʃər] *n* arquero.

**archery** ['ɑːtʃərɪ] *n* tiro con arco.

**archipelago** [ɑːkɪ'pelɪgəu] *n* archipiélago.
ⓘ *pl* archipelagos o archipelagoes.

**architect** ['ɑːkɪtekt] *n* arquitecto,-a.

**architecture** ['ɑːkɪtektʃər] *n* arquitectura.

**archives** ['ɑːkaɪvz] *n pl* archivo *m sing*.

**archivist** ['ɑːkaɪvɪst] *n* archivero,-a.

**Arctic** ['ɑːktɪk] *adj* ártico,-a.
▶ *n* the Arctic el Ártico. COMP the Arctic Circle el Círculo Polar Ártico. ▎the Arctic Ocean el océano Ártico.

**ardor** ['ɑːdər] *n* US → ardour.

**ardour** ['ɑːdər] *n* ardor *m*.

**arduous** ['ɑ:djʊəs] *adj* arduo,-a.

**are** [ɑ:ʳ, əʳ] *pres* → be.

**area** ['eərɪə] *n* **1** *(extent)* área, superficie *f*. **2** *(region)* región *f*; *(of town)* zona. **3** *(field)* campo.

**arena** [əˈriːnə] *n* **1** *(stadium)* estadio. **2** *(in amphitheatre)* arena. **3** *fig* ámbito.

☒ Arena no significa 'arena', que se traduce por sand.

**aren't** [ɑ:nt] *contr* → are not.

**Argentina** [ɑ:dʒənˈtiːnə] *n* Argentina.

**Argentine** ['ɑ:dʒəntaɪn] *adj* argentino,-a.
▶ *n* the Argentine Argentina.

**Argentinian** [ɑ:dʒənˈtɪnɪən] *adj* argentino,-a.
▶ *n* argentino,-a.

**argon** ['ɑ:gɒn] *n* argón *m*.

**argot** ['ɑ:gəʊ] *n* jerga.

**argue** ['ɑ:gjʊ:] *vi* **1** *(quarrel)* discutir (with, con). **2** *(reason)* argüir, argumentar, sostener.

**argument** ['ɑ:gjʊmənt] *n* **1** *(quarrel)* discusión *f*, disputa. **2** *(reasoning)* argumento. [LOC] **to have an argument with SB** discutir con ALGN.

**arid** ['ærɪd] *adj* árido,-a.

**aridity** [əˈrɪdɪtɪ] *n* aridez *f*.

**Aries** ['eəriːz] *n* Aries.

**arise** [əˈraɪz] *vi* surgir (from, de).
ⓘ *pt* arose [əˈrəʊz], *pp* arisen [əˈrɪzᵊn].

**aristocracy** [ærɪsˈtɒkrəsɪ] *n* aristocracia.
ⓘ *pl* aristocracies.

**aristocrat** ['ærɪstəkræt, US əˈrɪstəkræt] *n* aristócrata *mf*.

**arithmetic** [*(n)* əˈrɪθmətɪk; *(adj)* ærɪθ-ˈmetɪk] *n* aritmética.
▶ *adj* aritmético,-a.

**arithmetical** [ærɪθˈmetɪkᵊl] *adj* aritmético,-a. [COMP] **arithmetical progression** progresión *f* aritmética.

**ark** [ɑ:k] *n* arca.

**arm** [ɑ:m] *n* **1** ANAT brazo. **2** *(of coat, etc)* manga. **3** *(of chair)* brazo.
▶ *vt* armar.
▶ *n pl* arms *(weapons)* armas *fpl*.

**armadillo** [ɑ:məˈdɪləʊ] *n* armadillo.
ⓘ *pl* armadillos.

**armchair** [ɑ:mˈtʃeəʳ] *n* sillón *m*.

**Armenia** [ɑ:ˈmiːnɪə] *n* Armenia.

**Armenian** [ɑ:ˈmiːnɪən] *adj* armenio,-a.
▶ *n* **1** *(person)* armenio,-a. **2** *(language)* armenio.

**armistice** ['ɑ:mɪstɪs] *n* armisticio.

**armor** ['ɑ:məʳ] *n* US → armour.

**armour** ['ɑ:məʳ] *n* **1** armadura. **2** *(on vehicle)* blindaje *m*.

**armpit** ['ɑ:mpɪt] *n* sobaco, axila.

**armrest** ['ɑ:mrest] *n* brazo.

**army** ['ɑ:mɪ] *n* ejército.
ⓘ *pl* armies.

**aroma** [əˈrəʊmə] *n* aroma *m*.

**aromatic** [ærəˈmætɪk] *adj* aromático,-a.

**arose** [əˈrəʊz] *pt* → arise.

**around** [əˈraʊnd] *adv* **1** *(near, in the area)* alrededor: *is there anybody around?* ¿hay alguien cerca? **2** *(from place to place)*: *they cycle around together* van juntos en bicicleta. **3** *(approximately)* alrededor de: *it costs around £5,000* cuesta unas cinco mil libras.
▶ *prep* **1** *(near)*: *there aren't many shops around here* hay pocas tiendas por aquí. **2** *(all over)*: *there were clothes around the room* había ropa por toda la habitación. **3** *(in a circle or curve)* alrededor de: *he put his arms around her* la rodeó con los brazos. **4** *(at)* sobre, cerca de: *they came around seven* vinieron sobre las siete.

**arouse** [əˈraʊz] *vt* **1** *(awake)* despertar. **2** *(sexually)* excitar.

**arrange** [əˈreɪndʒ] *vt* **1** *(gen)* arreglar; *(furniture, etc)* colocar, ordenar. **2** *(plan)* planear, organizar. **3** *(marriage)* concertar.

**arrangement** [əˈreɪndʒmənt] *n* **1** *(agreement)* acuerdo, arreglo. **2** MUS arreglo.
▶ *n pl* arrangements *(plans)* planes *mpl*; *(preparations)* preparativos *mpl*.

**array** [əˈreɪ] *n* **1** *(selection)* surtido. **2** *(series)* serie *f*. **3** COMPUT matriz *f*.

**arrears** [əˈrɪəz] *n pl* atrasos *mpl*.

**arrest** [əˈrest] *n* arresto, detención *f*.

**arrival** [əˈraɪvᵊl] *n* llegada.

**arrive** [əˈraɪv] *vi* llegar.

**arrogant** ['ærəgənt] *adj* arrogante.

**arrow** ['ærəʊ] *n* flecha.

**arsenal** ['ɑ:sənᵊl] *n* arsenal *m*.

**arsenic** ['ɑːsᵊnɪk] n arsénico.

**arson** ['ɑːsᵊn] n incendio provocado.

**arsonist** ['ɑːsənɪst] n pirómano,-a.

**art** [ɑːt] n (painting, etc) arte m.
▸ n pl arts (branch of knowledge) letras fpl.
COMP art deco art deco m. ▮ art gallery 1 (museum) pinacoteca. 2 (commercial) galería de arte. ▮ art nouveau art nouveau m, modernismo.

**artefact** ['ɑːtɪfækt] n artefacto.

**arterial** [ɑːˈtɪərɪəl] adj 1 ANAT arterial. 2 (road) principal, importante.

**artery** ['ɑːtərɪ] n ANAT arteria.
① pl arteries.

**artesian well** [ɑːtiːzɪənˈwel] n pozo artesiano.

**arthritis** [ɑːˈθraɪtəs] n artritis f.

**arthropod** ['ɑːθrəpɒd] n artrópodo.

**artichoke** ['ɑːtɪtʃəʊk] n alcachofa.

**article** ['ɑːtɪkᵊl] n artículo. COMP article of clothing prenda de vestir. ▮ definite article artículo determinado. ▮ indefinite article artículo indeterminado. ▮ leading article editorial m.

**articulate** [(adj) ɑːˈtɪkjʊlət; (vb) ɑːˈtɪkjʊleɪt] adj (person) que se expresa con facilidad; (speech) claro,-a.
▸ vt 1 articular. 2 (pronounce) pronunciar.

**articulated** [ɑːˈtɪkjʊleɪtɪd] adj articulado,-a. COMP articulated lorry camión m articulado.

**articulation** [ɑːtɪkjʊˈleɪʃᵊn] n articulación f.

**artifact** ['ɑːtɪfækt] n US → artefact.

**artificial** [ɑːtɪˈfɪʃᵊl] adj artificial.

**artillery** [ɑːˈtɪlərɪ] n artillería.

**artisan** ['ɑːtɪzæn] n artesano,-a.

**artist** ['ɑːtɪst] n 1 artista mf. 2 (painter) pintor,-ra.

**artistic** [ɑːˈtɪstɪk] adj artístico,-a.

**artwork** ['ɑːtwɜːk] n ilustraciones fpl.

**as** [æz, unstressed əz] prep como: he works as a clerk trabaja de oficinista.
▸ adv (in comparatives): eat as much as you like come tanto como quieras.
▸ conj 1 (while) mientras; (when) cuando: as he painted, he whistled mientras pintaba, silbaba; as he grew older he became more tolerant a medida que iba envejeciendo se volvía más tolerante. 2 (because) ya que, como: as there were no seats we had to stand como no había asientos tuvimos que estar de pie. 3 (although) aunque: tall as he was, he still couldn't reach the shelf aunque era alto no podía alcanzar el estante.
LOC as far as hasta. ▮ as far as I know que yo sepa. ▮ as for en cuanto a. ▮ as if como si. ▮ as long as mientras. ▮ as of desde. ▮ as soon as tan pronto como. ▮ as though como si. ▮ as well as además de. ▮ as yet hasta ahora, de momento.

**asbestos** [æsˈbestəs] n amianto.

**ascend** [əˈsend] vt ascender, subir a.
▸ vi ascender, subir.

**ascendancy** [əˈsendənsɪ] n predominio, supremacía.
① pl ascendancies.

**ascension** [əˈsenʃᵊn] n ascensión f.

**ascent** [əˈsent] n 1 (slope) subida. 2 (climb) ascensión f.

**ascribe** [əsˈkraɪb] vt atribuir (to, a).

**aseptic** [əˈseptɪk] adj aséptico,-a.

**asexual** [eɪˈseksjʊəl] adj asexual.

**ash¹** [æʃ] n ceniza. COMP Ash Wednesday miércoles m de ceniza.
① pl ashes.

**ash²** [æʃ] n (tree) fresno.
① pl ashes.

**ashamed** [əˈʃeɪmd] adj avergonzado,-a.

**ashbin** ['æʃbɪn] n US cubo de la basura.

**ashtray** ['æʃtreɪ] n cenicero.

**Asia** ['eɪʃə, 'eɪʒə] n Asia.

**Asian** ['eɪʃᵊn, 'eɪʒᵊn] adj asiático,-a.
▸ n asiático,-a.

**Asiatic** [eɪʃɪˈætɪk, eɪʒɪˈætɪk] adj asiático,-a.

**aside** [əˈsaɪd] adv al lado, a un lado.
LOC aside from aparte de.

**ask** [ɑːsk] vt 1 (inquire) preguntar. 2 (request) pedir: we have to ask permission debemos pedir permiso. 3 (invite) invitar, convidar: he asked her to go out with him la invitó a salir con él.
◆ to ask after vt insep preguntar por.
◆ to ask for vt insep (thing) pedir; (person) preguntar por.
◆ to ask out vt sep invitar a salir.

**asleep** [ə'sli:p] *adj (person)* dormido,-a. ⎣LOC⎦ **to fall asleep** dormirse.

**asparagus** [æs'pærəgəs] *n (plant)* espárrago; *(shoots)* espárragos *mpl*. ⎣COMP⎦ **an asparagus tip** una punta de espárrago.

**aspect** ['æspekt] *n* **1** *(gen)* aspecto. **2** *(of building)* orientación *f*.

**asphalt** ['æsfælt] *n* asfalto.

**asphyxia** [əs'fɪksɪə] *n* asfixia.

**asphyxiate** [əs'fɪksɪeɪt] *vt* asfixiar.

**aspic** ['æspɪk] *n* CULIN gelatina.

**aspire** [əs'paɪəʳ] *vi* aspirar (**to**, a).

**aspirin®** ['æspɪrɪn] *n* aspirina®.

**ass** [æs] *n (animal)* burro,-a, asno,-a; *(person)* burro,-a, imbécil *mf*.

**assail** [ə'seɪl] *vt* **1** *(physically)* atacar. **2** *(doubts, problems, etc)* asaltar.

**assailant** [ə'seɪlənt] *n* atacante *mf*.

**assassin** [ə'sæsɪn] *n* asesino,-a.

**assassinate** [ə'sæsɪneɪt] *vt* asesinar.

**assassination** [əsæsɪ'neɪ(ə)n] *n* asesinato.

✎ Assassin, assassinate y assassination sólo se emplean cuando se trata del asesinato de un personaje importante. En los demás casos, se usan las palabras murderer, murder.

**assault** [ə'sɔ:lt] *n* **1** MIL asalto, ataque *m*. **2** JUR agresión *f*.
▶ *vt* JUR *(gen)* agredir; *(sexually)* abusar de.

**assemble** [ə'sembªl] *vt* **1** *(bring together)* reunir. **2** *(put together)* montar. **3** COMPUT ensamblar.
▶ *vi* reunirse.

**assembly** [ə'semblɪ] *n* **1** *(meeting)* reunión *f*. **2** *(group, body)* asamblea. **3** TECH *(putting together)* montaje *m*; *(unit)* unidad *f*. ⎣COMP⎦ **assembly hall** sala de actos. ⎣ **assembly line** cadena de montaje.
ⓘ *pl* assemblies.

**assent** [ə'sent] *n* asentimiento.
▶ *vi* asentir (**to**, a).

**assert** [ə'sɜ:t] *vt* aseverar, afirmar.

**assertion** [ə'sɜ:(ə)n] *n* afirmación *f*.

**assess** [ə'ses] *vt* **1** *(value)* tasar, valorar. **2** *(calculate)* calcular. **3** *fig* evaluar.

**assessment** [ə'sesmənt] *n* **1** *(valuation)* tasación *f*, valoración *f*. **2** *(calculation)* cálculo. **3** *fig* evaluación *f*.

**asset** ['æset] *n* calidad *f* positiva, ventaja.
▶ *n pl* **assets** COMM activo *m sing*.

**assign** [ə'saɪn] *vt* asignar, atribuir.

**assignment** [ə'saɪnmənt] *n* **1** *(mission)* misión *f*. **2** *(task)* tarea.

**assimilate** [ə'sɪmɪleɪt] *vt* asimilar.
▶ *vi* asimilarse.

**assist** [ə'sɪst] *vt & vi* ayudar.

☒ To assist no significa 'asistir, ir', que se traducen por to attend, to go.

**assistance** [ə'sɪstəns] *n* ayuda.

**assistant** [ə'sɪstənt] *n* **1** *(helper)* ayudante *mf*. **2** *(in shop)* dependiente *mf*.

**associate** [*(adj-n)* ə'səʊʃɪət; *(vb)* ə'səʊʃɪeɪt] *adj* **1** *(company)* asociado,-a. **2** *(member)* correspondiente.
▶ *n (partner)* socio,-a.
▶ *vt* asociar.
▶ *vi* relacionarse (**with**, con).

**association** [əsəʊsɪ'eɪ(ə)n] *n* asociación *f*.

**associative** [ə'səʊʃɪətɪv] *adj* asociativo,-a.

**associativity** [əsəʊʃɪə'tɪvɪtɪ] *n* propiedad *f* asociativa.

**assonance** ['æsənəns] *n* asonancia.

**assorted** [ə'sɔ:tɪd] *adj* surtido,-a, variado,-a.

**assortment** [ə'sɔ:tmənt] *n* surtido, variedad *f*.

**assume** [ə'sju:m] *vt* **1** *(suppose)* suponer. **2** *(power, responsibility)* tomar, asumir. **3** *(attitude, expression)* adoptar.

**assurance** [ə'ʃʊərəns] *n* **1** *(guarantee)* garantía. **2** *(confidence)* seguridad *f*, confianza. **3** *(insurance)* seguro. ⎣COMP⎦ **life assurance** seguro de vida.

**assure** [ə'ʃʊəʳ] *vt* asegurar.

**asterisk** ['æstərɪsk] *n* asterisco.

**asteroid** ['æstərɔɪd] *n* asteroide *m*.

**asthma** ['æsmə] *n* asma.

**astonish** [əs'tɒnɪʃ] *vt* asombrar, sorprender.

**astonishing** [əsˈtɒnɪʃɪŋ] *adj* asombroso,-a, sorprendente.

**astonishment** [əsˈtɒnɪʃmənt] *n* asombro.

**astound** [əsˈtaʊnd] *vt* asombrar.

**astral** [ˈæstrəl] *adj* astral.

**astray** [əˈstreɪ] *adv* extraviado,-a. LOC **to go astray 1** *(err)* descarriarse. **2** *(be lost)* extraviarse.

**astrolabe** [ˈæstrəleɪb] *n* astrolabio.

**astrologer** [əsˈtrɒlədʒəʳ] *n* astrólogo,-a.

**astrology** [əsˈtrɒlədʒɪ] *n* astrología.

**astronaut** [ˈæstrənɔːt] *n* astronauta *mf*.

**astronomer** [əsˈtrɒnəməʳ] *n* astrónomo,-a.

**astronomical** [æstrəˈnɒmɪkəl] *n* astronómico,-a.

**astronomy** [əsˈtrɒnəmɪ] *n* astronomía.

**astute** [əsˈtjuːt] *adj* astuto,-a, sagaz.

**asylum** [əˈsaɪləm] *n* **1** *(political)* asilo, refugio. **2** *(for mentally ill)* manicomio.

**asymmetric** [æsɪˈmetrɪk] *adj* asimétrico,-a. COMP **asymmetric bars** barras *fpl* asimétricas.

**at¹** [æt, *unstressed* ət] *prep* **1** *(position)* en, a: *at home/school/work/church* en casa/el colegio/el trabajo/la iglesia; *she's at the dentist's* ha ido al dentista. **2** *(time)* a: *at two o'clock* a las dos; *at night* por la noche. **3** *(direction, violence)* a, contra: *she's always shouting at them* no para de gritarles. **4** *(with numbers)* a: *at 50 miles an hour* a 50 millas la hora,.. **5** *(state)*: *he's at breakfast/lunch/dinner* está desayunando/comiendo/cenando; *men at work* hombres trabajando. **6** *(ability)*: *he's good at French* va bien en francés. LOC **at first** al principio. ‖ **at last!** ¡por fin! ‖ **at least** por lo menos. ‖ **at most** como máximo. ‖ **at the moment** ahora.

**at²** [æt] *n* *(Internet)* arroba

**ate** [et, eɪt] *pt* → **eat**.

**atheism** [ˈeɪθɪɪzəm] *n* ateísmo.

**atheist** [ˈeɪθɪɪst] *n* ateo,-a.

**Athens** [ˈæθənz] *n* Atenas.

**athlete** [ˈæθliːt] *n* atleta *mf*.

**athletic** [æθˈletɪk] *adj* **1** atlético,-a. **2** *(sporty)* deportista.

**athletics** [æθˈletɪks] *n* atletismo.

**Atlantic** [ətˈlæntɪk] *adj* atlántico,-a. COMP **the Atlantic (Ocean)** el (océano) Atlántico.

**atlas** [ˈætləs] *n* atlas *m inv*.

**atmosphere** [ˈætməsfɪəʳ] *n* **1** atmósfera. **2** *(ambience)* ambiente *m*, atmósfera.

**atmospheric** [ætməsˈferɪk] *adj* atmosférico,-a. COMP **atmospheric pressure** presión *f* atmosférica.

**atoll** [ˈætɒl] *n* atolón *m*.

**atom** [ˈætəm] *n* átomo. COMP **atom bomb** bomba atómica.

**atomic** [əˈtɒmɪk] *adj* atómico,-a.

**atrium** [ˈeɪtriːəm] *n* atrio.
  ① *pl* **atriums** o **atria** [ˈeɪtrɪə].

**atrocity** [əˈtrɒsɪtɪ] *n* atrocidad *f*.
  ① *pl* **atrocities**.

**attach** [əˈtætʃ] *vt* **1** *(fasten)* sujetar. **2** *(tie)* atar. **3** *(stick)* pegar. **4** *(document)* adjuntar.

**attachment** [əˈtætʃmənt] *n* **1** TECH accesorio. **2** *(to an e-mail)* anexo. **3** *(fondness)* cariño, apego.

**attack** [əˈtæk] *n* *(gen)* ataque *m*; *(terrorist)* atentado.
  ▶ *vt* **1** atacar.

**attain** [əˈteɪn] *vt* **1** *(goal)* lograr. **2** *(rank, age)* llegar a.

**attempt** [əˈtempt] *n* *(try)* intento, tentativa.
  ▶ *vt* intentar.

**attend** [əˈtend] *vt* **1** *(be present at)* asistir a: *all her friends attended the funeral* todos sus amigos asistieron al funeral. **2** *(care for)* atender, cuidar.
  ▶ *vi* asistir.
  ◆ **to attend to** *vt insep* **1** ocuparse de. **2** *(in shop)* despachar.

**attendance** [əˈtendəns] *n* **1** *(being present)* asistencia. **2** *(people present)* asistentes *mpl*.

**attendant** [əˈtendənt] *n* *(in car park, museum)* vigilante *mf*; *(in cinema)* acomodador,-ra.

**attention** [əˈtenʃən] *n* atención *f*.
  ▶ *interj* **attention!** MIL ¡firmes! LOC **to pay attention** prestar atención.

**attentive** [əˈtentɪv] *adj* **1** *(paying attention)* atento,-a. **2** *(helpful)* solícito,-a.

**attic** ['ætɪk] *n* desván *m*.

**attire** [ə'taɪəʳ] *n* atuendo, atavío.

**attitude** ['ætɪtjuːd] *n* **1** *(way of thinking)* actitud *f*. **2** *(pose)* postura, pose *f*.

**attorney** [ə'tɜːnɪ] *n* US abogado,-a. COMP **Attorney General** GB ≈ Ministro,-a de Justicia.

**attract** [ə'trækt] *vt* atraer.

**attraction** [ə'trækʃ°n] *n* atracción *f*.

**attractive** [ə'træktɪv] *adj* **1** *(person)* atractivo,-a. **2** *(offer)* interesante, tentador,-ra.

**attribute** [*(n)* æ'trɪbjuːt *(vb)* ə'trɪbjuːt] *n* atributo.
  ▶ *vt* atribuir.

**attribution** [ætrɪ'bjuːʃ°n] *n* atribución *f*.

**attributive** [ə'trɪbjutɪv] *adj* atributivo,-a.

**atypical** [eɪ'tɪpɪk°l] *adj* atípico,-a.

**aubergine** ['əʊbəʒiːn] *n* berenjena.

**auction** ['ɔːkʃ°n] *n* subasta.
  ▶ *vt* subastar.

**audacious** [ɔː'deɪʃəs] *adj* **1** *(daring)* audaz, intrépido,-a. **2** *(rude)* descarado,-a, osado,-a.

**audible** ['ɔːdɪb°l] *adj* audible.

**audience** ['ɔːdɪəns] *n* *(spectators)* público; *(radio)* audiencia; *(television)* telespectadores *mpl*.

**audio-visual** [ɔːdɪəʊ'vɪzjuəl] *adj* audiovisual.

**audit** ['ɔːdɪt] *n* auditoría.
  ▶ *vt* auditar.

**audition** [ɔː'dɪʃ°n] *n* prueba.

**auditor** ['ɔːdɪtəʳ] *n* auditor,-ra.

**auditorium** [ɔːdɪ'tɔːrɪəm] *n* auditorio.
  ⓘ *pl* **auditoriums** o **auditoria** [ɔːdɪ'tɔːrɪə].

**augment** [ɔːg'ment] *vt fml* aumentar.
  ▶ *vi fml* aumentarse.

**augmentative** [ɔːg'mentətɪv] *adj* aumentativo,-a.

**August** ['ɔːgəst] *n* agosto.

✎ Para ejemplos de uso, consulta **May**.

**aunt** [ɑːnt] *n* tía.

**auntie** ['ɑːntɪ] *n fam* tía, tita.

**au pair** [əʊ'peəʳ] *n* au pair *f*. COMP **au pair girl** au pair *f*.

**aura** ['ɔːrə] *n* aura.

**auricle** ['ɔrɪk°l] *n* **1** *(of heart)* aurícula. **2** *(of ear)* aurícula, pabellón *m* de la oreja.

**aurora** [ɔ'rɔːrə] *n* aurora. COMP **aurora australis** aurora austral. ▌**aurora borealis** aurora boreal.

**auscultate** ['ɔːskʌlteɪt] *vt* auscultar.

**auscultation** [ɔːskʌl'teɪʃ°n] *n* auscultación *f*.

**austere** [ɒs'tɪəʳ] *adj* austero,-a.

**austerity** [ɒs'terɪtɪ] *n* austeridad *f*.

**Australia** [ɒ'streɪlɪə] *n* Australia.

**Australian** [ɒ'streɪlɪən] *adj* australiano,-a.
  ▶ *n* australiano,-a.

**Austria** ['ɒstrɪə] *n* Austria.

**Austrian** ['ɒstrɪən] *adj* austríaco,-a, austriaco,-a.
  ▶ *n* austríaco,-a, austriaco,-a.

**authentic** [ɔː'θentɪk] *adj* auténtico,-a.

**author** ['ɔːθəʳ] *n* autor,-ra, escritor,-ra.

**authoritarian** [ɔːθɒrɪ'teərɪən] *adj* autoritario,-a.

**authority** [ɔː'θɒrɪtɪ] *n* **1** *(gen)* autoridad *f*. **2** *(permission)* autorización *f*, permiso.
  ⓘ *pl* **authorities**.

**authorisation** [ɔːθəraɪ'zeɪʃ°n] *n* → **authorization**.

**authorise** ['ɔːθəraɪz] *vt* → **authorize**.

**authorization** [ɔːθəraɪ'zeɪʃ°n] *n* autorización *f*.

**authorize** ['ɔːθəraɪz] *vt* autorizar.

**autism** ['ɔːtɪz°m] *n* autismo.

**autistic** [ɔː'tɪstɪk] *adj* autista.

**auto** ['ɔːtəʊ] *n* US *fam* coche *m*.
  ⓘ *pl* **autos**.

**autobiography** [ɔːtəbaɪ'ɒgrəfɪ] *n* autobiografía.
  ⓘ *pl* **autobiographies**.

**autograph** ['ɔːtəgrɑːf] *n* autógrafo.
  ▶ *vt* autografiar.

**automatic** [ɔːtə'mætɪk] *adj* automático,-a. COMP **automatic pilot** piloto automático.

**automation** [ɔːtə'meɪʃ°n] *n* automatización *f*.

**automobile** ['ɔ:təməbi:l] *n* automóvil *m*, coche *m*.

**autonomous** [ɔ:'tɒnəməs] *adj* autónomo,-a.

**autonomy** [ɔ:'tɒnəmɪ] *n* autonomía.
ⓘ *pl* autonomies.

**autopsy** ['ɔ:tɒpsɪ] *n* autopsia.
ⓘ *pl* autopsies.

**autumn** ['ɔ:təm] *n* otoño.

**auxiliary** [ɔ:g'zɪljərɪ] *adj* auxiliar. COMP **auxiliary verb** verbo auxiliar.

**available** [ə'veɪləbəl] *adj* disponible.

**avalanche** ['ævəlɑ:nʃ] *n* 1 alud *m*. 2 *fig* avalancha.

**avarice** ['ævərɪs] *n* avaricia.

**avenge** [ə'vendʒ] *vt* vengar.

**avenue** ['ævənju:] *n* 1 (street) avenida. 2 (means) vía.

**average** ['ævərɪdʒ] *n* promedio, media. LOC **above average** por encima de la media. ‖ **below average** por debajo de la media. ‖ **on average** por término medio.
▶ *adj* 1 medio,-a. 2 (not special) corriente, regular.
▶ *vt* hacer un promedio de: *I average 10 kilometres an hour* hago un promedio de 10 kilómetros por hora.

**aversion** [ə'vɜ:ʃən] *n* aversión *f*.

**avert** [ə'vɜ:t] *vt* (avoid) evitar. LOC **to avert one's eyes** apartar la vista.

**aviary** ['eɪvjərɪ] *n* pajarera.
ⓘ *pl* aviaries.

**aviation** [eɪvɪ'eɪʃən] *n* aviación *f*.

**aviator** ['eɪvɪeɪtə'] *n* aviador,-ra.

**avid** ['ævɪd] *adj* ávido,-a.

**avocado** [ævə'kɑ:dəʊ] [also **avocado pear**] *n* aguacate *m*.
ⓘ *pl* avocados.

**avoid** [ə'vɔɪd] *vt* 1 evitar. 2 (question) eludir. 3 (person) esquivar.

**awake** [ə'weɪk] *adj* despierto,-a.
▶ *vi* 1 despertar. 2 despertarse.
ⓘ *pt* awoke [ə'wəʊk], *pp* awoken [ə'wəʊkən].

**awaken** [ə'weɪkən] *vt-vi* → awake.
ⓘ *pt & pp* awakened.

**award** [ə'wɔ:d] *n* 1 (prize) premio; (medal) condecoración *f*; (trophy) tro-

feo. 2 (grant) beca. 3 (damages) indemnización *f*.
▶ *vt* 1 (prize, grant) otorgar, conceder. 2 (damages) adjudicar.

**aware** [ə'weə'] *adj* 1 consciente. 2 (informed) informado,-a, enterado,-a. LOC **to be aware of** ser consciente de. ‖ **to become aware of** darse cuenta de.

**away** [ə'weɪ] *adv* 1 lejos, fuera, alejándose: *he lives 4 km away* vive a 4 km (de aquí); *the wedding is 6 weeks away* faltan 6 semanas para la boda. 2 (indicating continuity): *they worked away all day* trabajaron todo el día. LOC **to go away** irse, marcharse. ‖ **to put away** guardar. ‖ **to run away** irse corriendo.

**awe** [ɔ:] *n* sobrecogimiento.

**awful** ['ɔ:fʊl] *adj* 1 (shocking) atroz, horrible. 2 *fam* (very bad) fatal, horrible, espantoso,-a.

**awfully** ['ɔ:fʊlɪ] *adv fam* terriblemente.

**awhile** [ə'waɪl] *adv* un rato.

**awkward** ['ɔ:kwəd] *adj* 1 (clumsy - person) torpe; (- expression) poco elegante. 2 (difficult) difícil; (uncooperative) poco cooperativo,-a: *it's an awkward place to get to* es difícil llegar hasta allí. 3 (embarrassing) embarazoso,-a, delicado,-a. 5 (uncomfortable) incómodo,-a.

**awning** ['ɔ:nɪŋ] *n* toldo.

**awoke** [ə'wəʊk] *pt* → awake.

**awoken** [ə'wəʊkən] *pp* → awake.

**ax** [æks] *n US* → axe.

**axe** [æks] *n* hacha.

**axiom** ['æksɪəm] *n* axioma *m*.

**axis** ['æksɪs] *n* eje *m*.

**axle** ['æksəl] *n* eje *m*.

**axon** ['æksən] *n* axón *m*.

**Azerbaijan** [æzəbaɪ'dʒɑ:n] *n* Azerbaiyán *m*.

**Azerbaijani** [æzəbaɪ'dʒɑ:nɪ] *adj* azerbaiyano,-a, azerí.
▶ *n* 1 (person) azerbaiyano,-a, azerí *mf*. 2 (language) azerí *m*, azerbaiyano.

**azimuth** ['æzɪməθ] *n* acimut *m*.

**Aztec** ['æztek] *adj* azteca.
▶ *n* 1 (person) azteca *mf*. 2 (language) azteca *m*.

# B

**B, b** [biː] *n* **1** *(the letter)* B, b *f.* **2** *(musical note)* si *m.* COMP **B road** carretera secundaria.

**babble** [ˈbæbəl] *vi* balbucear.
▸ *vt* farfullar.
▸ *n* murmullo, rumor *m.*

**baboon** [bəˈbuːn] *n* mandril *m,* babuino.

**baby** [ˈbeɪbɪ] *n* **1** bebé *m.* **2** *(of animal)* cría. LOC **to have a baby** dar a luz, tener un niño. COMP **baby carriage** US cochecito de niño. ‖ **baby tooth** diente *m* de leche.
ⓘ *pl* babies.

**baby-sit** [ˈbeɪbɪsɪt] *vi* hacer de canguro, cuidar niños.
ⓘ *pt & pp* baby-sat [ˈbeɪbɪsɪt], *ger* babysitting.

**baby-sitter** [ˈbeɪbɪsɪtəʳ] *n* canguro *mf.*

**baby-walker** [ˈbeɪbɪwɔːkəʳ] *n* andador *m,* tacataca *m,* tacatá *m.*

**bachelor** [ˈbætʃələʳ] *n* soltero. COMP **bachelor flat** piso de soltero.

☒ Bachelor no significa 'bachiller', que no tiene una traducción directa en inglés.

**bacillus** [bəˈsɪləs] *n* bacilo.
ⓘ *pl* bacilli [bəˈsɪlaɪ].

**back** [bæk] *n* **1** *(of person)* espalda. **2** *(of animal, book)* lomo. **3** *(of chair)* respaldo. **4** *(of hand)* dorso. **5** *(sport - player)* defensa *mf; (- position)* defensa.
▸ *adj* trasero,-a, de atrás.
▸ *adv (at the rear)* atrás; *(towards the rear)* hacia atrás. LOC **back to front** al revés.
▸ *vt* **1** *(support)* apoyar, respaldar. **2** *(finance)* financiar.
◆ **to back away** *vi* retirarse.
◆ **to back off** *vi* apartarse.
◆ **to back out** *vi* volverse atrás.

◆ **to back up** *vt sep (support)* apoyar; *(vehicle)* dar marcha atrás a.

✎ Cuando se combina con un verbo, la partícula back da el sentido de contrapartida a la acción normal del verbo. Así, to answer back, to be back, to come back, to give back, to phone back... significan 'contestar', 'estar de vuelta', 'volver', 'devolver', 'volver a llamar'...

**backache** [ˈbækeɪk] *n* dolor *m* de espalda.

**backbone** [ˈbækbəʊn] *n* columna vertebral.

**backbreaking** [ˈbækbreɪkɪŋ] *adj (work)* agotador,-ra.

**backcloth** [ˈbækklɒθ] *n* telón *m* de fondo.

**backdated** [bækˈdeɪtɪd] *adj* con efecto retroactivo.

**backer** [ˈbækəʳ] *n* **1** FIN promotor,-ra. **2** *(guarantor)* fiador,-ra. **3** *(supporter)* partidario,-a.

**backfire** [bækˈfaɪəʳ] *vi* fallar: *our plan backfired* nos salió el tiro por la culata.

**background** [ˈbækgraʊnd] *n* **1** fondo. **2** *fig (origins)* orígenes *mpl,* antecedentes *mpl.* COMP **background knowledge** conocimientos *mpl* previos. ‖ **background music** música de fondo.

**backhand** [ˈbækhænd] *n* revés *m.* COMP **backhand shot** revés *m.*

**backhanded** [bækˈhændɪd] *adj (compliment)* equívoco,-a.

**backhander** [bækˈhændəʳ] *n fam* soborno.

**backing** [ˈbækɪŋ] *n* **1** *(support)* apoyo, respaldo. **2** MUS acompañamiento.

**backlash** [ˈbæklæʃ] *n* reacción *f* violenta y repentina.
ⓘ *pl* backlashes.

**backlog** ['bæklɒg] *n* acumulación *f* de trabajo, trabajos *mpl* pendientes.

**backpack** ['bækpæk] *n* US mochila.
▶ *vi* viajar por un país o continente: *my sister's backpacking around Europe* mi hermana está de viaje por Europa.

**back-seat** ['bæksi:t] *n* asiento trasero.

**backside** [bæk'saɪd] *n fam* trasero.

**backslash** ['bækslæʃ] *n* barra inversa.

**backslide** ['bækslaɪd] *vi* reincidir.
① *pt & pp* backslid ['bækslɪd].

**backstage** [bæk'steɪdʒ] *n* **1** *(area)* bastidores *mpl*. **2** *(dressing-rooms)* camerinos *mpl*.

**backstroke** ['bækstrəʊk] *n* *(swimming)* espalda.

**backtrack** ['bæktræk] *vi* **1** *(retrace one's steps)* desandar lo andado, volverse atrás. **2** *(reverse opinion)* desdecirse.

**backup** ['bækʌp] *n* **1** *(moral support)* apoyo. **2** COMPUT copia de seguridad. COMP **backup file** archivo de seguridad.

**backward** ['bækwəd] *adj* **1** hacia atrás. **2** *(child)* atrasado,-a. **3** *(shy)* tímido,-a.
▶ *adv* → backwards.

**backwards** ['bækwədz] *adv* **1** hacia atrás. **2** *(the wrong way)* al revés: *he always does things backwards* siempre hace las cosas al revés.

**backyard** [bæk'jɑːd] *n* patio de atrás.

**bacon** ['beɪkən] *n* tocino, bacón *m*.

**bacteria** [bæk'tɪərɪə] *n pl* bacterias *fpl*.
① *sing* bacterium.

**bacterium** [bæk'tɪərɪəm] *n* bacteria.
① *pl* bacteria.

**bad** [bæd] *adj* **1** malo,-a; *(before masc noun)* mal: *he made a bad decision* tomó una mala decisión. **2** *(rotten)* podrido,-a. **3** *(serious)* grave: *they had a bad accident* tuvieron un accidente grave. **4** *(naughty)* malo,-a, travieso,-a. **5** *(aches, illnesses)* fuerte, intenso,-a: *he's got a bad headache* tiene un fuerte dolor de cabeza. LOC **to be bad at** *(skill, subject)* ser malo,-a en: *he's bad at English* es malo en inglés. ‖ **to come to a bad end** acabar mal. ‖ **to have a bad leg** tener la pierna lisiada. COMP **bad cheque** cheque *m* sin fondos.
① *comp* worse, *superl* worst.

▶ *adv* mal. LOC **to feel bad** encontrarse mal. ‖ **to look bad 1** *(person)* tener mala cara. **2** *(situation)* pintar mal.
▶ *n* lo malo. LOC **too bad!** ¡mala pata!, ¡qué lástima!

**baddy** ['bædɪ] *n fam* malo,-a de la película.
① *pl* baddies.

**bade** [beɪd] *pt* → bid.

**badge** [bædʒ] *n* **1** insignia, distintivo. **2** *(metallic)* chapa. COMP **lapel badge** pin *m*.

**badger** ['bædʒə'] *n* tejón *m*.

**badly** ['bædlɪ] *adv* **1** mal: *he behaved badly at the party* se portó mal en la fiesta. **2** *(seriously)* gravemente: *he was badly hurt in the bombing* fue gravemente herido en el atentado. **3** *(very much)* mucho,-a: *he badly needs your help* tiene mucha necesidad de tu ayuda.

**bad-mannered** [bæd'mænəd] *adj* maleducado,-a.

**bad-tempered** [bæd'tempəd] *adj* *(permanently)* de mal genio; *(temporarily)* malhumorado,-a, de mal humor.

**baffle** ['bæfəl] *vt* **1** *(perplex)* dejar perplejo,-a, desconcertar. **2** *(frustrate)* frustrar.

**bag** [bæg] *n* **1** *(paper, plastic)* bolsa; *(large)* saco. **2** *(handbag)* bolso. **3** *(for school)* cartera.
▶ *n pl* **bags** *(under eyes)* ojeras *fpl*. LOC **bags of** montones de.

**baggage** ['bægɪdʒ] *n* equipaje *m*.

**baggy** ['bægɪ] *adj* holgado,-a, ancho,-a.
① *comp* baggier, *superl* baggiest.

**bagpipes** ['bægpaɪps] *n pl* gaita *f sing*.

**bail¹** [beɪl] *n* fianza. LOC **to be on bail** estar en libertad bajo fianza.
◆ **to bail out** *vt sep* **1** pagar la fianza a. **2** *fig* sacar de un apuro.

**bail²** [beɪl] *vt* *(water)* achicar.

**bailiff** ['beɪlɪf] *n* *(court officer)* alguacil *m*.

**bait** [beɪt] *n* cebo.
▶ *vt* **1** cebar. **2** *(torment)* atosigar. LOC **to take the bait** picar.

**bake** [beɪk] *vt* cocer (en el horno).
▶ *vi* cocerse.

**baked** [beɪkt] *adj* cocido al horno. COMP **baked apple** manzana al horno. **baked beans** alubias *fpl* guisadas en salsa de tomate. **baked potato** patata asada.

**baker** ['beɪkəʳ] *n (of bread)* panadero,-a; *(of cakes)* pastelero,-a.

**bakery** ['beɪkərɪ] *n (for bread)* panadería; *(for cakes)* pastelería.
ⓘ *pl* bakeries.

**baking** ['beɪkɪŋ] *n* cocción *f.* COMP **baking powder** levadura en polvo. **baking soda** bicarbonato sódico.

**balaclava** [bælə'klɑːvə] *n* pasamontañas *m.*

**balance** ['bæləns] *n* **1** equilibrio. **2** *(scales)* balanza. **3** *(of account, etc)* saldo. **4** *(remainder)* resto.
▶ *vi* **1** mantenerse en equilibrio. **2** FIN cuadrar.

**balanced** ['bælənst] *adj* equilibrado,-a.

**balcony** ['bælkənɪ] *n* **1** balcón *m.* **2** *(in theatre)* anfiteatro; *(gallery)* gallinero.
ⓘ *pl* balconies.

**bald** [bɔːld] *adj* **1** calvo,-a. **2** *(tyre)* desgastado,-a. **3** *(style)* escueto,-a. **4** *(statement)* directo,-a, franco,-a.

**Balearic** [bælɪ'ærɪk] *adj* balear, baleárico,-a. COMP **the Balearic Islands** las (islas) Baleares.

**ball** [bɔːl] *n* **1** *(gen)* pelota; *(football, etc)* balón *m; (golf, billiards)* bola. **2** *(of paper)* bola; *(of wool)* ovillo. **3** *(of eye)* globo ocular. **4** *(dance)* baile *m,* fiesta. LOC **to play ball 1** US *(sport)* jugar a la pelota. **2** *(cooperate)* cooperar, colaborar. COMP **gala ball** baile *m* de etiqueta.

**ballad** ['bæləd] *n* balada.

**ball-and-socket** ['bɔːlən'sɒkɪt] COMP **ball-and-socket joint** articulación *f* de rótula.

**ballast** ['bæləst] *n (boat, balloon)* lastre *m.*

**ballerina** [bælə'riːnə] *n* bailarina.

**ballet** ['bæleɪ] *n* ballet *m.*

**ballistics** [bə'lɪstɪks] *n* balística.

**balloon** [bə'luːn] *n* **1** globo. **2** *(in cartoon)* bocadillo. **3** *(glass)* copa grande.

❎ Balloon no significa 'balón', que se traduce por ball.

**ballot** ['bælət] *n* **1** *(vote)* votación *f.* **2** *(votes recorded)* número de votos escrutados. LOC **to take a ballot on** STH someter algo a votación. COMP **ballot box** urna. **ballot paper** papeleta.

**ballpoint** ['bɔːlpɔɪnt] [también **ballpoint pen**] *n* bolígrafo.

**ballroom** ['bɔːlruːm] *n* sala de baile. COMP **ballroom dancing** baile *m* de salón.

**balm** [bɑːm] *n* bálsamo.

**balmy** ['bɑːmɪ] *adj* **1** *(weather)* suave. **2** *(soothing)* balsámico,-a.
ⓘ *comp* balmier, *superl* balmiest.

**balsam** ['bɔːlsəm] *n* → balm.

**balsamic** [bɔːl'sæmɪk] *adj* balsámico,-a.

**Baltic** ['bɔːltɪk] *adj* báltico,-a. COMP **the Baltic (Sea)** el (mar) Báltico.

**bamboo** [bæm'buː] *n* bambú *m.*

**ban** [bæn] *n* prohibición *f.*
▶ *vt* prohibir.
ⓘ *pt & pp* banned, *ger* banning.

**banal** [bə'nɑːl] *adj* banal, trivial.

**banality** [bə'nælɪtɪ] *n* banalidad *f.*
ⓘ *pl* banalities.

**banana** [bə'nɑːnə] *n* **1** *(fruit)* plátano, banana. **2** *(tree)* bananero, AM banano.

**band** [bænd] *n* **1** *(gen)* banda; *(pop)* conjunto; *(jazz)* orquesta. **2** *(strip)* tira. **3** *(around arm)* brazalete *m.* **4** *(wrapper)* faja. **5** PHYS banda, frecuencia. **7** TECH correa.

**bandage** ['bændɪdʒ] *n* venda, vendaje *m.*
▶ *vt* vendar.
◆ **to bandage up** *vt sep* vendar.

**Band-Aid®** ['bændeɪd] *n* tirita®.

**B and B** ['biː:ən'biː:] *abbr* (bed and breakfast) *casa de huéspedes que ofrece habitación con desayuno incluido.*

🌐 Los B and B son una alternativa por lo general más asequible a los hoteles. Tradicionalmente, estos establecimientos solían estar situados en casas grandes cuyos dueños obtenían así una fuente adicional de ingresos. Hoy en día, el concepto se ha ampliado y hay B and B para todos los gustos y bolsillos.

**bandit** ['bændɪt] *n* bandido,-a.

**bandstand** ['bændstænd] *n* quiosco de música.

**bandwidth** ['bændwɪdθ] *n* ancho de banda.

**bandy** ['bændɪ] *vt* SP *(ball)* pasarse. LOC **to bandy SB's name about** difamar ALGN, hablar mal de ALGN.

ⓘ *pt & pp* bandied, *ger* bandying.

**bandy-legged** ['bændɪlegᵊd] *adj* patizambo,-a.

**bang** [bæŋ] *n* **1** *(blow)* golpe *m*. **2** *(noise)* ruido; *(of gun)* estampido; *(explosion)* estallido; *(of door)* portazo.

▶ *vt* golpear, dar golpes en.

▶ *adv fam* justo: *bang in the middle* justo en medio. LOC **to bang the door** dar un portazo.

▶ *n pl* bangs US flequillo.

**banger** ['bæŋəʳ] *n* **1** *(firework)* petardo. **2** GB *fam (sausage)* salchicha. **3** *fam (car)* tartana, trasto.

**bangle** ['bæŋgəl] *n* brazalete *m*.

**banish** ['bænɪʃ] *vt (expel)* desterrar.

**banishment** ['bænɪʃmənt] *n* destierro, exilio.

**banister** ['bænɪstəʳ] *n* barandilla.

**bank¹** [bæŋk] *n* banco. COMP **bank holiday** GB festivo, día festivo.

▶ *vt (deposit money)* ingresar, depositar.

**bank²** [bæŋk] *n* **1** *(of river)* ribera; *(edge)* orilla: *on the banks of the Manzanares* a orillas del Manzanares. **2** *(mound)* loma; *(embankment)* terraplén *m*.

▶ *vt* **1** *(soil, earth)* amontonar. **2** *(river)* encauzar.

**bankbook** ['bæŋkbʊk] *n* libreta de ahorro, cartilla de ahorro.

**banker** ['bæŋkəʳ] *n* banquero,-a.

**banking** ['bæŋkɪŋ] *n* banca.

**banknote** ['bæŋknəʊt] *n* billete *m* de banco.

**bankruptcy** ['bæŋkrʌptsɪ] *n* quiebra, bancarrota.

ⓘ *pl* bankruptcies.

**banner** ['bænəʳ] *n* **1** *(flag)* bandera. **2** *(placard)* pancarta. **3** *(on web page)* banner *m*, anuncio.

▶ *adj* US excelente, de primera. COMP **banner headlines** grandes titulares *mpl*.

**banns** [bænz] *n pl* amonestaciones *fpl*.

**banquet** ['bæŋkwɪt] *n* banquete *m*.

**banter** ['bæntəʳ] *n* bromas *fpl*, guasa.

▶ *vi* bromear, estar de guasa.

**baptise** [bæp'taɪz] *vt* → baptize.

**baptism** ['bæptɪzəm] *n* bautismo.

**baptize** [bæp'taɪz] *vt* bautizar.

**bar** [bɑːʳ] *n* **1** *(iron, gold)* barra. **2** *(in prison)* barrote *m*. **3** *(soap)* pastilla. **4** *(obstacle)* obstáculo. **5** *(counter)* barra, mostrador *m*. **6** *(room)* bar *m*. **7** *(in court)* tribunal *m*: *the prisoner at the bar* el acusado, la acusada. COMP **bar chart** gráfica de barras.

▶ *vt* **1** *(door)* atrancar; *(road, access)* cortar. **2** *(ban)* prohibir, vedar; *(from a place)* prohibir la entrada. **3** *(prevent)* impedir.

ⓘ *pt & pp* barred, *ger* barring.

▶ *prep* excepto, salvo: *they all came, bar his parents* acudieron todos, excepto sus padres.

▶ *n* **the Bar** JUR el colegio de abogados.

**barbarian** [bɑː'beərɪən] *adj* bárbaro,-a.

▶ *n* bárbaro,-a.

**barbecue** ['bɑːbəkjuː] *n* barbacoa.

▶ *vt* asar a la parrilla.

ⓘ *ger* barbecuing.

**barbed** [bɑːbd] *adj* **1** con púas, punzante. **2** *fig* mordaz, incisivo,-a.

**barber** ['bɑːbəʳ] *n* barbero. COMP **barber's shop** barbería.

**barbiturate** [bɑː'bɪtʃərət] *n* barbitúrico.

**bare** [beəʳ] *adj* **1** *(naked)* desnudo,-a; *(head)* descubierto,-a; *(land)* raso,-a; *(tree, plant)* sin hojas. **3** *(empty)* vacío,-a; *(unfurnished)* sin muebles. **4** *(scant)* escaso,-a. **5** *(worn)* gastado,-a, raído,-a.

▶ *vt* desnudar; *(uncover)* descubrir.

**barefaced** ['beəfeɪst] *adj* descarado,-a.

**barefoot** ['beəfʊt] *adj* descalzo,-a.

▶ *adv* descalzo,-a.

**barely** ['beəlɪ] *adv* apenas.

**bargain** ['bɑːgən] *n* **1** *(agreement)* trato, acuerdo. **2** *(good buy)* ganga.

▶ *vi* **1** *(negotiate)* negociar. **2** *(haggle)* regatear. COMP **bargain offer** oferta especial. ▮ **bargain price** precio de oferta, precio de saldo.

**barge** [bɑːdʒ] *n* gabarra, barcaza.

**B**

**baritone** ['bærɪtəʊn] *n* barítono.

**barium** ['beərɪʌm] *n* bario.

**bark¹** [bɑːk] *n* **1** *(of dog)* ladrido. **2** *(cough)* tos *f* fuerte.
▶ *vi* ladrar.

**bark²** [bɑːk] *n* *(of tree)* corteza.

**barley** ['bɑːlɪ] *n* cebada.

**barmaid** ['bɑːmeɪd] *n* camarera.

**barman** ['bɑːmən] *n* camarero, barman *m*.
ⓘ *pl* barmen ['bɑːmen].

**barn** [bɑːn] *n* *(for grain)* granero.

**barnacle** ['bɑːnəkəl] *n* percebe *m*.

**barnyard** ['bɑːnjɑːd] *n* corral *m*.

**barometer** [bəˈrɒmɪtəʳ] *n* barómetro.

**baron** ['bærən] *n* barón *m*.

**baroness** ['bærənəs] *n* baronesa.

**baroque** [bəˈrɒk] *adj* barroco,-a.
▶ *n* barroco.

**barrack** ['bærək] *vt* *(jeer)* abuchear.

**barracks** ['bærəks] *n pl* cuartel *m*.

✎ Puede considerarse singular o plural: *where is/are the barracks* ¿dónde está el cuartel.

**barrage** ['bærɑːʒ] *n* presa, embalse *m*.

**barrel** ['bærəl] *n* **1** *(of beer)* barril *m*; *(of wine)* tonel *m*, cuba. **2** *(of gun)* cañón *m*. **3** *(of pen)* depósito. **4** TECH tambor *m*.

**barren** ['bærən] *adj* **1** *(land, woman)* estéril. **2** *(meagre)* escaso,-a.

**barricade** [bærɪˈkeɪd] *n* barricada.
▶ *vt* poner barricadas en.

**barrier** ['bærɪəʳ] *n* barrera. COMP **barrier reef** banco de coral, arrecife *m*.

**barrister** ['bærɪstəʳ] *n* abogado,-a *(capacitado,-a para actuar en tribunales superiores)*.

**barrow** ['bærəʊ] *n* *(wheelbarrow)* carretilla; *(for carrying goods)* carro.

**barstool** ['bɑːstuːl] *n* taburete *m* de bar.

**bartender** ['bɑːtendəʳ] *n* US camarero, barman *m*.

**barter** ['bɑːtəʳ] *n* trueque *m*.
▶ *vt* trocar.

**basalt** ['bæsɔːlt] *n* basalto.

**base¹** [beɪs] *n* **1** *(gen)* base *f*. **2** ARCH *(of column)* basa, base *f*. **3** *(of word)* raíz *f*.
▶ *vt* basar.

**base²** [beɪs] *adj* **1** bajo,-a, vil. **2** *(metal)* común, de baja ley.

**baseball** ['beɪsbɔːl] *n* béisbol *m*.

**baseline** ['beɪslaɪn] *n* **1** SP *(tennis)* línea de saque. **2** *(diagram)* línea cero. **3** ART punto de fuga.

**basement** ['beɪsmənt] *n* sótano.

**bash** [bæʃ] *vt fam* golpear, aporrear.
▶ *n* **1** *fam (blow)* golpe *m*. **2** *fam (try)* intento.

**bashful** ['bæʃfʊl] *adj* vergonzoso,-a, tímido,-a, modesto,-a.

**basic** ['beɪsɪk] *adj* **1** básico,-a. **2** *(elementary)* elemental, para principiantes.

**basil** ['bæzəl] *n* BOT albahaca.

**basilica** [bəˈzɪlɪkə] *n* basílica.

**basin** ['beɪsən] *n* **1** *(bowl)* cuenco; *(washbowl)* palangana. **2** *(washbasin)* lavabo. **3** GEOG cuenca.

**basis** ['beɪsɪs] *n* base *f*, fundamento. LOC **on the basis of ...** **1** *(according to)* según. **2** *(in accordance with)* de acuerdo con. **2** *(starting from)* a partir de. **2** *(because of)* por, a causa de.
ⓘ *pl* bases ['beɪsiːz].

✎ En ocasiones, basis puede traducirse al español mediante un adverbio: *on a temporary/regular/weekly basis* temporalmente/regularmente/semanalmente.

**bask** [bɑːsk] *vi* tumbarse al sol.

**basket** ['bɑːskɪt] *n* **1** cesta, cesto. **2** *(basketball)* canasta, cesta. **3** *(of balloon)* barquilla.

**basketball** ['bɑːskɪtbɔːl] *n* baloncesto.

**Basque** [bɑːsk] *adj* vasco,-a.
▶ *n* **1** *(person)* vasco,-a. **2** *(language)* vasco, euskera *m*.

**bas-relief** [bæsrɪˈliːf] *n* bajorrelieve *m*.

**bass¹** [beɪs] *n* **1** MUS *(singer)* bajo. **2** MUS *(notes)* graves *mpl*. **3** MUS *(guitar)* bajo.
▶ *adj* MUS bajo,-a.

**bass²** [bæs] *n* *(fish)* róbalo, lubina; *(freshwater)* perca.

**bassoon** [bəˈsuːn] *n* fagot *m*.

**bastard** ['bɑːstəd] *adj & n* bastardo,-a.

**baste** [beɪst] *vt* CULIN rociar, bañar.

**bastion** ['bæstɪən] *n* baluarte *m*.

**bat¹** [bæt] *n* ZOOL murciélago.

**bat²** [bæt] *n* SP bate *m*; *(table tennis)* pala.
▸ *vi* batear.
① *pt & pp* batted, *ger* batting.
**batch** [bætʃ] *n (gen)* lote *m*, remesa; *(of bread, etc)* hornada.
**bath** [bɑːθ] *n* **1** baño. **2** *(tub)* bañera.
▸ *vi* bañarse.
▸ *n pl* **baths** piscina *f sing* municipal.
LOC **to have a bath / take a bath** bañarse. ‖ **to run a bath** preparar un baño.
**bathe** [beɪð] *vt* **1** MED *(cut, wound)* lavar. **2** *(eyes)* bañarse. **3** *fig (with light)* bañar.
▸ *vi (in sea)* bañarse.

⊕ La diferencia entre los verbos bath y bathe es que este último se emplea para referirse a un baño en el mar, un río o un lago, es decir, sin un objetivo higiénico.

**bather** [ˈbeɪðəʳ] *n* bañista *mf*.
**bathing** [ˈbeɪðɪŋ] *n* baño. LOC **"No bathing"** «Prohibido bañarse». COMP **bathing costume** traje *m* de baño. ‖ **bathing suit** traje *m* de baño.
**bathrobe** [ˈbɑːθrəʊb] *n* albornoz *m*.
**bathroom** [ˈbɑːθruːm] *n* cuarto de baño.
**bathtub** [ˈbɑːθtʌb] *n* US bañera.
**bathyscaph** [ˈbæθɪskæf] *n* batiscafo.
**baton** [ˈbætən, ˈbætɒn] *n* **1** *(truncheon)* porra. **2** MUS batuta. **3** SP testigo.
**batrachian** [bəˈtreɪkjən] *adj* batracio,-a.
▸ *n* batracio.
**battalion** [bəˈtæljən] *n* batallón *m*.
**batter¹** [ˈbætəʳ] *n* CULIN rebozado.
**batter²** [ˈbætəʳ] *vt (person)* golpear, apalear; *(bruise)* magullar; *(object)* maltratar, estropear.
**batter³** [ˈbætəʳ] *n* SP *(baseball, cricket)* bateador,-ra.
**battery** [ˈbætərɪ] *n* **1** ELEC *(wet)* batería; *(dry)* pila. **2** MIL *(of artillery)* batería. **3** *(series)* batería.
① *pl* batteries.
**battle** [ˈbætəl] *n* batalla.
▸ *vi* pelearse, batirse.
**battlefield** [ˈbætəlfiːld] *n* campo de batalla.
**battleship** [ˈbætəlʃɪp] *n* acorazado.
**bauble** [ˈbɔːbəl] *n* **1** *(trinket)* baratija. **2** *(Christmas decoration)* bola de Navidad.

**bawl** [bɔːl] *vi* chillar, gritar.
**bay¹** [beɪ] *n* GEOG bahía; *(large)* golfo. COMP **Bay of Biscay** golfo de Vizcaya.
**bay²** [beɪ] *n (tree)* laurel *m*.
**bay³** [beɪ] *vi (howl)* aullar.
**bay⁴** [beɪ] *n* **1** ARCH *(recess)* hueco, nicho. **2** *(in factory)* nave *f*.
**bayonet** [ˈbeɪənət] *n* MIL bayoneta.
**bazaar** [bəˈzɑːʳ] *n* bazar *m*.
**BBC** [ˈbiːˈbiːˈsiː] *abbr* (British Broadcasting Corporation) compañía británica de radiodifusión; *(abbreviation)* BBC *f*.
**BC** [ˈbiːˈsiː] *abbr* (before Christ) antes de Cristo.
**be** [biː] *vi* **1** *(permanent or essential characteristic)* ser: *she's clever* es inteligente. **2** *(nationality, origin)* ser: *John's English* John es inglés. **3** *(occupation)* ser: *we are both teachers* los dos somos profesores. **4** *(ownership, authorship)* ser: *it's my pencil* es mi lápiz. **5** *(composition)* ser: *this cupboard is oak* este armario es de roble. **6** *(use)* ser: *this product is for tiles* este producto es para baldosas. **7** *(location)* estar: *Whitby is on the coast* Whitby está en la costa. **8** *(temporary state)* estar: *your supper's cold* tu cena está fría; *how are you?* ¿cómo estás? **9** *(age)* tener: *Philip is 22* Philip tiene 22 años. **10** *(price)* costar, valer: *a single ticket is £9.50* un billete de ida cuesta 9,50 libras. **11** tener: *he's hot/cold* tiene calor/frío; *he's right* tiene razón. LOC **to be about to + inf** estar para + inf, estar a punto de + inf: *the train is about to arrive* el tren está a punto de llegar.
▸ *aux* **1** be + *pres part (action in progress or near future)* estar: *it is raining* está lloviendo; *the train is coming* viene el tren; *I am going on Thursday* iré el jueves. **2** to be + *pp (passive)* ser: *she was arrested at the border* fue detenida en la frontera, la detuvieron en la frontera. **3** be + *to* + *inf (future)*: *the King is to visit Egypt* el Rey visitará Egipto. LOC **there is / there are** hay.
◆ **to be after** *vi* querer, estar buscando: *what are you after?* ¿qué estás buscando?
◆ **to be off** *vi (leave)* salir, marcharse; *(be stale, bad)* estar pasado,-a.
◆ **to be in** *vi* **1** *(at home)* estar en casa. **2** *(in fashion)* estar de moda.

◆ **to be out** *vi (away)* no estar, estar fuera: *John's out at the moment* John no está en estos momentos.

◆ **to be away** *vi* estar fuera.

◆ **to be back** *vi* estar de vuelta, haber vuelto.

◆ **to be over** *vi* haber acabado.

ⓘ *pres 1ª pers* am, *2ª pers sing y todas las del pl* are, *3ª pers sing* is; *pt 1ª y 3ª pers sing* was, *2ª pers sing y todas del pl* were; *pp* been.

**beach** [biːtʃ] *n* playa.

ⓘ *pl* beaches.

**beacon** ['biːkən] *n* **1** *(fire)* almenara. **2** *(light)* baliza. **3** *(lighthouse)* faro.

**bead** [biːd] *n* **1** *(on rosary, necklace)* cuenta; *(glass)* abalorio. **2** *(of liquid)* gota.

**beak** [biːk] *n* pico.

**beaker** ['biːkəʳ] *n* **1** taza alta. **2** *(for measuring, playing dice)* cubilete *m*. **3** CHEM vaso de precipitación.

**beam** [biːm] *n* **1** *(wooden)* viga. **2** *(of light)* rayo. **3** *(width of ship)* manga. **4** *(smile)* sonrisa radiante. **5** PHYS haz *m*.
► *vi* **1** *(shine)* brillar. **2** *(smile)* sonreír.
► *vt* irradiar, emitir. [COMP] **electron beam** haz *m* de electrones.

**bean** [biːn] *n* **1** *(vegetable)* alubia, judía, haba. **2** *(of coffee)* grano.

**beansprout** ['biːnspraʊt] *n* brote *m* de soja.

**bear¹** [beəʳ] *n* ZOOL oso. [COMP] **bear cub** ZOOL osezno. ❙ **grizzly bear** oso pardo. ❙ **the Great Bear** la Osa Mayor. ❙ **the Little Bear** la Osa Menor.

**bear²** [beəʳ] *vt* **1** *(gen)* llevar. **2** *(show signs of)* mostrar, revelar. **3** *(weight)* soportar, aguantar; *(responsibility, cost)* asumir. **4** *(fruit)* producir. **5** FIN *(interest)* devengar.
ⓘ *pt* bore [bɔːʳ], *pp* borne [bɔːⁿ].

**bearable** ['beərəbəl] *adj* soportable, llevadero,-a.

**beard** [bɪəd] *n* **1** *(on face)* barba. **2** *(of corn)* arista, raspa.

**bearded** ['bɪədɪd] *adj* barbudo,-a.

**bearing** ['beərɪŋ] *n* **1** *(posture)* porte *m*. **2** *(relevance)* relación *f*. **3** *(importance)* trascendencia. **4** TECH cojinete *m*. **5** ARCH soporte *m*, columna. **6** MAR rumbo, orientación *f*.

**bearskin** ['beəskɪn] *n (hat)* birretina.

**beast** [biːst] *n* bestia, animal *m*.

**beastly** ['biːstlɪ] *adj* **1** bestial. **2** *(unpleasant)* antipático,-a. **3** *sl (damn)* dichoso,-a, maldito,-a.
ⓘ *comp* beastlier, *superl* beastliest.

**beat** [biːt] *n* **1** *(of heart)* latido. **2** *(noise)* golpe *m*, ruido; *(of rain)* tamborileo; *(of wings)* aleteo. **3** MUS ritmo. **4** *(of policeman)* ronda.
► *adj fam* agotado,-a, rendido,-a.
► *vt* **1** *(hit)* golpear; *(metals)* martillear; *(person)* azotar; *(drum)* tocar. **2** CULIN batir. **3** *(defeat)* vencer, derrotar; *(in competition)* ganar.
► *vi* **1** *(heart)* latir. **2** *(wings)* batir.

◆ **to beat down** *vt sep* **1** *(door)* derribar, echar abajo. **2** *(price)* conseguir un precio más bajo.

◆ **to beat up** *vt sep* dar una paliza a.
ⓘ *pt* beat, *pp* beaten ['biːtən].

**beater** ['biːtəʳ] *n* **1** CULIN batidora. **2** *(in hunting)* ojeador,-ra.

**beating** ['biːtɪŋ] *n* **1** *(thrashing)* paliza. **2** *(defeat)* derrota. **3** *(of heart)* latidos *mpl*.

**beautician** [bjuːˈtɪʃən] *n* esteticista *mf*.

**beautiful** ['bjuːtɪfʊl] *adj* **1** *(person, object, place)* hermoso,-a, bonito,-a, precioso,-a; *(person)* guapo,-a. **2** *(wonderful)* maravilloso,-a, magnífico,-a. **3** *(delicious)* delicioso,-a.

**beauty** ['bjuːtɪ] *n* belleza. [COMP] **beauty spot 1** *(on face)* lunar *m*. **2** *(place)* lugar *m* pintoresco.
ⓘ *pl* beauties.

**beaver** ['biːvəʳ] *n* castor *m*.

**became** [bɪˈkeɪm] *pt* → become.

**because** [bɪˈkɒz] *conj* porque.
► *prep* **because of** a causa de: *they were late because of the snow* llegaron tarde a causa de la nieve.

**become** [bɪˈkʌm] *vi* **1** *(with noun)* convertirse en, hacerse, llegar a ser: *to become a doctor/teacher* hacerse médico,-a/maestro,-a; *to become friends* hacerse amigos. **2** *(change into)* convertirse en, transformarse en: *chrysalids become butterflies* las crisálidas se transforman en mariposas. **3** *(irrevocable state)* volverse; *(temporary state)* ponerse; *(involuntary state)* quedarse: *to become mad* volverse loco,-a, *to become fat* engordar; *to become sad* ponerse triste.

ⓘ *pt* became [bɪˈkeɪm], *pp* become.

**becoming** [bɪˈkʌmɪŋ] *adj* **1** *(dress, etc)* que sienta bien, favorecedor,-ra. **2** *(behaviour, language)* apropiado,-a.

**bed** [bed] *n* **1** cama. **2** *(for animals)* lecho. **3** *(of flowers)* arriate *m*, macizo. **4** *(of river)* lecho, cauce *m*; *(of sea)* fondo. **5** GEOL capa, yacimiento. LOC **to go to bed** acostarse. ▌**to put sb to bed** acostar a ALGN. ▌**to make the bed** hacer la cama. COMP **bunk bed** litera. ▌**double bed** cama de matrimonio. ▌**single bed** cama individual. ▌**twin beds** camas *fpl* separadas. ▌**bed and board** pensión *f* completa. ▌**bed and breakfast** alojamiento con desayuno incluido.

✎ Consulta B and B.

**bedbug** [ˈbedbʌg] *n* chinche *f*.

**bedclothes** [ˈbedkləʊðz] *n pl* ropa de cama.

**bedding** [ˈbedɪŋ] *n* **1** ropa de cama. **2** *(for animals)* lecho.

**bedpan** [ˈbedpæn] *n* cuña, orinal *m* de cama.

**bedridden** [ˈbedrɪdən] *adj* postrado,-a en cama.

**bedroom** [ˈbedrʊm] *n* dormitorio, habitación *f*.

**bedside** [ˈbedsaɪd] *n* cabecera.

**bedsit** [bedˈsɪt] *n* estudio.

⊕ El bedsit es un tipo de alojamiento de alquiler asequible típico del Reino Unido. Consiste en una sola habitación que hace de dormitorio, sala de estar y comedor. Se suele compartir el baño con otras personas y a veces se tiene derecho a cocina.

**bedsore** [ˈbedsɔː] *n* MED llaga, úlcera.

**bedspread** [ˈbedspred] *n* cubrecama.

**bedtime** [ˈbedtaɪm] *n* la hora de acostarse.

**bee** [biː] *n* abeja.

**beech** [biːtʃ] *n* *(wood)* haya. COMP **beech grove** hayal *m*, hayedo. ▌**beech tree** haya.

**bee-eater** [ˈbiːiːtər] *n* abejaruco.

**beef** [biːf] *n* **1** *(meat)* carne *f* de buey, carne *f* de vaca. **2** *(animal)* buey *m*, vaca; *(cattle)* ganado vacuno. COMP **corned beef** carne *f* de vaca en conserva.

**beefburger** [ˈbiːfbɜːgər] *n* hamburguesa.

**beefeater** [ˈbiːfiːtər] *n* alabardero de la Torre de Londres.

**beefsteak** [ˈbiːfsteɪk] *n* bistec *m*.

**beehive** [ˈbiːhaɪv] *n* colmena.

**beekeeper** [ˈbiːkiːpər] *n* apicultor,-ra.

**beekeeping** [ˈbiːkiːpɪŋ] *n* apicultura.

**beeline** [ˈbiːlaɪn] *n* línea recta. LOC **to make a beeline for...** irse directamente a…

**been** [biːn, bɪn] *pp* → be.

**beep** [biːp] *n* pitido.
▶ *vi* pitar, tocar el pito. LOC **to beep the horn** tocar el claxon.

**beer** [bɪər] *n* cerveza.

**beeswax** [ˈbiːzwæks] *n* cera de abejas.

**beet** [biːt] *n* remolacha.

**beetle** [ˈbiːtəl] *n* escarabajo.

**beetroot** [ˈbiːtruːt] *n* **1** [*pl* beet] remolacha azucarera. **2** US [*pl* beets] remolacha.

**before** [bɪˈfɔː] *prep* **1** *(earlier)* antes de. **2** *(in front of)* delante de; *(in the presence of)* ante; *(for the attention of)* ante: *he's before me in the queue* va delante de mi en la cola; *he appeared before the judge* compareció ante el juez. **3** *(rather than)* antes que. **4** *(ahead)* por delante. **5** *(first)* primero: *ladies before gentlemen* las señoras primero.
▶ *conj* **1** *(earlier than)* antes de + *inf*, antes de que + *subj*: *don't forget to say goodbye before you go* no te olvides de despedirte antes de irte. **2** *(rather than)* antes de + *inf*: *he would starve before he asked them for money* preferiría morir de hambre antes de pedirles dinero.
▶ *adv* **1** *(earlier)* antes. **2** *(previous)* anterior. **3** *(already)* ya: *we've seen it before* ya lo hemos visto.

**beforehand** [bɪˈfɔːhænd] *adv* **1** *(earlier)* antes. **2** *(in advance)* de antemano, con antelación: *payment must be made a month beforehand* los pagos deben efectuarse con un mes de antelación. **3** *(before)* antes: *they arrived two hours beforehand* llegaron dos horas antes.

**befriend** [bɪˈfrend] *vt* ofrecer su amistad a.

**beg** [beg] *vt* **1** mendigar. **2** *(ask for)* pedir. **3** *lit (beseech)* suplicar, rogar. LOC **I beg your pardon** ¿cómo ha dicho?
▸ *vi* **1** mendigar. **2** *(dog)* sentarse *(con las patas delanteras levantadas).*
ⓘ *pt & pp* **begged,** *ger* **begging.**

**began** [bɪˈgæn] *pt* → **begin.**

**beggar** [ˈbegəʳ] *n* **1** mendigo,-a, pordiosero,-a. **2** *fam* tipo, individuo,-a: *he's a funny beggar* es un tipo raro.

**begin** [bɪˈgɪn] *vt* empezar, comenzar.
ⓘ *pt* **began** [bɪˈgæn], *pp* **begun** [bɪˈgʌn], *ger* **beginning.**

**beginner** [bɪˈgɪnəʳ] *n* principiante *mf.*

**beginning** [bɪˈgɪnɪŋ] *n* **1** principio, comienzo. **2** *(cause)* origen *m,* causa.

**begrudge** [bɪˈgrʌdʒ] *vt* **1** *(envy)* envidiar. **2** *(disapprove)* desaprobar.

**beguile** [bɪˈgaɪl] *vt* **1** *(seduce)* seducir, atraer; *(bewitch)* embrujar. **2** *(cheat)* engañar.

**begun** [bɪˈgʌn] *pp* → **begin.**

**behalf** [bɪˈhɑːf] *phr* **on behalf of** *(acting for)* en nombre de, de parte de; *(in favour of)* por, en favor de; *(for the benefit of)* para, en beneficio de.

**behave** [bɪˈheɪv] *vi* **1** *(people)* comportarse, portarse. **2** *(equipment, machinery)* funcionar bien: *this computer won't behave* este ordenador no funciona bien.

**behavior** [bɪˈheɪvjəʳ] *n* US → **behaviour.**

**behaviour** [bɪˈheɪvjəʳ] *n* **1** *(of person)* conducta, comportamiento. **2** *(of equipment, machine)* funcionamiento. **3** *(treatment)* trato.

**behead** [bɪˈhed] *vt* decapitar.

**behind** [bɪˈhaɪnd] *prep* detrás de.
▸ *adv* **1** detrás, atrás. **2** *(late)* atrasado,-a. **3** *(with payment)* retrasado,-a: *he's behind with the payments* está retrasado en los pagos.
▸ *n fam (buttocks)* trasero.

**behindhand** [bɪˈhaɪndhænd] *adv* en retraso, retrasado,-a.

**beige** [beɪʒ] *n* beige *m.*

▸ *adj* (de color) beige.

**being** [ˈbiːɪŋ] *n* **1** *(living thing)* ser *m.* **2** *(existence)* existencia. LOC **being as** ya que, puesto que: *being as they arrived late …* puesto que llegaron tarde … **‖ for the time being** por ahora, de momento. COMP **human being** ser *m* humano.

**Belarus** [ˈbelərʌs] *n* Bielorrusia.

**belated** [bɪˈleɪtɪd] *adj fam* tardío,-a.

**belay** [bɪˈleɪ] *vt (boat)* amarrar; *(rope in mountaineering)* asegurar, fijar.

**belch** [beltʃ] *n* eructo.
▸ *vi* eructar. LOC **to belch (out)** vomitar, arrojar: *the burning building belched out smoke* el edificio en llamas arrojaba humo.

**beleaguer** [bɪˈliːgəʳ] *vt* **1** *(beseige)* sitiar, cercar. **2** *(harass)* perseguir, hostigar.

**belfry** [ˈbelfrɪ] *n* campanario.
ⓘ *pl* **belfries.**

**Belgian** [ˈbeldʒən] *adj* belga.
▸ *n* belga *mf.*

**Belgium** [ˈbeldʒəm] *n* Bélgica.

**belie** [bɪˈlaɪ] *vt* **1** *(contradict)* mostrar como falso. **2** *(misrepresent)* no reflejar, ocultar. **3** *(fail to justify)* defraudar.

**belief** [bɪˈliːf] *n* **1** *(gen)* creencia. **2** *(opinion)* opinión *f.* **3** *(confidence)* confianza: *he has no belief in the legal system* no tiene confianza en el sistema jurídico. LOC **to the best of my belief** que yo sepa. **‖ it is beyond belief** parece mentira.

**believable** [bɪˈliːvəbəl] *adj* creíble, verosímil.

**believe** [bɪˈliːv] *vt* **1** *(accept as true, think)* creer. **2** *(suppose)* suponer.
▸ *vi* **1** creer (in, en). **2** *(trust)* confiar (in, en). **3** *(support, be in favour of)* ser partidario,-a (in, de). **4** REL tener fe. LOC **it is believed that** se cree que.

**believer** [bɪˈliːvəʳ] *n* **1** creyente *mf.* **2** *(supporter)* partidario,-a.

**belittle** [bɪˈlɪtəl] *vt* menospreciar.

**bell** [bel] *n* **1** *(church, etc)* campana. **2** *(handbell)* campanilla. **3** *(on bicycle, door, etc)* timbre *m.* **4** *(on toy, hat)* cascabel *m.* **5** *(cowbell)* cencerro. **6** *(flower)* campanilla. LOC **to ring the bell** tocar el timbre.

**bell-bottoms** [bel'bɒtəmz] *n pl* pantalones *mpl* acampanados.

**bellboy** ['belbɔɪ] *n* botones *m*.

**bellhop** ['belhɒp] *n* US botones *m*.

**belligerent** [bɪ'lɪdʒərənt] *adj* beligerante.

**bellow** ['beləʊ] *n* bramido.
► *vi* bramar.
► *n pl* **bellows** fuelle *m sing*.

**belly** ['belɪ] *n* **1** *(person)* vientre *m*, barriga. **2** *(animal)* panza. COMP **belly button** ombligo. ❙ **belly laugh** carcajada.
ⓘ *pl* bellies.

**bellyache** ['belɪeɪk] *n fam* dolor *m* de barriga.
► *vi fam* quejarse.

**bellybutton** ['belɪbʌtən] *n fam* ombligo.

**belong** [bɪ'lɒŋ] *vi* **1** pertenecer (to, a), ser (to, de). **2** *(be a member of a club)* ser socio,-a (to, de); *(be a member of a political party)* ser miembro (to, de). **3** *(have suitable qualities)* ser apto,-a (in, para).

**belongings** [bɪ'lɒŋɪŋz] *n pl* pertenencias *fpl*, bártulos *mpl*.

**beloved** [*(adj)* bɪ'lʌvd; *(n)* bɪ'lʌvɪd] *adj* querido,-a, amado,-a.
► *n* amado,-a.

**below** [bɪ'ləʊ] *prep* **1** debajo de, bajo. **2** por debajo (de). **3** *(lower than)* bajo. LOC **below sea level** por debajo del nivel del mar.
► *adv* **1** abajo. **2** de abajo. LOC **see below** véase abajo.

**belt** [belt] *n* **1** cinturón *m*. **2** TECH correa. **3** *(area)* zona.
► *vt fam (hit)* arrear un tortazo.
◆ **to belt along** *vi fam* ir a todo gas.
◆ **to belt up** *vi fam* cerrar el pico.

**bemused** [bɪ'mju:zd] *adj* perplejo,-a.

**bench** [bentʃ] *n* **1** banco. **2** JUR tribunal *m*. **3** SP banquillo. LOC **to be on the bench** ser juez,-za.
ⓘ *pl* benches.

**bend** [bend] *n* **1** *(in road, etc)* curva. **2** *(in pipe)* ángulo.
► *vt* **1** doblar, curvar. **2** *(head)* inclinar; *(back)* doblar, encorvar; *(knee)* doblar, flexionar.
► *vi* **1** doblarse, combarse: *the legs of the chair bent when he sat down* las patas

de la silla se combaron cuando se sentó. **2** *(head)* inclinarse; *(back)* encorvarse. **3** *(road)* torcer.
◆ **to bend down** *vi* agacharse.
◆ **to bend over** *vi* inclinarse.
ⓘ *pt & pp* bent [bent].

**beneath** [bɪ'ni:θ] *prep* **1** bajo, debajo de. **2** por debajo de: *the underground line runs beneath our house* la línea de metro va por debajo de nuestra casa. **3** *fig* indigno,-a de, no digno,-a de: *it's beneath you to behave like this* es indigno de ti comportarte de esta manera.
► *adv* de abajo: *she lives in the flat beneath* vive en el piso de abajo.

**benefactor** ['benɪfæktə'] *n* benefactor *m*.

**beneficial** [benɪ'fɪʃəl] *adj* beneficioso,-a, provechoso,-a.

**beneficiary** [benɪ'fɪʃərɪ] *n* beneficiario,-a.
ⓘ *pl* beneficiaries.

**benefit** ['benɪfɪt] *n* **1** *(advantage)* beneficio, provecho. **2** *(good)* bien *m*. **3** *(allowance)* subsidio. **4** *(charity performance)* función *f* benéfica; *(charity game)* partido benéfico.
► *vt* beneficiar.
► *vi* beneficiarse (from, de).
ⓘ *pt & pp* benefited (US benefitted), *ger* benefiting (US benefitting).

**benevolence** [bɪ'nevələns] *n* benevolencia.

**benevolent** [bɪ'nevələnt] *adj* benévolo,-a. COMP **benevolent society** sociedad *f* benéfica.

**beneficence** [bɪ'nefɪsəns] *n* beneficencia.

**benign** [bɪ'naɪn] *adj* benigno,-a.

**bent** [bent] *pt & pp* → bend.
► *adj* **1** torcido,-a, doblado,-a. **2** *sl (corrupt)* corrupto,-a.
► *n (innate ability)* facilidad *f*, don *m*: *she's got a bent for maths* tiene facilidad para las matemáticas.

**benzene** ['benzi:n] *n* CHEM benceno.

**benzine** ['benzi:n] *n* CHEM bencina.

**bequest** [bɪ'kwest] *n* legado.

**bereaved** [bɪ'ri:vd] *adj* desconsolado,-a, afligido,-a: *his bereaved wife* su desconsolada esposa.

**bereavement** [bɪˈriːvmənt] n **1** *(loss)* pérdida. **2** *(mourning)* duelo.

**beret** [ˈbereɪ] n boina.

**berry** [ˈberɪ] n baya.
ⓘ pl berries.

> ✎ Hay muchas frutas cuyo nombre se forma con berry, ya que se trata de bayas. Por ejemplo: **blackberry** *(mora)*, **gooseberry** *(grosella espinosa)*, **raspberry** *(frambuesa)* o **strawberry** *(fresón)*.

**berserk** [bəˈzɜːk] adj enloquecido,-a.

**berth** [bɜːθ] n **1** *(in harbour)* amarradero. **2** *(on ship)* camarote m, litera.
▶ vi atracar.

**beryl** [ˈberəl] n GEOL berilo.

**beryllium** [bəˈrɪlɪəm] n CHEM berilio.

**beseech** [bɪˈsiːtʃ] vt *lit* implorar, suplicar.
ⓘ pt & pp besought [bɪˈsɔːt] o beseeched.

**beset** [bɪˈset] vt **1** *(attack, harass)* acosar, asaltar. **2** *(hem in, surround)* acorralar, cercar.
ⓘ pt & pp beset, ger besetting.

**beside** [bɪˈsaɪd] prep **1** al lado de. **2** *(compared to)* frente a, comparado,-a con. ⎡LOC⎤ **to be beside os** estar fuera de sí. ▌ **that's beside the point** esto no viene al caso.

**besides** [bɪˈsaɪdz] prep *(as well as)* además de, aparte de.
▶ adv además.

**besiege** [bɪˈsiːdʒ] vt **1** MIL sitiar. **2** *fig* asediar, inundar.

**besought** [bɪˈsɔːt] pt & pp → beseech.

**best** [best] adj *(superl of* good*)* mejor. ⎡LOC⎤ **the best part of** casi: *it cost me the best part of £5,000* me costó casi 5.000 libras. ⎡COMP⎤ **best man** padrino de boda. **the best one** el mejor, la mejor.
▶ adv **1** *(superl of* well*)* mejor. **2** *(to a greater extent)* más: *of all the girls she is the one he likes best* de todas las chicas ella es la que le gusta más. ⎡LOC⎤ **best before ...** consumir preferentemente antes de ...
▶ n **1** lo mejor: *the best is yet to come* lo mejor aún está por venir. **2** *(person)* el mejor, la mejor: *she's the best in the class at maths* es la mejor de la clase en mates. **3** *(in*

*sport)* plusmarca. ⎡LOC⎤ **all the best! 1** ¡que te vaya bien! **2** *(in letter)* un saludo. ▌ **it's for the best** más vale que sea así.

**bestial** [ˈbestɪəl] adj bestial, brutal.

**bestow** [bɪˈstəʊ] vt *(honour, award)* otorgar (on, a); *(favour)* hacer (on, a); *(title)* conferir (on, a).

**best-seller** [bestˈselər] n best seller m, superventas m.

**bet** [bet] n apuesta. ⎡LOC⎤ **to make a bet** hacer una apuesta.
▶ vt & vi apostar
ⓘ pt & pp bet o betted, ger betting.

**beta** [ˈbiːtə] n beta. ⎡COMP⎤ **beta rays** rayos mpl beta.

**betray** [bɪˈtreɪ] vt **1** traicionar. **2** *(secret)* revelar. **3** *(show signs of)* dejar ver, acusar. **4** *(deceive)* engañar.

**betrayal** [bɪˈtreɪəl] n **1** traición f. **2** *(deceit)* engaño.

**better**[1] [ˈbetər] adj **1** *(comp of* good*)* mejor: *his new novel is better than his last one* su última novela es mejor que la anterior. **2** *(more healthy)* mejor: *he's feeling better today* hoy se encuentra mejor. ⎡LOC⎤ **to get better** recuperarse, mejorarse. ▌ **better and better** cada vez mejor.
▶ adv **1** *(comp of* well*)* mejor. **2** *(to a greater extent)* más: *I like this one better* me gusta más éste. ⎡LOC⎤ **had better + inf** más vale que + subj: *we'd better be going* más vale que nos vayamos. ▌ **to like STH/SB better** preferir ALGO/a ALGN.
▶ vt **1** *(improve)* mejorar: *he has bettered their working conditions* ha mejorado sus condiciones de trabajo. **2** *(surpass)* superar: *he bettered his own record* superó su propio récord.
▶ n pl **betters** superiores mpl: *you must listen to your betters* debes escuchar a tus superiores.

**betting** [ˈbetɪŋ] n apuestas fpl. ⎡LOC⎤ **what's the betting that he "(she, it, etc)...?"** ¿qué te apuestas a que ...?: *what's the betting that he arrives late?* ¿qué te apuestas a que llega tarde? ⎡COMP⎤ **betting shop** GB administración f de apuestas hípicas.

**between** [bɪˈtwiːn] prep entre: *choose a number between one and ten* escoge un número entre uno y diez.

▸ *adv* [también **in between**] de en medio: *we could see the sea if it wasn't for the houses (in) between* podríamos ver el mar si no fuera por las casas de en medio.

**bevel** ['bevəl] *n* bebida.

**beverage** ['bevərɪdʒ] *n* bebida.

**bevy** ['bevɪ] *n (of birds)* bandada.
ⓘ *pl* **bevies**.

**beware** [bɪ'weəʳ] *vi* tener cuidado (**of**, con): *beware of the dog!* ¡cuidado con el perro!

**bewilder** [bɪ'wɪldəʳ] *vt* desconcertar, dejar perplejo,-a.

**bewitch** [bɪ'wɪtʃ] *vt* **1** hechizar, embrujar. **2** *fig* hechizar, fascinar.

**beyond** [bɪ'jɒnd] *prep* **1** más allá de: *they live beyond the mountains* viven más allá de las montañas. **2** *(outside)* fuera de: *it's beyond my jurisdiction* está fuera de mi jurisdicción. ⯀ **it's beyond doubt** es indudable, es seguro, no cabe duda.
▸ *adv* más allá, más lejos.
▸ *n* **the beyond** el más allá.

**bias** ['baɪəs] *n* **1** *(prejudice)* parcialidad *f*, prejuicio. **2** *(inclination)* tendencia, predisposición *f*. **3** *(in statistics)* margen *f* de error.
▸ *vt* predisponer, influenciar.
ⓘ *pt & pp* **biased** o **biassed**, *ger* **biasing** o **biassing**.

**biased** ['baɪəst] *adj* parcial.

**bib** [bɪb] *n* **1** *(for baby)* babero. **2** *(top of apron, overall)* peto.

**Bible** ['baɪbəl] *n* Biblia.

**bibliography** [bɪblɪ'ɒɡrəfɪ] *n* bibliografía.
ⓘ *pl* **bibliographies**.

**bicarbonate** [baɪ'kɑːbənət] *n* CHEM bicarbonato.

**biceps** ['baɪseps] *n* bíceps *m*.

**bicker** ['bɪkəʳ] *vi* discutir, porfiar.

**bicycle** ['baɪsɪkəl] *n* bicicleta. ⯀ **to ride a bicycle** montar en bicicleta. ⯀ **bicycle pump** bomba de bicicleta.

**bid** [bɪd] *n* **1** *(at auction)* puja. **2** *(attempt)* intento. **3** *(offer)* oferta.
▸ *vi (at auction)* pujar (**for**, por).
ⓘ *pt & pp* **bid**, *ger* **bidding**.

**bidder** ['bɪdəʳ] *n* postor,-ra, pujador,-ra, licitador,-ra.

**bidding** ['bɪdɪŋ] *n* **1** *(at auction)* puja, oferta. **2** *(order)* orden *f*.

**bide** [baɪd] *vt* **to bide one's time** esperar el momento oportuno.
ⓘ *pt* **bided** o **bode** [bəʊd], *pp* **bided**, *ger* **biding**.

**bidet** ['biːdeɪ] *n* bidé *m*.

**bifocal** [baɪ'fəʊkəl] *adj* bifocal.
▸ *n pl* **bifocals** lentes *fpl* bifocales.

**bifurcate** ['baɪfəkeɪt] *vi* bifurcarse.

**big** [bɪɡ] *adj* **1** *(size, importance)* grande; *(before sing noun)* gran. **2** *(older)* mayor.
ⓘ *comp* **bigger**, *superl* **biggest**.

**bigamy** ['bɪɡəmɪ] *n* bigamia.

**big-head** ['bɪɡhed] *n* sabihondo,-a, creído,-a.

**big-hearted** [bɪɡ'hɑːtɪd] *adj* de buen corazón, generoso,-a.

**bigmouth** ['bɪɡmaʊθ] *n* bocazas *mf*.

**bigot** ['bɪɡət] *n* fanático,-a.

⯀ Bigot no significa 'bigote', que se traduce por **moustache**.

**bigotry** ['bɪɡətrɪ] *n* fanatismo.

**bigwig** ['bɪɡwɪɡ] *n fam* pez *m* gordo.

**bike** [baɪk] *n* **1** *fam (bicycle)* bici *f*. **2** *(motorcycle)* moto *f*.

**bikeway** ['baɪkweɪ] *n* carril-bici *m*.

**bikini®** [bɪ'kiːnɪ] *n* biquini® *m*, bikini® *m*.

**bilateral** [baɪ'lætərəl] *adj* bilateral.

**bile** [baɪl] *n* bilis *f*, hiel *f*. ⯀ **bile duct** conducto biliar.

**biliary** ['bɪlɪərɪ] *adj* biliar.

**bilingual** [baɪ'lɪŋɡwəl] *adj* bilingüe.

**bilirubin** [bɪlɪ'ruːbɪn] *n* bilirrubina.

**bill¹** [bɪl] *n* **1** factura; *(in restaurant)* cuenta. **2** *(law)* proyecto de ley. **3** US *(banknote)* billete *m*. **4** *(poster)* cartel *m*. ⯀ **bill of exchange** letra de cambio. ∥ **Bill of Rights** declaración *f* de derechos.
▸ *vt* **1** facturar, pasar la factura. **2** THEAT programar.

**bill²** [bɪl] *n* **1** *(of bird)* pico. **2** *(headland)* cabo, promontorio.

**billboard** ['bɪlbɔːd] *n* US valla publicitaria.

**billfold** ['bɪlfəʊld] *n* US billetero, cartera.

**billing** ['bɪlɪŋ] *n* **1** *(invoicing)* facturación *f*. **2** THEAT *orden de aparición en cartel*.

**billion** ['bɪlɪən] *n* **1** mil millones *mpl*. **2** GB *(formerly)* billón *m*.

✎ En el uso actual, tanto en EE UU como en Gran Bretaña, un **billion** equivale a mil millones. Antiguamente, el **billion** británico tenía el mismo significado que en español, es decir, 'un millón de millones'

**billionaire** [bɪlɪə'neəʳ] *n* multimillonario,-a.

**billow** ['bɪləʊ] *n* **1** *(of water)* ola. **2** *(of smoke)* nube *f*.
▸ *vt* **1** *(sea)* ondear. **2** *(sail)* hincharse.

**billy goat** ['bɪlɪgəʊt] *n* macho cabrío.

**bin** [bɪn] *n* **1** *(for rubbish)* cubo de la basura; *(for paper)* papelera. **2** *(large container)* recipiente *m*.

**binary** ['baɪnərɪ] *adj* binario,-a. COMP **binary fission** bipartición *f*, fisión *f* binaria.

**bind** [baɪnd] *n fam* fastidio, molestia.
▸ *vt* **1** *(tie up)* atar; *(cereals, corn)* agavillar. **2** CULIN *(sauce)* ligar. **3** *(book, etc)* encuadernar. **4** *(bandage)* vendar. **5** *(require)* obligar.
ⓘ *pt & pp* **bound** [baʊnd].

**binder** ['baɪndəʳ] *n* **1** *(file)* carpeta. **2** *(of books)* encuadernador,-ra.

**binding** ['baɪndɪŋ] *n* **1** *(of book)* encuadernación *f*. **2** SEW ribete *m*. **3** *(of skis)* fijación *f*.
▸ *adj* obligatorio,-a (**on**, para).

**binge** [bɪndʒ] *n* *(drinking)* borrachera; *(eating)* atracón *m*.
▸ *vi* atiborrarse, hartarse de comida.

**bingo** ['bɪŋgəʊ] *n* bingo.
ⓘ *pl* **bingos**.

**binnacle** ['bɪnəkəl] *n* bitácora.

**binoculars** [bɪ'nɒkjʊləz] *n pl* prismáticos *mpl*, gemelos *mpl*.

**biochemistry** [baɪəʊ'kemɪstrɪ] *n* bioquímica.

**biodegradable** [baɪəʊdɪ'greɪdəbəl] *adj* biodegradable.

**biography** [baɪ'ɒgrəfɪ] *n* biografía.
ⓘ *pl* **biographies**.

**biological** [baɪə'lɒdʒɪkəl] *adj* biológico,-a.

**biologist** [baɪ'ɒlədʒɪst] *n* biólogo,-a.

**biology** [baɪ'ɒlədʒɪ] *n* biología.

**biomass** ['baɪəʊmæs] *n* biomasa.

**biomechanics** [baɪəʊmɪ'kænɪks] *n* biomecánica.

**biometry** [baɪ'ɒmətrɪ] *n* biometría.

**bionic** [baɪ'ɒnɪk] *adj* biónico,-a.

**biophysics** [baɪəʊ'fɪzɪks] *n* biofísica.

**biopsy** ['baɪɒpsɪ] *n* biopsia.
ⓘ *pl* **biopsies**.

**biorhythm** ['baɪərɪðəm] *n* biorritmo.

**biosphere** ['baɪəsfɪəʳ] *n* biosfera.

**biotope** ['baɪətəp] *n* biotopo.

**biped** ['baɪped] *adj* bípedo,-a.
▸ *n* bípedo.

**biplane** ['baɪpleɪn] *n* biplano.

**bipolar** [baɪ'pəʊləʳ] *adj* bipolar.

**birch** [bɜːtʃ] *n* **1** *(tree)* abedul *m*. **2** *(rod)* vara de abedul.
▸ *vt* azotar.

**bird** [bɜːd] *n* **1** *(large)* ave *f*; *(small)* pájaro. **2** GB *sl (girl)* chica. **3** *sl (person)* tipo. COMP **bird of prey** ave *f* de rapiña, ave *f* de presa.

**birdcage** ['bɜːdkeɪdʒ] *n* jaula de pájaro.

**birdie** ['bɜːdɪ] *n* **1** *(little bird)* pajarito. **2** *(in golf)* birdie *m*.

**birdseed** ['bɜːdsiːd] *n* BOT alpiste *m*.

**bird's-eye view** [bɜːdzaɪ'vjuː] *n* vista panorámica.

**bird-watcher** ['bɜːdwɒtʃəʳ] *n* ornitólogo,-a *(cuya afición es observar las aves)*.

**Biro®** ['baɪrəʊ] [also written **biro**] *n fam* boli *m*.
ⓘ *pl* **Biros**.

**birth** [bɜːθ] *n* **1** nacimiento. **2** MED parto. **3** *(descent)* linaje *m*. LOC **to give birth to 1** *(child)* dar a luz. **2** *fig* dar lugar a. COMP **birth certificate** partida de nacimiento. ▮ **birth control** control *m* de la natalidad. ▮ **birth rate** tasa de natalidad.

**birthday** ['bɜːθdeɪ] *n* cumpleaños *m*.

**birthmark** ['bɜːθmɑːk] *n* mancha de nacimiento, antojo.

**birthplace** ['bɜːθpleɪs] *n* lugar *m* de nacimiento.

**biscuit** ['bɪskɪt] *n* galleta.

**bisection** [baɪ'sekʃən] *n* bisección *f*.

**bisectrix** [baɪ'sektrɪks] *n* bisectriz *f*.
ⓘ *pl* **bisectrices** [baɪ'sektrɪsiːz].

**bisexual** [baɪ'seksjuəl] *adj* bisexual.
► *n* bisexual *mf*.

**bishop** ['bɪʃəp] *n* **1** obispo. **2** *(chess)* alfil *m*.

**bison** ['baɪsən] *n* bisonte *m*.

**bissextile** [baɪ'sekstaɪl] *adj* bisiesto,-a.

**bit¹** [bɪt] *n* **1** *(small piece)* trozo, pedacito. **2** *(small amount)* poco. **3** *fam (time)* un poco, un ratito. LOC **a bit** *fam (rather)* algo, un poco. ‖ **a bit of** algo de. ‖ **quite a bit / a good bit** *fam* bastante. **to come to bits** hacerse pedazos, romperse.

**bit²** [bɪt] *n* **1** *(of bridle)* bocado. **2** *(of drill)* broca.

**bit³** [bɪt] *n* COMPUT bit *m*.

**bit⁴** [bɪt] *pt* → bite.

**bite** [baɪt] *n* **1** *(act)* mordisco. **2** *(of insect)* picadura. **3** *(of dog, etc)* mordedura. **4** *(of food)* bocado.
► *vt* **1** morder. **2** *(insect, snake)* picar. **3** *(grip)* agarrar.
► *vi* **1** morder. **2** *(insect, snake)* picar. **3** *(fish)* picar.
① *pt* bit, *pp* bitten ['bɪtən].

**biting** ['baɪtɪŋ] *adj* **1** *(wind)* cortante, penetrante. **2** *(comment)* mordaz.

**bitten** ['bɪtən] *pp* → bite.

**bitter** ['bɪtər] *adj* **1** *(gen)* amargo,-a; *(fruit)* ácido,-a, agrio,-a. **2** *(weather)* glacial. **3** *(person)* amargado,-a. **4** *(fight)* enconado,-a.
► *n* cerveza amarga.

**bitterly** ['bɪtəlɪ] *adv* **1** con amargura, amargamente: *she complained bitterly* se quejó amargamente. **2** *(very)* muy: *it's bitterly cold* hace un frío glacial.

**bitterness** ['bɪtənəs] *n* **1** *(gen)* amargura; *(of fruit)* acidez *f*. **2** *(of weather)* crudeza. **3** *(resentment)* rencor *m*, resentimiento.

**bittersweet** ['bɪtəswiːt] *adj* agridulce.

**bitumen** ['bɪtjʊmɪn] *n* betún *m*.

**bivalent** [baɪ'veɪlənt] *adj* bivalente.

**bivalve** ['baɪvælv] *adj* bivalvo,-a.
► *n* bivalvo.

**bizarre** [bɪ'zɑːr] *adj* **1** raro,-a, extraño,-a.

**blab** [blæb] *vi* **1** *fam (gossip)* cotillear, chismear. **2** *fam (talk constantly)* rajar, parlotear.
① *pt & pp* blabbed, *ger* blabbing.

**black** [blæk] *adj* **1** negro,-a. **2** *(dirty)* sucio,-a. **3** *(threatening)* amenazador,-ra. LOC **black and white** blanco y negro. COMP **black economy** economía sumergida.
► *n* **1** *(colour)* negro. **2** *(person)* negro,-a.
► *vt* **1** *(make black)* ennegrecer. **2** *(boycott)* boicotear.
◆ **to black out** *vt sep* **1** *(windows of house)* tapar; *(electrical supply)* apagar el alumbrado. **2** *(cause power cut)* dejar sin luz, causar un apagón.
► *vi (faint)* desmayarse.

**blackberry** ['blækbərɪ] *n* zarzamora, mora. COMP **blackberry bush** zarza.
① *pl* blackberries.

**blackbird** ['blækbɜːd] *n* mirlo.

**blackboard** ['blækbɔːd] *n* pizarra.

**blackcurrant** [blæk'kʌrənt] *n* grosella negra.

**blacken** ['blækən] *vt* **1** ennegrecer. **2** *fig (defame)* manchar.

**blackhead** ['blækhed] *n* espinilla.

**blackjack** ['blækdʒæk] *n (card game)* veintiuna.

**blackleg** ['blækleg] *n* esquirol *m*.

**blacklist** ['blæklɪst] *n* lista negra.

**blackmail** ['blækmeɪl] *n* chantaje *m*.
► *vt* hacer chantaje a, chantajear.

**blackmailer** ['blækmeɪlər] *n* chantajista *mf*.

**blackout** ['blækaʊt] *n* **1** *(through electrical fault)* apagón *m*; *(in wartime)* oscurecimiento general de una ciudad. **2** *(fainting)* pérdida de conocimiento, desmayo.

**blacksmith** ['blæksmɪθ] *n* herrero. COMP **blacksmith's forge** herrería.

**blackthorn** ['blækθɔːn] *n* BOT endrino.

**bladder** ['blædər] *n* **1** vejiga. **2** *(in tyre, football)* cámara de aire.

**blade** [bleɪd] *n* **1** *(of sword, knife, etc)* hoja. **2** *(of ice skate)* cuchilla. **3** *(of propeller, fan, oar, hoe)* pala. **4** *(of grass)* brizna.

**blame** [bleɪm] *n* culpa.
► *vt* culpar, echar la culpa a.

**blanch** [blɑ:ntʃ] *vt* CULIN escaldar.
▶ *vi* palidecer.

**bland** [blænd] *adj* soso,-a.

❌ Bland no significa 'blando', que se traduce por **soft**.

**blank** [blæŋk] *adj* **1** *(page, etc)* en blanco. **2** *(look, etc)* vacío,-a. **3** *(cassette, tape)* virgen. COMP **blank cheque** cheque *m* en blanco.
▶ *n* **1** *(on paper)* espacio en blanco. **2** *(bullet)* bala de fogueo.

**blanket** ['blæŋkɪt] *n* **1** manta, AM frazada. **2** *(layer)* capa, manto: *a blanket of snow* una capa de nieve.

**blare** [bleəʳ] *n* **1** *(loud noise)* estruendo, fragor *m*. **2** *(of trumpet)* trompetazo.
▶ *vi* resonar, sonar.
◆ **to blare out** *vi* sonar muy fuerte.

**blaspheme** [blæsˈfi:m] *vi* blasfemar (against, contra).

**blasphemy** ['blæsfəmɪ] *n* blasfemia.
ⓘ *pl* blasphemies.

**blast** [blɑ:st] *n* **1** *(of wind)* ráfaga. **2** *(of water, air, etc)* chorro. **3** *(of horn)* toque *m*. **4** *(of trumpet)* trompetazo. **5** *(explosion)* explosión *f*, voladura. **6** *(shock wave)* onda expansiva. **7** *(reprimand)* bronca.
▶ *vt* **1** *(explode)* volar, hacer volar. **2** *(criticize)* criticar. **3** *(reprimand)* echar una bronca. **4** *(ruin, spoil)* echar a perder, dar al traste con. **5** *(shoot)* pegar un tiro a. **6** *(shrivel, wither)* marchitar.

**blasted** ['blɑ:stɪd] *adj* maldito,-a, dichoso,-a.

**blast-off** ['blɑ:stɒf] *n* *(of rocket, missile)* despegue *m*.

**blatant** ['bleɪtənt] *adj* descarado,-a.

**blaze** [bleɪz] *n* **1** *(fire)* incendio. **2** *(flame)* llamarada. **3** *(of light)* resplandor *m*. **4** *(outburst)* arranque *m*, acceso.
▶ *vi* **1** *(fire)* arder. **2** *(sun)* brillar con fuerza. **3** *(light)* resplandecer.

**blazer** ['bleɪzəʳ] *n* americana de sport, blazer *m*.

**bleach** [bli:tʃ] *n* lejía.
▶ *vt* blanquear.

**bleachers** ['bli:tʃəz] *n pl* US gradas *fpl*.

**bleak** [bli:k] *adj* **1** *(countryside)* desolado,-a. **2** *(weather)* desapacible. **3** *(future)* poco prometedor,-ra. **4** *(welcome, reception)* frío,-a.

**bleary** ['blɪərɪ] *adj* **1** *(from tears)* nubloso,-a. **2** *(from tiredness)* legañoso,-a.
ⓘ *comp* blearier, *superl* bleariest.

**bleat** [bli:t] *n* balido.
▶ *vi* balar.

**bled** [bled] *pt & pp* → **bleed**.

**bleed** [bli:d] *vi* MED sangrar.
ⓘ *pt & pp* **bled** [bled].

**bleep** [bli:p] *n* pitido.
▶ *vi* pitar.
▶ *vt* localizar con un busca.

**bleeper** ['bli:pəʳ] *n* busca *m*, buscapersonas *m*.

**blemish** ['blemɪʃ] *n* **1** desperfecto, imperfección *f*.
▶ *vt* **1** *(spoil)* estropear, desmejorar. **2** *fig (reputation)* manchar, tiznar. LOC **without a blemish** *fig* intachable.

**blench** [blenʃ] *vi* **1** *(recoil)* retroceder. **2** *(flinch)* pestañear, inmutarse.

**blend** [blend] *n* mezcla, combinación *f*.
▶ *vt* **1** *(mix)* mezclar, combinar. **2** *(match)* matizar, armonizar.

**blender** ['blendəʳ] *n* CULIN batidora, minipímer® *m*.

**bless** [bles] *vt* bendecir. LOC **bless you!** *(on sneezing)* ¡Jesús!

**blessed** ['blesɪd] *adj* **1** *(holy)* bendito,-a, santo,-a. **2** *(content, happy)* bienaventurado,-a.

**blessing** ['blesɪŋ] *n* bendición *f*.

**blew** [blu:] *pt* → **blow**.

**blight** [blaɪt] *n* **1** *(mildew)* tizón *m*. **2** *(calamity)* plaga.

**blind** [blaɪnd] *adj* ciego,-a.
▶ *n* *(on window)* persiana.
▶ *vt* **1** cegar, dejar ciego,-a. **2** *(dazzle)* deslumbrar.

**blindfold** ['blaɪndfəʊld] *n* venda.
▶ *vt* vendar los ojos a.
▶ *adv* con los ojos vendados.

**blink** [blɪŋk] *n* **1** parpadeo. **2** *(gleam, glimmer)* destello. LOC **on the blink** *fam* averiado,-a.

**blinkers** ['blɪŋkəz] *n pl* anteojeras *fpl*.

**bliss** [blɪs] *n* felicidad *f*, dicha.

**blister** ['blɪstə'] *n* **1** *(on skin)* ampolla. **2** *(on paint, surface)* burbuja.

**blizzard** ['blɪzəd] *n* tempestad *f* de nieve, ventisca.

**bloated** ['bləʊtɪd] *adj* hinchado,-a.

**blob** [blɒb] *n* **1** *(drop)* gota. **2** *(smudge)* borrón *m*. **3** *(of colour)* mancha.

**bloc** [blɒk] *n* POL bloque *m*.

**block** [blɒk] *n* **1** bloque *m*. **2** *(of wood, stone)* taco. **3** *(group of buildings)* manzana. **6** *(obstruction)* obstrucción *f*. COMP **block letters** mayúsculas *fpl*. ▌ **block of flats** bloque *m* de pisos. ▌ **note block** taco, bloc *m* de notas.
▸ *vt* **1** *(pipe, etc)* obstruir, atascar. **2** *(streets, etc)* bloquear.

**blockade** [blɒˈkeɪd] *n* MIL bloqueo.
▸ *vt* bloquear.

**blockage** ['blɒkɪdʒ] *n* obstrucción *f*, atasco.

**blockbuster** ['blɒkbʌstə'] *n* **1** *fig (novel)* best seller *m*, éxito de ventas. **2** *fig (film)* película de acción.

**bloke** [bləʊk] *n* GB *fam* tipo, tío.

**blond** [blɒnd] [suele escribirse **blonde** cuando se refiere a una mujer] *adj* rubio,-a.
▸ *n* rubio,-a.

**blonde** [blɒnd] *adj-n* → blond.

**blood** [blʌd] *n* sangre *f*. **2** *(ancestry)* parentesco, alcurnia. COMP **blood pressure** tensión *f* arterial. ▌ **blood vessel** vaso sanguíneo.

**bloodhound** ['blʌdhaʊnd] *n* sabueso.

**bloodshed** ['blʌdʃed] *n* derramamiento de sangre.

**bloodstream** ['blʌdstriːm] *n* corriente *f* sanguínea.

**bloodthirsty** ['blʌdθɜːstɪ] *adj* sanguinario,-a, ávido,-a de sangre.
ⓘ *comp* bloodthirstier, *superl* bloodthirstiest.

**bloody** ['blʌdɪ] *adj* **1** *(battle)* sangriento,-a. **2** *sl (damned)* puñetero,-a, mierda de.
ⓘ *comp* bloodier, *superl* bloodiest.

**bloody-minded** [blʌdɪˈmaɪndɪd] *adj* **1** *(stubborn)* tozudo,-a, terco,-a. **2** *(bad-tempered)* de malas pulgas.

**bloom** [bluːm] *n* **1** *(flower)* flor *f*. **2** *(on fruit)* pelusa.
▸ *vi* florecer.

**bloomer** ['bluːmə'] *n* GB *fam* metedura de pata, pifia.

**blossom** ['blɒsəm] *n* flor *f*.
▸ *vi* florecer.
◆ **to blossom out** *vi* alcanzar su plenitud.

🖎 Blossom se refiere a las flores de los árboles; para el resto de flores, se emplea la palabra flower.

**blot** [blɒt] *n* *(of ink)* borrón *m*; *(on reputation)* mancha.
▸ *vt* **1** *(stain)* manchar. **2** *(dry)* secar.
◆ **to blot out** *vt sep* **1** *(hide)* ocultar. **2** *(memory)* borrar.
ⓘ *pt & pp* blotted, *ger* blotting.

**blotch** [blɒtʃ] *n* mancha.
▸ *vi* **1** *(become stained)* mancharse. **2** *(skin)* salir manchas.

**blotting-paper** ['blɒtɪŋpeɪpə'] *n* papel *m* secante.

**blouse** [blaʊz] *n* blusa.

**blow¹** [bləʊ] *n* golpe *m*.

**blow²** [bləʊ] *vi* **1** *(wind)* soplar. **2** *(instrument)* tocar, sonar; *(whistle)* pitar. **3** *(fuse)* fundirse. **4** *(tyre)* reventarse.
▸ *vt fam (money)* despilfarrar, malgastar.
◆ **to blow away** *vt sep* **1** arrastrar. **2** *fam fig* mandar al otro barrio.
◆ **to blow in** *vt sep* derribar.
◆ **to blow off** *vi (lid, hat)* salir volando.
◆ **to blow out** *vt sep* **1** *(flame)* apagar; *(candle)* soplar. **2** *(cheeks)* hinchar.
◆ **to blow over** *vt sep* derribar.
▸ *vi* **1** derrumbarse. **2** *(storm)* amainar.
◆ **to blow up** *vt sep* **1** *(explode)* (hacer) volar: *they blew up the building* hicieron volar el edificio. **2** *(inflate)* hinchar. **3** *(photograph)* ampliar.
▸ *vi* **1** *(explode)* explotar. **2** *(lose one's temper)* salirse de sus casillas.
ⓘ *pt* blew [bluː], *pp* blown [bləʊn].

**blowhole** ['bləʊhəʊl] *n* **1** *(of whale)* orificio nasal. **2** *(hole, air vent)* respiradero.

**blowlamp** ['bləʊlæmp] *n* soplete *m*.

**blown** [bləʊn] *pp* → blow.

**blowout** ['bləʊaʊt] n **1** AUTO reventón m, pinchazo. **2** sl comilona, atracón m.

**blowtorch** ['bləʊtɔːtʃ] n soplete m.

**blow-up** ['bləʊʌp] n (photograph) ampliación f.

**blue** [bluː] adj **1** azul. **2** (sad) triste. **3** (depressed) deprimido,-a. **4** (obscene) verde: a blue joke un chiste verde.
▶ n azul m.
▶ n pl **blues** MUS blues m.
▶ n pl **the blues** la depresión f.

**bluebell** ['bluːbel] n BOT campanilla.

**blueberry** ['bluːbəri] n BOT arándano.
ⓘ pl blueberries.

**blue-collar** ['bluːkɒləʳ] adj obrero,-a.

**blueprint** ['bluːprint] n fig anteproyecto.

**blues** [bluːz] n pl → blue.

**blunder** ['blʌndəʳ] n metedura de pata.
▶ vi meter la pata.

**blunt** [blʌnt] adj **1** (knife) desafilado,-a; (pencil) despuntado,-a. **2** fig (person) que no tiene pelos en la lengua.
▶ vt desafilar, embotar; (pencil) despuntar. COMP **blunt angle** MATH ángulo obtuso.

**blur** [blɜːʳ] n borrón m, mancha.

**blurb** [blɜːb] n fam pej información f publicitaria.

**blurred** [blɜːd] adj **1** borroso,-a. **2** fig (memories) vago,-a, confuso,-a.

**blurt** [blɜːt] LOC **to blurt** STH **out** soltar ALGO bruscamente, espetar algo.

**blush** [blʌʃ] n rubor m, sonrojo.
▶ vi ruborizarse, sonrojarse.

**blusher** ['blʌʃəʳ] n colorete m.

**blustery** ['blʌstəri] adj (windy) ventoso,-a.

**boa** ['bəʊə] n ZOOL boa.

**boar** [bɔːʳ] n ZOOL verraco.

**board** [bɔːd] n **1** (piece of wood) tabla, tablero. **2** (food) comida, pensión f. **3** (committee) junta, consejo. **4** (company) compañía: the gas board la compañía del gas. LOC **on board** a bordo. **I to take on board 1** (responsibility) asumir. **2** (concept, idea) abarcar. COMP **board and lodging** pensión completa. **I board of directors** junta directiva. **I board of trade** US cámara de comercio.
▶ vt (ship, etc) subirse a, embarcar en.
▶ vi (lodge) alojarse; (at school) ser interno,-a.

**boarder** ['bɔːdəʳ] n **1** (gen) huésped mf. **2** (at school) interno,-a.

**boarding** ['bɔːdɪŋ] n **1** (ship, plane, etc) embarque m. **2** (lodging) pensión f, alojamiento. COMP **boarding card** tarjeta de embarque. **I boarding house** casa de huéspedes. **I boarding school** internado.

**boast** [bəʊst] n jactancia.
▶ vi jactarse (about, de), presumir (about, de).
▶ vt fig presumir de.

**boat** [bəʊt] n barco, nave f; (small) bote m, barca; (large) buque m, navío; (launch) lancha.

**boatswain** ['bəʊsən] n contramaestre m.

**boatyard** ['bəʊtjɑːd] n astillero.

**bob¹** [bɒb] n **1** (jerking movement) sacudida; (bouncing movement) rebote m. **2** (curtsy) reverencia.
▶ vi **1** (jerk) moverse a sacudidas; (bounce) rebotar. **2** (curtsy) hacer una reverencia.

**bobbin** ['bɒbɪn] n (for textiles, wire, etc) carrete m, bobina; (for lace) bolillo, palillo.

**bobby** ['bɒbi] n GB fam poli m.
ⓘ pl bobbies.

⊕ Este término, aunque hoy poco utilizado, se usa para referirse a los agentes de policía del Reino Unido. El nombre proviene del fundador del cuerpo, sir Robert Peel, ya que Bobby es el diminutivo de Robert.

**bobsleigh** ['bɒbsleɪ] n bobsleigh m.

**bode** [bəʊd] pt → bide.
▶ vt (foretell) presagiar, augurar. LOC **to bode ill/well** ser de buen/mal agüero.

**bodice** ['bɒdɪs] n corpiño.

**body** ['bɒdi] n **1** cuerpo. **2** (corpse) cadáver m. **3** (organization) organismo, entidad f, ente m; (association) agrupación f. **4** (of wine) cuerpo. **5** (of people) grupo, conjunto. **6** AUTO (of car) carrocería. **7** AV fuselaje m.
ⓘ pl bodies.

**body-blow** ['bɒdɪbləʊ] n revés m.

**body-building** [ˈbɒdɪbɪldɪŋ] n SP culturismo.

**bodyguard** [ˈbɒdɪɡɑːd] n guardaespaldas m.

**bodywork** [ˈbɒdɪwɜːk] n carrocería.

**bog** [bɒɡ] n **1** pantano, cenagal m. **2** sl (toilet) meódromo.

◆ **to bog down** vt sep atascar.

**bogey** [ˈbəʊɡɪ] n (golf) bogey m.

**bogus** [ˈbəʊɡəs] adj **1** (fake) falso,-a, apócrifo,-a. **2** (fictitious) ficticio,-a. **3** (sham) simulado,-a, fingido,-a.

**boil**[1] [bɔɪl] n MED furúnculo, forúnculo.

**boil**[2] [bɔɪl] vt (liquid) hervir; (food) hervir, cocer; (egg) pasar por agua, cocer.
▶ vi **1** (liquid) hervir; (food) hervir, cocerse. **2** fig (undulate, seethe) bullir.
◆ **to boil down to** vt insep fig reducirse a.

**boiler** [ˈbɔɪləʳ] n **1** caldera. **2** (fowl) gallina (que solo sirve para el caldo).

**boiling** [ˈbɔɪlɪŋ] adj hirviendo, hirviente. [COMP] **boiling point** punto de ebullición.

**boisterous** [ˈbɔɪstərəs] adj **1** (noisy, rowdy) bullicioso,-a, alborotador,-ra. **2** (weather) borrascoso,-a; (sea) agitado,-a.

**bold** [bəʊld] adj **1** (brave) valiente. **2** (daring) audaz, atrevido,-a. **3** (cheeky) descarado,-a, fresco,-a. **4** (vivid) vivo,-a. **5** (print) en negrita.

**Bolivia** [bəˈlɪvɪə] n Bolivia.

**Bolivian** [bəˈlɪvɪən] adj boliviano,-a.
▶ n boliviano,-a.

**bolster** [ˈbəʊlstəʳ] n **1** (pillow) cabezal m, travesaño. **2** TECH soporte m.
▶ vt reforzar.

**bolt** [bəʊlt] n **1** (on door, etc) cerrojo; (small) pestillo. **2** (screw) perno, tornillo. **3** (lightning) rayo.
▶ vt **1** (lock) cerrar con cerrojo, cerrar con pestillo. **2** (screw) sujetar con pernos, sujetar con tornillos. **3** fam (food) engullir.
▶ vi (person) escaparse; (horse) desbocarse.

**bolus** [ˈbəʊləs] n bolo alimenticio.

**bomb** [bɒm] n **1** bomba. **2** US (failure) fracaso.

▶ vt MIL bombardear; (terrorist) colocar una bomba en.
▶ vi US fam (fail) fracasar.

**bombard** [bɒmˈbɑːd] vt bombardear.

**bombardment** [bɒmˈbɑːdmənt] n bombardeo.

**bombastic** [bɒmˈbæstɪk] adj rimbombante, ampuloso,-a.

**bomber** [ˈbɒməʳ] n **1** MIL bombardero. **2** (terrorist) terrorista mf que coloca bombas.

❌ Bomber no significa 'bombero', que se traduce por fireman.

**bombing** [ˈbɒmɪŋ] n **1** MIL bombardeo. **2** (terrorist act) atentado con bomba.

**bombshell** [ˈbɒmʃel] n **1** fig bomba. **2** MIL (artillery bomb) obús m. **3** fam (attractive woman) mujer f explosiva.

**bona fide** [bəʊnəˈfaɪdɪ] adj genuino,-a, auténtico,-a.

**bond** [bɒnd] n **1** (link) lazo, vínculo; bonds of friendship vínculos de amistad. **2** FIN bono, obligación f. **3** JUR fianza. **4** (agreement) pacto, compromiso.
▶ vt **1** (stick, join) pegar, unir. **2** (deposit in customs) depositar.
▶ vi (stick, join) pegarse, unirse.

**bondage** [ˈbɒndɪdʒ] n esclavitud f, servidumbre f.

**bone** [bəʊn] n **1** hueso. **2** (of fish) espina, raspa. **3** (of whale) barba. **3** (of corset) ballena.
▶ vt (meat) deshuesar; (fish) quitar la espina.
▶ n pl bones (remains) huesos mpl, restos mpl mortales. [COMP] **bone marrow** médula ósea.
◆ **to bone up on** vt insep empollar.

**bonfire** [ˈbɒnfaɪəʳ] n hoguera. [COMP] **Bonfire night** GB la noche del cinco de noviembre; se celebra con hogueras y fuegos artificiales.

⊕ Es la noche del 5 de noviembre que se celebra en Inglaterra con hogueras y fuegos artificiales. Conmemora el intento fallido en el año 1605, de Guy Fawkes y otros conspiradores, de volar el edificio del parlamento. También se llama Guy Fawkes Night.

**bonkers** [ˈbɒŋkəz] adj GB sl chalado,-a.

**bonnet** ['bɒnɪt] *n* **1** *(child's, woman's)* gorro, gorra. **2** *(maid's)* cofia. **3** AUTO capó *m*.

**bonus** ['bəʊnəs] *n* **1** *(gratuity)* plus *m*, sobresueldo, prima. **2** *(benefit)* beneficio.
ⓘ *pl* bonuses.

**bony** ['bəʊnɪ] *adj* **1** *(thin)* esquelético,-a. **2** *(with a lot of bone)* huesudo,-a. **3** *(like bone)* óseo,-a. **4** *(meat)* lleno,-a de huesos; *(fish)* lleno,-a de espinas.
ⓘ *comp* bonier, *superl* boniest.

**bonze** [bɒnz] *n* bonzo.

**boo** [buː] *n* abucheo.
▶ *vi* abuchear.

**booby** ['buːbɪ] *n* alcatraz *m*.
ⓘ *pl* boobies.

**booby-trap** ['buːbɪtræp] *n* trampa explosiva.

**book** [bʊk] *n* **1** libro. **2** *(of tickets)* taco; *(of matches)* cajetilla.
▶ *vt* **1** *(table, room, holiday)* reservar; *(entertainer, speaker)* contratar. **2** *(police)* multar; *(football)* advertir, amonestar.
▶ *n pl* books COMM libros *mpl*, cuentas *fpl*. ⌐LOC⌐ to be booked up **1** *(hotel, restaurant)* estar completo. ⌐COMP⌐ savings book libreta de ahorro.
◆ to book in *vt sep (in hotel)* hacer la reserva.
▶ *vi* registrarse.

**bookcase** ['bʊkkeɪs] *n* librería, estantería.

**booking** ['bʊkɪŋ] *n (table, room, holiday)* reserva; *(entertainer, speaker)* contratación *f*. ⌐COMP⌐ booking office taquilla.

**bookkeeping** ['bʊkkiːpɪŋ] *n* contabilidad *f*, teneduría de libros.

**bookmaker** ['bʊkmeɪkəʳ] *n* GB corredor,-ra de apuestas.

**bookmark** ['bʊkmɑːk] *n (for book)* punto de libro; *(electronic)* marcador.
▶ *vt (electronically)* agregar un marcador.

**bookseller** ['bʊkseləʳ] *n* librero,-a.

**bookshelf** ['bʊkʃelf] *n* estante *m*.
▶ *n pl* bookshelves estantería.
ⓘ *pl* bookshelves.

**bookshop** ['bʊkʃɒp] *n* librería.

**bookstand** ['bʊkstænd] *n* **1** *(stall)* quiosco de periódicos. **2** *(bookrest)* atril *m*.

**bookstore** ['bʊkstɔːʳ] *n* US librería.

**bookworm** ['bʊkwɜːm] *n fig* ratón *m* de biblioteca.

**boom¹** [buːm] *n (noise)* estampido.
▶ *vi* tronar, retumbar.
▶ *interj* ¡bum!

**boom²** [buːm] *n* **1** MAR botalón *m*. **2** *(of microphone)* jirafa. **3** *(of crane)* brazo. **4** *(barrier)* barrera.

**boom³** [buːm] *n fig (prosperity, increase)* boom *m*, auge *m*.

**boomerang** ['buːməræŋ] *n* **1** bumerán *m*. **2** *fig* resultado contraproducente.

**boost** [buːst] *n* **1** *(incentive)* incentivo, estímulo. **2** *(promotion)* promoción *f*, fomento. **3** *(increase)* aumento.
▶ *vt* **1** *(create an incentive)* incentivar, estimular. **2** *(promote)* promocionar, fomentar. **3** *(increase)* aumentar.

**booster** ['buːstəʳ] *n* **1** ELEC elevador *m* de voltaje. **2** RAD repetidor *m*. **3** TECH motor *m* auxiliar de propulsión. ⌐COMP⌐ booster injection MED revacunación *f*.

**boot** [buːt] *n* **1** *(footwear)* bota. **2** GB *(of car)* maletero, portaequipajes *m*. **3** *(kick)* patada.
▶ *vt* **1** *(kick)* dar una patada a. **2** COMPUT cargar el sistema operativo.
◆ to boot out *vt sep* echar, echar a patadas.

**bootblack** ['buːtblæk] *n* US limpiabotas *m*, AM lustrabotas *m*.

**booth** [buːð] *n* **1** cabina. **2** *(at fair)* puesto. ⌐COMP⌐ telephone booth locutorio.

**bootleg** ['buːtleg] *n (illegal recording)* grabación *f* pirata.

**bootlegger** ['buːtlegəʳ] *n* contrabandista *mf* de licores.

**booty** ['buːtɪ] *n* botín *m*.
ⓘ *pl* booties.

**booze** [buːz] *n fam* trinque *m*, alcohol *m*.
▶ *vi fam* mamar.

**bop** [bɒp] *n* **1** *fam (dance)* baile *m*. **2** *fam (thump)* cachete *m*.
▶ *vi fam (dance)* bailar.
ⓘ *pt & pp* bopped, *ger* bopping.

**border** ['bɔːdəʳ] *n* **1** *(of country)* frontera. **2** *(edge)* borde *m*. **3** *(in sewing)* ribete *m*, orla. **4** *(of flowers, plants)* arriate *m*.
◆ **to border on** *vt insep* **1** lindar con. **2** *fig* rayar en.

**bore¹** [bɔːʳ] *pt* → **bear**.

**bore²** [bɔːʳ] *n* **1** *(of gun)* ánima, alma; *(calibre)* calibre *m*. **2** *(hole)* taladro.
▸ *vt & vi* perforar, taladrar.

**bore³** [bɔːʳ] *n* *(person)* pelmazo,-a, pesado,-a; *(thing)* lata, rollo, tostón *m*.
▸ *vt* aburrir, fastidiar.

**bored** [bɔːd] *adj* aburrido,-a. LOC **to get bored** aburrirse.

**boredom** ['bɔːdəm] *n* aburrimiento.

**borer** ['bɔːrəʳ] *n* **1** *(tool)* taladro, barrena. **2** *(machine)* taladradora.

**boric** ['bɔːrɪk] *adj* CHEM bórico,-a. COMP **boric acid** ácido bórico.

**boring** ['bɔːrɪŋ] *adj* aburrido,-a.

**born** [bɔːn] *adj* nato,-a: *she's a born leader* es una líder nata. LOC **to be born** nacer.

**borne** [bɔːn] *pp* → **bear²**.

**borough** ['bʌrə] *n* **1** *(district)* barrio, distrito. **2** *(town, city)* ciudad *f*.

**borrow** ['bɒrəʊ] *vt* pedir prestado,-a, tomar prestado,-a: *can I borrow my pen?* ¿me dejas tu boli?; *you can borrow it if you like* te lo presto si quieres.

**Bosnia** ['bɒznɪə] *n* Bosnia.

**Bosnian** ['bɒznɪən] *adj* bosnio,-a.
▸ *n* bosnio,-a.

**bosom** ['buzəm] *n* **1** pecho. **2** *(centre)* seno: *in the bosom of the family* en el seno de la familia. COMP **bosom friend** amigo,-a del alma.

**boss** [bɒs] *n* jefe,-a.
◆ **to boss around** *vt sep* mangonear.

**bosun** ['bəʊsən] *n* MAR contramaestre *m*.

**botanic** [bə'tænɪk] *adj* botánico,-a.

**botanical** [bə'tænɪkəl] *adj* botánico,-a. COMP **botanical gardens** jardín *m* botánico.

**botany** ['bɒtənɪ] *n* botánica.

**botch** [bɒtʃ] *n* chapuza.
▸ *vt* [also **to botch up**.] *(bungle)* pifiarla, fastidiarla.

**both** [bəʊθ] *adj* ambos,-as, los dos, las dos.

▸ *pron* ambos,-as, los dos, las dos: *both of us* nosotros,-as dos; *both of you* vosotros,-as dos; *both of them* los dos, las dos, ambos,-as. LOC **both ... and** tanto ... como: *both she and her sister are teachers* tanto ella como su hermana son profesoras.
▸ *adv* a la vez: *it's both cheap and good* es bueno y barato a la vez.

**bother** ['bɒðəʳ] *n* **1** *(nuisance)* molestia, fastidio. **2** *(problems)* problemas *mpl*.
▸ *vt* **1** *(be a nuisance)* molestar, fastidiar. **2** *(worry)* preocupar.
▸ *vi* **1** *(take trouble)* molestarse, tomar la molestia. **2** *(worry)* preocuparse.

**Botswana** [bɒt'swaːnə] *n* Botsuana.

**Botswanan** [bɒt'swaːnən] *adj* botsuanés,-esa, botsuano,-a.
▸ *n* botsuanés,-esa, bostuano,-a.

**bottle** ['bɒtəl] *n* **1** botella; *(small)* frasco; *(for baby)* biberón *m*; *(for gas)* bombona. **2** *sl* *(nerve)* agallas *fpl*.
▸ *vt* *(wine, etc)* embotellar; *(fruit)* envasar.

**bottle-bank** ['bɒtəlbæŋk] *n* contenedor *m* de vidrio.

**bottled** ['bɒtəld] *adj* *(wine, etc)* embotellado,-a; *(fruit)* envasado,-a. COMP **bottled gas** gas *m* butano.

**bottom** ['bɒtəm] *n* **1** *(gen)* fondo; *(of bottle)* culo; *(of hill, steps, page)* pie *m*; *(of ship)* quilla. **2** *(of dress)* bajo; *(of trousers)* bajos *mpl*. **3** *(buttocks)* trasero, culo. **4** *(last)* último,-a. **5** *(underneath)* parte *f* inferior, parte *f* de abajo.
▸ *adj* **1** *(position)* de abajo. **2** *(number, result)* más bajo,-a.

**bottomless** ['bɒtəmləs] *adj* sin fondo, insondable.

**boudoir** ['buːdwɑːʳ] *n* tocador *m*.

**bough** [baʊ] *n* rama.

**bought** [bɔːt] *pt & pp* → **buy**.

**bouillon** ['buːjɒn] *n* CULIN caldo.

**boulder** ['bəʊldəʳ] *n* canto rodado.

**boulevard** ['buːləvɑːd] *n* bulevar *m*.

**bounce** [baʊns] *n* bote *m*.
▸ *vi* *(ball)* rebotar, botar.
▸ *vt* **1** *(cheque)* ser rechazado por el banco. **2** *(ball)* hacer botar.

**bouncer** ['baʊnsəʳ] *n sl* gorila *m*.

**brain**

**bound¹** [baʊnd] *pt & pp* → **bind.**
► *adj* **1** *(tied)* atado,-a. **2** *(forced)* obligado,-a. **3** *(book)* encuadernado,-a. LOC **to be bound to** ser seguro que.

**bound²** [baʊnd] *adj (destined)* destinado,-a: *he knew he was bound to succeed* sabía que estaba destinado a tener éxito. LOC **to be bound for** ir con destino, navegar con rumbo a. ▐ **-bound** con rumbo a: *Paris-bound* con rumbo a París.

**bound³** [baʊnd] *n (jump)* salto, brinco.
► *vi* saltar.

**boundary** [ˈbaʊndərɪ] *n* límite *m*, frontera. COMP **boundary stone** hito, mojón *m*. ① *pl* **boundaries.**

**boundless** [ˈbaʊndləs] *adj* sin límites.

**bounds** [baʊndz] *n pl (border)* frontera; *(boundary)* límites *mpl.*

**bouquet** [buːˈkeɪ] *n* **1** *(flowers)* ramo. **2** *(wine)* aroma *m*, buqué *m.*

**bourgeois** [ˈbʊəʒwɑːʳ] *adj* burgués,-esa.
► *n* burgués,-esa.

**bourgeoisie** [bʊəʒwɑːˈziː] *n* burguesía.

**bout** [baʊt] *n* **1** *(period)* rato. **2** MED *(of flu, measles, etc)* ataque *m*. **3** *(boxing)* combate.

**boutique** [buːˈtiːk] *n* boutique *f*, tienda.

**bovine** [ˈbəʊvaɪn] *adj* bovino,-a.
► *n* bovino.

**bow¹** [bəʊ] *n* **1** *(for arrows)* arco. **2** *(of violin)* arco. **3** *(knot)* lazo. COMP **bow saw** sierra de arco.

**bow²** [baʊ] *n* MAR proa.

**bow³** [baʊ] *n (with body)* reverencia.
► *vt* inclinar: *he bowed his head* inclinó la cabeza.

**bowel** [ˈbaʊəl] *n* intestino.
► *n pl* **bowels** *(entrails)* entrañas *fpl.*

**bowl** [bəʊl] *n* **1** *(for food, etc)* cuenco, fuente *f*, bol *m*; *(large drinking bowl)* tazón *m*. **2** *(for washing)* palangana, barreño *m*. **3** *(of toilet)* taza.

**bow-legged** [bəʊˈlegd, bəʊˈlegɪd] *adj* patizambo,-a.

**bowler¹** [ˈbəʊləʳ] *n (hat)* bombín *m.*

**bowler²** [ˈbəʊləʳ] *n (cricket)* lanzador,-ra.

**bowling** [ˈbəʊlɪŋ] *n* bolos *mpl.* COMP **bowling alley** bolera.

**bow-tie** [bəʊˈtaɪ] *n* pajarita.

**box¹** [bɒks] *n* **1** caja; *(large)* cajón *m*. **2** *(of matches)* cajetilla. **3** THEAT palco. **4** *(for sentry)* garita. **5** *(of coach)* pescante *m*. **6** GB *fam (telly)* tele *f.* COMP **box number** número de apartado de correos. ▐ **box office** taquilla. ▐ **post-office box** apartado de correos.

**box²** [bɒks] *vi* boxear.

**boxcar** [ˈbɒkskɑːʳ] *n* US furgón *m.*

**boxer** [ˈbɒksəʳ] *n* **1** boxeador,-ra. **2** *(dog)* bóxer *m.*

**boxing** [ˈbɒksɪŋ] *n* boxeo. COMP **Boxing Day** GB *el día 26 de diciembre.*

⊕ El 26 de diciembre es festivo en Gran Bretaña. Las tiendas inician las rebajas, se disputan partidos de fútbol y se celebran carreras de caballos.

**boy** [bɔɪ] *n (baby)* niño; *(child)* chico, muchacho; *(youth)* joven *m.*

**boycott** [ˈbɔɪkɒt] *n* boicoteo, boicot *m.*
► *vt* boicotear.

**boyfriend** [ˈbɔɪfrend] *n* **1** *(fiancé)* novio. **2** *(male friend)* amigo.

**boyhood** [ˈbɔɪhʊd] *n* infancia, niñez *f.*
► *adj* de la infancia.

**bra** [brɑː] *n* sostén *m*, sujetador *m.*

**brace** [breɪs] *n* **1** *(clamp)* abrazadera. **2** ARCH *(support)* riostra. **3** *(drill)* berbiquí *m*. **4** *(on teeth)* aparato.
► *n pl* **braces** tirantes *mpl.*

**bracelet** [ˈbreɪslət] *n* pulsera, brazalete *m.*

**bracken** [ˈbrækən] *n* BOT helechos *mpl.*

**bracket** [ˈbrækɪt] *n* **1** *(round)* paréntesis *m*. **2** *(for shelf)* escuadra, soporte *m*. **3** *(group, category)* grupo, categoría *m.* COMP **square bracket** corchete *m.*

**brag** [bræg] *n* jactancia, fanfarria.
► *vi* jactarse (about, de).
① *pt & pp* **bragged**, *ger* **bragging.**

**braggart** [ˈbrægət] *n* fanfarrón,-ona.

**braid** [breɪd] *n* **1** *(on clothing)* galón *m*. **2** *(plait)* trenza.

**Braille** [breɪl] *n* braille *m.*

**brain** [breɪn] *n (organ)* cerebro, seso.

► *n pl* **brains 1** *(intellect)* cerebro, seso, inteligencia. **2** *(as food)* sesos *mpl.* LOC **to have brains** ser un cerebro, ser inteligente. LOC **brain death** muerte *f* cerebral. ‖ **brain drain** fuga de cerebros. ‖ **brain scan** electroencefalograma *m.*

**brain-dead** ['breɪndɛd] *adj* clínicamente muerto,-a.

**brainstorming** ['breɪnstɔːmɪŋ] *n* reunión *f* creativa, lluvia de ideas.

**brainy** ['breɪnɪ] *adj fam* inteligente, sesudo,-a.
① *comp* brainier, *superl* brainiest.

**braise** [breɪz] *vt* CULIN freír y luego cocer a fuego lento.

**brake** [breɪk] *n* freno. COMP **brake arm** palanca del freno. ‖ **brake block** pastilla de freno. ‖ **brake fluid** líquido de freno.
► *vt* frenar, hacer frenar.

**bramble** ['bræmbəl] *n* BOT zarzamora, mora. COMP **bramble bush** zarza.

**bran** [bræn] *n* salvado.

**branch** [brɑːntʃ] *n* **1** *(tree)* rama. **2** *(of family)* ramo. **3** *(road, railway)* ramal *m*; *(stream, river)* brazo. **4** *(of shop)* sucursal *f*; *(of bank)* oficina, sucursal *f*. **5** *(field of science, etc)* ramo. **6** *(of candelabra)* brazo.
► *vi (road)* bifurcarse.

**brand** [brænd] *n* **1** marca. **2** *(type)* clase *f*, tipo.

**brand-new** [bræn'njuː] *adj* flamante, de estreno.

**brandy** ['brændɪ] *n* brandy *m.*
① *pl* brandies.

**brass** [brɑːs] *n* **1** latón *m.* **2** *sl (money)* pasta. **3** MUS metales *mpl.*
► *adj* de cobre.

**brassiere** ['bræzɪəʳ] *n* sujetador *m*, sostén *m.*

**brat** [bræt] *n fam pej* mocoso,-a.

**brave** [breɪv] *adj* valiente.
► *n* guerrero indio.
► *vt* **1** *(defy)* desafiar. **2** *(confront)* afrontar, hacer frente a.

**bravo** [brɑː'vəʊ] *interj* ¡bravo!

**brawl** [brɔːl] *n* reyerta, pelea.
► *vi* pelearse.

**bray** [breɪ] *vi* **1** *(donkey, ass)* rebuznar. **2** *(laugh)* carcajearse.

**Brazil** [brə'zɪl] *n* Brasil.

**Brazilian** [brə'zɪlɪən] *adj* brasileño,-a.
► *n* brasileño,-a.

**breach** [briːtʃ] *n* **1** *(opening)* brecha, abertura. **2** *(in promise, undertaking)* incumplimiento; *(in law)* violación *f*, infracción *f*. **3** *(in relationship)* ruptura.

**bread** [bred] *n* pan *m.* COMP **wholemeal bread** pan *m* integral.

**bread-and-butter** ['bredənbʌtəʳ] *adj* *(commonplace)* rutinario,-a, corriente y moliente.

**breadth** [bredθ] *n* **1** *(broadness)* ancho, anchura. **2** *(space)* extensión *f*, amplitud *f.*

**break** [breɪk] *n* **1** *(in leg, etc)* rotura. **2** *(in relationship)* ruptura. **3** *(in meeting)* descanso, pausa; *(at school)* recreo. LOC **to take a break** tomarse un descanso. ‖ **without a break** sin descanso, sin parar. ‖ **at break of day** al amanecer.
► *vt* **1** romper. **2** *(record)* batir.
► *vi* **1** romperse. **2** *(storm)* estallar.
◆ **to break away** *vi (escape)* escaparse, darse a la fuga; *(leave family, job)* irse.
◆ **to break down** *vt sep* **1** *(door)* derribar, echar abajo. **2** *(resistance)* vencer.
► *vi* **1** *(car)* averiarse; *(driver)* tener una avería. **2** *(burst into tears)* romper a llorar. **3** *(talks, negotiations)* fracasar.
◆ **to break in** *vi (force entry)* entrar por la fuerza.
◆ **to break off** *vt sep* **1** *(relationship)* romper. **2** *(discussions, negotiations)* interrumpir.
◆ **to break out** *vi* **1** *(prisoners)* escaparse. **2** *(war, fire, etc)* estallar.
◆ **to break up** *vt sep (chair, table, etc)* romper; *(ship, boat)* desguazar.
► *vi* **1** *(couple)* separarse. **2** *(gathering, meeting)* disolverse. **3** *(school)* empezar las vacaciones.
① *pt* broke [brəʊk], *pp* broken ['brəʊkən].

**breakable** ['breɪkəbəl] *adj* frágil, rompible.

**breakage** ['breɪkɪdʒ] *n* rotura.

**breakdown** ['breɪkdaʊn] *n* **1** *(of car, machine)* avería. **2** MED crisis *f* nerviosa. **3** *(in negotiations)* ruptura. **4** *(chemical analysis)* análisis *m.* COMP **breakdown service** (servicio de) asistencia en carretera. ▌ **breakdown van / breakdown truck** grúa.

**breakfast** ['brekfəst] n desayuno. LOC **to have breakfast** desayunar.
▸ vi desayunar.

**break-in** ['breɪkɪn] n entrada forzada.

**breaking** ['breɪkɪŋ] n **1** (of leg, object) rotura. **2** (of relationship) ruptura.

**break-out** ['breɪkaʊt] n (from prison) fuga.

**breakthrough** ['breɪkθruː] n avance m importante.

**break-up** ['breɪkʌp] n (of relationship, negotiations) ruptura; (of couple) separación f.

**breakwater** ['breɪkwɔːtə'] n rompeolas m.

**bream** [briːm] n (river fish) brema. COMP **gilt-head bream** dorada. ▌ **red bream** besugo.

**breast** [brest] n **1** (chest) pecho; (of woman) pecho, seno. **2** (of chicken, etc) pechuga.

**breastbone** ['brestbəʊn] n ANAT esternón m.

**breast-feed** ['brestfiːd] vt amamantar, dar el pecho a.
ⓘ pt & pp **breast-fed** ['brestfed].

**breaststroke** ['breststrəʊk] n (swimming) braza.

**breath** [breθ] n **1** (of person) aliento. **2** (of air) soplo. **3** (breathing) resuello, respiración f. LOC **out of breath** sin aliento. COMP **breath test** GB prueba del alcohol.

**Breathalyser®** ['breθəlaɪzə'] n alcoholímetro.

**breathe** [briːð] vt (air, etc) respirar.
▸ vi **1** (air, etc) respirar. **2** (be alive) respirar, vivir: is he still breathing? ¿respira aún? LOC **to breathe in** aspirar. ▌ **to breathe out** espirar.

**breathing** ['briːðɪŋ] n respiración f.

**bred** [bred] pt & pp → breed.

**breeches** ['brɪtʃɪz] n pl **1** (knee-length trousers) calzones mpl. **2** fam (trousers) pantalones mpl.

**breed** [briːd] n (of animal) raza; (of plant) variedad f.
▸ vt (animals) criar.
▸ vi (animals) reproducirse.
ⓘ pt & pp **bred** [bred].

**breeze** [briːz] n METEOR brisa.

**brew** [bruː] n **1** (tea, etc) infusión f. **2** (potion) brebaje m.
▸ vt **1** (beer) elaborar. **2** (tea, etc) preparar.
▸ vi **1** (tea, etc) reposar. **2** (storm) prepararse, acercarse.

**brewer** ['bruːə'] n fabricante mf de cerveza, cervecero,-a. COMP **brewer's yeast** levadura de cerveza.

**brewery** ['bruːərɪ] n fábrica de cerveza, cervecería.
ⓘ pl breweries.

**briar** ['braɪə'] n BOT (heather) brezo.

**bribe** [braɪb] n soborno.
▸ vt sobornar.

**bribery** ['braɪbərɪ] n soborno.

**bric-a-brac** ['brɪkəbræk] n baratijas fpl.

**brick** [brɪk] n **1** ladrillo. **2** (toy) cubo (de madera).

**bricklayer** ['brɪkleɪə'] n albañil m.

**bridal** ['braɪdəl] adj nupcial. COMP **bridal gown** vestido de novia.

**bride** [braɪd] n novia, desposada. COMP **the bride and groom** los novios.

**bridegroom** ['braɪdgruːm] n novio.

✎ Bridegroom o groom sólo se emplean para referirse al novio durante el día de la boda.

**bridesmaid** ['braɪdzmeɪd] n dama de honor.

**bridge** [brɪdʒ] n **1** puente m. **2** (of nose) caballete m.

**bridle** ['braɪdəl] n brida.
▸ vt (horse) embridar.
▸ vi mostrar desagrado (at, por).

**brief** [briːf] adj (short) breve; (concise) conciso,-a; (scanty) diminuto,-a.
▸ n **1** (report) informe m. **2** JUR expediente m. **3** MIL instrucciones fpl.
▸ vt **1** (inform) informar (about, sobre). **2** (instruct) dar instrucciones a.

**briefcase** ['briːfkeɪs] n maletín m, cartera.

**briefing** ['briːfɪŋ] n reunión f informativa, briefing m.

**brigade** [brɪ'geɪd] n MIL brigada.
▸ vt MIL formar una brigada con.

**bright** [braɪt] adj **1** (gen) brillante. **2** METEOR (sky, day) claro,-a, despejado,-a;

*(sunny)* soleado,-a, de sol. **3** *(colour)* vivo,-a. **4** *(cheerful)* alegre, animado,-a.
◆ **to brighten up** *vt sep* **1** METEOR despejar. **2** *(room, house)* dar un aspecto más alegre a. **3** *(enliven)* alegrar, animar.

**brightness** ['braɪtnəs] *n* **1** *(light)* luminosidad *f*. **2** *(of sun)* resplandor *m*. **3** *(of day)* claridad *f*. **4** *(of colour)* viveza. **5** *(cleverness)* inteligencia.

**brilliant** ['brɪljənt] *adj* **1** *(gen)* brillante. **2** *(colour)* vivo,-a. **3** *fam* estupendo,-a, fantástico,-a.

**brim** [brɪm] *n* **1** *(of cup, glass, etc)* borde *m*. **2** *(of hat)* ala.
▶ *vi* rebosar (**with**, de): *he was brimming with pride* rebosaba de orgullo.

**brine** [braɪn] *n* salmuera.

**bring** [brɪŋ] *vt* **1** traer. **2** *(lead)* llevar, conducir.
◆ **to bring about** *vt sep (accident, change, etc)* provocar, causar.
◆ **to bring back** *vt sep* **1** *(book, record, etc)* devolver. **2** *(past experience, childhood, etc)* recordar, hacer recordar.
◆ **to bring down** *vt sep* **1** *(chair, book, etc)* bajar. **2** *(door, house, government)* derribar. **3** *(prices, temperature)* hacer bajar.
◆ **to bring forward** *vt sep* **1** *(meeting, appointment)* adelantar. **2** *(theme, question)* presentar, plantear.
◆ **to bring in** *vt sep* **1** *(person)* hacer pasar. **2** *(coal, food, etc into house)* traer. **3** JUR *(verdict)* emitir, pronunciar.
◆ **to bring off** *vt sep (victory, result)* conseguir, lograr.
◆ **to bring on** *vt sep (illness)* provocar.
◆ **to bring out** *vt sep (record)* sacar al mercado, sacar; *(book)* publicar.
◆ **to bring to** *vt sep* hacer volver en sí.
◆ **to bring up** *vt sep* **1** *(chair, book, etc)* subir. **2** *(child)* criar, educar. **3** *(subject, topic)* plantear. **4** *(vomit)* devolver.
ⓘ *pt & pp* **brought** [brɔːt].

**brink** [brɪŋk] *n* borde *m*.

**brisk** [brɪsk] *adj* enérgico,-a.

**bristle** ['brɪsəl] *n* cerda.
▶ *vi* **1** *(hair)* erizarse, ponerse de punta. **2** *(show annoyance)* mosquearse.

**Britain** ['brɪtən] *n* Gran Bretaña. COMP **Great Britain** Gran Bretaña.

**British** ['brɪtɪʃ] *adj* británico,-a.
▶ *n pl* **the British** los británicos *mpl*.

**Briton** ['brɪtən] *n* británico,-a.

**brittle** ['brɪtəl] *adj* quebradizo,-a, frágil.

**broach** [brəʊtʃ] *n* **1** *(drill bit)* broca. **2** *(roasting-spit)* espetón *m*.

**broad** [brɔːd] *adj* **1** *(street, avenue)* ancho,-a; *(surface, water, plateau)* extenso,-a. **2** *fig (field of study, debate)* amplio,-a. **3** *(measurement)* de ancho. **4** *(general)* general. **5** *(main)* principal. **6** *(accent)* marcado,-a, cerrado,-a. **7** *(vowel)* abierto,-a.

**broadcast** ['brɔːdkɑːst] *n* *(by TV, radio)* emisión *f*.
▶ *vt* **1** *(by TV, radio)* emitir, transmitir. **2** *(make known)* difundir.
ⓘ *pt & pp* **broadcast**.

**broadcasting** ['brɔːdkɑːstɪŋ] *n* **1** RAD radiodifusión *f*. **2** TV transmisión *f*.

**broaden** ['brɔːdən] *vt* ensanchar.

**broadly** ['brɔːdlɪ] *adv* en términos generales.

**broad-minded** [brɔːd'maɪndɪd] *adj* liberal, tolerante.

**broccoli** ['brɒkəlɪ] *n* brécol *m*, brócoli *m*.

**brochette** [brə'ʃet] *n* brocheta.

**brochure** ['brəʊʃər] *n* folleto.

**broil** [brɔɪl] *vt* US asar a la parrilla.

**broiler** ['brɔɪlər] *n* **1** CULIN pollo. **2** *(gridiron)* parrilla.

**broke** [brəʊk] *pt* → **break**.
▶ *adj fam* sin un duro, sin blanca.

**broken** ['brəʊkən] *pp* → **break**.
▶ *adj* **1** *(plate, window, etc)* roto,-a. **2** *(machine)* estropeado,-a. **3** *(bone)* fracturado,-a. **4** *(person)* destrozado,-a. **6** *(language)* chapurreado,-a: *he speaks broken Spanish* chapurrea el español.

**broker** ['brəʊkər] *n* COMM corredor,-ra, agente *mf* de Bolsa.

**brolly** ['brɒlɪ] *n* GB *fam* paraguas *m*.
ⓘ *pl* **brollies**.

**bromine** ['brəʊmaɪn] *n* CHEM bromo.

**bronchial** ['brɒŋkɪəl] *adj* ANAT bronquial. COMP **bronchial tubes** ANAT bronquios *mpl*.

**bronchitis** [brɒŋ'kaɪtəs] *n* MED bronquitis *f*.

**bronchus** ['brɒŋkəs] *n* bronquio.
ⓘ *pl* **bronchi** ['brɒŋkaɪ].

**brontosaurus** [brɒntə'sɔːrəs] *n* brontosaurio.

**bronze** [brɒnz] *n* bronce *m*. COMP **the Bronze Age** HIST la Edad del Bronce.
▶ *vi (get a suntan)* broncearse.

**brooch** [brəʊtʃ] *n* broche *m*.

**brood** [bruːd] *n* **1** *(birds)* nidada. **2** *fam fig (children)* prole *f*.
▶ *vi* **1** *(hen)* empollar. **2** *fig (worry)* apurarse, preocuparse.

**brook** [brʊk] *n* arroyo, riachuelo.

**broom** [bruːm] *n* **1** *(for sweeping)* escoba. **2** BOT hiniesta.

**broomstick** ['bruːmstɪk] *n* **1** *(handle)* palo de escoba. **2** *(of witch)* escoba.

**Bros** [brɒs] *abbr* (Brothers) Hermanos *mpl*; *(abbreviation)* Hnos: *Jones Bros* Hnos Jones.

**broth** [brɒθ] *n* CULIN caldo.

**brothel** ['brɒθəl] *n* burdel *m*.

**brother** ['brʌðəʳ] *n* **1** *(gen)* hermano. **2** US *fam (friend)* colega *m*, tío: *what's happening brother?* ¿qué pasa tío?

**brotherhood** ['brʌðəhʊd] *n* hermandad *f*, cofradía.

**brother-in-law** ['brʌðərɪnlɔː] *n* cuñado.
ⓘ *pl* **brothers-in-law** ['brʌðərɪnlɔː].

**brought** [brɔːt] *pt & pp* → **bring**.

**brow** [braʊ] *n* **1** *(eyebrow)* ceja. **2** *(forehead)* frente *f*. **3** *(of hill)* cresta.

**browbeat** ['braʊbiːt] *vt* intimidar.
ⓘ *pt* **browbeat**, *pp* **browbeaten** ['braʊbiːtən].

**brown** [braʊn] *adj* **1** marrón. **2** *(hair, etc)* castaño,-a. **3** *(skin)* moreno,-a.
▶ *vi* CULIN dorarse.

**brownie** ['braʊnɪ] *n* US *pastelito de chocolate y nueces.*

**browse** [braʊz] *vi* **1** *(grass)* pacer. **2** *(person in shop)* mirar.
◆ **to browse through** *vt insep (book, magazine)* hojear.

**browser** ['braʊzəʳ] *n* *(Internet)* navegador *m*, explorador *m*.

**bruise** [bruːz] *n* morado, magulladura, contusión *f*.
▶ *vt* magullar, contusionar.
▶ *vi* magullarse.

**bruiser** ['bruːzəʳ] *n fam* gorila *m*, matón *m*.

**brunch** [brʌntʃ] *n* brunch *m*.

✎ El brunch es una especie de copioso desayuno que se toma a última hora de la mañana y hace asimismo las veces de almuerzo.

**brunette** [bruː'net] *n* morena.
▶ *adj* moreno,-a.

**brush** [brʌʃ] *n* **1** *(for teeth, clothes, etc)* cepillo. **2** *(artist's)* pincel *m*; *(house painter's)* brocha. **3** *(unpleasant encounter)* roce *m*: *he had a brush with the police* tuvo un roce con la policía.
▶ *vt* **1** *(gen)* cepillar. **2** *(touch lightly)* rozar.
◆ **to brush away** *vt sep (dirt, dust)* quitar, limpiar.
◆ **to brush up** *vt sep (knowledge)* refrescar, repasar.

**brush-off** ['brʌʃɒf] *n (rebuff, snub)* desaire *m*.

**brushwood** ['brʌʃwʊd] *n* **1** *(twigs)* broza. **2** *(undergrowth)* maleza.

**brusque** [brʌsk] *adj* brusco,-a.

**Brussels** ['brʌsəlz] *n* Bruselas. COMP **Brussels sprouts** coles *fpl* de Bruselas.

**brutal** ['bruːtəl] *adj* brutal, cruel.

**brute** [bruːt] *n* bruto,-a, bestia *mf*.
▶ *adj* brutal, bruto,-a.

✖ Brute no se utiliza en el sentido de '(importe) bruto', que se traduce por gross.

**bubble** ['bʌbəl] *n (in liquid)* burbuja; *(of soap)* pompa.

**bubonic** [bjuː'bɒnɪk] *adj* MED bubónico,-a. COMP **bubonic plague** peste *f* bubónica.

**buck¹** [bʌk] *n (rabbit, hare)* macho; *(deer)* ciervo; *(goat)* macho cabrío.
▶ *adj (animal)* macho.

**buck²** [bʌk] *n* US *fam* dólar *m*.

**bucket** ['bʌkɪt] *n* cubo.

**buckle** ['bʌkəl] *n (on shoe, belt)* hebilla.
▶ *vt (belt)* abrochar.
▶ *vi* **1** *(metal, object)* torcerse, combarse. **2** *(knees)* doblarse.

**bucolic** [bjuː'kɒlɪk] *adj* bucólico,-a.

**bud¹** [bʌd] *n (on tree, plant)* brote *m*, yema; *(of flower)* botón *m*, capullo.

**bud²** [bʌd] n US fam colega mf.

**Buddhism** ['budɪzəm] n REL budismo.

**budding** ['bʌdɪŋ] adj en ciernes.

**buddy** ['bʌdɪ] n US fam amigote m, colega mf.
ⓘ pl buddies.

**budge** [bʌdʒ] vt **1** (move) mover. **2** (make change opinion) hacer cambiar de opinión.

**budgerigar** ['bʌdʒərɪgɑːʳ] n ZOOL periquito.

**budget** ['bʌdʒɪt] n presupuesto.
▶ adj (good-value) bien de precio.
▶ vt **to budget for** presupuestar.

**budgie** ['bʌdʒɪ] n ZOOL fam periquito.

**buff** [bʌf] n **1** (leather) piel f de ante. **2** (colour) color m de ante. **3** (enthusiast) aficionado,-a.

**buffalo** ['bʌfələu] n ZOOL búfalo.
ⓘ pl buffalo o buffaloes.

**buffer** ['bʌfəʳ] n **1** (for train) tope m. **2** COMPUT memoria intermedia. **3** CHEM regulador m.

**buffet** ['bʌfeɪ] n **1** (bar) bar m; (at station) bar m, cantina. **2** (meal) bufé m libre, bufé m. **3** (sideboard) aparador m.

**bug** [bʌg] n **1** (insect) bicho. **2** fam (microbe) microbio. **3** (microphone) micrófono oculto. **4** fam (interest) afición f. **5** (in computer program) error m.
▶ vt **1** fam ocultar micrófonos en. **2** US (annoy) molestar, fastidiar: what's bugging her? ¿qué mosca le ha picado?
ⓘ pt & pp bugged, ger bugging.

**bugle** ['bjuːgəl] n MUS corneta.

**build** [bɪld] n (physique) constitución f, complexión f: a strong build una complexión fuerte.
▶ vt construir.
ⓘ pt & pp built [bɪlt].

**builder** ['bɪldəʳ] n **1** (owner of company) constructor,-ra. **2** (bricklayer) albañil m.

**building** ['bɪldɪŋ] n **1** edificio. **2** (action) construcción f, edificación f. COMP building society sociedad f hipotecaria. ▌ the building industry / the building trade la construcción.

**build-up** ['bɪldʌp] n **1** (increase) aumento: a build-up in pollution un aumento de la contaminación. **2** (of gas) acumulación f.

**built** [bɪlt] pt & pp → build.

**built-in** [bɪlt'ɪn] adj **1** (as component) incorporado,-a. **2** (recessed) empotrado,-a.

**built-up** [bɪlt'ʌp] adj urbanizado,-a.

**bulb** [bʌlb] n **1** BOT bulbo. **2** ELEC bombilla.

**Bulgaria** [bʌl'geərɪə] n Bulgaria.

**Bulgarian** [bʌl'geərɪən] adj búlgaro,-a.
▶ n búlgaro.

**bulge** [bʌldʒ] n bulto.

**bulimia** [bjuː'liːmɪə] n bulimia.

**bulk** [bʌlk] n **1** (mass) masa, bulto; (amount, quantity) volumen m, cantidad f. **2** (greater part) mayor parte f.

**bulk-buying** ['bʌlkbaɪɪŋ] n compra en grandes cantidades.

**bull¹** [bul] n **1** toro. **2** (elephant, whale, etc) macho. **3** FIN alcista mf.
▶ adj **1** (elephant, whale, etc) macho. **2** FIN alcista, en alza.

**bull²** [bul] n REL (papal) bula.

**bulldog** ['buldɒg] n bulldog m.

**bulldozer** ['buldəuzəʳ] n bulldozer m.

**bullet** ['bulɪt] n bala.

**bulletin** ['bulɪtɪn] n **1** (publication) boletín m. **2** (medical, etc) parte m.

**bulletproof** ['bulɪtpruːf] adj antibalas. COMP **bulletproof vest** chaleco antibalas.

**bullfight** ['bulfaɪt] n corrida de toros.

**bullfighter** ['bulfaɪtəʳ] n torero,-a.

**bullfighting** ['bulfaɪtɪŋ] n los toros mpl (art) tauromaquia.

**bullion** ['buljən] n (gold) oro en lingotes; (silver) plata en lingotes.

**bullock** ['bulək] n buey m.

**bullring** ['bulrɪŋ] n plaza de toros.

**bull's-eye** ['bulzaɪ] n **1** (target) diana. **2** (score) acierto. **3** MAR (porthole) portilla. LOC **to score a bull's-eye** dar en el blanco.

**bullshit** ['bulʃɪt] n taboo (nonsense) chorradas fpl.

**bully** ['bulɪ] n matón,-ona.
ⓘ pl bullies.

**bum¹** [bʌm] n GB fam (bottom) culo.

**bum²** [bʌm] n **1** US fam (tramp) vagabundo,-a. **2** US fam (idler) vago,-a, holgazán,-ana.

▸ vt *fam (scrounge)* gorrear, sablear.

**bumblebee** ['bʌmbəlbiː] n ZOOL abejorro.

**bummer** ['bʌmə'] n *fam* lata, latazo.

**bump** [bʌmp] n **1** *(blow)* golpe m, batacazo. **2** *(on head)* chichón m; *(swelling)* hinchazón m; *(lump)* bulto. **4** *(dent)* abolladura. **5** *(on road)* bache m.

▸ vt **1** darse un golpe en: *he bumped his head* se dio un golpe en la cabeza. **2** dar un golpe a.

▸ vi **1** chocar (into, con), topar (into, contra). **2** *(collide)* chocar, colisionar.

◆ **to bump into** vt insep *fam* encontrar por casualidad, tropezar con.

◆ **to bump off** vt sep *sl* liquidar.

**bumper** ['bʌmpə'] n parachoques m.

▸ adj abundante.

**bumpy** ['bʌmpɪ] adj **1** *(surface)* desigual, accidentado,-a. **2** *(road)* lleno,-a de baches.

ⓘ comp bumpier, superl bumpiest.

**bun** [bʌn] n **1** *(bread)* panecillo; *(sweet)* bollo. **2** *(cake)* ma(g)dalena. **3** *(hair)* moño.

**bunch** [bʌntʃ] n **1** manojo. **2** *(flowers)* ramo. **3** *(fruit)* racimo. **4** *fam (group of people)* grupo; *(gang)* pandilla.

**bundle** ['bʌndəl] n **1** *(clothes)* fardo, bulto. **2** *(wood)* haz m. **3** *(papers, banknotes)* fajo. **4** *(keys)* manojo.

**bung** [bʌŋ] n *(stopper)* tapón m.

**bungalow** ['bʌŋgələʊ] n bungalow m.

**bungle** ['bʌŋgəl] vt chapucear.

**bungler** ['bʌŋglə'] n chapucero,-a.

**bunion** ['bʌnjən] n MED juanete m.

**bunk** [bʌŋk] n *(bed)* litera.

**bunk-bed** ['bʌŋkbed] n litera.

ⓘ pl bunk-beds.

**bunker** ['bʌŋkə'] n **1** MIL búnker m. **2** *(golf)* búnker m.

**bunny** ['bʌnɪ] n *fam* conejito.

ⓘ pl bunnies.

**buoy** [bɔɪ] n boya, baliza.

**buoyant** ['bɔɪənt] adj **1** flotante. **2** *(cheerful)* animado,-a. **3** *(optimistic)* optimista.

**burden** ['bɜːdən] n carga.

▸ vt cargar.

**bureau** ['bjʊərəʊ] n **1** *(desk)* escritorio. **2** US *(office)* oficina. **3** US *(agency)* agen-

cia. **4** US *(chest of drawers)* cómoda. **5** US departamento del estado.

ⓘ pl bureaus o bureaux ['bjʊərəʊ].

**bureaucracy** [bjʊəˈrɒkrəsɪ] n burocracia.

ⓘ pl bureaucracies.

**burger** ['bɜːgə'] n hamburguesa.

**burglar** ['bɜːglə'] n ladrón,-ona.

**burglary** ['bɜːglərɪ] n *(gen)* robo.

ⓘ pl burglaries.

**burgle** ['bɜːgəl] vt robar.

**burial** ['berɪəl] n entierro. COMP **burial ground** cementerio.

**burn¹** [bɜːn] n quemadura.

▸ vt quemar.

▸ vi **1** arder.

◆ **to burn down** vt sep incendiar.

◆ **to burn out** vi **1** *(fire)* extinguirse. **2** *(fuse, bulb)* fundirse.

ⓘ pt & pp burnt [bɜːnt] o burned.

**burn²** [bɜːn] n *(stream)* arroyo.

**burner** ['bɜːnə'] n quemador m.

**burning** ['bɜːnɪŋ] adj **1** *(on fire)* en llamas, ardiendo. **2** *(sun)* abrasador,-ra, de justicia; *(heat)* achicharrante. **3** *(desire, need)* ardiente. COMP **burning issue / burning question** cuestión f candente.

**burnt** [bɜːnt] pt & pp → **burn**.

**burnt-out** ['bɜːntaʊt] adj **1** *(building, car)* carbonizado,-a. **2** *fig (person)* quemado,-a, caduco,-a.

**burp** [bɜːp] n *fam* eructo.

▸ vi *fam* eructar.

**burrow** ['bʌrəʊ] n madriguera.

**bursary** ['bɜːsərɪ] n *(scholarship)* beca.

ⓘ pl bursaries.

**burst** [bɜːst] n **1** *(of balloon, pipe)* reventón m; *(of tyre)* pinchazo, reventón m. **2** *(explosion)* estallido, explosión f. **3** *(of applause)* salva. **4** *(of gunfire)* ráfaga.

▸ vi *(balloon, pipe)* reventarse; *(tyre)* pincharse, reventarse.

ⓘ pt & pp burst.

**bury** ['berɪ] vt enterrar.

ⓘ pt & pp buried, ger burying.

**bus** [bʌs] n **1** autobús m, bus m. **2** COMPUT bus m. COMP **bus conductor** cobrador. ‖ **bus conductress** cobradora. ‖ **bus lane** carril m de autobuses. ‖ **bus route** línea de autobús. ‖ **bus shelter**

parada de autobús cubierta. ▌**bus station** estación *f* de autobuses. ▌**bus stop** parada de autobús.
ⓘ *pl* buses (US busses).

**bush** [buʃ] *n* **1** *(plant)* arbusto. **2** *(land)* breña.
▶ *n pl* **bushes** matorral *m*, maleza.

**Bushman** ['buʃmən] *n & adj* bosquimano,-a.
ⓘ *pl* Bushmen ['buʃmen].

**bushy** ['buʃɪ] *adj* espeso,-a, tupido,-a.
ⓘ *comp* bushier, *superl* bushiest.

**business** ['bɪznəs] *n* **1** *(commerce)* negocios *mpl*: *the business world* el mundo de los negocios. **2** *(firm)* negocio, empresa: *he's got a small business on the coast* tiene un pequeño negocio en la costa. **3** *(affair)* asunto, tema *m*: *I've got business to discuss with the manager* tengo asuntos que tratar con el director. ⌑LOC⌑ **it's my "(your, etc)" business to ...** me *(te, etc)* incumbe .... ▌ **to go out of business** quebrar. ▌**to run a business** llevar un negocio. ▌**to set up a business** montar un negocio. ▌**mind your own business!** ¡no te metas donde no te llaman! ▌⌑LOC⌑ **business card** tarjeta de presentación, tarjeta comercial. ▌**business trip** viaje *m* de negocios.

**businesslike** ['bɪznəslaɪk] *adj* formal, serio,-a.

**businessman** ['bɪznəsmən] *n* hombre *m* de negocios, empresario.
ⓘ *pl* businessmen ['bɪznəsmen].

**businesswoman** ['bɪznəswumən] *n* mujer *m* de negocios, empresaria.
ⓘ *pl* businesswomen ['bɪznəswɪmɪn].

**busker** ['bʌskər] *n* GB músico callejero,-a.

**bust¹** [bʌst] *n* busto.

**bust²** [bʌst] *adj fam* roto,-a. ⌑LOC⌑ **to go bust** *fam* quebrar.
▶ *vt fam* romper.
▶ *vi* romperse.
ⓘ *pt & pp* bust [bʌst] o busted.

**bustard** ['bʌstəd] *n* avutarda.

**bustle** ['bʌsəl] *n* bullicio, ajetreo.

**busy** ['bɪzɪ] *adj* **1** *(person)* ocupado,-a, atareado,-a. **2** *(street, place)* concurrido,-a. **3** *(day)* ajetreado,-a. **4** US *(telephone)* comunicando: *the line was busy* estaba comunicando. ⌑LOC⌑ **to get busy 1** *fam (work)* ponerse a trabajar. **2** *(hurry)* darse prisa.
ⓘ *comp* busier, *superl* busiest.

**busybody** ['bɪzɪbɒdɪ] *n* entremetido,-a, fisgón,-ona.
ⓘ *pl* busybodies.

**but** [bʌt] *conj* **1** pero: *it's cold, but dry* hace frío, pero no llueve; *I'd like to, but I can't* me gustaría, pero no puedo. **2** *(after negative)* sino: *not two, but three* no dos, sino tres. **3** *(after negative with verb)* sino que: *she told him not to wait, but to go home* le dijo que no se esperara, sino que se fuera para casa. ⌑LOC⌑ **but for** de no ser por, si no fuera por: *but for him, we would have failed* de no ser por él, habríamos fracasado.
▶ *adv* (nada) más que, no ... sino, solamente, solo,: *he spoke nothing but the truth* no dijo nada más que la verdad.
▶ *prep* excepto, salvo, menos: *everyone but me* todos menos yo; *I can meet you any day but Friday* te puedo ver cualquier día excepto el viernes.
▶ *n* pero: *there are no buts about it* no hay pero que valga.

**butane** ['bjuːteɪn] *n* CHEM butano. ⌑COMP⌑ **butane bottle** bombona (de butano). ▌**butane gas** gas *m* butano.

**butcher** ['butʃər] *n* carnicero,-a.

**butcher's** ['butʃəz] *n* carnicería.

**butchery** ['butʃərɪ] *n* carnicería.

**butt¹** [bʌt] *n* *(with head)* cabezazo.

**butt²** [bʌt] *n* **1** *(of rifle)* culata. **2** *(of cigarette)* colilla. **3** US *fam (bottom)* culo.

**butt³** [bʌt] *n* *(target)* blanco.

**butt⁴** [bʌt] *n* **1** *(barrel)* tonel *m*. **2** *(for water)* aljibe *m*.

**butter** ['bʌtər] *n* mantequilla.
▶ *vt* untar con mantequilla. ⌑COMP⌑ **butter dish** mantequera. ▌
◆ **to butter up** *vt sep fam* dar coba a.

**buttercup** ['bʌtəkʌp] *n* BOT botón *m* de oro, ranúnculo.

**butterfingers** ['bʌtəfɪŋɡəz] *n* manazas *mf*, torpe *mf*.

**butterfly** ['bʌtəflaɪ] *n* **1** mariposa. **2** SP *(swimming)* mariposa.
ⓘ *pl* butterflies.

**buttock** ['bʌtək] *n* **1** *(of person)* nalga. **2** *(of animal)* anca.
▶ *n pl* **buttocks** *(bottom)* trasero, nalgas *fpl*.

**button** ['bʌtən] *n* **1** *(on clothing, machine)* botón *m*; *(on doorbell)* pulsador *m*, botón *m*: *press the button* pulse el botón. **2** BOT *(bud)* botón *m*, yema.
▶ *vi* abrocharse.
▶ *vt* **to button (up)** abrochar, abrocharse: *button (up) your coat* abróchate el abrigo.

**buttonhole** ['bʌtənhəʊl] *n* ojal *m*.

**buttress** ['bʌtrəs] *n* ARCH contrafuerte *m*.

**butty** ['bʌtɪ] *n fam* bocata *m*.
ⓘ *pl* **butties**.

**buy** [baɪ] *n* compra.
▶ *vt* **1** comprar: *they've just bought a new flat* acaban de comprar un piso nuevo. **2** *(bribe)* sobornar. **3** *fam (accept, believe)* tragárselo: *he's so gullible he bought it* es tan ingenuo que se lo tragó.
ⓘ *pt & pp* **bought** [bɔːt].

**buyer** ['baɪəʳ] *n* comprador,-ra.

**buying power** ['baɪɪŋpaʊəʳ] *n* poder *m* adquisitivo.

**buzz** [bʌz] *n* **1** zumbido. **2** *(of voices)* murmullo. **3** *fam* telefonazo, toque *m*: *give me a buzz* dame un toque.
▶ *vi* zumbar.

**buzzard** ['bʌzəd] *n* ratonero.

**buzzer** ['bʌzəʳ] *n* timbre *m*.

**buzzing** ['bʌzɪŋ] *n* zumbido.

**buzz-saw** ['bʌzsɔː] *n* sierra circular.

**buzz-word** ['bʌzwɜːd] *n* palabra pegadiza, palabra que está de moda.

**by** [baɪ] *prep* **1** *(agent)* por: *painted by Constable* pintado por Constable. **2** *(means)* por: *by air/sea* por avión/mar; *by car/train* en coche/tren; *by hand* a mano; *by heart* de memoria. **3** *(showing difference)* por: *I won by 3 points* gané por tres puntos; *better by far* muchísimo mejor. **4** *(not later than)* para: *I need it by ten* lo necesito para las diez. **5** *(during)* de: *by day/night* de día/noche. **6** *(near)* junto a, al lado de: *sit by me* siéntate a mi lado. **7** *(according to)* según: *by the rules* según las reglas. **8** *(measurements)* por: *6 metres by 4* 6 metros por 4. **9** *(rate)* por: *paid by the hour* pagado por horas. **10** MATH por: *12 divided by 3* 12 dividido por 3. **11** *(progression)* a: *day by day* día a día; *little by little* poco a poco. **12** *(in sets)* en: *two by two* de dos en dos. **13** *(introducing gerund)* : *you can find out by reading the papers* te enterarás leyendo los periódicos. LOC **to go by** pasar delante. I **by** os solo,-a.
▶ *adv* al lado, delante. LOC **to go by** pasar delante.

**bye** [baɪ] *interj fam* ¡adiós!, ¡hasta luego!

**bye-bye** ['baɪbaɪ] *interj fam* ¡adiós!, ¡hasta luego! LOC **to say bye-bye** *fam* decir adiós. I **to go to bye-byes** ir a dormir, ir a la cama.

**Byelorussia** [bjeləʊˈrʌʃə] *n* → Belarus.

**bygone** ['baɪgɒn] *adj* pasado,-a: *a bygone age* tiempos pasados.
▶ *n (object)* antigualla. LOC **in bygone times** antiguamente. I **let bygones be bygones** lo pasado, pasado está.

**bylaw** ['baɪlɔː] *n* ley *f* municipal.

**bypass** ['baɪpɑːs] *n* **1** AUTO variante *f*. **2** TECH tubo de desviación. **3** MED bypass *m*.
▶ *vt* **1** *(traffic, road)* desviar. **2** *(avoid)* esquivar, evitar.

**by-product** ['baɪprɒdʌkt] *n* **1** subproducto, derivado. **2** *fig* consecuencia.

**byre** ['baɪəʳ] *n* establo.

**by-road** ['baɪrəʊd] *n* carretera secundaria.

**bystander** ['baɪstændəʳ] *n* espectador,-ra, curioso,-a.

**byte** [baɪt] *n* COMPUT byte *m*.

**by-way** ['baɪweɪ] *n* **1** *(road)* carretera secundaria. **2** *(remote path)* camino poco frecuentado.

**byword** ['baɪwɜːd] *n* **1** arquetipo, mayor *mf* exponente. **2** *(proverb)* refrán *m*, proverbio. LOC **to be a byword in** ser sinónimo de: *their products are a byword in luxury* sus productos son sinónimo de lujo.

**Byzantine** [bɪˈzæntaɪn] *n* bizantino,-a.
▶ *adj* bizantino,-a.

**Byzantium** [bɪˈzæntɪəm] *n* Bizancio.

# C

**C, c** [si:] n **1** (the letter) C, c f. **2** MUS do.

**c.** ['sentʃərɪ] abbr (circa) hacia; (abbreviation) h.: *Ramses III c. (800 BC)* Ramsés III (h. 800 a. d. C.).

**cab** [kæb] n **1** (taxi) taxi m. **2** (in vehicle) cabina. COMP **cab driver** taxista mf. ▌ **cab rank** parada de taxis.

**cabaret** ['kæbəreɪ] n cabaret m.

**cabbage** ['kæbɪdʒ] n col f, repollo, berza.

**cabin** ['kæbɪn] n **1** (wooden house) cabaña. **2** (on ship) camarote m. **3** (on plane) cabina. COMP **cabin crew** personal m de cabina.

❌ Cabin no significa 'cabina (telefónica)', que se traduce por phone box.

**cabinet** ['kæbɪnət] n **1** (furniture - gen) armario; (glass fronted) vitrina. **2** POL gabinete m (ministerial), consejo de ministros. COMP **cabinet meeting** consejo de ministros.

**cable** ['keɪbəl] n **1** (rope, wire) cable m. **2** (telegram) cable m, telegrama m. COMP **cable television** televisión por cable.

**cacao** [kəˈkɑːəʊ] n BOT cacao.

**cache** [kæʃ] n **1** (store) alijo. **2** (computer memory) caché m. COMP **cache memory** memoria caché.

**cackle** ['kækəl] n **1** (of hen) cacareo. **2** (of person) risotada, carcajada.
▶ vi **1** (of hen) cacarear. **2** (of person) reírse a carcajadas.

**cacophony** [kəˈkɒfənɪ] n cacofonía.

**cactus** ['kæktəs] n cactus m.
ⓘ pl cacti ['kæktaɪ] o cactuses.

**caddie** ['kædɪ] n (in golf) cadi m. COMP **caddie car / caddie cart** carrito de golf.

**cadence** ['keɪdəns] n cadencia.

**cadet** [kəˈdet] n cadete m.

**cadge** [kædʒ] vt fam gorronear.
▶ vi fam gorronear (from/off, a).

**cadger** ['kædʒəʳ] n fam gorrón,-ona.

**cadmium** ['kædmɪəm] n cadmio.

**caecum** ['siːkəm] n ANAT intestino ciego.
ⓘ pl caeca ['siːkə].

**Caesarean** [sɪˈzeərɪən] [also Caesarean section] n cesárea.

**caesium** ['siːzɪəm] n cesio.

**café** ['kæfeɪ] n cafetería, café m.

**cafeteria** [kæfəˈtɪərɪə] n (in factory, college, etc) cafetería, cantina; (restaurant) autoservicio, self-service m.

**caffeine** ['kæfiːn] n cafeína.

**cage** [keɪdʒ] n (gen) jaula.
▶ vt enjaular.

**cagey** ['keɪdʒɪ] adj fam reservado,-a, cauteloso,-a, precavido,-a.
ⓘ comp cagier, superl cagiest.

**cagoule** [kəˈguːl] n chubasquero.

**cajole** [kəˈdʒəʊl] vt engatusar.

**cake** [keɪk] n **1** CULIN pastel m, tarta, torta. **2** (of soap) pastilla.

**calamity** [kəˈlæmɪtɪ] n calamidad f.
ⓘ pl calamities.

**calcite** ['kælsaɪt] n calcita.

**calcium** ['kælsɪəm] n calcio.

**calculate** ['kælkjəleɪt] vt & vi calcular.

**calculation** [kælkjəˈleɪʃən] n cálculo.

**calculator** ['kælkjəleɪtəʳ] n calculadora.

**calculus** ['kælkjələs] n **1** MATH cálculo matemático. **2** [pl calculi ['kælkjəlaɪ]] MED cálculo.

**calendar** ['kælɪndəʳ] n calendario.

**calf¹** [kɑːf] n ZOOL (of cattle) ternero,-a, becerro,-a; (of whale) ballenato; (of other animals) cría.
ⓘ pl calves.

**calf²** [kɑ:f] *n* ANAT pantorrilla.
ⓘ *pl* **calves**.

**caliber** [ˈkælɪbəʳ] *n* US → **calibre**.

**calibre** [ˈkælɪbəʳ] *n* calibre *m*.

**caliph** [ˈkeɪlɪf, ˈkælɪf] *n* califa *f*.

**call** [kɔ:l] *n* **1** *(shout, cry)* grito, llamada. **2** *(by telephone)* llamada (telefónica). **4** *(demand)* demanda; *(need)* motivo. LOC **to be on call** estar de guardia. ‖ **to give sb a call** llamar a ALGN. COMP **call box** GB cabina telefónica.
▶ *vt* **1** *(shout)* llamar. **2** *(by telephone)* llamar. **3** *(summon - meeting, strike, election)* convocar; *(announce - flight)* anunciar.
▶ *vi* **1** *(shout)* llamar. **2** *(by phone)* llamar. **3** *(visit)* pasar, hacer una visita: *I called round at Martin's this afternoon* he pasado por casa de Martin esta tarde. **4** *(train)* parar (at, en). LOC **to call for** STH/SB pasar a recoger ALGO/a ALGN.
◆ **to call back** *vi* *(by phone)* volver a llamar; *(visit)* volver a pasar.
◆ **to call on** *vt insep* visitar, ir a ver a.
◆ **to call out** *vt sep* *(summon - fire brigade)* llamar; *(doctor)* hacer venir; *(workers)* llamar a la huelga.

**caller** [ˈkɔ:ləʳ] *n* **1** *(visitor)* visita, visitante *mf*. **2** *(by telephone)* persona que llama.

**calligraphy** [kəˈlɪgrəfɪ] *n* caligrafía.

**calling** [ˈkɔ:lɪŋ] *n* *(vocation)* vocación *f*, llamada; *(profession)* profesión *f*. COMP **calling card** US tarjeta de visita.

**callous** [ˈkæləs] *adj* duro,-a, insensible.

❌ Callous no significa 'callos', que se traduce por **tripe**.

**callus** [ˈkæləs] *n* callo.
ⓘ *pl* **calluses**.

**calm** [kɑ:m] *adj* **1** *(sea, weather)* en calma, tranquilo,-a. **2** *(person)* tranquilo, -a, calmado,a: *keep calm!* ¡tranquilo!
▶ *n* **1** *(of sea, weather)* calma. **2** *(peace and quiet)* tranquilidad *f*.
▶ *vt* calmar, tranquilizar, sosegar.
◆ **to calm down** *vt* tranquilizar, calmar.
▶ *vi* tranquilizarse, calmarse.

**Calor Gas®** [ˈkælǝgæs] *n* (gas *m*) butano.

**caloric** [kəˈlɒrɪk] *adj* calórico,-a.

**calorie** [ˈkælərɪ] *n* caloría.

**calvary** [ˈkælvərɪ] *n* calvario.

**calves** [kɑ:vz] *npl* → **calf**.

**calyx** [ˈkeɪlɪks, ˈkælɪks] *n* cáliz *m*.
ⓘ *pl* **calices** o **calixes**.

**Cambodia** [kæmˈbǝʊdɪǝ] *n* Camboya.

**Cambodian** [kæmˈbǝʊdɪǝn] *adj* camboyano,-a.
▶ *n* **1** *(person)* camboyano,-a. **2** *(language)* camboyano.

**camcorder** [ˈkæmkɔ:dǝʳ] *n* videocámara.

**came** [keɪm] *pt* → **come**.

**camel** [ˈkæmªl] *n* ZOOL camello,-a.

**camellia** [kǝˈmi:lɪǝ] *n* BOT camelia.

**camera** [ˈkæmªrǝ] *n* cámara.

**cameraman** [ˈkæmªrǝmǝn] *n* cámara *mf*.

**Cameroon** [kæmǝˈru:n] *n* Camerún *m*.

**Cameroonian** [kæmǝˈru:nɪǝn] *adj & n* camerunés,-esa.

**camomile** [ˈkæmǝmaɪl] *n* BOT manzanilla, camomila.

**camouflage** [ˈkæmǝflɑ:ʒ] *n* camuflaje *m*.

**camp** [kæmp] *n* **1** *(gen)* campamento. **2** *(group, faction)* bando.
▶ *vi* acampar.

**campaign** [kæmˈpeɪn] *n* campaña.
▶ *vi* hacer una campaña (for, en favor de).

**camper** [ˈkæmpǝʳ] *n* **1** *(person)* campista *mf*. **2** *(vehicle)* caravana.

**campfire** [ˈkæmpfaɪǝʳ] *n* fogata, hoguera.

**camping** [ˈkæmpɪŋ] *n* camping *m*. LOC «**No camping**» «Prohibido acampar». ‖ **to go camping** ir de camping. COMP **camping site** camping *m*, campamento.

**campus** [ˈkæmpǝs] *n* campus *m*.
ⓘ *pl* **campuses**.

**can¹** [kæn] *n* **1** *(tin - for food, drinks)* lata, bote *m*. **2** *(container - for oil, petrol, etc)* bidón *m*.

**can²** [kæn] *aux* **1** *(gen)* poder: *can you come tomorrow?* ¿puedes venir mañana?. **2** *(know how to)* saber: *he can speak Chinese* sabe hablar chino; *can you swim?* ¿sabes nadar?. **3** *(be allowed to)* poder, estar permitido,-a: *you can't smoke here* no se puede fumar aquí; *you can go now* ya te puedes ir. **4** *(with verbs of perception or mental activity)*: *she couldn't see anything* no veía nada; *I can smell burning* huele a quemado.
ⓘ *pt & cond* **could** [kʊd].

**Canada** [ˈkænədə] *n* Canadá.

**Canadian** [kəˈneɪdɪən] *adj* canadiense.
▶ *n (person)* canadiense *mf*.

**canal** [kəˈnæl] *n* canal *m*.

**canapé** [ˈkænəpeɪ] *n* canapé *m*.

**canary** [kəˈneərɪ] *n* canario.
ⓘ *pl* canaries.

**cancel** [ˈkænsˀl] *vt* **1** *(gen)* cancelar. **2** *(stamp)* matasellar. **3** *(delete)* tachar. **6** MATH eliminar.
ⓘ *pt & pp* cancelled (US canceled), *ger* cancelling (US canceling).

**cancellation** [kænsˀleɪʃˀn] *n* **1** *(gen)* cancelación *f*. **2** *(of stamp)* matasellos *m*.

**cancer** [ˈkænsəʳ] *n* **1** MED cáncer *m*.
▶ *n* Cancer *(constellation, sign)* Cáncer *m*.

**cancerous** [ˈkænsərəs] *adj* canceroso,-a.

**candid** [ˈkændɪd] *adj* franco,-a, sincero,-a. COMP candid camera cámara indiscreta.

☒ Candid no significa 'cándido', que se traduce por ingenuous.

**candidacy** [ˈkændɪdəsɪ] *n* candidatura.
ⓘ *pl* candidacies.

**candidate** [ˈkændɪdət] *n* candidato,-a.

**candidature** [ˈkændɪdətʃəʳ] *n* candidatura.

**candle** [ˈkændˀl] *n (gen)* vela; *(in church)* cirio.

**candlestick** [ˈkændˀlstɪk] *n (gen)* candelero, palmatoria.

**candy** [ˈkændɪ] *n* US *(sweets)* caramelos *mpl*, golosinas *fpl*; *(a sweet)* caramelo.
ⓘ *pl* candies.

**candyfloss** [ˈkændɪflɒs] *n* GB algodón *m* de azúcar.

**cane** [keɪn] *n* **1** BOT caña. **2** *(stick)* bastón *m*. **3** *(furniture)* mimbre *m*.

**canine** [ˈkeɪnaɪn] *adj* ZOOL canino,-a. COMP canine tooth *(diente m)* canino, colmillo.

**canister** [ˈkænɪstəʳ] *n (for tea, coffee, etc)* bote *m*, lata.

**canned** [kænd] *adj* enlatado,-a. COMP canned food conservas *fpl*.

**cannelloni** [kænəˈləʊnɪ] *n pl* canelones *mpl*, canalones *mpl*.

**cannibal** [ˈkænɪbˀl] *n* caníbal *mf*.

**canning** [ˈkænɪŋ] *n* enlatado. COMP canning factory fábrica de conservas. I canning industry industria conservera.

**cannon** [ˈkænən] *n* **1** MIL cañón *m*. **2** *(in billiards)* carambola.
ⓘ *pl* cannon o cannons.

**cannonball** [ˈkænənbɔːl] *n* bala de cañón.

**cannot** [ˈkænɒt] *aux* = can not.

**canoe** [kəˈnuː] *n* canoa, piragua.

**canonization** [kænənaɪˈzeɪʃˀn] *n* canonización.

**can-opener** [ˈkænəʊpˀnəʳ] *n* abrelatas *m*.

**can't** [kɑːnt] *aux* = can not.

**canteen** [kænˈtiːn] *n* **1** *(restaurant)* cantina, comedor *m*. **2** *(set of cutlery)* juego de cubiertos. **3** *(flask)* cantimplora.

**cantilever** [ˈkæntɪliːvəʳ] *n* ARCH voladizo. COMP cantilever bridge puente *m* voladizo.

**canton** [ˈkæntɒn] *n* cantón *m*.

**canvas** [ˈkænvəs] *n* **1** *(cloth)* lona. **2** ART lienzo.

**canvass** [ˈkænvəs] *vi* POL hacer propaganda electoral (for, a favor de), hacer campaña (for, a favor de).

**canyon** [ˈkænjən] *n* GEOG cañón *m*.

**canyoning** [ˈkænjənɪŋ] *n* barranquismo.

**cap** [kæp] *n* **1** *(type of hat)* gorra. **2** *(cover - of pen)* capuchón *m*; *(- of bottle)* tapón *m*, chapa. **3** GEOG casquete *m*.

**capability** [keɪpəˈbɪlɪtɪ] *n* capacidad *f* (to, para/de).
ⓘ *pl* capabilities.

**capable** [ˈkeɪpəbˀl] *adj* **1** *(able)* capaz (of, de): he's capable of breaking the world record es capaz de batir el récord mundial. **2** *(competent)* competente, capaz: a very capable person una persona muy competente.

**capacity** [kəˈpæsɪtɪ] *n* capacidad *f*.
ⓘ *pl* capacities.

**cape¹** [keɪp] *n (garment)* capa.

**cape²** [keɪp] *n* cabo. COMP Cape Verde Cabo Verde.

**caper¹** [ˈkeɪpəʳ] *n* alcaparra.

**caper²** [ˈkeɪpəʳ] *n* **1** *(jump)* brinco. **2** *fam (prank)* travesura, broma.

**capillary** [kəˈpɪlərɪ] *n* capilar *m*.
ⓘ *pl* capillaries.

**capital** ['kæpɪtəl] n **1** (of country, etc) capital f. **2** FIN capital m: starting capital capital inicial. **3** (letter) mayúscula: write it in capitals escríbelo con mayúsculas.
▶ adj **1** (gen) capital. **2** (letter) mayúscula: capital A A mayúscula. COMP capital goods bienes mpl de equipo.

**capitalism** ['kæpɪtəlɪzəm] n capitalismo.

**capitol** ['kæpɪtəl] n capitolio.

**capitulation** [kəpɪtjʊ'leɪʃən] n capitulación f.

**Capricorn** ['kæprɪkɔːn] n (constellation, sign) Capricornio.

**capsicum** ['kæpsɪkəm] n pimiento.

**capsize** [kæp'saɪz] vi zozobrar.
▶ vt hacer zozobrar.

**capsule** ['kæpsjuːl] n cápsula.

**captain** ['kæptɪn] n capitán,-ana.

**caption** ['kæpʃən] n **1** (under picture) leyenda, pie m de foto. **2** CINEM subtítulo.

**captivate** ['kæptɪveɪt] vt cautivar, fascinar.

**captivating** ['kæptɪveɪtɪŋ] adj encantador,-ra, cautivador,-ra.

**captive** ['kæptɪv] adj & n cautivo,-a.

**captivity** [kæp'tɪvɪti] n cautiverio, cautividad f.

**capture** ['kæptʃər] n (seizure - of person) captura, apresamiento; (- of town) toma, conquista.
▶ vt **1** (seize - person) capturar, apresar; (- town) tomar. **2** fig (attract) captar.

**car** [kɑːr] n **1** AUTO coche m, automóvil m. **2** US (railway carriage) vagón m, coche m. LOC **to go by car** ir en coche.

**caramel** ['kærəməl] n **1** CULIN (burnt sugar) azúcar m quemado. **2** (toffee) caramelo.

**carapace** ['kærəpeɪs] n caparazón m.

**carat** ['kærət] n quilate m.

**caravan** [kærə'væn] n caravana.

**caravel** ['kærəvəl] n carabela.

**carbohydrate** [kɑːbəʊ'haɪdreɪt] n hidrato de carbono, carbohidrato.

**carbon** ['kɑːbən] n CHEM carbono. COMP **carbon dioxide** dióxido de carbono. I **carbon monoxide** monóxido de carbono. I **carbon paper** papel m carbón.

❌ Carbon no significa 'carbón', que se traduce por **coal**.

**carbonated** ['kɑːbəneɪtɪd] adj (fizzy) gaseoso,-a, con gas.

**Carboniferous** [kɑːbə'nɪfərəs] adj GEOL carbonífero,-a. COMP **the Carboniferous period** el carbonífero.

**carburettor** [kɑːbə'retər] n carburador m.

**carcass** ['kɑːkəs] n res f muerta.

**carcinogenic** [kɑːsɪnə'dʒenɪk] adj MED cancerígeno,-a, carcinógeno,-a.

**card** [kɑːd] n **1** (gen) tarjeta. **2** (greetings card) tarjeta de felicitación, felicitación f. **3** (of membership, identity) carnet m, carné m. **4** (stiff paper) cartulina. **5** carta, naipe m.

**cardboard** ['kɑːdbɔːd] n cartón m.

**cardiac** ['kɑːdɪæk] adj cardíaco,-a. COMP **cardiac arrest** paro cardíaco. I **cardiac sphincter** cardias.

**cardigan** ['kɑːdɪgən] n rebeca.

**cardinal** ['kɑːdɪnəl] adj (most important) capital, fundamental, principal.
▶ n REL cardenal m. COMP **cardinal number** número cardinal. I **cardinal point** punto cardinal. I **cardinal sin** pecado capital.

**cardiologist** [kɑːdɪ'ɒlədʒɪst] n cardiólogo,-a.

**cardiology** [kɑːdɪ'ɒlədʒɪ] n cardiología.

**care** [keər] n **1** (gen) cuidado: take care when driving at night (ten) cuidado al conducir de noche; I left the baby in the care of my mother dejé al bebé al cuidado de mi madre. **2** (worry, grief) preocupación f.
▶ vi (be worried, be concerned) preocuparse (about, por), importar: I don't care no me importa, me da igual.
▶ vt (feel concern, mind) importar: no-one cares if you're late a nadie le importa si llegas tarde. LOC «Handle with care» «Frágil». I **take care! 1** (be careful) ¡ten cuidado! **2** (look after yourself) ¡cuídate! COMP **medical care** asistencia médica.
◆ **to care for** vt insep **1** (look after) cuidar, atender. **2** (like) gustar; (feel affection for) querer, sentir cariño por.

**career** [kə'rɪər] n **1** (profession) carrera. **2** (working life) vida profesional.

**carefree** ['keəfriː] adj despreocupado,-a, libre de preocupaciones.

**careful** ['keəfʊl] *adj* **1** *(cautious)* pruden- te, cuidadoso,-a: *a careful driver* un con- ductor prudente. **2** *(painstaking)* cuidado- so,-a. `LOC` **to be careful** tener cuidado.

**carefully** ['keəfʊlɪ] *adv* **1** *(cautiously)* con cuidado, con precaución: *drive care- fully* conduce con cuidado. **2** *(with great attention)* cuidadosamente.

**careless** ['keələs] *adj* *(inattentive, thought- less - person)* descuidado; *(driving)* ne- gligente.

**caress** [kə'res] *n* caricia.
▶ *vt* acariciar.

**caretaker** ['keəteɪkəʳ] *n* conserje *m*, portero,-a.

**cargo** ['kɑːɡəʊ] *n* *(goods)* carga; *(load)* cargamento.
ⓘ *pl* **cargoes o cargos.**

> ❌ Cargo no significa 'cargo (empleo)', que se traduce por **position.**

**Caribbean** [kærɪ'bɪən, US kə'rɪbɪən] *adj* caribeño,-a. `COMP` **the Caribbean (Sea)** el (mar) Caribe.

**caribou** ['kærɪbuː] *n* caribú *m*.

**caricature** ['kærɪkətjʊəʳ] *n* caricatura.

**caries** ['keərɪz] *n* caries *f*.

**carnage** ['kɑːnɪdʒ] *n* carnicería.

**carnal** ['kɑːnᵊl] *adj* carnal.

**carnation** [kɑː'neɪʃᵊn] *n* clavel *m*.

**carnival** ['kɑːnɪvᵊl] *n* carnaval *m*.

**carnivore** ['kɑːnɪvɔːʳ] *n* carnívoro,-a.

**carnivorous** [kɑː'nɪvərəs] *adj* carnívoro,-a.

**carol** ['kærᵊl] *n* villancico.

**carotene** ['kærətiːn] *n* caroteno.

**carousel** [kærə'sel] *n* **1** US *(roundabout)* tiovivo, caballitos *mpl*, carrusel *m*. **2** *(for baggage)* cinta transportadora. **3** *(for slides)* carrete *m* de diapositivas.

**carp**¹ [kɑːp] *n* *(fish)* carpa.

**carp**² [kɑːp] *vi* *(complain)* quejarse (about/at, de).

**carpenter** ['kɑːpɪntəʳ] *n* carpintero,-a.

**carpentry** ['kɑːpɪntrɪ] *n* carpintería.

**carpet** ['kɑːpɪt] *n* **1** *(gen)* alfombra; *(fit- ted)* moqueta. **2** *fig* alfombra.

> ❌ Carpet no significa 'carpeta', que se traduce por **folder.**

**carriage** ['kærɪdʒ] *n* **1** HIST *(horse-drawn)* carruaje *m*. **2** GB *(railway vehicle)* vagón *m*, coche *m*. **3** *(of typewriter)* carro. **4** *(cost of transport)* porte *m*, transporte *m*.

**carriageway** ['kærɪdʒweɪ] *n* GB calzada.

**carrier** ['kærɪəʳ] *n* **1** *(company, person)* trans- portista *mf*. **2** AV compañía aérea, línea aérea. **3** MED *(of disease)* portador,-ra. `COMP` aircraft carrier MAR portaaviones *m*. ▌carrier pigeon paloma mensajera.

**carrion** ['kærɪən] *n* carroña.

**carrot** ['kærət] *n* zanahoria.

**carrousel** [kærə'sel] *n* **1** *(roundabout)* tiovi- vo, carrusel. **2** *(for baggage reclaim)* cinta.

**carry** ['kærɪ] *vt* **1** *(gen)* llevar. **2** *(goods, load, passengers)* transportar. **3** *(disease)* ser portador,-ra de. **4** *(blame, responsi- bility)* cargar con. **5** *(entail, involve)* con- llevar **8** MATH llevar(se).
◆ **to carry forward / carry over** *vt sep* llevar a la columna siguiente, llevar a la página siguiente: *carry this figure forward to the next page* lleva esta cifra a la página siguiente.
◆ **to carry off** *vt sep* **1** *(part, action, duty)* realizar con éxito, salir airoso,-a de: *she carried the speech off well* salió airosa del discurso. **2** *(prize)* llevarse, hacerse con.
◆ **to carry on** *vt insep* continuar con, seguir con.
◆ **to carry through** *vt sep* *(plan, etc)* lle- var a cabo.
ⓘ *pt & pp* **carried,** *ger* **carrying.**

**carry-out** ['kærɪaʊt] *n* **1** US *(food)* comida para llevar. **2** *(drink)* bebida para lle- var.

**carsick** ['kɑːsɪk] *adj* mareado,-a (al ir en coche). `LOC` **to get carsick** marearse en coche.

**cart** [kɑːt] *n* **1** *(horse-drawn)* carro, ca- rreta; *(handcart)* carretilla. **2** US *(for shopping)* carrito, carro.

**cartel** [kɑː'tel] *n* cártel *m*.

**Cartesian** [kɑː'tiːʒᵊn] *adj* cartesiano,-a.

**Carthaginian** [kɑːθə'dʒɪnɪən] *adj* car- taginense.
▶ *n* cartaginense *mf*.

**cartilage** ['kɑːtɪlɪdʒ] *n* cartílago.

**cartography** [kɑː'tɒɡrəfɪ] *n* cartografía.

**carton** ['kɑ:tᵊn] n (of cream, yoghurt) bote m; (of milk, juice, cigarettes) cartón m; (of cereals, etc) caja.

⊠ Carton no significa 'cartón', que se traduce por **cardboard**.

**cartoon** [kɑ:'tu:n] n 1 (drawing) viñeta, chiste m; (strip) tira cómica, historieta. 2 (animated) dibujos mpl animados.

**cartridge** ['kɑ:trɪdʒ] n 1 MIL cartucho. 2 (for pen) recambio.

**carve** [kɑ:v] vt 1 (wood, stone) tallar; (statue, etc) esculpir; (initials) grabar. 2 (meat) cortar, trinchar.

**cascade** [kæs'keɪd] n cascada.

**case¹** [keɪs] n 1 (gen) caso. 2 JUR (lawsuit) causa, litigio, pleito. LOC in case ... por si..., en caso de que... ∎ in no case bajo ninguna circunstancia.

**case²** [keɪs] n 1 (suitcase) maleta. 2 (box) caja, cajón m; (small, hard container) estuche m; (soft container) funda.

**cash** [kæʃ] n dinero (en) efectivo, metálico.
▶ vt (cheque) cobrar, hacer efectivo.

**cashier** [kæ'ʃɪəʳ] n cajero,-a.

**cashmere** [kæʃ'mɪəʳ] n cachemira.

**casino** [kə'si:nəʊ] n casino.
ⓘ pl casinos.

**cask** [kɑ:sk] n tonel m, barril m.

⊠ Cask no significa 'casco (para la cabeza)', que se traduce por **helmet**.

**casket** ['kɑ:skɪt] n 1 (box) cofre m. 2 (coffin) ataúd m.

**casserole** ['kæsərəʊl] n 1 (dish) cazuela. 2 (food) guiso, guisado.

**cassette** [kə'set] n casete f.

**cast** [kɑ:st] n 1 THEAT reparto. 2 TECH (mould) molde m; (product) pieza.
▶ vt 1 (gen) lanzar. 2 (shadow, light) proyectar. 3 (vote) emitir. 4 THEAT (part, role) asignar el papel a. LOC to be cast away naufragar. ∎ to cast a spell on STH/SB hechizar ALGO/a ALGN.
◆ to cast about for / cast around for vt insep buscar, andar buscando.
◆ to cast out vt sep fml expulsar.
ⓘ pt & pp cast.

**castaway** ['kɑ:stəweɪ] n náufrago,-a.

**caste** [kɑ:st] n casta.

**caster** ['kɑ:stəʳ] n (wheel) ruedecilla.

**Castilian** [kæ'stɪlɪən] adj castellano,-a.
▶ n 1 (person) castellano,-a. 2 (language) castellano.

**casting** ['kɑ:stɪŋ] n 1 TECH (process) fundición f; (object) pieza fundida. 2 THEAT (selection) selección f, casting m.

**cast-iron** ['kɑ:staɪən] adj de hierro fundido, de hierro colado.

**castle** ['kɑ:sᵊl] n 1 (gen) castillo. 2 (chess) torre f.
▶ vi (chess) enrocar.

**castor¹** ['kɑ:stəʳ] n → caster.

**castor²** ['kɑ:stəʳ] n COMP castor oil aceite m de ricino.

**castrate** [kæ'streɪt] vt castrar, capar.

**casual** ['kæʒjʊəl] adj 1 (chance - visit, visitor) ocasional; (- meeting) fortuito,-a, casual. 2 (superficial) superficial; (reader) ocasional. 3 (informal) informal.

**casually** ['kæʒjʊəlɪ] adv 1 (dress) de manera informal. 2 (unconcernedly) despreocupadamente.

⊠ Casually no significa 'casualmente', que se traduce por **by chance**.

**casualty** ['kæʒjʊəltɪ] n (of accident) herido,-a; MIL baja
ⓘ pl casualties.

⊠ Casualty no significa 'casualidad', que se traduce por **chance**.

**cat** [kæt] n (domestic) gato,-a; (lion, tiger) felino,-a

**Catalan** ['kætələn] adj catalán,-ana.
▶ n 1 (person) catalán,-ana. 2 (language) catalán m.

**catalogue** ['kætəlɒg] n catálogo.
▶ vt catalogar.

**catalyst** ['kætəlɪst] n catalizador m.

**catapult** ['kætəpʌlt] n 1 (gen) catapulta. 2 (toy) tirachinas m.

**cataract** ['kætərækt] n 1 (waterfall) catarata. 2 MED catarata.

**catarrh** [kə'tɑːʳ] n catarro.

**catastrophe** [kə'tæstrəfɪ] n catástrofe f.

**catch** [kætʃ] n 1 (of ball) parada. 2 (of fish) presa. 4 (fastener on door) pestillo.

▶ vt **1** *(gen)* coger, agarrar; *(fish)* pescar. **2** *(train, plane - take)* coger, tomar: *I just caught the last train* cogí el último tren con el tiempo justo. LOC **to catch a cold** resfriarse, coger un resfriado.

◆ **to catch on** vi **1** *(understand)* entender, darse cuenta (to, de). **2** *(become popular)* ponerse de moda, imponerse.

◆ **to catch out** vt sep *(doing something wrong)* pillar, sorprender; *(trick)* hacer que uno caiga.

◆ **to catch up** vt sep *(person)* alcanzar.
ⓘ pt & pp **caught** [kɔːt].

**catching** [ˈkætʃɪŋ] adj contagioso,-a.

**catchword** [ˈkætʃwɜːd] n eslogan m.

**catechism** [ˈkætəkɪzəm] n catecismo.

**categoric** [kætəˈgɒrɪk] adj categórico,-a.

**category** [ˈkætəgəri] n categoría.
ⓘ pl **categories**.

**cater** [ˈkeɪtər] vi *(food)* proveer comida (for, para).

◆ **to cater for** vt insep *(needs, interests, tastes)* atender a, satisfacer.

**caterer** [ˈkeɪtərər] n proveedor,-ra.

**catering** [ˈkeɪtərɪŋ] n *(business, course)* hostelería; *(service)* catering m.

**caterpillar** [ˈkætəpɪlər] n oruga.

**cathedral** [kəˈθiːdrəl] n catedral f.

**catheter** [ˈkæθətər] n catéter m.

**cathode** [ˈkæθəud] n cátodo. COMP **cathode ray** rayo catódico.

**Catholic** [ˈkæθəlɪk] adj & n REL católico,-a.

**Catholicism** [kəˈθɒlɪsɪzəm] n REL catolicismo.

**cattle** [ˈkætəl] n pl ganado (vacuno).

**caught** [kɔːt] pt & pp → **catch**.

**cauldron** [ˈkɔːldrən] n caldero.

**cauliflower** [ˈkɒlɪflaʊər] n coliflor f.

**cause** [kɔːz] n **1** *(gen)* causa **2** *(reason, grounds)* razón f, motivo.
▶ vt causar.

**caustic** [ˈkɔːstɪk] adj cáustico,-a. COMP **caustic soda** sosa cáustica.

**cauterize** [ˈkɔːtəraɪz] vt cauterizar.

**caution** [ˈkɔːʃən] n **1** *(care, prudence)* cautela, precaución f, prudencia. **2** *(warning)* aviso, advertencia.
▶ vt **1** *(warn)* advertir. **2** GB *(judge, etc)* amonestar.

**cautious** [ˈkɔːʃəs] adj cauteloso,-a, prudente, cauto,-a.

**cavalry** [ˈkævəlri] n caballería.
ⓘ pl **cavalries**.

**cave** [keɪv] n cueva. COMP **cave painting** pintura rupestre.

◆ **to cave in** vi *(roof, etc)* hundirse, derrumbarse; *(opposition, etc)* ceder.

**caveman** [ˈkeɪvmæn] n cavernícola m, hombre m de las cavernas.

**cavern** [ˈkævən] n caverna.

**caviar** [ˈkæviɑːr] n caviar m.

**caving** [ˈkeɪvɪŋ] n espeleología.

**cavity** [ˈkævɪti] n **1** *(hole)* cavidad f. **2** *(in tooth)* caries f.
ⓘ pl **cavities**.

**caw** [kɔː] n graznido.
▶ vi graznar.

**cayman** [ˈkeɪmən] n caimán m.

**CD** [ˈsiːˈdiː] abbr (compact disc) disco compacto; *(abbreviation)* CD m.

**CD-ROM** [ˈsiːˈdiːˈrɒm] abbr (compact disc read-only memory) CD-ROM m.

**cease** [siːs] vt suspender. LOC **to cease fire** MIL cesar el fuego.
▶ vi cesar.

**cease-fire** [siːsˈfaɪər] n alto el fuego.

**ceaseless** [ˈsiːsləs] adj incesante.

**cecum** [ˈsiːkəm] n US → caecum.

**cedar** [ˈsiːdər] n BOT cedro.

**ceiling** [ˈsiːlɪŋ] n **1** *(of room)* techo. **2** *(upper limit)* tope m, límite m.

**celebrate** [ˈselɪbreɪt] vt & vi celebrar.

**celebrated** [ˈselɪbreɪtɪd] adj célebre, famoso,-a.

**celebration** [selɪˈbreɪʃən] n *(event)* fiesta, festejo; *(activity)* celebración f.
▶ n pl **celebrations** festividades fpl, festejos mpl.

**celebrity** [səˈlebrɪti] n celebridad f, personaje m famoso.
ⓘ pl **celebrities**.

**celery** [ˈseləri] n apio.

**celestial** [sɪˈlestiəl] adj **1** *(heavenly)* celestial. **2** *(of the skies)* celeste.

**cell** [sel] n **1** *(in prison, monastery)* celda. **2** *(of honeycomb)* celdilla. **3** *(of organism)* célula. **4** ELEC *(in battery)* pila.

**cellar** ['selə<sup>r</sup>] *n* **1** *(basement)* sótano. **2** *(for wine)* bodega.

**cellist** ['tʃelɪst] *n* violoncelista *mf*.

**cello** ['tʃeləʊ] *n* violoncelo.
ⓘ *pl* cellos.

**Cellophane®** ['seləfeɪn] *n* celofán® *m*.

**cellphone** ['selfəʊn] *n* US teléfono móvil.

**cellular** ['seljʊlə<sup>r</sup>] *adj* celular. COMP cellular telephone teléfono móvil.

**cellulite** ['seljʊlaɪt] *n (fat)* celulitis *f*.

**celluloid®** ['seljələɪd] *n* celuloide® *m*.

**cellulose** ['seljələʊs] *n* celulosa.

**Celsius** ['selsɪəs] *adj* Celsius: *30 degrees Celsius* 30 grados Celsius.

**Celt** [kelt] *n* celta *mf*.

**cement** [sɪ'ment] *n* **1** *(in building)* cemento. **2** *(glue)* adhesivo; *(for filling teeth)* empaste *m*. COMP cement mixer hormigonera.

**cemetery** ['semətrɪ] *n* cementerio.
ⓘ *pl* cemeteries.

**censor** ['sensə<sup>r</sup>] *n* censor,-ra.
▶ *vt* censurar.

**censorship** ['sensəʃɪp] *n* censura.

**censure** ['senʃə<sup>r</sup>] *n fml* censura.
▶ *vt fml* censurar.

**census** ['sensəs] *n* censo, padrón *m*.

**cent** [sent] *n* centavo, céntimo.

**centenary** [sen'tiːnərɪ] *n* centenario.
ⓘ *pl* centenaries.

**centennial** [sen'tenɪəl] *n* US centenario.

**center** ['sentə<sup>r</sup>] *n & vb* US → centre.

**centigrade** ['sentɪgreɪd] *adj* centígrado,-a.

**centigram** ['sentɪgræm] *n* centigramo.

**centilitre** ['sentɪliːtə<sup>r</sup>] *n* centilitro.

**centimetre** ['sentɪmiːtə<sup>r</sup>] *n* centímetro.

**centipede** ['sentɪpiːd] *n* ciempiés *m*.

**central** ['sentrəl] *adj* **1** *(government, bank, committee)* central. **2** *(of, at or near centre)* céntrico,-a. COMP central nervous system sistema *m* nervioso central.

**centre** ['sentə<sup>r</sup>] *n* centro.
▶ *vt (put in centre)* centrar.
▶ *vi (focus on)* centrarse (on/upon, en).

**centrifugal** [sentrɪ'fjuːgəl] *adj* centrífugo,-a.

**centripetal** [sen'trɪpɪtəl] *adj* centrípeto,-a.

**century** ['sentʃərɪ] *n* siglo: *the twentieth century* el siglo veinte.
ⓘ *pl* centuries.

**ceramic** [sə'ræmɪk] *adj* de cerámica.
▶ *n* cerámica.

**ceramics** [sə'ræmɪks] *n (art)* cerámica; *(objects)* objetos *mpl* de cerámica.

**cereal** ['sɪərɪəl] *n (plant, grain)* cereal *m*; *(breakfast food)* cereales *mpl*.

**cerebellum** [serɪ'beləm] *n* cerebelo.

**cerebral** ['serɪbrəl] *adj* cerebral. COMP cerebral palsy parálisis *f* cerebral.

**cerebrum** ['serəbrəm] *n* cerebro.

**ceremony** ['serɪmənɪ] *n* ceremonia.
ⓘ *pl* ceremonies.

**certain** ['sɜːt<sup>ə</sup>n] *adj* **1** *(gen)* seguro,-a: *she's certain to pass* seguro que aprobará. **2** *(specific, particular)* cierto,-a. **4** *(named)* tal: *a certain Pedro Díaz* un tal Pedro Díaz.

**certainly** ['sɜːt<sup>ə</sup>nlɪ] *adv* **1** *(definitely, surely)* seguro. **2** *(when answering questions)* desde luego, por supuesto.

**certainty** ['sɜːt<sup>ə</sup>ntɪ] *n* certeza, seguridad *f*.
ⓘ *pl* certainties.

**certificate** [sə'tɪfɪkət] *n (gen)* certificado: *birth certificate* partida de nacimiento.

**certify** ['sɜːtɪfaɪ] *vt* certificar.
ⓘ *pt & pp* certified, *ger* certifying.

**cervical** ['sɜːvɪk<sup>ə</sup>l] *adj* **1** *(of neck)* cervical. **2** *(of uterus)* del (cuello del) útero. COMP cervical cancer cáncer *m* de útero. ▌cervical vertebrae vértebras cervicales.

**cervix** ['sɜːvɪks] *n* **1** *fml (neck)* cerviz *f*, cuello. **2** *(uterus)* cuello del útero.
ⓘ *pl* cervixes o cervices.

**cesium** ['siːzɪəm] *n* US → caesium.

**cesspit** ['sespɪt] *n* pozo negro.

**cetacean** [sɪ'teɪʃ<sup>ə</sup>n] *adj* cetáceo,-a.
▶ *n* cetáceo.

**chafe** [tʃeɪf] *vt* **1** *(make sore)* rozar, excoriar. **2** *(make warm)* frotar, friccionar.
▶ *vi* irritarse.

**chain** [tʃeɪn] *n* **1** *(metal rings)* cadena. **2** *(of shops, hotels, etc)* cadena; *(of events)* cadena, serie *f*. COMP chain reaction reacción en cadena. ▌mountain chain cordillera, cadena montañosa.
▶ *vt* encadenar, atar.

**chair** [tʃeəʳ] *n (gen)* silla; *(with arms)* sillón *m*, butaca. LOC **to address the chair** dirigirse al presidente, dirigirse a la presidencia. COMP **chair lift** telesilla.
▸ *vt (meeting)* presidir.

**chairman** [ˈtʃeəmən] *n* presidente *m*.
① *pl* **chairmen** [ˈtʃeəmen].

**chairmanship** [ˈtʃeəmənʃɪp] *n* presidencia.

**chairperson** [ˈtʃeəpɜːsən] *n* presidente,-a.

**chairwoman** [ˈtʃeəwumən] *n* presidenta.
① *pl* **chairwomen** [ˈtʃeəwɪmɪn].

**chaise longue** [ʃeɪzˈlɒŋ] *n* diván *m*.

**chalet** [ˈʃæleɪ] *n* chalet *m*, chalé *m*.

**chalice** [ˈtʃælɪs] *n* cáliz *m*.

**chalk** [tʃɔːk] *n* **1** *(mineral)* creta, roca caliza. **2** *(for writing)* tiza.
♦ **to chalk up** *vt insep fam (victory, success)* apuntarse.

**challenge** [ˈtʃælɪndʒ] *n* reto, desafío.
▸ *vt* **1** *(invite to compete)* retar, desafiar. **2** *(statement)* poner en duda, cuestionar.

**challenger** [ˈtʃælɪndʒəʳ] *n (for title, leadership)* aspirante *mf*; *(opponent, rival)* contrincante *mf*, rival *mf*.

**challenging** [ˈtʃælɪndʒɪŋ] *adj (task, job, problem)* que supone un reto; *(idea)* estimulante; *(look, tone)* desafiante.

**chamber** [ˈtʃeɪmbəʳ] *n* **1** *(gen)* cámara. **2** *(of gun)* recámara.

**chambermaid** [ˈtʃeɪmbəmeɪd] *n* camarera (de hotel).

**chameleon** [kəˈmiːlɪən] *n* camaleón *m*.

**champagne** [ʃæmˈpeɪn] *n (French)* champán *m*, champaña; *(Catalan)* cava *m*.

**champion** [ˈtʃæmpɪən] *n* **1** campeón, -ona. **2** *fig (defender)* defensor,-ra, paladín,-ina.
▸ *adj* premiado,-a.
▸ *vt fig* defender, abogar por.

**championship** [ˈtʃæmpɪənʃɪp] *n* SP campeonato.

**chance** [tʃɑːns] *n* **1** *(fate, fortune)* azar *m*, casualidad *f*. **2** *(opportunity)* oportunidad *f*, ocasión *f*: *you won't get another chance like this* no se te presentará otra oportunidad como ésta. **3** *(possibility, likelihood)* posibilidad *f*. LOC **by chance** por casualidad.
▸ *adj (meeting, discovery, occurrence)* fortuito,-a, casual.
▸ *vt (risk)* arriesgar.

**chancellor** [ˈtʃɑːnsələʳ] *n* **1** POL canciller *m*. **2** GB *(of university)* rector,-ra. COMP **Chancellor of the Exchequer** GB ministro,-a de Hacienda.

**chancy** [ˈtʃɑːnsɪ] *adj fam* arriesgado,-a.
① *comp* **chancier**, *superl* **chanciest**.

**chandelier** [ʃændəˈlɪəʳ] *n* araña.

**change** [tʃeɪndʒ] *n* **1** *(gen)* cambio. **2** *(of clothes)* muda. **3** *(coins)* cambio, monedas *fpl*; *(money returned)* cambio, vuelta.
▸ *vi* cambiar, cambiarse.

**changeable** [ˈtʃeɪndʒəbəl] *adj* variable.

**changeless** [ˈtʃeɪndʒləs] *adj* inmutable.

**changing** [ˈtʃeɪndʒɪŋ] *adj* cambiante. COMP **changing room** vestuario.
▸ *n* MIL cambio, relevo.

**channel** [ˈtʃænəl] *n* **1** *(gen)* canal *m*. **2** *(on television)* canal *m*, cadena.

**chant** [tʃɑːnt] *n* **1** REL canto litúrgico, cántico. **2** *(of crowd)* eslogan *m*, consigna.

**chaos** [ˈkeɪɒs] *n* caos *m*.

**chaotic** [keɪˈɒtɪk] *adj* caótico,-a.

**chap** [tʃæp] *n fam* tío, tipo.

**chapel** [ˈtʃæpəl] *n* capilla.

**chaplain** [ˈtʃæplɪn] *n* capellán *m*.

**chapter** [ˈtʃæptəʳ] *n* capítulo.

**char** [tʃɑːʳ] *vt* chamuscar, carbonizar.
① *pt & pp* **charred**, *ger* **charring**.

**character** [ˈkærəktəʳ] *n* **1** *(gen)* carácter *m*. **2** *(in film, book, play)* personaje *m*.

**characteristic** [kærəktəˈrɪstɪk] *adj* característico,-a.
▸ *n* característica.

**characterize** [ˈkærəktəraɪz] *vt (gen)* caracterizar; *(describe character of)* calificar (as, de).

**chard** [tʃɑːd] *n* acelgas *fpl*.

**charge** [tʃɑːdʒ] *n* **1** *(price)* precio; *(fee(s))* honorarios *mpl*. **2** *(responsibility)* cargo. **3** JUR cargo, acusación *f*. **4** MIL *(attack)* carga. **5** *(explosive)* carga explosiva. **6** ELEC carga.
▸ *vt* **1** *(ask as a price - customer, amount)* cobrar; *(record as debit)* cargar. **2** JUR

acusar (with, de). **3** ELEC cargar. **4** MIL cargar contra, atacar.

**charger** ['tʃɑːdʒəʳ] n **1** ELEC cargador m. **2** *(horse)* corcel m.

**chariot** ['tʃærɪət] n cuadriga, carro.

**charisma** [kə'rɪzmə] n carisma m.

**charitable** ['tʃærɪtəbəl] adj **1** *(person)* caritativo,-a. **2** *(organization)* benéfico,-a.

**charity** ['tʃærɪtɪ] n **1** *(gen)* caridad f. **2** *(organization)* institución f benéfica.
ⓘ pl charities.

**charlatan** ['ʃɑːlətən] n embaucador,-a.

❌ Charlatan no significa 'charlatán (que habla mucho)', que se traduce por chatterbox.

**charm** [tʃɑːm] n **1** *(quality)* encanto. **2** *(object)* amuleto. **3** *(spell)* hechizo.
▶ vt encantar.

**charmer** ['tʃɑːməʳ] n **1** *(charming person)* persona encantadora. **2** *(of snakes)* encantador,-ra.

**charming** ['tʃɑːmɪŋ] adj *(delightful)* encantador,-ra.

**chart** [tʃɑːt] n **1** *(table)* tabla; *(graph)* gráfico, carta, mapa m. **2** *(navigational)* carta de navegación.
▶ vt *(make a map of)* trazar un mapa de; *(plan, plot on map)* trazar.
▶ n pl **the charts** MUS la lista de éxitos, el hit parade m.

**charter** ['tʃɑːtəʳ] n **1** *(gen)* estatutos mpl; *(of town)* fuero. **2** *(constitution)* carta. **3** *(hiring of plane, etc)* fletamiento.
▶ vt **1** *(grant rights, privileges to)* aprobar los estatutos de. **2** *(hire plane, boat etc)* fletar, alquilar.

**chartered** ['tʃɑːtəd] adj *(qualified)* colegiado,-a. COMP **chartered accountant** contable mf diplomado,-a.

**chase** [tʃeɪs] n *(gen)* persecución f; *(hunt)* caza.
▶ vt *(gen)* perseguir; *(hunt)* cazar.

**chasm** ['kæzəm] n **1** GEOG sima. **2** fig abismo.

**chassis** ['ʃæsɪ] n chasis m.
ⓘ pl chassis.

**chaste** [tʃeɪst] adj **1** *(pure)* casto,-a, puro,-a. **2** *(not ornate)* sobrio,-a, sencillo,-a.

**chastise** [tʃæs'taɪz] vt fml castigar.

**chastity** ['tʃæstɪtɪ] n castidad f.

**chat** [tʃæt] n **1** *(in general)* charla. **2** *(on Internet)* charla, chat m.

**chatter** ['tʃætəʳ] n **1** *(rapid talk)* cháchara, parloteo. **2** *(of teeth)* castañeteo.
▶ vi **1** *(talk rapidly)* chacharear, parlotear, cotorrear. **2** *(teeth)* castañetear.

**chatterbox** ['tʃætəbɒks] n fam parlanchín,-ina, charlatán,-ana.

**chatty** ['tʃætɪ] adj *(person)* hablador,-ra, parlanchín,-ina.
ⓘ comp chattier, superl chattiest.

**chauffeur** ['ʃəʊfəʳ] n chófer mf, chofer mf.

**chauvinism** ['ʃəʊvɪnɪzəm] n chovinismo.

**cheap** [tʃiːp] adj **1** *(gen)* barato,-a. **2** *(of poor quality, shoddy)* ordinario,-a. **3** *(contemptible - trick, gibe, crook)* vil, bajo,-a; *(vulgar - joke, remark)* de mal gusto.
▶ adv barato.

**cheapen** ['tʃiːpən] vt **1** *(in price)* abaratar. **2** *(degrade)* degradar, rebajar.

**cheat** [tʃiːt] n **1** *(gen)* tramposo,-a; *(swindler)* estafador,-ra. **2** *(trick)* trampa; *(swindle)* estafa, timo.
▶ vt *(trick, deceive)* engañar; *(swindle)* estafar, timar.
▶ vi *(gen)* hacer trampa(s); *(in exam)* copiar.

**check** [tʃek] n **1** *(gen)* revisión f, control m; *(of machine)* verificación f, inspección f; *(of results, facts, information)* comprobación f, verificación f. **2** *(stop, restraint)* control m, freno. **3** US → **cheque**. **4** US *(bill)* cuenta, nota. **5** *(chess)* jaque m.
▶ vi *(make sure)* comprobar, verificar.
◆ **to check in** vi *(at airport)* facturar el equipaje; *(at hotel)* registrarse.
▶ vt sep facturar.
◆ **to check out** vi pagar la cuenta e irse, dejar el hotel.
▶ vt sep *(facts, information)* verificar, comprobar; *(place)* ir a ver; *(person)* hacer averiguaciones sobre.

**checked** [tʃekt] adj a cuadros.

**checkers** ['tʃekəz] n pl US damas fpl.

**checkmate** ['tʃekmeɪt] n (jaque m) mate m.
▶ vt dar (jaque) mate a.

**checkout** ['tʃekaʊt] n *(in supermarket)* caja.

**checkpoint** ['tʃekpɔɪnt] n control m.

**checkroom** ['tʃekruːm] *n* US guardarropa.

**check-up** ['tʃekʌp] *n* (by doctor) chequeo, reconocimiento médico.

**cheek** [tʃiːk] *n* **1** ANAT mejilla. **2** *fam* (nerve, impudence) descaro, cara.

**cheekbone** ['tʃiːkbəʊn] *n* pómulo.

**cheeky** ['tʃiːkɪ] *adj* (person) descarado, -a, fresco,-a; (remark) impertinente.
ⓘ *comp* cheekier, *superl* cheekiest.

**cheer** [tʃɪər] *n* **1** (shout of joy) viva *m*, vítor *m*, hurra *m*. **2** (happiness) alegría.
▶ *vt* **1** (applaud with shouts) vitorear, aclamar. **2** (gladden) animar, alegrar.
◆ **to cheer up** *vt sep* animar, alegrar.
▶ *vi* animarse, alegrarse: *cheer up!* ¡ánimo!

**cheerful** ['tʃɪəfʊl] *adj* alegre.

**cheerio** [tʃɪərɪ'əʊ] *interj* GB *fam* ¡adiós!, ¡hasta luego!

**cheerleader** ['tʃɪəliːdər] *n* animador, -ra (de un equipo deportivo).

**cheers** [tʃɪəz] *interj* **1** *fam* (as toast) ¡salud! **2** *fam* (thanks) ¡gracias! **3** *fam* (goodbye) ¡adiós!, ¡hasta luego!

**cheese** [tʃiːz] *n* queso.

**cheetah** ['tʃiːtə] *n* guepardo.

**chef** [ʃef] *n* chef *m*, jefe,-a de cocina.

**chemical** ['kemɪkəl] *adj* químico,-a.
▶ *n* sustancia química.

**chemist** ['kemɪst] *n* **1** CHEM químico, -a. **2** GB (pharmacist) farmacéutico,-a.
COMP chemist's (shop) GB farmacia.

**chemistry** ['kemɪstrɪ] *n* química.

**chemotherapy** [kiːməʊ'θerəpɪ] *n* quimioterapia.

**cheque** [tʃek] *n* cheque *m*, talón *m*.

**chequebook** ['tʃekbʊk] *n* talonario de cheques.

**chequered** ['tʃekəd] *adj* **1** (cloth, pattern) a cuadros. **2** *fig* (past, history, career) con altibajos, accidentado,-a.

**chequers** ['tʃekəz] *n pl* damas *fpl*.

**cherish** ['tʃerɪʃ] *vt* **1** (person) apreciar, querer. **2** (hope, memory, illusion) abrigar.

**cherry** ['tʃerɪ] *n* (fruit) cereza, guinda; (wood) cerezo. COMP cherry tree cerezo.
ⓘ *pl* cherries.

**chess** [tʃes] *n* ajedrez *m*: *a game of chess* una partida de ajedrez.

**chessboard** ['tʃesbɔːd] *n* tablero de ajedrez.

**chessmen** ['tʃesmən] *n pl* piezas *fpl* de ajedrez.

**chest** [tʃest] *n* **1** (large) arca, arcón *m*; (small) cofre *m*. **2** ANAT pecho.

**chestnut** ['tʃesnʌt] *n* **1** BOT (tree, wood) castaño; (nut) castaña. **2** (colour) castaño. **3** (horse) alazán,-ana.
▶ *adj* (colour) castaño,-a; (horse) alazán,-ana.

**chew** [tʃuː] *vt* (food) mascar, masticar; (nails, pencil) morder.

**chewing gum** ['tʃuːɪŋgʌm] *n* chicle *m*.

**chic** [ʃiːk] *adj* chic, elegante.
▶ *n* elegancia.

**chick** [tʃɪk] *n* polluelo.

**chicken** ['tʃɪkɪn] *n* **1** (hen) gallina; (food) pollo. **2** *fam* (coward) gallina *mf*.
▶ *adj* *fam* gallina.

**chickenpox** ['tʃɪkɪnpɒks] *n* varicela.

**chickpea** ['tʃɪkpiː] *n* garbanzo.

**chicory** ['tʃɪkərɪ] *n* achicoria, chicoria.

**chief** [tʃiːf] *n* (gen) jefe,-a; (of party) líder *mf*; (of tribe) cacique *m*.
▶ *adj* principal.

**chiefly** ['tʃiːflɪ] *adv* (mainly) principalmente; (especially) sobre todo.

**chieftain** ['tʃiːftən] *n* cacique *m*, jefe,-a.

**chiffon** ['ʃɪfɒn] *n* gasa.

**chilblain** ['tʃɪlbleɪn] *n* sabañón *m*.

**child** [tʃaɪld] *n* **1** (boy) niño; (girl) niña. **2** (son) hijo; (daughter) hija.
ⓘ *pl* children.

**childbirth** ['tʃaɪldbɜːθ] *n* parto.

**childhood** ['tʃaɪldhʊd] *n* infancia.

**childish** ['tʃaɪldɪʃ] *adj* (of a child) infantil; (immature) pueril, infantil.

**childlike** ['tʃaɪldlaɪk] *adj* infantil.

**children** ['tʃɪldrən] *n pl* → child.

**chili** ['tʃɪlɪ] *n* US → chilli.

**chill** [tʃɪl] *n* MED (cold) resfriado; (shiver) escalofrío.
▶ *adj* (wind, etc) frío,-a.
▶ *vt* enfriar.

**chilli** ['tʃɪlɪ] n chile m.

**chilling** ['tʃɪlɪŋ] adj **1** glacial. **2** fig espeluznante, escalofriante.

**chilly** ['tʃɪlɪ] adj (gen) frío,-a.
ⓘ comp chillier, superl chilliest.

**chime** [tʃaɪm] n (bells) carillón m; (sound of bells) repique m; (of clock) campanada; (of doorbell) campanilla.
▶ vi (bells) sonar, repicar; (clock) dar la hora, sonar.

**chimney** ['tʃɪmnɪ] n chimenea.

✎ Chimney sólo se refiere al conducto por donde sale el humo. El hogar se traduce por fireplace.

**chimpanzee** [tʃɪmpæn'zi:] n chimpancé m.

**chin** [tʃɪn] n barbilla, mentón m.

**china** ['tʃaɪnə] n **1** (white clay) loza; (fine) porcelana. **2** (crockery) vajilla, objetos mpl de porcelana, loza.

**China** ['tʃaɪnə] n China.

**Chinese** [tʃaɪ'ni:z] adj chino,-a.
▶ n **1** (person) chino,-a. **2** (language) chino.

**chink¹** [tʃɪŋk] n grieta, abertura.

**chink²** [tʃɪŋk] n (noise) tintineo.
▶ vt hacer tintinear, hacer sonar.

**chip** [tʃɪp] n **1** GB (fried potato) patata frita. **2** US patata frita (de bolsa). **3** COMPUT chip m. **4** (of wood) astilla; (of stone) lasca. **5** (flaw - in plate, glass) desportilladura. **6** (in gambling) ficha.
▶ vt **1** GB (potatoes) cortar. **2** (china, glass) desportillar; (paint) desconchar.
ⓘ pt & pp chipped, ger chipping.

**chipboard** ['tʃɪpbɔ:d] n aglomerado, madera aglomerada.

**chiropodist** [kɪ'rɒpədɪst] n podólogo, -a, pedicuro,-a, callista mf.

**chirp** [tʃɜ:p] vi (insect) chirriar; (bird) gorjear.

**chisel** ['tʃɪzəl] n (for stone) cincel m.
▶ vt (stone) cincelar; (wood, metal) labrar, tallar.
ⓘ pt & pp chiselled (US chiseled), ger chiselling (US chiseling).

**chit** [tʃɪt] n fam (note) nota.

**chitchat** ['tʃɪttʃæt] n fam palique m, cháchara.

**chives** [tʃaɪvz] n pl BOT cebollino, cebolleta.

**chloride** ['klɔ:raɪd] n cloruro.

**chlorine** ['klɔ:ri:n] n cloro.

**chloroform** ['klɒrəfɔ:m] n cloroformo.

**chlorophyll** ['klɒrəfɪl] n clorofila.

**chock** [tʃɒk] n calzo, cuña.

**chock-a-block** [tʃɒkə'blɒk] adj fam hasta los topes, de bote en bote.

**chock-full** [tʃɒk'fʊl] adj fam hasta los topes.

**chocolate** ['tʃɒkələt] n **1** (substance) chocolate m: a bar of chocolate una chocolatina, una tableta de chocolate. **2** (individual sweet) bombón m.

**choice** [tʃɔɪs] n **1** (act) elección f, opción f. **2** (person, thing chosen) elección f. **3** (variety, range) surtido, selección f.
▶ adj **1** (top quality) selecto,-a, de primera calidad.

**choir** ['kwaɪə'] n coro.

**choke** [tʃəʊk] vt **1** (person) ahogar, asfixiar, estrangular. **2** (block - pipe, drain, etc) atascar, obstruir.
▶ n estárter m.

☒ Choke no significa 'choque', que se traduce por collision.

**cholera** ['kɒlərə] n cólera m.

**cholesterol** [kə'lestərɒl] n colesterol m.

**choose** [tʃu:z] vt **1** (select) escoger, elegir; (elect) elegir. **2** (decide) decidir, optar por.
ⓘ pt chose [tʃəʊz], pp chosen ['tʃəʊzən], ger choosing.

**choosy** ['tʃu:zɪ] adj fam exigente.
ⓘ comp choosier, superl choosiest.

**chop** [tʃɒp] n **1** (blow) tajo, golpe m; (with axe) hachazo. **2** CULIN chuleta.
▶ vt cortar (up, -).
◆ to chop down vt sep (tree, etc) talar.
◆ to chop off vt sep cortar.
ⓘ pt & pp chopped, ger chopping.

**choppy** ['tʃɒpɪ] adj (sea) picado,-a.
ⓘ comp choppier, superl choppiest.

**chopsticks** ['tʃɒpstɪks] n pl palillos mpl.

**choral** ['kɔ:rəl] adj coral. COMP choral society coral f, orfeón m.

**chorale** [kə'rɑ:l] n coral f.

**chord¹** [kɔːd] n **1** MATH cuerda. **2** ANAT → cord.

**chord²** [kɔːd] n MUS acorde m.

**chore** [tʃɔːʳ] n (job) quehacer m, tarea; (boring job) lata.

**choreography** [kɒrɪˈɒgrəfɪ] n coreografía.

**chorister** [ˈkɒrɪstəʳ] n corista mf.

**chorus** [ˈkɔːrəs] n **1** (choir) coro. **2** (of song) estribillo.

**chose** [tʃəʊz] pt → choose.

**chosen** [ˈtʃəʊzˀn] pp → choose.
  ▶ adj elegido,-a, escogido,-a.

**Christ** [kraɪst] n Cristo, Jesucristo.

**christening** [ˈkrɪsˀnɪŋ] n (ritual) bautismo; (celebration) bautizo.

**Christian** [ˈkrɪstɪən] adj & n cristiano,-a.

**Christmas** [ˈkrɪsməs] n Navidad f, Navidades fpl. COMP **Christmas Eve** Nochebuena. ‖ **Christmas Day** día m de Navidad.

**chrome** [krəʊm] n cromo.

**chromosome** [ˈkrəʊməsəʊm] n cromosoma m.

**chronic** [ˈkrɒnɪk] adj **1** (disease, person, problem) crónico,-a. **2** GB fam (terrible) malísimo,-a, terrible.

**chronicle** [ˈkrɒnɪkˀl] n crónica.

**chronological** [krɒnəˈlɒdʒɪkˀl] adj cronológico,-a.

**chronology** [krəˈnɒlədʒɪ] n cronología.

**chronometer** [krəˈnɒmɪtəʳ] n cronómetro.

**chrysalis** [ˈkrɪsəlɪs] n crisálida.
  ① pl chrysalises.

**chrysanthemum** [krɪˈsænθəməm] n crisantemo.

**chubby** [ˈtʃʌbɪ] adj (person) regordete,-a, gordinflón,-ona.
  ① comp chubbier, superl chubbiest.

**chuck** [tʃʌk] vt **1** fam (throw) tirar. **2** fam (give up) dejar, plantar.
  ◆ **to chuck away** vt sep (rubbish) tirar; (money) derrochar.

**chuckle** [ˈtʃʌkˀl] vi reírse (entre dientes).
  ▶ n risita.

**chum** [tʃʌm] n fam compinche mf.

**church** [tʃɜːtʃ] n iglesia. COMP **Church of England** Iglesia Anglicana.

**churchyard** [ˈtʃɜːtʃjɑːd] n cementerio, camposanto.

**churn** [tʃɜːn] n **1** GB (for milk) lechera. **2** (for butter) mantequera.
  ▶ vt **1** (butter) hacer; (milk, cream) batir. **2** (water, earth) agitar (up, -), revolver (up, -).
  ◆ **to churn out** vt sep producir en serie, hacer como churros.

**chute** [ʃuːt] n (slide) tobogán m.

**cicada** [sɪˈkɑːdə] n cigarra.

**cider** [ˈsaɪdəʳ] n sidra.

**cigar** [sɪˈgɑːʳ] n puro, cigarro.

**cigarette** [sɪgəˈret] n cigarrillo.

**cinder** [ˈsɪndəʳ] n ceniza, pavesa.

**Cinderella** [sɪndəˈrelə] n (la) Cenicienta.

**cinema** [ˈsɪnəmə] n cine m.

**cinnamon** [ˈsɪnəmən] n canela.

**cipher** [ˈsaɪfəʳ] n **1** (code) código, clave f. **2** (zero) cero; (numeral) cifra.

**circle** [ˈsɜːkˀl] n círculo.
  ▶ vt (encircle) rodear, cercar; (move in a circle) dar vueltas alrededor de.

**circuit** [ˈsɜːkɪt] n **1** (route, journey round) recorrido; (of running track) vuelta. **2** ELEC circuito. **3** SP (series of tournaments) circuito.

**circular** [ˈsɜːkjələʳ] adj circular.

**circulate** [ˈsɜːkjəleɪt] vi circular.
  ▶ vt hacer circular.

**circulation** [sɜːkjəˈleɪʃˀn] n **1** (gen) circulación f. **2** (of newspaper, magazine) tirada.

**circulatory** [sɜːkjəˈleɪtərɪ] adj circulatorio,-a.

**circumcision** [sɜːkəmˈsɪʒˀn] n circuncisión f.

**circumference** [səˈkʌmfˀrəns] n circunferencia.

**circumflex** [ˈsɜːkəmfleks] n circunflejo.

**circumstance** [ˈsɜːkəmstəns] n (condition, fact) circunstancia.
  ▶ n pl **circumstances** (financial position) situación f económica.

**circus** [ˈsɜːkəs] n **1** (entertainment) circo. **2** GB (in town) glorieta, plaza redonda.

**cistern** [ˈsɪstən] n cisterna.

**cite** [saɪt] vt citar.

**citizen** [ˈsɪtɪzˀn] n ciudadano,-a.

**citizenship** [ˈsɪtɪzˀnʃɪp] n ciudadanía.

**citric** [ˈsɪtrɪk] adj cítrico,-a.

**C**

**city** ['sɪtɪ] *n* ciudad *f.* COMP **city council** GB ayuntamiento, municipio. ▌ **the City** GB el centro financiero de Londres.
ⓘ *pl* **cities**.

⊕ La City de Londres es el barrio original a partir del cual creció la actual metrópoli. Hoy en día, concentra las sedes de las grandes empresas y es unos de los centros económicos más importantes del mundo.

**civic** ['sɪvɪk] *adj (duty, pride)* cívico,-a; *(leader, event)* municipal.

**civics** ['sɪvɪks] *n* educación *f* cívica.

**civil** ['sɪvəl] *adj* **1** *(of citizens)* civil. **2** *(polite)* cortés,-esa, educado,-a. COMP **civil servant** funcionario,-a. ▌ **the Civil Service** la administración pública.

**civilian** [sɪ'vɪljən] *adj* civil. LOC **in civilian dress** de paisano.
▶ *n* civil *mf.*
▶ *n pl* **civilians** población *f sing* civil.

**civility** [sɪ'vɪlɪtɪ] *n* cortesía.

**civilization** [sɪvɪlaɪ'zeɪ[ə]n] *n* civilización *f.*

**civilize** ['sɪvɪlaɪz] *vt* civilizar.

**clad** [klæd] *pt & pp* → clothe.
▶ *adj* vestido,-a.

**claim** [kleɪm] *n* **1** *(demand - for insurance)* reclamación *f*; *(for benefit, allowance)* solicitud *f.* **2** *(assertion)* afirmación *f.*
▶ *vt* **1** *(gen)* reclamar. **2** *(apply for)* solicitar. **3** *(of disaster, accident, etc)* cobrar. **4** *(assert)* afirmar, sostener, decir.
▶ *vi* presentar un reclamación.

**claimant** ['kleɪmənt] *n* **1** *(of benefit, allowance)* solicitante *mf*; *(of insurance)* reclamante *mf.* **2** *(to throne)* pretendiente *mf.* **3** JUR demandante *mf.*

**clam** [klæm] *n* almeja.

**clamber** ['klæmbə'] *vi* trepar gateando (over, a).

**clammy** ['klæmɪ] *adj (weather)* bochornoso,-a; *(hands)* pegajoso,-a.
ⓘ *comp* **clammier**, *superl* **clammiest**.

**clamor** ['klæmə'] *n* US → clamour.

**clamour** ['klæmə'] *n* clamor *m.*
▶ *vi* clamar.

**clamp** [klæmp] *n* abrazadera.
▶ *vt* sujetar con abrazaderas.

◆ **to clamp down on** *vt insep* poner freno a, tomar medidas drásticas contra.

**clan** [klæn] *n* clan *m.*

**clandestine** [klæn'destɪn] *adj* clandestino,-a.

**clang** [klæŋ] *n* sonido metálico (fuerte).
▶ *vi* sonar.

**clap** [klæp] *n* **1** *(noise)* ruido seco. **2** *(applause)* aplauso. **3** *(slap)* palmada.
▶ *vt* **1** *(applaud)* aplaudir. **2** *(slap)* dar una palmada a.

◆ **to clap on** *vt sep (add)* agregar.

**clapperboard** ['klæpəbɔːd] *n* claqueta.

**clapping** ['klæpɪŋ] *n* aplausos *mpl.*

**claret** ['klærət] *n (wine)* clarete *m.*

**clarify** ['klærɪfaɪ] *vt* aclarar.
ⓘ *pt & pp* **clarified**, *ger* **clarifying**.

**clarinet** [klærɪ'net] *n* clarinete *m.*

**clarity** ['klærɪtɪ] *n* claridad *f.*

**clash** [klæʃ] *n* **1** *(fight)* enfrentamiento, choque *m*; *(disagreement, argument)* desacuerdo. **2** *(conflict - of interests)* conflicto; *(- of personalities, cultures, opinions)* choque *m.* **3** *(loud noise)* sonido.
▶ *vi* **1** *(opposing forces - fight)* chocar; *(- disagree)* discutir, enfrentarse (with, a). **2** *(interests)* estar en conflicto. **3** *(dates, events)* coincidir. **4** *(colours)* desentonar (with, con). **5** *(cymbals)* sonar.

**clasp** [klɑːsp] *n (on necklace)* broche *m*; *(on belt)* cierre *m*, hebilla.
▶ *vt* agarrar, sujetar.

**class** [klɑːs] *n* clase *f.*
▶ *vt* clasificar, catalogar.

**classic** ['klæsɪk] *adj* clásico,-a.
▶ *n (novel, film, play)* clásico.
▶ *n pl* **classics** *(literature)* clásicos *mpl*; *(languages)* clásicas *fpl.*

**classical** ['klæsɪk[ə]l] *adj (gen)* clásico,-a.

**classification** [klæsɪfɪ'keɪ[ə]n] *n* clasificación *f.*

**classified** ['klæsɪfaɪd] *adj* **1** *(categorized)* clasificado,-a. **2** *(secret)* secreto,-a, confidencial.

**classify** ['klæsɪfaɪ] *vt* clasificar.
ⓘ *pt & pp* **classified**, *ger* **classifying**.

**classmate** ['klɑːsmeɪt] *n* compañero,-a de clase.

**classroom** ['klɑːsruːm] *n* aula, clase *f.*

**classy** ['klɑːsɪ] *adj sl* con clase.
ⓘ *comp* **classier**, *superl* **classiest**.

**clatter** ['klætə'] *n* ruido.
► *vi* hacer ruido.

**clause** [klɔːz] *n* **1** *(in document)* cláusula. **2** LING oración *f*.

**claustrophobia** [klɔːstrəˈfəʊbɪə] *n* claustrofobia.

**claustrophobic** [klɔːstrəˈfəʊbɪk] *adj* claustrofóbico,-a.

**clavichord** ['klævɪkɔːd] *n* clavicordio.

**clavicle** ['klævɪkəl] *n* clavícula.

**claw** [klɔː] *n* **1** *(of lion, tiger, etc)* garra, zarpa; *(of cat)* uña; *(of bird)* garra; *(of crab, lobster)* pinza.
► *vi (scratch)* arañar (at, -).

**clay** [kleɪ] *n* arcilla.

**clean** [kliːn] *adj* limpio,-a.
► *vt (gen)* limpiar.
► *vi* limpiarse.
◆ **to clean out** *vt sep* **1** *(room, etc)* limpiar a fondo. **2** *fam (take all money)* dejar limpio,-a, dejar sin blanca.
◆ **to clean up** *vt sep* **1** *(room, mess, etc)* limpiar. **2** *fam (money, fortune)* hacer, sacar.
► *vi* **1** *(room, etc)* limpiar. **2** *fam (make money)* forrarse, barrer con todo.

**clean-cut** [kliːnˈkʌt] *adj (outline, feature)* bien definido,-a, nítido,-a; *(person, appearance)* limpio,-a, muy cuidado,-a.

**cleaner** ['kliːnə'] *n* **1** *(person)* encargado, -a de la limpieza. **2** *(product)* limpiador *m*.
► *n* **cleaner's** *(place, shop)* tintorería.

**cleanse** [klenz] *vt* limpiar (of, de).

**cleanser** ['klenzə'] *n (detergent)* producto de limpieza; *(lotion for skin)* leche *f* limpiadora, crema limpiadora.

**cleansing** ['klenzɪŋ] *n* limpieza.

**clear** [klɪə'] *adj* **1** *(glass, plastic, liquid)* transparente; *(sky, day, etc)* despejado,-a. **2** *(not blocked - road, desk)* despejado,-a; *(free - time)* libre. **3** *(picture, outline)* nítido, -a. **4** *(voice, sound, explanation)* claro,-a.
► *adv* **1** *(clearly - speak)* claramente; *(hear)* bien. **2** *(not touching)* a distancia.
► *vt* **1** *(table)* quitar; *(floor, road)* despejar; *(pipe, drain)* desatascar; *(building, room - of people)* desalojar, desocupar;

*(house, room - of furniture)* vaciar. **2** *(accused person)* absolver, exculpar; *(one's name)* limpiar. **3** *(debt)* liquidar, saldar. **4** *(obstacle)* salvar. **5** SP *(ball)* despejar.
◆ **to clear away** *vt sep (dishes, etc)* recoger, quitar.1
◆ **to clear off** *vi fam* largarse.
► *vt sep (debt)* liquidar.
◆ **to clear out** *vi fam* largarse.
► *vt sep (cupboard, drawers, room)* vaciar; *(old things)* tirar.
◆ **to clear up** *vt sep* **1** *(mystery, crime)* resolver, esclarecer; *(issue, misunderstanding)* aclarar; *(loose ends)* atar. **2** *(tidy)* recoger.
► *vi* **1** *(tidy)* ordenar. **2** *(weather)* despejar, mejorar.

**clearance** ['klɪərəns] *n* **1** SP despeje *m*. **2** *(permission)* autorización *f*. COMP **clearance sale** liquidación *f*.

**clear-cut** [klɪəˈkʌt] *adj* claro,-a, bien definido,-a.

**clear-headed** ['klɪəˈhedɪd] *adj* lúcido,-a, despejado,-a.

**clearing** ['klɪərɪŋ] *n (in wood)* claro.

**clearness** ['klɪənəs] *n* claridad *f*.

**clear-sighted** [klɪəˈsaɪtɪd] *adj* perspicaz, lúcido,-a.

**clef** [klef] *n* MUS clave *f*: *bass/treble clef* clave de fa/de sol.

**cleft** [kleft] *adj (chin, lip)* partido,-a.
► *n* hendidura, grieta.

**clementine** ['kleməntaɪn] *n* clementina.

**clench** [klentʃ] *vt* **1** *(teeth, fist)* apretar. **2** *(grip)* apretar, agarrar.

**clergy** ['klɜːdʒɪ] *n* clero.

**clergyman** ['klɜːdʒɪmən] *n* clérigo.
ⓘ *pl* **clergymen** ['klɜːdʒɪmən].

**clerical** ['klerɪkəl] *adj* **1** REL clerical, eclesiástico,-a. **2** *(of a clerk)* de oficina, administrativo,-a.

**clerk** [klɑːk, US klɜːrk] *n* **1** *(office worker)* oficinista *mf*, administrativo,-a. **2** US *(in a shop)* dependiente,-a *mf*.

**clever** ['klevə'] *adj* **1** *(person - intelligent)* listo,-a, inteligente; *(skilful)* hábil. **2** *(idea, plan, gadget)* ingenioso,-a; *(move)* hábil.

**cliché** ['kliːʃeɪ] *n* cliché *m*, tópico.

**click** [klɪk] n (sound - gen) clic m; (of tongue, fingers) chasquido.
▶ vt (tongue, fingers) chasquear.
▶ vi 1 (make noise) hacer clic. 2 (understand, realize) caer en la cuenta, darse cuenta de.

**client** ['klaɪənt] n cliente,-a.

**cliff** [klɪf] n acantilado, precipicio.

**cliffhanger** ['klɪfhæŋəʳ] n situación f de suspense.

**climate** ['klaɪmət] n 1 GEOG clima m. 2 fig clima m, situación f.

**climatic** [klaɪ'mætɪk] adj climático,-a.

**climatological** [klaɪmətə'lɒdʒɪkəl] adj climatológico,-a.

**climatology** [klaɪmə'tɒlədʒɪ] n climatología.

**climax** ['klaɪmæks] n clímax m.

**climb** [klaɪm] n 1 (gen) subida. 2 SP escalada.
▶ vt subir (a).
▶ vi trepar.
◆ to climb down vi 1 (descend) bajar. 2 fig (admit mistake, withdraw) ceder, volverse atrás.

**climber** ['klaɪməʳ] n 1 SP alpinista mf, escalador,-ra. 2 BOT enredadera.

**climbing** ['klaɪmɪŋ] n SP alpinismo, montañismo.

**clinch** [klɪntʃ] n 1 fam (embrace) abrazo apasionado. 2 SP (in boxing) cuerpo a cuerpo.
▶ vt fam (deal) cerrar; (argument) resolver; (title) hacerse con.
▶ vi SP (in boxing) abrazarse.

**cling** [klɪŋ] vi 1 (hold tightly) agarrarse (to, a). 2 (stick - clothes) pegarse, ceñirse; (- smell) pegarse.
① pt & pp clung [klʌŋ].

**clingfilm** ['klɪŋfɪlm] n film m transparente.

**clinic** ['klɪnɪk] n 1 (private, specialized) clínica. 2 (in state hospital) ambulatorio, dispensario.

**clink** [klɪŋk] n (noise) tintineo.
▶ vt hacer tintinear.
▶ vi tintinear.

**clip¹** [klɪp] n 1 (with scissors) tijeretada. 2 (of film) fragmento. 3 fam (blow) cachete m.
▶ vt 1 (cut - gen) cortar; (ticket) picar; (animals) esquilar. 2 (cut out) recortar. 3 fam (hit) dar un cachete a.
① pt & pp clipped, ger clipping.

**clip²** [klɪp] n 1 (for papers, etc) clip m; (for hair) pasador m, clip m. 2 (brooch) broche m, alfiler m de pecho.

**clipboard** ['klɪpbɔːd] n INFORM portapapeles m.

**clippers** ['klɪpəz] n pl (for nails) cortaúñas m sing; (for hair) maquinilla f sing.

**clipping** ['klɪpɪŋ] n (cutting) recorte m de periódico, recorte m de prensa.

**clique** [kliːk] n pej camarilla.

**clitoris** ['klɪtərɪs] n clítoris m.

**cloak** [kləʊk] n 1 (garment) capa. 2 fig (cover) capa, manto.

**cloakroom** ['kləʊkruːm] n 1 (gen) guardarropa. 2 GB euph (toilet) lavabo, servicios mpl.

**clock** [klɒk] n reloj m (de pared).
▶ vt 1 (time - athlete, race) cronometrar. 2 (register - speed, time) registrar, hacer.
◆ to clock in/on vi fichar (al llegar al trabajo).
◆ to clock out/off vi fichar (al salir del trabajo).
◆ to clock up vt insep (miles, hours) hacer.

**clockwise** ['klɒkwaɪz] adv en el sentido de las agujas del reloj.

**clog** [klɒg] n (shoe) zueco.
▶ vt [also clog up] obstruir, atascar.
▶ vi [also clog up] obstruirse, atascarse.
① pt & pp clogged, ger clogging.

**cloister** ['klɔɪstəʳ] n claustro.

**clone** [kləʊn] n clon m.
▶ vt clonar.

**close¹** [kləʊz] n 1 (end) fin m, final m. 2 (precincts) recinto.
▶ vt cerrar.
▶ vi 1 (gen) cerrar, cerrarse. 2 (end) concluir, terminar.
◆ to close up vi 1 (of wound) cicatrizar, cerrarse. 2 (shop, etc) cerrar.

**close²** [kləʊs] adj 1 (near) cercano,-a (to, a), próximo,-a (to, a). 2 (friend) íntimo,-a; (relation, family) cercano,-a.
▶ adv 1 (in position) cerca. 2 (in time) cerca.

**closed** [kləʊzd] adj cerrado,-a.

**close-knit** [kləʊsˈnɪt] *adj* unido,-a.

**closely** [ˈkləʊslɪ] *adv* **1** *(connect)* estrechamente, muy. **2** *(resemble)* mucho. **3** *(carefully - watch, listen)* atentamente; *(follow)* de cerca; *(question)* a fondo.

**closet** [ˈklɒzɪt] *n* US armario.

**close-up** [ˈkləʊsʌp] *n* primer plano.

**closing** [ˈkləʊzɪŋ] *n* cierre *m*.

**closure** [ˈkləʊʒəʳ] *n (gen)* cierre *m*; *(debate)* clausura.

**clot** [klɒt] *n* **1** *(of blood)* coágulo. **2** GB *fam* tonto,-a, bobo,-a.
▸ *vt* coagular.
▸ *vi (blood)* coagularse; *(cream)* cuajar.
ⓘ *pt & pp* clotted, *ger* clotting.

**cloth** [klɒθ] *n* **1** *(fabric)* tela; *(thick)* paño. **2** *(rag)* trapo.

✎ Consulta también **clothes**.

**clothe** [kləʊð] *vt* **1** *(dress, provide clothes for)* vestir (in/with, de). **2** *(cover)* revestir (in, de), cubrir (in, de).
ⓘ *pt & pp* clothed o clad [klæd], *ger* clothing.

**clothes** [kləʊðz] *n pl* ropa *f sing*.

**clothing** [ˈkləʊðɪŋ] *n* ropa.

**cloud** [klaʊd] *n* nube *f*.
◆ **to cloud over** *vi (sky)* nublarse; *(face, eyes)* empañarse.

**cloudy** [ˈklaʊdɪ] *adj* **1** *(sky, weather, day)* nublado,-a. **2** *(liquid)* turbio,-a.
ⓘ *comp* cloudier, *superl* cloudiest.

**clout** [klaʊt] *n* **1** *fam* tortazo. **2** *fam (influence)* influencia, peso.

**clove¹** [kləʊv] *n (spice)* clavo.

**clove²** [kləʊv] *n (of garlic)* diente *f*.

**clover** [ˈkləʊvəʳ] *n* trébol *m*.

**cloverleaf** [ˈkləʊvəliːf] *n* BOT hoja de trébol.

**clown** [klaʊn] *n* payaso, clown *m*.

**club** [klʌb] *n* **1** *(gen)* club *m*. **2** *(stick)* porra. **3** SP *(in golf)* palo. **5** *(in cards - English pack)* trébol *m*; *(- Spanish pack)* basto.

**cluck** [klʌk] *n* cloqueo.
▸ *vi* cloquear.

**clue** [kluː] *n* pista.

**clump** [klʌmp] *n* **1** *(of trees)* grupo; *(of plants)* mata, macizo. **2** *(of earth)* terrón *m*.

**clumsy** [ˈklʌmzɪ] *adj* **1** *(gen)* torpe. **2** *(tool, shape)* pesado,-a y difícil de manejar; *(furniture)* mal diseñado,-a.
ⓘ *comp* clumsier, *superl* clumsiest.

**clung** [klʌŋ] *pt & pp* → cling.

**cluster** [ˈklʌstəʳ] *n* **1** *(of trees, stars, buildings, people)* grupo; *(of berries, grapes)* racimo; *(of plants)* macizo.
▸ *vi* agruparse, apiñarse (round, alrededor de/en torno a).

**clutch** [klʌtʃ] *n* **1** AUTO embrague *m*. **2** *(grasp, grip)* agarrón *m*.
▸ *vt (seize)* agarrar; *(hold tightly)* estrechar, apretar.

**clutter** [ˈklʌtəʳ] *n (things)* cosas *fpl*, trastos *mpl*; *(untidy state)* desorden *m*.
▸ *vt* [also **to clutter up**] llenar, atestar, abarrotar.

**cm** [ˈsiːˈem] *symb* **(centimetre)** centímetro; *(symbol)* cm.

**coach** [kəʊtʃ] *n* **1** GB *(bus)* autocar *m*. **2** *(carriage)* carruaje *m*, coche *m* de caballos. **3** *(on train)* coche *m*, vagón *m*. **4** EDUC *(tutor)* profesor,-ra particular. **5** SP *(trainer)* entrenador,-ra.
▸ *vt* **1** EDUC dar clases particulares a, preparar. **2** SP entrenar.

**coagulate** [kəʊˈægjəleɪt] *vt* coagular.
▸ *vi* coagularse.

**coagulation** [kəʊægjəˈleɪʃ(ə)n] *n* coagulación *f*.

**coal** [kəʊl] *n* carbón *m*, hulla.

**coalition** [kəʊəˈlɪʃ(ə)n] *n* coalición *f*.

**coarse** [kɔːs] *adj* **1** *(fabric)* basto,-a; *(skin)* áspero,-a; *(sand, salt)* grueso,-a. **2** *(language, joke)* grosero,-a, vulgar.

**coast** [kəʊst] *n* costa, litoral *m*.
▸ *vi (in car)* ir en punto muerto; *(on bicycle)* ir sin pedalear.

**coastal** [ˈkəʊst(ə)l] *adj* costero,-a.

**coastguard** [ˈkəʊstgɑːd] *n* guardacostas *mf*.

**coat** [kəʊt] *n* **1** *(overcoat)* abrigo; *(short)* chaquetón *m*. **2** *(of paint)* capa, mano *f*; *(of dust)* capa. **3** *(of animal)* pelo, pelaje *m*.
▸ *vt* **1** cubrir (in/with, de).

**coating** [ˈkəʊtɪŋ] *n* **1** CULIN capa, baño. **2** *(of paint, dust, wax)* capa; *(of metal)* revestimiento.

**coax** [kəʊks] vt *(person)* engatusar.

**coaxial** [kəʊˈæksɪəl] adj coaxial.

**cob** [kɒb] n *(of corn)* mazorca (de maíz).

**cobble** [ˈkɒbəl] n adoquín m.
▶ vt *(street)* adoquinar.

**cobblestone** [ˈkɒbəlstəʊn] n adoquín m.

**cobweb** [ˈkɒbweb] n telaraña.

**cocaine** [kəˈkeɪn] n cocaína.

**coccyx** [ˈkɒksɪks] n coxis m, cóccix m.
ⓘ pl **coccyxes** o **coccyges**.

**cochineal** [kɒtʃɪˈniːl] n cochinilla.

**cochlea** [ˈkɒklɪə] n caracol m del oído.

**cock** [kɒk] n 1 *(rooster)* gallo; *(any male bird)* macho. 2 *(on firearm)* percutor m.

**cockle** [ˈkɒkəl] n berberecho.

**Cockney** [ˈkɒknɪ] adj *del barrio obrero del este de Londres.*
▶ n 1 *(person) persona del barrio obrero del este de Londres.* 2 *(dialect) dialecto que se habla en el barrio obrero del este de Londres.*

**cockpit** [ˈkɒkpɪt] n *(in plane)* cabina del piloto, carlinga; *(in racing car)* cabina.

**cockroach** [ˈkɒkrəʊtʃ] n cucaracha.

**cocktail** [ˈkɒkteɪl] n cóctel m.

**cocoa** [ˈkəʊkəʊ] n *(powder)* cacao; *(drink)* chocolate m.

**coconut** [ˈkəʊkənʌt] n coco.

**cocoon** [kəˈkuːn] n capullo.
▶ vt fig envolver, arropar.

**cod** [kɒd] n bacalao.
ⓘ pl **cod**.

**code** [kəʊd] n 1 *(gen)* código. 2 *(telephone)* prefijo; *(postal)* código (postal).
▶ vt poner en clave, cifrar.

**codification** [kəʊdɪfɪˈkeɪʃən] n codificación f.

**codify** [ˈkəʊdɪfaɪ] vt codificar.
ⓘ pt & pp **codified**, ger **codifying**.

**coeducation** [kəʊedjəˈkeɪʃən] n enseñanza mixta.

**coefficient** [kəʊɪˈfɪʃənt] n coeficiente m.

**coexist** [kəʊɪɡˈzɪst] vi coexistir.

**coffee** [ˈkɒfɪ] n café m.

**coffeepot** [ˈkɒfɪpɒt] n cafetera.

**coffer** [ˈkɒfəʳ] n arca, cofre m.

**coffin** [ˈkɒfɪn] n ataúd m, féretro.

**cog** [kɒg] n 1 *(on wheel)* diente m. 2 fig pieza.

**cogent** [ˈkəʊdʒənt] adj convincente, contundente.

**cognac** [ˈkɒnjæk] n coñac m.

**cognitive** [ˈkɒgnɪtɪv] adj cognitivo,-a.

**coherent** [kəʊˈhɪərənt] adj coherente.

**coil** [kɔɪl] n 1 *(of rope, wire)* rollo; *(of cable)* carrete m; *(of hair)* rizo, moño; *(of smoke)* espiral m, voluta. 2 *(single loop)* vuelta, lazada. 3 TECH bobina.
▶ vt *[also to coil up]* enrollar.

**coin** [kɔɪn] n moneda.
▶ vt acuñar.

**coincide** [kəʊɪnˈsaɪd] vi coincidir (with, con).

**coincidence** [kəʊˈɪnsɪdəns] n coincidencia, casualidad f.

**Coke®** [kəʊk] n Coca Cola®.

**coke** [kəʊk] n *(coal)* coque m.

**colander** [ˈkʌləndəʳ] n colador m.

**cold** [kəʊld] adj frío,-a.
▶ n 1 *(weather)* frío. 2 MED resfriado, catarro, constipado. COMP **cold cuts** US embutidos mpl, fiambres mpl.

**cold-blooded** [kəʊldˈblʌdɪd] adj 1 ZOOL de sangre fría. 2 fig *(person)* frío,-a, insensible; *(crime)* a sangre fría.

**coleslaw** [ˈkəʊlslɔː] n ensaladilla de col y zanahoria.

**colic** [ˈkɒlɪk] n cólico.

**coliseum** [kɒlɪˈsiːəm] n coliseo.

**collaborate** [kəˈlæbəreɪt] vi colaborar (with, con).

**collaborator** [kəˈlæbəreɪtəʳ] n 1 colaborador,-ra. 2 *(with enemy)* colaboracionista mf.

**collage** [ˈkɒlɑːdʒ] n ART collage m.

**collapse** [kəˈlæps] n 1 *(falling down)* derrumbamiento; *(falling in)* hundimiento. 2 *(failure, breakdown)* fracaso. 3 *(prices, currency)* caída en picado; *(business, company)* quiebra. 4 MED colapso.
▶ vi 1 *(building, bridge, etc)* derrumbarse, desplomarse; *(roof)* hundirse, venirse abajo. 2 MED *(person)* sufrir un colapso.
▶ vt *(table)* plegar.

**collapsible** [kəˈlæpsəbəl] adj plegable.

**collar** [ˈkɒləʳ] n **1** (of shirt, etc) cuello. **2** (for dog) collar m. **3** TECH collar m, abrazadera.
► vt fam pescar, pillar.

❌ Collar no significa 'collar (de persona)', que se traduce por necklace.

**collarbone** [ˈkɒləbəʊn] n clavícula.

**collateral** [kəˈlætᵊrəl] adj colateral. LOC collateral damage daños mpl colaterales.

**colleague** [ˈkɒliːg] n colega mf, compañero,-a.

**collect** [kəˈlekt] vt **1** (glasses, plates, belongings, etc) recoger; (information, data) reunir, recopilar. **2** (stamps, records, etc) coleccionar. **3** (taxes) recaudar; (rent) cobrar. **4** (pick up, fetch) ir a buscar, recoger.
► vi **1** (dust, water) acumularse; (people) reunirse, congregarse. **2** (for charity) recaudar dinero, hacer una colecta.

**collection** [kəˈlekʃᵊn] n **1** (of stamps, paintings, etc) colección f; (of poems, short stories) recopilación f; (of people) grupo. **2** (range of new clothes) colección f. **3** (for charity) colecta. **4** (of mail, of refuse) recogida. **5** (of taxes) recaudación f; (of rent) cobro.

**collective** [kəˈlektɪv] adj colectivo,-a.
► n (enterprise) cooperativa.

**collector** [kəˈlektəʳ] n **1** (of stamps, etc) coleccionista mf. **2** (of rent, debts, tickets) cobrador,-ra.

**college** [ˈkɒlɪdʒ] n **1** (for higher education) escuela, instituto mf. **2** US (university) universidad f, facultad f. **3** GB (within university) colegio universitario.

❌ College no significa 'colegio (de niños)', que se traduce por school.

**collide** [kəˈlaɪd] vi chocar.

**colliery** [ˈkɒljərɪ] n mina de carbón.
ⓘ pl collieries.

**collision** [kəˈlɪʒᵊn] n (between cars, trains, etc) colisión f, choque m; (between ships) abordaje m.

**colloquial** [kəˈləʊkwɪəl] adj coloquial.

**cologne** [kəˈləʊn] n colonia.

**Colombia** [kəˈlʌmbɪə] n Colombia.

**Colombian** [kəˈlʌmbɪən] adj & n colombiano,-a.

**colon¹** [ˈkəʊlən] n ANAT colon m.

**colon²** [ˈkəʊlən] n LING dos puntos mpl.

**colonel** [ˈkɜːnᵊl] n coronel m.

**colonial** [kəˈləʊnɪəl] adj colonial.
► n colono,-a.

**colonialism** [kəˈləʊnɪəlɪzᵊm] n colonialismo.

**colonist** [ˈkɒlənɪst] n (inhabitant) colono; (colonizer) colono,-a, colonizador,-ra.

**colonize** [ˈkɒlənaɪz] vt colonizar.

**colony** [ˈkɒlənɪ] n (gen) colonia.
ⓘ pl colonies.

**color** [ˈkʌləʳ] n US → colour.

**colossal** [kəˈlɒsᵊl] adj colosal.

**colossus** [kəˈlɒsəs] n coloso.

**colour** [ˈkʌləʳ] n color m.
► adj (television, film, etc) en color.
► vt **1** (with pen, paint, crayon) pintar, colorear; (dye) teñir. **2** fig (affect negatively, influence) influir en.
► vi **1** (blush) ruborizarse, sonrojarse, ponerse rojo,-a. **2** (of leaves) ponerse amarillo,-a; (fruit) coger color.
► n pl **colours** GB (worn by team, school) colores mpl; MIL (flag) bandera, enseña.
◆ to colour in vt sep pintar, colorear.

**colour-blind** [ˈkʌləblaɪnd] adj daltónico,-a.

**coloured** [ˈkʌləd] adj de color, de colores.

**colourful** [ˈkʌləful] adj **1** (full of colour, bright) lleno,-a de color, vistoso,-a; (brightly coloured) de colores vivos. **2** (person) pintoresco,-a.

**colouring** [ˈkʌlərɪŋ] n **1** (substance, dye) colorante m. **2** (person's skin, hair and eye colour) color m. **3** (of animal's skin, fur, plumage) color m.

**colourless** [ˈkʌlələs] adj **1** (without colour) incoloro,-a, sin color; (pale) pálido,-a. **2** fig (dull, uninteresting) soso,-a, anodino,-a, gris.

**colt** [kəʊlt] n potro.

**column** [ˈkɒləm] n (gen) columna.

**columnist** [ˈkɒləmnɪst] n columnista mf.

**coma** [ˈkəʊmə] n MED coma m. LOC to go into a coma caer en coma, entrar en coma.

**comb** [kəʊm] n **1** (for hair) peine m. **2** (for wool, cotton) carda. **3** (of bird) cresta. **4** (of honeycomb) panal m.
▶ vt **1** (hair) peinar. **2** (wool, cotton) cardar, peinar. **3** (search - area) rastrear, peinar.

**combat** ['kɒmbæt] n combate m.
▶ vt combatir, luchar contra.

**combination** [kɒmbɪ'neɪʃ°n] n combinación f.

**combine** [(vb) kəm'baɪn; (n) 'kɒmbaɪn] vt combinar.
▶ vi (gen) combinarse; (teams, forces) unirse; (companies) fusionarse.
▶ n COMM grupo industrial, asociación f.

**combined** [kəm'baɪnd] adj combinado,-a, conjunto,-a.

**combustible** [kəm'bʌstɪb°l] adj combustible, inflamable.

**combustion** [kəm'bʌst∫°n] n combustión f.

**come** [kʌm] vi **1** (gen) venir. **2** (arrive, reach) llegar. **3** (happen) suceder.
▶ vt (behave, play the part) hacerse: don't come the innocent with me no te hagas el inocente conmigo.
◆ **to come about** vi (happen) ocurrir, suceder.
◆ **to come across** vt insep (thing) encontrar, tropezar con.
▶ vi **1** (be understood) ser comprendido, -a. **2** (make an impression) causar una impresión.
◆ **to come after** vt insep seguir.
◆ **to come along** vi **1** (progress) ir, marchar. **2** (hurry up) darse prisa. **3** (arrive) venir, llegar; (appear) aparecer.
◆ **to come back** vi **1** (return) volver (from, de). **2** (remember) volver a la memoria. **3** (return to topic, question, idea) volver (to, a); (reply, retort) replicar, contestar.
◆ **to come before** vt insep **1** JUR comparecer ante. **2** (be more important than) ser más importante que.
◆ **to come down** vi **1** (gen) bajar; (collapse) caerse, hundirse, venirse abajo; (fall - rain, snow) caer. **2** (plane - land) aterrizar; (- fall) caer.
◆ **to come down with** vt insep (illness) caer enfermo,-a de, contraer, coger.

◆ **to come in** vi (enter) entrar.
◆ **to come on** vi **1** (make progress) avanzar. **2** (hurry up) darse prisa.
◆ **to come out** vi **1** (leave) salir (of, de); (tooth, hair) caerse; (stain) salir, quitarse; (colour, dye) desteñirse. **2** (sun, moon, stars) salir. **3** (new book, record, magazine, figures) salir, publicarse; (film) estrenarse.
◆ **to come through** vt insep (operation, accident) sobrevivir, salir con vida de; (illness) recuperarse de; (difficult period) pasar por, atravesar.
◆ **to come up to** vt insep **1** (equal) alcanzar, llegar a, estar a la altura de. **2** (approach - in space) acercarse a; (- in time) ser casi.
◆ **to come up with** vt insep (idea) tener, ocurrirse; (solution) encontrar; (plan) idear; (proposal) presentar, plantear.
◆ **to come upon** vt insep encontrarse con, encontrar.
ⓘ pt **came** [keɪm], pp **come**[kʌm], ger **coming**.

**comeback** ['kʌmbæk] n **1** fam (of person) reaparición f, vuelta, retorno. **2** (way of obtaining compensation) reclamación f. **3** (reply) réplica, respuesta.

**comedian** [kə'mi:dɪən] n cómico, humorista m.

**comedienne** [kəmi:dɪ'en] n cómica, humorista.

**comedy** ['kɒmədɪ] n comedia.
ⓘ pl **comedies**.

**comet** ['kɒmɪt] n cometa m.

**comfort** ['kʌmfət] n **1** (well-being) comodidad f, confort m, bienestar m. **2** (thing, luxury) comodidad f. **3** (consolation) consuelo.
▶ vt consolar.

**comfortable** ['kʌmf°təb°l] adj **1** (furniture, clothes, etc) cómodo,-a. **2** (life) desahogado,-a, acomodado,-a.

**comforting** ['kʌmfətɪŋ] adj reconfortante.

**comic** ['kɒmɪk] adj cómico,-a.
▶ n **1** (comedian) cómico,-a, humorista mf. **2** (magazine) tebeo, cómic m.

**coming** ['kʌmɪŋ] adj (gen) próximo,-a; (generation) venidero,-a, futuro,-a.
▶ n llegada.

**comma** [ˈkɒmə] *n* coma. LOC **inverted comma** comilla.

**command** [kəˈmɑːnd] *n* **1** *(order)* orden *f*. **2** *(control, authority)* mando. **3** *(knowledge, mastery)* dominio. **4** INFORM comando, instrucción *f*.
▸ *vt* **1** *(order)* mandar, ordenar. **2** MIL *(have authority over)* estar al mando de, comandar.

**commander** [kəˈmɑːndəʳ] *n* **1** MIL comandante *m*. **2** MAR capitán *m* de fragata.

**commanding** [kəˈmɑːndɪŋ] *adj* **1** *(voice, manner, appearance)* autoritario,-a. **2** *(position)* dominante, de superioridad.

**commandment** [kəˈmɑːndmənt] *n* REL mandamiento.

**commando** [kəˈmɑːndəʊ] *n* comando.
ⓘ *pl* **commandos** o **commandoes**.

**commemorate** [kəˈmeməreɪt] *vt* conmemorar.

**commend** [kəˈmend] *vt* *(praise)* alabar (for, por), elogiar (for, por); *(recommend)* recomendar.

**comment** [ˈkɒment] *n* comentario, observación *f*. LOC **no comment** sin comentarios.
▸ *vt* comentar, observar.

**commentary** [ˈkɒmənt°rɪ] *n* **1** *(spoken description)* comentario, comentarios *mpl*. **2** *(set of written remarks)* comentario, crítica.
ⓘ *pl* **commentaries**.

**commentator** [ˈkɒmənteɪtəʳ] *n* comentarista *mf*.

**commerce** [ˈkɒmɜːs] *n* comercio.

**commercial** [kəˈmɜːʃl] *adj* comercial.
▸ *n* *(advertisement)* anuncio, spot *m* publicitario.

**commercialization** [kəˈmɜːʃ°laɪzeɪʃ°n] *n* comercialización *f*.

**commercialize** [kəˈmɜːʃ°laɪz] *vt* comercializar.

**commission** [kəˈmɪʃ°n] *n* **1** COMM comisión *f*. **2** *(piece of work)* encargo.
▸ *vt* *(order)* encargar.

**commissioner** [kəˈmɪʃ°nəʳ] *n* **1** *(public official)* comisario. **2** *(member of a commission)* comisionado,-a.

**commit** [kəˈmɪt] *vt* **1** *(crime, error, sin)* cometer. **2** *(send to prison, etc)* internar. **3** *(bind)* comprometer, obligar; *(pledge)* asignar, consignar, destinar.
ⓘ *pt & pp* **committed**, *ger* **committing**.

**commitment** [kəˈmɪtmənt] *n* **1** *(undertaking, obligation)* compromiso, obligación *f*; *(responsibility)* responsabilidad *f*. **2** *(dedication)* dedicación *f*, entrega.

**committed** [kəˈmɪtɪd] *adj* *(to a cause)* comprometido,-a; *(dedicated)* dedicado,-a, entregado,-a.

**committee** [kəˈmɪtɪ] *n* comité *m*

**commode** [kəˈməʊd] *n* cómoda.

**commodity** [kəˈmɒdɪtɪ] *n* **1** COMM producto, artículo, mercancía. **2** FIN materia prima.
ⓘ *pl* **commodities**.

☒ Commodity no significa 'comodidad', que se traduce por comfort.

**common** [ˈkɒmən] *adj* **1** *(ordinary, average)* corriente. **2** *(usual, not scarce)* común, corriente. **3** *(shared, joint)* común. **4** *pej* *(vulgar)* ordinario,-a.
▸ *n* *(land)* tierras *fpl* comunales.

**commoner** [ˈkɒmənəʳ] *n* plebeyo,-a.

**commonplace** [ˈkɒmənpleɪs] *adj* común, corriente.
▸ *n* *(platitude)* lugar *m* común, tópico.

**Commons** [ˈkɒmənz] *n pl* **the Commons** GB los Comunes. COMP **the House of Commons** la Cámara de los Comunes.

⊕ La Cámara de los Comunes británica es el equivalente al Congreso español y es el órgano legislativo más importante del Reino Unido.

**Commonwealth** [ˈkɒmənwelθ] *n* GB Commonwealth *f*.

⊕ La Commonwealth es una organización compuesta por 53 naciones con fuertes vínculos con el Reino Unido por haber pertenecido en algún momento de su historia al Imperio británico.

**commotion** [kəˈməʊʃ°n] *n* *(scandal)* escándalo; *(noise, excitement)* alboroto, jaleo; *(confusion)* confusión *f*.

**communal** [ˈkɒmjənᵊl] *adj (shared)* comunal; *(of a community)* comunitario,-a.

**commune** [ˈkɒmjuːn] *n* comuna.

**communicate** [kəˈmjuːnɪkeɪt] *vt* **1** *(make known, convey)* comunicar. **2** MED transmitir, contagiar.
▶ *vi* comunicarse (**with**, con).

**communication** [kəmjuːnɪˈkeɪʃᵊn] *n* **1** *(gen)* comunicación *f*. **2** *(message)* comunicado.
▶ *n pl* **communications** comunicaciones *fpl*.

**communicative** [kəˈmjuːnɪkətɪv] *adj* comunicativo,-a.

**communion** [kəˈmjuːnjən] *n fml* comunión *f*.
▶ *n* **Communion** REL Comunión *f*.

**communiqué** [kəˈmjuːnɪkeɪ] *n* comunicado.

**communism** [ˈkɒmjənɪzᵊm] *n* comunismo.

**communist** [ˈkɒmjənɪst] *adj* comunista.
▶ *n* comunista *mf*.

**community** [kəˈmjuːnɪtɪ] *n* comunidad *f*.
ⓘ *pl* **communities**.

**commute** [kəˈmjuːt] *vi* desplazarse diariamente al lugar de trabajo.
▶ *vt* conmutar.

**commuter** [kəˈmjuːtəʳ] *n* persona que se desplaza diariamente a su lugar de trabajo. COMP **the commuter belt** los barrios *mpl* periféricos.

**compact** [*(adj-vb)* kəmˈpækt; *(n)* ˈkɒmpækt] *adj (gen)* compacto,-a; *(style)* conciso,-a.
▶ *n* **1** *(for powder)* polvera de bolsillo. **2** US coche *m* utilitario.
▶ *vt* compactar, comprimir.

**companion** [kəmˈpænjən] *n* **1** *(partner, friend)* compañero,-a. **2** *(person employed)* persona de compañía. **3** *(either of pair or set)* compañero,-a, pareja.

**companionship** [kəmˈpænjənʃɪp] *n* compañerismo, camaradería.

**company** [ˈkʌmpᵊnɪ] *n* **1** *(companionship)* compañía. **2** *(visitors)* visita. **3** *(business)* empresa, compañía, sociedad *f*. **4** THEAT compañía. **5** MIL compañía.
ⓘ *pl* **companies**.

**comparable** [ˈkɒmpᵊrəbᵊl] *adj* comparable (**to**, a) (**with**, con).

**comparative** [kəmˈpærətɪv] *adj* **1** *(relative)* relativo,-a. **2** *(making a comparison)* comparado,-a. **3** LING comparativo,-a.
▶ *n* LING comparativo.

**compare** [kəmˈpeəʳ] *vt* comparar (**to/ with**, con).

**comparison** [kəmˈpærɪsᵊn] *n* comparación *f*.

**compartment** [kəmˈpɑːtmənt] *n (in wallet, fridge, desk)* compartimento; *(in train)* departamento, compartimento.

**compass** [ˈkʌmpəs] *n* **1** *(magnetic)* brújula, compás *m*: *the points of the compass* los puntos cardinales. **2** [se usa como *sing* or *pl*] *(for drawing)* compás *m*: *a pair of compasses, a compass* un compás. COMP **compass rose** rosa de los vientos.

**compassion** [kəmˈpæʃᵊn] *n* compasión *f*.

**compassionate** [kəmˈpæʃᵊnət] *adj* compasivo,-a.

**compatibility** [kəmpætəˈbɪlɪtɪ] *n* compatibilidad *f*.

**compatible** [kəmˈpætɪbᵊl] *adj* compatible (**with**, con).

**compatriot** [kəmˈpætrɪət] *n* compatriota *mf*.

**compel** [kəmˈpel] *vt* **1** *(force)* obligar. **2** fig *(inspire)* infundir, inspirar.
ⓘ *pt & pp* **compelled**, *ger* **compelling**.

**compensate** [ˈkɒmpənseɪt] *vt* **1** *(recompense, indemnify)* indemnizar (**for**, por), compensar (**for**, por). **2** *(counterbalance)* compensar.
▶ *vi* compensar (**for**, -).

**compensation** [kɒmpənˈseɪʃᵊn] *n* **1** *(money, damages)* indemnización *f* (**for**, por). **2** *(way of compensating)* compensación *f* (**for**, por).

**compere** [ˈkɒmpeəʳ] *n* GB presentador, -ra.
▶ *vt* GB presentar.

**compete** [kəmˈpiːt] *vi (try to win)* disputarse; *(take part in)* competir, participar.

**competence** [ˈkɒmpɪtəns] *n* **1** *(ability)* competencia, capacidad *f*, aptitud *f*: *a fair level of competence in German* un buen nivel de alemán. **2** JUR *(legal authority)* competencia.

🅇 Competence no significa 'competencia (en el mercado)', que se traduce por competition.

**competent** [ˈkɒmpɪtənt] *adj* **1** *(person)* competente; *(work, novel, etc)* aceptable, bastante bien. **2** JUR competente.

**competition** [kɒmpəˈtɪʃⁿn] *n* **1** *(gen)* concurso *m*; *(race, sporting event)* competición *f*. **2** *(rivalry)* competencia.

**competitive** [kəmˈpetɪtɪv] *adj* competitivo,-a.

**competitor** [kəmˈpetɪtəʳ] *n* **1** COMM *(rival)* competidor,-ra, rival *mf*. **2** SP *(in race, etc)* participante *mf*; *(opponent)* contrincante *mf*. **3** *(in quiz, etc)* concursante *mf*, participante *mf*; *(in competitive examination)* opositor,-ra.

**compilation** [kɒmpɪˈleɪʃⁿn] *n* **1** *(gen)* compilación *f*. **2** *(record, etc)* recopilación *f*.

**compile** [kəmˈpaɪl] *vt* **1** *(produce book, list, etc)* compilar; *(collect information)* recopilar. **2** COMPUT compilar.

**complain** [kəmˈpleɪn] *vi* quejarse (about/of, de).

**complaint** [kəmˈpleɪnt] *n* **1** *(gen)* queja *(about, de)*; *(formal)* reclamación *f*. **2** MED enfermedad *f* (leve), achaque *m*.

**complement** [ˈkɒmplɪmənt] *n* *(gen)* complemento *(to, de)*.
▶ *vt* complementar.

**complementary** [kɒmplɪˈmentərɪ] *adj* *(gen)* complementario,-a.

**complete** [kəmˈpliːt] *adj* **1** *(entire)* completo,-a. **2** *(finished)* acabado,-a, terminado,-a.
▶ *vt* **1** *(make whole)* completar. **2** *(finish)* acabar, terminar. **3** *(fill in - form)* rellenar.

**completion** [kəmˈpliːʃⁿn] *n* *(act, state)* finalización *f*, terminación *f*.

**complex** [ˈkɒmpleks] *adj* complejo,-a.
▶ *n* complejo.

**complexion** [kəmˈplekʃⁿn] *n* *(quality of skin)* cutis *m*; *(colour or tone of skin)* tez *f*.

🅇 Complexion no significa 'complexión (física)', que se traduce por constitution.

**complexity** [kəmˈpleksɪtɪ] *n* complejidad *f*.
ⓘ *pl* complexities.

**complicate** [ˈkɒmplɪkeɪt] *vt* complicar.

**complicated** [ˈkɒmplɪkeɪtɪd] *adj* complicado,-a.

**complication** [kɒmplɪˈkeɪʃⁿn] *n* complicación *f*.
▶ *n pl* **complications** MED complicaciones *fpl*.

**complicity** [kəmˈplɪsɪtɪ] *n* complicidad *f* (in, en).

**compliment** [ˈkɒmplɪmənt] *vt* felicitar (on, por).
▶ *n* *(praise)* cumplido, halago.
▶ *n pl* **compliments** saludos *mpl*, felicitaciones *fpl*.

**comply** [kəmˈplaɪ] *vi* *(order)* obedecer (with, -), cumplir (with, con); *(request)* acceder (with, a); *(law)* acatar (with, -); *(standards)* cumplir (with, con).
ⓘ *pt & pp* complied, *ger* complying.

**component** [kəmˈpəʊnənt] *adj* componente.
▶ *n* **1** *(gen)* componente *m*. **2** AUTO pieza.

**compose** [kəmˈpəʊz] *vt* **1** *(music, poem)* componer; *(letter)* redactar. **2** *(constitute)* componer. **3** *(one's thoughts)* poner en orden.
▶ *vi* MUS componer.

**composed** [kəmˈpəʊzd] *adj* *(calm)* sereno,-a, sosegado,-a, tranquilo,-a.

**composer** [kəmˈpəʊzəʳ] *n* compositor,-ra.

**composite** [ˈkɒmpəzɪt] *adj* compuesto,-a.
▶ *n* combinación *f*, conjunto.

**composition** [kɒmpəˈzɪʃⁿn] *n* **1** *(gen)* composición *f*. **2** *(essay)* redacción *f*. **3** *(substance)* mezcla.

**compost** [ˈkɒmpɒst] *n* abono orgánico, abono vegetal, compost *m*.

**composure** [kəmˈpəʊʒəʳ] *n* calma, serenidad *f*, compostura.

**compound¹** *[(adj-n)* ˈkɒmpaʊnd; *(vb)* kəmˈpaʊnd] *adj* compuesto,-a.
▶ *n* **1** CHEM compuesto. **2** *(substance)* mezcla. **3** LING palabra compuesta.

▶ *vt* **1** *(mix)* componer, combinar, mezclar. **2** *(worsen, exacerbate - problem)* agravar; *(- difficulty)* aumentar.

**compound²** ['kɒmpaʊnd] *n (enclosed area)* recinto.

**comprehend** [kɒmprɪ'hend] *vt* **1** *(understand)* comprender. **2** *fml (include)* comprender, abarcar.

**comprehensible** [kɒmprɪ'hensəbəl] *adj* comprensible.

**comprehension** [kɒmprɪ'henʃən] *n* comprensión *f*.

**comprehensive** [kɒmprɪ'hensɪv] *adj (thorough)* detallado,-a, global, completo,-a; *(broad)* amplio,-a, extenso,-a.

☒ Comprehensive no significa 'comprensivo (tolerante)', que se traduce por understanding.

**compress** [(*n*) 'kɒmpres; (*vb*) kəm'pres] *n* compresa.

▶ *vt* **1** *(air, straw)* comprimir. **2** *(text, argument, speech)* condensar.

**compressibility** [kəmprəsɪ'bɪlɪtɪ] *n* compresibilidad *f*.

**compression** [kəm'preʃən] *n* compresión *f*.

**compressor** [kəm'presəʳ] *n* compresor *m*.

**comprise** [kəm'praɪz] *vt (consist of, be made up of)* comprender, constar de; *(constitute, form)* componer, constituir.

**compromise** ['kɒmprəmaɪz] *n* acuerdo mutuo, solución *f* de compromiso.

▶ *vi* llegar a un acuerdo, transigir.

▶ *vt (endanger, weaken)* comprometer.

☒ Compromise no significa 'compromiso (obligación o promesa de matrimonio)', que se traducen por commitment y engagement.

**compulsion** [kəm'pʌlʃən] *n* **1** *(force)* obligación *f*, coacción *f*. **2** *(urge)* compulsión *f*.

**compulsive** [kəm'pʌlsɪv] *adj* **1** *(compelling, fascinating)* fascinante, irresistible, absorbente. **2** *(obsessive)* obsesivo,-a.

**compulsory** [kəm'pʌlsərɪ] *adj (subject, military service)* obligatorio,-a; *(retirement, redundancy)* forzoso,-a.

**computation** [kɒmpjʊ'teɪʃən] *n* cálculo, cómputo.

**compute** [kəm'pjuːt] *vt* computar, calcular.

**computer** [kəm'pjuːtəʳ] *n* ordenador *m*, computadora.

**computerization** [kəmpjuːtərəɪ'zeɪʃən] *n (of data)* computerización *f*; *(of system, business)* informatización *f*.

**computerize** [kəm'pjuːtəraɪz] *vt (data)* computarizar, computerizar; *(system, business)* informatizar.

**computing** [kəm'pjuːtɪŋ] *n* informática.

**comrade** ['kɒmreɪd] *n* POL camarada *mf*, compañero,-a.

**con¹** [kɒn] *n fam* estafa, timo.

▶ *vt fam (money)* estafar, timar; *(person)* embaucar, engañar.

ⓘ *pt & pp* conned, *ger* conning.

**con²** [kɒn] *n (disadvantage)* contra *m*.

✎ Consulta también pro.

**concave** ['kɒnkeɪv] *adj* cóncavo,-a.

**concavity** [kɒn'kævɪtɪ] *n* concavidad *f*.

**conceal** [kən'siːl] *vt (gen)* ocultar; *(facts)* encubrir; *(feelings)* disimular.

**concede** [kən'siːd] *vt* **1** *(admit)* reconocer, admitir. **2** *(allow, give away)* conceder.

▶ *vi* ceder, rendirse.

**conceit** [kən'siːt] *n (pride)* vanidad *f*.

**conceivable** [kən'siːvəbəl] *adj* concebible, imaginable.

**conceive** [kən'siːv] *vt* **1** *(gen)* concebir. **2** *(understand)* entender.

**concentrate** ['kɒnsəntreɪt]

▶ *vt (gen)* concentrar (on, en).

▶ *vi* **1** *(person)* concentrarse (on, en).

**concentration** [kɒnsən'treɪʃən] *n* concentración *f* (on, en).

**concentric** [kən'sentrɪk] *adj* concéntrico,-a.

**concept** ['kɒnsept] *n* concepto.

**conception** [kən'sepʃən] *n* **1** *(of child, idea, plan)* concepción *f*. **2** *(idea)* concepto, idea, noción *f*.

**concern** [kən'sɜːn] *n* **1** *(worry)* preocupación *f*, inquietud *f*. **2** *(interest)* interés *m*; *(affair)* asunto. **3** COMM *(company, business)* negocio.

▶ vt **1** (affect, involve) afectar, concernir. (interest) interesar. **2** (worry) preocupar. **3** (book, film, article, etc) tratar de.

**concerned** [kən'sɜːnd] adj (worried) preocupado,-a (**about/for**, por).

**concerning** [kən'sɜːnɪŋ] prep referente a, con respecto a, en cuanto a.

**concert** ['kɒnsət] n concierto.

**concerted** [kən'sɜːtɪd] adj concertado,-a, coordinado,-a.

**concerto** [kən'tʃeətəʊ] n concierto.
ⓘ pl concertos o concerti [kən'tʃeətɪ].

✎ Concerto se refiere específicamente a conciertos de música clásica para uno o varios instrumentos solistas y una orquesta.

**concession** [kən'seʃən] n concesión f (**to**, a).

**concessionaire** [kənseʃə'neər] n concesionario,-a.

**conciliate** [kən'sɪlɪeɪt] vt & vi conciliar.

**concise** [kən'saɪs] adj conciso,-a.

**concision** [kən'sɪʒən] n concisión f.

**conclude** [kən'kluːd] vt **1** (end) concluir, finalizar. **2** (settle - deal) cerrar; (- agreement) llegar a; (- treaty) firmar. **3** (deduce) concluir, llegar a la conclusión de.
▶ vi concluir, terminar.

**conclusion** [kən'kluːʒən] n conclusión f.

**conclusive** [kən'kluːsɪv] adj concluyente.

**concoct** [kən'kɒkt] vt **1** (dish, sauce, drink) confeccionar, preparar. **2** (story, excuse, explanation) inventar, inventarse.

**concord** ['kɒŋkɔːd] n **1** fml (harmony) concordia. **2** LING concordancia.

**concourse** ['kɒŋkɔːs] n (hall) vestíbulo; (in station) explanada.

✗ Concourse no significa 'concurso (competición)', que se traduce por **competition**.

**concrete** ['kɒŋkriːt] adj **1** (definite, not abstract) concreto,-a. **2** (made of concrete) de hormigón.
▶ n hormigón m.

**concur** [kən'kɜː] vi (agree) estar de acuerdo, coincidir.
ⓘ pt & pp concurred, ger concurring.

**concurrence** [kən'kʌrəns] n acuerdo, coincidencia.

**concussion** [kən'kʌʃən] n MED conmoción f cerebral.

**condemn** [kən'dem] vt condenar.

**condemnation** [kɒndem'neɪʃən] n condena.

**condensation** [kɒnden'seɪʃən] n CHEM (process) condensación f; (on glass) vaho.

**condense** [kən'dens] vt condensar.

**condenser** [kən'densər] n condensador m.

**condescend** [kɒndɪ'send] vi **1** (deign) condescender, dignarse. **2** (patronize) tratar con condescendencia.

**condescending** [kɒndɪ'sendɪŋ] adj (attitude, answer) condescendiente.

**condiment** ['kɒndɪmənt] n condimento.

**condition** [kən'dɪʃən] n **1** (state) condición f, estado. **2** (requirement, provision) condición f. **3** MED afección f, enfermedad f.
▶ vt **1** (determine, accustom) condicionar. **2** (treat - hair) acondicionar, suavizar.

**conditional** [kən'dɪʃənəl] adj condicional.
▶ n **the conditional** LING el condicional m.

**conditioner** [kən'dɪʃənər] n (for hair) acondicionador m, suavizante m.

**condolences** [kən'dəʊlənsɪs] n pl pésame m sing.

**condom** ['kɒndəm] n condón m, preservativo.

**condominium** [kɒndə'mɪnɪəm] n **1** POL condominio. **2** US (apartment block) bloque m de pisos; (apartment) apartamento, piso.

**condone** [kən'dəʊn] vt (person) aprobar, consentir.

**condor** ['kɒndɔːr] n cóndor m.

**conducive** [kən'djuːsɪv] adj propicio,-a (**to**, para).

**conduct** [(n) 'kɒndʌkt; (vb) kɒn'dʌkt] n **1** (behaviour) conducta, comportamiento. **2** (management) dirección f, gestión f, administración f.
▶ vt **1** (direct - survey, campaign) llevar a cabo, realizar; (- business) administrar.

**2** *(lead, guide)* conducir, guiar. **3** *(transmit - heat, etc)* conducir. **4** MUS dirigir.
▶ *vi* MUS dirigir.

**conduction** [kənˈdʌkʃ°n] *n* PHYS conducción *f.*

❌ Conduction no significa 'conducción (de un vehículo)', que se traduce por **driving**.

**conductivity** [kənˈdʌktɪvɪtɪ] *n* conductividad *f.*

**conductor** [kənˈdʌktəʳ] *n* **1** *(of heat, electricity)* conductor *m.* **2** *(of orchestra)* director,-ra de orquesta. **3** *(on bus)* cobrador,-ra. **4** US *(on train)* jefe,-a de tren.

❌ Conductor no significa 'conductor (de un vehículo)', que se traduce por **driver**.

**conductress** [kənˈdʌktrəs] *n (on bus)* cobradora *f.*

**conduit** [ˈkɒndjʊɪt] *n* conducto.

**cone** [kəʊn] *n* **1** *(shape, for traffic)* cono. **2** *(for ice cream)* cucurucho. **3** BOT *(fruit of pine tree)* piña.

**confectioner** [kənˈfekʃ°nəʳ] *n* confitero,-a, pastelero,-a.

**confectionery** [kənˈfekʃ°nərɪ] *n* dulces *mpl.*

**confederacy** [kənˈfed°rəsɪ] *n* confederación *f.*
ⓘ *pl* confederacies.

**confederation** [kənfedəˈreɪʃ°n] *n* confederación *f.*

**confer** [kənˈfɜːʳ] *vt (award, grant, bestow)* conferir, conceder.
▶ *vi (consult, discuss)* consultar (with, con) (about/on, sobre).
ⓘ *pt & pp* conferred, *ger* conferring.

**conference** [ˈkɒnf°rəns] *n* **1** *(large event, convention)* congreso. **2** *(meeting)* reunión *f,* junta.

❌ Conference no significa 'conferencia (discurso)', que se traduce por **lecture**.

**confess** [kənˈfes] *vt & vi* confesar.

**confessed** [kənˈfest] *adj* declarado,-a.

**confession** [kənˈfeʃ°n] *n* confesión *f.*

**confessional** [kənˈfeʃən°l] *n* confesionario.

**confessor** [kənˈfesəʳ] *n* REL confesor *m.*

**confetti** [kənˈfetɪ] *n* confeti *m.*

**confidant** [ˈkɒnfɪdænt] *n* confidente *m.*

**confidante** [ˈkɒnfɪdænt] *n* confidenta.

**confide** [kənˈfaɪd] *vt* confiar.
◆ to confide in *vi* confiar en.

**confidence** [ˈkɒnfɪdəns] *n* **1** *(trust, faith)* confianza (in, en), fe *f* (in, en). **2** *(self-confidence)* confianza, seguridad *f.* **3** *(secrecy)* confianza. **4** *(secret)* confidencia.

**confident** [ˈkɒnfɪd°nt] *adj* **1** *(certain)* seguro,-a. **2** *(self-confident)* seguro,-a de sí mismo,-a.

**confidential** [kɒnfɪˈdenʃ°l] *adj* confidencial.

**confine** [kənˈfaɪn] *vt* **1** *(person)* confinar, recluir; *(animal)* encerrar. **2** *(limit, restrict)* limitar.

**confinement** [kənˈfaɪnmənt] *n* **1** *(imprisonment)* reclusión *f.* **2** MED *(in childbirth)* parto.

**confines** [ˈkɒnfaɪnz] *n pl* límites *mpl,* confines *mpl.*

**confirm** [kənˈfɜːm] *vt* confirmar.

**confirmation** [kɒnfəˈmeɪʃ°n] *n* confirmación *f.*

**confirmed** [kənˈfɜːmd] *adj (inveterate)* empedernido,-a.

**confiscate** [ˈkɒnfɪskeɪt] *vt* confiscar.

**conflict** [*(n)* ˈkɒnflɪkt; *(vb)* kənˈflɪkt] *n* conflicto.
▶ *vi* chocar (with, con), estar en conflicto (with, con).

**conflicting** [kənˈflɪktɪŋ] *adj (evidence, accounts)* contradictorio,-a; *(opinions, interests)* contrario,-a, opuesto,-a.

**confluence** [ˈkɒnflʊəns] *n* confluencia.

**conform** [kənˈfɔːm] *vi* **1** *(comply with rules, standards, regulations)* ajustarse (to/with, a), cumplir (to/with, con). **2** *(agree, be consistent with)* conformarse (to/with, con), concordar (with, con). **3** *(fit in, behave like other people)* ser conformista.

**conformist** [kənˈfɔːmɪst] *adj* conformista.
▶ *n* conformista *mf.*

**conformity** [kənˈfɔːmɪtɪ] *n* conformidad *f.*

**confront** [kənˈfrʌnt] *vt* hacer frente a, enfrentarse a.

**confuse** [kənˈfjuːz] *vt* confundir.

**confused** [kən'fjuːzd] *adj* **1** *(person)* confundido,-a. **2** *(mind, ideas, account)* confuso,-a.

**confusing** [kən'fjuːzɪŋ] *adj* confuso,-a.

**confusion** [kən'fjuːʒ°n] *n* confusión *f.*

**congeal** [kən'dʒiːl] *vi (blood)* coagularse; *(fat)* solidificarse.

**congenial** [kən'dʒiːnɪəl] *adj* agradable.

**congenital** [kən'dʒenɪt°l] *adj* MED congénito,-a.

**congested** [kən'dʒestɪd] *adj* congestionado,-a.

**congestion** [kən'dʒestʃ°n] *n* congestión *f.*

**conglomerate** [*(n)* kən'glɒmərət; *(vb)* kən'glɒməreɪt] *n* **1** COMM conglomerado (de empresas). **2** GEOL conglomerado.

**congratulate** [kən'grætjəleɪt] *vt* felicitar (on, por).

**congratulation** [kən'grætjəleɪʃ°nz] *n* felicitación *f.*
   ▶ *interj* **congratulations!** ¡felicidades! *fpl*, ¡enhorabuena!

**congregate** ['kɒŋgrɪgeɪt] *vi* congregarse.

**congregation** [kɒŋgrɪ'geɪʃ°n] *n* REL *(people gathered)* fieles *mpl*; *(parishioners)* feligreses *mpl*.

**congress** ['kɒŋgres] *n* congreso.
   ▶ *n* **Congress** US el Congreso.

**congruent** ['kɒŋgruənt] *adj* MATH congruente.

**conic** ['kɒnɪk] *adj* cónico,-a.

**conifer** ['kɒnɪfəʳ] *n* conífera.

**conjecture** [kən'dʒektʃəʳ] *n* conjetura, suposición *f.*
   ▶ *vi* hacer conjeturas.

**conjugal** ['kɒndʒəg°l] *adj* conyugal.

**conjugate** ['kɒndʒəgeɪt] *vt* conjugar.
   ▶ *vi* conjugarse.

**conjugation** [kɒndʒə'geɪʃ°n] *n* conjugación *f.*

**conjunction** [kən'dʒʌŋkʃ°n] *n* conjunción *f.* LOC **in conjunction with** conjuntamente con.

**conjure** ['kʌndʒəʳ] *vi* hacer magia, hacer juegos de manos.

◆ **to conjure up** *vt sep (evoke - memories)* evocar, traer a la memoria; *(summon - spirits)* invocar.

> ⊠ **Conjure** no significa 'conjura (conspiración)', que se traduce por **plot**.

**conjurer** ['kʌndʒərəʳ] *n* mago,-a, prestidigitador,-ra.

**connect** [kə'nekt] *vt* **1** *(gen)* conectar. **2** *(associate)* relacionar, asociar. **3** *(on telephone)* poner (with, con).

**connection** [kə'nekʃ°n] *n* **1** *(gen)* conexión *f.* **2** *(train, plane)* conexión *f,* enlace *m.*
   ▶ *n pl* **connections** *(professional)* contactos *mpl*; *(relatives)* familia, parientes *mpl.*

**connector** [kə'nektəʳ] *n* conector *m.*

**connoisseur** [kɒnə'sɜːʳ] *n* entendido,-a, conocedor,-ra.

**connotation** [kɒnə'teɪʃ°n] *n* connotación *f.*

**conquer** ['kɒŋkəʳ] *vt (country, mountain, heart)* conquistar; *(enemy, fear)* vencer.

**conqueror** ['kɒŋkərəʳ] *n* conquistador,-ra, vencedor,-ra.

**conquest** ['kɒŋkwest] *n* conquista.

**consanguinity** [kɒnsæŋ'gwɪnɪtɪ] *n* consanguinidad *f.*

**conscience** ['kɒnʃ°ns] *n* conciencia.

**conscientious** [kɒnʃɪ'enʃəs] *adj (work)* concienzudo,-a; *(person)* aplicado,-a, serio,-a.

**conscientiousness** [kɒnʃɪ'enʃəsnəs] *n* escrupulosidad *f.*

**conscious** ['kɒnʃəs] *adj* **1** MED consciente. **2** *(aware)* consciente. **3** *(intentional, deliberate)* deliberado,-a.

**conscript** [*(n)* 'kɒnskrɪpt; *(vb)* kən'skrɪpt] *n* recluta.
   ▶ *vt* reclutar.

**conscription** [kən'skrɪpʃ°n] *n* servicio militar obligatorio.

**consecrate** ['kɒnsɪkreɪt] *vt* consagrar.

**consecutive** [kən'sekjətɪv] *adj* consecutivo,-a.

**consensus** [kən'sensəs] *n* consenso.

**consent** [kən'sent] *n* consentimiento.
   ▶ *vi* consentir (to, en), acceder (to, en).

**consequence** ['kɒnsɪkwəns] n **1** (result) consecuencia. **2** (importance) importancia, trascendencia.

**consequent** ['kɒnsɪkwənt] adj consiguiente.

**conservation** [kɒnsə'veɪ[ə]n] n conservación f.

**conservationist** [kɒnsə'veɪ[ə]nɪst] n ecologista mf.

**conservatism** [kən'sɜ:vətɪz[ə]m] n POL conservadurismo.

**conservative** [kən'sɜ:vətɪv] adj **1** (traditional) conservador,-ra. **2** (cautious) cauteloso,-a, prudente.
 ▶ n (traditionalist) conservador,-ra.
 ▶ adj **Conservative** POL conservador,-ra.
 ▶ n **Conservative** POL conservador,-ra.

**conservatoire** [kən'sɜ:vətwɑ:ʳ] n conservatorio.

**conservatory** [kən'sɜ:vətrɪ] n **1** MUS conservatorio. **2** (greenhouse) invernadero.
 ① pl conservatories.

**conserve** [kən'sɜ:v] vt (nature, wildlife, etc) conservar, proteger; (save) conservar, ahorrar.
 ▶ n CULIN (jam) confitura.

**consider** [kən'sɪdəʳ] vt considerar.

**considerable** [kən'sɪd[ə]rəb[ə]l] adj considerable.

**considerate** [kən'sɪd[ə]rət] adj considerado,-a, atento,-a.

**consideration** [kənsɪdə'reɪ[ə]n] n **1** (gen) consideración f. **2** (factor to consider) factor m a tener en cuenta.

**considering** [kən'sɪdərɪŋ] prep teniendo en cuenta.
 ▶ conj teniendo en cuenta que.
 ▶ adv después de todo.

**consign** [kən'saɪn] vt **1** COMM (send - goods) consignar. **2** fml (entrust) confiar.

**consignment** [kən'saɪnmənt] n COMM remesa, envío.

**consist** [kən'sɪst] vi **1** fml (have as chief element) consistir (in, en). **2** (comprise, be composed of) constar (of, de), estar compuesto,-a (of, de).

**consistency** [kən'sɪstənsɪ] n (of actions, behaviour, policy) coherencia, lógica. **2** (of mixture) consistencia.

**consistent** [kən'sɪstənt] adj (of person, behaviour, beliefs) coherente (with, con), consecuente (with, con); (denial, improvement) constante.

**consolation** [kɒnsə'leɪ[ə]n] n consuelo.

**console¹** ['kɒnsəʊl] n (electrical) consola; (video games) consola.

**console²** [kən'səʊl] vt consolar.

**consolidate** [kən'sɒlɪdeɪt] vt **1** (gen) consolidar. **2** COMM (merge) fusionar.

**consolidation** [kənsɒlɪ'deɪ[ə]n] n **1** (gen) consolidación f. **2** COMM fusión f.

**consommé** ['kɒnsɒmeɪ] n consomé m.

**consonant** ['kɒns[ə]nənt] n consonante f.

**conspicuous** [kən'spɪkjuəs] adj (clothes) llamativo,-a; (mistake, difference, lack) evidente, obvio,-a.

**conspiracy** [kən'spɪrəsɪ] n conspiración f: a conspiracy to murder una conspiración de asesinato.
 ① pl conspiracies.

**conspirator** [kən'spɪrətəʳ] n conspirador,-ra.

**conspire** [kən'spaɪəʳ] vi conspirar.

**constable** ['kʌnstəb[ə]l] n policía mf, guardia mf, agente mf (de policía).

**constabulary** [kən'stæbjələrɪ] n GB policía.
 ① pl constabularies.

**constant** ['kɒnstənt] adj **1** (gen) constante. **2** (unchanging) constante.
 ▶ n constante f.

**constellation** [kɒnstə'leɪ[ə]n] n constelación f.

**consternation** [kɒnstə'neɪ[ə]n] n consternación f.

**constipated** ['kɒnstɪpeɪtɪd] adj estreñido,-a.

☒ To be constipated no significa ' estar constipado (acattarrado)', que se traduce por to have a cold.

**constipation** [kɒnstɪ'peɪ[ə]n] n estreñimiento.

☒ Constipation no significa 'constipado (catarro)', que se traduce por cold.

**constituency** [kən'stɪtjuənsɪ] n circunscripción f, distrito electoral.
 ① pl constituencies.

**constituent** [kənˈstɪtjuənt] *adj* constituyente.
▸ *n (component)* componente *m*.
**constitute** [ˈkɒnstɪtjuːt] *vt* constituir.
**constitution** [kɒnstɪˈtjuːʃ°n] *n* **1** *(gen)* constitución *f*. **2** *(of person)* constitución *f*, complexión *f*.
**constitutional** [kɒnstɪˈtjuːʃ°l] *adj* constitucional.
**constrain** [kənsˈtreɪn] *vt* **1** *(oblige, force)* constreñir, obligar, forzar. **2** *(restrict, hold back)* contener.
**constraint** [kənˈstreɪnt] *n* **1** *(compulsion, coercion)* coacción *f*, obligación *f*. **2** *(restriction)* restricción *f*, limitación *f*.
**constrict** [kənˈstrɪkt] *vt* **1** *(blood vessels)* estrangular; *(breathing, movement)* dificultar; *(neck)* apretar, oprimir. **2** *fig (action, behaviour)* limitar, coartar.
**construct** [kənsˈtrʌkt] *vt* construir.
**construction** [kənsˈtrʌkʃ°n] *n* **1** *(gen)* construcción *f*. **2** *fig (meaning)* interpretación *f*.
**constructive** [kənsˈtrʌktɪv] *adj* constructivo,-a.
**constructor** [kənsˈtrʌktər] *n* constructor,-ra.
**construe** [kənˈstruː] *vt* interpretar.
**consul** [ˈkɒns°l] *n* cónsul *mf*.
**consulate** [ˈkɒnsjələt] *n* consulado.
**consult** [kənˈsʌlt] *vt* consultar.
▸ *vi* consultar.
**consultant** [kənˈsʌltənt] *n* **1** *(expert, advisor)* asesor,-ra, consultor,-ra. **2** GB *(doctor)* especialista *mf*.
**consultation** [kɒnsəlˈteɪʃ°n] *n* cónsulta.
**consulting** [kənˈsʌltɪŋ] *adj (architect, engineer)* asesor,-ra, consultor,-ra. COMP **consulting room** MED consulta.
**consume** [kənˈsjuːm] *vt* consumir.
**consumer** [kənˈsjuːmər] *n* consumidor,-ra.
**consummate** [*(adj)* ˈkɒnsəmət; *(vb)* ˈkɒnsəmeɪt] *adj fml* consumado,-a.
▸ *vt fml* consumar.
**consumption** [kənˈsʌmpʃ°n] *n* consumo.
**contact** [ˈkɒntækt] *n* contacto. COMP **contact lenses** lentes *fpl* de contacto.
▸ *vt* ponerse en contacto con.

**contagion** [kənˈteɪdʒ°n] *n* contagio.
**contagious** [kənˈteɪdʒəs] *adj* contagioso,-a.
**contain** [kənˈteɪn] *vt* contener.
**container** [kənˈteɪnər] *n* **1** *(receptacle)* recipiente *m*; *(packaging)* envase *m*. **2** *(for transporting goods)* contenedor *m*, contáiner *m*.
**containment** [kənˈteɪnmənt] *n* contención *f*.
**contaminate** [kənˈtæmɪneɪt] *vt* contaminar.
**contamination** [kəntæmɪˈneɪʃ°n] *n* contaminación *f*.
**contemplate** [ˈkɒntempleɪt] *vt* contemplar.
**contemporaneous** [kɒntempəˈreɪnɪəs] *adj fml* contemporáneo,-a.
**contemporary** [kənˈtemp°rərɪ] *adj* contemporáneo,-a.
▸ *n* contemporáneo,-a.
ⓘ *pl* contemporaries.
**contempt** [kənˈtempt] *n* desprecio, desdén *m*, menosprecio.
**contemptible** [kənˈtemptəb°l] *adj* despreciable.
**contend** [kənˈtend] *vi* **1** *(compete)* contender, competir. **2** *(deal with, struggle against)* enfrentarse a, lidiar con.
▸ *vt (claim, state)* sostener, afirmar.
**contender** [kənˈtendər] *n* contendiente *mf* (for, por).
**content¹** [ˈkɒntent] *n* contenido.
▸ *n pl* **contents** contenido *m sing*.
**content²** [kənˈtent] *adj* contento,-a, satisfecho,-a: *he's content to watch the match at home* se conforma con ver el partido en casa.
▸ *n* contento.
▸ *vt* contentar, satisfacer.
**contented** [kənˈtentɪd] *adj* contento,-a, satisfecho,-a.
**contention** [kənˈtenʃ°n] *n* **1** *(opinion, assertion)* opinión *f*. **2** *(dispute, disagreement)* discusión *f*, controversia.
**contentious** [kənˈtenʃəs] *adj* polémico,-a.
**contest** [*(n)* ˈkɒntest; *(vb)* kənˈtest] *n* **1** *(competition - gen)* concurso; *(- sports)* com-

petición *f*; *(- boxing)* combate *m*. **2** *(struggle, attempt)* contienda, lucha.
▸ *vt* **1** *(championship, seat)* competir por, luchar por, disputarse; *(election)* presentarse como candidato,-a a. **2** *(dispute)* refutar, rebatir. **3** JUR *(appeal against)* impugnar.

☒ To contest no significa 'contestar', que se traduce por to answer.

**contestant** [kən'testənt] *n (in competition, quiz, game)* concursante *mf*; *(for post, position)* candidato,-a, aspirante *mf*.

**context** ['kɒntekst] *n* contexto.

**contiguous** [kən'tɪgjuəs] *adj* contiguo,-a.

**continent** ['kɒntɪnənt] *n* continente *m*.

**continental** [kɒntɪ'nentəl] *adj* continental.
▸ *adj* Continental GB europeo,-a.

**contingency** [kən'tɪndʒənsɪ] *n* contingencia. COMP contingency plan plan *m* de emergencia.

**contingent** [kən'tɪndʒənt] *adj* contingente.
▸ *n* contingente *m*.

**continual** [kən'tɪnjuəl] *adj* continuo,-a, constante.

**continuation** [kəntɪnju'eɪʃən] *n* continuación *f*.

**continue** [kən'tɪnjuː] *vt & vi* continuar, seguir.

**continuous** [kən'tɪnjuəs] *adj* continuo,-a.

**contort** [kən'tɔːt] *vt (face)* contraer.
▸ *vi* contraerse.

**contortion** [kən'tɔːʃən] *n* contorsión *f*.

**contour** ['kɒntuər] *n* contorno.

**contraband** ['kɒntrəbænd] *n* contrabando.

**contraception** [kɒntrə'sepʃən] *n* anticoncepción *f*.

**contraceptive** [kɒntrə'septɪv] *adj* anticonceptivo,-a.
▸ *n* anticonceptivo.

**contract** [*(n)* 'kɒntrækt; *(vb)* kən'trækt] *n (gen)* contrato; *(for public work, services)* contrata.
▸ *vt* **1** *(place under contract)* contratar. **2** *(make smaller)* contraer. **3** *fml (debt, habit, illness)* contraer.

**contraction** [kən'trækʃən] *n* contracción *f*.

**contractor** [kən'træktər] *n* contratista *mf*.

**contradict** [kɒntrə'dɪkt] *vt & vi* contradecir.

**contradiction** [kɒntrə'dɪkʃən] *n* contradicción *f*.

**contradictory** [kɒntrə'dɪktərɪ] *adj* contradictorio,-a.

**contraption** [kən'træpʃən] *n fam* cacharro, artefacto, artilugio.

**contrary** [*(adj)* 'kɒntrərɪ; *(n)* kən'treərɪ] *adj* **1** *(opposite)* contrario,-a. **2** *(stubborn)* terco,-a, obstinado,-a, tozudo,-a.
▸ the contrary lo contrario.

**contrast** [*(n)* 'kɒntrɑːst; *(vb)* kən'trɑːst] *n* contraste *m*.
▸ *vt & vi* contrastar.

**contribute** [kən'trɪbjuːt] *vt* **1** *(money)* contribuir (to, a; towards, para); *(ideas, information)* aportar. **2** *(article, poem, etc)* escribir.
▸ *vi* **1** *(gen)* contribuir (to, a; towards, para); *(in discussion)* participar (to, en). **2** *(to newspaper, magazine, etc)* colaborar (to, en), escribir (to, para).

**contributor** [kən'trɪbjətər] *n* **1** *(to charity, appeal, etc)* donante *mf*. **2** *(to newspaper, magazine, etc)* colaborador,-ra.

**contrive** [kən'traɪv] *vt* **1** *(way, device)* idear, inventar; *(meeting)* arreglar; *(meal, dress, etc)* improvisar. **2** *(manage)* conseguir.

**contrived** [kən'traɪvd] *adj* artificial.

**control** [kən'trəʊl] *vt* controlar.
▸ *n* **1** *(power, command)* poder *m*, dominio, mando; *(authority)* autoridad *f*. **2** *(restriction, means of regulating)* control *m*. **3** *(place, people in control)* control *m*. **4** *(switch, button)* botón *m*, mando. COMP control tower torre *f* de emergencia.
▸ *n pl* controls *(of vehicle)* mandos *mpl*.

**controller** [kən'trəʊlər] *n* **1** *(financial)* interventor,-ra. **2** *(in broadcasting)* director,-ra de programación.

**controversy** [kən'trɒvəsɪ] *n* controversia, polémica.
ⓘ *pl* controversies.

**contusion** [kən'tjuːʒən] *n* contusión *f*.
**convalesce** [kɒnvə'les] *vi* convalecer.
**convalescence** [kɒnvə'lesəns] *n* convalecencia.
**convalescent** [kɒnvə'lesənt] *adj* convaleciente.
**convenience** [kən'viːniəns] *n* conveniencia, comodidad *f*. COMP **convenience food** plato precocinado.
**convenient** [kən'viːniənt] *adj (time, arrangement)* conveniente, oportuno,-a; *(thing)* práctico,-a, cómodo,-a.
**convent** ['kɒnvənt] *n* convento.
**convention** [kən'venʃən] *n* convención *f*, congreso.
**converge** [kən'vɜːdʒ] *vi (lines, roads)* convergir (on, en), converger (on, en); *(people)* reunirse.
**conversant** [kən'vɜːsənt] *adj* familiarizado,-a (with, con), versado,-a (with, en).
**conversation** [kɒnvə'seɪʃən] *n* conversación *f*.
**converse** ['kɒnvɜːs] *adj* opuesto,-a, contrario,-a.
**conversion** [kən'vɜːʃən] *n* conversión *f* (to, a; into, en).
**convert** [*(vb)* kən'vɜːt; *(n)* 'kɒnvɜːt] *vt (gen)* convertir (into, en; to, a).
   ► *n* REL converso,-a.
**convertible** [kən'vɜːtəbəl] *adj (gen)* convertible; *(car)* descapotable.
   ► *n* AUTO descapotable *m*.
**convex** ['kɒnveks] *adj* convexo,-a.
**convey** [kən'veɪ] *vt* **1** *(goods, people, electricity)* transportar, conducir; *(sound)* transmitir, llevar. **2** *(opinion, feeling, idea)* comunicar, transmitir.
**conveyance** [kən'veɪəns] *n* **1** *(transport)* transporte *m*. **2** *fml (vehicle)* vehículo. **3** JUR traspaso, transferencia.
**conveyor belt** [kən'veɪə'belt] *n* cinta transportadora.
**convict** [*(n)* 'kɒnvɪkt; *(vb)* kən'vɪkt] *n* presidiario,-a, recluso,-a.
   ► *vt* JUR declarar culpable, condenar.
**conviction** [kən'vɪkʃən] *n* **1** *(belief)* convicción *f*, creencia. **2** JUR condena (for, por).
**convince** [kən'vɪns] *vt* convencer.

**convincing** [kən'vɪnsɪŋ] *adj* convincente.
**convoy** ['kɒnvɔɪ] *n* convoy *m*.
**cook** [kʊk] *n* cocinero,-a.
   ► *vt (food)* guisar, cocinar; *(meals)* preparar, hacer.
**cooker** ['kʊkə'] *n (stove)* cocina.
**cookery** ['kʊkəri] *n* cocina: *Spanish cookery* cocina española. COMP **cookery book** libro de cocina.
**cookie** ['kʊki] *n* **1** US *(biscuit)* galleta. **2** *(in computing)* cookie *m & f*, galleta.
**cooking** ['kʊkɪŋ] *n* cocina: *home cooking* cocina casera.
**cool** [kuːl] *adj* **1** *(gen)* fresco,-a. **2** *(unfriendly, reserved)* frío,-a. **3** *(calm)* tranquilo,-a, sereno,-a. **4** *fam (great)* guay.
**coop** [kuːp] *n* gallinero.
**cooperate** [kəʊ'ɒpəreɪt] [also written co-operate] *vi* cooperar, colaborar.
**coordinate** [*(vb)* kəʊ'ɔːdɪneɪt; *(n)* kəʊ'ɔːdɪnət] [also written co-ordinate] *vt* coordinar.
   ► *n* MATH coordenada.
**coordination** [kəʊɔːdɪ'neɪʃən] [also written co-ordination] *n* coordinación *f*.
**cop** [kɒp] *n sl (policeman)* poli *mf*.
**cope** [kəʊp] *vi* arreglárselas, poder.
**copious** ['kəʊpiəs] *adj* copioso,-a, abundante.
**copper** ['kɒpə'] *n* **1** *(metal)* cobre *m*. **2** GB *fam (coin)* penique *m*, pela, perra. **3** *sl (policeman)* poli *mf*.
**copse** [kɒps] *n* arboleda, bosquecillo.
**copulate** ['kɒpjəleɪt] *vi* copular.
**copy** ['kɒpi] *n* **1** *(reproduction)* copia. **2** *(of book, magazine, etc)* ejemplar *m*.
   ① *pl* copies.
   ► *vi* copiar.
**copycat** ['kɒpikæt] *n fam* copión,-ona.
   ► *adj (crime)* inspirado,-a en otro.
**copyright** ['kɒpirait] *n* copyright *m*, derechos *mpl* de autor.
**coral** ['kɒrəl] *n* coral *m*.
**cord** [kɔːd] *n* **1** *(string, rope)* cuerda. **2** ELEC cable *m*. **3** *(corduroy)* pana.
**cordon** ['kɔːdən] *n* cordón *m*.
**corduroy** ['kɔːdərɔɪ] *n* pana.

**core** [kɔː�<sup>r</sup>] n **1** (gen) núcleo. **2** (of apple, pear, etc) corazón m.

**coriander** [kɒrɪˈændə<sup>r</sup>] n cilantro.

**cork** [kɔːk] n (material) corcho.

**corkscrew** [ˈkɔːkskruː] n sacacorchos m.

**corm** [kɔːm] n bulbo.

**corn**[1] [kɔːn] n (gen) cereales mpl; (wheat) trigo; (oats) avena; (maize) maíz m.

**corn**[2] [kɔːn] n MED callo.

**corncob** [ˈkɔːnkɒb] n mazorca de maíz.

**cornea** [ˈkɔːnɪə] n córnea.

**corned beef** [kɔːndˈbiːf] n carne f en conserva.

**corner** [ˈkɔːnə<sup>r</sup>] n **1** (of street) esquina; (bend in road) curva; (of table, etc) esquina, punta. **2** (of room, cupboard, etc) rincón m; (of mouth) comisura; (of eye) rabillo; (of page, envelope) ángulo. **3** SP (kick - in football) córner m, saque m de esquina.
▶ vt arrinconar, acorralar; (person) arrinconar.

**cornet** [ˈkɔːnɪt] n **1** MUS corneta. **2** GB (for ice-cream) cucurucho.

**cornflakes** [ˈkɔːnfleɪks] npl copos de maíz.

**cornice** [ˈkɔːnɪs] n cornisa.

**corolla** [kəˈrɒlə] n corola.

**coronation** [kɒrəˈneɪʃ<sup>ə</sup>n] n coronación f.

**coroner** [ˈkɒrənə<sup>r</sup>] n juez mf de instrucción.

**corporal** [ˈkɔːp<sup>ə</sup>rəl] n MIL cabo.

**corporate** [ˈkɔːp<sup>ə</sup>rət] adj **1** (collective) colectivo,-a. **2** (of a corporation) de la empresa, de la compañía.

**corporation** [kɔːpəˈreɪʃ<sup>ə</sup>n] n corporación f.

**corps** [kɔː<sup>r</sup>] n cuerpo.
ⓘ pl corps [kɔːz].

**corpse** [kɔːps] n cadáver m.

**corpus** [ˈkɔːpəs] adj **1** (of texts) corpus m. **2** ANAT cuerpo. COMP ANAT **corpus callosum** cuerpo calloso.

**corpuscle** [ˈkɔːpəs<sup>ə</sup>l] n corpúsculo, glóbulo.

**correct** [kəˈrekt] adj correcto,-a.
▶ vt corregir.

**correspond** [kɒrɪsˈpɒnd] vi **1** (gen) corresponderse (with, con). **2** (write) escribirse (with, con).

**correspondence** [kɒrɪsˈpɒndəns] n correspondencia.

**correspondent** [kɒrɪsˈpɒndnt] n corresponsal mf.

**corridor** [ˈkɒrɪdɔː<sup>r</sup>] n pasillo.

**corrode** [kəˈrəʊd] vt corroer.
▶ vi corroerse.

**corrosion** [kəˈrəʊʒ<sup>ə</sup>n] n **1** (process) corrosión f. **2** (substance) herrumbre f, orín m.

**corrupt** [kəˈrʌpt] adj corrompido,-a, corrupto,-a.
▶ vt corromper; (bribe) sobornar.

**corruption** [kəˈrʌpʃ<sup>ə</sup>n] n corrupción f.

**corset** [ˈkɔːsɪt] n corsé m.

**cortex** [ˈkɔːteks] n corteza.

**cos** [ˈkəʊsaɪn] abbr (cosine) coseno; (abbreviation) cos.

**cosine** [ˈkəʊsaɪn] n MATH coseno.

**cosmetic** [kɒzˈmetɪk] adj cosmético,-a. COMP **cosmetic surgery** cirugía estética.

**cosmic** [ˈkɒzmɪk] adj cósmico,-a.

**cosmonaut** [ˈkɒzmənɔːt] n cosmonauta mf.

**cosmopolitan** [kɒzməˈpɒlɪt<sup>ə</sup>n] adj cosmopolita.

**cosmos** [ˈkɒzmɒs] n cosmos m.

**cost** [kɒst] vt costar, valer.
ⓘ pt & pp cost [kɒst].
▶ n (price) coste m, precio. COMP **cost of living** coste de la vida.

**costal** [ˈkɒztəl] adj costal.

**co-star** [ˈkəʊstɑː<sup>r</sup>] n coprotagonista mf.

**Costa Rica** [kɒstəˈriːkə] n Costa Rica.

**Costa Rican** [kɒstəˈriːkən] adj costarricense.
▶ n (person) costarricense mf.

**cost-effective** [kɒstɪˈfektɪv] adj rentable.

**costly** [ˈkɒstlɪ] adj costoso,-a.
ⓘ comp costlier, superl costliest.

**costume** [ˈkɒstjuːm] n traje m.
▶ n pl costumes THEAT vestuario.

**cosy** [ˈkəʊzɪ] adj **1** (room, house, atmosphere) acogedor,-ra. **2** (chat) íntimo,-a y agradable.
ⓘ comp cosier, superl cosiest.

**cot** [kɒt] n **1** (for baby) cuna. **2** US (camp bed) cama de campaña.

**cotton** [ˈkɒtən] *n* **1** *(cloth, plant)* algodón *m*. **2** *(thread)* hilo (de coser).
▶ *adj (shirt, etc)* de algodón. COMP **cotton bud** bastoncillo de algodón. ∥ **cotton wool** algodón *m* hidrófilo.

**couch** [kaʊtʃ] *n* *(sofa)* canapé *m*, sofá *m*.

**couchette** [kuːˈʃet] *n* litera.

> ✎ Couchette se refiere específicamente a las literas de los trenes. Las literas que puede haber en una casa se llaman **bunk beds**.

**cougar** [ˈkuːgəʳ] *n* puma *m*.

**cough** [kɒf] *n* tos *f*.
▶ *vi* toser.

**could** [kʊd] *pt* → **can**.

**council** [ˈkaʊnsəl] *n* **1** *(elected group)* consejo. **2** GB *(of town, city)* ayuntamiento. **3** REL concilio.

**councillor** [ˈkaʊnsələʳ] *n* concejal,-la.

**counsel** [ˈkaʊnsəl] *n* **1** *(advice)* consejo. **2** JUR abogado,-a.

**counsellor** [ˈkaʊnsələʳ] *n* **1** *(adviser)* consejero,-a, asesor,-ra. **2** US *(lawyer)* abogado,-a.

**count¹** [kaʊnt] *n* *(act of counting)* recuento; *(of votes)* escrutinio; *(total)* total *m*, suma.
▶ *vt* **1** *(gen)* contar. **2** *(consider)* considerar.

❌ To count no significa 'contar (relatar)', que se traduce por to tell.

**count²** [kaʊnt] *n* *(nobleman)* conde *m*.

**countable** [ˈkaʊntəbəl] *adj* contable.

**countdown** [ˈkaʊntdaʊn] *n* cuenta atrás.

**counter** [ˈkaʊntəʳ] *n* **1** *(in shop)* mostrador *m*; *(individual)* ventanilla. **2** *(in board games)* ficha.

**counteract** [kaʊntəˈrækt] *vt* contrarrestar.

**counterattack** [ˈkaʊntərətæk] *n* contraataque *m*.
▶ *vt* contraatacar.

**counterclockwise** [kaʊntəˈklɒkwaɪz] *adj* US en sentido contrario a las agujas del reloj.

**counterfeit** [ˈkaʊntəfɪt] *adj* falso,-a, falsificado,-a.
▶ *n* falsificación *f*.
▶ *vt* falsificar.

**counterfoil** [ˈkaʊntəfɔɪl] *n* matriz *f*.

**counterpart** [ˈkaʊntəpɑːt] *n* homólogo,-a.

**counterproductive** [kaʊntəprəˈdʌktɪv] *adj* contraproducente.

**countess** [ˈkaʊntəs] *n* condesa.

**countless** [ˈkaʊntləs] *adj* incontable, innumerable.

**country** [ˈkʌntri] *n* **1** *(state, nation)* país *m*; *(people)* pueblo. **2** [no se usa en *pl*] *(rural area)* campo. **3** [no se usa en *pl*] *(region, area of land)* región *f*, zona, territorio. **1** [también **country music**] MUS música country, country *m*.
ⓘ *pl* **countries**.
▶ *adj (rural - life, lane)* rural; *(- house)* de campo.

**countryman** [ˈkʌntrimən] *n* **1** *(man from country)* campesino. **2** *(compatriot)* compatriota *m*.
ⓘ *pl* **countrymen** [ˈkʌntrimən].

**countryside** [ˈkʌntrisaɪd] *n* *(area)* campo, campiña; *(scenery)* paisaje *m*.

**countrywoman** [ˈkʌntriwʊmən] *n* **1** *(woman from the country)* campesina. **2** *(compatriot)* compatriota.
ⓘ *pl* **countrywomen** [ˈkʌntriwɪmɪn].

**county** [ˈkaʊnti] *n* condado.
ⓘ *pl* **counties**.

**coup** [kuː] *n* golpe *m*. COMP **coup d'état** golpe *m* de estado.

**couple** [ˈkʌpəl] *n* **1** *(two things)* par *m*; *(a few)* unos,-as. **2** *(two people)* pareja.
▶ *vt* conectar, acoplar.

**coupon** [ˈkuːpɒn] *n* **1** COMM *(for discount, free gift, etc)* cupón *m*, vale *m*. **2** GB *(for competition, football pools)* boleto.

**courage** [ˈkʌrɪdʒ] *n* coraje *m*, valor *m*, valentía.

**courageous** [kəˈreɪdʒəs] *adj* valiente.

**courgette** [kʊəˈʒet] *n* calabacín *m*.

**courier** [ˈkʊəriəʳ] *n* **1** *(messenger)* mensajero,-a. **2** *(guide)* guía *mf* turístico,-a.

**course** [kɔːs] *n* **1** *(gen)* curso; *(of ship)* rumbo. **2** EDUC *(year - long)* curso; *(- short)* cursillo; *(at university)* carrera; *(individual subject)* asignatura. **3** *(of meal)* plato. **4** SP *(for golf)* campo. LOC **of course** desde luego, por supuesto. COMP **main course** segundo plato.

**court** [kɔːt] n **1** JUR (place, people) tribunal m; (building) juzgado. **2** (royal) corte f. **3** SP (tennis, squash, etc) pista, cancha. **4** (courtyard) patio.

**courteous** ['kɜːtɪəs] adj cortés.

**courtesy** ['kɜːtəsɪ] n **1** (good manners) cortesía, educación f. **2** (polite act or remark) favor m, atención f.
  ① pl courtesies.

**courthouse** ['kɔːthaʊs] n juzgado.

**courtroom** ['kɔːtruːm] n sala de justicia, tribunal m.

**courtyard** ['kɔːtjɑːd] n patio.

**cousin** ['kʌzən] n primo,-a.

**cove** [kəʊv] n cala, ensenada.

**covenant** ['kʌvənənt] n JUR (formal agreement) convenio, pacto; (clause) cláusula, provisión f.

**cover** ['kʌvər] n **1** (lid) tapa, cubierta. **2** (thing that covers - gen) funda. **3** (outside pages - of book) cubierta, tapa; (- of magazine) portada. **4** (insurance) cobertura. **5** (shelter, protection) abrigo, protección f.
  ▶ vt **1** (place over - gen) cubrir (with, de); (- floor, wall) revestir (with, de); (- sofa) tapizar; (- book) forrar. **2** (with lid, hands) tapar. **3** (hide) tapar.

**coverage** ['kʌvərɪdʒ] n cobertura.

**coveralls** ['kʌvərɔːlz] n pl US → overalls.

**covering** ['kʌvərɪŋ] n (protective) cubierta, envoltura; (layer) capa.

**covert** ['kʌvət] adj secreto,-a.

**cover-up** ['kʌvərʌp] n encubrimiento.

**covet** ['kʌvət] vt codiciar.

**cow** [kaʊ] n vaca.

**coward** ['kaʊəd] n cobarde mf.

**cowardly** ['kaʊədlɪ] adj cobarde.

**cowboy** ['kaʊbɔɪ] n vaquero.

**cox** [kɒks] n timonel mf.

**coy** [kɔɪ] adj tímido,-a, recatado,-a.

**coyote** [kaɪˈəʊtɪ] n coyote m.

**cozy** ['kəʊzɪ] adj US → cosy.
  ① comp cozier, superl coziest.

**crab** [kræb] n (shellfish) cangrejo.

**crack** [kræk] vt **1** (break - cup, glass, etc) rajar; (- bone) fracturar, romper. **2** (break open - safe) forzar; (- egg, nut) cascar; (- bottle) abrir, descorchar. **3** (hit) pegar, golpear.
  ▶ vi **1** (break - cup, glass) rajarse, resquebrarse; (- rock, plaster, paint, skin) agrietarse. **2** (relationship, system) venirse abajo; (person) sufrir una crisis nerviosa.
  ▶ n **1** (in cup, glass) raja; (in ice, wall, ground, pavement, etc) grieta. **2** (slit, narrow opening) rendija. **3** (of whip) restallido, chasquido.
  ▶ adj (troops, regiment, shot) de primera.

**cracked** [krækt] adj fam (mad, crazy) chiflado,-a, chalado,-a.

**cracker** ['krækər] n **1** (biscuit) galleta seca. **2** (firework) petardo m.

**cracking** ['krækɪŋ] adj fam (shot, goal) de primera; (pace) muy rápido,-a.

**crackle** ['krækəl] n (of twigs, etc) crujido, chasquido.
  ▶ vi (twigs, etc) chasquear; (fire) chisporrotear, crepitar; (radio, telephone) hacer ruido.

**cradle** ['kreɪdəl] n cuna f.
  ▶ vt (baby) acunar (en los brazos), mecer.

**craft** [krɑːft] n **1** (occupation) oficio. **2** (art) arte m; (skill) habilidad f, destreza. **3** (boat) embarcación f.
  ▶ vt trabajar.

**craftsman** ['krɑːftsmən] n artesano.
  ① pl craftsmen ['krɑːftsmən].

**craftswoman** ['krɑːftswʊmən] n artesana.
  ① pl craftswomen ['krɑːftswɪmɪn].

**crafty** ['krɑːftɪ] adj (person) astuto,-a; (child) pillo,-a; (method, idea, etc) hábil.
  ① comp craftier, superl craftiest.

**crag** [kræg] n peña, risco, peñasco.

**cram** [kræm] vt (stuff, fill) atestar (with, de), atiborrar (with, de).
  ▶ vi fam (learn for exam) empollar.
  ① pt & pp crammed, ger cramming.

**cramp¹** [kræmp] n MED calambre m.
  ▶ n pl cramps (gen) retortijones mpl.

**cramp²** [kræmp] vt obstaculizar.

**cranberry** ['krænbərɪ] n arándano.
  ① pl cranberries.

**crane** [kreɪn] n **1** ZOOL grulla común. **2** (machine) grúa.

**cranium** ['kreɪnɪəm] n cráneo.
  ① pl craniums o crania ['kreɪnɪə].

**crank** [kræŋk] n 1 (crankshaft) cigüeñal m. 2 (starting handle) manivela.

**crash** [kræʃ] n 1 (noise) estrépito; (of thunder) trueno, estallido. 2 (collision) choque m, accidente m. 3 COMM (collapse) quiebra.

**crate** [kreɪt] n caja, cajón m.
▶ vt embalar.

**crater** ['kreɪtəʳ] n cráter m.

**crave** [kreɪv] vt ansiar, tener ansias de.

**craving** ['kreɪvɪŋ] n (gen) ansia (for, de), ansias fpl (for, de); (in pregnancy) antojo (for, de).

**crawfish** ['krɔːfɪʃ] n → crayfish.

**crawl** [krɔːl] vi 1 (move slowly - person, snake) arrastrarse; (- baby) gatear. 2 (car, traffic) ir a paso de tortuga.
▶ n SP (in swimming) crol m.

**crayfish** ['kreɪfɪʃ] n cangrejo de río.
ⓘ pl crayfish.

**crayon** ['kreɪɒn] n lápiz m de cera.

**craze** [kreɪz] n (fashion) moda; (game, sport, hobby, etc) manía.

**crazy** ['kreɪzɪ] adj fam loco,-a.
ⓘ comp crazier, superl craziest.

**creak** [kriːk] vi (floorboard, stairs, joints) crujir, hacer un crujido; (door, hinge) chirriar.

**cream** [kriːm] n 1 (of milk) nata, crema (de leche). 2 (cosmetic) crema; (medical) pomada, crema.

**crease** [kriːs] n 1 (wrinkle) arruga; (fold) pliegue m; (ironed) raya. 2 SP (in cricket) línea.

**create** [kriːˈeɪt] vt 1 (gen) crear. 2 (cause) producir, causar.

**creation** [kriːˈeɪʃⁿn] n creación f.

**creature** ['kriːtʃəʳ] n 1 (animal) criatura. 2 (human being) ser m.

**credentials** [krɪˈdenʃlz] n pl 1 (qualifications) credenciales fpl. 2 (documents) cartas fpl credenciales.

**credible** ['kredɪbⁿl] adj creíble.

**credit** ['kredɪt] n 1 (praise, approval) mérito, reconocimiento. 2 (belief, trust, confidence) crédito. 3 FIN (gen) crédito; (in accountancy) haber m; (on statement) saldo acreedor. 5 EDUC crédito.
▶ n pl credits (of film, programme) ficha técnica.

**creditor** ['kredɪtəʳ] n acreedor,-ra.

**creed** [kriːd] n credo.

**creek** [kriːk] n 1 GB cala. 2 US riachuelo, arroyo.

**creep** [kriːp] vi 1 (move quietly) moverse sigilosamente, deslizarse. 2 (move with the body close to the ground) arrastrarse, reptar.
ⓘ pt & pp crept [krept].

**creeper** ['kriːpəʳ] n (planta) trepadora.

**cremate** [krɪˈmeɪt] vt incinerar.

**crematorium** [kreməˈtɔːrɪəm] n (horno) crematorio.
ⓘ pl crematoriums o crematoria [kreməˈtɔːrɪə].

**crepe** [kreɪp] n crepe m.

**crept** [krept] pt & pp → creep.

**crescent** ['kresⁿnt] n (shape) medialuna.
▶ adj creciente. COMP crescent moon luna creciente.

**cress** [kres] n berro.

**crest** [krest] n 1 (of cock) cresta. 2 (of hill) cima, cumbre f; (of wave) cresta.

**crestfallen** ['krestfɔːlⁿn] adj abatido,-a.

**crevice** ['krevɪs] n grieta, raja.

**crew¹** [kruː] n 1 (of ship, etc) tripulación f. 2 (working team) equipo.

**crew²** [kruː] pt → crow.

**crib** [krɪb] n 1 (manger) pesebre m; (Nativity scene) belén m, pesebre m. 2 (for baby) cuna. 3 (for cheating) chuleta.
▶ vt plagiar, copiar.
ⓘ pt & pp cribbed, ger cribbing.

**crick** [krɪk] n (in neck) tortícolis f.

**cricket¹** ['krɪkɪt] n (insect) grillo.

**cricket²** ['krɪkɪt] n SP cricket m.

**cried** [kraɪd] pp → cry.

**crime** [kraɪm] n crimen m.

**criminal** ['krɪmɪnⁿl] adj criminal.
▶ n delincuente mf, criminal mf.

**cringe** [krɪndʒ] vi encogerse, agacharse.

**crinkle** ['krɪŋkⁿl] n arruga.
▶ vt arrugar.

**cripple** ['krɪpⁿl] n lisiado,-a, tullido,-a.
▶ vt 1 (person) dejar cojo,-a, lisiar. 2 fig (industry, country) paralizar.

**crisis** ['kraɪsɪs] n crisis f.
ⓘ pl crises ['kraɪsiːs].

**crisp** [krɪsp] *adj* **1** *(pastry, biscuits, etc)* crujiente; *(lettuce)* fresco,-a. **2** *(weather, air)* frío,-a y seco,-a.
▶ *n* GB patata frita *(de bolsa o churrería)*.

✎ Son las patatas de bolsa o de churrería que se comen frías, pues las que se comen calientes se llaman **chips** en inglés británico y **french fries** en inglés americano.

**crisscross** ['krɪskrɒs] *vt* entrecruzar.
**critic** ['krɪtɪk] *n* *(reviewer)* crítico,-a.
**critical** ['krɪtɪkəl] *adj* crítico,-a.
**criticism** ['krɪtɪsɪzəm] *n* crítica.
**criticize** ['krɪtɪsaɪz] *vt* criticar.
**croak** [krəʊk] *n* **1** *(of raven)* graznido; *(of frog)* canto. **2** *(of person)* voz *f* ronca.
**Croatia** [krəʊˈeɪʃə] *n* Croacia.
**Croatian** [krəʊˈeɪʃən] *adj* croata.
▶ *adj (person)* croata *mf*; *(language)* croata *m*.
**crochet** ['krəʊʃeɪ] *n* ganchillo.
**crockery** ['krɒkərɪ] *n* loza, vajilla.
**crocodile** ['krɒkədaɪl] *n* cocodrilo.
**crocus** ['krəʊkəs] *n* azafrán *m*.
**crony** ['krəʊnɪ] *n* fam compinche *mf*.
ⓘ *pl* cronies.
**crook** [krʊk] *n* **1** cayado, gancho. **2** *fam (criminal)* sinvergüenza *mf*, delincuente *mf*.
▶ *vt (finger, arm)* doblar.
**crop** [krɒp] *n* **1** *(plant)* cultivo; *(harvest)* cosecha. **2** *(group, batch)* tanda. **3** *(hairstyle)* corte *m* al rape.
**cross** [krɒs] *n* **1** *(gen)* cruz *f*. **2** BIOL *(hybrid)* cruce *m*.
▶ *vt (street, river, bridge,)* cruzar, atravesar; *(arms, legs)* cruzar.
▶ *vi (walk across)* cruzar (over, -); *(intersect, pass each another)* cruzarse.
**crossbar** ['krɒsbɑːʳ] *n* **1** *(of goal)* travesaño, larguero; *(of bicycle)* barra.
**crossing** ['krɒsɪŋ] *n* **1** MAR travesía. **2** *(intersection, crossroads)* cruce *m*. COMP **border crossing** paso fronterizo.
**cross-reference** [krɒsˈrefərəns] *n* remisión *f*.
▶ *vt* remitir.
**crossroads** ['krɒsrəʊdz] *n* encrucijada, cruce *m*.

**crossword** ['krɒswɜːd] [también **crossword puzzle**] *n* crucigrama *m*.
**crotch** [krɒtʃ] *n* entrepierna.
**crotchet** ['krɒtʃɪt] *n* MUS negra.
**crouch** [kraʊtʃ] [también **crouch down**] *vi (person)* agacharse, ponerse en cuclillas; *(cat)* agazaparse.
**crow¹** [krəʊ] *n (bird)* cuervo.
**crow²** [krəʊ] *vi (cock)* cantar, cacarear.
ⓘ *pt* crowed o crew [kruː], *pp* crowed.
**crowbar** ['krəʊbɑːʳ] *n* palanca.
**crowd** [kraʊd] *n* **1** *(large number of people)* multitud *f*, muchedumbre *f*, gentío; *(at match, concert, etc)* público. **2** *(particular group)* gente *f*; *(clique)* pandilla.
**crowded** ['kraʊdɪd] *adj* abarrotado,-a de gente, concurrido,-a.
**crown** [kraʊn] *n* **1** *(of king, queen)* corona. **2** ANAT *(of head)* coronilla; *(of tooth)* corona. **3** *(top of hat, tree)* copa.
**crucial** ['kruːʃəl] *adj* crucial.
**crucifix** ['kruːsɪfɪks] *n* crucifijo.
**crucify** ['kruːsɪfaɪ] *vt* crucificar.
ⓘ *pt & pp* crucified, *ger* crucifying.
**crude** [kruːd] *n* **1** *(manners, style)* tosco,-a, grosero,-a; *(joke)* grosero,-a, ordinario,-a. **2** *(oil)* crudo,-a.

⊠ Crude no significa 'crudo (sin hacer)', que se traduce por raw.

**cruel** ['kruːəl] *adj* cruel.
ⓘ *comp* crueller, *superl* cruellest.
**cruelty** ['kruːəltɪ] *n* crueldad *f* (to, hacia).
ⓘ *pl* cruelties.
**cruise** [kruːz] *vi* MAR hacer un crucero.
▶ *n* crucero.
**cruiser** ['kruːzəʳ] *n* **1** *(warship)* crucero. **2** *(pleasure boat)* yate *m*.
**crumb** [krʌm] *n* miga, migaja.
**crumble** ['krʌmbəl] *vt (gen)* desmenuzar, deshacer; *(bread)* desmigajar.
**crumple** ['krʌmpəl] *vt (clothes)* arrugar; *(paper)* estrujar.
**crunch** [krʌntʃ] *vt* **1** *(food)* mascar. **2** *(with feet, tyres)* hacer crujir.
**crusade** [kruːˈseɪd] *n* cruzada.
**crush** [krʌʃ] *vt* **1** *(squash - gen)* aplastar; *(squeeze)* estrujar;. **2** *(smash, pound - gen)* triturar; *(- ice)* picar.

▶ *n* **1** *(of people)* aglomeración *f*. **2** GB *(soft drink)* refresco.
**crust** [krʌst] *n* corteza.
**crustacean** [krʌˈsteɪʃ⁰n] *n* crustáceo.
**crutch** [krʌtʃ] *n* **1** *(for walking)* muleta.
**crux** [krʌks] *n* quid *m*, meollo.
**cry** [kraɪ] *vt* **1** *(shout, call)* gritar. **2** *(weep)* llorar.
ⓘ *pt & pp* cried, *ger* crying.
**crying** [ˈkraɪɪŋ] *n (weeping)* llanto.
**crypt** [krɪpt] *n* cripta.
**crystal** [ˈkrɪst⁰l] *n* cristal *m*.
**crystallize** [ˈkrɪst⁰laɪz] *vt* cristalizar.
**cub** [kʌb] *n* ZOOL cachorro,-a
**cube** [kjuːb] *n* **1** *(shape)* cubo; *(of sugar)* terrón *m*; *(of ice)* cubito; *(of cheese, meat, etc)* dado. **2** MATH cubo. COMP **cube root** raíz *f* cúbica.
▶ *vt* MATH elevar al cubo.
**cubic** [ˈkjuːbɪk] *adj* cúbico,-a.
**cubism** [ˈkjuːbɪz⁰m] *n* cubismo.
**cuckoo** [ˈkʊkuː] *n* cuco.
ⓘ *pl* cuckoos.
**cucumber** [ˈkjuːkʌmbəʳ] *n* pepino.
**cuddle** [ˈkʌd⁰l] *vt* abrazar, acariciar.
**cue¹** [kjuː] *n* **1** *(for actor)* pie *m*; *(for musician)* entrada. **2** *(signal)* señal *f*. **3** *(example)* ejemplo.
**cue²** [kjuː] *n (in billiards, etc)* taco. COMP **cue ball** bola blanca.
**cuff¹** [kʌf] *n* **1** *(of sleeve)* puño. **2** US *(of trousers)* dobladillo.
▶ *n pl* **cuffs** *sl* esposas *fpl*.
**cuff²** [kʌf] *vt* dar un bofetada a.
▶ *n* bofetada, cachete *m*, bofetón *m*.
**cufflinks** [ˈkʌflɪŋks] *n pl* gemelos *mpl*.
**cuisine** [kwɪˈziːn] *n* cocina.
**cul-de-sac** [ˈkʌldəsæk] *n* calle *f* sin salida.
**culminate** [ˈkʌlmɪneɪt] *vi* culminar.
**culottes** [kjuːˈlɒts] *n pl* falda pantalón *f sing*.
**culprit** [ˈkʌlprɪt] *n* culpable *mf*.
**cult** [kʌlt] *n (gen)* culto; *(sect)* secta.
**cultivate** [ˈkʌltɪveɪt] *vt* cultivar.
ⓘ *pt & pp* cupped, *ger* cupping.
**culture** [ˈkʌltʃəʳ] *n* **1** *(gen)* cultura. **2** *(growth)* cultivo.

**cumbersome** [ˈkʌmbəsəm] *adj* **1** *(thing)* incómodo,-a, voluminoso,-a, pesado,-a. **2** *(procedure)* torpe, engorroso,-a.
**cumin** [ˈkʌmɪn] *n* comino.
**cunning** [ˈkʌnɪŋ] *adj* astuto,-a
▶ *n* astucia.
**cup** [kʌp] *n* **1** *(for drinking)* taza. **2** SP *(trophy)* copa.
**cupboard** [ˈkʌbəd] *n* armario.
**curator** [kjuˈreɪtəʳ] *n (of museum)* conservador,-ra.
**curb** [kɜːb] *n* **1** *(for horse)* barbada. **2** *(control)* freno. **3** US bordillo.
**curd** [kɜːd] *n (from milk)* cuajada. COMP **curd cheese** requesón *m*.
**curdle** [ˈkɜːd⁰l] *vi (form curds)* cuajarse; *(go bad)* cortarse.
**cure** [kjʊəʳ] *vt* curar.
▶ *n* cura.
**cure-all** [ˈkjʊərɑːl] *n* panacea.
**curfew** [ˈkɜːfjuː] *n* toque *m* de queda.
**curiosity** [kjʊərɪˈɒsətɪ] *n* curiosidad *f*.
ⓘ *pl* curiosities.
**curious** [ˈkjʊərɪəs] *adj* **1** *(inquisitive)* curioso,-a. **2** *(strange, odd)* curioso,-a, extraño,-a; *(interesting)* interesante.
**curl** [kɜːl] *vt* rizar.
▶ *vi* rizarse.
▶ *n (of hair)* rizo; *(ringlet)* bucle *m*, tirabuzón *m*; *(of smoke)* espiral *f*, voluta.
**curly** [ˈkɜːlɪ] *adj* rizado,-a.
ⓘ *comp* curlier, *superl* curliest.
**currant** [ˈkʌrənt] *n* **1** *(dried grape)* pasa (de Corinto). **2** *(fruit)* grosella.
**currency** [ˈkʌrənsɪ] *n* FIN moneda. COMP **foreign currency** divisa.
ⓘ *pl* currencies.
**current** [ˈkʌrənt] *adj* **1** *(present, existing - gen)* actual; *(- month, year)* en curso; *(most recent - issue)* último,-a. **2** *(generally accepted)* corriente, común, habitual, general. COMP **current account** cuenta corriente.
▶ *n (gen)* corriente *f*.
**currently** [ˈkʌrəntlɪ] *adv* **1** *(at present)* actualmente, en la actualidad. **2** *(commonly)* comúnmente.
**curriculum** [kəˈrɪkjələm] *n* EDUC plan *m* de estudios. COMP **curriculum vitae** currículum *m*, historial *m*.

**curry** ['kʌrɪ] n CULIN curry m.
ⓘ pl curries.

**curse** [kɜːs] n 1 (evil spell) maldición f. 2 (oath) palabrota.

**cursor** ['kɜːsəʳ] n cursor m.

**curt** [kɜːt] adj seco,-a, brusco,-a.

**curtain** ['kɜːtⁿn] n 1 (gen) cortina. 2 THEAT telón m.

**curvature** ['kɜːvətʃəʳ] n 1 (of surface) curvatura. 2 MED encorvamiento.

**curve** [kɜːv] n (gen) curva.
▶ vi (of road, river, ball) describir una curva, torcer.

**cushion** ['kʊʃⁿn] n (gen) cojín m; (large) almohadón m.
▶ vt fig suavizar, amortiguar.

**custard** ['kʌstəd] n (cold, set) natillas fpl; (hot, liquid) crema. COMP **custard apple** chirimoya.

**custom** ['kʌstəm] n costumbre f: it's a typical Spanish custom es una típica costumbre española.

**customary** ['kʌstəmərɪ] adj (habitual) acostumbrado,-a, habitual.

**customer** ['kʌstəməʳ] n cliente mf.

**customize** ['kʌstəmaɪz] vt hacer por encargo, hacer a la medida.

**custom-made** [kʌstəm'meɪd] adj (clothes, etc) hecho,-a a medida.

**customs** ['kʌstəmz] n aduana.
✎ Puede ser tanto singular como plural.

**cut** [kʌt] n 1 (ge) corte m; (knife wound) cuchillada. 3 (share) parte f, tajada. 4 (reduction - in budget, services, wages) recorte m; (- in level, number, price) reducción f. 6 ELEC corte m, apagón m.
▶ vt 1 (gen) cortar 2 (reduce - level, number) reducir; (- budget, spending) recortar; (- price) rebajar, reducir.
◆ **to cut down** vt sep (tree) talar, cortar; (kill) matar.
◆ **to cut off** vt sep 2 (disconnect, discontinue) cortar: our phone's been cut off nos han cortado el teléfono. 3 (isolate, separate) aislar: she felt cut off se sentía aislada.
◆ **to cut out** vt sep 1 (from newspaper) recortar; (in sewing) cortar. 2 (exclude) suprimir, eliminar.
ⓘ pt & pp cut, ger cutting.

**cutaneous** [kjuː'teɪnɪəs] adj cutáneo,-a.

**cute** [kjuːt] adj 1 (sweet) mono,-a, rico, -a; (good-looking) guapo,-a, lindo,-a. 2 US (clever) listo,-a.

**cutlery** ['kʌtlərɪ] n cubiertos mpl, cubertería.

**cutlet** ['kʌtlət] n CULIN chuleta.

**cutout** ['kʌtaʊt] n 1 (shape) recortable m. 2 (device, switch) cortacircuitos m.

**cutter** ['kʌtəʳ] n (tool) cúter m.

**cutting** ['kʌtɪŋ] n 1 (from newspaper) recorte m. 2 BOT esqueje m.

**cuttlefish** ['kʌtⁿlfɪʃ] n jibia, sepia.

**cyanide** ['saɪənaɪd] n cianuro.

**cybernetics** [saɪbə'netɪks] n cibernética.

**cycle** ['saɪkⁿl] n 1 (series of events, of songs, etc) ciclo; (of washing machine) programa m. 2 (bicycle) bicicleta; (motorcycle) moto f. COMP **cycle lane/path/way** carril m bici. ‖ **cycle track** velódromo.
▶ vi ir en bicicleta.

**cyclic** ['sɪklɪk, 'saɪklɪk] adj cíclico,-a.

**cyclical** ['sɪklɪkⁿl, 'saɪklɪkⁿl] adj cíclico,-a.

**cycling** ['saɪklɪŋ] n ciclismo.

**cyclist** ['saɪklɪst] n ciclista mf.

**cyclone** ['saɪkləʊn] n ciclón m.

**cygnet** ['sɪgnət] n pollo de cisne.

**cylinder** ['sɪlɪndəʳ] n 1 (gen) cilindro. 2 (for gas) bombona.

**cylindrical** [sɪ'lɪndrɪkⁿl] adj cilíndrico,-a.

**cymbal** ['sɪmbⁿl] n címbalo, platillo.

**cynic** ['sɪnɪk] n cínico,-a.

**cynical** ['sɪnɪkⁿl] adj cínico,-a.

**cynicism** ['sɪnɪsɪzⁿm] n cinismo.

**cypress** ['saɪprəs] n ciprés m.

**Cypriot** ['sɪprɪət] adj chipriota,-a.
▶ n 1 (person) chipriota mf. 2 (language) chipriota m.

**Cyprus** ['saɪprəs] n Chipre m.

**cyst** [sɪst] n quiste m.

**cystitis** [sɪ'staɪtɪs] n cistitis f.

**czar** [zɑːʳ] n zar m.

**Czech** [tʃek] adj checo,-a.
▶ n 1 (person) checo,-a. 2 (language) checo. COMP **Czech Republic** República Checa.

**Czechia** ['tʃekɪə] n Chequia.

# D

**D, d** [di:] n **1** (the letter) D, d f. **2** MUS re m.

**'d** [əd] aux **1** → would. I'd go iría. **2** → had: he'd seen había visto. **3** fam → did. what'd you do? ¿qué hiciste?

**dab** [dæb] n (of paint) toque m; (of perfume) gota; (of butter) poquito.
▸ vi dar ligeros toques (at, en).
▸ n pl **dabs** GB sl huellas fpl dactilares.

**dabble** ['dæbəl] vi (in activity) aficionarse (in, a), tener escarceos (in, con).
▸ vt (in water) chapotear.

**dad** [dæd] n fam papá m.

**daddy** ['dædɪ] n fam papá m, papi m.
ⓘ pl daddies.

**daffodil** ['dæfədɪl] n narciso.

**dagger** ['dægəʳ] n **1** (weapon) daga, puñal m. **2** (obelisk) cruz f.

**daguerreotype** [də'gerəutaɪp] n daguerrotipo.

**dahlia** ['deɪljə] n dalia.

**daily** ['deɪlɪ] adj (newspaper, prayers) diario,-a; (routine) diario,-a, cotidiano,-a.
▸ adv diariamente, a diario.
▸ n (newspaper) diario.
ⓘ pl dailies.

**dainty** ['deɪntɪ] adj **1** (delicate - thing) delicado,-a, fino,-a; (- person) precioso,-a, delicado,-a, refinado,-a.
ⓘ comp daintier, superl daintiest.
▸ n pl **dainties** (small cakes) pastelitos mpl.

**dairy** ['deərɪ] n **1** (on farm) vaquería. **2** (shop) lechería; (company) central f lechera. COMP **dairy products** productos lácteos. ‖ **dairy products** productos lácteos.
ⓘ pl dairies.

✎ No hay que confundir las palabras dairy con diary, que significa 'diario, agenda'.

**dairymaid** ['deərɪmeɪd] n lechera.

**dairyman** ['deərɪmən] n lechero.
ⓘ pl dairymen ['deərɪmən].

**dais** [deɪz] n tarima.
ⓘ pl daises.

**daisy** ['deɪzɪ] n margarita.
ⓘ pl daisies.

**daltonism** ['dɔːltənɪzəm] n daltonismo.

**dam¹** [dæm] n **1** (barrier) dique m. **2** (reservoir) embalse m, presa.
◆ **to dam up** vt sep **1** (river) represar, embalsar. **2** (emotions) reprimir, contener.
ⓘ pt & pp dammed, ger damming.

**dam²** [dæm] n ZOOL madre f.

**damage** ['dæmɪdʒ] n (gen) daño; (to reputation, cause, health) perjuicio, daños mpl; (destruction) destrozos mpl, daños mpl.

**dame** [deɪm] n **1** US fam mujer f, tía. **2** (in pantomime) vieja (representada por un hombre).
▸ n **Dame** GB (title) título honorífico concedido a una mujer.

**damn** [dæm] interj fam ¡mecachis!, ¡caray!
▸ adj fam maldito,-a, condenado,-a.
▸ adv fam muy, sumamente: you were damn lucky tuviste mucha suerte.
▸ vt **1** REL condenar. **2** (curse) maldecir: damn it! ¡maldita sea!

**damned** [dæmd] adj **1** fam maldito,-a, condenado,-a. **2** REL condenado,-a.

**damp** [dæmp] adj (gen) húmedo,-a; (wet) mojado,-a. COMP **damp course** aislante m hidrófugo.
▸ n humedad f.

**dampen** ['dæmpən] vt **1** (make damp) humedecer. **2** fig (enthusiasm, ardour, etc) hacer perder, apagar, enfriar; (person's spirits) desanimar.

**damsel** ['dæmzəl] *n* doncella.

**dance** [dɑːns] *n (gen)* baile *m*; *(classical, tribal)* danza.
▶ *vi* bailar.

**dancer** ['dɑːnsəʳ] *n* bailarín,-ina; *(flamenco)* bailaor,-ra.

**dandelion** ['dændɪlaɪən] *n* diente *m* de león.

**dandruff** ['dændrəf] *n* caspa.

**dandy** ['dændɪ] *n* dandy *m*, petimetre *m*.
ⓘ *pl* dandies.
▶ *adj* US *fam* estupendo,-a.

**danger** ['deɪndʒəʳ] *n (peril, hazard)* peligro; *(risk)* riesgo.

**dangerous** ['deɪndʒərəs] *adj (gen)* peligroso,-a; *(risky)* arriesgado,-a; *(illness)* grave.

**dangle** ['dæŋgəl] *vt (hang)* colgar; *(swing)* balancear.
▶ *vi* colgar, pender.

**Danish** ['deɪnɪʃ] *adj* danés,-esa.
▶ *n (language)* danés *m*.
▶ *n pl* the Danish los daneses *mpl*.

**dank** [dæŋk] *adj* húmedo,-a y frío,-a.

**dare** [deəʳ] *vi* atreverse (to, a), osar (to, -).
▶ *vt (challenge)* desafiar.
▶ *n* desafío, reto.

**daredevil** ['deədevəl] *n* atrevido,-a, temerario,-a.

**daring** ['deərɪŋ] *adj (bold, brave)* audaz, osado,-a, atrevido,-a.
▶ *n* osadía, atrevimiento, audacia.

**dark** [dɑːk] *adj* **1** *(without light)* oscuro,-a. **2** *(hair, skin)* moreno,-a; *(eyes)* negro,-a. **3** *(gloomy)* triste, sombrío,-a. **4** *(sinister)* siniestro,-a, tenebroso,-a. **5** *(secret)* misterioso,-a.
▶ *n* **1** *(darkness)* oscuridad *f*. **2** *(nightfall)* anochecer *m*.

**darken** ['dɑːkən] *vt* **1** oscurecer, hacer más oscuro,-a. **2** *fig* entristecer, ensombrecer.

**darkness** ['dɑːknəs] *n* oscuridad *f*.

**darling** ['dɑːlɪŋ] *n (lover)* querido,-a, amor *m*, cariño; *(popular person)* niño,-a mimado,-a.
▶ *adj* **1** *(loved)* querido,-a. **2** *fam (charming)* precioso,-a, encantador,-ra, mono,-a.

**darn** [dɑːn] *n* zurcido.
▶ *vt (sock, etc)* zurcir.

**darnel** ['dɑːnəl] *n* cizaña.

**dart** [dɑːt] *n* **1** *(object)* dardo, flechilla. **2** *(rush)* movimiento rápido. **3** SEW *(fold)* pinza.
▶ *vt (look, glance)* lanzar; *(tongue)* disparar.
▶ *vi (move quickly - person)* lanzarse, precipitarse; *(- butterfly, etc)* revolotear.

**dartboard** ['dɑːtbɔːd] *n* diana, blanco de tiro.

**dash** [dæʃ] *n* **1** *(sudden run)* carrera. **2** *(small amount)* poco; *(of salt, spice)* pizca; *(of liquid)* chorrito, gota. **3** *(horizontal mark)* raya; *(hyphen)* guion *m*; *(in Morse code)* raya. **4** *(style, panache)* elegancia; *(energy, vitality)* brío, dinamismo. **5** US *(dashboard)* salpicadero.
▶ *vt* **1** *(hit)* lanzar, arrojar; *(smash)* romper, estrellar. **2** *(hopes)* truncar.

**dashboard** ['dæʃbɔːd] *n* salpicadero.

**data** ['deɪtə] *n pl* datos *mpl*, información *f*.
ⓘ *sing* datum.

**database** ['deɪtəbeɪs] *n* COMPUT base *f* de datos.

**date¹** [deɪt] *n* **1** *(in time)* fecha. **2** *(appointment)* cita, compromiso: *I've got a date with David tonight* tengo una cita con David esta noche. **3** US *(person)* ligue *m*, amigo,-a, pareja. **4** *(performance, booking)* actuación *f*.
▶ *vt* **1** *(write a date on)* fechar. **2** *(determine the date of)* datar. **3** *(show the age of)* demostrar la edad de. **4** US *fam (go out with)* salir con.
▶ *vi* **1** *(have existed since)* datar (from, de), remontarse (back to, a). **2** *(go out of fashion)* pasar de moda. **3** US *(go out together)* salir juntos, ser novios.

**date²** [deɪt] *n (fruit)* dátil *m*.

**dated** ['deɪtɪd] *adj* anticuado,-a.

**dative** ['deɪtɪv] *n* LING dativo.

**datum** ['deɪtəm] *n* dato.
ⓘ *pl* data.

**daub** [dɔːb] *n* **1** *(small bit, smear)* mancha. **2** *(bad painting)* pintarrajo.
▶ *vt* embadurnar.

**daughter** ['dɔːtəʳ] *n* hija.

**daughter-in-law** ['dɔːtərɪnlɔː] *n* nuera.

D

**daunt** [dɔ:nt] *vt (frighten)* intimidar; *(dishearten)* desanimar, desalentar.

**dauphin** [ˈdɔ:fɪn] *n* delfín *m*.

**dawn** [dɔ:n] *n* alba, aurora, amanecer *m*.
▶ *vi* amanecer, alborear, clarear.

**day** [deɪ] *n* día *m*. LOC the day after tomorrow pasado mañana. ‖ the day before tomorrow anteayer. COMP day off día libre.
▶ *n pl* days *(period)* época, tiempos *mpl*.

**daybreak** [ˈdeɪbreɪk] *n* amanecer *m*, alba.

**daydream** [ˈdeɪdri:m] *n* ensueño, ensoñación *f*.
▶ *vi* soñar despierto,-a, fantasear.

**daytime** [ˈdeɪtaɪm] *n* día *m*.
▶ *adj (flight)* diurno,-a.

**daze** [deɪz] *n* aturdimiento.
▶ *vt* aturdir.

**D-day** [ˈdi:deɪ] *n* **1** *(in war)* día *m* D. **2** *(important date)* el día *m* señalado.

**deacon** [ˈdi:kⁿn] *n* diácono.

**deactivate** [di:ˈæktɪveɪt] *vt* desactivar.

**dead** [ded] *adj* **1** *(not alive)* muerto,-a. **2** *(obsolete - language)* muerto,-a; *(- custom)* desusado,-a, en desuso; *(finished with - topic, issue, debate)* agotado,-a, pasado,-a; *(- glass, bottle)* terminado,-a, acabado,-a. **3** *(numb)* entumecido,-a, dormido,-a. **4** *(not functioning - telephone)* desconectado,-a, cortado,-a; *(- machine)* averiado,-a; *(- battery)* descargado,-a, gastado,-a; *(- match)* gastado,-a. **5** *fam (very tired)* muerto,-a. **6** *(dull, quiet, not busy)* muerto,-a. **7** *(sounds)* sordo,-a; *(colours)* apagado,-a. **8** SP *(ball)* muerto,-a. **9** *(total)* total, completo,-a, absoluto,-a.
▶ *adv* **1** *(completely, absolutely)* completamente, sumamente; *(as intensifier)* muy: *I'm dead sure* estoy segurísimo. **2** *(exactly)* justo: *we arrived dead on time* llegamos puntualísimos.
▶ *n* the dead los,-las muertos,-as.

**deaden** [ˈdedən] *vt (pain)* calmar, aliviar; *(noise, blow)* amortiguar.

**deadline** [ˈdedlaɪn] *n (date)* fecha límite, fecha tope, plazo de entrega; *(time)* hora límite, hora tope.

**deadlock** [ˈdedlɒk] *n* punto muerto, impasse *m*.

**deaf** [def] *adj* sordo,-a.
▶ *n* the deaf los sordos *mpl*.

**deaf-aid** [ˈdefeɪd] *n* audífono.

**deafen** [ˈdefⁿn] *vt* ensordecer.

**deaf-mute** [ˈdefmju:t] *n* sordomudo,-a.

**deafness** [ˈdefnəs] *n* sordera.

**deal** [di:l] *n* **1** *(agreement)* trato, acuerdo, pacto; *(financial)* acuerdo. **2** *(treatment)* trato. **3** *(amount)* cantidad *f*. **4** *(in card games)* reparto.
▶ *vt* **1** *(cards)* repartir, dar. **2** *(drugs)* traficar.
◆ to deal with *vt insep* **1** COMM *(trade with)* tratar con, tener relaciones comerciales con. **2** *(tackle - problem, etc)* abordar, ocuparse de; *(- task)* encargarse de; *(- person)* tratar (con), lidiar con.
① *pt & pp* dealt [delt].

**dealer** [ˈdi:ləʳ] *n* **1** COMM comerciante *mf*, negociante *mf*. **2** *(illegal - in drugs)* traficante *mf*; *(- in stolen goods)* perista *mf*. **3** FIN corredor,-ra de bolsa, corredor,-ra de valores.

**dealt** [delt] *pt & pp* → deal.

**dean** [di:n] *n* **1** REL deán *m*. **2** EDUC decano,-a.

**deanery** [ˈdi:nərɪ] *n* decanato.

**dear** [dɪəʳ] *adj* **1** *(loved - person)* querido,-a; *(- thing)* preciado,-a. **2** *(as form of address)* querido,-a. **3** *fam (in letter)* querido,-a; *(more formally)* apreciado,-a, estimado,-a. **4** *(expensive)* caro,-a.
▶ *interj* ¡Dios mío!
▶ *adv* caro.

**dearly** [ˈdɪəlɪ] *adv* **1** *(very much)* mucho. **2** *(at a cost)* caro.

**death** [deθ] *n* **1** *(gen)* muerte *f*; *(decease, demise)* fallecimiento, defunción *f*. **2** *(end - of custom, institution)* fin *m*. COMP death penalty pena de muerte.

**deathtrap** [ˈdeθtræp] *n fam* lugar peligroso.

**debacle** [deɪˈbɑ:kəl] *n* debacle *m*.

**debate** [dɪˈbeɪt] *n* debate *m*.
▶ *vt* **1** *(discuss)* debatir, discutir. **2** *(consider, think over)* considerar, dar vueltas a.

**debit** ['debɪt] n FIN débito.
▶ vt cargar en cuenta.

**debrief** [di:'bri:f] vt interrogar.

**debris** ['deɪbri:] n (ruins) escombros mpl; (wreckage) restos mpl.

**debt** [det] n (something owed) deuda; (indebtedness) endeudamiento.

**debtor** ['detəʳ] n deudor,-ra.

**debug** [di:'bʌg] vt 1 (computer programme, system) depurar. 2 (room, building, etc) quitar los micrófonos ocultos de.
ⓘ pt & pp debugged, ger debugging.

**debunk** [di:'bʌŋk] vt fam (person) desmitificar, desenmascarar; (idea, belief) desacreditar, desprestigiar.

**debut** ['deɪbju:] n debut m.

**decade** ['dekeɪd] n década, decenio.

**decadence** ['dekədəns] n decadencia.

**decaffeinated** [di:'kæfɪneɪtɪd] adj descafeinado,-a.

**decagon** ['dekəgɒn] n decágono.

**decagonal** [dɪ'kægənəl] adj decagonal.

**decahedron** [dekə'hi:drən] n decaedro.

**decalitre** ['dekəli:təʳ] n decalitro.

**decanter** [dɪ'kæntəʳ] n decantador m.

**decapitation** [dɪkæpɪ'teɪʃən] n decapitación f.

**decapod** ['dekəpɒd] n decápodo.

**decasyllable** [dekə'sɪləbəl] n decasílabo.

**decathlete** [dɪ'kæθli:t] n decatleta m.

**decathlon** [dɪ'kæθlɒn] n decatlón m.

**decay** [dɪ'keɪ] n 1 (of organic matter) descomposición f; (of teeth) caries f. 2 (of building) deterioro, desmoronamiento. 3 fig (of culture, values) decadencia.

**decease** [dɪ'si:s] n fallecimiento, defunción f.

**deceit** [dɪ'si:t] n (trick) engaño; (deceiving) falsedad f.

**deceive** [dɪ'si:v] vt engañar.

**decelerate** [di:'seləreɪt] vi reducir la velocidad, desacelerar.

**December** [dɪ'sembəʳ] n diciembre m.

✎ Para ejemplos de uso, consulta May.

**decency** ['di:sənsɪ] n 1 (seemliness) decencia, decoro. 2 (politeness) buena educación f, cortesía, consideración f.
ⓘ pl decencies.

**decennial** [dɪ'senɪəl] n decenal.

**decent** ['di:sənt] adj decente.

**decentralize** [di:'sentrəlaɪz] vt descentralizar.

**deception** [dɪ'sepʃən] n (trick) engaño; (deceiving) falsedad f.

❌ Deception no significa 'decepción', que se traduce por **disappointment**.

**deceptive** [dɪ'septɪv] adj engañoso,-a: appearances can be deceptive las apariencias engañan.

**decibel** ['desɪbel] n decibelio.

**decide** [dɪ'saɪd] vt decidir.

**deciduous** [dɪ'sɪdjʊəs] adj de hoja caduca.

**decigram** ['desɪgræm] n decigramo.

**decilitre** ['desɪli:təʳ] n decilitro.

**decimal** ['desɪməl] n decimal m. COMP decimal point coma decimal.

**decimate** ['desɪmeɪt] vt diezmar.

**decimation** [desɪ'meɪʃən] n reducción f catastrófica, acción de diezmar.

**decimetre** ['desɪmi:təʳ] n decímetro.

**decipher** [dɪ'saɪfəʳ] vt descifrar.

**decision** [dɪ'sɪʒən] n 1 (choice, verdict) decisión f. 2 (resolution) resolución f, decisión f, determinación f.

**decisive** [dɪ'saɪsɪv] adj 1 (conclusive - gen) decisivo,-a; (- victory) contundente. 2 (firm, resolute - person) decidido,-a, resuelto,-a; (- reply, action) firme.

**deck** [dek] n 1 (of ship) cubierta. 2 (of bus, coach) piso. 3 US (of cards) baraja. 4 (of record player) plato. 5 US (raised roofless area) terraza.

**deckchair** ['dektʃeəʳ] n tumbona.

**declaim** [dɪ'kleɪm] vt declamar.
▶ vi declamar.

**declamation** [deklə'meɪʃən] n declamación f.

**declarant** [dɪ'kleərənt] n declarante mf.

**declaration** [deklə'reɪʃən] n declaración f.

**declare** [dɪ'kleəʳ] vt 1 (gen) declarar; (opinion) manifestar. 2 (at customs) declarar.

**declassify** [dɪ'klæsɪfaɪ] vt desclasificar.
ⓘ pt & pp declassified, ger declassifying.

**declination** [deklɪ'neɪʃ°n] *n* declinación *f*, variación *f*. COMP **magnetic declination** variación *f* magnética.

**decline** [dɪ'klaɪn] *n* **1** *(decrease)* disminución *f*, descenso. **2** *(deterioration - gen)* deterioro, declive *m*, decadencia; *(in health)* deterioro, empeoramiento.

**decode** [di:'kəʊd] *vt* decodificar, descodificar.

**decompose** [di:kəm'pəʊz] *vt* descomponer.
▶ *vi* **1** descomponerse, pudrirse. **2** CHEM descomponerse.

**decomposer** [di:kəm'pəʊzə'] *n* saprótrofo.

**decompress** [dɪkəm'pres] *vt* someter a descompresión.

**decompression** [dɪkəm'preʃ°n] *n* descompresión *f*.

**decongestion** [di:kən'dʒetʃ°n] *n* descongestión *f*.

**decontaminate** [di:kən'tæmɪneɪt] *vt* descontaminar.

**decor** ['deɪkɔ:'] *n* **1** *(furnishings)* decoración *f*. **2** THEAT decorado.

**decorate** ['dekəreɪt] *vt* **1** *(adorn, make beautiful)* decorar (with, con), adornar (with, con). **2** *(paint)* pintar; *(wallpaper)* empapelar. **3** *(honour)* condecorar (for, por).

**decoration** [dekə'reɪʃ°n] *n* **1** *(act, art)* decoración *f*. **2** *(ornament)* adorno. **3** *(medal)* condecoración *f*.

**decorator** ['dekəreɪtə'] *n* *(designer)* decorador,-ra, interiorista *mf*; *(painter)* pintor,-ra; *(wallpaperer)* empapelador,-ra.

**decoy** ['di:kɔɪ] *n* **1** *(bird)* cimbel *m*; *(in hunting)* señuelo, reclamo. **2** *fig (lure)* señuelo, carnada, gancho.

**decrease** [dɪ'kri:s] *n* disminución *f*, descenso.
▶ *vt* disminuir, reducir.

**decreasing** [dɪ'kri:sɪŋ] *adj* decreciente.

**decree** [dɪ'kri:] *n* **1** *(command)* decreto. **2** US *(judgement)* sentencia.
▶ *vt* decretar.

**decriminalize** [di:'krɪmɪn°laɪz] *vt* despenalizar.

**dedicate** ['dedɪkeɪt] *vt* dedicar.

**dedicatory** ['dedɪkət°rɪ] *adj* dedicatorio,-a.

**deduce** [dɪ'dju:s] *vt* deducir (from, de).

**deduct** [dɪ'dʌkt] *vt* *(gen)* descontar, deducir; *(from taxes)* desgravar.

**deduction** [dɪ'dʌkʃ°n] *n* **1** *(subtraction)* deducción *f*, descuento; *(from taxes)* desgravación *f*. **2** *(reasoning)* deducción *f*.

**deed** [di:d] *n* **1** *lit (act)* acto, acción *f*, obra; *(feat)* hazaña, proeza. **2** JUR escritura.

**deejay** ['di:dʒeɪ] *n* pinchadiscos *mf*, discjockey *mf*.

**deep** [di:p] *adj* **1** *(river, hole, well, etc)* hondo,-a, profundo,-a. **2** *(shelf, wardrobe)* de fondo; *(hem, border)* ancho,-a. **3** *(sound, voice)* grave, bajo,-a; *(note)* grave; *(breath)* hondo,-a.
▶ *adv* **1** *(to a great depth)* profundamente. **2** *(far from the outside)* lejos. **3** *(far in time, late)* tarde.

**deepen** ['di:p°n] *vt* **1** *(well, channel, river)* profundizar, hacer más profundo,-a. **2** *(knowledge)* profundizar, ahondar; *(sympathy)* aumentar; *(colour, emotion)* intensificar; *(sound, voice)* hacer más grave.

**deep-freeze** ['di:p'fri:z] *n* congelador *m*.
▶ *vt* *(at home)* congelar; *(commercially)* ultracongelar.
ⓘ *pt* deep-froze [di:p'frəʊz], *pp* deep-frozen [di:p'frəʊz°n].

**deep-sea** ['di:psi:] *n* *(fishing, diving)* de altura.

**deer** [dɪə'] *n* ciervo, venado.
ⓘ *pl* deer.

**default** [dɪ'fɔ:lt] *n* **1** *(failure to act)* omisión *f*, negligencia. **2** *(failure to pay)* incumplimiento de pago, mora, demora.
▶ *vi* **1** *(fail to act)* faltar a sus compromisos, incumplir un acuerdo. **2** *(fail to pay)* no pagar (on, -), demorarse (on, en).

**defeat** [dɪ'fi:t] *n* **1** *(of army, team)* derrota; *(of motion, bill)* rechazo. **2** *fig (of hopes, plans)* fracaso.
▶ *vt* **1** *(gen)* derrotar, vencer. **2** *fig (hopes, plans)* frustrar.

**defect** [*(n)* 'di:fekt; *(vb)* dɪ'fekt] *n* *(gen)* defecto; *(flaw)* desperfecto, tara.

▶ *vi (party, team)* desertar, pasarse al bando contrario; *(country)* huir.

**defective** [dɪˈfektɪv] *adj* **1** *(faulty)* defectuoso,-a; *(flawed)* con desperfectos; *(incomplete, lacking)* deficiente. **2** LING defectivo,-a.

**defence** [dɪˈfens] *n* defensa.

**defend** [dɪˈfend] *vt* defender.
▶ *vi* SP jugar de defensa.

**defendant** [dɪˈfendənt] *n* JUR *(in civil case)* demandado,-a; *(in criminal case)* acusado,-a.

**defender** [dɪˈfendəʳ] *n* **1** *(gen)* defensor,-ra. **2** SP defensa *mf*.

**defense** [dɪˈfens] *n* US → **defence**.

**defensive** [dɪˈfensɪv] *adj* defensivo,-a.

**defer¹** [dɪˈfɜːʳ] *vt (postpone)* aplazar, posponer, retrasar.
ⓘ *pt & pp* **deferred**, *ger* **deferring**.

**defer²** [dɪˈfɜːʳ] *vi (submit to)* deferir **(to,** a).
ⓘ *pt & pp* **deferred**, *ger* **deferring**.

**defiance** [dɪˈfaɪəns] *n* desafío.

**defiant** [dɪˈfaɪənt] *adj* desafiante.

**deficiency** [dɪˈfɪʃənsɪ] *n* **1** *(lack)* deficiencia; *(shortage)* escasez *f*, falta, déficit *m*. **2** *(fault, shortcoming)* defecto, deficiencia.
ⓘ *pl* **deficiencies**.

**deficient** [dɪˈfɪʃənt] *adj* deficiente.

**deficit** [ˈdefɪsɪt] *n* déficit *m*.

**define** [dɪˈfaɪn] *vt* definir.

**definite** [ˈdefɪnət] *adj* **1** *(final, fixed - gen)* definitivo,-a; *(- opinions)* fijo,-a. **2** *(clear, distinct)* claro,-a.

**definitely** [ˈdefɪnətlɪ] *adv* **1** *(without doubt)* sin duda, seguramente. **2** *(definitively)* definitivamente.
▶ *interj* ¡desde luego!, ¡claro que sí!

**definition** [defɪˈnɪʃən] *n* definición *f*.

**definitive** [dɪˈfɪnɪtɪv] *adj* **1** *(final, conclusive)* definitivo,-a. **2** *(ultimate - study, etc)* de mayor autoridad.

**deflate** [dɪˈfleɪt] *vt (balloon, tyre)* desinflar, deshinchar.

**deflation** [dɪˈfleɪʃən] *n* **1** *(of balloon, tyre)* desinflamiento. **2** *(economic)* deflación *f*.

**deflect** [dɪˈflekt] *vt* desviar.
▶ *vi* desviarse.

**deforest** [diːˈfɒrɪst] *vt* deforestar.

**deform** [dɪˈfɔːm] *vt* deformar.

**deformation** [diːfɔːˈmeɪʃən] *n* deformación *f*.

**deformed** [dɪˈfɔːmd] *adj* deforme.

**defraud** [dɪˈfrɔːd] *vt* estafar.

❎ To **defraud** no significa 'defraudar (decepcionar)', que se traduce por **to disappoint**.

**defrost** [diːˈfrɒst] *vt* **1** *(freezer, food)* descongelar. **2** US *(windscreen)* desempañar.

**deft** [deft] *adj* diestro,-a, hábil.

**defunct** [dɪˈfʌŋkt] *adj* difunto,-a.

**defy** [dɪˈfaɪ] *vt* **1** *(gen)* desafiar; *(disobey - law, order, authority)* desobedecer, desacatar. **2** *(make impossible)* ser imposible.
ⓘ *pt & pp* **defied**, *ger* **defying**.

**degenerate** [*(adj-n)* dɪˈdʒenərət; *(vb)* dɪˈdʒenəreɪt] *adj* degenerado,-a.
▶ *n* degenerado,-a.
▶ *vi* degenerar **(into,** en).

**degenerative** [dɪˈdʒenərətɪv] *adj* degenerativo,-a.

**degradation** [degrəˈdeɪʃən] *n* degradación *f*.

**degrade** [dɪˈgreɪd] *vt* degradar.

**degree** [dɪˈgriː] *n* **1** *(unit of measurement)* grado. **2** *(extent, level, point)* nivel *m*, punto; *(amount)* algo. **3** EDUC título.

**dehumanize** [diːˈhjuːmənaɪz] *vt* deshumanizar.

**dehydrate** [diːhaɪˈdreɪt] *vt* deshidratar.
▶ *vi* deshidratarse.

**de-icing** [diːˈaɪsɪŋ] *n* deshielo.

**deification** [diːɪfɪˈkeɪʃən] *n* deificación *f*.

**deign** [deɪn] *vi* dignarse **(to,** a).

**deity** [ˈdeɪtɪ] *n* deidad *f*.
ⓘ *pl* **deities**.

**dejection** [dɪˈdʒekʃən] *n* abatimiento, desaliento, desánimo.

**delay** [dɪˈleɪ] *n* retraso.
▶ *vt* **1** *(gen)* aplazar, retrasar. **2** *(make late - flight, train)* retrasar, demorar; *(person)* entretener.

**delayed** [dɪˈleɪd] *adj* con retraso.

**delegate** [*(adj-n)* ˈdelɪgət; *(vb)* ˈdelɪgeɪt] *n* delegado,-a.
▶ *vt (duties, responsibility, etc)* delegar **(to,** en).

**delegation** [delɪˈgeɪʃən] *n* delegación *f*.

**delete** [dɪˈliːt] *vt (remove)* eliminar, suprimir; *(cross out)* tachar.

**deliberate** [*(adj)* dɪˈlɪbᵊrət; *(vb)* dɪˈlɪbəreɪt] *adj* **1** *(intentional)* deliberado,-a, intencionado,-a; *(studied)* premeditado,-a. **2** *(slow, unhurried)* pausado,-a, lento,-a; *(careful)* reflexivo,-a.
▶ *vi* deliberar (on, sobre).

**delicacy** [ˈdelɪkəsɪ] *n* **1** *(softness, tenderness)* delicadeza. **2** *(fragility)* fragilidad *f*. **3** *(food)* exquisitez *f*.
ⓘ *pl* delicacies.

**delicate** [ˈdelɪkət] *adj* **1** *(fine - gen)* delicado,-a; *(- embroidery, handiwork)* fino,-a, esmerado,-a. **2** *(easily damaged)* frágil. **3** *(sensitive - instrument)* sensible; *(- sense of smell, taste)* fino,-a.

**delicatessen** [delɪkəˈtesᵊn] *n* charcutería.

**delicious** [dɪˈlɪʃəs] *adj* delicioso,-a.

**delight** [dɪˈlaɪt] *n* **1** *(great pleasure, joy)* placer *m*, gusto, alegría, deleite *m*. **2** *(source of pleasure)* encanto, delicia, placer *m*.
▶ *vi* deleitarse (in, en/con).

**delighted** [dɪˈlaɪtɪd] *adj (person)* encantado,-a, contentísimo,-a; *(smile, shout, look)* de alegría.

**delinquency** [dɪˈlɪŋkwənsɪ] *n* **1** *(behaviour)* delincuencia. **2** *(act)* delito.

**delinquent** [dɪˈlɪŋkwənt] *adj* **1** *(youth)* delincuente; *(activity)* delictivo,-a. **2** FIN *(person)* moroso,-a.
▶ *n* delincuente *mf*.

**delirious** [dɪˈlɪrɪəs] *adj* **1** MED delirante. **2** *fig (happy)* loco,-a de alegría.

**deliver** [dɪˈlɪvəʳ] *vt* **1** *(gen)* entregar; *(distribute)* repartir (a domicilio). **2** *(hit, kick, push)* dar; *(shot, fast ball)* lanzar. **3** *(say)* pronunciar. **4** *(produce, provide, fulfil)* cumplir. **5** MED *(baby)* asistir en el parto de, atender en el parto de.

**delivery** [dɪˈlɪvᵊrɪ] *n* **1** *(act - gen)* entrega, reparto; *(- of mail)* reparto. **2** *(consignment)* partida, remesa. **3** *(manner of speaking)* modo de hablar. **4** *(of baby)* parto. **5** *(throwing, launching - of ball, missile)* lanzamiento. ⬚COMP **delivery note** albarán de entrega.
ⓘ *pl* deliveries.

**delta** [ˈdeltə] *n* **1** GEOG delta *m*. **2** *(Greek letter)* delta.

**deltoid** [ˈdeltɔɪd] *adj* deltoides.
▶ *n* deltoides *m*.

**delude** [dɪˈluːd] *vt* engañar.

**deluge** [ˈdeljuːdʒ] *n* **1** *(rain)* diluvio; *(flood)* inundación *f*. **2** *fig* avalancha, alud *m*.

**delusion** [dɪˈluːʒᵊn] *n* **1** *(false belief)* falsa ilusión *f*; *(mistaken idea)* error *m*. **2** *(act, state)* engaño.

**de luxe** [dəˈlʌks] *adj* de lujo.

**demagogue** [ˈdeməgɒg] *n* demagogo,-a.

**demagogy** [ˈdeməgɒgɪ] *n* demagogia.

**demand** [dɪˈmɑːnd] *n* **1** *(request)* solicitud *f*, petición *f*; *(claim)* exigencia; *(for pay rise, rights, etc)* reclamación *f*. **2** COMM demanda. **3** *(note, warning)* aviso.
▶ *vt (call for, insist on)* exigir; *(rights, conditions, etc)* reclamar.

**demanding** [dɪˈmɑːndɪŋ] *adj* **1** *(person - gen)* exigente; *(awkward)* difícil. **2** *(tiring - job, etc)* agotador,-ra.

**dementia** [dɪˈmenʃɪə] *n* demencia.

**demise** [dɪˈmaɪz] *n* **1** *(death)* fallecimiento, defunción *f*. **2** *fig (end)* desaparición *f*; *(failure)* fracaso.

**demist** [diːˈmɪst] *vt* desempañar.

**demo** [ˈdeməʊ] *n* **1** *(recording, tape)* maqueta. **2** *fam (demonstration)* manifa *f*, manifestación *f*. **3** INFORM demo.
ⓘ *pl* demos.

**demobilize** [diːˈməʊbɪlaɪz] *vt* desmovilizar.

**democracy** [dɪˈmɒkrəsɪ] *n* democracia.
ⓘ *pl* democracies.

**democrat** [ˈdeməkræt] *n* demócrata *mf*.

**demography** [dɪˈmɒgrəfɪ] *n* demografía.

**demolish** [dɪˈmɒlɪʃ] *vt* derribar, demoler, echar abajo.

**demolition** [deməˈlɪʃᵊn] *n* demolición *f*, derribo.

**demon** [ˈdiːmən] *n* demonio, diablo.

**demonstrate** [ˈdemənstreɪt] *vt* demostrar.
▶ *vi (protest)* manifestarse.

**demonstration** [demənˈstreɪʃ°n] *n* **1** *(act of showing)* demostración *f*, muestra. **3** *(march)* manifestación *f*.

**demonstrative** [dɪˈmɒnstrətɪv] *adj* **1** *(person - showing feelings)* abierto,-a, expresivo,-a. **3** LING demostrativo,-a.

**demonstrator** [ˈdemənstreɪtər] *n* POL manifestante *mf*.

**demoralize** [dɪˈmɒrəlaɪz] *vt* desmoralizar.

**den** [den] *n* **1** *(of animals)* guarida *f*. **2** *(secret meeting-place)* antro. **3** *fam (room)* cuarto; *(for study)* estudio.

**denarius** [dɪˈneərɪəs] *n* denario.
ⓘ *pl* **denarii** [dɪˈneərɪɪ].

**denaturize** [diːˈneɪtʃəraɪz] *vt* desnaturalizar.

**dendrite** [ˈdendraɪt] *n* dendrita.

**denial** [dɪˈnaɪəl] *n* **1** *(of accusation)* mentís *m*, desmentido **2** *(of principle)* negación *f*. **3** *(of rights, justice)* denegación *f*. **4** *(of request)* negativa, rechazo.

**denim** [ˈdenɪm] *n* tela vaquera.
▶ *n pl* **denims** vaqueros *mpl*, tejanos *mpl*.

**Denmark** [ˈdenmɑːk] *n* Dinamarca.

**denominate** [dɪˈnɒmɪneɪt] *vt* denominar.

**denomination** [dɪnɒmɪˈneɪʃ°n] *n* **1** REL confesión *f*. **2** *(standard of value)* valor *m*. **3** *(classification)* denominación *f*.

**denominator** [dɪˈnɒmɪneɪtər] *n* MATH denominador *m*.

**denounce** [dɪˈnaʊns] *vt* denunciar.

**dense** [dens] *adj* denso,-a.

**density** [ˈdensɪtɪ] *n (gen)* densidad *f*.
ⓘ *pl* **densities**.

**dent** [dent] *n (in car, metal)* abolladura.
▶ *vt (car, metal)* abollar.

**dentist** [ˈdentɪst] *n* dentista *mf*.

**dentistry** [ˈdentɪstrɪ] *n* odontología.

**denture** [ˈdentʃər] *n (plate)* prótesis *f* dental.
▶ *n pl* **dentures** dentadura *f sing* postiza.

**deny** [dɪˈnaɪ] *vt* **1** *(repudiate - accusation, fact)* negar; *(rumour, report)* desmentir; *(charge)* rechazar. **2** *(refuse - request)* denegar; *(- rights, equality)* privar de; *(- access)* negar.
ⓘ *pt & pp* **denied**, *ger* **denying**.

**deodorant** [diːˈəʊdərənt] *n* desodorante *m*.

**deoxyribonucleic** [diːˌɒksɪraɪbəʊnjuːˈkleɪɪk] *n* desoxirribonucleico,-a.

**depart** [dɪˈpɑːt] *vi fml* partir, salir.

**department** [dɪˈpɑːtmənt] *n* **1** *(in shop)* sección *f*; *(in company, organization)* departamento, sección *f*; *(in government)* ministerio. **2** *fam (responsibility)* campo, esfera, terreno.

**departure** [dɪˈpɑːtʃər] *n* **1** *(of person)* partida, marcha; *(of plane, train, etc)* salida. **2** *fig (divergence)* desviación *f*; *(venture, type of activity)* innovación *f*.

**depend** [dɪˈpend] *vi* depender.
◆ **to depend on** *vt* confiar en.

**depict** [dɪˈpɪkt] *vt* **1** *(portray visually, in music)* pintar, representar, retratar. **2** *(describe in writing)* describir, retratar.

**deplore** [dɪˈplɔː] *vt* deplorar.

**deploy** [dɪˈplɔɪ] *vt* **1** MIL desplegar. **2** *(use effectively)* utilizar, hacer uso de.

**deport** [dɪˈpɔːt] *vt* deportar.

**deportee** [diːpɔːˈtiː] *n* deportado,-a.

**depose** [dɪˈpəʊz] *vt* **1** *(remove from power - leader, president)* deponer, destituir; *(- king)* destronar. **2** JUR declarar, deponer.

**deposit** [dɪˈpɒzɪt] *n* **1** *(sediment)* sedimento, depósito; *(layer)* capa. **2** *(mining - of gold, etc)* yacimiento. **3** FIN *(payment into account)* depósito, ingreso.

> ✕ Deposit no significa 'depósito (recipiente)', que se traduce por tank.

**depot** [ˈdepəʊ] *n (storehouse)* almacén *m*.

**depreciate** [dɪˈpriːʃɪeɪt] *vi* FIN depreciarse.
▶ *vt* FIN depreciar, amortizar.

**depress** [dɪˈpres] *vt* **1** *(make sad)* deprimir. **2** *(reduce - prices, sales, wages)* reducir, disminuir. **3** *fml (press down)* pulsar, apretar.

**depression** [dɪˈpreʃ°n] *n* depresión *f*.

**depressive** [dɪˈpresɪv] *adj* depresivo,-a.

**deprive** [dɪˈpraɪv] *vt* privar (of, de).

**depth** [depθ] *n (of hole, swimming pool, mine, etc)* profundidad *f*; *(of cupboard, shelf)* fondo; *(of hem, border)* ancho.

**deputation** [depjʊ'teɪʃ⁅ə⁆n] *n* delegación *f*.

**deputy** ['depjətɪ] *n* **1** *(substitute)* sustituto,-a, suplente *mf*. **2** POL diputado,-a. **3** US ayudante *mf* del shérif. COMP **deputy head** EDUC subdirector,-ra. ⓘ *pl* **deputies**.

**derby** ['dɑːbɪ] *n* **1** SP *(between two local teams)* derby *m*. **2** US *(horse race)* carrera (de caballos). **3** US *(bowler hat)* bombín *m*, sombrero (de) hongo. ⓘ *pl* **derbies**.

**derelict** ['derɪlɪkt] *adj (building)* abandonado,-a, en ruinas.

**deride** [dɪ'raɪd] *vt* burlarse de, ridiculizar, reírse de.

**derive** [dɪ'raɪv] *vt (get, obtain)* sacar, recibir.
▶ *vi* **1** LING *(word)* derivar, derivarse (from, de). **2** *(stem from - problem, attitude)* provenir (from, de).

**dermatitis** [dɜːmə'taɪtɪs] *n* dermatitis *f*.

**dermis** ['dɜːmɪs] *n* dermis *f*.

**derogatory** [dɪ'rɒgət⁅ə⁆rɪ] *adj (remark, attitude, article)* despectivo,-a; *(meaning, sense)* peyorativo,-a.

**derrick** ['derɪk] *n* **1** *(crane)* grúa. **2** *(tower over oil well)* torre *f* de perforación.

**descend** [dɪ'send] *vt* descender, bajar.

**descent** [dɪ'sent] *n (by plane, climbers, etc)* descenso, bajada; *(slope)* pendiente *f*, declive *m*.

**describe** [dɪ'skraɪb] *vt* **1** *(depict in words)* describir. **2** *(call, characterize)* calificar, definir. **3** *(move in shape)* describir; *(draw)* trazar.

**desert¹** ['dezət] *n* desierto.

**desert²** [dɪ'zɜːt] *vt (family, person, place)* abandonar; *(political party, idea)* desertar (from, de).

**deserve** [dɪ'zɜːv] *vt* merecer, merecerse.

**desiccation** [desɪ'keɪʃ⁅ə⁆n] *n* desecación *f*.

**design** [dɪ'zaɪn] *n* **1** ART *(gen)* diseño, dibujo. **2** *(plan, drawing)* plano, proyecto; *(sketch)* boceto; *(of dress)* patrón *m*; *(of product, model)* modelo. **3** *fig (purpose, intention)* plan *m*, intención, proyecto.
▶ *vt* **1** *(gen)* diseñar, proyectar; *(fashion, set, product)* diseñar; *(course, programme)* planear, estructurar. **2** *(develop for a purpose)* concebir, idear; *(intend, mean)* pensar, destinar.

**designate** [*(vb)* 'dezɪgneɪt; *(adj)* 'dezɪgnət] *vt* **1** *fml (indicate, mark, show)* indicar, señalar. **2** *(appoint)* designar, nombrar.

**desire** [dɪ'zaɪəʳ] *n* deseo.
▶ *vt fml* desear.

**desist** [dɪ'zɪst] *vi fml* desistir (from, de).

**desk** [desk] *n* **1** *(in school)* pupitre *m*; *(in office)* escritorio. **2** *(service area)* mostrador *m*. **3** *(newspaper office)* sección *f*.

**desktop** [desktɒp] *n* escritorio. COMP **desktop computer** ordenador de sobremesa. ▌ **desktop publishing** autoedición.

**desolate** ['desələt] *adj* **1** *(place)* deshabitado,-a, desierto,-a. **2** *(person - sad)* triste, desconsolado,-a; *(lonely)* solitario,-a.
▶ *vt* desolar.

**despair** [dɪs'peəʳ] *n* desesperación *f*.
▶ *vi* desesperar (of, de), desesperarse (of, por).

**desperado** [despə'rɑːdəʊ] *n* forajido,-a.

**desperate** ['desp⁅ə⁆rət] *adj (reckless, risky)* desesperado,-a.

**despicable** [dɪ'spɪkəb⁅ə⁆l] *adj (person, act)* despreciable, vil; *(behaviour)* indigno,-a.

**despise** [dɪ'spaɪz] *vt* despreciar, menospreciar.

**despite** [dɪ'spaɪt] *prep* a pesar de: *she went to work despite having a bad cold* se fue a trabajar a pesar de estar muy resfriada.

**despondent** [dɪ'spɒndənt] *adj* desalentado,-a, desanimado,-a, abatido,-a.

**despot** ['despɒt] *n* déspota *mf*.

**dessert** [dɪ'zɜːt] *n* postre *m*.

**destabilize** [diː'steɪbəlaɪz] *vt* desestabilizar.

**destination** [destɪ'neɪʃ⁅ə⁆n] *n* destino.

**destined** ['destɪnd] *adj* **1** *(intended, meant)* destinado,-a. **2** *(fated)* condenado,-a, destinado,-a. **3** *(bound)* con destino (for, a).

**destiny** ['destɪnɪ] *n* destino, sino.
ⓘ *pl* destinies.

❌ Destiny no significa 'destino (punto de llegada)', que se traduce por **destination**.

**destitute** ['destɪtjuːt] *adj* indigente, mísero,-a.

❌ To destitute no significa 'destituir', que se traduce por **to dismiss**.

**destroy** [dɪ'strɔɪ] *vt* destruir.

**destruction** [dɪ'strʌkʃ°n] *n* destrucción *f*.

**detach** [dɪ'tætʃ] *vt* **1** *(separate, remove)* separar, quitar; *(unstick)* despegar: *you can detach the collar from the coat* se puede quitar el cuello del abrigo. **2** MIL destacar.

**detached** [dɪ'tætʃt] *adj* **1** *(separated - gen)* separado,-a, suelto,-a. **2** *(person, manner - impartial)* objetivo,-a, imparcial; *(- aloof)* distante, indiferente. COMP **detached house** vivienda unifamiliar.

**detail** ['diːteɪl] *n* detalle *m*, pormenor *m*.
▶ *vt* **1** *(describe)* detallar. **2** MIL destacar.
▶ *n pl* **details** *(information)* información *f*; *(particulars)* datos *mpl*.

**detain** [dɪ'teɪn] *vt* **1** *(hold - in custody)* detener. **2** *(delay)* entretener, demorar.

**detainee** [diːteɪ'niː] *n* detenido,-a.

**detect** [dɪ'tekt] *vt* **1** *(gen)* detectar. **2** *(discover - crime, criminal, fraud)* descubrir.

**detective** [dɪ'tektɪv] *n* *(private)* detective *mf*; *(in police force)* agente *mf*, oficial *mf*.

**detector** [dɪ'tektə'] *n* detector *m*.

**detente** ['deɪtɒnt] *n* distensión *f*.

**detention** [dɪ'tenʃ°n] *n* **1** JUR *(of suspect)* detención *f*, arresto. **2** EDUC *(of pupil)* castigo.

**deter** [dɪ'tɜː'] *vt* **1** *(person - dissuade)* disuadir (from, de). **2** *(prevent, stop)* impedir.
ⓘ *pt & pp* deterred, *ger* deterring.

**detergent** [dɪ'tɜːdʒənt] *n* detergente *m*.

**deteriorate** [dɪ'tɪərɪəreɪt] *vi* *(economy, health, situation, relations, material)* deteriorarse; *(weather, work)* empeorar.

**deterioration** [dɪtɪərɪə'reɪʃ°n] *n* *(gen)* empeoramiento; *(of material)* deterioro.

**determination** [dɪtɜːmɪ'neɪʃ°n] *n* determinación *f*.

**determine** [dɪ'tɜːmɪn] *vt* determinar.

**determined** [dɪ'tɜːmɪnd] *adj* *(person)* decidido,-a, resuelto,-a; *(attempt, effort)* enérgico,-a, persistente.

❌ Determined no significa 'determinado (cierto)', que se traduce por **particular**.

**determiner** [dɪ'tɜːmɪnə'] *n* LING determinante *m*.

**deterrent** [dɪ'terənt] *adj* disuasivo,-a, disuasorio,-a.
▶ *n* fuerza disuasoria, fuerza disuasiva.

**detest** [dɪ'test] *vt* detestar, odiar, aborrecer: *I detest cooking* odio cocinar.

**detonate** ['detəneɪt] *vi* estallar, detonar, explotar.
▶ *vt* hacer estallar, hacer explotar.

**detonation** [detə'neɪʃ°n] *n* detonación *f*.

**detour** ['diːtʊə'] *n* *(in traffic)* desvío.

**detract** [dɪ'trækt] *vi* **to detract from** *(achievement)* quitar mérito(s) a, restar valor a; *(beauty)* deslucir.

**detractor** [dɪ'træktə'] *n* detractor,-ra.

**detritus** [dɪ'traɪtəs] *n* **1** GEOL detrito, detritus *m*. **2** *(debris)* deshechos *mpl*.

**deuce** [djuːs] *n* *(in tennis)* cuarenta *mpl* iguales.

**devaluation** [diːvæljuː'eɪʃ°n] *n* FIN devaluación *f*, desvaloración *f*.

**devalue** [diː'væljuː] *vt* **1** FIN *(currency)* devaluar, desvalorizar. **2** *(person, achievement)* subvalorar.

**devastate** ['devəsteɪt] *vt* **1** *(city, area, country)* devastar. **2** *fam fig (person)* anonadar, apabullar.

**devastation** [devə'steɪʃ°n] *n* devastación *f*

**develop** [dɪ'veləp] *vt* **1** *(gen)* desarrollar; *(foster - trade, arts)* fomentar, promover. **2** *(acquire - habit, quality, feature)* contraer, adquirir; *(- talent, interest)* mostrar; *(get - illness, disease)* contraer. **3** *(exploit - resources)* explotar; *(- site, land)* urbanizar. **4** *(film, photograph)* revelar.
▶ *vi* **1** *(gen)* desarrollarse; *(- system)* perfeccionarse. **2** *(evolve - emotion)* conver-

tirse (into, en), transformarse (into, en); *(plot, novel)* desarrollarse. **3** *(appear - problem, complication, symptom)* aparecer, surgir; *(situation, crisis)* producirse. **4** *(of film, photograph)* salir.

**developer** [dɪ'veləpəʳ] *n* **1** *(of land, property - company)* promotora inmobiliaria, empresa constructora; *(- person)* constructor,-ra. **2** *(for photographs)* revelador *m*.

**developing** [dɪ'veləpɪŋ] *adj (country)* en vías de desarrollo.

**development** [dɪ'veləpmənt] *n* **1** *(gen)* desarrollo; *(- of skill, system)* perfección *f*; *(fostering)* fomento, promoción *f*; *(evolution)* evolución *f*. **2** *(invention - of product)* creación *f*. **4** *(event, incident)* acontecimiento, suceso; *(advance)* avance *m*, conquista. **5** *(of resources)* explotación *f*; *(of site, land, etc)* urbanización *f*.

**deviance** ['di:vɪəns] *n* desviación *f*.

**deviant** ['di:vɪənt] *adj* anormal.
▶ *n* pervertido,-a.

**deviate** ['di:vɪeɪt] *vi* desviarse (from, de).

**device** [dɪ'vaɪs] *n* **1** *(object, equipment)* aparato, artefacto; *(mechanism)* mecanismo, dispositivo. **2** *(scheme, trick)* ardid *m*, estratagema.

**devil** ['devəl] *n* diablo, demonio.

**devious** ['di:vɪəs] *adj* tortuoso,-a, sinuoso,-a.

**devise** [dɪ'vaɪz] *vt (plan, scheme)* idear, concebir, crear; *(object, tool)* inventar.

**devoid** [dɪ'vɔɪd] *adj* carente (of, de), desprovisto,-a (of, de).

**devote** [dɪ'vəʊt] *vt (time, effort)* dedicar, consagrar.

**devoted** [dɪ'vəʊtɪd] *adj (loyal - friend)* fiel (to, a), leal (to, a); *(- couple)* unido,-a; *(- follower, supporter)* ferviente; *(selfless)* abnegado,-a: *your devoted daughter* tu hija que te quiere.

**devotion** [dɪ'vəʊʃ°n] *n* **1** *(loyalty)* lealtad *f*, fidelidad *f*; *(love)* cariño, afecto, amor *m*. **2** *(to work, research, cause)* dedicación *f*, entrega. **3** REL *(devoutness)* devoción *f*.

**devour** [dɪ'vaʊəʳ] *vt* devorar.

**dew** [dju:] *n* rocío.

**dexterity** [dek'sterɪtɪ] *n (manual)* destreza, maña; *(intellectual)* habilidad *f*.

**diabetes** [daɪə'bi:ti:z] *n* diabetes *f*.
ⓘ *pl* diabetes.

**diabolical** [daɪə'bɒlɪk°l] *adj* **1** *(evil)* diabólico,-a. **2** GB *fam (extremely bad)* espantoso,-a, atroz.

**diabolo** [dɪ'æbələʊ] *n* diábolo.

**diacritic** [daɪə'krɪtɪk] *adj* diacrítico,-a.
▶ *n* signo diacrítico.

**diadem** ['daɪədem] *n* diadema.

**diaeresis** [daɪ'erəsɪs] *n* diéresis *fpl*.
ⓘ *pl* diaereses [daɪ'erəsi:z].

**diagnose** ['daɪəgnəʊz] *vt* MED diagnosticar.

**diagnosis** [daɪəg'nəʊsɪs] *n* MED diagnóstico.
ⓘ *pl* diagnoses [daɪəg'nəʊsi:s].

**diagonal** [daɪ'ægən°l] *adj (line)* diagonal; *(path)* en diagonal.
▶ *n* diagonal *f*.

**diagram** ['daɪəgræm] *n (gen)* diagrama *m*; *(graph)* gráfico, gráfica; *(of process, system)* esquema *m*.

**dialect** ['daɪəlekt] *n* dialecto.

**dial** ['daɪəl] *n* **1** *(of clock)* esfera. **2** *(of radio)* dial *m*.
▶ *vt* marcar. COMP **dialling code** prefijo (telefónico). I **dialling tone** señal *f* de llamada.

**dialogue** ['daɪəlɒg] *n* diálogo.

**diameter** [daɪ'æmɪtəʳ] *n* diámetro.

**diamond** ['daɪəmənd] *n* **1** *(stone)* diamante *m*, brillante *m*. **2** *(shape)* rombo. **3** *(in cards)* diamante *m*.

**diaper** ['daɪəpəʳ] *n* US pañal *m*.

**diaphragm** ['daɪəfræm] *n* diafragma *m*.

**diarrhoea** [daɪə'rɪə] *n* diarrea.

**diary** ['daɪərɪ] *n* **1** *(of thoughts, events, etc)* diario. **2** *(for appointments)* agenda.
ⓘ *pl* diaries.

❌ Diary no significa 'diario (periódico)', que se traduce por **newspaper**.

**diastole** [daɪəs'təlɪ] *n* diástole *f*.

**dice** [daɪs] *n* dado.
ⓘ *pl* dice.

**dichotomy** [daɪ'kɒtəmɪ] *n* dicotomía.
ⓘ *pl* dichotomies.

**dictate** [*(vb)* dɪk'teɪt; *(n)* 'dɪkteɪt] *vt* **1** *(letter, etc)* dictar. **2** *(state, lay down - law, demands, trends)* ordenar; *(terms - conditions)* imponer.
 ▸ *vi (read out)* dictar.
 ▸ *n* mandato.

**dictation** [dɪk'teɪʃ°n] *n* dictado.

**dictator** [dɪk'teɪtə'] *n* dictador,-ra.

**dictatorship** [dɪk'teɪtəʃɪp] *n* dictadura.

**dictionary** ['dɪkʃ°n°rɪ] *n* diccionario.
 ① *pl* dictionaries.

**did** [dɪd] *pt* → do.

**didn't** [dɪdənt] *pt* → do.

**didactic** [dɪ'dæktɪk] *adj* didáctico,-a.

**die** [daɪ] *vi* morir, morirse.
 ◆ **to die away** *vi (noise)* desvanecerse, irse apagando; *(breeze)* amainar.

**die-hard** ['daɪhɑːd] *n* intransigente *mf*.

**dieresis** [daɪ'erəsɪs] *n* US → diaeresis.

**diesel** ['diːz°l] *n* **1** *(fuel)* gasóleo, gasoil *m*. **2** *(car)* coche *m* diesel.

**diet** ['daɪət] *n (food)* dieta (alimenticia), alimentación *f*. **2** *(restricted food)* régimen *m*, dieta. LOC **to be on a diet** estar a régimen. ‖ **to go on a diet** ponerse a régimen.
 ▸ *adj (food)* de régimen, bajo,-a en calorías.
 ▸ *vi* estar a régimen, estar a dieta, hacer régimen, hacer dieta.

**differ** ['dɪfə'] *vi* **1** *(be unlike)* ser distinto,-a (from, de), ser diferente (from, de), diferir (from, de). **2** *(disagree)* discrepar (about/on, en).

**difference** ['dɪf°rəns] *n* diferencia.

**different** ['dɪf°rənt] *adj* diferente (from, de), distinto,-a (from, de).

**differential** [dɪfə'renʃ°l] *adj* diferencial.
 ▸ *n* **1** FIN diferencial *m*. **2** [también differential gear] AUTO diferencial *m*.

**differentiate** [dɪfə'renʃɪeɪt] *vt* diferenciar (from, de), distinguir (from, de).
 ▸ *vi* distinguir (between, entre).

**difficult** ['dɪfɪk°lt] *adj* difícil.

**difficulty** ['dɪfɪk°ltɪ] *n* dificultad *f*.
 ① *pl* difficulties.

**diffuse** [*(adj)* dɪ'fjuːs; *(vb)* dɪ'fjuːz] *adj (light, gas)* difuso,-a.
 ▸ *vt (light, heat, news)* difundir.

**diffusion** [dɪ'fjuːʒ°n] *n* difusión *f*.

**dig** [dɪg] *n* **1** *(poke, prod)* codazo. **2** *fam (gibe)* pulla; *(hint)* indirecta. **3** *(by archaeologists)* excavación *f*.
 ▸ *vt (ground, garden)* cavar (en); *(by machine - tunnel, trench)* excavar; *(by hand - hole)* hacer, cavar; *(site)* excavar.
 ◆ **to dig into** *vt insep* **1** *(investigate, examine)* investigar. **2** *(resources, savings, reserves)* echar mano de.
 ◆ **to dig out** *vt sep (trapped person, car)* sacar, desenterrar.
 ① *pt & pp* dug, *ger* digging.

**digest** [*(n)* 'daɪdʒest; *(vb)* dɪ'dʒest] *n (summary)* resumen *m*, compendio.
 ▸ *vt* digerir.

**digestion** [dɪ'dʒestʃ°n] *n* digestión *f*.

**digestive** [daɪ'dʒestɪv] *adj* digestivo,-a.

**digger** ['dɪgə'] *n* excavadora.

**digit** ['dɪdʒɪt] *n* **1** MATH dígito. **2** ANAT *(finger)* dedo; *(thumb)* pulgar *m*.

**digital** ['dɪdʒɪtəl] *adj* **1** *(watch, display, recording)* digital. **2** ANAT dactilar, digital.

**dignify** ['dɪgnɪfaɪ] *vt* dignificar.
 ① *pt & pp* dignified, *ger* dignifying.

**dignitary** ['dɪgnɪtərɪ] *n* dignatario,-a.
 ① *pl* dignitaries.

**dignity** ['dɪgnɪtɪ] *n* dignidad *f*.

**dilapidated** [dɪ'læpɪdeɪtɪd] *adj (furniture)* desvencijado,-a, en mal estado; *(building)* ruinoso,-a; *(car)* desvencijado,-a, destartalado,-a.

☒ Dilapidated no significa 'dilapidado (malgastado)', que se traduce por **wasted**.

**dilate** [daɪ'leɪt] *vt* dilatar.

**dilation** [daɪ'leɪʃ°n] *n* dilatación *f*.

**dilemma** [dɪ'lemə] *n* dilema *m*.

**diligence** ['dɪlɪdʒəns] *n* diligencia.

**dill** [dɪl] *n* eneldo.

**dilute** [daɪ'luːt] *vt* **1** *(liquid, concentrate)* diluir. **2** *fig (criticism, effect, influence)* atenuar, suavizar.
 ▸ *adj* diluido,-a.

**dilution** [daɪ'luːʃ°n] *n* dilución *f*.

**dim** [dɪm] *adj* **1** *(light)* débil, tenue; *(room, corridor, corner)* oscuro,-a. **2** *fam (person)* tonto,-a, corto,-a (de luces).
 ① *comp* dimmer, *superl* dimmest.

▸ vt *(light)* atenuar, bajar; *(eyes)* nublar, empañar; *(memory)* borrar, difuminar.
ⓘ *pt & pp* dimmed, *ger* dimming.

**dime** [daɪm] *n* US moneda de diez centavos.

**dimension** [dɪˈmenʃ<sup>ə</sup>n] *n* dimensión f.
▸ *n pl* **dimensions** dimensiones fpl.

**diminish** [dɪˈmɪnɪʃ] *vt* disminuir, reducir.

**diminution** [dɪmɪˈnjuː<sup>ə</sup>n] *n* disminución f, reducción f.

**diminutive** [dɪˈmɪnjətɪv] *adj* **1** diminuto,-a. **2** LING diminutivo,-a.
▸ *n* LING diminutivo.

**dimmer** [ˈdɪmə<sup>r</sup>] [también dimmer switch] *n* regulador m de intensidad (de la luz).

**dimple** [ˈdɪmp<sup>ə</sup>l] *n* hoyuelo.

**din** [dɪn] *n (of voices)* barullo, alboroto; *(of traffic)* estruendo, ruido.

**dine** [daɪn] *vi fml (gen)* comer (on, -); *(in evening)* cenar (on, -).
◆ **to dine out** *vi* cenar fuera.

**diner** [ˈdaɪnə<sup>r</sup>] *n* **1** *(person)* comensal mf. **2** US restaurante m barato.

**dinghy** [ˈdɪŋgɪ] *n* bote m.
ⓘ *pl* dinghies.

**dingy** [ˈdɪndʒɪ] *adj (dark, depressing - room, house, street)* lúgubre, deprimente, sórdido,-a; *(drab - colour, wall, curtains)* deslucido,-a; *(dirty)* sucio,-a.
ⓘ *comp* dingier, *superl* dingiest.

**dining car** [ˈdaɪnɪŋkɑː<sup>r</sup>] *n* vagón m restaurante.

**dining room** [ˈdaɪnɪŋruːm] *n* comedor m.

**dinner** [ˈdɪnə<sup>r</sup>] *n (at midday)* comida; *(in evening)* cena. LOC **to have dinner** cenar. COMP **dinner jacket** esmoquin m, smoking m.

⊕ En los países anglosajones la cena se sirve mucho más temprano que en España (entre las 17 h 30 y las 19 h) y es la comida más importante del día.

**dinosaur** [ˈdaɪnəsɔː<sup>r</sup>] *n* dinosaurio.

**diocese** [ˈdaɪəsɪs] *n* diócesis f.

**dioxide** [daɪˈɒksaɪd] *n* dióxido.

**dip** [dɪp] *n* **1** *(downward slope)* declive m, pendiente f; *(drop - in prices, temperature, sales, production, profits)* caída, descen-

so. **2** *fam (quick swim)* chapuzón m. **3** CULIN *(sauce)* salsa.
▸ vt **1** *(put into liquid - pen, brush, bread)* mojar; *(- hand, spoon)* meter. **2** *(lower - head)* agachar, bajar.
▸ *vi* bajar.
ⓘ *pt & pp* dipped, *ger* dipping.

**diphthong** [ˈdɪfθɒŋ] *n* LING diptongo.

**diploma** [dɪˈpləʊmə] *n* diploma m.

**diplomacy** [dɪˈpləʊməsɪ] *n* diplomacia.

**diplomat** [ˈdɪpləmæt] *n* **1** *(ambassador, etc)* diplomático,-a. **2** *(tactful person)* persona diplomática.

**diplomatic** [dɪpləˈmætɪk] *adj* diplomático,-a.

**dire** [ˈdaɪə<sup>r</sup>] *adj* **1** *(desperate, extreme)* extremo,-a, urgente. **2** *(serious, ominous)* serio,-a, grave. **3** *(terrible, dreadful)* terrible, atroz.

**direct** [dɪˈrekt, daɪˈrekt] *adj* **1** *(gen)* directo,-a. **2** *(exact, complete)* exacto,-a. **3** *(straightforward - person)* franco,-a, sincero,-a; *(- question)* directo,-a; *(- answer)* claro,-a.
▸ *adv (go, write, phone)* directamente; *(broadcast)* en directo.
▸ vt **1** *(gen)* dirigir. **2** *(show the way)* indicar el camino a.

**direction** [dɪˈrekʃ<sup>ə</sup>n, daɪˈrekʃ<sup>ə</sup>n] *n* dirección f.
▸ *n pl* **directions** instrucciones f pl de uso. LOC **to ask for directions** preguntar cómo se va.

**directive** [dɪˈrektɪv] *n* directiva, directriz f.

**director** [dɪˈrektə<sup>r</sup>, daɪˈrektə<sup>r</sup>] *n* director,-ra.

**directory** [dɪˈrekt<sup>ə</sup>rɪ, daɪˈrekt<sup>ə</sup>rɪ] *n* **1** *(telephone)* guía telefónica, listín m (de teléfonos); *(book, lost, index)* directorio, guía. **2** [también street directory] callejero.
ⓘ *pl* directories.

**dirt** [dɜːt] *n* **1** *(dirtiness)* suciedad f. **2** *(earth)* tierra. **3** *fam (scandal, gossip)* chismes mpl, trapos mpl sucios.

**dirty** [ˈdɜːtɪ] *adj* **1** *(gen)* sucio,-a; *(stained)* manchado,-a. COMP **dirty word** palabrota.
ⓘ *comp* dirtier, *superl* dirtiest.
▸ vt ensuciar.

**disability** [dɪsəˈbɪlɪtɪ] *n (state)* invalidez *f*, discapacidad *f*, minusvalía; *(handicap)* desventaja, handicap *m*.
ⓘ *pl* disabilities.

**disabled** [dɪsˈeɪbəld] *adj* minusválido,-a. COMP **disabled access** acceso para minusválidos.
▸ *n pl* **the disabled** los minusválidos.

**disadvantage** [dɪsədˈvɑːntɪdʒ] *n (drawback)* desventaja; *(obstacle)* inconveniente *m*.

**disadvantaged** [dɪsədˈvɑːntɪdʒd] *adj* desfavorecido,-a.
▸ *n pl* **the disadvantaged** los desfavorecidos *mpl*.

**disagree** [dɪsəˈgriː] *vi* **1** *(not agree)* no estar de acuerdo (**on**, en), (**with**, con), disentir (**with**, de), discrepar (**with**, de), (**on**, en). **3** *(food)* sentar mal (**with**, a); *(weather)* no convenir (**with**, a).

**disagreeable** [dɪsəˈgriəbəl] *adj* desagradable.

**disagreement** [dɪsəˈgriːmənt] *n* **1** *(difference of opinion)* desacuerdo; *(argument)* discusión *f*, riña, altercado. **2** *(lack of similarity)* discrepancia.

**disappear** [dɪsəˈpɪəʳ] *vi* desaparecer.

**disappearance** [dɪsəˈpɪərəns] *n* desaparición *f*.

**disappoint** [dɪsəˈpɔɪnt] *vt* decepcionar, defraudar, desilusionar.

**disappointed** [dɪsəˈpɔɪntɪd] *adj* decepcionado,-a.

**disappointment** [dɪsəˈpɔɪntmənt] *n* desilusión *f*, decepción *f*.

**disapprove** [dɪsəˈpruːv] *vt* desaprobar (**of**, -).

**disarm** [dɪsˈɑːm] *vt* **1** *(gen)* desarmar; *(bomb)* desactivar.

**disarmament** [dɪsˈɑːməmənt] *n* desarme *m*.

**disaster** [dɪˈzɑːstəʳ] *n* desastre *m*.

**disbelief** [dɪsbɪˈliːf] *n* incredulidad *f*.

**disc** [dɪsk] *n* disco. COMP **disc jockey** pinchadiscos *m sing*.

**discard** [dɪsˈkɑːd] *vt* desechar, deshacerse de.

**discern** [dɪˈsɜːn] *vt* percibir, distinguir.

**discernment** [dɪˈsɜːnmənt] *n* (buen) criterio, discernimiento.

**discharge** [*(n)* ˈdɪstʃɑːdʒ; *(vb)* dɪsˈtʃɑːdʒ] *n* **1** descarga. **2** *(of prisoner)* liberación *f*, puesta en libertad; *(of patient)* alta. **3** *(of worker)* despido.
▸ *vt* **1** *(give, send out - sewage, waste, oil)* verter; *(smoke, fumes)* despedir; *(- electric current)* descargar. **2** *(prisoner)* liberar, poner en libertad; *(patient)* dar de alta. **3** *(dismiss)* despedir.

**disciple** [dɪˈsaɪpəl] *n* discípulo,-a.

**disciplinary** [ˈdɪsɪplɪnərɪ] *adj* disciplinario,-a.

**discipline** [ˈdɪsɪplɪn] *n* **1** *(behaviour)* disciplina. **2** *(punishment)* castigo.

**disclose** [dɪsˈkləʊz] *vt* **1** *(make known)* revelar, dar a conocer. **2** *(show)* mostrar, dejar ver.

**disco** [ˈdɪskəʊ] *n fam* disco *f*, discoteca.
ⓘ *pl* discos.

**discomfort** [dɪsˈkʌmfət] *n* **1** incomodidad *f*. **2** inquietud *f*, desasosiego.

**disconnect** [dɪskəˈnekt] *vt (from mains)* desconectar; *(gas, electricity, etc)* cortar.

**disconsolate** [dɪsˈkɒnsələt] *adj* desconsolado,-a.

**discontent** [dɪskənˈtent] *n* descontento.

**discontinue** [dɪskənˈtɪnjuː] *vt (service)* suspender, interrumpir; *(model)* dejar de fabricar.

**discotheque** [ˈdɪskətek] *n fml* discoteca.

**discount** [*(n)* ˈdɪskaʊnt; *(vb)* dɪsˈkaʊnt] *n* descuento.
▸ *vt (goods)* rebajar; *(price)* reducir; *(amount, bill of exchange)* descontar.

**discourage** [dɪsˈkʌrɪdʒ] *vt* **1** *(dishearten)* desanimar, desalentar. **2** *(dissuade)* disuadir (**from**, de).

**discouragement** [dɪsˈkʌrɪdʒmənt] *n* desaliento, desánimo.

**discover** [dɪˈskʌvəʳ] *vt (find - gen)* descubrir; *(mistake, loss, fact)* descubrir, darse cuenta de.

**discoverer** [dɪˈskʌvərəʳ] *n* descubridor,-ra.

**discovery** [dɪˈskʌvərɪ] *n* descubrimiento.
ⓘ *pl* discoveries.

**discredit** [dɪs'kredɪt] *n (dishonour, disgrace)* descrédito.

**discreet** [dɪ'skri:t] *adj (gen)* discreto,-a; *(distance)* prudencial.

**discrepancy** [dɪ'skrepənsɪ] *n* discrepancia.

ⓘ *pl* discrepancies.

**discrete** [dɪs'kri:t] *adj* diferenciado,-a, distinto,-a.

☒ Discrete no significa 'discreto', que se traduce por discreet.

**discretion** [dɪ'skreʃ°n] *n* **1** *(quality of being discreet)* discreción *f*; *(prudence)* prudencia. **2** *(judgement)* criterio, juicio.

**discriminate** [dɪ'skrɪmɪneɪt] *vi (treat differently)* discriminar (against, a; between, entre).

▸ *vt (see a difference)* distinguir (from, de), discriminar.

**discrimination** [dɪskrɪmɪ'neɪʃ°n] *n* **1** *(bias)* discriminación *f*. **2** *(distinction)* diferenciación *f*, distinción *f*. **3** *(judgement)* discernimiento, criterio.

**discus** ['dɪskəs] *n (object)* disco.

▸ *n* the discus *(event, sport)* el lanzamiento de disco.

ⓘ *pl* discuses o disci ['dɪskaɪ].

**discuss** [dɪ'skʌs] *vt (talk about - person)* hablar de; *(- subject, topic)* hablar de, tratar; *(- plan, problem)* discutir.

☒ To discuss no significa 'discutir (pelearse)', que se traduce por to argue.

**discussion** [dɪ'skʌʃ°n] *n* discusión *f*, debate *m*.

☒ Discussion no significa 'discusión (pelea)', que se traduce por argument.

**disdain** [dɪs'deɪn] *n* desdén *m*, desprecio.

▸ *vt* desdeñar, despreciar.

**disease** [dɪ'zi:z] *n* enfermedad *f*.

**disembark** [dɪsɪm'bɑ:k] *vt* desembarcar.

**disembarkation** [dɪsɪmbɑ:'keɪʃ°n] *n (of people)* desembarco; *(of goods)* desembarque *m*.

**disenchanted** [dɪsɪn'tʃɑ:ntɪd] *adj* desencantado,-a, desilusionado,-a.

**disenchantment** [dɪsɪn'tʃɑ:ntmənt] *n* desencanto, desilusión *f*.

**disengage** [dɪsɪn'geɪdʒ] *vt* **1** *(free - gen)* soltar (from, de); *(gears, mechanism)* desconectar. **2** MIL *(troops)* retirar (from, de).

**disentangle** [dɪsɪn'tæŋg°l] *vt (unravel)* desenredar, desenmarañar.

**disfavour** [dɪs'feɪvə'] *n* desaprobación *f*.

**disfigure** [dɪs'fɪgə'] *vt (face, person)* desfigurar; *(building, town, landscape)* afear, estropear.

**disgrace** [dɪs'greɪs] *n* **1** *(loss of favour)* desgracia; *(loss of honour)* deshonra, deshonor *m*. **2** *(shame)* escándalo, vergüenza.

▸ *vt* **1** *(bring shame on)* deshonrar. **2** *(discredit)* desacreditar.

**disgraceful** [dɪs'greɪsful] *adj* vergonzoso,-a: it's disgraceful es vergonzoso, es una vergüenza.

**disguise** [dɪs'gaɪz] *n* disfraz *m*. LOC in disguise disfrazado,-a.

▸ *vt (person)* disfrazar (as, de); *(voice, handwriting)* disimular.

**disgust** [dɪs'gʌst] *n (revulsion)* asco, repugnancia; *(strong disapproval)* indignación *f*.

▸ *vt (revolt)* repugnar, dar asco a; *(disapprove)* indignar.

☒ To disgust no significa 'disgusto', que se traduce por displeasure o sorrow.

**disgusting** [dɪs'gʌstɪŋ] *adj* asqueroso,-a, repugnante.

**dish** [dɪʃ] *n* **1** *(plate)* plato; *(for serving)* fuente *f*. **2** CULIN *(food)* plato. **3** TV antena parabólica.

▸ *n pl* dishes *(crockery)* platos *mpl*, vajilla *f sing*. LOC to do the dishes lavar los platos.

**dishcloth** ['dɪʃklɒθ] *n* trapo, bayeta.

**dishearten** [dɪs'hɑ:t°n] *vt* descorazonar, desanimar, desalentar.

**dishevel** [dɪ'ʃev°l] *vt* despeinar.

ⓘ *pt & pp* dishevelled (US disheveled), *ger* dishevelling (US disheveling).

**dishonest** [dɪs'ɒnɪst] *adj (person, answer)* deshonesto,-a, poco honrado,-a; *(means, etc)* fraudulento,-a.

**dishonour** [dɪsˈɒnəʳ] n deshonra, deshonor m.
▶ vt deshonrar.

**dishonourable** [dɪsˈɒnərəbəl] adj deshonroso,-a.

**dishwasher** [ˈdɪʃwɒʃəʳ] n (machine) lavaplatos m, lavavajillas m; (person) lavaplatos mf.

**disillusion** [dɪsɪˈluːʒən] vt desilusionar.

**disinfect** [dɪsɪnˈfekt] vt desinfectar.

**disinfection** [dɪsɪnˈfekʃən] n desinfección f.

**disinherit** [dɪsɪnˈherɪt] vt desheredar.

**disintegration** [dɪsɪntɪˈgreɪʃən] n desintegración f.

**disinter** [dɪsɪnˈtɜːʳ] vt fml desenterrar.
ⓘ pt & pp disinterred, ger disinterring.

**disk** [dɪsk] n (gen) disco. COMP disk drive COMPUT disquetera.

**diskette** [dɪsˈket] n COMPUT disquete m.

**dislike** [dɪsˈlaɪk] n aversión f, antipatía.

**dislocation** [dɪsləˈkeɪʃən] n MED dislocación f.

**dislodge** [dɪsˈlɒdʒ] vt **1** (object) sacar. **2** (person) desalojar (from , de).

**disloyal** [dɪsˈlɔɪəl] adj desleal (to, a/con).

**dismal** [ˈdɪzməl] adj sombrío,-a, deprimente, lúgubre.

**dismantle** [dɪsˈmæntəl] vt (take apart - machinery) desmontar; (- furniture) desarmar.

**dismay** [dɪsˈmeɪ] n consternación f.
▶ vt consternar.

✖ To dismay no significa 'desmayo', que se traduce por faint.

**dismiss** [dɪsˈmɪs] vt **1** descartar, desechar. **2** (sack) despedir.

**dismissal** [dɪsˈmɪsəl] n **1** descarte m, abandono. **2** (sacking - of employee) despido; (- of official, minister) destitución f.

**dismissive** [dɪsˈmɪsɪv] adj desdeñoso,-a.

**dismount** [dɪsˈmaunt] vi desmontarse (from, de), apearse (from, de).

**disobedience** [dɪsəˈbiːdɪəns] n desobediencia.

**disobedient** [dɪsəˈbiːdɪənt] adj desobediente.

**disobey** [dɪsəˈbeɪ] vt desobedecer.

**disorder** [dɪsˈɔːdəʳ] n desorden m.

**disordered** [dɪsˈɔːdəd] adj desordenado,-a.

**disorganisation** [dɪsɔːgənaɪˈzeɪʃən] n → disorganization.

**disorganization** [dɪsɔːgənaɪˈzeɪʃən] n desorganización f.

**disorganize** [dɪsˈɔːgənaɪz] vt desorganizar.

**disorganized** [dɪsˈɔːgənaɪzd] adj desorganizado,-a.

**disorientate** [dɪsˈɔːrɪənteɪt] vt desorientar.

**disorientation** [dɪsɔːrɪənˈteɪʃən] n desorientación f.

**disown** [dɪsˈəun] vt renegar de, repudiar.

**disparity** [dɪˈspærɪti] n fml (inequality) disparidad f; (difference) discrepancia.
ⓘ pl disparities.

**dispatch** [dɪˈspætʃ] n **1** mensaje, despacho. **2** (journalist's report) noticia, reportaje m.
▶ vt **1** (send) enviar, expedir. **2** (finish quickly) despachar.

✖ To dispatch no significa 'despachar (despedir)', que se traduce por to dismiss.

**dispel** [dɪˈspel] vt disipar.
ⓘ pt & pp dispelled, ger dispelling.

**dispensary** [dɪˈspensəri] n (in hospital) dispensario; (in school) enfermería.
ⓘ pl dispensaries.

**dispense** [dɪˈspens] vt **1** (distribute) distribuir, repartir. **2** JUR (justice) administrar. **3** fml (public service) suministrar, administrar.
◆ to dispense with vt insep prescindir de, pasar sin.

**dispenser** [dɪˈspensəʳ] n máquina expendedora.

**disperse** [dɪˈspɜːs] vt dispersar.

**dispersed** [dɪsˈpɜːst] adj disperso,-a.

**displace** [dɪsˈpleɪs] *vt* **1** *(gen)* desplazar; *(bone)* dislocar. **2** *(replace)* sustituir, reemplazar.

**display** [dɪˈspleɪ] *n* **1** exposición *f*, muestra. **2** COMPUT visualización *f*.
▶ *vt* **1** exhibir, exponer. **5** COMPUT visualizar.

**displease** [dɪsˈpliːz] *vt fml* disgustar.

**displeasure** [dɪsˈpleʒər] *n* disgusto.

**disposable** [dɪˈspəʊzəbəl] *adj* desechable, de usar y tirar.

**disposal** [dɪˈspəʊzəl] *n* **1** eliminación *f*. **2** disponibilidad *f*.

**dispose** [dɪˈspəʊz] *vt* **1** disponer, colocar. **2** *fml* predisponer (to/towards, hacia).
◆ **to dispose of** *vt insep* **1** tirar, deshacerse de.

☒ To dispose no significa 'disponer de (tener)', que se traduce por to have.

**disposition** [dɪspəˈzɪʃən] *n* **1** *fml* carácter *m*. **2** disposición *f*.

**dispossess** [dɪspəˈzes] *vt* desposeer, despojar.

**disproportionate** [dɪsprəˈpɔːʃənət] *adj* desproporcionado,-a (to, a).

**disprove** [dɪsˈpruːv] *vt (theory)* refutar, rebatir.

**disputable** [dɪˈspjuːtəbəl] *adj* discutible.

**dispute** [*(n)* ˈdɪspjuːt; *(vb)* dɪˈspjuːt] *n* discusión *f*.
▶ *vi* discutir.

**disqualification** [dɪskwɒlɪfɪˈkeɪʃən] *n* descalificación *f*.

**disqualify** [dɪsˈkwɒlɪfaɪ] *vt* descalificar.
ⓘ *pt & pp* disqualified, *ger* disqualifying.

**disregard** [dɪsrɪˈgɑːd] *n* indiferencia (for, hacia); despreocupación *f*.
▶ *vt (danger, difficulty)* ignorar, despreciar.

**disrespect** [dɪsrɪˈspekt] *n* falta de respeto.

**disrespectful** [dɪsrɪˈspektfʊl] *adj* irrespetuoso,-a; irreverente.

**disrupt** [dɪsˈrʌpt] *vt* interrumpir.

**disruption** [dɪsˈrʌpʃən] *n (of meeting)* interrupción *f*; *(of traffic)* problemas *mpl*.

**disruptive** [dɪsˈrʌptɪv] *adj* perjudicial, nocivo,-a; perturbador,-ra.

**dissatisfaction** [dɪssætɪsˈfækʃən] *n* insatisfacción *f*, descontento.

**dissatisfied** [dɪsˈsætɪsfaɪd] *adj* insatisfecho,-a, descontento,-a.

**dissect** [dɪˈsekt, daɪˈsekt] *vt* diseccionar.

**disseminate** [dɪˈsemɪneɪt] *vt fml* divulgar, difundir, diseminar.

**dissemination** [dɪsemɪˈneɪʃən] *n fml* diseminación *f*, difusión *f*.

**dissent** [dɪˈsent] *n* desacuerdo, disconformidad *f*.
▶ *vi* disentir, discrepar.

**dissenting** [dɪˈsentɪŋ] *adj* discrepante.

**dissertation** [dɪsəˈteɪʃən] *n* **1** *(formal discourse)* disertación *f*. **2** EDUC *(for lower degree, master's)* tesina; *(for PhD)* tesis (doctoral).

**dissidence** [ˈdɪsɪdəns] *n* disidencia.

**dissident** [ˈdɪsɪdənt] *adj* disidente.
▶ *n* disidente *mf*.

**dissimilar** [dɪˈsɪmɪlər] *adj* diferente (to, de), distinto,-a (to, de/a).

**dissimilarity** [dɪsɪmɪˈlærɪtɪ] *n* diferencia.

**dissimulate** [dɪˈsɪmjəleɪt] *vt fml* disimular; ocultar, encubrir.
▶ *vi fml* disimular.

**dissipate** [ˈdɪsɪpeɪt] *vt* dispersar; difundir.
▶ *vi* disiparse, desvanecerse.

**dissipated** [ˈdɪsɪpeɪtɪd] *adj* disoluto,-a, disipado,-a.

**dissociate** [dɪˈsəʊʃɪeɪt] *vt (separate)* disociar (from, de), separar (from, de).

**dissolve** [dɪˈzɒlv] *vt* disolver.

**dissuade** [dɪˈsweɪd] *vt* disuadir (from, de).

**dissuasion** [dɪˈsweɪʒən] *n* disuasión *f*.

**dissuasive** [dɪˈsweɪsɪv] *adj* disuasorio,-a.

**distance** [ˈdɪstəns] *n (gen)* distancia. LOC **from a distance** desde lejos. **in the distance** a lo lejos.
▶ *vt* distanciar.

**distant** [ˈdɪstənt] *adj* lejano,-a, distante.

**distaste** [dɪsˈteɪst] *n* aversión *f*, desagrado.

**distasteful** [dɪsˈteɪstful] *adj (idea, task)* desagradable; *(joke, remark)* de mal gusto.

**distend** [dɪˈstend] *vt* dilatar, hinchar.
▶ *vi* dilatarse, hincharse.

**distil** [dɪsˈtɪl] *vt* destilar.
ⓘ *pt & pp* distilled, *ger* distilling.

**distill** [dɪsˈtɪl] *vt* US → distil.

**distillation** [dɪstrɪˈleɪ(ə)n] *n* destilación *f*.

**distiller** [dɪsˈtɪlə(r)] *n* destilador,-ra.

**distillery** [dɪsˈtɪlərɪ] *n* destilería.
ⓘ *pl* distilleries.

**distinct** [dɪˈstɪŋkt] *adj* distinto,-a (from, a), diferente (from, de).

**distinction** [dɪˈstɪŋkʃ(ə)n] *n* **1** diferencia, distinción *f*. **3** GB ≈ matrícula de honor.

**distinctive** [dɪˈstɪŋktɪv] *adj* distintivo,-a, característico,-a; personal, inconfundible.

**distinctly** [dɪˈstɪŋktlɪ] *adv* con claridad.

✘ Distinctly no significa 'de forma distinta', que se traduce por differently.

**distinguish** [dɪˈstɪŋgwɪʃ] *vt* distinguir.
▶ *vi* distinguir (between, entre).

**distinguished** [dɪˈstɪŋgwɪʃt] *adj* distinguido,-a.

**distort** [dɪˈstɔːt] *vt* deformar.

**distortion** [dɪˈstɔːʃ(ə)n] *n* deformación *f*.

**distract** [dɪˈstrækt] *vt* distraer (from, de).

**distracting** [dɪˈstræktɪŋ] *adj (noise)* molesto,-a; *(presence)* que distrae.

**distraction** [dɪˈstrækʃ(ə)n] *n* distracción *f*. **2** desconsuelo, aflicción *f*.

**distraught** [dɪˈstrɔːt] *adj* afligido,-a.

**distress** [dɪˈstres] *n (mental)* aflicción *f*, angustia; *(physical)* dolor *m*; *(exhaustion)* agotamiento. COMP distress call señal de socorro.
▶ *vt (upset)* afligir; *(grieve)* consternar.

**distressing** [dɪˈstresɪŋ] *adj* penoso,-a, angustioso,-a.

**distribute** [dɪˈstrɪbjuːt] *vt* distribuir.

**distribution** [dɪstrɪˈbjuː(ə)n] *n* distribución *f*.

**distributor** [dɪˈstrɪbjətə(r)] *n* distribuidor,-ra.

**district** [ˈdɪstrɪkt] *n (of town, city)* distrito, barrio; *(of country)* región *f*, zona.

**distrust** [dɪsˈtrʌst] *n* desconfianza, recelo.
▶ *vt* desconfiar de, no fiarse de.

**disturb** [dɪˈstɜːb] *vt* molestar.

**disturbed** [dɪˈstɜːbd] *adj* perturbado,-a.

**disturbing** [dɪˈstɜːbɪŋ] *adj* inquietante.

**disuse** [dɪsˈjuːs] *n* desuso.

**ditch** [dɪtʃ] *n (gen)* zanja; *(at roadside)* cuneta; *(for irrigation)* acequia.
▶ *vt fam* deshacerse de.
▶ *vi* AV hacer un aterrizaje forzoso.

**dither** [ˈdɪðə(r)] *vi* vacilar, titubear.

**ditto** [ˈdɪtəu] *n (in list)* ídem *m*.

**diuretic** [daɪjəˈretɪk] *adj* diurético,-a.

**diurnal** [daɪˈɜːnəl] *adj* diurno,-a.

**divan** [dɪˈvæn] *n (couch)* diván *m*, canapé *m*.

**dive** [daɪv] *n* **1** *(into water)* zambullida; *(in competition)* salto (de trampolín); *(underwater)* buceo; *(whale)* inmersión *f*. **2** *(of plane, bird)* picado.
▶ *vi* [US *pt* dove [dəuv]] **1** *(into water)* zambullirse, tirarse (de cabeza); *(in competition)* saltar; *(underwater)* bucear; *(whale)* sumergirse. **2** *(birds, planes)* bajar en picado. **3** *(move suddenly)* precipitarse hacia.
◆ to dive in *vi* zambullirse, tirarse de cabeza.

**diver** [ˈdaɪvə(r)] *n* buzo, submarinista *mf*.

**diverge** [daɪˈvɜːdʒ] *vi (gen)* divergir; *(roads)* bifurcarse.

**divergence** [daɪˈvɜːdʒəns] *n* divergencia.

**divergent** [daɪˈvɜːdʒənt] *adj* divergente.

**diverse** [daɪˈvɜːs] *adj* diverso,-a, variado,-a.

**diversification** [daɪvɜːsɪfɪˈkeɪʃ(ə)n] *n* **1** *(variety)* variedad *f*. **2** COMM diversificación *f*.

**diversify** [daɪˈvɜːsɪfaɪ] *vt* diversificar.
ⓘ *pt & pp* diversified, *ger* diversifying.

**diversion** [daɪˈvɜːʃ(ə)n] *n* desvío, desviación *f*.

**diversity** [daɪˈvɜːsɪtɪ] *n* diversidad *f*.

**divert** [daɪˈvɜːt] *vt* **1** desviar. **2** divertir.

**divest** [daɪˈvest] *vt* despojar, privar (of, de).

**divide** [dɪˈvaɪd] *vt* dividir, separar.
▶ *vi* dividirse, bifurcarse.
▶ *n fml* división *f*, diferencia.

**divided** [dɪˈvaɪdɪd] *adj (opinion)* dividido,-a.

**dividend** [ˈdɪvɪdend] *n* dividendo.

**divider** [dɪˈvaɪdəʳ] *n (in file)* separador *m*; *(in room)* mampara.

**dividers** [dɪˈvaɪdəz] *n pl* compás *m* de punta (fija).

**divine** [dɪˈvaɪn] *adj* divino,-a.

**diviner** [dɪˈvaɪnəʳ] *n* zahorí *m*.

**diving** [ˈdaɪvɪŋ] *n* **1** buceo, submarinismo. **2** *(in competition)* saltos *mpl* (de trampolín). COMP **diving board** trampolín *m*. **▮ diving mask** gafas *f pl* de bucear.

**divinity** [dɪˈvɪnɪtɪ] *n* **1** *(quality, state)* divinidad *f*. **2** *(subject)* teología.
① *pl* divinities.

**divisible** [dɪˈvɪzəbəl] *adj* divisible.

**division** [dɪˈvɪʒ°n] *n* división *f*, reparto.

**divisor** [dɪˈvaɪzəʳ] *n* divisor *m*.

**divorce** [dɪˈvɔːs] *n* divorcio.
▶ *vi* divorciarse.

**divorced** [dɪˈvɔːst] *adj* divorciado,-a.

**divulge** [daɪˈvʌldʒ] *vt* divulgar, revelar.

**DIY** [ˈdiːaɪˈwaɪ] *abbr* GB **(do-it-yourself)** bricolaje *m*.

**dizziness** [ˈdɪzɪnəs] *n* mareo, vértigo.

**dizzy** [ˈdɪzɪ] *adj* **1** *(person)* mareado,-a. **2** *(speed, pace)* vertiginoso,-a; *(height)* de vértigo.
① *comp* dizzier, *superl* dizziest.

**DJ¹** [ˈdiːˈdʒeɪ] *abbr* GB *fam* **(dinner jacket)** esmoquin *m*, smoking *m*.

**DJ²** [ˈdiːˈdʒeɪ] *abbr* **(disc jockey)** pinchadiscos *m*, disc-jockey *m*.

**DNA** [ˈdiːˈenˈeɪ] *abbr* **(deoxyribonucleic acid)** ácido desoxirribonucleico; *(abbreviation)* ADN *m*.

**do** [duː] *vt* **1** *(gen)* hacer. **2** *(as job)* dedicarse. **3** *(be sufficient for)* ser suficiente *(be satisfactory for, acceptable to)* ir bien a. **4** *fam (cheat, swindle)* estafar, timar. LOC **how do you do?** *(greeting)* buenos días buenas tardes; *(answer)* mucho gusto.

✎ Do es el verbo auxiliar que se emplea en inglés con la mayoría de los verbos para formar las preguntas (do you like dancing? ¿te gusta bailar?; does she live in Spain? ¿vive en España?) y formar las frases negativas (I don't want to go no quiero ir; he doesn't play tennis no juega a tenis). También sirve para sustituir al verbo principal en las respuestas (did you see the film? – no I didn't ¿viste la película – no, no la vi) y para otros usos, como en las question tags o como manera de enfatizar una afirmación.

◆ **to do away with** *vt insep* abolir, su primir.

◆ **to do for** *vt insep (manage)* arreglárselas para conseguir.

◆ **to do in** *vt sep fam* matar, agotar.

◆ **to do up** *vt sep* **1** *fam (fasten, belt* abrochar(se). **2** *(wrap)* envolver. **3** *(dress up)* arreglar.

◆ **to do with** *vt insep (need)* venir bien a.

◆ **to do without** *vi* arreglárselas sin.
① *pt* did [dɪd], *pp* done [dʌn], *ger* doing

**doc** [dɒk] *n fam* doctor,-ra.

**docile** [ˈdəʊsaɪl] *adj* dócil.

**dock¹** [dɒk] *n* **1** MAR *(gen)* muelle *m*; *(fc cargo)* dársena. **2** JUR banquillo (de lo acusados).
▶ *vt (ship)* atracar (at, a); *(spaceship* acoplar.
▶ *n pl* docks puerto.

**dock²** [dɒk] *vt* **1** *(animal's tail)* cortar. *(wages)* descontar dinero de.

**docker** [ˈdɒkəʳ] *n* estibador,-ra, carga dor,-ra.

**dockland** [ˈdɒklænd] *n* zona del puer to, zona portuaria.

⊕ En Londres Docklands es la antigua zona portuaria cerca del río Támesis donde se han establecido muchas grandes empresas, sobre todo del sector financiero.

**lockside** ['dɒksaɪd] *n* dársena.

**lockyard** ['dɒkjɑːd] *n* astillero.

**loctor** ['dɒktə'] *n* médico,-a, doctor,-ra.
  ▸ *vt pej* falsificar, amañar.

**loctorate** ['dɒkt°rət] *n* doctorado.

**loctrine** ['dɒktrɪn] *n* doctrina.

**locument** ['dɒkjəmənt] *n* documento.
  ▸ *vt* documentar.

**locumentary** [dɒkjə'ment°rɪ] *adj* documental.
  ▸ *n* documental *m*.
  ① *pl* **documentaries.**

**locumentation** [dɒkjəmən'teɪʃ°n] *n* documentación *f*.

**lodder** ['dɒdə'] *vi fam* andar tambaleándose.

**loddery** ['dɒdərɪ] *adj fam* chocho,-a.

**loddle** ['dɒd°l] COMP **it's a doddle** *fam* es pan comido, está chupado.

**lodecagon** [dəʊ'dekəgɒn] *n* dodecágono.

**lodecahedron** [dəʊdekə'hiːdrən] *n* dodecaedro.

**lodecasyllable** [dəʊdekə'sɪləb°l] *n* dodecasílabo.

**lodge** [dɒdʒ] *n* **1** *(quick movement)* regate *m*. **2** *fam (trick)* truco, treta, artimaña.
  ▸ *vt* esquivar.

**lodgems** ['dɒdʒəmz] *n pl* coches *mpl* de choque, autos *mpl* de choque.

**lodgy** ['dɒdʒɪ] *adj* **1** *fam (risky)* arriesgado,-a. **2** *fam (person)* que no es de fiar.
  ① *comp* **dodgier,** *superl* **dodgiest.**

**oe** [dəʊ] *n (of deer)* gama; *(of rabbit)* coneja.

**oes** [dʌz] *pres* → **do.**

**oesn't** ['dʌz°nt] *contr (does + not)* → **do.**

**og** [dɒg] *n* perro,-a.
  ▸ *vt (pursue)* perseguir.
  ① *pt & pp* **dogged,** *ger* **dogging.**

**ogged** ['dɒgɪd] *adj* terco,-a, obstinado,-a.

**oggie** ['dɒgɪ] *n* → **doggy.**

**oggy** ['dɒgɪ] *n* perrito,-a.
  ① *pl* **doggies.**

**oghouse** ['dɒghaʊs] *n* US caseta del perro.

**dogma** ['dɒgmə] *n* dogma *m*.

**dogmatic** [dɒg'mætɪk] *adj* dogmático,-a.

**dogmatism** ['dɒgmətɪz°m] *n* dogmatismo.

**dog-tired** ['dɒgtaɪəd] *adj* rendido,-a, hecho,-a polvo.

**doh** [dəʊ] *n* MUS do.

**do-it-yourself** [duːɪtjɔː'self] *n* bricolaje *m*.

**dole** [dəʊl] *n* **the dole** GB *fam* el subsidio de desempleo, el paro.
  ◆ **to dole out** *vt sep* repartir, dar.

**doll** [dɒl] *n* muñeca.
  ◆ **to doll up** *vt sep fam* poner guapo,-a.

**dollar** ['dɒlə'] *n* dólar *m*.

**dolly** ['dɒlɪ] *n (doll)* muñeca.
  ① *pl* **dollies.**

**dolmen** ['dɒlmən] *n* dolmen *m*.

**dolphin** ['dɒlfɪn] *n* delfín *m*.

**domain** [də'meɪn] *n* **1** *(lands)* dominios *mpl*. **2** *(in computing)* dominio. **3** *(sphere of knowledge)* campo, esfera; *(area of activity)* ámbito.

**dome** [dəʊm] *n* ARCH *(roof)* cúpula; *(ceiling)* bóveda.

**domestic** [də'mestɪk] *adj* **1** doméstico,-a: *domestic animal* animal doméstico. **2** hogareño,-a, casero,-a. **3** *(news, flight)* nacional; *(trade, policy)* interior; *(affairs, policy, market)* interno,-a.

**domesticate** [də'mestɪkeɪt] *vt* domesticar.

**domicile** ['dɒmɪsaɪl] *n* JUR domicilio.

**dominance** ['dɒmɪnəns] *n* dominio.

**dominant** ['dɒmɪnənt] *adj* dominante.

**dominate** ['dɒmɪneɪt] *vt* dominar.
  ▸ *vi (predominate)* predominar.

**domination** [dɒmɪ'neɪʃ°n] *n* dominación *f*.

**domineer** [dɒmɪ'nɪə'] *vi* avasallar.

**domineering** [dɒmɪ'nɪərɪŋ] *adj* dominante.

**Dominica** [dɒmɪ'niːkə] *n* Dominica.

**Dominican** [də'mɪnɪkən] *adj* dominicano,-a.
  ▸ *n* dominicano,-a. COMP **Dominican Republic** República Dominicana.

**dominion** [dəˈmɪnjən] *n* dominio.
**domino** [ˈdɒmɪnəu] *n* ficha de dominó.
▶ *n pl* **dominoes** *(game)* dominó *m*.
ⓘ *pl* dominoes.
**donate** [dəuˈneɪt] *vt* donar.
**donation** [dəuˈneɪ(ə)n] *n* **1** *(act)* donación *f*. **2** *(gift)* donativo.
**done** [dʌn] *pp* → do.
▶ *adj* **1** *(finished)* terminado,-a, hecho,-a. **2** bien visto,-a.
**donkey** [ˈdɒŋkɪ] *n* burro,-a, asno.
**donor** [ˈdəunəʳ] *n* donante *m*.
**don't** [dəunt] *aux (do + not)* → do.
**donut** [ˈdəunʌt] *n* → doughnut.
**doodle** [ˈduːdəl] *vi* garabatear.
▶ *n* garabato.
**doom** [duːm] *n (fate)* destino; *(ruin)* fatalidad *f*; *(death)* muerte *f*.
▶ *vt (destine)* destinar; *(condemn)* condenar.
**door** [dɔːʳ] *n* **1** *(gen)* puerta. **2** *(entrance)* puerta, entrada.
**doorbell** [ˈdɔːbel] *n* timbre *m*.
**doorknob** [ˈdɔːnɒb] *n* pomo.
**doorman** [ˈdɔːmən] *n* portero.
**doormat** [ˈdɔːmæt] *phr* felpudo.
**doorstep** [ˈdɔːstep] *n* **1** peldaño, umbral *m*. **2** GB *fam (thick slice of bread)* rebanada gruesa de pan.
**doorstop** [ˈdɔːstɒp] *n* cuña, tope.
**door-to-door** [dɔːtəˈdɔː] *adj* de puerta en puerta, a domicilio.
**doorway** [ˈdɔːweɪ] *n* entrada, portal *m*.
**dope** [dəup] *vt* **1** *fam (food, drink)* adulterar con drogas, poner droga en. **2** SP *(athlete, horse)* dopar, drogar.
**doping** [ˈdəupɪŋ] *n* dopaje *m*, doping *m*.
**dormant** [ˈdɔːmənt] *adj* **1** *(volcano)* inactivo,-a; *(animal, plant)* aletargado,-a. **2** *fig (idea, emotion, rivalry)* latente.
**dormer** [ˈdɔːməʳ] *n* [también dormer window] *n* buhardilla.
**dormitory** [ˈdɔːmɪt(ə)rɪ] *n* **1** *(in boarding school, hostel)* dormitorio. **2** US residencia de estudiantes, colegio mayor.
ⓘ *pl* dormitories.

☒ Dormitory no significa 'dormitorio (de una casa)', que se traduce por bedroom.

**dormouse** [ˈdɔːmaus] *n* lirón *m*.
ⓘ *pl* dormice [ˈdɔːmaɪs].
**dorsal** [ˈdɔːsəl] *adj* dorsal.
**dosage** [ˈdəusɪdʒ] *n (amount)* dosis *f*; *(on medicine bottle)* posología.
**dose** [dəus] *n* dosis *f*.
▶ *vt* medicar.
**doss** [dɒs] *n fam (short sleep)* cabezada.
◆ **to doss down** *vi* GB *fam* echarse a dormir.
**dossier** [ˈdɒsɪeɪ] *n* expediente *m*, dossier *m*.
**dot** [dɒt] *n (spot)* punto.
▶ *vt* **1** *(letter)* poner el punto a. **2** *(scatter)* esparcir, salpicar.
ⓘ *pt & pp* dotted, *ger* dotting.
**dote** [dəut] *vi* **to dote on** adorar.
**dotted** [ˈdɒtɪd] *adj (line)* de puntos.
**dotty** [ˈdɒtɪ] *adj* GB *fam* chiflado,-a.
ⓘ *comp* dottier, *superl* dottiest.
**double** [ˈdʌbəl] *adj* doble. COMP **double bass** contrabajo. ▮ **double bed** cama de matrimonio. ▮ **double room** habitación doble.
▶ *n* doble.
▶ *vt* **1** *(increase twofold)* doblar, duplicar. **2** *(fold in half)* doblar por la mitad.
▶ *n pl* **doubles** *(tennis)* partido de dobles.
◆ **to double back** *vi* volver sobre sus pasos.
◆ **to double up** *vt sep* doblar.
▶ *vi* **1** *(with pain, laughter)* doblarse; *(with laughter)* partirse, mondarse. **2** *(share)* compartir la habitación.
**double-click** [dʌbəlˈklɪk] *vi* hacer doble clic.
**double-cross** [dʌbəlˈkrɒs] *vt fam* engañar, traicionar.
**double-dealing** [dʌbəlˈdiːlɪŋ] *n* doble juego.
**double-decker** [dʌbəlˈdekəʳ] *n* [también double-decker bus] GB autobús de dos pisos.

⊕ Double-decker es cualquier vehículo de dos pisos. Sin embargo el double-decker por antonomasia es el clásico autobús londinense que se retiró del servicio en 2005.

**double-edged** [dʌbəl'edʒd] *adj* de doble filo.

**double-park** [dʌbəl'pɑːk] *vt* aparcar en doble fila.

**doubt** [daʊt] *n* **1** *(gen)* duda; incertidumbre *f*.
▶ *vi* dudar.

**doubtful** ['daʊtfʊl] *adj* dudoso,-a, incierto,-a.

**doubtless** ['daʊtləs] *adv* sin duda, indudablemente.

**dough** [dəʊ] *n* **1** CULIN masa. **2** *sl (money)* pasta.

**doughnut** ['dəʊnʌt] *n* rosquilla, donut® *m*.

**Douro** ['dʊərəʊ] *n* el Duero.

**douse** [daʊs] *vt* **1** *(extinguish - light, candle)* apagar. **2** *(soak)* mojar, empapar.

**dove¹** [dʌv] *n* *(bird)* paloma (blanca).

**dove²** [dəʊv] *pt* US → **dive**.

**dovecote** ['dʌvkəʊt] *n* palomar *m*.

**dowdy** ['daʊdɪ] *adj pej* sin gracia, sin estilo
ⓘ *comp* dowdier, *superl* dowdiest.

**down¹** [daʊn] *prep* **1** *(to a lower level)* (hacia) abajo. **2** *(at a lower level)* abajo. **3** *(along)* por: *cut it down the middle* córtalo por la mitad.
▶ *adv* **1** *(to lower level)* (hacia) abajo. **2** *(on paper, in writing)*: *she wrote his phone number down* apuntó su teléfono.
▶ *vt* **1** *(knock over, force to ground)* derribar, tumbar. **2** *fam (drink)* beberse rápidamente: *he downed the glass in one* se bebió el vaso de un trago.

**down²** [daʊn] *n* *(on bird)* plumón *m*; *(on peach)* pelusa; *(on body)* vello.

**downcast** ['daʊnkɑːst] *adj* abatido,-a.

**downer** ['daʊnə'] *n* **1** *fam (drug)* calmante *m*, sedante *m*. **2** *(blow, depressing experience)* palo.

**downfall** ['daʊnfɔːl] *n* **1** *fig (of person)* perdición *f*, ruina. **2** *(of regime, dictator, etc)* caída.

**downgrade** ['daʊngreɪd] *vt* **1** *(demote)* bajar de categoría. **2** *(make seem unimportant)* restar importancia a.

**downhearted** [daʊn'hɑːtɪd] *adj* desanimado,-a, desmoralizado,-a.

**downhill** [daʊn'hɪl] *adv* cuesta abajo.
▶ *n (in skiing)* descenso.

**download** ['daʊn'ləʊd] *vt* bajar; *(internet)* descargar.

**downpour** ['daʊnpɔː'] *n* chaparrón *m*, aguacero.

**downright** ['daʊnraɪt] *adj fam* descarado,-a.
▶ *adv fam* muy, absolutamente.

**downs** [daʊnz] *n pl* GB colinas *fpl*.

**Down's syndrome** ['daʊnz sɪndrəʊm] *n* MED síndrome *m* de Down.

**downstairs** [daʊn'steəz] *adv (down the stairs)* abajo.
▶ *adj (room)* (del piso) de abajo.
▶ *n* planta baja.

**downstream** [daʊn'striːm] *adv* río abajo.

**downtown** [daʊn'taʊn] *adj* US céntrico,-a.
▶ *n* US centro de la ciudad.

**downward** ['daʊnwəd] *adj (movement)* descendente; *(direction, pressure)* hacia abajo.

**downwards** ['daʊnwədz] *adv* hacia abajo.

**downy** ['daʊnɪ] *adj* aterciopelado,-a.
ⓘ *comp* downier, *superl* downiest.

**dowry** ['daʊərɪ] *n* dote *f*.
ⓘ *pl* dowries.

**doze** [dəʊz] *n* cabezada.
▶ *vi* dormitar, echar una cabezada.
◆ **to doze off** *vi* quedarse dormido,-a.

**dozen** ['dʌzən] *n* docena.

**dozy** ['dəʊzɪ] *adj* **1** *(sleepy)* adormilado,-a. **2** GB *fam (stupid)* tonto,-a.
ⓘ *comp* dozier, *superl* dozier.

**Dr** ['dɒktə'] *abbr* (Doctor) Doctor,-ra; *(abbreviation)* Dr., Dra.

**drab** [dræb] *adj* **1** *(colour)* apagado,-a; *(appearance)* soso,-a, sin gracia. **2** *(dreary - life)* monótono,-a, gris.

**draft** [drɑːft] *n* **1** *(rough copy - of letter, speech, etc:* borrador *m*; *(of plot)* esbozo; *(of plan, project)* anteproyecto. **2** FIN *(bill of exchange)* letra de cambio, giro. **3** US *(conscription)* (reclutamiento para el) servicio militar obligatorio. **4** US → **draught.**

► *adj (version, copy)* preliminar.

**draftsman** ['drɑːftsmən] *n* US → **draughtsman.**

**drag** [dræg] *n (hindrance)* estorbo (on, para), carga (on, para).

► *vt (pull, cause to trail)* arrastrar, llevar a rastras.

◆ **to drag on** *vi* alargarse, prolongarse, hacerse interminable.

◆ **to drag out** *vt sep* alargar, prolongar.

◆ **to drag up** *vt sep (revive, recall)* sacar a relucir.

ⓘ *pt & pp* dragged, *ger* dragging.

**dragon** ['dræg°n] *n* **1** *(mythology)* dragón *m*. **2** *fam (woman)* bruja.

**dragonfly** ['dræganflaɪ] *n* libélula.

ⓘ *pl* dragonflies.

**drain** [dreɪn] *n* desagüe *m*, alcantarilla.

► *vt* **1** *(empty)* vaciar; *(- wound, blood)* drenar. **2** *(rice, pasta, vegetables, etc)* escurrir.

► *vi* **1** *(discharge - pipes, rivers)* desaguar. **2** *(dry out)* escurrir (off, -), escurrirse (off, -). **3** *fig (strength, energy, etc)* irse agotando.

► *n pl* **the drains** *(of town)* el alcantarillado *m sing*; *(of building)* las tuberías *fpl* del desagüe.

◆ **to drain away** *vi (liquid - empty)* vaciarse.

**drainage** ['dreɪnɪdʒ] *n* **1** drenaje, desagüe *m*. **2** *(drains - of town)* alcantarillado; *(of building)* desagüe *m*. COMP **drainage basin** cuenca hidrográfica.

**drainpipe** ['dreɪnpaɪp] *n (pipe)* tubo de desagüe.

**drake** [dreɪk] *n* pato (macho).

**drama** ['drɑːmə] *n* **1** THEAT *(play)* obra de teatro; *(plays, literature)* teatro, drama *m*. **2** *(as school subject)* expresión *f* corporal; *(at drama school)* arte *m* dramático.

**dramatic** [drə'mætɪk] *adj* dramático,-a, teatral, emocionante.

**dramatist** ['dræmətɪst] *n* dramaturgo,-a.

**drank** [dræŋk] *pt* → **drink.**

**drape** [dreɪp] *vt* **1** *(decorate)* drapear *(cover)* cubrir (in/with, con). **2** *(part o body)* descansar, acomodar.

► *n pl* **drapes** US *(curtains)* cortinas *fpl*.

**drastic** ['dræstɪk] *adj* drástico,-a.

**draught** [drɑːft] *n* **1** *(of cold air)* corrien te *f* (de aire). **2** *(swallow of beer, etc)* tra go. **3** *(medicine)* pócima. **4** *(piece in game* dama, pieza.

► *n pl* **draughts** GB damas *fpl*.

**draughtboard** ['drɑːftbɔːd] *n* tabler de damas.

**draughtsman** ['drɑːftsmən] *n* **1** *(artis* delineante *mf*. **2** GB *(in game)* ficha d damas.

ⓘ *pl* draughtsmen ['drɑːftsmən].

**draughtswoman** ['drɑːftswʊmən] ARCH delineante.

ⓘ *pl* draughtswomen ['drɑːftswɪmɪn]

**draw** [drɔː] *n* **1** *(raffle, lottery)* sorteo. SP *(tie - gen)* empate *m*. **3** *(attractior* atracción *f*.

► *vt* **1** *(sketch - picture)* dibujar; *(- plans* trazar. **2** *(move)* llevar. **3** *(pull out, tak out - gen)* sacar, extraer; *(bow)* tensar. SP *(tie)* empatar. **5** *(attract)* atraer. **6** *(pr* duce, elicit)* provocar, obtener; *(- praise* conseguir.

◆ **to draw back** *vi* **1** *(move away)* retira se, retroceder. **2** *(pull out)* echars atrás, volverse atrás.

◆ **to draw in** *vi* **1** *(of days)* acortarse. *(train)* llegar.

◆ **to draw off** *vt sep (liquid)* sacar, extrae

◆ **to draw on** *vt insep (make use of - exper ence, etc)* recurrir a, hacer uso de; *(- mor ey, savings)* utilizar, recurrir a.

► *vi (approach - winter, night, etc)* acercarse

◆ **to draw up** *vt sep (draft - contract, treat etc)* preparar, redactar; *(- list)* hacer; *plan)* esbozar.

► *vi (of vehicle)* detenerse, pararse.

ⓘ *pt* drew [druː], *pp* drawn [drɔːn].

**drawback** ['drɔːbæk] *n* inconvenien *m*, desventaja.

**drawbridge** ['drɔːbrɪdʒ] *n* puente levadizo.

**drawer** ['drɔːəʳ] *n* **1** *(in furniture)* cajón *n* **2** *(draughtsperson)* dibujante *mf*.

**drawing** ['drɔːɪŋ] *n* dibujo: *she's good at drawing* dibuja muy bien. LOC **to go back to the drawing board** volver a empezar, empezar de nuevo. COMP **drawing board** tablero de dibujo. ▌**drawing pin** GB chincheta. ▌**drawing room** sala de estar, salón *m*.

**drawn** [drɔːn] *pp* → draw.
▶ *adj* **1** *(face - tired, haggard)* ojeroso,-a, cansado,-a; *(- worried)* preocupado,-a. **2** SP *(match, etc)* empatado,-a.

**dread** [dred] *n* terror *m*, pavor *m*.
▶ *vt* temer, tener terror a: *he's dreading the exam* le teme al examen la de terror.

**dreadful** ['dredfʊl] *adj* **1** *(shocking)* terrible, espantoso,-a, atroz. **2** *fam (awful)* fatal, horrible, malísimo,-a: *how dreadful!* ¡qué horror!

**dream** [driːm] *n* **1** *(while asleep)* sueño: *I had a bad dream* tuve una pesadilla; *sweet dreams!* ¡felices sueños! **2** *(daydream)* ensueño, sueño: *he lives in a dream* vive en las nubes. **3** *(hope, fantasy)* sueño (dorado), deseo, ilusión *f*: *the house of your dreams* la casa de tus sueños.
▶ *adj (imaginary)* imaginario,-a; *(ideal)* ideal, de ensueño: *your dream holiday* las vacaciones de tus sueños.
▶ *vt* **1** *(while asleep)* soñar: *I dreamt that I was flying* soñé que volaba. **2** *(imagine)* imaginarse: *I never dreamt you'd actually do it* nunca me imaginé que lo harías de verdad.
▶ *vi* **1** *(while asleep)* soñar (about/of, con); *(daydream)* soñar (despierto,-a): *I dreamt about you last night* soñé contigo anoche; *dream on* sigue soñando. **2** *(imagine)* soñar (of, con); *(contemplate)* soñar despierto: *I dream of having my own business* sueño con tener mi propia empresa.
◆ **to dream up** *vt sep fam pej (excuse)* inventarse; *(plan)* idear.
ⓘ *pt & pp* dreamed o dreamt [dremt].

**dreamer** ['driːmə'] *n* soñador,-ra.

**dreamt** [dremt] *pt & pp* → dream.

**dreary** ['drɪərɪ] *adj* **1** *(gen)* triste, deprimente. **2** *fam (dull, uninteresting)* pesado,-a, aburrido,-a.
ⓘ *comp* drearier, *superl* dreariest.

**dredge¹** [dredʒ] *vt & vi (river, lake, etc)* dragar, rastrear.

**dredge²** [dredʒ] *vt* CULIN *(with sugar)* espolvorear; *(with flour)* enharinar, rebozar.

**drench** [drentʃ] *vt* empapar. LOC **to be/get drenched** empaparse. ▌**to be drenched to the skin** estar calado,-a hasta los huesos.

**dress** [dres] *n* **1** *(for women)* vestido. **2** *(clothing)* ropa, vestimenta.
▶ *adj (shirt, suit)* de etiqueta. COMP **dress rehearsal** THEAT ensayo general.
▶ *vt* **1** *(person)* vestir. **2** MED *(wound)* vendar. **3** CULIN *(poultry, crab)* aderezar, preparar; *(salad)* aliñar. **4** *(shop window)* arreglar, decorar; *(Christmas tree)* decorar, adornar; *(hair)* arreglar.
▶ *vi (gen)* vestirse; *(formally)* vestirse de etiqueta. LOC **to get dressed** vestirse.
◆ **to dress down** *vt sep (scold)* regañar; *(rebuke)* echar una bronca.
▶ *vi (dress informally)* vestirse informalmente.
◆ **to dress up** *vi (in fancy dress)* disfrazarse (as, de); *(dress formally)* ponerse de tiros largos.
▶ *vt sep fig (truth, facts, etc)* disfrazar.

**dresser** ['dresə'] *n* **1** GB *(in kitchen)* aparador *m*. **2** US *(chest of drawers)* tocador *m*.

**dressing** ['dresɪŋ] *n* **1** *(gen)* apósito; *(bandage)* vendaje *m*. **2** *(act of getting dressed)* el vestir(se) *m*. **3** CULIN *(for salad)* aliño. **4** US *(stuffing)* relleno. COMP **dressing gown** bata. ▌**dressing room** THEAT camerino. ▌**dressing table** tocador *m*.

**dressmaker** ['dresmeɪkə'] *n (woman)* modista *f*, modisto; *(man)* modista *m*, modisto.

**dressmaking** ['dresmeɪkɪŋ] *n* costura.

**drew** [druː] *pt* → draw.

**dribble** ['drɪbºl] *n* **1** *(saliva)* saliva, baba. **2** *(of water, blood)* gotas *fpl*, hilo, chorrito. **3** SP dribling *m*.
▶ *vi* **1** *(baby)* babear. **2** *(liquid)* gotear.
▶ *vt* driblar, regatear.

**dried** [draɪd] *pp* → dry.
▶ *adj (fruit)* seco,-a; *(milk)* en polvo.

**drier** ['draɪə'] *n* → dryer.

**drift** [drɪft] *n* **1** *(of snow)* ventisquero; *(of sand)* montón *m*. **2** MAR *(flow of water)* deriva. **3** *(movement)* movimiento; *(tendency)* tendencia. **4** *(meaning, gist)* significado, sentido, idea: *do you get my drift?* ¿entiendes lo que quiero decir?

▶ *vi* **1** *(float on water)* ir a la deriva. **2** *(pile up - of snow, sand, leaves, etc)* amontonarse.

**drill¹** [drɪl] *n* **1** *(handtool)* taladro; *(large machine)* barreno, perforadora; *(dentist's)* fresa; *(drill head, bit)* broca. **2** MIL instrucción *f*. **3** EDUC *(exercise)* ejercicio. **4** *(rehearsal, practice)* simulacro; *(procedures to be followed)* procedimiento: *fire drill* simulacro de incendio; *safety drill* instrucciones de seguridad.

▶ *vt* **1** *(wood, metal, etc)* taladrar, perforar; *(hole)* hacer, perforar. **2** MIL instruir.

▶ *vi* **1** *(for oil, coal)* perforar. **2** MIL entrenarse. [LOC] **to drill STH into SB** inculcarle ALGO a ALGN.

**drill²** [drɪl] *n (material)* dril *m*.

**drink** [drɪŋk] *n (gen)* bebida; *(alcoholic drink)* copa, trago; *(soft drink)* refresco: *let's go for a drink!* ¡vamos a tomar algo!, ¡vamos a tomar una copa!

▶ *vt (gen)* beber, tomar: *you haven't drunk your tea* no te has bebido el té; *what do you want to drink?* ¿qué quieres beber? [LOC] **to drink a toast to SB** brindar por ALGN. I **to drink to STH/SB** brindar por ALGO/ALGN. I **to have STH to drink** tomar(se) ALGO.

▶ *vi* beber: *she doesn't drink (alcohol)* no bebe (alcohol); *don't drink and drive* si bebes, no conduzcas.

◆ **to drink in** *vt sep (scene, sights, sounds, etc)* apreciar, empaparse de; *(success)* saborear.

ⓘ *pt* **drank** [dræŋk], *pp* **drunk** [drʌŋk].

**drinkable** ['drɪŋkəbl] *adj (water)* potable; *(wine, beer, etc)* aceptable.

**drinker** ['drɪŋkəʳ] *n* bebedor,-ra.

**drinking** ['drɪŋkɪŋ] *n (alcohol)* bebida; *(action)* beber *m*. [COMP] **drinking fountain** fuente *f* de agua potable. I **drinking water** agua potable.

**drip** [drɪp] *n* **1** *(drop of liquid)* goteo; *(sound)* gotear *m*. **2** MED gota a gota *m*: *they put him on a drip* le pusieron el gota a gota. **3** *fam (person)* soso,-a.

▶ *vi (fall in drops)* gotear, caer; *(fall heavily)* chorrear: *the tap drips* el grifo gotea.

▶ *vt* dejar caer gota a gota.

ⓘ *pt & pp* **dripped**, *ger* **dripping**.

**drive** [draɪv] *n* **1** *(trip)* paseo en coche; *(journey)* viaje *m*: *we went for a drive* dimos una vuelta en coche; *it's a two-hour drive* es un viaje de dos horas. **2** *(road)* calle *f*. **3** SP *(golf, tennis)* drive *m*. **4** *(campaign)* campaña: *sales drive* promoción; *membership drive* campaña para atraer socios; *a no-smoking drive* una campaña antitabaco. **5** *(energy, initiative)* energía. **6** *(propulsion system)* transmisión *f*, propulsión *f*; *(of wheeled vehicle)* tracción *f*: *front-wheel drive* tracción delantera; *four-wheel drive* tracción en las cuatro ruedas.

▶ *vt* **1** *(operate - vehicle)* conducir: *he drives a bus* es conductor de autobús. **2** *(take - person)* llevar (en coche). **3** *(cause to move - person)* hacer, obligar a; *(- animal)* arrear. **4** *(provide power for, keep going)* hacer funcionar, mover: *the river drives the waterwheel* el río mueve el molino. **5** *(force, compel to act)* forzar, obligar; *(cause to be in state)* llevar: *you're driving me crazy* me estás volviendo loco.

▶ *vi (vehicle)* conducir: *can you drive?* ¿sabes conducir?; *he's learning to drive* está aprendiendo a conducir; *I drove here* vine en coche.

◆ **to drive at** *vt insep* insinuar.

◆ **to drive away** *vt sep (fend off - attacker, animal)* ahuyentar; *(throw out)* alejar.

◆ **to drive off** *vt sep* ahuyentar.

▶ *vi (car, driver)* irse.

◆ **to drive out** *vt sep* expulsar.

ⓘ *pt* **drove** [drəʊv], *pp* **driven** ['drɪvªn].

**drivel** ['drɪvªl] *n* tonterías *fpl*, bobadas *fpl*, memeces *fpl*.

**driven** ['drɪvªn] *pp* → **drive**.

**driver** ['draɪvəʳ] *n* **1** *(of bus, car)* conductor,-ra; *(of taxi)* taxista *mf*; *(of lorry)* camionero,-a; *(of racing car)* piloto *mf*; *(of train)* maquinista *mf*: *he's a very good driver* conduce muy bien. **2** SP *(golf club)* madera número 1. [COMP] **driver's licence** US carnet *m* de conducir, permiso de conducir.

**driving** ['draɪvɪŋ] *n* AUTO conducción *f*: *we shared the driving* nos turnamos para conducir.
▶ *adj* COMP **driving licence** carnet *m* de conducir, permiso de conducir. ▪ **driving school** autoescuela. ▪ **driving test** examen *m* de conducir.

**drizzle** ['drɪzªl] *n* llovizna.
▶ *vi* lloviznar.

**droll** [drəʊl] *adj (amusing)* gracioso,-a, chistoso,-a; *(odd, quaint)* curioso,-a.

**dromedary** ['drɒmədªrɪ] *n* dromedario.
ⓘ *pl* dromedaries.

**drone¹** [drəʊn] *n (bee)* zángano.

**drone²** [drəʊn] *n* **1** *(noise)* zumbido. **2** *(monotonous talk)* cantinela, sonsonete *m*.
▶ *vi (bee, plane, engine)* zumbar.

**drool** [druːl] *n* **1** *(of baby)* baba, babas *fpl*. **2** *(drivel)* tonterías *fpl*, bobadas *fpl*.
▶ *vi (of baby, dog)* babear.

**droop** [druːp] *n (of shoulders)* caída, inclinación *f,*.
▶ *vi* **1** *(head)* inclinarse, caerse; *(shoulders)* encorvarse; *(eyelids)* cerrar. **2** *(flower)* marchitarse; *(branches)* inclinarse.

**drop** [drɒp] *n* **1** *(of liquid)* gota: *she carried the cup without spilling a drop* llevó la taza sin derramar ni una gota; *we could do with a drop of rain* nos iría bien un poco de lluvia. **2** *(sweet)* pastilla, caramelo. **3** *(descent, distance down)* desnivel *m*, caída. **4** *(fall - gen)* caída; *(in temperature)* descenso.
▶ *vt* **1** *(let fall - accidentally)* caérsele a uno: *he dropped the glass* se le cayó el vaso; *don't drop it!* ¡que no se te caiga!. **2** *(let fall - deliberately)* dejar caer, tirar; *(let go of)* soltar; *(launch - bomb, supplies)* lanzar: *she dropped her handkerchief by his chair* dejó caer su pañuelo al lado de su silla; *drop it!* ¡suéltalo! **3** *(lower - gen)* bajar; *(- speed)* reducir. **4** *fam (set down - passenger)* dejar (off, -); *(- delivery)* dejar, pasar a dejar (off, -): *where shall I drop you?* ¿dónde quieres que te deje? **5** *(give up, abandon)* dejar, abandonar. **6** *(omit, leave out - in speaking)* no pronunciar, comerse; *(in writing)* omitir: *don't drop your "h"s* no te comas las «haches». **7** SP *(player from team)* echar, sacar, no seleccionar; *(lose)* perder. LOC **to drop**

dead caerse muerto,-a. ▪ **to drop SB a line / drop SB a note** escribir cuatro/unas líneas a ALGN.
▶ *vi* **1** *(fall - object)* caer, caerse; *(- person)* dejarse caer, tirarse. **2** *(prices, temperature, voice)* bajar; *(wind)* amainar; *(speed)* reducirse, disminuir. **3** *(lapse)* dejar: *let it drop!* ¡déjalo ya!, ¡basta ya!
◆ **to drop away** *vi* **1** *(support, interest)* disminuir. **2** *(ground)* caer.
◆ **to drop by** *vi* pasar.
▶ *vt insep* pasar por.
◆ **to drop in** *vi (visit)* pasar.
◆ **to drop off** *vi* **1** *fam (fall asleep)* dormirse. **2** *(sales, interest, etc)* disminuir.
◆ **to drop out** *vi (of school, etc)* dejar los estudios; *(of group)* dejar el grupo; *(of race, competition)* abandonar; *(of society)* marginarse.
ⓘ *pt & pp* dropped, *ger* dropping.

**droplet** ['drɒplət] *n* gotita.

**drought** [draʊt] *n* sequía.

**drove** [drəʊv] *pt* → drive.
▶ *n* **1** *(of cattle)* manada. **2** *(of people)* multitud *f*.

**drown** [draʊn] *vt* **1** *(gen)* ahogar. **2** *(submerge - place)* inundar, anegar.
▶ *vi* ahogarse.

**drowse** [draʊz] *vi* dormitar.

**drowsy** ['draʊzɪ] *adj (person, look)* somnoliento,-a: *these tablets make me drowsy* estas pastillas me dan sueño. LOC **to feel drowsy** tener sueño.
ⓘ *comp* drowsier, *superl* drowsiest.

**drug** [drʌg] *n* **1** *(medicine)* medicamento. **2** *(narcotic)* droga: *hard/soft drugs* drogas duras/blandas. LOC **to be on/do/take drugs** drogarse. COMP **drug addict** drogadicto,-a, toxicómano,-a. ▪ **drug dealer** traficante *mf* de drogas. ▪ **drug pusher** camello *mf*.
▶ *vt* **1** *(person, animal)* drogar. **2** *(food, drink)* adulterar con drogas.
ⓘ *pt & pp* drugged, *ger* drugging.

**druggist** ['drʌgɪst] *n* US farmacéutico,-a.

**drugstore** ['drʌgstɔːʳ] *n* US *establecimiento donde se puede comprar medicamentos, cosméticos, periódicos y otras cosas.*

D

**drum** [drʌm] n **1** *(instrument)* tambor m. **2** *(container)* bidón m. **3** TECH tambor.
▶ vi **1** tocar el tambor.
ⓘ pt & pp **drummed**, ger **drumming**.
▶ n pl **drums** *(set)* batería.

**drummer** ['drʌmər] n *(in marching band)* tambor mf; *(in pop group, jazz band)* batería mf.

**drumstick** ['drʌmstɪk] n **1** MUS baqueta, palillo (de tambor). **2** CULIN muslo (de ave).

**drunk** [drʌŋk] pp → drink.
▶ adj borracho,-a. LOC **to get drunk** emborracharse.

**drunkard** ['drʌŋkəd] n borracho,-a.

**drunken** ['drʌŋkªn] adj borracho,-a.

**dry** [draɪ] adj **1** seco,-a. COMP **dry dock** dique m seco. ‖ **dry goods 1** GB comestibles mpl no perecederos. **2** US artículos mpl de mercería. ‖ **dry land** tierra firme.
ⓘ comp **drier**, superl **driest**.
▶ vt secar.
▶ vi secarse (off, -).
ⓘ pt & pp **dried**, ger **drying**.

**dry-clean** [draɪ'kliːn] vt limpiar en seco.

**dry-cleaner's** [draɪ'kliːnəz] n tintorería, tinte m.

**dryer** ['draɪər] n *(for clothes)* secadora; *(for hair)* secador m.

**dryness** ['draɪnəs] n sequedad f.

**dual** ['djuːəl] adj *(gen)* doble. COMP **dual carriageway** GB carretera de doble calzada.

**dub¹** [dʌb] vt *(soundtrack)* doblar (into, a).
ⓘ pt & pp **dubbed**, ger **dubbing**.

**dub²** [dʌb] vt *(give nickname)* apodar.
ⓘ pt & pp **dubbed**, ger **dubbing**.

**dub³** [dʌb] n MUS dub m.

**dubbing** ['dʌbɪŋ] n *(of soundtrack)* doblaje m.

**duchess** ['dʌtʃəs] n duquesa.

**duck¹** [dʌk] n pato,-a.

**duck²** [dʌk] vi *(bend down)* agacharse; *(hide)* esconderse: *she ducked behind the sofa* se escondió detrás del sofá.

**duckling** ['dʌklɪŋ] n patito.

**duct** [dʌkt] n conducto.

**ductile** ['dʌktaɪl] adj dúctil.

**ductility** [dʌk'tɪlətɪ] n ductilidad f.

**dud** [dʌd] n **1** fam *(object)* trasto inútil, engañifa; *(person)* desastre m, inútil mf. **2** *(grenade, bomb, firework, etc)* granada, bomba, fuego artificial, etc. que no estalla.
▶ adj *(defective)* defectuoso,-a; *(worthless, useless)* inútil,; *(valueless - note, coin)* falso,-a; *(grenade, bomb, firework)* que no estalla. COMP **dud cheque** cheque m sin fondos.

**due** [djuː] adj *(expected)* esperado,-a: *her new book is due out in December* su nuevo libro saldrá en diciembre; *the train is due (in) at five o'clock* el tren debe llegar a las cinco. LOC **due to** debido a. COMP **due date** (fecha de) vencimiento.
▶ n merecido.
▶ adv derecho hacia: *due north* derecho hacia el norte.
▶ n pl **dues** cuota.

**duel** ['djuːəl] n duelo.
▶ vi batirse en duelo (with, con).
ⓘ pt & pp **duelled** (US **dueled**), ger **duelling** (US **dueling**).

**duet** [djuː'et] n dúo.

**dug** [dʌg] pt & pp → dig.

**duke** [djuːk] n duque m.

**dull** [dʌl] adj **1** *(boring - job)* monótono,-a, pesado,-a; *(- person, life, film)* pesado,-a, aburrido,-a, soso,-a; *(- place, town)* aburrido,-a. **2** *(not bright - colours)* apagado,-a; *(weather, day)* gris, triste, feo,-a. **3** *(sound, pain)* sordo,-a. **4** *(slow-witted)* torpe, lerdo,-a.
▶ vt *(pain)* aliviar, calmar; *(sound)* amortiguar; *(hearing)* embotar.

**duly** ['djuːlɪ] adv **1** fml *(properly)* debidamente. **2** *(as expected)* como era de esperar.

**dumb** [dʌm] adj **1** *(unable to speak)* mudo,-a. **3** US fam *(stupid)* tonto,-a.

**dummy** ['dʌmɪ] n **1** *(in shop window, dressmaker's)* maniquí m. **2** *(fake)* imitación f. **3** GB *(for baby)* chupete m. **4** fam imbécil mf.
ⓘ pl **dummies**.

**dump** [dʌmp] n vertedero, basurero.
▶ vt *(drop, unload - rubbish)* verter, descargar; *(leave)* dejar, poner: *he dumped*

*his dirty washing on the floor* dejó su ropa sucia en el suelo.

**dumping** ['dʌmpɪŋ] *n* vertido. LOC «No dumping» «Prohibido arrojar basuras».

**dune** [dju:n] [también **sand dune**] *n* duna.

**dung** [dʌŋ] *n* estiércol *m*.

**dungarees** [dʌŋɡə'ri:z] *n (garment)* peto; *(overalls)* mono.

**dungeon** ['dʌndʒən] *n* mazmorra.

**duo** ['dju:əʊ] *n* dúo.
  ① *pl* duos.

**duodena** [dju:ə'di:nə] *n pl →* **duodenum**.

**duodenum** [dju:ə'di:nəm] *n* duodeno.
  ① *pl* duodenums o duodena [dju:ə'di:nə].

**dupe** [dju:p] *n* ingenuo,-a.
  ▶ *vt* engañar, embaucar.

**duplex** ['dju:pleks] *n* US *(house)* casa adosada; *(flat, apartment)* dúplex *m*.

**duplicate** [*(adj)* 'dju:plɪkət; *(n)* 'dju:plɪkeɪt] *adj* duplicado,-a.
  ▶ *n* copia, duplicado. LOC **in duplicate** por duplicado.
  ▶ *vt* duplicar, hacer copias de.

**durable** ['djʊərəbªl] *adj* duradero,-a.

**duration** [djʊə'reɪʃªn] *n* duración *f*.

**during** ['djʊərɪŋ] *prep* durante: *I lived in France during the war* viví en Francia durante la guerra; *she's out at work during the day* trabaja fuera de casa durante el día.

**dusk** [dʌsk] *n* anochecer *m*. LOC **at dusk** al anochecer.

**dust** [dʌst] *n* polvo.
  ▶ *vt* quitar el polvo a.

**dustbin** ['dʌstbɪn] *n* GB cubo de la basura. COMP **dustbin man** basurero.

**dustcart** ['dʌstkɑ:t] *n* camión *m* de la basura.

**duster** ['dʌstər] *n (for dusting)* paño, trapo (del polvo); *(for blackboard)* borrador *m*.

**dustman** ['dʌstmən] *n* GB basurero.

**dustpan** ['dʌstpæn] *n* recogedor *m*.

**Dutch** [dʌtʃ] *adj* holandés,-esa, neerlandés,-esa. LOC **to go Dutch (with SB)** pagar a escote.
  ▶ *n (language)* holandés *m*.

**Dutchman** ['dʌtʃmən] *n* holandés *m*, neerlandés *m*.
  ① *pl* Dutchmen ['dʌtʃmən].

**Dutchwoman** ['dʌtʃwʊmən] *n* holandesa.
  ① *pl* Dutchwomen ['dʌtʃwɪmɪn].

**duty** ['dju:tɪ] *n* **1** *(obligation)* deber *m*, obligación *f*: *I feel it's my duty to go* creo que es mi obligación ir. **2** *(task)* función *f*, cometido: *her duties include dealing with the public* sus funciones incluyen atender al público. **3** *(service)* guardia, servicio. **4** *(tax)* impuesto. LOC **to be off duty 1** *(doctor, nurse, etc)* no estar de guardia. **2** *(police, firefighter, etc)* no estar de servicio. I **to be on duty 1** *(doctor, nurse, etc)* estar de guardia. **2** *(police, firefighter)* estar de servicio. COMP **customs duties** derechos *mpl* de aduana, aranceles *mpl*.
  ① *pl* duties.

**duty-free** ['dju:tɪfri:] *adj & adv* libre de impuestos. COMP **duty-free shop** duty-free *m*, tienda libre de impuestos.

**duvet** ['du:veɪ] *n* GB edredón *m*. COMP **duvet cover** funda de edredón.

**DVD** ['di:vi:'di:] *n* (Digital Video Disc) DVD *m*. COMP **DVD player** lector *m* de DVD.

**dwarf** [dwɔ:f] *n* enano,-a.
  ① *pl* dwarfs o dwarves [dwɔ:z].
  ▶ *adj* enano,-a.

**dwell** [dwel] *vi fml* habitar, vivir.
  ① *pt & pp* dwelt [dwelt].

**dweller** ['dwelər] *n* habitante *mf*.

**dwelling** ['dwelɪŋ] *n fml* morada.

**dwelt** [dwelt] *pt & pp →* **dwell**.

**dye** [daɪ] *n* tinte *m*, tintura, colorante *m*.
  ▶ *vt* teñir.

**dying** ['daɪɪŋ] *adj* moribundo,-a.

**dyke** [daɪk] *n (bank)* dique *m*, barrera; *(causeway)* terraplén *m*.

**dynamic** [daɪ'næmɪk] *adj* dinámico,-a.

**dynamics** [daɪ'næmɪks] *n* dinámica.

**dynamite** ['daɪnəmaɪt] *n* dinamita.

**dynamo** ['daɪnəməʊ] *n* dinamo *f*.
  ① *pl* dynamos.

**dynasty** ['dɪnəstɪ] *n* dinastía.
  ① *pl* dynasties.

**dyne** [daɪn] *n* dina.

**dysentery** ['dɪsªntrɪ] *n* disentería.

**dyslexia** [dɪs'leksɪə] *n* dislexia.

**dyslexic** [dɪs'leksɪk] *adj* disléxico,-a.

**dystrophy** ['dɪstrəfɪ] *n* distrofia.

# E

**E, e** [i:] *n* **1** *(the letter)* E, e *f*. **2** MUS mi *m*.

**each** [i:tʃ] *adj* cada: *each day* cada día, todos los días.
▶ *pron* cada uno,-a: *they each have their own car* cada uno tiene su coche.
▶ *adv* cada uno,-a: *apples cost 15p each* las manzanas cuestan 15 peniques la pieza.

✎ Each y every tienen significados muy similares. Each se emplea cuando se considera cada cosa por separado. Every, cuando se considera cada cosa en función del todo del que forma parte.

**eager** [ˈiːɡəʳ] *adj (anxious)* ávido,-a (to, de), ansioso,-a (to, de); *(desirous)* deseoso,-a (to, de).

**eagle** [ˈiːɡəl] *n* **1** *(bird)* águila. **2** *(in golf)* eagle *m*.

**eaglet** [ˈiːɡlət] *n* aguilucho.

**ear¹** [ɪəʳ] *n* **1** ANAT oreja. **2** *(sense)* oído.
COMP **ear canal** conducto auditivo. ▮ **ear flap** orejera. ▮ **ear lobe** lóbulo. ▮ **ear, nose and throat specialist** otorrinolaringólogo,-a.

**ear²** [ɪəʳ] *n (of cereal)* espiga.

**earache** [ˈɪəreɪk] *n* dolor *m* de oídos.

**eardrum** [ˈɪədrʌm] *n* tímpano.

**earflap** [ˈɪəflæp] *n* orejera.

**earl** [ɜːl] *n* conde *m*.

**early** [ˈɜːlɪ] *adj* **1** *(before expected)* temprano,-a, pronto,-a: *we were early* llegamos temprano. **2** *(initial)* primero,-a: *take the early train* coge el primer tren de la mañana. **3** *(near beginning)*: *in the early 1960's* a principios de los sesenta.
① *comp* **earlier**, *superl* **earliest**.
▶ *adv* **1** *(before expected)* temprano, pronto; *(soon)* pronto: *she got up early* se levantó temprano. **2** *(in good time)* con tiempo, con anticipación: *we got there early to get a good seat* llegamos con tiempo para coger buen sitio.

**earn** [ɜːn] *vt* ganar, ganarse: *how much do you earn a month?* ¿cuánto ganas al mes?

✎ Cuando se habla de dinero, la diferencia entre earn y win (ambos, 'ganar') es que earn se refiere al dinero que se gana trabajando y win al que se obtiene por azar, como en la lotería.

**earner** [ˈɜːnəʳ] *n* **1** *(person)* persona que gana dinero: *I'm the only earner in the family* soy el único de la familia que gana un sueldo. **2** *(thing)* cosa rentable.

**earnest** [ˈɜːnɪst] *adj* serio,-a, formal.

**earnings** [ˈɜːnɪŋz] *n pl* **1** *(personal)* ingresos mpl. **2** *(of company)* ganancias fpl.

**earphones** [ˈɪəfəʊnz] *n pl* auriculares mpl.

**earplug** [ˈɪəplʌg] *n* tapón *m* para los oídos.

**earring** [ˈɪərɪŋ] *n* pendiente *m*.

**earth** [ɜːθ] *n* **1** *(gen)* tierra. **2** GB toma de tierra, tierra. **3** GB *(of fox, badger)* madriguera.

✎ Cuando se refiere al planeta Tierra se suele escribir con mayúscula: Earth.

**earthen** [ˈɜːðən] *adj* **1** *(of earth)* de tierra. **2** *(of baked clay)* de barro, de arcilla.

**earthquake** [ˈɜːθkweɪk] *n* terremoto.

**earthworm** [ˈɜːθwɜːm] *n* lombriz *f*.

**earwax** [ˈɪəwæks] *n* cerumen *m*, cera.

**earwig** [ˈɪəwɪg] *n* tijereta.

**ease** [iːz] *n* **1** *(lack of difficulty)* facilidad *f*. **2** *(natural manner)* soltura, naturalidad *f*. **3** *(freedom from pain)* alivio. **4** *(leisure, affluence)* comodidad *f*, desahogo.

▶ vt **1** *(relieve, alleviate)* aliviar (**of**, de), calmar. **2** *(improve)* mejorar, facilitar; *(make easier)* facilitar.

▶ vi **1** *(pain)* aliviarse, calmarse; *(tension, etc)* disminuir. **2** *(become easier)* mejorar.

◆ **to ease off / ease up** vi **1** *(pain)* aliviarse, calmarse; *(tension, etc)* disminuir; *(rain)* amainar. **2** *(slow down)* ir más despacio.

◆ **to ease up on** vt insep fam *(go easy, be more moderate)* aflojar, no pasarse con.

**easel** ['iːzəl] *n* caballete *m*.

**easily** ['iːzɪlɪ] *adv* **1** *(without difficulty)* fácilmente, con facilidad. **2** *(by far)* con mucho; *(without doubt)* sin duda.

**east** [iːst] *adj (gen)* este, oriental; *(wind)* del este.
▶ *adv* hacia el este.
▶ *n* este *m*.
▶ *n* **the East** *(Asia)* Oriente *m*; *(Eastern Europe)* el Este *m*.

**Easter** ['iːstəʳ] *n* **1** REL Pascua (de Resurrección). **2** *(holiday)* Semana Santa.

**easterly** ['iːstəlɪ] *adj* **1** *(to the east)* al este, hacia el este. **2** *(from the east)* del este.
▶ *n* viento del este.
ⓘ *pl* **easterlies**.

**eastern** ['iːstən] *adj* oriental, del este.

**eastward** ['iːstwəd] *adj* hacia el este.

**eastwards** ['iːstwədz] *adv* hacia el este.

**easy** ['iːzɪ] *adj* **1** *(not difficult)* fácil, sencillo. **2** *(comfortable)* cómodo,-a, holgado,-a. **3** *(unworried, relaxed)* tranquilo,-a.
ⓘ *comp* **easier**, *superl* **easiest**.
▶ *adv* con cuidado, con calma.

**easy-going** [iːzɪ'ɡəʊɪŋ] *adj (relaxed)* tranquilo,-a; *(easy to please)* fácil de complacer, poco exigente.

**eat** [iːt] *vt* comer.
▶ *vi* comer.
◆ **to eat away** vt sep *(mice)* roer; *(termites)* carcomer; *(acid)* corroer.
◆ **to eat out** vi *(lunch)* comer fuera; *(dinner)* cenar fuera.
◆ **to eat up** vt sep **1** *(finish food)* comerse: *eat it all up!* ¡cómetelo todo!. **2** *(consume)* consumir, tragar, devorar.
ⓘ *pt* **ate** [et, eɪt], *pp* **eaten** ['iːtən].

**eaten** ['iːtən] *pp* → **eat**.

**eavesdrop** ['iːvzdrɒp] *vi* escuchar a escondidas (**on**, -).
ⓘ *pt & pp* **eavesdropped**, *ger* **eavesdropping**.

**ebb** [eb] *n* reflujo.
▶ *vi* **1** *(water)* bajar. **2** *fig* disminuir.

**ebonite** ['ebənaɪt] *n* ebonita.

**ebony** ['ebənɪ] *n* ébano.

**eccentric** [ɪk'sentrɪk] *adj* excéntrico,-a.
▶ *n (person)* excéntrico,-a.

**echinoderm** [ɪ'kaɪnəʊdɜːm] *n* equinodermo.

**echo** ['ekəʊ] *n* eco.
ⓘ *pl* **echoes**.
▶ *vt* **1** repetir (back, -). **2** *fig (words)* repetir, imitar; *(opinions)* hacerse eco de.

**eclectic** [ɪ'klektɪk] *adj fml* ecléctico,-a.
▶ *n* ecléctico,-a.

**eclipse** [ɪ'klɪps] *n* eclipse *m*.
▶ *vt* eclipsar.

**ecofriendly** [ekəʊ'frendlɪ] *adj* que no perjudica el medio ambiente.

**ecological** [iːkə'lɒdʒɪkəl] *adj* ecológico,-a. COMP **ecological footprint** huella ecológica.

**ecologist** [ɪ'kɒlədʒɪst] *n* ecologista *mf*.

**ecology** [ɪ'kɒlədʒɪ] *n* ecología.

**economic** [ekə'nɒmɪk, iːkə'nɒmɪk] *adj* **1** *(gen)* económico,-a. **2** *(profitable)* rentable.

**economically** [ekə'nɒmɪklɪ, iːkə'nɒmɪklɪ] *adv* económicamente: *economically speaking* en términos económicos.

**economics** [ekə'nɒmɪks, iːkə'nɒmɪks] *n* **1** *(science)* economía. **2** EDUC económicas *fpl*, ciencias *fpl* económicas.

**economist** [ɪ'kɒnəmɪst] *n* economista *mf*.

**economize** [ɪ'kɒnəmaɪz] *vi* economizar (on, en), ahorrar (on, en).

**economy** [ɪ'kɒnəmɪ] *n* **1** *(saving)* economía, ahorro. **2** *(science)* economía.
ⓘ *pl* **economies**.

**ecosystem** ['iːkəʊsɪstəm] *n* ecosistema *m*.

**Ecuador** ['ekwədɔːʳ] *n* Ecuador *m*.

**Ecuadorian** [ekwə'dɔːrɪən] *adj* ecuatoriano,-a.
▶ *n* ecuatoriano,-a.

**eczema** ['eksɪmə] *n* eccema *m*.

**edema** [ɪ'diːmə] *n* US → **oedema**.

**Eden** ['iːdən] *n* el Edén *m*.

**edge** [edʒ] *n* **1** *(of cliff, wood, etc)* borde *m*. **2** *(of coin, step, etc)* canto. **3** *(of knife)* filo. **4** *(of water)* orilla. **5** *(of town)* afueras *fpl*. **6** *(of paper)* margen *m*.
▶ *vt* **1** *(supply with border)* bordear. **2** SEW ribetear.
◆ **to edge away** *vi* alejarse poco a poco.
◆ **to edge forward** *vi* avanzar lentamente, avanzar poco a poco.

**edible** ['edɪbəl] *adj* comestible.

**edict** ['iːdɪkt] *n* **1** edicto. **2** JUR decreto.

**edit** ['edɪt] *vt* **1** *(prepare for printing)* preparar para la imprenta. **2** *(correct)* corregir; *(put together)* editar. **3** *(run newspaper, etc)* dirigir. **4** *(film, programme)* montar, editar.
◆ **to edit out** *vt sep* cortar.

**edition** [ɪ'dɪʃən] *n* edición *f*.

**editor** ['edɪtər] *n* **1** *(of book)* editor,-ra; *(writer)* redactor,-ra; *(proofreader)* corrector,-ra. **2** *(of newspaper, etc)* director,-ra. **3** *(of film, programme)* montador,-ra.

**editorial** [edɪ'tɔːrɪəl] *adj* editorial.
▶ *n* editorial *m*. COMP **editorial staff** redacción *f*.

**educate** ['edjʊkeɪt] *vt* educar.

**educated** ['edjʊkeɪtɪd] *adj* culto,-a, cultivado,-a.

☒ Educated no significa 'educado (de buenos modales)', que se traduce por polite.

**education** [edjʊ'keɪʃən] *n* **1** *(system of teaching)* educación *f*, enseñanza. **2** *(training)* formación *f*, preparación *f*. **3** *(acquisition of knowledge)* estudios *mpl*, formación *f* académica. **4** *(theory of teaching)* pedagogía. **5** *(knowledge, culture)* cultura.

☒ Education no significa 'educación (buenos modales)', que se traduce por manners.

**educational** [edjʊ'keɪʃənəl] *adj* educativo,-a.

**eel** [iːl] *n* anguila.

**eerie** ['ɪərɪ] *adj* misterioso,-a.

**effect** [ɪ'fekt] *n* efecto.
▶ *vt fml* efectuar, provocar.
▶ *n pl* **effects** *(property)* efectos *mpl*.

**effective** [ɪ'fektɪv] *adj* **1** *(successful)* eficaz. **2** *(real, actual)* efectivo,-a. **3** *(operative)* vigente. **4** *(impressive)* impresionante; *(striking)* llamativo,-a.

**effervescent** [efə'vesənt] *adj* efervescente.

**efficiency** [ɪ'fɪʃənsɪ] *n* **1** *(of person)* eficiencia, competencia. **2** *(of system, product)* eficacia. **3** *(of machine)* rendimiento.

**efficient** [ɪ'fɪʃənt] *adj* **1** *(person)* eficiente, competente. **2** *(system, product)* eficaz. **3** *(machine)* de buen rendimiento.

**effigy** ['efɪdʒɪ] *n* efigie *f*.
① *pl* **effigies**.

**effort** ['efət] *n* **1** *(exertion)* esfuerzo. **2** *(attempt, struggle)* intento, tentativa. **3** *(achievement)* obra.

**egg¹** [eg] *n* **1** *(laid by birds, etc)* huevo. **2** BIOL *(ovum)* óvulo. COMP **boiled egg** huevo pasado por agua.

**egg²** [eg] *vt* **to egg on** animar, incitar.

**eggplant** ['egplɑːnt] *n* US berenjena.

**eggshell** ['egʃel] *n* cáscara de huevo.

**ego** ['iːgəʊ] *n* ego.
① *pl* **egos**.

**egocentric** [iːgəʊ'sentrɪk] *adj* egocéntrico,-a.

**egoism** ['iːgəʊɪzəm] *n* egoísmo.

**egoist** ['iːgəʊɪst] *n* egoísta *mf*.

**Egypt** ['iːdʒɪpt] *n* Egipto.

**Egyptian** [ɪ'dʒɪpʃən] *adj* egipcio,-a.
▶ *n* **1** *(person)* egipcio,-a. **2** *(language)* egipcio.

**eider** ['aɪdər] [also **eider duck**] *n* eider *m*.

**eiderdown** ['aɪdədaʊn] *n* edredón *m*.

**eight** [eɪt] *adj* ocho.
▶ *n* ocho.

✎ Consulta también six.

**eighteen** [eɪ'tiːn] *adj* dieciocho.
▶ *n* dieciocho.

✎ Consulta también six.

**eighteenth** [eɪ'tiːnθ] *adj* decimoctavo,-a.
▶ *adv* en decimoctavo lugar.

▶ *n* **1** *(in series)* decimoctavo,-a. **2** *(fraction)* decimoctavo; *(one part)* decimoctava parte *f*.

✎ Consulta también sixth.

**eighth** [eɪtθ] *adj* octavo,-a.
▶ *adv* en octavo lugar.
▶ *n* **1** *(in series)* octavo,-a. **2** *(fraction)* octavo; *(one part)* octava parte *f*.

✎ Consulta también sixth.

**eightieth** [ˈeɪtɪɪθ] *adj* octogésimo,-a.
▶ *adv* en octogésimo lugar.
▶ *n* **1** *(in series)* octogésimo,-a. **2** *(fraction)* octogésimo; *(one part)* octogésima parte *f*.

✎ Consulta también sixtieth.

**eighty** [ˈeɪtɪ] *adj* ochenta.
▶ *n* ochenta.

✎ Consulta también sixty.

**either** [ˈaɪðəʳ, ˈiːðəʳ] *pron* **1** *(affirmative)* cualquiera: *either of them* cualquiera de los dos. **2** *(negative)* ni el uno ni el otro, ni la una ni la otra, ninguno de los dos, ninguna de las dos: *I can't stand either* no aguanto ni el uno ni el otro.
▶ *adj* **1** cualquier. **2** *(both)* cada, los dos, las dos, ambos,-as. **3** *(neither)* ninguno de los dos, ninguna de las dos.
▶ *conj* **1** *(affirmative)* o: *he'll arrive either today or tomorrow* llegará u hoy o mañana. **2** *(negative)* ni: *I didn't go to either the wedding or the party* no fui ni a la boda ni a la fiesta.
▶ *adv* *(after negative)* tampoco: *Ann didn't come either* tampoco vino Ann.

**ejaculation** [ɪdʒækʊˈleɪʃən] *n* **1** *(ejection)* eyaculación *f*. **2** *(exclamation)* exclamación *f*.

**eject** [ɪˈdʒekt] *vt* expulsar, echar.
▶ *vi* AV eyectar(se).

**ejection** [ɪˈdʒekʃən] *n* **1** *(gen)* expulsión *f*. **2** *(from plane)* eyección *f*.

**elaborate** [*(adj)* ɪˈlæbərət; *(vb)* ɪˈlæbəreɪt] *adj* **1** *(detailed, extensive)* detallado,-a. **2** *(ornate, intricate)* muy trabajado,-a, esmerado,-a. **3** *(complex, intricate)* complicado,-a.
▶ *vt* *(work out in detail, refine)* elaborar.

▶ *vi* *(discuss in detail)* explicar detalladamente; *(expand)* ampliar, dar más detalles.

**elaboration** [ɪlæbəˈreɪʃən] *n* **1** *(working out in detail)* elaboración *f*. **2** *(additional detail)* complicación *f*, detalle *m*.

**elastic** [ɪˈlæstɪk] *adj* elástico,-a. COMP **elastic band** goma elástica.

**elasticity** [ɪlæˈstɪsətɪ] *n* elasticidad *f*.

**Elastoplast®** [ɪˈlæstəplɑːst] *n* tirita®.

**elbow** [ˈelbəʊ] *n* **1** ANAT codo. **2** *(bend)* recodo.

**elder** [ˈeldəʳ] *adj* mayor.
▶ *n* **1** mayor *m*. **2** REL anciano,-a.

**elderly** [ˈeldəlɪ] *adj* mayor, anciano,-a.
▶ *n* **the elderly** los ancianos *mpl*.

**eldest** [ˈeldɪst] *adj* mayor.
▶ *n* el mayor, la mayor.

**elect** [ɪˈlekt] *adj* electo,-a.
▶ *vt* **1** *(vote for)* elegir. **2** *(choose, decide)* decidir.

**election** [ɪˈlekʃən] *n* elección *f*.
▶ *adj* electoral.

**elector** [ɪˈlektəʳ] *n* elector,-ra.

**electoral** [ɪˈlektərəl] *adj* electoral. COMP **electoral college** colegio electoral. ‖ **electoral roll / electoral register** censo electoral.

**electorate** [ɪˈlektərət] *n* electorado.

**electric** [ɪˈlektrɪk] *adj* eléctrico,-a.

**electrical** [ɪˈlektrɪkəl] *adj* eléctrico,-a.

**electrician** [ɪlekˈtrɪʃən] *n* electricista *mf*.

**electricity** [ɪlekˈtrɪsɪtɪ] *n* electricidad *f*.

**electrocute** [ɪˈlektrəkjuːt] *vt* electrocutar.

**electrode** [ɪˈlektrəʊd] *n* electrodo.

**electrolysis** [ɪlekˈtrɒləsɪs] *n* electrólisis *f*.

**electrolyte** [ɪˈlektrəlaɪt] *n* electrolito, electrólito.

**electromagnet** [ɪlektrəʊˈmægnɪt] *n* electroimán *m*.

**electromagnetism** [ɪlektrəʊˈmægnɪtɪzəm] *n* electromagnetismo.

**electromagnetic** [ɪlektrəʊmægˈnetɪk] *adj* electromagnético,-a.

**electron** [ɪˈlektrɒn] *n* electrón *m*. COMP **electron microscope** microscopio electrónico.

**electronic** [ɪlek'trɒnɪk] *adj* electrónico,-a.

**electronics** [ɪlek'trɒnɪks] *n (science, technology)* electrónica.
▸ *n pl (circuits and devices)* componentes *mpl* electrónicos.

**elegance** ['elɪɡəns] *n* elegancia.

**elegant** ['elɪɡənt] *adj* elegante.

**element** ['elɪmənt] *n* **1** CHEM elemento. **2** *(necessary part of a whole)* parte *f*, componente *m*. **3** ELEC resistencia. **4** *(group, section)* fracción *f*.
▸ *n pl* **elements 1***(weather)* los elementos *mpl*. **2***(basics)* rudimentos *mpl*.

**elementary** [elɪ'mentərɪ] *adj* **1** *(basic)* elemental, básico,-a. **2** *(easy)* fácil, sencillo,-a. COMP **elementary education** enseñanza primaria.

**elephant** ['elɪfənt] *n* elefante *m*. COMP **elephant seal** elefante *m* marino.

**elevate** ['elɪveɪt] *vt fml (raise)* elevar; *(promote)* ascender, promover.

**elevated** ['elɪveɪtɪd] *adj fml (fine, noble)* elevado,-a, noble.

**elevation** [elɪ'veɪʃən] *n* **1** *fml (gen)* elevación *f*. **2** *fml (in rank)* ascenso. **3** *(height)* altitud *f*, altura. **4** ARCH alzado.

**elevator** ['elɪveɪtəʳ] *n* **1** US ascensor *m*. **2** *(machine)* montacargas *m*.

**eleven** [ɪ'levən] *adj* once.
▸ *n* once *m*.

✎ Consulta también **six**.

**eleventh** [ɪ'levənθ] *adj* undécimo,-a.
▸ *adv* en undécimo lugar.
▸ *n* **1** *(in series)* undécimo,-a, onceno,-a. **2** *(fraction)* onceavo, undécimo; *(one part)* onceava parte *f*, undécima parte *f*.

✎ Consulta también **sixth**.

**elicit** [ɪ'lɪsɪt] *vt* **1** *fml (facts, information)* sonsacar, obtener. **2** *(reaction, response)* provocar.

**elide** [ɪ'laɪd] *vt* elidir.
▸ *vi* elidirse.

**eligible** ['elɪdʒəbəl] *adj* **1** *(qualified, suitable)* idóneo,-a, apto,-a. **2** *(desirable)* deseable.

**eliminate** [ɪ'lɪmɪneɪt] *vt* eliminar.

**elision** [ɪ'lɪʒən] *n* elisión *f*.

**elite** [eɪ'li:t] *n* elite *f*.
▸ *adj* exclusivo,-a, selecto,-a.

**elk** [elk] *n* alce *m*.

**ellipse** [ɪ'lɪps] *n* elipse *f*.

**ellipsis** [ɪ'lɪpsɪs] *n* elipsis *f*.
① *pl* **ellipses** [ɪ'lɪpsi:z].

**elliptic** [ɪ'lɪptɪk] *adj* elíptico,-a.

**elm** [elm] *n* olmo.

**elongated** ['i:lɒŋɡeɪtɪd] *adj* alargado,-a.

**eloquence** ['eləkwəns] *n* elocuencia.

**eloquent** ['eləkwənt] *adj* elocuente.

**else** [els] *adv* más, otro,-a: *anything else? ¿*algo más?*; where else have you been? ¿*en qué otro(s) sitio(s) has estado?

**elsewhere** [els'weəʳ] *adv* en otro sitio, en otra parte.

**elude** [ɪ'lu:d] *vt* **1** *(escape from)* escaparse de. **2** *(avoid)* eludir. **3** *(not remember)* no recordar, no acordarse; *(not understand)* no entenderse.

**elusive** [ɪ'lu:sɪv] *adj* **1** *(difficult to capture)* huidizo,-a, esquivo,-a. **2** *(difficult to remember)* difícil de recordar; *(difficult to understand)* difícil de entender.

**e-mail** ['i:meɪl] *n* correo electrónico.

**emancipate** [ɪ'mænsɪpeɪt] *vt* emancipar.

**emancipation** [ɪmænsɪ'peɪʃən] *n* emancipación *f*.

**embankment** [ɪm'bæŋkmənt] *n* **1** *(wall, earth, etc)* terraplén *m*. **2** *(river bank)* dique *m*.

**embargo** [em'bɑ:ɡəʊ] *n* embargo.
① *pl* **embargoes**.
▸ *vt* **1** *(prohibit)* prohibir. **2** *(seize)* embargar.
① *pt & pp* **embargoed**, *ger* **embargoing**.

**embark** [ɪm'bɑ:k] *vt* embarcar.
◆ **to embark on** *vt insep* emprender.

**embarrass** [ɪm'bærəs] *vt (make ashamed)* avergonzar, hacer pasar vergüenza a; *(make awkward)* desconcertar.

**embarrassed** [ɪm'bærəst] *adj (behaviour, action)* embarazoso,-a; *(person)* avergonzado,-a, molesto,-a.

☒ **Embarrassed** no significa 'embarazada', que se traduce por **pregnant**.

**embarrassing** [ɪmˈbærəsɪŋ] *adj* embarazoso,-a, violento,-a, desconcertante.

**embarrassment** [ɪmˈbærəsmənt] *n* **1** *(state)* vergüenza, desconcierto. **2** *(person, object)* vergüenza, estorbo. **3** *(event, situation)* disgusto, vergüenza.

**embassy** [ˈembəsɪ] *n* embajada.
ⓘ *pl* embassies.

**embed** [ɪmˈbed] *vt (jewels, stones)* incrustar; *(weapon, nails)* clavar (in, en).
ⓘ *pt & pp* embedded, *ger* embedding.

**embellish** [ɪmˈbelɪʃ] *vt* adornar, embellecer.

**ember** [ˈembəʳ] *n* brasa, ascua.

**emblem** [ˈembləm] *n* emblema *m*.

**emblematic** [embləˈmætɪk] *adj* emblemático,-a.

**emboss** [ɪmˈbɒs] *vt (leather, metal)* repujar; *(initials)* grabar en relieve.

**embrace** [ɪmˈbreɪs] *n* abrazo.
▶ *vt* **1** *(hug)* abrazar, dar un abrazo a. **2** *(include)* abarcar, incluir. **3** *fml (accept - opportunity, etc)* aprovechar; *(- offer)* aceptar. **4** *fml (adopt - religion, etc)* convertirse a; *(- new idea)* abrazar.

**embroidery** [ɪmˈbrɔɪdəəɪ] *n* SEW bordado.

**embryo** [ˈembrɪəʊ] *n* embrión *m*.
ⓘ *pl* embryos.
▶ *adj* embrionario,-a.

**emerald** [ˈemərəld] *n* esmeralda *f*.
▶ *adj* (de color) esmeralda.

**emerge** [ɪˈmɜːdʒ] *vi* **1** *(come out)* emerger, aparecer, salir. **2** *(become known)* resultar.

**emergence** [ɪˈmɜːdʒəns] *n* aparición *f*.

**emergency** [ɪˈmɜːdʒənsɪ] *n* **1** emergencia. **2** MED urgencia.
ⓘ *pl* emergencies.
▶ *adj* de emergencia, de urgencia.

**emergent** [ɪˈmɜːdʒənt] *adj* **1** *(emerging)* emergente. **2** *(of countries, nations)* en vías de desarrollo.

**emery** [ˈemərɪ] *n* esmeril *m*.

**emigrant** [ˈemɪgrənt] *n* emigrante *mf*.

**emigrate** [ˈemɪgreɪt] *vi* emigrar.

**emigration** [emɪˈgreɪʃən] *n* emigración *f*.

**eminence** [ˈemɪnəns] *n* eminencia.

**eminent** [ˈemɪnənt] *adj* **1** *(of person)* eminente. **2** *(of qualities)* destacado,-a.

**emir** [eˈmɪəʳ] *n* emir *m*.

**emirate** [ˈemɪrət] *n* emirato. COMP
**United Arab Emirates** Emiratos *mpl* Árabes Unidos.

**emissary** [ˈemɪsərɪ] *n* emisario,-a.
ⓘ *pl* emissaries.

**emission** [ɪˈmɪʃən] *n* emisión *f*.

> ✖ Emission no significa 'emisión (de televisión)', que se traduce por programme.

**emit** [ɪˈmɪt] *vt (signal, heat, light, smoke)* emitir, producir; *(sound, noise)* producir; *(smell)* despedir; *(cry)* dar.
ⓘ *pt & pp* emitted, *ger* emitting.

**emoticon** [ɪˈmɒtɪkɒn] *n* COMPUT emoticón *m*, emoticono.

**emotion** [ɪˈməʊʃən] *n* **1** *(feeling)* sentimiento. **2** *(strong feeling)* emoción *f*.

**emotional** [ɪˈməʊʃənəl] *adj* **1** *(connected with feelings)* emocional, afectivo,-a. **2** *(moving)* conmovedor,-ra, emotivo,-a. **3** *(sensitive)* emotivo,-a, sentimental.

**emotive** [ɪˈməʊtɪv] *adj* emotivo,-a.

**emperor** [ˈempərəʳ] *n* emperador *m*.

**emphasis** [ˈemfəsɪs] *n* énfasis *m*.
ⓘ *pl* emphases [ˈemfəsiːs].

**emphasize** [ˈemfəsaɪz] *vt* enfatizar.

**emphatic** [emˈfætɪk] *adj* **1** *(forceful - tone, gesture)* enfático,-a, enérgico,-a. **2** *(insistent - refusal, rejection, assertion)* categórico,-a, rotundo,-a.

**empire** [ˈempaɪəʳ] *n* imperio: *the British Empire* el Imperio Británico.

**empirical** [emˈpɪrɪkəl] *adj* empírico,-a.

**employ** [ɪmˈplɔɪ] *n fml* empleo.
▶ *vt* **1** *(give work to)* emplear; *(appoint)* contratar. **2** *fml (make use of, use)* emplear, usar. **3** *(occupy)* ocupar.

**employed** [emˈplɔɪd] *adj* **1** *(in work)* empleado,-a. **2** *(busy)* ocupado,-a.

**employee** [emˈplɔɪiː, emplɔɪˈiː] *n* empleado,-a.

**employer** [emˈplɔɪəʳ] *n* **1** *(manager, boss)* empresario,-a; *(of domestic worker)* patrón,-ona. **2** *(company, organization)* empresa, organismo.

E

**employment** [em'plɔɪmənt] n **1** (work) trabajo; (availability of work) empleo. **2** (use) empleo, uso.

**empress** ['emprəs] n emperatriz f.

**empty** ['emptɪ] adj **1** (gen) vacío,-a; (place) desierto,-a; (house) desocupado,-a, deshabitado,-a; (seat, table, place) libre. **2** fam (hungry) hambriento,-a.
  ① comp **emptier**, superl **emptiest**.
  ▶ vt vaciar.
  ▶ n pl **empties** envases mpl, cascos mpl.

**emulsifier** [ɪ'mʌlsɪfaɪəʳ] n emulsionante m.

**emulsify** [ɪ'mʌlsɪfaɪ] vt emulsionar.
  ① pt & pp **emulsified**, ger **emulsifying**.

**emulsion** [ɪ'mʌlʃən] n emulsión f.

**enable** [ɪ'neɪbəl] vt permitir.

**enact** [ɪ'nækt] vt **1** (law) promulgar. **2** (play) representar.

**enamel** [ɪ'næməl] n esmalte m.
  ▶ vt esmaltar.
  ① pt & pp **enamelled** (US **enameled**), ger **enamelling** (US **enameling**).

**encephalic** [ensɪ'fælɪk] adj encefálico,-a.

**enchant** [ɪn'tʃɑːnt] vt **1** (delight) encantar, cautivar. **2** (cast spell on) hechizar.

**enchanted** [ɪn'tʃɑːntɪd] adj encantado,-a.

**enchanting** [ɪn'tʃɑːntɪŋ] adj encantador,-ra.

**enchantment** [ɪn'tʃɑːntmənt] n **1** (delight) encanto. **2** (spell) hechizo.

**encircle** [ɪn'sɜːkəl] vt rodear, cercar.

**enclitic** [en'klɪtɪk] adj enclítico,-a.

**enclose** [ɪn'kləʊz] vt **1** (surround) encerrar; (with wall or fence) cercar, rodear. **2** (include in letter) adjuntar.

**enclosure** [ɪn'kləʊʒəʳ] n **1** (land) cercado; (area) recinto. **2** (with letter) anexo, documento adjunto.

**encode** [ɪŋ'kəʊd] vt codificar.

**encore** ['ɒŋkɔːʳ] interj ¡otra!.
  ▶ n repetición f, bis m.

**encounter** [ɪn'kaʊntəʳ] n encuentro.
  ▶ vt (meet) encontrar, encontrarse con; (be faced with) tropezar con.

**encourage** [ɪn'kʌrɪdʒ] vt **1** (cheer, inspire) animar, alentar. **2** (develop, stimulate) fomentar, favorecer, estimular.

**encouragement** [ɪn'kʌrɪdʒmənt] n **1** (act) aliento, ánimo. **2** (development) fomento, estímulo.

**encrypt** [en'krɪpt] vt cifrar.

**encyclopaedia** [ensaɪklə'piːdɪə] n enciclopedia.

**encyclopedia** [ensaɪklə'piːdɪə] n enciclopedia.

**end** [end] n **1** (extremity - of rope) cabo; (- of street) final m; (- of table, sofa) extremo; (- of stick, tail) punta; (- of box) lado. **2** (final part, finish) fin m, final m. **3** (aim) objeto, objetivo, fin m. **4** (of cigarette) colilla.
  ▶ adj final, último,-a.
  ▶ vt **1** (conclude) acabar, terminar. **2** (stop) terminar, poner fin a, acabar con.
  ◆ **to end in** vi acabar en.
  ◆ **to end off** vt sep acabar.
  ◆ **to end up** vi acabar, terminar.

**endanger** [ɪn'deɪndʒəʳ] vt poner en peligro.

**endangered** [ɪn'deɪndʒəd] adj en peligro. COMP **endangered species** especie f en peligro (de extinción).

**endeavor** [ɪn'devəʳ] n US → endeavour.

**endeavour** [ɪn'devəʳ] n fml esfuerzo, empeño.
  ▶ vi esforzarse, intentar, procurar.

**endemic** [en'demɪk] adj endémico,-a.

**ending** ['endɪŋ] n **1** final m, conclusión f, desenlace m. **2** LING terminación f.

**endive** ['endaɪv] n **1** GB escarola. **2** US endibia.

**endless** ['endləs] adj interminable.

**endocarp** ['endəʊkɑːp] n endocarpio.

**endocrine** ['endəʊkrɪn] adj endocrino,-a. COMP **endocrine gland** glándula endocrina.

**endorse** [ɪn'dɔːs] vt **1** (of cheque, etc) endosar. **2** (approve) aprobar, apoyar.

**endow** [ɪn'daʊ] vt **1** (bless) dotar. **2** (give money) dotar (de fondos).

**endurance** [ɪn'djʊərəns] n resistencia, aguante m.
  ▶ adj de resistencia.

**endure** [ɪn'djʊəʳ] vt soportar, aguantar.

▶ vi *(continue to exist, survive)* durar.
**enemy** ['enəmɪ] n enemigo,-a.
ⓘ pl enemies.
▶ adj enemigo,-a.
**energetic** [enə'dʒetɪk] adj enérgico,-a.
**energy** ['enədʒɪ] n energía.
▶ n pl **energies** *(efforts)* energías fpl, fuerzas fpl.
ⓘ pl energies.
**enforce** [ɪn'fɔːs] vt **1** *(force to obey)* hacer cumplir. **2** *(impose)* imponer.
**engage** [ɪn'geɪdʒ] vt **1** *(hire)* contratar. **2** *(take up, occupy)* ocupar, entretener. **3** *(attract)* llamar, atraer, captar. **5** AUTO *(gear)* engranar, meter; *(clutch)* apretar. **6** TECH engranar con.
**engaged** [ɪn'geɪdʒd] adj **1** *(to be married)* prometido,-a. **2** *(busy)* ocupado,-a.
**engagement** [ɪn'geɪdʒmənt] n **1** *(to be married)* petición f de mano; *(period)* noviazgo. **2** *(appointment)* compromiso, cita. **3** MIL combate m. **4** *(employment)* contrato, empleo.
**engaging** [ɪn'geɪdʒɪŋ] adj atractivo,-a.
**engine** ['endʒɪn] n **1** motor m. **2** *(of train)* máquina, locomotora. COMP **engine driver** maquinista mf.
**engineer** [endʒɪ'nɪər] n **1** *(graduate)* ingeniero,-a; *(technician)* técnico,-a. **2** US maquinista mf.
▶ vt *(contrive)* maquinar, tramar, urdir.
**engineering** [endʒɪ'nɪərɪŋ] n ingeniería.
**England** ['ɪŋglənd] n Inglaterra.
**English** ['ɪŋglɪʃ] adj inglés,-esa.
▶ n *(language)* inglés m.
**Englishman** ['ɪŋglɪʃmən] n inglés m.
ⓘ pl Englishmen.
**English-speaking** ['ɪŋglɪʃspiːkɪŋ] adj de habla inglesa.
**Englishwoman** ['ɪŋglɪʃwumən] n inglesa.
ⓘ pl Englishwomen ['ɪŋglɪʃwɪmɪn].
**engrave** [ɪn'greɪv] vt grabar.
**engrossed** [ɪn'grəust] adj absorto,-a (in, en).
**engulf** [ɪn'gʌlf] vt envolver.
**enhance** [ɪn'hɑːns] vt **1** *(beauty, taste)* realzar; *(quality, chances)* mejorar; *(power, value)* aumentar. **2** COMPUT procesar.

**enigma** [ɪ'nɪgmə] n enigma m.
**enigmatic** [enɪg'mætɪk] adj enigmático,-a.
**enjoy** [ɪn'dʒɔɪ] vt **1** *(get pleasure from)* disfrutar de; *(like)* gustarle a uno. **2** *(benefit from)* gozar de.
**enjoyment** [ɪn'dʒɔɪmənt] n placer m.
**enlarge** [ɪn'lɑːdʒ] vt *(gen)* extender, aumentar; *(photograph)* ampliar.
**enlargement** [ɪn'lɑːdʒmənt] n **1** *(photograph)* ampliación f. **2** extensión f.
**enlighten** [ɪn'laɪtən] vt **1** *(free from ignorance)* iluminar, ilustrar. **2** *(inform)* informar, instruir.
**enlightenment** [ɪn'laɪtənmənt] n **1** fml *(act)* aclaración f, explicación f. **2** *(liberalism)* tolerancia.
▶ n the Enlightenment la Ilustración f.
**enliven** [ɪn'laɪvən] vt avivar, animar.
**enormous** [ɪ'nɔːməs] adj enorme.
**enough** [ɪ'nʌf] adj bastante, suficiente.
▶ adv bastante, suficientemente.
**enquire** [ɪŋ'kwaɪər] vt preguntar.
▶ vi **1** preguntar, informarse. **2** JUR investigar (into, -).
**enquiry** [ɪŋ'kwaɪərɪ] n **1** pregunta. **2** JUR investigación f.
ⓘ pl enquiries.
**enrage** [ɪn'reɪdʒ] vt enfurecer.
**enrich** [ɪn'rɪtʃ] vt enriquecer.
**enrol** [ɪn'rəul] vt matricular, inscribir.
▶ vi matricularse, inscribirse.
ⓘ pt & pp enrolled, ger enrolling.
**enroll** [ɪn'rəul] n US → enrol.
**enrollment** [ɪn'rəulmənt] n US → enrolment.
**enrolment** [ɪn'rəulmənt] n matrícula, inscripción f.
**ensemble** [ɒn'sɒmbəl] n conjunto.
**ensue** [ɪn'sjuː] vi **1** *(follow)* seguir. **2** *(result)* resultar (from, de).
**ensure** [ɪn'ʃuər] vt **1** *(make sure)* asegurarse. **2** *(assure)* asegurar.
**entail** [ɪn'teɪl] vt *(involve, mean)* suponer, implicar; *(make necessary)* ocasionar.
**entangle** [ɪn'tæŋgəl] vt enredar.
**enter** ['entər] vt **1** *(gen)* entrar en. **3** *(participate)* participar en; *(register)* inscribirse en. **4** *(write down, record)* anotar, apuntar.

**enterprise** ['entəpraɪz] n **1** *(venture)* empresa, proyecto. **2** *(initiative)* iniciativa. **3** *(firm)* empresa.

**entertain** [entə'teɪn] vt **1** *(amuse)* entretener, divertir. **2** *(suggestion, etc)* considerar, tener en cuenta; *(doubts, etc)* abrigar. **3** *(invite)* recibir, invitar.
▶ vi *(act as host)* tener invitados.

X To entertain no significa 'entretener (distraer)', que se traduce por to occupy.

**entertaining** [entə'teɪnɪŋ] adj divertido,-a, entretenido,-a.

**entertainment** [entə'teɪnmənt] n **1** *(amusement)* entretenimiento, diversión f. **2** THEAT espectáculo, función f.

**enthral** [ɪn'θrɔːl] vt cautivar.
ⓘ pt & pp enthralled, ger enthralling.

**enthrall** [ɪn'θrɔːl] vt US → enrol.

**enthrone** [ɪn'θrəʊn] vt entronizar.

**enthusiasm** [ɪn'θjuːzɪæzəm] n entusiasmo (about/for, por).

**enthusiast** [ɪn'θjuːzɪæst] n entusiasta mf.

**enthusiastic** [ɪnθjuːzɪ'æstɪk] adj **1** *(reaction)* entusiástico,-a, caluroso,-a. **2** *(person)* entusiasta.

**entice** [ɪn'taɪs] vt persuadir, tentar.

**entire** [ɪn'taɪəʳ] adj entero,-a.

**entitle** [ɪn'taɪtəl] vt **1** *(give right to)* dar derecho (to, a). **2** *(book, etc)* titular.

**entity** ['entɪtɪ] n entidad f.
ⓘ pl entities.

**entourage** [ɒntʊ'rɑːʒ] n séquito.

**entrails** ['entreɪlz] n pl entrañas fpl, tripas fpl, vísceras fpl.

**entrance** ['entrəns] n **1** *(gen)* entrada; *(door, gate)* puerta; *(hall)* vestíbulo, hall m. **2** *(admission)* entrada, admisión f; *(to school, university)* ingreso.

**entrant** ['entrənt] n *(competitor)* participante mf; *(applicant)* aspirante mf.

**entrepreneur** [ɒntrəprə'nɜːʳ] n *(business person)* empresario,-a.

**entrust** [ɪn'trʌst] vt confiar.

**entry** ['entrɪ] n **1** *(entrance)* entrada; *(joining)* ingreso. **2** *(right to enter)* admisión f. **3** US *(door, gate)* puerta. **4** *(item in accounts)* asiento; *(in diary)* anotación f; *(in diction-*

*ary)* entrada. **5** *(in competition - participant)* participante mf.
ⓘ pl entries.

**entryphone** ['entrɪfəʊn] n portero automático.

**enumerate** [ɪ'njuːməreɪt] vt enumerar.

**enunciate** [ɪ'nʌnsɪeɪt] vt **1** *(pronounce)* pronunciar, articular. **2** *(express)* expresar, enunciar.

**envelop** [ɪn'veləp] vt envolver.

**envelope** ['envələʊp] n *(of letter)* sobre m; *(covering)* envoltura.

**enviable** ['envɪəbəl] adj envidiable.

**envious** ['envɪəs] adj *(person)* envidioso,-a; *(look, etc)* de envidia.

**environment** [ɪn'vaɪrənmənt] n **1** *(ecology)* medio ambiente m: we need to protect the environment hemos de proteger el medio ambiente. **2** *(surroundings)* ambiente m, entorno; *(habitat)* hábitat m.

**environmental** [ɪnvaɪərən'mentəl] adj **1** *(ecological)* del medio ambiente, ambiental: environmental pollution contaminación del medio ambiente. **2** *(of surroundings)* ambiental.

**environs** [ɪn'vaɪərənz] n pl alrededores mpl.

**envisage** [ɪn'vɪzɪdʒ] vt **1** *(foresee)* prever. **2** *(imagine)* imaginarse.

**envoy** ['envɔɪ] n enviado,-a.

**envy** ['envɪ] n envidia (at/of, de).
ⓘ pl envies.
▶ vt envidiar, tener envidia de.
ⓘ pt & pp envied, ger envying.

**enzyme** ['enzaɪm] n enzima m & f.

**ephemeral** [ɪ'femərəl] adj efímero,-a.

**epic** ['epɪk] adj épico,-a.

**epicentre** ['epɪsentəʳ] n epicentro.

**epidemic** [epɪ'demɪk] n epidemia.
▶ adj epidémico,-a.

**epidermis** [epɪ'dɜːmɪs] n epidermis f.

**epiglottis** [epɪ'glɒtɪs] n epiglotis f.

**epigraph** ['epɪgrɑːf] n epígrafe m.

**epilepsy** ['epɪlepsɪ] n epilepsia.

**epileptic** [epɪ'leptɪk] adj epiléptico,-a.
▶ n epiléptico,-a.

**epilogue** ['epɪlɒg] n epílogo.

**episode** ['epɪsəʊd] n **1** episodio. **2** *(series)* capítulo.

**epitaph** ['epɪtɑːf] *n* epitafio.

**epithelial** [epɪˈθiːlɪəl] *adj* epitelial.

**epithet** ['epɪθet] *n* epíteto.

**epoch** ['iːpɒk] *n* época.

**equal** ['iːkwəl] *adj* **1** *(identical)* igual; *(same)* mismo,-a. **2** *(capable)* capaz.
▸ *n* igual *mf*.
▸ *vt* **1** MATH ser igual a, equivaler a. **2** *(match)* igualar.

**equality** [ɪˈkwɒlɪtɪ] *n* igualdad *f*.
ⓘ *pl* equalities.

**equalize** ['iːkwəlaɪz] *vi* SP empatar.
▸ *vt* igualar.

**equanimity** [ekwəˈnɪmɪtɪ] *n* ecuanimidad *f*.

**equate** [ɪˈkweɪt] *vt* equiparar (with, con), comparar (with, con).

**equation** [ɪˈkweɪʒən] *n* **1** MATH ecuación *f*. **2** *fml (relationship)* relación *f*.
COMP **simple equation** ecuación *f* de primer grado.

**equator** [ɪˈkweɪtər] *n* ecuador *m*.

**equestrian** [ɪˈkwestrɪən] *adj* ecuestre.
▸ *n* *(man)* jinete *m*; *(woman)* amazona.

**equidistant** [iːkwɪˈdɪstənt] *adj* equidistante.

**equilateral** [iːkwɪˈlætərəl] *adj* equilátero,-a. COMP **equilateral triangle** triángulo equilátero.

**equilibrium** [iːkwɪˈlɪbrɪəm] *n* equilibrio.

**equine** ['ekwaɪn] *adj* equino,-a.

**equinox** ['iːkwɪnɒks] *n* equinoccio.

**equip** [ɪˈkwɪp] *vt* **1** *(fit out, supply)* equipar (with, con), proveer (with, de). **2** *(prepare)* preparar (for/to, para).
ⓘ *pt & pp* equipped, *ger* equipping.

**equipment** [ɪˈkwɪpmənt] *n* **1** *(materials)* equipo, material *m*. **2** *(act of equipping)* equipamiento.

**equitable** ['ekwɪtəbəl] *adj fml* equitativo,-a.

**equivalence** [ɪˈkwɪvələns] *n* equivalencia.

**equivalent** [ɪˈkwɪvələnt] *adj* equivalente.
▸ *n* equivalente *m*.

**era** ['ɪərə] *n* era, época.

**eradicate** [ɪˈrædɪkeɪt] *vt* erradicar.

**eradication** [ɪrædɪˈkeɪʃən] *n* erradicación *f*.

**erase** [ɪˈreɪz] *vt* borrar.

**eraser** [ɪˈreɪzər] *n* goma de borrar.

**erect** [ɪˈrekt] *adj* **1** *(upright)* derecho,-a, erguido,-a. **2** ANAT erecto,-a.
▸ *vt (build)* erigir, levantar; *(put up - tent)* armar; *(- flagstaff)* izar.

**erection** [ɪˈrekʃən] *n* erección *f*.

**ergonomic** [ɜːgəˈnɒmɪk] *adj* ergonómico,-a.

**erode** [ɪˈrəʊd] *vt* **1** *(rock, soil)* erosionar. **2** *(metal)* corroer, desgastar.

**erosion** [ɪˈrəʊʒən] *n* **1** *(of rock, soil)* erosión *f*. **2** *(of metal)* corrosión *f*.

**erotic** [ɪˈrɒtɪk] *adj* erótico,-a.

**errand** ['erənd] *n* encargo, recado.

**error** ['erər] *n* error *m*, equivocación *f*.

**erupt** [ɪˈrʌpt] *vi* **1** *(volcano)* entrar en erupción. **2** *fig (war, violence, fire)* estallar. **3** MED *(rash, spots, etc)* brotar, salir; *(tooth)* salir.

**eruption** [ɪˈrʌpʃən] *n* **1** *(volcano)* erupción *f*. **2** *fig (war, anger)* estallido. **3** *(disease)* brote *m*, epidemia; *(rash, spots, etc)* erupción *f*.

**escalator** ['eskəleɪtər] *n* escalera mecánica.

**escalope** ['eskələp] *n* escalope.

**escapade** ['eskəpeɪd, eskəˈpeɪd] *n* aventura.

**escape** [ɪˈskeɪp] *n* **1** *(flight)* fuga, huida (from, de). **2** *(of gas)* fuga, escape *m*.
▸ *vi* **1** *(get free, get away)* escaparse, fugarse, huir. **2** *(gas, etc)* escapar.
▸ *vt* **1** *(avoid)* escapar a, librarse de. **2** *(be forgotten or unnoticed)* no recordar.

**escort** [*(n)* eˈskɔːt; *(vb)* ɪˈskɔːt] *n* **1** acompañante *mf*. MIL escolta.
▸ *vt* **1** acompañar: *I'll escort you home* te acompañaré a casa. **2** MIL escoltar.

**Eskimo** ['eskɪməʊ] *n* **1** *(person)* esquimal *mf*. **2** *(language)* esquimal *m*.
ⓘ *pl* Eskimos o Eskimo.
▸ *adj* esquimal.

**esophagus** [ɪˈsɒfəgəs] *n* US → **oesophagus**.

**esoteric** [esəʊˈterɪk] *adj* esotérico,-a.

**espadrille** [espəˈdrɪl] *n* alpargata.

**especial** [ɪˈspeʃəl] *adj* especial.

**especially** [ɪˈspeʃəlɪ] *adv* especialmente, sobre todo.

**espresso** [esˈpresəʊ] *n* café *m* exprés.
ⓘ *pl* espressos.

**essay** [ˈeseɪ] *n* **1** *(school)* redacción *f*; *(university)* trabajo. **2** *(literary)* ensayo. **3** *fml (attempt)* intento.
► *vt fml* intentar.

**essence** [ˈesəns] *n* esencia.

**essential** [ɪˈsenʃəl] *adj* esencial.
► *n (necessary thing)* necesidad *f* básica.
► *n pl* **essentials** lo esencial *m sing*, lo fundamental *m sing*.

**establish** [ɪˈstæblɪʃ] *vt* **1** *(gen)* establecer. **2** *(find out, determine)* determinar, averiguar.

**established** [ɪˈstæblɪʃt] *adj* **1** *(practice, custom)* consolidado,-a. **2** *(person - set up)* establecido,-a; *(- well known)* reconocido,-a. **3** *(fact)* comprobado,-a.

**establishment** [ɪˈstæblɪʃmənt] *n* **1** *(setting up)* establecimiento, fundación *f*. **2** *(premises)* establecimiento; *(business)* negocio. **3** *(staff)* plantilla, personal *m*.
► *n* the Establishment GB el sistema.

**estate** [ɪˈsteɪt] *n* **1** *(land)* finca. **2** GB *(with houses)* urbanización *f*. **3** *(money and property)* propiedad *f*, bienes *mpl*; *(inheritance)* herencia.

❌ Estate no significa 'estado', que se traduce por state o condition.

**esteem** [ɪˈstiːm] *vt* estimar.
► *n* aprecio, estima.

**esthetic** [iːsˈθetɪk] *adj* US → aesthetic.

**estimate** [*(n)* ˈestɪmət; *(vb)* ˈestɪmeɪt] *n* **1** *(calculation - of amount, size)* cálculo, estimación *f*; *(- of value, cost)* valoración *f*, estimación *f*; *(- for work)* presupuesto. **2** *(judgement)* evaluación *f*, juicio, opinión *f*.
► *vt* **1** *(calculate)* calcular. **2** *(judge, form opinion about)* pensar, creer, estimar.
► *vi (for work)* hacer un presupuesto (for, de).

❌ To estimate no significa 'estimar (querer)', que se traduce por to respect.

**estimation** [estɪˈmeɪʃən] *n* **1** opinión *f*, juicio. **2** *(esteem)* estima, aprecio.

**Estonia** [eˈstəʊnɪə] *n* Estonia.

**Estonian** [eˈstəʊnɪən] *adj* estonio,-a.
► *n* **1** *(person)* estonio,-a. **2** *(language)* estonio.

**estrogen** [ˈiːstrədʒən] *n* US → oestrogen.

**estuary** [ˈestjʊərɪ] *n* estuario.
ⓘ *pl* estuaries.

**etching** [ˈetʃɪŋ] *n* aguafuerte *m & f*.

**eternal** [ɪˈtɜːnəl] *adj* **1** *(everlasting)* eterno,-a. **2** *fam (unceasing)* incesante. **3** *(immutable)* inmutable.

**eternity** [ɪˈtɜːnətɪ] *n* eternidad *f*.

**ether** [ˈiːθəʳ] *n* éter *m*.

**ethic** [ˈeθɪk] *n* ética.

**ethical** [ˈeθɪkəl] *adj* ético,-a, moral.

**ethics** [ˈeθɪks] *n (science)* ética.
► *n pl (moral correctness)* moralidad *f*.

**Ethiopia** [iːθɪˈəʊpɪə] *n* Etiopía.

**Ethiopian** [iːθɪˈəʊpɪən] *adj* etíope.
► *n* **1** *(person)* etíope *mf*, etiope *mf*. **2** *(language)* etíope *m*.

**ethnic** [ˈeθnɪk] *adj* étnico,-a. COMP **ethnic minority** minoría étnica.

**ethnography** [eθˈnɒɡrəfɪ] *n* etnografía.

**ethnology** [eθˈnɒlədʒɪ] *n* etnología.

**ethyl** [ˈiːθaɪl, ˈeθɪl] *n* CHEM etilo. COMP **ethyl alcohol** alcohol *m* etílico.

**etiquette** [ˈetɪket] *n* protocolo, etiqueta.

❌ Etiquette no significa 'etiqueta (rótulo)', que se traduce por label.

**etymological** [etɪməˈlɒdʒɪkəl] *adj* etimológico,-a.

**etymology** [etɪˈmɒlədʒɪ] *n* etimología.
ⓘ *pl* etymologies.

**eucalyptus** [juːkəˈlɪptəs] *n* eucalipto. COMP **eucalyptus tree** eucalipto.

**EU** [ˈiːˈjuː] *abbr* (European Union) Unión *f* Europea; *(abbreviation)* UE *f*.

**euphemism** [ˈjuːfəmɪzəm] *n* eufemismo.

**euro** [ˈjʊərəʊ] *n* euro.

**Europe** [ˈjʊərəp] *n* Europa.

**European** [jʊərəˈpɪən] *adj* europeo,-a.
► *n (person)* europeo,-a. COMP **European Economic Community** Comunidad *f* Económica Europea. I **European Parliament** Parlamento Europeo. I **European Union** Unión *f* Europea.

**euthanasia** [juːθəˈneɪzɪə] *n* eutanasia.

**evacuate** [ɪˈvækjueɪt] *vt* **1** *(people)* evacuar. **2** *(place)* desalojar; *(mil)* desocupar.

**evacuation** [ɪvækjuˈeɪʃən] *n* **1** *(of people)* evacuación *f*. **2** *(of place)* desalojo.

**evade** [ɪˈveɪd] *vt* **1** evadir, eludir.

**evaluate** [ɪˈvæljueɪt] *vt* *(assess)* evaluar, juzgar; *(estimate value)* valorar, calcular (el valor de), tasar.

**evaluation** [ɪvæljuˈeɪʃən] *n* evaluación *f*.

**evaporate** [ɪˈvæpəreɪt] *vt* evaporar.
  ▶ *vi* evaporarse.

**evaporation** [ɪvæpəˈreɪʃən] *n* evaporación *f*.

**evasion** [ɪˈveɪʒən] *n* **1** *(gen)* evasión *f*. **2** *(excuse, etc)* evasiva.

**evasive** [ɪˈveɪsɪv] *adj* evasivo,-a.

**eve** [iːv] *n* víspera, vigilia. ⓁⓄⒸ on the eve of sth en vísperas de ALGO.

**even** [ˈiːvən] *adj* **1** *(level, flat)* llano,-a, plano,-a; *(smooth)* liso,-a: *this surface isn't even* esta superficie no es plana. **2** *(regular, steady)* uniforme, regular, constante. **3** *(evenly balanced)* igual, igualado,-a. **4** *(number)* par. **5** *(placid - character)* apacible. **7** *(on the same level as)* a nivel **(with, de)**.
  ▶ *adv* **1** hasta, incluso, aun: *it's always sunny, even in winter* siempre hace sol, incluso en invierno. **2** *(with negative)* siquiera, ni siquiera: *she never even said hello* ni siquiera me saludó. **3** *(before comparative)* aun, todavía: *she's even more beautiful than I remembered* es aun más guapa de lo que recordaba. ⓁⓄⒸ even if aun si, aunque. ▮ even so aun así. ▮ even though aunque, aun cuando.
  ▶ *vt* **1** *(level)* nivelar, allanar. **2** *(score)* igualar; *(situation)* equilibrar.
  ◆ to even out *vt sep (make level)* nivelar; *(make equal)* igualar; *(spread equally)* repartir equitativamente.

**evening** [ˈiːvənɪŋ] *n (early)* tarde *f*; *(late)* noche *f*. ⓁⓄⒸ good evening! ¡buenas tardes!, !buenas noches!

✎ Evening comprende la parte final de la tarde y el principio de la noche, antes de que anochezca del todo.

**evenly** [ˈiːvənlɪ] *adv* **1** *(uniformly)* uniformemente. **2** *(fairly, equally)* equitativamente, igualmente. **3** *(of voice)* en el mismo tono,.

**event** [ɪˈvent] *n* **1** *(happening)* suceso, acontecimiento. **2** SP prueba.

**eventual** [ɪˈventʃuəl] *adj* **1** *(final, ultimate)* final. **2** *(resulting)* consiguiente. **3** *(possible)* posible.

❎ Eventual no significa 'provisional', que se traduce por temporary.

**eventually** [ɪˈventʃuəlɪ] *adv* finalmente, con el tiempo.

**ever** [ˈevəʳ] *adv* **1** *(in negative sentences)* nunca, jamás. **2** *(in questions)* alguna vez. **3** *(always)* siempre. **4** *(after comparative and superlative)* nunca. **5** *(emphatic use)*: *how ever did you lose your coat?* ¿cómo has podido perder el abrigo? ⓁⓄⒸ for ever para siempre.

**evergreen** [ˈevəgriːn] *adj* BOT de hoja perenne.
  ▶ *n* árbol *m* de hoja perenne.

**everlasting** [evəˈlɑːstɪŋ] *adj* **1** *(eternal, lasting for ever)* eterno,-a. **2** *(lasting for a long time)* duradero,-a.

**every** [ˈevrɪ] *adj* **1** *(each)* cada; *(all)* todos,-as: *every day* cada día, todos los días. **3** *(all possible)*: *we encourage people to help in every way* animamos a la gente a que ayude de cualquier manera. ⓁⓄⒸ every other day un día sí un día no, cada dos días.

✎ Consulta también each.

**everybody** [ˈevrɪbɒdɪ] *pron* todos,-as, todo el mundo.

**everyday** [ˈevrɪdeɪ] *adj (day-to-day)* diario,-a; *(ordinary)* corriente, cotidiano,-a: *for everyday use* para uso diario.

**everyone** [ˈevrɪwʌn] *pron* → everybody.

**everyplace** [ˈevrɪpleɪs] *adv* → US everywhere.

**everything** [ˈevrɪθɪŋ] *pron* todo.

**everywhere** [ˈevrɪweəʳ] *adv* **1** *(place)* en todas partes, por todas partes: *he's been everywhere* ha estado en todas partes. **2** *(movement)* a todas partes.

**evidence** ['evɪdəns] n 1 (proof) prueba, pruebas fpl. 2 (sign, indication) indicio, indicios mpl, señal f. 3 JUR (testimony) testimonio, declaración f.
► vt 1 (prove) demostrar, probar. 2 (give proof of) justificar.

**evident** ['evɪdənt] adj evidente.

**evil** ['iːvəl] adj 1 (gen) malo,-a. 2 (foul-smell) fétido,-a, repugnante; (- temper, weather) terrible, de perros. 4 (unlucky) aciago,-a, de mal agüero.
► n (wickedness) mal m, maldad f.

**evoke** [ɪ'vəuk] vt 1 (bring to mind) evocar. 2 fml (produce, cause) provocar.

**evolution** [iːvə'luːʃən] n evolución f.

**evolve** [ɪ'vɒlv] vt 1 (develop) desarrollar. 2 (give off) desprender.
► vi evolucionar.

**ewe** [juː] n oveja.

**exact** [ɪg'zækt] adj 1 (precise) exacto,-a. 2 (meticulous) meticuloso,-a. 3 (accurate) preciso,-a. 4 (specific, particular) justo.
► vt (demand, insist on) exigir (from, a).

**exacting** [ɪg'zæktɪŋ] adj exigente.

**exaggerate** [ɪg'zædʒəreɪt] vt exagerar.

**exalt** [ɪg'zɔːlt] vt 1 fml (elevate) exaltar, elevar. 2 (praise, extol) ensalzar.

**exam** [ɪg'zæm] n fam examen m.

**examination** [ɪgzæmɪ'neɪʃən] n 1 EDUC examen m. 2 (inspection) inspección f, examen m; (of house, room) registro. 3 MED reconocimiento. 4 JUR interrogatorio.

**examine** [ɪg'zæmɪn] vt 1 (inspect) inspeccionar, examinar; (check) comprobar; (consider) examinar, estudiar. 2 (customs) registrar. 3 EDUC examinar (in/on, de). 4 MED hacer un reconocimiento a. 5 JUR interrogar.

**examiner** [ɪg'zæmɪnər] n examinador,-ra.

**example** [ɪg'zɑːmpəl] n (gen) ejemplo.

**exasperate** [ɪg'zɑːspəreɪt] vt exasperar, irritar. LOC for example por ejemplo.

**excavate** ['ekskəveɪt] vt excavar.

**excavation** [ekskə'veɪʃən] n excavación f.

**excavator** ['ekskəveɪtər] n (machine) excavadora.

**exceed** [ɪk'siːd] vt exceder.

**excel** [ɪk'sel] vt (surpass) superar.
► vi (be very good at) destacar (at/in, en), sobresalir (at/in, en).
① pt & pp excelled, ger excelling.

**excellence** ['eksələns] n excelencia.

**excellent** ['eksələnt] adj excelente.
► interj fam ¡estupendo!, ¡fantástico!.

**except** [ɪk'sept] prep excepto, salvo.
► vt fml excluir, exceptuar.

**exception** [ɪk'sepʃən] n excepción f.

**exceptional** [ɪk'sepʃənəl] adj excepcional.

**excerpt** ['eksɜːpt] n extracto.

**excess** [ɪk'ses] n 1 exceso. 2 COMM excedente m.
► adj excedente, sobrante.

**excessive** [ɪk'sesɪv] adj excesivo,-a.

**exchange** [ɪks'tʃeɪndʒ] n 1 (gen) cambio. 2 (of ideas, information, etc) intercambio. 3 (of prisoners) canje m. 4 FIN cambio. 5 EDUC (reciprocal visit) intercambio.
► vt 1 (gen) cambiar. 2 (ideas, information, etc) intercambiar. 3 (prisoners) canjear.

**exchequer** [ɪks'tʃekər] n (treasury) tesoro público.
► n the Exchequer Hacienda.

**excite** [ɪk'saɪt] vt 1 (enthuse, thrill) emocionar, apasionar. 2 fml (bring about) provocar. 3 (stimulate) excitar.

**excited** [ɪk'saɪtɪd] adj 1 emocionado,-a, ilusionado,-a. 2 (sexually) excitado,-a.

**excitement** [ɪk'saɪtmənt] n 1 (strong feeling) emoción f, entusiasmo, ilusión f. 2 (commotion) agitación f, conmoción f, revuelo.

**exciting** [ɪk'saɪtɪŋ] adj emocionante.

**exclaim** [ɪk'skleɪm] vt exclamar, gritar.
► vi exclamar.

**exclamation** [eksklə'meɪʃən] n exclamación f. COMP exclamation mark signo de admiración. ‖ exclamation point US signo de admiración.

**exclude** [ɪk'skluːd] vt 1 (leave out, not include) excluir, no incluir. 2 (debar, prevent from entering) no admitir.

**excluding** [ɪkˈsklu:dɪŋ] *prep (excepting)* excepto, con excepción de.

**exclusive** [ɪkˈsklu:sɪv] *adj* **1** *(gen)* exclusivo,-a. **2** *(press)* en exclusiva.
▸ *n (press)* exclusiva.

**excrement** [ˈekskrɪmənt] *n* excremento.

**excrete** [ɪkˈskri:t] *vt* excretar.

**excretory** [ɪkˈskrəɪ:təər] *adj* excretor,-ra. COMP **excretory system** sistema excretor.

**excruciating** [ɪkˈskru:ʃɪeɪtɪŋ] *adj* **1** insoportable. **2** *euph* fatal, horrible.

**excursion** [ɪkˈskɜ:ʒən] *n (outing)* excursión *f*, viaje *m*.

**excuse** [*(n)* ɪkˈskju:s; *(vb)* ɪkˈskju:z] *n* **1** *(apology)* disculpa. **2** *(pretext)* excusa.
▸ *vt* **1** perdonar, disculpar. **2** *(justify)* justificar. **3** *(exempt)* eximir.

**execute** [ˈeksɪkju:t] *vt* **1** *(put to death)* ejecutar. **2** *(carry out)* ejecutar; *(orders)* cumplir; *(tasks)* realizar. **3** *(music, etc)* interpretar.

**execution** [eksɪˈkju:ʃən] *n* **1** *(carrying out)* ejecución *f*; *(of order)* cumplimiento; *(of task)* realización *f*. **2** *(putting to death)* ejecución *f*. **4** *(of music, etc)* interpretación *f*.

**executioner** [eksɪˈkju:ʃənəʳ] *n* verdugo.

**executive** [ɪgˈzekjətɪv] *adj* ejecutivo,-a.
▸ *n (person)* ejecutivo,-a; *(committee)* ejecutiva.
▸ *n* **the executive** el (poder) ejecutivo.

**exemplify** [ɪgˈzemplɪfaɪ] *vt* ejemplificar.
ⓘ *pt & pp* **exemplified**, *ger* **exemplifying**.

**exempt** [ɪgˈzempt] *adj* exento,-a, libre (from, de).
▸ *vt* eximir, dispensar (from, de).

**exemption** [ɪgˈzempʃən] *n* exención *f* (from, de).

**exercise** [ˈeksəsaɪz] *n* ejercicio. COMP **exercise book** cuaderno.
▸ *vt* **1** *(employ, make use of)* ejercer, emplear. **2** *(give exercise to - dog)* sacar de paseo; *(- horse)* entrenar.
▸ *vi* hacer ejercicio, entrenarse.

**exert** [ɪgˈzɜ:t] *vt* ejercer.

**exhalation** [ekshəlˈeɪ[ə]n] *vt* exhalación *f*.

**exhale** [eksˈheɪl] *vt (breathe out)* exhalar.
▸ *vi (give off)* despedir.

**exhaust** [ɪgˈzɔ:st] *n* **1** *(pipe)* (tubo de) escape *m*. **2** *(fumes)* gases *mpl* de combustión.
▸ *vt* **1** *(gen)* agotar. **2** *(empty)* vaciar.

**exhausted** [ɪgˈzɔ:stɪd] *adj* agotado,-a.

**exhausting** [ɪgˈzɔ:stɪŋ] *adj* agotador,-ra.

**exhaustive** [ɪgˈzɔ:stɪv] *adj* exhaustivo,-a.

**exhibit** [ɪgˈzɪbɪt] *n* ART objeto expuesto.
▸ *vt* **1** *(display, show)* exponer, presentar. **2** *fml (manifest)* manifestar, mostrar.
▸ *vi (of artist)* exponer.

**exhibition** [eksɪˈbɪʃən] *n* **1** *(art, etc)* exposición *f*. **2** *(display)* demostración *f*, muestra.

**exhibitionist** [eksɪˈbɪʃənɪst] *n* exhibicionista *mf*.

**exhilarating** [ɪgˈzɪləreɪtɪŋ] *adj (invigorating)* estimulante; *(exciting)* emocionante.

**exhume** [eksˈhju:m] *vt* exhumar.

**exile** [ˈeksaɪl] *n* **1** *(action)* destierro, exilio. **2** *(person)* desterrado,-a, exiliado,-a.
▸ *vt* desterrar, exiliar.

**exist** [ɪgˈzɪst] *vi* **1** *(gen)* existir. **2** *(subsist)* subsistir (on, a base de).

**existence** [ɪgˈzɪstəns] *n* existencia.

**existent** [ɪgˈzɪstənt] *adj* existente.

**exit** [ˈeksɪt] *n* **1** *(gen)* salida. **2** THEAT mutis *m*.
▸ *vi* THEAT hacer mutis.

✗ Exit no significa 'éxito', que se traduce por **success**.

**exodus** [ˈeksədəs] *n* éxodo.

**exorbitant** [ɪgˈzɔ:bɪtənt] *adj* exorbitante.

**exorcism** [ˈeksɔ:sɪzəm] *n* exorcismo.

**exotic** [egˈzɒtɪk] *adj* exótico,-a.

**expand** [ɪkˈspænd] *vt* **1** *(enlarge - business)* ampliar; *(- number)* aumentar, incrementar. **2** *(gas, metal)* dilatar, expandir.
▸ *vi* **1** *(grow larger)* crecer, aumentar. **2** *(metal)* dilatarse; *(gas)* expandirse. **3** *(spread out)* extenderse.

◆ **to expand on** *vt insep* ampliar, desarrollar.

**expanse** [ɪk'spæns] *n* extensión *f*.

**expansion** [ɪk'spænʃən] *n* **1** crecimiento, aumento. **2** *(gas, metal)* dilatación *f*, expansión *f*. **3** *(trade)* desarrollo.

**expansive** [ɪk'spænsɪv] *adj* **1** *(friendly, talkative)* hablador,-ra, comunicativo,-a. **2** *(able to expand)* expansivo,-a.

**expect** [ɪk'spekt] *vt* **1** *(anticipate)* esperar: *I never expected to win* no esperaba ganar. **2** *(demand)* esperar, contar con. **3** GB *fam (suppose)* suponer, imaginar.

**expectancy** [ɪk'spektənsɪ] *n (anticipation)* expectación *f*, expectativa; *(hope)* ilusión *f*.

**expectation** [ekspek'teɪʃən] *n (hope, firm belief)* esperanza.

▸ *n pl* **expectations** *(confident feelings)* expectativas *fpl*.

⊠ Expectation no significa 'expectativa', que se traduce por **excitement**.

**expedient** [ɪk'spiːdɪənt] *adj* conveniente, oportuno,-a.

▸ *n* expediente *m*, recurso.

**expedition** [ekspɪ'dɪʃən] *n* **1** *(gen)* expedición *f*. **2** *fml (speed)* aceleración *f*, prontitud *f*.

**expel** [ɪk'spel] *vt* expulsar.

① *pt & pp* expelled, *ger* expelling.

**expend** [ɪk'spend] *vt* **1** *fml (spend, use)* gastar, emplear. **2** *fml (use up, exhaust)* agotar.

**expendable** [ɪk'spendəbəl] *adj fml* prescindible.

**expenditure** [ɪk'spendɪtʃəʳ] *n* gasto, desembolso.

**expense** [ɪk'spens] *n* gasto, desembolso.

▸ *n pl* **expenses** gastos *mpl*.

**expensive** [ɪk'spensɪv] *adj* caro,-a.

**experience** [ɪk'spɪərɪəns] *n* experiencia.

▸ *vt (sensation, situation, etc)* experimentar; *(difficulty)* tener; *(loss)* sufrir.

**experienced** [ɪk'spɪərɪənst] *adj* experimentado,-a, con experiencia.

**experiment** [ɪk'sperɪmənt] *n* experimento.

▸ *vi* experimentar, hacer experimentos.

**experimental** [ɪksperɪ'mentəl] *adj* experimental.

**expert** ['eksp3ːt] *n* experto,-a (at/in, on, en).

▸ *adj* experto,-a.

**expertise** [eksp3ː'tiːz] *n (skill)* pericia, habilidad *f*; *(knowledge)* conocimiento (práctico).

**expire** [ɪk'spaɪəʳ] *vi (come to end)* terminar, acabarse; *(die)* expirar, morir. **2** *(run out - contract)* vencer; *(- passport, ticket)* caducar. **3** MED *(breathe out)* espirar.

**expiry** [ɪk'spaɪərɪ] *n* **1** *(ending)* expiración *f*, terminación *f*. **2** *(of contract, bill of exchange)* vencimiento; *(of passport, driving licence, etc)* caducidad *f*.

**explanation** [eksplə'neɪʃən] *n* explicación *f*.

**explicit** [ɪk'splɪsɪt] *adj* explícito,-a.

**explode** [ɪk'spləʊd] *vt* **1** *(blow up - bomb, etc)* hacer estallar, explotar. **2** *(refute - theory)* refutar; *(- rumour)* desmentir.

▸ *vi* **1** *(blow up)* estallar, explotar. **2** *(react violently)* reventar, explotar, estallar.

**exploit** [*(n)* 'eksplɔɪt; *(vb)* ɪk'splɔɪt] *n* hazaña, proeza.

▸ *vt* **1** *(work, develop fully)* explotar. **2** *(use unfairly)* aprovecharse de, explotar.

**exploitation** [eksplɔɪ'teɪʃən] *n* explotación *f*.

**exploration** [eksplə'reɪʃən] *n* exploración *f*.

**explore** [ɪk'splɔːʳ] *vt* **1** *(gen)* explorar. **2** *(examine)* examinar.

▸ *vi* explorar.

**explorer** [ɪk'splɔːrəʳ] *n* explorador,-ra.

**explosion** [ɪk'spləʊʒən] *n* **1** *(gen)* explosión *f*, estallido. **2** *(violent outburst)* ataque *m*, arrebato.

**explosive** [ɪk'spləʊsɪv] *adj* explosivo,-a.

**exponent** [ɪk'spəʊnənt] *n* **1** *(gen)* exponente *m*; *(supporter)* defensor,-ra (of, de), partidario,-a (of, de). **2** *(performer)* intérprete *mf*; *(expert)* experto,-a. **3** MATH exponente *m*.

**exponential** [ekspə'nenʃəl] *adj* MATH exponencial.

**export** [(*n*) 'ekspɔ:t; (*vb*) ɪk'spɔ:t] *n* **1** *(trade)* exportación *f*. **2** *(article)* artículo de exportación.
▶ *vt* exportar.

**exporter** [ek'spɔ:təʳ] *n* exportador,-ra.

**expose** [ɪk'spəʊz] *vt* **1** *(uncover, make visible)* exponer. **2** *(make known - secret, etc)* revelar, descubrir; *(- person)* desenmascarar. **3** *fig (lay open)* exponerse. **4** *(photo)* exponer.

**exposure** [ɪk'spəʊʒəʳ] *n* **1** *(being exposed)* exposición *f*. **2** *(revelation, disclosure)* revelación *f*, descubrimiento. **3** *(in photography - picture)* fotografía; *(- time)* exposición *f*. **4** *(position of house, etc)* situación *f*, orientación *f*. **5** *(publicity)* publicidad *f*; *(coverage)* cobertura.

**express** [ɪk'spres] *adj* **1** *(explicit)* expreso,-a, claro,-a. **2** *(fast - mail)* urgente; *(- train, coach)* expreso.
▶ *adv* urgente.
▶ *n* *(rail)* (tren *m*) expreso.
▶ *vt* **1** expresar. **2** *fml (juice)* exprimir.

**expression** [ɪk'spreʃən] *n* **1** *(gen)* expresión *f*; *(manifestation)* manifestación *f*. **2** MATH expresión *f*.

**expressive** [ɪk'spresɪv] *adj* expresivo,-a.

**expressway** [ɪk'spreswei] *n* US autopista.

**expulsion** [ɪk'spʌlʃən] *n* expulsión *f*.

**exquisite** [ek'skwɪzɪt, 'ekskwɪzɪt] *adj* **1** *(delicate, etc)* exquisito,-a, perfecto,-a. **2** *fml (of emotion)* intenso,-a; *(of power to feel)* delicado,-a.

**extend** [ɪk'stend] *vt* **1** *(enlarge)* ampliar; *(lengthen - line, road)* prolongar, alargar. **2** *(over time)* prolongar, alargar; *(deadline)* prorrogar. **3** *(stretch out - arm, hand)* alargar, tender; *(- leg)* estirar; *(- wing)* desplegar, extender.
▶ *vi* **1** *(in space)* continuar, extenderse, llegar hasta. **2** *(in time)* prolongarse, alargarse, durar. **3** *(become extended - ladder, etc)* extenderse. **4** *(include, affect)* incluir, abarcar, extenderse a.

**extension** [ɪk'stenʃən] *n* **1** *(widening)* ampliación *f*, extensión *f*. **2** *(of line, road, etc)* prolongación *f*. **5** *(telephone line)* extensión *f*; *(telephone)* supletorio.

**extensive** [ɪk'stensɪv] *adj* **1** *(area)* extenso,-a, amplio,-a. **2** *(wide-ranging)* vasto,-a, amplio,-a, extenso,-a; *(thorough)* exhaustivo, minucioso,-a. **3** *(very great in effect, widespread)* importante, múltiple.

**extensor** [ɪk'stensəʳ] *n* extensor.

**extent** [ɪk'stent] *n* **1** *(expanse)* extensión *f*. **2** *(range, scale, scope)* amplitud *f*, alcance *m*. **3** *(point)* punto.

**extenuate** [ɪk'stenjʊeɪt] *vt fml* atenuar.

**exterior** [ɪk'stɪəəɪəʳ] *adj* exterior, externo,-a: *exterior walls* paredes exteriores.
▶ *n* **1** exterior *m*. **2** *(of person)* aspecto externo, apariencia.

**exterminate** [ɪk'stɜ:mɪneɪt] *vt* exterminar.

**extermination** [ɪkstɜ:mɪ'neɪʃən] *n* exterminación *f*, exterminio.

**external** [ek'stɜ:nəl] *adj* externo,-a, exterior. COMP **external ear** oído externo.

**extinct** [ɪk'stɪŋkt] *adj* **1** *(of animal)* extinguido,-a. **2** *(of volcano)* extinguido,-a, apagado,-a.

**extinction** [ɪk'stɪŋkʃən] *n* extinción *f*.

**extinguish** [ɪk'stɪŋgwɪʃ] *vt* extinguir.

**extinguisher** [ɪk'stɪŋgwɪʃəʳ] *n* extintor *m*.

**extort** [ɪk'stɔ:t] *vt (money)* sacar, conseguir a la fuerza; *(promise, confession)* arrancar, obtener.

**extortion** [ɪk'stɔ:ʃən] *n* extorsión *f*.

**extra** ['ekstəə] *adj (additional)* extra, más, otro,-a; *(spare)* de sobra; *(on top)* aparte.
▶ *adv (more than usually)* extra, muy; *(additional)* aparte.
▶ *n* **1** *(additional thing)* extra *m*, complemento; *(additional charge)* suplemento; *(luxury)* lujo. **2** CINEM extra *mf*. **3** *(press)* edición *f* especial.

**extract** [(*n*) 'ekstrækt; (*vb*) ɪk'strækt] *n* extracto.

► vt **1** *(pull out)* extraer, sacar. **2** *(obtain - confession, promise, etc)* arrancar, obtener; *(- information, passage, quotation)* extraer, sacar. **3** *(produce)* extraer, sacar.

**extraction** [ɪkˈstrækʃən] *n* **1** *(gen)* extracción *f*. **2** *(of tooth)* extracción *f*. **3** *(descent)* origen *m*.

**extractor** [ɪkˈstræktəʳ] *n* extractor *m*. COMP **extractor fan** extractor *m* de humos.

**extradite** [ˈekstrədaɪt] *vt* extraditar, extradir.

**extradition** [ekstrəˈdɪʃən] *n* extradición *f*.

**extramarital** [ekstrəˈmærɪtəl] *adj* extramatrimonial.

**extraordinary** [ɪkˈstrɔːdənəɪ] *adj* extraordinario,-a.

**extrasensory** [ekstrəˈsensəɪ] *adj* extrasensorial.

**extraterrestrial** [ekstrətəˈrestrɪəl] *adj* extraterrestre.

► *n* extraterrestre *mf*.

**extravagance** [ɪkˈstrævəgəns] *n (spending)* derroche *m*, despilfarro, lujo; *(behaviour)* extravagancia.

**extravagant** [ɪkˈstrævəgənt] *adj* **1** *(wasteful - person)* derrochador,-ra, despilfarrador,-ra; *(- thing)* ineficaz, ineficiente. **2** *(extreme)* extravagante. **3** *(luxurious)* lujoso,-a.

**extreme** [ɪkˈstriːm] *adj* **1** *(gen)* extremo,-a. **2** *(severe, unusual)* excepcional.

► *n* extremo.

**extremism** [ɪkˈstriːmɪzəm] *n* extremismo.

**extremist** [ɪkˈstriːmɪst] *n* extremista *mf*.

**extremity** [ɪkˈstremɪtɪ] *n* **1** *fml (furthest point)* extremo. **2** *fml (extreme degree, situation)* situación *f* extrema.

► *n pl* **extremities** ANAT extremidades *fpl*.
ⓘ *pl* extremities.

**extricate** [ˈekstrɪkeɪt] *vt fml* librar, sacar. LOC **to extricate os** lograr salir (from, de).

**extrinsic** [ɪkˈstrɪnzɪk] *adj* extrínseco,-a.

**extrovert** [ˈekstrəvɜːt] *adj* extrovertido,-a.

► *n* extrovertido,-a.

**exuberance** [ɪgˈzjuːbəəəns] *n (vigour)* exuberancia; *(high spirits)* euforia.

**exuberant** [ɪgˈzjuːbəəənt] *adj* **1** *(of person)* eufórico,-a. **2** *(of plants)* exuberante.

**exude** [ɪgˈzjuːd] *vt* **1** *fml (of sweat, etc)* exudar, rezumar. **2** *fig (of feeling)* rebosar: *she exudes confidence* rebosa de confianza.

► *vi (of sweat, etc)* exudar, rezumar.

**exultant** [ɪgˈzʌltənt] *adj* exultante.

**eye** [aɪ] *n* **1** ANAT ojo. **2** *(sense)* vista. **3** *(of needle, potato, storm)* ojo.

► *vt (observe)* mirar, observar; *(look at longingly)* echar el ojo a.

**eyeball** [ˈaɪbɔːl] *n* globo ocular.

**eyebolt** [ˈaɪbəʊlt] *n* armella, hembrilla.

**eyebrow** [ˈaɪbəʊ] *n* ceja.

**eye-catching** [ˈaɪkætʃɪŋ] *adj* llamativo,-a.

**eyelash** [ˈaɪlæʃ] *n* pestaña.

**eyelid** [ˈaɪlɪd] *n* párpado.

**eyeliner** [ˈaɪlaɪnəʳ] *n* lápiz *m* de ojos.

**eyesight** [ˈaɪsaɪt] *n* vista.

**eyesore** [ˈaɪsɔːʳ] *n* monstruosidad *f*.

**eyestrain** [ˈaɪstreɪn] *n* vista cansada.

**eyetooth** [aɪˈtuːθ] *n* colmillo.

**eyewash** [ˈaɪwɒʃ] *n* **1** MED colirio. **2** *fam (nonsense)* tonterías *fpl*: *it's all eyewash!* ¡eso son disparates!.

**eyewitness** [ˈaɪwɪtnəs] *n* testigo presencial, testigo ocular.

# F

**F, f** [ef] *n* **1** *(the letter)* F, f *f*. **2** MUS fa *m*.

**F** ['færənhaɪt] *abbr* (Fahrenheit) Fahrenheit; *(abbreviation)* F.

**fable** ['feɪbəl] *n* fábula.

**fabric** ['fæbrɪk] *n* **1** *(material)* tela, tejido. **2** *(structure)* fábrica, estructura.

⊠ Fabric no significa 'fábrica', que se traduce por **factory**.

**fabulous** ['fæbjələs] *adj* fabuloso,-a.

**façade** [fə'sɑːd] *n* fachada.

**face** [feɪs] *n* **1** *(gen)* cara. **2** *(surface)* superficie *f*. **3** *(of dial)* cuadrante *m*. **4** *(of watch)* esfera. LOC **face down** boca abajo. ▌**face up** boca arriba.
▶ *vt* **1** *(look towards)* mirar hacia. **2** *(look onto)* estar orientado,-a hacia, dar a. **3** *(be opposite to)* estar enfrente de. **4** *(confront)* presentarse, plantearse; *(deal with)* enfrentarse a. **5** *(tolerate)* soportar.
◆ **to face up to** *vt insep* afrontar, enfrentar, enfrentarse a.

**faceless** ['feɪsləs] *adj* anónimo,-a.

**facelift** ['feɪslɪft] *n* **1** lifting *m*. **2** *fig (building)* lavado de cara.

**facet** ['fæsɪt] *n* faceta.

**facial** ['feɪʃəl] *adj* facial.

**facilitate** [fə'sɪlɪteɪt] *vt* facilitar.

**facility** [fə'sɪlɪti] *n* facilidad *f*.
▶ *n pl* **facilities 1** *(equipment)* instalaciones *fpl*, servicios *mpl*. **2** *(means)* facilidades *fpl*.
ⓘ *pl* **facilities**.

**fact** [fækt] *n* **1** *(event, happening)* hecho. **2** *(the truth)* realidad *f*. LOC **as a matter of fact** en realidad. ▌**in fact** de hecho.

**faction** ['fækʃən] *n* facción *f*.

**factor** ['fæktər] *n* factor *m*.

**factorize** ['fæktəraɪz] *vt* descomponer en factores.

**factory** ['fæktəri] *n* fábrica.
ⓘ *pl* **factories**.

**faculty** ['fækəlti] *n* **1** *(power, ability)* facultad *f*. **2** *(at university)* facultad *f*. **3** US *(at university)* profesorado.
ⓘ *pl* **faculties**.

**fad** [fæd] *n* **1** *(fashion)* moda pasajera. **2** *(personal)* manía.

**fade** [feɪd] *vt* *(colour)* descolorar, descolorir, desteñir.
◆ **to fade away** *vi* **1** *(become less intense, strong, etc)* desvanecerse, esfumarse. **2** *(die)* morirse.

**faecal** ['fiːkəl] *adj* fecal.

**faeces** ['fiːsiːz] *n pl* heces *fpl*.

**fag** [fæg] *n* **1** GB *fam (cigarette)* pitillo. **2** *sl (drag)* lata, rollo.

**Fahrenheit** ['færənhaɪt] *adj* Fahrenheit.

**fail** [feɪl] *n* EDUC suspenso.
▶ *vt* **1** *(let down)* fallar, decepcionar; *(desert)* fallar, faltar. **2** EDUC suspender.
▶ *vi* **1** *(neglect)* dejar de. **2** *(not succeed)* fracasar, no hacer algo. **3** *(crops)* fallar, echarse a perder. **4** *(stop working)* fallar. **5** *(light)* acabarse, irse apagando. **6** *(become weak)* debilitarse, fallar. **7** COMM *(become bankrupt)* quebrar, fracasar.

**failing** ['feɪlɪŋ] *n* *(fault)* defecto, fallo; *(weakness)* punto débil.
▶ *prep* a falta de.

**fail-safe** ['feɪlseɪf] *adj (device, mechanism)* de seguridad; *(plan)* infalible.

**failure** ['feɪljər] *n* **1** *(lack of success)* fracaso. **2** COMM quiebra. **3** EDUC suspenso. **4** *(person)* fracasado,-a. **5** *(breakdown)* fallo, avería. **6** *(of crops)* pérdida.

**faint** [feɪnt] *adj* **1** *(sound, voice)* débil, tenue. **2** *(colour)* pálido,-a. **3** *(slight - memory, etc)* vago,-a.
▸ *n* mareo.
▸ *vi* desmayarse (from, de).

**fair¹** [feəʳ] *adj* **1** *(just)* justo,-a; *(impartial)* imparcial; *(reasonable)* razonable. **2** *(considerable)* considerable. **3** *(idea, guess, etc)* bastante bueno,-a. **4** *(weather)* bueno,-a. **5** *(hair)* rubio,-a; *(skin)* blanco,-a.

**fair²** [feəʳ] *n* **1** *(market)* mercado, feria. **2** *(show)* feria; *(funfair)* parque *m* de atracciones.

**fairground** [ˈfeəɡraʊnd] *n (site)* recinto ferial; *(show)* feria; *(funfair)* parque *m* de atracciones.

**fairly** [ˈfeəlɪ] *adv* **1** *(justly)* justamente. **2** *(moderately)* bastante. **3** *(completely)* completamente.

**fairway** [ˈfeəweɪ] *n* **1** *(golf)* calle *f*. **2** *(sea)* canal *m* navegable.

**fairy** [ˈfeərɪ] *n* hada. [COMP] **fairy story/ tale** cuento de hadas.
ⓘ *pl* fairies.

**faith** [feɪθ] *n* **1** fe *f*. **2** *(trust, confidence)* confianza (in, en), fe *f* (in, en). **3** REL fe *f*.

**faithful** [ˈfeɪθfʊl] *adj* **1** *(loyal)* fiel (to, a), leal (to, a/con). **2** *(accurate)* exacto,-a.

**faithfully** [ˈfeɪθfʊlɪ] *adv* fielmente. [LOC] **yours faithfully** *(in letter)* atentamente.

**fake** [feɪk] *n* **1** falsificación *f*. **2** *(person)* impostor,-ra, farsante *mf*.
▸ *adj* falso,-a, falsificado,-a.
▸ *vt* **1** *(falsify)* falsificar. **2** *(pretend)* fingir: *she faked illness* fingió estar enferma.

**falcon** [ˈfɔːlkən] *n* halcón *m*.

**fall** [fɔːl] *n* **1** *(act of falling)* caída. **2** *(of rock)* desprendimiento; *(of snow)* nevada. **3** *(decrease)* baja, descenso, disminución *f*. **4** *(defeat)* caída. **5** US *(autumn)* otoño.
▸ *vi* **1** *(gen)* caer, caerse. **2** *(decrease)* bajar, descender. **3** *(be defeated)* caer; *(be killed)* perecer. [LOC] **to fall asleep** quedarse dormido. ‖ **to fall in love** enamorarse.
▸ *n pl* **falls** *(waterfall)* cascada *f sing*, cataratas *fpl*.
◆ **to fall apart** *vi* romperse, deshacerse, caerse a pedazos.
◆ **to fall back** *vi (retreat)* retroceder, retirarse.

◆ **to fall back on** *vt insep (resort to)* recurrir a.
◆ **to fall behind** *vi (be overtaken)* retrasarse, rezagarse.
◆ **to fall down** *vi* **1** *(gen)* caer, caerse. **2** *(fail)* fallar.
◆ **to fall for** *vt insep* **1** *(be tricked)* dejarse engañar por, picar. **2** *fam (fall in love)* enamorarse de.
◆ **to fall off** *vi* **1** *(decrease in quantity)* bajar, disminuir; *(in quality)* empeorar. **2** *(become detached)* desprenderse, caerse.
◆ **to fall out** *vi (quarrel)* reñir (with, con), pelearse (with, con).
▸ *vi (drop)* caerse.
◆ **to fall over** *vt insep* caer, tropezar con.
ⓘ *pt* fell [fel], *pp* fallen [ˈfɔːlən].

**fallen** [ˈfɔːlən] *pp* → fall.
▸ *adj (not virtuous)* perdido,-a.

**Fallopian tube** [fələʊpɪənˈtjuːb] *n* trompa de Falopio.

**fallout** [ˈfɔːlaʊt] *n* lluvia radiactiva.

**fallow** [ˈfæləʊ] *adj* en barbecho.

**false** [fɔːls] *adj* **1** *(untrue)* falso,-a. **2** *(artificial)* postizo,-a. [COMP] **false alarm** falsa alarma. ‖ **false start** salida nula. ‖ **false teeth** dentadura postiza.

**falsify** [ˈfɔːlsɪfaɪ] *vt* **1** *(alter falsely)* falsificar. **2** *(misrepresent)* falsear.
ⓘ *pt & pp* falsified, *ger* falsifying.

**falter** [ˈfɔːltəʳ] *vi (person)* vacilar, titubear; *(voice)* fallar.

**fame** [feɪm] *n* fama.

**familiar** [fəˈmɪlɪəʳ] *adj* **1** *(well-known)* conocido,-a (to, a). **2** *(aware)* familiarizado,-a (with, con). **3** *(intimate)* íntimo,-a.

☒ Familiar no significa 'familiar (de la familia)', que se traduce por **family**.

**familiarity** [fəmɪlɪˈærɪtɪ] *n* familiaridad *f*.

**familiarize** [fəˈmɪlɪəraɪz] *vt (become acquainted)* familiarizarse (with, con).

**family** [ˈfæmɪlɪ] *n* familia.
ⓘ *pl* families.
▸ *adj* familiar. [COMP] **family name** apellido.

**famine** [ˈfæmɪn] *n* hambruna, hambre *f*.

**famous** [ˈfeɪməs] *adj* famoso,-a (for, por).

**famously** [ˈfeɪməslɪ] *adv fam* estupendamente.

**fan** [fæn] *n* **1** *(object)* abanico. **2** ELEC ventilador *m*. **3** *(follower)* aficionado,-a; *(of pop star, etc)* admirador,-ra, fan *mf*. **4** *(of football)* hincha *mf*.
▶ *vt (face)* abanicar; *(elec)* ventilar.
① *pt & pp* fanned, *ger* fanning.

**fanatic** [fə'nætɪk] *n* fanático,-a.
▶ *adj* fanático,-a (about, de).

**fancier** [fænsɪə'] *n* aficionado,-a.

**fanciful** ['fænsɪful] *adj* **1** *(idea)* imaginario,-a, fantástico,-a. **2** *(extravagant)* caprichoso,-a, estrafalario,-a.

**fancy** ['fænsɪ] *n* **1** *(imagination)* fantasía, imaginación *f*. **2** *(whim)* capricho, antojo.
① *pl* fancies.
▶ *adj* **1** *(jewels, goods, etc)* de fantasía. **2** *(high-class, posh)* elegante, de lujo.
▶ *vt* **1** *(want)* apetecer, querer. **2** *(find attractive)* encontrar atractivo,-a. **3** *(think)* creer, suponer.
① *pt & pp* fancied, *ger* fancying.

**fanfare** ['fænfeə'] *n* fanfarria.

**fang** [fæŋ] *n* colmillo.

**fantastic** [fæn'tæstɪk] *adj* fantástico,-a.

**fantasy** ['fæntəsɪ] *n* fantasía.
① *pl* fantasies.

**FAQ** ['efə'kjuː] *n* (frequently asked questions) preguntas frecuentes.

**far** [fɑː'] *adj* **1** *(distant)* lejano,-a, remoto,-a. **2** *(more distant)* opuesto,-a, extremo,-a.
① *comp* farther o further, *superl* farthest o furthest.
▶ *adv* **1** *(a long way)* lejos. **2** *(a long time)* lejos. **3** *(much)* mucho. LOC as far as hasta: *as far as I am concerned* por lo que a mí se refiere. ‖ far away lejos. ‖ so far hasta ahora.

**faraway** ['fɑːrəweɪ] *adj* lejano,-a, remoto,-a; *(look)* distraído,-a.

**farce** [fɑːs] *n* farsa.

**fare** [feə'] *n (price)* tarifa, precio del billete; *(boat)* pasaje *m*.
▶ *vi (progress, get on)* desenvolverse.

✎ Fare se refiere sólo a los billetes de transporte público.

**farewell** [feə'wel] *interj* ¡adiós!
▶ *n* despedida.

**farm** [fɑːm] *n* granja.
▶ *adj* agrícola, de granja.

▶ *vt* **1** *(use land)* cultivar, labrar. **2** *(breed animals)* criar.
▶ *vi (grow crops)* cultivar la tierra.

**farmer** ['fɑːmə'] *n* granjero,-a, agricultor,-ra.

**farmhouse** ['fɑːmhaʊs] *n* granja.

**farming** ['fɑːmɪŋ] *n* agricultura. LOC farming industry industria agropecuaria.

**farmland** ['fɑːmlænd] *n* tierra de cultivo.

**farmyard** ['fɑːmjɑːd] *n* corral *m*.

**far-reaching** [fɑː'riːtʃɪŋ] *adj* de gran alcance.

**farrier** ['færɪə'] *n* herrero.

**far-sighted** [fɑː'saɪtɪd] *adj* previsor,-ra.

**fart** [fɑːt] *n* **1** *fam* pedo. **2** *(fool)* carcamal *m*, carroza *m*.
▶ *vi* tirarse un pedo.

**farther** ['fɑːðə'] *adj comp → far: Santander is farther than Murcia* Santander está más lejos que Murcia.

**farthest** ['fɑːðɪst] *adj → far: Pluto is the farthest planet from the Sun* Plutón es el planeta más alejado del Sol.
▶ *adv → far: who lives farthest from the school?* ¿quién vive más lejos de la escuela?

**fascinate** ['fæsɪneɪt] *vt* fascinar.

**fascinating** ['fæsɪneɪtɪŋ] *adj* fascinante.

**fascination** [fæsɪ'neɪʃən] *n* fascinación *f*.

**fascism** ['fæʃɪzəm] *n* fascismo.

**fascist** ['fæʃɪst] *n* fascista *mf*.
▶ *adj* fascista.

**fashion** ['fæʃən] *n* **1** *(style)* moda. **2** *(way)* modo. LOC in fashion de moda. ‖ out of fashion pasado de moda.
▶ *vt (clay)* formar; *(metal)* labrar.

**fashionable** ['fæʃənəbəl] *adj* de moda.

**fast¹** [fɑːst] *adj* **1** *(gen)* rápido,-a. **2** *(tight, secure)* firme, seguro,-a. **3** *(clock)* adelantado,-a.
▶ *adv* **1** rápidamente, deprisa. **2** *(securely)* firmemente; *(thoroughly)* profundamente.

**fast²** [fɑːst] *n* ayuno.
▶ *vi* ayunar.

**fasten** ['fɑːsən] *vt* **1** *(attach)* fijar, sujetar. **2** *(tie)* atar. **3** *(box, door, window)* cerrar; *(belt, dress)* abrochar.
▶ *vi (box, door, etc)* cerrarse; *(dress, etc)* abrocharse.

**fastener** [ˈfɑːsənəʳ] *n* cierre *m*.

**fastidious** [fæˈstɪdɪəs] *adj* quisquilloso,-a, melindroso,-a.

☒ Fastidious no significa 'fastidioso (molesto)', que se traduce por **annoying**.

**fat** [fæt] *adj* gordo,-a.
ⓘ *comp* **fatter**, *superl* **fattest**.
▸ *n* **1** *(of meat)* grasa; *(of person)* carnes *fpl*. **2** *(for cooking)* manteca; *(lard)* lardo.

**fatal** [ˈfeɪtəl] *adj* **1** *(causing disaster)* fatal, funesto,-a; *(serious)* grave. **2** *(causing death)* mortal. **3** *(fateful)* fatídico,-a.

☒ Fatal no significa 'fatal (muy malo)', que se traduce por **awful**.

**fatality** [fəˈtælɪtɪ] *n* víctima mortal.
ⓘ *pl* **fatalities**.

**fate** [feɪt] *n* **1** *(destiny)* destino. **2** *(person's lot)* suerte *f*.

**fated** [ˈfeɪtɪd] *adj* predestinado,-a.

**fateful** [ˈfeɪtful] *adj* fatídico,-a.

**father** [ˈfɑːðəʳ] *n* **1** *(male parent)* padre *m*. **2** *(priest)* padre *m*.
▸ *vt* engendrar.

**father-in-law** [ˈfɑːðərɪnlɔː] *n* suegro.

**fatherland** [ˈfɑːðəlænd] *n* patria.

**fatherly** [ˈfɑːðəlɪ] *adj* paternal.

**fatigue** [fəˈtiːg] *n* **1** fatiga, cansancio. **2** TECH fatiga.
▸ *vt fml* fatigar, cansar.

**fat-soluble** [fætˈsɒljəbəl] *adj* liposoluble.

**fatten** [ˈfætən] *vt* **1** *(animal)* cebar (up, -). **2** *(person)* engordar (up, -).

**fattening** [ˈfætənɪŋ] *adj* que engorda: *biscuits are fattening* las galletas engordan.

**fatty** [ˈfætɪ] *adj (greasy)* graso,-a.
ⓘ *comp* **fattier**, *superl* **fattiest**.
▸ *n fam pej* gordinflón,-ona.
ⓘ *pl* **fatties**.

**faucet** [ˈfɔːsɪt] *n* US grifo.

**fault** [fɔːlt] *n* **1** *(gen)* defecto. **2** *(blame)* culpa. **4** *(mistake)* error *m*, falta. **5** *(in earth)* falla. **6** *(in tennis, etc)* falta.
▸ *vt* criticar, encontrar defectos a.

☒ Fault no significa 'falta (carencia)', que se traduce por **lack**.

**faultless** [ˈfɔːltləs] *adj* perfecto,-a, intachable, impecable.

**faulty** [ˈfɔːltɪ] *adj* defectuoso,-a.
ⓘ *comp* **faultier**, *superl* **faultiest**.

**fauna** [ˈfɔːnə] *n* fauna.

**faux pas** [fəʊˈpɑː] *n* metedura de pata.
ⓘ *pl* **faux pas**.

**favor** [ˈfeɪvəʳ] *n-vt* US → **favour**.

**favorite** [ˈfeɪvərɪt] *n* US → **favorite**.

**favour** [ˈfeɪvəʳ] *n* **1** *(kindness)* favor *m*. **2** *(approval)* aprobación *f*, favor *m*. **3** *(favouritism)* parcialidad *f*, favoritismo.
▸ *vt* **1** *(prefer)* preferir, inclinarse por. **2** *(benefit, aid)* favorecer.

**favourable** [ˈfeɪvərəbəl] *adj* favorable (to/towards, a).

**favourite** [ˈfeɪvərɪt] *n* favorito,-a.
▸ *adj* favorito,-a.

**favouritism** [ˈfeɪvərɪtɪzəm] *n* favoritismo.

**fawn** [fɔːn] *n* **1** ZOOL cervato. **2** *(colour)* beige *m*.
▸ *adj* beige.
◆ **to fawn on** *vt insep* adular, lisonjear.

**fax** [fæks] *n* fax *m*.
▸ *vt* enviar por fax. COMP **fax machine** fax *m*.

**fear** [fɪəʳ] *n* miedo, temor *m*.
▸ *vt* temer, tener miedo a.
▸ *vi* temer, tener miedo.
◆ **to fear for** *vt insep* temer por: *I fear for the children's safety* temo por la seguridad de los niños.

**fearful** [ˈfɪəful] *adj* **1** *(frightened)* temeroso,-a (of, de). **2** *(terrible)* terrible, espantoso,-a.

**fearless** [ˈfɪələs] *adj* audaz.

**fearsome** [ˈfɪəsəm] *adj* temible.

**feasibility** [fiːzəˈbɪlɪtɪ] *n* viabilidad *f*.

**feasible** [ˈfiːzəbəl] *adj* **1** *(viable)* factible, viable. **2** *(plausible)* verosímil.

**feast** [fiːst] *n* **1** festín *m*, banquete *m*. **2** *fam* comilona. **3** REL fiesta de guardar, día *m* de fiesta.
▸ *vi* banquetear, festejar.

**feat** [fiːt] *n* proeza, hazaña.

**feather** [ˈfeðəʳ] *n* pluma.

**feature** [ˈfiːtʃəʳ] *n* **1** *(of face)* rasgo, facción *f*. **2** *(characteristic)* rasgo, característica. **3** *(press)* artículo especial, especial *m*.
COMP **feature (film)** largometraje *m*.

▶ *vt (have)* tener; *(film)* tener como protagonista: *this car features the latest safety devices* este coche incorpora los últimos dispositivos de seguridad.
▶ *vi (appear)* figurar (in, en): *his name featured in the police report* su nombre figuró en el informe policial.

**February** ['februəri] *n* febrero.

✎ Para ejemplo de uso, consulta May.

**fecal** ['fiːkəl] *adj* US → faecal.

**feces** ['fiːsiːz] *n* US → faeces.

**fed** [fed] *pt & pp* → feed. LOC **to be fed up with** *fam* estar harto,-a de.

**federal** ['fedərəl] *adj* federal.

**federation** [fedəˈreɪʃən] *n* federación *f*.

**fee** [fiː] *n* 1 *(doctor's, etc)* honorarios *mpl*; *(for tuition)* derechos *mpl* (de matrícula). 2 *(membership)* cuota, cuota de socio. COMP **registration fee** matrícula.

**feeble** ['fiːbəl] *adj* 1 *(person)* débil. 2 *(light, sound)* tenue, débil. 3 *(argument, excuse)* de poco peso.

**feed** [fiːd] *n* 1 comida. 2 *fam* comilona. 3 *(for cattle)* pienso. 4 TECH alimentación *f*.
▶ *vt* 1 alimentar: *could you feed our cat while we're away?* ¿podrías dar de comer a nuestro gato mientras estamos fuera? 2 *(breastfeed)* dar de mamar a; *(bottle-feed)* dar el biberón a. 3 TECH alimentar, suministrar. 4 *(insert)* introducir; *(coins)* meter.
▶ *vi (people)* comer, alimentarse (on, de); *(animals)* pacer.
◆ **to feed up** *vt sep (animal)* cebar; *(person)* engordar.
① *pt & pp* fed [fed].

**feedback** ['fiːdbæk] *n* 1 TECH retroalimentación *f*, retroacción *f*. 2 *fig* reacción *f*, respuesta *f*.

**feeder** ['fiːdər] *n* 1 TECH alimentador *m*. 2 *(road)* ramal *m*, carretera.

**feel** [fiːl] *n* 1 *(sense, texture)* tacto. 2 *(atmosphere)* aire *m*, ambiente *m*.
▶ *vt* 1 *(touch)* tocar, palpar. 2 *(search with fingers)* buscar. 3 *(sense, experience)* sentir, experimentar. 4 *(believe)* creer.
▶ *vi* 1 *(be)* sentir(se), encontrarse. 2 *(seem)* parecer: *it feels like leather* parece piel. 3 *(perceive, sense)* sentir: *she could feel all eyes upon her* sentía que todos la miraban. 4 *(opinion)* opinar, pensar: *how do you feel about exams?* ¿qué opinas de los exámenes?
◆ **to feel for** *vt insep (have sympathy for)* compadecer a, compadecerse de.
① *pt & pp* felt [felt].

**feeler** ['fiːlər] *n* antena *f*.

**feeling** ['fiːlɪŋ] *n* 1 *(emotion)* sentimiento, emoción *f*. 2 *(sensation)* sensación *f*. 3 *(sense)* sensibilidad *f*. 4 *(impression)* impresión *f*: *I have the feeling that ...* tengo la impresión de que ...
▶ *adj* sensible, compasivo,-a.
▶ *n pl* **feelings** sentimientos *mpl*.

**feet** [fiːt] *n pl* → foot.

**feign** [feɪn] *vt* fingir, aparentar: *she feigned illness to get off school* fingió estar enferma para no ir a la escuela.

**feint** [feɪnt] *n fml (fencing)* finta; *(boxing)* treta, estratagema.
▶ *adj (paper)* rayado,-a.

**feldspar** ['feldspɑːr] *n* feldespato.

**feline** ['fiːlaɪn] *adj* felino,-a.
▶ *n* felino,-a.

**fell¹** [fel] *vt* 1 *(tree)* talar. 2 *(enemy)* derribar.

**fell²** [fel] *pt* → fall.

**fellow** ['feləʊ] *n* 1 *fam (chap)* tipo, tío: *old fellow* viejo amigo; *poor fellow!* ¡pobrecito! 2 *(companion, comrade)* compañero,-a, camarada *mf*. 3 *(member)* socio,-a.

**fellowship** ['feləʊʃɪp] *n* 1 *(group)* asociación *f*, sociedad *f*. 2 *(companionship)* compañerismo, camaradería *f*. 3 EDUC *(scholarship)* beca.

**felspar** ['felspɑːr] *n* feldespato.

**felt¹** [felt] *pt & pp* → feel.

**felt²** [felt] *n* fieltro.
▶ *adj* de fieltro.

**felt-tip** ['felttɪp] [also felt-tip pen] *n* rotulador *m*.

**female** ['fiːmeɪl] *n* 1 hembra. 2 *(woman)* mujer *f*; *(girl)* chica.
▶ *adj* 1 femenino,-a. 2 ZOOL hembra.

**feminine** ['femɪnɪn] *adj* femenino,-a.
▶ *n* femenino,-a.

**feminism** ['femɪnɪzəm] *n* feminismo.

**feminist** ['femɪnɪst] *n* feminista *mf*.

**femoral** ['fiːmərəl] *adj* femoral.

**femur** ['fi:mər] n fémur m.

**fence** [fens] n valla, cerca. LOC **to sit on the fence** ver los toros desde la barrera.
▶ vi **1** SP practicar la esgrima. **2** (land) cercar.

**fencing** ['fensɪŋ] n **1** SP esgrima. **2** (structure) cercado.

**fend** [fend] vi **to fend for os** valerse por uno mismo,-a.
◆ **to fend off** vt sep (blow) parar, desviar; (question) esquivar; (attack) rechazar, defenderse de.

**fender** ['fendər] n **1** (for fire) pantalla. **2** US (on automobile) parachoques m.

**fennel** ['fenəl] n hinojo.

**ferment** [(n) 'fɜ:mənt] (vb) fə'ment] n **1** (substance) fermento. **2** (unrest) agitación f.
▶ vt & vi fermentar.

**fermentation** [fɜ:men'teɪʃən] n fermentación f.

**fern** [fɜ:n] n helecho.

**ferocious** [fə'rəʊʃəs] adj feroz.

**ferocity** [fə'rɒsɪti] n ferocidad f.

**ferret** ['ferɪt] n hurón m.
◆ **to ferret out** vt sep descubrir.

**ferrous** ['ferəs] adj ferroso,-a.

**ferry** ['feri] n (small) barca de pasaje; (large) transbordador m, ferry m.
ⓘ pl **ferries**.
▶ vt transportar.
ⓘ pt & pp **ferried**, ger **ferrying**.

**ferryboat** ['feribəʊt] n → **ferry**.

**fertile** ['fɜ:taɪl] adj fértil.

**fertility** [fə'tɪlɪti] n fertilidad f.

**fertilization** [fɜ:təlaɪ'zeɪʃən] n **1** (soil) fertilización f. **2** (egg) fecundación f.

**fertilize** ['fɜ:tɪlaɪz] vt **1** (soil) fertilizar, abonar. **2** (egg) fecundar.

**fertilizer** ['fɜ:tɪlaɪzər] n fertilizante m, abono.

**ferule¹** ['feru:l] n férula.

**fervent** ['fɜ:vənt] adj fervoroso,-a.

**fervor** ['fɜ:və] n US → **fervour**.

**fervour** ['fɜ:və] n fervor m.

**fester** ['festər] vi **1** MED supurar, enconarse. **2** fig amargarse.

**festival** ['festɪvəl] n **1** (event) festival m. **2** (celebration) fiesta.

**fetal** ['fi:təs] n US → **foetal**.

**fetch** [fetʃ] vt **1** (go and get) ir por, ir a buscar, buscar; (bring) traer. **2** fam (sell for) venderse por, alcanzar.
◆ **to fetch up** vi ir a parar.

**fête** [feɪt] n (party) fiesta; (fair) feria.
▶ vt festejar.

**fetid** ['fetɪd] adj fétido,-a.

**fetish** ['fetɪʃ] n fetiche m.

**fetter** ['fetər] vt **1** encadenar. **2** fig estorbar, poner trabas a.
▶ n pl **fetters** grilletes mpl, cadenas fpl.

**fetus** ['fi:təs] n US → **foetus**.

**feud** [fju:d] n enemistad f (duradera): *there's been a feud between the two families for years* hace años que existe una enemistad entre ambas familias.
▶ vi disentir, reñir, pelear.

❌ **Feud** no significa 'feudo (dominio)', que se traduce por **fief**.

**feudal** ['fju:dəl] adj feudal.

**feudalism** ['fju:dəlɪzəm] n feudalismo.

**fever** ['fi:və] n fiebre f.

**feverish** ['fi:vərɪʃ] adj febril.

**few** [fju:] adj **1** (not many) poco,-a, pocos,-as: *very few cars* muy pocos coches. **2** (some) uno,-as cuantos,-as, algunos,-as: *in the next few days* en los próximos días.
▶ pron **1** (not many) pocos,-as: *many try but few succeed* muchos lo intentan pero pocos lo consiguen. **2** (some) unos,-as cuantos,-as, algunos,-as: *there are a few left* quedan unos cuantos.

**fiancé** [fɪ'ænseɪ] n prometido, novio.

**fiancée** [fɪ'ænseɪ] n prometida, novia.

**fiasco** [fɪ'æskəʊ] n fiasco, fracaso.
ⓘ pl **fiascos**.

**fib** [fɪb] n fam bola, trola.
▶ vi fam contar bolas, contar trolas.
ⓘ pt & pp **fibbed**, ger **fibbing**.

**fibre** ['faɪbə] n fibra. COMP **fibre optics** fibra óptica. ▌**man-made fibre** fibra artificial.

**fibreglass** ['faɪbəglɑ:s] n fibra de vidrio.

**fibrosis** [faɪ'brəʊsɪs] n fibrosis f.

**fibrous** ['faɪbrəs] adj fibroso,-a.

**fibula** ['fɪbjələ] n peroné m.

**fickle** ['fɪkəl] adj inconstante, voluble.

**fiction** ['fɪkʃən] n **1** *(novels)* novela, narrativa. **2** *(invention)* ficción f.

**fictitious** [fɪk'tɪʃəs] adj ficticio,-a.

**fiddle** ['fɪdəl] n **1** fam violín m. **2** fam *(fraud)* estafa, trampa.
▶ vi **1** tocar el violín. **2** fam *(play)* juguetear (with, con).
▶ vt fam *(cheat)* amañar, falsificar.
◆ **to fiddle about / fiddle around** vi fam perder el tiempo.

**fiddler** ['fɪdlər] n **1** fam *(violinist)* violinista mf. **2** fam *(cheat)* tramposo,-a.

**fidelity** [fɪ'delɪtɪ] n fidelidad f.

**fidget** ['fɪdʒɪt] n persona inquieta.
▶ vi *(move about)* moverse, no poder estar(se) quieto,-a; *(play about)* jugar (with, con).

**fief** [fi:f] n feudo.

**field** [fi:ld] n **1** *(gen)* campo. **2** *(for mining)* yacimiento. **3** *(subject, area)* campo, terreno. **4** SP *(competitors)* competidores mpl; *(horses)* participantes mpl.

**fierce** [fɪəs] adj **1** *(gen)* feroz. **2** fig *(heat, competition, etc)* fuerte, intenso,-a; *(argument)* acalorado,-a.

**fiery** ['faɪərɪ] adj **1** *(colour)* encendido,-a, rojo,-a. **2** *(burning)* ardiente. **3** *(food)* muy picante; *(drink)* muy fuerte.
ⓘ comp **fierier**, superl **fieriest**.

**fifteen** [fɪf'ti:n] adj quince.
▶ n quince m.
✎ Consulta también six.

**fifteenth** [fɪf'ti:nθ] adj decimoquinto,-a.
▶ adv en decimoquinto lugar.
▶ n **1** *(in series)* decimoquinto,-a. **2** *(fraction)* decimoquinto; *(one part)* decimoquinta parte f.
✎ Consulta también sixth.

**fifth** [fɪfθ] adj quinto,-a.
▶ adv quinto, en quinto lugar.
▶ n **1** *(in series)* quinto,-a. **2** *(fraction)* quinto; *(one part)* quinta parte f.
✎ Consulta también sixth.

**fiftieth** ['fɪftɪəθ] adj quincuagésimo,-a.
▶ adv en quincuagésimo lugar.

▶ n **1** *(in series)* quincuagésimo,-a. **2** *(fraction)* quincuagésimo; *(one part)* quincuagésima parte f.
✎ Consulta también sixtieth.

**fifty** ['fɪftɪ] adj cincuenta.
▶ n cincuenta m.
✎ Consulta también sixty.

**fifty-fifty** ['fɪftɪ'fɪftɪ] adv fam mitad y mitad, a medias.

**fig** [fɪg] n higo. COMP **fig tree** higuera.

**fight** [faɪt] n **1** *(struggle)* lucha. **2** *(physical violence)* pelea; *(quarrel)* riña; *(argument)* disputa. **3** *(boxing)* combate m.
▶ vi **1** *(quarrel)* pelear(se) (about/over, por), discutir (about/over, por). **2** *(in boxing)* pelear (against, contra). **3** *(with physical violence)* pelearse (with, con) (against, contra), luchar (with, con) (against, contra).
▶ vt **1** *(bull)* lidiar. **2** *(engage in - battle)* librar; *(- war)* hacer; *(- election)* presentarse a. **3** *(with physical violence)* pelearse, luchar.
◆ **to fight back** vi defenderse, resistir.
▶ vt sep *(tears)* contener.
◆ **to fight off** vt sep vencer, rechazar.
ⓘ pt & pp **fought** [fɔːt].

**fighter** ['faɪtər] n **1** *(war)* combatiente mf. **2** *(boxing)* boxeador,-ra. **3** fig luchador,-ra.

**fig-leaf** ['fɪgliːf] n hoja de parra.

**figurative** ['fɪgərətɪv] adj figurado,-a.

**figure** ['fɪgər] n **1** *(number, sign)* cifra, número. **2** *(money, price)* cantidad f, precio. **3** *(in art, shape, human form)* figura. **4** *(personality)* figura, personaje m.
▶ vi *(appear)* figurar, constar.
▶ vt US *(think)* suponer, imaginarse.
◆ **to figure out** vt sep fam *(gen)* comprender, enterarse; *(problem)* resolver, calcular.

**filament** ['fɪləmənt] n filamento.

**file** [faɪl] n **1** *(tool)* lima. **2** *(folder)* carpeta. **3** *(archive)* archivo, expediente m. **4** COMPUT archivo. **5** *(line)* fila.
▶ vt **1** *(smooth)* limar. **2** *(put away)* archivar; *(in card index)* fichar. **3** JUR presentar.
▶ vi *(walk in line)* desfilar.

**filigree** ['fɪlɪgriː] n filigrana.

**fill** [fɪl] *vt* **1** *(make full)* llenar (with, de). **2** *(time)* ocupar. **3** *(cover)* cubrir. **4** CULIN rellenar. **5** *(tooth)* empastar. **6** *(hold a position)* ocupar; *(appoint)* cubrir. **7** *(fulfil)* satisfacer.
▶ *vi* llenarse (with, de).
◆ **to fill in** *vt sep* **1** *(space, form)* rellenar. **2** *(inform)* poner al corriente (on, de).
◆ **to fill in for** *vt insep* sustituir a.
◆ **to fill up** *vt sep* llenar.
▶ *vi* llenarse.

**fillet** ['fɪlɪt] *n* filete *m*.

**filling** ['fɪlɪŋ] *n* **1** *(in tooth)* empaste *m*. **2** CULIN relleno. COMP **filling station** gasolinera.

**film** [fɪlm] *n* **1** CINEM película, filme *m*, film *m*. **2** *(coating of dust, etc)* capa, película. **3** *(of photos)* carrete *m*, rollo.
▶ *vt* **1** CINEM rodar, filmar; *(tv programme)* grabar. **2** *(event)* filmar.
▶ *vi* CINEM rodar.

**filter** ['fɪltə<sup>r</sup>] *n* filtro.
▶ *vt* filtrar.

**filth** [fɪlθ] *n* **1** *(dirt)* suciedad *f*, porquería. **2** *fig (obscenity)* obscenidades *fpl*, porquerías *fpl*.

**filthy** ['fɪlθɪ] *adj* **1** *(dirty)* sucio,-a, asqueroso,-a. **2** *(obscene)* obsceno,-a, grosero,-a, asqueroso,-a.
ⓘ *comp* **filthier**, *superl* **filthiest**.

**fin** [fɪn] *n* aleta.

**final** ['faɪnəl] *adj* final.
▶ *n* SP final *f*.
▶ *n pl* **finals** *(at university)* exámenes *mpl* finales.

**finale** [fɪ'nɑːlɪ] *n* final *m*.

**finalist** ['faɪnəlɪst] *n* finalista *mf*.

**finality** [faɪ'nælətɪ] *n* carácter *m* definitivo.

❌ **Finality** no significa 'finalidad (objetivo)', que se traduce por **purpose, aim**.

**finalize** ['faɪnəlaɪz] *vt* *(plans, arrangements)* ultimar; *(date)* fijar.

**finally** ['faɪnəlɪ] *adv* **1** *(at last)* por fin, al final. **2** *(lastly)* por último, finalmente.

**finance** ['faɪnæns] *n* *(management of money)* finanzas *fpl*.
▶ *vt* financiar.
▶ *n pl* **finances** *(money available)* fondos *mpl*.

**financial** [faɪ'nænsɪəl] *n* financiero,-a, económico,-a.

**find** [faɪnd] *n* *(act, thing found)* hallazgo.
▶ *vt* *(gen)* encontrar. **2** JUR declarar.
◆ **to find out** *vt sep* **1** *(enquire)* preguntar, averiguar; *(discover)* descubrir, enterarse de.
▶ *vi* **1** *(enquire)* informarse (about, sobre), averiguar. **2** *(discover)* enterarse (about, de), (llegar a) saber.
ⓘ *pt & pp* **found** [faʊnd].

**finding** ['faɪndɪŋ] *n* **1** *(of inquiry)* conclusión *f*, resultado. **2** JUR fallo, veredicto.

✎ Se usa en plural con el mismo significado.

**fine<sup>1</sup>** [faɪn] *adj* **1** *(gen)* fino,-a. **2** *(high-quality)* excelente. **3** *(weather)* bueno,-a. **4** *(healthy)* bien. **5** *fam (all right)* bien.
▶ *adv* **1** *(in small bits)* fino, finamente. **2** *fam (very well)* muy bien.

**fine<sup>2</sup>** [faɪn] *n* *(punishment)* multa.
▶ *vt* multar.

**finger** ['fɪŋgə<sup>r</sup>] *n* dedo.
▶ *vt* tocar.

**fingernail** ['fɪŋgəneɪl] *n* uña.

**fingerprint** ['fɪŋgəprɪnt] *n* huella digital, huella dactilar.

**fingertip** ['fɪŋgətɪp] *n* punta del dedo, yema del dedo.

**finish** ['fɪnɪʃ] *n* **1** fin *m*, final *m*. **2** SP llegada, meta. **3** *(for surface)* acabado.
▶ *vt* acabar, terminar.
◆ **to finish up** *vi* *(end up)* ir a parar a/en.

**finite** ['faɪnaɪt] *adj* finito,-a.

**Finland** ['fɪnlənd] *n* Finlandia.

**Finn** [fɪn] *n* *(person)* finlandés,-esa.

**Finnish** ['fɪnɪʃ] *adj* finlandés,-esa.
▶ *n* *(language)* finlandés *m*.

**fiord** [fɪ'ɔːd] *n* fiordo.

**fir** [fɜː<sup>r</sup>] *n* abeto.

**fire** [faɪə<sup>r</sup>] *n* **1** *(gen)* fuego. **2** *(blaze)* incendio, fuego. **3** *(heater)* estufa. **4** MIL fuego. LOC to **be on fire** estar ardiendo. **I to catch fire** prenderse. COMP **fire brigade** los bomberos. **I fire engine** coche de bomberos. **I fire escape** escalera de incendios. **I fire extinguisher** extintor *m*. **I fire hydrant** boca de incendios. **I fire station** parque *m* de bomberos.

▶ vt (weapon) disparar; (rocket) lanzar. **2** fam (dismiss) despedir.

▶ vi **1** (shoot) disparar (at, sobre), hacer fuego. **2** AUTO encenderse.

▶ interj ¡fuego!

**firearm** ['faɪərɑːm] n arma de fuego.

**firebreak** ['faɪəbreɪk] n cortafuego.

**firecracker** ['faɪəkrækəʳ] n petardo.

**firefighter** ['faɪəfaɪtəʳ] n bombero mf.

**firefly** ['faɪəflaɪ] n luciérnaga.
ⓘ pl fireflies.

**fireman** ['faɪəmən] n bombero.
ⓘ pl firemen ['faɪəmən].

**fireplace** ['faɪəpleɪs] n **1** (structure) chimenea. **2** (hearth) hogar m.

**fireproof** ['faɪəpruːf] adj a prueba de fuego.

**firewall** ['faɪəwɔːl] n cortafuego.

**firewood** ['faɪəwud] n leña.

**fireworks** ['faɪəwɜːks] n pl fuegos mpl artificiales, fuegos mpl de artificio.

**firing** ['faɪərɪŋ] n tiroteo.

**firm¹** [fɜːm] n (business) empresa.

☒ Firm no significa 'firma (escrita)', que se traduce por signature.

**firm²** [fɜːm] adj **1** (strong, solid, steady) firme, sólido,-a. **2** (strict, strong) duro,-a. **3** FIN (steady) firme, estable.

**first** [fɜːst] adj primero,-a.
▶ adv **1** (before anything else) primero. **2** (for the first time) por primera vez. **3** (in preference to) antes. LOC at first al principio. ‖ first of all primero.
▶ n **1** la primera vez. **2** (gear) primera: I can't put it into first no puedo meter primera.

**first-aid** [fɜːstˈeɪd] adj de primeros auxilios. COMP first-aid kit botiquín m.

**first-born** ['fɜːstbɔːn] adj primogénito,-a.
▶ n primogénito,-a.

**first-class** ['fɜːstklɑːs] adj **1** de primera clase. **2** fig de primera, excelente.
▶ adv en primera.

**first-hand** [fɜːstˈhænd] adj de primera mano.

**firstly** ['fɜːstlɪ] adv en primer lugar.

**first-rate** ['fɜːstreɪt] adj de primera.
▶ adv de primera.

**fiscal** ['fɪskəl] adj fiscal.

**fish** [fɪʃ] n **1** pez m. **2** CULIN pescado. COMP fish farm piscifactoría. ‖ fish finger palito de pescado rebozado. ‖ fish shop pescadería.
ⓘ pl fish o fishes.
▶ vi pescar (for, -).

✎ Cuando significa 'pez', fish es un nombre contable y su plural es fish, aunque también se puede emplear la forma menos frecuente fishes. Cuando significa 'pescado', es incontable y, por lo tanto, no tiene plural.

**fishbowl** ['fɪʃbəʊl] n pecera.

**fisherman** ['fɪʃəmən] n pescador m.
ⓘ pl fishermen ['fɪʃəmən].

**fish-hook** ['fɪʃhʊk] n anzuelo.

**fishing** ['fɪʃɪŋ] n pesca. LOC to go fishing ir de pesca. COMP fishing line sedal m. ‖ fishing net red f de pesca. ‖ fishing rod caña de pescar.

**fishmonger** ['fɪʃmʌŋgəʳ] n GB pescadero,-a. COMP fishmonger's pescadería.

**fission** ['fɪʃən] n fisión f.

**fissure** ['fɪʃəʳ] n fisura, grieta.

**fist** [fɪst] n puño.

**fistful** ['fɪstfʊl] n puñado.

**fit¹** [fɪt] n **1** MED ataque m, acceso. **2** (of laughter, rage) ataque m.

**fit²** [fɪt] adj **1** (suitable, appropriate) adecuado,-a, apropiado,-a; (qualified for) capacitado,-a, capaz. **2** (in good health) sano,-a, bien de salud; (physically) en forma. **3** fam (ready) a punto de.
ⓘ comp fitter, superl fittest.

▶ n **1** (of clothes) : it's a perfect fit me va perfectamente. **2** (in space): it'll be a tight fit vamos a estar muy apretados.

▶ vt **1** (be right size for) sentar bien, quedar bien. **2** (try (clothing) on sb) probar. **3** (key) abrir. **4** (install) instalar, poner. **5** (adapt) ajustar, adaptar, adecuar.

◆ to fit in vi **1** (get on) llevarse bien, integrarse. **2** (suit) encajar; (harmonize) pegar, quedar bien; (tally) cuadrar.

► *vt sep* **1** *(physically)* hacer sitio para. **2** *(in timetable)* hacer un hueco para. **3** *(harmonize)* encajar, cuadrar.

ⓘ *pt & pp* fitted, *ger* fitting.

**fitness** ['fɪtnəs] *n* **1** *(health)* buena forma física, buen estado físico. **2** *(suitability)* capacidad *f* (for, para).

**fitted** ['fɪtɪd] *adj (cupboard)* empotrado,-a; *(room)* amueblado,-a. COMP **fitted carpet** moqueta.

**fitting** ['fɪtɪŋ] *adj (appropriate, proper)* apropiado,-a, adecuado,-a.
► *n* SEW prueba.
► *n pl* **fittings 1** *(accessories)* accesorios *mpl.* **2** *(furnishings)* muebles, cortinas y alfombras.

**five** [faɪv] *n* cinco.
► *adj* cinco.

✎ Consulta también six.

**fix** [fɪks] *n* **1** *fam (difficult situation)* apuro, aprieto. **2** *(position of ship, aircraft)* posición *f.* **3** *(dishonest arrangement)* tongo.
► *vt* **1** *(gen)* fijar. **2** *(decide)* decidir; *(date, meeting, etc)* fijar. **3** *(organize)* arreglar, organizar. **4** *(dishonestly)* amañar. **5** *(repair)* arreglar.
◆ **to fix on** *vt insep (decide, select - person)* decidir, optar por, escoger; *(- date)* fijar.
◆ **to fix up** *vt sep* **1** *(accommodate, provide with)* proveer (with, de), conseguir. **2** *(organize)* arreglar, organizar. **3** *(repair, redecorate)* arreglar; *(install)* poner.

**fixation** [fɪk'seɪʃən] *n* obsesión *f.*

**fixture** ['fɪkstʃəʳ] *n* SP encuentro.
► *n pl* **fixtures** *(furniture)* muebles *mpl* empotrados.

**fizz** [fɪz] *n* burbujeo, efervesencia.
► *vi* burbujear.

**fizzle** ['fɪzəl] *vi* burbujear.
◆ **to fizzle out** *vi* esfumarse, perder fuerza, quedar en nada.

**fizzy** ['fɪzɪ] *adj (gen)* gaseoso,-a, con gas; *(wine)* espumoso,-a.
ⓘ *comp* fizzier, *superl* fizziest.

**fjord** [fɪ'ɔːd] *n* fiordo.

**flabbergasted** ['flæbəgɑːstɪd] *adj* pasmado,-a, atónito,-a.

**flabby** ['flæbɪ] *adj (part of body)* fofo,-a.
ⓘ *comp* flabbier, *superl* flabbiest.

**flaccid** ['flæksɪd] *adj* fláccido,-a.

**flag¹** [flæg] *n (paving slab)* → flagstone.

**flag²** [flæg] *n* **1** *(gen)* bandera. **2** MAR pabellón *m.* **3** *(for charity)* banderita.
◆ **to flag down** *vt sep* hacer señales para que un coche se detenga.

**flagellum** [flə'dʒələm] *n* flagelo.
ⓘ *pl* flagellums o flagella [flə'dʒələ].

**flagpole** ['flægpəʊl] *n* asta de bandera.

**flagship** ['flægʃɪp] *n* buque *m* insignia.

**flagstone** ['flægstəʊn] *n (large)* losa; *(small)* loseta.

**flair** [fleəʳ] *n* talento, don *m*, facilidad *f.*

**flake** [fleɪk] *n* **1** *(of snow, oats)* copo. **2** *(of skin, soap)* escama. **3** *(of paint)* desconchón *m*, trozo desprendido.
► *vi* **to flake away/off** *(gen)* descamarse; *(paint)* desconcharse.

**flamboyant** [flæm'bɔɪənt] *adj* llamativo,-a, extravagante.

**flame** [fleɪm] *n* llama.
► *vi* **1** *(burn)* arder. **2** *(glow, shine)* brillar. **3** *(become angry)* montar en cólera.

**flame-thrower** ['fleɪmθrəʊəʳ] *n* lanzallamas *m.*

**flamingo** [flə'mɪŋgəʊ] *n* flamenco.
ⓘ *pl* flamingos o flamingoes.

**flammable** ['flæməbəl] *adj* inflamable.

**flan** [flæn] *n* CULIN tarta rellena.

☒ Flan no significa 'flan', que se traduce por crème caramel.

**flange** [flændʒ] *n (on wheel)* pestaña; *(on pipe)* reborde *m.*

**flank** [flæŋk] *n* **1** *(of animal)* ijada, ijar *m.* **2** MIL flanco. **3** *(of building, mountain, etc)* lado, falda.

**flannel** ['flænəl] *n (material)* franela.

**flap** [flæp] *n* **1** *(of envelope, pocket)* solapa. **2** *(of tent)* faldón *m.* **3** *(of plane)* alerón *m.*
► *vt (wings)* batir; *(arms)* agitar.
► *vi* **1** *(wings)* aletear. **2** *(flag, sails)* ondear. **3** *fam* inquietarse.
ⓘ *pt & pp* flapped, *ger* flapping.

**flare** [fleəʳ] *n* **1** *(flame)* llamarada. **2** *(signal)* bengala.
► *vi* **1** llamear. **2** *fig* estallar, encenderse.
◆ **to flare up** *vi (blow up, erupt)* estallar, encenderse; *(get angry)* enfadarse, montar en cólera.

**flared** [fleəd] *adj* acampanado,-a.

**flash** [flæʃ] *n* **1** *(of light)* destello, centelleo; *(of lightning)* relámpago. **2** *(from firearm)* fogonazo. **3** *fig* destello, rayo. **4** *(photography)* flash *m*.
▶ *vi* brillar, destellar.
▶ *vt (shine - light)* dirigir, lanzar; *(- torch)* encender, dirigir.

**flashback** ['flæʃbæk] *n* flashback *m*.

**flashlight** ['flæʃlaɪt] *n* **1** *(torch)* linterna. **2** *(photo)* flash *m*.

**flashy** ['flæʃɪ] *adj* llamativo,-a.
ⓘ *comp* flashier, *superl* flashiest.

**flask** [flɑːsk] *n* **1** frasco. **2** CHEM matraz *m*.

**flat¹** [flæt] *n (apartment)* piso.

**flat²** [flæt] *adj* **1** *(level, even)* llano,-a, plano,-a; *(smooth)* liso,-a. **2** *(shoes)* sin tacón. **3** *(tyre, ball, etc)* desinflado,-a. **4** *(battery)* descargado,-a. **5** *(drink)* sin gas. **6** MUS *(key)* bemol; *(voice, instrument)* desafinado,-a.
ⓘ *comp* flatter, *superl* flattest.
▶ *n* **1** *(plain)* llano, llanura. **2** *(of hand)* palma. **3** MUS bemol *m*. **4** US *(tyre)* pinchazo.

**flatly** ['flætlɪ] *adv* **1** *(categorically)* categóricamente, rotundamente. **2** *(voice)* con voz monótona.

**flatten** ['flætən] *vt* **1** *(make flat)* allanar, aplanar (out, -); *(smooth)* alisar. **2** *(crush)* aplastar; *(knock down)* derribar, tumbar; *(knock over)* atropellar.

**flatter** ['flætə'] *vt* **1** *(praise)* halagar, adular. **2** *(suit)* favorecer.

**flattering** ['flætərɪŋ] *adj* **1** *(words)* lisonjero,-a, halagüeño,-a. **2** *(clothes, etc)* favorecedor,-ra.

**flattery** ['flætərɪ] *n* adulación *f*, halagos *mpl*.

**flaunt** [flɔ:nt] *vt* hacer alarde de, hacer ostentación de.

**flautist** ['flɔ:tɪst] *n* flautista *mf*.

**flavor** ['fleɪvə'] *n* US → flavour.

**flavour** ['fleɪvə'] *n* sabor *m*, gusto.
▶ *vt* sazonar, condimentar (with, con).

**flavouring** ['fleɪvərɪŋ] *n* condimento.

**flaw** [flɔ:] *n* **1** *(fault - in material, product, etc)* defecto, tara. **2** *(failing - in character)* defecto; *(- in argument)* error *m*.

**flawless** ['flɔ:ləs] *adj* sin defecto, impecable, perfecto,-a.

**flax** [flæks] *n* lino.

**fleck** [flek] *n* mota, punto.

**fled** [fled] *pt* → flee.

**flee** [fli:] *vt (run away)* huir de.
▶ *vi* **1** *(run away, escape)* huir. **2** *(vanish)* desaparecer.
ⓘ *pt & pp* fled [fled].

**fleece** [fli:s] *n* **1** *(sheep's coat, fabric)* lana. **2** *(sheared)* vellón *m*.

**fleet** [fli:t] *n* **1** *(of ships)* flota. **2** *(of vehicles)* flota, parque *m* móvil.

**fleeting** ['fli:tɪŋ] *adj* fugaz, efímero,-a.

**flesh** [fleʃ] *n* **1** *(of animals, humans)* carne *f*. **2** *(of fruit)* carne *f*, pulpa.

**flew** [flu:] *pt* → fly¹.

**flex** [fleks] *n* GB cable *m*.
▶ *vt (body, joints)* doblar; *(muscles)* flexionar.

**flexibility** [fleksɪ'bɪlɪtɪ] *n* flexibilidad *f*.

**flexible** ['fleksəbəl] *adj* flexible.

**flexor** ['fleksə'] *n* flexor.

**flexitime** ['fleksɪtaɪm] *n* horario flexible.

**flick** [flɪk] *n* **1** *(jerk)* movimiento rápido, movimiento brusco. **2** *(of fingers)* capirotazo; *(of whip)* latigazo, chasquido; *(of tail)* coletazo. **3** *(of pages)* hojeada.
◆ **to flick away** *vt sep* quitar, sacudirse.
◆ **to flick through** *vt insep* hojear.

**flicker** ['flɪkə'] *n* **1** *(of flame, eyelids)* parpadeo; *(of light)* titileo, parpadeo. **2** *fig (slight sign)* señal *f*, muestra; *(faint emotion)* chispa, pizca.
▶ *vi* **1** *(gen)* parpadear; *(shadow)* bailar. **2** *(eyelids)* parpadear. **3** *(smile)* esbozarse.

**flies** [flaɪs] *pt* → fly³.

**flight** [flaɪt] *n* **1** *(journey by air)* vuelo: *our flight has been delayed* nuestro vuelo se ha retrasado. **2** *(path)* trayectoria. **3** *(flock of birds)* bandada. **4** *(of stairs)* tramo. **5** *(escape)* huida, fuga. COMP **flight attendant** auxiliar *mf* de vuelo.

**flimsy** ['flɪmzɪ] *adj* **1** *(thin)* fino,-a, ligero,-a. **2** *(structure)* poco sólido,-a. **3** *fig (unconvincing)* flojo,-a, pobre, poco convincente.
ⓘ *comp* flimsier, *superl* flimsiest.

**flinch** [flɪntʃ] *vi* **1** *(wince)* estremecerse. **2** *(shun)* retroceder (from, ante).

**fling** [flɪŋ] n **1** (throw) lanzamiento. **2** (wild time) juerga. **3** (affair) aventura (amorosa), romance m.
▸ vt **1** (throw) arrojar, tirar, lanzar. **2** (move) echar, lanzar. **3** (say) lanzar.
ⓘ pt & pp flung [flʌŋ].

**flint** [flɪnt] n **1** (stone) sílex m; (piece) pedernal m. **2** (of lighter) piedra.

**flip** [flɪp] n **1** (light blow) golpecito. **2** (somersault) voltereta (en el aire).
▸ interj fam ¡ostras!
▸ vt **1** (toss - gen) echar, tirar al aire; (-coin) echar a cara o cruz. **2** (turn over) dar la vuelta a.
▸ vi fam (get angry) perder los estribos; (go mad) volverse loco,-a.
ⓘ pt & pp flipped, ger flipping.

**flip-flop** ['flɪpflɒp] n chancla.

**flipper** ['flɪpəʳ] n aleta.

**flirt** [flɜːt] n coqueto,-a, ligón,-ona.
▸ vi (coquette) flirtear (with, con), coquetear (with, con).

**float** [fləʊt] n **1** (for fishing) boya, flotador m. **2** (for swimming) flotador m. **3** (vehicle - in procession) carroza; (- for delivery) furgoneta.
▸ vi (gen) flotar.

**flock** [flɒk] n **1** (of sheep, goats) rebaño; (of birds) bandada. **2** fam (crowd) multitud f, tropel m.

**flood** [flʌd] n **1** (overflow of water) inundación f. **2** (of river) riada.
▸ vt **1** (gen) inundar, anegar; (engine) ahogar. **2** fig (with calls, applications, etc) llover, inundar (with, de).
▸ vi **1** (river) desbordarse. **2** fig (cover, fill) invadir, inundar.

**floodgate** ['flʌdgeɪt] n compuerta.

**flooding** ['flʌdɪŋ] n inundación f.

**floodlight** ['flʌdlaɪt] n foco.

**floor** [flɔːʳ] n **1** (surface) suelo. **2** GEOG fondo. **3** (storey) piso, planta. **4** (dance) pista.

❌ Floor no significa 'flor', que se traduce por flower.

**flop** [flɒp] n fam fracaso.
▸ vi **1** (fall clumsily) abalanzarse, arrojarse (into, en); (sit or lie clumsily) tumbarse, dejarse caer. **2** fam (fail) fracasar.
ⓘ pt & pp flopped, ger flopping.

**floppy** ['flɒpɪ] adj blando,-a, flexible.
COMP floppy disk COMPUT disco flexible, disquete m.
ⓘ comp floppier, superl floppiest.

**flora** ['flɔːrə] n flora.

**florist** ['flɒrɪst] n florista mf. COMP florist's (shop) floristería.

**flounce** [flaʊns] n SEW volante m.

**flounder** ['flaʊndəʳ] n (fish) platija.
▸ vi **1** (struggle, move with difficulty) forcejear. **2** fig (hesitate, dither) vacilar.

**flour** [flaʊəʳ] n harina.
▸ vt enharinar.

**flourish** ['flʌrɪʃ] n **1** (gesture) ademán m, gesto exagerado. **2** (signature) rúbrica.
▸ vt (wave about) agitar, blandir.
▸ vi **1** (be successful) florecer, prosperar. **2** (plant) crecer bien.

**flow** [fləʊ] n **1** (gen) flujo. **2** (of river) corriente f. **3** (of traffic) circulación f.
▸ vi **1** (gen) fluir. **2** (pour out - blood) manar; (- tears) correr. **3** (tide) subir. **4** (traffic) circular.
◆ to flow into vi (river) desembocar en: the Ebro flows into the sea at Amposta el Ebro desemboca en el mar en Amposta.

**flower** [flaʊəʳ] n flor f.
▸ vi florecer.

**flowerbed** ['flaʊəbed] n parterre m, macizo.

**flowerpot** ['flaʊəpɒt] n maceta, tiesto.

**flown** [fləʊn] pp → fly.

**flu** [fluː] n gripe f: he's got (the) flu tiene la gripe.

**fluctuate** ['flʌktjʊeɪt] vi fluctuar.

**fluency** ['fluːənsɪ] n **1** fluidez f. **2** (of language) dominio (in, de).

**fluent** ['fluːənt] adj **1** (gen) fluido,-a. **2** (language) fluido,-a: he speaks fluent English habla inglés con soltura.

**fluff** [flʌf] n **1** (down, material) pelusa, lanilla. **2** fam (mistake, blunder) pifia, fallo.
▸ vt fam (do badly, fail) hacer mal.

**fluffy** ['flʌfɪ] adj **1** (feathery) mullido,-a. **2** (toys) de peluche.
ⓘ comp fluffier, superl fluffiest.

**fluid** ['fluːɪd] adj **1** (not solid) fluido,-a, líquido,-a. **2** (smooth, graceful) natural, con soltura. **3** (not fixed) flexible.
▸ n fluido, líquido.

**fluke** [fluːk] *n fam* chiripa.

**flung** [flʌŋ] *pt & pp* → fling.

**fluorescent** [fluəˈresənt] *adj* fluorescente. COMP **fluorescent light/lamp** fluorescente *m*.

**flurry** [ˈflʌrɪ] *n* **1** (of wind) ráfaga; (of snow) nevisca. **2** *fig* (burst) nerviosismo.
ⓘ *pl* flurries.

**flush¹** [flʌʃ] *n* (in cards) color *m*.

**flush²** [flʌʃ] *n* **1** (blush) rubor *m*. **2** (of emotion) acceso, arrebato. **3** (of toilet) cisterna.
▶ *vt* **1** (cause to blush) ruborizar, sonrojar. **2** (clean) limpiar con agua. **3** (toilet) tirar (de) la cadena.
▶ *vi* **1** (blush) ruborizarse. **2** (toilet) funcionar.

**fluster** [ˈflʌstəʳ] *vt* poner nervioso,-a.
▶ *n* confusión *f*, agitación *f*.

**flute** [fluːt] *n* flauta.

**flutter** [ˈflʌtəʳ] *n* **1** (excitement) agitación *f*, emoción *f*. **2** (of wings) aleteo. **3** (of eyelashes) pestañeo. **4** *fam* (bet) apuesta.
▶ *vt* **1** (eyelashes) parpadear. **2** (wings) aletear.
▶ *vi* **1** (flag) ondear. **2** (wings) aletear. **3** (flit) revolotear. **4** (heart) palpitar.

**fluvial** [ˈfluːvɪəl] *adj* fluvial.

**fly¹** [flaɪ] *vi* **1** volar. **2** (go by plane) ir en avión. **3** (flag, hair) ondear. **4** *fam* (flee) largarse.
▶ *vt* **1** (plane) pilotar. **2** (send by plane) transportar. **3** (kite) hacer volar. **4** (flag) enarbolar.
ⓘ *pt* flew [fluː], *pp* flown [fləʊn], *ger* flying.
▶ *n pl* flies (on trousers) bragueta *f sing*.
◆ **to fly away / off** *vi* irse volando.

**fly²** [flaɪ] *adj* GB *fam* (smart) astuto,-a.
ⓘ *comp* flier, *superl* fliest.

**fly³** [flaɪ] *n* mosca.
ⓘ *pl* flies.

**flying** [ˈflaɪɪŋ] *n* **1** AV aviación *f*. **2** (action) vuelo.
▶ *adj* **1** (soaring) volante; (animal, machine) volador,-ra, que vuela. **2** (quick) rápido,-a.

**flyover** [ˈflaɪəʊvəʳ] *n* GB paso elevado.

**foal** [fəʊl] *n* potro,-a.
▶ *vi* parir.

**foam** [fəʊm] *n* espuma.

**foamy** [ˈfəʊmɪ] *adj* espumoso,-a.
ⓘ *comp* foamier, *superl* foamiest.

**fob** [fɒb] *vt* engañar, engatusar.
ⓘ *pt & pp* fobbed, *ger* fobbing.

**focal** [ˈfəʊkəl] *adj* focal.

**focus** [ˈfəʊkəs] *n* **1** foco. **2** (centre) centro.
ⓘ *pl* focuses o foci [ˈfəʊsaɪ].
▶ *vt* **1** (camera, etc) enfocar (on, -). **2** *fig* (concentrate) fijar (on, en), centrar (on, en).
ⓘ *pt & pp* focused o focussed, *ger* focusing o focussing.

**fodder** [ˈfɒdəʳ] *n* pienso, forraje *m*.

**foetal** [ˈfiːtəl] *adj* fetal.

**foetus** [ˈfiːtəs] *n* feto.

**fog** [fɒg] *n* niebla.
▶ *vt* **1** (mirror, etc) empañar. **2** (photo) velar. **3** *fig* complicar.
▶ *vi* empañarse (up/over, -).
ⓘ *pt & pp* fogged, *ger* fogging.

**foggy** [ˈfɒgɪ] *adj* **1** de niebla: *it's foggy* hay niebla. **2** (confused) confuso,-a.
ⓘ *comp* foggier, *superl* foggiest.

**foglamp** [ˈfɒglæmp] *n* faro antiniebla.

**foil¹** [fɔɪl] *vt* (prevent, frustrate) frustrar.

**foil²** [fɔɪl] *n* **1** (metal paper) papel *m* de plata. **2** (contrast) contraste *m*.

**fold¹** [fəʊld] *n* (for sheep) redil *m*, aprisco.

**fold²** [fəʊld] *n* **1** (crease) pliegue *m*, doblez *m*. **2** GEOG pliegue *m*.
▶ *vt* **1** doblar, plegar (up, -). **2** (wrap) envolver.
▶ *vi* **1** doblarse, plegarse. **2** (go bankrupt) quebrar.

**folder** [ˈfəʊldəʳ] *n* carpeta.

**folding** [ˈfəʊldɪŋ] *adj* plegable.

**folk** [fəʊk] *n pl* gente *f sing*.
▶ *adj* popular.
▶ *n pl* **folks** *fam* (family) familia *f sing*; (friends) amigos *mpl*.

**folklore** [ˈfəʊklɔːʳ] *n* folklor(e) *m*.

**follicle** [ˈfɒlɪkəl] *n* folículo.

**follow** [ˈfɒləʊ] *vt* **1** (gen) seguir. **2** (pursue) perseguir. **3** (take interest in) seguir, estar al corriente de.
▶ *vi* **1** (gen) seguir. **2** (understand) entender. **3** (be logical) resultar, derivarse.
◆ **to follow up** *vt sep* **1** (develop) profundizar en. **2** (investigate) investigar.

**following** ['fɒləʊɪŋ] *adj* siguiente.
► *prep* después de.
► *n (supporters)* seguidores *mpl*.

**folly** ['fɒlɪ] *n fml* locura, desatino.
ⓘ *pl* follies.

**fond** [fɒnd] *adj* 1 *(loving)* cariñoso,-a. 2 *(indulgent)* indulgente. 3 *(hope, belief)* vano,-a.

**fondle** ['fɒndəl] *vt* acariciar.

**fondness** ['fɒndnəs] *n* 1 cariño (for, a). 2 *(liking)* afición *f* (for, a/por).

**font** [fɒnt] *n* pila (bautismal).

**food** [fuːd] *n* comida, alimento.

**foodstuffs** ['fuːdstʌfs] *n pl* alimentos *mpl*, productos *mpl* alimenticios.

**fool** [fuːl] *n* 1 tonto,-a, loco,-a. 2 *(jester)* bufón,-ona. ⌊LOC⌋ **to make a fool of** poner en ridículo a. ‖ **to play the fool** hacer el tonto.
► *vt* engañar.
► *vi* bromear.
◆ **to fool about / fool around** *vi* 1 *(be stupid)* hacer el tonto, hacer el payaso. 2 *(waste time)* perder el tiempo neciamente.

**foolish** ['fuːlɪʃ] *adj* 1 *(silly)* tonto,-a. 2 *(stupid)* estúpido,-a; *(unwise)* imprudente. 3 *(ridiculous)* ridículo,-a.

**foolproof** ['fuːlpruːf] *adj* 1 *(plan, method, idea)* infalible. 2 *(machine)* seguro,-a.

**foot** [fʊt] *n* 1 ANAT pie *m*. 2 *(measurement)* pie *m*. 3 *(bottom)* pie *m*. 4 *(of animal)* pata. ⌊LOC⌋ **on foot** a pie.
ⓘ *pl* feet.

**football** ['fʊtbɔːl] *n* 1 *(game)* fútbol *m*. 2 *(ball)* balón *m*. ⌊COMP⌋ **football player** futbolista *mf*. ‖ **football pools** quinielas.

⊕ En inglés americano football a secas se refiere al 'fútbol americano'; el 'fútbol' tal como se conoce en Europa se suele llamar soccer.

**football** ['fʊtbɔːləʳ] *n* futbolista *mf*.

**footlights** ['fʊtlaɪts] *n pl* candilejas *fpl*.

**footloose** ['fʊtluːs] *adj* libre.

**footnote** ['fʊtnəʊt] *n* nota a pie de página.

**footpath** ['fʊtpɑːθ] *n* sendero, camino.

**footprint** ['fʊtprɪnt] *n* huella, pisada.

**footstep** ['fʊtstep] *n* paso, pisada.

**footwear** ['fʊtweəʳ] *n* calzado.

**for** [fɔːʳ] *prep* 1 *(intended)* para. 2 *(purpose)* para: what's this for? ¿para qué sirve esto? 3 *(destination)* para. 4 *(in order to help, on behalf of)* por: do it for me hazlo por mí. 5 *(because of, on account of)* por, a causa de. 6 *(past time)* durante; *(future time)* por; *(specific point in time)* para. 7 *(distance)*: I walked for five miles caminé cinco millas. 8 *(in exchange, as replacement of)* por. 9 *(in favour of, in support of)* por, a favor de. 10 *(despite)* a pesar de, para; *(considering, contrast)* para: she's very tall for her age es muy alta para su edad. 11 *(as)* de, como, por. 12 *(in order to obtain)* para: for further details ... para más información…
► *conj* 6 *fml lit* ya que, puesto que.

**forage** ['fɒrɪdʒ] *n (food)* forraje *m*.

**forbade** [fɔːˈbeɪd] *pt* → forbid.

**forbid** [fəˈbɪd] *vt* 1 *(prohibit)* prohibir. 2 *(make impossible)* impedir.
ⓘ *pt* forbade [fɔːˈbeɪd], *pp* forbidden [fɔːˈbɪdən], *ger* forbidding.

**forbidden** [fɔːˈbɪdən] *pp* → forbid.

**forbidding** [fəˈbɪdɪŋ] *adj (stern)* severo,-a; *(unfriendly)* formidable.

**force** [fɔːs] *n* 1 *(strength, power, violence)* fuerza. 2 PHYS fuerza. 3 MIL cuerpo.
► *vt (oblige)* forzar, obligar.

**forceful** ['fɔːsful] *adj (person, manner)* enérgico,-a; *(speech)* contundente; *(argument)* convincente.

**forceps** ['fɔːseps] *n pl* fórceps *m inv*.

**ford** [fɔːd] *n* vado.
► *vt* vadear.

**forearm** ['fɔːrɑːm] *n* antebrazo.

**foreboding** [fɔːˈbəʊdɪŋ] *n* presentimiento.

**forecast** ['fɔːkɑːst] *n* pronóstico, previsión *f*.
► *vt* pronosticar.
ⓘ *pt & pp* forecast o forecasted.

**forefinger** ['fɔːfɪŋgəʳ] *n* (dedo) índice *m*.

**forefront** ['fɔːfrʌnt] *n* vanguardia.

**forego¹** [fɔːˈgəʊ] *vt (precede)* preceder.
ⓘ *pt* forewent [fɔːˈwent], *pp* foregone ['fɔːgɒn], *ger* foregoing.

**forego²** [fɔːˈgəʊ] *vt* → forgo.
ⓘ *pt* forewent [fɔːˈwent], *pp* foregone ['fɔːgɒn], *ger* foregoing.

**foregoing** [fɔ:ˈɡəʊɪŋ] *adj* precedente.

**foregone** [ˈfɔ:ɡɒn] *pp* → **forego**.
 ▸ *adj* inevitable.

**foreground** [ˈfɔ:ɡraʊnd] *n* primer plano, primer término.

**forehead** [ˈfɒrɪd, ˈfɔ:hed] *n* frente *f*.

**foreign** [ˈfɒrɪn] *adj* **1** *(from abroad)* extranjero,-a. **2** *(dealing with other countries)* exterior. **3** *(strange)* ajeno,-a, extraño,-a.

**foreigner** [ˈfɒrɪnəʳ] *n* extranjero,-a.

**foreman** [ˈfɔ:mən] *n* **1** *(of workers)* capataz *m*. **2** *(of jury)* presidente *m* del jurado.
 ⓘ *pl* **foremen** [ˈfɔ:mən].

**foremost** [ˈfɔ:məʊst] *adj* principal.

**forename** [ˈfɔ:neɪm] *n* nombre *m* (de pila).

**forensic** [fəˈrensɪk] *adj* forense.

**forerunner** [ˈfɔ:rʌnəʳ] *n* precursor,-ra.

**foresaw** [fɔ:ˈsɔ:] *pt* → **foresee**.

**foresee** [fɔ:ˈsi:] *vt* prever.
 ⓘ *pt* **foresaw** [fɔ:ˈsɔ:], *pp* **foreseen** [fɔ:ˈsi:n], *ger* **foreseeing**.

**foreseen** [fɔ:ˈsi:n] *pp* → **foresee**.

**foresight** [ˈfɔ:saɪt] *n* previsión *f*.

**foreskin** [ˈfɔ:skɪn] *n* prepucio.

**forest** [ˈfɒrɪst] *n* **1** *(gen)* bosque *m*. **2** *(jungle)* selva.
 ▸ *adj* forestal.

**forestall** [fɔ:ˈstɔ:l] *vt* **1** *(preempt)* anticiparse a. **2** *(prevent)* prevenir.

**forestry** [ˈfɒrɪstrɪ] *n* silvicultura.

**foretell** [fɔ:ˈtel] *vt* predecir, pronosticar.
 ⓘ *pt & pp* **foretold** [fɔ:ˈtəʊld].

**forethought** [ˈfɔ:θɔ:t] *n* **1** previsión *f*. **2** JUR premeditación *f*.

**foretold** [fɔ:ˈtəʊld] *pt & pp* → **foretell**.

**forever** [fəˈrevəʳ] *adv* **1** *(all the time)* siempre. **2** *(for good)* para siempre.

**forewarn** [fɔ:ˈwɔ:n] *vt* prevenir.

**forewent** [fɔ:ˈwent] *pp* → **forego**.

**foreword** [ˈfɔ:wɜ:d] *n* prólogo.

**forfeit** [ˈfɔ:fɪt] *n* **1** *(penalty)* pena, multa. **2** *(in games)* prenda.
 ▸ *vt* perder, perder (el derecho de).

**forgave** [fəˈɡeɪv] *pt* → **forgive**.

**forge** [fɔ:dʒ] *n* **1** *(apparatus)* fragua. **2** *(smithy)* forja.

 ▸ *vt* **1** *(counterfeit)* falsificar. **2** *(metal)* forjar, fraguar.

**forgery** [ˈfɔ:dʒərɪ] *n* falsificación *f*.
 ⓘ *pl* **forgeries**.

**forget** [fəˈɡet] *vt* **1** *(gen)* olvidar, olvidarse de. **2** *(leave behind)* dejar.
 ⓘ *pt* **forgot** [fəˈɡɒt], *pp* **forgotten** [fəˈɡɒtən], *ger* **forgetting**.
 ▸ *vi* olvidarse de, no recordar.

**forgive** [fəˈɡɪv] *vt* **1** *(pardon)* perdonar. **2** *(let off debt)* perdonar.
 ⓘ *pt* **forgave** [fəˈɡeɪv], *pp* **forgiven** [fəˈɡɪvnən].

**forgiven** [fəˈɡɪvnən] *pp* → **forgive**.

**forgiveness** [fəˈɡɪvnəs] *n* perdón *m*.

**forgo** [fɔ:ˈɡəʊ] *vt* renunciar a, sacrificar.
 ⓘ *pt* **forwent** [fɔ:ˈwent], *pp* **forgone** [fɔ:ˈɡɒn], *ger* **forgoing**.

**forgone** [fɔ:ˈɡɒn] *pp* → **forgo**.

**forgot** [fəˈɡɒt] *pt* → **forget**.

**forgotten** [fəˈɡɒtən] *pp* → **forget**.

**fork** [fɔ:k] *n* **1** *(for eating)* tenedor *m*. **2** AGR horca, horquilla. **3** *(in road, river, etc)* bifurcación *f*.
 ▸ *vi* **1** *(road, river, etc)* bifurcarse. **2** *(person, car)* torcer, girar.
 ▸ *n pl* **forks** *(on bike)* horquilla.

**forlorn** [fəˈlɔ:n] *adj* **1** *(forsaken)* abandonado,-a. **2** *(desolate)* triste. **3** *(hopeless)* desesperado,-a.

**form** [fɔ:m] *n* **1** *(shape, mode, etc)* forma. **2** *(kind)* clase *f*, tipo. **3** *(formality)* formas *fpl*; *(behaviour)* educación *f*. **4** *(physical condition)* forma. **5** *(mood, spirit)* humor *m*. **6** *(document)* formulario, impreso, hoja. **7** EDUC *(age group)* curso; *(class)* clase *f*.
 ▸ *vt* **1** *(mould)* moldear; *(make)* hacer, formar. **2** *(be, constitute)* formar, constituir. **3** *fig (idea)* hacerse, formarse.

**formal** [ˈfɔ:məl] *adj* **1** *(gen)* formal. **2** *(dress, dinner)* de etiqueta.

 ⊠ Formal no significa 'formal (serio)', que se traduce por **serious**.

**formality** [fɔ:ˈmælɪtɪ] *n* *(correctness)* formalidad *f*; *(convention)* ceremonia.
 ⓘ *pl* **formalities**.

**format** [ˈfɔ:mæt] *n* formato.
 ▸ *vt* COMPUT formatear.
 ⓘ *pt & pp* **formatted**, *ger* **formatting**.

**formation** [fɔ:'meɪʃən] *n* **1** *(gen)* formación *f*. **2** *(establishment)* creación *f*.

**former** ['fɔ:mə<sup>r</sup>] *adj* **1** *(earlier)* antiguo,-a; *(person)* ex. **2** *(of two)* primero,-a.
► *pron* **the former** aquél, aquélla.

**formerly** ['fɔ:məlɪ] *adv* *(previously)* antiguamente, antes.

**formidable** ['fɔ:mɪdəbəl] *adj* **1** *(impressive)* formidable. **2** *(daunting)* temible, imponente.

❌ Formidable no significa 'formidable (magnífico)', que se traduce por **wonderful**.

**formula** ['fɔ:mjələ] *n* fórmula.
ⓘ *pl* formulas o formulae ['fɔ:mjuli:].

**formulate** ['fɔ:mjəleɪt] *vt* formular.

**formulation** [fɔ:mjə'leɪʃən] *n* formulación *f*.

**fort** [fɔ:t] *n* fuerte *m*.

**forth** [fɔ:θ] *adv* *(onwards)* en adelante.

**forthcoming** [fɔ:θ'kʌmɪŋ] *adj* **1** *fml (happening in near future)* próximo,-a. **2** *(available)* disponible. **3** *(communicative)* comunicativo,-a, dispuesto,-a a hablar.

**fortieth** ['fɔ:tɪəθ] *adj* cuadragésimo,-a.
► *adv* en cuadragésimo lugar.
► *n (fraction)* cuadragésimo; *(one part)* cuadragésima parte *f*.

✎ Consulta también **sixtieth**.

**fortification** [fɔ:tɪfɪ'keɪʃən] *n* fortificación *f*.

**fortify** ['fɔ:tɪfaɪ] *vt* **1** MIL fortificar. **2** *(strengthen)* fortalecer.
ⓘ *pt & pp* fortified, *ger* fortifying.

**fortnight** ['fɔ:tnaɪt] *n* GB quincena, quince días *mpl*.

**fortress** ['fɔ:trəs] *n* fortaleza.

**fortunate** ['fɔ:tʃənət] *adj* afortunado,-a.

**fortunately** ['fɔ:tʃənətlɪ] *adv* afortunadamente, por suerte.

**fortune** ['fɔ:tʃən] *n* **1** *(fate)* fortuna; *(luck)* suerte *f*. **2** *(money)* fortuna.

**fortune-teller** ['fɔ:tʃəntelə<sup>r</sup>] *n* adivino,-a.

**forty** ['fɔ:tɪ] *adj* cuarenta.
► *n* cuarenta *m*.

✎ Consulta también **sixty**.

**forum** ['fɔ:rəm] *n* foro.

**forward** ['fɔ:wəd] *adv* [como adverbio, también **forwards**] **1** *(gen)* hacia adelante. **2** *(time)* en adelante.
► *adj* **1** *(position)* delantero,-a, frontal; *(movement)* hacia delante. **2** *(future)* a largo plazo. **3** *(advanced)* adelantado,-a, precoz. **4** *(too bold, too eager)* atrevido,-a, descarado,-a, fresco,-a.
► *vt* **1** *(send on to new address)* remitir; *(send goods)* enviar, expedir. **2** *fml (further, advance)* adelantar, fomentar.

**forwent** [fɔ:'went] *pt* → **forgo**.

**fossil** ['fɒsəl] *n* fósil *m*.
► *adj* fósil.

**foster** ['fɒstə<sup>r</sup>] *vt* **1** *(child)* acoger temporalmente. **2** *(encourage)* fomentar, promover.
► *adj* adoptivo,-a.

**fought** [fɔ:t] *pt & pp* → **fight**.

**foul** [faul] *adj* **1** *(dirty, disgusting)* asqueroso,-a; *(smell)* fétido,-a. **2** *(language)* grosero,-a, obsceno,-a.
► *n* SP falta (on, contra).
► *vt* **1** *(dirty)* ensuciar; *(pollute)* contaminar. **2** *(snag)* enredar. **3** SP cometer una falta contra.

**found¹** [faund] *vt (metals)* fundir.

**found²** [faund] *vt* **1** *(establish)* fundar. **2** *(base)* basar (on, en).

**found³** [faund] *pt & pp* → **find**.

**foundation** [faun'deɪʃən] *n* **1** *(act, organization)* fundación *f*. **2** *(basis)* fundamento, base *f*. **3** *(make-up)* base *f*.
► *n pl* **foundations** cimientos *mpl*.

**founder¹** ['faundə<sup>r</sup>] *vi* **1** *(plan, etc)* fracasar, malograrse. **2** *(ship)* hundirse. **3** *(horse)* dar un traspié.

**founder²** ['faundə<sup>r</sup>] *n* fundador,-ra.

**foundry** ['faundrɪ] *n* fundición *f*.
ⓘ *pl* foundries.

**fountain** ['fauntən] *n* **1** fuente *f*. **2** *(jet)* surtidor *m*, chorro.

**four** [fɔ:<sup>r</sup>] *adj* cuatro.
► *n* cuatro.

✎ Consulta también **six**.

**fourteen** [fɔ:'ti:n] *adj* catorce.
► *n* catorce *m*.

✎ Consulta también **six**.

**fourteenth** [fɔː'tiːnθ] *adj* decimocuarto,-a.
► *adv* en decimocuarto lugar.
► *n* **1** *(in series)* decimocuarto,-a. **2** *(fraction)* decimocuarto; *(one part)* decimocuarta parte *f*.

✎ Consulta también sixth.

**fourth** [fɔːθ] *adj* cuarto,-a.
► *adv* cuarto, en cuarto lugar.
► *n* **1** *(in series)* cuarto,-a. **2** *(fraction)* cuarto; *(one part)* cuarta parte *f*.

✎ Consulta también sixth.

**fowl** [faʊl] *n* ave *f* de corral.
① *pl* fowl.

**fox** [fɒks] *n* zorro,-a.
► *vt* **1** *fam (trick)* engañar. **2** *(confuse)* dejar perplejo,-a, confundir, despistar.

**foxy** ['fɒksɪ] *adj fam* astuto,-a.
① *comp* foxier, *superl* foxiest.

**foyer** ['fɔɪeɪ, 'fɔɪə'] *n* vestíbulo.

**fraction** ['frækʃən] *n* **1** *(division)* fracción *f*. **2** *(small part, bit)* poquito.

**fractional** ['frækʃənəl] *adj* **1** *(in fractions)* fraccionario,-a. **2** *(very small)* muy pequeño,-a, ínfimo,-a.

**fracture** ['fræktʃə'] *n* fractura.
► *vt* fracturar.
► *vi* fracturarse.

**fragile** ['frædʒaɪl] *adj* **1** frágil. **2** *fig (health)* delicado,-a.

**fragility** [frə'dʒɪlɪtɪ] *n* fragilidad *f*.

**fragment** [*(n)* 'frægmənt; *(vb)* fræg'ment] *n* fragmento.
► *vi* fragmentarse.

**fragmentation** [frægmən'teɪʃən] *n* fragmentación *f*.

**fragrance** ['freɪgrəns] *n* fragancia.

**fragrant** ['freɪgrənt] *adj* fragante.

**frail** [freɪl] *adj* **1** frágil, delicado,-a. **2** *(morally weak)* débil.

**frame** [freɪm] *n* **1** *(of building, machine, tent)* armazón *f*. **2** *(of bed)* armadura. **3** *(of bicycle)* cuadro. **4** *(of spectacles)* montura. **5** *(of window, door, picture, etc)* marco. **6** CINEM fotograma *m*. **7** *(of comic)* viñeta.
► *vt* **1** *(picture)* enmarcar. **2** *(door)* encuadrar.

**framework** ['freɪmwɜːk] *n* **1** armazón *f*. **2** *fig* estructura, sistema *m*, marco.

**franc** [fræŋk] *n* franco.

**France** [frɑːns] *n* Francia.

**franchise** ['fræntʃaɪz] *n* **1** COMM concesión *f*, franquicia. **2** *(vote)* derecho de voto.

**frank** [fræŋk] *adj* franco,-a.
► *vt* franquear.

**frantic** ['fræntɪk] *adj* **1** *(hectic)* frenético,-a. **2** *(anxious)* desesperado,-a.

**fraternal** [frə'tɜːnəl] *adj* fraternal.

**fraternity** [frə'tɜːnɪtɪ] *n* **1** *(brotherhood)* fraternidad *f*. **2** *(society)* asociación *f*. **3** REL hermandad *f*, cofradía. **4** US *(university)* club *m* de estudiantes.
① *pl* fraternities.

**fraud** [frɔːd] *n* **1** *(act)* fraude *m*. **2** *(person)* impostor,-ra, farsante *mf*.

**fraught** [frɔːt] *adj* **1** *(filled, charged)* lleno,-a (with, de), cargado,-a (with, de). **2** *fam (worried)* nervioso,-a, alterado,-a, tenso,-a.

**fray¹** [freɪ] *vi* **1** *(cloth)* deshilacharse, raerse. **2** *(tempers, nerves, etc)* crisparse.

**fray²** [freɪ] *n* contienda, lucha.

**freak** [friːk] *n* *(monster)* monstruo; *(strange person)* bicho raro. **2** *fam (fan)* fanático,-a. **3** *(eccentric)* estrafalario,-a.
► *adj (unusual)* insólito,-a; *(unexpected)* inesperado,-a.
◆ **to freak out** *vt sep* flipar, alucinar.

**freckle** ['frekəl] *n* peca.

**free** [friː] *adj* **1** *(gen)* libre. **2** *(without cost)* gratuito,-a, gratis; *(exempt)* libre (from, de).
► *adv* **1** *(gratis)* gratis. **2** *(loose)* suelto,-a.
► *vt* **1** *(liberate, release - person)* poner en libertad, liberar; *(- animal)* soltar. **2** *(rid)* deshacerse (of/from, de), librarse (of/from, de). **3** *(loosen, untie)* soltar, desatar.

**freedom** ['friːdəm] *n* libertad *f*.

**freehand** ['friːhænd] *adj* a mano alzada.

**freelance** ['friːlɑːns] *adj* independiente, autónomo,-a.
► *n* persona que trabaja por cuenta propia.
► *vi* trabajar por cuenta propia.

**freestyle** ['fri:staɪl] *n (swimming)* estilo libre.

**freeway** ['fri:weɪ] *n* US autopista.

**freewheel** [fri:'wi:l] *vi (cycle)* ir a rueda libre; *(car)* ir en punto muerto.

**freeze** [fri:z] *n* **1** METEOR helada. **2** COMM congelación *f*.
▸ *vt (gen)* congelar.
▸ *vi* **1** *(liquid)* helarse; *(food)* congelarse. **2** METEOR helar.
ⓘ *pt* froze [frəʊz], *pp* frozen [frəʊzən], *ger* freezing.

**freezer** ['fri:zəʳ] *n* congelador *m*.

**freeze-up** ['fri:zʌp] *n* helada.

**freight** [freɪt] *n* **1** *(transport)* transporte *m*. **2** *(goods)* carga, flete *m*. **3** *(price)* flete *m*.
▸ *vt* transportar.

**freighter** ['freɪtəʳ] *n (ship)* buque *m* de carga; *(aircraft)* avión *m* de carga.

**French** [frentʃ] *adj* francés,-esa.
▸ *n (language)* francés *m*.
▸ *n pl* the French los franceses *mpl*.

**Frenchman** ['frentʃmən] *n* francés *m*.
ⓘ *pl* Frenchmen ['frentʃmən].

**Frenchwoman** ['frentʃwumən] *n* francesa.
ⓘ *pl* Frenchwomen ['frentʃwɪmɪn].

**frenzy** ['frenzɪ] *n* frenesí *m*.
ⓘ *pl* frenzies.

**frequency** ['fri:kwənsɪ] *n* frecuencia.
ⓘ *pl* frequencies.

**frequent** [*(adj)* 'fri:kwənt; *(vb)* frɪ'kwent] *adj* frecuente.
▸ *vt* frecuentar.

**fresco** ['freskəʊ] *n* fresco.
ⓘ *pl* frescos o frescoes.

**fresh** [freʃ] *adj* **1** *(gen)* fresco,-a. **2** *(water)* dulce. **3** *(air)* puro,-a.

**freshen** ['freʃən] *vt* refrescar.
▸ *vi* refrescarse.

**freshly** ['freʃlɪ] *adv* recién: *freshly baked bread* pan recién hecho.

**freshness** ['freʃnəs] *n* **1** *(brightness)* frescura. **2** *(cool)* frescor *m*. **3** *(newness)* novedad *f*. **4** *fam (cheek)* descaro.

**freshwater** ['freʃwæːɔːtəʳ] *adj* de agua dulce: *freshwater fish* pez de agua dulce.

**fret¹** [fret] *vi* preocuparse (about/at/over, por).

▸ *vt (wear away)* raer, desgastar.
ⓘ *pt & pp* fretted, *ger* fretting.
▸ *n (worry)* preocupación *f*.

**fret²** [fret] *n (on guitar)* traste *m*.

**friar** ['fraɪəʳ] *n* fraile *m*.

**fricative** ['frɪkətɪv] *adj* fricativo,-a.
▸ *n* fricativa.

**friction** ['frɪkʃən] *n* **1** *(conflict)* fricción *f*, roces *mpl*. **2** *(rubbing)* rozamiento, roce *m*.

**Friday** ['fraɪdɪ] *n* viernes *m*.

✎ Para ejemplos de uso, consulta Saturday.

**fridge** [frɪdʒ] *n* nevera, frigorífico.

**fried** [fraɪd] *pt & pp →* fry.
▸ *adj* frito,-a.

**friend** [frend] *n* **1** amigo,-a, compañero,-a. **2** *(helper, supporter)* amigo,-a (of/to, de).

**friendly** ['frendlɪ] *adj* **1** *(person)* simpático,-a, amable. **2** *(atmosphere)* acogedor,-ra. **3** *(smile, manner, etc)* amable.
ⓘ *comp* friendlier, *superl* friendliest.

**friendship** ['frendʃɪp] *n* amistad *f*.

**frieze** [fri:z] *n* **1** *(painted)* friso. **2** *(wallpaper)* cenefa.

**frigate** ['frɪgət] *n* fragata.

**fright** [fraɪt] *n* **1** *(shock)* susto. **2** *(fear)* miedo.

**frighten** ['fraɪtən] *vt* asustar, espantar.

**frightfully** ['fraɪtfʊlɪ] *adv fam* muchísimo.

**frigid** ['frɪdʒɪd] *adj* **1** *(sexually)* frígido,-a. **2** *(icy)* glacial, muy frío,-a.

**frill** [frɪl] *n (on dress)* volante *m*.
▸ *n pl* frills *(decorations)* adornos *mpl*.

**fringe** [frɪndʒ] *n* **1** *(decorative)* fleco. **2** *(of hair)* flequillo. **3** *(edge)* borde *m*.

**frisk** [frɪsk] *vt (search)* registrar, cachear.
▸ *vi (frolic)* brincar, retozar.

**frisky** ['frɪskɪ] *adj (child, animal)* juguetón,-ona; *(adult)* vivo,-a, vital.
ⓘ *comp* friskier, *superl* friskiest.

**fritter** ['frɪtəʳ] *n* CULIN buñuelo.

**frivolity** [frɪ'vɒlətɪ] *n* frivolidad *f*.
ⓘ *pl* frivolities.

**frizzy** ['frɪzɪ] *adj* crespo,-a, rizado,-a.
ⓘ *comp* frizzier, *superl* frizziest.

**frock** [frɒk] *n* vestido.

**frog** [frɒg] *n* rana.

**frolic** ['frɒlɪk] *vi* juguetear, retozar.
▸ *n* aventura.

**from** [frɒm] *prep* **1** *(starting at)* de; *(train, plane)* procedente de: *the train from Madrid* el tren procedente de Madrid. **2** *(origin, source)* de, desde. **9** *(because of)* por, a causa de. **10** *(considering, according to)* según, por. **11** *(indicating difference)* de; *(when distinguishing)* entre. **12** *(indicating position)* desde. LOC **from now on** de ahora en adelante, a partir de ahora.

**front** [frʌnt] *n* **1** *(forward part)* parte *f* delantera, frente *m*. **2** METEOR frente *m*. **3** *(facade)* fachada. **4** MIL frente *m*. **5** *(promenade)* paseo marítimo.
▶ *adj* delantero,-a, de delante.
▶ *vi* (face) dar (**on**/**onto**, a).
▶ *vt* **1** *(lead, head)* encabezar. **2** *(present)* presentar.

**frontalis** [frən'talɪs] *n* músculo frontal.

**frontier** [ˈfrʌntɪəʳ] *n* frontera.
▶ *adj* fronterizo,-a.

**front-page** [ˈfrʌntpeɪdʒ] *adj* de portada, de primera plana.

**frost** [frɒst] *n* **1** *(covering)* escarcha. **2** *(freezing)* helada.
▶ *vt* helar, cubrir de escarcha.

**frostbite** [ˈfrɒstbaɪt] *n* congelación *f*.

**frosted** [ˈfrɒstɪd] *adj* **1** *(glass)* esmerilado,-a. **2** CULIN recubierto,-a de azúcar glas, escarchado,-a.

**frosty** [ˈfrɒstɪ] *adj* **1** METEOR *(cold with frost)* de helada; *(very cold)* helado,-a, muy frío,-a. **2** METEOR *(covered with frost)* escarchado,-a, cubierto,-a de escarcha. **3** *fig (unfriendly)* glacial.
ⓘ *comp* **frostier**, *superl* **frostiest**.

**froth** [frɒθ] *n* *(gen)* espuma.

**frown** [fraʊn] *n* ceño.
▶ *vi* fruncir el ceño.

**froze** [frəʊz] *pt* → freeze.

**frozen** [ˈfrəʊzən] *pp* → freeze.
▶ *adj* **1** *(water, ground)* helado,-a. **2** *(food)* congelado,-a.

**fructose** [ˈfrʌktəʊz] *n* fructosa.

**frugal** [ˈfruːɡəl] *adj* frugal.

**fruit** [fruːt] *n* **1** *(food)* fruta. **2** BOT fruto. **3** *(result, reward)* fruto.
▶ *adj* de fruta. COMP **fruit juice** zumo de fruta. **‖ fruit salad** macedonia.
▶ *vi* dar fruto.

**fruitful** [ˈfruːtful] *adj* fructífero,-a.

**frustrate** [frʌˈstreɪt] *vt* **1** *(thwart)* frustrar. **2** *(upset)* frustrar.

**frustration** [frʌˈstreɪʃən] *n* frustración *f*.

**fry¹** [fraɪ] *vt* freír.
▶ *vi* **1** freírse. **2** *fig (in sun)* asarse, achicharrarse.
ⓘ *pt & pp* **fried**, *ger* **frying**.

**fry²** [fraɪ] *n pl (fish)* alevines *mpl*.

**fryer** [fraɪəʳ] *n (frying pan)* sartén *f*.

**frying pan** [ˈfraɪɪŋpæn] *n* sartén *f*.

**ft** [fʊt, 'fiːt] *abbr* (foot, feet) pie *m*, pies *mpl*.

**fuel** [fjʊəl] *n* **1** *(gen)* combustible *m*. **2** *(for motors)* carburante *m*.
▶ *vt* **1** *(plane)* abastecer de combustible; *(car)* echar gasolina. **2** *fig (make worse)* empeorar; *(encourage)* alimentar.

**fugitive** [ˈfjuːdʒɪtɪv] *n (from danger, war, etc)* fugitivo,-a; *(from justice)* prófugo,-a.
▶ *adj* fugitivo,-a.

**fulcrum** [ˈfʊlkrəm] *n* fulcro.

**fulfil** [fʊlˈfɪl] *vt* **1** *(promise, duty)* cumplir. **2** *(task, plan, ambition)* realizar. **3** *(role, function, order)* efectuar, desempeñar. **4** *(need, desire, wish)* satisfacer.
ⓘ *pt & pp* **fulfilled**, *ger* **fulfilling**.

**fulfill** [fʊlˈfɪl] *vt* US → fulfil.

**fulfilled** [fʊlˈfɪld] *pt & pp* → fulfill.
▶ *adj* realizado,-a, satisfecho,-a.

**full** [fʊl] *adj* **1** *(gen)* lleno,-a. **2** *(week, day)* cargado,-a, movido,-a. **3** *(entire, complete)* completo,-a. **4** *(highest or greatest possible)* máximo,-a. LOC **full time** a jornada completa. COMP **full board** pensión *f* completa. **‖ full stop** punto.
▶ *adv (directly)* justo, de lleno.

**full-length** [fʊlˈleŋθ] *adj* **1** *(mirror, portrait)* de cuerpo entero. **2** *(garment)* largo,-a. **3** *(film)* de largo metraje.

**full-scale** [fʊlˈskeɪl] *adj* **1** *(actual size)* de tamaño natural. **2** *(complete, total )* completo,-a, total.

**full-time** [fʊlˈtaɪm] *adj* a tiempo completo, de jornada completa.
▶ *adv* a tiempo completo.

**fumble** [ˈfʌmbəl] *vt* dejar caer.
▶ *vi* **to fumble for** buscar a tientas.
▶ *vi* **to fumble with** hacer torpemente.

F

**fume** [fjuːm] vi **1** (produce smoke, etc) echar humo. **2** fig (show anger) echar humo, subirse por las paredes.
▶ n pl **fumes** humos mpl.

❎ To fume no significa 'fumar', que se traduce por to smoke.

**fumigate** ['fjuːmɪɡeɪt] vt fumigar.
**fun** [fʌn] n **1** (enjoyment, pleasure) diversión f: it'll be good fun when we go camping lo pasaremos muy bien cuando nos vayamos de camping. **2** (amusement) gracia: it's no fun staying in alone on Saturday night no tiene gracia quedarse solo en casa el sábado por la noche.
▶ adj (humorous, amusing) divertido,-a.
**function** ['fʌŋkʃən] n **1** (purpose, use, duty) función f. **2** (ceremony) acto, ceremonia; (reception) recepción f. **3** MATH función f.
▶ vi funcionar. LOC **to fulfil a function** desempeñar una función. COMP **function key** tecla de función.
**functional** ['fʌŋkʃənəl] adj **1** (operational) funcional. **2** (practical, useful) práctico,-a.
**fund** [fʌnd] n **1** (sum of money) fondo. **2** (supply) fuente f.
▶ vt **1** (finance) patrocinar. **2** (debt) consolidar.
▶ n pl **funds** (financial resources) fondos mpl.
**fundamental** [fʌndəˈmentəl] adj fundamental.
▶ n pl **fundamentals** (essential part, basic rule) fundamentos mpl, reglas fpl básicas.
**fundamentalist** [fʌndəˈmentəlɪst] adj REL fundamentalista, integrista.
▶ n REL fundamentalista mf, integrista mf.
**funeral** ['fjuːnərəl] n entierro, funeral m.
▶ adj fúnebre.
**funfair** ['fʌnfeəʳ] n GB feria, parque m de atracciones.
**fungus** ['fʌŋɡəs] n hongo.
ⓘ pl funguses o fungi ['fʌŋdʒaɪ].
**funicular** [fjuːˈnɪkjələ] n funicular m.
**funk** [fʌŋk] n MUS funky m.
**funky** ['fʌŋkɪ] adj **1** MUS funky. **2** fam (fashionable) guay, chulo,-a.
ⓘ comp funkier, superl funkiest.
**funnel** ['fʌnəl] n **1** (for liquid) embudo. **2** (chimney) chimenea.

▶ vi verterse.
▶ vt fig (channel) encauzar.
**funny** ['fʌnɪ] adj **1** (amusing) gracioso,-a, divertido,-a: I don't find your remarks at all funny tus comentarios no son nada graciosos. **2** (strange) raro,-a, extraño,-a, curioso,-a: the funny thing is that... lo curioso es que ... **3** fam (slightly ill) rarillo,-a, malito,-a; (slightly mad) chiflado,-a: I feel funny no me encuentro bien.
ⓘ comp funnier, superl funniest.
**fur** [fɜː] n **1** (of living animal) pelo, pelaje m. **2** (of dead animal) piel f. **3** (garment) abrigo de piel. **4** (on tongue) sarro.
▶ adj de piel. COMP **fur coat** abrigo de pieles.
**furious** ['fjʊərɪəs] adj (very angry) furioso,-a: she'll be furious if we break anything se pondrá furiosa si rompemos algo; he's got a furious temper tiene muy mal genio.
**furnace** ['fɜːnəs] n horno.
**furnish** ['fɜːnɪʃ] vt **1** (house, etc) amueblar (with, de): I'd like to rent a furnished flat quisiera alquilar un piso amueblado. **2** fml (supply - material) suministrar, proveer; (- information, etc) facilitar, proporcionar.
**furnishings** ['fɜːnɪʃɪŋz] n pl muebles, cortinas y alfombras.
**furniture** ['fɜːnɪtʃə] n mobiliario, muebles mpl: I need some new furniture necesito unos muebles nuevos.
**furrow** ['fʌrəʊ] n **1** AGR surco. **2** (wrinkle) arruga.
▶ vt **1** AGR surcar. **2** (forehead) arrugar.
**furry** ['fɜːrɪ] adj **1** (hairy) peludo,-a. **2** (scaly) sarroso,-a.
ⓘ comp furrier, superl furriest.
**further** ['fɜːðə] adj **1** (farther) más lejos she lives further down the road vive más abajo de la calle. **2** (more, additional) más adicional; (new) nuevo,-a: I have just one further question tengo una pregunta más this office will remain closed until further notice esta oficina permanecerá cerrada hasta nuevo aviso; for further information please contact ... para más información póngase en contacto con ...
▶ adv **1** (farther) más lejos: is it much further? ¿queda mucho más?; don't go any further no vayas más lejos. **2** (more, to ...

*greater degree)* más: *the police want to take the matter further* la policía quiere investigar más el asunto; *I'd like to go further into this subject* me gustaría estudiar el tema más a fondo. **3** *fml (besides)* además: *further, I'd like to complain about the lack of parking spaces* además, quisiera quejarme de la falta de aparcamientos.

▶ *vt (advance, promote)* fomentar, promover: *he would have gone to any lengths to further his career* hubiera hecho cualquier cosa para promover su propia carrera. [LOC] **this must not go any further** esto tiene que quedar entre nosotros, esto no tiene que salir de aquí. ▪ **further to** con referencia a, referente a: *further to your letter of the 6th inst* con referencia a su carta del día 6 del corriente. [COMP] **further education** estudios *mpl* superiores.

✎ Consulta también far.

**furthermore** [fɜː'ðə'mɔːr] *adv fml* además.

**furthest** [ˈfɜːðɪst] *adj* → far, farthest, further.

▶ *adv* → far, further.

**furtive** [ˈfɜːtɪv] *adj* furtivo,-a.

**fury** [ˈfjʊərɪ] *n* furia. [LOC] **to be in a fury** estar furioso,-a. ▪ **to fly into a fury** ponerse hecho,-a una furia.

① *pl* furies.

**fuse** [fjuːz] *n* **1** ELEC fusible *m*, plomo: *the fuses blew* saltaron los fusibles, se fundieron los plomos. **2** *(wick)* mecha; *(detonator)* espoleta. [LOC] **to blow a fuse 1** *(appliance)* saltar el fusible de, fundirse el plomo de. **2** *(person)* estallar, explotar. [COMP] **fuse box** caja de fusibles.

▶ *vt* **1** *(cause to stop working, melt)* fundir.- **2** *fig (merge)* fusionar.

▶ *vi* **1** *(stop working, melt)* fundirse: *the lights have fused* se han fundido los plomos. **2** *fig (merge)* fusionarse: *the two companies fused* las dos empresas se fusionaron.

**fuselage** [ˈfjuːzəlɑːʒ] *n* fuselaje *m*.

**fusillade** [ˌfjuːzəˈleɪd] *n* tiroteo,.

**fusion** [ˈfjuːʒən] *n* fusión *f*.

**fuss** [fʌs] *n* **1** *(commotion, nervous excitement)* alboroto, jaleo. **2** *(angry scene, dispute)* escándalo, problemas *mpl*; *(complaints)* quejas *fpl*.

▶ *vt (pester, annoy, bother)* molestar: *stop fussing me* no me molestes.

▶ *vi* **1** *(worry, fret)* preocuparse, inquietarse: *don't fuss, we'll get there on time* no te preocupes, llegaremos a tiempo. **2** *(pay excessive attention to)* preocuparse excesivamente (over, de). [LOC] **to make a fuss / kick up a fuss** *(complain strongly)* armar un escándalo, montar una escena. ▪ **to make a fuss of** SB deshacerse por ALGN.

**fussy** [ˈfʌsɪ] *adj* **1** *(concerned with details)* quisquilloso,-a, exigente. **2** *(nervous about small things)* nervioso,-a. **3** *(too elaborate)* recargado,-a.

① *comp* fussier, *superl* fussiest.

**fusty** [ˈfʌstɪ] *adj* **1** *(musty)* mohoso,-a, rancio,-a; *(stale)* que huele a cerrado. **2** *(old-fashioned)* chapado,-a a la antigua.

① *comp* fustier, *superl* fustiest.

**futile** [ˈfjuːtaɪl] *adj* vano,-a, inútil: *a futile attempt to save him* un intento inútil de salvarlo.

**future** [ˈfjuːtʃər] *adj* futuro,-a: *my future husband* mi futuro marido; *we arranged to meet at some future time* quedamos para vernos en un futuro. [COMP] **future tense** futuro.

▶ *n* **1** futuro, porvenir *m*: *the future is promising* el futuro es prometedor. **2** *(verb tense)* futuro. [LOC] **in future** en el futuro, de aquí en adelante. ▪ **in the future** en el futuro. ▪ **in the distant future** en un futuro lejano. ▪ **in the near future** en un futuro próximo. ▪ **in the not too distant future** en un futuro no muy lejano.

**fuzz** [fʌz] *n (fluff)* pelusa; *(fine hair)* vello.

**fuzzy** [ˈfʌzɪ] *adj* **1** *(frizzy)* rizado,-a, crespo,-a; *(fluffy)* con pelusilla. **2** *(blurred)* borroso,-a, movido,-a.

① *comp* fuzzier, *superl* fuzziest.

# G

**G, g** [giː] n **1** (the letter) G, g f. **2** MUS sol m.

**g** [græm] symb (gram, gramme) gramo; (abbreviation) g.

**gab** [gæb] n labia, palique m. LOC **to have the gift of the gab** tener el pico de oro.
▸ vi charlar, parlotear.
ⓘ pt & pp **gabbed**, ger **gabbing**.

**gabardine** ['gæbədiːn] n gabardina.

**gabble** ['gæbəl] n chapurreo.
▸ vt farfullar, charlotear.

**gadfly** ['gædflaɪ] n ZOOL tábano.
ⓘ pl **gadflies**.

**gadget** ['gædʒɪt] n fam aparato, artilugio, chisme m.

**Gaelic** ['geɪlɪk] adj gaélico,-a.
▸ n (language) gaélico.

**gaffe** [gæf] n metedura de pata.

**gag** [gæg] n **1** (cover for the mouth) mordaza. **2** (joke) chiste m, gag m, broma.
▸ vt amordazar.
▸ vi tener náuseas.
ⓘ pt & pp **gagged**, ger **gagging**.

**gaily** ['geɪlɪ] adv alegremente.

**gain** [geɪn] n **1** (achievement) logro. **2** (profit) ganancia. **3** (increase) aumento.
▸ vt **1** (achieve) lograr, conseguir. **2** (obtain) ganar. **3** (increase) aumentar. **4** (clock) adelantar.
▸ vi **1** (clock) adelantar. **2** (shares) subir.

**gait** [geɪt] n andares mpl.

**gaiter** ['geɪtəʳ] n polaina.

**galactic** [gəˈlæktɪk] adj galáctico,-a.

**galaxy** ['gæləksɪ] n galaxia.
ⓘ pl **galaxies**.

**gale** [geɪl] n (wind) vendaval m; (storm) tempestad f.

**gall¹** [gɔːl] n fig descaro, caradura. COMP **gall bladder** vesícula biliar.

**gall²** [gɔːl] vt irritar, molestar.

**gallant** ['gælənt] adj **1** (brave) valiente. **2** (chivalrous) galante.

**galleon** ['gælɪən] n galeón m.

**gallery** ['gælərɪ] n **1** (gen) galería. **2** (in theatre) gallinero.
ⓘ pl **galleries**.

**galley** ['gælɪ] n **1** (ship) galera. **2** (kitchen on ships) cocina.

**gallon** ['gælən] n galón m.

> ✎ Equivale en GB a 4,55 litros y en US 3,78 litros.

**gallop** ['gæləp] n galope m.
▸ vi galopar.

**gallows** ['gæləʊz] n pl horca sing, patíbulo sing.

**galore** [gəˈlɔːʳ] adj en abundancia.

**galvanize** ['gælvənaɪz] vt galvanizar.

**gamble** ['gæmbəl] n **1** (risky undertaking) empresa arriesgada. **2** (risk) riesgo. **3** (bet) jugada, apuesta.
▸ vt jugar(se).
▸ vi **1** (bet) apostar. **2** (take a risk) arriesgarse, confiar.

**gambler** ['gæmbləʳ] n jugador,-ra.

**gambling** ['gæmblɪŋ] n juego.

**game** [geɪm] n **1** juego. **2** (match) partido. **3** (of cards, chess, etc) partida. **4** (hunting) caza. COMP **game reserve** coto de caza.
▸ adj dispuesto,-a, listo,-a.
▸ n pl **games** GB educación f sing física.

**gamekeeper** ['geɪmkiːpəʳ] n guarda bosque mf.

**gammon** ['gæmən] n GB jamón m (ahumado o curado a la sal).

**gamut** ['gæmət] n gama, serie f.

**gander** ['gændəʳ] n ganso.

**gang** [gæŋ] n **1** (criminals) banda. **2** (youths) pandilla.

**gangplank** [ˈgæŋplæŋk] n plancha.

**gangrene** [ˈgæŋgriːn] n gangrena.

**gangster** [ˈgæŋstəʳ] n gángster m.

**gangway** [ˈgæŋweɪ] n 1 GB (aisle, passage) pasillo. 2 (on ship) pasarela.

**gaol** [dʒeɪl] n GB cárcel f.

✎ Consulta también jail.

**gap** [gæp] n 1 (hole) abertura, hueco. 2 (crack) brecha. 3 (empty space) espacio. 4 (blank) blanco. 5 (time) intervalo.

**gape** [geɪp] vi 1 abrirse. 2 (stare) mirar boquiabierto,-a.

**garage** [ˈgærɑːʒ, ˈgærɪdʒ] n 1 garaje m. 2 (for repairs) taller m mecánico. 3 (for petrol, etc) gasolinera.

**garbage** [ˈgɑːbɪdʒ] n 1 US basura. 2 GB desperdicios mpl. 3 fig tonterías fpl, majaderías fpl, sandeces fpl.

**garbled** [ˈgɑːbəld] adj confuso,-a.

**garden** [ˈgɑːdən] n jardín m.
  ▶ vi cuidar el jardín.

**gardener** [ˈgɑːdənəʳ] n (gen) jardinero,-a; (of vegetables) hortelano,-a.

**gargle** [ˈgɑːgəl] vi hacer gárgaras.

**gargoyle** [ˈgɑːgɔɪl] n gárgola.

**garish** [ˈgeərɪʃ] adj (colour) chillón,-ona, llamativo,-a; (light) cegador,-ra, deslumbrante.

**garland** [ˈgɑːlənd] n guirnalda.

**garlic** [ˈgɑːlɪk] n ajo.

**garment** [ˈgɑːmənt] n (clothes) prenda.

**garnet** [ˈgɑːnɪt] n granate m.

**garnish** [ˈgɑːnɪʃ] n guarnición f.
  ▶ vt guarnecer.

**garrison** [ˈgærɪsən] n guarnición f.

**garter** [ˈgɑːtəʳ] n liga.

**gas** [gæs] n 1 (substance) gas m. 2 US gasolina. 3 (anaesthetic) anestesia. 4 US fig algo divertido. COMP **gas chamber** cámara de gas. ‖ **gas mask** máscara antigás. ‖ US **gas station** gasolinera.
  ① pl gases o gasses.
  ▶ vt asfixiar con gas.
  ▶ vi fam charlotear.

**gaseous** [ˈgæsɪəs] adj gaseoso,-a.

**gash** [gæʃ] n cuchillada.

**gasket** [ˈgæskɪt] n junta.

**gasoline** [ˈgæsəliːn] n US gasolina.

**gasp** [gɑːsp] vi 1 (in astonishment) quedar boquiabierto,-a. 2 (to pant) jadear.

**gassy** [ˈgæsɪ] adj gaseoso,-a.
  ① comp gassier, superl gassiest.

**gastric** [ˈgæstrɪk] adj gástrico,-a.

**gastronomy** [gæsˈtrɒnəmɪ] n gastronomía.

**gate** [geɪt] n 1 (door) puerta, verja. 2 (at airport) puerta; (at stadium) entrada. 3 GB (attendance) asistencia.

**gateau** [ˈgætəʊ] n pastel m, tarta.
  ① pl gateaux [ˈgætəʊz].

**gatecrash** [ˈgeɪtkræʃ] vt fam colarse en.
  ▶ vi fam colarse.

**gateway** [ˈgeɪtweɪ] n entrada, puerta.

**gather** [ˈgæðəʳ] vt 1 (collect) juntar. 2 (call together) reunir. 3 (pick up) recoger. 4 (taxes) recaudar. 5 (gain) ganar, cobrar.
  ▶ vi 1 (come together) reunirse, juntarse. 2 (build up) acumularse. 3 (form) formarse.

**gathering** [ˈgæðərɪŋ] n reunión f.

**gauche** [gəʊʃ] adj (awkward) torpe, desmañado,-a; (tactless) sin tacto.

**gaudy** [ˈgɔːdɪ] adj chillón,-ona.
  ① comp gaudier, superl gaudiest.

**gauge** [geɪdʒ] n 1 (device) indicador m, calibrador m. 2 (measure) medida estándar. 3 (railways) ancho de vía.
  ▶ vt 1 (measure) medir, calibrar. 2 fig apreciar, calcular.

**gaunt** [gɔːnt] adj 1 (lean) demacrado,-a. 2 fig (desolate) lúgubre; (grim) siniestro,-a.

**gauze** [gɔːz] n gasa.

**gave** [geɪv] pt → give.

**gay** [geɪ] adj 1 fam (homosexual) gay. 2 (happy, lively) alegre. 3 (bright) vistoso,-a.

**gaze** [geɪz] n mirada fija.
  ▶ vi mirar fijamente.

**gazelle** [gəˈzel] n gacela.

**gazette** [gəˈzet] n GB boletín oficial.

**GCSE** [ˈdʒiːsiːesˈiː] abbr GB (General Certificate of Secondary Education) ≈ Enseñanza Secundaria Obligatoria; (abbreviation) ESO f.

⊕ GCSE es el examen que se hace en Gran Bretaña al final de la enseñanza secundaria, a los 16 años aproximadamente.

**GDP** [ˈdʒiːˈdiːˈpiː] *abbr* (gross domestic product) producto interior bruto; *(abbreviation)* PIB *m*.

**gear** [ɡɪəʳ] *n* **1** TECH engranaje *m*. **2** AUTO marcha, velocidad *f*. **3** *(equipment)* equipo. **4** *fam (belongings)* efectos *mpl* personales, pertenencias *fpl*; *(clothes)* ropa. COMP **gear lever** palanca de cambios.

**gearbox** [ˈɡɪəbɒks] *n* caja de cambios.

**gearshift** [ˈɡɪəʃɪft] *n* AUTO US palanca de cambio.

**gearstick** [ˈɡɪəstɪk] *n* AUTO palanca de cambios.

**geese** [ɡiːs] *n pl* → goose.

**gel** [dʒel] *n* **1** gel *m*. **2** *(for hair)* gomina, fijador *m*.

**gelatine** [ˈdʒelətiːn] *n* gelatina.

**gem** [dʒem] *n* **1** *(jewel)* gema. **2** *fig (person, thing)* joya, alhaja.

**Gemini** [ˈdʒemɪnaɪ] *n* Géminis *m*.

**gender** [ˈdʒendəʳ] *n* género.

**gene** [dʒiːn] *n* gene *m*, gen *m*. COMP **gene pool** banco genético.

**genera** [ˈdʒenərə] *n pl* → genus.

**general** [ˈdʒenʳrəl] *adj* general. COMP **general election** elecciones *fpl* generales. ‖ **general knowledge** cultura general.
  ▶ *n* MIL general *m*.

**generalize** [ˈdʒenʳrəlaɪz] *vt & vi* generalizar.

**generate** [ˈdʒenəreɪt] *vt (gen)* generar.

**generation** [dʒenəˈreɪʃʳn] *n* generación *f*.

**generator** [ˈdʒenəreɪtəʳ] *n* generador *m*.

**generic** [dʒəˈnerɪk] *adj* genérico,-a.

**generosity** [dʒenəˈrɒsəti] *n* generosidad *f*.

**generous** [ˈdʒenʳrəs] *adj* generoso,-a.

**genetic** [dʒəˈnetɪk] *adj* genético,-a. COMP **genetic code** código genético.

**genetically** [dʒəˈnetɪkli] *adv* genéticamente. LOC **genetically modified** transgénico,-a.

**genetics** [dʒəˈnetɪks] *n* genética.

**genial** [ˈdʒiːnɪəl] *adj* afable, amable.

☒ Genial no significa 'genial (brillante)', que se traduce por **brilliant**.

**genital** [ˈdʒenɪtʳl] *adj* genital.
  ▶ *n pl* **genitals** (órganos *mpl*) genitales *mpl*.

**genitive** [ˈdʒenɪtɪv] *adj* genitivo,-a.
  ▶ *n* genitivo.

**genius** [ˈdʒiːnɪəs] *n* **1** *(person)* genio. **2** *(gift)* don *m*.
  ⓘ *pl* geniuses.

☒ Genius no significa 'genio (carácter)', que se traduce por **temper**.

**genocide** [ˈdʒenəsaɪd] *n* genocidio.

**genome** [ˈdʒiːnəʊm] *n* genoma *m*.

**genotype** [ˈdʒenətaɪp] *n* genotipo.

**genre** [ˈʒɑːnrə] *n* género.

**gent** [dʒent] *n fam* caballero, señor *m*.

**gentle** [ˈdʒentʳl] *adj* **1** *(person)* bondadoso,-a, dulce, tierno,-a. **2** *(breeze, movement, touch, etc)* suave. **3** *(hint)* discreto,-a. **4** *(noble)* noble.
  ⓘ *comp* gentler, *superl* gentlest.
  ▶ *n pl* **gents** servicio de caballeros.

**gentleman** [ˈdʒentʳlmən] *n* caballero, señor *m*.
  ⓘ *pl* gentlemen [ˈdʒentʳlmən].

**gently** [ˈdʒentlɪ] *adv* **1** *(smoothly)* suavemente. **2** *(slowly)* despacio, poco a poco. **3** *(kindly)* amablemente.

**genuine** [ˈdʒenjʊɪn] *adj* **1** *(authentic, true)* genuino,-a, auténtico,-a, verdadero,-a. **2** *(sincere)* sincero,-a.

**genus** [ˈdʒiːnəs] *n* género.
  ⓘ *pl* genera [ˈdʒenərə].

**geographic** [dʒɪəˈɡræfɪk] *adj* geográfico,-a.

**geography** [dʒɪˈɒɡrəfɪ] *n* geografía.

**geological** [dʒɪəˈlɒdʒɪkəl] *adj* geológico,-a.

**geology** [dʒɪˈɒlədʒɪ] *n* geología.

**geometric** [dʒɪəˈmetrɪk] *adj* geométrico,-a.

**geometry** [dʒɪˈɒmətrɪ] *n* geometría.

**geranium** [dʒəˈreɪnɪəm] *n* geranio.

**geriatric** [dʒerɪˈætrɪk] *adj* geriátrico,-a.

**germ** [dʒɜːm] *n* germen *m*.

**German** [ˈdʒɜːmən] *adj* alemán,-ana.
  ▶ *n* **1** *(person)* alemán,-ana. **2** *(language)* alemán *m*.

**Germany** [ˈdʒɜːmənɪ] *n* Alemania.

**germinate** [ˈdʒɜːmɪneɪt] *vi* germinar.
  ▶ *vt* hacer germinar.

**germination** [dʒɜ:mɪˈneɪʃ⁽ᵊ⁾n] *n* germinación *f*.

**gerund** [ˈdʒerənd] *n* gerundio.

**gestation** [dʒeˈsteɪʃ⁽ᵊ⁾n] *n* BIOL gestación *f*.

**gesticulate** [dʒesˈtɪkjəleɪt] *vi* gesticular.

**gesture** [ˈdʒestʃəʳ] *n* **1** ademán *m*, gesto. **2** *fig (token)* detalle *m*, gesto, muestra.
▶ *vi* hacer gestos, hacer ademanes.

❌ Gesture no significa 'gesto (de la cara)', que se traduce por grimace.

**get** [get] *vt* **1** *(obtain)* obtener, conseguir: *I want to get a job* quiero conseguir un trabajo; *he got a bank loan* le concedieron un crédito bancario; *what did you get in maths?* ¿qué sacaste en mates?. **2** *(receive)* recibir: *I got your letter yesterday* recibí tu carta ayer. **3** *(buy)* comprar: *where did you get your jeans?* ¿dónde compraste tus vaqueros? **4** *(fetch)* traer: *get the car* traiga el coche. **5** *(catch illnesses, means of transport)* coger: *she got the flu* cogió la gripe. **6** *(receive signal)* captar, recibir, coger. **7** *(ask)* pedir, decir; *(persuade)* persuadir, convencer: *get your brother to help you* pídele a tu hermano que te ayude. **8** *(have sth done)* hacer algo a uno: *she loves getting her hair done* le encanta que le arreglen el pelo.
▶ *vi* **1** *(become)* ponerse, volverse: *she gets very angry if we're late* se pone furiosa si llegamos tarde. **2** *(go)* ir: *how do you get there?* ¿cómo se va hasta allí? **3** *(arrive)* llegar: *how did you get home?* ¿cómo llegaste a casa? **4** *(come to)* llegar a. **5** *(start)* empezar a. LOC **to get dressed** vestirse. **I to get lost** perderse. **I to get married** casarse. **I to get old** envejecer, hacerse viejo. **I to get ready** prepararse. **I to get wet** mojarse.
◆ **to get across** *vt insep (cross - street, road)* cruzar; *(- bridge)* atravesar.
▶ *vi* hacerse entender.
◆ **to get ahead** *vi* adelantar, progresar.
◆ **to get along** *vi* **1** *(manage)* arreglárselas, apañárselas. **2** *(leave)* marcharse, irse.
◆ **to get along with** *vt insep* **1** *(person)* llevarse (bien) con. **2** *(progress)* marchar.
◆ **to get around** *vi* **1** *(person)* moverse; *(travel)* viajar. **2** *(news)* difundirse.
▶ *vt insep (avoid)* evitar, sortear.
◆ **to get around to** *vi* encontrar tiempo para.

◆ **to get away** *vi* escaparse, irse.
▶ *vt sep* alejar, quitar, sacar.
◆ **to get away with** *vt insep* salir impune de.
◆ **to get back** *vi* **1** *(return)* volver, regresar. **2** *(move backwards)* moverse hacia atrás, retroceder.
▶ *vt sep (recover)* recuperar: *did you get your money back?* ¿te devolvieron el dinero?
◆ **to get behind** *vi* atrasarse.
◆ **to get by** *vi* **1** *(manage)* arreglárselas. **2** *(pass)* pasar.
◆ **to get down** *vt sep* **1** *(depress)* deprimir, desanimar. **2** *(gen)* bajar. **3** *(write down)* apuntar, anotar. **4** *(swallow)* tragar.
▶ *vi (descend)* bajarse.
◆ **to get down to** *vi* ponerse a.
◆ **to get in** *vi* **1** *(arrive)* llegar. **2** *(enter)* entrar; *(car)* subir; *(be elected)* ser elegido,-a.
▶ *vt sep* **1** *(insert)* meter. **2** *(harvest)* cosechar; *(washing)* recoger; *(supplies)* comprar. **3** *(summon)* llamar.
◆ **to get into** *vt insep* **1** *(arrive)* llegar a. **2** *(enter)* entrar en; *(car)* subir a.
◆ **to get off** *vt sep (remove)* quitarse.
▶ *vt insep (vehicle, horse, etc)* bajarse de.
▶ *vi* **1** bajarse. **2** *(leave)* salir. **3** *(begin)* comenzar. **4** *(escape)* escaparse.
◆ **to get off with** *vt insep fam* ligar con.
◆ **to get on** *vt insep (vehicle)* subir a, subirse a; *(bicycle, horse, etc)* montar a.
▶ *vi* **1** *(make progress)* progresar, avanzar, ir. **2** *(succeed)* tener éxito. **3** *(be friendly)* llevarse bien, avenirse, entenderse. **4** *(continue)* seguir, continuar. **5** *(grow old)* hacerse mayor, envejecerse.
◆ **to get out** *vt sep (thing)* sacar; *(stain)* quitar.
▶ *vi* **1** *(leave)* salir. **2** *(of car, etc)* bajar de, bajarse de. **3** *(escape)* escapar(se). **4** *(news, rumours, etc)* llegar a saberse, hacerse público,-a.
◆ **to get out of** *vt insep (avoid)* librarse de.
▶ *vi (stop)* dejar, perder la costumbre.
◆ **to get over** *vt insep* **1** *(illness)* recuperarse de. **2** *(recover from)* sobreponerse a; *(forget)* olvidar. **3** *(obstacle)* salvar; *(difficulty)* vencer.
▶ *vt sep (idea, etc)* comunicar, hacer comprender.
◆ **to get over with** *vt sep* acabar con.

◆ **to get round** *vt insep* **1** *(obstacle)* salvar. **2** *(law, regulation)* evitar, soslayar. **3** *(person)* convencer, persuadir.
▶ *vi (news)* difundirse, hacerse público,-a, llegar a saber.

◆ **to get through** *vi* **1** *(gen)* llegar. **2** *(on phone)* conseguir hablar (to, con). **3** *(communicate)* hacerse comprender (to, a).
▶ *vt insep* **1** *(finish)* acabar, terminar. **2** *(consume)* consumir; *(money)* gastar; *(drink)* beber. **3** *(exam)* aprobar.

◆ **to get together** *vi (people)* reunirse, juntarse.
▶ *vt sep* **1** *(people)* juntar, reunir. **2** *(assemble)* montar; *(money)* recoger, reunir.

◆ **to get up** *vi* **1** *(rise)* levantarse; *(climb up)* subir. **2** *(become stronger - wind, storm)* levantarse.

◆ **to get up to** *vt insep* **1** hacer: *what have you been getting up to?* ¿qué has estado haciendo? **2** *(reach)* llegar a.
① *pt* **got** [gɒt], *pp* **got** [gɒt] (US **gotten** ['gɒtᵊn]), *ger* **getting**.

**getaway** ['getəweɪ] *n fam* fuga, huida.

**get-together** ['gettəgeðəʳ] *n fam (meeting)* reunión *f*; *(party)* fiesta.

**getup** ['getʌp] *n fam* atavío, atuendo.

**geyser** ['giːzəʳ, US 'gaɪzəʳ] *n* **1** *(natural spring)* géiser *m*. **2** *(water heater)* calentador *m* de agua.

**ghastly** ['gɑːstlɪ] *adj* **1** espantoso,-a, horrible, horroroso,-a. **2** *(pale)* pálido,-a, mortecino,-a.
① *comp* **ghastlier**, *superl* **ghastliest**.

**gherkin** ['gɜːkɪn] *n* pepinillo.

**ghetto** ['getəʊ] *n* gueto.
① *pl* **ghettos** o **ghettoes**.

**ghost** [gəʊst] *n* fantasma *m*, espectro.
⟨COMP⟩ **ghost train** tren *m* de la bruja.

**ghostwrite** ['gəʊstraɪt] *vt (literature)* hacer de negro, escribir para otro.

**giant** ['dʒaɪənt] *n* gigante,-a.
▶ *adj* gigante, gigantesco,-a.

**gibberish** ['dʒɪbərɪʃ] *n* galimatías *m*.

**Gibraltar** [dʒɪˈbrɔːltəʳ] *n* Gibraltar *m*.

**Gibraltarian** [dʒɪbrɔːlˈteərɪən] *adj* gibraltareño,-a.

**giddy** ['gɪdɪ] *adj (dizzy)* mareado,-a.
① *comp* **giddier**, *superl* **giddiest**.

**gift** [gɪft] *n* **1** *(present)* regalo, obsequio. **2** *(talent)* don *m*. **3** REL ofrenda. **4** JUR donación *f*. ⟨COMP⟩ **gift shop** tienda de regalos.

**gifted** ['gɪftɪd] *adj* dotado,-a.

**gigabyte** ['gɪgəbaɪt] *n* (giga)byte *m*.

**gigantic** [dʒaɪˈgæntɪk] *adj* gigantesco,-a.

**giggle** ['gɪgᵊl] *n* **1** risita, risa tonta. **2** GB *fam* broma, diversión *f*.

**gild** [gɪld] *vt* dorar.

**gill** [gɪl] *n (of fish)* agalla, branquia.

**gilt** [gɪlt] *adj* dorado,-a.
▶ *n* dorado.

**gin** [dʒɪn] *n* ginebra.

**ginger** ['dʒɪndʒəʳ] *n (spice)* jengibre *m*.
▶ *adj (hair)* rojo,-a; *(person)* pelirrojo,-a.
◆ **to ginger up** *vt sep* animar, estimular.

**gingerbread** ['dʒɪndʒəbred] *n* pan *m* de jengibre.

**gipsy** ['dʒɪpsɪ] *n* gitano,-a.
① *pl* **gipsies**.

**giraffe** [dʒɪˈrɑːf] *n* jirafa.

**girdle** ['gɜːdᵊl] *n* **1** *(clothes)* faja. **2** *fig* cinturón *m*.
▶ *vt fig* rodear.

**girl** [gɜːl] *n* **1** chica, muchacha, joven *f*; *(small)* niña. **2** *(daughter)* hija.

**girlfriend** ['gɜːlfrend] *n* **1** *(partner)* novia. **2** *(friend)* amiga, compañera.

**girlish** ['gɜːlɪʃ] *adj (of girl)* de niña; *(effeminate)* afeminado,-a.

**giro** ['dʒaɪrəʊ] *n GB* giro.
① *pl* **giros**.

**gist** [dʒɪst] *n (general idea)* idea general, sentido general; *(fundamental idea)* lo esencial.

**give** [gɪv] *n (flexibility)* elasticidad *f*, flexibilidad *f*.
▶ *vt* **1** *(gen)* dar, entregar. **2** *(as a gift)* dar, regalar: *he gave her a dress* le regaló un vestido. **3** *(perform a concert, etc)* dar; *(speech)* pronunciar. **4** *(dedicate)* dedicar, consagrar. ⟨LOC⟩ **to give way** ceder el paso.
▶ *vi (yield)* ceder; *(cloth, elastic)* dar de sí.
◆ **to give away** *vt sep* **1** *(gen)* distribuir, repartir; *(present)* regalar; *(prize)* entregar. **2** *(betray)* delatar, traicionar; *(disclose)* revelar, descubrir.
◆ **to give back** *vt sep (return)* devolver.

◆ **to give in** *vi (admit defeat)* darse por vencido,-a, rendirse; *(yield)* ceder.
▶ *vt sep (hand in)* entregar.

◆ **to give off** *vt sep (smell, heat, etc)* despedir, desprender, emitir.

◆ **to give onto** *vi* dar a.

◆ **to give over** *vt sep (hand over)* entregar; *(allocate)* dedicar, asignar.
▶ *vi fam (stop)* dejar de.

◆ **to give up** *vt sep* **1** *(renounce)* dejar; *(idea)* abandonar, renunciar a. **2** *(devote)* dedicar. **3** *(surrender)* entregarse.
▶ *vi (admit defeat)* darse por vencido,-a, rendirse.

◆ **to give up on** *vt insep* abandonar, desistir.
ⓘ *pt* gave [geɪv], *pp* given ['gɪvªn], *ger* giving.

**given** ['gɪvªn] *pp* → give.
▶ *adj* **1** *(fixed)* dado,-a, determinado,-a. **2** *(prone)* dado,-a, propenso,-a.
▶ *prep* **1** *(considering)* dado,-a, teniendo en cuenta. **2** *(if)* si.

**glacial** ['gleɪʃªl] *adj* **1** GEOL glaciar. **2** *(icy)* glacial.

**glacier** ['glæsɪəʳ, 'gleɪʃəʳ] *n* GEOL glaciar *m*.

**glad** [glæd] *adj (pleased)* contento,-a, alegre; *(happy)* feliz.
ⓘ *comp* gladder, *superl* gladdest.

**gladden** ['glædªn] *vt* alegrar.

**gladiator** ['glædɪeɪtəʳ] *n* HIST gladiador *m*.

**gladly** ['glædlɪ] *adv* de buena gana, con mucho gusto.

**glamorous** ['glæmərəs] *adj* **1** atractivo, -a. **2** *(charming)* encantador,-ra.

**glamour** ['glæməʳ] *n* **1** atractivo. **2** *(charm)* encanto.

**glance** [glɑːns] *n* vistazo, ojeada.
▶ *vi* echar un vistazo (at, a).

**gland** [glænd] *n* ANAT glándula.

**glare** [gleəʳ] *n* **1** *(light)* luz *f* deslumbrante. **2** AUTO deslumbramiento. **3** *(look)* mirada furiosa, mirada hostil.
▶ *vi* **1** *(dazzle)* deslumbrar. **2** *(look)* lanzar una mirada furiosa.

**glass** [glɑːs] *n* **1** *(material)* vidrio, cristal *m*. **2** *(for drinking)* vaso; *(with stem)* copa. **3** GB barómetro.
ⓘ *pl* glasses.
▶ *n pl* glasses gafas *fpl*.

**glassware** ['glɑːsweəʳ] *n* cristalería.

**glaze** [gleɪz] *n (for pottery)* vidriado; *(lustre)* brillo, lustre *m*; *(varnish)* barniz *m*, esmalte *m*.
▶ *vt* **1** *(pottery)* vidriar, esmaltar. **2** *(windows)* poner cristales a. **3** CULIN glasear.

**gleam** [gliːm] *n* **1** destello, rayo. **2** *fig* rayo, resquicio, vislumbre *m*.
▶ *vi* brillar, destellar, relucir.

**glean** [gliːn] *vt* **1** AGR espigar. **2** *fig* recoger, cosechar.

**glide** [glaɪd] *n* **1** deslizamiento. **2** AV planeo, vuelo sin motor. **3** LING semivocal *f*.
▶ *vi* **1** deslizarse. **2** AV planear.

**glider** ['glaɪdəʳ] *n* AV planeador *m*.

**glimmer** ['glɪməʳ] *n (light)* luz *f* tenue.
▶ *vi* brillar con luz tenue.

**glimpse** [glɪmps] *n* visión *f* fugaz.
▶ *vt* vislumbrar, entrever.

**glisten** ['glɪsªn] *vi* brillar, relucir.

**glitter** ['glɪtəʳ] *n* brillo.
▶ *vi* brillar, relucir.

**global** ['gləʊbªl] *adj* **1** mundial. **2** *(total)* global. COMP global warming calentamiento global.

**globalization** [gləʊbəlaɪˈzeɪʃªn] *n* globalización *f*.

**globe** [gləʊb] *n* globo

✖ Globe no significa 'globo (de niño)', que se traduce por balloon.

**globe-trotter** ['gləʊbtrɒtəʳ] *n fam* trotamundos *mf*.

**globule** ['glɒbjuːl] *n* glóbulo.

**gloom** [gluːm] *n* **1** *(darkness)* penumbra *f*. **2** *(sadness)* tristeza, melancolía. **3** *(hopelessness)* desolación *f*, pesimismo.

**gloomy** ['gluːmɪ] *adj* **1** *(dark)* lóbrego,-a, oscuro,-a, tenebroso,-a. **2** *(sad)* melancólico,-a, triste; *(depressing)* deprimente. **3** *(pessimistic)* pesimista. **4** *(weather)* gris, encapotado,-a.
ⓘ *comp* gloomier, *superl* gloomiest.

**glorious** ['glɔːrɪəs] *adj* **1** glorioso,-a. **2** *(wonderful)* espléndido,-a, magnífico,-a.

**glory** ['glɔːrɪ] *n* **1** *(gen)* gloria. **2** *fig* esplendor *m*.
ⓘ *pl* glories.

**gloss** [glɒs] n **1** lustre m, brillo. **2** (explanation) glosa. **3** fig oropel m.
▶ vt (text) glosar, comentar.
◆ **to gloss over** vt insep (play down) paliar, suavizar; (hide) encubrir; (ignore) pasar por alto.

**glossary** [ˈglɒsərɪ] n glosario.
ⓘ pl glossaries.

**glove** [glʌv] n guante m. COMP **glove compartment** guantera.

**glow** [gləʊ] n **1** (of lamp) luz f; (of jewel) brillo. **2** (of fire) calor m vivo; (of sky) arrebol m; (of fire, metal, etc) incandescencia. **3** (of face) rubor m. **4** fig sensación f de bienestar, satisfacción f.
▶ vi **1** (jewel, sun, etc) brillar; (of metal) estar al rojo vivo; (fire) arder. **2** fig rebosar de.

**glucose** [ˈgluːkəʊz] n glucosa.

**glue** [gluː] n cola, pegamento.
▶ vt encolar, pegar.

**gluten** [ˈgluːtən] n gluten m.

**gluteal** [ˈgluːtəl] adj glúteo,-a.

**gluteus** [ˈgluːtɪəs] n glúteo.

**glutton** [ˈglʌt°n] n glotón,-ona.

**glycerine** [ˈglɪsəˈriːn] n glicerina.

**GMT** [ˈdʒiːˈemˈdiː] abbr (Greenwich Mean Time) hora media de Greenwich; (abbreviation) GMT.

**gnat** [næt] n ZOOL mosquito.

**gnaw** [nɔː] vt **1** (bite) roer. **2** fig (worry) corroer.

**gnome** [nəʊm] n gnomo.

**GNP** [ˈdʒiːˈenˈpiː] abbr (gross national product) producto nacional bruto; (abbreviation) PNB m.

**gnu** [nuː] n ñu m.

**go** [gəʊ] n **1** (energy) energía, empuje m. **2** (turn) turno: it's my go me toca a mí. **3** (try) intento: I'd like to have a go at hang gliding me gustaría intentar vuelo con ala delta. **4** (start) principio.
▶ vi **1** (gen) ir: to go on holiday irse de vacaciones. **2** (leave) marcharse, irse; (bus, train, etc) salir: let's go! ¡vámonos! **3** (vanish) desaparecer. **4** (function) funcionar, marchar: his business is going very well su negocio marcha muy bien. **5** (become) volverse, ponerse, quedarse: to go deaf quedarse

sordo,-a. **6** (fit) entrar, caber: the bed won't go into the room la cama no cabrá en la habitación. **7** (break) romperse, estropearse; (yield) ceder; (blow) fundirse. **8** (progress) ir, marchar, andar: things aren't going too well for him no le van muy bien las cosas. **9** (be available) quedar, haber: is there any more meat going? ¿queda algo de carne?. **10** (make a noise, gesture, etc) hacer: go like this with your head haz así con la cabeza. **11** (time - pass) pasar; (- be remaining) faltar: the years went by slowly los años pasaron lentamente; only two weeks to go solo faltan dos semanas. **16** (say) decir: as the saying goes según el dicho.
▶ vt **1** (make a noise) hacer: it goes tick-tock hace tic-tac. **2** (travel) hacer, recorrer.
▶ interj go! (starting races) ¡ya!: ready, steady, go! ¡preparados, listos, ya!.
◆ **to go after** vt insep (pursue) perseguir, andar tras.
◆ **to go ahead** vi (proceed) proceder: go ahead! ¡adelante!.
◆ **to go along with** vt insep estar de acuerdo con.
◆ **to go around** vi → to go round.
◆ **to go away** vi marcharse.
◆ **to go back** vi (return) volver, regresar; (date from) datar de, remontarse a.
◆ **to go back on** vt insep (break) romper, no cumplir.
◆ **to go by** vi (time) pasar.
▶ vt insep (rules) atenerse a, seguir; (instinct) dejarse llevar por; (appearances) juzgar por.
◆ **to go down** vi **1** (gen) bajar; (tyre) deshincharse; (sun) ponerse; (ship) hundirse. **2** (be received) ser acogido,-a.
◆ **to go for** vt insep **1** (attack) atacar. **2** (fetch) ir a buscar. **3** fam (like) gustar. **4** fam (be valid) valer para.
◆ **to go in** vi entrar.
◆ **to go in for** vt insep (enter - race, competition) participar en; (- exam) presentarse a; (- career) dedicarse a; (like, agree with) ser partidario,-a de.
◆ **to go into** vt insep **1** (gen) entrar en. **2** (investigate) investigar. **3** (crash) chocar contra.
◆ **to go off** vi **1** (leave) marcharse. **2** (bomb) estallar; (alarm) sonar; (gun) dis-

pararse. **3** *(food)* estropearse, pasarse; *(milk)* cortarse. **4** *(stop operating)* apagarse.

▶ *vt insep (stop liking)* perder el gusto por, perder el interés por.

◆ **to go on** *vi* **1** *(continue)* seguir, continuar. **2** *(happen)* pasar, ocurrir: *what's going on?* ¿qué pasa?. **3** *(complain)* quejarse (about, de); *(talk at length)* hablar sin parar. **4** *(light, etc)* encenderse. **5** *(age)* estar a punto de cumplir: *she's ten going on eleven* está a punto de cumplir los once años.

◆ **to go out** *vi* **1** *(leave)* salir: *he goes out a lot* sale mucho. **2** *(fire, light)* apagarse.

◆ **to go over** *vt insep (check, revise)* revisar, repasar.

◆ **to go over to** *vt insep* **1** *(betray)* pasarse a. **2** *(change to)* cambiar a, pasar a.

◆ **to go round** *vi* **1** *(gyrate)* dar vueltas, girar. **2** *(visit)* pasar por casa de, visitar.

◆ **to go through** *vt insep (undergo)* pasar por, sufrir, padecer. **2** *(examine)* examinar; *(search)* registrar; *(spend)* gastar; *(explain)* explicar.

▶ *vi (act, law)* ser aprobado,-a.

◆ **to go through with** *vt insep* llevar a cabo.

◆ **to go under** *vi* **1** *(ship)* hundirse. **2** *fig* fracasar.

◆ **to go up** *vi* **1** *(gen)* subir; *(approach)* acercarse. **2** *(curtain in theatre)* levantarse. **3** *(explode)* estallar; *(burst into flames)* prenderse fuego.

ⓘ *pt* went [went], *pp* gone [gɒn], *ger* going.

**goal** [gəʊl] *n* **1** SP *(area)* meta, portería. **2** SP *(point)* gol *m*, tanto. **3** *(aim)* fin *m*, objetivo, meta.

**goalkeeper** ['gəʊlkiːpəʳ] *n* portero,-a, guardameta *mf*.

**goat** [gəʊt] *n (female)* cabra; *(male)* macho cabrío.

**goatee** ['gəʊtiː] *n (beard)* perilla.

**gobble** ['gɒbəl] *vt* engullir, zamparse.

**god** [gɒd] *n (deity, idol)* dios *m*.

▶ *n* God Dios *m*.

**godchild** ['gɒdtʃaɪld] *n* ahijado,-a.

ⓘ *pl* godchildren ['gɒdtʃɪldrən].

**goddaughter** ['gɒddɔːtəʳ] *n* ahijada.

**goddess** ['gɒdəs] *n* diosa.

**godfather** ['gɒdfɑːðəʳ] *n* padrino.

**godmother** ['gɒdmʌðəʳ] *n* madrina.

**godparents** ['gɒdpeərənts] *n pl* padrinos *mpl*.

**godsend** ['gɒdsend] *n* regalo llovido del cielo.

**godson** ['gɒdsʌn] *n* ahijado.

**goggle** ['gɒgəl] *vi* quedarse atónito,-a.

**goggles** ['gɒgəlz] *n pl* gafas *fpl* protectoras.

**going** ['gəʊɪŋ] *n* **1** *(departure)* ida, salida. **2** *(pace)* paso, ritmo. **3** *(path, road)* estado del camino.

▶ *adj* **1** *(price, rate)* actual, corriente. **2** *(business)* que marcha bien.

**gold** [gəʊld] *n (metal)* oro.

▶ *adj* **1** *(colour)* dorado,-a. **2** *(made of gold)* de oro.

**golden** ['gəʊldən] *adj* **1** de oro. **2** *(colour)* dorado,-a. **3** *(hair)* rubio,-a.

**goldfinch** ['gəʊldfɪntʃ] *n* jilguero.

**goldfish** ['gəʊldfɪʃ] *n* pez *m* de colores.

ⓘ *pl* goldfish ['gəʊldfɪʃ].

**goldsmith** ['gəʊldsmɪθ] *n* orfebre *mf*.

**golf** [gɒlf] *n* golf *m*.

▶ *vi* jugar al golf. COMP **golf course** campo de golf.

**golfer** ['gɒlfəʳ] *n* jugador,-ra de golf.

**gone** [gɒn] *pp* → go.

▶ *adj* **1** *(time)* pasado,-a. **2** *(dead)* muerto,-a.

**gong** [gɒŋ] *n* **1** gong *m*. **2** *fam fig (award, prize)* galardón *m*.

**good** [gʊd] *adj* **1** bueno,-a; *(before m sing noun)* buen. **2** *(healthy)* sano,-a. **3** *(kind)* amable. **4** *(useful)* servible. LOC **for good** para siempre. COMP **Good Friday** Viernes *m* Santo.

ⓘ *comp* better, *superl* best.

▶ *n* bien *m*: *its for your own good* es por tu propio bien.

▶ *n pl* goods *(property)* bienes *mpl*; COMM *(in shop)* género *m sing*, artículos *mpl*; COMM *(merchandise)* mercancías *fpl*.

**goodbye** [gʊdˈbaɪ] [also written good-bye] *n* adiós *m*.

▶ *interj* ¡adiós!

**good-for-nothing** [ˈgʊdfənʌθɪŋ] *n* golfo.

**good-hearted** [gʊdˈhɑːtɪd] *adj* de buen corazón.

**good-humoured** [gʊdˈhjuːməd] *adj* de buen humor, campechano,-a.

**good-looking** [gʊdˈlʊkɪŋ] *adj* guapo,-a, bien parecido,-a.

**good-natured** [gʊdˈneɪtʃəd] *adj* bondadoso,-a.

**goodness** [ˈgʊdnəs] *n* **1** *(virtue)* bondad *f*. **2** *(in food)* lo nutritivo.

**goodwill** [gʊdˈwɪl] *n* buena voluntad *f*.

**goose** [guːs] *n* ganso, oca.
ⓘ *pl* geese.

**gooseberry** [ˈgʊzbrɪ, ˈguːsbˀrɪ] *n* **1** BOT grosella espinosa. **2** GB *fam fig (person)* carabina.
ⓘ *pl* gooseberries.

**gooseflesh** [ˈguːsfleʃ] *n* piel *f* de gallina.

**gore¹** [gɔːʳ] *n* sangre *f* derramada.

**gore²** [gɔːʳ] *vt* dar una cornada a.

**gorge** [gɔːdʒ] *n* *(mountain pass)* desfiladero; *(ravine)* barranco.

**gorgeous** [ˈgɔːdʒəs] *adj* **1** magnífico,-a, espléndido,-a. **2** *(person)* guapísimo,-a.
▸ *n fam* guapo,-a.

**gorilla** [gəˈrɪlə] *n* ZOOL gorila *m*.

**go-slow** [gəʊˈsləʊ] *n* huelga de celo.

**gospel** [ˈgɒspˀl] *n* REL **1** evangelio. **2** MUS música gospel.

**gossip** [ˈgɒsɪp] *n* **1** *(talk)* cotilleo, chismorreo. **2** *(person)* cotilla *mf*, chismoso,-a. COMP **gossip column** crónica de sociedad.
▸ *vi* cotillear, chismorrear.

**got** [gɒt] *pt & pp* → **get**.

**Gothic** [ˈgɒθɪk] *adj* **1** godo,-a. **2** *(language, architecture, type)* gótico,-a.

**gotten** [ˈgɒtˀn] *pp* US → **get**.

**gourmet** [ˈgʊəmeɪ] *n* gastrónomo,-a, gurmet *mf*.

**govern** [ˈgʌvˀn] *vt* **1** gobernar, dirigir. **2** LING regir. **3** *(determine)* dictar.
▸ *vi* **1** gobernar. **2** *(predominate)* predominar, prevalecer.

**government** [ˈgʌvˀnmənt] *n* gobierno.
▸ *adj* **1** *(of government)* del gobierno, gubernamental. **2** *(of a governor)* del gobernador.

**governmental** [gʌvˀnˈmentˀl] *adj* gubernamental.

**governor** [ˈgʌvˀnəʳ] *n* **1** *(town, state, bank)* gobernador,-ra. **2** *(prison)* director,-ra. **3** *(school)* administrador,-ra. **4** GB *fam (employer)* jefe *m*.

**gown** [gaʊn] *n* **1** vestido largo. **2** *(judge's, academic's)* toga. **3** *(surgeon's)* bata.

**GP** [ˈdʒiːˈpiː] *abbr* (general practitioner) médico,-a de cabecera.
ⓘ *pl* GPs.

**grab** [græb] *vt* **1** *(seize, snatch)* coger, agarrar, asir. **2** *(capture, arrest)* pillar, coger. **3** *fam* entusiasmar.
ⓘ *pt & pp* grabbed, *ger* grabbing.

**grace** [greɪs] *n* **1** gracia, elegancia. **2** *(deportment)* garbo. **3** *(courtesy)* delicadeza, cortesía. **4** *(blessing)* bendición *f*. **5** REL gracia. **6** *(delay)* plazo.
▸ *vt* **1** *(adorn)* adornar. **2** *(honour)* honrar.

☒ Grace no significa 'gracia (chiste)', que se traduce por joke.

**gracious** [ˈgreɪʃəs] *adj* **1** gracioso,-a. **2** *(polite)* cortés. **3** *(kind)* amable. **4** *(benevolent)* benévolo,-a.
▸ *interj* ¡Dios mío!.

☒ Gracious no significa 'gracioso (divertido)', que se traduce por funny.

**grade** [greɪd] *n* **1** *(degree, level)* grado. **2** *(quality)* calidad *f*. **3** *(class, category)* clase *f*, categoría. **4** *(rank)* rango, grado. **5** *(mark)* nota. **6** US *(gradient)* pendiente *f*. **7** US *(form)* clase *f*.
▸ *vt* **1** *(sort, classify)* clasificar. **2** *(road)* nivelar. **3** *(student)* calificar, poner una nota. **4** *(colours)* degradar.
◆ **to grade up** *vt sep* subir de categoría.
◆ **to grade down** *vt sep* bajar de categoría.

**gradual** [ˈgrædjʊəl] *adj* gradual.

**graduate** [*(n)* ˈgrædjʊət; *(vb)* ˈgrædjʊeɪt] *n* EDUC *(after 3-year course)* diplomado,-a; *(after 5-year course)* licenciado,-a.
▸ *vt* *(grade, classify)* graduar.

▶ vi (after 3-year course) diplomarse (in, en); (after 5-year course) licenciarse (in, en).

**graduation** [grædjʊ'eɪʃ⁰n] n **1** EDUC graduación f. **2** TECH graduación f.

**graft** [grɑːft] n (of plant, tissue) injerto.
▶ vt injertar (onto, en).

**grain** [greɪn] n **1** (gen) grano. **2** (cereals) cereales mpl. **3** (in wood) veta, fibra; (in stone) filón m, veta; (of leather) flor f.
▶ vt (give granular texture) granular.

**grammar** ['græmə⁰] n gramática. LOC grammar school instituto de enseñanza media.

**gramme** [græm] n gramo.

**granary** ['grænərɪ] n granero.
ⓘ pl granaries.

**grand** [grænd] adj **1** (splendid) grandioso,-a, espléndido,-a, magnífico,-a. **2** (impressive) impresionante. **3** (important - person) distinguido,-a, importante. **4** fam (great) fenomenal. COMP grand piano piano de cola.

**grandchild** ['græntʃaɪld] n nieto,-a.
ⓘ pl grandchildren [grən'tʃɪldrən].

**granddad** ['grændæd] n fam abuelo.

**granddaughter** ['grændɔːtə⁰] n nieta.

**grandfather** ['grænfɑːðə⁰] n abuelo.

**grandma** ['grænmɑː] n fam abuela.

**grandmother** ['grænmʌðə⁰] n abuela.

**grandpa** ['grænpɑː] n fam abuelo.

**grandparents** ['grændpeərənts] n pl abuelos mpl.

**grandson** ['grændsʌn] n nieto.

**granite** ['grænɪt] n granito.
▶ adj de granito.

**granny** ['grænɪ] n fam abuela.
ⓘ pl grannies.

**grant** [grɑːnt] n **1** EDUC beca. **2** (subsidy) subvención f. **3** JUR (rights, property) cesión f.
▶ vt **1** conceder, otorgar. **2** JUR ceder, transferir. LOC to take STH for granted dar ALGO por sentado.

**granule** ['grænjuːl] n gránulo.

**grape** [greɪp] n uva.

**grapefruit** ['greɪpfruːt] n pomelo.
ⓘ pl grapefruits o grapefruit.

**grapevine** ['greɪpvaɪn] n (gen) parra; (vine) vid f.

**graph** [grɑːf] n gráfica, gráfico. COMP graph paper papel cuadriculado.

**graphic** ['græfɪk] adj **1** (gen) gráfico,-a. **2** (vivid) muy gráfico,-a, vívido,-a.

**graphite** ['græfaɪt] n grafito.

**grasp** [grɑːsp] vt **1** (seize - with hands) agarrar, asir; (opportunity, offer) aprovechar. **2** (understand) comprender, captar.

**grass** [grɑːs] n (plant) hierba, yerba; (lawn) césped m; (pasture) pasto; (dried) paja.

**grasshopper** ['grɑːshɒpə⁰] n saltamontes m.

**grassy** ['grɑːsɪ] adj cubierto,-a de hierba.
ⓘ comp grassier, superl grassiest.

**grate¹** [greɪt] vt **1** CULIN rallar. **2** (scrape - gen) rascar; (- teeth) hacer rechinar.

**grate²** [greɪt] n (metal frame) rejilla; (fireplace) chimenea.

**grateful** ['greɪtfʊl] adj (person) agradecido,-a; (letter, smile) de agradecimiento.

**grater** ['greɪtə⁰] n rallador m.

**gratification** [grætɪfɪ'keɪʃ⁰n] n gratificación f, satisfacción f, placer m.

**gratify** ['grætɪfaɪ] vt **1** (satisfy - desire, etc) satisfacer. **2** (give pleasure to) complacer, gratificar.
ⓘ pt & pp gratified, ger gratifying.

**gratitude** ['grætɪtjuːd] n gratitud f, agradecimiento.

**gratuitous** [grə'tjuːɪtəs] adj gratuito,-a.

✗ Gratuitous no significa 'gratuito (gratis)', que se traduce por free.

**grave¹** [greɪv] n tumba, sepultura.

**grave²** [greɪv] adj **1** (gen) grave. **2** [grɑːv] (accent) grave.

**gravel** ['græv⁰l] n grava, gravilla, guijo.

**gravestone** ['greɪvstəʊn] n lápida.

**graveyard** ['greɪvjɑːd] n cementerio.

**gravity** ['grævɪtɪ] n **1** PHYS gravedad f. **2** (seriousness) gravedad f; (of person, manner) gravedad f, circunspección f.

**gray** [greɪ] adj US → grey.

**graze¹** [greɪz] n rasguño, roce m.

**graze²** [greɪz] vt (sheep, cattle) pastar, pastorear, apacentar.

**grease** [griːs] n (gen) grasa.
▶ vt (part of car, machine, device) engrasar.

**greasy** ['griːsɪ] *adj* **1** *(oily - hands)* grasiento,-a. **3** *fam pej (smarmy)* pelota.
ⓘ *comp* greasier, *superl* greasiest.

**great** [greɪt] *adj* **1** *(gen)* grande; *(before sing noun)* gran. **2** *fam (excellent, wonderful)* estupendo,-a, fantástico,-a, sensacional, fabuloso,-a.
▶ *adv fam* muy bien, estupendamente, fenomenal.

**great-grandchild** [greɪt'græntʃaɪld] *n* bisnieto,-a, biznieto,-a.
ⓘ *pl* great-grandchildren [greɪtgrən'tʃɪldrən].

**great-grandfather** [greɪt'grændfɑːðəʳ] *n* bisabuelo.

**great-grandmother** [greɪt'grænmʌðəʳ] *n* bisabuela.

**Greece** [griːs] *n* Grecia.

**greed** [griːd] *n* **1** *(for money, power)* codicia, avaricia. **2** *(for food)* gula, glotonería.

**greedy** ['griːdɪ] *adj* **1** *(for money, power)* codicioso,-a. **2** *(for food)* glotón,-ona.
ⓘ *comp* greedier, *superl* greediest.

**Greek** [griːk] *adj* griego,-a.
▶ *n* **1** *(person)* griego,-a. **2** *(language)* griego.

**green** [griːn] *adj* **1** *(colour)* verde. **2** *(environment friendly)* ecológico,-a. **4** *(pale)* pálido,-a. **5** *(inexperienced)* novato,-a, verde; *(gullible)* ingenuo,-a, crédulo,-a. **6** *(jealous)* envidioso,-a.
▶ *n* **1** *(colour)* verde *m*. **2** *(stretch of grass)* césped *m*; *(in golf)* green *m*; *(in village)* césped público .
▶ *n pl* greens *(vegetables)* verduras *fpl*.
▶ *n pl* the Greens POL los verdes *mpl*.

**greenfly** ['griːnflaɪ] *n* pulgón *m*.
ⓘ *pl* greenflies.

**greengrocer** ['griːngrəʊsəʳ] *n* verdulero, -a. LOC greengrocer's (shop) verdulería.

**greenhouse** ['griːnhaʊs] *n* invernadero. COMP greenhouse effect efecto invernadero.

**Greenland** ['griːnlənd] *n* Groenlandia.

**Greenlander** ['griːnləndəʳ] *n* groenlandés,-esa.

**greet** [griːt] *vt* **1** *(wave at, say hello to)* saludar; *(welcome)* dar la bienvenida a; *(receive)* recibir. **2** *(react)* acoger, recibir. **3** *fig (meet)* llegar, presentarse.

**greeting** ['griːtɪŋ] *n* saludo.
▶ *n pl* greetings saludos *mpl*, recuerdos *mpl*.

**gregarious** [gre'geərɪəs] *adj* gregario,-a, sociable.

**gremlin** ['gremlɪn] *n* duende *m*.

**Grenada** [grə'neɪdə] *n* Granada.

**grenade** [grə'neɪd] *n* granada.

**grew** [gruː] *pt* → grow.

**grey** [greɪ] *adj* **1** *(colour)* gris; *(hair)* cano,-a; *(sky)* nublado,-a, gris. **2** *(gloomy)* triste, gris.
▶ *n* **1** *(colour)* gris *m*. **2** *(horse)* caballo tordo. LOC to go grey encanecer.

**greyhound** ['greɪhaʊnd] *n* galgo.

**grid** [grɪd] *n* **1** *(grating)* reja, parrilla, rejilla. **2** ELEC *(network)* red *f* nacional de tendido eléctrico. **3** *(on map)* cuadrícula.

**griddle** ['grɪdªl] *n* CULIN plancha.

**grief** [griːf] *n* dolor *m*, pena.

**grieve** [griːv] *vt* afligir, apenar, dar pena a, entristecer.
▶ *vi* apenarse, afligirse.

**grill** [grɪl] *n* CULIN *(over cooker)* gratinador *m*, grill *m*; *(on charcoal)* parrilla. **4** → grille.

**grille** [grɪl] *n* reja.

**grim** [grɪm] *adj* **1** *(serious)* austero,-a, severo,-a; *(look)* ceñudo,-a. **2** *(unpleasant)* horroroso,-a, pesimista; *(- prospect, outlook)* nefasto,-a, desalentador,-ra; *(- reality)* crudo,-a, duro,-a. **3** *(gloomy - landscape, place)* lúgubre, sombrío,-a.
ⓘ *comp* grimmer, *superl* grimmest.

**grimace** ['grɪməs] *n* mueca.

**grin** [grɪn] *n* *(genuine)* sonrisa (abierta); *(mocking)* sonrisa burlona.
▶ *vi* sonreír (abiertamente).
ⓘ *pt & pp* grinned, *ger* grinning.

**grind** [graɪnd] *vt* **1** *(mill)* moler; *(crush)* machacar, triturar; *(lens, mirror)* pulir; *(knife, blade)* afilar. **2** US *(mince - beef)* picar. **3** *(teeth)* rechinar. **4** *(press down hard on)* incrustar, aplastar; *(press in)* meter.
▶ *vi* **1** *(crush)* triturarse. **2** *(make harsh noise)* rechinar. **3** US *(swot)* empollar.
ⓘ *pt & pp* ground [graʊnd].
▶ *n* **1** *fam (work)* trabajo pesado; *(effort)* paliza. **2** US *fam (swot)* empollón,-ona.
◆ to grind down *vt sep* oprimir.
◆ to grind out *vt sep (music)* tocar.

**grinder** ['graɪndəʳ] *n (machine - for coffee)* molinillo; *(person - for knives, etc)* afilador,-ra.

**grindstone** ['graɪnstəʊn] *n* muela, piedra de afilar.

**gringo** ['grɪŋgəʊ] *n pej* gringo,-a.
ⓘ *pl* gringos.

**grip** [grɪp] *n* **1** *(tight hold)* asimiento. **2** *(of tyre)* adherencia, agarre *m*. **3** *fig (control, force)* control *m*, dominio. **4** *fig (way of holding)* la forma en que uno coge la raqueta, etc; *(part of handle)* asidero, empuñadura. **5** *(hairgrip)* horquilla.
▸ *vt* **1** *(hold tightly - gen)* agarrar, asir, sujetar. **2** *(adhere to)* tener agarre, agarrarse, adherirse. **3** *fig (film, story, play)* captar el interés de, captar la atención de.
▸ *vi* adherirse.
ⓘ *pt & pp* gripped, *ger* gripping.

**grit** [grɪt] *n* **1** *(fine)* arena; *(coarse)* gravilla; *(dirt)* polvo. **2** *fam (determination)* valor *m*, agallas *fpl*.

**grizzly** ['grɪzlɪ] [also grizzly bear] *n* oso pardo.

**groan** [grəʊn] *n* **1** gemido, quejido. **2** *(creak)* crujido.
▸ *vi* **1** *(in pain)* gemir, quejarse; *(with disapproval)* gruñir. **2** *(creak)* crujir.

**grocer** ['grəʊsəʳ] *n* tendero,-a. COMP grocer's (shop) tienda de comestibles.

**groceries** ['grəʊsərɪz] *n pl* comestibles *mpl*.

**grocery** ['grəʊsərɪ] *n* US tienda de ultramarinos, tienda de comestibles.
ⓘ *pl* groceries.

**groggy** ['grɒgɪ] *adj fam* grogui.
ⓘ *comp* groggier, *superl* groggiest.

**groin** [grɔɪn] *n* ANAT ingle *f*.

**groom** [gruːm] *n* **1** *(bridegroom)* novio. **2** *(for horses)* mozo de cuadra.

✎ Se usa para referirse al novio sólo durante el día de la boda. Es la forma abreviada de **bridegroom**.

**groove** [gruːv] *n* **1** *(gen)* ranura; *(for door)* guía; *(in column)* acanaladura. **2** *(on record)* surco.

**groovy** ['gruːvɪ] *adj fam* guay, genial.
ⓘ *comp* groovier, *superl* grooviest.

**grope** [grəʊp] *vi* andar a tientas.

**gross** [grəʊs] *adj* **1** *(flagrant - injustice)* flagrante; *(- ignorance)* craso,-a; *(- error)* grave. **2** *(fat)* muy gordo,-a, obeso,-a. **3** *(behaviour, manners)* grosero,-a, tosco,-a; *(- language)* soez; *(disgusting)* asqueroso,-a. **4** FIN *(total)* bruto,-a.
▸ *vt (person)* obtener unos ingresos brutos de; *(film, etc)* recaudar.

**grotesque** [grəʊ'tesk] *adj* grotesco,-a.

**grotto** ['grɒtəʊ] *n* gruta.
ⓘ *pl* grottoes o grottos.

**ground¹** [graʊnd] *n* **1** *(surface of earth)* suelo; *(soil, earth)* tierra; *(terrain, land)* campo, terreno. **2** US *(electrical)* tierra. **3** ART *(background)* fondo. **4** *(matter, subject)* aspecto, punto. COMP ground floor planta baja.
▸ *n pl* grounds *(reason, justification)* razón *f*, motivo; *(of coffee)* poso, posos *mpl*; *(gardens)* jardines *mpl*; *(area of land)* terreno.

**ground²** [graʊnd] *pt & pp* → **grind.**
▸ *adj* **1** *(coffee)* molido,-a. **2** US *(beef)* picado,-a.

**grounding** ['graʊndɪŋ] *n* base *f*, conocimientos *mpl*.

**groundwork** ['graʊndwɜːk] *n* trabajo preliminar, trabajo preparatorio.

**group** [gruːp] *n* grupo.
▸ *vt* agrupar.

**grouper** ['gruːpəʳ] *n* mero.

**groupie** ['gruːpɪ] *n fam* grupi *mf*.

**grow** [grəʊ] *vi* **1** *(gen)* crecer. **2** *(increase)* aumentar. **3** *(become)* hacerse, volverse. **4** *(begin gradually)* llegar a. LOC to grow old envejecer.
▸ *vt* **1** *(crop, plant, flower)* cultivar. **2** *(beard, etc)* dejarse (crecer); *(hair, nails)* dejarse crecer.
◆ to grow into *vt insep (become)* convertirse en, hacerse.
◆ to grow on *vt insep* llegar a gustar.
◆ to grow up *vi* **1** *(become adult)* hacerse mayor; *(spend childhood)* criarse, crecer. **2** *(spring up)* surgir, nacer, desarrollarse.
ⓘ *pt* grew ['gruː], *pp* grown [grəʊn].

**grower** ['grəʊəʳ] *n (farmer)* cultivador,-ra.

**growl** [graʊl] *n* gruñido.
▸ *vi* gruñir.

**grown** [grəʊn] *pp* → **grow.**
▸ *adj* adulto,-a.

**grown-up** [ˈgrəʊnʌp] *adj* mayor, adulto,-a.
▶ *n* persona mayor.

**growth** [grəʊθ] *n* **1** *(gen)* crecimiento; *(increase)* aumento; *(development)* desarrollo. **2** MED *(tumour)* bulto, tumor *m*. **3** *(of beard)* barba.

**grub** [grʌb] *n* *(larva)* larva, gusano.
▶ *vi* **1** *(by digging)* escarbar, hurgar. **2** *fig* rebuscar.
ⓘ *pt & pp* grubbed, *ger* grubbing.

**grudge** [grʌdʒ] *n* rencor *m*.
▶ *vt* **1** *(begrudge, resent)* dar a regañadientes, dar de mala gana. **2** *(envy)* envidiar.

**grumble** [ˈgrʌmbəl] *n* **1** *(complaint)* queja. **2** *(of thunder)* estruendo.
▶ *vi* **1** *(moan, complain)* refunfuñar, quejarse *(about,* de). **2** *(rumble - thunder)* retumbar; *(- stomach)* hacer ruido.

**grumpy** [ˈgrʌmpɪ] *adj* gruñón,-ona, malhumorado,-a, de mal humor.
ⓘ *comp* grumpier, *superl* grumpiest.

**grunge** [grʌndʒ] *n* MUS grunge *m*.

**grunt** [grʌnt] *n* gruñido.
▶ *vi* gruñir.

**guarantee** [gærənˈtiː] *n* **1** *(gen)* garantía; *(certificate)* certificado de garantía.
▶ *vt* **1** *(gen)* garantizar; *(assure, promise)* asegurar. **2** *(debt)* avalar, garantizar.

**guard** [gɑːd] *n* **1** *(sentry, soldier)* guardia *mf*; *(security guard)* guarda *mf*, guarda jurado,-a, guarda de seguridad; *(prison officer)* carcelero,-a. **2** *(duty)* guardia. **3** GB *(on train)* jefe,-a de tren. **4** *(on machine)* dispositivo de seguridad; *(on gun)* seguro. LOC to be on guard estar de guardia. ‖ to stand guard montar guardia.
▶ *vt* **1** *(watch over)* vigilar; *(protect - person, reputation)* proteger; *(keep - secret)* guardar. **2** *(control - tongue)* cuidar, controlar.

✖ To guard no significa 'guardar (en un sitio)', que se traduce por to put away.

**guardian** [ˈgɑːdɪən] *n* **1** *(defender)* guardián,-ana, defensor,-ra. **2** JUR *(of child)* tutor,-ra.

**guava** [ˈgwɑːvə] *n* *(fruit)* guayaba.

**guess** [ges] *n* *(conjecture)* conjetura; *(estimate)* cálculo. LOC to have a guess adivinar.
▶ *vt* **1** *(gen)* adivinar. **2** US *fam* *(suppose)* suponer, pensar, creer.
▶ *vi* adivinar.

**guesswork** [ˈgeswɜːk] *n* conjeturas *fpl*, suposiciones *fpl*.

**guest** [gest] *n* **1** *(at home, restaurant, etc)* invitado,-a; *(in hotel)* cliente,-a, huésped,-da. **2** *(on TV programme)* invitado,-a.

**guesthouse** [ˈgesthaʊs] *n* casa de huéspedes, pensión *f*.

**guestroom** [ˈgestruːm] *n* cuarto de (los) invitados.

**Guiana** [gaɪˈænə, gɪˈɑːnə] *n* Guayana.

**guidance** [ˈgaɪdəns] *n* *(help, advice)* orientación *f*, consejos *mpl*.

**guide** [gaɪd] *n* **1** *(person)* guía *mf*. **2** *(book)* guía. **3** *(indicator)* guía, modelo. COMP guide dog perro lazarillo.
▶ *vt* **1** *(show the way)* guiar; *(lead)* conducir. **2** *(advise, influence)* orientar, aconsejar.

**guidebook** [ˈgaɪdbʊk] *n* guía.

**guideline** [ˈgaɪdlaɪn] *n* pauta, directriz *f*.

**guiding** [ˈgaɪdɪŋ] *adj* que guía, que sirve de guía.

**guild** [gɪld] *n* *(of workers)* gremio; *(association)* asociación *f*, agrupación *f*.

**guillotine** [ˈgɪlətiːn] *n* guillotina.
▶ *vt* *(person, paper)* guillotinar.

**guilt** [gɪlt] *n* **1** JUR culpabilidad *f*. **2** *(blame)* culpa; *(remorse)* remordimiento.

**guilty** [ˈgɪltɪ] *adj* culpable *(of,* de). LOC to find SB guilty declarar culpable a ALGN.
ⓘ *comp* guiltier, *superl* guiltiest.

**Guinea** [ˈgɪnɪ] *n* Guinea. COMP Equatorial Guinea Guinea Ecuatorial. ‖ New Guinea Nueva Guinea.

**guinea** [ˈgɪnɪ] *n* *(coin)* guinea. COMP guinea fowl gallina de Guinea, pintada. ‖ guinea pig conejillo de Indias, cobaya.

**Guinea-Bissau** [gɪnɪbɪˈsaʊ] *n* Guinea Bissau.

**Guinean** [ˈgɪnɪən] *adj* guineano,-a.
▶ *n* guineano,-a.

**guitar** [gɪˈtɑːr] *n* guitarra.

**guitarist** [gɪˈtɑːrɪst] *n* guitarrista *mf*.

**gulf** [gʌlf] *n* **1** GEOG golfo. **2** *fig* abismo. COMP Gulf of Mexico golfo de Méjico. ‖ Persian Gulf golfo Pérsico. ‖ Gulf Stream corriente *f* del Golfo.

**gull** [gʌl] *n* gaviota.

**gulley** ['gʌlɪ] *n* → gully.

**gullible** ['gʌlɪbəl] *adj* crédulo,-a.

**gully** ['gʌlɪ] *n* **1** GEOG *(small valley, ravine)* barranco, torrentera. **2** *(deep ditch, waterway, channel)* surco, cauce *m*.
  ① *pl* gullies.

**gulp** [gʌlp] *n (of drink)* trago; *(of air)* bocanada: *he drank his glass in one gulp* se bebió todo el vaso de un trago.
  ▶ *vt (drink)* beberse de un trago (down, -); *(food)* engullir (down, -).
  ▶ *vi (swallow air)* tragar aire; *(with fear)* tragar saliva.
  ◆ **to gulp back** *vt insep* tragarse.

**gum¹** [gʌm] *n* ANAT encía.

**gum²** [gʌm] *n* **1** *(natural substance)* goma, resina. **2** *(chewing gum)* chicle *m*. **3** *(glue)* goma (de pegar), pegamento.
  ▶ *vt* pegar (con goma).
  ① *pt & pp* gummed, *ger* gumming.

**gumboil** ['gʌmbɔɪl] *n* flemón *m*.

**gumboot** ['gʌmbuːt] *n* bota de agua.

**gumtree** ['gʌmtriː] *n* gomero, árbol *m* del caucho.

**gun** [gʌn] *n* **1** *(gen)* arma de fuego; *(handgun)* pistola, revólver *m*; *(rifle)* rifle *m*, fusil *m*; *(shotgun)* escopeta; *(cannon)* cañón *m*. **2** SP pistola.

**gunboat** ['gʌnbəʊt] *n* (lancha) cañonera.

**gunfire** ['gʌnfaɪəʳ] *n (gen)* fuego, disparos *mpl*; *(shooting)* tiroteo; *(shellfire)* cañoneo, cañonazos *mpl*.

**gunman** ['gʌnmən] *n* pistolero.
  ① *pl* gunmen ['gʌnmən].

**gunner** ['gʌnəʳ] *n* artillero.

**gunpoint** ['gʌnpɔɪnt] LOC **at gunpoint** a punta de pistola.

**gunpowder** ['gʌnpaʊdəʳ] *n* pólvora.

**gunshot** ['gʌnʃɒt] *n* disparo, tiro.

**guru** ['gʊruː] *n* gurú *m*.

**gush** [gʌʃ] *n* chorro, borbotón *m*.
  ▶ *vi* **1** *(liquid)* salir a borbotones. **2** *(person)* ser efusivo,-a: *everyone was gushing over her new baby* todos se deshacían en elogios con su nuevo bebé.
  ▶ *vt* chorrear, derramar.

**gust** [gʌst] *n* **1** *(of wind)* ráfaga, racha; *(of rain)* chaparrón *m*. **2** *fig (of anger)* arrebato: *gust of laughter* carcajada.
  ▶ *vi* soplar.

**gut** [gʌt] *n* **1** ANAT intestino. **2** *fam (belly)* barriga, tripa.
  ▶ *n pl* **guts** *(entrails)* entrañas *fpl*, tripas *fpl*; *fam (courage)* agallas *fpl*: *it takes guts to do what you did* hay que tener agallas para hacer lo que hiciste.

**gutter** ['gʌtəʳ] *n (in street)* arroyo, cuneta; *(on roof)* canal *m*, canalón *m*. COMP **gutter press** prensa amarilla.

**guy** [gaɪ] *n* **1** *fam (man)* tipo, tío: *he's a great guy* es un tío estupendo; *a tough guy* un tipo duro. **2** US *fam (person)* tío,-a: *come on you guys* venga tíos. COMP **Guy Fawkes Night** → Bonfire night.

**Guyana** [gaɪˈænə] *n* Guyana, Guayana.

**Guyanan** [gaɪˈænən] *adj-n* → Guyanese.

**guzzle** ['gʌzəl] *vt fam (eat)* zamparse, engullirse; *(drink)* chupar, tragar.
  ▶ *vi fam (eat)* engullir; *(drink)* chupar, tragar.

**gym** [dʒɪm] *n* **1** *fam (gymnasium)* gimnasio. **2** *(gymnastics)* gimnasia.

**gymkhana** [dʒɪmˈkɑːnə] *n* gymkhana.

**gymnasium** [dʒɪmˈneɪzɪəm] *n* gimnasio.
  ① *pl* gymnasiums o gymnasia [dʒɪmˈneɪzɪə].

**gymnast** ['dʒɪmnæst] *n* gimnasta *mf*.

**gymnastics** [dʒɪmˈnæstɪks] *n* gimnasia.

**gymnosperm** ['dʒɪmnəʊspɜːm] *n* gimnospermo.

**gynaecological** [gaɪnəkəˈlɒdʒɪkəl] *adj* ginecológico,-a.

**gynaecologist** [gaɪnɪˈkɒlədʒɪst] *n* ginecólogo,-a.

**gynaecology** [gaɪnɪˈkɒlədʒɪ] *n* ginecología.

**gypsum** ['dʒɪpsəm] *n* yeso.

**gypsy** ['dʒɪpsɪ] *n* gitano,-a.
  ① *pl* gypsies.
  ▶ *adj* gitano,-a.

**gyroscope** ['dʒaɪrəskəʊp] *n* giroscopio, giróscopo.

G

# H

**H, h** [eɪtʃ] *n (the letter)* H, h *f*.
**habit** ['hæbɪt] *n* **1** *(custom)* hábito, costumbre *f*. **2** REL *(garment)* hábito.
**habitable** ['hæbɪtəbˀl] *adj* habitable.
**habitat** ['hæbɪtæt] *n* hábitat *m*.
**habitual** [hə'bɪtʃuəl] *adj* **1** *(usual)* habitual. **2** *(liar, etc)* empedernido,-a.
**hack** [hæk] *vt* **1** *(cut)* cortar. **2** COMPUT *(cut)* cortar.
**hacker** ['hækəʳ] *n fam (in computers)* pirata *mf*.
**had** [hæd] *pt & pp* → have.
**haddock** ['hædək] *n (fish)* eglefino.
**hadn't** [hæd] *pt* → have.
**haematoma** [hi:mə'təumə] *n* hematoma *mf*.
**haemorrhage** ['hemərɪdʒ] *n* hemorragia.
**haggis** ['hægɪs] *n* CULIN *plato típico escocés hecho con las asaduras del cordero.*
**haggle** ['hægˀl] *vi* regatear (**over**, -).
**hail¹** [heɪl] *n (greeting)* saludo; *(shout)* grito.
 ▶ *vi* **1** *(call a taxi)* llamar. **2** *(acclaim)* aclamar.
**hail²** [heɪl] *n* **1** METEOR granizo. **2** *fig* lluvia.
 ▶ *vi* METEOR granizar.
**hailstone** ['heɪlstəun] *n* granizo.
**hailstorm** ['heɪlstɔ:m] *n* granizada.
**hair** [heəʳ] *n* **1** *(on head)* cabello, pelo. **2** *(on body)* vello. **3** *(horse's mane)* crin *f*.
**hairbrush** ['heəbrʌʃ] *n* cepillo para el pelo.
**haircut** ['heəkʌt] *n* corte *m* de pelo. LOC **to have a haircut** cortarse el pelo.
**hairdresser** ['heədresəʳ] *n* peluquero,-a. COMP **hairdresser's** peluquería.
**hairdryer** ['heədraɪəʳ] *n* secador *m* (de pelo).

**hairspray** ['heəspreɪ] *n* laca para el pelo.
**hairstyle** ['heəstaɪl] *n* peinado.
**hairy** ['heərɪ] *adj* **1** peludo,-a. **2** *fig (scary)* espeluznante, espantoso,-a.
 ⓘ *comp* hairier; *superl* hairiest.
**Haiti** ['heɪtɪ] *n* Haití *m*.
**Haitian** ['heɪʃˀn] *adj* haitiano,-a.
 ▶ *n* haitiano,-a.
**hake** [heɪk] *n (fish)* merluza; *(young)* pescadilla.
**half** [hɑ:f] *n* **1** mitad *f*: *a kilo and a half* un kilo y medio. **2** SP *(period)* parte *f*, mitad *f*, tiempo. **3** *(beer)* media pinta.
 ⓘ *pl* halves.
 ▶ *adj* medio,-a: *he's been gone for half an hour* lleva fuera media hora. COMP **half board** media pensión *f*. ❙ **half term** *vacaciones que se hacen a mitad de trimestre.*
 ▶ *adv* medio, a medias: *she's half Spanish* es medio española. LOC **half past** y media: *it's half past two* son las dos y media.

⊕ Half term es una semana de vacaciones que los colegios británicos tienen a mediados de cada trimestre.

**half-day** [hɑ:fdeɪ] *n* media jornada.
**half-mast** [hɑ:fmɑ:st] *phr* **at half-mast** a media asta.
**half-note** [hɑ:fnəut] *n* US blanca.
**half-time** [hɑ:ftaɪm] *n* SP descanso, media parte *f*.
**halfway** ['hɑ:fweɪ] *adj* medio,-a, intermedio,-a.
 ▶ *adv* a medio camino.
**hall** [hɔ:l] *n* **1** *(entrance)* vestíbulo, entrada. **2** *(for concerts, etc)* sala. **3** *(mansion)* casa solariega, mansión *f*. **4** US *(corridor)* pasillo, corredor *m*.
**hallo** [hə'ləu] *interj* → hello.

**Halloween** [hæləʊ'i:n] *n* víspera de Todos los Santos.

⊕ Halloween es la fiesta de la víspera de Todos los Santos. Los niños se disfrazan y van de casa en casa. Cuando les abren la puerta dicen «trick or treat!» (truco o trato) y la gente les da golosinas.

**hallucinate** [hə'lʊ:sɪneɪt] *vi* alucinar.

**hallway** ['hɔ:lweɪ] *n* US vestíbulo.

**halo** ['heɪləʊ] *n* **1** *(round moon, etc)* halo. **2** REL aureola.

ⓘ *pl* haloes o halos.

**halogen** ['hælədʒen] *n* halógeno.

**halt** [hɔ:lt] *n* **1** alto, parada. **2** *(railway)* apeadero.
▸ *vt* parar, detener, interrumpir.

**halve** [hɑ:v] *vt* **1** *(cut in two)* partir en dos. **2** *(reduce)* reducir a la mitad. **3** *(share)* compartir. **4** *(golf)* empatar.

**halves** [hɑ:vz] *n pl* → half.

**ham** [hæm] *n (food)* jamón *m*.

**hamburger** ['hæmbɜ:gəʳ] *n (food)* hamburguesa.

✎ Lo más habitual es llamar burger a la hamburguesa.

**hamlet** ['hæmlət] *n* aldea.

**hammer** ['hæməʳ] *n* **1** *(tool, bone)* martillo. **2** *(gun)* percutor *m*.
▸ *vt* **1** *(gen)* martillar, martillear; *(nail)* clavar. **2** *fam (beat)* dar una paliza, machacar.

**hammock** ['hæmək] *n* **1** hamaca. **2** MAR coy *m*.

**hamster** ['hæmstəʳ] *n* ZOOL hámster *m*.

**hand** [hænd] *n* **1** mano *f*. **2** *(worker)* trabajador,-ra, operario,-a; *(sailor)* tripulante *mf*, marinero,-a. **3** *(of clock)* manecilla, aguja. **4** *(handwriting)* letra. **5** *(of cards)* mano *f*, cartas *fpl*. **6** *(applause)* aplauso. LOC at hand a mano. ∥ hands up! ¡manos arriba! ∥ on the one hand por un lado ∥ by hand a mano ∥ on the other hand por otro lado ∥ to lend a hand echar una mano.

◆ to hand back *vt sep* devolver.

◆ to hand in *vt sep (work, etc)* entregar; *(resignation, etc)* presentar, notificar.

◆ to hand on *vt sep (traditions, etc)* transmitir, heredar; *(give)* pasar, dar.

◆ to hand out *vt sep (distribute)* repartir, distribuir; *(give - gen)* dar; *(- punishment)* aplicar.

◆ to hand over *vt sep (give)* entregar; *(one's possessions, etc)* ceder.

**handbag** ['hændbæg] *n* bolso.

**handball** ['hændbɔ:l] *n* SP balonmano.

**handbook** ['hændbʊk] *n (guidebook)* guía; *(reference book)* manual *m*.

**handbrake** ['hændbreɪk] *n* freno de mano.

**handcuff** ['hændkʌf] *vt* esposar.
▸ *n pl* handcuffs esposas *fpl*.

**handful** ['hændfʊl] *n* puñado.

**handicap** ['hændɪkæp] *n* **1** *(physical)* discapacidad *f*; *(mental)* deficiencia, disminución *f* psíquica. **2** *(in sport)* handicap *m*. **3** *fig* obstáculo.
▸ *vt* obstaculizar, impedir.

ⓘ *pt & pp* handicapped, *ger* handicapping.

**handicapped** ['hændɪkæpt] *adj* **1** *(physically)* minusválido,-a, discapacitado,-a, disminuido,-a físico,-a; *(mentally)* disminuido,-a psíquico,-a. **2** *fig* desfavorecido,-a.

**handicraft** ['hændɪkrɑ:ft] *n* **1** *(job, art)* artesanía; *(objects)* objetos *mpl* de artesanía. **2** *(manual skill)* habilidad *f* manual.

**handkerchief** ['hæŋkətʃi:f] *n* pañuelo.

ⓘ *pl* handkerchiefs o handkerchieves.

**handle** ['hændəl] *n* **1** *(of door)* pomo, manilla. **2** *(of drawer)* tirador *m*. **3** *(of cup)* asa. **4** *(of knife)* mango. **5** *(lever)* palanca. **6** *(crank)* manivela.
▸ *vt* **1** *(gen)* manejar, manipular. **2** *(people)* tratar. **3** *(tolerate)* aguantar. **4** *(control)* controlar, dominar. **5** *(manage)* poder con, tener la capacidad para.

**handlebar** ['hændəlbɑ:ʳ] *n* manillar *m*.

**handmade** [hænd'meɪd] *adj* hecho,-a a mano.

**handout** ['hændaʊt] *n* **1** *(leaflet)* folleto, prospecto; *(political)* octavilla. **2** EDUC material *m*. **3** *(press)* nota de prensa.

H

**handshake** ['hændʃeɪk] n apretón m de manos.

**handsome** ['hænsəm] adj **1** (man) apuesto, guapo; (woman) bella, guapa. **2** (elegant) elegante. **3** (generous) considerable, generoso,-a.

**hands-on** ['hændzɒn] adj (for computers) práctico,-a.

**handstand** ['hændstænd] n LOC to do a handstand hacer el pino.

**handwriting** ['hændraɪtɪŋ] n letra, escritura.

**handy** ['hændɪ] adj **1** (person) hábil. **2** (close at hand) a mano, cercano,-a. **3** (useful) práctico,-a, cómodo,-a, útil. ① comp handier, superl handiest.

**handyman** ['hændɪmæn] n manitas mf. ① pl handymen ['hændɪmən].

**hang** [hæŋ] vt **1** [pt & pp hung [hʌŋ]] (gen) colgar. **2** [pt & pp hung [hʌŋ]] (wallpaper) colocar. **3** [pt & pp hanged.] JUR ahorcar.
▶ n (of dress, etc) caída.
◆ to hang about / hang around vi **1** esperar. **2** (waste time) perder el tiempo.
▶ vt insep frecuentar.
◆ to hang back vi **1** quedarse atrás. **2** fig vacilar.
◆ to hang down vi colgar, caer.
◆ to hang on vi **1** (hold tight) agarrarse. **2** (wait) esperar.
◆ to hang out vt sep (washing) tender.
▶ vi fam soler estar.
◆ to hang up vt sep colgar.

**hangar** ['hæŋəʳ] n hangar m.

**hanger** ['hæŋəʳ] n percha f.

**hang-glider** ['hæŋglaɪdəʳ] n ala delta.

**hang-gliding** ['hæŋglaɪdɪŋ] n ala m delta.

**hangover** ['hæŋəʊvəʳ] n **1** (after too much drinking) resaca. **2** (remains) resto, vestigio.

**happen** ['hæpən] vi **1** (occur) ocurrir, pasar, suceder. **2** (by chance) dar la casualidad de.

**happening** ['hæpənɪŋ] n acontecimiento.

**happily** ['hæpɪlɪ] adv **1** (in a happy way) felizmente, con alegría. **2** (luckily) afortunadamente.

**happiness** ['hæpɪnəs] n felicidad f, alegría.

**happy** ['hæpɪ] adj **1** (cheerful) feliz, alegre, dichoso,-a, afortunado,-a. **2** (glad) contento,-a, satisfecho,-a. LOC happy birthday! ¡feliz cumpleaños! ① comp happier, superl happiest.

**harass** ['hærəs] vt **1** acosar, hostigar. **2** (military) hostilizar, hostigar. **3** (worries, problems) atormentar, agobiar.

**harassment** ['hærəsmənt] n acoso, hostigamiento.

**harbor** ['hɑːbəʳ] n US → harbour.

**harbour** ['hɑːbəʳ] n puerto.
▶ vt **1** (criminal) encubrir. **2** (doubts) abrigar. **3** (suspicions) tener; (contain, hide) contener, esconder.

**hard** [hɑːd] adj **1** (gen) duro,-a; (solid) sólido,-a. **2** (difficult) difícil. **3** (harsh, severe,-a. **4** (work) arduo,-a, agotador,-ra. **5** (final decision) definitivo,-a, irrevocable; (person) severo,-a, inflexible. **6** LING fuerte. LOC hard of hearing duro,-a de oído. I to work hard trabajar mucho. COMP hard court pista dura. I hard disk disco duro. I hard labour trabajos forzados.
▶ adv (forcibly) fuerte; (diligently) mucho concienzudamente, con ahínco.

**harden** ['hɑːdən] vt **1** endurecer. **2** fig insensibilizar.

**hardly** ['hɑːdlɪ] adv (scarcely) apenas casi; (not easily) difícilmente.

**hardness** ['hɑːdnəs] n dureza.

**hardware** ['hɑːdweəʳ] n **1** (goods) artículos mpl de ferretería. **2** COMPUT hardware m, soporte m físico. COMP hardware store ferretería.

**hard-working** ['hɑːdwɜːkɪŋ] adj trabajador,-ra.

**hare** [heəʳ] n ZOOL liebre f.
▶ vi correr muy deprisa.

**haricot bean** [hærɪkəʊbiːn] n alubia judía.

**harm** [hɑːm] n mal m, daño.
▶ vt dañar, perjudicar. LOC to do s harm hacerle daño a ALGN. I there' no harm in... no se pierda nada...

**harmful** ['hɑːmfʊl] adj dañino,-a, nocivo,-a, perjudicial.

**harmless** ['hɑ:mləs] *adj* inocuo,-a, inofensivo,-a.

**harmonic** [hɑ:'mɒnɪk] *adj* armónico,-a.

**harmony** ['hɑ:mənɪ] *n* armonía.
  ① *pl* harmonies.

**harp** [hɑ:p] *n* MUS arpa.

**harpist** ['hɑ:pɪst] *n* MUS arpista *mf*.

**harpoon** [hɑ:'pu:n] *n* arpón *m*.
  ▶ *vt* arponear.

**harsh** [hɑ:ʃ] *adj* **1** *(cruel)* cruel, duro,-a, severo,-a. **2** *(sound)* discordante. **3** *(rough)* áspero,-a.

**harvest** ['hɑ:vɪst] *n* **1** *(gen)* cosecha, siega. **2** *(grapes)* vendimia.
  ▶ *vt* **1** cosechar, recoger. **2** *(grapes)* vendimiar.

**harvester** ['hɑ:vɪstəʳ] *n* **1** *(person)* segador,-ra. **2** *(machine)* segadora, cosechadora.

**has** [hæz] *pres* → have.

**haste** [heɪst] *n* prisa, precipitación *f*.

**hasten** ['heɪsᵊn] *vi* darse prisa.

**hastily** ['heɪstɪlɪ] *adv (quickly)* de prisa.

**hat** [hæt] *n* sombrero.

**hatch** [hætʃ] *n* **1** *(on ship)* escotilla. **2** *(of chickens, brood)* pollada.
  ▶ *vt* **1** *(eggs)* empollar, incubar. **2** *fig (plot, plan)* idear, tramar.
  ▶ *vi* salir del cascarón, salir del huevo.

**hate** [heɪt] *n* odio.
  ▶ *vt* **1** *fam (detest)* odiar, detestar, aborrecer. **2** *fam (regret)* lamentar, sentir.

**hatred** ['heɪtrəd] *n* odio.

**haul** [hɔ:l] *n* **1** *(distance)* recorrido, camino. **3** *(fish)* redada. **4** *(loot)* botín *m*.
  ▶ *vt* **1** *(drag)* tirar de, arrastrar. **2** *(boat)* halar; *(car, caravan, etc)* remolcar.

**haunt** [hɔ:nt] *n (of people)* sitio preferido; *(of criminals, animals)* guarida.
  ▶ *vt* **1** *(frequent - gen)* frecuentar; *(- ghost)* aparecer en, rondar por. **2** *(memory, thought)* obsesionar, perseguir.

**haunted** ['hɔ:ntɪd] *adj* encantado,-a.

**have** [hæv] *vt* **1** *(gen)* tener, poseer. **2** *(food)* comer, tomar; *(drink)* beber, tomar. **3** *(treatment)* recibir: *she's having physiotherapy* acude a fisioterapia. **4** *(invite)* recibir, invitar. **5** *(borrow)* pedir prestado, dejar. **6** *(party, meeting)* cele-

brar, tener, dar. **7** *(cause to happen)* hacer, mandar: *he had the house painted* hizo pintar la casa. **8** *fam (cheat)* timar.
  [LOC] **have got** tener: *he's got two sisters* tiene dos hermanas; *we haven't got any sugar* no tenemos azúcar. **▮ to have breakfast** desayunar. **▮ to have dinner** cenar. **▮ to have just** acabar de: *I have just seen him* acabo de verlo. **▮ to have lunch** comer, almorzar. **▮ to have a bath** bañarse. **▮ to have a shower** ducharse. **▮ to have a swim** darse un baño.
  ▶ *aux* haber: *I have seen her* la he visto.
  ◆ **to have on** *vt sep* **1** *(wear)* llevar puesto,-a. **2** *(tease)* tomar el pelo a.
  ◆ **to have out** *vt sep (tooth)* sacarse; *(appendix)* operarse de.
  ① *3rd pers pres sing* **has** [hæz], *pt & pp* **had** [hæd], *ger* **having**.

✎ Have es el verbo auxiliar que se emplea en inglés para conjugar los tiempos perfectos.

**haven** ['heɪvᵊn] *n* **1** *fig* refugio, asilo. **2** *(harbour)* puerto.

**havoc** ['hævək] *n* estragos *mpl*.

**hawk¹** [hɔ:k] *n* halcón *m*.

**hawk²** [hɔ:k] *vt* **1** *(in the street)* vender en la calle; *(door to door)* vender de puerta en puerta. **2** *(gossip, news)* divulgar, pregonar, difundir.
  ▶ *vi* carraspear.

**hay** [heɪ] *n* BOT heno. [COMP] **hay fever** fiebre *f* del heno.

**hazard** ['hæzəd] *n* **1** *(risk)* riesgo, peligro. **2** *(in sports in general)* obstáculo.
  ▶ *vt* **1** *fml* arriesgar, poner en peligro. **2** *fml (guess, remark)* aventurar, atreverse a hacer.

**hazardous** ['hæzədəs] *adj* arriesgado,-a, peligroso,-a, aventurado,-a.

**haze** [heɪz] *n* **1** neblina. **2** *fig* confusión *f*, vaguedad *f*.
  ▶ *vt* US hacer una novatada a.

**hazel** ['heɪzᵊl] *n* BOT avellano.
  ▶ *adj* (de color de) avellana.

**hazelnut** ['heɪzᵊlnʌt] *n* BOT avellana.

**hazy** ['heɪzɪ] *adj* con neblina.

H

**he** [hi:] *pron* **1** él: *he's my brother* (él) es mi hermano. **2** *(gen)* el que, quien.
▶ *n* **1** *(male animals)* macho. **2** *(man)* hombre *m*, varón *m*.

**head** [hed] *n* **1** *(gen)* cabeza; *(mind)* mente *f*. **2** *(on tape recorder, video)* cabezal *m*. **3** *(of bed, table)* cabecera. **4** *(of page)* principio. **5** *(on beer)* espuma. **6** *(cape)* cabo, punta. **7** *(of school, company)* director,-ra.
▶ *adj* principal, jefe.
▶ *vt* **1** *(company, list, etc)* encabezar. **2** *(ball)* rematar de cabeza, dar un cabezazo a, cabecear.
◆ **to head for** *vt insep* dirigirse hacia.
◆ **to head off** *vi* marcharse, irse.
▶ *vt sep (divert)* interceptar; *(avoid)* evitar.

**headache** [ˈhedeɪk] *n* dolor *m* de cabeza.

**head-first** [hedˈfɜːst] *adv* de cabeza.

**head-hunter** [hedˈhʌntəʳ] *n* **1** cazador,-ra de cabezas, jíbaro,-a. **2** *fam fig* cazatalentos *mf*.

**heading** [ˈhedɪŋ] *n* **1** *(of chapter)* encabezamiento, título. **2** *(letterhead)* membrete *m*.

**headlamp** [ˈhedlæmp] *n* AUTO faro.

**headlight** [ˈhedlaɪt] *n* AUTO faro.

**headline** [ˈhedlaɪn] *n* titular *m*.

**headmaster** [hedˈmɑːstəʳ] *n* director *m*.

**headmistress** [hedˈmɪstrəs] *n* directora.

**headphones** [ˈhedfəʊnz] *n pl* auriculares *mpl*, cascos *mpl*.

**headquarters** [ˈhedkwɔːtəz] *n* **1** *(of an organization)* sede *f*; *(main office)* oficina central. **2** *(of a firm)* domicilio social. **3** MIL cuartel *m* general.

✎ Headquarters puede considerarse tanto singular como plural: *our headquarters is/are in New York* nuestra sede está en Nueva York.

**headteacher** [hedˈtiːʳ] *adj* director,-a.

**headword** [ˈhedwɜːd] *n* entrada.

**heal** [hi:l] *vt* **1** *(disease, patient)* curar; *(wound)* cicatrizar, curar. **2** *fig* curar, remediar.

▶ *vi* **1** *(wounds)* cicatrizar, cicatrizarse; *(people)* curarse,. **2** *fig* remediarse.
◆ **to heal up** *vi* curarse, cicatrizarse.

**health** [helθ] *n* **1** salud *f*. **2** *(service)* sanidad *f*. **3** *fig* prosperidad *f*. COMP **health care** sanidad *f*. ▌ **health centre** centro de salud. ▌ **health food** alimentos *mpl* naturales.

**healthy** [ˈhelθɪ] *adj* **1** *(gen)* sano,-a. **2** *(good for health)* saludable. **3** *(appetite)* bueno,-a. **4** *(prosperous)* próspero,-a; *(disposition)* sensato,-a.
ⓘ *comp* healthier, *superl* healthiest.

**heap** [hi:p] *n* montón *m*.

**hear** [hɪəʳ] *vt* **1** *(gen)* oír. **3** *(lecture)* asistir a; *(a news item)* saber. **3** JUR *(case)* ver; *(witness, defendant)* oír.
ⓘ *pt & pp* heard [hɜːd].

**heard** [hɜːd] *pt & pp* → hear.

**hearer** [ˈhɪərəʳ] *n* oyente *mf*.

**hearing** [ˈhɪərɪŋ] *n* **1** *(sense)* oído. **2** *(act of hearing)* audición *f*. **3** JUR audiencia, vista.

**heart** [hɑːt] *n* **1** ANAT corazón *m*. **2** *(centre of feeling)* corazón *m*. **3** *(courage)* valor *m*, corazón *m*. **4** *(of lettuce, etc)* cogollo; *(of place)* corazón *m*, centro; *(of question)* fondo, quid *m*, meollo. LOC **to learn by heart** aprender de memoria. ▌ **to take heart** animarse. ▌ **to learn by heart** aprender de memoria. COMP **heart attack** ataque *m* de corazón.
▶ *n pl* **hearts** *(cards)* corazones *mpl*; *(Spanish cards)* copas *fpl*.

**heartbeat** [ˈhɑːtbiːt] *n* latido del corazón.

**heartburn** [ˈhɑːtbɜːn] *n* ardor *m* de estómago.

**hearten** [ˈhɑːtən] *vt* animar, alentar.

**heartless** [ˈhɑːtləs] *adj* cruel, insensible.

**heat** [hi:t] *n* **1** *(gen)* calor *m*. **2** *(heating)* calefacción *f*. **3** SP eliminatoria, serie *f*. **4** ZOOL celo.
▶ *vt* **1** calentar. **2** *fig* acalorar.
◆ **to heat up** *vi (warm up)* calentarse *(to raise excitement, etc)* acalorarse.

**heater** [ˈhiːtəʳ] *n* calentador *m*.

**heather** [ˈheðəʳ] *n* BOT brezo.

**heating** [ˈhiːtɪŋ] *n* calefacción *f*.

**heatstroke** ['hi:tstrəʊk] *n* MED insolación *f*.

**heatwave** ['hi:tweɪv] *n* ola de calor.

**heave** [hi:v] *n (pull)* tirón *m*; *(push)* empujón *m*.
▶ *vt* **1** *(pull)* tirar; *(lift)* levantar. **2** *(push)* empujar. **3** *fam (throw)* lanzar, arrojar.

**heaven** ['hevⁿn] *n* **1** cielo. **2** *fam* gloria, paraíso.
▶ *n pl* **heavens** cielo.

**heavily** ['hevɪlɪ] *adv* **1** *(fall, move, step, etc)* pesadamente; *(rain)* fuertemente, mucho. **2** *(sleep, etc)* profundamente; *(drink)* con exceso, mucho; *(breathe)* con dificultad *f*.

**heavy** ['hevɪ] *adj* **1** *(gen)* pesado,-a. **2** *(rain, blow)* fuerte, pesado,-a. **3** *(traffic)* denso,-a. **4** *(sleep)* profundo,-a. **5** *(crop)* abundante. **6** *(atmosphere)* cargado,-a. **7** *(loss, expenditure)* grande, considerable. COMP **heavy metal** rock *m* duro, heavy metal *m*.
ⓘ *comp* **heavier**, *superl* **heaviest**.

**heavy-duty** ['hevɪ'dju:tɪ] *adj (clothes, shoes, etc)* de faena, resistente; *(equipment, machinery, etc)* reforzado,-a, robusto,-a, para grandes cargas.

**heavyweight** ['hevɪweɪt] *n* **1** SP peso pesado. **2** *fig* peso pesado.

**Hebrew** ['hi:bru:] *adj* hebreo,-a.
▶ *n* **1** *(person)* hebreo,-a. **2** *(language)* hebreo.

**hectare** ['hektɑːʳ] *n* hectárea.

**hectic** ['hektɪk] *adj* agitado,-a, ajetreado,-a, movido,-a.

**he'd** [hi:z] *contr* **1** he had. **2** he would.

**hedge** [hedʒ] *n* **1** seto vivo. **2** *fig* protección *f*, barrera.
▶ *vi* contestar con evasivas.
▶ *vt* **1** cercar, separar con un seto. **2** *fig (protect)* proteger, guardar; *(protect os against)* protegerse.

**hedgehog** ['hedʒhɒg] *n* ZOOL erizo.

**heel** [hi:l] *n* **1** ANAT talón *m*. **2** *(on shoe)* tacón *m*; *(of sock)* talón *m*.
▶ *vt* **1** poner tacón a. **2** *(in rugby)* talonear. **3** MAR inclinar.
▶ *vi* MAR escorar.

**height** [haɪt] *n* **1** *(gen)* altura. **2** *(altitude)* altitud *f*. **3** *(of person)* estatura. **4** GEOG cumbre *f*, cima.

**heir** [eəʳ] *n* heredero.

**heiress** ['eəres] *n* heredera.

**held** [held] *pt & pp* → hold.

**helicopter** ['helɪkɒptəʳ] *n* helicóptero.

**heliport** ['helɪpɔːt] *n* helipuerto.

**helium** ['hi:lɪəm] *n* CHEM helio.

**helix** ['hi:lɪks] *n* hélice *f*.

**hell** [hel] *n* infierno.

**he'll** [hi:l] *contr* **1** he will. **2** he shall.

**hello** [he'ləʊ] *interj* **1** ¡hola! **2** *(on telephone - answering)* ¡diga!; *(- calling)* ¡oiga! **3** *(to get sb's attention)* ¡oiga!, ¡oye!

**helm** [helm] *n* MAR timón *m*.

**helmet** ['helmɪt] *n* casco.

**help** [help] *n* **1** *(gen)* ayuda. **2** *(servant)* asistenta, criada.
▶ *interj* ¡socorro!
▶ *vt* **1** *(gen)* ayudar. **2** *(be of use)* ayudar, servir. **3** *(to relieve)* aliviar. **4** *(avoid)* evitar.
◆ **to help out** *vt sep* ayudar.

**helper** ['helpəʳ] *n* **1** ayudante,-a *mf*, auxiliar *mf*. **2** *(collaborator)* colaborador,-ra.

**helpful** ['helpfʊl] *adj* **1** *(thing)* útil, práctico,-a,. **2** *(person)* amable.

**helping** ['helpɪŋ] *n* ración *f*, porción *f*.
▶ *adj* ayuda.

**helpless** ['helpləs] *adj* **1** *(unprotected)* desamparado,-a, indefenso,-a, desvalido,-a. **2** *(powerless)* impotente, incapaz, inútil.

**hem** [hem] *n* SEW dobladillo.
▶ *vt* hacer un dobladillo en.
ⓘ *pt & pp* **hemmed**, *ger* **hemming**.

**hematoma** [hi:mə'təʊmə] *n* US → haematoma.

**hemisphere** ['hemɪsfɪəʳ] *n* hemisferio.

**hemorrhage** ['hemərɪdʒ] *n* US → haemorrhage.

**hen** [hen] *n* *(chicken)* gallina; *(female bird)* hembra.

**hence** [hens] *adv* **1** *fml (so)* por eso, por lo tanto, de ahí. **2** *(from now)* de aquí a, dentro de.

**henceforth** [hens'fɔːθ] *adv fml* de ahora en adelante.

**henhouse** ['henhaʊs] *n* gallinero.

**henna** ['henə] *n* BOT alheña.

**heptagon** ['heptəgən] *n* heptágono.

**heptagonal** [hep'tægənˀl] *adj* heptagonal.

**her** [hɜːʳ] *pron* **1** *(direct object)* la: *I love her* la quiero. **2** *(indirect object)* le; *(with other third person pronouns)* se: *give it to her* dáselo. **3** *(after preposition)* ella: *go with her* vete con ella. **4** *fam (as subject)* ella: *listen, that's her!* ¡escucha, es ella!
► *adj* su, sus; *(emphatic)* de ella.

**heraldic** [he'rældɪk] *adj* heráldico,-a.

**herb** [hɜːb] *n* hierba.

**herbaceous** [hɜː'beɪʃəs] *adj* herbáceo,-a.

**herbal** ['hɜːbˀl] *adj* de hierbas.

**herbicide** ['hɜːbɪsaɪd] *n* herbicida *m*.

**herbivore** ['hɜːbɪvɔːʳ] *n* ZOOL herbívoro,-a.

**herd** [hɜːd] *n* **1** *(cattle)* manada; *(goats)* rebaño; *(pigs)* piara. **2** *fam (people)* montón *m*, multitud *f*.

**here** [hɪəʳ] *adv* aquí. LOC **here you are** aquí tienes.

**hereby** [hɪə'baɪ] *adv fml* por la presente.

**hereditary** [hɪ'redɪtˀrɪ] *adj* hereditario,-a.

**heredity** [hɪ'redɪtɪ] *n* herencia.

**heresy** ['herəsɪ] *n* herejía.
ⓘ *pl* heresies.

**heritage** ['herɪtɪdʒ] *n* herencia, patrimonio.

**hermaphrodite** [hɜː'mæfrədaɪt] *adj* hermafrodita.

**hernia** ['hɜːnɪə] *n* hernia.

**hero** ['hɪərəʊ] *n* **1** *(gen)* héroe *m*. **2** *(in novel)* protagonista *m*.
ⓘ *pl* heroes.

**heroic** [hɪ'rəʊɪk] *adj* heroico,-a.

**heroin** ['herəʊɪn] *n (drug)* heroína.

**heroine** ['herəʊɪn] *n* **1** heroína. **2** *(in novel)* protagonista.

**herpes** ['hɜːpiːz] *n* herpe *m*, herpes *m*.

**herring** ['herɪŋ] *n* arenque *m*.
ⓘ *pl* herring o herrings.

**hers** [hɜːz] *pron (sing)* (el) suyo, (la) suya; *(pl)* (los) suyos, (las) suyas; *(emphatic)* de ella: *this pencil is hers* este lápiz es suyo.

**herself** [hɜː'self] *pron* **1** *(reflexive use)* se: *she washed herself* se lavó. **2** *(emphatic)* ella misma: *she made it all herself* lo hizo todo ella misma. LOC **by herself** sola.

**hertz** [hɜːts] *n* hertz *m*, hercio.

**he's** [hiːz] *contr* **1** he is. **2** he has.

**hesitate** ['hezɪteɪt] *vi* vacilar, dudar.

**hesitation** [hezɪ'teɪʃˀn] *n* duda, indecisión.

**heterogeneous** [hetərəʊ'dʒiːnɪəs] *adj* heterogéneo,-a.

**heterosexual** [hetərəʊ'seksjʊəl] *adj* heterosexual.

**heterotrophic** [hetərəʊ'trɒfɪk] *adj* heterotrófico,-a.

**hexagon** ['heksəgən] *n* hexágono.

**hexagonal** [hek'sægənˀl] *adj* hexagonal.

**hi** [haɪ] *interj fam* ¡hola!

**hibernate** ['haɪbəneɪt] *vi* hibernar.

**hiccough** ['hɪkʌp] *n-vi* → **hiccup**.

**hiccup** ['hɪkʌp] *n* hipo: *to have hiccups* tener hipo.

**hid** [hɪd] *pt & pp* → **hide**.

**hidden** ['hɪdˀn] *pp* → **hide**.
► *adj* **1** escondido,-a. **2** *fig* oculto,-a.

**hide¹** [haɪd] *n (concealed place)* escondite *m*.
► *vt (conceal)* esconder; *(obscure)* ocultar, tapar.
ⓘ *pt* hid [hɪd], *pp* hid [hɪd] o hidden ['hɪdˀn].

**hide²** [haɪd] *n* **1** piel *f*, cuero. **2** *fig (of a person)* pellejo.

**hide-and-seek** [haɪdˀn'siːk] *n* escondite *m*.

**hideous** ['hɪdɪəs] *adj* **1** *(terrible)* horroroso,-a, atroz. **2** *(ugly)* horrendo,-a, espantoso.

**hide-out** ['haɪdaʊt] *n* escondrijo, escondite *m*, guarida.

**hierarchic** [haɪə'rɑːkɪk] *adj* jerárquico,-a.

**hierarchy** ['haɪərɑːkɪ] *n* jerarquía.
ⓘ *pl* hierarchies.

**hieroglyphics** [haɪərə'glɪfɪks] *n pl* jeroglíficos *mpl*.

**hi-fi** ['haɪfaɪ] *n* hifi *m*, alta fidelidad *f*.

**high** [haɪ] *adj* **1** alto,-a, elevado. **2** *(important)* alto,-a, importante; *(strong)* fuerte. **3** *(very good)* bueno,-a. **4** *(going rotten - food)* pasado,-a; *(- game)* manido,-a. **5** *(of time)* pleno,-a. `COMP` **high jump** salto de altura. ‖ **high school** instituto (de bachillerato). ‖ **high street** calle mayor. ‖ **high tide** marea alta.

⊕ El **high school** es el equivalente a los institutos de bachillerato, sobre todo en Estados Unidos.

**high-class** [haɪˈklɑːs] *adj (classy)* de categoría; *(superior)* de calidad *f.*

**higher** [ˈhaɪəʳ] *adj* **1** → **high**. **2** superior. **3** *(bigger)* más alto,-a; *(number, velocity, etc)* mayor. `COMP` **higher education** enseñanza superior.

**high-heeled** [ˈhaɪˈhiːld] *adj* de tacón alto.

**highlight** [ˈhaɪlaɪt] *vt* **1** destacar, hacer resaltar. **2** *(with pen)* marcar *(con un rotulador fosforescente).*
▸ *n* **1** ART toque *m* de luz. **2** *(hairdressing)* reflejo. **3** *fig (especially in show business)* atracción *f* principal; *(most outstanding)* punto culminante; *(aspect or feature)* característica notable.

**highly** [ˈhaɪlɪ] *adv (very)* muy; *(favourably)* muy bien.

**Highness** [ˈhaɪnəs] *n* Alteza *mf.*

**high-pitched** [ˈhaɪˈpɪtʃt] *adj (sound, voice)* agudo,-a; *(roof)* empinado,-a.

**high-tech** [ˈhaɪˈtek] *adj* de alta tecnología.

**highway** [ˈhaɪweɪ] *n* **1** US autovía. **2** JUR vía pública.

**hijack** [ˈhaɪdʒæk] *n* secuestro.
▸ *vt* secuestrar.

**hijacker** [ˈhaɪdʒækəʳ] *n* secuestrador,-a.

**hijacking** [ˈhaɪdʒækɪŋ] *n* secuestro.

**hike** [haɪk] *n* **1** *(walk)* excursión *f* a pie. **2** *fam* aumento de precio.
▸ *vi* ir de excursión, hacer una excursión.
▸ *vt fam* aumentar los precios.

**hiker** [ˈhaɪkəʳ] *n* excursionista.

**hiking** [ˈhaɪkɪŋ] *n* excursionismo a pie.

**hilarious** [hɪˈleərɪəs] *adj* graciosísimo,-a, hilarante, divertidísimo,-a.

**hill** [hɪl] *n* **1** colina, cerro. **2** *(slope)* cuesta.

**hillside** [ˈhɪlsaɪd] *n* ladera.

**hilltop** [ˈhɪltɒp] *n* cumbre *f,* cima.

**him** [hɪm] *pron* **1** *(direct object)* lo: *I love him* lo quiero. **2** *(indirect object)* le; *(with other pronouns)* se: *give him the money* dale el dinero; *give it to him* dáselo. **3** *(after preposition)* él: *we went with him* fuimos con él. **4** *fam (as subject)* él: *it's him!* ¡es él!

**himself** [hɪmˈself] *pron* **1** *(reflexive)* se; *(alone)* solo, por sí mismo: *he cut himself* se cortó; *he did it by himself* lo hizo solo. **2** *(emphatic)* él mismo, sí mismo, en persona.

**hinder** [ˈhɪndəʳ] *vt* dificultar, entorpecer, estorbar, impedir.

**Hindu** [hɪnˈduː, ˈhɪnduː] *n* hindú *mf.*
▸ *adj* hindú.

**Hinduism** [ˈhɪnduɪzəm] *n* hinduismo.

**hinge** [hɪndʒ] *n* **1** TECH gozne *m,* bisagra. **2** *(for stamps)* fijasello. **3** *fig* eje *m.*
▸ *vi* girar sobre goznes.

**hint** [hɪnt] *n* **1** insinuación *f,* indirecta. **2** *(advice)* consejo, sugerencia. **3** *(clue)* pista. **4** *(trace)* pizca. **5** *(sign)* sombra.
▸ *vt (imply)* insinuar, aludir a.

**hip¹** [hɪp] *n* ANAT cadera.

**hip²** [hɪp] `LOC` hip hip hooray! ¡hurra!

**hippie** [ˈhɪpɪ] *n fam* hippie *mf.*

**hippo** [ˈhɪpəʊ] *n fam* hipopótamo.

**hippopotamus** [hɪpəˈpɒtəməs] *n* ZOOL hipopótamo.

**hippy** [ˈhɪpɪ] *n fam* hippie *mf.*
ⓘ *pl* hippies.

**hire** [ˈhaɪəʳ] *n* alquiler *m.*
▸ *vt* **1** *(rent)* alquilar. **2** *(employ)* contratar.
◆ **to hire out** *vt sep (equipment, vehicles, etc)* alquilar; *(people)* contratar.

**his** [hɪz] *adj* **1** su, sus: *his dog* su perro. **2** *(emphatic)* de él.
▸ *pron* (el) suyo, (la) suya, (los) suyos, (las) suyas.

**Hispanic** [hɪsˈpænɪk] *adj* hispánico,-a.
▸ *n* US hispano,-a, latino,-a.

**hiss** [hɪs] *n* **1** *(gen)* siseo. **2** *(air, snake, steam, etc)* silbido. **3** *(protest)* silbido.
▸ *vt* **1** sisear, silbar. **2** *(in protest)* pitar, abuchear.

**historic** [hɪˈstɒrɪk] *adj* histórico,-a.

**historical** [hɪˈstɒrɪkəl] *adj* histórico,-a.

**history** ['hɪstºrɪ] *n* **1** *(in general)* historia. **2** COMPUT historial *m*.
ⓘ *pl* histories.

❎ History no significa 'historia (relato)', que se traduce por story.

**hit** [hɪt] *n* **1** *(blow)* golpe *m*. **2** *(success)* éxito, acierto. **3** *(shot)* impacto. **4** *(visit to web page)* acceso. **5** *fig (damaging remark)* pulla.
▶ *vt* **1** *(strike)* golpear, pegar. **2** *(crash into)* chocar contra. **3** *(affect)* afectar, perjudicar. **4** *(reach)* alcanzar.
◆ **to hit back** *vi (strike in return)* devolver golpe por golpe; *(reply to criticism)* defenderse.
ⓘ *pt & pp* hit, *ger* hitting.

**hitch** [hɪtʃ] *n* obstáculo, dificultad *f*.
▶ *vt (tie)* enganchar, atar.
▶ *vi fam* hacer autoestop, ir a dedo, hacer dedo.

**hitchhike** ['hɪtʃhaɪk] *vi* hacer autoestop.

**hitchhiking** ['hɪtʃhaɪkɪŋ] *vi* autoestop *m*, dedo.

**HIV** ['eɪtʃ'aɪ'viː] *abbr* (human immunodeficiency virus) virus *m* de inmunodeficiencia humana; *(abbreviation)* VIH *m*.

**hive** [haɪv] *n* **1** colmena. **2** *fig* lugar *m* muy activo.

**hoard** [hɔːd] *n* **1** *(provisions)* reserva. **2** *(money)* tesoro escondido.
▶ *vt* **1** *(objects)* acumular. **2** *(money)* atesorar.

**hoarse** [hɔːs] *adj* ronco,-a, áspero,-a.

**hoax** [həʊks] *n (trick)* trampa, engaño; *(joke)* broma pesada.
▶ *vt* engañar a, gastar una broma a.

**hob** [hɒb] *n (of cooker)* encimera; *(next to fireplace)* repisa.

**hobble** ['hɒbºl] *vi (limp)* cojear, andar con dificultad *f*.
▶ *vt* **1** *(tie)* trabar, manear. **2** *fig* poner trabas a, obstaculizar.

**hobby** ['hɒbɪ] *n* afición *f*, hobby *m*, pasatiempo favorito.
ⓘ *pl* hobbies.

**hockey** ['hɒkɪ] *n* SP hockey *m*.

**hoe** [həʊ] *n* azada, azadón *m*.

▶ *vt (earth)* azadonar, cavar; *(weeds)* sachar.

**hog** [hɒg] *n* **1** cerdo, puerco, marrano. **2** *fam pej (not a nice person)* indeseable *mf*.
▶ *vt* acaparar.
ⓘ *pt & pp* hogged, *ger* hogging.

**hoist** [hɔɪst] *n* **1** *(crane)* grúa. **2** *(lift)* montacargas *m*.
▶ *vt* **1** levantar, subir. **2** *(flag)* izar.

**hold** [həʊld] *n* **1** *(place to grip)* asidero. **2** *(in ship, plane)* bodega. ⌸ **to get hold of 1** *(grab)* agarrar, coger. **2** *(obtain)* hacerse con, encontrar.
▶ *vt* **1** *(keep in one's hand)* aguantar, sostener: *hold my bag* aguántame el bolso. **2** *(opinion)* sostener. **3** *(contain)* dar cabida a, tener capacidad para: *the stadium holds a lot of people* el estadio tiene capacidad para mucha gente. **4** *(meeting)* celebrar; *(conversation)* mantener: *political parties often hold meetings in parks* los partidos políticos celebran a menudo sus mítines en los parques. ⌸ **to hold SB** abrazar a ALGN.
◆ **to hold back** *vt sep* **1** *(suspect)* retener. **2** *(information)* ocultar; *(restrain)* contener; *(feelings)* reprimir; *(keep)* guardar.
▶ *vi (hesitate)* vacilar, no atreverse; *(abstain)* abstenerse.
◆ **to hold down** *vt sep (control)* dominar; *(job)* desempeñar.
◆ **to hold forth** *vi* hablar largo y tendido.
◆ **to hold off** *vt sep* mantener alejado,-a.
▶ *vi (refrain)* refrenarse.
◆ **to hold on** *vi* **1** *(grip tightly)* agarrarse fuerte, agarrarse bien. **2** *(wait)* esperar; *(on phone)* no colgar.
◆ **to hold over** *vt sep* aplazar.
◆ **to hold up** *vt sep* **1** *(rob)* atracar, asaltar. **2** *(delay)* retrasar. **3** *(raise)* levantar. **4** *(support)* aguantar, sostener.
▶ *vi* aguantar, resistir.
◆ **to hold with** *vt insep* estar de acuerdo con.
ⓘ *pt & pp* held [held].

**holder** ['həʊldºr] *n* **1** *(owner)* poseedor, -ra; *(of passport)* titular *mf*. **2** *(container)* recipiente *m*, receptáculo. **3** *(bearer - gen)* portador,-ra; *(- of bonds)* tenedor,-ra.

**4** *(handle)* asidero. **5** *(tenant - on land)* arrendatario,-a; *(- of a flat)* inquilino,-a.

**hold-up** [ˈhəʊldʌp] *n* **1** *(robbery)* atraco; *(of train, etc)* asalto. **2** *(delay)* retraso. **3** AUTO atasco.

**hole** [həʊl] *n* **1** *(gen)* agujero; *(in ground, golf)* hoyo. **2** *(in road)* bache *m*. **3** *(of rabbits)* madriguera; *(cavity)* cavidad *f*. **4** *fam (town)* pueblucho de mala muerte. **5** *fam (place to live)* cuchitril *m*; *(unsavoury place)* antro. **6** *(a tight spot)* aprieto, apuro.
▶ *vt* **1** *(make holes - small)* agujerear; *(large)* hacer un boquete en. **2** *(at golf)* meter en el hoyo.

**holiday** [ˈhɒlɪdeɪ] *n* **1** *(one day)* fiesta, día *m* de fiesta, día *m* festivo. **2** *(period)* vacaciones *fpl*. [LOC] **to be on holiday** estar de vacaciones. ‖ **to go on holiday** irse de vacaciones.
▶ *vi* GB *(gen)* pasar las vacaciones; *(in summer)* veranear.

**Holland** [ˈhɒlənd] *n* Holanda.

**hollow** [ˈhɒləʊ] *adj* **1** *(sound, thing)* hueco,-a. **2** *(cheeks, etc)* hundido,-a. **3** *fig (laugh)* falso,-a; *(promise)* vacío,-a.
ⓘ *comp* **hollower**, *superl* **hollowest**.
▶ *n* **1** hueco. **2** GEOG hondonada.

**holly** [ˈhɒlɪ] *n* acebo.
ⓘ *pl* **hollies**.

**holocaust** [ˈhɒləkɔːst] *n* holocausto.

**holy** [ˈhəʊlɪ] *adj* **1** REL *(sacred)* santo,-a, sagrado,-a. **2** *(blessed)* bendito,-a.
ⓘ *comp* **holier**, *superl* **holiest**.

**home** [həʊm] *n* **1** *(house)* hogar *m*, casa. **2** *fml* domicilio. **3** *(institution)* asilo. **4** *(country, village, etc)* patria, tierra. **5** ZOOL hábitat *m*. [LOC] **at home** en casa.
▶ *adj* **1** casero,-a. **2** POL (del) interior. **3** *(native)* natal.

**homeland** [ˈhəʊmlænd] *n* *(gen)* patria; *(birthplace)* tierra natal.

**homeless** [ˈhəʊmləs] *adj* sin hogar, sin techo.

**home-made** [ˈhəʊmˈmeɪd] *adj* casero,-a, de fabricación casera, hecho,-a en casa.

**homemaker** [ˈhəʊmˈmeɪkəʳ] *n* ama de casa.

**homesick** [ˈhəʊmsɪk] *adj* nostálgico,-a.

**homesickness** [ˈhəʊmsɪknəs] *n* añoranza, morriña, nostalgia.

**homework** [ˈhəʊmwɜːk] *n* deberes *mpl*.

**homogeneous** [hɒməˈdʒiːnɪəs] *adj* homogéneo,-a.

**homograph** [ˈhɒməgræf] *n* homógrafo.

**homonym** [ˈhɒmənɪm] *n* homónimo.

**homosexual** [həʊməʊˈseksjʊəl] *adj & n* homosexual.

**honest** [ˈɒnɪst] *adj* **1** *(trustworthy)* honrado,-a, honesto,-a. **2** *(frank)* sincero,-a, franco,-a. **3** *(fair)* justo,-a.
▶ *adv fam* de verdad.

**honestly** [ˈɒnɪstlɪ] *adv* **1** *(fairly)* honradamente. **2** *(frankly)* sinceramente, francamente. **3** *(truthfully)* de verdad, a decir verdad.
▶ *interj (question)* ¿de verdad?; *(exclamation)* ¡hay que ver!

**honesty** [ˈɒnɪstɪ] *n* honradez *f*.

**honey** [ˈhʌnɪ] *n* **1** miel *f*. **2** US *fam (dear)* cariño, cielo.

**honeycomb** [ˈhʌnɪkəʊm] *n* panal *m*.

**honeymoon** [ˈhʌnɪmuːn] *n* luna de miel, viaje *m* de novios.

**honor** [ˈɒnəʳ] *n* US → **honour**.

**honour** [ˈɒnəʳ] *n* **1** *(virtue)* honor *m*, honra. **2** *(title)* Su Señoría.
▶ *vt* **1** *(respect)* honrar. **2** *(cheque)* pagar, aceptar; *(promise, word, agreement)* cumplir.

**hood** [hʊd] *n* **1** *(of clothes)* capucha. **2** *(on pram, etc)* capota. **3** US *(car bonnet)* capó *m*. **4** *(of hawk)* capirote *m*.

**hoof** [huːf] *n* *(of sheep, cow, etc)* pezuña; *(of horse)* casco.
ⓘ *pl* **hoofs** o **hooves**.

**hook** [hʊk] *n* **1** *(gen)* gancho. **2** *(for fishing)* anzuelo.
▶ *vt* **1** *(catch)* enganchar. **2** *(fishing)* pescar, coger. **3** *(in boxing)* pegar un gancho.
◆ **to hook up** *vt sep (connect)* conectar.

**hooligan** [ˈhuːlɪgən] *n* gamberro,-a.

**hoop** [huːp] *n* *(gen)* aro; *(of barrel)* fleje *m*; *(of wheel)* llanta.

**hoot** [huːt] *n* **1** *(of owl)* ululato, grito. **2** *(of car)* bocinazo. **3** *fam (funny thing)* cosa divertida; *(funny person)* persona divertida.

**hooter** ['huːtəʳ] n **1** *(siren)* sirena. **2** *(on car)* bocina, claxon m. **3** GB *(nose)* narizota, napias *fpl.*

**Hoover®** ['huːvəʳ] n GB aspiradora.

**hooves** ['huːvz] *pl* → hoof.

**hop¹** [hɒp] n **1** salto, brinco. **2** *fam (dance)* baile m. **3** AV *fam* vuelo corto.
▸ *vi* saltar, dar brincos, dar saltos.
▸ *vt* **1** US *fam (train, etc)* coger. **2** AV cruzar.
ⓘ *pt & pp* hopped, *ger* hopping.

**hop²** [hɒp] n *(plant)* lúpulo.

**hope** [həʊp] n *(gen)* esperanza; *(false)* ilusión f.
▸ *vt* esperar.

**hopeful** ['həʊpfʊl] adj **1** *(promising)* esperanzador,-ra, prometedor,-ra, alentador,-ra. **2** *(confident)* optimista.

**hopefully** ['həʊpfʊlɪ] adv **1** *(confidently)* con esperanza, con ilusión, con optimismo. **2** *fam (all being well)* ojalá.

**hopeless** ['həʊpləs] adj **1** desesperado,-a. **2** *fam (useless)* inútil.

**hopelessly** ['həʊpləslɪ] adv sin esperanza, con desesperación, desesperadamente.

**horizon** [həˈraɪzᵊn] n horizonte m.

**horizontal** [hɒrɪˈzɒntᵊl] adj horizontal.

**hormonal** [hɔːˈməʊnᵊl] adj hormonal.

**hormone** ['hɔːməʊn] n hormona.

**horn** [hɔːn] n **1** ZOOL asta, cuerno. **2** AUTO bocina, claxon m. **3** MUS cuerno, trompa.

**horoscope** ['hɒrəskəʊp] n horóscopo.

**horrible** ['hɒrɪbᵊl] adj *(gen)* horrible, horroroso,-a; *(person)* antipático,-a.

**horrid** ['hɒrɪd] adj *(horrible)* horroroso,-a, horrible; *(unkind)* antipático,-a, odioso,-a; *(child)* inaguantable, insoportable.

**horrific** [həˈrɪfɪk] adj horrendo,-a, horroroso,-a.

**horrify** ['hɒrɪfaɪ] vt horrorizar, espantar.
ⓘ *pt & pp* horrified, *ger* horrifying.

**horrifying** ['hɒrɪfaɪɪŋ] adj escalofriante.

**horror** ['hɒrəʳ] n horror m, terror m.
COMP **horror film** película de terror.

**hors d'oeuvre** [ɔːˈdɜːvʳ] n CULIN entremés m.
ⓘ *pl* hors d'oeuvre o hors d'oeuvres.

**horse** [hɔːs] n **1** ZOOL caballo. **2** *(in gym)* potro. **3** TECH caballete m. **4** *sl (heroin)* caballo. COMP **horse riding** equitación f.

**horseback** ['hɔːsbæk] adj & adv a caballo. LOC **on horseback** a caballo.

**horsepower** ['hɔːspaʊəʳ] n **1** AUTO caballo de vapor, caballo. **2** potencia.

**horseshoe** ['hɔːsʃuː] n herradura.

**hose¹** [həʊz] n *(pipe)* manguera.
ⓘ *pl* hose.
▸ *vt* regar, lavar.

**hose²** [həʊz] n pl *(socks)* calcetines mpl; *(stockings)* medias fpl.

**hosepipe** ['həʊzpaɪp] n manguera.

**hospitable** [hɒˈspɪtəbᵊl] adj hospitalario,-a, acogedor,-ra.

**hospital** ['hɒspɪtᵊl] n hospital m.

**hospitality** [hɒspɪˈtælɪtɪ] n hospitalidad f.

**host¹** [həʊst] n **1** *(person)* anfitrión,-ona; *(place)* sede f. **2** *(TV presenter)* presentador,-ra. **3** *(animal, plant)* huésped m.
▸ *vt* **1** TV presentar. **2** celebrar,.

**host²** [həʊst] n *(large number)* multitud f.

**Host** [həʊst] n REL hostia.

**hostage** ['hɒstɪdʒ] n rehén mf.

**hostel** ['hɒstᵊl] n residencia, hostal m.

**hostess** ['həʊstəs] n **1** *(at home)* anfitriona. **2** *(on plane, etc)* azafata. **3** *(in club)* camarera. **4** TV presentadora.

**hostile** ['hɒstaɪl] adj hostil, enemigo,-a.

**hostility** [hɒˈstɪlɪtɪ] n hostilidad f.
ⓘ *pl* hostilities.

**hot** [hɒt] adj **1** *(gen)* caliente. **2** METEOR caluroso,-a, cálido,-a. **3** *(food - spicy)* picante.
ⓘ *comp* hotter, *superl* hottest.

**hotel** [həʊˈtel] n hotel m.

**hotline** ['hɒtlaɪn] n línea directa.

**hound** [haʊnd] n perro de caza.
▸ *vt (harass)* acosar, perseguir.

**hour** [aʊəʳ] n hora.

**hourly** ['aʊəlɪ] adj cada hora.
▸ *adv* a cada hora, por horas.

**house** [(n) haʊs; (vb) haʊz] n **1** *(gen)* casa; *(official use)* domicilio. **2** POL cámara. **3** THEAT sala. **4** *(company)* empresa, casa.
COMP **House of Commons** Cámara de los Comunes. ▌ **House of Lords** Cáma-

ra de los Lores. ▌ **House of Representatives** Cámara de Representantes. ▌ **Houses of Parliament** Parlamento.

▸ *vt* **1** *(gen)* alojar, albergar; *(supply housing)* proveer de vivienda. **2** *(store)* guardar, almacenar; *(fit)* dar cabida a.

⊕ Tanto el Reino Unido como Estados Unidos disponen, al igual que nosotros, de un sistema legislativo bicameral, con unas cámaras bajas (equivalentes al Congreso de los diputados), que se llaman **House of Commons** en el Reino Unido y **House of Representatives** en Estados Unidos, y unas cámaras altas (similares a nuestro Senado), que se llaman **House of Lords** en el Reino Unido y **Senate** en Estados Unidos.

**housemaster** [ˈhaʊsmɑːstəʳ] *n* EDUC tutor *m*.

**housemistress** [ˈhaʊsmɪstrəs] *n* EDUC tutora.

**housewife** [ˈhaʊswaɪf] *n* ama de casa.
ⓘ *pl* **housewives** [ˈhaʊswaɪvz].

**housework** [ˈhaʊswɜːk] *n* quehaceres *mpl* domésticos.

**housing** [ˈhaʊzɪŋ] *n* **1** vivienda. **2** TECH bastidor *m*, caja.

**hover** [ˈhɒvəʳ] *vi* **1** *(aircraft)* permanecer inmóvil *(en el aire)*. **2** *(bird)* cernerse, revolotear. **3** *(move around)* rondar. **4** *(hesitate)* dudar, vacilar.

**hovercraft** [ˈhɒvəkrɑːft] *n* aerodeslizador *m*.
ⓘ *pl* **hovercraft**.

**how** [haʊ] *adv* **1** *(in questions - direct)* ¿cómo?; *(- indirect)* cómo: *tell me how to do it* dime cómo se hace. **2** *(in exclamations)* qué: *how odd!* ¡qué extraño!, ¡qué raro! |LOC| **how about...?** ¿qué te parece si...? ▌ **how are you?** ¿cómo estás? ▌ **how many** cuántos,-as ▌ **how much** cuánto

✎ La expresión **How do you do?** se emplea en inglés formal cuando se encuentran dos personas por primera vez. La respuesta es la misma **How do you do?** El equivalente en español sería 'encantado'.

**however** [haʊˈevəʳ] *adv* **1** *(nevertheless)* sin embargo, no obstante. **2** *(with adj)*

por: *however hard it may be* por difícil que sea; *however much* por más que, por mucho que.

**howl** [haʊl] *n (cry)* aullido.
▸ *vi* aullar.
◆ **to howl down** *vt sep* abuchear.

**HP** [ˈeɪtʃˈpiː] *abbr* **(horsepower)** caballos *mpl* de vapor; *(abbreviation)* cv *mpl*.

**HQ** [ˈeɪtʃˈkjuː] *abbr* **1** **(headquarters)** cuartel *m* general. **2** *fig* centro de operaciones.

**HTML** [ˈeɪtʃˈtiːˈemˈel] *abbr* **(hypertext markup language)** HTML.

**hub** [hʌb] *n* **1** AUTO cubo. **2** *fig* centro, eje *m*.

**hubcap** [ˈhʌbkæp] *n* AUTO tapacubos *m*.

**huddle** [ˈhʌdəl] *n* grupo.
▸ *vi* **1** *(crouch)* acurrucarse, apiñarse, amontonarse. **2** *(cluster)* apiñarse.

**hug** [hʌg] *n* abrazo.
▸ *vt* **1** abrazar. **2** *fig (kerb, coast)* pegarse a, ceñirse a.
ⓘ *pt & pp* **hugged**, *ger* **hugging**.

**huge** [hjuːdʒ] *adj* enorme, inmenso,-a.

**hull** [hʌl] *n* **1** *(of ship)* casco. **2** BOT *(shell)* cáscara; *(pod)* vaina.
▸ *vt (peas, beans, etc)* desvainar.

**hullo** [hʌˈləʊ] *interj* → **hello.**

**hum** [hʌm] *n (of bees, engine)* zumbido.
▸ *vi* **1** *(bees, engine, etc)* zumbar. **2** *(sing)* tararear, canturrear. **3** *(bustling with activity)* hervir.
▸ *vt (tune)* tararear, canturrear.
ⓘ *pt & pp* **hummed**, *ger* **humming**.

**human** [ˈhjuːmən] *adj* humano,-a. |COMP| **human being** ser *m* humano.
▸ *n* ser *m* humano, humano.

**humanitarian** [hjuːmænɪˈteərɪən] *adj* humanitario,-a, filantrópico,-a.
▸ *n* filántropo,-a.

**humanity** [hjuːˈmænɪtɪ] *n* **1** *(virtue)* humanidad *f*. **2** *(mankind)* género humano, raza humana.
ⓘ *pl* **humanities.**

**humanize** [ˈhjuːmənaɪz] *vt* humanizar.

**humble** [ˈhʌmbəl] *adj* humilde.
▸ *vt* humillar.
ⓘ *comp* **humbler**, *superl* **humbliest.**

**humerus** ['hju:mərəs] *n* ANAT *(bone)* húmero.
ⓘ *pl* humeri ['hju:mərai].

**humid** ['hju:mɪd] *adj* húmedo,-a.

❌ Humid no significa 'húmedo (impregnado de agua)', que se traduce por damp, wet.

**humidity** [hju:'mɪdɪti] *n* humedad *f*.
**humiliate** [hju:'mɪlieɪt] *vt* humillar.
**humiliation** [hju:mɪli'eɪʃən] *n* humillación *f*.
**hummingbird** ['hʌmɪŋbɜːd] *n* colibrí *m*.
**humor** ['hju:mər] *n* US → humour.
**humorous** ['hju:mərəs] *adj* **1** *(funny)* gracioso,-a, divertido,-a. **2** *(writer)* humorístico,-a, humorista.
**humour** ['hju:mə'] *n* **1** humor *m*. **2** *(of a joke)* gracia. **3** *(whim)* capricho.
▶ *vt* complacer, seguir el humor a.

❌ Humour no significa 'humor (estado de ánimo)', que se traduce por mood.

**hump** [hʌmp] *n* **1** *(on back)* giba, joroba. **2** *(hillock)* montículo.
▶ *vt* **1** GB *fam (carry)* cargar.
**humus** ['hju:məs] *n* AGR mantillo, humus *m*.
**hunchback** ['hʌntʃbæk] *n* *(person)* jorobado,-a.
**hundred** ['hʌndrəd] *n* cien.
▶ *n pl* hundreds *(many)* centenares *mpl*, cientos *mpl*.
**hundredth** ['hʌndrədθ] *adj* centésimo,-a.
▶ *adv* en centésimo lugar.
**hung** [hʌŋ] *pt & pp* → hang.
**Hungarian** [hʌŋ'geəriən] *adj* húngaro,-a.
▶ *n* **1** *(person)* húngaro,-a. **2** *(language)* húngaro.
**Hungary** ['hʌŋgəri] *n* Hungría.
**hunger** ['hʌŋgə'] *n* **1** hambre *f*. **2** *fig* sed *f*. COMP **hunger strike** huelga de hambre.
◆ **to hunger after / hunger for** *vt insep* ansiar, anhelar, tener hambre de.
**hungry** ['hʌŋgri] *adj* **1** hambriento,-a. **2** *fig* ávido,-a, sediento,-a. LOC **to be hungry** tener hambre.
ⓘ *comp* hungrier, *superl* hungriest.

**hunt** [hʌnt] *n* **1** *(gen)* caza, cacería. **2** *(search)* búsqueda.
▶ *vt* cazar.
◆ **to hunt down** *vt sep (corner)* acorralar, perseguir; *(to find)* dar con, encontrar.
◆ **to hunt out / hunt up** *vt sep (to find)* encontrar; *(to look for)* buscar.
**hunter** ['hʌntə'] *n* **1** cazador,-ra *mf*. **2** ZOOL caballo de caza. **3** *(watch)* saboneta.
**hunting** ['hʌntɪŋ] *n* *(gen)* caza; *(expedition)* cacería, montería.
**hurdle** ['hɜːdəl] *n* **1** SP valla. **2** *fig* obstáculo.
▶ *vt* SP *(barrier)* saltar.
**hurdling** ['hɜːdlɪŋ] *n* SP carrera de vallas.
**hurl** [hɜːl] *vt* **1** lanzar, arrojar, tirar. **2** *(insults)* soltar.
**hurrah** [hʊ'rɑː] *interj* ¡hurra!: *hurrah for Peter!* ¡viva Peter!
▶ *vt* vitorear, aclamar.
**hurray** [hʊ'reɪ] *interj* ¡hurra!
**hurricane** ['hʌrɪkən, 'hʌrɪkeɪn] *n* huracán *m*.
**hurry** ['hʌri] *n* prisa: *are you in a hurry for the report?* ¿le corre prisa el informe? LOC **to be in a hurry** tener prisa.
▶ *vi* apresurarse, darse prisa.
◆ **to hurry up** *vi* darse prisa.
ⓘ *pt & pp* hurried, *ger* hurrying.
**hurt** [hɜːt] *n* **1** *(harm)* daño, dolor *m*, mal *m*. **2** *(wound)* herida. **3** *fig* daño, perjuicio.
▶ *adj* **1** *(physically)* herido,-a. **2** *(offended)* dolido,-a.
▶ *vt* **1** *(cause injury)* lastimar, hacer daño; *(to wound)* herir: *he has hurt his arm* se ha hecho daño en el brazo. **2** SP lesionar. **3** *(offend)* herir, ofender: *you hurt her feelings* la has ofendido, le has herido los sentimientos.
▶ *vi* **1** doler: *my eyes hurt* me duelen los ojos. **2** *fam* venir mal, ir mal.
ⓘ *pt & pp* hurt.
**husband** ['hʌzbənd] *n* marido, esposo.
**hush** [hʌʃ] *n* quietud *f*, silencio.
▶ *vt* callar, silenciar.

▶ *interj* ¡silencio! ¡cállate! ¡cállese! ¡chito! COMP **hush money** *fam* soborno *(que se paga para que alguien no hable)*.
◆ **to hush up** *vt sep (affair)* echar tierra a; *(person)* hacer callar.

**hustle** ['hʌsəl] *n* bullicio. COMP **hustle and bustle** ajetreo.

**hut** [hʌt] *n* **1** cabaña. **2** *(in garden)* cobertizo. **3** MIL barraca.

**hyacinth** ['haɪəsɪnθ] *n* BOT jacinto.

**hyaena** [haɪ'iːnə] *n* hiena.

**hybrid** ['haɪbrɪd] *adj* híbrido,-a.
▶ *n* híbrido.

**hydrant** ['haɪdrənt] *n* boca de riego.

**hydrate** [haɪ'dreɪt] *vt* hidratar.

**hydraulic** [haɪ'drɔːlɪk] *adj* hidráulico,-a. COMP **hydraulic brake** freno hidráulico.

**hydrocarbon** [haɪdrəʊ'kɑːbən] *n* CHEM hidrocarburo.

**hydrochloric** [haɪdrə'klɒrɪk] *adj* clorhídrico,-a. COMP **hydrochloric acid** ácido clorhídrico.

**hydroelectric** [haɪdrəʊɪ'lektrɪk] *adj* hidroeléctrico,-a. COMP **hydroelectric power station** central *f* hidroeléctrica.

**hydrogen** ['haɪdrədʒən] *n* CHEM hidrógeno. COMP **hydrogen bomb** bomba de hidrógeno.

**hydrography** [haɪ'drɒgrəfɪ] *n* hidrografía.

**hydrology** [haɪ'drɒlədʒɪ] *n* hidrología.

**hydroplane** ['haɪdrəpleɪn] *n* hidroavión *m*, hidroplano.

**hydrosphere** ['haɪdrəsfəˈ] *n* hidrosfera.

**hydroxide** [haɪ'drɒksaɪd] *n* hidróxido.

**hyena** [haɪ'iːnə] *n* ZOOL hiena.

**hygiene** ['haɪdʒiːn] *n* higiene *f*.

**hygienic** [haɪ'dʒiːnɪk] *adj* higiénico,-a.

**hymn** [hɪm] *n* himno. COMP **hymn book** cantoral *m*.

**hyperbola** [haɪ'pɜːbələ] *n* hipérbola.
ⓘ *pl* hyperbole [haɪ'pɜːbəlɪ] o hyperbolas.

**hyperbole** [haɪ'pɜːbəlɪ] *n* hipérbole *f*.

**hyperlink** ['haɪpəlɪŋk] *n* hiperenlace.

**hypermarket** ['haɪpəmɑːkɪt] *n* GB hipermercado.

**hypertension** [haɪpə'tenʃən] *n* MED hipertensión *f*.

**hypertext** ['haɪpətekst] *n* hipertexto.

**hyphen** ['haɪfən] *n* guion *m*.

**hypnosis** [hɪp'nəʊsɪs] *n* MED hipnosis *f*.

**hypnotise** ['hɪpnətaɪz] *vt* → hypnotize.

**hypnotize** ['hɪpnətaɪz] *vt* hipnotizar.

**hypochondriac** [haɪpə'kɒndriæk] *n* hipocondríaco,-a.
▶ *adj* hipocondríaco,-a.

**hypocrisy** [hɪ'pɒkrɪsɪ] *n* hipocresía.

**hypocrite** ['hɪpəkrɪt] *n* hipócrita *mf*.

**hypotension** [haɪpəʊ'tenʃən] *n* MED hipotensión *f*.

**hypotenuse** [haɪ'pɒtənjuːz] *n (geometry)* hipotenusa.

**hypothesis** [haɪ'pɒθəsɪs] *n* hipótesis *f*.
ⓘ *pl* hypotheses [haɪ'pɒθəsiːz].

**hypothetic** [haɪpə'θetɪk] *adj* hipotético,-a.

**hysteria** [hɪ'stɪərɪə] *n* histeria.

**hysterical** [hɪ'sterɪkəl] *adj* histérico,-a.

H

# I

**I, i** [aɪ] *n (the letter)* I, i *f.*

**I** [aɪ] *pron* yo.

**Iberian** [aɪˈbɪərɪən] *adj (modern)* ibérico,-a; *(historically)* ibero,-a, íbero,-a.
▶ *n* **1** *(person - now)* ibérico,-a; *(- historically)* ibero,-a, íbero,-a. **2** *(language)* ibero, íbero, -a. COMP **Iberian Peninsula** Península Ibérica.

**ice** [aɪs] *n* **1** *(frozen water)* hielo. **2** *(ice-cream)* helado. COMP **ice cube** cubito de hielo. **I ice hockey** hockey *m* sobre hielo. **I ice lolly** polo. **I ice ring** pista de hielo.

**iceberg** [ˈaɪsbɜːg] *n* **1** iceberg *m.* **2** *fig* persona fría.

**icebreaker** [ˈaɪsbreɪkəʳ] *n* rompehielos *m inv.*

**ice-cream** [ˈaɪskriːm] *n* helado.

**Iceland** [ˈaɪslənd] *n* Islandia.

**Icelander** [ˈaɪsləndəʳ] *n (person)* islandés,-esa.

**Icelandic** [aɪsˈlændɪk] *adj* islandés,-esa.
▶ *n (language)* islandés *m.*

**ice-skate** [ˈaɪsskeɪt] *vi* patinar sobre hielo.

**ice-skating** [ˈaɪskeɪtɪŋ] *n* patinaje *m* sobre hielo.

**icicle** [ˈaɪsɪkəl] *n* carámbano.

**icing** [ˈaɪsɪŋ] *n* cobertura.

**icon** [ˈaɪkən] *n* icono.

**iconography** [aɪkəˈnɒgrəfɪ] *n* iconografía.

**icy** [ˈaɪsɪ] *adj* **1** *(very cold - hand, etc)* helado,-a; *(- wind)* glacial. **2** *(covered with ice)* cubierto,-a de hielo. **3** *fig* glacial.
ⓘ *comp* **icier**, *superl* **iciest**.

**ID** [ˈaɪˈdiː] *abbr* **(identification)** identificación *f.* COMP **ID card** documento nacional de identidad, DNI *m.*

**I'd** [aɪd] *contr* **1** I would. **2** I had.

**idea** [aɪˈdɪə] *n* **1** *(gen)* idea; *(opinion)* opinión *f.* **2** *(intuition)* impresión *f*, sensación *f.* **3** *(concept)* concepto.
▶ *n* **the idea** *(aim, purpose)* idea, intención *f*, objetivo.

**ideal** [aɪˈdiːl] *adj* ideal, perfecto,-a.
▶ *n* **1** *(perfect example)* ideal *m.* **2** *(principle)* principio, ideal *m.*

**idealize** [aɪˈdɪəlaɪz] *vt* idealizar: *we tend to idealize the past* tendemos a idealizar el pasado.

**identical** [aɪˈdentɪkəl] *adj* **1** *(exactly alike)* idéntico,-a **(to/with,** a). **2** *(the same)* mismísimo,-a.

**identification** [aɪdentɪfɪˈkeɪʃən] *n* **1** *(gen)* identificación *f.* **2** *(papers)* documentación *f.*

**identify** [aɪˈdentɪfaɪ] *vt* **1** *(gen)* identificar. **2** *(associate)* asociar **(with,** con), relacionar **(with,** con).
ⓘ *pt & pp* **identified**, *ger* **identifying**.

**Identikit®** [aɪˈdentɪkɪt] COMP **Identikit picture** retrato robot.

**identity** [aɪˈdentɪtɪ] *n* identidad *f.* COMP **identity card** carnet *m* de identidad.
ⓘ *pl* **identities**.

**ideogram** [ˈɪdɪəʊgræm] *n* ideograma *m.*

**ideological** [aɪdɪəˈlɒdʒɪkəl] *adj* ideológico,-a.

**ideology** [aɪdɪˈɒlədʒɪ] *n* ideología.
ⓘ *pl* **ideologies**.

**idiom** [ˈɪdɪəm] *n* **1** *(phrase)* locución *f*, modismo, frase *f* hecha. **2** *(language)* lenguaje *m*, idioma *m*; *(style)* estilo.

❌ **Idiom** no significa 'idioma', que se traduce por **language**.

**idiomatic** [ɪdɪəˈmætɪk] *adj* idiomático,-a.

**idiot** ['ɪdɪət] n **1** fam idiota mf, tonto,-a. **2** MED idiota mf.

**idle** ['aɪd°l] adj **1** (lazy) perezoso,-a, vago,-a. **2** (not working - person) parado,-a, desempleado,-a; (- machinery) parado,-a; (- money) improductivo,-a.
ⓘ comp **idler**, superl **idlest**.
▸ vi (waste time) gandulear, holgazanear, perder el tiempo.

**idol** ['aɪd°l] n ídolo m.

**idolatry** [aɪ'dɒlətrɪ] n idolatría.
ⓘ pl **idolatries**.

**i.e.** ['aɪ'i:] abbr (id est) esto es, a saber; (abbreviation) i.e.

**if** [ɪf] conj **1** (supposing) si: if it rains, we'll stay at home si llueve, nos quedaremos en casa; you can come if you want puedes venir si quieres. **2** (whether) si: do you know if she got the job? ¿sabes si consiguió el trabajo? **3** (used after verbs expressing feelings) que: do you mind if I open the window? ¿te importa que abra la ventana? **4** (but) aunque, pero: it's good, if a little slow at times es bueno pero algo lento a veces. **5** (in exclamations): well, if it isn't Jimmy Jazz! vaya, ¡pero si es Jimmy Jazz!
LOC **if I were you** yo que tú, yo en tu lugar. ‖ **if only** (present or future time) ¡ojalá!, ¡si al menos...!

**igloo** ['ɪgluː] n iglú m.
ⓘ pl **igloos**.

**igneous** ['ɪgnɪəs] adj ígneo,-a.

**ignition** [ɪg'nɪʃ°n] n **1** ignición f. **2** AUTO encendido, arranque m.

**ignorance** ['ɪgnərəns] n ignorancia.

**ignorant** ['ɪgnərənt] adj **1** (unaware) ignorante (of, de). **2** fam (rude) descortés, maleducado,-a.

**ignore** [ɪg'nɔːʳ] vt **1** (order, warning) no hacer caso de, hacer caso omiso de; (behaviour, fact) pasar por alto. **2** (person) hacer como si no existiese.

☒ To ignore no significa 'ignorar (no saber)', que se traduce por not to know.

**iguana** [ɪ'gwɑːnə] n iguana.

**ilium** ['ɪlɪəm] n ilion m, íleon m.

**ill** [ɪl] adj **1** (sick) enfermo,-a. **2** (harmful, unpropitious) malo,-a.
▸ n fml (harm, evil) mal m.

▸ adv **1** (badly) mal. **2** (unfavourably) mal. **3** (with difficulty) mal, a duras penas.
▸ n pl ills (problems, misfortunes) desgracias fpl.

**I'll** [aɪl] contr **1** I will. **2** I shall.

**illegal** [ɪ'liːg°l] adj ilegal.

**illegality** [ɪlɪ'gælɪtɪ] n ilegalidad f.
ⓘ pl **illegalities**.

**illegible** [ɪ'ledʒɪb°l] adj ilegible.

**illegitimate** [ɪlɪ'dʒɪtɪmət] adj ilegítimo,-a.

**illicit** [ɪ'lɪsɪt] adj ilícito,-a.

**illiterate** [ɪ'lɪt°rət] adj **1** (unlettered) analfabeto,-a. **2** (uneducated) ignorante, inculto,-a. **3** (poor style) inculto,-a, pobre.
▸ n (unlettered person) analfabeto,-a.

**ill-mannered** [ɪl'mænəd] adj maleducado,-a, descortés.

**illness** ['ɪlnəs] n enfermedad f.
ⓘ pl **illnesses**.

**illogical** [ɪ'lɒdʒɪk°l] adj ilógico,-a.

**illuminate** [ɪ'luːmɪneɪt] vt iluminar.

**illuminated** [ɪ'luːmɪneɪt°d] adj (manuscript) iluminado,-a.

**illumination** [ɪluːmɪ'neɪʃ°n] n **1** (light) iluminación f. **2** (clarification) aclaración.

**illusion** [ɪ'luːʒ°n] n ilusión f, falsa impresión f.

☒ Illusion no significa 'ilusión (esperanza)', que se traduce por hope.

**illusionist** [ɪ'luːʒ°nɪst] n ilusionista mf.

**illustrate** ['ɪləstreɪt] vt ilustrar.

**illustrated** ['ɪləstreɪt] adj ilustrado,-a.

☒ Illustrated no significa 'ilustrado (culto)', que se traduce por learned.

**illustration** [ɪləs'treɪʃ°n] n **1** (gen) ilustración f. **2** (example) ejemplo.

**illustrative** ['ɪləstrətɪv] adj **1** (gen) ilustrativo,-a, ilustrador,-a. **2** (example) aclaratorio,-a.

**I'm** [aɪm] contr I am.

**image** ['ɪmɪdʒ] n **1** (gen) imagen f. **2** (reputation) imagen f, fama, reputación f.

**imaginary** [ɪ'mædʒɪnərɪ] adj imaginario,-a, inventado,-a.

**imagination** [ɪmædʒɪˈneɪʃ°n] n (gen) imaginación f; (inventiveness) inventiva.

**imaginative** [ɪˈmædʒɪnətɪv] adj (person) imaginativo,-a, de gran inventiva; (creation) lleno,-a de imaginación, lleno,-a de fantasía.

**imagine** [ɪˈmædʒɪn] vt 1 (visualize) imaginar. 2 (suppose) suponer, imaginar(se), figurarse.

**imam** [ɪˈmɑːm] n imán m.

**imbalance** [ɪmˈbæləns] n desequilibrio.

**IMF** [ˈaɪˈemˈef] abbr (International Monetary Fund) Fondo Monetario Internacional; (abbreviation) FMI m.

**imitate** [ˈɪmɪteɪt] vt (gen) imitar, copiar; (for fun) imitar.

**imitation** [ɪmɪˈteɪʃ°n] n 1 (gen) imitación f, copia; (for fun) imitación f. 2 (reproduction) reproducción f.
   ▶ adj de imitación.

**immaterial** [ɪməˈtɪərɪəl] adj 1 (unimportant) irrelevante. 2 (incorporeal) inmaterial, incorpóreo,-a.

**immature** [ɪməˈtjʊəʳ] adj 1 (gen) inmaduro,-a; (- plant) joven. 2 (childish) inmaduro,-a, pueril.

**immediate** [ɪˈmiːdɪət] adj 1 (instant) inmediato,-a; (urgent) urgente. 2 (nearest) inmediato,-a, más próximo,-a. 3 (direct) primero,-a, principal.

**immediately** [ɪˈmiːdɪətlɪ] adv (instantly, at once) inmediatamente, de inmediato, en seguida, en el acto.

**immense** [ɪˈmens] adj inmenso,-a, enorme.

**immensely** [ɪˈmenslɪ] adv enormemente, sumamente.

**immersion** [ɪˈmɜːʃ°n] n 1 inmersión f, sumersión f. 2 fig absorción f.

**immigrant** [ˈɪmɪɡrənt] adj inmigrante.
   ▶ n inmigrante mf.

**immigrate** [ˈɪmɪɡreɪt] vi inmigrar.

**immigration** [ɪmɪˈɡreɪʃ°n] n inmigración f.

**imminent** [ˈɪmɪnənt] adj inminente.

**immoral** [ɪˈmɒr°l] adj inmoral.

**immortal** [ɪˈmɔːt°l] adj 1 (god, soul, etc) inmortal. 2 fig (fame, memory, etc) imperecedero,-a, perdurable.
   ▶ n inmortal mf.

**immortality** [ɪmɔːˈtælɪtɪ] n inmortalidad f.

**immune** [ɪˈmjuːn] adj 1 (gen) inmune (to, a). 2 (exempt) exento,-a.

**immunity** [ɪˈmjuːnɪtɪ] n 1 (gen) inmunidad f. 2 (exemption) exención f.

**immunize** [ˈɪmjənaɪz] vt inmunizar (against, contra).

**immunodeficient** [ɪmjʊnəʊdɪˈfɪʃ°nt] adj inmunodeficiente.

**immunodeficiency** [ɪmjʊnəʊdɪˈfɪʃ°n-sɪ] n inmunodeficiencia.

**immunology** [ɪmjʊˈnɒlədʒɪ] n inmunología.

**impact** [(n) ˈɪmpækt; (vb) ɪmˈpækt] n 1 (gen) impacto; (crash) choque m. 2 (impression, effect) efecto, impresión f, impacto.
   ▶ vt US (have impact on) impresionar.

**impartial** [ɪmˈpɑːʃ°l] adj imparcial.

**impatience** [ɪmˈpeɪʃ°ns] n 1 (eagerness) impaciencia, ansiedad f. 2 (irritation) impaciencia, irritación f.

**impatient** [ɪmˈpeɪʃ°nt] adj 1 (eager) impaciente, ansioso,-a. 2 (irritable) irritable. 3 fml (intolerant) intolerante.

**impeachment** [ɪmˈpiːtʃmənt] n JUR (accusation) acusación f, denuncia; (trial) proceso.

**impeccable** [ɪmˈpekəb°l] adj (gen) impecable, perfecto,-a.

**impending** [ɪmˈpendɪŋ] adj inminente.

**imperative** [ɪmˈperətɪv] adj 1 (indispensable) imprescindible. 2 (authoritative) imperativo,-a, imperioso,-a. 3 LING imperativo,-a.

**imperfect** [ɪmˈpɜːfekt] adj 1 (gen) imperfecto,-a; (goods, sight) defectuoso,-a. 2 LING imperfecto,-a.
   ▶ n the imperfect LING el imperfecto.

**imperfection** [ɪmpəˈfekʃ°n] n (gen) perfección f; (defect) defecto, tara, tacha; (blemish) mancha.

**imperial** [ɪmˈpɪərɪəl] *adj* **1** *(gen)* imperial. **2** *(weight, measure)* del sistema métrico *británico*.

**imperialism** [ɪmˈpɪərɪəlɪzᵊm] *n* imperialismo.

**imperialist** [ɪmˈpɪərɪəlɪst] *n* imperialista *mf*.

**impersonal** [ɪmˈpɜːsᵊnəl] *adj* impersonal.

**impersonate** [ɪmˈpɜːsᵊneɪt] *vt* **1** *(imitate to deceive)* hacerse pasar por. **2** *(imitate to entertain)* imitar.

**impertinent** [ɪmˈpɜːtɪnənt] *adj* impertinente, descarado,-a.

**implant** [*(vb)* ɪmˈplɑːnt; *(n)* ˈɪmplɑːnt] *vt* **1** MED implantar, injertar. **2** *(ideas, etc)* inculcar (in, en).
▶ *n* MED implantación *f*, injerto.

**implement** [*(n)* ˈɪmpləmənt; *(vb)* ˈɪmplɪment] *n (instrument)* instrumento, utensilio; *(tool)* herramienta.
▶ *vt (plan, suggestion, etc)* llevar a cabo, poner en práctica; *(law, policy)* aplicar.

**implementation** [ɪmpləmənˈteɪʃᵊn] *n (of plan, etc)* puesta en práctica, desarrollo; *(of law, etc)* aplicación *f*.

**implicate** [ˈɪmplɪkeɪt] *vt* implicar, (in, en).

**implication** [ɪmplɪˈkeɪʃᵊn] *n* implicación *f*.

**implicit** [ɪmˈplɪsɪt] *adj* **1** *(implied)* implícito,-a, tácito,-a. **2** *(absolute)* absoluto,-a, incondicional.

**implied** [ɪmˈplaɪd] *adj* implícito,-a, tácito,-a.

**imply** [ɪmˈplaɪ] *vt* **1** *(involve, entail)* implicar, suponer, presuponer. **2** *(mean)* significar, querer decir; *(hint)* insinuar, dar a entender.
ⓘ *pt & pp* implied.

**impolite** [ɪmpəˈlaɪt] *adj* maleducado,-a, descortés.

**import** [ˈɪmpɔːt] *n* **1** *(article)* artículo de importación. **2** *(activity)* importación *f*.
▶ *vt* importar.

❌ To import no significa 'importar (tener importancia)', que se traduce por to matter.

**importance** [ɪmˈpɔːtᵊns] *n* importancia.

**important** [ɪmˈpɔːtᵊnt] *adj* **1** *(gen)* importante. **2** *(influential)* de categoría.

**importation** [ɪmpɔːˈteɪʃᵊn] *n* importación *f*.

**importer** [ɪmˈpɔːtəʳ] *n* importador,-ra.

**impose** [ɪmˈpəʊz] *vt (gen)* imponer (on, a).
◆ **to impose on** *vt insep (take advantage of)* abusar de, aprovecharse de.

**impossible** [ɪmˈpɒsɪbᵊl] *adj (gen)* imposible.

**impotence** [ˈɪmpətᵊns] *n* impotencia.

**impoverishment** [ɪmˈpɒvᵊrɪʃmənt] *n* empobrecimiento.

**imprecise** [ɪmprəˈsaɪs] *adj* impreciso,-a, inexacto,-a.

**imprecision** [ɪmprəˈsɪʒᵊn] *n* imprecisión *f*, falta de precisión.

**impress** [ɪmˈpres] *vt* **1** *(cause respect)* impresionar. **2** *(emphasize, stress)* subrayar, convencer, recalcar. **3** *fig* grabar.

**impression** [ɪmˈpreʃᵊn] *n* **1** *(gen)* impresión *f*. **2** *(imitation)* imitación *f*. **3** *(imprint, mark)* marca, señal *f*, impresión *f*; *(in wax, plaster)* molde *m*; *(of foot, etc)* huella. **4** *(reprint)* impresión *f*, edición *f*.

**impressionism** [ɪmˈpreʃᵊnɪzᵊm] *n* ART impresionismo.

**impressionist** [ɪmˈpreʃᵊnɪst] *adj* ART impresionista.
▶ *n* **1** ART impresionista. **2** *(mimic)* imitador,-ra.

**impressive** [ɪmˈpresɪv] *adj* impresionante.

**imprison** [ɪmˈprɪzᵊn] *vt* encarcelar, meter en la cárcel.

**imprisonment** [ɪmˈprɪzᵊnmənt] *n* encarcelamiento.

**improbable** [ɪmˈprɒbəbᵊl] *adj* **1** *(event)* improbable. **2** *(story, explanation)* inverosímil.

**improper** [ɪmˈprɒpəʳ] *adj* **1** *(behaviour)* impropio,-a; *(method, conditions)* inadecuado,-a. **3** *(language)* indecente. **2** *(proposal)* deshonesto,-a.

**improve** [ɪmˈpruːv] *vt* **1** *(quality, etc)* mejorar. **2** *(skill, knowledge)* perfeccionar. **3** *(mind)* cultivar. **4** *(property)* hacer mejoras en. **5** *(increase)* aumentar.
▶ *vi (get better)* mejorar, mejorarse.

◆ **to improve on** *vt insep (better)* superar.

**improvement** [ɪmˈpruːvmənt] *n* **1** *(gen)* mejora, mejoramiento; *(in health)* mejoría. **2** *(in knowledge)* perfeccionamiento. **3** *(increase)* aumento.

**improvise** [ˈɪmprəvaɪz] *vt* improvisar.

**imprudent** [ɪmˈpruːdənt] *adj fml (unwise)* imprudente; *(rash)* precipitado,-a.

**impudent** [ˈɪmpjʊdənt] *adj* insolente, fresco,-a, descarado,-a.

**impulse** [ˈɪmpʌls] *n* **1** *(sudden urge)* impulso, capricho; *(stimulus, drive)* impulso, estímulo, ímpetu *m*. **2** TECH impulso.

**impulsive** [ɪmˈpʌlsɪv] *adj* impulsivo,-a, irreflexivo,-a.

**impunity** [ɪmˈpjuːnɪtɪ] *n* impunidad *f*.

**impure** [ɪmˈpjʊəʳ] *adj* **1** *(contaminated)* contaminado,-a; *(adulterated)* adulterado,-a. **2** *(morally - act)* impuro,-a; *(- thought)* impúdico,-a, deshonesto,-a.

**in¹** [ɪn] *prep* **1** *(place)* en, dentro de: *it's in the box* está en la caja. **2** *(motion)* en, a: *we arrived in Bonn* llegamos a Bonn. **3** *(time - during)* en, durante: *in 1980* en 1980. **4** *(time - within)* en, dentro de. **5** *(wearing)* en, vestido,-a de: *the woman in black* la mujer vestida de negro. **6** *(state, condition)* en. **7** *(ratio, measurement, number)* varias traducciones: *in twos* de dos en dos; *she's in her thirties* tiene treinta y tantos años. **8** *(profession)* en: *she's in television* trabaja en la televisión. **9** *(weather, light)* varias traducciones: *walking in the rain* caminando bajo la lluvia. **10** *(after superlative)* de: *the tallest in the class* el más alto de la clase. LOC **in all** en total.
► *adv* **1** *(motion)* dentro. **2** *(tide)* alto,-a. **3** *(fashionable)* de moda: *hats are in* los sombreros están de moda. **4** *(on sale, obtainable)* disponible.
► *n pl* **ins and outs** *(details)* detalles *mpl*, pormenores *mpl*.
► *phr* **to be in** *(at home)* estar en casa; *(at work)* estar.

**inability** [ɪnəˈbɪlɪtɪ] *n* incapacidad *f*.

**inaccessible** [ɪnækˈsesəbəl] *adj* inaccesible.

**inaccuracy** [ɪnˈækjərəsɪ] *n* **1** *(gen)* inexactitud *f*. **2** *(error)* error *m*, incorrección *f*.
ⓘ *pl* inaccuracies.

**inaccurate** [ɪnˈækjərət] *adj* *(gen)* inexacto,-a; *(incorrect)* incorrecto,-a, erróneo,-a.

**inactive** [ɪnˈæktɪv] *adj* inactivo,-a.

**inactivity** [ɪnækˈtɪvɪtɪ] *n* inactividad *f*.

**inadequate** [ɪnˈædɪkwət] *adj* **1** *(not sufficient)* insuficiente; *(not appropriate)* inadecuado,-a. **2** *(person)* incapaz, incompetente. **3** *(defective)* defectuoso,-a, imperfecto,-a.

**inanimate** [ɪnˈænɪmət] *adj* inanimado,-a.

**inappropriate** [ɪnəˈprəʊprɪət] *adj* *(unsuitable - clothes, behaviour)* poco apropiado,-a, no apropiado,-a; *(- time, remark)* inoportuno,-a, inconveniente.

**inarticulate** [ɪnɑːˈtɪkjʊlət] *adj* **1** *(person)* incapaz de expresarse. **2** *(speech, words, writing)* mal expresado,-a, incoherente. **3** *(cry, sound)* inarticulado,-a. **4** *(joints)* inarticulado,-a.

**inattentive** [ɪnəˈtentɪv] *adj* *(not paying attention)* poco atento,-a, distraído,-a; *(not attentive)* poco atento,-a.

**inaudible** [ɪnˈɔːdəbəl] *adj* inaudible, imperceptible.

**inaugural** [ɪˈnɔːgjʊrəl] *adj* inaugural, de inauguración, de apertura.

**inaugurate** [ɪˈnɔːgjʊreɪt] *vt* **1** *(building, exhibition, etc)* inaugurar. **2** *(president, etc)* investir.

**inauguration** [ɪnɔːgjʊˈreɪʃən] *n* **1** *(of building, etc)* inauguración *f*. **2** *(of president, etc)* investidura, toma de posesión.

**inborn** [ˈɪnbɔːn] *adj* innato,-a.

**inbox** [ˈɪnbɒks] *n* bandeja de entrada.

**inbred** [ˈɪnbred] *adj* **1** *(innate)* innato,-a. **2** *(produced by inbreeding)* endogámico,-a.

**Inc** [ɪnˈkɔːpəreɪtɪd] *abbr* US **(Incorporated)** ≈ sociedad *f* anónima; *(abbreviation)* S.A.

**incantation** [ɪnkænˈteɪʃən] *n* conjuro, ensalmo.

**incapable** [ɪnˈkeɪpəbəl] *adj* **1** *(unable)* incapaz. **2** *(incompetent)* incompetente.

**3** *(helpless)* impotente, imposibilitado,-a.

**incapacity** [ɪnkəˈpæsɪtɪ] *n* incapacidad *f*.

**incense¹** [ˈɪnsens] *n* incienso.

**incense²** [ɪnˈsens] *vt (make angry)* enfurecer, poner furioso,-a.

**incentive** [ɪnˈsentɪv] *n* incentivo, estímulo, aliciente *m*.

**incest** [ˈɪnsest] *n* incesto.

**inch** [ɪntʃ] *n* **1** *(measurement)* pulgada. **2** *(small amount)* poco, pelo, ápice *m*.
ⓘ *pl* **inches**.

  ✎ Equivale a 2,54 cm.

**incidence** [ˈɪnsɪdəns] *n* **1** *(occurrence)* frecuencia, extensión *f*. **2** PHYS incidencia.

**incident** [ˈɪnsɪdənt] *n (event)* incidente *m*; *(violent episode)* altercado.

**incidentally** [ɪnsɪˈdentəlɪ] *adv* **1** *(by the way)* a propósito, por cierto, dicho sea de paso. **2** *(by chance)* por casualidad.

**incinerate** [ɪnˈsɪnəreɪt] *vt* incinerar, quemar.

**incineration** [ɪnsɪnəˈreɪʃən] *n* incineración *f*, quema.

**incision** [ɪnˈsɪʒən] *n* incisión *f*.

**incisive** [ɪnˈsaɪsɪv] *adj* **1** *(comment, wit)* incisivo,-a, mordaz. **2** *(mind)* penetrante.

**incisor** [ɪnˈsaɪzər] *n (diente m)* incisivo.

**inclination** [ɪnklɪˈneɪʃən] *n* **1** *(tendency)* inclinación *f*, tendencia; *(disposition)* disposición *f*, propensión *f*. **2** *(slope)* inclinación *f*, pendiente *f*. **3** *(bow)* inclinación *f*.

**incline** [*(n)* ˈɪnklaɪn; *(vb)* ɪnˈklaɪn] *n* pendiente *f*, inclinación *f*, cuesta.
▶ *vt* **1** *(bend forward)* inclinar. **2** *fml (persuade, influence)* inclinar, predisponer.
▶ *vi* **1** *(slope)* inclinarse, estar inclinado,-a. **2** *(tend)* tender a, tener tendencia a.

**inclined** [ɪnˈklaɪnd] *adj* **1** *(disposed, encouraged)* dispuesto,-a (to, a). **2** *(tending to)* propenso,-a. **3** *(having natural ability)* dotado,-a. **4** *(sloping)* inclinado,-a.

**include** [ɪnˈkluːd] *vt* incluir.

**including** [ɪnˈkluːdɪŋ] *prep* incluso, incluyendo.

**inclusion** [ɪnˈkluːʒən] *n* inclusión *f*.

**inclusive** [ɪnˈkluːsɪv] *adj* inclusive.

**incognito** [ɪnkɒgˈniːtəʊ] *adv* de incógnito.

**incoherence** [ɪnkəʊˈhɪərəns] *n* incoherencia.

**incoherent** [ɪnkəʊˈhɪərənt] *adj* incoherente.

**income** [ˈɪnkʌm] *n (from work)* ingresos *mpl*, renta; *(from investment)* réditos *mpl*.
COMP **income tax** impuesto sobre la renta.

**incompatibility** [ɪnkəmpætəˈbɪlɪtɪ] *n* incompatibilidad *f*.
ⓘ *pl* **incompatibilities**.

**incompatible** [ɪnkəmˈpætəbl] *adj* incompatible (**with**, con).

**incompetence** [ɪnˈkɒmpətəns] *n* incompetencia, ineptitud *f*, incapacidad *f*.

**incompetent** [ɪnˈkɒmpətənt] *adj* incompetente, inepto,-a, incapaz.
▶ *n* incompetente *mf*, inepto,-a.

**incomplete** [ɪnkəmˈpliːt] *adj* **1** *(not whole)* incompleto,-a; *(not finished)* inacabado,-a, sin terminar. **2** *(partial)* parcial.

**incomprehensible** [ɪnkɒmprɪˈhensəbl] *adj* incomprensible.

**inconceivable** [ɪnkənˈsiːvəbl] *adj* **1** inconcebible. **2** *fam* imposible, increíble.

**inconclusive** [ɪnkənˈkluːsɪv] *adj* **1** *(debate, vote, etc)* no decisivo,-a. **2** *(evidence, result, etc)* no concluyente.

**inconsequent** [ɪnˈkɒnsɪkwənt] *adj* **1** *(not following logically)* inconsecuente. **2** *(inconsequential)* de poca importancia, sin trascendencia.

**inconsiderate** [ɪnkənˈsɪdərət] *adj* desconsiderado,-a, inconsiderado,-a, poco atento,-a.

**inconsistent** [ɪnkənˈsɪstənt] *adj* **1** *(not agreeing with, at variance with)* inconsecuente; *(contradictory)* contradictorio,-a. **2** *(changeable - weather)* variable; *(- person)* inconstante, voluble, irregular; *(- behaviour)* imprevisible, irregular.

**inconstant** [ɪnˈkɒnstənt] *adj* **1** *(person)* inconstante, veleidoso,-a, mudable. **2** *(not fixed)* variable.

**incontinence** [ɪnˈkɒntɪnəns] *n* incontinencia.

**inconvenience** [ɪnkənˈviːnɪəns] *n (gen)* inconveniente *m*; *(trouble, difficulty)* molestia, dificultad *f*; *(hindrance)* estorbo, obstáculo; *(discomfort)* incomodidad *f*: *I'm sorry to cause you so much inconvenience* siento causarle tanta molestia.
▶ *vt* causar molestia a, molestar; *(cause difficulty)* incomodar.

**inconvenient** [ɪnkənˈviːnɪənt] *adj* **1** *(gen)* inconveniente, molesto,-a, incómodo,-a; *(place)* mal situado,-a; *(time)* mal, inoportuno,-a; *(arrangement)* poco práctico,-a. **2** *(fact)* incómodo,-a.

**incorporate** [ɪnˈkɔːpəreɪt] *vt* **1** *(make part of, include in)* incorporar (**in/into**, a), incluir (**in/into**, en); *(include, contain)* incluir, contener. **2** US *(company)* constituir, constituir en sociedad.
▶ *adj* US *(company)* constituido,-a, constituido,-a en sociedad.

❎ To incorporate no significa 'incorporarse (levantarse)', que se traduce por to sit up.

**incorrect** [ɪnkəˈrekt] *adj* **1** *(wrong, untrue)* incorrecto,-a, erróneo,-a, equivocado,-a. **2** *(- dress)* impropio,-a, inadecuado,-a.

**increase** [*(n)* ˈɪnkriːs; *(vb)* ɪnˈkriːs] *n (gen)* aumento, incremento; *(in price, temperature)* subida, alza.
▶ *vt (gen)* aumentar, incrementar; *(temperature)* subir.

**increasing** [ɪnˈkriːsɪŋ] *adj* creciente.

**increasingly** [ɪnˈkriːsɪŋlɪ] *adv* cada vez más.

**incredible** [ɪnˈkredɪbəl] *adj (unbelievable)* increíble, inverosímil; *(amazing)* fantástico,-a.

**incredulous** [ɪnˈkredjələs] *adj* incrédulo,-a.

**increment** [ˈɪnkrɪmənt] *n* aumento, incremento.

**incriminate** [ɪnˈkrɪmɪneɪt] *vt* incriminar.

**incubate** [ˈɪnkjʊbeɪt] *vt* incubar.
▶ *vi (of eggs)* incubar; *(of bird)* empollar.

**incubation** [ɪnkjʊˈbeɪʃən] *n* incubación *f*.

**incubator** [ˈɪnkjʊbeɪtər] *n* incubadora.

**incurable** [ɪnˈkjʊərəbəl] *adj* **1** *(disease)* incurable. **2** *fig (loss)* irremediable; *(habit, optimist)* incorregible.
▶ *n* enfermo,-a incurable.

**indebted** [ɪnˈdetɪd] *adj* **1** *(in debt)* endeudado,-a. **2** *fig (grateful)* agradecido,-a.

**indecent** [ɪnˈdiːsənt] *adj* **1** *(obscene)* indecente, indecoroso,-a, obsceno,-a. **2** *(improper)* impropio,-a, indebido,-a, injustificado,-a; *(undue)* excesivo,-a.

**indecisive** [ɪndɪˈsaɪsɪv] *adj* **1** *(hesitant)* indeciso,-a, irresoluto,-a. **2** *(inconclusive)* poco concluyente, no concluyente, no decisivo,-a.

**indeed** [ɪnˈdiːd] *adv* **1** *(yes, certainly)* efectivamente, en efecto: *are you Mr Fox? yes, indeed* ¿es el Sr Fox? sí, efectivamente. **2** *(intensifier)* realmente, de veras, de verdad: *thank you very much indeed* muchísimas gracias. **3** *fml (in fact)* realmente, en realidad, de hecho; *(what is more)* es más.

**indefinite** [ɪnˈdefɪnət] *adj* **1** *(vague, not precise)* indefinido,-a, vago,-a, impreciso,-a. **2** *(not fixed - period of time, amount, number)* indefinido,-a, indeterminado,-a.

**indefinitely** [ɪnˈdefɪnətlɪ] *adv* indefinidamente.

**indemnity** [ɪnˈdemnɪtɪ] *n* **1** *(insurance, guarantee)* indemnidad *f* (**against**, contra). **2** *(compensation)* indemnización *f* (**for**, por), reparación *f*, compensación *f*.
① *pl* indemnities.

**indent** [*(vb)* ɪnˈdent; *(n)* ˈɪndent] *vt (text)* sangrar.
▶ *vi* GB *(order)* hacer un pedido (**for**, de), encargar (**for**, -).
▶ *n* GB *(order)* pedido.

**indentation** [ɪndenˈteɪʃən] *n* **1** *(in text)* sangría. **2** *(notch in edge, mark)* mella, muesca.

**independence** [ɪndɪˈpendəns] *n* independencia (**from**, de).

**independent** [ɪndɪ'pendªnt] *adj (gen)* independiente.
▶ *n* POL (candidato,-a) independiente *mf*.

**in-depth** [ɪn'depθ] *adj* minucioso,-a, exhaustivo,-a, a fondo.

**indeterminate** [ɪndɪ'tɜ:mɪnət] *adj* indeterminado,-a.

**India** ['ɪndɪə] *n* (la) India. COMP **India rubber** caucho.

**index** ['ɪndeks] *n* índice. COMP **index finger** dedo índice.
ⓘ *pl* **indixes** o **indices** ['ɪndɪsi:z].

**Indian** ['ɪndɪən] *adj* indio,-a, hindú *mf*.
▶ *n* indio,-a, hindú. COMP **the Indian Ocean** el océano Índico.

**indicate** ['ɪndɪkeɪt] *vt* indicar, señalar, marcar.
▶ *vi* AUTO poner el intermitente.

**indication** [ɪndɪ'keɪʃªn] *n (gen)* indicio, señal *f*, indicación *f*.

**indicative** [ɪn'dɪkətɪv] *adj* **1** *fml* indicativo,-a (of, de). **2** LING indicativo,-a.
▶ *n* LING indicativo.

**indicator** ['ɪndɪkeɪtəʳ] *n* **1** *(gen)* indicador *m*. **2** AUTO intermitente *m*.

**indices** ['ɪndɪsi:z] *n pl* → **index**.

**indictment** [ɪn'daɪtmənt] *n* **1** JUR acusación *f*, sumario. **2** *fig (criticism)* crítica.

**indifference** [ɪn'dɪfªrəns] *n* indiferencia (to, ante).

**indifferent** [ɪn'dɪfªrənt] *adj* **1** *(gen)* indiferente (to, a). **2** *(mediocre, average)* mediocre, regular, pobre.

☒ Indifferent no significa 'indiferente (irrelevante)', que se traduce por immaterial.

**indigestion** [ɪndɪ'dʒestʃªn] *n* indigestión *f*, empacho.

**indignation** [ɪndɪg'neɪʃªn] *n* indignación *f* (about/over, por) (at, ante/por).

**indigo** ['ɪndɪgəʊ] *n* añil *m*.

**indirect** [ɪndɪ'rekt] *adj* indirecto,-a.

**indirectly** [ɪndɪ'rektlɪ] *adv* indirectamente.

**indissoluble** [ɪndɪ'sɒljəbªl] *adj fml (cannot be dissolved)* indisoluble; *(cannot be broken)* inseparable.

**individual** [ɪndɪ'vɪdjʊəl] *adj* **1** *(single, separate)* por separado. **2** *(for one person)* individual. **3** *(particular, personal)* personal, propio,-a. **4** *(different, unique)* personal, original.
▶ *n* **1** *(person)* individuo, persona. **2** *fam* individuo, tipo, tío,-a.

**individualism** [ɪndɪ'vɪdʒʊəlɪzªm] *n* individualismo.

**individualist** [ɪndɪ'vɪdʒʊəlɪst] *n* individualista *mf*.

**individually** [ɪndɪ'vɪdʒʊəlɪ] *adv (separately)* individualmente, por separado; *(one by one)* uno por uno.

**indivisible** [ɪndɪ'vɪzəbªl] *adj* indivisible.

**indoor** ['ɪndɔ:ʳ] *adj* **1** *(aerial, plant, photography, etc)* interior; *(clothes, etc)* de estar por casa. **2** SP *(swimming pool, running track)* cubierto,-a.

**indoors** [ɪn'dɔ:z] *adv (inside house)* dentro (de casa); *(at home)* en casa; *(inside building)* a cubierto, dentro.

**induction** [ɪn'dʌkʃªn] *n* **1** *(initiation - gen)* admisión *f*, ingreso; *(- of priest)* instalación *f*. **2** US *(recruitment)* reclutamiento. **3** *(logic)* inducción *f*.

**inductive** [ɪn'dʌktɪv] *adj* inductivo,-a.

**indulgence** [ɪn'dʌldʒªns] *n* **1** *(luxury)* (pequeño) lujo; *(bad habit)* vicio. **2** *(of desire, whim)* satisfacción *f*, complacencia; *(partaking - of food, drink)* abuso; *(of person)* consentimiento; *(of child)* mimo. **3** REL indulgencia.

**industrial** [ɪn'dʌstrɪəl] *adj* industrial.

**industrialize** [ɪn'dʌstrɪəlaɪz] *vt* industrializar.
▶ *vi* industrializarse.

**industrious** [ɪn'dʌstrɪəs] *adj (hard-working)* trabajador,-ra, laborioso,-a; *(diligent)* diligente, aplicado,-a.

**industry** ['ɪndəstrɪ] *n* **1** *(gen)* industria. **2** *fml (hard work)* diligencia.
ⓘ *pl* **industries**.

**inefficiency** [ɪnɪ'fɪʃªnsɪ] *n* **1** *(gen)* ineficacia. **2** *(of person)* incompetencia, ineficiencia, ineptitud *f*.

**inefficient** [ɪnɪ'fɪʃªnt] *adj* **1** *(gen)* ineficaz. **2** *(person)* incompetente, ineficiente, poco eficiente.

**inept** [ɪ'nept] *adj (person)* inepto,-a, incapaz; *(remark)* torpe.

**inequality** [ɪnɪ'kwɒlɪtɪ] *n* desigualdad *f*.
ⓘ *pl* inequalities.

**inequity** [ɪn'ekwɪtɪ] *n* injusticia.
ⓘ *pl* inequities.

**inertia** [ɪ'nɜ:ʃə] *n* **1** PHYS inercia. **2** *(lethargy)* inercia, letargo, apatía.

**inevitable** [ɪn'evɪtəbəl] *adj* **1** *(unavoidable)* inevitable. **2** *fam (usual)* sempiterno,-a, consabido,-a, de siempre.

**inexact** [ɪnɪg'zækt] *adj* inexacto,-a.

**inexpensive** [ɪnɪk'spensɪv] *adj* barato,-a, económico,-a.

**inexperience** [ɪnɪk'spɪərɪəns] *n* inexperiencia, falta de experiencia.

**inexpert** [ɪn'ekspɜ:t] *adj (person)* inexperto,-a (at, en).

**inexplicable** [ɪnɪk'splɪkəbəl] *adj* inexplicable.

**inexpressive** [ɪnɪk'spresɪv] *adj* inexpresivo,-a.

**infant** ['ɪnfənt] *n* **1** *(baby)* bebé *m*, niño,-a; *(at infant school)* niño,-a, párvulo,-a. **2** GB menor *mf* de edad.
COMP infant school escuela primaria.

**infanticide** [ɪn'fæntɪsaɪd] *n* **1** *(crime)* infanticidio. **2** *(person)* infanticida *mf*.

**infantry** ['ɪnfəntrɪ] *n* infantería.

**infect** [ɪn'fekt] *vt* **1** *(wound, cut, etc)* infectar; *(food, water, etc)* contaminar; *(person)* contagiar. **2** *fig (emotions)* contagiar. **3** *(poison)* envenenar.

**infection** [ɪn'fekʃən] *n* **1** *(of wound, cut, etc)* infección *f*; *(of food, water, etc)* contaminación *f*; *(with illness)* infección *f*, contagio. **2** *(disease)* infección *f*.

**infectious** [ɪn'fekʃəs] *adj* infeccioso,-a, contagioso,-a.

**inferior** [ɪn'fɪərɪər] *adj* inferior (to, a).
▶ *n* inferior *mf*.

**inferiority** [ɪnfɪərɪ'ɒrɪtɪ] *n* inferioridad *f*.

**infertility** [ɪnfə'tɪlɪtɪ] *n* esterilidad *f*.

**infidel** ['ɪnfɪdəl] *n* infiel *mf*.

❌ Infidel no significa 'infiel (con la pareja, un amigo)', que se traduce por unfaithful.

**infidelity** [ɪnfɪ'delɪtɪ] *n* infidelidad *f*.
ⓘ *pl* infidelities.

**infiltration** [ɪnfɪl'treɪʃən] *n* infiltración *f*.

**infinite** ['ɪnfɪnət] *adj (endless)* infinito,-a; *(very great)* sin límites.
▶ *n* the Infinite Dios *m*.

**infinitesimal** [ɪnfɪnɪ'tesɪməl] *adj* infinitesimal, infinitésimo,-a.

**infinitive** [ɪn'fɪnɪtɪv] *n* LING infinitivo.

**infinity** [ɪn'fɪnɪtɪ] *n* **1** *(gen)* infinidad *f*. **2** MATH infinito.

**infirmary** [ɪn'fɜ:mərɪ] *n* **1** *(hospital)* hospital *m*. **2** *(in school, etc)* enfermería.
ⓘ *pl* infirmaries.

**inflammable** [ɪn'flæməbəl] *adj* **1** inflamable. **2** *fam fig* explosivo,-a.

**inflammation** [ɪnflə'meɪʃən] *n* inflamación *f*.

**inflate** [ɪn'fleɪt] *vt* **1** inflar, hinchar. **2** *fig* inflar, hinchar, exagerar. **3** *(economy)* inflar.

**inflation** [ɪn'fleɪʃən] *n* inflación *f*.

**inflexible** [ɪn'fleksɪbəl] *adj* inflexible.

**inflict** [ɪn'flɪkt] *vt* **1** *(grief, suffering, pain)* causar (on, a); *(blow)* dar a, asestar a, propinar a; *(defeat, punishment)* infligir (on, a), imponer (on, a); *(grief, suffering, pain)* causar (on, a). **2** *fig (view, etc)* imponer (on, a).

**influence** ['ɪnflʊəns] *n (gen)* influencia.
▶ *vt (decision, etc)* influir en/sobre; *(person)* influenciar.

**influential** [ɪnflʊ'enʃəl] *adj* influyente.

**influenza** [ɪnflʊ'enzə] *n* gripe *f*.

**info** ['ɪnfəʊ] *n fam* información *f*.

**inform** [ɪn'fɔ:m] *vt* informar, notificar.

**informal** [ɪn'fɔ:məl] *adj (speech)* informal, familiar; *(discussion)* informal.

❌ Informal no significa 'informal (poco serio)', que se traduce por unreliable.

**information** [ɪnfə'meɪʃən] *n (gen)* información *f*; *(facts)* datos *mpl*.

**informative** [ɪn'fɔ:mətɪv] *adj* informativo,-a.

**infrared** [ɪnfrə'red] *adj* infrarrojo,-a.

**infrastructure** ['ɪnfrəstrʌktʃər] *n* infraestructura.

**infringe** [ɪn'frɪndʒ] *vt (law, rule, etc)* infringir, transgredir, violar; *(copyright,* *agreement, etc)* no respetar; *(liberty, rights)* violar, usurpar.

**infuriate** [ɪn'fjʊərɪeɪt] *vt* enfurecer, poner furioso,-a, sacar de quicio.

**ingenious** [ɪn'dʒiːnɪəs] *adj (person, thing)* ingenioso,-a; *(idea)* genial.

**ingenuity** [ɪndʒɪ'njuːɪtɪ] *n* ingenio, ingeniosidad *f*, inventiva.

**ingredient** [ɪn'griːdɪənt] *n* **1** CULIN ingrediente *m*. **2** *fig* componente *m*, elemento.

**inhabit** [ɪn'hæbɪt] *vt* habitar, vivir en, ocupar, poblar.

**inhabitable** [ɪn'hæbɪtəbəl] *adj* habitable.

> ☒ Inhabitable no significa 'inhabitable', que se traduce por **uninhabitable**.

**inhabitant** [ɪn'hæbɪtənt] *n* habitante *mf*.

**inhalation** [ɪnhə'leɪʃən] *n* inhalación *f*.

**inhale** [ɪn'heɪl] *vt (air)* aspirar, respirar; *(gas, vapour)* inhalar.

**inherit** [ɪn'herɪt] *vt* heredar (from, de).

**inheritance** [ɪn'herɪtəns] *n (money, property, etc)* herencia (from, de); *(succession)* sucesión *f*.

**inheritor** [ɪn'herɪtər] *n* heredero,-a.

**inhibit** [ɪn'hɪbɪt] *vt* **1** *(person)* inhibir, cohibir. **2** *(hold back - attempt)* inhibir. **3** *(prevent)* impedir, restringir.

**inhuman** [ɪn'hjuːmən] *adj* inhumano,-a.

**initial** [ɪ'nɪʃəl] *adj* inicial, primero,-a.
> ► *n* inicial *f*, letra inicial.
> ► *n pl* **initials** *(of name)* iniciales *fpl*; *(of abbreviation)* siglas *fpl*.

**initially** [ɪ'nɪʃəlɪ] *adv* al principio.

**initiate** [*(vb)* ɪ'nɪʃɪeɪt; *(n)* ɪ'nɪʃɪət] *vt* **1** *(gen)* iniciar; *(reform, plan, etc)* promover. **2** JUR entablar. **3** *(admit, introduce)* admitir (into, en).
> ► *n* iniciado,-a.

**initiative** [ɪ'nɪʃɪətɪv] *n* iniciativa.

**inject** [ɪn'dʒekt] *vt* **1** *(drug, etc)* inyectar; *(person)* poner una inyección a, pinchar. **2** *fig (new ideas, enthusiasm, etc)* infundir; *(money, resources, etc)* invertir.

**injection** [ɪn'dʒekʃən] *n* **1** inyección *f*.

**injure** ['ɪndʒər] *vt* **1** herir, lesionar, lastimar. **2** *fig (feelings)* herir; *(health, reputation, etc)* perjudicar.

**injured** ['ɪndʒəd] *adj* **1** *(hurt)* herido,-a, lesionado,-a, lastimado,-a. **2** *fig (offended - feeling)* herido,-a; *(- look, tone, etc)* ofendido,-a.
> ► *n pl* **the injured** los heridos.

**injury** ['ɪndʒərɪ] *n* **1** herida, lesión *f*. **2** *fig (to feelings, etc)* daño; *(to reputation, etc)* agravio.
> ① *pl* **injuries**.

> ☒ Injury no significa 'injuria', que se traduce por **insult**.

**injustice** [ɪn'dʒʌstɪs] *n* injusticia.

**ink** [ɪŋk] *n* tinta.
> ► *vt* entintar.

**inkblot** ['ɪŋkblɒt] *n* borrón *m*.

**inkjet printer** ['ɪŋkdʒet 'prɪntər] *n* impresora de chorro de tinta.

**inkpad** ['ɪŋkpæd] *n* tampón *m* de entintar, almohadilla.

**inland** [*(adj)* 'ɪnlənd; *(adv)* ɪn'lænd] *adj* (del) interior.
> ► *adv (travel)* tierra adentro, hacia el interior; *(live)* en el interior. COMP **Inland Revenue** GB Hacienda.

**inn** [ɪn] *n (with lodgings)* posada, fonda, mesón *m*; *(in country)* venta; *(pub)* taberna.

**innate** [ɪ'neɪt] *adj* innato,-a.

**inner** ['ɪnər] *adj* **1** *(room, region, etc)* interior; *(organization)* interno,-a. **2** *(feelings, etc)* interior, íntimo,-a.

**innocence** ['ɪnəsəns] *n* inocencia.

**innocent** ['ɪnəsənt] *adj (gen)* inocente; *(harmless)* inocuo,-a, inofensivo,-a; *(naive)* ingenuo,-a.

**innovate** ['ɪnəveɪt] *vi* innovar.

**innumerable** [ɪ'njuːmərəbəl] *adj* innumerable.

**inopportune** [ɪn'ɒpətjuːn] *adj* inoportuno,-a.

**inorganic** [ɪnɔː'gænɪk] *adj* inorgánico,-a.

**input** ['ɪnpʊt] *n (of power)* entrada; *(of money, resources)* inversión *f*; *(of data)* input *m*.
> ► *vt* COMPUT entrar, introducir.
> ① *pt & pp* **input** o **inputted**.

**inquire** [ɪnˈkwaɪəʳ] *vi fml* preguntar, informarse.

◆ **to inquire into** *vt insep* investigar.

**inquiry** [ɪnˈkwaɪʳrɪ] *n* **1** *fml (question)* pregunta. **2** *(investigation)* investigación *f*.

ⓘ *pl* inquiries.

**inquisition** [ɪnkwɪˈzɪʃ*ᵊ*n] *n* investigación *f*, inquisición *f*. COMP **the Inquisition** HIST la Inquisición *f*.

**inquisitive** ɪnkwɪˈzɪtɪv] *adj (person)* curioso,-a.

**inroads** [ˈɪnrəʊds] *n pl (raid)* incursión *f sing.*

▶ *n fig (encroachment)* intrusión *f*.

**insalubrious** [ɪnsəˈluːbrɪəs] *adj fml* insalubre.

**insane** [ɪnˈseɪn] *adj* **1** *(person)* loco,-a, demente; *(act)* insensato,-a. **2** *fam (idea, etc)* loco,-a. LOC **to go insane** volverse loco,-a.

⊠ Insane no significa 'insano', que se traduce por **unhealthy**.

**inscription** [ɪnˈskrɪpʃ*ᵊ*n] *n (gen)* inscripción *f*; *(in book)* dedicatoria.

**insect** [ˈɪnsekt] *n* insecto.

**insecticide** [ɪnˈsektɪsaɪd] *n* insecticida *m*.

**insecure** [ɪnsɪˈkjʊəʳ] *adj* inseguro,-a.

**insecurity** [ɪnsɪˈkjʊərɪtɪ] *n* inseguridad *f*.

**inseminate** [ɪnˈsemɪneɪt] *vt* inseminar.

**insensitive** [ɪnˈsensətɪv] *adj* insensible.

**insert** [(*vb*) ɪnˈsɜːt; (*n*) ˈɪnsɜːt] *vt (gen)* introducir en, meter en; *(comment, clause, paragraph, etc)* incluir (in, en), insertar (in, en); *(advertisement)* poner (in, en).

▶ *n (in book, newspaper)* encarte *m*; *(in clothing)* añadido.

**inside** [ɪnˈsaɪd] *n* **1** interior *m*, parte *f* interior. **2** *(driving on left)* la izquierda; *(driving on right)* la derecha.

▶ *adv (position)* dentro; *(movement)* adentro. LOC **inside out** del revés.

▶ *prep* dentro de.

▶ *n pl* **insides** *fam* entrañas *fpl*, tripas *fpl*.

**insight** [ˈɪnsaɪt] *n* **1** *(deep understanding, perception)* perspicacia, penetración *f*. **2** *(sudden understanding)* idea.

**insignificant** [ɪnsɪgˈnɪfɪkənt] *adj* insignificante.

**insincere** [ɪnsɪnˈsɪəʳ] *adj* poco sincero,-a, insincero,-a, falso,-a.

**insinuate** [ɪnˈsɪnjʊeɪt] *vt* **1** *(hint, suggest)* insinuar, dar a entender. **2** *(worm, install)* insinuarse (into, en).

**insist** [ɪnˈsɪst] *vt* **1** *(declare firmly)* insistir en. **2** *(demand forcefully)* exigir.

**insolence** [ˈɪnsələns] *n* insolencia.

**insolent** [ˈɪnsələnt] *adj* insolente.

**insoluble** [ɪnˈsɒljəb*ᵊ*l] *adj* **1** *(of substances)* insoluble, indisoluble. **2** *fig* sin solución, insoluble.

**insomnia** [ɪnˈsɒmnɪə] *n* insomnio.

**inspect** [ɪnˈspekt] *vt (gen)* inspeccionar, examinar, revisar.

**inspection** [ɪnˈspekʃ*ᵊ*n] *n* **1** *(gen)* inspección *f*, examen, revisión *f* **2** *(of luggage)* registro.

**inspector** [ɪnˈspektəʳ] *n (gen)* inspector,-ra; *(on train)* revisor,-ra; *(in police)* inspector,-ra de policía.

**inspiration** [ɪnspɪˈreɪʃ*ᵊ*n] *n* **1** *(gen)* inspiración *f*. **2** *fam (good idea)* genialidad *f*.

**inspire** [ɪnˈspaɪəʳ] *vt* **1** *(gen)* inspirar. **2** *(encourage)* estimular, animar, mover. **3** *(fill with - fear)* infundir; *(- confidence, respect)* inspirar.

⊠ To inspire no significa 'inspirar (aire)', que se traduce por **to breathe, to inhale.**

**install** [ɪnˈstɔːl] [also **instal**] *vt* **1** *(equipment, etc)* instalar. **2** *(person)* instalar, colocar.

**installation** [ɪnstəˈleɪʃ*ᵊ*n] *n* instalación *f*.

**installment** [ɪnˈstɔːlmənt] *n* US→ **instalment**

**instalment** [ɪnˈstɔːlmənt] *n* **1** *(of payment)* plazo. **2** *(of book, story, etc)* entrega; *(of collection)* fascículo.

**instance** [ˈɪnstᵊns] *n* ejemplo, caso. LOC **for instance** por ejemplo.

▶ *vt* poner por caso, citar como ejemplo.

⊠ Instance no significa 'instancia (formulario)', que se traduce por **form.**

**instant** [ˈɪnstᵊnt] *n* instante *m*, momento.

▶ *adj* **1** *(at once)* inmediato,-a. **2** *(coffee, etc)* instantáneo,-a. **3** *fml (urgent)* urgente. **4** COMM *(of the present month)* del corriente.

**instantly** ['ɪnstəntlɪ] *adv* al instante, inmediatamente.

**instead** [ɪn'sted] *adv* en cambio, en su lugar: *Mrs Jones couldn't do the class so I did it instead* la Señora Jones no pudo dar la clase así que yo la di en su lugar.

▶ *prep* **instead of** en vez de, en lugar de: *we should eat more fish instead of meat* deberíamos comer más pescado en lugar de carne.

**instinct** ['ɪnstɪŋkt] *n* instinto.

**instinctive** [ɪn'stɪŋktɪv] *adj* instintivo,-a.

**institute** ['ɪnstɪtjuːt] *n* **1** *(gen)* instituto, centro. **2** *(professional body)* colegio, asociación *f*; *(educational)* escuela.

▶ *vt fml (organize, establish)* instituir, establecer, fundar; *(initiate - enquiry)* iniciar, empezar; *(- proceedings)* entablar.

**institution** [ɪnstɪ'tjuːʃən] *n* **1** *(gen)* institución *f* **3** *(home)* asilo; *(asylum)* hospital *m* psiquiátrico, manicomio; *(orphanage)* orfanato.

**instruct** [ɪn'strʌkt] *vt* **1** *(teach)* instruir, enseñar; *(inform)* informar. **2** *(order)* ordenar, mandar, dar instrucciones. **3** JUR *(solicitor, barrister)* dar instrucciones a; *(jury)* instruir.

**instruction** [ɪn'strʌkʃən] *n* **1** *(teaching)* instrucción *f*, enseñanza. **2** *(order)* orden *f*, mandato.

**instructor** [ɪn'strʌktər] *n* *(gen)* instructor,-ra; *(of driving)* profesor,-ra; *(of sport)* monitor,-ra.

**instrument** ['ɪnstrəmənt] *n* instrumento.

**insufficient** [ɪnsə'fɪʃənt] *adj* insuficiente.

**insulate** ['ɪnsjəleɪt] *vt* **1** TECH aislar (against/from, de). **2** *fig (protect)* proteger (against, contra), (from, de).

**insulation** [ɪnsjə'leɪʃən] *n* TECH aislamiento.

**insulator** ['ɪnsjəleɪtər] *n* TECH aislante *m*, aislador *m*.

**insulin** ['ɪnsjəlɪn] *n* insulina.

**insult** [*(n)* 'ɪnsʌlt; *(vb)* ɪn'sʌlt] *n* insulto.

▶ *vt* insultar, ofender, injuriar.

**insurance** [ɪn'ʃuərəns] *n* **1** seguro. **2** *fig (safeguard)* salvaguarda, protección *f*, garantía.

**insure** [ɪn'ʃuər] *vt* **1** asegurar (against, contra). **2** US *(ensure)* asegurar.

**insurgent** [ɪn'sɜːdʒənt] *adj* insurgente, insurrecto,-a.

**insurrection** [ɪnsə'rekʃən] *n* insurrección *f*.

**intact** [ɪn'tækt] *adj* intacto,-a.

**intake** ['ɪnteɪk] *n* **1** *(of food, etc)* consumo; *(of breath)* inhalación *f*. **2** TECH *(of air, water)* entrada; *(of electricity, gas, water)* toma. **3** *(number of people)* número de personas inscritas.

**integer** ['ɪntɪdʒər] *n* MATH entero, número entero.

**integral** ['ɪntɪgrəl] *adj* **1** *(intrinsic, essential)* integral, esencial, fundamental. **2** *(built-in)* incorporado,-a. **3** MATH integral.

**integrity** [ɪn'tegrətɪ] *n* **1** *(honesty)* integridad *f*, honradez *f*. **2** *(completeness)* totalidad *f*.

**intellect** ['ɪntəlekt] *n* **1** *(intelligence)* intelecto, inteligencia. **2** *(person)* intelectual *mf*.

**intellectual** [ɪntə'lektjuəl] *adj* intelectual.

▶ *n* intelectual *mf*.

**intelligence** [ɪn'telɪdʒəns] *n* **1** *(gen)* inteligencia. **2** *(information)* información *f*, espionaje *m*.

**intelligent** [ɪn'telɪʒənt] *adj* inteligente.

**intend** [ɪn'tend] *vt* **1** *(plan, mean, have in mind)* tener la intención de, tener el propósito de, proponerse, pensar, querer. **2** *(destine for)* ir dirigido,-a a.

**intense** [ɪn'tens] *adj* **1** *(gen)* intenso,-a, fuerte; *(stare)* penetrante. **2** *(emotions)* profundo,-a, grande, vivo,-a. **3** *(person)* muy serio,-a.

**intensify** [ɪn'tensɪfaɪ] *vt (search, campaign)* intensificar; *(effort)* redoblar; *(production, pollution, pain)* aumentar.
ⓘ *pt & pp* intensified, *ger* intensifying.

**intensity** [ɪn'tensɪtɪ] *n* **1** intensidad *f*. **2** *(of person)* seriedad *f*.
ⓘ *pl* intensities.

**intensive** [ɪnˈtensɪv] *adj* **1** *(course, training, etc)* intensivo,-a. **2** *(search)* minucioso,-a; *(study)* profundo,-a. COMP **intensive care** cuidados *mpl* intensivos.

**intention** [ɪnˈtenʃ°n] *n* *(purpose, aim, plan, determination)* intención *f*, propósito.

**interact** [ɪntərˈækt] *vi* **1** *(people)* relacionarse, interaccionar. **2** CHEM reaccionar.

**interaction** [ɪntərˈækʃ°n] *n* interacción *f*.

**interactive** [ɪntərˈæktɪv] *adj* interactivo,-a.

**inter-city** [ɪntəˈsɪti] *adj* interurbano,-a, de largo recorrido.

**intercom** [ˈɪntəkɒm] *n* interfono.

**interconnection** [ɪntəkəˈnekʃ°n] *n* interconexión *f*.

**intercontinental** [ɪntəkɒntɪˈnent°l] *adj* intercontinental.

**intercostal** [ɪntəˈkɒst°l] *adj* intercostal.

**intercourse** [ˈɪntəkɔːs] *n* **1** *(dealings)* trato. **2** *(sexual)* coito, relaciones *fpl* sexuales.

**interest** [ˈɪntrəst] *n* **1** *(gen)* interés *m*. **2** *(hobby)* afición *f*, interés *m*. **3** *(advantage, benefit)* provecho, beneficio. **4** COMM *(share, stake)* participación *f*, interés *m*. **5** FIN *(money)* interés *m*, rédito.
▶ *vt* interesar.

**interested** [ˈɪntrəstɪd] *adj* interesado,-a (in, en).

**interesting** [ˈɪntrəstɪŋ] *adj* interesante.

**interface** [ˈɪntəfeɪs] *n* **1** COMPUT interface *f*, interfaz *f*. **2** *fig* terreno común.

**interfere** [ɪntəˈfɪəʳ] *vi* *(meddle)* entrometerse (in, en), inmiscuirse (in, en).

**interference** [ɪntəˈfɪərəns] *n* **1** *(meddling)* intromisión *f*, entrometimiento, injerencia. **2** *(with broadcast)* interferencia.

**interior** [ɪnˈtɪərɪəʳ] *adj* interior.
▶ *n* interior *m*, parte *f* interior.

**interjection** [ɪntəˈdʒekʃ°n] *n* **1** *(part of speech)* interjección *f*. **2** *(comment)* interposición *f*.

**intermediate** [ɪntəˈmiːdɪət] *adj* intermedio,-a.

**internal** [ɪnˈtɜːn°l] *adj* interno,-a.

**international** [ɪntəˈnæʃnəl] *adj* internacional.

**internationalize** [ɪntəˈnæʃnəlaɪz] *vt* internacionalizar.

**Internet** [ˈɪntənet] *n* Internet *f*.

**interpret** [ɪnˈtɜːprət] *vt* *(gen)* interpretar; *(understand)* interpretar, entender.

**interpretation** [ɪntɜːprəˈteɪʃ°n] *n* interpretación *f*.

**interpreter** [ɪnˈtɜːprətəʳ] *n* intérprete *mf*.

**interrogate** [ɪnˈterəgeɪt] *vt* interrogar.

**interrogation** [ɪnterəˈgeɪʃ°n] *n* interrogatorio.

**interrogative** [ɪntəˈrɒgəætɪv] *adj* *fml* interrogativo,-a.
▶ *n* LING *(word)* palabra interrogativa; *(phrase)* oración *f* interrogativa.

**interrupt** [ɪntəˈrʌpt] *vt* interrumpir.
▶ *vi* interrumpir.

**interruption** [ɪntəˈrʌpʃ°n] *n* interrupción *f*.

**interstate** [ˈɪntəsteɪt] *adj* *(esp us)* interestatal, entre estados.

**interval** [ˈɪntəv°l] *n* **1** *(in time, space)* intervalo (between, entre). **2** *(in play, film, etc)* intermedio, descanso; *(in play)* entreacto. **3** *(pause, break)* pausa; *(silence)* silencio; *(rest)* descanso. **4** MUS intervalo.

**intervene** [ɪntəˈviːn] *vi* **1** *(person)* intervenir (in, en). **2** *(event, etc)* sobrevenir, ocurrir. **3** *fml* *(time)* transcurrir, mediar.

☒ To intervene no significa 'intervenir (operar)', que se traduce por to operate on.

**interview** [ˈɪntəvjuː] *n* *(gen)* entrevista; *(press)* entrevista.
▶ *vt* entrevistar, hacer una entrevista a, entrevistarse con.

**interviewee** [ɪntəvjuːˈiː] *n* entrevistado,-a.

**interviewer** [ˈɪntəvjuːəʳ] *n* entrevistador,-ra.

**intervocalic** [ɪntəvəˈkælɪk] *adj* intervocálico,-a.

**intestinal** [ɪnˈtestɪn°l] *adj* intestinal.

**intestine** [ɪn'testɪn] *n* intestino. COMP
**large intestine** intestino grueso. ‖ **small
intestine** intestino delgado.

**intimate¹** ['ɪntɪmət] *adj* **1** *(gen)* íntimo,-a;
*(link, etc)* estrecho,-a. **2** *(knowledge)* profundo,-a.
▶ *n (friend)* amigo,-a íntimo,-a.

**intimate²** ['ɪntɪmeɪt] *vi fml* insinuar,
dar a entender.

☒ To intimate no significa 'intimar (conocerse mejor)', que se traduce por **to become close.**

**intimidate** [ɪn'tɪmɪdeɪt] *vt* intimidar.

**into** ['ɪntu] *prep* **1** *(indicating movement)*
en, dentro de, a; *(in direction of)* a, hacia; *(against)* contra, con. **2** *(time, age)*
hasta. **3** *(indicating change)* en, a: *he
turned water into wine* transformó el agua
en vino. **4** MATH entre: *what's four into
twenty?* ¿cuánto son veinte entre cuatro?

**intolerant** [ɪn'tɒlərənt] *adj* intolerante,
intransigente.

**intonation** [ɪntə'neɪʃ°n] *n* entonación *f.*

**intoxicate** [ɪn'tɒksɪkeɪt] *vt* **1** *fml* embriagar, emborrachar. **2** *fig* embriagar.

☒ To intoxicate no significa 'intoxicar',
que se traduce por **to poison.**

**intoxication** [ɪntɒksɪ'keɪʃ°n] *n* embria-
guez *f.*

☒ Intoxicate no significa 'intoxicación',
que se traduce por **poisoning.**

**intranet** ['ɪntrənet] *n* red *f* local.

**intransitive** [ɪn'trænsɪtɪv] *adj* LING intransitivo,-a.

**intrauterine** [ɪntrə'juːtəraɪn] *adj* MED
intrauterino,-a.

**introduce** [ɪntrə'djuːs] *vt* **1** *(person, programme)* presentar. **2** *(bring in - gen)* introducir; *(- new product, etc)* presentar,
lanzar; *(law, procedure, etc)* instituir. **3**
*(to hobby, habit)* iniciar (to, en). **4** *(bring
up)* proponer, sugerir, plantear. **5** *fml
(insert)* introducir, meter, insertar.

**introduction** [ɪntrə'dʌkʃ°n] *n* **1** *(of person,
programme)* presentación *f.* **2** *(to book,
speech, etc)* introducción *f.* **3** *(- of new
product, etc)* presentación *f,* lanzamiento; *(- of law, procedure, etc)* introducción
*f,* institución *f.* **4** *(first experience)* iniciación *f.* **5** MUS introducción *f.*

**introvert** ['ɪntrəvɜːt] *n* introvertido,-a.

**intruder** [ɪn'truːdə^r] *n* intruso,-a.

**intuition** [ɪntjuː'ɪʃ°n] *n* intuición *f.*

**intuitive** [ɪn'tjuːɪtɪv] *adj* intuitivo,-a.

**invade** [ɪn'veɪd] *vt (gen)* invadir.

**invader** [ɪn'veɪdə^r] *n* invasor,-ra.

**invalid¹** ['ɪnvəlɪd] *n (disabled person)*
inválido,-a, minusválido,-a; *(sick person)* enfermo,-a.

**invalid²** [ɪn'vælɪd] *adj (gen)* inválido,-a,
no válido,-a, nulo,-a; *(out of date)* caducado,-a.

**invalidate** [ɪn'vælɪdeɪt] *vt (result, rule,
etc)* invalidar, anular; *(argument)* refutar, demostrar el error de.

**invasion** [ɪn'veɪʒ°n] *n (gen)* invasión *f.*

**invent** [ɪn'vent] *vt* inventar, inventarse.

**invention** [ɪn'venʃ°n] *n* **1** *(gen)* invento,
invención *f;* *(lying)* invención *f,* mentira. **2** *(capacity for inventing)* inventiva.

**inventive** [ɪn'ventɪv] *adj* inventivo,-a.

**inventor** [ɪn'ventə^r] *n* inventor,-ra.

**inventory** ['ɪnvəntrɪ] *n* inventario.
ⓘ *pl* inventories.

**inversion** [ɪn'vɜːʒ°n] *n* inversión *f.*

☒ Inversion no significa 'inversión (de
dinero)', que se traduce por **investment.**

**invert** [ɪn'vɜːt] *vt* invertir. COMP **inverted commas** comillas.

☒ To invert no significa 'invertir (dinero)', que se traduce por **to invest.**

**invertebrate** [ɪn'vɜːtɪbrət] *adj* invertebrado,-a.

**invest** [ɪn'vest] *vt* **1** *(money)* invertir (in,
en). **2** *(time, effort, etc)* emplear (in, en),
invertir (in, en). **3** *fml (right, rank, power,
etc)* investir (with, con), conferir (with,
-), otorgar (with, -). **4** *fml (quality, characteristic, etc)* revestir (with, con), envolver
(with, de). **5** MIL *dated* sitiar, cercar.

**investigate** [ɪn'vestɪgeɪt] *vt (crime)* investigar; *(cause, possibility)* examinar,
estudiar.
▶ *vi fam (check)* mirar.

**investigation** [ɪnvestɪˈɡeɪʃᵊn] *n (of crime)* investigación *f* (into, sobre); *(of cause, possibility)* examen *m* (into, de), estudio (into, de).

**investigator** [ɪnˈvestɪɡeɪtəʳ] *n* investigador,-ra.

**investment** [ɪnˈvestmənt] *n* **1** *(of money)* inversión *f*. **2** *(investiture)* investidura.

**investor** [ɪnˈvestəʳ] *n* inversor,-ra, inversionista *mf*.

**invidious** [ɪnˈvɪdɪəs] *adj* **1** *(task, job, etc)* odioso,-a, ingrato,-a. **2** *(comparison, choice, etc)* injusto,-a.

> ☒ Invidious no significa 'envidioso', que se traduce por envious.

**invisible** [ɪnˈvɪzəbᵊl] *adj* invisible.

**invitation** [ɪnvɪˈteɪʃᵊn] *n* invitación *f*.

**invite** [*(vb)* ɪnˈvaɪt; *(n)* ˈɪnvaɪt] *vt* **1** *(guest, etc)* invitar, convidar; *(candidate, participant)* pedir, invitar. **2** *(comment, suggestion, etc)* solicitar. **3** *(criticism, disaster, etc)* provocar, incitar.

**invoice** [ˈɪnvɔɪs] *n* COMM factura.

**invoke** [ɪnˈvəʊk] *vt* invocar.

**involuntary** [ɪnˈvɒləntərɪ] *adj* involuntario,-a.

**involve** [ɪnˈvɒlv] *vt* **1** *(entail)* suponer, implicar, conllevar; *(give rise to)* acarrear, ocasionar. **2** *(include, affect, concern)* tener que ver con, afectar a. **3** *(implicate)* implicar, involucrar, meter.

**inward** [ˈɪnwəd] *adj* interior.
▸ *adv* hacia dentro.

**inwards** [ˈɪnwədz] *adv* hacia dentro.

**iodine** [ˈaɪədiːn] *n* yodo.

**ion** [aɪən] *n* ion *m*.

**ionize** [ˈaɪənaɪz] *vt* ionizar.

**ionosphere** [aɪˈɒnəsfɪəʳ] *n* ionosfera.

**IQ** [ˈaɪˈkjuː] *abbr* (intelligence quotient) coeficiente *m* de inteligencia; *(abbreviation)* CI *m*.

**Iran** [ɪˈrɑːn] *n* Irán.

**Iraq** [ɪˈrɑːk] *n* Irak.

**Ireland** [ˈaɪələnd] *n* Irlanda. COMP Northern Ireland Irlanda del norte.

**iris** [ˈaɪˈrɪs] *n* **1** *(of eye)* iris *m inv*. **2** BOT lirio.

**Irish** [ˈaɪrɪʃ] *adj* irlandés,-esa.

**Irishman** [ˈaɪrɪʃmən] *n* irlandés *m*.
① *pl* Irishmen [ˈaɪrɪʃmən].

**Irishwoman** [ˈaɪrɪʃwumən] *n* irlandesa.
① *pl* Irishwomen [ˈaɪrɪʃwɪmɪn].

**iron** [ˈaɪən] *n* **1** *(metal)* hierro. **2** *(appliance)* plancha. **3** *(for golf)* hierro, palo de hierro.
▸ *adj* de hierro.
▸ *vt (clothes)* planchar.
▸ *n pl* irons *(fetters)* grilletes *mpl*.
◆ to iron out *vt sep* **1** *(clothes)* planchar. **2** *fig (problem, difficulty, etc)* resolver, solucionar.

**ironing** [ˈaɪrɒnɪŋ] *n* planchado. LOC to do the ironing planchar. COMP ironing board tabla de planchar.

**ironic** [aɪˈrɒnɪk] *adj* irónico,-a.

**ironmonger** [ˈaɪənmʌŋɡəʳ] *n* GB ferretero,-a. COMP ironmonger's (shop) ferretería.

**ironmongery** [ˈaɪənmʌŋɡərɪ] *n* GB ferretería.

**irony** [ˈaɪrənɪ] *n* ironía.
① *pl* ironies.

**irregular** [ɪˈreɡjələʳ] *adj* **1** *(gen)* irregular; *(uneven)* desigual. **2** *(unusual, abnormal)* raro,-a, anormal; *(against the rules)* inadmisible. **3** *(troops)* irregular.

**irrelevant** [ɪˈrelɪvənt] *adj* **1** *(unimportant - fact, detail, etc)* irrelevante. **2** *(out of place)* que no viene al caso: *that's irrelevant* eso no tiene nada que ver, eso no viene al caso.

**irresistible** [ɪrɪˈzɪstəbᵊl] *adj* **1** *(temptation, impulse, etc)* irresistible: *an irresistible urge* un impulso irrefrenable. **2** *(person, thing)* irresistible.

**irresponsibility** [ɪrɪspɒnsəˈbɪlətɪ] *n* irresponsabilidad *f*, falta de seriedad.

**irresponsible** [ɪrɪˈspɒnsəbᵊl] *adj* irresponsable, poco serio,-a.

**irrigable** [ˈɪrɪɡəbᵊl] *adj* irrigable, regadío,-a.

**irrigate** [ˈɪrɪɡeɪt] *vt* **1** AGR regar, irrigar. **2** MED irrigar.

**irrigated** [ˈɪrɪɡeɪtɪd] *vt* **1** AGR irrigado,-a. **2** MED irrigar.

**irrigation** [ɪrɪˈɡeɪʃᵊn] *n* AGR riego, irrigación *f*. COMP irrigation channel acequia, canal *m* de riego. ❙ **irrigation farming** cultivo de regadío. ❙ **irrigation system** sistema *m* de regadío.

**irritate** ['ɪrɪteɪt] *vt* **1** *(annoy)* irritar, molestar, fastidiar. **2** MED *(cause discomfort)* irritar; *(make inflamed)* inflamar.

**irritating** ['ɪrɪteɪtɪŋ] *adj* **1** *(annoying)* irritante, molesto,-a, fastidioso,-a, pesado,-a. **2** MED irritante.

**irritation** [ɪrɪ'teɪ[ə]n] *n* **1** MED irritación *f*. **2** *(cause of annoyance)* molestia, fastidio. **3** *(anger)* mal humor *m*, enfado, irritación *f*.

**is** [ɪz] *pres* → be.

**Islam** ['ɪzlɑːm] *n* islam *m*.

**Islamic** [ɪz'læmɪk] *adj* islámico,-a.

**island** ['aɪlənd] *n* isla.
▶ *adj* isleño,-a. COMP **safety island** US isla de peatones, isleta, refugio. ❙ **traffic island** isla de peatones, isleta, refugio.

**isle** [aɪl] *n* isla.

**islet** ['aɪlət] *n* islote *m*.

**isobar** ['aɪsəbɑːʳ] *n* isobara.

**isolate** ['aɪsəleɪt] *vt* aislar (from, de): *scientists have isolated the germ* los científicos han aislado el microbio.

**isolated** ['aɪsəleɪtɪd] *adj* **1** *(solitary)* aislado,-a, apartado,-a: *an isolated house* una casa aislada; *I live a very isolated life* llevo una vida muy solitaria. **2** *(single)* aislado,-a, único,-a, excepcional: *an isolated case* un caso aislado.

**isosceles** [aɪ'spsəliːz] *adj* isósceles. COMP **isosceles triangle** triángulo isósceles.

**isotherm** ['aɪsəθɜːm] *n* isotermo.

**isotope** ['aɪsətəʊp] *n* isótopo.

**Israel** ['ɪzrɪəl] *n* Israel.

**Israeli** [ɪz'reɪlɪ] *adj* israelí.
▶ *n* israelí *mf*.

**Israelite** ['ɪzrɪəlaɪt] *adj* israelita.
▶ *n* israelita *mf*.

**issue** ['ɪʃuː] *n* **1** *(subject, topic)* tema *m*, cuestión *f*, asunto. **2** *(of newspaper, magazine, etc)* número. **3** *(of stamps, shares, back notes, etc)* emisión *f*; *(of book)* publicación *f*. **4** *(of passport, licence)* expedición *f*. **5** *(of equipment, supplies, etc)* distribución *f*, reparto, suministro.

**6** *fml (emergence - of water, blood)* flujo. **7** *fml (children)* descendencia. **8** *fml (result, outcome)* resultado, consecuencia, desenlace *m*.
▶ *vt* **1** *(book, article)* publicar. **2** *(stamps, shares, banknotes, etc)* emitir. **3** *(passport, visa)* expedir. **4** *(equipment, supplies, etc)* distribuir, repartir, suministrar, proporcionar. **5** *(order, instruction)* dar; *(statement, warning)* dar, hacer público; *(writ, summons)* dictar, expedir; *(decree)* promulgar; *(warrant)* expedir.
▶ *vi* **1** *fml (liquid, blood)* fluir, manar; *(smell, etc)* salir. **2** *fml (result)* resultar (from, de), provenir (from, de), derivar(se) (from, de).

**isthmus** ['ɪsməs] *n* istmo.

**it** [ɪt] *pron* **1** *(subject)* él, ella, ello: *where's my supper? it's in the oven!* ¿dónde está mi cena? ¡está en el horno!; *whose is this coat? it's mine!* ¿de quién es este abrigo? ¡es mío!; *is it a boy or a girl?* ¿es niño o niña?; *who's that? who is it? it's me!* ¿quién eres? ¿quién es? ¡soy yo! **2** *(object - direct)* lo, la; *(- indirect)* le: *I doubt it* lo dudo; *I've just got this letter. Can you read it for me?* acabo de recibir esta carta. ¿Me la puedes leer?; *do you like skiing? yes, I love it* ¿te gusta esquiar? sí, me encanta; *she went up to the horse and patted it* se acercó al caballo y lo acarició; *can you manage that bag? Give it to me* ¿puedes con esa bolsa? Dámela. **3** *(after prep)* él, ella, ello: *a vase with flowers in it* un florero con flores dentro; *the train was still there so I ran for it* el tren aún estaba allí así que corrí para cogerlo; *you're not frightened of it, are you?* no le tienes miedo, ¿verdad?; *tell me about it* explícamelo, cuéntamelo. **4** *(abstract)* ello: *let's get on with it* vamos a por ello. **5** *(impersonal)* no se traduce: *it's cold* hace frío; *it's too early* es demasiado temprano; *it's six o'clock* son las seis; *it's Wednesday* es miércoles; *it's cloudy* está nublado; *it's not far* no está lejos; *it's impossible* es imposible; *it's important* es importante; *it's worth it* vale la pena; *it doesn't matter* no importa; *what's it like?* ¿cómo es?; *it cost a fiver* costó cinco libras; *it's true* es verdad; *it seems (that) she failed* parece que suspendió.

**Italian** [ɪˈtælɪən] *adj* italiano,-a.
► *n* **1** *(person)* italiano,-a. **2** *(language)* italiano.

**italic** [ɪˈtælɪks] *adj* (letra) cursiva.

**itch** [ɪtʃ] *n* **1** MED picazón *f*, picor *m*. **2** *fam fig (strong desire)* deseo, anhelo, ansia: *an itch to travel* un deseo de viajar.
► *vi* picar: *my feet itch* me pican los pies; *I'm itching all over* me pica todo; *this blanket itches* esta manta pica.

**it'd** [ˈɪtəd] *contr* **1** it had. **2** it would.

**item** [ˈaɪtəm] *n* **1** *(on list)* artículo, cosa; *(in collection)* pieza. **2** *(on agenda)* asunto, punto. **3** *(on bill)* partida, asiento. **4** *(in show)* número. COMP **item of clothing** prenda de vestir.
► *adv* también.

**itinerary** [aɪˈtɪnəˈrərɪ] *n* itinerario, ruta.
ⓘ *pl* itineraries.

**it'll** [ˈɪtəl] *contr* it will.

**its** [ɪts] *adj* *(one thing)* su; *(more than one thing)* sus: *the cat cleaned its paws* el gato se limpió las patas; *the baby's in its pram* el bebé está en su cochecito; *the film has its good points* la película tiene sus puntos buenos.

**it's** [ɪts] *contr* **1** → it is. **2** → it has.

**itself** [ɪtˈself] *pron* **1** *(reflexive)* se: *the bird preened itself* el pájaro se arregló las plumas; *Barcelona has opened itself up to the sea* Barcelona se ha abierto al mar. **2** *(emphatic)* en sí: *the house itself is quite old* la casa en sí es bastante vieja; *the job itself isn't that difficult* el trabajo en sí no es muy difícil; *she is politeness itself* es la cortesía personificada. **3** *(after prep)* sí: *the committee wants to keep all the profits for itself* el comité quiere guardar todos los beneficios para sí; *each dog has a kennel to itself* cada perro tiene su propia casita; *the idea in itself isn't bad* la idea en sí no está mal; *the first course was a meal in itself* el primer plato ya era una comida de por sí. LOC **by itself** solo,-a: *it switches off by itself* se apaga solo, se apaga automáticamente; *the baby did it all by itself* el niño lo hizo él solo.

**I've** [aɪv] *contr* I have.

**ivory** [ˈaɪvərɪ] *n (substance)* marfil *m*; *(colour)* color *m* marfil.
► *adj* de marfil.
► *n pl* **ivories** *(objects)* objetos *mpl* de marfil; *(piano keys)* teclas *fpl*. LOC **an ivory tower** una torre de marfil. COMP **Ivory Coast** Costa de Marfil.

**ivy** [ˈaɪvɪ] *n* hiedra, yedra. COMP **Ivy League** *ocho prestigiosas universidades privadas del nordeste de los Estados Unidos.*

⊕ La Ivy League reúne a las ocho universidades más prestigiosas de Estados Unidos que, además, son de las más antiguas. Un título de cualquiera de estos centros suele ser sinónimo de una excelente formación académica.

# J

**J, J** [dʒeɪ] *n (the letter)* J, j *f.*

**jab** [dʒæb] *n* **1** pinchazo; *(with elbow)* codazo. **2** *fam (of pain)* pinchazo: *a flu jab* una inyección contra la gripe. **3** *(in boxing)* gancho.
▶ *vt* pinchar; *(with elbow)* dar un codazo a.
ⓘ *pt & pp* jabbed, *ger* jabbing.

**jack** [dʒæk] *n* **1** AUTO gato. **2** *(in cards)* jota; *(Spanish pack)* sota. **3** *(in bowls)* boliche *m*. **4** ELEC enchufe *m*. COMP **jack plug** ELEC jack *m*, clavija.

**jackal** ['dʒækɔːl] *n* chacal *m*.

**jacket** ['dʒækɪt] *n* **1** *(in general)* chaqueta; *(of suit)* americana; *(leather, etc)* cazadora. **2** *(of book)* sobrecubierta. **3** US *(of record)* funda. COMP **jacket potato** patata asada *(con su piel)*.

**jackknife** ['dʒæknaɪf] *n* navaja.

**jackpot** ['dʒækpɒt] *n* (premio) gordo. LOC **to hit the jackpot** tocarle a ALGN el gordo.

**Jacuzzi®** [dʒə'kuːzɪ] *n* jacuzzi® *m*.

**jade** [dʒeɪd] *n* jade *m*.

**jagged** ['dʒægɪd] *adj* irregular, dentado,-a.

**jaguar** ['dʒægjʊəʳ] *n* jaguar *m*.

**jail** [dʒeɪl] *n* cárcel *f*, prisión *f*.
▶ *vt* encarcelar: *he was jailed for life* lo condenaron a cadena perpetua.

**jailer** ['dʒeɪləʳ] *n* carcelero,-a.

**jailhouse** ['dʒeɪlhaʊs] *n* US cárcel *f*.

**jam¹** [dʒæm] *n* mermelada, confitura. COMP **jam jar** bote *m* de mermelada.

**jam²** [dʒæm] *n (tight spot)* aprieto, apuro. LOC **to get into a jam** meterse en un apuro. COMP **jam session** sesión improvisada de jazz o rock.

▶ *vt* **1** *(fill)* abarrotar, atestar: *thousands of people jammed the streets* miles de personas abarrotaban las calles. **2** *(cram)* embutir, meter a la fuerza: *she jammed all her things into the bag* embutió todas sus cosas en la bolsa. **3** *(block)* bloquear: *the switchboard was jammed with calls of complaint* las llamadas de protesta bloquearon la centralita.
ⓘ *pt & pp* jammed, *ger* jarring.

**Jamaica** [dʒə'meɪkə] *n* Jamaica.

**Jamaican** [dʒə'meɪkⁿn] *adj* jamaicano,-a.
▶ *n* jamaicano,-a.

**jangle** ['dʒæŋgⁿl] *vi* sonar de un modo discordante.
▶ *vt* hacer sonar de un modo discordante.
▶ *n* sonido discordante.

**January** ['dʒænjʊərɪ] *n* enero.

✎ Para ejemplos de usos, consulta May.

**Japan** [dʒə'pæn] *n* (el) Japón *m*.

**Japanese** [dʒæpə'niːz] *adj* japonés,-esa.
▶ *n* **1** *(person)* japonés,-esa. **2** *(language)* japonés *m*.

**jar** [dʒɑːʳ] *n* **1** *(glass)* tarro, bote *m*: *a jar of strawberry jam* un tarro de mermelada de fresa. **2** *(earthenware)* vasija, tinaja. **3** *(shake, shock)* sacudida: *it gave me a bit of a jar* me chocó bastante. **4** *fam (drink)* copa: *let's go and have a few jars!* ¡vamos a tomar unas copas!

**jargon** ['dʒɑːgⁿn] *n* jerga, jerigonza.

**jasmine** ['dʒæzmɪn] *n* jazmín *m*.

**jaundice** ['dʒɔːndɪs] *n* ictericia.

**jaunty** ['dʒɔːntɪ] *adj* garboso,-a.
ⓘ *comp* jauntier, *superl* jauntiest.

**javelin** ['dʒævⁿlɪn] *n* jabalina. LOC **to throw the javelin** lanzar la jabalina.

COMP **javelin competition** lanzamiento de jabalina.

**jaw** [dʒɔ:] n **1** ANAT mandíbula. COMP **upper jaw** maxilar m superior. I **lower jaw** maxilar m inferior. **2** ZOOL mandíbula, quijada, carrillera.
▶ vi fam (talk) charlar.

**jazz** [dʒæz] n jazz m. LOC **and all that jazz** y demás, y toda la pesca, y todo el rollo.
▶ adj de jazz, jazzístico,-a. COMP **jazz band** conjunto de jazz.
◆ **to jazz up** vt sep (in general) hacer más alegre, dar vida a; (party) animar.

**jealous** ['dʒeləs] adj **1** celoso,-a. **2** (envious) envidioso,-a. LOC **to be jealous of** SB tener celos de ALGN, estar celoso,-a de ALGN. I **to make** SB **jealous** poner celoso,-a a ALGN.

**jealousy** ['dʒeləsɪ] n **1** celos mpl. **2** (envy) envidia.
ⓘ pl jealousies.

**jeans** [dʒi:nz] n pl vaqueros mpl, tejanos mpl.

**jeep®** [dʒi:p] n jeep® m, todoterreno.

**jeer** [dʒɪəʳ] vi (mock) burlarse (at, de), mofarse (at, de).
▶ vt (boo) abuchear.
▶ vi (boo) abuchear.
▶ n pl **jeers** (booing) abucheos mpl; (mocking) burlas fpl, mofas fpl, befas fpl.

**jelly** ['dʒelɪ] n **1** (in general) jalea. **2** (fruit) gelatina.
ⓘ pl jellies.

**jellyfish** ['dʒelɪfɪʃ] n medusa.
ⓘ pl jellyfishes.

**jeopardy** ['dʒepədɪ] n peligro. LOC **to be in jeopardy** estar en peligro, peligrar. I **to put in jeopardy** poner en peligro, hacer peligrar.

**jerk** [dʒɜ:k] n **1** (pull) tirón m; (jolt) sacudida. **2** fam imbécil mf, subnormal mf. LOC **with a jerk** bruscamente.
▶ vt dar una sacudida a, tirar de.
▶ vi dar una sacudida.

**jerrycan** ['dʒerɪkæn] n bidón m.

**jersey** ['dʒɜ:zɪ] n jersey m, suéter m.

**jest** [dʒest] n broma. LOC **in jest** en broma.
▶ vi bromear.

**jester** ['dʒestəʳ] n HIST bufón m.

**Jesus** ['dʒi:zəs] n Jesús m, Jesucristo.
COMP **Jesus Christ** Jesucristo.

**jet** [dʒet] n **1** (aircraft) reactor m. **2** (stream) chorro. **3** (outlet) boquilla, mechero. COMP **jet engine** reactor m, propulsor m a chorro. I **jet foil** deslizador m. I **jet lag** jet lag m, desarreglo horario. I **jet set** la jet set f, la jet f. I **jet propulsion** propulsión f a chorro.

**jetty** ['dʒetɪ] n (stone) malecón m; (wooden) embarcadero.
ⓘ pl jetties.

**Jew** [dʒu:] n REL judío,-a.

**jewel** ['dʒu:əl] n **1** joya, alhaja. **2** (stone) piedra preciosa. **3** (in watch) rubí m.

**jewelled** ['dʒu:əld] adj adornado,-a con piedras preciosas.

**jeweller** ['dʒu:ələʳ] n joyero,-a.

**jewellery** ['dʒu:əlrɪ] n joyas fpl.

**Jewish** ['dʒu:ɪʃ] adj judío,-a.

**jigsaw** ['dʒɪgsɔ:] n **1** (saw) sierra de vaivén. **2** (puzzle) rompecabezas m, puzzle m.

**jingle** ['dʒɪŋgəl] n **1** tintineo. **2** TV tonadilla publicitaria.
▶ vi tintinear.
▶ vt hacer sonar.

**jinx** [dʒɪŋks] n **1** (person) gafe mf. **2** (bad luck) mala suerte f: there's a jinx on this computer este ordenador está gafado.
▶ vt gafar.

**job** [dʒɒb] n **1** (employment) empleo, (puesto de) trabajo: what's your job? ¿en qué trabajas? **2** (piece of work) trabajo; (task) tarea: he did a good job (of work) hizo un buen trabajo. LOC **it's a good job that ...** menos mal que... I **on the job** trabajando. I **out of a job** parado, -a. I **to make the best of a bad job** poner a mal tiempo buena cara. COMP **job centre** oficina de empleo. I **job hunting** búsqueda de trabajo.

**jobless** ['dʒɒbləs] adj parado,-a.

**jockey** ['dʒɒkɪ] n jockey m.

**jog** [dʒɒg] n **1** (push) empujoncito, sacudida. **2** (pace) trote m.
▶ vt empujar, sacudir.

▶ *vi* hacer footing. LOC **at a jog trot** a trote corto. ▌ **to go for a jog** (ir a) hacer footing.

◆ **to jog along** *vi* **1** andar a trote corto. **2** *fig* ir tirando.

ⓘ *pt & pp* **jogged**, *ger* **jogging**.

**jogging** ['dʒɒgɪŋ] *n* footing *m*. LOC **to go jogging** hacer footing.

**join** [dʒɔɪn] *vt* **1** (*bring together*) juntar, unir. **2** (*connect*) unir, conectar: *the two cities are joined by a bridge* las dos ciudades están unidas por un puente. **3** (*company, etc*) incorporarse a: *Mr Osuna joined the company last year* el Sr Osuna se incorporó a la empresa el año pasado. **4** (*armed forces*) alistarse en; (*police*) ingresar en. **5** (*club*) hacerse socio,-a de. **6** (*party*) afiliarse a, ingresar en. **7** (*be with sb*) reunirse con, unirse a: *would you like to join us for the evening?* ¿les gustaría pasar la tarde con nosotros? LOC **join the club!** ¡ya somos dos *etc*! ▌ **to join forces** aunar esfuerzos. ▌ **to join hands** cogerse de las manos.

▶ *vi* **1** juntarse, unirse. **2** (*rivers*) confluir; (*roads*) juntarse, empalmar.

◆ **to join in** *vi* participar.

▶ *vt insep* (*debate*) intervenir en.

◆ **to join up** *vi* alistarse.

**joiner** ['dʒɔɪnəʳ] *n* carpintero *que se dedica a puertas, ventanas, etc*.

**joint** [dʒɔɪnt] *n* **1** junta, unión *f*. **2** ANAT articulación *f*. **3** *sl* (*drugs*) porro. LOC **to put out of joint** (*elbow, shoulder, etc*) dislocar: *she put her shoulder out of joint* se dislocó el hombro.

▶ *adj* colectivo,-a, mutuo,-a. COMP **joint account** cuenta conjunta, cuenta indistinta. ▌ **joint owner** copropietario,-a.

▶ *vt* CULIN descuartizar.

**jointed** ['dʒɔɪntɪd] *adj* **1** articulado,-a. **2** (*chicken, etc*) cortado,-a a piezas.

**jointly** ['dʒɔɪntlɪ] *adv* conjuntamente.

**joke** [dʒəʊk] *n* **1** chiste *m*: *shall I tell you a joke?* ¿te cuento un chiste? **2** (*practical*) broma: *John can't take a joke* John no aguanta una broma. **3** (*person*) payaso. LOC **to make a joke of** STH reírse de ALGO. ▌ **to play a joke on** SB gastar una

broma a ALGN. ▌ **to tell a joke** contar un chiste.

▶ *vi* bromear. LOC **you must be joking!** ¡venga ya!

**joker** ['dʒəʊkəʳ] *n* **1** bromista *mf*: *some joker put salt in the sugar* algún gracioso ha puesto sal en el azúcar. **2** (*card*) comodín *m*. **3** *fam* idiota *mf*. COMP **the joker in the pack** un elemento desconocido.

**jolly** ['dʒɒlɪ] *adj* (*cheerful*) alegre, animado,-a: *she was a very jolly person* era una persona muy animada.

ⓘ *comp* **jollier**, *superl* **jolliest**.

▶ *adv* GB *fam* muy: *it's jolly difficult* es la mar de difícil; *they played jolly well* jugaron fenomenal.

◆ **to jolly along** *vt sep* dar ánimos a, animar.

ⓘ *pt & pp* **jollied**, *ger* **jollying**.

**jolt** [dʒəʊlt] *n* **1** sacudida. **2** (*fright*) susto.

▶ *vt* sacudir.

▶ *vi* dar tumbos.

**Jordan** ['dʒɔːdən] *n* **1** (*country*) Jordania.

**Jordanian** [dʒɔːˈdeɪnɪən] *adj* jordano,-a.

▶ *n* jordano,-a.

**jot** [dʒɒt] *n* pizca: *there isn't a jot of truth in it* no hay pizca de verdad en esto; *I don't care a jot* me importa un bledo.

▶ *vt* apuntar, anotar.

◆ **to jot down** *vt sep* apuntar.

ⓘ *pt & pp* **jotted**, *ger* **jotting**.

**joule** [dʒuːl] *n* julio.

**journal** ['dʒɜːnəl] *n* **1** (*magazine*) revista. **2** (*diary*) diario.

**journalism** ['dʒɜːnəlɪzəm] *n* periodismo.

**journalist** ['dʒɜːnəlɪst] *n* periodista *mf*.

**journey** ['dʒɜːnɪ] *n* viaje *m*: *it's a 100 mile journey* es un viaje de 100 millas.

▶ *vi* viajar.

**joy** [dʒɔɪ] *n* **1** alegría, júbilo: *her face was a picture of joy* estaba radiante de alegría; *he's a joy to work with* da gusto trabajar con él. **2** *fam* (*satisfaction*) satisfacción *f*; (*luck*) suerte *f*; (*success*) éxito: *you can complain all you like, but you'll get no joy* quéjate todo lo que quieras, pero no te servirá de nada.

**joyful** ['dʒɔɪfʊl] *adj* jubiloso,-a, alegre.

**joystick** ['dʒɔɪstɪk] *n* **1** AV palanca de mando. **2** COMPUT joystick *m*.

**jubilation** [dʒu:bɪ'leɪ(ə)n] *n* júbilo.

☒ Jubilation no significa 'jubilación', que se traduce por retirement.

**jubilee** ['dʒu:bɪli:] *n* **1** festejos *mpl*. **2** *(anniversary)* aniversario.

**Judaism** ['dʒu:deɪɪzəm] *n* judaísmo.
► *n* vibración *f (violenta)*.

**judge** [dʒʌdʒ] *n* **1** *(man)* juez *m*; *(woman)* juez *f*, jueza. **2** *(in competition)* jurado, miembro del jurado.
► *vt* **1** *(court case)* juzgar. **2** *(calculate)* calcular: *it's hard to judge how much we need* es difícil juzgar cuánto necesitamos.

**judgement** ['dʒʌdʒmənt] [también se escribe judgment.] *n* **1** *(ability)* (buen) juicio, (buen) criterio. **2** *(opinion)* juicio, opinión *f*: *my personal judgement is that...* mi opinión es que ...; *in my judgement...* a mi juicio... **3** *(decision)* fallo. **4** *(criticism)* crítica.

**judicial** [dʒu:'dɪʃ(ə)l] *adj* judicial. COMP judicial inquiry investigación *f* judicial.

**judo** ['dʒu:dəʊ] *n* yudo, judo.

**jug** [dʒʌg] *n* **1** jarra, jarro. **2** *sl (prison)* chirona.

**juggle** ['dʒʌg(ə)l] *vi* **1** hacer juegos malabares (with, con). **2** *fig (figures, etc)* jugar (with, con).

**juggler** ['dʒʌg(ə)ləʳ] *n* malabarista *mf*.

**jugular** ['dʒʌgjələʳ] *adj* yugular. COMP jugular vein vena yugular.
► *n* yugular *f*. LOC to go for the jugular saltarle a ALGN a la yugular.

**juice** [dʒu:s] *n* **1** *(gen)* jugo. **2** *(of fruit)* zumo, AM jugo. **3** *fam (petrol)* gasolina; *(electricity)* fuerza, luz *f*. COMP juice extractor licuadora.

**juicy** ['dʒu:sɪ] *adj* **1** jugoso,-a. **2** *fam (gossip, etc)* picante, escabroso,-a.
ⓘ *comp* juicier, *superl* juiciest.

**jukebox** ['dʒu:kbɒks] *n* máquina de discos.

**July** [dʒu:'laɪ] *n* julio.

✎ Para ejemplos de usos, consulta May.

**jumble** ['dʒʌmb(ə)l] *n* revoltijo, mezcolanza. COMP jumble sale rastrillo benéfico.
► *vt* desordenar.

**jumbo** ['dʒʌmbəʊ] *adj* gigante.
► *n* [Also jumbo jet.] *(plane)* jumbo.

**jump** [dʒʌmp] *n* **1** salto: *a parachute jump* un salto en paracaídas. **2** *(in prices, etc)* salto, aumento importante, disparo: *there's been a tremendous jump in profits* ha habido un aumento importante de los beneficios. **3** *(fence)* valla, obstáculo: *the horse refused at the first jump* el caballo se plantó en el primer obstáculo. COMP jump seat asiento plegable. ‖ jump suit mono.
► *vi* **1** saltar. **2** *(rise sharply)* dar un salto: *inflation jumped 2% last month* la inflación dio un salto de un 2% el mes pasado. LOC to jump to conclusions llegar a conclusiones precipitadas.
► *vt* saltar: *he tried to jump the wall, but it was too high* intentó saltar el muro, pero era demasiado alto. LOC to jump rope US saltar a la comba. ‖ to jump the gun precipitarse, adelantarse. ‖ to jump the lights saltarse el semáforo en rojo. ‖ to jump the queue colarse.
◆ to jump at *vt insep* aceptar sin pensarlo: *when they offered him the job, he jumped at it* cuando le ofrecieron el trabajo lo aceptó sin pensar.

**jumper**[1] ['dʒʌmpəʳ] *n* **1** GB jersey *m*. **2** US *(dress)* pichi *m*.

**jumper**[2] ['dʒʌmpəʳ] *n* SP saltador,-ra.

**junction** ['dʒʌŋkʃ(ə)n] *n* **1** *(railways)* empalme *m*. **2** *(roads)* cruce *m*. **3** *(motorway - entry)* acceso; *(- exit)* salida.

**June** [dʒu:n] *n* junio.

✎ Para ejemplos de usos, consulta May.

**jungle** ['dʒʌŋg(ə)l] *n* selva, jungla.

**junior** ['dʒu:nɪəʳ] *adj* **1** *(in rank)* subalterno,-a. **2** *(in age)* menor, más joven. **3** US *(after name)* hijo.
► *n* **1** *(in rank)* subalterno,-a. **2** *(in age)* menor *mf*: *she is three years my junior* tiene tres años menos que yo. **3** GB alumno,-a de EGB. **4** US hijo: *where's your mom, Junior?* ¿dónde está tu mamá,

hijo? COMP **junior college** US *colegio universitario para los dos primeros cursos.* I **junior high school** US instituto de enseñanza secundaria. I **junior school** GB escuela primaria.

**junk** [dʒʌŋk] *n* trastos *mpl.* COMP **junk food** comida basura. I **junk mail** correo basura. I **junk shop** chamarilería.

**Jupiter** ['dʒuːpɪtəʳ] *n* Júpiter *m.*

**Jurassic** [dʒuˈræsɪk] *adj* jurásico,-a.

**jury** ['dʒʊərɪ] *n* jurado.
ⓘ *pl* **juries.**

**just¹** [dʒʌst] *adj* **1** *(fair)* justo,-a. **2** *(justifiable)* fundado,-a, justificado,-a. **3** *(deserved)* merecido,-a. LOC **to get one's just desserts** llevar su merecido.

**just²** [dʒʌst] *adv* **1** *(exactly)* exactamente, precisamente, justo: *this is just what I needed* esto es justo lo que necesitaba. **2** *(only)* solamente, solo: *no sugar for me, please, just milk* no quiero azúcar, gracias, solo leche. **3** *(barely)* apenas, por poco: *I ran all the way and (only) just caught the bus* fui corriendo y cogí el autobús por poco. **4** *(right now)* en este momento: *I'm just finishing it* lo acabo ahora mismo. **5** *(simply)* sencillamente:

*we could just stay here and wait for her* pues, sencillamente podríamos quedarnos aquí y esperarla. **6** *(for emphasis)*: *he's just as clever as you are* él es tan inteligente como tú. **7** *(used to interrupt)*: *just shut up, will you?* ¡cállese, por favor! **8** *fam (really)* realmente, verdaderamente: *the weather's just marvellous* hace un tiempo realmente maravilloso. LOC **just about** prácticamente. I **just in case** por si acaso. I **just like that!** ¡sin más! I **just so 1** *(tidy)* ordenado,-a, arreglado,-a. **2** *(as a reply)* sí, exactamente. I **just then** en ese momento. I **just the same 1** *(not different)* exactamente igual. **2** *(nevertheless)* sin embargo, no obstante.

▶ *phr* **to have just + pres part** acabar de + *infin*: *he has just telephoned* acaba de telefonear.

**justice** ['dʒʌstɪs] *n* **1** justicia. **2** *(judge-man)* juez *m*; *(- woman)* juez *f*, jueza. LOC **to bring to justice** llevar ante los tribunales. I **to do justice to** SB hacer justicia a ALGN.

**justify** ['dʒʌstɪfaɪ] *vt* justificar.
ⓘ *pt & pp* **justified,** *ger* **justifying.**

# K

**K, k** [keɪ] *n (the letter)* K, k *f.*

**kaleidoscope** [kəˈlaɪdəskəʊp] *n* calidoscopio.

**kangaroo** [kæŋgəˈruː] *n* canguro.
ⓘ *pl* kangaroos.

**karaoke** [kærɪˈəʊkɪ] *n* karaoke *m.*

**karate** [kəˈrɑːtɪ] *n* kárate *m.*

**karstic** [ˈkɑːstɪk] *adj* kárstico,-a.

**Kazakh** [kæˈzæk] *adj* kazajio,-a.
▶ *n* **1** *(person)* kazajio,-a. **2** *(language)* kazajio.

**Kazakhstan** [kæzækˈstæn] *n* Kazajstán.

**keen** [kiːn] *adj* **1** *(eager)* entusiasta, aficionado,-a: *he's a very keen pupil* es un alumno muy entusiasta. **2** *(sharp - mind, senses, etc)* agudo,-a, vivo,-a; *(- look)* penetrante; *(- wind)* cortante; *(- edge, point)* afilado,-a. **3** *(feeling)* profundo, -a, intenso,-a. **4** *(competition)* fuerte, reñido,-a. **5** *(price)* competitivo,-a.
ᴸᴼᶜ **to be keen on** sᴛʜ ser aficionado,-a a ᴀʟɢᴏ, gustarle ᴀʟɢᴏ a ᴀʟɢɴ. ▌**to be keen on** sʙ gustarle ᴀʟɢɴ a ᴀʟɢɴ. ▌**to take a keen interest in** mostrar un gran interés por.

**keep** [kiːp] *n* **1** *(board)* sustento, mantenimiento: *to earn one's keep* ganarse el pan. **2** *(of castle)* torreón *m*, torre *f* del homenaje.
▶ *vt* **1** *(not throw away)* guardar. **2** *(not give back)* quedarse con: *keep the change* quédese con el cambio. **3** *(have)* tener; *(carry)* llevar. **4** *(look after, save)* guardar: *can you keep me a loaf of bread for Friday?* ¿me guarda una barra de pan para el viernes?. **5** *(put away, store)* guardar: *where do you keep the glasses?* ¿dónde guardas los vasos? **6** *(secret)* guardar: *can you keep a secret?* ¿sabes guardar un secreto? **7** *(with adj, verb, etc)* mantener:

*these doors must be kept locked* estas puertas deben mantenerse cerradas.
▶ *vi* **1** *(do repeatedly)* no dejar de; *(do continuously)* seguir, continuar: *she was exhausted but kept swimming* estaba agotada pero siguió nadando. **2** *(stay fresh)* conservarse. **3** *(continue in direction)* continuar, seguir: *keep left/right* circula por la izquierda/derecha. **4** *(with adj, verb, etc)* quedarse, permanecer: *we must keep calm* debemos mantener la calma. ᴸᴼᶜ **to keep going** seguir (adelante). ▌**to keep one's head** no perder la cabeza. ▌**to keep quiet** callarse, no hacer ruido. ▌**to keep** sʙ **from doing** sᴛʜ impedir que ᴀʟɢɴ haga ᴀʟɢᴏ. ▌**to keep** sᴛʜ **from** sʙ ocultar ᴀʟɢᴏ a ᴀʟɢɴ.
◆ **to keep off** *vi (stay away)* mantenerse a distancia; *(of rain)* no llover: *if the rain keeps off, we'll be able to play tennis* si no llueve, podremos jugar a tenis.
▶ *vt sep (make stay away)* no dejar entrar, no dejar acercarse; *(avoid)* no tocar, no hablar de: *"Keep off the grass"* «No pisar la hierba».
◆ **to keep out** *vt sep* no dejar entrar, no dejar pasar.
▶ *vi* no entrar.
◆ **to keep up** *vt sep* **1** *(gen)* mantener, seguir. **2** *(from sleeping)* mantener despierto,-a, tener en vela.
▶ *vi* **1** *(not fall behind)* aguantar el ritmo. **2** *(stay in touch)* mantenerse al día.
ⓘ *pt & pp* **kept** [kept].

**keeper** [ˈkiːpəʳ] *n* **1** *(in zoo)* guardián, -ana. **2** *(in park)* guarda *mf.* **3** *(in museum)* conservador,-ra; *(in archives)* archivador,-ra.

**kennel** [ˈkenəl] *n* caseta del perros.
▶ *n pl* **kennels** *(boarding)* residencia *f sing* canina.

**Kenya** [ˈkenjə] *n* Kenia.

**Kenyan** [ˈkenjən] *adj* keniano,-a.
  ▶ *n* keniano,-a.

**kerb** [kɜːb] *n* bordillo.

**kept** [kept] *pt & pp* → **keep**.

**kernel** [ˈkɜːnəl] *n* **1** *(of nut, fruit)* semilla.
  **2** *fig* núcleo, grano.

**kerosene** [ˈkerəsiːn] *n* US queroseno.

**ketchup** [ˈketʃəp] *n* ketchup *m*, catsup *m*.

**kettle** [ˈketəl] *n* tetera *(para hervir agua)*:
  *will you put the kettle on to make some tea?*
  ¿quieres poner el agua a hervir para hacer té? [LOC] *that's a different kettle of*
  *fish* eso es harina de otro costal.

**key** [kiː] *n* **1** *(of door, car, etc)* llave *f*. **2** *(of*
  *clock, mechanical)* llave *f*. **3** *fig (to problem,*
  *map, code)* clave *f*; *(to exercises)* respuestas *fpl*. **4** *(on computer, piano, etc)* tecla. **5**
  MUS *(on wind instrument)* llave *f*, pistón
  *m*; *(set of notes)* clave *f*; *(tone, style)* tono.
  ▶ *adj* clave, principal: *tourism is the*
  *country's key industry* el turismo es la industria principal del país. [COMP] **key ring**
  llavero.
  ◆ **to key in** *vt sep* introducir, teclear:
  *she keyed in the data* introdujo los datos.

**keyboard** [ˈkiːbɔːd] *n* teclado. [COMP]
  **keyboard player** teclista *mf*.
  ▶ *n pl* **keyboards** teclados *mpl*.

**keyhole** [ˈkiːhəʊl] *n* ojo de la cerradura.

**khaki** [ˈkɑːkɪ] *n* caqui *m*.
  ▶ *adj* caqui.

**kick** [kɪk] *n* **1** *(by person)* puntapié *m*, patada. **2** SP golpe *m*, tiro. **3** *(by animal)*
  coz *f*. **4** *fam (pleasure)* diversión *f*, emoción *f*: *he gets a kick out of playing basketball* se divierte jugando al baloncesto.
  ▶ *vt* **1** *(hit ball)* dar un puntapié a, golpear con el pie; *(score)* marcar. **2** *(hit*
  *person)* dar una patada a; *(move legs)* patalear. **3** *(by animal)* dar coces a, cocear.
  ◆ **to kick off** *vi* SP sacar, hacer el saque
  inicial; *(begin)* empezar, comenzar.
  ▶ *vt sep* **1** *(begin)* empezar, comenzar,
  iniciar. **2** *(remove - shoes)* quitarse.
  ◆ **to kick out** *vt sep* echar.

**kick-off** [ˈkɪkɒf] *n* SP saque *m* inicial.

**kid¹** [kɪd] *n* **1** *fam* crío,-a, niño,-a, chico,-a, chaval,-la. **2** *(animal)* cabrito. **3**
  *(leather)* cabritilla. [LOC] **to treat SB with**

**kid gloves** tratar a ALGN con guantes
  de seda.
  ▶ *adj (brother, sister)* menor.

**kid²** [kɪd] *vt* **1** *(deceive, tease)* tomar el
  pelo a, engañar. **2** *(fool os)* engañarse
  a sí mismo, hacerse ilusiones.
  ▶ *vi* estar de broma: *you're kidding!* ¡estás de broma!, ¡no me digas!; *no kidding!*
  ¡en serio!

**kidnap** [ˈkɪdnæp] *vt* secuestrar, raptar.
  ⓘ *pt & pp* kidnapped, *ger* kidnapping.

**kidnapper** [ˈkɪdnæpər] *n* secuestrador,-ra.

**kidnapping** [ˈkɪdnæpɪŋ] *n* secuestro.

**kidney** [ˈkɪdnɪ] *n* riñón *m*. [COMP] **kidney**
  **machine** riñón *m* artificial.

**kill** [kɪl] *n (act)* matanza; *(animal)* pieza.
  ▶ *vt* **1** matar, asesinar. **2** *fig (hope, conversation, etc)* destruir, acabar con;
  *(pain)* aliviar. **3** *(hurt)* doler mucho: *my*
  *back's killing me* me duele mucho la espalda. [LOC] **to kill os** matarse, suicidarse. **I to kill os laughing** morirse de risa. **I to kill time** pasar el rato, matar
  el tiempo. **I to kill two birds with one**
  **stone** matar dos pájaros de un tiro. **I**
  ◆ **to kill off** *vt sep* exterminar, rematar.

**killer** [ˈkɪlər] *n (person)* asesino,-a; *(thing)*
  mortal, que mata. [COMP] **killer whale**
  orca.

**killing** [ˈkɪlɪŋ] *n* matanza; *(of person)*
  asesinato. [LOC] **to make a killing** ganar
  una fortuna, hacer el negocio del
  siglo.
  ▶ *adj fig* agotador,-ra, duro,-a.

**kiln** [kɪln] *n* horno.

**kilo** [ˈkiːləʊ] *n* kilo.
  ⓘ *pl* kilos.

**kilobyte** [ˈkɪləbaɪt] *n* kilobyte.

**kilocalorie** [ˈkɪləkælərɪ] *n* kilocaloría.

**kilogram** [ˈkɪləgræm] *n* kilogramo.

**kilogramme** [ˈkɪləgræm] *n* US → **kilogram**.

**kilometer** [kɪˈlɒmɪtər] *n* US → **kilometer**.

**kilometre** [kɪˈlɒmɪtər] *n* kilómetro.

**kilt** [kɪlt] *n* falda escocesa.

**kimono** [kɪˈməʊnəʊ] *n* quimono.
  ⓘ *pl* kimonos.

K

**kin** [kɪn] *n* parientes *mpl*, familia. COMP **next of kin** pariente *m* más próximo.

**kind** [kaɪnd] *adj* (*person*) amable: *she is the sweetest, kindest person I know* es la persona más dulce y amable que conozco; *that's very kind of you* eres muy amable.
▶ *n* (*sort*) tipo, género, clase *f*: *what kind of...?* ¿qué clase de ...? LOC **to be two of a kind** ser tal para cual. ‖ **to pay in kind 1** pagar en especie. **2** (*treatment*) pagar con la misma moneda.
▶ *adv fam* **kind of** bastante, algo, un poco: *it's kind of difficult* es un poco difícil; *have you finished? – Kind of...* ¿has acabado? –Más o menos; *... and that kind of thing ...* y cosas por el estilo.

**kindergarten** [ˈkɪndəgɑːtⁿn] *n* parvulario, guardería.

**kind-hearted** [kaɪndˈhɑːtɪd] *adj* bondadoso,-a.

**kindly** [ˈkaɪndlɪ] *adj* amable.
① *comp* kindlier, *superl* kindliest.
▶ *adv* **1** con amabilidad: *she very kindly lent me £5* tuvo la amabilidad de prestarme cinco libras. **2** (*please*) por favor: *kindly shut up!* ¡haz el favor de callarte!

**kindness** [ˈkaɪndnəs] *n* **1** bondad *f*, amabilidad *f*. **2** (*favour*) favor *m*.

**kinetics** [kɪˈnetɪks] *n* cinética.

**king** [kɪŋ] *n* rey *m*. COMP **the king and queen** los reyes *mpl*. ‖ **the Three Kings** los Reyes *mpl* Magos.

**kingdom** [ˈkɪŋdəm] *n* reino.

**kingfisher** [ˈkɪŋfɪʃəʳ] *n* martín pescador *m*.

**king-size** [ˈkɪŋsaɪz] *adj* extragrande, extralargo,-a.

**kiosk** [ˈkiːɒsk] *n* **1** quiosco. **2** (*telephone*) cabina telefónica.

**kipper** [ˈkɪpəʳ] *n* arenque *m*.

**Kiribati** [kɪrɪˈbætɪ] *n* Kiribati.

**kiss** [kɪs] *n* beso.
① *pl* kisses.
▶ *vt* besar, dar un beso a: *he kissed her on the cheek* le dio un beso en la mejilla.
▶ *vi* besarse, darse un beso.

**kit** [kɪt] *n* **1** (*equipment, gear*) equipo, equipaje *m*. **2** (*clothes*) ropa. **3** (*model*) maqueta, kit *m*.
◆ **to kit out** *vt sep* equipar.

**kitchen** [ˈkɪtʃɪn] *n* cocina. COMP **kitchen garden** huerto.

**kite** [kaɪt] *n* **1** (*bird*) milano. **2** (*toy*) cometa: *to fly a kite* hacer volar una cometa.

**kitten** [ˈkɪtⁿn] *n* gatito,-a. LOC **to have kittens** tener un ataque: *I nearly had kittens!* ¡por poco me da un ataque!

**kitty** [ˈkɪtɪ] *n* **1** *fam* (*cat*) minino,-a. **2** (*in card games*) bote *m*; (*for bills, drinks*) fondo común.
① *pl* kitties.

**kiwi** [ˈkiːwiː] *n* **1** (*bird*) kiwi *m*. **2** (*fruit*) kiwi *m*.

**klaxon** [ˈklæksⁿn] *n* claxon *m*.

**knack** [næk] *n* maña, truco. LOC **to get the knack of doing sth** cogerle el tranquillo a ALGO.

**knapsack** [ˈnæpsæk] *n* mochila.

**knead** [niːd] *vt* amasar.

**knee** [niː] *n* **1** ANAT rodilla: *on one's knees* de rodillas. **2** (*of trousers*) rodillera.
▶ *vt* dar un rodillazo a.

**kneecap** [ˈniːkæp] *n* rótula.

**kneel** [niːl] *vi* arrodillarse.
① *pt & pp* knelt [nelt].

**kneepad** [ˈniːpæd] *n* rodillera.

**knelt** [nelt] *pt & pp* → kneel.

**knew** [njuː] *pt* → know.

**knickers** [ˈnɪkəz] *n pl* bragas *fpl*: *she bought three pairs of knickers* compró tres bragas.

**knife** [naɪf] *n* (*gen*) cuchillo; (*folding*) navaja.
① *pl* knives.
▶ *vt* apuñalar, acuchillar.

**knight** [naɪt] *n* **1** *arch* caballero. **2** (*chess*) caballo. **3** caballero, (*hombre que lleva el título de* Sir). COMP **knight in shining armour** príncipe *m* azul.

**knit** [nɪt] *vt* tejer.
▶ *vi* **1** hacer punto, hacer media. **2** MED soldarse. **3** *fig* unirse. LOC **to knit one's brow** fruncir.
① *pt & pp* knit o knitted, *ger* knitting.

**knitting** [ˈnɪtɪŋ] *n* (*material*) punto; (*activity*) labor *f* de punto. COMP **knitting machine** tricotosa. ‖ **knitting needle** aguja de tejer.

**knives** [naɪvz] *pl* → knife.

**knitwear** [ˈnɪtweəʳ] *n* género de punto.

**knob** [nɒb] *n* **1** *(on door - large)* pomo; *(- small)* tirador *m*. **2** *(on stick)* puño. **3** *(natural)* bulto, protuberancia. **4** *(on radio, etc)* botón *m*.

**knock** [nɒk] *n* **1** *(blow)* golpe *m*. **2** *(on door)* llamada: *was that a knock at the door?* ¿han llamado a la puerta? **3** *fig (bad luck)* revés *m*.
► *vt* **1** *(to hit)* golpear, darse un golpe en. **2** *fam (criticize)* criticar, hablar mal de: *the newspapers are forever knocking the England manager* los periódicos siempre critican al entrenador de la selección inglesa.
► *vi* **1** *(at door)* llamar: *please knock before entering* por favor, llamen antes de entrar. **2** *(of car engine)* golpear, martillear.
◆ **to knock down** *vt sep* **1** *(building)* derribar. **2** *(person - with a car)* atropellar; *(- with a blow)* derribar. **3** *(price)* rebajar.
◆ **to knock out** *vt sep* **1** *(make unconscious)* dejar sin conocimiento; *(put to sleep)* dejar dormido,-a; *(boxing)* dejar K.O. **2** *(from competition)* eliminar.
◆ **to knock over** *vt sep* **1** *(overturn)* volcar, tirar. **2** *(run over)* atropellar.

**knockdown** ['nɒkdaʊn] *adj* rebajado. COMP **knockdown price** precio de saldo.

**knocker** ['nɒkəʳ] *n* **1** aldaba. **2** *(critic)* detractor,-ra.

**knockout** ['nɒkaʊt] *n* **1** SP knock-out *m*, fuera de combate *m*. **2** *fam* maravilla: *it's a knockout!* ¡es alucinante!

**knot** [nɒt] *n* **1** *(gen)* nudo. **2** *(people)* corrillo, grupo.
► *vt* anudar.
ⓘ *pt & pp* knotted, *ger* knotting.

**know** [nəʊ] *vt* **1** *(be acquainted with)* conocer: *do you know Colin?* conoces a Colin? **2** *(recognize)* reconocer: *I'd know him if I saw him again* lo reconocería si lo volviera a ver. **3** *(have knowledge of)* saber: *I don't know the answer* no sé la respuesta. LOC **as far as I know** que yo sepa. ‖ **I don't know it!** ¿y me lo dices a mí?, ¡ni que lo digas! ‖ **how should I know?** ¡yo qué sé! ‖ **if only I'd known!** ¡haberlo sabido! ‖ **not that I know of** que yo sepa, no. ‖ **you never know** nunca se sabe. ‖ **I know what!** ¡ya lo tengo! ‖ **to be in the know** estar enterado,-a.

‖ **you know best** tú sabes mejor que yo, sabes lo que más te conviene. ‖ **to know better** tener más juicio. ‖ **to know by sight** conocer de vista. ‖
◆ **to know about** *vt insep* **1** saber de, entender de.
◆ **to know of** *vt insep* saber de, haber oído hablar de.
ⓘ *pt* knew [njuː], *pp* known [nəʊn].

**know-all** ['nəʊɔːl] *n* sabelotodo *mf*.

**know-how** ['nəʊhaʊ] *n* saber hacer *m*, conocimiento práctico.

**knowledge** ['nɒlɪdʒ] *n* **1** *(learning, information)* conocimientos *mpl*: *his knowledge of football is amazing* sus conocimientos de fútbol son increíbles. **2** *(awareness)* conocimiento: *at that time I had no knowledge of what was happening* entonces no tenía conocimiento de lo que estaba pasando. LOC **to my knowledge** que yo sepa. ‖ **to be common knowledge that ...** ser notorio que ..., todo el mundo sabe que ... ‖ **it has come to my knowledge that ...** he llegado a saber que ... ‖ **to have a good knowledge of sth** conocer algo bien.

**knowledgeable** ['nɒlɪdʒəbəl] *adj* entendido,-a: *he's very knowledgeable about music* es muy entendido en música.

**known** [nəʊn] *pp* → **know**.

**knuckle** ['nʌkəl] *n* nudillo.
◆ **to knuckle down** *vi fam* ponerse a trabajar en serio.
◆ **to knuckle under** *vi* pasar por el aro.

**koala** [kəʊˈɑːlə] *n* koala *m*.

**Koran** [kɔːˈrɑːn] *n* Alcorán *m*, Corán *m*.

**Korea** [kəˈrɪə] *n* Corea. COMP **North Korea** Corea del Norte. ‖ **South Korea** Corea del Sur.

**Korean** [kəˈrɪən] *adj* coreano,-a.
► *n* **1** *(person)* coreano,-a. **2** *(language)* coreano. COMP **North Korean** norcoreano,-a. ‖ **South Korean** surcoreano,-a.

**kudos** ['kjuːdɒs] *n* prestigio.

**Kurd** [kɜːd] *adj* kurdo,-a.
► *n (person)* kurdo,-a.

**Kurdish** ['kɜːdɪʃ] *adj* kurdo,-a.
► *n (language)* kurdo.

**Kuwait** [kuˈweɪt] *n* Kuwait.

**Kuwaiti** [kuˈweɪtɪ] *adj* kuwaití.
► *n* kuwaití *mf*.

**K**

**L, l** [el] *n (the letter)* L, l *f*.

**l** [ˈliːtəʳ] *symb* (litre, US liter) litro; *(symbol)* l.

**lab** [læb] *n fam (abbr of laboratory)* laboratorio.

**label** [ˈleɪbəl] *n* **1** etiqueta. **2** *(record company)* casa discográfica.
▶ *vt* **1** etiquetar, poner etiqueta a. **2** *fig* calificar (as, de).
ⓘ *pt & pp* labelled (US labeled), *ger* labelling (US labeling).

**laboratory** [ləˈbɒrətərɪ, US ˈlæbrətɔːrɪ] *n* laboratorio.
ⓘ *pl* laboratories.

**labor** [ˈleɪbəʳ] *n* US → labour.

⊕ El **Labor Day** es el día del trabajo en Estados Unidos. Se celebra del primer lunes de septiembre y marca el final del verano y el inicio del curso escolar.

**labour** [ˈleɪbəʳ] *n* **1** *(work)* trabajo. **2** *(task)* labor *f*, tarea, faena. **3** *(workforce)* mano *f* de obra. **4** *(childbirth)* parto.
COMP **labour camp** campo de trabajos forzados. ‖ **Labour Day** día del trabajo. ‖ **labour force** mano *f* de obra.
▶ *vi* **1** *(work hard)* trabajar duro. **2** *(move slowly)* avanzar penosamente; *(engine)* funcionar con dificultad.
▶ *n* **Labour** GB los laboristas *mpl*, el Partido Laborista.

**laborer** [ˈleɪbərəʳ] *n* US → labourer.

**labourer** [ˈleɪbərəʳ] *n* peón *m*, jornalero,-a, bracero. COMP **farm labourer** peón *m* agrícola.

**labyrinth** [ˈlæbərɪnθ] *n* laberinto.

**lace** [leɪs] *n* **1** *(material)* encaje *m*. **2** *(shoestring)* cordón *m*.
▶ *vt (pull string through)* poner los cordones a.

**lachrymal** [ˈlækrɪməl] *adj* lagrimal, lacrimal.

**lack** [læk] *n* falta, carencia, escasez *f*: *she has no lack of self-confidence* no le falta confianza en sí misma. LOC **for lack of** por falta de.
▶ *vt* carecer de.

**lacquer** [ˈlækəʳ] *n* laca.
▶ *vt (metal, wood)* lacar; *(hair)* poner laca a.

**lacrimal** [ˈlækrɪməl] *adj* → lachrymal.

**lactic** [ˈlæktɪk] *adj* láctico,-a.

**lactose** [ˈlæktəʊs] *n* lactosa.

**lad** [læd] *n* **1** GB *fam* muchacho, chaval *m*, chico. **2** GB *fam* diablillo, pillo: *John's a bit of a lad.* John es un poco pillo. **3** *(stable boy)* mozo de cuadra.

**ladder** [ˈlædəʳ] *n* **1** escalera (de mano). **2** GB *(in stocking)* carrera. **3** *fig* escala.
COMP **rope ladder** escalera de cuerda.
▶ *vi* GB hacerse una carrera.
▶ *vt* GB hacerse una carrera en.

**laden** [ˈleɪdən] *adj* cargado,-a (with, de). LOC **to be fully laden** estar lleno,-a hasta el tope.

**ladies** [ˈleɪdɪz] *n* GB *(toilet)* lavabo (de señoras). COMP **ladies room** US lavabo (de señoras).

**ladle** [ˈleɪdəl] *n* cucharón *m*.
▶ *vt* servir con cucharón.
◆ **to ladle out** *vt sep* repartir.

**lady** [ˈleɪdɪ] *n* señora; *(of high social position)* dama.
ⓘ *pl* ladies.

**ladybird** [ˈleɪdɪbɜːd] *n* mariquita.

**ladybug** [ˈleɪdɪbʌg] *n* US mariquita.

**lag** [læg] *n* **1** retraso. **2** GB *sl* preso.
COMP **time lag** retraso.

**lager** [ˈlɑːgəʳ] *n* cerveza rubia.

**laid** [leɪd] *pt & pp* → lay².

**lain** [leɪn] *pp* → **lie²**.

**lake** [leɪk] *n* lago.

**lama** ['lɑːmə] *n* lama *m*.

**lamb** [læm] *n* **1** *(animal)* cordero,-a. **2** *(meat)* carne *f* de cordero. **3** *fam (person)* cordero,-a: *poor lamb!* ¡pobrecito,-a!

**lame** [leɪm] *adj* **1** cojo,-a: *lame in one leg* cojo,-a de una pierna. **2** *fig* débil; *(excuse)* poco convincente; *(business)* fallido,-a. COMP **lame duck** inútil *mf*.

**lamp** [læmp] *n* **1** lámpara. **2** *(on car, train)* faro.

**lamppost** ['læmppəʊst] *n* (poste *m* de) farol *m*.

**lampshade** ['læmpʃeɪd] *n* pantalla (de lámpara).

**land** [lænd] *n* **1** *(gen)* tierra: *by land and sea* por tierra y por mar. **2** *(soil)* suelo, tierra. **3** *(country, region)* tierra: *in foreign lands* en tierras extranjeras. **4** *(property)* terreno, tierras *fpl*. LOC **land ahoy!** ¡tierra a la vista! COMP **farm land** tierras *fpl* de cultivo. ‖ **land-agent** GB encargado,-a de una granja.
▶ *vi* **1** *(plane, etc)* aterrizar, tomar tierra; *(bird)* posarse. **2** *(disembark)* desembarcar. **3** *(fall)* caer.
◆ **to land in** *vt sep* causar, traer: *he's bound to land you in trouble* seguro que te traerá problemas.
◆ **to land up** *vi* acabar.

**landing** ['lændɪŋ] *n* **1** *(plane)* aterrizaje *m*. **2** *(on stairs)* descansillo, rellano. **3** *(of people)* desembarco. COMP **crash landing** aterrizaje *m* de emergencia. ‖ **landing field** pista de aterrizaje. ‖ **landing gear** tren *m* de aterrizaje.

**landlady** ['lændleɪdɪ] *n* *(of flat)* propietaria, dueña; *(of house)* casera.
① *pl* **landladies**.

**landlord** ['lændlɔːd] *n* **1** *(of flat)* propietario, dueño; *(of house)* casero.

**landowner** ['lændəʊnəʳ] *n* propietario,-a, terrateniente *mf*, hacendado,-a.

**landscape** ['lændskeɪp] *n* paisaje *m*. COMP **landscape gardener** jardinista *mf*, arquitecto,-a paisajista. ‖ **landscape painter** paisajista *mf*.
▶ *vt* ajardinar.

**lane** [leɪn] *n* **1** *(in country)* camino, sendero; *(in town)* callejuela, callejón *m*. **2** *(on road)* carril *m*. **3** *(in athletics, swimming)* calle *f*.

**language** ['læŋgwɪdʒ] *n* **1** *(faculty, way of speaking)* lenguaje *m*. **2** *(tongue)* idioma *m*, lengua. **3** *(school subject)* lengua. LOC **to use bad language** ser mal hablado,-a. COMP **language laboratory** laboratorio de idiomas. ‖ **language school** escuela de idiomas.

**lantern** ['læntən] *n* linterna, farol *m*.

**Laos** [laʊz, laʊs] *n* Laos.

**Laotian** ['laʊʃɪən] *adj* laosiano,-a.
▶ *n* laosiano,-a.

**lap¹** [læp] *n* regazo; *(knees)* rodillas *fpl*; *(skirt)* falda.

**lap²** [læp] *n* **1** SP vuelta. **2** *fig (stage)* etapa.
▶ *vt* SP *(overtake)* doblar.
▶ *vi (go round)* dar la vuelta.
① *pt & pp* **lapped**, *ger* **lapping**.

**lap³** [læp] *vt* **1** *(animal)* beber a lengüetadas. **2** *(waves)* lamer, besar.
① *pt & pp* **lapped**, *ger* **lapping**.

**lapel** [ləˈpel] *n* solapa.

**Lapland** ['læplænd] *n* Laponia.

**lapse** [læps] *n* **1** *(in time)* intervalo, lapso. **2** *(slip)* desliz *m*. **3** *(when speaking)* lapsus *m*; *(of memory)* fallo.

**laptop** ['læptɒp] *[also* **laptop computer***]* *n* ordenador *m* portátil.

**lard** [lɑːd] *n* manteca de cerdo.

**larder** ['lɑːdəʳ] *n* despensa.

**large** [lɑːdʒ] *adj* **1** grande; *(before sing noun)* gran; *(sum, amount)* importante; *(meal)* abundante. **2** *(family)* numeroso,-a. **3** *(extensive)* amplio,-a, extenso,-a. LOC **at large** *(as a whole)* en general. ‖ **by and large** por lo general.

**large-scale** ['lɑːdʒskeɪl] *adj* **1** de gran escala. **2** *(map)* a gran escala.

**lark¹** [lɑːk] *n (bird)* alondra.

**lark²** [lɑːk] *n fam (bit of fun)* broma.
◆ **to lark about / lark around** *vi fam* hacer el indio.

**larva** ['lɑːvə] *n* larva.
① *pl* **larvae** ['lɑːviː].

**laryngitis** [lærɪnˈdʒaɪtəs] *n* laringitis *f*.

**larynx** ['lærɪŋks] *n* laringe *f*.
① *pl* **larynxes** o **larynges** ['lærɪdʒiːz].

**L**

**lasagna** [ləˈzɑːnjə] *n* lasaña.

**laser** [ˈleɪzəʳ] *n* láser *m*.

**lash** [læʃ] *n* **1** *(blow with whip)* latigazo, azote *m*; *(with tail)* coletazo. **2** *(whip)* látigo; *(thong)* tralla. **3** *(eyelash)* pestaña.
ⓘ *pl* lashes.
▶ *vt* **1** *(in general)* azotar. **2** *(fasten)* sujetar.
◆ **to lash out** *vi* **1** arremeter (against/at, contra). **2** *(splurge)* gastarse un montón (de dinero) (on, en).

**lass** [læs] *n fam* chica, chavala.
ⓘ *pl* lasses.

**lasso** [læˈsuː] *n* lazo.
ⓘ *pl* lassos o lassoes.

**last** [lɑːst] *adj* **1** *(final)* último,-a. **2** *(most recent)* último,-a: *the last time* la última vez. **3** *(past)* pasado,-a; *(previous)* anterior: *last Monday* el lunes pasado; *the night before last* anteanoche.
▶ *adv* **1** por última vez: *when he last came to see me* cuando vino a verme por última vez. **2** *(at the end)* en último lugar; *(in race)* en última posición. LOC at last al fin, por fin. ▌at long last por fin.
▶ *n (person)* el/la último,-a; *(thing)* lo último: *are you the last?* ¿eres tú el último? LOC last but one penúltimo,-a.
▶ *vi (continue)* durar; *(hold out)* aguantar, resistir.
▶ *vt* durar.
◆ **to last out** *vi* resistir, aguantar.

**lasting** [ˈlɑːstɪŋ] *adj* duradero,-a.

**lastly** [ˈlɑːstlɪ] *adv* por último, finalmente.

**latch** [lætʃ] *n* pestillo: *come in, the door's on the latch* entra, el pestillo no está echado.

**late** [leɪt] *adj* **1** *(not on time)* tardío,-a: *you're ten minutes late* llegas diez minutos tarde. **2** *(far on in time)* tarde: *in late May* a finales de mayo. **3** *euph (dead)* difunto,-a, fallecido,-a. **4** *(former)* anterior. **5** *(last-minute)* de última hora. LOC to get late hacerse tarde.
▶ *adv* **1** tarde: *I stayed up late last night* anoche me acosté muy tarde. **2** *(recently)* recientemente: *as late as yesterday* ayer mismo. LOC of late últimamente.

**lately** [ˈleɪtlɪ] *adv* últimamente, recientemente.

**later** [ˈleɪtəʳ] *adj* **1** más tardío,-a: *we'll discuss that at a later date* hablaremos de eso más adelante. **2** *(more recent)* más reciente.
▶ *adv* **1** más tarde: *five minutes later* cinco minutos más tarde; *see you later!* ¡hasta luego! **2** *(afterwards)* después, luego. LOC later on más adelante, más tarde.

**lateral** [ˈlætʳrəl] *adj* lateral.

**latest** [ˈleɪtɪst] *adj* último,-a, más reciente.
▶ *n* lo último. LOC at the latest como máximo.

**latex** [ˈleɪteks] *n* látex *m*.

**lather** [ˈlɑːðəʳ] *n* **1** *(of soap)* espuma. **2** *(sweat)* sudor *m*.
▶ *vt* enjabonar.

**Latin** [ˈlætɪn] *adj* latino,-a.
▶ *n* **1** *(person)* latino,-a. **2** *(language)* latín *m*. COMP Latin American latinoamericano,-a.

**latitude** [ˈlætɪtjuːd] *n* latitud *f*.

**latter** [ˈlætəʳ] *adj* **1** *(last)* último,-a: *the latter days of his life were very happy* los últimos días de su vida fueron muy felices. **2** *(second)* segundo,-a.
▶ *pron* the latter éste,-a, este,-a último,-a.

**lattice** [ˈlætɪs] *n* celosía, enrejado.

**Latvia** [ˈlætvɪə] *n* Letonia.

**Latvian** [ˈlætvɪən] *adj* letón,-ona.
▶ *n* **1** *(person)* letón,-ona. **2** *(language)* letón *m*.

**laugh** [lɑːf] *vi* reír, reírse: *it makes me laugh* me da risa. LOC he who laughs last laughs longest quien ríe último ríe mejor. ▌to laugh one's head off *fam* partirse de risa, troncharse de risa, desternillarse de risa.
▶ *n* risa: *we had a really good laugh* nos reímos muchísimo.
◆ **to laugh at** *vt insep* reírse de.
◆ **to laugh off** *vt sep* tomar a risa.

**laughter** [ˈlɑːftəʳ] *n* risas *fpl*: *a fit of laughter* un ataque de risa.

**launch** [lɔːntʃ] *vt* **1** lanzar: *it will be launched on the market next year* se lanzará al mercado el año que viene. **2** *(ship)* botar; *(lifeboat)* echar al mar. **3** *(film, etc)* estrenar; *(book)* presentar. **4** *(company)* fundar. **5** *(scheme, attack)* iniciar. COMP **launch pad** plataforma de lanzamiento.

▶ *n (boat)* lancha.

ⓘ *pl* launches.

**launching** ['lɔ:ntʃɪŋ] *n* **1** lanzamiento. **2** *(of ship)* botadura. **3** *(of film)* estreno; *(of book)* presentación *f.* COMP **launching pad** plataforma de lanzamiento.

**launder** ['lɔ:ndəʳ] *vt* **1** *(clothes)* lavar (y planchar). **2** *fig (money)* blanquear.

**launderette** [lɔ:n'd⁰ret] *n* lavandería automática.

**laundry** ['lɔ:ndrɪ] *n* **1** *(place)* lavandería. **2** *(dirty)* ropa sucia, colada; *(clean)* ropa limpia, ropa lavada. LOC **to do the laundry** lavar la ropa.

ⓘ *pl* laundries.

**lava** ['lɑ:və] *n* lava.

**lavatory** ['lævət⁰rɪ] *n* **1** váter *m.* **2** *(room)* lavabo, baño.

ⓘ *pl* lavatories.

**lavender** ['lævɪndəʳ] *n* espliego, lavanda.

▶ *adj (colour)* de color lavanda.

**law** [lɔ:] *n* **1** ley *f.* **2** EDUC derecho. LOC **against the law** contra la ley. ▌ **by law** por ley. ▌ **to keep within the law** obrar según la ley. COMP **law and order** orden *m* público. ▌ **law court** tribunal *m* de justicia.

**lawful** ['lɔ:fʊl] *adj* legal.

**lawn** [lɔ:n] *n* césped *m.*

**lawnmower** ['lɔ:nməʊəʳ] *n* cortacésped *m & f.*

**lawsuit** ['lɔ:sju:t] *n* pleito, juicio.

**lawyer** ['lɔ:jəʳ] *n* abogado,-a.

**laxative** ['læksətɪv] *adj* laxante.

▶ *n* laxante *m.*

**lay¹** [leɪ] *adj* **1** REL laico,-a, seglar. **2** *(non-professional)* lego,-a, no profesional.

**lay²** [leɪ] *vt* **1** *(gen)* poner, colocar; *(spread out)* extender. **2** *(bricks, carpet)* poner; *(cable, pipe)* tender; *(foundations, basis)* echar; *(bomb)* colocar. **3** *(prepare)* preparar; *(curse)* lanzar. **4** *(eggs)* poner.

**5** *(bet)* apostar. **6** *(charge)* formular. LOC **to lay the table** poner la mesa.

▶ *vi (hen)* poner huevos.

◆ **to lay by** *vt sep* guardar; *(money)* ahorrar.

◆ **to lay down** *vt sep* **1** *(let go)* dejar, soltar. **2** *(give up)* entregar. **3** *(establish)* imponer, fijar.

◆ **to lay off** *vt sep (worker)* despedir.

▶ *vt insep fam (stop)* dejar en paz.

▶ *vi fam* parar: *lay off!* ¡ya está bien!, ¡para ya!

◆ **to lay on** *vt sep (provide)* suministrar.

▶ *vt insep (burden)* cargar.

◆ **to lay out** *vt sep* **1** *(spread out)* tender, extender. **2** *(arrange)* disponer, colocar. **3** *(present)* presentar, exponer. **4** *(town, etc)* hacer el trazado de; *(garden)* diseñar.

◆ **to lay over** *vi* US *(gen)* hacer una parada (at/in, en); *(plane)* hacer escala (at/in, en).

ⓘ *pt & pp* laid [leɪd].

**lay³** [leɪ] *pp* → lie².

**lay-by** ['leɪbaɪ] *n* área de descanso.

ⓘ *pl* lay-bys.

**layer** ['leɪəʳ] *n* **1** capa. **2** *(of rock)* estrato. **3** *(hen)* gallina ponedora.

**layout** ['leɪaʊt] *n* **1** *(arrangement)* disposición *f*; *(presentation)* presentación *f.* **2** *(printing)* composición *f*, formato. **3** *(plan)* trazado.

**laze** [leɪz] *vi* gandulear, holgazanear.

◆ **to laze about / laze around** *vi* hacer el vago.

**laziness** ['leɪzɪnəs] *n* pereza.

**lazy** ['leɪzɪ] *adj* **1** gandul,-la, vago,-a, perezoso,-a. **2** *(river)* perezoso,-a.

ⓘ *comp* lazier, *superl* laziest.

**lazybones** ['leɪzɪbəʊnz] *n* perezoso,-a, gandul,-la.

ⓘ *pl* lazybones.

**lb** [paʊnd] *abbr* (pound) libra.

ⓘ *pl* lb o lbs.

**lead¹** [led] *n* **1** *(metal)* plomo. **2** *(in pencil)* mina. LOC **to swing the lead** *fam* hacer el vago.

**lead²** [li:d] *vt* **1** *(guide)* llevar, conducir: *our tour guide led the way to the cathedral* la guía nos llevó a la catedral. **2** *(be leader*

*of)* liderar, dirigir. **3** *(be first in)* ocupar el primer puesto en. **4** *(influence)* llevar: *he is easily led* se deja llevar fácilmente.
▶ *vi* **1** *(road)* conducir, llevar (to, a). **2** *(command)* tener el mando. **3** *(go first)* ir primero,-a.
ⓘ *pt & pp* led [led].
▶ *n* **1** *(front position)* delantera. **2** SP liderato; *(difference)* ventaja. **3** THEAT primer papel *m*.

**leader** ['liːdəʳ] *n* POL líder *mf*, dirigente *mf*. **2** *(in race)* líder *mf* (of/in, de).

**leadership** ['liːdəʃɪp] *n* **1** *(position)* liderato, liderazgo. **2** *(qualities)* dotes *mpl* de mando. **3** *(leaders)* dirección *f*.

**lead-free** ['ledfriː] *adj* sin plomo.

**leading** ['liːdɪŋ] *adj* destacado,-a, principal.

**leaf** [liːf] *n* **1** *(of plant)* hoja. **2** *(of book)* hoja, página.
ⓘ *pl* leaves [liːvz].

**leaflet** ['liːflət] *n* *(folded)* folleto; *(single sheet)* octavilla, hoja suelta.
▶ *vi* GB repartir folletos, repartir octavillas.

**league** [liːg] *n* liga. ⓁⓄⒸ **to be in league with** SB estar conchabado,-a con ALGN.

**leak** [liːk] *vi* **1** *(container)* tener un agujero; *(pipe)* tener un escape. **2** *(roof)* gotear. **3** *(gas, fluid)* escaparse.
▶ *n* **1** *(hole)* agujero. **2** *(in roof)* gotera. **3** *(of gas)* fuga, escape *m*; *(of liquid)* escape *m*. **4** *fig (of information, etc)* filtración *f*.
◆ **to leak out** *vi* **1** *(gas, fluid)* escaparse. **2** *fig* filtrarse.

**leakage** ['liːkɪdʒ] *n* fuga, escape *m*.

**leaky** ['liːkɪ] *adj* **1** *(container)* agujereado,-a; *(pipe)* con un escape. **2** *(roof)* que tiene goteras. **3** *(pipe)* que tiene escapes.
ⓘ *comp* lcakier, *superl* leakiest.

**lean¹** [liːn] *adj* **1** *(person)* delgado,-a, flaco,-a. **2** *(meat)* magro,-a. **3** *(harvest)* malo,-a, escaso,-a; *(year)* malo,-a, pobre: *it was a lean year for car sales* fue un mal año para la venta de coches.
▶ *n* *(meat)* carne *f* magra.

**lean²** [liːn] *vi* **1** inclinarse. **2** *(for support)* apoyarse (on, en) (against, contra).
▶ *vt* apoyar.
◆ **to lean on** *vt insep* **1** *(depend on)* depender de. **2** *(pressure)* presionar a.
◆ **to lean towards** *vt insep* estar a favor de, tirar hacia.
ⓘ *pt & pp* leaned o leant [lent].

**leaning** ['liːnɪŋ] *adj* inclinado,-a.
▶ *n* inclinación *f*, tendencia.

**leant** [lent] *pt & pp* → **lean²**.

**leap** [liːp] *vi* saltar, brincar.
ⓘ *pt & pp* leaped o leapt [lept].
▶ *n* **1** salto, brinco. ⒸⓄⓂⓅ **leap year** año bisiesto.

**leapfrog** ['liːpfrɒg] *n* pídola.
▶ *vt fig (skip)* saltarse.
ⓘ *pt & pp* leapfrogged, *ger* leapfrogging.

**leapt** [lept] *pt & pp* → **leap**.

**learn** [lɜːn] *vt* **1** aprender: *I'd love to learn (how) to ice-skate* me encantaría aprender a patinar sobre hielo. **2** *(find out about)* enterarse de, saber.
▶ *vi* **1** aprender. **2** *(find out)* enterarse (about/of, de).
ⓘ *pt & pp* learned o learnt [lɜːnt].

**learned** ['lɜːnəd] *adj* erudito,-a.

**learner** ['lɜːnəʳ] *n* estudiante *mf*. ⒸⓄⓂⓅ **learner driver** conductor,-a en prácticas.

**learnt** [lɜːnt] *pt & pp* → **learn**.

**leash** [liːʃ] *n* correa.

**leasing** ['liːsɪŋ] *n* **1** arrendamiento, arriendo. **2** FIN leasing *m*.

**least** [liːst] *adj* menor, menos: *he makes the least money* es el que gana menos dinero.
▶ *adv* menos: *when you least expect it* cuando menos lo esperas.
▶ *n* lo menos: *it's the least I can do* es lo menos que puedo hacer. ⓁⓄⒸ **at (the) least** por lo menos.

**leather** ['leðəʳ] *n* piel *f*, cuero.
▶ *adj* de piel, de cuero.

**leave¹** [liːv] *vt* **1** *(go away from)* dejar, abandonar; *(go out of)* salir de: *she left home when she was 16* se marchó de casa a los 16 años. **2** *(stop being with)* irse de, marcharse de. **3** *(forget)* dejarse, olvidar, olvidarse. **4** *(allow to remain)* dejar: *please leave the door open* por favor, deja la puerta abierta. **5** *(cause to remain)* dejar: *the glass left a ring on the table* el vaso dejó un cerco en la mesa. **6** *(bequeath)* dejar, legar. **7** MATH dar: *two from six leaves four* seis menos dos dan cuatro.

▶ *vi* marcharse, irse, partir: *he left for Rome this morning* esta mañana salió hacia Roma.

◆ **to leave off** *vt insep* dejar de: *there was so much noise that I had to leave off studying* había tanto ruido que tuve que dejar de estudiar.

▶ *vi* acabar, terminar.

◆ **to leave out** *vt sep* omitir, excluir.

ⓘ *pt & pp* left, *ger* leaving.

**leave²** [liːv] *n* **1** *(time off)* permiso. **2** *(permission)* permiso. LOC **to be on leave** MIL estar de permiso.

**leaven** ['levən] *n* levadura.

**leaves** [liːvz] *pl* → leaf.

**Lebanese** [lebəˈniːz] *adj* libanés,-esa.

▶ *n* libanés,-esa.

▶ *n pl* **the Lebanese** los libaneses *mpl*.

**Lebanon** ['lebənən] *n* Líbano.

**lectern** ['lektən] *n* atril *m*; *(in church)* facistol *m*.

**lecture** ['lektʃəʳ] *n* **1** conferencia. **2** *(in university)* clase *f*. **3** *(telling-off)* reprimenda, sermón *m*.

▶ *vi* **1** dar una conferencia (on, sobre). **2** *(in university)* dar clase.

▶ *vt* *(scold)* sermonear, echar una reprimenda a.

☒ Lecture no significa 'lectura', que se traduce por reading.

**lecturer** ['lektʃərəʳ] *n* **1** conferenciante *mf*. **2** *(in university)* profesor,-ra.

☒ Lecturer no significa 'lector', que se traduce por reader.

**led** [liːvz] *pp & pt* → lead².

**ledge** [ledʒ] *n* **1** *(shelf)* repisa; *(of window)* antepecho, alféizar *m*. **2** *(of rock)* saliente *m*.

**lee** [liː] *n* **1** MAR sotavento, socaire *m*. **2** *(shelter)* abrigo. LOC **in the lee of** al abrigo de.

**leech** [liːtʃ] *n* sanguijuela.

**leek** [liːk] *n* puerro.

**left¹** [left] *adj* **1** izquierdo,-a. **2** POL de izquierdas: *the left wing of the party* el ala izquierda del partido.

▶ *adv* a la izquierda, hacia la izquierda.

▶ *n* **1** izquierda: *keep to the left* manténgase a la izquierda. **2** *(punch)* golpe *m* de la izquierda. LOC **on the left** a mano izquierda.

**left²** [left] *pt & pp* → leave¹. LOC **to be left** quedar: *is there any milk left?* ¿queda leche? **‖ to be left over** sobrar, quedar. COMP **left luggage office** consigna.

**left-hand** ['lefthænd] *adj* izquierdo,-a: *the shop is on the left-hand side* la tienda está a mano izquierda.

**leftover** ['leftəʊvəʳ] *adj* sobrante, restante.

▶ *n pl* **leftovers** sobras *fpl*, restos *mpl*.

**leg** [leg] *n* **1** ANAT pierna; *(of animal)* pata. **2** CULIN *(lamb, etc)* pierna; *(chicken, etc)* muslo. **3** *(of furniture)* pata, pie *m*. **4** *(of trousers)* pernera. **5** *(stage)* etapa. LOC **to pull sb's leg** *fam* tomarle el pelo a ALGN.

**legal** ['liːgəl] *adj* **1** legal, lícito,-a. **2** *(relating to the law)* jurídico,-a, legal: *the legal profession* la abogacía. LOC **to take legal action** entablar un pleito (against, contra).

**legalize** ['liːgəlaɪz] *vt* legalizar.

**legend** ['ledʒənd] *n* leyenda.

**legendary** ['ledʒəndəri] *adj* legendario,-a.

**leggings** ['legɪnz] *n pl* *(whole leg)* mallas *fpl*; *(below knee)* polainas *fpl*.

**legible** ['ledʒəbəl] *adj* legible.

**legion** ['liːdʒən] *n* legión *f*.

**legionary** ['liːdʒənəri] *n* legionario.

ⓘ *pl* legionarios.

**legionnaire** [liːdʒəˈneəʳ] *n* legionario. COMP **legionnaire's disease** enfermedad *f* del legionario.

**legislation** [ledʒɪsˈleɪʃən] *n* legislación *f*.

**legislative** ['ledʒɪslətɪv] *adj* legislativo,-a.

**legitimate** [lɪˈdʒɪtɪmət] *adj* legítimo,-a.

**legume** ['legju:m] *n* legumbre *f*.

**leisure** ['leʒəʳ, US 'li:ʒəʳ] *n* ocio, tiempo libre. LOC **at leisure 1** *(with free time)* en su tiempo libre. **2** *(calmly)* tranquilamente. COMP **leisure centre** centro recreativo.

**lemon** ['lemən] *n* limón *m*.
▸ *adj (colour)* de color limón. COMP **lemon squeezer** exprimidor *m*. ‖ **lemon tree** limonero.

**lemonade** [lemə'neɪd] *n* **1** *(fizzy - plain)* gaseosa; *(- lemony-flavoured)* limonada. **2** *(still)* limonada.

**lend** [lend] *vt* **1** dejar, prestar: *could you lend me some money?* ¿me dejas un poco de dinero? **2** *fig (add)* dotar de, prestar. LOC **to lend os to STH** prestarse a ALGO, prestarse para ALGO. ‖ **to lend (SB) a hand** echar una mano (a ALGN).
① *pt & pp* lent [lent].

**length** [leŋθ] *n* **1** longitud *f*. **2** *(of time)* duración *f*. **3** *(piece)* trozo; *(of cloth)* largo. **4** *(of road)* tramo; *(of swimming pool)* largo.

**lengthen** ['leŋθ*ə*n] *vt* **1** *(skirt, etc)* alargar. **2** *(lifetime)* prolongar.
▸ *vi* **1** *(skirt, etc)* alargarse. **2** *(lifetime)* prolongarse; *(days)* crecer.

**lengthy** ['leŋθɪ] *adj (in general)* largo,-a.
① *comp* lengthier, *superl* lengthiest.

**lens** [lenz] *n* **1** *(of glasses)* lente *m & f*. **2** *(of camera)* objetivo. **3** ANAT cristalino.
① *pl* lenses.

**lent** [lent] *pt & pp* → **lend**.

**lentil** ['lent*ə*l] *n* lenteja.

**Leo** ['li:əʊ] *n* Leo.

**leopard** ['lepəd] *n* leopardo.

**leotard** ['li:ətɑ:d] *n* malla.

**Lesotho** [lɪ'su:tu:] *n* Lesotho.

**less** [les] *adj* menos.
▸ *pron* menos: *the less you buy, the less you'll spend* cuánto menos compres, menos gastarás. LOC **no less** nada menos.
▸ *adv* menos: *less and less* cada vez menos; *he was being less than sincere* no fue nada sincero. LOC **much less** menos aún.
▸ *prep* menos.

**lessen** ['les*ə*n] *vt* disminuir, reducir.
▸ *vi* disminuir, reducirse.

**lesser** ['lesəʳ] *adj* menor.

**lesson** ['les*ə*n] *n* **1** *(class)* clase *f*. **2** *(warning)* lección *f*.

**let** [let] *vt (allow)* dejar: *he lets the children watch cartoon videos* a los niños les deja mirar vídeos de dibujos animados. LOC **to let SB alone** dejar a ALGN en paz, no molestar a ALGN. ‖ **to let SB know** hacer saber a ALGN, avisar a ALGN.
▸ *aux que + subjuntivo*: *let him come* que venga; *let's go!* ¡vamos!, ¡vámonos!
▸ *vt* GB *(rent)* alquilar: *«House to let»* «Se alquila casa».
▸ *n* GB *(renting)* alquiler *m*.
◆ **to let down** *vt sep* **1** *(lower)* bajar. **2** *(lengthen)* alargar. **3** *(deflate)* desinflar. **4** *(disappoint)* fallar, defraudar.
◆ **to let in** *vt sep* dejar entrar: *her father let me in* me abrió su padre.
◆ **to let into** *vt sep* **1** dejar entrar a: *this key will let you into the garage* con esta llave podrás entrar en el garaje. **2** *(reveal)* revelar.
◆ **to let off** *vt sep* **1** *(leave off)* dejar. **2** *(bomb)* hacer explotar; *(fireworks)* hacer estallar. **3** *(person - forgive)* perdonar; *(- let leave)* dejar marcharse; *(- free)* dejar en libertad.
◆ **to let on** *vi fam (tell)* decir, descubrir.
▸ *vt insep fam (pretend)* hacer ver.
◆ **to let out** *vt sep* **1** *(in general)* dejar salir; *(release)* soltar (**from**, de). **2** *(utter)* soltar.
◆ **to let through** *vt sep* dejar pasar.
◆ **to let up** *vi* parar.
◆ **to let up on** *vt insep fam* dejar en paz.
① *pt & pp* let, *ger* letting.

**let's** [lets] *v aux* → **let**.

**letter** ['letəʳ] *n* **1** *(of alphabet)* letra. **2** *(message)* carta. LOC **to the letter** al pie de la letra. COMP **capital letter** mayúscula. ‖ **letter box** buzón *m*. ‖ **small letter** minúscula.

**lettuce** ['letɪs] *n* lechuga.

**leukaemia** [lʊ'ki:mɪə] *n* leucemia.

**leukemia** [lʊ'ki:mɪə] *n* US → **leukaemia**.

**leukocyte** ['lʊ:kəsaɪt] *n* leucocito.

**level** ['levªl] *adj* **1** *(horizontal)* llano,-a, plano,-a. **2** *(even)* a nivel, nivelado,-a; *(spoonful, etc)* raso,-a: *the table's not level* la mesa no está nivelada. **3** *(equal)* igual, igualado,-a. **4** *(steady)* estable; *(voice)* llano,-a. COMP **level crossing** paso a nivel.
▶ *n* **1** nivel *m*: *above sea level* sobre el nivel del mar. **2** *(flat ground)* llano, llanura. LOC **to be on a level with** estar al mismo nivel que.
▶ *vt* **1** *(make level, survey)* nivelar. **2** *(raze)* arrasar, rasar. **3** *(aim)* apuntar.
▶ *adv* a ras (with, de).
ⓘ *pt & pp* levelled (US leveled), *ger* levelling (US leveling).

**lever** ['li:vər] *n* **1** palanca. **2** *(in lock)* guarda.

**levy** ['levɪ] *vt* recaudar; *(fine)* imponer.
ⓘ *pt & pp* levied, *ger* levying.
▶ *n* recaudación *f*; *(of fine)* imposición *f*.
ⓘ *pl* levies.

**lexical** ['leksɪkªl] *adj* léxico,-a.

**liable** ['laɪəbªl] *adj* **1** *(likely, susceptible)* propenso,-a (to, a): *the car is liable to stall* el coche tiende a calarse. **2** *(susceptible)* susceptible (to, a).

**liar** ['laɪə'] *n* mentiroso,-a, embustero,-a: *he's such a liar!* ¡menudo embustero está hecho!

**liberal** ['lɪbªrªl] *adj* **1** *(in general)* liberal. **2** *(abundant)* abundante.

**Liberal** ['lɪbªrªl] *adj* POL liberal.
▶ *n* POL liberal *mf*.

**liberalize** ['lɪbªrəlaɪz] *vt* liberalizar.

**liberation** [lɪbəˈreɪʃªn] *n* liberación *f*.

**Liberia** [laɪˈbɪərɪə] *n* Liberia.

**Liberian** [laɪˈbɪərɪən] *adj* liberiano,-a.
▶ *n* liberiano,-a.

**liberty** ['lɪbətɪ] *n* libertad *f*.
ⓘ *pl* liberties. LOC **at liberty** en libertad, libre (to, de). ▌ **to take liberties with sb/sth** tomarse libertades con ALGN/ALGO.

**Libra** ['li:brə] *n* Libra *m*.

**librarian** [laɪˈbreərɪən] *n* bibliotecario,-a.

**library** ['laɪbrərɪ] *n* **1** biblioteca. **2** *(collection)* colección *f*. COMP **newspaper library** hemeroteca.
ⓘ *pl* libraries.

Library no significa 'librería (tienda)', que se traduce por **bookshop**, ni 'librería (mueble)', que se traduce por **bookcase**.

**libretto** [lɪˈbretəʊ] *n* libreto.
ⓘ *pl* librettos o libretti [lɪˈbreti:].

**Libya** ['lɪbɪə] *n* Libia.

**Libyan** ['lɪbɪən] *adj* libio,-a.
▶ *n* libio,-a.

**lice** [laɪs] *pl* → louse.

**licence** ['laɪsªns] *n* **1** *(permit)* licencia, permiso. **2** *(freedom)* libertad *f*; *(excessive freedom)* licencia. COMP **licence number** matrícula.

**license** ['laɪsªns] *n* US → licence.
▶ *vt* autorizar, dar licencia a.

**licensed** ['laɪsªnst] *adj* autorizado,-a.

**lichen** ['laɪkªn, 'lɪtʃªn] *n* liquen *m*.

**lick** [lɪk] *vt* **1** lamer. **2** *fam (defeat - team)* vencer a, derrotar; *(- problem)* superar, solucionar. LOC **to lick one's lips** relamerse.
▶ *n* **1** lamedura, lengüetada. **2** *fam (of paint)* mano *f*.

**licorice** ['lɪkªrɪs, 'lɪkªrɪʃ] *n* regaliz *m*.

**lid** [lɪd] *n* **1** *(cover)* tapa. **2** *(of eye)* párpado. LOC **to take the lid off sth** *fig* destapar ALGO.

**lie¹** [laɪ] *vi* mentir.
ⓘ *pt & pp* lied, *ger* lying.
▶ *n* mentira. LOC **to tell lies** mentir.

**lie²** [laɪ] *vi* **1** *(adopt a flat position)* acostarse, tumbarse. **2** *(be situated)* estar (situado,-a), encontrarse. **3** *(be buried)* yacer. **4** *(remain)* quedarse, permanecer.
◆ **to lie back** *vi* recostarse.
◆ **to lie down** *vi* acostarse, tumbarse, echarse.
◆ **to lie up** *vi* guardar cama.
ⓘ *pt* lay [leɪ], *pp* lain [leɪn], *ger* lying.

**Liechtenstein** ['lɪktªnstaɪn] *n* Liechtenstein.

**lie-down** ['laɪdaʊn] *n* siesta.

**lieutenant** [lefˈtenənt, US lu:ˈtenənt] *n* **1** MIL teniente *m*. **2** *(non-military)* lugarteniente *m*.

**life** [laɪf] *n* **1** vida. **2** *(of battery)* duración *f*. LOC **it's a matter of life and death** es

cuestión de vida o muerte. ∎ **not on your life!** *fam* ¡ni hablar! ∎ **to come to life** cobrar vida. ∎ **to lose one's life** perder la vida. ∎ **to take one's own life** suicidarse, quitarse la vida. ∎ **to take sb's life** matar a ALGN. COMP **life belt / life buoy** salvavidas *m*. ∎ **life jacket** chaleco salvavidas. ∎ **life style** estilo de vida.
ⓘ *pl* lives [laɪvz].

**lifeboat** ['laɪfbəʊt] *n* **1** *(on shore)* lancha de socorro. **2** *(on ship)* bote *m* salvavidas.

**lifeguard** ['laɪfgɑːd] *n* socorrista *mf*.

**lifelong** ['laɪflɒŋ] *adj* de toda la vida.

**life-saver** ['laɪfseɪvəʳ] *n* socorrista *mf*.

**lifestyle** ['laɪfstaɪl] *n* estilo de vida.

**lifetime** ['laɪftaɪm] *n* **1** vida: *in her lifetime* en su vida. **2** *fam* eternidad *f*.

**lift** [lɪft] *vt* **1** *(in general)* levantar, coger. **2** *(by plane)* transportar.
▸ *vi (of movable parts)* levantarse:.
▸ *n* GB ascensor *m*. LOC **to give sb a lift 1** *(in car)* llevar a ALGN en coche. **2** *(cheer up)* animar.

**liftoff** ['lɪftɒf] *n* despegue *m*.

**ligament** ['lɪgəmənt] *n* ligamento.

**light¹** [laɪt] *n* **1** *(gen)* luz *f*. **2** *(lamp)* luz *f*, lámpara; *(traffic light)* semáforo. **3** *(for cigarette, fire)* fuego. LOC **in (the) light of** GB en vista de, teniendo en cuenta. ∎ **to come to light** salir a luz. ∎ **to throw light on sth** aclarar ALGO. COMP **light bulb** bombilla. ∎ **light switch** interruptor *m* de la luz. ∎ **light year** año luz.
▸ *vt* **1** *(ignite)* encender. **2** *(illuminate)* iluminar, alumbrar.
ⓘ *pt & pp* lighted o lit [lɪt].
▸ *adj* **1** *(colour)* claro,-a; *(complexion)* blanco,-a. **2** *(bright)* con mucha claridad.

**light²** [laɪt] *adj* **1** *(not heavy)* ligero,-a; *(rain)* fino,-a; *(breeze)* suave. **2** *(sentence, wound)* leve. COMP **light aircraft** avioneta.

**lighten¹** ['laɪtⁿn] *vt* **1** *(colour)* aclarar. **2** *(room)* iluminar.
▸ *vi (colour)* aclararse.

**lighten²** ['laɪtⁿn] *vt (make less heavy)* aligerar.
▸ *vi (mood, etc)* alegrarse.

**lighter** ['laɪtəʳ] [also cigarette lighter] *n* encendedor *m*, mechero.

**lighthouse** ['laɪthaʊs] *n* faro.

**lighting** ['laɪtɪŋ] *n* **1** *(in general)* iluminación *f*. **2** *(system)* alumbrado.

**lightly** ['laɪtlɪ] *adv* **1** *(not heavily)* ligeramente. **2** *(not seriously)* a la ligera.

**lightning** ['laɪtⁿnɪŋ] *n* rayo; *(flash only)* relámpago.

**lights-out** ['laɪtsaʊt] *n* la hora de apagar las luces.

**lightweight** ['laɪtweɪt] *n (boxing)* peso ligero.

**lignite** ['lɪgnaɪt] *n* lignita.

**like¹** [laɪk] *prep* **1** *(the same as)* como: *the flat looks like new* el piso está como nuevo. **2** *(typical of)* propio,-a de: *it isn't like her to make a scene* no es propio de ella armar un escándalo. LOC **to look like sb** parecerse a ALGN. ∎ **something like that** ALGO así, ALGO por el estilo.
▸ *adj* **1** *(such as)* como. **2** *fml* parecido,-a.
▸ *conj fam* como.
▸ *n* ALGO parecido: *I've never seen the like of it* nunca he visto cosa igual.

**like²** [laɪk] *vt* **1** *(enjoy)* gustar. **2** *(want)* querer, gustar: *I'd like a cup of coffee* me gustaría tomar un café. LOC **to like sth better** preferir ALGO.
▸ *vi* querer: *if you like* si quieres.
▸ *n pl* likes gustos *mpl*.

**likeable** ['laɪkəbⁿl] *adj* simpático,-a.

**likelihood** ['laɪklɪhʊd] *n* probabilidad *f*.

**likely** ['laɪklɪ] *adj* probable: *he's likely to leave late* es probable que salga tarde.
▸ *adv* probablemente. LOC **as likely as not** *fam* lo más seguro.
ⓘ *comp* likelier, *superl* likeliest.

**likeness** ['laɪknəs] *n* **1** *(similarity)* semejanza, parecido. **2** *(portrait)* retrato.

**likewise** ['laɪkwaɪz] *adv* **1** *(the same)* lo mismo, igualmente: *to do likewise* hacer lo mismo.

**liking** ['laɪkɪŋ] *n (for thing)* gusto, afición *f*; *(for person)* simpatía; *(for friend)* cariño.

**lilac** ['laɪlək] *n* **1** BOT lila. **2** *(colour)* lila *m*.
▸ *adj* (de color) lila.

**lily** ['lɪlɪ] *n* lirio, azucena.
ⓘ *pl* lilies.

**limb** [lɪmb] *n* **1** ANAT miembro. **2** *(branch)* rama.
◆ **to limber up** *vi* SP entrar en calor.
▶ *vt sep* calentar.

**lime** [laɪm] *n* **1** *(citrus fruit)* lima. **2** *(citrus tree)* limero. **3** *(linden)* tilo.

**limestone** ['laɪmstəʊn] *n* piedra caliza.

**limit** ['lɪmɪt] *n* límite *m*. LOC **that's the limit!** *fam* ¡eso es el colmo! ▌ **to be off limits** estar en zona prohibida (**to**, para). ▌ **within limits** dentro de ciertos límites.
▶ *vt* limitar, restringir (**to**, a)

**limitation** [lɪmɪ'teɪᵉn] *n* limitación *f*.

**limousine** [lɪmə'zi:n] *n* limusina.

**limp¹** [lɪmp] *vi* cojear.
▶ *n* cojera.

**limp²** [lɪmp] *adj* **1** *(floppy)* flojo,-a, fláccido,-a; *(lettuce)* mustio,-a. **2** *(weak)* débil.

**limpet** ['lɪmpɪt] *n* lapa.

**linden** ['lɪndᵉn] *n* tilo.

**line** [laɪn] *n* **1** *(in general)* línea: *in a straight line* en línea recta. **2** *(drawn on paper)* raya. **3** *(of text)* línea, renglón *m*; *(of poetry)* verso: *new line* punto y aparte. **4** *(row)* fila, hilera. **5** US *(queue)* cola. **6** *(cord)* cuerda, cordel *m*; *(fishing)* sedal *m*; *(wire)* cable *m*. **7** *(route)* vía. LOC **all along the line 1** *(from the beginning)* desde el principio. **2** *(in detail)* con todo detalle. ▌ **in line with** *fig* conforme a. ▌ **to stand in line** US hacer cola. COMP **dotted line** línea de puntos. ▌ **line drawing** dibujo lineal.
▶ *vt* **1** *(draw lines on)* dibujar rayas en. **2** *(mark with wrinkles)* arrugar. **3** *(form rows along)* bordear.
◆ **to line up** *vi* ponerse en fila; *(in queue)* hacer cola.

**linen** ['lɪnɪn] *n* **1** *(material)* lino, hilo. **2** *(sheets, etc)* ropa blanca, lencería. COMP **bed linen** ropa de cama. ▌ **table linen** mantelería.

**liner** ['laɪnər] *n* *(mar)* transatlántico.

**linesman** ['laɪnzmən] *n* juez *mf* de línea, linier *m*.
ⓘ *pl* **linesmen** ['laɪnzmən].

**line-up** ['laɪnʌp] *n* *(of people)* alineación *f*, formación *f*.

**lingerie** ['lɑ:nʒəri:] *n fml* lencería.

**linguist** ['lɪŋgwɪst] *n* **1** lingüista *mf*. **2** *(fam)* políglota *mf*.

**linguistic** [lɪŋ'gwɪstɪk] *adj* lingüístico,-a.

**linguistics** [lɪŋ'gwɪstɪks] *n* lingüística.

**lining** ['laɪnɪŋ] *n* forro.

**link** [lɪŋk] *n* **1** *(in chain)* eslabón *m*. **2** *(connection)* enlace *m*. **3** *fig* vínculo, lazo.
▶ *vt* **1** unir, conectar. **2** *fig* vincular, relacionar.

**linkage** ['lɪŋkɪdʒ] *n* conexión *f*.

**lintel** ['lɪntᵉl] *n* dintel *m*.

**lion** ['laɪən] *n* león *m*.

**lioness** ['laɪənəs] *n* leona.
ⓘ *pl* **lionesses**.

**lip** [lɪp] *n* **1** labio. **2** *(of cup, etc)* borde *m*.

**lipid** ['lɪpɪd] *n* lípido.

**lip-read** ['lɪpri:d] *vt* leer en los labios.
▶ *vi* leer en los labios.
ⓘ *pt & pp* **lip-read** ['lɪpred].

**lipstick** ['lɪpstɪk] *n* *(stick)* barra de labios, lápiz *m* de labios; *(substance)* pintura de labios.

**liquefaction** [lɪkwɪ'fækʃᵉn] *n* licuefacción *f*, licuación *f*.

**liquefy** ['lɪkwɪfaɪ] *vt* licuar.
▶ *vi* licuarse.
ⓘ *pt & pp* **liquefied**, *ger* **liquefying**.

**liqueur** [lɪ'kjʊər, US lɪ'kɜ:r] *n* licor *m*.

**liquid** ['lɪkwɪd] *n* **1** líquido.
▶ *adj* **1** líquido,-a.

**liquidate** ['lɪkwɪdeɪt] *vt* liquidar.

**liquor** ['lɪkər] *n* US licor *m*.

**liquorice** ['lɪkərɪs, 'lɪkərɪʃ] *n* regaliz *m*.

**lira** ['lɪərə] *n* lira.
ⓘ *pl* **liras** o **lire** ['lɪərə].

**list** [lɪst] *n* lista.
▶ *vt* hacer una lista de: *he listed the contents of the house* hizo una lista de las cosas que había en la casa.

**listen** ['lɪsᵉn] *vi* escuchar (**to**, -): *listen to me!* ¡escúchame!
◆ **to listen in** *vi* *(radio)* escuchar (**to**, -).
◆ **to listen out** *vi fam* estar a la escucha, estar en escucha (**for**, de).

**listener** ['lɪsᵉnər] *n* **1** *(in general)* oyente *mf*. **2** RAD radioyente *mf*.

| listing 222 |

**listing** ['lɪstɪŋ] n listado.

**lit** [lɪt] pt & pp → **light**.

**liter** ['li:tər] n US → **litre**.

**literacy** ['lɪtʰrəsɪ] n **1** (ability to read) alfabetización f. **2** (knowledge) conocimientos mpl, nociones fpl.

**literal** ['lɪtʰrəl] adj literal.

**literary** ['lɪtʰrərɪ] adj literario,-a.

**literature** ['lɪtʰrətʃər] n **1** literatura. **2** (bibliography) bibliografía.

**lithium** ['lɪθɪəm] n litio.

**lithograph** ['lɪθəgrɑːf] n litografía.

**lithosphere** ['lɪθəsfɪər] n litosfera.

**Lithuania** [lɪθjʊ'eɪnɪə] n Lituania.

**Lithuanian** [lɪθjʊ'eɪnɪən] adj lituano,-a.
▶ n **1** (person) lituano,-a. **2** (language) lituano.

**litre** ['li:tər] n litro.

**litter** ['lɪtər] n **1** (rubbish) basura, desperdicios mpl; (paper) papeles mpl. **2** (of kittens, etc) camada. COMP **litter bin** GB papelera.

**little** ['lɪtʰl] adj **1** (small) pequeño,-a: a little cup una tacita. **2** (not much) poco,-a: a little milk un poco de leche. COMP **little finger** dedo meñique.
ⓘ comp less, superl least.
▶ pron poco: more tea? -just a little, please ¿quieres más té? -un poco, por favor.
▶ adv poco: I'm a little (bit) tired estoy un poco cansada. LOC **little by little** poco a poco.

**liturgy** ['lɪtədʒɪ] n liturgia.
ⓘ pl liturgies.

**live¹** [lɪv] vi vivir: he lives in the country vive en el campo.
▶ vt vivir: the old woman had lived a life of luxury la vieja había llevado una vida llena de lujos. LOC **to live it up** fam pasárselo bomba.
◆ **to live down** vt sep lograr que se olvide.
◆ **to live in** vi (student) estar internado,-a; (servant) vivir con la familia.
◆ **to live off** vt insep vivir de.
◆ **to live on** vi sobrevivir; (memory) seguir vivo,-a.
◆ **to live through** vt insep sobrevivir.

**live²** [laɪv] adj **1** (not dead) vivo,-a: it's a real live snake es una serpiente de verdad. **2** (still burning) vivo,-a, candente; (issue) candente. **3** (broadcast) en directo: a live concert un concierto en directo.
▶ adv en directo, en vivo.

**livelihood** ['laɪvlɪhʊd] n sustento.

**lively** ['laɪvlɪ] adj **1** vivo,-a, animado,-a; (interest) entusiasmado,-a. **2** (colour) vivo,-a.
ⓘ comp livelier, superl liveliest.

**liven** ['laɪvʰn] vt **to liven up** animar.
▶ vi **liven up** animarse.

**liver** ['lɪvər] n ANAT hígado.

**lives** [laɪvz] pl → **life**.

**livestock** ['laɪvstɒk] n ganado. LOC **livestock farming** ganadería.

**living** ['lɪvɪŋ] adj vivo,-a: every living creature todo bicho viviente.
▶ n vida: what do you do for a living? ¿cómo te ganas la vida? COMP **living room** salón m, sala de estar. ▮ **living thing** ser m vivo.

**lizard** ['lɪzəd] n lagarto; (small) lagartija.

**'ll** [l] v aux → **will, shall**.

**llama** ['lɑːmə] n ZOOL llama.

**load** [ləʊd] n **1** (in general) carga: a lorry shed its load on the motorway yesterday ayer un camión perdió su carga en la autopista. **2** (weight) peso. LOC **a load of ... / loads of ...** fam montones de…, un montón de…
▶ vt cargar (with, de): they loaded up the van with furniture cargaron la furgoneta de muebles.
▶ vi cargar.
◆ **to load down** vt sep cargar (with, de); (with worries, etc) agobiar (with, de/por).

**loaf** [ləʊf] n pan m; (French) barra; (sliced) pan m de molde.
ⓘ pl loaves [ləʊvz].

**loan** [ləʊn] n (of money) préstamo, crédito. LOC **on loan** prestado,-a.

**loathe** [ləʊð] vt odiar, aborrecer.

**loaves** [ləʊvz] pl → **loaf**.

**lobby** ['lɒbɪ] n **1** (hall) vestíbulo. **2** POL grupo de presión.
ⓘ pl lobbies.

▶ *vi* presionar (**for**, para) (**against**, en contra de).

▶ *vt* POL presionar, ejercer presión sobre.

**lobe** [ləʊb] *n* lóbulo.

**lobster** [ˈlɒbstəʳ] *n* bogavante *m*.

**local** [ˈləʊkəl] *adj* **1** (in general) local. **2** (person) del barrio, de la zona.

▶ *n* **1** *fam* (person) vecino,-a. **2** GB *fam* bar *m*, pub *m* (del barrio). **3** US (train) tren *m* de cercanías; (bus) autobús *m*.

☒ Local no significa 'local (establecimiento)', que se traduce por premises.

**locality** [ləʊˈkælɪtɪ] *n fml* localidad *f*.
ⓘ *pl* localities.

**locate** [ləʊˈkeɪt] *vt* **1** *fml* (find) localizar. **2** *fml* (situate) situar, ubicar.

**location** [ləʊˈkeɪʃən] *n* **1** lugar, ubicación *m*. **2** CINEM exteriores *mpl*.

**loch** [lɒk] *n* (in Scotland) lago.

**lock¹** [lɒk] *n* **1** (gen) cerradura; (padlock) candado. **2** (in canal) esclusa. **3** (in wrestling) llave *f*.

▶ *vt* (with key) cerrar con llave; (with padlock) cerrar con candado.

▶ *vi* **1** (door, etc) cerrarse (con llave).

**lock²** [lɒk] *n* (of hair) mecha, mechón *m*.

**locker** [ˈlɒkəʳ] *n* armario, taquilla.

**locksmith** [ˈlɒksmɪθ] *n* cerrajero.

**locomotion** [ləʊkəˈməʊʃən] *n* locomoción *f*.

**locomotive** [ləʊkəˈməʊtɪv] *n* locomotora.

▶ *adj* locomotor,-ra.

**locomotor** [ləʊkəˈmətəʳ] *adj* locomotor,-a.

**locust** [ˈləʊkəst] *n* langosta.

✎ La palabra locust se refiere al insecto; el marisco se llama lobster.

**lodge** [lɒdʒ] *n* **1** (in general) casita; (hunter's) refugio. **2** (porter's) portería. **3** (masonic) logia.

▶ *vi* **1** (as guest) alojarse, hospedarse. **2** (become fixed) quedarse atrapado,-a.

▶ *vt* (complaint) presentar.

**lodger** [ˈlɒdʒəʳ] *n* huésped,-da.

**lodging** [ˈlɒdʒɪŋ] *n* alojamiento. COMP lodging house casa de huéspedes.

**loft** [lɒft] *n* desván *m*, buhardilla.

▶ *vt* SP lanzar al aire.

**log** [lɒg] *n* **1** tronco; (for fire) leño. **2** (on ship) cuaderno de bitácora; (on plane) diario de vuelo. **3** MATH *fam* (abbr of logarithm) logaritmo.

▶ *vt* **1** registrar, anotar. **2** (cover) recorrer.

◆ **to log in** *vi* COMPUT entrar (en el sistema).

◆ **to log out** *vi* COMPUT salir (del sistema).

ⓘ *pt & pp* logged, *ger* logging.

**logarithm** [ˈlɒgərɪðəm] *n* logaritmo.

**logic** [ˈlɒdʒɪk] *n* lógica.

**logical** [ˈlɒdʒɪkəl] *adj* lógico,-a: the logical thing would be to say yes lo lógico sería decir que sí.

**logistics** [ləˈdʒɪstɪks] *n* logística.

**logo** [ˈləʊgəʊ] *n* logotipo.
ⓘ *pl* logos.

**loin** [lɔɪn] *n* CULIN (of pork) lomo; (of beef) solomillo.

**lollipop** [ˈlɒlɪpɒp] *n* **1** pirulí *m*, piruleta. **2** GB (iced) polo.

**lolly** [ˈlɒlɪ] *n* **1** GB *fam* pirulí *m*, piruleta. **2** GB *fam* (iced) polo.
ⓘ *pl* lollies.

**loneliness** [ˈləʊnlɪnəs] *n* soledad *f*.

**lonely** [ˈləʊnlɪ] *adj* **1** (person) solo,-a. **2** (place) solitario,-a, aislado,-a.
ⓘ *comp* lonelier, *superl* loneliest.

**lonesome** [ˈləʊnsəm] *adj* US→ lonely.

**long¹** [lɒŋ] *adj* largo,-a: a long journey un largo viaje. COMP long jump salto de longitud.

▶ *adv* mucho tiempo: it takes a long time to climb the mountain se tarda mucho en escalar la montaña. LOC as long as (while) mientras. ‖ long ago hace mucho tiempo.

**long²** [lɒŋ] *phr* to long to do STH tener muchos deseos de hacer ALGO.

◆ **to long for** *vt insep* (yearn) anhelar; (nostalgically) añorar.

**long-distance** [lɒŋˈdɪstəns] *adj* de larga distancia.

**longing** [ˈlɒŋɪŋ] *n (yearning)* ansia, anhelo; *(nostalgia)* nostalgia.

**longitude** [ˈlɒndʒɪtjuːd] *n* longitud *f*.

**long-life** [ˈlɒŋlaɪf] *adj (battery)* de larga duración; *(milk)* UHT, uperizado,-a.

**long-range** [ˈlɒŋreɪndʒ] *adj* **1** *(distance)* de largo alcance. **2** *(plans, forecast)* a largo plazo.

**long-term** [lɒŋˈtɜːm] *adj* a largo plazo, de largo plazo.

**long-wearing** [lɒŋˈweərɪŋ] *adj* US duradero,-a, resistente.

**loo** [luː] *n* GB *fam* váter *m*.
ⓘ *pl* loos.

**look** [lʊk] *vi* **1** mirar *(at, -)*. **2** *(seem)* parecer: *he looks tired* parece cansado. LOC **look out!** ¡cuidado!
▸ *vt* **1** mirar: *I can't look him in the face* no puedo mirarle a la cara. **2** *(seem)* parecer: *he doesn't look his age* no aparenta la edad que tiene.
▸ *n* **1** *(glance)* mirada: *have a look at this* mira esto. **2** *(appearance)* aspecto, apariencia. **4** *(fashion)* moda: *I'm not into the punk look* no me va la moda punk.
▸ *interj* ¡mira!
◆ **to look after** *vt insep (deal with)* ocuparse de, atender a; *(take care of)* cuidar (de).
◆ **to look at** *vt insep* **1** *(consider)* mirar, considerar. **2** *(examine)* mirar.
◆ **to look back** *vi* mirar atrás.
◆ **to look for** *vt insep* buscar: *what are you looking for?* ¿qué buscas?
◆ **to look forward to** *vt insep* esperar (con ansia).
◆ **to look on** *vt insep* considerar.
◆ **to look like** *vt insep* parecerse a: *he looks like his father* se parece a su padre.
◆ **to look out** *vi (be careful)* ir con cuidado.
◆ **to look through** *vt insep (check)* revisar (bien); *(quickly)* ojear.
◆ **to look up** *vi fam (improve)* mejorar.
▸ *vt sep* **1** *(in dictionary, etc)* consultar, buscar.

**lookalike** [ˈlʊkəlaɪk] *n fam* doble *mf*, sosia *m*.

**loom¹** [luːm] *n* telar *m*.

**loom²** [luːm] *vi* vislumbrarse; *(causing fear)* amenazar.
◆ **to loom up** *vi* surgir.

**loony** [ˈluːnɪ] *adj fam* chiflado,-a, chalado,-a.
ⓘ *comp* loonier, *superl* looniest.

**loop** [luːp] *n (in string, etc)* lazo.
▸ *vi* formar un lazo. LOC **to loop the loop** rizar el rizo.

**loose** [luːs] *adj* **1** *(in general)* suelto,-a. **2** *(not tight)* flojo,-a; *(clothes)* holgado,-a.
▸ *vt lit* soltar.

**loose-fitting** [luːsˈfɪtɪŋ] *adj* holgado,-a, amplio,-a.

**loosen** [ˈluːsən] *vt (gen)* soltar, aflojar; *(belt)* desabrochar.
▸ *vi* **1** soltarse, aflojarse.
◆ **to loosen up** *vi (relax)* relajarse.

**loot** [luːt] *n* botín *m*.

**lord** [lɔːd] *n* **1** señor *m*. **2** GB *(title)* lord *m*. **3** *(judge)* señoría *mf*. LOC **good Lord!** ¡ay Dios!, ¡Dios mío! COMP **the Lord** REL el Señor.

**lorry** [ˈlɒrɪ] *n* GB camión *m*.
ⓘ *pl* lorries.

**lose** [luːz] *vt* **1** *(in general)* perder: *don't lose it* no lo pierdas. **2** *(clock)* atrasar.
▸ *vi* **1** *(in general)* perder: *Liverpool lost to United* el Liverpool perdió ante el United. **2** *(clock)* atrasarse. LOC **to lose one's way** perderse. ‖ **to lose sight of** STH perder ALGO de vista.
ⓘ *pt & pp* lost [lɒst], *ger* losing.

**loser** [ˈluːzər] *n* perdedor,-ra.

**loss** [lɒs] *n* **1** *(in general)* pérdida. **2** MIL *(death)* baja.
ⓘ *pl* losses.

**lost** [lɒst] *pt* → lose.
▸ *adj* perdido,-a. LOC **to get lost** perderse. COMP **lost property** objetos perdidos.

**lost-and-found** [lɒstənˈfaʊnd] [also lost-and-found department] *n* US oficina de objetos perdidos.

**lot** [lɒt] *n* **1** *(large number)* cantidad *f*: *he talks a lot* habla mucho. **2** *(group)* grupo: *the next lot of passengers* el próximo grupo de pasajeros. **3** *(fate)* suerte *f*. LOC **thanks a lot!** ¡muchísimas gracias!
▸ *n* **the lot** todo,-a, todos,-as.

▶ *phr* **lots of** mucho,-a, muchos,-as, cantidad de: *there were lots of people* había mucha gente.

**lotion** [ˈləʊʃᵊn] *n* loción *f*.

**lottery** [ˈlɒtᵊrɪ] *n* lotería.
ⓘ *pl* lotteries.

**loud** [laʊd] *adj* **1** *(sound)* fuerte. **2** *(voice)* alto,-a. **3** *(colour)* chillón,-ona.
▶ *adv* fuerte, alto. LOC **out loud** en voz alta.

**loudly** [ˈlaʊdlɪ] *adv (speak)* alto; *(shout)* fuerte; *(complain)* a voz en grito.

**loudness** [ˈlaʊdnəs] *n (of sound)* fuerza, intensidad *f*; *(noisiness)* bullicio.

**loudspeaker** [laʊdˈspiːkəʳ] *n* altavoz *m*.

**lounge** [laʊndʒ] *n* salón *m*. COMP **lounge suit** *fam* traje *m*.
▶ *vi* **1** *(on sofa, etc)* repantigarse. **2** *(idle)* holgazanear.

**lounger** [ˈlaʊndʒəʳ] *n (chair)* tumbona.

**louse** [laʊs] *n* **1** piojo. **2** *fam* canalla *mf*.
ⓘ *pl* lice.

**lousy** [ˈlaʊzɪ] *adj* **1** *fam* fatal, malísimo,-a: *he felt lousy* se encontraba fatal.
ⓘ *comp* lousier, *superl* lousiest.

**lovable** [ˈlʌvəbᵊl] *adj* adorable.

**love** [lʌv] *n* **1** *(in general)* amor *m*; *(affection)* cariño; *(liking)* afición *f* (for, a). **2** GB *fam (person)* guapo,-a, chato,-a. **3** *(regards)* recuerdos mpl: *(give my)* love to your parents muchos recuerdos a tus padres. LOC **to be in love with** estar enamorado,-a de. ▮ **to fall in love** enamorarse. ▮ **to make love** hacer el amor (to, a). COMP **love affair** aventura amorosa, lío.
▶ *vt* **1** amar, querer: *do you love him?* ¿lo quieres? **2** *(like a lot)* encantarle a uno, gustarle a uno mucho: *I love playing tennis* me encanta jugar a tenis.

**lovely** [ˈlʌvlɪ] *adj* **1** *(wonderful)* estupendo,-a, maravilloso,-a. **2** *(beautiful)* hermoso,-a, precioso,-a; *(charming)* encantador,-ra.
ⓘ *comp* lovelier, *superl* loveliest.

**lover** [ˈlʌvəʳ] *n* amante *mf*.:

**loving** [ˈlʌvɪŋ] *adj* cariñoso,-a: *your loving son, Paul* tu hijo que te quiere, Paul.

**low** [ləʊ] *adj* **1** *(in general)* bajo,-a; *(neckline)* escotado,-a: *low clouds* nubes bajas. **2** *(battery)* gastado,-a. **3** *(depressed)* deprimido,-a, abatido,-a. **4** MUS grave. LOC **to keep a low profile** ser discreto,-a. COMP **low tide** marea baja. ▮ **the Low Countries** los Países Bajos.
▶ *adv* bajo: *we're running low on petrol* se nos acaba la gasolina.
▶ *n (low level)* punto bajo.

**low-calorie** [ləʊˈkælərɪ] *adj* bajo,-a en calorías, hipocalórico,-a.

**lower** [ˈləʊəʳ] *adj* inferior. COMP **lower case** caja baja, minúscula.
▶ *vt* **1** *(in general)* bajar; *(price)* rebajar. **2** *(flag)* arriar.

**lower-class** [ləʊəˈklɑːs] *adj* de clase baja.

**lowest** [ˈləʊɪst] *adj* más bajo,-a; *(price, speed)* mínimo,-a.
▶ *n* mínimo: *at the lowest* como mínimo.

**low-fat** [ləʊˈfæt] *adj* de bajo contenido graso.

**loyal** [ˈlɔɪəl] *adj* leal, fiel.

**loyalty** [ˈlɔɪəltɪ] *n* lealtad *f*, fidelidad *f*.
ⓘ *pl* loyalties.

**lozenge** [ˈlɒzɪndʒ] *n* **1** pastilla. **2** *(geometry)* rombo.

**LP** [ˈelˈpiː] *abbr* **(long player)** elepé *m*; *(abbreviation)* LP.

**lubricant** [ˈluːbrɪkənt] *n* lubricante *m*.

**lucerne** [luːˈsɜːn] *n* GB alfalfa.

**luck** [lʌk] *n* suerte *f*. LOC **bad luck! / hard luck! / tough luck!** ¡mala suerte! ▮ **good luck! / best of luck!** ¡suerte! ▮ **to be in luck** estar de suerte. ▮ **to try one's luck** probar fortuna.

**luckily** [ˈlʌkɪlɪ] *adv* afortunadamente.

**lucky** [ˈlʌkɪ] *adj (in general)* afortunado,-a; *(timely)* oportuno,-a: *how lucky you were!* ¡qué suerte tuviste! COMP **lucky charm** amuleto.
ⓘ *comp* luckier, *superl* luckiest.

**lucrative** [ˈluːkrətɪv] *adj* lucrativo,-a.

**ludo** [ˈluːdəʊ] *n* GB parchís *m*.

**luggage** [ˈlʌgɪdʒ] *n* GB equipaje *m*. COMP **luggage rack** portaequipajes *m*. ▮ **luggage van** furgón *m* de equipaje.

L

**lukewarm** ['luːkwɔːm] *adj* tibio,-a, templado,-a.

**lullaby** ['lʌləbaɪ] *n* canción *f* de cuna, nana.
ⓘ *pl* lullabies.

**lumbar** ['lʌmbəʳ] *adj* lumbar.

**luminous** ['luːmɪnəs] *adj* luminoso,-a.

**lump** [lʌmp] *n* **1** *(chunk)* pedazo, trozo; *(in sauce)* grumo. **2** *(swelling)* bulto, protuberancia; *(in throat)* nudo. **3** *(of sugar)* terrón *m*. **4** *fam (idiot)* burro,-a.

**lumpy** ['lʌmpɪ] *adj* lleno,-a de bultos; *(sauce)* grumoso,-a.
ⓘ *comp* lumpier, *superl* lumpiest.

**lunar** ['luːnəʳ] *adj* lunar. COMP lunar landing alunizaje *m*. ‖ lunar month mes *m* lunar.

**lunatic** ['luːnətɪk] *adj* loco,-a.
▶ *n* loco,-a, lunático,-a. COMP lunatic asylum manicomio. ‖ the lunatic fringe los fanáticos *mpl*.

**lunch** [lʌntʃ] *n* comida, almuerzo: *we'll have lunch at one* comeremos a la una. COMP business lunch almuerzo de trabajo. ‖ lunch break hora de comer. ‖ lunch hour hora de comer.
▶ *vi fml* comer, almorzar.

**lunchtime** ['lʌntʃtaɪm] *n* hora de comer, hora de almorzar.

**lung** [lʌŋ] *n* pulmón *m*: *her little girl has a good pair of lungs!* ¡su hijita tiene buenos pulmones! COMP lung cancer cáncer *m* de pulmón.

**lurk** [lɜːk] *vi* **1** *(wait)* estar al acecho. **2** *(hide)* esconderse.

**lust** [lʌst] *n* **1** *(sexual)* lujuria. **2** *(greed)* codicia; *(strong desire)* ansia.

**lute** [luːt] *n* laúd *m*.

**Luxembourg** ['lʌksᵉmbɜːg] *n* Luxemburgo.

**Luxembourger** ['lʌksᵉmbɜːgəʳ] *n* luxemburgués,-esa.

**luxuriant** [lʌgˈzjuəriənt] *adj* **1** *(vegetation)* exuberante; *(hair)* abundante.

**luxurious** [lʌgˈzjuərɪəs] *adj* lujoso,-a.

**luxury** ['lʌkʃərɪ] *n* lujo.
ⓘ *pl* luxuries.

**lychee** ['laɪtʃiː] *n* lichi *m*.

**lying** ['laɪɪŋ] *adj (deceitful)* mentiroso,-a.
▶ *n (lies)* mentiras *fpl*.

**lymph** [lɪmf] *n* linfa.

**lymphatic** [lɪmˈfætɪk] *adj* linfático,-a.

**lynch** [lɪntʃ] *vt* linchar.

**lynx** [lɪŋks] *n* lince *m*.

**lyre** [laɪəʳ] *n* lira.

**lyric** ['lɪrɪk] *adj* lírico,-a.
▶ *n* poema *m* lírico.
▶ *n pl* lyrics *(of song)* letra *f sing*.

**M, m** [em] *n (the letter)* M, m *f*.
**mac** [mæk] *n* GB *fam (mackintosh)* impermeable *m*.
**macaroni** [mækə'rəuni] *n* macarrones *mpl*.
**macaw** [mə'kɔ:] *n* guacamayo, ara *m*.
**mace** [meɪs] *n (club, staff)* maza.
**macerate** ['mæsəreɪt] *vt* macerar.
  ► *vi* macerarse.
**machine** [mə'ʃi:n] *n* **1** *(gen)* máquina. **2** *(organization, system)* organización *f*, aparato. COMP **machine gun** ametralladora.
  ► *n pl* **machines** *(machinery)* maquinaria *f sing*.
**machinery** [mə'ʃi:nəri] *n* **1** *(machines)* maquinaria. **2** *(workings)* mecanismo.
**mackerel** ['mæk⁹rəl] *n* caballa.
**mackintosh** ['mækɪntɒʃ] *n* impermeable *m*.
**macro** ['mækrəu] *n* COMPUT macro *f*.
**macroeconomics** [mækrəui:kə'nɒmɪks] *n* macroeconomía.
**macroscopic** [mækrə'skɒpɪk] *adj* macroscópico,-a.
**mad** [mæd] *adj* **1** *(insane)* loco,-a: *she's quite mad* está completamente loca. **2** *fam (person)* loco,-a; *(crazy - idea, plan)* disparatado,-a, descabellado,-a. **3** *fam (enthusiastic)* loco,-a *(about,* por), chiflado,-a: *he's mad about her* está loco por ella. **4** *fam (angry)* enfadado,-a, furioso,-a *(at/with,* con). LOC **to drive SB mad / send SB mad** volver a ALGN loco,-a, traer loco,-a a ALGN. ‖ **to get mad** enfadarse. ‖ **to go mad** volverse loco,-a, enloquecer.
  ① *comp* **madder**, *superl* **maddest**.
**Madagascan** [mædə'gæsk⁹n] *adj* malgache.
  ► *n (person)* malgache *mf*.
**Madagascar** [mædə'gæskə^r] *n* Madagascar.
**madam** ['mædəm] *n fml* señora.
**made** [meɪd] *pt & pp* → make.
  ► *adj (produced)* hecho,-a, fabricado,-a: *made in England* hecho,-a en Inglaterra. LOC **to be made from** STH estar hecho, -a de ALGO. ‖ **to be made of** STH ser de ALGO, estar hecho,-a de ALGO, estar compuesto,-a de ALGO.
**madly** ['mædlɪ] *adv* como un loco.
**madness** ['mædnəs] *n* **1** *(insanity)* locura, demencia. **2** *(foolishness)* locura: *it is madness to drive in this weather* es una locura conducir con el tiempo que hace.
**magazine** [mægə'zi:n] *n* **1** *(periodical)* revista. **2** *(on TV, radio)* magacín *m*, magazine *m*. COMP **magazine rack** revistero.
**maggot** ['mægət] *n* larva, gusano.
**magic** ['mædʒɪk] *n* magia.
  ► *adj* mágico,-a. COMP **magic wand** varita mágica.
**magical** ['mædʒɪk⁹l] *adj* mágico,-a.
**magician** [mə'dʒɪʃ⁹n] *n* **1** *(conjurer)* prestidigitador,-ra, ilusionista *mf*. **2** *(wizard)* mago,-a.
**magistrate** ['mædʒɪstreɪt] *n* JUR magistrado,-a, juez *mf*.
**magma** ['mægmə] *n* magma.
**magnesite** ['mægnesɪt] *n* magnesita.
**magnesium** [mæg'ni:zɪəm] *n* magnesio.
**magnet** ['mægnət] *n* imán *m*.
**magnetic** [mæg'netɪk] *adj* **1** *(force, etc)* magnético,-a. **2** *fig (personality, charm)* carismático,-a.
**magnetism** ['mægnɪtɪz⁹m] *n* magnetismo.

**magnetized** ['mægnɪtaɪzd] *adj* magnetizado,-a. **2** *fig (person)* magnetizar, cautivar.

**magnification** [mægnɪfɪ'keɪʃ°n] *n* **1** *(increase)* aumento, ampliación *f*. **2** *(power of lens, etc)* aumento.

**magnificent** [mæg'nɪfɪs°nt] *adj (splendid)* magnífico,-a, espléndido,-a.

**magnify** ['mægnɪfaɪ] *vt* **1** *(enlarge)* aumentar, ampliar. **2** *fig (exaggerate)* exagerar, agrandar.
  ⓘ *pt & pp* magnified, *ger* magnifying.

**magnifying glass** ['mægnɪfaɪɪŋglɑːs] *n* lupa.
  ⓘ *pl* magnifying glasses.

**magnitude** ['mægnɪtjuːd] *n (size)* magnitud *f*; *(importance)* magnitud *f*, envergadura.

**magnolia** [mæg'nəʊlɪə] *n* **1** *(tree)* magnolio, magnolia. **2** *(flower)* magnolia.

**magpie** ['mægpaɪ] *n* urraca.

**mahogany** [mə'hɒgənɪ] *n (wood, tree)* caoba; *(colour)* color *m* caoba.

**maid** [meɪd] *n (servant)* criada, sirvienta; *(in hotel)* camarera.

**maiden** ['meɪd°n] *n (unmarried woman, girl)* doncella.
  ▶ *adj (first of its kind - speech, voyage)* inaugural.

**mail** [meɪl] *n* **1** *(system)* correo: *send it by mail* envíalo por correo. **2** *(letters, etc)* correo, cartas *mpl*, correspondencia.
  ▶ *vt (send)* mandar por correo.

**mailbox** ['meɪlbɒks] *n* buzón *m*.

**mailman** ['meɪlmæn] *n* US cartero.
  ⓘ *pl* mailmen ['meɪlmæn].

**maim** [meɪm] *vt* mutilar, lisiar.

**main** [meɪn] *adj (most important)* principal: *be careful when you cross the main road* ten cuidado al cruzar la carretera principal. COMP **main course** plato principal, segundo plato. ‖ **main road** carretera principal.

**mainframe** ['meɪnfreɪm] [also mainframe computer] *n* unidad *f* central, ordenador *m* central.

**mainland** ['meɪnlənd] *n continente o isla grande en contraposición a una isla cercana más pequeña*.

**mainly** ['meɪnlɪ] *adv (chiefly)* principalmente, sobre todo; *(mostly)* en su mayoría.

**maintain** [meɪn'teɪn] *vt* **1** *(preserve, keep up - gen)* mantener; *(- silence, appearances)* guardar. **2** *(support financially)* mantener, sostener.

**maintenance** ['meɪntənəns] *n* **1** *(gen)* mantenimiento. **2** *(upkeep of family)* manutención *f*.

**maize** [meɪz] *n* maíz *m*.

**majesty** ['mædʒəstɪ] *n* majestad *f*.
  ⓘ *pl* majesties.

**major** ['meɪdʒəʳ] *adj* **1** *(more important, greater)* mayor, principal: *tourism is the major industry* el turismo es la industria principal. **2** *(important - gen)* importante; *(- issue)* de gran envergadura; *(- illness)* grave. **3** MUS *(key, scale)* mayor.
  ▶ *n* **1** MIL comandante *m*.

**majorette** [meɪdʒər'et] *n* majorette *f*.

**majority** [mə'dʒɒrɪtɪ] *n* mayoría: *the great majority of students* la gran mayoría de los estudiantes. LOC **to be in a/the majority** ser mayoría.
  ⓘ *pl* majorities.
  ▶ *adj* mayoritario,-a.

**make** [meɪk] *n (brand)* marca: *what make is your watch?* ¿de qué marca es tu reloj?
  ▶ *vt* **1** *(produce - gen)* hacer; *(construct)* construir; *(manufacture)* fabricar; *(create)* crear; *(prepare)* preparar: *she made some sandwiches* hizo unos bocadillos, preparó unos bocadillos; *stop making all that noise!* ¡dejad de hacer tanto ruido! **2** *(carry out, perform)* hacer: *I must make a phone call* tengo que hacer una llamada. **3** *(cause to be)* hacer, poner, volver: *the gift made him happy* el regalo lo hizo feliz. **4** *(force, compel)* hacer, obligar; *(cause to do)* hacer: *they make me go to bed early* me obligan a acostarme temprano. **5** *(be, become)* ser, hacer; *(cause to be)* hacer, convertir en: *she'll make a good singer* será buena cantante, tiene madera de cantante.
  ▶ *vi (to be about to)* hacer como, simular: *he made as if to kiss her* hizo como si la besara. LOC **to make sense** tener sentido. ‖ **to make sure (of** STH**)** asegurarse (de ALGO).

◆ **to make for** *vt insep* **1** *(move towards)* dirigirse hacia. **2** *(result in, make possible)* contribuir a, crear, conducir a.

◆ **to make out** *vt sep* **1** *(write - list, receipt)* hacer; *(- cheque)* extender, hacer; *(- report)* redactar. **2** *(see)* distinguir, divisar; *(writing)* descifrar. **3** *(understand)* entender, comprender.

▸ *vt insep fam* *(pretend, claim)* pretender, hacerse pasar por.

◆ **to make up** *vt sep* **1** *(invent)* inventar. **2** *(put together)* hacer; *(assemble)* montar; *(bed, prescription)* preparar; *(page)* componer; *(clothes, curtains)* confeccionar, hacer. **3** *(complete)* completar. **4** *(constitute)* componer, formar, integrar; *(represent)* representar. **5** *(cosmetics)* maquillar.

▸ *vi* **1** maquillarse, pintarse. **2** *(become friends again)* hacer las paces, reconciliarse.

ⓘ *pt & pp* made, *ger* making.

**maker** ['meɪkə<sup>r</sup>] *n* *(of product)* fabricante *mf*; *(of film, etc)* creador,-ra.

**make-up** ['meɪkʌp] *n* **1** *(cosmetics)* maquillaje *m*: she never wears make-up nunca se maquilla, nunca se pone maquillaje. **2** *(composition, combination)* composición *f*. **3** *(of person)* carácter *m*.

**malaria** [mə'leərɪə] *n* malaria, paludismo.

**Malawi** [mə'lɑːwɪ] *n* Malawi.

**Malawian** [mə'lɑːwɪən] *adj* malawiano,-a.

▸ *n* malawiano,-a.

**Malaysia** [mə'leɪzɪə] *n* Malaysia, Malasia.

**Malaysian** [mə'leɪzɪən] *adj* malasio,-a.

▸ *n* malasio,-a.

**Maldives** ['mɔːldaɪvz] *n* Maldivas.

**Maldivian** [mɔːl'dɪvɪən] *adj* maldivo,-a.

▸ *n* maldivo,-a.

**male** [meɪl] *adj* **1** *(animal, plant)* macho; *(person, child)* varón; *(sex, hormone, character, organ)* masculino,-a. **2** *(manly)* varonil, viril.

▸ *n* *(man, boy)* varón *m*; *(animal, plant)* macho.

**Mali** ['mɑːlɪ] *n* Malí.

**Malian** ['mɑːlɪən] *adj* maliense.

▸ *n* maliense *mf*.

**mall** [mæl, mɔːl] *n* US *(covered)* centro comercial; *(street)* zona comercial.

**malleability** ['mælɪəbɪlɪtɪ] *n* **1** *(metal)* maleabilidad *f*. **2** *fig* *(person)* docilidad *f*.

**malleable** ['mælɪəb<sup>ə</sup>l] *adj* **1** *(metal)* maleable. **2** *fig* *(person)* dócil.

**mallet** ['mælət] *n* mazo.

**malnutrition** [mælnjuː'trɪʃ<sup>ə</sup>n] *n* desnutrición *f*.

**malt** [mɔːlt] *n* *(grain)* malta.

**Malta** ['mɔːltə] *n* Malta.

**Maltese** [mɔːl'tiːz] *adj* maltés,-esa.

▸ *n* **1** *(person)* maltés,-esa. **2** *(language)* maltés *m*.

▸ *n pl* **the Maltese** los malteses *mpl*.

**maltreatment** [mæl'triːtmənt] *n* malos tratos *mpl*.

**mammal** ['mæm<sup>ə</sup>l] *n* mamífero.

**mammary** ['mæmərɪ] *adj* mamario,-a.

COMP **mammary gland** mama.

**mammography** [mæ'mɒgrəfɪ] *n* mamografía.

ⓘ *pl* mammographies.

**mammoth** ['mæməθ] *n* ZOOL mamut *m*.

**mammy** ['mæmɪ] *n fam* mamá.

ⓘ *pl* mammies.

**man** [mæn] *n* **1** *(adult male)* hombre *m*, señor *m*: an old man un hombre mayor, un señor mayor, un viejo. **2** *(human being, person)* ser *m* humano, el hombre *m*: all men are born equal todos los hombres nacen iguales. **3** *(husband)* marido, hombre *m*; *(boyfriend)* novio; *(partner)* pareja: man and wife marido y mujer.

ⓘ *pl* men.

**manage** ['mænɪdʒ] *vt* **1** *(run - business, company)* dirigir; *(- property)* administrar: she manages a shop es la encargada de una tienda, lleva una tienda. **2** *(handle, cope with - child, person)* llevar, manejar; *(- animal)* domar; *(- work, luggage, etc)* poder con. **3** *(succeed)* conseguir, lograr: we managed it! ¡lo conseguimos! **4** *(have room for, have time for)* poder.

▸ *vi* **1** poder: can you manage? ¿puedes? **2** *(financially)* arreglárselas, apañarse.

**manager** ['mænɪdʒə<sup>r</sup>] *n* **1** *(of company, bank)* director,-ra, gerente *mf*. **2** *(of shop, restaurant)* encargado,-a; *(of depart-*

**M**

*ment)* jefe,-a. **3** *(of actor, group, etc)* representante *mf*, manager *mf*. **4** SP *(of football team)* entrenador *m*, míster *m*.

**mandarin** [ˈmændərɪn] *n* **1** mandarina. **2** GB *pej (government official)* mandarín *m*.
▸ *n* Mandarin *(language)* mandarín *m*.

**mandatory** [ˈmændətˀrɪ] *adj (compulsory)* obligatorio,-a.

**mandible** [ˈmændɪbˀl] *n* mandíbula.

**mane** [meɪn] *n (of horse)* crin *f*; *(of lion)* melena.

**maneuver** [məˈnuːvəʳ] *n & v* US → **manoeuvre.**

**manganese** [ˈmæŋgəniːz] *n* manganeso.

**manger** [ˈmeɪndʒəʳ] *n* pesebre *m*.

**mangle** [ˈmæŋgˀl] *vt* **1** *(cut to pieces)* destrozar, despedazar; *(crush)* aplastar.

**mango** [ˈmæŋgəʊ] *n* mango.
ⓘ *pl* mangoes o mangos.

**mangrove** [ˈmæŋgrəʊv] *n* manglar *m*.

**maniac** [ˈmeɪnɪæk] *n* **1** *fam (wild person)* loco,-a. **2** *fam (fan)* entusiasta *mf*, fanático,-a.

**manifestation** [mænɪfeˈsteɪˀn] *n fml* manifestación *f*.

❌ Manifestation no significa 'manifestación (de protesta)', que se traduce por demonstration.

**manifesto** [mænɪˈfestəʊ] *n* manifiesto.
ⓘ *pl* manifestos o manifestoes.

**manioc** [ˈmænɪɒk] *n* mandioca, yuca.

**manipulate** [məˈnɪpjəleɪt] *vt* **1** *(work-machine)* manejar; *(- knob, lever)* accionar. **2** *(control, influence)* manipular.

**mankind** [mænˈkaɪnd] *n* la humanidad *f*, el género humano, los hombres *mpl*.

**man-made** [mænˈmeɪd] *adj* **1** *(lake, etc)* artificial. **2** *(fabric, etc)* sintético,-a.

**mannequin** [ˈmænɪkɪn] *n* **1** *(dummy)* maniquí *m*. **2** *dated (model)* modelo *f*.

**manner** [ˈmænəʳ] *n* **1** *(way, method)* manera, modo: *in this manner* de esta manera. **2** *(way of behaving)* forma de ser, comportamiento, aire *m*: *she has a pleasant manner* tiene una forma de ser agradable. LOC **in a manner of speaking** por decirlo así, hasta cierto punto.

▸ *n pl* **manners** *(social behaviour)* maneras *fpl*, modales *mpl*; *(customs)* costumbres *fpl*. COMP **bad manners** falta de educación. **I good manners** buenos modales *mpl*.

**manoeuvre** [məˈnuːvəʳ] *n* maniobra.
▸ *vt* **1** *(gen)* maniobrar. **2** *(person)* manipular, manejar.
▸ *vi* maniobrar.

**manometer** [məˈnɒmɪtəʳ] *n* manómetro.

**manor** [ˈmænəʳ] *n* señorío. COMP **manor house** casa solariega.

**manpower** [ˈmænpaʊəʳ] *n* mano *f* de obra.

**mansion** [ˈmænʃˀn] *n (gen)* casa grande; *(country)* casa solariega.

**mantelpiece** [ˈmæntˀlpiːs] *n* repisa de chimenea.

**mantis** [ˈmæntɪs] *n* mantis *f*.
ⓘ *pl* mantis.

**manual** [ˈmænjuəl] *adj* manual.
▸ *n* manual *m*.

**manufacture** [mænjəˈfæktʃəʳ] *n (gen)* fabricación *f*; *(of clothing)* confección *f*; *(of foodstuffs)* elaboración *f*.
▸ *vt* **1** *(gen)* fabricar; *(clothing)* confeccionar; *(foodstuffs)* elaborar. **2** *fig (excuse, etc)* inventar.

**manufactured** [mænjəˈfæktʃərəd] *adj* manufacturado,-da.

**manufacturer** [mænjəˈfæktʃərəʳ] *adj* fabricante *mf*.

**manure** [məˈnjʊəʳ] *n* abono, estiércol *m*.

**manuscript** [ˈmænjəskrɪpt] *n* **1** *(historic handwritten book)* manuscrito. **2** *(original copy of text)* original *m*, texto original.

**many** [ˈmenɪ] *adj* mucho,-a, muchos,-as: *many people never go abroad* mucha gente nunca va al extranjero.
ⓘ *comp* more, *superl* most. LOC **as many ... as** tantos,-as... como. I **how many?** ¿cuántos,-as? I **not many** pocos,-as, no muchos,-as. I **too many** demasiados,-as.
▸ *pron* muchos,-as: *I don't want many* no quiero muchos.

🔊 Many se usa sobre todo en las frases negativas y en las preguntas; en las frases afirmativas se usa más a lot of.

**map** [mæp] n *(of country, region)* mapa m; *(of town, bus, tube)* plano. COMP **map of the world** mapamundi m.

▶ vt *(area)* trazar un mapa de.

ⓘ pt & pp **mapped**, ger **mapping**.

**maple** ['meɪpªl] n *(tree, wood)* arce m.

**marathon** ['mærəθªn] n maratón m.

▶ adj fig maratoniano,-a, larguísimo,-a.

**marble** ['mɑːbªl] n **1** *(stone, statue)* mármol m. **2** *(glass ball)* canica.

▶ n pl **marbles** *(game)* canicas fpl. ART mármoles mpl.

**March** [mɑːtʃ] n marzo.

✎ Para ejemplos de uso, consulta May.

**march** [mɑːtʃ] n **1** MIL marcha. **2** *(walk)* caminata. **3** *(demonstration)* manifestación f. **4** MUS marcha.

▶ vi **1** MIL marchar, hacer una marcha. **2** *(walk)* caminar, marchar.

▶ vt hacer marchar.

**mare** [meəʳ] n yegua.

**margarine** [mɑːdʒəˈriːn] n margarina.

**marge** [mɑːdʒ] n GB fam margarina.

**margin** ['mɑːdʒɪn] n **1** *(gen)* margen m. **2** *(difference, leeway)* margen m: *there is no margin for error* no hay margen de error.

**marginal** ['mɑːdʒɪnªl] adj **1** *(small, minor)* menor, pequeño,-a, mínimo,-a. **2** *(artist)* marginal.

**marihuana** [mærɪˈhwɑːnə] n marihuana.

**marina** [məˈriːnə] n puerto deportivo.

**marinate** ['mærɪneɪt] vt adobar.

**marine** [məˈriːn] n *(life, flora, etc)* marino,-a, marítimo,-a.

▶ adj *(law, stores, etc)* marítimo,-a.

▶ n soldado de infantería de marina.

▶ n pl **the Marines** GB la infantería de marina.

**marionette** [mærɪəˈnet] n marioneta, títere m.

**marital** ['mærɪtªl] adj *(relations, problems)* matrimonial, marital; *(bliss)* conyugal. COMP **marital status** estado civil.

**maritime** ['mærɪtaɪm] adj marítimo,-a.

**mark** [mɑːk] n **1** *(imprint, trace)* huella; *(from blow)* señal f; *(stain)* mancha: *there's a mark on this blouse* esta blusa tie-

ne una mancha. **2** *(sign, symbol)* marca, señal f: *I've put a mark by the things I'm interested in* he señalado las cosas que me interesan. **3** EDUC nota, calificación f: *he got a good mark in maths* sacó una buena nota en mates. LOC **on your marks, get set, go!** ¡preparados, listos, ya!

▶ vt **1** *(gen)* marcar. **2** EDUC *(correct)* corregir; *(grade - student)* poner nota a; *(- exam, essay, etc)* puntuar, calificar.

▶ vi *(stain)* mancharse.

◆ **to mark down** vt sep **1** *(reduce price of)* rebajar el precio de. **2** *(reduce marks of)* bajar la nota de. **3** *(note in writing)* apuntar.

◆ **to mark out** vt sep **1** *(area)* marcar, delimitar; *(boundary)* marcar, trazar. **2** *(choose)* señalar, seleccionar.

**market** ['mɑːkɪt] n **1** *(selling fruit, vegetables, etc)* mercado; *(selling clothes, etc)* mercadillo; *(marketplace)* plaza: *I always go to the market on Saturdays* siempre voy a la plaza los sábados. **2** *(trade)* mercado: *the property market* el mercado inmobiliario. LOC **to be on the market** estar en venta. COMP **market day** día m de mercado. ▌**market garden** GB huerta. ▌**market price** precio de mercado.

**marketing** ['mɑːkɪtɪŋ] n marketing m, mercadotecnia.

**marketplace** ['mɑːkɪtpleɪs] n mercado; *(square)* plaza.

**marksman** ['mɑːksmən] n tirador m.

ⓘ pl **marksmen** ['mɑːksmən].

**marmalade** ['mɑːməleɪd] n mermelada (de cítricos).

✎ La palabra **marmalade** sólo se refiere a las mermeladas de cítricos y en especial a la de naranja. Las demás mermeladas se llaman **jam**.

**maroon** [məˈruːn] adj granate.

▶ n *(color m)* granate m.

**marquee** [mɑːˈkiː] n *(large tent)* carpa.

**marriage** ['mærɪdʒ] n **1** *(state, institution)* matrimonio. **2** *(act, wedding)* boda, casamiento, enlace m matrimonial. LOC **to take SB in marriage** casarse con ALGN. COMP **marriage bureau** agencia matrimonial. ▌**marriage certificate** certificado de matrimonio.

**M**

**married** ['mærɪd] *adj* **1** *(person, status)* casado,-a (**to**, con): *a married couple* un matrimonio. **2** *(life, bliss)* matrimonial, conyugal.

**marrow** ['mærəʊ] *n* **1** ([also bone marrow] ANAT *(of bone)* tuétano, médula. *fig (inner meaning)* meollo. **2** [also vegetable marrow] GB calabacín *m* grande.

**marry** ['mærɪ] *vt* **1** *(take in marriage)* casarse con. **2** *(unite in marriage)* casar.
▸ *vi* **1** casarse. **2** *fig* unirse. LOC **to get married** casarse (**to**, con).
ⓘ *pt & pp* **married**, *ger* **marrying**.

**Mars** [mɑːz] *n* Marte *m*.

**marsh** [mɑːʃ] *n* **1** *(bog)* pantano. **2** *(area)* zona con pantanos, pantanal *m*.

**marshal** ['mɑːʃəl] *n* **1** MIL mariscal *m*. **2** *(at sports event, demonstration)* oficial *mf*, organizador,-ra.

**martial** ['mɑːʃəl] *adj* marcial.

**Martian** ['mɑːʃən] *n* marciano,-a.
▸ *adj* marciano,-a.

**martyr** ['mɑːtəʳ] *n* **1** mártir *mf*. **2** *fam* víctima (**to**, de).

**martyrdom** ['mɑːtədəm] *n* martirio.

**marvel** ['mɑːvəl] *n* **1** *(wonder)* maravilla: *it's a marvel no-one was hurt* es un milagro que no hubiera heridos. **2** *(person)* maravilla. LOC **to do marvels / work marvels** hacer maravillas.
▸ *vi* **1** *fml* maravillarse (**at**, con), asombrarse (**at**, de).
ⓘ *pt & pp* **marvelled** (US **marveled**), *ger* **marvelling** (US **marveling**).

**marvellous** ['mɑːvələs] *adj* maravilloso,-a, magnífico,-a, estupendo,-a.

**marzipan** ['mɑːzɪpæn] *n* mazapán *m*.

**mascara** [mæˈskɑːrə] *n* rímel *m*.

❎ Mascara no significa 'máscara', que se traduce por mask.

**mascot** ['mæskɒt] *n* mascota.

**masculine** ['mɑːskjəlɪn] *adj* masculino,-a.
▸ *n* LING masculino.

**mash** [mæʃ] *n* CULIN *fam* puré *m* de patatas.
▸ *vt* **1** *(beat, crush)* triturar (**up**, -), machacar (**up**, -). **2** CULIN *(potatoes)* hacer un puré de. COMP **mashed potatoes** puré *m* de patatas.

**mask** [mɑːsk] *n* *(gen)* máscara; *(disguise)* careta, carátula; *(around eyes)* antifaz *m*. COMP **diving mask** gafas *fpl* de bucear.
▸ *vt* *(gen)* enmascarar.

**masked** [mɑːskt] *adj* enmascarado,-a. COMP **masked ball** baile *m* de disfraces, baile *m* de máscaras.

**masking tape** ['mɑːskɪŋteɪp] *n* cinta adhesiva.

**masochism** ['mæsəkɪzəm] *n* masoquismo.

**masochist** ['mæsəkɪst] *n* masoquista.
▸ *adj* masoquista.

**mason** ['meɪsən] *n* *(builder)* albañil *m*.

**mass** [mæs] *n* **1** *(large quantity)* montón *m*, masa; *(of people)* masa, multitud *f*, muchedumbre *f*: *a mass of books* un montón de libros. **2** *(majority)* mayoría.
▸ *vi* *(crowd)* congregarse, reunirse en gran número.
▸ *vt* reunir.
▸ *adj* masivo,-a, multitudinario,-a, de masas: *there was a mass meeting* se celebró un mitin multitudinario. COMP **mass media** medios *mpl* de comunicación (de masas).
▸ *n pl* **masses** *fam* *(lots)* cantidad *f*, montones *mpl*, mogollón *m*.

**Mass** [mæs] *n* REL misa.

**massage** ['mæsɑːʒ] *n* masaje *m*.
▸ *vt* **1** *(person, body)* dar un masaje a; *(part of body)* dar un masaje en.

**masseter** ['mæsətəʳ] *n* masetero.

**masseur** [mæˈsɜːʳ] *n* masajista *m*.

**masseuse** [mæˈsɜːz] *n* masajista *f*.

**massif** [mæˈsiːf] *n* macizo.

**massive** ['mæsɪv] *adj* **1** *(huge)* enorme, gigantesco. **2** *(solid, weighty)* sólido,-a, macizo,-a.

**mast** [mɑːst] *n* **1** MAR mástil *m*, palo. **2** *(transmitter)* torre *f*, poste *m*.

**master** ['mɑːstəʳ] *n* **1** *(of slave, servant, dog)* amo; *(of household)* señor *m*; *(owner)* dueño. **2** MAR *(of ship)* capitán *m*; *(of fishing boat)* patrón *m*. **3** GB *(teacher - infant school)* maestro, profesor *m*; *(- secondary)* profesor *m*. COMP **master bedroom** dormitorio principal. ∥ **master copy** original *m*.
▸ *n* **Master's (degree)** EDUC máster *m*.

▶ *adj (expert, skilled)* maestro,-a, experto,-a.

▶ *vt (learn - subject, skill)* llegar a dominar; *(- craft)* llegar a ser experto,-a en.

**mastermind** ['mɑːstəmaɪnd] *n (person)* cerebro, genio.

**masterpiece** ['mɑːstəpiːs] *n* obra maestra.

**mastodon** ['mæstədɒn] *n* mastodonte *m*.

**masturbation** [mæstəˈbeɪʃ⁰n] *n* masturbación *f*.

**mat** [mæt] *n* **1** *(rug)* alfombrilla; *(doormat)* felpudo. **2** *(rush mat)* estera; *(beach mat)* esterilla. **3** SP colchoneta.

**match¹** [mætʃ] *n (light)* cerilla, fósforo.

**match²** [mætʃ] *n* **1** SP *(football, hockey, etc)* partido, encuentro. **2** *(equal)* igual *mf*: *when it comes to chess, she's no match for you* ella no puede competir contigo al ajedrez. **3** *(marriage)* casamiento, matrimonio. **4** *(clothes, colour, etc)* juego, combinación *f*.
ⓘ *pl* matches.

▶ *vt* **1** *(equal)* igualar: *nobody can match him* nadie lo iguala. **2** *(go well with)* hacer juego (con), combinar (con): *her shoes match her dress* los zapatos hacen juego con el vestido. **3** *(be like, correspond to)* corresponder a, ajustarse a.

▶ *vi* **1** *(go together)* hacer juego, combinar. **2** *(tally)* coincidir, concordar. **3** *(people)* llevarse bien, avenirse.

**matchbox** ['mætʃbɒks] *n* caja de cerillas.
ⓘ *pl* matchboxes.

**matching** ['mætʃɪŋ] *adj* que hace juego, a juego.

**mate** [meɪt] *n* **1** *(school friend, fellow worker, etc)* compañero,-a, colega *mf*; *(friend)* amigo,-a, colega *mf*, compinche *mf*. **2** *(assistant)* ayudante *mf*, aprendiz,-za. **3** ZOOL pareja; *(male)* macho; *(female)* hembra.

✎ Mate entra también en la formación de palabras como classmate (compañero de clase), flatmate (persona con la que se comparte un piso), roommate (persona con la que se comparte una habitación) o teammate (compañero de equipo).

**material** [məˈtɪərɪəl] *n* **1** *(physical substance)* materia, material *m*; *raw material* materia prima; *building materials* materiales de construcción. **2** *(cloth)* tela, tejido.

▶ *adj* **1** *(physical)* material. **2** *(important)* importante.

**materialism** [məˈtɪərɪəlɪz⁰m] *n* materialismo.

**maternity** [məˈtɜːnɪtɪ] *n* maternidad *f*.

**math** [mæθ] *n fam* US mates *fpl*.

**mathematical** [mæθəˈmætɪk⁰l] *adj* matemático,-a.

**mathematician** [mæθ⁰məˈtɪʃ⁰n] *n* matemático,-a.

**mathematics** [mæθ⁰ˈmætɪks] *n* matemáticas *fpl*.

**maths** [mæθs] *n fam* mates *fpl*.

**mating** ['meɪtɪŋ] *n* ZOOL acoplamiento, apareamiento. COMP **mating call** reclamo. ▌**mating season** época de celo.

**matrix** ['meɪtrɪks] *n* matriz *f*.
ⓘ *pl* matrixes o matrices ['meɪtrɪsiːz].

**matter** ['mætə⁰] *n* **1** *(affair, subject)* asunto, cuestión *f*: *it's a personal matter* es un asunto personal. **2** *(trouble, problem)* problema *m*: *what's the matter?* ¿qué pasa? **3** PHYS *(physical substance)* materia, sustancia. **4** *(type of substance, things of a particular kind)* materia. LOC **as a matter of fact** en realidad, de hecho. ▌**to be another matter** ser otra cosa.

▶ *vi (be important)* importar (to, a): *it doesn't matter* no importa, es igual, da igual. LOC **no matter** no importa: *no matter what* pase lo que pase; *no matter what I say* diga lo que diga.

**matting** ['mætɪŋ] *n* estera.

**mattress** ['mætrəs] *n* colchón *m*.
ⓘ *pl* mattresses.

**mature** [məˈtʃʊə⁰] *adj (gen)* maduro,-a.
▶ *vt* madurar.
▶ *vi & vt* madurar.

**maturity** [məˈtʃʊərətɪ] *n* madurez *f*.

**Mauritania** [mɒrɪˈteɪnɪə] *n* Mauritania.

**Mauritanian** [mɒrɪˈteɪnɪən] *adj* mauritano,-a.
▶ *n* mauritano,-a.

**mausoleum** [mɔːsəˈlɪəm] *n* mausoleo.

**mauve** [məʊv] *adj* malva.
▶ *n* malva *m*.

**maverick** ['mæv°rɪk] n inconformista mf, independiente mf.
▶ adj inconformista, independiente.

**maxilla** ˈmæksɪlə] n maxilar m.
① pl maxillae.

**maximum** ['mæksɪməm] adj máximo,-a.
▶ n máximo, máximum m. LOC to the maximum al máximo.

**May** [meɪ] n mayo: his birthday is on the twentieth of May su cumpleaños es el veinte de mayo; at the beginning/end of May a principios/finales de mayo; in the middle of May a mediados de mayo; last May en mayo del año pasado; next May en mayo del año que viene.

**may** [meɪ] aux 1 (possibility, probability) poder, ser posible: he may come es posible que venga, puede que venga; you may laugh, but I think it's serious tú bien puedes reír, pero yo creo que es grave. 2 (permission) poder: may I help you? ¿en qué puedo servirle?; may I go? ¿puedo irme? 3 (wish) ojalá: may it be so ojalá sea así.

✎ Cuando may expresa una posibilidad se puede traducir por 'quizá', 'quizás', 'a lo mejor', 'tal vez' o 'puede que'; cuando se usa para pedir o conceder permiso se traduce sencillamente por 'poder'. Consulta también might.

**maybe** ['meɪbi:] adv quizá, quizás, tal vez: maybe it'll rain tal vez llueva; maybe you're right quizás tengas razón, a lo mejor tienes razón.

**mayday** ['meɪdeɪ] n señal f de socorro, S.O.S. m.

**mayonnaise** [meɪə'neɪz] n mayonesa, mahonesa.

**mayor** [meəʳ] n (man) alcalde m; (woman) alcaldesa.

**mayoress** ['meəres] n alcaldesa.

**maze** [meɪz] n laberinto.

**me¹** [mi:] n MUS mi m.

**me²** [mi:] pron 1 (as object of verb) me: follow me sígueme; give it to me dámelo; he looked at me me miró. 2 (after prep) mí: it's for me es para mí; are you talking to me? ¿me lo dices a mí? 3 (emphatic) yo: it's me! ¡soy yo!; it's me, David soy David.

**meadow** ['medəu] n prado, pradera.

**meal¹** [mi:l] n (flour) harina.

**meal²** [mi:l] n (gen) comida: three meals a day tres comidas al día. LOC to have a meal 1 (lunch) comer. 2 (supper) cenar.

✎ Meal se refiere a cualquiera de las tres comidas principales que se toman a lo largo del día.

**mealtime** ['mi:ltaɪm] n hora de comer.

**mean¹** [mi:n] adj 1 (miserly, selfish - person) mezquino,-a, tacaño,-a, agarrado, -a. 2 (unkind) malo,-a, antipático,-a; (petty) mezquino,-a; (ashamed) avergonzado,-a. 3 fam (skilful, great) excelente, de primera, genial. LOC to be no mean ser todo,-a un,-a: she's no mean singer es una cantante genial.

**mean²** [mi:n] vt 1 (signify, represent) significar, querer decir; (to be a sign of, indicate) ser señal de, significar: what does «mug» mean? ¿qué significa «mug»?, ¿qué quiere decir «mug»? 2 (have in mind) pensar, tener la intención de: she didn't mean to do it lo hizo sin querer. 3 (involve, entail) suponer, implicar; (have as result) significar: that means we can't go on holiday eso significa que no podemos irnos de vacaciones. LOC to be meant for 1 (be intended for) ser para. 2 (be destined for) estar dirigido,-a a, ir dirigido,-a a: these shoes are meant for light walking estos zapatos son para pasear.
① pt & pp meant [ment].

**mean³** [mi:n] adj (average) medio,-a: mean temperature temperatura media.
▶ n 1 (average) promedio. 2 MATH media. 3 (middle term) término medio.

**meander** [mɪ'ændəʳ] vi 1 (river, etc) serpentear. 2 (person) vagar, deambular, andar sin rumbo fijo. 3 fig (conversation) divagar.
▶ n (of river, etc) meandro.

**meaning** ['mi:nɪŋ] n 1 (sense) sentido, significado. what's the meaning of «draft»? ¿qué significa «draft»?, ¿qué quiere decir «draft»? 2 (significance, importance) sentido; (purpose, intention) intención f: a glance full of meaning una mirada llena de intención.

**meaningless** ['miːnɪŋləs] *adj* **1** *(word, phrase, etc)* sin sentido. **2** *(futile)* sin sentido, inútil, vano,-a.

**means** [miːnz] *n (way, method)* medio, manera: *there's no means of escape* no hay escapatoria, no hay manera de escapar; *a means of transport* un medio de transporte. ► *n pl (resources)* medios *mpl* de vida, recursos *mpl*. LOC **a means to an end** un medio de conseguir un objetivo, un medio para lograr un fin. ❙ **by all means** naturalmente, por supuesto. ❙ **by means of** por medio de, mediante. ❙ **by no means / not by any means** de ninguna manera, de ningún modo. ❙ **to live beyond one's means** vivir por encima de sus posibilidades.
ⓘ *pl* means.

**meant** [mærɪˈhwɑːnə] *pp & pt* → **mean**.

**meantime** ['miːntaɪm] *adv* mientras tanto, entretanto. LOC **in the meantime** mientras tanto.

**meanwhile** ['miːnwaɪl] *adv* mientras tanto, entretanto.

**measles** ['miːzəlz] *n* MED sarampión *m*.

**measurable** ['meʒərəbəl] *adj* mensurable.

**measure** ['meʒər] *n* **1** *(system)* medida: *liquid measure* medida para líquidos. **2** *(indicator)* indicador *m*: *it's a measure of her popularity* es un indicador de su popularidad. **3** *(ruler)* regla. **4** *(measured amount, unit)* medida. **5** *(amount, degree, extent)* grado, cantidad *f*: *some measure of happiness* cierta felicidad. **6** *(method, step, remedy)* medida, disposición *f*: *safety measures* medidas de seguridad. LOC **in large measure** en gran parte, en gran medida. ❙ **in some measure** hasta cierto punto, en cierta medida. ❙ **to take measures** tomar medidas, adoptar medidas.
► *vt* **1** *(area, object, etc)* medir. **2** *(person)* tomar las medidas de. **3** *fig (assess)* evaluar; *(consider carefully)* sopesar, pensar bien.
► *vi (be)* medir: *it measures 3 feet by 6 feet* mide 1 metro por 2 metros.

☒ Measure no significa 'mesura', que se traduce por **moderation**.

⊕ Tanto los británicos como los americanos utilizan un sistema de medidas diferente del sistema métrico decimal, en el que empleamos nosotros. En la páginas centrales de este diccionario encontrarás las equivalencias entre estos dos sistemas de medición.

**measurement** ['meʒəmənt] *n* **1** *(act)* medición *f*. **2** *(length, etc)* medida.

**measuring** ['meʒərɪŋ] *n (act)* medición *f*. COMP **measuring tape** cinta métrica, metro.

**meat** [miːt] *n* carne *f*: *I prefer meat to fish* me gusta más la carne que el pescado. COMP **cold meat / cooked meat** fiambre *m*.

**meatball** ['miːtbɔːl] *n* albóndiga.

**mechanic** [məˈkænɪk] *n (person)* mecánico,-a.

**mechanical** [məˈkænɪkəl] *adj* mecánico,-a.

**mechanics** [məˈkænɪks] *n (science)* mecánica. COMP **the mechanics** *(working parts)* el mecanismo. *(processes)* el funcionamiento.

**mechanism** ['mekənɪzəm] *n* mecanismo.

**medal** ['medəl] *n* medalla.

**medallist** ['medəlɪst] *n* medalla *mf*, campeón,-ona.

**media** ['miːdɪə] *n pl* **the media** los medios *mpl* de comunicación.

✎ Consulta también media.

**mediaeval** [medɪˈiːvəl] *adj* medieval.

**median** ['miːdɪən] *adj* MATH mediano,-a. ► *n* MATH *(line)* mediana; *(quantity)* valor *m* mediano.

**mediator** ['miːdɪeɪtər] *n* mediador,-ra.

**medical** ['medɪkəl] *adj (treatment, care, examination)* médico,-a; *(book, student)* de medicina. ► *n fam (check-up)* chequeo, reconocimiento médico, revisión *f* médica.

**medicinal** [məˈdɪsɪnəl] *adj* medicinal.

**medicine** ['medɪsən] *n* **1** *(science)* medicina. **2** *(drugs, etc)* medicina, medicamento.

**medieval** [medɪˈiːvəl] *adj* medieval.

**mediocrity** [miːdɪˈɒkrətɪ] *n* mediocridad *f*.

**M**

**meditation** [medɪˈteɪ[ə]n] *n* meditación *f*.
**Mediterranean** [medɪtəˈreɪnɪən] *adj* mediterráneo,-a.
▸ *n* the Mediterranean el Mediterráneo.
**medium** [ˈmiːdɪəm] *adj (average)* mediano,-a, regular, normal. COMP **medium wave** onda media.
▸ *n* **1** [*pl* **media**] *(means)* medio. **2** [*pl* **media.**] *(environment)* medio (ambiente). **3** [*pl* **media**] *(middle position)* punto medio, término medio. **4** [*pl* **mediums**] *(spiritualist)* médium *mf*.
**medium-sized** [ˈmiːdɪəmˈsaɪzd] *adj (thing)* de tamaño mediano.
**meet** [miːt] *vt* **1** *(by chance)* encontrar, encontrarse con: *she met an old friend* se encontró con un viejo amigo. **2** *(by arrangement)* reunirse con, quedar con; *(informally)* ver: *I'm meeting Rob tomorrow* he quedado con Rob para mañana. **3** *(meet for first time)* conocer: *I met him at a party* lo conocí en una fiesta. **4** *(collect)* ir a buscar, pasar a buscar; *(await arrival of)* esperar; *(receive)* ir a recibir: *he'll meet me at the station* me vendrá a buscar a la estación.
▸ *vi* **1** *(by chance)* encontrarse: *we'll meet again* nos volveremos a encontrar. **2** *(by arrangement)* reunirse, verse, quedar; *(formally)* entrevistarse: *we arranged to meet on Saturday* quedamos para el sábado., **3** *(get acquainted)* conocerse: *I think we've already met* creo que ya nos conocemos.
① *pt & pp* met [met].
▸ *n* **1** SP encuentro.
**meeting** [ˈmiːtɪŋ] *n* **1** *(gen - prearranged)* reunión *f*; *(- formal)* entrevista; *(- date)* cita. **2** *(chance encounter)* encuentro. **3** *(of club, committee, etc)* reunión *f*; *(of assembly)* sesión *f*; *(of shareholders, creditors)* junta. **4** POL *(rally)* mitin *m*. COMP **meeting place** lugar *m* de encuentro, lugar *m* de reunión.
**megabyte** [ˈmegəbaɪt] *n* COMPUT megabyte *m*, megaocteto.
**megalith** [ˈmegəlɪθ] *n* megalito.
**megaphone** [ˈmegəfəʊn] *n* megáfono, altavoz *m*.

**megawatt** [ˈmegəwɒt] *n* megavatio.
**melamine** [ˈmeləmiːn] *n* melamina.
**melodramatic** [melədrəˈmætɪk] *adj* melodramático,-a.
**melody** [ˈmelədɪ] *n* melodía.
① *pl* **melodies**.
**melon** [ˈmelən] *n (honeydew, etc)* melón *m*; *(watermelon)* sandía.
**melt** [melt] *vt* **1** *(ice, snow, butter, etc)* derretir. **2** *(metal)* fundir (down, -). **3** *(sugar, chemical)* disolver. **4** *fig* ablandar.
▸ *vi* **1** *(ice, snow)* derretirse (away, -). **2** *(metal)* fundirse. **3** *(sugar, chemical)* disolverse.
◆ **to melt away** *vi* **1** *(money, crowd, person)* desaparecer. **2** *fig (confidence, etc)* desvanecerse, esfumarse; *(anger)* disiparse, desaparecer.
**melting** [ˈmeltɪŋ] *n (of metal)* fundición *f*; *(of snow)* derretimiento. COMP **melting point** punto de fusión. ▌ **melting pot** crisol *m*.
**member** [ˈmembər] *n* **1** *(gen)* miembro *mf*; *(of club)* socio,-a; *(of union, party)* afiliado,-a: *the youngest member of the family* el miembro más joven de la familia. **2** POL *(of Parliament)* diputado,-a; *(of European Parliament)* eurodiputado,-a. **3** ANAT miembro.
▸ *adj (country, state)* miembro,-a.
**membership** [ˈmembəʃɪp] *n* **1** *(of club - state)* calidad *f* de socio,-a, pertenencia; *(- entry)* ingreso. **2** *(of political party, union - state)* afiliación *f*; *(- entry)* ingreso. **3** *(members - of club)* miembros *mpl*, socios *mpl*; *(- of political party)* afiliados *mpl*.
**membrane** [ˈmembreɪn] *n* membrana.
**memo** [ˈmeməʊ] *n* **1** *(official)* memorándum *m*. **2** *(personal note)* nota, apunte *m*. COMP **memo pad** bloc *m* de notas.
① *pl* **memos**.
**memorandum** [meməˈrændəm] *n* **1** *(official note)* memorándum *m*, memorando. **2** *(personal note)* nota, apunte *m*.
① *pl* **memorandums** o **memoranda** [meməˈrændə].
**memorial** [məˈmɔːrɪəl] *adj (plaque, etc)* conmemorativo,-a.
▸ *n (monument)* monumento conmemorativo; *(ceremony)* homenaje *m*.

⊕ El Memorial Day es una fiesta que se celebra en Estados Unidos el último lunes de mayo en honor de todos los soldados muertos en las distintas guerras en las que ha participado el país americano.

**memorize** ['meməraɪz] *vt* memorizar, aprender de memoria.

**memory** ['memərɪ] *n* **1** *(ability, computers)* memoria: *she's got a good memory for names* tiene buena memoria para los nombres. **2** *(recollection)* recuerdo. LOC **to lose one's memory** perder la memoria. ▮ **within living memory** que se recuerde.

ⓘ *pl* memories.

**men** [men] *pl* → man.

**menace** ['menəs] *n* **1** *(threat)* amenaza (to, para); *(danger)* peligro (to, para). **2** *fam (nuisance - person)* pesado,-a; *(- thing)* lata, molestia.
▸ *vt* amenazar (with, de).

**mend** [mend] *vt* **1** *(repair - gen)* reparar, arreglar; *(sew)* coser; *(patch)* remendar; *(darn)* zurcir: *can you mend my watch?* ¿me puedes arreglar el reloj? **2** *(improve)* mejorar. LOC **to be on the mend** ir mejorando.
▸ *n (patch)* remiendo; *(darn)* zurcido.

**meninges** [me'nɪdʒəs] *n pl* MED meninges *fpl*.

**meningitis** [menɪn'dʒaɪtəs] *n* MED meningitis *f*.

**meniscus** [mɪ'nɪskəs] *n* menisco.
ⓘ *pl* meniscuses o menisci [mɪ'nɪskaɪ].

**menopause** ['menəʊpɔ:z] *n* menopausia.

**menstrual** ['menstruəl] *adj* menstrual. COMP **menstrual cycle** ciclo menstrual. ▮ **menstrual period** regla, período.

**menstruation** [menstru'eɪʃ⁰n] *n* menstruación *f*, regla.

**menswear** ['menzweəʳ] *n* ropa de caballero, ropa de hombres.

**mental** ['ment⁰l] *adj* mental: *mental effort* esfuerzo mental; *mental health* salud mental; *mental arithmetic* cálculo mental. COMP **mental age** edad *f* mental. ▮ **mental handicap** disminución *f* psíquica. ▮

**mental home / mental hospital** (hospital *m*) psiquiátrico.

**mentality** [men'tælətɪ] *n* mentalidad *f*.
ⓘ *pl* mentalities.

**mention** ['menʃ⁰n] *n* mención *f*: *she made no mention of your visit* no mencionó tu visita.
▸ *vt* mencionar, hacer mención de, aludir a: *he never mentioned the money* no mencionó el dinero. LOC **don't mention it!** ¡de nada!, ¡no hay de qué!

**menu** ['menju:] *n* **1** carta, menú *m*. **2** COMPUT menú *m*. COMP **menu bar** barra de menús.
ⓘ *pl* menus.

**meow** [mɪ'aʊ] *n* maullido, miau *m*.
▸ *vi* maullar.

**mercenary** ['mɜ:s⁰nərɪ] *adj* mercenario,-a.
▸ *n* mercenario,-a.
ⓘ *pl* mercenaries.

**merchandise** ['mɜ:tʃ⁰ndaɪz] *n* mercancías *fpl*, géneros *mpl*.
▸ *vt (sell)* vender, poner en venta; *(promote)* promocionar.

**merchant** ['mɜ:tʃ⁰nt] *n (trader)* comerciante *mf*; *(dealer, businessperson)* negociante *mf*. COMP **merchant bank** banco comercial. ▮ **merchant navy** marina mercante.

**Mercury¹** ['mɜ:kjərɪ] *n (planet)* Mercurio.

**mercury²** ['mɜ:kjərɪ] *n (metal)* mercurio.

**mercy** ['mɜ:sɪ] *n* **1** *(compassion)* misericordia, clemencia, piedad *f*: *have mercy upon me!* ¡tenga piedad de mí! **2** *fam (good fortune)* suerte *f*, milagro; *(blessing)* bendición *f*.
LOC **to be at the mercy of** SB/STH estar a merced de ALGN/ALGO.
ⓘ *pl* mercies.
▸ *adj* de ayuda, de socorro. COMP **mercy killing** eutanasia.

**mere** [mɪəʳ] *adj* mero,-a, simple, puro,-a.
▸ *adj* merest *(slightest)* el/la más mínimo,-a.

**merge** [mɜ:dʒ] *vt (combine - gen)* unir (with, a), combinar (with, con); *(- road)* empalmar (into, con); *(- river)* desem-

M

bocar (into, en); *(- firms, businesses)* fusionar.

**meridional** [məˈrɪdɪənᵊl] *adj* meridional.

**meringue** [məˈræŋ] *n* merengue *m*.

**merit** [ˈmerɪt] *n* mérito.
▶ *vt (deserve)* merecer.

**mermaid** [ˈmɜːmeɪd] *n* sirena.

**merry** [ˈmerɪ] *adj* **1** *(cheerful)* alegre; *(amusing)* divertido,-a, gracioso,-a. **2** *fam (slightly drunk)* alegre, achispado, -a. [LOC] **merry Christmas!** ¡felices Navidades!
ⓘ *comp* merrier; *superl* merriest.

**merry-go-round** [ˈmerɪɡəʊraʊnd] *n* tiovivo, caballitos *mpl*.

**mess** [mes] *n* **1** *(untidy state)* desorden *m*, revoltijo: *your room is a complete mess!* ¡tu habitación está toda desordenada! **2** *(confusion, mix-up)* confusión *f*, lío, follón *m*; *(person, thing)* desastre *m*: *what a mess!* ¡vaya lío!
▶ *vt (untidy)* desordenar; *(dirty)* ensuciar.
◆ **to mess about / mess around** *vi* **1** *(idle)* gandulear; *(kill time)* pasar el tiempo; *(potter about)* entretenerse. **2** *(act the fool)* hacer el primo, tontear.
◆ **to mess up** *vt sep* **1** *fam (untidy)* desordenar; *(dirty)* ensuciar. **2** *(spoil)* estropear, echar a perder.

**message** [ˈmesɪdʒ] *n* **1** *(communication)* recado, mensaje *m*: *could you give her a message?* ¿podrías darle un recado? **2** *(of story, film, etc)* mensaje *m*. [LOC] **to get the message** *(understand)* entender, darse cuenta.

**messenger** [ˈmesɪndʒəʳ] *n* mensajero,-a. [COMP] **messenger boy** recadero.

**Messiah** [məˈsaɪə] *n* REL Mesías *m*.

**messy** [ˈmesɪ] *adj* **1** *(untidy)* desordenado,-a, en desorden; *(- dirty)* sucio,-a. **2** *(confused)* complicado,-a, enredado,-a; *(awkward)* difícil; *(unpleasant)* desagradable.
ⓘ *comp* messier; *superl* messiest.

**met** [met] *pp & pt* → meet.

**metabolism** [məˈtæbəlɪzᵊm] *n* metabolismo.

**metal** [ˈmetᵊl] *n* metal *m*.
▶ *adj* metálico,-a, de metal.

**metallic** [məˈtælɪk] *adj* metálico,-a. [COMP] **metallic paint** pintura metalizada.

**metallurgy** [məˈtælədʒɪ] *n* metalurgia.

**metamorphic** [metəˈmɔːfɪk] *adj* metamórfico,-a

**metamorphosis** [metəˈmɔːfəsɪs] *n* metamorfosis *f*.
ⓘ *pl* metamorphoses [metəˈmɔːfəsiːz].

**metaphor** [ˈmetəfɔːʳ] *n* metáfora.

**metaphysics** [metəˈfɪzɪks] *n* metafísica.

**metatarsus** [metəˈtɑːsəs] *n* metatarso.
ⓘ *pl* metatarsi [metəˈtɑːsaɪ].

**meteorite** [ˈmiːtɪəraɪt] *n* meteorito.

**meteorological** [miːtɪərəˈlɒdʒɪkᵊl] *adj* meteorológico,-a.

**meteorologist** [miːtɪəˈrɒlədʒɪst] *n* meteorólogo,-a.

**meteorology** [miːtɪəˈrɒlədʒɪ] *n* meteorología.

**meter** [ˈmiːtəʳ] *n* **1** US → metre. **2** contador *m*.
▶ *vt* medir.

**methacrylate** [meθˈækrɪleɪt] *n* metacrilato.

**methane** [ˈmiːθeɪn] *n* metano.

**method** [ˈmeθəd] *n* **1** *(manner, way)* método, forma. **2** *(system, order)* sistema *m*, orden *m*, lógica.

**metonymy** [meˈtɒnɪmɪ] *n* metonimia.

**metre** [ˈmiːtəʳ] *n* **1** *(measure)* metro. **2** *(in poetry)* metro. [COMP] **cubic metre** metro cúbico.

**metric** [ˈmetrɪk] *adj* métrico,-a. [COMP] **metric system** sistema métrico. ❙ **metric ton** tonelada métrica.

**metropolis** [məˈtrɒpəlɪs] *n* metrópoli *f*, metrópolis *f*.
ⓘ *pl* metropolises.

**metropolitan** [metrəˈpɒlɪtᵊn] *adj* metropolitano,-a.

**mew** [mjuː] *vi* maullar.
▶ *n* maullido.

**Mexican** [ˈmeksɪkᵊn] *adj* mejicano,-a.
▶ *n* mejicano,-a.

**Mexico** [ˈmeksɪləʊ] *n* Méjico.

**mi** [miː] *n* MUS mi *m*.

**miaow** [miːˈaʊ] *n* maullido.
▶ *vi* maullar.

**mica** [ˈmaɪkə] *n* mica.

**mice** [maɪs] *pl* → mouse.

**micro** [ˈmaɪkrəʊ] *n fam* microordenador *m*.
ⓘ *pl* micros.

**microbe** [ˈmaɪkrəʊb] *n* microbio.

**microbiology** [maɪkrəʊbaɪˈɒlədʒɪ] *n* microbiología.

**microchip** [ˈmaɪkəʊtʃɪp] *n* microchip *m*.

**microclimate** [ˈmaɪkrəʊklaɪmət] *n* microclima *mf*.

**microfilm** [ˈmaɪkrəʊfɪlm] *n* microfilme *m*.

**micron** [ˈmaɪkrɒn] *n* micra.

**microphone** [ˈmaɪkrəfəʊn] *n* micrófono.

**microprocessor** [maɪkrəʊˈprəʊsesəʳ] *n* microprocesador *m*.

**microscope** [ˈmaɪkrəskəʊp] *n* microscopio.

**microscopic** [maɪkrəˈskɒpɪk] *adj* microscópico,-a.

**microwave** [ˈmaɪkrəweɪv] *n* microonda. [COMP] **microwave oven** horno de microondas, microondas *m inv*.
▶ *vt* cocinar en el microondas.

**midday** [mɪdˈdeɪ] *n* mediodía *m*.
▶ *adj* de mediodía. [LOC] **at midday** al mediodía.

**middle** [ˈmɪdəl] *adj (central)* de en medio, central; *(medium)* mediano,-a, medio,-a: *he's the middle son* él es el hijo mediano. [LOC] **in the middle of nowhere** en el quinto pino. [COMP] **middle age** mediana edad *f*. ▌ **middle class** clase *f* media. ▌ **middle finger** dedo corazón. ▌ **the Middle Ages** la Edad Media.
▶ *n* **1** *(centre)* medio, centro: *there's a pond in the middle of the garden* hay un estanque en medio del jardín. **2** *(halfway point of period, activity)* mitad *f*: *in the middle of a storm* en medio de una tormenta. **3** *fam (waist)* cintura.

✎ El apellido se traduce por **surname** o **family name** y el nombre de pila, por **Christian name** o **first name**. Casi todo el mundo tiene dos **Christian names**, aunque se utilice sólo uno. Ese segundo nombre de pila es el **middle name**, que se suele escribir sólo con la inicial.

**middle-aged** [mɪdəlˈeɪdʒd] *adj* de mediana edad.

**middle-class** [mɪdəlˈklɑːs] *adj* de la clase media.

**middleman** [ˈmɪdəlmən] *n* intermediario.
ⓘ *pl* middlemen [ˈmɪdəlmen].

**middleweight** [ˈmɪdəlweɪt] *n (boxing)* peso medio.

**midnight** [ˈmɪdnaɪt] *n* medianoche *f*: *we got home at midnight* llegamos a casa a medianoche.

**midwife** [ˈmɪdwaɪf] *n* comadrona, partera, matrona.
ⓘ *pl* midwives [ˈmɪdwaɪvz].

**might** [maɪt] *aux* **1** *(possibility)* poder: *it might rain* podría llover. **2** *(in suggestions or requests)* poder: *you might try the hardware shop* podrías probar en la ferretería. **3** *(permission)* poder: *he asked if he might come in* pidió permiso para entrar. [LOC] **I might have known!** ¡debí imaginármelo!, ¡típico! ▌ **I might (just) as well** más vale que.

✎ Como expresa una posibilidad también se puede traducir por 'quizá', 'quizás', 'a lo mejor', 'tal vez' o 'puede que'. Consulta también **may**.

**mighty** [ˈmaɪtɪ] *adj* **1** *(very strong)* muy fuerte; *(powerful)* potente. **2** *(great, imposing)* enorme.
ⓘ *comp* mightier, *superl* mightiest.
▶ *adv US fam (very)* muy.

**migraine** [ˈmaɪɡreɪn] *n* jaqueca, migraña.

**migrant** [ˈmaɪɡrənt] *adj* migratorio,-a.
▶ *n (person)* emigrante *mf*; *(bird)* ave *f* migratoria.

**migrate** [maɪˈɡreɪt] *vi* migrar.

**migration** [maɪˈɡreɪʃən] *n* migración *f*.

**migratory** [ˈmaɪɡrətərɪ] *adj* migratorio,-a.

**mike** [maɪk] *n fam* micro.

**mild** [maɪld] *adj* **1** *(person, character)* apacible, afable, dulce. **2** *(climate, weather)* benigno,-a, templado,-a, suave, blando,-a; *(soap, detergent)* suave. **3** *(protest, attempt)* ligero,-a; *(punishment, fever)* leve;

*(illness, attack)* ligero,-a, leve; *(criticism, rebuke)* suave, leve.

**mile** [maɪl] *n* milla (1,6 kms).
► ► *n pl* **miles** *(much)* mucho, muchísimo: *I'm miles better* estoy mucho mejor; *it's miles away* está muy lejos.

**mileage** ['maɪlɪdʒ] *n* **1** AUTO *(miles travelled by a car)* ≈ kilómetros *mpl*, kilometraje *m*. **2** *fam fig (benefit, advantage, use)* jugo, partido.

**mileometer** [maɪˈlɒmɪtəʳ] *n* AUTO cuentakilómetros *m*.

**milestone** ['maɪlstəʊn] *n* **1** hito, mojón *m*. **2** *fig* hito.

**militant** ['mɪlɪtənt] *adj* POL militante.
► ► *n* POL militante *mf*.

**military** ['mɪlɪtˀrɪ] *adj* militar.
► ► *n* **the military** los militares, las fuerzas armadas.

**milk** [mɪlk] *n (gen)* leche *f*. COMP **milk shake** batido. ▌ **milk tooth** diente *m* de leche.
► ► *adj (bottle, production)* de leche; *(product)* lácteo,-a.

**milkman** ['mɪlkmən] *n* lechero, repartidor *m* de la leche.
① *pl* **milkmen** ['mɪlkmen].

**milky** ['mɪlkɪ] *adj* **1** *(liquid, jewel)* turbio,-a. **2** *(coffee, tea)* con mucha leche; *(substance)* lechoso,-a. **3** *(colour)* pálido,-a. COMP **Milky Way** Vía Láctea.
① *comp* **milkier**, *superl* **milkiest**.

**mill** [mɪl] *n* **1** *(machinery)* molino. **2** *(for coffee, pepper, etc)* molinillo. **3** *(factory)* fábrica.
► ► *vt (crush, grind)* moler.

**millennium** [mɪˈlenɪəm] *n* milenio, milenario.
① *pl* **millenniums** o **millennia** [mɪˈlenɪə].

**millet** ['mɪlɪt] *n* mijo.

**millimetre** ['mɪlɪmiːtəʳ] *n* milímetro.

**million** ['mɪljən] *n* millón *m*: *one million dollars* un millón de dólares.
► ► *n pl* **millions** *fam (lots)* millones *mpl*.

**millionaire** [mɪljəˈneəʳ] *n* millonario,-a.

**millionth** ['mɪljənθ] *adj* millonésimo,-a.
► ► *n* millonésima parte, millonésimo.

**millipede** ['mɪlɪpiːd] *n* milpiés *m inv*.

**millstone** ['mɪlstəʊn] *n* muela, rueda de molino.

**mime** [maɪm] *n* **1** *(art)* mimo. **2** *(performance)* pantomima, representación *f* de mimo.
► ► *vt (express by mime)* expresar haciendo mímica.

**mimic** ['mɪmɪk] *n* imitador,-ra.
► ► *vt (copy)* imitar, remedar.
① *pt & pp* **mimicked**, *ger* **mimicking**.

**mince** [mɪns] *n* GB *(meat)* carne *f* picada.
COMP **mince pie** pastelito.
► ► *vt (chop, cut)* picar.

**mind** [maɪnd] *n* **1** *(intellect)* mente *f*. **2** *(mentality)* mentalidad *f*. **3** *(brain, thoughts)* cabeza, cerebro: *her mind was very confused* estaba confusa.
► ► *vt* **1** *(heed, pay attention to)* hacer caso de; *(care about)* importar, preocupar: *I mind what people say* me importa lo que dice la gente. **2** *(be careful with)* tener cuidado con: *mind the step!* ¡cuidado con el escalón! **3** *(look after - child)* cuidar, cuidar de; *(- house)* vigilar; *(- shop)* atender; *(- seat, place)* guardar. **4** *(object to, be troubled by)* tener inconveniente en, importar: *I don't mind staying* no tengo inconveniente en quedarme. **5** *(fancy, quite like)* venir bien: *I wouldn't mind a coffee* me vendría bien un café.
► ► *vi* **1** *(be careful)* tener cuidado: *mind (out)!* ¡cuidado!, ¡ojo! **2** *(object to)* importar, molestar: *do you mind if I open the window?* ¿le importa que abra la ventana?
LOC **never mind 1** *(it doesn't matter)* no importa, da igual. **2** *(don't worry)* no te preocupes. **3** *(let alone)* ni hablar de. ▌ **to be out of one's mind** estar loco,-a. ▌ **to change one's mind** cambiar de opinión, cambiar de parecer. ▌ **to make up one's mind** decidirse. ▌ **to sb's mind** en la opinión de ALGN.

**mine¹** [maɪn] *n (gen)* mina.
► ► *vt* **1** *(coal, gold, etc)* extraer; *(area)* explotar. **2** MIL sembrar minas en, minar.
► ► *vi* explotar una mina.

**mine²** [maɪn] *pron* (el) mío, (la) mía, (los) míos, (las) mías, lo mío: *hey! that's mine!* ¡ey! ¡eso es mío!; *a friend of mine* un/una amigo,-a mío,-a.

**miner** ['maɪnər] *n* minero,-a.

**mineral** ['mɪnərəl] *adj* mineral.
▶ *n* mineral *m*. COMP **mineral water** agua mineral. ‖ **mineral oil** GB petróleo.

**miniature** ['mɪnɪtʃər] *n* miniatura.
▶ *adj* (en) miniatura.

**minibus** ['mɪnɪbʌs] *n* microbús *m*.
ⓘ *pl* minibuses.

**minicab** ['mɪnɪkæb] *n* GB taxi *m*.

**minicomputer** [mɪnɪkəm'pjuːtər] *n* microordenador *m*.

**minimal** ['mɪnɪməl] *adj* mínimo,-a.

**minimum** ['mɪnɪməm] *adj* mínimo,-a.
▶ *n* mínimo: *a minimum of 20 people* un mínimo de 20 personas.

**mining** ['maɪnɪŋ] *n* minería, explotación *f* de minas: *coal mining* extracción de carbón.
▶ *adj* (*area, town, industry*) minero,-a. COMP **mining engineer** ingeniero,-a de minas.

**miniseries** ['mɪnɪsɪəriːz] *n* TV miniserie *f*.

**miniskirt** ['mɪnɪskɜːt] *n* minifalda.

**minister** ['mɪnɪstər] *n* **1** (*gen*) ministro, -a (for, de). **2** GB (*priest*) pastor,-ra.
▶ *vi* atender (to, a), cuidar (to, a).

**ministry** ['mɪnɪstri] *n* (*gen*) ministerio.
▶ *n* the ministry
ⓘ *pl* ministries. GB (*priesthood*) el clero.

**minor** ['maɪnər] *adj* **1** (*unimportant*) menor; (*secondary*) secundario,-a. **2** MUS menor.
▶ *n* JUR menor *mf*.

**minority** [maɪ'nɒrɪti] *n* **1** minoría. **2** JUR minoría de edad.
ⓘ *pl* minorities.
▶ *adj* minoritario,-a.

**mint¹** [mɪnt] *n* FIN (*place*) casa de la moneda.
▶ *vt* (*coins, words*) acuñar.

**mint²** [mɪnt] *n* **1** BOT menta. **2** (*sweet*) caramelo de menta.

**minus** ['maɪnəs] *prep* **1** MATH menos: *four minus three equals one* cuatro menos tres es igual a uno. **2** METEOR bajo cero: *minus five degrees* cinco grados bajo cero.
▶ *adj* negativo,-a. COMP **minus sign** signo de menos *m*.

▶ *n* **1** MATH menos *m*. **2** (*disadvantage*) desventaja *m*.

**minuscule** ['mɪnəskjuːl] *adj* minúsculo.

**minute¹** [maɪ'njuːt] *adj* (*tiny*) diminuto,-a, minúsculo,-a.

**minute²** ['mɪnɪt] *n* **1** (*of time*) minuto: *it's a five minute walk* es un paseo de cinco minutos. **2** *fam* (*moment*) momento; (*instant*) instante *m*: *I'll be back in a minute* ahora vuelvo, vuelvo en un momento.
▶ *n pl* **minutes** (*notes*) acta *f sing*, actas *fpl*. LOC **(at) any minute now** en cualquier momento. ‖ **at the last minute** en el último momento, a última hora.

**miracle** ['mɪrəkəl] *n* (*gen*) milagro.

**mirage** [mɪ'rɑːʒ] *n* espejismo.

**mirror** ['mɪrər] *n* (*gen*) espejo: *stop looking at yourself in the mirror* deja de mirarte en el espejo. COMP **driving mirror** espejo (retrovisor).
▶ *vt* reflejar.

**misbehave** [mɪsbɪ'heɪv] *vi* portarse mal, comportarse mal.

**miscarriage** [mɪs'kærɪdʒ] *n* MED aborto (espontáneo).

**miscarry** [mɪs'kæri] *vi* **1** MED abortar (espontáneamente), tener un aborto. **2** (*plans, etc*) fracasar, frustrarse, malograrse.
ⓘ *pt & pp* miscarried, *ger* miscarrying.

**miscellaneous** [mɪsɪ'leɪniəs] *adj* (*mixed, varied*) variado,-a, vario,-a, diverso,-a, misceláneo,-a.

**mischief** ['mɪstʃɪf] *n* **1** (*naughtiness*) travesura, diablura: *I know you're up to some mischief* sé que estás haciendo alguna travesura. **2** *fml* daño, mal *m*.

**miserable** ['mɪzərəbəl] *adj* **1** (*person - unhappy*) abatido,-a, triste, deprimido, -a; (*- bad-tempered*) antipático,-a. **2** (*place, etc*) deprimente, triste; (*weather*) horrible. **3** (*paltry*) miserable, mezquino,-a; (*pathetic*) lamentable.

**misery** ['mɪzəri] *n* **1** (*wretchedness, unhappiness*) desgracia, desdicha, tristeza. **2** (*suffering*) sufrimiento, dolor *m*, suplicio. **3** (*poverty*) pobreza, miseria.
ⓘ *pl* miseries.

**misfortune** [mɪsˈfɔːtʃ(ə)n] *n* infortunio, desgracia, mala fortuna.

**miss¹** [mɪs] *n* señorita.

✎ Miss se emplea delante del apellido de una mujer soltera.

**miss²** [mɪs] *n* (*catch, hit, etc*) fallo; (*shot*) tiro errado.

▶ *vt* **1** (*not to hit, score, etc*) fallar: *he missed a penalty* falló un penalti. **2** (*not catch*) perder: *I missed the bus* perdí el autobús. **3** (*not experience*) perderse: *don't miss this concert!* ¡no te pierdas este concierto! **4** (*not see*) perderse: *she doesn't miss anything* no se le escapa nada. **5** (*not attend - meeting, etc*) no asistir a; (*- class, work*) faltar a. **7** (*long for - person*) echar de menos; (*- place*) añorar: *she misses her family* echa de menos a su familia.

▶ *vi* **1** (*catch, kick, etc*) fallar; (*shot*) errar el tiro. **2** (*engine*) fallar. **3** (*fail*) fallar.

◆ **to miss out** *vt sep* (*omit, fail to include*) saltarse, omitir; (*overlook, disregard*) pasar por alto, dejarse.

▶ *vi* (*lose opportunity*) dejar pasar, perderse.

**missile** [ˈmɪsaɪl] *n* **1** (*explosive weapon*) misil *m*. **2** (*object thrown*) proyectil *m*.

**missing** [ˈmɪsɪŋ] *adj* **1** (*object - lost*) perdido,-a, extraviado,-a. **2** (*person - disappeared*) desaparecido,-a; (*- absent*) ausente: *she's been missing for a week* hace una semana que desapareció. ⌊LOC⌋ **to be missing** faltar. ⌊COMP⌋ **missing person** desaparecido,-a.

**mission** [ˈmɪʃ(ə)n] *n* misión *f*.

**missionary** [ˈmɪʃ(ə)nərɪ] *n* misionero,-a. ① *pl* missionaries.

**misspell** [mɪsˈspel] *vt* escribir mal. ① *pt & pp* misspelled o misspelt [mɪsˈspelt], *ger* misspelling.

**misspend** [mɪsˈspend] *vt* malgastar. ① *pt & pp* misspent [mɪsˈspent].

**mist** [mɪst] *n* **1** (*gen*) neblina; (*sea*) bruma; (*haze*) calima. **2** (*on window, mirror, etc*) vaho.

**mistake** [mɪsˈteɪk] *n* (*error*) equivocación *f*, error *m*; (*in test*) falta; (*oversight*) descuido: *there must be some mistake* debe haber algún error. ⌊LOC⌋ **by mistake 1**

(*in error*) por error. **2** (*unintentionally*) sin querer. ‖ **to make a mistake** equivocarse, cometer un error.

▶ *vt* **1** (*misunderstand*) entender mal. **2** (*confuse*) confundir (**for**, con). ① *pt* mistook [mɪsˈtʊk], *pp* mistaken [mɪsˈteɪk(ə)n].

**mistaken** [mɪsˈteɪk(ə)n] *pp* → mistake.

▶ *adj* (*wrong, incorrect*) equivocado,-a, erróneo,-a. ⌊LOC⌋ **to be mistaken** equivocarse.

**mister** [ˈmɪstər] *n* señor *m*.

**mistletoe** [ˈmɪsˈltəʊ] *n* muérdago.

**mistook** [mɪsˈtʊk] *pt* → mistake.

**mistreat** [mɪsˈtriːt] *vt* maltratar, tratar mal.

**mistress** [ˈmɪstrəs] *n* **1** (*owner - gen*) dueña, ama, señora; (*of dog*) ama, dueña. **2** (*lover*) amante *f*. **3** GB maestra, profesora.

**mistrust** [mɪsˈtrʌst] *n* desconfianza, recelo.

▶ *vt* desconfiar de.

**misty** [ˈmɪstɪ] *adj* **1** METEOR neblinoso,-a: *it's misty* hay neblina. **2** (*window, glasses, etc*) empañado,-a. ① *comp* mistier, *superl* mistiest.

**misunderstand** [mɪsʌndəˈstænd] *vt* (*gen*) entender mal; (*misinterpret*) malinterpretar. ① *pt & pp* misunderstood [mɪsʌndəˈstʊd].

**misunderstanding** [mɪsʌndəˈstændɪŋ] *n* malentendido (**about**, sobre).

**mite** [maɪt] *n* (*insect*) ácaro, acárido.

**miter** [ˈmaɪtər] *n* US → mitre.

**mitigating** [ˈmɪtɪɡeɪtɪŋ] *adj* mitigador,-ra. ⌊COMP⌋ **mitigating circumstances** JUR circunstancias *fpl* atenuantes.

**mitre** [ˈmaɪtər] *n* **1** REL mitra. **2** TECH inglete *m*.

**mitten** [ˈmɪt(ə)n] *n* (*fingers covered*) manopla; (*fingers exposed*) mitón *m*.

**mix** [mɪks] *n* **1** (*mixture - gen*) mezcla. **2** CULIN preparado.

▶ *vt* **1** (*combine*) mezclar, combinar: *mix the sugar with the butter* mezclar el azúcar con la mantequilla. **2** (*make, prepare - plaster, cement*) amasar; (*- cocktail, salad, medicine*) preparar.

▸ *vi* **1** *(substances)* mezclarse. **2** *(clothes, colours, food)* combinar bien, ir bien juntos,-as. **3** *(people - come together)* mezclarse con la gente; *(- get on)* llevarse bien (**with**, con).

◆ **to mix up** *vt sep* **1** *(ingredients)* mezclar bien. **2** *(confuse)* confundir. **3** *(mess up, put in disorder)* desordenar, revolver.

**mixed** [mɪkst] *adj* **1** *(of different kinds)* variado,-a: *mixed biscuits* galletas surtidas. **2** *(ambivalent)* desigual. **3** *(for both sexes)* mixto,-a.

**mixer** [ˈmɪksə<sup>r</sup>] *n (for food)* batidora.

**mixture** [ˈmɪkstʃə<sup>r</sup>] *n (gen)* mezcla.

**mix-up** [ˈmɪksʌp] *n fam (confusion)* lío, confusión *f*; *(misunderstanding)* malentendido.

**mm** [ˈmɪlimiːtə<sup>r</sup>] *symb (millimetre)* milímetro; *(abbreviation)* mm.

**moan** [məʊn] *n* **1** *(groan)* gemido, quejido. **2** *(complaint)* queja, protesta.
▸ *vi* **1** *(groan)* gemir. **2** *(complaint)* quejarse (**about**, de), protestar (**about**, por).

**moaner** [ˈməʊnə<sup>r</sup>] *n* quejica *m & f*.

**moat** [məʊt] *n* foso.

**mobile** [ˈməʊbaɪl] *adj (object, troops, etc)* móvil, movible. COMP **mobile home** caravana, remolque *m*. ‖ **mobile phone** teléfono móvil.
▸ *n (hanging ornament)* móvil *m*.

**mock** [mɒk] *adj* **1** *(object)* de imitación. **2** *(feeling)* fingido,-a, simulado,-a; *(modesty)* falso,-a.
▸ *vt (laugh at, make fun of)* burlarse de, mofarse de.
▸ *vi* burlarse (**at**, de).

**mockery** [ˈmɒkəri] *n* **1** *(ridicule)* burla, mofa. **2** *(farce)* farsa; *(travesty)* parodia. LOC **to make a mockery of** STH poner ALGO en ridículo.

**modal** [ˈməʊd<sup>ə</sup>l] *adj* modal. COMP **modal auxiliary** auxiliar *m* modal. ‖ **modal verb** verbo modal.

**model** [ˈmɒd<sup>ə</sup>l] *n* modelo.
▸ *adj* **1** *(miniature)* en miniatura, a escala; *(toy)* de juguete. **2** *(exemplary)* ejemplar; *(ideal)* modelo.
▸ *vt (clay, etc)* modelar.
ⓘ *pt & pp* modelled (US modeled), *ger* modelling (US modeling).

**modem** [ˈməʊdem] *n* COMPUT modem *m*.

**moderate** [ˈmɒd<sup>ə</sup>rət] *adj* **1** *(average)* mediano,-a, regular: *moderate size* tamaño mediano. **2** *(not extreme)* moderado,-a; *(reasonable)* razonable. **3** *(talent, ability, performance)* mediocre, regular.
▸ *vt* moderar.
▸ *vi* moderarse.

**moderation** [mɒdəˈreɪʃ<sup>ə</sup>n] *n* moderación *f*.

**modern** [ˈmɒd<sup>ə</sup>n] *adj* **1** *(up-to-date)* moderno,-a. **2** *(history, literature, etc)* contemporáneo,-a. COMP **modern language** lengua moderna.

**modernize** [ˈmɒd<sup>ə</sup>naɪz] *vt* modernizar.
▸ *vi* modernizarse.

**modest** [ˈmɒdɪst] *adj* **1** *(gen)* modesto,-a, humilde. **2** *(improvement, increase)* modesto,-a; *(- price)* módico,-a.

**modesty** [ˈmɒdɪsti] *n* **1** *(humility)* modestia, humildad *f*. **2** *(chastity)* pudor *m*, recato.

**modify** [ˈmɒdɪfaɪ] *vt (change)* modificar.
ⓘ *pt & pp* modified, *ger* modifying.

**module** [ˈmɒdjuːl] *n* módulo.

**moist** [mɔɪst] *adj (damp)* húmedo,-a; *(slightly wet)* ligeramente mojado,-a: *a moist sponge cake* un bizcocho tierno.

**moisture** [ˈmɔɪstʃə<sup>r</sup>] *n* humedad *f*.

**mold** [məʊld] *n* → mould.

**mole¹** [məʊl] *n (on skin)* lunar *m*.

**mole²** [məʊl] *n* **1** ZOOL topo. **2** *fam (spy)* topo *mf*, espía *mf*.

**molecular** [məˈlekjələ<sup>r</sup>] *adj* molecular.

**molecule** [ˈmɒlɪkjuːl] *n* molécula.

**molest** [məˈlest] *vt* **1** *(attack - person)* atacar, asaltar; *(- dog)* perseguir, atacar. **2** *(sexually)* abusar sexualmente.

✖ To molest no significa 'molestar', que se traduce por to bother.

**mollusc** [ˈmɒləsk] *n* molusco.

**molt** [məʊlt] *n* US → moult.

**mom** [mɒm] *n* US *fam* mamá *f*.

**moment** [ˈməʊmənt] *n* **1** *(instant)* momento, instante *m*: *just a moment* un momentito; *I didn't believe that story for a moment* no me creí ese cuento ni por un momento. LOC **at any moment** de un momento a otro, en cualquier momento. **at the moment** en este momento. **at the last moment** a última hora. **for the moment** de momento, por el momento. **in a moment** dentro de un momento.

**mommy** ['mɒmɪ] *n* US *fam* mamá.
ⓘ *pl* mommies.

**Monaco** ['mɒnəkəʊ] *n* Mónaco.

**monarch** ['mɒnək] *n* monarca *m*.

**monarchy** ['mɒnəkɪ] *n* monarquía.
ⓘ *pl* monarchies.

**monastery** ['mɒnəstªrɪ] *n* monasterio.
ⓘ *pl* monasteries.

**Monday** ['mʌndɪ] *n* lunes *m inv.*

⊛ Para ejemplos de uso, consulta Saturday.

**Monegasque** ['mɒnəgæsk] *n* monegasco,-a.

**monetary** ['mʌnɪtªrɪ] *adj* monetario,-a.

**money** ['mʌnɪ] *n* **1** *(gen)* dinero: *how much money have you got?* ¿cuánto dinero tienes? **2** *(currency)* moneda. ⌐LOC¬ **to make money 1** *(person)* ganar dinero, hacer dinero. **2** *(business)* dar dinero. **to put money on** STH apostar por ALGO.

**moneybox** ['mʌnɪbɒks] *n* hucha.
ⓘ *pl* moneyboxes.

**Mongol** ['mɒŋgɒl] *n* mongol,-la, mogol,-la.

**Mongolia** [mɒŋ'gəʊlɪə] *n* Mongolia.

**Mongolian** [mɒŋ'gəʊlɪən] *adj* mongol, -la, mogol,-la.
▶ *n* **1** *(person)* mongol,-la, mogol,-la. **2** *(language)* mongol *m*, mogol *m*.

**monitor** ['mɒnɪtəʳ] *n* **1** *(screen)* monitor *m*. **2** *(school pupil)* responsable *mf*, encargado,-a.
▶ *vt (check)* controlar; *(follow)* seguir de cerca; *(watch)* observar.

**monk** [mʌŋk] *n* monje *m*.

**monkey** ['mʌŋkɪ] *n (gen)* mono,-a; *(long-tailed)* mico,-a. ⌐COMP¬ **monkey nut** cacahuete *m*. **monkey wrench** llave *f* inglesa.

**monogamy** [mə'nɒgəmɪ] *n* monogamia.

**monographic** [mɒnə'græfɪk] *adj* monográfico,-a.

**monolith** ['mɒnəlɪθ] *n* monolito.

**monologue** ['mɒnəlɒg] *n* monólogo.

**monopoly** [mə'nɒpəlɪ] *n* monopolio.
ⓘ *pl* monopolies.

**monorail** ['mɒnəʊreɪl] *n* monorraíl *m*, monocarril *m*.

**monotheism** ['mɒnəʊθɪɪzªm] *n* monoteísmo.

**monotonous** [mə'nɒtənəs] *adj* monótono,-a.

**monotony** [mə'nɒtənɪ] *n* monotonía.

**monoxide** [mə'nɒksaɪd] *n* monóxido.

**monsoon** [mɒn'suːn] *n* **1** *(wind)* monzón *m* **2** *(rainy season)* estación *f* lluviosa. ⌐COMP¬ **monsoon rains** lluvias *fpl* monzónicas.

**monster** ['mɒnstəʳ] *n (gen)* monstruo.
▶ *adj fam (huge)* enorme, gigantesco,-a.

**Montenegrin** [mɒntɪ'niːgrɪn] *adj* montenegrino,-a.
▶ *n* montenegrino,-a.

**Montenegro** [mɒntɪ'niːgrəʊ] *n* Montenegro.

**month** [mʌnθ] *n* mes *m*: *I'm going on holiday at the end of the month* me voy de vacaciones a final de mes.

**monthly** ['mʌnθlɪ] *adj* mensual.
▶ *adv* mensualmente, cada mes.
▶ *n (magazine)* revista mensual.

**monument** ['mɒnjəmənt] *n* monumento (to, a).

**monumental** [mɒnjə'mentªl] *adj* **1** *(gen)* monumental. **2** *fam (lie, blunder, etc)* garrafal, monumental.

**moo** [muː] *n (of cow)* mugido.
▶ *vi* mugir.
◆ **to mooch about / mooch around** *vi* dar vueltas, deambular.
ⓘ *pt & pp* mooed, *ger* mooing.

**mood¹** [muːd] *n* LING modo.

**mood²** [muːd] *n* **1** *(humour)* humor *m*: *her moods change very quickly* cambia de humor de repente. ⌐LOC¬ **to be in a good/ bad mood** estar de buen/mal humor.

**moon** [muːn] *n* luna: *full moon* luna llena. ⌐LOC¬ **to be over the moon** estar en el séptimo cielo.

**moonlight** ['muːnlaɪt] *n* claro de luna, luz *f* de luna.

**Moor** [mʊəʳ] *n* moro,-a.

**moor**[1] [mʊəʳ] *n (heath)* brezal *m*.

**moor**[2] [mʊəʳ] *vt (with rope)* amarrar; *(with anchor)* anclar.
► *vi (with anchor)* anclar; *(with rope)* echar amarras.

**mooring** [ˈmʊərɪŋ] *n (place)* amarradero.
► *n pl* **moorings** *(ropes, etc)* amarras *fpl*.

**Moorish** [ˈmʊərɪʃ] *adj* moro,-a.

**moorland** [ˈmʊərlənd] *n* páramo.

**moose** [muːs] *n* alce *m*.

**mop** [mɒp] *n* **1** *(for floor)* fregona. **2** *fam (of hair)* mata de pelo.
► *vt* **1** *(floor)* fregar, limpiar. **2** *(brow, tears)* enjugarse (with, con), secarse.
◆ **to mope about / mope around** *vi* andar abatido,-a, andar deprimido,-a.
① *pt & pp* **mopped**, *ger* **mopping**.

**moped** [ˈməʊped] *n* ciclomotor *m*.

**moral** [ˈmɒrəl] *adj* moral.
► *n (of story)* moraleja.
► *n pl* **morals** moral *f sing*, moralidad *f sing*.

⊠ Moral no significa 'moral (estado de ánimo)', que se traduce por **morale**.

**morale** [məˈrɑːl] *n* moral *f*, estado de ánimo.

**morality** [məˈrælɪtɪ] *n* moralidad *f*, moral *f*.

**morally** [ˈmɒrəlɪ] *adv* moralmente.

**more** [mɔːʳ] *adj* más: *more than half an hour* más de media hora.
► *pron* más: *we need some more* necesitamos más. ⎣LOC⎦ **the more ..., the more ...** cuanto más …, más … ▌ **what is more** además, lo que es más.
► *adv* más: *it's more expensive* es más caro. ⎣LOC⎦ **more and more** cada vez más. ▌ **more or less 1** *(approximately)* más o menos. **2** *(almost)* casi.

✎ Consulta también **many** y **much**.

**moreover** [mɔːˈrəʊvəʳ] *adv fml* además, por otra parte.

**morgue** [mɔːg] *n* depósito de cadáveres.

**morning** [ˈmɔːnɪŋ] *n (gen)* mañana; *(early)* madrugada: *at eight o'clock in the morning* a las ocho de la mañana; *the following morning* a la mañana siguiente.

⎣LOC⎦ **good morning!** ¡buenos días! ▌ **in the morning** *(tomorrow before noon)* mañana por la mañana.
► *adv* **mornings** por la mañana, por las mañanas.

**Moroccan** [məˈrɒkən] *adj* marroquí, -ina.
► *n* marroquí,-ina.

**Morocco** [məˈrɒkəʊ] *n* Marruecos.

**morose** [məˈrəʊs] *adj* malhumorado, -a, hosco,-a, taciturno,-a.

⊠ Morose no significa 'moroso', que se traduce por **defaulting**.

**morpheme** [ˈmɔːfiːm] *n* LING morfema *m*.

**morphine** [ˈmɔːfiːn] *n* morfina.

**morphological** [mɔːfəˈlɒdʒɪkəl] *adj* morfológico,-a.

**morphology** [mɔːˈfɒlədʒɪ] *n (gen)* morfología.

**Morse** [mɔːs] *n* Morse *m*. ⎣COMP⎦ **Morse code** alfabeto Morse.

**mortal** [ˈmɔːtəl] *adj (gen)* mortal.
► *n* mortal *mf*.

**mortality** [mɔːˈtælɪtɪ] *n* mortalidad *f*.

**mortgage** [ˈmɔːgɪdʒ] *n* hipoteca.
► *adj* hipotecario,-a.
► *vt* hipotecar.

**mosaic** [məˈzeɪɪk] *adj* mosaico.

**Moslem** [ˈmʌzləm] *adj* musulmán, -ana.
► *n* musulmán,-ana.

**mosque** [mɒsk] *n* mezquita.

**mosquito** [məsˈkiːtəʊ] *n* mosquito.
⎣COMP⎦ **mosquito bite** picadura de mosquito. ▌ **mosquito net** mosquitero, mosquitera.
① *pl* mosquitoes o mosquitos.

**moss** [mɒs] *n* BOT musgo.

**most** [məʊst] *adj* **1** *(greatest in quantity)* más: *Simon's got the most points* Simon tiene más puntos. **2** *(majority)* la mayoría de, la mayor parte de: *most people live in flats* la mayoría de la gente vive en pisos.
► *adv* más: *the most difficult question* la pregunta más difícil.
► *pron* **1** *(greatest part)* la mayor parte: *it rained most of the time* llovió durante la mayor parte del tiempo. **2** *(greatest number*

**M**

*or amount)* lo máximo. **3** *(the majority of people)* la mayoría.

▶ *adv* **1** *(superlative)* más: *the most beautiful girl* la chica más guapa. **3** *(very)* muy, de lo más: *it was most kind of you* ha sido muy amable de su parte; *a most delightful evening* una tarde muy agradable. **3** US *(almost)* casi. LOC **for the most part** por lo general. ‖ **most of all** sobre todo.

✎ Consulta también **many** y **much**.

**mostly** ['məʊstlɪ] *adv* **1** *(mainly)* principalmente, en su mayor parte. **2** *(generally)* generalmente; *(usually)* normalmente.

**moth** [mɒθ] *n* mariposa nocturna. COMP **clothes moth** polilla.

**mother** ['mʌðəʳ] *n* madre *f*: *a single mother* una madre soltera.
▶ *vt* **1** *(care for)* cuidar como una madre; *(rear)* criar. **2** *(spoil)* mimar. COMP **Mother Nature** la Madre *f* Naturaleza. ‖ **mother ship** buque *m* nodriza. ‖ **mother tongue** lengua materna.

**mother-in-law** ['mʌðərɪnlɔː] *n* suegra.
① *pl* **mothers-in-law**.

**mother-of-pearl** [mʌðərəvˈpɜːl] *n* madreperla, nácar *m*.

**motif** [məʊˈtiːf] *n* **1** *(pattern, design)* motivo. **2** *(in music, literature - theme)* tema *m*.

**motion** ['məʊʃ⁰n] *n* **1** *(movement)* movimiento. **2** *(gesture)* gesto, ademán *m*. **3** POL *(proposal)* moción *f*. LOC **in motion** en movimiento. ‖ **in slow motion** CINEM a cámara lenta. COMP **motion picture** película. ‖ **motion pictures** el cine *m*.

**motivate** ['məʊtɪveɪt] *vt* motivar.

**motive** ['məʊtɪv] *n* **1** *(reason)* motivo. **2** JUR móvil *m*.
▶ *adj* motor,-ra, motriz. COMP **motive force / motive power** fuerza motriz.

**motocross** ['məʊtəkrɒs] *n* SP motocross *m*.

**motor** ['məʊtəʳ] *n* **1** *(engine)* motor *m*. **2** GB *fam (car)* coche *m*, automóvil *m*. COMP **motor racing** carreras *fpl* de coches. ‖ **motor vehicle** vehículo a motor.
▶ *adj* **1** TECH motor,-ra. **2** BIOL motor,-ra, motriz.

**motorbike** ['məʊtəbaɪk] *n fam* motocicleta, moto *f*.

**motorboat** ['məʊtəbəʊt] *n* lancha motora, motora.

**motorcycle** ['məʊtəsaɪk⁰l] *n* motocicleta, moto *f*.

**motorcycling** ['məʊtəsaɪk⁰lɪŋ] *n* motociclismo.

**motorcyclist** ['məʊtəsaɪk⁰lɪst] *n* motociclista *mf*, motorista *mf*.

**motorist** ['məʊtərɪst] *n* automovilista *mf*, conductor,-ra (de coche).

**motorway** ['məʊtəweɪ] *n* GB autopista.

**motto** ['mɒtəʊ] *n* lema *m*.
① *pl* **mottos** o **mottoes**.

**mould¹** [məʊld] *n* *(growth)* moho.

**mould²** [məʊld] *n* **1** *(cast)* molde *m*. **2** *fig (type)* carácter *m*, temple *m*.
▶ *vt* **1** *(figure)* moldear; *(clay)* modelar.

**moult** [məʊlt] *vi* ZOOL mudar.
▶ *n* ZOOL muda.

**mound** [maʊnd] *n* **1** *(small hill)* montículo. **2** *(pile, heap)* montón *m*.

**mount¹** [maʊnt] *n* *(mountain)* monte *m*.

**mount²** [maʊnt] *n* **1** *(horse, etc)* montura. **2** *(for machine, gun, trophy)* soporte *m*, base *f*; *(for photo, picture)* fondo; *(for jewel)* engaste *m*, engarce *m*; *(for slide)* marquito.
▶ *vt* **1** montar. *(stairs)* subir.
▶ *vi* **1** *(go up)* subir, ascender.
◆ **to mount up** *vi* *(accumulate)* amontonarse, acumularse.

**mountain** ['maʊnt⁰n] *n* **1** GEOG montaña. **2** *fig (large amount)* montaña, montón *m*. COMP **mountain bike** bicicleta de montaña. ‖ **mountain range** cordillera, sierra.
▶ *adj* de montaña.

**mountaineer** [maʊntəˈnɪəʳ] *n* montañero,-a, alpinista *mf*, AM andinista *mf*.

**mountaineering** [maʊntəˈnɪərɪŋ] *n* montañismo, alpinismo, AM andinismo.

**mountainous** ['maʊnt⁰nəs] *adj* **1** *(region)* montañoso,-a. **2** *(huge)* enorme, gigantesco,-a.

**mourn** [mɔːn] *vt* *(person)* llorar la muerte de; *(thing)* llorar, añorar.

**mourning** ['mɔːnɪŋ] *n* luto, duelo. LOC **to be in mourning for** SB estar de luto por ALGN.

**mouse** [maʊs] *n (gen)* ratón *m*.
ⓘ *pl* **mice**.

**mousse** [muːs] *n* CULIN mousse *f*.

**moustache** [məsˈtɑːʃ] *n* bigote *m*.

**mouth** [*(n)* maʊθ; *(vb)* maʊð] *n* **1** ANAT boca. **2** *(of river)* desembocadura; *(of bottle)* boca; *(of tunnel, cave)* boca, entrada. **3** *(person to feed)* boca. LOC **to keep one's mouth shut** mantener la boca cerrada, no decir nada. COMP **mouth organ** armónica.

**mouthful** ['maʊθfʊl] *n* **1** *(of food)* bocado; *(of drink)* trago; *(of air)* bocanada. **2** *fam (long word, phrase)* trabalenguas *m*.

**mouth-to-mouth** [maʊθtəˈmaʊθ] [also mouth-to-mouth resuscitation] *n* boca a boca *m*.

**movable** ['muːvəbəl] *adj* movible, móvil.

**move** [muːv] *n* **1** *(act of moving, movement)* movimiento: *he watched my every move* observó todos mis movimientos. **2** *(to new home)* mudanza; *(to new job)* traslado. **3** *(in game)* jugada; *(turn)* turno: *whose move is it?* ¿a quién le toca jugar? **4** *(action, step)* paso, acción *f*, medida; *(decision)* decisión *f*; *(attempt)* intento.
▶ *vt* **1** *(gen)* mover; *(furniture, etc)* cambiar de sitio, trasladar; *(transfer)* trasladar; *(out of the way)* apartar: *you've moved the furniture!* ¡habéis cambiado los muebles de sitio! **2** *(affect emotionally)* conmover. **3** *(in games)* mover, jugar.
▶ *vi* **1** *(gen)* moverse; *(change - position)* trasladarse, desplazarse; *(- house)* mudarse; *(- post, department)* trasladarse: *she was so scared she couldn't move* tenía tanto miedo que no podía moverse.
◆ **to move away** *vi* **1** *(move aside, etc)* alejarse, apartarse. **2** *(change house)* mudarse de casa.
◆ **to move in** *vi* **1** *(into new home)* instalarse. **2** *(prepare to take control, attack, etc)* acercarse.
◆ **to move over** *vt sep (step aside)* apartarse.
▶ *vi (make room)* correrse, moverse.

**movement** ['muːvmənt] *n* **1** *(act, motion)* movimiento; *(gesture)* gesto, ademán *m*. **2** *(of goods)* traslado; *(of troops)* desplazamiento; *(of population)* movimiento. **3** *(political, literary)* movimiento. **4** *(trend)* tendencia, corriente *f*.
▶ *n pl* **movements** *(activities)* movimientos *mpl*, actividades *fpl*.

**movie** ['muːvɪ] *n* US película.
▶ *n pl* **the movies** el cine *m sing*. LOC **to go to the movies** ir al cine.

**moving** ['muːvɪŋ] *adj* **1** *(that moves)* móvil; *(in motion)* en movimiento, en marcha. **2** *(causing motion)* motor,-ra, motriz. **3** *(causing action, motivating)* instigador,-ra, promotor,-ra. **4** *(emotional)* conmovedor,-ra.

**mow** [məʊ] *vt (lawn)* cortar, segar; *(corn, wheat)* segar.
ⓘ *pt* **mowed**, *pp* **mowed** o **mown** [məʊn].

**mower** ['məʊəʳ] *n (for lawn)* cortacésped *m & f*; *(for fields)* segadora.

**mown** [məʊn] *pp* → **mow**.

**Mozambique** [məʊzæmˈbiːk] *n* Mozambique.

**Mozambiquean** [məʊzæmˈbiːkən] *adj* mozambiqueño,-a.
▶ *n* mozambiqueño,-a.

**MP** ['emˈpiː] *abbr* (member of Parliament) diputado,-a.

**mph** ['emˈpiːˈeɪtʃ] *abbr* (miles per hour) millas por hora.

**Mr** *abbr* (Mister) señor; *(abbreviation)* sr.

**Mrs** *abbr* señora; *(abbreviation)* sra.

**Ms** *abbr* (Miss) señorita; *(abbreviation)* srta.

**much** [mʌtʃ] *adj* mucho,-a: *we haven't got much bread* no tenemos mucho pan; *he didn't have much time* no tenía mucho tiempo; *we've made too much jam* hemos hecho demasiada mermelada; *why is there so much traffic?* ¿por qué hay tanto tráfico?; *take as much time as you need* tómate tanto tiempo como necesites; *how much money have you got?* ¿cuánto dinero tienes?
ⓘ *comp* **more**, *superl* **most**.
▶ *pron* mucho: *there's not much to do round here* no hay mucho que hacer por aquí; *how much is it?* ¿cuánto vale? LOC **a bit much** un poco demasiado, un po-

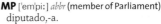

co excesivo,-a. ▌ **as much 1** *(equal)* equivalente a. **2** *(the same)* lo mismo.
▶ *adv* mucho: *he felt much better* se encontraba mucho mejor.

✎ Much se emplea sobre todo en las frases negativas e interrogativas, en las frases afirmativas se emplea **a lot**.

**mucus** [ˈmjuːkəs] *n* mucosidad *f*.

**mud** [mʌd] *n (gen)* barro, lodo; *(thick)* fango.

**muddle** [ˈmʌdəl] *n* **1** *(mess)* desorden *m*: *everything's in a muddle* todo está en desorden. **2** *(confusion, mix-up)* confusión *f*, embrollo, lío.
▶ *vt* [also to muddle up] *(untidy)* revolver, desordenar; *(confuse mentally)* liar, confundir, embarullar; *(confuse, mix up)* confundir.
◆ **to muddle through** *vi* arreglárselas.

**muddy** [ˈmʌdɪ] *adj* **1** *(gen)* fangoso,-a, barroso,-a, lodoso,-a. **2** *(colour)* sucio,-a. **3** *(thinking, idea, etc)* confuso,-a, turbio,-a.
ⓘ *comp* muddier, *superl* muddiest.

**mudguard** [ˈmʌdɡɑːd] *n* guardabarros *m inv*.

**muesli** [ˈmjuːzlɪ] *n* muesli *m*.

**muffin** [ˈmʌfɪn] *n* **1** GB panecillo redondo que se come tostado y con mantequilla. **2** US tipo de magdalena.

**mug** [mʌɡ] *n (large cup)* taza alta, tazón *m*.

**mugger** [ˈmʌɡər] *n* atracador,-ra, asaltante *mf*.

**mugging** [ˈmʌɡɪŋ] *n* atraco, asalto.

**mule** [mjuːl] *n* ZOOL mulo,-a.

**mullet** [ˈmʌlɪθ] COMP **grey mullet** mújol *m*. ▌ **red mullet** salmonete *m*.

**multicultural** [ˌmʌltɪˈkʌltʃərəl] *adj* multicultural.

**multilateral** [ˌmʌltɪˈlætərəl] *adj* multilateral.

**multinational** [ˌmʌltɪˈnæʃənəl] *adj* multinacional.
▶ *n* multinacional *f*.

**multiple** [ˈmʌltɪpəl] *adj* múltiple.
▶ *n* MATH múltiplo.

**multiple-choice** [ˌmʌltɪpəlˈtʃɔɪs] *adj* tipo test.

**multiplex** [ˈmʌltɪpleks] *adj* **1** *(cinema)* multicines *mpl*. **2** TECH múltiple.

**multiplication** [ˌmʌltɪplɪˈkeɪʃən] *n* multiplicación *f*. COMP **multiplication sign** signo de multiplicar. ▌ **multiplication table** tabla de multiplicar.

**multiply** [ˈmʌltɪplaɪ] *vt* MATH multiplicar (by, por).
ⓘ *pt & pp* multiplied, *ger* multiplying.
▶ *vi* multiplicarse.

**multipurpose** [ˌmʌltɪˈpɜːpəs] *adj* multiuso *inv*.

**mum** [mʌm] *n* GB *fam* mamá *f*.

**mumble** [ˈmʌmbəl] *vt (gen)* decir entre dientes, mascullar; *(prayer)* musitar.
▶ *vi* hablar entre dientes, farfullar.

**mummify** [ˈmʌmɪfaɪ] *vt* momificar.
ⓘ *pt & pp* mummified, *ger* mummifying.

**mummy¹** [ˈmʌmɪ] *n (dead body)* momia *f*.
ⓘ *pl* mummies.

**mummy²** [ˈmʌmɪ] *n* GB *fam (mother)* mamá *f*.
ⓘ *pl* mummies.

**mumps** [mʌmps] *n* MED paperas *fpl*.

**mundane** [mʌnˈdeɪn] *adj* **1** *(worldly)* mundano,-a. **2** *pej (banal)* rutinario,-a, banal.

**municipal** [mjuːˈnɪsɪpəl] *adj* municipal.

**municipality** [mjuːnɪsɪˈpælɪtɪ] *n* municipio.
ⓘ *pl* municipalities.

**mural** [ˈmjʊərəl] *n* pintura mural, mural *m*.

**murder** [ˈmɜːdər] *n* **1** asesinato, homicidio. **2** *fam fig (difficult experience)* pesadilla. COMP **murder story** novela negra, novela policíaca.
▶ *vt* **1** *(kill)* asesinar, matar. **2** *fam fig (be angry with)* matar.

**murderer** [ˈmɜːdərər] *n* asesino, homicida *mf*.

**murmur** [ˈmɜːmər] *n* **1** *(of voice)* murmullo, susurro. **2** *(of traffic)* rumor *m*; *(of insects)* zumbido; *(of wind)* murmullo; *(of water)* susurro. **3** MED soplo.
▶ *vt* murmurar: *they murmured their approval* hubo un murmullo de aprobación.

▶ *vi* **1** murmurar, susurrar. **2** *(complain)* quejarse (**against/at**, de).

❌ To murmur no significa 'murmurar (hablar mal)', que se traduce por to gossip.

**muscle** ['mʌsəl] *n* **1** ANAT músculo. **2** *(muscle power)* fuerza. **3** *fig (strength, power)* poder *m*, fuerza. ⸤LOC⸥ **to not move a muscle** no inmutarse.

◆ **to muscle in** *vi (situation)* entrometerse (**on**, en); *(place)* introducirse por la fuerza.

**muscular** ['mʌskjələʳ] *adj* **1** *(pain, tissue)* muscular. **2** *(person)* musculoso,-a.

**musculature** ['mʌskjələtʃəʳ] *n* **1** musculatura. **2** *(person)* musculoso,-a.

**muse¹** [mjuːz] *vi* meditar (**on/over**, -), reflexionar (**on/over**, sobre).

**muse²** [mjuːz] *n* musa.
▶ *n pl* **the Muses** las Musas *fpl*.

**museum** [mjuːˈzɪəm] *n* museo.

**mushroom** ['mʌʃruːm] *n* **1** BOT seta, hongo. **2** CULIN *(button mushroom)* champiñón *m*; *(wild)* seta. ⸤COMP⸥ **mushroom cloud** hongo nuclear.

✎ La palabra mushroom se usa para designar cualquier seta u hongo comestible; las setas no comestibles se llaman toadstools.

**music** ['mjuːzɪk] *n* música. ⸤COMP⸥ **music box** caja de música. ‖ **music centre** equipo de música. ‖ **music hall** teatro de variedades. ‖ **music score** partitura. ‖ **music stand** atril *m*.

**musical** ['mjuːzɪkəl] *adj* **1** *(gen)* musical. **2** *(person - gifted)* dotado,-a para la música; *(- fond of music)* aficionado,-a a la música, melómano,-a. ⸤COMP⸥ **musical box** caja de música. ‖ **musical instrument** instrumento musical.
▶ *n* musical *m*.

**musician** [mjuːˈzɪʃən] *n* músico,-a.

**musk** [mʌsk] *n (substance)* almizcle *m*.

**musket** ['mʌskɪt] *n* mosquete *m*.

**musketeer** [mʌskəˈtɪəʳ] *n* mosquetero.

**Muslim** ['mʌzlɪm] *adj* musulmán,-ana.
▶ *n* musulmán,-ana.

**muslin** ['mʌzlɪn] *n* muselina.

**mussel** ['mʌsəl] *n* mejillón *m*.

**must¹** [mʌst] *aux* **1** *(necessity, obligation)* deber, tener que: *I must leave now* tengo que marcharme ahora; *must you play your music so loud?* ¿es necesario poner la música tan fuerte? **2** *(probability)* deber de: *she must be tired* debe de estar cansada; *but someone must have seen her* pero alguien debe de haberla visto. ⸤LOC⸥ **if I must** si no hay más remedio. ‖ **if you must know,** ... si te empeñas en saberlo, ...
▶ *n (need)* necesidad *f*: *it's an absolute must for all film buffs* es imprescindible para todos los cinéfilos.

**mustache** [məsˈtɑːʃ] *n* US → **moustache**.

**mustard** ['mʌstəd] *n (gen)* mostaza. ⸤COMP⸥ **mustard gas** gas *m* mostaza.

**mutant** ['mjuːtənt] *n* mutante *mf*.
▶ *adj* mutante.

**mutation** [mjuːˈteɪʃən] *n* mutación *f*.

**mute** [mjuːt] *adj (dumb, silent)* mudo,-a. ⸤COMP⸥ **deaf mute** sordomudo,-a.
▶ *n* **1** LING mudo,-a. **2** *(dumb person)* mudo,-a. **3** MUS sordina.

**mutilate** ['mjuːtɪleɪt] *vt* mutilar.

**mutilation** [mjuːtɪˈleɪʃən] *n* mutilación *f*.

**mutiny** ['mjuːtɪnɪ] *n* motín *m*, amotinamiento, sublevación *f*, rebelión *f*.
ⓘ *pl* mutinies.
▶ *vi* amotinarse.
ⓘ *pt & pp* mutinied, *ger* mutinying.

**mutter** ['mʌtəʳ] *n* murmullo, refunfuño.
▶ *vt (mumble)* murmurar, mascullar, decir entre dientes, refunfuñar.
▶ *vi* **1** *(mumble)* murmurar, hablar entre dientes. **2** *(complain)* refunfuñar, rezongar, quejarse.

**mutton** ['mʌtən] *n* carne *f* de oveja.

**mutual** ['mjuːtʃuəl] *adj* **1** *(help, love, etc)* mutuo,-a, recíproco,-a. **2** *(friend, interest, etc)* común.

**mutually** ['mjuːtʃuəlɪ] *adv* mutuamente.

**muzzle** ['mʌzəl] *n* **1** *(snout)* hocico. **2** *(guard)* bozal *m*. **3** *(of gun)* boca.

▸ *vt* **1** *(dog)* poner un bozal a. **2** *fig (person, press, etc)* amordazar.

**muzzy** ['mʌzɪ] *adj* **1** *(blurred)* borroso,-a. **2** *(groggy)* atontado,-a, espeso,-a.
ⓘ *comp* muzzier, *superl* muzziest.

**my** [maɪ] *adj* mi, mis: *my book* mi libro; *my records* mis discos; *one of my friends* un amigo mío.
▸ *interj* ¡caramba!, ¡caray!

**myopia** [maɪ'əʊpɪə] *n* miopía.

**myopic** [maɪ'ɒpɪk] *adj* miope.

**myrtle** ['mɜːtəl] *n* BOT arrayán *m*, mirto.

**myself** [maɪ'self] *pron* **1** *(reflexive)* me: *I cut myself* me corté; *I helped myself* me serví. **2** *(after preposition)* mí (mismo,-a): *I kept it for myself* lo guardé para mí; *I said to myself* me dije a mí mismo. **3** *(emphatic)* yo mismo,-a: *I did it by myself* lo hice yo mismo,-a. LOC **all by myself 1** *(alone)* solo,-a. **2** *(without help)* yo solo,-a. ▌ **to myself** *(private)* para mí solo,-a.

**mysterious** [mɪ'stɪərɪəs] *adj* misterioso,-a.

**mysteriously** [mɪ'stɪərɪəslɪ] *adv* misteriosamente.

**mystery** ['mɪstərɪ] *n* misterio.
ⓘ *pl* mysteries.

**mystic** ['mɪstɪk] *adj* místico,-a.
▸ *n* místico,-a.

**mystical** ['mɪstɪkəl] *adj* místico,-a.

**myth** [mɪθ] *n* **1** *(ancient story)* mito. **2** *(fallacy)* falacia.

**mythical** ['mɪθɪkəl] *adj* **1** *(of a myth)* mítico,-a. **2** *(not real, imagined)* imaginario,-a, fantástico,-a.

**mythological** [mɪθə'lɒdʒɪkəl] *adj* mitológico,-a.

**mythology** [mɪ'θɒlədʒɪ] *n* mitología.

**N, n** [en] *n (the letter)* N, n *f*.

**N** [nɔːθ] *abbr* (**north**) norte *m*; *(abbreviation)* N.

**naff** [næf] *adj fam* hortera.

**nag** [næg] *vt* **1** *(annoy)* molestar, fastidiar. **2** *(complain)* dar la tabarra a.
▸ *vi* quejarse.
ⓘ *pt & pp* nagged, *ger* nagging.

**nail** [neɪl] *n* **1** *(on finger, toe)* uña: *to bite/cut/trim one's nails* morderse/cortarse/arreglarse las uñas. **2** *(metal)* clavo.
▸ *vt* **1** clavar, fijar con clavos. **2** *fam* pillar, coger. [COMP] **nail clippers** cortaúñas *m*. ∎ **nail polish** esmalte *m* para las uñas. ∎ **nail varnish** esmalte *m* para las uñas. ∎ **nail varnish remover** quitaesmaltes *m*.
◆ **to nail down** *vt sep* **1** *(thing)* clavar, sujetar con clavos. **2** *fig (person)* conseguir que ALGN se comprometa: *I couldn't nail him down to a price* no pude conseguir que me concretara un precio.

**naive** [naɪˈiːv] *adj* ingenuo,-a.

**naked** [ˈneɪkɪd] *adj* desnudo,-a.

**name** [neɪm] *n* **1** *(first name)* nombre *m*; *(surname)* apellido: *his name's Richard* se llama Richard; *what's your name?* ¿cómo te llamas? **2** *(fame)* fama, reputación *f*: *she made her name in the theatre* se hizo famosa en el teatro.
▸ *vt* **1** llamar: *they named the child Dominic after his uncle* al niño le pusieron Dominic por su tío. **2** *(appoint)* nombrar: *he was named Minister of Transport* lo nombraron Ministro de Transportes. [LOC] **in the name of...** en nombre de... [COMP] **big name** pez *m* gordo. ∎ **name day** santo.

**namely** [ˈneɪmlɪ] *adv* a saber.

**Namibia** [nəˈmɪbɪə] *n* Namibia.

**Namibian** [nəˈmɪbɪən] *adj* namibio,-a.
▸ *n* namibio,-a.

**nanny** [ˈnænɪ] *n* **1** *(carer)* niñera. **2** GB *fam (grandmother)* yaya, abuela.
ⓘ *pl* nannies.

**nap** [næp] *n* siesta.
▸ *vi* dormir la siesta. [LOC] **to have a nap / take a nap** echar la siesta.
ⓘ *pt & pp* napped, *ger* napping.

**nape** [neɪp] *n* nuca, cogote *m*.

**napkin** [ˈnæpkɪn] *n* servilleta. [COMP] **napkin ring** servilletero.

**nappy** [ˈnæpɪ] *n* GB pañal *m*.
ⓘ *pl* nappies.

**narcissus** [nɑːˈsɪsəs] *n* narciso.
ⓘ *pl* narcissi o narcissuses.

**narcotic** [nɑːˈkɒtɪk] *adj* narcótico,-a.
▸ *n* narcótico.

**narrate** [nəˈreɪt] *vt* narrar.

**narrative** [ˈnærətɪv] *adj* narrativo,-a.
▸ *n* **1** narración *f*. **2** *(genre)* narrativa.

**narrator** [nəˈreɪtəʳ] *n* narrador,-ra.

**narrow** [ˈnærəʊ] *adj* **1** estrecho,-a: *a narrow road* una carretera estrecha. **2** *(restricted)* reducido,-a, restringido,-a: *a narrow circle of friends* un círculo reducido de amigos. **3** *(by very little)* escaso,-a: *by a narrow majority* por una escasa mayoría.
ⓘ *comp* narrower, *superl* narrowest.
▸ *vt* **1** *(make narrower)* estrechar. **2** *(reduce)* reducir, acortar: *Leeds narrowed Hull's lead to only 1 point* el Leeds redujo la ventaja del Hull a 1 solo punto.

**nasal** [ˈneɪzºl] *adj* **1** nasal. **2** *(way of speaking)* gangoso,-a.

**nasty** [ˈnɑːstɪ] *adj* **1** *(unpleasant)* desagradable, repugnante, horrible: *what a nasty smell!* ¡qué olor más desagradable! **2** *(malicious)* malintencionado,-a; *(unkind)*

antipático,-a: *she was really nasty to everyone* se mostró muy antipática con todos. **3** *(dangerous)* peligroso,-a: *this bend is really nasty* esta curva es muy peligrosa. **4** *(tricky)* peliagudo,-a: *it's quite a nasty little problem* es un problemita bastante peliagudo. **5** *(serious)* grave: *a nasty cold* un resfriado de cuidado.
① *comp* **nastier**, *superl* **nastiest**.

**nation** ['neɪʃ°n] *n* **1** *(country)* nación *f*, país *m*. **2** *(ethnic group)* pueblo, nación *f*.

**national** ['næʃ°nəl] *adj* nacional. COMP **national anthem** himno nacional.
▶ *n* súbdito,-a, ciudadano,-a.

**nationalism** ['næʃ°nəlɪz°m] *n* nacionalismo.

**nationalist** ['næʃ°nəlɪst] *adj* nacionalista.
▶ *n* nacionalista *mf*.

**nationality** [næʃ°nælɪtɪ] *n* nacionalidad *f*.
① *pl* **nationalities**.

**native** ['neɪtɪv] *adj* **1** *(place)* natal; *(language)* materno,-a: *her native country* su país natal; *his native tongue is Danish* su lengua materna es el danés; *we need a native speaker of English* necesitamos un hablante de inglés que sea nativo. **2** *(plant, animal)* originario,-a: *it's native to Australia* es originario de Australia; *native varieties of grape* variedades autóctonas de vid.
▶ *n* **1** natural *mf*, nativo,-a: *she's a native of Orense* es natural de Orense. **2** *(original inhabitant)* indígena *mf*. COMP **Native American** indio,-a americano,-a.

⊕ Se llama **Native American** a los descendientes de las tribus aborígenes que habitaban Estados Unidos antes de la llegada de los europeos. Se trata de una multitud de pueblos con lenguas y tradiciones diferentes que fueron diezmados durante la colonización y, posteriormente, recluidos en reservas.

**nativity** [nə'tɪvɪtɪ] *n* natividad *f*.
① *pl* **nationalities**.

**NATO** ['neɪtəʊ] [also written Nato] *abbr* **(North Atlantic Treaty Organization)** Organización *f* del Tratado del Atlántico Norte; *(abbreviation)* OTAN *f*.

**natural** ['nætʃ°rəl] *adj* natural. **3** *(usual)* natural, normal: *it's only natural to feel afraid* es normal tener miedo. COMP **natural childbirth** parto natural. ‖ **natural gas** gas *m* natural. ‖ **natural history** historia natural. ‖ **natural resources** recursos *mpl* naturales. ‖ **natural science** ciencias *fpl* naturales. ‖ **natural selection** selección *f* natural.

**naturally** ['nætʃ°rəlɪ] *adv* **1** *(by nature)* por naturaleza. **2** *(unaffectedly)* con naturalidad. **3** *(not artificially)* de manera natural. **4** *(of course)* naturalmente, por supuesto.

**nature** ['neɪtʃ°r] *n* **1** *(gen)* naturaleza. **2** *(character)* carácter *m*, forma de ser: *it's in her nature to be like that* es así por naturaleza. LOC **by nature** por naturaleza. COMP **nature conservation** conservación *f* de la naturaleza. ‖ **nature reserve** reserva natural. ‖ **nature study** ciencias *fpl* naturales.

**naughty** ['nɔːtɪ] *adj* **1** travieso,-a, malo,-a. **2** *(risqué)* atrevido,-a.
① *comp* **naughtier**, *superl* **naughtiest**.

**Nauru** ['naʊruː, 'nɑːuːruː] *n* Nauru.

**Nauruan** [naʊ'ruːən] *adj* nauruano,-a.
▶ *n* nauruano,-a.

**nausea** ['nɔːzɪə] *n* **1** *(physical)* náusea. **2** *(disgust)* asco, repugnancia.

**nauseating** ['nɔːzɪeɪtɪŋ] *adj* **1** *(physically)* nauseabundo,-a. **2** *(disgusting)* asqueroso,-a, repugnante.

**nautical** ['nɔːtɪk°l] *adj* náutico,-a. COMP **nautical mile** milla náutica.

**Navajo** ['nævəhəʊ] *adj-n* → **Navaho**.

**naval** ['neɪv°l] *adj* naval. COMP **naval battle** batalla naval. ‖ **naval base** base *f* naval.

**navel** ['neɪv°l] *n* ombligo.

**navigate** ['nævɪgeɪt] *vt* **1** *(river, sea)* navegar por. **2** *(steer - ship)* gobernar; *(- plane)* pilotar.
▶ *vi (when sailing, flying)* dirigir; *(when driving)* guiar: *you drive, I'll navigate* tu conduce, yo te guiaré.

**navigation** [nævɪ'geɪʃ°n] *n* navegación *f*.

**navigator** ['nævɪgeɪtə°r] *n* MAR navegante *mf*.

**navy** ['neɪvɪ] *n* marina de guerra, armada. COMP **navy blue** azul marino.
ⓘ *pl* **navies**.

**Nazi** ['nɑːtsɪ] *adj* nazi.
▸ *n* nazi *mf*.

**Nazism** ['nɑːtsɪzᵊm] *n* nazismo.

**Neanderthal** [nɪˈændətɑːl] *adj* de Neanderthal. COMP **Neanderthal man** hombre *m* de Neanderthal.

**near** [nɪəʳ] *adj* **1** cercano,-a: *where is the nearest bank?* ¿dónde está el banco más cercano?; *a near relative* un pariente cercano. **2** *(time)* próximo,-a: *in the near future* en un futuro próximo.
ⓘ *comp* **nearer**, *comp* **nearest**.
▸ *adv* cerca: *I live quite near (by)* vivo bastante cerca.
▸ *prep* **1** cerca de: *it's near the market* está cerca del mercado. **2** *[also near to.]* a punto de: *she was near to crying* estuvo a punto de llorar.
▸ *vt* acercarse a: *we are nearing the day when…* nos acercamos al día en que…

**nearby** [*(adj)* 'nɪəbaɪ; *(adv)* nɪəˈbaɪ] *adj* cercano,-a: *a nearby hotel* un hotel cercano.
▸ *adv* cerca: *is there one nearby?* ¿hay alguno cerca?

**nearly** ['nɪəlɪ] *adv* casi. LOC **not nearly** ni mucho menos, ni con mucho: *there's not nearly enough time to finish* el tiempo para acabar es del todo insuficiente.

**neat** [niːt] *adj* **1** *(room)* ordenado,-a; *(garden)* bien arreglado,-a. **2** *(person)* pulcro,-a; *(in habits)* ordenado,-a. **3** *(writing)* claro,-a. **4** *(clever)* ingenioso,-a, apañado,-a. **5** *(drinks)* solo,-a. **6** US fantástico,-a, estupendo,-a, chulo,-a, guay.

**neatness** ['niːtnəs] *n* esmero.

**necessarily** [nesəˈserɪlɪ] *adv* **1** necesariamente. **2** *(inevitably)* inevitablemente, forzosamente.

**necessary** ['nesɪsᵊrɪ] *adj* **1** necesario,-a. **2** *(inevitable)* inevitable, forzoso,-a. LOC **to do the necessary** hacer lo necesario.
▸ *n pl* **necessaries** lo necesario, cosas *fpl* necesarias.

**necessity** [nɪˈsesɪtɪ] *n* **1** necesidad *f*: *it's a necessity* es indispensable. **2** *(item)* requisito indispensable.
ⓘ *pl* **necessities**.

**neck** [nek] *n* cuello. LOC **to be in STH up to one's neck** estar metido,-a en ALGO hasta el cuello. **‖ to break one's neck** desnucarse. **‖ to risk one's neck** jugarse el tipo.

**necklace** ['nekləs] *n* collar *m*.

**neckline** ['neklaɪn] *n* escote *m*. LOC **with a low neckline** muy escotado,-a.

**nectarine** ['nektərɪn] *n* nectarina.

**née** [neɪ] *adj* de soltera: *Mrs Hastings, née Lawley* la Sra. Hastings, de soltera Lawley.

**need** [niːd] *n* **1** necesidad *f*: *there's no need for all of you to come with me* no hace falta que me acompañéis todos; *I have enough to satisfy my needs* tengo suficiente para satisfacer mis necesidades. **2** *(poverty)* necesidad *f*, infortunio: *to help SB in time of need* ayudar a ALGN en tiempos de necesidad. LOC **if need be** si hace falta. **‖ to be in need of** necesitar. **‖ to have need of** necesitar, tener necesidad de.
▸ *vt* necesitar: *you'll need a pencil* necesitarás un lápiz; *I need to see you* tengo que verte.
▸ *aux* hacer falta: *need we all go?* ¿hace falta que vayamos todos?; *need you drive so fast?* ¿tienes que conducir tan deprisa?; *you needn't come in tomorrow* no hace falta que vengas mañana; *you needn't have bought me a present* no hacía falta que me compraras ningún regalo.

**needle** ['niːdᵊl] *n* **1** *(gen)* aguja. **2** GB *fam (friction)* pique *m*. **3** US *fam (injection)* inyección *f*. **4** *(leaf)* hoja: *pine needles* hojas de pino. LOC **it's like looking for a needle in a haystack** es como buscar una aguja en un pajar.
▸ *vt fam* pinchar.

**needless** ['niːdləs] *adj* innecesario,-a.

**needn't** ['niːdᵊnt] *v* → **need**.

**negative** ['negətɪv] *adj* negativo,-a.
▸ *n* **1** LING negación *f*. **2** *(answer)* negativa. **3** *(photograph)* negativo.

**neglect** [nɪˈglekt] *n* **1** *(of thing)* descuido, desatención *f*: *the house was in a state of neglect* la casa estaba totalmente descuidada, la casa se encontraba en un estado de abandono. **2** *(of duty)* incumplimiento.

▶ *vt* **1** *(not take care of)* tener abandonado,-a, desatender: *I've been neglecting my friends recently* tengo abandonados a mis amigos. **2** *(fail to attend to)* descuidar: *with so much sport you've been neglecting your academic work* con tanto deporte tienes los estudios muy descuidados. **3** *(forget to do)* olvidar: *she neglected to lock the safe* olvidó cerrar la caja con llave.

**neglected** [nɪˈglektɪd] *adj* descuidado,-a.

**negligence** [ˈneglɪdʒəns] *n* negligencia.

**negotiate** [nɪˈgəʊʃɪeɪt] *vt* negociar.

**negotiation** [nɪgəʊʃɪˈeɪʃ(ə)n] *n* negociación *f*: *the agreement is under negotiation* el acuerdo se está negociando.

**negotiator** [nɪˈgəʊʃɪeɪtəʳ] *n* negociador,-ra.

**neigh** [neɪ] *n* relincho.
▶ *vi* relinchar.

**neighbor** [ˈneɪbəʳ] *n* US → neighbour.

**neighbour** [ˈneɪbəʳ] *n* **1** vecino,-a. **2** *(fellow man)* prójimo,-a.

**neighbourhood** [ˈneɪbəhʊd] *n* **1** vecindad *f*, barrio. **2** *(people)* vecindario. COMP **neighbourhood watch** grupo de vigilancia vecinal.

**neither** [ˈnaɪðəʳ, ˈniːðəʳ] *adj* ninguno de los dos, ninguna de las dos: *neither boy knew the answer* ninguno de los dos chicos sabía la respuesta.
▶ *pron* ninguno de los dos, ninguna de las dos: *neither is here* ninguno de los dos está aquí.
▶ *adv* **1** ni: *he's neither fat nor thin* no es ni gordo ni delgado. **2** tampoco: *I don't like it and neither does my wife* no me gusta a mí, y a mi mujer tampoco. LOC **neither... nor...** ni... ni...: *she neither smokes nor drinks* ni fuma ni bebe.

**neolithic** [nəʊˈlɪθɪk] *adj* neolítico,-a.

**neon** [ˈniːɒn] *n* neón *m*. COMP **neon light** luz *f* de neón. ▌ **neon sign** rótulo con tubos de neón.

**Nepal** [nəˈpɔːl] *n* Nepal.

**Nepalese** [nepəˈliːz] *adj* nepalés,-esa, nepalí.
▶ *n* **1** *(person)* nepalés,-esa, nepalí *mf*. **2** *(language)* nepalés *m*, nepalí *m*.

**Nepali** [nəˈpɔːlɪ] *adj* → Nepalese.

**nephew** [ˈnevjuː] *n* sobrino.

**Neptune** [ˈneptjuːn] *n* Neptuno.

**nerve** [nɜːv] *n* **1** nervio. **2** *(daring)* valor *m*. **3** *(cheek)* descaro, cara: *what a nerve!* ¡qué cara! LOC **to be a bundle of nerves** estar hecho,-a un manojo de nervios. ▌ **to get on SB's nerves** crispar los nervios a ALGN. ▌ **to lose one's nerve** rajarse. COMP **nerve cell** neurona. ▌ **nerve centre** centro neurálgico. ▌ **nerve gas** gas *m* nervioso.

**nervous** [ˈnɜːvəs] *adj* **1** nervioso,-a. **2** *(afraid)* miedoso,-a; *(timid)* tímido,-a. **3** *(apprehensive)* aprensivo,-a. COMP **nervous breakdown** crisis *f* nerviosa. ▌ **nervous system** sistema *m* nervioso. ▌ **nervous wreck** manojo de nervios.

**nest** [nest] *n* **1** nido; *(hen's)* nidal *m*. **2** *(wasp's)* avispero; *(animal's)* madriguera. **3** *fig* nido, refugio.
▶ *vi* anidar, nidificar.
▶ *vt* COMPUT anidar.

**net¹** [net] *n* red *f*.
▶ *vt* coger con red.
① *pt & pp* netted, *ger* netting.

**net²** [net] *adj* FIN neto,-a: *they made a net profit of £1.5M* tuvieron beneficios netos de un millón y medio de libras. COMP **net result** resultado final. ▌ **net weight** peso neto.

**nether** [ˈneðəʳ] *adj lit* inferior, de abajo.

**Netherlander** [ˈneðəlændəʳ] *n* neerlandés,-esa.

**Netherlands** [ˈneðələndʒ] *n* **the Netherlands** los Países *mpl* Bajos.

**netsurfer** [ˈnetsɜːfəʳ] *n* internauta *mf*.

**nettle** [ˈnet°l] *n* ortiga. LOC **to grasp the nettle** coger el toro por los cuernos. COMP **nettle rash** urticaria.

**network** [ˈnetwɜːk] *n* red *f*.
▶ *vt* COMPUT conectar en red.

**neuron** [ˈnjʊərɒn] *n* neurona.

**neuter** [ˈnjuːtəʳ] *adj* neutro,-a.
▶ *n* LING neutro.

**neutral** [ˈnjuːtrəl] *adj* **1** *(in general)* neutro,-a: *a neutral colour/shampoo* un color/ champú neutro. **2** POL neutral: *a neutral country* un país neutral. **3** *(impartial)* neutral, imparcial: *a neutral judgment* un juicio imparcial.

▶ *n* AUTO **punto muerto**: *leave the car in neutral* deja el coche en punto muerto.

**neutron** [ˈnjuːərɒn] *n* neutrón *m*.

**never** [ˈnevəʳ] *adv* nunca, jamás: *I have never been there* jamás he estado allí; *we never go there any more* ya no vamos allí nunca; *never have I heard such rubbish* en mi vida he oído tales tonterías; *he never so much as thanked me* ni siquiera me dio las gracias. Loc **never again** nunca más. **I never mind!** ¡no importa!

**never-ending** [nevəˈrendɪŋ] *adj* interminable.

**nevertheless** [nevəðəˈles] *adv* sin embargo.

**new** [njuː] *adj* **1** *(following - in order)* nuevo,-a: *a new car* un coche nuevo; *new bread* pan recién hecho. **2** *(baby)* recién nacido,-a: *she's got a new baby* acaba de tener un hijo. Loc **what's new?** ¿qué hay de nuevo? COMP **new moon** luna nueva. **I New Testament** Nuevo Testamento. **I new wave** nueva ola. **I New World** Nuevo Mundo. **I New Year** Año Nuevo. **I New Year's Day** día *m* de Año Nuevo. **I New Year's Eve** Nochevieja. **I New York** Nueva York. **I New Zealand** Nueva Zelanda. **I New Zealander** neozelandés,-esa.

**newborn** [ˈnjuːbɔːn] *adj* recién nacido,-a.

**newcomer** [ˈnjuːkʌməʳ] *n* recién llegado,-a.

**Newfoundland** [ˈnjuːfəndlənd] *n* Terranova.

**news** [njuːz] *n* noticias *fpl*. Loc **bad news travels fast** las malas noticias corren deprisa. **I it's news to me** *fam* ahora me entero. **I no news is good news** la falta de noticias son buenas noticias. **I to break the news to SB** dar la noticia a ALGN. COMP **a piece of news** una noticia. **I news agency** agencia de noticias. **I news bulletin** boletín *m* de noticias. **I news conference** conferencia de prensa. **I news item** noticia.

**newsagent** [ˈnjuːzeɪdʒənt] *n* vendedor,-ra de periódicos. COMP

**newsagent's (shop)** quiosco, puesto de periódicos.

**newsdealer** [ˈnjuːzdiːləʳ] *n* US vendedor,-ra de periódicos.

**newsflash** [ˈnjuːzflæʃ] *n* noticia de última hora.

**newsgroup** [ˈnjuːzgruːp] *n* grupo de discusión.

**newsletter** [ˈnjuːzletəʳ] *n* hoja informativa, boletín *m*.

**newspaper** [ˈnjuːspeɪpəʳ] *n* diario, periódico.

**newsstand** [ˈnjuːzstænd] *n* quiosco, puesto de periódicos.

**newt** [njuːt] *n* tritón *m*.

**newton** [ˈnjuːtən] *n* newton *m*.

**next** [nekst] *adj* **1** *(following - in order)* próximo,-a, siguiente; *(- in time)* próximo,-a, que viene: *the next street on the left* la próxima calle a la izquierda; *it's on the next page* está en la página siguiente; *not this stop, the next* esta parada no, la siguiente; *next Thursday «(Friday, etc)»* el próximo jueves *(viernes, etc)*, el jueves *(viernes, etc)* que viene; *next week/month/ year* la semana/el mes/el año que viene. **2** *(room, house, etc)* de al lado: *they live in the next house* viven en la casa de al lado.

▶ *adv* luego, después, a continuación: *what did you say next?* ¿qué dijiste luego?; *what do you want to do next?* ¿qué quieres hacer ahora?

▶ *prep* **next to** al lado de: *it's next to the cinema* está al lado del cine. Loc **next to nothing** casi nada. **I next door** al lado, la casa de al lado: *they live next door* viven (en la casa de) al lado.

**next-door** [ˈnekstdɔːʳ] *adj* de al lado, de la casa de al lado: *my next-door neighbours* los vecinos de al lado.

**NGO** [ˈenˈdʒiːˈəʊ] *abbr* (Non-Governmental Organization) Organización *f* no gubernamental; *(abbreviation)* ONG *f*.

**nibble** [ˈnɪbəl] *n* **1** *(action)* mordisco. **2** *(piece)* bocadito.

▶ *vi* picar.

**Nicaragua** [nɪkəˈrægjuə] *n* Nicaragua.

**Nicaraguan** [nɪkəˈrægjuən] *adj* nicaragüense.

▶ *n* nicaragüense.

N

**nice** [naɪs] *adj* **1** *(person)* amable, simpático: *he's such a nice boy!* ¡es un chico tan simpático! **2** *(thing)* bueno,-a, agradable: *nice day today, isn't it?* hace buen día, ¿verdad? **3** *(food)* delicioso,-a, bueno,-a. **4** *(pretty)* bonito,-a, mono,-a, guapo,-a.

**nicely** ['naɪslɪ] *adv* **1** *(well)* bien: *she was very nicely dressed* iba muy bien vestida. **2** *(properly)* bien: *behave nicely, dear* compórtate bien, cariño. **3** *fam (very well)* perfecto, estupendo: *Friday would suit me nicely* el viernes me iría perfecto.

**nickel** ['nɪkəl] *n* **1** níquel *m.* **2** US moneda de cinco centavos.

**nickname** ['nɪkneɪm] *n* apodo.
▶ *vt* apodar: *he was nicknamed "Lanky"* lo apodaron «Lanky».

**niece** [niːs] *n* sobrina.

**Niger** [niːˈʒeəʳ] *n* Níger.

**Nigeria** [naɪˈdʒɪərɪə] *n* Nigeria.

**Nigerian** [naɪˈdʒɪərɪən] *adj* nigeriano,-a.
▶ *n* nigeriano,-a.

**night** [naɪt] *n* noche *f.* LOC **all night long** toda la noche. ❙ **at night** de noche. ❙ **by night** de noche. ❙ **last night** anoche. ❙ **late at night** a altas horas de la noche. ❙ **night and day** noche y día. ❙ **to have a bad night** pasar una mala noche. ❙ **to have a good night 1** *(sleep well)* dormir bien. **2** *(have fun)* pasárselo bien. ❙ **to have a late night** acostarse tarde. ❙ **to have a night out** salir por la noche. COMP **night shift** turno de noche. ❙ **night watchman** vigilante *m* nocturno.

**nightdress** ['naɪtdres] *n* camisón *m.*
ⓘ *pl* nightdresses.

**nightfall** ['naɪtfɔːl] *n* anochecer *m.*

**nightie** ['naɪtɪ] *n* camisón *m.*

**nightgown** ['naɪtgaʊn] *n* camisón *m.*

**nightingale** ['naɪtɪŋgeɪl] *n* ruiseñor *m.*

**nightmare** ['naɪtmeəʳ] *n* pesadilla.

**nighttime** ['naɪttaɪm] *n* noche *f.*

**nil** [nɪl] *n* **1** cero, nada: *costs have been reduced to practically nil* los costes se han reducido prácticamente a cero. **2** SP cero: *Lincoln beat Grantham two goals to nil* Lincoln ganó a Grantham por dos goles a cero.

**nine** [naɪn] *adj* nueve.
▶ *n* nueve *m.*

✎ Consulta también six.

**nineteen** [naɪnˈtiːn] *adj* diecinueve.
▶ *n* diecinueve *m.*

✎ Consulta también six.

**nineteenth** [naɪnˈtiːnθ] *adj* decimonono,-a.
▶ *adv* en decimonono lugar.
▶ *n* **1** *(in series)* decimonono,-a. **2** *(fraction)* decimonono; *(one part)* decimonona parte *f.*

✎ Consulta también sixth.

**ninetieth** ['naɪntɪəθ] *adj* nonagésimo,-a.
▶ *adv* en nonagésimo lugar.
▶ *n* **1** *(in series)* nonagésimo,-a. **2** *(fraction)* nonagésimo; *(one part)* nonagésima parte *f.*

✎ Consulta también sixtieth.

**ninety** ['naɪntɪ] *adj* noventa.
▶ *n* noventa *m.*

✎ Consulta también sixty.

**ninth** [naɪnθ] *adj* nono,-a, noveno,-a.
▶ *adv* en nono lugar, en noveno lugar.
▶ *n* **1** *(in series)* nono,-a, noveno,-a. **2** *(fraction)* noveno; *(one part)* novena parte *f.*

✎ Consulta también sixth.

**nip** [nɪp] *n* **1** *(pinch)* pellizco: *she gave him a nip* le pegó un pellizco. **2** *(bite)* mordisco, mordedura: *the dog gave me a nip on the ankle* el perro me pegó un mordisco en el tobillo. **3** *(drink)* trago: *a nip of whisky* un trago de whisky.
▶ *vt* **1** *(pinch)* pellizcar: *a crab nipped my finger* un cangrejo me pellizcó el dedo. **2** *(bite)* morder *(con poca fuerza)*: *the dog nipped me* el perro me mordió.
ⓘ *pt & pp* nipped, *ger* nipping.

**nipple** ['nɪpəl] *n* **1** *(female)* pezón *m.* **2** *(male)* tetilla. **3** *(teat)* tetilla. **4** TECH pezón *m.*

**nit** [nɪt] *n* **1** liendre *f.* **2** GB *fam* imbécil *mf.*

**niter** ['naɪtəʳ] *n* US→ nitre.

**nitre** ['naɪtəʳ] *n* salitre *m.*

**nitrogen** ['naɪtrədʒən] *n* nitrógeno *m.*

**no** [nəʊ] *adv* no: *have you seen it? –no!* ¿lo has visto? –¡no!; *he's no better than a thief* no es más que un ladrón. LOC **no way!** ¡ni hablar!

▶ *adj* ninguno,-a; *(before masc sing)* ningún: *I have no time* no tengo tiempo; *«No smoking»* «Prohibido fumar»; *«No motorcycles»* «Motos no».

▶ *n* no: *there were two noes, nine yeses and one abstention* hubo dos noes, nueve síes y una abstención.

**nobility** [nəʊˈbɪlɪtɪ] *n* nobleza.

**noble** [ˈnəʊbəl] *adj* noble.
ⓘ *comp* **nobler,** *superl* **noblest.**
▶ *n* noble *mf.*

**nobleman** [ˈnəʊbəlmən] *n* noble *m.*
ⓘ *pl* **noblemen** [ˈnəʊbəlmən].

**noblewoman** [ˈnəʊbəlwʊmən] *n* noble *f.*
ⓘ *pl* **noblewomen** [ˈnəʊbəlwɪmɪn].

**nobody** [ˈnəʊbədɪ] *pron* nadie: *nobody went to the party* no fue nadie a la fiesta.
▶ *n* don nadie *m.*

**nod** [nɒd] *n* **1** saludo *con la cabeza.* **2** *(in agreement)* señal *f* de asentimiento.
▶ *vi* **1** saludar *con la cabeza.* **2** *(agree)* asentir *con la cabeza).*
ⓘ *pt & pp* **nodded,** *ger* **nodding.**

**noise** [nɔɪz] *n* ruido, sonido.
▶ *n pl* **noises** comentarios *mpl.* LOC **to make a noise** hacer ruido. COMP **big noise** *fam* pez *m* gordo.

**noisy** [ˈnɔɪzɪ] *adj* ruidoso,-a.
ⓘ *comp* **noisier,** *superl* **noisiest.**

**nomad** [ˈnəʊmæd] *n* nómada *mf.*

**no-man's-land** [ˈnəʊmænzlænd] *n* tierra de nadie.

**nominal** [ˈnɒmɪnəl] *adj* **1** nominal. **2** *(price)* simbólico,-a.

**nominate** [ˈnɒmɪneɪt] *vt* **1** nombrar: *he was nominated team captain* lo nombraron capitán del equipo. **2** *(propose)* proponer: *I nominate Neil as captain* yo propongo a Neil como capitán.

**nonconformist** [nɒnkənˈfɔːmɪst] *adj* disidente.

**none** [nʌn] *pron* ninguno,-a: *none of the keys opens the door* ninguna de las llaves abre la puerta; *none of them could do it* nadie supo hacerlo; *I wanted nutmeg, but they had none* quería nuez moscada, pero no tenían.
▶ *adv* de ningún modo: *he's none the worse for his ordeal* no le ha afectado esa

mala experiencia. LOC **none but** únicamente, solamente, solo: *none but the strongest survived* sobrevivieron solo los más fuertes..

**nonsense** [ˈnɒnsəns] *n* tonterías *fpl:* *don't talk nonsense!* ¡no digas tonterías!

**nonstick** [ˈnɒnstɪk] *adj* antiadherente.

**nonstop** [ˈnɒnstɒp] *adj* **1** *(continuous)* continuo,-a. **2** *(flight, etc)* directo,-a, sin escalas.
▶ *adv* sin parar.

**noodle** [ˈnuːdəl] *n* fideo.

**noon** [nuːn] *n* mediodía *m.*

**no-one** [ˈnəʊwʌn] *[also written no one] pron* nadie: *no-one went to the party* no fue nadie a la fiesta.

**no-place** [ˈnəʊpleɪs] *adv* US→ **nowhere.**

**nor** [nɔːr] *conj* **1** ni: *neither you nor I* ni tú ni yo; *I neither know nor care* ni lo sé ni me importa. **2** tampoco: *nor do I* yo tampoco.

**Nordic** [ˈnɔːdɪk] *adj* nórdico,-a.

**normal** [ˈnɔːməl] *adj* normal.

**normally** [ˈnɔːməlɪ] *adv* normalmente.

**normality** [nɔːˈmælɪtɪ] *n* normalidad *f.*

**north** [nɔːθ] *n* norte *m:* *to the north of London* al norte de Londres; *in the north of Scotland* en el norte de Escocia.
▶ *adj* del norte: *I live in north London* vivo en el norte de Londres.
▶ *adv* al norte, hacia el norte: *we're travelling north* viajamos hacia el norte; *they've moved north* se han trasladado al norte; *it's north of Cambridge* está al norte de Cambridge. COMP **North Pole** Polo Norte.

**northeast** [nɔːθˈiːst] *n* nordeste *m,* noreste *m.*
▶ *adj* del nordeste.
▶ *adv* al nordeste, hacia el nordeste.

**northern** [ˈnɔːθən] *adj* norte, del norte.

**northwest** [nɔːθˈwest] *n* noroeste *m.*
▶ *adj* del noroeste.
▶ *adv* al noroeste, hacia el noroeste.

**Norway** [ˈnɔːweɪ] *n* Noruega.

**Norwegian** [nɔːˈwiːdʒən] *adj* noruego,-a.
▶ *n* **1** *(person)* noruego,-a. **2** *(language)* noruego.

**nose** [nəʊz] *n* **1** nariz *f.* **2** *(of animal)* hocico. **3** *(sense)* olfato. **4** *(of car, etc)* morro.

N

LOC **to blow one's nose** sonarse. ▌ **to get up** sb's **nose** GB *fam* fastidiar a ALGN. ▌ **under** sb's **very nose / right under** sb's **nose** ante las propias narices de ALGN.

**nosebleed** [ˈnəʊzbliːd] *n* hemorragia nasal.

**nostril** [ˈnɒstrəl] *n* fosa nasal.

**nosy** [ˈnəʊzɪ] *adj fam* curioso,-a, entrometido,-a.
ⓘ *comp* **nosier**, *superl* **nosiest**.

**not** [nɒt] [la forma contracta es n't: isn't, aren't, doesn't.] *adv* no: *I did not steal it* no lo robé; *she told me not to tell anyone* me dijo que no lo dijera a nadie; *I hope/suppose not* espero/supongo que no; *are you coming or not?* ¿vienes o no? LOC **not likely!** ¡ni hablar! ▌ **I not that...** no es que...: *where is he?, not that I mind, of course* ¿dónde está?, no es que me importe, claro está. ▌ **not to say...** por no decir…

✎ Not acompaña al auxiliar del verbo en las oraciones negativas. En el inglés hablado y en los textos escritos informales se suele contraer a -n't: *she isn't English; he doesn't like it.* También se usa para la forma negativa de los verbos subordinados.

**notary** [ˈnəʊtərɪ] *n* notario,-a.
ⓘ *pl* **notaries**.

**note** [nəʊt] *n* **1** MUS nota; *(key)* tecla. **2** *(message)* nota. **3** *(money)* billete *m*.
▶ *vt* **1** *(notice)* notar, advertir: *I noted a certain reluctance on John's part* noté cierta reticencia por parte de John. **2** *(pay special attention)* fijarse en: *note that the plural of «child» is «children»* fijaos en que el plural de «child» es «children». **3** *(write down)* apuntar, anotar.
▶ *n pl* **notes** apuntes *mpl*.
◆ **to note down** *vt sep* apuntar.

☒ Note no significa 'nota (calificación)', que se traduce por **mark**.

**notebook** [ˈnəʊtbʊk] *n* **1** *(book)* libreta, cuaderno. **2** *(computer)* ordenador *m* portátil.

**notepad** [ˈnəʊtpæd] *n* bloc *m* de notas.

**nothing** [ˈnʌθɪŋ] *n* nada: *there's nothing left* no queda nada; *it's nothing special* no es nada del otro jueves. LOC **for nothing** *fam* gratis. ▌ **nothing but...** únicamente..., solo…
▶ *adv* de ningún modo, de ninguna manera: *it's nothing like a pheasant* no se parece en nada a un faisán.

**notice** [ˈnəʊtɪs] *n* **1** *(sign)* letrero: *there's a notice which says «No parking»* hay un letrero que pone «Prohibido aparcar». **2** *(announcement)* anuncio: *there's a notice in the paper about a lost dog* hay un anuncio en el diario acerca de un perro extraviado. **3** *(warning)* aviso: *they gave him a month's notice to quit the flat* le dieron un plazo de un mes para abandonar el piso. LOC **to take no notice of** no hacer caso de. ▌ **until further notice** hasta nuevo aviso. ▌ **without notice** sin previo aviso.
▶ *vt* notar, fijarse en, darse cuenta de.
▶ *vi fam (show)* verse: *don't worry, the stain doesn't notice* no te preocupes, la mancha no se ve.

☒ Notice no significa 'noticia', que se traduce por **news**.

**noticeable** [ˈnəʊtɪsəbªl] *adj* que se nota, evidente.

**noticeboard** [ˈnəʊtɪsbɔːd] *n* tablón *m* de anuncios.

**notify** [ˈnəʊtɪfaɪ] *vt* notificar, avisar.
ⓘ *pt & pp* **notified**, *ger* **notifying**.

**notion** [ˈnəʊʃªn] *n* noción *f*, idea, concepto.
▶ *n pl* **notions** US mercería *f sing*.

**notorious** [nəʊˈtɔːrɪəs] *adj pej* célebre: *a notorious criminal* un conocido criminal.

☒ Notorious no significa 'notorio (conocido)', que se traduce por **well-known**.

**nougat** [ˈnuːgɑː] *n* turrón *m* blando.

**nought** [nɔːt] *n* cero: *nought point sixty-six* cero coma sesenta y seis. COMP **noughts and crosses** tres en raya *m*.

**noun** [naʊn] *n* nombre *m*, sustantivo. COMP **noun phrase** sintagma *m* nominal.

**nourish** [ˈnʌrɪʃ] *vt* nutrir, alimentar.

**nourishing** [ˈnʌrɪʃɪŋ] *adj* nutritivo,-a.

**novel¹** [ˈnɒvªl] *adj* original, novedoso,-a: *what a novel idea!* ¡qué idea más original!

**novel²** [ˈnɒvªl] *n* novela.

**novelist** [ˈnɒvªlɪst] *n* novelista *mf*.

**novelty** ['nɒvəltɪ] *n* **1** novedad *f*: *the novelty soon wore off* pronto dejó de ser novedad. **2** *(trinket)* chuchería.
ⓘ *pl* **novelties**.

**November** [nəʊˈvembəʳ] *n* noviembre *m*.

🐦 Para ejemplos de uso, consulta May.

**novice** ['nɒvɪs] *n* **1** novato,-a. **2** REL novicio,-a.

**now** [naʊ] *adv* **1** *(at the present)* ahora; *(used contrastively)* ya: *where do you work now?* ¿dónde trabajas ahora?; *I'm ready now* ya estoy listo. **2** *(immediately)* ya, ahora mismo: *do it now!* ¡hazlo ya! **3** *(in past)* ya, entonces. **4** *(introductory)* bueno, vamos a ver, veamos: *now, let's begin* bueno, empecemos. LOC **by now** ya: *she'll be in Mexico by now* ya debe de estar en Méjico. **‖ for now** por el momento. **‖ from now on** de ahora en adelante. **‖ just now 1** *(at this moment)* en estos momentos, ahora mismo. **2** *(a short while ago)* hace un momento, ahora mismo: *I can't help you just now* ahora mismo no puedo ayudarte; **‖ now and then** de vez en cuando. **‖ right now** ahora mismo.
▸ *conj* [also **now that**] ahora que, ya que: *now (that) we're all here, we can begin* ya que estamos todos, podemos empezar.

**nowadays** ['naʊədeɪz] *adv* hoy día, hoy en día, actualmente.

**nowhere** ['nəʊweəʳ] *adv (position)* en ninguna parte, en ningún sitio, en ningún lugar; *(direction)* a ninguna parte, a ningún sitio: *where are you going? – nowhere special* ¿dónde vas? –a ningún sitio en especial; *there's nowhere to hide* no hay donde esconderse. LOC **in the middle of nowhere** en el quinto pino. **‖ nowhere near** muy lejos de.

**nozzle** ['nɒzəl] *n (of hose)* boquilla; *(of oilcan)* pitorro; *(large calibre)* tobera.

**nuclear** ['njuːklɪəʳ] *adj* nuclear. COMP **nuclear bomb** bomba nuclear. **‖ nuclear energy** energía nuclear. **‖ nuclear fission** fisión *f* nuclear. **‖ nuclear fusion** fusión *f* nuclear. **‖ nuclear power** energía nuclear. **‖ nuclear power station** central *f* nuclear. **‖ nuclear reactor** reactor *m* nu-

clear. **‖ nuclear waste** residuos nucleares. **‖ nuclear weapon** arma nuclear.

**nucleus** ['njuːklɪəs] *n* núcleo.
ⓘ *pl* **nuclei** [njuːˈklɪaɪ].

**nude** [njuːd] *adj* desnudo,-a.
▸ *n* desnudo.

**nudge** [nʌdʒ] *n* **1** *(with elbow)* codazo. **2** empujón *m* suave.
▸ *vt* dar un codazo a.

**nuisance** ['njuːsəns] *n* **1** molestia, fastidio, lata. **2** *(person)* pesado,-a. LOC **to make a nuisance of os** dar la lata.

**numb** [nʌm] *adj* entumecido,-a, insensible. LOC **to be numb with cold** estar helado,-a de frío.

**number** ['nʌmbəʳ] *n* número. LOC **a number of...** varios,-as… **‖ any number of...** muchísimos,-as… **‖ without number** un sinfín de… COMP **number plate** placa de matrícula..
◆ **to number off** *vi* numerarse.

**numeral** ['njuːmərəl] *n* número, cifra.

**numerous** ['njuːmərəs] *adj* numeroso,-a.

**nun** [nʌn] *n* monja, religiosa.

**nurse** [nɜːs] *n* **1** enfermero,-a. **2** *(children's)* niñera.
▸ *vt* **1** *(look after)* cuidar. **2** *(suckle)* amamantar. **3** *(hold)* acunar. **4** *(feeling)* guardar.

**nursery** ['nɜːsərɪ] *n* **1** *(in house)* cuarto de los niños. **2** *(kindergarten)* guardería. **3** *(for plants)* vivero. COMP **nursery rhyme** canción *f* infantil, poema *m* infantil. **‖ nursery school** parvulario.
ⓘ *pl* **nurseries**.

**nut** [nʌt] *n* **1** BOT fruto seco. **2** TECH tuerca. **3** *fam (head)* coco. **4** *fam (nutcase)* chalado,-a, chiflado,-a.

**nutcrackers** ['nʌtkrækəz] *n pl* cascanueces *m inv*.

**nutmeg** ['nʌtmeg] *n* nuez *f* moscada.

**nutrient** [njuːˈtrɪənt] *n* nutriente *m*.

**nutrition** [njuːˈtrɪʃən] *n* nutrición *f*.

**nutritious** [njuːˈtrɪʃəs] *adj* nutritivo,-a.

**nutshell** ['nʌtʃel] *n* cáscara. LOC **in a nutshell** en pocas palabras.

**nylon®** ['naɪlɒn] *n* nailon *m*.
▸ *n pl* **nylons** medias *fpl* de nailon.

**nymph** [nɪmf] *n* ninfa.

**N**

**O**

**O, o** [əʊ] *n (the letter)* O, o *f.*
**O** [əʊ] *n (as number)* cero.
**oak** [əʊk] *n* **1** BOT roble *m.* **2** *(wood)* roble *m.*
  ▸ *adj* de roble.
**oar** [ɔːʳ] *n* remo.
**oarsman** [ˈɔːzmən] *n* remero.
  ① *pl* oarsmen [ˈɔːzmən].
**oasis** [əʊˈeɪsɪs] *n* oasis *m.*
  ① *pl* oases [əʊˈeɪsiːz].
**oats** [əʊts] *n pl* avena.
**oath** [əʊθ] *n* **1** JUR juramento. **2** *(swearword)* palabrota, juramento. LOC **on my oath** lo juro. ‖ **to be on oath / be under oath** estar bajo juramento.
**obedience** [əˈbiːdɪəns] *n* obediencia.
**obedient** [əˈbiːdɪənt] *adj* obediente.
**obelisk** [ˈɒbəlɪsk] *n* obelisco.
**obese** [əʊˈbiːs] *adj* obeso,-a.
**obesity** [əʊˈbiːsɪtɪ] *n* obesidad *f.*
**obey** [əˈbeɪ] *vt* **1** *(gen)* obedecer; *(orders)* acatar. **2** *(law)* cumplir.
  ▸ *vi (gen)* obedecer.
**object** [*(n)* ˈɒbdʒekt; *(vb)* əbˈdʒekt] *n* **1** *(thing)* objeto, cosa. **2** *(aim, purpose)* objetivo, fin *m.* **3** *(focus of feelings)* objeto: *he was an object of ridicule* fue objeto de burlas. **4** LING complemento: *direct/indirect object* complemento directo/indirecto. COMP **object glass / object lens** objetivo.
  ▸ *vt* objetar.
  ▸ *vi* **1** *(oppose)* oponerse (to, a), poner reparos (to, a).
**objection** [əbˈdʒekʃ[ə]n] *n* objeción *f,* reparo, inconveniente.
**objective** [əbˈdʒektɪv] *adj* objetivo,-a.
  ▸ *n* **1** *(purpose)* objetivo, fin *m.* **2** *(lens)* objetivo.
**objectivity** [ɒbdʒekˈtɪvɪtɪ] *n* objetividad *f.*

**obligation** [ɒblɪˈgeɪ[ə]n] *n* obligación *f.*
**oblige** [əˈblaɪdʒ] *vt* **1** *(compel)* obligar: *I felt obliged to attend* me veía obligado a asistir. **2** *(do a favour)* hacer un favor a, ayudar a. LOC **much obliged!** ¡muy agradecido,-a!
  ▸ *vi (do a favour)* hacer un favor, ayudar.
**oblong** [ˈɒblɒŋ] *adj* oblongo,-a, alargado,-a.
  ▸ *n* rectángulo.
**oboe** [ˈəʊbəʊ] *n* oboe *m.*
**obscene** [ɒbˈsiːn] *adj* obsceno,-a, indecente.
**obscenity** [əbˈsenɪtɪ] *n* obscenidad *f.*
  ① *pl* obscenities.
**obscure** [əbsˈkjʊəʳ] *adj* **1** *(unclear)* oscuro,-a, poco claro,-a. **2** *(vague, indistinct)* vago,-a, confuso,-a; *(hidden)* recóndito,-a.

> ☒ Obscure no significa 'oscuro (un color)', que se traduce por dark.

**obsequious** [əbˈsiːkwɪəs] *adj* servil.

> ☒ Obsequious no significa 'obsequioso', que se traduce por obliging.

**observant** [əbˈzɜːv[ə]nt] *adj* observador,-ra.
**observation** [ɒbzəˈveɪ[ə]n] *n* **1** *(watching, study)* observación *f*; *(surveillance)* vigilancia. **2** *(remark)* observación *f*, comentario.
**observatory** [əbˈzɜːvət[ə]rɪ] *n* observatorio.
  ① *pl* observatories.
**observe** [əbˈzɜːv] *vt* **1** *(see, watch)* observar, ver; *(in surveillance)* vigilar. **2** *(law)* cumplir, respetar. **3** *fml (say)* señalar.
  ▸ *vi* observar.
**obsess** [əbˈses] *vt* obsesionar.

**obsession** [əb'seʃ⁽ə⁾n] *n* obsesión *f* (with/about, con).

**obsessive** [əb'sesɪv] *adj* obsesivo,-a.
▶ *n* obsesivo,-a.

**obstacle** ['ɒbstək⁽ə⁾l] *n* **1** obstáculo. **2** *fig* obstáculo, impedimento. COMP **obstacle race** carrera de obstáculos.

**obstetrics** [ɒb'stetrɪks] *n* obstetricia, tocología.

**obstinate** ['ɒbstɪnət] *adj* obstinado,-a.

**obstruct** [əb'strʌkt] *vt* **1** *(block - gen)* obstruir; *(- pipe, etc)* atascar, bloquear; *(- view)* tapar. **2** *(make difficult)* dificultar.

**obstruction** [əb'strʌkʃ⁽ə⁾n] *n* **1** *(gen)* obstrucción *f*. **2** *(hindrance)* estorbo, obstáculo.

**obtain** [əb'teɪn] *vt* obtener, conseguir.

**obtuse** [əb'tjuːs] *adj fml (stupid)* obtuso,-a. COMP **obtuse angle** ángulo obtuso.

**obvious** ['ɒbvɪəs] *adj (clear)* obvio,-a: *for obvious reasons* por razones obvias.

**obviously** ['ɒbvɪəslɪ] *adv* obviamente, evidentemente.

**occasion** [ə'keɪʒ⁽ə⁾n] *n* **1** *(time)* ocasión *f*; *(event)* acontecimiento. **2** *(opportunity)* ocasión *f*, oportunidad *f*: *if the occasion arises* si se presenta la ocasión. LOC **on occasion** de vez en cuando. ∎ **on the occasion of** con motivo de. ∎ **to rise to the occasion** estar a la altura de las circunstancias, dar la talla.

**occasional** [ə'keɪʒ⁽ə⁾nəl] *adj (not frequent)* esporádico,-a, eventual.

**occasionally** [ə'keɪʒ⁽ə⁾nəlɪ] *adv* de vez en cuando, ocasionalmente.

**occipital** [ɒk'spɪt⁽ə⁾l] *adj* occipital.

**occult** ['ɒkʌlt] *adj* oculto,-a.

❌ Occult no significa 'oculto (escondido)', que se traduce por **hidden**.

**occupant** ['ɒkjəpənt] *n (gen)* ocupante *mf*; *(tenant)* inquilino,-a.

**occupation** [ɒkjə'peɪʃ⁽ə⁾n] *n* **1** *(job)* ocupación *f*, profesión *f*. **2** *(pastime)* pasatiempo. **3** *(act, state of occupying)* ocupación *f*.

**occupied** ['ɒkjəpaɪd] *adj* ocupado,-a.

**occupy** ['ɒkjəpaɪ] *vt* ocupar.
ⓘ *pt & pp* occupied, *ger* occupying.

**occur** [ə'kɜːʳ] *vi* **1** *(happen - event, incident)* ocurrir, suceder; *(- change)* producirse. **2** *fml (be found, exist)* existir, darse. **3** *(come to mind)* ocurrir, ocurrirse: *it never occurred to me to ask* no se me ocurrió preguntar.
ⓘ *pt & pp* occurred, *ger* occurring.

**occurrence** [ə'kʌrəns] *n* **1** *(event, incident)* suceso. **2** *fml (frequency)* incidencia, frecuencia; *(existing amount)* cantidad *f*.

❌ Occurrence no significa 'ocurrencia', que se traduce por **idea**.

**ocean** ['əʊʃ⁽ə⁾n] *n* océano.
▶ *adj* oceánico,-a: *ocean currents* corrientes oceánicas.

**oceanic** [əʊʃɪ'ænɪk] *adj fml* oceánico,-a.

**oceanography** [əʊʃən'ɒgrəfɪ] *n* oceanografía.

**ocher** ['əʊkəʳ] *adj* US → ochre.

**ochre** ['əʊkəʳ] *adj* (de color) ocre.
▶ *n* ochre *m*.

**o'clock** [ə'klɒk] *adv*: *it's one o'clock* es la una; *at three o'clock* a las tres.

**octagon** ['ɒktəgən] *n* octágono, octógono.

**octagonal** [ɒk'tægən⁽ə⁾l] *adj* octagonal, octogonal.

**octahedron** [ɒktə'hiːdrən] *n* octaedro.

**October** [ɒk'təʊbəʳ] *n* octubre *m*.
Para ejemplos de uso, consulta May.

**octopus** ['ɒktəpəs] *n* pulpo.
ⓘ *pl* octopuses.

**O**

**odd** [ɒd] *adj* **1** *(strange)* extraño,-a, raro,-a: *the odd thing is that...* lo raro es que... **2** *(number)* impar. **3** *(approximately)* y pico: *thirty odd people* unas treinta y pico personas. **4** *(shoe, glove, etc)* suelto,-a, desparejado,-a. LOC **to be the odd man out 1** *(be over)* estar de más. **2** *(be different)* ser la excepción. COMP **odd jobs** trabajillos *mpl*.
▶ *n pl* **odds 1** *(probability, chances)* probabilidades *fpl*: *the odds are that...* lo más probable es que... **2** *(in betting)* apuestas *fpl*. LOC **against (all) the odds** contra todo pronóstico.

**odontology** [ɒdɒn'tɒlədʒɪ] *n* odontología.

**odor** ['əʊdəʳ] *adj* US → odour.

**odorless** ['əʊdələs] *adj* US → odourless.

**odour** ['əʊdər] n (smell) olor m; (fragrance) perfume m, fragancia.

**odourless** ['əʊdələs] adj inodoro,-a.

**odyssey** ['ɒdɪsɪ] n odisea.

**oesophagus** [iːˈsɒfəgəs] n esófago.
ⓘ pl oesophagi [iːˈsɒfəgaɪ].

**oestrogen** ['iːstrədʒ³n] n estrógeno.

**of** [ɒv, unstressed əv] prep 1 (belonging to) de: a friend of mine un amigo mío. 2 (made from) de: Spanish-leather shoes zapatos de piel española. 3 (containing) de: a bag of crisps una bolsa de patatas. 4 (showing a part, a quantity) de: a kilo of apples un kilo de manzanas. 5 (partitive use) de: the two of us nosotros dos. 6 (dates, distance) de: the 7th of August el 7 de agosto. 7 (apposition) de: the city of London la ciudad de Londres. 8 (by) de: the works of Shakespeare las obras de Shakespeare. 9 (with, having) de: a child of five un niño de cinco años. 10 (after superlative) de: best of all was the food lo mejor de todo fue la comida.

**off** [ɒf] prep 1 (movement) de: he got off the bus bajó del autobús. 2 (indicating removal) de: he cut a branch off the tree cortó una rama del árbol. 3 (distance, situation) diferentes traducciones: a narrow street off the main road una callejuela que sale a la carretera; the ship sank off Malpica el barco se hundió a la altura de Malpica. 4 (away from) diferentes traducciones: the ship went off course el barco se desvió de su rumbo; we're a long way off finding a cure estamos lejos de encontrar una cura. 5 (not wanting): I'm off coffee ya no tomo café. 6 (not at work): she comes off duty at 10.00pm acaba el turno a las 10.00. 7 fam (from) a: I bought it off Eva se lo compré a Eva.

▶ adv 1 (departure): he ran off se fue corriendo; I'm off me voy. 2 (showing distance) a: the village is three miles off el pueblo está a tres millas. 3 (reduced in price) menos: 70% off! ¡70% menos! 4 (disconnected, not working) diferentes traducciones: turn the light off apaga la luz; she turned the tap off cerró el grifo. 7 (free, on holiday) libre: can I have the afternoon off? ¿puedo tomarme la tarde libre? LOC off and on / on and off de vez en cuando, a ratos. ▌ right off / straight off acto seguido.

▶ adj 1 (event) cancelado,-a, suspendido,-a: the wedding's off la boda se ha suspendido. 2 (not turned on - gas, water) cerrado,-a; (- electricity) apagado,-a. COMP off season temporada baja.

**offence** [əˈfens] n 1 JUR delito, infracción f: a traffic offence una infracción de tráfico. 2 (insult) ofensa. LOC to take offence at sth ofenderse por algo, sentirse ofendido,-a por algo.

**offend** [əˈfend] vt (insult, hurt) ofender: she'll be offended if we don't go se ofenderá si no vamos.
▶ vi 1 fml (do wrong to) atentar (against, a). 2 JUR fml (commit crime) cometer un delito.

**offender** [əˈfendər] n 1 JUR (gen) infractor,-ra; (criminal) delincuente mf. 2 (culprit) culpable mf.

**offensive** [əˈfensɪv] adj 1 (insulting) ofensivo,-a, insultante. 2 (disgusting - gen) repugnante; (- smell) desagradable. 3 (attacking) ofensivo,-a.
▶ n MIL ofensiva.

**offer** ['ɒfər] vt 1 (gen) ofrecer: she offered us a coffee nos ofreció un café. 2 (show willingness) ofrecerse (to, para): he offered me a lift to the airport se ofreció para llevarme al aeropuerto. 3 (propose) proponer, sugerir.
▶ n 1 (gen) oferta, ofrecimiento; (proposal) propuesta. 2 COMM oferta. LOC to be on offer 1 (at reduced price) estar de oferta. 2 (available) disponible.

**office** ['ɒfɪs] n 1 (room) despacho, oficina; (building) oficina; (staff) oficina. 2 GB ministerio: the Foreign Office el Ministerio de Asuntos Exteriores. 3 (post, position) cargo. LOC to hold office ocupar un cargo. COMP office block edificio de oficinas. ▌ office boy recadero. ▌ office junior auxiliar mf de oficina. ▌ office worker oficinista mf.

**officer** ['ɒfɪsər] n 1 MIL oficial mf. 2 (police officer) agente mf. 3 (in government) funcionario,-a. 4 (of club, society) directivo,-a.

**official** [əˈfɪʃ³l] adj (gen) oficial.
▶ n funcionario,-a, oficial mf.

❌ Official no significa 'oficial (militar)', que se traduce por officer.

**officially** [əˈfɪʃˀlɪ] *adv* oficialmente.

**officious** [əˈfɪʃəs] *adj (too eager)* oficioso,-a; *(interfering)* entrometido,-a.

❌ Officious no significa 'oficioso (no oficial)', que se traduce por **unofficial**.

**off-licence** [ˈɒflaɪsˀns] *n* GB tienda de bebidas alcohólicas.

**offshoot** [ˈɒfʃuːt] *n* BOT retoño, vástago.

**offshore** [ɒfˈʃɔːʳ] *adj* **1** *(at sea)* a poca distancia de la costa. **2** *(breeze)* terral, de tierra. **3** *(overseas)* en el extranjero.
▶ *adv* mar adentro.

**offside** [ɒfˈsaɪd] *adj* **1** SP fuera de juego. **2** GB *(part of vehicle)* del lado del conductor.
▶ *adv* SP en fuera de juego.
▶ *n* GB *(of vehicle)* lado del conductor.

**offspring** [ˈɒːfsprɪŋ] *n* **1** *fml (child)* descendiente *mf; (children)* descendencia, prole *f*. **2** *(animal - one)* cría; *(- several)* crías *fpl*.
ⓘ *pl* offspring.

**off-the-record** [ɒfðəˈrekɔːd] *adj* extraoficial, confidencial.

**often** [ˈɒfˀn, ˈɒftˀn] *adv (frequently)* a menudo, con frecuencia: *we often go to the theatre* vamos al teatro a menudo.

**oh** [əʊ] *interj* ¡oh!, ¡ay!, ¡vaya!: *oh, really?* ¿de veras?; *oh, look!* ¡eh, mira!

**ohm** [əʊm] *n* ohmio, ohm *m*.

**oil** [ɔɪl] *n* **1** *(gen)* aceite *m: sunflower oil* aceite de girasol. **2** *(petroleum)* petróleo: *crude oil* crudo. **3** ART *(painting)* óleo, pintura al óleo.
▶ *vt* engrasar, lubricar, lubrificar.
▶ *n pl* oils *(paints)* óleo: *she paints in oils* pinta al óleo. COMP **oil painting** cuadro al óleo, óleo. ‖ **oil rig** plataforma petrolífera. ‖ **oil slick** marea negra. ‖ **oil tanker** petrolero. ‖ **oil well** pozo petrolífero.

**oilcan** [ˈɔɪlkæn] *n* aceitera.

**oilcloth** [ˈɔɪlklɒθ] *n* hule *m*.

**oilfield** [ˈɔɪlfiːld] *n* yacimiento petrolífero.

**oily** [ˈɔɪlɪ] *adj* **1** *(food)* aceitoso,-a, grasiento,-a; *(skin, hair)* graso,-a. **2** *pej (manner)* empalagoso,-a.
ⓘ *comp* oilier, *superl* oiliest.

**ointment** [ˈɔɪntmənt] *n* ungüento, pomada.

**okay** [əʊˈkeɪ] *interj* ¡vale!, ¡de acuerdo!
▶ *adj* correcto,-a, bien: *are you okay?* ¿estás bien?
▶ *adv* bien, bastante bien: *he's doing okay at school* va bien en el colegio.
▶ *n* visto bueno, aprobación *f*.

**old** [əʊld] *adj* **1** *(gen)* viejo,-a: *an old man* un anciano, un hombre mayor; *the old part of the city* el casco antiguo de la ciudad; *he's an old friend* es un viejo amigo. **2** *(former)* antiguo,-a: *in my old job* en mi antiguo trabajo. LOC **how old are you?** ¿cuántos años tienes?, ¿qué edad tienes? ‖ **to be... years old** tener... años. COMP **old age** vejez *f*. ‖ **the Old World** el viejo mundo.
▶ *n* **the old** las personas *fpl* mayores, los ancianos *mpl*.

**older** [ˈəʊldəʳ] *adj* **1** *(comparative)* → old. **2** *(elder)* mayor.

**old-fashioned** [əʊldˈfæʃˀnd] *adj (outdated - gen)* anticuado,-a, pasado,-a de moda; *(- person)* chapado,-a a la antigua.

**olfactory** [ɒlˈfæktˀrɪ] *adj* olfativo,-a, olfatorio,-a. COMP **olfactory epithelium** epitelio olfativo. ‖ **olfactory nerve** nervio olfativo.

**oligarchy** [ˈɒlɪgɑːkɪ] *n* oligarquía.
ⓘ *pl* oligarchies.

**olive** [ˈɒlɪv] *n* **1** *(tree, wood)* olivo. **2** *(fruit)* aceituna, oliva. **3** *(colour)* verde *m* oliva. COMP **olive grove** olivar. ‖ **olive oil** aceite *m* de oliva. ‖ **olive tree** olivo.
▶ *adj (paint)* color aceituna; *(skin)* aceitunado,-a.

**Olympiad** [əˈlɪmpiæd] *n* Olimpíada, Olimpiada.

**Olympic** [əˈlɪmpɪk] *adj* olímpico,-a.
▶ *n pl* **the Olympics** los Juegos Olímpicos, la Olimpíada *f sing*. COMP **Olympic Games** Juegos *mpl* Olímpicos.

**omega** [ˈəʊmɪgə] *n* omega.

**omelette** [ˈɒmlət] *n* tortilla. COMP **plain omelette** tortilla francesa.

**omit** [əʊˈmɪt] *vt* **1** *(not include, leave out)* omitir, suprimir; *(forget to include)* olvi-

O

dar incluir. **2** *(fail to do)* omitir, dejar de; *(forget)* olvidarse.
ⓘ *pt & pp* omitted, *ger* omitting.

**omnivore** ['ɒmnɪvɔːʳ] *n* omnívoro.

**omnivorous** [ɒm'nɪvərəs] *adj* ZOOL *fml* omnívoro,-a.

**on** [ɒn] *prep* **1** *(covering or touching)* sobre, encima de, en: *it's on the table* está encima de la mesa. **2** *(supported by, hanging from)* en: *she put the picture on the wall* colgó el cuadro en la pared. **3** *(to, towards)* a, hacia: *on the right/left* a la derecha/izquierda. **4** *(at the edge of)* en: *a village on the coast* un pueblo de la costa. **5** *(days, dates, times)* no se traduce: *on Saturday* el sábado. **6** *(at the time of, just after)* al: *on arriving* al llegar. **7** *(as means of transport)* a, en: *on foot* a pie; *on the train* en el tren. **8** *(regarding, about)* sobre, de: *a book on art* un libro de arte. **9** *(in possession of)* con: *have you got any money on you?* ¿llevas dinero?
▶ *adv* **1** *(not stopping)* sin parar: *she kept on talking* siguió hablando. **2** *(movement forward)* diferentes traducciones: *walk on until you get to the church* sigue hasta que llegues a la iglesia; *it's time we were moving on* es hora de que nos vayamos. **3** *(clothes - being worn)* puesto,-a: *she had a cap on* llevaba puesta una gorra. **4** *(working)* diferentes traducciones: *who left the TV on?* ¿quién dejó la TV encendida?; *don't leave the tap on!* ¡no dejes el grifo abierto! **5** *(happening)* diferentes traducciones: *what time is the film on?* ¿a qué hora ponen la película?; *have we got anything on this weekend?* ¿tenemos plan para este fin de semana? LOC **and so on** y así sucesivamente. ▎ **from that day on** a partir de aquel día.
▶ *adj* **1** *(in use)* diferentes traducciones: *is the heating on?* ¿está puesta la calefacción?; *all the lights were on* todas las luces estaban encendidas. **2** *(happening)* diferentes traducciones: *the strike's on* la huelga sigue convocada; *is the party still on?* ¿se hace la fiesta?; *the match is on after all* después de todo, el partido se celebra. **3** *(performing)* diferentes traducciones: *you're on next!* ¡sales tú el próximo!; *they're bringing the sub on* hacen salir a jugar al suplente. LOC **it's not on** no hay derecho, eso no vale. ▎ **you're on!** ¡trato hecho!

**once** [wʌns] *adv* **1** *(one time)* una vez: *once a week* una vez por semana. **2** *(formerly)* antes, en otro tiempo: *I was a cook once* antes era cocinero. LOC **at once 1** *(at the same time)* a la vez. **2** *(immediately)* en seguida, inmediatamente, ahora mismo. ▎ **once again** otra vez. ▎ **once and for all** de una vez para siempre, de una vez por todas. ▎ **once in a while** de vez en cuando. ▎ **once more** una vez más. ▎ **once upon a time** érase una vez.
▶ *conj* una vez que, en cuanto: *once everyone gets here, we can start* una vez que lleguen todos, empezamos.
▶ *n* vez *f*: *just this once* solo esta vez.

**oncoming** ['ɒnkʌmɪŋ] *adj* **1** *(traffic)* que viene en dirección contraria. **2** *(event, season)* venidero,-a, futuro,-a.

**one** [wʌn] *adj* **1** *(stating number)* un, una: *I've got one brother* tengo un hermano. **2** *(unspecified, a certain)* un, una, algún, -una: *one day in January* un día de enero. **3** *(only, single)* único,-a: *it's my one chance* es mi única oportunidad. **4** *(same)* mismo, -a: *in one direction* en la misma dirección.
▶ *pron* **1** *(thing)* uno,-a: *a red one* uno,-a rojo,-a; *this one* éste,-a. **2** *(person)* él, la: *he's the one who I was telling you about* es él de quien te estaba hablando. **3** *(any person, you)* uno, una: *one can't think of everything* uno no puede pensar en todo. LOC **one after another** uno,-a detrás de otro,-a. ▎ **one another** el uno al otro. ▎ **one at a time** de uno en uno. ▎ **one by one** de uno,-a en uno,-a.
▶ *n* *(number)* uno: *my son is one today* mi hijo cumple un año hoy.

**oneself** [wʌn'self] *pron* **1** *(reflexive)* se; *(emphatic)* uno,-a mismo,-a; *(after prep)* sí mismo,-a: *to wash oneself* lavarse. **2** *(alone)* solo,-a: *one can't do everything oneself* uno no puede hacerlo todo solo. LOC **(all) by oneself** solo,-a. ▎ **to oneself** para sí, para sí solo,-a.

**one-way** ['wʌnweɪ] *adj* **1** *(street)* de sentido único, de dirección única. **2** *(ticket)* de ida.

**onion** ['ʌnɪən] *n* cebolla.

**online** ['ɒnlaɪn] *adj* COMPUT en línea.
▶ *adv* COMPUT en línea.

**onlooker** [ˈɒnlukəʳ] n espectador,-ra, curioso,-a.

**only** [ˈəʊnlɪ] adj (sole) único,-a: the only problem is that... el único problema es que... COMP only child hijo,-a único,-a.
▶ adv 1 (just, merely) solo, solamente: he's only a child solo es un niño. 2 (exclusively) solo, solamente, únicamente: only my mother knows mi madre es la única que lo sabe. LOC not only... but also no solamente... sino también. I only just 1 (a moment before) acabar de. 2 (almost not, scarcely) por poco. I only too... muy...
▶ conj pero: it's like yoghurt, only better es como el yogur, pero mejor.

**onshore** [ɒnˈʃɔːʳ] adj (on land) en tierra.
▶ adv (towards land) tierra adentro.

**onto** [ˈɒntu] prep 1 (movement) a, en: it fell onto the floor cayó al suelo. 2 (new subject) a: let's move onto a different subject cambiemos de tema.

**onwards** [ˈɒnwədz] adv GB adelante, hacia adelante: from now onwards de ahora en adelante.

**ooze¹** [uːz] vi rezumar.
▶ vt 1 rezumar. 2 fig rebosar.

**ooze²** [uːz] n cieno, lodo.

**opacity** [əʊˈpæsɪtɪ] n 1 (non-transparency) opacidad f. 2 (obscurity) oscuridad f.

**opal** [ˈəʊpəl] n ópalo.

**opaque** [əʊˈpeɪk] adj 1 (not transparent) opaco,-a. 2 (difficult to understand, obscure) obscuro,-a, oscuro,-a, poco claro,-a.

**open** [ˈəʊpən] adj 1 (gen) abierto,-a; I can't keep my eyes open no puedo mantener los ojos abiertos. 2 (not covered) descubierto,-a: an open car un coche descapotable. COMP open day jornada de puertas abiertas. I open letter carta abierta. I open season temporada de caza.
▶ n SP (competition) open m.
▶ vt abrir: open your mouth abre la boca. LOC to open fire abrir fuego (on/at, contra).
▶ vi 1 (gen) abrir, abrirse: the door opened la puerta se abrió. 2 (spread out, unfold) abrirse: the roses are opening las rosas se están abriendo. 3 (start - conference, play, book) comenzar, empezar;

(film) estrenarse. 4 (begin business) abrir.
▶ adj open to (susceptible) susceptible a, expuesto,-a a; (receptive) abierto,-a a.
▶ n the open (the outdoors, open air) campo, aire m libre.
◆ to open into / open onto vt insep dar a: the back door opens onto the patio la puerta trasera da al patio.

**open-air** [ˈəʊpˈneəʳ] adj al aire libre.

**opener** [ˈəʊpˈnəʳ] n abridor m.

**opening** [ˈəʊpˈnɪŋ] n 1 (ceremony - gen) inauguración f, comienzo. 2 (first night) estreno. 3 (process of opening, unfolding) apertura. 4 (hole) abertura; (space) hueco; (gap) brecha; (clearing) claro. 5 (chance) oportunidad f (for, para). 6 (vacancy) vacante f (for, para). COMP opening hours horario de apertura. I opening night noche f de estreno.
▶ adj (initial) inicial.

**openly** [ˈəʊpˈnlɪ] adv (not secretly) abiertamente; (publicly) públicamente, en público.

**open-minded** [əʊpˈnˈmaɪndɪd] adj abierto,-a, de actitud abierta.

**openness** [ˈəʊpˈnnəs] n (frankness) franqueza; (receptiveness) actitud f abierta.

**opera** [ˈɒpʳrə] n ópera.

**operate** [ˈɒpʳreɪt] vt 1 (machine, etc) hacer funcionar, manejar,. 2 (manage, run - business) dirigir, llevar.
▶ vi 1 (function - machine, etc) funcionar. 2 (carry on trade) operar; (work) trabajar. 3 MED operar (on, a), intervenir (on, a).

**operating** [ˈɒpʳreɪtɪŋ] adj COMM (losses, costs) de explotación. COMP operating room US quirófano. I operating system COMPUT sistema m operativo. I operating theatre GB quirófano.

**operation** [ɒpʳreɪˈʃən] n 1 MED operación f, intervención f. 2 (of machine - gen) funcionamiento; (- by person) manejo; (of system) uso. 3 (activity) operación f; (planned campaign) campaña. 4 MIL operación f. 5 MATH operación f.

**operator** [ˈɒpʳreɪtəʳ] n 1 (of equipment, machine) operario,-a. 2 (of switchboard) operador,-ra, telefonista mf.

O

**ophthalmologist** [ɒfθæl'mɒlədʒɪst] *n* oftalmólogo,-a, oculista *mf*.

**opinion** [ə'pɪnɪən] *n* **1** *(belief)* opinión *f*, parecer *m*. **2** *(evaluation, estimation)* opinión *f*, concepto. ⃞ **in my opinion** en mi opinión, a mi juicio. ⃞ ⃞ **opinion poll** encuesta.

**opium** ['əʊpɪəm] *n* opio.

**opponent** [ə'pəʊnənt] *n* adversario,-a, oponente *mf*.

**opportunity** [ɒpə'tjuːnɪtɪ] *n* **1** *(gen)* oportunidad *f*, ocasión *f*. **2** *(prospect)* perspectiva.
ⓘ *pl* opportunities.

**oppose** [ə'pəʊz] *vt* oponerse a.

**opposite** ['ɒpəzɪt] *adj* **1** *(facing)* de enfrente: *she lives on the opposite side of the road* vive al otro lado de la calle. **2** *(contrary, different)* opuesto,-a, contrario,-a.
▶ *prep* enfrente de, frente a: *the building opposite the cinema* el edificio enfrente del cine.
▶ *adv* enfrente: *the family who live opposite* la familia que vive enfrente.
▶ *n* lo contrario, lo opuesto: *the opposite of big is small* lo contrario a grande es pequeño.

**opposition** [ɒpə'zɪʃən] *n* **1** *(resistance)* oposición *f*, resistencia. **2** *(rivals - in sport)* adversarios *mpl*; *(- in business)* competencia.
▶ *n* **the Opposition** POL la oposición *f*.

**oppress** [ə'pres] *vt* oprimir.

**oppression** [ə'preʃən] *n* opresión *f*.

**oppressor** [ə'presər] *n* opresor,-ra.

**opt** [ɒpt] *vi* optar **(for,** por).
◆ **to opt out** *vi (person)* abandonar, dejar de participar.

**optic** ['ɒptɪk] *adj* óptico,-a.

**optical** ['ɒptɪkəl] *adj* óptico,-a.

**optician** [ɒp'tɪʃən] *n* óptico,-a, oculista *mf*. ⃞ ⃞ **optician's (shop)** óptico.

**optics** ['ɒptɪks] *n* óptica.

**optimism** ['ɒptɪmɪzəm] *n* optimismo.

**optimist** ['ɒptɪmɪst] *n* optimista *mf*.

**optimistic** [ɒptɪ'mɪstɪk] *adj* optimista.

**option** ['ɒpʃən] *n* **1** *(choice)* opción *f*, posibilidad *f*. **2** EDUC *(optional subject)* asignatura optativa.

**optional** ['ɒpʃənəl] *adj* opcional.

**or** [ɔːr] *conj* **1** *(alternative - gen)* o; *(- before word beginning with* o *or* ho) u: *tea or coffee* té o café. **2** *(with negative)* ni: *she can't sing or dance* no sabe cantar ni bailar. **3** *(otherwise)* o: *come on, or we'll be late!* ¡date prisa o llegaremos tarde! ⃞ **or so** más o menos.

**oral** ['ɔːrəl] *adj* **1** *(spoken - gen)* oral; *(tradition)* transmitido,-a oralmente. **2** MED *(contraceptive)* oral; *(hygiene)* bucal.
▶ *n (exam)* examen *m* oral.

**orange** ['ɒrɪndʒ] *n* **1** *(fruit)* naranja. **2** *(colour)* naranja *m*. ⃞ ⃞ **orange blossom** azahar *m*. ▌ **orange juice** zumo de naranja. ▌ **orange tree** naranjo.
▶ *adj* naranja, de color naranja.

**orang-utan** [ɔː'ræŋuː'tæn] *n* orangután *m*.

**orbicularis** [ɔːbɪkə'lærɪs] *adj* **1** ANAT orbicular. **2** *fml lit (sphere)* esfera; *(sun)* el sol *m*; *(moon)* la luna.

**orbit** ['ɔːbɪt] *n* **1** *(of satellite)* órbita. **2** *(area of influence)* órbita, esfera de influencia, ámbito. ⃞ **to go into orbit** entrar en órbita.
▶ *vt* girar alrededor de, orbitar alrededor de.

**orbital** ['ɔːbɪtəl] *adj* orbital, orbitario,-a. ⃞ ⃞ **orbital road** carretera de circunvalación.

**orchard** ['ɔːtʃəd] *n* huerto.

**orchestra** ['ɔːkɪstrə] *n* orquesta.

**orchid** ['ɔːkɪd] *n* BOT orquídea.

**order** ['ɔːdər] *n* **1** *(gen)* orden *m*: *in alphabetical/chronological order* por orden alfabético/cronológico. *she put her affairs in order* puso sus asuntos en orden. **2** *(fitness for use)* condiciones *fpl*, estado: *the car's in good working order* el coche funciona bien. **3** *(obedience, authority, discipline)* orden *m*, disciplina. **4** *(rules, procedures, etc)* orden *m*, procedimiento. **5** *(command)* orden *f*. **6** COMM *(request, goods)* pedido: *the waiter took our order* el camarero tomó nota de lo que queríamos. **7** *(group, society)* orden *f*; *(badge, sign worn)* condecoración *f*, orden *f*: *the monastic orders* las órdenes monásticas. ⃞ **in order that** para que, a fin de que. ▌ **in order to** para, a fin de. ▌ **out of order** *(not working)* que no funciona. COMP **order book** libro de pedidos. ∎ **order form** hoja de pedido.

▸ *vt* **1** *(command)* ordenar, mandar. **2** *(ask for)* pedir, encargar: *I've ordered a cake for his birthday* he encargado un pastel para su cumpleaños. **3** *(arrange, put in order, organize)* ordenar, poner en orden.

▸ *vi (request to bring, ask for)* pedir.

**ordinal** [ˈɔːdɪnəl] *adj* ordinal.

▸ *n* ordinal *m*.

**ordinarily** [ˈɔːdənərɪlɪ] *adv* generalmente.

**ordinary** [ˈɔːdɪnˈrɪ] *adj (usual, normal)* normal, usual, habitual; *(average)* normal, común. COMP **ordinary seaman** marinero.

⊠ Ordinary no significa 'ordinario (vulgar)', que se traduce por **vulgar**.

**ordinate** [ˈɔːdɪnət] *n* MATH ordenada.

**ore** [ɔːʳ] *n* mineral *m*, mena.

⊠ Ore no significa 'oro', que se traduce por **gold**.

**oregano** [ɒrɪˈɡɑːnəʊ] *n* orégano.

**organ** [ˈɔːɡən] *n* órgano.

**organic** [ɔːˈɡænɪk] *adj* **1** *(living)* orgánico,-a. **2** *(without chemicals)* biológico,-a, ecológico,-a.

**organism** [ˈɔːɡənɪzəm] *n* organismo.

**organization** [ɔːɡənaɪˈzeɪʃən] *n* organización *f*.

**organize** [ˈɔːɡənaɪz] *vt* organizar, ordenar.

▸ *vi* organizar.

**organized** [ˈɔːɡənaɪzd] *adj (gen)* organizado,-a.

**organizer** [ˈɔːɡənaɪzəʳ] *n* organizador, -ra.

**orgy** [ˈɔːdʒɪ] *n (wild party)* orgía.
ⓘ *pl* orgies.

**Orient** [ˈɔːrɪənt] *n* **the Orient** el oriente *m*.

**oriental** [ɔːrɪˈentəl] *adj* oriental.

▸ *n* oriental *mf*.

**orientate** [ˈɔːrɪənteɪt] *vt* orientar.

**orientation** [ɔːrɪənˈteɪʃən] *n* orientación *f*.

**origin** [ˈɒrɪdʒɪn] *n* origen *m*.

▸ *n pl* **origins** origen *m sing*.

**original** [əˈrɪdʒɪnəl] *adj* original, originario,-a, primero,-a.

▸ *n* original *m*.

**originally** [əˈrɪdʒɪnəlɪ] *adv* **1** *(in the beginning)* originariamente, en un principio. **2** *(in a new way)* con originalidad.

**originate** [əˈrɪdʒɪneɪt] *vt (create)* originar, crear, dar lugar a.

▸ *vi (arise)* tener su origen (in, en), originarse (in, en), provenir (in, de).

**ornament** [ˈɔːnəmənt] *n (decoration)* ornamento, adorno; *(object)* adorno.

**ornithology** [ɔːnɪˈθɒlədʒɪ] *n* ornitología.

**orography** [ɒˈrɒɡrəfɪ] *n* orografía.

**orphan** [ˈɔːfən] *n* huérfano,-a.

▸ *vt* dejar huérfano,-a. LOC **to be orphaned** quedar huérfano,-a.

**orphanage** [ˈɔːfənɪdʒ] *n* orfanato.

**orthodox** [ˈɔːθədɒks] *adj* ortodoxo,-a.

**orthography** [ɔːˈθɒɡrəfɪ] *n* ortografía.

**orthopaedic** [ɔːθəʊˈpiːdɪk] *adj* MED ortopédico,-a.

**osmosis** [ɒzˈməʊsɪs] *n* ósmosis *f*, osmosis *f*.

**osseous** [ˈɒzɪəʊz] *adj* óseo,-a.

**ostensible** [ɒˈstensɪbəl] *adj (apparent)* aparente; *(alleged)* pretendido,-a, fingido,-a.

⊠ Ostensible no significa 'ostensible', que se traduce por **obvious**.

**ostrich** [ˈɒstrɪtʃ] *n* avestruz *m*.

**other** [ˈʌðəʳ] *adj* **1** *(additional)* otro,-a: *I have one other idea* tengo otra idea. **2** *(different)* otro,-a: *people from other countries* gente de otros países. **3** *(second, remaining)* otro,-a: *it's on the other side of the street* está al otro lado de la calle. LOC **every other day** un día sí, otro no. ∎ **the other day** el otro día.

▸ *pron* otro,-a. LOC **one after the other** uno tras otro.

▸ *prep* **other than** *(except)* aparte de, salvo: *there was nobody other than the teacher* aparte del profesor, no había nadie.

**otherwise** [ˈʌðəwaɪz] *adv* **1** *(differently)* de otra manera, de manera distinta: *she couldn't do otherwise* no podía obrar

**O**

de otra manera. **2** *(apart from that, in other respects)* aparte de eso, por lo demás.
▶ *conj (if not)* si no, de no ser así, de lo contrario.
▶ *adj* distinto,-a.

**otitis** [əʊˈtaɪtɪs] *n* otitis *f*.

**otter** [ˈɒtəʳ] *n* nutria.

**ouch** [aʊtʃ] *interj* ¡ay!

**ought** [ɔ:t] *aux* ought to **1** *(moral obligation)* deber: *you ought to have helped them* debiste ayudarles. **2** *(recommendation)* deber, tener que. **3** *(expectation)* deber de: *they ought to be home by now* seguramente ya estarán en casa.

**ounce** [aʊns] *n* **1** *(weight)* onza. **2** *fam (small quantity)* pizca.

✎ La onza equivale a 28,35 gramos.

**our** [aʊəʳ] *adj* nuestro,-a: *our house* nuestra casa; *our children* nuestros hijos.

**ours** [aʊəz] *pron* (el) nuestro, (la) nuestra: *a friend of ours* un amigo nuestro.

**ourselves** [aʊəˈselvz] *pron* **1** *(reflexive)* nos: *we made ourselves comfortable* nos pusimos cómodos. **2** *(emphatic)* nosotros,-as mismos,-as: *we did it ourselves* lo hicimos nosotros mismos.

**out** [aʊt] *adv* **1** *(gen)* fuera, afuera: *could you wait out there?* ¿podrías esperar allí fuera?; *she ran out* salió corriendo. **2** *(expressing distance)* en: *they live out in the country* viven en el campo. **3** *(expressing removal)* diferentes traducciones: *I've had a tooth out* me han sacado una muela; *she got out a handkerchief* sacó un pañuelo. **4** *(available, existing)* diferentes traducciones: *the film comes out next month* la película se estrenará el mes que viene; *it's the best sandwich out* es el mejor bocadillo que hay. **5** *(protruding)* que se sale: *a nail sticking out* un clavo que sobresale. **6** *(clearly, loudly)* en voz alta: *he called out to me* me llamó en voz alta.
▶ *prep* out of **1** *(gen)* fuera de: *out of danger* fuera de peligro; *they are out of the cup* han quedado fuera de la copa. **2** *(from among)* de: *she got five out of ten in French* sacó (un) cinco sobre diez en francés. **3** *(without)* sin: *out of money* sin dinero. **6** *(using, made from)* de: *made out of wood* hecho,-a de madera.

**outboard motor** [aʊtbɔ:dˈməʊtəʳ] *n* MAR motor *m* fueraborda, fuoraborda *m*.

**outbreak** [ˈaʊtbreɪk] *n* **1** *(of violence, fighting)* brote *m*. **2** *(of disease)* brote *m*, epidemia; *(of spots)* erupción *f*.

**outburst** [ˈaʊtbɜ:st] *n* **1** *(of emotion)* explosión *f*, arrebato *m*. **2** *(of activity)* explosión *f*.

**outcast** [ˈaʊtkɑ:st] *n* marginado,-a.

**outclass** [ˈaʊtklɑ:s] *vt* superar.

**outcome** [ˈaʊtkʌm] *n* resultado.

**outdated** [aʊtˈdeɪtɪd] *adj* anticuado,-a.

**outdoor** [ˈaʊtdɔ:ʳ] *adj (gen)* exterior.

**outdoors** [aʊtˈdɔ:ʳz] *adv* fuera, al aire libre.

**outer** [ˈaʊtəʳ] *adj* exterior, externo,-a.
COMP outer space espacio exterior. I outer suburbs afueras *fpl*.

**outgrow** [aʊtˈgrəʊ] *vt (clothes, etc)* hacerse demasiado grande para: *he's outgrown his shoes* se le han quedado pequeños los zapatos.
① *pt* outgrew [aʊtˈgru:], *pp* outgrown [aʊtˈgrəʊn].

**outing** [ˈaʊtɪŋ] *n (trip)* salida, excursión *f*.

**outlaw** [ˈaʊtlɔ:] *n* forajido,-a, proscrito,-a.
▶ *vt* prohibir, declarar ilegal.

**outlet** [ˈaʊtlet] *n* **1** *(opening - gen)* salida; *(for water)* desagüe *m*. **2** *fig (for emotions)* válvula de escape. **3** COMM *(shop)* punto de venta.

**outline** [ˈaʊtlaɪn] *n* **1** *(outer edge)* contorno; *(shape)* perfil *m*. **2** *(draft)* bosquejo, esquema *m*; *(summary)* resumen *m*.
▶ *vt* **1** *(draw lines of)* perfilar; *(sketch)* bosquejar. **2** *(summarize)* resumir.

**outnumber** [aʊtˈnʌmbəʳ] *vt* superar en número, ser más que.

**out-of-date** [aʊtəvˈdeɪt] *adj (fashion)* pasado,-a de moda; *(technology)* desfasado,-a, obsoleto,-a; *(food, ticket)* caducado,-a.

**output** [ˈaʊtpʊt] *n* **1** *(gen)* producción *f*; *(of machine)* rendimiento. **2** COMPUT salida.

**outrageous** [aʊtˈreɪdʒəs] *adj* **1** *(shocking - gen)* escandaloso,-a; *(crime)* atroz; *(language)* injurioso,-a. **2** *(unconventional)* extravagante.

**outside** [(n) aʊt'saɪd; (prep) 'aʊtsaɪd] n **1** (exterior part) exterior m, parte f exterior: from the outside desde fuera. **2** GB (when driving) derecha.

▶ prep **1** (gen) fuera de. **2** (beyond) más allá de, fuera de: outside working hours fuera del horario laboral. **3** (other than) aparte de, fuera de.

▶ adv (gen) fuera, afuera.

▶ adj **1** (exterior) exterior. **2** (external) externo,-a. **3** (remote) remoto,-a. ⓛⓞⓒ at the outside como máximo, como mucho.

**outsider** [aʊt'saɪdə^r] n **1** (person- stranger) extraño,-a, forastero,-a, desconocido,-a. **2** (unlikely winner - athlete, etc) competidor,-ra con pocas probabilidades de ganar.

**outskirts** ['aʊtskɜːts] n pl afueras fpl, alrededores mpl, extrarradio m sing.

**outstanding** [aʊt'stændɪŋ] adj **1** (excellent) destacado,-a, notable, sobresaliente; (exceptional) excepcional, extraordinario,-a, singular. **2** (gen) sin pagar, pendiente.

**outstretched** [aʊt'stretʃt] adj extendido,-a.

**outward** ['aʊtwəd] adj **1** (appearance) exterior; (sign) externo,-a, show. **2** (journey, flight) de ida.

**outwards** ['aʊtwədʒ] adv (gen) hacia fuera, hacia afuera; (attention, etc) hacia el exterior.

**oval** ['əʊvəl] adj oval, ovalado,-a.

▶ n óvalo.

**ovary** ['əʊvərɪ] n ovario.

ⓘ pl ovaries.

**ovation** [əʊ'veɪʃ^ən] n ovación f.

**oven** ['ʌv^ən] n horno.

**over** ['əʊvə^r] adv **1** (down) diferentes traducciones: the boy fell over el niño se cayó; I knocked the glass over tiré la copa (de un golpe). **2** (from one side to another) diferentes traducciones: turn over the page dar la vuelta a la página; he bent over se inclinó. **3** (across) diferentes traducciones: let's cross over crucemos al otro lado; over here/there aquí/allí. **5** (too much) de más: it's 50 grams over pesa 50 gramos de más. ⓛⓞⓒ over here aquí. ▮ over there allí.

▶ prep **1** (gen) encima de: a sign over the door un letrero encima de la puerta; he wore a jacket over his sweater llevaba una americana encima del jersey. **2** (across) sobre; (on the other side of) al otro lado de: he lives over the border vive al otro lado de la frontera. **3** (during) durante: over the past 25 years durante los últimos 25 años. **4** (throughout) por: we travelled all over Italy viajamos por toda Italia. **5** (more than) más de: she's over thirty tiene más de treinta años. **6** (about) por: an argument over money una discusión por dinero. ⓛⓞⓒ all over en todas partes. ▮ over and above además de.

▶ adj (ended) acabado,-a, terminado,-a: the game is over la partida ha acabado.

**overact** [əʊvər'ækt] vi exagerar, sobreactuar.

**overall** [(adj) 'əʊvərɔːl; (adv) əʊvər'ɔːl] adj (general) global, total.

▶ adv (generally, on the whole) en conjunto, por lo general.

▶ n GB (work coat) guardapolvo, bata.

▶ n pl **overalls** mono m sing.

**overambitious** [əʊvəræm'bɪʃəs] adj demasiado ambicioso,-a.

**overboard** ['əʊvəbɔːd] adv por la borda. ⓛⓞⓒ to fall overboard caer al agua. ▮ to go overboard pasarse.

**overbooking** [əʊvə'bʊkɪŋ] n sobrecontratación f.

**overcame** [əʊvə'keɪm] pt → overcome.

**overcoat** ['əʊvəkəʊt] n abrigo.

**overcome** [əʊvə'kʌm] vt **1** (defeat) vencer. **2** (overwhelm) agobiar, abrumar, invadir, apoderarse de, vencer: he was overcome by sleep el sueño se apoderó de él.

ⓘ pt overcame [əʊvə'keɪm], pp overcome [əʊvə'kʌm].

**overdose** ['əʊvədəʊs] n sobredosis f.

**overflow** [(n) 'əʊvəfləʊ; (vb) əʊvə'fləʊ] n **1** (of river, etc) desbordamiento. **2** (pipe) tubo de desagüe; (hole) rebosadero.

▶ vi **1** (river) desbordarse; (bath, etc) rebosar. **2** (people) rebosar. **3** (be full of) rebosar (with, de). ⓛⓞⓒ to be full to overflowing estar lleno,-a hasta el borde.

▶ vt (liquid) salirse de.

**O**

**overhead** [*(adj)* 'əʊvəhed; *(adv)* əʊvə'hed] *adj (cable)* aéreo,-a; *(railway)* elevado,-a.
▸ *adv* arriba, por encima de la cabeza.

**overhear** [əʊvə'hɪəʳ] *vt* oír por casualidad.
ⓘ *pt & pp* overheard [əʊvə'hɜːd].

**overheard** [əʊvə'hɜːd] *pt & pp* → overhear.

**overland** [*(adj)* 'əʊvəlænd; *(adv)* əʊvə'lænd] *adj* por tierra.
▸ *adv* por tierra.

**overlap** [əʊvə'læp] *vi* superponerse, solaparse.
ⓘ *pt & pp* overlapped, *ger* overlapping.
▸ *n* superposición *f*, coincidencia.

**overlook** [əʊvə'lʊk] *vt* 1 *(not notice)* pasar por alto;. 2 *(excuse)* disculpar. 3 *(have a view of)* tener vistas a.

**overnight** [əʊvə'naɪt] *adv* 1 *(during the night)* durante la noche; *(at night)* por la noche: *it rained overnight* llovió durante la noche. 2 *fam (suddenly)* de la noche a la mañana.
▸ *adj* 1 *(during the night)* de la noche; *(for the night)* de una noche. 2 *fam (sudden)* repentino,-a.

**oversaw** [əʊvə'sɔː] *pt* → oversee.

**overseas** [əʊvə'siːz] *adj (person)* extranjero,-a; *(trade)* exterior.
▸ *adv* en ultramar.

**oversee** [əʊvə'siː] *vt* supervisar.
ⓘ *pt* oversaw [əʊvə'sɔː], *pp* overseen [əʊvə'siːn].

**overseen** [əʊvə'siːn] *pp* → oversee.

**oversized** [əʊvə'saɪzd] *adj* demasiado grande.

**oversleep** [əʊvə'sliːp] *vi* quedarse dormido,-a, no despertarse a tiempo.
ⓘ *pt & pp* overslept [əʊvə'slept].

**overslept** [əʊvə'slept] *pt & pp* → oversleep.

**overtake** [əʊvə'teɪk] *vt* 1 GB *(a vehicle)* adelantar, pasar, AM rebasar: *we overtook a sports car* adelantamos un coche deportivo. 2 *(surpass)* superar. 3 *(happen suddenly to)* adelantarse a; *(surprise)* sorprender.
ⓘ *pt* overtook [əʊvə'teɪkən], *pp* overtaken [əʊvə'tʊk].

**overtaken** [əʊvə'teɪkən] *pp* → overtake.

**overtime** ['əʊvətaɪm] *n (extra work, extra hours)* horas *fpl* extras.

**overtook** [əʊvə'tʊk] *pt* → overtake.

**overturn** [əʊvə'tɜːn] *vt* 1 *(vehicle)* volcar; *(boat)* hacer zozobrar; *(furniture)* dar la vuelta a. 2 *(government)* derrocar. 3 *fig (ruling)* anular.
▸ *vi (vehicle)* volcar; *(boat)* zozobrar.

**overview** ['əʊvəvjuː] *n* perspectiva general.

**overweight** [əʊvə'weɪt] *adj (thing)* demasiado pesado,-a; *(person)* demasiado gordo,-a.

**overwhelm** [əʊvə'welm] *vt* 1 *(physically - defeat)* arrollar, aplastar. 2 *fig (emotionally)* abrumar.

**overwhelming** [əʊvə'welmɪŋ] *adj (defeat, victory)* aplastante, arrollador,-ra; *(generosity)* abrumador,-ra.

**ovine** [əʊ'vɪn] *adj* ovino,-a.

**oviparous** [əʊ'vɪpərəs] *adj* ovíparo,-a.

**ovulate** ['ɒvjəleɪt] *vi* ovular.

**ovulation** [ɒvjə'leɪʃᵊn] *n* ovulación *f*.

**ovule** ['ɒvjuːl] *n* óvulo.

**owe** [əʊ] *vt (gen)* deber: *you owe me 10 pounds* me debes 10 libras.

**owing** ['əʊɪŋ] *adj (due)* debido,-a.
▸ *prep* owing to debido a, a causa de.

**owl** [aʊl] *n* búho, lechuza.

**own** [əʊn] *adj* propio,-a: *they grow their own vegetables* cultivan sus propios verduras.
▸ *pron* propio,-a: *would you like to borrow mine or do you have your own?* ¿quieres que te deje el mío o ya tienes uno propio? LOC on one's own 1 *(alone)* solo,-a. 2 *(without help)* uno,-a mismo,-a.
▸ *vt (possess)* poseer, ser dueño,-a de.
◆ to own up *vi* confesarlo.

**owner** ['əʊnəʳ] *n* dueño,-a, propietario,-a.

**ox** [ɒks] *n* buey *m*.
ⓘ *pl* oxen [ɒksᵊn].

**oxen** ['ɒksən] *npl* → ox.

**oxidation** [ɒksɪ'deɪʃᵊn] *n* oxidación *f*.

**oxide** ['ɒksaɪd] *n* óxido.

**oxygen** ['ɒksɪdʒᵊn] *n* oxígeno.

**oyster** ['ɔɪstəʳ] *n (shellfish)* ostra.

**ozone** ['əʊzəʊn] *n* ozono. COMP ozone layer capa de ozono.

**ozone-friendly** ['əʊzəʊnfrendlɪ] *adj* que no daña la capa de ozono.

# P

**P, p** [piː] *n (the letter)* P, p *f*.

**pace** [peɪs] *n* **1** *(rate, speed)* marcha, ritmo, velocidad *f*. **2** *(step)* paso.
▶ *vt* **1** *(room, floor)* ir de un lado a otro de. **2** *(set speed for)* marcar el ritmo a.

**pacemaker** [ˈpeɪsmeɪkəʳ] *n* **1** SP liebre *f*. **2** MED marcapasos *m*.

**pachyderm** [ˈpækɪdɜːm] *n* paquidermo.

**pacifism** [ˈpæsɪfɪzəm] *n* pacifismo.

**pacifist** [ˈpæsɪfɪst] *n* pacifista *mf*.

**pacify** [ˈpæsɪfaɪ] *vt* **1** *(person)* calmar, tranquilizar. **2** *(country)* pacificar.
ⓘ *pt & pp* pacified, *ger* pacifying.

**pack** [pæk] *n* **1** *(parcel)* paquete *m*; *(bundle)* fardo, bulto; *(rucksack)* mochila. **2** US *(packet - gen)* paquete *m*; *(of cigarettes)* paquete *m*, cajetilla. **3** GB *(of cards)* baraja. **4** *pej (of thieves)* banda, partida. **5** *(of lies)* sarta. **6** *(of wolves, dogs)* manada; *(of hounds)* jauría.
▶ *vt* **1** *(goods)* empaquetar, envasar. **2** *(suitcase)* hacer; *(clothes, etc)* poner, meter. **3** *(fill)* atestar, abarrotar, llenar: *the disco was packed with young people* la discoteca estaba abarrotada de jóvenes. **4** *(press down)* apretar.
▶ *vi* **1** *(suitcase, etc)* hacer las maletas, hacer el equipaje: *he hasn't packed yet* aún no ha hecho las maletas. **2** *(people)* apiñarse, apretarse, meterse.
◆ **to pack up** *vi* **1** *(stop, give up)* dejarlo. **2** *(machine)* estropearse; *(car)* averiarse.
▶ *vt sep (belongings - in case)* meter en la maleta; *(gather together)* recoger.

**package** [ˈpækɪdʒ] *n* **1** *(parcel)* paquete *m*. **2** *(proposals)* paquete *m*; *(agreement)* acuerdo. COMP **package holiday** viaje *m* organizado.
▶ *vt (goods)* empaquetar, envasar.

**packaging** [ˈpækɪdʒɪŋ] *n* embalaje *m*.

**packed** [pækt] *adj (with people)* lleno,-a, abarrotado,-a, repleto,-a; *(with facts, information, etc)* lleno,-a.

**packet** [ˈpækɪt] *n* **1** *(small box - gen)* paquete *m*, cajita; *(of cigarettes)* paquete *m*, cajetilla; *(envelope)* sobre *m*. **2** *fam (large amount of money)* dineral *m*.

**packing** [ˈpækɪŋ] *n (material)* embalaje *m*.

**pact** [pækt] *n* pacto.

**pad** [pæd] *n* **1** *(cushioning)* almohadilla, cojinete *m*. **2** *(inkpad)* tampón *m*. **3** *(of paper)* taco, bloc *m*. **4** *(of animal)* almohadilla. **5** *(platform)* plataforma. COMP **knee pad** rodillera. ‖ **sanitary pad** compresa.
▶ *vt (chair, etc)* acolchar, rellenar, guatear; *(garment)* poner hombreras a.
ⓘ *pt & pp* padded, *ger* padding.

**paddle¹** [ˈpædəl] *n (oar)* pala, remo.
▶ *vt (boat, canoe)* remar con pala.
▶ *vi* remar con pala.

**paddle²** [ˈpædəl] *vi (walk or play in water)* mojarse los pies, chapotear.
▶ *n* chapoteo.

**paddling pool** [ˈpædəlɪŋpuːl] *n* piscina para niños, piscina infantil.

**padlock** [ˈpædlɒk] *n* candado.
▶ *vt* cerrar con candado.

**padre** [paːdreɪ] *n (priest)* padre *m*.

**paediatrician** [piːdʒæetrɪʃən] *n* pediatra *mf*.

**paedophile** [ˈpiːdəfaɪl] *n* pedófilo,-a.

**pagan** [ˈpeɪɡən] *adj* pagano,-a.
▶ *n* pagano,-a.

**page¹** [peɪdʒ] *n (of book)* página; *(of newspaper)* plana, página. LOC **on the front page** en primera plana.

**page²** [peɪdʒ] *n* **1** *(boy servant, at wedding)* paje *m*; *(in hotel, club)* botones *m*. **2** HIST escudero.

**pagoda** [pə'gəudə] *n* pagoda.
**paid** [peɪd] *pp & pt* → **pay**.
▸ *adj (purchase, holiday)* pagado,-a; *(work)* remunerado,-a.
**pail** [peɪl] *n* cubo.
**pain** [peɪn] *n* **1** *(physical)* dolor *m*: *I've got a pain in my stomach* me duele el estómago. **2** *(mental suffering)* sufrimiento, dolor *m*. **3** *(annoying thing)* lata, fastidio; *(person)* pesado,-a, pelmazo. LOC **to be a pain in the neck** ser un,-a pesado,-a.
▸ *vt* doler, dar pena a, apenar.
▸ *n pl* **pains** *(effort)* esfuerzos *mpl*.

   ❌ Pain no significa 'pena (tristeza)', que se traduce por **grief**, **sorrow**.

**painful** ['peɪnful] *adj (physically)* doloroso,-a; *(mentally)* angustioso,-a.
**painkiller** ['peɪnkɪlə'] *n* calmante *m*.
**painless** ['peɪnləs] *adj* **1** *(without pain)* indoloro,-a, sin dolor. **2** *(without distress)* sencillo,-a, sin complicaciones.
**paint** [peɪnt] *n* **1** pintura: *a tin of paint* una lata de pintura. LOC **"Wet paint"** «Recién pintado».
▸ *vt (gen)* pintar: *we're going to paint the walls yellow* vamos a pintar las paredes de amarillo.
▸ *vi* pintar: *she paints in oils* pinta al óleo.
**paintbrush** ['peɪntbrʌʃ] *n* **1** *(for walls, etc)* brocha. **2** *(artist's)* pincel *m*.
**painter** ['peɪntə'] *n* **1** ART pintor,-ra. **2** *(decorator)* pintor,-ra de brocha gorda.
**painting** ['peɪntɪŋ] *n* **1** ART *(picture)* pintura, cuadro. **2** *(activity)* pintura.
**pair** [peə'] *n* **1** *(of shoes, socks, gloves, etc)* par *m*; *(of cards)* pareja: *a pair of brown eyes* dos ojos castaños. **2** *(of people, animals)* pareja. LOC **in pairs** de dos en dos. COMP **a pair of scissors** unas tijeras. ‖ **a pair of trousers** unos pantalones.
▸ *vt (people)* emparejar; *(animals)* aparear.
▸ *vi (animals)* aparearse.
**pajamas** [pə'dʒæməz] *n pl* US → **pyjamas**.
**Pakistan** [pɑːkɪ'stɑːn] *n* Pakistán *m*.
**Pakistani** [pɑːkɪ'stɑːnɪ] *adj* pakistaní.
▸ *n* pakistaní *mf*.
**pal** [pæl] *n fam* amigo,-a, colega *mf*.
**palace** ['pæləs] *n* palacio.

**Palaeolithic** [pælɪəu'lɪθɪk] *adj* paleolítico,-a.
**palate** ['pælət] *n (gen)* paladar *m*.
**pale** [peɪl] *adj (complexion, skin)* pálido,-a; *(colour)* claro,-a, pálido,-a; *(light)* débil. LOC **to turn pale** ponerse pálido,-a.
▸ *vi* palidecer.
**Paleolithic** [pælɪəu'lɪθɪk] *adj* US → **Palaelothic**.
**Palestine** ['pælɪstaɪn] *n* Palestina.
**Palestinian** [pælɪ'stɪnɪən] *adj* palestino,-a.
▸ *n* palestino,-a.
**palette** ['pælət] *n* paleta.
**palfrey** ['pɔːlfrɪ] *n* palafrén *m*.
**palm¹** [pɑːm] *n* BOT *(tree)* palmera; *(leaf)* palma. COMP **palm tree** palmera.
**palm²** [pɑːm] *n* ANAT palma.
**pamphlet** ['pæmflət] *n* folleto.
**pan** [pæn] *n (saucepan)* cacerola, cazuela, cazo; *(cooking pot)* olla.
**Panama** ['pænəmɑː] *n* Panamá.
**Panamanian** [pænə'meɪnɪən] *adj* panameño,-a.
▸ *n* panameño,-a.
**pancake** ['pænkeɪk] *n* tortita, crepe *f*.
**pancreas** ['pæŋkrɪəs] *n* páncreas *m*.
**panda** ['pændə] *n (oso)* panda *m*.
**pane** [peɪn] *n* cristal *m*, vidrio.
**panel** ['pænəl] *n* **1** *(of door, wall, car body, etc)* panel *m*; *(on ceiling)* artesón *m*. **2** *(of controls, instruments)* tablero. **3** *(group of people)* panel *m*; *(team)* equipo.
**panic** ['pænɪk] *n* pánico: *panic spread throughout the crowd* el pánico cundió entre la gente. LOC **to get into a panic** dejarse llevar por el pánico.
▸ *vt* infundir pánico a.
▸ *vi* entrarle el pánico a, aterrarse.
   ⓘ *pt & pp* **panicked**, *ger* **panicking**.
**panic-stricken** ['pænɪkstrɪkən] *adj* preso,-a de pánico, aterrorizado,-a.
**panorama** [pænə'rɑːmə] *n (view)* panorama *m*.
**panoramic** [pænə'ræmɪk] *adj* panorámico,-a.
**pant** [pænt] *vi* jadear, resoplar.
**pantheon** ['pænθɪən] *n* ARCH panteón *m*.
**panther** ['pænθə'] *n* pantera.

**pantomime** ['pæntəmaɪm] n **1** (mime) pantomima. **2** GB (play) representación musical navideña basada en cuentos de hadas.

⊕ Es una representación teatral cómica y musical que se hace por Navidades y que suele contar historias tradicionales como, por ejemplo, Aladdin (*Aladino y la lámpara maravillosa*), Puss in Boots (*El gato con botas*) o Cinderella (*La Cenicienta*).

**pantry** ['pæntrɪ] n despensa.
ⓘ pl pantries.

**pants** [pænts] n pl **1** GB (underpants - men's) calzoncillos mpl; (- women's) bragas fpl. **2** US (trousers) pantalón m, pantalones mpl.

**papaya** [pəˈpaɪə] n papaya.

**paper** ['peɪpəʳ] n **1** (material) papel m: take a sheet of paper coge una hoja de papel. **2** (newspaper) periódico, diario. **3** (examination) examen m. **4** (essay, written work) trabajo (escrito); (for conference) ponencia. LOC **on paper** por escrito. COMP **paper mill** fábrica de papel. ❙ **paper money** papel m moneda. ❙ **paper shop** quiosco.
▶ vt empapelar.
▶ n pl **papers** (documents) documentos mpl.

☒ Paper no significa 'papel (en el teatro o el cine)', que se traduce por **role, part**.

**paperclip** ['peɪpəklɪp] n clip m.

**paprika** ['pæprɪkə] n pimentón m dulce.

**Papua** ['pæpjʊə] n Papúa. COMP **Papua New Guinea** Papúa Nueva Guinea.

**Papuan** ['pæpjʊən] adj papú,-úa.
▶ n papú,-úa.

**parabola** [pəˈræbələ] n MATH parábola.

**parachute** ['pærəʃuːt] n paracaídas m.
▶ vi saltar en paracaídas.

**parade** [pəˈreɪd] n **1** (procession) desfile m: fashion parade desfile de modelos. **2** MIL desfile m.
▶ vt **1** MIL hacer desfilar. **2** (flaunt - knowledge, wealth) alardear, hacer alarde de.
▶ vi **1** (gen) desfilar. **2** MIL pasar revista.

☒ Parade no significa 'parada (detención)', que se traduce por **stop**.

**paradise** ['pærədaɪs] n paraíso.

**paradox** ['pærədɒks] n paradoja.

**paraffin** ['pærəfɪn] n GB queroseno. COMP **paraffin wax** parafina.

**paragraph** ['pærəgrɑːf] n párrafo. COMP **full stop, new paragraph** punto y aparte.

**Paraguay** ['pærəgwaɪ] n Paraguay.

**Paraguayan** [pærəˈgwaɪən] adj paraguayo,-a.
▶ n paraguayo,-a.

**parallel** ['pærəlel] adj **1** paralelo,-a (to/with, a). **2** fig (similar) paralelo,-a (to/with, a), análogo,-a (to/with, a).
▶ n **1** MATH paralela. **2** GEOG paralelo. **3** (similarity) paralelo, paralelismo.

**paralyse** ['pærəlaɪz] vt (gen) paralizar.

**paralysis** [pəˈræləsɪs] n **1** MED parálisis f. **2** fig paralización f.

**paralytic** [pærəˈlɪtɪk] adj MED paralítico,-a.
▶ n MED paralítico,-a.

**parameter** [pəˈræmɪtəʳ] n parámetro.

**paranoia** [pærəˈnɔɪə] n paranoia.

**paraplegia** [pærəˈpliːdʒə] n MED paraplejía.

**parasite** ['pærəsaɪt] n parásito,-a.

**parasol** ['pærəsɒl] n sombrilla.

**paratrooper** ['pærətruːpəʳ] n MIL paracaidista mf.

**parcel** ['pɑːsəl] n **1** (package) paquete m. **2** (piece of land) parcela. LOC **parcel post** servicio de paquetes postales.

**parchment** ['pɑːtʃmənt] n pergamino.

**pardon** ['pɑːdən] n **1** (forgiveness) perdón m. **2** JUR indulto. LOC **I beg your pardon!** fml ¡perdone! ❙ **I beg your pardon?** fml ¿cómo dice?
▶ vt **1** (forgive) perdonar: pardon me for interrupting perdone que le interrumpa. **2** JUR indultar. COMP **pardon?** (for repetition) ¿cómo dice?, ¿cómo? ❙ **pardon me!** (sorry) ¡perdón!, ¡perdone!, ¡Vd. perdone!

**parent** ['peərənt] n (father) padre m; (mother) madre f.
▶ n pl **parents** padres mpl.

☒ Parent no significa 'pariente', que se traduce por **relative**.

**parietal** [pəˈraɪətəl] adj parietal.

P

**parish** ['pærɪʃ] *n* **1** REL parroquia. **2** GB *(civil)* municipio.

**parishioner** [pə'rɪʃ°nəʳ] *n* feligrés,-esa.

**park** [pɑːk] *n* parque *m*, jardín *m* público.
▶ *vt (car)* aparcar, estacionar: *I'm parked opposite* he aparcado enfrente.
▶ *vi* aparcar, estacionar.

**parking** ['pɑːkɪŋ] *n (act)* estacionamiento. LOC "No parking" «Prohibido aparcar». COMP parking meter parquímetro.

**parliament** ['pɑːləmənt] *n (assembly)* parlamento.
▶ *n* Parliament GB *(body)* Parlamento; *(period)* legislatura.

**parlor** ['pɑːləʳ] *adj* US → parlour.

**parlour** ['pɑːləʳ] *n* **1** US *(shop)* salón *m*, tienda. **2** *dated (room in house)* salón *m*. COMP parlour game juego de salón.

**parody** ['pærədɪ] *n* parodia.
① *pl* parodies.
▶ *vt* parodiar.
① *pt & pp* parodied, *ger* parodying.

**parole** [pə'rəʊl] *n* libertad *f* condicional.
▶ *vt* poner en libertad condicional.

**parquet** ['pɑːkeɪ] *n* parqué *m*.

**parrot** ['pærət] *n* loro, papagayo.

**parsimonious** [pɑːsɪ'məʊɪəs] *adj fml* mezquino,-a, tacaño,-a.

Parsimonious no significa 'parsimonioso (lento)', que se traduce por slow.

**parsley** ['pɑːslɪ] *n* perejil *m*.

**parsnip** ['pɑːsnɪp] *n* chirivía.

**part** [pɑːt] *n* **1** *(gen)* parte *f*: *we spent part of the day on the beach* pasamos parte del día en la playa. **2** *(component)* pieza. **3** *(of serial, programme)* capítulo. **4** *(measure)* parte *f*. **5** *(in play, film)* papel *m*: *she plays the part of Scarlett* hace el papel de Scarlett. **6** *(role, share, involvement)* papel *m*, parte *f*: *I want no part in your dodgy deals* no quiero saber nada de tus negocios sucios. LOC for my part por mi parte, en cuanto a mí. I in part en parte. I the best part of / the better part of la mayor parte de, casi todo,-a. I to play a part in desempeñar un papel en.
▶ *adv* en parte.
▶ *adj* parcial.
▶ *vt (separate)* separar (from, de).

▶ *vi* **1** *(separate)* separarse; *(say goodbye)* despedirse: *they parted as friends* se separaron amistosamente. **2** *(open - lips, curtains)* abrirse.
▶ *n pl* parts *(area)* zona, parajes *mpl*.
◆ **to part with** *vt insep* desprenderse de, separarse de.

**partial** ['pɑːʃ°l] *adj* **1** *(not complete)* parcial. **2** *(biased)* parcial. LOC to be partial to STH ser aficionado,-a a ALGO.

**participant** [pɑː'tɪsɪpənt] *n (gen)* participante *mf*; *(in competition)* concursante *mf*.

**participate** [pɑː'tɪsɪpeɪt] *vi* participar (in, en).

**participation** [pɑːtɪsɪ'peɪʃ°n] *n* participación *f*.

**participle** ['pɑːtɪsɪp°l] *n* participio.

**particle** ['pɑːtɪk°l] *n* partícula.

**particular** [pə'tɪkjʊləʳ] *adj* **1** *(special)* particular, especial: *for no particular reason* por nada en especial. **2** *(specific)* concreto, particular. **3** *(fussy)* exigente, especial.
▶ *n pl* particulars *(of event, thing)* detalles *mpl*; *(of person)* datos *mpl* personales.

Particular no significa 'particular (privado)', que se traduce por private.

**particularly** [pə'tɪkjʊləlɪ] *adv* especialmente, particularmente.

**partly** ['pɑːtlɪ] *adv* en parte.

**partner** ['pɑːtnəʳ] *n* **1** *(in an activity)* compañero,-a; *(in dancing, tennis, cards, etc)* pareja. **2** COMM socio,-a, asociado,-a. **3** *(spouse)* cónyuge *mf*; *(husband)* marido; *(wife)* mujer *f*; *(in relationship)* pareja, compañero,-a.

**partnership** ['pɑːtnəʃɪp] *n* **1** COMM *(company)* sociedad *f*. **2** *(working relationship)* asociación *f*.

**partridge** ['pɑːtrɪdʒ] *n* perdiz *f*.
① *pl* partridges o partridge.

**part-time** [pɑːt'taɪm] *adj (work, job)* de media jornada, a tiempo parcial.
▶ *adv* media jornada, a tiempo parcial.

**part-timer** [pɑːt'taɪməʳ] *n* trabajador, -ra a tiempo parcial.

**party** ['pɑːtɪ] *n* **1** *(celebration)* fiesta: *birthday party* fiesta de cumpleaños. **2** POL partido. **3** *(group)* grupo.
① *pl* parties.

▶ adj **1** (dress) de fiesta; (mood, atmosphere) festivo,-a. **2** POL (member, leader) del partido.

▶ vi (go to parties) ir a fiestas; (have fun) divertirse.

ⓘ pt & pp **partied**, ger **partying**.

**pass** [pɑ:s] n **1** GEOG (in mountains - gen) puerto, paso (de montaña); (narrow) desfiladero. **2** (official permit) pase m, permiso. **3** (in exam) aprobado. **4** SP pase m. COMP **bus pass** abono de autobús.

▶ vt **1** (go past - gen) pasar; (person) cruzarse con: *I passed her in the street* me crucé con ella en la calle. **2** (overtake) adelantar. **3** (cross - border, frontier) pasar, cruzar. **4** (give, hand) pasar: *pass me that screwdriver* pásame ese destornillador. **5** SP (ball) pasar. **6** (exam, test, examinee) aprobar; (bill, law, proposal, motion) aprobar; (censor) pasar. **7** (time) pasar.

▶ vi **1** (go past - gen) pasar; (procession) desfilar; (people) cruzarse: *I was just passing* pasaba por aquí. **2** (overtake) adelantar. **3** (move, go) pasar: *we passed through Zaragoza* pasamos por Zaragoza. **4** SP hacer un pase. **5** (exam, test) aprobar; (bill, motion) ser aprobado,-a. **6** (happen) ocurrir, acontecer, suceder: *it came to pass that ...* sucedió que…

◆ **to pass away** vi (die) pasar a mejor vida.

◆ **to pass by** vi pasar: *she watched the people passing by* miraba pasar a la gente.

▶ vt sep pasar de largo.

◆ **to pass out** vi **1** (faint) desmayarse. **2** MIL graduarse.

▶ vt sep (distribute) repartir.

**passage** ['pæsɪdʒ] n **1** (in street) pasaje m; (alleyway) callejón m; (narrow) pasadizo. **2** (in building - corridor) pasillo. **3** (way, movement - gen) paso; (of vehicle) tránsito, paso. **4** (of time) paso, transcurso. **5** MAR (journey) travesía, viaje m; (fare) pasaje m. **6** (writing, music) pasaje m.

**passenger** ['pæsɪndʒəʳ] n pasajero,-a.

**passer-by** [pɑ:səʳ'baɪ] n transeúnte mf.
ⓘ pl **passers-by**.

**passion** ['pæʃ°n] n pasión f. COMP **passion fruit** granadilla, maracuyá m.

**passionate** ['pæʃ°nət] adj apasionado,-a.

**passionately** ['pæʃ°nətlɪ] adv apasionadamente, fervientemente.

**passive** ['pæsɪv] adj (gen) pasivo,-a.
▶ n LING voz f pasiva.

**passivity** [pæ'sɪvətɪ] n pasividad f.

**passport** ['pɑ:spɔ:t] n pasaporte m.

**password** ['pɑ:swɜ:d] n contraseña.

**past** [pɑ:st] adj **1** (gone by in time) pasado,-a; (former) anterior. **2** (gone by recently) último,-a: *the past few days* los últimos días. **3** (finished, over) acabado,-a, terminado,-a: *summer is past* el verano ha terminado. **4** LING pasado,-a. COMP **past participle** participio pasado. **| past tense** pasado.

▶ n **1** (former times) pasado: *in the past* en el pasado, antes, antiguamente. **2** (of person) pasado; (of place) historia.

▶ prep **1** (farther than, beyond) más allá de; (by the side of) por (delante de): *it's just past the cinema* está un poco más allá del cine. **2** (in time) y: *it's five past six* son las seis y cinco. **3** (older than) más de: *he's past forty* pasa de los cuarenta (años). **4** (beyond the limits of): *it's past my comprehension* me resulta incomprensible.

▶ adv: *a few joggers ran past* pasaron unos haciendo footing.

**pasta** ['pæstə] n pasta, pastas fpl.

**paste** [peɪst] n **1** (mixture) pasta; (glue) engrudo. **2** CULIN pasta, paté m.
▶ vt (stick) pegar; (put paste on) encolar.

**pasteboard** ['peɪstbɔ:d] n cartón m.

**pastel** ['pæst°l] n **1** (chalk) pastel m; (drawing) dibujo al pastel. **2** (colour) color m pastel.
▶ adj (drawing) al pastel; (colour, tone, shade, etc) pastel.

✗ Pastel no significa 'pastel (tarta)', que se traduce por **cake**, **pie**.

**pastime** ['pɑ:staɪm] n pasatiempo.

**pastry** ['peɪstrɪ] n **1** (dough) masa. **2** (cake) pasta, bollo.
ⓘ pl **pastries**.

**pasture** ['pɑ:stʃəʳ] n pasto.

**pasty¹** ['pæstɪ] n CULIN empanadilla.
ⓘ pl **pasties**.

**pasty²** ['peɪstɪ] adj **1** (pale) pálido,-a. **2** (like paste) pastoso,-a.
ⓘ comp **pastier**, superl **pastiest**.

P

**pat** [pæt] n **1** *(tap)* golpecito, palmadita; *(touch)* toque m; *(caress)* caricia. **2** *(of butter)* porción f.
► vt *(tap)* dar palmaditas a; *(touch)* tocar; *(caress)* acariciar.
ⓘ pt & pp **patted**, ger **patting**.

**patch** [pætʃ] n **1** *(to mend clothes)* remiendo, parche m. **2** *(over eye)* parche m. **3** *(area on surface - gen)* trozo, lugar m, zona; *(- of colour, damp, etc)* mancha. **4** *(plot of land)* parcela.
► vt *(mend)* remendar; *(put patch on)* poner un parche a.

**patchwork** ['pætʃwɜːk] n **1** labor f de retales. **2** fig *(of fields)* mosaico.
► adj de retales.

**pâté** ['pæteɪ] n paté m.

**patella** [pə'telə] n rótula.

**patent** ['peɪtªnt] n COMM patente f.
► adj *(obvious)* patente, evidente. COMP
**patent leather** charol m.
► vt COMM patentar.

**paternity** [pə'tɜːnɪtɪ] n paternidad f.

**path** [pɑːθ] n **1** *(track)* camino, sendero: *keep to the path* seguir el camino. **2** *(course of bullet, missile)* trayectoria; *(of flight)* rumbo. LOC **to be on the right path** ir bien encaminado,-a.

**pathetic** [pə'θetɪk] adj patético,-a.

**pathology** [pə'θɒlədʒɪ] n patología.

**pathway** ['pɑːθweɪ] n camino, sendero.

**patience** ['peɪʃªns] n **1** *(quality)* paciencia: *I lost my patience* perdí la paciencia. **2** *(card game)* solitario.

**patient** ['peɪʃªnt] adj *(person - gen)* paciente; *(long-suffering)* sufrido,-a: *be patient with him* ten paciencia con él.
► n paciente mf, enfermo,-a.

**patiently** ['peɪʃªntlɪ] adv pacientemente.

**patio** ['pætɪəʊ] n patio.
ⓘ pl patios.

**patriarch** ['peɪtrɪɑːk] n patriarca m.

**patrician** [pə'trɪʃªn] adj patricio,-a.
► n patricio.

**patrimony** ['pætrɪmənɪ] n patrimonio.

**patriot** ['peɪtrɪət] n patriota mf.

**patriotic** [pætrɪ'ɒtɪk] adj patriótico,-a.

**patrol** [pə'trəʊl] n patrulla. LOC **to be on patrol** patrullar, estar de patrulla.

► vt *(area)* patrullar por, estar de patrulla en.
ⓘ pt & pp **patrolled** (US **patroled**), ger **patrolling** (US **patroling**).

**patron** ['peɪtrən] adj **1** *(customer)* cliente, -a habitual, parroquiano,-a. **2** *(sponsor)* patrocinador,-ra, mecenas m. COMP **patron saint** patrón m.

❎ Patron no significa 'patrón (jefe)', que se traduce por boss.

**pattern** ['pætªn] n **1** *(decorative design)* diseño, dibujo; *(on fabric)* diseño, estampado. **2** *(way something develops)* orden m, estructura: *behaviour pattern* patrón de conducta. **3** *(example, model)* ejemplo, modelo. **4** *(for sewing, knitting)* patrón m; *(sample)* muestra.

**pause** [pɔːz] n **1** *(gen)* pausa; *(silence)* silencio; *(rest)* descanso. **2** MUS pausa.
► vi *(gen)* hacer una pausa; *(stop moving)* detenerse.

**pavement** ['peɪvmənt] n GB acera. **2** US calzada, pavimento.

**paving** ['peɪvɪŋ] n pavimento. COMP **paving stone** baldosa, losa.

**paw** [pɔː] n **1** ZOOL *(foot)* pata; *(claw - of big cats)* zarpa, garra. **2** fam *(person's hand)* manaza.

**pawn** [pɔːn] n **1** *(in chess)* peón m. **2** *(unimportant person)* juguete m, marioneta, títere m.

**pawnshop** ['pɔːnʃɒp] n casa de empeños.

**pawpaw** ['pɔːpɔː] n papaya.

**pay** [peɪ] n *(wages)* paga, sueldo, salario. COMP **pay phone** teléfono público.
► vt **1** *(gen)* pagar; *(bill, debt)* pagar, saldar: *I paid him 10 pounds to mend my bike* le pagué 10 libras para que me arreglara la bici. **2** *(make, give - attention)* prestar; *(homage, tribute)* rendir; *(respects)* presentar, ofrecer; *(compliment, visit, call)* hacer. **3** FIN *(make, give - interest, dividends)* dar. **4** *(be worthwhile)* compensar, convenir: *it'll pay you to keep your mouth shut* te conviene no decir ni pío. LOC **to pay attention** prestar atención.
► vi **1** *(gen)* pagar: *you don't have to pay to go in* no hay que pagar para entrar. **2** fig

*(suffer)* pagar **(for, -)**: *he'll pay for this!* ¡me las pagará! **3** *(be profitable - business, etc)* ser rentable, ser factible. **4** *(be worthwhile)* compensar, convenir. [LOC] **to get paid** cobrar. I **to pay in advance** pagar por adelantado. I **to pay cash / pay in cash** pagar al contado, pagar en efectivo.

◆ **to pay back** *vt sep* **1** *(money)* devolver, reembolsar; *(loan, mortgage)* pagar. **2** *fig (take revenge on)* hacer pagar a: *I'll pay you back for this!* ¡te haré pagar por esto!

◆ **to pay off** *vt sep* **1** *(debt)* saldar, liquidar, cancelar; *(loan)* pagar; *(mortgage)* acabar de pagar. **2** *(worker)* dar el finiquito a.

▶ *vi (be successful)* dar resultado; *(prove worthwhile)* valer la pena.

ⓘ *pt & pp* **paid** [peɪd].

**payment** ['peɪmənt] *n* **1** *(paying)* pago. **2** *(instalment)* plazo.

**payroll** ['peɪrəʊl] *n* nómina.

**pea** [piː] *n* guisante *m*.

**peace** [piːs] *n* **1** *(not war)* paz *f*. **2** *(tranquillity)* paz *f*, tranquilidad *f*: *I just want a bit of peace and quiet* solo quiero un poco de paz y de tranquilidad. [LOC] **at peace / in peace** en paz. I **to make one's peace with SB** hacer las paces con ALGN.

**peaceful** ['piːsfʊl] *adj* **1** *(non-violent)* pacífico,-a. **2** *(calm)* tranquilo,-a.

**peacefully** ['piːsfʊlɪ] *adv (quietly)* tranquilamente; *(non violently)* pacíficamente.

**peacetime** ['piːstaɪm] *n* tiempos *mpl* de paz.

**peach** [piːtʃ] *n* **1** *(fruit)* melocotón *m*. **2** *(colour)* (color *m*) melocotón *m*.

▶ *adj* de color melocotón. [COMP] **peach tree** melocotonero.

**peacock** ['piːkɒk] *n* pavo real.

**peak** [piːk] *n* **1** GEOG *(of mountain)* pico; *(summit)* cima, cumbre *f*. **2** *fig (highest point)* cumbre *f*, punto álgido; *(climax)* apogeo. **3** *(of cap)* visera. [LOC] **peak hours** horas *fpl* punta.

▶ *adj (maximum)* máximo,-a.

▶ *vi* alcanzar el punto máximo.

**peaked** [piːkt] *adj (cap)* con visera.

**peanut** ['piːnʌt] *n* cacahuete *m*.

▶ *n pl* **peanuts** *(small amount)* una miseria.

**pear** [peər] *n (fruit)* pera. [COMP] **pear tree** peral *m*.

**pearl** [pɜːl] *n* perla.

**peasant** ['pezənt] *adj* campesino,-a, rural.

▶ *n* **1** *(gen)* campesino,-a. **2** *pej (uncultured person)* inculto,-a, palurdo,-a.

**pebble** ['pebəl] *n* guija, guijarro, china.

**peck** [pek] *n (of bird)* picotazo; *(kiss)* besito.

▶ *vt (bird)* picotear; *(kiss)* dar un besito a.

▶ *vi (bird)* picotear **(at, -)**.

**pectin** ['pektɪn] *n* pectina.

**pectoral** ['pektərəl] *adj* pectoral.

**peculiar** [pɪ'kjuːlɪər] *adj* **1** *(strange)* extraño,-a, raro,-a; *(unwell)* indispuesto,-a. **2** *(particular)* característico,-a **(to, de)**, propio,-a **(to, de)**.

**pedagogy** ['pedəgɒdʒɪ] *n* pedagogía.

**pedal** ['pedəl] *n (gen)* pedal *m*. [COMP] **pedal bin** cubo de la basura con pedal.

▶ *vi* pedalear.

ⓘ *pt & pp* **pedalled** *(US pedaled)*, *ger* **pedalling** *(US pedaling)*.

**pedalo** ['pedələʊ] *n* patín *m*.

ⓘ *pl* **pedalos** o **pedaloes**.

**peddle** ['pedəl] *vt* COMM vender de puerta en puerta.

**pederast** ['pedəræst] *n* pederasta *m*.

**pedestal** ['pedɪstəl] *n* pedestal *m*.

**pedestrian** [pə'destrɪən] *n* peatón, -ona. [COMP] **pedestrian crossing** paso de peatones. I **pedestrian precinct** zona peatonal.

▶ *adj (dull)* pedestre.

**pediatrician** [piːdɪə'trɪʃən] *n* US → **paediatrician**.

**pedigree** ['pedɪgriː] *n (of animals)* pedigrí *m*; *(of people)* linaje *m*.

▶ *adj* de raza.

**pedophile** ['piːdəfaɪl] *n* US → **paedophile**.

**pee** [piː] *n fam* pis *m*, pipí *m*.

▶ *vi fam* hacer pis, hacer pipí.

**peel** [piːl] *n (skin - gen)* piel *f*; *(- of orange, lemon, etc)* corteza, cáscara, monda, mondadura.

▶ *vt* pelar, quitar la piel de.

**P**

► *vi (skin)* pelarse; *(paint)* desconcharse; *(wallpaper)* despegarse.

**peeler** ['piːlər] [also potato peeler] *n* pelapatatas *m*.

**peep¹** [piːp] *n (look)* ojeada, vistazo.
► *vi* espiar, mirar a hurtadillas.

**peep²** [piːp] *n (noise)* pío: *I don't want to hear another peep out of you!* ¡que no te oiga decir ni pío!

**peephole** ['piːphəʊl] *n* mirilla.

**peer** [pɪər] *vi (look closely)* mirar detenidamente (at, -).

**peg** [peg] *n* **1** *(for hanging clothes on)* percha, colgador *m*. **2** TECH clavija.
► *vt* **1** *(clothes)* tender (out, -); *(tent)* fijar con estacas (down, -). **2** *(prices)* fijar, estabilizar.
ⓘ *pt & pp* pegged, *ger* pegging.

**pejorative** [pəˈdʒɒrətɪv] *adj* peyorativo,-a, despectivo,-a.

**pelican** ['pelɪkən] *n* pelícano.

**pelvis** ['pelvɪs] *n* pelvis *f*.

**pen¹** [pen] *n (gen)* pluma; *(ballpoint)* bolígrafo *m*.
► *vt (write - gen)* escribir.
ⓘ *pt & pp* penned, *ger* penning.

> 🖉 Pen es el nombre general que se da a cualquier instrumento que escriba con tinta, por ejemplo, la estilográfica (**fountain pen**), el bolígrafo (**ballpoint pen**) o el rotulador (**felt tip pen**).

**pen²** [pen] *n* corral *m*.

**penal** ['piːnəl] *adj* penal.

**penalty** ['penəltɪ] *n* **1** *(gen)* pena, castigo; *(fine)* multa. **2** SP *(gen)* castigo (máximo); *(football)* penalti *m*. **3** *(disadvantage)* desventaja, inconveniente *m*.
ⓘ *pl* penalties.

**pence** [pens] *n* → penny

**pencil** ['pensəl] *n* lápiz *m*: *write in pencil* escribir con lápiz. COMP **pencil case** plumero, estuche *m* de lápices. ‖ **pencil sharpener** sacapuntas *m*.

**pending** ['pendɪŋ] *adj (waiting to be decided or settled)* pendiente; *(imminent)* próximo,-a, inminente.
► *prep (while awaiting)* en espera de.

**penetrate** ['penɪtreɪt] *vt* **1** *(gen)* penetrar en; *(clothing)* atravesar, traspasar; *(organization)* infiltrarse en. **2** *(understand)* penetrar, entender.
► *vi (sink in)* causar impresión.

**penfriend** ['penfrend] *n* amigo,-a por correspondencia.

**penguin** ['peŋgwɪn] *n* pingüino.

**penicillin** [penɪˈsɪlɪn] *n* penicilina.

**peninsula** [pəˈnɪnsjʊlə] *n* península.

**penis** ['piːnɪs] *n* ANAT pene *m*.
ⓘ *pl* penises o penes ['piːniːs].

**penknife** ['pennaɪf] *n* cortaplumas *m*, navaja.
ⓘ *pl* penknives ['pennaɪvz].

**pennant** ['penənt] *n* banderín *m*.

**penny** ['penɪ] *n* **1** GB penique *m*: *a fifty pence piece* una moneda de cincuenta peniques. **2** US centavo.
ⓘ *pl* penises o pence [pens].

**pennyroyal** [penɪˈrɔɪəl] *n* poleo.

**pension** ['penʃən] *n* pensión *f*.

**pensioner** ['penʃənər] *n* jubilado,-a, pensionista *mf*.

**pentagon** ['pentəgən] *n* pentágono.

> 🌐 El Pentagon (Pentágono) es la sede de la secretaría de Defensa de los Estados Unidos y es sinónimo del poderío militar del país. Fue uno de los objetivos de los famosos atentados perpetrados con aviones de pasajeros el 11 de septiembre de 2001.

**pentathlon** [penˈtæθlən] *n* pentatlón *m*.

**penthouse** ['penthaʊs] *n* ático.

**penultimate** [pɪˈnʌltɪmət] *adj* penúltimo,-a.

**people** ['piːpəl] *n pl* **1** *(gen)* gente *f*, personas *fpl*: *a lot of people* mucha gente; *over a hundred people* más de cien personas; *people say that...* dicen que…, se dice que… **2** *(citizens)* ciudadanos *mpl*; *(inhabitants)* habitantes *mpl*. COMP **old people** los viejos *mpl*, los ancianos *mpl*, la gente *f* mayor. ‖ **the common people** la gente *f* corriente. ‖ **young people** los jóvenes *mpl*, la juventud *f*, la gente *f* joven.
► *n (nation, race)* pueblo, nación *f*.
► *vt* poblar.

> 🖉 Consulta también person.

**pepper** ['pepə$^r$] n **1** *(spice)* pimienta. **2** *(vegetable)* pimiento.
▶ vt CULIN echar pimienta a.

**peppermint** ['pepəmɪnt] n **1** BOT menta. **2** *(sweet)* caramelo de menta.

**per** [pɜ:$^r$] prep por: *100 miles per hour* 100 millas por hora. LOC **as per** de acuerdo con, según. ∥ **per annum** por año, al año. ∥ **per cent** por ciento.

**perceive** [pə'si:v] vt *(see)* percibir, ver; *(notice)* notar; *(realize)* darse cuenta de.

⊠ To perceive no significa 'percibir (dinero)', que se traduce por receive.

**percentage** [pə'sentɪdʒ] n porcentaje m.

**perception** [pə'sepʃ$^ə$n] n **1** *(sense)* percepción f. **2** *(insight)* perspicacia, agudeza. **3** *(way of understanding)* idea.

**perch¹** [pɜ:tʃ] n *(fish)* perca.
ⓘ pl perch o perches.

**perch²** [pɜ:tʃ] n **1** *(for bird)* percha. **2** *(high position)* posición f elevada, posición f privilegiada; *(pedestal)* pedestal m.
▶ vi *(bird)* posarse (on, en); *(person)* sentarse (on, en).

**percolator** ['pɜ:kəleɪtə$^r$] n cafetera eléctrica.

**percussion** [pɜ:'kʌʃ$^ə$n] n percusión f.

**percussionist** [pe'kʌʃ$^ə$nɪst] n percusionista nf.

**perennial** [pə'renɪəl] adj perenne.

**perfect** [*(adj)* 'pɜ:fɪkt; *(vb)* pə'fekt] adj **1** *(gen)* perfecto,-a. **2** *(absolute, utter - fool)* perdido,-a, redomado,-a; *(- gentleman)* consumado; *(- waste of time)* auténtico,-a: *he's a perfect stranger to me* me es totalmente desconocido. **3** LING perfecto,-a.
▶ n LING perfecto.
▶ vt perfeccionar.

**perfection** [pə'fekʃ$^ə$n] n **1** *(state, quality)* perfección f. **2** *(act)* perfeccionamiento. LOC **to do STH to perfection** hacer ALGO a la perfección.

**perfectionist** [pə'fekʃ$^ə$nɪst] n perfeccionista mf.

**perfectly** ['pɜ:fektlɪ] adv **1** *(exactly, faultlessly)* perfectamente. **2** *(absolutely)* totalmente.

**perform** [pə'fɔ:m] vt **1** *(task)* ejecutar, llevar a cabo; *(function)* desempeñar,

hacer, cumplir. **2** *(piece of music)* interpretar, tocar; *(song)* cantar; *(play)* representar, dar; *(role)* interpretar.
▶ vi **1** *(actor)* actuar; *(singer)* cantar; *(musician)* tocar, interpretar; *(dancer)* bailar. **2** *(machine)* funcionar, marchar; *(person)* trabajar.

**performance** [pə'fɔ:məns] n **1** *(of task)* ejecución f, realización f; *(of function, duty)* ejercicio. **2** *(session - at theatre)* representación f, función f; *(- of circus, show, etc)* número, espectáculo. **3** *(action - of song, of musician)* interpretación f; *(- of play)* representación f; *(- of actor)* interpretación f, actuación f. **4** *(of machine)* funcionamiento.

**performer** [pə'fɔ:mə$^r$] n *(gen)* artista mf, actor m, actriz f; *(musician)* intérprete mf.

**perfume** ['pɜ:fju:m] n perfume m.
▶ vt perfumar.

**perhaps** [pə'hæps] adv quizá, tal vez: *perhaps they've got lost* quizá se hayan perdido.

**perimeter** [pə'rɪmɪtə$^r$] n perímetro.

**period** ['pɪərɪəd] n **1** *(length of time)* período, periodo. **2** *(epoch)* época. **3** GEOL período. **4** EDUC *(lesson)* clase f. **5** *(menstruation)* regla, período. **6** US *(full stop)* punto.
▶ adj *(dress, furniture)* de época.

**periodic** [pɪərɪ'ɒdɪk] adj periódico,-a. COMP **periodic table** CHEM tabla periódica.

**periodical** [pɪərɪ'ɒdɪk$^ə$l] adj periódico,-a.
▶ n publicación f periódica.

**peripheral** [pə'rɪfər$^ə$l] adj **1** *(zone, etc)* periférico,-a. **2** *(secondary)* secundario,-a.

**periphery** [pə'rɪfərɪ] n **1** *(of city)* periferia. **2** *(of society)* margen m.

**periscope** ['perɪskəup] n periscopio.

**perish** ['perɪʃ] vi **1** *(die)* perecer, fallecer. **2** *(decay)* estropearse.
▶ vt *(rubber)* deteriorar.

**perishable** ['perɪʃəb$^ə$l] adj perecedero,-a.

**peritonitis** [perɪtə'naɪtəs] n MED peritonitis f.

**perm** [pɜ:m] n fam *(in hair)* permanente f.

**permanent** ['pɜ:mənənt] adj **1** *(lasting - gen)* permanente; *(dye, ink)* indeleble; *(damage)* irreparable. **2** *(job, address)* fijo,-a.

**permission** [pəˈmɪʃᵊn] *n (gen)* permiso; *(authorization)* autorización *f.* LOC **to ask for permission to do STH** pedir permiso para hacer ALGO.

**permit** [*(n)* ˈpɜːmɪt; *(vb)* pɜːˈmɪt] *n* permiso.
▸ *vt (gen)* permitir; *(authorize)* autorizar: *he was not permitted access to the meeting* no se le permitió la entrada a la reunión.
▸ *vi* permitir: *weather permitting* si el tiempo lo permite.
ⓘ *pt & pp* **permitted**, *ger* **permitting**.

**permutation** [pɜːmjuˈteɪʃᵊn] *n* **1** MATH permutación *f.* **2** GB *fam (in football pools)* combinación *f.*

**perpendicular** [pɜːpənˈdɪkjʊləʳ] *adj* **1** MATH perpendicular (to, a). **2** *(upright)* vertical.
▸ *n* perpendicular *f.*

**perpetuity** [pɜːprˈtjuːtɪ] *n* perpetuidad *f.*

**perplexity** [pəˈpleksɪtɪ] *n* perplejidad *f.*

**persecution** [pɜːsɪˈkjuːʃᵊn] *n* persecución *f.*

**perseverance** [pɜːsɪˈvɪərəns] *n* perseverancia.

**persistent** [pəˈsɪstənt] *adj* **1** *(person)* insistente. **2** *(cough, pain, fog)* persistente; *(rain)* continuo,-a, persistente; *(denials, rumours, warnings)* continuo,-a, constante, repetido,-a.

**person** [ˈpɜːsᵊn] *n* **1** *(gen)* persona: *he's a really nice person* es una persona muy simpática. **2** LING persona. LOC **in person** personalmente.

✎ El plural más usual es **people**, pero **persons** se emplea en el lenguaje jurídico.

**personal** [ˈpɜːsᵊnəl] *adj* **1** *(private)* personal, privado,-a: *for personal reasons* por motivos personales. **2** *(own)* particular, personal. **3** *(individual)* personal. **4** *(physical - appearance)* personal; *(hygiene)* íntimo,-a, personal. **5** *(in person)* en persona. LOC **to get personal** hacer alusiones personales. COMP **personal computer** ordenador personal.

**personality** [pɜːsᵊˈnælɪtɪ] *n* **1** *(nature)* personalidad *f.* **2** *(famous person)* personaje *m.*
ⓘ *pl* **personalities**.

**personally** [ˈpɜːsᵊnəlɪ] *adv* **1** *(in person)* personalmente, en persona. **2** *(for my part)* personalmente. **3** *(as a person)* como persona. LOC **to take STH personally** ofenderse.

**personify** [pɜːˈsɒnɪfaɪ] *vt* personificar.
ⓘ *pt & pp* **personified**, *ger* **personifying**.

**perspective** [pəˈspektɪv] *n* **1** ART perspectiva. **2** *fig (view, angle)* perspectiva.

**persuade** [pəˈsweɪd] *vt* persuadir, convencer: *she's easily persuaded* se deja convencer fácilmente.

**persuasion** [pəˈsweɪʒᵊn] *n* **1** *(act)* persuasión *f.* **2** *(ability)* persuasiva.

**perturb** [pəˈtɜːb] *vt* perturbar.

**Peru** [pəˈruː] *n* Perú.

**Peruvian** [pəˈruːvɪən] *adj* peruano,-a.
▸ *n (person)* peruano,-a.

**perversion** [pəˈvɜːʃᵊn] *n* **1** *(sexual)* perversión *f.* **2** *(distortion)* tergiversación *f*, distorsión *f.*

**perversity** [pəˈvɜːsɪtɪ] *n (wickedness)* perversidad *f*; *(stubbornness)* terquedad *f.*
ⓘ *pl* **perversities**.

**pessimist** [ˈpesɪmɪst] *n* pesimista *mf.*

**pessimistic** [pesɪˈmɪstɪk] *adj* pesimista.

**pest** [pest] *n* **1** plaga: *greenfly and other pests* pulgones y otras plagas. **2** *fam (person)* pelma *mf*, pesado,-a; *(thing)* lata, rollo.

☒ Pest no significa 'peste (mal olor)', que se traduce por **stink**.

**pester** [ˈpestəʳ] *vt* molestar.

**pesticide** [ˈpestɪsaɪd] *n* pesticida.

**pet** [pet] *n (tame animal)* animal *m* de compañía, mascota. COMP **teacher's pet** enchufado,-a.
▸ *adj* **1** *(kind person)* sol, cielo; *(term of affection)* cariño, cielo. **2** *(tame)* domesticado,-a. **3** *(favourite - theory, subject, etc)* favorito,-a. COMP **pet name** nombre *m* cariñoso.
▮ **pet shop** tienda de animales.
▸ *vt (animal)* acariciar.
▸ *vi fam* tocarse y besuquearse.
ⓘ *pt & pp* **petted**, *ger* **petting**.

**petal** [ˈpetᵊl] *n* pétalo.

**petiole** [ˈpetɪəʊl] *n* pecíolo.

**petition** [pəˈtɪʃᵊn] *n* **1** petición *f*, solicitud *f.* **2** JUR demanda.

▶ *vt* presentar una solicitud a.
▶ *vi* solicitar (for, -).

**petrochemical** [petrəʊˈkemɪkᵊl] *adj* petroquímico,-a.

**petrol** [ˈpetrəl] *n* gasolina. COMP **petrol pump** surtidor *m* de gasolina. ‖ **petrol station** gasolinera.

⊠ Petrol no significa 'petróleo', que se traduce por **oil**.

**petroleum** [pəˈtrəʊlɪəm] *n* petróleo. COMP **petroleum jelly** vaselina.

**petticoat** [ˈpetɪkəʊt] *n* (underskirt) enaguas *fpl*; (slip) enagua, combinación *f*.

**petty** [ˈpetɪ] *adj* **1** (trivial) insignificante, sin importancia. **2** (mean) mezquino, -a. COMP **petty cash** dinero para gastos *mpl* menores.
ⓘ *comp* **pettier**, *superl* **pettiest**.

**petulant** [ˈpetjʊlənt] *adj* malhumorado,-a.

⊠ Petulant no significa 'petulante', que se traduce por **vain**.

**pew** [pjuː] *n* banco de iglesia.

**phalange** [ˈfælændʒ] *n* falange *f*.

**phallus** [ˈfæləs] *n* falo.

**phantom** [ˈfæntəm] *n* (ghost) fantasma *m*.
▶ *adj* (imaginary) ilusorio,-a.

**Pharaoh** [ˈfeərəʊ] *n* faraón *m*.

**pharmaceutical** [fɑːməˈsjuːtɪkᵊl] *adj* farmacéutico,-a.

**pharmacist** [ˈfɑːməsɪst] *n* farmacéutico,-a.

**pharmacy** [ˈfɑːməsɪ] *n* farmacia.
ⓘ *pl* **pharmacies**.

✎ Cuando se trata del establecimiento donde se expenden medicamentos, la palabra más usual es **chemist's**.

**pharyngitis** [færɪnˈdʒaɪtɪs] *n* faringitis *f*.

**pharynx** [ˈfærɪŋks] *n* faringe *f*.

**phase** [feɪz] *n* (gen) fase *f*; (stage) etapa.
▶ *vt* escalonar, realizar por etapas.

**pheasant** [ˈfezᵊnt] *n* faisán *m*.

**phenomenon** [fɪˈnɒmɪnən] *n* fenómeno.
ⓘ *pl* **phenomenons** o **phenomena** [fɪˈnɒmɪnə].

**philately** [fɪˈlætəlɪ] *n* filatelia.

**philharmonic** [fɪlɑːˈmɒnɪk] *adj* filarmónico,-a.

**philology** [fɪˈlɒlədʒɪ] *n* filología.

**philosopher** [fɪˈlɒsəfəʳ] *n* filósofo,-a.

**philosophical** [fɪləˈsɒfɪkᵊl] *adj* filosófico,-a.

**philosophy** [fɪˈlɒsəfɪ] *n* filosofía.

**phobia** [ˈfəʊbɪə] *n* fobia.

**Phoenician** [fəˈniːʃən] *adj* fenicio,-a.
▶ *n* **1** (person) fenicio,-a. **2** (language) fenicio.
▶ *n* fenicio,-a.

**phone** [fəʊn] *n fam* teléfono. COMP **phone book** listín *m*, guía telefónica. ‖ **phone box** cabina telefónica. ‖ **phone call** llamada telefónica. ‖ **phone number** número de teléfono.
▶ *vt* llamar (por teléfono), telefonear.
▶ *vi* llamar (por teléfono), telefonear.

**phonecard** [ˈfəʊnkɑːd] *n* tarjeta telefónica.

**phonetic** [fəˈnetɪk] *adj* fonético,-a.

**phonetics** [fəˈnetɪks] *n* fonética.

**phosphorus** [ˈfɒsfərəs] *n* fósforo.

**photo** [ˈfəʊtəʊ] *n fam* foto *f*.

**photocopier** [ˈfəʊtəʊkɒpɪəʳ] *n* fotocopiadora.

**photocopy** [ˈfəʊtəʊkɒpɪ] *n* fotocopia.
ⓘ *pl* **photocopies**.
▶ *vt* fotocopiar.
ⓘ *pt & pp* **photocopied**, *ger* **photocopying**.

**photoelectric** [fəʊtəʊɪˈlektrɪk] *adj* fotoeléctrico,-a. COMP **photoelectric cell** célula fotoeléctrica, fotocélula.

**photograph** [ˈfəʊtəgrɑːf] *n* fotografía, foto *f*: colour photograph fotografía en color. LOC **to take a photograph of** STH/SB fotografiar ALGO/a ALGN, hacer/sacar/tomar una fotografía de ALGO/ALGN.
▶ *vt* fotografiar.

**photographer** [fəˈtɒgrəfəʳ] *n* fotógrafo,-a.

**photographic** [fəʊtəˈgræfɪk] *adj* fotográfico,-a.

**photography** [fəˈtɒgrəfɪ] *n* fotografía.

**photosynthesis** [fəʊtəʊˈsɪnθəsɪs] *n* fotosíntesis *f*.

**P**

**phrasal verb** [freɪzˤəlˈvɜːb] n verbo compuesto.

✎ Los phrasal verbs son verbos seguidos de una partícula (adverbio, preposición) cuyo significado es muy distinto del significado del verbo por sí solo. Existen multitud de phrasal verbs y su traducción suele plantear bastantes problemas a los estudiantes de inglés. En algunos casos, el verbo es separable, es decir, se pueden colocar complementos entre el verbo y la partícula, y en otros no.

**phrase** [freɪz] n **1** LING frase f, locución f. **2** (expression) frase f, expresión f.
▶ vt (express) expresar.

**physical** [ˈfɪzɪkˤəl] adj **1** (gen) físico,-a, material. **2** (of physics) físico,-a. **3** fam euph (rough) duro,-a: it was a very physical game fue un partido muy duro. LOC physical education educación f física.
▌ physical geography geografía f física.
▶ n (medical examination) reconocimiento médico.

**physician** [fɪˈzɪʃˤən] n médico,-a.

**physicist** [ˈfɪzɪsɪst] n físico,-a.

**physics** [ˈfɪzɪks] n física.

**physiology** [fɪzɪˈblədʒɪ] n fisiología.

**physiotherapist** [fɪzɪəʊˈθerəpɪst] n fisioterapeuta mf.

**physiotherapy** [fɪzɪəʊˈθerəpɪ] n fisioterapia.

**pianist** [ˈpɪənɪst] n pianista mf.

**piano** [pɪˈænəʊ] n (instrument) piano.
ⓘ pl pianos.

**piccolo** [ˈpɪkələʊ] n flautín m.
ⓘ pl piccolos.

**pick¹** [pɪk] n (tool) pico, piqueta.

**pick²** [pɪk] n (choice) elección f, selección f: take your pick elige el que quieras, escoge el que quieras. COMP the pick of the bunch el/la mejor de todos,-as.
▶ vt **1** (choose - gen) elegir, escoger; (team) seleccionar. **2** (flowers, fruit, cotton, etc) coger, recoger. **3** (remove pieces from - gen) escarbar, hurgar; (spots) tocarse. **4** (remove from - hair, etc) quitar. **5** (open - lock) forzar, abrir con una ganzúa. **6** (of birds) picotear.

◆ **to pick on** vt insep (victimize) meterse con; (choose for task) elegir, escoger.

◆ **to pick up** vt sep **1** (lift) levantar; (from floor) recoger; (take) coger; (stitch) coger; (telephone) descolgar: don't forget to pick up all your litter no os olvidéis de recoger toda la basura. **2** (learn - language) aprender; (- habit) adquirir, coger; (- news, gossip) descubrir, enterarse de. **3** (illness, cold) pescar, pillar. **4** (acquire, get) conseguir, encontrar. **5** (collect - person) recoger, pasar a buscar; (- hitchhiker) coger; (- thing) recoger: I'll pick you up at 9.00 pm te vendré a buscar a las nueve.

**pickaxe** [ˈpɪkæks] n GB pico, piqueta.

**picket** [ˈpɪkɪt] n **1** (industry) piquete m. **2** (stick) estaca.

**pickle** [ˈpɪkˤəl] vt encurtir, conservar en vinagre.
▶ n pl **pickles** (vegetables) encurtidos mpl.

**pickpocket** [ˈpɪkpɒkɪt] n carterista mf.

**pick-up** [ˈpɪkʌp] n (on record player) brazo (del tocadiscos). COMP pick-up truck furgoneta, camioneta.

**picnic** [ˈpɪknɪk] n picnic m.
▶ vi (go on a picnic) ir de picnic; (eat) hacer un picnic.
ⓘ pt & pp picnicked, ger picnicking.

**picnicker** [ˈpɪknɪkər] n excursionista mf.

**picture** [ˈpɪktʃər] n **1** (painting) pintura, cuadro; (portrait) retrato; (drawing) dibujo, grabado; (illustration) ilustración f, lámina; (photograph) fotografía, foto f: he painted her picture la retrató; I took a picture of them les saqué una foto. **2** (account, description) descripción f; (mental picture) imagen f, idea, impresión f. **3** TV (quality of image) imagen f. **4** GB (film) película. LOC to take a picture hacer una foto. COMP picture book libro ilustrado. ▌ picture window ventanal m.
▶ vt **1** (imagine) imaginarse, verse: I can't picture them married no me los imagino casados. **2** (paint) pintar; (draw) dibujar.
▶ n pl the **pictures** GB el cine: we went to the pictures fuimos al cine.

**pie** [paɪ] n CULIN (sweet) pastel m, tarta; (savoury) pastel m, empanada.

**piece** [piːs] n **1** (bit - large) trozo, pedazo; (small) cacho; (of broken glass) fragmento.

**2** *(part, component)* pieza, parte *f: a thirty-piece dinner service* una vajilla de treinta piezas. **3** *(coin)* moneda. **4** *(in board games)* ficha. **5** *(in newspaper)* artículo. **6** *(item, example of)* pieza: *a piece of advice* un consejo; *a piece of chalk* una tiza; *a piece of furniture* un mueble; *a piece of news* una noticia; *a piece of paper* un papel; *a piece of work* un trabajo. [LOC] **in one piece** *(unharmed)* sano,-a y salvo,-a. ‖ **to be in pieces 1** *(broken)* estar hecho,-a pedazos. **2** *(dismantled)* estar desmontado,-a. ‖ **to break STH in pieces** hacer ALGO pedazos.

**pier** [pɪəʳ] *n* **1** *(landing place)* muelle *m*, embarcadero. **2** ARCH *(pillar)* pilar *m*, estribo.

**pierce** [pɪəs] *vt* **1** *(make hole in)* perforar, agujerear; *(go through)* atravesar, traspasar. **2** *(of light, sound)* penetrar, traspasar.

**piercing** ['pɪəsɪŋ] *adj (sound)* agudo,-a; *(scream)* desgarrador,-ra; *(look)* penetrante; *(wind)* cortante.

**piety** ['paɪətɪ] *n* piedad *f*.

**pig** [pɪg] *n* **1** ZOOL cerdo, puerco, marrano. **2** *pej (ill-mannered person)* cerdo, puerco, cochino; *(glutton)* glotón,-ona, tragón,-ona, comilón,-ona.

**pigeon** ['pɪdʒɪn] *n (bird)* paloma; *(for eating)* pichón *m*.

**pigeonhole** ['pɪdʒɪnhəʊl] *n* casilla.
▸ *vt* encasillar.

**piggy** ['pɪgɪ] *n* cerdito. [COMP] **piggy bank** hucha (en forma de cerdito).
ⓘ *pl* piggies.

**piglet** ['pɪglət] *n* cerdito, cochinillo.

**pigment** ['pɪgmənt] *n* pigmento.

**pigsty** ['pɪgstaɪ] *n* pocilga.
ⓘ *pl* pigsties.

**pigtail** ['pɪgteɪl] *n* coleta.

**pilchard** ['pɪltʃəd] *n* sardina.

**pile¹** [paɪl] *n* **1** *(heap)* montón *m*, pila. **2** *fam (a lot of)* montón *m*, pila: *I've got a pile of essays to mark* tengo que corregir un montón de redacciones.
▸ *vt* **1** *(form a pile)* amontonar, apilar. **2** *(fill)* llenar, colmar: *the sink was piled high with dishes* el fregadero estaba lleno de platos.
▸ *n pl* **piles of** montones *mpl* de.

**pile²** [paɪl] *n* ARCH pilote *m*, pilar *m*.

**pilgrim** ['pɪlgrɪm] *n* peregrino,-a.

**pilgrimage** ['pɪlgrɪmɪdʒ] *n* peregrinación *f*.

**pill** [pɪl] *n (gen)* píldora, pastilla.

**pillow** ['pɪləʊ] *n* almohada.

**pillowcase** ['pɪləʊkeɪs] *n* funda de almohada.

**pilot** ['paɪlət] *n* **1** AV piloto *mf*. **2** MAR práctico *mf*. **3** *(TV or radio programme)* programa *m* piloto. [COMP] **pilot light** piloto.
▸ *adj* piloto, experimental.
▸ *vt* **1** *(ship, etc)* pilotar. **2** *(guide)* dirigir. **3** *(test)* poner a prueba.

**pimento** [pɪ'mentəʊ] *n* pimiento morrón.
ⓘ *pl* pimentos.

**pimp** [pɪmp] *n* chulo, proxeneta *mf*.

**pimple** ['pɪmpªl] *n (spot)* grano.

**pin** [pɪn] *n* **1** *(gen)* alfiler *m*. **2** *(badge, brooch)* insignia, pin *m*, alfiler *m*. **3** TECH *(peg, dowel)* clavija, espiga. **4** ELEC polo: *a two-pin plug* una clavija de dos patillas. [COMP] **pins and needles** hormigueo.
▸ *vt* **1** *(garment, hem, seam)* prender (con alfileres); *(papers, etc together)* sujetar (con un alfiler); *(notice on board, etc)* clavar (up, -); *(hair)* recoger (up,-). **2** *(person)* inmovilizar; *(arms)* sujetar.
▸ *n pl* **pins** *fam (legs)* patas *fpl*.
◆ **to pin up** *vt sep* clavar (con chinchetas), sujetar (con alfileres).
ⓘ *pt & pp* pinned, *ger* pinning.

**pinafore** ['pɪnəfɔːʳ] *n (apron)* delantal *m*. [COMP] **pinafore dress** pichi *m*.

**pinball** ['pɪnbɔːl] *n* flipper *m*.

**pincer** ['pɪnsəʳ] *n (of crab, etc)* pinza.
▸ *n pl* **pincers** *(tool)* tenaza, tenazas *fpl*.

**pinch** [pɪntʃ] *n* **1** *(nip)* pellizco. **2** *(small amount)* pizca.
▸ *vt* **1** *(nip)* pellizcar; *(shoes)* apretar. **2** *fam (steal)* birlar, afanar, robar.

ⓧ To pinch no significa 'pinchar', que se traduce por **to prick**.

**pine¹** [paɪn] *n* BOT *(tree, wood)* pino.
▸ *adj* de pino. [COMP] **pine cone** piña. ‖ **pine nut** piñón *m*.
◆ **to pine away** *vi* consumirse, morirse de pena.

**pineapple** ['paɪnæpªl] *n* piña.

**ping-pong** ['pɪŋpɒn] *n* tenis *m* de mesa, ping-pong *m*.

**pinion**['pɪnɪən] *n* TECH piñón *m*.

**pink** [pɪŋk] *adj* (de color) rosa, rosado,-a. LOC **to go pink / turn pink** ponerse colorado,-a.
  ► *n* **1** *(colour)* (color *m*) rosa *m*. **2** BOT clavel *m*, clavellina.

**pint** [paɪnt] *n (measurement)* pinta.
  ► *n* **a pint** *fam (of beer)* una cerveza, una jarra. LOC **to go for a pint** ir a tomar una cerveza.

✎ En Gran Bretaña equivale a 0,57 litros; en Estados Unidos equivale a 0,47 litros.

**pioneer** [paɪə'nɪəʳ] *n* pionero,-a.
  ► *vt (policy, industry)* promover; *(technique)* iniciar.

**pious** ['paɪəs] *adj* piadoso,-a.

**pip¹** [pɪp] *n (seed)* pepita.

**pip²** [pɪp] *n (sound)* señal *f* (corta).

**pipe** [paɪp] *n* **1** *(for water, gas, etc)* tubería, cañería, conducto. **2** *(for smoking)* pipa: *he smokes a pipe* fuma en pipa.
  ► *n pl* **pipes** gaita *f sing.*

**pipeline** ['paɪplaɪn] *n (for water)* tubería, cañería; *(for gas)* gasoducto; *(for oil)* oleoducto.

**piper** ['paɪpəʳ] *n* gaitero,-a.

**piping** ['paɪpɪŋ] *n* tubería, cañería.

**piracy** ['paɪʳrəsɪ] *n* piratería.

**piranha** [pɪ'rɑːnə] *n (fish)* piraña.

**pirate** ['paɪʳrət] *n* pirata *m*.
  ► *adj* pirata.
  ► *vt* piratear.

**pirouette** [pɪrʊ'et] *n* pirueta.

**Pisces** ['paɪsiːz] *n* piscis.
  ► *vi* hacer piruetas, piruetear.

**pistachio** [pɪs'tɑːʃɪəʊ] *n* pistacho. COMP **pistachio tree** pistachero.
  ① *pl* **pistachios**.

**pistil** ['pɪstɪl] *n* pistilo.

**pistol** ['pɪstᵊl] *n* pistola.

**piston** ['pɪstᵊn] *n* TECH pistón *m*, émbolo.

**pit¹** [pɪt] *n* **1** *(hole)* hoyo, foso; *(grave)* fosa. **2** *(mine)* mina, pozo. **3** *(mark - on metal, glass)* señal *f*, marca; *(- on skin)* picadura, cicatriz *f*. **4** THEAT *(for orchestra)* foso de la orquesta.
  ► *n pl* **the pits** *(in motor racing)* los boxes *mpl.*

**pit²** [pɪt] *n* US *(seed)* pepita; *(stone)* hueso.

**pitch¹** [pɪtʃ] *n* **1** MUS *(of sound)* tono; *(of instrument)* diapasón *m*. **2** SP *(field)* campo, terreno; *(throw)* lanzamiento. **3** *(degree, level)* grado, punto, extremo. **4** *(position, site)* lugar *m*, sitio; *(in market)* puesto. **5** MAR *(movement)* cabezada. **6** *(slope of roof)* pendiente *f*.
  ► *vt* **1** MUS *(note, sound)* entonar. **2** *fig (aim, address)* dirigir (at, a); *(set)* dar un tono a. **3** *(throw)* tirar, arrojar; *(in baseball)* lanzar. **4** *(tent)* plantar, montar; *(camp)* montar.
  ► *vi* **1** *(fall)* caerse. **2** *(ship, plane)* cabecear. **3** SP *(in baseball)* lanzar.

**pitch²** [pɪtʃ] *n (tar)* brea, pez *f*.

**pitched** [pɪtʃt] *adj (roof)* en pendiente, inclinado,-a. COMP **pitched battle** batalla campal.

**pitcher¹** ['pɪtʃəʳ] *n (of clay)* cántaro.

**pitcher²** ['pɪtʃəʳ] *n* SP pítcher *mf*, lanzador,-ra.

**pitchfork** ['pɪtʃfɔːk] *n* AGR horca.

**pith** [pɪθ] *n* **1** *(of bone, plant)* médula; *(of orange)* piel *f* blanca. **2** *fig* meollo.

**pitiful** ['pɪtɪfʊl] *adj* **1** *(arousing pity - sight)* lastimoso,-a; *(cry)* lastimero,-a. **2** *(arousing contempt)* lamentable.

**pituitary** [pɪ'tjuːɪtᵊrɪ] *adj* pituitario,-a. LOC **pituitary gland** glándula pituitaria.

**pity** ['pɪtɪ] *n* **1** *(compassion)* piedad *f*, compasión *f*: *she gave him some money out of pity* le dio dinero por compasión. **2** *(regret)* lástima, pena. LOC **for pity's sake!** ¡por amor de Dios! ▐ **what a pity!** ¡qué lástima!, ¡qué pena!
  ① *pl* **pities**.
  ► *vt (feel pity for)* compadecerse de, tener lástima de, dar lástima.
  ① *pt & pp* **pitied**, *ger* **pitying**.

**pivot** ['pɪvət] *n* **1** pivote *m*. **2** *fig* eje *m*.

**pixel** ['pɪksəl] *n* píxel *m*.

**pizza** ['piːtsə] *n* pizza.

**pizzeria** [piːtsə'rɪə] *n* pizzería.

**placard** ['plækɑːd] *n* pancarta.

**place** [pleɪs] *n* **1** *(particular position, part)* lugar *m*, sitio: *we visited lots of different places* fuimos a muchos sitios diferentes. **2** *(proper position)* lugar *m*, sitio; *(suitable place)* lugar *m* adecuado, sitio adecuado: *put the book back in its place* devuelve el libro a su sitio. **3** *(building)* lugar *m*, sitio; *(home)* casa, piso: *let's go to my place* vamos a mi casa. **4** *(in book)* página *f*. **5** *(seat)* asiento, sitio; *(at table)* cubierto. **6** *(position, role, rank)* lugar *m*; *(duty)* obligación *f*: *if I were in your place* yo en tu lugar. **7** *(in race, contest)* puesto, lugar *m*, posición *f*; *(in queue)* turno. **8** *(job)* puesto; *(at university, on course)* plaza; *(on team)* puesto. ⎡LOC⎤ **all over the place** por todas partes, por todos lados. ‖ **in place** en su sitio. ‖ **in place of** SB / **in** SB's **place** en el lugar de ALGN. ‖ **out of place** fuera de lugar. ‖ **to take place** tener lugar.
▶ *vt* **1** *(put - gen)* poner; *(- carefully)* colocar: *she placed the vase on the shelf* puso el florero en la estante. **2** *(find home, job for)* colocar. **3** *(rank, class)* poner, situar. **4** *(remember - face, person)* recordar; *(- tune, accent)* identificar. ⎡LOC⎤ **to place an order** hacer un pedido.

**placenta** [pləˈsentə] *n* placenta.
⓵ *pl* placentas o placentae [pləˈsenti:].

**plague** [pleɪg] *n* **1** *(of insects, etc)* plaga. **2** MED peste *f*.
▶ *vt* **1** *(pester)* acosar, asediar. **2** *(afflict)* afligir, asolar, plagar, atormentar.

**plain** [pleɪn] *adj* **1** *(clear)* claro,-a, evidente: *he made it quite plain* lo dejó muy claro. **2** *(straightforward)* franco,-a, directo,-a: *tell me in plain language* dímelo en lenguaje corriente. **3** *(simple, ordinary)* sencillo,-a; *(without pattern)* liso,-a. **4** *(unattractive)* poco agraciado,-a, feúcho,-a. **5** *(chocolate)* sin leche. ⎡LOC⎤ **in plain clothes** vestido,-a de paisano.
▶ *adv* **1** *(absolutely)* totalmente. **2** *(clearly)* claramente, francamente.
▶ *n* GEOG llanura.

**plait** [plæt] *n* trenza.
▶ *vt* trenzar.

**plan** [plæn] *n* **1** *(scheme, arrangement)* plan *m*, proyecto: *a change of plan* un cambio de planes. **2** *(map, drawing, diagram)* plano; *(design)* proyecto; *(for essay)* esquema *m*.
▶ *vt* **1** *(make plans)* planear, proyectar, planificar; *(intend)* pensar, tener pensado: *they plan to get married next year* tienen planeado casarse el año que viene. **2** *(make a plan of - house, garden, etc)* hacer los planos de, diseñar; *(- economy, strategy)* planificar.
⓵ *pt & pp* planned, *ger* planning.

**plane¹** [pleɪn] *n* **1** MATH *(surface)* plano. **2** *fig (level, standard)* nivel *m*. **3** *fam (aircraft)* avión *m*: *they went by plane* fueron en avión.
▶ *adj* plano,-a.

**plane²** [pleɪn] *n* *(tool)* cepillo.
▶ *vt* cepillar.

**plane³** [pleɪn] *n* *(tree)* plátano.

**planet** [ˈplænət] *n* planeta *m*.

**planetarium** [plænɪˈteərɪəm] *n* planetario.
⓵ *pl* planetariums o planetaria [plænɪˈteərɪə].

**plank** [plæŋk] *n* *(of wood)* tablón *m*, tabla.

**plankton** [ˈplæŋktən] *n* plancton *m*.

**planning** [ˈplænɪŋ] *n* planificación *f*.

**plant¹** [plɑ:nt] *n* BOT planta.
▶ *vt* **1** *(flowers, trees)* plantar; *(seeds, vegetables)* sembrar; *(bed, garden, etc)* plantar (with, de). **2** *(bomb)* colocar; *(blow)* plantar; *(kiss)* dar, plantar. **3** *(ideas, doubt)* inculcar, meter.

**plant²** [plɑ:nt] *n* *(factory)* planta, fábrica; *(machinery)* equipo, maquinaria.

**plantation** [plænˈteɪʃən] *n* *(for crops)* plantación *f*.

**plasma** [ˈplæzmə] *n* plasma *m*.

**plaster** [ˈplɑ:stər] *n* **1** *(powder, mixture - gen)* yeso; *(for walls)* revoque *m*, enlucido. **2** MED escayola: *he's got his arm in plaster* tiene el brazo escayolado.
▶ *vt* **1** *(wall, ceiling)* enyesar, enlucir. **2** *(cover, spread)* cubrir (with, de).

**plastic** [ˈplæstɪk] *adj* **1** *(bag, cup, spoon, etc)* de plástico,-a. **2** *(malleable)* moldeable. ⎡COMP⎤ **plastic surgery** cirugía plástica. ‖ **the plastic arts** las artes *fpl* plásticas.
▶ *n* **1** plástico. **2** *fam (credit cards)* tarjetas de crédito.

**Plasticine®** [ˈplæstɪsi:n] *n* GB plastilina.

P

| plate                                                                 286 |

**plate** [pleɪt] *n* **1** *(dish, plateful)* plato. **2** *(sheet of metal, glass)* placa; *(thin layer)* lámina. **3** *(illustration)* grabado, lámina. COMP **number plate** matrícula. ‖ **plate rack** escurreplatos.

**plateau** [ˈplætəʊ] *n* **1** GEOG meseta. **2** *(state)* estancamiento.
ⓘ *pl* plateaus o plateaux [ˈplætəʊz].

**platform** [ˈplætfɔːm] *n* **1** *(gen)* plataforma; *(for speaker)* tribuna, estrado; *(for band)* estrado. **2** *(railway)* andén *m*, vía.

**platinum** [ˈplætɪnəm] *n* platino.

**platonic** [pləˈtɒnɪk] *adj* platónico,-a.

**platoon** [pləˈtuːn] *n* MIL pelotón *m*.

**platypus** [ˈplætɪpəs] *n* ornitorrinco.

**play** [pleɪ] *n* **1** *(recreation)* juego: *children at play* niños jugando. **2** SP *(action)* juego; *(match)* partido; *(move)* jugada. **3** THEAT obra *(de teatro)*, pieza *(teatral)*.
▶ *vt* **1** *(game, sport)* jugar a. **2** SP *(compete against)* jugar contra; *(in position)* jugar de; *(ball)* pasar; *(card)* jugar; *(piece)* mover. **3** MUS tocar. **4** *(joke, trick)* gastar, hacer. **5** THEAT *(part)* hacer el papel de, hacer de; *(play)* representar, dar: *she plays the part of Juliet* hace de Julieta. LOC **to play it cool** hacer como si nada. ‖ **to play the game** jugar limpio.
▶ *vi* **1** *(amuse oneself)* jugar (at, a), (with, con). **2** SP *(at game)* jugar. **3** THEAT *(cast)* actuar, trabajar; *(show)* ser representado,-a. **4** MUS tocar.
◆ **to play about** *vi* juguetear.
◆ **to play around** *vi* *(gen)* juguetear; *(have affairs)* tener líos.

**player** [ˈpleɪəʳ] *n* **1** SP jugador,-ra. **2** THEAT *(actor)* actor *m*; *(actress)* actriz *f*.

**playful** [ˈpleɪfʊl] *adj* juguetón,-ona, travieso,-a.

**playground** [ˈpleɪgraʊnd] *n* patio de recreo.

**playhouse** [ˈpleɪhaʊs] *n* **1** *(theatre)* teatro. **2** *(for children)* casita.

**playing card** [ˈpleɪɪŋkɑːd] *n* carta, naipe *m*.

**playing field** [ˈpleɪɪŋfiːld] *n* campo deportivo.

**playmate** [ˈpleɪmeɪt] *n* compañero,-a de juego, amiguito,-a.

**play-off** [ˈpleɪɒf] *n* SP partido de desempate.

**playpen** [ˈpleɪpen] *n* parque *m* (para niños).

**playtime** [ˈpleɪtaɪm] *n* recreo.

**plead** [pliːd] *vi* suplicar (with, -).
▶ *vt* *(give as excuse)* alegar.

**pleading** [ˈpliːdɪŋ] *adj* *(tone, voice, look)* suplicante.
▶ *n* súplica, ruego.

**pleasant** [ˈplezənt] *adj* **1** *(gen)* agradable; *(surprise)* grato,-a. **2** *(person)* simpático, -a, amable.
ⓘ *comp* pleasanter, *superl* pleasantest.

**please** [pliːz] *vt* *(make happy, be agreeable to)* agradar, gustar, complacer; *(satisfy)* contentar, complacer: *you can't please everyone* no se puede complacer a todos.
▶ *vi* **1** *(satisfy)* contentar, complacer, satisfacer. **2** *(choose, want, like)* querer: *you can do as you please* puedes hacer lo que quieras.
▶ *interj* por favor: *quiet, please* silencio, por favor.

**pleased** [pliːzd] *adj* *(happy)* contento,-a; *(satisfied)* satisfecho,-a. LOC **pleased to meet you!** ¡encantado,-a!, ¡mucho gusto!

**pleasing** [ˈpliːzɪŋ] *adj* agradable, grato,-a.

**pleasure** [ˈpleʒəʳ] *n* placer *m*: *it's a pleasure to be here* es un placer estar aquí. LOC **my pleasure** ha sido un placer. ‖ **to have the pleasure of...** tener el placer de…, tener gusto de… ‖ **with pleasure** con mucho gusto.

**plebeian** [plɪˈbiːən] *adj* **1** HIST plebeyo, -a. **2** *pej* ordinario,-a.

**plentiful** [ˈplentɪfʊl] *adj* abundante.

**plenty** [ˈplentɪ] *n* abundancia.
▶ *pron* mucho,-a, muchos,-as: *we've got plenty of time* tenemos tiempo de sobra.

**pliers** [ˈplaɪəz] *n pl* alicates *mpl*, tenazas *fpl*.

**plinth** [plɪnθ] *n* *(of column, pillar)* plinto; *(of statue)* peana.

**plod** [plɒd] *vi* **1** *(walk slowly)* andar con paso lento. **2** *(work steadily)* hacer laboriosamente.
ⓘ *pt & pp* plodded, *ger* plodding.

**plot¹** [plɒt] *n* **1** *(conspiracy)* conspiración *f*, complot *m*. **2** *(of book, film, etc)* trama, argumento.
▶ *vt* **1** *(plan secretly)* tramar, urdir. **2** *(course, position)* trazar.
▶ *vi* conspirar, tramar, maquinar.
ⓘ *pt & pp* plotted, *ger* plotting.

**plot²** [plɒt]

**plough** [plaʊ] *n* AGR arado.
▶ *vt (land, etc)* arar.

**plow** [plaʊ] *adj* US → plough.

**plug** [plʌg] *n* **1** *(for bath, sink, etc)* tapón *m*. **2** ELEC *(on lead)* enchufe *m*, clavija; *(socket)* enchufe *m*, toma de corriente. **3** *(publicity)* publicidad *f*.
▶ *vt* **1** *(hole, etc)* tapar (up, -). **2** *(publicize)* dar publicidad a, promocionar.
◆ **to plug away** *vt insep* perseverar (at, en).
◆ **to plug in** *vt sep* enchufar.
▶ *vi* enchufarse.
◆ **to plug into** *vt sep* enchufar a.
ⓘ *pt & pp* plugged, *ger* plugging.

**plug-in** [ˈplʌgɪn] *n* plug-in *m*, conector *m*.

**plum** [plʌm] *n* **1** *(fruit)* ciruela. **2** *(colour)* color *m* ciruela. COMP **plum tree** ciruelo.
▶ *adj fam* fantástico,-a.
◆ **to plumb in** *vt sep* instalar, conectar.

**plumber** [ˈplʌməʳ] *n* fontanero,-a.

**plumbing** [ˈplʌmɪŋ] *n* **1** *(occupation)* fontanería. **2** *(system)* tubería, cañería.

**plump** [plʌmp] *adj* regordete, rollizo,-a.

**plunder** [ˈplʌndəʳ] *n* **1** *(action)* pillaje *m*, saqueo. **2** *(loot)* botín *m*.
▶ *vt* saquear, pillar.

**plunge** [plʌndʒ] *n* **1** *(dive)* zambullida, chapuzón *m*. **2** *(fall)* caída, descenso.
▶ *vi* **1** *(dive)* lanzarse, zambullirse; *(fall)* caer, hundirse. **2** *(drop - prices, etc)* caer en picado.
▶ *vt (immerse)* sumergir, hundir; *(thrust)* clavar, meter; *(in despair, poverty, etc)* sumir.

**plural** [ˈplʊərəl] *adj* plural.
▶ *n* plural *m*.

**plus** [plʌs] *prep* más: *four plus five is nine* cuatro más cinco son nueve.
▶ *adj* **1** *(ion, number)* positivo,-a. **2** *(and more)* más de, ALGO más de. **3** *(advantageous)* positivo,-a.
▶ *n* **1** MATH *(sign)* signo más. **2** *(advantage)* ventaja, factor *m* positivo, pro.

**Pluto** [ˈpluːtəʊ] *n* Plutón *m*.

**plutonium** [pluːˈtəʊnɪəm] *n* plutonio.
◆ **to ply with** *vt sep (drink, food)* no parar de ofrecer; *(questions)* asediar a, acosar a.

**ply** [plaɪ] *n (of wood)* chapa; *(of paper)* capa.
ⓘ *pl* plies.

**plywood** [ˈplaɪwʊd] *n* contrachapado.

**pm** [ˈpiːem] *abbr* **(post meridiem)** de la tarde. *it is 5.10 p.m.* son las cinco y diez de la tarde.

**pneumatic** [njuːˈmætɪk] *adj* neumático,-a.

**pneumonia** [njuːˈməʊnɪə] *n* pulmonía.

**poach** [pəʊtʃ] *vt* CULIN *(fish)* hervir; *(eggs)* escalfar.

**poacher** [ˈpəʊtʃəʳ] *n (of game)* cazador,-ra furtivo,-a; *(of fish)* pescador,-ra furtivo,-a.

**pocket** [ˈpɒkɪt] *n* **1** *(gen)* bolsillo. **2** *(small area - of air)* bolsa; *(- of resistance)* foco.
▶ *adj (dictionary, camera, etc)* de bolsillo.
LOC **pocket money** *(for children)* paga, semanada.

**pocketknife** [ˈpɒkɪtnaɪf] *n* navaja.
ⓘ *pl* pocketknives.

**pod** [pɒd] *n* BOT vaina.

**podium** [ˈpəʊdɪəm] *n* podio.
ⓘ *pl* podiums o podia [ˈpəʊdɪə].

**poem** [ˈpəʊɪm] *n* poema *m*, poesía.

**poet** [ˈpəʊɪt] *n* poeta *mf*.

**poetic** [pəʊˈetɪk] *adj* poético,-a.

**poetry** [ˈpəʊətrɪ] *n* poesía.

**point** [pɔɪnt] *n* **1** *(sharp end - of knife, nail, pencil)* punta. **2** *(place)* punto, lugar *m*: *meeting point* punto de encuentro. **3** *(moment)* momento, instante *m*: *at this point* en este momento. **4** *(state, degree)* punto, extremo. **5** *(on scale, graph, compass)* punto; *(on thermometer)* grado. **6** SP *(score, mark)* punto, tanto. **8** *(item, matter, idea, detail)* punto. **9** *(central idea, meaning)* idea, significado: *you've missed the point* no has captado la idea. **10** *(purpose, use)* sentido, propósito: *what's the point?* ¿para qué? **11** *(quality, ability)* cualidad *f*. **12** GEOG punta, cabo. **13** MATH *(in geometry)* punto (de intersección). **14** *(in decimals)* coma: *five point six* cinco coma seis. LOC **to come to the point** ir al grano. COMP **point of view** punto de vista.

**P**

► vi **1** *(show)* señalar: *the girl pointed at the clown* la niña señaló al payaso con el dedo. **2** *fig (indicate)* indicar.

► vt **1** *(with weapon)* apuntar. **2** *(direct)* señalar, indicar.

◆ **to point out** vt sep **1** *(show)* señalar. **2** *(mention)* señalar, hacer notar; *(warn)* advertir.

✎ En el sistema inglés, los millares se separan con una coma y los decimales con un punto, así que *tres mil ochocientos treinta y cinco* se escribiría 3,835 y *treinta y ocho coma veinticinco* se escribiría 38.25.

**pointed** ['pɔɪntɪd] *adj* puntiagudo,-a, en punta.

**pointless** ['pɔɪntləs] *adj (meaningless)* sin sentido; *(useless)* inútil.

**poison** ['pɔɪzᵊn] *n* veneno.

► vt *(harm, kill - person, animal)* envenenar; *(make ill)* intoxicar; *(river)* contaminar.

**poisoning** ['pɔɪzᵊnɪŋ] *n* envenenamiento.

**poisonous** ['pɔɪzᵊnəs] *adj* **1** *(plant, berry, snake)* venenoso,-a; *(drugs, gas)* tóxico, -a. **2** *fig* pernicioso,-a.

**poke** [pəʊk] *n (jab)* empujón *m*, golpe *m*; *(with elbow)* codazo; *(with sharp object)* pinchazo.

**poker** ['pəʊkəʳ] *n (card game)* póquer *m*.

**Poland** ['pəʊlənd] *n* Polonia.

**polar** ['pəʊləʳ] *adj* polar. COMP **polar bear** oso polar.

**polarity** [pəʊ'lærɪtɪ] *n* polaridad *f*.
ⓘ *pl* polarities.

**Pole** [pəʊl] *n* polaco,-a.

**pole¹** [pəʊl] *n (stick, post)* poste *m*, pértiga. COMP **pole vault** salto con pértiga.

**pole²** [pəʊl] *n (electrical, geographical)* polo. LOC **to be poles apart** ser polos opuestos.

**police** [pə'liːs] *n pl (body)* policía *f sing*; *(officers)* policías *mpl*. COMP **police station** comisaría.

✎ Recuerda que el verbo que acompaña a police va en plural.

**policeman** [pə'liːsmən] *n* policía *m*, agente *m* de policía, guardia *m*.
ⓘ *pl* policemen [pə'liːsmən].

**policewoman** [pə'liːswʊmən] *n* policía, agente *f* de policía, guardia.
ⓘ *pl* policewomen [pə'liːswɪmɪn].

**policy** ['pɒlɪsɪ] *n* **1** POL política. **2** *(course of action, plan)* política, estrategia. **3** *(insurance)* póliza (de seguros).
ⓘ *pl* policies.

**polish** ['pɒlɪʃ] *n* **1** *(for furniture)* cera (para muebles); *(for shoes)* betún *m*; *(for floors)* cera, abrillantador *m* (de suelos); *(for nails)* esmalte *m*. **2** *(shine)* lustre *m*, brillo. **3** *fig (refinement)* refinamiento, brillo.

► vt *(floor, furniture)* sacar brillo a, encerar; *(shoes)* limpiar; *(silver, cutlery)* sacar brillo a; *(nails)* pintar con esmalte; *(stone)* pulir.

**Polish** ['pəʊlɪʃ] *adj* polaco,-a.

► *n* **1** *(person)* polaco,-a. **2** *(language)* polaco.

► *n pl* **the Polish** los polacos *mpl*.

**polite** [pə'laɪt] *adj* cortés, educado,-a, cumplido,-a, correcto,-a: *he was very polite to me* me trató con cortesía.
ⓘ *comp* politer, *superl* politest.

**politely** [pə'laɪtlɪ] *adv* cortésmente, educadamente, correctamente.

**politeness** [pə'laɪtnəs] *n* cortesía, educación *f*.

**political** [pə'lɪtɪkᵊl] *adj (gen)* político,-a.

**politician** [pɒlɪ'tɪʃᵊn] *n* político,-a.

**politics** ['pɒlɪtɪks] *n* **1** *(gen)* política: *he's active in politics* es militante (político). **2** *(science)* ciencias *fpl* políticas.

► *n pl (view, opinions)* ideas *fpl* políticas.

**polka** ['pɒlkə] *n (dance)* polca. COMP **polka dot** lunar *m*.

**poll** [pəʊl] *n* **1** *(voting)* votación *f*. **2** *(survey)* encuesta, sondeo.

► vt **1** *(votes - obtain)* obtener. **2** *(ask opinion)* sondear, encuestar.

► *n pl* **the polls** las elecciones *fpl*, los comicios *mpl*. LOC **to go to the polls** acudir a las urnas.

**pollen** ['pɒlən] *n* polen *m*.

**pollination** [pɒlɪ'neɪʒᵊn] *n* polinización *f*.

**polling** ['pəʊlɪŋ] *n* votación *f*. COMP **polling station** colegio electoral.

**pollute** [pə'luːt] *vt* contaminar.

**pollution** [pəˈluːʃ*ə*n] *n* contaminación *f*.

**polo** [ˈpəʊləʊ] *n* SP polo.

**polo-neck** [ˈpəʊləʊnek] *adj (sweater)* de cuello alto, de cuello cisne.

**polyester** [pɒlɪˈestə*r*] *n* poliéster *m*.

**polygamy** [pəˈlɪgəmɪ] *n* poligamia.

**polygon** [ˈpɒlɪgɒn] *n* polígono.

**polytechnic** [pɒlɪˈteknɪk] *n* escuela politécnica, politécnico.

**pond** [pɒnd] *n* estanque *m*.

**pony** [ˈpəʊnɪ] *n* póney *m*, poni *m*.
  ⓘ *pl* ponies.

**ponytail** [ˈpəʊnɪteɪl] *n* cola de caballo.

**pool¹** [puːl] *n* **1** *(of water, oil, blood, etc)* charco; *(of light)* foco. **2** *(pond)* estanque *m*; *(in river)* pozo.

**pool²** [puːl] *n* **1** *(common fund of money)* fondo común; *(in gambling)* bote *m*. **2** *(common supply of services)* servicios *mpl* comunes. **3** US *(snooker)* billar *m* americano.
  ▶ *vt (funds, money)* reunir, juntar; *(ideas, resources)* poner en común.
  ▶ *n pl* **the pools** las quinielas *fpl*.

**poor** [pʊə*r*] *adj* **1** *(person, family, country)* pobre. **2** *(inadequate)* pobre, escaso,-a; *(bad quality)* malo,-a; *(inferior)* inferior: *you've got a poor memory* tienes mala memoria. **3** *(unfortunate)* pobre: *poor Edward* el pobre Edward.
  ▶ *n pl* **the poor** los pobres *mpl*.

**poorly** [ˈpʊəlɪ] *adj (ill)* indispuesto,-a.
  ▶ *adv (badly)* mal: *poorly dressed* mal vestido,-a.

**pop¹** [pɒp] *n* **1** *(of cork)* taponazo. **2** *fam (drink)* gaseosa.
  ▶ *vt* **1** *(burst)* hacer reventar; *(cork)* hacer saltar. **2** *(put)* poner, meter.
  ▶ *vi* **1** *(burst)* estallar, reventar; *(cork)* saltar. **2** *(go quickly)* ir rápidamente.
  ⓘ *pt & pp* popped, *ger* popping.

**pop²** [pɒp] *n* **1** *fam (music)* música pop.
  [COMP] **pop art** pop-art *m*. ‖ **pop star** estrella del pop.

**popcorn** [ˈpɒpkɔːn] *n* palomitas *fpl* de maíz.

**pope** [pəʊp] *n* papa *m*.

**poplar** [ˈpɒplə*r*] *n* BOT álamo.

**poppy** [ˈpɒpɪ] *n* amapola.
  ⓘ *pl* poppies.

**popular** [ˈpɒpjʊlə*r*] *adj* **1** *(well-liked - gen)* popular; *(- person)* estimado,-a; *(- resort, restaurant)* muy frecuentado,-a; *(fashionable)* de moda: *she's popular with her workmates* les cae muy bien a sus compañeras de trabajo. **2** *(of or for general public)* popular; *(prices)* popular, económico,-a.

**popularity** [pɒpjʊˈlærɪtɪ] *n* popularidad *f*.

**population** [pɒpjʊˈleɪʃ*ə*n] *n* población *f*.

**porcelain** [ˈpɔːs*ə*lɪn] *n* porcelana.
  ▶ *adj* de porcelana.

**porch** [pɔːtʃ] *n* **1** *(of church)* pórtico; *(of house)* porche *m*, entrada. **2** US *(veranda)* terraza.

**porcine** [ˈpɔːsaɪn] *adj* porcino,-a.

**porcupine** [ˈpɔːkjʊpaɪn] *n* puerco espín.

**pore** [pɔː*r*] *n* ANAT poro.

**pork** [pɔːk] *n* carne *f* de cerdo. [COMP] **pork butcher** charcutero,-a.

**pornography** [pɔːˈnɒgrəfɪ] *n* pornografía.

**porridge** [ˈpɒrɪdʒ] *n* gachas *fpl* de avena.

**port¹** [pɔːt] *n* *(harbour, town)* puerto.
  ▶ *adj* portuario,-a.

**port²** [pɔːt] *n* *(left side)* babor *m*.

**portable** [ˈpɔːtəb*ə*l] *adj* portátil.

**porter** [ˈpɔːtə*r*] *n* **1** *(in hotel, block of flats)* portero,-a; *(in public building, school)* conserje *m*; *(in hospital)* camillero. **2** *(at station, airport)* mozo, maletero.

**portion** [ˈpɔːʃ*ə*n] *n* *(gen)* porción *f*, parte *f*; *(of food)* ración *f*.
  ◆ **to portion out**

**portrait** [ˈpɔːtreɪt] *n* retrato.

**portray** [pɔːˈtreɪ] *vt* **1** *(painting)* representar, retratar. **2** *(describe)* describir, retratar. **3** *(act)* interpretar.

**portrayal** [pɔːˈtreɪəl] *n* **1** *(painting)* representación *f*. **2** *(description)* descripción *f*. **3** *(acting)* interpretación *f*.

**Portugal** [ˈpɔːtjʊg*ə*l] *n* Portugal.

P

**Portuguese** [pɔ:tjˈgiːz] *adj* portugués, -esa.

▸ *n* **1** *(person)* portugués,-esa. **2** *(language)* portugués *m*.

▸ *n pl* **the Portuguese** los portugueses *mpl*.

**pose** [pəʊz] *n* **1** *(position, stance)* postura, actitud *f*. **2** *pej (affectation)* pose *f*, afectación *f*.

▸ *vt (problem, question, etc)* plantear; *(threat)* representar.

▸ *vi* **1** *(for painting, photograph)* posar. **2** *pej (behave affectedly)* presumir, hacer pose.

[LOC] **to pose as** hacerse pasar por.

**posh** [pɒʃ] *adj* **1** GB *fam (place, area)* elegante, de lujo; *(accent)* refinado,-a. **2** GB *fam (upper-class)* pijo,-a.

**position** [pəˈzɪʃ°n] *n* **1** *(place)* posición *f*. **2** *(right place)* sitio, lugar *m*: they manoeuvred the piano into position colocaron el piano en su lugar. **3** *(posture)* postura, posición *f*. **4** *(on scale, in competition)* posición *f*, lugar *m*, puesto; *(social standing)* categoría social, posición *f*. **5** *(job)* puesto. **6** *(situation, circumstances)* situación *f*, lugar *m*. **7** *(opinion, point of view)* postura, posición *f*. **8** SP posición *f*.

▸ *vt (put in place)* colocar, poner.

**positive** [ˈpɒzɪtɪv] *adj* **1** *(gen)* positivo,-a. **2** *(definite - proof, evidence)* concluyente, definitivo,-a; *(- refusal, decision)* categórico,-a; *(- instruction, order)* preciso,-a. **3** *(effective - criticism, advice)* constructivo,-a; *(- attitude, experience)* positivo,-a. **4** *(quite certain)* seguro,-a (**about**, de): I'm absolutely positive estoy segurísimo.

▸ *n* positivo.

**possess** [pəˈzes] *vt* **1** *(own)* poseer, tener. **2** *(take over - anger, fear)* apoderarse de.

**possession** [pəˈzeʃ°n] *n* **1** *(ownership)* posesión *f*, poder *m*. **2** *(thing owned)* bien *m*, posesión *f*.

**possessive** [pəˈzesɪv] *adj* **1** *(person)* posesivo,-a; *(selfish)* egoísta. **2** LING posesivo,-a.

▸ *n* LING posesivo.

**possessor** [pəˈzesəʳ] *n* poseedor,-ra.

**possibility** [pɒsɪˈbɪlɪtɪ] *n* **1** *(likelihood)* posibilidad *f*. **2** *(something possible)* posibilidad *f*.

ⓘ *pl* possibilities.

**possible** [ˈpɒsɪb°l] *adj* posible. [LOC] **as much as possible** todo lo posible. ▌ **as soon as possible** cuanto antes, lo antes posible.

▸ *n* posible candidato,-a.

**possibly** [ˈpɒsɪblɪ] *adv* **1** *(reasonably, conceivably)* posiblemente: you can't possibly have finished already! ¡no es posible que ya hayas acabado! **2** *(in requests)*: could you possibly give me a lift to the station? ¿me podría llevar a la estación? **3** *(perhaps)* posiblemente, quizás.

**post¹** [pəʊst] *n (of wood)* estaca, poste *m*.

**post²** [pəʊst] *n* **1** *(job)* puesto, empleo; *(important position)* cargo. **2** MIL puesto.

▸ *vt* **1** MIL destinar, apostar. **2** *(employee)* destinar, mandar.

**post³** [pəʊst] *n* GB *(mail)* correo; *(collection)* recogida; *(delivery)* reparto: it's in the post ya está enviado.

▸ *vt* **1** GB *(send - letter, parcel)* mandar por correo, echar al correo; *(put in postbox)* echar al buzón. [COMP] **post office** Correos, oficina de correos.

**postage** [ˈpəʊstɪdʒ] *n* franqueo, porte *m*.

**postal** [ˈpəʊst°l] *adj* postal.

**postbag** [ˈpəʊstbæg] *n* **1** *(sack)* saca (de correos). **2** GB *(letters)* correspondencia.

**postbox** [ˈpəʊstbɒks] *n* GB buzón *m*.

**postcard** [ˈpəʊstkɑ:d] *n* tarjeta postal *f*.

**postcode** [ˈpəʊstkəʊd] *n* GB código postal.

**poster** [ˈpəʊstəʳ] *n* póster *m*, cartel *m*.

**postgraduate** [pəʊstˈgrædjʊət] *n* postgraduado,-a.

▸ *adj* de postgrado.

**postman** [ˈpəʊstmən] *n* cartero. ⓘ *pl* postmen [ˈpəʊstmən].

**postmark** [ˈpəʊstmɑ:k] *n* matasellos *m*.

▸ *vt* timbrar, matasellar.

**postpone** [pəsˈpəʊn] *vt* posponer.

**posture** [ˈpɒstʃəʳ] *n* **1** *(position of body)* postura, pose *f*. **2** *(attitude)* postura.

▸ *vi* hacer poses, adoptar poses.

**postwar** [ˈpəʊstwɔ:ʳ] *adj* de la posguerra.

**postwoman** [ˈpəʊstwʊmən] *n* cartera. ⓘ *pl* postwomen [ˈpəʊstwɪmɪn].

**pot** [pɒt] *n* **1** CULIN *(container)* pote *m*, tarro; *(for cooking)* olla, puchero; *(earthen-*

*ware)* vasija; *(teapot)* tetera; *(coffee pot)* cafetera. **2** *(of paint)* bote *m.* **3** *(flowerpot)* maceta, tiesto.
▶ *vt (plant)* plantar en una maceta.
▶ *n* **the pot** *(in card games)* el bote.

**potassium** [pəˈtæsɪəm] *n* potasio.

**potato** [pəˈteɪtəʊ] *n* patata.
ⓘ *pl* potatoes.

**potential** [pəˈtenʃ[ə]l] *adj* potencial.
▶ *n* potencial *m.*

**potholer** [ˈpɒthəʊlər] *n* GB espeleólo-go,-a.

**potholing** [ˈpɒthəʊlɪŋ] *n* GB espeleolo-gía.

**potter** [ˈpɒtər] *n* alfarero,-a.

**pottery** [ˈpɒtərɪ] *n* alfarería.

**potty** [ˈpɒtɪ] *n* orinal *m.*
ⓘ *pl* potties.

**pouch** [paʊtʃ] *n* **1** *(gen)* bolsa (peque-ña); *(for tobacco)* petaca. **2** ZOOL bolsa abdominal.

**poultry** [ˈpəʊltrɪ] *n* aves *fpl* de corral.

**pounce** [paʊns] *n* salto.
▶ *vi* saltar (on, sobre), abalanzarse (on, sobre).

**pound¹** [paʊnd] *vt* **1** *(crush)* machacar. **2** *(strike, beat)* aporrear, golpear.
▶ *vi* **1** *(strike, beat)* aporrear (at/on, -), golpear (at/on, -); *(of waves)* batir (against, contra). **2** *(heart)* palpitar, la-tir con fuerza.

**pound²** [paʊnd] *n* **1** FIN libra: *a five-pound note* un billete de cinco libras. **2** *(weight)* libra: *half a pound of tomatoes* media libra de tomates.

✎ Como medida de peso equivale a 454 gr.

**pound³** [paʊnd] *n (enclosure - for dogs)* pe-rrera; *(- for cars)* depósito.

**pour** [pɔːr] *vt (liquid)* verter, echar; *(sub-stance)* echar; *(drink)* servir: *she poured the orange juice into a jug* vertió el zumo de naranja en una jarra.
▶ *vi* **1** *(blood)* manar, salir; *(water, sweat)* chorrear. **2** *fig* moverse en tropel. COMP **to pour (down/with rain)** llover a cánta-ros: *it's pouring* está lloviendo a cántaros.

**pouring** [ˈpɔːrɪŋ] *adj (rain)* torrencial.

**poverty** [ˈpɒvətɪ] *n (gen)* pobreza.

**powder** [ˈpaʊdər] *n (dust)* polvo; *(cosmetic, medicine)* polvos *mpl.*
▶ *vt* **1** *(put powder on)* poner polvos, empolvar. **2** *(pulverize)* pulverizar, re-ducir a polvo.

**power** [ˈpaʊər] *n* **1** *(strength, force)* fuerza; *(of sun, wind)* potencia, fuerza; *(of argu-ment)* fuerza. **2** *(ability, capacity)* poder *m,* capacidad *f: it's beyond his power* no está en sus manos. **3** *(faculty)* facultad *f.* **4** *(con-trol, influence, authority)* poder *m; (of country)* poderío, poder *m: the power of the media* el poder de los medios de comunicación. **5** *(nation)* potencia; *(person, group)* fuerza. **6** PHYS *(capacity, performance)* potencia; *(en-ergy)* energía. **7** ELEC electricidad *f,* corriente *f.* **8** MATH potencia: *six to the pow-er of four* seis elevado a la cuarta potencia.
▶ *vt* propulsar, impulsar: *it's powered by electricity* funciona con electricidad.

**powerful** [ˈpaʊəful] *adj* **1** *(strong - athlete, body, current)* fuerte; *(- blow, engine, ma-chine)* potente. **2** *(influential - enemy, na-tion, ruler)* poderoso,-a. **3** *(effective )* im-pactante.

**powerless** [ˈpaʊələs] *adj* impotente.

**practical** [ˈpræktɪk[ə]l] *adj* **1** *(gen)* prác-tico,-a. **2** *(good with hands)* hábil.
▶ *n (lesson)* clase *f* práctica. COMP practi-cal joke broma.

**practically** [ˈpræktɪk[ə]lɪ] *adv* **1** *(almost)* ca-si, prácticamente. **2** *(in a practical way)* de manera práctica.

**practice** [ˈpræktɪs] *n* **1** *(repeated exercise)* práctica; *(training)* entrenamiento: *I'm out of practice* me falta práctica. **2** *(action, reality)* práctica: *in practice* en la práctica. **3** *(custom, habit)* costumbre *f.* LOC **to be out of practice** haber perdido práctica.
▶ *vt & vi* US → **practise**.

**practise** [ˈpræktɪs] *vt* **1** GB *(do repeatedly - language, serve, scales)* practicar; *(song, act)* ensayar. **2** GB *(religion, belief, economy)* practicar. **3** GB *(profession)* ejercer.
▶ *vi* **1** GB *(gen)* practicar. **2** GB *(sports team)* entrenar; *(actors)* ensayar. **3** GB *(profes-sionally)* ejercer (as, de/como).

**pragmatic** [prægˈmætɪk] *adj* pragmá-tico,-a.

**prairie** [ˈpreərɪ] *n* pradera, llanura.

**praise** [preɪz] n **1** alabanza, elogio, loa. **2** REL alabanza.
▸ vt **1** elogiar. **2** REL alabar.

**pram** [præm] n GB cochecito de niño.

**prank** [præŋk] n (trick) broma; (of child) travesura. LOC **to play a prank on SB** gastar una broma a ALGN.

**prawn** [prɔːn] n (large) langostino; (medium) gamba; (small) camarón m.

**pray** [preɪ] vi REL orar, rezar.

**prayer** [preəʳ] n REL (request) oración f, rezo, plegaria; (action) oración f, rezo.

**preach** [priːtʃ] vt **1** REL (gospel) predicar; (sermon) dar, hacer. **2** (advocate) aconsejar.
▸ vi REL predicar.

**preacher** ['priːtʃəʳ] n predicador,-ra.

**precaution** [prɪ'kɔːʃˤn] n precaución f.

**precedent** ['presɪdˤnt] n precedente m.

**preceding** [prɪ'siːdɪŋ] adj anterior.

**precinct** ['priːsɪŋkt] n **1** (of cathedral, hospital, etc) recinto. **2** GB (part of town) zona.
▸ n pl **precincts** recinto m sing.

☒ Precinct no significa 'precinto', que se traduce por seal.

**precious** ['preʃəs] adj **1** (jewel, stone, metal) precioso,-a. **2** (moment, memory, possession) preciado,-a, querido,-a. COMP **precious little** poquísimo,-a.

☒ Precious no significa 'precioso (bonito)', que se traduce por beautiful.

**precipice** ['presɪpɪs] n precipicio.

**precipitation** [prɪsɪpɪ'teɪʃˤn] n **1** fml (haste) precipitación f. **2** METEOR precipitación.

**precise** [prɪ'saɪs] adj preciso,-a.

**precisely** [prɪ'saɪslɪ] adv (exactly) precisamente; (accurately) con precisión. LOC **precisely!** ¡exacto!, ¡eso es!

**precision** [prɪ'sɪʒˤn] n precisión f.

**precocious** [prɪ'kəʊʃəs] adj precoz.

**precooked** [priː'kʊkt] adj precocinado,-a.

**predator** ['predətəʳ] n ZOOL depredador m.

**predecessor** ['priːdɪsesəʳ] n predecesor,-ra, antecesor,-ra.

**predict** [prɪ'dɪkt] vt predecir.

**prediction** [prɪ'dɪkʃˤn] n predicción f.

**predominate** [prɪ'dɒmɪneɪt] vi predominar.

**prefect** ['priːfekt] n **1** (official) prefecto. **2** GB (in school) monitor,-ra.

**prefer** [prɪ'fɜːʳ] vt preferir: she prefers coffee to tea prefiere el café al té.
ⓘ pt & pp **preferred**, ger **preferring**.

**preferable** ['prefˤrəbˤl] adj preferible (to, a).

**preference** ['prefˤrəns] n preferencia (for, por).

**prefix** ['priːfɪks] n LING prefijo.

**pregnancy** ['pregnənsɪ] n embarazo.
ⓘ pl **pregnancies**.

**pregnant** ['pregnənt] n (woman) embarazada; (animal) preñada: she's six months pregnant está embarazada de seis meses.

**preheat** [priː'hiːt] vt precalentar.

**prehistoric** [priːhɪ'stɒrɪk] adj prehistórico,-a.

**prehistory** [priː'hɪstˤrɪ] n prehistoria.

**prejudice** ['predʒədɪs] n **1** (unfavourable bias) prejuicio; (favourable) predisposición f.
▸ vt **1** (influence, bias) predisponer (against, contra), (in favour of, a favor de). **2** (harm) perjudicar.

**prejudiced** ['predʒʊdɪst] adj parcial.

**premature** [premə'tjʊəʳ] adj (gen) prematuro,-a.

**premiere** ['premɪeəʳ] n estreno.

**premises** ['premɪsɪz] n pl local m. LOC **on the premises** dentro del local.

**preoccupy** [priː'ɒkjʊpaɪ] vt (worry) preocupar; (think about too much) pensar demasiado en.
ⓘ pt & pp **preoccupied**, ger **preoccupying**.

**preparation** [prepə'reɪʃˤn] n **1** (action) preparación f. **2** (substance) preparado.
▸ n pl **preparations** preparativos mpl (for, para).

**preparatory** [prɪ'pærətˤrɪ] adj preparatorio,-a, preliminar.

**prepare** [prɪ'peəʳ] vt (gen) preparar; (report) redactar.
▸ vi prepararse (for, para).

**prepared** [prɪ'peəd] adj **1** (gen) preparado,-a. **2** (willing) dispuesto,-a (to, a).

**preposition** [prepə'zɪʃˤn] n preposición f.

**prescribe** [prɪsˈkraɪb] vt **1** (medicine, drugs, etc) recetar; (holiday, rest) recomendar. **2** fml (order) prescribir.

**prescription** [prɪsˈkrɪpʃ°n] n receta (médica).

**presence** [ˈprez°ns] n **1** (gen) presencia; (attendance) asistencia. **2** (spirit) espíritu m.

**present¹** [ˈprez°nt] adj **1** (in attendance) presente. **2** (current) actual. **3** LING presente.
▸ n (now) presente m, actualidad f. LOC **at present** actualmente, en este momento.
▸ n **the present** LING presente m. COMP **present continuous** presente continuo. I **present perfect** presente perfecto. I **present tense** presente.

**present²** [(vb) prɪˈzent; (n) ˈprez°nt] vt **1** (make presentation) entregar, hacer entrega de; (give - as gift) regalar. **2** (offer - report, petition, bill, cheque) presentar; (- argument, ideas, case) presentar, exponer. **3** fml (offer - apologies, respects) presentar; (- compliments, greetings) dar. **4** (give - difficulty, problem) plantear; (constitute) suponer, constituir, ser. **5** (introduce) presentar. **6** (play) representar; (programme) presentar.
▸ n (gift) regalo; (formal) obsequio: he gave me a present me hizo un regalo.

**presentation** [prez°nˈteɪʃ°n] n **1** (of awards, prizes, gifts) entrega. **2** (way of presenting) presentación f. **3** (of play) representación f.

**presenter** [prɪˈzentəʳ] n (on radio) presentador,-ra, locutor,-ra; (on TV) presentador,-ra.

**presently** [ˈprez°ntlɪ] adv **1** GB (soon) pronto, enseguida. **2** US (at present) actualmente.

**preservation** [prezəˈveɪʃ°n] n (of wildlife) conservación f, preservación f; (of food, works of art, buildings) conservación f.

**preservative** [prɪˈzɜːvətɪv] n CULIN conservante m.

**preserve** [prɪˈzɜːv] n CULIN (fruit) conserva; (jam) confitura, mermelada.
▸ vt conservar, proteger.

**preset** [priːˈset] vt programar.
ⓘ pt & pp **preset**, ger **presetting**.

**presidency** [ˈprezɪdənsɪ] n presidencia.
ⓘ pl **presidencies**.

**president** [ˈprezɪd°nt] n presidente,-a.

**press** [pres] n **1** (newspapers) prensa. **2** (machine) prensa, imprenta. **3** (act of pressing) presión f; (of hand) apretón m; (act of ironing) planchado. COMP **press agency** agencia de prensa. I **press conference** conferencia de prensa, rueda de prensa.
▸ vt **1** (push down - button, switch) pulsar, apretar, presionar; (- accelerator) pisar; (- key on keyboard) pulsar; (- trigger) apretar. **2** (squeeze - hand) apretar. **3** (crush - fruit) exprimir, estrujar; (- grapes, olives, flowers) prensar. **4** (clothes) planchar, planchar a vapor. **5** (record) imprimir. **6** (urge, put pressure on) presionar, instar; (insist on) insistir en, exigir.
▸ vi **1** (push) apretar, presionar. **2** (crowd) apretujarse, apiñarse. **3** (urge, pressurize) presionar, insistir; (time) apremiar.

**pressing** [ˈpresɪŋ] adj urgente, apremiante.

**pressure** [ˈpreʃəʳ] n **1** (gen) presión f. **5** (stress) tensión f: he's under a lot of pressure está sometido a una gran presión. COMP **pressure cooker** olla a presión, olla exprés.

**prestige** [presˈtiːʒ] n prestigio.

**prestigious** [presˈtɪdʒəs] adj prestigioso,-a.

**presume** [prɪˈzjuːm] vt suponer, imaginarse, presumir: I presume so supongo que sí.
▸ vi **1** suponer. **2** (venture to) atreverse a.

☒ To presume no significa 'presumir (vanagloriarse)', que se traduce por to boast.

**pretend** [prɪˈtend] vt (feign) fingir, aparentar: the children pretended to be asleep los niños fingían estar dormidos.
▸ vi (feign) fingir.
▸ adj (make-believe) de mentirijillas.

☒ To pretend no significa 'pretender', que se traduce por to want to, to try to.

**pretension** [prɪˈtenʃ°n] n pretensión f.

**pretentious** [prɪˈtenʃəs] adj pretencioso,-a.

**preterite** [ˈpret°rɪt] n LING pretérito.

**pretty** [ˈprɪtɪ] adj (girl, baby) bonito,-a, guapo,-a, mono,-a; (thing) bonito,-a

P

mono,-a: *what a pretty little girl!* ¡qué niña más bonita!

① *comp* **prettier**, *superl* **prettiest**.

▶ *adv* bastante: *I'm pretty sure* estoy bastante seguro,-a. [LOC] **pretty much** más o menos. ❚ **pretty well** casi.

**prevailing** [prɪ'veɪlɪŋ] *adj* predominante.

**prevent** [prɪ'vent] *vt (gen)* impedir; *(avoid - accident)* evitar; *(- illness)* prevenir. [LOC] **to prevent** SB **from doing** STH impedir a ALGN hacer ALGO.

**prevention** [prɪ'venʃ°n] *n* prevención *f*.

**preview** ['priːvjuː] *n* preestreno.

**previous** ['priːvɪəs] *adj* previo,-a, anterior: *the previous day* el día anterior.

**prey** [preɪ] *n* **1** *(animal)* presa. **2** *fig* presa, víctima.

**price** [praɪs] *n* **1** *(gen)* precio; *(amount)* importe *m*; *(value)* valor *m*: *what's the price of this jacket?* ¿qué precio tiene esta chaqueta? **2** *fig (cost, sacrifice)* precio. [LOC] **at any price** a toda costa, cueste lo que cueste.

▶ *vt (fix price of)* tener un precio; *(value)* valorar, tasar; *(mark price on)* poner el precio a.

**priceless** ['praɪsləs] *adj* que no tiene precio, inestimable.

**pricey** ['praɪsɪ] *adj fam* caro,-a.

① *comp* **pricier**, *superl* **priciest**.

**prick** [prɪk] *n (pain)* pinchazo; *(hole)* agujero.

▶ *vt (with needle, pin, fork)* pinchar.

▶ *vi (pin, thorn)* pinchar; *(itch, sting)* escocer, picar.

**prickly** ['prɪkl°ɪ] *adj* **1** *(plant)* espinoso,-a; *(animal)* con púas; *(wool, sweater)* que pica. **2** *(irritable, touchy)* enojadizo,-a, irritable, difícil.

① *comp* **pricklier**, *superl* **prickliest**.

**pride** [praɪd] *n* **1** *(gen)* orgullo; *(self-respect)* amor *m* propio. **2** *(arrogance)* soberbia, orgullo.

**priest** [priːst] *n* sacerdote *m*, cura *m*.

**priestess** ['priːstes] *n* sacerdotisa.

**priesthood** ['priːsθ°ʊd] *n (clergy)* clero; *(office)* sacerdocio.

**primary** ['praɪmərɪ] *adj* **1** *(main)* principal, fundamental. **2** *(first, basic)* prima-

rio,-a. [COMP] **primary school** escuela primaria.

**primate** ['praɪmeɪt] *n* ZOOL primate *m*.

**prime** [praɪm] *adj* **1** *(main, chief)* principal, primero,-a. **2** *(first-rate - meat)* de primera (calidad); *(example, location)* excelente.

▶ *n (best time of life)* flor *f* de la vida. [COMP] **Prime Minister** primer,-a ministro,-a.

▶ *vt* **1** *(engine, pump, bomb)* cebar; *(surface, wood)* imprimar, preparar. **2** *fig (person)* preparar, enseñar.

**primitive** ['prɪmɪtɪv] *adj (man, tribe, culture)* primitivo,-a; *(tool, method, shelter)* rudimentario,-a, primitivo,-a.

**prince** [prɪns] *n* príncipe *m*.

**princess** ['prɪnses] *n* princesa.

① *pl* **princesses**.

**principal** ['prɪnsɪp°l] *adj* principal.

▶ *n* **1** EDUC director,-ra. **2** THEAT protagonista *mf*, primera figura.

**principle** ['prɪnsɪp°l] *n* **1** *(basic idea, rule, law)* principio; *(basis)* base *f*. **2** *(moral rule)* principio: *it's a matter of principle* es cuestión de principios.

**print** [prɪnt] *n* **1** *(lettering)* letra: *in large print* en letra grande. **2** *(photo)* copia. **3** *(printed fabric)* estampado. **4** *(mark - of finger, foot)* huella.

▶ *vt* **1** *(book, page, poster, etc)* imprimir; *(publish)* publicar, editar. **2** *(photo - negative)* imprimir; *(- copy)* sacar una copia de. **3** *(write clearly)* escribir con letra de imprenta. **4** *(fabric)* estampar. **5** *(make impression)* marcar.

◆ **to print out** *vt sep* imprimir.

**printer** ['prɪntər] *n (person)* impresor,-ra; *(machine)* impresora.

**printing** ['prɪntɪŋ] *n (act, process)* impresión *f*; *(industry)* imprenta. [COMP] **printing press** prensa.

**print-out** ['prɪntaʊt] *n* COMPUT impresión *f*.

**prior** ['praɪər] *adj* anterior, previo,-a. [LOC] **prior to** antes de.

**priority** [praɪ'ɒrɪtɪ] *n* prioridad *f*.

① *pl* **priorities**.

▶ *adj* prioritario,-a.

**prism** [prɪz°m] *n* prisma.

**prison** ['prɪzᵊn] *n* prisión *f*, cárcel *f*: *he's in prison* está en la cárcel.

**prisoner** ['prɪzᵊnəʳ] *n* (*in jail*) preso,-a, recluso,-a; (*captive*) prisionero,-a.

**privacy** ['praɪvəsɪ] *n* privacidad *f*.

**private** ['praɪvət] *adj* **1** (*own, for own use - property, house, class*) particular; (*- letter, income*) personal. **2** (*confidential*) privado, -a, confidencial. **3** (*not state-controlled*) privado,-a. **4** (*not official*) privado,-a, personal. **5** (*person*) reservado,-a. COMP
**private eye** detective *mf* privado,-a.
▶ *n* MIL soldado raso.

**privatize** ['praɪvətaɪz] *vt* privatizar.

**privilege** ['prɪvɪlɪdʒ] *n* privilegio.

**prize** [praɪz] *n* (*gen*) premio.
▶ *adj* (*having won a prize*) premiado,-a; (*excellent*) de primera, selecto,-a.

**probability** [prɒbə'bɪlɪtɪ] *n* probabilidad *f*.
ⓘ *pl* probabilities.

**probable** ['prɒbəbᵊl] *adj* probable.

**probably** ['prɒbəblɪ] *adv* probablemente: *it'll probably rain* es probable que llueva.

**probation** [prə'beɪʃᵊn] *n* **1** JUR libertad *f* condicional. **2** (*in employment*) período de prueba.

**probe** [prəʊb] *n* **1** MED sonda. **2** (*investigation*) investigación *f*.
▶ *vt* **1** MED sondar. **2** (*investigate - gen*) investigar; (*public opinion*) sondear.

✗ To probe no significa 'probar (demostrar o catar)', que se traducen por **to prove** o **to taste**.

**problem** ['prɒbləm] *n* problema *m*: *no problem!* ¡no hay problema!, ¡ningún problema!

**procedure** [prə'siːdʒəʳ] *n* (*set of actions*) procedimiento; (*step*) trámite *m*, gestión *f*.

**proceed** [prə'siːd] *vi* **1** (*continue*) seguir, continuar. **2** (*progress*) marchar. **3** *fml* (*go along*) avanzar, circular; (*go towards*) dirigirse a.

✗ To proceed no significa 'proceder (venir de)', que se traduce por **to come from**.

**proceedings** [prə'siːdɪŋz] *n pl* **1** (*events at meeting, ceremony, etc*) actos *mpl*. **2** JUR (*lawsuit*) proceso *sing*.

**process** ['prəʊses] *n* **1** (*set of actions, changes*) proceso: *the process of growing old* el envejecimiento. **2** (*method*) procedimiento, proceso.
▶ *vt* **1** (*raw material, food*) procesar, tratar; (*film*) revelar. **2** (*deal with*) ocuparse de, tramitar. **3** COMPUT procesar, tratar.

**processing** ['prəʊsesɪŋ] *n* **1** (*treatment*) procesamiento, tratamiento; (*of film*) revelado. **2** (*in business, law*) tramitación *f*. **3** COMPUT procesamiento.

**procession** [prə'seʃᵊn] *n* **1** (*gen*) desfile *m*. **2** REL procesión *f*.

**processor** ['prəʊsesəʳ] *n* **1** (*for food*) robot *m* de cocina. **2** COMPUT procesador *m*.

**proclaim** [prə'kleɪm] *vt* proclamar, declarar.

**procure** [prə'kjʊəʳ] *vt* (*obtain*) conseguir, obtener.

✗ To procure no significa 'procurar (intentar)', que se traduce por **to try**.

**prodigy** ['prɒdɪdʒɪ] *n* prodigio.
ⓘ *pl* prodigies.

**produce** [(*vb*) prə'djuːs; (*n*) 'prɒdjuːs] *vt* **1** (*gen*) producir, fabricar. **2** (*give birth to*) tener. **3** (*show*) enseñar, presentar. **4** (*cause*) producir, causar. **5** (*play*) poner en escena, dirigir.
▶ *n* productos *mpl*: *produce of Spain* productos de España.

**producer** [prə'djuːsəʳ] *n* **1** (*gen*) productor,-ra, fabricante. **2** (*play*) director,-ra de escena.

**product** ['prɒdʌkt] *n* producto.

**production** [prə'dʌkʃᵊn] *n* **1** (*gen*) producción *f*, fabricación *f*. **2** (*of film*) producción *f*; (*of play*) producción *f*, puesta en escena. COMP **production line** cadena de montaje.

**productive** [prə'dʌktɪv] *adj* productivo,-a.

**productivity** [prɒdʌk'tɪvɪtɪ] *n* productividad *f*.

**profession** [prə'feʃᵊn] *n* (*occupation*) profesión *f*: *he's a baker by profession* es panadero de profesión.

**professional** [prə'feʃᵊnəl] *adj* (*gen*) profesional.
▶ *n* profesional *mf*.

P

**professor** [prəˈfesər] *n* **1** GB catedrático, -a. **2** US profesor,-ra universitario,-a.

**proficiency** [prəˈfɪʃənsɪ] *n* competencia.

**profile** [ˈprəʊfaɪl] *n* **1** *(side view)* perfil *m*. **2** *(description)* perfil *m*; *(written)* reseña.

**profit** [ˈprɒfɪt] *n* **1** COMM ganancia, beneficio. **2** *fml (advantage)* provecho. |LOC| **to make a profit** sacar beneficios, tener ganancias.

**profitable** [ˈprɒfɪtəbəl] *adj* **1** COMM rentable. **2** *(beneficial)* provechoso,-a.

**profit-making** [ˈprɒfɪtmeɪkɪŋ] *adj (business)* rentable; *(charity)* con fines lucrativos.

**profound** [prəˈfaʊnd] *adj* profundo,-a.

**program** [ˈprəʊgræm] *n* COMPUT programa *m*.
▶ *vt* COMPUT programar.
ⓘ *pt & pp* programmed, *ger* programming.

**programme** [ˈprəʊgræm] *n (gen)* programa *m*; *(plan)* plan *m*.
▶ *vt (gen)* programar; *(activities)* planear.

**programmer** [ˈprəʊgræmər] *n* programador,-ra.

**programming** [ˈprəʊgræmɪŋ] *n* programación *f*.

**progress** [*(n)* ˈprəʊgres; *(vb)* prəʊˈgres] *n* *(advance)* progreso, avance *m*; *(development)* desarrollo.
▶ *vi* **1** *(advance)* progresar, avanzar, adelantar; *(develop)* desarrollar. **2** *(improve)* mejorar, hacer progresos. |LOC| **to be in progress** *(work)* estar en curso, estar en marcha.

**progression** [prəˈgreʃən] *n* **1** *(development)* evolución *f*, avance *m*. **2** *(series)* serie *f*.

**prohibit** [prəˈhɪbɪt] *vt* prohibir.

**prohibition** [prəʊɪˈbɪʃən] *n* prohibición *f*.

**project** [*(n)* ˈprɒdʒekt; *(vb)* prəˈdʒekt] *n* **1** *(gen)* proyecto. **2** EDUC trabajo, estudio.
▶ *vt* **1** *(gen)* proyectar. **2** *(extrapolate)* extrapolar.
▶ *vi* sobresalir, resaltar.

**projectile** [prəˈdʒektaɪl] *n* proyectil *m*.

**projection** [prəˈdʒekʃən] *n* **1** *(gen)* proyección *f*. **2** *(protuberance)* saliente *m*, resalto.

**proletariat** [prəʊləˈteərɪət] *n* proletariado.

**prologue** [ˈprəʊlɒg] *n* prólogo.

**prolong** [prəˈlɒŋ] *vt* prolongar, alargar.

**promenade** [prɒməˈnɑːd] *n* **1** GB *(at seaside)* paseo marítimo. **2** *fml (walk)* paseo.

**prominent** [ˈprɒmɪnənt] *adj (important)* importante; *(projecting)* prominente, saliente.

**promise** [ˈprɒmɪs] *n* **1** *(pledge)* promesa. **2** *(expectation, hope)* esperanza, esperanzas *fpl*. |LOC| **to break a promise** romper una promesa. **❙ to keep a promise** mantener una promesa.
▶ *vt* **1** prometer: *you promised to help me* prometiste ayudarme. **2** *(seem likely)* prometer.
▶ *vi (gen)* prometer; *(swear)* jurar: *I promise* te lo prometo.

**promote** [prəˈməʊt] *vt* **1** *(in rank)* promover, ascender. **2** *(encourage)* promover, fomentar.

**promotion** [prəˈməʊʃən] *n* promoción *f*.

**prompt** [prɒmpt] *adj (quick)* pronto,-a, rápido,-a; *(punctual)* puntual.
▶ *adv* en punto.
▶ *vt* **1** *(cause, incite)* instar, incitar, mover. **2** THEAT apuntar.
▶ *n* THEAT *(line)* apunte *m*.

**promptly** [ˈprɒmptlɪ] *adv* rápidamente.

**prone** [prəʊn] *adj (face down)* boca abajo. |LOC| **to be prone to** STH ser propenso,-a A ALGO.

**pronoun** [ˈprəʊnaʊn] *n* LING pronombre *m*.

**pronounce** [prəˈnaʊns] *vt* **1** LING pronunciar. **2** *(declare)* declarar.
▶ *vi* pronunciarse (on, sobre).

**pronunciation** [prənʌnsɪˈeɪʃən] *n* pronunciación *f*.

**proof** [pruːf] *n* **1** *(evidence)* prueba. **2** *(trial copy, print)* prueba.

**propaganda** [prɒpəˈgændə] *n* propaganda.

⊠ Propaganda no significa 'propaganda (publicidad)', que se traduce por **advertising**.

**propagation** [prɒpəˈgeɪʃən] *n* propagación *f*.

**propane** [ˈprəʊpeɪn] *n* propano.

**propel** [prə'pel] *vt* propulsar, impulsar.
  ⓘ *pt & pp* **propelled**, *ger* **propelling**.

**propeller** [prə'pelə'] *n* hélice *f*.

**propelling pencil** [prəpelɪŋ'pensəl] *n* portaminas *m*.

**proper** ['prɒpə'] *adj* **1** *(suitable)* adecuado,-a, apropiado,-a; *(correct)* correcto, -a. **2** *fam (real, genuine)* verdadero,-a, de verdad. **3** *fam (thorough)* auténtico,-a. **4** *(respectable)* correcto,-a, decente. COMP **proper name / proper noun** nombre propio.

  ✗ Proper no significa 'propio (de uno)', que se traduce por **own**.

**properly** ['prɒpəlɪ] *adv* **1** *(properly)* bien, adecuadamente. **2** *(correctly)* bien; *(as one should)* como es debido.

**property** ['prɒpətɪ] *n* **1** *(possessions, ownership)* propiedad *f*. **2** *(buildings, land)* propiedad *f*, bienes *mpl*; *(estate)* finca *f*. **3** *fml (building)* inmueble *m*.
  ⓘ *pl* **properties**.

**prophecy** ['prɒfəsɪ] *n* profecía.
  ⓘ *pl* **prophecies**.

**prophet** ['prɒfɪt] *n* profeta *m*.

**prophetic** [prə'fetɪk] *adj* profético,-a.

**proportion** [prə'pɔːʃən] *n* **1** *(ratio)* proporción *f*. **2** *(part)* parte *f*; *(percentage)* porcentaje *m*. **3** *(correct relation)* proporción *f*.
  ▸ *n pl* **proportions** dimensiones *fpl*, proporciones *fpl*.

**proportional** [prə'pɔːʃənəl] *adj* proporcional (**to**, a).

**proposal** [prə'pəʊzəl] *n* propuesta.

**propose** [prə'pəʊz] *vt* **1** *(suggest)* proponer. **2** *(intend)* pensar.
  ▸ *vi* declararse, proponer matrimonio a.

**prose** [prəʊz] *n* LIT prosa.

**prosecute** ['prɒsɪkjuːt] *vt* JUR procesar.
  ▸ *vi* JUR *(bring a charge)* entablar una acción judicial; *(be prosecutor)* llevar la acusación.

**prosecution** [prɒsɪ'kjuːʃən] *n* JUR *(action)* procesamiento, acción *f* judicial.
  ▸ *n* **the prosecution** JUR *(person)* la acusación.

**prosecutor** ['prɒsɪkjuːtə'] *n* JUR fiscal *mf*, acusador,-ra.

**prospect** [*(n)* 'prɒspekt; *(vb)* prə'spekt] *n* **1** *(picture in mind)* perspectiva. **2** *(possibility, hope)* posibilidad *f*, probabilidad *f*. **3** *fml (wide view)* panorama *m*, vista, perspectiva.
  ▸ *vt* prospectar, explorar.
  ▸ *vi* buscar (**for**, -).
  ▸ *n pl* **prospects** perspectivas *fpl*.

  ✗ Prospect no significa 'prospecto', que se traduce por **leaflet**.

**prosper** ['prɒspə'] *vi* prosperar.

**prosperity** [prɒ'sperɪtɪ] *n* prosperidad *f*.

**prosperous** ['prɒspərəs] *adj* próspero,-a.

**prostate** ['prɒsteɪt] *n* próstata.

**prosthesis** ['prɒsθəsɪs] *n* prótesis *f*.

**prostitute** ['prɒstɪtjuːt] *n* prostituta.

**protect** [prə'tekt] *vt* *(gen)* proteger; *(interests)* proteger, salvaguardar.

**protection** [prə'tekʃən] *n* *(gen)* protección *f*; *(shelter)* protección *f*, amparo.

**protective** [prə'tektɪv] *adj* protector,-ra.

**protector** [prə'tektə'] *n* protector,-ra.

**protein** ['prəʊtiːn] *n* proteína.

**protest** [*(n)* 'prəʊtest; *(vb)* prə'test] *n* *(gen)* protesta; *(complaint)* queja; *(demonstration)* manifestación *f* de protesta.
  ▸ *vt* protestar de.
  ▸ *vi* protestar (**about**, de), (**against**, contra), (**at**, por): *they protested about the working conditions* protestaron de las condiciones de trabajo.

**Protestant** ['prɒtɪstənt] *adj* protestante.
  ▸ *n* protestante *mf*.

**proton** ['prəʊtɒn] *n* protón *m*.

**proud** [praʊd] *adj* orgulloso,-a: *I'm proud of you* estoy orgulloso de ti.

**proudly** ['praʊdlɪ] *adv* *(with satisfaction)* orgullosamente, con orgullo; *(arrogantly)* arrogantemente, con arrogancia.

**prove** [pruːv] *vt* **1** *(show to be true)* probar, demostrar. **2** *(turn out to be)* demostrar.
  ⓘ *pt* **proved**, *pp* **proved** o **proven** [pruːvən], *ger* **proving**.

  ✗ To prove no significa 'probar (comida)', que se traduce por **to taste**.

**proven** ['pruːvən] *pp* → **prove**.
  ▸ *adj* probado,-a, comprobado,-a.

**proverb** ['prɒvɜ:b] *n* proverbio, refrán *m*.

**provide** [prə'vaɪd] *vt* **1** *(supply)* proveer, suministrar, proporcionar: *he provided us with all the information* nos facilitó toda la información. **2** *fig (answer, example)* ofrecer, dar.

**provided** [prə'vaɪdɪd] [also provided that] *conj* siempre que, con tal que.

**province** ['prɒvɪns] *n* **1** *(region)* provincia. **2** *fig* terreno, campo, competencia.

**provincial** [prə'vɪnʃəl] *adj* **1** *(government)* provincial; *(town)* de provincia(s). **2** *pej* provinciano,-a, pueblerino,-a.

**provision** [prə'vɪʒən] *n* **1** *(supply)* suministro, abastecimiento. **2** *(preparation)* previsiones *fpl*.
▶ *n pl* **provisions** *(food)* provisiones *fpl*, víveres *mpl*.

**provisional** [prə'vɪʒənəl] *adj* provisional.

**provoke** [prə'vəʊk] *vt* **1** *(make angry)* provocar, irritar: *he's not easily provoked* no se irrita fácilmente. **2** *(cause)* provocar.

**prowl** [praʊl] *vi* merodear, rondar.
▶ *vt* merodear por, rondar por.
▶ *n* merodeo.

**proximity** ['prɒksɪmɪtɪ] *n fml* proximidad *f*.

**prune** [pruːn] *n* ciruela pasa.

**psalm** [sɑːm] *n* salmo.

**pseudonym** ['suːdənɪm] *n* seudónimo.

**psychedelic** [saɪkɪ'delɪk] *adj* psicodélico,-a.

**psychiatric** [saɪkɪ'ætrɪk] *adj* psiquiátrico,-a.

**psychiatrist** [saɪ'kaɪətrɪst] *n* psiquiatra *mf*.

**psychiatry** [saɪ'kaɪətrɪ] *n* psiquiatría.

**psychic** ['saɪkɪk] *adj (mental)* psíquico,-a.

**psychoanalyst** [saɪkəʊ'ænəlɪst] *n* psicoanalista *mf*.

**psychological** [saɪkə'lɒdʒɪkəl] *adj* psicológico,-a.

**psychologist** [saɪ'kɒlədʒɪst] *n* psicólogo,-a.

**psychology** [saɪ'kɒlədʒɪ] *n* psicología.

**psychosis** [saɪ'kəʊsɪs] *n* psicosis *f*.
ⓘ *pl* **psychoses** [saɪ'kəʊsiːz].

**pub** [pʌb] *n* bar *m*, pub *m*, taberna.

**puberty** ['pjuːbətɪ] *n* pubertad *f*.

**pubis** ['pjuːbɪs] *n* pubis *m*.

**public** ['pʌblɪk] *adj* público,-a. COMP **public convenience** servicios *mpl*, aseos *mpl*. ‖ **public holiday** fiesta nacional. ‖ **public house** bar *m*, pub *m*. ‖ **public school 1** GB colegio privado. **2** US colegio público.
▶ *n* **the public** el público.

⊕ En el Reino Unido, los **public schools** son colegios privados de prestigio y de mucha tradición; suelen ser internados. Los colegios públicos británicos se llaman **state schools**. En Estados Unidos los **public schools** son, sencillamente, colegios públicos.

**publication** [pʌblɪ'keɪʃən] *n* publicación *f*.

**publicity** [pʌ'blɪsɪtɪ] *n* publicidad *f*.

**publish** ['pʌblɪʃ] *vt* **1** *(book, newspaper)* publicar, editar. **2** *(make known)* divulgar.

**publisher** ['pʌblɪʃəʳ] *n* *(person)* editor,-ra. *(company)* editorial *f*.

**pudding** ['pʊdɪŋ] *n* **1** CULIN *(sweet)* budín *m*, pudín *m*; *(savoury)* pastel *m*. **2** GB *fam (dessert)* postre *m*.

**puddle** ['pʌdəl] *n* charco.

**Puerto Rican** [pweətəʊriːkən] *adj* puertorriqueño,-a, portorriqueño,-a.
▶ *n* puertorriqueño,-a, portorriqueño,-a.

**Puerto Rico** [pweətəʊriːkəʊ] *n* Puerto Rico.

**puff** [pʌf] *n* **1** *(of wind, air)* soplo, racha, ráfaga; *(of smoke)* bocanada. **2** *(action)* soplo, soplido; *(at cigarette, pipe)* calada, chupada.
▶ *vt (blow - gen)* soplar; *(- smoke)* echar.
▶ *vi* **1** *(pipe, cigarette)* chupar (at/on, -), dar caladas (at/on, a). **2** *(pant)* jadear, resoplar. **3** *(train)* echar humo, echar vapor.

**puke** [pjuːk] *vi fam* devolver, vomitar.

**pull** [pʊl] *n* **1** *(tug)* tirón *m*. **2** *(of moon, current)* fuerza. **3** *(attraction)* atracción *f*; *(influence)* influencia.
▶ *vt* **1** *(draw)* tirar de; *(drag)* arrastrar: *the horse was pulling a cart* el caballo tiraba de una carreta. **2** *(tug forcefully)* tirar de, dar un tirón a: *don't pull my hair!* ¡no me tires del pelo! **3** *(remove, draw out)* sacar. **4** *(damage - muscle)* sufrir un tirón. **5**

*fam (attract - crowd, audience)* atraer; *(boy, girl)* ligarse, ligar con.

▶ *vi* **1** *(tug)* tirar (at/on, de). **2** *(on pipe, cigarette)* chupar, dar caladas a. **3** *(of vehicle - veer)* tirar.

◆ **to pull down** *vt sep* derribar, tirar (abajo).

◆ **to pull in** *vt sep* **1** *(crowd)* atraer. **2** *(money)* sacar, ganar.

▶ *vi (train)* entrar en la estación; *(bus, car)* parar.

◆ **to pull out** *vt sep (gun, tooth, plug, etc)* sacar; *(troops)* retirar.

▶ *vi* **1** *(train)* salir de la estación; *(bus, car)* salir. **2** *(withdraw)* retirarse.

**pulley** ['pʊlɪ] *n* polea.

**pullover** ['pʊləʊvəʳ] *n* pullover *m*, jersey *m*.

**pulmonary** ['pʌlmənᵊrɪ] *adj* pulmonar.

**pulse¹** [pʌls] *n* **1** ANAT pulso. **2** PHYS pulsación *f*.

▶ *vi* palpitar, latir.

**pulse²** [pʌls] *n* BOT legumbre *f*.

**puma** ['pjuːmə] *n* puma *m*.

**pumice stone** ['pʌmɪsstəʊn] *n* piedra pómez.

**pump¹** [pʌmp] *n (machine)* bomba: *bicycle pump* bomba de aire, bombín *m*.

▶ *vt* bombear.

▶ *vi (of heart)* latir.

◆ **to pump up** *vt sep* inflar.

**pump²** [pʌmp] *n (plimsoll)* zapatilla de lona, playera; *(for dancing)* zapatilla de ballet.

**pumpkin** ['pʌmpkɪn] *n* calabaza.

**punch¹** [pʌntʃ] *n* **1** *(blow)* puñetazo, golpe *m*; *(in boxing)* pegada. **2** *fig* fuerza, empuje *m*.

▶ *vt* dar un puñetazo a, pegar a.

**punch²** [pʌntʃ] *n (for making holes)* perforadora, taladro; *(in leather)* punzón *m*; *(for tickets)* máquina de picar billetes.

▶ *vt (make a hole in)* perforar; *(leather)* punzar; *(ticket)* picar.

**punch³** [pʌntʃ] *n (drink)* ponche *m*.

**punctual** ['pʌŋktjʊəl] *adj* puntual.

**punctuality** ['pʌŋktjʊəlɪtɪ] *n* puntualidad *f*.

**punctuate** ['pʌŋktjʊeɪt] *vt* **1** LING puntuar. **2** *(interrupt)* interrumpir.

**punctuation** [pʌŋktjʊ'eɪʃᵊn] *n* puntuación *f*. COMP **punctuation mark** signo de puntuación.

**puncture** ['pʌŋktʃəʳ] *n* pinchazo.

▶ *vt (tyre, ball, etc)* pinchar.

**punish** ['pʌnɪʃ] *vt* castigar.

**punishment** ['pʌnɪʃmənt] *n* castigo.

**punk** [pʌŋk] *n (person)* punk *mf*; *(music)* punk *m*.

**pupil¹** ['pjuːpᵊl] *n* EDUC alumno,-a.

**pupil²** ['pjuːpᵊl] *n* ANAT pupila.

**puppet** ['pʌpɪt] *n* **1** títere *m*. **2** *fig* títere *m*. COMP **puppet show** teatro de títeres.

**puppy** ['pʌpɪ] *n* cachorro,-a.

ⓘ *pl* puppies.

**purchase** ['pɜːtʃəs] *n fml* compra.

▶ *vt fml* comprar, adquirir.

**pure** ['pjʊəʳ] *adj (gen)* puro,-a: *it was pure chance* fue pura casualidad.

**purée** ['pjʊəreɪ] *n* puré *m*.

**purification** [pjʊərɪfɪ'keɪʃᵊn] *n* purificación *f*.

**purify** ['pjʊərɪfaɪ] *vt (gen)* purificar; *(water)* depurar, purificar.

ⓘ *pt & pp* purified, *ger* purifying.

**puritan** ['pjʊərɪtᵊn] *adj* puritano,-a.

▶ *n* puritano,-a.

**purple** ['pɜːpᵊl] *adj* morado,-a.

▶ *n (color m)* púrpura, (color *m*) morado.

**purpose** ['pɜːpəs] *n* **1** *(aim, intention)* propósito, intención *f*, fin *m*; *(reason)* razón *f*, motivo: *what is the purpose of your visit?* ¿cuál es el motivo de su visita? **2** *(use)* uso, utilidad *f*. **3** *(determination)* resolución *f*. LOC **to no purpose** inútilmente, en vano. ‖ **on purpose** a propósito, adrede, a posta.

**purr** [pɜːʳ] *n (of cat)* ronroneo.

▶ *vi (of cat)* ronronear.

**purse** [pɜːs] *n* **1** GB monedero, portamonedas *m*. **2** US bolso.

▶ *vt (lips)* fruncir.

**pursue** [pə'sjuː] *vt* **1** *(chase)* perseguir; *(follow)* seguir. **2** *(seek)* buscar; *(strive for)* esforzarse por conseguir, luchar por. **3** *(carry out - policy)* llevar a cabo; *(- mat-*

**P**

*ter)* investigar. **4** *(continue with)* seguir, dedicarse a, ejercer.

**pursuit** [pə'sjuːt] *n* **1** *(chase)* persecución *f*; *(hunt)* caza. **2** *(search)* búsqueda; *(striving)* lucha. **3** *(activity)* actividad *f*.

**pus** [pʌs] *n* pus *m*.

**push** [puʃ] *n* *(shove)* empujón *m*.
  ▶ *vt* **1** *(gen)* empujar. **2** *(press - button, bell, etc)* pulsar, apretar.
  ▶ *vi* **1** *(shove)* empujar. **2** *(move forward)* abrirse paso. **3** *(pressurize)* presionar, exigir.

**pushchair** ['puʃtʃeəʳ] *n* GB cochecito de niño, sillita de niño.

**push-up** ['puʃʌp] *n* US flexión *f*.

**pussycat** ['pusɪkæt] *n* *fam* minino,-a, gatito,-a.

**put** [put] *vt* **1** *(gen)* poner; *(place)* colocar; *(add)* echar, añadir; *(place inside)* meter, poner. **2** *(express)* expresar, decir: *you put that very well* lo has expresado muy bien. **3** *(calculate, estimate)* calcular: *I'd put the cost at 100 pounds* yo diría que cuesta 100 libras. LOC **to put STH right** arreglar ALGO. ‖ **to put the blame on SB** echar la culpa a ALGN.
  ◆ **to put down** *vt sep* **1** *(set down - gen)* dejar; *(- phone)* colgar. **2** *(payment)* entregar, dejar (en depósito); *(deposit)* dejar. **3** *(rebellion)* sofocar. **4** *(write)* apuntar, anotar, escribir.
  ▶ *vi* AV aterrizar.
  ◆ **to put forward** *vt sep* **1** *(idea, theory, plan)* proponer, presentar. **2** *(clock, meeting, wedding)* adelantar.
  ◆ **to put in** *vt sep* **1** *(install, fit)* instalar, poner. **2** *(include, insert)* poner, incluir; *(say)* agregar. **3** *(enter, submit - claim, request, bid)* presentar. **4** *(spend time working)* trabajar, hacer.
  ▶ *vi* *(ship)* hacer escala.
  ◆ **to put off** *vt sep* **1** *(postpone)* aplazar, posponer. **2** *(distract)* distraer. **3** *(discourage)* desanimar, disuadir, quitar las ganas a.
  ◆ **to put on** *vt sep* **1** *(clothes)* ponerse: *put your coat on* ponte el abrigo. **2** *(expression, attitude)* fingir, adoptar. **3** *(gain, increase)* aumentar. **4** *(present - show)* presentar, montar; *(- exhibition)* organizar. **5** *(switch on - light, television)* encender; *(- music, radio)* poner.
  ◆ **to put out** *vt sep* **1** *(fire, light, cigarette)* apagar. **2** *(put outside - cat, washing, rubbish)* sacar. **3** *(extend - hand)* tender, alargar; *(- tongue)* sacar; *(dislocate)* dislocar. **4** *(inconvenience)* molestar; *(upset, offend, annoy)* molestar, ofender. **5** *(publish, issue)* publicar; *(broadcast)* difundir.
  ◆ **to put up** *vt sep* **1** *(provide accommodation for)* alojar, hospedar. **2** *(erect - tent)* armar; *(- building, fence)* levantar, construir. **3** *(shelves, picture, decorations)* colocar; *(curtains, notice, poster)* colgar. **4** *(raise - hand)* levantar; *(flag)* izar; *(hair)* recoger; *(umbrella)* abrir. **5** *(increase - price, etc)* aumentar, subir. **6** *(present - candidate)* presentar, proponer.
  ▶ *vt insep* **1** *(resistence, struggle)* ofrecer, oponer: *they put up a good fight* ofrecieron mucha resistencia. **2** *(money)* poner, aportar.
  ◆ **to put up with** *vt insep* soportar, aguantar.
  ① *pt & pp* **put**, *ger* **putting**.

**putt** [pʌt] *n* tiro al hoyo.
  ▶ *vt* tirar al hoyo.

**puzzle** ['pʌzəl] *n* **1** *(jigsaw)* puzzle *m*; *(toy)* rompecabezas *m*; *(riddle)* adivinanza, acertijo; *(crossword)* crucigrama *m*. **2** *(mystery)* misterio, enigma *m*.
  ▶ *vt* dejar perplejo,-a, extrañar.
  ◆ **to puzzle out** *vt sep* *(problem)* resolver; *(mystery)* descifrar.

**pygmy** ['pɪgmɪ] *adj* pigmeo,-a, enano,-a.
  ▶ *n* *(small person)* pigmeo,-a, enano,-a.

**pyjamas** [pə'dʒɑːməz] *n pl* pijama *m sing*.

**pylon** ['paɪlən] *n* **1** ELEC torre *f* (de tendido eléctrico). **2** ARCH pilón *m*, pilar *m*.

**pylorus** [paɪlərəs] *n* píloro *m*.

**pyramid** ['pɪrəmɪd] *n* pirámide *f*.

**pyrites** [paɪ'raɪtiːz] *n* pirita *f*.

**pyromaniac** [paɪrəʊ'meɪnɪæk] *n* pirómano,-a.

**pyrotechnics** [paɪrəʊ'teknɪks] *n* pirotecnia.
  ▶ *n pl* fuegos *mpl* artificiales.

**python** ['paɪθən] *n* pitón *m*.

**Q, q** [kjuː] *n (the letter)* Q, q *f*.
**quack** [kwæk] *vi* graznar.
**Qatar** [kæˈtɑːʳ] *n* Qatar.
**quadriceps** [ˈkwɒdrɪseps] *n* ANAT cuádriceps *m*.
**quail** [kweɪl] *n* codorniz *f*.
**quake** [kweɪk] *n fam* terremoto.
**qualification** [kwɒlɪfɪˈkeɪʃⁿn] *n* **1** *(for job)* requisito. **2** *(ability)* aptitud *f*, capacidad *f*. **3** *(paper)* diploma *m*, título. **4** *(reservation)* reserva, salvedad *f*. **5** *(restriction)* limitación *f*.

☒ Qualification no significa 'calificación (nota)', que se traduce por mark.

**qualified** [ˈkwɒlɪfaɪd] *adj* **1** *(for job)* capacitado,-a. **2** *(with qualifications)* titulado,-a. *qualified nurse* enfermero,-a titulado,-a. **3** *(limited, modified)* limitado,-a, restringido,-a.
**qualify** [ˈkwɒlɪfaɪ] *vt* **1** *(entitle, make eligible)* capacitar, dar derecho. **2** *(modify)* modificar, matizar, puntualizar. **3** LING calificar.
ⓘ *pt & pp* qualified, *ger* qualifying.
**quality** [ˈkwɒlɪtɪ] *n* **1** *(degree of excellence)* calidad *f*: *of good quality* de buena calidad; *of poor quality* de poca calidad. **2** *(attribute)* cualidad *f*: *she has many qualities* tiene muchas cualidades. COMP **quality control** control *m* de calidad. ‖ **quality newspapers** prensa de calidad.
ⓘ *pl* qualities.
**quantity** [ˈkwɒntɪtɪ] *n* **1** cantidad *f*. **2** MATH cantidad *f*.
ⓘ *pl* quantities.
**quarrel** [ˈkwɒrəl] *n* **1** riña, disputa, pelea. **2** *(disagreement)* desacuerdo. **3** *(complaint)* queja: *I have no quarrel with him* no tengo ninguna queja de él, no tengo nada contra él. LOC **to pick a quar-**

**rel with** SB meterse con ALGN, buscar pelea con ALGN.
▶ *vi (argue)* reñir, pelearse, disputar, discutir: *she is always quarrelling with her mother* siempre está discutiendo con su madre.
ⓘ *pt & pp* quarrelled (US quarreled), *ger* quarrelling (US quarreling).
**quarry** [ˈkwɒrɪ] *n* **1** cantera. **2** *(in hunting)* presa.
ⓘ *pl* quarries.
▶ *vt* extraer.
ⓘ *pt & pp* quarried, *ger* quarrying.
**quart** [kwɔːt] *n* cuarto de galón.

🖎 En Gran Bretaña equivale a 1,14 litros; en Estados Unidos equivale a 0,95 litro.

**quarter** [ˈkwɔːtəʳ] *n* **1** cuarto. **2** *(area)* barrio: *the old quarter* el casco antiguo. **3** *(time)* cuarto: *it's a quarter to one* es la una menos cuarto. **4** *(of moon)* cuarto. **5** *(three months)* trimestre *m*. **6** US *(amount)* veinticinco centavos; *(coin)* moneda de veinticinco centavos. COMP **first quarter** cuarto creciente. ‖ **last quarter** cuarto menguante.
▶ *n pl* **quarters** alojamiento *m sing*. COMP **at close quarters** desde muy cerca. ‖ **to give no quarter** no dar cuartel.
**quartz** [kwɔːts] *n* cuarzo. COMP **quartz watch** reloj *m* de cuarzo.
**quay** [kiː] *n* muelle *m*.
**queen** [kwiːn] *n* **1** reina. **2** *(cards, chess)* dama, reina; *(chess)* reina. COMP **queen bee** abeja reina. ‖ **Queen Mother** reina madre.
**queer** [kwɪəʳ] *adj* **1** raro,-a, extraño,-a. **2** *(ill)* malucho,-a. **3** *fam* gay. **4** *(mad)* loco,-a, chiflado,-a.
**quench** [kwentʃ] *vt* **1** *(thirst)* saciar. **2** *(fire)* apagar.

**query** [ˈkwɪərɪ] n **1** pregunta, duda. **2** LING signo de interrogación. **3** fig interrogante m.
ⓘ pl queries.
▶ vt **1** (doubt) poner en duda. **2** (ask) preguntar.
ⓘ pt & pp queried, ger querying.

**quest** [kwest] n búsqueda, busca. LOC in quest of en busca de: in quest of the Holy Grail en busca del Santo Grial.

**question** [ˈkwestʃ°n] n **1** pregunta. **2** (in exam) pregunta, problema m. **3** (problem, issue) cuestión f, problema m. **4** (topic, matter) cuestión f, asunto. LOC it's a question of se trata de, es cuestión de: it's a question of time es cuestión de tiempo. ❙ out of the question imposible, impensable. ❙ that is the question de eso se trata. ❙ without question sin rechistar: she did it without question lo hizo sin rechistar. COMP question mark **1** (punctuation mark) signo de interrogación, interrogación f, interrogante m. **2** (doubt) interrogante m. ❙ question tag coletilla.
▶ vt **1** hacer preguntas a, interrogar. **2** (cast doubt on) cuestionar, poner en duda.

**questionnaire** [kwestʃəˈneəʳ] n cuestionario.

**queue** [kjuː] n GB cola. LOC to jump the queue colarse.
▶ vi hacer cola.

**quick** [kwɪk] adj **1** (fast) rápido,-a: let's have a quick look echemos un vistazo. **2** (clever) espabilado,-a, listo,-a.

**quickly** [ˈkwɪklɪ] adv (speed up) rápido
▶ vi (speed up) acelerarse.

**quicksand** [ˈkwɪksænd] n arenas fpl movedizas.

**quiet** [ˈkwaɪət] adj **1** (silent) callado,-a, silencioso,-a: he kept quiet all night estuvo callado toda la noche. **2** (peaceful, calm) tranquilo,-a, sosegado,-a: this is a very quiet village éste es un pueblo muy tranquilo. **3** (unobtrusive) callado,-a, reservado,-a. **4** (tranquil, without fuss) tranquilo,-a. LOC be quiet! ¡cállate!
▶ n **1** (silence) silencio. **2** (calm) tranquilidad f, calma, sosiego.
▶ vt US calmar, silenciar: she quieted the baby down calmó a la criatura.

▶ vi US calmarse. LOC on the quiet a la chita callando, a hurtadillas: he did it on the quiet lo hizo en secreto.

**quietly** [ˈkwaɪətlɪ] adv **1** (silently) silenciosamente, sin hacer ruido; (not loudly) bajo: she always speaks quietly siempre habla en voz baja. **2** (calmly) tranquilamente. **3** (discreetly) discretamente, con discreción. **4** (simply) sencillamente, con sencillez.

**quilt** [kwɪlt] n edredón m.

**quince** [kwɪns] n membrillo.

**quit** [kwɪt] vt **1** dejar, abandonar: he quit his job dejó el trabajo. **2** (stop) dejar de: she quit smoking dejó de fumar.
▶ vi marcharse, irse.
ⓘ pt & pp quit, ger quitting.

✗ To quit no significa 'quitar', que se traduce por to remove.

**quite** [kwaɪt] adv **1** (rather) bastante: they played quite well jugaron bastante bien; they're quite difficult exercises son ejercicios bastante difíciles. **2** (totally) completamente, del todo: I quite understand lo entiendo perfectamente. **3** (exceptional) excepcional, increíble, original: it's been quite a year ha sido un año excepcional. **4** (exactly) exactamente: it isn't quite what I was looking for no es exactamente lo que buscaba.

**quiver¹** [ˈkwɪvəʳ] n **1** (tremble of lips, voice) temblor m; (of eyelids) parpadeo; (shiver) estremecimiento.
▶ vi temblar, estremecerse.

**quiz** [kwɪz] n **1** (competition) concurso. **2** (enquiry) encuesta; (exam) examen m.
▶ vt preguntar, interrogar.

**quotation** [kwəʊˈteɪʃ°n] n **1** LING cita. **2** FIN cotización f. **3** COMM presupuesto. COMP quotation marks comillas fpl.

**quote** [kwəʊt] n **1** LING cita. **2** (price - gen) presupuesto; (- for shares) cotización f.
▶ vt **1** citar, entrecomillar. **2** (price) dar, ofrecer. **3** FIN cotizar.

**quotient** [ˈkwəʊʃ°nt] n **1** (in mathematics) cociente m. **2** (degree) coeficiente m, grado. COMP intelligence quotient coeficiente intelectual m, coeficiente m de inteligencia.

# R

**R, r** [ɑː] *n* **1** *(the letter)* R, r *f*.

**rabbit** ['ræbɪt] *n* conejo.

**raccoon** [rə'kuːn] *n* mapache *m*.

**race¹** [reɪs] *n (people)* raza.

**race²** [reɪs] *n* **1** SP carrera. **2** *(current)* corriente *f* fuerte; *(channel)* canal *m*. LOC to **run a race** participar en una carrera.
▶ *vt* **1** *(person)* competir con, echar una carrera a. **2** *(engine)* acelerar.

**racecourse** ['reɪskɔːs] *n* GB hipódromo.

**racehorse** ['reɪhɔːs] *n* caballo de carreras.

**racial** ['reɪʃəl] *adj* racial.

**racing** ['reɪsɪŋ] *n* carreras *fpl*.
▶ *adj* de carreras. COMP **racing car** coche *m* de carreras. ‖ **racing driver** piloto de carreras.

**racism** ['reɪsɪzəm] *n* racismo.

**racist** ['reɪsɪst] *adj* racista.
▶ *n* racista *mf*.

**rack** [ræk] *n* **1** estante *m*. **2** AUTO baca. **3** *(on train)* rejilla. **4** *(for torture)* potro.

**racket¹** ['rækɪt] *n* SP raqueta.

**racket²** ['rækɪt] *n* **1** *(din)* alboroto, ruido. **2** *fam (fraud)* timo. **3** *fam (business)* asunto, negocio.

**racoon** [rə'kuːn] *n* mapache *m*.

**racquet** ['rækɪt] *n* raqueta.

**radar** ['reɪdɑː'] *n* radar *m*. COMP **radar trap** control *m* de velocidad por radar.

**radiation** [reɪdɪ'eɪʃən] *n* radiación *f*.

**radiator** ['reɪdɪeɪtə'] *n* radiador *m*.

**radical** ['rædɪkəl] *adj* radical.
▶ *n* radical *mf*.

**radii** ['reɪdɪaɪ] *n pl* → radius.

**radio** ['reɪdɪəʊ] *n* radio *f*. COMP **radio cassette** radiocasete *m*.
ⓘ *pl* radios.

**radioactive** [reɪdɪəʊ'æktɪv] *adj* radiactivo,-a. LOC **radioactive waste** residuos *mpl* radiactivos.

**radioactivity** [reɪdɪəʊæk'tɪvɪtɪ] *n* radiactividad *f*.

**radiography** [reɪdɪ'ɒgrəfɪ] *n* radiografía.
ⓘ *pl* radiographies.

**radiologist** [reɪdɪ'ɒlədʒɪst] *n* radiólogo,-a.

**radiology** [reɪdɪ'ɒlədʒɪ] *n* radiología.

**radish** ['rædɪʃ] *n* rábano.

**radium** ['reɪdɪəm] *n* radio.

**radius** ['reɪdɪəs] *n* radio.
ⓘ *pl* radii ['reɪdɪaɪ].

**radon** ['reɪdɒn] *n* radón *m*.

**raffle** ['ræfəl] *n* rifa.
▶ *vt* rifar, sortear.

**raft** [rɑːft] *n* **1** balsa. **2** US *fam* montón *m*.

**rag** [ræg] *n* **1** harapo, andrajo,. **2** *(for cleaning)* trapo.

**rage** [reɪdʒ] *n* rabia, furor *m*, cólera.
▶ *vi* **1** *(person)* estar hecho,-a una furia. **2** *(fire, etc)* arder sin control; *(storm, sea)* rugir; *(debate, etc)* seguir candente.

**ragout** [ræ'guː] *n* ragú *m*.

**raid** [reɪd] *n* **1** MIL incursión *f*, ataque *m*. **2** *(by police)* redada. **3** *(robbery)* atraco.
▶ *vt* **1** MIL hacer una incursión en. **2** *(police)* hacer una redada en. **3** *(rob)* atracar, asaltar.

**rail** [reɪl] *n* **1** barra. **2** *(handrail)* pasamano, barandilla, baranda. **3** *(for train)* raíl *m*, carril *m*, riel *m*. **4** *(the railway)* ferrocarril *m*. LOC **by rail** por ferrocarril.

**railing** ['reɪlɪŋz] *n* verja.

**railroad** ['reɪlrəʊd] *n* US → railway.
▶ *vt* **1** *(person)* presionar. **2** *(measure, bill)* tramitar sin debate.

**railway** ['reɪlweɪ] *n* ferrocarril *m*. COMP
railway **carriage** vagón *m*. I railway **engine** locomotora. I railway **line** vía
férrea. I railway **station** estación *f* de
ferrocarril. I railway **track** vía férrea.

**rain** [reɪn] *n* lluvia. COMP rain **forest** selva tropical. I rain **gauge** pluviómetro.
▶ *vi* llover: *it's raining* está lloviendo.

**rainbow** ['reɪnbəʊ] *n* arco iris *m*.

**raincoat** ['reɪnkəʊt] *n* impermeable *m*.

**raindrop** ['reɪndrɒp] *n* gota de lluvia.

**rainfall** ['reɪnfɔːl] *n* **1** precipitación *f*.
**2** *(quantity)* pluviosidad *f*.

**rainforest** ['reɪnfɒrɪst] *n* selva tropical.

**rainy** ['reɪnɪ] *adj* lluvioso,-a.
ⓘ *comp* rainier, *superl* rainiest.

**raise** [reɪz] *vt* **1** *(lift up)* levantar: *raise
your hands* levantad la mano. **2** *(move to a
higher position)* subir. **3** *(build, erect)* erigir, levantar. **4** *(increase)* subir, aumentar. **5** *(improve)* mejorar. **6** *(laugh,
smile, etc)* provocar; *(doubt, fear)* suscitar. **7** *(children)* criar, educar; *(animals)*
criar. **8** *(matter, point)* plantear. **9** *(funds)*
recaudar.
▶ *n* US aumento de sueldo.

> ✎ Raise en el sentido de 'levantar' siempre va seguido de un complemento. Mientras que rise (subir), nunca lleva complemento.

**raisin** ['reɪzən] *n* pasa.

**rake** [reɪk] *n* *(tool)* rastrillo.

**rally** ['rælɪ] *n* **1** *(public gathering)* reunión
*f*; *(political)* mitin *m*; *(demonstration)* manifestación *f*. **2** *(car race)* rally *m*. **3** *(in
tennis)* intercambio (de golpes).
ⓘ *pl* rallies.
▶ *vi* *(recover)* reponerse, recuperarse.
▶ *vt* *(bring together)* unir.
ⓘ *pt & pp* rallied, *ger* rallying.

**ram** [ræm] *n* ZOOL carnero.

**ramp** [ræmp] *n* **1** *(slope)* rampa. **2** *(steps)*
escalerilla. **3** GB *(speed bump)* badén *m*.
**4** US *(slip road)* vía de acceso.

**ran** [ræn] *pt* → run.

**ranch** [ræntʃ] *n* rancho, hacienda. COMP
ranch **house 1** *(type of house)* bungalow
*m*. **2** *(house on ranch)* hacienda.

**random** ['rændəm] *adj* aleatorio,-a. LOC
at **random** al azar. COMP random **access
memory** memoria de acceso directo.

**rang** [ræŋ] *pt* → ring.

**range** [reɪndʒ] *n* **1** *(choice)* gama, surtido; *(of products)* gama; *(of clothes)* línea.
**2** *(reach)* alcance *m*. **3** *(of mountains)* cordillera, sierra. **4** US *(prairie)* pradera.
▶ *vi* **1** variar, oscilar: *they range from ...
to...* van desde ... hasta ... **2** *(wander)* vagar (over, por).
▶ *vt* **1** *(arrange)* colocar, disponer. **2**
*(travel)* recorrer, viajar por.

**rank** [ræŋk] *n* **1** *(line)* fila. **2** MIL *(in hierarchy)* graduación *f*, rango.
▶ *vi* *(be)* figurar, estar
▶ *vt* *(classify)* clasificar, considerar.

**ranking** ['ræŋkɪŋ] *n* clasificación *f*,
ranking *m*.

**ransom** ['rænsəm] *n* rescate *m*. LOC to
hold to **ransom 1** pedir rescate por. **2**
*fig* chantajear. LOC ransom **money** rescate *m*.
▶ *vt* rescatar.

**rap** [ræp] *n* **1** golpe *m* seco. **2** MUS rap *m*.
▶ *vi* **1** golpear. **2** MUS cantar rap.
ⓘ *pt & pp* rapped, *ger* rapping.

**rape¹** [reɪp] *n* violación *f*.
▶ *vt* violar.

**rape²** [reɪp] *n* BOT colza.

**rapid** ['ræpɪd] *adj* rápido,-a.
▶ *n pl* rapids rápidos *mpl*.

**rapper** ['ræpəʳ] *n* cantante *mf* de rap,
rapero,-a.

**rare** [reəʳ] *adj* **1** *(uncommon)* poco común, raro,-a. **2** *(air)* enrarecido,-a. **3**
CULIN poco hecho,-a. COMP rare **earth**
tierra rara. I rare **gas** gas *m* raro.

> ✗ Rare no significa 'raro (extraño)', que se traduce por strange.

**rarely** ['reəlɪ] *adv* rara vez, pocas veces.

**rascal** ['rɑːskəl] *n* bribón *m*, pillo.

**rash¹** [ræʃ] *n* **1** MED sarpullido, erupción *f* cutánea. **2** *(series)* sucesión *f*, serie *f*.

**rash²** [ræʃ] *adj* imprudente, precipitado,-a.

**raspberry** ['rɑːzbˀrɪ] n **1** frambuesa. **2** fam (noise) pedorreta.
ⓘ pl raspberries.

**rat** [ræt] n **1** rata. **2** fam canalla m.

**rate** [reɪt] n **1** tasa, índice m **2** (speed) velocidad f, ritmo **3** (price) tarifa, precio. LOC at any rate **1** (anyway) de todos modos. **2** (at least) por lo menos, al menos. ▮ at the rate of a razón de. ▮ first/second rate de primera/segunda (categoría). COMP rate of exchange tipo de cambio.
▸ vt **1** (consider) considerar **2** (deserve) merecer. **3** (fix value) tasar.
▸ n pl rates GB contribución f sing urbana.

**rather** ['rɑːðəʳ] adv **1** (a little) algo; (fairly) bastante; (very) muy. **2** (showing preference): I'd rather go out preferiría salir. **3** (more precisely) o mejor dicho: there was a river, or rather a stream había un río, o mejor dicho un arroyo

**ratify** ['rætɪfaɪ] vt ratificar.
ⓘ pt & pp ratified, ger ratifying.

**ratings** ['reɪtɪŋs] n pl TV índice m sing de audiencia.

**ratio** ['reɪʃɪəʊ] n razón f, relación f, proporción f.
ⓘ pl ratios.

**ration** ['ræʃˀn] n ración f.
▸ vt racionar.
▸ n pl rations víveres mpl.

☒ Ration no significa 'ración (de comida)', que se traduce por portion.

**rational** ['ræʃˀnəl] adj racional.

**rattle** ['rætˀl] n **1** (object) carraca, matraca; (baby's) sonajero; (rattlesnake's) cascabel m. **2** (noise) ruido; (of train) traqueteo; (vibration) vibración f.
▸ vt hacer sonar, hacer vibrar.
▸ vi sonar, vibrar.

**rattlesnake** ['rætˀlsneɪk] n serpiente f de cascabel.

**ravage** ['rævɪdʒ] vt devastar, asolar.
▸ n pl ravages estragos mpl.

**rave** [reɪv] n GB fiesta con música de baile y que puede durar toda la noche.

**raven** ['reɪvˀn] n cuervo.

**ravine** [rəˈviːn] n barranco.

**raw** [rɔː] adj **1** (uncooked) crudo,-a. **2** (unprocessed) bruto,-a; (unrefined) sin refinar; (untreated) sin tratar. **3** (inexperienced) novato,-a. **4** (weather) crudo,-a.
COMP raw material materia prima.

**ray¹** [reɪ] n (of light) rayo.

**ray²** [reɪ] n (fish) raya.

**razor** ['reɪzəʳ] n **1** (cutthroat) navaja de afeitar; (safety) maquinilla de afeitar. **2** (electric) máquina de afeitar. COMP razor blade hoja de afeitar.

**reach** [riːtʃ] n alcance m. LOC beyond the reach of fuera del alcance de. ▮ out of reach of fuera del alcance de. ▮ within reach of **1** (at hand) al alcance de. **2** (near) cerca de
▸ vt **1** (arrive in/at, get to) llegar a. **2** (rise to, fall to) alcanzar. **3** (be able to touch) alcanzar, llegar a. **4** (contact) contactar, localizar. **5** (pass) alcanzar
▸ vi **1** (be long enough) llegar. **2** (extend) extenderse. **3** (take) extender la mano, tender la mano.

**react** [rɪˈækt] vi reaccionar.

**reaction** [rɪˈækʃˀn] n reacción f.

**reactor** [rɪˈæktəʳ] n reactor m.

**read** [riːd] vt **1** (gen) leer. **2** (instrument) indicar, marcar. **3** (sign, notice) decir, poner.
◆ to read out vt sep leer en voz alta.
ⓘ pt & pp read [red].

**readable** ['riːdəbˀl] adj **1** (handwriting) legible. **2** (style) ameno,-a.

**reader** ['riːdəʳ] n **1** (person - gen) lector,-ra; (- of proofs) corrector,-ra. **2** (at university) profesor,-ra adjunto,-a. **3** (apparatus) lector m.

**readily** ['redɪlɪ] adv **1** (easily) fácilmente. **2** (willingly) de buena gana.

**reading** ['riːdɪŋ] n **1** lectura. **2** (of bill, law) presentación f. **3** (of instrument) indicación f, lectura. **4** (interpretation) interpretación f.

**readjust** [riːəˈdʒʌst] vt reajustar.
▸ vi (readapt) readaptarse.

**ready** ['redɪ] adj **1** (prepared) preparado,-a, listo,-a. **2** (willing) dispuesto,-a. **3** (quick) rápido,-a; (easy) fácil. LOC to get ready prepararse. ▮ to get STH ready

**R**

preparar ALGO. ∎ **to make ready** preparar.

**ready-made** [redɪˈmeɪd] *adj* hecho,-a, confeccionado,-a.

**reafforestation** [rɪəfɒrɪˈsteɪʃ°n] *n* GB reforestación *f*, repoblación *f* forestal.

**reagent** [riːˈeɪdʒənt] *n* reactivo.

**real** [rɪəl] *adj* **1** real, verdadero,-a. **2** *(genuine)* auténtico,-a. COMP **real estate** bienes *mpl* inmuebles.
▸ *adv* US *fam* muy

**realise** [ˈrɪəlaɪz] *vt* → realize.

**reality** [rɪˈælɪtɪ] *n* realidad *f*.

**realize** [ˈrɪəlaɪz] *vt* **1** *(understand)* darse cuenta de, comprender. **2** *(know)* saber. **3** *(carry out)* realizar. **4** *(sell)* realizar, vender; *(fetch)* reportar

☒ To realize no significa 'realizar', que se traduce por **to carry out**.

**really** [ˈrɪəlɪ] *adv* **1** *(in fact)* en realidad. **2** *(very)* muy, realmente. **3** *(showing interest)* ¿ah sí?, ¿en serio? ¿de verdad?; *(showing surprise)* ¿de verdad?, ¡no me digas!; *(showing annoyance)* ¡vaya!

**reap** [riːp] *vt* cosechar.

**rear¹** [rɪəʳ] *adj* trasero,-a, de atrás.
▸ *n* **1** *(back part)* parte *f* de atrás. **2** *(of room)* fondo. **3** *fam (of person)* trasero.

**rearmament** [riːˈɑːməment] *n* rearme *m*.

**rearrange** [riːəˈreɪndʒ] *vt* **1** *(objects)* colocar de otra manera. **2** *(event)* cambiar la fecha de, cambiar la hora de.

**rear-view mirror** [rɪəvjuːˈmɪrə] *n* retrovisor *m*.

**reason** [ˈriːz°n] *n* **1** *(cause)* razón *f*, motivo. **2** *(faculty)* razón *f*.
▸ *vt* deducir, llegar a la conclusión de que
▸ *vi* razonar.

**reasonable** [ˈriːzənəb°l] *adj* **1** *(gen)* razonable. **2** *(acceptable)* aceptable.

**reasonably** [ˈriːz°nəblɪ] *adv* **1** *(gen)* razonablemente. **2** *(quite)* bastante.

**reassure** [riːəˈʃʊəʳ] *vt* **1** *(comfort)* tranquilizar. **2** *(assure again)* volver a asegurar.

**rebate** [ˈriːbeɪt] *n* **1** *(of tax)* devolución *f*. **2** *(discount)* descuento.

**rebel** [*(adj-n)* ˈreb°l; *(vb)* rɪˈbel] *adj* rebelde.
▸ *n* rebelde *mf*.
▸ *vi* rebelarse (**against**, contra).
ⓘ *pt & pp* **rebelled**, *ger* **rebelling**.

**rebellion** [rɪˈbelɪən] *n* rebelión *f*.

**rebound** [*(n)* ˈriːbaʊnd; *(vb)* rɪˈbaʊnd] *n* rebote *m*
▸ *vi* rebotar.

**recall** [*(n)* riːkɔːl; *(vb)* rɪˈkɔːl] *n* **1** *(memory)* memoria. **2** *(withdrawal)* retirada.
▸ *vt* **1** *(remember)* recordar. **2** *(withdraw)* retirar.

**receipt** [rɪˈsiːt] *n* **1** *(document)* recibo. **2** *(act of receiving)* recepción *f*, recibo.
▸ *n pl* **receipts** COMM ingresos *mpl*, recaudación *f sing*.

**receive** [rɪˈsiːv] *vt* **1** *(gen)* recibir. **2** *(wound)* sufrir. **3** *(radio signal)* recibir. **4** *(stolen goods)* comerciar con
▸ *vt* *(welcome)* recibir, acoger.

**receiver** [rɪˈsiːvəʳ] *n* **1** *(of telephone)* auricular *m*. **2** *(of stolen goods)* perista *mf*. **3** JUR síndico,-a, síndico,-a de quiebras. **4** *(of radio signal)* receptor *m*. **5** *(in American football)* receptor,-ra.

**recent** [ˈriːs°nt] *adj* reciente: *in recent months/years* en los últimos meses/años.

**recently** [ˈriːs°ntlɪ] *adv* **1** *(lately)* recientemente, últimamente. **2** *(a short time ago)* hace poco

**reception** [rɪˈsepʃ°n] *n* **1** *(gen)* recepción *f*. **2** *(welcome)* acogida. **3** *(party)* recepción *f*; *(after wedding)* banquete *m*. COMP **reception desk** recepción *f*.

**receptionist** [rɪˈsepʃ°nɪst] *n* recepcionista *m & f*.

**recharge** [riːˈtʃɑːdʒ] *vt* recargar.

**rechargeable** [riːˈtʃɑːdʒəb°l] *adj* recargable.

**recipe** [ˈresəpɪ] *n* **1** receta. **2** *fig* fórmula. COMP **recipe book 1** *(personal collection)* recetario. **2** *(cookery book)* libro de cocina.

**reckless** [ˈrekləs] *adj* **1** *(hasty)* precipitado,-a. **2** *(careless)* imprudente, temerario,-a. COMP **reckless driving** conducción *f* temeraria.

**reckon** [ˈrek°n] *vt* **1** *(estimate)* calcular. **2** *(calculate)* calcular. **3** *(regard)* considerar. **4** *(think)* creer, considerar.

**reckoning** ['rekənɪŋ] *n* cálculos *mpl*: *by my reckoning, ...* según mis cálculos,…

**recognise** ['rekəgnaɪz] *vt* → **recognize.**

**recognition** [rekəg'nɪʃən] *n* reconocimiento.

**recognize** ['rekəgnaɪz] *vt* reconocer.

**recollect** [rekə'lekt] *vt* recordar.

☒ To recollect no significa 'recolectar', que se traduce por to harvest.

**recollection** [rekə'lekʃən] *n* recuerdo.

☒ Recollection no significa 'recolección', que se traduce por harvest.

**recommend** [rekə'mend] *vt* recomendar.

**recommendation** [rekəmen'deɪʃən] *n* recomendación *f*.

**reconstruct** [ri:kəns'trʌkt] *vt* reconstruir.

**record** [(*n*) 'rekɔ:d; (*vb*) rɪ'kɔ:d] *n* **1** *(written evidence)* constancia escrita **2** *(note)* relación *f*. **3** *(facts about a person)* historial *m*. **4** MUS disco. **5** SP récord *m*, marca, plusmarca. ⎣LOC⎦ **to break a record** batir un récord. ⎣COMP⎦ **medical record** historial *m* médico. ▌ **record holder** plusmarquista *mf*. ▌ **record player** tocadiscos *m sing*.
▸ *vt* **1** *(write down)* anotar, apuntar. **2** *(voice, music)* grabar. **3** *(instrument, gauge)* registrar
▸ *adj* récord.
▸ *n pl* **records** *(files)* archivos *mpl*

☒ Record no significa 'recordar', que se traduce por to remember.

**recorded** [rɪ'kɔ:dɪd] *adj (written)* anotado,-a; *(on tape, etc)* grabado,-a. ⎣COMP⎦ **recorded delivery** correo certificado.

**recorder** [rɪ'kɔ:də<sup>r</sup>] *n* MUS flauta. ⎣COMP⎦ **cassette recorder** casete *m*.

**recording** [rɪ'kɔ:dɪŋ] *n* grabación *f*. ⎣COMP⎦ **recording studio** estudio de grabación.

**recover** [rɪ'kʌvə<sup>r</sup>] *vt (gen)* recuperar; *(dead body)* rescatar.
▸ *vi* recuperarse, reponerse.

**recovery** [rɪ'kʌvərɪ] *n* recuperación *f*.

**recreation** [rekrɪ'eɪʃən] *n* **1** *(free time)* esparcimiento. **2** *(hobby)* pasatiempo. **3** *(in school)* recreo.

**recruit** [rɪ'kru:t] *n (soldier)* recluta *m*.
▸ *vt (soldier)* reclutar.

**recruitment** [rɪ'kru:tmənt] *n (of soldiers)* reclutamiento; *(of employees)* contratación *f*.

**recta** ['rektə] *n pl* → **rectum.**

**rectangle** ['rektæŋgəl] *n* rectángulo.

**rectangular** [rekt'æŋgjulə<sup>r</sup>] *adj* rectangular.

**rectify** ['rektɪfaɪ] *vt* rectificar.

**rectum** ['rektəm] *n* recto.
ⓘ *pl* rectums o recta ['rektə].

**recur** [rɪ'kɜ:<sup>r</sup>] *vi* repetirse, reproducirse.
ⓘ *pt & pp* recurred, *ger* recurring.

☒ To recur no significa 'recurrir a', que se traduce por to resort to, to turn to.

**recurrent** [rɪ'kʌrənt] *adj* **1** MATH periódico,-a. **2** MED recurrente.

**recycle** [ri:'saɪkəl] *vt* reciclar.

**recycling** [ri:'saɪkəlɪŋ] *n* reciclaje *m*.

**red** [red] *n* **1** *(colour)* rojo. **2** *(left-winger)* rojo,-a.
▸ *adj* **1** rojo,-a **2** *(hair)* pelirrojo,-a.
ⓘ *comp* redder, *superl* reddest.

**redbreast** ['redbrest] *n* petirrojo.

**redcurrant** [red'kʌrənt] *n* grosella.

**redemption** [rɪ'dempʃən] *n* **1** *(of debt)* pago. **2** *(of voucher)* canje *m*. **3** REL redención *f*.

**red-haired** ['red'heəd] *adj* pelirrojo,-a.

**redhead** ['redhed] *n* pelirrojo,-a.

**redid** [ri:'dɪd] *pt* → **redo.**

**redo** [ri:'du:] *vt* rehacer, volver a hacer.
ⓘ *pt* redid [ri:'dɪd], *pp* redone [ri:'dʌn], *ger* redoing.

**redone** [ri:'dʌn] *pp* → **redo.**

**redskin** ['redskɪn] *n* piel roja *mf*.

**reduce** [rɪ'dju:s] *vt* **1** *(gen)* reducir, disminuir. **2** *(price, etc)* rebajar.

**reduction** [rɪ'dʌkʃən] *n* *(gen)* reducción *f*; *(fall)* disminución *f*; *(in price)* rebaja.

**redundancy** [rɪ'dʌndənsɪ] *n* **1** *(dismissal)* despido. **2** *(superfluity)* superfluidad *f*. **3** LING redundancia.
ⓘ *pl* redundancies.

**R**

**redundant** [rɪ'dʌndənt] *adj* **1** *(dismissed)* despedido,-a. **2** *(superfluous)* super-fluo,-a. **3** LING redundante.

**redwood** ['redwʊd] *n* secuoya.

**reed** [riːd] *n* **1** *(plant)* caña, junco. **2** MUS lengüeta.

**reef** [riːf] *n* arrecife *m*.

**reel** [riːl] *n* **1** *(of thread, cotton)* carrete *m*; *(of camera film)* carrete *m*, rollo; *(of cine film)* bobina; *(of wire, tape)* rollo *m*. **2** *(for fishing)* carrete *m*.
◆ **to reel in** *vt sep (line)* recoger, cobrar; *(fish)* cobrar, sacar del agua.

**refer** [rɪ'fɜːr] *vt (send)* mandar, enviar
▸ *vi* **1** *(allude to)* referirse (**to**, a). **2** *(mention, name)* hacer referencia (**to**, a).
ⓘ *pt & pp* referred, *ger* referring.

**referee** [refə'riː] *n* SP árbitro,-a.
▸ *vt* arbitrar.

**reference** ['refərəns] *n* **1** referencia, mención **2** *(for job)* referencias *fpl*. COMP **reference book** libro de consulta.

**referendum** [refə'rendəm] *n* referéndum *m*.
ⓘ *pl* referendums o referenda [refə-'rendə].

**refill** [*(n)* 'riːfɪl; *(vb)* riː'fɪl] *n (for pen, etc)* recambio; *(for lighter)* carga.
▸ *vt (glass, pen)* volver a llenar; *(lighter)* recargar.

**refinery** [rɪ'faɪnərɪ] *n* refinería.
ⓘ *pl* refineries.

**reflect** [rɪ'flekt] *vt* reflejar.
▸ *vi (think)* reflexionar (**on**, sobre).
◆ **to reflect on** *vt insep* perjudicar.

**reflection** [rɪ'flekʃ°n] *n* **1** *(image)* reflejo. **2** *(thought)* reflexión *f*. **3** *(aspersion)* descrédito. LOC **on reflection,** ... pensándolo bien, ...

**reflector** [rɪ'flektər] *n (gen)* reflector *m*; *(on car)* catafaro *m*.

**reflex** ['riːfleks] *n* reflejo.
ⓘ *pl* reflexes.

**reflexive** [rɪ'fleksɪv] *adj* reflexivo,-a.

**reforest** [riː'fɒrɪst] *vt* reforestar.

**reforestation** [riːfɒrɪ'steɪʃ°n] *n* reforestación *f*, repoblación *f* forestal.

**reform** [rɪ'fɔːm] *n* reforma.
▸ *vt* reformar.

**refraction** [rɪ'frækʃ°n] *n* refracción *f*.

**refrain¹** [rɪ'freɪn] *n* MUS estribillo.

☒ Refrain no significa 'refrán', que se traduce por proverb, saying.

**refrain²** [rɪ'freɪn] *vi* abstenerse (**from**, de)

**refresh** [rɪ'freʃ] *vt* refrescar.

**refreshing** [rɪ'freʃɪŋ] *adj (gen)* refrescante; *(rest, sleep)* reparador,-ra.

**refreshment** [rɪ'freʃmənt] *n* refresco.

**refrigerator** [rɪ'frɪdʒəreɪtər] *n* frigorífico, nevera.

**refuge** ['refjuːdʒ] *n* refugio.

**refugee** [refjuː'dʒiː] *n* refugiado,-a.

**refund** [*(n)* 'riːfʌnd; *(vb)* riː'fʌnd] *n* reembolso.
▸ *vt* reembolsar.

**refusal** [rɪ'fjuːzəl] *n* **1** *(negative reply)* negativa, respuesta negativa. **2** *(rejection)* rechazo.

**refuse¹** ['refjuːs] *n* basura. COMP **refuse collection** recogida de basuras.

**refuse²** [rɪ'fjuːz] *vt* **1** *(reject)* rehusar, rechazar, no aceptar. **2** *(withhold)* negar, denegar, no conceder
▸ *vi* negarse (**to**, a)

**regard** [rɪ'gɑːd] *n* respeto, consideración. LOC **to hold in high regard** tener en gran estima. **I without regard to** sin hacer caso de.
▸ *vt* **1** *(consider)* considerar. **2** *(look at)* mirar. **3** *(heed)* hacer caso a.
▸ *n pl* **regards** recuerdos *mpl*.

**regarding** [rɪ'gɑːdɪŋ] *prep* tocante a, respecto a.

**regardless** [rɪ'gɑːdləs] *adv fam* a pesar de todo.
▸ *prep* **regardless of** *fam* sin tener en cuenta.

**regime** [reɪ'ʒiːm] *n* [also written régime] régimen *m*.

**regiment** ['redʒɪmənt] *n* regimiento.
▸ *vt* **1** MIL regimentar. **2** *fig* disciplinar, reglamentar.

**region** ['riːdʒ°n] *n* región *f*.

**regional** ['riːdʒ°nəl] *adj* regional.

**register** ['redʒɪstər] *n (gen)* registro; *(in school)* lista. COMP **register office** registro civil.

▶ *vt* **1** *(put on record, list)* registrar; *(car, student)* matricular; *(birth, death, marriage)* inscribir en el registro. **2** *(show - reading)* indicar, marcar; *(- feeling)* mostrar, reflejar. **3** *(make known)* hacer constar. **4** *(letter)* certificar.
▶ *vi* **1** *(for classes)* matricularse; *(at congress, with doctor)* inscribirse; *(at hotel)* registrarse.

⊠ To register no significa 'registrar (cachear)', que se traduce por to frisk.

**registered** ['redʒɪstəd] *adj* **1** *(person)* inscrito,-a; *(student)* matriculado,-a. **2** *(letter)* certificado,-a. **3** *(car, etc)* matriculado,-a; *(ship)* de bandera. [COMP] **registered trademark** marca registrada.

**registration** [redʒɪs'treɪʃ°n] *n* **1** *(of birth, death, marriage)* inscripción *f*; *(of patent, etc)* registro. **2** *(enrolment)* inscripción *f*; *(of student)* matrícula. [COMP] **registration number** AUTO matrícula.

**registry** ['redʒɪstrɪ] *n* registro. [COMP] **registry office** registro civil

**regret** [rɪ'gret] *n* **1** *(remorse)* remordimiento. **2** *(sadness)* pesar *m*.
▶ *vt* **1** *(feel sorry)* lamentar, arrepentirse de. **2** *(express one's sadness)* lamentar. **3** *(miss)* echar de menos, echar en falta.
▶ *n pl* **regrets** excusas *mpl*

**regular** ['regjʊlə<sup>r</sup>] *adj*. **1** *(gen)* regular. **2** *(normal)* normal. **3** *(habitual)* habitual. **4** *(normal in size)* de tamaño normal. **5** US *(pleasant)* simpático,-a.
▶ *n fam* cliente *mf* habitual.

⊠ Regular no significa 'regular (pasable)', que se traduce por so-so, not bad.

**regularity** [regjʊ'lærətɪ] *n* regularidad *f*.
**regularly** ['regjʊləlɪ] *adv* regularmente, con regularidad.
**regulate** ['regjʊleɪt] *vt* regular.
**regulation** [regjʊ'leɪʃ°n] *n* **1** *(control)* regulación *f*. **2** *(rule)* regla.
**rehearsal** [rɪ'hɜ:s°l] *n* ensayo.
**rehearse** [rɪ'hɜ:s] *vt* ensayar.
**reign** [reɪn] *n* reinado.
▶ *vi* reinar.
**rein** [reɪn] *n* rienda.
▶ *n pl* **reins** *(child's)* andadores *mpl*.

**reindeer** ['reɪndɪə<sup>r</sup>] *n* reno.
ⓘ *pl* reindeer o reindeers.

**reject** [*(n)* 'ri:dʒekt; *(vb)* rɪ'dʒekt] *n* *(thing)* artículo defectuoso; *(person)* marginado,-a.
▶ *vt* *(gen)* rechazar, no aceptar; *(in law)* desestimar.

**rejection** [rɪ'dʒekʃ°n] *n* *(gen)* rechazo; *(negative reply)* respuesta negativa.

**rejoice** [rɪ'dʒɔɪs] *vi* alegrarse.

**relapse** [rɪ'læps] *n* **1** MED recaída. **2** *(crime)* reincidencia.
▶ *vi* **1** MED recaer. **2** *(crime)* reincidir. [LOC] **to suffer a relapse** tener una recaída.

**relate** [rɪ'leɪt] *vt* **1** *(tell)* relatar, contar. **2** *(connect)* relacionar (**to**, con).
▶ *vi* *(connect)* relacionarse.

**related** [rɪ'leɪtɪd] *adj* **1** *(connected)* relacionado,-a. **2** *(relatives)* emparentado,-a.

**relation** [rɪ'leɪʃ°n] *n* **1** *(connection)* relación *f*. **2** *(family)* pariente *mf*.

**relationship** [rɪ'leɪʃ°nʃɪp] *n* **1** *(connection)* relación *f*. **2** *(between people)* relaciones *fpl*.

**relative** ['relətɪv] *adj* relativo,-a.
▶ *n* pariente *mf*, familiar *mf*.

**relatively** ['relətɪvlɪ] *adv* relativamente.
**relativity** [relə'tɪvɪtɪ] *n* relatividad *f*.

**relaunch** [*(vb)* ri:'lɔ:ntʃ; *(n)* 'ri:lɔ:ntʃ] *vt* relanzar.
▶ *n* relanzamiento.

**relax** [rɪ'læks] *vt* **1** *(gen)* relajar. **2** *(grip, hold)* aflojar. **3** *(rules, control)* suavizar.
▶ *vi* **1** *(gen)* relajarse. **2** *(grip, hold)* aflojarse.

**relaxation** [ri:læk'seɪʃ°n] *n* **1** *(gen)* relajación *f*. **2** *(of grip, hold)* aflojamiento. **3** *(of rules, control)* suavización *f*.

**relaxed** [rɪ'lækst] *adj* **1** *(person)* relajado,-a. **2** *(atmosphere)* distendido,-a.

**relaxing** [rɪ'læksɪŋ] *adj* relajante.

**relay** ['ri:leɪ] *n* **1** relevo. **2** ELEC relé *m*. [COMP] **relay race** carrera de relevos. ▌ **relay station** estación *f* repetidora.

**release** [rɪ'li:s] *n* **1** *(setting free)* liberación *f*, puesta en libertad. **2** *(relief)* alivio. **3** *(of film)* estreno; *(of record)* lanzamiento. **4** *(of gas, etc)* emisión *f*.

R

**5** *(new thing - film)* estreno, novedad *f* cinematográfica; *(- record)* nuevo disco, novedad *f* discográfica. **6** *(statement)* comunicado.
▶ *vt* **1** *(set free)* liberar, poner en libertad. **2** *(let go of)* soltar. **3** *(bring out - film)* estrenar; *(- record)* sacar. **4** *(gas, etc - give out)* emitir. **5** *(statement, information)* hacer público, dar a conocer.

**relevant** ['reləvənt] *adj* **1** *(connected)* pertinente. **2** *(important)* relevante.

**reliable** [rɪˈlaɪəbəl] *adj* fiable.

**relief** [rɪˈliːf] *n* **1** *(from pain, etc)* alivio. **2** *(help)* auxilio, socorro, ayuda. **3** *(person)* relevo. **4** *(lifting of siege)* liberación *f*. **5** GEOG relieve *m*.

**relieve** [rɪˈliːv] *vt* **1** *(lessen)* aliviar. **2** *(take over from)* relevar. **3** *(help)* socorrer, ayudar. **4** *(lift siege of)* liberar.

**religion** [rɪˈlɪdʒən] *n* religión *f*.

**religious** [rɪˈlɪdʒəs] *adj* religioso,-a.

**reload** [riːˈləʊd] *vt* **1** *(gun)* volver a cargar; *(program, page)* recargar.

**reluctant** [rɪˈlʌktənt] *adj* reacio,-a.

**reluctantly** [rɪˈlʌktəntlɪ] *adv* muy a mi *(tu, su, etc)* pesar.

**rely on** [rɪˈlaɪ ɒn] *vt (trust)* confiar en.
ⓘ *pt & pp* relied.

**remade** [riːˈmeɪd] *pt & pp* → remake.

**remain** [rɪˈmeɪn] *vi* **1** *(stay)* quedarse, permanecer. **2** *(be left)* quedar, sobrar. **3** *(continue)* seguir, continuar.
▶ *n pl* remains restos *mpl*.

**remainder** [rɪˈmeɪndər] *n* resto.

**remake** [*(n)* ˈriːmeɪk; *(vb)* riːˈmeɪk] *n* nueva versión *f*.
▶ *vt* hacer una nueva versión de.
ⓘ *pt & pp* remade [riːˈmeɪd].

**remark** [rɪˈmɑːk] *n* observación *f*.
▶ *vt* **1** *(say)* observar, comentar. **2** *(notice)* advertir.
◆ **to remark on** *vt insep* comentar.

**remarkable** [rɪˈmɑːkəbəl] *adj* **1** *(exceptional)* extraordinario,-a, excepcional. **2** *(odd)* extraño,-a; *(surprising)* sorprendente, curioso,-a.

**remedy** [ˈremədɪ] *n* remedio.
ⓘ *pl* remedies.
▶ *vt* remediar.

**remember** [rɪˈmembər] *vt* **1** recordar, acordarse de. **2** *(commemorate)* recordar.
▶ *vi* acordarse, recordar.

> ✎ La diferencia entre remember y remind es que remember se refiere al acto de recordar algo (acordarse de) y remind se emplea cuando se le recuerda algo a alguien.

**remind** [rɪˈmaɪnd] *vt* recordar.

> ✎ Consulta también remember.

**reminder** [rɪˈmaɪndər] *n* **1** *(note)* recordatorio. **2** *(of payment due)* aviso. **3** *(keepsake)* recuerdo.

**remorse** [rɪˈmɔːs] *n* remordimiento.

**remote** [rɪˈməʊt] *adj* **1** *(far away)* remoto,-a, lejano,-a. **2** *(lonely)* aislado,-a, apartado,-a. **3** *(person)* distante. COMP **remote control** mando a distancia.

**removal** [rɪˈmuːvəl] *n* **1** *(getting rid of)* eliminación *f*; *(surgically)* extirpación *f*. **2** *(moving)* traslado; *(to another house)* traslado, mudanza. **3** *(from post)* destitución *f*.

**remove** [rɪˈmuːv] *vt* **1** *(get rid of - gen)* quitar, eliminar; *(- surgically)* extirpar. **2** *(take out, take off)* quitar. **3** *(move)* trasladar. **4** *(dismiss)* destituir.
▶ *vi (change houses)* trasladarse.

**renaissance** [rəˈneɪsəns] *n* renacimiento. COMP **the Renaissance** el Renacimiento.
▶ *adj* **Renaissance** renacentista.

**rename** [riːˈneɪm] *vt* renombrar.

**rendezvous** [ˈrɒndɪvuː] *n* **1** cita. **2** *(place)* lugar *m* de reunión.
ⓘ *pl* rendezvous.

**renew** [rɪˈnjuː] *vt* **1** *(gen)* renovar; *(contract, permit, etc)* prorrogar. **2** *(start again)* reanudar. **3** *(replace)* sustituir.

**renewable** [rɪˈnjuːəbəl] *adj* renovable. COMP **renewable energy** energía renovable.

**renounce** [rɪˈnaʊns] *vt* renunciar a.

**rent** [rent] *n* **1** *(for flat, etc)* alquiler *m*. **2** *(for land)* arriendo.
▶ *vt* **1** *(flat)* alquilar. **2** *(land)* arrendar.
LOC **"For rent"** «Se alquila».

> ✘ Renta no significa 'renta (ingresos)', que se traduce por income.

**rental** ['rentəl] *n* **1** *(for flat, etc)* alquiler *m*. **2** *(for land)* arriendo.

**rented** ['rentɪd] *adj* de alquiler.

**reorganise** [ri:'ɔ:gənaɪz] *vt* → **reorganize**.

**reorganize** [ri:'ɔ:gənaɪz] *vt* reorganizar.

**repaid** [ri:'peɪd] *pt & pp* → **repay**.

**repair** [rɪ'peəʳ] *n* reparación *f*.
▶ *vt* reparar, arreglar.

**repay** [ri:'peɪ] *vt* devolver.
ⓘ *pt & pp* **repaid**, *ger* **repaying**.

**repeat** [rɪ'pi:t] *n* **1** *(gen)* repetición *f*. **2** *(on television)* reposición *f*.
▶ *vt & vi* repetir.

**repel** [rɪ'pel] *vt* **1** *(gen)* repeler. **2** *(disgust)* repugnar, repeler.
ⓘ *pt & pp* **repelled**, *ger* **repelling**.

**repellent** [rɪ'pelənt] *n* repelente *m*.
▶ *vt* arrepentirse de.

**repetition** [repə'tɪʃən] *n* repetición *f*.

**repetitive** [rɪ'petɪtɪv] *adj* repetitivo,-a.

**replace** [rɪ'pleɪs] *vt* **1** *(put back)* devolver a su sitio. **2** *(substitute)* reemplazar, sustituir; *(change)* cambiar.

**replacement** [rɪ'pleɪsmənt] *n* **1** *(act)* sustitución *f*, reemplazo. **2** *(person)* sustituto,-a. **3** *(thing)* otro,-a. **4** *(spare part)* recambio, pieza de recambio.

**replay** [*(n)* 'ri:pleɪ; *(vb)* ri:'pleɪ] *n* **1** *(of film sequence)* repetición *f* de la jugada. **2** *(match)* partido de desempate.
▶ *vt* **1** *(tape, film)* volver a poner. **2** *(match)* volver a jugar.

**reply** [rɪ'plaɪ] *n* respuesta, contestación *f*. LOC **in reply to** en respuesta a.
ⓘ *pl* **replies**.
▶ *vi* responder (to, a), contestar (to, a).
ⓘ *pt & pp* **replied**.

**report** [rɪ'pɔ:t] *n* **1** *(informative document)* informe *m*. **2** *(school report)* boletín *m* escolar, informe *m* escolar. **3** *(piece of news)* noticia. **4** *(news story)* reportaje *m*. **5** *(rumour)* rumor *m*. **6** *(of gun)* estampido.
▶ *vi* **1** *(give information)* informar (on, sobre). **2** *(go in person)* presentarse.
▶ *vt* **1** *(say, inform)* decir. **2** *(to authority)* informar de. **3** *(to police - crime)* denunciar; *(- accident)* dar parte de

**reported speech** [rɪpɔ:tɪd'spi:tʃ] *n* estilo indirecto.

**reporter** [rɪ'pɔ:təʳ] *n* reportero,-a.

**represent** [reprɪ'zent] *vt* representar.

**representative** [reprɪ'zentətɪv] *adj* representativo,-a.
▶ *n* **1** representante *mf*. **2** US diputado,-a.

**reproach** [rɪ'prəʊtʃ] *n* reproche *m*.
▶ *vt* reprochar (for, -).

**reproduce** [ri:prə'dju:s] *vt* reproducir.
▶ *vi* reproducirse.

**reproduction** [ri:prə'dʌkʃən] *n* reproducción *f*.

**reproductive** [ri:prə'dʌktɪv] *adj* reproductor,-ra.

**reptile** ['reptaɪl] *n* reptil *m*.

**republic** [rɪ'pʌblɪk] *n* república.

**republican** [rɪ'pʌblɪkən] *adj* republicano,-a.
▶ *n* republicano,-a.

**repugnant** [rɪ'pʌgnənt] *adj* repugnante.

**repulsion** [rɪ'pʌlʒən] *vt* **1** *(reject)* rechazar. **2** *(drive back)* repulsar.

**repulsive** [rɪ'pʌlsɪv] *adj* repulsivo,-a.

**reputation** [repjʊ'teɪʃən] *n* reputación *f*, fama. LOC **to have a reputation for …** tener fama de…

**request** [rɪ'kwest] *n* **1** solicitud *f*, petición *f*. **2** *(on radio)* canción *f*.
▶ *vt* **1** *(gen)* pedir, solicitar; *(officially)* rogar. **2** *(on radio)* pedir.

**require** [rɪ'kwaɪəʳ] *vt* **1** requerir, exigir. **2** *(need)* necesitar, requerir. LOC **to be required to do sth** estar obligado,-a a hacer ALGO.

**requirement** [rɪ'kwaɪəmənt] *n* **1** *(demand)* requisito. **2** *(need)* necesidad *f*.

**reran** [ri:'ræn] *pt* → **rerun**.

**rerun** [*(n)* 'ri:rʌn; *(vb)* ri:'rʌn] *n* *(repetition)* repetición *f*; *(TV programme)* reposición *f*; *(film)* reestreno.
▶ *vt* *(repeat)* repetir; *(TV programme)* reponer; *(film)* reestrenar.
ⓘ *pt* **reran** [ri:'ræn], *pp* **rerun** [ri:'rʌn], *ger* **rerunning**.

**resat** ['ri:sæt] *pt & pp* → **resit**.

**rescue** ['reskju:] *n* rescate *m*.
▶ *vt* rescatar (from, de).

**research** [rɪ'sɜ:tʃ] *n* investigación *f*.
▶ *vi* investigar (into, -).
▶ *vt* documentar.

**R**

**researcher** [rɪ'sɜːtʃəʳ] *n* investigador,-ra.

**resemblance** [rɪ'zembləns] *n* parecido, semejanza.

**resemble** [rɪ'zembᵊl] *vt* parecerse a.

**resent** [rɪ'zent] *vt* ofenderse por.

**resentment** [rɪ'zentmənt] *n* resentimiento, rencor *m*.

**reservation** [rezə'veɪʃᵊn] *n* reserva.

**reserve** [rɪ'zɜːv] *n* (gen) reserva.
▸ *vt* reservar.

**reservoir** ['rezəvwɑːʳ] *n* **1** (lake) embalse *m*. **2** (store) reserva.

**reset** [riːˈset] *vt* **1** (programmer, computer) reinicializar. **2** (mechanism) rearmar. **2** (clock) poner en hora. **3** (bone) componer. **4** (book) recomponer.
ⓘ *pt & pp* reset, *ger* resetting.

**residence** ['rezɪdəns] *n* residencia.

**resident** ['rezɪdᵊnt] *adj* residente.
▸ *n* (gen) residente *mf*; (of area) vecino, -a; (in hotel) huésped,-da.

**residential** [resɪ'denʃᵊl] *adj* residencial.

**residual** [rɪ'zɪdjuəl] *adj* residual.

**resign** [rɪ'zaɪn] *vi* dimitir (from, de), presentar la dimisión.
▸ *vt* dimitir de. ⌐ᴸᴼᶜ¬ **to resign os to** sᴛʜ resignarse a ALGO.

**resignation** [rezɪg'neɪʃᵊn] *n* **1** (from post) dimisión *f*. **2** (acceptance) resignación *f*. ⌐ᴸᴼᶜ¬ **to hand in one's resignation** presentar la dimisión.

**resilience** [rɪ'zɪliəns] *n* **1** (flexibility) elasticidad *f*. **2** (strength) fuerza, resistencia.

**resin** ['rezɪn] *n* resina.

**resist** [rɪ'zɪst] *vt* **1** (not give in to) resistir. **2** (oppose) oponer resistencia a.

**resistance** [rɪ'zɪstəns] *n* **1** (gen) resistencia. **2** (opposition) oposición *f*. ⌐ᴸᴼᶜ¬ **to put up resistance** oponer resistencia.

**resistant** [rɪ'zɪstənt] *adj* resistente.

**resit** [(n) 'riːsɪt; (vb) riː'sɪt] *n* examen *m* de repesca.
▸ *vt* volver a presentarse a.
ⓘ *pt & pp* resat [riː'sɪt], *ger* resitting.

**resolution** ['rezəluːʃən] *n* resolución *f*.

**resort** [rɪ'zɔːt] *n* **1** (place) lugar *m* de vacaciones. **2** (recourse) recurso.
▸ *vi* recurrir (to, a).

**resource** [rɪ'zɔːs] *n* recurso.

**respect** [rɪ'spekt] *n* **1** (admiration, consideration) respeto. **2** (aspect) respecto.
▸ *vt* respetar.

**respectable** [rɪ'spektəbᵊl] *adj* **1** (gen) respetable. **2** (decent) decente.

**respiration** [respɪ'reɪʃən] *n* respiración *f*.

**respiratory** ['respᵊrətᵊrɪ] *adj* respiratorio,-a. ⌐ᶜᴼᴹᴾ¬ **respiratory system** sistema *m* respiratorio.

**respond** [rɪ'spɒnd] *vi* responder.

**response** [rɪ'spɒns] *n* **1** (gen) respuesta. **2** (reaction) reacción *f*.

**responsibility** [rɪspɒnsɪ'bɪlɪtɪ] *n* responsabilidad *f*. ⌐ᶜᴼᴹᴾ¬ **to accept responsibility for** responsabilizarse de.
ⓘ *pl* responsibilities.

**responsible** [rɪ'spɒnsəbᵊl] *adj* **1** (gen) responsable. **2** (position) de responsabilidad

**rest¹** [rest] *n* **1** (repose) descanso, reposo. **2** (peace) paz *f*, tranquilidad *f*. **3** (support) soporte *m*; (for head) reposacabezas *m*; (for arms) apoyabrazos *m*.
▸ *vt* **1** (relax) descansar. **2** (lean) apoyar.
▸ *vi* **1** (relax) descansar. **2** (be calm) quedarse tranquilo,-a. **3** (depend) depender (on, de).
▸ *vt* (lean) apoyar.

☒ To rest no significa 'restar', que se traduce por to substract.

**rest²** [rest] *vi* quedar así.
▸ *n* **the rest** el resto.

**restaurant** ['restᵊrɒnt] *n* restaurante *m*.

**restless** ['restləs] *adj* inquieto,-a. ⌐ᴸᴼᶜ¬ **to grow restless** impacientarse.

**restoration** [restə'reɪʃᵊn] *n* **1** (gen) restauración *f*. **2** (return) devolución *f*.

**restore** [rɪ'stɔːʳ] *vt* **1** (gen) restaurar. **2** (return) devolver. **3** (order) restablecer.

**restrain** [rɪ'streɪn] *vt* contener.

**restrict** [rɪ'strɪkt] *vt* restringir, limitar.

**restriction** [rɪ'strɪkʃən] *n* (limited) restricción *f*.

**result** [rɪ'zʌlt] *n* **1** resultado. **2** (consequence) consecuencia.
▸ *vi* **to result from** resultar de.
◆ **to result in** *vt insep* producir.

**resume** [rɪˈzjuːm] *vt* **1** *(begin again)* reanudar. **2** *(take over again)* volver a asumir.
▶ *vi* continuar.

❌ To resume no significa 'resumir', que se traduce por to summarize.

**résumé** [ˈrezjuːmeɪ] *n* **1** *(summary)* resumen *m*. **2** US *(curriculum vitae)* currículo, currículum vitae *m*.

**resuscitate** [rɪˈsʌsɪteɪt] *vt* reanimar.

**retail** [ˈriːteɪl] *n* venta al detalle, venta al por menor.
▶ *vt* vender al detalle, vender al por menor.
▶ *adv* al detalle, al por menor.

**retailer** [ˈriːteɪləʳ] *n* detallista *mf*, minorista *mf*.

**retain** [rɪˈteɪn] *vt* **1** *(keep - power, moisture)* retener; *(- heat, charge)* conservar. **2** SP *(lead)* mantener; *(title)* revalidar. **3** *(possessions)* guardar. **4** *(remember)* retener, recordar. **5** *(hold back)* contener. **6** *(employ)* contratar.

**retaliate** [rɪˈtælɪeɪt] *vi* tomar represalias (against, contra).

**retard** [rɪˈtɑːd] *vt* retardar, retrasar.

**retina** [ˈretɪnə] *n* retina.
ⓘ *pl* retinas o retinae [ˈretɪniː].

**retinue** [ˈretɪnjuː] *n* séquito.

**retire** [rɪˈtaɪəʳ] *vt* *(from work)* jubilar.
▶ *vi* **1** *(from work)* jubilarse. **2** *(withdraw)* retirarse. **3** *(go to bed)* acostarse.

**retired** [rɪˈtaɪəd] *adj* jubilado,-a.

**retirement** [rɪˈtaɪənt] *n* jubilación *f*.

**retrace** [rɪˈtreɪs] *vt* desandar, volver sobre. LOC to retrace one's steps volver sobre sus pasos.

**retreat** [rɪˈtriːt] *n* **1** *(withdrawal)* retirada. **2** *(place)* retiro, refugio.
▶ *vi* **1** *(withdraw)* retirarse. **2** *(back down)* dar marcha atrás.

**retribution** [retrɪˈbjuːʃən] *n* justo castigo.

❌ Retribution no significa 'retribución (pago)', que se traduce por pay.

**retrospective** [retrəˈspektɪv] *adj* **1** *(exhibition, etc)* retrospectivo,-a. **2** *(law)* retroactivo,-a.

**return** [rɪˈtɜːn] *n* **1** *(coming or going back)* vuelta, regreso. **2** *(giving back)* devolución *f*. **3** SP *(of ball)* devolución *f*; *(of service)* resto. **4** *(on keyboard)* retorno. **5** *(ticket)* billete *m* de ida y vuelta. COMP return ticket billete *m* de ida y vuelta.
▶ *vi* **1** *(come back, go back)* volver, regresar. **2** *(reappear)* reaparecer.
▶ *vt* **1** *(give back)* devolver. **2** SP *(ball)* devolver; *(serve)* restar. **3** POL *(elect)* elegir. **4** *(verdict)* pronunciar. **5** *(interest)* producir.
▶ *n pl* returns resultados *mpl* electorales.

**returnable** [rɪˈtɜːnəbəl] *adj* retornable.

**reunion** [riːˈjuːnɪən] *n* reencuentro.

❌ Reunion no significa 'reunión', que se traduce por meeting.

**reunite** [riːjuːˈnaɪt] *vt* *(parts)* reunir.

**reuse** [riːjuːˈz] *vt* *(parts)* reutilizar.

**reveal** [rɪˈviːl] *vt* **1** *(make known)* revelar. **2** *(show)* dejar ver, mostrar.

❌ To reveal no significa 'revelar (una foto)', que se traduce por to develop.

**revenge** [rɪˈvendʒ] *n* venganza.
▶ *vt* vengar. LOC to revenge os vengarse.

**revenue** [ˈrevənjuː] *n* ingresos *mpl*.

**reverberation** [rɪˈvɜːbəreɪʃən] *vt* resonar, retumbar.

**reverse** [rɪˈvɜːs] *adj* inverso,-a.
▶ *n* **1** *(back - coin, paper)* reverso; *(- of cloth)* revés *m*. **2** AUTO marcha atrás. **3** *(setback)* revés *m*. COMP reverse gear marcha atrás. ▌ the reverse side **1** *(of coin, paper)* reverso. **2** *(of cloth)* revés *m*.
▶ *vt* **1** *(positions, roles)* invertir. **2** *(decision)* revocar. **3** *(vehicle)* dar marcha atrás a.
▶ *vi* AUTO poner marcha atrás, dar marcha atrás.
▶ *n* the reverse lo contrario.

**revert** [rɪˈvɜːt] *vi* **1** volver (to, a). **2** JUR revertir.

**review** [rɪˈvjuː] *n* **1** *(magazine, show)* revista. **2** MIL revista. **3** *(examination)* examen *m*. **4** *(of film, book, etc)* crítica.
▶ *vt* **1** *(troops)* pasar revista a. **2** *(examine)* examinar. **3** *(film, book, etc)* hacer una crítica de. LOC under review bajo revisión.

R

**revise** [rɪˈvaɪz] *vt* **1** revisar. **2** *(correct)* corregir. **3** *(change)* modificar. **4** *(examination topic)* repasar.
▶ *vi (for exam)* repasar.

**revision** [rɪˈvɪʒᵊn] *n* **1** revisión *f.* **2** *(correction)* corrección *f.* **3** *(change)* modificación *f.* **4** *(for exam)* repaso.

**revival** [rɪˈvaɪvᵊl] *n* **1** *(rebirth)* renacimiento. **2** *(of economy)* reactivación *f.* **3** *(of play)* reestreno.

**revive** [rɪˈvaɪv] *vt* **1** reanimar, reavivar, despertar. **2** *(economy)* reactivar. **3** *(play)* reestrenar. **4** MED reanimar.
▶ *vi* MED volver en sí.

**revolt** [rɪˈvəʊlt] *n (rising)* revuelta, rebelión *f.*
▶ *vi (rise)* sublevarse (**against**, contra), rebelarse (**against**, contra).
▶ *vt (disgust)* repugnar.

**revolting** [rɪˈvəʊltɪŋ] *adj* repugnante, asqueroso,-a.

**revolution** [revəˈluːʃᵊn] *n* revolución *f.*

**revolutionary** [revəˈluːʃᵊnərɪ] *adj* revolucionario,-a.
▶ *n* revolucionario,-a.

**revolve** [rɪˈvɒlv] *vi* girar.
▶ *vt* hacer girar.

**revolver** [rɪˈvɒlvəʳ] *n* revólver *m.*

**revolving** [rɪˈvɒlvɪŋ] *adj* giratorio,-a.
COMP **revolving door** puerta giratoria.

**reward** [rɪˈwɔːd] *n* recompensa.
▶ *vt* recompensar.

**rewind** [riːˈwaɪnd] *vt* rebobinar.
ⓘ *pt & pp* rewound [riːˈwaʊnd].

**rewound** [riːˈwaʊnd] *pt & pp* → rewind.

**rewrite** [*(vb)* riːˈraɪt; *(n)* ˈriːraɪt] *vt* volver a escribir.
ⓘ *pt* rewrote [riːˈrəʊt], *pp* rewritten [riːˈrɪtən].
▶ *n* nueva versión *f.*

**rewritten** [riːˈrɪtən] *pp* → rewrite.

**rewrote** [riːˈrəʊt] *pt* → rewrite.

**rheumatism** [ˈruːmətɪzᵊm] *n* reumatismo, reuma *m*, reúma *m.*

**rhinoceros** [raɪˈnɒsərəs] *n* rinoceronte *m.*
ⓘ *pl* rhinoceroses o rhinoceros.

**rhizome** [ˈraɪzəʊm] *n* rizoma *m.*

**rhombus** [ˈrɒmbəs] *n* rombo.
ⓘ *pl* rhombuses o rhombi [ˈrɒmbaɪ].

**rhubarb** [ˈruːbɑːb] *n* ruibarbo.

**rhyme** [raɪm] *n* rima.
▶ *vi* rimar (**with**, con).

**rhythm** [ˈrɪðᵊm] *n* ritmo.

**rhythmic** [ˈrɪðmɪk] *adj* rítmico,-a. COMP **rhythmic gymnastics** gimnasia rítmica.

**rib** [rɪb] *n* costilla. COMP **rib cage** caja torácica.

**ribbon** [ˈrɪbᵊn] *n* **1** cinta. **2** *(for hair)* lazo.

**ribonucleic** [raɪbəʊnjuˈkleɪk] *adj* ribonucleico,-a.

**rice** [raɪs] *n* arroz *m.* COMP **rice field** arrozal *m.* **▌ rice pudding** arroz *m* con leche.

**rich** [rɪtʃ] *adj* **1** rico,-a. **2** *(luxurious)* suntuoso,-a, lujoso,-a. **3** *(fertile)* fértil. **4** *(food)* fuerte, pesado,-a.
▶ *n pl* **riches** riqueza *f sing.*

❎ Rich no significa 'rico (sabroso)', que se traduce por tasty.

**richness** [ˈrɪtʃnəs] *n* **1** *(wealth)* riqueza. **2** *(fertility)* fertilidad *f.* **3** *(of voice)* sonoridad *f.* **4** *(of colour)* viveza.

**rid** [rɪd] *vt* librar. LOC **to get rid of** deshacerse de.
ⓘ *pt & pp* rid o ridded, *ger* ridding.

**ridden** [ˈrɪdən] *pp* → ride.

**riddle** [ˈrɪdᵊl] *n* acertijo, adivinanza.
▶ *vt* **1** cribar. **2** *(with bullets)* acribillar.

**ride** [raɪd] *n* **1** *(on bicycle, horse)* paseo. **2** *(in car)* paseo, vuelta; *(on bus, train)* viaje *m*, trayecto.
▶ *vi* **1** *(on horse)* montar a caballo; *(on bicycle)* ir en bicicleta. **2** *(in vehicle)* viajar.
▶ *vt* **1** *(horse)* montar. **2** *(bicycle)* montar en, andar en.
ⓘ *pt* rode [rəʊd], *pp* ridden [ˈrɪdən], *ger* riding.

**rider** [ˈraɪdəʳ] *n* **1** *(on horse - man)* jinete *m*, *(woman)* amazona. **2** *(on bicycle)* ciclista *mf.* **3** *(on motorcycle)* motorista *mf.* **4** *(clause)* cláusula adicional.

**ridge** [rɪdʒ] *n* **1** GEOG cresta. **2** *(of roof)* caballete *m.*

**ridiculous** [rɪˈdɪkjʊləs] *adj* ridículo,-a.

**ridicule** [ˈrɪdɪkjuːl] *n* ridículo.
▶ *vt* ridiculizar, poner en ridículo.

**riding** [ˈraɪdɪŋ] *n* equitación *f.*

**rifle** [ˈraɪfᵊl] *n* rifle *m*, fusil *m.*

**rig** [rɪg] *n* plataforma petrolífera.
▶ *vt* **1** MAR aparejar. **2** *fam (fix)* amañar.
ⓘ *pt & pp* **rigged**, *ger* **rigging**.

**right** [raɪt] *adj* **1** *(not left)* derecho,-a. **2** *(correct)* correcto,-a. **3** *(just)* justo,-a. **4** *(suitable)* apropiado,-a, adecuado,-a. **5** *fam (total)* auténtico,-a, total. **6** *fam (okay)* bien. LOC **all right!** ¡bien!, ¡conforme!, ¡vale! ‖ **right away** en seguida. ‖ **right now** ahora mismo. ‖ **to be right** tener razón. ‖ **to get it right** acertar. ‖ **to put right** arreglar, corregir. COMP **right angle** ángulo recto. ‖ **right wing** POL derecha.
▶ *adv* **1** a la derecha. **2** *(correctly)* bien, correctamente. **3** *(exactly)* justo. **4** *(well)* bueno, bien.
▶ *n* **1** *(not left)* derecha. **2** *(entitlement)* derecho.
▶ *vt* **1** corregir. **2** MAR enderezar.

**right-hand** [ˈraɪthænd] *adj* derecho,-a.

**right-handed** [raɪtˈhændɪd] *adj* diestro,-a.

**right-wing** [ˈraɪtwɪŋ] *adj* POL de derechas, derechista.

**rigid** [ˈrɪdʒɪd] *adj* rígido,-a.

**rim** [rɪm] *n* **1** *(gen)* borde *m*, canto *m*. **2** *(of wheel)* llanta. **3** *(of spectacles)* montura.

**rind** [raɪnd] *n* corteza.

**ring¹** [rɪŋ] *n* **1** *(for finger)* anillo, sortija. **2** *(hoop)* anilla, aro. **3** *(circle)* círculo; *(of people)* corro; *(of criminals)* red *f*. **4** *(of circus)* pista, arena. **5** *(for boxing)* ring *m*, cuadrilátero; *(for bullfighting)* ruedo.
COMP **ring road** cinturón *m* de ronda.
▶ *vt* **1** *(put a ring on)* anillar. **2** *(draw a ring round)* marcar con un círculo. **3** *(encircle)* rodear.

**ring²** [rɪŋ] *n* **1** *(of bell)* tañido, toque *m*; *(of doorbell)* llamada. **2** *(phone call)* llamada.
▶ *vi* **1** *(bell)* sonar. **2** *(ears)* zumbar.
▶ *vt* **1** *(call)* llamar. **2** *(bell)* tocar.
◆ **to ring off** *vt sep* colgar el teléfono.
◆ **to ring up** *vt sep* llamar por teléfono, telefonear.
ⓘ *pt* **rang** [ræŋ], *pp* **rung** [rʌŋ].

**ringing** [ˈrɪŋɪŋ] *n* **1** campaneo, repique *m*. **2** *(in ears)* zumbido.

**rink** [rɪŋk] *n* pista de patinaje. COMP **ice rink** pista de hielo.

**rinse** [rɪns] *vt* **1** *(clothes, hair)* aclarar. **2** *(dishes, mouth)* enjuagar.
▶ *n* **1** *(of clothes)* aclarado. **2** *(of dishes)* enjuague *m*. **3** *(for hair)* tinte *m*.

**riot** [ˈraɪət] *n* **1** *(in street)* disturbio. **2** *(in prison)* motín *m*. COMP **riot police** policía antidisturbios.
▶ *vi* **1** *(in street)* provocar disturbios. **2** *(in prison)* amotinarse.

**rip** [rɪp] *n* rasgón *m*, desgarrón *m*.
▶ *vt* rasgar, desgarrar.
ⓘ *pt & pp* **ripped**, *ger* **ripping**.

**ripe** [raɪp] *adj* maduro,-a.

**rip-off** [ˈrɪpɒf] *n fam* timo.

**ripple** [ˈrɪpəl] *n* **1** *(on water)* onda. **2** *(sound)* murmullo.
▶ *vt* rizar.
▶ *vi* rizarse.

**rise** [raɪz] *n* **1** ascenso, subida. **2** *(increase)* aumento. **3** *(slope)* subida, cuesta.
▶ *vi* **1** ascender, subir. **2** *(increase)* aumentar. **3** *(stand up)* ponerse de pie. **4** *(get up)* levantarse. **5** *(sun)* salir. **6** *(river)* nacer. **7** *(level of river)* crecer. **8** *(mountains)* elevarse.
ⓘ *pt* **rose** [rəʊz], *pp* **risen** [ˈrɪzən].

**risen** [ˈrɪzən] *pp* → **rise**.

**rising** [ˈraɪzɪŋ] *n* *(rebellion)* levantamiento.
▶ *adj* **1** *(prices)* en aumento. **2** *(sun)* naciente. **3** *(land)* en pendiente.

**risk** [rɪsk] *n* riesgo, peligro. LOC **to take a risk** correr un riesgo.
▶ *vt* arriesgar.

**risky** [ˈrɪskɪ] *adj* arriesgado,-a.
ⓘ *comp* **riskier**, *superl* **riskiest**.

**ritual** [ˈrɪtjʊəl] *adj* risorio.

**rite** [raɪt] *n* rito.

**rival** [ˈraɪvəl] *adj* competidor,-ra, rival.
▶ *n* competidor,-ra, rival *mf*.
▶ *vt* competir con, rivalizar con.

**river** [ˈrɪvəʳ] *n* río.

**river-bed** [ˈrɪvəbed] *n* lecho.

**riverside** [ˈrɪvəsaɪd] *n* ribera, orilla.

**rivet** [ˈrɪvɪt] *n* remache *m*.
▶ *vt* **1** remachar. **2** *fig* fijar, absorber.

**road** [rəʊd] *n* **1** carretera. **2** *(way)* camino. COMP **road sign** señal *f* de tráfico.

**R**

**roadway** ['rəʊdweɪ] *n* calzada.

**roadworks** ['rəʊdweːks] *n pl* obras.

**roam** [rəʊm] *vt* vagar por.
▶ *vi* vagar.

**roar** [rɔːʳ] *n* **1** *(of bull, person)* bramido. **2** *(of lion, sea)* rugido. **3** *(of traffic)* estruendo. **4** *(of crowd)* griterío, clamor *m*.
▶ *vi* **1** *(bull, person)* bramar. **2** *(lion, sea)* rugir.

**roast** [rəʊst] *adj* asado,-a. COMP **roast beef** rosbif *m*. ‖ **roast potato** patata al horno.
▶ *n* asado.
▶ *vt* **1** *(meat)* asar. **2** *(coffee, nuts, etc)* tostar.
▶ *vi* asarse.

**rob** [rɒb] *vt* **1** robar. **2** *(bank)* atracar; *(shop)* asaltar, robar.
① *pt & pp* **robbed**, *ger* **robbing**.

✎ Rob no es lo mismo que steal: rob se usa con la persona robada o con un sitio que se atraca; steal se usa con el dinero u objetos robados. Consulta también steal.

**robber** ['rɒbəʳ] *n* atracador,-a.

**robbery** ['rɒbəri] *n* atraco.

**robin** ['rɒbɪn] *n* petirrojo.

**robot** ['rəʊbɒt] *n* robot *m*.

**rock** [rɒk] *n* **1** *(gen)* roca. **2** US piedra. **3** MUS rock *m*, música rock.
▶ *vt* **1** *(chair)* mecer. **2** *(baby)* acunar. **3** *(upset)* sacudir, convulsionar.
▶ *vi* *(chair)* mecerse.

**rocket** ['rɒkɪt] *n* **1** *(missile)* cohete *m*. COMP **rocket launcher** lanzacohetes *m*.
▶ *vi* *(rise)* dispararse.

**rocking-chair** ['rɒkɪŋtʃeəʳ] *n* mecedora.

**rocky** ['rɒki] *adj* rocoso,-a.
① *comp* **rockier**, *superl* **rockiest**.

**rod** [rɒd] *n* **1** *(thin)* vara. **2** *(thick)* barra. **3** *(for fishing)* caña.

**rode** [rəʊd] *pt* → **ride**.

**rodent** ['rəʊdᵊnt] *n* roedor *m*.

**roebuck** ['rəʊbʌk] *n* corzo.

**rogue** [rəʊg] *n* bribón,-ona, pillo,-a.

**role** [rəʊl] *n* papel, interpretación *m*.

**roll** [rəʊl] *n* **1** *(gen)* rollo. **2** *(of film)* carrete *m*. **3** *(list)* lista. **4** *(of bread)* bollo, panecillo; *(sandwich)* bocadillo. COMP **to call the roll** pasar lista.
▶ *vt* **1** *(ball, coin)* hacer rodar. **2** *(flatten)* allanar, apisonar. **3** *(into a ball)* enroscar. **4** *(paper)* enrollar.
◆ **to roll up** *vt sep* **1** enrollar. **2** *(into a ball)* enroscar.
▶ *vi* enrollarse.

**roller** ['rəʊləʳ] *n* **1** *(for painting)* rodillo. **2** *(wave)* ola grande. **3** *(for hair)* rulo. COMP **roller coaster** montaña rusa. ‖ **roller skating** patinaje *m* sobre ruedas.

**rollerblades** ['rəʊləbleɪdz] *n pl* patines *mpl* en línea.

**ROM** [rɒm] *abbr* (read-only memory) memoria solo de lectura; *(abbreviation)* ROM *f*.

**Roman** ['rəʊmən] *adj* romano,-a.
▶ *n* romano,-a. COMP **Roman numeral** número romano.

**Romance** [rəʊ'mæns] *adj* románico,-a.

**romance** [rəʊ'mæns] *n* **1** romance *m*. **2** *(novel)* novela romántica.

**Romania** [ruː'meɪnɪə] *n* Rumanía.

**Romanian** [ruː'meɪnɪən] *adj* rumano,-a.
▶ *n* **1** *(person)* rumano,-a. **2** *(language)* rumano.

**romanise** ['rəʊmənaɪz] *vt* romanizar.

**romantic** [rəʊ'mæntɪk] *adj* romántico,-a.

**roof** [ruːf] *n* **1** tejado; *(tiled)* techado. **2** *(of mouth)* cielo. **3** *(of car, etc)* techo. COMP **flat roof** azotea. ‖ **roof rack** baca. ‖ **roof tiles** tejas *fpl*.
▶ *vt* techar.

**rooftop** ['ruːftɒp] *n* tejado.

**rookie** ['rʊki] *n fam* novato,-a.

**room** [ruːm] *n* **1** habitación *f*, pieza. **2** *(space)* espacio, sitio, lugar *m*. COMP **room temperature** temperatura ambiente.
▶ *vi* **1** *(lodge)* alojarse. **2** *(share a room)* compartir una habitación.

**roomy** ['ruːmi] *adj* espacioso,-a.
① *comp* **roomier**, *superl* **roomiest**.

**rooster** ['ruːstəʳ] *n* gallo.

**root¹** [ruːt] *n* raíz *f*.
▶ *vt* arraigar.
▶ *vi* arraigar.

**rope** [rəʊp] *n* *(gen)* cuerda; *(thicker)* soga.
▶ *vt* atar *(con cuerdas)*, amarrar.
◆ **to rope off** *vt sep* acordonar.

**rosary** ['rəʊzəri] *n* rosario.
ⓘ *pl* rosaries.

**rose¹** [rəʊz] *n* **1** (*flower*) rosa. **2** (*bush*) rosal *m*. **3** (*colour*) rosa *m*. **4** (*of shower, etc*) alcachofa. COMP **rose garden** rosaleda. ‖ **rose window** rosetón *m*.

**rose²** [rəʊz] *pt* → rise.

**rosé** ['rəʊzeɪ] *n* vino rosado.

**rosebud** ['rəʊzbʌd] *n* capullo de rosa.

**rosebush** ['rəʊzbʌʃ] *n* rosal *m*.

**rosemary** ['rəʊzmərɪ] *n* romero.

**rot** [rɒt] *n* **1** (*decay*) putrefacción *f*. **2** (*rubbish*) tonterías *fpl*.
▸ *vt* pudrir.
▸ *vi* pudrirse.
ⓘ *pt & pp* rotted, *ger* rotting.

**rotate** [rəʊˈteɪt] *vt* **1** (*spin*) hacer girar, dar vueltas a. **2** (*alternate*) alternar.
▸ *vi* **1** (*spin*) girar, dar vueltas. **2** (*alternate*) alternarse.

**rotation** [rəʊˈteɪʃən] *n* rotación *f*.

**rotten** [rɒtən] *adj* podrido,-a.

**rough** [rʌf] *adj* **1** (*not smooth*) áspero,-a, basto,-a. **2** (*road*) lleno,-a de baches. **3** (*edge*) desigual. **4** (*rude*) rudo,-a. **5** (*approximate*) aproximado,-a.

**roughly** ['rʌflɪ] *adv* **1** (*about*) aproximadamente; (*more or less*) más o menos. **2** (*not gently*) bruscamente.

**round** [raʊnd] *adj* redondo,-a.
▸ *n* **1** (*circle*) círculo. **2** (*series*) serie *f*, tanda; (*one of a series*) ronda. **3** SP (*stage of competition*) ronda; (*boxing*) asalto; (*of golf*) partido. **4** (*of drinks*) ronda. **5** (*of policeman, etc*) ronda. **6** (*for gun*) cartucho. **7** (*of bread*) rebanada. COMP **round trip** viaje *m* de ida y vuelta. ‖ **round number** número redondo.
▸ *adv* **1** (*in circles*): it goes round and round da vueltas y vueltas. **2** (*about*) por ahí. **3** (*to somebody's house*) a casa.
▸ *prep* alrededor de.
▸ *vt* doblar.

**roundabout** ['raʊndəbaʊt] *n* **1** tiovivo. **2** AUTO rotonda.

**route** [ruːt] *n* **1** ruta, camino. **2** (*of bus*) línea, trayecto.
▸ *vt* mandar.

**router** ['ruːtər] *n* COMPUT direccionador *m*, enrutador *m*.

**routine** [ruːˈtiːn] *n* rutina.

**row¹** [raʊ] *n* **1** (*fight*) riña, pelea. **2** (*din, racket*) jaleo.
▸ *vi* pelearse.

**row²** [rəʊ] *n* (*line*) fila, hilera.

**row³** [rəʊ] *vi* (*in a boat*) remar.

**rowing** ['rəʊɪŋ] *n* remo. COMP **rowing boat** bote *m* de remos.

**royal** ['rɔɪəl] *adj* real.

**royalty** ['rɔɪəltɪ] *n* **1** realeza. **2** (*people*) miembros *mpl* de la familia real.
ⓘ *pl* royalties.
▸ *n pl* **royalties** (*gen*) royalties *mpl*; (*of writer*) derechos *mpl* de autor.

**rub** [rʌb] *n* friega.
▸ *vt* (*gen*) frotar; (*hard*) restregar.
▸ *vi* rozar.
◆ **to rub out** *vt sep* borrar.
▸ *vi* borrarse.
ⓘ *pt & pp* rubbed, *ger* rubbing.

**rubber** ['rʌbər] *n* **1** caucho, goma. **2** (*eraser*) goma de borrar. COMP **rubber band** goma elástica. ‖ **rubber ring** flotador *m*.

**rubbish** ['rʌbɪʃ] *n* **1** (*refuse*) basura. **2** (*nonsense*) tonterías *fpl*. COMP **rubbish bin** cubo de la basura. ‖ **rubbish dump** vertedero, basurero.

**rubella** [ruːˈbelə] *n* rubéola.

**ruby** ['ruːbɪ] *n* rubí *m*.
ⓘ *pl* rubies.

**rucksack** ['rʌksæk] *n* mochila.

**rudder** ['rʌdər] *n* timón *m*.

**rude** [ruːd] *adj* **1** (*person*) maleducado, -a, grosero,-a; (*behaviour*) grosero,-a; (*word*) malsonante. **2** (*improper*) grosero,-a. **3** (*crude*) rudo,-a, tosco,-a.

**rug** [rʌg] *n* alfombra, alfombrilla.

**rugby** ['rʌgbɪ] *n* rugby *m*.

**ruin** ['ruːɪn] *n* ruina.
▸ *vt* **1** arruinar. **2** (*spoil*) estropear.

**ruined** ['ruːɪnd] *adj* **1** arruinado,-a. **2** (*spoilt*) estropeado,-a. **3** (*building*) en ruinas.
◆ **to rule out** *vt sep* excluir, descartar.

**ruler** ['ruːlər] *n* **1** gobernante *mf*, dirigente *mf*. **2** (*monarch*) soberano,-a, monarca *mf*. **3** (*instrument*) regla.

R

**ruling** ['ruːlɪŋ] *adj (in charge)* dirigente; *(governing)* en el poder; *(reigning)* reinante.
▶ *n* JUR fallo.

**rum** [rʌm] *n* ron *m*.

**Rumania** [ruːˈmeɪnɪə] *n* → **Romania**.

**Rumanian** [ruːˈmeɪnɪən] *adj-n* → **Romanian**.

**rumble** ['rʌmbəl] *n (gen)* ruido sordo; *(of thunder)* estruendo.
▶ *vi (gen)* hacer un ruido sordo; *(thunder)* retumbar.

**ruminant** ['ruːmɪnənt] *adj* rumiante.
▶ *n* rumiante *m*.

**run** [rʌn] *n* **1** carrera. **2** *(trip)* viaje *m*; *(for pleasure)* paseo. **3** *(ski)* pista. **4** *(in stocking)* carrera. **4** *(in cricket)* carrera. **9** *(in printing)* tirada. **10** *(at cards)* escalera.
LOC **to go for a run** ir a correr.
▶ *vi* **1** *(gen)* correr. **2** *(flow)* correr. **3** *(operate)* funcionar. **4** *(trains, buses)* circular. **5** *(in election)* presentarse. **6** *(play)* estar en cartel; *(contract, etc)* seguir vigente. **7** *(colour)* correrse.
▶ *vt* **1** *(gen)* correr. **2** *(race)* correr en, participar en. **3** *(take by car)* llevar, acompañar. **4** *(manage)* dirigir, regentar. **5** *(organize)* organizar. **6** *(operate)* hacer funcionar. **7** *(pass, submit to)* pasar. **8** *(publish)* publicar. **9** *(water)* dejar correr.
◆ **to run after** *vt insep* perseguir.
◆ **to run away** *vi* **1** *(gen)* irse corriendo. **2** *(from home, etc)* fugarse, escaparse.
◆ **to run down** *vt sep* **1** *(knock down)* atropellar. **2** *(criticize)* criticar. **3** *(battery)* agotar.
▶ *vt insep* bajar corriendo.
▶ *vi* **1** bajar corriendo. **2** *(battery)* agotarse. **3** *(clock)* pararse.
◆ **to run into** *vt insep* **1** entrar corriendo en. **2** *(car)* chocar con. **3** *(meet)* tropezar con.
◆ **to run off** *vt sep (print)* imprimir.
▶ *vi* irse corriendo.
◆ **to run out** *vi* **1** salir corriendo. **2** *(be used up - gen)* acabarse; *(- stocks)* agotarse. **3** *(contract)* caducar.
ⓘ *pt* ran [ræn], *pp* run [rʌn], *ger* running.

**rung¹** [rʌŋ] *n* escalón *m*.

**rung²** [rʌŋ] *pp* → **ring**.

**runner** ['rʌnəʳ] *n* **1** corredor,-ra. **2** *(of sledge)* patín *m*; *(of skate)* cuchilla. **3** *(carpet)* alfombrilla. **4** *(on furniture)* tapete *m*. COMP **runner bean** judía verde.

**running** ['rʌnɪŋ] *n* **1** *(action)* el correr; *(sport)* atletismo. **2** *(management)* dirección *f*.
▶ *adj* **1** *(water)* corriente. **2** *(continuous)* continuo,-a.

**runny** ['rʌnɪ] *adj* **1** *(liquid)* líquido,-a; *(egg)* poco hecho..
ⓘ *comp* runnier, *superl* runniest.

**run-up** ['rʌnʌp] *n* **1** *(period before)* etapa preliminar. **2** *(before jumping, etc)* carrerilla.

**runway** ['rʌnweɪ] *n* pista de aterrizaje.

**rural** ['ruərəl] *adj* rural.

**rush¹** [rʌʃ] *n* **1** prisa. **2** *(movement)* movimiento impetuoso. COMP **rush hour** hora punta. ‖ **rush job** trabajo urgente.
▶ *vt* **1** *(hurry - person)* apresurar, dar prisa a, meter prisa a. **2** *(send quickly)* enviar urgentemente. **3** *(attack)* abalanzarse sobre.
▶ *vi* ir deprisa, precipitarse.
◆ **to rush in** *vi* entrar corriendo.
◆ **to rush out** *vi* salir corriendo.

**rush²** [rʌʃ] *n (plant)* junco *m*.

**Russia** ['rʌʃə] *n* Rusia.

**Russian** ['rʌʃən] *adj* ruso,-a.
▶ *n* **1** *(person)* ruso,-a. **2** *(language)* ruso.

**rust** [rʌst] *n* óxido, herrumbre *m*.
▶ *vt* oxidar.
▶ *vi* oxidar.

**rustle** ['rʌsəl] *n (of leaves, etc)* crujido; *(of silk)* frufrú *m*.
▶ *vt (leaves, etc)* hacer crujir.
▶ *vi (leaves, etc)* crujir.
▶ *vt (cattle)* robar.
▶ *vi (cattle)* robar ganado.

**rusty** ['rʌstɪ] *adj* **1** *(metal)* oxidado,-a. **2** *fig* oxidado,-a, olvidado,-a.
ⓘ *comp* rustier, *superl* rustiest.

**ruthless** ['ruːθləs] *adj* cruel, despiadado,-a.

**Rwanda** [ruˈændə] *n* Ruanda.

**Rwandan** [ruˈændən] *adj* ruandés,-esa.
▶ *n* ruandés,-esa.

**rye** [raɪ] *n* centeno. COMP **rye bread** pan *m* de centeno. ‖ **rye grass** ballica.

# S

**S, s** [es] *n (the letter)* S, s *f.*

**saber** ['seɪbəʳ] *n* US → sabre.

**sabotage** ['sæbəta:ʒ] *n* sabotaje *m.*
▸ *vt* sabotear.

**saboteur** [sæbə'tɜ:ʳ] *n* saboteador,-ra.

**sabre** ['seɪbəʳ] *n* sable *m.*

**saccharin** ['sækərɪn] *n* sacarina.

**sachet** ['sæʃeɪ] *n* bolsita, sobrecito.

**sack¹** [sæk] *n (bag)* saco.
▸ *vt* GB *fam* despedir a, echar a. LOC **to get the sack** ser despedido,-a. ▌ **to give sb the sack** despedir a ALGN.

**sack²** [sæk] *vt* MIL saquear.
▸ *n* MIL saqueo.

⚠ To sack no significa 'sacar', que se traduce por **to take out**.

**sacrament** ['sækrəmənt] *n* sacramento.

**sacred** ['seɪkrəd] *adj* sagrado,-a.

**sacrifice** ['sækrɪfaɪs] *n* **1** *(gen)* sacrificio. **2** *(offering)* ofrenda.
▸ *vt* sacrificar.

**sacrum** ['sækrəm] *n* ANAT sacro.
ⓘ *pl* sacra ['sækrə].

**sad** [sæd] *adj* **1** *(unhappy)* triste: *you look very sad* estás muy triste. **2** *(deplorable)* lamentable.
ⓘ *comp* sadder, *superl* saddest.

**sadden** ['sædən] *vt* entristecer.
▸ *vi* entristecerse.

**saddle** ['sædəl] *n (for horse)* silla (de montar); *(of bicycle, etc)* sillín *m.*
▸ *vt* ensillar (up, -).

**sadism** ['seɪdɪzəm] *n* sadismo.

**sadist** ['seɪdɪst] *n* sádico,-a.

**sadly** ['sædlɪ] *adv* tristemente.

**sadness** ['sædnəs] *n* tristeza.

**safari** [sə'fɑ:rɪ] *n* safari *m.*

**safe** [seɪf] *adj* **1** *(gen)* seguro,-a; *(out of danger)* a salvo, fuera de peligro: *it's not safe to play in the road* es peligroso jugar en la calle. **2** *(unharmed)* ileso,-a, indemne. **3** *(not risky - method, investment, choice)* seguro,-a; *(subject)* no polémico,-a. LOC **safe and sound** sano,-a y salvo,-a.
▸ *n* caja fuerte, caja de caudales.

**safe-conduct** [seɪf'kɒndʌkt] *n* salvoconducto.

**safely** ['seɪflɪ] *adv* **1** *(for certain)* con toda seguridad: *we can safely say that...* podemos decir con toda seguridad que .... **2** *(without mishap)* sin contratiempos, sin accidentes. **3** *(securely)* de manera segura.

**safety** ['seɪftɪ] *n* seguridad *f.* COMP **safety belt** cinturón *m* de seguridad. ▌ **safety match** cerilla, fósforo. ▌ **safety pin** imperdible *m.*

**saffron** ['sæfrən] *n (plant, condiment)* azafrán *m.*

**sag** [sæg] *vi* **1** *(shelf, branch, beam, ceiling)* combarse; *(roof, bed)* hundirse. **2** *(demand, prices, etc)* caer, bajar. **3** *fig (spirits)* flaquear, decaer.
ⓘ *pt & pp* sagged, *ger* sagging.

**sage¹** [seɪdʒ] *adj* sabio,-a.
▸ *n* sabio,-a.

**sage²** [seɪdʒ] *n* BOT salvia.

**Sagittarius** [sædʒɪ'teərɪəs] *n* Sagitario.

**said** [sed] *pt & pp* → say.

**sail** [seɪl] *n* **1** *(canvas)* vela. **2** *(of windmill)* aspa.
▸ *vt* **1** *(travel)* navegar; *(cross)* cruzar en barco: *she sailed the Atlantic single-handed* cruzó el Atlántico sola. **2** *(control ship)* gobernar. LOC **in full sail** a toda vela. ▌ **to set sail** zarpar, hacerse a la mar.
▸ *vi* **1** *(ship, boat)* navegar. **2** *(begin journey)* zarpar, hacerse a la mar.

S

**sailing** ['seɪlɪŋ] *n* **1** *(skill)* navegación *f*. **2** *(sport)* vela: *we go sailing every weekend* hacemos vela todos los fines de semana. **3** *(departure)* salida; *(crossing)* travesía. COMP **sailing boat** barco de vela, velero.

**sailor** ['seɪləʳ] *n* marinero.

**saint** [seɪnt] *n (person)* santo,-a.

**sake** [seɪk] *n* bien *m*: *for your own sake* por tu propio bien; *for the kids' sake* por los niños. LOC **for God's sake!** ¡por el amor de Dios!, ¡por Dios! ∎ **for Heaven's sake!** ¡por el amor de Dios!

**salad** ['sæləd] *n* ensalada. COMP **salad bowl** ensaladera. ∎ **salad dressing** aliño, aderezo.

**salamander** ['sæləmændəʳ] *n* salamandra.

**salami** [sə'lɑːmɪ] *n* salami *m*.

**salary** ['sælərɪ] *n* sueldo, salario.
ⓘ *pl* salaries.

**sale** [seɪl] *n* **1** *(act, transaction)* venta. **2** *(special offer)* rebajas *fpl*, liquidación *f*: *I bought it in a sale* lo compré en las rebajas.
▶ *n pl* **sales** *(amount sold)* venta, ventas *fpl*; *(reductions)* rebajas *fpl*. LOC **for sale** en venta. ∎ **"For sale"** *(sign on house, etc)* «Se vende». ∎ **on sale 1** *(available)* en venta, a la venta. **2** *(reduced)* rebajado,-a. COMP **clearance sale** liquidación *f*. ∎ **sale goods** artículos *mpl* rebajados. ∎ **sales assistant** dependiente,-a.

**salesclerk** ['seɪlzklɑːk] *n* US dependiente,-a.

**salesman** ['seɪlzmən] *n* **1** *(gen)* vendedor *m*; *(in shop)* dependiente *m*. **2** *(travelling)* representante *m*.
ⓘ *pl* salesmen ['seɪlzmən].

**saleswoman** ['seɪlzwʊmən] *n* **1** *(gen)* vendedora; *(in shop)* dependienta. **2** *(travelling)* representante *f*.
ⓘ *pl* saleswomen ['seɪlzwɪmɪn].

**saline** ['seɪlaɪn] *adj* salino,-a.

**saliva** [sə'laɪvə] *n* saliva.

**salivary** [sə'laɪvərɪ] *adj* salival.

**salmon** ['sæmən] *n* **1** *(fish)* salmón *m*. **2** *(colour)* color *m* salmón.
ⓘ *pl* salmon.

**salmonella** [sælmə'nelə] *n* **1** *(bacteria)* salmonella. **2** *(food poisoning)* intoxicación *f*.

**saloon** [sə'luːn] *n* **1** US taberna, bar *m*. **2** *(public room)* sala; *(on ship)* salón *m*.

**salt** [sɔːlt] *n (gen)* sal *f*. LOC **to be the salt of the earth** ser la sal de la tierra.▶ *adj* salado,-a.
▶ *vt* **1** *(preserve, cure)* salar. **2** *(season)* echar sal a.
▶ *n pl* **salts** sales *fpl*.

**salted** ['sɔːltɪd] *adj* salado,-a.

**salpeter** [sɔːlt'piːtəʳ] *n* US → saltpetre.

**saltpetre** [sɔːlt'piːtəʳ] *n* salitre *m*.

**salty** ['sɔːltɪ] *adj* salado,-a.
ⓘ *comp* saltier, *superl* saltiest.

**salute** [sə'luːt] *n* MIL saludo; *(firing of guns)* salva.
▶ *vt* MIL saludar.

✗ To salute no significa 'saludar (decir hola)', que se traduce por **to say hello**.

**Salvadorian** [sælvə'dɔːrɪən] *adj* salvadoreño,-a.
▶ *n* salvadoreño,-a.

**samba** ['sæmbə] *n (dance)* samba.

**same** [seɪm] *adj* **1** *(not different)* mismo,-a: *the same day* el mismo día. **2** *(alike)* mismo,-a, igual, idéntico,-a: *he's wearing the same tie as you* lleva una corbata igual que la tuya. LOC **at the same time 1** *(simultaneously)* a la vez, al mismo tiempo. **2** *(however)* sin embargo, aun así.
▶ *pron* **the same** lo mismo: *it won't be the same without you* no será lo mismo sin ti.
▶ *adv* **the same** igual, del mismo modo: *they talk the same* hablan igual. LOC COMP **all the same** a pesar de todo. ∎ **it's all the same to me** me da igual, me da lo mismo. ∎ **the same as** igual que, como. ∎ **the same to you** ¡igualmente!

**Samoa** [sə'məʊə] *n* Samoa.

**Samoan** [sə'məʊən] *adj* samoano,-a.
▶ *n* **1** *(person)* samoano,-a. **2** *(language)* samoano.

**sample** ['sɑːmpəl] *n* muestra.
▶ *vt* probar.

**sanatorium** [sænə'tɔːrɪəm] *n* sanatorio.
ⓘ *pl* sanatoriums o sanatoria [sænə'tɔːrɪə].

**sanction** ['sæŋkʃən] *n* sanción *f*.
▶ *vt fml* sancionar.

**sanctuary** ['sæŋktjʊərɪ] *n* **1** REL *(sacred place)* santuario. **2** *(gen)* refugio, protección *f*. **3** *(for animals)* reserva.
ⓘ *pl* sanctuaries.

**sand** [sænd] *n (gen)* arena.
▶ *vt (smooth)* lijar (down, -).
▶ *n pl* sands *(beach)* playa *f sing;* *(sand-bank)* banco *m sing* de arena.

**sandal** ['sændəl] *n* sandalia.

**sandbank** ['sændbæŋk] *n* banco de arena.

**sandcastle** ['sænka:səl] *n* castillo de arena.

**sander** ['sændəʳ] *n (machine)* lijadora.

**sandpaper** ['sændpeɪpəʳ] *n* papel *m* de lija.
▶ *vt* lijar.

**sandwich** ['sænwɪdʒ] *n (French bread)* bocadillo; *(sliced bread)* sándwich *m*.
ⓘ *pl* sandwiches.

**sandy** ['sændɪ] *adj* **1** *(beach, etc)* arenoso,-a, de arena. **2** *(hair)* rubio,-a oscuro,-a.
ⓘ *comp* sandier, *superl* sandiest.

**sane** [seɪn] *adj* **1** *(person)* cuerdo,-a; *(mind)* sano,-a. **2** *fig (solution, decision, etc)* sensato,-a.

ⓧ Sane no significa 'sano (con salud)', que se traduce por healthy.

**sang** [sæŋ] *pt* → sing.

**sanitary** ['sænɪtərɪ] *adj* **1** *(to do with health)* sanitario,-a, de sanidad. **2** *(hygienic)* higiénico,-a. COMP **sanitary napkin / sanitary pad / sanitary towel** compresa.

**sanitation** [sænɪ'teɪʃən] *n (public health)* sanidad *f* (pública); *(hygiene)* higiene *f*.

**sank** [sæŋk] *pt* → sink.

**Santa Claus** [sæntə'klɔːz] *n* Papá *m* Noel.

**sap** [sæp] *n* BOT savia.

**sapphire** ['sæfaɪəʳ] *n* zafiro.

**sarcasm** ['sɑːkæzəm] *n* sarcasmo.

**sarcastic** [sɑː'kæstɪk] *adj* sarcástico,-a.

**sarcophagus** [sɑː'kɒfəgəs] *n* sarcófago.
ⓘ *pl* sarcophaguses o sarcophagi [sɑː'kɒfəgaɪ].

**sardine** [sɑː'diːn] *n* sardina. COMP **to be packed like sardines** estar como sardinas en lata.

**sat** [sæt] *pt & pp* → sit.

**satanic** [sə'tænɪk] *adj* satánico,-a.

**satchel** ['sætʃəl] *n* cartera *(de colegial)*, mochila *(de colegial)*.

**satellite** ['sætəlaɪt] *n* satélite *m*. COMP **satellite dish** TV antena parabólica. I **satellite television** televisión *f* vía satélite.

**satin** ['sætɪn] *n* satén *m*, raso.
▶ *adj (made of satin)* de satén, de raso.

**satisfaction** [sætɪs'fækʃən] *n* satisfacción *f*.

**satisfactory** [sætɪs'fæktərɪ] *adj* **1** satisfactorio,-a. **2** EDUC suficiente.

**satisfied** ['sætɪsfaɪd] *adj* **1** satisfecho, -a, complacido,-a, contento,-a. **2** *(convinced)* convencido,-a.

**satisfy** ['sætɪsfaɪ] *vt* **1** *(please, make happy)* satisfacer, complacer, contentar: **does nothing satisfy you?** ¿no hay nada que te satisfaga? **2** *(fulfil)* satisfacer. **3** *(convince)* convencer.
ⓘ *pt & pp* satisfied, *ger* satisfying.

**satisfying** ['sætɪsfaɪɪŋ] *adj (gen)* satisfactorio,-a; *(meal)* bueno,-a, delicioso,-a.

**satsuma** [sæt'suːmə] *n* mandarina.

**saturate** ['sætʃəreɪt] *vt* saturar (with, de).

**saturation** [sætʃə'reɪʃən] *n* saturación *f*.

**Saturday** ['sætədɪ] *n* sábado: **next Saturday** el sábado que viene, el próximo sábado; **on Saturday morning** el sábado por la mañana; **the following Saturday** el sábado siguiente.

**Saturn** ['sætɜːn] *n* Saturno.

**sauce** [sɔːs] *n* CULIN salsa.

**saucepan** ['sɔːspən] *n* cazo, cacerola.

**saucer** ['sɔːsəʳ] *n* platillo.

**Saudi** ['saʊdɪ] *adj* saudí, saudita.
▶ *n* saudí *mf*, saudita *mf*. COMP **Saudi Arabia** Arabia Saudita.

**sauna** ['sɔːnə] *n* sauna.

**sausage** ['sɒsɪdʒ] *n* salchicha.

**sauté** ['səʊteɪ] *vt* saltear.
ⓘ *pt & pp* sautéed o sauté, *ger* sautéing.
▶ *adj* salteado,-a.

S

**savage** ['sævɪdʒ] *adj* **1** *(ferocious)* feroz; *(cruel)* cruel; *(violent)* violento,-a, salvaje: *a savage attack* un ataque duro. **2** *pej (primitive)* salvaje.

**savanna** [sə'vænə] *n* sabana.

**save** [seɪv] *vt* **1** *(gen)* salvar (from, de), rescatar (from, de): *you saved my life!* ¡me has salvado la vida! **2** *(not spend)* ahorrar: *I've saved $200 towards my holidays* he ahorrado 200 dólares para las vacaciones. **3** *(keep, put by - food, strength)* guardar, reservar; *(- stamps)* coleccionar. **4** SP *(goal)* parar. **5** COMPUT guardar, archivar.
▶ *vi (not spend)* ahorrar (up, -): *we're saving up to buy a flat* ahorramos para comprar un piso.
▶ *n* SP parada.

**saving** ['seɪvɪŋ] *n (of time, money)* ahorro, economía.
▶ *n pl* **savings** ahorros *mpl*. COMP **savings account** cuenta de ahorros.

**savor** ['seɪvəʳ] *n* US → savour.

**savory** ['seɪvərɪ] *adj* US → savoury.

**savour** ['seɪvəʳ] *vt* saborear.

**savoury** ['seɪvərɪ] *adj* **1** *(salty)* salado, -a; *(tasty)* sabroso,-a. **2** *(respectable, wholesome)* saludable, sano,-a.
▶ *n* entrante *m* salado, canapé *m*.

**saw¹** [sɔː] *n (tool)* sierra, serrucho.
▶ *vt* serrar.
▶ *vi* serrar, cortar.
ⓘ *pt* sawed, *pp* sawed o sawn [sɔːn].

**saw²** [sed] *pt* → see.

**sawdust** ['sɔːdʌst] *n* serrín *m*.

**sawn** [sɔːn] *pp* → saw¹.

**saxophone** ['sæksəfəʊn] *n* saxofón *m*.

**saxophonist** [sæk'sɒfənɪst] *n* saxofonista *mf*, saxo *mf*.

**say** [seɪ] *vt* **1** *(gen)* decir: *what did he say?* ¿qué dijo?, ¿qué ha dicho? **2** *(prayer)* rezar; *(poem, lines)* recitar. **3** *(think)* pensar, opinar, decir: *I say we keep looking* creo que deberíamos seguir buscando. **5** *(suppose)* suponer, poner, decir: *come round at, say, 8.00 pm* pásate hacia las 8.00, ¿te parece? LOC **it is said that ...** dicen que ..., se dice que .... ▌**not to say ...** por no decir .... ▌**that is to say** es decir.
ⓘ *pt & pp* said [sed].

**saying** ['seɪɪŋ] *n* dicho, decir *m*.

**scab** [skæb] *n* MED costra, postilla.

**scabies** ['skeɪbiːz] *n* MED sarna.

**scaffold** ['skæfəʊld] *n* **1** *(framework)* andamio. **2** *(for execution)* patíbulo, cadalso.

**scaffolding** ['skæfəldɪŋ] *n* andamiaje *m*.

**scald** [skɔːld] *n* escaldadura.
▶ *vt* escaldar.

**scale¹** [skeɪl] *n* **1** *(of fish, reptile)* escama. **2** *(on skin)* escama.

**scale²** [skeɪl] *n* **1** *(measure)* escala: *a metric scale* una escala métrica. **2** *(size, amount)* escala, magnitud *f*. **3** MUS escala. LOC **on a large scale** a gran escala. COMP **scale model** maqueta.

**scale³** [skeɪl] *n (pan)* platillo.
▶ *vi* SP *(weigh)* pesar.
▶ *n pl* **scales** *(for weighing in shop, kitchen)* balanza; *(bathroom, large weights)* báscula.

**scallop** ['skɒləp] *n (mollusc)* vieira, concha de peregrino.

**scalp** [skælp] *n* ANAT cuero cabelludo.

**scalpel** ['skælpəl] *n* **1** *(surgeon's)* bisturí *m*; *(for dissecting)* escalpelo. **2** *(tool)* escoplo, gubia.

**scamper** ['skæmpəʳ] *vi* corretear.

**scampi** ['skæmpɪ] *n* colas *fpl* de cigala rebozadas.

**scan** [skæn] *vt* **1** *(examine)* escrutar, escudriñar. **2** *(glance at)* echar un vistazo a. **3** TECH *(with radar)* explorar. **4** MED, INFORM escanear.
ⓘ *pt & pp* scanned, *ger* scanning.
▶ *n* **1** TECH *(with radar)* exploración *f*. **2** MED *(gen)* exploración *f* ultrasónica; *(in gynaecology, etc)* ecografía.

**scandal** ['skændəl] *n* **1** *(outrage)* escándalo; *(disgrace)* vergüenza. **2** *(gossip)* chismorreo.

❌ Scandal no significa 'escándalo (alboroto)', que se traduce por racket.

**scandalous** ['skændələs] *adj* escandaloso,-a.

❌ Scandalous no significa 'escandaloso (ruidoso)', que se traduce por noisy.

**scanner** ['skænəʳ] *n* **1** TECH *(radar)* antena direccional. **2** MED, INFORM escáner *m*.

**scapula** ['skæpjʊlə] *n* ANAT escápula.

**scar** [skɑːˈ] *n* **1** cicatriz *f*. **2** *fig* marca, señal *f*.

**scarce** [skeəs] *adj* (*not plentiful*) escaso,-a.

**scarcely** ['skeəslɪ] *adv* **1** (*hardly*) apenas: *I scarcely know them* apenas los conozco. **2** (*surely not*) ni mucho menos.

**scare** [skeəˈ] *n* **1** (*fright*) susto: *what a scare you gave me!* ¡vaya susto me has dado! **2** (*widespread alarm*) alarma, pánico.
▶ *vt* asustar, espantar: *did I scare you?* ¿te he asustado?
▶ *vi* asustarse, espantarse.

**scarecrow** ['skeəkrəʊ] *n* espantapájaros *m*.

**scared** ['skeəd] *adj* asustado,-a, espantado,-a. [LOC] **to be scared** tener miedo (**of**, a/de): *I'm scared of spiders* tengo miedo a las arañas, las arañas me dan miedo.

**scarf** [skɑːf] *n* **1** (*small*) pañuelo; (*silk*) fular *m*; (*long, woollen*) bufanda.
ⓘ *pl* **scarfs** o **scarves** [skɑːvz].

**scarlet** ['skɑːlət] *adj* escarlata.
▶ *n* escarlata *m*.

**scary** ['skeərɪ] *adj fam* (*situation, etc*) espantoso,-a; (*film, story*) de miedo, de terror.
ⓘ *comp* scarier, *superl* scariest.

**scatter** ['skætəˈ] *vt* **1** (*crowd, birds*) dispersar. **2** (*papers, cushions, etc*) esparcir, desparramar; (*money*) derrochar.
▶ *vi* dispersarse.

**scenario** [sɪˈnɑːrɪəʊ] *n* **1** (*of film*) guion *m*; (*in theatre*) argumento. **2** (*situation*) (posible) situación *f*, panorama *m*.
ⓘ *pl* scenarios.

❎ Scenario no significa 'escenario', que se traduce por **stage**.

**scene** [siːn] *n* **1** (*place*) lugar *m*, escenario; (*sight, picture*) escena. **2** (*in play, book*) escena. **3** (*stage setting*) decorado, escenario.

**scenery** ['siːnərɪ] *n* **1** (*landscape*) paisaje *m*. **2** THEAT (*on stage*) decorado.

**scent** [sent] *n* **1** (*gen*) olor *m*; (*pleasant smell*) aroma *m*. **2** (*perfume*) perfume *m*. **3** (*track, trail*) pista, rastro.
▶ *vt* **1** (*animal*) olfatear. **2** *fig* (*suspect*) intuir. **3** (*perfume*) perfumar (**with**, de).

**scepter** ['septəˈ] *n* US → sceptre.

**sceptical** ['skeptɪkəl] *adj* escéptico,-a.

**sceptre** ['septəˈ] *n* cetro.

**schedule** [ˈʃedjuːl, US ˈskedjuəl] *n* **1** (*programme*) programa *m*: *a work schedule* un programa de trabajo. **2** (*list - gen*) lista. **3** US (*timetable*) horario. [LOC] **on schedule 1** (*flight*) a la hora (prevista). **2** (*work*) al día. ∥ **to be ahead of schedule** ir adelantado,-a. ∥ **to be behind schedule** ir retrasado,-a.
▶ *vt* programar, fijar.

**schematic** [skiːˈmætɪk] *adj* esquemático,-a.

**scheme** [skiːm] *n* **1** (*plan*) plan *m*; (*project*) proyecto. **2** (*system, order*) sistema *m*, orden *m*; (*arrangement*) disposición *f*, combinación *f*: *a colour scheme* una combinación de colores. **3** (*plot*) complot *m*, conspiración *f*.
▶ *vi* (*plot*) conspirar, intrigar, confabularse.
▶ *vt* (*plan deviously*) tramar, maquinar.

❎ Scheme no significa 'esquema (resumen)', que se traduce por **outline**.

**schism** ['skɪzəm] *n* cisma *m*.

**schizophrenia** [skɪtsəʊˈfriːnɪə] *n* esquizofrenia.

**schizophrenic** [skɪtsəʊˈfrenɪk] *adj* esquizofrénico,-a.

**scholar** ['skɒləˈ] *n* **1** (*learned person*) erudito,-a; (*specialist*) especialista *mf*: *Latin scholar* latinista. **2** (*scholarship holder*) becario,-a. **3** (*good learner*) estudiante *mf*.

❎ Scholar no significa 'escolar (alumno)', que se traduce por **pupil**.

**scholarship** ['skɒləʃɪp] *n* **1** (*grant, award*) beca. **2** (*learning*) erudición *f*.

**school¹** [skuːl] *n* **1** (*gen*) escuela, colegio: *what are you going to do when you leave school?* ¿qué harás cuando dejes el colegio? **2** (*lessons*) clase *f*: *let's meet after school* quedemos después de clase. **3** (*university department*) facultad *f*. **4** (*group of artists, etc*) escuela: *the Dutch school of painting* la escuela pictórica holandesa. [COMP] **school age** edad *f* escolar.
▶ *vt* **1** (*teach*) enseñar; (*train*) educar, formar. **2** (*discipline*) disciplinar.

**S**

**school²** [sku:l] *n (of fish)* banco.

**schoolbook** ['sku:lbuk] *n* libro de texto.

**schoolboy** ['sku:lbɔɪ] *n* alumno, escolar *m*.

**schoolchild** ['sku:ltʃaɪld] *n* alumno,-a, escolar *mf*.
ⓘ *pl* schoolchildren ['sku:ltʃɪldrən].

**schoolgirl** ['sku:lgɜ:l] *n* alumna, escolar *f*.

**school-leaver** ['sku:lli:və<sup>r</sup>] *n alumno,-a que está a punto de dejar la escuela.*

**schoolteacher** ['sku:lti:tʃə<sup>r</sup>] *n (secondary school)* profesor,-ra; *(primary school)* maestro,-a.

**science** ['saɪəns] *n* **1** *(gen)* ciencia. **2** *(subject)* ciencias *fpl*. ‖COMP‖ **science fiction** ciencia ficción.

**scientific** [saɪən'tɪfɪk] *adj* científico,-a.

**scientist** ['saɪəntɪst] *n* científico,-a.

**scissors** ['sɪzəz] *n pl* tijeras *fpl*. ‖COMP‖ **a pair of scissors** unas tijeras.

**scold** [skəʊld] *vt* reñir, regañar.

**scone** [skəʊn, skɒn] *n* CULIN *bollo (que se suele comer con mantequilla, mermelada, nata, etc)*.

**scoop** [sku:p] *n* **1** *(for flour, rice, etc)* pala; *(for ice-cream)* cucharón *m*. **2** *(amount)* palada, cucharada. **3** *(news story)* primicia.
▶ *vt* **1** *(take out)* sacar con una pala. **2** *(beat rival)* vencer, pisar; *(get news first)* dar la primicia. **3** *(win)* ganar; *(make profit)* forrarse.

**scooter** ['sku:tə<sup>r</sup>] *n (child's)* patinete *m*, patineta; *(motorized)* escúter *m*, Vespa.

**scope** [skəʊp] *n* alcance *m: that is beyond the scope of this report* eso queda fuera del alcance de este informe.

**scorch** [skɔ:tʃ] *vt* **1** *(singe)* chamuscar,. **2** *(burn)* quemar, abrasar.
▶ *vi* **1** *(singe)* chamuscarse. **2** GB *fam (travel fast)* ir a toda velocidad.

**score** [skɔ:<sup>r</sup>] *n* **1** SP *(gen)* tanteo; *(in golf, cards)* puntuación *f: what's the score?* ¿cómo van? **2** *(in exam, test)* nota, calificación *f*. **3** MUS *(written version)* partitura; *(of film, play, etc)* música.
▶ *vt* **1** SP *(goal)* marcar, hacer, meter; *(point)* ganar; *(run)* hacer, realizar: *he scored the winning goal* marcó el gol decisivo. **2** *(in exam, test)* sacar, obtener,

conseguir. **3** *(give points to)* dar, puntuar: *this question scores 10 points* esta pregunta vale 10 puntos.
▶ *vi* SP *(gen)* marcar (un tanto); *(goal)* marcar (un gol); *(point)* puntuar, conseguir puntos.

**scoreboard** ['skɔ:bɔ:d] *n* marcador *m*.

**scorer** ['skɔ:rə<sup>r</sup>] *n* **1** *(scorekeeper)* encargado,-a del marcador. **2** *(goal striker)* goleador,-ra.

**scorn** [skɔ:n] *n* desdén *m*, desprecio.
▶ *vt* desdeñar, despreciar, menospreciar.

**Scorpio** ['skɔ:pɪəʊ] *n* Escorpión *mf*.

**scorpion** ['skɔ:pɪən] *n* escorpión *m*, alacrán *m*.

**Scot** [skɒt] *n* escocés,-esa.

**Scotland** ['skɒtlənd] *n* Escocia.

**Scottish** ['skɒtɪʃ] *adj* escocés,-esa.

**scourer** ['skaʊrə<sup>r</sup>] *n* estropajo.

**scout** [skaʊt] *n* **1** MIL *(person)* explorador,-ra; *(plane)* avión *m* de reconocimiento. **2** *(boy)* scout *m*.

**scowl** [skaʊl] *vi* fruncir el ceño.
▶ *n* ceño (fruncido).

**scrabble** ['skræbəl] *vi (among stones, etc)* escarbar; *(in bag, etc)* hurgar; *(on floor, etc)* rebuscar.

**scramble** ['skræmbəl] *vi* trepar (over, por) (up, a), subir gateando. *(clamber)* moverse rápidamente.
▶ *vt* **1** *(mix, jumble)* revolver, mezclar. **2** *(eggs)* revolver.

**scrambled eggs** [skræmbəld 'egz] *n pl* huevos revueltos.

**scrap** [skræp] *n* **1** *(of paper, cloth, etc)* trozo, pedazo; *(of news, conversation)* fragmento, migaja. **2** *(of metal)* chatarra. **3** *(in negatives)* pizca, ápice *m*.
▶ *vt* **1** *(throw away)* desechar; *(cars, etc)* desguazar. **2** *fig (idea)* descartar; *(plan)* abandonar.
ⓘ *pt & pp* scrapped, *ger* scrapping.
▶ *n pl* scraps *(gen)* restos *mpl*.

**scrapbook** ['skræpbuk] *n* álbum *m* de recortes.

**scrape** [skreɪp] *vt* **1** *(surface, paint, etc)* raspar (away/off, -), rascar (away/off, -): *he scraped the paint off the door* raspó la pintura de la puerta. **2** *(graze skin)* arañarse. **3** *(rub against)* rozar, raspar, rascar.

▶ *vi* **1** *(grate)* chirriar. **2** *(rub against)* raspar, rozar. **3** *(economize)* hacer economías, ahorrar.

**scratch** [skrætʃ] *n* arañazo, rasguño: *there's a scratch on this record* este disco está rayado.

▶ *adj* **1** *(improvised)* improvisado,-a.
ⓘ *comp* scratchier, *superl* scratchiest.

▶ *vt* **1** *(with nail, claw)* arañar, rasguñar; *(paintwork, furniture, record)* rayar. **2** *(part of body)* rascar: *she scratched her leg* se rascó la pierna.

▶ *vi* **1** *(animal)* arañar, rascar, rasguñar; *(pen)* raspear; *(wool, sweater, towel)* raspar, picar. **2** *(itch)* rascarse.

**scream** [skri:m] *n* **1** *(of pain, fear)* grito, chillido, alarido; *(of laughter)* carcajada. **2** *fig (screech)* chirrido. **3** *fam (funny person)* persona divertida; *(funny thing)* cosa divertida: *your cousin's a scream* tu primo es la monda, tu primo es divertidísimo.

▶ *vi* **1** *(gen)* gritar, chillar,; *(wind, siren, etc)* aullar: *she screamed for help* pidió socorro a gritos; *he was screaming with laughter* se mondaba de risa, se tronchaba de risa. **2** *fig (need)* pedir (a gritos), clamar (a gritos).

**screech** [skri:tʃ] *n* *(of person)* grito, alarido, chillido; *(of tyres, brakes, birds, etc)* chirrido; *(of siren)* aullido. COMP **screech owl** lechuza.

▶ *vt* gritar, decir a gritos, chillar.

▶ *vi* *(person)* chillar; *(tyres, brakes, bird, etc)* chirriar; *(siren)* aullar; *(gate)* rechinar.

**screen** [skri:n] *n* **1** *(partition)* biombo, mampara. **2** *(for window)* mosquitera. **3** *(protection, cover)* cortina, pantalla. **4** *(of TV, for projection)* pantalla.

▶ **the screen** la pantalla, el cine.

**screenplay** ['skri:npleɪ] *n* guion *m*.

**screensaver** ['skri:nseɪvəʳ] *n* salvapantallas *m*.

**screw** [skru:] *n* **1** *(metal pin)* tornillo. **2** *(propeller)* hélice *f*. **3** *(turn)* vuelta.

▶ *vt* **1** *(fasten with screws)* atornillar; *(tighten)* enroscar, apretar: *screw the two pieces together* une las dos piezas con tornillos. **2** *(crumple)* arrugar. **3** *(cheat,*

*swindle)* timar; *(overcharge)* clavar; *(get money out of)* sacar.

▶ *vi* *(turn, tighten)* atornillarse, enroscarse.

**screwdriver** ['skru:draɪvəʳ] *n* *(tool)* destornillador *m*.

**scribble** ['skrɪbəl] *n* garabato, garabatos *mpl*.

▶ *vt* garabatear, garrapatear.

**scribe** [skraɪb] *n* **1** *(copier)* escribiente *mf*, amanuense *mf*. **2** *(in Biblical times)* escriba *m*.

**script** [skrɪpt] *n* **1** *(of film, etc)* guion *m*. **2** *(writing)* escritura; *(text)* texto; *(handwriting)* letra.

**scroll** [skrəʊl] *n* COMPUT barra de desplazamiento.

◆ **to scroll down** *vi* COMPUT desplazarse hacia abajo.

◆ **to scroll up** *vi* COMPUT desplazarse hacia arriba.

**scrooge** [skru:dʒ] *n* *fam pej* tacaño,-a.

**scrotum** ['skrəʊtəm] *n* ANAT escroto.
ⓘ *pl* scrotums o scrota ['skrəʊtə].

**scrounge** [skraʊndʒ] *vi* *fam* gorrear (from/off, a), vivir de gorra.

▶ *vt* *(gen)* gorrear (from/off, a), gorronear (from/off, a): *he scrounges fags off his friends* gorronea pitillos a los amigos.

**scrub¹** [skrʌb] *n* *(undergrowth)* maleza.

**scrub²** [skrʌb] *vt* **1** *(clean)* fregar bien, restregar. **2** *fam (cancel)* cancelar.
ⓘ *pt & pp* scrubbed, *ger* scrubbing.

**scruffy** ['skrʌfɪ] *adj* desaliñado,-a.
ⓘ *comp* scruffier, *superl* scruffiest.

**scrupulous** ['skru:pjʊləs] *adj* *(meticulous)* escrupuloso,-a.

**scrutinize** ['skru:tɪnaɪz] *vt* escudriñar.

**scrutiny** ['skru:tɪnɪ] *n* **1** *(examination)* examen *m* profundo. **2** GB *(of votes)* escrutinio. LOC **to be under scrutiny** ser analizado,-a.

**scuba** ['skju:bə] *n* equipo de submarinismo. COMP **scuba diving** submarinismo, buceo con botellas de oxígeno.

**sculptor** ['skʌlptəʳ] *n* escultor,-ra.

**sculpture** ['skʌlptʃəʳ] *n* escultura.

▶ *vt* esculpir (in, en).

**S**

**scythe** [saɪð] *n* guadaña.

**sea** [si:] *n* **1** mar *m & f*: *we love swimming in the sea* nos encanta nadar en el mar. **2** *fig* mar *m*, multitud *f*: *a sea of faces* un mar de caras. LOC **at sea** en el mar. **I by sea** por mar, en barco. **I by the sea** a orillas del mar. **I out to sea** mar adentro. **I to go by sea** ir en barco. COMP **sea bird** ave *f* marina. **I sea lion** león marino. **I sea mile** milla marina. **I sea wall** dique *m*, rompeolas *m*.
▶ *adj* marítimo,-a, de mar.

**seabed** ['si:bed] *n* fondo marino.

**seafood** ['si:fu:d] *n* marisco, mariscos *mpl*.

**seagull** ['si:gʌl] *n* gaviota.

**seahorse** ['si:hɔ:s] *n* caballito de mar, hipocampo.

**seal¹** [si:l] *n* ZOOL foca.

**seal²** [si:l] *n* **1** *(official stamp)* sello: *wax seal* sello de lacre. **2** *(on letter)* sello; *(on bottle, etc)* precinto.

**seam** [si:m] *n* **1** SEW costura. **2** GEOL *(of mineral)* veta, filón *m*: *coal seam* veta de carbón.

**seaman** ['si:mən] *n* marinero, marino. ① *pl* seamen ['si:mən].

**search** [sɜ:tʃ] *n* *(gen)* búsqueda (for, de); *(of building)* registro; *(of person)* cacheo. LOC **in search of** en busca de. LOC **search warrant** orden *f* de registro.
▶ *vt* *(gen)* buscar (for, -); *(building, suitcase, etc)* registrar; *(person)* cachear, registrar: *they searched the house for clues* registraron la casa buscando pistas.
▶ *vi* *(gen)* buscar (through, entre); *(pockets)* registrar.

**seashell** ['si:ʃel] *n* concha (de mar).

**seashore** ['si:ʃɔ:ʳ] *n* *(coast)* orilla del mar.

**seasick** ['si:sɪk] *adj* mareado,-a.

**seasickness** ['si:sɪknəs] *n* mareo.

**seaside** ['si:saɪd] *n* playa, costa. LOC COMP **seaside resort** lugar *m* de veraneo en la costa.

**season** ['si:zən] *n* *(of year)* estación *f*; *(time)* época *f*; *(for sport, theatre, social activity)* temporada: *the tourist season* la temporada turística. LOC **to be in season 1** *(fresh food)* estar en sazón. **2** *(game)* ser temporada de: *strawberries are in season* es temporada de fresas. **I to go in season** ir en temporada alta. **I to go off/out of season** ir en temporada baja.
▶ *vt* **1** *(food)* sazonar (with, con), condimentar (with, con).

**seasonal** ['si:zənəl] *adj* estacional.

**seasoning** ['si:zənɪŋ] *n* CULIN condimento.

**seat** [si:t] *n* **1** *(chair - gen)* asiento; *(- in cinema, theatre)* butaca: *I'd like a window seat* quisiera un asiento al lado de la ventanilla. **2** *(place)* plaza; *(at theatre, opera, stadium)* localidad *f*. **3** POL *(in parliament)* escaño. LOC **to take a seat** sentarse, tomar asiento. COMP **seat belt** cinturón *m* de seguridad.
▶ *vt* **1** *(sit)* sentar. **2** *(accommodate)* tener sitio para; *(theatre, hall, etc)* tener cabida para. LOC **please be seated** siéntese/siéntense por favor. **I to seat os** sentarse.

**seaweed** ['si:wi:d] *n* alga (marina).

**second¹** ['sekənd] *n* **1** *(time)* segundo: *Powell's time was 9.77 seconds* Powell hizo un tiempo de 9,77 segundos. **2** *fam* momento, momentito: *I'll be back in a second* enseguida vuelvo. COMP **second hand** *(of watch)* segundero. **I second name** apellido.

**second²** ['sekənd] *adj* **1** *(gen)* segundo,-a; *(another)* otro,-a: *it's the second largest city in England* es la segunda ciudad más grande de Inglaterra. LOC **to have second helpings** repetir. **I to have second thoughts (about STH)** entrarle dudas a uno (sobre ALGO), cambiar de idea (sobre ALGO). COMP **second floor 1** GB segundo piso. **2** US primer piso. **I second name** apellido.
▶ *pron* segundo,-a.
▶ *n* **1** *(in series)* segundo,-a. **2** GB *(degree)* ≈ notable *m*.
▶ *adv* segundo, en segundo lugar: *he came second* llegó segundo, quedó en segundo lugar.

🔍 Consulta también **sixth**.

**secondary** ['sekəndərɪ] *adj* secundario,-a. COMP **secondary school** colegio de enseñanza secundaria, instituto de bachillerato .

**second-class** [sekənd'klɑːs] *adj* de segunda (clase).

**second-degree** [sekənddrˈgriː] *adj* MED de segundo grado. COMP **second-degree burns** quemaduras *fpl* de segundo grado.

**second-hand** [sekənd'hænd] *adj* **1** *(used, not new)* de segunda mano, usado,-a, viejo,-a: *we bought a second-hand car* compramos un coche de segunda mano.
▸ *adv* **1** *(buy)* de segunda mano. **2** *(learn, find out)* por terceros.

**secret** ['siːkrət] *adj* *(gen)* secreto,-a: *this is my secret hiding-place* éste es mi escondite secreto.
▸ *n* **1** *(gen)* secreto; *(something confided)* secreto, confidencia. **2** *(method, key)* secreto, clave *f*. LOC **in secret** en secreto. ▮ **to keep a secret** guardar un secreto.

**secretary** ['sekrətərɪ] *n* **1** secretario,-a. **2** *(non-elected official)* ministro,-a; *(representative below ambassador)* ministro,-a plenipotenciario,-a.
ⓘ *pl* secretaries.

**secrete** [sɪˈkriːt] *vt* **1** *(emit liquid)* secretar, segregar. **2** *fml (hide)* ocultar, esconder.

**secretion** [sɪˈkriːʃən] *n* *(of liquid)* secreción *f*.

**secretly** ['siːkrətlɪ] *adv* en secreto.

**sect** [sekt] *n* secta.

**section** ['sekʃən] *n* sección *f*.

**sector** ['sektə] *n* *(gen)* sector *m*.

**secular** ['sekjʊlə] *(education)* laico,-a; *(art, music)* profano,-a.

ⓧ Secular no significa 'secular (antiguo)', que se traduce por ancient.

**secure** [sɪˈkjʊə] *adj* **1** *(job, income, etc)* seguro,-a; *(relationship, etc)* estable. **2** *(ladder, shelf, foothold)* firme; *(stronghold)* seguro,-a; *(base, foundation)* sólido,-a.
▸ *vt* **1** *(make safe)* asegurar; *(protect)* proteger (from, de), (against, contra). **2** *(fasten)* cerrar bien. **3** *(obtain)* obtener, conseguir.

ⓧ Secure no significa 'seguro', que se traduce por sure.

**securely** [sɪˈkjʊəlɪ] *adv* bien.

**security** [sɪˈkjʊərətɪ] *n* **1** *(safety, confidence)* seguridad *f*. **2** *(protection)* seguridad *f*. COMP **security guard** guarda *mf* de seguridad. ▮ **security service** servicio de seguridad. ▮ **security van** furgoneta blindada.
ⓘ *pl* securities.

**sedan** [sɪˈdæn] *n* US *(car)* berlina.

**sedate** [sɪˈdeɪt] *vt* MED sedar.

**sedative** ['sedətɪv] *n* sedante *m*, calmante *m*.
▸ *adj* sedante.

**sedentary** ['sedəntərɪ] *adj* sedentario,-a.

**sediment** ['sedɪmənt] *n* sedimento.

**sedimentary** [sedɪˈmentərɪ] *adj* sedimentario,-a.

**sedimentation** [sedɪmenˈteɪʃən] *n* sedimentación *f*.

**seduction** [sɪˈdʌkʃən] *n* *(sexual)* seducción *f*.

**see** [siː] *vt* **1** *(gen)* ver: *you can see the sea from here* desde aquí se ve el mar; *see page 123* véase la página 123. **2** *(meet, visit)* ver; *(receive)* ver, atender; *(go out with)* salir con: *I'm seeing Pat on Friday* he quedado con Pat el viernes. **3** *(understand)* comprender, entender, ver: *I can see your point* entiendo tu punto de vista. **4** *(visualize, imagine)* imaginarse, ver; *(envisage)* creer: *I can't see him working in a factory* no me lo imagino trabajando en una fábrica. **5** *(find out, discover)* ver; *(learn)* oír, leer: *I'll see what I can do* veré lo que puedo hacer. **6** *(ensure, check)* asegurarse de, procurar: *see that you arrive on time* procura llegar a la hora. **7** *(accompany)* acompañar: *he saw me home* me acompañó a casa.
▸ *vi* **1** *(gen)* ver: *she can't see without her glasses* no ve sin las gafas. **2** *(find out, discover)* ver: *we'll have to see* ya veremos. **3** *(understand)* entender, ver: *oh, I see* ah, ya veo. LOC **I'll be seeing you!** ¡hasta luego! ▮ **let me see/let's see** a ver, vamos a ver. ▮ **seeing is believing** ver para creer. ▮ **see you around** ya nos veremos. ▮ **see you later/soon/Monday!** ¡hasta luego/pronto/el lunes! ▮ **you see 1** *(in explanations)* verás. **2** *(in questions)* ¿sabes?, ¿ves?
ⓘ *pt* saw [sɔː], *pp* seen [siːn], *ger* seeing.

**seed** [siːd] *n* BOT *(gen)* semilla; *(of fruit)* pepita: *sunflower seeds* pipas.
  ▶ *vt* **1** *(plant seeds)* sembrar (with, de). **2** *(remove seed)* despepitar.

**seek** [siːk] *vt* **1** *(look for, try to obtain)* buscar: *the homeless seek food and shelter* la gente sin techo busca comida y alojamiento. **2** *(ask for)* pedir, solicitar. **3** *(attempt, try)* tratar de, intentar.
  ▶ *vi (look for, try to obtain)* buscar (after/for, -), ir en busca de.
  ⓘ *pt & pp* sought [sɔːt].

**seem** [siːm] *vi (appear)* parecer: *she seems nice* parece maja; *it seems like there's going to be a storm* parece que va a haber una tormenta. LOC **so it seems** eso parece.

**seemingly** ['siːmɪŋlɪ] *adv* **1** *(used with adjective)* aparentemente. **2** *(used separately)* al parecer, según parece.

**seen** [siːn] *pp* → see.

**seep** [siːp] *vi* filtrarse.

**seesaw** ['siːsɔː] *n (for children)* balancín *m*, subibaja *m*.

**see-through** ['siːθruː] *adj* transparente.

**segment** ['segmənt] *n (gen)* segmento; *(of orange)* gajo.

**seize** [siːz] *vt* **1** *(grab)* asir, agarrar, coger: *he seized my arm* me agarró del brazo. **2** *(opportunity)* aprovechar. **3** *(take control of)* tomar, apoderarse de. **4** *(person - arrest)* detener; *(- take hostage)* secuestrar. LOC **to be seized with** STH *(pain, fear, panic, etc)* apoderarse ALGO de uno.

**seldom** ['seldəm] *adv* raramente, pocas veces: *we seldom eat out* pocas veces comemos fuera.

**select** [sɪ'lekt] *vt (thing)* escoger, elegir; *(team, player, candidate)* seleccionar.
  ▶ *adj* selecto,-a, escogido,-a.

**selection** [sɪ'lekʃən] *n* **1** *(people or things chosen)* selección *f*; *(choosing)* elección *f*. **2** *(range to choose from)* surtido, gama.

**selective** [sɪ'lektɪv] *adj* selectivo,-a.

**self** [self] *n* **1** ser *m*, uno,-a mismo,-a, sí mismo,-a: *he was his usual self again* volvió a ser él mismo. **2** *(in psychology)* yo: *my other self* mi otro yo.
  ⓘ *pl* selves.

**self-adhesive** [selfəd'hiːsɪv] *adj* autoadhesivo,-a, autoadherente.

**self-catering** [self'keɪtərɪŋ] *adj* sin servicio de comidas.

**self-confident** [self'kɒnfɪdənt] *adj* seguro,-a de sí mismo,-a.

**self-control** [selfkən'trəʊl] *n* dominio de sí mismo,-a, autocontrol *m*.

**self-defence** [selfdɪ'fens] *n* defensa personal, autodefensa. LOC **to act in self-defence** actuar en defensa propia.

**self-employed** [selfɪm'plɔɪd] *adj* autónomo,-a, que trabaja por cuenta propia.

**self-esteem** [selfɪ'stiːm] *n* amor *m* propio.

**self-government** [self'gʌvənmənt] *n* autonomía, autogobierno.

**self-help** [self'help] *n* autoayuda.

**selfish** ['selfɪʃ] *adj* egoísta.

**selfishness** ['selfɪʃnəs] *n* egoísmo.

**self-made** [selfmeɪd] *adj (man, woman)* que ha llegado donde está por sus propios esfuerzos, que se ha hecho a sí mismo,-a .

**self-portrait** [self'pɔːtreɪt] *n* autorretrato.

**self-respect** [selfrɪ'spekt] *n* amor *m* propio, dignidad *f*.

**self-service** [self'sɜːvɪs] *adj* de autoservicio.
  ▶ *n* autoservicio.

**self-sufficient** [selfsə'fɪʃənt] *adj* autosuficiente.

**sell** [sel] *vt* **1** *(gen)* vender: *he sold his bike to his neighbour* vendió la bici a su vecino. **2** *fam (convince)* convencer de.
  ▶ *vi (product)* venderse: *these plants sell at a pound each* estas plantas se venden a una libra cada una. LOC **to be sold out** estar agotado,-a.
  ◆ **to sell off** *vt sep* liquidar.
  ◆ **to sell out** *vi* **1** *(be disloyal)* claudicar, venderse. **2** COMM *(sell all of)* agotarse (of, -), acabarse (of, -).
  ▶ *vt sep* COMM *(sell all of)* agotar, agotar las existencias de.
  ⓘ *pt & pp* sold [səʊld].

**sell-by date** ['selbaɪdeɪt] *n* fecha límite de venta, fecha de caducidad.

**seller** ['selə<sup>r</sup>] *n (person)* vendedor,-ra.

**Sellotape®** ['seləteɪp] *n* celo®.

**sell-out** ['selaut] *n* **1** *(performance)* éxito de taquilla. **2** *fam (betrayal)* traición *f*, engaño.

**semantic** [sɪˈmæntɪk] *adj* semántico,-a.

**semen** ['siːmən] *n* semen *m*.

**semester** [sɪˈmestə<sup>r</sup>] *n* semestre *m*.

**semiautomatic** [semɪɔːtəˈmætɪk] *adj* semiautomático,-a.

**semicircle** ['semɪsɜːkəl] *n* semicírculo.

**semicolon** [semɪˈkəʊlən] *n* punto y coma *m*.

**semidetached** [semɪdɪˈtætʃt] *adj* pareado,-a.
▶ *n (house)* casa pareada.

**semifinal** [semɪˈfaɪnəl] *n* semifinal *f*.

**semifinalist** [semɪˈfaɪnəlɪst] *n* semifinalista *mf*.

**seminal** ['semɪnəl] *adj* seminal.

**semiskimmed** [semɪˈskɪmd] *adj* semidesnatado,-a, semidescremado,-a.

**semolina** [seməˈliːnə] *n* sémola.

**senate** ['senət] *n* POL senado.

**senator** ['senətə<sup>r</sup>] *n* senador,-ra.

**send** [send] *vt* **1** *(gen)* enviar, mandar; *(telex, telegram)* enviar, poner; *(radio signal, radio message)* transmitir, emitir: *he sent me some flowers* me mandó flores. **2** *(order to go)* mandar, enviar: *the doctor sent me to a specialist* el médico me mandó a un especialista. **3** *(cause to become)* volver, hacer: *the noise sent her mad* el ruido la volvió loca.
▶ *vi (send a message)* avisar.
◆ **to send away** *vt sep* despachar.
◆ **to send back** *vt sep* **1** *(goods, etc)* devolver. **2** *(person)* hacer volver.
◆ **to send for** *vt insep* **1** *(person)* llamar a, hacer llamar a. **2** *(thing)* pedir, encargar.
◆ **to send in** *vt sep (application, request)* mandar, enviar.
① *pt & pp* **sent** [sent].

**sender** ['sendə<sup>r</sup>] *n* remitente *mf*.

**Senegal** [senɪˈgɔːl] *n* Senegal.

**Senegalese** [senɪgəˈliːz] *adj* senegalés,-esa.
▶ *n* senegalés,-esa.
▶ *n pl* **the Senegalese** los senegaleses *mpl*.

**senile** ['siːnaɪl] *adj* senil.

**senior** ['siːnɪə<sup>r</sup>] *adj* **1** *(in age)* mayor: *he's five years senior to me* es cinco años mayor que yo. **2** *(in rank)* superior; *(with longer service)* más antiguo,-a, de mayor antigüedad. COMP **senior citizen** jubilado,-a.
▶ *n* **1** *(in age)* mayor *mf*; *(in rank)* superior *fm*. **2** GB *(pupil)* mayor *mf*. **3** US estudiante *mf* del último curso.

☒ To accord no significa 'acordar', que se traduce por to agree.

**sensation** [senˈseɪʃən] *n (gen)* sensación *f*; *(ability to feel)* sensibilidad *f*.

**sensational** [senˈseɪʃənəl] *adj* **1** *fam (wonderful)* sensacional. **2** *(exaggerated)* sensacionalista.

**sensationalist** [senˈseɪʃənəlɪst] *adj* sensacionalista.

**sense** [sens] *n* **1** *(faculty)* sentido: *sense of smell* sentido del olfato. **2** *(feeling - of well-being, loss)* sensación *f*; *(awareness, appreciation - of justice, duty)* sentido. **3** *(wisdom, judgement)* sentido común. **4** *(meaning - gen)* sentido; *(- of word)* significado, acepción *f*: *in every sense of the word* en todos los sentidos. LOC **in a sense** hasta cierto punto, en cierto sentido. ∎ **in no sense** de ninguna manera. ∎ **to make sense 1** *(have clear meaning)* tener sentido. **2** *(be sensible)* ser razonable, ser sensato,-a. ∎ **to talk sense** hablar con juicio. COMP **sense of humour** sentido del humor.

**senseless** ['sensləs] *adj* **1** *(unconscious)* inconsciente. **2** *(foolish, pointless)* absurdo,-a, sin sentido, insensato,-a.

**sensibility** [sensɪˈbɪlətɪ] *n* sensibilidad *f*.
▶ *n pl* **sensibilities** susceptibilidad *f sing*.

**sensible** ['sensɪbəl] *adj* **1** *(person)* sensato,-a; *(behaviour, decision)* razonable, prudente; *(choice)* acertado,-a. **2** *(clothes)* cómodo,-a.

☒ Sensible no significa 'sensible', que se traduce por sensitive.

**sensitive** ['sensɪtɪv] *adj* **1** *(person - perceptive)* sensible (to, a), consciente (to, de). **2** *(person - touchy)* susceptible (to, a), preocupado,-a (about, por). **3** *(teeth, paper, instrument, film)* sensible (to,-a).

**sensitivity** [sensɪ'tɪvətɪ] *n* **1** *(gen)* sensibilidad *f* (to, a/frente a). **2** *(touchiness)* susceptibilidad *f* (to, a). **3** *(of skin, issue)* delicadeza.

**sensor** ['sensə<sup>r</sup>] *n* TECH sensor *m*, detector *m*.

**sent** [sent] *pt & pp* → **send**.

**sentence** ['sentəns] *n* **1** *(gen)* frase *f*; *(in grammar)* oración *f*. **2** JUR sentencia, fallo.
  ▶ *vt* JUR condenar.

❎ Sentence no significa 'sentencia (máxima)', que se traduce por **saying**.

**sentimental** [sentɪ'mentəl] *adj* sentimental.

**sentry** ['sentrɪ] *n* centinela *m*.
  ① *pl* sentries.

**sepal** ['sepəl] *n* BOT sépalo.

**separate** [*(vb)* 'sepəreɪt; *(adj)* 'sepərət] *vt* separar (from, de).
  ▶ *vi* **1** *(gen)* separarse.
  ▶ *adj* **1** *(apart)* separado,-a: *keep the sheep separate from the goats* mantén a las ovejas separadas de las cabras. **2** *(not shared)* separado,-a, individual: *we had separate rooms* cada uno tenía su habitación. **3** *(different)* distinto,-a, diferente.

**separately** ['sepərətlɪ] *adv* por separado, aparte.

**separation** [sepə'reɪʃən] *n* separación *f*.

**sepia** ['si:pɪə] *adj* sepia.

**September** [səp'tembə<sup>r</sup>] *n* septiembre *m*, setiembre *m*.

✎ Para ejemplos de uso, consulta **May**.

**septic** ['septɪk] *adj* séptico,-a.

**septum** ['septəm] *n* ANAT septo.
  ① *pl* septa ['septə].

**sepulcher** ['sepəlkə<sup>r</sup>] *n* US → **sepulchre**.

**sepulchre** ['sepəlkə<sup>r</sup>] *n* sepulcro.

**sequel** ['si:kwəl] *n* **1** *(result, consequence)* secuela. **2** *(book, film, etc)* segunda parte *f*.

**sequence** ['si:kwəns] *n* secuencia, orden *m*.

**sequoia** [sɪ'kwɔɪə] *n* secoya, secuoya.

**Serb** [sɜ:b] *n* *(person)* serbio,-a.
  ▶ *adj* serbio,-a.

**Serbia** ['sɜ:bɪə] *n* Serbia.

**Serbian** ['sɜ:bɪən] *n* **1** *(person)* serbio, -a. **2** *(dialect)* serbio.
  ▶ *adj* serbio,-a.

**serf** [sɜ:f] *n* siervo,-a.

**sergeant** ['sɑ:dʒənt] *n* **1** MIL sargento *mf*. **2** *(of police)* cabo *mf*.

**serial** ['sɪərɪəl] *adj* **1** consecutivo,-a, en serie. **2** *(in parts)* seriado,-a, en capítulos.
  ▶ *n* *(gen)* serie *f*, serial *m*.

**series** ['sɪəri:z] *n* *(gen)* serie *f*, sucesión *f*. LOC **in series** TECH en serie.
  ① *pl* series.

**serious** ['sɪərɪəs] *adj* **1** *(solemn, earnest)* serio,-a: *you can't be serious!* ¡no lo dices en serio! **2** *(causing concern, severe)* grave, serio,-a: *no serious damage was caused* no hubo daños importantes.

**seriously** ['sɪərɪəslɪ] *adv* **1** *(in earnest)* en serio. **2** *(severely)* seriamente, gravemente.

**seriousness** ['sɪərɪəsnəs] *n* **1** *(severity)* seriedad *f*. **2** *(earnestness, solemnity)* seriedad *f*. LOC **in all seriousness** hablando (muy) en serio.

**sermon** ['sɜ:mən] *n* sermón *m*.

**serum** ['sɪərəm] *n* MED suero.
  ① *pl* serums o sera ['sɪərə].

**servant** ['sɜ:vənt] *n* sirviente *mf*.

**serve** [sɜ:v] *vt* **1** *(work for)* servir (as, de). **2** *(customer)* servir: *dinner is served at 8.00 pm* se sirve la cena a les 8.00. **3** *(be useful to)* servir, ser útil: *it serves many different purposes* sirve para varias cosas. **4** *(provide with service)* prestar servicio a: *the new hospital will serve the whole region* el nuevo hospital prestará servicio a toda la región.
  ▶ *vi* **1** *(work for)* servir: *my father served in the army* mi padre sirvió en el ejército. **2** *(in shop)* atender; *(food, drink)* servir. **3** *(be useful to)* servir (as, de): *this will serve as an example* esto servirá de ejemplo.
  ▶ *n* *(tennis)* saque *m*.

**server** ['sɜ:və<sup>r</sup>] *n* *(computer)* servidor *m*.

**service** ['sɜ:vɪs] *n* **1** *(gen)* servicio. **2** *(maintenance of car, machine)* revisión *f*. **3** REL oficio. **4** *(tennis)* saque *m*, servicio.

▶ adj *(for use of workers)* de servicio: *service entrance* entrada de servicio. COMP
**service area** área de servicio. ▎ **service charge 1** *(on bill)* servicio. **2** *(in banking)* comisión *f.* ▎ **service station** estación *f* de servicio.

▶ *n pl* **services** *(work, act, help)* servicios *mpl.*

**serviette** [sɜ:vɪˈet] *n* GB servilleta.

**sesame** [ˈsesəmɪ] *n* BOT sésamo, ajonjolí *m.*

**session** [ˈseʃən] *n* **1** *(gen)* sesión *f.* **2** EDUC *(term)* trimestre *m.*

**set¹** [set] *n* **1** *(of golf clubs, brushes, tools, etc)* juego *(books, poems)* colección *f; (of turbines)* equipo, grupo: *chess set* juego de ajedrez; *set of dishes* vajilla. **2** ELEC *(apparatus)* aparato: *they bought a TV set* compraron un televisor. **3** MATH conjunto. **4** SP *(tennis)* set *m.*

**set²** [set] *n* **1** *(in hairdressing)* marcado. **2** *(scenery)* decorado; *(place of filming)* plató *m.* **3** *(position, posture)* postura. COMP
**set square** cartabón *m,* escuadra.

▶ *vt* **1** *(put, place)* poner, colocar. **2** *(prepare - trap)* tender, preparar; *(- table)* poner; *(- camera, video)* preparar; *(- clock, watch, oven, etc)* poner: *set the table for dinner* pon la mesa para la cena. **3** *(date, time)* fijar, señalar, acordar: *have you set a date for the wedding?* ¿has fijado una fecha para la boda? **4** *(price)* fijar; *(value)* poner. **5** *(exam, test, problem)* poner; *(homework)* mandar, poner. **6** *(story, action)* ambientar: *the novel is set in Madrid* la novela está ambientada en Madrid.

◆ **to set off** *vi (begin journey)* salir.

▶ *vt sep* **1** *(bomb)* hacer estallar; *(alarm)* hacer sonar; *(firework)* lanzar, tirar. **2** *(cause, start)* provocar.

① *pt & pp* set.

◆ **to set up** *vt sep* **1** *(business)* establecer, montar. **2** *(machine)* instalar.

**setback** [ˈsetbæk] *n* revés *m,* contratiempo.

**settee** [seˈti:] *n* sofá *m.*

**settle¹** [ˈsetəl] *vt* **1** *(establish)* instalar, colocar; *(make comfortable)* poner cómodo,-a *he settled himself on the sofa* se puso cómodo en el sofá. **2** *(decide on, fix)* acordar, decidir, fijar. **3** *(sort out - problem, dispute)* resolver, solucionar; *(- differences)* resolver, arreglar; *(- score)* arreglar, ajustar: *we need to settle an argument* tenemos que resolver una discusión. **4** *(calm - nerves)* calmar; *(- stomach)* asentar.

▶ *vi* **1** *(make one's home in)* establecerse, instalarse. **2** *(make os comfortable)* ponerse cómodo,-a *(into,* en). **3** *(bird, fly, etc)* posarse. **4** *(sediment, dregs)* precipitarse. **5** *(calm down)* calmarse. **6** *(pay)* pagar, saldar la deuda.

◆ **to settle down** *vi* **1** *(establish a home)* instalarse, afincarse, establecerse; *(lead settled way of life)* empezar a llevar una vida asentada. **2** *(calm down)* calmarse, tranquilizarse. **3** *(get comfortable)* ponerse cómodo,-a.

◆ **to settle in** *vi* **1** *(get used to)* acostumbrarse, adaptarse. **2** *(move in)* instalarse.

**settle²** [ˈsetəl] *n (wooden bench)* banco.

**settlement** [ˈsetəlmənt] *n* **1** *(village)* poblado, pueblo, asentamiento; *(colony)* colonia. **2** *(agreement)* acuerdo, convenio.

**setup** [ˈsetʌp] *n* **1** *(arrangement, organization)* sistema *m,* situación *f.* **2** *fam (trick)* montaje *m.*

**seven** [ˈsevən] *adj* siete.
▶ *n* siete *m.*

✎ Consulta también six.

**seventeen** [sevənˈti:n] *adj* diecisiete.
▶ *n* diecisiete *m.*

✎ Consulta también six.

**seventeenth** [sevənˈti:nθ] *adj* decimoséptimo,-a.
▶ *adv* en decimoséptimo lugar.
▶ *n* **1** *(in series)* decimoséptimo,-a. **2** *(fraction)* decimoséptimo; *(one part)* decimoséptima parte *f.*

✎ Consulta también sixth.

**seventh** [ˈsevənθ] *adj* séptimo,-a.
▶ *adv* en séptimo lugar.
▶ *n* **1** *(in series)* séptimo,-a. **2** *(fraction)* séptimo; *(one part)* séptima parte *f.*

✎ Consulta también sixth.

**seventieth** [ˈsevəntɪəθ] *adj* septuagésimo,-a.

S

► *adv* en septuagésimo lugar.
► *n* **1** *(in series)* septuagésimo,-a. **2** *(fraction)* septuagésimo; *(one part)* septuagésima parte *f*.

✎ Consulta también **sixtieth**.

**seventy** ['sevəntɪ] *adj* setenta.
► *n* setenta *m*.

✎ Consulta también **sixty**.

**several** ['sevərəl] *adj (some)* varios,-as: *we've been there several times* hemos ido varias veces.
► *pron (some)* varios,-as.

**severe** [sɪ'vɪə'] *adj* **1** *(person, punishment, treatment)* severo,-a. **2** *(pain)* agudo,-a; *(injury, illness, damage)* grave, serio,-a.

**severity** [sɪ'verətɪ] *n* **1** *(of person, punishment, criticism)* severidad *f*. **2** *(of pain)* agudeza, intensidad *f*; *(of illness, wound)* gravedad *f*.

**sew** [səʊ] *vt* coser (onto, a).
► *vi* coser.
◆ **to sew up** *vt sep* **1** *(hole, tear, etc)* coser; *(mend)* remendar. **2** *fam (arrange, settle)* arreglar, acordar: *you've got everything sewn up!* ¡lo tienes todo arreglado!
ⓘ *pt* sewed, *pp* sewed o sewn [səʊn].

**sewage** ['sjuːɪdʒ] *n* aguas *fpl* residuales.

**sewer** [sjʊə'] *n* alcantarilla, cloaca.

**sewing** ['səʊɪŋ] *n* costura. COMP **sewing machine** máquina de coser.

**sewn** [səʊn] *pp* → sew.

**sex** [seks] *n* sexo: *the opposite sex* el sexo opuesto. LOC **to have sex with** SB tener relaciones sexuales con ALGN.

**sexism** ['seksɪzəm] *n* sexismo.

**sexist** ['seksɪst] *adj* sexista.
► *n* sexista *mf*.

**sexual** ['seksjʊəl] *adj* sexual.

**sexuality** [seksjʊ'ælətɪ] *n* sexualidad *f*.

**sexy** ['seksɪ] *adj (sexually attractive)* sexy; *(erotic)* erótico,-a.
ⓘ *comp* sexier, *superl* sexiest.

**shabby** ['ʃæbɪ] *adj* **1** *(clothes)* gastado,-a, raído,-a, desharrapado,-a; *(furniture)* de aspecto lastimoso. **2** *(person)* mal vestido,-a, desaseado,-a.
ⓘ *comp* shabbier, *superl* shabbiest.

**shack** [ʃæk] *n* choza.

**shade** [ʃeɪd] *n* **1** *(shadow)* sombra: *a temperature of 30 degrees in the shade* una temperatura de 30 grados a la sombra. **2** *(for lamp)* pantalla; *(for eye)* visera; *(blind)* persiana. **3** *(of colour)* tono, matiz *m*.
► *vt* **1** *(shelter from light)* proteger de la luz. **2** ART *(darken)* sombrear (in, -).
► *vi (change gradually)* convertirse (into, en).
► *n pl* **shades** *fam* gafas *fpl* de sol.

**shadow** ['ʃædəʊ] *n* **1** *(dark shape)* sombra. **2** *(trace)* sombra, vestigio. **3** *(follower)* sombra.
► *adj* GB en la sombra.

**shady** ['ʃeɪdɪ] *adj* **1** *(place)* a la sombra; *(tree)* que da sombra. **2** *fam (person)* sospechoso,-a; *(deal, past)* turbio,-a.
ⓘ *comp* shadier, *superl* shadiest.

**shaft** [ʃɑːft] *n* **1** *(of axe, tool, golf club)* mango; *(of arrow)* astil *m*; *(of lance, spear)* asta. **2** *(of mine)* pozo; *(of lift)* hueco. **3** *(of light)* rayo.

**shake** [ʃeɪk] *n* **1** sacudida. **2** US *fam (milkshake)* batido.
► *vt* **1** *(move - carpet, person)* sacudir; *(- bottle, dice)* agitar: *shake well before use* agítese bien antes de usar. **2** *(upset, shock)* afectar, impresionar: *the news shook her badly* la noticia le afectó mucho. LOC **to shake hands** estrecharse la mano. ‖ **to shake one's head** negar con la cabeza.
► *vi (gen)* temblar: *she was shaking with fear* temblaba de miedo.
ⓘ *pt* shook [ʃʊk], *pp* shaken ['ʃeɪkən].

**shaken** ['ʃeɪkən] *pp* → shake.
► *adj (liquid)* agitado,-a.

**shaker** ['ʃeɪkə'] *n (for cocktails)* coctelera; *(for salt)* salero.

**shaky** ['ʃeɪkɪ] *adj* **1** *(hand, voice)* tembloroso,-a; *(writing)* temblón,-ona; *(step)* inseguro,-a. **2** *fig (argument, etc)* sin fundamento; *(government, currency)* débil.
ⓘ *comp* shakier, *superl* shakiest.

**shall** [ʃæl, *unstressed* ʃəl] *aux* **1** [usado con la primera persona del *sing* y el *pl*] *(future)*: *I shall go tomorrow* iré mañana; *I shan't mention any names* no daré nombres. **2** [usado con la primera persona del *sing* y el *pl*] *(questions, offers, suggestions)*: *shall I close the window?* ¿cierro la ventana?; *I'll carry it, shall I?* lo llevaré yo, ¿quieres?

**3** *fml (emphatic, command)*: *you shall leave immediately* te irás enseguida.

**shallow** ['ʃæləʊ] *adj* **1** *(water, pond, etc)* poco profundo,-a; *(dish, bowl)* llano, -a, plano,-a. **2** *fig* superficial.
ⓘ *comp* shallower, *superl* shallowest.
▶ *n pl* **shallows** bajío *m sing.*

**shame** [ʃeɪm] *n* **1** *(disgrace, humiliation)* vergüenza; *(dishonour)* deshonra. **2** *(pity)* pena, lástima: *what a shame you couldn't go* qué pena que no pudieras ir.
▶ *vt* avergonzar, deshonrar.

**shameful** ['ʃeɪmfʊl] *adj* vergonzoso,-a.

**shameless** ['ʃeɪmləs] *adj* desvergonzado,-a.

**shammy** ['ʃæmɪ] *n* gamuza.
ⓘ *pl* shammies.

**shampoo** [ʃæm'puː] *n* **1** *(product)* champú *m.* **2** *(act)* lavado.
ⓘ *pl* shampoos.

**shandy** ['ʃændɪ] *n* GB cerveza con limonada.
ⓘ *pl* shandies.

**shan't** [ʃɑːnt] *aux* → shall.

**shanty** ['ʃæntɪ] *n (shack)* chabola.
ⓘ *pl* shanties.

**shantytown** ['ʃæntɪtaʊn] *n* chabolas *fpl,* barrio de chabolas.

**shape** [ʃeɪp] *n* **1** *(form, appearance)* forma: *in the shape of a heart* en forma de corazón. **2** *(outline, shadow)* figura. **3** *(state - of thing)* estado; *(- of person)* forma, condiciones *fpl: the team is in good shape* el equipo está en buena forma. **4** *(framework, character)* configuración *f.*
LOC in shape *(fit)* en forma. ‖ in the shape of **1** *(physically)* bajo la forma de. **2** *(figuratively)* en forma de. ‖ to take shape tomar forma.
▶ *vt* **1** *(gen)* dar forma a; *(clay)* modelar: *he shaped the dough into a ball* formó una bola con la masa. **2** *(character)* formar; *(future, destiny)* decidir, determinar.
◆to shape up *vi* desarrollarse.

**share** [ʃeəʳ] *n* **1** *(portion)* parte *f.* **2** FIN acción *m*
▶ *vt* **1** *(have or use with others)* compartir: *can you share one book between two?* ¿podéis compartir un libro entre los dos? **2** *(tell news, feelings, etc)* compartir. **3** *(divide)* repartir, dividir.
▶ *vi* compartir: *there's only one bed so you'll have to share* solo hay una cama, así que tendréis que compartirla.

**shareholder** ['ʃeəhəʊldəʳ] *n* accionista *mf.*

**shareware** ['ʃeəweəʳ] *n* programas *mpl* compartidos.

**shark** [ʃɑːk] *n* ZOOL tiburón *m.*

**sharp** [ʃɑːp] *adj* **1** *(knife, etc)* afilado,-a; *(needle, pencil)* puntiagudo,-a. **2** *(angle)* agudo,-a; *(bend)* cerrado,-a; *(slope)* empinado,-a. **3** *(outline)* definido,-a; *(photograph, etc)* nítido,-a; *(contrast)* marcado,-a. **4** *(mind, wit)* perspicaz; *(eyes, ears)* agudo,-a, bueno,-a: *keep a sharp eye on those two* ten bien vigilados a esos dos. **5** *(person - clever)* listo,-a, vivo,-a. **6** *(pain)* agudo,-a, fuerte; *(cry, noise)* agudo,-a, estridente; *(frost)* fuerte; *(wind)* cortante, penetrante. **7** *(taste)* ácido,-a; *(smell)* acre. **8** *(change, etc)* brusco,-a, repentino,-a, súbito,-a. **9** MUS *(key)* sostenido, -a; *(too high)* desafinado,-a.
▶ *adv* **1** *(exactly)* en punto: *at ten o'clock sharp* a las diez en punto. **2** *(abruptly)* bruscamente.

**sharpen** ['ʃɑːpən] *vt* **1** *(knife, claws)* afilar; *(pencil)* sacar punta a. **2** *fig (feeling, intelligence)* agudizar; *(desire)* avivar; *(appetite)* abrir.
▶ *vi (voice)* agudizarse.

**sharpener** ['ʃɑːpənəʳ] *n (for knife)* afilador *m; (for pencil)* sacapuntas *m.*

**sharply** ['ʃɑːplɪ] *adv* **1** *(abruptly, suddenly)* repentinamente. **2** *(acutely)* agudamente. **3** *(clearly)* marcadamente, claramente.

**shatter** ['ʃætəʳ] *vt* **1** *(break into small pieces)* romper, hacer añicos, hacer pedazos. **2** *fig (health)* destrozar, quebrantar, minar; *(nerves)* destrozar.

**shave** [ʃeɪv] *n* afeitado. LOC to have a shave afeitarse.
▶ *vt* **1** *(face, legs, underarms)* afeitar; *(head)* rapar. **2** *(wood)* cepillar.
▶ *vi (person)* afeitarse: *he shaves every morning* se afeita cada mañana.

**shaver** ['ʃeɪvəʳ] *n* máquina de afeitar.

S

**shaving** [ˈʃeɪvɪŋ] n (of face) afeitado. COMP **shaving brush** brocha de afeitar. ‖ **shaving cream** crema de afeitar. ‖ **shaving foam** espuma de afeitar.
▸ n pl **shavings** (wood) virutas fpl.

**shawl** [ʃɔːl] n chal m, mantón m.

**she** [ʃiː] pron ella: she's called Nina se llama Nina; she's happy está contenta.
▸ n (animal) hembra; (baby) niña.

**she-** [ʃiː] pref hembra: she-bear osa.

**shear** [ʃɪəʳ] vt 1 (sheep) esquilar.
① pt **sheared**, pp **sheared o shorn** [ʃɔːn].
▸ n pl **shears** (gen) tijeras fpl (grandes); (for hedges) podadera f sing.

**shearer** [ˈʃɪərəʳ] n esquilador,-ra.

**shed¹** [ʃed] n (in garden, for bicycles) cobertizo.

**shed²** [ʃed] vt 1 (leaves, horns, skin) mudar; (clothes) quitarse, despojarse de; (workers, jobs) deshacerse de; (load, weight) perder: the snake sheds its skin la serpiente muda la piel. 2 fig (inhibitions, etc) liberarse de. 3 (water) repeler. 4 (blood, tears, etc) derramar.
① pt & pp **shed**, ger **shedding**.

**she'd** [ʃiːd] contr 1 she had. 2 she would.

**sheep** [ʃiːp] n oveja.
① pl **sheep**.

**sheepdog** [ˈʃiːpdɒg] n perro pastor.

**sheepfold** [ˈʃiːpfəʊld] n redil m, aprisco.

**sheer** [ʃɪəʳ] adj 1 (total, utter) total, absoluto,-a, puro,-a: by sheer coincidence por pura casualidad. 2 (cliff) escarpado,-a; (drop) vertical.

**sheet** [ʃiːt] n 1 (on bed) sábana: bottom/top sheet sábana bajera/encimera. 2 (of paper) hoja; (of metal) lámina, chapa; (of glass) lámina, placa; (of tin) hoja. COMP **sheet music** hojas pl de partitura, papel pautado.

**shelf** [ʃelf] n estante. COMP **(set of) shelves** estantería.
① pl **shelves**.

**shell** [ʃel] n 1 (of egg, nut) cáscara; (of pea) vaina; (of tortoise, lobster, etc) caparazón m; (of snail, oyster, etc) concha: the children were collecting shells on the beach los niños recogían conchas en la playa. 2 (of building) armazón m, esqueleto,

estructura; (of vehicle) armazón m; (of ship) casco. 3 MIL (for explosives) proyectil m, obús m.

**she'll** [ʃiːl] contr 1 she will. 2 she shall.

**shellfish** [ˈʃelfɪʃ] n (individual) marisco; (as food) marisco, mariscos mpl.
① pl **shellfish**.

**shelter** [ˈʃeltəʳ] n 1 (protection) abrigo, protección f, cobijo: the climbers sought shelter from the storm los montañeros buscaron abrigo para protegerse de la tormenta. 2 (place) refugio, cobijo.
▸ vt (protect) proteger, resguardar; these trees should shelter us from the rain esos árboles nos resguardarán de la lluvia.
▸ vi (from weather, etc) resguardarse, guarecerse; (from danger) refugiarse.

**shelve** [ʃelv] vt 1 (put on shelf) poner en el estante, poner en la estantería. 2 fig (postpone, abandon) aparcar, archivar.

**shepherd** [ˈʃepəd] n pastor m.
▸ vt (guide, direct) guiar, conducir.

**shelves** [ʃelvz] pl → shelf.

**sheriff** [ˈʃerɪf] n 1 US sheriff mf, alguacil,-la. 2 GB gobernador,-ra civil.

**sherry** [ˈʃerɪ] n jerez m.
① pl **sherries**.

**she's** [ʃiːz] contr 1 she is. 2 she has.

**shield** [ʃiːld] n 1 (for protection) escudo. 2 TECH pantalla protectora. 3 (of animal) caparazón m.
▸ vt (protect) proteger (from, de).

**shift** [ʃɪft] n 1 (change) cambio: a shift in policy un cambio de política. 2 (of work, workers) turno: the day/night shift el turno de día/de noche. COMP **shift key** tecla de las mayúsculas.
▸ vt 1 (change) cambiar; (move) desplazar, mover: he shifted his feet movió sus pies. 2 (transfer) traspasar, transferir. 3 US (change gear) cambiar.
▸ vi 1 (change) cambiar: the wind shifted el viento cambió de dirección. 2 US (change gear) cambiar de marcha.

**shilling** [ˈʃɪlɪŋ] n chelín m.

**shin** [ʃɪn] n ANAT espinilla, canilla. COMP **shin guard / shin pad** espinillera.

**shinbone** [ˈʃɪnbəʊn] n ANAT tibia.

**shine** [ʃaɪn] n brillo, lustre m: *he gave his shoes a good shine* sacó brillo a sus zapatos.

▶ vi **1** *(sun, light, eyes)* brillar; *(metal, glass, shoes)* relucir, brillar; *(face)* resplandecer, irradiar: *her eyes shone with happiness* le brillaban los ojos de alegría. **2** *fig (excel)* sobresalir (at, en), destacar (at, en), brillar (at, en): *he shines at tennis* destaca en tenis.

ⓘ *pt & pp* shone [ʃɒn].

**shiny** [ˈʃaɪni] adj brillante.

ⓘ *comp* shinier, *superl* shiniest.

**ship** [ʃɪp] n *(gen)* barco, buque m, embarcación f. ᴄᴏᴍᴾ **passenger ship** buque m de pasajeros. ❙ **ship's company** tripulación f.

▶ vt *(send - gen)* enviar, mandar; *(- by ship)* enviar por barco: *we had our luggage shipped to England* mandamos nuestro equipaje a Inglaterra por barco.

ⓘ *pt & pp* shipped, *ger* shipping.

**shipbuilding** [ˈʃɪpbɪldɪŋ] n construcción f naval.

**shipment** [ˈʃɪpmənt] n *(act)* embarque m, envío, transporte m *(marítimo)*.

**shipowner** [ˈʃɪpəʊnəʳ] n armador,-ra.

**shipwreck** [ˈʃɪprek] n naufragio. ʟᴏᴄ **to be shipwrecked** naufragar.

**shipyard** [ˈʃɪpjɑːd] n astillero.

**shirk** [ʃɜːk] vt *(duty, etc)* esquivar, eludir.

**shirt** [ʃɜːt] n *(gen)* camisa; *(for sport)* camiseta.

**shirtsleeve** [ˈʃɜːtsliːv] n manga de camisa. ʟᴏᴄ **in shirtsleeves** en mangas de camisa.

**shiver** [ˈʃɪvəʳ] n *(with cold)* escalofrío.

▶ vi *(with cold)* temblar, tiritar; *(with fear)* estremecerse.

▶ n pl **the shivers** escalofríos mpl.

**shivery** [ˈʃɪvəri] adj *(with cold)* estremecido,-a; *(feverish)* destemplado,-a.

**shoal¹** [ʃəʊl] n *(underwater sandbank)* banco de arena.

**shoal²** [ʃəʊl] n *(of fish)* banco, cardumen m.

▶ n pl **shoals** fam montones mpl.

**shock¹** [ʃɒk] n **1** *(jolt, blow)* choque m, impacto, golpe m; *(of explosion, etc)* sa-

cudida; *(electric)* descarga. **2** *(upset, distress)* conmoción f, golpe m; *(fright, scare)* susto: *you gave me quite a shock* me has dado un buen susto. **3** ᴍᴇᴅ shock m, choque m. ᴄᴏᴍᴾ **shock absorber** amortiguador m. ❙ **shock therapy / shock treatment** electrochoque m.

▶ vt **1** *(upset)* conmocionar, conmover, afectar. **2** *(startle)* asustar, sorprender; *(scandalize)* escandalizar, horrorizar.

▶ vi impresionar, impactar.

**shock²** [ʃɒk] n *(of hair)* mata.

**shocked** [ʃɒkt] adj horrorizado,-a, escandalizado,-a.

**shocking** [ˈʃɒkɪŋ] adj **1** *(disgraceful, offensive)* chocante, escandaloso,-a, vergonzoso,-a. **2** fam *(very bad)* espantoso,-a, pésimo,-a.

**shoe** [ʃuː] n **1** zapato: *I need a new pair of shoes* necesito unos zapatos nuevos. **2** *(for horse)* herradura. ʟᴏᴄ **to put os in sb else's shoes** ponerse en el lugar de ᴀʟɢɴ. ᴄᴏᴍᴾ **shoe polish** betún m.

❙ **shoe shop** zapatería.

**shoebrush** [ˈʃuːbrʌʃ] n cepillo para los zapatos.

**shoehorn** [ˈʃuːhɔːn] n calzador m.

**shoelace** [ˈʃuːleɪs] n cordón m *(de zapato)*.

**shoemaker** [ˈʃuːmeɪkəʳ] n zapatero,-a.

**shoeshine** [ˈʃuːʃaɪn] n limpieza de zapatos. ᴄᴏᴍᴾ **shoeshine boy** limpiabotas m.

**shone** [ʃɒn] pt → shine.

**shook** [ʃʊk] pt → shake.

**shoot** [ʃuːt] n ʙᴏᴛ *(gen)* brote m, retoño, renuevo; *(of vine)* sarmiento.

▶ vt **1** *(person, animal)* pegar un tiro a, pegar un balazo a; *(hit, wound)* herir (de bala); *(kill)* matar de un tiro, matar a tiros; *(hunt)* cazar: *she was shot in the back* recibió un balazo en la espalda. **2** *(fire - missile)* lanzar; *(- arrow, bullet, weapon)* disparar; *(- glance)* lanzar: *they shot questions at her* la bombardearon a preguntas. **3** *(film)* rodar, filmar; *(photograph)* fotografiar. ʟᴏᴄ **to shoot pool** jugar al billar. ❙ **to shoot sb dead** matar a ᴀʟɢɴ a tiros.

**S**

► *vi* **1** *(fire weapon)* disparar (at, a/sobre); *(hunt with gun)* cazar. **2** SP *(aim at goal)* tirar, disparar, chutar. **3** CINEM rodar, filmar. **5** BOT brotar.

◆ **to shoot down** *vt sep* **1** *(aircraft)* derribar, abatir; *(person)* matar a tiros. **2** *fig (argument, idea, etc)* rebatir.

① *pt & pp* shot [ʃɒt].

**shooting** [ˈʃuːtɪŋ] *n* **1** *(shots)* disparos *mpl*, tiros *mpl*; *(killing)* asesinato. **2** *(hunting)* caza. **3** CINEM rodaje *m*.

► *adj (pain)* punzante. COMP **shooting star** estrella fugaz.

**shop** [ʃɒp] *n* **1** *(gen)* tienda; *(business)* comercio, negocio: *I'm going to the shop* voy a la tienda. **2** *(workshop)* taller *m*. LOC **to keep shop** tener una tienda. COMP **repair shop** taller *m* de reparaciones. ▌ **shop assistant** dependiente,-a. ▌ **shop window** escaparate *m*.

► *vi (gen)* hacer la compra, comprar: *we usually shop on Saturday mornings* normalmente hacemos la compra los sábados por la mañana.

◆ **to shop around** *vi* ir de tienda en tienda y comparar precios.

① *pt & pp* shopped, *ger* shopping.

**shopkeeper** [ˈʃɒpkiːpəʳ] *n* tendero,-a.

**shoplifter** [ˈʃɒplɪftəʳ] *n* mechero,-a.

**shoplifting** [ˈʃɒplɪftɪŋ] *n* hurto (en las tiendas).

**shopper** [ˈʃɒpəʳ] *n* comprador,-ra.

**shopping** [ˈʃɒpɪŋ] *n* *(purchases)* compra, compras *fpl*; *(activity)* compra: *I had a bit of shopping to do* tuve que hacer unas compras. LOC **to do the shopping** hacer la compra. ▌ **to go shopping** ir de compras. COMP **shopping bag** cesta de la compra. ▌ **shopping basket** bolsa de la compra. ▌ **shopping centre** centro comercial. ▌ **shopping list** lista de la compra. ▌ **shopping mall** US centro comercial. ▌ **shopping precinct** zona comercial. ▌ **shopping trolley** carrito (de la compra).

**shore** [ʃɔːʳ] *n (of sea, lake)* orilla; *(coast)* costa; *(beach)* playa. LOC **on shore** en tierra.

**shorn** [ʃɔːn] *pp* → shear.

**short** [ʃɔːt] *adj* **1** *(not long)* corto,-a; *(not tall)* bajo,-a: *he's got short hair* lleva el pe-

lo corto; *Jo is short for Joanne* Jo es el diminutivo de Joanne. **2** *(brief - of time)* breve, corto,-a: *the days are shorter in winter* los días son más cortos en invierno **3** *(deficient)* escaso,-a: *water was short* escaseaba el agua. **4** *(curt)* seco,-a, brusco,-a. LOC **for short** para abreviar. ▌ **in short** en pocas palabras. ▌ **short of** a menos que, salvo que. ▌ **to be short of** STH andar escaso,-a de ALGO, estar falto,-a de ALGO: *I'm a bit short of money* ando ALGO escaso de dinero. ▌ **to run short of** STH acabarse ALGO: *we're running short of coffee* se nos está acabando el café. COMP **short circuit** cortocircuito. ▌ **short cut 1** *(route)* atajo. **2** *(method)* método fácil, fórmula mágica. ▌ **short order** US comida rápida. ▌ **short story** cuento.

► *adv (abruptly)* bruscamente: *the car stopped short* el coche se paró bruscamente.

► *n* **1** *(drink)* copa, chupito. **2** CINEM cortometraje *m*, corto. **3** ELEC cortocircuito.

**shortage** [ˈʃɔːtɪdʒ] *n* falta, escasez *f*.

**shorten** [ˈʃɔːtən] *vt* acortar.

► *vi* acortarse.

**shorthand** [ˈʃɔːthænd] *n* taquigrafía.

**shortly** [ˈʃɔːtlɪ] *adv* **1** *(soon)* dentro de poco, en breve: *shortly after/before* poco después/antes. **2** *(impatiently)* bruscamente.

**shorts** [ʃɔːts] *n pl* **1** pantalones *mpl* cortos, shorts *mpl*: *a pair of shorts* un pantalón corto. **2** US *(underpants)* calzoncillos *mpl*.

**short-sighted** [ˈʃɔːtsaɪtɪd] *adj* **1** MED miope, corto,-a de vista. **2** *(plan, policy, etc)* corto,-a de miras, estrecho,-a de miras.

**short-sleeved** [ˈʃɔːtsliːvd] *adj* de manga corta.

**shot¹** [ʃɒt] *n* **1** *(act, sound)* tiro, disparo, balazo: *I thought I heard a shot* creo haber oído un disparo. **2** *(projectile)* bala, proyectil *m*. **3** *(person)* tirador,-ra. **4** SP *(in football)* chut *m*, chute *m*; *(in tennis, golf, cricket, etc)* golpe *m*; *(in basketball)* tiro. **5** *(attempt, try)* intento. **6** *fam (injection)* inyección *f*, pinchazo. **7** *(drink)* trago, chupito. **8** (photo) foto f; (cinema) toma. LOC **like a shot** (without hesitation) sin pensarlo dos veces, sin dudar.

**shot²** [sed] pt & pp → **shoot**.

**shotgun** ['ʃɒtgʌn] n escopeta.

**should** [ʃʊd] aux **1** (duty, advisability, recommendation) deber: you should see the dentist deberías ir al dentista. **2** (probability) deber de: the clothes should be dry now la ropa ya debe de estar seca. **3** (subjunctive, conditional): if you should see Janet by any chance si por casualidad vieras a Janet. **4** (conditional, 1st person) : I should like to ask a question quisiera hacer una pregunta. **5** (tentative statement) : I should think so me imagino que sí. **6** (disbelief, surprise): how should I know! ¡yo qué sé! LOC **I should have thought ...** hubiera pensado...

✎ Should, cuando expresa el condicional para la primera persona, equivale a would.

**shoulder** ['ʃəʊldər] n **1** ANAT hombro: she looked over her shoulder miró por encima del hombro. **2** (of meat) paletilla. **3** (of hill, mountain) ladera; (of road) arcén m, andén m. LOC **a shoulder to cry on** un paño de lágrimas. ‖ **to rub shoulders with SB** codearse con ALGN. COMP **shoulder bag** bolso (de bandolera). ‖ **shoulder blade** omóplato. ‖ **shoulder strap 1** (of garment) tirante m. **2** (of bag) correa.
▸ n pl **shoulders** ANAT hombros mpl, espalda f sing.

**shout** [ʃaʊt] n grito.
▸ vt gritar (out, -): get out! he shouted ¡fuera! gritó.
▸ vi gritar: I don't like it when you shout at me no me gusta que me grites.
◆ **to shout down** vt sep abuchear.

**shouting** ['ʃaʊtɪŋ] n gritos mpl.

**shove** [ʃʌv] n empujón m: we had to give the car a shove tuvimos que dar un empujón al coche.
▸ vt **1** (push) empujar: she shoved the plate away apartó el plato de un empujón. **2** (put casually) meter.
▸ vi (push) empujar, dar empujones.

**shovel** ['ʃʌvəl] n **1** (tool) pala. **2** (machine) excavadora, pala mecánica.

**show** [ʃəʊ] n **1** THEAT (entertainment) espectáculo; (performance) función f: let's go and see a show vayamos a ver un espectáculo. **2** (on TV, radio) programa m, show m. **3** (exhibition) exposición f. **4** (display) muestra, demostración f: a show of strength una demostración de fuerza, una exhibición de fuerza. **5** (outward appearance, pretence) apariencia. LOC **the show must go on** el espectáculo debe continuar. ‖ **time will show** el tiempo lo dirá. COMP **fashion show** desfile m de modelos. ‖ **quiz show** programa m concurso. ‖ **show business** el mundo del espectáculo.
▸ vt **1** (gen) enseñar: I showed her my photos le enseñé mis fotos. **2** (point out) indicar, señalar. **3** (reveal - feelings) demostrar, expresar; (- interest, enthusiasm, etc) demostrar, mostrar: she rarely shows his feelings raras veces demuestra sus sentimientos. **4** (allow to be seen) dejar ver: black doesn't show the dirt el negro no deja ver la suciedad. **5** (prove, demonstrate) demostrar. **6** (guide) llevar, acompañar: I'll show you to your room te acompañaré a tu habitación. **7** (painting, etc) exponer, exhibir; (film) dar, poner, pasar, proyectar; (slides) pasar, proyectar; (on TV) dar, poner.
▸ vi **1** (be perceptible) verse, notarse: the stain doesn't show no se ve la mancha. **2** CINEM poner, dar, echar, proyectar, exhibir: what's showing at the Odeon? ¿qué dan en el Odeon?, ¿qué echan en el Odeon?
◆ **to show off** vi (gen) fanfarronear, presumir, lucirse; (child) hacerse el/la graciosa,-a.
▸ vt sep **1** (set off) hacer resaltar, realzar. **2** (flaunt, parade) hacer alarde de, presumir de.
◆ **to show up** vt sep **1** (make visible) hacer resaltar, hacer destacar. **2** fam (embarrass) dejar en ridículo, poner en evidencia.
▸ vi **1** (be visible) notarse, verse. **2** fam (arrive) acudir, presentarse, aparecer.
ⓘ pt **showed**, pp **showed** o **shown** [ʃəʊn].

S

**shower** ['ʃaʊəʳ] n **1** METEOR chubasco, chaparrón m. **2** (of stones, blows, insults, etc) lluvia. **3** (in bathroom) ducha. LOC **to have a shower / take a shower** ducharse. COMP **shower cap** gorro de baño. ▌ **shower gel** gel m de baño, gel m de ducha.
▸ vt **1** (sprinkle) espolvorear; (spray) rociar. **2** fig (bestow, heap) inundar, colmar, llover.
▸ vi **1** (rain) llover; (objects) caer, llover. **2** (in bath) ducharse.

**showing** ['ʃaʊɪŋ] n **1** (of film) pase m, sesión f, proyección f; (of paintings) exhibición f. **2** (performance) actuación f; (result) resultado.

**showman** ['ʃaʊmən] n **1** (manager) empresario (de espectáculos). **2** (entertainer) artista m, showman m.
① pl **showmen** ['ʃaʊmən].

**shown** [ʃaʊn] pp → show.

**show-off** ['ʃaʊɒf] n fam fanfarrón, -ona.

**showroom** ['ʃaʊruːm] n sala de exposiciones (de concesionario de coches).

**showy** ['ʃaʊɪ] adj (thing) llamativo,-a, vistoso,-a; (person) ostentoso,-a.
① comp **showier**, superl **showiest**.

**shrank** [ʃræŋk] pt → shrink.

**shrapnel** ['ʃræpnəl] n metralla.

**shred** [ʃred] n **1** (gen) triza; (of cloth) jirón m; (of paper) tira; (of tobacco) brizna, hebra. **2** fig (bit) pizca: not a shred of truth ni pizca de verdad. LOC **to tear STH/ sb to shreds** hacer trizas ALGO/a ALGN.
▸ vt (paper) hacer trizas, triturar; (vegetables - cut in strips) cortar en tiras; (- grate) rallar.
① pt & pp **shredded**, ger **shredding**.

**shrew** [ʃruː] n ZOOL musaraña.

**shrewd** [ʃruːd] adj **1** (person) astuto,-a, sagaz. **2** (decision) muy acertado,-a; (move) hábil, inteligente.

**shrewdness** ['ʃruːdnəs] n (gen) astucia, sagacidad f.

**shriek** [ʃriːk] n chillido, grito agudo.
▸ vi chillar, gritar. LOC **to shriek with laughter** reírse a carcajadas.
▸ vt chillar, gritar.

**shrill** [ʃrɪl] adj **1** (voice, words, people) agudo,-a, estridente; (sound, whistle) agudo,-a, estridente, penetrante. **2** (demand, protest, criticism) frenético,-a, estridente.
▸ vi (whistle) pitar; (phone, alarm) sonar; (person, voice) chillar.

**shrimp** [ʃrɪmp] n camarón m, gamba.

**shrine** [ʃraɪn] n REL (holy place) santuario, lugar m sagrado.

**shrink** [ʃrɪŋk] vt (clothes, etc) encoger.
▸ vi **1** (clothes) encoger, encogerse; (meat) achicarse, reducirse. **2** (savings, numbers, profits, etc) disminuir, reducirse. **3** (move back) retroceder, echarse atrás.
① pt **shrank** [ʃræŋk], pp **shrunk** [ʃrʌŋk].

**shroud** [ʃraʊd] n **1** REL mortaja, sudario. **2** fig (of mist, secrecy) velo.

**Shrove Tuesday** [ʃraʊv'tjuːzdɪ] n martes m de carnaval.

**shrub** [ʃrʌb] n arbusto, mata.

**shrug** [ʃrʌg] vt encoger. LOC **to shrug one's shoulders** encogerse de hombros.
① pt & pp **shrugged**, ger **shrugging**.

**shrunk** [ʃrʌŋk] pp → shrink.

**shudder** ['ʃʌdəʳ] n **1** (of person) escalofrío. **2** (of machine, engine) vibración f, sacudida.
▸ vi **1** (person) estremecerse, temblar (with, de): I shudder to think of it me dan escalofríos solo de pensarlo. **2** (machinery, vehicle) vibrar, dar sacudidas.

**shuffle** ['ʃʌfəl] n **1** (walk) arrastre m. **2** (of cards) baraje m, barajadura.
▸ vt **1** (feet - drag) arrastrar; (- move) mover. **2** (cards) barajar; (papers) revolver.
▸ vi (walk) andar arrastrando los pies; (in seat) revolverse.

**shut** [ʃʌt] vt (gen) cerrar: shut your eyes cierra los ojos.
▸ vi (gen) cerrar, cerrarse.
◆ **to shut down** vt sep (factory, business) cerrar.
▸ vi (factory, business) cerrar.
◆ **to shut up** vt sep **1** (close) cerrar. **2** (confine) encerrar. **3** fam (quieten) callar, hacer callar.
▸ vi **1** (close) cerrar. **2** (keep quiet) callarse: shut up! ¡cállate!
① pt & pp **shut**, ger **shutting**.

**shutdown** ['ʃʌtdaʊn] n (of factory, etc) cierre m.

**shutter** ['ʃʌtər] n 1 (on window) postigo, contraventana; (of shop) cierre m. 2 (of camera) obturador m.

**shuttle** ['ʃʌtəl] n 1 AV puente m aéreo. 2 (bus, train) servicio regular de enlace. 3 (in weaving) lanzadera. COMP shuttle service servicio regular de enlace.

**shuttlecock** ['ʃʌtəlkɒk] n volante m.

**shy** [ʃaɪ] adj 1 (person) tímido,-a, vergonzoso,-a: don't be shy no seas tímido, no tengas vergüenza. 2 (animal) asustadizo,-a.
ⓘ comp shyer o shier, superl shyest o shiest.
▸ vi (horse) espantarse (at, de), respingar, asustarse.

**shyness** ['ʃaɪnəs] n timidez f.

**sick** [sɪk] adj 1 (ill) enfermo,-a. 2 (nauseated, queasy) mareado,-a. 3 (fed up) harto,-a; (worried) preocupado,-a: I'm sick and tired of your moaning estoy más que harto de tus quejas. LOC to be sick vomitar, devolver. ‖ to feel sick estar mareado,-a, tener náuseas. COMP sick leave baja por enfermedad.

**sickle** ['sɪkəl] n hoz f.

**sickly** ['sɪklɪ] adj 1 (person) enfermizo,-a. 2 (smell, taste) empalagoso,-a, dulzón, -ona; (colour) horrible, asqueroso,-a.
ⓘ comp sicklier, superl sickliest.

**sickness** ['sɪknəs] n 1 (illness) enfermedad f. 2 (nausea) náuseas fpl, ganas fpl de vomitar.

**side** [saɪd] n 1 (gen) lado; (of coin, cube, record) cara: there's a garage at the side of the house hay un garaje al lado de la casa; write on one side of the paper only solo escribir en una cara del papel. 2 (of hill, mountain) ladera, falda. 3 (of body) lado, costado: she was lying on her side estaba echada de lado. 4 (edge - gen) borde m; (- of lake, river, etc) orilla; (- of page) margen m. LOC side by side juntos,-as, uno,-a al lado del/de la otro,-a. ‖ to keep on the right side of SB tratar de llevarse bien con ALGN.
▸ adj lateral. COMP side dish guarnición f, acompañamiento. ‖ side drum tambor m. ‖ side effect efecto secundario. ‖ side street callejuela. ‖ side view vista de perfil.

**sideboard** ['saɪdbɔːd] n (furniture) aparador m.

**sideboards** ['saɪdbɔːdz] n pl patillas fpl.

**sideburns** ['saɪdbɜːnz] n pl patillas fpl.

**sidecar** ['saɪdkɑːr] n sidecar m.

**sidelight** ['saɪdlaɪt] n AUTO luz f de posición.

**sidereal** [saɪ'dɪərɪəl] adj sideral.

**sidewalk** ['saɪdwɔːk] n US acera.

**sideways** ['saɪdweɪz] adj (movement, step) lateral; (look, glance) de soslayo, de reojo.
▸ adv de lado.

**siege** [siːdʒ] n 1 MIL sitio, cerco. 2 (by criminals, journalists) asedio. LOC to be under siege estar sitiado,-a.

**Sierra Leone** [sɪeərəlɪ'əʊn] n Sierra Leona.

**Sierra Leonean** [sɪeərəlɪ'əʊnɪən] adj sierraleonés,-esa.
▸ n sierraleonés,-esa.

**sieve** [sɪv] n (fine) tamiz m; (coarse) criba; (for liquids) colador m.
▸ vt (fine) tamizar; (coarse) cribar.

**sigh** [saɪ] n (of person) suspiro.
▸ vi (person) suspirar (for, por); (wind) susurrar, gemir: she sighed with relief suspiró aliviada.

**sight** [saɪt] n 1 (gen) vista: his sight is failing le está fallando la vista; we waited until he was out of sight esperamos hasta que hubo desaparecido; it was her first sight of the countryside fue la primera vez que veía el campo. 2 (thing seen, spectacle) espectáculo. LOC in/within sight a la vista. ‖ to come into sight aparecer. ‖ to know SB by sight conocer a ALGN de vista.
▸ vt ver, divisar.
▸ adv a sight fam (a great deal) mucho: a sight better mucho mejor.
▸ n pl sights (of city) monumentos mpl, lugares mpl de interés.

**sightseeing** ['saɪtsiːɪŋ] n visita turística, turismo. LOC to go sightseeing visitar los monumentos y lugares de interés.

**sign** [saɪn] n 1 (symbol) signo, símbolo. 2 (gesture) gesto, seña; (signal) señal f:

*wait until I give the sign* espera hasta que dé la señal. ᴸᴼᶜ **as a sign of** como muestra de. ᶜᴼᴹᴾ **sign language** lenguaje *m* por señas.

▶ *vt* **1** *(letter, document, cheque, etc)* firmar: *sign your name here, please* firme aquí, por favor. **2** *(player, group)* fichar **(on/up, -)**. **3** *(gesture)* hacer una seña/señal.

▶ *vi* **1** *(write name)* firmar. **2** *(player, group)* fichar **(for/with, por)**. **3** ᴜꜱ *(use sign language)* comunicarse por señas, hablar por señas.

◆ **to sign up** *vt sep* *(soldier)* reclutar; *(worker)* contratar.

▶ *vi* *(soldier)* alistarse; *(student)* matricularse.

**signal** ['sɪɡnəl] *n* señal *f*: *traffic signal* señal de tráfico.

▶ *adj* *(achievement, triumph, success, etc)* señalado,-a, destacado,-a, notable.

▶ *vt* **1** *(indicate)* indicar, señalar, marcar; *(forecast)* pronosticar. **2** *(gesture)* hacer señas, hacer una seña: *he signalled the waiter to bring the bill* le hizo una seña al camarero para que trajera la cuenta.

▶ *vi* **1** *(gesture)* hacer señas, hacer una seña. **2** ᴀᴜᴛᴏ poner el intermitente.

**signature** ['sɪɡnɪtʃəʳ] *n* *(name)* firma.

**significance** [sɪɡ'nɪfɪkəns] *n* **1** *(meaning)* significado. **2** *(importance)* importancia: *it's of no significance* no tiene importancia.

**significant** [sɪɡ'nɪfɪkənt] *adj* **1** *(meaningful - gen)* significativo,-a. **2** *(important)* importante, trascendente, considerable.

**signify** ['sɪɡnɪfaɪ] *vt fml* significar.
ⓘ *pt & pp* **signified**, *ger* **signifying**.

**signpost** ['saɪnpəʊst] *n* poste *m* indicador.

**silence** ['saɪləns] *n* *(gen)* silencio: *we walked in silence* caminamos en silencio. ᴸᴼᶜ **to reduce ꜱʙ to silence** dejar a ᴀʟɢɴ sin habla.

▶ *vt* *(person)* acallar, hacer callar; *(protest, opposition, criticism)* apagar, silenciar.

**silencer** ['saɪlənsəʳ] *n* silenciador *m*.

**silent** ['saɪlənt] *adj* **1** *(thing, place, taciturn person)* silencioso,-a. **2** *(not speaking)* callado,-a: *he was silent for a moment* se quedó callado un momento. **3** *(film, con-*

*sonant)* mudo,-a; *(prayer)* silencioso,-a. ᴸᴼᶜ **to be silent** callarse.

**silhouette** [sɪluːˈet] *n* silueta.

**silicon** ['sɪlɪkən] *n* silicio.

**silicone** ['sɪlɪkəʊn] *n* silicona.

**silk** [sɪlk] *n* seda.
▶ *adj* de seda.

**silken** ['sɪlkən] *adj* *(like silk)* sedoso,-a; *(of silk)* de seda.

**silkworm** ['sɪlkwɜːm] *n* gusano de seda.

**silky** ['sɪlkɪ] *adj* *(cloth, hair, fur, etc)* sedoso,-a; *(voice)* aterciopelado,-a; *(skin)* suave.
ⓘ *comp* **silkier**, *superl* **silkiest**.

**sill** [sɪl] *n* *(of window)* alféizar *m*, antepecho.

**silly** ['sɪlɪ] *adj* **1** *(stupid)* tonto,-a, estúpido,-a: *how silly of me!* ¡qué tonto soy! **2** *(unimportant)* trivial, sin importancia.
ⓘ *comp* **sillier**, *superl* **silliest**.

▶ *n* tonto,-a, bobo,-a.

**silver** ['sɪlvəʳ] *n* **1** *(metal)* plata: *sterling silver* plata de ley. **2** *(coins)* monedas *fpl* (de plata). **3** *(articles, ornaments, etc)* plata.

▶ *adj* **1** *(made of silver)* de plata. **2** *(in colour)* plateado,-a; *(hair)* canoso,-a, cano,-a. ᶜᴼᴹᴾ **silver foil / silver paper** papel *m* de plata. ❙ **silver medal** medalla de plata. ❙ **silver screen** el cine *m*.

▶ *vt* *(metal)* dar un baño de plata a, platear.

**similar** ['sɪmɪləʳ] *adj* parecido,-a **(to, a)**, similar **(to, a)**, semejante **(to, a)**: *those boys are very similar* esos chicos se parecen mucho.

**similarity** [sɪmɪˈlærətɪ] *n* *(likeness)* semejanza, parecido, similitud *f*.
ⓘ *pl* **similarities**.

**simile** ['sɪmɪlɪ] *n* símil *m*.

**simmer** ['sɪməʳ] *vt* ᴄᴜʟɪɴ hervir a fuego lento.
▶ *vi* ᴄᴜʟɪɴ hervir a fuego lento.

**simple** ['sɪmpəl] *adj* **1** *(gen)* sencillo,-a, simple: *a simple solution* una solución sencilla. **2** *(plain, pure, nothing more than)* sencillo,-a, puro,-a, mero,-a: *for the simple reason that...* por la sencilla razón que ...
ⓘ *comp* **simpler**, *comp* **simplest**.

**simplicity** [sɪm'plɪsətɪ] *n* **1** *(easiness, incomplexity)* sencillez *f*, simplicidad *f*. **2** *(lack of sophistication)* sencillez *f*, naturalidad *f*.

**simplify** ['sɪmplɪfaɪ] *vt* simplificar.
ⓘ *pt & pp* simplified, *ger* simplifying.

**simply** ['sɪmplɪ] *adv* **1** *(easily, plainly, modestly)* simplemente, sencillamente: *she lives very simply* vive muy sencillamente. **2** *(only)* simplemente, solamente, solo; *(just, merely)* meramente: *I simply don't know* sencillamente, no lo sé. **3** *(really, absolutely)* francamente, realmente.

**simulate** ['sɪmjəleɪt] *vt* simular.

**simultaneous** [sɪməl'teɪnɪəs] *adj* simultáneo,-a: *simultaneous translation* traducción simultánea.

**sin** [sɪn] *n* pecado.
▶ *vi* pecar (against, contra).
ⓘ *pt & pp* sinned, *ger* sinning.

**since** [sɪns] *adv* desde entonces: *she arrived in 1988 and has lived here ever since* llegó en 1988 y vive aquí desde entonces.
▶ *prep* desde: *I've been here since four o'clock* llevo aquí desde las cuatro.
▶ *conj* **1** *(time)* desde que: *it's years since I went to the theatre* hace años que no voy al teatro. **2** *(because, seeing that)* ya que, puesto que: *since you're going to the shop ...* ya que vas a la tienda ...

**sincere** [sɪn'sɪə<sup>r</sup>] *adj* sincero,-a.

**sincerely** [sɪn'sɪəlɪ] *adv* sinceramente.
LOC **Yours sincerely** *(in letter)* (le saluda) atentamente.

**sincerity** [sɪn'serətɪ] *n* sinceridad *f*.

**sinew** ['sɪnjuː] *n* tendón *m*.

**sing** [sɪŋ] *vt* *(gen)* cantar.
▶ *vi (person, bird)* cantar; *(wind, kettle, bullet)* silbar; *(ears, insect)* zumbar.
ⓘ *pt* sang [sæŋ], *pp* sung [sʌŋ].

**singer** ['sɪŋə<sup>r</sup>] *n* *(gen)* cantante *mf*; *(in choir)* cantor,-ra: *jazz singer* cantante de jazz.

**singing** ['sɪŋɪŋ] *n* *(act)* canto, cantar *m*; *(songs)* canciones *fpl*: *he loves singing in the shower* le encanta cantar en la ducha.

**single** ['sɪŋɡəl] *adj* **1** *(only one)* solo,-a, único,-a: *we heard a single scream* oímos un solo grito. **2** *(composed of one part)* simple, sencillo,-a: *single figures* cifras de un solo dígito. **3** *(for one person)* indi-

vidual. **4** *(separate, individual)* cada: *every single day* todos los días. **5** *(unmarried)* soltero,-a. LOC **in single file** en fila india. COMP **single cream** nata líquida. **single parent 1** *(mother)* madre *f* soltera. **2** *(father)* padre *m* soltero. **single room** habitación *f* individual.
▶ *n* **1** GB *(single ticket)* billete *m* de ida, billete *m* sencillo. **2** *(record)* (disco) sencillo, single *m*.
▶ *n pl* **singles** SP *(in tennis, badminton)* individuales *mpl*.

**single-parent** ['sɪŋɡəlpeərənt] *adj* *(family)* monoparental.

**singular** ['sɪŋɡjulə<sup>r</sup>] *adj* **1** *(in grammar)* singular. **2** *fml (outstanding)* extraordinario,-a.
▶ *n* LING singular *m*.

**sinister** ['sɪnɪstə<sup>r</sup>] *adj* siniestro,-a.

**sink** [sɪŋk] *n* *(in kitchen)* fregadero, pila; *(in bathroom)* lavabo, lavamanos *m*.
▶ *vt* **1** *(ship)* hundir. **2** *fig (hopes, plans)* acabar con.
▶ *vi* **1** *(gen)* hundirse. **2** *(sun, moon)* ponerse.
ⓘ *pt* sank [sæŋk], *pp* sunk [sʌŋk].

**sinner** ['sɪnə<sup>r</sup>] *n* pecador,-ra.

**sip** [sɪp] *n* sorbo.
▶ *vt* sorber, beber a sorbos.
ⓘ *pt & pp* sipped, *ger* sipping.

**siphon** ['saɪfən] *n* *(gen)* sifón *m*.

**sir** [sɜː<sup>r</sup>] *n* **1** *fml (gen)* señor *m*: *yes, sir* sí, señor. **2** *(title)* sir *m*. LOC **Dear Sir** *(in letter)* muy señor mío, muy señores míos, estimado señor.

**siren** ['saɪərən] *n* *(gen)* sirena.

**sirloin** ['sɜːlɔɪn] *n* solomillo.

**sister** ['sɪstə<sup>r</sup>] *n* **1** *(relative)* hermana. **2** *(comrade)* hermana, compañera.

**sister-in-law** ['sɪstərɪnlɔː] *n* cuñada.
ⓘ *pl* sisters-in-law.

**sit** [sɪt] *vt* **1** *(child, etc)* sentar (down, -): *she sat him down on the table* lo sentó en la mesa. **2** *(room, hall, etc)* tener cabida para; *(table)* ser para. **3** GB *(exam)* presentarse a.
▶ *vi* **1** *(action)* sentarse (down, -): *I sat next to Anna* me senté junto a Anna. **2** *(be seated)* estar sentado,-a: *they were sitting on the floor* estaban sentados en el

**S**

suelo. **3** *(village, building)* estar, situarse; *(clothes)* sentar, quedar: *that dress sits well on you* aquel vestido te sienta bien.
▸ *vi fam (baby-sit)* hacer de canguro (for, a).
◆ **to sit back** *vi (lean back)* recostarse; *(relax)* ponerse cómodo,-a. **2** *(take no active part)* cruzarse de brazos.
◆ **to sit out** *vt sep* **1** *(stay until end)* aguantar (hasta el final). **2** *(not dance)* no bailar.
◆ **to sit up** *vi* **1** *(in bed)* incorporarse (en la cama). **2** *(stay up late)* quedarse levantado,-a.
▸ *vt sep (child, etc)* sentar.
① *pt & pp* **sat** [sæt], *ger* **sitting**.

**site** [saɪt] *n (location)* situación *f*, emplazamiento, colocación *f*. COMP **archaeological site** yacimiento arqueológico.
▸ *vt* situar, ubicar, emplazar.

**sit-in** ['sɪtɪn] *n (protest)* sentada.

**sitting** ['sɪtɪŋ] *n (of meal)* turno; *(of committee, for portrait)* sesión *f*.
▸ *adj (position)* sentado,-a. COMP **sitting room** sala de estar.

**situated** ['sɪtjʊeɪtɪd] *adj (building, etc)* situado,-a, ubicado,-a.

**situation** [sɪtjʊ'eɪʃən] *n* **1** *(circumstances)* situación *f*: *we're in a difficult situation* estamos en una situación difícil. **2** *(location)* situación *f*, ubicación *f*.

**sit-up** ['sɪtʌp] *n SP* abdominal *m*.

**six** [sɪks] *adj* seis: *it costs six pounds* cuesta seis libras; *six hundred* seiscientos,-as; *six thousand* seis mil.
▸ *n* seis *m*: *she's six years old* tiene seis años; *it's six o'clock* son las seis.

**sixteen** [sɪks'ti:n] *adj* dieciséis.
▸ *n* dieciséis *m*.

✎ Consulta también **six**.

**sixteenth** [sɪks'ti:nθ] *adj* decimosexto,-a.
▸ *adv* en decimosexto lugar.
▸ *n* **1** *(in series)* decimosexto,-a. **2** *(fraction)* decimosexto; *(one part)* decimosexta parte *f*.

✎ Consulta también **sixth**.

**sixth** [sɪksθ] *adj* sexto,-a: *the sixth floor* la sexta planta, el sexto piso.
▸ *adv* sexto, en sexto lugar: *he came sixth* llegó en sexto lugar.
▸ *n* **1** *(in series)* sexto,-a; *(day)* el seis, el día seis: *the sixth of June* el seis de junio. **2** *(fraction)* sexto; *(one part)* sexta parte *f*. COMP **sixth form** GB ≈ segundo de bachillerato. ▌ **sixth form college** GB ≈ *instituto para estudiantes de segundo de bachillerato.*

**sixtieth** ['sɪkstɪəθ] *adj* sexagésimo,-a.
▸ *adv* en sexagésimo lugar.
▸ *n* **1** *(in series)* sexagésimo,-a. **2** *(fraction)* sexagésimo; *(one part)* sexagésima parte *f*.

**sixty** ['sɪkstɪ] *adj* sesenta: *there were about sixty people* había unas sesenta personas.
▸ *n* sesenta *m*.

**size** [saɪz] *n* **1** *(gen)* tamaño; *(magnitude)* magnitud *f*: *it's the size of an egg* es del tamaño de un huevo. **2** *(of clothes)* talla; *(of shoes)* número; *(of person)* talla, estatura: *she's a size 12* gasta la talla 12.

**skate¹** [skeɪt] *n* patín *m*.
▸ *vi* patinar.

**skate²** [skeɪt] *n (fish)* raya.

**skateboard** ['skeɪtbɔ:d] *n* monopatín *m*.

**skater** ['skeɪtə'] *n* patinador,-ra.

**skating** ['skeɪtɪŋ] *n* patinaje *m*. COMP **ice skating** patinaje *m* sobre hielo. ▌ **skating rink** pista de patinaje.

**skeleton** ['skelɪtən] *n* **1** *(of person, animal)* esqueleto. **2** *(of building, ship)* armazón *m*, estructura.

**sketch** [sketʃ] *n* **1** *(drawing)* dibujo; *(preliminary drawing)* bosquejo, esbozo. **2** *(outline, rough idea)* esquema *m*, esbozo.
▸ *vt (draw)* dibujar; *(preliminary drawing)* bosquejar, hacer un bosquejo de.
▸ *vi* hacer bosquejos, hacer bocetos.
◆ **to sketch in/out**

**skewer** ['skjʊə'] *n* CULIN pincho, brocheta.

**ski** [ski:] *n (equipment)* esquí *m*.
▸ *vi* esquiar. LOC **to ski down** bajar esquiando. COMP **ski jump 1** *(slope)* pista de saltos, trampolín *m*. **2** *(competition)* saltos *mpl* de esquí. ▌ **ski lift** telesquí *m*.

**ski resort** estación *f* de esquí. **ski slope** pista de esquí.

**skid** [skɪd] *n* AUTO patinazo, derrapaje *m*. **skid row** US barrios *mpl* bajos, barriadas *fpl*.

**skier** ['skɪəʳ] *n* esquiador,-ra.

**skies** [skaɪz] *pl* → **sky**.

**skiing** ['skɪɪŋ] *n* esquí *m*.

**skilful** ['skɪlfʊl] *adj* (*gen*) diestro,-a, hábil. LOC **to be skilful at** STH ser hábil para ALGO.

**skilfully** ['skɪlfʊlɪ] *adv* hábilmente.

**skill** [skɪl] *n* **1** (*ability*) habilidad *f*, destreza; (*talent*) talento, don *m*, dotes *fpl*. **2** (*technique*) técnica, arte *m*.
▶ *n pl* **skills** (*expertise*) capacidad *f sing*, aptitudes *fpl*: *a person with computer skills* una persona que sepa informática.

**skilled** [skɪld] *adj* **1** (*specialized*) cualificado,-a, especializado,-a. **2** (*able*) hábil, diestro,-a; (*expert*) experto,-a.

**skillful** ['skɪlfʊl] *adj* US → **skilful**.

**skillfully** ['skɪlfʊlɪ] *adv* US → **skilfully**.

**skimmed** [skɪmd] *adj* (*milk*) desnatado,-a.

**skimmer** ['skɪməʳ] *n* (*spoon*) espumadera.

**skin** [skɪn] *n* **1** (*of person*) piel *f*; (*of face*) cutis *m*, piel *f*: *she has light/dark skin* tiene la piel clara/morena. **2** (*of animal*) piel *f*, pellejo. **3** (*of fruit, vegetable*) piel *f*. **4** (*on paint*) telilla, capa fina; (*on milk, custard, etc*) nata.

**skinflint** ['skɪnflɪnt] *n fam* tacaño,-a.

**skinhead** ['skɪnhed] *n* cabeza *mf* rapada, skin *mf*.

**skinny** ['skɪnɪ] *adj fam* flaco,-a.
ⓘ *comp* skinnier, *superl* skinniest.

**skip¹** [skɪp] *n* salto, brinco.
▶ *vi* **1** (*move, jump*) saltar, brincar; (*with rope*) saltar a la comba. **2** (*jump, flit*) saltar.
▶ *vt* (*miss, omit*) saltarse: *she skipped a few pages* se saltó unas páginas.
ⓘ *pt & pp* skipped, *ger* skipping.

**skip²** [skɪp] *n* (*container*) contenedor *m*.

**skipper** ['skɪpəʳ] *n* **1** MAR patrón,-ona, capitán,-ana. **2** SP capitán,-ana.

**skipping** ['skɪpɪŋ] *n* COMP **skipping rope** comba, cuerda de saltar.

**skirt** [skɜːt] *n* (*garment*) falda.

**skirting** ['skɜːtɪŋ] *n* [also **skirting board**] *n* GB zócalo, rodapié *m*.

**skittle** ['skɪtəl] *n* (*wooden pin*) bolo.
▶ *n pl* **skittles** bolos *mpl*, boliche *m sing*.

**skull** [skʌl] *n* **1** ANAT cráneo. **2** (*symbol*) calavera. COMP **skull and crossbones** bandera pirata.

**skunk** [skʌŋk] *n* ZOOL mofeta.

**sky** [skaɪ] *n* (*gen*) cielo; (*firmament*) firmamento.
ⓘ *pl* skies.

**sky-blue** ['skaɪblu:] *adj* azul celeste.

**skylark** ['skaɪlɑ:k] *n* alondra.

**skylight** ['skaɪlaɪt] *n* tragaluz *m*, claraboya.

**skyline** ['skaɪlaɪn] *n* **1** (*horizon*) horizonte *m*. **2** (*of city*) perfil *m*.

**skyscraper** ['skaɪskreɪpəʳ] *n* rascacielos *m*.

**slab** [slæb] *n* (*of stone*) losa; (*of cake*) trozo; (*of chocolate*) tableta.

**slack¹** [slæk] *adj* **1** (*not taut*) flojo,-a: *a slack rope* una cuerda floja. **2** (*careless, lax*) descuidado,-a. **3** (*not busy - trade, demand*) flojo,-a.
▶ *n* (*part of rope, wire, etc*) parte *f* floja.
◆ **to slack off**

**slack²** [slæk] *n* (*in coal*) cisco.

**slacken** ['slækən] *vt* **1** (*rope, grip*) aflojar; (*reins*) soltar. **2** (*speed*) reducir, disminuir.
▶ *vi* (*speed*) reducirse, disminuir.

**slalom** ['slɑ:ləm] *n* SP slalom *m*, eslalon *m*.

**slam** [slæm] *n* (*of lid, book, etc*) golpe *m*; (*of door*) portazo.
▶ *vt* **1** (*shut forcefully*) cerrar de golpe: *she slammed the door in my face* me dio con la puerta en las narices. **2** (*throw noisily*) arrojar, lanzar. **3** *fig* (*criticize*) criticar duramente. **4** (*defeat*) dar una paliza a. LOC **to slam on the brakes** AUTO dar un frenazo. **to slam the phone down** colgar de golpe.
ⓘ *pt & pp* slammed, *ger* slamming.

**slang** [slæŋ] *n* argot *m*, jerga.
▶ *adj* de jerga, de argot.

**S**

**slant** [slɑ:nt] n **1** (gen) inclinación f. **2** (point of view) enfoque m, punto de vista.
▶ vt **1** (slope) inclinar. **2** fig (news, report, etc) presentar tendenciosamente.
▶ vi (slope) inclinarse.

**slap** [slæp] n (gen) palmada; (smack) cachete m; (in face) bofetada, bofetón m. COMP **a slap in the face** (rebuff) un desaire, una bofetada.
▶ adv **1** (straight) de lleno: we drove slap into a wall dimos de lleno contra una pared. **2** (right) justo.
▶ vt (gen) pegar (con la mano).
ⓘ pt & pp **slapped**, ger **slapping**.

**slash** [slæʃ] n **1** (with sword) tajo; (with knife) cuchillada. **2** fam (oblique) barra oblicua.
▶ vt **1** (with sword) dar un tajo a; (with knife) acuchillar, rajar. **2** fig (prices, wages) rebajar, reducir: prices slashed precios de remate.

**slate** [sleɪt] n (gen) pizarra. LOC **to wipe the slate clean** hacer borrón y cuenta nueva.

**slaughter** [ˈslɔːtər] n matanza.
▶ vt (animals) matar, sacrificar; (people) matar brutalmente.

**slaughterhouse** [ˈslɔːtəhaʊs] n matadero.

**slave** [sleɪv] n esclavo,-a. COMP **slave trade** trata de esclavos.

**slavery** [ˈsleɪvəri] n esclavitud f.

**sledge** [sledʒ] n GB trineo.
▶ vi ir en trineo.

**sleep** [sliːp] n sueño: I'm going to have a little sleep voy a dormir un poco. LOC **to go to sleep 1** (fall asleep) dormirse. **2** (become numb) dormirse, entumecerse.
▶ vi (gen) dormir: I slept well he dormido bien.
◆ **to sleep in** vi (sleep late) quedarse en la cama, dormir hasta tarde.
ⓘ pt & pp **slept** [slept].

**sleeping** [ˈsliːpɪŋ] adj durmiente, dormido,-a. COMP **sleeping bag** saco de dormir. ‖ **Sleeping Beauty** la Bella Durmiente. ‖ **sleeping car** coche cama m.

**sleepless** [ˈsliːpləs] adj insomne. LOC **to have a sleepless night** pasar la noche en blanco.

**sleepy** [ˈsliːpɪ] adj **1** (drowsy) soñoliento,-a. **2** (quiet, not busy) tranquilo,-a.
ⓘ comp **sleepier**, superl **sleepiest**.

**sleet** [sliːt] n aguanieve f.
▶ vi caer aguanieve.

**sleeve** [sliːv] n **1** (of garment) manga. **2** (of record) funda. LOC **to have STH up one's sleeve** guardarse una carta en la manga.

**sleigh** [sleɪ] n trineo. COMP **sleigh bell** cascabel m.

**slender** [ˈslendər] adj **1** (person) delgado,-a, esbelto,-a. **2** fig (hope, chance) ligero,-a, remoto,-a; (income, majority) escaso,-a.
ⓘ comp **slenderer**, comp **slenderest**.

**slept** [slept] pt & pp → sleep.

**slice** [slaɪs] n **1** (of bread) rebanada; (thin - ham, etc) lonja, loncha; (- meat) tajada; (- of salami, lemon, etc) rodaja. **2** (portion - cake, pie) porción f, trozo; (- of melon, etc) raja. **3** fig (share) parte f; (proportion) proporción f. COMP **sliced bread** pan m de molde.
▶ vt **1** (cut up) cortar a rebanadas, cortar a lonjas, cortar a rodajas: she sliced up the ham cortó el jamón en lonchas. **2** (cut off) cortar: can you slice me a piece of cake? ¿puedes cortarme un trozo de pastel?
◆ **to slick down** vt sep (hair) alisar.

**slid** [slɪd] pt & pp → slide.

**slide** [slaɪd] n **1** (act of sliding) deslizamiento, desliz m; (slip) resbalón m. **2** (in playground) tobogán m. **3** (photo) diapositiva. **4** (of microscope) platina, portaobjetos m. COMP **slide projector** proyector m de diapositivas.
▶ vt (gen) deslizar, pasar; (furniture) correr.
▶ vi **1** (slip deliberately) deslizar, deslizarse; (slip accidentally) resbalar: she slid on the ice resbaló en el hielo. **2** (move quietly) deslizarse: the drawer slid open el cajón se abrió con facilidad.
ⓘ pt & pp **slid** [slɪd].

**slight** [slaɪt] adj **1** (small in degree) pequeño,-a, ligero,-a; (not serious, unim-

*portant)* leve, insignificante: *a slight change of plan* un pequeño cambio de planes. **2** *(person)* menudo,-a. LOC **not in the slightest** en absoluto.
▶ *n (affront)* desaire *m*, desprecio.

**slightly** ['slaɪtlɪ] *adv (a little)* ligeramente, un poco, ALGO: *I know him slightly* apenas lo conozco. LOC **to be slightly built** ser de complexión menuda.

**slim** [slɪm] *adj* **1** *(person, build)* delgado,-a, esbelto,-a. **2** *(chance, hopes, prospect)* remoto,-a.
ⓘ *comp* slimmer, *superl* slimmest.
▶ *vi* adelgazar, hacer régimen: *I'm slimming* estoy a régimen.
ⓘ *pt & pp* slimmed, *ger* slimming.

**sling** [slɪŋ] *n* **1** MED cabestrillo. **2** *(catapult)* honda; *(child's)* tirador *m*. **3** *(device for lifting, carrying)* cuerda; *(for baby)* canguro.
▶ *vt* **1** *fam (throw)* tirar, arrojar: *sling it in the bin* tíralo a la basura. **2** *(lift, support)* colgar.
ⓘ *pt & pp* slung [slʌŋ].

**slingshot** ['slɪŋʃɒt] *n* tirachinas *m*.

**slip** [slɪp] *n* **1** *(slide)* resbalón *m*; *(trip)* traspiés *m*, tropezón *m*. **2** *(mistake)* error *m*, equivocación *f*; *(moral)* desliz *m*. **3** *(women's underskirt)* combinación *f*; *(petticoat)* enaguas *fpl*. COMP **a slip of the pen** un lapsus. ▌ **a slip of the tongue** un lapsus linguae.
▶ *vi* **1** *(slide)* resbalar; *(fall, get away, escape)* caer: *my foot slipped* se me fue el pie. **2** AUTO *(clutch, tyre)* patinar.
▶ *vt* **1** *(pass, give, put)* pasar, deslizar, dar a escondidas: *she slipped the note into her bag* disimuladamente metió la nota en el bolso. **2** *(overlook, forget)* escaparse.
◆ **to slip out** *vi (secret, comment, etc)* escaparse.
ⓘ *pt & pp* slipped, *ger* slipping.

**slipper** ['slɪpə<sup>r</sup>] *n* zapatilla.

**slippery** ['slɪpərɪ] *adj (surface)* resbaladizo,-a
ⓘ *comp* slipperier, *superl* slipperiest.

**slit** [slɪt] *n (opening)* abertura, hendedura; *(cut)* corte *m*, raja: *light came*

*through the slits in the blind* entraba la luz por las ranuras de la persiana.
▶ *vt (cut)* cortar, rajar, hender.
ⓘ *pt & pp* slit, *ger* slitting.

**slither** ['slɪðə<sup>r</sup>] *vi* deslizarse.

**slogan** ['sləʊgən] *n* eslogan *m*, lema *m*.

**slope** [sləʊp] *n* **1** *(incline)* cuesta, pendiente *f*; *(upward)* subida; *(downward)* bajada, declive *m*: *a steep slope* una cuesta empinada. **2** *(of mountain)* ladera, falda, vertiente *f*; *(of roof)* vertiente *f*.
▶ *vi* inclinarse.

**sloppy** ['slɒpɪ] *adj* **1** *(messy, careless - gen)* descuidado,-a; *(- manual work)* chapucero,-a; *(- appearance, dress)* desaliñado,-a, dejado,-a. **2** *(sentimental)* empalagoso,-a.
ⓘ *comp* sloppier, *superl* sloppiest.

**slot** [slɒt] *n* **1** *(for coin)* ranura; *(groove)* muesca; *(opening)* rendija, abertura. **2** *(programme)* espacio; *(position, place)* puesto, hueco. COMP **slot machine 1** *(vending machine)* distribuidor *m* automático. **2** *(for gambling)* máquina tragaperras.
▶ *vt (insert)* insertar, introducir: *slot the coin in the machine* insertar la moneda en la máquina.
ⓘ *pt & pp* slotted, *ger* slotting.

**Slovak** ['sləʊvæk] *adj* eslovaco,-a.
▶ *n* **1** *(person)* eslovaco,-a. **2** *(language)* eslovaco.

**Slovakia** [sləʊ'vækɪə] *n* Eslovaquia.

**Slovene** ['sləʊviːn] *adj* esloveno,-a.
▶ *n* **1** *(person)* esloveno,-a. **2** *(language)* esloveno.

**Slovenia** [sləʊ'viːnə] *n* Eslovenia.

**slow** [sləʊ] *adj* **1** *(gen)* lento,-a: *a slow recovery* una recuperación lenta. **2** *(clock, watch)* atrasado,-a: *my watch is slow* mi reloj va atrasado. **3** *(dull, not active)* aburrido,-a. **4** *(not quick to learn)* lento,-a, torpe; *(thick)* corto,-a de alcances: *he's a slow learner* le cuesta aprender. COMP **to be slow about/in doing** STH tardar en hacer ALGO.
▶ *adv* despacio, lentamente: *drive slow!* ¡conduce despacio!
▶ *vt (vehicle, machine)* reducir la marcha de.

**S**

▶ *vi (gen)* ir más despacio.

◆ **to slow down** *vt sep* hacer ir más despacio.

▶ *vi (gen)* ir más despacio.

**slowdown** ['sləʊdaʊn] *n* US *(workers)* huelga de celo.

**slowly** ['sləʊlɪ] *adv* despacio, lentamente.

**sludge** [slʌdʒ] *n* **1** *(mud)* fango, cieno, lodo, barro. **2** *(sewage)* aguas *fpl* residuales.

**slug** [slʌg] *n* ZOOL babosa.

**slum** [slʌm] *n* **1** *(place, house, etc)* casuca, casucha, tugurio. **2** *fam (tip)* pocilga.
▶ *vi fam* visitar los barrios bajos.
ⓘ *pt & pp* slummed, *ger* slumming.
▶ *n pl* **slums** *(area)* barrios *mpl* bajos.

**slump** [slʌmp] *n (recession)* crisis *f* económica; *(drop in demand, etc)* bajón *m*, baja repentina.

**slung** [slʌŋ] *pt & pp* → sling.

**slurp** [slɜːp] *vt* sorber ruidosamente.

**sly** [slaɪ] *adj* **1** *(cunning)* astuto,-a, ladino,-a; *(deceitful)* tramposo,-a. **2** *(secretive, knowing)* furtivo,-a: *a sly smile* una sonrisa maliciosa. **3** *(mischievous, playful)* travieso,-a, pícaro,-a. LOC **on the sly** a escondidas.
ⓘ *comp* slyer o slier, *superl* slyest o sliest.

**smack¹** [smæk] *n* **1** *(slap)* bofetada, tortazo, azote *m*; *(blow)* golpe *m*. **2** *fam (loud kiss)* besote *m*, beso sonoro.
▶ *vt* **1** *(slap)* dar una bofetada a, abofetear, pegar a. **2** *(strike)* golpear.

**smack²** [smæk] *n* **1** *(flavour)* sabor *m*; *(smell)* olor *m*. **2** *(hint, suggestion)* pizca.

**small** [smɔːl] *adj* **1** *(not large)* pequeño, -a, chico,-a: *we live in a small flat* vivimos en un piso pequeño. **2** *(in height)* bajo,-a, pequeño,-a: *he's a small man* es un hombre bajito. **3** *(young)* joven, pequeño,-a: *when I was small* cuando era pequeño. LOC **in the small hours** a altas horas de la madrugada. ‖ COMP **small ads** anuncios *mpl* por palabras, pequeños anuncios *mpl*. ‖ **small change** cambio, monedas *fpl* sueltas. ‖ **small letter** letra minúscula. ‖ **small print** letra pequeña.
ⓘ *comp* smaller, *comp* smallest.

▶ *adv* pequeño: *cut it up small* córtalo en trocitos.

**smallpox** ['smɔːlpɒks] *n* viruela.

**smart** [smɑːt] *adj* **1** *(elegant)* elegante, fino,-a; *(chic)* fino,-a, de buen tono. **2** US *(clever)* listo,-a, inteligente; *(sharp)* agudo,-a, vivo,-a; *(impudent)* fresco,-a, descarado,-a: *he thinks he's so smart* se cree muy listo. **3** *(quick, brisk)* rápido,-a, ligero,-a.

**smash** [smæʃ] *n* **1** *(noise)* estrépito, estruendo. **2** *(collision)* choque *m* violento, colisión *f*. **3** *(blow)* golpe *m*. **4** SP *(tennis)* smash *m*, mate *m*. **5** *(success, hit)* exitazo, gran éxito. COMP **smash hit** gran éxito, exitazo.
▶ *vt* **1** *(break)* romper; *(shatter)* hacer pedazos, hacer añicos; *(destroy - car, room, etc)* destrozar: *the vandals smashed the place up* los vándalos destrozaron el local. **2** *(hit forcefully)* romper; *(crash, throw violently)* estrellar *(into*, contra). **3** *(defeat)* vencer, aplastar; *(destroy)* destrozar. **4** SP *(in tennis)* hacer un mate.
▶ *vi* **1** *(break)* romperse; *(shatter)* hacerse añicos: *the mirror smashed into tiny pieces* el espejo se hizo añicos. **2** *(crash)* estrellarse *(into*, contra), chocar *(into*, contra).

**smashing** ['smæʃɪŋ] *adj* GB *fam* estupendo,-a, fantástico,-a, genial, fenomenal.

**smear** [smɪəʳ] *n* **1** *(smudge, stain)* mancha. **2** *fig (defamation)* calumnia.
▶ *vt* **1** *(spread - butter, ointment)* untar; *(grease, paint)* embadurnar: *he smeared butter on the bread* untó el pan con mantequilla. **2** *(make dirty)* manchar. **3** *fig (defame)* calumniar, difamar.

**smell** [smel] *n* **1** *(sense)* olfato. **2** *(odour)* olor *m*; *(perfume)* perfume *m*, aroma *m*.
▶ *vt* **1** oler. **2** *fig* olfatear.
▶ *vi* **1** oler. **2** *(have particular smell)* oler (a).
ⓘ *pt & pp* smelled o smelt [smelt].

**smelly** ['smelɪ] *adj* apestoso,-a, maloliente.

**smelt¹** [smelt] *vt (melt)* fundir.

**smelt²** [smelt] *pp* → smell.

**smile** [smaɪl] *n* sonrisa.
▶ *vi (gen)* sonreír.

▶ *vt (say with a smile)* decir sonriendo.
◆ **to smile on** *vi* sonreír a.

**smiley** ['smaɪlɪ] *n* COMPUT emoticón *m*.

**smith** [smɪθ] *n* herrero,-a.

**smog** [smɒg] *n* niebla tóxica, smog *m*.

**smoke** [sməʊk] *n* **1** *(gen)* humo. **2** *fam (cigarette)* cigarrillo, cigarro, pitillo.
▶ *vt* **1** *(person)* fumar. **2** *(meat, fish)* ahumar.
▶ *vi* **1** *(person)* fumar. **2** *(fire, chimney, etc)* echar humo, humear.

**smoker** ['sməʊkəʳ] *n* **1** *(person)* fumador,-ra. **2** *(on train)* vagón *m* de fumadores.

**smoking** ['sməʊkɪŋ] *adj* humeante.
▶ *n* fumar *m*.

**smoky** ['sməʊkɪ] *adj* lleno,-a de humo.
ⓘ *comp* smokier, *comp* smokiest.

**smooth** [smuːð] *adj* **1** *(surface, texture, tyre)* liso,-a; *(skin)* suave; *(road)* llano,-a, uniforme; *(sea)* tranquilo,-a, en calma. **2** *(liquid mixture, sauce)* sin grumos. **3** *(wine, beer, etc)* suave.
▶ *vt (gen)* alisar; *(with sandpaper)* lijar; *(polish)* pulir.

**smother** ['smʌðəʳ] *vt* **1** *(asphyxiate)* asfixiar, ahogar. **2** *(put out - fire)* sofocar, extinguir, apagar. **3** *(stifle - yawn, cough, laughter)* contener, reprimir; *(suppress - opposition)* acallar. **4** *(cover)* cubrir (in/with, de); *(heap)* colmar (in/with, de).
▶ *vi (asphyxiate)* asfixiarse, ahogarse.

**smudge** [smʌdʒ] *n* *(stain - gen)* mancha; *(- of ink)* borrón *m*.
▶ *vt (gen)* manchar; *(writing)* emborronar.
▶ *vi (ink, paint, etc)* correrse.

**smuggle** ['smʌgəl] *vt* **1** *(illegally)* pasar de contrabando. **2** *(sneak)* pasar a escondidas.

**smuggler** ['smʌgləʳ] *n* contrabandista *mf*.

**snack** [snæk] *n (light meal)* bocado, piscolabis *m*, tentempié *m*, refrigerio; *(in afternoon)* merienda.
▶ *vi* comer, comerse. [LOC] **to have a snack** picar ALGO. [COMP] **snack bar** cafetería.

▶ *n pl* **snacks** *(gen)* cosas *fpl* para picar; *(in bar)* tapas *fpl*.

**snail** [sneɪl] *n* caracol *m*.

**snake** [sneɪk] *n (big)* serpiente *f*; *(small)* culebra.
▶ *vi fig (river, road, etc)* serpentear.

**snap** [snæp] *n* **1** *(sharp noise)* ruido seco; *(of fingers, branch)* chasquido. **2** *fam (snapshot)* foto *f*, instantánea.
▶ *vt* **1** *(break)* partir en dos, romper en dos. **2** *(close)* cerrar de golpe. **3** *(click)* chasquear. **4** *(say sharply)* decir bruscamente.
▶ *vi* **1** *(break)* romperse, partirse. **2** *fig (person)* perder los nervios, sufrir una crisis nerviosa. **3** *(speak sharply)* regañar (at, a), hablar con brusquedad (at, a).
ⓘ *pt & pp* snapped, *ger* snapping.

⊕ Snap es también un juego de cartas en el que los jugadores van poniendo cartas sobre la mesa, y si salen dos del mismo número el primero que cante snap se las lleva todas. El que se quede sin cartas es eliminado; gana el que queda cuando los demás están eliminados.

**snapshot** ['snæpʃɒt] *n* foto *f*, instantánea.

**snarl** [snɑːl] *n (growl)* gruñido.
▶ *vi (growl)* gruñir (at, a).
▶ *vt (say)* gruñir.

**snatch** [snætʃ]
*vt* **1** *(grab)* arrebatar, arrancar, coger; *(steal)* robar; *(kidnap)* secuestrar. **2** *(sleep, food, etc)* coger, pillar; *(opportunity, etc)* aprovechar.
▶ *vi* arrebatar, quitar.

**sneak** [sniːk] *n fam* acusica *mf*, acusón,-ona, chivato,-a, soplón,-ona.
▶ *vt (take out)* sacar (a escondidas); *(take in)* pasar (a escondidas), colar (de extranjis).
▶ *vi* **1** *(move)* moverse sigilosamente. **2** *(tell tales)* acusar (on, a), chivarse (on, de).

**sneakers** ['sniːkəz] *n pl* US zapatillas *fpl* de deporte.

**sneer** [snɪəʳ] *n* **1** *(look)* cara de desprecio; *(smile)* sonrisa burlona. **2** *(remark)* comentario desdeñoso.

**S**

► *vi (mock)* burlarse (at, de), mofarse (at, de); *(scorn)* desdeñar, despreciar.

**sneeze** [sni:z] *n* estornudo.

► *vi* estornudar.

**sniff** [snɪf] *n* **1** aspiración. **2** *(inhalation)* aspiración *f* (por la nariz), inhalación *f*.

► *vt* **1** *(person - gen)* oler; *(animal)* olfatear, husmear. **3** *(drugs)* esnifar.

◆ **to snip off** *vt sep* cortar con tijeras.

**snob** [snɒb] *n* esnob *mf*.

**snooker** ['snu:kəʳ] *n* snooker *m*.

**snoop** [snu:p] *vi* **1** *(search, investigate)* husmear, fisgar. **2** *(pry)* entrometerse, meterse (into, en).

► *n (person)* fisgón,-ona.

**snooze** [snu:z] *n fam* cabezada, siestecilla.

► *vi fam* dormitar, echar una cabezada.

**snore** [snɔ:ʳ] *n* ronquido.

► *vi* roncar.

**snorkel** ['snɔ:kəl] *n (of swimmer)* tubo de respiración; *(of submarine)* esnórquel *m*.

► *vi* bucear con tubo de respiración.

ⓘ *pt & pp* snorkelled (US snorkeled), *ger* snorkelling (US snorkeling).

**snorkelling** ['snɔ:kəlɪŋ] *n* buceo (con tubo de respiración).

**snort** [snɔ:t] *vi* **1** *(make noise - person)* resoplar, bufar; *(- animal)* resoplar. **2** *(say angrily, etc)* bramar, gruñir.

► *vt (drugs)* esnifar.

► *n* **1** *(person)* resoplido, bufido; *(animal)* resoplido. **2** *fam (drink)* trago.

**snout** [snaut] *n* **1** *(of animal)* morro, hocico. **2** GB *fam (of person)* napias *mf*, narizotas *mf*. **3** *(of gun, bottle, etc)* morro. **4** GB *sl (tobacco)* tabaco. **5** GB *sl (informer)* soplón,-ona, chivato,-a.

**snow** [snəu] *n* **1** METEOR *(gen)* nieve *f*; *(snowfall)* nevada. **2** TV nieve *f*.

► *vi* nevar: *it's snowing* está nevando.

**snowball** ['snəubɔ:l] *n* bola de nieve.

**snowboard** ['snəubɔ:d] *n* snowboard.

**snowdrop** ['snəudrɒp] *n* BOT campanilla de invierno.

**snowflake** ['snəufleɪk] *n* copo de nieve.

**snowman** ['snəumæn] *n* muñeco de nieve.

**snowplough** ['snəuplau] *n* quitanieves *m*.

**snowshoe** ['snəuʃu:] *n* raqueta (de nieve).

**snowstorm** ['snəustɔ:m] *n* tormenta de nieve.

**snowy** ['snəuɪ] *adj* de nieve, nevado,-a.

ⓘ *comp* snowier, *superl* snowiest.

◆ **to snuff out** *vt sep (rebellion)* sofocar; *(hopes)* acabar con.

**so** [səu] *conj* **1** *(therefore)* así que, por lo tanto, de manera que. **2** *(to express purpose)* para, para que.

► *adv* **1** *(introductory)* así que, pues, bueno: *so you've decided to come* así que has decidido venir. **2** *(very - before adj or adv)* tan; *(- before noun or with verb)* tanto,-a: *she's so bored* está tan aburrida. **3** *(unspecified number or amount, limit)* tanto,-a: *I can only do so much* no puedo hacer más. **4** *(thus, in this way)* así, de esta manera, de este modo: *he's about so tall* es así de alto. **5** *(to avoid repetition)* que sí: *I think/hope so* creo/espero que sí. **6** *(to express agreement, also)* también: *so am I/so do I/so can I/so have I* yo también.

► *adj (factual, true)* así: *it can't be so* no puede ser. LOC **and so on (and so forth)** y así sucesivamente. **‖ if so** de ser así. **‖ or so** más o menos. **‖ so far** hasta ahora. **‖ so long!** ¡hasta luego! **‖ so many** tantos,-as. **‖ so much** tanto. **‖ so much for STH**: *so much for your advice!* ¡vaya consejo que me diste! **‖ so that** para que. **‖ so what?** ¿y qué?

**soak** [səuk] *vt (put in liquid)* poner en remojo, remojar; *(saturate)* empapar.

► *vi* **1** *(washing, dried pulses)* estar en remojo. **2** *(bathe)* bañarse. **3** *(penetrate)* empapar, calar.

► *n* **1** remojón *m*. **2** *fam (drunkard)* borracho,-a.

**soap** [səup] *n* jabón *m*: *a bar/cake/tablet of soap* una pastilla de jabón. COMP **soap opera** culebrón *m*, telenovela. **‖ soap powder** detergente *m* en polvo.

► *vt* enjabonar, jabonar.

**soar** [sɔːˀ] vi **1** (bird, plane - fly) volar; (- rise) remontar el vuelo, remontarse; (- glide) planear. **2** fig (prices, costs, etc) dispararse. **3** (building) elevarse, alzarse.

**sob** [sɒb] n sollozo.
► vi sollozar.
► vt decir sollozando, decir entre sollozos.
ⓘ pt & pp **sobbed**, ger **sobbing**.

**sober** [ˈsəʊbəˀ] adj **1** (not drunk) sobrio,-a. **2** (person) serio,-a, formal; (attitude) sobrio,-a, moderado,-a, sensato,-a. **3** (colour) discreto,-a, sobrio,-a.

**so-called** [ˈsəʊkɔːld] adj llamado,-a, supuesto,-a.

**soccer** [ˈsɒkəˀ] n fútbol m.

⊕ El soccer es la denominación que se utiliza en Estados Unidos para hablar nuestro fútbol. La palabra football está reservada al fútbol americano, uno de los deportes rey del país.

**sociable** [ˈsəʊʃəbəl] adj sociable.

**social** [ˈsəʊʃᵊl] adj **1** (gen) social. **2** fam (sociable) sociable.
► n (informal meeting) acto social, reunión f (social); (party) fiesta; (dance) baile m.

**socialism** [ˈsəʊʃəlɪzəm] n socialismo.

**socialist** [ˈsəʊʃəlɪst] adj & n socialista mf.

**socialize** [ˈsəʊʃᵊlaɪz] vi (mix socially) relacionarse, alternar; (at party) mezclarse con la gente, hacer vida social.
► vt **1** TECH (adapt to society) socializar. **2** US (nationalize) nacionalizar.

**society** [səˈsaɪətɪ] n **1** (community, people) sociedad f. **2** (fashionable group, upper class) (alta) sociedad f. **3** (organization, club) sociedad f, asociación f, club m, círculo. **4** fml (company) compañía.
ⓘ pl **societies**.

**sociology** [səʊsɪˈɒlədʒɪ] n sociología.

**sock** [sɒk] n calcetín m.

**socket** [ˈsɒkɪt] n **1** ANAT (of eye) cuenca, órbita; (of joint) glena. **2** ELEC (for plug) enchufe m, toma de corriente; (for light bulb) portalámparas m. COMP **socket wrench** llave f de tubo.

**soda** [ˈsəʊdə] n **1** CHEM sosa, soda. **2** (soda water) soda, sifón m. **3** US (pop) refresco. **4** (ice-cream soda) soda con helado y almíbar.

**sodium** [ˈsəʊdɪəm] n CHEM sodio. COMP **sodium bicarbonate** bicarbonato sódico.

**sofa** [ˈsəʊfə] n sofá m.

**soft** [sɒft] adj **1** (not hard) blando,-a; (spongy) esponjoso,-a; (flabby) fofo,-a. **2** (skin, hair, fur, etc) suave. **3** (light, music, colour) suave; (words) tierno,-a; (breeze, steps, knock) ligero,-a; (outline) difuminado,-a; (voz) baja. **4** fam (easy) fácil. COMP **soft copy** datos mpl contenidos en la memoria del ordenador. ‖ **soft drink** refresco. ‖ **soft palate** velo del paladar.

**soft-boiled** [ˈsɒftˈbɔɪld] adj (egg) pasado por agua.

**soften** [ˈsɒfᵊn] vt suavizar, ablandar.
► vi (leather, heart, butter) ablandarse; (skin) suavizarse.

**softener** [ˈsɒfənəˀ] n suavizante m.

**software** [ˈsɒftweəˀ] n COMPUT software m.

**soggy** [ˈsɒgɪ] adj **1** (wet) empapado,-a, saturado,-a. **2** (too soft) pastoso,-a, gomoso,-a.
ⓘ comp **soggier**, superl **soggiest**.

**soil** [sɔɪl] n **1** (earth) tierra. **2** fml (country, territory) tierra.
► vt **1** (dirty) ensuciar; (stain) manchar. **2** fig (reputation) manchar.
► vi ensuciarse.

**soiled** [sɔɪld] adj (dirty) sucio,-a; (stained) manchado,-a.

**solar** [ˈsəʊləˀ] adj solar. COMP **solar cell** célula solar. ‖ **solar corona** corona solar. ‖ **solar energy** energía solar. ‖ **solar plexus** plexo solar.‖ **solar year** año solar. ‖ **the solar system** el sistema m solar.

**sold** [səʊld] pt & pp → **sell**.

**solder** [ˈsɒldəˀ] n soldadura.
► vt soldar.

**soldier** [ˈsəʊldʒəˀ] n (not officer) soldado; (military man) militar m. COMP **a soldier of fortune** un mercenario.

**sole¹** [səʊl] n (fish) lenguado.

S

**sole²** [səʊl] *adj* **1** *(only, single)* único,-a. **2** *(exclusive)* exclusivo,-a.

**sole³** [səʊl] *n (of foot)* planta; *(of shoe, sock)* suela.
► *vt* poner suela a.

**solicitor** [səˈlɪsɪtəʳ] *n* GB abogado,-a. **2** US oficial *mf* de justicia.

**solid** [ˈsɒlɪd] *adj* **1** *(not liquid or gas)* sólido,-a. **2** *(not hollow)* macizo,-a. **3** *(dense, compact)* compacto,-a. **4** *(unmixed)* puro,-a, macizo,-a. **5** *(strong)* sólido,-a, fuerte. **6** *(reliable)* sólido,-a, de confianza, de fiar. **7** *(unanimous)* unánime. **8** *(continuous)* seguido,-a, entero, -a; *(unbroken)* continuo,-a. **9** TECH *(three-dimensional)* tridimensional.
► *n (substance)* sólido.

**solidarity** [sɒlɪˈdærətɪ] *n* solidaridad *f*.

**solidification** [səlɪdɪfɪˈkeɪ∫ᵊn] *n* solidificación *f*.

**solidify** [səˈlɪdɪfaɪ] *vt* solidificar.
► *vi* solidificarse.
ⓘ *pt & pp* solidified, *ger* solidifying.

**solitary** [ˈsɒlɪtᵊrɪ] *adj* **1** *(alone)* solitario,-a. **2** *(secluded, remote)* apartado,-a, retirado,-a. **3** *(only, sole)* solo,-a, único,-a.

**solitude** [ˈsɒlɪtjuːd] *n* soledad *f*.

**solo** [ˈsəʊləʊ] *n* **1** MUS solo. **2** AV vuelo en solitario. **3** *(card game)* solitario.
ⓘ *pl* solos.
► *adj* **1** MUS *(performance, album)* en solitario; *(instrument)* solo; *(piece)* para solista. **2** *(attempt, flight)* en solitario.
► *adv* **1** MUS *(play, sing)* solo,-a. **2** *(fly)* en solitario.

**soloist** [ˈsəʊləʊɪst] *n* MUS solista *mf*.

**solstice** [ˈsɒlstɪs] *n* solsticio.

**soluble** [ˈsɒljəbᵊl] *adj* soluble.

**solution** [səˈljuː∫ən] *n* solución *m*.

**solve** [sɒlv] *vt (problem)* resolver, solucionar; *(case, equation)* resolver.

**solvent** [ˈsɒlvənt] *adj* **1** *(not in debt)* solvente. **2** *(that can dissolve)* soluble.
► *n* solvente *m*, disolvente *m*.

**Somali** [səˈmɑːlɪ] *adj* somalí.
► *n* somalí *mf*.

**Somalia** [səˈmɑːlɪə] *n* Somalia.

**some** [sʌm] *adj* **1** *(with plural noun)* unos, -as, algunos,-as; *(a few)* unos,-as

cuantos,-as, unos,-as pocos,-as: *there were some flowers on the table* había unas flores en la mesa. **2** *(with singular noun)* algún, alguna; *(a little)* algo de, un poco de: *would you like some coffee?* ¿quieres un poco de café? **3** *(certain)* cierto,-a, alguno,-a: *some days are better than others* algunos días son mejores que otros. **4** *(unknown, unspecified)* algún, alguna: *some day* un día de éstos. **5** *(quite a lot of)* bastante: *she's been gone some time* hace ya bastante tiempo que se ha ido. **6** *fam iron (none, not at all)* valiente, menudo,-a: *some help that was!* ¡valiente ayuda! **7** *fam (quite a, a fine)* menudo,-a: *that was some meal!* ¡menuda comida!
► *pron* **1** *(unspecified number)* unos,-as, algunos,-as: *I'll have to buy some potatoes* tendré que comprar patatas. **2** *(unspecified amount)* no se traduce: *if you want more paper, there's some in the drawer* si te hace falta más papel, hay en el cajón. **3** *(certain ones)* ciertos,-as, algunos,-as; *(a certain part)* algo, un poco, parte *f*: *some of my friends* algunos amigos míos.
► *adv* **1** *(approximately, about)* unos,-as, alrededor de, aproximadamente: *there were some twenty people* había unas veinte personas. **2** US *fam (rather, a little)* un poco: *they waited some* esperaron un poco.

**somebody** [ˈsʌmbədɪ] *pron* alguien: *somebody must have lost it* alguien debe haberlo perdido. LOC **somebody else** otro,-a, otra persona.

**somehow** [ˈsʌmhaʊ] *adv* **1** *(in some way)* de algún modo, de alguna manera. **2** *(for some reason)* por alguna razón.

**someone** [ˈsʌmwʌn] *pron* → **somebody**.

**someplace** [ˈsʌmpleɪs] *adv* US → **somewhere**.

**somersault** [ˈsʌməsɔːlt] *n (by acrobat)* salto mortal; *(by child)* voltereta; *(by car)* vuelta de campana.
► *vi (acrobat)* dar un salto mortal; *(child)* dar volteretas; *(car)* dar una vuelta de campana.

**something** [ˈsʌmθɪŋ] *pron* **1** algo. **2** *(a thing of value)* algo. **3** *(in vague or ill-defined statements)* algo.

▶ *adv*: *it costs something like 100 pounds* cuesta unas cien libras.

**sometime** ['sʌmtaɪm] *adv* algún día.
▶ *adj fml (former)* antiguo,-a, ex-.

**sometimes** ['sʌmtaɪmz] *adv* a veces, de vez en cuando.

**somewhat** ['sʌmwɒt] *adv* algo, un tanto.

**somewhere** ['sʌmweəʳ] *adv* **1** *(in some place)* en alguna parte; *(to some place)* a alguna parte. **2** *(approximately)* más o menos, alrededor de.
▶ *pron* un lugar, un sitio. ⸤LOC⸥ **somewhere else 1** *(in)* en otra parte, en otro sitio. **2** *(to)* a otra parte, a otro sitio.

**son** [sʌn] *n* hijo.

**song** [sɒŋ] *n (gen)* canción *f*; *(art, of bird)* canto.

**songbird** ['sɒŋbɜːd] *n* pájaro cantor, ave *f* canora.

**songbook** ['sɒŋbʊk] *n* cancionero.

**songwriter** ['sɒŋraɪtəʳ] *n* compositor, -ra (de canciones).

**son-in-law** ['sʌnɪnlɔː] *n* yerno.
ⓘ *pl* sons-in-law.

**soon** [suːn] *adv* **1** *(within a short time)* pronto, dentro de poco. **2** *(early)* pronto, temprano. **3** *(expressing preference, readiness, willingness)*: *I'd (just) as soon eat in as...* preferiría comer en casa que... ⸤LOC⸥ **as soon as** tan pronto como. **I as soon as possible** cuanto antes. **I soon afterwards** poco después.

**sooner** ['suːnəʳ] *adv* **1** *(earlier)* más temprano. **2** *(rather)* antes. ⸤LOC⸥ **no sooner said than done** dicho y hecho. **I sooner or later** tarde o temprano. **I the sooner the better** cuanto antes mejor.

**soot** [sʊt] *n* hollín *m*.

**soothe** [suːð] *vt* **1** *(calm)* calmar, tranquilizar, aplacar; *(quieten)* acallar. **2** *(ease pain)* aliviar, calmar.

**sorcerer** ['sɔːsərəʳ] *n* hechicero, brujo.

**sorcery** ['sɔːsəri] *n* hechicería, brujería.

**sore** [sɔːʳ] *adj* **1** *(aching)* dolorido,-a; *(painful)* doloroso,-a; *(inflamed)* inflamado,-a. **2** *US fam (angry)* enfadado,-a (about, por), picado,-a (about, por).

**3** *lit (great)* enorme, gran; *(serious)* grave; *(urgent)* urgente.
▶ *n* MED llaga, úlcera.

**sorrow** ['sɒrəʊ] *n* **1** *(grief)* pena, pesar *m*, dolor *m*. **2** *(cause of sadness)* disgusto.
▶ *vi* llorar (at/over/for, por).

**sorry** ['sɒrɪ] *adj* *(pitiful, wretched)* triste, lamentable. ⸤LOC⸥ **to be sorry** *(grieved, feeling sadness)* sentir. **I to feel sorry for** sʙ compadecer. **I to say sorry** disculparse, pedir perdón.
ⓘ *comp* sorrier, *superl* sorriest.
▶ *interj* **1** *(apology)* ¡perdón!, ¡disculpe! **2** GB *(for repetition)* ¿perdón?, ¿cómo?

**sort** [sɔːt] *n* **1** *(type, kind)* clase *f*, tipo, género, suerte *f*; *(make, brand)* marca. **2** *fam (person)* tipo,-a, tío,-a. ⸤LOC⸥ **a sort of** una especie de. **I of a sort / of sorts** una especie de. **I nothing of the sort** nada semejante. **I sort of** en cierto modo.
▶ *vt* **1** *(classify)* clasificar. **2** *(repair)* arreglar.
▶ *vi (check)* revisar (through, -).
◆ **to sort out** *vt sep* **1** *(classify)* clasificar; *(put in order)* ordenar, poner en orden. **2** *(separate)* separar (from, de). **3** *(solve - problem)* arreglar, solucionar; *(- misunderstanding)* aclarar. **4** *(arrange)* organizar, arreglar; *(set - date)* fijar. **5** *(deal with - person)* meter en vereda.

**so-so** ['səʊsəʊ] *adv fam* así así, regular.

**sought** [sɔːt] *pt & pp* → seek.

**soul** [səʊl] *n* **1** REL alma, espíritu *m*. **2** *(spirit)* espíritu *m*; *(feeling, character)* carácter *m*, personalidad *f*. **3** *(person)* alma, persona. **4** MUS soul *m*, música soul.

**sound¹** [saʊnd] *adj* **1** *(healthy)* sano,-a. **2** *(solid)* sólido,-a, firme; *(in good condition)* en buen estado. **3** *(sensible)* sensato,-a, acertado,-a; *(valid)* sólido,-a, lógico,-a, razonable; *(responsible)* responsable, formal, de fiar; *(reliable, safe)* seguro,-a. **4** *(thorough)* completo,-a; *(severe)* severo,-a. **5** *(of sleep)* profundo,-a. ⸤LOC⸥ **to be sound asleep** estar dormido como un tronco.

**sound²** [saʊnd] *vt* **1** MAR sondar. **2** MED *(gen)* sondar; *(chest)* auscultar.
▶ *n* MED sonda.

**S**

**sound³** [saʊnd] n GEOG estrecho, brazo de mar.

**sound⁴** [saʊnd] n 1 (gen) sonido; (noise) ruido. 2 TV (volume) volumen m. 3 (impression, idea) idea. COMP **sound effects** efectos sonoros.
▸ vt 1 (bell, horn, trumpet) tocar, hacer sonar; (alarm) dar (la señal de); (retreat) tocar. 2 LING pronunciar.
▸ vi 1 (bell, horn, alarm, etc) sonar, resonar. 2 (seem) parecer; (give impression) sonar. 3 LING pronunciarse, sonar.

**soundtrack** [ˈsaʊndtræk] n banda sonora.

**soup** [suːp] n CULIN (gen) sopa; (clear, thin) caldo, consomé m.

**sour** [ˈsaʊəʳ] adj 1 (fruit) ácido,-a, agrio, -a; (milk) cortado,-a, agrio,-a; (wine) agrio,-a. 2 (person) amargado,-a, avinagrado,-a; (behaviour, expression) agrio,-a, avinagrado,-a.
▸ vt 1 (milk) agriar, cortar. 2 (person, relationship) amargar.
▸ vi 1 (milk) agriarse, cortarse; (wine) agriarse. 2 (person, character) amargarse, avinagrarse.

**source** [sɔːs] n 1 (of river) fuente f, nacimiento. 2 (origin, cause) fuente f, origen m.

**south** [saʊθ] n sur m.
▸ adj sur, del sur, meridional. COMP **South American** sudamericano,-a. ‖ **the South Pole** el Polo Sur.
▸ adv (direction) hacia el sur; (location) al sur.
▸ n **the South** el Sur m, el sur m.

**southeast** [saʊθˈiːst] n sudeste m.
▸ adj sudeste, del sudeste.
▸ adv (direction) hacia el sudeste; (location) al sudeste.

**southern** [ˈsʌðən] adj del sur, meridional, austral. COMP **Southern Europe** Europa del Sur.

**southward** [ˈsaʊθwəd] adj hacia el sur, en dirección sur.
▸ adv al sur, hacia el sur.

**southwards** [ˈsaʊθwədz] adv (direction) hacia el sur; (location) al sur.

**southwest** [saʊθˈwest] n suroeste m.
▸ adj suroeste, del suroeste.
▸ adv al suroeste, hacia el suroeste.

**souvenir** [suːvəˈnɪəʳ] n recuerdo (of, de).

**sovereign** [ˈsɒvrɪn] n 1 soberano,-a. 2 GB (coin) soberano.
▸ adj soberano,-a.

**sow¹** [saʊ] n ZOOL cerda, puerca.

**sow²** [səʊ] vt (gen) sembrar (with, de).
① pt sowed, pp sowed o sown [səʊn].

**sown** [səʊn] pp → sow.

**soy** [sɔɪ] n US soja.

**soya** [ˈsɔɪə] n GB soja. COMP **soya bean** soja.

**spa** [spɑː] n 1 (resort) balneario; (baths) baños mpl, termas fpl. 2 US (jacuzzi) jacuzzi m. 3 US (gymnasium) gimnasio.

**space** [speɪs] n 1 PHYS espacio. 2 (continuous expanse) espacio. 3 (room, unoccupied area) espacio, sitio, lugar m. 4 (gap, empty place) espacio, hueco. 5 (in time) espacio, lapso. COMP **space lab** laboratorio espacial. ‖ **space probe** sonda espacial. ‖ **space ship** nave f espacial. ‖ **space shuttle** transbordador m espacial.

**space-bar** [ˈspeɪsbɑːʳ] n barra espaciadora m.

**spacecraft** [ˈspeɪskrɑːft] n nave f espacial.
① pl spacecraft.

**spaceship** [ˈspeɪsʃɪp] n nave f espacial.

**spade¹** [speɪd] n (playing card - international pack) pica; (- Spanish pack) espada.

**spade²** [speɪd] n (for digging) pala.

☒ Spade no significa 'espada', que se traduce por sword.

**spaghetti** [spəˈgetɪ] n espagueti m.

**Spain** [speɪn] n España.

**span¹** [spæn] pt → spin.

**span²** [spæn] n 1 (of wings) envergadura; (of arch, bridge) luz f, ojo; (of hand) palmo. 2 (of time) período, lapso.
▸ vt 1 (cross) atravesar, cruzar. 2 (extend over) abarcar, extenderse a.
① pt & pp spanned, ger spanning.

**Spaniard** [ˈspænjəd] n (person) español,-la.

**Spanish** ['spænɪʃ] *adj* español,-la. COMP **Spanish America** Hispanoamérica. ▪ **Spanish guitar** guitarra clásica.
▶ *n* **1** *(person)* español,-la. **2** *(language)* español *m*, castellano.
▶ *n pl* **the Spanish** los españoles *mpl*.

**spanner** ['spænər] *n* llave *f* de tuerca.

**spare** [speər] *adj* **1** *(reserve)* de repuesto; *(free)* libre; *(extra)* de sobra. **2** *(thin, lean)* enjuto,-a.
▶ *n (spare part)* recambio, repuesto. COMP **spare room** habitación *f* de invitados. ▪ **spare time** tiempo libre. ▪ **spare tyre 1** *(wheel)* rueda de recambio. **2** *(stomach)* michelín *m*. ▪ **spare wheel** rueda de recambio.
▶ *vt* **1** *(do without)* prescindir de, pasar sin. **2** *(begrudge)* escatimar. **3** *(save, relieve)* ahorrar, evitar.

**spark** [spɑːk] *n* **1** *(from fire, electrical)* chispa. **2** *(trace)* chispa, pizca. **3** *(cause, trigger)* chispazo. COMP **spark plug** bujía.
▶ *vi* echar chispas, chispear.

**sparking plug** ['spɑːkɪŋplʌg] *n* AUTO bujía.

**sparkle** ['spɑːkəl] *n* **1** *(of diamond, glass)* centelleo, destello, brillo; *(of eyes)* brillo. **2** *fig (liveliness)* viveza; *(wit)* brillo.
▶ *vi* **1** *(gen)* brillar; *(firework)* echar chispas, chispear. **2** *fig (person)* brillar, lucirse; *(conversation)* brillar.

**sparkler** ['spɑːkələr] *n* **1** *(firework)* bengala. **2** *fam (gem)* brillante *m*.

**sparrow** ['spærəʊ] *n* gorrión *m*.

**sparse** [spɑːs] *adj (vegetation)* escaso,-a, poco denso,-a; *(population)* disperso,-a, esparcido,-a; *(hair)* ralo,-a; *(information)* escaso,-a.

**spasm** ['spæzəm] *n* **1** MED espasmo. **2** *(of coughing, laughing, etc)* ataque *m*, acceso; *(of anger)* arrebato, acceso.

**spat** [spæt] *pt & pp* → spit².

**spatter** ['spætər] *vt (splash)* salpicar (with, de); *(sprinkle)* rociar (with, de).
▶ *vi* salpicar.
▶ *n (spattered spot)* salpicadura, manchita; *(small amount)* pizca.

**speak** [spiːk] *vi* **1** *(gen)* hablar. **2** *(make speech)* pronunciar un discurso. **3** *(on phone)* hablar.

▶ *vt* **1** *(utter, say)* decir. **2** *(language)* hablar. LOC **generally/roughly speaking** en términos generales. ▪ **personally speaking** personalmente. ▪ **speaking of...** a propósito de...
◆ **to speak for** *vt insep (state views, wishes of)* hablar en nombre de.
◆ **to speak out** *vi (speak openly)* hablar claro.
◆ **to speak up** *vi* **1** *(speak more loudly)* hablar más fuerte. **2** *(give opinion)* defender.
① *pt* **spoke** [spəʊk], *pp* **spoken** [spəʊkən].

**speaker** ['spiːkər] *n* **1** *(gen)* persona que habla, el que habla, la que habla; *(in dialogue)* interlocutor,-ra; *(in public)* orador,-ra; *(lecturer)* conferenciante *mf*. **2** *(of language)* hablante *mf*. **3** *(loudspeaker)* altavoz *m*.
▶ *n* **the Speaker 1** GB el/la presidente,-a de la Cámara de los Comunes. **2** US el/la presidente,-a de la Cámara de los Representantes.

**spear** [spɪər] *n* **1** *(gen)* lanza; *(javelin)* jabalina; *(harpoon)* arpón *m*. **2** BOT punta.
▶ *vt (with fork)* pinchar; *(with harpoon)* arponear; *(impale with spear)* atravesar con una lanza.

**special** ['speʃəl] *adj* **1** *(not ordinary or usual)* especial; *(exceptional)* extraordinario,-a. **2** *(specific)* específico,-a, particular.
▶ *n* **1** *(train)* tren *m* especial. **2** *(TV programme)* programa *m* especial. **3** US *(special offer)* oferta especial.

**speciality** [speʃɪˈælɪtɪ] *n* especialidad *f*.
① *pl* **specialities**.

**specialize** ['speʃəlaɪz] *vi* especiliazarse.

**species** ['spiːʃiːz] *n* especie *f*.
① *pl* **species**.

**specific** [spəˈsɪfɪk] *adj* **1** *(particular, not general)* específico,-a; *(definite)* concreto,-a. **2** *(exact, detailed, precise)* preciso,-a; *(clear in meaning)* explícito,-a.
▶ *n* MED *(drug)* específico.
▶ *n pl* **specifics** *(particulars, details)* datos *mpl* (concretos).

**specify** ['spesɪfaɪ] *vt* especificar, precisar, concretar.
① *pt & pp* **specified**, *ger* **specifying**.

**specimen** ['spesɪmən] *n* **1** *(sample)* es-pécimen *m*, muestra. **2** *(example)* ejemplar *m*. **3** *fam pej (person)* tipo,-a.

**speck** [spek] *n* **1** *(of dust, soot)* mota; *(stain)* manchita; *(dot)* punto negro. **2** *(trace)* pizca.

**spectacle** ['spektəkᵊl] *n (show, display)* espectáculo.
▸ *n pl* **spectacles** gafas *fpl*.

**spectacular** [spek'tækjələʳ] *adj* espectacular.

**spectator** [spek'teɪtəʳ] *n* espectador,-ra.
▸ *n pl* **the spectators** el público *m sing*.

**specter** ['spektəʳ] *n* US → **spectre**.

**spectre** ['spektəʳ] *n* espectro.

**spectrum** ['spektrəm] *n* **1** PHYS espec-tro. **2** *(range)* espectro, gama.
ⓘ *pl* **spectra** ['spektrə].

**sped** [sped] *pt & pp* → **speed**.

**speech** [spiːtʃ] *n* **1** *(faculty, act)* habla. **2** *(spoken language, way of speaking)* habla, manera de hablar. **3** *(formal talk)* discur-so, alocución *f*; *(informal talk)* charla; *(lectura)* conferencia; *(lines in play)* diálo-go. COMP **direct speech** estilo directo. ▌**indirect speech** estilo indirecto. ▌**part of speech** parte de la oración.
ⓘ *pl* **speeches**.

**speed** [spiːd] *n* **1** *(rate of movement)* velo-cidad *f*; *(quickness)* rapidez *f*; *(haste)* prisa. **2** *(sensitivity of film)* sensibilidad *f*, velocidad *f*; *(time of shutter)* tiempo de exposición, abertura. **3** *(gear)* mar-cha, velocidad *f*. **4** *sl (drug)* speed *m*, anfetas *fpl*. COMP **speed limit** límite *m* de velocidad.
▸ *vi* **1** *(go fast)* ir corriendo, ir a toda prisa, ir a toda velocidad. **2** *(break limit)* ir a exceso de velocidad.
**1** *(hurry - process, matter)* acelerar. **2** *(take quickly)* hacer llegar rápidamente.
◆ **to speed up** *vt sep (process, matter, pro-duction)* acelerar; *(person)* apresurar, meter prisa a.
▸ *vi (vehicle)* acelerar; *(person, process, production)* acelerarse, apresurarse, darse prisa.
ⓘ *pt & pp* **speeded** o **sped** [sped].

**speedboat** ['spiːdbəʊt] *n* lancha rápida.

**speeding** ['spiːdɪŋ] *n* AUTO exceso de velocidad.

**speedometer** [spɪ'dɒmɪtəʳ] *n* velocí-metro.

**speedway** ['spiːdweɪ] *n* **1** *(racing)* ca-rreras *fpl* de moto. **2** *(track)* pista de carreras, circuito.

**speedy** ['spiːdɪ] *adj (quick)* rápido,-a, veloz; *(prompt)* pronto,-a, rápido,-a.
ⓘ *comp* **speedier**, *superl* **speediest**.

**speleology** [spiːlɪ'ɒlədʒɪ] *n* espeleología.

**spell¹** [spel] *n (magical)* hechizo, en-canto.

**spell³** [spel] *vt* **1** *(orally)* deletrear; *(writ-ten)* escribir correctamente. **2** *fig (mean)* significar, representar; *(bring)* traer, acarrear; *(foretell)* anunciar, au-gurar, presagiar.
▸ *vi* saber escribir correctamente.
◆ **to spell out** *vt sep* **1** *(word)* deletrear. **2** *(explain in detail)* explicar con deta-lle, detallar, pormenorizar.
ⓘ *pt & pp* **spelled** o **spelt** [spelt].

**spelling** ['spelɪŋ] *n* ortografía. COMP **spelling mistake** falta de ortografía.

**spelt** [spelt] *pt & pp* → **spell**.

**spend** [spend] *vt* **1** *(money)* gastar (on, en). **2** *(pass time)* pasar. **3** *(devote time/en-ergy)* dedicar (on, a), invertir (on, en). **4** *(use up, exhaust)* gastar, agotar.
▸ *vi (money)* gastar.
ⓘ *pt & pp* **spent** [spent].

**spent** [spent] *pt & pp* → **spend**.
▸ *adj* **1** *(used)* usado,-a, gastado,-a. **2** *(exhausted)* agotado,-a; *(finished)* aca-bado,-a.

**sperm** [spɜːm] *n* esperma *mf*. COMP **sperm whale** cachalote *m*.

**sphere** [sfɪəʳ] *n* **1** *(shape)* esfera. **2** *(area, range, extent)* esfera, ámbito.

**spherical** ['sferɪkəl] *adj* esférico,-a.

**sphincter** ['sfɪŋktəʳ] *n* esfínter *m*.

**sphinx** [sfɪŋks] *n* esfinge *f*.

**spice** [spaɪs] *n* **1** especia. **2** *fig* sazón *m*, sal *f*, salsa, sabor *m*.
▸ *vt* **1** CULIN sazonar, condimentar. **2** *(story, etc)* echar salsa a (up, -).

**spicy** ['spaɪsɪ] *adj* **1** CULIN *(seasoned)* sazonado,-a, condimentado,-a; *(hot)* picante. **2** *fig (story, etc)* picante.
ⓘ *comp* spicier, *superl* spiciest.

**spider** ['spaɪdəʳ] *n* araña. COMP spider's web telaraña.

**spied** [spaɪd] *pt & pp* → spy.

**spike¹** [spaɪk] *n* **1** *(sharp point)* punta, pincho; *(sharp-pointed object)* objeto puntiagudo. **2** *(on running shoe)* clavo.
▶ *vt* **1** *(with shoes)* clavar. **2** *(drink)* echar alcohol a.

**spike²** [spaɪk] *n* BOT espiga.

**spill** [spɪl] *vt (liquid)* derramar, verter; *(knock over)* volcar.
▶ *vi* **1** *(liquid)* derramarse, verterse. **2** *(people)* salir en tropel.
◆ **to spill over** *vi (liquid)* salirse, desbordarse; *(people)* rebosar; *(conflict)* extenderse.
ⓘ *pt & pp* spilled o spilt [spɪlt].

**spilt** [spɪlt] *pt & pp* → spill.

**spin** [spɪn] *n* **1** *(turn)* vuelta, giro, revolución *f*. **2** *(of washing machine)* centrifugado. **3** SP *(of ball)* efecto. **4** *(of plane)* barrena; *(of car)* patinazo. **5** *(ride, trip)* vuelta, paseo (en coche o en moto).
▶ *vt* **1** *(make turn)* hacer girar, dar vueltas a. **2** *(washing)* centrifugar. **3** *(ball)* darle efecto a. **4** *(cotton, wool, etc)* hilar; *(spider's web)* tejer.
▶ *vi* **1** *(turn)* girar, dar vueltas. **2** *(washing machine)* centrifugar. **3** *(cotton, wool, etc)* hilar. **4** *(plane)* caer en barrena; *(car)* patinar. **5** *(move rapidly)* girar(se), darse la vuelta.
ⓘ *pt* spun [spʌn] o span [spæn], *pp* spun [spʌn], *ger* spinning.

**spinach** ['spɪnɪdʒ] *n* **1** BOT espinaca. **2** CULIN espinacas *fpl*.

**spinal** ['spaɪnəl] *adj* espinal, vertebral. COMP spinal column columna vertebral. ▮ spinal cord médula espinal.

**spin-dryer** [spɪn'draɪəʳ] *n* secador *m* centrífugo, centrifugadora.

**spine** [spaɪn] *n* **1** ANAT columna vertebral, espina dorsal, espinazo. **2** *(of book)* lomo. **3** ZOOL *(of hedgehog, etc)* púa. **4** BOT espina.

**spinning** ['spɪnɪŋ] *n (action)* hilado; *(art)* hilandería. COMP spinning top peonza, trompo. ▮ spinning wheel rueca, torno de hilar.

**spiny** ['spaɪnɪ] *adj* espinoso,-a.
ⓘ *comp* spinier, *superl* spiniest.

**spiral** ['spaɪərəl] *n* espiral *f*.
▶ *adj* espiral, en espiral.
▶ *vi* **1** *(move in a spiral)* moverse en espiral. **2** *(increase rapidly)* dispararse.

**spire** [spaɪəʳ] *n* aguja.

**spirit¹** ['spɪrɪt] *n* CHEM alcohol *m*.
▶ *n pl* spirits *(alcoholic drink)* bebidas *fpl* alcohólicas, licores *mpl*.

**spirit²** ['spɪrɪt] *n* **1** *(soul)* espíritu *m*, alma; *(ghost)* fantasma *m*. **2** *(person)* ser *m*, alma. **3** *(force, vigour)* vigor *m*, energía; *(personality)* carácter *m*; *(courage)* valor *m*.

**spiritual** ['spɪrɪtjʊəl] *adj* espiritual.
▶ *n (song)* espiritual *m* negro.

**spit¹** [spɪt] *n* **1** CULIN asador *m*, espetón *m*. **2** GEOG *(of sand)* banco; *(of land)* punta, lengua.

**spit²** [spɪt] *n (saliva)* saliva, esputo.
▶ *vt (gen)* escupir.
▶ *vi* **1** *(gen)* escupir (at, a), (on, en). **2** *(rain)* chispear. **3** *(sputter)* chisporrotear.
◆ **to spit out** *vt sep* **1** *(gen)* escupir. **2** *fig (say sharply)* soltar.
ⓘ *pt & pp* spat [spæt].

**spite** [spaɪt] *n (ill will)* rencor *m*, ojeriza. LOC in spite of a pesar de, pese a
▶ *vt* fastidiar.

**spiteful** ['spaɪtfʊl] *adj (person)* rencoroso,-a, malévolo,-a; *(comment)* malicioso,-a.

**spittle** ['spɪtəl] *n* saliva, baba.

**splash** [splæʃ] *n* **1** *(noise)* chapoteo. **2** *(spray)* salpicadura, rociada. **3** *(small amount)* gota, chorrito, poco. **4** *fig (light, colour, etc)* mancha.
▶ *vt* **1** *(gen)* salpicar (with, de), rociar (with, de). **2** *fam (of news, story, etc)* sacar, salir.
ⓘ *pl* splashes.
▶ *vi* **1** *(of liquid)* salpicar, esparcirse. **2** *(move noisily)* chapotear (about/around, -).
◆ **to splash down** *vi* amarar, amerizar.

**S**

◆ **to splash out** *vi fam* darse un lujo, gastarse un dineral.

**spleen** ['spli:n] *n* ANAT bazo.

**splendid** ['splendɪd] *adj* **1** *(excellent)* estupendo,-a, maravilloso,-a. **2** *(magnificent)* espléndido,-a, magnífico,-a.

☒ Splendid no significa 'espléndido (generoso)', que se traduce por lavish.

**splinter** ['splɪntər] *n (of wood)* astilla; *(of metal, bone, stone)* esquirla; *(of glass)* fragmento.

**split** [splɪt] *n* **1** *(crack, cut, break)* grieta, raja. **2** *(tear - in garment)* desgarrón *m*, rasgón *m*; *(- in seam)* descosido. **3** *(division)* división *f*, ruptura. **4** *(division, sharing out)* reparto.
▶ *adj* **1** *(cracked)* partido,-a, rajado,-a; *(torn)* desgarrado,-a, rasgado,-a. **2** *(divided)* dividido,-a.
▶ *vt* **1** *(crack, break)* agrietar; *(cut)* partir. **2** *(tear - garment)* rajar, desgarrar; *(- seam)* descoser. **3** PHYS *(atom)* desintegrar. **4** *(divide, separate)* dividir (up, -).
▶ *vi* **1** *(crack)* agrietarse, rajarse; *(in two parts)* partirse. **2** *(tear - garment)* rajarse, desgarrarse; *(- seams)* descoserse. **3** *(divide)* dividirse (up, -).
◆ **to split up** *vt sep (friends, lovers)* separar.
▶ *vi (crowd, meeting)* dispersarse; *(couple)* separarse, romper.
① *pt & pp* split, *ger* splitting.

**spoil** [spɔɪl] *vt* **1** *(ruin)* estropear, echar a perder, arruinar. **2** *(invalidate)* anular. **3** *(make child selfish)* mimar, consentir; *(indulge)* complacer.
▶ *vi (food)* estropearse, echarse a perder.
① *pt & pp* spoiled o spoilt [spɔɪlt].

**spoilt** [spɔɪlt] *pp* → **spoil**.
▶ *adj* **1** *(food, etc)* estropeado,-a. **2** *(child)* mimado,-a, consentido,-a. **3** *(ballot paper)* nulo,-a.

**spoke¹** [spəʊk] *n (of wheel)* radio, rayo.

**spoke²** [spəʊk] *pt* → **speak**.

**spoken** ['spəʊkən] *pt & pp* → **speak**.
▶ *adj* hablado,-a, oral.

**spokesman** ['spəʊksmən] *n* portavoz *m*.
① *pl* spokesmen ['spəʊksmən].

**spokesperson** ['spəʊkspɜːsən] *n* portavoz *mf*.
① *pl* spokespersons o spokespeople ['spəʊkspiːpəl].

**spokeswoman** ['spəʊkswʊmən] *n* portavoz *f*.
① *pl* spokeswomen ['spəʊkswɪmɪn].

**sponge** [spʌndʒ] *n* **1** *(gen)* esponja. **2** GB *(cake)* bizcocho. COMP **sponge cake** bizcocho.

**sponsor** ['spɒnsər] *n* **1** *(gen)* patrocinador,-ra, sponsor *mf*; *(for arts)* mecenas *mf*. **2** FIN avalador,-ra, garante *mf*.
▶ *vt* **1** *(gen)* patrocinar; *(studies, research)* subvencionar. **2** *(support)* apoyar, respaldar. **3** FIN avalar, garantizar.

**spontaneous** [spɒn'teɪnɪəs] *adj* espontáneo,-a.

**spooky** ['spuːkɪ] *adj fam* escalofriante, espeluznante, horripilante.
① *comp* spookier, *superl* spookiest.

**spool** [spuːl] *n* carrete *m*, bobina.

**spoon** [spuːn] *n* cuchara.

**spoonful** ['spuːnfʊl] *n* cucharada.
① *pl* spoonfuls o spoonsful.

**sport** [spɔːt] *n* **1** *(gen)* deporte *m*. **2** *(person)* buena persona. **3** *(fun)* diversión *f*. **4** *fam (fellow)* amigo,-a.
▶ *vt (wear proudly)* lucir.
▶ *vi (frolic)* retozar, juguetear.

**sports** [spɔːts] *n pl* deportes *mpl*.
▶ *n (meeting)* competición *f* deportiva.
▶ *adj* deportivo,-a, de deportes. COMP
**sports car** (coche *m*) deportivo. ‖ **sports centre/complex** polideportivo. ‖ **sports club** club deportivo. ‖ **sports commentator** comentarista deportivo. ‖ **sports event** evento deportivo. ‖ **sports ground** campo de deportes. ‖ **sports jacket** chaqueta (de) sport.

**sportsman** ['spɔːtsmən] *n* deportista *m*.
① *pl* sportsmen ['spɔːtsmən].

**sportswear** ['spɔːtsweər] *n (for sport)* ropa de deporte; *(casual)* ropa (de) sport.

**sportswoman** ['spɔːtswʊmən] *n* deportista.
① *pl* sportswomen ['spɔːtswɪmɪn].

**sporty** ['spɔːtɪ] *adj* deportivo,-a, aficionado,-a a los deportes.
① *comp* sportier, *superl* sportiest.

**spot** [spɒt] n 1 (dot) punto; (on fabric) lunar m, mota; (on animal) mancha. 2 (mark, stain) mancha. 3 (blemish, pimple) grano. 4 (place) sitio, lugar m. 5 (area of body) punto; (flaw) mancha. 6 (fix, trouble) lío, aprieto, apuro. 7 (place in broadcast) espacio. 8 fam (small amount) poquito, poquitín m; (drop) gota. 9 (position) puesto. 10 fam (spotlight) foco. ⓁⓄⒸ on the spot 1 (at once, then and there) en el acto, allí mismo. 2 (at the place of the action) en el lugar del los hechos. 3 (without moving away) en el lugar.
▶ vt 1 (notice) darse cuenta de, notar; (see) ver; (recognize) reconocer; (find) encontrar, descubrir; (catch out) pillar. 2 (mark with spots) motear; (stain) manchar, salpicar.
▶ vi GB (rain) chispear, lloviznar.
ⓘ pt & pp spotted, ger spotting.
▶ adj (price, cash) contante, al contado.

**spotlight** ['spɒtlaɪt] n (lamp) foco, proyector m, reflector m; (beam) luz f de foco.
▶ vt 1 iluminar, enfocar. 2 (draw attention to) poner de relieve, destacar.

**spotted** ['spɒtɪd] adj (with dots) con puntos; (fabric) de lunares; (speckled) moteado,-a; (stained) manchado,-a; (animal) con manchas.

**spotty** ['spɒtɪ] adj (person, face, complexion) con granos, lleno,-a de granos.
ⓘ comp spottier, superl spottiest.

**spout** [spaʊt] n 1 (of jug) pico; (of fountain) surtidor m, caño; (of roof-gutter) canalón m; (of teapot) pitorro m. 2 (jet of water) chorro.

**sprain** [spreɪn] n MED torcedura.
▶ vt torcer.

**sprang** [spræn] pt → spring.

**spray¹** [spreɪ] n (of flowers) ramillete m.

**spray²** [spreɪ] n 1 (of water) rociada; (from sea) espuma; (from aerosol) pulverización f. 2 (aerosol) spray m; (atomizer) atomizador m, vaporizador m. ⒸⓄⓂⓅ spray can aerosol m. ▮ spray paint pintura spray.
▶ vt (water) rociar; (crops) fumigar; (paint) pintar a pistola.
▶ vi (water) rociar.

**spread** [spred] vt 1 (lay out) extender, tender; (unfold) desplegar; (scatter) esparcir. 2 (butter, etc) untar, extender; (paint, glue, etc) extender, repartir. 3 (news, ideas, etc) difundir, divulgar; (rumour) hacer correr; (disease, fire) propagar; (panic, terror) sembrar. 4 (wealth, work, cost) distribuir, repartir.
▶ vi 1 (stretch out) extenderse; (open out, unfold) desplegarse; (widen) ensancharse. 2 (butter, etc) extenderse. 3 (news, ideas, etc) difundirse, divulgarse; (rumour) correr; (disease, fire) propagarse. 4 (in time) extenderse.
ⓘ pt & pp spread.

**spreadsheet** ['spredʃiːt] n hoja de cálculo.

**spring** [sprɪŋ] n 1 (season) primavera. 2 (of water) manantial m, fuente f. 3 (of mattress, seat) muelle m; (of watch, lock, etc) resorte m; (of car) ballesta. 4 (elasticity) elasticidad f; (active, healthy quality) energía, brío. 5 (leap, jump) salto, brinco. ⒸⓄⓂⓅ spring onion cebolleta.
▶ vi 1 (jump) saltar. 2 (appear) aparecer (de repente),
▶ vt 1 (operate mechanism) accionar. 2 fig (news, surprise) espetar (on, a), soltar. 3 fam (help escape, set free) soltar.
ⓘ pt sprang [spræn], pp sprung [sprʌn].

**springboard** ['sprɪŋbɔːd] n trampolín m.

**sprinkle** ['sprɪŋkəl] vt 1 (with water) rociar (with, de/con), salpicar (with, de/con). 2 (with flour, sugar, etc) espolvorear (with, de/con). 3 fig salpicar (with, de/con).

**sprint** [sprɪnt] (dash) carrera corta.
▶ vi (dash) correr a toda velocidad.

**sprocket** ['sprɒkɪt] n TECH diente m de engranaje. ⒸⓄⓂⓅ sprocket wheel rueda dentada.

**sprout** [spraʊt] n BOT (shoot) brote m, retoño. ⒸⓄⓂⓅ (Brussels) sprouts coles fpl de Bruselas.
▶ vi brotar, salir.
▶ vt (leaves, shoots) echar; (beard, etc) salir.

**sprung** [sprʌn] pp → spring.

**spud** [spʌd] n fam patata.

**spun** [spʌn] pt & pp → spin.

**spur** [spɜːʳ] n **1** (horse rider's) espuela. **2** ZOOL (of cock) espolón m.
  ▶ vt **1** (horse) espolear. **2** fig (stimulate) estimular, incitar.
  ① pt & pp **spurred**, ger **spurring**.

**spy** [spaɪ] n (gen) espía mf.
  ① pl **spies**.
  ▶ vi espiar (on, a).
  ① pt & pp **spied**, ger **spying**.

**spyhole** ['spaɪhəʊl] n mirilla.

**squabble** ['skwɒbəl] n riña, pelea.
  ▶ vi reñir, pelearse (over, por) (about, sobre).

**squad** [skwɒd] n **1** MIL pelotón m. **2** (of police) brigada. **3** SP (team) equipo m; (national) selección f.

**squadron** ['skwɒdrən] n (of soldiers) escuadrón m; (of planes) escuadrilla; (of ships) escuadra.

**square** [skweəʳ] n **1** (shape) cuadrado; (on fabric) cuadro; (on chessboard, graph paper, crossword) casilla. **2** (in town) plaza; (block of houses) manzana. **3** MATH cuadrado. **4** (tool) escuadra.
  ▶ adj **1** (in shape) cuadrado,-a; (forming right angle) en ángulo recto, a escuadra. **2** MATH cuadrado,-a. **3** fam (fair) justo, -a, equitativo,-a; (honest) honesto,-a, franco,-a. **4** (equal in points) igual, empatado,-a; (not owing money) en paz. COMP
  **square metre** metro cuadrado. ‖ **square root** raíz f cuadrada.
  ▶ adv directamente.

**squared** ['skweəd] adj (paper) cuadriculado,-a.

**squash¹** [skwɒʃ] n **1** (drink) concentrado de frutas. **2** SP squash m.
  ▶ vt **1** (crush, flatten) aplastar, chafar. **2** (squeeze) apretar, apiñar.
  ▶ vi **1** (crush, flatten) aplastarse, chafarse. **2** (squeeze) apretujarse.

**squash²** [skwɒʃ] n BOT calabaza.

**squat** [skwɒt] adj (person) rechoncho, -a y bajo,-a, achaparrado,-a; (building) achaparrado,-a.
  ① comp **squatter**, superl **squattest**.
  ▶ vi **1** (crouch) agacharse, ponerse en cuclillas. **2** (in building) ocupar ilegalmente.
  ① pt & pp **squatted**, ger **squatting**.

**squatter** ['skwɒtəʳ] n ocupante mf ilegal, okupa m.

**squeak** [skwiːk] n (of mouse) chillido; (of wheel, hinge, etc) chirrido, rechinamiento; (of shoes) crujido.
  ▶ vi (mouse) chillar; (wheel, hinge, etc) chirriar, rechinar; (shoes) chirriar.

**squeal** [skwiːl] n (of animal, person) chillido, grito; (of tyres, brakes) chirrido.
  ▶ vi **1** (animal, person) chillar; (tyres, brakes) chirriar. **2** fam (inform on) cantar, chivarse.
  ▶ vt (say) decir chillando, gritar.

**squeeze** [skwiːz] vt **1** (gen) apretar; (lemon, orange) exprimir. **2** (fit in) meter. **3** (force out) extraer, sacar.

**squeezer** ['skwiːzəʳ] n exprimidor m.

**squid** [skwɪd] n (gen) calamar m; (small) chipirón m.
  ① pl **squid** o **squids**.

**squint** [skwɪnt] n **1** MED bizquera, estrabismo. **2** fam (quick look) vistazo, ojeada, miradita.
  ▶ vi **1** MED bizquear, ser bizco,-a. **2** (in sunlight) entrecerrar los ojos.

**squire** [skwaɪəʳ] n **1** HIST (knight's armour-carrier) escudero. **2** GB fam jefe m.

**squirrel** ['skwɪrəl] n ardilla.

**Sri Lanka** [sriːˈlæŋkə] n Sri Lanka.

**stab** [stæb] n **1** (with knife) puñalada, navajazo. **2** (of pain) punzada.
  ▶ vt (with knife) apuñalar, acuchillar.
  ① pt & pp **stabbed**, ger **stabbing**.

**stability** [stəˈbɪlɪtɪ] n estabilidad f.

**stabilizer** ['steɪbəlaɪzəʳ] n **1** (on plane, ship, bicycle) estabilizador m. **2** (in food) estabilizante m.

**stable¹** ['steɪbəl] adj **1** estable.
  ① comp **stabler**, comp **stablest**.

**stable²** ['steɪbəl] n (for horses) cuadra; (for other animals) establo.

**stack** [stæk] n **1** (pile, heap) montón m. **2** (of grass, grain, etc) almiar m. **3** (chimney) cañón de chimenea.
  ▶ vt **1** (pile up) apilar, amontonar; (fill) llenar. **2** fam (in cards) arreglar.
  ▶ n pl **stacks** fam montón m, montones mpl.
  ▶ n pl **stacks** (in library) estanterías fpl.

**stadium** ['steɪdɪəm] *n* estadio.
ⓘ *pl* stadiums o stadia ['steɪdɪə].

**staff** [stɑːf] *n* **1** *(personnel - gen)* personal *m*, plantilla; *(- teachers)* profesorado. **2** MIL estado mayor. **3** *(stick)* bastón *m*; *(of shepherd)* cayado; *(of bishop)* báculo; *(flagpole)* asta. **4** [*n* staves ['steɪdɪə] MUS pentagrama *m*.

**stag** [stæg] *n* ZOOL ciervo, venado.

**stage** [steɪdʒ] *n* **1** *(point, period)* etapa, fase *f*. **2** *(of journey, race)* etapa; *(day's journey)* jornada. **3** *(in theatre)* escenario, escena; *(raised platform)* plataforma, tablado, estrado. **4** *fig (scene of action)* escena. **5** *(of rocket)* fase *f*. **6** *fam (stagecoach)* diligencia. LOC **by stages / in stages** por etapas.
▶ *vt* **1** THEAT poner en escena, montar. **2** *(hold, carry out)* llevar a cabo, efectuar; *(arrange)* organizar, montar.
▶ *n* **the stage** *(the theatre)* el teatro, las tablas *fpl*.

**stagecoach** ['steɪdʒkəʊtʃ] *n* diligencia.

**stagger** ['stægəʳ] *vi (walk unsteadily)* tambalearse.
▶ *vt* **1** *(hours, work)* escalonar. **2** *(amaze)* asombrar, pasmar.
▶ *n (unsteady walk)* tambaleo.

**stagnation** [stæg'neɪʃ°n] *n (of water)* estancamiento; *(person)* anquilosamiento.

**stain** [steɪn] *n* **1** *(gen)* mancha. **2** *(dye)* tinte *m*, tintura.
▶ *vt* **1** *(gen)* manchar. **2** *(dye)* teñir. COMP **stain remover** quitamanchas *m*.
▶ *vi* mancharse.

**stainless** ['steɪnləs] *adj (spotless)* sin mancha. COMP **stainless steel** acero inoxidable.

**stair** [steəʳ] *n* **1** *(single step)* escalón *m*, peldaño. **2** *lit* escalera.
▶ *n pl* **stairs** escalera *f sing*.

**staircase** ['steəkeɪs] *n* escalera.

**stairway** ['steəweɪ] *n* escalera.

**stake** [steɪk] *n* **1** *(bet)* apuesta. **2** *(investment, share)* interés *m*, participación *f*.
▶ *vt* **1** *(bet)* apostar, jugar(se); *(risk)* arriesgar, jugarse. **2** *(give financial support to)* invertir en.

**stale** [steɪl] *adj* **1** *(food - gen)* no fresco, -a, pasado,-a; *(- bread, cake)* duro,-a; *(tobacco)* rancio,-a; *(wine, beer)* picado, -a. **2** *(air)* viciado,-a; *(smell)* a cerrado. **3** *(news)* viejo,-a, pasado,-a; *(joke)* trillado,-a.

**stalemate** ['steɪlmeɪt] *n* **1** *(chess)* tablas *fpl*. **2** *fig* punto muerto, impasse *m*.

**stalk** [stɔːk] *n* **1** BOT *(of plant)* tallo; *(of fruit)* rabo, rabillo; *(of cabbage)* troncho. **2** ZOOL pedúnculo.

**stall²** [stɔːl] *n* **1** *(in market)* puesto, tenderete *m*; *(at fair)* caseta, barraca. **2** *(for animal - stable)* establo; *(- stable compartment)* compartimiento (en un establo). **3** *(row of seats)* sillería. **4** *(small room, compartment)* compartimiento.
▶ *vi* AUTO calarse, pararse.
▶ *n pl* **stalls** *(in theatre)* platea *f sing*.

**stallion** ['stælɪən] *n* semental *m*.

**stamen** ['steɪmən] *n* BOT estambre *m*.

**stamina** ['stæmɪnə] *n (endurance)* resistencia, aguante *m*.

**stammer** ['stæməʳ] *n* tartamudeo.
▶ *vi* tartamudear.
▶ *vt (say with a stammer)* decir tartamudeando, farfullar.

**stamp** [stæmp] *n* **1** *(postage)* sello; *(fiscal)* timbre *m*; *(trading stamp)* cupón *m*, vale *m*. **2** *(tool - gen)* sello; *(- rubber)* sello de goma, tampón *m*; *(- metal)* cuño, troquel *m*. **3** *(seal, mark)* sello. **4** *(with foot - act)* patada, pisotón *m*; *(- sound)* paso.
COMP **stamp collecting** filatelia.
▶ *vt* **1** *(letter)* franquear. **2** *(passport, document)* sellar, marcar con sello; *(metal, coin)* acuñar, troquelar.

❌ Stamp no significa 'estampa', que se traduce por **picture**.

**stand** [stænd] *n* **1** *(position)* lugar *m*, sitio; *(attitude, opinion)* posición *f*, postura; *(defence, resistance)* resistencia. **2** *(of lamp, sculpture, etc)* pie *m*, pedestal *m*, base *f*. **3** *(stall - in market)* puesto, tenderete *m*; *(- at exhibition)* stand *m*; *(- at fair)* caseta, barraca. **4** *(for taxis)* parada. **5** SP *(in stadium)* tribuna. **6** US *(witness box)* estrado.

S

▶ vi **1** *(person - be on one's feet)* estar de pie, estar; *(- get up)* ponerse de pie, levantarse; *(- remain on one's feet)* quedarse de pie; *(- take up position)* ponerse. **2** *(measure - height)* medir; *(- value, level)* marcar, alcanzar. **3** *(thing - be situated)* estar, encontrarse.

▶ vt **1** *(place)* poner, colocar. **2** fam *(bear, tolerate)* aguantar, soportar. **3** fam *(invite)* invitar: *I'll stand you a drink* te invitaré a una copa. LOC **not to stand a chance** no tener ni la más remota posibilidad. ▮ **to stand clear (of STH)** apartarse (de algo). ▮ **to stand in the way of** impedir, obstaculizar, poner trabas a. ▮ **to stand to reason** ser lógico,-a. ▮ **to stand trial** ser procesado,-a.

◆ **to stand back** vi *(move back)* apartarse, echarse hacia atrás, alejarse; *(be objective)* distanciarse (from, de).

◆ **to stand by** vi **1** *(do nothing)* cruzarse de brazos, quedarse sin hacer nada. **2** *(be ready for action - gen)* estar preparado,-a, estar listo,-a; *(- troops)* estar en estado de alerta.

▶ vt insep **1** *(not desert)* no abandonar, respaldar, apoyar, defender. **2** *(keep to - decision)* atenerse a; *(- promise)* cumplir.

◆ **to stand for** vt insep **1** *(mean)* significar, querer decir; *(represent)* representar. **2** *(support, be in favour of)* defender, apoyar, ser partidario,-a de. **3** *(tolerate)* tolerar, permitir, consentir.

◆ **to stand in for** vt insep *(substitute, deputize)* sustituir, suplir.

◆ **to stand up** vi **1** *(get up)* ponerse de pie, levantarse; *(be standing)* estar de pie. **2** *(withstand)* resistir (to, -), soportar (to, -).

▶ vt sep **1** *(place upright)* poner en posición vertical. **2** fam *(fail to keep appointment)* dejar plantado,-a a, dar un plantón a.

◆ **to stand up for** vt insep *(defend)* defender; *(support)* apoyar.

ⓘ pt & pp **stood** [stʊd].

**standard** ['stændəd] n **1** *(level, degree)* nivel m; *(quality)* cualidad f. **2** *(criterion, yardstick)* criterio, valor m. **3** *(norm, rule)* norma, regla, estándar m. **4** *(flag)* estandarte m, bandera; *(of ship)* pabellón m. **5** *(official measure)* patrón m. COMP **standard of living** nivel m de vida.

▶ adj normal, estándar.

▶ n pl **standards** *(moral principles)* principios mpl, valores mpl.

**standardize** ['stændədaɪz] vt normalizar, estandarizar.

**standby** ['stændbaɪ] n **1** *(person)* suplente mf, sustituto,-a, reserva mf. **2** *(thing)* recurso.

**stank** [stæŋk] pt → stink.

**stanza** ['stænzə] n estrofa.

**staple¹** ['steɪpəl] adj **1** *(food, ingredient)* básico,-a; *(product, export)* principal. **2** *(usual)* típico,-a, de siempre.

▶ n *(main food)* alimento básico; *(main product)* producto principal; *(main thing)* elemento principal.

**staple²** ['steɪpəl] n *(fastener)* grapa.

▶ vt grapar.

**stapler** ['steɪpələʳ] n grapadora.

**star** [stɑːʳ] n *(gen)* estrella; *(person)* estrella, astro. COMP **Stars and Stripes** la bandera de los Estados Unidos.

▶ vi CINEM protagonizar (in, -).

ⓘ pt & pp **starred**, ger **starring**.

⊕ La bandera de Estados Unidos se conoce como Stars and Stripes (barras y estrellas) porque está compuesta por 13 barras horizontales rojas y lleva en una esquina 50 estrellas blancas sobre un fondo azul.

**starboard** ['stɑːbəd] n MAR estribor m.

**starch** [stɑːtʃ] n *(for laundry, in rice)* almidón m; *(in potatoes)* fécula.

▶ vt *(laundry)* almidonar.

**stare** [steəʳ] n mirada fija.

▶ vi mirar fijamente (at, -), clavar la vista (at, en).

**starfish** ['stɑːfɪʃ] n estrella de mar.

**starlet** ['stɑːlət] n aspirante f a estrella.

**starling** ['stɑːlɪŋ] n estornino.

**start** [stɑːt] n **1** *(gen)* principio, comienzo, inicio. **2** SP *(of race)* salida; *(advantage)* ventaja. **3** *(fright, jump)* susto, sobresalto.

▶ vt **1** *(begin - gen)* empezar, comenzar, iniciar; *(- conversation)* entablar. **2** *(cause to begin - fire, epidemic)* provocar; *(- argu-*

ment, *fight, war, etc)* empezar, iniciar. **3**
*(set up - business)* montar, poner; *(- organization)* fundar, establecer, crear. **4**
*(set in motion - machine)* poner en marcha;
*(- vehicle)* arrancar, poner en marcha.
▸ *vi* **1** *(begin)* empezar, comenzar. **2**
*(be set up - business)* ser fundado,-a,
fundarse, crearse. **3** *(begin to operate)*
ponerse en marcha; *(car)* arrancar.
◆ **to start off** *vi* **1** *(begin)* empezar, comenzar. **2** *(leave)* salir, ponerse en
camino.
▸ *vt sep* empezar, ayudar a empezar.
◆ **to start up** *vt sep (car)* arrancar; *(engine)* poner en marcha; *(business)*
montar, poner en marcha; *(conversation)* entablar.

**starter** ['stɑːtə'] *n* **1** SP *(official)* juez *mf*
de salida. **2** SP *(competitor)* competi-
dor,-ra, participante *mf*. **3** AUTO motor *m* de arranque. **4** CULIN *fam* primer plato, entrante *m*.

**startle** ['stɑːt<sup>ə</sup>l] *vt* asustar, sobresaltar:
*you startled me!* ¡me has asustado!

**starvation** [stɑː'veɪʃ<sup>ə</sup>n] *n* hambre *f*,
inanición *f*.

**starve** [stɑːv] *vi (feel hungry)* pasar
hambre; *(die)* morirse de hambre.
▸ *vt* **1** *(deprive of food)* privar de comida
a, hacer pasar hambre a. **2** *fig* privar
*(of, de)*.

**starving** ['stɑːvɪŋ] *adj* muerto,-a de
hambre, famélico,-a.

**state** [steɪt] *n* **1** *(condition)* estado. **2** POL
*(government)* estado. **3** *(country, division of
country)* estado. **4** *(ceremony, pomp)* ceremonia, pompa, solemnidad *f*.
▸ *adj* POL estatal, del estado.
▸ *vt* **1** *(say, declare, express)* exponer, declarar, afirmar. **2** *(specify)* fijar.

**stated** ['steɪtɪd] *adj (specified)* indicado,-a, señalado,-a.

**statement** ['steɪtmənt] *n* **1** *(gen)* declaración *f*, afirmación *f*; *(official)* comunicado. **2** FIN estado de cuentas, extracto de cuenta. COMP **to make a
statement** JUR prestar declaración.

**statesman** ['steɪtsmən] *n* estadista *m*,
hombre *m* de estado.
ⓘ *pl* **statesmen** ['steɪtsmən].

**static** ['stætɪk] *adj* **1** TECH estático,-a. **2**
*(not moving, not changing)* estaciona-
rio,-a. COMP **static electricity** electricidad *f* estática.
▸ *n (interference)* interferencias *fpl*, pa-
rásitos *mpl*.
▸ *n* **statics** PHYS estática.

**station** ['steɪʃ<sup>ə</sup>n] *n* **1** *(railway)* estación *f*
*(de ferrocarril)*; *(underground)* estación
*f* de metro; *(bus, coach)* estación *f*, terminal *f*. **2** *(radio)* emisora, estación *f*,
radio *f*; *(TV)* canal *m*. **3** AGR granja. **4**
*(social rank)* condición *f* social, posición *f* social.

**stationary** ['steɪʃ<sup>ə</sup>n<sup>ə</sup>rɪ] *adj* estacionario,-a.

**stationer** ['steɪʃ<sup>ə</sup>nə'] *n* dueño,-a de
una papelería. COMP **stationer's (shop)**
papelería.

**stationery** ['steɪʃ<sup>ə</sup>n<sup>ə</sup>rɪ] *n (paper)* papel
*m* de escribir; *(pen, ink, etc)* artículos
*mpl* de escritorio.

**statistics** [stə'tɪstɪks] *n (science)* estadística.
▸ *n pl (data)* estadísticas *fpl*.

**statue** ['stætjuː] *n* estatua.

**statuette** [stætjʊ'et] *n* estatuilla.

**stature** ['stætʃə'] *n* **1** *(height)* estatura,
talla. **2** *fig (standing)* talla.

**statute** ['stætjuːt] *n* estatuto.

**staves** [steɪvz] *n pl* → **staff**.

**stay¹** [steɪ] *n* **1** *(prop, support)* sostén *m*, soporte *m*, puntal *m*. **2** *(in corset)* ballena.

**stay²** [steɪ] *n (time)* estancia, permanencia.
▸ *vi (remain)* quedarse, permanecer.
▸ *vt (continue to be)* seguir.
▸ *vi (reside temporarily)* alojarse, hospedarse.
▸ *vt fml (stop)* detener; *(delay)* aplazar,
suspender; *(calm)* calmar.
◆ **to stay in** *vi* quedarse en casa, no
salir.

**steadily** ['stedɪlɪ] *adv* **1** *(grow, improve,
rise)* constantemente, a un ritmo
constante; *(rain, work)* sin parar. **2**
*(gaze, stare)* fijamente; *(walk)* con paso
seguro, decididamente; *(speak)* firmemente.

**S**

**steady** ['stedɪ] *adj* **1** *(table, ladder, etc)* firme, seguro,-a; *(gaze)* fijo,-a; *(voice)* tranquilo,-a, firme. **2** *(regular, constant - heartbeat, pace)* regular; *(- demand, speed, improvement, decline, increase)* constante; *(- flow, rain)* continuo,-a; *(rhythm)* regular, constante; *(- prices, currency)* estable. **3** *(regular - job)* fijo,-a, estable; *(- income)* regular, fijo,-a. **4** *(student)* aplicado,-a; *(worker, person)* serio,-a, formal.
ⓘ *comp* steadier, *superl* steadiest.
▸ *interj* ¡cuidado!, ¡ojo!
▸ *n (boyfriend)* novio; *(girlfriend)* novia.
▸ *vt* **1** *(hold firm - ladder, table, etc)* sujetar, sostener; *(stabilize)* estabilizar. **2** *(person, nerves)* calmar, tranquilizar.
ⓘ *pt & pp* steadied, *ger* steadying.

**steak** [steɪk] *n* **1** *(of beef)* bistec *m*, filete *m*; *(of salmon)* rodaja. **2** *(meat for stewing)* carne *f* de vaca para estofar.

**steal** [stiːl] *vt* robar, hurtar.
▸ *vi* **1** *(rob)* robar, hurtar. **2** *(move quietly, creep)* moverse con sigilo.
ⓘ *pt* stole [stəʊl], *pp* stolen ['stəʊlən].

**steam** [stiːm] *n* vapor *m*. COMP steam engine **1** *(locomotive)* locomotora de vapor, máquina de vapor. **2** *(engine)* motor *m* de vapor. ❙ steam iron plancha de vapor.
▸ *vt* CULIN *(vegetables)* cocer al vapor.
▸ *vi (boat)* echar vapor; *(soup, drink, etc)* humear.

**steamboat** ['stiːmbəʊt] *n* vapor *m*.

**steamer** ['stiːmə'] *n* **1** MAR vapor *m*, buque *m* de vapor. **2** CULIN olla a vapor.

**steamship** ['stiːmʃɪp] *n* vapor *m*, buque *m* de vapor.

**steel** [stiːl] *n (gen)* acero.
▸ *adj (knife, girder, etc)* de acero. COMP steel industry industria del acero ❙ steel mill acerería, acería. ❙ steel wool estropajo de acero.

**steelworks** ['stiːlwɜːks] *n pl* acería, acerería.

**steep¹** [stiːp] *vt (soak - washing)* remojar; *(- dried food)* poner en remojo; *(- fruit)* macerar.
▸ *vi (fruit)* macerarse.

**steep²** [stiːp] *adj* **1** *(hill, slope, stairs)* empinado,-a; *(rise, drop)* abrupto,-a,

brusco,-a. **2** *fam (price, fee)* excesivo,-a; *(demand)* excesivo,-a, poco razonable.

**steeple** ['stiːpªl] *n* aguja, chapitel *m*.

**steeplechase** ['stiːpªlʃeɪs] *n* carrera de obstáculos.

**steer¹** [stɪə'] *n* buey *m*.

**steer²** [stɪə'] *vt (gen)* dirigir, guiar; *(vehicle)* conducir, dirigir; *(ship)* gobernar; *(conversation)* llevar.
▸ *vi (vehicle)* ir al volante; *(ship)* llevar el timón, estar al timón.

**steering** ['stɪərɪŋ] *n* dirección *f*. COMP steering column columna de (la) dirección. ❙ steering lock **1** *(device)* seguro antirrobo. **2** *(when turning)* radio de giro. ❙ steering wheel volante *m*.

**stem** [stem] *n* **1** BOT *(of plant, flower)* tallo; *(of leaf)* pecíolo; *(of fruit)* pedúnculo. **2** *(of glass)* pie *m*; *(of tobacco pipe)* boquilla, caña. **3** LING raíz *f*, radical *m*.
▸ *vt (stop - gen)* frenar, detener, parar; *(- bleeding)* contener, parar.
ⓘ *pt & pp* stemmed, *ger* stemming.

**stench** [stentʃ] *n* hedor *m*, peste *f*, fetidez *f*.

**stencil** ['stensªl] *n* **1** *(template)* plantilla; *(design, pattern)* estarcido. **2** *(for typewriter)* cliché *m*, matriz *f*.

**stenography** [stə'nɒgrəfɪ] *n* US taquigrafía.

**step** [step] *n* **1** *(gen)* paso. **2** *(measure)* medida; *(formality)* gestión *f*, trámite *m*. **3** *(stair)* escalón *m*, peldaño; *(of vehicle)* estribo.
▸ *vi* **1** *(move, walk)* dar un paso, andar. **2** *(tread)* pisar.
▸ *n pl* steps GB *(stepladder)* escalera de tijera. *(outdoor)* escalinata; *(indoor)* escalera; *(of plane)* escalerilla.
ⓘ *pt & pp* stepped, *ger* stepping.

**stepbrother** ['stepbrʌðə'] *n* hermanastro.

**stepchild** ['steptʃaɪld] *n* hijastro,-a.
ⓘ *pl* stepchildren ['steptʃɪldrən].

**stepdaughter** ['stepdɔːtə'] *n* hijastra.

**stepfather** ['stepfɑːðə'] *n* padrastro.

**stepladder** ['steplædə'] *n* escalera de tijera.

**stepmother** ['stepmʌðə'] *n* madrastra.

**steppe** [step] *n* GEOG estepa.

**stepsister** ['stepsɪstər] *n* hermanastra.

**stepson** ['stepsʌn] *n* hijastro.

**stereo** ['steriəʊ] *n* estéreo.

**stereotype** ['steriətaip] *n* estereotipo.
▶ *vt* estereotipar.

**sterile** ['stərail] *adj* 1 *(barren)* estéril. 2 *(germfree)* esterilizado,-a.

**sterility** [stə'rɪlɪtɪ] *n* esterilidad *f*.

**sterilize** ['sterəlaiz] *vt* esterilizar.

**sterling** ['stɜːlɪŋ] *n* FIN libra esterlina, libras *fpl* esterlinas. [LOC] the pound sterling la libra esterlina.

**stern¹** [stɜːn] *adj* severo,-a, austero,-a.

**stern²** [stɜːn] *n* MAR popa.

**sternum** ['stɜːnəm] *n* ANAT esternón *m*.
ⓘ *pl* sternums o sterna ['stɜːnə].

**steroid** ['sterɔid] *n* esteroide *m*.

**stethoscope** ['steθəskəʊp] *n* estetoscopio.

**stew** [stjuː] *n* CULIN estofado, guisado.
▶ *vt (meat)* estofar, guisar; *(fruit)* hacer una compota de.

**steward** ['stjuːəd] *n* 1 *(on ship)* camarero; *(on plane)* auxiliar *m* de vuelo. 2 *(manager of estate)* administrador *m*. 3 *(of club, hotel)* mayordomo. 4 GB *(in horse racing)* comisario de carreras; *(in athletics)* juez *m*; *(at demonstration, etc)* oficial *mf*.

**stewardess** ['stjuːədes] *n* *(on ship)* camarera; *(on plane)* azafata, auxiliar *f* de vuelo.
ⓘ *pl* stewardesses.

**stick¹** [stɪk] *vt* 1 *(insert pointed object)* clavar, hincar. 2 *fam* poner, meter. 3 *(fix)* colocar, fijar; *(with glue)* pegar, fijar. 4 *fam (bear)* aguantar, soportar.
▶ *vi* 1 *(penetrate)* clavarse. 2 *(fix, become attached)* pegarse. 3 *(jam - drawer, key in lock)* atascarse; *(- machine part, lock)* atrancarse, encasquillarse; *(- vehicle in mud)* atascarse. 4 *(in cards)* plantarse.
◆ to stick out *vi* 1 *(project, protrude)* salir, sobresalir; *(be noticeable)* resaltar, destacarse. 2 *fam (be obvious)* ser obvio,-a, ser evidente.
▶ *vt sep* 1 *(tongue, hand)* sacar. 2 *(endure)* aguantar.
ⓘ *pt & pp* stuck [stʌk].

**stick²** [stɪk] *n* 1 *(piece of wood)* trozo de madera, palo; *(twig)* ramita; *(for punishment)* palo, vara. 2 *(for walking)* bastón *m*. 3 *(for plants)* rodrigón *m*, tutor *m*. 4 MUS *(baton)* batuta; *(drumstick)* palillo. 5 SP *(for hockey)* palo.

**sticker** ['stɪkər] *n* 1 *(label)* etiqueta adhesiva; *(with slogan, picture)* pegatina. 2 *(person)* persona tenaz.

**sticking** ['stɪkɪŋ] [COMP] sticking plaster *(small)* tirita®; *(on roll)* esparadrapo.

**sticky** ['stɪkɪ] *adj* pegajoso,-a. [COMP] sticky tape cinta adhesiva.
ⓘ *comp* stickier, *comp* stickiest.

**stiff** [stɪf] *adj* 1 *(hair, fabric)* rígido,-a, tieso,-a; *(card, collar, brush, lock)* duro,-a. 2 *(joint)* entumecido,-a; *(muscle)* agarrotado,-a. 3 *(door, window)* difícil de abrir, difícil de cerrar. 4 *(not liquid)* espeso,-a, consistente. 5 *(person, manner)* estirado,-a, tieso,-a; *(smile)* forzado,-a. 6 *fig (climb, test, etc)* difícil, duro,-a; *(breeze)* fuerte; *(sentence, punishment)* severo,-a. 7 *fam (price, fee)* excesivo,-a. 8 *fam (drink)* fuerte, cargado,-a. [LOC] to be stiff tener agujetas.

**stifle** ['staifəl] *vt* ahogar, sofocar.

**still** [stɪl] *adj* 1 *(not moving)* quieto,-a, inmóvil; *(stationary)* parado,-a; *(water)* manso,-a; *(air)* en calma. 2 *(tranquil, calm)* tranquilo,-a; *(peaceful)* sosegado,-a; *(subdued)* callado,-a, apagado, -a; *(silent)* silencioso,-a. 3 *(not fizzy - water)* sin gas; *(soft drink)* sin burbujas.
▶ *adv* 1 *(so far)* todavía, aún. 2 *(even)* aún, todavía. 3 *(even so, nevertheless)* a pesar de todo, con todo, no obstante, sin embargo. 4 *fml (besides, yet, in addition)* aún, todavía. 5 *(quiet, without moving)* quieto,-a. [COMP] still life ART naturaleza muerta *m*.

**stilt** [stɪlt] *n* zanco.

**stilted** ['stɪltɪd] *adj* afectado,-a.

**stimulant** ['stɪmjʊlənt] *n* estimulante *m*.

**stimulate** ['stɪmjəleit] *vt (activate)* estimular; *(encourage)* animar, alentar.

**stimulating** ['stɪmjəleitɪŋ] *adj (gen)* estimulante; *(inspiring)* inspirador,-ra.

**stimulation** [stɪmjə'leiʃən] *n (stimulus)* estímulo; *(action)* estimulación *f*.

S

**stimulus** ['stɪmjələs] *n* estímulo.
ⓘ *pl* stimuli ['stɪmjəlɪ:].

**sting** [stɪŋ] *n* **1** *(organ - of bee, wasp)* aguijón *m*; *(- of scorpion)* uña; *(- of plant)* pelo urticante. **2** *(action, wound)* picadura. **3** *(pain)* escozor *m*, picazón *f*. **4** *fig (of remorse)* punzada. **5** US *(trick)* timo, golpe *m*.
▶ *vt* **1** *(gen)* picar. **2** *fig (remark)* herir en lo más hondo; *(conscience)* remorder. **3** *(provoke)* incitar, provocar (into/to, a). **4** *(overcharge, swindle)* clavar.
▶ *vi* **1** *(insects, nettles, etc)* picar; *(substance)* escocer. **2** *(be painful)* escocer.
ⓘ *pt & pp* stung [stʌŋ].

**stink** [stɪŋk] *n* **1** *(smell)* peste *f*, hedor *m*, hediondez *f*, fetidez *f*. **2** *fam (fuss, trouble)* escándalo, lío, follón *m*.
▶ *vi* **1** apestar (of, a), heder (of, a). **2** *fam (seem bad or dishonest)* dar asco.
ⓘ *pt* stank [stæŋk] o stunk [stʌŋk], *pp* stunk [stʌŋk].

**stinking** ['stɪŋkɪŋ] *adj* apestoso,-a.

**stipulate** ['stɪpjəleɪt] *vt* estipular, especificar.

**stipulation** [stɪpjə'leɪʃ(ə)n] *n* estipulación *f*, condición *f*.

**stir** [stɜːʳ] *vt* **1** *(liquid, mixture)* remover, revolver. **2** *(move slightly)* mover, agitar. **3** *(curiosity, interest, etc)* despertar, excitar; *(anger)* provocar; *(imagination)* avivar, estimular; *(emotions)* conmover.
▶ *vi* **1** *(move)* moverse, agitarse; *(wake up)* despertarse; *(get up)* levantarse. **2** *(feelings)* despertarse. **3** *fam (cause trouble)* armar lío, meter cizaña.
ⓘ *pt & pp* stirred, *ger* stirring.

**stirring** ['stɜːrɪŋ] *adj (moving)* conmovedor,-ra; *(rousing, exciting)* emocionante.

**stirrup** ['stɪrəp] *n* **1** *(for riding)* estribo. **2** *(on trousers)* trabilla. COMP stirrup pump bomba de mano.

**stitch** [stɪtʃ] *n* **1** *(in sewing)* puntada; *(in knitting)* punto. **2** MED punto (de sutura). **3** *(sharp pain)* punzada; *(when running, etc)* flato.
▶ *vt* **1** SEW coser (on, a), (up, -). **2** MED suturar (up, -).
▶ *vi* SEW coser.

**stoat** [stəʊt] *n* armiño.

**stock** [stɒk] *n* **1** *(supply)* reserva. **2** COMM *(goods)* existencias *fpl*, stock *m*; *(variety)* surtido. **3** FIN *(company's capital)* capital *m* social. **4** AGR *(livestock)* ganado. **5** CULIN *(broth)* caldo. LOC in stock en existencia. ‖ out of stock agotado,-a. COMP stock exchange bolsa. ‖ stock market mercado bursátil.
▶ *vt* COMM *(keep supplies of)* tener en stock; *(sell)* vender.
▶ *n pl* stocks FIN *(shares)* acciones *fpl*, valores *mpl*.

**stockbroker** ['stɒkbrəʊkəʳ] *n* corredor,-ra de bolsa, agente *mf* de bolsa, bolsista *mf*.

**stockholder** ['stɒkhəʊldəʳ] *n* US accionista *mf*.

**stocking** ['stɒkɪŋ] *n* media.

**stoic** ['stəʊɪk] *n* estoico,-a.

**stoical** ['stəʊɪkªl] *adj* estoico,-a.

**stoicism** ['stəʊɪsɪzªm] *n* estoicismo.

**stole¹** [stəʊl] *pt* → steal.

**stole²** [stəʊl] *n (garment)* estola.

**stolen** ['stəʊlən] *pp* → steal.

**stomach** ['stʌmək] *n* **1** ANAT estómago. **2** *fam (belly)* barriga; *(abdomen)* abdomen *m*, vientre *m*.
▶ *vt fig (bear, endure)* aguantar, soportar, tragar; *(eat, drink)* tolerar.

**stomachache** ['stʌməkeɪk] *n* dolor *m* de estómago.

**stoma** [s'təʊmə] *n* estoma *m*.
ⓘ *pl* stomas o stomata [s'təʊmətə].

**stomp** [stɒmp] *vi fam* pisar fuerte.

**stone** [stəʊn] *n* **1** *(gen)* piedra. **2** *(on grave)* lápida. **3** *(of fruit)* hueso. **4** MED cálculo, piedra. **5** GB *(measure of weight)* unidad de peso que equivale a 6,348 kg.
▶ *adj* de piedra, pétreo,-a. COMP Stone Age Edad *f* de Piedra.
▶ *vt* **1** *(person)* apedrear, lapidar. **2** *(fruit)* deshuesar.

**stoneware** ['stəʊnweəʳ] *n* gres *m*, cerámica de gres.

**stonework** ['stəʊnwɜːk] *n* mampostería.

**stood** [stʊd] *pt & pp* → stand.

**stooge** [stuːdʒ] *n* **1** THEAT comparsa *mf*. **2** *pej (person)* títere *mf*, pelele *mf*.

**stool** [stuːl] *n* **1** *(seat)* taburete *m*, banqueta. **2** MED *(faeces)* deposición *f*, heces *fpl*.

**stoop¹** [stuːp] *n* US *(porch)* entrada.

**stoop²** [stuːp] *n* *(of person)* encorvamiento, encorvadura; *(of shoulders)* espaldas *fpl* encorvadas.
▸ *vi* **1** *(bend)* inclinarse (down, -), agacharse (down, -). **2** *(have a stoop)* andar encorvado,-a.

**stop** [stɒp] *n* **1** *(halt)* parada, alto. **2** *(stopping place)* parada. **3** *(on journey)* parada; *(break, rest)* descanso, pausa. **4** *(punctuation mark)* punto; *(in telegram)* stop *m*. **5** MUS *(on organ)* registro; *(knob)* botón *m* de registro; *(on wind instrument)* llave *f*. **6** *(in camera)* diafragma *m*.
▸ *vt* **1** *(halt - vehicle, person)* parar, detener; *(- machine, ball)* parar. **2** *(end, interrupt - production)* parar; *(- inflation, advance)* parar, contener; *(- conversation, play)* interrumpir; *(- pain, etc)* poner fin a, acabar con. **3** *(pay, match, holidays)* suspender; *(cheque)* cancelar; *(money from wages)* retener. **4** *(cease)* dejar de, parar de. **5** *(prevent)* impedir, evitar. **6** *(block - hole)* tapar, taponar (up, -); *(- gap)* rellenar (up, -); *(- tooth)* empastar (up, -). **7** MUS *(string, key)* apretar; *(hole)* cubrir.
▸ *vi* **1** *(halt)* parar, pararse, detener, detenerse. **2** *(cease)* acabarse, terminar, cesar. **3** GB *fam* *(stay)* quedarse.
◆ **to stop over** *vi* **1** *(interrupt journey)* parar; *(overnight)* pasar la noche, hacer noche. **2** *(on flight)* hacer escala.
ⓘ *pt & pp* stopped, *ger* stopping.

**stopcock** [ˈstɒpkɒk] *n* llave *f* de paso.

**stopover** [ˈstɒpəʊvəʳ] *n* *(stop)* parada; *(on flight)* escala; *(stay)* estancia.

**stopper** [ˈstɒpəʳ] *n* tapón *m*.

**stopping** [ˈstɒpɪŋ] *adj* GB *(of train)* que para en todas las estaciones.

**stop-press** [stɒpˈpres] *adj* *(news)* de última hora.

**stopwatch** [ˈstɒpwɒtʃ] *n* cronómetro.
ⓘ *pl* stopwatches.

**storage** [ˈstɔːrɪdʒ] *n* **1** *(act)* almacenaje *m*, almacenamiento. **2** *(place)* almacén *m*, depósito, guardamuebles *m*.

**3** *(cost)* (gastos *mpl* de) almacenaje *m*. **4** COMPUT almacenamiento.

**store** [stɔːʳ] *n* **1** *(supply - gen)* reserva, provisión *f*; *(- of wisdom, knowledge)* reserva; *(- of jokes, etc)* colección *f*. **2** *(warehouse)* almacén *m*, depósito. **3** US *(shop)* tienda.
▸ *vt* **1** *(put away)* almacenar (up, -); *(keep)* guardar; *(amass)* acumular, hacer acopio de. **2** COMPUT almacenar. **3** *(put in storage)* guardar, almacenar, mandar a un depósito. **4** *fig* *(trouble, etc)* ir acumulando (up, -), ir almacenando (up, -). **5** *(fill with supplies)* abastecer (with, de).
▸ *n pl* **stores** *(provisions)* provisiones *fpl*, víveres *mpl*, MIL *(supplies, equipment)* pertrechos *mpl*; *(place)* intendencia *f sing*.

**storehouse** [ˈstɔːhaʊs] *n* almacén *m*, depósito.

**storekeeper** [ˈstɔːkiːpəʳ] *n* US tendero,-a.

**storeroom** [ˈstɔːruːm] *n* *(gen)* almacén *m*, depósito; *(for food)* despensa.

**storey** [ˈstɔːri] *n* piso, planta.

**stork** [stɔːk] *n* cigüeña.

**storm** [stɔːm] *n* **1** *(thunderstorm)* tormenta; *(at sea)* tempestad *f*, temporal *m*; *(with wind)* borrasca. **2** *fig* *(uproar)* revuelo, escándalo; *(of missiles, insults)* lluvia, torrente *m*.

**stormy** [ˈstɔːmi] *adj* **1** *(weather)* tormentoso,-a. **2** *fig* *(meeting, discussion)* acalorado,-a; *(relationship)* tormentoso,-a, con muchos altibajos.
ⓘ *comp* stormier, *superl* stormiest.

**story¹** [ˈstɔːri] *n* US → storey.

**story²** [ˈstɔːri] *n* **1** *(gen)* historia; *(tale)* cuento, relato; *(account)* relato. **2** *(anecdote)* anécdota; *(joke)* chiste *m*. **3** *(rumour)* rumor *m*; *(lie)* mentira, cuento. **4** *(newspaper article)* artículo; *(newsworthy item)* artículo de interés periodístico. **5** *(storyline, narrative, plot)* argumento, trama.
ⓘ *pl* stories.

**storybook** [ˈstɔːrɪbʊk] *n* libro de cuentos.

**storyteller** [ˈstɔːrɪteləʳ] *n* cuentista *mf*.

**stout** [staʊt] *adj* **1** *euph* *(fat)* corpulento,-a, robusto,-a. **2** *(strong)* sólido,-a, fuerte. **3** *(determined, resolute)* firme, resuelto,-a, tenaz; *(brave)* valiente.

**S**

► *n (beer)* cerveza negra.

**stove** [stəʊv] *n* **1** *(for heating)* estufa. **2** *(cooker)* cocina; *(cooking ring)* hornillo; *(oven)* horno.

**straight** [streɪt] *adj* **1** *(not curved - gen)* recto,-a; *(- hair)* liso,-a. **2** *(level, upright)* derecho,-a, recto,-a. **3** *(tidy, neat)* en orden. **4** *(honest - person)* honrado,-a, de confianza; *(sincere)* sincero,-a. **5** *(direct - question)* directo,-a; *(- refusal, rejection)* categórico,-a, rotundo,-a. **6** *(correct, accurate)* correcto,-a. **7** *(consecutive)* seguido,-a. **8** *(drink)* solo,-a.

► *adv* **1** *(in a straight line)* recto,-a. **2** *(not in a curve)* derecho,-a, recto,-a. **3** *(directly)* directamente. **4** *(immediately)* en seguida. **5** *(frankly)* francamente, con franqueza. **6** *(clearly)* claro, con claridad: LOC **straight away** en seguida. ‖ **straight off** en el acto. ‖ **straight up** en serio. ‖ **to go straight** *(criminal)* reformarse.

**straightaway** [streɪtəˈweɪ] *adv* en seguida, inmediatamente.

**straighten** [ˈstreɪtᵊn] *vt* **1** *(wire)* enderezar; *(- tie, skirt, picture)* poner bien, poner recto,-a; *(- hair)* estirar, alisar. **2** *(tidy)* ordenar (up, -), arreglar (up, -).

► *vi (road)* hacerse recto,-a.

**straightforward** [streɪtˈfɔ:wəd] *adj* **1** *(honest)* honrado,-a; *(sincere, open)* sincero,-a, franco,-a, abierto,-a. **2** *(simple, easy)* sencillo,-a, simple; *(clear)* claro,-a.

**strain¹** [streɪn] *n* **1** *(race, breed)* raza; *(descent)* linaje *m*; *(of plant, virus)* cepa. **2** *(streak)* vena.

**strain²** [streɪn] *n* **1** PHYS *(tension)* tensión *f*; *(pressure)* presión *f*; *(weight)* peso. **2** *(stress, pressure)* tensión *f*, estrés *m*; *(effort)* esfuerzo; *(exhaustion)* agotamiento. **3** *(tension)* tirantez *f*, tensión *f*. **4** MED torcedura, esguince *m*.

► *vt* **1** *(stretch)* estirar, tensar. **2** *(damage, weaken - muscle)* torcer(se), hacerse un esguince en; *(- back)* hacerse daño en; *(- voice, eyes)* forzar; *(ears)* aguzar; *(- heart)* cansar. **3** *(stretch - patience, nerves, credulity)* poner a prueba; *(- resources)* estirar al máximo; *(- relations)* someter a demasiada tensión, crear tirantez en. **4** *(filter - liquid)* colar; *(- vegetables, rice)* escurrir.

**strainer** [ˈstreɪnər] *n* colador *m*.

**strait** [streɪt] *n* GEOG estrecho.

► *n pl* **straits** *(difficulties)* aprietos *mpl*, apuros *mpl*.

**straitjacket** [ˈstreɪtdʒækɪt] *n* **1** camisa de fuerza. **2** *fig* control *m*, limitaciones *fpl*.

**strand¹** [strænd] *n lit (beach)* playa.

**strand²** [strænd] *n* **1** *(of thread)* hebra, hilo; *(of rope, string)* ramal *m*; *(of hair)* pelo; *(of pearls)* sarta. **2** *fig (of story, argument)* hilo, línea.

**strange** [streɪndʒ] *adj* **1** *(odd, bizarre)* extraño,-a, raro,-a. **2** *(unknown)* desconocido,-a; *(unfamiliar)* nuevo,-a. COMP **strange to say** aunque parezca mentira.

**strangely** [ˈstreɪndʒlɪ] *adv* extrañamente.

**stranger** [ˈstreɪndʒər] *n (unknown person)* extraño,-a, desconocido,-a; *(outsider)* forastero,-a.

☒ Stranger no significa 'extranjero', que se traduce por foreigner.

**strangle** [ˈstræŋgᵊl] *vt* **1** *(kill)* estrangular. **2** *fig (stifle)* sofocar, ahogar.

**stranglehold** [ˈstræŋgᵊlhəʊld] *n* **1** SP *(wrestling)* llave *f* al cuello. **2** *pej (firm control)* poder *m*, dominio.

**strap** [stræp] *n (on watch, camera)* correa; *(on bag)* asa; *(on shoe)* tira; *(on dress, etc)* tirante *m*.

► *vt* **1** *(fasten)* atar con correa. **2** *(bandage)* vendar.
ⓘ *pt & pp* strapped, *ger* strapping.

**strapless** [ˈstræpləs] *adj* sin tirantes.

**strapping** [ˈstræpɪŋ] *adj (big, strong)* fornido,-a, robusto,-a.

**stratagem** [ˈstrætədʒəm] *n* estratagema.

**strategic** [strəˈti:dʒɪk] *adj* estratégico,-a.

**strategist** [ˈstrætədʒɪst] *n* estratega *mf*.

**strategy** [ˈstrætədʒɪ] *n* estrategia.
ⓘ *pl* strategies.

**stratosphere** [ˈstrætəsfɪər] *n* estratosfera.

**stratum** [ˈstrɑ:təm] *n* **1** GEOL estrato. **2** *(level, class)* estrato, nivel *m*.
ⓘ *pl* strata [ˈstrɑ:tə].

**straw** [strɔ:] *n* **1** *(dried stalk(s))* paja. **2** *(for drinking)* paja, pajita.
▶ *adj* de paja.

**strawberry** ['strɔ:bərɪ] *n* *(gen)* fresa; *(large)* fresón *m*. COMP **strawberry jam** mermelada de fresa. ▌ **strawberry tree** madroño.
ⓘ *pl* strawberries.

**stray** [streɪ] *adj* **1** *(lost)* perdido,-a, extraviado,-a; *(animal)* callejero,-a. **2** *(isolated, odd)* perdido,-a.
▶ *n* *(animal)* animal *m* extraviado.
▶ *vi* **1** *(get lost)* extraviarse, perderse; *(wander away)* desviarse, apartarse, alejarse; *(from group)* separarse, apartarse, alejarse. **2** *fig* *(digress, wander)* divagar, apartarse del tema, desviarse del tema.

**stream** [stri:m] *n* **1** *(brook)* arroyo, riachuelo. **2** *(current)* corriente *f*. **3** *(flow of liquid)* flujo, chorro, río; *(of blood, air)* chorro; *(of lava, tears)* torrente *m*; *(of light)* raudal *m*. **4** *fig* *(of people)* oleada, torrente *m*; *(of vehicles, traffic)* desfile *m* continuo, caravana; *(of abuse, excuses, insults)* torrente *m*, sarta. **5** GB *(class, pupils)* clase *f*, grupo, nivel *m* *(de alumnos seleccionados según su nivel académico)*.
▶ *vi* **1** *(flow, pour out)* manar, correr, chorrear; *(gush)* salir a chorros. **2** *fig* *(people, vehicles, etc)* desfilar. **3** *(hair, banner, scarf)* ondear.
▶ *vt* **1** *(liquid)* derramar. **2** GB poner en grupos según su nivel académico.

**streamer** ['stri:məʳ] *n* *(decoration)* serpentina; *(flag)* banderín *m*.

**street** [stri:t] *n* calle *f*. LOC **at street level** a nivel de la calle. ▌ **to walk the streets 1** *(homeless)* estar sin techo. **2** *(prostitute)* trabajar la calle. COMP **one-way street** calle de sentido único. ▌ **street cleaner** barrendero,-a. ▌ **street corner** esquina. ▌ **street directory** callejero. ▌ **street lamp** farola. ▌ **street lighting** alumbrado público. ▌ **street plan** plano de la ciudad. ▌ **street market** mercadillo. ▌ **street value** valor *m* (en el mercado).

**streetcar** ['stri:tka:] *n* US tranvía.

**streetlamp** ['stri:tlæmp] *n* farol *m*, farola.

**streetlight** ['stri:tlaɪt] *n* farol *m*, farola.

**strength** [streŋθ] *n* **1** *(of person - physical)* fuerza, fuerzas *fpl*, fortaleza; *(- stamina)* resistencia, aguante *m*. **2** *(intellectual, spiritual)* fortaleza, entereza, firmeza. **3** *(of machine, object)* resistencia; *(of wind, current)* fuerza; *(of light, sound, magnet, lens)* potencia. **4** *(of solution)* concentración *f*; *(of drug)* potencia; *(of alcohol)* graduación *f*. **5** *(of currency)* valor *m*, fortaleza; *(of economy)* solidez *f*, fortaleza. **6** *(of argument, evidence, story)* fuerza, validez *f*, credibilidad *f*; *(of emotion, conviction, colour)* intensidad *f*; *(of protest)* energía. **7** *(strong point)* punto fuerte, virtud *f*; *(ability, capability)* capacidad *f*; *(advantage)* ventaja. **8** *(power, influence)* poder *m*, potencia. **9** *(force in numbers)* fuerza numérica, número.

**strengthen** ['streŋθən] *vt* **1** *(wall, glass, defence, etc)* reforzar; *(muscle)* fortalecer. **2** *(character, faith, love)* fortalecer; *(support)* aumentar; *(relationship, ties)* consolidar, fortalecer; *(resolve, determination)* redoblar, intensificar.
▶ *vi* **1** *(muscle)* fortalecerse. **2** *(economy, currency)* reforzarse, fortalecerse; *(relationship)* consolidarse, reforzarse, fortalecerse; *(support, opposition, feeling)* intensificarse, aumentar.

**stress** [stres] *n* **1** MED tensión *f* (nerviosa), estrés *m*. **2** *(pressure)* presión *f*, tensión *f*. **3** TECH tensión *f*. **4** *(emphasis)* hincapié *m* (on, en), énfasis *m* (on, en). **5** LING *(on word)* acento (tónico).
COMP **stress mark** acento.
▶ *vt* **1** *(emphasize)* hacer hincapié en, poner énfasis en, subrayar, enfatizar. **2** LING *(word)* acentuar.

**stressed** [strest] *adj* **1** MED *(person)* estresado,-a. **2** PHYS *(object)* tensado,-a.

**stressful** ['stresful] *adj* estresante, de mucho estrés.

**stretch** [stretʃ] *n* **1** *(of land, water)* extensión *f*; *(of road)* tramo, trecho. **2** *(elasticity)* elasticidad *f*. **3** *(act of stretching)* estiramiento. **4** *(period of time)* período, tiempo, intervalo; *(in prison)* condena. **5** SP *(of racetrack)* recta.
▶ *vt* **1** *(extend - elastic, clothes, rope)* estirar; *(- canvas)* extender; *(- shoes)* ensanchar;

S

*(- arm, leg)* alargar, estirar, extender; *(-wings)* desplegar, extender. **2** *(make demands on, make to use all abilities)* exigir a. **3** *(strain - money, resources)* estirar, emplear al máximo; *(- patience)* abusar; *(- meaning)* forzar, distorsionar.

▸ *vi* **1** *(elastic)* estirarse; *(fabric)* dar de sí; *(shoes)* ensancharse, dar de sí; *(person, animal - gen)* estirarse; *(person - when tired)* desperezarse. **2** *(extend - land, sea, etc)* extenderse *(out, -)*; *(- in time)* alargarse, prolongarse. **3** *(reach)* llegar *(to, para)*, alcanzar *(to, para)*.

▸ *adj (material, jeans, etc)* elástico,-a.

◆ **to stretch out** *vi (person - gen)* estirarse; *(- lie down)* tumbarse.

▸ *vt sep* **1** *(arm, leg)* alargar, estirar, extender. **2** *(money, resources)* estirar.

❌ To stretch no significa 'estrechar', que se traduce por to tighten, to narrow.

**stretcher** ['stretʃəʳ] *n* camilla.

**stretchy** ['stretʃɪ] *adj* elástico,-a.
ⓘ *comp* **stretchier**, *superl* **stretchier**.

**strew** [struː] *vt lit (scatter)* esparcir, desparramar; *(lie scattered)* sembrar, cubrir.
ⓘ *pt* strewed, *pp* strewed o strewn [struːn].

**strict** [strɪkt] *adj* **1** *(severe - person)* severo,-a, estricto,-a; *(- discipline)* riguroso,-a, severo,-a, estricto,-a; *(- rule, law, order, etc)* estricto,-a, riguroso,-a, rígido,-a. **2** *(exact, precise)* estricto,-a, riguroso,-a; *(complete, total)* absoluto,-a.

**strictly** ['strɪktlɪ] *adv* **1** *(severely)* severamente, estrictamente, de manera estricta. **2** *(rigorously, rigidly)* estrictamente; *(categorically)* terminantemente. **3** *(exactly, precisely)* estrictamente, exactamente; *(completely)* totalmente, del todo. **4** *(exclusively)* exclusivamente. ⎣LOC⎦ **strictly speaking** en realidad.

**stride** [straɪd] *n* **1** *(long step)* zancada; *(gait)* paso, manera de andar. **2** *(advance, development)* progresos *mpl*.

▸ *vi* andar a zancadas.
ⓘ *pt* strode [strəʊd], *pp* stridden ['strɪdən].

▸ *n pl* **strides** *fam (trousers)* pantalón *m sing*, pantalones *mpl*.

**stridden** ['strɪdən] *pp* → **stride**.

**strike** [straɪk] *n* **1** *(by workers, students, etc)* huelga. **2** SP *(blow - gen)* golpe *m*; *(- in tenpin bowling)* pleno; *(- in baseball)* strike *m*. **3** *(find)* hallazgo; *(of oil, gold, etc)* descubrimiento. **4** MIL ataque *m*: air strike ataque aéreo.

▸ *vt* **1** *(hit)* pegar, golpear. **2** *(knock against, collide with)* dar contra, chocar contra; *(ball, stone)* pegar contra, dar contra; *(lightning, bullet, torpedo)* alcanzar. **3** *(disaster, earthquake)* golpear, sobrevenir; *(disease)* atacar, golpear. **4** *(gold, oil)* descubrir, encontrar, dar con; *(track, path)* dar con. **5** *(coin, medal)* acuñar. **6** *(match)* encender. **7** *(of clock)* dar, tocar. **8** MUS *(note)* dar; *(chord)* tocar. **9** *(bargain, deal)* cerrar, hacer; *(balance)* encontrar, hallar; *(agreement)* llegar a. **10** *(pose, attitude)* adoptar. **11** *(give impression)* parecer, dar la impresión de. **12** *(occur to)* ocurrírsele a; *(remember)* acordarse de. **13** *(render)* dejar. **14** *(cause fear, terror, worry)* infundir. **15** *(take down - sail, flag)* arriar; *(- tent, set)* desmontar. **16** *(cutting)* plantar.

▸ *vi* **1** *(attack - troops, animal, etc)* atacar; *(- disaster, misfortune)* sobrevenir, ocurrir; *(- disease)* atacar, golpear; *(- lightning)* alcanzar, caer. **2** *(workers, etc)* declararse en huelga, hacer huelga. **3** *(clock)* dar la hora.

◆ **to strike back** *vi* **1** *(gen)* devolver el golpe. **2** MIL contraatacar.

◆ **to strike down** *vt sep (by illness, disease)* abatir, fulminar.

◆ **to strike off** *vt sep* **1** *(name from list)* tachar. **2** JUR *(doctor, lawyer, etc)* inhabilitar para ejercer.

◆ **to strike on** *vt insep (discover)* dar con, encontrar.

◆ **to strike out** *vt sep (remove, cross out)* tachar.

▸ *vi* **1** *(attack, hit out)* arremeter *(at, contra)*. **2** *(set off)* emprender el camino.

◆ **to strike up** *vt insep (friendship)* entablar, trabar; *(conversation)* entablar, iniciar.

▸ *vi (band)* empezar a tocar.
ⓘ *pt & pp* struck [strʌk].

**strikebreaker** ['straɪkbreɪkəʳ] *n* esquirol *mf*, rompehuelgas *mf*.

**striker** ['straɪkə'] n **1** (worker) huelguista mf. **2** SP (football) delantero,-a; (cricket) bateador,-ra.

**striking** ['straɪkɪŋ] adj **1** (eye-catching) llamativo,-a; (stunning) atractivo,-a. **2** (similarity, resemblance) sorprendente, asombroso,-a; (feature, etc) impresionante, destacado,-a. **3** (on strike) en huelga.

**string** [strɪŋ] n **1** (cord) cuerda, cordel m; (lace) cordón m; (of puppet) hilo. **2** (on instrument, racket) cuerda. **3** (of garlic, onions) ristra; (of pearls, beads) sarta, hilo. **4** (of vehicles) fila, hilera; (of hotels) cadena; (of events) serie f, cadena, sucesión f; (of lies, complaints) sarta; (of insults) retahíla. COMP
**string orchestra** orquesta de cuerda. ‖ **string quartet** cuarteto de cuerda.
▶ vt **1** (beads) ensartar, enhebrar. **2** (guitar, racket) encordar. **3** (beans) quitar la hebra.
ⓘ pt & pp **strung** [strʌŋ].
▶ n pl **the strings** MUS los instrumentos mpl de cuerda.

**strip¹** [strɪp] vt **1** (person) desnudar, quitarle la ropa a; (bed) quitar la ropa de; (room, house) vaciar; (wallpaper, paint) quitar; (leaves, bark) arrancar. **2** (property, rights, titles) despojar (of, de). **3** (engine) desarmar, desmontar (down, -); (ship) desaparejar.
▶ vi (undress) desnudarse (off, -), quitarse la ropa; (perform striptease) hacer un strip-tease.
ⓘ pt & pp **stripped**, ger **stripping**.
▶ n (striptease) strip-tease m.

**strip²** [strɪp] n **1** (of paper, leather) tira; (of land) franja; (of metal) tira, cinta. **2** SP (colours, kit) equipo. **3** (airstrip) pista (de aterrizaje). **4** [also **strip** (cartoon)] historieta, tira cómica. COMP **strip lighting** alumbrado fluorescente. ‖ **strip mining** US explotación f a cielo abierto.

**stripe** [straɪp] n **1** (gen) raya, lista. **2** MIL galón m. **3** (kind, type) tipo, clase f.
▶ vt pintar a rayas, dibujar a rayas.

**striped** [straɪpt] adj rayado,-a, a rayas: a striped shirt una camisa a rayas.

**stripy** ['staɪpɪ] adj rayado,-a, a rayas.
ⓘ comp **stripier**, superl **stripiest**.

**strive** [straɪv] vi esforzarse, procurar.
ⓘ pt **strove** [strəʊv], pp **striven** ['strɪvən].

**striven** ['strɪvən] pt → strive.

**strode** [strəʊd] pt → stride.

**stroke** [strəʊk] n **1** (blow) golpe m. **2** (caress) caricia. **3** SP (in tennis, cricket, golf) golpe m, jugada; (in billiards) tacada; (in rowing) palada; (in swimming - movement) brazada; (- style) estilo. **4** SP (oarsman) cabo. **5** (of pen) trazo; (of brush) pincelada. **6** (of bell) campanada. **7** (of engine) tiempo; (of piston) carrera. **8** MED ataque m de apoplejía, derrame m cerebral. **9** (oblique) barra (oblicua).
▶ vt **1** (caress) acariciar. **2** (ball) dar un golpe a.

**stroll** [strəʊl] n paseo, vuelta.
▶ vi dar un paseo, dar una vuelta.

**stroller** ['strəʊlə'] n **1** (pushchair) cochecito, sillita de niño. **2** (person) paseante mf.

**strong** [strɒŋ] adj **1** (physically - person) fuerte; (- consitution) robusto,-a. **2** (material, furniture, shoes, etc) fuerte, resistente. **3** (country, army) poderoso,-a, fuerte. **4** (beliefs, views, principles) firme; (faith) firme, sólido,-a; (support) mucho, firme. **5** (argument, evidence) contundente, convincente; (influence) grande; (protest) enérgico,-a. **6** (colour) fuerte, intenso,-a, vivo,-a; (smell, food, drink) fuerte; (tea, coffee) fuerte, cargado,-a; (light) brillante. **7** (resemblance, accent) fuerte, marcado,-a. **8** (chance, likelihood, probability) bueno,-a. **9** (wind, current) fuerte. **10** (good - team) fuerte; (- cast) sólido,-a. **11** (currency, etc) fuerte.
▶ adv fuerte.

**strongbox** ['strɒŋbɒks] n caja fuerte.

**stronghold** ['strɒŋhəʊld] n **1** MIL fortaleza. **2** fig baluarte m.

**strongroom** ['strɒŋruːm] n cámara acorazada.

**stroppy** ['strɒpɪ] adj GB fam borde, de mala uva.
ⓘ comp **stroppier**, superl **stroppiest**.

**strove** [strəʊv] pt → strive.

**struck** [strʌk] pt & pp → strike.

**structural** ['strʌktʃərəl] adj (gen) estructural. COMP **structural engineer** ingeniero,-a de estructuras.

**S**

**structure** ['strʌktʃəʳ] n 1 *(organization, composition)* estructura. 2 *(thing constructed)* construcción f; *(building)* edificio.
▶ vt *(arguemnt, essay, report, etc)* estructurar; *(event)* planificar.

**struggle** ['strʌgəl] n *(gen)* lucha; *(physical fight)* pelea, forcejeo.
▶ vi 1 *(fight)* luchar; *(physically)* forcejear. 2 *(strive)* luchar (for, por), esforzarse (for, por); *(suffer)* pasar apuros; *(have difficulty)* costar, tener problemas.

**strum** [strʌm] vt rasguear.
▶ vi rasguear (on, -).
ⓘ pt & pp strummed, ger strumming.

**strung** [strʌŋ] pt & pp → string. LOC to be highly strung estar muy nervioso, -a, estar muy tenso,-a.

**strut** [strʌt] n 1 ARCH *(rod, bar)* puntal m, riostra. 2 *(way of walking)* contoneo, pavoneo.
▶ vi pavonearse, contonearse.
ⓘ pt & pp strutted, ger strutting.

**stub** [stʌb] n *(of cigarette)* colilla; *(of pencil, candle)* cabo; *(of cheque, etc)* matriz f.
▶ vt darse un golpe.
ⓘ pt & pp stubbed, ger stubbing.
◆ to stub out vt sep apagar.

**stubborn** ['stʌbən] adj 1 *(person, animal)* terco,-a, testarudo,-a, tozudo,-a, obstinado,-a; *(refusal, resistance)* obcecado,-a. 2 *(stain, cough, etc)* rebelde.

**stubbornly** ['stʌbənlɪ] adv tercamente, cabezudamente.

**stubby** ['stʌbɪ] adj corto,-a y rechoncho,-a.
ⓘ comp stubbier, superl stubbiest.

**stucco** ['stʌkəʊ] n estuco.
ⓘ pl stuccoes o stuccos.

**stuck** [stʌk] pt & pp → stick.
▶ adj 1 *(unable to move)* atascado,-a. 2 *(trapped)* atrapado,-a; *(in routine)* estancado,-a. 3 *fam (stumped)* atascado,-a; *(in difficulties)* en apuros.

**stuck-up** [stʌk'ʌp] adj fam creído,-a, estirado,-a.

**stud** [stʌd] n semental m. COMP stud farm cuadra.

**student** ['stjuːdənt] n 1 *(university)* estudiante mf, universitario,-a; *(school)* alumno,-a. 2 *fml (scholar)* estudioso,-a.
▶ adj estudiantil.

**studio** ['stjuːdɪəʊ] n 1 *(TV, radio)* estudio. 2 *(artist's)* estudio, taller m.
ⓘ pl studios.
▶ n pl studios CINEM estudios mpl.

**studious** ['stjuːdɪəs] adj 1 *(fond of studying)* estudioso,-a, aplicado,-a. 2 *fml (careful)* esmerado,-a; *(deliberate)* deliberado,-a.

**study** ['stʌdɪ] n 1 *(act of studying)* estudio; *(investigation, research)* investigación f, estudio. 2 *(room)* despacho, estudio.
ⓘ pl studies.
▶ vt 1 *(gen)* estudiar; *(university subject)* estudiar, cursar; *(investigate, research)* estudiar, investigar. 2 *(scrutinize)* estudiar, examinar.
▶ vi estudiar.
ⓘ pt & pp studied, ger studying.
▶ n pl studies *(work)* estudios mpl; *(subjects)* estudios mpl, asignaturas fpl.

**stuff** [stʌf] n 1 *fam (matter, material, substance)* materia, material m. 2 *fam (things, possesions)* cosas fpl, trastos mpl. 3 *fam (content)* cuento, rollo, cosas fpl.
▶ vt 1 *(fill - container, bag, box)* llenar (with, de); *(- cushion, toy, food)* rellenar (with, de); *(- hole)* tapar. 2 *(dead animal)* disecar. 3 *(push carelessly, shove)* meter, poner. 4 *fam (beat, thrash)* dar una paliza a. 5 *sl (sod)* meter.

**stuffed** [stʌft] adj 1 *(full)* relleno,-a; *(crammed)* atiborrado,-a. 2 *(animal)* disecado,-a.

**stuffing** ['stʌfɪŋ] n relleno.

**stuffy** ['stʌfɪ] adj 1 *(room)* mal ventilado,-a; *(atmosphere)* cargado,-a. 2 *(person)* estirado,-a, remilgado,-a; *(institution)* tradicional; *(ideas, manners)* formal, serio,-a, convencional.
ⓘ comp stuffier, superl stuffiest.

**stumble** ['stʌmbəl] n tropezón m, traspié m, trompicón m.
▶ vi 1 *(trip)* tropezar (on/over, con), dar un traspié. 2 *(walk unsteadily)* tambalearse. 3 *(while speaking)* atrancarse, atascarse.
◆ to stumble across / stumble on vi insep dar con, tropezar con.

**stun** [stʌn] vt 1 *(make unconscious)* dejar sin sentido; *(daze)* aturdir, atontar, pas-

mar. **2** *(surprise)* sorprender, dejar atónito,-a, dejar pasmado,-a; *(shock)* atolondrar, aturdir, dejar anonadado,-a.
ⓘ *pt & pp* stunned, *ger* stunning.

**stung** [stʌŋ] *pt & pp* → sting.

**stunk** [stʌŋk] *pt & pp* → stink.

**stunning** ['stʌnɪŋ] *adj* **1** *(surprising)* alucinante, apabullante; *(shocking)* asombroso,-a. **2** *(beautiful, impressive)* impresionante, imponente, fenomenal.

**stunt¹** [stʌnt] *vt (growth)* atrofiar.

**stunt²** [stʌnt] *n* **1** *(dangerous act)* proeza; *(in film)* escena peligrosa. **2** *(trick)* truco, maniobra. COMP **stunt man** especialista *m*. ‖ **stunt woman** especialista *f*.

**stunted** ['stʌntɪd] *adj (tree, body)* raquítico,-a; *(growth)* atrofiado,-a.

**stupefy** ['stjuːpɪfaɪ] *vt* **1** *(alcohol, drugs)* atontar, aturdir, aletargar. **2** *(amaze)* dejar pasmado,-a, dejar estupefacto,-a.
ⓘ *pt & pp* stupefied, *ger* stupefying.

**stupid** ['stjuːpɪd] *adj* **1** tonto,-a, bobo,-a, imbécil, estúpido,-a. **2** *(senseless)* atontado,-a. **3** *fam (annoying)* maldito,-a.
ⓘ *comp* stupider, *comp* stupidest.
▸ *n* tonto,-a, imbécil *mf*.

**stupidity** [stjuːˈpɪdɪtɪ] *n* estupidez *f*, tontería.

**stupidly** ['stjuːpɪdlɪ] *adv* estúpidamente, tontamente.

**stupor** ['stjuːpəʳ] *n* estupor *m*.

**sturdy** ['stɜːdɪ] *adj* **1** *(strong)* robusto,-a, fuerte; *(solid)* sólido,-a. **2** *(opposition, resistence, defence)* enérgico,-a, férreo,-a, tenaz, inquebrantable.
ⓘ *comp* sturdier, *superl* sturdiest.

**sturgeon** ['stɜːdʒən] *n* esturión *m*.

**stutter** ['stʌtəʳ] *n* tartamudeo.
▸ *vi* tartamudear.
▸ *vt* decir tartamudeando, balbucear.

**sty¹** [staɪ] *n (for pigs)* pocilga.
ⓘ *pl* sties.

**sty²** [staɪ] *n* → stye.
ⓘ *pl* sties.

**stye** [staɪ] *n (in eye)* orzuelo.

**style** [staɪl] *n* **1** *(gen)* estilo. **2** *(type, model)* modelo, diseño. **3** *(of hair)* peinado. **4** *(fashion)* moda. **5** *fml (correct title)* título. **6** BOT estilo.

▸ *vt* **1** *(gen)* diseñar; *(hair)* peinar. **2** *fml (name, title)* llamar.

**stylish** ['staɪlɪʃ] *adj* **1** *(elegant)* elegante, con mucho estilo. **2** *(fashionable)* a la moda, de última moda.

**stylist** ['staɪlɪst] *n* **1** *(hairdresser)* estilista *mf*, peluquero,-a. **2** *(writer)* estilista *mf*.

**stylized** ['staɪlaɪzd] *adj* estilizado,-a.

**stylus** ['staɪləs] *n* **1** *(of record player)* aguja. **2** *(for writing)* estilo.
ⓘ *pl* styluses o styli .

**suave** [swɑːv] *adj (charming, polite)* afable, cortés; *(slick, ingratiating)* zalamero,-a.

❌ Suave no significa 'suave', que se traduce por soft.

**sub** [sʌb] *n* **1** *(submarine)* submarino. **2** SP *(substitute)* sustituto,-a, suplente *mf*. **3** *(subscription)* cuota, subscripción *f*, suscripción *f*. **4** *(subeditor)* redactor,-ra. **5** GB *(advance from wages)* anticipo.
▸ *vi (act as substitute)* sustituir (for, a).
▸ *vt* **1** GB *(give an advance)* anticipar, dar un anticipo. **2** *(subedit)* corregir, revisar.
ⓘ *pt & pp* subbed, *ger* subbing.

**subconscious** [sʌbˈkɒnʃəs] *adj* subconsciente.
▸ *n* **the subconscious** el subconsciente *m*.

**subcontinent** [sʌbˈkɒntɪnənt] *n* subcontinente *m*.

**subcontract** [*(n)* sʌbˈkɒntrækt; *(vb)* sʌbkənˈtrækt] *n* subcontrato.
▸ *vt* subcontratar (to, a).

**subculture** ['sʌbkʌltʃəʳ] *n* subcultura.

**subdivide** [sʌbdɪˈvaɪd] *vt* subdividir (into, en).

**subgroup** ['sʌbɡruːp] *n* subgrupo.

**subhuman** [sʌbˈhjuːmən] *adj* infrahumano,-a.

**subject** [*(n-adj)* 'sʌbdʒekt; *(vb)* səbˈdʒekt] *n* **1** *(theme, topic)* tema *m*. **2** EDUC asignatura. **3** *(citizen)* súbdito, ciudadano,-a. **4** LING sujeto. **5** *(cause)* objeto (of/for, de). **6** *(of experiment)* sujeto.
▸ *vt (bring under control)* someter, sojuzgar (to, a).
▸ *adj (subordinate, governed)* sometido,-a.
**subject to** *(bound by)* sujeto,-a a; *(prone to - floods, subsidence)* expuesto,-a a; *(- change, delay)* susceptible de, suje-

**S**

to,-a a; *(- illness)* propenso,-a a. COMP
**subject matter 1** *(topic)* tema *m*, materia. **2** *(contents)* contenido.

▸ *prep* **subject to** *(conditional on)* previo, -a, supeditado,-a a.

◆ **to subject to** *vt sep* someter a.

**subjective** [səbˈdʒɛktɪv] *adj* subjetivo,-a.

**subjunctive** [səbˈdʒʌŋktɪv] *adj* LING subjuntivo,-a.

▸ *n* LING subjuntivo.

**sublet** [sʌbˈlet] *vt* realquilar, subarrendar.

▸ *vi* realquilar, subarrendar.

ⓘ *pt & pp* **sublet**, *ger* **subletting**.

**sublime** [səˈblaɪm] *adj* **1** *(beauty, music, compliment, etc)* sublime. **2** *fam (food, performance)* maravilloso,-a, sensacional. **3** *pej (indifference, ignorance, etc)* sumo,-a, supremo,-a, absoluto,-a, total.

▸ *n* **the sublime** lo sublime.

**subliminal** [sʌbˈlɪmɪnəl] *adj* subliminal.

**sub-machine-gun** [sʌbməˈʃiːngʌn] *n* ametralladora, metralleta.

**submarine** [ˈsʌbməriːn] *n* submarino.

▸ *adj* submarino,-a.

**submerge** [səbˈmɜːdʒ] *vt* sumergir (in, en).

▸ *vi* sumergirse.

**submission** [səbˈmɪʃən] *n* **1** *(subjection)* sumisión *f* (to, a). **2** SP *(in wrestling)* rendición *f*. **3** *(presentation)* presentación *f*. **4** *(report)* informe *m*; *(proposal)* propuesta.

**submit** [səbˈmɪt] *vt* **1** *(present)* presentar. **2** *(subject)* someter (to, a). **3** JUR *(suggest)* sostener.

▸ *vi (admit defeat, surrender)* rendirse, ceder; *(to demand, wishes)* acceder.

ⓘ *pt & pp* **submitted**, *ger* **submitting**.

**subnormal** [sʌbˈnɔːməl] *adj* **1** *(person)* subnormal, retrasado,-a. **2** *(temperatures)* por debajo de lo normal.

**subordinate** [(*adj-n*) səˈbɔːdɪnət; *(vb)* səˈbɔːdɪneɪt] *adj* **1** *(lower, less important)* subordinado,-a (to, a), secundario, -a. **2** LING subordinado,-a. COMP **subordinate clause** oración *f* subordinada.

▸ *n (person)* subordinado,-a, subalterno,-a.

▸ *vt* subordinar (to, a), supeditar (to, a).

**subordination** [səbɔːdɪˈneɪʃən] *n* subordinación *f*.

**subscribe** [səbˈskraɪb] *vi* **1** *(to newspaper, etc)* suscribirse (to, a), abonarse (to, a). **2** *(to charity)* hacer donaciones, contribuir con donativos (to, a). **3** *(to opinion, theory)* suscribir (to, -), estar de acuerdo (to, con). **4** FIN *(shares)* suscribir (for, -).

▸ *vt* **1** *(contribute)* contribuir, donar. **2** *fml (sign)* suscribir.

**subscriber** [səbˈskraɪbəʳ] *n (to newspaper, etc)* suscriptor,-ra, abonado,-a; *(to telephone service, cable television)* abonado,-a.

**subscription** [səbˈskrɪpʃən] *n (to newspaper, etc)* suscripción *f*, abono; *(to club)* cuota; *(to charity)* donativo, donación *f*.

**subsection** [ˈsʌbsekʃən] *n* JUR *(in document, text)* artículo.

**subsequent** [ˈsʌbsɪkwənt] *adj* subsiguiente, posterior. LOC **subsequent to** posterior a.

**subside** [səbˈsaɪd] *vi* **1** *(land, building, road)* hundirse. **2** *fig (person)* dejarse caer. **3** *(storm, wind)* amainar; *(floods)* decrecer, bajar; *(pain, fever)* disminuir; *(noise, applause)* irse apagando; *(anger, excitement)* calmarse.

**subsidiary** [səbˈsɪdɪərɪ] *adj* **1** *(role, interest, issue)* secundario,-a. **2** *(income)* adicional, extra; *(payment, loan)* subsidiario,-a.

▸ *n* COMM filial *f*.

ⓘ *pl* **subsidiaries**.

**subsidize** [ˈsʌbsɪdaɪz] *vt (gen)* subvencionar; *(exports)* primar.

**subsidy** [ˈsʌbsɪdɪ] *n* subvención *f*, subsidio.

ⓘ *pl* **subsidies**.

**subsist** [səbˈsɪst] *vi* subsistir.

**subsistence** [səbˈsɪstəns] *n* subsistencia.

**subsoil** [ˈsʌbsɔɪl] *n* subsuelo.

**substance** [ˈsʌbstəns] *n* **1** *(matter)* sustancia. **2** *(real matter, solid content)* sustancia, solidez *f*. **3** *(essence, gist)* esencia, sustancia. **4** *(wealth)* riqueza.

**substantial** [səbˈstænʃəl] *adj* **1** *(solid)* sólido,-a, fuerte. **2** *(large - sum, increase, loss, damage)* importante, considerable; *(- difference, change)* sustancial, notable. **3** *(meal - large)* abundante; *(nourishing)* sustancioso,-a. **4** *(wealthy)* acaudalado,-a. **5** *fml (real, tangible)* sustancial.

**substantiate** [səb'stænʃɪeɪt] *vt (gen)* confirmar, corroborar; *(accusation)* probar.

**substantive** ['sʌbstəntɪv] *adj fml (research, information, evidence)* sustantivo, -a; *(matter, issue)* fundamental.
▶ *n* LING sustantivo.

**substitute** ['sʌbstɪtjuːt] *n* **1** *(person)* sustituto,-a, suplente *mf*. **2** *(thing)* sucedáneo *(for, de)*.
▶ *vt* sustituir, reemplazar.
▶ *vi* sustituir, suplir *(for, a)*.

**substitution** [sʌbstɪ'tjuːʃ°n] *n* sustitución *f*.

**subterranean** [sʌbtə'reɪnɪən] *adj* subterráneo,-a.

**subtitle** ['sʌbtaɪt°l] *n* subtítulo.
▶ *vt* subtitular, poner subtítulos a.

**subtle** ['sʌt°l] *adj* **1** *(person - tactful)* delicado,-a, discreto,-a. **2** *(colour, difference, hint, joke)* sutil; *(taste)* delicado,-a, ligero,-a; *(lighting)* tenue, sutil. **3** *(remark, mind)* agudo,-a, perspicaz; *(plan, argument, analysis)* ingenioso,-a; *(irony)* fino,-a.
ⓘ *comp* subtler, *comp* subtlest.

**subtotal** [sʌb'təʊt°l] *n* subtotal *m*.

**subtract** [səb'trækt] *vt* restar *(from, de)*.

**subtraction** [səb'træk[°n] *n* resta.

**subtropical** [sʌb'trɒpɪk°l] *adj* subtropical.

**suburb** ['sʌbɜːb] *n* barrio residencial.
COMP **the suburbs** las afueras *fpl*.

❌ Suburb no significa 'suburbio (barrio desfavorecido', que se traduce por **slums**.

**suburban** [sə'bɜːb°n] *adj (area)* de los barrios residenciales; *(attitude)* convencional.

**suburbia** [sə'bɜːbɪə] *n* los barrios *mpl* residenciales.

**subversion** [sʌb'vɜːʃ°n] *n* subversión *f*.

**subversive** [sʌb'vɜːsɪv] *adj* subversivo,-a.
▶ *n (person)* elemento subversivo.

**subway** ['sʌbweɪ] *n* **1** GB *(underpass)* paso subterráneo. **2** US *(underground)* metro.

**succeed** [sək'siːd] *vi* **1** *(be successful - person)* tener éxito, triunfar; *(- plan, marriage)* salir bien; *(- strike)* surtir efecto, dar resultado. **2** *(manage)* lograr, conseguir. **3** *(throne)* subir *(to, a)*; *(title)* heredar *(to, -)*.
▶ *vt* **1** *(take place of)* suceder a. **2** *fml (follow after)* suceder a.

❌ To succeed no significa 'suceder', que se traduce por **to happen**.

**succeeding** [sək'siːdɪŋ] *adj* subsiguiente.

**success** [sək'ses] *n* **1** *(good result, achievement)* éxito. **2** *(successful person, thing)* éxito.

❌ Success no significa 'suceso', que se traduce por **event**.

**successful** [sək'sesfʊl] *adj (person, career, film)* de éxito; *(plan, performance, attempt)* acertado,-a, logrado,-a; *(business)* próspero,-a; *(marriage)* feliz; *(meeting)* satisfactorio,-a, positivo,-a.

**successfully** [sʌk'sesfʊlɪ] *adv* con éxito, satisfactoriamente.

**succession** [sək'se[°n] *n* **1** *(act of following)* sucesión *f*. **2** *(series)* serie *f*, sucesión *f*. **3** *(to post, throne)* sucesión *f*.

**successive** [sək'sesɪv] *adj* sucesivo,-a, consecutivo,-a.

**successor** [sək'sesəʳ] *n* sucesor,-ra.

**succulent** ['sʌkjələnt] *adj* **1** *(juicy)* suculento,-a. **2** BOT carnoso,-a.
▶ *n* BOT planta carnosa, suculenta.

**such** [sʌtʃ] *adj* **1** *(of that sort)* tal, semejante. **2** *(so much, so great)* tal, tanto,-a.
▶ *adv (so very)* tan.
▶ *pron (of that specified sort)* tal. LOC **as such** **1** *(strictly speaking)* propiamente dicho. **2** *(that way)* como tal. ‖ **in such a way that...** de tal manera que... ‖ **such as** *(like, for example)* como. ‖ **such as?** ¿por ejemplo?

**suck** [sʌk] *vt* **1** *(person - liquid)* sorber; *(- lollipop, pencil, thumb, etc)* chupar; *(insect - blood, nectar)* chupar, succionar. **2** *(vacuum cleaner)* aspirar *(in, -)*; *(pump)* succionar, aspirar *(in, -)*; *(plant)* absorber *(up, -)*. **3** *(draw powerfully)* arrastrar.
▶ *vi* **1** *(person)* chupar *(at/on, -)*; *(baby)* mamar *(at, -)*; *(vacuum cleaner)* aspirar *(up,-)*; *(pump)* succionar, aspirar.

S

**sucker** [ˈsʌkəʳ] n 1 ZOOL ventosa. 2 BOT chupón m, mamón m. 3 (rubber disc) ventosa.

**suckle** [ˈsʌkəl] vt amamantar, dar de mamar a.
▶ vi mamar.

**sucrose** [ˈsjuːkrəʊz] n sacarosa.

**suction** [ˈsʌkʃən] n (sticking together) succión f; (of water, air) aspiración f. COMP suction cup ventosa. ▌ suction pump bomba de aspiración.

**Sudan** [suːˈdæn] [also the Sudan] n Sudán.

**Sudanese** [suːdəˈniːz] adj sudanés, -esa.
▶ n sudanés,-esa.
▶ n pl the Sudanese los sudaneses mpl.

**sudden** [ˈsʌdən] adj 1 (quick) súbito,-a, repentino,-a. 2 (unexpected) inesperado,-a, imprevisto,-a. 3 (abrupt) brusco,-a. LOC all of a sudden de repente. COMP sudden death muerte f súbita.

**suddenly** [ˈsʌdənlɪ] adv 1 (unexpectedly) de repente, de pronto. 2 (abruptly) bruscamente.

**suds** [sʌdz] n pl jabonaduras fpl, espuma f sing (de jabón).

**sue** [suː] vt JUR demandar.
▶ vi JUR entablar una demanda (for, por).

**suede** [sweɪd] n ante m, gamuza f.
▶ adj de ante, de gamuza.

**suet** [ˈsuːɪt] n sebo.

**suffer** [ˈsʌfəʳ] vt 1 (gen) sufrir; (pain) padecer, sufrir; (hunger) padecer, pasar; (losses) sufrir, registrar. 2 (bear, tolerate) aguantar, soportar, tolerar.
▶ vi 1 (gen) sufrir. 2 (be affected - work, studies, etc) verse afectado,-a; (- health) resentirse: LOC to suffer from 1 (illness) sufrir de, padecer. 2 (shock) sufrir los efectos de. 3 (effects) resentirse de.

**sufferer** [ˈsʌfərəʳ] n enfermo,-a.

**suffering** [ˈsʌfərɪŋ] n (affliction) sufrimiento, aflicción f; (grief) pena, dolor m; (pain) dolor m.

**sufficient** [səˈfɪʃənt] adj suficiente, bastante. LOC to be sufficient bastar.

**suffix** [ˈsʌfɪks] n sufijo.

**suffocate** [ˈsʌfəkeɪt] vt asfixiar, ahogar.
▶ vi asfixiarse, ahogarse.

⊠ To suffocate no significa 'sofocar (un incendio)', que se traduce por to put out.

**suffocation** [sʌfəˈkeɪʃən] n asfixia, ahogo.

**suffrage** [ˈsʌfrɪdʒ] n sufragio.

**sugar** [ˈʃʊgəʳ] n 1 azúcar m & f. 2 US fam (form of address) cariño, cielo. COMP sugar beet remolacha azucarera.
▶ vt azucarar.

**sugar-coated** [ʃʊgəˈkəʊtɪd] adj cubierto,-a de azúcar.

**suggest** [səˈdʒest] vt 1 (propose) sugerir, proponer; (advise) sugerir, aconsejar. 2 (imply) insinuar. 3 (indicate) indicar. 4 (evoke) evocar, sugerir.

**suggestion** [səˈdʒestʃən] n 1 (proposal) sugerencia, propuesta. 2 (insinuation) insinuación f. 3 (indication, hint) indicio; (slight trace) sombra, traza, asomo, nota. 4 (in psychology) sugestión f.

**suggestive** [səˈdʒestɪv] adj (with sexual connotations) provocativo,-a, insinuante.

**suicidal** [suːɪˈsaɪdəl] adj suicida.

**suicide** [ˈsuːɪsaɪd] n 1 (act) suicidio. 2 (person) suicida mf. 3 fig suicidio. COMP to commit suicide suicidarse.

**suit** [suːt] n 1 (man's) traje m; (woman's) traje m de chaqueta. 2 JUR pleito, juicio. 3 (in cards) palo.
▶ vt 1 (be convenient, acceptable) convenir a, venir bien a; (please) satisfacer, agradar, contentar. 2 (be right for) ir bien a, sentar bien a; (look good on) quedar bien a, favorecer. 3 (adapt) adaptar (to, a), ajustar (to, a).

**suitable** [ˈsuːtəbəl] adj 1 (appropriate) adecuado,-a (for, para), apropiado, -a (for, para); (for job, post) adecuado,-a, indicado,-a, idóneo,-a. 2 (acceptable, proper) apropiado,-a, apto,-a. 3 (convenient) conveniente.

**suitcase** [ˈsuːtkeɪs] n maleta.

**suite** [swiːt] n 1 (of furniture) juego. 2 (in hotel) suite f. 3 MUS suite f. 4 (retinue) séquito, comitiva. 5 COMPUT juego.

**suited** ['suːtɪd] *adj* apropiado,-a (for, para), adecuado,-a (for, para).

**sulk** [sʌlk] *vi* enfurruñarse, estar de mal humor.
▶ *n* malhumor *m*.

**sulky** ['sʌlkɪ] *adj* (look, mood) malhumorado,-a; (person) con tendencia a enfurruñarse.
ⓘ *comp* sulkier, *superl* sulkiest.

**sullen** ['sʌlən] *adj* **1** (person, mood) hosco,-a, arisco,-a, huraño,-a; (face) adusto,-a.

**sully** ['sʌlɪ] *vt* **1** (dirty) ensuciar. **2** *fig* (tarnish, spoil) manchar, mancillar.
ⓘ *pt & pp* sullied, *ger* sullying.

**sultan** ['sʌltⁿn] *n* sultán *m*.

**sultry** ['sʌltrɪ] *adj* **1** (weather) bochornoso,-a, sofocante. **2** (person) sensual.
ⓘ *comp* sultrier, *superl* sultriest.

**sum** [sʌm] *n* **1** MATH (calculation) cuenta; (addition) suma, adición *f*. **2** (amount of money) suma (de dinero), cantidad *f* (de dinero). **3** (total amount) suma, total *m*. [COMP] **in sum** en resumen. ‖ [LOC] **the sum total** total *m*.
▶ *n pl* **sums** aritmética *f sing*, cálculos *mpl*.
◆ **to sum up** *vt sep* **1** (summarize) resumir, hacer un resumen de, sintetizar. **2** (size up - situation) evaluar; (- person) catalogar.
▶ *vi* (summarize) resumir; (of judge) recapitular.
ⓘ *pt & pp* summed, *ger* summing.

**summarize** ['sʌmərɑɪz] *vt* resumir, hacer un resumen de.

**summary** ['sʌmərɪ] *n* (gen) resumen *m*.
ⓘ *pl* summaries.
▶ *adj* **1** JUR (justice, punishment) sumario, -a: *summary trial* juicio sumario. **2** (immediate - dismissal) inmediato,-a. **3** (brief - account) breve, corto,-a. [LOC] **in summary** en resumen.

**summer** ['sʌmə'] *n* **1** (gen) verano. **2** *lit* abril *m*.
▶ *adj* (gen) de verano; (summery) veraniego,-a.

**summertime** ['sʌmətɑɪm] *n* verano, estío *m*.

**summit** ['sʌmɪt] *n* **1** (of mountain, career) cumbre *f*, cima *f*. **2** (meeting) cumbre *f*.

**summon** ['sʌmən] *vt* **1** (person) llamar; (meeting, parliament) convocar. **2** JUR citar, emplazar.
◆ **to summon up** *vt insep* **1** (courage) armarse de; (strength) reunir, cobrar; (support) lograr, obtener; (resources, help) reunir, conseguir. **2** (memories, thoughts) evocar.

**sumptuous** ['sʌmptjʊəs] *adj* (gen) suntuoso,-a; (meal) opíparo,-a.

**sun** [sʌn] *n* (gen) sol *m*.

**sunbathe** ['sʌnbeɪð] *vi* tomar el sol.

**sunbeam** ['sʌnbiːm] *n* rayo de sol.

**sunbed** ['sʌnbed] *n* cama solar.

**sunburn** ['sʌnbɜːn] *n* quemadura de sol.

**sunburnt** ['sʌnbɜːnt] *adj* (burnt) quemado,-a (por el sol); (tanned) bronceado, -a, moreno,-a.

**Sunday** ['sʌndɪ] *n* domingo.

✎ Para ejemplos de uso, consulta **Saturday**.

**sundial** ['sʌndaɪəl] *n* reloj *m* de sol.

**sundown** ['sʌndaʊn] *n* US puesta de(l) sol.

**sun-dried** ['sʌndraɪd] *adj* secado,-a al sol.

**sunflower** ['sʌnflaʊə'] *n* girasol *m*. [COMP] **sunflower seed** semilla de girasol, pipa.

**sung** [sʌŋ] *pp* → **sing**.

**sunglasses** ['sʌnglɑːsɪz] *n pl* gafas *fpl* de sol.

**sunhat** ['sʌnhæt] *n* pamela, sombrero de ala ancha.

**sunk** [sʌŋk] *pp* → **sink**.

**sunken** ['sʌŋkən] *adj* **1** (ship, treasure) hundido,-a, sumergido,-a; (eyes, cheeks) hundido,-a. **2** (terrace, bath) a un nivel más bajo.

**sunlight** ['sʌnlaɪt] *n* sol *m*, luz *f* del sol.

**sunlit** ['sʌnlɪt] *adj* soleado,-a.

**sunny** ['sʌnɪ] *adj* **1** (room, house, etc) soleado,-a; (day) de sol. **2** *fig* (person) alegre, risueño,-a; (future) risueño,-a.
ⓘ *comp* sunnier, *superl* sunniest.

**sunrise** ['sʌnraɪz] *n* (sun-up) salida del sol; (dawn) amanecer *m*, alba *m*.

**sunroof** ['sʌnruːf] *n* **1** AUTO capota, techo corredizo. **2** (on building) azotea.

**S**

**sunset** ['sʌnset] *n (sundown)* puesta de(l) sol, ocaso; *(twilight)* crepúsculo, atardecer *m*.

**sunshade** ['sʌnʃeɪd] *n* **1** *(parasol)* sombrilla. **2** *(awning)* toldo.

**sunshine** ['sʌnʃaɪn] *n* **1** sol *m*, luz *f* de sol. **2** fig alegría. **3** GB fam *(friendly form of address)* corazón, majo,-a; *(sarcastic)* guapo,-a.

**sunstroke** ['sʌnstrəʊk] *n* insolación *f*.

**suntan** ['sʌntæn] *n* bronceado, moreno. COMP **suntan lotion** bronceador *m*.

**sun-tanned** ['sʌntænd] *adj* bronceado,-a, moreno,-a.

**super** ['suːpəʳ] *adj* fam genial, súper, fenomenal, de primera.
▸ *n* **1** GB *(superintendent)* comisario,-a de policía. **2** US *(superintendent)* portero,-a.

**superb** [suːˈpɜːb] *adj* estupendo,-a, magnífico,-a, espléndido,-a, soberbio,-a.

**superbly** [suːˈpɜːblɪ] *adv* estupendamente, magníficamente, espléndidamente, soberbiamente.

**supercilious** [suːpəˈsɪlɪəs] *adj (condescending)* altanero,-a; *(disdainful)* desdeñoso,-a.

**superficial** [suːpəˈfɪʃəl] *adj (gen)* superficial.

**superfluous** [suːˈpɜːflʊəs] *adj (gen)* superfluo,-a; *(remark, comment)* de más.

**superhuman** [suːpəˈhjuːmən] *adj* sobrehumano,-a.

**superintendent** [suːpərɪnˈtendənt] *n* **1** *(person in charge - gen)* director,-ra, inspector,-ra, supervisor,-ra. **2** GB *(in police)* comisario,-a de policía. **3** US *(in apartment building)* portero,-a, conserje *mf*. **4** *(of park)* encargado,-a.

**superior** [suːˈpɪərɪəʳ] *adj* **1** *(gen)* superior (to, a). **2** *pej (attitude, tone, smile)* de superioridad.
▸ *n (senior)* superior *mf*.

**superiority** [suːpɪərɪˈbrɪtɪ] *n* superioridad *f*.

**superlative** [suːˈpɜːlətɪv] *adj* **1** *(excellent)* superlativo,-a, de primera, excelente, excepcional. **2** LING superlativo,-a.
▸ *n* LING superlativo.

**superman** ['suːpəmæn] *n* superhombre *m*.
ⓘ *pl* **supermen** ['suːpəmən].

**supermarket** [suːpəˈmɑːkɪt] *n* supermercado, autoservicio.

**supernatural** [suːpəˈnætʃ³rəl] *adj* sobrenatural.
▸ *n* **the supernatural** lo sobrenatural *m*.

**superpower** ['suːpəpaʊəʳ] *n* superpotencia.

**supersonic** [suːpəˈsɒnɪk] *adj* supersónico,-a.

**superstar** ['suːpəstɑːʳ] *n* superestrella.

**superstition** [suːpəˈstɪʃ³n] *n* superstición *f*.

**superstitious** [sjuːpəˈstɪʃəs] *adj* supersticioso,-a.

**superstore** ['suːpəstɔːʳ] *n* hipermercado.

**superstructure** ['suːpəstrʌktʃəʳ] *n* superestructura.

**supertanker** ['suːpətæŋkəʳ] *n* superpetrolero.

**supervise** ['suːpəvaɪz] *vt* **1** *(watch over)* vigilar. **2** *(keep check on)* supervisar; *(run)* dirigir.

**supervision** [suːpəˈvɪʒ³n] *n* supervisión *f*.

**supervisor** ['suːpəvaɪzəʳ] *n* **1** *(gen)* supervisor,-ra. **2** GB *(of thesis)* director,-ra de tesis.

**superwoman** ['suːpəwʊmən] *n* supermujer *f*.
ⓘ *pl* **superwomen** ['suːpəwɪmɪn].

**supper** ['sʌpəʳ] *n* cena. LOC **to have supper** cenar.

**supper-time** ['sʌpətaɪm] *n* hora de cenar.

**supplement** [*(n)* 'sʌplɪmənt]; *(vb)* 'sʌplɪment] *n* **1** *(charge)* suplemento. **2** *(dietary)* complemento. **3** LIT suplemento.
▸ *vt* complementar.

**supplementary** [sʌplɪˈment³rɪ] *adj* **1** *(gen)* suplementario,-a, adicional. **2** MATH suplementario,-a.

**supplier** [səˈplaɪəʳ] *n* COMM proveedor, -ra, abastecedor,-ra.

**supply** [səˈplaɪ] *n* **1** *(provision)* suministro. **2** COMM *(provision - to markets, areas, etc)* abastecimiento; *(- to individuals,* *houses, shops, etc)* suministro. **3** *(amount available)* reserva.

ⓘ *pl* supplies.

▶ *vt* **1** *(goods, materials)* suministrar. **2** *(a person, company, city, etc)* abastecer (with, de), proveer (with, de). **3** *(give - information, proof, facts)* facilitar, proporcionar. **4** MIL *(with provisions)* aprovisionar. **5** *fml (need, requirement)* satisfacer.

ⓘ *pt & pp* supplied, *ger* supplying.

▶ *n pl* supplies *(food)* provisiones *fpl*, víveres *mpl*; *(stock)* existencias *fpl*, stock *m*. MIL pertrechos *mpl*.

**support** [sə'pɔːt] *n* **1** *(physical - gen)* apoyo, sostén *m*; *(- thing worn on body)* protector *m*. **2** *(of building)* soporte *m*, puntal *m*. **3** *(moral)* apoyo, respaldo. **4** *(financial)* ayuda económica, apoyo económico; *(sustenance)* sustento; *(person)* sostén *m*. **5** *(supporters)* afición *f*. **6** *(evidence)* pruebas *fpl*.

▶ *vt* **1** *(roof, bridge, etc)* sostener; *(weight)* aguantar, resistir; *(part of body)* sujetar. **2** *(back, encourage)* apoyar, respaldar, ayudar; *(cause, motion, proposal)* apoyar, estar de acuerdo con. **3** SP *(follow)* seguir; *(encourage)* animar. **4** *(keep, sustain)* mantener, sustentar, sostener; *(feed)* alimentar. **5** *(corroborate, substantiate)* confirmar, respaldar, apoyar, respaldar. **6** *fml (endure)* soportar, tolerar.

✖ To support no significa 'soportar (sufrir)', que se traduce por to bear.

**supporter** [sə'pɔːtəʳ] *n* **1** POL partidario,-a. **2** SP *(gen)* seguidor,-ra; *(fan)* hincha *mf*, forofo,-a.

▶ *n pl* supporters SP la afición *f sing*.
COMP supporters' club peña deportiva.

**supporting** [sə'pɔːtɪŋ] *adj (part, role)* secundario,-a.

**suppose** [sə'pəʊz] *vt* **1** *(assume, imagine)* suponer, imaginarse. **2** *(in polite requests)*: I don't suppose you could lend me £10, could you? no podrías dejarme 10 libras, ¿no? **3** *(believe)* creer. **4** *(postulate)* suponer. **5** *fml (presuppose)* suponer. LOC I suppose not supongo que no. ‖ I suppose so supongo que sí.

▶ *conj* **1** *(hypothesis)* ¿y si…?, pongamos por caso, supongamos. **2** *(making suggestions)* ¿y si…?, ¿qué tal si…?

**supposed** [sə'pəʊzd] *adj* supuesto,-a.
LOC to be supposed to **1** *(supposition, reputation)* se supone que, dicen que. **2** *(obligation, responsibility)* deber, tener que. **3** *(intention)* se supone que.

**supposing** [sə'pəʊzɪŋ] *conj* **1** *(hypothesis)* ¿y si…?, suponiendo. **2** *(making suggestions)* ¿y si…?, ¿qué tal si…?

**suppository** [sə'pɒzɪtᵊrɪ] *n* supositorio.
ⓘ *pl* suppositories.

**supremacy** [suː'preməsɪ] *n* supremacía.

**supreme** [suː'priːm] *adj (highest)* supremo,-a, sumo,-a; *(greatest)* supremo,-a.

**supremo** [sʊ'priːməʊ] *n* GB *fam* gran jefe,-a.
ⓘ *pl* supremos.

**surcharge** ['sɜːtʃɑːdʒ] *n* recargo, sobretasa.

▶ *vt (person)* aplicar un recargo a.

**sure** [ʃʊəʳ] *adj* **1** *(positive, certain)* seguro,-a (about/of, de); *(convinced)* convencido,-a. **2** *(certain, inevitable)* seguro,-a. **3** *(reliable)* seguro,-a.

▶ *adv* **1** *(of course)* claro, por supuesto. **2** US *(as intensifier)* realmente, de verdad.

**surely** ['ʃʊəlɪ] *adv* **1** *(doubtless)* seguramente, sin duda. **2** *(as intensifier)*: surely you haven't forgotten! ¡no se te habrá olvidado! **3** *(in a sure manner)* con seguridad. **4** US *(certainly)* por supuesto, desde luego, claro (que sí).

**surf** [sɜːf] *n (waves)* olas *fpl*, oleaje *m*; *(foam)* espuma.

▶ *vi* hacer surf. LOC to surf the net navegar en Internet.

**surface** ['sɜːfɪs] *n* **1** *(gen)* superficie *f*; *(of road)* firme *m*. **2** *fig (exterior)* apariencia.

▶ *adj (gen)* superficial.

▶ *vt (cover road)* pavimentar; *(with asphalt)* asfaltar.

▶ *vi* **1** *(submarine, etc)* salir a la superficie; *(problems, etc)* aflorar, aparecer, surgir. **2** *(from bed)* asomarse, dejarse ver; *(after disappearance)* reaparecer.

**surfboard** ['sɜːfbɔːd] *n* tabla de surf.

**surfer** ['sɜːfəʳ] *n* surfista *mf*.

**surfing** ['sɜːfɪŋ] *n* surf *m*.

**S**

**surgeon** ['sɜ:dʒ°n] *n* cirujano,-a.

**surgery** ['sɜ:dʒərɪ] *n* **1** *(operating)* cirugía. **2** GB *(place)* consultorio, consulta; *(time)* consulta.
ⓘ *pl* surgeries.

**surgical** ['sɜ:dʒɪk°l] *adj (instrument, treatment)* quirúrgico,-a.

**Surinam** ['sʊərɪ'næm] *n* Surinam.

**surmount** [sɜ:'maʊnt] *vt* **1** *(overcome)* superar, vencer. **2** ARCH rematar, coronar.

**surname** ['sɜ:neɪm] *n* apellido.

**surpass** [sɜ:'pɑ:s] *vt (better)* superar; *(exceed)* superar, sobrepasar.

**surplus** ['sɜ:pləs] *n (of goods, produce)* excedente *m*, sobrante *m*; *(of budget)* superávit *m*.
▶ *adj* sobrante, excedente.

**surprise** [sə'praɪz] *n* sorpresa.
▶ *adj (visit, result)* inesperado,-a; *(attack, party)* sorpresa.
▶ *vt* **1** *(cause surprise to)* sorprender. **2** *(catch unawares)* sorprender, coger desprevenido,-a.

**surprised** [sə'praɪzd] *adj (person)* sorprendido,-a; *(look)* de sorpresa.

**surprising** [sə'praɪzɪŋ] *adj* sorprendente.

**surreal** [sə'rɪəl] *adj* surrealista.

**surrealism** [sə'rɪəlɪz°m] *n* surrealismo.

**surrealist** [sə'rɪəlɪst] *n* surrealista *mf*.
▶ *adj* surrealista.

**surrender** [sə'rendə'] *n* **1** *(capitulation)* rendición *f*; *(submission)* sumisión *f*, claudicación *f*. **2** *(giving up - of arms)* entrega; *(- of rights)* renuncia.
▶ *vt* **1** MIL *(weapons, town)* rendir, entregar. **2** *fml (passport, ticket, etc)* entregar; *(claim, right, privilege)* renunciar a, ceder.
▶ *vi* rendirse, entregarse.

**surround** [sə'raʊnd] *vt (encircle)* rodear (with, de).
▶ *n* marco, borde *m*.

**surrounding** [sə'raʊndɪŋ] *adj* circundante.
▶ *n pl* **surroundings** *(of town, city, etc)* alrededores *mpl fpl. (environment)* entorno, ambiente *m*.

**surveillance** [sɜ:'veɪləns] *n* vigilancia.

**survey** [(n) 'sɜ:veɪ; (vb) sə'veɪ] *n* **1** *(investigation - of opinion)* sondeo, encuesta; *(- of prices, trends, etc)* estudio; *(written report)* informe *m*. **2** *(of land)* inspección *f*, reconocimiento; *(in topography)* medición *f*. **3** *(general view)* visión *f* general, visión *f* de conjunto. **4** GB *(of house, building)* inspección *f*, peritaje *m*.
▶ *vt* **1** *(contemplate, look at)* contemplar, mirar. **2** *(study - gen)* examinar, analizar; *(- prices, trends, etc)* estudiar, hacer una encuesta sobre; *(investigate - people)* encuestar, hacer un sondeo de. **3** *(- land)* hacer un reconocimiento de; *(in topography)* medir. **4** *(house, building)* inspeccionar, hacer un peritaje de.

**surveyor** [sə'veɪə'] *n (of land)* agrimensor,-ra, topógrafo,-a; *(of house, building)* perito,-a.

**survival** [sə'vaɪv°l] *n* **1** *(gen)* supervivencia. **2** *(relic)* reliquia, vestigio (from, de).

**survive** [sə'vaɪv] *vi* **1** *(gen)* sobrevivir; *(custom, tradition)* sobrevivir, perdurar; *(book, painting)* conservarse. **2** *fam (cope, get by)* ir tirando, arreglárselas.
▶ *vt* **1** *(disaster)* sobrevivir a. **2** *(person)* sobrevivir a.

**survivor** [sə'vaɪvə'] *n* superviviente *mf*, sobreviviente *mf*.

**suspect** [(adj-n) 'sʌspekt; (vb) sə'spekt] *adj (suspicious)* sospechoso,-a; *(dubious, questionable)* dudoso,-a.
▶ *n (person)* sospechoso,-a.
▶ *vt* **1** *(believe guilty)* sospechar de; *(mistrust)* recelar de, desconfiar de, dudar de. **2** *(think true)* sospechar. **3** *(suppose, guess)* imaginarse, creer.

**suspend** [sə'spend] *vt* **1** *(stop temporarily)* suspender; *(postpone)* posponer, aplazar. **2** *(remove)* suspender. **3** *(hang)* suspender, colgar.

❌ To suspend no significa 'suspender (un examen)', que se traduce por to fail.

**suspense** [səs'spens] *n (anticipation)* incertidumbre *f*; *(intrigue)* suspense *m*, intriga.

**suspension** [sə'spenʃ°n] *n* **1** *(halt)* suspensión *f*; *(postponement)* aplazamiento, postergación *f*. **2** *(of employee, player)* suspensión *f*; *(of pupil)* expulsión *f*. **3**

CHEM suspensión *f*. **4** TECH suspensión *f*. COMP **suspension points** puntos suspensivos.

**suspicion** [sə'spɪʃ°n] *n* **1** *(gen)* sospecha; *(mistrust)* recelo, desconfianza; *(doubt)* duda; *(hunch)* presentimiento. **2** *(slight trace)* pizca, asomo, atisbo.

**suspicious** [sə'spɪʃəs] *adj* **1** *(arousing suspicion)* sospechoso,-a. **2** *(distrustful, wary)* desconfiado,-a, suspicaz.

**sustain** [sə'steɪn] *vt* **1** *(keep alive - gen)* sustentar; *(- spirits, hope)* mantener. **2** *(maintain - gen)* sostener; *(- interest, conversation)* mantener; *(- work)* continuar. **3** MUS *(note)* sostener. **4** *fml (suffer - loss, injury, wound, etc)* sufrir. **5** *fml (hold up)* sostener. **6** JUR admitir.

**sustainable** [sə'steɪnəb°l] *adj* sostenible.

**suture** ['sʌtʃə'] *n (thread)* hilo de sutura; *(stitch)* punto de sutura.
▸ *vt* suturar.

**swab** [swɒb] *n* **1** MED *(cotton wool)* algodón *m*; *(gauze)* gasa. **2** MED *(specimen)* frotis *m*, muestra. **3** *(cleaning cloth)* paño, bayeta, trapo; *(mop)* fregona.
▸ *vt* **1** MED *(wound)* limpiar, fregar. **2** MAR *(deck)* limpiar, fregar.
ⓘ *pt & pp* swabbed, *ger* swabbing.

**swallow¹** ['swɒləʊ] *n (of drink, food)* trago.
▸ *vt* **1** *(food, etc)* tragar. **2** *fig (be taken in by)* tragarse.
▸ *vi* tragar.
◆ **to swallow up** *vt sep* **1** *(engulf)* tragarse, engullir. **2** *(use up)* consumir, tragarse, comerse, absorber.

**swallow²** ['swɒləʊ] *n (bird)* golondrina.

**swam** [swæm] *pt* → swim.

**swamp** [swɒmp] *n* pantano, ciénaga.
▸ *vt* **1** *(land)* inundar, anegar; *(boat)* hundir. **2** *fig (inundate)* inundar (**with/by**, de); *(overwhelm)* agobiar, abrumar (**with/by**, de).

**swan** [swɒn] *n (bird)* cisne *m*.
▸ *vi* pavonearse.
ⓘ *pt & pp* swanned, *ger* swanning.

**swap** [swɒp] *n* canje *m*, cambalache *m*.
▸ *vt* cambiar, intercambiar.
▸ *vi* hacer un intercambio, cambiar.
ⓘ *pt & pp* swapped, *ger* swapping.

**swarm** [swɔːm] *n* **1** *(of bees)* enjambre *m*. **2** *fig (of people)* enjambre *m*, nube *f*, multitud *f*.
▸ *vi* **1** *(bees)* enjambrar. **2** *fig (people)* aglomerarse, apiñarse, arremolinarse.
◆ **to swarm with** *vt insep* rebosar de, estar plagado,-a de.

**swathe¹** [sweɪð] *n* → swath.

**swathe²** [sweɪð] *vt (wrap)* envolver, vendar.
◆ **to swathe in** *vt sep fig* envolver.

**sway** [sweɪ] *n* **1** *(movement)* balanceo, vaivén *m*, movimiento. **2** *fig (influence)* dominio, influencia (**over**, sobre).
▸ *vt* **1** *(swing)* balancear, bambolear. **2** *fig (influence)* influir en, influenciar, convencer.
▸ *vi* **1** *(person, tree, ladder)* balancearse, bambolearse; *(tower)* bambolearse; *(crops)* mecerse; *(person - totter)* tambalearse. **2** *fig (waver)* vacilar (**between**, entre), oscilar (**between**, entre).

**swear** [sweə'] *vt* **1** *(declare formally)* jurar; *(vow)* juramentar. **2** *fam (state firmly)* jurar.
▸ *vi* **1** *(declare formally)* jurar, prestar juramento. **2** *(curse)* decir palabrotas, soltar tacos; *(blaspheme)* jurar, blasfemar.
◆ **to swear by** *vt insep fam* tener una fe absoluta en.
◆ **to swear in** *vt sep (in court)* tomarle juramento a.
◆ **to swear to** *vt insep* jurar.
ⓘ *pt* swore [swɔː'], *pp* sworn [swɔːn].

**swearword** ['sweə'wɜːd] *n* palabrota.

**sweat** [swet] *n* **1** *(perspiration)* sudor *m*. **2** *fam (hard work)* paliza. **3** *fam (anxious state)* nerviosismo. COMP **sweat gland** glándula sudorípara.
▸ *vi* **1** *(perspire)* sudar. **2** *(cheese)* exudar humedad. **3** *(work hard)* sudar la gota gorda. **4** *fam (worry)* estar preocupado,-a, sufrir.
▸ *vt* GB *(cook gently)* rehogar.
◆ **to sweat out** *vt sep (illness, cold)* quitarse sudando; *(toxins)* eliminar.

**sweater** ['swetə'] *n* suéter *m*, jersey *m*.

**sweatshirt** ['swetʃɜːt] *n* sudadera.

**Swede** [swiːd] *n (person)* sueco,-a.

**Sweden** ['swiːd°n] *n* Suecia.

**Swedish** ['swiːdɪʃ] *adj* sueco,-a.

▶ *n (language)* sueco.

▶ *n pl* **the Swedish** los suecos *mpl*.

**sweep** [swi:p] *n* **1** *(with broom)* barrido. **2** *(of arm)* movimiento amplio, gesto amplio; *(with weapon)* golpe *m*. **3** *(curve)* curva; *(area, stretch)* extensión *f*. **4** *fig (range, extent)* abanico, alcance *m*. **5** *(by police, rescuers)* peinado, rastreo. **6** *fam (chimney cleaner)* deshollinador,-ra.

▶ *vt* **1** *(room, floor)* barrer; *(chimney)* deshollinar. **2** *(with hand)* quitar de un manotazo. **3** *(move over)* azotar, barrer. **4** *(remove by force)* arrastrar, llevarse. **5** *(pass over)* recorrer. **6** *fig (spread through)* recorrer, extenderse por. **7** *(touch lightly)* rozar, pasar por.

▶ *vi* **1** *(with broom)* barrer. **2** *(move quickly)* pasar rápidamente. **3** *(extend)* recorrer, extenderse.

◆ **to sweep aside** *vt sep* **1** *(objection, etc)* rechazar; *(suggestion)* descartar. **2** *(object)* apartar (bruscamente).

◆ **to sweep away** *vt sep* **1** *(privilege, etc)* erradicar. **2** *(by flood, storm)* arrastrar, llevarse.

◆ **to sweep up** *vt sep* **1** *(room, etc)* barrer; *(dust, etc)* (barrer y) recoger. **2** *(object, person)* recoger, levantar.

▶ *vi* barrer, limpiar.

ⓘ *pt & pp* **swept** [swept].

**sweeping** ['swi:pɪŋ] *adj* **1** *(broad)* amplio,-a; *(very general)* muy general. **2** *(overwhelming)* arrollador,-ra, aplastante; *(far-reaching)* radical; *(huge)* enorme. COMP **sweeping brush** escoba.

**sweet** [swi:t] *adj* **1** *(taste)* dulce; *(sugary)* azucarado,-a. **2** *(pleasant)* agradable; *(smell)* fragante, bueno,-a; *(sound, music, voice)* melodioso,-a, suave, dulce. **3** *(air)* limpio,-a; *(water)* dulce. **4** *(charming)* encantador,-ra, simpático,-a; *(cute)* rico,-a, mono,-a; *(gentle)* dulce. COMP **sweet corn** maíz *m* tierno. ▪ **sweet pea** guisante *m* de olor. ▪ **sweet pepper** pimiento morrón. ▪ **sweet potato** boniato, batata.

▶ *n* **1** GB *(candy)* caramelo, golosina; *(chocolate)* bombón *m*. **2** GB *(dessert)* postre *m*. **3** *(form of address)* cariño, cielo, amor *m*, vida.

**sweet-and-sour** ['swi:tⁿsaʊəʳ] *adj* CULIN agridulce.

**sweetcorn** ['swi:tkɔ:n] *n* maíz *m* tierno.

**sweeten** ['swi:tⁿn] *vt* **1** *(drink, etc)* endulzar, azucarar; *(air, breath)* refrescar. **2** *fig (person)* endulzar (el carácter de); *(temper)* aplacar, calmar. **3** *fam (make more attractive)* hacer más apetecible.

◆ **to sweeten up** *vt sep* ablandar.

**sweetener** ['swi:tⁿnəʳ] *n* **1** *(in food, drink)* edulcorante *m*, dulcificante *m*. **2** *fam (bribe)* soborno.

**sweetheart** ['swi:thɑ:t] *n* **1** *(dear, love)* cariño, tesoro, amor *m*. **2** *(loved one)* novio,-a.

**sweetness** ['swi:tnəs] *n* *(taste)* dulzor *m*; *(smell)* fragancia; *(sound)* suavidad *f*; *(character)* dulzura, simpatía.

**swell** [swel] *n* **1** *(of sea)* marejada, oleaje *m*. **2** MUS *(crescendo)* crescendo.

▶ *vi* **1** *(gen)* hincharse (up, -); *(sea)* levantarse; *(river)* crecer, subir. **2** *(grow in number)* crecer, aumentar; *(- louder)* hacerse más fuerte.

▶ *vt* **1** *(gen)* hinchar; *(river)* hacer crecer. **2** *(increase in number)* aumentar, engrosar.

ⓘ *pt & pp* **swelled** o **swollen** ['swəʊlən].

**swelling** ['swelɪŋ] *n* *(swollen place)* hinchazón *f*, bulto; *(condition)* tumefacción *f*.

**swept** [swept] *pt & pp* → **sweep**.

**swerve** [swɜ:v] *n* **1** AUTO viraje *m* brusco, desvío brusco. **2** SP *(by player)* regate *m*; *(of ball)* efecto.

▶ *vi* **1** AUTO virar bruscamente, dar un viraje brusco. **2** SP *(player)* dar un regate, regatear; *(ball)* llevar efecto. **3** *fig (veer, deviate)* desviarse *(from, de)*.

**swift** [swɪft] *adj* **1** *(runner, horse)* rápido,-a, veloz. **2** *(reaction, reply)* pronto,-a, rápido,-a.

▶ *n (bird)* vencejo común.

**swim** [swɪm] *n* baño. LOC **to go for a swim** ir a nadar. ▪ **to have a swim** bañarse, nadar.

▶ *vi* **1** *(gen)* nadar. **2** *(be covered in liquid)* nadar (in, en), flotar (in, en); *(be overflowing)* estar cubierto,-a (with, de), estar inundado,-a. **3** *(spin, whirl)* dar vueltas.

▶ *vt (cross river)* cruzar a nado, cruzar nadando; *(cover distance)* nadar, hacer; *(use particular stroke)* nadar.

ⓘ *pt* swam [swæm], *pp* swum [swʌm], *ger* swimming.

**swimmer** ['swɪməʳ] *n* nadador,-ra.

**swimming** ['swɪmɪŋ] *n* natación *f*. LOC **to go swimming** ir a nadar. COMP **swimming baths** piscina cubierta. ∎ **swimming costume** bañador *m*. ∎ **swimming pool** piscina. ∎ **swimming trunks** bañador *m* (de hombre).

**swimsuit** ['swɪmsuːt] *n* bañador *m*.

**swimwear** ['swɪmweəʳ] *n* bañadores *mpl*.

**swindle** ['swɪndəl] *n (fiddle)* estafa; *(con)* timo.

▶ *vt* estafar, timar.

**swine** [swaɪn] *n* **1** [*pl* swine] *arch (pig)* cerdo, puerco, cochino. **2** [*pl* swines] *fam (person)* cerdo,-a, canalla *mf*, marrano,-a.

**swing** [swɪŋ] *n* **1** *(movement)* balanceo, vaivén *m*; *(of pendulum)* oscilación *f*, vaivén *m*; *(of hips)* contoneo. **2** *(plaything)* columpio. **3** *(change, shift)* giro, viraje *m*, cambio. **4** SP *(in golf, boxing)* swing *m*. **5** MUS *(jazz style)* swing *m*; *(rhythm)* ritmo. COMP **swing bridge** puente *m* giratorio. ∎ **swing door** puerta giratoria.

▶ *vi* **1** *(hanging object)* balancearse, bambolearse; *(pendulum)* oscilar; *(arms, legs)* menearse; *(child on swing)* columpiarse; *(on a pivot)* mecerse. **2** *(drive)* girar, doblar; *(walk)* caminar con energía; *(jump)* saltar. **3** *(shift)* cambiar, oscilar, virar. **4** *(music, band)* tener ritmo; *(party)* estar muy animado,-a.

▶ *vt* **1** *(gen)* balancear. **2** *(cause to move)* hacer girar. **3** *(change)* cambiar. **4** *fam (arrange, achieve)* arreglar.

ⓘ *pt & pp* swung [swʌŋ].

**swipe** [swaɪp] *n* **1** *(blow)* golpe *m*. **2** *(verbal attack)* ataque *m*. COMP **swipe card** tarjeta magnética.

▶ *vt* **1** pegarle a, darle a. **2** *fam (pinch)* birlar, mangar, afanar.

▶ *vi* asestar un golpe (at, a), intentar darle (at, a).

**swirl** [swɜːl] *n* **1** *(gen)* remolino; *(of smoke, cream)* voluta; *(of skirt)* vuelo. **2** *(pattern)* espiral *f*.

▶ *vi (whirl)* arremolinarse; *(person)* girar, dar vueltas.

▶ *vt* arremolinar.

**Swiss** [swɪs] *adj* suizo,-a.

▶ *n* suizo,-a.

▶ *n pl* **the Swiss** los suizos *mpl*.

**switch** [swɪtʃ] *n* **1** ELEC interruptor *m*, conmutador *m*. **2** US *(on railway)* agujas *fpl*. **3** *(change, shift)* cambio; *(turnaround)* viraje *m*. **4** *(exchange, swap)* intercambio, trueque *m*.

▶ *vt* **1** *(change)* cambiar de; *(move)* trasladar; *(attention)* desviar. **2** *(exchange)* intercambiar. **3** *(setting)* poner; *(channel)* cambiar de. **4** *(train)* desviar, cambiar de vía.

▶ *vi (gen)* cambiar (to, a).

◆ **to switch off** *vt sep (light, TV, etc)* apagar; *(current, gas, electricity)* cortar, desconectar; *(engine)* parar.

▶ *vi (light, machine, heating)* apagarse; *(engine)* parar; *(person)* distraerse, desconectar, dejar de prestar atención.

◆ **to switch on** *vt sep (light, machine, engine)* encender; *(light, radio, TV)* poner.

▶ *vi (gen)* encenderse.

◆ **to switch over** *vi (gen)* cambiar (to, a); *(channel)* cambiar de canal.

**switchboard** ['swɪtʃbɔːd] *n* centralita.

**Switzerland** ['swɪtsələnd] *n* Suiza.

**swivel** ['swɪvəl] *vi* girarse, volverse.

ⓘ *pt & pp* swivelled (US swiveled), *ger* swivelling (US swiveling).

▶ *vt (head)* girar; *(chair)* hacer girar. COMP **swivel chair** silla giratoria.

**swollen** ['swəʊlən] *pp* → swell.

▶ *adj (ankle, face)* hinchado,-a; *(glands)* inflamado,-a; *(river, lake)* crecido,-a.

**swoop** [swuːp] *vi* **1** *(bird)* abalanzarse (down on, sobre), abatirse (down on, sobre); *(plane)* bajar en picado. **2** *fam (police)* hacer una redada (on, en).

▶ *n* **1** *(of bird, plane)* descenso (en picado). **2** *fam (by police)* redada.

**sword** [sɔːd] *n* espada.

**swordfish** ['sɔːdfɪʃ] *n* pez *m* espada.

**swore** [swɔːʳ] *pt* → swear.

S

**sworn** [swɔːn] *pp* → swear.
**swot** [swɒt] *n* empollón,-ona.
▸ *vi* empollar.
ⓘ *pt & pp* swotted, *ger* swotting.
**swum** [swʌm] *pp* → swim.
**swung** [swʌŋ] *pt & pp* → swing.
**sybarite** ['sɪbəraɪt] *n lit* sibarita *mf*.
**syllable** ['sɪləbəl] *n* sílaba.
**syllabus** ['sɪləbəs] *n* programa *m* de estudios.
ⓘ *pl* syllabuses o syllabi.
**sylph** [sɪlf] *n* sílfide *f*.
**symbiosis** [sɪmbɪ'əʊsɪs] *n* simbiosis *f*.
**symbol** ['sɪmbəl] *n* símbolo (of, de).
**symbolize** ['sɪmbəlaɪz] *vt* simbolizar.
**symmetrical** [sɪ'metrɪkəl] *adj* simétrico,-a.
**symmetry** ['sɪmɪtrɪ] *n* simetría.
**sympathetic** [sɪmpə'θetɪk] *adj* **1** *(showing pity, compassion)* compasivo,-a; *(understanding)* comprensivo,-a (to, con); *(kind)* amable. **2** *(showing agreement, approval)* favorable (to, a).

☒ Sympathetic no significa 'simpático', que se traduce por nice.

**sympathize** ['sɪmpəθaɪz] *vi* **1** *(show pity, commiserate)* compadecer, compadecerse (with, de); *(understand)* comprender (with, -). **2** *(support - cause)* simpatizar (with, con).
**sympathizer** ['sɪmpəθaɪzər] *n* simpatizante *mf*.
**sympathy** ['sɪmpəθɪ] *n* **1** *(pity, compassion)* compasión *f*, lástima; *(condolences)* condolencia, pésame *m*. **2** *(understanding)* comprensión *f*; *(affinity)* afinidad *f*. **3** *(agreement, support)* acuerdo *m*.
ⓘ *pl* sympathies.
▸ *n pl* sympathies *(condolences)* condolencia *f sing*, pésame *m sing*. *(loyalties, leanings)* simpatías *fpl*, tendencias *fpl*.

☒ Sympathy no significa 'simpatía (amabilidad)', que se traduce por pleasantness.

**symphony** ['sɪmfənɪ] *n* sinfonía. [COMP] symphony orchestra orquesta sinfónica.
ⓘ *pl* symphonies.

**symposium** [sɪm'pəʊzɪəm] *n* simposio.
ⓘ *pl* symposiums o symposia.
**symptom** ['sɪmptəm] *n* **1** MED síntoma *m*. **2** *(sign)* síntoma *m*, señal *f*, indicio.
**synagogue** ['sɪnəgɒg] *n* sinagoga.
**synchronize** ['sɪŋkrənaɪz] *vt* sincronizar.
**syncopation** [sɪŋkə'peɪʃən] *n* síncopa.
**syndicalism** ['sɪndɪkəlɪzəm] *n* sindicalismo.
**syndicalist** ['sɪndɪkəlɪst] *n* sindicalista *mf*.
**syndicate** ['sɪndɪkət] *n* **1** *(gen)* corporación *f*, agrupación *f*, empresa. **2** *(news agency)* agencia (de prensa).
▸ *vt (distribute)* distribuir; *(publish)* publicar.

☒ Syndicate no significa 'sindicato', que se traduce por trade union.

**syndrome** ['sɪndrəʊm] *n* síndrome *m*.
**synonym** ['sɪnənɪm] *n* sinónimo.
**synopsis** [sɪ'nɒpsɪs] *n* sinopsis *f*, resumen *m*.
ⓘ *pl* synopses.
**syntactic** [sɪn'tæktɪk] *adj* sintáctico,-a.
**syntax** ['sɪntæks] *n* sintaxis *f inv*.
**synthesis** ['sɪnθəsɪs] *n* síntesis *f inv*.
ⓘ *pl* syntheses.
**synthesize** ['sɪnθəsaɪz] *vt* sintetizar.
**synthesizer** ['sɪnθəsaɪzər] *n* sintetizador *m*.
**synthetic** [sɪn'θetɪk] *adj* sintético,-a.
▸ *n* fibra sintética.
**syphilis** ['sɪfɪlɪs] *n* sífilis *f*.
**Syria** ['sɪrɪə] *n* Siria.
**Syrian** ['sɪrɪən] *adj* sirio,-a.
▸ *n* sirio,-a.
**syringe** [sɪ'rɪndʒ] *n* MED jeringa, jeringuilla.
▸ *vt* MED *(ear)* hacer un lavado de.
**syrup** ['sɪrəp] *n* **1** MED jarabe *m*. **2** CULIN almíbar *m*.
**system** ['sɪstəm] *n* **1** *(gen)* sistema *m*: **2** *(body)* cuerpo, organismo.
**systematic** [sɪstə'mætɪk] *adj* sistemático,-a, metódico,-a.
**systematize** ['sɪstɪmətaɪz] *vt* sistematizar.
**systemize** ['sɪstəmaɪz] *vt* sistematizar.
**systole** ['sɪstəlɪ] *n* sístole *m*.

**T, t** [tiː] *n (the letter)* T, t *f*.

**tab** [tæb] *n* **1** *(flap)* lengüeta; *(on can)* anilla. **2** *(label)* etiqueta. **3** US *(bill)* cuenta. **4** *(on computer)* tabulador *m*.

**table** ['teɪbəl] *n* **1** *(gen)* mesa. **2** *(chart)* tabla, cuadro. **3** SP clasificación *f*. [COMP]
▶ **table football** futbolín *m*. ∎ **table of contents** índice *m* de materias. ∎ **table tennis** tenis *m* de mesa, pingpong *m*.
▶ *vt* GB *(motion, report, etc)* presentar.
▶ *n pl* **tables** tablas *fpl* de multiplicar.

[✗] Table no significa 'tabla (de madera)', que se traduce por **board, plank**.

**tablecloth** ['teɪbəlklɒθ] *n* mantel *m*.

**tablespoon** ['teɪbəlspuːn] *n* **1** cucharón *m*. **2** cuchara grande.

**tablet** ['tæblɪt] *n* **1** MED pastilla, comprimido. **2** *(of soap)* pastilla.

**tabloid** ['tæblɔɪd] *n* periódico de formato pequeño.

**tabulate** ['tæbjʊleɪt] *vt* tabular.

**tachycardia** [tækɪ'kɑːdɪə] *n* taquicardia.

**tack** [tæk] *n* **1** *(nail)* tachuela. **2** MAR bordada, viraje *m*. **3** *(approach)* táctica. **4** SEW hilván *m*.

**tackle** ['tækəl] *n* **1** *(equipment)* equipo, aparejos *mpl*. **2** MAR polea, aparejo. **3** SP *(football)* entrada; *(rugby)* placaje *m*.
▶ *vt* **1** *(deal with - problem)* abordar, encarar; *(- task)* emprender; *(person)* hablar con. **2** SP *(football)* entrarle a; *(rugby)* placar.

**tact** [tækt] *n* tacto, discreción *f*.

[✗] Tact no significa 'tacto (sentido)', que se traduce por **touch**.

**tactful** ['tæktfʊl] *adj* diplomático,-a.

**tactic** ['tæktɪk] *n* táctica.

**tactical** ['tæktɪkəl] *adj* táctico,-a.

**tactics** ['tæktɪks] *n pl* MIL táctica *f sing*.

**tactless** ['tæktləs] *adj (person)* falto,-a de tacto, poco diplomático,-a; *(remark, question)* indiscreto,-a.

**tadpole** ['tædpəʊl] *n* renacuajo.

**Tadzhik** ['tædʒɪk] *adj* tadjiko,-a.
▶ *n (person)* tadjiko,-a.
① *pl* Tadzhik.

**Tadzhiki** [tæ'dʒiːkɪ] *n (language)* tadjiko.

**Tadzhikistan** [tædʒiːkɪ'stæn] *n* Tadjikistán.

**tag** [tæg] *n* **1** *(label)* etiqueta. **2** *(phrase)* coletilla. **3** *(game)* el corre que te pillo.
▶ *vt* etiquetar.

**Tahiti** [tə'hiːtɪ] *n* Tahití.

**Tahitian** [tə'hiːʃən] *adj* tahitiano,-a.
▶ *n* **1** *(person)* tahitiano,-a. **2** *(language)* tahitiano.
**4** ['teɪfə] *n* taifa.

**tail** [teɪl] *n (gen)* cola; *(of some four-legged animals)* cola, rabo.
▶ *n pl* **tails** *(of coin)* cruz *f sing*.

**tailback** ['teɪlbæk] *n (traffic jam)* caravana, cola, retención *f*.

**tailbone** ['teɪlbəʊn] *n* cóccix *m*.

**tailor** ['teɪlər] *n* sastre,-a.

**Taiwan** [taɪ'wæn] *n* Taiwan.

**Taiwanese** [taɪwæ'niːz] *adj* taiwanés,-esa.
▶ *n* taiwanés,-esa.

**take** [teɪk] *n* CINEM toma.
▶ *vt* **1** *(gen)* llevar. **2** *(remove)* llevarse, quitar, coger. **3** *(hold, grasp)* tomar, coger. **4** *(accept - money, etc)* aceptar. **5** *(win prize, competition)* ganar. **6** *(medicine, drugs)* tomar. **7** *(subject)* estudiar; *(course of study)* seguir, cursar. **8** *(bus, train, etc)* tomar, coger. **9** *(time)* tardar, llevar.
[LOC] **not to take no for an answer** no

aceptar una respuesta negativa.
▌**take it or leave it** lo tomas o lo dejas. ▌**to take place** ocurrir. ▌**to take sth for granted** dar ALGO por sentado.

▸ vi **1** (work - dye) coger; (- fire) prender; (- cutting) prender; (- seed) germinar. **2** (fish) picar. **3** (in draughts, etc) comer.

◆ **to take after** vi parecerse.

◆ **to take apart** vt sep **1** (machine, etc) desmontar, deshacer. **2** (argument) echar por tierra.

◆ **to take away** vt sep **1** (remove) llevarse, quitar. **2** (subtract) restar.

▸ vi (food) llevar.

◆ **to take back** vt sep **1** (accept back) recibir otra vez, aceptar algo devuelto; (employee) readmitir. **2** (return) devolver. **3** (retract) retirar, retractar. **4** (in time) hacer recordar.

◆ **to take off** vt sep **1** (clothes) quitarse. **2** (remove, detach) quitar, sacar. **3** (force to go) llevar. **4** (have as holiday) tomarse. **5** (imitate) imitar. **6** (deduct, discount) descontar, rebajar.

▸ vi **1** (plane) despegar. **2** (leave hurriedly) irse, marcharse. **3** (become popular) tener éxito, ponerse de moda.

◆ **to take over** vt sep **1** (country, party, etc) tomar (posesión de), apoderarse de; (building) ocupar. **2** (company, business) absorber, adquirir; (job, post) hacerse cargo de; (duty, responsibility) asumir.
ⓘ pt **took** [tʊk], pp **taken** ['teɪkən].

**take-away** ['teɪkəweɪ] n **1** (food) comida para llevar. **2** (restaurant) restaurante m de comida para llevar.

**taken** ['teɪkⁿn] pp → take.
▸ adj (seat) ocupado,-a.

**take-off** ['teɪkə:f] n **1** (aviation) despegue m. **2** SP salto.

**take-out** ['teɪkaʊt] n US (food) comida para llevar.

**takeover** ['teɪkəʊvəʳ] n **1** POL toma de posesión. **2** (of company) adquisición f.

**talc** [tælk] n talco.

**talcum powder** ['tælkəmpaʊdəʳ] n polvos mpl de talco.

**tale** [teɪl] n (story) cuento.

**talent** ['tælənt] n **1** (special ability) talento, dotes mpl. **2** (talented people) gente f

de talento, gente f dotada. **3** fam (attractive people) gente f guapa.

**talented** ['tæləntɪd] adj de talento.

**talk** [tɔːk] vi **1** (gen) hablar (to, con/a). **2** (negotiate) negociar.
▸ vt hablar (about/of, de).
▸ n **1** (conversation) conversación f. **2** (lecture) charla, conferencia.
▸ n pl **talks** negociaciones fpl.

◆ **to talk back** vi contestar, contestar de mala manera.

◆ **to talk down** vt insep **1** (person) hacer callar. **2** (aircraft) dirigir por radio.

**talkative** ['tɔːkətɪv] adj hablador,-ra, parlanchín,-ina, charlatán,-ana.

**tall** [tɔːl] adj alto,-a. COMP **tall story** cuento chino.

**tallow** ['tæləʊ] n sebo.

**talon** ['tælən] n garra.

**tambourine** [tæmbəˈriːn] n pandereta.

**tame** [teɪm] adj **1** (by nature) manso,-a, dócil. **2** (tamed) domesticado,-a.
▸ vt domar, domesticar.

**tampon** ['tæmpɒn] n tampón m.

**tan¹** [tæn] n **1** (colour) color m marrón claro. **2** (suntan) bronceado, moreno. LOC **to get a tan** ponerse moreno.
▸ adj marrón claro.
▸ vt **1** (leather) curtir. **2** (skin) broncear, poner moreno,-a.
▸ vi broncearse, ponerse moreno,-a.
ⓘ pt & pp **tanned**, ger **tanning**.

**tangent** ['tændʒənt] n tangente f.

**tangerine** [tændʒəˈriːn] n **1** (fruit) clementina, mandarina. **2** (colour) naranja.
▸ adj naranja.

**tangle** ['tæŋgⁿl] n (confused mass) enredo, embrollo; (confusion) enredo, lío.
▸ vt enredar, enmarañar.
▸ vi enredarse.

**tank** [tæŋk] n **1** (for water) depósito, tanque m; (for fuel) depósito. **2** MIL tanque m. COMP **think tank** grupo de expertos.

**tanker** ['tæŋkəʳ] n **1** (ship) buque m cisterna. **2** (for oil) petrolero. **3** (lorry) camión m cisterna.

**tanned** [tænd] adj (person) moreno,-a, bronceado,-a; (leather) curtido,-a.

**tantrum** ['tæntrəm] *n* berrinche *m*, rabieta.

**Tanzania** [tænzə'nɪə] *n* Tanzania.

**Tanzanian** [tænzə'nɪən] *adj* tanzano,-a.
▸ *n* tanzano,-a.

**tap¹** [tæp] *n* **1** grifo. **2** *(light blow)* golpecito. **3** *(on phone)* micrófono de escucha. **4** *(on barrel)* espita; *(for gas)* llave *f*.
COMP **tap water** agua del grifo.
▸ *vt* **1** *(strike lightly)* dar un golpecito a. **2** *(on keyboard)* teclear, pulsar. **3** *(liquid)* sacar. **4** *(resources)* explotar, utilizar. **5** *(telephone)* pinchar, intervenir.
◆ **to tap out** *vt sep* **1** teclear, escribir a máquina. **2** *(in Morse code)* enviar.
ⓘ *pt & pp* **tapped**, *ger* **tapping**.

❌ Tap no significa 'tapa', que se traduce por lid.

**tap²** [tæp] *n* claqué *m*. COMP **tap dance** claqué *m*.

**tape** [teɪp] *n* **1** *(audio, visual)* cinta. **2** *(recorded material)* grabación *f*. **3** SP cinta de llegada. **4** *(sticky)* cinta adhesiva.
COMP **tape measure** cinta métrica. ‖ **tape recorder** magnetófono.
▸ *vt* **1** *(fasten)* pegar con cinta adhesiva. **2** *(record)* grabar.

**tapestry** ['tæpəstrɪ] *n* **1** *(art)* tapicería. **2** *(cloth)* tapiz *m*.
ⓘ *pl* **tapestries**.

**tar** [tɑː] *n* **1** *(for roads, in cigarettes)* alquitrán *m*. **2** *(in soap, etc)* brea.
▸ *vt* alquitranar.
ⓘ *pt & pp* **tarred**, *ger* **tarring**.

**target** ['tɑːgɪt] *n* **1** *(of missile, goal, aim)* objetivo. **2** *(in shooting, of criticism)* blanco. **3** *(board)* diana.
▸ *vt* **1** *(aim at target)* apuntar. **2** *(cause to have effect on)* dirigir a, destinar a.
▸ *adj* *(date, figure)* fijado,-a; *(audience, market)* objetivo.

**tariff** ['tærɪf] *n* **1** *(list of fixed charges)* tarifa. **2** *(duty to be paid on imports)* arancel *m*.
▸ *adj* arancelario,-a.

**tarmac** ['tɑːmæk] *n* **1** asfalto. **2** *(area)* pista.
▸ *vt* asfaltar.

**tarpaulin** [tɑːˈpɔːlɪn] *n* lona.

**tarsus** ['tɑːsəs] *n* ANAT tarso.
ⓘ *pl* **tarsi**.

**tart** [tɑːt] *adj* **1** *(sour)* acre, agrio,-a. **2** *(reply)* mordaz, áspero,-a, acre.
▸ *n* **1** *(pie)* tarta, pastel *m*.
◆ **to tart up** *vt sep* *(building)* renovar, remodelar; *(person)* emperifollar.

**tartan** ['tɑːtən] *n* tartán *m*.

**tartar** ['tɑːtə'] *n* **1** *(on teeth)* sarro. **2** *(in wine)* tártaro.

**task** [tɑːsk] *n* tarea, labor *f*.

**Tasmania** [tæz'meɪnɪə] *n* Tasmania.

**Tasmanian** [tæz'meɪnɪən] *adj* tasmano,-a.
▸ *n* tasmano,-a.

**taste** [teɪst] *n* **1** *(faculty)* gusto. **2** *(flavour)* sabor *m*. **3** *(small sample)* muestra, poquito; *(experience)* experiencia. **4** *(ability to make good judgements)* gusto; *(liking)* afición *f* (for, a), gusto (for, por). COMP **taste buds** papilas gustativas.
▸ *vt* **1** *(try food)* probar; *(wine)* catar, degustar. **2** *(eat, drink)* probar. **3** *(experience)* conocer. **4** *(perceive flavour)* notar.
▸ *vi* saber (of/like, a).

**tasteful** ['teɪstfʊl] *adj* de buen gusto, elegante.

**tasteless** ['teɪstləs] *adj* **1** de mal gusto. **2** *(insipid)* insípido,-a, soso,-a.

**tasty** ['teɪstɪ] *adj* sabroso,-a, rico,-a.
ⓘ *comp* **tastier**, *superl* **tastiest**.

**tattoo** [tə'tuː] *n* **1** MIL retreta. **2** *(on skin)* tatuaje *m*.
ⓘ *pl* **tattoos**.
▸ *vt* tatuar.
ⓘ *pt & pp* **tattooed**, *ger* **tattooing**.

**taught** [tɔːt] *pt & pp* → **teach**.

**taunt** [tɔːnt] *n* mofa, pulla, insulto.
▸ *vt* *(mock)* burlarse de, mofarse de; *(provoke)* hostigar, provocar.

**Taurus** ['tɔːrəs] *n* Tauro.

**taut** [tɔːt] *adj* tirante, tenso,-a.

**tavern** ['tævə°n] *n* taberna, mesón *m*.

**tax** [tæks] *n* **1** impuesto, contribución *f*. **2** *fig (burden, strain)* carga (on, sobre), esfuerzo (on, para).
ⓘ *pl* **taxes**.
▸ *vt* **1** *(impose a tax on - goods, profits)* gravar; *(- business, person)* imponer contribuciones a. **2** *fig (strain, test)* poner a prueba.

T

**taxation** [tæk'seɪʃ°n] n (taxes) impuestos mpl; (system) sistema m tributario.

**tax-deductible** ['tæksdɪ'dʌktəb°l] adj desgravable.

**tax-free** ['tæks'friː] adj libre de impuestos, exento,-a de impuestos.

**taxi** ['tæksɪ] n taxi m. COMP **taxi driver** taxista mf.
ⓘ pl taxis.

**taxonomy** [tæk'sɒnəmɪ] n taxonomía.
ⓘ pl taxonomies.

**taxpayer** ['tækspeɪəʳ] n contribuyente mf.

**tea** [tiː] n 1 (gen) té m. 2 (infusion) infusión f.

**tea-break** ['tiːbreɪk] n descanso para tomar el té.

**teach** [tiːtʃ] vt (gen) enseñar; (subject) dar clases. LOC **that'll teach you** así aprenderás.
► vi ser profesor,-ra, dar clases
ⓘ pt & pp taught [tɔːt].

**teacher** ['tiːtʃəʳ] n maestro,-a, profesor,-ra.

**teaching** ['tiːtʃɪŋ] n enseñanza.
► adj docente. COMP **teaching staff** profesorado.
► n pl **teachings** enseñanzas fpl.

**teacup** ['tiːkʌp] n taza para té.

**teak** [tiːk] n teca.

**team** [tiːm] n 1 (gen) equipo. 2 (of horses) tiro; (of oxen) yunta.
► adj de equipo.
► vi combinar (with, con).

**teamwork** ['tiːmwɜːk] n trabajo de equipo.

**teapot** ['tiːpɒt] n tetera.

**tear¹** [teəʳ] n (rip) rasgón m, desgarrón m.
► vt 1 (rip, make a hole) rasgar, desgarrar; (pull apart, into pieces) romper, hacer pedazos. 2 (remove by force) arrancar.
► vi 1 romperse, rasgarse. 2 (rush) ir a toda velocidad, lanzarse, precipitarse. COMP **wear and tear** desgaste m.
◆ **to tear apart** vt sep 1 (rip up) despedazar, desgarrar; (destroy) destrozar. 2 fig destrozar, desgarrar.

◆ **to tear up** vt sep (paper) hacer pedazos; (plant) arrancar de raíz.
ⓘ pt tore [tɔːʳ], pp torn [tɔːn].

**tear²** [tɪəʳ] n lágrima.

**teardrop** ['tɪəd rɒp] n lágrima.

**tearoom** ['tiːrʊm] n salón m de té.

**tease** [tiːz] vt 1 (make fun of - playfully) tomar el pelo a, burlarse de; (- annoyingly, unkindly) molestar. 2 (wool, etc) cardar.
► vi tomar el pelo.
► n 1 (joker) bromista mf. 2 fam (flirt) coqueta.

**teasel** ['tiːz°l] n cardencha.

**teashop** ['tiːʃɒp] n salón m de té.

**teaspoon** ['tiːspuːn] n cucharilla.

**teat** [tiːt] n 1 ZOOL tetilla. 2 (on bottle) tetina.

**teatime** ['tiːtaɪm] n hora del té, hora de la merienda.

**technical** ['teknɪk°l] adj técnico,-a. COMP **technical college** instituto de formación profesional.

**technician** [tek'nɪʃ°n] n técnico,-a.

**technique** [tek'niːk] n técnica.

**technological** [teknə'lɒdʒɪk°l] adj tecnológico,-a.

**technology** [tek'nɒlədʒɪ] n tecnología.
ⓘ pl technologies.

**teddy bear** ['tedɪbeəʳ] [also **teddy**] n osito de peluche.

**tedious** ['tiːdɪəs] adj tedioso,-a, aburrido,-a.

**teenage** ['tiːneɪdʒ] adj adolescente.

**teenager** ['tiːneɪdʒəʳ] n quinceañero,-a.

**teens** [tiːnz] n pl adolescencia.

**tee-shirt** ['tiːʃɜːt] n camiseta.

**teeth** [tiːθ] n pl → tooth.

**teethe** [tiːð] vi echar los dientes.

**teetotaller** [tiː'təʊt°ləʳ] n abstemio,-a.

**telecommunications** [telɪkəmjuːnɪ-'keɪʃ°nz] n pl telecomunicaciones fpl.

**telegram** ['telɪgræm] n telegrama m.

**telegraph** ['telɪgrɑːf] n telégrafo.
► vi telegrafiar.

**telepathy** [tɪ'lepəθɪ] n telepatía.

**telephone** ['telɪfəʊn] n teléfono. COMP **telephone box** cabina telefónica.
**telephone call** llamada telefónica.

**telephone directory** listín *m* telefónico. ▌ **telephone number** número telefónico.

▸ *vt* telefonear, llamar por teléfono.

▸ *vi* hacer una llamada telefónica.

**telephonist** [təˈlefənɪst] *n* telefonista *mf*.

**telephoto lens** [telɪfəutəuˈlenz] *n* teleobjetivo.

**teleprinter** [ˈtelɪprɪntəʳ] *n* teletipo.

**telescope** [ˈtelɪskəup] *n* telescopio.

**telescopic** [telɪˈskɒpɪk] *adj (aerial)* telescópico,-a; *(umbrella)* plegable.

**televise** [ˈtelɪvaɪz] *vt* televisar.

**television** [ˈtelɪvɪʒ°n] *n* **1** *(gen)* televisión *f*. **2** *(set)* televisor *m*.

**telex**® [ˈteleks] *n* télex *m*.

▸ *vt* enviar por télex.

**tell** [tel] *vt* **1** *(gen)* decir. **2** *(story, joke)* contar; *(truth, lies, secret)* decir. **3** *(talk about)* hablar de. **4** *fml* comunicar, informar. **5** *(distinguish)* distinguir.

◆ **to tell apart** *vt sep* (saber) distinguir.

◆ **to tell off** *vt sep* **1** regañar, reñir. **2** MIL destacar.

◆ **to tell on** *vt insep (inform on)* chivarse de.

ⓘ *pt & pp* told [təuld].

**teller** [ˈteləʳ] *n (in bank)* cajero,-a.

**telling-off** [telɪŋˈɒf] *n fam* bronca.

**telltale** [ˈtelteɪl] *n* chivato,-a, acusica *mf*.

▸ *adj* revelador,-ra.

**telly** [ˈtelɪ] *n fam* tele *f*.

ⓘ *pl* tellies.

**temper** [ˈtempəʳ] *n* **1** *(mood)* humor *m*; *(nature)* genio. **2** *(of metal)* temple *m*.

▸ *vt* **1** *(metal)* templar. **2** *fig* atenuar.

**tempera** [ˈtempərə] *n* temple *m*. COMP **tempera paints** témperas.

**temperate** [ˈtemprɪt] *adj (gen)* moderado,-a; *(climate)* templado,-a.

**temperature** [ˈtemp°rɪt∫əʳ] *n* temperatura. LOC **to have/run a temperature** tener fiebre.

**tempered** [ˈtempəd] *adj* templado,-a.

**tempest** [ˈtempɪst] *n* tempestad *f*.

**template** [ˈtempleɪt] *n* plantilla.

**temple** [ˈtemp°l] *n* **1** *(building)* templo. **2** ANAT sien *f*.

**temporary** [ˈtemp°rərɪ] *adj* temporal.

**tempt** [tempt] *vt* tentar.

**temptation** [tempˈteɪʃ°n] *n* tentación *f*. LOC **to yield to temptation** caer en la tentación.

**tempting** [ˈtemptɪŋ] *adj* tentador,-ra.

**ten** [ten] *n* diez *m*.

▸ *adj* diez.

✎ Consulta también **six**.

**tenable** [ˈtenəb°l] *adj* **1** *(theory, etc)* sostenible, defendible. **2** *(post, office)*: *how long is the post tenable for?* ¿durante cuántos años se puede ocupar el puesto?

**tenacity** [təˈnæsɪtɪ] *n* tenacidad *f*.

**tenant** [ˈtenənt] *n* inquilino,-a.

**tend** [tend] *vt (person)* cuidar de, atender; *(other)* ocuparse de.

▸ *vi (have tendency)* tender (**to**, a), tener tendencia (**to**, a).

◆ **to tend to** *vt insep* ocuparse de.

**tendency** [ˈtendənsɪ] *n* tendencia.

ⓘ *pl* tendencies.

**tender**¹ [ˈtendəʳ] *adj* **1** *(meat, etc)* tierno,-a. **2** *(loving)* tierno,-a, cariñoso,-a. **3** *(sore)* dolorido,-a. **4** *(delicate)* delicado,-a, sensible.

ⓘ *comp* tenderer, *comp* tenderest.

**tender**² [ˈtendəʳ] *n* COMM *(offer)* oferta.

▸ *vt* presentar, ofrecer.

▸ *vi* hacer una oferta (**for**, para).

**tenderness** [ˈtendənəs] *n* ternura.

**tendon** [ˈtendən] *n* tendón *m*.

**tennis** [ˈtenɪs] *n* tenis *m*. COMP **tennis court** pista de tenis. ▌ **tennis player** jugador,-a de tenis.

**tenon** [ˈtenən] *n* espiga.

▸ *vt* despatillar.

**tenor** [ˈtenəʳ] *n* tenor *m*.

**tense** [tens] *adj* **1** *(anxious)* tenso,-a. **2** *(taut)* tirante, tenso,-a.

▸ *n (of verb)* tiempo verbal.

▸ *vt* tensar.

**tension** [ˈtenʃ°n] *n* tensión *f*.

**tent** [tent] *n* tienda de campaña.

**tentacle** [ˈtentək°l] *n* tentáculo.

**tenth** [tenθ] *adj* décimo,-a.

▸ *adv* en décimo lugar.

▸ *n (fraction)* décimo; *(one part)* décima parte *f*.

✎ Consulta también **sixth**.

**T**

**tepee** ['ti:pi:] *n* tipi *m*.

**tepid** ['tepɪd] *adj* tibio,-a.

**term** [tɜːm] *n* 1 EDUC trimestre *m*. 2 *(period of time)* período. 3 *(expression, word)* término.
▶ *n pl* **terms** *(sense)* términos *mpl*. COMM condiciones *fpl*, *(relations)* relaciones *fpl*.

**terminal** ['tɜːmɪnəl] *adj* terminal.
▶ *n* 1 ELEC borne *m*. 2 COMPUT terminal *m*. 3 *(at airport, etc)* terminal *f*.

**terminate** ['tɜːmɪneɪt] *vt* 1 *(gen)* terminar, poner fin a; *(contract)* rescindir. 2 *(pregnancy)* interrumpir.
▶ *vi* terminarse.

**termini** ['tɜːmɪnaɪ] *n pl* → terminus.

**terminology** [tɜːmɪ'nɒlədʒɪ] *n* terminología.

**terminus** ['tɜːmɪnəs] *n* término.
ⓘ *pl* terminuses o termini ['tɜːmɪnaɪ].

**termite** ['tɜːmaɪt] *n* termita.

**terrace** ['terəs] *n* 1 *(of house, café, bar, etc)* terraza. 2 *(on hillside)* terraza, bancal *m*.
▶ *n pl* **terraces** SP gradas *fpl*.

**terraced house** [terəst'haʊs] *n* casa adosada.

**terrain** [tə'reɪn] *n* terreno.

**terrible** ['terɪbəl] *adj* 1 terrible, espantoso,-a. 2 *fam (as intensifier)* mucho,-a.

**terribly** ['terɪblɪ] *adv* 1 terriblemente. 2 *fam (very)* muy.

**terrific** [tə'rɪfɪk] *adj* 1 *(wonderful)* fabuloso,-a, estupendo,-a. 2 *(huge)* tremendo,-a.

☒ Terrific no significa 'terrorífico', que se traduce por terrifying.

**terrify** ['terɪfaɪ] *vt* aterrar, aterrorizar.
ⓘ *pt & pp* terrified, *ger* terrifying.

**terrifying** ['terɪfaɪɪŋ] *adj* aterrador,-ra, espantoso,-a.

**territory** ['terɪtərɪ] *n* 1 *(gen)* territorio. 2 *(zone)* zona, área.
ⓘ *pl* territories.

**terror** ['terər] *n* 1 *(gen)* terror *m*, espanto. 2 *fam (child)* diablillo.

**terrorism** ['terərɪzəm] *n* terrorismo.

**terrorist** ['terərɪst] *n* terrorista *mf*.
▶ *adj* terrorista.

**tertiary** ['tɜːʃərɪ] *adj* terciario,-a.

**test** [test] *n* 1 *(trial)* prueba. 2 EDUC *(gen)* examen *m*; *(multiple choice)* test *m*. 3 MED análisis *m*. COMP test tube probeta.
▶ *vt* probar.

**testicle** ['testɪkəl] *n* testículo.

**testify** ['testɪfaɪ] *vt* JUR declarar.
▶ *vi* 1 *(bear witness)* dar fe (to, de). 2 JUR prestar declaración, testificar.
ⓘ *pt & pp* testified, *ger* testifying.

**testimony** ['testɪmənɪ] *n* testimonio.
ⓘ *pl* testimonies.

**test-tube baby** [testtjuːb'beɪbɪ] *n* niño,-a probeta.

**tetanus** ['tetənəs] *n* tétanos *m inv*.

**text** [tekst] *n* texto.

**textbook** ['tekstbʊk] *n* libro de texto.

**textile** ['tekstaɪl] *adj* textil.
▶ *n* textil *m*.

**texture** ['tekstʃər] *n* textura.

**Thai** [taɪ] *adj* tailandés,-esa.
▶ *n* 1 *(person)* tailandés,-esa. 2 *(language)* tailandés *m*.

**Thailand** ['taɪlænd] *n* Tailandia.

**Thames** [temz] *n* el Támesis *m*.

**than** [ðæn, *unstressed* ðən] *conj* 1 que: *he is taller than you are* él es más alto que tú. 2 *(with numbers)* de: *more than fifty* más de cincuenta. 3 *(followed by clause)* de lo que: *this is easier than we thought* esto es más fácil de lo que pensábamos.

**thank** [θæŋk] *vt* dar las gracias a, agradecer. LOC no, thank you no, gracias. ▮ I thank you gracias.

**thankful** ['θæŋkfʊl] *adj* agradecido,-a.

**thankless** ['θæŋkləs] *adj* ingrato,-a.

**thanks** [θæŋks] *interj* gracias: *thanks to* gracias a. LOC no, thanks no, gracias.
▶ *n pl (gratitude)* agradecimiento.

**thanksgiving** [θæŋks'gɪvɪŋ] *n* acción *f* de gracias. COMP Thanksgiving Day Día *m* de Acción de Gracias.

⊕ Thanksgiving Day (Día de Acción de Gracias) se celebra en Estados Unidos el cuarto jueves de noviembre. Recuerda el día de 1621 en que los colonos ingleses dieron gracias a Dios por la cosecha que les permitiría sobrevivir su segundo invierno en el Nuevo Mundo.

**that** [ðæt *unstressed* ðət] *adj* ese, esa; *(remote)* aquel, aquella.
ⓘ *pl* those.
► *pron* **1** ése *m*, ésa; *(remote)* aquél *m*, aquélla. **2** *(indefinite)* eso; *(remote)* aquello. **3** *(relative)* que. **4** *(with preposition)* que, el/la que, el/la cual. LOC that is to say es decir. ‖ that's it **1** *(that's all)* eso es todo. **2** *(that's right)* eso es. **3** *(that's enough)* se acabó. ‖ that's right así es. ‖ that's that se acabó. ‖ who's that? *(on 'phone)* ¿quién es?
ⓘ *pl* those.
► *adv fam* tan, tanto,-a, tantos,-as.

**thatch** [θætʃ] *n* **1** *(straw)* paja; *(roof)* tejado de paja. **2** *(hair)* mata.

**thaw** [θɔ:] *n* deshielo.
► *vt (food)* descongelar; *(snow, ice)* derretir.
► *vi* **1** *(food)* descongelarse; *(snow, ice)* derretirse. **2** *(person)* ablandarse; *(relations)* distenderse, mejorar.
◆ **to thaw out** *vi* descongelarse.
► *vt sep* descongelar.

**the** [ðə] [delante de una vocal se pronuncia [ðɪ]; con énfasis [ði:]] *def art* **1** el, la; *(plural)* los, las. **2** *(per)* por: *we are paid by the hour* nos pagan por horas. **3** *(emphasis)* el, la, los, las: *you're not the Paul Newman, are you?* no serás el auténtico Paul Newman, ¿verdad?
► *adv (with comparatives)*: *the more you have, the more you want* cuanto más se tiene, más se quiere.

**theater** ['θɪətər] *n* US → **theatre**.

**theatre** ['θɪətər] *n* **1** *(gen)* teatro. **2** MED quirófano. **3** US cine *m*. **4** *(scene of action)* escenario.
► *adj* teatral, de teatro.

**theft** [θeft] *n* robo, hurto.

**their** [ðeər] *adj* su; *(plural)* sus: *they took their children and their dog* se llevaron a sus hijos y al perro.

**theirs** [ðeəz] *pron* (el) suyo, (la) suya; *(plural)* (los) suyos, (las) suyas: *that house is theirs* aquella casa es suya.

**them** [ðem, *unstressed* ðəm] *pron* **1** *(direct object)* los, las; *(indirect object)* les; *(before another pronoun)* se: *the Smiths are coming, do you know them?* vienen los Smith, ¿los conoces?; *take these flowers and give them to Mary* coge estas flores y se las das a Mary. **2** *(with preposition, stressed)* ellos, ellas: *don't speak to them* no hables con ellos. **3** *fam (used with singular meaning)* lo, la, le: *if anyone arrives, tell them to wait* si llega alguien, dile que espere.

**thematic** [θɪ'mætɪk] *adj* temático,-a.

**theme** [θi:m] *n* tema *m*. COMP **theme park** parque *m* temático.

**themselves** [ðəm'selvz] *pron* **1** *(subject)* ellos/ellas mismos(as): *they made it themselves* lo hicieron ellos mismos. **2** *(object)* se: *they looked at themselves in the mirror* se miraron en el espejo. **3** *(after preposition)* sí mismos,-as: *they are old enough to look after themselves* son lo bastante mayores como para cuidar de sí mismos. LOC **by themselves** solos,-as: *don't leave the children by themselves* no dejes a los niños solos.

**then** [ðen] *adv* entonces, luego: *I was born in 1963, life was different then* nací en 1963, entonces la vida era distinta; *I'll have soup first and then steak* primero tomaré sopa y luego un filete.

**theology** [θɪ'blədʒɪ] *n* teología.

**theorem** ['θɪərəm] *n* teorema *m*.

**theoretic** [θɪə'retɪk] *adj* teórico,-a.

**theoretical** [θɪə'retɪkəl] *adj* teórico,-a.

**theory** ['θɪərɪ] *n* teoría. LOC **in theory** en teoría.
ⓘ *pl* theories.

**therapist** ['θerəpɪst] *n* terapeuta *mf*.

**therapy** ['θerəpɪ] *n* terapia, terapéutica: *she's having therapy* está recibiendo terapia.
ⓘ *pl* therapies.

**there** [ðeər] *adv* **1** allí, allá, ahí: *I often go there on holiday* voy de vacaciones allí a menudo. **2** *(in discussion)* acerca de eso: *I agree with you there* estoy de acuerdo contigo en eso. LOC **there and then** en el momento. ‖ **there is/are, etc** → be. ‖ **there you are** aquí tiene. ‖ **there you go** ya está.

**thereafter** [ðeər'ɑ:ftər] *adv* a partir de entonces.

**thereby** ['ðeəbaɪ] *adv* por eso, por ello.

**therefore** [ˈðeəfɔːʳ] *adv* por tanto, por lo tanto, por consiguiente.

**thermal** [ˈθɜːməl] *adj* **1** *(stream, bath, spring)* termal; *(underwear)* térmico,-a. **2** PHYS térmico,-a.
▶ *n* corriente *f* térmica.

**thermometer** [θəˈmɒmɪtəʳ] *n* termómetro.

**thermos®** [ˈθɜːmɒs] *n* termo.

**thermostat** [ˈθɜːməstæt] *n* termostato.

**thesaurus** [θɪˈsɔːrəs] *n* diccionario ideológico.

**these** [ðiːz] *adj* estos,-as: *these apples are cheaper than those* estas manzanas son más baratas que aquellas.
▶ *pron* éstos,-as: *which ones do you prefer? –these* ¿cuáles prefieres? –éstos.

**they** [ðeɪ] *pron* **1** *(plural)* ellos,-as: *where are the children? –they're in the garden* ¿dónde están los niños? –están en el jardín. **2** *fam (singular - substitutes* he *or* she*)* él, ella: *if anyone saw the accident, they should go to the police* si alguien vio el accidente, que vaya a la policía. LOC **they say that...** se dice que…

**thick** [θɪk] *adj* **1** *(solid things)* grueso,-a: *it's a thick book* es un libro grueso. **2** *(liquid, gas, vegetation, etc)* espeso,-a. **3** *(beard, eyebrows)* poblado,-a. **4** *(cloud, smoke, fog, forest)* denso,-a, espeso,-a. **5** *(fur, hedge)* tupido,-a. **6** *fam (stupid)* corto,-a, corto,-a de alcances; *(unable to think)* espeso,-a. **7** *(accent)* marcado,-a, cerrado, -a; *(of speech, voice)* poco claro,-a.
▶ *adv* espesamente, gruesamente.

**thicken** [ˈθɪkən] *vt* espesar.
▶ *vi* espesarse, hacerse más denso,-a.

**thickness** [ˈθɪknəs] *n* **1** *(in size)* espesor *m*, grosor *m*. **2** *(density - of liquid)* espesura; *(- of fog)* densidad *f*. **3** *(layer)* capa.

**thief** [θiːf] *n (gen)* ladrón,-ona; *(mugger)* atracador,-ra.
ⓘ *pl* **thieves** [θiːvz].

**thieves** [θiːvz] *pl* → **thief**.

**thigh** [θaɪ] *n* muslo.

**thighbone** [ˈθaɪbəʊn] *n* fémur *m*.

**thimble** [ˈθɪmbəl] *n* dedal *m*.

**thin** [θɪn] *adj* **1** *(gen)* delgado,-a, fino,-a, **2** *(liquid - soup, sauce)* poco espeso,-a, claro,-a; *(- rain)* fino,-a. **3** *(audience, crowd)* poco numeroso,-a; *(response, attendance)* escaso,-a. **4** *(voice)* débil. **5** *(excuse, argument)* pobre, poco convincente.
ⓘ *comp* **thinner**, *superl* **thinnest**.
▶ *adv* finamente.
▶ *vt (paint)* diluir; *(sauce)* hacer menos espeso,-a.
▶ *vi* **1** *(fog, mist)* disiparse. **2** *(audience, crowd, traffic)* hacerse menos denso,-a, disminuir.
◆ **to thin down** *vi* adelgazar.
▶ *vt sep (sauce)* hacer menos espeso,-a, aclarar; *(paint)* diluir.
◆ **to thin out** *vt insep (crowd, traffic)* mermar, disminuir.
▶ *vt sep (crops, plants)* entresacar.

**thing** [θɪŋ] *n* **1** *(object)* cosa, objeto. **2** *(non-material)* cosa. **3** *(affair)* asunto. **4** *(person, creature)*: *you poor little thing!* ¡pobrecito! **5** *(with negative)* nada: *I can't understand a thing you're saying* no entiendo nada de lo que dices.
▶ *n* **the thing** *(what)* lo que: *the thing I like most in life* lo que más me gusta en la vida.
▶ *n pl* **things** *(belongings)* cosas *fpl*, ropa *f sing*, equipaje *m sing*.

**think** [θɪŋk] *vi* **1** *(gen)* pensar. **2** *(remember)* acordarse *(of, de)*, recordar. **3** *(imagine)* imaginarse, pensar.
▶ *vt* **1** *(gen)* pensar. **2** *(believe)* creer. **3** *(remember)* recordar, acordarse de.
◆ **to think ahead** *vi* prevenir.
◆ **to think back** *vi* hacer memoria.
◆ **to think out** *vt sep (consider carefully)* estudiar, pensar bien.
ⓘ *pt & pp* **thought** [θɔːt].

**thinking** [ˈθɪŋkɪŋ] *n* **1** *(opinion)* opinión *f*, parecer *m*. **2** *(thought)* pensamiento.
▶ *adj* pensante, inteligente.

**third** [θɜːd] *adj* tercero,-a. COMP **third person** LING tercera persona.
▶ *adv (in series)* tercero, en tercer lugar.
▶ *n* **1** tercero,-a. **2** *(fraction)* tercio; *(one part)* tercera parte *f*.
✎ Consulta también **sixth**.

**third-party** [ˈθɜːdpɑːtɪ] *adj (insurance)* a terceros.

**third-world** ['θɜ:dwɜ:ld] *adj (in general)* del tercer mundo; *(pejorative use)* tercermundista.

**thirst** [θɜ:st] *n* sed *f*.

**thirsty** ['θɜ:stɪ] *adj* **1** sediento,-a: *I'm thirsty* tengo sed. **2** *(work, etc)* que da sed. **3** *fig (eager)* ansioso,-a (for, por). LOC **to be thirsty** tener sed.
ⓘ *comp* thirstier, *superl* thirstiest.

**thirteen** [θɜ:'ti:n] *n* trece *m*.
▶ *adj* trece.
✎ Consulta también six.

**thirteenth** [θɜ:'ti:nθ] *adj* decimotercero,-a.
▶ *adv* en decimotercero lugar.
▶ *n (fraction)* decimotercero; *(one part)* decimotercera parte *f*.
✎ Consulta también sixth.

**thirties** ['θɜ:tɪz] *n pl* **the thirties** los años *mpl* treinta. LOC **to be in one's thirties** tener treinta y tantos años.
✎ Consulta también sixties.

**thirtieth** ['θɜ:tɪəθ] *adj* trigésimo,-a.
▶ *adv* en trigésimo lugar.
▶ *n (fraction)* trigésimo; *(one part)* trigésima parte *f*.
✎ Consulta también sixtieth.

**thirty** ['θɜ:tɪ] *n* treinta *m*.
▶ *adj* treinta.
✎ Consulta también sixty.

**this** [ðɪs] *adj* este, esta: *whose is this book?* ¿de quién es este libro?
ⓘ *pl* these [ði:s].
▶ *pron* **1** éste, ésta; *(indefinite)* esto: *I prefer this one* prefiero éste. **2** *(on 'phone)*: *this is Laura* soy Laura.
ⓘ *pl* these [ði:s].
▶ *adv* tan, tanto,-a: *I didn't think it was this far* no creía que fuera tan lejos. LOC **this is** *(introducing)* te presento a.

**thistle** ['θɪsᵊl] *n* cardo.

**thoracic** [θəræsɪk] *adj* torácico,-a.

**thorax** ['θɔ:ræks] *n* tórax *m inv*.

**thorn** [θɔ:n] *n* espina, pincho.

**thorough** ['θʌrə] *adj* **1** *(deep)* profundo,-a, a fondo. **2** *(careful)* cuidadoso,-a,

minucioso,-a. **3** *(person)* concienzudo, -a. **4** *(utter, complete)* total, verdadero,-a.

**thoroughgoing** ['θʌrəgəʊɪŋ] *adj* profundo,-a, minucioso,-a.

**thoroughly** ['θʌrəlɪ] *adv* **1** *(carefully)* a fondo, meticulosamente. **2** *(completely)* totalmente, absolutamente.

**those** [ðəʊz] *adj* esos,-as; *(remote)* aquellos,-as: *could you pass me those plates?* ¿me podrías pasar esos platos?
▶ *pron* ésos,-as; *(remote)* aquéllos,-as: *if these are my books, whose are those?* si estos libros son míos, ¿de quién son aquellos?

**though** [ðəʊ] *conj* aunque, si bien, a pesar de que: *though he doesn't earn very much, he loves his job* aunque no gana mucho, le encanta su trabajo.
▶ *adv* sin embargo, a pesar de todo: *it's expensive –it's worth it though* es caro –sin embargo, vale lo que cuesta. LOC **even though** como si. ▌ **even though** aun cuando, a pesar de que.

**thought** [θɔ:t] *pt & pp* → think.
▶ *n* **1** pensamiento **2** *(consideration)* consideración *f*. **3** *(idea, opinion)* idea, opinión *f*. **4** *(intention)* intención *f*.

**thoughtful** ['θɔ:tfʊl] *adj* **1** *(considerate)* atento,-a, considerado,-a. **2** *(pensive)* pensativo,-a, meditabundo,-a. **3** *(considered)* serio,-a.

**thoughtless** ['θɔ:tləs] *adj* **1** *(unthinking)* irreflexivo,-a, descuidado,-a. **2** *(inconsiderate)* desconsiderado,-a, poco considerado,-a.

**thousand** ['θaʊzᵊnd] *n* mil *m*: *there were thousands of people* había miles de personas.
▶ *adj* mil: *it costs a thousand euros* cuesta mil euros.

**thousandth** ['θaʊzᵊnθ] *adj* milésimo,-a.
▶ *adv* en milésimo lugar.
▶ *n (fraction)* milésimo; *(one part)* milésima parte *f*.

**thrash** [θræʃ] *vt* **1** *(beat)* azotar. **2** *(defeat)* derrotar, dar una paliza a. **3** *(arm, leg, etc)* sacudir.

**thread** [θred] *n* **1** SEW hilo, hebra. **2** *(of screw, bolt)* rosca. **3** *(of story)* hilo.
▶ *vt* **1** *(needle)* enhebrar. **2** *(beads)* ensartar.

**threat** [θret] *n* amenaza.

**threaten** ['θretᵊn] *vt* amenazar (with/ to, con).
▶ *vi* amenazar.

**threatening** ['θretᵊnɪŋ] *adj* amenazador,-ra, intimidatorio,-a.

**three** [θriː] *n* tres *m*.
▶ *adj* tres. COMP **three quarters** tres cuartos. ‖ **Three Wise Men** los Reyes Magos.

✎ Consulta también six.

**three-dimensional** [θriːdɪ'menʃənəl] *adj* tridimensional.

**thresh** [θreʃ] *vt* trillar.

**thresher** ['θreʃəʳ] *n (machine)* trilladora.

**threshold** ['θreʃəʊld] *n* **1** umbral *m*. **2** *fig* umbral *m*, límite *m*.

**threw** [θruː] *pt* → **throw**.

**thrill** [θrɪl] *n (excitement)* emoción *f*, ilusión *f*.
▶ *vt (excite)* entusiasmar, hacer ilusión a, ilusionar.
▶ *vi (de excited)* entusiasmarse.

**thriller** ['θrɪləʳ] *n (novel)* novela de suspense; *(film)* película de suspense; *(play)* obra de suspense.

**thrilling** ['θrɪlɪŋ] *adj* emocionante, apasionante.

**throat** [θrəʊt] *n* garganta.

**thrombosis** [θrɒm'bəʊsɪs] *n* trombosis *f inv*.

**throne** [θrəʊn] *n* trono.

**throttle** ['θrɒtᵊl] *n* **1** válvula reguladora. **2** *fam* acelerador *m*. LOC **at full throttle** a toda pastilla.

**through** [θruː] *prep* **1** por, a través de. **2** *(because of)* por, a causa de. **3** *(from beginning to the end)* hasta el final de.
▶ *adv* **1** de un lado a otro. **2** *(to the end)* hasta el final. **3** GB *(on phone)* conectado,-a. **4** US terminado,-a, acabado,-a.
▶ *adj (train)* directo,-a; *(traffic)* de paso.

**throughout** [θruː'aʊt] *prep* **1** por todo,-a, en todo,-a. **2** *(time)* a lo largo de.
▶ *adv* **1** *(all over)* por/en todas partes. **2** *(completely)* completamente. **3** *(time)* todo el tiempo.

**throw** [θrəʊ] *n* **1** lanzamiento, tiro. **2** *(of dice)* tirada, lance *m*; *(in game)* jugada, turno.
▶ *vt* **1** *(gen)* tirar, arrojar, lanzar. **2** *fig (kiss)* echar, tirar; *(glance, look)* lanzar, dirigir.
◆ **to throw away** *vt sep* **1** *(get rid of, discard)* tirar. **2** *(waste)* desaprovechar, perder; *(money)* malgastar, derrochar. **3** *(speech)* lanzar al aire.
◆ **to throw back** *vt sep* **1** *(ball, etc)* devolver. **2** *(bedclothes)* echar atrás.
◆ **to throw in** *vt sep* **1** *fam (include)* incluir gratis. **2** SP sacar de banda.
◆ **to throw out** *vt sep* **1** *(expel)* echar, expulsar. **2** *(reject)* rechazar. **3** *(discard)* tirar.
◆ **to throw up** *vi* vomitar, devolver.
ⓘ *pt* threw [θruː], *pp* thrown [θrəʊn].

**throwaway** ['θrəʊəweɪ] *adj* de usar y tirar.

**throw-in** ['θrəʊɪn] *n* SP saque *m* de banda.

**thrown** [θrəʊn] *pp* → **throw**.

**thru** [θruː] *prep-adv* US → **through**.
◆ **to thrust on** *vt sep* imponer.

**thud** [θʌd] *n* ruido sordo.
▶ *vi* caer con un ruido sordo.
ⓘ *pt & pp* thudded, *ger* thudding.

**thumb** [θʌm] *n* pulgar *m*.
▶ *vt* hacer autostop.
◆ **to thumb through** *vt insep* hojear.

**thumbtack** ['θʌmtæk] *n* US chincheta.

**thump** [θʌmp] *n (blow)* golpe *m*, puñetazo; *(sound)* golpazo.
▶ *vt* golpear, pegar un puñetazo.
▶ *vi (gen)* golpear; *(heart)* latir con fuerza; *(feet)* caminar con pasos pesados.

**thunder** ['θʌndəʳ] *n* trueno.
▶ *vi* tronar.
▶ *vt (shout)* bramar, rugir.

**thunderstorm** ['θʌndəstɔːm] *n* tormenta.

**Thursday** ['θɜːzdɪ] *n* jueves *m*.

✎ Para ejemplos de uso, consulta Saturday.

**thus** [ðʌs] *adv* **1** *(in this way, like this)* así, de este modo. **2** *(consequently)* así que, por lo tanto, por consiguiente. **3** *(to this extent)* hasta.

**thwart** [θwɔːt] *vt* desbaratar, frustrar.

**thyme** [taɪm] *n* tomillo.

**thyroid** ['θaɪrɔɪd] *n* tiroides *m*. COMP **thyroid gland** glándula tiroides.

**Tibet** [tɪ'bet] *n* Tíbet.

**Tibetan** [tɪˈbetᵊn] *adj* tibetano.
▸ *n* **1** *(person)* tibetano,-a. **2** *(language)* tibetano.

**tibia** [ˈtɪbɪə] *n* tibia.

**tick¹** [tɪk] *n* ZOOL garrapata.

**tick²** [tɪk] *n* **1** *(noise)* tictac *m*. **2** *(mark)* marca, señal *f*.
▸ *vi (clock)* hacer tictac.
▸ *vt* señalar, marcar.

**ticket** [ˈtɪkɪt] *n* **1** *(for transport)* billete *m*. **2** *(for concert, cinema, etc)* entrada. **3** *(for library, etc)* carnet *m*. **4** *(label)* etiqueta. **5** *(for item deposited)* resguardo. **6** *fam (fine)* multa. **7** POL lista de candidatos. [COMP] **ticket collector** revisor,-a. **∥ ticket inspector** revisor,-a. **∥ ticket office** taquilla.

**tickle** [ˈtɪkᵊl] *n* cosquilleo.
▸ *vi (touch lightly)* hacer cosquillas; *(itch)* picar.

**tidal** [ˈtaɪdᵊl] *adj* de la marea. [COMP] **tidal wave 1** *(gen)* maremoto. **2** *fig* oleada.

**tide** [taɪd] *n* **1** marea. **2** *fig (trend)* corriente *f*. [COMP] **high tide** pleamar *f*. **∥ low tide** bajamar *f*.

**tidy** [ˈtaɪdɪ] *adj* **1** *(place)* ordenado,-a, bien arreglado. **2** *(person - appearance)* arreglado,-a; *(- habits)* metódico,-a.
ⓘ *comp* **tidier**, *superl* **tidiest**.
▸ *n* organizador *m*.
▸ *vt* [also **tidy up**] ordenar.
▸ *vi* [also **tidy up**] poner las cosas en orden.
◆ **to tidy away** *vt sep* recoger, guardar.
◆ **to tidy out** *vt sep* limpiar, ordenar.
ⓘ *pt & pp* **tidied**, *ger* **tidying**.

**tie** [taɪ] *n* **1** *(of shirt)* corbata. **2** *(for fastening)* cierre *m*. **3** *(rod, beam)* tirante *m*. **4** *fig (bond)* lazo, vínculo: *family ties are strong* los lazos del parentesco son fuertes. **5** *fig (restriction)* atadura. **6** SP *(draw)* empate *m*; *(match)* partido.
▸ *vt* **1** *(fasten)* atar; *(knot, bow)* hacer. **2** *fig* ligar, vincular, relacionar. **3** *(restrict)* atar. **4** MUS ligar.
▸ *vi* **1** *(fasten)* atarse. **2** SP empatar.
◆ **to tie down** *vt sep* **1** atar, sujetar. **2** *(restrict)* atar; *(commit oneself)* comprometerse.
◆ **to tie up** *vt sep* **1** *(fasten)* atar; *(boat)* amarrar. **2** *(link)* conectar, ligar, rela-

cionar. **3** *(occupy)* liar, ocupar. **4** FIN *(capital)* inmovilizar, invertir. **5** *(finalize)* finalizar, concluir, cerrar.
ⓘ *pt & pp* **tied**, *ger* **tying**.

**tier** [tɪəʳ] *n* **1** *(in stadium)* grada. **2** *(of cake)* piso. **3** *(in hierarchy)* nivel *m*.

**tiger** [ˈtaɪgəʳ] *n* tigre *m*.

**tight** [taɪt] *adj* **1** *(firmly fastened)* apretado,-a, duro,-a. **2** *(taut)* tirante, tenso, -a. **3** *(clothes)* ajustado,-a, ceñido,-a. **4** *(not leaky)* hermético,-a, impermeable. **5** *(hold)* estrecho,-a, fuerte. **6** *(packed together)* apretado,-a. **7** *(strict - schedule)* apretado,-a; *(- security)* estricto,-a, riguroso,-a. **8** *fam (mean)* agarrado,-a, tacaño,-a. **9** *fam (drunk)* borracho,-a. **10** *(bend)* cerrado,-a.
▸ *adv* firmemente, fuerte.

**tighten** [ˈtaɪtᵊn] *vt* **1** *(gen)* apretar, ajustar; *(rope)* tensar. **2** *(make stricter - security)* hacer más estricto, reforzar; *(- credit)* restringir.
▸ *vi (gen)* apretarse; *(rope, muscles)* tensarse.
◆ **to tighten up** *vt sep* intensificar, hacer más estricto,-a.
▸ *vi* ponerse más estricto,-a.

**tightrope** [ˈtaɪtrəʊp] *n* cuerda floja. [COMP] **tightrope walker** funámbulo.

**tights** [taɪts] *n pl* **1** *(gen)* pantys *mpl*, medias *fpl*. **2** *(thick)* leotardos *mpl*, mallas *fpl*.

**tigress** [ˈtaɪgrəs] *n* tigresa.

**tile** [taɪl] *n* *(wall)* azulejo; *(floor)* baldosa; *(roof)* teja.
▸ *vt* **1** *(wall)* alicatar, poner azulejos a. **2** *(floor)* embaldosar. **3** *(roof)* tejar.

**till** [tɪl] *prep* hasta.
▸ *conj* hasta que.
▸ *n (for cash)* caja.
▸ *vt (cultivate)* labrar, cultivar.

**tiller** [ˈtɪləʳ] *n* caña del timón.

**tilt** [tɪlt] *n* **1** inclinación *f*, ladeo. **2** *(with lance)* acometida.
▸ *vt* inclinar, ladear.
▸ *vi* **1** *(slope, shift)* inclinarse. **2** *(with lance)* acometer.

**timber** [ˈtɪmbəʳ] *n* **1** *(wood)* madera (de construcción). **2** *(beam)* viga. **3** *(trees)*

T

árboles *mpl* maderables. COMP **timber mill** aserradero.

▸ *interj* ¡cuidado, que cae!, ¡allá va!

**time** [taɪm] *n* **1** *(period)* tiempo. **2** *(short period)* rato. **3** *(of day)* hora. **4** *(age, period, season)* época. **5** *(occasion)* vez *f*. **6** *(suitable moment)* momento. **7** MUS compás *m*. **8** GB la hora de cerrar.

▸ *vt* **1** *(measure time)* medir la duración de, calcular; *(races, etc)* cronometrar. **2** *(schedule)* estar previsto,-a. LOC **(and) about time** ya era hora. ▎ **all the time** todo el tiempo. ▎ **at any time** en cualquier momento. ▎ **at no time** nunca. ▎ **at one time** en un tiempo. ▎ **at the same time** al mismo tiempo. ▎ **for the time being** de momento. ▎ **from time to time** de vez en cuando. ▎ **in time 1** *(in the long run)* con el tiempo. **2** *(not late)* a tiempo. ▎ **on time** puntual. ▎ **time after time** una y otra vez. ▎ **time's up** se acabó el tiempo. ▎ **to be ahead of one's time** adelantarse a su época. ▎ **to give** sb **a hard time** ponérselo difícil a ALGN. ▎ **to have a bad time** pasarlas negras. ▎ **to have a good time** pasarlo bien. ▎ **to take one's time 1** *(not hurry)* hacer ALGO con calma. **2** *(be slow)* tardar mucho. ▎ **to tell the time** decir la hora.

▸ *n pl* **times** veces *fpl*. LOC **at times** a veces. ▎ **to keep up with the times** estar al día.

**timeless** ['taɪmləs] *adj* eterno,-a.

**timely** ['taɪmlɪ] *adj* oportuno,-a.

**timer** ['taɪmər] *n* temporizador *m*.

**time-share** ['taɪmʃeər] *adj (property)* en multipropiedad.

**timetable** ['taɪmteɪbəl] *n* horario.

**timid** ['tɪmɪd] *n* tímido,-a.

**timing** ['taɪmɪŋ] *n* **1** *(time chosen)* momento escogido; *(judgement)* sentido de la oportunidad. **2** SP *(measurement of time)* cronometraje *m*.

**tin** [tɪn] *n* **1** *(metal)* estaño. **2** *(can)* lata, bote *m*. **3** *(for baking)* molde *m*.

▸ *vt* enlatar.

ⓘ *pt & pp* **tinned**, *ger* **tinning**.

**tinfoil** ['tɪnfɔɪl] *n* papel *m* de estaño.

**tinkle** ['tɪŋkəl] *n* tintineo.

▸ *vt* hacer tintinear.

▸ *vi* **1** *(ring)* tintinear. **2** GB *fam (urinate)* hacer pipí.

**tinned** [tɪnd] *adj* enlatado,-a. COMP **tinned food** comida de lata.

**tin-opener** ['tɪnəʊpənər] *n* abrelatas *m inv*.

**tinsel** ['tɪnsəl] *n* espumillón *m*.

**tiny** ['taɪnɪ] *adj* diminuto,-a.

ⓘ *comp* **tinier**, *superl* **tiniest**.

**tip¹** [tɪp] *n (gen)* extremo, punta, cabo; *(of cigarette)* boquilla, filtro. LOC **from tip to toe** de pies a cabeza.

**tip²** [tɪp] *n* **1** *(gratuity)* propina. **2** *(advice)* consejo, truco; *(confidential information)* soplo, confidencia; *(prediction)* pronóstico.

▸ *vt* **1** *(give gratuity to)* dar una propina a. **2** *(predict)* pronosticar.

**tip³** [tɪp] *n (for rubbish)* vertedero, basurero; *(dirty place)* porquería, desorden *m*.

▸ *vt* **1** *(lean, tilt)* inclinar, ladear. **2** *(pour)* verter; *(throw)* tirar; *(empty)* vaciar. **3** *(rubbish)* verter.

◆ **to tip over** *vi (overturn)* volcarse, caerse; *(boat)* zozobrar.

▸ *vt sep* volcar.

ⓘ *pt & pp* **tipped**, *ger* **tipping**.

**tipsy** ['tɪpsɪ] *adj* achispado,-a, piripi.

ⓘ *comp* **tipsier**, *superl* **tipsiest**.

**tiptoe** ['tɪptəʊ] *vi* caminar de puntillas. LOC **on tiptoe** de puntillas.

**tire¹** [taɪər] *vt* cansar.

▸ *vi* cansarse *(of, de)*.

◆ **to tire out** *vt sep* agotar.

**tire²** [taɪər] *n* US → **tyre**.

**tired** [taɪəd] *adj* **1** *(weary)* cansado,-a. **2** *(fed up)* harto,-a *(of, de)*. LOC **to get tired** cansarse.

**tireless** ['taɪələs] *adj* incansable.

**tiresome** ['taɪəsəm] *adj* molesto,-a, pesado,-a.

**tiring** ['taɪərɪŋ] *adj* cansado,-a, agotador,-ra.

**tissue** ['tɪʃuː] *n* **1** *(cloth)* tisú *m*. **2** *(handkerchief)* pañuelo de papel, kleenex. **3** BIOL tejido. COMP **tissue paper** papel *m* de seda.

**title** ['taɪtəl] *n* título.

▸ *vt* titular.

▸ *n pl* **titles** *(film credits)* créditos *mpl*.

**titleholder** ['taɪtəlhəʊldəʳ] *n* campeón,-ona.

**to** [tu, *unstressed* tə] *prep* **1** *(with place)* a: *we're going to a concert* vamos a un concierto. **2** *(towards)* hacia: *the Labour party has moved to the right* el partido laborista se ha desplazado hacia la derecha. **3** *(as far as, until)* a, hasta: *from beginning to end* desde el principio hasta el final. **4** *(of time)* menos: *it's ten to two* son las dos menos diez. **5** *(with indirect object)* a: *I showed the letter to my mother* le enseñé la carta a mi madre. **6** *(indicating comparison)* a: *I prefer tea to coffee* prefiero el té al café. **7** *prep (ratio)* a: *they won by fourteen points to ten* ganaron por catorce puntos a diez. **8** *(in order to)* para, a fin de: *I worked overtime to earn some extra money* hice horas extras para ganar más dinero. **9** *(substituting infinitive)*: *would you like to dance? -I'd love to* ¿te gustaría bailar? -me encantaría.
► *adv (of door)* ajustada: *push the door to* ajusta la puerta. LOC **to and fro** ir y venir.

✎ Cuando se usa con la raíz del verbo para formar el infinitivo no se traduce: *I want to help you* quiero ayudarte.

**toad** [təʊd] *n* sapo.

**toadstool** ['təʊdstuːl] *n* hongo venenoso.

✎ Toadstool es el nombre en general de las setas no comestibles, las que sí se pueden comer se llaman **mushrooms**.

**toast** [təʊst] *n* **1** *(food)* pan *m* tostado, tostada. **2** *(drink)* brindis *m*.
► *vt* **1** *(cook)* tostar. **2** *(drink)* brindar por, beber a la salud de.

**toaster** ['təʊstəʳ] *n* tostadora.

**tobacco** [təˈbækəʊ] *n* tabaco.
① *pl* tobaccos o tobaccoes.

**tobacconist's** [təbækənɪsts] *n* estanco.

**Tobago** [təˈbeɪgəʊ] *n* Tobago.

**toboggan** [təˈbɒgən] *n* trineo.

**today** [təˈdeɪ] *n* hoy *m*.
► *adv* **1** hoy. **2** *(nowadays)* hoy en día.
◆ **to toddle off** *vi* marcharse, irse.

**toddler** ['tɒdləʳ] *n* niño,-a (que empieza a andar).

**toe** [təʊ] *n* **1** ANAT dedo del pie. **2** *(of shoe)* puntera; *(of sock)* punta.

**toecap** ['təʊkæp] *n* puntera.

**toenail** ['təʊneɪl] *n* uña del dedo del pie.

**toffee** ['tɒfɪ] *n* caramelo.
◆ **to tog out / tog up** *vt sep* vestir.
► *vi* vestirse.

**together** [təˈgeðəʳ] *adv* **1** *(gen)* juntos, -as. **2** *(simultaneously)* a la vez, al mismo tiempo. **3** *(nonstop)* seguido,-a. LOC **to bring together** reunir. ‖ **to come together** juntarse.‖ **together with** junto con.
► *adj fam (confident, organized, capable)* seguro,-a de sí mismo,-a.

**Togo** ['təʊgəʊ] *n* Togo.

**Togolese** [təʊgəˈliːz] *adj* togolés,-esa.
► *n* togolés,-esa.

**toilet** ['tɔɪlət] *n* **1** *(appliance)* váter *m*, inodoro; *(room)* lavabo, baño. **2** *(public)* servicios *mpl*, aseos *mpl*. **3** *(washing)* aseo personal, higiene *m* personal.
COMP **toilet paper** papel *m* higiénico.

**toiletries** ['tɔɪlətrɪz] *n pl* artículos *mpl* de aseo.

**token** ['təʊkən] *n* **1** *(sign, proof)* señal *f*, prueba. **2** *(memento, souvenir)* detalle *m*, recuerdo. **3** *(coupon)* vale *m*. **4** *(coin)* ficha. LOC **in token of** en recuerdo de.
► *adj* simbólico,-a.

**told** [təʊld] *pt & pp* → **tell**.

**tolerance** ['tɒlərəns] *n* tolerancia.

**tolerant** ['tɒlərənt] *adj* tolerante *(of/ towards,* con).

**tolerate** ['tɒləreɪt] *vt* tolerar, aguantar, soportar.

**toll¹** [təʊl] *n* **1** *(payment)* peaje *m*. **2** *(loss)* mortalidad *f*, número de víctimas mortales. LOC **to take its toll on** afectar negativamente.

**toll²** [təʊl] *n (of bell)* tañido.
► *vt* tañer, doblar.
► *vi* doblar.

**tollgate** ['təʊlgeɪt] *n* peaje *m*.

**tom** [tɒm] *n* gato (macho).

**tomahawk** ['tɒməhɔːk] *n* hacha de guerra.

**tomato** [təˈmɑːtəʊ, US təˈmeɪtəʊ] *n* tomate *m*.
① *pl* tomatoes.

**tomb** [tu:m] *n* tumba, sepulcro.
**tombstone** ['tu:mstəʊn] *n* lápida (sepulcral).
**tomcat** ['tɒmkæt] *n* gato (macho).
**tomorrow** [tə'mɒrəʊ] *n* mañana.
▶ *adv* mañana: *tomorrow morning/afternoon* mañana por la mañana/tarde; *see you tomorrow!* ¡hasta mañana!
**ton** [tʌn] *n* tonelada.
▶ *n pl* **tons** *fam* montones *mpl*.
**tone** [təʊn] *n* tono.
**Tonga** ['tɒŋgə] *n* Tonga.
**Tongan** ['tɒŋgən] *adj* tongano,-a.
▶ *n* **1** *(person)* tongano,-a. **2** *(language)* tongano.
**tongs** [tɒŋz] *n pl* tenacillas *fpl*, pinzas *fpl*.
**tongue** [tʌŋ] *n* **1** ANAT lengua. **2** *(language)* lengua, idioma *m*. **3** *(of shoe)* lengüeta. **4** *(of bell)* badajo. **5** *(of land, flame)* lengua. LOC **to stick one's tongue out** sacar la lengua. COMP **tongue twister** trabalenguas *m*.
**tonic** ['tɒnɪk] *n* **1** MED tónico. **2** MUS tónica. **3** *(drink)* tónica.
▶ *adj* tónico,-a. COMP **tonic water** tónica.
**tonight** [tə'naɪt] *n* esta noche *f*.
▶ *adv* esta noche *f*.
**tonne** [tʌn] *n* tonelada.
**tonsil** ['tɒnsl] *n* amígdala.
**tonsillitis** [tɒnsə'laɪtəs] *n* amigdalitis *f*.
**too** [tu:] *adv* **1** *(excessively)* demasiado. **2** *(also)* también. **3** *(besides)* además. **4** *(very)* muy. LOC **too many** demasiados,-as. ∎ **too much** demasiado,-a.
**took** [tʊk] *pt* → take.
**tool** [tu:l] *n* *(gen)* herramienta; *(instrument)* instrumento.
▶ *vt* *(book)* estampar; *(leather)* labrar.
▶ *n pl* **tools** *(gardening, etc)* útiles *mpl*.
◆ **to tool up** *vt sep* equipar.
**toolbar** ['tu:lbɑː'] *n* barra de herramientas.
**toolbox** ['tu:lbɒks] *n* caja de herramientas.
**toolkit** ['tu:lkɪt] *n* juego de herramientas.

**tooth** [tu:θ] *n* **1** *(gen)* diente *m*; *(molar)* muela; *(front tooth)* incisivo. **2** *(of comb)* púa. **3** *(of saw)* diente *m*.
① *pl* teeth.
**toothache** ['tu:θeɪk] *n* dolor *m* de muelas.
**toothbrush** ['tu:θbrʌʃ] *n* cepillo de dientes.
**toothless** ['tu:θləs] *adj* desdentado,-a.
**toothpaste** ['tu:θpeɪst] *n* pasta de dientes.
**toothpick** ['tu:θpɪk] *n* mondadientes *m inv*, palillo.
**top¹** [tɒp] *n* **1** *(highest/upper part)* parte *f* superior. **2** *(far end - of street)* final *m*; *(- of table)* cabecera. **3** *(of mountain)* cumbre *m*. **4** *(of tree)* copa. **5** *(surface)* superficie *f*. **6** *(of bottle)* tapón *m*; *(of pen)* capuchón *m*. **7** *(highest position)*: *she was top of the class* fue la primera de la clase. **8** *(of list)* cabeza. **9** *(of car)* capota. **10** *(clothes)* top *m*; *(of bikini)* parte de arriba. **11** *(beginning)* principio. **12** *(gear)* directa.
▶ *adj* **1** *(highest)* de arriba, superior, más alto,-a. **2** *(best, highest, leading)* mejor, principal. **3** *(highest, maximum)* principal, máximo,-a. COMP **top brass** altos mandos *mpl*. ∎ **top gear** directa.
▶ *vt* **1** *(cover)* cubrir, rematar. **2** *(remove top of plant/fruit)* quitar los rabillos. **3** *sl (kill)* cargarse. **4** *(come first, head)* encabezar. **5** *(better, surpass, exceed)* superar.
① *pt & pp* topped, *ger* topping.
▶ *n* **tops** *(of plant)* hojas *fpl*.
**top²** [tɒp] *n* peonza. LOC **to sleep like a top** dormir como un tronco.
**topaz** ['təʊpæz] *n* topacio.
**topic** ['tɒpɪk] *n* tema *m*.

⊠ Tópico no significa 'tópico', que se traduce por **commonplace**.

**topography** [tə'pɒɡrəfɪ] *n* topografía.
**toponym** ['tɒpənɪm] *n* topónimo.
**topping** ['tɒpɪŋ] *n* *(for pizza)* ingrediente *m*; *(for ice-cream)* cubierta.
▶ *adj* excelente.
**topple** ['tɒpəl] *vt* **1** *(overturn)* volcar. **2** *fig (overthrow)* derribar, derrocar.
▶ *vi* *(fall)* caerse; *(lose balance)* tambalearse, perder el equilibrio.

**torch** [tɔːtʃ] *n* **1** *(with naked flame)* antorcha. **2** *(electric)* linterna.
▶ *vt* quemar, prender fuego a.

**tore** [tɔːʳ] *pt* → **tear**.

**torment** [*(n)* 'tɔːmənt; *(vb)* tɔː'ment] *n* *(gen)* tormento; *(suffering)* angustia.
▶ *vt* **1** *(cause to suffer)* atormentar, torturar. **2** *(annoy)* molestar.

**torn** [tɔːn] *pp* → **tear**.

**tornado** [tɔː'neɪdəʊ] *n* tornado.
ⓘ *pl* tornados o tornadoes.

**torpedo** [tɔː'piːdəʊ] *n* torpedo.
ⓘ *pl* torpedos o torpedoes.

**torrent** ['tɒrənt] *n* torrente *m*.

**torrential** [tə'renʃəl] *adj* torrencial.

**torso** ['tɔːsəʊ] *n* torso.
ⓘ *pl* torsos.

**tort** [tɔːt] *n* JUR agravio.

**tortoise** ['tɔːtəs] *n* tortuga (de tierra).

**torture** ['tɔːtʃəʳ] *n* tortura.

**Tory** ['tɔːrɪ] *n* GB conservador,-ra.
ⓘ *pl* Tories.
▶ *adj* GB conservador,-ra.

**toss** [tɒs] *n* **1** *(shake)* sacudida, movimiento. **2** *(of coin)* sorteo a cara o cruz.
▶ *vt* **1** *(move, shake)* mover, agitar, sacudir; *(pancake)* dar la vuelta a; *(salad)* mezclar. **2** *(throw)* arrojar, lanzar, tirar.
ⓁⓄⒸ **to toss a coin** echarlo a cara o cruz.
ⓘ *pt & pp* totted, *ger* totting.

**total** ['təʊtəl] *adj* *(overall)* total; *(complete)* completo,-a, rotundo,-a.
▶ *n* total *m*, suma. ⓁⓄⒸ **in total** en total.
▶ *vt* sumar.
▶ *vi* sumar, ascender a.

**totalitarian** [təʊtælɪ'teərɪən] *adj* totalitario,-a.

**totally** ['təʊtəlɪ] *adv* totalmente, completamente.

**totem** ['təʊtəm] *n* tótem *m*. ⒸⓄⓂⓅ **totem pole** tótem *m*.

**touch** [tʌtʃ] *n* **1** *(gen)* toque *m*; *(light touch)* roce *m*. **2** *(detail)* detalle *m*, toque *m*. **3** *(sense)* tacto. **4** *(connection)* contacto, comunicación *f*. **5** *(slight quantity)* poquito, pizca. **6** *fam (skill, ability)* habilidad *f*. **7** *(manner, style)* toque *m*, sello. **9** SP toque *m*. ⓁⓄⒸ **to be in touch with** STH estar al corriente de ALGO. ❙

**to get in touch** ponerse en contacto (with, con).
▶ *vt* **1** *(gen)* tocar; *(lightly)* rozar. **2** *(eat)* probar. **3** *(move)* conmover. **4** *(equal, rival)* igualar.
▶ *vi* tocarse.
◆ **to touch down** *vi* **1** *(plane)* aterrizar.
◆ **to touch on / touch upon** *vi* mencionar.
◆ **to touch up** *vt sep* ART retocar.

**touching** ['tʌtʃɪŋ] *adj* conmovedor,-ra.

**touch-screen** ['tʌtʃskriːn] *n* pantalla táctil.

**tough** [tʌf] *adj* **1** *(strong)* fuerte, resistente. **2** *(difficult)* duro,-a, arduo,-a. **3** *(rough, violent)* violento,-a. **4** *(severe)* duro,-a, severo,-a. **5** *(meat)* duro,-a.
▶ *n* tipo duro.

**tour** [tʊəʳ] *n* **1** viaje *m*, excursión *f*. **2** *(round building)* visita. **3** *(by performers)* gira; *(cycling)* vuelta.
▶ *vt* **1** *(gen)* recorrer, viajar por. **2** *(building)* visitar. ⒸⓄⓂⓅ **tour operator** agente *m* de viajes.
▶ *vi* *(by performers)* hacer una gira.

**tourism** ['tʊərɪzəm] *n* turismo.

**tourist** ['tʊərɪst] *n* turista *mf*.
▶ *adj* turístico,-a. ⒸⓄⓂⓅ **tourist class** clase *f* turista. ❙ **tourist office** oficina de turismo.

**tournament** ['tʊənəmənt] *n* torneo.

**tow** [təʊ] *vt* remolcar.
▶ *n* remolque *m*. ⓁⓄⒸ **on tow** de remolque.

**toward** [tə'wɔːd] *prep* US → **towards**.

**towards** [tə'wɔːdz] *prep* **1** *(in direction of)* hacia. **2** *(attitude)* con, para con. **3** *(payment)* para. **4** *(of time)* hacia, cerca de.

**towel** ['taʊəl] *n* toalla.

**tower** ['taʊəʳ] *n* **1** *(gen)* torre *f*. **2** *(of church)* campanario. ⒸⓄⓂⓅ **tower block** bloque *m* (de pisos).

**town** [taʊn] *n* **1** *(large)* ciudad *f*; *(small)* población *f*, municipio, pueblo. **2** *(city centre)* centro. **3** *(people)* ciudadanos *mpl*, ciudad *f*.
▶ *adj* urbano,-a, municipal. ⒸⓄⓂⓅ **town council** ayuntamiento. ❙ **town hall** ayuntamiento.

**township** ['taʊnʃɪp] n **1** (gen) municipio, pueblo. **2** (in South Africa) distrito segregado.

**toxic** ['tɒksɪk] n tóxico,-a.

**toy** [tɔɪ] n juguete m.
▶ adj **1** de juguete. **2** (dog) enano,-a.
COMP **toy shop** juguete m.

**toyshop** ['tɔɪʃɒp] n juguetería.

**trace** [treɪs] n **1** (mark, sign) indicio, rastro. **2** (small amount - material) pizca, vestigio; (- non-material) dejo, asomo, nota. COMP **trace element** oligoelemento.
▶ vt **1** (sketch) trazar, esbozar. **2** (copy) calcar. **3** (find) encontrar, localizar; (follow) seguir la pista de. **4** (describe development) describir.

**tracer** ['treɪsəʳ] n **1** MIL trazadora. **2** MED trazador m. COMP **tracer bullet** bala trazadora.

**trachea** [trə'kɪə] n ANAT tráquea.

**tracing** ['treɪsɪŋ] n calco. COMP **tracing paper** papel m de calco.

**track** [træk] n **1** (mark) pista, huellas fpl, rastro; (of wheels) rodada. **2** (of rocket, bullet, etc) trayectoria. **3** (path) camino, senda, sendero. **4** SP pista. **5** (for motor-racing) circuito. **6** (of railway) vía; (platform) andén m. **7** (on record, etc) tema m, corte m, canción f. LOC **to be on the right track** ir por buen camino. **I to keep track of** seguir. COMP **track and field** atletismo.
▶ vt **1** (person, animal) seguir la pista de. **2** TECH seguir la trayectoria de.
◆ **to track down** vt sep localizar.

**tracksuit** ['træksuːt] n chándal m.

**tract¹** [trækt] n (treatise) tratado; (pamphlet) folleto.

**traction** ['trækʃ[ə]n] n tracción f.

**tractor** ['træktəʳ] n tractor m.

**trade** [treɪd] n **1** (commerce) comercio. **2** (business) negocio; (industry) industria. **3** (occupation) oficio, profesión f.
▶ adj comercial. COMP **trade gap** déficit m comercial. **I trade fair** feria de muestras. **I trade name** nombre m comercial. **I trade union** sindicato. **I trade winds** vientos mpl alisios.
▶ vi (do business) comerciar.
▶ vt (exchange) cambiar.

**trademark** ['treɪdmɑːk] n marca registrada, marca.

**trader** ['treɪdəʳ] n comerciante mf.

**tradesman** ['treɪdzmən] n **1** (businessman) comerciante m; (shopkeeper) tendero. **2** (deliveryman) repartidor m.
ⓘ pl **tradesmen** ['treɪdɪn].

**trading** ['treɪdɪŋ] n comercio.

**tradition** [trə'dɪʃən] n tradición f.

**traditional** [trə'dɪʃənəl] adj tradicional.

**traffic** ['træfɪk] n tráfico.
▶ adj de la circulación, del tráfico. COMP **traffic circle** US rotonda. **I traffic jam** atasco, embotellamiento. **I traffic lights** semáforo. **I traffic warden** guardia mf de tráfico.
▶ vi traficar (in, con).

⊕ Un **traffic warden** es un especie de guardia urbano que vigila que los coches estén bien aparcados y regula el tráfico de las ciudades.

**tragedy** ['trædʒədɪ] n tragedia.
ⓘ pl **tragedies**.

**tragic** ['trædʒɪk] adj trágico,-a.

**trail** [treɪl] n **1** (path) camino, sendero. **2** (track, mark, scent) rastro, pista, huellas fpl. **3** (of rocket, comet) cola; (of dust, vapour) estela; (of blood) reguero.
▶ vt **1** (follow) seguir la pista de. **2** (drag) arrastrar.
▶ vi **1** (lag behind) ir rezagado,-a, quedarse atrás. **2** (drag) arrastrarse.

**trailer** ['treɪləʳ] n **1** AUTO remolque m. **2** US caravana. **3** CINEM tráiler m, avance m.

**train** [treɪn] n **1** (transport) tren m. **2** (of dress) cola. **3** (line - of animals) recua; (- of vehicles) convoy m.
▶ vt **1** SP entrenar, preparar. **2** (teach) enseñar. **3** (animal) amaestrar, adiestrar. COMP **train driver** maquinista m. **I train station** estación f de tren.
▶ vi **1** SP entrenarse, prepararse. **2** (teach) estudiar. **3** MIL adiestrarse.

**trained** [treɪnd] adj **1** (worker - skilled) calificado,-a, cualificado,-a. **2** (animal) amaestrado,-a, adiestrado,-a.

**trainee** [treɪ'niː] *n* **1** *(manual work)* aprendiz,-za. **2** *(professional work)* *persona que está haciendo prácticas.*

**trainer** ['treɪnəʳ] *n* **1** SP entrenador,-ra. **2** *(of dogs)* amaestrador,-ra; *(of circus animals)* domador,-ra; *(of race horses)* preparador,-ra. **3** *(shoe)* zapatilla de deporte.

**training** ['treɪnɪŋ] *n* **1** formación *f* (profesional), capacitación *f*. **2** SP entrenamiento, preparación *f* física.
▶ *vi* MIL instrucción *f*.

**traitor** ['treɪtəʳ] *n* traidor,-ra.

**tram** [træm] *n* tranvía *m*.

**tramcar** ['træmkɑː'] *n* tranvía *m*.

**tramp** [træmp] *n* vagabundo,-a.

☒ Tramp no significa 'trampa', que se traduce por trap.

**trample** ['træmpəl] *vt* pisotear.
▶ *vi* pisotear (on/over, -).

**trampoline** ['træmpəliːn] *n* cama elástica.

**tranquilliser** ['træŋkwɪlaɪzəʳ] *n* → **tranquilizer.**

**tranquillizer** ['træŋkwɪlaɪzəʳ] *n* tranquilizante *m*, calmante *m*.

**transcend** [træn'send] *vt* **1** *(go beyond)* trascender. **2** *(surpass)* superar.

**transept** ['trænsept] *n* crucero.

**transfer** [*(n)* 'trænsfɜːʳ; *(vb)* træns'fɜːʳ] *n* **1** FIN transferencia. **2** JUR *(of property)* traspaso. **3** *(of employee)* traslado. **4** SP *(of player)* traspaso; *(player)* fichaje *m*. **5** *(drawing)* cromo, calcomanía. **6** *(of airline passenger)* transbordo, trasbordo.
▶ *vt* **1** FIN transferir. **2** JUR *(property)* traspasar. **3** *(employee, prisoner)* trasladar. **4** SP *(player)* traspasar. **5** *(data, information, phone call)* pasar.
ⓘ *pt & pp* transferred, *ger* transferring.

**transform** [træns'fɔːm] *vt* transformar.
▶ *vi* transformarse (into, en), convertirse (into, en).

**transistor** [træn'zɪstəʳ] *n* transistor.

**transition** [træn'zɪʃən] *n* transición *f*.

**transitive** ['trænsɪtɪv] *adj* transitivo,-a.

**translate** [træns'leɪt] *vt* **1** *(gen)* traducir (from, de) (into, a). **2** *(express, explain)* expresar. **3** *(transform)* transformar.
▶ *vi* *(person)* traducir; *(word, book, etc)* traducirse.

**translation** [træns'leɪʃən] *n* traducción *f*.

**translator** [træns'leɪtəʳ] *n* traductor,-ra.

**translucent** [trænz'luːsənt] *adj* translúcido,-a.

**transmission** [trænz'mɪʃən] *n* transmisión *f*.

**transmit** [trænz'mɪt] *vt* transmitir (to, a).
ⓘ *pt & pp* transmitted, *ger* transmitting.

**transmitter** [trænz'mɪtəʳ] *n* transmisor *m*.

**transparency** [træns'peərənsɪ] *n* **1** *(quality)* transparencia. **2** *(slide)* diapositiva; *(acetate)* transparencia.
ⓘ *pl* transparencies.

**transparent** [træns'peərənt] *adj* **1** transparente. **2** *fig* claro,-a, evidente.

**transplant** [*(n)* 'trænsplɑːnt; *(vb)* træns'plɑːnt] *n* trasplante *m*.
▶ *vt* trasplantar.

**transport** [*(n)* 'trænspɔːt; *(vb)* træns'pɔːt] *n* transporte *m*.
▶ *vt* **1** transportar. **2** HIST deportar.

**trap** [træp] *n* **1** *(gen)* trampa. **2** *(vehicle)* coche *m* ligero de dos ruedas. **3** *(of drain)* sifón *m*. LOC **to set a trap** tender una trampa.
▶ *vt* **1** *(catch - gen)* atrapar; *(snare - animal)* cazar; *(imprison)* entrampar; *(part of body)* pillar. **2** SP *(in football)* parar con el pie. **3** *fig (trick)* engañar, tender una trampa a. **4** *(heat, light, etc)* retener.
ⓘ *pt & pp* trapped, *ger* trapping.

**trapdoor** ['træpdɔːʳ] *n* *(gen)* trampilla; *(in theatre)* escotillón *m*.

**trapeze** [trə'piːz] *n* *(of circus)* trapecio.

**trapezium** [trə'piːzɪəm] *n* trapecio.
ⓘ *pl* trapeziums o trapezia [trə'piːzɪə].

**trapezoid** ['træpɪzɔɪd] *n* **1** GB trapecio *m*. **1** US trapezoide.

**trash** [træʃ] *n* basura. COMP **trash can 1** *(on computer)* papelera de reciclaje. **2** *(for waste)* US cubo de la basura.

**trauma** ['trɔːmə] *n* trauma *m*.

T

**travel** ['trævᵊl] *n* viajes *mpl*, viajar *m*. COMP **travel agency** agencia de viajes. ‖ **travel sickness** mareo.
▶ *vt* viajar por, recorrer.
▶ *vi* **1** *(make a journey)* viajar; *(go)* ir. **2** *(move, go)* ir. **3** *(go fast)* ir rápido, ir a toda velocidad. **4** *(as salesperson)* ser viajante, ser representante. **5** *(wine, food, etc)* poderse transportar.
ⓘ *pt & pp* travelled (US traveled), *ger* travelling (US traveling).
▶ *n pl* **travels** *(journeys)* viajes *mpl*.

**traveler** ['trævᵊləʳ] *n* US → **traveller**.

**traveller** ['trævᵊləʳ] *n* **1** *(gen)* viajero,-a. **2** *(representative)* viajante *mf*, representante *mf*. COMP **traveller's cheque** cheque *m* de viaje.

**trawler** ['trɔːləʳ] *n* pesquero de arrastre.

**tray** [treɪ] *n* **1** *(for food)* bandeja. **2** *(for papers)* caja, cesta. **3** *(in photography)* cubeta.

**treachery** ['tretʃərɪ] *n* traición *f*.
ⓘ *pl* treacheries.

**tread** [tred] *n* **1** *(manner or sound of walking)* paso, pasos *mpl*. **2** *(on stair)* escalón *m*.
▶ *vt* **1** *(gen)* pisar, pisotear. **2** *(walk on)* andar por; *(make)* hacer.
ⓘ *pt* trod [trɒd], *pp* trodden [trɒdən] o trod [trɒd].

**treason** ['triːzᵊn] *n* traición *f*.

**treasure** ['treʒəʳ] *n* *(gen)* tesoro.

**treasurer** ['treʒərəʳ] *n* tesorero,-a.

**treasury** ['treʒərɪ] *n* tesorería.
ⓘ *pl* treasuries.

**treat** [triːt] *n* **1** *(meal, drink)* convite *m*. **2** *(present)* regalo. **3** *(pleasure)* placer *m*, gusto, deleite *m*.
▶ *vt* **1** *(gen)* tratar. **2** *(invite)* invitar; *(give)* regalar.

**treatment** ['triːtmənt] *n* **1** MED tratamiento, cura. **2** *(manner of treating)* trato. **3** *(process)* tratamiento.

❌ Treatment no significa 'tratamiento (forma de dirigirse alguien)', que se traduce por form of address.

**treaty** ['triːtɪ] *n* tratado.
ⓘ *pl* treaties.

**treble** ['trebᵊl] *adj* **1** *(threefold)* triple. **2** MUS de tiple. COMP **treble clef** clave *f* de sol.
▶ *n* MUS tiple *mf*.

▶ *vt* triplicar.
▶ *vi* triplicarse.

**tree** [triː] *n* árbol *m*.

**tree-top** ['triːtɒp] *n* copa.

**trekking** ['trekɪŋ] *n* senderismo.

**tremble** ['trembᵊl] *n* temblor *m*.
▶ *vi* temblar.

**tremendous** [trɪ'mendəs] *adj* **1** *(huge)* tremendo,-a, inmenso,-a. **2** *fam (great)* fantástico,-a, estupendo,-a.

**trench** [trentʃ] *n* **1** *(ditch)* zanja. **2** MIL trinchera.

**trend** [trend] *n* **1** *(tendency)* tendencia (to/towards, hacia), tónica. **2** *(fashion)* moda.

**trendy** ['trendɪ] *adj fam* moderno,-a, de moda.
ⓘ *comp* trendier, *superl* trendiest.

**trespass** ['trespəs] *n* **1** entrada ilegal. **2** REL pecado.
▶ *vi* **1** *(on land)* entrar sin autorización; *(in affairs)* entrometerse. **2** REL pecar (against, contra). LOC **"No trespassing"** «Prohibido el paso».

❌ To trespass no significa 'traspasar', que se traduce por to go through.

**trespasser** ['trespəsəʳ] *n* intruso,-a.

**tress** [tres] *n* mechón *m*.
▶ *n pl* **tresses** melena *f sing*, cabellera *f sing*.

**trestle** ['tresᵊl] *n* caballete *m*.

**trial** ['traɪəl] *n* **1** JUR proceso, juicio. **2** *(test)* prueba. **3** *(suffering)* aflicción *f*, sufrimiento; *(trouble)* molestia.
▶ *n pl* **trials** SP pruebas *fpl*.

**triangle** ['traɪæŋgᵊl] *n* triángulo.

**triangular** [traɪ'æŋgjʊləʳ] *adj* triangular.

**tribal** ['traɪbᵊl] *adj* tribal.

**tribe** [traɪb] *n* **1** tribu *f*. **2** *fam (family)* tribu *f*, familia.

**tribune** ['trɪbjuːn] *n* **1** ARCH tribuna. **2** *(Roman magistrate)* tribuno.

**tributary** ['trɪbjʊtrəɪ] *n* afluente *m*.
ⓘ *pl* tributaries.
▶ *adj* tributario,-a.

**tribute** ['trɪbjuːt] *n* **1** *(homage)* homenaje *m*, tributo. **2** *(payment)* tributo.

**triceps** ['traɪseps] *n pl* tríceps *m inv*.

**trick** [trɪk] n **1** (gen) truco. **2** (prank, joke) broma. **3** (cards won) baza. LOC **to play a trick on SB** gastarle una broma a ALGN. ∎ **trick or treat** US frase de los niños que en Halloween van por las casas pidiendo un regalo a cambio de no hacer una jugarreta.
▶ adj de juguete, de mentira.
▶ vt (deceive) engañar, burlar.

**trickle** ['trɪkəl] n **1** goteo, hilo. **2** fig pequeña cantidad f, poco.
▶ vi **1** (liquid) gotear, salir gota a gota. **2** fig salir (entrar, llegar, etc) poco a poco.

**tricky** ['trɪkɪ] adj **1** (person) astuto,-a. **2** (problem, situation - difficult) difícil; (- delicate) delicado,-a.
① comp **trickier**, superl **trickiest**.

**tricycle** ['traɪsɪkəl] n triciclo.

**trident** ['traɪdənt] n tridente m.

**trier** [traɪəʳ] n persona que se esfuerza.

**trifle** ['traɪfəl] n **1** (unimportant thing) nimiedad f. **2** (little money) poco dinero. **3** GB postre de bizcocho. LOC **a trifle** un poco, algo.

**trigger** ['trɪgəʳ] n **1** (of gun) gatillo. **2** (of camera, machine) disparador m.

**trigonometry** [trɪgə'nɒmətrɪ] n trigonometría.

**trillion** ['trɪlɪən] n **1** billón m. **2** GB (formerly) trillón m.

🖉 En el uso actual, tanto en EE UU como en Gran Bretaña, un **trillion** equivale al billón español, es decir, un millón de millones.

**trim** [trɪm] adj **1** (neat, tidy) (bien) arreglado,-a, ordenado,-a, cuidado,-a. **2** (person, figure) esbelto,-a, delgado,-a.
① comp **trimmer**, superl **trimmest**.
▶ n **1** (cut) recorte m. **2** (decoration - on clothes) adornos mpl; (- along edges) ribete m; (upholstery) tapicería.
▶ vt **1** (make neat) arreglar; (cut - hair) cortar, recortar; (- hedge, etc) podar. **2** (reduce by cutting back) recortar, reducir. **3** (decorate) adornar (with, con); (upholster) tapizar.
◆ **to trim off** vt sep recortar, quitar.
① pt & pp **trimmed**, ger **trimming**.

**trimmings** ['trɪmɪŋz] n pl **1** CULIN (accompaniments) guarnición f sing. **2** (decorations) adornos mpl. **3** (after cutting) recortes mpl.

**Trinidad** ['trɪnɪdæd] n Trinidad. COMP **Trinidad and Tobago** Trinidad y Tobago.

**trip** [trɪp] n **1** (journey) viaje m. **2** (excursion) excursión f.
▶ vi **1** (stumble) tropezar (over, con). **2** (move lightly) ir con paso ligero.
① pt & pp **tripped**, ger **tripping**.

**tripe** [traɪp] n **1** CULIN callos mpl. **2** fam tonterías fpl, bobadas fpl.

**triple** ['trɪpəl] adj triple.

**triplet** ['trɪplət] n (child) trillizo,-a.

**triumph** [traɪəmf] n **1** triunfo, éxito. **2** (joy) júbilo, alegría.
▶ vi triunfar (over, de/sobre), vencer.

**trivial** ['trɪvɪəl] adj trivial.

**trod** [trɒd] pt → tread.

**trodden** ['trɒdən] pp → tread.

**troll** [trəʊl] n duende m.

**trolley** ['trɒlɪ] n **1** (in supermarket, at airport) carro, carrito. **2** (in hospital) cama con ruedas. **3** (for food) mesita de ruedas. **4** US tranvía. COMP **trolley bus** trolebús mf. ∎ **trolley car** tranvía mf.

**trombone** [trɒm'bəʊn] n trombón m.

**trophy** ['trəʊfɪ] n trofeo.
① pl **trophies**.

**tropic** ['trɒpɪk] n trópico.
▶ n pl **the tropics** los trópicos mpl.

**tropical** ['trɒpɪkəl] adj tropical.

**tropism** [trə'pɪzəm] n tropismo.

**troposphere** ['trɒpəsfɪəʳ] n troposfera.

**trot** [trɒt] n trote m.
▶ vi (gen) trotar, ir al trote; (on horse) cabalgar al trote.
① pt & pp **trotted**, ger **trotting**.
▶ n pl **the trots** fam diarrea f sing.

**trouble** ['trʌbəl] n **1** (problems) problema m, problemas mpl. **2** (inconvenience, bother) molestia, esfuerzo. **3** (unrest, disturbance) conflictos mpl, disturbios mpl. LOC **to be in trouble** tener problemas. ∎ **to get in trouble** meterse en un lío.
▶ vt **1** (cause worry, distress) preocupar, inquietar. **2** (hurt) dar problemas a, doler. **3** (bother) molestar, incomodar.
▶ vi molestarse, preocuparse (about, por).

**T**

**troublemaker** [ˈtrʌbəlmeɪkəʳ] n alborotador,-ra.

**trough** [trɒf] n (for drinking) abrevadero; (for eating) comedero, pesebre m.

**trousers** [ˈtraʊzəz] n pl pantalón m sing, pantalones mpl.

**trout** [traʊt] n trucha.

**trowel** [ˈtraʊəl] n 1 (bricklaying tool) paleta. 2 (garden tool) desplantador m.

**truant** [ˈtruːənt] n (from school) persona que hace novillos. LOC **to play truant** hacer novillos.

**truce** [truːs] n tregua.

**truck** [trʌk] n 1 (lorry) camión m. 2 GB (railway wagon) vagón m.

**trucker** [ˈtrʌkəʳ] n US camionero,-a.

**true** [truː] adj 1 (not false) verdadero,-a, cierto,-a. 2 (genuine, real) auténtico,-a, genuino,-a, real. 3 (faithful) fiel, leal. 4 (exact) exacto,-a. LOC **to come true** hacerse realidad.
  ▶ adv 1 (truthfully) sinceramente. 2 (accurately) bien.

**truffle** [ˈtrʌfəl] n trufa.

**truly** [ˈtruːlɪ] adv 1 (really) verdaderamente, de verdad, realmente. 2 (sincerely) sinceramente. 3 (faithfully) fielmente, lealmente. LOC **yours truly** (in letters) atentamente.
  ◆ **to trump up** vt sep inventar, falsificar.

**trumpet** [ˈtrʌmpɪt] n MUS trompeta.
  ▶ vi 1 fanfarronear. 2 (elephant) barritar.

**truncheon** [ˈtrʌntʃən] n porra (de policía).

**trunk** [trʌŋk] n 1 (of tree, body) tronco. 2 (large case) baúl m. 3 (elephant's) trompa. 4 US (of car) maletero.

**trunks** [trʌŋks] n pl bañador m sing (de hombre).

**trust** [trʌst] n 1 (confidence) confianza. 2 (responsibility) responsabilidad f. 3 FIN (money, property) fondo de inversión.
  ▶ vt 1 (have faith in, rely on) confiar en, fiarse de. 2 (hope, expect) esperar.
  ▶ vi confiar (in, en), tener confianza (in, en).

**trustful** [ˈtrʌstful] adj confiado,-a.

**trustworthy** [ˈtrʌstwɜːðɪ] adj 1 (person) digno,-a de confianza, honrado,-a. 2 (news, etc) fidedigno,-a.

**truth** [truːθ] n verdad f.

**truthful** [ˈtruːθful] adj 1 (account, etc) verídico,-a, veraz. 2 (person) sincero,-a, veraz.

**try** [traɪ] n 1 intento. 2 SP (rugby) ensayo.
  ⓘ pl **tries**.
  ▶ vt 1 (attempt) intentar. 2 (test, use) probar, ensayar; (food) probar. 3 JUR juzgar, procesar.
  ▶ vi (make an attempt) intentar.
  ◆ **to try for** vi tratar de obtener.
  ◆ **to try on** vt sep (clothes) probarse.
  ◆ **to try out** vt sep probar, ensayar.
  ⓘ pt & pp **tried**, ger **trying**.

**tsar** [zɑːʳ] n zar m.

**tsarina** [zɑːˈriːnə] n zarina.

**tsetse fly** [ˈtsetsɪflaɪ] n mosca tsetsé.

**T-shirt** [ˈtiːʃɜːt] n camiseta.

**tub** [tʌb] n 1 (for washing clothes) balde m. 2 (bath) bañera. 3 (food container) tarrina.

**tuba** [ˈtjuːbə] n tuba.

**tube** [tjuːb] n 1 (pipe, container) tubo. 2 AUTO cámara de aire.
  ▶ n **the tube** la televisión f.
  ▶ n **the Tube** (underground) el metro.

⊕ **The Tube** es el nombre con el que se conoce al metro de Londres.

**tuck** [tʌk] n 1 (fold) pliegue m. 2 GB (sweets, etc) golosinas fpl, chucherías fpl.

**Tuesday** [ˈtjuːzdɪ] n martes m inv.

✎ Para ejemplos de uso, consulta **Saturday**.

**tuft** [tʌft] n 1 (of feathers) penacho. 2 (of hair) mechón m. 3 (of grass) mata.

**tug** [tʌg] n 1 (pull) tirón m, estirón m. 2 (boat) remolcador m.
  ▶ vt 1 (pull) tirar de, dar un estirón de. 2 (boat) remolcar.
  ⓘ pt & pp **tugged**, ger **tugging**.
  ▶ vi tirar (at, de).
  ⓘ pt & pp **tugged**, ger **tugging**.

**tuition** [tjuːˈɪʃən] n enseñanza, instrucción f. COMP **private tuition** clases fpl particulares. ▌ **tuition fees** EDUC matrícula.

**tulip** [ˈtjuːlɪp] n tulipán m.

**tumble** [ˈtʌmbəl] n caída, tumbo. COMP **tumble drier** secadora.
  ▶ vi 1 (fall) caerse. 2 (in acrobatics) dar volteretas.

**tumbler** ['tʌmbᵊləʳ] *n* **1** *(glass)* vaso. **2** *(acrobat)* volteador,-ra. **3** *(toy)* tentetieso.

**tummy** ['tʌmɪ] *n* barriga.
ⓘ *pl* **tummies.**

**tumor** ['tjuːməʳ] *n* US → **tumour.**

**tumour** ['tjuːməʳ] *n* barriga.

**tuna** ['tjuːnə] *n* atún *m*, bonito.
ⓘ *pl* **tuna** o **tunas.**

**tune** [tjuːn] *n* melodía. LOC **in tune** afinado,-a. ‖ **out of tune** desafinado,-a.
▶ *vt* **1** MUS afinar. **2** *(radio, etc)* sintonizar. **3** *(engine)* poner a punto.

**tuner** ['tjuːnəʳ] *n* **1** *(of piano)* afinador, -ra. **2** *(on radio)* sintonizador *m*.

**tungsten** ['tʌŋstən] *n* tungsteno.

**tunic** ['tjuːnɪk] *n* túnica.

**tuning** ['tjuːnɪŋ] *n* **1** *(of instrument)* afinación *f*. **2** *(of radio)* sintonización *f*. **3** *(of engine)* puesta a punto. COMP **tuning fork** diapasón *m*.

**Tunis** ['tjuːnɪs] *n* Túnez.

**Tunisia** [tjuːˈnɪsɪə] *n* Túnez.

**Tunisian** [tjuːˈnsɪən] *adj* tunecino,-a.
▶ *n* tunecino,-a.

**tunnel** ['tʌnᵊl] *n* túnel *m*.
▶ *vt* excavar un túnel.
ⓘ *pt & pp* **tunnelled** (US **tunneled**), ger **tunnelling** (US **tunneling**).

**turban** ['tɜːbᵊn] *n* turbante *m*.

**turbojet** ['tɜːbəʊdʒet] *n* turborreactor *m*.

**turbot** ['tɜːbət] *n* rodaballo.
ⓘ *pl* **turbot** o **turbots.**

**turbulence** ['tɜːbjʊləns] *n* turbulencia.

**turf** [tɜːf] *n* césped *m*. COMP **the turf** las carreras de caballos, el turf *m*.
◆ **to turf out** *vt sep fam* poner de patitas en la calle, echar.

**Turk** [tɜːk] *n* *(person)* turco,-a.

**Turkey** ['tɜːkɪ] *n* Turquía.

**turkey** ['tɜːkɪ] *n* pavo. LOC **to talk turkey** hablar a las claras.

**Turkish** ['tɜːkɪʃ] *adj* turco,-a.
▶ *n* *(language)* turco.
▶ *n pl* **the Turkish** los turcos *mpl*.

**turn** [tɜːn] *n* **1** *(gen)* vuelta. **2** *(change of direction)* giro, vuelta; *(bend)* curva, recodo. **3** *(chance, go)* turno. **4** *(change)* cambio, giro.
LOC **to turn a corner** doblar la esquina.

▶ *vt* **1** *(rotate)* girar, hacer girar. **2** *(page)* pasar, volver; *(soil)* revolver; *(ankle)* torcer. **3** *(change)* convertir, transformar; *(milk)* agriar; *(stomach)* revolver.
▶ *vi* **1** *(revolve)* girar, dar vueltas. **2** *(change direction - person)* girarse, volverse. **3** *(become)* hacerse, ponerse, volverse; *(milk)* agriarse, cortarse.
◆ **to turn back** *vt sep* **1** *(make return)* hacer volver. **2** *(clock)* retrasar.
▶ *vi* *(return)* volverse atrás.
◆ **to turn down** *vt sep* **1** *(reject)* rechazar; *(request)* denegar. **2** *(radio, etc)* bajar. **3** *(fold)* doblar.
◆ **to turn into** *vt sep* convertir.
◆ **to turn off** *vt sep* **1** *(electricity)* desconectar; *(light, gas, appliance)* apagar; *(tap)* cerrar. **2** *(dislike)* repugnar, dar asco a.
▶ *vt insep* *(off road)* salir de.
▶ *vi* **1** *(switch off)* apagarse. **2** *(off road)* salir.
◆ **to turn on** *vt sep* **1** *(electricity)* conectar; *(light, gas, appliance)* encender; *(tap)* abrir; *(engine)* poner en marcha, encender. **2** *(attack)* atacar, arremeter contra; *(aim, point at)* apuntar, dirigir. **3** *fam (excite)* excitar, entusiasmar.
▶ *vt insep* *(hinge on)* depender de, girar en torno a.
▶ *vi* encenderse.
◆ **to turn out** *vt sep* **1** *(light)* apagar. **2** *(produce)* producir, fabricar. **3** *(empty)* vaciar; *(cake, jelly, etc)* desmoldar. **4** *(expel)* expulsar, echar.
▶ *vi* **1** *(prove to be, happen)* salir, resultar. **2** *(go out)* salir; *(attend)* asistir, acudir; *(crowds)* salir a la calle.
◆ **to turn round** *vi* dar la vuelta.
◆ **to turn up** *vi* *(arrive)* llegar, presentarse; *(appear)* aparecer.
▶ *vt sep* **1** *(fold upwards)* doblar hacia arriba, levantar; *(shorten)* acortar. **2** *(radio, gas, heat, etc)* subir.
▶ *vt insep* *(find)* descubrir, encontrar.

**turnabout** ['tɜːnəbaʊt] *n* giro, cambio.

**turning** ['tɜːnɪŋ] *n* bocacalle *f*, esquina. COMP **turning lathe** torno *m*.

**turnip** ['tɜːnɪp] *n* nabo.

**turnover** ['tɜːnəʊvəʳ] *n* **1** *(sales, business)* facturación *f*. **2** *(movement of employees)* movimiento; *(of stock)* rotación *f*. **3** CULIN pastelito relleno.

**turnpike** ['tɜːnpaɪk] n US autopista de peaje.

**turquoise** ['tɜːkwɔɪz] n **1** (gem) turquesa. **2** (colour) azul m turquesa.
▶ adj azul turquesa.

**turtle** ['tɜːtᵊl] n tortuga marina.

**tusk** [tʌsk] n colmillo.

**tutor** ['tjuːtəʳ] n **1** (private teacher) profesor,-ra particular. **2** (at university) profesor,-ra, tutor,-ra.
▶ vt dar clases particulares a (in, de).

**Tuvalu** [tuːvəˈluː] n Tuvalu.

**tuxedo** [tʌkˈsiːdəʊ] n US esmoquin m.
ⓘ pl tuxedos.

**TV** ['tiːbjuːləns] abbr (television) televisión f, tele f.

**tweezers** ['twiːzəz] n pl pinzas fpl.

**twelfth** [twelfθ] adj duodécimo,-a.
▶ adv en duodécimo lugar.
▶ n (fraction) duodécimo; (one part) duodécima parte f.

✎ Consulta también sixth.

**twelve** [twelv] n doce m.
▶ adj doce.

✎ Consulta también six.

**twenties** ['twentɪz] n pl the twenties los años mpl veinte. ⌊LOC⌋ to be in one's twenties tener veintitantos años.

✎ Consulta también sixties.

**twentieth** ['twentɪəθ] adj vigésimo,-a.
▶ adv en vigésimo lugar.
▶ n (fraction) vigésimo; (one part) vigésima parte f.

✎ Consulta también sixtieth.

**twenty** ['twentɪ] n veinte m.
▶ adj veinte.

✎ Consulta también sixty.

**twice** [twaɪs] adv dos veces. ⌊LOC⌋ twice over dos veces.

**twig¹** [twɪg] n ramita.

**twilight** ['twaɪlaɪt] n crepúsculo.

**twin** [twɪn] n gemelo,-a, mellizo,-a.
▶ adj gemelo,-a, mellizo,-a. ⌊COMP⌋ twin bed cama doble.
▶ vt hermanar.
ⓘ pt & pp twinned, ger twinning.

**twinkle** ['twɪŋkᵊl] n **1** (of light, stars) centelleo. **2** (in eye) brillo.
▶ vi **1** (lights, stars) centellear, destellar. **2** (eyes) brillar.

**twirl** [twɜːl] n giro, vuelta.
▶ vt **1** girar rápidamente, dar vueltas a. **2** (twist, fiddle with) retorcer, juguetear con.
▶ vi girar rápidamente, dar vueltas.

**twist** [twɪst] n **1** (in road) recodo, vuelta. **2** (action) torsión m. **3** MED torcedura, esguince m. **4** (dance) twist m.
▶ vt **1** (sprain) torcer. **2** (screw, coil) retorcer. **3** (turn, wind) girar, dar vueltas a.
▶ vi **1** (turn) girarse. **2** (wind, coil) enroscarse, enrollarse. **3** (road) serpentear.

**twitch** [twɪtʃ] n **1** (pull) tirón m. **2** (nervous tic) tic m nervioso.
▶ vt mover.
▶ vi moverse nerviosamente.

**twitter** ['twɪtəʳ] n gorjeo.
▶ vt gorjear.

**two** [tuː] n dos m. ⌊LOC⌋ in two por la mitad. ❙ in twos de dos en dos. ❙ it takes two es cosa de dos. ❙ to put two and two together atar cabos. ❙ that makes two of us ya somos dos.
▶ adj dos.

**tycoon** [taɪˈkuːn] n magnate m.

**type** [taɪp] n **1** (kind) tipo, clase f. **2** (letter) letra, carácter m.
▶ vt & vi escribir a máquina.
◆ to type up vt sep pasar a máquina.

☒ Type no significa 'tipo (persona)', que se traduce por guy.

**typewriter** ['taɪpraɪtəʳ] n máquina de escribir.

**typhoid** ['taɪfɔɪd] n fiebre f tifoidea.

**typhus** ['taɪfəs] n tifus m.

**typical** ['tɪpʊkəl] adj típico,-a.

**typing** ['taɪpɪŋ] n mecanografía.

**typist** ['taɪpɪst] n mecanógrafo,-a.

**tyranny** ['tɪrənɪ] n tiranía.
ⓘ pl tyrannies.

**tyrant** ['taɪᵊrənt] n tirano,-a.

**tyre** [taɪəʳ] n neumático.

**Tyrrhenian** [tɪˈriːnɪən] adj tirreno,-a. ⌊COMP⌋ the Tyrrhenian Sea el (mar) m Tirreno.

**tzar** [zɑːʳ] n zar m, czar m.

**U, u** [juː] *n (the letter)* U, u *f.*

**udder** [ˈʌdəʳ] *n* ubre *f.*

**UFO** [ˈjuːˈefəʊ] *abbr* (unidentified flying object) ovni *m f,* objeto volador no identificado.

**Uganda** [juːˈgændə] *n* Uganda.

**Ugandan** [juːˈgændən] *adj* ugandés, -esa.
  ► *n* ugandés,-esa.

**ugly** [ˈʌglɪ] *adj* **1** feo,-a. **2** *(situation, etc)* desagradable. **3** *(custom, vice)* repugnante.
  ⓘ *comp* uglier, *superl* ugliest.

**Ukraine** [juːˈkreɪn] *n* Ucrania.

**Ukranian** [juːˈkeɪnɪən] *adj* ucraniano,-a.
  ► *n* **1** *(person)* ucraniano,-a. **2** *(language)* ucraniano.

**ulcer** [ˈʌlsəʳ] *n* **1** *(external)* llaga. **2** *(in stomach)* úlcera.

**ulna** [ˈʌlnə] *n* cúbito.
  ⓘ *pl* ulnae [ˈʌlniː].

**ultimate** [ˈʌltɪmət] *adj* **1** *(final)* final. **2** *(basic)* esencial, fundamental.
  ► *n* the ultimate *(good)* el último grito; *(bad)* el colmo.

☒ Ultimate no significa último', que se traduce por last.

**ultrasound** [ˈʌltrəsaʊnd] *n* ultrasonido.

**ultraviolet** [ˌʌltrəˈvaɪələt] *adj* ultravioleta.

**umbilical** [ʌmˈbɪlɪkəl] *adj* umbilical.
  COMP **umbilical cord** cordón *m* umbilical.

**umbrella** [ʌmˈbrelə] *n* **1** paraguas *m.* **2** *fig (protection)* manto *f; (patronage)* patrocinio.

**umpire** [ˈʌmpaɪəʳ] *n* árbitro,-a.

► *vt* arbitrar.

**unable** [ʌnˈeɪbəl] *adj* incapaz.

**unacceptable** [ˌʌnəkˈseptəbəl] *adj* inaceptable, inadmisible.

**unaccountable** [ˌʌnəˈkaʊntəbəl] *adj* inexplicable.

**unaccustomed** [ˌʌnəˈkʌstəmd] *adj* desacostumbrado,-a.

**unaffected** [ˌʌnəˈfektɪd] *adj* **1** *(unchanged)* no afectado,-a. **2** *(for person)* afable, campechano. **3** *(indifferent)* inmutable. **4** *(style)* llano,-a.

**unanimous** [juːˈnænɪməs] *adj* unánime.

**unashamed** [ˌʌnəˈʃeɪmd] *adj* descarado,-a.

**unattended** [ˌʌnəˈtendɪd] *adj* **1** *(children)* sin vigilar. **2** *(not looked after)* desatendido,-a. **3** *(alone)* solo,-a.

**unavailable** [ˌʌnəˈveɪləbəl] *adj* **1** no disponible. **2** *(busy)* ocupado,-a. **3** *(out of print)* agotado,-a. **4** *(not for sale)* que no está en venta.

**unaware** [ˌʌnəˈweəʳ] *adj* ignorante, inconsciente.

**unbearable** [ʌnˈbeərəbəl] *adj* inaguantable, insoportable, intolerable.

**unbeatable** [ʌnˈbiːtəbəl] *adj* **1** *(competition)* invencible. **2** *(price, quality)* insuperable, inigualable, inmejorable.

**unbelievable** [ˌʌnbɪˈliːvəbəl] *adj* increíble.

**unbiased** [ʌnˈbaɪəst] *adj* imparcial.

**unbiassed** [ʌnˈbaɪəst] *adj* → unbiased.

**unblock** [ʌnˈblɒk] *vt* **1** *(pipe, drain)* desatascar. **2** *(street, road)* desobstruir. **3** *(nose)* destaponar.

**unbreakable** [ʌnˈbreɪkəbəl] *adj* **1** irrompible. **2** *fig* inquebrantable. **3** *(horse)* indomable.

**unbutton** [ʌnˈbʌtən] *vt* desabrochar.
▸ *vi fam* relajarse.

**uncertain** [ʌnˈsɜːtən] *adj* **1** *(not certain)* incierto,-a, dudoso,-a. **2** *(unspecified)* indeterminado,-a. **3** *(indecisive)* indeciso,-a. **4** *(changeable)* variable.

**unchanged** [ʌnˈtʃeɪndʒd] *adj* igual, sin alterar.

**unchecked** [ʌnˈtʃekt] *adj* **1** no comprobado,-a. **2** *(unrestrained)* libre, libremente.

**uncivilized** [ʌnˈsɪvəlaɪzd] *adj* **1** *(tribe)* salvaje. **2** *(not cultured)* inculto,-a. **3** *fig* poco ortodoxo,-a.

**uncle** [ˈʌŋkəl] *n* tío.

**unclear** [ʌnˈklɪəʳ] *adj* confuso,-a.

**uncoil** [ʌnˈkɔɪl] *vt* desenrollar.
▸ *vi* **1** *(snake)* desenroscarse. **2** *(rope)* desenrollarse.

**uncomfortable** [ʌnˈkʌmfətəbəl] *adj* **1** *(physical)* incómodo,-a. **2** *(worrying)* inquietante. **3** *(unpleasant)* desagradable.

**uncommon** [ʌnˈkɒmən] *adj* **1** *(rare)* poco común. **2** *(strange)* insólito,-a; *(unusual)* extraordinario,-a. **3** *(excessive)* desmesurado,-a.

**unconcerned** [ʌnkənˈsɜːnd] *adj* despreocupado, indiferente.

**unconscious** [ʌnˈkɒnʃəs] *adj* **1** MED inconsciente. **2** *(unaware)* inconsciente. **3** *(not on purpose)* involuntario,-a.
▸ *n* **the unconscious** el inconsciente.

✖ Unconscious no significa 'inconsciente (irresponsable)', que se traduce por thoughtless.

**uncontrollable** [ʌnkənˈtrəʊləbəl] *adj* **1** *(general)* incontrolable. **2** *(people)* ingobernable. **3** *(desire)* irresistible. **4** *(child)* indisciplinado,-a.

**uncountable** [ʌnˈkaʊntəbəl] *adj* incontable.

**uncover** [ʌnˈkʌvəʳ] *vt* **1** destapar. **2** *(secret)* revelar, descubrir.

**unction** [ˈʌŋkʃən] *n* **1** REL *(act, ointment)* unción *f*. **2** *(balm)* ungüento.

**uncultivated** [ʌnˈkʌltɪveɪtɪd] *adj* **1** *(land)* yermo,-a, baldío,-a. **2** *(person)* inculto,-a.

**undamaged** [ʌnˈdæmɪdʒd] *adj* **1** *(goods)* sin desperfectos, intacto,-a. **2** *(person)* indemne, ileso,-a.

**undefeated** [ʌndɪˈfiːtɪd] *adj* invicto,-a.

**undeniable** [ʌndɪˈnaɪəbəl] *adj* innegable.

**under** [ˈʌndəʳ] *prep* **1** *(below)* bajo, debajo de. **2** *(less than)* menos de. **3** *(controlled, affected, influenced by)* bajo. **4** *(suffering, subject to)* bajo. **5** *(according to)* conforme a, según. **6** *(known by)* con, bajo.
▸ *adv* **1** *(below)* debajo. **2** *(less)* menos.

**undercarriage** [ˈʌndəkærɪdʒ] *n* tren *m* de aterrizaje.

**underclothes** [ˈʌndəkləʊðz] *n pl* ropa *f sing* interior.

**undercover** [ʌndəˈkʌvəʳ] *adj* clandestino,-a, secreto,-a,.
▸ *adv* en la clandestinidad.

**underdeveloped** [ʌndədɪˈveləpt] *adj* **1** subdesarrollado,-a. **2** *(of photo)* insuficientemente revelado,-a.

**underestimate** [(n) ʌndərˈestɪmət; (vb) ʌndərˈestɪmeɪt] *n* menosprecio.
▸ *vt* infravalorar, subestimar.

**undergo** [ʌndəˈgeʊ] *n* cúbito.
ⓘ *pt* **underwent** [ʌndəˈwent], *pp* **undergone** [ʌndəˈgɒn].

**undergone** [ʌndəˈgɒn] *pp* → **undergo**.

**underground** [(adj-n) ˈʌndəgraʊnd; (adv) ʌndəˈgraʊnd] *adj* **1** subterráneo,-a. **2** *fig* clandestino,-a. **3** *fig (cinema, music)* underground.
▸ *n* **1** *(railway)* metro. **2** *(resistance)* resistencia.
▸ *adv* **1** bajo tierra. **2** *fig (secretly)* en la clandestinidad, clandestinamente.

**undergrowth** [ˈʌndəgrəʊθ] *n* maleza, monte *m* bajo.

**underline** [ʌndəˈlaɪn] *vt* subrayar.

**underneath** [ʌndəˈniːθ] *prep* bajo, debajo de.
▸ *adv* abajo, debajo, por debajo.
▸ *adj* de abajo, inferior.
▸ *n* parte *f* inferior, fondo.

**undernourished** [ʌndəˈnʌrɪʃt] adj desnutrido,-a, subalimentado,-a.

**underpants** [ˈʌndəpænts] n pl calzoncillos mpl, eslip m sing.

**understand** [ʌndəˈstænd] vt **1** entender. **2** (believe) tener entendido. **3** (to get on with sb) entenderse. **4** (take for granted) sobreentender.
ⓘ pt & pp understood [ʌndəˈstʊd].

**understanding** [ʌndəˈstændɪŋ] n comprensión.

**understatement** [ʌndəˈsteɪtmənt] n eufemismo.

**understood** [ʌndəˈstʊd] pt & pp → understand.

**undertake** [ʌndəˈteɪk] vt (take on - job, task) emprender; (- responsibility) asumir.
▶ vi (promise) comprometerse (to, a).
ⓘ pt undertook [ʌndəˈtʊk], pp undertaken [ʌndəˈteɪkən].

**undertaken** [ʌndəˈteɪkən] pp → undertake.

**undertaker** [ˈʌndəteɪkəʳ] n empresario,-a de pompas fúnebres.
▶ n pl (undertaker's) funeraria, pompas fpl fúnebres.

**undertook** [ʌndəˈtʊk] pt → undertake.

**undervalue** [ʌndəˈvæljuː] vt subvalorar.

**underwater** [ʌndəˈwɔːtəʳ] adj submarino,-a, subacuático,-a.
▶ adv bajo el agua.

**underwear** [ˈʌndəwɛəʳ] n ropa interior.

**underwent** [ʌndəˈwent] pt → undergo.

**underworld** [ˈʌndəwɜːld] n (of criminals) hampa, bajos fondos mpl, inframundo.

**undesirable** [ʌndɪˈzaɪərəbəl] adj indeseable.
▶ n indeseable mf.

**undetermined** [ʌndɪˈtɜːmaɪnd] adj indeterminado,-a, indefinido,-a.

**undid** [ʌnˈdɪd] pt → undo.

**undisputed** [ʌndɪsˈpjuːtɪd] adj **1** (unquestionable) indiscutible, incuestionable. **2** (unchallenged) incontestable.

**undo** [ʌnˈduː] vt **1** (knot) deshacer, desatar. **2** (button) desabrochar. **3** (arrange-

ment) anular. **4** (destroy) deshacer, destruir. **5** (to set right) enmendar, reparar.
ⓘ pt undid [ʌnˈdɪd], pp undone [ʌnˈdʌn].

**undone** [ʌnˈdʌn] pp → undid.
▶ adj (incomplete) inacabado,-a.

**undoubted** [ʌnˈdaʊtɪd] adj indudable.

**undress** [ʌnˈdres] vt desnudar.
▶ vi desnudarse.

**undrinkable** [ʌnˈdrɪŋkəbəl] adj imbebible.

**uneasy** [ʌnˈiːzɪ] adj **1** (worried) intranquilo,-a, inquieto,-a, preocupado,-a; (disturbing) inquietante. **2** (annoying) incómodo,-a.
ⓘ comp uneasier, superl uneasiest.

**unemployed** [ʌnɪmˈplɔɪd] adj parado, -a, sin trabajo, en paro.

**unemployment** [ʌnɪmˈplɔɪmənt] n **1** paro, desempleo. **2** (percentage) número de parados.

**unequal** [ʌnˈiːkwəl] adj **1** (not the same) desigual, distinto,-a; (pulse) irregular. **2** (not adequate) poco apto, inadecuado,-a.

**unequivocal** [ʌnɪˈkwɪvəkəl] adj inequívoco,-a, claro,-a.

**uneven** [ʌnˈiːvən] adj **1** (not level) desigual; (bumpy) accidentado,-a. **2** (varying) irregular, variable. **3** (road) lleno, -a de baches. **4** (unfairly matched) desigual. **5** MATH impar.

**unexpected** [ʌnɪkˈspektɪd] adj **1** inesperado,-a. **2** (event) imprevisto,-a.

**unfair** [ʌnˈfeəʳ] adj injusto,-a.

**unfaithful** [ʌnˈfeɪθfʊl] adj **1** (husband, wife) infiel. **2** (friend) desleal.

**unfamiliar** [ʌnfəˈmɪlɪəʳ] adj (unknown) desconocido,-a.

**unfashionable** [ʌnˈfæʃənəbəl] adj (fashion, trends, etc) pasado,-a de moda; (ideas, measures) poco popular.

**unfasten** [ʌnˈfɑːsən] vt **1** (vest, button) desabrochar. **2** (untie) desatar. **3** (open) abrir.

**unfavorable** [ʌnˈfeɪvərəbəl] adj US → unfavourable.

**unfavourable** [ʌnˈfeɪvərəbəl] adj **1** (gen) desfavorable; (criticism) adverso,-a. **2** (winds) contrario,-a.

U

**unfinished** [ʌnˈfɪnɪʃt] *adj* inacabado, -a, incompleto,-a, sin acabar.

**unfit** [ʌnˈfɪt] *adj* **1** *(person)* no apto,-a, incapaz. **2** *(physically)* incapacitado,-a, inútil. **3** *(injured)* lesionado,-a. **4** *(incompetent)* incompetente. [LOC] **to be unfit** no estar en forma.

**unfold** [ʌnˈfəʊld] *vt* **1** *(paper)* desplegar; *(sheet)* desdoblar. **2** *(newspaper)* abrir; *(map)* extender. **3** *(outline)* exponer; *(reveal)* revelar. **4** *(secret)* descubrir.
▶ *vi* **1** *(open up)* desdoblarse; *(landscape)* extenderse. **2** *(ideas, etc)* desarrollarse. **3** *(secret)* descubrirse, revelarse.

**unforgettable** [ʌnfəˈgetəbəl] *adj* inolvidable.

**unfortunate** [ʌnˈfɔːtʃənət] *adj* **1** *(person, event)* desgraciado,-a. **2** *(remark)* desafortunado,-a.

**unfriendly** [ʌnˈfrendlɪ] *adj* poco amistoso,-a, antipático,-a, hostil.
ⓘ *comp* **unfriendlier**, *superl* **unfriendliest**.

**unfulfilled** [ʌnfʊlˈfɪld] *adj* **1** *(not carried out)* incumplido,-a, frustrado,-a. **2** *(not satisfied)* insatisfecho,-a. **3** *(ambition)* frustrado,-a; *(dream)* irrealizado,-a.

**ungrateful** [ʌnˈgreɪtfʊl] *adj* **1** *(unthankful)* desagradecido,-a. **2** *(thankless)* ingrato,-a.

**unhappy** [ʌnˈhæpɪ] *adj* **1** *(sad)* infeliz. **2** *(miserable)* desdichado,-a. **3** *(unsuitable)* desafortunado,-a, poco afortunado,-a.
ⓘ *comp* **unhappier**, *superl* **unhappiest**.

**unharmed** [ʌnˈhɑːmd] *adj* ileso,-a.

**unhealthy** [ʌnˈhelθɪ] *adj* **1** *(place)* malsano,-a, insalubre. **2** *(ill)* enfermizo, -a, enfermo,-a. **3** *fig (unnatural)* morboso,-a, malsano,-a.
ⓘ *comp* **unhealthier**, *superl* **unhealthiest**.

**unhelpful** [ʌnˈhelpfʊl] *adj (advice)* inútil, vano,-a; *(person)* poco servicial.

**unhurt** [ʌnˈhɜːt] *adj* ileso,-a, indemne.

**unicorn** [ˈjuːnɪkɔːn] *n* unicornio.

**uniform** [ˈjuːnɪfɔːm] *adj* **1** uniforme. **2** *(temperature)* constante.
▶ *n* uniforme *m*.

**unify** [ˈjuːnɪfaɪ] *vt* unificar.
ⓘ *pt & pp* **unified**, *ger* **unifying**.

**unimportant** [ʌnɪmˈpɔːtənt] *adj* insignificante, sin importancia, poco importante.

**uninhabited** [ʌnɪnˈhæbɪtɪd] *adj* **1** deshabitado,-a. **2** *(deserted)* despoblado,-a.

**uninteresting** [ʌnˈɪntrəstɪŋ] *adj* sin interés.

**union** [ˈjuːnɪən] *n* **1** unión *f*. **2** *fig (marriage)* enlace *m*. **3** *(of workers)* sindicato. **4** TECH unión *f*.
▶ *adj* sindical, del sindicato. [COMP] **Union Jack** la bandera del Reino Unido.

⊕ La **Union Jack** es la bandera del Reino Unido y está formada por la combinación de las enseñas de Inglaterra, Escocia e Irlanda.

**unionize** [juːnjəˈnaɪz] *vt* sindicalizar.
▶ *vi* agremiarse, sindicalizarse.

**unirrigated** [ʌnɪrɪgeɪtəd] *adj* de secano.

**unique** [juːˈniːk] *adj* **1** *(singular)* único, -a. **2** *(outstanding)* extraordinario,-a.

**unit** [ˈjuːnɪt] *n* **1** unidad *f*. **2** *(furniture)* módulo, elemento. **3** MIL unidad *f*. **4** MATH unidad *f*. **5** TECH grupo. **6** *(centre)* centro; *(department)* servicio. **7** *(team)* equipo.

**unite** [juːˈnaɪt] *vt (join)* unir; *(assemble)* reunir.
▶ *vi* unirse, reunirse.

**unity** [ˈjuːnɪtɪ] *n (union)* unidad *f*; *(harmony)* armonía.

**universal** [juːnɪˈvɜːsəl] *adj* universal.

**universe** [ˈjuːnɪvɜːs] *n* universo.

**university** [juːnɪˈvɜːsətɪ] *n* universidad *f*.
ⓘ *pl* **universities**.
▶ *adj* universitario,-a.

**unkempt** [ʌnˈkempt] *adj* **1** *(general)* descuidado,-a. **2** *(hair)* despeinado,-a. **3** *(appearance)* desaliñado,-a.

**unkind** [ʌnˈkaɪnd] *adj* **1** *(unpleasant)* desconsiderado,-a. **2** *(cruel)* cruel; *(criticism)* despiadado,-a.

**unknown** [ʌnˈnəʊn] *adj* desconocido,-a.
▶ *n* lo desconocido.

**unleash** [ʌnˈliːʃ] *vt* **1** *(dog)* soltar. **2** *fig (free - gen)* liberar; *(- passions)* desatar. **3** *(fury)* provocar.

**unless** [ənˈles] *conj* a menos que, a no ser que.
▶ *prep* salvo, excepto.

**unlike** [ʌnˈlaɪk] *adj (different)* diferente a, distinto de; *(not characteristic)* impropio,-a.
▶ *prep* a diferencia de

**unlikely** [ʌnˈlaɪklɪ] *adj (improbable)* improbable, poco probable; *(unexpected, unusual)* inverosímil.
ⓘ *comp* unlikelier, *superl* unlikeliest.

**unlimited** [ʌnˈlɪmɪtɪd] *adj* ilimitado,-a.

**unload** [ʌnˈləʊd] *vt* **1** *(gen)* descargar. **2** *(get rid of)* deshacerse de.
▶ *vi* descargar.

**unlock** [ʌnˈlɒk] *vt* **1** *(door)* abrir (con llave). **2** *fig (secret)* revelar; *(enigma)* resolver.

**unlucky** [ʌnˈlʌkɪ] *adj* **1** *(unfortunate)* desafortunado,-a, desgraciado,-a. **2** *(fateful)* aciago,-a, nefasto,-a.
ⓘ *comp* unluckier, *superl* unluckiest.

**unmarried** [ʌnˈmærɪd] *adj* soltero,-a.

**unmistakable** [ʌnmɪsˈteɪkəbəl] *adj* inconfundible, inequívoco,-a.

**unnecessary** [ʌnˈnesəsərɪ] *adj* innecesario,-a.

**unnoticed** [ʌnˈnəʊtɪst] *adj* inadvertido,-a, desapercibido,-a.

**unoccupied** [ʌnˈɒkjʊpaɪd] *adj* **1** *(house)* deshabitado,-a. **2** *(person)* desocupado,-a. **3** *(post)* vacante. **4** *(area)* despoblado,-a. **5** *(seat)* libre. **6** MIL no ocupado,-a.

**unofficial** [ʌnəˈfɪʃəl] *adj* extraoficial, oficioso,-a.

**unpack** [ʌnˈpæk] *vt* **1** *(objects)* desempaquetar, desenvolver. **2** *(suitcase)* deshacer. **3** *(boxes)* desembalar.
▶ *vi* deshacer las maletas.

**unpardonable** [ʌnˈpɑːdənəbəl] *adj* imperdonable.

**unpleasant** [ʌnˈplezənt] *adj* **1** *(disagreeable, nasty)* desagradable, molesto,-a. **2** *(unfriendly)* antipático,-a. **3** *(words)* grosero,-a, mal educado,-a.

**unplug** [ʌnˈplʌg] *vt* desenchufar.
ⓘ *pt & pp* unplugged, *ger* unplugging.

**unpopular** [ʌnˈpɒpjələʳ] *adj* impopular.

**unpredictable** [ʌnprɪˈdɪktəbəl] *adj* **1** imprevisible. **2** *(of person)* de reacciones imprevisibles. **3** *(whimsical)* antojadizo,-a.

**unproductive** [ʌnprəˈdʌktɪv] *adj* **1** *(inefficient)* improductivo,-a. **2** *fig (fruitless)* infructuoso,-a.

**unprovable** [ʌnˈpruːvəbəl] *adj* indemostrable.

**unpublished** [ʌnˈpʌblɪʃt] *adj* inédito,-a, no publicado,-a.

**unreachable** [ʌnˈriːtʃəbəl] *adj* inalcanzable.

**unreadable** [ʌnˈriːdəbəl] *adj* **1** *(handwriting)* ilegible. **2** *(book)* imposible de leer; *(understand)* incomprensible.

**unreal** [ʌnˈrɪəl] *adj* irreal.

**unrealistic** [ʌnrɪəˈlɪstɪk] *adj* poco realista.

**unreasonable** [ʌnˈriːzənəbəl] *adj* **1** irrazonable. **2** *(irrational)* irracional. **3** *(excessive)* desmesurado,-a; *(prices)* exorbitante. **4** *(hour)* inoportuno,-a.

**unrecognizable** [ʌnrekəgˈnaɪzəbəl] *adj* irreconocible.

**unreliable** [ʌnrɪˈlaɪəbəl] *adj* **1** *(person)* de poca confianza, poco formal, que no es de fiar. **2** *(information)* que no es de fiar, poco seguro,-a. **3** *(machine)* poco fiable, poco seguro,-a. **4** *(news)* poco fidedigno,-a.

**unrest** [ʌnˈrest] *n* **1** *(uneasiness)* malestar *m*. **2** *(restlessness)* inquietud *f*; *(political disturbance)* agitación *f*, disturbios *mpl*.

**unroll** [ʌnˈrəʊl] *vt* desenrollar.
▶ *vi* desenrollarse.

**unsaddle** [ʌnˈsædəl] *vt* **1** *(horse)* desensillar. **2** *(horseman)* desmontar.

**unsafe** [ʌnˈseɪf] *adj* **1** *(risky)* inseguro,-a, arriesgado,-a. **2** *(dangerous)* peligroso,-a.

**unsatisfactory** [ʌnsætɪsˈfæktərɪ] *adj* insatisfactorio,-a, poco satisfactorio,-a.

**unsavory** [ʌnˈseɪvərɪ] *adj* US → unsavoury.

**unsavoury** [ʌnˈseɪvərɪ] *adj* **1** *(taste, etc)* desagradable; *(tasteless)* insípido,-a. **2** *(morally not right)* deshonroso,-a, infame, sospechoso,-a; *(person)* indeseable.

**U**

**unscrew** [ʌnˈskruː] vt destornillar, desatornillar.

**unseen** [ʌnˈsiːn] adj (invisible) no visto, -a, invisible; (unnoticed) inadvertido,-a.

**unselfish** [ʌnˈselfɪʃ] adj desinteresado,-a.

**unsettled** [ʌnˈsetʰld] adj 1 (weather) inestable. 2 (person) nervioso,-a, intranquilo; (situation) inestable. 3 (country, etc) agitado,-a. 4 (question, matter) pendiente; (account, etc) sin saldar. 5 (land) sin colonizar, sin poblar.

**unshaven** [ʌnˈʃeɪvʰn] adj sin afeitar.

**unsheathe** [ʌnˈʃiːð] vt desenvainar.

**unshrinkable** [ʌnˈʃrɪŋkəbʰl] adj inencogible, que no encoge.

**unskilled** [ʌnˈskɪld] adj 1 (worker) no cualificado,-a. 2 (job) no especializado,-a. 3 (untalented) inexperto,-a.

**unsolved** [ʌnˈsɒlvd] adj sin resolver.

**unstable** [ʌnˈsteɪbʰl] adj inestable.

**unsteady** [ʌnˈstedɪ] adj 1 (not firm) inseguro,-a, inestable; (furniture) cojo,-a, inestable. 2 (voice, hand) tembloroso, -a, poco firme. 3 (weather conditions) variable; (pulse) irregular.

ⓘ comp unsteadier, superl unsteadiest.

**unstressed** [ʌnˈstrest] adj LING átono,-a.

**unsuccessful** [ʌnsəkˈsesful] adj 1 fracasado,-a, sin éxito. 2 (useless) inútil, infructuoso,-a; (examination) suspendido,-a. 3 (candidate in elections) derrotado,-a, vencido,-a.

**unsuited** [ʌnˈsuːtɪd] adj 1 (person) no apto,-a; (thing) impropio,-a, inadecuado,-a. 2 (people) incompatible.

**unsure** [ʌnˈʃʊəʳ] adj inseguro,-a, poco seguro,-a.

**unsympathetic** [ʌnsɪmpəˈθetɪk] adj (unfeeling) poco compasivo,-a, sin compasión f, indiferente; (lacking understanding) poco comprensivo,-a.

**untamable** [ʌnˈteɪməbʰl] adj indomable.

**untangle** [ʌnˈtæŋgʰl] vt desenredar.

**untidy** [ʌnˈtaɪdɪ] adj 1 (room, person) desordenado,-a. 2 (scruffy) desaliñado,-a, desaseado,-a; (hair) despeinado,-a.

ⓘ comp untidier, superl untidiest.

**untie** [ʌnˈtaɪ] vt 1 (unfasten) desatar. 2 (liberate) soltar, desligar.

**until** [ʌnˈtɪl] prep hasta.
▶ conj hasta que.

**untrue** [ʌnˈtruː] adj 1 falso,-a. 2 (unfaithful) infiel, desleal. 3 (inexact) inexacto,-a, erróneo,-a.

**unusable** [ʌnˈjuːzəbʰl] adj inservible.

**unused** adj 1 [ʌnˈjuːzd] (new) nuevo,-a, sin estrenar; (not in use) que no se utiliza. 2 [ʌnˈjuːst] (unaccustomed) desacostumbrado,-a.

**unusual** [ʌnˈjuːʒʊəl] adj 1 (rare, strange) insólito,-a, poco común. 2 (different) original; (exceptional) extraordinario,-a.

**unveil** [ʌnˈveɪl] vt 1 (uncover) descubrir. 2 fig (reveal) descubrir, desvelar; (secret) revelar.

**unwanted** [ʌnˈwɒntɪd] adj 1 (child) no deseado,-a. 2 (advice, etc) no solicitado,-a, no pedido,-a. 3 (superfluous) superfluo,-a.

**unwelcome** [ʌnˈwelkəm] adj 1 (guest) inoportuno,-a, molesto,-a; (news) desagradable. 2 (uncomfortable) incómodo,-a.

**unwell** [ʌnˈwel] adj (sick, ill) indispuesto,-a, malo,-a.

**unwilling** [ʌnˈwɪlɪŋ] adj reacio,-a, poco dispuesto,-a.

**unwind** [ʌnˈwaɪnd] vt desenrollar.
▶ vi 1 desenrollarse. 2 fam (relax) relajarse.

ⓘ pt & pp unwound [ʌnˈwaʊnd].

**unwise** [ʌnˈwaɪz] adj 1 (foolish) imprudente; (senseless) insensato,-a. 2 (ill-advised) desaconsejable, poco aconsejable.

**unwound** [ʌnˈwaʊnd] pt & pp → unwind.

**unwrap** [ʌnˈræp] vt (present) desenvolver; (parcel, package) abrir, deshacer.

ⓘ pt & pp unwrapped, ger unwrapping.

**unzip** [ʌnˈzɪp] vt 1 bajar la cremallera de. 2 COMPUT descomprimir.

ⓘ pt & pp unzipped, ger unzipping.

**up** [ʌp] adv 1 (upwards) hacia arriba, arriba. 2 (out of bed) levantado,-a. 3 (sun, moon): the sun is up ha salido el sol. 4 (roadworks) levantado,-a, en obras. 5 (towards)

hacia. **6** *(northwards)* ir hacia el norte. **7** *(totally finished)* acabado,-a. **8** *(into pieces)* a trozos, a porciones, a raciones.
▶ *prep* **1** *(movement)*: *to go up the stairs* subir la escalera. **2** *(position)* en lo alto de.
▶ *vt* subir, aumentar.
ⓘ *pt & pp* upped, *ger* upping.

**up-and-coming** [ʌpənˈkʌmɪŋ] *adj* prometedor,-ra, que promete mucho.

**up-and-down** [ʌpənˈdaʊn] *adj* **1** *(motion)* vertical; *(varying)* variable. **2** *(eventful)* accidentado,-a; *(period)* con altibajos.

**upbringing** [ˈʌpbrɪŋɪŋ] *n* educación *f*.

**upcoming** [ˈʌpkʌmɪŋ] *adj* próximo,-a.

**update** [*(n)* ˈʌpdeɪt; *(vb)* ʌpˈdeɪt] *n* actualización *f*, puesta al día.
▶ *vt* actualizar, modernizar.

**upfront** [ʌpˈfrʌnt] *adj* sincero,-a, franco,-a.

**upgrade** [*(vb)* ʌpˈɡreɪd; *(n)* ˈʌpɡreɪd] *vt* **1** *(promote)* ascender; subir de categoría. **2** *(improve)* mejorar.
▶ *n* mejora.

**uphekd** [ʌpˈhəʊld] *pt & pp* → uphold.

**uphill** [*(adj)* ˈʌphɪl; *(adv)* ʌpˈhɪl] *adj* **1** ascendente. **2** *fig (task, struggle)* arduo,-a, difícil, duro,-a, penoso,-a.
▶ *adv* cuesta arriba.

**uphold** [ʌpˈhəʊld] *vt* **1** *(opinion)* sostener, mantener; *(to support)* apoyar. **2** *(defend)* defender. **3** *(confirm)* confirmar.
ⓘ *pt & pp* upheld [ʌpˈheld].

**upholster** [ʌpˈhəʊlstəʳ] *vt* tapizar.

**upkeep** [ˈʌpkiːp] *n* *(maintenance)* conservación *f*; *(costs)* gastos *mpl* de mantenimiento.

**uplift** [ʌpˈlɪft] *vt* *(lift up)* elevar, levantar; *(soul, voice)* inspirar, elevar, alzar.
▶ *n fig* edificación *f*, inspiración *f*.

**upload** [ʌpˈləʊd] *vt* *(Internet)* publicar en la red, subir a la red.

**up-market** [ˈʌpmɑːkɪt] *adj* de calidad *f* superior, de categoría.

**upon** [əˈpɒn] *prep fml* en, sobre.
Consulta también on.

**upper** [ˈʌpəʳ] *adj* **1** *(position)* superior. **2** *(in geography)* alto,-a; superior.
▶ *n (of shoe)* pala.

**uppermost** [ˈʌpəməʊst] *adj* **1** más alto,-a. **2** *fig* principal, dominante.

**upright** [ˈʌpraɪt] *adj* **1** derecho,-a, vertical. **2** *(honest)* recto,-a, honrado,-a.
▶ *adv* derecho, en posición *f* vertical.
▶ *n* SP poste *m*, palo.

**uprising** [ʌpˈraɪzɪŋ] *n* alzamiento, levantamiento, sublevación *f*.

**uproar** [ˈʌprɔːʳ] *n* alboroto, tumulto.

**uproot** [ʌpˈruːt] *vt* **1** *(plant, etc)* desarraigar, arrancar; *(people)* desarraigar. **2** *(eliminate)* eliminar, extirpar.

**upset** [*(adj-vb)* ʌpˈset; *(n)* ˈʌpset] *adj* **1** *(angry)* disgustado,-a, contrariado,-a. **2** *(mentally or physically)* trastornado,-a; *(worried)* preocupado,-a. **3** *(nerves)* desquiciado,-a; *(a little unwell)* indispuesto,-a. **4** *(stomach)* trastornado,-a. **5** *(overturned)* volcado,-a; *(spoiled)* desbaratado,-a.
▶ *n* **1** *(reversal)* revés *m*, contratiempo; *(slight ailment)* malestar *m*. **2** *(emotion, stomach, etc)* trastorno; *(plans, etc)* trastorno. **3** *(trouble, difficulty)* molestia *f*. **4** *(sport)* un resultado inesperado.
▶ *vt* **1** *(overturn)* volcar; *(capsize)* hacer zozobrar. **2** *(spill)* derramar. **3** *(shock)* trastornar. **4** *(person)* contrariar; *(worry)* preocupar; *(displease)* disgustar. **5** *(stomach)* sentar mal. **6** *(plans)* desbaratar. **7** *(to cause disorder)* desordenar, revolver.
ⓘ *pt & pp* upset [ʌpˈset], *ger* upsetting.

**upsetting** [ʌpˈsetɪŋ] *adj* desconcertante, inquietante, preocupante.

**upside down** [ʌpsaɪdˈdaʊn] *adv* **1** al revés. **2** *fig (disorder)* patas arriba.

**upstairs** [*(adv)* ʌpˈsteəz; *(n)* ˈʌpsteəz] *adv* *(direction)* al piso de arriba; *(position)* en el piso de arriba.
▶ *adj* de arriba.
▶ *n* piso de arriba, piso superior.

**upstream** [ʌpˈstriːm] *adv* **1** aguas arriba. **2** *(against the current)* a contracorriente.

**upsurge** [ˈʌpsɜːdʒ] *n* **1** *(increase)* aumento; *(anger)* acceso. **2** *fig (strong increase in feelings, etc)* resurgimiento; *(of violence)* ola.

**up-to-date** [ʌptəˈdeɪt] *adj* **1** al día. **2** *(modern)* moderno,-a, a la moda; *(informed)* al tanto, al corriente, al día.

U

**upward** [ˈʌpwəd] *adj* hacia arriba.
  ▸ *adv* hacia arriba.
  ▸ *adj* COMM *(tendency)* al alza *m*.
**upwards** [ˈʌpwədz] *adv* **1** hacia arriba.
  **2** *fam* algo más de.
**uranium** [jʊˈreɪnɪəm] *n* CHEM uranio.
**Uranus** [jʊˈreɪnəs] *n* Urano.
**urban** [ˈɜːbən] *adj* urbano,-a.
**urbane** [ɜːˈbeɪn] *adj* cortés, urbano,-a.
**ureter** [jʊəˈriːtər] *n* uréter *m*.
**urethra** [jʊˈriːθrə] *n* uretra.
**urge** [ɜːdʒ] *n* impulso, deseo.
  ▸ *vt* **1** encarecer, preconizar, instar, insistir. **2** *(incite)* incitar; *(plead)* exhortar. **3** *(encourage)* animar.
**urgency** [ˈɜːdʒənsɪ] *n* urgencia.
**urgent** [ˈɜːdʒənt] *adj* urgente.
**urinary** [ˈjʊərɪnərɪ] *adj* urinario,-a.
  COMP **urinary tract** tracto urinario.
**urinate** [ˈjʊərɪneɪt] *vi* orinar.
**urine** [ˈjʊərɪn] *n* orina.
**urn** [ɜːn] *n* urna.
**urology** [jʊˈrɒlədʒɪ] *n* MED urología.
**Ursa** [ˈɜːrsə] *(constellation) n* la Osa.
**Uruguay** [ˈjʊərəgwaɪ] *n* Uruguay.
**Uruguayan** [jʊərəˈgwaɪən] *adj* uruguayo,-a.
  ▸ *n* uruguayo,-a.
**us** [ʌs, ʌz] *pron* **1** nos; *(with preposition)* nosotros,-as. **2** *fam* me.
**usable** [ˈjuːzəbəl] *adj* utilizable, aprovechable.
**usage** [ˈjuːsɪdʒ] *n* **1** uso, manejo. **2** *(custom)* uso, costumbre *f*, usanza. **3** LING uso. **4** *(way of speaking)* habla *m*, lenguaje *m*.
**use** [(n)] juːs; *(vb)* juːz] *n* **1** uso, empleo, utilización *f*. **2** *(handling)* manejo. **3** *(usefulness)* utilidad *f*. **4** *(right to use, power to use)* uso.
  ▸ *vt* **1** utilizar. **2** *(consume)* gastar, consumir. **3** *(exploit unfairly)* aprovecharse de. **4** *fam (need)* necesitar.

  ▸ *aux* **to use to** *(past habits)* soler, acostumbrar: *we used to go fishing in the lake* solíamos ir a pescar al lago.

  ✎ Como auxiliar, si la frase no indica una costumbre, se debe traducir con el imperfecto.

  ◆ **to use up** *vt sep* gastar, acabar.
**useable** [ˈjuːzəbəl] *adj* → usable.
**used** [ˈjuːst] *adj* **1** [juːzd] *(second-hand)* usado,-a. **2** [juːst] *(accustomed)* acostumbrado,-a. COMP **to be used to** estar acostumbrado,-a a. ‖ **to get used to** acostumbrarse a.

  ✎ Consulta también use.

**useful** [ˈjuːsfʊl] *adj* útil.
**useless** [ˈjuːsləs] *adj* **1** inútil. **2** *fam (person)* inepto,-a, incompetente.
**user** [ˈjuːzər] *n* usuario,-a.
**usual** [ˈjuːʒʊəl] *adj* habitual, corriente.
  ▸ *n* **1** lo habitual. **2** *fam (drink, etc)* lo de siempre.
**utensil** [juːˈtensəl] *n* utensilio.
**uterus** [ˈjuːtərəs] *n* útero.
  ① *pl* **uteruses** o **uteri** [ˈjuːtəraɪ].
**utility** [juːˈtɪlɪtɪ] *n* **1** utilidad *f*. **2** *(company)* empresa de servicio público.
  ① *pl* **utilities**.
**utmost** [ˈʌtməʊst] *adj* sumo,-a, extremo,-a.
  ▸ *n* máximo.
**utter** [ˈʌtər] *adj* completo,-a, total.
  ▸ *vt* **1** *(words)* pronunciar, articular; *(feelings)* expresar. **2** *(lies curses, etc)* soltar; *(shouts, cries, etc)* lanzar, dar. **3** *(theatre)* proferir; *(sounds)* emitir.
**utterly** [ˈʌtəlɪ] *adv* totalmente.
**uvula** [ˈjuːvjʊlə] *n* úvula, campanilla.
  ① *pl* **uvulas** o **uvulae** [ˈjuːvjʊliː].
**Uzbek** [ˈʊzbek] *adj* uzbeco,-a.
  ▸ *n* **1** *(person)* uzbeco,-a. **2** *(language)* uzbeco.
**Uzbekistan** [ʊzbekɪˈstæn] *n* Uzbekistán.

# V

**V, v** [viː] *n (the letter)* V, v *f*.

**vacancy** ['veɪkˀnsɪ] *n* **1** *(job)* vacante *f*. **2** *(room)* habitación *f* libre. LOC "No vacancies" «Completo».
ⓘ *pl* vacancies.

**vacant** ['veɪkˀnt] *adj* **1** *(gen)* vacío. **2** *(job)* vacante. **3** *(room)* libre. **4** *(mind, expression)* vacío,-a.

**vacation** [vəˈkeɪʃˀn] *n* vacaciones *fpl*.

**vaccinate** ['væksɪneɪt] *vt* vacunar.

**vaccination** [væksɪˈneɪʃˀn] *n* vacunación *f*.

**vaccine** ['væksiːn] *n* vacuna.

**vacuum** ['vækjuəm] *n* **1** vacío. **2** *fam (vacuum cleaner)* aspiradora. COMP **vacuum cleaner** aspirador *m*. ▮ **vacuum flask** termo.
▸ *vt* limpiar con aspiradora, pasar la aspiradora por.

**vacuum-packed** ['vækjuəmpækt] *adj* envasado,-a al vacío.

**vagina** [vəˈdʒaɪnə] *n* vagina.
ⓘ *pl* vaginas o vaginae [vəˈdʒaɪniː].

**vaginae** [vəˈdʒaɪniː] *n pl* → vagina.

**vague** [veɪg] *adj* **1** *(imprecise)* vago,-a, impreciso,-a. **2** *(indistinct)* borroso,-a.

❌ Vague no significa 'vago (holgazán)', que se traduce por **lazy**.

**vain** [veɪn] *adj* **1** *(conceited)* vanidoso,-a. **2** *(hopeless)* vano,-a, inútil. LOC **in vain** en vano.

**valence** ['veɪləns] *n* US valencia.

**valency** ['veɪlənsɪ] *n* GB valencia.
ⓘ *pl* valencies.

**valid** ['vælɪd] *adj* **1** válido,-a. **2** *(ticket)* valedero,-a.

**validate** ['vælɪdeɪt] *vt fml* validar.

**valley** ['vælɪ] *n* valle *m*.

**valor** ['vælər] *n* US → valour.

**valour** ['vælər] *n* valor *m*, valentía.

❌ Valour no significa 'valor (valía)', que se traduce por **value**.

**valuation** [væljuˈeɪʃˀn] *n* **1** *(act)* valoración *f*. **2** *(price)* valor *m*.

**value** ['væljuː] *n* valor *m*.
▸ *vt* **1** *(estimate value of)* valorar, tasar. **2** *(appreciate)* valorar, apreciar.

**valve** [vælv] *n* **1** *(in general)* válvula. **2** RAD lámpara. **3** ZOOL valva. **4** MUS llave *f*.

**vampire** ['væmpaɪər] *n* urgencia.

**van** [væn] *n* **1** camioneta, furgoneta. **2** GB *(on train)* furgón *m*.

**vanadium** [vəˈneɪdɪəm] *n* vanadio.

**Vandal** ['vændˀl] *adj* vándalo,-a.
▸ *n* vándalo,-a.

**vandalism** ['vændəlɪzəm] *n* vandalismo.

**vandalize** ['vændəlaɪz] *n* urgencia.

**vane** [veɪn] *n* **1** *(weather, etc)* veleta. **2** *(of fan, etc)* aspa.

**vanilla** [vəˈnɪlə] *n* vainilla.

**vanish** ['vænɪʃ] *vi* desaparecer.

**vanity** ['vænɪtɪ] *n* vanidad *f*.

**vapor** ['veɪpər] *n* US → vapour.

**vapour** ['veɪpər] *n* **1** vapor *m*. **2** *(on windowpane)* vaho.

**variable** ['veərɪəbˀl] *adj* variable.
▸ *n* variable *f*.

**variant** ['veərɪənt] *n* variante *f*.

**varicose** ['værɪkəʊs] *adj* varicoso,-a.
COMP **varicose veins** varices *fpl*.

**varied** ['veərɪd] *adj* variado,-a, diverso,-a.

**variety** [vəˈraɪətɪ] *n* **1** *(diversity)* variedad *f*. **2** *(assortment)* surtido.
ⓘ *pl* varieties.

**various** ['veərɪəs] adj **1** (different) diverso,-a, distinto,-a. **2** (several) varios,-as.

**varnish** ['vɑːnɪʃ] n **1** (for wood, metals) barniz m. **2** (for nails) esmalte m.
► vt **1** (wood, metals) barnizar. **2** (nails) pintar.

**vary** ['veərɪ] vi variar.
► vt variar de.
① pt & pp varied, ger varying.

**vascular** ['væskjələʳ] adj vascular.

**vas deferens** ['væs 'defərenz] n ANAT conducto deferente.

**vase** [vɑːz, US veɪz] n jarrón m, florero.

**vassal** ['væsəl] n vasallo,-a.

**vast** [vɑːst] adj (extensive) vasto,-a, inmenso,-a; (huge) inmenso,-a, enorme.

**Vatican** ['vætɪkən] adj vaticano,-a.
COMP **Vatican City** Ciudad f del Vaticano.
► n the Vatican el Vaticano.

**vault¹** [vɔːlt] n **1** (ceiling) bóveda. **2** (in bank) cámara acorazada. **3** (for dead) panteón m; (in church) cripta. **4** (cellar) sótano; (for wine) bodega.

**vault²** [vɔːlt] vt saltar.
► vi saltar.
► n (gymnastics) salto.

**veal** [viːl] n ternera.

**vector** ['vektəʳ] n vector m.

**vegetable** ['vedʒtəbəl] n **1** (as food) verdura, hortaliza. **2** (as plant) vegetal m. **3** fam (person) vegetal m.

**vegetarian** [vedʒɪ'teərɪən] adj vegetariano,-a.
► n vegetariano,-a.

**vegetation** [vedʒɪ'teɪʃən] n vegetación f.

**vehicle** ['viːəkəl] n **1** TECH vehículo. **2** fig medio, vehículo.

**veil** [veɪl] n velo.
► vt velar.

**vein** [veɪn] n **1** ANAT vena. **2** BOT vena, nervio. **3** (of mineral) veta, vena, filón m. **4** (mood) humor m, vena.

**velum** ['viːləm] n velo (del paladar).
① pl vela ['viːlə].

**velvet** ['velvɪt] n terciopelo.

**vena cava** ['viːnə 'keɪvə] n ANAT vena cava.

**vending machine** ['vendɪŋməʃiːn] n máquina expendedora.

**vendor** ['vendəʳ] n vendedor,-ra.

**Venezuela** [venə'zweɪlə] n Venezuela.

**Venezuelan** [venə'zweɪlən] adj venezolano,-a.
► n venezolano,-a.

**vengeance** ['vendʒəns] n venganza.

**venous** ['viːnəs] adj venoso,-a.

**ventilate** ['ventɪleɪt] vt ventilar.

**ventricle** ['ventrɪkəl] n ventrículo.

**venture** ['ventʃəʳ] vt arriesgar, aventurar.
► vi arriesgarse.
► n aventura, empresa arriesgada.
COMP **business venture** empresa comercial. ‖ **joint venture** empresa conjunta. ‖ **venture capital** capital m riesgo.

**venue** ['venjuː] n **1** (place) local m. **2** (scene) escenario.

**Venus** ['viːnəs] n Venus f. COMP **Venus flytrap** dionea.

**veranda** [və'rændə] n porche m.

**verb** [vɜːb] n verbo.

**verbal** ['vɜːbəl] adj verbal. COMP **verbal noun** gerundio.

**verdict** ['vɜːdɪkt] n **1** veredicto, fallo. **2** (opinion) opinión f, juicio.

**verge** [vɜːdʒ] n **1** borde m, margen m. **2** (of road) arcén m.
◆ **to verge on** vt insep **1** (condition) rayar en. **2** (age) rondar.

**verify** ['verɪfaɪ] vt verificar, comprobar.
① pt & pp verified, ger verifying.

**vermicelli** [vɜːmɪ'selɪ] n fideos mpl.

**vermin** ['vɜːmɪn] n pl **1** (small animals) alimañas fpl. **2** (insects) bichos mpl, sabandijas fpl. **3** (people) gentuza f sing, chusma f sing.

**verruca** [və'ruːkə] n verruga.
① pl verrucas o verrucae [və'ruːkiː].

**verse** [vɜːs] n **1** (poetry) versos mpl, poesía. **2** (set of lines) estrofa. **3** (song, set of lines) estrofa. **4** (in Bible) versículo.

✕ Verse no significa 'verso (parte del poema)', que se traduce por line.

**version** ['vɜːʒ³n] *n* **1** versión *f.* **2** MUS interpretación *f.* **3** AUTO modelo. COMP **stage version** THEAT adaptación *f* teatral.

**versus** ['vɜːsəs] *prep* **1** *(against)* contra. **2** *(as opposed to)* frente a.

**vertebra** ['vɜːtɪbrə] *n* vértebra.
ⓘ *pl* vertebrae ['vɜːtɪbriː].

**vertebral** ['vɜːtɪbrəl] *adj* vertebral.

**vertebrate** ['vɜːtɪbrət, 'vɜːtɪbreɪt] *adj* vertebrado,-a.
▶ *n* vertebrado.

**vertex** ['vɜːteks] *n* vértice *m.*
ⓘ *pl* vertexes o vertices ['vɜːtɪsiːz].

**vertical** ['vɜːtɪkəl] *adj* vertical.

**very** ['verɪ] *adv* **1** *(extremely)* muy. **2** *(emphatic)* muy.
▶ *adj* **1** *(extreme)* de todo. **2** *(precise)* mismo,-a, exacto,-a. LOC **the very best** el/la mejor, lo mejor.

**vesicle** ['vesɪk³l] *n* vesícula.

**vessel** ['ves³l] *n* **1** *(ship)* nave *f,* buque *m.* **2** *(container)* recipiente *m,* vasija. **3** ANAT vaso. COMP **cargo vessel** buque *m* de carga.

**vest** [vest] *n* **1** GB camiseta. **2** US chaleco.

**vestibule** ['vestɪbjuːl] *n* **1** *(entrance hall)* vestíbulo, entrada. **2** ANAT vestíbulo.

**vet** [vet] *n fam* veterinario,-a.

**veteran** ['vet³rən] *adj* veterano,-a.
▶ *n* **1** veterano,-a. **2** *(soldier, etc)* excombatiente *mf.*

**veterinary** ['vet³rɪn³rɪ] *adj* veterinario,-a. COMP **veterinary surgeon** veterinario,-a.

**veto** ['viːtəu] *n* veto.
ⓘ *pl* vetoes.
▶ *vt* vetar; *(forbid)* prohibir, vedar.
ⓘ *pt & pp* vetoed, *ger* vetoing.

**vexed** [vekst] *adj* disgustado,-a. COMP **vexed question** tema *m* controvertido.

**via** ['vaɪə] *prep* **1** *(through)* vía, por. **2** *(by means of)* por medio de, a través de.

**vibrate** [vaɪˈbreɪt, US 'vaɪbreɪt] *vi* vibrar (with, con).
▶ *vt* hacer vibrar.

**vibration** [vaɪˈbreɪʃ³n] *n* vibración *f.*

**vicar** ['vɪkə'] *n* párroco.

**vice¹** [vaɪs] *n* vicio.

**vice²** [vaɪs] *n (tool)* torno de banco, tornillo de banco.

**vice³** [vaɪs] *pref* vice-. COMP **vice admiral** MIL vicealmirante *m.* ▌ **vice chancellor** EDUC rector,-ra. ▌ **vice president** vicepresidente,-ta.

**vicereine** [vaɪsˈreɪn] *n* virreina.

**viceroy** ['vaɪsrɔɪ] *n* virrey *m.*

**vicinity** [vəˈsɪnətɪ] *n* **1** inmediaciones *fpl.* **2** *fml* proximidad *f.*

**vicious** ['vɪʃəs] *adj* **1** *(cruel)* cruel; *(malicious)* malintencionado,-a. **2** *(violent)* virulento,-a, violento,-a. **3** *(dangerous)* peligroso,-a.

☒ Vicious no significa 'vicioso', que se traduce por depraved.

**victim** ['vɪktɪm] *n* víctima.

**victory** ['vɪkt³rɪ] *n* victoria, triunfo.
ⓘ *pl* victories.

**victuals** ['vɪt³lz] *n pl* vituallas *fpl,* víveres *mpl.*

**vicuna** [vɪˈkjuːnə] *n* vicuña.

**video** ['vɪdɪəu] *n* **1** *(in general)* vídeo. **2** *(pop video)* videoclip *m.* COMP **video game** videojuego.
ⓘ *pl* videos.

**videoconference** [vɪdɪəukˈkɒnf³rəns] *n* videoconferencia.

**videodisc** ['vɪdɪəudɪsk] *n* videodisco.

**videorecorder** [vɪdɪəurɪˈkɔːdə'] *n* vídeo.

**videotape** ['vɪdɪəuteɪp] *n* cinta de video
▶ *vt* grabar en vídeo.

**videotext** ['vɪdɪəutekst] *n* videotexto.

**Vietnam** [vɪetˈnæm] *n* Vietnam.

**Vietnamese** [vɪetnəˈmiːz] *adj* vietnamita.
▶ *n* **1** *(person)* vietnamita *mf.* **2** *(language)* vietnamita *m.*
▶ *n pl* **the Vietnamese** los vietnamitas *mpl.*

**view** [vjuː] *n* **1** vista, panorama *m.* **2** *(opinion)* opinión *f,* parecer *m.*
▶ *vt* **1** *(consider)* considerar, ver. **2** *(regard, think about)* enfocar. **3** *(examine)* ver; *(visit)* visitar. **4** *(watch)* ver; *(critically)* visionar.

V

**viewer** ['vjuːəʳ] *n* **1** TV telespectador,-ra, televidente *mf*. **2** *(photography)* visionadora.

**viewpoint** ['vjuːpɔɪnt] *n* punto de vista.

**vignette** [vɪnˈjet] *n* **1** *(artwork)* viñeta. **2** *(description)* estampa.

**vigor** ['vɪgəʳ] *n* US → vigour.

**vigour** ['vɪgəʳ] *n* vigor *m*, energía.

**Viking** ['vaɪkɪŋ] *adj* vikingo,-a.
▶ *n* vikingo,-a.

**villa** ['vɪlə] *n* **1** *(for holidays)* chalet *m*; *(in country)* casa de campo. **2** *(Roman)* villa. **3** GB *(large house)* villa, quinta.

**village** ['vɪlɪdʒ] *n* *(gen)* pueblo; *(small)* pueblecito. COMP **village idiot** el tonto del pueblo. ‖ **village life** la vida de pueblo.

**villager** ['vɪlɪdʒəʳ] *n* habitante *m* del pueblo, aldeano,-a.

**villain** ['vɪlən] *n* **1** *(bad character)* malo,-a, malo,-a de la película. **2** GB *fam* malvado,-a. LOC **the villain of the piece** *fam* el malo de la película.

**vine** [vaɪn] *n* **1** vid *f*. **2** *(made to climb)* parra. COMP **vine grower** viticultor,-ra. ‖ **vine growing** viticultura. ‖ **vine leaf** hoja de parra. ‖ **vine shoot** sarmiento.

**vinegar** ['vɪnɪgəʳ] *n* vinagre *m*. COMP **vinegar bottle** vinagrera. ‖ **wine vinegar** vinagre *m* de vino.

**vineyard** ['vɪnjəd] *n* viña, viñedo.

**vintage** ['vɪntɪdʒ] *n* cosecha.
▶ *adj* **1** *(wine)* de añada. **2** *(classic)* clásico,-a; *(high-quality)* glorioso,-a, maravilloso,-a. **3** *fam* lo mejor de. COMP **vintage car** coche *m* de época *construido entre 1919 y 1930*.

**viola¹** [vaɪˈəʊlə] *n* MUS viola.

**viola²** [vaɪˈəʊlə] *n* BOT violeta.

**violate** ['vaɪəleɪt] *vt* violar; *(law)* infringir, transgredir.

**violation** [vaɪəˈleɪʃ³n] *n* violación *f*; *(of law)* infracción *f*, transgresión *f*.

**violence** ['vaɪələns] *n* violencia.

**violet** ['vaɪələt] *n* **1** BOT violeta *f*. **2** *(colour)* violeta *m*, violado,-a, violáceo,-a.
▶ *adj* (de color) violeta, violado,-a.

**violin** [vaɪəˈlɪn] *n* violín *m*.

**violinist** [vaɪəˈlɪnɪst] *n* violinista *mf*.

**viper** ['vaɪpəʳ] *n* víbora.

**viral** ['vaɪr³l] *adj* viral, vírico,-a.

**virgin** [vaɪəˈlɪnɪst] *adj* virgen.
▶ *n* virgen *f*.

**Virgo** ['vɜːgəʊ] *n* Virgo.

**virtual** ['vɜːtʃʊəl] *adj* virtual. COMP **virtual reality** realidad *f* virtual.

**virtue** ['vɜːtʃuː] *n* **1** virtud *f*. **2** *(advantage)* ventaja. LOC **by virtue of** en virtud de. ‖ **in virtue of** en virtud de.

**virus** ['vaɪr³əs] *n* virus *m*. COMP **virus infection** infección *f* vírica.
ⓘ *pl* viruses.

**visa** ['viːzə] *n* visado, *am* visa. COMP **entry visa** visado de entrada. ‖ **exit visa** visado de salida.

**viscosity** [vɪsˈkɒsɪti] *n* viscosidad *f*.

**visibility** [vɪzɪˈbɪləti] *n* visibilidad *f*.

**visible** ['vɪzɪbəl] *adj* visible.

**Visigoth** ['vɪzɪgɒθ] *n* visigodo,-a.

**Visigothic** ['vɪzɪgɒθɪk] *adj* visigodo,-a.

**vision** ['vɪʒ³n] *n* **1** *(gen)* visión *f*. **2** *(eyesight)* vista. LOC **a man of vision** un hombre con visión de futuro.

**visit** ['vɪzɪt] *vt* **1** *(person)* visitar, hacer una visita a. **2** *(place)* visitar, ir a.
▶ *vi* estar de visita.
▶ *n* visita. LOC **to pay sb a visit** hacer una visita a algn. ‖ **to visit with sb** US charlar con algn.

**visiting** ['vɪzɪtɪŋ] *adj* **1** *(for visiting)* de visita. **2** *(guest)* visitante. COMP **visiting card** tarjeta de visita. ‖ **visiting hours** horas *fpl* de visita. ‖ **visiting lecturer** profesor,-ra invitado,-a. ‖ **visiting team** equipo visitante.

**visitor** ['vɪzɪtəʳ] *n* **1** *(at home)* invitado,-a, visita. **2** *(tourist)* turista *mf*, visitante *mf*. COMP **visitors' book** libro de visitas.

**visor** ['vaɪzəʳ] *n* visera.

**visual** ['vɪʒʊəl] *adj* visual. COMP **visual aid** medio visual. ‖ **visual arts** artes *mpl* visuales. ‖ **visual display unit** pantalla.

**vital** ['vaɪt³l] *adj* **1** vital. **2** *(essential)* esencial, imprescindible. COMP **vital organ** órgano vital. ‖ **vital signs** señales *fpl* de vida.

▶ *n pl* órganos *mpl* vitales. LOC **of vital importance** de suma importancia.

**vitamin** ['vɪtəmɪn, 'vaɪtəmɪn] *n* vitamina. COMP **vitamin C** vitamina C. ▮ **vitamin content** contenido vitamínico. ▮ **vitamin deficiency** avitaminosis *f*.

**vitro** ['vi:trəʊ] LOC **in vitro** in vitro.

**viva** ['vaɪvə] *n* GB *fam* (*abbr of* **viva voce**) examen *m* oral.

**vivid** ['vɪvɪd] *adj* **1** vivo,-a, intenso,-a. **2** (*description*) gráfico,-a. LOC **to have a vivid imagination** tener mucha imaginación.

**viviparous** [vɪ'vɪpərəs] *adj* vivíparo,-a.

**vixen** ['vɪksⁿn] *n* zorra.

**V-neck** ['vi:nek] *n* cuello de pico.

**vocabulary** [və'kæbjʊlərɪ] *n* vocabulario.
ⓘ *pl* vocabularies.

**vocal** ['vəʊkⁿl] *adj* **1** vocal. **2** *fam* (*noisy*) escandaloso,-a. COMP **vocal cords** cuerdas *fpl* vocales.

**vocational** [vəʊ'keɪ[ⁿnəl] *adj* profesional. COMP **vocational guidance** orientación *f* profesional.

**vocative** ['vɒkətɪv] *n* vocativo.
▶ *adj* vocativo,-a.

**vogue** [vəʊg] *n* boga, moda. LOC **to be all the vogue** estar muy en boga. COMP **to be in vogue** estar en boga.

**voice** [vɔɪs] *n* voz *f*. LOC **at the top of one's voice** a voz en grito. ▮ **in a loud voice** en voz alta. ▮ **in a low/soft voice** en voz baja, a media voz. ▮ **to lose one's voice** quedarse afónico,-a, quedarse sin voz. ▮ **to lower/raise one's voice** bajar/levantar la voz. ▮ **with one voice** de una voz, a una, a coro. COMP **voice box** laringe *f*. ▮ **voice offstage** THEAT voz *f* en off.
▶ *vt* **1** expresar. **2** LING sonorizar.

**voiceless** ['vɔɪsləs] *adj* **1** (*hoarse*) afónico,-a. **2** LING sordo,-a.

**voice-over** [vɔɪs'əʊvəʳ] *n* voz *f* en off.

**void** [vɔɪd] *adj* **1** vacío,-a (of, de): *void of interest* falto,-a de interés. **2** JUR nulo, -a, inválido,-a.
▶ *n* vacío.
▶ *vt* **1** (*empty*) vaciar. **2** JUR anular.

**volcano** [vɒl'keɪnəʊ] *n* volcán *m*.
ⓘ *pl* volcanos o volcanoes.

**volley** ['vɒlɪ] *n* **1** MIL descarga. **2** *fig* (*of stones*) aluvión *m*; (*of blows*) tanda; (*of applause*) salva. **3** (*tennis*) volea.
▶ *vi* **1** MIL lanzar una descarga. **2** (*tennis*) hacer una volea.
▶ *vt* (*sp*) volear.

**volleyball** ['vɒlɪbɔːl] *n* voleibol *m*.

**volt** [vəʊlt] *n* voltio.

**voltage** ['vəʊltɪdʒ] *n* voltaje *m*, tensión *f*.

**voltmeter** ['vəʊltmi:təʳ] *n* voltímetro.

**voluble** ['vɒljəbⁿl] *adj* locuaz, hablador,-ra.

❌ Voluble no significa 'voluble', que se traduce por changeable.

**volume** ['vɒljuːm] *n* **1** volumen *m*. **2** (*book*) tomo. LOC **to speak volumes** decirlo todo. ▮ **to turn down/up the volume** bajar/subir el volumen.

**voluntary** ['vɒləntⁿrɪ] *adj* voluntario,-a. COMP **voluntary organization** organización *f* benéfica. ▮ **voluntary society** sociedad *f* benéfica. ▮ **voluntary work** obras *fpl* benéficas. ▮ **voluntary helper/worker** voluntario,-a.

**volunteer** [vɒlən'tɪəʳ] *n* voluntario,-a.
▶ *vt* ofrecer.
▶ *vi* **1** ofrecerse (for, para). **2** MIL alistarse como voluntario,-a (for, en).

**vomit** ['vɒmɪt] *n* vómito.
▶ *vi* vomitar, devolver.
▶ *vt* vomitar, devolver.

**vote** [vəʊt] *n* **1** voto. **2** (*voting*) voto, votación *f*. **3** (*right to vote*) sufragio.
▶ *vi* votar. COMP **vote of censure** voto de censura. ▮ **vote of confidence** voto de confianza.
▶ *vt* **1** votar. **2** (*elect*) elegir. **3** *fam* considerarse: *the party was voted a complete flop* la fiesta se consideró un desastre total. LOC **to be voted into/out of office** ganar/perder las elecciones. ▮ **to vote by a show of hands** votar a mano alzada. ▮ **to vote on sth / take a vote on sth** someter algo a votación.
◆ **to vote down** *vt sep* rechazar.
◆ **to vote through** *vt sep* aprobar.

**voter** ['vəʊtəʳ] *n* votante *mf*.

**voucher** ['vaʊt[əʳ] *n* GB vale *m*, bono. JUR comprobante *m*, justificante *m*.

**V**

**vow** [vaʊ] *n* **1** promesa solemne. **2** REL voto. LOC **to take a vow of chastity/ poverty** hacer voto de castidad/pobreza. ▌ **to take one's vows** pronunciar sus votos. COMP **vow of silence** voto de silencio.

**vowel** ['vaʊəl] *n* vocal *f*.

**voyage** ['vɔɪɪdʒ] *n* viaje *m*; *(by sea)* viaje *m* en barco; *(crossing)* travesía.
▶ *vi fml* viajar.

✎ Voyage se refiere a un viaje generalmente largo por mar o en el espacio. La palabra más usual para 'viaje' es journey.

**vulgar** ['vʌlgəʳ] *adj* **1** *(in poor taste)* de mal gusto. **2** *(coarse)* grosero,-a, ordinario,-a. **3** LING vulgar. COMP **vulgar fraction** fracción *f* común.

☒ Vulgar no significa 'vulgar (corriente)', que se traduce por common.

**vulgarity** [vʌlˈgærɪtɪ] *n* **1** *(poor taste)* mal gusto. **2** *(coarseness)* vulgaridad *f*, ordinariez *f*, grosería.

**vulnerable** ['vʌlnəʳrəbəl] *adj* vulnerable.

**vulture** ['vʌltʃəʳ] *n* buitre *m*.

**vulva** ['vʌlvə] *n* vulva.
ⓘ *pl* vulvas o vulvae ['vʌlviː].

**W, w** [ˈdjʌbəlju:] *n (the letter)* W, w *f.*

**W** [west] *abbr* (**west**) oeste *m; (abbreviation)* O.

**wade** [weɪd] *vi* caminar por el agua.
▸ *vt* vadear.

**wafer** [ˈweɪfəʳ] *n (for ice cream)* barquillo; *(biscuit)* galleta de barquillo.

**wage** [weɪdʒ] *n* sueldo, salario.
▸ *n pl* **wages** sueldo *m sing*, salario *m sing*.

**waggon** [ˈwægən] *n* GB → **wagon**.

**wagon** [ˈwægən] *n* **1** *(cart)* carro; *(covered)* carromato. **2** GB *(railway truck)* vagón *m*. **3** US *(trolley)* carrito, mesa camarera.

**wagon-lit** [vægɒnˈliː] *n* coche-cama *m*.
ⓘ *pl* wagons-lits.

**wail** [weɪl] *n (of pain, grief)* lamento, gemido; *(of siren)* aullido.
▸ *vi* **1** *(person - cry)* gemir, llorar; *(- complain)* quejarse (about/over, de), lamentarse (about/over, de). **2** *(siren)* aullar, ulular; *(wind)* ulular.

**waist** [weɪst] *n* **1** ANAT cintura. **2** *(of garment)* talle *m*. **3** *(of guitar, etc)* parte estrecha.

**waistcoat** [ˈweɪskəʊt] *n* chaleco.

**waistline** [ˈweɪstlaɪn] *n* **1** ANAT cintura. **2** SEW talle *m*.

**wait** [weɪt] *n (gen)* espera; *(delay)* demora.
▸ *vi* esperar (for, -), aguardar (for, -).
LOC **to wait at table** servir la mesa.
▸ *vt* esperar, aguardar.
◆ **to wait about / wait around** *vi* esperar, perder el tiempo.
◆ **to wait on** *vt insep* servir.

**waiter** [ˈweɪtəʳ] *n* camarero. COMP **head waiter** maitre *m*.

**waiting** [ˈweɪtɪŋ] *n* espera. COMP **waiting room** sala de espera.

**waitress** [ˈweɪtrəs] *n* camarera.
ⓘ *pl* waitresses.

**wake** [weɪk] *vt* despertar (up, -).
▸ *vi* despertarse (up, -).
◆ **to wake up to** *vt insep (become aware)* darse cuenta de.
ⓘ *pt* woke [wəʊk], *pp* woken [ˈwəʊkᵊn].

**Wales** [weɪlz] *n* País *m* de Gales.

**walk** [wɔːk] *n* **1** *(gen)* paseo; *(distance)* camino; *(long)* caminata, excursión *f; (sport)* marcha. **2** *(path, route)* paseo, ruta; *(long)* excursión *f*. **3** *(gait)* modo de andar *mpl*.
▸ *vi* andar, caminar, pasear.
▸ *vt* **1** *(cover on foot)* ir a pie, ir andando, andar. **2** *(person)* acompañar; *(animal)* pasear.
◆ **to walk away** *vi* alejarse.
◆ **to walk into** *vt insep* **1** *(get caught)* caer en. **2** *(bump into)* tropezar con.
◆ **to walk out** *vi* **1** *(leave suddenly)* marcharse. **2** *(go on strike)* ir a la huelga.
◆ **to walk out on** *vt insep (abandon)* abandonar a.

**walker** [ˈwɔːkəʳ] *n* **1** *(gen)* paseante *mf; (hiker)* excursionista *mf*. **2** *(athlete)* marchador,-ra. **3** *(for babies)* andador *m; (for disabled)* andador *m*.

**walkie-talkie** [wɔːkɪˈtɔːkɪ] *n* walkie-talkie *m*.

**walkman®** [ˈwɔːkmən] *n* walkman® *m*.
ⓘ *pl* walkmen [ˈwɔːkmən].

**wall** [wɔːl] *n* **1** *(exterior)* muro; *(defensive, city)* muralla; *(garden)* tapia; *(sea)* dique *m*. **2** *(interior)* pared *f; (partition)* tabique *m*. **3** ANAT *(of artery, blood vessel)* pared *f; (of abdomen)* pared *f* abdominal. **4** SP barrera.

**wallet** ['wɒlɪt] *n* cartera.

**wallpaper** ['wɔ:lpeɪpə'] *n* **1** papel *m* pintado. **2** *(for computer screen)* papel *m* tapiz.
▸ *vt* empapelar.

**wally** ['wɒlɪ] *n fam* idiota *mf*, inútil *mf*.
① *pl* wallies.

**walnut** ['wɔ:lnʌt] *n (fruit)* nuez *f*; *(wood)* nogal *m*. COMP **walnut tree** nogal *m*.

**walrus** ['wɔ:lrəs] *n* morsa.
① *pl* walruses.

**waltz** [wɔ:ls] *n* vals *m*.
① *pl* waltzes.

**wand** [wɒnd] *n* varita.

**wander** ['wɒndə'] *vi* **1** *(roam)* deambular, errar, vagar; *(stroll)* pasear, caminar. **2** *(stray)* apartarse, desviarse, alejarse; *(get lost)* extraviarse.
▸ *n* vuelta, paseo.

**want** [wɒnt] *n* **1** *(lack)* falta, carencia. **2** *(desire, need)* necesidad *f.*
▸ *vt* **1** *(gen)* querer. **2** *fam (need)* necesitar. **3** *fam (ought to)* deber. **4** *fml (lack)* necesitar, carecer de,.

**wanted** ['wɒntɪd] *adj* **1** *(for work)* necesario,-a. **2** *(by police)* buscado,-a.

**war** [wɔ:'] *n* guerra.

**ward** [wɔ:d] *n* **1** *(in hospital)* sala. **2** GB *(for elections)* distrito electoral.

**warden** ['wɔ:d°n] *n* **1** *(of hostel, home)* encargado,-a. **2** US *(of prison)* alcaide *m*, director,-ra. **3** *(of university)* rector,-ra.

**wardrobe** ['wɔ:drəʊb] *n* **1** armario (ropero), guardarropa *m*. **2** *(clothes)* vestuario. **3** *(theatre)* vestuario.

**warehouse** ['weəhaʊs] *n* almacén *m*, depósito.
▸ *vt* almacenar, depositar.

**warfare** ['wɔ:feə'] *n* **1** *(war)* guerra. **2** *(conflict, struggle)* lucha, batalla.

**warhead** ['wɔ:hed] *n* ojiva, cabeza.

**warm** [wɔ:m] *adj* **1** *(climate, wind)* cálido,-a; *(day)* caluroso,-a, de calor. **2** *(hands, etc)* caliente; *(liquid)* tibio,-a, templado,-a. **3** *(clothing)* de abrigo, que abriga. **4** *(colour)* cálido,-a. **5** *(welcome, applause, etc)* cálido,-a, caluroso,-a. **6** *(character)* afectuoso,-a.
▸ *vt (gen)* calentar.

▸ *vi* calentarse.
◆ **to warm up** *vt sep* **1** *(food)* calentar, recalentar; *(engine)* calentar. **2** *(audience, party)* animar.
▸ *vi* **1** *(food, engine, etc)* calentarse. **2** *(audience, party)* animarse. **3** SP hacer ejercicios de calentamiento.

**warm-blooded** ['wɔ:m'blʌdɪd] [se escribe warm blooded cuando no se usa para calificar a un nombre] *adj* de sangre caliente.

**warmly** ['wɔ:mlɪ] *adv* **1** *(with heat)* con ardor. **2** *(thank)* con efusión; *(recommend)* con entusiasmo; *(welcome, greet)* calurosamente. **3** *(dress)* con ropa de abrigo.

**warmth** [wɔ:mθ] *n* **1** *(heat)* calor *m*. **2** *fig* afecto, cordialidad *f.*

**warm-up** ['wɔ:mʌp] *n* SP calentamiento, precalentamiento.

**warn** [wɔ:n] *vt* **1** avisar (of, de), advertir (of, de), prevenir (about, sobre), (against, contra). **2** *(instead of punishing)* amonestar.

**warning** ['wɔ:nɪŋ] *n* **1** *(of danger)* aviso, advertencia. **2** *(instead of punishment)* amonestación *f*. **3** *(advance notice)* aviso.
▸ *adj (shot, glance)* de aviso, de advertencia.

**warrant** ['wɒrənt] *n* **1** JUR orden *f* judicial, mandamiento judicial. **2** *(voucher)* bono, vale *m*. **3** *fml (justification)* justificación *f*. COMP **warrant officer** suboficial *m*.
▸ *vt* **1** *fml (justify)* justificar; *(deserve)* merecer, ser digno,-a de. **2** *(guarantee)* garantizar.

**warranty** ['wɒrəntɪ] *n* **1** COMM *(guarantee)* garantía. **2** *fml (authority)* autorización *f.*
① *pl* warranties.

**warrior** ['wɒrɪə'] *n* guerrero,-a.

**warship** ['wɔ:ʃɪp] *n* buque *m* de guerra.

**wart** [wɔ:t] *n* verruga.

**warthog** [wɔ:thɔ:g] *n* jabalí *m* verrugoso.

**wartime** ['wɔ:taɪm] *n* tiempos *mpl* de guerra.
▸ *adj* de guerra.

**was** [wɒz, *unstressed* wəz] *pt* → **be.**

**wash** [wɒʃ] *n* **1** *(act)* lavado. **2** *(laundry)* ropa sucia, colada. **3** *(of ship)* estela; *(of water)* remolinos *mpl*; *(sound)* chapoteo.
▸ *vt* **1** *(gen)* lavar; *(dishes)* fregar. **2** *(carry)* llevar, arrastrar.
▸ *vi* **1** *(gen)* lavarse. **2** *(flow, lap)* batir.
◆ **to wash away** *vt sep* **1** *(destroy and carry away)* llevarse, arrastrar. **2** *(remove)* borrar.
◆ **to wash up** *vt sep* **1** fregar. **2** arrastrar a la playa.
▸ *vi* **1** fregar los platos. **2** US lavarse las manos y la cara, lavarse rápidamente.

**washable** [ˈwɒʃəbəl] *adj* lavable.

**washbasin** [ˈwɒʃbeɪsᵊn] *n* *(fixed to wall)* lavabo; *(bowl)* palangana.

**washbowl** [ˈwɒʃbəʊl] *n* US palangana.

**washer** [ˈwɒʃəʳ] *n* **1** TECH *(metal)* arandela; *(rubber)* junta. **2** *fam* *(machine)* lavadora.

**washing** [ˈwɒʃɪŋ] *n* **1** *(action)* lavado, el lavar *m*. **2** *(dirty clothes)* colada, ropa sucia; *(clean clothes)* colada; *(clothes hanging out)* ropa tendida. LOC **to do the washing** hacer la colada. LOC **washing machine** lavadora. ǀ **washing powder** detergente *m*.

**washing-up** [wɒʃɪŋˈʌp] *n* **1** *(action)* fregado, el fregar *m*. **2** *(dishes)* platos *mpl*. LOC **to do the washing-up** fregar los platos. COMP **washing-up liquid** lavavajillas *m*.

**wasp** [wɒsp] *n* avispa. COMP **wasp's nest** avispero.

**waste** [weɪst] *n* **1** *(gen)* derroche *m*; *(of money, energy)* despilfarro; *(of time)* pérdida,. **2** *(matter)* desechos *mpl*, desperdicios *mpl*; *(rubbish)* basura.
▸ *adj* **1** *(unwanted)* desechado,-a. **2** *(land)* yermo,-a, baldío,-a.
▸ *vt* *(gen)* desperdiciar, malgastar; *(resources)* derrochar; *(time, chance)* desaprovechar, perder.

**wastepaper basket** [weɪstˈpeɪpə-bɑː-kɪt] *n* papelera.

**watch** [wɒtʃ] *n* **1** *(timepiece)* reloj *m*. **2** *(look-out)* vigilancia, guardia; *(person)* vigilante *mf*, guardia *mf*, centinela *mf*, guarda *mf*. **3** MAR *(period, body)* guardia; *(individual)* vigía. **4** HIST ronda.
① *pl* watches.
▸ *vt* **1** *(look at, observe)* mirar, observar; *(television, sport)* ver. **2** *(keep an eye on)* vigilar, observar; *(spy on)* espiar, vigilar. **3** *(be careful about)* tener cuidado con, cuidar de.
▸ *vi* *(look)* mirar, observar. LOC **watch out!** ¡cuidado!
◆ **to watch out for** *vt insep* **1** *(look out for, be alert)* estar alerta, estar pendiente de. **2** *(be careful of)* tener cuidado con.

**watchdog** [ˈwɒtʃdɒg] *n* **1** perro guardián. **2** *fig* guardián,-ana.

**watcher** [ˈwɒtʃəʳ] *n* observador,-ra, espectador,-ra.

**water** [ˈwɔːtəʳ] *n* **1** *(gen)* agua: *drinking water* agua potable; *mineral water* agua mineral; *running water* agua corriente; *spring water* agua de manantial. **2** *(tide)* marea. COMP **water bottle** *(flask)* cantimplora. ǀ **water polo** waterpolo.ǀ **water power** energía hidráulica. ǀ **water supply** abastecimiento de agua, suministro de agua. ǀ **water tank** depósito de agua. ǀ **water vapour** vapor *m* de agua. ǀ **water wheel** **1** *(for power)* rueda hidráulica. **2** *(for irrigation)* noria.
▸ *vt* **1** *(plant, river)* regar. **2** *(animals)* abrevar.
◆ **to water down** *vt sep* **1** *(drink)* aguar, mezclar con agua. **2** *fig* descafeinar.

**watercolor** [ˈwɔːtəkʌləʳ] *n* → **watercolour.**

**watercolour** [ˈwɔːtəkʌləʳ] *n* acuarela.
▸ *n pl* **watercolours** acuarelas *fpl*.

**watercress** [ˈwɔːtkres] *n* berro.

**waterfall** [ˈwɔːtəfɔːl] *n* cascada, salto de agua, catarata.

**watering** [ˈwɔːtᵊrɪŋ] *n* riego.

**watermark** [ˈwɔːtəmɑːk] *n* filigrana.

**watermelon** [ˈwɔːtəmelən] *n* sandía.

**watermill** [ˈwɔːtəmɪl] *n* molino de agua.

**waterpark** [ˈwɔːtəpɑːk] *n* parque *m* acuático.

**waterpipe** [ˈwɔːtəpaɪp] *n* cañería.

**waterproof** ['wɔːtəpruːf] adj 1 (material) impermeable. 2 (watch) sumergible.
  ► n (coat) impermeable m.
  ► vt impermeabilizar.

**water-ski** ['wɔːtəskiː] n esquí m acuático.
  ► vi hacer esquí acuático.

**water-skiing** ['wɔːtəskiːɪŋ] n esquí m acuático.

**watersports** ['wɔːtəspɔːts] n pl deportes mpl acuáticos.

**watertight** ['wɔːtətaɪt] adj 1 estanco,-a, hermético,-a. 2 fig irrefutable, irrebatible.

**water-wheel** ['wɔːtəwiːl] n 1 (for power) rueda hidráulica. 2 (for irrigation) noria.

**waterworks** ['wɔːtəwɜːks] n depuradora, planta de tratamiento de aguas.
  ► n pl GB fam euph aparato urinario.

**watt** [wɒt] n ELEC watt m, vatio.

**wave** [weɪv] n 1 (in sea) ola. 2 (in hair) onda. 3 PHYS onda. 4 (of hand) ademán m, movimiento; (in greeting) saludo con la mano. 5 (steady increase) ola, oleada. 6 (influx) oleada; (sudden increase) olcada, ola.
  ► vi 1 (greet) saludar (con la mano). 2 (flag) ondear; (corn) ondular. 3 (hair) ondular.
  ► vt 1 (brandish) agitar. 2 (direct) indicar con la mano. 3 (hair) marcar, ondular.

**wavelength** ['weɪvleŋθ] n RAD longitud f de onda.

**wavy** ['weɪvɪ] adj ondulado,-a.
  ① comp wavier, superl waviest.

**wax** [wæks] n 1 (gen) cera. 2 (in ear) cerumen m.
  ► vt (polish) encerar. COMP paraffin wax parafina. ▌sealing wax lacre m. ▌wax candle vela. ▌wax crayons ceras fpl. ▌wax paper papel m encerado.

**way** [weɪ] n 1 (right route, road, etc) camino. 2 (direction) dirección f. 3 (distance) distancia. 4 (manner, method) manera, modo.
  ► adv fam muy. LOC all the way 1 (distance) todo el viaje. 2 (completely) totalmente. ▌by the way (incidentally) a pro-

pósito, por cierto. ▌in a way en cierto modo, en cierta manera. ▌in some ways en algunos aspectos. ▌in this way (thus) de este modo, de esta manera. ▌one way or the other (somehow) de algún modo, de una manera u otra, como sea. ▌out of the way 1 (remote) apartado,-a, remoto,-a. 2 (exceptional) excepcional, particular, original. ▌that way 1 (direction) por allá. 2 (like that) así. ▌the right way round bien puesto. ▌the wrong way round al revés. ▌to be in the way estorbar, estar por en medio. ▌to be on the way (coming) estar en camino, estar al llegar, avecinarse. ▌to get out of the way apartarse. ▌to find your way encontrar el camino. ▌to give way 1 (collapse) ceder, hundirse. 2 (yield) ceder (to, a). 3 (when driving) ceder el paso. ▌to loose your way perderse. LOC way in entrada. ▌way out 1 (exit) salida. 2 (solution) solución f, remedio.
  ► n pl ways (customs) costumbres fpl; (habits, behaviour) manías fpl.

**WC** ['wɔːtəskiːɪŋ] abbr water closet váter m, retrete m.

**we** [wiː, unstressed wɪ] pron nosotros, -as.

**weak** [wiːk] adj 1 (gen) débil. 2 (tea, coffee, etc) aguado,-a, poco cargado,-a.
  ► n pl the weak los necesitados mpl, los inválidos mpl.

**weaken** ['wiːkən] vt 1 (gen) debilitar. 2 (argument) quitar fuerza a; (morale) socavar.
  ► vi 1 (person) debilitarse, desfallecer. 2 (resolve, influence) flaquear. 3 (currency) aflojar, caer. 4 (give in) ceder.

**weakness** ['wiːknəs] n 1 (gen) debilidad f, flaqueza. 2 (lack of conviction) falta de peso, pobreza. 3 (defect, fault, flaw) flaqueza, punto flaco.
  ① pl weaknesses.

**wealth** [welθ] n 1 (riches) riqueza. 2 fig abundancia, profusión f.

**wealthy** ['welθɪ] adj rico,-a, adinerado,-a, acaudalado,-a.
  ① comp wealthier, superl wealthiest.

**weapon** ['wepən] n arma.

**wear** [weə<sup>r</sup>] z **1** *(clothing)* ropa: *evening wear* traje de noche; *ladies' wear* ropa para señoras; *men's wear* ropa para hombres. **2** *(use)* uso: *for everyday wear* para todos los días. **3** *(deterioration)* desgaste *m*, deterioro. **4** *(capacity for being used)* durabilidad *f*. COMP **wear and tear** desgaste *m*.
▶ *vt* **1** *(clothing, jewellery, etc)* llevar, vestir; *(shoes)* calzar. **2** *fam (accept, tolerate)* tolerar, aceptar, soportar. **3** *(damage by use)* desgastar.
▶ *vi* **1** *(become damaged by use)* desgastarse. **2** *(endure)* durar.
◆ **to wear out** *vt sep* **1** *(shoes, etc)* gastar, desgastar, romper con el uso. **2** *(person)* agotar, rendir.
▶ *vi* *(shoes, etc)* gastarse, desgastarse, romperse con el uso.
① *pt* **wore** [wɔː<sup>r</sup>], *pp* **worn** [wɔːn].

**wearable** ['weərəb<sup>ə</sup>l] *adj* que se puede llevar, que se puede poner.

**weary** ['wɪərɪ] *adj* **1** *(exhausted)* cansado, -a, agotado,-a. **2** *(fed up)* cansado,-a, harto,-a.
① *comp* **wearier**, *superl* **weariest**.
▶ *vt* cansar.
▶ *vi* cansarse de.

**weasel** ['wiːz<sup>ə</sup>l] *n* comadreja.

**weather** ['weðə<sup>r</sup>] *n (gen)* tiempo. COMP **weather forecast** parte *m* meteorológico.

**weather-vane** ['weðəveɪn] *n (clothing)* veleta.

**weave** [wiːv] *n* tejido.
▶ *vt* **1** *(gen)* tejer. **2** *fig (plot, story)* tramar, urdir.
① *pt* **wove** [wəʊv], *pp* **woven** ['wəʊv<sup>ə</sup>n], *ger* **weaving**.

**weaver** ['wiːvə<sup>r</sup>] *n* tejedor,-ra.

**web** [web] *n* **1** *(spider's)* telaraña. **2** *fig* red *f*, sarta, embrollo. **3** *(of animals' feet)* membrana interdigital. **4** *(Internet)* web *f*.

**webmaster** ['webmɑːstə<sup>r</sup>] *n* administrador,-ra de web.

**website** ['websaɪt] *n* web *f*, sitio web.

**wed** [wed] *vt* casarse con.
① *pt & pp* **wedded** o **wed**, *ger* **wedding**.

**we'd** [wiːd] *contr* (we had, we would) → have, would.

**wedding** ['wedɪŋ] *n* boda, casamiento. COMP **wedding anniversary** aniversario de bodas. ▮ **wedding ring** anillo de bodas.

**wedge** [wedʒ] *n* **1** *(gen)* cuña, calza. **2** *(of cake, cheese)* trozo grande. **3** *(golf)* wedge *m*.
▶ *vt* **1** *(force apart)* acuñar, calzar. **2** *(pack tightly)* apretar.

**Wednesday** ['wenzdɪ] *n* miércoles *m inv*.

✎ Para ejemplos de uso, consulta **Saturday**.

**weed** [wiːd] *n* **1** BOT *(in garden)* mala hierba; *(in water)* algas *fpl*. **2** *fam pej (person)* debilucho,-a, canijo,-a.

**weedkiller** ['wiːdkɪlə<sup>r</sup>] *n* herbicida *m*.

**week** [wiːk] *n* semana.

**weekend** ['wiːkend, wiːk'end] *n* fin *m* de semana. COMP **long weekend** puente *m*.
▶ *vi* pasar el fin de semana.

**weekly** ['wiːklɪ] *adj* semanal.
▶ *adv* semanalmente, cada semana: *twice weekly* dos veces por semana.
▶ *n (press)* semanario.

**weep** [wiːp] *vi* **1** *fml (person)* llorar. **2** *(wound)* supurar.
① *pt & pp* **wept** [wept].

**weigh** [weɪ] *vt* **1** *(gen)* pesar. **2** *fig (consider carefully)* ponderar, sopesar (up, -); *(compare carefully)* contraponer (with/ against, a).
▶ *vi* **1** *(gen)* pesar. **2** *(be important to, have influence on)* influir en, pesar.

**weight** [weɪt] *n* **1** *(gen)* peso. **2** *(of scales, clock, gym)* pesa; *(heavy object)* peso, cosa pesada. **3** *fig (burden, worry)* peso, carga. **4** *fig (importance, influence)* peso, importancia, influencia. LOC **to lose weight** perder peso, adelgazar. ▮ **to put on weight** engordar, ganar peso. COMP **weights and measures** pesos *mpl* y medidas.
▶ *vt* **1** *(make heavy)* cargar con peso, poner peso en, añadir peso a; *(fishing net)* lastrar. **2** *fig (statistics, etc)* ponderar.

W

**weightlifter** ['weɪtlɪftə'] n SP levantador,-ra de pesas, halterófilo,-a.

**weird** [wɪəd] adj **1** (bizarre) raro,-a, extraño,-a. **2** (eerie) siniestro,-a.

**welcome** ['welkəm] adj **1** (gen) bienvenido,-a. **2** (news, sight, etc) grato,-a, agradable; (change) oportuno,-a, beneficioso,-a. LOC **you're welcome** (not at all) no hay de qué, de nada.
► interj bienvenido,-a (to, a).
► n bienvenida, acogida.
► vt **1** (greet) acoger, recibir; (officially) dar la bienvenida a. **2** (approve of, support) aplaudir, acoger con agrado.

**welcoming** ['welkəmɪŋ] adj (smile) acogedor,-ra; (speech) de bienvenida.

**weld** [weld] n soldadura.
► vt **1** soldar. **2** fig soldar, unir.
► vi soldarse.

**welfare** ['welfeə'] n **1** (well-being) bienestar m; (health) salud f. **2** (care, help) protección f. **3** US (money) seguridad f social. COMP **welfare state** estado de bienestar. ‖ **welfare worker** asistente mf social.

**well¹** [wel] n **1** (for water) pozo. **2** (of staircase) hueco de la escalera; (of lift) hueco del ascensor. **3** GB (in court) área de los abogados.
► vi (tears, blood) brotar (up, -), manar (up, -).

**well²** [wel] adj **1** (in good health) bien. **2** (satisfactory, right) bien.
► adv **1** (gen) bien. **2** (with modals) bien. **3** (much, quite) bien. LOC **as well** (also, too) también. ‖ **as well as** además de. ‖ **very well** muy bien, bueno. ‖ **well done!** ¡muy bien!, ¡así se hace! ‖ **well I never!** ¡vaya!, ¡habráse visto! ‖ **well off** (comfortable, rich) acomodado,-a.
► interj **1** (gen) bueno, bien, pues. **2** (surprise) ¡vaya!

**well-balanced** ['wel'bælənst] [se escribe well balanced cuando no se usa para calificar a un nombre] adj equilibrado,-a.

**well-behaved** ['welbɪ'heɪvd] [se escribe well behaved cuando no se usa para calificar a un nombre] adj formal, educado,-a.

**well-being** [wel'biːɪŋ] n bienestar m.

**well-done** ['wel'dʌn] [se escribe well done cuando no se usa para calificar a un nombre] adj muy hecho,-a.

**well-founded** ['wel'faʊndɪd] [se escribe well founded cuando no se usa para calificar a un nombre.] adj bien fundado,-a.

**wellington** ['welɪŋtən] [a veces Wellington] n botas de agua.

**well-known** [wel'nəʊn] adj (bien) conocido,-a.

**well-off** ['wel'ɒf] [se escribe well off cuando no se usa para calificar a un nombre] adj rico,-a, acomodado,-a, pudiente.

**Welsh** [welʃ] adj galés,-esa.
► n (language) galés m.
► n pl **the Welsh** los galeses mpl.

**Welshman** ['welʃmən] n galés m.
ⓘ pl Welshmen ['welʃmən].

**Welshwoman** ['welʃwʊmən] n galesa.
ⓘ pl Welshwomen ['welʃwɪmɪn].

**went** [went] pt → go.

**wept** [wept] pt & pp → weep.

**were** [wɜː'] pt → be.

**we're** [wɪə'] contr (we are) → be.

**werewolf** ['wɪəwʊlf] n hombre m lobo.
ⓘ pl werewolves ['wɪəwʊlvz].

**west** [west] n oeste m, occidente m.
► adj occidental, del oeste. COMP **West Indies** las Antillas. ‖ **West Indian** antillano,-a.
► adv al oeste, hacia el oeste.
► n **the West** POL Occidente m, los países mpl occidentales.

**western** ['westən] adj del oeste, occidental.
► n (cinema) western m.

**westerner** ['westənə'] n occidental mf.

**westward** ['westwəd] adj hacia el oeste.

**westwards** ['westwəds] adv hacia el oeste.

**wet** [wet] adj **1** (gen) mojado,-a; (damp) húmedo,-a. **2** (weather) lluvioso,-a. **3** (paint, ink) fresco,-a. **4** fam (person) apocado,-a, soso,-a.
ⓘ comp wetter, superl wettest.
► n **1** (damp) humedad f. **2** (rain) lluvia. **3** fam (person) apocado,-a; (politician) moderado,-a.

► *vt* mojar, humedecer.
ⓘ *pt & pp* wet o wetted, *ger* wetting.

**wetness** ['wetnəs] *n* humedad *f*.

**wetsuit** ['wetsuːt] *n* traje *m* isotérmico.

**we've** [wiːv] *contr* (we have) → have.

**whale** [weɪl] *n* ballena.

**whalebone** ['weɪlbəʊn] *n* (barba de) ballena.

**whaler** ['weɪləʳ] *n* (gen) ballenero,-a.

**whaling** ['weɪlɪŋ] *n* caza de ballenas.
[COMP] **whaling industry** industria ballenera.

**wharf** [wɔːf] *n* muelle *m*, embarcadero.
ⓘ *pl* wharfs o wharves.

**wharves** [wɔːvz] *pl* → wharf.

**what** [wɒt] *adj* **1** *(direct questions)* qué: *what time is it?* ¿qué hora es?. **2** *(indirect questions)* qué: *I don't know what to do* no sé qué hacer. **3** *(exclamations)* qué: *what a man!* ¡qué hombre! **4** *(all the)* todo,-a: *what money we have is in the drawer* todo el aceite que tenemos está aquí.
► *pron* **1** *(direct questions)* qué: *what is it?* ¿qué es?. **2** *(indirect questions)* qué: *he didn't know what to say* no sabía qué decir. **3** lo que: *that's what he told me* eso es lo que me dijo. [LOC] **guess what?** ¿sabes qué? ▌ **what about...?** ¿qué te parece…?. ▌ **what for?** **1** *(why)* ¿por qué? **2** *(for what purpose)* ¿para qué? ▌ **what if...?** ¿y si…? ▌ **what is it?** **1** *(what's wrong?)* ¿qué pasa? **2** *(definition)* ¿qué es?

► *interj* ¡cómo!: *what! you've lost it!* ¡cómo! ¡lo has perdido!

**whatever** [wɒt'evəʳ] *adj* **1** *(any)* cualquiera que. **2** *(at all)* en absoluto.
► *pron* **1** *(anything, all that)* (todo) lo que. **2** *(no matter what)*: *whatever happens* pase lo que pase. **3** *(surprise)* qué. **4** *fam (show indifference)* lo que sea.

**whatsoever** [wɒtsəʊ'evəʳ] *adj* en absoluto.

**wheat** [wiːt] *n* trigo.

**wheatmeal** ['wiːtmiːl] *n* [COMP] **wheatmeal flour** harina integral de trigo.

**wheel** [wiːl] *n* **1** rueda. **2** *(steering wheel)* volante *m*.
► *vt (push)* empujar.

► *vi* **1** girar. **2** *(birds)* revolotear.
► *n pl* **wheels** *fam* coche *m sing*.

**wheelbarrow** ['wiːlbærəʊ] *n* carretilla de mano.

**wheelchair** ['wiːltʃeəʳ] *n* silla de ruedas.

**when** [wen] *adv* **1** *(direct questions)* cuándo: *when did it happen?* ¿cuándo pasó? **2** *(indirect questions)* cuándo: *tell me when you're ready* dime cuándo estés listo. **3** *(at which, on which)* cuando, en que: *there are times when I can't cope* hay momentos en que no puedo más.
► *conj* **1** *(at the time that)* cuando: *when I arrived* cuando llegué yo. **2** *(whenever)* cuando, siempre que: *when I have a free moment* cuando tenga un momento libre. **3** *(considering)* cuando, si: *why do you want to move?* ¿por qué te quieres mudar? **4** *(although)* cuando, aunque: *they said it was red when in fact it was blue* dijeron que era roja cuando en realidad era azul.
► *pron* cuando: *that was when it broke* fue entonces cuando se rompió.

**whenever** [wen'evəʳ] *conj* **1** *(at any time, when)* cuando quiera que. **2** *(every time that)* siempre que.
► *adv (surprise)* cuándo.

**where** [weəʳ] *adv* **1** *(direct question - place)* dónde; *(- direction)* adónde: *where is it?* ¿dónde está?. **2** *(indirect question)* dónde, adónde: *tell me where it is* dime dónde está. **3** *(at, in or which)* donde, en que; *(to which)* adonde, a donde: *this is where it all happened* es aquí donde pasó todo.
► *conj* **1** donde: *where I come from we don't do that* de donde soy yo eso no se hace. **2** *(when)* cuando: *where possible* cuando sea posible.

**whereabouts** [*(n)* 'weərəbaʊts; *(adv)* weərə'baʊts] *n* paradero.
► *adv* (por) dónde.

**whereas** [weər'æz] *conj* **1** mientras que. **2** JUR considerando que.

**whereby** [weə'baɪ] *adv fml* por el/la/lo cual.

**wherein** [weə'rɪn] *adv* en donde.

**whereupon** ['weərəpɒn] *adv* con lo cual.

**wherever** [weərˈevəʳ] *conj* **1** *(in any place, where)* dondequiera que. **2** *(everywhere)* dondequiera.

▸ *adv* **1** *(in questions)* dónde, adónde. **2** *(unspecified place)* en cualquier parte.

**whether** [ˈweðəʳ] *conj* **1** si. **2** *(no matter if)* aunque.

**which** [wɪtʃ] *adj* **1** *(direct questions)* qué, cuál, cuáles: *which size?* ¿qué tamaño/ talla? **2** *(indirect questions)* qué: *I can't remember which department she's in* no recuerdo en qué sección trabaja.

▸ *pron* **1** *(questions)* cuál, cuáles: *which do you want?* ¿cuál quieres? **2** *(indirect questions)* cuál: *ask him which is his* pregúntale cuál es el suyo. **3** *(defining relative)* que; *(with preposition)* que, el/la que, el/la cual, los/las que, los/las cuales: *the shoes which I bought* los zapatos que compré. **4** *(non-defining relative)* el/la cual, los/las cuales: *two glasses, one of which was dirty* dos copas, una de las cuales estaba sucia. **5** *(referring to a clause)* lo que, lo cual: *he lost, which was sad* perdió, lo cual era triste.

**whichever** [wɪtʃˈevəʳ] *adj* **1** *(any one)* cualquier, el/la que. **2** *(no matter which)* cualquiera que, no importa. **3** *(interrogative)* cuál.

▸ *pron* **1** cualquiera, el/la que. **2** *(interrogative)* cuál.

**while** [waɪl] *n (time)* rato, tiempo: *we talked for a while* charlamos durante un rato.

▸ *conj* **1** *(when)* mientras: *somebody stole our car while we were on holiday* nos robaron el coche mientras estábamos de vacaciones. **2** *(although)* aunque: *while I sympathize with the cause, I cannot support your methods* aunque simpatizo con la causa, no puedo apoyar tus métodos. **3** *(whereas)* mientras que: *he prefers to go out, while I like staying in* él prefiere salir mientras que a mí me gusta quedarme en casa.

**whim** [wɪm] *n* antojo, capricho.

**whimsical** [ˈwɪmsɪkəl] *adj (person, idea, etc)* caprichoso,-a; *(smile)* enigmático,-a; *(story, etc)* fantástico,-a.

**whip** [wɪp] *n* **1** *(for animals)* látigo; *(for punishment)* azote *m*; *(for riding)* fusta. **2** CULIN *(desert)* batido.

▸ *vt* **1** *(person)* azotar; *(horse)* fustigar. **2** *(wind)* azotar. **3** CULIN *(ingredients)* batir; *(cream, egg whites)* montar. **4** GB *fam (steal)* birlar, mangar. **5** *(act quickly)* hacer algo deprisa.

ⓘ *pt & pp* whipped, *ger* whipping.

**whipping** [ˈwɪpɪŋ] *n* azotaina, paliza. COMP **whipping cream** nata para montar.

**whirl** [wɜːl] *n* **1** *(movement)* giro, vuelta. **2** *fig* torbellino.

▸ *vi* **1** *(move round)* girar, dar vueltas; *(of dust, leaves, etc)* arremolinarse. **2** *(move quickly)* ir como un relámpago.

**whisk** [wɪsk] *n* **1** *(quick movement)* movimiento brusco, sacudida. **2** CULIN *(hand)* batidor *m*; *(electric)* batidora.

▸ *vt* **1** *(of animal's tail)* sacudir (la cola). **2** CULIN batir. **3** *(take quickly)* llevar rápidamente.

**whisker** [ˈwɪskəʳ] *n (single hair)* pelo (de la barba).

▸ *n pl* whiskers *(man's)* patillas *fpl*. *(of cat, etc)* bigote *m*, bigotes *mpl*.

**whiskey** [ˈwɪskɪ] *n* → whisky.

**whisky** [ˈwɪskɪ] *n* whisky *m*.

ⓘ *pl* whiskies.

**whisper** [ˈwɪspəʳ] *n* **1** *(quiet voice)* susurro. **2** *(rumour)* rumor *m*, voz *f*.

▸ *vt* **1** *(gen)* susurrar, decir en voz baja. **2** *(rumour)* correr la voz, rumorearse.

**whispering** [ˈwɪspərɪŋ] *n (gen)* cuchicheo; *(of leaves)* murmullo.

**whistle** [ˈwɪsəl] *n* **1** *(instrument)* silbato, pito. **2** *(noise)* silbido, pitido; *(of train)* pitido; *(of wind)* silbido.

▸ *vt (tune)* silbar.

▸ *vi (person, kettle, wind)* silbar; *(referee, police, train)* pitar.

**white** [waɪt] *adj* **1** blanco,-a. **2** *(pale)* pálido,-a.

▸ *n* **1** blanco, color *m* blanco. **2** *(person)* blanco,-a. **3** *(of egg)* clara. **4** *(of eye)* blanco. COMP **white (blood) cell** glóbulo blanco. ‖ **the White House** la Casa Blanca.

▸ *n pl* **whites** *(linen)* ropa *f sing* blanca; *(for tennis)* ropa *f sing* de jugar al tenis.

⊕ La White House es la residencia oficial del presidente de Estados Unidos y se usa como sinónimo del gobierno de este país.

**white-collar** [waɪtˈkɒləʳ] *adj* administrativo,-a; oficinista *mf*.

**whiten** [ˈwaɪtⁿ] *vt* blanquear, emblanquecer.

◆ **to whittle away** *vt sep* mermar, ir reduciendo, ir disminuyendo.

◆ **to whittle down** *vt sep* reducir.

**whiz** [wɪz] *n* → whizz.

**whizz** [wɪz] *n (sound)* zumbido, silbido.

▸ *vi* **1** *(make sound)* zumbar, silbar. **2** *(car, bullet)* pasar zumbando, pasar silbando; *(time)* pasar volando.

**who** [huː] *pron* **1** *(direct questions)* quién, quiénes: *who is it?* ¿quién es? **2** *(indirect questions)* quién, quiénes: *I don't know who they are* no sé quiénes son. **3** *(defining relative)* que: *you're the only one who can help me* eres el único que puede ayudarme. **4** *(non-defining relative)* que, quien, quienes, el/la cual, los/las cuales: *the workers, who were on strike,...* los trabajadores, los cuales estaban en huelga,…

**whoever** [huːˈevəʳ] *pron* **1** *(the person who)* quien, quienquiera que, el que. **2** *(no matter who)* quienquiera que, cualquiera que. **3** *(questions, exclamations)* ¿quién?

**whole** [həʊl] *adj* **1** *(entire, all (the), the full amount of)* entero,-a, íntegro,-a, todo,-a. **2** *(intact, not broken)* intacto,-a, sano,-a; *(in one piece, complete)* entero,-a. COMP **whole number** número entero.

▸ *n* conjunto, todo. LOC **as a whole** en conjunto, en su totalidad. ∥ **on the whole** en general.

**wholemeal** [ˈhəʊlmiːl] *adj* integral.

**wholesale** [ˈhəʊlseɪl] *adj* **1** COMM al por mayor. **2** *(complete, indiscriminate)* total,

general, masivo,-a, sistemático,-a, absoluto,-a, indiscriminado,-a.

▸ *adv* **1** COMM al por mayor. **2** *(on a large scale)* de modo general, en su totalidad, en masa, de manera sistemática.

▸ *n* COMM venta al por mayor.

**whom** [huːm] *pron* **1** *fml (direct questions)* a quién/quiénes: *to whom should I address it?* ¿a quién debería ir dirigido? **2** *fml (relative - defining)* que, quien, quienes; *(- after preposition)* quien, quienes, el cual, la cual, los cuales, las cuales: *pupils whom I have taught* alumnos a quienes he dado clase. **3** *(relative - non-defining)* quien, quienes, el cual, la cual, los cuales, las cuales: *our guest, of whom you must all have heard,...* nuestro invitado, de quien todos deben haber oído hablar,…

**whopper** [ˈwɒpəʳ] *n* **1** *fam (large thing)* cosa enorme, cosa descomunal. **2** *fam (lie)* trola, bola.

**whose** [huːz] *pron* **1** *(direct questions)* de quién/quiénes: *whose is this?* ¿de quién es esto? **2** *(indirect questions)* de quién/quiénes: *I don't know whose it is* no sé de quién es.

▸ *adj* **1** *(direct questions)* de quién/quiénes: *whose dog is this?* de quién es este perro? **2** *(indirect questions)* de quién/quiénes: *I wonder whose books these are* me pregunto de quién serán estos libros. **3** *(relative)* cuyo,-a, cuyos,-as: *the woman whose car was stolen* la mujer cuyo coche fue robado.

**why** [waɪ] *adv* **1** *(direct questions - for what reason)* por qué; *(- for what purpose)* para qué: *why didn't you go?* ¿por qué no fuiste? **2** *(indirect questions - for what reason)* por qué; *(- for what purpose)* para qué: *I asked him why he did it* le pregunté por qué lo hizo. **3** *(relative)* por eso: *that is why he left* por eso se fue. COMP **why not?** ¿por qué no?

▸ *interj* ¡vaya!, ¡anda!, ¡toma!

▸ *n* porqué *m*.

**wick** [wɪk] *n* mecha.

**wicked** [ˈwɪkɪd] *adj* **1** *(evil - person)* malvado,-a, malo,-a; *(- action)* malo,-a,

**W**

perverso,-a, inicuo,-a. **2** *(harmful)* peligroso,-a, dañino,-a, nocivo,-a. **3** *(mischievous)* travieso,-a, pícaro,-a. **4** *fam fig (very bad - gen)* malísimo,-a; *(- weather)* feo,-a, horrible; *(- temper, price)* terrible; *(- waste)* vergonzoso,-a; *(humour)* cruel.

▶ *n pl* **the wicked** los malos.

**wicker** ['wɪkəʳ] *n* mimbre *m*.
▶ *adj* de mimbre.

**wide** [waɪd] *adj* **1** *(broad)* ancho,-a; *(space, hole, gap)* grande. **2** *(having specified width)* de ancho. **3** *(large - area)* amplio,-a, extenso,-a; *(- knowledge, experience, repercussions)* amplio,-a; *(- coverage, range, support)* extenso,-a; *(- eyes, smile)* abierto,-a. **5** *(off target)* desviado,-a.
▶ *adv* **1** *(fully - gen)* completamente. **2** *(off target)* desviado.

**wide-angle** ['waɪdæŋgəl] *adj* amplio,-a. COMP **wide-angle lens** objetivo gran angular.

**widely** ['waɪdlɪ] *adv* **1** *(over wide area or range of things)* extensamente; *(generally)* generalmente. **2** *(to a large degree)* mucho.

**widen** ['waɪdən] *vt* **1** *(road, etc)* ensanchar. **2** *fig (knowledge, etc)* ampliar, extender.
▶ *vi* **1** *(road, etc)* ensancharse; *(eyes)* abrirse. **2** *(project, etc)* extenderse; *(difference, gap)* aumentar.

**widescreen** ['waɪdskriːn] *adj* TV pantalla panorámica.

**widespread** ['waɪdspred] *adj (concern, confusion, unrest, use, belief)* generalizado,-a; *(damage, disease, news)* extenso, -a, extendido,-a. LOC **to become widespread 1** *(gen)* generalizarse. **2** *(illness, news)* extenderse, difundirse.

**widow** ['wɪdəʊ] *n* viuda.

**widower** ['wɪdəʊəʳ] *n* viudo.

**width** [wɪdθ] *n* **1** *(gen)* anchura. **2** *(of material)* ancho. **3** *(of swimming pool)* ancho.

**wield** [wiːld] *vt* **1** *(weapon, tool, etc)* empuñar, blandir, manejar. **2** *fig (power, control, etc)* ejercer.

**wife** [waɪf] *n* esposa, mujer *f*.
① *pl* **wives**.

**wig** [wɪg] *n* **1** *(gen)* peluca. **2** JUR peluquín *m*.

**wild** [waɪld] *adj* **1** *(gen)* salvaje. **2** *(plant, flower)* silvestre; *(vegetation)* salvaje. **3** *(country, landscape)* agreste. **4** *(weather - wind)* borrascoso,-a; *(- sea)* bravo,-a; *(- night)* tempestuoso,-a. **5** *(very excited - person)* loco,-a *(with,* de*)*, alocado, -a. **6** *(showing lack of thought - thoughts, talk)* disparatado,-a; *(- guess)* al azar; *(- idea, scheme)* descabellado,-a. **7** *fam (fantastic, crazy)* bárbaro,-a, salvaje. LOC **wild boar** jabalí *m*.

▶ *n* **the wild** estado salvaje, estado natural, naturaleza.

**wildcat** ['waɪldkæt] *n* gato,-a montés. COMP **wildcat strike** huelga espontánea.

**wildebeest** ['wɪldəbiːst] *n* ñu *m*.

**wildlife** ['waɪldlaɪf] *n* fauna. COMP **wildlife park** reserva natural.

**will¹** [wɪl] *n* **1** *(control, volition)* voluntad *f*; *(free will)* albedrío. **2** JUR testamento, últimas *fpl* voluntades. LOC **against one's will** contra su voluntad. COMP **last will and testament** última voluntad *f*.

▶ *vt* **1** *(make or intend to happen by power of mind)* desear, querer. **2** *fml (intend, desire)* querer, ordenar, mandar. **3** JUR legar, dejar en testamento.

**will²** [wɪl] *aux* **1** *(future)*: *she will be here tomorrow* estará aquí mañana. **2** *(be disposed to, be willing to)*: *(no), I won't* no quiero. **3** *(requests)* querer: *will you do me a favour?* ¿quieres hacerme un favor? **4** *(general truths, custom)*: *accidents will happen* siempre habrá accidentes. **5** *(orders, commands)*: *will you be quiet!* ¡quieres callarte! **6** *(insistence, persistence)* insistir en: *she will play her music at full volume* insiste en poner la música a tope. **7** *(can, possibility)* poder: *this phone will accept credit cards* este teléfono va con tarjetas de crédito. **8** *(supposition, must, probability)* deber de: *that'll be John* será John, debe de ser John.

**willing** ['wɪlɪŋ] *adj* **1** *(without being forced)* complaciente, de gran voluntad, dispuesto,-a; *(eager)* entusiasta. **2**

*(ready, prepared, disposed)* dispuesto,-a (to, a). **3** *(given/done gladly)* voluntario, -a. COMP **to show willing** dar pruebas de buena voluntad.

**willingly** [ˈwɪlɪŋlɪ] *adv* de buena gana, de buen grado.

**willow** [ˈwɪləʊ] *n* sauce *m*.

**willpower** [ˈwɪlpaʊəʳ] *n* (fuerza de) voluntad *f*.

**wilt** [wɪlt] *vt* marchitar, secar.
▶ *vi* **1** *(plant)* marchitarse, secarse. **2** *(person - become weak or tired)* debilitarse, decaer, languidecer; *(- lose confidence)* desanimarse.

**wimp** [wɪmp] *n fam pej* debilucho,-a, esmirriado,-a, canijo,-a.

**win** [wɪn] *n* victoria,
▶ *vt* **1** *(gen)* ganar; *(victory)* conseguir, ganar. **2** *(prize, cup, etc)* ganar, llevarse. **3** *(gain, obtain, achieve - gen)* conseguir, obtener, ganar; *(- friendship, respect)* granjearse; *(- sympathy, affection)* ganarse, granjearse; *(- support)* atraer, captar; *(- heart, love)* conquistar.
▶ *vi* ganar.
ⓘ *pt & pp* **won**, *ger* **winning**.

**wind¹** [wɪnd] *n* **1** METEOR viento, aire *m*. **2** *(breath)* aliento. **3** *(flatulence)* gases *mpl*, flato; *(air)* gases *mpl* del estómago. **4** *pej (talk)* palabrería.
▶ *adj* MUS de viento. COMP **wind instrument** instrumento de viento.
▶ *vt* **1** dejar sin aliento, cortar la respiración. **2** *(baby)* hacer eructar.

**wind²** [waɪnd] *vt* **1** *(handle)* dar vueltas a, girar. **2** *(on reel)* arrollar, devanar. **3** *(tape, film)* bobinar. **4** *(clock)* dar cuerda a (up, -). **5** *(bandage, scarf)* envolver; *(wool)* ovillar.
▶ *vi (road, river)* serpentear, zigzaguear; *(staircase)* formar una espiral.
ⓘ *pt & pp* **wound** [waʊnd].
▶ *n (bend)* curva, recodo, vuelta.

**windlass** [ˈwɪndləs] *n* torno.

**windmill** [ˈwɪndmɪl] *n* molino de viento.

**window** [ˈwɪndəʊ] *n* **1** *(gen)* ventana. **2** *(in vehicle, bank, theatre, etc)* ventanilla. **3** *(of shop)* escaparate *m*. **4** *(glass)* cristal *m*. **5** COMPUT ventana.

**window-dressing** [ˈwɪndəʊdresɪŋ] *n* **1** decoración *f* de escaparates, escaparatismo. **2** *fig* fachada, apariencias *fpl*.

**windowpane** [ˈwɪndəʊpeɪn] *n* cristal *m*.

**windpipe** [ˈwɪndpaɪp] *n* tráquea.

**windscreen** [ˈwɪndskriːn] *n* AUTO parabrisas *m inv*. COMP **windscreen wiper** limpiaparabrisas *m*.

**windshield** [ˈwɪndʃiːld] *n* US→ **windscreen**.

**windsurf** [ˈwɪndsɜːf] *vi* hacer windsurfing.

**windsurfing** [ˈwɪndsɜːfɪŋ] *n* windsurf *m*.

**windy** [ˈwɪndɪ] *adj* **1** *(day, weather)* ventoso,-a; *(place)* expuesto,-a al viento. **2** *(speech)* rimbombante.
ⓘ *comp* **windier**, *superl* **windiest**.

**wine** [waɪn] *n* **1** *(colour)* vino: red/rosé/white wine vino tinto/rosado/blanco. **2** *(colour)* (color *m*) morado, granate *m*. COMP **wine cellar** bodega. ▌ **wine grower** vinicultor,-ra. ▌ **wine taster** catavinos *mf*.

**winery** [ˈwaɪnərɪ] *n* bodega.
ⓘ *pl* **wineries**.

**wineskin** [ˈwaɪnskɪn] *n* odre *m*, bota.

**wing** [wɪŋ] *n* **1** *(gen)* ala. **2** AUTO aleta. **3** SP *(side)* banda; *(player)* extremo,-a.
▶ *vi* volar.
▶ *n pl* **wings** THEAT bastidores *mpl*.

**winged** [wɪŋd] *adj* alado,-a, con alas.

**winger** [ˈwɪŋəʳ] *n* SP extremo,-a.

**wingspan** [ˈwɪŋspæn] *n* envergadura.

**wink** [wɪŋk] *n* guiño.
▶ *vi* **1** *(person)* guiñar el ojo. **2** *(of light, star)* titilear, parpadear..
◆ **to wink at** *vt insep (pretend not to notice)* hacer la vista gorda.

**winker** [ˈwɪŋkəʳ] *n* GB *(indicator)* intermitente *m*.

**winkle** [ˈwɪŋkᵊl] *n* bígaro, bigarro.

**winner** [ˈwɪnəʳ] *n* **1** ganador,-ra, vencedor,-ra. **2** *fam (idea, etc)* éxito.

**winning** [ˈwɪnɪŋ] *adj* **1** *(person, team, etc)* ganador,-ra. **2** *(ticket, number, etc)* premiado,-a. **3** *(stroke, goal)* decisivo,-a. **4** *(smile, ways)* atractivo,-a, encantador,-ra.
▶ *n pl* **winnings** ganancias *fpl*.

**W**

**winter** ['wɪntər] *n* invierno.
▶ *vi fml* invernar, pasar el invierno.
COMP **winter solstice** solsticio de invierno.

**wipe** [waɪp] *vt (clean)* limpiar; *(dry)* enjugar.
▶ *vi (dishes)* enjugar.
▶ *n* **1** *(clean)* lavado, fregado. **2** *(cloth)* paño, trapo.
◆ **to wipe out** *vt sep* **1** *(destroy - army)* aniquilar; *(- population, species)* exterminar. **2** *(clean inside)* limpiar el interior de. **3** *(cancel - debts)* saldar, liquidar, cancelar; *(- profit)* borrar, anular.

**wiper** ['waɪpər] *n* AUTO limpiaparabrisas *m inv*.

**wire** ['waɪər] *n* **1** *(metal)* alambre *m*. **2** ELEC cable *m*, hilo. **3** *(fence)* alambrada, valla. **4** US telegrama *m*. COMP **wire cutters** cortaalambres *m inv*.
▶ *vt* **1** *(fasten, join)* atar con alambre. **2** *(house)* hacer la instalación eléctrica de; *(equipment, appliance)* conectar (a la toma eléctrica). **3** US *(telegram)* enviar un telegrama a; *(money)* mandar un giro telegráfico a.

**wired** ['waɪəd] *adj* conectado,-a.

**wireless** ['waɪələs] *n* **1** *(set)* radio *f*. **2** *(system)* radiofonía. COMP **wireless operator** radiotelegrafista *mf*.

**wiring** ['waɪrɪŋ] *n* cableado.

**wisdom** ['wɪzdəm] *n* **1** *(knowledge)* sabiduría, saber *m*. **2** *(good sense - of person)* cordura, (buen) juicio, tino; *(- of action)* prudencia, sabiduría, sensatez *f*. COMP **wisdom tooth** muela del juicio.

**wise** [waɪz] *adj* **1** *(learned, knowledgeable)* sabio,-a. **2** *(sensible, prudent - person)* prudente, sensato,-a; *(- action, remark)* prudente; *(- advice)* sabio,-a; *(- decision, choice, move)* atinado,-a, acertado,-a. COMP **the Three Wise Men** los Reyes Magos. ‖ **wise guy** sabelotodo.

✎ Consulta **three**.

◆ **to wise up** *vi (realize, become aware)* darse cuenta; *(become informed)* enterarse; *(wake up)* espabilarse.

**wish** [wɪʃ] *vt* **1** *(want)* querer, desear. **2** *fml (demand, want)* querer. **3** *(hope)* desear.
▶ *vi* **1** desear (for, -). **2** *fml (want)* querer.
▶ *n* deseo.
▶ *n pl* **wishes** *(greeting)* deseos *mpl*; *(in letter)* saludos *mpl*, recuerdos *mpl*.
◆ **to wish on** *vt sep*: *I wouldn't wish that on anyone* eso no se lo desearía a nadie.

**wishful** ['wɪʃful] *adj fml* de ensueño. COMP **wishful thinking** ilusiones *fpl*.

**wisp** [wɪsp] *n* **1** *(of grass, straw, etc)* brizna; *(of hair, wool, etc)* mechón *m*; *(of smoke, cloud)* voluta. **2** *(person)* persona menuda.

**wistful** ['wɪstful] *adj* pensativo,-a, nostálgico,-a, melancólico,-a.

**wit** [wɪt] *n* **1** *(clever humour)* agudeza, ingenio. **2** *(intelligence)* inteligencia. **3** *(person)* persona salada, chistoso,-a.

**witch** [wɪtʃ] *n* bruja. COMP **witch doctor** hechicero.
ⓘ *pl* **witches**.

**witchcraft** ['wɪtʃkrɑːft] *n* brujería.

**witch-hunt** ['wɪtʃhʌnt] *n* caza de brujas.

**with** [wɪð, wɪθ] *prep* **1** *(accompanying)* con: *come with me* ven conmigo. **2** *(having, possessing)* con, de; *(including, and also)* con, incluido: *the man with the beard* el hombre de la barba. **3** *(using, by means of)* con: *cut it with a knife* córtalo con un cuchillo. **4** *(cover, fill, contain)* de: *you fill it with water* lo llenas de agua. **5** *(agreeing, in support of)* con: *we're with you all the way!* ¡estamos contigo hasta el final! **6** *(against)* con: *I've had a row with Daniel* he discutido con Daniel. **7** *(because of, on account of)* de: *trembling with fear* temblando de miedo. **8** *(indicating manner)* con: *with pleasure* con mucho gusto. **9** *(in same direction as)* con: *with the flow* con la corriente. **10** *(at the same time and rate as)* con: *wine improves with age* el vino mejora con los años. **11** *(regarding, concerning)* con: *this has nothing to do with you* esto no tiene nada que ver contigo. **12** *(in the case of, as regards)* con respecto a, en cuanto a: *with Mrs Smith what happened was that...* en el caso de la Señora Smith lo que pasó fue que… **13** *(as an employee or client of)* en: *she's with the council now* trabaja en el ayuntamiento ahora. **14** *(remaining): with only half an hour to go* cuando tan solo falta media hora. **15** *(despite, in spite of)* con: *with all his faults* con todos sus defectos. **16** *(in comparisons)* con: *if we compare this brand with a cheaper one* si comparamos esta marca con una más barata. **17** *(illness)* con: *he's in bed with flu* está en cama con la gripe. **18** *(according to)* según, de acuerdo con: *prices vary with the seasons* los precios varían según la temporada.

**withdraw** [wɪð'drɔ:] *vt* **1** *(take out)* retirar, sacar. **2** *fml (retract, take back - statement)* retractarse de, retirar; *(- offer)* renunciar a; *(- charge, support)* retirar.
ⓘ *pt* **withdrew** [wɪð'dru:], *pp* **withdrawn** [wɪð'drɔ:n].
▸ *vi (retire, not take part in)* retirarse. COMP
**to withdraw into oneself** retraerse.

**withdrawal** [wɪð'drɔ:əl] *n* **1** *(gen)* retirada. **2** *(of words)* retractación *f*. **3** *(psychology, behaviour)* retraimiento. COMP
**withdrawal symptoms** síndrome *m* de abstinencia.

**withdrawn** [wɪð'drɔ:n] *pp* → **withdraw**.

**withdrew** [wɪð'dru:] *pt* → **withdraw**.

**wither** ['wɪðəʳ] *vt* **1** *(plant)* marchitar, secar. **2** *(crush)* fulminar, aplastar, intimidar.
▸ *vi* **1** *(plant)* marchitarse (away, -), secarse (away, -). **2** *fig (hopes, etc)* desvanecerse, menguar.

**within** [wɪ'ðɪn] *prep* **1** *fml (inside)* dentro de. **2** *(inside range or limits of)* al alcance de. **3** *(less than - distance)* a menos de. **4** *(less than - time)* dentro de.
▸ *adv fml* dentro, en el interior.

**without** [wɪ'ðaʊt] *prep* **1** sin. **2** *arch* fuera de.
▸ *adv* **1** fuera. **2** sin.

**withstand** [wɪð'stænd] *vt (gen)* resistir; *(pain)* aguantar, soportar.
ⓘ *pt & pp* **withstood** [wɪð'stʊd].

**withstood** [wɪð'stʊd] *pt & pp* → **withstand**.

**witness** ['wɪtnəs] *n* **1** *(person)* testigo *mf*. **2** *fml (testimony, evidence)* testimonio.
ⓘ *pl* **witnesses**.
▸ *vt* **1** *(see)* presenciar, ver. **2** *(document)* firmar como testigo. **3** *(be a sign or proof of)* testimoniar; *(look at the example of)* ver, notar, considerar.
▸ *vi* JUR *fml (give evidence, testify)* atestiguar (to, -), declarar (to, -).

**witty** ['wɪtɪ] *adj (person)* ingenioso,-a, agudo,-a, salado,-a; *(remark)* agudo, -a; *(speech)* gracioso,-a.
ⓘ *comp* **wittier**, *superl* **wittiest**.

**wives** [waɪvz] *n pl* → **wife**.

**we'd** [wi:d] *contr* (we had, we would) → **have, would**.

**wizard** ['wɪzəd] *n* **1** *(male witch)* brujo, hechicero. **2** *(genius)* lince *mf*, genio, experto,-a.

**woeful** ['wəʊfʊl] *adj* **1** *fml (very sad)* afligido,-a, apenado,-a, triste. **2** *(deplorable)* lamentable, deplorable, penoso,-a, malísimo,-a.

**woke** [wəʊk] *pt* → **wake**.

**woken** ['wəʊkən] *pp* → **have, wake**.

**wolf** [wʊlf] *n* lobo. COMP **wolf cub** lobezno.
ⓘ *pl* **wolves**.
▸ *vt* [also **wolf down**] tragarse, zamparse, devorar.

**wolfhound** ['wʊlfhaʊnd] *n* perro lobo.

**wolfram** ['wʊlfrəm] *n* wolframio, volframio, wolfram *m*.

**wolves** [wʊlvz] *pl* → **wolf**.

**woman** ['wʊmən] *n* mujer *f*, señora.
ⓘ *pl* **women** ['wɪmɪn].

**womb** [wu:m] *n* útero, matriz *f*.

**women** ['wɪmɪn] *n pl* → **woman**.

**won** [wʌn] *pt & pp* → **win**.

**wonder** ['wʌndəʳ] *n* **1** *(thing)* maravilla, milagro. **2** *(feeling)* admiración *f*, asombro.
▸ *adj* milagroso,-a.
▸ *vt* **1** *fml (be surprised)* sorprenderse, extrañarse. **2** *(ask oneself)* preguntarse. **3** *(polite request): I wonder if you can help me* a ver si puede ayudarme.

W

▶ *vi* **1** *(reflect, ponder)* pensar (about, en); *(doubt)* tener dudas. **2** *fml (marvel)* asombrarse, maravillarse, admirarse. [COMP] **I shouldn't wonder if +** *indic* no me extrañaría que **+** *subj.* **I it's a wonder (that) +** *indic* es un milagro que **+** *subj.* **I no/little/small wonder (that) +** *indic* no es de extrañar que **+** *subj.*

**wonderful** [ˈwʌndəfʊl] *adj* maravilloso,-a, estupendo,-a.

**wont** [wəʊnt] *n* costumbre *f*, hábito.

**won't** [wəʊnt] *contr* (will not) → will.

**wood** [wʊd] *n* **1** *(material)* madera. **2** *(for fire)* leña. **3** *(forest)* bosque *m*. **4** SP *(golf)* palo de madera; *(bowling)* bola.
▶ *n pl* **woods** bosque *m sing*.

**wooden** [ˈwʊdən] *adj* **1** de madera. **2** *fig (expression, style)* rígido,-a; *(movement)* tieso,-a; *(acting)* sin expresión.

**woodland** [ˈwʊdlənd] *n* bosque *m*, arbolado, monte *m*.

**woodpecker** [ˈwʊdpekəʳ] *n* pico, pájaro carpintero.

**woodwork** [ˈwʊdwɜːk] *n* **1** *(craft)* carpintería. **2** *(of building)* maderaje *m*, maderamen *m*.

**woodworm** [ˈwʊdwɜːm] *n* carcoma: *it has woodworm* está carcomido,-a.

**woody** [ˈwʊdɪ] *adj* **1** *(wooded)* arbolado,-a. **2** *(like wood)* leñoso,-a.
① *comp* **woodier**, *superl* **woodiest**.

**wool** [wʊl] *n* lana.
▶ *adj* **1** *(made of wool)* de lana. **2** COMM lanero,-a.

**woolen** [ˈwʊlən] *adj-n* US → **woollen**.

**woollen** [ˈwʊlən] *adj* **1** *(made of wool)* de lana. **2** COMM lanero,-a.
▶ *n pl* **woollens** géneros *mpl* de lana.

**word** [wɜːd] *n* **1** *(gen)* palabra: *tell me what happened in your own words* explícame con tus propias palabras lo que pasó. **2** *(message, news)* noticia: *word came that...* llegó noticia (de) que… **3** *(promise)* palabra: *I give you my word* te doy mi palabra. **4** *(command)* orden *f*: *wait until I give the word* espera hasta que dé la orden. **5** LING palabra, vocablo, voz *f*. **6 the word** *(rumour)* voz *f*, rumor *m*: *the word is that Macy is pregnant* corre la voz de que Macy

está embarazada. [LOC] **in a word** en una palabra. **I in other words** o sea, es decir. **I not in so many words** no exactamente. **I to keep one's word** cumplir su palabra. **I to put sth into words** expresar ALGO con palabras. **I word for word** palabra por palabra. [COMP] **a word of advice** un consejo. **I a word of warning** una advertencia. **I word processor** procesador *m* de textos.
▶ *n pl* **words** *(lyrics)* letra *f sing. (discussion, talk)* palabras *fpl*.
▶ *vt* expresar, formular, redactar: *a well-worded letter* una carta bien redactada.

**wording** [ˈwɜːdɪŋ] *n* redacción *f*, expresión *f*, palabras *fpl*, términos *mpl*.

**wore** [wɔːʳ] *pt* → wear.

**work** [wɜːk] *n* **1** *(gen)* trabajo. **2** *(employment)* empleo, trabajo. **3** *(building work, roadworks)* obras *fpl*. **4** *(product, results)* trabajo, obra. **5** *(literary, etc)* obra.
▶ *vt* **1** *(person)* hacer trabajar. **2** *(machine)* manejar; *(mechanism)* accionar. **3** *(mine, oil well)* explotar; *(land, fields)* trabajar, cultivar. **4** *(produce)* hacer. **5** *(wood, metal, clay)* trabajar; *(dough)* amasar. **6** *(make by work or effort)* trabajar. **7** *fam (arrange)* arreglar. **8** *(move gradually)*: *work the butter into the flour* vaya mezclando la mantequilla con la harina. [COMP] **to be in work** tener trabajo. **I to be out of work** estar en el paro. **I to get down/set to work** ponerse a trabajar. **I to get worked up** exaltarse.
▶ *vi* **1** *(gen)* trabajar. **2** *(machine, system)* funcionar. **3** *(medicine, cleaner)* surtir efecto; *(plan)* tener éxito. **4** *(move)*: *they eventually worked round to my way of thinking* finalmente coincidieron con mi parecer.
▶ *n pl* **works** *(factory)* fábrica *f sing*.
◆ **to work out** *vt sep* **1** *(calculation, sum)* calcular, hacer. **2** *(plan, scheme)* planear, elaborar, pensar; *(itinerary)* planear; *(details, idea)* desarrollar. **3** *(problem)* solucionar, resolver; *(solution)* encontrar. **4** *(person)* calar, entender.
▶ *vi* **1** *(calculation)* salir (at, por), resultar. **2** *(turn out well - things)* salir bien;

(- *problem*) resolverse. **3** SP hacer ejercicio.

**workaholic** [wɜːkəˈhɒlɪk] *n fam* adicto,-a al trabajo.

**workbench** [ˈwɜːkbentʃ] *n* banco de trabajo.

**workbook** [ˈwɜːkbʊk] *n* cuaderno, libreta de ejercicios.

**workday** [ˈwɜːkdeɪ] *n* US día *m* laborable.

**worker** [ˈwɜːkəʳ] *n* (*gen*) trabajador,-ra; (*manual*) obrero,-a, operario,-a; (*office*) oficinista *mf*, administrativo,-a. COMP worker bee abeja obrera.

**workforce** [ˈwɜːkfɔːs] *n* (*of company, factory, etc*) personal *m*, plantilla; (*of country*) población *f* activa.

**working** [ˈwɜːkɪŋ] *adj* **1** (*clothes, conditions, surface*) de trabajo; (*week, day, life*) laborable. **2** (*population, partner, etc*) activo,-a; (*person, mother*) que trabaja. COMP the working class la clase trabajadora.

▶ *n* (*machine, model*) que funciona; (*part*) móvil.

▶ *adj* **1** (*majority*) suficiente. **2** (*hypothesis, etc*) de trabajo.

▶ *n* (*of machine*) funcionamiento; (*of pit*) explotación *f*.

▶ *n pl* **workings** (*of mine, quarry*) pozos *mpl*. (*mechanics*) funcionamiento.

**working-class** [wɜːkɪŋˈklɑːs] *adj* (*person*) de clase obrera, de clase trabajadora; (*area*) obrero,-a.

**workman** [ˈwɜːkmən] *n* (*gen*) trabajador *m*; (*manual*) obrero, operario.
ⓘ *pl* workmen [ˈwɜːkmən].

**workmate** [ˈwɜːkmeɪt] *n* compañero, -a de trabajo.

**workplace** [ˈwɜːkpleɪs] *n* lugar *m* de trabajo.

**workshop** [ˈwɜːkʃɒp] *n* taller *m*.

**worktop** [ˈwɜːktɒp] *n* encimera.

**world** [wɜːld] *n* **1** (*earth*) mundo: *I'd love to travel round the world* me encantaría dar la vuelta al mundo. **2** (*sphere*) mundo: *the world of show business* el mundo del espectáculo. **3** (*life*) mundo, vida: *in this world* en esta vida. **4** (*people*) mundo: *in the eyes of the world* a los ojos del

mundo. **5** (*large amount, large number*): *this will make a world of difference to the disabled* esto cambiará totalmente la vida de los minusválidos. LOC out of this world fenomenal.

▶ *adj* (*population, peace*) mundial; (*politics, trade*) internacional: *world record* récord mundial; *world power* potencia mundial. COMP World Bank Banco Mundial. ▌ world champion campeón,-ona mundial. ▌ World Cup el Mundial, los Mundiales. ▌ world fair exposición *f* internacional. ▌ world music música étnica. ▌ World Wusic guerra mundial.

**worldwide** [wɜːldwaɪd] *adj* mundial, universal.

▶ *adv* mundialmente.

**worm** [wɜːm] *n* **1** (*grub, maggot*) gusano; (*earthworm*) lombriz *f*. **2** *pej* (*person*) gusano, canalla. **3** TECH (*of screw*) tornillo.

▶ *vt* **1** (*make one's way*) deslizarse; (*insinuate*) insinuarse (into, en). **2** MED quitar las lombrices a, desparasitar.

▶ *n pl* **worms** MED lombrices *fpl*.

**worn** [wɔːn] *pp* → wear.

**worn-out** [ˈwɔːnˈaʊt] [se escribe worn out cuando no se usa para calificar a un nombre] *adj* **1** (*thing*) gastado,-a, estropeado,-a. **2** (*person*) rendido,-a, agotado,-a.

**worried** [ˈwʌrɪd] *adj* (*person*) inquieto,-a, preocupado,-a (about, por); (*look, voice*) de preocupación.

**worry** [ˈwʌrɪ] *n* (*state, feeling*) preocupación *f*, inquietud *f*, intranquilidad *f*; (*problem*) preocupación *f*, problema *m*; (*responsibility*) responsabilidad *f*.
ⓘ *pl* worries.

▶ *vt* **1** inquietar, preocupar. **2** (*annoy, disturb*) molestar. **3** (*of dog*) acosar, perseguir.

▶ *vi* inquietarse, preocuparse (about/ over, por).

ⓘ *pt & pp* worried, *ger* worrying.

**worrying** [ˈwʌrɪŋ] *adj* inquietante, preocupante, desconcertante.

W

**worse** [wɜːs] *adj (comp of* **bad**) peor.
▸ *adv (comp of badly)* peor; *(more intensely)* más. [LOC] **to be worse off 1** *(financially)* andar peor de dinero. **2** *(physically)* estar peor. | **to get worse** empeorar. | **to get worse and worse** ir de mal en peor. | **to go from bad to worse** ir de mal en peor. | **to make matters worse** por si fuera poco. | **worse still** lo que es peor.
▸ *n* lo peor.

**worsen** [ˈwɜːsən] *vt* empeorar.
▸ *vi* empeorarse.

**worship** [ˈwɜːʃɪp] *n* **1** REL adoración *f*, veneración *f*, culto; *(service)* culto, oficio. **2** *(devotion, love)* amor *m*, culto, idolatría.
▸ *vt* **1** REL adorar, venerar. **2** *(idolize)* rendir culto a, idolatrar.
ⓘ *pt & pp* worshipped, *ger* worshipping.

**worst** [wɜːst] *adj (superl of* **bad**) peor.
▸ *adv (superl)* peor.
▸ *n (indefinite)* lo peor; *(person)* el/la peor, los/las peores. [LOC] **at (the) worst** en el peor de los casos. | **if the worst comes to the worst** si pasa lo peor.

**worth** [wɜːθ] *n* **1** *(in money)* valor *m*. **2** *(of person)* valía; *(of thing)* valor *m*.
▸ *adj* **1** *(having certain value)* que vale, que tiene un valor de. **2** *(deserving of)* que vale la pena, que merece la pena. [LOC] **to get one's money's worth** sacarle jugo al dinero. | **to be worth** SB's **while** valer la pena.

**worthless** [ˈwɜːθləs] *adj* **1** *(gen)* sin valor. **2** *(useless)* inútil, sin ningún valor. **3** *(person)* despreciable.

**worthwhile** [wɜːθˈwaɪl] *adj (gen)* que vale la pena, que merece la pena.

**worthy** [ˈwɜːðɪ] *adj* **1** *(deserving)* digno,-a *(of,* de), merecedor,-ra *(of,* de); *(winner, opponent, successor)* digno,-a. **2** *(action, cause)* meritorio,-a, bueno,-a, justo,-a.
ⓘ *comp* worthier, *superl* worthiest.

**would** [wʊd] *aux* **1** *(conditional)*: I would love to me encantaría. **2** *(polite requests)*: would you be so kind as to close the window? ¿me haría usted el favor de cerrar la ven-

tana? **3** *(offers, invitations)*: would you like a drink? ¿quieres tomar algo? **4** *(willingness)*: he wouldn't help me se negó a ayudarme, no quiso ayudarme. **5** *(giving advice)*: I wouldn't dwell on it yo que tú no pensaría en ello. **6** *(conjecture)*: that would have been in 1978 eso debe haber sido en 1978. **7** *(past habit, custom)* soler: we would often go out together a menudo salíamos juntos. **8** *(insistence, persistence)*: you would say that! ¡es típico de ti decir eso!

**wound**¹ [wuːnd] *n* herida.
▸ *vt* herir.

**wound**² [waʊnd] *pt & pp* → **wind**²

**wounded** [ˈwuːndɪd] *adj* herido,-a.
▸ *n pl* **the wounded** los heridos.

**wove** [wəʊv] *pt* → **weave**.

**woven** [ˈwəʊvən] *pp* → **weave**.

**wrap** [ræp] *vt* **1** *(cover)* envolver. **2** *fig (surround, immerse)* envolver (in, de), rodear (in, de).
◆ **to wrap up** *vi* **1** *(wear warm clothes)* abrigarse. **2** *(shut up)* callarse, cerrar el pico.
▸ *vt sep (complete)* conseguir; *(conclude)* concluir, dar fin a.
ⓘ *pt & pp* wrapped, *ger* wrapping.

**wrapper** [ˈræpər] *n (of food)* envoltorio, envoltura; *(of book)* sobrecubierta.

**wrapping** [ˈræpɪŋ] *n* envoltura, envoltorio. [COMP] **wrapping paper 1** *(plain)* papel *m* de envolver. **2** *(fancy)* papel *m* de regalo.

**wrath** [rɒθ] *n* cólera, ira.

**wreak** [riːk] *vt* causar, provocar, sembrar. [COMP] **to wreak damage/havoc on** STH hacer estragos en ALGO.

**wreath** [riːθ] *n (of flowers)* corona.

**wreck** [rek] *n* **1** MAR *(action)* naufragio; *(ship)* barco naufragado o hundido. **2** *(of car, plane)* restos *mpl*; *(of building)* ruinas *fpl*, escombros *mpl*. **3** *fig (person)* ruina.
▸ *vt* **1** MAR *(ship)* hacer naufragar. **2** *(car, plane)* destrozar; *(machine)* desbaratar, estropear. **3** *fig (health, career)* arruinar; *(life, marriage)* destrozar; *(hopes)* destruir, echar por tierra; *(plans)* estropear, desbaratar; *(chances)* echar a perder.

**wreckage** ['rekɪdʒ] *n* **1** *(of vehicle)* restos *mpl*; *(of building)* ruinas *fpl*, escombros *mpl*. **2** *fig* ruina.

**wrecked** [rekt] *adj* **1** MAR *(ship)* naufragado,-a; *(sailor)* náufrago,-a. **2** *(car, plane)* destrozado,-a; *(building)* destruido,-a.
 ▸ *n fig (life, career, hopes)* arruinado,-a, destrozado,-a; *(plans)* estropeado,-a.
 ▸ *adj fam fig (stoned)* ciego,-a, colocado,-a, pasado,-a.

**wrench** [rentʃ] *n* **1** *(pull)* tirón *m*, arranque *m*. **2** MED torcedura. **3** *fig* separación *f* dolorosa. **4** GB *(tool)* llave *f* inglesa. **5** US *(tool)* llave *f*.
 ⓘ *pl* wrenches.
 ▸ *vt* **1** *(pull)* arrancar (de un tirón), arrebatar. **2** MED torcer.

**wrestle** ['resºl] *vi* **1** *(fight)* luchar (with, con/contra). **2** *fig (problem, conscience)* luchar (with, con), lidiar (with, con).
 ▸ *vt* luchar contra.
 ▸ *n* lucha.

**wrestler** ['resºləʳ] *n* SP luchador,-ra.

**wrestling** ['resəlɪŋ] *n* lucha.

**wretch** [retʃ] *n* **1** *(unfortunate person)* desdichado,-a, infeliz, desgraciado,-a. **2** *fam (rascal)* pillo,-a, pícaro,-a, granuja *mf*. **3** *(bad person)* canalla *mf*, malvado,-a.

**wriggle** ['rɪgºl] *vi* retorcerse, menearse, moverse.
 ▸ *vt* menear, mover.
 ▸ *n* meneo.

**wriggly** ['rɪgºlɪ] *adj* sinuoso,-a.
 ⓘ *comp* wrigglier, *superl* wriggliest.

**wring** [rɪŋ] *vt* **1** *(one's hands)* torcer, retorcer; *(bird's neck)* retorcer. **2** *(clothes)* escurrir (out, -), retorcer (out, -). **3** *fig (heart)* partir. **4** *fig (confession, truth, etc)* sonsacar, arrancar, sacar.
 ⓘ *pt & pp* wrung [rʌŋ].
 ▸ *n (of clothes)*: *give it a good wring* escúrrelo bien.

**wringer** ['rɪŋəʳ] *n* escurridor *m*, rodillo.

**wrinkle** ['rɪŋkºl] *n* arruga.
 ▸ *vt* arrugar.
 ▸ *vi* arrugarse.

**wrinkled** ['rɪŋkºld] *adj* arrugado,-a.

**wrist** [rɪst] *n* **1** ANAT muñeca. **2** *(of clothes)* puño.

**wristband** ['rɪstbænd] *n* **1** *(of clothes)* puño. **2** *(sweatband)* muñequera.

**wristwatch** ['rɪstwɒtʃ] *n* reloj *m* de pulsera.
 ⓘ *pl* wristwatches.

**write** [raɪt] *vt (gen)* escribir; *(article)* redactar; *(cheque)* extender.
 ▸ *vi (gen)* escribir (about, sobre).
 ◆ **to write back** *vi* contestar (por carta).
 ◆ **to write down** *vt sep (note)* anotar, apuntar.
 ⓘ *pt* wrote [rəʊt], *pp* written ['rɪtən], *ger* writing.

**writer** ['raɪtəʳ] *n* **1** *(by profession)* escritor,-ra; *(of book, letter)* autor,-ra. **2** *(of handwriting)*: *she's a neat writer* tiene buena letra.

**writhe** [raɪð] *vi (physically)* retorcerse, contorsionarse.

**writing** ['raɪtɪŋ] *n* **1** *(script)* escritura; *(handwriting)* letra. **2** *(written work)* composición *f*, trabajo. **3** *(occupation)* profesión *f* de escritor,-ra, trabajo literario; *(activity)* escribir *m*. LOC **in writing** por escrito. COMP **writing desk** escritorio. ❙ **writing materials** objetos *mpl* de escritorio. ❙ **writing paper** papel *m* de escribir.
 ▸ *n pl* writings obra, escritos *mpl*.

**written** ['rɪtºn] *pp* → write.
 ▸ *adj* escrito,-a. LOC **the written word** la palabra escrita. COMP **written consent** consentimiento por escrito. ❙ **written exam** examen *m* escrito.

**wrong** [rɒŋ] *adj* **1** *(erroneous)* erróneo,-a, equivocado,-a, incorrecto,-a: *a wrong answer* una respuesta incorrecta. **2** *(mistaken)* equivocado,-a: *we proved him wrong* demostramos que estaba equivocado. **3** *(evil, immoral)* malo,-a; *(unacceptable, unfair)* injusto,-a: *stealing is wrong* robar es malo. **4** *(amiss)* mal: *is anything wrong?* ¿pasa algo? **5** *(unsuitable)* inadecuado,-a, impropio,-a; *(time)* inoportuno,-a: *she's the wrong person for the job* no es la persona adecuada para el puesto; *I think I said the wrong thing* creo que

**W**

he dicho algo que no debía; *he was in the wrong place at the wrong time* estaba en el sitio equivocado en el momento inoportuno. ⎣LOC⎦ **to be in the wrong 1** *(mistaken)* estar equivocado,-a. **2** *(at fault)* tener la culpa. ‖ **to be wrong** *(person)* estar equivocado,-a, no tener razón, equivocarse. ‖ **to have/get the wrong number** *(tel)* confundirse de número, equivocarse de número. ‖ **to get** sb **wrong** malinterpretar a ALGN. ‖ **to get sth wrong** equivocarse, no acertar. ‖ **to go wrong 1** *(things in general)* salir mal. **2** *(make a mistake)* equivocarse. **3** *(go wrong way)* equivo-carse de camino. *(machine, device)* romperse, estropearse. *(plan)* fallar, fracasar. ‖ **wrong side out** al revés. ‖ **you can't go wrong** *(giving directions)* no tiene pérdida.
  ▸ *adv* mal, incorrectamente, equivo-cadamente.
  ▸ *n* **1** *(evil, bad action)* mal *m*. **2** *(injustice)* injusticia; *(offence)* agravio.
  ▸ *vt (treat unfairly)* ser injusto,-a con; *(judge unfairly)* juzgar mal; *(offend)* agra-viar.

**wrote** [rəʊt] *pt* → write.

**wrung** [rʌŋ] *pt & pp* → wring.

**wry** [raɪ] *adj* irónico,-a, sardónico,-a.

**X, x** [eks] *n (the letter)* X, x *f.*
**xenon** [ˈzenɒn] *n* xenón *m.*
**xenophobia** [zenəˈfəubɪə] *n* xenofobia.
**xenophobic** [zenˈfəubɪk] *adj* xenófobo,-a.
**xerography** [zɪˈrɒɡrəfɪ] *n* xerografía.
**Xerox®** [ˈzɪərɒks] *n* xerocopia, fotocopia.
▶ *vt* xerocopiar, fotocopiar.
**X-ray** [ˈeksreɪ] *n* **1** rayo X. **2** *(photograph)* radiografía.
▶ *vt* radiografiar.
**xylene** [ˈzaɪliʌn] *n* xileno.
**xylography** [zaɪˈlɒɡrəfɪ] *n* xilografía.
**xylophone** [ˈzaɪləfəun] *n* xilófono.

# Y

**Y, y** [waɪ] *n (the letter)* Y, y *f*.

**yacht** [jɒt] *n* **1** yate *m*. **2** *(with sails)* velero, yate *m*. ⟨COMP⟩ **yacht club** club *m* náutico. ▌ **yacht race** regata.

**yachting** [ˈjɒtɪŋ] *n* deporte *m* de la vela, vela.

**yak** [jæk] *n* yac *m*, yak *m*.

**yank** [jæŋk] *n fam* tirón *m*.
▶ *vt fam* tirar de.
◆ **to yank out** *vt sep* arrancar, sacar de un tirón.

**yard** [jɑːd] *n* **1** *(measure)* yarda. **2** GB *(of house)* patio. **3** US *(of house)* jardín *m*. **4** *(industrial)* almacén *m*. **5** *(naut)* verga. ⟨COMP⟩ **Scotland Yard** oficina central de la policía británica en Londres.

✎ Una yarda equivale a 0,914 metros.

**yarn** [jɑːn] *n* **1** hilo. **2** *(story)* cuento. ⟨COMP⟩ **to spin a yarn 1** *(story)* contar un cuento. **2** *(lie)* venir con cuentos.

**yawn** [jɔːn] *vi* **1** bostezar. **2** *(gap, etc)* abrirse.
▶ *n* **1** bostezo. **2** *fam (boring event)* rollo.

**year** [jɪəʳ] *n* **1** año. **2** EDUC curso. ⟨LOC⟩ **all the year round** durante todo el año. ▌ **year in, year out** año tras año.

**yearbook** [ˈjɪəbʊk] *n* anuario.

**yearly** [ˈjɪəlɪ] *adj* anual.
▶ *adv* anualmente.

**yearn** [jɜːn] *vi (desire)* anhelar (for, -), ansiar (for, -); *(nostalgically)* añorar. ⟨LOC⟩ **to yearn to do** STH suspirar por hacer ALGO.

**yearning** [ˈjɜːnɪŋ] *n (desire)* anhelo (for, de); *(nostalgia)* añoranza (for, de).
▶ *adj* anhelante.

**yeast** [jiːst] *n* levadura.

**yell** [jel] *n* grito, alarido.
▶ *vi* gritar, dar alaridos.

**yellow** [ˈjeləʊ] *adj* **1** amarillo,-a. **2** *(cowardly)* cobarde.
▶ *n* amarillo.
▶ *vt* ponerse amarillo.
▶ *vi* amarillear. ⟨COMP⟩ **yellow card** *(sp)* tarjeta amarilla. ▌ **yellow fever** fiebre *f* amarilla. ▌ **yellow jersey** *(sp)* maillot *m* amarillo. ▌ **Yellow Pages** páginas amarillas. ▌ **yellow press** prensa sensacionalista.

**yelp** [jelp] *n* gañido.
▶ *vi* gañir.

**Yemen** [ˈjemən] *n* Yemen.

**Yemeni** [ˈjemənɪ] *adj* yemení.
▶ *n* yemení *mf*.

**yeoman** [ˈjəʊmən] *n* HIST pequeño terrateniente *m*. ⟨COMP⟩ **yeoman of the guard** alabardero de la Torre de Londres.

**yes** [jes] *adv* **1** sí. **2** *(answering person)* dime; *(answering phone)* ¿dígame?
▶ *n* sí *m*. ⟨LOC⟩ **to say yes** decir que sí.

**yesterday** [ˈjestədɪ] *adv* ayer.
▶ *n* ayer *m*. ⟨LOC⟩ **the day before yesterday** anteayer.

**yesteryear** [ˈjestəjɪəʳ] *adv lit* antaño.

**yet** [jet] *adv* **1** todavía, aún. **2** *(until now)* hasta la fecha, hasta ahora. **3** *(even)* aún, todavía. **4** *(expressing future possibility, hope, etc)* aún: *don't give up, you may win yet* no te rindas, aún puedes ganar. ⟨COMP⟩ **yet again** otra vez. ▌ **yet another...** otro,-a...: más: *yet another gold medal for Broddle* otra medalla de oro más para Broddle.
▶ *conj* pero, aunque: *a cheap yet effective solution to the problem* una solución barata pero efectiva para el problema.

**yew** [juː] *n* tejo.

**yield** [jiːld] *n* **1** *(harvest)* cosecha. **2** FIN *(return)* rendimiento, rédito.

► *vt* **1** *(produce)* producir, dar. **2** *(give, hand over)* entregar. **3** FIN rendir.

► *vi* **1** *(surrender)* rendirse (to, ante), ceder (to, a). **2** *(break)* ceder. **3** US ceder el paso.

◆ **to yield up** *vt sep (secrets)* revelar.

**yoghourt** ['jɒgət] *n* → yoghurt.

**yoghurt** ['jɒgət] *n* yogur *m*. COMP **yoghurt maker** yogurtera.

**yogurt** ['jɒgət] *n* → yoghurt.

**yoke** [jəʊk] *n* **1** *(for carrying, pulling)* yugo. **2** *(pair of oxen)* yunta. **3** SEW canesú *m*.

► *vt* **1** *(oxen)* uncir. **2** *fig* unir.

**yolk** [jəʊk] *n* yema.

**you** [juː] *pron* **1** *(subject, familiar, singular)* tú: *and what did you say?* y tú, ¿qué dijiste? **2** *(subject, familiar, plural - men)* vosotros; *(- women)* vosotras: *you two, where are you going?* vosotros dos, ¿adónde vais? **3** *(subject, polite, singular)* usted, Vd., Ud.: *you must wait here until the doctor arrives* usted debe esperar aquí hasta que llegue el médico. **4** *(subject, polite, plural)* ustedes, Vds., Uds.: *you must both wait here* ustedes dos deben esperar aquí. **5** *(subject, impersonal)* se, uno: *you can go by coach or train* se puede ir en tren o en autocar. **6** *(object, familiar, singular)* te; *(with prep)* ti; *(if prep is* con) contigo: *I'm going with you* voy contigo. **7** *(object, familiar, plural)* os; *(with preposition)* vosotros,-as: *I'll go with you* iré con vosotros. **8** *(direct object, polite, singular - man)* lo, le; *(- woman)* la; *(with preposition)* usted: *good morning, sir, can I help you?* buenos días, señor, ¿puedo ayudarlo? **9** *(direct object, polite, plural - men)* los; *(- women)* las; *(with preposition)* ustedes: *I wanted to talk to you two ladies* quería hablar con ustedes dos. **10** *(indirect object, polite, singular)* le: *I'll send you a letter* te mandaré una carta. **11** *(indirect object, polite, plural)* les: *I sent both of you a card* les mandé una felicitación a los dos. **12** *(object, impersonal)*: *cyanide kills you* el cianuro mata.

**young** [jʌŋ] *adj (gen)* joven; *(brother, sister)* menor. LOC **to be young at heart** ser joven de espíritu. COMP **young lady 1** *(woman)* señorita. **2** *(girlfriend)* novia. ▮ **young man 1** *(man)* joven *m*, muchacho. **2** *(boyfriend)* novio. ▮ **young woman** joven *f*, muchacha.

► *n* **the young** *(humans)* los jóvenes *mpl*, la juventud *f*, la gente *f* joven; *(animals)* las crías *fpl*.

**youngish** ['jʌŋɪʃ] *adj* bastante joven, juvenil.

**youngster** ['jʌŋstəʳ] *n* joven *mf*.

**your** [jɔːʳ] *adj* **1** *(familiar, singular)* tu, tus; *(plural)* vuestro,-a, vuestros,-as. **2** *(polite)* su, sus. **3** *fml (address)* Su: *Your Majesty* Su Majestad.

**yours** [jɔːz] *pron* **1** *(familiar, singular)* (el) tuyo, (la) tuya, (los) tuyos, (las) tuyas; *(plural)* (el) vuestro, (la) vuestra, (los) vuestros, (las) vuestras. **2** *(polite)* (el) suyo, (la) suya, (los) suyos, (las) suyas. **3** *(letters)* le saluda…: *Yours sincerely…* le saluda atentamente…

**yourself** [jɔːˈself] *pron* **1** *(familiar singular)* te; *(emphatic)* tú mismo,-a. **2** *(polite singular)* se; *(emphatic)* usted mismo,-a.

**yourselves** [jɔːˈselvz] *pron* **1** *(familiar plural)* os; *(emphatic)* vosotros,-as mismos,-as. **2** *(polite plural)* se; *(emphatic)* ustedes mismos,-as.

**youth** [juːθ] *n* **1** *(period)* juventud *f*. **2** *(young person)* joven *mf*. **3** *(young people)* juventud *f*, los jóvenes *mpl*. COMP **youth club** club *m* juvenil. ▮ **youth hostel** albergue *m* juvenil.

**youthful** ['juːθfʊl] *adj* joven, juvenil.

**yowl** [jaʊl] *n* aullido.

► *vi* aullar.

**yucca** ['jʌkə] *n* yuca.

**Yugoslav** ['juːgəslɑːv] *n (person)* yugoslavo,-a.

**Yugoslavia** [juːgəˈslɑːvɪə] *n* Yugoslavia.

**Yugoslavian** [juːgəˈslɑːvɪən] *adj* yugoslavo,-a.

► *n* yugoslavo,-a.

**yuppie** ['jʌpɪ] *n* yuppie *mf*.

# Z

**Z, z** [zed] *n (the letter)* Z, z *f.*

**Zaire** [zɑːˈɪə] *n* Zaire.

**Zairean** [zɑːˈɪrɪən] *adj* zaireño,-a.
▸ *n* zaireño,-a.

**Zambia** [ˈzæmbɪə] *n* Zambia.

**Zambian** [ˈzæmbɪən] *adj* zambiano,-a.
▸ *n* zambiano,-a.

**zap** [zæp] *vt* **1** *fam (kill)* cargarse. **2** *(attack)* atacar.
▸ *vi (hurry)* apresurarse.
① *pt & pp* zapped, *ger* zapping.
▸ *n* marcha.

**zeal** [ziːl] *n* celo, entusiasmo.

**zebra** [ˈziː brə, ˈzebrə] *n* cebra. COMP **zebra crossing** paso de peatones, paso de cebra.

**zebu** [ˈziː buː, ˈziː bjuː ] *n* cebú *m.*

**zed** [zed] *n* GB zeta.

**zee** [ziː ] *n* US zeta.

**zenith** [ˈzenɪθ] *n* cenit *m.*

**zephyr** [ˈzefəʳ] *n* céfiro *m.*

**zeppelin** [ˈzepəlɪn] *n* zepelín *m.*

**zero** [ˈzɪərəʊ] *n* cero.
① *pl* zeros o zeroes.

**zest** [zest] *n* **1** *(eagerness)* brío, entusiasmo. **2** *(spice)* emoción *f.* **3** *(of lemon, etc)* cáscara.

**zigzag** [ˈzɪgzæg] *n* zigzag *m.*
▸ *vi* zigzaguear.
① *pt & pp* zigzagged, *ger* zigzagging.

**Zimbabwe** [zɪmˈbɑː bweɪ] *n* Zimbabwe.

**Zimbabwean** [zɪmˈbɑː bwɪən] *adj* zimbabwense, zimbabuo,-a.
▸ *n* zimbabwense *mf*, zimbabuo,-a.

**zinc** [zɪŋk] *n* cinc *m*, zinc *m.*

**zip** [zɪp] *n* **1** cremallera. **2** *fam (energy)* vigor *m*, energía. **3** *fam (hiss)* zumbido.
▸ *vt* COMPUT comprimir. COMP **zip code** US código postal. **l zip fastener** cremallera.
◆ **to zip by** *vt insep* pasar como un rayo.
▸ *vi* pasar como un rayo.
◆ **to zip past** *vt-vi* → **zip by**.
◆ **to zip up** *vt sep* cerrar con cremallera.

**zipped** [zɪpt] *adj* COMPUT comprimido,-a.

**zipper** [ˈzɪpəʳ] *n* US cremallera.

**zodiac** [ˈzəʊdɪæk] *n* zodiaco, zodíaco.

**zombie** [ˈzɒmbɪ] *n* zombi *mf*, zombie *mf.*

**zonal** [ˈzəʊnəl] *adj* zonal.

**zone** [zəʊn] *n* zona.
▸ *vt* dividir en zonas.

**zoo** [zuː ] *n* zoo *m*, parque *m* zoológico, zoológico.
① *pl* zoos.

**zoological** [ʒuːəˈlɒdʒɪkəl] *adj* zoológico,-a.

**zoologist** [zuːˈɒlədʒɪst] *n* zoólogo,-a.

**zoology** [zuːˈɒlədʒɪ] *n* zoología.

**zucchini** [zuːˈkiː nɪ] *n* US calabacín *m.*
① *pl* zucchini o zucchinis.

**zygote** [ˈzaɪgəʊt] *n* cigoto.

# LEARNING IN SPANISH

## La comunicación en clase

- ¡Buenos días a todos!
- ¿Cómo estáis esta mañana?
- ¿Qué quiere decir...?
- ¿Cómo se pronuncia esta palabra?
- ¿Podrías repetir eso, por favor?
- ¿Podría hablar más despacio?
- Lo siento, no lo entiendo

## Communication in class

- Good morning everybody!
- How are you this morning?
- What does... mean?
- How do you pronounce this word?
- Could you repeat that, please?
- Could you speak more slowly?
- Sorry, I don't understand

## Pasando lista

- Voy a pasar lista
- ¿Dónde está Pedro? Hoy no ha venido...
- Kevin no ha venido porque está enfermo
- Marta no está porque ha ido al médico

## Taking the roll

- I'm going to take the roll
- Where's Peter? –He's not here today...
- Kevin isn't here because he's ill
- Marta is absent because she's gone to the doctor's

## Vocabulario / Vocabulary

| | | | |
|---|---|---|---|
| lista de alumnos de clase | roll | silla | chair |
| tiempo climatológico | weather | limpiar | clean |
| | | borrar | rub off |
| caliente | hot | leer | read |
| frío | cold | responder | answer |
| estufa | heater | repartir | hand out |
| aparato de aire acondicionado | air conditioner | sacar | take out |
| | | encender | switch on |
| | | apagar | switch off |
| | | abrir | open |
| pizarra | blackboard | cerrar | close |

## Preguntando sobre cosas que se hacen en clase

- ► ¿Podrías limpiar la pizarra?
- ► ¿Podrías borrar esas frases?

- ► Por favor, levantad esas sillas

## Requesting Actions in Class

- ► Would you clean the blackboard?
- ► Could you erase those sentences?

- ► Please, lift those chairs up

## Organizar la clase

- ► Sacad los libros de matemáticas, por favor
- ► ¿Podrías repartir estas hojas, por favor?
- ► Colocaos en grupos de 2,3,4...
- ► Voy a dividir la clase en dos grupos

## Organizing the Class

- ► Take your math books out, please
- ► Could you hand out these papers, please?
- ► Put yourselves into groups of 2,3,4...
- ► I'm going to divide the class in two groups

## Poner deberes

- ► En casa, leed este fragmento
- ► Revisad estos ejercicios
- ► Completad las siguientes actividades...

## Assigning Homework

- ► Read this passage at home
- ► Go over these exercises
- ► Complete the following activities...

## Hablar sobre la lección

- ► En unos minutos vamos a practicar...
- ► Al final de la clase vamos a leer una historia
- ► María, por favor, ¿podrías responder a esta pregunta?
- ► ¿Podrías traerme los diccionarios?
- ► ¿Podrías pasarme la goma?

## Talking About the Lesson

- ► In a few minutes we're going to practice...
- ► At the end of the class we're going to read a story
- ► Mary, please, could you answer this question?
- ► Could you bring me the dictionaries?
- ► Could you pass me the eraser?

## Vocabulario / Vocabulary

| | |
|---|---|
| papel de lija | sandpaper |
| papel higiénico | toilet paper |
| papel de periódico | newspaper |
| papel de colores | colored paper |
| papel charol | glazed paper |
| maqueta | model |
| retrato | portrait |
| dibujo | drawing |
| contorno | outline |
| esquema | diagram |
| fondo | background |
| paisaje | landscape |

## Diseños / Patterns

| | |
|---|---|
| tela vaquera | denim |
| liso | plain |
| a rayas | striped |
| a cuadros | checked |
| de lunares | spotted |

## Texturas / Textures

| | |
|---|---|
| liso | smooth |
| rugoso | rough |
| suave | soft |
| áspero | coarse |
| duro | hard |

marquetería
marquetry

tejer
knitting

cerámica
pottery

bordado
embroidery

costura
sewing

collage
collage

mosaicos
mosaics

decoración de huevos
egg decorating

encuadernado de libros
bookbinding

construcción de collares
beadwork

diseño de postales
cardmaking

## FRASES COMUNICATIVAS EN CLASE DE MANUALIDADES

## COMMUNICATIVE SENTENCES IN THE ARTS & CRAFTS CLASS

- ► Vete a buscar las ceras, por favor
- ► Fetch the crayons, please

- ► Que los responsables repartan los pinceles, por favor
- ► Students in charge, please, hand out the brushes

- ► ¡Arreglad ese desorden!
- ► Tidy up that mess!

- ► ¿Puedo sacar punta a los lápices de colores?
- ► May I sharpen the crayons?

- ► Hoy vamos a hacer dos talleres en clase
- ► Today we are going to do two workshops in class

- ► Traed toallas para secar la mesa
- ► Fetch some towels to dry the table

- ► Calcad la plantilla en la cartulina
- ► Trace round the template onto the card

- ► Colgad esos dibujos para que se sequen
- ► Hang up those printings to dry them

- ► Este pegamento se seca enseguida
- ► This glue sets right away

- ► Lavaos las manos antes de salir de clase
- ► Wash your hands before leaving the class

### Verbos en la clase de manualidades

| | | | |
|---|---|---|---|
| pegar | stick | cortar | cut out |
| calcar | trace | doblar | fold |
| sombrear | shade | difuminar | diffuse |
| mirar | look | acabar | finish |
| dibujar | draw | crear | create |
| colorear | color | pulir | polish |
| seguir | follow | pintar | paint |
| completar | complete | hacer punto | knit |
| comenzar de nuevo | start over | bordar | embroider |
| | | coser | sew |

## FRASES COMUNICATIVAS EN CLASE DE MATEMÁTICAS

▸ ¿Puedes resolver esta multiplicación?
  • 7 × 3 = (siete por tres igual a ____)

▸ Dime el resultado de esta suma

▸ ¿Cuál es el dividendo de esta división?
  • ¿y el resto?

▸ ¿Cuántas caras tiene un hexágono?

▸ Dibuja una línea recta

▸ Coge una regla y comprueba esta medida

▸ ¿Cómo se leen estos números?
  • 6.5 seis coma cinco
  • 1 $^2/_3$ uno y dos tercios
  • 8$^2$ ocho al cuadrado
  • 5$^3$ cinco al cubo
  • 3$^4$ tres elevado a cuatro

## COMMUNICATIVE SENTENCES IN THE MATH CLASS

▸ Can you solve this multiplication?
  • 7 × 3 = (seven times three equals ____)

▸ Tell me the answer to this sum

▸ What is the dividend of this division?
  • and the remainder?

▸ How many sides does a hexagon have?

▸ Draw a straight line

▸ Take a ruler and check this measurement

▸ How do you read these numbers?
  • six point five
  • one and two thirds
  • eight squared
  • five cubed
  • three to the power of four

### Vocabulario / Vocabulary

| | |
|---|---|
| operación | operation |
| resultado | result |
| problema | problem |
| conmutativa | commutative |
| asociativa | associative |
| distributiva | distributive |
| resto | remainder |
| divisor | divisor |
| cociente | quotient |

### Don't forget

In English we use a comma (,) to separate thousands, but in Spanish we use a period (.):

**1.532.620**          1,532,620

However, the Spanish use a comma to separate decimals, not a period, like we do:

**23,45**          23.45

| | | | |
|---|---|---|---|
| **+** | más<br>plus | $7+2=9$<br>**suma** / addition | |
| **–** | menos<br>minus | $7-2=5$<br>**resta** / subtraction | |
| **X** | multiplicado por<br>multiplied by | $7\times2=14$<br>**multiplicación** / multiplication | |
| **/** | dividido entre<br>divided by | $7/2=3,5$<br>**división** / division | |
| **=** | es igual a<br>is equal to | **≠** | no es igual a<br>is not equal to |
| **1/2** | fracción<br>fraction | **3.5** | parte decimal<br>decimal part |
| **()** | paréntesis<br>parenthesis | **√** | raíz cuadrada de<br>square root of |
| **%** | porcentaje<br>percentage | **∅** | conjunto vacío<br>empty set |
| **>** | es mayor que<br>is greater than | **≥** | es igual o mayor que<br>is equal to or greater than |
| **<** | es menor que<br>is less than | **≤** | es igual o menor que<br>is equal to or less than |
| **∈** | pertenece a<br>belongs to | **π** | pi<br>pi |

## Números / Numbers

| | | | | | |
|---|---|---|---|---|---|
| 1 | uno | one | 21 | veintiuno | twenty-one |
| 2 | dos | two | 22 | veintidós | twenty-two |
| 3 | tres | three | 30 | treinta | thirty |
| 4 | cuatro | four | 31 | treinta y uno | thirty-one |
| 5 | cinco | five | 40 | cuarenta | forty |
| 6 | seis | six | 50 | cincuenta | fifty |
| 7 | siete | seven | 60 | sesenta | sixty |
| 8 | ocho | eight | 70 | setenta | seventy |
| 9 | nueve | nine | 80 | ochenta | eighty |
| 10 | diez | ten | 90 | noventa | ninety |
| 11 | once | eleven | 100 | cien | one hundred |
| 12 | doce | twelve | 101 | ciento uno | one hundred one |
| 13 | trece | thirteen | | | |
| 14 | catorce | fourteen | 200 | doscientos | two hundred |
| 15 | quince | fifteen | 300 | trescientos | three hundred |
| 16 | dieciséis | sixteen | | | |
| 17 | diecisiete | seventeen | 1.000 | mil | one thousand |
| 18 | dieciocho | eighteen | | | |
| 19 | diecinueve | nineteen | 1.000.000 | un millón | one million |
| 20 | veinte | twenty | | | |

## Ordinales / Ordinal numbers

| | | | |
|---|---|---|---|
| primero | first | undécimo | eleventh |
| segundo | second | duodécimo | twelfth |
| tercero | third | decimotercero | thirteenth |
| cuarto | fourth | decimocuarto | fourteenth |
| quinto | fifth | decimoquinto | fifteenth |
| sexto | sixth | vigésimo | twentieth |
| séptimo | seventh | vigésimo primero | twenty-first |
| octavo | eighth | | |
| noveno | ninth | trigésimo | thirtieth |
| décimo | tenth | centésimo | hundredth |

| | unidad / unit |
| 1.345.36**5** | |
| 1.345.3**6**5 | decenas / tens |
| 1.345.**3**65 | centenas / hundreds |
| 1.34**5**.365 | millares / thousands |
| **1**.345.365 | millones / millions |

| 1/2 | medio / a half |
| 1/3 | un tercio / a third |
| 1/4 | un cuarto / a quarter |
| 3/4 | tres cuartos / three quarters |

## Medidas de longitud / Linear measures

| 1 milímetro | 1 millimeter | = 0.04 inches |
| 1 centímetro | 1 centimeter | = 0.39 inches |
| 1 metro | 1 meter | = 1.09 yards |
| 1 kilómetro | 1 kilometer | = 1,093.61 yards / 0.62 miles |

## Medidas de capacidad / Measures of capacity

| 1 mililitro | 1 mililiter | = 0.002 pints |
| 1 centilitro | 1 centiliter | = 0.02 pints |
| un litro | 1 liter | = 2.113 pints |

## Pesos / Weights

| 1 gramo | 1 gram | = 0,035 ounces |
| 1 kilo | 1 kilogram | = 2.204 pounds |
| 1 tonelada | 1 ton | = 2204 pounds |

## FRASES COMUNICATIVAS EN FÚTBOL Y BALONCESTO

- ► Venga, hagamos diez flexiones
- ► Botad el balón
- ► Haz una finta y lanza el balón
- ► Penalización por más de 3 segundos
- ► Parad el partido
- ► Id a la línea de tiros libres
- ► Bloquead el tiro
- ► ¡Pasos!
- ► Dobles
- ► Id al punto de penalty
- ► Id a la línea de banda
- ► Id a la línea de fondo
- ► Pasad el balón
- ► Coged el rebote
- ► Salto entre dos
- ► Detén el balón en la línea de medio campo

## COMMUNICATIVE SENTENCES IN SOCCER AND BASKETBALL

- ► Come on! Let's do ten push-ups
- ► Bounce the ball
- ► Fake and shoot the ball
- ► Three-second violation
- ► Stop the game
- ► Go to the free-throw line
- ► Block the shot
- ► Traveling!
- ► Double dribble
- ► Go to the penalty spot
- ► Go to the side line
- ► Go to the end line
- ► Pass the ball
- ► Get the rebound
- ► Jump ball
- ► Stop the ball at the midfield line

---

**pista de atletismo**
athletic track

**estadio**
stadium

**pabellón deportivo**
arena

**gradas**
stands

**pista de juego**
pitch

**terreno de juego**
field

## Verbos en la clase de educación física

| | | | |
|---|---|---|---|
| caminar | walk | usar | blow a |
| hacer | jog | el silbato | whistle |
| footing | | arrodillarse | kneel |
| nadar | swim | hacer una finta | fake |
| bucear | dive | hacer | do push-ups |
| saltar | jump | flexiones | |
| placar | tackle | | |
| patinar | skate | hacer el pino | do a |
| esquiar | ski | | handstand |
| hacer esquí | water-ski | botar | bounce |
| acuático | | lanzar | throw |
| apuntar | aim | coger | catch |
| correr | run | balancearse | swing |
| golpear | punch | escalar | climb |
| pedalear | cycle | hacer | stretch |
| montar | ride | estiramientos | |
| chutar | hit (the ball) | flexionar hacia | bend over |
| chutar | kick | delante | |
| saltar a la comba | jump rope | flexionar | bend |
| caer | fall | hacia atrás | backwards |

cuerda
rope

balón
ball

colchoneta
mat

palo de hockey
hockey stick

raqueta
racket

potro
vaulting-horse

silbato
whistle

bate
bat

## Frases comunicativas

- ¡Mirad, está lloviendo a cántaros!

- Ayer un rayo cayó en la antena

- Vamos a mirar la estación meteorológica y comprobar la humedad

- ¡Estamos a dos grados bajo cero!

- Hala! ¡Acaba de salir un arco iris!

- Se aproxima un frente frío

## Communicative sentences

- Look, it's pouring down rain!

- Yesterday, lightning struck the antenna

- Let's look at the weather station and check the humidity

- It's two degrees below zero!

- Wow, a rainbow has just appeared!

- A cold front is approaching

### Estaciones / Seasons

| | |
|---|---|
| primavera | spring |
| verano | summer |
| otoño | fall |
| invierno | winter |

### Temperatura / Temperature

| | |
|---|---|
| cálido | hot |
| templado | warm |
| fresco | cool |
| frío | cold |
| helado | freezing |

### Vocabulario / Vocabulary

| | | | |
|---|---|---|---|
| soleado | sunny | atardecer | dusk |
| lluvioso | rainy | nubes | clouds |
| nevado | snowy | nieve | snow |
| ventoso | windy | lluvia | rain |
| nebuloso | foggy | granizo | hail |
| nublado | cloudy | niebla | fog |
| tormentoso | stormy | trueno | thunder |
| amanecer | dawn | arco iris | rainbow |

## FRASES COMUNICATIVAS EN EL LABORATORIO

## COMMUNICATIVE SENTENCES AT THE LAB

▶ Examinad ese insecto con el microscopio

▶ Look at that insect under the microscope

▶ Ajustad el objetivo si está borroso

▶ Adjust the lens if it's blurred

▶ Tened mucho cuidado con esas probetas

▶ Be very careful with those test tubes

▶ Colocad bien los taburetes

▶ Put those stools back properly

▶ No os llevéis las batas a casa

▶ Don't take the lab coats home

▶ Conectad esos electrodos

▶ Connect those electrodes

### El microscopio / The microscope

| | |
|---|---|
| prismáticos binoculares | prismatic binoculars |
| rueda de enfoque | focusing wheel |
| lente convexa | convex lens |
| lente cóncava | concave lens |

### Vocabulario / Vocabulary

| | | | |
|---|---|---|---|
| probeta | test tube | alambre | wire |
| llama | flame | electrodo | electrode |
| frasco | flask | imán | magnet |
| embudo | funnel | espátula | spatula |
| filtro de papel | filter paper | pipeta | pipette |
| pinzas | tongs | peso | weight |
| lupa | magnifying glass | batería | battery |
| | | temporizador | timer |
| jeringuilla | syringe | microscopio | microscope |
| termómetro | thermometer | ocular | eyepiece |
| gasa | gauze | transparencia | slide |
| trípode | tripod | báscula | balance/scales |
| bata de laboratorio | lab coat | objetivo | objective lens |

## La cara / The face

| | |
|---|---|
| ojo | eye |
| nariz | nose |
| oreja | ear |
| boca | mouth |
| mejilla | cheek |
| barbilla | chin |
| frente | forehead |
| mandíbula | jaw |
| bigote | mustache |
| barba | beard |
| diente | tooth |
| labio | lip |
| lengua | tongue |

## El ojo / The eye

| | |
|---|---|
| globo ocular | eyeball |
| ceja | eyebrow |
| párpado | eyelid |
| pestaña | eyelash |
| pupila | pupil |
| iris | iris |

## Los órganos / The organs

| | |
|---|---|
| cerebro | brain |
| tráquea | windpipe |
| intestino | bowel |
| vejiga | bladder |

## Peinados / Hairstyles

| | | | |
|---|---|---|---|
| rubio | blonde/fair | calvo | bald |
| moreno | dark | entradas | receding hairline |
| gris, canoso | gray | | |
| liso | straight | trenzas | plaits |
| rizado | curly | coleta | ponytail |
| ondulado | wavy | flequillo | bangs |
| en punta | spiky | | |
| a la altura de los hombros | shoulder-length | | |
| largo | long | perilla | goatee |
| corto | short | barba de 3 días | stubble |

### FRASES COMUNICATIVAS

► ¿Cuántos huesos crees que tiene el cuerpo humano?

► ¿Eres miope/hipermétrope?

► ¿Te han operado alguna vez?

### COMMUNICATIVE SENTENCES

► How many bones do you think the human body has?

► Are you near-/far-sighted?

► Have you ever had surgery?

## FRASES COMUNICATIVAS EN CLASE DE INFORMÁTICA

## COMMUNICATIVE SENTENCES IN THE COMPUTER SCIENCE CLASS

- ▶ Imprimid los textos después de corregirlos
- ▶ Print the texts after you've corrected them

- ▶ Encended los monitores
- ▶ Switch the monitors on

- ▶ Id a la carpeta 'Mis documentos' y abridla
- ▶ Go to the 'My documents' folder and open it

- ▶ Preparad una breve presentación visual
- ▶ Prepare a short visual presentation

- ▶ Ahora no hay conexión a Internet
- ▶ There's no Internet connection available now

| Partes de un e-mail / Parts of an email | |
|---|---|
| correo basura | spam |
| tema | subject |
| herramientas | tools |
| borrador | draft |
| archivo | file |
| adjuntar | attach |
| guardar | save |
| eliminar | delete |
| enviar | send |
| archivo adjunto | attachment |
| libreta de direcciones | address book |

| Vocabulario / Vocabulary | | | |
|---|---|---|---|
| dominio | domain | palanca de mando | joystick |
| enlace | link | | |
| contraseña | password | impresora de inyección | inkjet printer |
| motor de búsqueda | search engine | | |
| | | impresora láser | laser printer |
| descarga | download | cartucho | cartridge |

## Meses / Months

| | |
|---|---|
| enero | January |
| febrero | February |
| marzo | March |
| abril | April |
| mayo | May |
| junio | June |
| julio | July |
| agosto | August |
| septiembre | September |
| octubre | October |
| noviembre | November |
| diciembre | December |

## Días / Days

| | |
|---|---|
| lunes | Monday |
| martes | Tuesday |
| miércoles | Wednesday |
| jueves | Thursday |
| viernes | Friday |
| sábado | Saturday |
| domingo | Sunday |

### Don't forget

In Spanish, never write days and months with a capital letter.

## FRASES COMUNICATIVAS

- ▶ ¿Qué fecha es hoy?
- ▶ El año 2013 no es un año bisiesto
- ▶ ¿Qué día de la semana es el 13?
- ▶ El último fin de semana de marzo iremos de excursión
- ▶ Nos quedan 10 minutos
- ▶ Tenemos que cambiar las pilas al reloj de pared
- ▶ ¿Qué hora es?

## COMMUNICATIVE SENTENCES

- ▶ What's today's date?
- ▶ The year 2013 is not a leap year
- ▶ What day of the week is the 13th?
- ▶ We're going on a field trip on the last weekend in March
- ▶ We have 10 minutes left
- ▶ We need to replace the batteries in the clock
- ▶ What's the time? / What time is it?

## Vocabulario / Vocabulary

| | | | |
|---|---|---|---|
| reloj de pulsera | watch | agujas del reloj | the hands of a clock |
| reloj de pared | clock | calendario | calendar |
| | | año bisiesto | leap year |

son las nueve
en punto
it's nine o'clock

son las 9 y cinco
it's five past nine

son las 9 y diez
it's ten past nine

son las nueve y cuarto
it's a quarter past nine

son las nueve
y media
it's half past nine

son las diez
menos veinte
it's twenty to ten

son las diez
menos cuarto
it's a quarter to ten

son las diez
menos diez
it's ten to ten

09:15 son las nueve
y quince
it's nine fifteen

09:10 son las nueve y diez
it's nine ten

09:30 son las nueve treinta
it's nine thirty

son las nueve y cuarenta 09:40
it's nine forty

## Carta informal / Informal letter

**tu dirección** → Calle de la Luna, 55
28108 Alcobendas
Madrid
España

**la fecha** → 22 de abril, 2012

**saludo** →

Hola Pedro:

Hace tiempo que no sé nada de ti. ¿Qué es de tu vida? ¿Sigues viviendo con tus padres? Te escribo esta carta porque perdí tu número de teléfono, bueno, perdí todos mis números de teléfono porque me robaron el móvil un día en la playa. Hacía mucho calor y me fui a bañar. Solo estuve en el agua un par de minutos, pero cuando volví a la toalla, mi bolsa había desaparecido, ¡vaya cabreo! Tu dirección de correo electrónico debe de haber cambiado también, ¿verdad? Te mandé un correo el otro día y tuve un mensaje de error. Bueno, si recibes esto, ponte en contacto por favor, tengo muchas ganas de volverte a ver. Mi dirección postal, ya la tienes, pero te doy mi número de teléfono también: es el 65567554

**despedida**

Espero tus noticias. Un fuerte abrazo,

**tu nombre**

María

---

Dear Pedro,

I haven't heard from you for ages. What are you doing with yourself? Are you still living with your parents? I'm writing this letter because I lost your phone number. Well, in fact I lost all my phone numbers because my cellphone was stolen one day at the beach. It was hot and I went for a swim. I was only in the water for a couple of minutes, but when I came back, my bag had disappeared. I was so annoyed! Your email address must have changed too, right? I sent you an email the other day and got an error message.

Well, if you get this, please get in touch. I'd really like to see you again. You've got my postal address, but here's my cellphone number too, it's 65567554.

Looking forward to hearing from you.

Love,

María

# FRASES ÚTILES EN CARTAS Y CORREOS ELECTRÓNICOS / USEFUL PHRASES IN LETTERS AND EMAILS

## SALUDOS FORMALES

- Estimado Sr. García
- Apreciada Sra. Gutiérrez
- Muy Sr mío / Muy Sra. mía
- Muy Sres. míos

## FORMAL GREETINGS

- Dear Mr. García
- Dear Mrs Gutiérrez
- Dear Sir / Dear Madam
- Dear Sirs

## SALUDOS INFORMALES

- Querida Paloma
- Hola Felipe

## INFORMAL GREETINGS

- Dear Paloma
- Hi Felipe, Dear Felipe

## DESPEDIDAS FORMALES

- Le agradezco de antemano su atención
- Le saluda atentamente
- Reciba un cordial saludo
- Quedo a la espera de recibir sus noticias

## FORMAL CLOSING PHRASES

- I thank you in advance for your attention
- Yours faithfully, Yours sincerely
- Yours faithfully, Yours sincerely
- I look forward to hearing from you.

## DESPEDIDAS INFORMALES

- Saludos cordiales
- Un saludo / Saludos
- Un abrazo
- Hasta pronto

## INFORMAL CLOSING PHRASES

- Kind regards
- Yours / Yours
- Best wishes
- See you soon

## DESPEDIDAS ENTRE AMIGOS Y FAMILIARES

- Con cariño / Con amor
- Un (fuerte) abrazo
- Un beso / Besos
- Un besazo / Un besote

## CLOSING PHRASES FOR FRIENDS AND FAMILY

- Yours affectionately / Love
- Best wishes / Love
- Love / Lots of love
- Love / Lots of love

## OTRAS EXPRESIONES

- Me dirijo a Usted ...
- Dale recuerdos a ...
- Saludos a ...
- María te manda recuerdos

## OTHER EXPRESSIONS

- I am writing to you ...
- Give my greetings to ...
- Give my love to ...
- María sends her greetings/love

## Al teléfono

- ▸ ¿Puedo hablar con Juan? / ¿Está Juan?
- ▸ ¿Podría dejarle un mensaje, por favor?
- ▸ ¿De parte de quién?
- ▸ Hola, soy Belén
- ▸ Un momento, por favor
- ▸ Ahora no está
- ▸ Te has equivocado de número
- ▸ ¿Puede deletrear su nombre?
- ▸ Está comunicando / Comunica
- ▸ No hay línea
- ▸ Mi dirección de correo electrónico es I, N, F, O, 'arroba', A, B, C, 'punto' E, S

## On the phone

- ▸ Can I speak to John, please? / Is John there, please?
- ▸ Could I leave a message for him, please?
- ▸ Who's calling?
- ▸ Hello, it's Belén speaking
- ▸ Hold on, please
- ▸ He/she's not in at the moment
- ▸ Wrong number / You've dialled the wrong number
- ▸ Could you spell your name?
- ▸ The line's engaged / The line's busy
- ▸ There's no tone
- ▸ My email address is info@abc.es

## SMS / SMS

| | | |
|---|---|---|
| **xa** | para | for |
| **xo** | pero | but |
| **xq, xk** | porque | because |
| **ad+** | además | what's more / also |
| **nls** | no lo sé | I don't know |
| **tkm** | te quiero mucho | I love you a lot |
| **a2** | adiós | bye |
| **salu2** | saludos | regards |
| **tvl** | te veo luego | see you later |

In general, Spanish words are pronounced as they are written, there is a closer correspondence between the pronunciation and the written word than there is in English. So, if you learn a few easy rules, you will be able to pronounce Spanish correctly when you read it.

Of course, people from different countries have different pronunciations, but the differences do not usually prevent understanding. Here we give you both European and Latin American Spanish, although the main differences in pronunciation, as opposed to accent, are confined to the letters **c** and **z**.

## VOCALES / VOWELS

Spanish has 5 pure vowels:

| | |
|---|---|
| **a** | **casa** – similar to the *a* in *father*, but shorter |
| **e** | **Pepe** – similar to the *e* in *went*, but a little longer |
| **i** | similar to *ee* in *feel*, but a little shorter |
| **o** | similar to the *o* in British English *lost* |
| **u** | similar to *oo* in *root* |

## DIPTONGOS / DIPHTHONGS

| | |
|---|---|
| **ai** | like the *y* in *pylon*. |
| **au** | like *ow* in *cow*. |
| **ei** | like *ay* in *day*. |
| **eu** | this does now exist in English, it is similar to a combination of *e* as in *get* and *w* as in *wet*. |
| **oi /oy** | like *oy* in *boy*. |
| **ui /uy** | like *wee* in *sweet*. |
| **uo** | similar to *wo* in *woke*. |

## CONSONANTES / CONSONANTS

| | |
|---|---|
| **b, v** | these are pronounced exactly the same, but they do have two pronunciations:<br>– at the start of a sentence and after **m**, like the *b* in *bubble*<br>– in other positions, the lips vibrate, but do not close entirely. It's like an English *v*, but with the top and bottom lips instead of the top teeth and bottom lips. |
| **c** | – before **a**, **o** and **u**, like the *c* in *cat*.<br>– before **e** and **i**, like *th* in *thin* [in American Spanish like *s* in *sister*] |
| **d** | – at the start of a sentence, and after **l**, like *d* in *dad*.<br>– in all other positions, like *th* in *this*. |

| | |
|---|---|
| f | as in English. |
| g | – before **a**, **o** and **u**, like *g* in *gang*. |
| | – before **e** and **i**, like Scottish *ch* as in *loch*. |
| | – remember that in the combinations **gue** and **gui**, the **u** is not pronounced unless it is written with a diaresis (**ü**), so in **guerra**, the first syllable **gue** is pronounced like *ge* in *get*, and in **guitarra**, **gui** is pronounced like *gi* in *give*. |
| h | always silent. |
| j | like Scottish *ch* as in *loch*. |
| k | as in English. |
| l | as in English. |
| ll | like *lli* as in *billion* [in some pronunciations, like *y* in *yes*]. |
| m | as in English. |
| n | as in English. |
| ñ | like *ny* as in *canyon*. |
| p | as in English. |
| qu | like *c* in *cat* |
| r | a single tap of the tongue behind the teeth. |
| rr | a strongly trilled *r*, as in Scottish pronunciation. |
| s | as in English. |
| t | as in English. |
| w | this only occurs in foreign words, it is pronounced like *b* and *v* (see above). |
| z | like *th* in *thin* [in American Spanish like *s* in *sister*]. |

## Acentuación / Accentuation

To pronounce Spanish properly, you also need to know which syllable to stress, a change in stress can sometimes change the meaning of a word! Here are the basic rules:
– words ending in a consonant except **–n** or **–s** are stressed on the last syllable: co<u>mer</u> (to eat), ciu<u>dad</u> (city), continen<u>tal</u> (continental).
– words ending in a vowel or **–n** or **–s** are stressed on the next to last syllable: <u>co</u>men (they eat), ciu<u>da</u>des (cities), te<u>rra</u>za (terrace), ja<u>ra</u>be (syrup).

All words which are exceptions to these two rules have a written accent over the stressed vowel; the accent shows you where the stress falls, it does not change the quality of the vowel: <u>ár</u>bol (tree), <u>á</u>guila (eagle), aca<u>bé</u> (I finished), ja<u>món</u> (ham).

Spanish verbs are conjugated in three moods: the indicative, the subjunctive and the imperative. In the indicative and subjunctive there are simple tenses and compound tenses. Compound tenses for all verbs are formed with the auxiliary verb *haber*, which accompanies the invariable participle of the verb to be conjugated.

The following table shows the conjugation of compound tenses, which is, as stated above, the same for all verbs, the only difference being the participle which follows the auxiliary. Following on from that come the simple tenses; firstly the three regular conjugations and then the models for the conjugation of the irregular verbs.

## Tiempos compuestos / Compound Tenses

| AMAR / TEMER / PARTIR | | | | | |
|---|---|---|---|---|---|
| **indicative** | | | **subjunctive** | | |
| **Present Perfect** | he | amado / temido / partido | **Present Perfect** | haya | amado / temido / partido |
| | has | amado / temido / partido | | hayas | amado / temido / partido |
| | ha | amado / temido / partido | | haya | amado / temido / partido |
| | hemos | amado / temido / partido | | hayamos | amado / temido / partido |
| | habéis | amado / temido / partido | | hayáis | amado / temido / partido |
| | han | amado / temido / partido | | hayan | amado / temido / partido |
| **Pluperfect** | había | amado / temido / partido | **Pluperfect** | hubiera o hubiese | amado / temido / partido |
| | habías | amado / temido / partido | | hubieras o hubieses | amado / temido / partido |
| | había | amado / temido / partido | | hubiera o hubiese | amado / temido / partido |
| | habíamos | amado / temido / partido | | hubiéramos o hubiésemos | amado / temido / partido |
| | habíais | amado / temido / partido | | hubierais o hubieseis | amado / temido / partido |
| | habían | amado / temido / partido | | hubieran o hubiesen | amado / temido / partido |
| **Past Anterior** | hube | amado / temido / partido | | | |
| | hubiste | amado / temido / partido | | | |
| | hubo | amado / temido / partido | | | |
| | hubimos | amado / temido / partido | | | |
| | hubisteis | amado / temido / partido | | | |
| | hubieron | amado / temido / partido | | | |
| **Future Perfect** | habré | amado / temido / partido | **Future Perfect** | hubiere | amado / temido / partido |
| | habrás | amado / temido / partido | | hubieres | amado / temido / partido |
| | habrá | amado / temido / partido | | hubiere | amado / temido / partido |
| | habremos | amado / temido / partido | | hubiéremos | amado / temido / partido |
| | habréis | amado / temido / partido | | hubiereis | amado / temido / partido |
| | habrán | amado / temido / partido | | hubieren | amado / temido / partido |
| **Future Perfect** | habría | amado / temido / partido | | | |
| | habrías | amado / temido / partido | | | |
| | habría | amado / temido / partido | | | |
| | habríamos | amado / temido / partido | | | |
| | habríais | amado / temido / partido | | | |
| | habría | amado / temido / partido | | | |

## Tiempos simples / Simple Tenses
## Modelos de conjugación de los verbos regulares / Models for the Conjugation of Regular Verbs

| -AR VERB AMAR | | | |
|---|---|---|---|
| **indicative** | | **subjunctive** | |
| Present | am–o | Present | am–e |
| | am–as / (vos) am–ás | | am–es |
| | am–a | | am–e |
| | am–amos | | am–emos |
| | am–áis | | am–éis |
| | am–an | | am–en |
| Imperfect | am–aba | Imperfect | am–ara o am–ase |
| | am–abas | | am–aras o am–ases |
| | am–aba | | am–ara o am–ase |
| | am–ábamos | | am–áramos o am–ásemos |
| | am–abais | | am–arais o am–aseis |
| | am–aban | | am–aran o am–asen |
| Preterite | am–é | Future | am–are |
| | am–aste | | am–ares |
| | am–ó | | am–are |
| | am–amos | | am–áremos |
| | am–asteis | | am–aréis |
| | am–aron | | am–aren |
| Future | am–aré | | |
| | am–arás | | |
| | am–ará | | |
| | am–aremos | | |
| | am–aréis | | |
| | am–arán | | |
| Conditional | am–aría | | |
| | am–arías | | |
| | am–aría | | |
| | am–aríamos | | |
| | am–aríais | | |
| | am–arían | | |
| **imperative** | | **non–personal forms** | |
| Imperativo | am–a (tú) | Infinitve | am–ar |
| | am–e (él/Vd.) | | |
| | am–emos (nos.) | Gerund | am–ando |
| | am–ad (vos.) | | |
| | am–en (ellos/Vds.) | Past participle | am–ado |

| -ER VERB TEMER | | | |
|---|---|---|---|
| **indicative** | | **subjunctive** | |
| **Present** | tem–o | **Present** | tem–a |
| | tem–es / (vos) tem–és | | tem–as |
| | tem–e | | tem–a |
| | tem–emos | | tem–amos |
| | tem–éis | | tem–áis |
| | tem–en | | tem–an |
| **Imperfect** | tem–ía | **Imperfect** | tem–iera *o* tem–iese |
| | tem–ías | | tem–ieras *o* tem–ieses |
| | tem–ía | | tem–iera *o* tem–iese |
| | tem–íamos | | tem–iéramos *o* tem–iésemos |
| | tem–íais | | tem–ierais *o* tem–ieseis |
| | tem–ían | | tem–ieran *o* tem–iesen |
| **Preterite** | tem–í | **Future** | tem–iere |
| | tem–iste | | tem–ieres |
| | tem–ió | | tem–iere |
| | tem–imos | | tem–iéremos |
| | tem–isteis | | tem–iereis |
| | tem–ieron | | tem–ieren |
| **Future** | tem–eré | | |
| | tem–erás | | |
| | tem–erá | | |
| | tem–eremos | | |
| | tem–eréis | | |
| | tem–erán | | |
| **Conditional** | tem–ería | | |
| | tem–erías | | |
| | tem–ería | | |
| | tem–eríamos | | |
| | tem–eríais | | |
| | tem–erían | | |
| **imperative** | | **non-personal forms** | |
| **Imperativo** | tem–e (tú) | **Infinitve** | tem–er |
| | tem–a (él/Vd.) | | |
| | tem–amos (nos.) | **Gerund** | tem–iendo |
| | tem–ed (vos.) | | |
| | tem–an (ellos/Vds.) | **Past participle** | tem–ido |

| -IR VERB PARTIR | | | |
|---|---|---|---|
| **indicative** | | **subjunctive** | |
| Present | part–o | Present | part–a |
| | part–es / (vos)part–ís | | part–as |
| | part–e | | part–a |
| | part–imos | | part–amos |
| | part–ís | | part–áis |
| | part–en | | part–an |
| Imperfect | part–ía | Imperfect | part–iera o part–iese |
| | part–ías | | part–ieras o part–ieses |
| | part–ía | | part–iera o part–iese |
| | part–íamos | | part–iéramos o part–iésemos |
| | part–íais | | part–ierais o part–ieseis |
| | part–ían | | part–ieran o part–iesen |
| Preterite | part–í | Future | part–iere |
| | part–iste | | part–ieres |
| | part–ió | | part–iere |
| | part–imos | | part–iéremos |
| | part–isteis | | part–iereis |
| | part–ieron | | part–ieren |
| Future | part–iré | | |
| | part–irás | | |
| | part–irá | | |
| | part–iremos | | |
| | part–iréis | | |
| | part–irán | | |
| Conditional | part–iría | | |
| | part–irías | | |
| | part–iría | | |
| | part–iríamos | | |
| | part–iríais | | |
| | part–irían | | |
| **imperative** | | **non–personal forms** | |
| Imperativo | part–e (tú) | Infinitve | part–ir |
| | part–a (él/Vd.) | | |
| | part–amos (nos.) | Gerund | part–iendo |
| | part–id (vos.) | | |
| | part–an (ellos/Vds.) | Past participle | part–ido |

# ESPAÑOL
## INGLÉS

**A**

**A, a** *nf (la letra)* A, a.

**a** *prep* **1** *(dirección)* to, on , in: *girar a la derecha* to turn (to the) right; *irse a casa* to go home; *subir al autobús* to get on the bus; *llegar a Barcelona* to arrive in Barcelona. **2** *(destino)* to, towards. **3** *(distancia)* away: *a diez kilómetros de casa* ten kilometres (away) from home. **4** *(lugar)* at, on: *a la entrada* at the entrance; *a la izquierda* on the left. **5** *(tiempo)* at: *a las once* at eleven; *a tiempo* in time; *al final* in the end. **6** *(modo)* by, in: *a ciegas* blindly; *a oscuras* in the dark. **7** *(instrumento)* by, in: *a mano* by hand; *a pie* on foot. **8** *(precio)* a: *a tres euros el kilo* three euros a kilo. **9** *(medida)* at: *a 90 kilómetros por hora* at 90 kilometres an hour. **10** *(finalidad)* to: *él vino a vernos* he came to see us. **11** *(complemento directo persona)*: *vi a Juanita* I saw Juanita. **12** *(complemento indirecto)* to: *dámelo* give it to me. **13** *verbo + a + inf* to: *aprender a nadar* to learn (how) to swim.

✎ Consulta también al.

**ábaco** *nm* abacus.

**abad** *nm* abbot.

**abadesa** *nf* abbess.

**abadía** *nf* abbey.

**abajo** *adv* **1** *(lugar)* below, down: *ahí abajo* down there. **2** *(en una casa)* downstairs. **3** *(dirección)* down, downward: *calle abajo* down the street.
  ▶ *interj* down with!: *¡abajo el dictador!* down with the dictator!

**abalanzarse** *vpr* **1** *(lanzarse)* to rush forward, spring forward. **2** abalanzarse sobre to rush at; *(león, tigre)* to pounce on; *(águila, etc)* to swoop down on.

**abandonado,-a** *pp* → abandonar.
  ▶ *adj* **1** abandoned: *un barco abandonado* an abandoned ship. **2** *(descuidado)* neglected: *tiene el despacho abandonado* his office hasn't been looked after. **3** *(desaseado)* untidy, unkempt.

**abandonar** *vt* **1** *(desamparar)* to abandon, forsake: *la suerte le ha abandonado* luck has forsaken him. **2** *(lugar)* to leave, quit: *abandonar el barco* to abandon ship. **3** *(descuidar)* to neglect. **4** DEP *(retirarse)* to withdraw from.
  ▶ *vpr* abandonarse to neglect OS.

**abanicar** *vt* to fan.

**abanico** *nm* **1** fan. **2** *fig* range: *un abanico de posibilidades* a range of possibilities.

**abaratar** *vt* to reduce the price of, make cheaper.
  ▶ *vpr* abaratarse *(precio)* to come down; *(artículo)* to become cheaper.

**abarcar** *vt* **1** *(englobar)* to cover, embrace: *sus conocimientos abarcan el campo de la psicología* her knowledge covers the field of psychology. **2** *(abrazar)* to embrace.

**abarrotado,-a** *adj* packed (de, with).

**abastecer** *vt* to supply, provide.

**abastecimiento** *nm* supplying.

**abasto** LOC dar abasto *fam* to be sufficient for: *no doy abasto para corregir tantos ejercicios* I've got so many exercises to correct that I just can't cope.

**abatible** *adj* folding, collapsible: *asiento abatible* folding seat.

**abatido,-a** *pp* → abatir.
  ▶ *adj (deprimido)* dejected, depressed.

**abatir** *vt* **1** *(derribar)* to knock down, pull down. **2** *(matar)* to kill; *(herir)* to wound. **3** *(bajar)* to lower, take down.

**abdicar** *vt & vi* to abdicate, renounce.

**abdomen** *nm* abdomen.

**abdominal** *adj* abdominal.

▸ *nm pl* **abdominales** *(ejercicios)* sit-ups.

**abductor** *adj* abductor.

**abecedario** *nm* alphabet.

**abedul** *nm* birch tree, birch.

**abeja** *nf* bee. COMP **abeja obrera** worker bee. ❙ **abeja reina** queen bee.

**abejorro** *nm* bumblebee.

**abertura** *nf* **1** *(agujero)* opening, gap; *(grieta)* crack, slit. **2** *(en óptica)* aperture.

**abeto** *nm* fir tree, fir.

**abierto,-a** *pp* → abrir.

▸ *adj* **1** open, unlocked. **2** *(grifo)* (turned) on: *dejó el grifo abierto* she left the tap running. **3** *fig (sincero)* open, frank. **4** *(tolerante)* open-minded.

**abisal** *adj* abyssal.

**abismo** *nm* abyss.

**ablación** *nf* ablation.

**ablandar** *vt* **1** to soften. **2** *fig (persona)* to soothe, soften up.

▸ *vpr* **ablandarse** to soften, get softer.

**ablativo** *nm* ablative (case).

**abofetear** *vt* to slap.

**abogacía** *nf* legal profession.

**abogado,-a** *nm & nf* lawyer, solicitor; *(tribunal supremo)* barrister. COMP **abogado de oficio** legal-aid lawyer. ❙ **abogado defensor** counsel for the defence. ❙ **abogado del diablo** devil's advocate.

**abolición** *nf* abolition.

**abolir** *vt* to abolish.

**abolladura** *nf (hundimiento)* dent; *(bollo)* bump.

**abollar** *vt* to dent.

**abominable** *adj* abominable, loathsome.

**abonado,-a** *pp* → abonar.

▸ *adj* **1** *(tierra)* fertilized. **2** FIN paid.

▸ *nm & nf (al teléfono, a revista)* subscriber; *(a teatro, tren, etc)* season ticket holder.

**abonar** *vt* **1** FIN to pay. **2** *(tierra)* to fertilize. **3** *(subscribir)* to subscribe.

▸ *vpr* **abonarse** *(a una revista)* to subscribe (a, to); *(al teatro, tren, etc)* to buy a season ticket (a, for).

**abono** *nm* **1** *(pago)* payment. **2** *(fertilizante)* fertilizer; *(acción)* fertilizing. **3**

*(a revista)* subscription; *(a teatro, tren, etc)* season-ticket.

**abordaje** *nm* boarding. LOC **¡al abordaje!** stand by to board!

**abordar** *vt* **1** MAR *(chocar)* to run foul of, collide with; *(atacar)* to board. **2** *fig (persona)* to approach; *(asunto, tema)* to tackle.

**aborigen** *adj* aboriginal, native.

▸ *nm* aborigine, native.

**aborrecer** *vt* **1** to abhor, hate, detest. **2** *(aves)* to abandon.

**abortar** *vi (voluntariamente)* to abort, have an abortion; *(involuntariamente)* to miscarry, have a miscarriage.

▸ *vt (interrumpir)* to stop; *(frustrar)* to foil, thwart.

**aborto** *nm* **1** *(provocado)* abortion; *(espontáneo)* miscarriage. **2** *pey (persona)* ugly person, freak; *(cosa)* abortion.

**abotonar** *vt (ropa)* to button, button up.

▸ *vpr* **abotonarse** to do one's buttons up.

**abovedado,-a** *adj* vaulted, arched.

**abrasador,-ra** *adj* burning, scorching.

**abrasar** *vt (quemar)* to burn, scorch.

▸ *vi* to burn (up): *esta sopa abrasa* this soup is scalding hot.

▸ *vpr* **abrasarse** to burn. LOC **abrasarse de calor** *fig* to be sweltering.

**abrazadera** *nf* clamp, brace.

**abrazar** *vt* to embrace, hug.

**abrazo** *nm* hug, embrace. LOC **dar un abrazo a ALGN** to embrace SB. ❙ **un abrazo (de)** *(en carta)* with best wishes from.

**abrebotellas** *nm inv* bottle opener.

**abrecartas** *nm inv* letter-opener, paper knife.

**abrelatas** *nm inv* tin-opener, US can-opener.

**abrevadero** *nm* drinking trough.

**abreviar** *vt* **1** *(acortar)* to shorten, cut short. **2** *(texto)* to abridge; *(palabra)* to abbreviate.

**abreviatura** *nf* abbreviation.

**abridor** *nm* opener.

**abrigar** *vt* **1** *(contra el frío)* to wrap up; *(ropa)* to be warm. **2** *(proteger)* to shelter, protect. **3** *fig (sospechas)* to harbour (US harbor), have.

**A**

▶ *vpr* **abrigarse** *(uso reflexivo)* to wrap os up.

**abrigo** *nm* **1** *(prenda)* coat, overcoat. **2** *(refugio)* shelter. LOC **ropa de abrigo** warm clothing, warm clothes *pl*.

**abril** *nm* April.

> ✎ Para ejemplos de uso, consulta marzo.

**abrillantador** *nm* polish.

**abrillantar** *vt* to polish, make shine, burnish.

**abrir** *vt* **1** *(gen)* to open. **2** *(cremallera)* to undo: *abrió la cremallera de la maleta* she undid the zip on the case, she unzipped the case. **3** *(luz)* to switch on, turn on; *(gas, grifo)* to turn on.
▶ *vpr* **abrirse 1** *(gen)* to open. **2** *(dar)* to open (a, onto), look (a, onto): *la casa se abre al mar* the house looks onto the sea. **3** *fig (sincerarse)* to open out. **4** *argot (largarse)* to clear off, be off. LOC **abrir fuego** MIL to open fire. **I abrir paso** to make way. **I en un abrir y cerrar de ojos** *fam* in the twinkling of an eye.

**abrochar** *vt* **1** *(camisa)* to button (up); *(zapato)* to tie up. **2** *(botones)* to do up; *(broche, corchete)* to fasten: *abróchense los cinturones* please fasten your seat belts.

**absceso** *nm* abscess.

**abscisa** *nf* abscissa.

**ábside** *nm* apse.

**absolución** *nf* **1** REL absolution. **2** JUR acquittal.

**absolutismo** *nm* absolutism.

**absoluto,-a** *adj* absolute. LOC **en absoluto** not at all, by no means. **I nada en absoluto** nothing at all.

**absolver** *vt* **1** REL to absolve. **2** JUR to acquit.

**absorbente** *adj* **1** absorbent. **2** *fig (trabajo)* absorbing; *(exigente)* demanding. **3** *fig (persona)* overbearing.
▶ *nm* absorbent.

**absorber** *vt* to absorb, soak up.

**absorción** *nf* absorption.

**absorto,-a** *adj* **1** *(pasmado)* amazed. **2** *(ensimismado)* absorbed (en, in).

**abstemio,-a** *adj* abstemious, teetotal.
▶ *nm & nf* teetotaller.

**abstención** *nf* abstention.

**abstenerse** *vpr* to abstain (de, from), refrain (de, from).

**abstinencia** *nf* abstinence. COMP **síndrome de abstinencia** withdrawal symptoms *pl*.

**abstracción** *nf* abstraction.

**abstracto,-a** *adj* abstract.

**absurdo,-a** *adj* absurd.

**abuchear** *vt* to boo, jeer at.

**abuela** *nf* grandmother; *(familiarmente)* grandma, granny.

**abuelo** *nm* grandfather; *(familiarmente)* granddad, grandpa.
▶ *nm pl* **abuelos** grandparents.

**abundancia** *nf* abundance, plenty.

**abundante** *adj* abundant, plentiful.

**abundar** *vi* to abound, be plentiful.

**aburrido,-a** *pp* → aburrir.
▶ *adj* **1** *(con ser)* boring, tedious. **2** *(con estar)* bored, weary; *(cansado)* tired of; *(harto)* fed up with.

**aburrimiento** *nm* boredom.

**aburrir** *vt* **1** to bore. **2** *(cansar)* to tire.
▶ *vpr* **aburrirse** to get bored (con/de/por, with).

**abusar** *vi* **1** *(propasarse)* to go too far, abuse (de, -): *abusar de algn* to take unfair advantage of sb. **2** *(usar mal)* to misuse (de, -): *abusar de la comida* to eat too much.

**abusivo,-a** *adj* excessive, exorbitant.

**abuso** *nm* **1** abuse, misuse. **2** *(injusticia)* injustice.

**a.C.** *abrev* (antes de Cristo) before Christ; *(abreviatura)* BC.

**acá** *adv* **1** *(lugar)* here, over here. **2** *(tiempo)* now, at this time. LOC **de acá para allá** to and fro, up and down.

**acabado,-a** *pp* → acabar.
▶ *adj* **1** *(terminado)* finished; *(perfecto)* perfect, complete: *acabado,-a de hacer* freshly made. **2** *fig (malparado)* worn-out, spent: *una persona acabada* a has-been; *un actor acabado* a burnt-out actor.
▶ *nm* **acabado** finish.

**acabar** *vt* **1** *(gen)* to finish; *(completar)* to complete. **2** *(consumir)* to use up.

▶ *vi* **1** *(gen)* to finish, end; *acaba en punta* it has a pointed end. **2** *acabar por + gerundio* to end up + *-ing*: *acabé por comprar el vestido* I ended up buying the dress.
▶ *vpr* **acabarse** to end, finish, come to an end; *(no quedar)* to run out. LOC **acabar bien** to have a happy ending. ∥ **acabar con 1** *(destruir)* to destroy, put an end to. **2** *(terminar)* to finish, finish off. ∥ **acabar de +** *inf* to have just + *pp*: *no lo toques, acabo de pintarlo ahora mismo* don't touch it, I've just painted it. ∥ **acabar mal 1** *(cosa)* to end badly. **2** *(persona)* to come to a bad end. ∥ **¡se acabó!** that's it!

**academia** *nf* **1** *(institución)* academy. **2** *(escuela)* school, academy.

**acalorado,-a** *adj* **1** hot; *(cara)* flushed. **2** *fig (persona)* excited, worked up; *(debate)* heated, angry.

**acampada** *nf* camping.

**acampar** *vt & vi* to camp.

**acantilado** *nm* cliff.

**acaparar** *vt* **1** *(productos)* to hoard; *(mercado)* to corner, buy up. **2** *(monopolizar)* to monopolize, keep for os.

**acariciar** *vt* **1** to caress, fondle. **2** *(pelo, animal)* to stroke. **3** *fig (esperanzas, etc)* to cherish; *(idea, plan)* to have in mind.

**ácaro** *nm* mite.

**acarrear** *vt* **1** *(transportar)* to carry, transport. **2** *fig (producir)* to cause, bring, give rise to.

**acaso** *adv* perhaps, maybe: *acaso esté enfermo* maybe he's ill. LOC **por si acaso** just in case.

**acatar** *vt* **1** *(leyes, etc)* to obey, observe, comply with. **2** *(respetar)* to respect.

**acatarrarse** *vpr* to catch a cold.

**acceder** *vi* **1** *(consentir)* to consent (a, to), agree (a, to). **2** *(tener entrada)* to enter. **3** *(alcanzar)* to accede (a, to).

**accesible** *adj* accessible; *(persona)* approachable.

**acceso** *nm* **1** *(entrada)* access, entry. **2** *(de tos)* fit; *(de fiebre)* attack, bout. **3** INFORM access: *acceso aleatorio* random access.

**accidental** *adj* accidental: *no fue más que un encuentro accidental* it was nothing but a chance meeting.

**accidente** *nm* **1** accident: *sufrir un accidente* to have an accident. **2** *(terreno)* unevenness, irregularity. LOC **por accidente** by chance. COMP **accidente de trabajo** industrial accident. ∥ **accidente de tráfico** road accident. ∥ **accidentes geográficos** geographical features.

**acción** *nf* **1** action; *(acto)* act, deed. **2** COM share. **3** TEAT plot. LOC **entrar en acción** MIL to go into action. ∥ **ponerse en acción** to start doing sth. COMP **película de acción** adventure film.

**accionar** *vt* *(máquina)* to drive, work, activate.

**accionista** *nm o nf* shareholder, stockholder.

**acechar** *vt* **1** *(vigilar)* to watch, spy on; *(esperar)* to lie in wait for. **2** *(caza)* to stalk.

**acecho** LOC **estar al acecho de 1** *(vigilar)* to be on the lookout for. **2** *(esperar)* to lie in wait for.

**aceite** *nm* oil. COMP **aceite de girasol** sunflower oil. ∥ **aceite de maíz** corn oil. ∥ **aceite de oliva** olive oil. ∥ **aceite de ricino** castor oil.

**aceitera** *nf* **1** oil bottle. **2** AUTO oil can.
▶ *nf pl* **aceiteras** oil and vinegar set *sing*, cruet *sing*.

**aceituna** *nf* olive.

**aceleración** *nf* acceleration. COMP **poder de aceleración** AUTO acceleration.

**acelerador,-ra** *adj* accelerating.
▶ *nm* **acelerador** AUTO accelerator.

**acelerar** *vt* **1** to accelerate; *(paso)* to quicken. **2** *fig* to speed up.

**acelga** *nf* chard.

**acento** *nm* **1** *(tilde)* accent (mark). **2** *(tónico)* stress. **3** *(pronunciación)* accent: *acento andaluz* Andalusian accent. **4** *(énfasis)* emphasis, stress. COMP **acento ortográfico** written accent, accent.

**acentuación** *nf* accentuation.

**acentuar** *vt* **1** *(tilde)* to accentuate; *(tónico)* to stress. **2** *(resaltar)* to emphasize, stress.

▶ *vpr* **acentuarse** to become more pronounced, become more marked.

**acepción** *nf* meaning, sense.

**aceptable** *adj* acceptable.

**aceptación** *nf* **1** acceptance. **2** *(aprobación)* approval; *(éxito)* success: *la película tuvo poca aceptación* the film wasn't popular, the film met with little success.

**aceptar** *vt* **1** to accept, receive. **2** *(aprobar)* to approve of.

**acequia** *nf* irrigation channel, ditch.

**acera** *nf* pavement, US sidewalk.

**acerca de** *adv* about, concerning, on.

**acercar** *vt* to bring near, bring nearer, draw up: *acércate* come closer; *¿me acercas el agua?* can you pass the water?
▶ *vpr* **acercarse 1** *(aproximarse)* to be near: *se acerca el verano* summer is near. **2** *(ir)* to go: *acércate a la esquina* go to the corner. **3** *(visitar)* to drop in, drop by.

**acero** *nm* steel. COMP **acero inoxidable** stainless steel.

**acertado,-a** *pp* → acertar.
▶ *adj* **1** *(opinión, etc)* right, correct; *(comentario)* fitting; *(idea, decisión)* clever; *(palabra)* exact. **2** *(conveniente)* suitable. LOC **estar acertado,-a** to be wise.

**acertante** *nm o nf* winner.

**acertar** *vt* **1** *(en un objetivo)* to hit. **2** *(dar con lo cierto)* to get right: *solo acertó cinco preguntas* she only got five questions right. **3** *(por azar)* to guess correctly; *(concurso, quinielas)* to win.
▶ *vi* to get right, be right.

**acertijo** *nm* riddle.

**acético,-a** *adj* acetic.

**acetileno** *nm* acetylene.

**achacar** *vt* to impute, attribute.

**achaque** *nm* ailment, complaint.

**achatado,-a** *adj* flattened.

**achicar** *vt* **1** *(hacerse más pequeño)* to diminish, reduce, make smaller. **2** *(agua)* to drain; *(en barco)* to bale out.
▶ *vpr* **achicarse 1** *(amenguarse)* to get smaller. **2** *(amilanarse)* to lose heart.

**achicharrar** *vt* to scorch; *(comida)* to burn.
▶ *vpr* **achicharrarse** to roast.

**achicoria** *nf* chicory.

**achuchar** *vt* **1** *(azuzar)* to nag at. **2** *(abrazar)* to hug, squeeze: *había una pareja achuchándose en el rincón* there was a couple having a cuddle in the corner. **3** *(empujar)* to shove.

**achuchón** *nm* **1** *fam (empujón)* push, shove. **2** *fam (indisposición)* ailment: *le dio un achuchón* he had a funny turn. **3** *fam (abrazo)* hug, squeeze.

**acicalarse** *vpr* to dress up, smarten up.

**acicate** *nm* spur.

**acidez** *nf* **1** *(sabor)* sourness, sharpness. **2** QUÍM acidity. COMP **acidez de estómago** heartburn.

**ácido,-a** *adj* **1** *(sabor)* sharp, tart. **2** QUÍM acidic. **3** *(tono)* harsh.
▶ *nm* **ácido** QUÍM acid. COMP **ácido sulfúrico** sulphuric acid. ‖ **ácido úrico** uric acid.

**acierto** *nm* **1** *(adivinación)* correct guess, right answer. **2** *(buena idea)* good choice/idea.

**aclamar** *vt* to acclaim.

**aclaración** *nf* explanation.

**aclarar** *vt* **1** *(cabello, color)* to lighten, make lighter. **2** *(líquido)* to thin (down). **3** *(enjuagar)* to rinse. **4** *(explicar)* to explain.
▶ *vi* *(mejorar el tiempo)* to clear (up).
▶ *vpr* **aclararse 1** *(entender)* to understand: *no me aclaro con esta lección* I can't understand this lesson. **2** *(decidirse)* to make up one's mind.

**aclimatación** *nf* acclimatization, US acclimation.

**aclimatarse** *vpr* to become acclimatized (a, to), become US acclimated (a, to).

**acné** *nf* acne.

**acobardarse** *vpr* to become frightened, lose one's nerve, shrink back (ante, from).

**acogedor,-ra** *adj* **1** *(persona)* welcoming, friendly. **2** *(lugar)* cosy, warm.

**acoger** *vt* *(recibir)* to receive; *(a invitado)* to welcome.

**acogida** *nf* **1** reception, welcome. **2** *(aceptación)* popularity. LOC **tener buena acogida** to be welcomed.

**acometer** *vt* **1** *(embestir)* to attack. **2** *(emprender)* to undertake.

**acometida** *nf* **1** *(ataque)* attack, assault. **2** *(derivación)* connection.

**acomodado,-a** *adj* *(rico)* well-to-do, well off.

**acomodador,-ra** *nm & nf (hombre)* usher; *(mujer)* usherette.

**acompañamiento** *nm* **1** accompaniment. **2** *(guarnición de plato)* accompaniment to a main dish, side dish. **3** MÚS accompaniment.

**acompañante** *nm o nf* **1** companion, escort. **2** MÚS accompanist.

**acompañar** *vt* **1** to accompany, go with: *te acompaño a la puerta* I'll see you to the door; *nos acompañó al cine* she came with us to the cinema. **2** *(adjuntar)* to enclose, attach. **3** MÚS to accompany. LOC **acompañar en el sentimiento** *fml* to express one's condolences to.

**acondicionado,-a** *pp →* acondicionar.
▶ *adj* equipped, fitted-out.

**acondicionador** *nm* conditioner. COMP **acondicionador de aire** air conditioner. ▌ **acondicionador del cabello** hair conditioner.

**acondicionar** *vt* **1** to fit up, set up. **2** *(mejorar)* to improve.

**aconsejable** *adj* advisable.

**aconsejar** *vt* to advise.

**acontecimiento** *nm* event, happening.

**acopio** LOC **hacer acopio de** to store up.

**acoplamiento** *nm* **1** fitting, adaptation. **2** *(de naves espaciales)* docking.

**acoplar** *vt* **1** *(juntar)* to fit (together), join, adjust. **2** TÉC to couple, connect.
▶ *vpr* **acoplarse 1** to fit, join. **2** *(naves espaciales)* to dock.

**acorazado,-a** *adj* armoured (US armored), armour-plated (US armor-plated).
▶ *nm* **acorazado** battleship.

**acordar** *vt* **1** to agree. **2** *(decidir)* to decide.
▶ *vpr* **acordarse** to remember (de, -): *no se acuerda de nada* she can't remember anything.

**acorde** *adj* in agreement, agreed.
▶ *nm* MÚS chord.

**acordeón** *nm* accordion.

**acorralar** *vt* to corner.

**acortar** *vt & vi* to shorten, make shorter.

**acosar** *vt* to pursue, chase.

**acoso** *nm* **1** pursuit, chase. **2** *fig* hounding. COMP **acoso sexual** sexual harassment.

**acostarse** *vpr* **1** *(estirarse)* to lie down. **2** *(irse a dormir)* to go to bed: *es hora de acostarse* it's bedtime. LOC **acostarse con** *fam* to sleep with, go to bed with.

**acostumbrado,-a** *pp →* acostumbrar.
▶ *adj* **1** *(persona)* accustomed (a, to), used (a, to). **2** *(hecho)* usual, customary: *es lo acostumbrado* it is the custom.

**acostumbrar** *vt* **1** *(habituar)* to accustom to. **2** *(soler)* to be in the habit of.
▶ *vpr* **acostumbrarse** *(habituarse)* to become accustomed (a, to), get used (a, to).

**acre** *nm (medida)* acre.

**acreditado,-a** *adj* **1** *(prestigioso)* reputable, well-known, prestigious. **2** *(representante, embajador)* accredited.

**acreedor,-ra** *adj* deserving: *ser/hacerse acreedor a* to be worthy of.
▶ *nm & nf* FIN creditor.

**acribillar** *vt* to riddle, pepper.

**acrílico,-a** *adj* acrylic.

**acrobacia** *nf* acrobatics.

**acróbata** *nm o nf* acrobat.

**acta** *nf* **1** *(relación)* minutes *pl*, record (of proceedings); *(publicación)* transactions *pl*. **2** *(certificado)* certificate, official document. LOC **levantar acta** to draw up the minutes. COMP **acta notarial** affidavit.

**actinia** *nf* sea anemone.

**actitud** *nf (disposición)* attitude; *(postura)* position.

**activar** *vt* **1** TÉC to activate. **2** INFORM to enable. **3** *fig (avivar)* to liven up, quicken.

**actividad** *nf* activity.

**activo,-a** *adj* active: *estar en activo* to be on active service.
▶ *nm* **activo** FIN asset, assets *pl*.

**acto** *nm* **1** act, action. **2** *(ceremonia)* ceremony. **3** TEAT act. LOC **en el acto** at once.

**actor** *nm* actor.

**actriz** *nf* actress.

**actuación** *nf* **1** *(en cine, teatro)* performance. **2** *(intervención)* intervention, action.

**actual** *adj* **1** present, current: *dadas las circunstancias actuales* under the present circumstances. **2** *(actualizado)* up-to-date: *tiene un diseño muy actual* it has a very up-to-date design.

**actualidad** *nf* **1** present (time). **2** *(hechos)* current affairs *pl*; *(estado)* the current state of things: *este programa te da toda la actualidad cinematográfica* this programme gives you all the latest cinema news. LOC **en la actualidad** at present.

**actualizar** *vt* **1** *(poner al día)* to bring up to date, update. **2** *(filosofía)* to actualize.

**actualmente** *adv* *(hoy en día)* nowadays, these days; *(ahora)* at present, at the moment.

**actuar** *vi* **1** *(gen)* to act (como/de, as). **2** *(en obra, película)* to perform, act.

**acuarela** *nf* watercolour (US watercolor).

**acuario** *nm* aquarium.

**Acuario** *nm inv* Aquarius.

**acuático,-a** *adj* aquatic, water.

**acudir** *vi* **1** *(ir)* to go; *(venir)* to come, arrive. **2** *(presentarse)* to come back.

**acueducto** *nm* aqueduct.

**acuerdo** *nm* agreement. LOC **¡de acuerdo!** all right!, O.K.! ▌ **de acuerdo con** in accordance with. ▌ **estar de acuerdo** to agree (con, with). ▌ **llegar a un acuerdo** to come to an agreement. ▌ **ponerse de acuerdo** to agree.

**acumulación** *nf* accumulation.

**acumular** *vt* to accumulate; *(datos)* to gather; *(dinero)* to amass.

**acunar** *vt* to rock.

**acuñar** *vt* **1** *(monedas)* to strike, coin, mint. **2** *(una frase)* to coin.

**acupuntura** *nf* acupuncture.

**acurrucarse** *vpr* to curl up, snuggle up.

**acusación** *nf* **1** accusation. **2** JUR charge.

**acusado,-a** *pp* → acusar.
▶ *nm & nf* accused, defendant.

**acusar** *vt* **1** *(echar la culpa)* to accuse (de, of). **2** JUR to charge (de, with). **3** *(manifestar)* to give away.

**acusativo** *nm* accusative.

**acuse** COMP **acuse de recibo** acknowledgement of receipt.

**acústica** *nf* acoustics.

**acutángulo** COMP **triángulo acutángulo** acute triangle.

**adaptación** *nf* adaptation.

**adaptar** *vt* **1** *(acomodar)* to adapt. **2** *(ajustar)* to adjust, fit.
▶ *vpr* **adaptarse** *(persona)* to adapt OS (a, to); *(cosa)* to fit, adjust.

**adecuado,-a** *pp* → adecuar.
▶ *adj* adequate, suitable.

**adecuar** *vt* to adapt, make suitable.

**a. de J.C.** *abrev* *(antes de Jesucristo)* before Christ; *(abreviatura)* BC.

**adelantado,-a** LOC **por adelantado** in advance.

**adelantamiento** *nm* overtaking. LOC **hacer un adelantamiento** to overtake.

**adelantar** *vt* **1** to move forward. **2** *(reloj)* to put forward. **3** *(pasar delante)* to pass. **4** AUTO to overtake. **5** *(dinero)* to pay in advance.
▶ *vi (reloj)* to be fast.
▶ *vpr* **adelantarse 1** *(ir delante)* to go ahead. **2** *(llegar temprano)* to be early. **3** *(anticiparse)* to get ahead (a, of). **4** *(reloj)* to gain, be fast.

**adelante** *adv* forward, further.
▶ *interj* **1** *(pase)* come in! **2** *(siga)* go ahead!, carry on! LOC **de aquí en adelante** from here on. ▌ **en adelante** henceforth. ▌ **más adelante 1** *(tiempo)* later on. **2** *(espacio)* further on.

**adelanto** *nm* **1** *(avance)* advance. **2** *(tiempo)* advance. **3** *(pago)* advance; *(técnicamente)* advance payment.

**adelgazar** *vt* *(afinar)* to make slim.
▶ *vi (perder peso)* to slim, lose weight.

**ademán** *nm* *(gesto)* gesture.
▶ *nm pl* **ademanes** manners.

**además** *adv* **1** *(también)* also, as well. **2** *(es más)* furthermore, what is more: *¡y además, el coche es mío!* and what's more, the car's mine! LOC **además de** as well as, in addition to: *además de amable es guapo* as well as being kind, he's handsome.

**adenoides** *nm* adenoids.

**adentro** *adv* inside.
▶ *nm pl* **adentros** inward mind *sing*: *para sus adentros* in his heart. LOC **mar adentro** out to sea.

**adepto,-a** *nm & nf* follower, supporter.

**aderezar** *vt* *(condimentar)* to season; *(ensalada)* to dress.

**adeudar** *vt* **1** *(deber)* to owe, have a debt of. **2** FIN to debit, charge.

**adherente** *adj* adherent, adhesive.

**adherir** *vt* *(pegar)* to stick on.
▶ *vi* *(pegarse)* to stick (a, to).
▶ *vpr* **adherirse 1** *(pegarse)* to stick (a, to). **2** *fig* *(unirse)* to adhere to, follow.

**adhesivo,-a** *adj* adhesive.
▶ *nm* **adhesivo** adhesive.

**adición** *nf* addition.

**adicción** *nf* addition. LOC **crear adicción** to be addictive.

**adicional** *adj* additional.

**adictivo,-a** *adj* addictive.

**adicto,-a** *adj* addicted (a, to).
▶ *nm & nf* **1** *(drogas)* addict. **2** *(partidario)* supporter, follower.

**adiestrar** *vt* to train, instruct.

**adinerado,-a** *adj* rich, wealthy.

**adiós** *interj* **1** *(gen)* goodbye!; *(familiarmente)* bye!, bye-bye! **2** *(al cruzarse con alguien)* hello!
▶ *nm* goodbye.

**adiposo,-a** *adj* adipose.

**aditivo,-a** *adj* additive.
▶ *nm* **aditivo** additive.

**adivinanza** *nf* riddle, puzzle.

**adivinar** *vt* **1** *(descubrir)* to guess: *le adivinó el pensamiento* she read his mind. **2** *(predecir)* to forecast, foretell. **3** *(enigma)* to solve.

**adivino,-a** *nm & nf* fortune-teller.

**adjetivo,-a** *adj* adjective, adjectival.
▶ *nm* **adjetivo** adjective.

**adjudicar** *vt* **1** *(premio)* to award. **2** *(venta)* to sell, knock down: *¡adjudicado!* sold! **3** *(obras)* to award a contract to.
▶ *vpr* **adjudicarse 1** *(apropiarse)* to appropriate, take over. **2** *(obtener)* to win.

**adjunto,-a** *adj* **1** *(en carta)* enclosed. **2** *(asistente)* assistant.

**administración** *nf* **1** *(gen)* administration. **2** *(de medicamento)* administering. COMP **administración de lotería** lottery office. ▌ **administración pública** public administration.

**administrador,-ra** *nm & nf* **1** administrator. **2** *(manager)* manager. COMP **administrador,-ra de fincas** estate agent. ▌ **administrador de web** webmaster.

**administrar** *vt* **1** *(bienes, justicia)* to administer. **2** *(dirigir)* to manage, run. **3** *(suministrar)* to give: *le administró una aspirina* she gave him an aspirin.
▶ *vpr* **administrarse** to manage one's own money, manage one's own affairs.

**administrativo,-a** *adj* administrative.
▶ *nm & nf* *(funcionario)* official, civil servant; *(de empresa, banco)* office worker.

**admirable** *adj* admirable.

**admiración** *nf* **1** admiration. **2** *(signo)* exclamation mark.

**admirador,-ra** *nm & nf* admirer.

**admirar** *vt* **1** *(estimar)* to admire. **2** *(sorprender)* to amaze, surprise, astonish.

**admisión** *nf* **1** admission. **2** *(aceptación)* acceptance. **3** TÉC inlet, intake. LOC «Reservado el derecho de admisión» "The management reserves the right to refuse admission". COMP **plazo de admisión** closing date.

**admitir** *vt* **1** *(dar entrada)* to admit, let in. **2** *(aceptar)* to accept, admit: *«No se admiten propinas»* "No tipping", "Tipping not allowed". **3** *(permitir)* to allow: *su obra admite varias interpretaciones* his work is open to various interpretations. **4** *(reconocer)* to admit. **5** *(tener capacidad)* to hold.

**ADN** *abrev* MED *(ácido desoxirribonucleico)* desoxyribonucleic acid; *(abreviatura)* DNA.

**adobar** *vt* **1** CULIN to marinate, marinade. **2** *(pieles)* to tan.

**adobe** *nm* adobe.

**adolescencia** *nf* adolescence.

**adolescente** *adj* adolescent.
▶ *nm o nf* adolescent.

**adonde** *adv* where.

**adónde** *adv* where.

**adopción** *nf* adoption.

**adoptar** *vt* to adopt.

**adoptivo,-a** *adj* adoptive.

**adoquín** *nm* cobble, paving stone.

**adorable** *adj* adorable.

**adoración** *nf* adoration, worship.

**adorar** *vt* **1** REL to worship. **2** *fig* to adore.

**adormecerse** *vpr* to doze off.

**adormilarse** *vpr* to doze, drowse.

**adornar** *vt* to adorn, decorate.

**adorno** *nm* decoration, adornment. LOC **de adorno** decorative.

**adosado,-a** *adj* semidetached: *casas adosadas* semidetached houses.

**adquirir** *vt* to acquire; *(comprar)* to buy.

**adquisición** *nf* acquisition; *(compra)* buy, purchase.

**adrede** *adv* deliberately, on purpose, purposely.

**adrenalina** *nf* adrenalin.

**aduana** *nf* **1** customs *pl*. **2** *(oficinas)* customs building. LOC **pasar (por) la aduana** to go through customs.

**aducir** *vt* to adduce, allege.

**adueñarse** *vpr* to take possession (de, of).

**adulación** *nf* adulation, flattery.

**adular** *vt* to adulate, flatter.

**adulterar** *vt* to adulterate.

**adulterio** *nm* adultery.

**adulto,-a** *adj* adult.
▶ *nm & nf* adult.

**adverbio** *nm* adverb.

**adversario,-a** *adj* opposing.
▶ *nm & nf* adversary, opponent.

**adversidad** *nf* adversity, misfortune.

**adverso,-a** *adj* adverse.

**advertencia** *nf* **1** warning. **2** *(consejo)* piece of advice.

**advertir** *vt* **1** *(darse cuenta)* to notice, realize. **2** *(llamar la atención)* to warn: *ya te lo advertí* I told you. **3** *(aconsejar)* to advise.

**adviento** *nm* Advent.

**adyacente** *adj* adjacent.

**aéreo,-a** *adj* **1** aerial. **2** AV air.

**aerobic** *nm* aerobics.

**aerobio,-a** *adj* aerobic.

**aerodeslizador** *nm* hovercraft.

**aerodinámico,-a** *adj* aerodynamic.

**aeródromo** *nm* aerodrome, US airfield.

**aeroespacial** *adj* aerospace.

**aerofagia** *nf* aerophagia.

**aerógrafo** *nm* airbrush.

**aerolínea** *nf* airline.

**aeronáutica** *nf* aeronautics.

**aeronaval** *adj* air-sea.

**aeronave** *nf* airship. COMP **aeronave espacial** spaceship.

**aeroplano** *nm* aeroplane, US airplane.

**aeropuerto** *nm* airport.

**aerosol** *nm* aerosol, spray.

**aerostático,-a** *adj* aerostatic.

**aerotaxi** *nm* air taxi.

**afable** *adj* affable, kind.

**afamado,-a** *adj* famous, well-known.

**afán** *nm* **1** *(celo)* zeal; *(interés)* keenness, eagerness. **2** *(esfuerzo)* effort.

**afanar** *vt* *fam (robar)* to nick, pinch.
▶ *vpr* **afanarse** to work with zeal. LOC **afanarse en** to work hard at. ‖ **afanarse por** to strive to, do one's best to.

**afección** *nf* *(enfermedad)* complaint, disease.

**afectado,-a** *pp* → **afectar**.
▶ *adj* affected.

**afectar** *vt* **1** *(impresionar)* to move. **2** *(dañar)* to damage. **3** *(concernir)* to concern.

**afectivo,-a** *adj* **1** *(sensible)* sensitive. **2** *(psicología)* affective.

**afecto** *nm* affection: *con todo mi afecto* with all my love. LOC **tomarle afecto a** ALGN to become fond of SB.

**afectuoso,-a** *adj* affectionate.

**afeitar** *vt* to shave.

**afeminado,-a** *adj* effeminate.

**aferrarse** *vpr* to clutch (a, to), cling (a, to).

**Afganistán** *nm* Afghanistan.

**afgano,-a** *adj* Afghan.
► *nm & nf (persona)* Afghan.
► *nm* **afgano** *(idioma)* Afghan.

**afianzar** *vt 1 (sujetar)* to strengthen, reinforce. **2** *fig* to support, back.
► *vpr* **afianzarse** *(estabilizarse)* to steady OS.

**afición** *nf 1 (inclinación)* liking, penchant: *tener afición por algo* to be fond of sth. **2 la afición** the fans *pl*, the supporters *pl*.

**aficionado,-a** *pp* → aficionarse.
► *adj 1* keen, fond: *ser aficionado a algo* to be fond of STH. **2** *(no profesional)* amateur.
► *nm & nf 1* fan, enthusiast. **2** *(no profesional)* amateur.

**aficionarse** *vpr* to become fond (a, of), take a liking (a, to).

**afijo** *nm* affix.

**afilar** *vt* to sharpen.

**afiliarse** *vpr* to join (a, to), become affiliated (a, to).

**afín** *adj 1 (semejante)* similar, kindred. **2** *(relacionado)* related. **3** *(próximo)* adjacent, next.

**afinar** *vt 1* MÚS to tune. **2** *(puntería)* to sharpen.

**afinidad** *nf 1* affinity. **2** QUÍM similarity.

**afirmación** *nf* statement, assertion.

**afirmar** *vt 1 (afianzar)* to strengthen, reinforce. **2** *(aseverar)* to state, say, declare.
► *vpr* **afirmarse** *(ratificarse)* to maintain (en, -).

**afirmativo,-a** *adj* affirmative. LOC **en caso afirmativo** if the answer is yes.

**aflicción** *nf* affliction, grief, suffering.

**afligir** *vt* to afflict, grieve, trouble.
► *vpr* **afligirse** to grieve, be distressed.

**aflojar** *vt 1 (soltar)* to loosen. **2** *fig (esfuerzo)* to relax. **3** *fam fig (dinero)* to pay up.

**aflorar** *vi 1 (mineral)* to crop out/up, outcrop. **2** *fig (aparecer)* to come up to the surface, appear.

**afluencia** *nf* inflow, influx: *afluencia de público* flow of people.

**afluente** *nm (río)* tributary.

**afonía** *nf* loss of voice.

**afónico,-a** *adj* hoarse, voiceless. LOC **estar afónico** to have lost one's voice.

**aforo** *nm (capacidad)* seating capacity.

**afortunado,-a** *adj 1* lucky, fortunate: *fue una pregunta poco afortunada* it was a rather inappropriate question. **2** *(dichoso)* happy.

**afrenta** *nf fml* affront, outrage.

**africano,-a** *adj* African.
► *nm & nf* African.

**afrontar** *vt* to face, confront.

**afterhours** *nm* after-hours club.

**afuera** *adv* outside: *la parte de afuera* the outside; *salir afuera* to come/go out.
► *nm pl* **afueras** outskirts.

**agacharse** *vpr 1 (encogerse)* to cower. **2** *(agazaparse)* to crouch (down), squat.

**agalla** *nf 1 (de pez)* gill. **2** *(de ave)* temple. **3** BOT gall, oak apple.
► *nf pl* **agallas** *fam* courage *sing*, guts, pluck *sing*: *tener agallas* to have guts.

**agarrado,-a** *pp* → agarrar.
► *adj fam* stingy, tight. LOC **bailar agarrado** to dance cheek to cheek.

**agarrar** *vt 1 (con la mano)* to clutch, seize, grasp: *agárrala fuerte* hold it tight. **2** *fam (pillar)* to catch.
► *vpr* **agarrarse** *(cogerse)* to hold on, cling (a, to).

**agarrotado,-a** *adj (músculo)* stiff.

**ágata** *nf* agate.

**agencia** *nf* agency; *(sucursal)* branch. COMP **agencia de turismo** tourist office. ▌**agencia de viajes** travel agency.

**agenda** *nf 1 (libro)* diary. **2** *(orden del día)* agenda.

**agente** *nm o nf* agent.
► *nm* agent. COMP **agente de cambio y bolsa** stockbroker. ▌**agente de policía 1** *(hombre)* policeman. **2** *(mujer)* policewoman.

**ágil** *adj* agile.

**agilidad** *nf* agility.

**agilizar** *vt* to speed up.

**agitar** *vt 1 (mover)* to agitate, shake; *(pañuelo)* to wave: *«Agítese antes de usarlo»* «Shake before use». **2** *(intranquilizar)* agitate, excite.

**aglomeración** *nf 1* agglomeration. **2** *(de gente)* crowd.

**aglomerado** *nm (madera)* chipboard.

**agnosticismo** *nm* agnosticism.

**agobiado,-a** *pp* → agobiar.
▸ *adj fig (abrumado)* overwhelmed: *agobiado de trabajo* up to one's eyes in work.

**agobiar** *vt (abrumar)* to overwhelm.
▸ *vpr* **agobiarse** *(angustiarse)* to worry too much, get worked up.

**agobio** *nm* burden, fatigue, suffocation.

**agonía** *nf* **1** dying breath, last gasp: *murió después de una larga agonía* she died after a long illness; *en su agonía* on her deathbed. **2** *(sufrimiento)* agony, grief, sorrow.

**agonizar** *vi* to be dying: *está agonizando* she could die any moment now.

**agosto** *nm* August. [LOC] **hacer su agosto** *fig* to make a packet/pile, feather one's nest.

✎ Para ejemplos de uso, consulta marzo.

**agotado,-a** *pp* → agotar.
▸ *adj* **1** *(cansado)* exhausted, worn out. **2** *(libros)* out of print; *(mercancías)* sold out.

**agotador,-ra** *adj* exhausting.

**agotamiento** *nm* exhaustion. [COMP] agotamiento físico physical strain.

**agotar** *vt* to exhaust, tire/wear out.
▸ *vpr* **agotarse** **1** *(cansarse)* to become exhausted, become tired out. **2** COM to be sold out.

**agraciado,-a** *adj* **1** *(bello)* attractive, beautiful. **2** *(ganador)* winning.
▸ *nm & nf* lucky winner. [LOC] **ser poco agraciado, -a** to be unattractive/plain.

**agradable** *adj* nice, pleasant.

**agradar** *vi* to please.

**agradecer** *vt* **1** to thank for, be grateful for. **2** *(uso impersonal)* to be welcome: *siempre se agradece una ayuda* help is always welcome.

**agradecido,-a** *pp* → agradecer.
▸ *adj* grateful, thankful: *le quedaría muy agradecido si...* I should be very much obliged if...

**agradecimiento** *nm* gratefulness, gratitude, thankfulness.

**agrado** *nm* pleasure: *no es de su agrado* it isn't to his liking.

**agrandar** *vt* to enlarge, make larger.

**agrario,-a** *adj* agrarian, land, agricultural.

**agravante** *adj* aggravating.
▸ *nm & nf* **1** added difficulty. **2** JUR aggravating circumstance.

**agravar** *vt* to aggravate, worsen.
▸ *vpr* **agravarse** to get worse, worsen.

**agravio** *nm* offence, insult.

**agredir** *vt* to attack.

**agregar** *vt* to add.

**agresión** *nf* aggression, attack.

**agresividad** *nf* aggressiveness.

**agresivo,-a** *adj* aggressive.

**agresor,-ra** *nm & nf* aggressor, attacker.

**agreste** *adj* **1** *(salvaje)* wild. **2** *(abrupto)* rugged; *(rocoso)* rocky. **3** *(sin cultivar)* uncultivated.

**agrícola** *adj* agricultural, farming.

**agricultor,-ra** *nm & nf* farmer.

**agricultura** *nf* agriculture, farming.

**agridulce** *adj* **1** bittersweet. **2** CULIN sweet and sour.

**agrietarse** *vpr* to crack; *(piel)* to get chapped.

**agrio,-a** *adj* sour.
▸ *nm pl* **agrios** citrus fruits.

**agronomía** *nf* agronomy.

**agrónomo,-a** *adj* farming.
▸ *nm & nf* agronomist.

**agropecuario,-a** *adj* agricultural, farming.

**agrupación** *nf* **1** grouping, group. **2** *(asociación)* association.

**agrupar** *vt* to group, put into groups.
▸ *vpr* **agruparse** **1** to group together, form a group. **2** *(asociarse)* to associate.

**agua** *nf* **1** water: *echarse al agua* to dive in. **2** *(lluvia)* rain. **3** ARQUIT slope of a roof: *tejado a dos aguas* pitched roof. [COMP] **agua dulce** fresh water. ❙ **agua corriente** running water. ❙ **agua de colonia** (eau de) cologne. ❙ **agua del grifo** tap water. ❙ **agua mineral con gas** sparkling mineral water. ❙ **agua oxigenada** hydrogen peroxide. ❙ **agua potable** drinking water. ❙ **aguas jurisdiccionales** territorial waters.

**aguacate** *nm (árbol)* avocado; *(fruto)* avocado (pear).

**aguacero** *nm* heavy shower, downpour.

**aguado,-a** *pp* → aguar.
▶ *adj* watered down, wishy-washy.

**aguafiestas** *nm o nf inv* killjoy, spoilsport, wet blanket.

**aguafuerte** *nm & nf* **1** ARTE etching. **2** QUÍM nitric acid.

**aguamarina** *nf* aquamarine.

**aguanieve** *nf* sleet.

**aguantar** *vt* **1** *(contener)* to hold (back). **2** *(sostener)* to hold, support. **3** *(soportar)* to tolerate: *no aguanto más* I can't stand any more, I can't take any more.
▶ *vpr* **aguantarse 1** *(contenerse)* to keep back; *(risa, lágrimas)* to hold back. **2** *(resignarse)* to resign OS.

**aguante** *nm* **1** *(paciencia)* patience, endurance. **2** *(fuerza)* strength. LOC **tener mucho aguante 1** *(paciente)* to be very patient. **2** *(resistente)* to be strong, have a lot of stamina.

**aguar** *vt* to water down, add water to. LOC **aguar la fiesta a ALGN** to spoil SB's fun.

**aguardar** *vt* to wait (for), await.
▶ *vi* to wait.

**aguardiente** *nm* eau de vie, spirit, liquor.

**aguarrás** *nm* turpentine.

**agudo,-a** *adj* **1** *(afilado)* sharp. **2** *(dolor)* acute. **3** *fig (ingenioso)* witty; *(mordaz)* sharp. **4** *(voz)* high-pitched. **5** *(sonido)* treble, high. **6** LING *(palabra)* oxytone; *(acento)* acute. **7** MAT *(ángulo)* acute.

**agüero** *nm* omen, presage. LOC **ser de mal agüero** to be ill-omened. **I ser pájaro de mal agüero** *fig* to be bird of ill omen.

**aguijón** *nm* **1** ZOOL sting. **2** BOT thorn, prickle. **3** *fig (estímulo)* sting, spur.

**águila** *nf* eagle.

**aguilucho** *nm* *(cría del águila)* eaglet.

**aguinaldo** *nm* Christmas bonus/box.

**aguja** *nf* **1** needle; *(de tricotar)* knitting needle. **2** *(de reloj)* hand; *(de tocadiscos)* stylus. **3** *(de arma)* firing pin. **4** *(de tren)* point, US switch.

**agujerear** *vt* to make holes in.

**agujero** *nm* **1** hole. **2** *fig (falta de dinero)* shortfall: *encontraron un agujero de varios millones de euros* they found that several million euros were missing. COMP **agujero negro** black hole.

**agujetas** *nf pl* stiffness *sing*: *tener agujetas* to be stiff.

**ah** *interj* **1** *(caer en la cuenta)* ah!, oh! **2** *(sorpresa, admiración)* oh!

**ahí** *adv* there, in that place. LOC **de ahí que** hence, therefore. **I por ahí 1** *(lugar)* round there. **2** *(aproximadamente)* more or less.

**ahijado,-a** *nm & nf* **1** godchild; *(chico)* godson; *(chica)* goddaughter. **2** *(adoptivo)* adopted child.

**ahínco** *nm* eagerness.

**ahogado,-a** *pp* → ahogar.
▶ *adj* **1** drowned. **2** *(asfixiado)* asphyxiated, suffocated.
▶ *nm & nf* drowned person.

**ahogar** *vt* **1** *(asfixiar)* to choke, suffocate. **2** *(en el agua)* to drown. **3** *(motor)* to flood.
▶ *vpr* **ahogarse 1** to be drowned, drown: *se cayó al río y se ahogó* he fell into the river and drowned. **2** *(sofocarse)* to choke, suffocate. **3** *(motor)* to flood. LOC **ahogarse en un vaso de agua** *fig* to make a mountain out of a molehill.

**ahora** *adv* **1** *(en este momento)* now: *ahora no tengo tiempo* I haven't got time now. **2** *(hace un momento)* just a moment ago: *lo acabo de ver ahora* I've just seen it. **3** *(dentro de un momento)* in a minute, shortly: *ahora te lo preparo* I'll get it ready for you in a minute. LOC **de ahora en adelante** from now on. **I hasta ahora** until now, so far. **I por ahora** for the time being.

**ahorcar** *vt* to hang.
▶ *vpr* **ahorcarse** to hang oneself.

**ahorrador,-ra** *adj* thrifty.
▶ *nm & nf* thrifty person.

**ahorrar** *vt* to save.
▶ *vpr* **ahorrarse** to save OS: *te ahorrarás problemas si lo haces como yo te digo* you'll save yourself problems if you do it the way I say.

**ahorro** *nm* saving: *me supone un ahorro de 60 euros al mes* it represents a saving of 60 euros a month.
  ▶ *nm pl* **ahorros** savings.
**ahumado,-a** *pp* → ahumar.
  ▶ *adj* smoked; *(bacon)* smoky.
**ahumar** *vt* to smoke.
**ahuyentar** *vt* **1** to drive away, scare away. **2** *fig* to dismiss.
**airbag®** *nm* airbag®.
**aire** *nm* **1** air. **2** *(viento)* wind; *(corriente)* draught. **3** *fig (aspecto)* air, appearance: *tiene un aire cansado* she looks tired. **4** *fig (parecido)* resemblance, likeness: *tienen un aire de familia* there's a family likeness to them. **5** *fig (estilo)* style, manner, way: *lo hizo a su aire* he did it his way. **6** MÚS air, melody. LOC **al aire libre** in the open air, outdoors. ▎**tomar el aire** to take the air, get some fresh air. COMP **aire acondicionado** air conditioning. ▎**aire puro** clean air.
**airear** *vt* **1** *(ventilar)* to air. **2** *fig (un asunto)* to publicize.
  ▶ *vpr* **airearse** to get some fresh air.
**airoso,-a** LOC **salir airoso,-a** to do well, be successful: *salió airoso de la entrevista* he did well in the interview.
**aislado,-a** *pp* → aislar.
  ▶ *adj* **1** *(suelto)* isolated. **2** TÉC insulated.
**aislante** *adj* insulating.
  ▶ *nm* insulator.
**aislar** *vt* **1** *(dejar separado)* to isolate. **2** TÉC to insulate.
**a. J.C.** *abrev* → a. de J.C.
**ajedrez** *nm* **1** *(juego)* chess. **2** *(tablero y piezas)* chess set.
**ajeno,-a** *adj* **1** *(de otro)* another's, belonging to other people. **2** *(extraño)* not involved.
**ajetreo** *nm* activity, bustle.
**ajo** *nm* garlic. LOC **estar en el ajo** *fam fig* to be involved, be in the thick of it. COMP **ajo tierno** young garlic.
**ajustado,-a** *pp* → ajustar.
  ▶ *adj* **1** *(precio)* very low, rock-bottom; *(presupuesto)* tight. **2** *(apretado)* tight-fitting, tight.

**ajustar** *vt* **1** *(adaptar)* to adjust, regulate. **2** *(apretar)* to tighten. **3** *(encajar)* to fit, fit tight.
**ajuste** *nm* **1** *(unión)* adjustment, fitting. **2** TÉC assembly. **3** COM settlement, fixing. COMP **ajuste de cuentas** *fig* settling of scores.
**al** *contr* → a. LOC **al + inf** on + ger: *me lo encontré al salir de casa* I met him when I was leaving, I met him on leaving.
**ala** *nf* **1** wing. **2** DEP winger.
  ▶ *nf pl* **alas** *(atrevimiento)* daring *sing*. COMP **ala delta 1** *(aparato)* hang glider. **2** *(deporte)* hang gliding.
**alabanza** *nf* praise.
**alabar** *vt* *(elogiar)* to praise.
**alabastro** *nm* alabaster.
**alacena** *nf* cupboard.
**alacrán** *nm* scorpion.
**alambique** *nm* still.
**alambre** *nm* wire.
**alameda** *nf* **1** poplar grove. **2** *(paseo)* avenue, promenade, boulevard.
**álamo** *nm* poplar.
**alano,-a** *adj* mastiff, wolfhound.
**alarde** *nm* display, bragging, boasting. LOC **hacer alarde de** to flaunt, show off, parade.
**alardear** *vi* to boast, brag, show off.
**alargador** *nm* extension lead.
**alargar** *vt* **1** to lengthen. **2** *(estirar)* to stretch. **3** *(prolongar)* to prolong. **4** *(dar)* to hand, pass.
**alarido** *nm* screech, yell, shriek.
**alarma** *nf* alarm. LOC **dar la alarma** to give the alarm, raise the alarm.
**alarmante** *adj* alarming.
**alarmar** *vt* to alarm.
  ▶ *vpr* **alarmarse** to be alarmed, alarm OS.
**alarmista** *nm o nf* alarmist.
**alazán,-ana** *adj* light chestnut, sorrel.
**alba** *nf* dawn, daybreak.
**albacea** *nm o nf* JUR *(hombre)* executor; *(mujer)* executrix.
**albahaca** *nf* basil.
**albanés,-esa** *adj* Albanian.
  ▶ *nm & nf (persona)* Albanian.
  ▶ *nm* **albanés** *(idioma)* Albanian.

**Albania** *nf* Albania.

**albañil** *nm* (de ladrillos) bricklayer; (en general) building worker.

**albarán** *nm* delivery note, despatch note.

**albaricoque** *nm* **1** (fruta) apricot. **2** (árbol) apricot tree.

**alberca** *nf* reservoir.

**albergar** *vt* **1** (alojar) to lodge, house, accommodate. **2** fig (sentimientos) to cherish, harbour (US harbor).

**albergue** *nm* **1** (hostal) hostel. **2** (refugio) shelter, refuge. COMP **albergue juvenil** youth hostel.

**albino,-a** *adj* albino.
▶ *nm & nf* albino.

**albóndiga** *nf* meatball.

**albornoz** *nm* bathrobe.

**alborotador,-ra** *nm & nf* troublemaker, agitator.

**alborotar** *vt* **1** (agitar) to agitate, excite. **2** (desordenar) to make untidy, turn upside down. **3** (sublevar) to incite to rebel.
▶ *vi* to make a racket.

**alboroto** *nm* **1** (gritería) din, racket, row. **2** (desorden) uproar, commotion, disturbance.

**albufera** *nf* lagoon.

**álbum** *nm* album.

**albúmina** *nf* albumin.

**alcachofa** *nf* **1** (planta) artichoke. **2** (pieza) rose, sprinkler.

**alcalde** *nm* mayor.

**alcaldesa** *nf* **1** (cargo) lady mayor, mayoress. **2** (mujer del alcalde) mayoress.

**alcaldía** *nf* **1** (cargo) mayorship. **2** (oficina) mayor's office, mayoralty.

**alcalino,-a** *adj* alkaline.

**alcaloide** *nm* alkaloid.

**alcance** *nm* **1** reach, grasp: está al alcance de todo el mundo it's within everyone's reach. **2** (de arma) range. **3** (trascendencia) scope, importance. **4** (inteligencia) intelligence: persona de pocos alcances person of low intelligence.

**alcanfor** *nm* camphor.

**alcantarilla** *nf* **1** (conducto) sewer. **2** (boca) drain.

**alcantarillado** *nm* sewer system.

**alcanzar** *vt* **1** (gen) to reach. **2** (persona) to catch up, catch up with. **3** (pasar) to pass, hand over: alcánzame el agua pass me some water. **4** (conseguir) to attain, achieve: alcanzamos los objetivos we achieved the goals.
▶ *vi* **1** (ser suficiente) to be sufficient (para, for), be enough (para, for): eso no alcanza para todos that's not enough for all of us. **2** (ser capaz) to manage, succeed: no alcanzo a verlo I can't see it.

**alcaparra** *nf* **1** (fruto) caper. **2** (planta) caper bush.

**alcayata** *nf* hook.

**alcázar** *nm* **1** (fortaleza) fortress, citadel. **2** (palacio) palace, castle.

**alce** *nm* elk, moose.

**alcoba** *nf* bedroom.

**alcohol** *nm* **1** (sustancia) alcohol. **2** (bebida) alcohol, spirits *pl*.

**alcoholemia** *nf* alcohol: tasa/nivel de alcoholemia blood alcohol level.

**alcohólico,-a** *adj* alcoholic.
▶ *nm & nf* alcoholic.

**alcoholímetro** *nm* breathalyzer®.

**alcoholismo** *nm* alcoholism.

**alcornoque** *nm* **1** BOT cork oak. **2** fig blockhead, idiot, dimwit.

**aldaba** *nf* **1** (llamador) door knocker. **2** (barra) bar. **3** (pestillo) bolt.

**aldea** *nf* hamlet, small village.

**aldeano,-a** *nm & nf* villager.

**aldehído** *nm* aldehyde.

**aleación** *nf* alloy.

**aleatorio,-a** *adj* random, chance.

**alegar** *vt* to allege, plead, claim.

**alegoría** *nf* allegory.

**alegórico,-a** *adj* allegorical, allegoric.

**alegrar** *vt* **1** (causar alegría) to make happy, make glad, cheer up. **2** fig (avivar) to brighten (up), enliven. **3** fam (achispar) to make tipsy.
▶ *vpr* **alegrarse 1** to be pleased, be glad. **2** fam (achisparse) to get tipsy.

**alegre** *adj* **1** (contento) happy, glad. **2** (color) bright. **3** (música) lively. **4** (espacio) cheerful, pleasant. **5** fam (achispado) tipsy.

**alegría** *nf* happiness, joy.

**alejar** *vt* to remove, move away.
▶ *vpr* **alejarse** to go/move away.

**alemán,-ana** *adj* German.
▶ *nm & nf (persona)* German.
▶ *nm* **alemán** *(idioma)* German.

**Alemania** *nf* Germany.

**alentar** *vt* **1** *(animar)* to encourage. **2** *(tener)* to harbour (US harbor), cherish.

**alérgeno** *nm* allergen.

**alergia** *nf* allergy.

**alérgico,-a** *adj* allergic (a, to).

**alero** *nm* **1** ARQUIT eaves *pl.* **2** DEP forward.

**alerta** *adv (vigilante)* on the alert.
▶ *nf (atención)* alert.
▶ *interj* look/watch out!

**alertar** *vt* to alert (de, to).

**aleta** *nf* **1** *(de pez)* fin; *(de mamífero, de nadador)* flipper. **2** *(de nariz)* wing, ala. **3** *(de avión)* aileron; *(de coche)* wing.

**aletear** *vi* **1** *(ave)* to flutter, flap its wings. **2** *(pez)* to move its fins.

**alfabetizar** *vt* **1** *(enseñar)* to teach to read and write. **2** *(ordenar)* to alphabetize, put in alphabetic order.

**alfabeto** *nm* **1** *(abecedario)* alphabet. **2** *(código)* code. COMP **alfabeto Morse** Morse code.

**alfalfa** *nf* alfalfa, lucerne.

**alfarería** *nf* **1** *(arte)* pottery. **2** *(taller)* potter's workshop.

**alféizar** *nm* sill, windowsill.

**alférez** *nm* second lieutenant.

**alfil** *nm* bishop.

**alfiler** *nm* **1** *(costura)* pin. **2** *(joya)* brooch, pin. **3** *(del pelo)* clip. **4** *(de corbata)* tiepin.

**alfombra** *nf* **1** carpet, rug. **2** *(de baño)* bath mat.

**alfombrilla** *nf* **1** rug, mat. **2** *(de ordenador)* mousemat, mousepad.

**alforja** *nf* saddlebag.

**alga** *nf* alga; *(marina)* seaweed.

**algarroba** *nf* **1** *(fruto)* carob bean. **2** *(planta)* vetch.

**algarrobo** *nm* carob tree.

**álgebra** *nf* algebra.

**algo** *pron (afirmación)* something; *(negación, interrogación)* anything: *vamos a tomar algo* let's have something to drink; *¿quieres algo?* do you want anything? LOC **algo es algo** something is better than nothing.
▶ *adv (un poco)* a bit, a little, somewhat: *te queda algo grande* it's a bit too big for you.

**algodón** *nm* cotton. COMP **algodón dulce/ de azúcar** candyfloss, (US cotton candy). ‖ **algodón hidrófilo** cotton wool.

**algoritmo** *nm* algorithm.

**alguacil** *nm* bailiff.

**alguien** *pron (afirmativo)* somebody, someone; *(interrogativo, negativo)* anybody, anyone: *preguntemos a alguien* let's ask someone; *¿hay alguien?* is anyone there?

**algún** *adj* → alguno,-a.

**alguno,-a** *adj (afirmativo)* some; *(interrogativo, negativo)* any: *alguna noche voy al cine* some nights I go to the cinema; *¿ha habido alguna llamada?* has anyone phoned?, have there been any phone calls?; *el ministro no facilitó dato alguno* the minister didn't provide any information.
▶ *pron (afirmativo)* someone, somebody; *(interrogativo, negativo)* anybody: *que venga alguno que sepa francés* get someone who speaks French. LOC **alguno que otro** some, a few.

**alhaja** *nf* **1** jewel, gem. **2** fig *(cosa, persona)* gem, treasure.

**aliado,-a** *pp* → aliar.
▶ *adj* allied.
▶ *nm & nf* ally.

**alianza** *nf* **1** *(pacto)* alliance. **2** *(anillo)* wedding ring.

**aliar** *vt* to ally.
▶ *vpr* **aliarse** to become allies, form an alliance (con, with).

**alias** *adv* alias.
▶ *nm inv* alias.

**alicates** *nm pl* pliers.

**aliciente** *nm* incentive, inducement.

**alienígena** *nm o nf* alien.

**aliento** *nm* **1** *(respiración)* breath, breathing. **2** fig *(ánimo)* spirit, courage. LOC **quedarse sin aliento 1** *(respi-*

*rando mal)* to be breathless, be out of breath. **2** *(sorprendido)* to gasp.

**alijo** *nm* consignment: *un alijo de armas* a consignment of smuggled arms, an arms cache.

**alimaña** *nf* pest.

**alimentación** *nf* **1** *(acción)* feeding. **2** *(alimento)* food; *(dieta)* diet. **3** TÉC feed. COMP **bomba de alimentación** feed pump.

**alimentar** *vt* **1** *(dar alimento)* to feed. **2** *(mantener)* to keep, support. **3** *(uso técnico)* to feed.
▶ *vpr* **alimentarse** to live (de/con, on).

**alimento** *nm* **1** *(comida)* food. **2** *(valor nutritivo)* nutritional value, nourishment.

**alineación** *nf* **1** *(colocación)* alignment, lining up. **2** *(equipo)* line-up.

**alinear** *vt* **1** *(poner en línea)* to align, line up. **2** DEP to pick, select.

**aliñar** *vt (gen)* to season, flavour (us flavor); *(ensalada)* to dress.

**aliño** *nm (gen)* seasoning; *(para ensalada)* dressing.

**alisar** *vt* to smooth.

**alistarse** *vpr* to enlist, join up, enrol (us enroll).

**aliviar** *vt* **1** fig *(enfermedad, dolor)* to relieve, ease, alleviate, soothe. **2** *(consolar)* to comfort, console.

**alivio** *nm* **1** *(mejoría)* relief: *¡qué alivio!* what a relief! **2** *(consuelo)* comfort, consolation.

**aljibe** *nm* cistern, tank.

**allá** *adv* **1** *(lugar)* there, over there: *más allá* further (on); *allá va tu madre* there goes your mother. **2** *(tiempo)* back: *allá por los años sesenta* back in the sixties.

**allanamiento** COMP **allanamiento de morada 1** unlawful entry. **2** *(robo)* housebreaking, breaking and entering.

**allanar** *vt* **1** *(aplanar)* to level, flatten. **2** *(dificultad, etc)* to smooth out, solve, resolve.

**allegado,-a** *adj* close, related.
▶ *nm & nf (familia)* relative; *(amigo)* close friend.

**allí** *adv* **1** *(lugar)* there, over there: *allí abajo/arriba* down/up there; *por allí* over

there, round there. **2** *(tiempo)* then, at that moment.

**alma** *nf* soul. LOC **no había ni una alma** there wasn't a soul, there was nobody there. **I no poder** ALGN **con su alma** to be absolutely exhausted.

**almacén** *nm* **1** *(local)* warehouse, storehouse. **2** *(habitación)* storeroom.
▶ *nm pl* **almacenes** department store *sing*. COMP **grandes almacenes** department store *sing*.

**almacenar** *vt* **1** to store, warehouse. **2** *(acumular)* to store up, keep.

**almeja** *nf* clam.

**almena** *nf* merlon.
▶ *nf pl* **almenas** battlements.

**almendra** *nf* almond.

**almendro** *nm* almond tree.

**almíbar** *nm* syrup.

**almidón** *nm* starch.

**almirante** *nm* admiral.

**almizcle** *nm* musk.

**almohada** *nf* pillow. LOC **consultar** ALGO **con la almohada** *fam* to sleep on STH.

**almohadilla** *nf* **1** *(gen)* small cushion. **2** COST *(para coser)* sewing cushion; *(para alfileres)* pincushion. **3** *(de teclado)* number sign, pound. **4** *(de animal)* pad. **5** ARQUIT *(de capitel)* volute cushion.

**almohadón** *nm* cushion, large pillow.

**almorrana** *nf fam* pile.

**almorzar** *vi (al mediodía)* to have lunch; *(de desayuno)* to have breakfast; *(a media mañana)* to have elevenses, have a mid-morning snack.
▶ *vt (al mediodía)* to have for lunch; *(de desayuno)* to have for breakfast; *(a media mañana)* to have for elevenses, have for a mid-morning snack.

**almuerzo** *nm* **1** *(a mediodía)* lunch. **2** *(a media mañana)* mid-morning snack, elevenses *pl*. **3** *(desayuno)* breakfast.

**alojamiento** *nm* lodging, accommodation.

**alojar** *vt* **1** *(hospedar)* to lodge, put up, accommodate; *(dar vivienda a)* to house. **2** *(meter)* to put, place.
▶ *vpr* **alojarse** *(persona)* to stay; *(bala, etc)* to be lodged.

**alondra** *nf* lark.

**alopecia** *nf* alopecia.

**alpaca¹** *nf (animal, tela)* alpaca.

**alpaca²** *nf (metal)* nickel silver, German silver, alpaca.

**alpargata** *nf* rope-soled sandal, espadrille.

**Alpes** *nm pl* los Alpes the Alps.

**alpinismo** *nm* mountaineering, mountain climbing.

**alpinista** *nm o nf* mountaineer, mountain climber.

**alpiste** *nm* birdseed, canary grass.

**alquilar** *vt* **1** *(dar en alquiler - período largo)* to rent, rent out, let; *(- período corto)* to hire out. **2** *(recibir en alquiler - período largo)* to rent; *(- período corto)* to hire. LOC «Se alquila» "To let".

**alquiler** *nm* **1** *(acción - de casa)* renting, letting; *(- de coche)* hire. **2** *(cuota - de casa)* rent; *(- de TV, etc)* rental. LOC «En alquiler» "To let", US "For rent".

**alquimia** *nf* alchemy.

**alquitrán** *nm* tar.

**alrededor** *adv* **1** *(lugar)* round, around: *mira alrededor* look around. **2** alrededor de *(tiempo)* around: *alrededor de las cuatro* around four o'clock. **3** *(aproximadamente)* about: *alrededor de veinte* about twenty.
▶ *nm pl* **alrededores** surrounding area *sing*: *en los alrededores de Sevilla* in the vicinity of Seville, just outside Seville.

**alta** *nf* **1** *(de un enfermo)* discharge: *dieron de/el alta al enfermo* the patient was discharged from hospital. **2** *(de un empleado)* registration *with Social Security*. **3** *(entrada, admisión)* admission; *(ingreso)* membership.

**altar** *nm* altar.

**altavoz** *nm* loudspeaker.

**alteración** *nf* **1** *(cambio)* alteration, change. **2** *(excitación)* agitation, uneasiness, restlessness. COMP **alteración del orden público** breach of the peace, disturbance of the peace.

**alterar** *vt* **1** *(cambiar)* to change, modify, alter. **2** *(enfadar)* to annoy, upset.
▶ *vpr* **alterarse 1** *(cambiar)* to change. **2** *(enfadarse)* to lose one's temper, get upset.

**altercado** *nm* argument, quarrel.

**alternar** *vt (gen)* to alternate.
▶ *vi* **1** *(turnar)* to alternate. **2** *(relacionarse)* to meet people, socialize (con, with), mix (con, with). **3** *(en salas de fiesta, bar)* to entertain.

**alternativa** *nf* alternative, option, choice.

**alternativo,-a** *adj* alternative.

**alterno,-a** *adj* alternate, alternating: *días alternos* alternate days.

**Alteza** *nf* Highness. LOC **Su Alteza Real 1** *(hombre)* His Royal Highness. **2** *(mujer)* Her Royal Highness.

**altibajos** *nm pl* ups and downs.

**altiplano** *nm* high plateau.

**altitud** *nf* height, altitude.

**alto¹** *nm (parada)* stop: *hicieron un alto para comer* they stopped for lunch.
▶ *interj* halt!; *(policía)* stop!

**alto,-a²** *adj* **1** *(persona, edificio, árbol)* tall. **2** *(montaña, pared, techo, precio)* high. **3** *(elevado)* top, upper: *viven en los pisos altos* they live on the upper floors. **4** *(voz, sonido)* loud: *lo dijo en voz alta* she said it aloud. LOC **a altas horas de la noche** late at night. COMP **alta cocina** haute cuisine.
❚ **alta sociedad** high society.
▶ *adv* **alto 1** high (up). **2** *(voz)* loud, loudly. LOC **pasar por alto** to pass over.
▶ *nm* **1** *(altura)* height: *solo hace dos metros de alto* it's only two metres high. **2** *(elevación)* hill, high ground. LOC **en lo alto de** on the top of. ❚ **por todo lo alto** *fig* in a grand way.

**altramuz** *nm* lupin.

**altruismo** *nm* altruism.

**altura** *nf* **1** *(gen)* height: *el edificio tiene una altura de 80 metros* the building is 80 metres high. **2** *(altitud)* altitude. **3** *(nivel)* level, par; *(punto)* point: *¿a qué altura de la calle vives?* how far up the street do you live? LOC **estar a la altura de** to measure up to, match up to, be on a par with. ❚ **a estas alturas** by now, at this stage.

**alubia** *nf* bean.

**alucinación** *nf* hallucination.

**alucinado,-a** *pp* → alucinar.
▶ *adj argot* amazed, stunned, gobsmacked.

**alucinante** *adj* **1** hallucinatory. **2** *argot (extraordinario)* brilliant, fantastic, amazing, incredible, mind-blowing.

**alucinar** *vt* **1** *(producir sensaciones)* to hallucinate. **2** *fig (cautivar)* to fascinate, amaze, astound, flip out, stun.
  ▶ *vi argot* to be amazed, be gobsmacked: ¡alucinas! you're out of your mind!, you're crazy!

**alud** *nm* avalanche.

**aludido,-a** *pp* → aludir.
  ▶ *adj* above-mentioned, in question. LOC darse por aludido,-a to take the hint.

**aludir** *vi* to allude (a, to), mention (a, -), refer (a, to).

**alumbrado,-a** *nm* lighting, lights *pl*; *(coche)* lights *pl*.

**alumbramiento** *nm* afterbirth.

**alumbrar** *vt* **1** *(iluminar)* to light, give light to, illuminate. **2** *fig (enseñar)* to enlighten.
  ▶ *vi* **1** *(iluminar)* to give light. **2** *(parir)* to give birth to.

**aluminio** *nm* aluminium, US aluminum.

**alumnado** *nm* *(de colegio)* pupils *pl*; *(de universidad)* student body.

**alumno,-a** *nm & nf (de colegio)* pupil; *(de universidad)* student. COMP alumno externo day pupil. ▌ alumno interno boarder. ▌ antiguo alumno **1** *(de colegio)* old boy, former pupil. **2** *(de universidad)* old student, former student.

**alunizar** *vi* to land on the moon.

**alusión** *nf* allusion, reference.

**aluvión** *nm* **1** alluvion: *tierra de aluvión* alluvium, alluvial soil. **2** *fig* flood: *un aluvión de insultos* a barrage of insults.

**alveolar** *adj* alveolar.

**alveolo** *nm* **1** ANAT alveolus. **2** *(de panal)* cell.

**alza** *nf (aumento)* rise, increase. LOC al alza / en alza rising.

**alzamiento** *nm* **1** *(aumento)* raising, lifting. **2** *(rebelión)* uprising, insurrection.

**alzar** *vt* **1** *(levantar)* to raise, lift. **2** *(construir)* to build, erect. **3** *(un plano)* to draw up, make out. LOC alzar el vuelo to take off.
  ▶ *vpr* **alzarse 1** *(levantarse)* to rise up, get up. **2** *(sublevarse)* to rise, rebel.

**a.m.** *abrev* (ante meridiem) ante meridiem; *(abreviatura)* a.m.

**ama** *nf (propietaria)* landlady. COMP ama de casa housewife.

**amabilidad** *nf* kindness, affability.

**amable** *adj* kind, nice: ¿seria usted tan amable de...? would you be so kind as to...?

**amaestrar** *vt (adiestrar)* to train; *(domar)* to tame.

**amainar** *vi (viento)* to die down, drop.

**amamantar** *vt* to breast-feed, suckle.

**amanecer** *vi* **1** to dawn, get light: *en verano amanece pronto* day breaks early in summer. **2** *(estar)* to be at dawn, be at daybreak: *amanecimos en Barcelona* we were in Barcelona at dawn.
  ▶ *nm* dawn, daybreak. LOC al amanecer at daybreak.

**amanerado,-a** *adj* affected, mannered.

**amante** *adj* loving, fond (de, of).
  ▶ *nm o nf* lover.

**amañar** *vt (falsear)* to fiddle, fix; *(cuentas)* to cook; *(elecciones)* to rig.

**amapola** *nf* poppy.

**amar** *vt* to love.
  ▶ *vpr* **amarse** to love each other, be in love (with each other).

**amarar** *vi (hidroavión)* to land at sea; *(nave espacial)* to splash down.

**amargado,-a** *pp* → amargar.
  ▶ *adj* embittered, resentful: *estar amargado,-a* to feel very bitter.
  ▶ *nm & nf* bitter person.

**amargar** *vi (tener sabor amargo)* to taste bitter.
  ▶ *vt* **1** *(hacer amargo)* to make bitter. **2** *fig (disgustos, etc)* to embitter, make bitter. **3** *fig (estropear)* to spoil, ruin: *la lluvia nos amargó el día* the rain put a damper on our day.
  ▶ *vpr* **amargarse** *fig* to become embittered, become bitter. LOC a nadie le amarga un dulce a gift is always welcome.

**amargo,-a** *adj* **1** *(sabor)* bitter. **2** *fig (carácter)* sour; *(experiencia)* bitter, sour, painful.

**amargura** *nf* **1** bitterness. **2** *(dolor)* sorrow, grief, sadness.

**amarillo,-a** *adj* yellow.
▶ *nm* **amarillo** yellow. COMP **prensa amarilla** sensationalist press.

**amarra** *nf* mooring rope.
▶ *nf pl* **amarras** *fam fig* connections. LOC **soltar las amarras 1** MAR to cast off, let go. **2** *fig* to break loose.

**amarrar** *vt* **1** *(atar)* to tie (up), fasten. **2** MAR to moor, tie up.

**amarre** *nm* mooring.

**amasar** *vt* **1** CULIN to knead. **2** *fig (reunir)* to amass.

**amasijo** *nm fam (mezcolanza)* hotchpotch, jumble.

**amateur** *adj* amateur.
▶ *nm o nf* amateur.

**amatista** *nf* amethyst.

**amazona** *nf* **1** *(mitología)* Amazon. **2** *(jinete)* horsewoman.

**Amazonas** *nm* **el Amazonas** the Amazon.

**amazónico,-a** *adj* Amazonian.

**ámbar** *nm* amber.

**ambición** *nf* ambition, aspiration.

**ambicioso,-a** *adj (plan, etc)* ambitious; *(persona)* ambitious, enterprising.

**ambidextro,-a** *adj* ambidextrous.
▶ *nm & nf* ambidextrous person.

**ambientación** *nf* **1** *(ambiente)* atmosphere. **2** *(localización)* setting.

**ambientador** *nm* air freshener.

**ambiental** *adj* **1** *(del ambiente)* environmental. **2** *(de fondo)* background.

**ambientar** *vt* **1** *(dar ambiente)* to give atmosphere to. **2** *(localizar)* to set.
▶ *vpr* **ambientarse** to adapt, get used (a, to).

**ambiente** *nm* **1** *(aire)* air, atmosphere. **2** *(entorno)* environment, atmosphere: *no hay mucho ambiente de noche* there is not much going on at night. LOC **cambiar de ambiente** to have a change of scene.

**ambigüedad** *nf* ambiguity.

**ambiguo,-a** *adj* ambiguous.

**ámbito** *nm* **1** *(espacio)* sphere, space. **2** *(marco)* field: *en el ámbito de la informática* in the computer science field.

**ambivalente** *adj* ambivalent.

**ambos,-as** *adj* both: *por ambos lados* on both sides.
▶ *pron* both: *me gustan ambos* I like both of them, I like them both.

**ambulancia** *nf* ambulance.

**ambulante** *adj* itinerant, travelling.

**ambulatorio,-a** *adj* ambulatory.
▶ *n* **ambulatorio** surgery, clinic.

**ameba** *nf* amoeba (US ameba).

**amedrentar** *vt* to frighten, scare.
▶ *vpr* **amedrentarse** *(asustarse)* to be frightened, be scared; *(acobardarse)* to become intimidated.

**amén** *nm* REL amen. LOC **decir amén a todo/todos** *fam* to agree with everything/everybody.

**amenaza** *nf* threat, menace.

**amenazar** *vt & vi* to threaten.

**amenizar** *vt* to liven up, make entertaining, make enjoyable.

**ameno,-a** *adj* lively, entertaining, enjoyable.

**América** *nf* America. COMP **América Central** Central America. ❙ **América del Norte** North America. ❙ **América del Sur** South America. ❙ **América Latina** Latin America.

**americana** *nf* jacket.

**americano,-a** *adj* American.
▶ *nm & nf* American.

**amerizar** *vi* → amarar.

**ametralladora** *nf* machine gun.

**ametrallar** *vt* **1** to machine-gun. **2** *fig (acosar)* to chase, pursue, besiege.

**amianto** *nm* asbestos.

**amígdala** *nf* tonsil.

**amigdalitis** *nf inv* tonsillitis.

**amigo,-a** *adj* **1** *(amigable)* friendly: *es muy amigo de Julio* he's very friendly with Julio. **2** *(aficionado)* fond (de, of): *no es muy amiga de discotecas* she's not keen on discos.
▶ *nm & nf* **1** friend: *una amiga mía* a friend of mine; *son amigos íntimos* they are close friends. **2** *(novio)* boyfriend; *(novia)* girlfriend. **3** *(amante)* lover.

**amigote** *nm fam* pal, mate, chum.

**amiguismo** *nm* contacts *pl*, string-pulling.

**aminoácido** *nm* amino acid.

**aminorar** *vt* to reduce, decrease. LOC aminorar el paso to slow down.

**amistad** *nf* friendship.
▸ *nf pl* **amistades** friends. LOC hacer amistades to make friends.

**amistoso,-a** *adj* friendly: *partido amistoso* friendly match.

**amnesia** *nf* amnesia.

**amniótico,-a** *adj* amniotic.

**amnistía** *nf* amnesty.

**amo** *nm* 1 *(señor)* master. 2 *(dueño)* owner. 3 *(jefe)* boss.

**amoldarse** *vpr* to adapt, adjust (a, to).

**amonestación** *nf* 1 *(reprensión)* reprimand, admonition, admonishment. 2 DEP caution, booking.

**amonestar** *vt* 1 *(reprender)* to reprimand, admonish. 2 DEP to caution, book.

**amoníaco** *nm* ammonia.

**amontonar** *vt* 1 to heap up, pile up. 2 *(juntar)* to collect, gather, accumulate.
▸ *vpr* **amontonarse** 1 to heap up, pile up. 2 *(gente)* to crowd together.

**amor** *nm* 1 *(gen)* love. 2 *(cuidado)* loving care; *(devoción)* devotion. LOC con/de mil amores *fam* willingly, with pleasure. ‖ hacer el amor to make love. COMP amor propio self-esteem.

**amoral** *adj* amoral.

**amoratado,-a** *adj* 1 *(de frío)* blue with cold. 2 *(de un golpe)* bruised, black and blue.

**amordazar** *vt (persona)* to gag; *(perro)* to muzzle.

**amorfo,-a** *adj* amorphous.

**amoroso,-a** *adj* loving, affectionate.

**amortiguador** *nm* 1 AUTO shock absorber. 2 TÉC damper.

**amortiguar** *vt (golpe)* to cushion; *(dolor)* to alleviate, ease, soothe; *(ruido)* to muffle; *(luz)* to subdue, dim.

**amotinarse** *vpr* 1 to rebel, rise up, riot. 2 MIL to mutiny.

**amparar** *vt* to protect, shelter.

▸ *vpr* **ampararse** 1 *(protegerse)* to take shelter, protect OS. 2 *(acogerse)* to avail OS of the protection (en, of), seek protection (en, in).

**amparo** *nm* protection, shelter.

**amperio** *nm* ampere.

**ampliación** *nf* 1 enlargement, extension. 2 ARQUIT extension. 3 *(fotografía)* enlargement.

**ampliar** *vt* 1 to enlarge, extend. 2 ARQUIT to build an extension onto. 3 *(fotografía)* to enlarge. 4 *(capital)* to increase. 5 *(estudios)* to further. 6 *(tema, idea)* to develop, expand on.

**amplificación** *nf* amplification.

**amplio,-a** *adj* 1 *(extenso)* large. 2 *(espacioso)* roomy, spacious. 3 *(ancho)* wide, broad. 4 *(holgado)* loose.

**amplitud** *nf* 1 *(extensión)* extent, range. 2 *(espacio)* room, space, spaciousness. 3 *(anchura)* width. 4 *(holgadura)* looseness. 5 FÍS amplitude.

**ampolla** *nf* 1 MED blister. 2 *(burbuja)* bubble. 3 *(tubito)* ampoule, phial.

**amputar** *vt* to amputate.

**amueblar** *vt* to furnish. LOC sin amueblar unfurnished.

**amuleto** *nm* amulet, charm.

**amurallar** *vt* to wall.

**anabolizante** *adj* anabolic.

**anaconda** *nf* anaconda.

**anacoreta** *nm o nf* anchorite.

**anacronismo** *nm* anachronism.

**anaerobio,-a** *adj* anaerobic.

**anagrama** *nm* anagram.

**anal** *adj* anal.

**analfabetismo** *nm* illiteracy.

**analfabeto,-a** *adj* 1 illiterate. 2 *fig* stupid.
▸ *nm & nf* 1 illiterate person. 2 *fig* stupid person, ignoramus.

**analgésico,-a** *adj* analgesic.
▸ *nm* **analgésico** analgesic, painkiller.

**análisis** *nm inv* analysis. COMP análisis de orina urine test. ‖ análisis de sangre blood test.

**analizar** *vt* to analyse (US analyze).

**analogía** *nf* analogy.

**analógico,-a** *adj* analogical.

**análogo,-a** *adj* analogous, similar.

**anaquel** *nm* shelf.

**anarquía** *nf* anarchy.

**anárquico,-a** *adj* anarchic, anarchical.

**anarquista** *adj* anarchist.
  ▶ *nm o nf* anarchist.

**anatomía** *nf* anatomy.

**anca** *nf* haunch. COMP **ancas de rana** frogs' legs.

**ancestral** *adj* ancestral, ancient.

**ancho,-a** *adj* **1** *(gen)* broad, wide. **2** *(prenda - holgada)* loose-fitting; *(- grande)* too big.
  ▶ *nm* ancho **1** *(anchura)* breadth, width: *¿qué ancho tiene?* how wide is it?; *tiene cuatro metros de ancho* it's four metres wide. **2** *(en costura)* width. LOC **a sus anchas** comfortable, at ease. ∎ **estar más ancho,-a que largo,-a** to be full of os. ∎ **quedarse tan ancho,-a** *fam* to behave as if nothing had happened, not bat an eyelid.

**anchoa** *nf* anchovy.

**anchura** *nf* breadth, width.

**anciano,-a** *adj* very old, elderly, aged.
  ▶ *nm & nf* old person, elderly person.

**ancla** *nf* anchor.

**anclar** *vi* MAR to anchor.
  ▶ *vt* TÉC to anchor.

**andadas** LOC **volver a las andadas** to go back to one's old tricks.

**Andalucía** *nf* Andalusia.

**andaluz,-za** *adj* Andalusian.
  ▶ *nm & nf (persona)* Andalusian.
  ▶ *nm* andaluz *(dialecto)* Andalusian.

**andamio** *nm* scaffold.

**andanada** *nf* MAR broadside.

**andante** COMP **caballero andante** knight errant.

**andanzas** *nf pl* adventures.

**andar** *vi* **1** *(moverse)* to walk. **2** *(funcionar)* to work, run, go: *este reloj no anda* this watch doesn't work. **3** *(estar)* to be: *¿cómo andas?* how are you?, how's it going? **4** *(juntarse)* to mix (con, with). LOC **andar a gatas** to crawl. ∎ **andar de puntillas** to tiptoe. ∎ **andar con rodeos** to beat about the bush. ∎ **andar con cui-**dado / **andarse con cuidado** to be careful. ∎ **andarse por las ramas** *fig* to beat about the bush.
  ▶ *interj* **¡anda!** well!, oh!: *¡anda ya!* come off it!.

**andén** *nm* platform.

**Andes** *nm pl* **los Andes** the Andes.

**andino,-a** *adj* Andean.
  ▶ *nm & nf* Andean.

**Andorra** *nm* Andorra.

**andorrano,-a** *adj* Andorran.
  ▶ *nm & nf* Andorran.

**androide** *nm* android.

**anécdota** *nf* anecdote.

**anélido** *nm* annelid.

**anemia** *nf* anaemia (US anemia).

**anemona** *nf* anemone. COMP **anemona de mar** sea anemone.

**anestesia** *nf* anaesthesia (US anesthesia).

**anestésico,-a** *adj* anaesthetic (US anesthetic).
  ▶ *nm* **anestésico** anaesthetic (US anesthetic).

**anexión** *nf* annexation.

**anexo,-a** *adj* adjoining, attached (a, to).
  ▶ *nm* **anexo** annexe (US annex).

**anfetamina** *nf* amphetamine.

**anfibio,-a** *adj* amphibious.
  ▶ *nm* **anfibio** amphibian.
  ▶ *nm pl* **los anfibios** amphibia *pl.*

**anfiteatro** *nm* **1** amphitheatre (US amphitheater). **2** *(en universidad)* lecture theatre (US theater). **3** *(en teatro, cine)* circle.

**anfitrión,-ona** *nm & nf (hombre)* host; *(mujer)* hostess.

**ángel** *nm* angel.

**angina** *nf* angina. LOC **tener anginas** to have a sore throat. COMP **angina de pecho** angina pectoris.

**anglosajón,-ona** *adj* Anglo-Saxon.
  ▶ *nm & nf (persona)* Anglo-Saxon.
  ▶ *nm* **anglosajón** *(idioma)* Anglo-Saxon.

**Angola** *nf* Angola.

**angosto,-a** *adj* narrow.

**ángstrom** *nm* angstrom.

**anguila** *nf* eel.

**angula** *nf* elver.

**ángulo** *nm* 1 angle. 2 *(rincón)* corner. COMP **ángulo recto** right angle.

**angustia** *nf* anguish, distress.

**angustiar** *vt* 1 *(afligir)* to distress, upset. 2 *(preocupar)* to worry, make anxious.

**angustioso,-a** *adj (situación)* distressing, worrying; *(mirada)* anguished.

**anhelar** *vt* to long for, yearn for.

**anhelo** *nm* longing, yearning.

**anhídrido** *nm* anhydride.

**anilla** *nf (aro)* ring.
  ▶ *nf pl* **anillas** DEP rings.

**anillo** *nm* 1 ring. 2 ARQUIT annulet. 3 *(de gusano)* annulus; *(de culebra)* coil. LOC **venir como anillo al dedo** to be just what SB needed, suit SB fine.

**animación** *nf* 1 *(actividad)* activity, movement, bustle. 2 *(viveza)* liveliness. 3 CINE animation.

**animado,-a** *pp* → animar.
  ▶ *adj* 1 *(movido)* animated, lively, jolly. 2 *(concurrido)* bustling, full of people. 3 *(alegre)* cheerful, in high spirits, excited.

**animador,-ra** *nm & nf* 1 *(artista)* entertainer. 2 *(de un equipo)* cheerleader.

**animadversión** *nf* antagonism, hostility, ill will, animosity.

**animal** *adj* animal.
  ▶ *nm* 1 animal. 2 *fig (basto)* rough person, brute, lout; *(necio)* dunce. COMP **animal doméstico** pet. ‖ **reino animal** animal kingdom.

**animar** *vt* 1 *(alegrar a algn)* to cheer up. 2 *(alegrar algo)* to brighten up, liven up. 3 *(alentar)* to encourage.
  ▶ *vpr* **animarse** 1 *(persona)* to cheer up. 2 *(fiesta, etc)* to brighten up, liven up. 3 *(decidirse)* to make up one's mind.

**ánimo** *nm* 1 *(espíritu)* spirit; *(mente)* mind; *(alma)* soul. 2 *(intención)* intention, purpose: *sin ánimo de ofender* no offence intended. 3 *(valor)* courage: *no tengo ánimos de nada* I don't feel up to anything. 4 *(aliento)* encouragement.
  ▶ *interj* cheer up!

**anión** *nm* anion.

**aniquilar** *vt* to annihilate, destroy.

**anís** *nm* 1 *(planta)* anise; *(grano)* aniseed. 2 *(bebida)* anisette.

**aniversario** *nm* anniversary.

**ano** *nm* anus.

**anoche** *adv (late)* last night; *(early)* yesterday evening.

**anochecer** *vi* 1 to get dark: *cuando anocheció* when it got dark. 2 to be at nightfall, reach at nightfall.
  ▶ *nm* nightfall, dusk, evening. LOC **al anochecer** at nightfall, at dusk.

**ánodo** *nm* anode.

**anofeles** *nm inv* anopheles.

**anomalía** *nf* anomaly.

**anómalo,-a** *adj* anomalous.

**anonimato** *nm* anonymity.

**anónimo,-a** *adj* 1 *(desconocido)* anonymous. 2 *(sociedad)* limited, US incorporated.
  ▶ *nm* **anónimo** *(carta)* anonymous letter.

**anorak** *nm* anorak.

**anorexia** *nf* anorexia.

**anormal** *adj* 1 *(no normal)* abnormal. 2 *(inhabitual)* unusual. 3 MED subnormal.

**anotación** *nf* 1 *(acotación)* annotation. 2 *(nota)* note. 3 *(apunte)* noting.

**anotar** *vt* 1 *(acotar)* to annotate, add notes to. 2 *(apuntar)* to take down, jot down, make a note of.

**ansia** *nf* 1 *(ansiedad)* anxiety; *(angustia)* anguish. 2 *(deseo)* eagerness, longing, yearning: *tener ansia de poder* to be longing for power.

**ansiar** *vt* to long for, yearn for.

**ansiedad** *nf* 1 anxiety. 2 MED nervous tension.

**ansioso,-a** *adj* 1 *(desasosegado)* anguished, anxious, desperate. 2 *(deseoso)* eager, longing (**por/de**, to).

**antagónico,-a** *adj* antagonistic.

**antaño** *adv* formerly, in olden times, long ago.

**antártico,-a** *adj* Antarctic.

**Antártida** *nf* Antarctica.

**ante¹** *prep* 1 before, in the presence of. 2 *(considerando)* in the face of: *ante estas circunstancias* under the circumstances. LOC **ante todo** 1 *(primero)* first of all. 2 *(por encima de)* above all.

**ante²** *nm* **1** ZOOL elk, moose. **2** *(piel)* suede.

**anteayer** *adv* the day before yesterday.

**antebrazo** *nm* forearm.

**antecedente** *nm* **1** precedent. **2** GRAM antecedent. **3** MED history.
▶ *nm pl* **antecedentes** record *sing*.

**antecesor,-ra** *nm & nf* **1** *(en un cargo)* predecessor. **2** *(antepasado)* ancestor.

**antelación** *nf* precedence: *con cinco días de antelación* five days beforehand. LOC **con antelación** in advance.

**antemano** LOC **de antemano** beforehand, in advance.

**antena** *nf* **1** RAD TV aerial, antenna. **2** ANAT antenna, feeler. LOC **estar en antena** to be on the air. COMP **antena parabólica** satellite dish.

**anteojos** *nm pl* **1** *(binóculos)* binoculars, field glasses. **2** *(gafas)* glasses, spectacles.

**antepasado** *nm* ancestor.
▶ *nm pl* **antepasados** forefathers, forbears.

**antepenúltimo,-a** *adj* antepenultimate.

**anteponer** *vt* **1** *(poner delante)* to place in front (a, of), put in front (a, of); *(poner antes)* to put before. **2** *(preferir)* to prefer (a, to).

**antera** *nf* anther.

**anterior** *adj* **1** *(tiempo)* previous, preceding, before: *el día anterior* the day before. **2** *(lugar)* front: *la parte anterior* the front part.
▶ *nm o nf* the previous one.

**anterioridad** *nf* priority. LOC **con anterioridad** previously. ‖ **con anterioridad a** prior to, before.

**antes** *adv* **1** *(tiempo)* before, earlier: *llámame antes de salir* ring me before you leave; *deberías estar allí antes de las nueve* you should be there before nine. **2** *(en el pasado)* before, in the past. **3** *(lugar)* in front, before. LOC **antes de nada** first of all. ‖ **lo antes posible** as soon as possible.
▶ *adj* before.

**antesala** *nf* anteroom, antechamber.

**antiadherente** *adj* nonstick.

**antiaéreo,-a** *adj* anti-aircraft.

**antibalas** *adj* bullet-proof.

**antibiótico,-a** *adj* antibiotic.
▶ *nm* **antibiótico** antibiotic.

**anticaspa** *adj* anti-dandruff: *champú anticaspa* dandruff shampoo.

**anticiclón** *nm* anticyclone, high pressure area.

**anticipación** *nf* anticipation, advance. LOC **con anticipación** in advance.

**anticipado,-a** *pp* → anticipar.
▶ *adj* brought forward; *(temprano)* early: *gracias anticipadas* thanks in advance; *pago anticipado* payment in advance. LOC **por anticipado** in advance.

**anticipar** *vt* **1** to anticipate, advance, bring forward. **2** *(dinero)* to advance.
▶ *vpr* **anticiparse 1** *(llegar antes)* to come early. **2** *(adelantarse)* to beat it to it: *él se me anticipó* he beat me to it.

**anticipo** *nm* **1** *(gen)* foretaste, preview. **2** *(pago)* advance, advance payment.

**anticlinal** *nm* anticline.

**anticonceptivo,-a** *adj* contraceptive.
▶ *nm* **anticonceptivo** contraceptive.

**anticongelante** *adj* antifreeze.
▶ *nm* **anticongelante** antifreeze.

**anticorrosivo,-a** *adj* anticorrosive.
▶ *nm* **anticorrosivo** anticorrosive.

**anticuado,-a** *adj* antiquated, old-fashioned, obsolete, out-of-date.

**anticuario** *nm* *(conocedor)* antiquary, antiquarian; *(comerciante)* antique dealer.

**anticuerpo** *nm* antibody.

**antidepresivo,-a** *adj* antidepressant.
▶ *nm* **antidepresivo** antidepressant.

**antidisturbios** *adj* riot. COMP **material antidisturbios** riot gear. ‖ **policía antidisturbios** riot police.

**antidoping** *adj* anti-doping, anti-drug.

**antídoto** *nm* antidote.

**antifaz** *nm* mask.

**antígeno** *nm* antigen.

**antigüedad** *nf* **1** *(período)* antiquity. **2** *(en empleo)* seniority. **3** *(objeto)* antique. LOC **en la antigüedad** in olden days, in former times. COMP **tienda de antigüedades** antique shop.

**antiguo,-a** *adj* **1** *(gen)* ancient, old; *(coche)* vintage, old. **2** *(en empleo)* senior. **3** *(pasado)* old-fashioned. **4** *(anterior)* former: *el antiguo primer ministro* the former Prime Minister.

**antihéroe** *nm* antihero.

**antihistamínico** *nm* antihistamine.

**antiinflamatorio** *nm* anti-inflammatory.

**antílope** *nm* antelope.

**antimonio** *nm* antimony.

**antiniebla** *adj inv* anti-fog. COMP **faros antiniebla** foglamps. ‖ **luces antiniebla** foglamps.

**antipatía** *nf* antipathy, dislike.

**antipático,-a** *adj* unfriendly, unpleasant, unkind.
▸ *nm & nf* unpleasant person.

**antípoda** *nm & nf (punto)* antipode, antipodes *pl*.

**antirrobo** *adj inv* anti-theft.

**antisemitismo** *nm* anti-Semitism.

**antiséptico,-a** *adj* antiseptic.
▸ *nm* **antiséptico** antiseptic.

**antiterrorista** *adj* antiterrorist.

**antítesis** *nf inv* antithesis.

**antitetánico,-a** *adj* anti-tetanus.

**antitranspirante** *adj* antiperspirant.
▸ *nm* antiperspirant.

**antivirus** *nm* **1** *(fármaco)* antivirus drug. **2** INFORM antivirus.

**antojo** *nm* **1** *(capricho)* whim, fancy; *(de embarazada)* craving. **2** *(en la piel)* birthmark.

**antología** *nf* anthology.

**antónimo** *nm* antonym.

**antonomasia** *nf* antonomasia. LOC **por antonomasia** par excellence.

**antorcha** *nf* torch.

**antracita** *nf* anthracite.

**ántrax** *nm inv* anthrax.

**antro** *nm* **1** *(caverna)* cavern. **2** *(tugurio)* dump, hole, dive.

**antropoide** *nm o nf* anthropoid.

**antropología** *nf* anthropology.

**anual** *adj* annual, yearly.

**anuario** *nm* yearbook.

**anudar** *vt (atar)* to knot, tie, fasten.

**anulación** *nf* **1** *(gen)* annulment, cancellation; *(de ley)* repeal; *(de sentencia)* quashing, overturning. **2** DEP *(de gol)* disallowing. COMP **anulación de matrimonio** annulment of marriage.

**anular¹** *adj* ring-shaped.
▸ *nm* ring finger.

**anular²** *vt* **1** *(matrimonio)* to annul; *(una ley)* to repeal; *(una sentencia)* to quash. **2** *(un pedido, viaje)* to cancel; *(un contrato)* to invalidate, cancel. **3** DEP *(un gol)* to disallow.

**anunciar** *vt* **1** *(avisar)* to announce, make public. **2** *(hacer publicidad)* to advertise.
▸ *vpr* **anunciarse** to put an advert (en, in).

**anuncio** *nm* **1** *(aviso)* announcement; *(signo)* sign. **2** *(publicidad)* advertisement, advert, ad. **3** *(valla publicitaria)* hoarding, US billboard. COMP **anuncios por palabras** classified adverts, small ads.

**anverso** *nm* **1** *(de moneda)* obverse. **2** *(de página)* recto.

**anzuelo** *nm* **1** fish-hook. **2** *fig* lure, bait. LOC **tragar/morder/picar el anzuelo** to swallow the bait.

**añadidura** *nf* addition, addendum. LOC **por añadidura** besides, in addition.

**añadir** *vt* to add (a, to).

**añejo,-a** *adj* **1** *(vino, queso)* mature; *(jamón)* cured. **2** *(viejo)* old.

**añicos** *nm pl* bits, pieces. LOC **hacer añicos** to smash to pieces. ‖ **hacerse añicos** to shatter, smash to bits.

**año** *nm* year: *el año pasado* last year; *el año que viene* next year; *los años sesenta* the sixties. COMP **año escolar** school year. ‖ **año luz** light year.
▸ *nm pl* years, age *sing*: *¿cuántos años tienes?* how old are you?; *tengo 20 años* I'm 20 years old. LOC **hace años** a long time ago, years ago.

**añorar** *vt* **1** *(gen)* to long for, miss, yearn for. **2** *(país)* to be homesick for, miss.

**aorta** *nf* aorta.

**aovar** *vi* to lay eggs.

**apacible** *adj* *(persona)* gentle, calm, placid; *(vida)* quiet, peaceful; *(clima, tiempo)* mild; *(mar)* calm.

**apaciguar** *vt* to pacify, appease, placate, calm down.

**apadrinar** *vt* **1** *(en bautizo)* to act as godfather to. **2** *(en boda)* to be the best man for. **3** *(artista)* to sponsor.

**apagar** *vt* **1** *(fuego)* to extinguish, put out. **2** *(luz)* to turn out, turn off, put out. **3** *(televisión, etc)* to switch off, turn off. **4** *fig (sed)* to quench.

**apagón** *nm* power cut, blackout.

**apaisado,-a** *adj* **1** oblong. **2** INFORM landscape.

**apalancarse** *vpr argot* to settle OS, settle down.

**apalear** *vt (pegar)* to beat, cane, thrash.

**apañarse** LOC apañárselas to manage, get by.

**apaño** *nm* **1** *(remiendo, compostura)* repair, mend, patch. **2** *(acuerdo)* agreement, deal.

**aparador** *nm* **1** *(escaparate)* shop window. **2** *(mueble)* sideboard, cupboard, buffet.

**aparato** *nm* **1** *(mecanismo)* (piece of) apparatus, set; *(eléctrico)* appliance. **2** *(dispositivo)* device; *(instrumento)* instrument. **3** *(teléfono)* telephone: *está al aparato* he's on the phone. COMP **aparato de radio** radio set. ‖ **aparato digestivo** ANAT digestive system.

**aparcamiento** *nm* **1** *(acción)* parking. **2** *(en la calle)* place to park, parking place. **3** *(parking)* car park, US parking lot.

**aparcar** *vt* to park.
  ▶ *vi* to park. LOC «Prohibido aparcar» «No parking».

**aparearse** *vpr* to mate.

**aparecer** *vi* **1** to appear: *no aparece en la lista de invitados* she's not on the guest list. **2** *(dejarse ver)* to show up, turn up: *espero que no aparezca por mi casa* I hope he doesn't show his face near my house.

**aparejador,-ra** *adj & nf (de obras)* clerk of works; *(perito)* quantity surveyor.

**aparentar** *vt* **1** *(simular)* to pretend, affect: *aparenta indiferencia* she pretends not to care, she affects indifference. **2** *(tener aspecto de)* to look: *no aparenta la edad que tiene* he doesn't look his age.
  ▶ *vi* to show off.

**aparente** *adj* apparent.

**aparición** *nf* **1** appearance. **2** *(visión)* apparition.

**apariencia** *nf* appearance, aspect. LOC **en apariencia** apparently, by all appearances. ‖ **guardar las apariencias** *fig* to keep up appearances.

**apartado,-a** *pp* → apartar.
  ▶ *adj* **1** *(alejado)* remote, distant; *(aislado)* isolated, cut off. **2** *(retirado)* retired.
  ▶ *nm* **apartado 1** post office box. **2** *(párrafo)* section.

**apartamento** *nm* small flat, apartment.

**apartar** *vt* **1** *(alejar)* to move away. **2** *(reservar)* to put aside, set aside.
  ▶ *vpr* **apartarse 1** *(alejarse)* to move away. **2** *(separarse)* to withdraw, move away.

**aparte** *adv* apart, aside, separately.
  ▶ *adj (distinto)* special: *eso es caso aparte* that's completely different.
  ▶ *nm* **1** TEAT aside. **2** LING paragraph: *punto y aparte* full stop, new paragraph. LOC **aparte de** *(excepto)* apart from. *(además de)* as well as, besides.

**apasionante** *adj* exciting, fascinating.

**apasionarse** *vpr* to get excited, become enthusiastic (**por/de**, about).

**apatía** *nf* apathy.

**apátrida** *adj* stateless.
  ▶ *nm o nf* stateless person.

**apeadero** *nm* halt.

**apearse** *vpr (del tren, autobús, etc.)* to get off; *(del coche)* to get out of; *(del caballo)* to dismount.

**apedrear** *vt* **1** *(tirar piedras)* to throw stones at. **2** *(matar a pedradas)* to stone (to death).

**apego** *nm* attachment, affection, liking, fondness.

**apelación** *nf* **1** JUR appeal. **2** *(llamamiento)* appeal, call.

**apelar** *vi* **1** JUR to appeal. **2** *fig (recurrir)* to resort to.

**apelativo** *nm* appellative, name.

**apellidarse** *vpr* to be called, have as a surname.

**apellido** *nm* family name, surname, (US last name).

**apenas** *adv* 1 *(casi no)* scarcely, hardly: *apenas lo conozco* I hardly know him. 2 *(con dificultad)* only just. 3 *(tan pronto como)* as soon as, no sooner: *apenas entramos, sonó el teléfono* no sooner had we had come in than the phone rang.

**apéndice** *nm* 1 *(órgano interno)* appendix. 2 *(de libro)* appendix.

**apendicitis** *nf inv* appendicitis.

**aperitivo** *nm* 1 *(bebida)* apéritif. 2 *(comida)* appetizer, snack.

**apertura** *nf* 1 *(comienzo)* opening, beginning. 2 POL. liberalization.

**apestar** *vi (oler mal)* to stink.

**apetecer** *vi (agradar)* to feel like, fancy: *¿te apetece ir al teatro?* do you fancy going to the theatre?

**apetecible** *adj* 1 *(empleo)* desirable; *(idea)* appealing. 2 *(comida)* tasty, appetizing.

**apetito** *nm* appetite. LOC **abrir el apetito** to whet one's appetite.

**apetitoso,-a** *adj* 1 *(aspecto de comida)* appetizing; *(comida)* tasty, delicious. 2 *(oferta)* tempting.

**apiadarse** *vpr* to take pity (de, on).

**ápice** *nm* 1 *(punta)* apex. 2 *fig* tiny bit, speck, iota. LOC **ni un ápice** not one bit.

**apicultura** *nf* beekeeping, apiculture.

**apilar** *vt* to pile up, heap up.

**apio** *nm* celery.

**apisonadora** *nf* steamroller, roadroller.

**aplacar** *vt* to placate, calm, soothe.

**aplanar** *vt* to smooth, level, make even.

**aplastante** *adj* crushing, overwhelming. COMP **triunfo/victoria aplastante** *(electoral)* landslide victory.

**aplastar** *vt* 1 *(gen)* to flatten, squash, crush. 2 *fig (destruir)* to crush, destroy.

**aplaudir** *vt* to clap, applaud.

**aplauso** *nm* applause.

**aplazamiento** *nm (gen)* adjournment, postponement; *(de pago)* deferment.

**aplazar** *vt (gen)* to adjourn, postpone, put off; *(un pago)* to defer.

**aplicación** *nf* application.

**aplicado,-a** *pp* → aplicar.
▶ *adj (estudioso)* studious, diligent, hard-working.

**aplicar** *vt* to apply.
▶ *vpr* **aplicarse** *(esforzarse)* to apply OS, work hard.

**aplique** *nm* 1 *(adorno)* appliqué. 2 *(lámpara)* wall light, wall lamp.

**aplomo** *nm* composure, self-possession.

**apocado,-a** *adj* 1 *(intimidado)* intimidated, frightened. 2 *(tímido)* shy, timid.

**apocalipsis** *nm inv* apocalypse.

**apócope** *nm* apocope.

**apodarse** *vpr* to be nicknamed.

**apoderado,-a** *pp* → apoderarse.
▶ *nm & nf* 1 agent, representative. 2 *(de torero, deportista)* manager.

**apoderarse** *vpr* to take possession (de, of), seize (de, -): *el miedo se apoderó de él* he was seized by fear.

**apodo** *nm* nickname.

**apogeo** *nm* 1 *(de órbita)* apogee. 2 *fig (punto culminante)* summit, height, climax, peak.

**apolítico,-a** *adj* apolitical.

**apología** *nf* apology, defence (US defense).

**apoplejía** *nf* apoplexy, stroke.

**aporrear** *vt (persona)* to beat, hit, thrash; *(puerta)* to bang on; *(piano)* to bang (away) on.

**aportación** *nf* contribution.

**aportar** *vt* 1 *(contribuir)* to contribute. 2 *(proporcionar)* to give, provide.

**aposento** *nm* 1 *(cuarto)* room. 2 *(hospedaje)* lodgings *pl*.

**apósito** *nm* dressing.

**aposta** *adv* on purpose, deliberately, intentionally.

**apostar** *vt* to bet (por, on).
▶ *vpr* **apostarse** to bet.

**apóstol** *nm* 1 apostle. 2 *fig (defensor)* apostle, champion.

**apóstrofe** *nm & nf* 1 GRAM apostrophe. 2 *(reprimenda)* reprimand, rebuke.

**apotema** *nf* apothem.

**apoteósico,-a** *adj* enormous, tremendous.

**apoyar** *vt* **1** to lean, rest. **2** *(fundar)* to base, found. **3** *fig (defender algo)* to support; *(defender a alguien)* to back, support.
▶ *vpr* **apoyarse 1** *(descansar)* to lean (en, on), rest (en, on), stand (en, on). **2** *fig (basarse)* to be based (en, on).

**apoyo** *nm* support.

**apreciable** *adj* **1** *(perceptible)* appreciable, noticeable. **2** *(estimable)* valuable, precious.

**apreciar** *vt* **1** *(valorar)* to appraise (en, at). **2** *(sentir aprecio)* to regard highly, hold in high esteem. **3** *(reconocer valor)* to appreciate. **4** *(percibir)* to notice, see, perceive.

**aprecio** *nm* esteem, regard. LOC **sentir aprecio por ALGN** to be fond of SB.

**aprender** *vt* **1** to learn. **2** *(memorizar)* to learn by heart.
▶ *vpr* **aprenderse** learn by heart.

**aprendiz,-za** *nm & nf* apprentice, trainee.

**aprendizaje** *nm* **1** *(situación)* apprenticeship. **2** *(tiempo)* training period. **3** *(en pedagogía)* learning.

**aprensión** *nf (miedo)* apprehension; *(asco)* squeamishness.

**aprensivo,-a** *adj* apprehensive.

**apresar** *vt* **1** *(tomar por fuerza)* to seize, capture. **2** *(asir)* to clutch.

**apresurarse** *vpr* to hurry, hurry up.

**apretar** *vt* **1** *(estrechar)* to squeeze, hug. **2** *(tornillo)* to tighten; *(cordones, nudo)* to do up tight. **3** *(comprimir)* to compress, press together, pack tight. **4** *(botón)* to press, push.
▶ *vi* **1** *fig (aumentar)* to increase, get worse: *el calor aprieta* it's getting hotter and hotter. **2** *(prendas)* to fit tight, be tight on.

**apretón** COMP **apretón de manos** handshake.

**aprieto** *nm* tight spot, difficulty, scrape, fix. LOC **poner a ALGN en un aprieto** to put SB in an awkward situation.

**aprisa** *adv* quickly.

**aprobación** *nf (gen)* approval; *(ley)* passing.

**aprobado,-a** *pp* → aprobar.
▶ *adj* approved, passed.
▶ *nm* **aprobado** EDUC pass (mark). LOC **sacar/tener un aprobado** to get a pass.

**aprobar** *vt* **1** *(gen)* to approve; *(ley)* to pass. **2** *(estar de acuerdo)* to approve of. **3** EDUC *(examen, asignatura)* to pass.
▶ *vi* to pass.

**apropiación** *nf* appropriation. COMP **apropiación indebida** JUR theft.

**apropiado,-a** *pp* → apropiarse.
▶ *adj* suitable, fitting, appropriate.

**apropiarse** *vpr* to appropriate (de, -), take possession (de, of).

**aprovechable** *adj* usable.

**aprovechado,-a** *pp* → aprovechar.
▶ *adj* **1** *(espacio)* well-planned. **2** *pey (egoísta)* selfish; *(gorrón)* sponging, scrounging. LOC **mal aprovechado,-a** wasted.
▶ *nm & nf fam (gorrón)* sponger, scrounger; *(oportunista)* opportunist.

**aprovechamiento** *nm* **1** *(uso)* use, exploitation: *el aprovechamiento de los recursos naturales* the exploitation of natural resources. **2** *(provecho)* improvement, progress.

**aprovechar** *vt* **1** *(emplear útilmente)* to make good use of, make the most of. **2** *(sacar provecho)* to benefit from, take advantage of.
▶ *vpr* **aprovecharse** *(de alguien)* to take advantage (de, of); *(de algo)* to make the most (de, of). LOC **¡que aproveche!** enjoy your meal!

**aproximación** *nf* **1** *(gen)* approximation. **2** *(acercamiento)* bringing together; *(de países)* rapprochement.

**aproximado,-a** *pp* → aproximar.
▶ *adj* approximate, estimated. COMP **cálculo aproximado** rough estimate.

**aproximar** *vt* to bring near, put near.
▶ *vpr* **aproximarse** to come near, come closer.

**aptitud** *nf* aptitude, ability.

**apto,-a** *adj* **1** *(apropiado)* suitable, appropriate: *no es apto para este trabajo* he's not suitable for this job. **2** *(capaz)* capable, able.

**apuesta** *nf* bet, wager.

**apuesto,-a** *adj (gen)* good-looking; *(hombre)* handsome.

**apuntador,-ra** *nm & nf* TEAT prompter.

**apuntar** *vt* **1** *(señalar)* to point (a, at). **2** *(arma)* to aim. **3** *(anotar)* to note down, make a note of. **4** TEAT to prompt.
▶ *vpr* **apuntarse 1** *(inscribirse)* to enrol. **2** *fam (participar)* to take part (a, in): ¿te apuntas? are you game?

**apunte** *nm* **1** note. **2** *(dibujo)* sketch.
▶ *nm pl* **apuntes** *(de clase)* notes.

**apuñalar** *vt* to stab.

**apurar** *vt* **1** *(terminar)* to finish up. **2** AM *(dar prisa)* to hurry, rush.
▶ *vpr* **apurarse 1** *(preocuparse)* to get worried, be worried. **2** AM *(darse prisa)* to hurry, rush.

**apuro** *nm* **1** fix, tight spot; *(de dinero)* hardship. **2** *(vergüenza)* embarrassment. LOC **estar/encontrarse en un apuro** to be in a tight spot. ‖ **pasar apuros 1** *(económicos)* to be hard up. **2** *(dificultades)* to be in a tight spot.

**aquejado,-a** *adj* suffering (de, from).

**aquel,-ella** *adj* **1** that. **2** **aquellos,-as** those.

**aquél,-élla** *pron* **1** that one; *(el anterior)* the former: aquél es el mío that one is mine. **2** **aquéllos,-as** those; *(los anteriores)* the former. LOC **aquél que...** he who... ‖ **todo aquél que...** anyone who..., whoever...

**aquella** *adj* → aquel.

**aquélla** *pron* → aquél.

**aquello** *pron* that, it.

**aquellos,-as** *adj* → aquel,-ella.

**aquéllos,-as** *pron* → aquél,-éllas.

**aquí** *adv* **1** *(lugar)* here: por aquí por favor this way please. **2** *(tiempo)* now: de aquí en adelante from now on.

**árabe** *adj (gen)* Arab; *(de Arabia)* Arabian.
▶ *nm & nf* Arab.

**Arabia** *nf* Arabia. COMP **Arabia Saudita** Saudi Arabia.

**arácnido** *nm* arachnid.

**arado** *nm* plough (US plow).

**arancel** *nm* tariff, customs duty.

**arándano** *nm* bilberry, blueberry.

**arandela** *nf* washer.

**araña** *nf* **1** *(arácnido)* spider. **2** *(pez)* weever. **3** *(lámpara)* chandelier. COMP **araña de mar** spider crab. ‖ **tela de araña** spider's web.

**arañar** *vt* **1** *(raspar)* to scratch. **2** *fig (recoger)* to scrape together.
▶ *vpr* **arañarse** to scratch.

**arañazo** *nm* scratch.

**arar** *vt* to plough (US plow).

**arbitraje** *nm* **1** *(en un desacuerdo)* arbitration. **2** DEP *(en fútbol, boxeo)* refereeing; *(en cricket, tenis)* umpiring.

**arbitrar** *vt* **1** to arbitrate. **2** DEP *(en fútbol, boxeo)* to referee; *(en cricket, tenis)* to umpire.

**arbitrario,-a** *adj* arbitrary.

**árbitro,-a** *nm & nf* **1** arbiter, arbitrator. **2** DEP *(fútbol, boxeo)* referee; *(cricket, tenis)* umpire.

**árbol** *nm* **1** BOT tree. **2** TÉC axle, shaft. **3** MAR mast. **4** *(gráfico)* tree (diagram).

**arboleda** *nf* grove, wood, copse.

**arbusto** *nm* shrub, bush.

**arca** *nf* chest. COMP **arca de Noé** Noah's ark. ‖ **arcas públicas** Treasury *sing*.

**arcada** *nf* **1** *(conjunto de arcos)* arcade. **2** *(de puente)* arch. **3** *(vómitos)* retching.

**arcaico,-a** *adj* archaic.

**arce** *nm* maple (tree).

**arcén** *nm* side of the road, verge; *(de autopista)* hard shoulder.

**archipiélago** *nm* archipelago.

**archivador** *nm* *(mueble)* filing cabinet; *(carpeta)* file.

**archivar** *vt* **1** *(ordenar)* to file (away). **2** INFORM to save. **3** *(arrinconar)* to shelve.

**archivo** *nm* **1** *(informe, ficha)* file. **2** *(documentos)* files *pl*, archives *pl*. **3** INFORM file. **4** *(lugar)* archive. **5** *(archivador)* filing cabinet.

**arcilla** *nf* clay.

**arco** *nm* **1** ARQUIT arch. **2** *(en geometría)* arc. **3** *(arma)* bow. **4** *(de violín, etc)* bow. COMP **arco de medio punto** semicircular arch. ‖ **arco iris** rainbow. ‖ **arco voltaico** electric arc.

**arder** *vi* to burn; *(completamente)* to burn down; *(sin llama)* to smoulder.

**ardid** *nm* scheme, trick.

**ardilla** *nf* squirrel.

**ardor** *nm* **1** burning sensation, burn; *(calor)* heat. **2** *fig (ansia)* ardour (US ardor), fervour (US fervor). COMP **ardor de estómago** heartburn.

**arduo,-a** *adj* arduous.

**área** *nf* **1** *(zona)* area, zone. **2** *(medida)* are. **3** *(superficie)* area.

**arena** *nf* sand. COMP **arenas movedizas** quicksand *sing*.

**arenisca** *nf* sandstone.

**arenoso,-a** *adj* sandy.

**arenque** *nm* herring.

**argamasa** *nf* mortar.

**Argelia** *nm* Algeria.

**argelino,-a** *adj* Algerian.
▶ *nm & nf* Algerian.

**Argentina** *nf* Argentina, the Argentine.

**argentino,-a** *adj* Argentinian.
▶ *nm & nf* Argentinian.

**argón** *nm* argon.

**argot** *nm* **1** *(popular)* slang. **2** *(técnico)* jargon.

**argucia** *nf* sophism, subtlety.

**argumentación** *nf* **1** *(proceso)* arguing, argument. **2** *(argumento)* argument.

**argumentar** *vt* to deduce.

**argumento** *nm* **1** argument. **2** *(de novela, obra, etc)* plot.

**aria** *nf* aria.

**aridez** *nf* **1** aridity. **2** *fig* dryness.

**árido,-a** *adj* **1** arid. **2** *fig* dry.
▶ *nm pl* **áridos** dry goods.

**Aries** *nm inv* Aries.

**ariete** *nm* **1** *(fútbol)* centre (US center) forward. **2** *(máquina)* battering ram.

**ario,-a** *adj* Aryan.

**arisco,-a** *adj* **1** *(persona - altiva)* unsociable, unfriendly; *(- áspera)* surly, gruff; *(- huidiza)* shy. **2** *(animal)* unfriendly.

**arista** *nf* **1** *(línea)* edge. **2** *(filamento del trigo)* beard. **3** ARQUIT *(de viga)* arris; *(de bóveda)* groin. **4** *(de montaña)* arête.

**aristocracia** *nf* aristocracy.

**aristócrata** *nm o nf* aristocrat.

**aritmético,-a** *adj* arithmetical, arithmetic.

**arma** *nf* weapon, arm. LOC **alzarse en armas** to rise up in arms. ∎ **ser de armas tomar** *fig* to be formidable. COMP **arma blanca** knife. ∎ **arma de fuego** firearm.

**armada** *nf* navy, naval forces *pl*.

**armadillo** *nm* armadillo.

**armador,-ra** *nm & nf* shipowner.

**armadura** *nf* **1** *(traje)* suit of armour (US armor). **2** *(armazón)* frame. **3** ARQUIT framework.

**armamento** *nm* *(acción)* armament, arming.

**armar** *vt* **1** *(dar armas)* to arm. **2** *(cargar)* to load; *(bayoneta)* to fix. **3** *(montar - mueble)* to assemble. **4** *fam (causar, originar)* to cause, kick up, create: *armó un lío tremendo* he kicked up a tremendous fuss. LOC **armarla** *fam* to cause trouble, kick up a fuss.
▶ *vpr* **armarse 1** *(proveerse)* to provide OS (de, with), arm OS (de, with): *se armó de pintura y pincel y se puso a pintar* he provided himself with paint and paintbrush and began to paint. **2** *(producirse)* to be, break out: *se armó un jaleo* there was a right row. LOC **armarse de paciencia** to summon up patience. ∎ **armarse de valor** to pluck up courage.

**armario** *nm* *(para ropa)* wardrobe, US closet; *(de cocina)* cupboard. COMP **armario empotrado** built-in wardrobe, built-in cupboard.

**armatoste** *nm* *(cosa)* monstrosity; *(máquina)* useless contraption.

**armazón** *nm & nf* **1** frame, framework; *(de madera)* timberwork. **2** ARQUIT shell; *(de escultura)* armature.

**armiño** *nm* ermine.

**armisticio** *nm* armistice.

**armonía** *nf* harmony.

**armónica** *nf* harmonica, mouth organ.

**armonioso,-a** *adj* harmonious.

**aro** *nm* **1** hoop, ring. **2** *(juego)* hoop.

**aroma** *nm* aroma; *(del vino)* bouquet.

**aromático,-a** *adj* aromatic, fragrant.

**arpa** *nf* harp.

**arpón** *nm* harpoon.

**arqueología** *nf* archaeology (US archeology).

**arqueólogo,-a** *nm & nf* archaeologist (US archeologist).

**arquero,-a** *nm & nf* archer.

**arquetipo** *nm* archetype.

**arquitecto,-a** *nm & nf* architect.

**arquitectura** *nf* architecture.

**arquitrabe** *nm* architrave.

**arquivolta** *nf* archivolt.

**arrabales** *nm pl* outskirts.

**arraigar** *vi* to take root.
▸ *vpr* **arraigarse** *(establecerse)* to settle down.

**arraigo** *nm* **1** *(acción)* act of taking root. **2** *fig* *(raíces)* roots: *con mucho arraigo* deeply-rooted.

**arrancar** *vt* **1** *(árbol)* to uproot; *(flor)* to pull up. **2** *(plumas, cejas)* to pluck; *(cabello, diente)* to pull out; *(con violencia - página)* to tear out. **3** *(obtener - aplausos, sonrisa)* to get; *(- confesión, información)* to extract. **4** *(coche)* to start.
▸ *vi* **1** *(partir)* to begin, start. **2** *(salir)* to go, leave. **3** *(coche)* to start; *(tren)* to pull out.

**arranque** *nm* **1** TÉC starting mechanism. **2** *(comienzo)* start. **3** *fig* *(arrebato)* outburst, fit.

**arrasar** *vt* **1** *(destruir)* to raze, destroy. **2** *(allanar)* to level, smooth.
▸ *vi* *(disco, libro, película)* to be a smash hit, sweep the board; *(deportista)* to sweep to victory.

**arrastrar** *vt* **1** *(gen)* to drag, pull, **2** *(corriente, aire)* to sweep along. **3** *(traer como consecuencia)* to cause, bring, lead to.
▸ *vpr* **arrastrarse 1** to drag OS, crawl. **2** *fig* *(humillarse)* to creep, crawl.

**arrastre** *nm* **1** *(acción)* dragging, pulling. **2** *(telesquí)* drag lift. **3** *(en naipes)* lead.

**arre** *interj* gee up!, giddy up!

**arrear** *vt* **1** *(animales)* to spur on, urge on. **2** *(apresurar)* to hurry up. **3** *fam* *(pegar)* to hit: *le arreó una bofetada* she slapped him round the face.

**arrebatar** *vt* **1** *(quitar)* to grab, snatch. **2** *fig* *(cautivar)* to captivate, fascinate.

**arrebato** *nm* *(arranque)* fit, outburst.

**arreciar** *vi* to get stronger, get worse.

**arrecife** *nm* reef.

**arreglado,-a** *pp* → arreglar.
▸ *adj* **1** *(solucionado)* settled, fixed, sorted out. **2** *(ordenado)* tidy, neat, arranged, orderly. **3** *(bien vestido)* well-dressed, smart.

**arreglar** *vt* **1** *(gen)* to settle, sort out, fix. **2** *(ordenar)* to tidy up, clear up. **3** *(reparar)* to mend, fix, repair. **4** MÚS to arrange. **5** *fam* to sort out: *¡ya te arreglaré!* I'll teach you!, I'll sort you out.
▸ *vpr* **arreglarse 1** *(componerse)* to get ready, dress up; *(cabello)* to do. **2** *(solucionarse)* to get sorted out, work out; *(pareja)* to get back together again. LOC **arreglárselas** to manage, cope: *arréglatelas como puedas* do the best you can.

**arreglo** *nm* **1** *(acuerdo)* arrangement, agreement, settlement. **2** *(reparación)* repair. **3** MÚS arrangement. COMP **arreglo de cuentas** settling of scores, settling-up.

**arremangarse** *vpr* to roll up one's sleeves.

**arremeter** *vi* **1** *(gen)* to attack, charge; *(el toro)* to charge. **2** *(verbalmente)* to attack.

**arrendamiento** *nm* **1** renting, leasing, letting. **2** *(precio)* rent.

**arrendar** *vt* *(dar en alquiler)* to let, lease; *(tomar en alquiler)* to rent, lease.

**arrendatario,-a** *nm & nf* **1** *(que da en arriendo)* leaseholder, lessee. **2** *(inquilino)* tenant.

**arrepentido,-a** *pp* → arrepentirse.
▸ *adj* regretful, repentant.
▸ *nm & nf* penitent.

**arrepentimiento** *nm* regret, repentance.

**arrepentirse** *vpr* **1** *(gen)* to regret (de, -). **2** REL to repent (de, of).

**arrestar** *vt* **1** to arrest, detain. **2** *(poner en prisión)* to imprison, jail, put in prison.

**arresto** *nm* arrest.

**arriar** *vt* **1** *(velas)* to lower. **2** *(bandera)* to strike.

**arriba** *adv* **1** up; *(encima)* on (the) top: *ponlo más arriba* put it higher up. **2** *(piso)* upstairs: *vive arriba* he/she lives upstairs. **3** *(en escritos)* above: *véase más arriba* see above.

▶ *interj* up!: ¡arriba la República! long live the Republic!, up the Republic! LOC **de arriba abajo** from top to bottom. ‖ hacia arriba upwards.

**arriesgado,-a** *pp* → arriesgar.
▶ *adj* **1** *(peligroso)* risky, dangerous. **2** *(temerario)* bold, daring, fearless.

**arriesgar** *vt* **1** to risk; *(dinero)* to stake. **2** *(aventurar)* to venture.
▶ *vpr* **arriesgarse** to risk.

**arrimar** *vt (acercar)* to move closer.
▶ *vpr* **arrimarse** to move close, get close.

**arrinconar** *vt* **1** *(poner en un rincón)* to put in a corner. **2** *(retirar)* to lay aside, put away. **3** *(acorralar)* to corner.

**arritmia** *nf* arrhythmia.

**arroba** *nf* **1** *(medida de peso)* measure of weight equal to 11.502 kg, 25.3 lbs; *(medida de capacidad)* variable liquid measure. **2** *(Internet)* at, @.

**arrodillarse** *vpr* to kneel down, get down on one's knees.

**arrogancia** *nf* arrogance.

**arrogante** *adj* arrogant.

**arrojar** *vt* **1** *(tirar)* to throw, fling. **2** *(echar con violencia)* to throw out, kick out. **3** *(vomitar)* to vomit, throw up. **4** *(cuentas, etc)* to show, produce, give.
▶ *vpr* **arrojarse** to throw OS.

**arrojo** *nm* boldness, dash, bravery, daring.

**arrollador,-ra** *adj* overwhelming, irresistible.

**arrollar** *vt* **1** *(envolver)* to roll (up). **2** *(al enemigo)* to crush, rout.

**arropar** *vt* to wrap up.

**arroyo** *nm* **1** *(corriente de agua)* stream, brook. **2** *(en la calle)* gutter.

**arroz** *nm* rice. COMP **arroz blanco 1** *(seco)* white rice. **2** *(hervido)* boiled rice. ‖ **arroz con leche** rice pudding. ‖ **arroz integral** brown rice.

**arruga** *nf* *(piel)* wrinkle; *(ropa)* crease.

**arrugar** *vt* *(piel)* to wrinkle; *(ropa)* to crease; *(papel)* to crumple (up).
▶ *vpr* **arrugarse 1** *(piel)* to wrinkle; *(ropa)* to crease; *(papel)* to crumple (up). **2** *fam (acobardarse)* to get the wind up.

**arruinar** *vt* **1** to bankrupt, ruin. **2** *(estropear)* to damage: la tormenta ha arruinado la cosecha the storm has ruined the crops.
▶ *vpr* **arruinarse** to be bankrupt, be ruined.

**arrullar** *vt* **1** *(ave)* to coo. **2** *(adormecer)* to lull.

**arsenal** *nm* **1** MAR shipyard. **2** *(de armas)* arsenal. **3** *fig (cantidad)* storehouse, mine.

**arsénico** *nm* arsenic.

**arte** *nm* **1** art. **2** *(habilidad)* craft, skill. **3** *(astucia)* cunning. **4** *(pesca)* fishing gear.

**artefacto** *nm* device, appliance; *(explosivo)* explosive device.

**arteria** *nf* artery. COMP **arteria carótida** carotid artery. ‖ **arteria coronaria** coronary artery.

**artesa** *nf* trough.

**artesanal** *adj (objeto)* handmade; *(comida)* home-made.

**artesanía** *nf* **1** *(calidad)* craftsmanship. **2** *(arte, obra)* crafts *pl*, handicrafts *pl*.

**artesano,-a** *adj* handmade.
▶ *nm & nf (hombre)* craftsman; *(mujer)* craftswoman.

**artesonado** *nm* panelled ceiling, coffered ceiling.

**ártico,-a** *adj* Arctic.
▶ *nm* **el Ártico** the Arctic. COMP **el Círculo Ártico** the Arctic Circle. ‖ **el océano Ártico** the Arctic Ocean.

**articulación** *nf* **1** LING articulation. **2** ANAT joint, articulation. **3** TÉC joint.

**articulado,-a** *pp* → articular.
▶ *adj* **1** *(lenguaje)* articulate. **2** *(objeto)* articulated.

**articular** *adj* articulated.
▶ *vt* **1** to articulate. **2** JUR to article.

**artículo** *nm* **1** article. **2** *(mercancía)* article, product. COMP **artículos de primera necesidad** basic commodities.

**artífice** *nm o nf* **1** *(artista)* craftsman, artist. **2** *(autor)* author: Pepe ha sido el artífice de todo esto this is all Pepe's doing.

**artificial** *adj* artificial.

**artificioso,-a** *adj* affected.

**artillería** *nf* artillery.

**artilugio** *nm* device, gadget.

**artimaña** *nf* artifice, trick, ruse.

**artista** *nm o nf* artist.

**artístico,-a** *adj* artistic.

**artritis** *nf inv* arthritis.

**artrópodo** *nm* arthropod.

**artrosis** *nf inv* arthrosis.

**arzobispo** *nm* archbishop.

**as** *nm* **1** *(naipes)* ace. **2** *(dados)* one. **3** *fig* ace, star, wizard.

**asa** *nf* handle.

**asado,-a** *pp* → asar.
▶ *adj* roast, roasted.
▶ *nm* **asado** roast.

**asador** *nm* **1** *(utensilio)* roaster. **2** *(establecimiento)* grill room, grill house.

**asalariado,-a** *nm & nf* wage earner, salaried worker.

**asalmonado,-a** *adj* salmon-pink.

**asaltante** *adj* assaulting, attacker.
▶ *nm o nf* attacker; *(en robo)* raider, robber.

**asaltar** *vt* **1** to assault, attack; *(para robar)* to raid, rob. **2** *(abordar)* to approach, come up to.

**asalto** *nm* **1** assault, attack; *(con robo)* raid, robbery. **2** *(boxeo)* round.

**asamblea** *nf* assembly, meeting.

**asar** *vt* to roast.
▶ *vpr* **asarse 1** *(cocerse)* to roast. **2** *fig* *(pasar calor)* to be roasting, be boiling hot. LOC **asar a la parrilla** to grill. ▌ **asar al horno** to roast.

**ascendencia** *nf* **1** ancestry, ancestors *pl*: *era alemán, pero de ascendencia polaca* he was German, but of Polish descent. **2** *(influencia)* ascendancy.

**ascender** *vt* to promote.
▶ *vi* **1** *(subir)* to climb. **2** *(de categoría)* to be promoted (a, to). **3** *(sumar)* to amount (a, to).

**ascendiente** *nm o nf (antepasado)* ancestor.
▶ *nm (influencia)* ascendancy, power.

**ascensión** *nf (subida)* climb, climbing.

**ascenso** *nm* **1** *(subida)* climb, ascent. **2** *(aumento)* rise (de, in). **3** *(promoción)* promotion.

**ascensor** *nm* lift, US elevator.

**asco** *nm* disgust, repugnance. LOC **dar asco** to be disgusting. ▌ **hacer ascos a AL-**GO to turn up one's nose at STH. ▌ **¡qué asco!** how disgusting!, how revolting!

**ascua** *nf* live coal.

**asear** *vt (adecentar)* to clean, tidy up.
▶ *vpr* **asearse** *(arreglarse)* to wash, get washed.

**asediar** *vt* to besiege.

**asedio** *nm* siege.

**asegurado,-a** *pp* → asegurar.
▶ *adj* **1** *(con seguro)* insured. **2** *(garantizado)* secure: *tiene el futuro asegurado* his future is secure.

**asegurar** *vt* **1** *(fijar)* to secure. **2** COM to insure. **3** *(garantizar)* to assure, guarantee.
▶ *vpr* **asegurarse 1** *(cerciorarse)* to make sure. **2** COM to insure OS.

**asemejarse** *vpr* to look like, be like.

**asentir** *vi* to assent, agree; *(con la cabeza)* to nod.

**aseo** *nm* **1** *(acción)* cleaning, tidying up. **2** *(limpieza)* cleanliness, tidiness. **3** *(habitación)* bathroom, toilet.

**aséptico,-a** *adj* **1** aseptic. **2** *fig* cold, indifferent.

**asequible** *adj* accessible: *a un precio asequible* at a reasonable price, at an affordable price.

**aserrar** *vt* to saw (up).

**asesinar** *vt* **1** to kill, murder. **2** *(a un personaje importante)* to assassinate.

**asesinato** *nm* **1** killing, murder. **2** *(de un pesonaje importante)* assassination.

**asesino,-a** *nm & nf* killer; *(hombre)* murderer; *(mujer)* murderess.

**asesor,-ra** *adj* advisory.
▶ *nm & nf* adviser, consultant.

**asesorar** *vt* **1** *(dar consejo)* to advise, give advice. **2** COM to act as a consultant to.
▶ *vpr* **asesorarse** *(tomar consejo)* to take advice, consult (de, -).

**asesoría** *nf* **1** *(cargo)* consultancy. **2** *(oficina)* consultant's office.

**aseveración** *nf* asseveration, assertion.

**asfalto** *nm* asphalt.

**asfixia** *nf* asphyxia, suffocation.

**asfixiar** *vt* to asphyxiate, suffocate.

▶ *vpr* **asfixiarse** to asphyxiate, suffocate.

**así** *adv* **1** *(de esta manera)* thus, (in) this way. **2** *(de esa manera)* (in) that way: *por decirlo así* so to speak; *y así sucesivamente* and so on. **3** *(tanto)* as: *así usted como yo* both you and I. **4** *(por tanto)* therefore. **5** *(tan pronto como)* as soon as: *así que lo sepa* as soon as I know. LOC **así así** so-so. ‖ **así que** so.
▶ *adj* such: *un hombre así* a man like that, such a man.

**Asia** *nf* Asia.

**asiático,-a** *adj* Asian.
▶ *nm & nf* Asian.

**asiduidad** *nf* assiduity, frequency.

**asiduo,-a** *adj* assiduous, frequent.

**asiento** *nm* **1** *(silla, etc)* seat. **2** *(emplazamiento)* site. **3** COM entry, registry. LOC **tomar asiento** to take a seat.

**asignación** *nf* **1** *(acción)* assignment, allocation. **2** *(nombramiento)* appointment, assignment. **3** *(remuneración)* allocation, allowance; *(sueldo)* wage, salary.

**asignar** *vt* **1** to assign, allot, allocate. **2** *(nombrar)* to appoint, assign.

**asignatura** *nf* subject.

**asilo** *nm* **1** *(institución)* asylum, home, institution. **2** *fig (protección)* protection, assistance. LOC **dar asilo** to shelter. COMP **asilo de ancianos** old people's home. ‖ **asilo político** political asylum.

**asimetría** *nf* asymmetry.

**asimilar** *vt* to assimilate.

**asimismo** *adv* **1** *(también)* also, as well. **2** *(de esta manera)* likewise. **3** *(además)* moreover.

**asir** *vt* *(agarrar)* to grab, seize, grasp, take hold of.

**asistencia** *nf* **1** *(presencia)* attendance, presence. **2** *(público)* audience. **3** *(ayuda)* assistance, help, aid. COMP **asistencia médica** medical assistance. ‖ **asistencia técnica** technical backup. ‖ **falta de asistencia** absence.

**asistenta** *nf* cleaning lady.

**asistente** *adj* **1** *(que está)* attending. **2** *(que ayuda)* assistant.

▶ *nm o nf* **1** *(que está)* member of the audience. **2** *(que ayuda)* assistant. COMP **asistente social** social worker.

**asistir** *vi* to attend, be present.
▶ *vt* *(ayudar)* to help, assist; *(a los enfermos)* to attend, care for.

**asma** *nf* asthma.

**asno** *nm* ass, donkey.

**asociación** *nf* association.

**asociado,-a** *pp* → asociar.
▶ *adj* associated, associate.
▶ *nm & nf* associate, partner.

**asociar** *vt* to associate (a/con, with), connect, link.
▶ *vpr* **asociarse 1** *(relacionarse)* to be associated (a/con, with). **2** COM to form a partnership, become partners.

**asociativo,-a** *nf* associative. COMP **propiedad asociativa** associativity.

**asomar** *vi* *(empezar a aparecer)* to appear, begin to show, come out.
▶ *vt* *(mostrar)* to stick out.
▶ *vpr* **asomarse 1** *(a ventana)* to stick one's head out (a, of), lean out (a, of); *(a balcón)* to come out (a, onto). **2** *(aparecer)* to appear.

**asombrar** *vt* to amaze, astonish.
▶ *vpr* **asombrarse** to be astonished, be amazed, be surprised.

**asombro** *nm* amazement, astonishment, surprise.

**asombroso,-a** *adj* amazing, astonishing, surprising.

**asomo** *nm* sign, trace, hint. LOC **ni por asomo** by no means.

**asonante** *adj* assonant.

**aspa** *nf* **1** *(cruz)* cross. **2** *(de molino)* sail; *(de ventilador)* blade; *(armazón)* arms *pl*.

**aspaviento** *nm* fuss. LOC **hacer aspavientos** to make a great fuss.

**aspecto** *nm* **1** *(faceta)* aspect, side, angle. **2** *(apariencia)* look, appearance: *¿qué aspecto tenía?* what did he look like?

**aspereza** *nf* roughness, coarseness.

**áspero,-a** *adj* **1** *(cosa)* rough, coarse. **2** *fig (persona)* surly.

**aspersión** *nf* sprinkling.

**aspersor** *nm* sprinkler.

**aspiración** *nf* **1** *(al respirar)* inhalation, breathing in. **2** LING aspiration. **3** TÉC intake. **4** *fig (ambición)* aspiration, ambition.

**aspirador** *nm* vacuum cleaner, Hoover.

**aspirante** *nm o nf* candidate, applicant.

**aspirar** *vt* **1** *(al respirar)* to inhale, breathe in. **2** *(absorber)* to suck in, draw in. **3** LING to aspirate.
▶ *vi fig (desear)* to aspire (a, to).

**aspirina®** *nf* aspirin.

**asquear** *vt* to disgust, revolt.

**asqueroso,-a** *adj* **1** *(sucio)* dirty, filthy. **2** *(desagradable)* disgusting, revolting, foul.
▶ *nm & nf (sucio)* filthy person, revolting person.

**asta** *nf* **1** *(de bandera)* staff, pole. **2** *(de lanza)* shaft; *(pica)* lance, pike. **3** *(cuerno)* horn.

**asterisco** *nm* asterisk.

**asteroide** *adj* asteroid.
▶ *nm* asteroid.

**astigmatismo** *nm* astigmatism.

**astilla** *nf* splinter, chip.

**astillero** *nm* shipyard, dockyard.

**astrágalo** *nm* **1** ANAT astragalus. **2** ARQUIT astragal.

**astro** *nm* star.

**astrofísica** *nf* astrophysics.

**astrología** *nf* astrology.

**astrólogo,-a** *nm & nf* astrologer.

**astronauta** *nm o nf* astronaut.

**astronomía** *nf* astronomy.

**astrónomo,-a** *nm & nf* astronomer.

**astucia** *nf* **1** astuteness, cunning, shrewdness. **2** *(treta)* trick, ruse.

**astuto,-a** *adj* astute, cunning, shrewd.

**asumir** *vt* to assume, take on, take upon OS.

**asunto** *nm* **1** *(cuestión)* matter, issue; *(tema)* subject; *(de obra)* theme: *no quiero hablar del asunto* I don't want to discuss the matter. **2** *(negocio)* affair, business: *no es asunto tuyo* it's none of your business. **3** *(aventura)* affair, love affair. COMP **asuntos exteriores** POL Foreign Affairs.

**asustado,-a** *adj* frightened, scared.

**asustar** *vt* to frighten, scare.
▶ *vpr* **asustarse** to be frightened, be scared.

**atacar** *vt* to attack.

**atajar** *vi* to take a short cut.

**atajo** *nm* **1** *(camino)* short cut. **2** *fig (grupo)* bunch.

**atalaya** *nf* *(torre)* watchtower, lookout; *(mirador)* vantage point.

**ataque** *nm* **1** attack. **2** MED fit. COMP **ataque de nervios** nervous breakdown.

**atar** *vt* to tie. LOC **atar cabos** *fig* to put two and two together.

**atardecer** *vi* to get dark, grow dark.
▶ *nm* evening, dusk.

**atareado,-a** *adj* busy, occupied.

**atascar** *vt* **1** *(bloquear)* to block up, clog. **2** *fig (obstaculizar)* to hamper, hinder, obstruct.
▶ *vpr* **atascarse 1** *(bloquearse)* to get blocked. **2** *(mecanismo)* to get stuck.

**atasco** *nm* **1** *(acción)* obstruction, blockage. **2** *(de tráfico)* traffic jam.

**ataúd** *nm* coffin.

**ataviar** *vt* **1** *(arreglar)* to dress up. **2** *(adornar)* to adorn, deck.

**ateísmo** *nm* atheism.

**atemorizar** *vt* to frighten, scare.

**atención** *nf* **1** *(gen)* attention. **2** *(detalle)* nice thought: *fue una atención por su parte* it was a nice thought, it was very kind of him. LOC **a la atención de** ALGN *(en cartas)* for the attention of SB. ‖ **llamar la atención** to attract attention. ‖ **llamar la atención a** ALGN to take SB to task. ‖ **prestar atención** to pay attention (a, to).
▶ *interj* **¡atención!** *(gen)* your attention please!; *(cuidado)* watch out!, look out!

**atender** *vt* **1** *(servir - cliente)* to serve, attend to, see to: *¿ya la atienden?* are you being served? **2** *(cuidar)* to take care of, look after. **3** *(negocio)* to take care of; *(teléfono)* to answer. **4** *(consejo, advertencia)* to heed, pay attention to; *(ruego, deseo, protesta)* to attend to; *(instrucción)* to follow, carry out.

▶ *vi* **1** *(prestar atención)* to pay attention (a, to), attend (a, to). **2** *(tener en cuenta)* to bear in mind.

**atenerse** *vpr* **1** *(ajustarse)* to abide (a, by), comply (a, with). **2** *(acogerse)* to rely (a, on).

**atentado** *nm* **1** *(ataque)* attack, assault. **2** *(afrenta)* affront. ⬛COMP⬛ **atentado terrorista** terrorist attack.

**atentamente** *adv* **1** attentively, carefully. **2** *(amablemente)* politely; *(en carta)* sincerely, faithfully: *«Le saluda atentamente»* "Yours sincerely", "Yours faithfully".

**atentar** *vi (físicamente - a una institución)* to attack (a/contra, -), make an attack (a/contra, on); *(- a una persona)* to attempt to kill, make an attempt on sb's life.

**atento,-a** *adj* **1** attentive. **2** *(amable)* polite, courteous.

**atenuante** *adj* **1** attenuating. **2** JUR extenuating.
▶ *nm* JUR extenuating circumstance.

**atenuar** *vt* **1** to attenuate. **2** JUR to extenuate.

**ateo,-a** *adj* atheistic.
▶ *nm & nf* atheist.

**aterrador,-ra** *adj* terrifying, frightful.

**aterrizaje** *nm* landing. ⬛COMP⬛ **aterrizaje forzoso** emergency landing.

**aterrizar** *vi* to land.

**aterrorizar** *vt* to terrify.

**atesorar** *vt* **1** *(acumular)* to hoard, accumulate, store up. **2** *fig* to possess.

**atestado¹** *nm* JUR affidavit, statement.

**atestado,-a²** *adj* packed (de, with), crammed (de, with).

**atestiguar** *vt* **1** JUR to testify to, bear witness to, give evidence of. **2** *(ofrecer muestras)* to attest, testify, vouch for.

**atiborrarse** *vpr fam (de comida)* to stuff OS (de, with).

**ático** *nm* **1** *(vivienda)* penthouse, attic flat. **2** ARQUIT attic, loft.

**atinar** *vi* **1** *(dar con)* to hit upon, find. **2** *(acertar)* to get it right, be right, succeed.

**atípico,-a** *adj* atypical.

**atisbo** *nm* **1** *(acción)* spying, watching. **2** *fig (indicio)* inkling, slight sign.

**atizar** *vt* **1** *(fuego)* to poke; *(vela)* to snuff. **2** *fig (pasiones)* to rouse, excite; *(rebelión)* to stir up. **3** *(dar - golpe)* give, deal.

**atlántico,-a** *adj* Atlantic. ⬛COMP⬛ **el (océano) Atlántico** the Atlantic (Ocean).

**atlas** *nm inv* atlas.

**atleta** *nm o nf* athlete.

**atlético,-a** *adj* athletic.

**atletismo** *nm* athletics.

**atmósfera** *nf* atmosphere.

**atolondrado,-a** *adj* **1** *(desatinado)* scatterbrained, reckless, silly. **2** *(aturdido)* stunned, bewildered.

**atómico,-a** *adj* atomic.

**atomizador** *nm* atomizer, spray.

**átomo** *nm* atom.

**atónito,-a** *adj* astonished, amazed.

**átono,-a** *adj* atonic, unstressed.

**atontado,-a** *adj* **1** *(aturdido)* stunned, confused, bewildered. **2** *(tonto)* stupid, silly, foolish.

**atormentar** *vt* **1** *(torturar)* to torture. **2** *fig (causar disgusto)* to torment, harass.
▶ *vpr* **atormentarse** *(sufrir)* to torment OS.

**atornillar** *vt* to screw on, screw down.

**atracador,-ra** *nm & nf (de banco)* (bank) robber; *(en la calle)* attacker, mugger, thief.

**atracar** *vt (robar - banco, tienda)* to hold up, rob; *(- persona)* to mug.
▶ *vi* MAR *(a otra nave)* to come alongside; *(a tierra)* to tie up, dock, berth.
▶ *vpr* **atracarse** *(de comida)* to gorge OS (de, on), stuff OS (de, with).

**atracción** *nf (gen)* attraction.
▶ *nf pl* **atracciones** *(de feria)* rides *pl*.

**atraco** *nm* hold-up, robbery.

**atracón** *nm fam* binge, blowout.

**atractivo,-a** *adj* attractive, charming.
▶ *nm* **atractivo** attraction, charm, appeal.

**atraer** *vt* to attract.

**atragantarse** *vpr (no poder tragar)* to choke (con, on), swallow the wrong way.

**atrapar** *vt* to seize, capture, catch.

**atrás** *adv* **1** back: *dio un salto atrás* she jumped back. **2** *(tiempo)* ago: *días atrás* several days ago.

**atrasado,-a** *pp* → atrasar.
▶ *adj* **1** *(desfasado)* outdated. **2** *(pago)* overdue. **3** *(reloj)* slow. **4** *(país)* backward, underdeveloped; *(alumno)* slow, backward.

**atrasar** *vt* *(gen)* to delay, postpone, put back; *(reloj)* to put back.
▶ *vi (reloj)* to be slow.
▶ *vpr* **atrasarse 1** *(tren, etc)* to be late. **2** *(quedarse atrás)* to fall behind.

**atraso** *nm* **1** delay. **2** *(de reloj)* slowness: *el tren lleva mucho atraso* the train is very late. **3** *(de un país)* backwardness.

**atravesar** *vt* **1** *(cruzar)* to cross, go across, go over; *(pasar por)* to go through, pass through. **2** *(experimentar - gen)* to go through, experience; *(enfermedad, etc)* to suffer. **3** *(poner oblicuamente)* to put across, lay across. **4** *(con bala, etc)* to go through; *(con espada)* to run through. **5** *(situación)* to go through.

**atrayente** *adj* attractive.

**atreverse** *vpr* to dare, venture.

**atrevido,-a** *pp* → atreverse.
▶ *adj* **1** *(osado)* daring, bold. **2** *(insolente)* insolent, impudent. **3** *(indecoroso)* daring, risqué.

**atribuir** *vt* to attribute (a, to), ascribe.

**atributo** *nm* attribute, quality.

**atril** *nm* *(para libros)* lectern, bookrest; *(para música)* music stand.

**atrio** *nm* **1** *(patio)* atrium. **2** *(vestíbulo)* vestibule, entrance hall.

**atrocidad** *nf* **1** *(barbaridad)* atrocity, outrage. **2** *(disparate - acción)* something stupid, foolish thing; *(- dicho)* silly remark, stupid remark.

**atropellar** *vt* **1** AUTO to knock down, run over. **2** *(arrollar)* to trample over.

**atropello** *nm* **1** *(accidente)* accident, collision; *(de coche)* knocking down, running over. **2** *(apresuramiento)* haste. **3** *fig (agravio)* outrage, abuse; *(de derecho)* violation.

**atroz** *adj* atrocious, outrageous.

**atuendo** *nm* attire, dress, outfit.

**atún** *nm* tuna, tuna fish, tunny.

**aturdido,-a** *adj* **1** *(confundido)* stunned, dazed, bewildered. **2** *(atolondrado)* reckless, harebrained.

**audacia** *nf* audacity, boldness, daring.

**audaz** *adj* audacious, bold, daring.

**audición** *nf* **1** *(acción)* hearing; *(radio, televisión)* reception. **2** TEAT audition. **3** MÚS concert.

**audiencia** *nf* **1** *(recepción)* audience, hearing. **2** *(entrevista)* formal interview. **3** JUR high court. **4** *(público)* audience.

**audífono** *nm* hearing aid, deaf aid.

**audiovisual** *adj* audio-visual.
▶ *nm* audio-visual.

**auditar** *vt* to audit.

**auditivo,-a** *adj* auditory.

**auditor,-ra** *nm & nf* FIN auditor.

**auditorio** *nm* **1** *(público)* audience. **2** *(lugar)* auditorium, hall.

**auge** *nm* **1** *(del mercado)* boom. **2** *(de precios)* boost. **3** *(de fama, etc)* peak, summit.

**augurio** *nm* augury.

**aula** *nf* *(en escuela)* classroom; *(en universidad)* lecture room.

**aullar** *vi* to howl, yell, bay.

**aullido** *nm* howl, yell.

**aumentar** *vt* **1** to augment, increase; *(precios)* to put up; *(producción)* to step up. **2** *(óptica)* to magnify. **3** *(fotos)* to enlarge. **4** *(sonido)* to amplify.

**aumento** *nm* **1** increase, growth. **2** *(óptica)* magnification. **3** *(fotos)* enlargement. **4** *(sonido)* amplification. **5** *(salario)* rise, US raise.

**aun** *adv* even: *aun los tontos lo saben* even a fool knows that.
▶ *conj (+ gerundio o participio)* although, even though: *aun llegando tarde, lo recibieron amablemente* although he was late, he was given a warm reception. LOC **aun así** even so, even then. ∎ **aun cuando** although, even though.

**aún** *adv* *(afirmación)* still; *(negación, interrogación)* yet: *aún no ha llamado* he hasn't phoned yet. LOC **aún más** even more.

**aunque** *conj* **1** *(valor concesivo)* although, though; *(con énfasis)* even if, even though. **2** *(valor adversativo)* but.

**aupar** *vt* to help up.

**aureola** *nf* aureole, halo.

**aurícula** *nf* auricle.

**auricular** *adj* auricular, of the ear.
▶ *nm* **1** *(teléfono)* receiver, earpiece. **2** *(dedo)* little finger.
▶ *nm pl* **auriculares** earphones, headphones.

**aurora** *nf* dawn, daybreak. COMP **aurora boreal/borealis** aurora borealis, northern lights *pl*.

**auscultar** *vt* to sound.

**ausencia** *nf* absence.

**ausentarse** *vpr* **1** *(faltar)* to be absent. **2** *(irse)* to leave.

**ausente** *adj* **1** absent. **2** *(distraído)* lost in thought.
▶ *nm o nf* absentee.

**austeridad** *nf* austerity.

**austero,-a** *adj* austere.

**Australia** *nf* Australia.

**australiano,-a** *adj* Australian.
▶ *nm & nf (persona)* Australian.

**australopiteco** *nm* australopithecine.

**Austria** *nf* Austria.

**austríaco,-a** *adj* Austrian.
▶ *nm & nf* Austrian.

**auténtico,-a** *adj* authentic, genuine, real.

**auto¹** *nm (coche)* car. COMP **autos de choque** bumper cars.

**auto²** *nm* **1** JUR decree, writ. **2** LIT mystery play, religious play.

**autoadhesivo,-a** *adj* self-adhesive.

**autobiografía** *nf* autobiography.

**autobús** *nm* bus.

**autocar** *nm* coach.

**autocontrol** *nm* self-control.

**autóctono,-a** *adj* indigenous.

**autodefensa** *nf* self-defence (US self-defense).

**autodeterminación** *nf* self-determination.

**autodidacta** *nm o nf* self-taught person.

**autoescuela** *nf* driving school, school of motoring.

**autoestop** *nm* → autostop.

**autoestopista** *nm o nf* → autostopista.

**autógrafo,-a** *nm* autograph.

**autómata** *nm* automaton.

**automático,-a** *adj* automatic.

**automóvil** *nm* automobile, car.

**automovilismo** *nm* **1** motoring. **2** DEP motor racing.

**automovilista** *nm o nf* motorist, driver.

**automovilístico,-a** *adj* car.

**autonomía** *nf* **1** *(gen)* autonomy. **2** *(capacidad para funcionar sin recargar)* range.

**autonómico,-a** *adj* autonomous, self-governing.

**autónomo,-a** *adj* **1** *(región)* autonomous. **2** *(trabajador)* self-employed.
▶ *nm & nf* COM self-employed person.

**autopista** *nf* motorway, US highway.

**autopsia** *nf* **1** autopsy, postmortem. **2** *fig* postmortem.

**autor,-ra** *nm & nf* **1** *(escritor)* writer, author; *(hombre)* author; *(mujer)* authoress. **2** *(responsable - gen)* person responsible; *(- de delito)* perpetrator.

**autoridad** *nf* authority.

**autoritario,-a** *adj* authoritarian.

**autorización** *nf* authorization.

**autorizado,-a** *pp* → autorizar.
▶ *adj* **1** *(oficial)* authorized, official. **2** *(experto)* authoritative, expert.

**autorizar** *vt* **1** to authorize. **2** JUR to legalize. **3** *(aprobar)* to approve of, give authority to.

**autorretrato** *nm* self-portrait.

**autoservicio** *nm* **1** *(restaurante)* self-service restaurant, cafeteria. **2** *(supermercado)* supermarket.

**autostop** *nm* hitchhiking.

**autostopista** *nm o nf* hitch-hiker.

**autosuficiencia** *nf* self-sufficiency.

**autovía** *nf* dual carriageway, US highway.

**auxiliar** *adj* auxiliary, assistant.
▶ *nm* **1** *(persona)* auxiliary, assistant. **2** GRAM *(verbo)* auxiliary.
▶ *vt (ayudar)* to help, assist; *(a un enfermo)* to attend; *(a un país)* to give aid to. COMP **auxiliar administrativo** administrative assistant.

**auxilio** *nm* help, aid, assistance, relief.
▶ *interj* help! COMP **primeros auxilios** first aid *sing*.

**aval** *nm* endorsement, guarantee.

**avalancha** *nf* avalanche.

**avalar** *vt* to guarantee, endorse.

**avance** *nm* **1** *(acción)* advance. **2** *(pago)* advance payment. **3** *(de película)* trailer. COMP **avance informativo** TV news preview, US news brief.

**avanzar** *vi* to advance, go forward.
▶ *vt* **1** *(mover adelante)* to advance, move forward. **2** *(dinero)* to advance. **3** *(una propuesta)* to put forward.

**avaricia** *nf* avarice.

**avaro,-a** *adj (tacaño)* avaricious, miserly, mean; *(codicioso)* greedy, avaricious.
▶ *nm & nf (tacaño)* miser; *(codicioso)* greedy person.

**avasallar** *vt* to subjugate, subdue.

**ave** *nf* bird. COMP **ave de rapiña** bird of prey. ‖ **aves de corral** poultry *sing.*

**avecinarse** *vpr* to approach (a, -).

**avellana** *nf* hazelnut.

**avemaría** *nf* Ave Maria, Hail Mary.

**avena** *nf* oats *pl.*

**avenida** *nf* **1** *(calle)* avenue. **2** *(riada)* flood, spate.

**aventajar** *vt* **1** *(exceder)* to surpass, beat. **2** *(ir en cabeza)* to lead, be ahead; *(llegar)* to come first, come ahead (a, of).

**aventura** *nf* **1** adventure. **2** *(riesgo)* hazard, risk. **3** *(relación amorosa)* (love) affair.

**aventurado,-a** *pp* → aventurar.
▶ *adj* **1** *(arriesgado)* dangerous, risky. **2** *(atrevido)* daring, bold.

**aventurar** *vt (idea, opinión, etc)* to venture, dare, hazard.
▶ *vpr* **aventurarse** to venture, dare.

**aventurero,-a** *nm & nf (hombre)* adventurer; *(mujer)* adventuress.

**avergonzado,-a** *pp* → avergonzar.
▶ *adj* embarrassed, ashamed.

**avergonzar** *vt (causar vergüenza)* to shame, put to shame; *(turbar)* to embarrass.
▶ *vpr* **avergonzarse** to be ashamed (de, of), be embarrassed (de, about).

**avería** *nf* **1** *(en productos)* damage. **2** TÉC failure. **3** AUTO breakdown.

**averiado,-a** *pp* → averiar.
▶ *adj* **1** *(en productos)* damaged. **2** TÉC faulty, not working, out of order. **3** AUTO broken down.

**averiar** *vt* **1** *(productos)* to damage, spoil. **2** TÉC to cause to malfunction. **3** AUTO to cause a breakdown to.
▶ *vpr* **averiarse 1** *(productos)* to get damaged. **2** TÉC to malfunction, go wrong. **3** AUTO to break down.

**averiguación** *nf* inquiry, investigation.

**averiguar** *vt* to inquire, investigate, find out about: *averigua quién viene* find out who's coming.

**aversión** *nf* aversion. LOC **sentir aversión por** to loathe.

**avestruz** *nm* ostrich.

**aviación** *nf* **1** aviation. **2** MIL air force. COMP **accidente de aviación** air crash.

**aviador,-ra** *nm & nf* aviator, flier; *(hombre)* airman; *(mujer)* airwoman.

**avidez** *nf* avidity, eagerness.

**ávido,-a** *adj* avid, eager: *el chico estaba ávido de aventuras* the boy was thirsty for adventure.

**avión** *nm* aeroplane (US airplane), plane, aircraft.

**avioneta** *nf* light plane, light aircraft.

**avisar** *vt* **1** *(informar)* to inform, notify, announce. **2** *(advertir)* to warn. **3** *(mandar llamar)* to call for.

**aviso** *nm* **1** *(información)* notice. **2** *(advertencia)* warning. LOC **hasta nuevo aviso** until further notice. ‖ **sin previo aviso** without prior notice.

**avispa** *nf* wasp.

**avispero** *nm* **1** *(conjunto de avispas)* swarm of wasps. **2** *(nido de avispas)* wasp's nest. **3** *fig (lío)* tight spot, mess.

**avivar** *vt* **1** *(fuego)* to stoke (up). **2** *(anhelos, deseos)* to enliven. **3** *(pasiones, dolor)* to intensify. **4** *(paso)* to quicken. **5** *(colores, luz)* to brighten up.

**axial** *adj* axial.

**axila** *nf* **1** *(del cuerpo)* armpit, underarm. **2** MED axilla. **3** *(de planta)* axil.

**axioma** *nm* axiom.

**ay** *interj* **1** *(dolor)* ouch!, ow! **2** *(pena)* alas!: *¡ay de mí!* woe is me!, poor me! **3** *(temor)* oh!

**ayer** *adv* **1** *(el día anterior)* yesterday. **2** *(en el pasado)* in the past, formerly.
▶ *nm* past. LOC **ayer por la mañana/tarde** yesterday morning/afternoon. ▮ **ayer por la noche** last night.

**ayuda** *nf* **1** help, aid, assistance. **2** *(lavativa)* enema. LOC **ir en ayuda de** ALGN to come to SB's assistance. ▮ **prestar ayuda** to help (a, -).

**ayudar** *vt* to help, aid, assist: *¿en qué podemos ayudarte?* how can we help you?
▶ *vpr* **ayudarse** *(apoyarse)* to make use (de/con, of).

**ayunar** *vi* to fast.

**ayunas** LOC **en ayunas** on an empty stomach: *tómalo en ayunas* take it on an empty stomach.

**ayuno** *nm* fast, fasting.

**ayuntamiento** *nm* **1** *(corporación)* town council, city council. **2** *(edificio)* town hall, city hall.

**azabache** *nm* jet. LOC **negro,-a como el azabache** jet-black.

**azada** *nf* hoe.

**azafata** *nf* **1** *(de avión)* air hostess, stewardess. **2** *(de congresos)* hostess.

**azafrán** *nm* saffron.

**azahar** *nm (de naranjo)* orange blossom; *(de limonero)* lemon blossom. COMP **agua de azahar** orange flower water.

**azalea** *nf* azalea.

**azar** *nm* **1** chance. **2** *(percance)* misfortune, accident. **3** *(en probabilidad)* event. LOC **al azar** at random. ▮ **por puro azar** by pure chance.

**azotar** *vt* **1** *(con látigo)* to whip, flog. **2** *(golpear)* to beat down on. **3** *(viento, olas)* to lash. **4** *fig (peste, hambre, etc)* to ravage.

**azote** *nm* **1** *(instrumento)* whip, scourge. **2** *(golpe)* lash, stroke (of the whip). **3** *(manotada)* smack. **4** *(del viento, del agua)* lashing. **5** *fig* scourge.

**azotea** *nf* flat roof. LOC **estar mal de la azotea** *fam* to have a screw loose.

**azteca** *adj* Aztec.
▶ *nm o nf* Aztec.

**azúcar** *nm & nf* sugar. COMP **azúcar blanco** refined sugar. ▮ **azúcar moreno/negro** brown sugar.

**azucarado,-a** *pp* → azucarar.
▶ *adj* **1** *(con azúcar)* sugared, sweetened. **2** *(como el azúcar)* sugar-like; *(dulce)* sweet. **3** *fig* sugary.

**azucarero** *nm (vasija)* sugar bowl.

**azucarillo** *nm (terrón)* sugar lump.

**azucena** *nf* white lily.

**azufre** *nm* sulphur (US sulfur).

**azul** *adj* blue.
▶ *nm* blue. COMP **azul celeste** sky blue, light blue. ▮ **azul cielo** sky blue, light blue. ▮ **azul eléctrico** electric blue. ▮ **azul marino** navy blue. ▮ **azul turquesa** turquoise. ▮ **sangre azul** blue blood.

**azulejo** *nm (baldosa)* tile, glazed tile.

**azuzar** *vt* to egg on.

# B

**B, b** *nf (la letra)* B, b.

**baba** *nf* **1** *(de animal, adulto)* spittle, saliva; *(de niño)* dribble. **2** *(de caracol, babosa)* slime. loc **caérsele a uno la baba** *fam* to drool.

**babear** *vi* **1** *(adulto, animal)* to slobber, slaver; *(niño)* to dribble. **2** *fig* to drool, slobber.

**babero** *nm* **1** bib. **2** *(babi)* child's overall.

**babosa** *nf* slug.

**baca** *nf* rack, roof rack, luggage rack.

**bacalao** *nm* cod.

**bache** *nm* **1** *(en carretera)* pothole. **2** *(de aire)* air pocket. **3** *fig* bad patch.

**bachillerato** *nm* **1** Spanish certificate of secondary education. **2** Spanish non-compulsory secondary education.

**bacilo** *nm* bacillus.

**bacón** *nm* bacon.

**bacteria** *nf* bacterium.

**bádminton** *nm* badminton.

**bafle** *nm* loudspeaker.

**Bahamas** *nf pl* **las Bahamas** the Bahamas.

**bahía** *nf* bay.

**bailaor,-ra** *nm & nf* flamenco dancer.

**bailar** *vt* **1** to dance. **2** *(hacer girar)* to spin: *bailó una moneda en la mesa* she spun a coin on the table.
▶ *vi* **1** to dance: *¿bailas?* do you want to dance?, would you like to dance? **2** *(girar)* to spin. **3** *(ser grande)* to be too big: *me bailan estos zapatos* these shoes are too big for me. **4** *(moverse - cosa)* to wobble; *(- persona)* to move about, fidget: *esta silla baila* this chair wobbles.

**5** *(estar suelto)* to be loose: *este tornillo baila* this screw is loose.

**bailarín,-ina** *nm & nf* dancer.

**baile** *nm* **1** dance. **2** *(de etiqueta)* ball. **3** *(sala)* dance hall.

**baja** *nf* **1** *(descenso)* fall, drop. **2** *(por enfermedad)* sick leave.

**bajada** *nf* **1** *(disminución)* drop, fall. **2** *(descenso)* descent; *(de telón, barrera)* lowering. **3** *(camino)* way down. **4** *(en carretera, etc)* slope, hill.

**bajar** *vt* **1** *(coger algo de un lugar alto)* to get down. **2** *(dejar más abajo)* to lower. **3** *(reducir)* to lower, reduce, bring down. **4** *(recorrer de arriba abajo)* to go down. **5** *(en informática)* to download.
▶ *vi* **1** to come down. **2** *(reducirse)* to fall, drop: *ha bajado la temperatura* the temperature has dropped. **3** *(marea)* to go out. **4** *(apearse - de coche)* to get out (de, of); *(de bicicleta, caballo)* to get off (de, -).
▶ *vpr* **bajarse** to come down, to get out (de, -), to get off (de, -).

**bajo,-a** *adj* **1** *(gen)* low: *precios bajos* low prices. **2** *(persona)* short, not tall. **3** *(cabeza)* bowed, held low; *(ojos)* lowered, downcast. **4** *(marea)* out: *la marea está baja* the tide is out. **5** *(época)* late: *la Baja Edad Media* the late Middle Ages.

**bajo** *nm* **1** *(piso)* ground floor, US first floor. **2** *(de prenda)* bottoms *pl*, US cuff. **3** MÚS *(instrumento)* bass; *(contrabajo)* double bass.
▶ *nm o nf* MÚS *(músico)* bass player.
▶ *adv* low, softly, quietly.
▶ *prep* under, below.
▶ *nm pl* **bajos** ground floor;

**bajura** loc **de bajura** inshore.

**bala** *nf* **1** bullet. **2** *(paquete)* bale.

**balada** *nf* ballad.

**balancear** *vt* to rock, swing.
 ▸ *vi* to rock, to swing.
 ▸ *vpr* **balancearse** *(mecerse)* to rock; *(columpio, brazo)* to swing.

**balanceo** *nm* *(gen)* swinging.

**balancín** *nm* **1** *(mecedora)* rocking chair. **2** *(columpio)* seesaw.

**balanza** *nf* *(aparato)* scales *pl*.

**balar** *vi* to bleat, baa.

**balcón** *nm* *(en edificio)* balcony.

**balde** *nm* bucket, pail. [LOC] **de balde** free, for nothing.

**baldío,-a** *adj* uncultivated, barren.
 ▸ *nm* **baldío** wasteland.

**baldosa** *nf* floor tile.

**baldosín** *nm* tile, wall tile.

**balido** *nm* bleat, baa.

**balín** *nm* pellet.

**baliza** *nf* **1** *(de mar)* buoy. **2** *(de tierra)* beacon.

**ballena** *nf* whale.

**ballesta** *nf* *(arma)* crossbow.

**ballet** *nm* ballet.

**balneario,-a** *adj* spa.

**balón** *nm* DEP ball.

**baloncesto** *nm* basketball.

**balonmano** *nm* handball.

**balonvolea** *nm* volleyball.

**balsa** *nf* **1** pool. **2** MAR raft.

**bálsamo** *nm* balsam, balm.

**bambolear** *vi* to sway.
 ▸ *vpr* **bambolearse** to sway.

**bamboleo** *nm* swaying.

**bambú** *nm* bamboo.

**banal** *adj* trivial.

**banana** *nf* banana.

**banca** *nf* **1** COM banking; *(bancos)* (the) banks *pl*. **2** *(en juego)* bank.

**bancada** *nf* **1** *(banco)* long bench. **2** *(superficie)* work surface.

**bancal** *nm* **1** *(en pendiente)* terrace. **2** *(en llano)* plot.

**bancarrota** *nf* bankruptcy. [LOC] **estar en bancarrota** to be bankrupt.

**banco** *nm* **1** bank. **2** *(asiento)* bench; *(de iglesia)* pew. **3** *(mesa)* bench, work bench. **4** *(de peces)* shoal. [COMP] **banco de datos** data bank.

**banda¹** *nf* **1** *(faja)* sash. **2** *(lista)* band. **3** *(tira)* strip. **4** *(lado)* side. **5** *(en billar)* cushion. [COMP] **banda magnética** magnetic strip.

**banda²** *nf* **1** *(músicos)* band. **2** *(maleantes)* gang.

**bandada** *nf* **1** *(de pájaros)* flock; *(de insectos)* swarm; *(de peces)* shoal. **2** *(de personas)* horde.

**bandeja** *nf* *(gen)* tray; *(para diapositivas)* magazine.

**bandera** *nf* flag. [COMP] **bandera nacional** national flag.

**banderilla** *nf* **1** *(tauromaquia)* banderilla *(barbed dart stuck into the bull's back)*. **2** *(tapa)* pickled onion, carrot, gherkin, pepper, etc on a cocktail stick.

**banderín** *nm* pennant.

**bandido,-a** *nm & nf* bandit.

**bando** *nm* **1** *(facción)* faction, party, camp. **2** *(de aves)* flock; *(de insectos)* swarm; *(de peces)* shoal.

**bandolera** *nf* bandolier.

**bandolero** *nm* bandit.

**banjo** *nm* banjo.

**banquero,-a** *nm & nf* banker.

**banqueta** *nf* **1** *(taburete)* stool; *(para los pies)* footstool. **2** *(banco)* little bench.

**banquete** *nm* banquet, feast.

**bañador** *nm* *(gen)* swimsuit; *(de mujer)* swimming costume; *(de hombre)* swimming trunks *pl*.

**bañar** *vt* **1** *(lavar)* to bath: *me baño cada mañana* I have a bath every morning. **2** *(cubrir)* to coat: *bañó los pasteles en chocolate* she coated the cakes in chocolate.
 ▸ *vpr* **bañarse** to bathe; *(nadar)* to have a swim, go for a swim.

**bañera** *nf* bath, bathtub.

**bañista** *nm o nf* bather, swimmer.

**baño** *nm* **1** *(gen)* bath; *(en piscina, mar)* dip, swim. **2** *(cuarto)* bathroom; *(servicio)* toilet. **3** *(bañera)* bath, bathtub.
 ▸ *nm pl* **baños** *(balneario)* spa *sing*.

**bar** *nm* **1** *(cafetería)* café, snack bar; *(de bebidas alcohólicas)* bar. **2** FÍS bar.

**baraja** *nf* *(naipes)* pack, deck.

**barajar** *vt* (*naipes*) to shuffle.

**baranda** *nf* handrail, banister.

**barandilla** *nf* handrail, banister.

**barato,-a** *adj* cheap.
  ▶ *adv* **barato** cheaply, cheap.

**barba** *nf* 1 ANAT chin. 2 (*pelo*) beard.

**barbacoa** *nf* barbecue.

**barbaridad** *nf* 1 (*crueldad - cualidad*) cruelty; (*- acto*) atrocity, act of cruelty. 2 (*disparate*) piece of nonsense.

**barbarismo** *nm* barbarism.

**bárbaro,-a** *adj* 1 HIST barbarian. 2 (*cruel*) barbaric, savage, cruel. 3 *fam* (*espléndido*) fantastic, terrific.
  ▶ *nm & nf* HIST barbarian.
  ▶ *adv* **bárbaro**: *lo pasamos bárbaro* we had a great time.

**barbecho** *nm* fallow land.

**barbería** *nf* barber's shop, barber's.

**barbero** *nm* barber.

**barbilla** *nf* chin.

**barbo** *nm* barbel.

**barca** *nf* boat, small boat.

**barcaza** *nf* lighter.

**barco** *nm* (*gen*) boat; (*grande*) ship.

**bardo** *nm* bard.

**baremo** *nm* 1 (*para calcular*) ready reckoner. 2 (*tarifas*) scale, table.

**barítono** *nm* baritone.

**barman** *nm* barman, US bartender.

**barniz** *nm* (*para madera*) varnish; (*para cerámica*) glaze.

**barnizar** *vt* (*madera*) to varnish; (*cerámica*) to glaze.

**barómetro** *nm* barometer.

**barón** *nm* baron.

**barquero,-a** *nm & nf* (*hombre*) boatman; (*mujer*) boatwoman.

**barquillo** *nm* (*gen*) wafer; (*cucurucho*) cornet.

**barra** *nf* 1 (*en bar, cafetería*) bar. 2 (*vara*) bar; (*para cortinas*) rod; (*de bicicleta*) crossbar. 3 (*de helado*) block. 4 (*de pan*) loaf. COMP **barra de labios** lipstick.

**barrabasada** *nf* dirty trick.

**barraca** *nf* 1 (*casita*) cottage (*typical in Valencia and Murcia*). 2 (*puesto*) stall; (*caseta de feria*) booth. 3 (*chabola*) shack.

**barracón** *nm* hut, large hut.

**barranco** *nm* 1 (*precipicio*) precipice. 2 (*torrentera*) gully; (*más profunda*) ravine.

**barranquismo** *nm* canyoning.

**barrendero,-a** *nm & nf* road sweeper.

**barreno** *nm* 1 (*barrena*) large drill. 2 (*agujero*) drill hole, bore hole.

**barreño** *nm* large bowl.

**barrer** *vt* 1 (*suelo*) to sweep; (*hojas, migas, etc*) to sweep up. 2 (*limpiar*) to sweep away: *el viento barrió las nubes del cielo* the wind swept the clouds from the sky.

**barrera** *nf* 1 (*gen*) barrier. 2 (*en plaza de toros - valla*) barrier; (*- asientos*) front row. 3 *fig* obstacle.

**barricada** *nf* barricade.

**barriga** *nf* belly, stomach, tummy.

**barril** *nm* barrel, keg.

**barrio** *nm* neighbourhood (US neighborhood); (*zona*) district, area.

**barrizal** *nm* quagmire.

**barro** *nm* 1 (*lodo*) mud. 2 (*arcilla*) clay: *objetos de barro* earthenware *sing*. 3 (*objeto*) earthenware object.

**barroco,-a** *adj* 1 ARTE baroque. 2 *fig* ornate.

**barrote** *nm* 1 bar. 2 (*de escalera, silla*) rung.

**barullo** *nm* noise, din, racket.

**basar** *vt* to base (en, on).
  ▶ *vpr* **basarse** (*cosa*) to be based (en, on); (*persona*) to base oneself on.

**báscula** *nf* (*gen*) scales *pl*; (*de farmacia*) weighing machine.

**bascular** *vi* 1 to tilt. 2 (*oscilar*) to swing. 3 (*variar*) to swing, alternate.

**base** *nf* 1 (*gen*) base. 2 *fig* basis. 3 QUÍM base, alkali. 4 MAT base. 5 (*en béisbol*) base. COMP **base de datos** database.
  ▶ *nf pl* **bases** 1 (*de concurso*) rules. 2 **las bases** (*de partido, etc*) grass roots.

**básico,-a** *adj* (*gen*) basic.

**basílica** *nf* basilica.

**basta¹** *nf* tacking stitch.

**basta²** *interj* enough!, stop it!

**bastante** *adj* **1** enough, sufficient. **2** *(abundante)* quite a lot of: *había bastante gente* there were quite a lot of people.
▶ *adv* **1** enough: *son lo bastante ricos como para poder permitírselo* they're rich enough to be able to afford it. **2** *(un poco)* fairly, quite: *es bastante alto* it's fairly high. **3** *(tiempo)* some time, quite a while.

**bastar** *vi* to be enough, be sufficient, suffice: *mi sueldo no basta para pagar el alquiler* my salary is not enough to pay the rent. LOC **bastar con** to be enough: *es muy concentrado, basta con una gota* it's highly concentrated, one drop is enough.

**bastidor** *nm* **1** frame. **2** *(de lienzo)* stretcher. **3** *(de coche)* chassis. **4** TEAT wing.

**basto¹** *nm* ≈ club.
▶ *nm pl* **bastos** ≈ clubs: *el as de bastos* ≈ the ace of clubs.

**basto,-a²** *adj* **1** *(grosero)* coarse, rough. **2** *(sin pulimentar)* rough, unpolished.

**bastón** *nm* **1** stick, walking stick, US cane. **2** *(de esquí)* stick, ski stick.

**basura** *nf* **1** *(cosa)* rubbish, US garbage. **2** *(persona despreciable)* swine. LOC **sacar la basura** to put the rubbish out.

**basurero** *nm* **1** *(persona)* dustman, US garbage man. **2** *(lugar)* tip, rubbish dump.

**bata** *nf* **1** *(prenda ligera)* housecoat; *(albornoz)* dressing gown, US robe. **2** *(de trabajo)* overall; *(de médicos, etc)* white coat.

**batalla** *nf* battle.

**batallar** *vi* to battle, fight.

**batallón** *nm* **1** MIL battalion. **2** *(multitud)* horde.

**batata** *nf* BOT sweet potato.

**bate** *nm* bat.

**batear** *vi* to bat.
▶ *vt* to hit.

**batería** *nf* **1** *(eléctrica)* battery. **2** TEAT footlights *pl*. **3** *(conjunto de cosas)* set; *(de preguntas)* barrage. **4** MÚS drums *pl*.
▶ *nm o nf* drummer. LOC **recargar las baterías** to recharge one's batteries. COMP **batería de cocina** pots and pans *pl*.

**batido,-a** *nm* batido **1** CULIN beaten eggs. **2** *(bebida)* milk shake.

**batidor,-ra** *nm* CULIN *(manual)* whisk.

**batidora** *nf* blender, mixer.

**batir** *vt* **1** *(huevos)* to beat; *(nata, claras)* to whip. **2** *(palmas)* to clap. **3** *(metales)* to beat. **4** *(alas)* to flap, beat. **5** *(derribar)* to knock down. **6** *(vencer)* to beat, defeat. **7** DEP *(marca, récord)* to break.
▶ *vpr* **batirse** to fight.

**batracio,-a** *adj* batrachian.
▶ *nm* batracio batrachian.

**batuta** *nf* baton. LOC **llevar la batuta** to be the boss.

**baúl** *nm* *(cofre)* chest; *(de viaje)* trunk.

**bautismo** *nm* baptism, christening.

**bautizar** *vt* **1** to baptize, christen. **2** *(poner nombre a)* to name.

**bautizo** *nm* baptism, christening.

**bauxita** *nf* bauxite.

**baya** *nf* berry.

**bayeta** *nf* **1** baize. **2** *(paño)* cloth.

**bayo,-a** *adj* bay, whitish yellow.
▶ *nm* bayo *(caballo)* bay.

**baza** *nf* **1** *(naipes)* trick. **2** *(ventaja)* asset, advantage. **3** *(ocasión)* chance. LOC **meter baza** *fig* to butt in, stick one's oar in.

**bazar** *nm* **1** *(oriental)* bazaar. **2** *(tienda)* electrical goods and hardware shop.

**beatificar** *vt* to beatify.

**beato,-a** *adj* **1** *(beatificado)* blessed. **2** *(devoto)* devout. LOC

**bebé** *nm* baby. COMP **bebé probeta** test-tube baby.

**bebedero,-a** *nm* **1** *(abrevadero)* water trough. **2** *(vasija)* drinking dish.

**beber** *vt* to drink.
▶ *vi* **1** to drink. **2** *(emborracharse)* to drink, drink heavily: *bebe mucho* he's a heavy drinker.

**bebida** *nf* drink, beverage.

**beca** *nf* *(gen)* grant; *(concedida por méritos)* scholarship, award.

**becar** *vt* *(gen)* to award a grant to; *(por méritos)* to award a scholarship to.

**becario,-a** *nm & nf* grant holder, scholarship holder.

**becerro,-a** *nm & nf* calf *(up to one year old)*.

**bechamel** *nf* béchamel sauce, white sauce.

**bedel,-la** *nm & nf* porter.

**beduino,-a** *nm & nf* Bedouin.

**begonia** *nf* begonia.

**beicon** *nm* bacon.

**beige** *adj* beige.
► *nm* beige.

**béisbol** *nm* baseball.

**belén** *nm* REL nativity scene, crib.

**belga** *adj* Belgian.
► *nm & nf* Belgian.

**Bélgica** *nf* Belgium.

**Belice** *nm* Belize.

**bélico,-a** *adj* military. COMP **conflicto bélico** armed conflict, war.

**belleza** *nf* beauty.

**bello,-a** *adj* beautiful.

**bellota** *nf* acorn.

**bemol** *adj* MÚS flat.
► *nm* MÚS flat.

**bencina** *nf* benzine.

**bendecir** *vt* to bless.

**bendición** *nf* blessing.
► *nf pl* **bendiciones** wedding ceremony *sing*.

**bendito,-a** *adj* **1** *(bienaventurado)* blessed. **2** *(feliz)* happy: *¡bendita la hora en que la conocí!* happy the hour I met her! **3** *(poco inteligente)* simple.
► *nm & nf* simple soul.

**benefactor,-ra** *adj* beneficent.
► *nm & nf (hombre)* benefactor; *(mujer)* benefactress.

**beneficiar** *vt* **1** to benefit, favour (US favor). **2** *(mina)* to work. **3** COM to sell below par.
► *vpr* **beneficiarse 1** to benefit. **2** COM to profit. LOC **beneficiarse de** ALGO to do well out of STH, benefit from STH.

**beneficiario,-a** *nm & nf* beneficiary.

**beneficio** *nm* **1** *(ganancia)* profit. **2** *(bien)* benefit. LOC **a beneficio de** in aid of.
**❙ sacar beneficio de** to profit from.

**beneficioso,-a** *adj* beneficial.

**benéfico,-a** *adj* charitable. COMP **función benéfica** charity performance.

**benevolencia** *nf* **1** benevolence, kindness. **2** *(comprensión)* understanding.

**benévolo,-a** *adj* **1** benevolent, kind. **2** *(comprensivo)* understanding.

**bengala** *nf (para fiestas, etc)* sparkler.

**benigno,-a** *adj* **1** *(persona)* benign, gentle. **2** *(tumor)* benign. **3** *(clima)* mild.

**benjamín,-ina** *nm & nf (en familia - gen)* youngest child.
► *adj* DEP of the youngest age group (9 or 10 years old).

**berberecho** *nm* cockle, common cockle.

**berenjena** *nf* aubergine, US eggplant.

**berilo** *nm* beryl.

**bermudas** *nm pl* Bermudas, Bermuda shorts.

**berrear** *vi* **1** *(becerro)* to bellow. **2** *(persona)* to bawl; *(niño)* to howl, bawl.

**berrido** *nm* **1** *(de becerro)* bellow. **2** *(de persona)* howl.

**berrinche** *nm* rage, tantrum, anger. LOC **coger un berrinche** to throw a tantrum.

**berro** *nm* watercress.

**berza** *nf* cabbage.

**besamel** *nf* bechamel, white sauce.

**besar** *vt* to kiss.
► *vpr* **besarse** *(uso recíproco)* to kiss.

**beso** *nm* kiss.

**bestia** *nf (animal)* beast.
► *nm o nf (persona - bruto)* brute; *(- ignorante)* ignorant fool; *(- torpe)* clumsy oaf.
► *adj* **1** *(bruto)* brutish. **2** *(ignorante)* ignorant; *(grosero)* rude; *(torpe)* clumsy. **3** *(asombroso)* fantastic, amazing. LOC **a lo bestia 1** *(fuerte)* hard. **2** *(a lo loco)* like a madman. **3** *(en cantidad)* in enormous amounts.

**bestial** *adj* **1** *(brutal)* beastly, bestial. **2** *fam (enorme)* enormous.

**bestiario** *nm* bestiary.

**best-seller** *nm* best-seller.

**besucón,-ona** *adj* fond of kissing.

**besugo** *nm* *(pez)* sea bream.

**besuquear** *vt* to kiss again and again.

**betún** *nm* *(para zapatos)* shoe polish.

**bianual** *adj* biannual.

**biberón** *nm* baby's bottle, bottle.

**Biblia** *nf* Bible.

**bibliografía** *nf* bibliography.

**biblioteca** *nf* **1** library. **2** *(mueble)* bookcase, bookshelf.

**bibliotecario,-a** *nm & nf* librarian.

**bicarbonato** *nm* bicarbonate.

**bicentenario,-a** *nm* bicentenary, US bicentennial.

**bíceps** *nm inv* biceps.

**bicho** *nm* *(animal)* animal, creature; *(insecto)* bug, creepy-crawly.

**bici** *nf fam* bike.

**bicicleta** *nf* bicycle. COMP **bicicleta de carreras** racing bike. ‖ **bicicleta de montaña** mountain bike.

**bicolor** *adj* two-coloured (US two-colored).

**bidé** *nm* bidet.

**bidón** *nm* drum.

**biela** *nf* AUTO connecting rod.

**bien** *adv* **1** *(gen)* well: *canta bien* she sings well. **2** *(como es debido)* properly, right: *si no pronuncias bien, no te van a entender* if you don't pronounce the words properly, they won't understand you. **3** *(acertadamente)* right, correctly: *contestó bien a todas las preguntas* she answered all the questions correctly. **4** *(de acuerdo)* O.K., all right: -*ven mañana a las dos, -bien* -come tomorrow at two, -all right. **5** *(mucho)* very: *es bien sencillo* it's really simple. **6** *(de gusto, olor, aspecto, etc)* good, nice, lovely: *esta cerveza está muy bien* this beer's very good. **7** *(de salud)* well: *¿te encuentras bien?* are you feeling all right? **8** *(físicamente)* good-looking: *su novio está muy bien* her boyfriend's very good-looking. LOC **hacer bien** to do good. ‖ **¡ya está bien!** that's enough!

▶ *nm pl* **bienes** property *sing*, possessions. COMP **bienes inmuebles** real estate *sing*.

▶ *conj* **bien... bien** either... or: *se lo enviaremos bien por correo, bien por mensajero*

we'll send it to you either by post or by messenger.

**bienal** *adj* biennial.

▶ *nf* biennial exhibition, biennial festival.

**bienestar** *nm* wellbeing, welfare: *bienestar social* social welfare.

**bienhechor,-ra** *adj* beneficent, beneficial.

**bienio** *nm* *(periodo)* two-year period, biennium.

**bienvenido,-a** *adj* welcome.

**bífido,-a** *adj* forked.

**bifocal** *adj* bifocal. COMP **gafas bifocales** bifocals.

**bifurcación** *nf* *(de la carretera)* fork; *(de ferrocarril)* junction.

**bigamia** *nf* bigamy.

**bigote** *nm* **1** moustache (US mustache). **2** *(de gato)* whiskers *pl*.

**bigotudo,-a** *adj* mustachioed.

**bikini®** *nm* → biquini®.

**bilabial** *adj* bilabial.

**bilateral** *adj* bilateral.

**biliar** *adj* biliary, bile.

**bilingüe** *adj* bilingual.

**bilingüismo** *nm* bilingualism.

**bilis** *nf inv* **1** bile. **2** *fig* spleen.

**billar** *nm* **1** billiards. **2** *(mesa)* billiard table. COMP **billar americano** pool.

▶ *nm pl* **billares** billiard room.

**billete** *nm* **1** *(moneda)* note, US bill: *un billete de cincuenta euros* a fifty-euro note. **2** *(de transporte, sorteo, teatro, etc)* ticket. COMP **billete de ida y vuelta** return ticket, US round-trip ticket.

**billetera** *nf* wallet, US billfold.

**billetero** *nm* purse, US change purse.

**billón** *nm* trillion.

✎ El uso español coincide con el antiguo significado británico en el que un billion era a million million.

**binario,-a** *adj* binary.

**bingo** *nm* **1** *(juego)* bingo. **2** *(sala)* bingo hall. LOC **¡bingo!** bingo!

**binóculo** *nm* pince-nez.

**binomio** *nm* binomial.

**biodegradable** *adj* biodegradable.

**biografía** *nf* biography.

**biográfico,-a** *adj* biographical.

**biógrafo,-a** *nm & nf* biographer.

**biología** *nf* biology.

**biológico,-a** *adj* biological.

**biólogo,-a** *nm & nf* biologist.

**biomasa** *nf* biomass.

**biombo** *nm* screen, folding screen.

**biopsia** *nf* biopsy.

**bioquímica** *nf* biochemistry.

**biosfera** *nf* biosphere.

**bióxido** *nm* dioxide.

**bípedo,-a** *adj* biped.

**biplaza** *nm* two-seater.

**bipolar** *adj* bipolar.

**biquini** *nm (traje de baño)* bikini.

**Birmania** *nf* Burma.

**birria** *nf* rubbish.

**bis** *adv* **1** *(en dirección):* viven en el 23 bis they live at 23A. **2** MÚS repeat, bis.

**bisabuelo,-a** *nm & nf* great-grandparent; *(hombre)* great-grandfather; *(mujer)* great-grandmother.

**bisagra** *nf* hinge.

**biscote** *nm* piece of Melba toast.

**bisección** *nf* bisection.

**bisectriz** *nf* bisector.

**bisel** *nm* bevel.

**biselado,-a** *adj* bevelled (US beveled).

**bisiesto** *adj* leap. COMP **año bisiesto** leap year.

**bisílabo,-a** *adj* two-syllabled.

**bismuto** *nm* bismuth.

**bisnieto,-a** *nm & nf* great-grandchild; *(chico)* great-grandson; *(chica)* great-granddaughter.

**bisonte** *nm* bison.

**bistec** *nm* steak.

**bisturí** *nm* scalpel.

**bisutería** *nf* costume jewellery (US jewelry).

**bit** *nm* bit.

**biunívoco,-a** *adj* one-to-one.

**bivalente** *adj* bivalent.

**bivalvo,-a** *adj* bivalve, bivalvular.

**bizco,-a** *adj* cross-eyed.

**bizcocho** *nm* sponge, sponge cake.

**biznieto,-a** *nm & nf* → bisnieto,-a.

**bizquear** *vi* to squint, be cross-eyed.

**blanco,-a** *adj* white.
► *nm & nf (gen)* white; *(hombre)* white man; *(mujer)* white woman.
► *nm* **blanco 1** *(color)* white. **2** *(objetivo)* target, mark. **3** *fig* object: *fue el blanco de todas sus críticas* he was the target of all their criticism. **4** *(hueco)* blank, gap; *(en escrito)* blank space. **5** *(vino)* white wine.

**blancura** *nf* whiteness.

**blando,-a** *adj (gen)* soft.

**blandura** *nf* softness.

**blanquear** *vt* **1** to whiten, make white. **2** *(con cal)* to whitewash. **3** *(con lejía)* to bleach.
► *vi* to whiten, turn white.

**blanquecino,-a** *adj* whitish, off-white.

**blanqueo** *nm* **1** whitening. **2** *(con cal)* whitewashing.

**bledo** *nm* common amaranth. LOC **me importa un bledo** *fam* I don't care less, I couldn't give a damn.

**blindado,-a** *adj* armoured (US armored). COMP **puerta blindada** reinforced door.

**blindaje** *nm* **1** armour (US armor), armour-plating (US armor-plating). **2** *(de puerta)* reinforcing.

**blindar** *vt* **1** to armour-plate (US armor-plate). **2** *(puerta)* to reinforce.

**bloc** *nm* notepad, pad.

**bloque** *nm* **1** block. **2** *(papel)* pad, notepad. LOC **en bloque** en bloc.

**bloquear** *vt (gen)* to block: *esto podría bloquear el proceso de paz* this could block the peace process.
► *vpr* **bloquearse** *(persona)* to have a mental block.

**bloqueo** *nm* **1** *(gen)* blocking. **2** MIL blockade. **3** *(precios, cuenta)* freezing.

**blues** *nm inv* blues.

**blusa** *nf* blouse.

**boa** *nf (serpiente)* boa.

**bobada** *nf* silliness, foolishness. LOC **decir bobadas** to talk nonsense.

**bobina** *nf* **1** reel, bobbin. **2** ELEC coil.

**bobo,-a** *adj* silly, foolish.
▶ *nm & nf* fool.

**boca** *nf* **1** ANAT mouth. **2** *(abertura)* entrance, opening: *hay una boca de metro en la esquina* there's an entrance to the underground on the corner. LOC **boca abajo** face downwards. ‖ **callarse la boca** to shut up, shut one's mouth. COMP **boca a boca** kiss of life.

**bocacalle** *nf* entrance to a street.

**bocadillo** *nm* sandwich.

**bocado** *nm* **1** mouthful. **2** *(piscolabis)* snack, bite to eat. **3** *(mordedura)* bite.

**bocajarro** LOC **a bocajarro 1** *(disparar)* at point-blank range. **2** *(decir algo)* point-blank.

**bocata** *nm fam* sandwich, sarnie.

**boceto** *nm* sketch; *(proyecto)* outline.

**bochorno** *nm* **1** *(calor)* sultry weather, close weather; *(viento)* hot wind. **2** *fig (rubor)* embarrassment, shame.

**bochornoso,-a** *adj* **1** *(sofocante)* hot, sultry. **2** *fig (vergonzoso)* disgraceful, shameful.

**bocina** *nf* horn.

**boda** *nf* marriage, wedding.

**bodega** *nf* **1** *(almacén)* wine cellar. **2** *(tienda)* wine shop. **3** *(de barco)* hold.

**bodegón** *nm* still life.

**body** *nm* body.

**bofetada** *nf* slap, slap in the face.

**bofetón** *nm* hard slap.

**boga** *nf* vogue.

**bogavante** *nm* lobster.

**bohemio,-a** *adj (vida, etc)* bohemian.
▶ *nm & nf (artista, etc)* bohemian.

**boicot** *nm (no participación)* boycott.

**boicotear** *vt (no participar)* to boycott.

**boina** *nf* beret.

**boj** *nm* **1** *(árbol)* box tree. **2** *(madera)* boxwood.

**bol** *nm* bowl.

**bola** *nf* **1** *(gen)* ball. **2** *fam* fib, lie.

**bolera** *nf* bowling alley.

**boletín** *nm* **1** *(revista)* periodical. **2** *(de noticias)* bulletin, news bulletin. **3** *(impreso)* form. **4** *(de colegio)* report.

**boleto** *nm* **1** ticket. **2** *(quiniela)* coupon.

**boli** *nm fam* ballpen, biro.

**bólido** *nm fam (coche)* racing car.

**bolígrafo** *nm* ballpoint pen.

**bolívar** *nm* bolivar *(monetary unit of Venezuela)*.

**Bolivia** *nf* Bolivia.

**boliviano,-a** *adj* Bolivian.
▶ *nm & nf* Bolivian.

**bollo** *nm* **1** *(dulce)* pastry, bun. **2** *(abolladura)* dent.

**bolo** *nm* skittle, ninepin.
▶ *nm pl* **bolos** skittles.

**bolsa¹** *nf (gen)* bag: *¿tiene una bolsa de plástico?* have you got a plastic bag? COMP **bolsa de aseo** toilet bag. ‖ **bolsa de deportes** sports bag.

**bolsa²** *nf* stock exchange.

**bolsillo** *nm* pocket. LOC **de bolsillo** pocket: *una calculadora de bolsillo* a pocket calculator.

**bolso** *nm* handbag, US purse.

**bomba** *nf* **1** *(explosivo)* bomb. **2** *(noticia)* bombshell. **3** pump. LOC **pasarlo bomba** to have a whale of a time.

**bombardear** *vt* **1** *(desde el aire)* to bomb. **2** *fig* to bombard: *me bombardearon a preguntas* they bombarded me with questions.

**bombardeo** *nm (desde el aire)* bombing.

**bombardero** *nm* bomber.

**bombear** *vt (agua)* to pump.

**bombero,-a** *nm (gen)* firefighter; *(hombre)* fireman; *(mujer)* firewoman.

**bombilla** *nf* light bulb, bulb.

**bombín** *nm (sombrero)* bowler hat.

**bombo** *nm (tambor)* bass drum.

**bombón** *nm* chocolate.

**bombona** *nf* cylinder. COMP **bombona de butano** butane cylinder.

**bonachón,-ona** *adj* kind.

**bondad** *nf* kindness.

**bondadoso,-a** *adj* kind, good.

**boniato** *nm* sweet potato.

**bonito** *nm (pez)* bonito.

**bonito,-a** *adj* lovely, nice.

**bono** *nm* **1** *(vale)* voucher. **2** *(billete)* ticket.

**bonobús** *nm* multiple-journey bus ticket.

**bonoloto** *nm* Spanish state-run lottery.

**boñiga** *nf* cow dung.

**boquerón** *nm* *(pez)* anchovy.

**boquete** *nm* hole.

**boquiabierto,-a** *adj* open-mouthed, agape.

**boquilla** *nf* **1** *(de pipa, instrumento)* mouthpiece. **2** *(filtro de cigarrillo)* tip.

**borbotear** *vi* to bubble.

**borbotón** *nm* bubbling.

**bordado,-a** *nm* embroidery.

**bordar** *vt* to embroider.

**borde¹** *adj* *(antipático)* unpleasant.

**borde²** *nm* **1** *(extremo)* edge. **2** *(de vaso, taza)* rim.

**bordear** *vt* to skirt, go round.

**bordillo** *nm* kerb, US curb.

**bordo** *nm* MAR board. LOC **a bordo** on board.

**boreal** *adj* boreal, northern.

**bórico,-a** *adj* boric.

**borla** *nf* tassel.

**borrachera** *nf* drunken state.

**borracho,-a** *adj* *(persona)* drunk.
▶ *nm & nf* drunkard, drunk.

**borrador** *nm*. **1** *(de pizarra)* duster. **2** *(goma)* eraser, GB rubber.

**borrar** *vt* **1** to erase, rub out. **2** INFORM to delete.

**borrasca** *nf* *(tormenta)* storm.

**borrego,-a** *nm & nf* lamb.

**borrón** *nm* blot, ink blot.

**borroso,-a** *adj* *(visión)* blurred, hazy.

**Bosnia** *nf* Bosnia. COMP **Bosnia-Herze-govina** Bosnia Herzegovina.

**bosnio,-a** *adj* Bosnian.
▶ *nm & nf* Bosnian.

**bosque** *nm* wood, forest.

**bosquejar** *vt* to sketch, outline.

**bosquejo** *nm* *(dibujo)* sketch; *(plan, etc)* outline.

**bostezar** *vi* to yawn.

**bostezo** *nm* yawn.

**bota¹** *nf* boot. COMP **botas de agua** gum boots, US rubber boots.

**bota²** *nf* *(de vino)* wineskin.

**botánico,-a** *adj* botanical.

**botar** *vi* **1** *(pelota)* to bounce. **2** *(persona)* to jump, jump up and down.

**bote¹** *nm* MAR small boat. COMP **bote salvavidas** lifeboat.

**bote²** *nm* *(salto)* bounce.

**bote³** *nm* **1** *(lata)* tin, can. **2** *(tarro)* jar. **3** *(para propinas)* jar for tips, box for tips. **4** *(fondo)* kitty.

**botella** *nf* **1** bottle. **2** *(de gas)* cylinder.

**botellín** *nm* small bottle.

**botijo** *nm* earthenware jar *(with spout and handle for drinking)*.

**botín¹** *nm* *(zapato)* ankle boot.

**botín²** *nm* **1** *(de guerra)* spoils *pl*, booty. **2** *(de robo)* haul.

**botiquín** *nm* first-aid kit.

**botón** *nm* *(gen)* button.

**bóveda** *nf* vault.

**boxeador,-ra** *nm & nf* boxer.

**boxear** *vi* to box.

**boxeo** *nm* boxing.

**bóxer** *nm* *(perro)* boxer.

**boya** *nf* **1** MAR buoy. **2** *(corcho)* float.

**boyante** *adj* *fig* prosperous.

**bozal** *nm* muzzle.

**bracear** *vi* *(nadar)* to swim.

**braga** *nf* *(prenda)* panties *pl*, knickers *pl*.

**bragueta** *nf* fly, flies *pl*.

**braille** *nm* Braille.

**bramar** *vi* to bellow.

**branquia** *nf* gill.

**brasa** *nf* ember, live coal.

**brasero** *nm* brazier.

**Brasil** *nm* Brazil.

**brasileño,-a** *adj* Brazilian.
▶ *nm & nf* Brazilian.

**bravío,-a** *adj* *(animal)* wild, fierce.

**bravo,-a** *adj* *(fiero)* fierce, ferocious.
▶ *interj* ¡bravo! well done!, bravo!

**bravura** *nf* *(fiereza)* fierceness.

**braza** *nf* *(natación)* breaststroke.

**brazada** *nf* *(natación)* stroke.

**brazalete** *nm* bracelet, bangle.

**brazo** *nm* *(de persona)* arm.
▶ *nm pl* **brazos** hands, workers.

**brea** *nf* tar, pitch.

**brebaje** *nm* brew, potion.

**brecha** *nf* **1** break, opening. **2** *fig* breach.

**breve** *adj* short, brief. LOC **en breve** soon, shortly.

**brevedad** *nf* brevity, briefness.

**brezo** *nm* heather, heath.

**bricolaje** *nm* do-it-yourself, DIY.

**brida** *nf* *(de caballo)* bridle.

**bridge** *nm* bridge.

**brigada** *nf* *(unidad militar)* brigade.

**brillante** *adj* **1** *(extraordinario)* brilliant: *un alumno brillante* a brilliant student. **2** *(pelo, metal, zapatos)* shiny; *(ojos)* sparkling; *(luz, color)* bright; *(pintura)* gloss.
▶ *nm (diamante)* diamond.

**brillantina** *nf* brilliantine.

**brillar** *vi* **1** *(luz, sol, luna, pelo, zapatos)* to shine. **2** *(ojos)* to sparkle; *(estrella)* to twinkle; *(metal, dientes)* to gleam; *(cosa húmeda)* to glisten. **3** *fig* to be outstanding.

**brillo** *nm* **1** *(gen)* shine. **2** *(de estrella)* twinkling; *(de ojos)* sparkle; *(de pelo, zapatos)* shine. **3** *(en televisor)* brightness.

**brincar** *vi* *(cabra, etc)* to skip; *(persona)* to leap, bound.

**brinco** *nm (de cabra)* skip, hop; *(de persona)* leap, bound.

**brindar** *vi* to toast (por, to), drink (por, to): *¡brindemos por el futuro!* let's drink to the future!
▶ *vt (ofrecer)* to offer, provide.
▶ *vpr* **brindarse** to offer (a, to), volunteer (a, to).

**brindis** *nm inv* toast.

**brisa** *nf* breeze.

**británico,-a** *adj* British.
▶ *nm & nf* British person, Briton, Britisher.

**brizna** *nf (gen)* bit; *(de hierba)* blade.

**broca** *nf (barrena)* drill, bit.

**brocha** *nf* brush, paintbrush.

**brochazo** *nf* brushstroke.

**broche** *nm* **1** *(cierre)* fastener. **2** *(joya)* brooch.

**broma** *nf* joke: *no es broma* It's not a joke.

**bromear** *vi* to joke.

**bromista** *nm o nf* joker.

**bronca** *nf* **1** *(lío)* row. **2** *(riña)* quarrel; *(discusión)* argument. **3** *(reprimenda)* telling-off.

**bronce** *nm* bronze.

**bronceado,-a** *adj* bronzed.
▶ *nm* **bronceado** tan, suntan.

**bronceador,-ra** *nm* suntan lotion.

**broncear** *vt (persona)* to tan, suntan.
▶ *vpr* **broncearse** to tan, get a tan.

**bronquio** *nm* bronchus.

**bronquitis** *nf inv* bronchitis.

**brotar** *vi (plantas - nacer)* to sprout; *(- echar brotes)* to come into bud.

**brote** *nm* shoot, sprout.

**broza** *nf* **1** *(hojas)* dead leaves; *(ramitas)* dead twigs. **2** *(maleza)* scrub, brush.

**bruces** LOC **caerse de bruces** to fall flat on one's face.

**bruja** *nf (hechicera)* witch.

**brujería** *nf* witchcraft, sorcery.

**brujo,-a** *nm* wizard, sorcerer.

**brújula** *nf* compass.

**bruma** *nf* mist.

**bruñido,-a** *adj* burnished.

**brusco,-a** *adj* **1** *(repentino)* sudden. **2** *(persona)* abrupt.

**brusquedad** *nf* **1** *(de carácter)* abruptness. **2** *(rapidez)* suddenness.

**brutal** *adj (cruel)* brutal, savage.

**brutalidad** *nf (crueldad)* brutality.

**bruto,-a** *adj* **1** *(cruel)* brutal. **2** *(necio)* stupid, thick. **3** *(tosco)* rough, coarse.
▶ *nm & nf (persona - violenta)* brute, beast; *(necio)* ignoramus.

**bucal** *adj* oral, mouth.

**bucanero** *nm* buccaneer.

**bucear** *vi* to dive.

**bucle** *nm* **1** curl. **2** INFORM loop.

**bucólico,-a** *adj* bucolic.

**budismo** *nm* Buddhism.

**budista** *adj* Buddhist.
▶ *nm o nf* Buddhist.

**buen** *adj* → bueno,-a.

**bueno,-a** *adj* **1** *(gen)* good. **2** *(persona - amable)* kind; *(- agradable)* nice. **3** *(tiempo)* good, nice. **4** *(apropiado)* right, suitable. **5** *(de salud)* well.
▸ *interj* **¡bueno!** *(sorpresa)* well, very well; *(de acuerdo)* all right!

**buey** *nm* ox, bullock.

**búfalo** *nm* buffalo.

**bufanda** *nf* scarf.

**bufar** *vi (toro)* to snort.

**bufé** *nm* buffet.

**bufete** *nm (de abogado)* lawyer's office.

**bufido** *nm* snort.

**bufón,-ona** *nm & nf* buffoon, jester.

**buhardilla** *nf* attic.

**búho** *nm* owl.

**buitre** *nm* vulture.

**bujía** *nf (de motor)* spark plug.

**bulbo** *nm* bulb.

**bulevar** *nm* boulevard.

**Bulgaria** *nf* Bulgaria.

**búlgaro,-a** *adj* Bulgarian.
▸ *nm & nf (persona)* Bulgarian.
▸ *nm* **búlgaro** *(idioma)* Bulgarian.

**bulldozer** *nm* bulldozer.

**bullicio** *nm* **1** *(ruido)* noise, racket. **2** *(tumulto)* bustle, hustle and bustle.

**bullicioso,-a** *adj (ruidoso)* noisy.

**bulto** *nm* **1** *(tamaño)* volume, size, bulk. **2** *(forma)* shape, form. **3** *(abultamiento - en cosa)* bulge; *(- en piel)* lump.

**bum** *interj* boom!

**bumerán** *nm* boomerang.

**bungalow** *nm* bungalow.

**búnker** *nm* bunker.

**buñuelo** *nm* fritter.

**BUP** *abrev* EDUC (Bachillerato Unificado Polivalente) former General Certificate of Secondary Education studies.

**buque** *nm* MAR ship, vessel.

**burbuja** *nf* bubble. LOC **con burbujas** *(bebida)* fizzy.

**burbujear** *vi* to bubble.

**burdo,-a** *adj* **1** *(tejido)* coarse, rough. **2** *(persona)* coarse, crude.

**burgués,-esa** *nm & nf* middle-class.

**burguesía** *nf* middle class.

**burla** *nf* **1** *(mofa)* mockery, gibe. **2** *(broma)* joke. **3** *(engaño)* deception, trick.

**burlar** *vt* **1** to deceive, trick. **2** *(eludir)* to dodge, evade.
▸ *vpr* **burlarse** to mock (de, -), make fun (de, of), laugh (de, at).

**burlón,-ona** *nm & nf* joker.

**burocracia** *nf* bureaucracy.

**burócrata** *nm o nf* bureaucrat.

**burrada** *nf* **1** drove of asses. **2** *fam* a lot: *me gusta una burrada* I love it.

**burro,-a** *adj* stupid.
▸ *nm & nf* **1** *(animal)* donkey, ass. **2** *(persona ignorante)* ass.

**bus** *nm* **1** AUTO bus. **2** INFORM bus.

**busca** *nf* search, hunt.

**buscapersonas** *nm* bleeper, pager.

**buscar** *vt* **1** *(gen)* to look for, search for. **2** *(en lista, índice, etc)* to look up: *búscalo en el diccionario* look it up in the dictionary. **3** *(ir a coger)* to go and get, fetch. **4** *(recoger)* to pick up.

**búsqueda** *nf* search.

**busto** *nm (figura)* bust.

**butaca** *nf (sillón)* armchair.

**butacón** *nm* easy chair.

**butano** *nm* butane.

**buzo** *nm* diver.

**buzón** *nm* letter box, US mailbox.

**byte** *nm* INFORM byte.

**C**

**C, c** *nf (la letra)* C, c.

**C¹** *sím* (Celsius) Celsius; *(símbolo)* C.

**C²** *sím* (centígrado) centigrade; *(símbolo)* C.

**cabal** *adj* **1** *(exacto)* exact, precise. **2** *fig (persona)* honest, upright.

**cábala** *nf* **1** *(ciencia oculta)* cabala, cabbala. **2** [en este sentido, también se usa en plural con el mismo significado] *fig (conjetura)* guess, divination. **3** *fig (intriga)* plot.

**cabalgar** *vi* to ride **(en/sobre, -).**

**cabalgata** *nf* cavalcade.

**caballa** *nf* mackerel.

**caballería** *nf* **1** MIL cavalry. **2** HIST knighthood.

**caballero,-a** *nm* **1** gentleman, sir. **2** HIST knight.

**caballete** *nm* easel.

**caballito** *nm* small horse. COMP **caballito de mar** sea horse.

▸ *nm pl* **caballitos** *(tiovivo)* merry-go-round *sing*, US carrousel *sing*.

**caballo** *nm* **1** ZOOL horse. **2** *(ajedrez)* knight.

**cabaña** *nf (choza)* cabin, hut, shack.

**cabecear** *vi* **1** to move one's head, shake one's head. **2** *(dar cabezadas)* to nod.

**cabecera** *nf* **1** *(gen)* top, head. **2** *(de un periódico)* headline.

**cabecilla** *nm o nf* leader.

**cabellera** *nf* hair, head of hair.

**cabello** *nm* hair.

**caber** *vi* **1** *(encajar)* to fit **(en, into):** *cabe ahí arriba* it'll fit up there. **2** *(pasar)* to fit, go. **3** MAT to go: *ocho entre dos caben a cuatro* two into eight goes four times, eight divided by two is four.

**cabeza** *nf* **1** *(gen)* head: *diez mil por cabeza* ten thousand a head. **2** *fig (juicio)* good judgement; *(talento)* talent, intelligence. LOC **cabeza abajo** upside down. ‖ **estar mal de la cabeza** *fig* not to be right in the head. ‖ **meterse** ALGO **en la cabeza** *fam* to get STH into one's head. COMP **cabeza cuadrada** *fam* bigot. ‖ **cabeza de ajo** bulb of garlic. ‖ **cabeza rapada** skinhead.

**cabezada** *nf (golpe recibido)* blow on the head; *(golpe dado)* butt, head butt. LOC **dar cabezadas** *fam* to nod.

**cabezal** *nm* TÉC head, headstock.

**cabina** *nf (gen)* cabin, booth. COMP **cabina telefónica** telephone box, US telephone booth.

**cable** *nm (maroma)* cable.

**cabo** *nm* **1** *(extremo)* end, stub. **2** *fig* end: *al cabo de un mes* in a month's time. **3** *(cuerda)* rope, line. **4** GEOG cape. LOC **al cabo** finally. ‖ **llevar a cabo** to carry out.

**cabra** *nf* goat. LOC **estar como una cabra** *fam* to be off one's rocker, be nuts.

**cabrito** *nm* ZOOL kid.

**caca** *nf* **1** *fam euf (excremento)* pooh. **2** *fam (en lenguaje infantil)* dirt.

**cacahuete** *nm (fruto)* peanut.

**cacao** *nm* **1** BOT cacao. **2** *(polvo, bebida)* cocoa. **3** *fam (jaleo)* mess, cockup.

**cacarear** *vi (gallina)* to cluck; *(gallo)* to crow.

**cacatúa** *nf (ave)* cockatoo.

**cacería** *nf* hunting, hunt.

**cacerola** *nf* saucepan, casserole.

**cachalote** *nm* sperm whale.

**cacharro** *nm* **1** *(de cocina)* crock, piece of crockery. **2** *fam (cosa)* piece of junk. **3** *fam pey (coche)* banger.

**cachemira** *nf (tejido)* cashmere.

**cachete** *nm (bofetada)* slap.

**cacho** *nm fam* bit, piece.

**cachorro,-a** *nm & nf (de perro)* pup, puppy; *(de gato)* kitten; *(de león, oso, zorro, tigre)* cub; *(de otros mamíferos)* young.

**cacique** *nm* **1** *(jefe indio)* chief, cacique. **2** POL local political boss.

**caco** *nm fam* thief.

**cacto** *nm* cactus.

**cada** *adj* **1** *(de dos)* each; *(de varios)* every. **2** *fam (intensificador)* such: *¡dice cada cosa!* he says such strange things! LOC **cada día** every day.

**cadáver** *nm* corpse, cadaver, body, dead body.

**cadena** *nf* **1** *(gen)* chain; *(de perro)* leash, lead. **2** *(montañosa)* range. **3** *(musical)* music centre (US center). **4** TV channel. **5** RAD chain of stations. COMP **trabajo en cadena** assembly-line work.

**cadera** *nf* hip.

**caducar** *vi* **1** *(documento, etc)* to expire: *mi pasaporte caduca este año* my passport expires this year. **2** *(alimento)* to pass its sell-by date.

**caducidad** *nf* expiry.

**caer** *vi* **1** *(gen)* to fall: *caer de espalda* to fall on one's back. **2** *(derrumbar)* to fall down, collapse. **3** *(hallarse)* to be: *el camino cae a la derecha* the road is on the right. **4** *(coincidir fechas)* to fall on, be: *el día cuatro cae en jueves* the fourth falls on a Thursday. LOC **dejar caer** to drop: *dejé caer el vaso* I dropped the glass.
► *vpr* **caerse 1** *(gen)* to fall, fall down. **2** *(desprenderse)* to fall out: *se le cae el pelo* he's losing his hair. LOC **caerse de sueño** *fig* to be dead on one's feet, be ready to drop.

**café** *nm* **1** *(gen)* coffee. **2** *(cafetería)* café, coffee bar, coffee shop. COMP **café con leche** white coffee.

**cafeína** *nf* caffeine.

**cafetera** *nf* **1** *(para hacer café)* coffee-maker. **2** *(para servir café)* coffeepot.

**cafetería** *nf (gen)* snack bar, coffee bar.

**caimán** *nm* alligator, cayman.

**caja** *nf* **1** *(gen)* box. **2** *(de madera)* chest; *(grande)* crate. **3** *(de bebidas)* case. **4** *(en comercio)* cash desk, till; *(en banco)* cashier's desk; *(en supermercado)* checkout. **5** *(banco)* bank: *caja de ahorros* savings bank. COMP **caja registradora** cash register.

**cajero,-a** *nm & nf* cashier. COMP **cajero automático** cash point, automatic cash dispenser.

**cajetilla** *nf* **1** *(de tabaco)* packet, US pack. **2** *(de cerillas)* box.

**cajón** *nm* **1** *(en mueble)* drawer. **2** *(caja grande)* crate.

**cal** *nf* lime. COMP **cal viva** quicklime.

**cala** *nf* **1** *(ensenada)* cove, creek. **2** *(planta)* arum lily.

**calabacín** *nm* **1** *(pequeño)* courgette, US zucchini. **2** *(grande)* marrow, US squash.

**calabaza** *nf* gourd, pumpkin.

**calabozo** *nm* **1** *(prisión)* jail, prison. **2** *(celda)* cell.

**calamar** *nm* squid.

**calambre** *nm* **1** *(contracción)* cramp. **2** *(descarga eléctrica)* electric shock.

**calamidad** *nf (desgracia)* calamity, disaster.

**calar** *vt (mojar)* to soak through, soak, drench.
► *vpr* **calarse 1** *(mojarse)* to get soaked. **2** AUTO to stop, stall.

**calavera** *nf (cabeza del esqueleto)* skull.

**calcetín** *nm* sock.

**cálcico,-a** *adj* calcium, calcic.

**calcinar** *vt* **1** to calcine. **2** *fig* to burn.

**calcio** *nm* calcium.

**calcita** *nf* calcite.

**calcomanía** *nf* transfer.

**calculador,-ra** *adj* calculating.
► *nm & nf* calculator. COMP **calculadora de bolsillo** pocket calculator.

**calcular** *vt* **1** to calculate, work out: *calcular una suma* to calculate a figure. **2** *(suponer)* to think, suppose, figure, guess.

**cálculo** *nm* calculation, estimate.

**caldera** *nf* boiler.

**calderilla** *nf* small change.

**caldo** *nm* **1** CULIN stock, broth. **2** *(sopa)* consommé.

**calefacción** *nf* heating. COMP **calefacción central** central heating.

**calefactor** *nm (máquina)* heater.

**calendario** *nm* calendar. COMP **calendario académico** school year.

**calentador,-ra** *nm* heater.

**calentar** *vt* **1** *(comida, habitación, cuerpo)* to warm up; *(agua, horno)* to heat. **2** DEP to warm up, tone up.

**calibre** *nm* **1** *(de arma)* calibre. **2** *fig (importancia)* importance.

**calidad** *nf* **1** quality. **2** *(cualidad)* kind, types. LOC **de primera calidad** first-class.

**cálido,-a** *adj* warm: *un clima cálido* a warm climate.

**caliente** *adj (mayor intensidad)* hot; *(menor intensidad)* warm.

**calificación** *nf (nota)* mark.

**calificar** *vt* **1** *(determinar las cualidades)* to describe, qualify. **2** EDUC to mark, grade.

**caligrafía** *nf* **1** *(arte)* calligraphy. **2** *(escritura de una persona)* handwriting. COMP **ejercicios de caligrafía** handwriting exercises.

**cáliz** *nm* **1** REL chalice. **2** BOT calyx. **3** *lit (copa)* cup.

**caliza** *nf* limestone.

**callar** *vi (no hablar)* to be quiet, keep quiet. LOC **¡cállate!** keep quiet!, be quiet!

**calle** *nf* **1** street, road. **2** DEP lane. LOC **dejar a** ALGN **en la calle 1** *(sin trabajo)* to fire SB. **2** *(sin casa)* to leave SB homeless.

**callejero,-a** *adj (que gusta de callejear)* fond of wandering about.
  ▶ *nm* **callejero** *(de calles)* street directory.

**callo** *nm* MED callus, corn.

**calma** *nf* calmness, calm, tranquillity (US tranquility). LOC **tomárselo con calma** to take it easy.

**calmante** *adj* soothing, sedative, tranquillizing (US tranquilizing).

**calmar** *vt* **1** *(persona)* to calm (down). **2** *(dolor)* to relieve, soothe.
  ▶ *vpr* **calmarse 1** *(persona)* to calm down. **2** *(dolor, etc)* to abate, ease off.

**calor** *nm* heat, warmth: *hace calor* it is hot.

**caloría** *nf* calorie.

**caluroso,-a** *adj* **1** *(tiempo)* warm, hot. **2** *fig* warm, enthusiastic.

**calva** *nf* **1** *(de la cabeza)* bald patch. **2** *(de un bosque)* clearing.

**calvo,-a** *adj (persona)* bald.

**calzada** *nf* road, US pavement.

**calzado** *nm* footwear, shoes *pl*.

**calzar** *vt* **1** *(poner calzado)* to put shoes on. **2** *(llevar calzado)* to wear: *¿qué número calzas?* what size do you take?
  ▶ *vpr* **calzarse** *(forma reflexiva)* to put (one's shoes) on.

**calzoncillos** *nm pl* pants.

**cama** *nf (gen)* bed. LOC **guardar cama** to be confined to bed, stay in bed. ▎ **hacer la cama** to make the bed. ▎ **irse a la cama** to go to bed. COMP **cama de matrimonio** double bed. ▎ **cama individual** single bed.

**camada** *nf (gen)* litter.

**camaleón** *nm* chameleon.

**cámara** *nf* **1** *(de parlamento)* house. **2** *(de rueda)* inner tube. **3** TÉC chamber. **4** *(fotográfica, de cine)* camera. **5** ANAT cavity. COMP **cámara alta** POL upper house. ▎ **cámara baja** POL lower house. ▎ **cámara de aire** air chamber. ▎ **cámara de cine** cine camera, (US movie camera).
  ▶ *nm o nf (hombre)* cameraman; *(mujer)* camerawoman.

**camarero,-a** *nm & nf (de bar, restaurante - hombre)* waiter; *(mujer)* waitress.

**camarón** *nm* common prawn.

**camarote** *nm* cabin.

**cambiar** *vt* **1** *(gen)* to change: *han cambiado las sillas* the chairs have been changed. **2** *(intercambiar)* to exchange. **3** *(moneda extranjera)* to change, exchange.

▶ *vi* **1** *(gen)* to change: *has cambiado mucho* you have changed a lot.
▶ *vpr* **cambiarse 1** *(mudarse de ropa)* to change, get changed. **2** *(mudarse de casa)* to move.

**cambio** *nm* **1** change, changing. **2** *(intercambio)* exchange, exchanging. LOC **a cambio de** in exchange for. ▌ **en cambio** on the other hand, but, whereas.

**camelia** *nf* camellia.

**camello** *nm* ZOOL camel.

**camerino** *nm* dressing room.

**camilla** *nf* *(para enfermos)* stretcher.

**caminar** *vi* *(andar)* to walk.
▶ *vt* *(recorrer)* to cover, travel: *he caminado cinco kilómetros* I have covered five kilometres.

**caminata** *nf* long walk, trek.

**camino** *nm* **1** *(vía)* path, track. **2** *(ruta)* way, route. LOC **ir camino de** to be on one's way to. ▌ **ponerse en camino** to set off (on a journey).

**camión** *nm* lorry, US truck. COMP **camión de mudanzas** removal van.

**camionero,-a** *nm & nf* lorry driver, US truck driver.

**camioneta** *nf* van.

**camisa** *nf* shirt.

**camiseta** *nf* **1** *(ropa interior)* vest, US undershirt. **2** *(niqui)* T-shirt. **3** DEP shirt, jersey.

**camisón** *nm* nightdress, nightie.

**campamento** *nm* **1** *(acción de acampar)* camping. **2** *(lugar)* camp.

**campana** *nf* **1** *(gen)* bell. **2** *fam (extractora)* extractor hood, (US stove extractor hood).

**campanada** *nf* stroke of a bell.

**campanario** *nm* belfry, bell tower.

**campanilla** *nf* **1** *(gen)* small bell. **2** ANAT uvula. **3** *(flor)* morning glory.

**campaña** *nf* **1** campaign: *campaña electoral* election campaign.

**campechano,-na** *adj fam* frank.

**campeón,-ona** *nm & nf* champion.

**campeonato** *nm* championship.

**campesino,-a** *nm & nf (gen)* peasant; *(hombre)* countryman; *(mujer)* countrywoman.

**camping** *nm* camp site. LOC **hacer camping / ir de camping** to go camping.

**campiña** *nf* countryside.

**campo** *nm* **1** *(campiña)* country, countryside: *vivir en el campo* to live in the country. **2** *(agricultura)* field. **3** *(de deportes)* field, pitch. **4** *(espacio)* space: *en el campo de la medicina* in the field of medicine.

**campus** *nm inv* campus.

**camuflaje** *nm* camouflage.

**cana** *nf* grey hair, white hair.

**Canadá** *nm* Canada.

**canadiense** *adj* Canadian.
▶ *nm & nf* Canadian.

**canal** *nm* **1** *(artificial)* canal. **2** *(natural)* channel.
▶ *nm & nf* TÉC channel.

**canalizar** *vt* to channel.

**canalla** *nm o nf* swine.

**canalón** *nm* *(por el borde del tejado)* gutter.

**Canarias** *fpl* **las (islas) Canarias** the Canary Islands, the Canaries.

**canario,-a** *adj* Canarian.
▶ *nm & nf* Canarian.
▶ *nm* **canario** *(pájaro)* canary.

**canasto** *nm* *(cesto)* basket, hamper.

**cancelar** *vt* **1** *(anular)* to cancel. **2** *(saldar una deuda)* to settle, pay.

**cáncer** *nm* cancer.

**cancerígeno,-a** *adj* carcinogenic.

**cancha** *nf* *(gen)* ground; *(tenis)* court.

**canciller** *nm* chancellor.

**canción** *nf* song. COMP **canción de cuna** lullaby.

**candado** *nm* padlock.

**candidato,-a** *nm & nf* candidate.

**candidatura** *nf* **1** *(aspiración)* candidacy, candidature: *presentó su candidatura* she put forward her candidature. **2** *(lista de candidatos)* list of candidates.

**candidez** *nf* ingenuousness, innocence.

**cándido,-a** *adj* ingenuous, innocent.

**candil** *nm* oil lamp.

**canela** *nf* cinnamon.

**cangrejo** *nm* *(de mar)* crab.

**canguro** *nm* ZOOL kangaroo.
▶ *nm o nf fam* baby-sitter.

**caníbal** *nm o nf* cannibal.

**canica** *nf* marble: *jugar a las canicas* to play marbles.

**canino,-a** *adj* canine.

**canjear** *vt* to exchange.

**canoa** *nf* canoe; *(bote)* boat.

**canon** *nm* 1 *(regla)* canon, norm. 2 *(cantidad de dinero)* tax.

**canoso,-a** *adj* grey-haired (US grayhaired).

**cansado,-a** *adj* 1 *(gen)* tired, weary: *estoy cansada* I'm tired. 2 *(que fatiga)* tiring: *es un trabajo muy cansado* it's a very tiring job. 3 *(harto)* tired (de, of), fed up (de, with).

**cansancio** *nm* tiredness, weariness.

**cansar** *vt* 1 *(causar cansancio)* to tire, tire out, make tired. 2 *(molestar)* to annoy; *(aburrir)* to tire, bore.
▶ *vi (causar cansancio)* to be tiring.
▶ *vpr* **cansarse** *(padecer cansancio)* to get tired, tire: *se cansó de correr* he got tired of running.

**cantante** *nm o nf* singer.

**cantaor,-ra** *nm & nf* flamenco singer.

**cantar** *vt* 1 to sing: *cantó una canción preciosa* she sang a beautiful song. 2 *(en juegos de naipes)* to call.
▶ *vi* 1 to sing. 2 *(pájaros)* to sing, chirp; *(insectos)* to chirp.

**cántaro** *nm (vasija)* pitcher. LOC **llover a cántaros** *fig* to rain cats and dogs.

**cante** *nm* MÚS singing.

**cantera** *nf (de piedra)* quarry.

**cantero** *nm* stonemason.

**cántico** *nm* canticle.

**cantidad** *nf (gen)* quantity; *(de dinero)* amount, sum.
▶ *adv fam* a lot: *llovía cantidad* it was pouring with rain.

**cantimplora** *nf* water bottle.

**cantina** *nf* 1 *(comedor)* canteen. 2 *(de estación)* buffet.

**canto** *nm* 1 *(arte)* singing. 2 *(canción)* song. 3 *(de cuchillo)* blunt edge. 4 *(esquina)* corner. 5 *(piedra)* stone, pebble. COMP **canto rodado** 1 *(grande)* boulder. 2 *(pequeño)* pebble.

**cantor,-ra** *adj* singing. LOC **pájaro cantor** songbird.
▶ *nm & nf* singer.

**caña** *nf* 1 *(planta)* reed. 2 *(tallo)* cane, stem. 3 *(de pescar)* rod. 4 *(de cerveza)* small glass of draught beer. COMP **caña de azúcar** sugar cane.

**cañada** *nf* 1 GEOG glen, dell, hollow. 2 *(sendero)* cattle track.

**cáñamo** *nm* BOT hemp.

**cañería** *nf* piping.

**caño** *nm (tubo)* tube.

**cañón** *nm* 1 *(de artillería)* gun; *(antiguamente)* cannon. 2 *(de arma)* barrel. 3 GEOG canyon.

**caoba** *nf* mahogany.

**caolín** *nm* kaolin.

**caos** *nm inv* chaos.

**caótico,-a** *adj* chaotic.

**capa** *nf* 1 *(prenda)* cloak, cape. 2 GEOL stratum, layer. 3 *(de pintura)* coat; *(de polvo)* layer; *(de chocolate, etc)* coating, layer.

**capacidad** *nf* 1 *(gen)* capacity: *hay capacidad para cinco personas* there's room for five people. 2 *fig (habilidad)* capability, ability.

**capacitar** *vt* 1 *(instruir)* to train, qualify. 2 *(autorizar)* to qualify, entitle.

**caparazón** *nm* shell, carapace.

**capataz,-za** *nm & nf (hombre)* foreman; *(mujer)* forewoman.

**capaz** *adj* 1 *(competente)* capable, able: *es una persona muy capaz* she's very capable. 2 *(cualificado)* qualified. 3 *(capaz)* capable (de, of): *no es capaz de eso* he's incapable of doing that.

**capazo** *nm* 1 *(cesto)* basket. 2 *(para bebé)* carry cot.

**capellán** *nm* chaplain.

**capicúa** *adj* reversible.

**capilla** *nf (iglesia)* chapel.

**capital** *nf* capital, chief town.

**capitalismo** *nm* capitalism.

**capitalista** *adj* capitalist.
▶ *nm o nf* capitalist.

**capitán,-ana** *nm & nf* 1 *(oficial)* captain. 2 *(jefe)* leader, chief. 3 DEP captain.

**capitanear** vt **1** *(gen)* to lead; *(tropas)* to command. **2** *(equipo)* to captain. **3** *(buque)* to captain.

**capitel** nm capital, chapter.

**capítulo** nm **1** *(gen)* chapter. **2** fig *(tema)* subject, matter.

**capó** nm bonnet, US hood.

**capota** nf *(cubierta plegadíza)* folding hood, folding top.

**capricho** nm *(deseo)* whim, fancy.

**caprichoso,-a** adj capricious, whimsical, fanciful.
▶ nm & nf whimsical person.

**cápsula** nf *(gen)* capsule.

**captar** vt **1** *(ondas)* to receive. **2** *(entender)* to understand, grasp. **3** *(atraer a personas)* to attract, recruit.

**captura** nf capture.

**capturar** vt to capture, seize.

**capucha** nf hood.

**capuchón** nm *(de estilográfica, etc)* cap.

**capullo** nm **1** *(de insectos)* cocoon. **2** BOT bud.

**caqui** adj khaki.

**cara** nf **1** *(rostro)* face. **2** *(expresión)* face, expression. **3** *(lado)* side; *(de moneda)* right side. **4** *(superficie)* face. **5** fig *(aspecto)* look. **6** fam fig *(desvergüenza)* cheek, nerve: *¡vaya cara!* what a cheek! LOC **dar la cara** fig to face the consequences. ‖ **poner buena cara** to look pleased. ‖ COMP **cara de circunstancias** fig serious look. ‖ **cara dura** fig cheek, nerve.

**carabina** nf *(arma)* carbine, rifle.

**caracol** nm *(de tierra)* snail.

**caracola** nf conch.

**carácter** nm **1** *(personalidad)* character. **2** *(condición)* nature, kind. LOC **tener buen carácter** to be good-natured.

**característico,-a** adj characteristic.

**carambola** nf *(billar)* cannon, US carom.

**caramelo** nm *(dulce)* sweet, US candy.

**caravana** nf *(expedición)* caravan. *(atasco)* traffic jam, tailback.

**caray** interj good heavens!, God!

**carbón** nm *(gen)* coal.

**carboncillo** nm charcoal.

**carbónico,-a** adj carbonic. COMP **anhídrido carbónico** carbon dioxide.

**carbonífero,-a** adj carboniferous.

**carbonilla** nf *(residuo de carbón)* coal dust.

**carbonizar** vt **1** *(reducir a carbón)* to carbonize. **2** *(quemar)* to burn, char.

**carbono** nm carbon. COMP **dióxido de carbono** carbon dioxide.

**carburador** nm carburettor (US carburetor).

**carcajada** nf burst of laughter, guffaw. LOC **reír(se) a carcajadas** to laugh one's head off, roar with laughter.

**cárcel** nf jail, gaol, prison.

**carcelero,-a** adj prison, goal, jail.

**carcoma** nf *(insecto)* woodworm.

**cardamomo** nm cardamom.

**cardenal** *(hematoma)* bruise. nm REL cardinal.

**cardiaco,-a** adj cardiac, heart.

**cardinal** adj cardinal.

**cardiología** nf cardiology.

**cardiólogo,-a** nm & nf cardiologist.

**cardo** nm **1** BOT *(espinoso)* thistle; *(comestible)* cardoon.

**carecer** vi to lack (de, -).

**carencia** nf lack (de, of).

**careta** nf *(máscara)* mask. COMP **careta antigás** gas mask.

**carey** nm **1** *(animal)* sea turtle. **2** *(concha)* tortoiseshell.

**carga** nf **1** *(acción)* loading. **2** *(lo cargado)* load; *(de avión, barco)* cargo, freight.

**cargado,-a** adj **1** *(atmósfera)* heavy, dense. **2** strong. **3** fig burdened, weighed down: *cargado,-a de responsabilidades* weighed down with responsibility.

**cargador,-ra** nm **1** *(de arma)* magazine. **2** *(de batería)* battery charger. **3** *(de pluma, etc)* filler.

**cargamento** nm *(gen)* load; *(de avión, barco)* cargo, freight.

**cargar** vt **1** *(poner peso)* to load. **2** *(arma, máquina de fotos)* to load. **3** ELEC to charge: *cargar las pilas* to charge the batteries. **4** *(pluma, etc)* to fill. **5** INFORM to load.
▶ vi **1** *(gen)* to load. **2** *(batería)* to charge. **3** *(toro, elefante, etc)* to charge. **4** *(atacar)* to charge (contra/sobre, -). **5**

**cargar con** *(algo que pesa)* to carry; *(una obligación)* to shoulder, take on.
▶ *vpr* **cargarse 1** *(llenarse)* to load os (de, with): *cargarse de trabajo* to burden os with work. **2** ELEC to become charged. **3** EDUC *fam (suspender)* to fail. **4** *fam (destrozar)* to smash, ruin. **5** *fam (matar)* to knock off.

**cargo** *nm* **1** *(peso)* load, weight. **2** *(empleo)* post, position. **3** *(gobierno, custodia)* charge, responsibility. [LOC] **hacerse cargo de 1** *(responsabilizarse de)* to take charge of. **2** *(entender)* to realize: *me hago cargo* I realize that.

**caricatura** *nf* caricature.

**caricia** *nf* caress, stroke.

**caridad** *nf* charity.

**caries** *nf inv (enfermedad)* tooth decay, caries *pl*; *(lesión)* cavity.

**cariño** *nm* **1** *(amor)* love, affection. **2** *(esmero)* loving care. **3** *(apelativo)* darling, love, US honey. [LOC] **coger/tomar cariño a** ALGN/ALGO to grow fond of SB/STH.

**cariñoso,-a** *adj* loving, affectionate.

**carisma** *nm* charisma.

**carismático,-a** *adj* charismatic.

**carmín** *nm (pintalabios)* lipstick.

**carnada** *nf* bait.

**carnaval** *nm* carnival.

**carne** *nf* **1** ANAT flesh. **2** CULIN meat. **3** *(de fruta)* pulp. **4** *fig (cuerpo)* flesh. [COMP] **carne de cerdo** pork. **I carne de cordero** lamb. **I carne de ternera** veal. **I carne de vaca** beef. **I carne picada** mince, mincemeat, US ground meat, loose meat.

**carné** *nm* card. [COMP] **carné de conducir** driving licence. **I carné de identidad** identity card..

**carnicería** *nf* butcher's, butcher's shop.

**carnicero,-a** *nm & nf (profesión)* butcher.

**carnívoro,-a** *adj* carnivorous.
▶ *nm & nf* carnivore.

**caro,-a** *adj (costoso)* expensive, dear.
▶ *adv* **caro** at a high price. [LOC] **costar caro,-a / salir caro,-a 1** *(ser costoso)* to cost a lot. **2** *(causar daño)* to cost dear.

**carpa** *nf* **1** *(pez)* carp. **2** *(de circo)* big top, marquee.

**carpeta** *nf (archivador)* folder, file; *(informática)* folder.

**carpintería** *nf (obra y oficio)* carpentry.

**carpintero,-a** *nm & nf* carpenter.

**carraca** *nf (instrumento)* rattle.

**carrera** *nf* **1** *(acción)* run. **2** *(trayecto - de desfile)* route; *(- de taxi)* ride, journey. **3** *(camino)* road. **4** DEP race. **5** *(estudios)* degree course, university education. [COMP] **carrera contra reloj** race against the clock. **I carrera diplomática** diplomatic career.

**carreta** *nf* cart.

**carrete** *nm* **1** *(de hilo)* bobbin, reel. **2** ELEC coil. **3** *(de caña de pescar)* reel. **4** *(de película)* spool; *(de fotos)* film, roll of film. **5** *(de máquina de escribir)* cartridge.

**carretera** *nf* road. [COMP] **carretera nacional** A road, main road. **I carretera de circunvalación** ring road.

**carretilla** *nf* wheelbarrow.

**carril** *nm* **1** *(de ferrocarril)* rail. **2** *(de carretera)* lane. [COMP] **carril bus** bus lane.

**carrillo** *nm* cheek.

**carrito** *nm (para la compra)* trolley, US cart.

**carro** *nm* **1** *(vehículo)* cart. **2** *(de supermercado, aeropuerto)* trolley, US cart.

**carrocería** *nf* body, bodywork.

**carromato** *nm* covered wagon.

**carroña** *nf* carrion.

**carroñero,-a** *adj* carrion-eating.

**carroza** *adj fam* old, old-fashioned.
▶ *nf (tirado por caballos)* coach, carriage.

**carruaje** *nm* carriage, coach.

**carrusel** *nm (tiovivo)* merry-go-round, US carrousel.

**carta** *nf* **1** *(misiva)* letter. **2** *(naipe)* card. **3** *(minuta)* menu. [LOC] **a la carta** à la carte. **I echar una carta** to post a letter, US mail a letter.

**cartabón** *nm* set square, triangle.

**cartel** *nm* poster, bill.

**cartelera** *nf (en periódicos)* entertainment section. [LOC] **en cartelera** running, on.

**cartera** *nf* **1** *(monedero)* wallet. **2** *(de colegial)* satchel, school bag. **3** *(de ejecutivo)* briefcase.

**carterista** *nm o nf* pickpocket.

**cartero,-a** *nm & nf* *(hombre)* postman; *(mujer)* postwoman.

**cartílago** *nm* cartilage.

**cartilla** *nf* **1** *(para aprender)* first reader. **2** *(cuaderno)* book.

**cartón** *nm* **1** *(material)* cardboard. **2** *(de cigarrillos)* carton. COMP **cartón piedra** papier-mâché.

**cartucho** *nm* *(de explosivo)* cartridge.

**cartulina** *nf* thin cardboard.

**casa** *nf* **1** *(vivienda)* house. **2** *(piso)* flat. **3** *(edificio)* building. **4** *(hogar)* home: *nos quedamos en casa* we stayed at home. **5** *(empresa)* firm, company. LOC **buscar casa** to go house-hunting.

**casaca** *nf* fitted short coat.

**casado,-a** *adj* married.

**casar** *vt* to marry.
▶ *vi (casarse)* to marry (con, -), get married (con, to).
▶ *vpr* **casarse** to get married (con, to) marry (con, -).

**cascabel** *nm* bell.

**cascada** *nf* cascade, waterfall.

**cascanueces** *nm inv* nutcrackers *pl*.

**cascar** *vt (romper)* to crack.
▶ *vpr* **cascarse** *(romperse)* to crack.

**cáscara** *nf* **1** *(de huevo, nuez)* shell. **2** *(de fruta)* skin, peel.

**cascarón** *nm* eggshell.

**cascarrabias** *nm o nf inv* fam grumpy person, bad-tempered person.

**casco** *nm* **1** *(para la cabeza)* helmet. **2** *(envase)* empty bottle. **3** *(de barco)* hull. **4** *(de caballería)* hoof.

**caserío** *nm* **1** *(casa)* country house. **2** *(pueblo)* hamlet, small village.

**casero,-a** *adj* **1** *(persona)* home-loving. **2** *(productos)* home-made: *pan casero* home-made bread.
▶ *nm & nf* *(dueño - hombre)* landlord; *(mujer)* landlady.

**caseta** *nf* **1** *(casita)* hut, booth. **2** *(de feria)* stall, stand. **3** *(de bañistas)* bathing hut, US bath house. **4** *(de perro)* kennel, doghouse.

**casete** *nm* *(magnetófono)* cassette player, cassette recorder.
▶ *nf (cinta)* cassette, cassette tape.

**casi** *adv* almost, nearly: *había casi cincuenta personas* there were almost fifty people. LOC **casi nunca** hardly ever.

**casilla** *nf* **1** *(casita)* hut, lodge. **2** *(de casillero)* pigeonhole. **3** *(cuadrícula)* square.

**casillero** *nm* pigeonholes *pl*.

**casino** *nm* casino.

**casis** *nm inv* blackcurrant bush.

**caso** *nm* **1** *(ocasión)* case, occasion. **2** *(gramatical)* case. LOC **en caso de que** if: *en caso de que te pierdas, llámame* if you get lost, call me. ▮ **en cualquier caso** in any case. ▮ **en todo caso** anyhow, at any rate.

**caspa** *nf* dandruff.

**casquete** *nm* *(prenda)* skullcap.

**casquillo** *nm* **1** TÉC ferrule, metal tip. **2** *(de cartucho)* case.

**casta** *nf (linaje)* lineage, descent.

**castaña** *nf* BOT chestnut.

**castañetear** *vi (dientes)* to chatter.

**castaño,-a** *adj (pelo)* brown.
▶ *nm* **castaño** **1** BOT *(árbol)* chestnut tree. **2** *(madera)* chestnut.

**castañuela** *nf* castanet.

**castellano,-a** *adj* Castilian.
▶ *nm & nf (persona)* Castilian.
▶ *nm* **castellano** *(idioma)* Castilian, Spanish.

**castigar** *vt (aplicar una pena)* to punish.

**castigo** *nm* **1** *(gen)* punishment. **2** *(en deporte)* penalty.

**castillo** *nm* castle.

**casting** *nm* casting, audition.

**castizo,-a** *adj* pure, authentic.

**casto,-a** *adj* chaste.

**castor** *nm* beaver.

**casual** *adj* accidental, chance.

**casualidad** *nf* **1** chance, accident. **2** *(coincidencia)* coincidence. LOC **de casualidad / por casualidad** by chance.

**cataclismo** *nm* cataclysm.

**catacumbas** *nf pl* catacombs.

**catalán,-ana** *adj* Catalan, Catalonian.
▶ *nm & nf (persona)* Catalan.
▶ *nm* **catalán** *(idioma)* Catalan.

**catalejo** *nm* telescope.

**catalogar** *vt* **1** to catalogue (US catalog). **2** *fig* to classify, class.

**catálogo** *nm* catalogue (US catalog).

**catamarán** *nm* catamaran.

**cataplasma** *nf* poultice, cataplasm.

**catapulta** *nf* catapult.

**catar** *vt* **1** *(probar)* to taste. **2** *(examinar)* to examine, inspect.

**catarata** *nf* **1** waterfall. **2** MED cataract.

**catarro** *nm* cold, catarrh: *cogí un catarro* I caught a cold.

**catástrofe** *nf* catastrophe.

**catastrófico,-a** *adj* catastrophic.

**catear** *vt* EDUC *fam* to fail, US flunk.

**catecismo** *nm* catechism.

**cátedra** *nf (cargo de universidad)* professorship; *(de instituto)* post of head of department.

**catedral** *nf* cathedral.

**catedrático,-a** *nm & nf (de universidad)* professor; *(de instituto)* head of department.

**categoría** *nf* category, class; *(social)* class: *un restaurante de primera categoría* a first-class restaurant.

**catequesis** *nf inv* catechism.

**cateto** *nm (de triángulo)* side of a right-angled triangle forming the right angle.

**catolicismo** *nm* Catholicism.

**católico,-a** *adj* Catholic.

**catorce** *adj (cardinal)* fourteen; *(ordinal)* four

**catorceavo,-a** *adj* fourteenth.
▶ *nm & nf* fourteenth.

✎ Consulta también **sexto,-a**.

**catre** *nm (cama plegable)* folding bed; *(de campaña)* camp bed.

**cauce** *nm* **1** *(de río)* bed. **2** *fig (canal)* channel, way.

**caucho** *nm* rubber.

**caudal** *nm (de río)* flow.

**caudaloso,-a** *adj (río)* deep, plentiful.

**causa** *nf* **1** *(gen)* cause. **2** *(motivo)* cause, reason, motive. LOC **a causa de** because of, on account of.

**causar** *vt* **1** *(provocar)* to cause, bring about. **2** *(proporcionar)* to make, give.

**cáustico,-a** *adj* caustic.

**cautela** *nf* caution, cautiousness.

**cauteloso,-a** *adj* cautious, wary.

**cauterizar** *vt* to cauterize, fire.

**cautivar** *vt* to take prisoner, capture.

**cautivo,-a** *adj* captive.

**cauto,-a** *adj* cautious, wary.

**cava** *nm (bebida)* cava, champagne.

**cavar** *vt* to dig.

**caverna** *nf* cavern, cave.

**cavernícola** *nm o nf* cave dweller, caveman.

**caviar** *nm* caviar.

**cavidad** *nf* cavity.

**cavilar** *vi* think about, brood over.

**caza** *nf* **1** *(acción)* hunting. **2** *(de animales)* game. LOC **ir de caza** to go hunting.

**cazador,-ra** *nm & nf* hunter.

**cazadora** *nf (chaqueta)* jacket.

**cazar** *vt* **1** to hunt. **2** *fam (conseguir)* to catch, land.

**cazo** *nm* **1** *(cucharón)* ladle. **2** *(cacerola)* saucepan.

**cazuela** *nf* **1** *(utensilio)* casserole, saucepan. **2** *(guiso)* casserole, stew.

**CE** *abrev* **(Comunidad Europea)** European Community; *(abreviatura)* EC.

**cebada** *nf* barley.

**cebar** *vt* **1** *(animal)* to fatten, fatten up. **2** *(poner cebo)* to bait.
▶ *vpr* **cebarse** *fig (ensañarse)* to show no mercy **(en/con,** towards), take it out **(en/con,** on), vent one's anger **(en/con,** on).

**cebo** *nm* **1** *(para animales)* food. **2** *(para pescar)* bait.

**cebolla** *nf* **1** onion. **2** *(bulbo)* bulb. **3** *(de ducha)* rose, nozzle.

**cebolleta** *nf* **1** *(especia)* chives *pl*. **2** *(cebolla)* spring onion.

**cebollino** *nm* **1** *(especia)* chives *pl.* **2** *(cebolla)* spring onion.

**cebra** *nf* zebra. [COMP] **paso cebra** zebra crossing, US crosswalk.

**ceceo** *nm* lisp.

**cecina** *nf* cured meat.

**ceder** *vt* **1** *(dar)* to cede, give: **2** DEP *(balón)* to pass.
▶ *vi* **1** *(rendirse)* to yield (a, to), give way (a, to). **2** *(disminuir)* to diminish, slacken, go down: *la fiebre ha cedido* his temperature has gone down. [LOC] **ceder el paso** AUTO to give way, US yield.

**cedro** *nm* cedar.

**CEE** *abrev* (Comunidad Económica Europea) European Economic Community; *(abreviatura)* EEC.

**cefalópodo,-a** *adj* cephalopod.
▶ *nm* **cefalópodo** cephalopod.

**cefalotórax** *nm* cephalothorax.

**cegar** *vt* *(gen)* to blind: *el sol me cegó* the sun blinded me.
▶ *vpr* **cegarse** *fig* to become blind, be blinded.

**ceguera** *nf* blindness.

**ceja** *nf* eyebrow. [LOC] **tener** ALGO **entre ceja y ceja** *fig* to have STH in one's head.

**celda** *nf* cell.

**celebración** *nf* *(fiesta)* celebration.

**celebrar** *vt* **1** *(festejar)* to celebrate. **2** *(organizar)* to hold: *celebraron el debate ayer* the debate was held yesterday.
▶ *vpr* **celebrarse** *(tener lugar)* to take place, be held.

**célebre** *adj* famous, celebrated.

**celeste** *adj (color)* sky-blue.
▶ *nm (color)* sky blue.

**celestial** *adj* celestial, heavenly.

**celibato** *nm* celibacy.

**celo®¹** *nm fam* sellotape, US Scotch tape.

**celo²** *nm* **1** *(cuidado)* zeal, fervour (US fervor). **2** BIOL *(macho)* rut; *(hembra)* heat.
▶ *nm pl* **celos** jealousy *sing.* [LOC] **dar celos** to make jealous.

**celofán®** *nm* cellophane®.

**celosía** *nf* **1** *(reja)* lattice. **2** *(ventana)* lattice window.

**celoso,-a** *adj (envidioso)* jealous.

**Celsius** *nm* Celsius.

**célula** *nf* cell.

**celular** *adj* cell, cellular.

**celulosa** *nf* cellulose.

**cementerio** *nm* cemetery.

**cemento** *nm (gen)* concrete, cement. [COMP] **cemento armado** reinforced concrete.

**cena** *nf (gen)* supper; *(formal)* dinner.

**cenar** *vi* to have supper, have dinner.
▶ *vt* to have for supper, have for dinner.

**cencerro** *nm* cowbell. [LOC] **estar como un cencerro** to be nuts, be crackers.

**cenefa** *nf* **1** *(sobre tejido)* edging, trimming. **2** *(sobre muro, pavimento, etc)* ornamental border, frieze.

**cenicero** *nm* ashtray.

**cenit** *nm* zenith.

**ceniza** *nf* ash, ashes *pl.*

**censar** *vt (hacer el censo)* to take a census of.

**censo** *nm (padrón)* census. [COMP] **censo electoral** electoral roll.

**censura** *nf* **1** censorship.

**censurar** *vt* to censor: *el libro fue censurado* the book was censored.

**centavo,-a** *nm* **1** *(parte)* hundredth, hundredth part. **2** *(moneda)* cent, centavo.

✎ Consulta también **sexto,-a**.

**centella** *nf* **1** *(rayo)* lightning. **2** *(chispa)* spark, flash.

**centellear** *vi* **1** *(gen)* to sparkle, flash. **2** *(estrellas)* to twinkle.

**centena** *nf* hundred.

**centenar** *nm* hundred. [LOC] **a centenares / por centenares** in hundreds.

**centenario,-a** *nm & nf (persona)* centenarian.
▶ *nm* **centenario** *(aniversario)* centenary, centennial, hundredth anniversary.

**centeno** *nm* rye.

**centésimo,-a** *adj* hundredth.
▶ *nm & nf* hundredth.

▶ *nm* **centésimo** *(moneda)* cent, centesimo.

✎ Consulta también **sexto,-a.**

**centígrado,-a** *adj* centigrade.

**centigramo** *nm* centigram, centigramme.

**centilitro** *nm* centilitre (US centiliter).

**centímetro** *nm* centimetre (US centimeter).

**céntimo** *nm* cent, centime. LOC **estar sin un céntimo** *fam* to be penniless.

**centinela** *nm & nf* **1** MIL sentry. **2** *(guardián)* watch, lookout.

**centollo** *nm* spider crab.

**central** *adj* central.
▶ *nf* **1** *(oficina principal)* head office, headquarters *pl*. **2** *(eléctrica)* power station. COMP **central telefónica** telephone exchange.

**centralita** *nf* switchboard.

**centralizar** *vt* to centralize.

**centrar** *vt* **1** *(gen)* to centre (US center). **2** *fig (atención, etc)* to centre (US center), focus.
▶ *vpr* **centrarse** to centre (US center) (en, on), focus (en, on): *se centró en el tema principal* he focused on the main topic.

**céntrico,-a** *adj* central, US downtown.

**centrifugadora** *nf (para ropa)* spindryer.

**centrifugar** *vt (ropa)* to spin-dry.

**centrífugo,-a** *adj* centrifugal.

**centrípeto,-a** *adj* centripetal.

**centro** *nm* **1** centre (US center), middle. **2** *(de ciudad)* town centre, city centre, US downtown area. **3** *(asociación)* centre (US center), association, institution. COMP **centro comercial** shopping centre, US mall. ‖ **centro cultural** cultural centre (US center).

**centrocampista** *nm o nf* midfield player.

**céntuplo,-a** *adj* centuple, hundredfold.
▶ *nm* **céntuplo** centuple, hundredfold.

**centuria** *nf* century.

**ceñir** *vt* **1** *(estrechar)* to cling to, be tight on. **2** *(rodear)* to surround, encircle.
▶ *vpr* **ceñirse 1** *(atenerse)* to keep (a, to), limit OS (a, to): *ceñirse al tema* to keep to the subject. **2** *(ajustarse una prenda)* to cling.

**ceño** *nm* frown. LOC **fruncir el ceño** to frown.

**cepa** *nf (de vid)* vine.

**cepillar** *vt (gen)* to brush.

**cepillo** *nm* **1** brush. **2** *(de carpintería)* plane. COMP **cepillo de dientes** toothbrush. ‖ **cepillo del pelo** hairbrush.

**cepo** *nm* **1** *(rama)* bough, branch. **2** *(de yunque)* stock. **3** *(de reo)* pillory, stocks *pl*. **4** *(trampa)* trap. **5** *(para auto)* clamp.

**cera** *nf* **1** wax; *(de abeja)* beeswax. **2** *(pulimento)* wax, polish.

**cerámica** *nf* **1** *(arte)* ceramics, pottery. **2** *(objeto)* piece of pottery.

**ceramista** *nm o nf* ceramist, potter.

**cerca¹** *nf (vallado)* fence, wall.

**cerca²** *adv (lugar y tiempo)* near, close: *aquí cerca* near here. LOC **cerca de 1** *(cercano a)* near, close. **2** *(aproximadamente)* nearly, about, around.

**cercado** *nm* **1** *(lugar)* enclosure. **2** *(cerca)* fence, wall.

**cercano,-a** *adj* **1** *(inmediato)* near, close: *el fin está cercano* the end is near. **2** *(vecino)* nearby, neighbouring (US neighboring). **3** *(pariente)* close.

**cercar** *vt (poner una cerca)* to fence in, enclose: *cercaron la hacienda* they fenced in the property.

**cerco** *nm* **1** *(lo que rodea)* circle, ring. **2** *(aureola)* halo. **3** *(asedio)* siege.

**cerdo,-a** *nm & nf fam pey (persona sucia)* pig, slob.
▶ *nm* **cerdo 1** *(animal)* pig. **2** *(carne)* pork.

**cereal** *nm* cereal.

**cerebro** *nm* **1** ANAT brain. **2** *fig* brains *pl*: *es el cerebro de la banda* he's the brains behind the gang.

**ceremonia** *nf* ceremony.

**ceremonial** *adj* ceremonial.

**ceremonioso,-a** *adj* ceremonious, formal.

**cereza** *nf* cherry.

**cerezo** *nm* cherry tree.

**cerilla** *nf (fósforo)* match.

**cero** *nm* **1** MAT zero. **2** *(cifra)* nought, zero. **3** DEP nil: *ganamos tres a cero* we won three nil.

**cerrado,-a** *adj* **1** shut, closed. **2** LING close, closed: *vocal cerrada* close vowel. **3** *(acento)* broad, thick. **4** *(curva)* tight, sharp. **5** *fig (persona introvertida)* uncommunicative, reserved.

**cerradura** *nf* lock.

**cerrajería** *nf (negocio)* locksmith's shop.

**cerrajero,-a** *nm & nf* locksmith.

**cerrar** *vt* **1** to close, shut: *cierra la puerta* close the door. **2** *(grifo, gas)* to turn off; *(luz)* to turn off, switch off. **3** *(cremallera)* to zip (up). **4** *(frontera, puerto)* to close; *(camino)* to block. **5** *(en dominó)* to block.
▶ *vi* **1** to close, shut. **2** *(punto)* to cast off. **3** *(una herida)* to close up, heal.
▶ *vpr* **cerrarse 1** to close, shut. **2** *(una herida)* to close up, heal.

**cerro** *nm* hill.

**cerrojo** *nm* bolt. LOC **correr el cerrojo** to bolt.

**certamen** *nm* competition, contest.

**certeza** *nf* certainty.

**certificado,-a** *adj (envío)* registered.
▶ *nm* **certificado 1** *(documento)* certificate. **2** *(carta)* registered letter.

**certificar** *vt* **1** *(gen)* to certify. **2** *(carta, paquete)* to register.

**cerumen** *nm* earwax, cerumen.

**cervato** *nm* fawn.

**cervecería** *nf* **1** *(bar)* pub, bar. **2** *(destilería)* brewery.

**cerveza** *nf* beer, ale. COMP **cerveza de barril** draught (US draft) beer. ‖ **cerveza negra** stout.

**cervical** *adj* cervical, neck.

**cesar** *vi* to cease, stop: *cesó de llover* it stopped raining. LOC **sin cesar** incessantly.

**cesárea** *nf* caesarean (US Cesarean), Caesarean (US Cesarean) section.

**cese** *nm* **1** cessation. **2** *(despido)* dismissal.

**cesión** *nf* cession.

**césped** *nm* lawn, grass.

**cesta** *nf* **1** basket. **2** DEP *(baloncesto)* basket. COMP **cesta de la compra** shopping basket.

**cesto** *nm* basket. COMP **cesto de los papeles** wastepaper basket.

**cetáceo,-a** *nm* cetacean.

**cetro** *nm* sceptre (US scepter).

**CFC** *abrev* **(clorofluorocarbono)** chlorofluorocarbon; *(abreviatura)* CFC.

**cg** *sím* **(centigramo)** centigram, centigramme; *(símbolo)* cg.

**chabola** *nf* shack: *un barrio de chabolas* a shanty town.

**chacal** *nm* jackal.

**chacha** *nf* **1** *fam (niñera)* nanny, nursemaid. **2** *fam (sirvienta)* maid.

**chacinería** *nf* pork butcher's shop.

**chador** *nm* chuddar, chudder, chuddah.

**chafar** *vt* **1** *(aplastar)* to squash, crush, flatten. **2** *(arrugar)* to crumple, crease.
▶ *vpr* **chafarse** *(aplastarse)* to be squashed, be crushed, be flattened; *(arrugarse)* to become creased, become crumpled.

**chaflán** *nm* **1** *(bisel)* chamfer. **2** *(esquina)* corner.

**chal** *nm* shawl.

**chalado,-a** *adj (loco)* mad, crazy, nuts.

**chalar** *vt fam (enloquecer)* to drive crazy.
▶ *vpr* **chalarse** *fam* to go mad, go crazy, go nuts.

**chaleco** *nm* waistcoat, US vest. COMP **chaleco salvavidas** life jacket.

**chalet** *nm* **1** *(casa individual)* house, detached house. **2** *(adosado)* semidetached house.

**chalupa** *nf (embarcación)* boat, launch.

**chamán** *nm* sorcerer, wizard, shaman.

**chamarra** *nf (zamarra)* sheepskin jacket.

**champaña** *nm* champagne.

**champiñón** *nm* mushroom.

**champú** *nm* shampoo.

**chamuscar** *vt* to singe, scorch.
▶ *vpr* **chamuscarse** to be singed, get scorched.

**chamusquina** *nf* scorching, singeing.

**chancho** *nm* AM *(animal)* pig; *(carne)* pork.

**chanchullo** *nm fam* fiddle, wangle, racket.

**chancla** *nf (chancleta)* flip-flop.

**chancleta** *nf* flip-flop.

**chándal** *nm* track suit, jogging suit.

**chanquete** *nm* transparent goby.

**chantaje** *nm* blackmail.

**chantajear** *vt* to blackmail.

**chao** *interj fam* bye-bye!, cheerio!, so long!, ciao!

**chapa** *nf* 1 *(de metal)* sheet, plate. 2 *(de madera)* panel, sheet; *(contrachapado)* plywood. 3 *(tapón)* bottle top, cap. 4 *(medalla)* badge, disc.
▶ *nf pl* **chapas** game *sing* of tossing up coins.

**chapado,-a** *adj* 1 *(metal)* plated: *chapado,-a en plata* silver-plated. 2 *(madera)* veneered, finished.

**chaparrón** *nm (lluvia)* downpour, heavy shower: *cayó un buen chaparrón* there was a downpour.

**chapista** *nm o nf* 1 sheet metal worker. 2 AUTO panel beater.

**chapotear** *vi (agitar en el agua)* to splash about.

**chapurrear** *vt* to speak a little, have a smattering of: *chapurreo el inglés* I have a smattering of English, I speak a little English.

**chapuza** *nf* 1 *(trabajo sin importancia)* odd job. 2 *(trabajo mal hecho)* botched job, shoddy piece of work.

**chapuzón** *nm (baño)* dip. LOC **darse un chapuzón** to have a dip.

**chaqueta** *nf* jacket. COMP **chaqueta de punto** cardigan.

**chaquetón** *nm* winter jacket.

**charanga** *nf* 1 brass band. 2 *fam (bulla)* din, racket.

**charca** *nf* pool, pond.

**charco** *nm* puddle, pond.

**charcutería** *nf* pork butcher's shop, delicatessen.

**charla** *nf* 1 *(conversación)* talk, chat. 2 *(conferencia)* talk, informal lecture.

**charlar** *vi* to chat, talk.

**charlatán,-ana** *adj* 1 *(hablador)* talkative. 2 *(chismoso)* gossipy.
▶ *nm & nf* 1 *(parlanchín)* chatterbox. 2 *(chismoso)* gossip.

**charloteo** *nm fam* chatter, prattle.

**chárter** *adj inv* charter.
▶ *nm* charter.

**chasco** *nm fig (decepción)* disappointment. LOC **llevarse un chasco** to be disappointed.

**chasis** *nm (del coche)* chassis.

**chasquear** *vi* 1 *(lengua)* to click; *(dedos)* to snap. 2 *(látigo, madera)* to crack.

**chasquido** *nm* 1 *(de la lengua)* click; *(de los dedos)* snap. 2 *(de látigo, madera)* crack.

**chat** *nm* INFORM chat.

**chatarra** *nf* 1 *(hierro viejo)* scrap iron, scrap. 2 *fam pey (calderilla)* small change.

**chatear** *vi* INFORM *fam* to chat (con, with/to).

**chateo** *nm* INFORM *fam* chat, chatting.

**chato,-a** *adj (nariz)* snub; *(persona)* snub-nosed.

**chaval,-la** *nm & nf (joven)* kid, youngster; *(chico)* lad, boy; *(chica)* lass, girl.

**chavo** *nm pl* **chavos** *(dinero)* money *sing*, cash *sing*.

**checo,-a** *adj* Czech.
▶ *nm & nf (persona)* Czech.
▶ *nm* **checo** *(idioma)* Czech. COMP **República Checa** Czech Republic.

**chef** *nm* chef.

**chelín** *nm* shilling.

**cheque** *nm* cheque (US check). LOC **cobrar un cheque** to cash a cheque (US check).

**chequear** *vt* **1** *(controlar)* to check. **2** *(comprobar)* to check up on.

**chequeo** *nm* MED checkup.

**Chequia** *nf* Czechia.

**chica** *nf* girl.

**chicharra** *nf (cigarra)* cicada.

**chicharro** *nm* **1** *(chicharrón)* pork crackling, fried pork rind. **2** *(pez)* scad, horse mackerel.

**chicharrón** *nm (de cerdo)* pork crackling, fried pork rind.

**chichón** *nm* bump, lump.

**chicle** *nm* chewing gum.

**chico,-a** *nm & nf (gen)* kid, youngster.

**chiflado,-a** *adj fam* mad, crazy, barmy, nuts, bonkers.

**chiflar** *vi (silbar)* to hiss, whistle.
▶ *vt* **1** *(silbar)* to hiss, boo. **2** *fam (gustar)* to fascinate, enchant.

**chiflido** *nm* whistle, whistling.

**chií** *adj* Shiite.
▶ *nm o nf* Shiite.

**chiíta** *adj-nm o nf* → **chií**.

**chilaba** *nf* jellabah, jellaba.

**chile** *nm (pimiento)* chili, chili pepper.

**Chile** *nm* Chile.

**chileno,-a** *adj* Chilean.
▶ *nm & nf* Chilean.

**chillar** *vi* **1** *(persona)* to scream, shriek, shout: **2** *(cerdo)* to squeal; *(ratón)* to squeak; *(pájaro)* to squawk, screech. **3** *(radio)* to blare; *(frenos)* to screech, squeal. **4** *(colores)* to be loud, be gaudy, clash. **5** *fam (reñir)* to tell off.

**chillido** *nm* **1** *(de persona)* shriek, scream, cry. **2** *(de cerdo)* squeal; *(de ratón)* squeak; *(de pájaro)* squawk, screech.

**chillón,-ona** *adj* **1** *(que chilla mucho)* screaming, loud. **2** *(voz)* shrill, high-pitched; *(sonido)* harsh, strident. **3** *fig (color)* loud, gaudy.

**chimenea** *nf* **1** chimney. **2** *(hogar)* fireplace, hearth. **3** *(de barco)* funnel, stack.

**chimpancé** *nm* chimpanzee.

**china** *nm (piedrecita)* pebble.

**China** *nf* China.

**chinchar** *vt fam* to annoy, pester, bug.
▶ *vpr* **chincharse** *fam* to grin and bear it, put up with it, lump it. LOC ¡**chínchate!** *fam* hard luck!, tough luck!

**chinche** *nm & nf* ZOOL bedbug, bug.

**chincheta** *nf* drawing pin, US thumbtack.

**chinchilla** *nf* chinchilla.

**chino,-a** *adj* Chinese.
▶ *nm & nf (persona)* Chinese person.
▶ *nm* **chino** **1** *(idioma)* Chinese. **2** *(colador)* sieve.
▶ *nm pl* **chinos** guessing game *sing*.

**chip** *nm* INFORM chip.

**chipirón** *nm* baby squid.

**Chipre** *nm* Cyprus.

**chipriota** *adj* Cypriot.
▶ *nm o nf* Cypriot.

**chiquillo,-a** *nm & nf* kid, youngster.

**chiquito,-a** *adj* tiny, very small, weeny.
▶ *nm & nf* tiny tot, kid.

**chirimoya** *nf* custard apple.

**chiringuito** *nm fam (en playa)* refreshment stall, refreshment stand; *(en carretera)* roadside snack bar, hot food stand.

**chirla** *nf* small clam.

**chirriar** *vi* **1** *(al freír comida, etc)* to sizzle. **2** *(rueda, frenos)* to screech, squeal; *(puerta)* to creak. **3** *(aves)* to squawk.

**chirrido** *nm* **1** *(de rueda, frenos)* screech; *(de puerta)* creak, creaking. **2** *(de aves)* squawk, squawking.

**chisme** *nm* **1** *(comentario)* piece of gossip. **2** *(trasto)* knick-knack; *(de cocina, etc)* gadget; *(cosa)* thing, thingamajig.

**chismoso,-a** *nm & nf* gossip.

**chispa** *nf* **1** *(de lumbre, eléctrica, etc)* spark. **2** *fig (ingenio, gracia)* wit, sparkle; *(inteligencia)* intelligence; *(viveza)* liveliness.

**chispear** *vi* **1** *(echar chispas)* to spark, throw out sparks. **2** [en este sentido se usa sólo en tercera persona; no lleva sujeto] METEOR to drizzle, spit.

**chistar** *vi* to speak. LOC **sin chistar** without saying a word.

**chiste** *nm* **1** *(dicho)* joke, funny story. **2** *(dibujo)* cartoon. LOC **contar un chiste** to tell a joke.

**chistera** *nf fig (sombrero)* top hat.

**chistoso,-a** *adj* **1** *(persona)* witty, funny, fond of joking. **2** *(suceso)* funny, amusing.

**chivar** *vt* **1** *fam (molestar)* to annoy, pester. **2** *fam (delatar)* to squeal on, tell on.
▶ *vpr* **chivarse** *fam* to tell, squeal, split.

**chivato,-a** *nm & nf fam (acusica)* telltale.

**chivo,-a** *nm & nf (cría macho)* kid, young goat; *(cría hembra)* kid, young she-goat.

**choc** *nm* shock.

**chocar** *vi* **1** *(colisionar con algo)* to collide (contra/con, with), crash (contra/con, into), run (contra/con, into). **2** *(una pelota)* to hit (contra, -), strike (contra, -).
▶ *vt* **1** *fig (sorprender)* to surprise; *(extrañar)* to shock. **2** *(las manos)* to shake.

**choco** *nm* small cuttlefish.

**chocolate** *nm* **1** *(sólido)* chocolate. **2** *(líquido)* drinking chocolate, cocoa. COMP **chocolate con leche** milk chocolate.

**chocolatería** *nf* **1** *(fábrica)* chocolate factory. **2** *(tienda)* chocolate shop. **3** *(donde se toma)* café specializing in drinking chocolate.

**chocolatero,-a** *adj (aficionado al chocolate)* fond of chocolate, chocolate-loving.
▶ *nm & nf* **1** *(fabricante)* chocolate maker. **2** *(vendedor)* chocolate seller.

**chocolatina** *nf* bar of chocolate.

**chófer** *nm* **1** *(particular)* chauffeur. **2** *(de autocar, etc)* driver.

**chollo** *nm* **1** *fam (ganga)* bargain, snip, gift. **2** *(trabajo)* cushy job.

**chopera** *nf* poplar grove.

**chopo** *nm (árbol)* poplar.

**choque** *nm* **1** *(gen)* collision, impact; *(de coche, tren, etc)* crash, smash, collision. **2** *(discusión)* dispute, quarrel. **3** MED shock.

**chorizo,-a** *nm* chorizo *(highly-seasoned pork sausage)*.

**chorrear** *vi* **1** *(caer a chorro)* to spout, gush, spurt. **2** *(gotear)* to drip.

**chorro** *nm* **1** *(de líquido)* jet, spout, spurt, gush. **2** *(de gas)* jet, blast. LOC **a chorros** in abundance: *tiene dinero a chorros* he's got plenty of money, he's loaded (with money).

**choto,-a** *nm & nf* **1** *(cabrito)* kid, young goat; *(cabrita)* female kid, young she-goat. **2** *(ternero)* sucking calf.

**choza** *nf* hut, shack.

**christmas** *nm inv* Christmas card.

**chubasco** *nm (chaparrón)* heavy shower, downpour.

**chubasquero** *nm* raincoat.

**chuche** *nm fam* sweet, US candy.

**chuchería** *nf fam (golosina)* sweet, US candy.

**chucho,-a** *nm & nf fam (perro)* mutt, US pooch.

**chucrut** *nm* sauerkraut.

**chufa** *nf (planta)* chufa; *(fruto)* tiger nut.

**chulear** *vi fam (presumir)* to brag, show off: *mira a Felipe cómo chulea con su coche nuevo* look at Felipe showing off his new car.

**chuleta** *nf* **1** *(costilla)* chop, cutlet. **2** *fam fig (entre estudiantes)* crib, crib note, US trot.

**chulo,-a** *adj* **1** *fam (descarado)* cocky, cheeky. **2** *fam (vistoso)* showy, flashy. **3** *fam (bonito)* nice, pretty.

**chupado,-a** *adj* **1** *fig (muy flaco)* skinny, thin; *(mejillas, cara)* hollow. **2** *argot fig (muy fácil)* dead easy.

**chupar** *vt* **1** to suck. **2** *(absorber)* to absorb, soak up, suck up.

**chupete** *nm* dummy, US pacifier.

**churrería** *nf* fritter shop.

**churro** *nm (dulce)* fritter, US cruller.

**chusma** *nf* riffraff, rabble, mob.

**chut** *nm* DEP shot, kick.

**chutar** *vi* DEP to shoot, kick.

**chute** *nm argot* fix.

**cianita** *nf* cyanite.

**cianuro** *nm* cyanide. COMP **cianuro potásico** potassium cyanide.

**cibercafé** *nm* Internet café.

**ciberespacio** *nm* cyberspace.

**cibernauta** *nm o nf* Net user.

**cibernética** *nf* cybernetics.

**cicatriz** *nf* scar.

**cicatrizar** *vi* to heal, cicatrize.

**cíclico,-a** *adj* cyclic, cyclical.

**ciclismo** *nm* cycling.

**ciclista** *adj* cycle, cycling.
▶ *nm o nf* cyclist.

**ciclomotor** *nm* moped.

**ciclón** *nm* cyclone.

**ciego,-a** *adj (persona)* blind. LOC **a ciegas 1** *(sin ver)* blindly. **2** *(sin pensar)* without thinking.

**cielo** *nm* **1** *(gen)* sky. **2** *(clima)* weather, climate. **3** REL heaven.
▶ *interj* **cielos** good heavens! LOC **llovido,-a del cielo** *fig* heaven-sent. **ser un cielo (de persona)** *fam* to be an angel.

**ciempiés** *nm inv* centipede.

**cien** *adj* [se usa sólo antes de los nombres en plural] one hundred, a hundred.
▶ *nm* one hundred, a hundred. LOC **cien por cien** one hundred per cent.

✎ Consulta también **ciento y seis**.

**ciénaga** *nf* marsh, bog.

**ciencia** *nf (disciplina)* science. COMP **ciencia ficción** science fiction. **ciencias naturales** natural sciences.

**cienmilésimo,-a** *adj* hundred thousandth.
▶ *nm & nf* hundred thousandth.

✎ Consulta también **sexto,-a**.

**cienmillonésimo,-a** *adj* hundred millionth.
▶ *nm & nf* hundred millionth.

✎ Consulta también **sexto,-a**.

**científico,-a** *adj* scientific.
▶ *nm & nf* scientist.

**ciento** *adj* one hundred, a hundred:
▶ *nm* **1** *(número)* hundred. **2** **un ciento** *(centena)* about a hundred. LOC **por ciento** per cent.

✎ Consulta también **cien**.

**cierre** *nm* **1** *(acción)* closing, shutting; *(de fábrica)* shutdown; *(de radio, etc)* close-down. **2** *(de prenda)* fastener; *(de bolso)* clasp; *(de cinturón)* buckle, clasp. COMP **cierre patronal** lockout.

**cierto,-a** *adj* **1** *(seguro)* certain, sure. **2** *(verdadero)* true: *no es cierto* that's not true. LOC **estar en lo cierto** to be right. **por cierto** by the way.
▶ *adv* **cierto** certainly.

**ciervo,-a** *nm & nf (gen)* deer; *(macho)* stag, hart; *(hembra)* doe, hind.

**cifra** *nf* **1** *(número)* figure, number. **2** *(cantidad)* amount, number. **3** *(código)* cipher, code.

**cifrar** *vt (codificar)* to encode; *(en informática)* to encrypt.

**cigala** *nf* Dublin Bay prawn.

**cigarra** *nf* cicada.

**cigarrillo** *nm* cigarette.

**cigarro** *nm* **1** *(puro)* cigar. **2** *(cigarrillo)* cigarette.

**cigoto** *nm* zygote.

**cigüeña** *nf (ave)* stork.

**cilindrada** *nf* cylinder capacity.

**cilíndrico,-a** *adj* cylindric, cylindrical.

**cilindro** *nm* cylinder.

**cima** *nf* **1** *(de montaña)* summit, top; *(de árbol)* top. **2** *fig (cumbre)* summit, peak.

**cimentar** *vt* **1** ARQUIT to lay the foundations of. **2** *fig (afianzar)* to strengthen, consolidate.

**cimiento** [se usa sólo en plural con el mismo significado] *nm* **1** ARQUIT foundation, foundations *pl*. **2** *fig* basis, origin. LOC **poner los cimientos** to lay the foundations.

**cinabrio** *nm* cinnabar.

**cinc** *nm* zinc.

**cincel** *nm* chisel.

**cincelar** *vt* to chisel, engrave.

**cincha** *nf (de caballo)* girth, US cinch.

**cinco** *adj (cardinal)* five; *(ordinal)* fifth.
▶ *nm (número)* five. LOC **¡choca esos cinco!** *fam* put it there!, give me five!

✎ Consulta también **seis**.

**cincuenta** *adj (cardinal)* fifty; *(ordinal)* fiftieth.
► *nm (número)* fifty.

✎ Consulta también seis.

**cincuentavo,-a** *adj* fiftieth.
► *nm & nf* fiftieth.

✎ Consulta también sexto,-a.

**cine** *nm* **1** *(local)* cinema, US movie theater: *ir al cine* to go to the cinema, US go to the movies. **2** *(arte)* cinema.

**cineasta** *nm o nf* film director, filmmaker.

**cineclub** *nm* **1** *(organización)* film society, film club. **2** *(local)* cinema, US movie theater.

**cinematografía** *nf* film-making, cinematography, US movie-making.

**cinematográfico,-a** *adj* cinematographic.

**cinematógrafo** *nm* film projector, US movie projector.

**cinética** *nf* kinetics.

**cinético,-a** *adj* kinetic.

**cínico,-a** *adj* cynical.
► *nm & nf* cynic.

**cinismo** *nm* cynicism.

**cinta** *nf* **1** *(gen)* band, strip; *(decorativa)* ribbon. **2** COST braid, edging. **3** TÉC tape. **4** *(de máquina de escribir)* ribbon. **5** *(casete)* tape. COMP **cinta adhesiva** adhesive tape. I **cinta magnética** magnetic tape. I **cinta métrica** tape measure.

**cintura** *nf* waist.

**cinturilla** *nf* waistband.

**cinturón** *nm* belt. COMP **cinturón de seguridad** safety belt, seat belt.

**ciprés** *nm* cypress.

**circo** *nm* **1** *(gen)* circus. **2** GEOG cirque.

**circonita** *nf* zirconite.

**circuito** *nm* **1** *(eléctrico)* circuit. **2** *(recorrido)* tour, circuit. **3** *(de carreras)* track, circuit.

**circulación** *nf* **1** *(gen)* circulation. **2** *(de vehículos)* traffic. COMP **circulación sanguínea** blood circulation. I **código de (la) circulación** highway code.

**circular** *adj* circular.
► *vi* **1** *(gen)* to circulate, move, go round. **2** *(líquido, electricidad)* to circulate, flow. **3** *(coche)* to drive; *(trenes, autobuses)* to run; *(peatón)* to walk. **4** *fig (rumor, etc)* to spread, get round.

**círculo** *nm* *(gen)* circle. COMP **círculo familiar** family circle. I **círculo polar antártico** Antarctic Circle. I **círculo polar ártico** Arctic Circle. I **círculo vicioso** *fig* vicious circle.

**circunferencia** *nf* circumference.

**circunflejo,-a** *adj* circumflex.
► *nm* **circunflejo** circumflex.

**circunscribir** *vt* to circumscribe.
► *vpr* **circunscribirse** *(ceñirse)* to confine OS (a, to), limit OS (a, to).

**circunscripción** *nf* district, area. COMP **circunscripción electoral** constituency.

**circunstancia** *nf* circumstance. LOC **en estas circunstancias** under the circumstances.

**circunstancial** *adj* circumstantial.

**circunvalar** *vt* to go round.

**cirio** *nm* long wax candle. LOC **armar un cirio** *fam* to kick up a rumpus.

**cirrosis** *nf inv* cirrhosis.

**ciruela** *nf* plum. COMP **ciruela claudia** greengage. I **ciruela pasa** prune.

**ciruelo** *nm* plum tree.

**cirugía** *nf* surgery. COMP **cirugía estética** plastic surgery.

**cirujano,-a** *nm & nf* surgeon.

**cisma** *nm* REL schism.

**cisne** *nm* swan.

**cisterna** *nf* cistern, tank.

**cita** *nf* **1** *(para negocios, médico, etc)* appointment: *tengo una cita con mi abogado* I have an appointment with my lawyer. **2** *(amorosa)* date. **3** *(mención)* quotation. LOC **tener una cita** to have an appointment, have an engagement.

**citación** *nf* **1** *(mención)* quotation. **2** JUR citation, summons.

**citar** *vt* **1** *(dar cita)* to make an appointment with, arrange to meet. **2** *(mencionar)* to quote.

**citoplasma** *nm* cytoplasm.

**cítrico,-a** *adj* citric.
▶ *nm pl* **cítricos** citrus fruits.

**ciudad** *nf* city, town. [COMP] **ciudad dormitorio** dormitory town. ▌ **ciudad universitaria** university campus.

**ciudadanía** *nf* citizenship.

**ciudadano,-a** *adj* civic.
▶ *nm & nf* citizen.

**ciudadela** *nf* citadel, fortress.

**cívico,-a** *adj* civic.

**civil** *adj* **1** civil. **2** *(no militar)* civilian. **3** *(no eclesiástico)* lay, secular.

**civilización** *nf* civilization.

**civilizar** *vt* to civilize.

**civismo** *nm* **1** good citizenship, community spirit. **2** *(al servicio de los demás)* civility.

**cizalla** [también se usa en plural con el mismo significado.] *nf (tijeras)* metal shears *pl*, wire cutters *pl*.

**cl** *sím* **(centilitro)** centilitre (US centiliter); *(símbolo)* cl.

**clamor** *nm (griterío)* shouting, din, noise.

**clan** *nm* clan.

**clandestino,-a** *adj* clandestine, underground, secret.

**claqué** *nm* tap dancing.

**claraboya** *nf* skylight.

**claridad** *nf (luminosidad)* light, brightness. [LOC] **con claridad** clearly.

**clarín** *nm (instrumento)* bugle.
▶ *nm o nf (músico)* bugler.

**clarinete** *nm (instrumento)* clarinet.

**clarinetista** *nm o nf* clarinettist, clarinetist.

**claro,-a** *adj* **1** *(gen)* clear. **2** *(iluminado)* bright, well-lit. **3** *(color)* light: *azul claro* light blue. **4** *(salsa, etc)* thin; *(café, chocolate, etc)* weak. [LOC] **dejar** ALGO **claro** to make STH clear. ▌ **estar claro** to be clear.
▶ *adv* clearly.
▶ *interj* **¡claro!** of course!.

**clase** *nf* **1** *(grupo, categoría)* class. **2** *(aula)* classroom; *(de universidad)* lecture hall. **3** *(tipo)* type, sort. [LOC] **asistir a clase** to attend class. [COMP] **clase me-** dia middle class. ▌ **clase particular** private class, private lesson. ▌ **primera clase** first class.

**clasicismo** *nm* classicism.

**clásico,-a** *adj* **1** *(de los clásicos)* classical: *literatura clásica* classical literature. **2** *(tradicional)* classic.
▶ *nm* **clásico** classic: *este libro es un clásico de la ciencia ficción* this book is a science-fiction classic.

**clasificación** *nf* **1** *(gen)* classification. **2** *(distribución)* sorting, filing. **3** DEP league, table. **4** *(de discos)* top twenty, hit parade.

**clasificar** *vt* **1** to class, classify. **2** *(distribuir)* to sort, file.
▶ *vpr* **clasificarse 1** DEP to qualify. **2** *(llegar)* to come.

**claustro** *nm* ARQUIT cloister.

**claustrofobia** *nf* claustrophobia.

**claustrofóbico,-a** *adj* claustrophobic.

**cláusula** *nf* clause.

**clausura** *nf* **1** *(cierre)* closure. **2** *(acto)* closing ceremony, closing session.

**clausurar** *vt* **1** *(poner fin)* to close, conclude. **2** *(cerrar)* to close (down).

**clavar** *vt* **1** *(con clavos)* to nail. **2** *(un clavo)* to bang, hammer in; *(estaca)* to drive. **3** *fig (atención)* to fix; *(ojos)* to rivet.
▶ *vpr* **clavarse** *(gen)* to stick.

**clave** *nf* **1** *(de un enigma, etc)* key, clue: *la clave del éxito* the key to success. **2** *(de signos)* code, key, cipher: *un mensaje en clave* a coded message. **3** MÚS key: **4** ARQUIT keystone.
▶ *nm (instrumento)* harpsichord.

**clavel** *nm* carnation.

**clavicémbalo** *nm* harpsichord.

**clavicordio** *nm* clavichord.

**clavícula** *nf* clavicle, collarbone.

**clavija** *nf* **1** TÉC peg. **2** ELEC *(de enchufe)* pin.

**clavo** *nm* **1** nail. **2** BOT clove. [LOC] **dar en el clavo** *fig* to hit the nail on the head.

**claxon®** *nm* horn, hooter.

**clemencia** *nf* clemency, mercy.

**clerical** *adj* clerical.

**clérigo** *nm* priest.

**clero** *nm* clergy.

**clic** *nm* click. LOC **hacer clic 1** *(hacer ruido)* to click, go click. **2** INFORM to click.

**clicar** *vt* to click on.
▸ *vi* to click.

**clienta** *nf* client, customer.

**cliente** *nm o nf* client, customer.

**clientela** *nf* customers *pl*, clients *pl*, clientele.

**clima** *nm* climate.

**climático,-a** *adj* climatic, climatical.

**climatizado,-a** *adj* air-conditioned.

**climatizar** *vt* to air-condition.

**climatología** *nf* climatology.

**clínica** *nf* *(hospital)* clinic, private hospital.

**clínico,-a** *adj* clinical: *muerte clínica* clinical death.

**clip** *nm* **1** *(para papel)* paper clip. **2** *(para pelo)* hair-grip, US bobby pin. **3** *(pendiente)* clip-on earring.

**cloaca** *nf* sewer, drain.

**clon** *nm* clone.

**clonación** *nf* cloning.

**clonar** *vt* to clone.

**clónico,-a** *adj* cloned.
▸ *nm* **clónico** *(ordenador)* clone.

**cloquear** *vi* to cluck.

**cloro** *nm* chlorine.

**clorofila** *nf* chlorophyll.

**clorofílico,-a** *adj* chlorophyllous.

**cloroformo** *nm* chloroform.

**clown** *nm* clown..

**club** *nm* club, society. COMP **club de fútbol** football club. ‖ **club de tenis** tennis club. ‖ **club náutico** yacht club.

**cm** *sím* *(centímetro)* centimetre (US centimeter); *(símbolo)* cm.

**coaccionar** *vt* to coerce, compel.

**coagular** *vt* *(gen)* to coagulate, clot; *(leche)* to curdle.
▸ *vpr* **coagularse** to coagulate, clot; *(leche)* to curdle.

**coágulo** *nm* coagulum, clot.

**coala** *nm* koala, koala bear.

**coartada** *nf* alibi.

**coba** *nf fam* soft soap. LOC **dar coba a ALGN** *fam* to soft-soap SB.

**cobalto** *nm* cobalt.

**cobarde** *adj* cowardly.
▸ *nm o nf* coward.

**cobardía** *nf* cowardice.

**cobaya** *nm* guinea pig.

**cobertizo** *nm* shed, shack.

**cobertura** *nf* **1** *(gen)* cover. **2** *(de una red, servicio)* coverage. COMP **cobertura de chocolate** chocolate coating. ‖ **cobertura de seguros** insurance cover.

**cobijar** *vt* **1** *(cubrir)* to cover. **2** *fig* to shelter.
▸ *vpr* **cobijarse** to take shelter.

**cobijo** *nm* **1** *(hospedaje)* lodging. **2** *(refugio)* shelter. **3** *fig* protection, refuge.

**cobol** *nm* INFORM COBOL.

**cobra** *nf* *(serpiente)* cobra.

**cobrador,-ra** *nm & nf* **1** *(de luz, etc)* collector. **2** *(de transporte - hombre)* conductor; *(- mujer)* conductress.

**cobrar** *vt* **1** *(fijar precio por)* to charge; *(cheques)* to cash; *(salario)* to earn. **2** to get: *si no te estás quieto vas a cobrar una torta* if you don't keep still you'll get a smack. **3** *fig* *(adquirir)* to gain, get.
▸ *vi* to be in for it.
▸ *vpr* **cobrarse 1** *(dinero)* to take, collect. **2** *(víctimas)* to claim. **3** *(recuperar)* to recover (de, from); *(volver en sí)* to come round.

**cobre** *nm* *(metal)* copper.

**cobro** *nm* **1** *(pago)* payment. **2** *(cobranza)* collection; *(de cheque)* cashing. COMP **cobro revertido** reverse-charge, US collect.

**coca** *nf* **1** *(arbusto)* coca. **2** *argot* coke. **3** *fam* *(bebida)* Coke®.

**cocción** *nf* *(gen)* cooking; *(en agua)* boiling; *(en horno)* baking.

**cóccix** *nm inv* coccyx.

**cocear** *vi* to kick.

**cocer** *vt* *(gen)* to cook; *(hervir)* to boil; *(al horno)* to bake.
▸ *vpr* **cocerse 1** *(gen)* to cook; *(hervir)* to boil; *(al horno)* to bake. **2** *fam* *(de calor)* to be roasting, be boiling.

**coche** *nm* **1** *(automóvil)* car, automobile, motorcar: *fuimos en coche* we went by car. **2** *(de tren, de caballos)* carriage, coach. **3** *(de niño)* pram, US baby carriage. COMP **coche cama** sleeping car. ▎ **coche de alquiler** hired car, US rented car. ▎ **coche de bomberos** fire engine. ▎ **coche de carreras** racing car.

**cochera** *nf* depot.

**cochino,-a** *adj* *(sucio)* filthy, disgusting.
▶ *nm & nf* **1** ZOOL *(gen)* pig; *(macho)* swine; *(hembra)* sow. **2** *fam* *(persona)* dirty person, filthy person, pig.

**cocido,-a** *adj* cooked; *(en agua)* boiled; *(al horno)* baked.
▶ *nm* **cocido** CULIN stew.

**cociente** *nm* quotient.

**cocina** *nf* **1** *(lugar)* kitchen. **2** *(gastronomía)* cooking: *cocina española* Spanish cooking, Spanish cuisine. **3** *(aparato)* cooker, US stove. COMP **cocina casera** home cooking. ▎ **cocina de gas** gas cooker, US gas stove. ▎ **cocina de mercado** seasonal produce. ▎ **cocina eléctrica** electric cooker, US electric stove.

**cocinar** *vt* to cook.
▶ *vi* to cook.

**cocinero,-a** *nm & nf* cook. COMP **primer cocinero** chef.

**coco¹** *nm* **1** BOT *(árbol)* coconut palm. **2** *(fruta)* coconut. COMP **coco rallado** desiccated coconut.

**coco²** *nm* **1** *fam* *(fantasma)* bogeyman. **2** *argot* *(cabeza)* noddle, noggin, nut. LOC **comerse el coco** *fam* to get worked up, worry about it.

**cocodrilo** *nm* crocodile.

**cocotero** *nm* coconut palm.

**cóctel** *nm* *(bebida)* cocktail.

**codazo** *nm* *(golpe)* poke with one's elbow, blow with one's elbow: *le pegó un codazo* she poked him with her elbow. LOC **abrirse paso a codazos** to elbow one's way through.

**codear** *vi* *(empujar)* to elbow.
▶ *vpr* **codearse** to rub shoulders (con, with), hobnob (con, with).

**codera** *nf* elbow patch.

**codicia** *nf* greed, coveting.

**codiciar** *vt* to covet, desire, crave for.

**codicioso,-a** *adj* covetous, greedy.

**codificación** *nf* **1** *(de mensajes)* encoding. **2** INFORM coding, code.

**codificar** *vt* **1** *(leyes)* to codify. **2** *(mensajes)* to encode. **3** INFORM to code.

**código** *nm* code. COMP **código de barras** bar code. ▎ **código de la circulación** highway code. ▎ **código de señales** MAR flag signals. ▎ **código Morse** Morse code.

**codillo** *nm* **1** *(del brazo)* elbow. **2** *(en cocina)* shoulder. **3** *(de tubería)* elbow.

**codo** *nm* **1** ANAT elbow. **2** TÉC bend. LOC **alzar el codo / empinar el codo** *fam* to have a few drinks, knock them back. ▎ **codo a codo / codo con codo** *fig* side by side, closely. ▎ **de codos** on one's elbows. ▎ **hablar por los codos** *fam* to talk nineteen to the dozen, talk nonstop. ▎ **romperse los codos** *fig* to study a lot, swot, cram.

**codorniz** *nf* quail.

**coeficiente** *nm* **1** MAT coefficient. **2** *(grado)* degree, rate. COMP **coeficiente de inteligencia** intelligence quotient, IQ.

**cofia** *nf* bonnet.

**coexistir** *vi* to coexist.

**cofradía** *nf* **1** *(hermandad)* brotherhood. **2** *(asociación)* association. **3** *(gremio)* guild.

**cofre** *nm* *(grande)* trunk, chest; *(pequeño)* box, casket.

**coger** *vt* **1** *(asir)* to seize, take hold of: *coge al bebé* hold the baby. **2** *(apresar)* to capture, catch. **3** *(tomar)* to take: *coge algo para beber* take a drink. **4** *(tren, etc)* to catch. **5** *(tomar prestado)* to borrow: *te he cogido el libro* I've borrowed your book. **6** *(recolectar frutos, etc)* to pick; *(del suelo)* to gather. **7** *(enfermedad, balón)* to catch: *cogí un resfriado* I caught a cold. **8** *(velocidad, fuerza)* to take. **9** *(emisora, canal)* to pick up, get: *coger la BBC* to get the BBC. **10** *(notas)* to take, take down. **11** *(entender)* to understand, get: *no cogí el final* I didn't get the end. LOC **coger cariño a** ALGO/ALGN to become fond of STH/SB, take a liking to STH/SB. **I coger por sorpresa** to catch by surprise.

▸ *vpr* **cogerse** *(agarrarse)* to hold on: *cógete fuerte* hold on tight. LOC **cogerse un cabreo** *fam* to get very angry.

**cogollo** *nm (de lechuga, etc)* heart.

**cogote** *nm* back of the neck.

**coherencia** *nf* coherence, coherency.

**coherente** *adj* coherent, connected.

**cohete** *nm* rocket.

**cohibir** *vt* to inhibit, restrain.

▸ *vpr* **cohibirse** to feel inhibited, feel embarrassed.

**coincidir** *vi* **1** *(estar de acuerdo)* to agree (en, on), coincide (en, in). **2** *(ajustarse)* to coincide. **3** *(ocurrir al mismo tiempo)* to be at the same time (con, as), coincide (con, with); *(en el mismo lugar)* to meet.

**cojear** *vi* **1** *(persona)* to limp, hobble. **2** *(muebles)* to wobble. LOC **cojear del mismo pie** *fam* to have the same faults.

**cojera** *nf* limp, lameness.

**cojín** *nm* cushion.

**cojo,-a** *adj* **1** *(persona)* lame, crippled. **2** *(mueble)* wobbly. **3** *fig (defectuoso)* faulty, incomplete.

**col** *nf* cabbage. COMP **col de Bruselas** Brussels sprout.

**cola¹** *nf* **1** *(gen)* tail. **2** *(de vestido)* train; *(de chaqueta)* tail. **3** *(fila)* queue, US line. LOC **hacer cola** to queue up, US stand in line. **I** COMP **cola de caballo** *(peinado)* ponytail.

**cola²** *nf (pegamento)* glue.

**colaboración** *nf* **1** collaboration. **2** *(prensa)* contribution.

**colaborador,-ra** *adj* collaborating.

▸ *nm & nf* **1** collaborator. **2** *(prensa)* contributor.

**colaborar** *vi* **1** to collaborate (con, with). **2** *(prensa)* to contribute (en, to).

**colada** *nf* **1** *(lavado)* washing, laundry; *(con lejía)* bleaching. **2** *(ropa)* washing, wash. **3** *(volcánica)* outflow. LOC **hacer**

**la colada** to do the washing, do the laundry.

**colador** *nm* **1** *(de té, café)* strainer. **2** *(de caldo, alimentos)* colander, sieve.

**colapsar** *vt (ciudad, aeropuerto, etc)* to paralyse; *(tráfico)* to bring to a standstill, bring to a halt.

▸ *vi* to collapse.

**colar** *vt (líquido)* to strain, filter.

▸ *vi fam* to wash: *veremos si cuela* we'll see if it washes.

▸ *vpr* **colarse 1** *(escabullirse)* to slip in, gatecrash. **2** *(en una cola)* to push in, jump the queue, US jump the line. **3** *fam (equivocarse)* to slip up, make a mistake.

**colcha** *nf* bedspread.

**colchón** *nm* mattress. COMP **colchón neumático** air mattress.

**colchoneta** *nf* small mattress.

**cole** *nm fam* school.

**colear** *vi (perro, etc)* to wag its tail; *(vaca, caballo, etc)* to swish its tail.

**colección** *nf* collection.

**coleccionar** *vt* to collect.

**coleccionista** *nm o nf* collector.

**colectividad** *nf* community.

**colectivo,-a** *adj* collective, group.

▸ *nm* **colectivo 1** *(asociación)* association, guild. **2** LING collective noun.

**colegio** *nm (escuela)* school: *van al colegio en autobús* they go to school by bus. COMP **colegio público** state school.

**coleóptero** *nm* coleopteran.

**cólera** *nf* **1** *(bilis)* bile. **2** *fig (ira)* anger, rage.

▸ *nm* MED cholera.

**colérico,-a** *adj* furious, irascible.

**colesterol** *nm* cholesterol.

**coleta** *nf* pigtail, ponytail.

**colgado,-a** *adj* hanging (de, from).

**colgador** *nm* (coat) hanger.

**colgante** *adj* hanging.

▸ *nm* **1** ARQUIT festoon. **2** *(joya)* pendant.

**colgar** *vt* **1** *(gen)* to hang (up). **2** *(la colada)* to hang out. **3** *(atribuir)* to pin. **4** *(el teléfono)* to put down.

▶ *vi* **1** *(estar colgado)* to hang (de, from): *cuelga del techo* it hangs from the ceiling. **2** *(una prenda)* to hang down, be crooked. **3** *(teléfono)* to hang up, ring off: *¡no cuelgue!* please hold!, hold the line, please!

**colibrí** *nm* humming bird.

**cólico** *nm* colic.

**coliflor** *nf* cauliflower.

**colilla** *nf* cigarette end, cigarette butt, butt.

**colina** *nf* hill, slope.

**colirio** *nm* eye drops *pl.*

**colisión** *nf (de vehículos)* collision, crash.

**colisionar** *vi (chocar)* to collide (con/contra, with), crash (con/contra, into).

**colitis** *nf inv* colitis.

**collar** *nm* **1** *(adorno)* necklace. **2** *(de animal)* collar.

**colmar** *vt (gen)* to fill (de, with); *(vaso, copa)* to fill to the brim.

**colmena** *nf* beehive.

**colmillo** *nm* **1** eye tooth, canine tooth. **2** *(de carnívoro)* fang; *(de jabalí, elefante, morsa)* tusk.

**colmo** *nm* height, summit. LOC *¡esto es el colmo!* this is the last straw!, this is the limit!

**colocar** *vt* **1** *(gen)* to place, put. **2** *(dar empleo)* to get a job for.
▶ *vpr* **colocarse 1** *(situarse)* to place os, put os, find os a place. **2** *(trabajar)* to find a job (de, as), get a job (de, as).

**Colombia** *nf* Colombia.

**colombiano,-a** *adj* Colombian.
▶ *nm & nf* Colombian.

**colon** *nm* ANAT colon.

**colonia** *nf* **1** *(grupo)* colony. **2** [normalmente en plural] *(vacaciones infantiles)* summer camp. **3** *(perfume)* cologne.

**colonial** *adj* POL colonial.

**colonialismo** *nm* colonialism.

**colonización** *nf* colonization.

**colonizar** *vt* to colonize, settle.

**colono** *nm* **1** *(habitante)* colonist, settler. **2** AGR tenant farmer.

**coloquial** *adj* colloquial.

**coloquio** *nm* talk, discussion.

**color** *nm* **1** colour (US color): *es de color verde* it's green. LOC **de color 1** *(en color)* in colour (US color), coloured (US colored). **2** *(persona)* coloured (US colored). ▮ **en color / en colores** *(cine, foto)* in colour (US color).

**colorado,-a** *adj* **1** coloured (US colored). **2** *(rojo)* red. LOC **ponerse colorado,-a** to blush, go red.

**colorante** *nm* colouring (US coloring), dye.

**colorear** *vt* to colour (US color).

**colorete** *nm* rouge, blusher.

**colorido** *nm* colour (US color).

**coloso** *nm* colossus.

**columna** *nf* **1** *(gen)* column. **2** ANAT spine. **3** *(elemento central)* backbone. COMP **columna vertebral** vertebral column, spinal column.

**columpiar** *vt* to swing.
▶ *vpr* **columpiarse** to swing (de, on).

**columpio** *nm* swing.

**colza** *nf* rape. COMP **aceite de colza** rapeseed oil, US canola oil.

**coma¹** *nf* **1** *(puntuación)* comma. **2** *(en música)* comma. **3** MAT point: *cuatro coma cinco* four point five.

**coma²** *nm* MED coma. LOC **entrar en coma** to go into a coma.

**comadreja** *nf* weasel.

**comadrona** *nm & nf* midwife.

**comandante** *nm* **1** *(oficial)* commander, commanding officer. **2** *(graduación)* major. **3** *(piloto)* pilot.

**comando** *nm* **1** MIL commando. **2** INFORM command.

**comarca** *nf* area, region.

**comba** *nf* **1** *(de cuerda, cable)* bend, curve. **2** *(cuerda)* skipping rope. **3** *(juego)* skipping. LOC **saltar a la comba** to skip, US skip rope.

**combar** *vt* to bend.
▶ *vpr* **combarse** *(una cuerda)* to bend; *(viga, pared)* to sag, bulge.

**combate** *nm* **1** *(gen)* combat, battle. **2** MIL battle. **3** *(boxeo)* fight, contest.

**combatiente** *adj* fighting.
▶ *nm o nf* fighter, combatant.

**combatir** *vi* to fight (contra, against /-), struggle (contra, against).
▶ *vt* **1** *(luchar contra)* to fight: *combatir el cáncer* to fight cancer. **2** *fig* to combat, fight. **3** *fig (batir, golpear)* to beat, lash.

**combativo,-a** *adj* spirited, aggressive.

**combinación** *nf* **1** combination. **2** *(prenda)* slip.

**combinar** *vt* **1** *(gen)* to combine. **2** QUÍM to combine. **3** *(colores)* to match (con, -), go (con, with).

**combustible** *adj* combustible.
▶ *nm* fuel.

**comedero** *nm* feeding trough, manger.

**comedia** *nf* **1** TEAT comedy, play. **2** *fig* farce, pretence (US pretense).

**comediante,-a** *nm & nf* **1** *(hombre)* actor; *(mujer)* actress. **2** *fig* hypocrite, comedian.

**comedor,-ra** *nm (sala)* dining room; *(en una fábrica, un colegio, etc)* canteen.

**comensal** *nm o nf* person at the table, diner.

**comentar** *vt* **1** *(texto)* to comment on. **2** *(expresar una opinión)* to talk about, discuss.

**comentario** *nm* **1** *(observación)* remark, comment. **2** *(explicación, narración)* commentary.
▶ *nm pl* **comentarios** *(murmuración)* gossip *sing*.

**comentarista** *nm o nf* commentator.

**comenzar** *vt* to begin, start.
▶ *vi* to begin, start: *comenzó a reír* he began to laugh, he began laughing. LOC **comenzar con** to begin with. I **comenzar + *ger*** to start by + *ger*: *comenzó explicando...* he started by explaining...

**comer** *vt* **1** to eat. **2** *(en ajedrez)* to take, capture.
▶ *vi (gen)* to eat; *(a mediodía)* to have lunch, lunch; *(por la noche)* to have dinner, dine.
▶ *nm* eating.
▶ *vpr* **comerse 1** to eat. **2** *fig (saltarse)* to omit; *(párrafo)* to skip; *(palabra)* to swallow.

**comercial** *adj* **1** *(del comercio)* commercial. **2** *(de tiendas)* shopping.
▶ *nm o nf (vendedor)* seller; *(hombre)* salesman; *(mujer)* saleswoman.

**comerciante** *adj* business-minded.
▶ *nm o nf* **1** merchant. **2** *(interesado)* moneymaker.

**comerciar** *vi* **1** *(comprar y vender)* to trade, deal, buy and sell. **2** *(hacer negocios)* to do business (con, with).

**comercio** *nm* **1** *(ocupación)* commerce, trade. **2** *(tienda)* shop, store. LOC **comercio al por mayor** wholesale trade. COMP **comercio exterior** foreign trade. I **libre comercio** free trade.

**comestible** *adj* edible, eatable.
▶ *nm pl* **comestibles** groceries, food *sing*, foodstuffs *pl*.

**cometa** *nm (cuerpo celeste)* comet.
▶ *nf (juguete)* kite.

**cometer** *vt (crimen)* to commit; *(falta, error)* to make.

**cómic** *nm* comic.

**cómico,-a** *adj* **1** *(divertido)* comic, comical, funny. **2** *(de comedia)* comedy.
▶ *nm & nf (actor)* comedian, comic.

**comida** *nf* **1** *(alimento)* food: **2** *(desayuno, etc)* meal. **3** *(almuerzo)* lunch.

**comienzo** *nm* start, beginning. LOC **a comienzos de** at the beginning of. I **dar comienzo** to begin, start.

**comillas** *nf pl* inverted commas. LOC **entre comillas** in inverted commas.

**comilona** *nf* big meal, blowout.

**comino** *nm* BOT cumin, cummin. LOC **me importa un comino** *fam* I don't give a damn.

**comisaría** *nf (de policía)* police station.

**comisario** *nm (de policía)* police inspector.

**comisión** *nf* **1** *(retribución)* commission. **2** *(comité)* committee. LOC **a comisión / con comisión** on a commission basis. COMP **comisión bancaria** service charge, bank commission.

**comité** *nm* committee.

**comitiva** *nf* suite, retinue.

**como** *adv* **1** *(modo)* how: *lo hizo como quiso* he did it the way he wanted to. **2** *(com-*

*paración)* as, like: *negro como la noche* as dark as night. **3** *(en calidad de)* as: *como invitado* as a guest. **4** *(según)* as: *como dice tu amigo* as your friend says. **5** *fam (aproximadamente)* about: *había como unos cien* there were about a hundred. LOC **como quiera que 1** *(no importa cómo)* however. **2** *(ya que)* since, as, inasmuch as. **I como sea** whatever happens, no matter what. **I hacer como si** to pretend to +*inf*: *hace como si no viese nada* he's pretending not to see anything.

▶ *conj* **1** *(así que)* as: *como llegaban se presentaban* they introduced themselves as they arrived. **2** *(si)* if: *como lo vuelvas a hacer...* if you do it again.... **3** *(porque)* as, since: *como llegamos tarde no pudimos entrar* since we arrived late we couldn't get in.

**cómo** *adv* **1** *(interrogativo)* how. **2** *(por qué)* why. **3** *(admiración)* how: *¡cómo pasa el tiempo!* how time flies! LOC **¿cómo?** *fam* what? **I ¿cómo es que...?** how is it that...? **I ¡cómo no!** but of course!, certainly!

**cómoda** *nf* chest of drawers, commode.

**comodidad** *nf* **1** *(confort)* comfort. **2** *(facilidad)* convenience. LOC **con comodidad** comfortably.

**comodín** *nm* *(mono)* joker; *(otra carta)* wild card.

**cómodo,-a** *adj* **1** comfortable, cosy. **2** *(útil)* convenient, handy.

**compactar** *vt* to compact, compress.

**compadecer** *vt* to pity, feel sorry for.
▶ *vpr* **compadecerse** to take pity (de, on), pity (de, -), feel sorry (de, for).

**compaginar** *vt* *(combinar)* to combine, make compatible.
▶ *vpr* **compaginarse** to go together, be compatible.

**compañerismo** *nm* companionship, fellowship, comradeship.

**compañero,-a** *nm & nf* **1** *(sentimental, pareja)* partner. **2** *(colega)* companion, mate; *(camarada)* comrade. **3** *fig (guante, zapato, etc)* the other one, the one that goes with this one. COMP **compa-**

**ñero,-a de colegio** schoolmate. **I compañero,-a de piso** flatmate. **I compañero,-a de trabajo** workmate, colleague.

**compañía** *nf* company. LOC **en compañía de** in the company of. **I hacer compañía a** ALGN to keep SB company.

**comparación** *nf* comparison. LOC **en comparación con** compared to, in comparison to.

**comparar** *vt* to compare:

**comparativo,-a** *adj* comparative.

**compartimento** *nm* compartment: *compartimento de primera clase* first-class compartment.

**compartir** *vt* **1** *(dividir)* to divide (up), split, share (out). **2** *(poseer en común)* to share.

**compás** *nm* **1** *(instrumento)* compass, compasses *pl*. **2** *(brújula)* compass. **3** MÚS *(división)* time; *(intervalo)* beat; *(ritmo)* rhythm. LOC **al compás de** in time to. **I llevar el compás 1** *(con la mano)* to beat time. **2** *(al bailar)* to keep time. **I perder el compás** to lose the beat.

**compasión** *nf* compassion, pity.

**compasivo,-a** *adj* compassionate, sympathetic.

**compatibilidad** *nf* compatibility.

**compatibilizar** *vt* to make compatible.

**compatible** *adj* compatible.

**compendio** *nm* summary, digest, précis, synopsis.

**compenetrarse** *vpr* *(uso recíproco)* to understand each other.

**compensar** *vt* **1** *(pérdida, error)* to make up for. **2** *(indemnizar)* to compensate, indemnify. **3** TÉC to balance, compensate. **4** *fam (merecer la pena)* to be worth one's while.

**competencia** *nf* **1** *(rivalidad)* competition, rivalry: **2** *(competidores)* competitors *pl*, rival company. **3** *(habilidad)* competence, ability, proficiency. **4** *(incumbencia)* responsibility.

**competente** *adj* **1** *(capaz)* competent, capable, proficient. **2** *(adecuado)* adequate.

**competición** *nf* competition, contest.

**competidor,-ra** *adj* **1** *(que compite)* competing. **2** *(rival)* rival.
▶ *nm & nf* **1** *(rival)* competitor. **2** *(en competición deportiva)* competitor.

**competir** *vi* to compete.

**competitividad** *nf* competitiveness.

**competitivo,-a** *adj* competitive.

**complacer** *vt* **1** *(satisfacer)* to satisfy, gratify, oblige. **2** *(agradar)* to please. **3** *fml* to please, give pleasure.

**complejo,-a** *adj* complex.
▶ *nm* **complejo** complex.

**complementar** *vt* to complement.
▶ *vpr* **complementarse** to complement each other, be complementary to each other.

**complementario,-a** *adj* complementary.

**complemento** *nm* **1** *(gen)* complement. **2** GRAM object, complement. COMP **complemento circunstancial** adverbial complement. **I complemento directo** direct object. **I complemento indirecto** indirect object.

**completamente** *adv* completely.

**completar** *vt* **1** *(gen)* to complete. **2** *(acabar)* to finish; *(perfeccionar)* to round off.

**completo,-a** *adj* **1** *(terminado)* finished, completed. **2** *(lleno)* full. LOC **al completo** full up, filled to capacity. **I por completo** completely.

**complexión** *nf* constitution, build: *su hermano es de complexión fuerte* his brother is well-built.

**complicación** *nf* complication.

**complicado,-a** *adj* **1** *(gen)* complicated, complex. **2** *(carácter)* complex.

**complicar** *vt* **1** *(gen)* to complicate, make complicated. **2** *(implicar)* to involve (en, in).

**cómplice** *nm o nf* accomplice.

**complicidad** *nf* complicity.

**complot** *nm* plot, conspiracy.

**componente** *adj* component, constituent.
▶ *nm* **1** *(pieza)* component, constituent; *(ingrediente)* ingredient. **2** *(miembro)* member.

**componer** *vt* **1** *(formar)* to compose, make up, form. **2** *(reparar)* to fix, repair, mend. **3** *(adornar)* to adorn, decorate. **4** *(música, versos)* to compose.
▶ *vpr* **componerse** *(consistir)* to consist (de, of), be made up (de, of): *las palabras se componen de sílabas* words are made up of syllables.

**comportamiento** *nm* behaviour (US behavior), conduct.

**comportar** *vt* *(implica)* to involve, entail: *eso comporta un cambio de planes* that involves a change of plan.
▶ *vpr* **comportarse** *(portarse)* to behave: *se comportó mal* she misbehaved.

**composición** *nf* **1** *(gen)* composition. **2** *(arreglo)* arrangement.

**compositor,-ra** *nm & nf* composer.

**compota** *nf* compote.

**compra** *nf* purchase, buy. LOC **hacer la compra** to do the shopping, go shopping. **I ir de compras** to go shopping. COMP **compra a plazos** hire purchase, US instalment buying.

**comprador,-ra** *nm & nf* purchaser, buyer, shopper.

**comprar** *vt* to buy.

**compraventa** *nf* buying and selling, dealing.

**comprender** *vt* **1** *(entender)* to understand: *lo comprendiste mal* you misunderstood it. **2** *(contener)* to comprise, include. LOC **¿comprendes?** *(en conversación)* you see?

**comprensión** *nf* understanding.

**comprensivo,-a** *adj* **1** *(tolerante)* understanding. **2** *(que comprende o incluye)* comprehensive.

**compresa** *nf* **1** *(higiénica)* sanitary towel. **2** *(vendaje)* compress.

**comprimido,-a** *adj* compressed.
▶ *nm* **comprimido** tablet.

**comprimir** *vt (apretar)* to compress; *(gente)* to cram together.

**comprobante** *nm (recibo)* receipt, voucher.

**comprobar** *vt* **1** *(verificar)* to verify, check. **2** *(observar)* to see, observe: *como podrán ustedes comprobar* as you can see for yourselves. **3** *(confirmar)* to confirm.

**comprometer** *vt* **1** *(exponer a riesgo)* to endanger, jeopardize, risk; *(a una persona)* to compromise. **2** *(implicar)* to involve, implicate. **3** *(obligar)* to commit. **4** *(poner en un aprieto)* to embarrass.
▶ *vpr* **comprometerse 1** *(contraer una obligación)* to commit os, pledge. **2** *(involucrarse)* to get involved. **3** *(establecer relaciones formales)* to get engaged. LOC **comprometerse a hacer** ALGO to undertake to do STH.

**comprometido,-a** *adj* **1** *(difícil, arriesgado)* difficult, in jeopardy. **2** *(escritor, artista, etc)* committed. **3** *(involucrado)* involved. **4** *(para casarse)* engaged.

**compromiso** *nm* **1** *(obligación)* commitment, obligation: *cumplió sus compromisos* she fulfilled her obligations. **2** *(cita)* appointment; *(amorosa)* date. **3** *(apuro)* difficult situation, bind. **4** *(matrimonial)* engagement.

**compuesto,-a** *adj (gen)* compound.

**compulsar** *vt* **1** *(cotejar)* to collate. **2** JUR to make a certified true copy of.

**compulsivo,-a** *adj* compelling, compulsive.

**compungido,-a** *adj* **1** *(arrepentido)* remorseful. **2** *fig (triste)* sorrowful, sad.

**compungir** *vt fml (entristecer)* to sadden, make sad.
▶ *vpr* **compungirse** *(entristecerse)* to be saddened, feel sad.

**computación** *nf* computing.

**computador** *nm* computer.

**computadora** *nf* computer.

**computar** *vt* **1** *(calcular)* to compute, calculate. **2** *fml (tomar en cuenta)* to take into account, count.

**computarizar** *vt* to computerize.

**computerizar** *vt* to computerize.

**cómputo** *nm* computation, calculation.

**comulgar** *vi* REL to receive Holy Communion.

**común** *adj* **1** *(gen)* common: *eso es poco común* that's unusual. **2** *(compartido)* shared, communal.

**comuna** *nf* commune.

**comunal** *adj* communal.

**comunicación** *nf* **1** *(gen)* communication. **2** *(comunicado)* communication; *(oficial)* communiqué. **3** *(telefónica)* connection. **4** *(unión)* link, connection.
▶ *nf pl* **comunicaciones** communications.

**comunicado,-a** *adj* served. COMP **comunicado de prensa** press release.

**comunicar** *vt* **1** *(hacer partícipe)* to communicate, convey, transmit. **2** *(hacer saber)* to communicate, make known, tell. **3** *(conectar)* to connect.
▶ *vi* **1** *(ponerse en comunicación)* to communicate; *(por carta)* to correspond. **2** *(teléfono)* to be engaged, US be busy. **3** *(estar conectado)* to communicate, be connected.
▶ *vpr* **comunicarse 1** *(tener relación)* to communicate; *(ponerse en contacto)* to get in touch, get in contact (con, with). **2** *(estar conectado)* to be connected (con, to).

**comunicativo,-a** *adj* **1** *(actitud, sentimiento)* catching, infectious. **2** *(persona)* communicative, sociable, open.

**comunidad** *nf* community. COMP **comunidad autónoma** autonomous region. ‖ **Comunidad Económica Europea** European Economic Community.

**comunión** *nf* **1** communion, fellowship. **2** REL Holy Communion.

**comunismo** *nm* communism.

**comunista** *adj* communist.
▶ *nm o nf* communist.

**comunitario,-a** *adj (gen)* of the community, relating to the community.

**con** *prep* **1** *(instrumento, medio)* with. **2** *(modo, circunstancia)* in, with. **3** *(juntamente, en compañía)* with. **4** *(contenido)* with. **5** *(relación)* to. **6** *(comparación)* compared to. **7 con +** *inf* by + *ger.* **8** *(aunque)* in spite of. loc **con que / con tal de que / con tal que** provided, as long as. ‖ **con todo (y eso)** nevertheless, even so.

**concavidad** *nf* concavity.

**cóncavo,-a** *adj* concave.

**concebir** *vt* **1** *(engendrar)* to conceive. **2** *fig* *(comprender)* to understand.
▶ *vi* *(quedarse embarazada)* to become pregnant, conceive.

**conceder** *vt* **1** *(otorgar)* to grant, concede; *(premio)* to award. **2** *(atribuir)* to give, attach. **3** *(oportunidad, tiempo)* to give. **4** *(admitir)* to concede, admit.

**concejal,-la** *nm & nf* town councillor.

**concejo** *nm* town council, council.

**concentración** *nf* **1** *(gen)* concentration. **2** *(de gente)* gathering, rally.

**concentrar** *vt* to concentrate.
▶ *vpr* **concentrarse 1** *(reunirse)* to concentrate. **2** *(fijar la atención)* to concentrate (en, on).

**concéntrico,-a** *adj* concentric.

**concepción** *nf* conception.

**concepto** *nm* **1** *(idea)* concept, conception, idea. **2** *(opinión)* opinion, view. loc **bajo ningún concepto** under no circumstances. ‖ **en concepto de** by way of.

**conceptual** *adj* conceptual.

**concernir** *vi* [se usa sólo en tercera persona de presente de indicativo, imperfecto de indicativo y presente de subjuntivo; y en formas impersonales] *(afectar)* to concern, touch. loc **en lo que a mí** *(ti, él, etc)* **concierne** as far as I am *(you are, he is, etc)* concerned.

**concertado,-a** *adj* concerted.

**concertar** *vt* **1** *(planear)* to plan, coordinate. **2** *(entrevista)* to arrange; *(acuerdo)* to reach; *(tratado, negocio)* to conclude, settle. **3** *(precio)* to agree on.
▶ *vi* **1** *(concordar)* to agree, match up; *(números)* to tally. **2** LING to agree.

**concertino** *nm* first violin.

**concertista** *nm o nf* soloist.

**concesión** *nf* **1** concession, granting. **2** *(de premio)* awarding.

**concesionario,-a** *nm & nf* concessionaire, licence holder, licensee.
▶ *nm* **concesionario** *(de coches)* dealer.

**concesivo,-a** *adj* LING concessive.

**concha** *nf* **1** *(caparazón)* shell. **2** *(carey)* tortoiseshell. **3** *(ostra)* oyster.

**conciencia** *nf* **1** *(moral)* conscience. **2** *(conocimiento)* consciousness, awareness. loc **a conciencia** conscientiously. ‖ **remorderle a** ALGN **la conciencia** to weigh on SB's conscience.

**concienciar** *vt* to make aware (de, of).
▶ *vpr* **concienciarse** to become aware (de, of).

**concienzudo,-a** *adj* conscientious.

**concierto** *nm* **1** MÚS *(sesión)* concert; *(composición)* concerto. **2** *(acuerdo)* agreement. **3** *(armonía)* concert, concord.

**conciliación** *nf* conciliation, reconciliation.

**conciliador,-ra** *adj* conciliatory, conciliating.

**conciliar** *adj* conciliar.
▶ *vt* **1** *(gen)* to conciliate, bring together. **2** *(enemigos)* to reconcile.

**concilio** *nm* council.

**concisión** *nf* concision, conciseness.

**conciso,-a** *adj* concise, brief.

**conciudadano,-a** *nm & nf* fellow citizen.

**concluir** *vt* **1** *(terminar)* to finish. **2** *(trato, negocio)* to close.
▶ *vi* *(finalizar)* to finish, come to an end, conclude.

**conclusión** *nf* **1** *(final)* conclusion, end. **2** *(deducción)* conclusion. loc **en conclusión** in conclusion. ‖ **llegar a una conclusión** to come to a conclusion.

**concluyente** *adj* conclusive, decisive.

**concordancia** *nf* **1** concordance, agreement. **2** LING agreement.

**concordante** *adj* concordant.

**concordar** *vt* **1** *(poner de acuerdo)* to bring into agreement, reconcile. **2** LING to make agree.

▶ *vi* **1** *(convenir)* to agree, coincide, match. **2** LING to agree.

**concordia** *nf* concord, harmony.

**concreción** *nf* *(concisión)* concision, conciseness.

**concretar** *vt* **1** *(precisar)* to specify, state explicitly. **2** *(hora, precio)* to fix, set. **3** *(resumir)* to sum up.

▶ *vpr* **concretarse** *(tomar forma)* to take shape.

**concreto,-a** *adj* **1** *(real)* concrete, real. **2** *(particular)* particular, specific. LOC **en concreto** *(en particular)* in particular, specifically.

**concurrencia** *nf* **1** *(confluencia)* combination, concurrence. **2** *(participación)* participation.

**concurrido,-a** *adj* **1** *(lugar público)* busy, crowded. **2** *(espectáculo)* well-attended, popular.

**concurrir** *vi* **1** *(juntarse en un lugar - gente)* to gather, come together, meet. **2** *(tomar parte - concurso, etc)* to compete, take part.

**concursante** *nm o nf* **1** *(a concurso)* contestant, participant, competitor. **2** *(a empleo)* candidate.

**concursar** *vi* **1** *(competir)* to compete, take part. **2** *(para un empleo)* to be a candidate.

**concurso** *nm* **1** *(gen)* competition; *(de belleza, deportivo)* contest; *(en televisión)* quiz. **2** *(para puestos)* public examination: **3** *fml (concurrencia)* gathering.

**condado** *nm* county.

**conde** *nm* count.

**condecoración** *nf* decoration.

**condecorar** *vt* to decorate.

**condena** *nf* JUR sentence.

**condenado,-a** *adj* **1** JUR convicted. **2** *(sin remedio)* hopeless.

**condenar** *vt* **1** JUR *(declarar culpable)* to convict, find guilty. **2** JUR *(decretar condena)* to sentence, condemn. **3** *(desaprobar)* to condemn.

**condensación** *nf* **1** *(acción)* condensing. **2** *(efecto)* condensation.

**condensado,-a** *adj* condensed.

**condensador,-ra** *adj* condensing.

**condensar** *vt* to condense.

**condescender** *vi* *(adaptarse)* to comply (a, with), consent (a, to).

**condescendiente** *adj* *(complaciente)* obliging.

**condición** *nf* **1** *(naturaleza)* nature, condition. **2** *(carácter)* nature, character. **3** *(circunstancia)* circumstance, condition. **4** *(estado social)* status, position. **5** *(calidad)* capacity. **6** *(exigencia)* condition. LOC **a condición de que...** provided (that)... ∥ **con la condición de que...** on the condition that...

▶ *nf pl* **condiciones 1** *(estado)* condition *sing*, state *sing*. **2** *(aptitud)* aptitude *sing*, talent *sing*. LOC **estar en condiciones de hacer** ALGO **1** *(físicas)* to be fit to do STH. **2** *(posición, autoridad)* to be in a position to do STH.

**condicionado,-a** *adj* conditioned.

**condicional** *adj* conditional.

▶ *nm* conditional.

**condicionar** *vt* **1** *(influir en)* to condition, determine. **2** *(supeditar)* to make conditional.

**condimentar** *vt* to season, flavour (US flavor).

**condimento** *nm* seasoning, flavouring (US flavoring).

**condolerse** *vpr* to sympathize (de, with), feel sorry (de, for), feel pity (de, for).

**cóndor** *nm* condor.

**conducir** *vt* **1** *(guiar)* to lead, take, show. **2** *(coche, animales)* to drive.

▶ *vi* **1** *(un coche)* to drive. **2** *(llevar)* to lead (a, -).

**conducta** *nf* conduct, behaviour (US behavior).

**conductividad** *nf* conductivity.

**conductivo,-a** *adj* conductive.

**conducto** *nm* *(tubería)* pipe, conduit.

**conductor,-ra** *adj* FÍS conductive.

▶ *nm & nf* AUTO driver.

▶ *nm* **conductor** FÍS conductor.

**conectar** *vt* *(gen)* to connect (up).

▶ *vi* **1** RAD TV *(coger)* to tune in (con, to); *(dar conexión)* to tune in (con, with). **2** *fam (llevarse bien)* to hit it off, get on well.

**conector** *nm* connector.

**conejera** *nf* **1** *(conejal)* rabbit hutch. **2** *(madriguera)* rabbit warren, rabbit burrow.

**conejero,-a** *nm & nf* rabbit breeder.

**conejillo** *nm* young rabbit. COMP **conejillo de Indias** guinea pig.

**conejo,-a** *nm & nf* rabbit.

**conexión** *nf* TÉC connection.

**conexo,-a** *adj* connected, related.

**confabulación** *nf* conspiracy, plot.

**confabular** *vi* to confabulate, discuss.
  ▶ *vpr* **confabularse** to conspire, plot.

**confección** *nf* **1** *(acción)* dressmaking, tailoring; *(ropa)* off-the-peg clothes *pl*, ready-to-wear clothes *pl*. **2** *(realización)* making, making up.

**confeccionar** *vt (vestido)* to make, make up; *(plato)* to prepare.

**confederación** *nf* confederation, confederacy.

**confederar** *vt* to confederate.

**conferencia** *nf* **1** *(charla)* talk, lecture. **2** POL conference, meeting. **3** *(teléfono)* long-distance call. LOC **dar una conferencia sobre ALGO** to lecture on STH, give a lecture on STH.

**conferenciante** *nm o nf* lecturer.

**conferenciar** *vi* to confer.

**conferir** *vt* **1** *(conceder)* to confer, bestow, award. **2** *(dar)* to give.

**confesar** *vt (reconocer)* to confess, admit.
  ▶ *vpr* **confesarse** to go to confession, confess.

**confesión** *nf (expresión)* confession, admission.

**confesional** *adj* denominational.

**confesionario** *nm* confessional.

**confeso,-a** *adj* JUR self-confessed.

**confesor** *nm* confessor.

**confeti** *nm* confetti.

**confiado,-a** *adj* **1** *(crédulo)* unsuspecting, gullible. **2** *(seguro)* confident, self-confident.

**confianza** *nf* **1** *(seguridad)* confidence. **2** *(familiaridad)* familiarity, intimacy. **3** *(presunción)* conceit. LOC **de confianza 1** *(fiable)* reliable. **2** *(de responsabilidad)* trustworthy. ▌ **en confianza** confidentially, in confidence. ▌ **tener confianza en uno mismo** to be self-confident.

**confiar** *vi* **1** *(tener fe)* to trust (en, -), confide (en, in). **2** *(estar seguro)* to be confident, trust. **3** *(contar)* to count (en, on), rely (en, on).
  ▶ *vt* **1** *(depositar)* to entrust. **2** *(secretos, problemas, etc)* to confide.
  ▶ *vpr* **confiarse** *(entregarse)* to entrust os.

**confidencia** *nf* confidence, secret.

**confidencial** *adj* confidential.

**confidencialidad** *nf* confidentiality.

**configurar** *vt* **1** to form, shape. **2** INFORM to configure.

**confinar** *vt (recluir)* to confine.

**confirmación** *nf* confirmation.

**confirmar** *vt* to confirm.

**confiscar** *vt* to confiscate.

**confitado,-a** *adj (fruta)* candied, glacé. COMP **frutas confitadas** candied fruit *sing*.

**confitar** *vt (frutas)* to candy; *(carne)* to preserve.

**confitería** *nf* confectioner's, sweet shop, US candy shop.

**confitero,-a** *nm & nf* confectioner.

**confitura** *nf* preserve, jam.

**conflictividad** *nf* disputes *pl*.

**conflictivo,-a** *adj (situación)* difficult; *(tema)* controversial.

**conflicto** *nm* **1** *(choque)* conflict. **2** *fig (apuro)* dilemma. COMP **conflicto laboral** industrial dispute.

**confluencia** *nf* confluence.

**confluir** *vi (personas)* to converge, come together; *(ríos, caminos, etc)* to meet, converge.

**conformar** *vt* **1** *(dar forma)* to shape. **2** *(adaptar)* to conform, adjust.
  ▶ *vpr* **conformarse** *(contentarse)* to resign os (con, to), be content (con, with), make do (con, with).

**conforme** *adj* **1** *(satisfecho)* satisfied. **2** *(de acuerdo)* in accordance with, in keeping with. **3** *(resignado)* resigned. LOC **conforme a** in accordance with, according to.
► *adv* **1** *(según, como)* as. **2** *(en cuanto)* as soon as. **3** *(a medida que)* as.

**conformidad** *nf* *(aprobación)* approval, consent. LOC **en conformidad con** ALGO in conformity with STH, in agreement with.

**conformismo** *nm* conformism.

**conformista** *nm o nf* conformist.

**confort** *nm* comfort.

**confortable** *adj* comfortable.

**confraternizar** *vi* to fraternize.

**confrontación** *nf* *(enfrentamiento)* confrontation.

**confrontar** *vt* **1** *(gen)* to confront; *(carear)* to bring face to face. **2** *(cotejar)* to compare (con, with), collate (con, with).

**confundir** *vt* **1** *(equivocar)* to confuse (con, with), mistake (con, for). **2** *(turbar)* to confound, embarrass.
► *vpr* **confundirse 1** *(mezclarse)* to mingle; *(colores, formas)* to blend. **2** *(equivocarse)* to get mixed up, make a mistake. **3** *(turbarse)* to be confused, be embarrassed.

**confusión** *nf* **1** *(desorden)* confusion, chaos. **2** *(equivocación)* mistake, confusion.

**confuso,-a** *adj* **1** *(ideas)* confused. **2** *(estilo, etc)* obscure, confused. **3** *fig (turbado)* confused, embarrassed.

**congelación** *nf* **1** *(gen)* freezing. **2** *(precios, salarios, etc)* freeze. **3** MED *(gen)* exposure; *(extremidades)* frostbite.

**congelado,-a** *adj* **1** *(gen)* frozen. **2** MED frostbitten.
► *nm pl* **congelados** frozen food *sing*.

**congelador** *nm* freezer.

**congelar** *vt* **1** *(gen)* to freeze. **2** MED to cause frostbite on.
► *vpr* **congelarse 1** to freeze. **2** MED to get frostbite.

**congeniar** *vi* to get on.

**congénito,-a** *adj* **1** congenital. **2** *fig* innate.

**congestión** *nf* congestion.

**congestionar** *vt* to congest.
► *vpr* **congestionarse** to become congested.

**conglomerado** *nm* **1** TÉC conglomerate. **2** *fig* conglomeration, collection.

**conglomerar** *vt* to conglomerate.

**congratular** *vt fml* to congratulate on.
► *vpr* **congratularse** *fml* to congratulate OS (de/por, on).

**congregación** *nf* **1** *(reunión)* assembly. **2** REL congregation.

**congregar** *vt* to congregate, assemble.
► *vpr* **congregarse** to congregate, assemble.

**congresista** *nm o nf* **1** *(que asiste a un congreso)* congress participant. **2** *(diputado)* member of congress; *(hombre)* congressman; *(mujer)* congresswoman.

**congreso** *nm* congress. COMP **congreso de los Diputados** Parliament, US Congress.

**congrio** *nm* conger, conger eel.

**congruencia** *nf* **1** *(conveniencia)* congruity. **2** MAT congruence.

**congruente** *adj* **1** *(coherente)* coherent, suitable. **2** MAT congruent.

**cónico,-a** *adj* **1** conical. **2** *(en geometría)* conic.

**conífera** *nf* conifer.

**conjetura** *nf* conjecture. LOC **hacer conjeturas** to make conjectures.

**conjeturar** *vt* to conjecture.

**conjugación** *nf* conjugation.

**conjugado,-a** *adj* *(enlazado)* combined.

**conjugar** *vt* to conjugate.

**conjunción** *nf* conjunction.

**conjuntamente** *adv* jointly, together.

**conjuntar** *vt* to coordinate.

**conjuntivitis** *nf inv* conjunctivitis.

**conjunto,-a** *adj* **1** *(compartido)* joint. **2** *(combinado)* combined. LOC **en conjunto** altogether, on the whole.

▸ *nm* **conjunto 1** *(grupo)* group, collection. **2** *(todo)* whole: **3** *(prenda)* outfit, ensemble. **4** MÚS *(clásico)* ensemble; *(pop)* band, group. **5** MAT set. **6** DEP team.

**conjura** *nf* plot, conspiracy.

**conjuración** *nf* plot, conspiracy.

**conjurar** *vt (gen)* to exorcise; *(peligro)* to avert, stave off, ward off.
▸ *vi (conspirar)* to conspire (**contra**, against).
▸ *vpr* **conjurarse** to conspire (**contra**, against).

**conjuro** *nm* **1** *(exorcismo)* exorcism. **2** *(encantamiento)* spell, incantation.

**conmemorar** *vt* to commemorate.

**conmemorativo,-a** *adj* commemorative.

**conmigo** *pron* with me, to me.

**conmoción** *nf* **1** commotion, shock: *causar conmoción* to cause a commotion. **2** MED concussion. **3** *(levantamiento)* riot. COMP **conmoción cerebral** concussion.

**conmocionar** *vt* **1** to shock. **2** MED to concuss. **3** *fig* to trouble, disturb.

**conmovedor,-ra** *adj* moving, touching.

**conmover** *vt* **1** *(persona)* to move, touch. **2** *(cosa)* to shake.

**conmutador** *nm* switch.

**conmutar** *vt* **1** *(cambiar)* to exchange. **2** JUR to commute. **3** ELEC to commutate.

**conmutativo,-a** *adj* commutative.

**connivencia** *nf* connivance, collusion.

**cono** *nm* cone.

**conocedor,-ra** *nm & nf* expert (**de**, on), connoisseur (**de**, of).

**conocer** *vt* **1** *(gen)* to know; *(noticia)* to hear. **2** *(persona)* to meet, get to know. **3** *(reconocer)* to recognize. **4** *(país, lugar)* to have been to. LOC **dar a conocer** to make known.
▸ *vi* **1** *(saber)* to know (**de**, about). **2** JUR to hear (**de**, -).
▸ *vpr* **conocerse** *(a sí mismo)* to know os; *(dos o más personas)* to know each other; *(por primera vez)* to meet, get to know.

**conocido,-a** *adj* **1** known. **2** *(famoso)* well-known.

**conocimiento** *nm* **1** [en 1, también se usa en plural con el mismo significado] *(saber)* knowledge. **2** *(sensatez)* good sense. **3** *(conciencia)* consciousness. LOC **tener conocimiento de** ALGO to know about STH.

**conquista** *nf* conquest. LOC **hacer una conquista** *(amorosa)* to make a conquest.

**conquistador,-ra** *adj* conquering.

**conquistar** *vt (con las armas)* to conquer.

**consagración** *nf* **1** *(artista, etc)* recognition. **2** *(de una costumbre)* establishment. **3** *(dedicación)* dedication.

**consagrado,-a** *adj (reconocido)* recognized, established.

**consagrar** *vt* **1** *(palabra, expresión)* to establish. **2** *(dedicar)* to dedicate. **3** *(artista, etc)* to confirm, establish.

**consanguíneo,-a** *adj* consanguineous.
▸ *nm & nf* blood relation.

**consanguinidad** *nf* consanguinity, blood relationship.

**consciente** *adj* **1** conscious, aware. **2** MED conscious. **3** *(responsable)* reliable, responsible. LOC **estar consciente** to be conscious. ▌ **ser consciente de** ALGO to be aware of STH.

**consecuencia** *nf* **1** consequence, result. **2** *(coherencia)* consistency. LOC **a consecuencia de** as a consequence of, as a result of. ▌ **como consecuencia de** as a consequence of, as a result of.

**consecuente** *adj* **1** *(siguiente)* consequent. **2** *(resultante)* resulting. **3** *(coherente)* consistent.

**consecutivamente** *adv* consecutively.

**consecutivo,-a** *adj* consecutive.

**conseguir** *vt* **1** *(cosa)* to obtain, get; *(objetivo)* to attain, achieve. **2** *(lograr)* to manage, succeed in.

C

**consejería** *nf* **1** *(lugar)* Council. **2** *(cargo)* councillor.

**consejero,-a** *nm & nf* **1** *(asesor)* adviser, advisor, counsellor. **2** POL councillor.

**consejo** *nm* **1** *(recomendación)* advice. **2** *(junta)* council, board. LOC **pedir consejo a** ALGN to ask SB for advice. COMP **consejo de ministros** cabinet.

**consenso** *nm* **1** *(acuerdo)* consensus. **2** *(consentimiento)* consent, assent.

**consensuar** *vt* to reach a consensus on.

**consentido,-a** *adj* *(mimado)* spoiled, spoilt.
▶ *nm & nf* *(persona)* spoiled person, spoilt person; *(niño)* spoiled child, spoilt child.

**consentimiento** *nm* consent.

**consentir** *vt* **1** *(tolerar)* to allow, permit, tolerate. **2** *(mimar)* to spoil.
▶ *vi* **1** *(admitir)* to consent (en, to), agree (en, to). **2** *(ceder)* to weaken.

**conserje** *nm* **1** *(portero)* porter; *(de hotel)* hall porter. **2** *(de escuela)* caretaker.

**conserva** [también se usa en plural con el mismo significado] *nf* **1** *(en lata)* tinned food, canned food. **2** *(dulces)* preserves *pl*.

**conservación** *nf* *(de alimentos)* preservation.

**conservador,-ra** *adj* POL conservative.
▶ *nm & nf* **1** POL conservative. **2** *(de museos)* curator.

**conservadurismo** *nm* conservatism.

**conservante** *nm* preservative.

**conservar** *vt* **1** *(alimentos)* to preserve. **2** *(guardar)* to keep, save.
▶ *vpr* **conservarse 1** *(tradición, etc)* to survive. **2** *fig (mantenerse)* to keep well.

**conservatorio** *nm* conservatory, conservatoire, school of music.

**conservero,-a** *adj* canning: *industria conservera* canning industry.

**considerable** *adj* considerable.

**considerablemente** *adv* considerably.

**consideración** *nf* **1** *(reflexión)* consideration, attention: *este tema merece nuestra consideración* this subject deserves our attention. **2** *(respeto)* regard. LOC **con consideración** *(respeto)* respectfully. **I en consideración a** considering.

**considerar** *vt* *(reflexionar)* to consider, think over, think about.

**consigna** *nf* *(en estación, etc)* left-luggage office, US check-room.

**consignar** *vt* **1** *(mercancías)* to consign, ship, dispatch. **2** *(destinar - dinero, etc)* to allocate. **3** *(anotar)* to note down.

**consigo** *pron* **1** *(3ª persona singular - hombre)* with him; *(- mujer)* with her; *(- cosa, animal)* with it. **2** *(usted)* with you. **3** *(3ª persona plural)* with them. **4** *(ustedes)* with you.

**consiguiente** *adj* consequent, resulting, resultant. LOC **por consiguiente** therefore, consequently.

**consistencia** *nf* *(dureza)* consistency.

**consistente** *adj* **1** *(firme)* firm, solid. **2** *fig* sound, solid. **3** CULIN thick. LOC **consistente en** consisting of.

**consistir** *vi* **1** *(estribar)* to lie (en, in), consist (en, in). **2** *(estar formado)* to consist (en, of).

**consistorial** *adj* REL consistorial. COMP **casa consistorial** town hall.

**consola** *nf* **1** *(mueble)* console table. **2** *(de ordenador, etc)* console. COMP **consola de videojuegos** games console.

**consolar** *vt* to console, comfort.

**consolidación** *nf* consolidation.

**consolidar** *vt* to consolidate.

**consomé** *nm* clear soup, consommé.

**consonante** *nf* consonant.

**consonántico,-a** *adj* consonantal, consonant.

**conspiración** *nf* conspiracy, plot.

**conspirador,-ra** *nm & nf* conspirator.

**conspirar** *vi* to conspire, plot.

**constancia** *nf* **1** *(perseverancia)* constancy, perseverance. **2** *(evidencia)* evidence, proof. LOC **dejar constancia de** ALGO *(probar)* to prove STH.

**constante** *adj* **1** *(invariable)* constant. **2** *(persona)* steadfast.
▶ *nf* MAT constant.

**constantemente** *adv* constantly.

**constar** vi 1 (consistir en) to consist (de, of), be made up (de, of), comprise (de, -). 2 (figurar) to figure, be included, appear. 3 (ser cierto) to be a fact. 4 (quedar claro) to be clear, be known. LOC **hacer constar 1** (señalar) to point out, state. 2 (escribir) to put down, include.

**constatar** vt to verify, confirm.

**constelación** nf constellation.

**consternar** vt to dismay, shatter.

**constipado,-a** nm MED cold. LOC **estar constipado,-a** to have a cold.

**constiparse** vpr to catch a cold.

**constitución** nf constitution.

**constitucional** adj constitutional.

**constituyente** adj constituent.

**construcción** nf 1 construction: la industria de la construcción the construction industry. 2 (edificio) building. LOC **en construcción** under construction.

**constructivo,-a** adj constructive.

**constructor,-ra** adj construction, building.
▶ nm & nf (de edificios) builder; (de barcos) shipbuilder.

**construir** vt to construct, build.

**consuelo** nm consolation, comfort.

**cónsul** nm o nf consul.

**consulado** nm 1 (oficina) consulate. 2 (cargo) consulship.

**consular** adj consular.

**consulta** nf 1 (acción) consultation. 2 MED surgery, US doctor's office; (consultorio) consulting room. LOC **pasar consulta** to see patients, hold surgery.

**consultar** vt 1 (pedir opinión) to consult (con, with/-), seek advice (con, from): consulté con mis padres I consulted with my parents. 2 (buscar en un libro) to look up. LOC **consultar con un abogado** to consult a lawyer, take legal advice.

**consultor,-ra** nm & nf consultant.

**consultorio** nm MED (consulta) surgery, US doctor's office; (habitación) consulting room.

**consumar** vt (terminar) to complete, carry out.

**consumición** nf 1 consumption. 2 (bebida) drink.

**consumidor,-ra** nm & nf consumer.

**consumir** vt 1 (gastar, usar) to consume, use. 2 (destruir) to destroy, consume.
▶ vpr **consumirse 1** (extinguirse) to burn out. 2 fig (afligirse) to waste away.

**consumismo** nm consumerism.

**consumista** nm o nf consumerist.

**consumo** nm consumption.

**contabilidad** nf 1 (profesión) accountancy; (carrera) accounting. 2 (de empresa, etc) accounting, bookkeeping. LOC **llevar la contabilidad** to keep the books.

**contabilizar** vt to enter in the books.

**contable** nm o nf bookkeeper, accountant.
▶ adj countable.

**contactar** vt to contact, get in touch (con, with).

**contacto** nm 1 contact. 2 AUTO ignition. LOC **ponerse en contacto con** to get in touch with, get in contact with.

**contado,-a** adj few. COMP **en contadas ocasiones** seldom, rarely.

**contador,-ra** nm meter.

**contagiar** vt 1 (enfermedad) to transmit, pass on. 2 fig to infect, pass on, give.
▶ vpr **contagiarse 1** (enfermar) to get infected. 2 (transmitirse) to be contagious: esta enfermedad no se contagia this disease is not contagious.

**contagio** nm MED contagion, infection.

**contagioso,-a** adj infectious, contagious: enfermedad contagiosa infectious disease; risa contagiosa infectious laugh.

**contáiner** nm container.

**contaminación** nf contamination; (de agua, aire) pollution.

**contaminante** nm polluting agent.

**contaminar** vt to contaminate; (agua, aire) to pollute.

**contar** vt 1 (calcular) to count. 2 (explicar) to tell: me contó un cuento she told me a story.
► vi to count: los niños saben contar the children know how to count.

**contemplación** nf (acción) contemplation.

**contemplar** vt (mirar) to contemplate.

**contemplativo,-a** adj contemplative.

**contemporáneo,-a** adj contemporary.

**contenedor,-ra** adj containing.
► nm contenedor container.

**contener** vt 1 (incluir) to contain, hold. 2 (detener) to hold back, restrain. 3 (respiración) to hold.

**contenido,-a** adj (moderado) moderate, reserved.
► nm contenido content, contents pl.

**contentar** vt (satisfacer) to please, content.
► vpr contentarse (conformarse) to make do (con, with), be satisfied (con, with).

**contento,-a** adj happy, pleased: estoy contento de conocerle I'm pleased to meet you.

**contestación** nf (respuesta) answer, reply.

**contestador** nm answering machine.

**contestar** vt (responder) to answer.

**contienda** nf contest, dispute, struggle.

**contigo** pron with you.

**contiguo,-a** adj contiguous (a, to), adjoining, adjacent (a, to).

**continental** adj continental.

**continente** nm GEOG continent.

**continuación** nf continuation, follow-up. LOC a continuación next.

**continuador,-ra** adj continuing.
► nm & nf continuator.

**continuamente** adv continuously.

**continuar** vt (proseguir) to continue, carry on.

**continuidad** nf continuity.

**continuo,-a** adj 1 (seguido) continuous. 2 (continuado) continual, constant.

**contornar** vt 1 (dar vueltas) to skirt. 2 (hacer los perfiles) to trace the outline of.

**contorno** nm 1 (perfil) outline; (perímetro) perimeter. 2 (canto) rim, edge.

**contorsionarse** vpr to contort os, twist os.

**contorsionista** nm o nf contortionist.

**contra** prep 1 (against): tres contra uno three against one. 2 for: un producto contra las picaduras de mosquitos a product for mosquito bites. LOC en contra against: estaba en contra he was against it.

**contraatacar** vt to counterattack.

**contraataque** nm counterattack.

**contrabajo** nm (instrumento) double bass.

**contrabandista** nm o nf smuggler.

**contrabando** nm 1 smuggling, contraband. 2 (mercancías) smuggled goods pl, contraband. LOC pasar ALGO de contrabando to smuggle STH in.

**contracción** nf contraction.

**contrachapado** nm plywood.

**contracorriente** nf crosscurrent.

**contractura** nf contracture.

**contradecir** vt (decir lo contrario) to contradict.

**contradicción** nf contradiction. LOC estar en contradicción con to be inconsistent with, contradictory to.

**contradictorio,-a** adj contradictory.

**contraer** vt 1 (encoger) to contract: contraer un músculo to contract a muscle. 2 (enfermedad) to catch. 3 (deuda) to contract, incur; (hábito) to pick up. 4 LING to contract.

**contrafuerte** nm ARQUIT buttress.

**contrahecho,-a** adj deformed, hunchbacked.

**contraindicación** nf MED contraindication.

**contraindicar** vt MED to contraindicate.

**contralto** nm o nf contralto.

**contraluz** nm o nf view against the light, back light.
LOC a contraluz against the light.

**contraofensiva** *nf* counteroffensive.

**contraorden** *nf* countermand.

**contrapartida** *nf* **1** COM balancing entry. **2** *fig* compensation.

**contrapesar** *vt* **1** to counterbalance, counterpoise. **2** *fig* to balance, offset.

**contrapeso** *nm* **1** counterweight. **2** *fig* counterbalance.

**contraponer** *vt* **1** (*oponer*) to set in opposition (a, to). **2** *fig* (*contrastar*) to contrast (a, with).

**contraportada** *nf* back page, back cover.

**contraposición** *nf* **1** (*contraste*) contrast. **2** (*oposición*) conflict, clash: *contraposición de intereses* conflict of interests. LOC **estar en contraposición** to clash.

**contraprestación** *nf* contractual obligation.

**contraproducente** *adj* counterproductive.

**contrapuesto,-a** *adj* opposed.

**contrapunto** *nm* counterpoint.

**contra-reloj** *adj* against the clock.
► *nm* (*en ciclismo*) time trial.

**contrariamente** *adv* contrary (a, to).

**contrariar** *vt* **1** (*oponerse*) to oppose, go against. **2** (*disgustar*) to annoy, upset: *no quería contrariarte* I didn't want to upset you.

**contrario,-a** *adj* **1** (*opuesto*) contrary, opposite: *iba en sentido contrario* he was going in the opposite direction. **2** (*perjudicial*) harmful (a, to), bad (a, for): *el fumar es contrario a la salud* smoking is bad for your health. LOC **al contrario** on the contrary. **de lo contrario** otherwise. **llevar la contraria a** ALGN to oppose SB. **por el contrario** on the contrary. **todo lo contrario** quite the opposite.
► *nm & nf* opponent, adversary, rival.

**contrarreloj** *adj* against the clock.
► *nf* race against the clock. COMP **(etapa) contrarreloj** time trial.

**contrarrestar** *vt* (*hacer frente*) to resist, oppose.

**contrasentido** *nm* **1** (*contradicción*) contradiction. **2** (*disparate*) piece of nonsense: *eso es un contrasentido* that's nonsense.

**contraseña** *nf* (*seña*) secret sign; (*palabra*) password.

**contrastar** *vt* (*comprobar*) to check, verify.
► *vi* (*oponerse*) to contrast (con, with).

**contraste** *nm* (*oposición*) contrast.

**contratación** *nf* **1** (*contrato - obrero*) hiring; (- *empleado*) engagement. **2** (*pedido*) total orders *pl*, volume of business.

**contratar** *vt* **1** (*servicio, etc*) to sign a contract for. **2** (*obrero*) to hire; (*empleado*) to engage.

**contratiempo** *nm* (*contrariedad*) setback, hitch; (*accidente*) mishap.

**contratista** *nm o nf* contractor. COMP **contratista de obras** building contractor.

**contrato** *nm* contract. COMP **contrato de alquiler** lease, leasing agreement. **contrato de compraventa** contract of sale. **contrato de trabajo** work contract. **contrato temporal** temporary contract.

**contraventana** *nf* shutter.

**contrayente** *adj* contracting.
► *nm o nf* (*en matrimonio*) contracting party.

**contribución** *nf* **1** contribution. **2** (*impuesto*) tax.

**contribuir** *vt* (*pagar*) to pay.
► *vi* **1** (*aportar*) to contribute: *contribuir a los gastos* to contribute to the expenses. **2** (*pagar impuestos*) to pay taxes.

**contribuyente** *nm o nf* taxpayer.

**contrincante** *nm* opponent, rival.

**control** *nm* **1** (*gen*) control. **2** (*comprobación*) check. **3** (*sitio*) checkpoint. LOC **estar bajo control** to be under control. **estar fuera de control** to be out of control. COMP **control a distancia** remote control. **control de natalidad** birth control.

**controlador,-ra** *adj* control.
► *nm & nf* (*aéreo*) air traffic controller.

**controlar** *vt* **1** *(gen)* to control. **2** *(comprobar)* to check.
▶ *vpr* **controlarse** *(moderarse)* to control os.

**contundente** *adj fig (categórico)* convincing, overwhelming, weighty: *un «no» contundente* a firm «no».

**contusión** *nf* contusion, bruise.

**contusionar** *vt* to contuse, bruise.

**convalecencia** *nf* convalescence.

**convalecer** *vi* to convalesce (de, after), recover (de, from).

**convaleciente** *adj* convalescent.
▶ *nm o nf* convalescent.

**convalidación** *nf* **1** EDUC validation. **2** *(documentos)* ratification, authentication.

**convalidar** *vt* **1** EDUC to validate. **2** *(documentos)* to ratify, authenticate.

**convencer** *vt* **1** *(de algo)* to convince; *(para hacer algo)* to persuade: *lo convencieron de su error* they convinced him of his mistake. **2** *fam (en frases negativas)* to like, be keen on: *ese color no me acaba de convencer* I'm not sure about that colour.
▶ *vi* to be convincing: *el equipo local no convenció con su actuación* the local team's performance was not very convincing.
▶ *vpr* **convencerse** to become convinced, be convinced, convince os: *se convenció de que era guapo* he convinced himself that he was good-looking.

**convencimiento** *nm* conviction. LOC **llegar al convencimiento de que...** to be convinced that...

**convención** *nf* **1** *(congreso)* convention, congress. **2** *(acuerdo)* convention, treaty. **3** *(costumbre)* convention.

**convencional** *adj* conventional.

**convencionalismo** *nm* conventionalism, conventionality.

**conveniencia** *nf* **1** *(utilidad)* usefulness. **2** *(oportunidad)* suitability, advisability: *la conveniencia de estas medidas* the advisability of these measures. **3** *(provecho)* interest, benefit: *solo se preocupa de su propia conveniencia* he only looks out for his own interests. COMP **conve-**niencia sociales social conventions. **I matrimonio de conveniencia** marriage of convenience.

**conveniente** *adj* **1** *(útil)* useful. **2** *(oportuno)* suitable, convenient. **3** *(ventajoso)* advantageous. **4** *(aconsejable)* advisable. **5** *(precio)* good, fair. LOC **creer conveniente** to think advisable, be better.

**convenientemente** *adv (adecuadamente)* suitably; *(bien)* properly.

**convenio** *nm* agreement, treaty. COMP **convenio colectivo / convenio laboral** collective agreement.

**convenir** *vt (acordar)* to agree, arrange: *convenimos el precio* we agreed the price.
▶ *vi* **1** *(acordar)* to agree: *convinimos en la fecha* we agreed on the date. **2** *(ser oportuno o conveniente)* to be good for: *no te conviene hacer esfuerzos* it's not good for you to exert yourself. **3** *(ser adecuado o propio)* to suit: *ese chico no te conviene* that boy is not right for you. LOC **conviene + inf** it is as well to + inf: *conviene mencionar que...* it's as well to mention that... **I conviene que + subj** it is better that, it is advisable + inf: *conviene que te vayas* it is better that you go.

**convento** *nm (de monjas)* convent; *(de monjes)* monastery.

**converger** *vi* to converge, come together.

**convergir** *vi* to converge, come together.

**conversación** *nf* conversation, talk. LOC **dar conversación a** ALGN to talk to SB, keep SB chatting. **I entablar conversación con** ALGN to get into conversation with SB, engage SB in conversation.

**conversador,-ra** *adj* talkative.
▶ *nm & nf* conversationalist, talker.

**conversar** *vi* to converse (con, with), talk (con, to).

**conversión** *nf* conversion.

**convertir** *vt (transformar)* to change, turn, transform, convert.
▶ *vpr* **convertirse 1** *(transformarse)* to turn (en, into), change (en, into). **2** *(volverse)* to become (en, -), turn (en,

into): *su sueño se convirtió en realidad* his dream came true.

**convexo,-a** *adj* convex.

**convicción** *nf* conviction: *tengo la convicción de que vendrán* I firmly believe that they'll come.

**convidado,-a** *adj* invited.
▸ *nm & nf* guest.

**convidar** *vt* **1** *(invitar)* to invite: *me convidó a una fiesta* he invited me to a party. **2** *(ofrecer)* to offer: *nos convidó a pastel* he offered us some cake.

**convincente** *adj* convincing.

**convincentemente** *adv* convincingly.

**convite** *nm* **1** *(invitación)* invitation. **2** *(comida)* meal; *(fiesta)* party.

**convivencia** *nf* **1** living together. **2** *fig* coexistence.

**convivir** *vi* **1** to live together. **2** *fig* to coexist. [LOC] **saber convivir** to give and take.

**convocar** *vt* to convoke, summon, call together. [LOC] **convocar una reunión** to call a meeting.

**convocatoria** *nf* **1** *(citación)* convocation, summons *sing*, call to a meeting. **2** EDUC examination: *convocatoria de septiembre* (September) resits *pl*.

**convoy** *nm* **1** *(escolta)* convoy. **2** *(tren)* train.

**conyugal** *adj* conjugal. [COMP] **vida conyugal** married life.

**cónyuge** *nm o nf* *(gen)* spouse, partner; *(marido)* husband; *(mujer)* wife.
▸ *nm pl* **cónyuges** husband and wife, married couple *sing*.

**coñac** *nm* cognac, brandy.

**cooperación** *nf* cooperation.

**cooperar** *vi* to cooperate.

**cooperativa** *nf* cooperative.

**coordenada** *nf* coordinate.

**coordinación** *nf* coordination.

**coordinador,-ra** *adj* coordinating.
▸ *nm & nf* coordinator.

**coordinadora** *nf* *(comité)* coordinating committee.

**coordinar** *vt* to coordinate: *coordinaron la compaña* they coordinated the campaign.

**copa** *nf* **1** *(vaso)* glass; *(bebida)* drink: *¿te apetece una copa?* do you fancy a drink? **2** *(de árbol)* top. **3** *(trofeo)* cup.
▸ *nf pl* **copas** *(naipes)* hearts.

**copete** *nm* **1** *(cabello)* tuft. **2** *(penacho)* crest. **3** *(de montaña, helado)* top.

**copia** *nf* **1** *(gen)* copy. **2** *(de fotografía)* print. **3** *fig (persona)* image: *es la copia de su padre* he's the image of his father. [LOC] **sacar una copia** to make a copy.

**copiadora** *nf* photocopier.

**copiar** *vt* **1** *(gen)* to copy: *lo copió del libro* he copied it from the book. **2** EDUC to cheat, copy. **3** *(escribir)* to take down. [LOC] **copiar al pie de la letra** to copy word for word.

**copiloto** *nm* **1** AV copilot. **2** AUTO co-driver.

**copioso,-a** *adj* **1** *fml (abundante)* plentiful, abundant, copious. **2** *fml (lluvia)* heavy; *(cabello)* long.

**copista** *nm o nf* copyist.

**copla** *nf* **1** *(verso, estrofa)* verse, stanza. **2** *(canción)* popular folk song.

**copo** *nm* *(gen)* flake; *(de nieve)* snowflake; *(de algodón)* ball (of cotton). [COMP] **copos de avena** rolled oats.

**coproducción** *nf* co-production, joint production.

**coproductor,-ra** *nm & nf* co-producer.

**copropiedad** *nf* joint ownership.

**coprotagonizar** *vt* to co-star (-, in).

**copulativo,-a** *adj* copulative.

**coque** *nm* coke.

**coqueta** *nf* **1** *(mujer)* flirt, coquette. **2** *(mueble)* dressing table.

**coquetear** *vi* to flirt.

**coqueteo** *nm* flirtation.

**coquetería** *nf* coquetry, flirting, flirtation.

**coraje** *nm* **1** *(valor)* courage, toughness. **2** *(ira)* anger. [LOC] **dar coraje** *fam* to infuriate, make furious: *me da coraje que haya ganado él* it makes me furious that he won. **I echarle coraje a** ALGO to put some spirit into STH.

**coral¹** *adj* MÚS choral.
▸ *nf* MÚS *(grupo)* choir, choral society.
▸ *nm* MÚS *(composición)* choral, chorale.

**coral²** *nm* ZOOL coral.
▸ *nm pl* **corales** coral beads.

**coralina** *nf* coralline.

**coralino,-a** *adj* coral.

**Corán** *nm* Koran.

**coránico,-a** *adj* Koranic.

**coraza** *nf* 1 *(armadura)* armour (US armor), cuirass. 2 *(caparazón)* shell, carapace. 3 *fig (protección)* armour (US armor), protection.

**corazón** *nm* 1 ANAT heart. 2 *fig (parte central)* heart, core: *en el corazón de la ciudad* in the heart of the city. 3 *(de fruta)* core. 4 *(apelativo)* darling, dear, sweetheart. LOC **abrir el corazón a** ALGN *fig* to open one's heart to SB. **I de todo corazón** *fig* sincerely, in all sincerity. **I estar con el corazón en un puño** *fig* to have one's heart in one's mouth. **I estar enfermo del corazón** to have heart trouble.
▸ *nm pl* **corazones** *(naipes)* hearts.

**corazonada** *nf (sentimiento)* hunch, feeling, inkling: *tuve la corazonada de que él no estaba* I had a hunch that he wasn't there.

**corbata** *nf* tie, US necktie: *iba con corbata* he was wearing a tie.

**corcel** *nm lit* steed, charger.

**corchea** *nf* quaver.

**corchete** *nm* 1 COST hook and eye, snap fastener. 2 *(signo impreso)* square bracket.

**corcho** *nm* 1 cork; *(corteza)* cork bark. 2 *(tapón)* cork. 3 *(para pescar, nadar)* float. 4 *(tabla)* cork mat. 5 *(tablón para anuncios, notas)* cork board.

**cordada** *nf* rope.

**cordel** *nm* rope, cord.

**cordelería** *nf* 1 *(oficio)* ropemaking. 2 *(cuerdas)* ropes *pl*.

**cordero,-a** *nm & nf* 1 lamb. 2 *fig (persona dócil)* lamb, angel.

▸ *nm* **cordero** 1 *(piel)* lambskin. 2 *(carne - joven)* lamb; *(- crecido)* mutton. LOC **ser manso como un cordero** to be as gentle as a lamb.

**cordial** *adj (afectuoso)* cordial, friendly, warm: *una bienvenida cordial* a warm welcome.

**cordialidad** *nf* cordiality, warmth, friendliness.

**cordialmente** *adv* 1 cordially, warmly. 2 *(despedida en carta)* sincerely.

**cordillera** *nf* mountain range, mountain chain.

**cordón** *nm* 1 *(cuerda)* string. 2 *(de zapatos)* shoelace, shoestring.

**cordoncillo** *nm* 1 *(en tejido)* rib, ribbing. 2 *(bordado)* braid, piping.

**cordura** *nf* good sense. LOC **con cordura** sensibly, prudently, wisely.

**Corea** *nf* Korea. COMP **Corea del Norte** North Korea. **I Corea del Sur** South Korea.

**coreano,-a** *adj* Korean.
▸ *nm & nf (persona)* Korean.
▸ *nm* **coreano** *(idioma)* Korean.

**corear** *vt* 1 *(cantar)* to chorus, sing in chorus. 2 *(hablar)* to chorus, speak in chorus. 3 *fig (aclamar)* to applaud.

**coreografía** *nf* choreography.

**coreografiar** *vt* to choreograph.

**coreógrafo,-a** *nm & nf* choreographer.

**corindón** *nm* corundum.

**corinto,-a** *adj* maroon.
▸ *nm* **corinto** *(color)* maroon.

**cormorán** *nm* cormorant.

**cornada** *nf* goring.

**cornalina** *nf* cornelian, carnelian.

**cornamenta** *nf (gen)* horns *pl*; *(del ciervo)* antlers *pl*.

**cornamusa** *nf* bagpipe.

**córnea** *nf* cornea.

**cornear** *vt* to gore.

**corneja** *nf* crow.

**cornejo** *nm* dogwood.

**córneo,-a** *adj* hornlike, corneous.

**córner** *nm* DEP *(lugar)* corner; *(golpe)* corner, corner kick. LOC **lanzar un córner**

/ sacar un córner / tirar un córner to take a corner.

**corneta** *nf (instrumento)* bugle.

**cornisa** *nf* ARQUIT cornice.

**coro** *nm* **1** MÚS choir. **2** TEAT chorus. LOC **a coro** *fig* all together. I **hacer coro** *fig* to join in the chorus.

**corola** *nf* corolla.

**corona** *nf* **1** *(aro, cerco)* crown. **2** *(de flores, etc)* wreath, garland, crown. **3** *fig (dignidad real)* King's, Queen's: *el discurso de la corona* the King's speech. **4** *fig (reino)* crown, kingdom. **5** *(aureola)* halo. **6** *(en geometría)* annulus, ring. COMP **corona solar** solar corona.

**coronación** *nf* **1** coronation. **2** *fig (culminación)* crowning.

**coronar** *vt* to crown.
▶ *vi* to crown.

**coronel** *nm* colonel.

**coronilla** *nf (parte de la cabeza)* crown of the head. LOC **estar hasta la coronilla** *fam* to be fed up (de, with).

**corpiño** *nm* bodice.

**corporación** *nf* corporation. COMP **corporación metropolitana** city corporation.

**corporativo,-a** *adj* corporative, corporate. COMP **imagen corporativa** corporate image.

**corpulencia** *nf* corpulence, stoutness.

**corpulento,-a** *adj* corpulent, stocky, stout.

**corral** *nm* **1** *(de casa)* yard, courtyard. **2** *(de granja)* farmyard, I corral.

**correa** *nf* **1** *(tira de piel)* strap, leather strip. **2** *(de perro)* lead, leash. **3** *(de reloj)* watchstrap. **4** *(cinturón)* belt. **5** TÉC belt.

**corrección** *nf* **1** *(rectificación)* correction. **2** *(educación)* courtesy, correctness, politeness, good manners *pl*. LOC **tratar con corrección** to be polite.

**correccional** *adj* correctional.
▶ *nm* detention centre, reformatory.

**correctamente** *adv* **1** *(sin errores)* correctly, accurately. **2** *(con educación)* correctly, politely, properly.

**correcto,-a** *adj* **1** *(sin errores)* correct, accurate. **2** *(adecuado)* suitable. **3** *(educado)* polite, courteous. **4** *(conducta)* proper.

**corrector,-ra** *adj* corrective.
▶ *nm & nf (de pruebas impresas)* proofreader.

**corredero,-a** *adj* sliding: *ventana corredera* sliding window.

**corredor,-ra** *adj* **1** running. **2** *(ave)* flightless: *ave corredora* flightless bird.
▶ *nm & nf* **1** DEP runner; *(de coches)* driver. **2** FIN broker. COMP **corredor,-ra de bolsa** stockbroker. I **corredor,-ra de coches** racing driver. I **corredor,-ra de fondo** long-distance runner.▶ *nm* **corredor** *(pasillo)* corridor, gallery.

**corregir** *vt* **1** *(amendar)* to correct, rectify. **2** *(reprender)* to reprimand, scold, tell off. **3** EDUC to mark.

**correlación** *nf* correlation.

**correlativo,-a** *adj* correlative.

**correo** *nm* **1** *(servicio, correspondencia)* post, US mail. **2** *(persona)* courier. LOC **echar al correo** to post, US mail. I **por correo** by post, US by mail. COMP **apartado de correos** (post office) box. I **correo aéreo** airmail. I **correo certificado** registered post, US registered mail. I **correo electrónico** electronic mail, e-mail. I **correo urgente** special delivery.
▶ *nm pl* **correos** *(oficina)* post office *sing*.

**correr** *vi* **1** *(gen)* to run: *se marchó corriendo* she ran off. **2** *(darse prisa)* to rush, hurry: *¡corre, es tarde!* hurry up, it's late! **3** *(viento)* to blow. **4** *(agua)* to flow, run. **5** *(tiempo)* to pass, fly. **6** *(conductor)* to drive fast. **7** *(coche)* to go fast. **8** *(puerta, ventana)* to slide.
▶ *vt* **1** *(distancia)* to cover; *(país)* to travel through. **2** *(carrera)* to run; *(caballo)* to race, run. **3** *(echar)* to close; *(cortina)* to draw; *(cerrojo)* to bolt. **4** *(mover)* to pull up, move, draw up: *corre la mesa* move the table. **5** *(estar expuesto)* to run: *correr un peligro* to run a risk. **6** *(aventura)* to have. LOC **a todo correr** at full speed. I **correr mundo** to be a globe-

trotter. **I correr un peligro** to be in danger.

▶ *vpr* **correrse 1** *(persona)* to move over; *(objeto)* to shift, slide. **2** *(color, tinta)* to run. **3** *(media)* to ladder. **4** *(avergonzarse)* to blush, go red.

**correspondencia** *nf* **1** *(gen)* correspondence. **2** *(cartas)* post, US mail. **3** *(de trenes, etc)* connection. LOC **mantener correspondencia con ALGN** to correspond with SB. COMP **curso por correspondencia** correspondence course.

**corresponder** *vi* **1** *(ser adecuado)* to become, befit; *(color, aspecto)* to match, go with: *los zapatos no corresponden al vestido* the shoes don't go with the dress. **2** *(encajar)* to correspond (a, to), tally (a, with); *(descripción)* to fit. **3** *(pertenecer)* to belong, pertain: *esta mesa corresponde a mi habitación* this table belongs in my bedroom.

▶ *vt* **1** *(ser el turno)* to be one's turn: *me corresponde a mi* it's my turn. **2** *(en un reparto)* to get. **3** *(incumbir)* to be the job of, be the responsibility of: *eso te corresponde a ti* that's your job. **4** *(devolver)* to return; *(amabilidad)* to repay.

▶ *vpr* **corresponderse 1** *(ajustarse)* to correspond; *(cifras)* to tally: *la dirección que te dio no se corresponde con la que yo tengo* the address he gave you doesn't correspond to the one I have. **2** *(armonizar)* to be in harmony, go with. **3** *(amarse)* to love each other.

**correspondiente** *adj* **1** *(que corresponde)* corresponding (a, to). **2** *(apropiado)* suitable, appropriate. **3** *(respectivo)* own.

**corresponsal** *nm o nf* correspondent.

**corretear** *vi* **1** *fam (correr)* to run about. **2** *fam (vagar)* to hang about.

**corrida** *nf* **1** *(carrera)* run, race. **2** *(de toros)* bullfight.

**corriente** *adj* **1** *(común)* ordinary, average: *personas corrientes* ordinary people. **2** *(agua)* running. **3** *(fecha)* current, present: *el cinco del corriente mes* the fifth of this month. **4** *(cuenta)* current. LOC **al corriente 1** *(actualizado)* up to date. **2** *(enterado)* aware. **3** *(informado)*

informed, in the know: *¿estás al corriente de lo que ha pasado?* do you know what's happened? **I ir a contra corriente** *fig* to go against the tide. **I seguirle la corriente a ALGN** to humour (US humor) SB. **I tener al corriente** to keep informed. **I corriente sanguínea** bloodstream.

▶ *nm (mes)* current month, this month.

▶ *nf* **1** *(masa de agua)* current, stream, flow. **2** *(de aire)* draught (US draft). **3** ELEC current.

**corrientemente** *adv* usually, normally.

**corro** *nm* **1** *(cerco)* circle, ring. **2** *(juego)* ring-a-ring o'roses. **3** *(en la bolsa)* round enclosure.

**corroer** *vt* **1** *(desgastar)* to corrode. **2** GEOL to erode.

**corromper** *vt* **1** *(pudrir)* to turn bad. **2** *(pervertir)* to corrupt, pervert. **3** *(sobornar)* to bribe.

▶ *vpr* **corromperse 1** *(pudrirse)* to go bad, rot. **2** *(pervertirse)* to become corrupted.

**corrosivo,-a** *adj* **1** corrosive. **2** *fig* caustic.

▶ *nm* **corrosivo** corrosive.

**corrupción** *nf* **1** *(putrefacción)* rot, decay. **2** *fig* corruption, degradation. **3** *fig (soborno)* bribery.

**corrupto,-a** *adj* corrupt.

**corruptor,-ra** *adj* corrupting.

▶ *nm & nf* corrupter, perverter.

**corsario,-a** *adj* privateer.

▶ *nm* **corsario** privateer.

**corsé** *nm* corset.

**corsetería** *nf* ladies' underwear shop.

**corta** *nf* tree felling.

**cortacésped** *nm & nf* lawnmower.

**cortacircuitos** *nm inv* circuit breaker.

**cortado,-a** *adj* **1** *(troceado)* cut; *(en lonchas)* sliced. **2** *(leche)* sour. **3** *fam (aturdido)* dumbfounded. LOC **quedarse cortado,-a 1** *fam (sin palabras)* to be speechless, be lost for words. **2** *(avergonzado)* to become embarrassed.

▶ *nm* **cortado** *(café)* coffee with a dash of milk.

**cortador,-ra** *adj* cutting.
▶ *nm & nf (sastre, zapatero)* cutter.

**cortadora** *nf* cutting machine.

**cortafrío** *nm* cold chisel.

**cortafuego** *nm* **1** *(en el campo)* firebreak. **2** *(en un edificio)* firewall. **3** INFORM firewall.

**cortante** *adj* **1** *(que corta)* cutting, sharp. **2** *fig (aire)* biting. **3** *fig (persona, estilo)* sharp, brusque.

**cortaplumas** *nm inv* penknife.

**cortar** *vt* **1** *(gen)* to cut. **2** *(pelo)* to cut, trim. **3** *(árbol)* to cut down. **4** *(carne)* to carve. **5** *(pastel)* to cut up. **6** *(cabeza, teléfono, gas)* to cut off. **7** *(mayonesa, leche)* to curdle. **8** *(piel)* to chap, crack. **9** *(viento, frío)* to chill, bite. **10** COST to cut out. **11** *(interrumpir)* to cut off, interrupt. **12** *(bloquear)* to block: *cortaron la carretera* the road was blocked. **13** *(suprimir)* to cut out. **14** *fig (separar)* to divide, split, cut. LOC **¡corta el rollo!** *fam* knock it off! ▌ **cortar con ALGN** *fam* to split up with SB. ▌ **cortar el bacalao** *fam* to be the boss. ▌ **cortar en seco** *fig* to cut short. ▌ **cortar la digestión** to give one indigestion, upset one's stomach. ▌ **cortar la palabra** to interrupt. ▌ **cortar por lo sano** *fam* to take drastic measures.
▶ *vpr* **cortarse 1** to cut: *este metal se corta fácilmente* this metal cuts easily. **2** *(herirse)* to cut, cut os: *me he cortado* I've cut myself. **3** *(el pelo - por otro)* to have one's hair cut; *(- uno mismo)* to cut one's hair: *¿te has cortado el pelo?* have you had your hair cut? **4** *(piel)* to become chapped. **5** *(leche)* to go off, curdle; *(mayonesa)* to curdle. **6** *(comunicación)* to be cut off.

**cortaúñas** *nm inv* nail clippers.

**corte¹** *nf* **1** *(del rey, etc)* court. **2** *(séquito)* retinue. **3** AM *(tribunal)* court.
▶ *nf pl* **las Cortes** the Spanish Parliament *sing*.

**corte²** *nm* **1** *(gen)* cut: *me he hecho un corte en el dedo* I've cut my finger. **2** *(filo)* edge. **3** *(sección)* section: *corte horizontal* horizontal section. **4** *(de pelo)* cut, haircut. **5** *(de helado)* wafer, US ice-cream sandwich. **6** *fam fig (vergüenza)* embarrassment: *le daba corte entrar y se quedó fuera* he was too embarrassed to go in so he stayed outside. LOC **dar un corte a ALGN** *fam* to cut SB dead.

**cortejar** *vt* to court.

**cortejo** *nm* **1** *(acompañantes)* entourage, retinue. **2** *(galanteo)* courting.

**cortés** *adj* courteous, polite.

**cortesano,-a** *adj* **1** *(de la corte)* court. **2** *(cortés)* courteous, courtly.
▶ *nm & nf (de la corte)* courtier.

**cortesía** *nf* **1** *(educación)* courtesy, politeness. **2** *(en cartas)* formal ending. **3** *(tratamiento)* title. **4** *(reverencia)* bow, curtsy. **5** *(regalo)* present: *esta bolsa es una cortesía de la empresa* this bag is courtesy of the company.

**cortina** *nf* **1** curtain. **2** *fig* curtain, screen. LOC **correr las cortinas** to draw the curtains. COMP **cortina de humo** *fig* smoke screen.

**cortinaje** *nm* drapery.

**corto,-a** *adj* **1** *(extensión)* short: *distancia corta* short distance. **2** *(duración)* short, brief: *una película corta* a short film. **3** *(escaso)* scant, meagre (US meager). **4** *fig (tonto)* thick, dim. **5** *fig (tímido)* shy, timid. LOC **corto,-a de miras** *fam* narrow-minded. ▌ **corto,-a de vista** short-sighted. ▌ **quedarse corto,-a 1** *(ropa)* to become too short: *el pantalón se me ha quedado corto* my trousers have become too short for me. **2** *(calcular mal)* to underestimate, miscalculate: *te quedaste corto con los bocadillos* you didn't make enough sandwiches.
▶ *nm* **corto** short film, short.

**cortocircuito** *nm* short circuit.

**cortometraje** *nm* short film, short.

**corva** *nf* back of the knee.

**corzo,-a** *nm & nf (macho)* roe buck; *(hembra)* roe deer.

**cosa** *nf* **1** *(gen)* thing: *coge tus cosas* take your things, take your stuff. **2** *(asunto)* matter, business: *es cosa tuya* it's your business. **3** *(nada)* nothing, not anything: *no hay cosa igual* there's nothing like it. **LOC** **como cosa tuya** as if it were your idea. **I como si tal cosa** just like that. **I es cosa de... 1** *(tiempo)* it's time to… **2** *(cuestión)* it's a matter of… **I no valer gran cosa** not to be worth much. **I ser cosa hecha** *fam* to be no sooner said than done.

▶ *nf pl* **cosas** *fam (manías)* hang-ups: *son cosas de niños* kids do that kind of thing.

**cosaco,-a** *adj* Cossack.
▶ *nm* **cosaco** Cossack.

**coscorrón** *nm* blow on the head, knock on the head.

**cosecante** *nf* cosecant.

**cosecha** *nf* **1** harvest, crop. **2** *(tiempo)* harvest time. **3** *(año del vino)* vintage. **LOC** **de cosecha propia 1** *(hortalizas, fruta)* home-grown. **2** *fig (ideas, etc)* of one's own invention.

**cosechadora** *nf* combine harvester.

**cosechar** *vi* to harvest, reap.
▶ *vt* **1** *(recoger)* to harvest. **2** *(cultivar)* to grow.

**coseno** *nm* cosine.

**coser** *vt* **1** *(unir)* to sew; *(un botón)* to sew on; *(pespuntes, etc)* to stitch: *le cosí los pantalones* I sewed up her trousers. **2** MED to stitch up. **3** *(grapar)* to staple together. **4** *fig (unir)* to join.

**cosido** *nm* **1** sewing. **2** MED stitching.

**cosificar** *vt* to trivialize, belittle.

**cosmética** *nf* cosmetics *pl*.

**cosmético,-a** *adj* cosmetic.
▶ *nm* **cosmético** cosmetic.

**cósmico,-a** *adj* cosmic.

**cosmogonía** *nf* cosmogony.

**cosmografía** *nf* cosmography.

**cosmográfico,-a** *adj* cosmographic, cosmographical.

**cosmología** *nf* cosmology.

**cosmológico,-a** *adj* cosmologic, cosmological.

**cosmonauta** *nm o nf* cosmonaut.

**cosmonave** *nf* spaceship, spacecraft.

**cosmopolita** *adj* cosmopolitan.
▶ *nm o nf* cosmopolitan.

**cosmos** *nm inv* cosmos.

**cosquillas** *nf pl* tickling *sing*. **LOC** **hacer cosquillas a** ALGN to tickle SB. **I tener cosquillas** to be ticklish. **I buscarle las cosquillas a** ALGN *fam* to needle SB, annoy SB.

**cosquilleo** *nm* tickling.

**costa**[1] *nf (litoral)* coast, coastline; *(playa)* beach, seaside, US shore: *tenemos una casa en la costa* we have a house at the seaside, US we have a house on the shore.

**costa**[2] *nf* FIN cost, price. **LOC** **a costa de 1** *(aprovechándose)* at the expense of. **2** *(a base de)* by, by dint of, by means of: *lo consiguió a costa de muchos sacrificios* he managed it by making a lot of sacrifices. **I a toda costa** at all costs, at any price.
▶ *nf pl* **costas** JUR costs.

**Costa de Marfil** *nf* Ivory Coast.

**costado** *nm* side.
▶ *nm pl* **costados** lineage *sing*. **LOC** **por los cuatro costados** through and through.

**costar** *vi* **1** *(valer)* to cost: *¿cuánto costó?* how much was it? **2** *(ser difícil)* to be hard, be difficult; *(resultar difícil)* to be difficult for: *cuesta encontrar trabajo* it's hard to find a job. **3** *(tiempo)* to take: *me costó cuatro horas* it took me four hours. **LOC** **costar barato,-a** to be cheap. **I costar caro,-a 1** to be expensive, cost a lot. **2** to pay dearly for STH: *esa afirmación le costará cara* he'll pay dearly for saying that. **I costar mucho / costar trabajo** to be difficult, be hard work.

**Costa Rica** *nf* Costa Rica.

**costarricense** *adj* Costa Rican.
▶ *nm o nf* Costa Rican.

**coste** *nm* cost, price, expense. **COMP** **coste de la vida** cost of living.

**costear** *vt (pagar)* to pay for, afford: *su padre le costeó el viaje* his father paid for his journey.
▶ *vpr* **costearse** to pay one's way.

**costero,-a** *adj* coastal, coast.

**costilla** *nf* **1** ANAT rib. **2** CULIN cutlet.
▶ *nf pl* **costillas** *fam (espalda)* back *sing*.

**costillar** *nm* ribs *pl*.

**costo** *nm* cost, price.

**costoso,-a** *adj* **1** *(caro)* costly, expensive. **2** *(difícil)* hard, difficult.

**costra** *nf* **1** crust. **2** MED scab.

**costumbre** *nf* **1** *(hábito)* habit: *tengo la costumbre de comer temprano* I'm in the habit of having lunch early. **2** *(tradición)* custom: *es una costumbre rusa* it's a Russian custom. **3** JUR usage. LOC **como de costumbre** as usual. ∎ **tener por costumbre +** *inf* to be in the habit of + *ger*. COMP **la fuerza de la costumbre** the force of habit.
▶ *nf pl* **costumbres** *(personales)* ways, manner *sing*; *(de un pueblo)* customs.

**costumbrismo** *nm* folk literature.

**costumbrista** *adj* about local customs.
▶ *nm o nf* writer of folk literature.

**costura** *nf* **1** *(cosido)* sewing. **2** *(línea de puntadas)* seam: *medias sin costura* seamless stockings. **3** *(confección)* dressmaking. COMP **cesto de la costura** sewing basket.

**costurera** *nf* seamstress.

**costurero** *nm* **1** *(estuche)* sewing basket, sewing kit. **2** *(mueble)* workbox.

**cota¹** *nf* *(traje)* tabard. COMP **cota de malla** coat of mail.

**cota²** *nf* **1** *(altura)* height above sea level: *la cota mil* one thousand metres above sea level. **2** *(número en mapa)* spot height. **3** *fig (nivel)* level: *la xenofobia está llegando a cotas muy altas* xenophobia is showing an alarming increase.

**cotangente** *nf* cotangent.

**cotejar** *vt (gen)* to compare; *(textos)* to collate, compare.

**cotejo** *nm (gen)* comparison; *(textos)* collation, comparison.

**cotidiano,-a** *adj* daily, everyday: *la vida cotidiana* everyday life.

**cotiledón** *nm* cotyledon.

**cotilla** *nf (faja)* corset.
▶ *nm o nf fam* busybody, gossip.

**cotillear** *vi fam* to gossip, tittle-tattle.

**cotilleo** *nm fam* gossip, gossiping, tittle-tattle.

**cotillón** *nm* **1** *(danza)* cotillion, cotillon. **2** *(fiesta)* party, celebration *especially on New Year's Eve*.

**cotización** *nf* **1** FIN quotation, market price. **2** *(cuota)* membership fee, subscription.

**cotizar** *vt* FIN to quote, price.
▶ *vi (pagar cuota)* to pay a subscription.
▶ *vpr* **cotizarse** **1** *(acciones)* to sell (a, at): *las acciones del banco se cotizan a diez euros con veintitrés* the bank's shares are selling at ten euros twenty-three. **2** *fig (valorarse)* to be valued, be in demand: *este pintor se cotiza mucho* this painter is in great demand.

**coto¹** *nm* **1** *(terreno)* enclosure, reserve. **2** *(poste)* boundary mark. **3** *(límite)* restriction. LOC **poner coto a** ALGO to put a stop to STH. COMP **coto de caza** game preserve.

**coto²** *nm (pez)* miller's thumb.

**cotorra** *nf* **1** *(ave)* parrot. **2** *fam fig* chatterbox. LOC **hablar como una cotorra** to be a chatterbox.

**cotorrear** *vi fam fig* to chatter, prattle (on).

**cotorreo** *nm fam fig* chatter, prattle.

**COU** *abrev* EDUC (Curso de Orientación Universitaria) ≈ *former pre-university course.*

**cowboy** *nm* cowboy.

**coxis** *nm inv* coccyx.

**coyote** *nm* coyote.

**coyuntura** *nf* **1** ANAT joint, articulation. **2** *fig (circunstancia)* moment, juncture. COMP **coyuntura económica** economic situation.

**coz** *nf* kick. LOC **dar una coz** to kick.

**crac** *nm* **1** *(quiebra)* crash, bankruptcy: *el crac de la bolsa de Nueva York* the Wall Street crash. **2** *(onomatopeya)* crack, snap: *el brazo me hizo crac* my arm gave a crack.

**crack** *nm (persona)* star, ace: *es un auténtico crack del fútbol* he's a crack football player.

**craneal** *adj* cranial.

**craneano,-a** *adj* cranial.

**cráneo** *nm* cranium, skull. LOC **ir de cráneo** *fam* to have a lot on one's plate, have one's work cut out.

**cráter** *nm* crater.

**crawl** *nm* crawl.

**creación** *nf* **1** *(gen)* creation. **2** *(fundación)* foundation, establishment, setting up.

**creador,-ra** *adj* creative.
▶ *nm & nf* creator, maker.

**crear** *vt* **1** *(gen)* to create: *crear problemas* to create problems. **2** *(fundar)* to found, establish; *(partido)* to set up. **3** *(inventar)* to invent.
▶ *vpr* **crearse** to make, make for os: *crearse enemigos* to make enemies for os.

**creatividad** *nf* creativity.

**creativo,-a** *adj* creative.

**crecer** *vi* **1** *(persona, planta)* to grow: *has crecido mucho* you've grown a lot. **2** *(incrementar)* to increase, grow, get bigger: *la población ha crecido un uno por ciento* the population has grown by one per cent. **3** *(corriente, marea)* to rise. **4** *(luna)* to wax.
▶ *vpr* **crecerse** *(tomar mayor fuerza)* to grow in confidence: *se crece ante las dificultades* he comes into his own when faced with problems.

**crecido,-a** *adj* **1** *(persona)* grown, grown-up. **2** *(cantidad)* big, large. **3** *(río)* in flood, in spate.

**creciente** *adj* **1** *(que crece)* growing; *(que aumenta)* increasing: *un interés creciente* an increasing interest. **2** *(precios)* rising. **3** *(luna)* crescent (in the first quarter).
▶ *nf* *(de agua)* flood, spate.

**crecimiento** *nm* **1** *(desarrollo)* growth, increase. **2** *(subida)* rise. **3** *(de un río)* flooding, rising.

**credibilidad** *nf* credibility.

**crédito** *nm* **1** COM credit. **2** *(confianza)* credit, belief, credence. **3** *(fama)* reputation, standing. LOC **a crédito** on credit. ∎ **dar crédito a** *(creer)* to believe (in): *no doy crédito a mis oídos* I can't believe what I'm hearing. ∎ **ser digno,-a de crédito** to be reliable. COMP **crédito hi-** potecario debt secured by a mortgage.

**credo** *nm* *fig (creencias)* credo, creed.

**credulidad** *nf* credulity, gullibility.

**crédulo,-a** *adj* credulous, gullible.

**creencia** *nf* belief.

**creer** *vt* **1** *(dar por cierto)* to believe: *si no lo veo no lo creo* I've got to see it to believe it. **2** *(suponer, opinar)* to think, suppose: *¿y tú que crees?* what do you think? **3** *(tener fe)* to believe. LOC **creer a ciencia cierta** to be convinced. ∎ **¡no creas!** do you really think so?, I'm not so sure. ∎ **¡ya lo creo!** of course!
▶ *vpr* **creerse 1** *(aceptar)* to believe: *no me lo creo* I don't believe it, I can't believe it. **2** *(considerarse)* to think: *¿quién te has creído que eres?* who do you think you are? LOC **¡que te crees tú eso!** that's what you think!

**creíble** *adj* credible, believable.

**creído,-a** *adj* arrogant, vain, conceited. LOC **ser un creído,-a** to be full of os.

**crema** *nf* **1** *(de leche, licor, ungüento)* cream. **2** *(natillas)* custard. **3** *(betún)* shoe polish. **4** *fig (lo mejor)* cream. COMP **crema bronceadora** suntan cream. ∎ **crema de afeitar** shaving cream. ∎ **crema hidratante** moisturizing cream.
▶ *adj* cream, cream coloured (US cream colored).

**cremación** *nf* cremation.

**crematorio** *nm* crematorium.

**cremoso,-a** *adj* creamy: *queso cremoso* full-fat cheese.

**crepe** *nf (torta)* pancake, crepe.

**crepé** *nm (tejido, caucho)* crepe.

**crepería** *nf* creperie.

**crepitar** *vi* to crackle.

**crepúsculo** *nm* twilight.

**cresta** *nf* **1** *(de ave)* crest; *(de gallo)* comb. **2** *(de pelo)* toupée. **3** *(de montaña, ola)* crest. LOC **estar en la cresta de la ola** *fam* to be on the crest of a wave.

**Creta** *nf* Crete.

**cretense** *adj* Cretan.
▶ *nm o nf* Cretan.

**cretino,-a** *adj* stupid, cretinous.
▶ *nm & nf* cretin, idiot.

**creyente** *adj* believing.
▶ *nm o nf* believer.

**cría** *nf* **1** *(acto de criar)* nursing; *(de animal)* breeding, raising. **2** *(cachorro)* young. **3** *(camada - ovíparos)* brood; *(- mamíferos)* litter.

**criada** *nf* maid.

**criadero** *nm* **1** *(de plantas)* nursery; *(de animales)* breeding farm; *(de peces)* hatchery. **2** *(mina)* seam. COMP **criadero de ostras** oyster bed.

**criado,-a** *adj* *(animal)* reared, raised; *(persona)* bred, brought up.
▶ *nm & nf* servant.

**criador** *nm & nf* breeder.

**criar** *vt* **1** *(educar niños)* to bring up, rear, care for: *lo crió una tía* his aunt brought him up. **2** *(nutrir)* to feed (con, -); *(con pecho)* to suckle, nurse, breast-feed. **3** *(animales)* to breed, raise, rear. **4** *(producir)* to have, grow; *(vinos)* to make, mature.
▶ *vpr* **criarse 1** *(crecer)* to grow; *(formarse)* to be brought up. **2** *(producirse)* to grow.

**criatura** *nf* **1** creature. **2** *(niño)* baby, child. **3** *fig* baby.

**cribar** *vt* **1** *(colar)* to sift, sieve. **2** *fig (seleccionar)* to screen.

**cric** *nm* jack.

**cricquet** *nm* cricket.

**crimen** *nm* **1** *(delito)* crime. **2** *(asesinato)* murder.

**criminal** *adj* **1** criminal. **2** *fam (muy malo)* awful, criminal, appalling.
▶ *nm o nf* criminal.

**criminalista** *nm o nf (abogado)* criminal lawyer.

**criminología** *nf* criminology.

**crin** [también se usa en plural con el mismo significado] *nf* mane.

**crío,-a** *nm & nf fam* kid, child.
▶ *adj fam* young: *todavía eres muy crío* you're still too young. LOC **ser un crío,-a** *fam* to be childish.

**criollo,-a** *adj* Creole.
▶ *nm & nf (persona)* Creole.
▶ *nm (idioma)* Creole.

**cripta** *nf* crypt.

**críquet** *nm* cricket.

**crisálida** *nf* chrysalis.

**crisantemo** *nm* chrysanthemum.

**crisis** *nf inv* **1** *(dificultad)* crisis. **2** *(ataque)* fit, attack: *crisis de asma* asthma attack. **3** *(escasez)* shortage: *crisis de alimentos* food shortage. LOC **estar en crisis** to be in crisis, reach crisis point. COMP **crisis de gobierno** cabinet crisis. ‖ **crisis nerviosa** nervous breakdown.

**crisma** *nm & nf fam (cabeza)* head, nut.

**crisol** *nm* **1** crucible. **2** *fig* melting pot.

**crispación** *nf fig* tension: *un clima de crispación* a tense atmosphere.

**crispar** *vt fig (irritar)* to irritate, annoy, infuriate: *ese tipo me crispa* that guy infuriates me. LOC **crispar los nervios a ALGN** *fig* to get on SB's nerves.
▶ *vpr* **crisparse** *fig (irritarse)* to get annoyed, get angry.

**cristal** *nm* **1** *(mineral)* crystal. **2** *(vidrio)* glass. **3** *(de ventana)* window pane, pane. **4** *(de lente)* lens. **5** *(de coche)* window.
▶ *nm pl* **cristales 1** *(trozos)* glass *sing*: *ten cuidado, hay cristales por el suelo* be careful, there's some broken glass on the floor. **2** *(ventanas)* windows. COMP **botella de cristal** glass bottle. ‖ **cristal de cuarzo** quartz crystal.

**cristalera** *nf* **1** *(mueble)* display cabinet. **2** *(escaparate)* window, shop window. **3** *(conjunto de cristales)* windows *pl*; *(puertas)* glass doors *pl*; *(techo)* glass roof.

**cristalería** *nf* **1** *(fábrica)* glassworks. **2** *(tienda)* glassware shop. **3** *(conjunto)* glassware; *(vasos)* glasses *pl*.

**cristalero,-a** *nm & nf* glazier.

**cristalino,-a** *adj* transparent, crystal-clear.
▶ *nm* **cristalino** crystalline lens.

**cristalización** *nf* **1** crystallization. **2** *fig* consolidation.

**cristalizar** *vt* to crystallize.
▶ *vi* **1** to crystallize. **2** *fig* to crystallize (en, into).
▶ *vpr* **cristalizarse** to crystallize.

**cristalografía** *nf* crystallography.
**cristiandad** *nf* Christendom.
**cristianismo** *nm* Christianity.
**cristiano,-a** *adj* Christian.
► *nm* Christian.
**criterio** *nm* **1** *(en lógica)* criterion. **2** *(juicio)* judgement, discernment. **3** *(opinión)* opinion, point of view.
**criticar** *vt* to criticize.
► *vi (murmurar)* to gossip.
**crítico,-a** *adj* critical.
► *nm & nf* critic.
**Croacia** *nf* Croatia.
**croar** *vi* to croak.
**croata** *adj* Croatian, Croat.
► *nm o nf (persona)* Croat, Croatian.
► *nm (idioma)* Croat, Croatian.
**crocante** *nm* almond brittle.
**crocanti** *nm* almond brittle.
**croché** *nm* crochet.
**croissant** *nm* croissant.
**croissantería** *nf* croissant shop.
**crol** *nm* crawl.
**cromado,-a** *adj* chrome.
► *nm* **cromado** chroming.
**cromar** *vt* to chrome.
**cromático,-a** *adj* chromatic.
**cromatismo** *nm* chromatism.
**cromo** *nm* **1** *(metal)* chromium, chrome. **2** *(estampa)* picture card, sticker: *un álbum de cromos* a picture-card album. ⌐LOC¬ **ir hecho,-a un cromo** *fam* to look a sight.
**cromosoma** *nm* chromosome.
**crónica** *nf* **1** *(gen)* account, chronicle. **2** *(en periódico)* article, column, feature. **3** RAD TV *(programa)* programme (US program); *(reportaje)* feature, report. **4** HIST chronicle.
**crónico,-a** *adj* **1** chronic. **2** *fig* deeply rooted.
**cronista** *nm o nf* **1** HIST chronicler. **2** *(de prensa)* columnist, feature writer. **3** RAD TV commentator.
**cronología** *nf* chronology.
**cronológico,-a** *adj* chronological.
**cronometrar** *vt* to time.

**cronómetro** *nm* **1** chronometer. **2** DEP stopwatch.
**croqueta** *nf* croquette.
**croquis** *nm inv* sketch, outline.
**cros** *nm inv (a pie)* cross-country race; *(en moto)* motocross race.
**cruasán** *nm* croissant.
**cruce** *nm* **1** cross, crossing. **2** AUTO crossroads. **3** *(de razas)* crossbreeding. **4** *(interferencia telefónica, etc)* crossed line: *hay un cruce* there's a crossed line. **5** ELEC short circuit.
**crucero** *nm* **1** *(buque)* cruiser. **2** *(viaje)* cruise.
**crucial** *adj* **1** crucial. **2** *fig* crucial, critical.
**crucifijo** *nm* crucifix.
**crucifixión** *nf* crucifixion.
**crucigrama** *nm* crossword (puzzle).
**crudeza** *nf* **1** *(rudeza)* crudeness, rudeness, coarseness. **2** *(del clima)* harshness.
**crudo,-a** *adj* **1** *(sin cocer)* raw; *(poco hecho)* underdone: *la carne está cruda* the meat is underdone, the meat isn't cooked enough. **2** *fig (duro)* crude, coarse. **3** *(color)* natural, unbleached. **4** *(clima)* harsh. ⌐LOC¬ **verlo muy crudo** *fam* not to hold out much hope.
► *nm* **crudo** *(petróleo)* crude oil, crude.
**cruel** *adj (persona)* cruel (con/para, to).
**crueldad** *nf* **1** cruelty. **2** *(dureza)* harshness, severity.
**cruelmente** *adv* cruelly.
**crujido** *nm* **1** *(de puerta)* creak, creaking. **2** *(de patatas fritas)* crunching. **3** *(seda, papel)* rustle, rustling. **4** *(de dientes)* grinding.
**crujiente** *adj* **1** *(alimentos)* crunchy. **2** *(seda)* rustling.
**crujir** *vi* **1** *(puerta)* to creak. **2** *(patatas fritas)* to crunch. **3** *(seda, hojas)* to rustle. **4** *(dientes)* to grind.
**crustáceo** *nm* crustacean.
**cruz** *nf* **1** *(gen)* cross. **2** *(de moneda)* tails *pl*: *¿cara o cruz?* heads or tails?
**cruzada** *nf* **1** HIST crusade. **2** *(campaña)* campaign.

**cruzar** *vt* **1** *(gen)* to cross: *cruzar una calle* to cross a street. **2** *(poner atravesado)* to lay across; *(estar atravesado)* to lie across. **3** *(en geometría)* to intersect. **4** *(animales)* to cross. **5** *(miradas, palabras)* to exchange. LOC **cruzar a nado** to swim across. ▪ **cruzar los brazos** to fold one's arms.
▶ *vpr* **cruzarse 1** *(encontrarse)* to crosseach other. **2** *(intercambiarse)* to exchange.

**cuaderno** *nm (libreta)* notebook, journal; *(escolar)* exercise book.

**cuadra** *nf* **1** *(establo)* stable. **2** AM *(manzana)* block, block of houses.

**cuadrado,-a** *adj* **1** *(forma)* square. **2** *fam (persona)* broad, stocky. **3** *fig (mente)* rigid, one-track.
▶ *nm* **cuadrado** square. LOC **elevar al cuadrado** to square.

**cuadragésimo,-a** *adj* fortieth.
▶ *nm & nf* fortieth.
✎ Consulta también sexto,-a.

**cuadrangular** *adj* quadrangular.

**cuadrángulo** *nm* quadrangle.

**cuadrante** *nm* **1** *(reloj)* sundial. **2** *(instrumento)* quadrant. **3** *(cojín)* square pillow.

**cuadrar** *vt* **1** *(dar figura cuadrada)* to square, make square. **2** *(geometría, matemáticas)* to square. **3** COM to balance.
▶ *vi* **1** *(coincidir)* to square, agree. **2** COM to tally, add up: *las cuentas de este mes no cuadran* the accounts don't add up this month. **3** *fig (ir bien)* to suit: *el estilo no cuadra con el tema* the style doesn't suit the subject.

**cuádriceps** *nm inv* quadriceps.

**cuadrícula** *nf* squares *pl*, grid.

**cuadriculado,-a** *adj* squared.
▶ *nm* **cuadriculado** squares *pl*, grid.

**cuadricular** *vt* to square, divide into squares.
▶ *adj* squared.

**cuadrienio** *nm* quadrennium.

**cuadriga** *nf* chariot.

**cuadrilátero,-a** *adj* quadrilateral, four-sided.
▶ *nm* **cuadrilátero** *(boxeo)* ring.

**cuadrilla** *nf* **1** *(grupo)* party, gang. **2** *(de bandidos, etc)* gang, band. **3** *(de obreros)* gang, team.

**cuadro** *nm* **1** *(cuadrado)* square. **2** *(pintura)* painting, picture. **3** TEAT scene. **4** *(descripción)* description, picture. **5** *(dirigentes)* leaders *pl*; *(personal)* staff. **6** *(conjunto de datos)* chart, graph. LOC **a cuadros** checked, US checkered: *tela a cuadros* checked (US checkered) cloth. COMP **cuadro clínico** clinical pattern. ▪ **cuadro sinóptico** diagram, chart.

**cuadrúpedo,-a** *adj* quadruped.
▶ *nm* **cuadrúpedo** quadruped.

**cuádruple** *adj* quadruple, fourfold.

**cuadruplicar** *vt* to quadruple.
▶ *vi* to quadruple.

**cuajada** *nf (leche)* curd; *(requesón)* cottage cheese.

**cuajar** *vt* **1** *(gen)* to coagulate; *(leche)* to curdle; *(sangre)* to clot. **2** *(huevo)* to set.
▶ *vi* **1** *(nieve)* to lie. **2** *fig (tener éxito)* to be a success, come off: *la cosa no cuajó* it didn't come off.
▶ *vpr* **cuajarse 1** to coagulate; *(leche)* to curdle; *(sangre)* clot. **2** *(huevo)* to set.

**cual** *pron* **1** *(precedido de artículo - persona)* who, whom: *la gente a la cual preguntamos* the people whom we asked. **2** *(precedido de artículo - cosa)* which: *la ciudad en la cual nací* the city where I was born. LOC **cada cual** everyone, everybody.
▶ *adv fml* as, like: *se enamoró cual si tuviese quince años* he fell in love like a teenager.

**cuál** *pron* **1** *(interrogativo)* which, which one, what: *¿cuál es el más alto?* which one is the tallest? **2** *(valor distributivo)* some. **3** *(exclamativo)* how, what: *¡cuál no sería mi asombro!* imagine my amazement! LOC **a cuál más** equally: *a cuál más listo* each as clever as the other.
▶ *adj (interrogativo)* which.

**cualidad** *nf* **1** *(de persona)* quality, attribute. **2** *(de cosa)* quality, property.

**cualitativo,-a** *adj* qualitative.

**cualquier** *adj (indefinido)* any: *cualquier otro día* any other day; *cualquier cosa* anything; *cualquier persona* anyone.
✎ Consulta también cualquiera.

**cualquiera** *adj* **1** *(indefinido)* any: *un día cualquiera* any day. **2** *(ordinario)* ordinary: *no es una corbata cualquiera* it's not an ordinary tie.
▶ *pron* **1** *(persona indeterminada)* anybody, anyone; *(cosa indeterminada)* any, any one: *cualquiera lo compraría* anybody would buy it. **2** *(nadie)* nobody: *¡cualquiera lo coge!* nobody would take it!
▶ *nf* **cualquiera que** *(persona)* whoever; *(cosa)* whatever, whichever: *cualquiera que diga eso, miente* whoever says that is lying.

**cuan** *adv* [se usa sólo antes de adjetivo y de adverbio] *fml* as: *cayó cuan largo era* he fell flat on the floor.

✎ Consulta también **cuanto**.

**cuán** *adv* [se usa sólo antes de adjetivo y de adverbio] *(interrogativo)* how: *¡cuán idiota!* how stupid!

✎ Consulta también **cuanto**.

**cuando** *adv* *(tiempo)* when: *cuando tenía diez años* when he was ten.
▶ *conj* **1** *(temporal)* when, whenever: *ven a verme cuando quieras* come and see me whenever you want. **2** *(condicional)* if: *cuando él lo dice* if he says so. **3** *(causal)* since. LOC **de vez en cuando** now and then, from time to time. ∎ **hasta cuando** until.
▶ *prep* during, at the time of: *cuando la guerra* during the war.

**cuándo** *adv* *(interrogativo)* when: *¿cuándo es tu cumpleaños?* when is your birthday?
▶ *nm* when: *no sé el cómo ni el cuándo* I don't know how or when.

**cuantía** *nf* **1** *(cantidad)* quantity; *(importe)* amount: *la cuantía de una factura* the amount of a bill. **2** *(dimensión)* extent: *la cuantía del desastre ecológico* the extent of the ecological disaster.

**cuantitativo,-a** *adj* quantitative.

**cuanto** *nm* Fís quantum: *la teoría de los cuantos* the quantum theory.

**cuánto,-a** *adj* **1** *(pregunta - singular)* how much; *(- plural)* how many: *¿cuántos años tienes?* how old are you? **2** *(exclama-*

*ción)* what a lot of, so many, so much: *¡cuánta gente!* there are so many people!, what a lot of people!
▶ *pron (singular)* how much; *(plural)* how many: *¿cuánto es?* how much is it?
▶ *adv* how, how much: *¡cuánto me alegro!* I'm so glad!

**cuanto,-a³** *adj (singular)* as much as; *(plural)* as many as: *puedes beber cuanta agua quieras* you can drink as much water as you want. LOC **cuanto antes** as soon as possible. ∎ **en cuanto** as soon as, when: *en cuanto llegue dile...* as soon as he arrives tell him... ∎ **unos,-as cuantos,-as** some, a few.
▶ *pron* **1** *(singular)* everything, all: *escribe cuanto quieras* write as much as you want. **2** *(plural)* all who, everybody who: *cuantos entraron se asustaron* everybody who came in was frightened.

**cuarcita** *nf* quartzite.

**cuarenta** *adj (cardinal)* forty; *(ordinal)* fortieth. LOC **cantarle las cuarenta a** ALGN to give SB a piece of one's mind.
▶ *nm (número)* forty.

✎ Consulta también **seis**.

**cuarentavo,-a** *adj* fortieth.
▶ *nm & nf* fortieth.

✎ Consulta también **sexto,-a**.

**cuarentena** *nf* **1** *(exacto)* forty; *(aproximado)* about forty. **2** MED quarantine. LOC **poner a** ALGN **en cuarentena** MED to quarantine SB, put SB in quarantine.

**cuaresma** *nf* Lent.

**cuarta** *nf* **1** *(palmo)* span. **2** *(cuadrante)* quadrant.

✎ Consulta también **cuarto,-a**.

**cuartear** *vt* **1** *(dividir en cuatro)* to quarter, divide into four. **2** *(descuartizar)* to quarter. **3** *(rajar)* to crack.
▶ *vpr* **cuartearse** *(rajarse)* to crack, split.

**cuartel** *nm* MIL barracks *pl*.

**cuarteto** *nm* quartet.

**cuartilla** *nf* sheet of paper.

**cuarto** *nm* **1** *(parte)* quarter: *un cuarto de hora* a quarter of an hour. **2** *(de animal)* quarter. **3** *(de ropa)* quarter: *un chaquetón tres cuartos* a three-quarter length jacket. **4** *(habitación)* room. ⎣LOC⎦ **de tres al cuarto** *fam* worthless, third-rate. ▎ **estar sin un cuarto** *fam* to be broke. ▎ **tres cuartos de lo mismo** *fam* almost exactly the same. ⎣COMP⎦ **cuarto creciente** first quarter. ▎ **cuarto de baño** bathroom. ▎ **cuartos de final** DEP quarter finals.
▸ *nm pl* **cuartos** *fam (dinero)* money *sing*, dough *sing*.

**cuarto,-a** *adj (ordinal)* fourth: *llegó cuarto* he arrived in fourth place, he came fourth.
▸ *nm & nf* fourth.

✎ Consulta también **sexto,-a.**

**cuarzo** *nm* quartz.
**cuaternario,-a** *adj* quaternary.
▸ *nm* **el cuaternario** the quaternary.
**cuatrienio** *nm* quadrennium, four-year period.
**cuatrimestral** *adj (en frecuencia)* four-monthly; *(en duración)* four-month.
**cuatrimestre** *nm* four-month period: *en el primer cuatrimestre de 2007* in the first four months of 2007.
**cuatrisílabo,-a** *adj* quadrisyllabic.
▸ *nm* **cuatrisílabo** quadrisyllable.
**cuatro** *adj (cardinal)* four; *(ordinal)* fourth. ⎣LOC⎦ **caer cuatro gotas** *fam* to rain very lightly, spit. ▎ **decirle cuatro cosas a** ALGN to tell SB off. ⎣COMP⎦ **cuatro gatos** *fam* just a few people, hardly anyone.
▸ *nm (número)* four.

✎ Consulta también **seis.**

**cuatrocientos,-as** *adj* four hundred.
▸ *nm* **cuatrocientos** *(número)* four hundred.

✎ Consulta también **seis.**

**cuba** *nf* cask, barrel.
**Cuba** *nf* Cuba.
**cubano,-a** *adj* Cuban.
▸ *nm & nf* Cuban.

**cubertería** *nf* cutlery.
**cubeta** *nf* **1** *(rectangular)* tray, tank, dish. **2** *(cubo)* bucket.
**cúbico,-a** *adj* cubic: *raíz cúbica* cube root.
**cubierta** *nf* **1** *(gen)* cover, covering. **2** *(de libro)* cover. **3** ARQUIT roof. **4** *(de neumático)* tyre (US tire). **5** *(de barco, avión)* deck. ⎣LOC⎦ **en cubierta** on deck.
**cubierto,-a** *adj* **1** *(gen)* covered. **2** *(cielo)* overcast. **3** *(plaza)* filled.
▸ *nm* **cubierto 1** *(techumbre)* cover. **2** *(en la mesa)* place setting. ⎣LOC⎦ **ponerse a cubierto** to take cover. ▎ **tener las espaldas cubiertas** *fam* to be well-heeled.
▸ *nm pl* **cubiertos** cutlery *sing*.
**cubilete** *nm* **1** *(molde)* mould (US mold). **2** *(de dados)* dice cup, dice shaker; *(juego)* cup.
**cubismo** *nm* cubism.
**cubista** *adj* cubist.
▸ *nm o nf* cubist.
**cubito** *nm* **1** little cube. **2** *(de hielo)* ice cube.
**cúbito** *nm* cubitus.
**cubo¹** *nm* **1** *(recipiente)* bucket. **2** *(de rueda)* hub. ⎣COMP⎦ **cubo de la basura** rubbish bin, US garbage can.
**cubo²** *nm* MAT cube. ⎣LOC⎦ **elevar al cubo** to cube.
**cubrecama** *nm* bedspread.
**cubrir** *vt* **1** *(gen)* to cover. **2** CULIN to coat (de, with). **3** *(poner tejado)* to put a roof on. **4** *(niebla, etc)* to shroud (de, in), cloak. **5** *(ocultar)* to hide. **6** *(llenar)* to fill (de, with), cover (de, with): *cubrir de agua* to fill with water. **7** *(alcanzar)* to come up: *el agua le cubría hasta los tobillos* the water came up to his ankles.
▸ *vpr* **cubrirse 1** *(abrigarse)* to cover os. **2** *(la cabeza)* to put one's hat on. **3** *fig (protegerse)* to protect os. **4** *(cielo)* to become overcast. **5** *(llenarse)* to be filled.
**cucaña** *nf* *(palo, juego)* greasy pole.
**cucaracha** *nf* cockroach.
**cuchara** *nf* spoon.

**cucharada** *nf* spoonful. COMP **cucharada colmada** heaped spoonful. ▌ **cucharada rasa** level spoonful.

**cucharadita** *nf* teaspoonful.

**cucharilla** *nf* teaspoon. COMP **cucharilla de café** coffee spoon.

**cucharita** *nf* teaspoon.

**cucharón** *nm* ladle.

**cuchichear** *vi* to whisper.

**cuchicheo** *nm* whispering.

**cuchilla** *nf (hoja)* blade. COMP **cuchilla de afeitar** razor blade.

**cuchillada** *nf (golpe)* stab, slash; *(herida)* stab wound, knife wound.

**cuchillería** *nf* cutler's shop.

**cuchillo** *nm* **1** knife. **2** ARQUIT support.

**cuclillas** LOC **en cuclillas** crouching. ▌ **ponerse en cuclillas** to crouch down.

**cuclillo** *nm* cuckoo.

**cuco** *nm (insecto)* caterpillar.

**cuco,-a** *adj* **1** *fam (coquetón)* cute. **2** *(taimado)* shrewd, crafty.
▶ *nm* **cuco** *(ave)* cuckoo.

**cucú** *nm* **1** *(canto)* cuckoo. **2** *(reloj)* cuckoo clock.

**cucurucho** *nm* **1** *(de papel)* paper cone. **2** *(helado)* cornet, cone. **3** *(capirote)* pointed hood.

**cuello** *nm* **1** ANAT neck. **2** *(de camisa, vestido, abrigo)* collar; *(de jersey)* neck: *un jersey de cuello alto* a polo neck jumper, US a turtleneck jumper. **3** *(de botella)* bottleneck.

**cuenca** *nf* **1** *(escudilla)* wooden bowl. **2** ANAT socket. **3** GEOG basin. **4** *(minera)* coalfield.

**cuenco** *nm (vasija)* earthenware bowl.

**cuenta** *nf* **1** *(bancaria)* account. **2** *(factura)* bill. **3** *(cálculo)* count, counting. **4** *(de collar, etc)* bead. LOC **caer en la cuenta** to realize: *y entonces caí en la cuenta de que...* and then I realized that..., and then it dawned on me that.... ▌ **en resumidas cuentas** in short. ▌ **hacer cuentas** to do sums. ▌ **más de la cuenta** too much, too many: *comió más de la cuenta* she ate too much. ▌ **pedir cuentas** to ask for an explanation. ▌ **por la cuenta que le trae** in one's own interest. ▌ **sacar cuentas** to work out. ▌ **tener en cuenta** to take into account. COMP **cuenta atrás** countdown. ▌ **cuenta corriente** current account. ▌ **cuenta de correo electrónico** e-mail account.

**cuentagotas** *nm inv* dropper.

**cuentakilómetros** *nm inv (de velocidad)* speedometer; *(de distancia)* mileometer.

**cuentarrevoluciones** *nm inv* rev counter.

**cuentavueltas** *nm inv* rev counter.

**cuentista** *adj fam* overdramatic.
▶ *nm o nf* **1** *(autor)* story writer; *(narrador)* storyteller. **2** *fam (que exagera)* over-dramatic person; *(que miente)* fibber, liar.

**cuento** *nm* **1** *(relato)* story, tale. **2** LIT short story. **3** *fam (chisme)* gossip. **4** *fam (embuste)* fib, story. LOC **dejarse de cuentos 1** *fam (ir al grano)* to get to the point. **2** *(decir mentiras)* to stop telling fibs. ▌ **ir con el cuento a** ALGN to go and tell SB. ▌ **tener mucho cuento** *fam* to make a lot of fuss. ▌ **venir a cuento** to be pertinent. COMP **cuento chino** tall story. ▌ **cuento de hadas** fairy tale.

**cuerda** *nf* **1** *(cordel)* rope, string. **2** *(instrumento)* string, cord; *(voz)* voice. **3** *(de reloj)* spring: *dar cuerda a un reloj* to wind up a watch. **4** *(en geometría)* chord. **5** DEP interior. COMP **cuerdas vocales** vocal chords.
▶ *nf pl* **cuerdas 1** *(boxeo)* ropes. **2** MÚS strings.

**cuerdo,-a** *adj* **1** *(persona)* sane. **2** *(acción)* prudent, sensible.
▶ *nm & nf (persona)* sane person, person in one's right mind.

**cuerno** *nm* **1** horn; *(de ciervo)* antlers *pl.* **2** *(de antena)* antlers *pl.* **3** MÚS horn.
▶ *interj* golly!, gosh!

**cuero** *nm* **1** *(de animal)* skin, hide. **2** *(curtido)* leather: *pantalón de cuero* leather trousers. **3** *(odre)* wineskin. **4** *(balón)* ball. LOC **quedarse en cueros** *fam* to strip off.

**cuerpo** *nm* **1** ANAT body. **2** *(constitución)* build. **3** *(figura)* figure. **4** *(tronco)* trunk.

**5** *(grupo)* body, force, corps: *el cuerpo de bomberos* the fire brigade (US the fire department). **6** *(cadáver)* corpse, body. **7** QUÍM substance. **8** FÍS body. **9** DEP length. LOC **cuerpo a cuerpo** hand-to-hand. ▐ **de cuerpo entero** full-length. ▐ **en cuerpo y alma** *fig* heart and soul, body and soul. COMP **cuerpo diplomático** diplomatic corps. ▐ **cuerpo geométrico** regular solid. ▐ **cuerpos celestes** heavenly bodies.

**cuervo** *nm (córvido en general)* crow; *(específico)* raven.

**cuesta** *nf (pendiente)* slope. LOC **a cuestas** on one's back, on one's shoulders. ▐ **hacérsele a uno** ALGO **cuesta arriba** *fig* to find STH an uphill struggle, find STH very difficult. ▐ **ir cuesta abajo** *fig* to go downhill.

**cuestión** *nf* **1** *(pregunta)* question. **2** *(asunto)* business, matter, question. **3** *(discusión)* dispute, quarrel, argument. LOC **en cuestión** in question. ▐ **en cuestión de...** *(tiempo)* in just a few..., in a matter of... ▐ **eso es otra cuestión** that's a whole different matter.

**cuestionable** *adj* questionable.

**cuestionar** *vt* to question.

**cuestionario** *nm* questionnaire.

**cueva** *nf* cave.

**cuidado** *nm* **1** *(atención)* care, carefulness. **2** *(recelo)* worry.
▸ *interj* look out!, watch out!: *¡cuidado con la moto!* mind the motorbike! LOC **andarse con cuidado** to go carefully. ▐ «**Cuidado con el perro**» «Beware of the dog». ▐ **con cuidado** carefully. ▐ **tener cuidado** to be careful. ▐ **traer sin cuidado** not to care. COMP **cuidados intensivos** intensive care *sing*.

**cuidador,-ra** *nm & nf* keeper.

**cuidadoso,-a** *adj* **1** *(atento)* careful. **2** *(celoso)* cautious.

**cuidar** *vt* to look after, take care of, care for.
▸ *vpr* **cuidarse** to take care of os, look after os: *¡cuídate mucho!* take good care of yourself!

**culebra** *nf* snake.

**culinario,-a** *adj* culinary, cooking: *arte culinario* cuisine.

**culminación** *nf* culmination, climax.

**culminante** *adj (momento)* culminating, climatic; *(punto)* highest.

**culminar** *vi* **1** to reach a peak. **2** *fig (acabar)* to finish, end.

**culpa** *nf* **1** *(culpabilidad)* guilt, blame. **2** *(falta)* fault: *esto es culpa mía* it's my fault. LOC **echar la culpa a** ALGN to put the blame on SB. ▐ **tener la culpa** to be to blame (de, for): *yo no tengo la culpa* I'm not to blame, it's not my fault.

**culpabilidad** *nf* guilt, culpability.

**culpable** *adj* guilty.
▸ *nm o nf* offender, culprit.

**culpar** *vt* **1** *(gen)* to blame (de, for). **2** *(de un delito)* to accuse (de, of).

**cultivar** *vt* **1** to cultivate, farm. **2** *(ejercitar facultades)* to work at, practise (US practice), improve: *cultivar la memoria* to improve one's memory. **3** *(en biología)* to produce. LOC **cultivar las amistades** *fig* to cultivate friendships.

**cultivo** *nm* **1** *(acción)* cultivation, farming. **2** *(cosecha)* crop. **3** BIOL culture. **4** *fig (desarrollo)* development, growth.

**culto,-a** *adj* **1** *(persona)* cultured, educated. **2** *(estilo)* refined.
▸ *nm* **culto** worship.

**cultura** *nf* culture. LOC **de cultura** educated.

**cultural** *adj* cultural.

**cumbre** *nf* **1** *(de montaña)* summit, top. **2** *fig (culminación)* pinnacle. **3** *(reunión)* summit conference, summit meeting.

**cumpleaños** *nm inv* birthday.

**cumplido,-a** *adj* **1** *(completo)* complete, full. **2** *(abundante)* large, ample. **3** *(perfecto)* perfect. **4** *(educado)* polite, courteous.
▸ *nm* **cumplido** compliment. LOC **sin cumplidos** informally.

**cumplidor,-ra** *adj (que cumple)* who delivers the goods: *es una chica muy cumplidora* she always delivers the goods, she always fulfils her promises.

C

**cumplir** vt **1** (orden) to carry out; (deseo) to fulfil (US fulfill); (deber) to do. **2** (promesa) to keep. **3** JUR (ley) to observe, abide by; (pena) to serve. **4** (años) to be, turn: ¡que cumplas muchos más! many happy returns! **5** (satisfacer) to do, carry out, fulfil (US fulfill). LOC **cumplir con el deber** to do one's duty. ▌**cumplir con su palabra** to keep one's word. ▌**para cumplir** as a formality.
► vi **1** (plazo) to expire, end. **2** (deuda, pago) to fall due.
► vpr **cumplirse 1** (realizarse) to be fulfilled, come true: se cumplió la profecía the prophecy came true. **2** (fecha) to be: se cumple una semana del comienzo del curso it's a week since the course began.

**cúmulo** nm **1** (montón) load, pile, heap; (cantidad) series, host, string: un cúmulo de desgracias a series of misfortunes. **2** METEOR cumulus.

**cumulonimbo** nm cumulonimbus.

**cuna** nf **1** (cama) cradle. **2** (linaje) birth, lineage, stock. **3** fig (origen) cradle, birthplace: la cuna de la filosofía the cradle of philosophy. **4** (lugar de nacimiento) birthplace.

**cundir** vi **1** (extenderse) to spread: cundió el pánico panic spread. **2** (dar de sí) to go a long way, go far: una hora cunde muy poco you can't do much in an hour. **3** (aumentar de volumen) to swell, expand: los fideos cunden al cocerse noodles expand when cooked.

**cuneta** nf **1** (de carretera) verge. **2** (zanja) ditch.

**cuña** nf (pieza) wedge.

**cuñado,-a** nm & nf (hombre) brother-in-law; (mujer) sister-in-law.

**cuño** nm **1** (troquel) die, stamp. **2** (sello) stamp, mark.

**cuota** nf **1** (pago) membership fee, dues pl. **2** (porción) quota, share.

**cupo** nm (cuota) quota.

**cupón** nm **1** (vale) coupon, voucher. **2** (de lotería) ticket.

**cúpula** nf cupola, dome.

**cura** nm REL priest.
► nf **1** cure, healing. **2** (tratamiento) treatment: cura de adelgazamiento slim-

ming treatment. LOC **hacer las primeras curas** to give first aid.

**curable** adj curable.

**curación** nf **1** (gen) cure. **2** (de herida) healing. **3** (recuperación) recovery.

**curandero,-a** nm & nf **1** (charlatán) quack. **2** (curador) folk healer.

**curar** vt **1** (sanar) to cure. **2** (herida) to dress; (enfermedad) to treat.
► vi **1** (cuidar) to take care (de, of). **2** (recuperarse) to recover, get well. **3** (herida) to heal (up).
► vpr **curarse 1** (recuperarse) to recover (de, from), get well. **2** (herida) to heal up.

**curativo,-a** adj curative: poder curativo healing power.

**curia** nf **1** REL curia. **2** JUR Bar.

**curiosamente** adv **1** (con curiosidad) curiously, strangely. **2** (limpiamente) cleanly.

**curiosear** vi **1** (fisgar) to pry, nose around. **2** (mirar) to look around.
► vt (fisgar) to pry into.

**curiosidad** nf **1** (gen) curiosity. **2** (aseo) cleanliness, tidiness. **3** (cuidado) care. LOC **tener curiosidad de ALGO** to be curious about STH.

**currículo** nm curriculum, curriculum vitae.

**curry** nm curry.

**cursar** vt **1** (estudiar) to study. **2** (enviar) to send, dispatch; (orden) to give. **3** (tramitar) to make an application.

**cursi** adj fam (afectado) pretentious, affected, twee.
► nm o nf fam pretentious person, affected person.

**cursilada** nf **1** (cualidad) affectation, pretentiousness. **2** (hecho) pretentious thing to do, posh thing to do. **3** (obra, cosa) pretentious thing: las películas románticas me parecen una cursilada for me romantic films are just sentimental slush.

**cursillo** nm short course, training course.

**cursiva** nf (escritura) cursive; (tipografía) italics pl.

**curso** *nm* **1** *(dirección)* course, direction: *el curso de los acontecimientos* the course of events. **2** EDUC *(nivel)* year, class; *(materia)* course; *(escolar)* school year: *vamos al mismo curso* we are in the same class. **3** *(río)* flow, current. COMP **curso acelerado** crash course.

**cursor** *nm* **1** INFORM cursor. **2** TÉC slide.

**curtido,-a** *adj* **1** *(por el sol)* tanned, sunburnt. **2** *(cuero)* tanned. **3** *fig (endurecido)* hardened.
▶ *nm* **curtido** *(operación)* tanning.
▶ *nm pl* **curtidos** tanned leather *sing*.

**curtidor,-ra** *nm & nf* tanner.

**curtir** *vt* **1** *(piel)* to tan. **2** *fig (acostumbrar)* to harden, toughen.
▶ *vpr* **curtirse 1** *(por el sol)* to get tanned. **2** *fig (acostumbrarse)* to become hardened.

**curva** *nf* **1** *(gen)* curve. **2** *(de carretera)* bend. **3** *(gráfico)* curve, graph. LOC **trazar una curva** to draw a curve.

**curvar** *vt* **1** *(gen)* to curve, bend. **2** *(espalda)* to arch.

**curvilíneo,-a** *adj* **1** curvilinear, curvilineal. **2** *fam (del cuerpo)* curvaceous, shapely.

**curvo,-a** *adj* curved, bent.

**cuscús** *nm* couscous.

**cúspide** *nf* **1** *(cumbre)* summit, peak. **2** *(en geometría)* apex. **3** *fig* peak.

**custodia** *nf* **1** custody, care. **2** REL monstrance. LOC **bajo custodia** in custody.

**custodiar** *vt* **1** *(proteger)* to keep, take care of. **2** *(vigilar)* to guard, watch over.

**cutáneo,-a** *adj* cutaneous, skin: *enfermedad cutánea* skin disease.

**cúter** *nm* **1** *(barco)* cutter. **2** *(cuchillo)* cutter.

**cutícula** *nf* cuticle.

**cutis** *nm inv* skin, complexion.

**cuyo,-a** *pron* **1** *(personas)* whose, of whom: *esta mujer, cuya hermana trabaja en Alemania...* this woman, whose sister works in Germany..., this woman, the sister of whom works in Germany... **2** *(cosas)* whose, of which: *un árbol cuyas hojas presentan esta enfermedad* a tree with leaves that show signs of this disease. LOC **en cuyo caso** in which case.

**CV¹** *sím* (caballos de vapor) horse power; *(símbolo)* HP.

**CV²** *abrev* (currículum vítae) curriculum vitae; *(abreviatura)* CV.

C

# D

**D, d** *nf (la letra)* D, d.

**dado** *nm* **1** *(para jugar)* die. **2** TÉC block. **3** ARQUIT dado. LOC **echar los dados** to throw the dice.

**dado,-a** *adj* **1** *given*: *dada la base y la altura, hallar la superficie* given the base and the height, find the area. **2** *(en vista de)* in view of: *dada su experiencia* in view of his experience. LOC **dado que** since, as, given that: *dado que llueve no saldremos* as it's raining we won't go out.

**daga** *nf* dagger.

**dalai lama** *nm* Dalai Lama.

**dalia** *nf* dahlia.

**dálmata** *adj* Dalmatian.
▸ *nm* Dalmatian.

**daltónico,-a** *adj* colour-blind, daltonic.

**daltonismo** *nm* colour (US color) blindness, daltonism.

**dama** *nf* **1** *(señora)* lady. **2** *(en el juego de damas)* king; *(en ajedrez)* queen.
▸ *nf pl* **damas** draughts, (US checkers). COMP **tablero de damas** draughtboard, (US checkerboard).

**damero** *nm* draughtboard, US checkerboard.

**damnificar** *vt* **1** *(a una persona)* to injure, harm. **2** *(cosa)* to damage.

**dandy** *nm* dandy.

**danés,-esa** *adj* Danish.
▸ *nm & nf (persona)* Dane.
▸ *nm* **danés** *(idioma)* Danish.

**danza** *nf* **1** *(baile)* dance. **2** *fig (negocio sucio)* shady business, shady deal; *(lío)* mess: *no te metas en esa danza* don't get mixed up in a deal like that. **3** *fam fig (riña)* row.

**danzante** *adj* dancing.
▸ *nm o nf* dancer.

**danzar** *vt (bailar)* to dance.
▸ *vi (bailar)* to dance (con, with).

**danzarín,-ina** *nm & nf* dancer.

**dañado,-a** *adj* damaged, spoiled.

**dañar** *vt* **1** *(causar dolor)* to hurt, harm. **2** *(estropear)* to damage, spoil. **3** *fig* to damage, stain: *ese asunto dañará su reputación* that affair will damage his reputation.
▸ *vpr* **dañarse** *(estropearse)* to get damaged, spoil; *(alimentos)* to go bad, go off.

**dañino,-a** *adj* harmful (para, to), damaging (para, to).

**daño** *nm* **1** *(a una persona)* harm, injury; *(a cosa)* damage; *(perjuicio)* wrong. LOC **hacer daño 1** *(doler)* to hurt. **2** *(causar dolor a ALGN)* to hurt. **3** *(ser malo para ALGN)* to damage, harm. *(ser malo para ALGN)* to do SB harm: *me hizo daño con sus palabras* her words hurt me. ▌**hacerse daño** to hurt OS: *se hizo daño en la mano* she hurt her hand.

**dar** *vt* **1** *(gen)* to give: *te daré un libro* I'll give you a book. **2** *(poner en las manos, entregar)* to deliver, hand over; *(poner al alcance)* to pass, hand: *dame la sal* pass me the salt. **3** *(proporcionar, ofrecer, procurar algo no material a una persona - noticia)* to tell, announce, report; *(- consejo)* to give; *(- recuerdos, recado)* to pass on, give. **4** *(permitir tener algo, conceder)* to give. **5** *(pagar a cambio)* to give, pay: *¿cuánto me daría por esto?* how much would you give me for it? **6** *(realizar una acción)*. **7** *(producir - cosecha)* to produce, yield; *(- fruto, flores)* to bear, produce; *(- beneficio)* to produce, yield: *la higuera da higos* the fig tree bears figs. **8** *(celebrar,* *tener lugar - película)* to show, screen; *(- obra de teatro)* to perform, put on; *(- concierto)* to give, perform, put on; *(- fiesta)* to give, throw: *daremos una fiesta* we'll have a party. **9** *(pegar)* to hit. **10** *(sonar el reloj las horas)* to strike. **11** *(untar, recubrir una superficie)* to apply, give. **12** *(abrir el paso de conductos)* to turn on: *he dado el gas* I've turned the gas on. LOC **dar a entender que...** to give to understand that..., imply that...: *dio a entender que no vendría* she implied she wouldn't come. **‖ dar a luz** to give birth (a, to). **‖ dar ALGO por** to assume, consider. **‖ dar de sí 1** *(ropa)* to stretch, give. **2** *(dinero, comida)* to go a long way. **‖ dar igual** to be all the same, not matter: *le daba igual* it didn't matter to him, he didn't care. **‖ dar la mano a** ALGN to shake hands with SB.

▶ *vi* **1** *(pegar, golpear)* to hit: *la pelota le dio en toda la cara* the ball hit him right in the face. **2** *(en naipes)* to deal. **3 dar a** *(botón, interruptor)* to press: *dale al botón* press the button. **4** *(mirar una cosa hacia una parte)* to look out onto, overlook. **5 dar de** *(caer)* to fall: *dio de narices en el suelo* he fell flat on his face. **6 dar de** *(suministrar)* to give. **7 dar en** *(acertar)* to find, hit on. **8 dar para** *(ser suficiente)* to be enough for, be sufficient for: *la sopa da para cuatro* the soup serves four.

**dardo** *nm (arma)* dart, arrow.

**dársena** *nf* dock, basin.

**darvinismo** *nm* Darwinism.

**datar** *vt (poner la data)* to date, put a date on.
▶ *vi (tener origen)* to date (de, from), date back (de, to): *esa iglesia data del siglo XI* that church dates from the eleventh century.

**dátil** *nm* date.

**datilera** *nf* date palm.

**dativo,-a** *adj* dative.
▶ *nm* **dativo** dative. LOC **en dativo** in the dative.

**dato** *nm (información)* fact, piece of information, datum. COMP **datos personales** personal details.

**dB** *sím* (decibelio) decibel; *(símbolo)* dB.

**d.C.** *abrev* (después de Cristo) Anno Domini; *(abreviatura)* AD.

**DDT** *abrev* (diclorodifeniltricloroetano) dichlorodiphenyltrichloroethane; *(abreviatura)* DDT.

**de** *prep* **1** *(posesión, pertenencia)* of, in: *la mesa de mi habitación* the table in my bedroom. **2** *(procedencia, origen)* from, in: *viene de Barcelona* she comes from Barcelona. **3** *(descripción)* with: *el señor del abrigo azul* the man in the blue coat. **4** *(tema)* of, on, about: *hablaron del tiempo* they talked about the weather. **5** *(materia)* made of, of: *un anillo de oro* a gold ring. **6** *(contenido)* of: *un vaso de agua* a glass of water. **7** *(oficio)* by, as: *trabaja de profesor* he works as a teacher. **8** *(modo)* on, in, as: *de pie* standing up. **9** *(tiempo)* at, by, in: *de día* by day, during the day. **10** *(lugar) varias traducciones*: *la vecina de arriba* our upstairs neighbour. **11** *(medida)* measuring: *una botella de dos litros* a two litre bottle. **12** *(causa)* with, because of, of: *llorar de alegría* to cry with joy. **13** *(agente)* by: *es una obra de Lope* a play by Lope. **14** *(con superlativo)* in, of: *el mayor de los tres* the eldest of the three. **15** *(en una aposición)* of: *la ciudad de Barcelona* the city of Barcelona.

✎ Consulta también del.

**deambular** *vi* to saunter, stroll.

**debajo** *adv* below, underneath: *el libro verde está debajo* the green book is underneath. LOC **por debajo** underneath: *tuvieron que pasar por debajo* they had to go underneath.

**debate** *nm* debate, discussion.

**debatir** *vt* to debate, discuss.

**debe** *nm* debit side.

**deber** *vt* **1** *(estar obligado a algo)* to owe: *debemos respeto a nuestros padres* we owe respect to our parents. **2** *(dinero, cosa)* to owe: *te debo cincuenta euros* I owe you fifty euros.
▶ *aux* **1** *(obligación presente)* must, have to, have got to: *debo ir a comprar* I must go shopping. **2** *(obligación pasada)* should, ought to: *debía haberlo comprado ayer* I should have bought it yester-

day. **3** *(obligación futura)* must, have to, have got to: *deberás tenerlo a las cinco* you must have it ready for five o'clock. **4** *(obligación moral)* should, ought to: *no deberías haberlo hecho* you shouldn't have done it. **5 deber de** *(probabilidad)* must; *(negativa)* can't: *deben de ser las seis* it must be six o'clock; *no deben de haber llegado* they can't have arrived.

▶ *vpr* **deberse 1** *(ser consecuencia)* to be due (a, to). **2** *(tener una obligación)* to have a duty (a, to).

▶ *nm* **deber** *(obligación)* duty, obligation. LOC **cumplir con su deber** to do one's duty. ‖ **hacer los deberes** to do one's homework.

▶ *nm pl* **deberes** *(escolares)* homework *sing.*

**debidamente** *adv* duly, properly.

**debido,-a** *adj* **1** *(merecido)* due: *con el debido respeto,...* with all due respect,... **2** *(conveniente)* right. LOC **como es debido 1** *(correctamente)* right, properly. **2** *(como es merecido)* deservedly: *siéntate en la silla como es debido* sit properly on the chair.

**débil** *adj* **1** *(persona)* weak, feeble. **2** *(ruido)* faint; *(luz)* dim, feeble. **3** LING weak.

▶ *nm o nf* weak person.

**debilidad** *nf* **1** *(de una persona)* weakness, feebleness. **2** *fig* weakness: *los coches de carreras son su debilidad* he has a weakness for racing cars. LOC **tener debilidad por 1** *(algo)* to have a weakness for. **2** *(alguien)* to have a soft spot for.

**debilitamiento** *nm* weakening.

**debilitar** *vt* to weaken, debilitate.

▶ *vpr* **debilitarse** to weaken, get weak, become weak.

**debut** *nm* debut, début.

**debutante** *nm o nf* *(actor)* first-time actor; *(actriz)* first-time actress.

**debutar** *vi* to make one's debut, make one's début.

**década** *nf* decade.

**decadencia** *nf* decadence, decline, decay.

**decadente** *adj* decadent.

**decaedro** *nm* decahedron.

**decaer** *vi* *(perder fuerzas)* to weaken; *(- entusiasmo, interés)* to flag; *(- salud)* to go down, deteriorate, decay; *(- belleza, etc)* to lose: *su interés está decayendo* his interest is flagging.

**decagonal** *adj* decagonal.

**decágono** *nm* decagon.

**decagramo** *nm* decagram, decagramme.

**decaído,-a** *adj* **1** *(débil)* weak. **2** *(triste)* sad, depressed, low.

**decalitro** *nm* decalitre (US decaliter).

**decálogo** *nm* Decalogue.

**decámetro** *nm* decametre (US decameter).

**decano,-a** *nm & nf* *(cargo)* dean.

**decantar¹** *vt* *(verter)* to decant, pour off.

**decantar²** *vt* *(alabar)* to praise, laud.

▶ *vpr* **decantarse** *(preferir)* to prefer (hacia/por, -): *el público se decantó por el equipo local* the spectators were on the side of the local team.

**decapar** *vt* *(pintura)* to strip (off).

**decapitar** *vt* to behead, decapitate.

**decápodo** *nm* decapod.

**decasílabo,-a** *adj* decasyllabic.

**decatlón** *nm* decathlon.

**decena** *nf* **1** *(exacto)* ten. **2** *(aproximado)* about ten: *he invitado a una decena de personas* I have invited ten or so people.

**decenal** *adj* ten-year, decennial.

**decencia** *nf* **1** *(decoro)* decency, propriety. **2** *(honestidad)* honesty.

**decenio** *nm* decade.

**decente** *adj* **1** *(decoroso)* decent, proper. **2** *(honesto)* honest, upright; *(respetable)* decent, respectable.

**decentemente** *adv* decently.

**decepción** *nf* disappointment.

**decepcionado,-a** *adj* disappointed.

**decepcionar** *vt* to disappoint, let down: *no nos decepciones* don't disappoint us.

**decibelio** *nm* decibel.

**decididamente** *adv* *(con determinación)* resolutely, with determination: *soli-*

*citó el trabajo decididamente* he applied for the job with determination.

**decidido,-a** *adj* determined, resolute: *está decidido a acabar el trabajo* he's determined to finish the job.

**decidir** *vt (gen)* to decide; *(asunto)* to settle.

▶ *vi* to decide, choose: *tuvo que decidir entre los dos* she had to decide between the two.

▶ *vpr* **decidirse** to make up one's mind. LOC **decidirse por** to decide on: *se decidió por la falda roja* she decided on the red skirt.

**decigramo** *nm* decigram, decigramme.

**decilitro** *nm* decilitre (US deciliter).

**décima** *nf* LIT stanza of ten octosyllabic lines. LOC **tener (unas) décimas** *fam* to have a slight temperature.

**decimal** *adj* decimal.
▶ *nm* decimal.

**decímetro** *nm* decimetre (US decimeter).

**décimo,-a** *adj* tenth.
▶ *nm & nf* tenth.

✎ Consulta también **sexto,-a**.

**decimoctavo,-a** *adj* eighteenth.
▶ *nm & nf* eighteenth.

✎ Consulta también **sexto,-a**.

**decimocuarto,-a** *adj* fourteenth.
▶ *nm & nf* fourteenth.

✎ Consulta también **sexto,-a**.

**decimonónico,-a** *adj* nineteenth-century: *un escritor decimonónico* a nineteenth-century writer.

**decimonono,-a** *adj* nineteenth.
▶ *nm & nf* nineteenth.

✎ Consulta también **sexto,-a**.

**decimonoveno,-a** *adj-nm & nf →* decimonono,-a.

✎ Consulta también **sexto,-a**.

**decimoquinto,-a** *adj* fifteenth.
▶ *nm & nf* fifteenth.

✎ Consulta también **sexto,-a**.

**decimoséptimo,-a** *adj* seventeenth.
▶ *nm & nf* seventeenth.

✎ Consulta también **sexto,-a**.

**decimosexto,-a** *adj* sixteenth.
▶ *nm & nf* sixteenth.

✎ Consulta también **sexto,-a**.

**decimotercero,-a** *adj* thirteenth.
▶ *nm & nf* thirteenth.

✎ Consulta también **sexto,-a**.

**decir** *vt* **1** *(gen)* to say. **2** *(contar, revelar)* to tell: *dijo la verdad* she told the truth. **3** *(nombrar, llamar)* to call: *le dicen Cuca* she's called Cuca. **4** *(opinar)* to have to say. **5** *(un texto)* to read, say: *el texto dice lo siguiente* the text reads as follows. LOC **digo yo** in my opinion, I think. ∎ **el qué dirán** what people say. ∎ **es decir** that is (to say). ∎ **¡no me digas!** really! ∎ **querer decir** to mean: *quiero decir,...* I mean,... ∎ **se dice...** they say..., it is said...

**decisión** *nf* **1** *(resolución)* decision: *sus padres tuvieron que tomar una decisión* his parents had to make a decision. **2** *(determinación)* determination, resolution.

**decisivo,-a** *adj (importante)* decisive.

**declamar** *vi* to declaim, recite.
▶ *vt* to declaim, recite.

**declamatorio,-a** *adj* declamatory.

**declaración** *nf* **1** *(gen)* declaration: *declaración de renta* income tax return. **2** [también se usa en plural con el mismo significado] *(explicación pública)* statement, comment. **3** JUR evidence. **4** *(en bridge)* bid. LOC **prestar declaración** JUR to give evidence.

**declarar** *vt* **1** *(gen)* to declare; *(manifestar)* to state: *lo declararon vencedor* he was declared the winner. **2** JUR to find.
▶ *vi* **1** to declare. **2** JUR to testify.
▶ *vpr* **declararse 1** *(amor)* to declare one's love (a, for). **2** *(fuego, guerra, etc)* to break out, start: *se declaró un incendio en el monte* a fire broke out on the mountain.

**declinación** *nf (gramatical)* declension.

**declinar** *vi* **1** *(disminuir)* to decline, come down. **2** *(acercarse al fin)* to end, draw to an end.
▶ *vt* GRAM to decline.

**declive** *nm* fig *(decadencia)* decline. LOC **en declive** *fig* on the decline.

**decodificar** *vt* to decode.

**decolorar** *vt* *(perder el color)* to discolour (US discolor).
▶ *vpr* **decolorarse** *(perder el color)* to fade, become discoloured (US discolored).

**decoración** *nf* **1** *(gen)* decoration. **2** TEAT scenery, set.

**decorador,-ra** *nm & nf* **1** decorator. **2** TEAT set designer.

**decorar** *vt* *(gen)* to decorate, adorn, embellish; *(una casa)* to decorate.

**decorativo,-a** *adj* decorative.

**decoroso,-a** *adj* **1** *(digno)* decent, respectable. **2** *(respetable)* respectable, honourable (US honorable): *un trabajo decoroso* an honourable job.

**decrecer** *vi* *(gen)* to decrease, diminish; *(aguas)* to subside, go down.

**decretar** *vt* **1** *(con decreto)* to decree. **2** *(ordenar)* to ordain, order.

**decreto** *nm* decree, order.

**décuplo,-a** *adj* tenfold.
▶ *nm* **décuplo** ten times.

**dedal** *nm* thimble.

**dedicación** *nf* dedication, devotion. LOC **de dedicación exclusiva** full-time.

**dedicar** *vt* **1** *(una dedicatoria)* to dedicate, inscribe. **2** *(tiempo, dinero)* to devote (a, to). **3** *(palabras)* to address.

**dedicatoria** *nf* dedication, inscription.

**dedo** *nm* **1** *(de la mano)* finger; *(del pie)* toe. **2** *(medida)* finger, digit. LOC **hacer dedo** *fam* to hitchhike. ‖ **no tener dos dedos de frente** *fig* to be as thick as two short planks. COMP **dedo anular** ring finger, third finger. ‖ **dedo gordo 1** *(de la mano)* thumb. **2** *(del pie)* big toe. ‖ **dedo índice** forefinger, index finger. ‖ **dedo meñique** little finger. ‖ **dedo pulgar** thumb. ‖ **yema del dedo** fingertip.

**deducción** *nf* deduction.

**deducir** *vt* **1** to deduce, infer. **2** *(dinero)* to deduct, subtract.
▶ *vpr* **deducirse** to follow: *de aquí se deduce que...* from this it follows that...

**deductivo,-a** *adj* deductive.

**defecto** *nm* **1** *(gen)* defect, fault; *(de una joya)* imperfection, flaw. **2** *(de persona - moral)* fault, shortcoming; *(- física)* handicap. LOC **por defecto** INFORM default: *la impresora por defecto* the default printer.

**defectuoso,-a** *adj* defective, faulty.

**defender** *vt* **1** *(gen)* to defend (contra/de, against). **2** *(mantener una opinión, afirmación)* to defend, uphold; *(respaldar a ALGN)* to stand up for, support. **3** *(proteger)* to protect (contra/de, against/from). **4** JUR *(algo)* to argue, plead; *(a alguien)* to defend.
▶ *vpr* **defenderse** *(espabilarse)* to manage, get by, get along: *¿qué tal se defiende en inglés?* how does she get by in English?, what's her English like?

**defensa** *nf* defence (US defense).
▶ *nm o nf* DEP *(jugador)* back, defender.

**defensiva** *nf* defensive. LOC **estar a la defensiva** to be on the defensive.

**defensor,-ra** *adj* defending.
▶ *nm & nf* **1** defender. **2** JUR counsel for the defence (US defense). COMP **defensor del pueblo** ombudsman.

**deficiente** *adj* **1** *(defectuoso)* deficient, faulty. **2** *(insuficiente)* lacking, insufficient.
▶ *nm o nf* mentally retarded person. COMP **deficiente mental** mentally retarded person.

**déficit** *nm inv* COM deficit.

**deficitario,-a** *adj* showing a deficit.

**definición** *nf* definition. LOC **por definición** by definition.

**definir** *vt* to define.

**definitivamente** *adv* *(para siempre)* for good, once and for all: *se marchó definitivamente* she left for good.

**definitivo,-a** *adj* definitive, final. LOC **en definitiva** finally, in short, all in all.

**deforestación** *nf* deforestation.

**deforestar** *vt* to deforest.

**deformación** *nf* deformation, distortion.

**deformar** *vt (gen)* to deform, put out of shape; *(cara)* to disfigure; *(realidad, imagen, etc)* to distort.

**deforme** *adj (persona)* deformed; *(cosa)* misshapen, out of shape; *(imagen, cara)* distorted.

**deformidad** *nf* deformity, malformation.

**defraudar** *vt* **1** *(estafar)* to defraud, cheat. **2** *(decepcionar)* to disappoint, deceive. **3** *fig (frustrar)* to betray: *defraudar las esperanzas* to dash one's hopes.

**defunción** *nf fml* death, decease.

**degenerar** *vi* to degenerate.

**degenerativo,-a** *adj* degenerative.

**deglutir** *vt* to swallow.
▶ *vi* to swallow.

**degradante** *adj* degrading, humiliating.

**degradar** *vt* to degrade, debase.
▶ *vpr* **degradarse** to demean OS, degrade OS.

**degustación** *nf* tasting.

**degustar** *vt* to taste, sample, try.

**dehesa** *nf* pasture, meadow.

**deidad** *nf* deity, divinity.

**dejadez** *nf* **1** *(negligencia)* negligence, carelessness. **2** *(pereza)* laziness, apathy.

**dejado,-a** *adj* **1** *(descuidado)* untidy, slovenly. **2** *(perezoso)* lazy.
▶ *nm & nf* untidy person, slovenly person.

**dejar** *vt* **1** *(colocar)* to leave, put. **2** *(abandonar - persona, lugar)* to leave; *(- hábito, cosa, actividad)* to give up: *dejó el tabaco* he gave up smoking. **3** *(permitir)* to allow, let: *déjale jugar* let him play. **4** *(prestar)* to lend. **5** *(ceder)* to give. **6** *(aplazar)* to put off: *dejémoslo hasta mañana* let's leave it till tomorrow. **7** *(causar un efecto)* to make: *le película me ha dejado triste* the film made me sad. **8** *(legar)* to bequeath, leave.

▶ *aux* **1** dejar de + *inf (cesar - voluntariamente)* to stop + *ger*, give up + *ger*; *(-involuntariamente)* to stop + *ger*: *ha dejado de llover* it's stopped raining. **2** no dejar de + *inf* not to fail *to + inf*: *no deja de sorprenderme* she never fails to surprise me. **3** dejar + *pp*: *lo dejó escrito en su agenda* he wrote it down in his diary.

▶ *vpr* **dejarse** *(olvidar)* to forget, leave behind: *me he dejado las llaves en casa* I've left my keys at home.

▶ *vpr* **dejarse de** *(cesar)* to stop: *déjate de tonterías* don't be silly. LOC **dejar** ALGO **por imposible** to give up on STH. ▌ **dejar en paz** to leave alone. ▌ **dejar preocupado,-a** to worry. ▌ **dejarse llevar por** ALGN to be influenced by SB.

**del** *contr (de + el)→* de.

**delantal** *nm* apron, pinafore.

**delante** *adv* **1** *(enfrente)* in front; *(adelantado)* in front, ahead. **2** de delante in front. **3** delante de in front of, ahead of, before: *delante de mis ojos* before my eyes. **4** por delante in front, ahead: *tenemos mucho tiempo por delante* we've got plenty of time ahead.

**delantera** *nf* **1** *(frente)* front (part). **2** DEP forward line, forwards *pl*. **3** *(ventaja)* lead, advantage. LOC **llevar la delantera** to be in the lead, be ahead.

**delantero,-a** *adj* front, front part: *el asiento delantero* the front seat.
▶ *nm* **delantero** DEP forward. COMP **delantero centro** centre (US center) forward.

**delatar** *vt* to inform on.
▶ *vpr* **delatarse** to give OS away.

**delator,-ra** *adj* accusing, denouncing.
▶ *nm & nf* accuser, denouncer.

**delegación** *nf* **1** *(gen)* delegation. **2** *(cargo)* office.

**delegado,-a** *nm & nf* **1** delegate. **2** COM representative.

**delegar** *vt* to delegate.

**deletrear** *vt* to spell, spell out.

**deletreo** *nm* spelling (out).

**delfín** *nm (animal)* dolphin.

**delgado,-a** *adj* **1** *(poco ancho)* thin. **2** *(esbelto)* slim, slender. **3** *(flaco)* thin.

**deliberación** *nf* deliberation.
**deliberadamente** *adv* deliberately.
**deliberar** *vt* to decide.
▶ *vi* to deliberate (**sobre**, on).
**delicadeza** *nf* **1** *(finura)* delicacy, daintiness. **2** *(tacto)* thoughtfulness; *(refinamiento)* refinement.
**delicado,-a** *adj* **1** *(fino)* delicate; *(refinado)* refined. **2** *(difícil)* delicate, difficult: *una situación delicada* a delicate situation. **3** *(frágil)* fragile.
**delicia** *nf* delight, pleasure.
**delicioso,-a** *adj* delightful, charming; *(una comida)* delicious.
**delimitar** *vt* **1** *(terreno)* to delimit, mark off. **2** *(definir)* to define, specify.
**delincuencia** *nf* delinquency.
**delincuente** *nm o nf* delinquent.
**delineante** *nm o nf (hombre)* draughtsman; *(mujer)* draughtswoman.
**delinear** *vt* to delineate, outline, sketch.
**delirar** *vi* to be delirious.
**delirio** *nm* **1** *(desvarío)* delirium. **2** *fig (disparate)* nonsense.
**delito** *nm* offence (US offense), crime.
**delta** *nf (letra)* delta. **2** *(ala delta)* hang-gliding.
▶ *nm* GEOG delta.
**demacrado,-a** *adj (gen)* emaciated; *(cara)* haggard, drawn.
**demagogia** *nf* demagoguery, demagogy.
**demagógico,-a** *adj* demagogic, demagogical.
**demagogo,-a** *nm & nf* demagogue.
**demanda** *nf* **1** *(petición)* petition, request. **2** COM *(pedido de mercancías)* demand. **3** JUR lawsuit. [LOC] **en demanda de** asking for.
**demandado,-a** *nm & nf* defendant.
**demandante** *nm o nf* **1** JUR plaintiff. **2** *(persona que busca)* seeker, hunter. *(persona que compra)* buyer. [COMP] **demandante de empleo** job hunter.
**demandar** *vt* **1** *(pedir)* to request, ask for; *(desear)* to desire. **2** JUR to sue.
**demarcar** *vt* to demarcate.
**demás** *adj* other, rest of.

▶ *pron* the other, the rest: *los demás llegaron tarde* the others arrived late.
▶ *adv* besides, moreover. [LOC] **por lo demás** apart from that, otherwise. **I todo lo demás** everything else.
**demasiado,-a** *adj (singular)* too much; *(plural)* too many.
▶ *adv (modificador de adjetivo)* too; *(modificador de verbo)* too much: *es demasiado gordo* he's too fat.
**demencia** *nf* **1** insanity, madness, dementia. **2** *fig (disparate)* silly thing. [COMP] **demencia senil** senile dementia.
**demente** *adj* mad, insane.
▶ *nm o nf* **1** *(persona enferma)* mental patient. **2** *(loco, chalado)* lunatic.
**democracia** *nf* democracy.
**demócrata** *nm o nf* democrat.
**democrático,-a** *adj* democratic.
**demografía** *nf* demography.
**demográfico,-a** *adj* demographic.
**demoler** *vt* to demolish, pull down, tear down.
**demolición** *nf* demolition.
**demoniaco,-a** *adj* demoniacal, demonic, possessed by the devil.
**demonio** *nm* demon, devil. [LOC] **¡demonios!** *fam* hell!, damn!
**demora** *nf* delay.
**demorar** *vt (retrasar)* to delay, hold up.
▶ *vpr* **demorarse** *(retrasarse)* to be delayed, be held up.
**demostración** *nf* **1** *(gen)* demonstration. **2** MAT proof.
**demostrar** *vt* **1** *(probar)* to prove, show. **2** *(hacer una demostración)* to demonstrate, show. **3** MAT to prove.
**demostrativo,-a** *adj* demonstrative.
▶ *nm* demonstrative.
**denegar** *vt (desestimar)* to refuse; *(negar)* to deny.
**denigrante** *adj* denigrating, disparaging.
**denigrar** *vt* **1** to denigrate, disparage, run down. **2** *(insultar)* to insult, revile.
**denominación** *nf* **1** *(acción)* denomination, naming. **2** *(nombre)* denomi-

nation, name. COMP **denominación de origen** *(vinos)* guarantee of origin.

**denominador,-ra** *adj* denominative.
▶ *nm* **denominador** MAT denominator. COMP **mínimo común denominador** lowest common denominator.

**denominar** *vt* to denominate, name.

**densidad** *nf* **1** *(gen)* density. **2** *fig (espesura)* thickness, denseness. COMP **densidad de población** population density.

**denso,-a** *adj (gen)* dense; *(espeso)* dense, thick.

**dentado,-a** *adj* **1** *(con dientes)* toothed. **2** BOT dentate.

**dentadura** *nf* teeth *pl*, set of teeth. COMP **dentadura postiza** false teeth *pl*, dentures *pl*.

**dental** *adj* dental. COMP **cepillo dental** toothbrush.

**dentellada** *nf* **1** *(mordisco)* bite. **2** *(señal)* tooth mark.

**dentera** *nf fig (envidia)* envy. LOC **dar dentera a** ALGN **1** *(dar grima)* to set SB's teeth on edge. **2** *(dar envidia)* to make SB green with envy.

**dentición** *nf* **1** *(acción de dentar)* teething, dentition, cutting of the teeth. **2** *(época en que dentan los niños)* dentition.

**dentífrico,-a** *adj* tooth.
▶ *nm* **dentífrico** toothpaste. COMP **pasta dentífrica** toothpaste.

**dentista** *nm o nf* dentist. LOC **ir al dentista** to go to the dentist's.

**dentro** *adv* inside; *(de edificio)* indoors, inside: *está ahí dentro* it's in there. LOC **dentro de 1** *(lugar)* in, inside: *dentro de la casa* in the house; *dentro de una semana* in a week, in a week's time. **2** *(tiempo)* in. ▌ **dentro de lo posible** as far as possible. ▌ **dentro de poco** soon, shortly. ▌ **por dentro 1** *(de una cosa)* (on the) inside. **2** *(de una persona)* deep down, inside, inwardly.

**denuncia** *nf* **1** *(acusación)* accusation, formal complaint, report. **2** JUR *(acción)* reporting; *(documento)* report. LOC **presentar una denuncia contra** ALGN to

lodge a complaint against SB, bring an action against SB, report SB.

**denunciar** *vt* **1** *(poner una denuncia)* to report. **2** *(dar noticia)* to denounce.

**deparar** *vt* **1** *(presentar)* to bring, hold in store: *nadie sabe lo que el destino nos deparará* nobody knows what fate holds in store for us. **2** *(proporcionar)* to give, afford.

**departamento** *nm* **1** *(sección)* department, section. **2** *(de tren)* compartment.

**dependencia** *nf* **1** *(hecho de depender)* dependence. **2** *(habitación)* room, outbuilding.

**depender** *vi* **1** to depend (de, on): *depende de ti* it's up to you. **2** *(estar bajo el mando o autoridad)* to be under, be answerable to; *(necesitar)* to be dependent on: *aún depende de sus padres* she's still dependent on her parents.

**dependienta** *nf* shop assistant, salesgirl, saleswoman.

**dependiente** *adj* dependent (de, on).
▶ *nm o nf* shop assistant, salesman.

**depilación** *nf* depilation, hair removal. LOC **depilación a la cera** waxing.

**depilar** *vt* to depilate, remove the hair from; *(cejas)* to pluck.

**depilatorio,-a** *adj* depilatory. COMP **crema depilatoria** hair-removing cream.

**deplorable** *adj* deplorable, regrettable.

**deplorar** *vt* to deplore, lament, regret deeply.

**deponer** *vt* **1** *(dejar)* to lay down, set aside. **2** *(destituir)* to remove from office; *(a un rey)* to depose.

**deportación** *nf* deportation.

**deportar** *vt* to deport.

**deporte** *nm* sport: *¿practicas algún deporte?* do you do any sport?, do you play any sport? LOC **hacer deporte** to do some sport.

**deportista** *adj* sporty, keen on sport.
▶ *nm o nf (hombre)* sportsman; *(mujer)* sportswoman.

**deportividad** *nf* sportsmanship.

**deportivo,-a** *adj* **1** *(aficionado al deporte)* sporting, sporty. **2** *(relacionado con el deporte)* sports: *club deportivo* sports club. **3** *(informal)* casual: *ropa deportiva* casual clothes.
▶ *nm* **deportivo** *(coche)* sports car.

**depositar** *vt* **1** *(dinero, joyas)* to deposit. **2** *(colocar)* to place, put. **3** *(sedimentar)* to deposit.
▶ *vpr* **depositarse** *(caer en el fondo)* to settle.

**depositario,-a** *nm & nf (de algo material)* depositary, trustee; *(de algo inmaterial)* repository.

**depósito** *nm* **1** *(recipiente)* tank. **2** *(almacén)* store, warehouse, depot. **3** *(sedimento)* deposit, sediment. ⎾LOC⏌ **en depósito** in bond. ⎾COMP⏌ **depósito de gasolina** petrol tank.

**depreciar** *vt* to depreciate.
▶ *vpr* **depreciarse** to depreciate.

**depredador,-ra** *adj* depredatory.
▶ *nm & nf* depredator, pillager.

**depredar** *vt* to depredate, pillage.

**depresión** *nf* depression: *depresión atmosférica* atmospheric depression. ⎾COMP⏌ **depresión nerviosa** nervous breakdown.

**depresivo,-a** *adj* **1** *(deprimente)* depressing. **2** MED depressive.

**deprimente** *adj* depressing.

**deprimido,-a** *adj* depressed.

**deprimir** *vt* to depress.
▶ *vpr* **deprimirse** to get depressed.

**deprisa** *adv* quickly.

**depuración** *nf (del agua)* purification; *(de la sangre)* cleansing.

**depurador,-ra** *adj* purifying.
▶ *nm* **depurador** *(sustancia)* depurative; *(aparato)* purifier.

**depurar** *vt* **1** *(purificar agua)* to purify, depurate; *(sangre)* to cleanse. **2** POL to purge. **3** *fig (perfeccionar)* to purify, refine.

**derecha** *nf* **1** *(mano)* right hand. **2** *(lugar)* right: *dame el de la derecha* give me the one on the right. **3** **la derecha** POL the right, the right wing.

**derechista** *adj* right-wing, rightist.

**derecho,-a** *adj* **1** right: *la mano derecha* the right hand. **2** *(recto)* straight, upright.
▶ *adv* **derecho** straight: *se fue derecho a la cama* he went straight to bed.
▶ *nm* **derecho 1** *(leyes)* law. **2** *(privilegio)* right: *todos los niños tienen derecho a la enseñanza gratuita* all children have a right to free education. **3** *(de una tela, calcetín, etc)* right side.
▶ *nm pl* **derechos** *(impuestos)* duties, taxes; *(tarifa)* fees. ⎾LOC⏌ **¡no hay derecho!** it's not fair! ∎ **tener derecho a** to be entitled to, have the right to. ⎾COMP⏌ **derecho civil** civil law. ∎ **derecho de admisión** right *sing* to refuse admission. ∎ **derechos de matrícula** registration fees. ∎ **derechos humanos** human rights.

**deriva** *nf* drift. ⎾LOC⏌ **ir a la deriva** to drift.

**derivada** *nf* MAT derivative.

**derivado,-a** *adj* derived, derivative.
▶ *nm* **derivado 1** LING derivative. **2** *(subproducto)* derivative, byproduct.

**derivar** *vi* **1** *(proceder)* to spring, arise, come, stem. **2** MAR to drift. **3** LING to be derived (de, from), derive (de, from).
▶ *vt* **1** *(dirigir)* to direct, divert. **2** LING to derive. **3** MAT to derive.
▶ *vpr* **derivarse 1** *(proceder)* to result (de, from), stem (de, from). **2** LING to be derived (de, from).

**dermatología** *nf* dermatology.

**dermatólogo,-a** *nm & nf* dermatologist.

**dérmico,-a** *adj* dermal, dermic, skin.

**dermis** *nf inv* dermis.

**dermoprotector,-ra** *adj* which is kind to the skin.

**derogar** *vt* **1** JUR to abolish, repeal. **2** *(contrato)* to rescind, cancel.

**derramar** *vt* to pour out, spill.

**derrame** *nm* pouring out, spilling. ⎾COMP⏌ **derrame cerebral** MED brain haemorrhage.

**derrapar** *vi* to skid.

**derredor** *nm* surroundings *pl*. ⎾LOC⏌ **al/en derredor** round, around.

✎ Consulta también **alrededor**.

**derretir** *vt (gen)* to melt; *(hielo, nieve)* to melt, thaw; *(metal)* to melt down.
▶ *vpr* **derretirse** *(fundirse)* to melt; *(hielo, nieve)* to melt, thaw.

**derribar** *vt* **1** *(demoler)* to pull down, demolish, knock down. **2** *(hacer caer a una persona)* to knock over; *(de un caballo)* to throw.

**derribo** *nm (demolición)* demolition, knocking down, pulling down.

**derrocar** *vt* **1** *(demoler)* to pull down, demolish, knock down. **2** *(gobierno)* to overthrow, bring down.

**derrochar** *vt (dilapidar)* to waste, squander.

**derroche** *nm (despilfarro)* waste, squandering.

**derrota** *nm* **1** *(de un ejército)* defeat. **2** *(fracaso)* failure, setback.

**derrotar** *vt* to defeat, beat: *me derrotó al tenis* he beat me at tennis.

**derruido,-a** *adj* in ruins.

**derruir** *vt* to pull down, demolish, knock down.

**derrumbar** *vt (demoler)* to pull down, demolish, knock down.
▶ *vpr* **derrumbarse** **1** *(un edificio)* to collapse, fall down; *(un techo)* to fall in, cave in. **2** *fig* to collapse.

**desabotonar** *vt (desabrochar)* to unbutton, undo.

**desabrigar** *vt (ropa)* to take someone's coat off.
▶ *vpr* **desabrigarse** *(uso reflexivo)* to take off one's coat.

**desabrochar** *vt* to undo, unfasten.
▶ *vpr* **desabrocharse** *(una prenda)* to come undone, come unfastened.

**desacato** *nm* **1** *(falta de respeto)* lack of respect (a, for), disrespect (a, for). **2** JUR contempt (a, for). LOC **desacato a la autoridad** contempt.

**desacelerar** *vi* to decelerate.

**desaconsejar** *vt* to advise against.

**desacostumbrado,-a** *adj* unusual, strange.

**desacostumbrar** *vt (hacer perder un uso)* to break of a habit, get out of a habit.
▶ *vpr* **desacostumbrarse** *(perder la costumbre)* to get out of the habit (de, of), lose the habit (de, of), give up (de, -).

**desacreditar** *vt* to discredit, bring discredit on, bring into discredit.

**desactivar** *vt* to defuse.

**desacuerdo** *nm* disagreement. LOC **estar en desacuerdo con** to be in disagreement with.

**desafiar** *vt* **1** *(gen)* to defy. **2** *(no hacer caso a)* to flout; *(no obedecer)* to defy. **3** *(plantar cara a - persona)* to defy, stand up to; *(- dificultad)* to brave. LOC **desafiar a ALGN a hacer ALGO** to challenge SB to do STH, dare SB to do STH.

**desafilar** *vt* to blunt.

**desafinado,-a** *adj* out of tune.

**desafinar** *vi (gen)* to be out of tune; *(cantar)* to sing out of tune; *(tocar)* to play out of tune.
▶ *vt* to put out of tune.

**desafío** *nm* **1** *(reto)* challenge. **2** *(provocación)* provocation, defiance.

**desafortunadamente** *adv* unfortunately.

**desafortunado,-a** *adj (sin suerte)* unlucky, unfortunate.

**desagradable** *adj* disagreeable, unpleasant.

**desagradar** *vi* to displease: *me desagrada su música* I don't like her music.

**desagradecido,-a** *adj* ungrateful.

**desagrado** *nm* displeasure, discontent. LOC **con desagrado** reluctantly.

**desagraviar** *vt (reparar el agravio)* to make amends for, make up for.

**desagravio** *nm* amends *pl*, compensation.

**desagüe** *nm* **1** *(acción)* draining, drainage. **2** *(cañería)* waste pipe, drainpipe.

**desahogado,-a** *adj* **1** *(espacioso)* roomy, spacious. **2** *(con dinero)* well-off, well-to-do, comfortable: *una posición desahogada* comfortable circumstances.

**desahogar** *vt* **1** *(consolar)* to comfort; *(aliviar)* to relieve. **2** *fig (mostrar)* to

vent, pour out: *desahogó sus penas* he vented his grief.
▶ *vpr* **desahogarse** *(desfogarse)* to let off steam: *¡desahógate!* don't bottle it up!

**desahogo** *nm* **1** *(alivio)* relief. **2** *fig (económico)* comfort, ease: *viven con desahogo* they live comfortably.

**desahuciado,-a** *adj* **1** *(enfermo)* hopeless. **2** *(inquilino)* evicted.

**desahuciar** *vt* **1** to deprive of all hope. **2** JUR *(inquilino)* to evict.

**desahucio** *nm* eviction.

**desajuste** *nm (mal funcionamiento)* maladjustment; *(avería)* breakdown.

**desalar** *vt* to desalt.

**desalentador,-ra** *adj* discouraging, disheartening.

**desalentar** *vt* fig *(quitar el ánimo)* to discourage, dishearten.
▶ *vpr* **desalentarse** get discouraged.

**desaliento** *nm* discouragement.

**desalinear** *vt* to put out of line.

**desaliñado,-a** *adj* untidy, unkempt, scruffy.

**desalojar** *vt* **1** *(marcharse)* to evacuate, clear, move out of. **2** *(inquilino)* to evict (de, from).

**desamortización** *nf* disentailment.

**desamortizar** *vt* to disentail.

**desamparado,-a** *adj (persona)* helpless, unprotected.

**desamparar** *vt* to abandon, desert, leave helpless.

**desamparo** *nm* **1** *(abandono)* abandonment, desertion. **2** *(falta de ayuda)* helplessness.

**desandar** *vt* to go back over, retrace.

**desangrar** *vt (sangrar)* to bleed.
▶ *vpr* **desangrarse** to bleed heavily, lose blood.

**desanimado,-a** *adj (decaído)* dejected, downhearted.

**desanimar** *vt* to discourage, dishearten.
▶ *vpr* **desanimarse** to be discouraged, be disheartened, lose heart.

**desánimo** *nm* despondency, discouragement, dejection.

**desaparecer** *vi (dejar de estar)* to disappear.

**desaparecido,-a** *adj* missing.
▶ *nm & nf* missing person: *había diez desaparecidos* there were ten missing.

**desaparición** *nf* disappearance.

**desapasionado,-a** *adj* dispassionate, objective, impartial.

**desapego** *nm* **1** *(indiferencia)* indifference. **2** *(falta de afecto)* coolness, lack of affection.

**desapercibido,-a** *adj (inadvertido)* unnoticed. LOC **pasar desapercibido,-a** to go unnoticed.

**desaprensivo,-a** *adj* unscrupulous.
▶ *nm & nf* unscrupulous person.

**desaprobación** *nf* disapproval.

**desaprobar** *vt* to disapprove of.

**desaprovechado,-a** *adj (desperdiciado)* wasted.

**desaprovechar** *vt* **1** *(no sacar suficiente provecho)* not to take advantage of. **2** *(desperdiciar)* to waste. LOC **desaprovechar una ocasión** to miss an opportunity, waste an opportunity.

**desarmado,-a** *adj* **1** *(sin armas)* unarmed. **2** *(desmontado)* dismantled, taken to pieces.

**desarmar** *vt* **1** *(quitar las armas)* to disarm. **2** *(desmontar)* to dismantle, take apart, take to pieces: *el mecánico desmontó el motor* the mechanic stripped the engine down.

**desarme** *nm* disarmament. COMP **desarme nuclear** nuclear disarmament.

**desarraigado,-a** *adj* fig *(persona)* rootless, without roots, uprooted.

**desarraigar** *vt (árbol, persona)* to uproot.
▶ *vpr* **desarraigarse** fig *(persona)* to pull up one's roots.

**desarraigo** *nm (de árbol, persona)* uprooting.

**desarreglar** *vt (desordenar)* make untidy, mess up, untidy.

**desarrollado,-a** *adj* developed: *es un país desarrollado* it's a developed country.

**desarrollar** *vt* **1** *(gen)* to develop. *(deshacer un rollo)* to unroll, unfold. **2** *(exponer)* to expound, explain. **3** *(llevar a cabo)* to carry out: *desarrollar un proyecto* to carry out a project. **4** MAT to expand, develop.
▶ *vpr* **desarrollarse** *(crecer)* to develop.

**desarrollo** *nm* **1** *(gen)* development. **2** MAT expansion.

**desarticulado,-a** *adj* disjointed.

**desarticular** *vt* **1** MED to disarticulate, put out of joint, dislocate. **2** *(un mecanismo)* to take to pieces.

**desaseado,-a** *adj* **1** *(sucio)* untidy, dirty. **2** *(dejado)* untidy, slovenly, unkempt, scruffy.

**desasosegado,-a** *adj* restless, anxious.

**desasosegar** *vt* to make restless, make uneasy.
▶ *vpr* **desasosegarse** to become restless, become uneasy.

**desasosiego** *nm* uneasiness, anxiety, restlessness.

**desastrado,-a** *adj* *(desaseado)* untidy, slovenly, unkempt, scruffy.

**desastre** *nm* **1** *(catástrofe)* disaster, catastrophe. **2** *fam* *(calamidad)* disaster, flop: *la excursión fue un desastre* the trip was a washout.

**desastroso,-a** *adj* disastrous.

**desatar** *vt* **1** *(soltar - gen)* to untie, undo, unfasten; *(- perro, etc)* to let loose: *desata al perro* let the dog loose. **2** *fig* *(desencadenar)* to spark off, give rise to; *(pasiones)* to unleash.
▶ *vpr* **desatarse 1** *(soltarse)* to come untied, come undone, come unfastened. **2** *fig* *(desencadenarse)* to break, explode: *se desató una gran tormenta* a great storm broke.

**desatascador** *nm* plunger.

**desatascar** *vt* to unblock, clear.

**desatender** *vt* *(no prestar atención)* to pay no attention to.

**desatento,-a** *adj* *(descortés)* discourteous, impolite.
▶ *nm & nf* *(descortés)* impolite person, discourteous person.

**desatornillar** *vt* to unscrew.

**desautorización** *nf* disapproval.

**desautorizado,-a** *adj* unauthorized.

**desautorizar** *vt* **1** *(desaprobar)* to disapprove. **2** *(prohibir)* to ban, forbid: *el gobierno desautorizó la manifestación* the Government banned the demonstration.

**desavenencia** *nf* *(desacuerdo)* disagreement, discord.

**desavenir** *vt* to cause to quarrel.
▶ *vpr* **desavenirse** to quarrel.

**desayunar** *vi* to have breakfast, breakfast.
▶ *vt* to have for breakfast.

**desayuno** *nm* breakfast.

**desazón** *nf* *fig* *(disgusto)* grief, affliction, worry.

**desazonado,-a** *adj* **1** *fig* *(disgustado)* upset. **2** *fig* *(inquieto)* anxious, uneasy.

**desazonar** *vt* **1** *fig* *(disgustar)* to annoy, upset. *fig* *(inquietar)* to make uneasy, worry.
▶ *vpr* **desazonarse 1** *fig* *(disgustarse)* to get upset. **2** *fig* *(inquietarse)* to worry.

**desbandada** *nf* scattering.

**desbandarse** *vpr* to scatter, disperse.

**desbaratar** *vt* *(frustrar)* to spoil, ruin: *nos desbarató los planes* she spoilt our plans.

**desbloquear** *vt* **1** TÉC to free. **2** FIN to unfreeze.

**desbloqueo** *nm* **1** TÉC freeing. **2** FIN unfreezing.

**desbocado,-a** *adj* *(caballo)* runaway.

**desbocar** *vi* *(desembocar)* to flow (en, into).
▶ *vpr* **desbocarse** *(caballo)* to run away, bolt.

**desbordar** *vt* **1** *(sobrepasar)* to overflow. **2** *fig* *(exceder)* to surpass, exceed: *eso desborda mis conocimientos* that's way over my head.
▶ *vi* *(salirse)* to overflow: *el río desbordó* the river overflowed.
▶ *vpr* **desbordarse 1** *(salirse)* to overflow, flood. **2** *fig* to burst.

**desbrozar** *vt* *(terreno)* to clear of weeds, clear of undergrowth.

**descabalgar** *vi* to dismount.

**descabellado,-a** *adj fig* wild, crazy: *una idea descabellada* a crackpot idea.

**descacharrar** *vt fam (romper)* to break; *(estropear)* to ruin, mess up, spoil.

**descafeinado,-a** *adj* decaffeinated.
▶ *nm* **descafeinado** decaffeinated coffee.

**descalabrar** *vt (herir)* to injure; *(en la cabeza)* to injure in the head.
▶ *vpr* **descalabrarse** to injure one's head.

**descalabro** *nm* misfortune, damage, loss.

**descalcificación** *nf* decalcification.

**descalcificar** *vt* to decalcify.

**descalificación** *nf* **1** disqualification. **2** *(descrédito)* discredit.

**descalificar** *vt* **1** to disqualify. **2** *(desacreditar)* to discredit.

**descalzar** *vt (zapatos)* to take off SB's shoes.
▶ *vpr* **descalzarse** to take off one's shoes.

**descalzo,-a** *adj* barefoot, barefooted.

**descamación** *nf* desquamation.

**descamarse** *vpr* to desquamate.

**descampado,-a** *nm* open space, open field.

**descansado,-a** *adj* **1** rested, refreshed. **2** *(tranquilo)* easy, effortless.

**descansar** *vi* **1** *(gen)* to rest, have a rest; *(un momento)* to take a break. **2** *(dormir)* to sleep: *¡que descanses!* sleep well!

**descansillo** *nm* landing.

**descanso** *nm* **1** rest, break. **2** *(en un espectáculo)* interval; *(en un partido)* interval, half-time. **3** *(alivio)* relief, comfort: *¡qué descanso!* what a relief! **4** *(rellano)* landing.

**descapitalizar** *vt (perder el capital)* to undercapitalize.

**descapotable** *adj* convertible.
▶ *nm* convertible.

**descarado,-a** *adj (actitud)* shameless, brazen, insolent; *(persona)* cheeky.
▶ *nm & nf* shameless person, cheeky person.

**descarga** *nf* **1** *(acción)* unloading. **2** *(eléctrica)* discharge. **3** INFORM download.

**descargar** *vt* **1** *(disparar una arma)* to fire, discharge, shoot; *(vaciar una arma)* to unload. **2** INFORM to download.
▶ *vi (tormenta)* to break; *(nubes)* to burst.
▶ *vpr* **descargarse** *(pilas, baterías)* to discharge.

**descargo** *nm (descarga)* unloading.

**descaro** *nm* impudence, cheek, nerve. LOC *¡qué descaro!* what a cheek!

**descarriado,-a** *adj fig* lost. LOC **ser la oveja descarriada** *fig* to be the lost sheep.

**descarriar** *vt* **1** *(apartar del camino)* to send the wrong way, put on the wrong road, misdirect. **2** *fig* to lead astray.
▶ *vpr* **descarriarse 1** *(perderse)* to lose one's way, get lost, go the wrong way. **2** *fig* to go astray.

**descarrilar** *vi* to be derailed, run off the rails, go off the rails .

**descartar** *vt* to discard, reject, rule out: *descartamos esa posibilidad* we ruled out that possibility.

**descastado,-a** *adj (poco cariñoso)* unaffectionate, cold.
▶ *nm & nf (poco cariñoso)* unaffectionate person.

**descendencia** *nf* offspring, descendants *pl.*

**descender** *vi* **1** to descend, go down, come down. **2** *(temperatura, nivel, etc)* to drop, fall, go down. **3** *(ser descendiente)* to descend (de, from), issue (de, from).
▶ *vt (bajar)* to go down: *descendió la escalera muy rápidamente* he went down the stairs very quickly.

**descendiente** *nm o nf* descendant; *(hijos)* offspring.

**descenso** *nm* **1** *(acción)* descent, lowering. **2** *(de temperatura)* drop, fall. **3** *fig (declive)* decline, fall. **4** DEP *(de división)* relegation.

**descentralización** *nf* decentralization.

**descentralizar** *vt* to decentralize.

**descentrar** *vt fig* to disorientate, throw, put off.
▶ *vpr* **descentrarse** *fig* to become disorientated.

**descifrar** *vt* **1** to decipher, decode. **2** *fig (llegar a comprender)* to solve, figure out.

**desclavar** *vt (desprender)* to take off.

**descodificar** *vt* to decode.

**descolgar** *vt* **1** *(cuadro, etc)* to take down. **2** *(bajar)* to lower, let down. **3** *(el teléfono)* to pick up, lift: *dejó el teléfono descolgado* she left the telephone off the hook.

**descollar** *vi* to stand out, excel.

**descolonización** *nf* decolonization.

**descolonizar** *vt* to decolonize.

**descolorar** *vt* to discolour (US discolor), fade.

**descolorido,-a** *adj* discoloured (US discolored), faded.

**descombro** *nm* clearing.

**descompensar** *vt* to unbalance, upset, throw out of kilter.

**descomponer** *vt* **1** *(separar)* to break down, split up. **2** *(estropear)* to break. **3** FÍS to resolve. **4** QUÍM to decompose. **5** MAT to split up. **6** *fig (molestar)* to disturb, upset; *(irritar)* irritate. **7** *(pudrir)* to rot.
▶ *vpr* **descomponerse 1** *(pudrirse)* to decompose, rot. **2** *(estropearse)* to break down. **3** FÍS to resolve. **4** QUÍM to decompose. **5** MAT to split.

**descomposición** *nf* **1** *(pudrimiento)* decomposition, decay. **2** *fam (diarrea)* diarrhoea (US diarrhea).

**descompresión** *nf* decompression.

**descomprimir** *vt* to decompress, depressurize.

**descompuesto,-a** *adj* **1** *(podrido)* decomposed, decayed, rotten. **2** *(estropeado)* out of order, broken down. **3** *fig (alterado)* upset. LOC **estar descompuesto,-a** to have diarrhoea (US diarrhea).

**descomunal** *adj* huge, enormous.

**desconcertado,-a** *adj* disconcerted, confused, upset.

**desconcertante** *adj* disconcerting, upsetting.

**desconcertar** *vt (perturbar)* to disconcert, upset, disturb.
▶ *vpr* **desconcertarse** *(perturbarse)* to be disconcerted.

**desconchado,-a** *nm (pared)* flaking, peeling; *(loza)* chipping.

**desconchar** *vt (pared)* to peel off, flake; *(loza)* to chip.
▶ *vpr* **desconcharse** to peel off, flake off; *(loza)* to chip.

**desconchón** *nm (en pared)* bare patch.

**desconcierto** *nm* disorder, confusion, chaos.

**desconectado,-a** *adj fig* cut off (de, from).

**desconectar** *vt* **1** ELEC to disconnect. **2** *(un aparato)* to switch off, turn off. **3** *(desenchufar)* to unplug. **4** *fam fig* to turn off, switch off.

**desconexión** *nf* disconnection.

**desconfiado,-a** *adj* distrustful, suspicious, wary.
▶ *nm & nf* distrustful person, suspicious person, wary person.

**desconfianza** *nf* distrust, mistrust, suspicion.

**desconfiar** *vi* **1** *(faltar la confianza)* to distrust (de, -), mistrust (de, -), be suspicious (de, of). **2** *(tener cuidado)* to beware (de, of).

**descongelar** *vt* **1** *(comida)* to thaw, thaw out. **2** *(nevera)* to defrost.

**descongestión** *nf (nasal)* unblocking, clearing, decongestion.

**descongestionar** *vt* to clear.

**desconocer** *vt* not to know, be unaware of: *desconozco su nombre* I don't know her name.

**desconocido,-a** *adj* **1** *(no conocido)* unknown. **2** *(extraño)* strange, unfamiliar.
▶ *nm & nf* stranger, unknown person.
▶ *nm* **lo desconocido** the unknown.

**desconocimiento** *nm* ignorance (de, of).

**desconsideración** *nf* thoughtlessness .

**desconsiderado,-a** *adj* thoughtless.
▶ *nm & nf* thoughtless person.

**desconsolado,-a** *adj* disconsolate, grief-stricken, inconsolable.

**desconsolar** *vt* to distress, grieve.

**desconsuelo** *nm* affliction.

**descontar** *vt (restar)* to deduct, take off, knock off.

**descontento,-a** *adj* displeased, unhappy, dissatisfied, discontented.
▶ *nm & nf* malcontent.

**descontrol** *nm fam* lack of control, chaos.

**descontrolado,-a** *adj* 1 uncontrolled, out of control. 2 *fam fig* out of control, wild.

**descontrolarse** *vpr (persona)* to lose control.

**desconvocar** *vt* to cancel, call off.

**descorazonador,-ra** *adj* disheartening, discouraging.

**descorazonar** *vt* to dishearten, discourage.
▶ *vpr* **descorazonarse** to lose heart, get discouraged.

**descorchar** *vt* to uncork.

**descorrer** *vt (cortinas)* to draw; *(cerrojo)* to unbolt.

**descortés** *adj* impolite, rude, discourteous.

**descortesía** *nf* impoliteness, rudeness, discourtesy.

**descoser** *vt* to unpick.
▶ *vpr* **descoserse** to come unstitched.

**descosido,-a** *nm* open seam.

**descoyuntar** *vt* 1 *(hueso)* to dislocate, disjoint. 2 *fig (cansar)* to exhaust, tire out.
▶ *vpr* **descoyuntarse** to become dislocated. LOC **descoyuntarse de risa** *fam* to split one's sides laughing.

**descreído,-a** *adj* disbelieving, unbelieving.
▶ *nm & nf* disbeliever, unbeliever.

**descremado,-a** *adj* skimmed. COMP **yogur descremado** low-fat yoghurt.

**describir** *vt* to describe.

**descripción** *nf* description.

**descriptivo,-a** *adj* descriptive.

**descrito,-a** *adj* described.

**descuartizar** *vt (persona)* to quarter; *(animal)* to quarter, cut up.

**descubierto,-a** *adj* open, uncovered: *el cielo está descubierto* the sky is clear.

**descubrimiento** *nm* discovery.

**descubrir** *vt* 1 *(gen)* to discover; *(petróleo, oro, minas)* to find; *(conspiración)* to uncover; *(crimen)* to bring to light. 2 *(averiguar)* to find out, discover: *descubrimos sus intenciones* we found out his intentions.
▶ *vpr* **descubrirse** *(la cabeza)* to take off one's hat.

**descuento** *nm* 1 discount, reduction, deduction. 2 DEP injury time. LOC **con descuento** at a discount, on offer.

**descuidado,-a** *adj* 1 *(negligente)* careless, negligent. 2 *(desprevenido)* unprepared.

**descuidar** *vt* 1 to neglect, overlook. 2 *(distraer)* to distract.
▶ *vpr* **descuidarse** *(no tener cuidado)* to be careless. LOC **¡descuida!** don't worry!

**descuido** *nm* 1 *(negligencia)* negligence, carelessness, neglect. 2 *(distracción)* oversight, slip, mistake. LOC **por descuido** inadvertently, by mistake.

**desde** *prep* 1 *(tiempo)* since: *desde 1992* since 1992. 2 *(lugar)* from: *desde allí* from there. LOC **desde ahora** from now on. ‖ **desde luego** 1 *(en realidad)* really. 2 *(como respuesta)* of course, certainly.

**desdentado,-a** *adj* toothless.

**desdibujar** *vt* to blur.
▶ *vpr* **desdibujarse** to become blurred, become faint.

**desdicha** *nf* misfortune, misery, adversity.

**desdichado,-a** *adj* unfortunate, wretched, unlucky.

**desdoblar** *vt* to unfold.

**desdramatizar** *vt* to make less traumatic, play down.

**deseado,-a** *adj* desired: *en el momento deseado* at the right time.

**desear** *vt* **1** *(querer)* to want: *deseo que venga* I want him to come. **2** *(anhelar)* to long for, wish for, desire; *(para alguien)* to wish: *¿qué desea?* can I help you?, what can I do for you?

**desecar** *vt* **1** *(gen)* to dry up. **2** *(pantano, laguna, etc)* to drain.
▶ *vpr* **desecarse** to dry up.

**desechable** *adj* disposable.

**desechar** *vt* **1** *(tirar)* to discard, throw out, throw away. **2** *(rechazar)* to refuse, reject; *(proyecto, idea)* to drop, discard.

**desecho** *nm* *(residuo)* reject.
▶ *nm pl* **desechos** waste *sing*, rubbish *sing*.

**desembalar** *vt* to unpack.

**desembarazar** *vt* *(dejar libre)* to free.
▶ *vpr* **desembarazarse** *(librarse)* to rid os (de, of), get rid (de, of).

**desembarcar** *vi* to disembark, land, go ashore.
▶ *vt* *(mercancías)* to unload; *(personas)* to disembark, put ashore.

**desembarco** *nm* *(mercancías)* landing, unloading; *(personas)* disembarkation, landing.

**desembocadura** *nf* *(de río)* mouth, outlet.

**desembocar** *vi* **1** *(río)* to flow (en, into). **2** *(calle)* to end (en, at), lead (en, into).

**desembolso** *nm* *(gasto)* expense, outlay, expenditure.

**desembozar** *vt fig* to uncover, bring out into the open.

**desembrujar** *vt* to remove a spell from.

**desembuchar** *vi* to come clean, spill the beans: *¡desembucha de una vez!* come out with it once and for all!

**desempañar** *vt* to wipe the steam from, demist.

**desempaquetar** *vt* to unpack, unwrap.

**desemparejar** *vt* to separate.

**desempatar** *vt* to break a tie between.
▶ *vi* DEP *(desempatar un resultado)* to break the deadlock.

**desempate** *nm* **1** tie-break, tiebreaker. **2** DEP play-off, tie-break. [COMP] **partido de desempate** play off, deciding match.

**desempeñar** *vt* **1** *(cumplir una obligación)* to discharge, fulfil (US fulfill); *(un cargo)* to fill, hold, occupy. **2** *(papel)* to play: *desempeña un papel vital* she plays a vital role.

**desempeño** *nm* **1** *(obligaciones, cargo)* carrying out, fulfilment (US fulfillment). **2** TEAT performance, acting.

**desempleado,-a** *adj* unemployed, out of work.
▶ *nm & nf* unemployed person.

**desempleo** *nm* unemployment. [LOC] **cobrar el desempleo** to be on the dole, (US be on welfare).

**desempolvar** *vt* **1** *(quitar el polvo)* to dust. **2** *fig* *(volver a usar)* to unearth.

**desencadenar** *vt fig* *(producir)* to spark off, give rise to.
▶ *vpr* **desencadenarse** **1** *(desatarse)* to break loose. **2** *(guerra, tormenta)* to break out: *se desencadenó una tormenta* a storm broke. **3** *(acontecimientos)* to start.

**desencajar** *vt* *(desunir)* to take apart, disjoint.
▶ *vpr* **desencajarse** *(desunirse)* to come apart, come loose.

**desencallar** *vt* to refloat.

**desencantar** *vt* *(desilusionar)* to disillusion, disappoint.
▶ *vpr* **desencantarse** to be disappointed, be disillusioned.

**desencanto** *nm* *(desilusión)* disillusionment, disappointment.

**desenchufar** *vt* to unplug, disconnect.

**desencolar** *vt* to unglue, unstick.
▶ *vpr* **desencolarse** to come unglued, come unstuck.

**desencuadernar** *vt* to unbind.
▶ *vpr* **desencuadernarse** to come unbound.

**desenfadado,-a** *adj* **1** *(despreocupado)* free and easy, carefree. **2** *(ropa)* casual.

**desenfadar** *vt* to calm down.
▶ *vpr* **desenfadarse** to calm down.

**desenfado** *nm* **1** *(soltura)* self-confidence, assurance. **2** *(franqueza)* frankness, openness.

**desenfocado,-a** *adj* out of focus.

**desenfocar** *vt* to take out of focus.

**desenfoque** *nm* incorrect focusing.

**desenfrenado,-a** *adj (gen)* frantic, uncontrolled, wild.

**desenfreno** *nm (falta de control)* lack of control, wild abandon.

**desenfundar** *vt (quitar)* to draw out, pull out.

**desenganchar** *vt (gen)* to unhook, unfasten; *(despegar)* to unstick.

**desengañado,-a** *adj* **1** *(desilusionado)* disillusioned. **2** *(decepcionado)* disappointed, let down.

**desengañar** *vt* **1** *(decepcionar)* to disappoint. **2** *(desilusionar)* to disillusion.
▶ *vpr* **desengañarse** **1** *(ver la verdad)* to have one's eyes opened (de, about). **2** *(tener una decepción)* to be disappointed.

**desengaño** *nm (desilusión)* disillusion; *(decepción)* disappointment. LOC **sufrir un desengaño** to be disappointed.

**desengrasar** *vt* to remove the grease from.

**desenhebrar** *vt* to unthread.

**desenjaular** *vt* to let out of a cage, release.

**desenlace** *nm* **1** *(resultado)* outcome, result. **2** *(final)* end.

**desenlazar** *vt (desatar)* to untie, undo.

**desenmarañar** *vt* **1** *(desenredar)* to untangle, unravel. **2** *fig (poner en claro)* to unravel, clear up; *(un asunto)* to sort out.

**desenmascarar** *vt* to unmask.

**desenredar** *vt* to untangle, disentangle.
▶ *vpr* **desenredarse** to get out (de, of), extricate OS (de, from).

**desenrollar** *vt* to unroll, unwind.

**desenroscar** *vt* to unscrew, uncoil.

**desentenderse** *vpr (afectar ignorancia)* to pretend not to know (de, -/about), ignore (de, -), feign ignorance (de, of): *se desentiende de mí* she ignores me.

**desenterrar** *vt (un objeto)* to unearth, dig up; *(cadáver)* to disinter, exhume.

**desentonar** *vi* **1** MÚS *(instrumento)* to be out of tune; *(cantante)* to sing out of tune. **2** *fig (combinar)* not to match (con, -).

**desentrenado,-a** *adj* out of training.

**desentrenarse** *vpr* to be out of training, get out of training.

**desenvainar** *vt* to unsheathe, draw.

**desenvoltura** *nf fig (soltura)* confidence, assurance.

**desenvolver** *vt* **1** *(quitar lo que envuelve)* to unwrap. **2** *(aclarar)* to clear up.
▶ *vpr* **desenvolverse** *(manejarse)* to manage, cope: *se desenvuelve muy bien en los negocios* he manages very well in business.

**desenvuelto,-a** *adj (seguro)* confident, self-assured.

**deseo** *nm* wish, desire. LOC **formular un deseo** to make a wish. COMP **buenos deseos** good intentions.

**deseoso,-a** *adj* desirous, eager, anxious. LOC **estar deseoso,-a de hacer ALGO** to be eager to do STH.

**desequilibrado,-a** *adj* **1** unbalanced, out of balance. **2** *(persona)* mentally unbalanced.

**desequilibrar** *vt* **1** to unbalance, throw off balance. **2** *fig* to unbalance.
▶ *vpr* **desequilibrarse** *fig* to become unbalanced.

**desequilibrio** *nm* **1** lack of balance, imbalance. **2** *fig (mental)* unbalanced state of mind.

**desertar** *vi* **1** MIL to desert. **2** *fig (abandonar)* to abandon, desert.

**desértico,-a** *adj* desert.

**desertización** *nf* desertification.

**desertor,-ra** *nm & nf* deserter.

**desesperación** *nf* despair, desperation.

**desesperadamente** *adv* desperately, frantically.

**desesperado,-a** *adj (sin esperanza)* hopeless, desperate.

**desesperanza** *nf* despair, desperation, hopelessness.

**desesperanzar** *vt* to drive to despair.
▶ *vpr* **desesperanzarse** to despair, lose hope, give up hope (de, of).

**desesperar** *vt* 1 *(hacer perder la paciencia)* to drive to despair. 2 *(exasperar)* to exasperate.
▶ *vpr* **desesperarse** 1 *(desesperanzar)* to lose hope, despair. 2 *(irritarse)* to get irritated, become exasperated: *se desespera por todo* everything exasperates her.

**desestabilización** *nf* destabilization.

**desestabilizar** *vt* to destabilize.

**desestimar** *vt* to disregard, underestimate.

**desfachatez** *nf* cheek, nerve.

**desfalco** *nm* embezzlement.

**desfallecer** *vt (disminuir las fuerzas)* to weaken.
▶ *vi* 1 *(debilitar)* to weaken, lose strength. 2 *(decaer)* to lose heart.

**desfallecido,-a** *adj* weak, faint.

**desfallecimiento** *nm* faintness.

**desfasado,-a** *adj* outdated, out of date; *(persona)* old-fashioned, behind the times.

**desfasar** *vt* TÉC to phase out.
▶ *vpr* **desfasarse** 1 TÉC to change phase. 2 *(persona)* to be out of synch.

**desfase** *nm* 1 *(diferencia)* imbalance, gap. 2 TÉC phase difference. COMP **desfase horario** 1 *(entre países)* time difference. 2 *(al volar en avión)* jet lag.

**desfavorable** *adj* unfavourable (US unfavorable).

**desfavorecer** *vt (perjudicar)* to disadvantage, put at a disadvantage.

**desfigurado,-a** *adj (persona)* disfigured.

**desfigurar** *vt (cara)* to disfigure.
▶ *vpr* **desfigurarse** *(descomponerse)* to become distorted.

**desfiladero** *nm* defile, gorge, narrow pass.

**desfilar** *vi* 1 *(gen)* to march. 2 MIL to march, march past, parade. 3 *(moda)* to parade, walk up and down.

**desfile** *nm* 1 *(gen)* parade, procession. 2 MIL parade. 3 *(moda)* fashion show.

**desfogar** *vt (descargar)* to give vent to, vent.
▶ *vpr* **desfogarse** to let off steam, vent one's anger.

**desgajar** *vt* 1 *(rama)* to tear off; *(página)* to rip out, tear out. 2 *(romper)* to break.

**desgana** *nf (inapetencia)* lack of appetite. LOC **con desgana** reluctantly.

**desganado,-a** *adj* 1 *(sin gana)* not hungry: *está desganado* he has no appetite. 2 *(apático)* apathetic, half-hearted.

**desganar** *vt* 1 *(quitar el apetito)* to spoil the appetite of. 2 *(quitar las ganas)* to turn off.
▶ *vpr* **desganarse** 1 *(perder el apetito)* to lose one's appetite. 2 *(perder el interés)* to lose interest (de, in), go off (de, -).

**desgañitarse** *vpr fam* to shout OS hoarse, shout one's head off.

**desgarbado,-a** *adj* ungainly, ungraceful, clumsy.

**desgarrador,-ra** *adj* heartbreaking, heart-rending.

**desgarrar** *vt (rasgar)* to tear, rip.
▶ *vpr* **desgarrarse** *(rasgarse)* to tear, rip.

**desgarro** *nm (rompimiento)* tear, rip.

**desgastar** *vt (ropa)* to wear out, wear away; *(tacones)* to wear down.
▶ *vpr* **desgastarse** *(gastarse)* to wear out, get worn.

**desgaste** *nm (gen)* wear.

**desglosar** *vt* 1 *(escrito)* to detach. 2 *(gastos)* to break down.

**desglose** *nm* breakdown, separation.

**desgracia** *nf* 1 *(desdicha)* misfortune. 2 *(mala suerte)* bad luck, mischance. LOC **por desgracia** unfortunately.

**desgraciado,-a** *adj* **1** *(sin suerte)* unfortunate, unlucky. **2** *(infeliz)* unhappy.
▶ *nm & nf* wretch, unfortunate person.

**desgraciar** *vt* *(echar a perder)* to spoil.
▶ *vpr* **desgraciarse** *(malograrse)* to fail, be spoiled; *(plan, proyecto)* to fall through.

**desgranar** *vt* *(guisante, maíz)* to shell; *(trigo)* to thresh.

**desgravar** *vt* to deduct.

**desguace** *nm* **1** *(de barco)* breaking up; *(coche)* car breaking, scrapping. **2** *(lugar)* breaker's yard, scrapyard.

**desguazar** *vt* *(barco)* to break up; *(coche)* to scrap.

**deshabitado,-a** *adj* *(pueblo, lugar)* uninhabited; *(casa, piso)* unoccupied.

**deshabitar** *vt* to leave, abandon, vacate.

**deshabituar** *vt* *(hacer perder el hábito)* to break from the habit.
▶ *vpr* **deshabituarse** to get out of the habit (a, of), give up (a, -).

**deshacer** *vt* **1** *(estropear)* to ruin, damage; *(romper)* to break; *(desordenar)* to upset. **2** *(nudo)* to untie, loosen; *(paquete)* to undo, unwrap; *(cama)* to strip; *(equipaje)* to unpack; *(puntadas)* to unpick. **3** *(romper un acuerdo)* to break off. **4** *(disolver)* to dissolve; *(derretir)* to melt. **5** *(desandar)* to retrace. **6** *(planes, proyectos)* to spoil, ruin.
▶ *vpr* **deshacerse 1** *(nudo)* to come undone, come untied; *(puntada)* to come unsewn. **2** *(disolverse)* to dissolve; *(derretirse)* to melt.

**desharrapado,-a** *adj* ragged, in tatters.

**deshecho,-a** *adj* **1** *(destruido)* destroyed. **2** *(estropeado)* damaged, ruined. **3** *(nudo)* untied, undone; *(paquete)* unwrapped; *(cama)* unmade; *(equipaje)* unpacked. **4** *(disuelto)* dissolved; *(derretido)* melted.

**deshelar** *vt* **1** to thaw, melt. **2** *(congelador)* to defrost. **3** *(coche)* to de-ice.
▶ *vpr* **deshelarse** to thaw out, melt.

**desherbar** *vt* to weed.

**desheredar** *vt* to disinherit.

**deshidratación** *nf* dehydration.

**deshidratado,-a** *adj* dehydrated.

**deshidratar** *vt* to dehydrate.
▶ *vpr* **deshidratarse** to become dehydrated.

**deshielo** *nm* thaw; *(de congelador)* defrosting; *(de parabrisas)* de-icing.

**deshilachado,-a** *adj* frayed.

**deshilachar** *vt* to fray.

**deshilvanar** *vt* to untack.

**deshinchado,-a** *adj* **1** *(neumático, etc)* flat, deflated. **2** *(sin hinchazón)* not swollen: *la rodilla ya la tienes deshinchada* the swelling in your knee has gone down.

**deshinchar** *vt* **1** *(neumático, etc)* to deflate, let down. **2** *(reducir la hinchazón)* to reduce the swelling of.
▶ *vpr* **deshincharse 1** to deflate, go down. **2** *(reducirse la hinchazón)* to go down.

**deshojar** *vt* *(flor)* to strip the petals off; *(árbol)* to strip the leaves off.
▶ *vpr* **deshojarse** *(flor)* to lose its petals; *(árbol)* to lose its leaves.

**deshollinador** *nm* chimney sweep.

**deshollinar** *vt* to sweep.

**deshonestidad** *nf* *(sin honestidad)* dishonesty.

**deshonesto,-a** *adj* *(sin honestidad)* dishonest.

**deshonra** *nf* dishonour (US dishonor), disgrace.

**deshonrar** *vt* *(gen)* to dishonour (US dishonor), disgrace.

**deshonroso,-a** *adj* dishonourable (US dishonorable).

**desidia** *nf* negligence.

**desierto,-a** *adj* *(sin habitantes)* uninhabited, deserted: *una isla desierta* a desert island.
▶ *nm* **desierto** desert.

**designar** *vt* **1** *(denominar)* to designate. **2** *(nombrar para un cargo)* to appoint, name, assign.

**desigual** *adj* **1** *(gen)* unequal, uneven. **2** *(diferente)* different, unequal. **3** *(irregular)* uneven, irregular. **4** *(no liso)* uneven, rough. **5** *(variable)* changeable:

*tiene un carácter muy desigual* she is very changeable.

**desigualdad** *nf* (gen) inequality, difference.

**desilusión** *nf* disappointment.

**desilusionar** *vt* to disappoint.
▶ *vpr* **desilusionarse** to be disappointed.

**desincrustar** *vt* to descale.

**desinencia** *nf* ending, desinence.

**desinfectante** *adj* disinfectant.
▶ *nm* disinfectant.

**desinfectar** *vt* to disinfect.

**desinflamar** *vt* to reduce the inflammation in.
▶ *vpr* **desinflamarse** to go down.

**desinflar** *vt* (gen) to deflate; (una rueda) to let down.
▶ *vpr* **desinflarse** to go down.

**desinformar** *vi* to misinform.

**desinsectar** *vt* to fumigate.

**desintegrar** *vt* **1** to disintegrate. **2** *fig* to disintegrate, break up. **3** FÍS to split.
▶ *vpr* **desintegrarse 1** to disintegrate. **2** *fig* to break up. **3** FÍS to split.

**desinterés** *nm* (falta de interés) lack of interest, indifference.

**desinteresarse** *vpr* **1** (perder el interés) to lose interest (de, in), go off (de, -). **2** (desentenderse) to have nothing to do (de, with).

**desintoxicación** *nf* detoxication.

**desintoxicar** *vt* to detoxicate.

**desistir** *vi* (gen) to desist, give up.

**deslavar** *vt* to half-wash.

**desleal** *adj* disloyal.

**deslealtad** *nf* disloyalty.

**deslenguado,-a** *adj fig* (descarado) insolent, cheeky.

**desligar** *vt* **1** (desatar) to untie, unfasten. **2** *fig* (separar) to separate (de, from). **3** *fig* (librar de una obligación) to release (de, from), free (de, from).
▶ *vpr* **desligarse 1** (desatarse) to break away (de, from). **2** (librarse) to release OS (de, from), free OS (de, from).

**deslindar** *vt* to delimit, mark the boundaries of.

**desliz** *nm* **1** (resbalón) slide, slip. **2** *fig* (error) slip, mistake error. LOC **tener un desliz** *fig* to slip up, make a slip.

**deslizamiento** *nm* slipping, slip. COMP **deslizamiento de tierra** landslide.

**deslizar** *vt* (pasar) to slide, slip.
▶ *vi* (resbalar) to slide, slip.
▶ *vpr* **deslizarse** (gen) to slide; (sobre agua) to glide.

**deslucir** *vt fig* (quitar la gracia) to mar, spoil.

**deslumbrar** *vt* to dazzle.

**deslustrar** *vt* (metal) to tarnish.

**desmadejar** *vt fig* to tire out, exhaust.

**desmagnetizar** *vt* to demagnetize.

**desmantelar** *vt* to dismantle.

**desmaquillar** *vt* to remove make-up from.
▶ *vpr* **desmaquillarse** to remove one's make-up.

**desmarcarse** *vpr* **1** DEP to get into an unmarked position. **2** (distanciarse) to distance OS (de, from), disassociate OS (de, from) .

**desmayar** *vt* (causar desmayo) to make faint.
▶ *vpr* **desmayarse** (perder el sentido) to faint.

**desmayo** *nm* (pérdida del conocimiento) faint, fainting fit. LOC **sufrir/tener un desmayo** to faint.

**desmejorar** *vt* to spoil, make worse, damage.
▶ *vi* to deteriorate, get worse, go downhill.
▶ *vpr* **desmejorarse** to deteriorate, get worse, go downhill.

**desmelenar** *vt* (desgreñar) to tousle, dishevel.
▶ *vpr* **desmelenarse** *fam* (desmadrarse) to let one's hair down.

**desmemoriado,-a** *adj* forgetful, absent-minded.

**desmentir** *vt* **1** (negar) to deny. **2** (contradecir) to contradict, belie.

**desmenuzar** *vt* (gen) to break into little pieces.

**desmirriado,-a** *adj fam* weedy, puny.

D

**desmitificar** *vt* to demystify.

**desmoldar** *vt* to remove from a mould, turn out.

**desmontable** *adj* that can be taken to pieces.

**desmontar** *vt* **1** *(desarmar)* to take to pieces, take down, dismantle. **2** *(motor)* to strip.
▸ *vi (del caballo)* to dismount (de, -).

**desmoralizar** *vt* to demoralize.
▸ *vpr* **desmoralizarse** to become demoralized.

**desmoronamiento** *nm* crumbling, disintegration, fall.

**desmoronar** *vt* to crumble, destroy.
▸ *vpr* **desmoronarse** to crumble, collapse, fall to pieces.

**desnatado,-a** *adj (leche)* skimmed; *(yogur)* low-fat.

**desnaturalización** *nf* **1** QUÍM denaturation. **2** *(adulteración)* adulteration.

**desnaturalizar** *vt* **1** *(adulterar)* to adulterate. **2** QUÍM to denature, denaturize.

**desnivel** *nm* **1** unevenness. **2** *(cuesta)* slope, drop. **3** *fig* difference.

**desnivelar** *vt* **1** *(sacar de nivel)* to make uneven. **2** *(desequilibrar)* to throw out of balance; *(balanza)* to tip.

**desnudar** *vt* **1** to undress. **2** *fig (despojar)* to strip.
▸ *vpr* **desnudarse** *(persona)* to get undressed, take one's clothes off.

**desnudez** *nf* nudity, nakedness.

**desnudo,-a** *adj (persona)* naked, nude; *(parte del cuerpo)* bare.

**desnutrición** *nf* malnutrition, undernourishment.

**desnutrido,-a** *adj* undernourished.

**desobedecer** *vt* to disobey.

**desobediente** *adj* disobedient.

**desocupado,-a** *adj* **1** *(ocioso)* free, not busy. **2** *(desempleado)* unemployed, out of work.

**desocupar** *vt* to vacate, leave, empty.

**desodorante** *nm* deodorant.

**desolación** *nf* **1** desolation. **2** *(tristeza)* affliction, grief.

**desolado,-a** *adj (triste)* distressed, heartbroken.

**desolador,-ra** *adj (desconsolador)* heartbreaking, devastating.

**desorden** *nm* disorder, disarray, mess, untidiness.

**desordenado,-a** *adj* **1** *(habitación, etc)* untidy, messy. **2** *(persona)* slovenly.

**desordenar** *vt* to untidy, disarrange, mess up.

**desorganizar** *vt* to disorganize, disrupt.

**desorientar** *vt* **1** to disorientate. **2** *fig (confundir)* to confuse.
▸ *vpr* **desorientarse** to lose one's bearings, lose one's sense of direction, get lost.

**desovar** *vi (insectos)* to lay eggs; *(peces)* to spawn.

**desove** *nm (insectos)* egg-laying; *(peces)* spawning.

**desoxidante** *adj* deoxidizing.

**desoxirribonucleico,-a** *adj* deoxyribonucleic.

**despabilado,-a** *adj fig (listo)* smart, sharp, quick.

**despabilar** *vt fig (despertar)* to wake up.
▸ *vpr* **despabilarse** **1** *(despertarse)* to wake up. **2** *(avivarse)* to wise up.

**despachar** *vt* **1** *(resolver)* to resolve, get through; *(tratar un asunto)* to deal with, attend. **2** *(despedir)* to dismiss, sack, fire. **3** *(en tienda)* to serve; *(vender)* to sell.

**despacho** *nm (oficina)* office; *(estudio)* study. COMP **despacho de billetes/localidades** ticket/box office.

**despacio** *adv (gen)* slowly.

**desparasitar** *vt (piojos)* to delouse; *(lombrices)* to worm.

**desparramar** *vt* to spread, scatter; *(un líquido)* to spill.

**despectivo,-a** *adj* **1** contemptuous, disparaging. **2** GRAM pejorative, derogatory.

**despedida** *nf* farewell, goodbye.

**despedir** *vt* **1** *(echar)* to throw out. **2** *(del trabajo)* to dismiss, fire, sack. **3**

*(decir adiós)* to see off, say goodbye to.

▶ *vpr* **despedirse** *(decirse adiós)* to say goodbye (de, to).

**despegar** *vt (desenganchar)* to unstick, take off, detach.

▶ *vi (avión)* to take off.

▶ *vpr* **despegarse** *(separarse)* to come unstuck.

**despegue** *nm (avión)* takeoff.

**despeinar** *vt* to dishevel, ruffle.

▶ *vpr* **despeinarse** to mess up one's hair.

**despejar** *vt* 1 *(desalojar)* to clear. 2 MAT to find. 3 INFORM to clear.

▶ *vpr* **despejarse** 1 METEOR to clear up. 2 *(espabilarse)* to wake OS up, clear one's head.

**despenalizar** *vt* to legalize.

**despensa** *nf (lugar)* pantry, larder.

**despeñar** *vt* to throw over a cliff.

▶ *vpr* **despeñarse** *(caer)* to fall over a cliff.

**desperdiciar** *vt* to waste, squander; *(oportunidad)* to throw away.

**desperdicio** *nm* waste.

▶ *nm pl* **desperdicios** *(basura)* rubbish sing; *(desechos)* scraps, leftovers.

**desperdigar** *vt* to scatter, disperse.

**desperezarse** *vpr* to stretch.

**desperfecto** *nm* 1 *(daño)* damage. 2 *(defecto)* flaw, defect.

**despertador** *nm* alarm clock.

**despertar** *vt* to wake, wake up, awaken.

▶ *vi* to wake up, awake.

▶ *vpr* **despertarse** to wake up, awake.

**despiadado,-a** *adj* ruthless, merciless.

**despido** *nm* dismissal, sacking.

**despierto,-a** *adj* 1 awake. 2 *(espabilado)* lively, smart, sharp, bright.

**despilfarrar** *vt* to waste, squander.

**despilfarro** *nm* waste.

**despistado,-a** *adj (distraído)* absentminded.

**despistar** *vt fig (desorientar)* to mislead, confuse.

▶ *vpr* **despistarse** 1 *(perderse)* to get lost.. 2 *(distraerse)* to get confused.

**despiste** *nm* 1 *(distracción)* absentmindedness. 2 *(error)* mistake, slip.

**desplazamiento** *nm (traslado)* moving, removal.

**desplazar** *vt* 1 *(mover)* to move, shift. 2 *fig (sustituir)* to replace, take over from.

▶ *vpr* **desplazarse** to travel.

**desplegar** *vt (extender)* to unfold, spread (out).

**despliegue** *nm fig (exhibición)* display, show, manifestation.

**desplomar** *vt (hacer perder la verticalidad)* to put out of plumb.

▶ *vpr* **desplomarse** *(caer algo de peso)* to fall down, collapse, topple over.

**despoblar** *vt* to depopulate.

▶ *vpr* **despoblarse** to become depopulated, become deserted.

**despojar** *vt (quitar)* to deprive (de, of), strip.

▶ *vpr* **despojarse** *(desposeerse voluntariamente)* to forsake (de, -), give up (de,-).

**despojo** *nm (botín)* plunder, booty.

▶ *nm pl* **despojos** *(sobras)* leavings, scraps, leftovers.

**desposeer** *vt (gen)* to dispossess.

**déspota** *nm o nf* despot, tyrant.

**despreciar** *vt* 1 *(desdeñar)* to despise, scorn, look down on. 2 *(ignorar)* to disregard, ignore.

**desprecio** *nm (desestima)* contempt, scorn, disdain.

**desprender** *vt* 1 *(soltar)* to release. 2 *(emanar)* to give off.

▶ *vpr* **desprenderse** *(soltarse)* to come off, come away.

**desprendimiento** *nm (acción de desprenderse)* detachment, loosening.

**despreocupado,-a** *adj (tranquilo)* unconcerned, unworried.

**despreocuparse** *vpr* 1 *(dejar de preocuparse)* to stop worrying. 2 *(desentenderse)* to be unconcerned (de, about), be indifferent (de, to).

**desprestigiar** *vt* to discredit, ruin the reputation of.

**desprevenido,-a** *adj* unprepared, unready. LOC **coger/pillar a** ALGN **desprevenido,-a** to catch SB unawares, take SB by surprise.

**desproporcionado,-a** *adj* disproportionate, out of proportion.

**después** *adv* **1** afterwards, later. **2** *(entonces)* then. **3** *(luego)* next. LOC **después de 1** *(tiempo)* after. **2** *(desde)* since. **3** (+ *pp*) after, once: *después de la cena* after supper. ∥ **después de todo** after all: *después de todo no está tan mal* it's not that bad after all.

**despuntar** *vt (quitar la punta)* to blunt, make blunt.

**destacamento** *nm* detachment.

**destacar** *vi (despuntar)* to stand out.
  ▶ *vt fig (dar énfasis)* to point out, emphasize.
  ▶ *vpr* **destacarse** to stand out.

**destajo** *nm* piecework. LOC **a destajo** by the piece.

**destapar** *vt* **1** *(gen)* to open: *destapé la caja y vi que estaba vacía* I opened the box and saw it was empty. **2** *(tapón)* to uncork; *(tapa)* to take the lid off. **3** *fig (descubrir)* to reveal, uncover.
  ▶ *vpr* **destaparse** *(en la cama)* to take the covers off.

**destellar** *vi (estrella)* to twinkle.

**destello** *nm (resplandor)* sparkle, flash; *(brillo)* gleam, shine.

**destemplado,-a** *adj* **1** *(carácter)* irritable, tetchy. **2** *(tiempo)* unpleasant.

**desteñir** *vt* to discolour (US discolor), fade.
  ▶ *vi* to lose colour (US color), fade, run.

**desternillarse** LOC **desternillarse de risa** *fam* to split one's sides laughing, be in stitches.

**desterrar** *vt* to exile, banish.

**destiempo** LOC **a destiempo** inopportunely, at the wrong moment: *llegó a destiempo* he arrived at the wrong moment.

**destierro** *nm* **1** *(pena)* banishment, exile. **2** *(lugar)* place of exile.

**destilar** *vt* to distil (US distill).

**destilería** *nf* distillery.

**destinar** *vt* **1** *(asignar)* to assign, set aside, destine; *(dinero)* to allocate, set aside. **2** *(persona)* to assign, post.

**destinatario,-a** *nm & nf* **1** *(de carta)* addressee. **2** *(de mercancías)* consignee.

**destino** *nm* **1** *(sino)* destiny, fate. **2** *(uso)* purpose, use. **3** *(lugar)* destination. LOC **con destino a** bound for, going to.

**destitución** *nf* dismissal, removal.

**destituir** *vt* to dismiss.

**destornillador** *nm* screwdriver.

**destornillar** *vt* to unscrew.

**destrabar** *vt (quitar las trabas)* to unfetter.

**destreza** *nf* skill.

**destronar** *vt* **1** to dethrone. **2** *fig* to overthrow, unseat.

**destrozar** *vt* **1** *(romper)* to destroy, wreck; *(despedazar)* to tear to pieces, tear to shreds. **2** *fig (causar daño moral)* to crush, shatter, devastate.

**destrozo** *nm (acción)* destruction.

**destrucción** *nf* destruction.

**destruir** *vt* to destroy.

**desunir** *vt (separar)* to divide, separate.

**desuso** *nm* disuse: *eso está en desuso* that's obsolete, that's outdated.

**desvalido,-a** *adj* needy, destitute.

**desvalijar** *vt* **1** *(a alguien)* to rob. **2** *(un lugar)* to burgle.

**desván** *nm* loft, attic.

**desvanecer** *vt* **1** *(hacer desaparecer)* to clear, dispel, disperse. **2** *fig (recuerdo, etc)* to dispel, banish.
  ▶ *vpr* **desvanecerse 1** *(disiparse)* to disperse, clear. **2** *fig (desaparecer)* to vanish, disappear; *(recuerdos)* to fade.

**desvanecimiento** *nm (desmayo)* faint, fainting fit.

**desvariar** *vi* to be delirious, rave.

**desvarío** *nm* **1** *(delirio)* delirium, raving. **2** *(disparate)* nonsense, act of madness. **3** *(capricho)* fancy, whim.

**desvelar** *vt* **1** *(quitar el sueño)* to keep awake. **2** *fig (revelar)* to reveal, disclose: *nos desveló el secreto* she revealed the secret to us.

▶ *vpr* **desvelarse 1** to be unable to sleep. **2** *fig (dedicarse)* to devote OS (por, to): *siempre se ha desvelado por su familia* she has always devoted herself to her family.

**desvelo** *nm (dedicación)* devotion, dedication.

**desventaja** *nf* **1** disadvantage, drawback. **2** *(problema)* problem. LOC **estar en desventaja** to be at a disadvantage.

**desvergonzado,-a** *adj (sinvergüenza)* shameless, brazen.

**desvergüenza** *nf (falta de decoro)* shamelessness.

**desvestir** *vt* to undress.

▶ *vpr* **desvestirse** to undress, get undressed.

**desviación** *nf* **1** deviation. **2** *(de carretera)* diversion, detour.

**desviar** *vt* **1** *(gen)* to deviate, change the course of: *desvió la mirada* she looked away. **2** *(golpe, balón)* to deflect. **3** *(carretera, río, barco, avión)* to divert. **4** *fig (tema)* to change.

▶ *vpr* **desviarse 1** *(avión, barco)* to go off course; *(coche)* to make a detour. **2** *(golpe, balón)* to be deflected. **3** *(persona, camino)* to leave.

**desvío** *nm* diversion, detour.

**desvivirse** *vpr* **1** *(desvelarse)* to do one's utmost (por, for), be devoted (por, to). **2** *(desear)* to be mad (por, about).

**detallado,-a** *adj* detailed, thorough.

**detallar** *vt* **1** to detail, give the details of, tell in detail. **2** *(especificar)* to specify.

**detalle** *nm* **1** *(pormenor)* detail, particular. **2** *(delicadeza)* nice gesture, nice thought. **3** *(toque decorativo)* touch. LOC **al detalle** COM retail. ‖ **tener un detalle** to be considerate, be thoughtful.

**detallista** *nm o nf* COM retailer, retail trader.

**detectar** *vt* to detect.

**detective** *nm o nf* detective.

**detener** *vt* **1** *(parar)* to stop, halt; *(proceso, negociación)* to hold up. **2** *(retener)* to keep, delay, detain.

▶ *vpr* **detenerse 1** *(pararse)* to stop, halt: *el tren se detuvo* the train stopped. **2** *(entretenerse)* to hang about, linger.

**detenidamente** *adv* carefully, thoroughly.

**detenido,-a** *adj* **1** *(parado)* held up. **2** JUR under arrest: *está detenido* he's under arrest.

▶ *nm & nf* JUR prisoner.

**detergente** *nm* detergent.

**deteriorar** *vt (estropear)* to damage, spoil; *(gastar)* to wear out.

▶ *vpr* **deteriorarse** *(estropearse)* to get damaged; *(gastarse)* to wear out.

**deterioro** *nm* **1** *(daño)* damage, deterioration; *(desgaste)* wear and tear. **2** *fig (empeoramiento)* deterioration, worsening.

**determinado,-a** *adj* **1** *(preciso)* definite, precise, certain, given, particular. **2** *(día, hora, etc)* fixed, set, appointed. **3** GRAM definite. **4** MAT determinate.

**determinante** *adj* decisive, determinant.

▶ *nm* MAT determinant.

**determinar** *vt* **1** *(decidir)* to resolve, decide, determine. **2** *(fijar)* to fix, set, appoint. **3** *(estipular)* to stipulate, specify.

▶ *vpr* **determinarse** *(decidirse)* to make up one's mind, decide.

**detestar** *vt* to detest, hate, abhor.

**detonación** *nf* detonation.

**detonador** *nm* detonator.

**detonante** *adj* detonating, explosive.

▶ *nm* **1** detonator. **2** *fig* trigger.

**detrás** *adv* **1** behind: *detrás de la puerta* behind the door. **2** *(en la parte posterior)* at the back, in the back. **3** *(después)* then, afterwards. LOC **ir detrás de** to go after.

**deuda** *nf* **1** debt. **2** REL trespass. COMP **deuda pública** national debt.

**deudor,-ra** *nm & nf* debtor.

**devaluación** *nf* devaluation.

**devaluar** *vt* to devalue.

**devoción** *nf* **1** devotion, devoutness. **2** *(afición)* devotion, dedication.

**devolver** *vt* **1** *(volver algo a un estado anterior)* to put back, return. **2** *(por correo)* to send back, return. **3** *(restituir un dinero)* to refund, return. **4** *(una visita, un cumplido, etc)* to return, pay back. **5** *fam (vomitar)* to vomit, throw up, bring up.
▶ *vi fam (vomitar)* to throw up, be sick.

**devorar** *vt* to devour.

**devuelto,-a** *nm (vómito)* vomit.

**Dg** *sím (decagramo)* decagram; *(símbolo)* Dg.

**dg** *sím (decigramo)* decigram; *(símbolo)* dg.

**día** *nm* **1** day. **2** *(con luz)* daylight, daytime: *ya es de día* it's daylight. **3** *(tiempo)* day, weather.
▶ *nm pl* **días** *(vida)* days. [LOC] **al día siguiente** the following day. ‖ **¡buenos días!** good morning! ‖ **todos los días** each day, every day. ‖ **dar los buenos días** to say good morning. ‖ **de día** during the day. ‖ **estar al día** *fig* to be up to date. ‖ **hacer buen/mal día** to be a nice/horrible day. ‖ **ser de día** to be daylight. [COMP] **día de año nuevo** New Year's Day. ‖ **día de descanso** day off. ‖ **día festivo** holiday, bank holiday. ‖ **día de paga** payday. ‖ **día entre semana** weekday.

**diabetes** *nf inv* diabetes.

**diabético,-a** *adj* diabetic.

**diablo** *nm* devil, demon. [COMP] **un diablillo** a little devil.

**diablura** *nf* mischief, naughtiness.

**diacrítico,-a** *adj* diacritic, diacritical.

**diadema** *nf* **1** *(joya)* diadem. **2** *(adorno para el pelo)* hairband.

**diafragma** *nm* **1** ANAT diaphragm. **2** *(en fotografía)* aperture. **3** MED diaphragm, cap.

**diagnóstico,-a** *nm* diagnosis.

**diagonal** *adj* diagonal. [LOC] **en diagonal** diagonally.

**diagrama** *nm* diagram. [COMP] **diagrama de flujo** INFORM flow chart.

**dial** *nm* dial.

**dialecto** *nm* dialect.

**dialogar** *vi* **1** *(conversar)* to talk, have a conversation. **2** *fig (negociar)* to negotiate, hold talks (**sobre**, on).

**diálogo** *nm* dialogue, conversation.

**diamante** *nm* diamond.

**diámetro** *nm* diameter.

**diana** *nf* DEP *(objeto)* target; *(para dardos)* dartboard; *(blanco)* bull's eye.

**diapositiva** *nf* slide.

**diario,-a** *adj* daily, everyday.
▶ *nm* **diario** **1** *(prensa)* daily, paper, daily newspaper. **2** *(íntimo)* diary, journal. [LOC] **a diario** daily, every day.

**diarrea** *nf* diarrhoea (US diarrhea).

**dibujante** *nm o nf* **1** artist, drawer. **2** *(de dibujos animados)* cartoonist. **3** TÉC *(hombre)* draughtsman (US draftsman); *(mujer)* draughtswoman (US draftswoman).

**dibujar** *vt* **1** to draw, sketch. **2** TÉC to design. **3** *fig (describir)* to describe.

**dibujo** *nm* **1** *(arte)* drawing, sketching. **2** *(imagen)* drawing. **3** *(motivo)* pattern, design. [COMP] **dibujo artístico** artistic drawing. ‖ **dibujo lineal** draughtsmanship (US draftsmanship). ‖ **dibujos animados** cartoons.

**diccionario** *nm* dictionary.

**dicho,-a** *adj* said, mentioned: *dicha casa...* the said house...; *dicho esto se marchó* having said this he left. [LOC] **dicho y hecho** no sooner said than done.

**diciembre** *nm* December.

✎ Consulta también **marzo**.

**dictado,-a** *nm* dictation.

**dictador,-ra** *nm & nf* dictator.

**dictadura** *nf* dictatorship.

**dictar** *vt* **1** to dictate. **2** JUR *(ley)* to enact, decree, announce; *(sentencia)* to pronounce, pass.

**didáctico,-a** *adj* didactic.

**diecinueve** *adj (cardinal)* nineteen; *(ordinal)* nineteenth.

▶ *nm* **1** *(número)* nineteen. **2** *(fecha)* nineteenth.

✎ Consulta también seis.

**dieciocho** *adj (cardinal)* eighteen; *(ordinal)* eighteenth.
▶ *nm* **1** *(número)* eighteen. **2** *(fecha)* eighteenth.

✎ Consulta también seis.

**dieciséis** *adj (cardinal)* sixteen; *(ordinal)* sixteenth.
▶ *nm* **1** *(número)* sixteen. **2** *(fecha)* sixteenth.

✎ Consulta también seis.

**diecisiete** *adj (cardinal)* seventeen; *(ordinal)* seventeenth.
▶ *nm* **1** *(número)* seventeen. **2** *(fecha)* seventeenth.

✎ Consulta también seis.

**diente** *nm* **1** *(gen)* tooth. **2** *(de ajo)* clove. [LOC] **echar los dientes** to teethe. ‖ **hablar entre dientes** *fig* to mumble, mutter. [COMP] **diente de leche** milk tooth.

**diéresis** *nf inv* diaeresis, dieresis.

**diesel** *adj* diesel.

**diestro,-a** *adj* **1** *lit* right. **2** *(hábil)* skilful (US skillful).

**dieta** *nf (régimen, alimentación)* diet.

**diez** *adj (cardinal)* ten; *(ordinal)* tenth.
▶ *nm* **1** *(número)* ten. **2** *(fecha)* tenth.

✎ Consulta también seis.

**diezmilésimo,-a** *adj* ten-thousandth.
▶ *nm & nf* ten-thousandth.

✎ Consulta también sexto,-a.

**diferencia** *nf* difference.

**diferenciar** *vt (distinguir)* to differentiate, distinguish (**entre**, between).
▶ *vpr* **diferenciarse** to differ, be different (**por**, because of).

**diferente** *adj* different.

**difícil** *adj* difficult, hard.

**dificultad** *nf* **1** difficulty. **2** *(obstáculo)* obstacle; *(problema)* trouble, problem.

**difunto,-a** *nm & nf* deceased.

**difusión** *nf* **1** *(de luz, calor)* diffusion. **2** *fig (de noticia, enfermedad, etc)* spreading. **3** RAD broadcast, broadcasting.

**digestión** *nf* digestion.

**digestivo,-a** *adj* digestive.

**digital** *adj* digital.

**dígito** *nm* digit.

**dignarse** *vpr* to deign (**a**, to), condescend (**a**, to).

**dignidad** *nf* **1** *(cualidad)* dignity. **2** *(cargo)* rank, office, post.

**digno,-a** *adj* **1** *(merecedor)* worthy, deserving. **2** *(respetable)* worthy, honourable (US honorable). [LOC] **digno,-a de admiración** worthy of admiration, admirable.

**dilatado,-a** *adj* **1** dilated. **2** *(vasto)* vast, extensive, large. **3** FÍS expanded.

**dilatar** *vt* **1** to dilate. **2** FÍS to expand. **3** *(prolongar)* to prolong, extend.

**diligencia** *nf* **1** *(cuidado)* diligence, care. **2** *(rapidez)* rapidity, speed. **3** *(carreta)* stagecoach.

**diluir** *vt* **1** *(un sólido)* to dissolve. **2** *(un líquido)* to dilute.
▶ *vpr* **diluirse 1** *(un sólido)* to dissolve. **2** *(un líquido)* to dilute.

**diluviar** *vi* [se emplea sólo en tercera persona del singular; no lleva sujeto] to pour with rain, pour down.

**diluvio** *nm* flood.

**dimensión** *nf* **1** [también se usa en plural con el mismo significado] dimension, size. **2** *fig (importancia)* importance.

**diminutivo,-a** *adj* diminutive.
▶ *nm* **diminutivo** diminutive.

**diminuto,-a** *adj* tiny, minute.

**dimisión** *nf* resignation.

**dimitir** *vi* to resign (**de**, from).

**Dinamarca** *nf* Denmark.

**dinamita** *nf* dynamite.

**dinastía** *nf* dynasty.

**dinero** *nm* **1** money. **2** *(fortuna)* wealth. [LOC] **andar mal/escaso,-a de dinero** to be short of money. ‖ **tirar el dinero por la ventana** to throw money down the drain. [COMP] **dinero en metálico** cash.

**dinosaurio** *nm* dinosaur.

**D**

**dioptría** *nf* dioptre (US diopter).

**dios** *nm* god.

**diosa** *nf* goddess.

**diploma** *nm* diploma.

**diplomacia** *nf* diplomacy.

**diplomático,-a** *adj* diplomatic.
▶ *nm & nf* diplomat.

**diptongo** *nm* diphthong.

**diputado,-a** *nm & nf (miembro del Congreso)* deputy, *member of the Spanish Parliament*.

**dique** *nm (muro)* dike, breakwater.

**dirección** *nf* **1** *(acción de dirigir)* management, running. **2** *(cargo)* directorship, position of manager. **3** *(sentido)* direction, way. **4** *(destino)* destination: *salió con dirección a Cádiz* he left for Cádiz. **5** *(domicilio)* address. **6** TÉC steering. COMP **calle de dirección única** one-way street.

**directivo,-a** *adj* directive, managing.
▶ *nm & nf* director, manager, board member.

**directo,-a** *adj* direct, straight.
▶ *nm* **directo** DEP straight hit. LOC **en directo** TV live.

**director,-ra** *nm & nf* **1** director, manager. **2** *(de colegio - hombre)* headmaster; *(- mujer)* headmistress. **3** *(de orquesta)* conductor. COMP **director,-ra de cine** film director.

**directorio,-a** *nm* **1** *(gobierno)* governing body. **2** *(de direcciones)* directory, guide. **3** INFORM directory.

**dirigente** *adj* leading, directing.
▶ *nm o nf* **1** leader. **2** *(de empresa)* manager.

**dirigir** *vt* **1** *(empresa)* to manage; *(negocio, escuela)* to run; *(un periódico)* to edit. **2** *(orquesta)* to conduct; *(película)* to direct. **3** *(coche)* to drive, steer; *(barco)* to steer; *(avión)* to pilot. **4** *(un partido)* to lead. **5** *(carta, protesta)* to address.
▶ *vpr* **dirigirse 1** *(ir)* to go (a, to), make one's way (a, to), make (a, for). **2** *(hablar)* to address (a, -), speak (a, to): *se dirigió a su padre* she addressed her father.

**discapacitado,-a** *adj* handicapped, disabled.

**disciplina** *nf* **1** *(conjunto de reglas)* discipline. **2** *(doctrina)* doctrine. **3** *(asignatura)* subject.

**disciplinado,-a** *adj* disciplined.

**discípulo,-a** *nm & nf* **1** *(seguidor)* disciple, follower. **2** *(alumno)* pupil, student.

**disc-jockey** *nm o nf* disc jockey, DJ.

**disco** *nm* **1** disc. **2** DEP discus. **3** *(de música)* record. **4** INFORM disk. COMP **disco duro** hard disk.

**discoteca** *nf (local)* discotheque, nightclub.

**discreción** *nf* **1** *(sensatez)* discretion, tact. **2** *(agudeza)* wit. LOC **a discreción** *(a voluntad)* at one's discretion.

**discreto,-a** *adj (prudente)* discreet, prudent, tactful.

**discriminación** *nf* discrimination. COMP **discriminación racial** racial discrimination.

**discriminar** *vt* **1** *(diferenciar)* to discriminate, distinguish. **2** *(por raza, religión, etc)* to discriminate against.

**disculpa** *nf* excuse, apology. LOC **pedir disculpas a ALGN** to apologize to SB.

**disculpar** *vt* **1** *(descargar de culpa)* to excuse: *disculpe el retraso* please excuse the delay. **2** *(perdonar)* to excuse, forgive: *¡disculpe!* excuse me!
▶ *vpr* **disculparse** to apologize (por, for), excuse OS.

**discurrir** *vi* **1** *(andar)* to walk, wander. **2** *(fluir)* to flow, run. **3** *(transcurrir)* to pass, go by. **4** *fig (reflexionar)* to think (sobre, about), ponder (sobre, on/over), meditate (sobre, on).

**discurso** *nm (conferencia)* speech.

**discusión** *nf* **1** *(charla)* discussion. **2** *(disputa)* argument.

**discutir** *vi* **1** *(examinar)* to discuss (de, -). **2** *(contender)* to argue.

**diseminar** *vt* to disseminate, scatter, spread.
▶ *vpr* **diseminarse** to spread.

**diseñador,-ra** *nm & nf* designer.

**diseñar** *vt* to design.

**diseño** *nm* design.

**disfraz** *nm* **1** *(para engañar)* disguise. **2** *(para una fiesta, etc)* fancy dress outfit, fancy dress costume.

**disfrazar** *vt (persona)* to disguise, dress up.
▸ *vpr* **disfrazarse 1** *(para engañar)* to disguise os **(de**, as). **2** *(para una fiesta, etc)* to dress up **(de**, as).

**disfrutar** *vt* **1** *(poseer)* to own, enjoy, possess; *(pensión, renta)* to receive. **2** *(aprovechar)* to make the most of.
▸ *vi* **1** *(poseer)* to enjoy **(de**, -), have **(de**, -), possess **(de**, -): *disfruta de buena salud* he enjoys good health. **2** *(gozar)* to enjoy, enjoy os: *disfruté mucho en el cine* I enjoyed myself very much at the cinema.

**disgustar** *vt* **1** *(molestar)* to displease, annoy, upset. **2** *(desagradar)* to dislike: *me disgusta ese sabor dulce* I don't like that sweet taste.
▸ *vpr* **disgustarse 1** *(enfadarse)* to get angry, get upset. **2** *(pelearse)* to quarrel **(con**, with).

**disgusto** *nm* **1** *(enfado)* displeasure, annoyance, anger. **2** *fig (pelea)* argument, quarrel. LOC **a disgusto** against one's will, reluctantly, unwillingly. ‖ **dar un disgusto** to upset. ‖ **llevarse un disgusto** to get upset.

**disimular** *vt (ocultar)* to hide, conceal.
▸ *vi* to pretend, dissemble: *no disimules* stop pretending.

**disimulo** *nm* pretence (US pretense), dissemblance.

**dislocar** *vt (sacar de lugar)* to dislocate.

**disminución** *nf* decrease, reduction.

**disminuido,-a** *adj* disabled.

**disminuir** *vt* **1** *(gen)* to decrease. **2** *(medidas, velocidad)* to reduce.
▸ *vi* **1** *(gen)* to diminish. **2** *(temperatura, precios)* to drop, fall.

**disolución** *nf* **1** *(gen)* dissolution. **2** QUÍM solution, dissolution.

**disolver** *vt (gen)* to dissolve.
▸ *vpr* **disolverse 1** *(gen)* to dissolve. **2** *fig* to be dissolved.

**dispar** *adj* unlike, different.

**disparar** *vt* **1** *(arma)* to fire; *(bala, flecha)* to shoot. **2** *(lanzar)* to hurl, throw. **3** DEP to shoot.

**disparatado,-a** *adj* absurd, foolish, ridiculous.

**disparo** *nm* **1** *(acción)* firing. **2** *(efecto)* shot. **3** DEP shot.

**dispersar** *vt (gen)* to disperse, scatter.
▸ *vpr* **dispersarse** *(gen)* to disperse, scatter.

**disperso,-a** *adj (esparcido)* scattered.

**disponer** *vt* **1** *(colocar)* to dispose, arrange, set out. **2** *(preparar)* to prepare, get ready. **3** *(ordenar)* to order, decree.
▸ *vi* **1** *(tener)* to have **(de**, -). **2** *(hacer uso)* to make use **(de**, of), have the use **(de**, of).
▸ *vpr* **disponerse** *(prepararse)* to get ready **(a**, to), prepare **(a**, to).

**disponibilidad** *nf* availability.

**disponible** *adj (gen)* available.

**dispositivo** *nm* device, gadget.

**dispuesto,-a** *adj* **1** *(decidido)* determined. **2** *(preparado)* prepared, ready, willing.

**disputa** *nf (discusión)* dispute, argument, quarrel.

**disputar** *vt* **1** *(competir)* to compete for, contend for. **2** DEP to play: *los equipos disputaron un partido amistoso* the teams played a friendly match.

**disquete** *nm* diskette, floppy disk.

**disquetera** *nf* disk drive.

**distancia** *nf* **1** distance. **2** *fig (diferencia)* difference, gap. LOC **a distancia** from a distance: *lo vimos a distancia* we saw it from a distance.

**distanciar** *vt* to distance, separate.
▸ *vpr* **distanciarse** to move away, become separated.

**distante** *adj* **1** *(en el espacio)* distant, far; *(en el tiempo)* distant, remote. **2** *fig* distant.

**distinción** *nf* **1** *(gen)* distinction. **2** *(elegancia)* distinction, elegance, refinement.

**distinguido,-a** *adj* **1** distinguished. **2** *(elegante)* elegant.

**distinguir** vt 1 (diferenciar) to distinguish. 2 (caracterizar) to mark, distinguish. 3 (ver) to see, make out.
 ▸ vpr **distinguirse** (destacar) to stand out, distinguish os.

**distinto,-a** adj (diferente) different.
 ▸ adj vpr **distintos,-as** various, several.

**distracción** nf 1 (divertimiento) amusement, pastime, recreation, entertainment. 2 (despiste) distraction, absent-mindedness.

**distraer** vt 1 (divertir) to amuse, entertain. 2 (atención) to distract.
 ▸ vpr **distraerse 1** (divertirse) to amuse os, enjoy os. 2 (despistarse) to get distracted, be inattentive, be absent-minded .

**distraído,-a** adj 1 (desatento) absent-minded. 2 (entretenido) entertaining, fun.

**distribuir** vt 1 (repartir) to distribute. 2 (correo) to deliver; (trabajo) to share, allot.

**distrito** nm district.

**disturbio** nm disturbance, riot.

**diurno,-a** adj daily, daytime.

**divagar** vi to digress, ramble.

**diván** nm divan, couch.

**divergente** adj divergent, diverging.

**divergir** vi to diverge.

**diversidad** nf diversity, variety.

**diversificar** vt to diversify, vary.

**diversión** nf fun, amusement, entertainment.

**diverso,-a** adj different.
 ▸ adj vpr **diversos,-as** several, various.

**divertido,-a** adj 1 (gracioso) funny, amusing. 2 (entretenido) fun, entertaining, enjoyable.

**divertir** vt to amuse, entertain.
 ▸ vpr **divertirse** to enjoy os, have a good time: ¡diviértete! enjoy yourself!

**dividir** vt 1 to divide. 2 (separar) to divide, separate: el río divide las dos comarcas the river separates the two counties. 3 (repartir) to divide, split.
 ▸ vpr **dividirse** (separarse) to divide, split up.

**divino,-a** adj divine.

**divisible** adj 1 dividable. 2 MAT divisible.

**división** nf 1 división. 2 fig division, divergence.

**divisor** nm 1 divider. 2 MAT divisor.
 COMP máximo común divisor MAT highest common factor, (US highest common denominator). ∎ mínimo común divisor MAT lowest common factor, (US lowest common denominator) .

**divo,-a** nm & nf star.

**divorciado,-a** adj divorced.
 ▸ nm & nf (hombre) divorcé; (mujer) divorcée.

**divorciar** vt to divorce.
 ▸ vpr **divorciarse** to get divorced (de, from).

**divorcio** nm divorce.

**divulgar** vt 1 (difundir) to divulge, spread, disclose. 2 (por radio) to broadcast. 3 (propagar) to popularize.
 ▸ vpr **divulgarse** to become known, spread.

**Djibouti** nm Djibouti, Jibouti.

**dl** sím (decilitro) decilitre (US deciliter); (símbolo) dl.

**Dl** sím (decalitro) decalitre (US decaliter); (símbolo) Dl.

**dm** sím (decímetro) decimetre (US decimeter); (símbolo) dm.

**Dm** sím (decámetro) decametre (US decameter); (símbolo) Dm.

**do** nm (de solfa) doh, do; (de escala diatónica) C.

**dobladillo** nm 1 (de vestido, etc) hem. 2 (de pantalones) turn-up, US cuff.

**doblaje** nm dubbing.

**doblar** vt 1 (duplicar) to double: le doblo la edad I'm twice as old as she is. 2 (plegar) to fold. 3 (torcer) to bend: doblar un dedo to bend a finger. 4 (esquina) to turn, go round. 5 (película) to dub.
 ▸ vpr **doblarse** (plegarse) to fold.

**doble** adj 1 double. 2 (nacionalidad) dual.
 ▸ nm 1 double: tiene el doble que yo he's got twice as much as I have. 2 (duplicado)

duplicate. LOC **ver doble** to see double.

▶ *nm o nf* CINE stand-in, double; *(hombre)* stunt man; *(mujer)* stunt woman.

▶ *adv* double.

▶ *nm pl* **dobles** *(tenis)* doubles.

**doce** *adj (cardinal)* twelve; *(ordinal)* twelfth.

▶ *nm* **1** *(número)* twelve. **2** *(fecha)* twelfth.

✎ Consulta también **seis**.

**docena** *nf* dozen. LOC **a docenas** COM by the dozen.

**dócil** *adj* docile, obedient.

**doctor,-ra** *nm & nf* doctor.

**doctrina** *nf* **1** doctrine. **2** *(enseñanza)* teachings *pl*.

**documentación** *nf* **1** documentation, documents *pl*. **2** *(para identificar)* papers *pl*, identification.

**documental** *adj* documentary.

▶ *nm* documentary.

**documento** *nm* document.

**dodecaedro** *nm* dodecahedron.

**dodecasílabo,-a** *nm* dodecasyllable, Alexandrine.

**dólar** *nm* dollar.

**doler** *vi* **1** to ache, hurt. **2** *(afligir)* to distress, sadden, upset, hurt: *me duele tal pobreza* such poverty distresses me. **3** *(sentir)* to be sorry, be sad: *me duele habérselo dicho* I'm sorry I told her about it.

**dolido,-a** *adj fig* hurt.

**dolor** *nm* **1** pain, ache. **2** *fig* pain, sorrow, grief. COMP **dolor de cabeza** headache.

**dolorido,-a** *adj* sore, aching.

**doloroso,-a** *adj* **1** painful. **2** *fig* painful, distressing.

**domador,-ra** *nm & nf* tamer; *(de caballos)* horse breaker.

**domar** *vt* **1** to tame; *(caballos)* to break in. **2** *fig* to tame, control.

**domesticar** *vt* **1** to domesticate, tame. **2** *(adiestrar)* to train. **3** *fig* to subdue.

**doméstico,-a** *adj* domestic.

**domicilio** *nm* **1** residence, home, abode. **2** *(dirección)* address.

**dominante** *adj* dominant, dominating.

**dominar** *vt* **1** *(tener bajo dominio)* to dominate. **2** *(conocer a fondo)* to master: *domina el inglés* she has a good command of English.

▶ *vi* **1** *(ser superior)* to dominate. **2** *(destacar)* to stand out: *domina mucho el rojo* red is the predominant colour. **3** *(predominar)* to predominate.

▶ *vpr* **dominarse** *(controlarse)* to control OS, restrain OS.

**domingo** *nm* Sunday.

✎ Consulta también **jueves**.

**Dominica** *nf* Dominica.

**dominicano,-a** *adj* Dominican.

▶ *nm & nf* Dominican. COMP **República Dominicana** Dominican Republic.

**dominio** *nm* **1** *(soberanía)* dominion. **2** *(poder)* power, control. **3** *(supremacía)* supremacy. **4** *(de conocimientos)* mastery, good knowledge; *(de un idioma)* good command. **5** *(territorio)* domain. **6** INFORM domain.

**dominó** *nm* **1** *(juego)* dominoes *pl*. **2** *(fichas)* set of dominoes.

**don¹** *nm* *(talento)* talent, natural gift.

**don²** *nm* Mr: *Señor Don Juan Pérez* Mr Juan Pérez.

**donante** *nm o nf* donor. COMP **donante de sangre** blood donor.

**donar** *vt fml* to donate, give.

**donativo** *nm* donation.

**donde** *adv* where, in which. LOC **de donde / desde donde** from where, whence.

**dónde** *pron* where: *¿dónde está?* where is it?; *no sé dónde está* I don't know where it is; *¿a dónde va?* where is he going?; *¿hasta dónde?* how far?

**dondequiera** *adv (en cualquier parte)* anywhere; *(en todas partes)* everywhere: *dondequiera que esté lo encontraremos* wherever he is we'll find him.

**dónut®** *nm* doughnut.

**doña** *nf* Mrs: *Doña Elena Suárez* Mrs Elena Suárez.

**dorado,-a** *adj* golden.

**dormido,-a** *adj* **1** asleep. **2** *(soñoliento)* sleepy: *tengo el brazo dormido* my arm has gone numb, my arm has gone to sleep. LOC **quedarse dormido,-a 1** *(dormir)* to fall asleep. **2** *(dormirse más de la cuenta)* to oversleep.

**dormir** *vi* **1** to sleep: *tengo ganas de dormir* I feel sleepy. **2** *(pernoctar)* to spend the night.
▶ *vt* to put to sleep.
▶ *vpr* **dormirse 1** to fall asleep, nod off. **2** *fig* to go to sleep: *se me ha dormido el pie* my foot has gone to sleep. LOC **¡a dormir!** to bed! ▌ **dormir como un lirón** *fam* to sleep like a log. ▌ **dormir la siesta** to have a nap.

**dormitorio** *nm* **1** *(en una casa)* bedroom. **2** *(colectivo)* dormitory.

**dorsal** *adj* **1** dorsal, back. **2** LING dorsal.
▶ *nm* DEP number.

**dorso** *nm* back, reverse. COMP **dorso de la mano** back of the hand.

**dos** *adj (cardinal)* two; *(ordinal)* second: *entre ellas dos* between the two of them.
▶ *nm (número)* two; *(fecha)* second. LOC **cada dos por tres** *fam* every five minutes. COMP **dos veces** twice: *es dos veces mayor que su hermana* she's twice as old as her sister.

✎ Consulta también seis.

**doscientos,-as** *adj (numeral)* two hundred; *(cardinal)* two-hundredth.
▶ *nm & nf* two hundred.

✎ Consulta también seis.

**dosificar** *vt* **1** *(gen)* to dose. **2** *(esfuerzos, etc)* to measure.

**dosis** *nf inv* dose.

**dotado,-a** *adj* **1** *(equipado)* equipped, provided: *está dotado con airbag* it's equipped with an airbag. **2** *(con dotes)* gifted: *está muy dotado para las matemáticas* he has a talent for mathematics.

**dotar** *vt* **1** *(proveer de personal)* to staff (de, with); *(de material)* to equip (de, with). **2** *(bienes, dinero)* to assign. **3** *fig (dones y cualidades)* to endow (de,

with), provide (de, with): *la naturaleza la dotó de un sexto sentido* nature endowed her with a sixth sense.

**dragón** *nm* **1** *(reptil)* flying dragon. **2** *(animal fabuloso)* dragon.

**drama** *nm* drama.

**dramático,-a** *adj* dramatic.

**drenar** *vt* to drain.

**drive** *nm* drive.

**droga** *nf* **1** drug. **2** *fig (cosa desagradable)* nuisance. COMP **droga blanda/dura** soft/hard drug.

**drogadicto,-a** *nm & nf* drug addict.

**drogar** *vt* to drug.
▶ *vpr* **drogarse** to take drugs.

**droguería** *nf* hardware shop.

**dromedario** *nm* dromedary.

**dualidad** *nf* duality.

**ducentésimo,-a** *adj* two-hundredth.
▶ *nm & nf* two-hundredth.

**ducha** *nf* shower. LOC **darse/tomar una ducha** to take a shower, have a shower.

**duchar** *vt* to give a shower.
▶ *vpr* **ducharse** to take a shower, have a shower.

**duda** *nf* doubt. LOC **no hay duda** there is no doubt. ▌ **salir de dudas** to shed one's doubts. ▌ **sin duda** no doubt, without a doubt.

**dudar** *vi* **1** to doubt, have doubts. **2** *(titubear)* to hesitate: *dudo entre quedarme o marcharme* I'm not sure whether to stay or leave.
▶ *vt* to doubt: *lo dudo* I doubt it. LOC **dudar de** ALGN to doubt SB, mistrust SB.

**dudoso,-a** *adj* **1** *(incierto)* doubtful, uncertain. **2** *(vacilante)* hesitant, undecided. **3** *(poco seguro)* questionable.

**duende** *nm (espíritu travieso)* goblin, elf.

**dueño,-a** *nm & nf (propietario)* owner: *¿quién es la dueña?* who is the owner? **2** *(de casa, piso - hombre)* landlord; *(mujer)* landlady. LOC **ser dueño,-a de sí mismo,-a** to be self-possessed.

**dulce** *adj* **1** *(gen)* sweet. **2** *fig* soft, gentle.

▶ *nm* CULIN *(caramelo)* sweet; *(pastel)* cake. COMP **dulce de membrillo** quince jelly.

**dulzura** *nf* **1** sweetness. **2** *fig* softness, gentleness, sweetness.

**duna** *nf* dune.

**dúo** *nm* duet.

**duodécimo,-a** *adj* twelfth.
▶ *nm & nf* twelfth.

✎ Consulta también **sexto,-a.**

**duodeno** *nm* duodenum.

**duplicar** *vt (gen)* to duplicate; *(cantidad)* to double.
▶ *vpr* **duplicarse** to double.

**duque** *nm* duke.

**duquesa** *nf* duchess.

**duración** *nf* **1** duration, length: *¿cuál es la duración de la obra?* how long is the play? **2** *(coche, máquina, etc)* life. LOC **de larga duración 1** *(periodo de tiempo)* long, long-term. **2** *(bombilla, etc)* long-life.

**duradero,-a** *adj* durable, lasting.

**duramente** *adv* **1** *(con dificultad)* hard. **2** *(con severidad)* harshly.

**durante** *adv* during, in, for: *viví allí durante un año* I lived there for a year.

**durar** *vi* **1** to last, go on for: *la película duró tres horas* the film went on for three hours. **2** *(ropa, calzado)* to wear well, last: *ese abrigo le duró mucho* he got a lot of wear out of that coat.

**durazno** *nm* **1** *(fruto)* peach. **2** *(árbol)* peach tree.

**dureza** *nf* **1** hardness, toughness. **2** *fig (de carácter)* toughness, harshness, severity. **3** *(callosidad)* corn.

**duro,-a** *adj* **1** hard. **2** *(carne)* tough; *(pan)* stale. **3** *(difícil)* hard, difficult.
▶ *nm* **duro** *(antiguamente)* five pesetas; *(moneda)* five-peseta coin.
▶ *adv* hard: *dale duro* hit him hard.

**DVD** *nm* (Disco Versátil Digital) DVD.

**D**

# E

**E, e** *nf (la letra)* E, e.
**e** *conj* and.

> 📎 Usado en vez de y antes de palabras que empiezan por i o hi: *compramos manzanas e higos* we bought some apples and figs.

**EAU** *abrev* (Emiratos Árabes Unidos) United Arab Emirates; *(abreviatura)* UAE.
**ebanista** *nm o nf* cabinet-maker.
**ebullición** *nf (hervor)* boil, boiling.
**echado,-a** *adj (tumbado)* lying down.
**echar** *vt* **1** *(lanzar)* to throw. **2** *(dejar caer)* to put, drop. **3** *(líquido)* to pour; *(comida)* to give; *(sal)* to add, put in. **4** *(carta)* to post, US mail. **5** *(expulsar)* to throw out: *lo han echado del cine* he was thrown out of the cinema. **6** *(despedir de empleo)* to sack, dismiss, fire. **7** *(brotar, salir - plantas)* to sprout; *(- dientes)* to cut; *(- pelo)* to grow. **8** *(decir)* to tell. **9** *(emanar)* to give out, give off: *la caja de fusibles echa chispas* sparks are coming out of the fuse box. **10** *(suponer, calcular)* to guess: *yo le echo 40* I think she's 40. **11** *(poner, aplicar)* to put on, apply. **12** *(llave)* to lock, turn; *(cerrojo)* to bolt, fasten. **13** *fam (en el cine, teatro)* to show, put on: *echan una buena película en la tele* there's a good film on TV.
▶ *vi* **1 echar a** + *inf (empezar)* to begin to: *echó a correr* she ran off. **2 echar de** + *inf (dar)*: *echar de comer* to feed.
▶ *vpr* **echarse 1** *(arrojarse)* to throw os. **2** *(tenderse)* to lie down. **3** *(ponerse)* to put on. **4** *(novio, novia)* to get os. **5 echarse a** + *inf (empezar)* to begin to: *se echó a reír* he burst out laughing.

**eclipsar** *vt* **1** *(astro)* to eclipse. **2** *fig* to eclipse, outshine.
**eclipse** *nm* eclipse.
**eco** *nm* echo.
**ecografía** *nf* ultrasound scan.
**ecología** *nf* ecology.
**ecológico,-a** *adj* ecological.
**ecologista** *adj* ecological.
▶ *nm o nf* ecologist.
**economato** *nm* company store.
**economía** *nf* **1** *(administración)* economy. **2** *(ciencia)* economics. **3** *(ahorro)* economy, saving.
**económico,-a** *adj* **1** *(gen)* economic. **2** *(barato)* cheap, economical, inexpensive. COMP **crisis económica** economic crisis, recession.
**economista** *nm o nf* economist.
**economizar** *vt (ahorrar)* to economize, save.
▶ *vi* to economize, save.
**ecosistema** *nm* ecosystem.
**ecuación** *nf* equation. COMP **ecuación de primer grado** simple equation. ‖ **ecuación de segundo grado** quadratic equation.
**ecuador** *nm* GEOG equator.
**Ecuador** *nm* Ecuador.
**ecuatoguineano,-a** *adj* of Equatorial Guinea, from Equatorial Guinea.
▶ *nm & nf* person from Equatorial Guinea, inhabitant of Equatorial Guinea.
**ecuatorial** *adj* equatorial.
**ecuatoriano,-a** *adj* Ecuadorian.
▶ *nm & nf* Ecuadorian.
**ecuestre** *adj* equestrian.
**edad** *nf* **1** age. **2** *(tiempo, época)* time, period.
**edén** *nm* **1** Eden. **2** *fig* paradise, heaven.

**edición** *nf* **1** *(ejemplares)* edition. **2** *(publicación)* publication. **3** INFORM editing.

**edificar** *vt (construir)* to build, construct.

**edificio** *nm* building.

**edil,-la** *nm & nf (concejal)* town councillor.
  ▶ *nm* **edil** *(magistrado romano)* aedile.

**edredón** *nm* eiderdown, US comforter.

**educación** *nf* **1** *(preparación)* education. **2** *(crianza)* upbringing, breeding. **3** *(modales)* manners *pl*, politeness.

**educado,-a** *adj* polite.

**educar** *vt* **1** *(enseñar)* to educate, teach. **2** *(criar)* to bring up. **3** *(en la cortesía, etc)* to teach manners.

**educativo,-a** *adj* educational: *sistema educativo* education system.

**edulcorar** *vt* **1** to sweeten. **2** *fig* to soften, alleviate.

**EE UU** *abrev (Estados Unidos)* the United States of America; *(abreviatura)* USA.

**efe** *nf* name of the letter **f**.

**efectivamente** *adv* **1** *(realmente)* in fact, actually. **2** *(de verdad)* indeed.

**efectivo,-a** *adj (que tiene efecto)* effective.
  ▶ *nm* **efectivo** *(dinero)* cash.

**efecto** *nm* **1** *(resultado)* effect, result, end. **2** *(impresión)* impression: *la escena le hizo un gran efecto* the scene made a great impression on her. **3** DEP spin: *dio efecto a la pelota* he put some spin on the ball.

**efectuar** *vt* **1** *(gen)* to carry out, perform, make, do. **2** *(pago)* to make; *(pedido)* to place. **3** *(suma, etc)* to do. **4** *(viaje, visita, etc)* to make.

**efervescente** *adj* **1** *(gen)* effervescent. **2** *(bebida)* sparkling, fizzy. **3** *(pastilla)* soluble.

**eficacia** *nf* **1** *(persona)* efficiency, effectiveness; *(cosas)* efficacy, effectiveness. **2** *(rendimiento)* efficiency.

**eficaz** *adj* **1** *(eficiente)* efficient. **2** *(cosa)* efficacious, effective. **3** *(que produce rendimiento)* efficient.

**eficiente** *adj* efficient.

**EGB** *abrev* EDUC *(Enseñanza General Básica)* ≈ *former Primary School Education.*

**egipcio,-a** *adj* Egyptian.
  ▶ *nm & nf (persona)* Egyptian.
  ▶ *nm* **egipcio** *(idioma)* Egyptian.

**Egipto** *nm* Egypt.

**egoísmo** *nm* selfishness, egoism.

**egoísta** *adj* selfish, egoistic, egoistical.
  ▶ *nm o nf* egoist, selfish person.

**eje** *nm* **1** *(línea, recta)* axis. **2** TÉC shaft, spindle. **3** AUTO axle.

**ejecución** *nf* **1** *(de una orden, etc)* carrying out, execution. **2** MÚS performance. **3** *(ajusticiamiento)* execution.

**ejecutar** *vt* **1** *(una orden, etc)* to carry out. **2** MÚS to perform, play. **3** *(ajusticiar)* to execute. **4** INFORM to run.

**ejecutivo,-a** *adj* executive.
  ▶ *nm & nf* executive.
  ▶ *nm* **el ejecutivo** *(gobierno)* the government. COMP **poder ejecutivo** the executive.

**ejemplar** *nm (copia)* copy, number, issue.

**ejemplo** *nm* **1** example. **2** *(modelo)* model. LOC **dar ejemplo** to set an example. ∎ **por ejemplo** for example, for instance.

**ejercer** *vt* **1** *(profesión, etc)* to practise (US practice), be in practice as. **2** *(influencia)* to exert.

**ejercicio** *nm* **1** *(de profesión)* practice; *(de derecho)* use, exercise; *(de función)* performance. **2** EDUC exercise; *(examen)* test; *(pregunta de examen)* question; *(deberes)* homework. **3** DEP exercise.

**ejército** *nm* army.

**el** *determinante* **1** the: *el agua* water. **2 el de** the one: *el de hoy* today's. **3 el que** *(persona - sujeto)* the one who; *(- objeto)* the one, the one that, the one whom: *el que vi* the one I saw. **4** *(cosa)* the one, the one that, the one which: *el que me diste* the one (that) you gave me.

**él** *pron* **1** *(sujeto - persona)* he; *(- cosa, animal)* it: *él vive aquí* he lives here. **2** *(objeto - persona)* him; *(- cosa, animal)* it: *comió con él* she had lunch with him. LOC **de él** *(posesivo)* his: *es de él* it's his. ∎ **él mismo** himself.

**elaborar** *vt* **1** *(producto)* to make, manufacture, produce. **2** *(madera, metal, etc)* to work.

**elástico,-a** *adj* elastic.
  ▶ *nm* **elástico** elastic.

**ele** *nf* name of the letter l.

**elección** *nf* **1** *(nombramiento)* election. **2** *(opción)* choice: *lo dejamos a tu elección* we'll leave it up to you.
► *nf pl* **elecciones** elections.

**electricidad** *nf* electricity.

**electricista** *nm o nf* electrician.

**eléctrico,-a** *adj* electric, electrical.

**electrodoméstico** *nm* electrical appliance.

**electrón** *nm* electron.

**electrónica** *nf* electronics.

**electrónico,-a** *adj* electronic.

**elefante,-a** *nm & nf (macho)* elephant; *(hembra)* cow elephant, female elephant. COMP **elefante marino** elephant seal.

**elegancia** *nf* elegance.

**elegante** *adj* elegant, smart, stylish.

**elegir** *vt* **1** *(escoger)* to choose. **2** POL to elect.

**elemental** *adj* **1** *(del elemento)* elemental. **2** *(obvio)* elementary, basic.

**elemento** *nm* **1** *(gen)* element. **2** *(parte)* component, part. **3** *(individuo)* type, sort. LOC **¡menudo elemento!** *fam* he's a right one!

**elevación** *nf* **1** *(de terreno)* elevation, rise. **2** *(precios)* rise, raising, increasing; *(voz, tono)* raising; *(peso)* raising, lifting. **3** MAT raising.

**elevado,-a** *adj (gen)* high. LOC **elevado,-a a** MAT raised to: *elevado a la quinta potencia* raised to the power of five; *elevado al cubo* cubed.

**elevalunas** *nm inv* window winder. COMP **elevalunas eléctrico** electric window.

**elevar** *vt* **1** *(peso, etc)* to elevate, raise, lift. **2** *(precios)* to raise, increase, put up; *(tono, voz)* to raise. **3** MAT to raise.
► *vpr* **elevarse 1** *(subir)* to rise (up): *el humo se elevaba* the smoke was rising up. **2** *(alcanzar)* to reach: *se eleva hasta el techo* it reaches the ceiling.

**eliminación** *nf* elimination.

**eliminar** *vt* **1** *(gen)* to eliminate, exclude. **2** *(esperanzas, miedos, etc)* to get rid of, cast aside. **3** *fam (matar)* to kill, eliminate.

**eliminatoria** *nf* heat, qualifying round.

**eliminatorio,-a** *adj* eliminatory.

**elipse** *nf* ellipse.

**elíptico,-a** *adj* elliptic, elliptical.

**elite** *nf* elite.

**ella** *pron* **1** *(sujeto - persona)* she; *(- cosa, animal)* it. **2** *(objeto - persona)* her; *(- cosa, animal)* it: *vino con ella* he came with her.

**elle** *nf* name of the digraph ll.

**ello** *pron* it: *no me digas nada de ello* don't tell me anything about it.

**ellos,-as** *pron* **1** *(sujeto)* they. **2** *(objeto)* them: *vino con ellos* she came with them. LOC **de ellos,-as** theirs: *el coche es de ellos* the car is theirs. **▮ ellos,-as mismos,-as** themselves.

**elocuente** *adj* eloquent.

**elogiar** *vt* to praise, eulogize.

**elogio** *nm* praise, eulogy.

**eludir** *vt* **1** *(responsabilidad, justicia, etc)* to evade. **2** *(pregunta)* to avoid, evade; *(persona)* to avoid.

**emanar** *vi* **1** *(olor, etc)* to emanate. **2** *(derivar)* to derive (de, from), come (de, from).

**emancipar** *vt* to emancipate, free.
► *vpr* **emanciparse** to become emancipated, become free.

**embajada** *nf (edificio)* embassy.

**embajador,-ra** *nm & nf* ambassador.

**embalar** *vt (empaquetar)* to pack, wrap.
► *vpr* **embalarse** *(acelerar)* to speed up.

**embalse** *nm* **1** *(acción)* damming. **2** *(presa)* dam, reservoir.

**embarazada** *adj-nf* pregnant woman.

**embarazo** *nm (preñez)* pregnancy.

**embarazoso,-a** *adj* embarrassing.

**embarcación** *nf (nave)* boat, vessel, craft.

**embarcadero** *nm* pier, jetty, quay.

**embarcar** *vt (personas)* to embark, put on board; *(mercancías)* to load.
► *vpr* **embarcarse** *(en barco)* to embark, go on board; *(en avión)* to board.

**embargar** *vt* **1** JUR to seize, sequestrate, impound. **2** *(emociones)* to overcome.

**embargo** *nm (de bienes)* seizure of property, sequestration. LOC **sin embargo** nevertheless, however.

**embarque** *nm (de personas)* boarding; *(de mercancías)* loading.

**embaucar** *vt* to deceive, trick, dupe, cheat, swindle.

**embelesar** *vt* to charm, delight, fascinate.

**embellecer** *vt* to make beautiful, beautify.
▶ *vpr* **embellecerse** to make os beautiful, beautify os.

**embestir** *vt (toro)* to charge.

**émbolo** *nm* TÉC piston; *(de cafetera)* plunger.

**emborrachar** *vt* to make drunk.
▶ *vpr* **emborracharse** to get drunk.

**emboscada** *nf* ambush. LOC **tender una emboscada** to lay an ambush.

**embotellamiento** *nm* AUTO *fig* traffic jam.

**embrague** *nm* clutch.

**embrión** *nm* **1** embryo. **2** *fig (idea, etc)* beginnings *pl*, embryo.

**embrujar** *vt* **1** *(persona)* to bewitch; *(lugar)* to haunt. **2** *fig (fascinar)* to bewitch, enchant.

**embrujo** *nm* **1** spell, charm. **2** *fig (fascinación)* fascination, attraction.

**embudo** *nm* funnel.

**embuste** *nm (mentira)* lie; *(engaño)* trick.

**embustero,-a** *nm & nf* liar.

**embutido** *nm (alimento)* processed cold meat, cold cut.

**eme** *nf name of the letter* m.

**emergencia** *nf* **1** *(imprevisto)* emergency. **2** *(salida)* emergence. LOC **en caso de emergencia** in case of emergency.

**emerger** *vi* to emerge.

**emigración** *nf* **1** emigration. **2** *(aves, pueblo)* migration.

**emigrante** *nm o nf* emigrant.

**emigrar** *vi* to emigrate; *(aves, pueblo)* to migrate.

**emirato** *nm* emirate. COMP **Emiratos Árabes Unidos** United Arab Emirates.

**emisión** *nf* **1** *(gen)* emission. **2** *(bonos, sellos, monedas)* issue. **3** RAD TV *(programa)* broadcast; *(transmisión)* transmission.

**emisora** *nf* radio station.

**emitir** *vt* **1** *(sonido, luz)* to emit; *(olor)* to give off. **2** *(manifestar)* to express. **3** *(bonos, monedas, sellos)* to issue. **4** RAD TV to broadcast, transmit.
▶ *vi* RAD TV to transmit.

**emoción** *nf* **1** *(sentimiento)* emotion, feeling. **2** *(excitación)* excitement.

**emocionado,-a** *adj* (deeply) moved, (deeply) touched.

**emocionante** *adj* **1** *(conmovedor)* moving, touching. **2** *(excitante)* exciting, thrilling.

**emocionar** *vt* **1** *(conmover)* to move, touch. **2** *(excitar)* to excite, thrill.
▶ *vpr* **emocionarse 1** *(conmoverse)* to be moved, be touched. **2** *(excitarse)* to get excited.

**emoticono** *nm* INFORM emoticon.

**emotivo,-a** *adj (persona)* emotional; *(acto, etc)* moving, touching; *(palabras)* emotive.

**empachar** *vt (comer demasiado)* to give indigestion.
▶ *vpr* **empacharse** *(de comer)* to have indigestion, get indigestion.

**empacho** *nm (indigestión)* indigestion.

**empalagoso,-a** *adj* **1** *(dulces)* too sweet, sickly. **2** *fig (persona)* sickly sweet, cloying.

**empalmar** *vt (unir)* to join, connect.
▶ *vi* **1** *(enlazar)* to join, connect. **2** *(seguir)* to follow on from.

**empanada** *nf* pasty, pie.

**empanadilla** *nf* pasty.

**empañar** *vt (cristal)* to steam up.
▶ *vpr* **empañarse** *(cristal)* to steam up.

**empapar** *vt* **1** *(humedecer)* to soak; *(penetrar)* to soak, drench. **2** *(absorber)* to soak up.

▶ *vpr* **empaparse 1** *(humedecerse)* to get soaked. **2** *(persona)* to get soaked, get drenched, be soaked, be drenched.

**empapelar** *vt (una pared)* to wallpaper.

**empaquetar** *vt (hacer paquetes)* to pack (up), wrap (up).

**empastar** *vt (diente)* to fill.

**empaste** *nm (de diente)* filling.

**empatar** *vt* to draw.

**empate** *nm (en fútbol, rugby)* draw, US tie; *(en carrera, votación)* tie: *el gol del empate* the equalizer.

**empedrado,-a** *adj (calle)* cobbled.
▶ *nm* **empedrado 1** *(adoquines)* cobbles *pl*, cobblestones *pl*. **2** *(acción)* cobbling, paving.

**empeine** *nm (pie, zapato)* instep.

**empeñar** *vt* **1** *(objetos)* to pawn, US hock. **2** *(palabra)* to pledge.
▶ *vpr* **empeñarse 1** *(endeudarse)* to get into debt. **2** *(insistir)* to insist (en, on).

**empeño** *nm (insistencia)* determination.

**empeorar** *vi* to worsen, deteriorate.

**emperador** *nm* **1** emperor. **2** *(pez)* swordfish.

**emperatriz** *nf* empress.

**empezar** *vt* to begin, start.

**empinado,-a** *adj (alto)* very high.

**emplazar** *vt (situar)* to locate, place, situate.

**empleado,-a** *nm & nf* employee, clerk.

**emplear** *vt* **1** *(dar empleo)* to employ. **2** *(usar)* to use: *empleó un cuchillo* he used a knife. **3** *(dinero)* to spend. **4** *(tiempo)* to invest, spend.
▶ *vpr* **emplearse 1** *(usarse)* to be used: *este tipo de ordenador ya no se emplea* this type of computer is no longer used. **2** *(tener trabajo)* to be employed.

**empleo** *nm* **1** *(trabajo)* occupation, job. **2** POL. employment. **3** *(uso)* use.

**empobrecer** *vi* to impoverish.
▶ *vpr* **empobrecerse** to become poor, become impoverished.

**empollar** *vt* **1** *(huevos)* to hatch. **2** *fam (estudiar)* to swot, swot up, US bone up on.

**empollón,-ona** *nm & nf fam pey* swot.

**emprendedor,-ra** *adj* enterprising, resourceful.

**emprender** *vt* **1** *(gen)* to start. **2** *(misión)* to tackle; *(viaje)* to set off on; *(tarea)* to undertake. LOC **emprender el vuelo** to take flight.

**empresa** *nf (compañía)* firm, company. COMP **empresa multinacional** multinational company.

**empresario,-a** *nm & nf (gen)* employer, manager; *(hombre)* businessman, manager; *(mujer)* businesswoman, manageress.

**empujar** *vt* to push, shove, thrust.

**empuje** *nm* **1** push, thrust, drive. **2** *fig (energía)* energy, drive.

**empujón** *nm* push, shove. LOC **abrirse paso a empujones** to push one's way through.

**en** *prep* **1** *(lugar - gen)* in, at: *en Valencia* in Valencia; *en casa* at home; *en el trabajo* at work. **2** *(- en el interior)* in, inside: *en el cajón* in the drawer. **3** *(lugar - sobre)* on: *en la mesa* on the table. **4** *(año, mes, estación)* in; *(día)* on; *(época, momento)* at: *en 1994* in 1994; *en aquel momento* at that moment. **5** *(dirección)* into: *entró en su casa* he went into his house. **6** *(transporte)* by: *ir en coche* to go by car. **7** *(tema, materia)* at, in: *experto en economía* expert in economics; *bueno en ajedrez* good at chess. **8** *(modo, manera)* in: *en inglés* in English. LOC **en cuanto** as soon as. ▮ **en camino** on the way.

**enajenar** *vt (propiedad)* to alienate.

**enamorado,-a** *nm & nf* lover, sweetheart.

**enamoramiento** *nm* infatuation, falling in love.

**enamorar** *vt* to win the heart of.
▶ *vpr* **enamorarse** to fall in love (de, with).

**enano,-a** *adj* dwarf.
▶ *nm & nf* dwarf.

**encabezamiento** *nm* **1** *(gen)* heading. **2** *(fórmula)* form of address.

**encabezar** *vt* **1** *(carta, lista)* to head. **2** *(acaudillar)* to lead. **3** DEP *(carrera)* to lead; *(clasificación)* to head, top.

**encadenar** *vt* **1** *(poner cadenas)* to chain (up). **2** *fig (enlazar)* to connect, link up.

**encajar** *vt* **1** *(ajustar)* to fit. **2** *(recibir)* to take, withstand. **3** *(soportar)* to bear. **4** *(indirecta, comentario)* to get in. **5** *(dar un golpe)* to land: *le encajó un golpe* he landed him a blow. **6** TÉC to gear.

**encaje** *nm* **1** *(acto)* fit, fitting. **2** *(hueco)* socket; *(caja)* housing. **3** COST lace.

**encalar** *vt* to whitewash.

**encallar** *vi* **1** MAR to run aground. **2** *fig* to flounder, fail.

**encaminar** *vt* *(guiar, orientar)* to direct, guide, set on the right road, put on the right road.
▶ *vpr* **encaminarse** *(dirigirse)* to head (a, for) (hacia, towards). LOC **estar bien encaminado,-a** to be on the right track.

**encantador,-ra** *adj* enchanting, charming, delightful.

**encantar** *vt* **1** *(hechizar)* to cast a spell on, bewitch. **2** *fam (gustar)* to delight, love.

**encanto** *nm* **1** *(hechizo)* spell, enchantment, charm. **2** *fig (cosa)* delight, enchantment; *(persona)* charm.

**encapricharse** *vpr* **1** *(empeñarse)* to set one's mind (con/en, to). **2** *(encariñarse)* to take a fancy (con, to).

**encarar** *vt* *(afrontar)* to face, face up to, confront.
▶ *vpr* **encararse 1** *(situación, problema)* to face up (a/con, to). **2** *(persona)* to stand up (a/con, to).

**encarcelar** *vt* to imprison.

**encarecer** *vt* *(precios)* to put up the price of.

**encargado,-a** *adj* in charge.
▶ *nm & nf* **1** COM *(hombre)* manager; *(mujer)* manageress. **2** *(empleado)* person in charge.

**encargar** *vt* **1** *(encomendar)* to entrust, put in charge of. **2** *(recomendar)* to recommend, advise. **3** COM *(pedir)* to order, place an order for: *encargó 4 kilos de naranjas* he ordered 4 kilos of oranges.
▶ *vpr* **encargarse de** to take charge of, look after, see to, deal with.

**encargo** *nm* **1** *(recado)* errand. **2** COM order, commission. LOC **hacer un encargo** *(recado)* to run an errand.

**encariñarse** *vpr* to become fond (con, of), get attached (con, to).

**encauzar** *vt* **1** to channel. **2** *fig* to direct, guide.

**encéfalo** *nm* encephalon.

**encendedor** *nm* lighter.

**encender** *vt* **1** *(hacer arder)* to light, set fire to; *(cerilla)* to strike, light; *(vela)* to light. **2** *(luz, radio, tv)* to turn on, switch on, put on; *(gas)* to turn on, light.
▶ *vpr* **encenderse** *(luz)* to go on, come on; *(llama)* to flare up.

**encerado** *nm* *(pizarra)* blackboard.

**encerar** *vt* to wax, polish.

**encerrar** *vt* **1** *(gen)* to shut in, shut up. **2** *(con llave)* to lock in, lock up.

**encestar** *vt* to score a basket.

**enchufado,-a** *adj fam* well-connected, with friends in the right places.
▶ *nm & nf fam (gen)* person with friends in the right places, US wirepuller; *(en la escuela)* teacher's pet.

**enchufar** *vt* **1** ELEC to connect, plug in. **2** *(unir)* to join, connect, fit. **3** *fam fig* to pull strings for: *enchufó a su hija en la empresa* he got his daughter a job in the company.

**enchufe** *nm* **1** ELEC *(hembra)* socket; *(macho)* plug. **2** *fam fig (trabajo)* easy job; *(influencias)* contacts *pl*, friends *pl* in high places. LOC **tener enchufe** *fam* to have contacts.

**encía** *nf* gum.

**enciclopedia** *nf* encyclopaedia, encyclopedia.

**encima** *adv* **1** *(más arriba)* above, overhead; *(sobre)* on top. **2** *(ropa, etc)* on, on top: *ponte algo encima* put something on. **3** *(además)* in addition, besides. **4** *fam (por si fuera poco)* what's more, on top of that, besides. LOC **encima de 1** *(a más altura)* over, above. **2** *(sobre)* on. **3** *(además)* besides, as well as, on top of that. **‖ por encima de 1** *(más importante)* above. **2** *(más allá)* beyond: *está por encima de sus posibilidades* it's beyond her capabilities.

**encina** *nf* holm oak, evergreen oak.

**encoger** *vt* **1** *(contraer)* to contract. **2** *(tejido)* to shrink.

▶ *vi (tejido)* to shrink.

▶ *vpr* **encogerse 1** *(contraerse)* to contract. **2** *(tejido)* to shrink.

**encolar** *vt (dar cola)* to glue.

**encontrar** *vt* **1** *(gen)* to find. **2** *(una persona sin buscar)* to come across, meet, bump into. **3** *(dificultades)* to run into, come up against.

▶ *vpr* **encontrarse 1** *(estar)* to be: *se encuentra enfermo* he's ill. **2** *(persona)* to meet; *(por casualidad)* to bump into, run into, meet: *nos encontraremos allí* we'll meet there. **3** *(dificultades)* to run into. **4** *fig (sentirse)* to feel, be: *me encuentro mal* I feel bad.

**encrucijada** *nf* **1** crossroads, intersection. **2** *fig* crossroads.

**encuadernación** *nf (arte)* bookbinding.

**encuadernar** *vt* to bind.

**encuadrar** *vt* **1** *(cuadro, etc)* to frame. **2** *fig (encajar)* to fit in, insert.

▶ *vpr* **encuadrarse** *(incorporarse)* to join.

**encuadre** *nm* framing.

**encubrir** *vt* **1** *(ocultar)* to conceal, hide. **2** JUR *(delito)* to cover up; *(criminal)* to cover up for.

**encuentro** *nm* **1** *(de personas)* meeting. **2** DEP meeting, clash; *(partido)* match, game.

**encuesta** *nf (sondeo)* poll, survey. LOC **hacer una encuesta** to carry out an opinion poll.

**encuestador,-ra** *nm & nf* pollster.

**encuestar** *vt* to poll.

**encurtidos** *nm pl* pickles.

**endecasílabo,-a** *adj* hendecasyllabic.

**enderezar** *vt* **1** *(poner derecho)* to straighten out. **2** *(poner vertical)* to set upright. **3** *fig (situación, etc)* to put right.

▶ *vpr* **enderezarse** *(ponerse recto)* to straighten up.

**endeudarse** *vpr* to get into debt, fall into debt.

**endibia** *nf* endive.

**endulzar** *vt* to sweeten.

**endurecer** *vt* **1** to harden, make hard. **2** *fig* to harden, toughen.

**ene** *nf name of the letter* n.

▶ *adj (indeterminado)* n: *ene veces* n times.

**enebro** *nm* juniper.

**eneldo** *nm* dill.

**enemigo,-a** *adj* enemy, hostile.

▶ *nm & nf* enemy, foe.

**enemistar** *vt* to make enemies of, set at odds, cause a rift between.

▶ *vpr* **enemistarse** to become enemies.

**energía** *nf* **1** energy, power. **2** *fig* vigour (US vigor). COMP **energía cinética** kinetic energy.

**enérgico,-a** *adj* **1** energetic, vigorous. **2** *fig (decisión)* firm; *(palabra)* strong.

**enero** *nm* January.

✎ Consulta también marzo.

**enervar** *vt* **1** MED to enervate. **2** *fam (irritar)* to irritate, exasperate, get on one's nerves.

▶ *vpr* **enervarse** *fam* to get flustered, get worked up.

**enfadado,-a** *adj* angry, cross, annoyed, US mad.

**enfadar** *vt* to make angry, make cross, annoy.

▶ *vpr* **enfadarse 1** to get angry (con, with), get cross (con, with). **2** *(pelearse)* to fall out (con, with) (por, about).

**enfado** *nm* anger, irritation.

**énfasis** *nm & nf inv* emphasis, stress.

**enfermar** *vi* to fall ill, become ill, be taken ill.

**enfermedad** *nf* illness, disease, sickness. COMP **enfermedad contagiosa** contagious disease.

**enfermería** *nf* infirmary, sick bay.

**enfermero,-a** *nm & nf (hombre)* male nurse; *(mujer)* nurse.

**enfermizo,-a** *adj* sickly, unhealthy.

**enfermo,-a** *adj* sick, ill.

**enfilar** *vt* **1** *(poner en fila)* to line up. **2** *(una calle)* to go along, go down.

**enfocar** *vt* **1** to focus, focus on, get into focus. **2** *(luz)* to shine a light on.

**3** *fig (problema, etc)* to focus on, approach, look at.

**enfoque** *nm (acción)* focus, focusing. **2** *fig* focus, approach, angle.

**enfrascarse** *vpr* **1** *fig* to become absorbed (en, in), become engrossed (en, in). **2** *fig (en lectura)* to bury os (en, in).

**enfrentamiento** *nm* confrontation.

**enfrentar** *vt* **1** *(poner frente a frente)* to bring face to face, confront. **2** *(encarar)* to face, confront.
▶ *vpr* **enfrentarse** **1** *(hacer frente)* to face (a/con, -), confront (a/con, -). **2** DEP to meet (a/con, -). **3** *(pelearse)* to have an argument (a, with), fall out (a, with); *(chocar)* to clash (a/con, with).

**enfrente** *adv* opposite, in front, facing.

**enfriar** *vt* to cool (down), chill. **2** *fig* to cool down.
▶ *vpr* **enfriarse** **1** *(lo demasiado caliente)* to cool down. **2** *(tener frío)* to get cold; *(resfriarse)* to catch a cold, get a cold.

**enfurecer** *vt* to infuriate, enrage.
▶ *vpr* **enfurecerse** **1** to get furious, lose one's temper. **2** *(mar)* to become rough.

**enfurruñarse** *vpr fam* to sulk, get in a huff.

**engalanar** *vt (cosa)* to festoon, deck out.
▶ *vpr* **engalanarse** *(persona)* to dress up, get dressed up.

**enganchar** *vt* **1** *(agarrar con gancho)* to hook. **2** *(colgar)* to hang, hang up. **3** *(vagones)* to couple.
▶ *vpr* **engancharse** **1** to get caught (en, on), snag (en, on). **2** MIL to enlist, join up. **3** *argot (drogas)* to get hooked (a, on).

**engañar** *vt* **1** *(gen)* to deceive, mislead, fool, take in. **2** *(estafar)* to cheat, trick.
▶ *vpr* **engañarse** **1** *(ilusionarse)* to deceive os. **2** *(equivocarse)* to be mistaken, be wrong.

**engaño** *nm* **1** deceit, deception. **2** *(estafa)* fraud, trick, swindle. **3** *(mentira)* lie.

**engañoso,-a** *adj (gen)* deceptive.

**engarzar** *vt* **1** *(perlas, etc)* to string, thread. **2** *fig (palabras, frases)* to string together.

**engatusar** *vt fam* to get round, coax, cajole.

**engendrar** *vt* to engender, beget.

**engendro** *nm* **1** *(feto)* foetus (US fetus). **2** *fam fig (persona)* freak. **3** *fig (cosa)* monstrosity.

**englobar** *vt* **1** *(incluir)* to include, comprise. **2** *(reunir)* to bring together, lump together.

**engomar** *vt* to gum, glue, stick.

**engominarse** *vpr (brillantina)* to put hair cream on; *(fijador)* to gel one's hair, put hair gel on.

**engordar** *vt* to fatten, fatten up, make fat.
▶ *vi* **1** *(persona)* to put on weight, get fatter. **2** *(alimento)* to be fattening.

**engorroso,-a** *adj fam* bothersome, annoying, awkward.

**engranaje** *nm* **1** TÉC gears *pl*. **2** *(de reloj)* cogs *pl*. **3** *fig* machinery.

**engrasar** *vt (dar grasa)* to grease, oil, lubricate.

**engrescar** *vt (incitar)* to cause trouble between; *(animar)* to get going, arouse, excite.
▶ *vpr* **engrescarse** to get embroiled.

**engrosar** *vt* **1** *(hacer grueso)* to thicken. **2** *fig (aumentar)* to increase, swell.

**engullir** *vt* to swallow.

**enharinar** *vt (cubrir)* to flour; *(manchar)* to sprinkle with flour.

**enhebrar** *vt* **1** to thread. **2** *fig* to connect, link.

**enhorabuena** *nf* congratulations *pl*.
▶ *adv* thank God.

**enigma** *nm* enigma, puzzle, mystery.

**enigmático,-a** *adj* enigmatic, mysterious, puzzling.

**enjabonar** *vt* **1** to soap. **2** *fig* to soft-soap, butter-up.

**enjambre** *nm* **1** swarm. **2** *fig* swarm, throng, crowd.

**enjaular** *vt* **1** to cage. **2** *fam fig* to put in jail, put inside.

**enjoyar** *vt* to adorn with jewels.

▶ *vpr* **enjoyarse** *fam* to put on lots of jewellery (US jewelry), be dripping with jewels.

**enjuagar** *vt* to rinse.

▶ *vpr* **enjuagarse** to rinse one's mouth out.

**enjugar** *vt* *(secar)* to dry, wipe (away), mop up.

**enjuiciar** *vt* **1** *(juzgar)* to judge; *(examinar)* to examine. **2** JUR *(civil)* to sue; *(criminal)* to indict, prosecute.

**enlace** *nm* **1** *(conexión)* link, connection. **2** *(boda)* marriage. **3** *(tren, etc)* connection. **4** QUÍM bond.

**enlatado,-a** *adj* canned, tinned.

**enlatar** *vt* to can, tin.

**enlazar** *vt* **1** *(unir)* to link, connect, tie (together). **2** *(ideas, etc)* to link, connect, relate. **3** *(carreteras, etc)* to connect.

▶ *vi (trenes, etc)* to connect (con, with).

▶ *vpr* **enlazarse 1** *(unirse)* to be linked, be connected. **2** *(casarse)* to get married, marry.

**enlodar** *vt* to muddy, cover with mud.

**enloquecedor,-ra** *adj* maddening.

**enloquecer** *vt* **1** *(volver loco)* to drive mad. **2** *fam (gustar)* to be mad/crazy about, be wild about.

▶ *vi (volverse loco)* to go mad/crazy, go out of one's mind.

**enlosado** *nm (de losas)* paving; *(de baldosas)* tiling.

**enlosar** *vt (losas)* to pave; *(baldosas)* to tile.

**enlucir** *vt (paredes, etc)* to plaster.

**enmadrado,-a** *adj* tied to one's mother's apron strings.

**enmadrarse** *vpr* to be tied to one's mother's apron strings.

**enmarañar** *vt* **1** *(enredar)* to tangle. **2** *fig* to embroil, muddle up, confuse.

▶ *vpr* **enmarañarse 1** *(enredarse)* to get tangled. **2** *fig* to get into a muddle, get confused.

**enmarcar** *vt* to frame.

**enmascarado,-a** *adj* masked.

▶ *nm & nf* masked person.

**enmascarar** *vt* **1** to mask. **2** *fig* to mask, disguise, conceal.

**enmendar** *vt* **1** to correct, put right. **2** *(un daño)* to repair, put right.

▶ *vpr* **enmendarse** to reform, mend one's ways.

**enmienda** *nf* **1** correction. **2** *(de daño)* repair, indemnity, compensation. LOC **hacer propósito de enmienda** to turn over a new leaf.

**enmohecer** *vt (pan, queso, etc)* to make mouldy (US moldy); *(metal)* to rust.

▶ *vpr* **enmohecerse** *(pan, queso, etc)* to go mouldy (US moldy); *(metal)* to rust, go rusty.

**enmoquetar** *vt* to carpet.

**enmudecer** *vt (hacer callar)* to silence.

▶ *vi* **1** *(quedar mudo)* to be struck dumb; *(perder la voz)* to lose one's voice. **2** *(callar)* to fall silent, keep quiet.

**enojado,-a** *adj* angry, cross.

**enojar** *vt* to anger, annoy, make angry.

▶ *vpr* **enojarse** to get angry (con, with), get annoyed (con, with), lose one's temper (con, with).

**enojo** *nm* anger, annoyance.

**enojoso,-a** *adj* annoying, irritating.

**enorgullecer** *vt* to fill with pride.

▶ *vpr* **enorgullecerse** to be proud (de, of), pride os (de, on).

**enorme** *adj (grande)* enormous, huge, vast.

**enormidad** *nf (grandeza)* enormity, hugeness.

**enquistarse** *vpr* to encyst.

**enrabiar** *vt* to enrage, infuriate.

▶ *vpr* **enrabiarse** to become enraged.

**enraizar** *vi* **1** BOT to take root. **2** *fig (persona)* to put down roots.

▶ *vpr* **enraizarse** *(planta, árbol)* to take root; *(persona)* to put down roots.

**enredadera** *nf* creeper, climbing plant.

**enredar** *vt* **1** *(engatusar)* to involve, implicate. **2** *(meter cizaña)* to sow discord, cause trouble. **3** *(enmarañar)* to tangle up, entangle. **4** *fig (asunto, etc)* to confuse, complicate.

▸ *vpr* **enredarse 1** *(hacerse un lío)* to get tangled up, get entangled, get into a tangle.

**enredo** *nm* **1** *(maraña)* tangle. **2** *(confusión)* mess, muddle, confusion, mix-up. **3** *(engaño)* deceit. **4** *(travesura)* mischief.

**enrejado** *nm* *(reja)* railings *pl*, grating.

**enrejar** *vt* **1** *(puerta, ventana)* to put a grating on. **2** *(vallar)* to fence, put railings round.

**enrevesado,-a** *adj* complicated, difficult.

**enriquecer** *vt* **1** *(hacer rico)* to make rich. **2** *fig* to enrich.
▸ *vpr* **enriquecerse** to get rich.

**enriquecimiento** *nm* enrichment.

**enrocar** *vi* *(ajedrez)* to castle.
▸ *vt* *(ajedrez)* to castle.

**enrojecimiento** *nm* *(rostro)* blushing.

**enrollado,-a** *adj* **1** *(papel)* rolled up; *(cable)* coiled. **2** *fam* *(guay)* cool, great.

**enrollar** *vt* **1** *(papel)* to roll up; *(hilo)* to wind up. **2** *(a alguien)* to involve.
▸ *vpr* **enrollarse 1** *fam fig (hablar)* to go on and on (con, to), chatter (con, to). **2** *fam fig (tener relaciones)* to have an affair (con, with). **3** *fam fig (liarse)* to get involved (con, with).

**enroque** *nm* castling.

**enroscar** *vt* *(tornillo)* to screw in.
▸ *vpr* **enroscarse** to wind, coil; *(cable)* to roll up; *(serpiente)* to coil itself (up).

**ensaimada** *nf* spiral-shaped pastry made of light dough.

**ensalada** *nf* salad.

**ensaladera** *nf* salad bowl.

**ensaladilla** *nf* vegetable salad.

**ensamblar** *vt* to join, assemble.

**ensanchar** *vt* **1** *(gen)* to widen, enlarge, extend. **2** COST to let out.
▸ *vpr* **ensancharse** to get wider, expand, spread, stretch.

**ensanche** *nm* **1** *(gen)* widening, enlargement, extension. **2** *(de ciudad)* urban development.

**ensartar** *vt* *(cuentas)* to string (together), thread; *(aguja)* to thread.

**ensayar** *vt* **1** TEAT to rehearse. **2** MÚS to practise (US practice). **3** *(probar)* to try out, test.

**ensayo** *nm* **1** TEAT rehearsal. **2** MÚS practice. **3** *(prueba)* test, experiment, trial, attempt. **4** *(literario, etc)* essay.

**enseguida** *adv* at once, straight away, immediately.

✎ También se escribe en seguida.

**enseñante** *nm o nf* teacher.

**enseñanza** *nf* **1** *(educación)* education, teaching. **2** *(doctrina)* teaching, doctrine. COMP **enseñanza general básica** general basic education. ▌**enseñanza primaria** primary education.

**enseñar** *vt* **1** *(en escuela, etc)* to teach, train, instruct. **2** *(educar)* to educate. **3** *(mostrar, dejar ver)* to show: *me enseñó el libro* he showed me the book.

**ensillar** *vt* put a saddle on.

**ensimismado,-a** *adj* engrossed, absorbed, lost.

**ensimismarse** *vpr* *(abstraerse)* to become lost in thought.

**ensoñar** *vt* to daydream about.

**ensordecedor,-ra** *adj* deafening.

**ensordecer** *vt* to deafen.
▸ *vi* to go deaf.

**ensortijado,-a** *adj* curly.

**ensuciar** *vt* to dirty, make dirty.
▸ *vpr* **ensuciarse** *(mancharse)* to get dirty.

**ensueño** *nm* dream, fantasy. LOC **de ensueño** dream.

**entablar** *vt* **1** *(poner tablas)* to plank, board. **2** *(conversación)* to begin, start, open; *(amistad)* to strike up.

**entallar** *vt* COST to take in at the waist.

**entarimado** *nm* parquet floor.

**ente** *nm* *(ser)* being.

**entender** *nm* *(opinión)* understanding, opinion.
▸ *vt* **1** *(comprender)* to understand. **2** *(darse cuenta)* to realize. **3** *(discurrir)* to think, believe: *entiendo que sería mejor ir* I think it would be better to go. **4** *(interpretar)* to understand, take it.

**entendido** ▶ *vi (tener conocimiento)* to know (de, about).

▶ *vpr* **entenderse 1** *(comprenderse)* to be understood. **2** *fam (conocerse)* to know what one is doing: *yo ya me entiendo* I have my reasons. **3** *fam (llevarse bien)* to get along.

**entendido,-a** *nm & nf* expert.

**entendimiento** *nm* **1** *(comprensión)* understanding, comprehension. **2** *(sentido común)* understanding, sense, judgement. **3** *(inteligencia)* intelligence.

**enterado,-a** *nm & nf fam* expert, authority. ⌐LOC⌐ **darse por enterado,-a de** ALGO to be aware of STH. ▮ **estar enterado,-a** to be in the know.

**enterar** *vt* to inform (de, about/of); *(poner al corriente)* to acquaint (de, with), tell (de, about).

▶ *vpr* **enterarse 1** *(averiguar)* to find out (de, about). **2** *(tener conocimiento)* to learn, hear. **3** *(darse cuenta)* to realize.

**enternecer** *vt (conmover)* to move, touch.

▶ *vpr* **enternecerse** to be moved, be touched.

**entero,-a** *adj (completo)* entire, whole, complete.

▶ *nm* **entero** MAT whole number.

**enterrar** *vt* **1** to bury, inter. **2** *fig (olvidar)* to forget, give up.

**entierro** *nm* **1** *(acción)* burial. **2** *(ceremonia)* funeral.

**entonar** *vt* **1** *(nota)* to pitch; *(canción)* to sing, intone. **2** *(colores)* to match.

▶ *vi* **1** MÚS to intone. **2** *(colores)* to match. **3** *fig (armonizar)* to be in harmony (con, with), be in tune (con, with).

**entonces** *adv* **1** *(en aquel momento)* then. **2** *(en tal caso)* so, then: *entonces no lo quieres* so you don't want it. ⌐LOC⌐ **desde entonces** since then.

**entornado,-a** *adj (ojos, etc)* half-closed; *(puerta)* ajar.

**entornar** *vt* **1** *(ojos, etc)* to half-close. **2** *(puerta)* to leave ajar.

**entorno** *nm* **1** environment, surroundings *pl*. **2** INFORM environment.

**entorpecer** *vt* **1** to make numb, make dull. **2** *fig (dificultar)* to obstruct.

**entorpecimiento** *nm* **1** dullness, numbness. **2** *fig (obstrucción)* obstruction, hindrance.

**entrada** *nf* **1** *(gen)* entrance, entry. **2** *(vestíbulo)* hall, entrance. **3** *(billete)* ticket, admission. **4** *(público)* audience. **5** *(de libro, oración, etc)* opening; *(de año, mes)* beginning: *la entrada de la primavera* the beginning of spring. **6** *(pago inicial)* down payment, deposit. **7** CULIN entrée, starter. **8** INFORM input. **9** DEP tackle. ⌐LOC⌐ **de entrada 1** *(desde el principio)* straight away, from the outset. **2** *(en comida)* for starters. ▮ «**Prohibida la entrada**» "No admittance".

**entramado** *nm* wooden framework.

**entrante** *adj* entering, coming, incoming: *el año entrante* the coming year; *el mes entrante* next month.

▶ *nm* CULIN starter.

**entrañable** *adj* **1** *(amistad)* intimate, close. **2** *(amigo)* dear. **3** *(recuerdo)* fond.

**entrar** *vi* **1** *(ir adentro)* to come in, go in. **2** *(tener entrada)* to be welcome. **3** *(en una sociedad, etc)* to join; *(en una profesión)* to take up, join. **4** *(encajar, caber)* to fit: *este tornillo no entra* this screw doesn't fit. **5** *(empezar - año, estación)* to begin, start; *(- período, época)* to enter; *(- libro, carta)* to begin, open: *ya ha entrado el verano* summer has begun. **6** *(venir)* to come over, come on: *me entraron ganas de llorar* I felt like crying. **7** *(alcanzar)* to reach: *ha entrado en los cuarenta* he has reached forty. **8** INFORM to access.

▶ *vt (meter)* to put.

**entre** *prep* **1** *(dos términos)* between. **2** *(varios)* among, amongst: *entre los periódicos* among the newspapers. **3** *(entremedio)* somewhere between: *entre azul y verde* somewhere between blue and green. ⌐LOC⌐ **de entre** from among, out of: ▮ **entre tanto** meanwhile, in the meantime.

**entreabierto,-a** *adj (ojos, etc)* half-open; *(puerta)* ajar.

**entreabrir** *vt* **1** *(ojos)* to half open. **2** *(puerta, etc)* to leave ajar.

**entreacto** *nm* interval.

**entrecejo** *nm* space between the eyebrows; *(ceño)* frown.

**entrecot** *nm* entrecôte.

**entredicho** *nm (duda)* doubt, question. LOC **poner** ALGO **en entredicho** to have one's doubts about STH.

**entrega** *nf* **1** *(gen)* handing over. **2** *(de premios)* presentation. **3** COM delivery. **4** *(de posesiones)* surrender. **5** *(fascículo)* instalment (US installment), part. **6** DEP pass. COMP **entrega a domicilio** home delivery.

**entregar** *vt* **1** *(dar)* to hand over. **2** *(deberes, ejercicios)* to hand in, give in; *(premios)* to present, award. **3** COM to deliver.
▶ *vpr* **entregarse 1** *(rendirse)* to give in (a, to), surrender. **2** *(dedicarse)* to devote os (a, to), be devoted (a, to). **3** *pey (caer en)* to give os over (a, to), take (a, to).

**entrelazar** *vt* to entwine, interweave, interlace.

**entremedias** *adv* **1** in between. **2** *(mientras tanto)* meanwhile, in the meantime. LOC **entremedias de** between, among.

**entremés** *nm* hors d'oeuvre *pl*.

**entremezclar** *vt* to intermingle.
▶ *vpr* **entremezclarse** to intermingle.

**entrenador,-ra** *nm & nf* trainer, coach.

**entrenamiento** *nm* training.

**entrenar** *vt* to train, coach.
▶ *vpr* **entrenarse** to train.

**entreno** *nm* training.

**entresijo** *nm fig* secret, mystery. LOC **conocer todos los entresijos** *fig* to know all the ins and outs.

**entresuelo** *nm* mezzanine, GB first floor, US second floor.

**entretanto** *adv* meanwhile.

**entretejer** *vt* to interweave, intertwine.

**entretener** *vt* **1** *(detener)* to hold up, detain; *(retrasar)* to delay. **2** *(ocupar)* to keep busy. **3** *(distraer)* to occupy, keep occupied. **4** *(divertir)* to entertain, amuse, distract.
▶ *vpr* **entretenerse 1** *(retrasarse)* to be delayed, be held up. **2** *(distraerse)* to keep os occupied. **3** *(divertirse)* to amuse os.

**entretenido,-a** *adj (divertido)* entertaining, amusing.

**entretenimiento** *nm (distracción)* entertainment, distraction, amusement.

**entretiempo** *nm* period between seasons; *(primavera)* spring; *(otoño)* autumn. LOC **un traje de entretiempo** a lightweight suit.

**entrevista** *nf* **1** *(prensa)* interview. **2** *(reunión)* meeting. LOC **hacer una entrevista a** ALGN to interview SB.

**entrevistador,-ra** *nm & nf* interviewer.

**entrevistar** *vt* to interview.
▶ *vpr* **entrevistarse 1** *(prensa)* to have an interview (con, with). **2** *(reunirse)* to have a meeting (con, with).

**entristecer** *vt* to make sad.
▶ *vpr* **entristecerse** to be sad (por, about).

**entrometerse** *vpr* to meddle, interfere.

**entrometido,-a** *adj* nosy.
▶ *nm & nf* meddler, nosy parker.

**entroncar** *vt* to relate, link, connect.
▶ *vi (parentesco)* to be related.

**entumecido,-a** *adj* numb.

**entumecimiento** *nm* numbness.

**enturbiar** *vt* **1** to make muddy, make cloudy, cloud. **2** *fig* to cloud, muddle, obscure.
▶ *vpr* **enturbiarse 1** to get muddy, become cloudy. **2** *fig* to get confused, get muddled.

**entusiasmado,-a** *adj* excited.

**entusiasmar** *vt* **1** *(causar entusiasmo)* to fill with enthusiasm, excite. **2** *(gustar)* to like, love: *me entusiasma la ópera* I love opera.
▶ *vpr* **entusiasmarse 1** to get enthusiastic (con, about), get excited (con, about). **2** *(gustar)* to love (con, -), like (con, -).

**E**

**entusiasmo** *nm* enthusiasm. LOC **con entusiasmo** keenly, enthusiastically.

**entusiasta** *adj* enthusiastic.

**enumeración** *nf (cómputo)* enumeration, count, reckoning.

**enumerar** *vt* to enumerate.

**enunciado** *nm* **1** *(teoría, etc)* enunciation. **2** LING statement. **3** *(problema, etc)* wording.

**enunciar** *vt* **1** *(teoría)* to enunciate. **2** *(expresar)* to express, state, word.

**envalentonar** *vt* to make bold, make daring.
  ▶ *vpr* **envalentonarse** *(volverse valiente)* to become bold, become daring.

**envasado,-a** *adj (bebidas)* bottled; *(conservas)* canned, tinned; *(paquetes)* packed.
  ▶ *nm* **envasado** *(bebidas)* bottling; *(conservas)* canning; *(paquetes)* packing. COMP **envasado al vacío** vacuum-packed.

**envasar** *vt (botellas)* to bottle; *(latas)* to can, tin; *(paquetes)* to pack.

**envase** *nm* **1** *(acción - paquetes)* packing; *(- botellas)* bottling; *(- latas)* canning. **2** *(recipiente)* container. **3** *(botella vacía)* empty. COMP **envase de cartón** carton. **I envase de plástico** plastic container. **I envase sin retorno** nonreturnable bottle.

**envejecer** *vt* to age, make look old.
  ▶ *vi* to get old, grow old.

**envejecido,-a** *adj* aged, old, old-looking: *Pablo está muy envejecido* Pablo looks very old.

**envejecimiento** *nm* ageing.

**envenenamiento** *nm* poisoning.

**envenenar** *vt* to poison.

**envés** *nm inv* **1** *(de página)* back, reverse. **2** *(de tela)* wrong side. **3** BOT reverse.

**enviado,-a** *nm & nf* messenger, envoy. COMP **enviado,-a especial** special correspondent.

**enviar** *vt* **1** *(gen)* to send. **2** COM to dispatch, remit; *(por barco)* to ship.

**enviciar** *vt (pervertir)* to corrupt, pervert.
  ▶ *vi* BOT to produce too many leaves and not enough fruit.

  ▶ *vpr* **enviciarse** *(pervertirse)* to become corrupted, fall into bad habits.

**envidar** *vi* to bid, bet.

**envidia** *nf* envy. LOC **dar envidia** to make envious. **I tener envidia de** ALGO/ALGN to envy STH/SB.

**envidiable** *adj* enviable.

**envidiar** *vt* to envy.

**envidioso,-a** *adj* envious.

**envío** *nm* **1** *(acción)* sending, dispatch. **2** COM dispatch, shipment. **3** *(paquete)* parcel. **4** *(mensaje electrónico)* posting. LOC **hacer un envío** COM to dispatch an order. **I envío contra reembolso** cash on delivery. **I** COMP **gastos de envío** postage and packing.

**envite** *nm (apuesta)* bet.

**enviudar** *vi (hombre)* to become a widower, lose one's wife; *(mujer)* to become a widow, lose one's husband.

**envoltorio** *nm (de caramelo, etc)* wrapper.

**envolver** *vt (con papel)* to wrap, wrap up.

**enyesado** *nm* **1** plastering. **2** MED plaster cast.

**enyesar** *vt* **1** to plaster. **2** MED to put in plaster.

**enzarzar** *vt* **1** *(de zarzas)* to cover with brambles. **2** *fig (engrescar)* to sow discord among, set at odds.
  ▶ *vpr* **enzarzarse** **1** *(enredarse en zarzas)* to get entangled in brambles. **2** *fig (discusión, asunto)* to get involved (en, in).

**enzima** *nm & nf* enzyme.

**eñe** *nf name of the letter* ñ.

**eoceno,-a** *adj* Eocene.
  ▶ *nm* **eoceno** Eocene.

**eólico,-a** *adj* wind: *energía eólica* wind power.

**épica** *nf* epic poetry.

**epiceno** *adj* epicene.

**epicentro** *nm* epicentre (US epicenter).

**épico,-a** *adj* epic, heroic.

**epicureísmo** *nm* Epicureanism.

**epicúreo,-a** *adj* Epicurean.

**epidemia** *nf* epidemic.

**epidémico,-a** *adj* epidemic.

**epidérmico,-a** *adj* epidermic, skin: *enfermedad epidérmica* skin disease.

**epidermis** *nf inv* epidermis, skin.

**epígrafe** *nm* **1** *(cita)* epigraph. **2** *(título)* title, heading.

**epilepsia** *nf* epilepsy.

**epiléptico,-a** *adj* epileptic.

**epílogo** *nm* *(parte final)* epilogue (US epilog).

**episcopado** *nm* *(obispos)* episcopacy.

**episcopal** *adj* episcopal.

**episodio** *nm* **1** *(literario)* episode. **2** *(suceso)* incident, event.

**epístola** *nf fml* epistle, letter.

**epitelio** *nm* epithelium.

**epíteto** *nm* epithet.

**época** *nf* **1** time, age. **2** HIST period, epoch: *muebles de época* period furniture. **3** AGR season, time: *la época de la recolección* harvest time. LOC **por aquella época** about that time. **l ser de su época** to be with the times.

**epopeya** *nf* **1** LIT epic poem. **2** *(hecho)* heroic deed.

**equidad** *nf* *(moderación)* fairness, reasonableness.

**equidistancia** *nf* equidistance.

**equidistante** *adj* equidistant.

**equidistar** *vi* to be equidistant (de, from).

**equilátero,-a** *adj* equilateral.

**equilibrado,-a** *adj* **1** balanced. **2** *(persona)* sensible, well-balanced.

**equilibrar** *vt* **1** to balance, poise. **2** *fig* to balance, adjust.
▶ *vpr* **equilibrarse 1** to balance (en, on). **2** *fig* to recover one's balance.

**equilibrio** *nm* **1** *(estabilidad)* balance: *perdió el equilibrio* he lost his balance. **2** FÍS equilibrium. **3** *fig (armonía)* balance, harmony. LOC **hacer equilibrios** *fig* to perform a balancing act. **l mantener el equilibrio** to keep one's balance.

**equilibrismo** *nm* *(gen)* balancing act; *(de funámbulo)* tightrope walking.

**equilibrista** *nm o nf (funámbulo)* tightrope walker.

**equino,-a** *adj* equine, horse.

**equinoccio** *nm* equinox.

**equinodermo** *nm* echinoderm.

**equipaje** *nm* luggage, baggage. COMP **equipaje de mano** hand luggage.

**equipar** *vt* to equip, furnish.
▶ *vpr* **equiparse** *(uso reflexivo)* to kit os out (con/de, with), equip os (con/de, with).

**equiparable** *adj* comparable (a/con, to/with).

**equiparar** *vt* to compare (a/con, with), liken (a/con, to).

**equipo** *nm* **1** *(prestaciones)* equipment. **2** *(ropas, utensilios)* outfit, kit. **3** *(de personas)* team. COMP **equipo de alta fidelidad** hi-fi system. **l equipo de fútbol** football team. **l equipo de música** music centre, stereo system.

**equis** *nf inv* **1** *name of the letter* x. **2** MAT x, unknown quantity.

**equitación** *nf* horsemanship, horse riding, US horseback riding.

**equitativo,-a** *adj* equitable, fair.

**equivalencia** *nf* **1** *(igualdad)* equivalence. **2** *(sustitución)* compensation.

**equivalente** *adj (igual)* equivalent.
▶ *nm* equivalent.

**equivaler** *vi* **1** *(ser igual)* to be equivalent (a, to), be equal (a, to). **2** *(significar)* to be tantamount (a, to), amount (a, to), mean (a, -).

**equivocación** *nf* **1** *(error)* mistake, error. **2** *(malentendido)* misunderstanding. LOC **cometer una equivocación** to make a mistake.

**equivocado,-a** *adj* mistaken, wrong.

**equivocar** *vt* **1** to mistake, get wrong. **2** *(cambiar)* to get mixed up: *equivoqué vuestros regalos* I got your presents mixed up.
▶ *vpr* **equivocarse** to make a mistake, be mistaken, be wrong; *(de dirección, camino, etc)* to go wrong, get wrong: *me equivoqué de calle* I got the wrong street.

**equívoco,-a** *adj* equivocal, misleading, ambiguous.
▶ *nm* **equívoco 1** ambiguity, double meaning. **2** *(malentendido)* misunderstanding.

**era** *nf (tiempo)* era, age.

**erario** *nm* exchequer, treasury.

**erasmismo** *nm* Erasmianism.

**ere** *nf* name of the letter r.

**erecto,-a** *adj* erect.

**eremita** *nm* hermit, eremite.

**ergonómico,-a** *adj* ergonomic.

**erguido,-a** *adj* erect, upright, straight.

**erguir** *vt* to raise (up straight), erect, lift up.
▶ *vpr* **erguirse** *(ponerse derecho)* to straighten up, stand up straight.

**erial** *adj* uncultivated, untilled.
▶ *nm* uncultivated land.

**erigir** *vt (alzar)* to erect, build.

**Eritrea** *nf* Eritrea.

**eritreo,-a** *adj* Eritrean.
▶ *nm & nf (persona)* Eritrean.

**erizado,-a** *adj* bristly, prickly.

**erizar** *vt (pelo - animal)* to bristle; *(- persona)* make stand on end.
▶ *vpr* **erizarse** *(pelo - de animal)* to bristle; *(- de persona)* to stand on end: *el pelo se le erizó* his hair stood on end.

**erizo** *nm (animal)* hedgehog. COMP **erizo de mar** sea urchin.

**ermita** *nf* hermitage, shrine.

**ermitaño,-a** *adj* recluse.
▶ *nm & nf (persona solitaria)* hermit.
▶ *nm* **ermitaño** ZOOL hermit crab.

**erosión** *nf* erosion, wearing away.

**erosionar** *vt* to erode.

**erosivo,-a** *adj* erosive.

**erradicar** *vt* 1 to eradicate. 2 *(enfermedad)* to stamp out.

**errado,-a** *adj* mistaken, wrong.

**errante** *adj* wandering, errant.

**errar** *vt (objetivo)* to miss, get wrong.
▶ *vi* 1 *(vagar)* to wander, rove, roam. 2 *(equivocarse)* to be mistaken, be wrong.

**errata** *nf* erratum, misprint.

**errático,-a** *adj* erratic.

**erre** *nf* name of the digraph rr.

**erróneo,-a** *adj* erroneous, wrong, mistaken, unsound: *explicación errónea* wrong explanation.

**error** *nm* error, mistake.

**eructar** *vi* to belch, burp.

**eructo** *nm* belch, burp.

**erudición** *nf* erudition, learning.

**erudito,-a** *adj* erudite, learned.
▶ *nm & nf* scholar, expert.

**erupción** *nf* 1 *(volcánica)* eruption. 2 *(cutánea)* rash. LOC **entrar en erupción** to erupt.

**eruptivo,-a** *adj* eruptive.

**esbelto,-a** *adj* slim, slender.

**esbozar** *vt* to sketch, outline. LOC **esbozar una sonrisa** *fig* to force a smile, smile weakly.

**esbozo** *nm* sketch, outline.

**escabechado,-a** *adj* pickled, in brine.

**escabechar** *vt* to pickle, preserve in brine; *(arenque)* to souse, pickle.

**escabeche** *nm* brine, pickle.

**escabechina** *nf fam* massacre.

**escabroso,-a** *adj* 1 *(desigual)* uneven, rough: *terreno escabroso* rough terrain. 2 *fig (difícil)* tough, difficult.

**escabullirse** *vpr* 1 *(entre las manos)* to slip through. 2 *fig (persona)* to slip away, sneak off, disappear.

**escacharrar** *vt* 1 *fam (romper)* to break. 2 *fam (estropear)* to ruin, spoil.

**escafandra** *nf* diving suit.

**escafandrista** *nm o nf* diver.

**escala** *nf* 1 *(escalera - de mano)* ladder; *(- de tijera)* stepladder. 2 *(mapa, plano, etc)* scale: *lo dibujó a escala* he drew it to scale. 3 *(puerto)* port of call; *(aeropuerto)* stopover. 4 MÚS scale.

**escalada** *nf (montaña)* climb, climbing.

**escalador,-ra** *nm & nf* climber.

**escalafón** *nm (de personas)* roll, promotion list.

**escalar** *vt (montaña)* to climb.

**escaldado,-a** *adj* scalded.

**escaleno** *adj* scalene.

**escalera** *nf* 1 stairs *pl*, staircase. 2 *(escala)* ladder.

**escalerilla** *nf (de barco)* gangway; *(de avión)* steps *pl*.

**escalfar** *vt* to poach: *huevos escalfados* poached eggs.

**escalinata** *nf* outside steps *pl*.

**escalofriante** *adj* chilling, bloodcurdling, hair-raising.

**escalofrío** *nm* *(de frío)* shiver. LOC tener escalofríos to shiver.

**escalón** *nm* **1** *(peldaño)* step, stair; *(de escala)* rung. **2** *fig* *(grado)* degree, level, grade. **3** *fig* *(paso, medio)* stepping stone.

**escalonado,-a** *adj* *(espaciado)* spaced out, at regular intervals.

**escalonar** *vt* **1** *(espaciar)* to place at intervals, space out. **2** *(cabello)* cut in layers.

**escama** *nf* **1** scale. **2** *fig* *(de piel, de jabón)* flake.

**escamado,-a** *adj* *fam fig* wary, suspicious.

**escamar** *vt* **1** *(quitar escamas)* to scale, remove the scales from. **2** *fam fig* to make suspicious, make wary.

**escampar** *vt* to clear out.
▶ *vi* [se emplea sólo en tercera persona; no lleva sujeto] METEOR to stop raining, clear up.

**escandalizar** *vt* to shock.
▶ *vpr* **escandalizarse** to be shocked (de/por, at), be scandalized (de/por, by).

**escándalo** *nm* **1** scandal. **2** *(alboroto)* racket, fuss, din, uproar. LOC armar un escándalo to kick up a fuss.

**escandaloso,-a** *adj* **1** scandalous, shocking, outrageous. **2** *(alborotado)* noisy, rowdy.

**Escandinavia** *nf* Scandinavia.

**escandinavo,-a** *adj* Scandinavian.
▶ *nm & nf* Scandinavian.

**escanear** *vt* to scan.

**escáner** *nm* scanner.

**escaño** *nm* **1** *(banco)* bench. **2** POL seat.

**escapada** *nf* **1** *fam* *(salida)* quick trip. **2** *(huida)* escape.

**escapar** *vi* **1** *(huir)* to escape, get away, run away. **2** *(librarse)* to escape.
▶ *vpr* **escaparse 1** *(huir)* to escape, run away, get away. **2** *(librarse)* to escape, avoid. **3** *(gas, etc)* to leak.

**escaparate** *nm* shop window.

**escapatoria** *nf* **1** *(huida)* escape, flight. **2** *(excusa)* excuse, way out.

**escape** *nm* **1** *(huida)* escape, flight, getaway. **2** *(de gas, etc)* leak.

**escarabajo** *nm* beetle.

**escaramujo** *nm* **1** *(rosal)* wild rose, dog rose. **2** *(fruto)* rosehip.

**escaramuza** *nf* *(riña)* run-in, squabble.

**escarbar** *vt* **1** *(suelo)* to scratch. **2** *(bolsillo, papeles)* to rummage in.

**escarcha** *nf* frost, hoarfrost.

**escarlata** *adj* scarlet.

**escarlatina** *nf* scarlet fever.

**escarmentar** *vt* teach a lesson to.
▶ *vi* to learn one's lesson: *a ver si escarmientas* that'll teach you (a lesson).

**escarmiento** *nm* lesson.

**escarola** *nf* curly endive.

**escarpado,-a** *adj* **1** *(inclinado)* steep, sheer. **2** *(abrupto)* craggy.

**escarpia** *nf* spike, hook.

**escasear** *vi* *(faltar)* to be scarce.

**escasez** *nf* *(carencia)* scarcity, lack, shortage.

**escaso,-a** *adj* **1** *(insuficiente)* scarce, scant, very little, small. **2** *(recursos)* slender; *(dinero)* tight; *(público)* small; *(lluvias, salario)* low; *(tiempo)* very little. **3** *(poco de algo)* few: *escasos días* few days. **4** *(que le falta poco)* hardly, scarcely, barely: *un kilo escaso* barely a kilo.

**escayola** *nf* **1** *(yeso)* plaster of Paris; *(estuco)* stucco. **2** MED plaster.

**escayolar** *vt* to put in plaster, plaster.

**escena** *nf* **1** TEAT *(parte)* scene; *(lugar)* stage. **2** *fig* scene.

**escenario** *nm* **1** TEAT stage. **2** CINE scenario. **3** *fig* scene, setting.

**escenificar** *vt* **1** *(novela)* to dramatize. **2** *(obra de teatro)* to stage.

**escenografía** *nm* **1** CINE set design. **2** TEAT stage design.

**escenógrafo,-a** *nm & nf* **1** CINE set designer. **2** TEAT stage designer.

**escepticismo** *nm* scepticism (US skepticism).

**escéptico,-a** *adj* sceptic (US skeptic).

**escindir** *vt* to split, divide.
▶ *vpr* **escindirse** to split (off) (en, into).

**escisión** *nf* **1** split, division. **2** FÍS fission. **3** MED excision.

**esclavitud** *nf* slavery, servitude.

**esclavizar** *vt* to enslave.

E

**esclavo,-a** *adj* enslaved.
▸ *nm & nf (gen)* slave.

**esclusa** *nf* lock, sluicegate, floodgate.

**escoba** *nf* brush, broom.

**escobilla** *nf* small brush.

**escobón** *nm* large brush.

**escocer** *vi* **1** to smart, sting: *le escuecen sus heridas* his cuts sting. **2** *fig* to hurt.

**escocés,-a** *adj* Scottish.
▸ *nm & nf (persona)* Scot; *(hombre)* Scotsman; *(mujer)* Scotswoman.
▸ *nm* **escocés** *(idioma)* Scottish Gaelic.

**Escocia** *nf* Scotland. COMP **Nueva Escocia** Nova Scotia.

**escoger** *vt* to choose, pick out, select.

**escogido,-a** *adj* chosen, selected; *(selecto)* choice, select.

**escolar** *adj* school, scholastic.
▸ *nm o nf (chico)* schoolboy; *(chica)* schoolgirl.

**escolástico,-a** *adj* scholastic.

**escollera** *nf* breakwater, jetty.

**escollo** *nm fig* difficulty, pitfall, snag.

**escolopendra** *nf* centipede.

**escolta** *nf* escort.

**escoltar** *vt* **1** to escort. **2** MAR to convoy.

**escombros** *nm pl* rubble *sing*, debris *sing*.

**esconder** *vt* to hide, conceal.
▸ *vpr* **esconderse** to hide.

**escondidas** LOC **hacer** ALGO **a escondidas de** ALGN to do STH behind SB's back.

**escondite** *nm* **1** *(lugar)* hiding place. **2** *(juego)* hide-and-seek.

**escopeta** *nf* shotgun.

**escorpión** *nm* scorpion.

**escorzo** *nm* foreshortening.

**escote** *nm* COST low neckline.

**escozor** *nm* **1** stinging, smarting. **2** *fig* pain, grief.

**escribir** *vt* **1** *(gen)* to write. **2** *(deletrear)* to spell, write.
▸ *vi* to write.
▸ *vpr* **escribirse 1** *(deletrear)* to spell, be spelt: *¿cómo se escribe?* how do you spell it? **2** *(uso recíproco)* to write to each other. LOC **escribir a mano** to write in longhand, write by hand. ▮ **escribir a máquina** to type.

**escrito,-a** *adj* written; *(mencionado)* stated.
▸ *nm* **escrito 1** *(documento)* writing, document, text. **2** *(obra)* work, writing: *los escritos de Orwell* Orwell's writings.

**escritor,-ra** *nm & nf* writer.

**escritorio** *nm* **1** *(mueble)* writing desk, bureau. **2** *(oficina)* office.

**escritura** *nf* **1** *(gen)* writing: *escritura fonética* phonetic script. **2** *(caligrafía)* handwriting, writing. **3** JUR deed, document.

**escrúpulo** *nm* **1** [también se usa en plural con el mismo significado] *(recelo)* scruple, doubt, qualm. **2** [también se usa en plural con el mismo significado] *(aprensión)* fussiness: *eso me da escrúpulos* I'm finicky about it, I'm fussy about it. **3** *fig (cuidado)* extreme care: *lo hizo con escrúpulo* he did it with extreme care.

**escrupuloso,-a** *adj* **1** scrupulous. **2** *(aprensivo)* finicky, fussy. **3** *fig (exacto)* scrupulous, meticulous.

**escrutinio** *nm* **1** *(examen)* scrutiny, examination. **2** *(de votos)* count.

**escuadra** *nf* **1** *(instrumento -de dibujo)* set square; *(-de carpintería)* square; *(pieza de metal)* bracket. **2** *(de tropas)* squad; *(de buques)* squadron, fleet. **3** *(fútbol)* angle.

**escuadrilla** *nf* squadron.

**escuadrón** *nm* squadron.

**escuálido,-a** *adj* **1** *(delgado)* emaciated, extremely thin, skinny. **2** *(sucio)* squalid, filthy.

**escucha** *nf (acción)* listening. LOC **estar a la escucha de** to be listening out for. ▮ COMP **escuchas telefónicas** phone tapping *sing*.

**escuchar** *vt* **1** to listen to; *(oír)* to hear. **2** *(atender)* to listen to, pay attention to: *no escuchaba mis consejos* he didn't listen to my advice.

**escudo** *nm* **1** *(arma)* shield. **2** *(de armas)* coat of arms. **3** *(moneda)* escudo. **4** *fig (amparo)* protection, shield.

**escuela** *nf* **1** *(gen)* school. **2** *(experiencia)* experience, instruction.

**esculpir** *vt (gen)* to sculpt, sculpture; *(madera)* to carve; *(metal)* to engrave.

**escultor,-ra** *nm & nf (hombre)* sculptor; *(mujer)* sculptress.

**escultura** *nf (gen)* sculpture; *(en madera)* carving; *(en metal)* engraving.

**escupir** *vi* to spit.
▸ *vt* **1** to spit out. **2** *fig (despedir)* to belch out: *la fábrica escupía humo* the factory belched out smoke.

**escurreplatos** *nm inv* plate rack.

**escurridizo,-a** *adj* **1** slippery. **2** *fig* slippery, elusive.

**escurridor** *nm* **1** *(colador)* strainer, colander. **2** *(de platos)* plate rack. **3** *(para ropa)* wringer, mangle.

**escurrir** *vt (platos, etc)* to drain; *(ropa)* to wring out; *(comida)* to strain.
▸ *vi* **1** *(destilar)* to drip, trickle. **2** *(deslizar)* to slip, slide.
▸ *vpr* **escurrirse 1** *(platos, etc)* to drain. **2** *(líquido)* to drip, trickle. **3** *(deslizarse)* to slip, slide. **4** *fam (escapar)* to run away, slip away.

**esdrújulo,-a** *adj* proparoxytone, stressed on the antepenultimate syllable.

**ese** *nf* name of the letter s.
▸ *nf pl* **eses** zigzags.

**ese,-a** *adj* that; *(plural)* those.

**ése,-a** *pron* **1** *(cosa)* that one. **2** *(hombre - sujeto)* he; *(mujer - sujeto)* she: *ése me lo dijo* he told me. **3** *(hombre - complemento)* him; *(mujer - complemento)* her: *se lo dio a ésa* he gave it to her. **4** *(anterior)* the former.

✎ Cuando no se produzca confusión con el adjetivo se puede omitir el acento.

**esencia** *nf* **1** essence. **2** *(perfume)* essence, perfume, scent.

**esencial** *adj* essential. ⌊LOC⌋ **lo esencial** the main thing.

**esfera** *nf* **1** sphere, globe. **2** *(de reloj)* dial, face. **3** *fig (campo)* field, sphere; *(ambiente)* sphere, circle.

**esférico,-a** *adj* spherical.
▸ *nm* **esférico** *(balón)* ball.

**esfinge** *nf* sphinx.

**esforzar** *vt* **1** *(forzar)* to strain. **2** *(animar)* to encourage, spur on.
▸ *vpr* **esforzarse** *(físicamente)* to make an effort, exert os; *(moralmente)* to try hard, strive: *se ha esforzado para llegar a la cumbre* she has striven to get to the top.

**esfuerzo** *nm* **1** effort, endeavour (US endeavor). **2** *(valor)* courage, spirit. ⌊LOC⌋ **sin esfuerzo** effortlessly.

**esfumar** *vt* **1** *(esfuminar)* to stump, blend. **2** *(colores)* to tone down.
▸ *vpr* **esfumarse** *fam (largarse)* to disappear, fade away.

**esgrima** *nf* fencing.

**esguince** *nm* MED sprain.

**eslabón** *nm* link.

**eslalon** *nm* slalom.

**eslip** *nm* **1** *(ropa interior)* men's briefs *pl*, underpants *pl*. **2** *(bañador)* trunks *pl*. s *pl* eslips.

**eslogan** *nm* slogan. ⌊COMP⌋ **eslogan publicitario** advertising slogan.

**eslovaco,-a** *adj* Slovak.
▸ *nm & nf (persona)* Slovak.
▸ *nm* **eslovaco** *(idioma)* Slovak.

**Eslovaquia** *nf* Slovakia.

**Eslovenia** *nf* Slovenia.

**esloveno,-a** *adj* Slovene.
▸ *nm & nf (persona)* Slovene.
▸ *nm* **esloveno** *(idioma)* Slovene.

**esmaltar** *vt* **1** to enamel. **2** *(uñas)* to varnish. **3** *fig (adornar)* to decorate, adorn.

**esmalte** *nm* **1** *(gen)* enamel. **2** *(de uñas)* nail varnish, nail polish. **3** *(objeto esmaltado)* enamelled object. **4** *(color)* smalt.

**esmeralda** *nf* emerald.

**esmerar** *vt (pulir)* to polish.
▸ *vpr* **esmerarse** to do one's best (en/por, to), take great pains (en/por, over).

**esmero** *nm* great care, neatness.

**esnob** *adj (persona)* snobbish; *(lugar, etc)* posh.
▸ *nm o nf* snob.

**esnobismo** *nm* snobbery, snobbishness.

**eso** *pron* that: *eso es lo que dijo* that's what she said.

**ESO** *abrev* EDUC (Enseñanza Secundaria Obligatoria) *compulsory secondary education up to 16.*

**esófago** *nm* oesophagus (US esophagus), gullet.

**esos,-as** *adj* those.

✎ Consulta también ese,-a.

**ésos,-as** *pron* those (ones).

✎ Consulta también ése,-a.

**espacial** *adj* 1 MAT spatial, spacial. 2 *(del cosmos)* space.

**espaciar** *vt* to space out.

**espacio** *nm* 1 *(gen)* space. 2 *(que se ocupa)* space, room: *necesitamos más espacio* we need more room. 3 *(de tiempo)* period, space. 4 *(programa)* programme (US program).

**espacioso,-a** *adj* *(ancho)* spacious, roomy.

**espada** *nf* 1 *(arma)* sword. 2 *(naipe)* spade.
▶ *nf pl* **espadas** *(palo de baraja)* spades.

**espaguetis** *nm pl* spaghetti *sing.*

**espalda** *nf* 1 [también se usa en plural con el mismo significado] *(gen)* back. 2 *(natación)* backstroke.

**espantapájaros** *nm inv* scarecrow.

**espantar** *vt* 1 *(asustar)* to frighten, scare, scare off. 2 *(ahuyentar)* to frighten away.
▶ *vpr* **espantarse** 1 *(asustarse)* to be frightened, be scared. 2 *(asombrarse)* to be amazed, be astonished.

**espanto** *nm* 1 *(miedo)* fright, dread, terror. 2 *(asombro)* astonishment, amazement. LOC **¡qué espanto!** how awful!

**espantoso,-a** *adj* 1 *(terrible)* frightful, dreadful. 2 *(asombroso)* astonishing, amazing. 3 *(desmesurado)* dreadful, terrible.

**España** *nf* Spain.

**español,-la** *adj* Spanish.
▶ *nm & nf (persona)* Spaniard.
▶ *nm* **español** *(idioma)* Spanish, Castilian.

**esparadrapo** *nm* sticking plaster.

**esparcir** *vt* 1 *(desparramar)* to scatter. 2 *fig (divulgar)* to spread.
▶ *vpr* **esparcirse** 1 *(desparramarse)* to scatter, be scattered. 2 *fig (divulgarse)* to spread out.

**espárrago** *nm* asparagus.

**esparto** *nm* esparto grass.

**espátula** *nf* 1 *(gen)* spatula. 2 *(de pintor)* palette knife; *(de cristalero)* putty knife. 3 TÉC stripping knife. 4 *(ave)* spoonbill.

**especia** *nf* spice.

**especial** *adj* 1 *(gen)* special. 2 *(remilgado)* fussy (para, about), finicky (para, about): *es un poco especial para la comida* she's a bit finicky about food. LOC **en especial** especially.

**especialidad** *nf* 1 *(gen)* speciality (US specialty). 2 EDUC main subject, specialized field.

**especialista** *adj* specialist.
▶ *nm o nf* 1 specialist. 2 CINE stand-in; *(hombre)* stunt man; *(mujer)* stunt woman.

**especialización** *nf* specialization.

**especialmente** *adv* 1 *(exclusivamente)* specially. 2 *(particularmente)* especially.

**especie** *nf* 1 *(de animales, plantas)* species. 2 *(tipo)* kind, sort. 3 *(tema)* matter, notion, idea; *(noticia)* piece of news. LOC **en especie** in kind: *pagar en especie* to pay in kind.

**especiero,-a** *nm & nf* grocer.
▶ *nm* **especiero** spice rack.

**especificar** *vt* to specify.

**específico,-a** *adj* specific.
▶ *nm* **específico** *(medicamento)* specific; *(especialidad)* patent medicine. COMP **peso específico** specific gravity.

**espécimen** *nm* specimen.

**espectacular** *adj* spectacular.

**espectáculo** *nm* 1 spectacle, sight. 2 *(diversión)* entertainment. 3 *(TV, radio, etc)* performance, show.

**espectador,-ra** *nm & nf* 1 *(de deportes)* spectator. 2 *(de obra, película)* member of the audience; *(de televisión)* viewer.

▶ *nm pl* **espectadores** *(de obra, película)* audience *sing*; *(de programa televisivo)* viewers.

**espectro** *nm* **1** FÍS spectrum. **2** *(fantasma)* spectre (US specter), ghost, apparition. **3** *fig (persona)* ghost. **4** *(conjunto, serie)* range.

**especulador,-ra** *adj* speculating.
▶ *nm & nf* speculator.

**especular** *vt fig (reflexionar)* to speculate about.
▶ *vi* **1** *(comerciar)* to speculate (en, in); *(en bolsa)* to speculate (en, on). **2** *(conjeturar)* to speculate (sobre, about).

**espejismo** *nm* **1** mirage. **2** *fig* mirage, illusion.

**espejo** *nm* **1** mirror. **2** *fig (imagen)* mirror, reflection.

**espeleología** *nf* potholing, speleology.

**espeleólogo,-a** *nm & nf* potholer, speleologist.

**espeluznante** *adj* hair-raising, terrifying, horrifying.

**espeluznar** *vt* to horrify, terrify, make one's hair stand on end.

**espera** *nf* **1** wait, waiting. **2** *(paciencia)* patience. LOC **en espera de...** waiting for.... ‖ **estar a la espera** to be waiting, be expecting.

**esperanza** *nf* hope, expectance. LOC **con la esperanza de...** in the hope of.... ‖ **tener muchas esperanzas** to have high hopes. COMP **esperanza de vida** life expectancy.

**esperanzador,-ra** *adj* encouraging.

**esperanzar** *vt* to give hope to.
▶ *vpr* **esperanzarse** to have hope.

**esperar** *vt* **1** *(tener esperanza)* to hope for, expect: *esperan un milagro* they're hoping for a miracle. **2** *(contar, creer)* to expect: *no te esperábamos hasta mañana* we didn't expect you till tomorrow. **3** *(aguardar)* to wait for, await: *espera un momento* wait a moment. **4** *(desear)* to hope: *espero verlo* I hope to see him. **5** *fig (bebé)* to expect.
▶ *vi* to wait: *esperaré hasta que lleguen* I'll wait until they get here.

▶ *vpr* **esperarse** **1** *(aguardar)* to wait: *espérense en recepción* please wait in reception. **2** *(creer, contar)* to expect: *se espera que seas puntual* you're expected to be punctual. **3** *(desear)* to hope: *se espera que lo hayan pasado bien* we hope you've had a good time.

**espermatozoide** *nm* spermatozoon, sperm.

**espesar** *vt (salsa, etc)* to thicken; *(tejido, etc)* to make thicker.
▶ *vpr* **espesarse** **1** *(gen)* to get thicker. **2** *(salsa, etc)* to thicken.

**espeso,-a** *adj* **1** *(líquido, sustancia, objeto)* thick. **2** *(bosque, niebla)* thick, dense. **3** *(pasta, masa)* stiff. LOC **estar espeso,-a** *fam* not to be able to think straight.

**espesor** *nm* thickness.

**espesura** *nf* **1** *(de líquido, objeto)* thickness. **2** *(de niebla, etc)* denseness. **3** *fig (en bosque)* thicket, dense wood.

**espía** *nm o nf* spy.

**espiar** *vt* to spy on, watch.

**espiga** *nf* **1** *(gen)* spike; *(de trigo)* ear. **2** *(de tejido)* herringbone. **3** *(clavija)* peg, pin.

**espigado,-a** *adj* **1** BOT ripe. **2** *(en forma de espiga)* ear-shaped. **3** *fig (persona)* tall, lanky.

**espigón** *nm* **1** MAR breakwater, jetty. **2** *(punta)* sharp point, spike.

**espina** *nf* **1** *(de planta)* thorn. **2** *(de pez)* fishbone. **3** *(columna vertebral)* spine, backbone. **4** *fig (pesar)* sadness, sorrow, grief.

**espinaca** *nf* spinach.

**espinal** *adj* spinal: *médula espinal* spinal marrow.

**espinilla** *nf* **1** *(de la pierna)* shinbone. **2** *(grano)* blackhead.

**espino** *nm* **1** *(árbol)* hawthorn. **2** *(alambre)* barbed wire. COMP **espino albar** common hawthorn. ‖ **espino negro** blackthorn.

**espinoso,-a** *adj* **1** *(planta)* thorny. **2** *(pez)* spiny. **3** *fig* thorny, prickly, difficult, tricky.

**espionaje** *nm* spying, espionage: *película de espionaje* spy film.

**espiral** *adj* spiral: *escalera espiral* spiral staircase.
  ▶ *nf* **1** spiral. **2** *(de reloj)* hairspring.
**espirar** *vt* to exhale, breathe out.
  ▶ *vi* to breathe.
**espiritismo** *nm* spiritualism.
**espiritista** *adj* spiritualistic.
  ▶ *nm o nf* spiritualist.
**espíritu** *nm* **1** *(gen)* spirit. **2** *(alma)* soul, spirit. **3** *(fantasma)* ghost, spirit. **4** *(licores)* spirits *pl*. **5** *fig (idea central)* spirit, essence, soul.
**espiritual** *adj* spiritual.
**espiritualidad** *nf* spirituality.
**espléndido,-a** *adj* **1** *(magnífico)* splendid, magnificent. **2** *(generoso)* generous, lavish.
**esplendor** *nm* **1** *(resplandor)* brilliance, shining. **2** *fig (magnificencia)* magnificence, splendour (US splendor). **3** *(auge)* glory.
**esplendoroso,-a** *adj* **1** *(resplandeciente)* brilliant, radiant, shining. **2** *(grandioso)* magnificent, lavish.
**espliego** *nm* lavender.
**espolear** *vt* **1** to spur on. **2** *fig* to spur on, encourage.
**espolón** *nm* **1** *(de ave)* spur. **2** *(de caballería)* fetlock. **3** *(de nave)* ram. **4** *(malecón)* sea wall. **5** *fam (sabañón)* chilblain.
**espolvorear** *vt* **1** *(despolvorear)* to dust. **2** *(esparcir)* to powder, sprinkle.
**esponja** *nf* **1** sponge. **2** *fig (gorrón)* sponger.
**esponjar** *vt* *(ahuecar)* to fluff up; *(tierra)* to loosen.
  ▶ *vpr* **esponjarse 1** *fig (envanecerse)* to swell with pride. **2** *fig (físicamente)* to glow with health.
**esponjoso,-a** *adj (gen)* spongy; *(bizcocho)* light.
**espontáneamente** *adv* spontaneously.
**espontaneidad** *nf* spontaneity.
**espontáneo,-a** *adj* **1** *(cosa)* spontaneous; *(discurso)* impromptu, unprepared. **2** *(persona)* natural, unaffected.
**espora** *nf* spore.
**esporádicamente** *adv* sporadically.

**esporádico,-a** *adj* sporadic.
**esposa** *nf* wife.
**esposado,-a** *adj* **1** *(casado)* married. **2** *(con esposas)* handcuffed.
**esposar** *vt* to handcuff, put handcuffs on.
**esposas** *nf pl* handcuffs.
**esposo** *nm* husband.
**esprint** *nm* sprint.
**esprintar** *vi* to sprint.
**esprínter** *nm o nf* sprinter.
**espuela** *nf* **1** spur. **2** *fig* spur, stimulus.
**espuerta** *nf* two-handled rush basket.
**espuma** *nf* **1** *(gen)* foam; *(de jabón)* lather; *(de cerveza)* froth, head; *(olas)* surf. **2** *(impurezas)* scum. **3** *(tejido)* foam.
**espumadera** *nf* skimmer.
**espumar** *vt* *(quitar espuma)* to skim.
  ▶ *vi (hacer espuma - jabón)* to lather; *(- cerveza)* to froth; *(- vino)* to sparkle; *(- olas)* to foam.
**espumillón** *nm* tinsel.
**espumoso,-a** *adj (ola)* foamy, frothy; *(jabón)* lathery; *(vino)* sparkling.
**esqueje** *nm* cutting.
**esquela** *nf* **1** *(carta)* short letter. **2** *(mortuoria)* obituary notice.
**esqueleto** *nm* **1** ANAT skeleton. **2** ARQUIT framework.
**esquema** *nm* **1** *(gráfica)* diagram. **2** *(plan)* outline, plan.
**esquemático,-a** *adj* schematic, diagrammatic.
**esquematizar** *vt* **1** *(plan, idea)* to outline. **2** *(plano, etc)* to sketch.
**esquí** *nm* **1** *(tabla)* ski. **2** DEP skiing. s *pl* esquís. [COMP] **esquí acuático** waterskiing. ▌ **esquí alpino** alpine skiing. ▌ **esquí náutico** water-skiing.
**esquiador,-ra** *nm & nf* skier.
**esquiar** *vi* to ski.
**esquilador,-ra** *nm & nf* sheepshearer.
**esquiladora** *nf* shears *pl*.
**esquilar** *vt* **1** *(pelo)* to clip. **2** *(ovejas)* to shear.
**esquimal** *adj* Eskimo.
  ▶ *nm o nf* Eskimo.
  ▶ *nm (idioma)* Eskimo.

**esquina** *nf* corner.
▸ *vt* **1** *(hacer esquina)* to form a corner with, be on the corner of. **2** *(poner en esquina)* to put in a corner.

**esquinazo** *nm* corner. LOC **dar el esquinazo a ALGN** *fam* to give SB the slip.

**esquirla** *nf* splinter.

**esquirol** *nm* blackleg, scab.

**esquisto** *nm* shale.

**esquivar** *vt* **1** *(persona)* to avoid, shun. **2** *(golpe)* to dodge, elude.

**esquivo,-a** *adj* cold, aloof.

**esquizofrenia** *nf* schizophrenia.

**esquizofrénico,-a** *adj* schizophrenic.
▸ *nm & nf* schizophrenic.

**estabilidad** *nf* stability.

**estabilización** *nf* stabilization.

**estabilizar** *vt* to stabilize, make stable.
▸ *vpr* **estabilizarse** to become stable, become stabilized.

**estable** *adj* stable, steady.

**establecer** *vt* **1** *(gen)* to establish; *(fundar)* to found, set up. **2** *(récord)* to set. **3** *(ordenar)* to state, lay down, establish.
▸ *vpr* **establecerse** *(en un lugar)* to settle; *(en un negocio)* to set up in business.

**establecimiento** *nm* **1** *(acto)* establishment, founding, setting-up. **2** *(de gente)* settlement. **3** *(local)* establishment, shop, store.

**establo** *nm* **1** stable, cowshed, stall. **2** *fig* filthy place, pigsty.

**estabular** *vt* to stable.

**estaca** *nf* **1** *(palo con punta)* stake, post; *(para tienda de campaña)* peg. **2** *(garrote)* stick, cudgel. **3** *(rama)* cutting. **4** *(clavo)* spike.

**estacada** *nf* *(obra)* fence, fencing.

**estacazo** *nm* blow with a stick.

**estación** *nf* **1** *(del año, temporada)* season. **2** *(de tren, radio)* station.

**estacional** *adj* seasonal.

**estacionamiento** *nm* **1** AUTO *(acción)* parking; *(lugar)* car park, US parking lot. **2** *fig (estancamiento)* impasse.

**estacionar** *vt* **1** *(colocar)* to position, place. **2** AUTO to park.
▸ *vpr* **estacionarse 1** *(estancarse)* to be stationary, remain in the same place. **2** AUTO to park.

**estacionario,-a** *adj* stationary, stable.

**estadio** *nm* **1** *(lugar)* stadium. **2** *(fase)* stage, phase. **3** *arc (medida)* stadium, furlong.

**estadista** *nm o nf* **1** POL *(hombre)* statesman; *(mujer)* stateswoman. **2** MAT statistician.

**estadística** *nf* **1** *(ciencia)* statistics. **2** *(dato)* statistic, figure.

**estadístico,-a** *adj* statistical.
▸ *nm & nf* statistician.

**estado** *nm* **1** *(situación)* state, condition: *su estado es delicado* his condition is delicate. **2** *(en orden social)* status. **3** HIST estate. **4** POL state.

**Estados Unidos** *nm pl* The United States.

**estadounidense** *adj* American, from the United States.
▸ *nm o nf* American, person from the United States.

**estafa** *nf* fraud, swindle.

**estafador,-ra** *nm & nf* racketeer, swindler, trickster.

**estafar** *vt* to swindle, trick, cheat, defraud.

**estafilococo** *nm* staphylococcus.

**estalactita** *nf* stalactite.

**estalagmita** *nf* stalagmite.

**estallar** *vi* **1** *(reventar)* to explode, blow up. **2** *(neumático)* to burst; *(bomba)* to explode, go off; *(cristal)* to shatter. **3** *(volcán)* to erupt. **4** *(látigo)* to crack. **5** *fig (rebelión, epidemia)* to break out. **6** *fig (pasión, sentimientos)* to burst: *estallar en lágrimas* to burst into tears.

**estallido** *nm* **1** *(explosión)* explosion. **2** *(de trueno)* crash; *(de látigo)* crack. **3** *fig* outbreak.

**estambre** *nm* **1** COST worsted, woollen yarn (US woolen yarn). **2** BOT stamen.

**estamento** *nm* class, stratum.

**estampa** *nf* **1** *(imagen)* picture. **2** *fig (aspecto)* appearance, look, aspect.

**estampación** *nf* printing.

**estampado,-a** *adj (gen)* patterned, print; *(tela)* printed; *(metal)* stamped.
▶ *nm* **estampado** *(tela)* print.

**estampar** *vt* **1** *(imprimir)* to print. **2** *(metales)* to stamp. **3** *(dejar huella)* to stamp. |LOC| **estampar la firma** to sign.

**estampida** *nf* **1** *(ruido)* bang. **2** *(de animales)* stampede.

**estampilla** *nf* stamp, rubber stamp.

**estampita** *nf* religious print.

**estancado,-a** *adj* **1** *(agua)* stagnant. **2** *fig (asunto, negocio)* at a standstill; *(negociaciones)* deadlocked; *(persona)* stuck, bogged down.

**estancamiento** *nm* **1** stagnation. **2** *fig* deadlock, standstill.

**estancar** *vt* **1** *(aguas)* to hold up, hold back, dam; *(flujo)* to check. **2** *fig (progreso)* to check, block, hold up.
▶ *vpr* **estancarse 1** *(líquido)* to stagnate, become stagnant. **2** *fig* to stagnate, get bogged down.

**estanco,-a** *adj* watertight.
▶ *nm* **estanco** *(tienda)* tobacconist's.

**estándar** *adj* standard, standardized: *modelo estándar* standard model; *reglas estándar* set rules.

**estandarte** *nm* standard, banner.

**estanque** *nm* **1** *(de peces, etc)* pool, pond. **2** *(para proveer agua)* reservoir, tank.

**estanquero,-a** *nm & nf* tobacconist.

**estante** *nm* **1** *(anaquel)* shelf; *(para libros)* bookcase. **2** *(de máquina)* stand.

**estantería** *nf* shelving, shelves *pl*.

**estaño** *nm* tin.

**estar** *vi* **1** *(lugar, posición)* to be: *estamos en casa* we are at home. **2** *(permanecer)* to be, stay: *estuvimos allí diez días* we stayed there for ten days. **3** *(cualidades transitorias)* to be: *está cansado* he's tired. **4** *(una prenda)* to suit, be: *te está grande* it's too big for you.
▶ *aux* **1 estar + gerundio** to be: *estaban cantando* they were singing. **2 estar a** *(precio)* to be, sell at; *(fecha)* to be: *estamos a 15 de marzo* it's the 15th of March. **3**

**estar con** *(tener)* to have; *(estar de acuerdo)* to agree with: *estoy con Ana* I agree with Ana. **4 estar de** *(gen)* to be; *(trabajar)* to be, be working as; *(ir vestido)* to be, be dressed in: *estar de vacaciones* to be on holiday; *está de uniforme* he's in uniform. **5 estar en** *(consistir)* to be, lie; *(entender)* to understand; *(creer)* to think, believe; *(depender de uno)* to be up to. **6 estar para** *(estar a punto)* to be about to; *(estar acabado)* to be finished, be ready; *(estar de humor)* to feel like, be in the mood for. **7 estar por** *(no haberse ejecutado)* to remain to be; *(estar determinado)* to be for; *(ir a)* to be going to; *(a favor)* to be for. **8 estar que** *fam* to be nearly, be really, be practically: *está que se hunde* it's practically ruined. **9 estar sin + inf** not to have been + *pp*: *el coche está sin lavar* the car hasn't been washed, the car still needs washing.
▶ *vpr* **estarse** *(permanecer)* to spend, stay: *se estuvo todo el día leyendo* she spent all day reading.

**estarcido** *nm* stencil.

**estarcir** *vt* to stencil.

**estasis** *nf inv* stasis.

**estatal** *adj* state.

**estático,-a** *adj* static.

**estatua** *nf* statue.

**estatuilla** *nf* statuette, figurine.

**estatura** *nf* height, stature.

**estatuto** *nm* statute. |COMP| **estatuto de autonomía** statute of autonomy.

**este** *adj* **1** east, eastern. **2** *(dirección)* easterly; *(viento)* east, easterly.
▶ *nm* **1** east. **2** *(viento)* east wind.

**este,-a** *adj* this; *(plural)* these: *este libro* this book; *estas manzanas* these apples.

**éste,-a** *pron* **1** *(cosa)* this one: *dame éste* give me this one. **2** *(hombre - sujeto)* he; *(mujer - sujeto)* she: *ésta me lo dijo* she told me. **3** *(hombre - complemento)* him; *(mujer - complemento)* her: *se lo dio a éste* she gave it to him. **4** *(este último)* the latter. **5** *pey* this one.

✎ Cuando no se produzca confusión con el adjetivo se puede omitir el acento.

**estela¹** *nf* **1** *(de barco)* wake, wash; *(de avión)* vapour (US vapor) trail; *(de cometa)* tail. **2** *fig* trail.

**estela²** *nf* *(monumento)* stela, stele.

**estelar** *adj* **1** *(sideral)* stellar. **2** *fig* star.

**estenordeste** *nm* **1** east-northeast. **2** *(viento)* east-northeast wind.

**estepa¹** *nf* *(llanura)* steppe.

**estepa²** *nf* *(planta)* rockrose.

**estepario,-a** *adj* steppe, from the steppes.

**éster** *nm* ester.

**estera** *nf* rush mat.

**estercolero** *nm* **1** dunghill, dung heap. **2** *fig* pigsty.

**estéreo** *nm* stereo.

**estereofónico,-a** *adj* stereo, stereophonic.

**estereoscopio** *nm* stereoscope.

**estereotipado,-a** *adj fig* stereotyped, standard, set.

**estereotipo** *nm* stereotype.

**estéril** *adj* **1** *(tierra)* sterile, barren. **2** *(hombre)* sterile; *(mujer)* sterile, infertile. **3** *(aséptico)* sterile. **4** *fig* futile, useless.

**esterilidad** *nf* **1** *(de terreno)* sterility, barrenness. **2** *(de hombre)* sterility; *(de mujer)* sterility, infertility. **3** *fig* futility, uselessness.

**esterilización** *nf* sterilization.

**esterilizador,-ra** *nm* sterilizer.

**esterilizar** *vt* to sterilize.

**esterilla** *nf* **1** *(felpudo)* small mat. **2** *(de cañamazo)* rush matting, wickerwork.

**esterlina** *adj* sterling.
▶ *nf* sterling.

**esternocleidomastoideo** *nm* sternocleidomastoid.

**esternón** *nm* sternum, breastbone.

**estesudeste** *nm* **1** east-southeast. **2** *(viento)* east-southeast wind.

**esteta** *nm o nf* aesthete (US esthete).

**estética** *nf* aesthetics (US esthetics).

**estéticamente** *adv* aesthetically.

**estético,-a** *adj* aesthetic (US esthetic).

**estetoscopio** *nm* stethoscope.

**estiércol** *nm* dung, manure.

**estilete** *nm* **1** *(punzón)* stylus. **2** *(puñal)* stiletto. **3** MED probe.

**estilismo** *nm* stylism.

**estilista** *nm o nf* **1** *(escritor)* stylist. **2** *(diseñador)* stylist, designer.

**estilístico,-a** *adj* stylistic.

**estilización** *nf* stylization.

**estilizar** *vt* **1** to stylize. **2** *(hacer delgado)* to make thinner.

**estilo** *nm* **1** *(gen)* style. **2** *(modo)* manner, fashion. **3** GRAM speech. **4** *(natación)* stroke.

**estilográfica** *nf* fountain pen.

**estima** *nf* esteem, respect.

**estimable** *adj* **1** esteemed, reputable, worthy. **2** *(cantidad)* considerable.

**estimación** *nf* **1** *(afecto)* esteem, respect. **2** *(valoración)* estimation, evaluation. **3** *(cálculo)* estimate. COMP **propia estima** self-esteem.

**estimado,-a** *adj* **1** *(apreciado)* esteemed, respected. **2** *(valorado)* valued, estimated: *el precio estimado* the estimated price.

**estimar** *vt* **1** *(apreciar)* to esteem, respect, hold in esteem, admire. **2** *(valorar)* to value. **3** *(juzgar, creer)* to consider, think, reckon.

**estimulación** *nf* stimulation.

**estimulante** *adj* stimulating, encouraging.
▶ *nm* stimulant.

**estimular** *vt* **1** *(animar)* to encourage, stimulate. **2** *(apetito, pasiones)* to whet.

**estímulo** *nm* **1** stimulus, stimulation. **2** *fig* encouragement. **3** COM incentive.

**estío** *nm* summer.

**estipendio** *nm* stipend, fee, remuneration.

**estipular** *vt* to stipulate.

**estirado,-a** *adj* **1** *fig (en el vestir)* stiff, formal, starchy. **2** *fig (orgulloso)* stiff, conceited, haughty.
▶ *nm* **estirado** **1** *(textil)* drawing. **2** *(del pelo)* straightening; *(de la piel)* lift.

**estiramiento** *nm* stretch.

**estirar** vt **1** (gen) to stretch. **2** (cuello) to crane. **3** (medias) to pull up; (falda) to pull down. **4** fig (dinero) to spin out, make go further.
▶ vi (crecer) to shoot up.
▶ vpr **estirarse 1** (crecer) to shoot up. **2** (desperezarse) to stretch.

**estirón** nm pull, jerk, tug.

**estirpe** nf stock, lineage, race.

**estival** adj summer.

**esto** pron this: esto me gusta I like this.

**estocada** nf stab, thrust.

**estofa** nf fig class, type.

**estofado** nm CULIN stew.

**estofar** vt CULIN to stew.

**estoicismo** nm stoicism.

**estoico,-a** adj stoic, stoical.
▶ nm & nf stoic.

**estoma** nm stoma.

**estomacal** adj **1** (del estómago) stomach, of the stomach. **2** (digestivo) digestive.
▶ nm (bebida) digestive liqueur.

**estómago** nm stomach. COMP dolor de estómago stomachache.

**Estonia** nf Estonia.

**estonio,-a** adj Estonian.
▶ nm & nf (persona) Estonian.
▶ nm **estonio** (idioma) Estonian.

**estopa** nf **1** (fibra) tow. **2** (tela) burlap. COMP estopa de acero steel wool.

**estoque** nm (espada) sword.

**estor** nm roller blind.

**estorbar** vt **1** (dificultar) to hinder, get in the way; (obstruir) to obstruct, block, hold up. **2** fig (molestar) to annoy, bother, disturb.
▶ vi (ser obstáculo) to be in the way.

**estorbo** nm **1** (obstáculo) obstruction, obstacle. **2** (molestia) hindrance, encumbrance; (persona) nuisance.

**estornino** nm starling.

**estornudar** vi to sneeze.

**estornudo** nm sneeze.

**estos,-as** adj these.

✎ Consulta también este,-a.

**éstos,-as** pron these (ones).

✎ Consulta también éste,-a.

**estrabismo** nm strabismus, squint: tengo estrabismo I have a squint.

**estrado** nm stage, platform; (tarima) dais.
▶ nm pl **estrados** JUR courtrooms.

**estrago** nm havoc, ruin, ravage.

**estragón** nm tarragon.

**estrangular** vt **1** (ahogar) to strangle. **2** MED to strangulate. **3** AUTO to throttle.

**estratagema** nf **1** MIL stratagem. **2** fam fig trick.

**estratega** nm o nf strategist.

**estrategia** nf strategy.

**estratégicamente** adv strategically.

**estratégico,-a** adj strategic.

**estratificar** vt to stratify.
▶ vpr **estratificarse** to be stratified.

**estrato** nm **1** GEOL stratum. **2** (capa) stratum. **3** (nivel social) stratum, class. **4** (nube) stratus.

**estratosfera** nf stratosphere.

**estraza** nf rag, piece of cloth.

**estrechamente** adv **1** (con estrechez) narrowly, tightly. **2** fig (con intimidad) closely, intimately: están estrechamente unidos they're very close.

**estrechar** vt **1** (carretera) to make narrower. **2** (prenda) to take in. **3** (abrazar) to squeeze, hug; (mano) to shake: nos estrechamos las manos we shook hands. **4** fig (obligar) to compel, constrain. **5** fig (relaciones, lazos) to strengthen.
▶ vpr **estrecharse 1** (valle, etc) to narrow, become narrower. **2** (apretarse) to squeeze together, squeeze up. **3** fig (relaciones, etc) to strengthen, get stronger.

**estrechez** nf **1** (poco ancho) narrowness. **2** (falta espacio) lack of space. **3** (prendas) tightness. **4** fig (económica) want, need. **5** fig (amistad) closeness, intimacy. **6** fig (apuro) tight spot. LOC pasar estrecheces fig to be hard up.

**estrecho,-a** adj **1** (poco ancho) narrow. **2** (ropa) tight; (calzado) tight, small. **3** (habitación) cramped, poky, small. **4** (sin espacio) packed, jam-packed. **5** fig (amistad, etc) close, intimate.
▶ nm **estrecho** GEOG strait, straits pl.

**estrella** *nf* **1** *(gen)* star. **2** *fig (destino)* destiny, fate.

**estrellado,-a** *adj* **1** *(cielo)* starry, star-spangled, full of stars. **2** *(forma)* star-shaped. **3** *(hecho pedazos)* smashed, shattered.

**estrellar** *vt* **1** *(llenar de estrellas)* to cover with stars. **2** *fam (hacer pedazos)* to smash (to pieces), shatter. **3** *(freír)* to fry.
▶ *vpr* **estrellarse 1** *(llenarse de estrellas)* to be full of stars. **2** *(hacerse pedazos)* to smash, shatter. **3** *(chocar)* to crash.

**estremecedor,-ra** *adj* **1** startling. **2** *(grito)* bloodcurdling.

**estremecer** *vt* **1** *(gen)* to shake. **2** *fig (asustar)* to startle, frighten.
▶ *vpr* **estremecerse 1** *(temblar)* to shake. **2** *(de miedo)* to tremble, shudder; *(de frío)* to shiver, tremble. **3** *fig* to shudder.

**estrenar** *vt* **1** *(gen)* to use for the first time; *(ropa)* to wear for the first time. **2** *(obra)* to perform for the first time, give the first performance of; *(película)* to release, put on release.
▶ *vpr* **estrenarse** to make one's debut.

**estreno** *nm* **1** *(de algo)* first use. **2** *(persona)* début, first appearance. **3** *(de obra)* first performance; *(de película)* premiere.

**estreñido,-a** *adj* **1** constipated. **2** *fig* mean, stingy.

**estreñimiento** *nm* constipation.

**estreñir** *vt* to constipate, make constipated.
▶ *vpr* **estreñirse** to become constipated.

**estrépito** *nm* **1** din, racket, clatter. **2** *fig* ostentation, fuss.

**estrepitoso,-a** *adj* **1** noisy, clamorous. **2** *(ruido)* deafening. **3** *fig (éxito)* resounding; *(fracaso)* spectacular.

**estreptococo** *nm* streptococcus.

**estrés** *nm* stress.

**estresado,-a** *adj* under stress.

**estresante** *adj* stressful.

**estría** *nf* **1** *(ranura)* groove. **2** ARQUIT flute. **3** *(en la piel)* stretch mark.

**estriar** *vt* **1** *(hacer ranuras)* to groove. **2** ARQUIT to flute. **3** *(piel)* to give stretch marks.
▶ *vpr* **estriarse** *(piel)* to get stretch marks.

**estribillo** *nm* **1** *(de poesía)* refrain; *(de canción)* chorus. **2** *(muletilla)* pet phrase, pet saying.

**estribo** *nm* **1** *(de jinete)* stirrup. **2** *(de carruaje, tren)* step. **3** AUTO running board; *(de moto)* footrest. **4** ARQUIT buttress; *(de puente)* pier, support. **5** *(del oído)* stirrup bone.

**estribor** *nm* starboard.

**estricto,-a** *adj* strict, rigorous.

**estridencia** *nf* **1** *(ruido)* stridency, shrillness. **2** *(color, etc)* loudness, garishness, gaudiness.

**estridente** *adj* **1** *(ruido)* strident, shrill. **2** *(color, etc)* loud, garish, gaudy.

**estroboscópico,-a** *adj* stroboscopic.

**estroboscopio** *nm* stroboscope, strobe.

**estrofa** *nf* stanza, verse.

**estrógeno** *nm* oestrogen (US estrogen).

**estropajo** *nm* **1** *(para fregar)* scourer. **2** *fig (desecho)* useless thing.

**estropajoso,-a** *adj* **1** *(lengua)* furry. **2** *(carne, etc)* gristly, tough. **3** *(pelo)* straw-like.

**estropear** *vt* **1** *(máquina)* to damage, break, ruin. **2** *(cosecha)* to spoil, ruin. **3** *(plan, etc)* to spoil, ruin.
▶ *vpr* **estropearse 1** *(máquina)* to break down. **2** *(cosecha)* to be spoiled, get damaged. **3** *(plan, etc)* to fail, fall through, go wrong. **4** *(comida)* to go bad.

**estropicio** *nm* **1** *fam (rotura)* breakage, damage; *(ruido producido)* crash, clatter, smash. **2** *fam (desorden)* mess; *(jaleo)* fuss, rumpus.

**estructura** *nf* **1** *(gen)* structure. **2** *(armazón)* frame, framework.

**estructurado,-a** *adj* structured, organized.

**estructurar** *vt* to structure, organize.
▶ *vpr* **estructurarse** to be structured, be organized.

**estruendo** *nm* **1** *(ruido)* great noise, din. **2** *(confusión)* uproar, tumult.

**estruendoso,-a** *adj (ruido)* noisy, deafening; *(aplauso)* thunderous.

**estrujar** *vt* **1** *(exprimir)* to squeeze. **2** *(apretar - alguien)* to crush; *(- algo)* to screw up. **3** *(ropa)* to wring. **4** *fig (sacar partido)* to drain, bleed dry.
▶ *vpr* **estrujarse** *(apretujarse)* to crowd, throng.

**estuario** *nm* estuary.

**estucado** *nm* stucco, stucco work.

**estucar** *vt* to stucco.

**estuche** *nm* **1** *(caja)* case, box. **2** *(conjunto)* set.

**estuco** *nm* stucco.

**estudiante** *nm o nf* student.

**estudiar** *vt* to study, learn.
▶ *vi* to study: *estudia para maestro* he's training to be a teacher.
▶ *vpr* **estudiarse** to consider.

**estudio** *nm* **1** *(gen)* study. **2** *(apartamento)* studio flat (US apartment), bedsit.
▶ *nm pl* **estudios** *(conocimientos)* studies, education *sing*.

**estudioso,-a** *adj* studious.

**estufa** *nf (calentador)* heater, stove; *(de gas, eléctrica)* fire.

**estupa** *nf argot (grupo)* drug squad.
▶ *nm o nf (oficial)* drug-squad officer.

**estupefaciente** *adj* stupefying.
▶ *nm* drug, narcotic.

**estupefacto,-a** *adj* astounded, dumbfounded, flabbergasted.

**estupendamente** *adv* marvellously (US marvelously), wonderfully.

**estupendo,-a** *adj* marvellous (US marvelous), wonderful, super.

**estupidez** *nf* stupidity, stupid thing.

**estúpido,-a** *adj* stupid, silly.
▶ *nm & nf* berk, idiot.

**estupor** *nm* stupor, amazement, astonishment. LOC **causar estupor** to astonish.

**esturión** *nm* sturgeon.

**etapa** *nf* **1** period, stage. **2** *(parada)* stop, stage. **3** DEP leg, stage.

**éter** *nm* QUÍM ether.

**etéreo,-a** *adj* ethereal.

**eternamente** *adv* eternally.

**eternidad** *nf* **1** eternity. **2** *fam* ages *pl*.

**eternizar** *vt* **1** to eternize, eternalize. **2** *fam* to prolong endlessly.
▶ *vpr* **eternizarse 1** *fam (ser interminable)* to be interminable, be endless; *(discusión)* to drag on. **2** *fam (tardar mucho)* to take ages.

**eterno,-a** *adj* eternal, everlasting, endless.

**ética** *nf* ethics *pl*, ethic.

**éticamente** *adv* ethically.

**ético,-a** *adj* ethical.

**etílico,-a** *adj* ethylic.

**etimología** *nf* etymology.

**etimológico,-a** *adj* etymological.

**etíope** *adj* Ethiopian.
▶ *nm o nf (persona)* Ethiopian.
▶ *nm* **etíope** *(idioma)* Ethiopian, Ethiopic.

**Etiopía** *nf* Ethiopia.

**etiqueta** *nf* **1** *(rótulo)* label, tag. **2** *(formalidad)* etiquette, formality, ceremony.

**etiquetar** *vt* to label, put a label on.

**etnia** *nf* ethnic group.

**étnico,-a** *adj* ethnic.

**etnografía** *nf* ethnography.

**etnología** *nf* ethnology.

**etnólogo,-a** *nm & nf* ethnologist.

**eucalipto** *nm* eucalyptus.

**eufemismo** *nm* euphemism.

**euforia** *nf* euphoria, elation.

**eufórico,-a** *adj* euphoric, elated.

**eunuco** *nm* eunuch.

**eureka** *interj* eureka!

**euritmia** *nf* eurythmics.

**euro** *nm* euro.

**euroasiático,-a** *adj* Eurasian.
▶ *nm & nf* Eurasian.

**eurodiputado,-a** *nm & nf* Member of the European Parliament, MEP, Euro MP.

**Europa** *nf* Europe.

**europeísta** *adj* pro-European.
▶ *nm o nf* pro-European.
**europeo,-a** *adj* European.
▶ *nm & nf* European. COMP **Comunidad Europea** European Community. I **Unión Europea** European Union.
**eurovisión** *nf* Eurovision.
**Euskadi** *nm* the Basque Country.
**euskera** *nm (idioma)* Basque.
**eutanasia** *nf* euthanasia.
**evacuación** *nf* evacuation.
**evacuar** *vt* 1 *(lugar)* to evacuate. 2 ANAT to empty.
**evadir** *vt* 1 *(peligro, respuesta)* to avoid; *(responsabilidad)* to shirk. 2 *(capital, impuestos)* to evade.
▶ *vpr* **evadirse** *(escaparse)* to escape.
**evaluación** *nf* 1 evaluation, assessment. 2 EDUC *(acción)* assessment; *(examen)* exam.
**evaluar** *vt* to evaluate, assess.
**evangélico,-a** *adj* evangelical.
**evangelio** *nm* gospel.
**evangelista** *nm* evangelist.
**evaporación** *nf* evaporation.
**evaporar** *vt* to evaporate.
▶ *vpr* **evaporarse** 1 to evaporate. 2 *fig* to vanish, disappear.
**evasión** *nf* 1 *(fuga)* escape, flight. 2 *fig* escape, escapism.
**evasivo,-a** *adj* evasive.
**eventual** *adj* 1 *(casual)* chance; *(probable)* possible. 2 *(trabajo)* casual, temporary, provisional. 3 *(ingresos, gastos)* incidental.
▶ *nm o nf* casual worker, temporary worker.
**eventualidad** *nf* eventuality, contingency.
**evidencia** *nf (claridad)* obviousness, clearness; *(certeza)* certainty.
**evidenciar** *vt* to show, make evident, prove, make obvious.
**evidente** *adj* evident, obvious.
**evidentemente** *adv* evidently, obviously.
**evitar** *vt* 1 *(gen)* to avoid. 2 *(impedir)* to prevent, avoid. 3 *(ahorrar)* to spare, save.

**evocar** *vt* 1 *(recuerdo)* to evoke, call up. 2 *(recordar)* to evoke, bring to mind.
**evolución** *nf* 1 *(cambio)* evolution; *(desarrollo)* development. 2 *(vuelta)* turn.
**evolucionar** *vi* 1 *(gen)* to evolve, develop. 2 *(dar vueltas)* to turn.
**evolucionismo** *nm* evolutionism.
**evolutivo,-a** *adj* evolutionary, evolving.
**ex-** *pref* ex-, former: *el ex primer ministro* the former prime minister.
**exacerbar** *vt* 1 *(agravar)* to exacerbate, aggravate, make worse. 2 *(irritar)* to exacerbate, exasperate, irritate.
**exactamente** *adv* exactly, precisely.
**exactitud** *nf (fidelidad)* exactness; *(precisión)* accuracy.
**exacto,-a** *adj* 1 *(fiel)* faithful, true; *(preciso)* accurate, exact. 2 *(verdad)* true: *eso no es exacto* that's not true.
**exageración** *nf* exaggeration.
**exagerado,-a** *adj* exaggerated.
**exagerar** *vt* to exaggerate.
▶ *vi* 1 to exaggerate. 2 *(abusar)* to overdo it, do too much.
**exaltado,-a** *adj* 1 *(discusión, etc)* heated, impassioned. 2 *(persona)* hot-headed, worked up.
**exaltar** *vt* 1 *(elevar)* to raise, promote. 2 *fig (alabar)* to exalt, praise, extol.
▶ *vpr* **exaltarse** *(excitarse)* to get overexcited, get worked up, get carried away.
**examen** *nm* 1 examination, exam. 2 *(estudio)* consideration, examination, study. COMP **examen final** final examination. I **examen oral** oral examination.
**examinar** *vt (gen)* to examine.
▶ *vpr* **examinarse** to take an examination, sit an examination.
**exasperante** *adj* exasperating.
**exasperar** *vt* to exasperate.
▶ *vpr* **exasperarse** to get exasperated.
**excavación** *nf* 1 excavation, digging. 2 *(arqueológica)* dig.
**excavadora** *nf (máquina)* digger.
**excavar** *vt* to excavate, dig.

E

**excedencia** *nf* **1** *(de funcionario, etc)* leave. **2** *(de profesor)* sabbatical leave.

**excedente** *adj (sobrante)* excess, surplus.
▶ *nm* COM surplus, excess.

**exceder** *vt* **1** *(superar)* to excel, surpass. **2** *(sobrepasar)* to exceed, be in excess of.
▶ *vpr* **excederse 1** *(pasarse)* to overdo it, go too far. **2** *(en atenciones, etc)* to be extremely kind.

**excelente** *adj* excellent, first-rate.

**excentricidad** *nf* eccentricity.

**excéntrico,-a** *adj* eccentric.

**excepción** *nf* exception. LOC **a excepción de** with the exception of, except for. ‖ **de excepción** exceptional.

**excepcional** *adj* **1** *(extraordinario)* exceptional, outstanding. **2** *(raro)* exceptional, unusual.

**excepto** *adv* except (for), apart from, excepting.

**exceptuar** *vt* to except, leave out, exclude.

**excesivo,-a** *adj* excessive.

**exceso** *nm* **1** excess. **2** COM surplus. COMP **exceso de equipaje** excess baggage.

**excipiente** *nm* excipient.

**excisión** *nf* excision.

**excitación** *nf* **1** *(acción)* excitation. **2** *(sentimiento)* excitement.

**excitante** *adj* **1** exciting. **2** MED stimulating.

**excitar** *vt* **1** to excite. **2** *(emociones)* to stimulate, arouse.
▶ *vpr* **excitarse** to get excited, get worked up, get carried away.

**exclamación** *nf* exclamation; *(grito)* cry.

**exclamar** *vt* to exclaim, cry out.
▶ *vi* to exclaim, cry out.

**exclamativo,-a** *adj* exclamatory.

**exclamatorio,-a** *adj* exclamatory.

**excluir** *vt* **1** to exclude, shut out. **2** *(rechazar)* to reject; *(descartar)* to rule out; *(expulsar)* to throw out.

**exclusión** *nf* exclusion, shutting out.

**exclusiva** *nf* COM **1** sole right. **2** *(prensa)* exclusive, scoop.

**exclusividad** *nf* exclusiveness, exclusivity.

**exclusivo,-a** *adj* exclusive.

**excluyente** *adj* exclusive.

**excremento** *nf* excrement.

**excretor,-ra** *adj* excretory.

**exculpar** *vt* **1** to exonerate. **2** JUR to acquit.

**excursión** *nf* excursion, trip.

**excursionismo** *nm* hiking, rambling.

**excursionista** *nm o nf* tripper; *(a pie)* hiker, rambler.

**excusa** *nf* **1** *(pretexto)* excuse. **2** *(disculpa)* excuse, apology.

**excusar** *vt* **1** *(justificar)* to excuse. **2** *(disculpar)* to pardon, forgive, excuse.
▶ *vpr* **excusarse** *(justificarse)* to excuse os; *(disculparse)* to apologize.

**exención** *nf* exemption.

**exento,-a** *adj* **1** free (de, from), exempt (de, from). **2** *(descubierto)* open.

**exfoliación** *nf* exfoliation.

**exfoliar** *vt* to exfoliate.
▶ *vpr* **exfoliarse** to exfoliate.

**exhalación** *nf* **1** exhalation. **2** *(estrella)* shooting star; *(rayo)* flash of lightning.

**exhalar** *vt* **1** *(gases, vapores, etc)* to give off; *(aire)* to exhale, breathe out. **2** *fig (suspiros, etc)* to heave, let out; *(quejas)* to utter.

**exhaustivo,-a** *adj* exhaustive, thorough, comprehensive.

**exhausto,-a** *adj* exhausted.

**exhibición** *nf* **1** *(exposición)* exhibition, show. **2** CINE showing.

**exhibicionismo** *nm* exhibitionism.

**exhibir** *vt* **1** to exhibit, show, display. **2** *(ostentar)* to show off.
▶ *vpr* **exhibirse** *(ostentar)* to show off, make an exhibition of os.

**exhortar** *vt* to exhort.

**exhumación** *nf* exhumation.

**exhumar** *vt* **1** to exhume. **2** *fig* to revive, recall.

**exigencia** *nf* **1** demand, exigency. **2** *(requisito)* requirement.

**exigente** *adj* demanding, exacting.

**exigir** *vt* **1** *(pedir por derecho)* to demand. **2** *fig (necesitar)* to require, call for.

**exilado,-a** *nm & nf* exile.

**exilio** *nm* exile.

**existencia** *nf (vida)* existence, life.
▶ *nf pl* **existencias** stock *sing*, stocks.

**existencial** *adj* existential.

**existencialismo** *nm* existentialism.

**existencialista** *adj* existentialist.
▶ *nm o nf* existentialist.

**existente** *adj* **1** existing, existent. **2** COM in stock.

**existir** *vi* to exist, be.

**éxito** *nm* success.

**exitoso,-a** *adj* successful.

**éxodo** *nm* exodus.

**exogamia** *nf* exogamy.

**exorcismo** *nm* exorcism.

**exorcista** *nm o nf* exorcist.

**exotérico,-a** *adj* exoteric.

**exótico,-a** *adj* exotic.

**exotismo** *nm* exoticism.

**expandir** *vt* **1** *(dilatar)* to expand. **2** *fig (divulgar)* to spread.
▶ *vpr* **expandirse 1** *(dilatarse)* to expand. **2** *fig (divulgarse)* to spread.

**expansión** *nf* **1** *(dilatación)* expansion. **2** *(difusión)* spreading. **3** *(aumento)* expansion, increase, growth.

**expansionista** *adj* expansionist.

**expansivo,-a** *adj (gas, etc)* expansive. **2** *fig (franco)* expansive, open, frank.

**expatriar** *vt* to expatriate, banish.
▶ *vpr* **expatriarse** *(emigrar)* to emigrate, become an expatriate; *(exilarse)* to go into exile.

**expectativa** *nf* **1** *(esperanza)* expectation, hope. **2** *(posibilidad)* prospect.

**expectoración** *nf* **1** *(acción)* expectoration. **2** *(flema)* sputum, phlegm.

**expectorar** *vt* to expectorate.
▶ *vi* to expectorate.

**expedición** *nf* **1** *(gen)* expedition. **2** *(grupo de personas)* expedition, party.

**3** *(acción de expedir)* dispatch, shipping; *(remesa)* shipment.

**expedientar** *vt* to take disciplinary action against, open a file on.

**expediente** *nm* **1** JUR proceedings *pl*, action: *expediente judicial* legal proceedings. **2** *(informe)* dossier, record; *(ficha)* file. **3** *(recurso)* expedient.

**expedir** *vt* **1** *(mercancías)* to send, dispatch, ship; *(correo)* to send, dispatch. **2** *(pasaporte, título)* to issue. **3** *(contrato, documento)* to draw up.

**expeditivamente** *adv* expeditiously.

**expeditivo,-a** *adj* expeditious.

**expendedor,-ra** *adj* selling, retailing, retail.
▶ *nm & nf* dealer, retailer, seller.

**expender** *vt* **1** *(gastar)* to spend. **2** *(vender)* to sell. **3** *(vender al menudeo)* to retail, sell.

**expensas** *nf pl* expenses, charges, costs.

**experiencia** *nf* **1** *(gen)* experience. **2** *(experimento)* experiment.

**experimentación** *nf* experimentation, experimenting, testing.

**experimentado,-a** *adj* **1** *(persona)* experienced. **2** *(método)* tested, tried.

**experimental** *adj* experimental.

**experimentar** *vt* **1** *(hacer experimentos)* to experiment, test. **2** *(probar)* to test, try out. **3** *(sentir, notar)* to experience, feel; *(- cambio)* to undergo; *(- aumento)* to show; *(- pérdida, derrota)* to suffer.

**experimento** *nm* experiment, test.

**experto,-a** *adj* expert.
▶ *nm & nf* expert.

**expiar** *vt* to expiate, atone for.

**expirar** *vi* to expire.

**explanada** *nf* esplanade.

**explayar** *vt fml (extender)* to extend, spread out.
▶ *vpr* **explayarse** *(dilatarse al hablar)* to dwell (en, on), talk at length (en, about).

**explicable** *adj* explicable, explainable.

**explicación** *nf* **1** explanation. **2** *(motivo)* reason.

**explicar** *vt* **1** *(gen)* to explain, expound, tell. **2** *(justificar)* to justify.
▶ *vpr* **explicarse** *(expresarse)* to explain os, make os understood, make os clear.

**explicativo,-a** *adj* explanatory.

**explícito,-a** *adj* explicit.

**exploración** *nf* **1** *(gen)* exploration. **2** TÉC scanning. **3** MIL reconnaissance.

**explorador,-ra** *nm & nf* **1** *(persona)* explorer. **2** *(niño)* boy scout; *(niña)* girl guide, US girl scout.

**explorar** *vt* **1** *(gen)* to explore. **2** MED to probe. **3** MIL to reconnoitre. **4** TÉC to scan. **5** *(de mina)* to drill, prospect.

**exploratorio,-a** *adj* **1** exploratory. **2** MED exploratory, probing.

**explosión** *nf* **1** explosion, blast, blowing up. **2** *fig* outburst.

**explosionar** *vt* to explode.
▶ *vi* to explode, blow up.

**explosiva** *nf* LING plosive.

**explosivo,-a** *adj* **1** explosive. **2** LING plosive.
▶ *nm* **explosivo** explosive.

**explotación** *nf* **1** *(gen)* exploitation. **2** *(de terreno)* cultivation, farming. **3** *(de industria)* running, operating. **4** *(de recursos)* tapping, exploitation.

**explotador,-ra** *nm & nf pey* exploiter.

**explotar** *vt* **1** *(sacar provecho)* to exploit; *(mina)* to work; *(tierra)* to cultivate; *(industria)* to operate, run; *(recursos)* to tap, exploit.
▶ *vi* *(explosionar)* to explode, blow up.

**expoliación** *nf* plundering, pillaging, despoiling.

**expoliar** *vt* to plunder, pillage, despoil.

**expolio** *nm* **1** *(acción)* plundering, pillaging, despoiling. **2** *(botín)* loot, booty.

**exponencial** *adj* exponential.

**exponente** *adj* exponent, expounding.
▶ *nm* **1** MAT index, exponent. **2** *(prototipo)* exponent.

**exponer** *vt* **1** *(explicar)* to expound, explain; *(propuesta)* to put forward; *(hechos)* to state, set out. **2** *(mostrar)* to show, exhibit; *(mercancías)* to display. **3** *(arriesgar)* to expose, risk, endanger.
▶ *vpr* **exponerse** *(arriesgarse)* to expose os (a, to), run the risk (a, of).

**exportable** *adj* exportable, for exportation.

**exportación** *nf* export, exportation.

**exportador,-ra** *adj* exporting.
▶ *nm & nf* exporter.

**exportar** *vt* to export.

**exposición** *nf* **1** *(de arte)* exhibition, show; *(de mercancías)* display. **2** *(explicación)* account, explanation; *(hechos, ideas)* exposé. **3** *(al sol, etc)* exposure.

**expositivo,-a** *adj* explanatory.

**exprés** *adj* **1** *(tren)* express. **2** *(café)* expresso. **3** *(olla)* pressure.

**expresar** *vt* **1** *(gen)* to express. **2** *(manifestar)* to state; *(comunicar)* to convey.
▶ *vpr* **expresarse** to express os.

**expresión** *nf* expression.

**expresionismo** *nm* expressionism.

**expresionista** *adj* expressionist.
▶ *nm o nf* expressionist.

**expresividad** *nf* expressivity.

**expresivo,-a** *adj* **1** *(elocuente)* expressive. **2** *(mirada)* meaningful; *(silencio)* eloquent.

**expreso,-a** *adj* *(especificado)* express.

**exprimidor** *nm* lemon squeezer, US juicer.

**exprimir** *vt* *(fruto)* to squeeze; *(zumo)* to squeeze out.

**expropiación** *nf* expropriation.

**expropiar** *vt* to expropriate.

**expuesto,-a** *adj* *(peligroso)* dangerous, risky; *(sin protección)* exposed.

**expulsar** *vt* **1** *(expeler)* to expel, eject, throw out; *(humo, etc)* to belch out. **2** DEP to send off.

**expulsión** *nf* **1** expulsion, ejection. **2** DEP sending off. **3** *(alumno)* expulsion.

**expurgar** *vt* **1** to expurgate. **2** *fig* to purge.

**exquisitez** *nf* **1** exquisiteness. **2** *(manjar)* delicacy.

**exquisito,-a** *adj* **1** *(gen)* exquisite. **2** *(gusto)* refined; *(sabor)* delicious, exquisite.

**extasiado,-a** *adj* ecstatic.

**extasiar** *vt* to enrapture.
  ▶ *vpr* **extasiarse** to go into ecstasies, go into raptures.

**éxtasis** *nm inv* ecstasy, rapture.

**extático,-a** *adj* extatic.

**extender** *vt* **1** *(mapa, papel)* to spread (out), open (out). **2** *(brazo, etc)* to stretch (out); *(alas)* to spread. **3** *(mantequilla, etc)* to spread. **4** *(documento)* to draw up; *(cheque)* to make out; *(pasaporte, certificado)* to issue.
  ▶ *vpr* **extenderse 1** *(durar)* to extend, last. **2** *(terreno)* to stretch. **3** *fig (difundirse)* to spread, extend.

**extendido,-a** *adj* **1** *(difundido)* widespread. **2** *(mano, etc)* outstretched.

**extensible** *adj* extendable.

**extensión** *nf* **1** *(gen)* extension. **2** *(dimensión)* extent, size; *(superficie)* area, expanse. **3** *(duración)* duration, length.

**extensivo,-a** *adj* extendable, extensive.

**extenso,-a** *adj* **1** *(amplio)* extensive, vast; *(grande)* large. **2** *(largo)* lengthy, long.

**extenuado,-a** *adj* **1** *(agotado)* exhausted. **2** *(débil)* weak. **3** *(flaco)* emaciated.

**extenuante** *adj* exhausting.

**extenuar** *vt* **1** *(agotar)* to exhaust. **2** *(debilitar)* to weaken.
  ▶ *vpr* **extenuarse** *(agotarse)* to exhaust os, wear os out.

**exterior** *adj* **1** *(gen)* exterior, outer, external. **2** *(ventana, puerta)* outside; *(pared)* outer. **3** *(aspecto)* outward. **4** *(extranjero)* foreign.
  ▶ *nm* **1** *(superficie externa)* exterior, outside. **2** *(extranjero)* abroad, overseas. **3** *(de una persona)* appearance. **4** DEP outside.
  ▶ *nm pl* **exteriores** CINE location shots.

**exteriorización** *nf* manifestation, externalization.

**exteriorizar** *vt* to show, reveal, express outwardly.

**exterminación** *nf* *(supresión)* extermination, wiping out; *(destrucción)* destruction.

**exterminador,-ra** *adj* exterminating.
  ▶ *nm & nf* exterminator.

**exterminar** *vt* *(suprimir)* to exterminate, wipe out; *(destruir)* to destroy.

**exterminio** *nm* extermination, wiping out; *(destrucción)* destruction.

**externado** *nm* day school.

**externo,-a** *adj* **1** external, outward: *parte externa* outside. **2** *(alumno)* day.

**extinción** *nf* extinction.

**extinguir** *vt* **1** *(fuego, etc)* to extinguish, put out. **2** *(especie, deuda, epidemia)* to wipe out.
  ▶ *vpr* **extinguirse 1** *(fuego, etc)* to go out. **2** *(especie, etc)* to become extinct, die out. **3** *(plazo)* to expire, run out.

**extintor** *nm* fire extinguisher.

**extirpación** *nf* **1** MED removal, extraction. **2** *fig* eradication, wiping out, stamping out.

**extirpar** *vt* **1** MED to remove, extract. **2** *fig* to eradicate, wipe out, stamp out.

**extorsión** *nf* **1** *(usurpación)* extortion. **2** *fig (molestia)* inconvenience, trouble.

**extorsionar** *vt* **1** *(usurpar)* to extort, exact. **2** *fig (molestar)* to inconvenience, cause inconvenience to.

**extra** *adj* **1** *fam* extra. **2** *fam (superior)* top-quality, best-quality. **3** *(paga)* bonus.
  ▶ *nm* **1** *fam (gasto)* additional expense. **2** *fam (plus)* bonus.

**extracción** *nf* **1** *(gen)* extraction; *(de lotería)* draw. **2** *(origen)* descent, extraction. COMP **extracción de datos** INFORM data retrieval.

**extracto** *nm* **1** *(sustancia)* extract. **2** *(trozo)* extract, excerpt. **3** *(resumen)* summary.

**extractor** *nm* extractor.

**extradición** *nf* extradition.

**extraditar** *vt* to extradite.

**extraer** vt **1** (gen) to extract. **2** (conclusión) to draw.

**extraescolar** adj out of school, extracurricular. [COMP] **actividades extraescolares** extracurricular activities.

**extrafino,-a** adj superfine, best quality.

**extralargo,-a** adj king-size.

**extralimitarse** vpr fig to go too far, overstep.

**extranjero,-a** adj foreign, alien.
▶ nm & nf foreigner.
▶ nm **extranjero** foreign countries pl, abroad.

**extrañar** vt **1** (sorprender) to surprise. **2** (notar extraño) to find strange, not to be used to.
▶ vpr **extrañarse 1** (desterrarse) to go into exile. **2** (sorprenderse) to be surprised (de/por, at).

**extraño,-a** adj **1** (no conocido) alien, foreign. **2** (particular) strange, peculiar, odd, funny.

**extraordinaria** nf (paga) bonus payment.

**extraordinariamente** adv extraordinarily, unusually.

**extraordinario,-a** adj **1** (fuera de lo común) extraordinary, unusual; (sorprendente) surprising; (admirable) outstanding, exceptional. **2** (raro) queer, odd. **3** (gastos, etc) additional, extra; (paga) bonus. **4** (revista, etc) special.
▶ nm **extraordinario 1** (correo) special delivery. **2** (revista, etc) special issue.

**extraplano,-a** adj slimline.

**extrapolar** vt to extrapolate.

**extrarradio** nm outskirts pl, suburbs pl.

**extraterrestre** adj extramundane, extraterrestrial.
▶ nm o nf alien.

**extravagancia** nf extravagance, eccentricity.

**extravagante** adj extravagant outrageous.

**extraviado,-a** adj **1** (disoluto) dissolute. **2** (perdido - persona, objeto) missing, lost; (- perro, niño) stray.

**extraviar** vt **1** (persona) to mislead. **2** (objeto) to mislay, lose.
▶ vpr **extraviarse 1** (persona) to get lost, lose one's way. **2** (objeto) to get mislaid.

**extravío** nm (persona) misleading; (cosa) loss, mislaying.

**extremado,-a** adj extreme.

**extremar** vt to carry to extremes, carry to the limit, overdo.
▶ vpr **extremarse** to do one's best, do one's utmost, take great pains.

**extremidad** nf **1** (parte extrema) extremity; (punta) end, tip. **2** ANAT limb, extremity.

**extremismo** nm extremism.

**extremista** adj extremist.
▶ nm o nf extremist.

**extremo,-a** adj **1** (exagerado) extreme. **2** (distante) further. **3** fig (intenso) utmost.
▶ nm **extremo 1** (punta) extreme, end. **2** (asunto, materia) matter, question. **3** DEP wing.

**extrínseco,-a** adj extrinsic.

**extrovertido,-a** adj extroverted.
▶ nm & nf extrovert.

**exuberante** adj **1** exuberant. **2** (vegetación) lush, abundant.

# F

**F, f** *nf (la letra)* F, f.

**F** *sím* (Fahrenheit) Fahrenheit; *(símbolo)* F.

**fa** *nm* F.

**fabada** *nf* bean stew *including pork sausage and bacon.*

**fábrica** *nf* **1** *(industria)* factory, plant. **2** *(fabricación)* manufacture.

**fabricación** *nf* manufacture, production, making.

**fabricante** *nm o nf* manufacturer, maker.

**fabricar** *vt* **1** *(producir)* to make, manufacture, produce. **2** *fig (inventar)* to fabricate, invent.

**fábula** *nf* **1** LIT fable. **2** *(mito)* myth, legend. **3** *(mentira)* invention.

**fabular** *vt* **1** *(contar fábulas)* to fable. **2** *(imaginar)* to imagine.

**fabuloso,-a** *adj* **1** *(fantástico)* fabulous, fantastic. **2** LIT fabulous, mythical.

**faceta** *nf* facet.

**fachada** *nf* **1** ARQUIT façade, front. **2** *fam (apariencia)* outward show.

**facial** *adj* facial.

**fácil** *adj* **1** easy. **2** *(probable)* probable, likely.

**facilidad** *nf* **1** *(simplicidad)* ease, facility. **2** *(aptitud)* talent, gift: *tiene facilidad para la música* he has a gift for music. COMP **facilidad de palabra** fluency.
  ▶ *nf pl* **facilidades** *(medios que facilitan)* facilities.

**facilitar** *vt* **1** *(simplificar)* to make easy, make easier, facilitate. **2** *(proporcionar)* to provide with, supply with.

**factor** *nm (gen)* factor.

**factoría** *nf* **1** COM trading post. **2** *(fábrica)* factory, mill.

**factura** *nf* invoice, bill.

**facturación** *nf* **1** COM invoicing. **2** *(de equipajes)* registration, check-in.

**facturar** *vt* **1** COM to invoice, charge for. **2** *(equipaje)* to register, check in.

**facultad** *nf* **1** *(capacidad)* faculty, ability. **2** *(poder)* faculty, power. **3** *(universitaria)* faculty, school.

**faena** *nf* **1** *(tarea)* task, job. **2** *fam (mala pasada)* dirty trick.

**fagocito** *nm* phagocyte.

**fagot** *nm (instrumento)* bassoon.
  ▶ *nm o nf (músico)* bassoonist.

**faisán** *nm* pheasant.

**faja** *nf* **1** *(cinturón)* band, belt. **2** *(ropa interior)* corset, girdle.

**fajo** *nm* bundle; *(de billetes)* wad.

**falda** *nf* **1** *(prenda)* skirt. **2** *(regazo)* lap. **3** *(ladera)* slope. **4** *(corte de carne)* brisket.

**faldón** *nm* **1** *(de traje)* coat-tail; *(de camisa)* shirt-tail. **2** *(prenda de bebé)* wraparound skirt. **3** *(de tejado)* gable.

**falible** *adj* fallible.

**falla** *nf* **1** *(defecto)* defect, fault. **2** GEOG fault.

**fallar** *vi* **1** *(premio)* to award a prize. **2** *(fracasar, no funcionar)* to fail. **3** *(puntería)* to miss; *(plan)* to go wrong.
  ▶ *vt (premio)* to award.

**fallecer** *vi fml* to pass away, die.

**fallo** *nm* **1** *(en concurso)* decision. **2** *(error)* mistake, blunder; *(fracaso)* failure. **4** *(defecto)* fault, defect.

**falsear** *vt (falsificar)* to counterfeit, forge.

**falsedad** *nf* **1** *(hipocresía)* falseness, hypocrisy. **2** *(mentira)* falsehood, lie.

**falsete** *nm* falsetto.

**falsificador,-ra** *adj (de firma, cuadro)* forging; *(de dinero)* counterfeiting.

▶ *nm & nf (de firma, cuadro)* forger; *(de dinero)* counterfeiter.

**falsificar** *vt* **1** *(gen)* to falsify. **2** *(firma, cuadro)* to forge; *(dinero)* to counterfeit, forge.

**falso,-a** *adj* **1** *(no verdadero)* false, untrue. **2** *(moneda)* false, counterfeit. **3** *(persona)* insincere, false.

**falta** *nf* **1** *(carencia)* lack: *falta de sensibilidad* lack of sensitivity. **2** *(escasez)* shortage: *existe una falta de agua* there is a water shortage. **3** *(ausencia)* absence. **4** *(error)* mistake: *has hecho una falta de ortografía* you've made a spelling mistake. **5** *(defecto)* fault, defect. **6** DEP *(fútbol)* foul; *(tenis)* fault. [LOC] **echar en falta** to miss. ∎ **sin falta** without fail.

**faltar** *vi* **1** *(haber poco)* to be lacking, be needed: *falta (más) leche* we need (more) milk. **2** *(no tener)* to lack, not have (enough). **3** *(quedar)* to remain, be left: *falta poco para que...* it won't be long till...

**falto,-a** [LOC] **estar falto,-a de** to lack, be short of, be without: *estamos faltos de dinero* we're short of money.

**fama** *nf (renombre)* fame, renown.

**famélico,-a** *adj* starving, famished.

**familia** *nf* **1** family. **2** *(prole)* children *pl*, family.

**familiar** *adj* **1** *(de la familia)* family, of the family. **2** *(conocido)* familiar, well-known. **3** LING colloquial.
▶ *nm o nf* relation, relative.

**familiaridad** *nf* familiarity.

**familiarizar** *vt* to familiarize (con, with), make familiar (con, with).
▶ *vpr* **familiarizarse** to get to know: *familiarízate con el teclado* get to know the keyboard.

**familiarmente** *adv* familiarly.

**famoso,-a** *adj* famous, well-known.

**fan** *nm o nf* fan, admirer. [LOC] **ser un,-a fan de** ALGO to be mad about STH.

**fanático,-a** *adj* fanatic, fanatical.

**fanatismo** *nm* fanaticism.

**fanerógamo,-a** *adj* phanerogamic, phanerogamous.

**fanfarrón,-ona** *adj fam* swanky.

**fanfarronear** *vi fam (chulear)* to show off, swank.

**fango** *nm (barro)* mud, mire.

**fantasear** *vi* **1** *(forjar en la imaginación)* to daydream, dream. **2** *(presumir)* to boast, show off.
▶ *vt (imaginar)* dream.

**fantasía** *nf* **1** fantasy. **2** fancy.

**fantasioso,-a** *adj* imaginative.

**fantasma** *nm* **1** *(espectro)* phantom, ghost. **2** *fam (fanfarrón)* braggart, show-off.

**fantasmal** *adj* ghostly.

**fantástico,-a** *adj* **1** fantastic. **2** *(estupendo)* wonderful.

**fantoche** *nm* **1** *(títere)* puppet, marionette. **2** *pey (fanfarrón)* braggart.

**faquir** *nm* fakir.

**faradio** *nm* farad.

**farándula** *nf* **1** *(compañía de teatro)* group of strolling players. **2** *(profesión, mundo del teatro)* acting, the stage.

**faraón** *nm* Pharaoh.

**faraónico,-a** *adj* Pharaonic.

**fardar** *vi argot (presumir)* to show off, swank.

**fardo** *nm (paquete)* bundle, pack.

**fardón,-ona** *adj argot* classy, flash.

**farero,-a** *nm & nf* lighthouse keeper.

**faringe** *nf* pharynx.

**faringitis** *nf inv* pharyngitis.

**farmacéutico,-a** *adj* pharmaceutical.
▶ *nm & nf* pharmacist.

**farmacia** *nf* **1** *(estudios)* pharmacy. **2** *(tienda)* chemist's (shop), US drugstore, pharmacy.

**fármaco** *nm* medicine, medication.

**farmacología** *nf* pharmacology.

**faro** *nm* **1** *(torre)* lighthouse, beacon. **2** *(coche)* headlight. **3** *fig (guía)* guiding light, guide.

**farol** *nm* **1** *(farola)* streetlamp, streetlight. **2** *argot (fardada)* bragging, swank.

**farola** *nf* streetlight, streetlamp; *(de gas)* gas lamp.

**farolero,-a** *adj fam* boastful.
▶ *nm & nf fam (fanfarrón)* show-off.
▶ *nm* farolero *(de profesión)* lamplighter.

**farolillo** *nm* **1** *(farol de papel)* Chinese lantern. **2** BOT Canterbury bell.

**farra** *nf fam* binge, spree.

**farruco,-a** *adj fam* conceited, cocky.

**farsa** *nf* TEAT farce.

**farsante** *adj* lying, deceitful.

**fascículo** *nm* instalment (US installment), fascicule, fascicle.

**fascinación** *nf* fascination.

**fascinante** *adj* fascinating.

**fascinar** *vt* to fascinate, captivate.

**fascismo** *nm* fascism.

**fascista** *adj* fascist.

**fase** *nf (etapa)* phase, stage.

**fastidiado,-a** *adj* **1** *(hastiado)* sickened, disgusted. **2** *(molesto)* annoyed. **3** *fam (estropeado)* ruined, spoilt. **4** *fam (mal de salud)* ill, sick, in a bad way.

**fastidiar** *vt* **1** *(hastiar)* to sicken, disgust. **2** *(molestar)* to annoy, bother. **3** *(partes del cuerpo)* to hurt: *le fastidia el estómago* he's got a bad stomach. **4** *fam (estropear)* to damage, ruin; *(planes)* to spoil.
▶ *vpr* **fastidiarse** **1** *(aguantarse)* to put up with, grin and bear it. **2** *fam (estropearse)* to go wrong, break down: *se ha fastidiado la tele* the telly has gone wrong.

**fastidio** *nm* **1** *(molestia)* bother, nuisance. **2** *(aburrimiento)* boredom.

**fastidioso,-a** *adj* **1** *(molesto)* annoying, irksome. **2** *(aburrido)* boring, tedious.

**fastuoso,-a** *adj* **1** *(cosa)* splendid, lavish. **2** *(persona)* lavish, ostentatious.

**fatal** *adj* **1** *(inexorable)* fateful. **2** *(mortal)* deadly, fatal.
▶ *adv fam* awfully, terribly.

**fatalidad** *nf* **1** *(destino)* fate. **2** *(desgracia)* misfortune.

**fatalismo** *nm* fatalism.

**fatalista** *adj* fatalistic.

**fatídico,-a** *adj (desastroso)* disastrous, calamitous.

**fatiga** *nf (cansancio)* fatigue.

**fatigar** *vt* **1** *(cansar)* to wear out, tire. **2** *(molestar)* to annoy.

**fatigoso,-a** *adj (cansado)* tiring, exhausting.

**fauces** *nf pl (en anatomía)* gullet *sing*.

**fauna** *nf* fauna.

**fauvismo** *nm* fauvism.

**fauvista** *nm o nf* fauvist.

**favor** *nm* favour (US favor). LOC **a favor de** in favour (US favor) of. ‖ **hacer un favor** to do a favour (US favor). ‖ **por favor** please.

**favorable** *adj* favourable (US favorable). LOC **mostrarse favorable a ALGO** to be in favour (US favor) of STH.

**favorecer** *vt* **1** *(ayudar)* to favour (US favor), help. **2** *(agraciar)* suit: *el azul no me favorece* blue doesn't suit me.

**favoritismo** *nm* favouritism (US favoritism).

**favorito,-a** *adj* favourite (US favorite).

**fax** *nm (sistema, documento)* fax.

**fe** *nf* faith.

**fealdad** *nf* ugliness.

**febrero** *nm* February.

✎ Para ejemplos de uso consulta marzo.

**febril** *adj* MED feverish.

**fecha** *nf* **1** date: *¿qué fecha es hoy?* what's the date today? **2** *(día)* day. LOC **fijar la fecha** to fix a date. COMP **fecha de nacimiento** date of birth.
▶ *nf pl* **fechas** *(época)* time *sing*: *por esas fechas* at that time.

**fécula** *nf* starch.

**fecundación** *nf* fertilization.

**fecundar** *vt* to fertilize.

**fecundidad** *nf (fertilidad)* fertility.

**federación** *nf* federation.

**federal** *adj* federal.

**federalismo** *nm* federalism.

**federalista** *adj* federalist.

**federar** *vt* to federate.

**feldespato** *nm* feldspar, felspar.

**felicidad** *nf* happiness. LOC **¡(muchas) felicidades!** **1** *(éxitos)* congratulations! **2** *(cumpleaños)* happy birthday!

**felicitación** *nf* **1** *(acción)* congratulation. **2** *(tarjeta)* greetings card.

**felicitar** *vt* to congratulate (**por**, on).

**felino,-a** *adj* feline.

**feliz** *adj* happy.

**felizmente** *adv (con felicidad)* happily.

**felpa** *nf* plush.

**felpudo,-a** *adj (textil)* plushy, velvety.

**femenino,-a** *adj* **1** feminine. **2** *(sexo)* female; *(equipo, asociación)* women's.

**feminidad** *nf* femininity.

**feminismo** *nm* feminism.

**feminista** *nmf* feminist.

**femoral** *adj* femoral.

**fémur** *nm* femur.

**fenomenal** *adj fam (fantástico)* great, terrific.
▶ *adv* wonderfully, marvellously.

**fenómeno** *nm* phenomenon.
▶ *adj fam (fantástico)* fantastic, terrific.

**fenotipo** *nm* phenotype.

**feo,-a** *adj* **1** *(persona - nada atractiva)* ugly; *(- poco atractiva)* plain. **2** *(aspecto, situación, tiempo, etc)* nasty, horrible, unpleasant, awful.

**féretro** *nm* coffin.

**feria** *nf* **1** COM fair. **2** *(fiesta)* fair.

**fermentación** *nf* fermentation.

**fermentar** *vi* to ferment.

**fermento** *nm* ferment.

**ferocidad** *nf* ferocity, fierceness.

**feroz** *adj* fierce, ferocious.

**ferretería** *nf* ironmonger's.

**ferretero,-a** *nm & nf* ironmonger.

**férrico,-a** *adj* ferric.

**ferrocarril** *nm* railway, US railroad.

**ferroviario,-a** *adj* railway.

**fértil** *adj* fertile, rich.

**fertilidad** *nf* fertility, fecundity.

**fertilización** *nf* fertilization.

**fertilizante** *adj* fertilizing.
▶ *nm (abono)* fertilizer.

**fertilizar** *vt* to fertilize.

**ferviente** *adj* fervent, passionate.

**fervor** *nm* fervour (US fervor).

**festejar** *vt (celebrar)* to celebrate.

**festejo** *nm* feast, entertainment.

**festival** *nm* festival.

**festividad** *nf* **1** *(fiesta)* festivity, celebration. **2** *(día)* feast day, holiday.

**festivo,-a** *adj* **1** *(alegre)* festive, merry. **2** *(humorístico)* witty.

**fétido,-a** *adj* stinking, fetid.

**feto** *nm* foetus (US fetus).

**feudal** *adj* feudal.

**feudalismo** *nm* feudalism.

**feudo** *nm* fief, feud.

**fiable** *adj* reliable, trustworthy.

**fiambre** *nm* **1** CULIN cold meat, cold cut. **2** *fam (cadáver)* stiff, corpse.

**fiambrera** *nf* lunch box.

**fianza** *nf (depósito)* deposit.

**fiar** *vt* **1** *(vender)* to sell on credit. **2** *(confiar)* to confide, entrust. LOC **de fiar** trustworthy, reliable.
▶ *vpr* **fiarse** *(confiarse)* to trust (de, -).

**fibra** *nf* fibre (US fiber). COMP **fibra óptica** optical fibre (US fiber).

**fibroso,-a** *adj* fibrous.

**ficción** *nf* fiction.

**ficha** *nf* **1** *(tarjeta)* index card, file card. **2** *(de teléfono)* token. **3** *(en juegos)* counter; *(naipes)* chip; *(ajedrez)* piece, man; *(dominó)* domino.

**fichaje** *nm* signing (up).

**fichar** *vt* **1** *(anotar)* to put on an index card; *(registrar)* to open a file on. **2** DEP to sign up, sign on.
▶ *vi* DEP to sign up (por, with): *finalmente fichó por el Barcelona* he finally signed up with Barcelona F.C.

**fichero** *nm* **1** *(archivo)* card index. **2** *(mueble)* filing cabinet, file. **3** INFORM file.

**ficticio,-a** *adj* fictitious.

**ficus** *nm inv* rubber plant.

**fidelidad** *nf* **1** *(lealtad)* fidelity, faithfulness. **2** *(exactitud)* accuracy. COMP **alta fidelidad** high fidelity, hi-fi.

**fideo** *nm* noodle.

**fiebre** *nf (enfermedad)* fever, temperature. LOC **tener fiebre** to have a temperature.

**fiel** *adj* **1** *(leal)* faithful, loyal. **2** *(exacto)* accurate.

**fieltro** *nm* felt.

**fiera** *nf* wild animal, wild beast.

**fiero,-a** *adj* wild, fierce, ferocious.

**fiesta** *nf* **1** *(día no laborable)* holiday: *el viernes es fiesta* Friday's a holiday. **2** *(reunión)* party.
▶ *nf pl* **fiestas** festivity, fiesta.

**figura** *nf* **1** *(gen)* figure. **2** *(forma)* shape.

**figurar** *vi* **1** *(encontrarse)* to appear, be, figure: *figura como director* he appears as director. **2** *(destacar)* to stand out, be important.
▶ *vpr* **figurarse** *(imaginarse)* to imagine, suppose.

**fijador,-ra** *nm* *(para pelo)* hairspray, hair gel.

**fijar** *vt* *(sujetar)* to fix, fasten; *(puerta)* to hang; *(ventana)* to put in.
▶ *vpr* **fijarse 1** *(darse cuenta)* to notice. **2** *(poner atención)* to pay attention, watch: *fíjate cómo se hace* watch how it's done.

**fijo,-a** *adj* **1** *(sujeto)* fixed, fastened. **2** *(establecido)* set, definite, firm: *fecha fija* set date. **3** *(firme)* steady, stable, firm. **4** *(permanente)* permanent.

**fila** *nf* *(línea)* file, line, row.
▶ *nf pl* **filas** *(de ejército, partido)* ranks.

**filamento** *nm* filament.

**filete** *nm* *(de carne, pescado)* fillet (US filet).

**Filipinas** *nf pl* **las Filipinas** the Philippines.

**filipino,-a** *adj* Filipino.
▶ *nm & nf (persona)* Filipino.
▶ *nm* **filipino** *(idioma)* Filipino.

**film** *nm* film, US movie.

**filmar** *vt* to film, shoot.

**filmina** *nf* slide, transparency.

**filmoteca** *nf* film institute.

**filo** *nm* cutting edge, edge.

**filo-** *pref* philo-.

**filología** *nf* philology.

**filólogo,-a** *nm & nf* philologist.

**filón** *nm* *(mineral)* seam, vein.

**filosofar** *vi* to philosophize.

**filosofía** *nf* philosophy.

**filósofo,-a** *nm & nf* philosopher.

**filoxera** *nf* phylloxera.

**filtrar** *vt* to filter, to leak.
▶ *vpr* **filtrarse** *(pasar a través)* to filter.

**filtro** *nm* *(material)* filter.

**fin** *nm* **1** *(final)* end. **2** *(objetivo)* purpose, aim. LOC **a fin de** in order to, so as to. ▌**a fin de que** so that. ▌**en fin** anyway. COMP **fin de semana** weekend.

**final** *adj* *(último)* final, last.
▶ *nm* end. COMP **final feliz** happy ending.
▶ *nf* DEP final.

**finalidad** *nf* purpose, aim.

**finalista** *nm o nf* finalist.

**finalizar** *vt* to end, finish.
▶ *vi* to end, finish.

**financiación** *nf* financing.

**financiar** *vt* to finance.

**finanzas** *nf pl* finances.

**finca** *nf* property, estate. COMP **finca rústica** country property.

**fingir** *vt* to feign, pretend: *fingió indiferencia* he feigned indifference.

**finito,-a** *adj* finite.

**finlandés,-esa** *adj* Finnish.
▶ *nm & nf (persona)* Finn.
▶ *nm* **finlandés** *(idioma)* Finnish.

**Finlandia** *nf* Finland.

**fino,-a** *adj* **1** *(delicado)* fine, delicate. **2** *(delgado)* thin. **3** *(educado)* refined, polite.

**fiordo** *nm* fiord, fjord.

**firma** *nf* **1** *(acto)* signing. **2** *(empresa)* firm.

**firmamento** *nm* firmament.

**firmar** *vt* to sign.

**firme** *adj* *(estable)* firm, steady.

**firmeza** *nf* firmness, steadiness.

**fiscal** *adj* fiscal, tax.
▶ *nm o nf* JUR public prosecutor, US district attorney.

**fisco** *nm* exchequer, US treasury.

**fisgar** *vt* *fam* to pry, snoop.

**fisgón,-ona** *adj* snooper, busybody.

**fisgonear** *vt* to pry, snoop.

**física** *nf* physics.

**físico,-a** *adj* physical.
▶ *nm & nf (profesión)* physicist.
▶ *nm* **físico** *(aspecto)* physique.

**fisioterapeuta** *nm o nf* physiotherapist.

**fisioterapia** *nf* physiotherapy.

**fisonomía** *nf* appearance.

**fisura** *nf* fissure.

**fito-** *pref* phyto-.

**Fiyi** *nm* Fiji.

**fiyiano,-a** *adj* Fijian.
▶ *nm & nf (persona)* Fijian.
▶ *nm* **fiyiano** *(idioma)* Fijian.

**fláccido,-a** *adj* flaccid, flabby.

**flaco,-a** *adj* **1** *(delgado)* thin, skinny. **2** *(débil)* weak, frail.

**flagelo** *nm* **1** whip. **2** BIOL flagellum.

**flamenco,-a** *adj* **1** *(gitano)* Andalusian gypsy. **2** *(música)* flamenco.
▶ *nm* **flamenco 1** *(idioma)* Flemish. **2** *(música)* flamenco music. **3** *(ave)* flamingo.

**flan** *nm* *(dulce)* crème caramel. LOC **estar como un flan** to be shaking like a leaf.

**flanco** *nm* flank, side.

**flanera** *nf* mould (US mold).

**flaquear** *vi* to weaken, give in, to fail.

**flaqueza** *nf* weakness, frailty.

**flash** *nm* flash, flashlight.

**flato** *nm* *(dolor)* stitch.

**flauta** *nf* flute.

**flautista** *nm o nf* flute player.

**flecha** *nf* arrow.

**flechazo** *nm* fig *(enamoramiento)* love at first sight.

**fleco** *nm* *(adorno)* fringe.

**flemón** *nm* abscess.

**flequillo** *nm* fringe, US bangs *pl.*

**flexibilidad** *nf* flexibility.

**flexible** *adj* flexible.

**flexionar** *vt* *(cuerpo)* to bend.

**flexo** *nm* adjustable table lamp.

**flipar** *vt* argot *(gustar)* to drive wild.
▶ *vi* **1** *(asombrarse)* to be amazed, be stunned. **2** *(pasárselo bien)* to freak out.

**flirtear** *vi* to flirt.

**flojear** *vi* **1** *(disminuir)* to go down. **2** *(debilitarse)* to weaken, grow weak.

**flojera** *nf* fam weakness, faintness.

**flojo,-a** *adj* **1** *(suelto)* loose; *(no tensado)* slack. **2** *(débil)* weak. **3** *(mediocre)* poor: *es un estudiante flojo* he's a poor student.

**flor** *nf* BOT flower, bloom. LOC **en flor** in bloom.

**florecer** *vi* **1** *(plantas)* to flower, bloom; *(árboles)* to blossom. **2** *(prosperar)* to flourish, thrive.

**floreciente** *adj* prosperous.

**florería** *nf* florist's (shop).

**florero** *nm* vase.

**florista** *nm o nf* florist.

**floristería** *nf* florist's (shop).

**flota** *nf* fleet.

**flotador** *nm* *(de niño)* rubber ring.

**flotar** *vi* to float.

**flote** LOC **a flote** afloat.

**fluctuar** *vi* *(variar)* to fluctuate.

**fluido,-a** *adj* *(sin obstáculos)* fluid.
▶ *nm* **fluido** FÍS fluid. COMP **fluido eléctrico** current, power.

**fluir** *vi* to flow.

**flúor** *nm* fluorine.

**fluorescente** *adj* fluorescent.
▶ *nm* fluorescent light.

**fluvial** *adj* fluvial, river.

**fobia** *nf* phobia.

**foca** *nf* seal.

**foco** *nm* **1** *(en física)* focus. **2** *(lámpara)* spotlight, floodlight.

**fofo,-a** *adj* flabby.

**fogata** *nf* bonfire.

**fogón** *nm* *(de cocina)* kitchen range, stove.

**fogueo** LOC **de fogueo** blank.

**folclore** *nm* folklore.

**folclórico,-a** *adj* folkloric, popular.

**folio** *nm* folio, leaf.

**folk** *nm* folk music.

**folleto** *nm* pamphlet, leaflet, brochure; *(explicativo)* instruction leaflet.

**follón** *nm* **1** fam *(alboroto)* rumpus, shindy. **2** fam *(enredo, confusión)* mess, trouble. LOC **armar (un) follón** fam to kick up a rumpus.

**fomentar** *vt* to promote.

**fonda** *nf* inn.

**fondo** *nm* **1** *(parte más baja)* bottom: *en el fondo del pozo* at the bottom of the well. **2** *(parte más lejana)* end, back: *al fondo de la sala* at the back of the hall. **3** *(segundo término)* background. LOC **a fondo 1** *(adjetival)* thorough. **2** *(adverbial)* thoroughly. ▌**en el fondo** fig deep down, at heart. COMP **fondo del mar** sea bed.
▶ *nm pl* **fondos** funds, money *sing.*

**fonema** *nm* phoneme.

**fonético,-a** *adj* phonetic.

**fónico,-a** *adj* phonic.

**fono-** *pref* phono-.

**fonología** *nf* phonology.

**fonoteca** *nf* record library.

**fontanería** *nf* plumbing.

**fontanero,-a** *nm & nf* plumber.

**footing** *nm* jogging. [LOC] **hacer footing** to go jogging.

**forastero,-a** *nm & nf* stranger.

**forcejear** *vi* to wrestle, struggle.

**forcejeo** *nm* struggle, struggling.

**forestal** *adj* forest.

**forja** *nf* *(fragua)* forge.

**forjado** *nm* ARQUIT framework.

**forjar** *vt* *(metales)* to forge.

**forma** *nf* **1** *(gen)* form, shape: *en forma de X* X-shaped. **2** *(manera)* way. **3** DEP form. [LOC] **de todas formas** anyway, in any case. ▎**estar en forma** to be in shape, be fit.

**formación** *nf* **1** *(gen)* formation. **2** *(educación)* upbringing. [COMP] **formación profesional** vocational training.

**formal** *adj* **1** *(con los requisitos necesarios)* formal. **2** *(serio)* serious, serious-minded. **3** *(cumplidor)* reliable, dependable.

**formalizar** *vt* to make formal.

**formalmente** *adv* formally.

**formar** *vt* **1** *(gen)* to form. **2** *(integrar, constituir)* to form, constitute: *formar parte de algo* to be a part of sth. **3** *(educar)* to bring up.
  ▸ *vpr* **formarse** *(educarse)* to be educated, be trained.

**formatear** *vt* to format.

**formato** *nm* *(gen)* format.

**formidable** *adj* tremendous, formidable.

**formón** *nm* firmer chisel.

**fórmula** *nf* *(gen)* formula.

**formular** *vt* **1** *(una teoría)* to formulate. **2** *(quejas, peticiones)* to express, make.
  ▸ *vi* QUÍM to write formulae.

**formulario,-a** *nm* *(documento)* form: *formulario de solicitud* application form.

**forofo,-a** *nm & nf fam* fan, supporter.

**forraje** *nm* *(pienso)* fodder, forage.

**forrar** *vt* **1** *(por dentro)* to line. **2** *(por fuera)* to cover. **3** *(tapizar)* to upholster.
  ▸ *vpr* **forrarse** *fam (de dinero)* to make a fortune, make a packet.

**forro** *nm* **1** *(interior)* lining. **2** *(funda)* cover, case. **3** *(tapizado)* upholstery.

**fortalecer** *vt* to fortify, strengthen.
  ▸ *vpr* **fortalecerse** to strengthen.

**fortaleza** *nf* **1** *(vigor)* strength. **2** *(recinto fortificado)* fortress.

**fortificación** *nf* fortification.

**fortuito,-a** *adj* chance, fortuitous.

**fortuna** *nf* **1** *(destino)* fortune, fate. **2** *(suerte)* luck.

**forzado,-a** *adj* **1** *(obligado)* forced. **2** *(rebuscado)* forced, strained. [COMP] **risa forzada** forced laugh.

**forzar** *vt* **1** *(persona)* to force, compel. **2** *(cosa)* to force open, break open.

**forzoso,-a** *adj* **1** *(inevitable)* inevitable, unavoidable. **2** *(obligatorio)* obligatory, compulsory.

**forzudo,-a** *adj* strong, brawny.

**fosa** *nf* **1** *(sepultura)* grave. **2** *(hoyo)* pit, hollow. **3** ANAT cavity, fossa. **4** *(en el océano)* trench, deep. [COMP] **fosas nasales** nostrils.

**fosfato** *nm* phosphate. [COMP] **fosfato de cal** calcium phosphate.

**fosforescente** *adj* phosphorescent.

**fósforo** *nm* **1** QUÍM phosphorus. **2** *(cerilla)* match.

**fósil** *nm* fossil.

**foso** *nm* **1** *(hoyo)* hole, pit. **2** *(de fortaleza)* moat.

**foto** *nf fam* photo, picture.

**fotocopia** *nf* photocopy.

**fotocopiadora** *nf* photocopier, photocopying machine.

**fotocopiar** *vt* to photocopy.

**fotografía** *nf* **1** *(proceso)* photography. **2** *(retrato)* photograph. [LOC] **hacer fotografías** to take photographs.

**fotografiar** *vt* to photograph, take a photograph of.

**fotógrafo,-a** *nm & nf* photographer.

**fotón** *nm* photon.

**fotosíntesis** *nf inv* photosynthesis.

**FP** *abrev* EDUC (Formación Profesional) Professional Formation *(vocational training)*.

**fracasar** *vi* to fail, be unsuccessful, fall through.

**fracaso** *nm* failure.

**fracción** *nf* **1** *(gen)* fraction. **2** POL faction.

**fraccionar** *vt* to divide, break up, split up.

**fractura** *nf* fracture.

**fragancia** *nf* fragrance.

**fragata** *nf* frigate.

**frágil** *adj* **1** *(quebradizo)* fragile, breakable. **2** *(débil)* frail, weak.

**fragilidad** *nf* **1** *(cualidad)* fragility. **2** *(debilidad)* frailty, weakness.

**fragmento** *nm* **1** *(pedazo)* fragment, piece. **2** *(literario)* passage.

**fragua** *nf* forge.

**fraguar** *vt* **1** *(metal)* to forge. **2** *fig (plan)* to dream up, fabricate; *(conspiración)* to hatch.
▸ *vi (endurecerse)* to set, harden.

**fraile** *nm* friar, monk.

**frambuesa** *nf* raspberry.

**francamente** *adv* frankly.

**francés,-esa** *adj* French.
▸ *nm & nf (persona)* French person; *(hombre)* Frenchman; *(mujer)* Frenchwoman.
▸ *nm* **francés** *(idioma)* French.

**Francia** *nf* France.

**franco,-a¹** *nm & nf* HIST *(persona)* Frank.
▸ *nm* **franco** HIST *(idioma)* Frankish; *(moneda)* franc.

**franco,-a²** *adj* **1** *(persona)* frank, open. **2** *(cosa)* clear, obvious. **3** COM free.

**francotirador,-ra** *nm & nf* sniper.

**franela** *nf* flannel.

**franja** *nf* **1** *(banda)* band, strip. **2** *(de tierra)* strip. **3** COST fringe, border.

**franquear** *vt* **1** *(dejar libre)* to free, clear. **2** *(atravesar)* to cross. **3** *(obstáculo)* to overcome. **4** *(carta)* to frank.

**franqueo** *nm* postage.

**franqueza** *nf* **1** *(sinceridad)* frankness, openness. **2** *(confianza)* familiarity, intimacy.

**frasco** *nm* flask.

**frase** *nf* **1** *(oración)* sentence. **2** *(expresión)* phrase. COMP **frase hecha** set phrase, set expression, idiom.

**fraternal** *adj* fraternal, brotherly.

**fraternidad** *nf* fraternity, brotherhood.

**fraude** *nm* fraud. COMP **fraude fiscal** tax evasion.

**fray** *nm* Brother.

**frecuencia** *nf* frequency. LOC **con frecuencia** frequently, often.

**frecuentar** *vt* to frequent, visit.

**frecuente** *adj* **1** *(repetido)* frequent. **2** *(usual)* common.

**frecuentemente** *adv* frequently, often.

**fregadero** *nm* kitchen sink.

**fregar** *vt* **1** *(lavar)* to wash. **2** *(el suelo)* to mop. LOC **fregar los platos** to wash the dishes, GB do the washing up, wash up.

**fregona** *nf (utensilio)* mop.

**freidora** *nf* fryer, deep fryer.

**freír** *vt* **1** *(guisar)* to fry. **2** *fig* to annoy, exasperate.

**frenar** *vt* **1** to brake. **2** *fig* to restrain, check.
▸ *vi* to brake: *frenó de golpe* he jammed on the brakes.

**frenazo** *nm* sudden braking. LOC **dar un frenazo** to jam on the brakes.

**freno** *nm* **1** *(de auto)* brake. **2** *fig (contención)* curb, check. LOC **poner freno a ALGO** *fig* to curb STH.

**frente** *nm* **1** *(gen)* front. **2** MIL front, front line.
▸ *nf* ANAT forehead. LOC **de frente 1** *(hacia adelante)* straight ahead. **2** *(sin rodeos)* straight. ǀ **ponerse al frente de ALGO** to take command of STH.

**fresa** *nf* **1** *(planta)* strawberry plant. **2** *(fruto)* strawberry.
▸ *adj* strawberry.

**fresco,-a** *adj* **1** *(temperatura)* cool, cold: *viento fresco* cool wind; *agua fresca* cold water. **2** *(tela, vestido)* light, cool. **3** *(comida)* fresh. **4** *(reciente)* fresh, new: *noticias frescas* latest news *sing*. **5** *(desvergonzado)* cheeky, shameless.
▸ *nm* **fresco 1** *(frescor)* fresh air, cool air. **2** ARTE fresco. LOC **al fresco** in the cool. ǀ **quedarse tan fresco,-a** not to

bat an eyelid. ∎ **tomar el fresco** to get some fresh air.

**frescor** *nm* coolness, freshness.

**frescura** *nf* **1** *(frescor)* freshness, coolness. **2** *(desvergüenza)* cheek, nerve. [LOC] **¡qué frescura!** what a nerve!

**fresno** *nm* ash tree.

**frialdad** *nf* **1** *(frío)* coldness. **2** *(indiferencia)* coldness, indifference.

**fricativo,-a** *adj* fricative.

**fricción** *nf* **1** *(roce)* friction. **2** *(desacuerdo)* friction, discord.

**frigorífico** *nm* **1** *(electrodoméstico)* refrigerator, fridge. **2** *(cámara frigorífica)* cold store.

**frijol** *nm* bean, kidney bean.

**frío,-a** *adj* **1** *(gen)* cold. **2** *(indiferente)* cold, cool, indifferent; *(pasmado)* stunned: *la película me dejó frío* the film left me cold.
▶ *nm* **frío** cold. [LOC] **coger a ALGN en frío** *fig* to catch SB on the hop. ∎ **hace un frío que pela** *fam* it's freezing cold. ∎ **hacer frío** to be cold. ∎ **tener frío / pasar frío** to be cold.

**friolero,-a** *adj* sensitive to the cold.

**friso** *nm* **1** ARQUIT frieze. **2** *(zócalo)* skirting board.

**frito,-a** *adj* **1** CULIN fried. **2** *fam* fed up, sick: *este niño me tiene frita* I'm sick and tired of this kid.
▶ *nm* **frito** piece of fried food. [LOC] **quedarse frito,-a** *fam* *(dormido)* to fall fast asleep.

**frívolo,-a** *adj* frivolous.

**frondoso,-a** *adj* leafy, luxuriant.

**frontera** *nf* **1** frontier, border. **2** *fig* limit, bounds *pl*, borderline.

**frontón** *nm* **1** *(juego)* pelota. **2** *(edificio)* pelota court. **3** ARQUIT pediment.

**frotar** *vt* to rub. [LOC] **frotarse las manos** to rub one's hands together.

**fruncir** *vt* COST to gather. [LOC] **fruncir el ceño** to frown, knit one's brow.

**frustración** *nf* frustration.

**frustrar** *vt* **1** *(cosa)* to frustrate, thwart. **2** *(persona)* to disappoint.

▶ *vpr* **frustrarse 1** *(proyectos, planes)* to fail, come to nothing. **2** *(persona)* to get frustrated, get disappointed.

**fruta** *nf* fruit.

**frutería** *nf* fruit shop.

**frutero,-a** *nm & nf* fruit seller, fruiterer.
▶ *nm* **frutero** fruit dish, fruit bowl.

**fruto** *nm* **1** *(fruta)* fruit. **2** *(resultado)* fruit, result, product. [LOC] **dar fruto** to bear fruit. ∎ **sacar fruto de ALGO** to profit from STH. [COMP] **frutos secos 1** *(almendras, etc)* nuts. **2** *(pasas, etc)* dried fruit *sing*.

**fucsia** *nf* fuchsia.

**fuego** *nm* **1** fire. **2** *(lumbre)* light. **3** *(cocina)* burner, ring. [LOC] **a fuego lento 1** on a low flame. **2** *(al horno)* in a slow oven. ∎ **poner las manos en el fuego por ALGO/ALGN** to stake one's life on STH/SB. ∎ **prender fuego a ALGO** to set fire to STH. [COMP] **fuegos artificiales** fireworks.

**fuel** *nm* fuel oil.

**fuelle** *nm* *(aparato)* bellows *pl*.

**fuente** *nf* **1** *(manantial)* spring. **2** *(artificial)* fountain. **3** *(recipiente)* serving dish, dish. **4** *fig* source.

**fuera** *adv* **1** *(exterior)* out, outside: *salimos fuera* we went out, we went outside. **2** *(alejado)* away; *(en el extranjero)* abroad.
▶ *interj* get out!
▶ *prep* **fuera de** *(un lugar)* out of; *(más allá de)* outside, beyond; *(excepto)* except for, apart from. [LOC] **estar fuera de sí** to be beside os. ∎ **fuera de lo normal** extraordinary, very unusual. ∎ **fuera de serie** extraordinary. [COMP] **fuera de juego** offside.

**fuerte** *adj* **1** *(gen)* strong: *tiene un sabor fuerte* it has a strong taste. **2** *(en asignatura)* strong, good: *está muy fuerte en historia* she's very strong on history. **3** *(viento)* strong; *(lluvia, nevada)* heavy; *(tormenta, seísmo)* severe; *(calor)* intense. **4** *(dolor, enfermedad)* severe, bad. **5** *(golpe)* hard, heavy. **6** *(sonido)* loud. **7** *(subida)* steep, sharp; *(bajada)* sharp: *un fuerte descenso en el precio del petróleo* a sharp fall in the price of oil. **8** *(discusión)*

heated, violent; *(aplauso)* loud, thunderous. **9** *(comida - pesado)* heavy; *(- cargado)* rich. **10** *(color)* intense.
▸ *nm* **1** *(fortificación)* fort. **2** *(punto fuerte)* forte, strong point.
▸ *adv* **1** *(mucho)* a lot. **2** *(con fuerza)* hard: *empuja fuerte* push hard. **3** *(volumen)* loud: *la música sonaba fuerte* the music was loud.

**fuerza** *nf* **1** *(gen)* strength. **2** *(violencia)* force, violence. **3** *(militar)* force. **4** *(en física)* force. **5** *(electricidad)* power, electric power. **6** *(poder)* power. `LOC` a **fuerza de** by dint of, by force of. ▌ **a la fuerza** by force. ▌ **con fuerza 1** *(gen)* strongly. **2** *(llover)* heavily. **3** *(apretar, agarrar)* tightly; *(pegar, empujar)* hard. ▌ **por fuerza** by force. `COMP` **fuerza de voluntad** willpower.

**fuga** *nf* **1** *(huida)* flight, escape. **2** *(escape)* leak.

**fugarse** *vpr* *(gen)* to flee, escape; *(de casa)* to run away from home.

**fugaz** *adj* fleeting, brief.

**fugitivo,-a** *adj* *(en fuga)* fleeing.
▸ *nm & nf* fugitive, runaway.

**fulano,-a** *nm & nf* so-and-so; *(hombre)* what's his name; *(mujer)* what's her name.
▸ *nm* **fulano** *fam pey* guy, GB bloke.

**fulminar** *vt* **1** to strike with lightning. **2** *fig* to strike dead. `LOC` **fulminar a** ALGN **(con la mirada)** to look daggers at SB.

**fumador,-ra** *nm & nf* smoker. `LOC` **los no fumadores** nonsmokers.

**fumar** *vt* to smoke.

**fumigar** *vt* to fumigate.

**funámbulo,-a** *nm & nf* tightrope walker.

**función** *nf* **1** *(gen)* function. **2** *(cargo)* duty. **3** *(espectáculo)* performance, show. `LOC` **en función de** according to. ▌ **en funciones** acting. ▌ **entrar en función** *(persona)* to take up one's post. ▌ **estar en funciones** to be in office. `COMP` **función de noche** evening performance. ▌ **función de tarde** matinée.

**funcional** *adj* functional.

**funcionamiento** *nm* operation, working.

**funcionar** *vi* *(desempeñar una función)* to work, function: *funciona con gasolina/diesel* it runs on petrol/diesel.

**funcionario,-a** *nm & nf* functionary, employee. `COMP` **funcionario,-a público,-a** civil servant, government employee.

**funda** *nf* **1** *(flexible)* cover. **2** *(rígida)* case. **3** *(de disco)* sleeve. `COMP` **funda de almohada** pillowcase.

**fundación** *nf* foundation.

**fundador,-ra** *nm & nf* founder.

**fundamental** *adj* fundamental.

**fundamentalismo** *nm* fundamentalism.

**fundamentalista** *adj* fundamentalist.
▸ *nm o nf* fundamentalist.

**fundamentalmente** *adv* fundamentally, basically.

**fundamento** *nm* **1** *(base)* basis, grounds *pl*. **2** *(seriedad)* seriousness; *(confianza)* reliability. `LOC` **sin fundamento** unfounded.

**fundar** *vt* **1** *(crear)* to found; *(erigir)* to raise: *su padre fundó la empresa* her father founded the company. **2** *(basar)* to base, found.
▸ *vpr* **fundarse 1** *(crearse)* to be founded. **2** *(teoría, afirmación)* to be based (en, on); *(persona)* to base os (en, on).

**fundición** *nf* **1** *(derretimiento)* melting. **2** *(de metales)* smelting. **3** *(lugar)* foundry, smelting works.

**fundir** *vt* **1** *(derretir)* to melt: *el sol funde la nieve* the sun melts the snow. **2** *(separar mena y metal)* to smelt. **3** *(dar forma)* to cast: *fundir una figura en bronce* to cast a figure in bronze. **4** *(bombilla, plomos)* to blow.
▸ *vpr* **fundirse 1** *(derretirse)* to melt: *la nieve se funde* snow melts. **2** *(bombilla, plomos)* to fuse, go, blow, burn out: *se han fundido los plomos* the fuses have gone. **3** *(unirse)* to merge.

**fúnebre** *adj* **1** *(mortuorio)* funeral. **2** *(lúgubre)* mournful, lugubrious.

**funeral** *nm* [también se usa en plural con el mismo significado] **1** *(entierro)* funeral. **2** *(conmemoración)* memorial service.

**funerala** COMP ojo a la funerala *fam* black eye.

**funeraria** *nf* undertaker's, US funeral parlor.

**funerario,-a** *adj* funerary, funeral.

**funesto,-a** *adj* ill-fated, fatal.

**fungicida** *adj* fungicidal.
▶ *nm* fungicide.

**funicular** *nm* funicular, funicular railway.

**furgón** *nm* **1** AUTO van, truck. **2** *(de tren)* (goods) wagon, US boxcar. COMP **furgón de cola** guard's van.

**furgoneta** *nf* van.

**furia** *nf* fury, rage.

**furibundo,-a** *adj* furious, enraged.

**furiosamente** *adv* furiously.

**furioso,-a** *adj* **1** *(colérico)* furious. **2** *(tempestad, vendaval)* raging. LOC **ponerse furioso,-a** to get angry.

**furor** *nm* fury, rage. LOC **hacer furor** *fig* to be all the rage.

**furtivamente** *adv* furtively.

**furtivo,-a** *adj* furtive.

**furúnculo** *nm* boil.

**fusa** *nf* demisemiquaver, US thirty-second note.

**fuseaux** *nm* ski pants *pl*.

**fuselaje** *nm* fuselage.

**fusible** *nm* fuse.

**fusil** *nm* rifle, gun.

**fusilamiento** *nm* shooting, execution.

**fusilar** *vt* **1** *(ejecutar)* to shoot, execute. **2** *(plagiar)* to plagiarize.

**fusión** *nf* **1** *(de metales)* fusion, melting; *(de hielo)* thawing, melting. **2** *(de intereses, partidos, ideas)* fusion. **3** *(de empresas)* merger, amalgamation.

**fusionar** *vt* **1** *(fundir)* to fuse. **2** *(unir)* to join, unite. **3** COM to merge: *proponen fusionar ambas empresas* they propose to merge the two companies.
▶ *vpr* **fusionarse** *(unir)* to join, unite; *(empresas)* to merge.

**fusta** *nf* riding whip.

**fuste** *nm* **1** *(palo)* stick. **2** *(de columna)* shaft.

**futbito** *nm* five-a-side football.

**fútbol** *nm* football, soccer. COMP **fútbol americano** American football.

**futbolín®** *nm* table football.

**futbolista** *nm o nf* footballer, football player, soccer player.

**futbolístico,-a** *adj* football.

**futón** *nm* futon.

**futurista** *adj* futuristic.

**futuro,-a** *adj* future.
▶ *nm* **futuro** future. LOC **en un futuro próximo** in the near future. COMP **futuro imperfecto** future. **I futuro perfecto** future perfect.

**G**

**G, g** *nf (la letra)* G, g.

**g** *sím (gramo)* gram, gramme; *(símbolo)* g.

**gabán** *nm* overcoat.

**gabardina** *nf (impermeable)* raincoat.

**gabinete** *nm* **1** *(habitación)* study. **2** POL cabinet. **3** *(despacho)* office.

**Gabón** *nm* Gabon.

**gabonés,-esa** *adj* Gabonese.
▶ *nm & nf* Gabonese.

**gacela** *nf* gazelle.

**gacha** *nf (masa)* paste.
▶ *nf pl* **gachas** *(papilla)* porridge *sing*.

**gafas** *nf pl* **1** spectacles, glasses. **2** *(de motorista, esquí, natación)* goggles. COMP **gafas de bucear** diving mask *sing*. ▌ **gafas de sol** sunglasses.

**gafe** *adj fam* jinx.
▶ *nm o nf fam* jinx.

**gaita** *nf* **1** bagpipes *pl*, pipes *pl*. **2** *fam* bother, drag, pain.

**gaitero,-a** *nm & nf* MÚS piper, bagpipe player.

**gajo** *nm (de fruta)* segment.

**gala** *nf* **1** *(espectáculo)* gala. **2** *(vestido)* best dress. LOC **hacer gala de** to make a show of. COMP **cena de gala** gala dinner.
▶ *nf pl* **galas** *(adorno)* finery *sing*. LOC **lucir sus mejores galas** to be dressed in all one's finery.

**galáctico,-a** *adj* galactic.

**galán** *nm (atractivo)* handsome young man; *(mujeriego)* ladies' man.

**galardón** *nm* prize.

**galaxia** *nf* galaxy.

**galera** *nf (mar)* galley.

**galería** *nf* **1** *(gen)* gallery. **2** *(corredor descubierto)* balcony, verandah. **3** TEAT gallery, balcony. COMP **galerías comerciales** shopping centre *sing*.

**galés,-a** *adj* Welsh.
▶ *nm & nf (persona)* Welsh person; *(hombre)* Welshman; *(mujer)* Welshwoman.
▶ *nm* galés *(idioma)* Welsh.

**Gales** *nm* Wales. COMP **País de Gales** Wales.

**galgo,-a** *nm & nf* greyhound.

**galleta** *nf* CULIN biscuit, US cookie.

**gallina** *nf* hen.
▶ *nm o nf fam* chicken, coward. LOC **jugar a la gallina ciega** to play blind man's buff.

**gallinero** *nm* **1** henhouse. **2** *fam* bedlam, madhouse. **3 el gallinero** TEAT the gods *pl*.

**gallo** *nm* **1** cock, rooster. **2** *(pez)* John Dory. **3** *fig (al cantar)* false note; *(al hablar)* squeak. LOC **en menos que canta un gallo** in a flash.

**galón**¹ *nm* **1** *(cinta)* braid. **2** MIL stripe, chevron.

**galón**² *nm (medida)* gallon.

**galopar** *vi* to gallop.

**galope** *nm* gallop. LOC **a galope / al galope 1** at a gallop. **2** *fig* in a rush. ▌ **a galope tendido** at full gallop.

**gama** *nf* **1** MÚS scale. **2** *(gradación, variedad)* range.

**gamba**¹ *nf* ZOOL prawn; *(pequeña)* shrimp.

**gamba**² *nf argot (pierna)* leg. LOC **meter la gamba** *fam* to put one's foot in it.

**gamberrada** *nf* act of hooliganism.

**gamberro,-a** *adj* loutish, rowdy.
▶ *nm & nf* vandal, hooligan, lout.

**Gambia** *nf* Gambia.

**gambiano,-a** *adj* Gambian.
▶ *nm & nf* Gambian.

**gamo** *nm* fallow deer.

**gamuza** *nf* **1** ZOOL chamois. **2** *(piel)* chamois leather. **3** *(paño)* duster.

**gana** *nf* **1** *(deseo)* wish (de, for), desire. **2** *(apetito)* appetite; *(hambre)* hunger. LOC **dar a** ALGN **la gana de hacer** ALGO *fam* to feel like doing STH. ∎ **tener ganas de (hacer)** ALGO to feel like (doing) STH.

**ganadería** *nf* **1** *(crianza)* cattle raising, stockbreeding. **2** *(ganado)* cattle, livestock.

**ganadero,-a** *nm & nf* **1** *(propietario)* cattle breeder, stockbreeder. **2** *(cuidador de ganado)* herdsman, US herder.

**ganado** *nm* livestock, stock; *(vacas)* cattle. COMP **ganado bovino** cattle *pl.* ∎ **ganado vacuno** cattle *pl.*

**ganador,-ra** *adj* winning.
▶ *nm & nf* winner.

**ganancia** *nf* gain, profit.

**ganar** *vt* **1** *(partido, concurso, premio)* to win. **2** *(dinero)* to earn: *¿cuánto ganas al año?* how much do you earn a year? **3** *(alcanzar)* to reach. **4** *(lograr)* to win.
▶ *vi* **1** *(mejorar)* to improve. **2** *(cambiar favorablemente)* to gain.
▶ *vpr* **ganarse 1** to earn. **2** *(ser merecedor)* to deserve: *se lo han ganado* they deserve it. LOC **ganar a** ALGN **en** ALGO to be better than SB at STH.

**ganchillo** *nm* **1** *(aguja)* crochet hook. **2** *(labor)* crochet work. LOC **hacer ganchillo** to crochet.

**gancho** *nm* **1** hook. **2** *(para ropa)* peg. **3** *fam (atractivo)* attractiveness, charm. *(en boxeo)* hook. **4** *(en baloncesto)* hook shot. LOC **tener gancho** *fam* to be attractive, have charm.

**gandul,-la** *adj* lazy, idle.
▶ *nm & nf* idler, loafer, lazybones.

**gandulear** *vi* to idle, loaf around.

**ganga** *nf (algo barato)* bargain, good buy. COMP **precio de ganga** bargain price.

**gángster** *nm* gangster.

**gansada** *nf fam* silly thing to say, silly thing to do.

**ganso,-a** *nm & nf* ZOOL goose; *(macho)* gander.

**ganzúa** *nf* **1** *(garfio)* picklock. **2** *(ladrón)* burglar.

**garabatear** *vt (escribir)* to scribble, scrawl; *(dibujar)* to doodle.

**garabato** *nm* **1** *(gancho)* hook. **2** *(dibujo)* doodle; *(escritura)* scrawl, scribble.

**garaje** *nm* garage.

**garantía** *nf* **1** *(seguridad)* guarantee, security. **2** COM guarantee, warranty.

**garantizado,-a** *adj* guaranteed.

**garantizar** *vt* **1** to guarantee. **2** COM to warrant.

**garbanzo** *nm* chickpea.

**garbeo** *nm fam* walk, stroll.

**garbo** *nm* **1** *(airosidad al andar)* gracefulness. **2** *(gracia)* grace, stylishness.

**garboso,-a** *adj (airoso)* graceful.

**gardenia** *nf* gardenia.

**garfio** *nm* hook, grapple.

**garganta** *nf* **1** *(cuello)* throat. **2** *(desfiladero)* gorge, narrow pass.

**gargantilla** *nf* short necklace.

**gárgola** *nf* gargoyle.

**garita** *nf* **1** *(caseta)* box, cabin, hut; *(de centinela)* sentry box. **2** *(portería)* porter's lodge.

**garito** *nm* **1** *(casa de juego)* gambling dene. **2** *(antro de diversión)* dive, joint.

**garra** *nf (de mamífero)* paw, claw; *(de ave)* talon.
▶ *nf pl* **garras** *(poder)* clutches. LOC **caer en las garras de** ALGN *fig* to fall into SB's clutches. ∎ **tener garra 1** *(relato, etc)* to be compelling. **2** *(persona)* to have charisma.

**garrafa** *nf* carafe.

**garrafal** *adj* monumental, huge.

**garrafón** *nm* demijohn, large carafe.

**garrapata** *nf* tick.

**garrotazo** *nm* blow with a stick.

**garrote** *nm* thick stick, cudgel, club.

**garza** *nf* heron. COMP **garza real** grey heron.

**gas** *nm (gen)* gas.

▸ *nm pl* **gases** *(flatulencias)* wind *sing*, flatulence *sing*, US gas *sing*.

**gasa** *nf* gauze.

**gaseosa** *nf* GB lemonade, US soda.

**gasóleo** *nm* diesel oil.

**gasolina** *nf* petrol, US gasoline, gas. LOC **poner gasolina** to get some petrol.

**gasolinera** *nf* **1** petrol station, US gas station. **2** *(lancha)* motorboat.

**gastado,-a** *adj* **1** *(desgastado)* worn-out. **2** *(acabado)* finished, empty, used up.

**gastador,-ra** *adj (derrochador)* spendthrift.

**gastar** *vt* **1** *(consumir dinero, tiempo)* to spend; *(gasolina, electricidad)* to use (up), consume: *este coche gasta mucha gasolina* this car uses a lot of petrol. **2** *(malgastar)* to waste. **3** *(usar perfume, jabón)* to use; *(ropa)* to wear.
▸ *vpr* **gastarse 1** *(desgastarse)* to wear out. **2** *(consumirse)* to run out.

**gasto** *nm* expenditure, expense. COMP **gastos de mantenimiento** running costs, maintenance costs. ‖ **gastos diarios** daily expenses.

**gastronomía** *nf* gastronomy.

**gastronómico,-a** *adj* gastronomic, gastronomical.

**gata** *nf* she-cat, cat.

✎ Véase también **gato**.

**gatas** LOC **a gatas** on all fours. ‖ **andar a gatas** to crawl.

**gatear** *vi (andar a gatas)* to crawl.

**gatera** *nf* cat door, cat flap.

**gatillo** *nm* trigger.

**gatito,-a** *nm & nf fam* kitty, pusy.

**gato** *nm* **1** cat, tomcat. **2** *(de coche)* jack. LOC **buscarle tres/cinco pies al gato** *fam* to split hairs, complicate things. ‖ **dar gato por liebre** *fam* to take SB in, con SB. ‖ **hay gato encerrado** *fam* there's something fishy going on.

**gatuno,-a** *adj* catlike, feline.

**gavilán** *nm* sparrowhawk.

**gavilla** *nf (de ramas, etc)* sheaf.

**gaviota** *nf* seagull, gull.

**gay** *adj* gay, homosexual.
▸ *nm* gay, homosexual.

**gaznate** *nm* gullet.

**gazpacho** *nm* cold soup made of tomatoes and other vegetables.

**ge** *nf* name of the letter **g**.

**gel** *nm* gel.

**gelatina** *nf* **1** *(sustancia)* gelatine. **2** *(preparado alimenticio)* jelly.

**gelatinoso,-a** *adj* gelatinous, jellylike.

**gélido,-a** *adj* icy, icy cold.

**gema** *nf* **1** BOT bud. **2** *(piedra)* gem.

**gemelo,-a** *adj* twin.
▸ *nm & nf* twin.
▸ *nm* **gemelo** *(músculo)* calf muscle.
▸ *nm pl* **gemelos 1** *(botones)* cufflinks. **2** *(anteojos)* binoculars.

**gemido** *nm (quejido)* groan, moan.

**gemir** *vi (quejarse)* to moan, groan.

**gen** *nm* gene.

**genciana** *nf* gentian.

**generación** *nf* generation.

**generacional** *adj* generation, generational.

**generador,-ra** *nm (máquina)* generator.

**general** *adj* **1** general. **2** *(común)* common, usual, widespread.
▸ *nm (oficial)* general. LOC **en general** in general, generally.

**generalidad** *nf* **1** *(gen)* generality. **2** *(mayoría)* majority. **3** *(generalización)* general statement.
▸ *nf pl* **generalidades** *(nociones)* basic knowledge *sing*.

**generalización** *nf* **1** *(gen)* generalization. **2** *(extensión)* spread, spreading.

**generalizado,-a** *adj* widespread, common.

**generalizar** *vt* **1** *(gen)* to generalize. **2** *(extender)* to spread, popularize.
▸ *vpr* **generalizarse** to spread, become widespread, become common.

**generalmente** *adv* usually.

**generar** *vt* to generate.

**genéricamente** *adv* generically.

**genérico,-a** *adj* generic.

**género** *nm* **1** *(clase)* kind, sort. **2** *(tela)* cloth. **3** *(mercancía)* article. **4** GRAM gender. **5** BIOL genus.

**generosamente** *adv* generously.

**generosidad** *nf* generosity, unselfishness.

**generoso,-a** *adj* generous (con/para, to).

**génesis** *nf inv* genesis.

**genética** *nf* genetics *sing*.

**genial** *adj* **1** brilliant, inspired. **2** *fam* terrific, great, smashing.
▶ *adv fam* great.

**genialidad** *nf* **1** *(idea)* brilliant idea, stroke of genius. **2** *(cualidad)* genius.

**genio** *nm* **1** *(carácter)* temper, disposition. **2** *(facultad)* genius: *Einstein fue un genio* Einstein was a genius. **3** *(espíritu)* spirit: *el genio del Renacimiento* the Renaissance spirit. LOC **estar de mal genio** to be in a bad mood. ‖ **tener mal genio** to have a bad temper.

**genital** *adj* genital.
▶ *nm pl* **genitales** genitals.

**genocidio** *nm* genocide.

**gente** *nf* **1** people *pl*. **2** *(familia)* family, folks *pl*, people *pl*: *me gusta estar con mi gente* I like being with my family. COMP **gente menuda** *fam* nippers *pl*, kids *pl*.

**gentil** *adj* *(amable)* kind.

**gentileza** *nf* **1** *(gracia)* grace, elegance. **2** *(cortesía)* politeness, kindness.

**gentilicio** *adj* gentile.
▶ *nm* gentile.

**gentío** *nm* crowd.

**gentuza** *nf pey* mob, rabble, riffraff.

**genuino,-a** *adj* genuine, authentic.

**geografía** *nf* geography.

**geógrafo,-a** *nm & nf* geographer.

**geología** *nf* geology.

**geológico,-a** *adj* geologic, geological.

**geólogo,-a** *nm & nf* geologist.

**geometría** *nf* geometry.

**geométrico,-a** *adj* geometric, geometrical.

**Georgia** *nf* Georgia.

**georgiano,-a** *adj* Georgian.
▶ *nm & nf (persona)* Georgian.
▶ *nm* **georgiano** *(idioma)* Georgian.

**geranio** *nm* geranium.

**gerencia** *nf (actividad)* management.

**gerente** *nm o nf (hombre)* manager; *(mujer)* manageress.

**geriatría** *nf* geriatrics *sing*.

**geriátrico,-a** *adj* geriatric.
▶ *nm* **geriátrico** *(sanatorio)* geriatric hospital; *(residencia)* old people's home.

**germano,-a** *adj* Germanic.

**germen** *nm* germ.

**germinar** *vi* to germinate.

**gerundio** *nm* gerund.

**gesta** *nf arc* heroic deed, exploit.

**gestación** *nf* **1** gestation. **2** *(período)* gestation period.

**gestante** *adj* gestating.
▶ *nf* expectant mother.

**gesticular** *vi* to gesticulate.

**gestión** *nf* [también se usa en plural con el mismo significado] *(trámite)* step, measure, move. COMP **gestión de datos** data management.

**gestionar** *vt* **1** *(negociar)* to negotiate. **2** *(administrar)* to manage, run.

**gesto** *nm* **1** *(movimiento)* gesture. **2** *(mueca)* grimace. LOC **hacer gestos a** *fam* to make gestures at.

**gestor,-ra** *nm & nf* **1** *(administrador)* manager, director. **2** *person who transacts official business on his clients' behalf*, ≈ solicitor.

**Ghana** *nf* Ghana.

**ghanés,-a** *adj* Ghanaian.
▶ *nm & nf* Ghanaian.

**giba** *nf* hump, hunch.

**giga** *nf (gigabyte)* giga, gigabyte.

**gigabyte** *nm* gigabyte.

**gigante** *nm & nf (hombre)* giant; *(mujer)* giantess.
▶ *adj* giant, gigantic, huge.

**gigantesco,-a** *adj* giant, gigantic.

**gimnasia** *nf* gymnastics *sing*.

**gimnasio** *nm* gymnasium, gym.

**gincana** *nf* gymkhana.

G

**ginebra** *nf* gin.

**ginecología** *nf* gynaecology.

**ginecólogo,-a** *nm & nf* gynaecologist.

**gineta** *nf* genet.

**gira** *nf* tour.

**girar** *vi* 1 *(dar vueltas)* to rotate, whirl, spin. 2 *(torcer)* to turn: *girar a la izquierda* to turn left. 3 *fig (versar)* to deal with: *la conversación giró en torno al teatro* the conversation evolved around theatre.
▶ *vt* 1 COM to issue: *girar una letra* to issue a draft. 2 *(cambiar de sentido)* to turn, turn around: *girar el cuerpo* to turn one's body.

**girasol** *nm* sunflower.

**giratorio,-a** *adj* rotating, gyratory.

**giro** *nm* 1 *(vuelta)* turn, turning. 2 *(dirección)* course, direction. 3 COM draft. COMP **giro postal** money order.

**gitano,-a** *nm & nf* gypsy, gipsy.

**glaciación** *nf* glaciation.

**glacial** *adj* 1 glacial. 2 *fig* glacial, icy: *tuvo un recibimiento glacial* he had an icy reception.

**glaciar** *nm* glacier.

**gladiador** *nm* gladiator.

**gladiolo** *nm* gladiolus.

**glándula** *nf* gland.

**glicerina** *nf* glycerin, glycerine.

**global** *adj* global, comprehensive.

**globo** *nm* 1 *(esfera)* globe, sphere. 2 *(tierra)* globe. 3 *(de aire)* balloon.

**glóbulo** *nm* globule. COMP **glóbulo blanco** white corpuscle. I **glóbulo rojo** red corpuscle.

**gloria** *nf* 1 *(bienaventuranza)* glory. 2 *(fama)* fame, honour (US honor).

**glorieta** *nf* 1 *(en un jardín)* arbour. 2 *(plazoleta)* small square.

**glorificar** *vt* to glorify.

**glorioso,-a** *adj* glorious.

**glosar** *vt* 1 *(explicar)* to gloss. 2 *(interpretar)* to interpret.

**glosario** *nm* glossary.

**glotón,-ona** *adj* greedy, gluttonous.
▶ *nm & nf* glutton.

**glotonería** *nf* gluttony, greed.

**glúcido** *nm* glucide.

**glucosa** *nf* glucose.

**gluten** *nm* gluten.

**gnomo** *nm* gnome.

**gobernador,-ra** *nm & nf* governor.

**gobernante** *adj* ruling, governing.
▶ *nm o nf* ruler, leader.

**gobernar** *vt* 1 *(gen)* to govern. 2 *(un país)* to rule. 3 *(un negocio)* to run, handle. 4 *(un barco)* to steer.

**gobierno** *nm* 1 POL government. 2 *(mando)* command, running, handling. 3 *(conducción)* direction, control; *(de un barco)* steering; *(de timón)* rudder.

**goce** *nm* pleasure, enjoyment.

**godo,-a** *adj* Gothic.
▶ *nm & nf (persona)* Goth.

**gofre** *nm* waffle.

**gol** *nm* goal.

**goleador,-ra** *nm & nf* scorer. COMP **el máximo goleador** the top scorer.

**golear** *vt* to hammer.

**golf** *nm (deporte)* golf.

**golfista** *nm o nf* golfer.

**golfo** *nm* gulf, large bay.

**golfo,-a** *nm & nf (holgazán)* good-for-nothing; *(niño)* rascal, little devil.

**golondrina** *nf (ave)* swallow.

**golosina** *nf* sweet, US candy.

**goloso,-a** *adj* sweet-toothed.

**golpe** *nm* 1 blow, knock; *(puñetazo)* punch: *le dio un golpe* he hit him. 2 *(de coche)* collision; *(fuerte)* bang; *(ligero)* bump. 3 *fig (desgracia)* blow, misfortune. LOC **de golpe** suddenly, all of a sudden. I **no dar golpe** *fam* not to lift a finger, not do a blessed thing. COMP **golpe bajo** *fig* punch below the belt. I **golpe de Estado** coup, coup d'état. I **golpe de vista** quick glance.

**golpear** *vt (gen)* to hit, strike; *(personas)* to thump, hit, punch; *(puerta)* to knock on.

**golpista** *nm o nf* person involved in a coup d'état.

**goma** *nf* 1 *(material)* gum, rubber. 2 *(de borrar)* rubber, US eraser. 3 *(de pegar)* glue, gum. 4 *(banda elástica)* rubber band. COMP **goma arábiga** gum arabic. I **goma de mascar** chewing gum.

**gomaespuma** *nf* foam rubber.

**gomina** *nf* hair cream.

**gominola** *nf* jelly bean, jelly.

**gong** *nm* gong.

**gordo,-a** *adj* **1** *(carnoso)* fat: *se puso gordo* he got fat. **2** *(grueso)* thick. **3** *(grave)* serious. **4** *(importante)* big: *¡qué mentira tan gorda!* what a big lie!
▶ *nm & nf* fat person, fatty.
▶ *nm* **gordo 1** *fam (grasa)* fat. **2 el gordo** the first prize *in the lottery*.

**gordura** *nf* fatness.

**gorila** *nm* *(animal)* gorilla.

**gorjear** *vi* to chirp, twitter.

**gorra** *nf* **1** *(gen)* cap. **2** *(con visera)* peaked cap. LOC **de gorra** *fam* free.

**gorrión,-ona** *nm & nf* sparrow.

**gorro** *nm* **1** cap. **2** *(de bebé)* bonnet. **3** *(de cocinero)* chef's hat.

**gorrón,-ona** *adj* *fam* scrounging, sponging.
▶ *nm & nf* sponger, scrounger.

**gorronear** *vi* to scrounge.

**gota** *nf* **1** drop. **2** *(de sudor)* bead. **3** *(de aire)* breath. LOC **caer cuatro gotas** to be spitting with rain. ‖ **gota a gota** drop by drop. ‖ **ni gota** not a bit, nothing at all. COMP **gota fría** cold air pool.

**gotear** *vi* **1** *(grifo)* to drip; *(tejado)* to leak. **2** [sólo se usa en tercera persona; no lleva sujeto] *(lluvia)* to drizzle.

**gotera** *nf* **1** *(agujero)* leak. **2** *(agua)* drip.

**gótico,-a** *adj* Gothic.

**gozar** *vi* **1** *(poseer, disfrutar)* to enjoy (de, -): *goza de muy buena salud* he enjoys very good health. **2** *(sentir placer)* to enjoy os: *gozamos con su presencia* we really enjoy her company.

**gozne** *nm* hinge.

**gozo** *nm* joy, delight, pleasure.

**grabación** *nf* recording.

**grabado,-a** *nm* **1** *(arte)* engraving. **2** *(dibujo)* picture, drawing.

**grabar** *vt* **1** ARTE to engrave. **2** *(registrar)* to record. **3** INFORM to save. LOC **grabarse en la memoria** *fig* to be engraved on one's memory.

**gracia** *nf* **1** *(favor)* favour (US favor). **2** *(atractivo)* grace, charm. **3** *(chiste)* joke. LOC **hacer gracia, tener gracia** *(diversión)* to be funny. ‖ **¡qué gracia!** how funny!
▶ *nf pl* **gracias** thank you, thanks. LOC **dar gracias a ALGN** to thank SB. ‖ **gracias a** thanks to.

**gracioso,-a** *adj* **1** *(atractivo)* graceful, charming. **2** *(bromista)* witty, facetious. **3** *(divertido)* funny, amusing.
▶ *nm & nf* TEAT jester, clown, fool. LOC **hacerse el gracioso** to try to be funny.

**grada** *nf* **1** *(peldaño)* step, stair. **2** *(gradería)* tier.
▶ *nf pl* **gradas** stands, terraces.

**gradería** *nf* stands *pl*, terraces *pl*.

**grado** *nm* **1** *(gen)* degree: *estábamos a 27 grados* it was 27 degrees. **2** *(estado)* stage. **3** EDUC *(curso)* class, year. **4** EDUC *(título)* degree. **5** *(peldaño)* step.

**graduación** *nf* **1** *(gen)* graduation. **2** *(de alcohol)* strength. **3** EDUC graduation.

**graduado,-a** *nm & nf* EDUC graduate. COMP **gafas graduadas** prescription glasses. ‖ **graduado escolar** *certificate of elementary school studies*.

**gradual** *adj* gradual.

**graduar** *vt* **1** *(termómetro)* to graduate, calibrate. **2** *(regular)* to adjust, regulate. **3** *(conceder un diploma)* to confer a degree on, US graduate. **4** *(medir)* to gauge, measure; *(la vista)* to test, check.
▶ *vpr* **graduarse** to graduate, get one's degree. LOC **graduarse la vista** to have one's eyes tested.

**grafía** *nf* **1** *(signo)* graphic symbol. **2** *(escritura)* writing. **3** *(ortografía)* spelling.

**gráficamente** *adv* graphically.

**grafía** *nf* graph, diagram.

**gráfico,-a** *adj* graphic.
▶ *nm* **gráfico** *(dibujo)* sketch, chart.

**grafiti** *nm pl* graffiti.

**grafito** *nm* graphite.

**gragea** *nf* pill, tablet.

**grajo,-a** *nm & nf* rook.

**gramática** *nf* grammar.

**gramo** *nm* gram, gramme.

**gramófono** *nm* gramophone.

**gramola®** *nf* gramophone.

**gran** *adj* [se usa delante de nombres masculinos en singular] **1** *(fuerte, intenso)* great: *se llevaron un gran susto* they were terribly shocked. **2** *(excelente)* great: *aquél era un gran libro* that was a great book.

✎ Consulta también **grande**.

**granada** *nf* BOT pomegranate.

**granate** *adj* maroon, claret.
▶ *nm* **1** *(color)* maroon, claret. **2** *(mineral)* garnet.

**grande** *adj* **1** *(tamaño)* large, big. **2** *(fuerte, intenso)* great: *su partida les produjo una pena muy grande* his departure caused them great sorrow. **3** *(mayor)* grown-up, old, big.
▶ *nm* *(de elevada jerarquía)* great. [LOC] **a lo grande** on a grand scale, in a big way. ‖ **estar grande una cosa a** ALGN to be too big on SB. ‖ **pasarlo en grande** *fam* to have a great time.

✎ Consulta también **gran**.

**grandeza** *nf* **1** *(tamaño)* size. **2** *(generosidad)* generosity.

**grandioso,-a** *adj* grandiose, grand, magnificent.

**granel** [LOC] **a granel 1** *(sin envase)* in bulk. **2** *(en abundancia)* lots of.

**granero** *nm* granary, barn.

**granito** *nm* granite.

**granizada** *nf* **1** hailstorm. **2** *fig (lluvia)* hail, shower.

**granizado,-a** *nm* iced drink.

**granizar** *vi* [sólo se usa en tercera persona; no lleva sujeto] to hail.

**granizo** *nm* hail, hailstone.

**granja** *nf* farm.

**granjero,-a** *nm & nf* farmer.

**grano** *nm* **1** grain; *(de café)* bean. **2** MED pimple, spot. [LOC] **ir al grano** *fam* to come to the point, get to the point.
▶ *nm pl* **granos** cereals.

**granuja** *nm* **1** *(pilluelo)* ragamuffin, urchin. **2** *(estafador)* crook, trickster.

**granulado,-a** *adj* granulated.

**granuloso,-a** *adj* **1** *(superficie)* granular. **2** *(piel)* pimply.

**grapa** *nf (para papel)* staple.

**grapadora** *nf* stapler.

**grapar** *vt* to staple.

**grasa** *nf* grease, fat.

**grasiento,-a** *adj* greasy, oily.

**graso,-a** *adj* greasy, oily, fatty.

**gratamente** *adv* pleasantly.

**gratén** *nm* gratin.

**gratificación** *nf* **1** *(satisfacción)* gratification. **2** *(recompensa)* reward.

**gratificador,-ra** *adj* gratifying, rewarding.

**gratificante** *adj* gratifying, rewarding.

**gratificar** *vt* **1** *(satisfacer)* to gratify. **2** *(recompensar)* to reward, tip.

**gratinador** *nm* grill.

**gratinar** *vt* to brown under the grill.

**gratis** *adv* free.

**gratitud** *nf* gratitude.

**grato,-a** *adj* pleasant, pleasing (para, to).

**gratuidad** *nf* gratuitousness.

**gratuitamente** *adv (de balde)* free of charge, free.

**gratuito,-a** *adj (de balde)* free.

**grava** *nf* **1** *(guijas)* gravel. **2** *(piedra machacada)* crushed stone.

**gravable** *adj* taxable.

**gravar** *vt* to tax.

**grave** *adj* **1** *(pesado)* heavy. **2** *(serio)* grave, serious. **3** *(voz, nota)* deep, low. [LOC] **estar grave** to be seriously ill.

**gravedad** *nf* **1** FÍS gravity. **2** *(importancia)* gravity, seriousness.

**gravemente** *adv* **1** *(seriamente)* seriously. **2** *(solemnemente)* solemnly, gravely.

**gravilla** *nf* fine gravel.

**gravitar** *vi* **1** FÍS to gravitate. **2** *(apoyarse en)* to rest (sobre, on).

**graznar** *vi* **1** *(cuervo)* to caw, croak. **2** *(oca)* to honk. **3** *(pato)* to quack.

**graznido** *nm* **1** *(de cuervo)* caw, croak. **2** *(de oca)* honk. **3** *(de pato)* quack.

**greca** *nf* fret, fretwork.

**Grecia** *nf* Greece.

**greda** *nf* fuller's earth, clay.

**gregario,-a** *adj* gregarious.

**gremial** *adj* **1** trade union, union. **2** HIST guild.

**gremio** *nm* **1** HIST guild, corporation. **2** *(sindicato)* union. **3** *(profesión)* profession.

**greña** *nf* lock of entangled hair.
  ▶ *nf pl* **greñas** untidy mop of hair.

**gres** *nm* stoneware.

**gresca** *nf* **1** *(bulla)* racket. **2** *(riña)* row.

**griego,-a** *adj* Greek.
  ▶ *nm & nf (persona)* Greek.
  ▶ *nm* **griego** *(idioma)* Greek.

**grieta** *nf* crack, crevice.

**grifería** *nf* taps *pl*, US faucets *pl*.

**grifo** *nm (llave)* tap, US faucet.

**grill** *nm* grill.

**grillete** *nm* shackle.

**grillo** *nm* ZOOL cricket.

**grima** *nf* displeasure, disgust.

**gripal** *adj* related to flu.

**gripe** *nf* flu, influenza. LOC **tener la gripe** to have (the) flu.

**griposo,-a** *adj* flu. LOC **estar griposo** to have (the) flu.

**gris** *adj* **1** grey (US gray). **2** *fig (mediocre)* mediocre, third-rate. **3** *fig (triste)* grey (US gray), gloomy.
  ▶ *nm (color)* grey (US gray).

**grisáceo,-a** *adj* greyish.

**gritar** *vi (gen)* to shout; *(chillar)* cry out, scream: *¡no me grites!* don't shout at me!

**griterío** *nm* shouting, uproar.

**grito** *nm* shout; *(chillido)* cry, scream. LOC **a grito limpio** at the top of one's voice. ∎ **dar un grito 1** to shout. **2** *(chillar)* to scream. ∎ **el último grito** *fig* the latest thing, the last word. ∎ **pedir** ALGO **a gritos** *fig* to be crying out for STH, be badly in need of STH. ∎ **pegar un grito 1** to shout. **2** *(chillar)* to scream.

**gritón,-ona** *adj* noisy, loudmouthed.
  ▶ *nm & nf* loudmouth.

**grogui** *adj* **1** DEP punch-drunk, groggy. **2** *fig* groggy, half-asleep.

**grosella** *nf* redcurrant.

**grosellero** *nm* redcurrant bush.

**groseramente** *adv* crudely, rudely.

**grosería** *nf* **1** *(ordinariez)* rude word, rude expression. **2** *(rusticidad)* rudeness, coarseness. LOC **decir una grosería** to say something rude.

**grosero,-a** *adj* **1** *(tosco)* coarse, crude. **2** *(maleducado)* rude.
  ▶ *nm & nf* rude person.

**grosor** *nm* thickness.

**grotesco,-a** *adj* ridiculous.

**grúa** *nf* **1** *(construcción)* crane, derrick. **2** AUTO breakdown van, US tow truck.

**gruesa** *nf (doce docenas)* gross.

**grueso,-a** *adj* **1** *(objeto)* thick. **2** *(persona)* fat, stout.
  ▶ *nm* **grueso 1** *(grosor)* thickness. **2** *(parte principal)* bulk.

**grulla** *nf* crane.

**grumete** *nm* cabin boy.

**grumo** *nm* lump; *(de sangre)* clot; *(de leche)* curd.

**grumoso,-a** *adj* lumpy, clotted.

**gruñido** *nm* grunt, growl.

**gruñir** *vi* to grunt.

**gruñón,-ona** *adj* grumbling, grumpy.

**grupa** *nf* croup, hindquarters *pl*.

**grupo** *nm* **1** group. **2** TÉC unit, set. COMP **grupo electrógeno** power plant. ∎ **grupo sanguíneo** blood group.

**gruta** *nf* cavern, grotto, cave.

**gua** *nm* **1** *(juego)* marbles *pl*. **2** *(hoyo)* hole for the marbles.

**guacamayo** *nm* macaw.

**guache** *nm* gouache.

**guadaña** *nf* scythe.

**guantada** *nf* slap.

**guantazo** *nm* slap.

**guante** *nm* glove. LOC **echar el guante a** ALGO *fam* to nick STH.

**guantera** *nf* glove compartment.

**guaperas** *adj inv fam* good-looking.
  ▶ *nm o nf* good looker, looker.

**guapetón,-ona** *adj fam* good-looking.

**guapo,-a** *adj* **1** good-looking; *(hombre)* handsome; *(mujer)* beautiful, pretty. **2** *argot (bonito)* nice, smart.

**guapote,-a** *adj fam* good-looking.

**guapura** *nf fam* good looks *pl*.

**guarda** *nm o nf (persona)* guard, keeper.
▶ *nf* **1** *(custodia)* custody, care. **2** *(de la ley, etc)* observance. **3** *(de libro)* flyleaf.

**guardabarrera** *nm o nf* gatekeeper.

**guardabarros** *nm inv* mudguard, US fender.

**guardabosque** *nm* forester.

**guardacoches** *nm o nf inv* parking attendant.

**guardacostas** *nm o nf inv (persona)* coastguard.
▶ *nm* coastguard vessel.

**guardaespaldas** *nm o nf inv* bodyguard.

**guardafrenos** *nm o nf inv* guard.

**guardagujas** *nm o nf inv (hombre)* pointsman, US switchman; *(mujer)* pointswoman, US switchwoman.

**guardameta** *nm o nf* goalkeeper.

**guardamuebles** *nm inv* furniture warehouse.

**guardapolvo** *nm* **1** *(cubierta)* dust cover. **2** *(mono)* overalls *pl*.

**guardar** *vt* **1** *(cuidar)* to keep, watch over, keep an eye on. **2** *(conservar)* to keep, hold. **3** *(la ley)* to observe, obey; *(un secreto)* to keep. **4** *(poner en un sitio)* to put away: *guárdatelo en el bolsillo* put it in your pocket. **5** *(reservar)* to save, keep: *le guardaron el mejor sitio* they saved the best seat for him. **6** INFORM to save. **7 guardarse de** *(precaverse, evitar)* to guard against, avoid, be careful not to. LOC **guardar las formas** to be polite.

**guardarropa** *nm* **1** *(armario)* wardrobe. **2** *(cuarto)* cloakroom.

**guardarropía** *nf* wardrobe for props.

**guardavía** *nm (hombre)* signalman.

**guardería** *nf* **1** crèche, nursery. **2** *(oficio de guarda)* keeping. COMP **guardería infantil** nursery, nursery school.

**guardia** *nf* **1** *(vigilancia)* watch, lookout. **2** *(servicio)* duty, call.
▶ *nm o nf (hombre)* policeman; *(mujer)* policewoman. LOC **estar de guardia 1** *(doctor)* to be on duty, be on call. **2** *(soldado)* to be on guard duty. **3** *(marino)* to be on watch. COMP **farmacia de guardia** duty chemist's. ▌ **médico de guardia** doctor on duty.

**guardián,-ana** *nm & nf* guardian, keeper, custodian.

**guarecer** *vt* to take shelter (de, from), shelter (de, from).

**guarida** *nf* ZOOL haunt, den, lair.

**guarnecer** *vt* **1** *(decorar)* to adorn, decorate; *(en cocina)* to garnish. **2** *(proveer)* to provide (de, with).

**guarnición** *nf* **1** *(gen)* decoration, trimmings *pl*. **2** CULIN accompaniment to a main dish. **3** MIL garrison.

**guarrada** *nf* **1** *fam* something dirty, disgusting thing: *¡no hagas guarradas!* don't do such filthy things! **2** *fam (mala pasada)* dirty trick.

**guarro,-a** *adj* dirty, filthy.
▶ *nm & nf* pig, dirty pig.

**guasa** *nf* jest, fun, mockery. LOC **estar de guasa** to be joking.

**guasón,-ona** *adj* funny, joking.
▶ *nm & nf* jester, joker.

**guata** *nf* **1** *(algodón)* raw cotton. **2** *(relleno)* padding.

**guateado,-a** *adj* padded, quilted.

**Guatemala** *nf* Guatemala.

**guatemalteco,-a** *adj* Guatemalan.
▶ *nm & nf* Guatemalan.

**guateque** *nm* party.

**guay** *adj fam* great, cool.

**gubernamental** *adj* government, governmental.

**gubernativo,-a** *adj* government, governmental.

**gubia** *nf* gouge.

**guepardo** *nm* cheetah.

**guerra** *nf* war. LOC **dar guerra** *fam* to cause trouble. ▌ **declarar la guerra a** to declare war on. COMP **guerra civil** civil war. ▌ **guerra fría** cold war. ▌ **guerra mundial** world war.

**guerrear** *vi* to war.

**guerrera** *nf (chaqueta)* army jacket.

**guerrero,-a** *adj* **1** warlike. **2** *fam (niño)* difficult.
▶ *nm & nf* warrior, soldier.

**guerrilla** *nf* **1** *(guerra)* guerrilla warfare. **2** *(banda)* guerrilla band.

**guerrillero,-a** *nm & nf* guerrilla.

**gueto** *nm* ghetto.

**guía** *nm o nf (persona)* guide, leader.
▶ *nf* **1** *(norma)* guidance, guideline. **2** *(libro)* guidebook. [COMP] **guía de teléfonos** telephone directory, phone book.

**guiar** *vt* **1** to guide, lead. **2** *(conducir automóvil)* to drive; *(barco)* to steer; *(avión)* to pilot; *(caballo, bici)* to ride.
▶ *vpr* **guiarse** to be guided.

**guijarro** *nm* pebble, stone.

**guillotina** *nf* guillotine.

**guillotinar** *vt* to guillotine.

**guinda** *nf* **1** *(fruta)* sour cherry, morello cherry. **2** *(remate)* final touch.

**guindilla** *nf* **1** red pepper, chilli. **2** *fam (policía)* cop.

**guindo** *nm* morello cherry tree. [LOC] **caerse ALGN del guindo** *fam* to cotton on, twig.

**guinea** *nf* guinea.

**Guinea** *nf* Guinea. [COMP] **Guinea Ecuatorial** Equatorial Guinea. ▌ **Guinea-Bissau** Guinea-Bissau. ▌ **Nueva Guinea** New Guinea.

**guineano,-a** *adj* Guinean.
▶ *nm & nf* Guinean.

**guiñapo** *nm* **1** *(andrajo)* rag, tatter. **2** *fig (persona)* wreck.

**guiñar** *vt* **1** to wink: *me guiñó un ojo* he winked at me. **2** MAR to yaw.

**guiño** *nm* wink.

**guiñol** *nm* puppet theatre.

**guion** *nm* **1** *(esquema)* notes *pl*, sketch, outline. **2** GRAM hyphen, dash. **3** CINE script.

**guionista** *nm o nf* scriptwriter.

**guirigay** *nm* **1** *(lenguaje)* gibberish. **2** *(griterío)* racket, noise, din.

**guirlache** *nm* almond brittle.

**guirnalda** *nf* garland, wreath.

**guisa** *nf* manner, way.

**guisado,-a** *adj* cooked, stewed.
▶ *nm* **guisado** stew.

**guisante** *nm* pea.

**guisar** *vt* to cook, stew.
▶ *vpr* **guisarse** to cook, stew.

**guiso** *nm* stew.

**guitarra** *nf* guitar.

**guitarrero,-a** *nm & nf* **1** *(vendedor)* guitar seller. **2** *(fabricante)* guitar maker.

**guitarrista** *nm o nf* guitarist.

**gula** *nf* gluttony.

**gurú** *nm* guru.

**gusanillo** *nm* **1** little worm. **2** *(espiral)* spiral binding. **3** *(intranquilidad)* niggling doubt. [LOC] **matar el gusanillo** *fam* to have a snack.

**gusano** *nm* **1** worm; *(oruga)* caterpillar. **2** *fig (persona)* worm. [COMP] **gusano de seda** silkworm.

**gustar** *vt* **1** *(agradar)* to like. **2** *(probar)* to taste, try.

**gustativo,-a** *adj* gustative. [COMP] **papila gustativa** taste bud.

**gustillo** *nm* **1** *fam (regusto)* aftertaste. **2** *fam (satisfacción)* satisfaction, pleasure.

**gusto** *nm* **1** *(sentido, sabor)* taste. **2** *(inclinación)* liking, taste. **3** *(placer)* pleasure: *tengo el gusto de presentarle a mi hermano* may I introduce you to my brother? **4** *(capricho)* whim, fancy. [LOC] **con mucho gusto** with pleasure. ▌ **dar gusto** to please, delight: *me da gusto verla comer* I enjoy watching her eat. ▌ **estar a gusto** to feel comfortable, feel at ease. ▌ **hacer ALGO a gusto** to enjoy doing STH. ▌ **hacer ALGO por gusto** to do STH for fun. ▌ **¡qué gusto!** how lovely! ▌ **tanto gusto** pleased to meet you. ▌ **tener buen gusto** to have good taste.

**gustosamente** *adv* with pleasure, gladly, willingly.

**gustoso,-a** *adj* **1** *(sabroso)* tasty, savoury, palatable. **2** *(agradable)* agreeable, pleasant. **3** *(con gusto)* glad, willing, ready: *aceptó gustosa* she accepted willingly.

**gutural** *adj* guttural.

**Guyana** *nf* Guyana.

**guyanés,-esa** *adj* Guyanese.
▶ *nm & nf* Guyanese.

**G**

# H

**H, h** *nf (la letra)* H, h.
**haba** *nf (legumbre)* broad bean.
**haber** *vi (impersonal)* to be: *hay un coche* there's a car.
  ▸ *aux* **1** *(en tiempos compuestos)* to have: *lo has hecho* you have done it. **2** haber **de** + *inf (obligación)* to have to, must, should: *han de venir hoy* they must come today. **3** haber que + *inf (obligación)* must, have to: *habrá que hacerlo* we'll have to do it. LOC ¡haberlo dicho! why didn't you say so! ▌había una vez... once upon a time there was... ▌¡habráse visto! what a cheek! ▌¡hay que ver! well, really!, well, I never! ▌no hay de qué you're welcome, don't mention it. ▌no hay (nada) como... there's nothing like... ▌¿qué hay? hello!, hi!, how are you doing?
  ▸ *nm* COM credit, assets *pl.*
  ▸ *nm pl* haberes *(posesiones)* property *sing,* assets.
**habichuela** *nf (gen)* bean; *(judía blanca)* haricot bean; *(judía verde)* French bean, green bean.
**hábil** *adj* **1** *(diestro)* skilful (US skillful). **2** *(despabilado)* clever, smart. **3** *(acto)* clever. **4** *(apto, adecuado)* good, suitable. LOC ser hábil en ALGO / ser hábil para ALGO *(persona)* to be good at STH. COMP día hábil working day.
**habilidad** *nf* **1** *(aptitud)* skill. **2** *(astucia)* cleverness, smartness. LOC tener habilidad para ALGO to be good at STH.
**habilidoso,-a** *adj* skilful (US skillful).
**habilitar** *vt* **1** *(espacio)* to fit out; *(tiempo)* to set aside: *habilitó una habitación para consulta* he fitted a bedroom out as a consulting room. **2** *(capacitar)* to entitle, qualify; *(autorizar)* to empower.

**habitable** *adj* habitable, liveable.
**habitación** *nf* **1** *(gen)* room. **2** *(dormitorio)* bedroom. COMP habitación doble double room. ▌habitación individual single room.
**habitante** *nm o nf* inhabitant.
**habitar** *vt* to live in, inhabit.
  ▸ *vi* to live.
**hábitat** *nm* habitat.
**hábito** *nm* **1** *(costumbre)* habit, custom. **2** *(vestido)* habit. LOC tener el hábito de... to be in the habit of...
**habitual** *adj* usual, habitual.
**habitualmente** *adv (repetidamente)* usually; *(regularmente)* regularly.
**habituar** *vt* to accustom (a, to).
  ▸ *vpr* habituarse to become accustomed (a, to), get used (a, to).
**habla** [va precedido de el en singular] *nf* **1** *(facultad)* speech. **2** *(idioma)* language; *(dialecto)* dialect. LOC de habla española / de habla hispana Spanish-speaking. ▌estar al habla con ALGN to be in touch with SB. ▌perder el habla to lose one's power of speech.
**hablado,-a** *adj* spoken, oral: *francés hablado* spoken French.
**hablador,-ra** *adj* **1** *(parlanchín)* talkative. **2** *(chismoso)* gossipy.
**habladuría** [también se usa en plural con el mismo significado] *nf (chisme)* piece of gossip; *(rumor)* rumour (US rumor).
**hablante** *nm o nf* speaker.
**hablar** *vi* **1** *(gen)* to speak, talk: *habló conmigo* he spoke to me. **2** *(mencionar)* to talk, mention: *no me habló de eso* she didn't mention that. LOC hablar a solas to talk to os. ▌hablar bajo to speak softly. ▌hablar claro to speak plainly.

**hablar en broma** to be joking. **¡quién fue a hablar!** look who's talking!▶ *vt* **1** *(idioma)* to speak: *habla francés* he speaks French. **2** *(tratar)* to talk over, discuss: *ya lo hablaremos después* we'll discuss it later. ⌐LOC¬ «**Se habla inglés**» "English spoken".

▶ *vpr* **hablarse** *(uso recíproco)* to speak, talk: *ayer nos hablamos por teléfono* we spoke on the 'phone yesterday. ⌐LOC¬ **no hablarse con** ALGN not to be on speaking terms with SB.

**hacendado,-a** *nm & nf* landowner.

**hacendoso,-a** *adj* house-proud.

**hacer** *vt* **1** *(producir, fabricar, crear)* to make: *hice un pastel* I made a cake. **2** *(arreglar, disponer - uñas)* to do; *(- barba)* to trim; *(- cama)* to make; *(- maleta)* to pack. **3** *(obrar, ejecutar)* to do: *haz lo que quieras* do what you want. **4** *(conseguir - amigos, dinero)* to make. **5** *(obligar)* to make: *nos hizo leer* she made us read. **6** *(recorrer)* to do: *hacer noventa kilómetros por hora* to do ninety kilometres per hour. **7** *(en suma)* to make: *con esta hacen ochenta* that makes eighty. **8** *(ocupar un lugar)* to be: *él hace el número cuatro* he's the fourth on the list. **9** *(hacer parecer)* to make look: *ese vestido te hace mayor* that dress makes you look older. **10** *(acostumbrar)* to accustom. **11** *(practicar)* to do: *¿haces deporte?* do you do any sport? ⌐LOC¬ **a medio hacer** half-done, half-finished. **¡así se hace!** that's it! **hace mucho** a long time ago. **hacer bien en...** to be right to...: *hice bien en ir* I was right to go. **hacer mal** to do the wrong thing. **hacer tiempo** to kill time.

▶ *vi* **1** *(actuar)* to play (de, -); *(representar)* to act: *hizo de abuela* she played the grandmother. **2** *(comportarse)* to pretend to be, act: *hacer el tonto* to act the fool. **3** *(clima)* to be: *hace buen día* it's a fine day. **4** *(tiempo pasado)* ago: *hace tres años* three years ago. ⌐LOC¬ **hacer como que +** *ind* to pretend, act as if: *hizo como que no sabía nada* he acted as if he knew nothing. **hacer como si +** *subj* to pretend, act as if.

▶ *vpr* **hacerse 1** *(volverse)* to become, get: *hacerse rico* to get rich. **2** *(crecer)* to grow: *se ha hecho mucho* he's grown a lot. **3** *(resultar)* to become, go on, seem: *la película se hizo muy larga* the film went on too long. **4** *(simular)* to pretend: *se hizo la elegante* she pretended to be elegant. **5** *(mandar hacer)* to have made, have done: *me hice un vestido en la modista* I had a dress made at the dressmaker's. ⌐LOC¬ **hacerse el/la sordo,-a** *fig* to turn a deaf ear. **hacerse una idea de** ALGO to imagine STH.

**hacha** [va precedido de el en singular] *nf* *(instrumento)* axe (US ax).

**hache** *nf* *(la letra)* aitch.

**hacia** *prep* **1** *(dirección)* towards, to. **2** *(tiempo)* at about, at around: *estaremos ahí hacia las dos* we'll be there at about two. ⌐LOC¬ **hacia abajo** downward(s), down. **hacia acá** this way. **hacia adelante** forward(s): *inclínate hacia delante* lean forward. **hacia allá** that way. **hacia atrás** backward(s), back. **hacia casa** home, homeward.

**hacienda** *nf* **1** *(bienes)* property, wealth, possessions *pl.* **2** *(finca)* estate, property, US ranch. **3** FIN Treasury. ⌐COMP¬ **hacienda pública** public funds *pl*, public finances *pl.*

**hada** [va precedido de el en singular] *nf* fairy.

**Haití** *nm* Haiti.

**haitiano,-a** *adj* Haitian.
▶ *nm & nf* Haitian.

**halagador,-ra** *adj* flattering.

**halagar** *vt* **1** *(lisonjear)* to flatter. **2** *(satisfacer)* to please.

**halago** *nm* compliment, flattery.

**halcón** *nm* falcon.

**hallar** *vt* **1** *(encontrar)* to find. **2** *(averiguar)* to find out.
▶ *vpr* **hallarse** *(estar)* to be: *se hallaba enfermo* he was ill.

**hallazgo** *nm* **1** *(descubrimiento)* finding, discovery. **2** *(cosa descubierta)* find.

**halo** *nm* halo, aura.

**halógeno,-a** *adj* halogenous.

H

**hamaca** *nf* **1** *(de red)* hammock. **2** *(tumbona)* deck chair.

**hambre** [va precedido de el en singular] *nf* hunger, starvation, famine. `LOC` **matar el hambre** *fig* to stave off hunger. ‖ **ser más listo,-a que el hambre** *fig* to be a cunning devil. ‖ **tener hambre** to be hungry.

**hambriento,-a** *adj* **1** hungry, starving. **2** *fig* hungry, longing: *hambriento de justicia* longing for justice.

**hambruna** *nf* famine.

**hamburguesa** *nf* hamburger.

**hamburguesería** *nf* hamburger restaurant.

**hámster** *nm* hamster.

**harapiento,-a** *adj* ragged, tattered.

**harapo** *nm* rag, tatter.

**hardware** *nm* hardware.

**harén** *nm* harem.

**harina** *nf* flour.

**hartar** *vt* **1** *(atiborrar)* to satiate, fill up. **2** *fig (deseo, etc)* to satisfy. **3** *(fastidiar)* to annoy, irritate: *me harta con sus tonterías* his silly remarks get on muy nerves. **4** *(cansar)* to tire, bore.
▶ *vpr* **hartarse 1** *(atiborrarse)* to eat one's fill, stuff os. **2** *(cansarse)* to get fed up (de, with), get tired (de, of): *me harté de esperarla* I got tired of waiting for her. `LOC` **hasta hartarse** to repletion.

**harto,-a** *adj* **1** *(repleto)* full, satiated. **2** *fam (cansado)* tired (de, of), fed up (de, with).

**hasta** *prep* **1** *(tiempo)* until, till, up to: *hasta el sábado* until Saturday; *desde las diez hasta las dos* from ten to two. **2** *(lugar)* as far as, up to, down to. **3** *(cantidad)* up to, as many as. **4** *(incluso)* even: *hasta sabe escribir* she even knows how to write. **5** *(como despedida)* see you: *¡hasta mañana!* see you tomorrow! `LOC` **desde... hasta...** from... to... ¿**hasta cuándo?** until when?, how long? ‖ **hasta que** until.

**hastiar** *vt* to bore.
▶ *vpr* **hastiarse** to get sick (de, of), get tired (de, of).

**hastío** *nm* **1** *(repugnancia)* disgust. **2** *fig (aburrimiento)* boredom.

**hatajo** *nm fig* heap, lot, bunch: *un hatajo de disparates* a load of nonsense.

**hatillo** *nm* small bundle.

**haya** *nf* BOT beech.

**hayedo** *nm* beech groove.

**haz** *nm* **1** *(de cosas)* bundle. **2** *(de luz)* shaft, beam.

**hazaña** *nf* deed, exploit, heroic feat.

**hazmerreír** *nm* laughing stock.

**hebilla** *nf* buckle.

**hebra** *nf* **1** *(de hilo)* thread. **2** *(de carne)* sinew; *(de legumbre)* string; *(de madera)* grain; *(de planta)* strand.

**hebreo,-a** *adj* Hebrew.
▶ *nm & nf (persona)* Hebrew.
▶ *nm* **hebreo** *(idioma)* Hebrew.

**hechicería** *nf* **1** *(arte)* sorcery, witchcraft. **2** *(hechizo)* spell, charm.

**hechicero,-a** *nm & nf (hombre)* sorcerer, wizard; *(mujer)* sorceress, witch.

**hechizar** *vt* **1** *(embrujar)* cast a spell on. **2** *fig (cautivar)* to charm, bewitch.

**hechizo** *nm* **1** *(embrujo)* charm, spell. **2** *fig (embelesamiento)* fascination, charm.

**hecho,-a** *adj* **1** *(carne)* done. **2** *(persona)* mature. **3** *(frase, expresión)* set. **4** *(ropa)* ready-made. `LOC` **muy hecho,-a 1** *(carne)* well-cooked. **2** *(pasada)* overdone. ‖ **ser un hombre hecho y derecho** to be a real man.
▶ *nm* **hecho 1** *(realidad)* fact. **2** *(suceso)* event. `LOC` **de hecho** in fact.

**hectárea** *nf* hectare.

**hectogramo** *nm* hectogramme.

**hectolitro** *nm* hectolitre.

**hectómetro** *nm* hectometre.

**hediondo,-a** *adj (apestoso)* stinking, foul-smelling, smelly.

**hedor** *nm* stink, stench.

**helada** *nf* METEOR frost.

**heladería** *nf* ice-cream parlour.

**helado,-a** *adj* **1** *(gen)* frozen: *estoy helado* I'm frozen. **2** *(muy frío)* icy, freezing cold. **3** *(café, té)* iced.

▶ *nm* **helado** ice-cream. LOC **dejar a** ALGN **helado,-a** to stun SB.

**helador,-ra** *adj* icy, freezing.

**helar** *vt* (*congelar*) to freeze.

▶ *vi* [sólo se usa en tercera persona; no lleva sujeto] METEOR to freeze: *anoche heló* it froze last night.

▶ *vpr* **helarse 1** (*congelarse*) to freeze: *el estanque se ha helado* the pond has frozen over. **2** (*persona*) to freeze, freeze to death: *me estoy helando* I'm freezing.

**helecho** *nm* fern.

**hélice** *nf* **1** (*espiral*) helix. **2** (*propulsor*) propeller.

**helicóptero** *nm* helicopter.

**helio** *nm* helium.

**helipuerto** *nm* heliport.

**hematoma** *nm* bruise.

**hembra** *nf* **1** (*animal*) female. **2** (*mujer*) woman. **3** TÉC female.

**hemeroteca** *nf* newspaper library.

**hemiciclo** *nm* (*parlamento*) floor.

**hemisferio** *nm* hemisphere.

**hemorragia** *nf* haemorrhage. COMP **hemorragia nasal** nosebleed.

**hemorroide** *nf* haemorrhoid.

▶ *nf pl* **hemorroides** piles, haemorrhoids.

**henchir** *vt* (*llenar*) to fill (de, with), stuff (de, with), cram (de, with).

**hender** *vt* (*cortar*) to cleave, split, crack.

**hendidura** *nf* cleft, crack.

**heno** *nm* hay.

**hepatitis** *nf inv* hepatitis.

**heptaedro** *nm* heptahedron.

**heptagonal** *adj* heptagonal.

**heptágono,-a** *adj* heptagonal.

▶ *nm* **heptágono** heptagon.

**heráldica** *nf* heraldry.

**herbario,-a** *adj* herbal.

▶ *nm & nf* (*botánico*) botanist.

▶ *nm* **herbario** (*colección*) herbarium.

**herbicida** *nm* weedkiller, herbicide.

**herbívoro,-a** *adj* herbivorous, grass-eating.

▶ *nm & nf* herbivore.

**herbolario,-a** *nm & nf* (*persona*) herbalist.

▶ *nm* **herbolario** (*tienda*) herbalist's (shop).

**herboristería** *nf* herbalist's (shop).

**hercio** *nm* hertz.

**heredad** *nf* (*terreno*) country estate.

**heredar** *vt* **1** to inherit. **2** *fig* to inherit: *ha heredado los ojos de su padre* he's got his father's eyes.

**heredero,-a** *nm & nf* (*hombre*) heir; (*mujer*) heiress.

**hereditario,-a** *adj* hereditary.

**hereje** *nm o nf* heretic.

**herejía** *nf* heresy.

**herencia** *nf* **1** inheritance, legacy. **2** (*genética*) heredity.

**herético,-a** *adj* heretical.

**herida** *nf* wound.

**herido,-a** *adj* **1** (*físicamente*) wounded, injured, hurt: *el niño resultó herido* the boy was injured. **2** *fig* (*emocionalmente*) hurt, wounded. LOC **herido,-a de gravedad** badly injured.

▶ *nm & nf* wounded person, injured person.

**herir** *vt* **1** (*dañar*) to wound, injure, hurt. **2** *fig* (*ofender*) to hurt, offend.

**hermafrodita** *adj* hermaphrodite.

**hermanado,-a** *adj* (*ciudad, pueblo*) twinned.

**hermanar** *vt* **1** (*unir*) to unite, join. **2** (*combinar*) to combine. **3** (*personas*) to unite spiritually. **4** (*ciudades*) to twin.

**hermanastro,-a** *nm & nf* (*hombre*) stepbrother; (*mujer*) stepsister.

**hermandad** *nf* (*de hermanos*) fraternity, brotherhood; (*de hermanas*) fraternity, sisterhood.

**hermano,-a** *nm & nf* (*hombre*) brother; (*mujer*) sister: *¿cuántos hermanos tienes?* how many brothers and sisters have you got?

**hermético,-a** *adj* **1** hermetic, airtight. **2** *fig* impenetrable, secretive.

**hermoso,-a** *adj* **1** (*gen*) beautiful, lovely: *hace un día hermoso* it's a lovely day. **2** (*hombre*) handsome.

**H**

**hermosura** *adj* *(cualidad - de mujer, lugar)* beauty, loveliness; *(- de hombre)* handsomeness.
▶ *nf* **1** *(mujer hermosa)* beautiful woman, beauty. **2** *(persona, cosa)* beautiful thing.

**hernia** *nf* hernia, rupture.

**héroe** *nm* hero.

**heroicamente** *adv* heroically.

**heroico,-a** *adj* heroic.

**heroína** *nf* **1** *(mujer)* heroine. **2** *(droga)* heroin.

**heroísmo** *nm* heroism.

**herpes** *nm inv* herpes, shingles.

**herradura** *nf* horseshoe.

**herraje** *nm* iron fittings *pl*, ironwork.

**herramienta** *nf* tool.

**herrar** *vt* *(caballo)* to shoe.

**herrería** *nf* **1** *(fábrica)* ironworks *pl*. **2** *(taller)* forge, smithy, blacksmith's.

**herrero** *nm* blacksmith, smith.

**herrumbre** *nf* *(óxido)* rust.

**hervir** *vt* to boil.
▶ *vi* **1** to boil: *el agua ya hierve* the water is boiling. **2** *fig* *(el mar)* to surge.

**hervor** *nm* boiling, bubbling. LOC **dar un hervor a** ALGO to blanch STH.

**heterogéneo,-a** *adj* heterogeneous.

**heterosexual** *adj* heterosexual.
▶ *nm o nf* heterosexual.

**hexaedro** *nm* hexahedron.

**hexagonal** *adj* hexagonal.

**hexágono** *nm* hexagon.

**hexámetro** *nm* hexameter.

**hiato** *nm* hiatus.

**hibernación** *nf* hibernation.

**hibernar** *vi* to hibernate.

**hibisco** *nm* hibiscus.

**híbrido,-a** *adj* hybrid.
▶ *nm & nf* hybrid.

**hidalgo,-a** *nm* nobleman.

**hidratante** *adj* moisturizing.

**hidratar** *vt* **1** to hydrate. **2** *(piel)* to moisturize.

**hidráulico,-a** *adj* hydraulic.

**hídrico,-a** *adj* hydric.

**hidroavión** *nm* seaplane.

**hidrocarburo** *nm* hydrocarbon.

**hidroeléctrico,-a** *adj* hydroelectric.

**hidrógeno** *nm* hydrogen.

**hidromasaje** COMP **bañera de hidromasaje** Jacuzzi®, whirlpool bath.

**hidroterapia** *nf* hydrotherapy.

**hiedra** *nf* ivy.

**hiel** *nf* **1** bile. **2** *fig* bitterness, gall.

**hielo** *nm* **1** ice. **2** *fig* *(frialdad)* coldness. COMP **cubito de hielo** ice cube.

**hiena** *nf* hyaena, hyena.

**hierático,-a** *adj* *(rígido)* rigid.

**hierba** *nf* **1** grass. **2** CULIN herb. COMP **finas hierbas** mixed herbs.

**hierbabuena** *nf* mint.

**hierro** *nm* *(metal)* iron. COMP **hierro forjado** wrought iron. ▮ **hierro fundido** cast iron.

**hígado** *nm* liver.

**higiene** *nf* hygiene.

**higiénico,-a** *adj* hygienic.

**higo** *nm* fig. LOC **de higos a brevas** *fig* once in a blue moon. COMP **higo chumbo** prickly pear.

**higuera** *nf* fig tree.

**hijastro,-a** *nm & nf* *(niño, niña)* stepchild; *(hijo)* stepson; *(hija)* stepdaughter.

**hijo,-a** *nm & nf* *(niño, niña)* child; *(chico)* son; *(chica)* daughter: *tiene dos hijos y dos hijas* he has two sons and two daughters. COMP **hijo,-a único,-a 1** *(niño, niña)* only child. **2** *(chico)* only son. **3** *(chica)* only daughter.
▶ *nm pl* **hijos** children: *tiene cuatro hijos* she has four children.

**hilacha** *nf* **1** *(hilacho)* loose thread. **2** *(resto)* rest.

**hilado,-a** *adj* spun.
▶ *nm* **hilado 1** *(operación)* spinning. **2** *(hilo)* thread.

**hilandería** *nf* **1** *(arte)* spinning. **2** *(fábrica)* spinning mill.

**hilandero,-a** *nm & nf* spinner.

**hilar** *vt* **1** to spin. **2** *fig* to work out.

**hilarante** *adj* hilarious.

**hilaridad** *nf fml* hilarity, mirth.

**hilatura** *nf* **1** *(arte)* spinning. **2** *(industria)* spinning mill.

**hilera** *nf* *(línea)* line, row.

**hilo** *nm* **1** thread; *(grueso)* yarn. **2** *(lino)* linen. **3** *(alambre, cable)* wire. **4** *fig (de luz)* thread, thin beam; *(de líquido)* trickle, thin stream. **5** *fig (de historia, discurso)* thread; *(de pensamiento)* train. [LOC] **estar pendiente de un hilo** *fig* to be hanging by a thread. ❚ **mover los hilos** *fig* to pull the strings. ❚ **perder el hilo** *fig* to lose the thread.

**hilvanar** *vt* **1** to tack, baste. **2** *fig* to put together, outline.

**himno** *nm* hymn. [COMP]

**hincapié** [LOC] **hacer hincapié** *(insistir)* to insist on. *(subrayar)* to emphasize (en, -), stress (en, -).

**hincar** *vt (clavar)* to drive (in).

**hincha** *nm o nf* DEP fan, supporter.

**hinchado,-a** *adj* **1** *(inflado)* blown up. **2** *(piel)* swollen, puffed up.

**hinchar** *vt* **1** *(inflar)* to blow up; *(con bomba)* to pump up: *hinchar un globo* to blow up a balloon. **2** *fig (exagerar)* to blow up.
  ▶ *vpr* **hincharse 1** MED to swell (up): *se me ha hinchado el pie* my foot has swollen up. **2** *fam (comer)* to stuff os.

**hinchazón** *nf* swelling, inflation.

**hindú** *adj* Hindu.
  ▶ *nm o nf* Hindu.

**hinduismo** *nm* Hinduism.

**hinojo** *nm* BOT fennel.

**hipar** *vi (tener hipo)* to hiccup, have the hiccups.

**hiperactivo,-a** *adj* hyperactive.

**hipermercado** *nm* hypermarket.

**hipersensible** *adj* hypersensitive.

**hipertensión** *nf* high blood pressure.

**hipertenso,-a** *adj* hypertensive.
  ▶ *nm & nf* hypertensive.

**hípica** *nf* horse riding.

**hípico,-a** *adj* horse, equestrian.

**hipnosis** *nf inv* hypnosis.

**hipnótico,-a** *adj* hypnotic.

**hipnotismo** *nm* hypnotism.

**hipnotizador,-ra** *adj* hypnotizing.
  ▶ *nm & nf* hypnotist.

**hipnotizar** *vt* to hypnotize.

**hipo** *nm* hiccup. [LOC] **quitar el hipo** *fig* to take one's breath away.

**hipocondríaco,-a** *adj* hypochondriac.

**hipocresía** *nf* hypocrisy.

**hipócrita** *adj* hypocritical.
  ▶ *nm o nf* hypocrite.

**hipódromo** *nm* racetrack, racecourse.

**hipopótamo** *nm* hippopotamus.

**hipoteca** *nf* mortgage.

**hipotecar** *vt* to mortgage.

**hipotecario,-a** *adj* mortgage.

**hipotensión** *nf* low blood pressure.

**hipotenso,-a** *adj* hypotensive.

**hipotenusa** *nf* hypotenuse.

**hipótesis** *nf inv* hypothesis.

**hipotético,-a** *adj* hypothetic, hypothetical.

**hippie** *adj* hippy.
  ▶ *nm o nf* hippy.

**hiriente** *adj* **1** wounding. **2** *fig* hurtful, cutting, wounding.

**hirsuto,-a** *adj* **1** hairy; *(cerdoso)* bristly. **2** *fig (persona)* rough, brusque, surly.

**hispánico,-a** *adj* Hispanic, Spanish.

**hispano,-a** *adj* **1** *(de España)* Spanish, Hispanic. **2** *(de América)* Spanish-American.
  ▶ *nm & nf* **1** *(de España)* Spaniard. **2** *(de América)* Spanish American, US Hispanic.

**hispanoamericano,-a** *adj* Spanish American, Latin American.

**Hispanoamérica** *nf* Spanish America, Latin America.

**hispanohablante** *adj* Spanish-speaking.
  ▶ *nm o nf* Spanish speaker.

**histeria** *nf* hysteria.

**histérico,-a** *adj* hysterical.
  ▶ *nm & nf* hysteric. [LOC] **poner histérico,-a a ALGN** *fam* to drive SB mad.

**histerismo** *nm* hysteria.

**historia** *nf* **1** *(estudio)* history. **2** *(narración)* story, tale. [LOC] **pasar a la historia** to go down in history. [COMP] **historia natural** natural history. ❚ **historia universal** world history.

**historiado,-a** *adj fig* overelaborate.

H

**historiador,-ra** *nm & nf* historian.

**historial** *nm* **1** MED medical record, case history. **2** *(currículo)* curriculum vitae.

**historiar** *vt* **1** *(contar)* to tell the story of; *(acontecimientos)* to recount. **2** *(escribir)* to write the history of.

**histórico,-a** *adj* **1** *(relativo a la historia)* historical. **2** *(importante)* historic, memorable. **3** *(cierto)* factual, true.

**historieta** *nf* **1** *(cuento)* short story, anecdote. **2** *(viñetas)* comic strip.

**hito** *nm* **1** *(mojón)* milestone. **2** *fig (hecho importante)* milestone, landmark.

**hobby** *nm* hobby.

**hocico** *nm (de animal)* snout, muzzle.

**hockey** *nm* hockey. COMP **hockey sobre hielo** ice hockey.

**hogar** *nm* **1** *(de chimenea)* hearth, fireplace. **2** *fig (casa)* home. **3** *fig (familia)* family.

**hogareño,-a** *adj* **1** *(vida)* family. **2** *(persona)* home-loving, stay-at-home.

**hogaza** *nf* large loaf (of bread).

**hoguera** *nf* **1** bonfire. **2** *fig* blaze.

**hoja** *nf* **1** *(gen)* leaf. **2** *(pétalo)* petal. **3** *(de papel)* sheet. **4** *(de libro)* leaf, page. **5** *(de cuchillo, etc)* blade. **6** *(de puerta, ventana)* leaf: *una ventana de dos hojas* a double-leaf window. LOC **de hoja perenne** BOT evergreen. ‖ COMP **hoja de afeitar** razor blade.

**hojalata** *nf* tin, tin plate.

**hojalatería** *nf (taller, tienda)* tinsmith's.

**hojalatero** *nm* tinsmith.

**hojaldrado,-a** *adj* puff: *pasta hojaldrada* puff pastry.

**hojaldre** *nm & nf* [suele utilizarse más como masculino] puff pastry.

**hojarasca** *nf* dead leaves *pl*.

**hojeada** *nf* flick.

**hojear** *vt* to leaf through.

**hola** *interj fam* hello!, hullo!, US hi!

**Holanda** *nf* Holland.

**holandés,-esa** *adj* Dutch.
► *nm & nf (persona)* Dutch person; *(hombre)* Dutchman; *(mujer)* Dutchwoman.
► *nm* **holandés** *(idioma)* Dutch.

**holandesa** *nf (papel)* quarto sheet.

**holgado,-a** *adj* **1** *(ropa)* loose. **2** *(espacio)* roomy. **3** *(posición)* comfortable.

**holgar** *vi* **1** *(descansar)* to rest. **2** *(estar ocioso)* to be idle. LOC **huelga decir que...** needless to say (that)...

**holgazán,-ana** *adj* idle, lazy.
► *nm & nf* lazybones, layabout.

**holgazanear** *vi* to laze around.

**holgazanería** *nf* idleness, laziness.

**holgura** *nf* **1** *(ropa)* looseness. **2** *(espacio)* room, spaciousness. **3** *fig (bienestar)* affluence, comfort.

**hollar** *vt (comprimir)* to tread (on).

**hollín** *nm* soot.

**holocausto** *nm* holocaust.

**hombre** *nm* **1** *(individuo)* man. **2** *(especie)* man, mankind. **3** *fam (marido)* husband.
► *interj (asombro)* hey!, hey there!, well!: *¡hombre, Pedro, no te esperaba!* hey, Pedro, I didn't expect you! COMP **hombre orquesta** one-man band. ‖ **hombre rana** frogman.

**hombrera** *nf* shoulder pad.

**hombría** *nm* manliness, virility.

**hombro** *nm* shoulder. LOC **a hombros** on one's shoulders. ‖ **arrimar el hombro** to help out, lend a hand.

**hombruno,-a** *adj* mannish, manly.

**homenaje** *nm* homage, tribute. LOC **en homenaje a** in honour of. ‖ **rendir homenaje a** ALGN to pay tribute to SB.

**homenajear** *vt* to pay tribute to.

**homeopatía** *nf* homeopathy.

**homicida** *adj* homicidal, murder: *el arma homicida* the murder weapon.
► *nm o nf (hombre)* murderer; *(mujer)* murderess.

**homicidio** *nm* homicide, murder.

**homínido** *nm* hominid, hominoid.

**homogéneo,-a** *adj* homogeneous.

**homologado,-a** *adj* **1** *(centro, estudios)* officially approved, officially recognized. **2** *(productos)* authorized.

**homologar** *vt (comprobar)* to approve, recognize, authorize.

**homosexual** *adj* homosexual.
► *nm o nf* homosexual.

**homosexualidad** *nf* homosexuality.

**honda** *nf* sling.

**hondo,-a** *adj* **1** deep. **2** *fig* profound.

**hondonada** *nf* hollow, depression.

**hondura** *nf* depth.

**Honduras** *nm* Honduras.

**hondureño,-a** *adj* Honduran.
  ▶ *nm & nf* Honduran.

**honestidad** *nf* **1** *(honradez)* honesty, uprightness. **2** *(decencia)* decency.

**honesto,-a** *adj* **1** *(honrado)* honest, upright. **2** *(decente)* decent.

**hongo** *nm* *(gen)* fungus; *(comestible)* mushroom; *(venenoso)* toadstool.

**honor** *nm* *(virtud)* honour. LOC **en honor a la verdad** to be fair, in all fairness. **I hacer honor a** to live up to.
  ▶ *nm pl* **honores** *(agasajo)* honours.

**honorable** *adj* honourable.

**honorario,-a** *adj* honorary.
  ▶ *nm pl* **honorarios** fees.

**honorífico,-a** *adj* honorary.

**honra** *nf* **1** *(honor)* honour. **2** *(buena reputación)* reputation, good name.
  ▶ *nf pl* **honras** *(fúnebres)* last honours.

**honradez** *nf* honesty, integrity.

**honrado,-a** *adj* *(honesto)* honest.

**honrar** *vt* *(gen)* to honour: *nos honró con su presencia* he honoured us with his presence.
  ▶ *vpr* **honrarse** to be honoured.

**honroso,-a** *adj* **1** *(que honra)* honourable. **2** *(decoroso)* respectable.

**hora** *nf* **1** *(unidad de tiempo)* hour: *media hora* half an hour. **2** *(tiempo)* time: *¿qué hora es?* what time is it? **3** *(cita)* appointment: *tengo hora para las cuatro y media* I have an appointment at half past four. LOC **a altas horas** in the small hours. **I ¡a buenas horas!** and about time too! **I a la hora** at the proper time, on time. **I a primera hora** first thing in the morning. **I dar la hora** to strike the hour. **I de última hora** last-minute: *una noticia de última hora* some last-minute news. **I pedir hora** to make an appointment. **I por horas** by the hour: *cobro por horas* I get paid by the

hour. COMP **hora de comer** lunch time, dinner time. **I hora punta** rush hour.

**horadar** *vt* **1** *(perforar)* to pierce. **2** *(taladrar)* to bore (through).

**horario,-a** *adj* time.
  ▶ *nm* **horario 1** timetable. **2** *(jornada laboral)* hours *pl*, timetable: *tengo horario de mañana* I work mornings. COMP **horario comercial** *(tienda)* opening hours *pl*. **I horario laboral** working hours *pl*.

**horca** *nf* **1** *(patíbulo)* gallows *pl*, gibbet. **2** AGR hayfork, pitchfork.

**horcajadas** LOC **a horcajadas** astride.

**horchata** *nf* sweet milky drink made from tiger nuts or almonds.

**horchatería** *nf* bar where *horchata* is sold.

**horda** *nf* **1** horde, mob. **2** *fig* gang.

**horizontal** *adj* horizontal.

**horizonte** *nm* horizon.

**horma** *nf* **1** mould. **2** *(de zapato)* last.

**hormiga** *nf* ant.

**hormigón** *nm* concrete. COMP **hormigón armado** reinforced concrete.

**hormigonera** *nf* concrete mixer.

**hormiguear** *vi* to itch, tingle: *me hormigueaba la mano* I had pins and needles in my hand.

**hormigueo** *nm* pins and needles *pl*.

**hormiguero** *nm* ant hill, ant's nest.

**hormona** *nf* hormone.

**hormonal** *adj* hormonal.

**hornacina** *nf* niche.

**hornada** *nf* **1** batch. **2** *fig* set, batch.

**hornear** *vt* to bake.

**hornillo** *nm* **1** TÉC small furnace. **2** *(para cocinar)* stove.

**horno** *nm* **1** *(de cocina)* oven. **2** TÉC furnace. **3** *(cerámica, ladrillos)* kiln. **4** *(panadería)* bakery. COMP **horno (de) micro-ondas** microwave oven. **I horno eléctrico** electric oven.

**horóscopo** *nm* horoscope.

**horquilla** *nf* *(de pelo)* hairgrip, hairclip.

**horrendo,-a** *adj* horrible, awful.

**hórreo** *nm* granary.

**horrible** *adj* horrible, awful.

H

**horripilante** *adj* hair-raising, horrifying, terrifying.

**horripilar** *vt* to horrify, scare stiff.

**horror** *nm* **1** *(repulsión)* horror, terror. **2** *(temor)* hate. **3** *fig (atrocidad)* atrocity. LOC ¡qué horror! how awful!

**horrorizar** *vt (causar horror)* to horrify, terrify.
  ▶ *vpr* **horrorizarse** to be horrified.

**horroroso,-a** *adj* **1** *(que causa miedo)* horrifying. **2** *fam (feo)* hideous.

**hortaliza** *nf* vegetable.

**hortelano,-a** *nm & nf* market gardener.

**hortensia** *nf* hydrangea.

**hortera** *adj fam* common, tasteless.

**hortícola** *adj* horticultural.

**horticultor,-ra** *nm & nf* horticulturist.

**horticultura** *nf* horticulture.

**hosco,-a** *adj* **1** *(insociable)* sullen, surly. **2** *(lugar)* gloomy, dark.

**hospedaje** *nm* **1** *(acción)* lodging; *(precio)* cost of lodging. **2** *(lugar)* lodgings *pl*, accommodation.

**hospedar** *vt* to lodge, put up.
  ▶ *vpr* **hospedarse** to stay (en, at).

**hospicio** *nm* **1** *(de huérfanos)* orphanage. **2** *(de pobres)* poorhouse.

**hospital** *nm* hospital, infirmary.

**hospitalidad** *nf* hospitality.

**hospitalizar** *vt* to send into hospital, hospitalize.

**hostal** *nm* hostel, hotel.

**hostelería** *nf* catering.

**hostia** *nf* **1** REL host. **2** *tabú (choque)* bump, bash; *(torta)* slap, punch.

**hostigar** *vt* **1** *(azotar)* to whip. **2** *fig (perseguir)* to plague, persecute.

**hostil** *adj* hostile.

**hostilidad** *nf* hostility.
  ▶ *nf pl* **hostilidades** hostilities.

**hotel** *nm (establecimiento)* hotel.

**hotelero,-a** *adj* hotel.
  ▶ *nm & nf* hotel manager, hotelier.

**hoy** *adv* **1** *(día)* today. **2** *fig (actualmente)* now, nowadays. LOC de hoy en adelante from now on. ▮ hoy (en) día nowadays, today, these days.

**hoyo** *nm* **1** *(agujero)* hole, pit. **2** *(sepultura)* grave.

**hoyuelo** *nm* dimple.

**hoz¹** *nf* agr sickle.

**hoz²** *nf* geog ravine, gorge.

**hucha** *nf* moneybox, piggy bank.

**hueco,-a** *adj* **1** hollow: *pared hueca* hollow wall, stud wall. **2** *(vacío)* empty. **3** *(cóncavo)* concave.
  ▶ *nm* **hueco** **1** *(cavidad)* hollow, hole. **2** *(de tiempo)* slot, free time; *(de espacio)* empty space. **3** *(vacante)* vacancy.

**huelga** *nf* strike. LOC estar en huelga / estar de huelga to be on strike. COMP huelga de brazos caídos go-slow. ▮ huelga de celo work-to-rule. ▮ huelga general general strike. ▮ huelga de hambre hunger strike.

✎ Consulta también holgar.

**huelguista** *nm o nf* striker.

**huella** *nf* **1** *(de pie)* footprint; *(de ruedas)* track. **2** *fig (vestigio)* trace, sign: *las huellas del tiempo* the traces of time. LOC dejar huella to leave one's mark (en, on). COMP huella dactilar fingerprint.

**huérfano,-a** *adj* orphan, orphaned.
  ▶ *nm & nf* orphan.

**huerta** *nf (terreno)* market garden.

**huerto** *nm (de verduras)* vegetable garden; *(de frutas)* orchard.

**hueso** *nm* **1** ANAT bone. **2** *(de fruta)* stone, US pit. **3** *fam fig (cosa difícil)* struggle, problem: *las mates son un hueso para mí* I find maths really hard. LOC ser un hueso duro de roer *fig* to be a hard nut to crack.

**huésped,-da** *nm & nf (invitado)* guest.

**hueste** *nf* [también se usa en plural con el mismo significado] MIL army, host.

**huesudo,-a** *adj* bony.

**hueva** *nf* roe, spawn.

**huevera** *nf* **1** *(copa)* egg cup. **2** *(cartón)* egg box.

**huevería** *nf* egg shop.

**huevero,-a** *nm & nf (persona)* egg seller.

**huevo** *nm* egg. COMP huevo duro hard-boiled egg. ▮ huevo frito fried egg. ▮ huevo pasado por agua soft-boiled egg.

**huida** *nf* flight, escape.

**huidizo,-a** *adj* fleeting, elusive.

**huir** *vi* **1** *(escapar)* to flee, run away. **2** *(evitar)* to avoid (de, -).

**hule** *nm* oilcloth, oilskin.

**hulla** *nf* coal.

**humanidad** *nf* **1** *(género humano)* humanity, mankind. **2** *(cualidad)* humanity, humaneness.
▶ *nf pl* **humanidades** EDUC humanities.

**humanismo** *nm* humanism.

**humanista** *nm o nf* humanist.

**humanístico,-a** *adj* humanistic.

**humanitario,-a** *adj* humanitarian.

**humanizar** *vt* to humanize.
▶ *vpr* **humanizarse** to become more human.

**humano,-a** *adj* **1** human. **2** *(benigno)* humane.

**humareda** *nf* cloud of smoke.

**humeante** *adj* **1** *(de humo)* smoky, smoking. **2** *(de vaho)* steaming.

**humear** *vi* **1** *(humo)* to smoke. **2** *(vaho)* to steam.

**humectante** *adj* moistening.

**humedad** *nf* **1** humidity. **2** *(de vapor)* moisture.

**humedecer** *vt* to moisten, dampen.
▶ *vpr* **humedecerse** to become moist.

**húmedo,-a** *adj* **1** *(clima)* humid, damp. **2** *(impregnado)* damp, moist, wet.

**húmero** *nm* humerus.

**humidificador** *nm* humidifier.

**humidificar** *vt* to humidify.

**humildad** *nf* humility, humbleness.

**humilde** *adj* humble, modest.

**humildemente** *adv* humbly.

**humillación** *nf* humiliation.

**humillante** *adj* humiliating.

**humillar** *vt* to humiliate, humble.
▶ *vpr* **humillarse** to humble os.

**humo** *nm* **1** smoke. **2** *(gas)* fumes *pl*. **3** *(vapor)* steam.
▶ *nm pl* **humos** *fig* airs. LOC **bajarle los humos a** ALGN *fig* to put SB in his/her place.

**humor** *nm* **1** *(ánimo)* mood. **2** *(carácter)* temper. **3** *(gracia)* humour. LOC **estar de buen humor** to be in a good mood.

**humorada** *nf* joke, witticism.

**humorismo** *nm* humour.

**humorista** *adj* humorous.
▶ *nm o nf (cómico)* comedian.

**humorístico,-a** *adj* humorous.

**humus** *nm inv* humus.

**hundible** *adj* sinkable.

**hundido,-a** *adj* **1** *(barco, etc)* sunken. **2** *(ojos)* deep-set; *(mejillas)* hollow.

**hundimiento** *nm* **1** *(barco)* sinking. **2** *(tierra)* subsidence. **3** *(edificio)* collapse.

**hundir** *vt* **1** *(sumir)* plunge: *hundió la mano en la arena* she plunged her hand into the sand. **2** *(barco)* to sink. **3** *(derrumbar)* to demolish, ruin: *el terremoto hundió el edificio* the earthquake caused the building to collapse.
▶ *vpr* **hundirse 1** *(barco)* to sink. **2** *(derrumbarse)* to collapse, fall down.

**húngaro,-a** *adj* Hungarian.
▶ *nm & nf (persona)* Hungarian.
▶ *nm* **húngaro** *(idioma)* Hungarian.

**Hungría** *nf* Hungary.

**huracán** *nm* hurricane.

**huracanado,-a** *adj* hurricane: *vientos huracanados* hurricane winds.

**huraño,-a** *adj* sullen, unsociable.

**hurgar** *vt* **1** *(remover)* to poke, rake. **2** *(bolsillo, bolso, etc)* to rummage in.
▶ *vpr* **hurgarse** to pick.

**hurón,-ona** *nm (animal)* ferret.

**hurra** *interj* hurray!, hurrah!

**hurraca** *nf* magpie.

**hurtadillas** LOC **a hurtadillas** stealthily, on the sly.

**hurtar** *vt (robar)* to steal, pilfer.

**hurto** *nm* petty theft, pilfering.

**husmeador,-ra** *adj* **1** *(con la nariz)* sniffing. **2** *fig (fisgón)* prying.

**husmear** *vt* **1** *(con el olfato)* to sniff, scent. **2** *fig (indagar)* to pry (en, into).
▶ *vi* **1** to sniff. **2** *fig* to snoop around.

**huso** *nm (para hilar)* spindle, bobbin. COMP **huso horario** time zone.

H

**I, i** *nf* (la letra) I, i.
COMP **i griega** *name of the letter* y. ▌**i latina** *name of the letter* i.

**ibérico,-a** *adj* Iberian.

**íbero,-a** *adj* Iberian.
▶ *nm & nf* (*persona*) Iberian.

**iberoamericano,-a** *adj* Latin American.
▶ *nm & nf* Latin American.

**iceberg** *nm* iceberg.

**icono** *nm* icon.

**ida** *nf* (*acción*) going; (*salida*) departure. LOC **de ida sola** single. ▌**de ida y vuelta** (*billete*) return.

**idea** *nf* **1** idea. **2** (*noción*) notion. **3** (*ingenio*) imagination.

**ideal** *adj* ideal.
▶ *nm* ideal.

**idealismo** *nm* idealism.

**idealista** *adj* idealistic.
▶ *nm o nf* idealist.

**idealizar** *vt* to idealize.

**idear** *vt* **1** (*concebir*) to conceive. **2** (*inventar*) to design.

**ideario** *nm* ideology.

**idéntico,-a** *adj* identical.

**identidad** *nf* identity. COMP **carnet de identidad** identity card.

**identificar** *vt* to identify.
▶ *vpr* **identificarse** (*solidarizarse*) to identify (con, with).

**ideología** *nf* ideology.

**ideólogo,-a** *nm & nf* ideologist.

**idílico,-a** *adj* idyllic.

**idilio** *nm* **1** *lit* idyll. **2** *fam* romance.

**idioma** *nm* language.

**idiosincrasia** *nf* idiosyncrasy.

**idiota** *adj* **1** MED idiotic. **2** *fam* (*tonto*) stupid.
▶ *nm o nf* idiot.

**idiotez** *nf* **1** MED idiocy. **2** (*estupidez*) stupid thing to say, stupid thing to do.

**idiotizar** *vt* to turn into an idiot.

**ido,-a** *adj* **1** (*loco*) mad. **2** (*despistado*) absent-minded. LOC **estar ido,-a 1** *fam* (*loco*) to be mad. **2** (*despistado*) to be miles away.

**idolatrar** *vt* **1** to worship. **2** *fig* to idolize.

**ídolo** *nm* idol.

**idóneo,-a** *adj* suitable.

**iglesia** *nf* **1** (*edificio*) church. **2** (*institución*) Church.

**iglú** *nm* igloo.

**ignorancia** *nf* ignorance.

**ignorante** *adj* ignorant.
▶ *nm o nf* ignoramus.

**ignorar** *vt* **1** (*desconocer*) not to know, not be aware of. **2** (*no hacer caso*) to ignore.

**igual** *adj* **1** (*parte*) equal. **2** (*lo mismo*) the same. **3** (*muy parecido*) just like.
▶ *nm* (*persona*) equal.
▶ *adv* **1** (*en comparativas*) the same. **2** *fam* maybe, perhaps: *igual no vienen* they may well not come.

**igualar** *vt* **1** to make equal. **2** (*allanar*) to level; (*pulir*) to smooth. **3** (*comparar*) to match: *no hay nadie que lo iguale* nobody can match him, he has no equal.
▶ *vpr* **igualarse 1** (*ser iguales*) to be equal. **2** (*compararse*) to be compared.

**igualdad** *nf* equality.

**iguana** *nf* iguana.

**ilegal** *adj* illegal.

**ilegalidad** *nf* illegality.

**ilegible** *adj* unreadable, illegible.

**ilegítimo,-a** *adj* illegitimate.

**ileso,-a** *adj* unharmed, unhurt. LOC
salir ileso,-a to escape unharmed.

**iletrado,-a** *adj* illiterate.

**ilícito,-a** *adj* unlawful, illicit.

**ilimitado,-a** *adj* unlimited.

**ilógico,-a** *adj* illogical.

**iluminación** *nf (de una sala)* lighting;
*(de una feria)* illumination; *(de una película, un espectáculo)* lighting.

**iluminar** *vt* to light, light up.

**ilusión** *nf* **1** *(no real)* illusion. **2** *(esperanza)* hope. **3** *(emoción)* excitement.

**ilusionado,-a** *adj* excited.

**ilusionar** *vt* **1** *(crear ilusiones)* to raise hopes. **2** *(entusiasmar)* to excite.
▶ *vpr* **ilusionarse** **1** *(esperanzarse)* to build up one's hopes. **2** *(entusiasmarse)* to be excited (**con**, about).

**ilusionismo** *nm* conjuring.

**ilusionista** *nm o nf* conjurer, illusionist.

**iluso,-a** *adj* naive, gullible.

**ilustración** *nf* **1** *(de un texto)* illustration. **2** *(erudición)* learning. **3** **la Ilustración** HIST the Enlightenment.

**ilustrado,-a** *adj* **1** *(texto)* illustrated. **2** *(culto)* learned. **3** HIST of the Enlightenment.

**ilustrar** *vt* **1** *(texto)* to illustrate. **2** *(instruir)* to enlighten.

**ilustre** *adj* **1** *(célebre)* renowned, illustrious. **2** *(distinguido)* distinguished.

**imagen** *nf* **1** image. **2** TV picture. LOC
ser la viva imagen de ALGN to be the spitting image of SB.

**imaginación** *nf* imagination, fantasy.

**imaginar** *vt* **1** *(gen)* to imagine. **2** *(idear)* to devise, think up.

> ✎ También se usa la forma **imaginarse**, sobre todo en el lenguaje coloquial.

**imaginario,-a** *adj* imaginary.

**imaginativo,-a** *adj* imaginative.

**imán**¹ *nm* magnet.

**imán**² *nm* REL imam.

**imantar** *vt* to magnetize.

**imbatible** *adj* unbeatable.

**imbécil** *adj* **1** MED *(retrasado)* imbecile. **2** *fam* stupid, imbecile.
▶ *nm o nf* **1** MED imbecile. **2** *fam* idiot.

**imbecilidad** *nf* **1** MED imbecility. **2** *fam* stupid thing to do.

**imberbe** *adj* beardless.

**imborrable** *adj* indelible.

**imbuir** *vt* to imbue.

**imitación** *nf* **1** *(copia)* imitation. **2** *(parodia)* impression.

**imitador,-ra** *adj* imitative.
▶ *nm & nf* **1** imitator. **2** *(cómico)* impressionist.

**imitar** *vt* to copy, imitate; *(gestos)* to mimic; *(persona)* to mimic, do an impression of.

**impaciencia** *nf* impatience.

**impacientar** *vt* to make lose one's patience, exasperate.
▶ *vpr* **impacientarse** to get impatient.

**impaciente** *adj* impatient, anxious.

**impactado,-a** *adj* impacted.

**impactante** *adj* striking, powerful.

**impactar** *vt* **1** *(físicamente)* to hit. **2** *(impresionar)* to make an impression on:
*esa escena me impactó mucho* that scene made a deep impression on me.

**impacto** *nm* **1** *(choque)* impact. **2** *(marca)* mark; *(agujero)* hole.

**impar** *adj* odd.

**imparable** *adj* unstoppable.

**imparcial** *adj* impartial, fair.

**imparcialidad** *nf* impartiality.

**impartir** *vt (lección)* to give.

**impasible** *adj* impassive.

**impávido,-a** *adj* dauntless.

**impecable** *adj* impeccable, faultless.

**impedido,-a** *adj* disabled.
▶ *nm & nf* disabled person.

**impedimento** *nm* impediment, obstacle.

**impedir** *vt (hacer imposible)* to prevent, stop: *¿hay algo que te lo impida?* is there anything stopping you?

**impeler** *vt* to drive forward, propel.

**impenetrable** *adj* impenetrable.

**impensable** *adj* unthinkable.

**imperar** *vi* to rule, prevail.

**imperativo,-a** *adj* imperative.
▸ *nm* **imperativo** LING imperative.
**imperceptible** *adj* imperceptible.
**imperdible** *nm* safety pin.
**imperdonable** *adj* unforgivable.
**imperfección** *nf* **1** imperfection. **2** *(defecto)* defect, fault.
**imperfecto,-a** *adj* **1** imperfect. **2** LING imperfect.
▸ *nm* **imperfecto** imperfect.
**imperialismo** *nm* imperialism.
**imperio** *nm* empire.
**imperioso,-a** *adj* **1** *(autoritario)* imperious. **2** *(necesario)* urgent, pressing.
**impermeabilizar** *vt* to waterproof.
**impermeable** *adj* waterproof.
▸ *nm* raincoat.
**impersonal** *adj* impersonal.
**impertérrito,-a** *adj* imperturbable.
**impertinencia** *nf* **1** impertinence. **2** *(palabras)* impertinent remark.
**impertinente** *adj* impertinent.
▸ *nm pl* **impertinentes** lorgnette *sing*.
**imperturbable** *adj* imperturbable.
**ímpetu** *nm* **1** *(fuerza)* vigour; *(entusiasmo)* enthusiasm; *(energía)* energy. **2** *(impulso)* impetus; *(fuerza)* force.
**impetuoso,-a** *adj* **1** *(persona)* impetuous. **2** *(viento)* violent.
**implacable** *adj* implacable, relentless.
**implantar** *vt* **1** to introduce. **2** MED to implant.
**implante** *nm* implant.
**implicar** *vt* **1** *(conllevar)* to imply. **2** *(involucrar)* to involve (en, in).
**implícito,-a** *adj* implicit.
**implorar** *vt* to implore, entreat, beg.
**impoluto,-a** *adj* spotless.
**imponderable** *adj* *(factor)* imponderable; *(valor)* incalculable.
**imponente** *adj* impressive.
**imponer** *vt* **1** *(ley, límite, sanción)* to impose. **2** *(respeto)* to inspire.
▸ *vi* *(asustar)* to be frightening.
▸ *vpr* **imponerse 1** to impose one's authority (a, on). **2** *(obligarse)* to force os to. **3** *(prevalecer)* to prevail.

**impopular** *adj* unpopular.
**importación** *nf* **1** *(acción)* importation, import. **2** *(productos)* imports *pl*.
**importancia** *nf* importance.
**importante** *adj* **1** *(gen)* important; *(por su gravedad)* serious; *(por su cantidad)* considerable.
**importar** *vt* **1** COM *(traer de fuera)* to import. **2** *(valer)* to amount to.
▸ *vi* **1** *(tener importancia)* to matter. **2** *(molestar)* to mind.
**importe** *nm* *(gen)* price, cost.
**importunar** *vt* *(molestar)* to pester.
**imposible** *adj* impossible.
**imposición** *nf* *(gen)* imposition.
**impostor,-ra** *nm & nf* **1** *(farsante)* impostor. **2** *(difamador)* slanderer.
**impotencia** *nf* impotence.
**impotente** *adj* impotent.
**impreciso,-a** *adj* imprecise, vague.
**impredecible** *adj* *(persona)* unpredictable; *(circunstancia)* unforeseeable.
**imprenta** *nf* **1** *(arte)* printing. **2** *(taller)* printer's, printing house.
**imprescindible** *adj* essential, indispensable.
**impresión** *nf* **1** *(en imprenta)* printing. **2** *(huella)* impression, imprint. **3** *fig (efecto)* impression; *(negativo)* shock.
**impresionable** *adj* impressionable.
**impresionante** *adj* **1** *(admirable)* impressive. **2** *fam (gen)* incredible; *(enorme)* tremendous.
**impresionar** *vt* **1** *(causar admiración)* to impress: *me impresionó el paisaje* the scenery impressed me. **2** *(afectar)* to affect; *(inquietar)* to disturb.
**impresionismo** *nm* impressionism.
**impresionista** *adj* impressionist.
▸ *nm o nf* impressionist.
**impreso,-a** *adj* printed.
▸ *nm* **impreso** *(formulario)* form.
**impresor,-ra** *nm & nf* *(persona)* printer.
**impresora** *nf* *(máquina)* printer.
**imprevisible** *adj* *(hecho)* unforeseeable; *(persona)* unpredictable.
**imprevisto,-a** *adj* unexpected.

▸ *nm pl* **imprevistos** *(gastos)* incidental expenses.

**imprimir** *vt* **1** *(gen)* to print. **2** *(dejar huella)* to stamp. **3** *fig (grabar)* to fix.

**improbable** *adj* improbable, unlikely.

**improductivo,-a** *adj* unproductive.

**improperio** *nm* insult.

**impropio,-a** *adj (inadecuado)* unsuitable, inappropriate. [LOC] **ser impropio,-a de ALGN** not to be worthy of SB.

**improvisado,-a** *adj (gen)* improvised.

**improvisar** *vt* to improvise.
▸ *vi* to improvise.

**improviso** [LOC] **de improviso** suddenly, unexpectedly.

**imprudencia** *nf* **1** *(falta de prudencia)* carelessness. **2** *(acción imprudente)* rash move; *(indiscreción)* indiscretion.

**imprudente** *adj* careless.
▸ *nm o nf (imprudente)* careless person; *(indiscreto)* indiscreet person.

**impúdico,-a** *adj (indecente)* immodest, indecent.

**impuesto,-a** *nm* **impuesto** tax, duty.

**impugnar** *vt* **1** *(resultado)* to contest. **2** *(teoría)* to refute.

**impulsar** *vt* **1** to impel. **2** TÉC to drive forward. **3** *(incitar)* to drive.

**impulsivo,-a** *adj* impulsive.
▸ *nm & nf* impulsive person.

**impulso** *nm* **1** impulse. **2** *(fuerza, velocidad)* momentum.

**impune** *adj* unpunished.

**impunidad** *nf* impunity.

**impureza** *nf* impurity.

**impuro,-a** *adj* impure.

**imputación** *nf* accusation.

**imputar** *vt* to impute.

**inabarcable** *adj* huge, vast.

**inaccesible** *adj* inaccessible.

**inaceptable** *adj* unacceptable.

**inadaptado,-a** *adj* maladjusted.
▸ *nm & nf* misfit.

**inadvertido,-a** *adj* unnoticed.

**inagotable** *adj* inexhaustible.

**inaguantable** *adj* unbearable.

**inalámbrico,-a** *adj* cordless.

**inanición** *nf* starvation.

**inanimado,-a** *adj* inanimate, lifeless.

**inapreciable** *adj* **1** *(insignificante)* imperceptible. **2** *(valioso)* invaluable.

**inaudible** *adj* inaudible.

**inaudito,-a** *adj (nunca oído)* unheard-of.

**inauguración** *nf* opening, inauguration.

**inaugurar** *vt* to inaugurate, open.

**inca** *adj* Inca.
▸ *nm o nf* Inca.

**incalculable** *adj* incalculable.

**incalificable** *adj (intolerable)* unspeakable.

**incandescente** *adj* incandescent.

**incansable** *adj* tireless.

**incapacidad** *nf* **1** *(gen)* incapacity, inability. **2** *(insuficiencia)* disability.

**incapacitado,-a** *adj (físicamente)* disabled; *(mentalmente)* incapacitated, unfit.

**incapacitar** *vt* **1** *(impedir)* to incapacitate.

**incapaz** *adj* **1** incapable (de, of). **2** *(incompetente)* incompetent.

**incauto,-a** *adj (crédulo)* gullible.
▸ *nm & nf* gullible person.

**incendiar** *vt* to set on fire, set fire to.
▸ *vpr* **incendiarse** to catch fire.

**incendiario,-a** *adj* incendiary.
▸ *nm & nf* arsonist.

**incendio** *nm* fire.

**incentivo** *nm* incentive.

**incertidumbre** *nf* uncertainty.

**incesto** *nm* incest.

**incestuoso,-a** *adj* incestuous.

**incidente** *nm* incident, event.

**incidir** *vi* **incidir en 1** *(repercutir en)* to have an effect on, affect. **2** *(incurrir en)* to fall into. **3** *(tratar)* to touch upon; *(insistir en)* to stress.

**incienso** *nm* incense.

**incierto,-a** *adj* uncertain, doubtful.

**incinerar** *vt (basura)* to incinerate; *(cadáveres)* to cremate.

**incipiente** *adj* incipient.

**incisión** *nf* incision.

**inciso,-a** *nm* passing remark.

**incitante** *adj* **1** *(estimulante)* inciting. **2** *(provocativo)* provocative.

**incitar** *vt* to incite (a, to).

**inclemencia** *nf* harshness.

**inclinación** *nf* **1** *(desviación)* slant. **2** *(tendencia)* leaning. **3** *(afición)* penchant.

**inclinar** *vt* **1** *(ladear)* to tilt. **2** *fig (persuadir)* to dispose, move.
▶ *vpr* **inclinarse 1** *(doblarse)* to bend, lean; *(como saludo)* to bow. **2 inclinarse a** *fig (propender a)* to incline to. **3 inclinarse por** *(escoger)* to choose, opt for.

**incluir** *vt* **1** to include. **2** *(adjuntar - en carta, etc)* to enclose.

**incluso** *adv* even.
▶ *prep* even.

**incógnita** *nf fig (misterio)* mystery.

**incógnito,-a** *adj* unknown.

**incoherencia** *nf (falta de coherencia)* incoherence.

**incoherente** *adj* incoherent.

**incomodar** *vt* **1** *(causar molestia)* to inconvenience. **2** *(fastidiar)* to annoy, bother. **3** *(enojar)* to anger.
▶ *vpr* **incomodarse** *(enfadarse)* to get annoyed, get angry.

**incómodo,-a** *adj* uncomfortable. LOC sentirse incómodo,-a to feel awkward.

**incomparable** *adj* incomparable.

**incompetencia** *nf* incompetence.

**incompetente** *adj* incompetent.

**incompleto,-a** *adj* **1** incomplete. **2** *(inacabado)* unfinished.

**incomprensión** *nf* lack of understanding.

**incomunicado,-a** *adj* **1** *(por la nieve)* cut off. **2** *(preso)* in solitary confinement.

**inconcebible** *adj* inconceivable.

**incondicional** *adj (rendición)* unconditional.
▶ *nm o nf* staunch supporter.

**inconexo,-a** *adj* disconnected.

**inconformista** *adj* nonconformist.
▶ *nm o nf* nonconformist.

**inconfundible** *adj* unmistakable.

**incongruencia** *nf* incongruity.

**inconsciencia** *nf* **1** MED unconsciousness. **2** *(irreflexión)* thoughtlessness.

**inconsciente** *adj* **1** MED unconscious. **2** *(irreflexivo)* thoughtless.

**inconstante** *adj (variable)* inconstant, changeable.

**incontable** *adj* countless.

**incontinencia** *nf* incontinence.

**incontrolable** *adj* uncontrollable.

**inconveniente** *adj* inappropriate.
▶ *nm (desventaja)* drawback.

**incordiar** *vt* to pester, bother.

**incorporación** *nf (llegada)* arrival; *(inclusión)* inclusion; *(unión)* joining.

**incorporar** *vt* **1** *(añadir)* to incorporate, include. **2** CULIN *(añadir)* to add.
▶ *vpr* **incorporarse 1** *(levantarse)* to sit up. **2** *(a un trabajo)* to start; *(a una empresa, equipo, etc)* to join.

**incorrección** *nf* **1** *(falta de corrección)* incorrectness. **2** *(error)* mistake.

**incorrecto,-a** *adj* **1** *(inexacto)* incorrect. **2** *(descortés)* impolite.

**incorregible** *adj* incorrigible.

**incrédulo,-a** *adj* incredulous.

**increíble** *adj* incredible.

**incrementar** *vt* to increase.

**incremento** *nm* increase, rise.

**increpar** *vt (insultar)* to abuse.

**incriminar** *vt* to incriminate.

**incrustar** *vt* **1** to incrust, encrust. **2** *(arte)* to inlay.

**incubar** *vt* to incubate.

**inculcar** *vt* to inculcate, instil: *les inculcaron la necesidad de tener estudios* they instilled in them the need to study.

**inculpar** *vt* to accuse (de, of).

**inculto,-a** *adj (persona)* uneducated.
▶ *nm & nf (persona)* ignoramus.

**incumbir** *vi* to be incumbent (a, upon).

**incumplir** *vt (promesa)* to break; *(deber)* to fail to fulfil; *(contrato)* to break; *(orden)* to disobey, fail to comply with.

**incurable** *adj* incurable.

**incurrir** *vi* incurrir en *(error)* to fall into; *(delito)* to commit.

**indagar** *vt* to investigate, inquire into.

**indecencia** *nf* **1** indecency. **2** *(acción indecente)* scandal, outrage.

**indecente** *adj* **1** *(impúdico)* indecent. **2** *(indigno)* miserable.

**indecible** *adj* indescribable.

**indecisión** *nf* indecision.

**indeciso,-a** *adj* **1** *(persona)* indecisive, undecided. **2** *(asunto no resuelto)* undecided.

**indecoroso,-a** *adj* indecorous.

**indefenso,-a** *adj* defenceless.

**indefinido,-a** *adj* **1** *(periodo de tiempo)* indefinite; *(contrato)* open-ended. **2** *(impreciso)* indefinite. **3** LING indefinite.

**indemne** *adj* unharmed, unhurt.

**indemnización** *nf* compensation, indemnity.

**indemnizar** *vt* to compensate (de/por, for), indemnify (de/por, for).

**independencia** *nf* independence.

**independiente** *adj* **1** independent. **2** *(individualista)* self-sufficient.

**independizar** *vt* to make independent.
▶ *vpr* **independizarse** to become independent (de, of).

**indeterminado,-a** *adj* **1** *(gen)* indeterminate; *(en tiempo, número)* indefinite. **2** *(impreciso)* vague.

**India** *nf* India.

**indicación** *nf* **1** *(gesto, señal)* sign. **2** *(instrucción)* instruction.

**indicado,-a** *adj* appropriate, suitable.

**indicador,-ra** *adj* *(gen)* indicating.
▶ *nm* *(gen)* indicator; *(con aguja, escala)* gauge.

**indicar** *vt* to indicate, point out.

**indicativo,-a** *adj* indicative.
▶ *nm* **indicativo** LING indicative.

**índice** *nm* **1** *(gen)* index. **2** *(de un libro)* index, table of contents; *(catálogo)* catalogue. **3** *(dedo)* index finger.

**indicio** *nm* **1** *(señal)* sign. **2** *(resto)* trace.

**indiferencia** *nf* indifference.

**indiferente** *adj* indifferent.

**indigente** *nm o nf* poor person: *los indigentes* the needy.

**indigestión** *nf* indigestion.

**indigesto,-a** *adj* *(alimento)* indigestible.

**indignación** *nf* indignation.

**indignar** *vt* to infuriate.
▶ *vpr* **indignarse** to become indignant (por, at/about).

**indigno,-a** *adj* **1** unworthy (de, of). **2** *(vil)* low, contemptible.

**indio,-a** *adj* Indian.
▶ *nm & nf* Indian. LOC **hacer el indio** *fam* to play the fool.

**indirecto,-a** *adj* indirect.

**indiscreción** *nf* indiscretion.

**indiscreto,-a** *adj* indiscreet.
▶ *nm & nf* indiscreet person.

**indispensable** *adj* essential.

**indisponer** *vt* MED to upset, make unwell.
▶ *vpr* **indisponerse** *(enfermarse)* to be unwell.

**indispuesto,-a** *adj* MED indisposed, unwell.

**individual** *adj* individual.
▶ *nm pl* **individuales** DEP singles.

**individualista** *adj* individualistic.
▶ *nm o nf* individualist.

**individuo,-a** *nm & nf pey (gen)* character, individual.
▶ *nm* **individuo** person.

**indocumentado,-a** *adj* *(sin documentación)* without means of identification.

**índole** *nf* **1** *(carácter)* disposition, nature. **2** *(tipo)* type, kind.

**indolente** *adj* indolent.

**indoloro,-a** *adj* painless.

**indómito,-a** *adj* indomitable.

**Indonesia** *nf* Indonesia.

**indonesio,-a** *adj* Indonesian.
▶ *nm & nf* Indonesian.

**inducir** *vt* **1** to induce. **2** ELEC to induce.

**indulgencia** *nf* indulgence, leniency.

**indultar** *vt* JUR to pardon.

**indulto** *nm* pardon, amnesty.

**indumentaria** *nf* clothing, clothes *pl*.

**industria** *nf* **1** *(gen)* industry. **2** *(fábrica)* factory.

**industrial** *adj* industrial.
▶ *nm o nf* industrialist, manufacturer.

**industrializar** *vt* to industrialize.

**inédito,-a** *adj* *(libro)* unpublished.

**inepto,-a** *adj* *(persona)* incompetent.
▶ *nm & nf* incompetent person.

**inercia** *nf* inertia.

**inerte** *adj* **1** *(materia, gas)* inert. **2** *(cadáver)* lifeless.

**inesperado,-a** *adj* unexpected.

**inestable** *adj* unstable, unsteady.

**inevitable** *adj* inevitable.

**inexistente** *adj* nonexistent.

**inexorable** *adj* inexorable.

**inexperto,-a** *adj* inexperienced.

**inexplicable** *adj* inexplicable.

**inexpresivo,-a** *adj* expressionless.

**infalible** *adj* infallible.

**infame** *adj* *(vil)* despicable, vile.

**infamia** *nf* disgrace.

**infancia** *nf* **1** *(gen)* childhood. **2** *(los niños)* children *pl*.

**infante** *nm* **1** *lit (niño)* infant. **2** *(soldado)* infantryman.

**infantería** *nf* infantry.

**infantil** *adj* **1** *(literatura, juego)* children's; *(equipo)* junior. **2** *(inmaduro)* childish.

**infarto** *nm* *(de miocardio)* heart attack. [COMP] **infarto de miocardio** heart attack.

**infatigable** *adj* indefatigable, tireless.

**infección** *nf* infection.

**infectar** *vt* to infect (de, with).
▶ *vpr* **infectarse** to become infected (de, with).

**infeliz** *adj* **1** *(desdichado)* unhappy. **2** *(ingenuo)* ingenuous.

**inferior** *adj* **1** *(situado debajo)* lower. **2** *(cantidad)* less, lower. **3** *(en calidad)* inferior (a, to).
▶ *nm o nf (en rango)* subordinate; *(en calidad)* inferior.

**inferioridad** *nf* inferiority.

**infernal** *adj* infernal.

**infidelidad** *nf* **1** *(sexual)* infidelity, unfaithfulness. **2** *(de un amigo)* disloyalty.

**infiel** *adj* *(esposo)* unfaithful (a/con/para, to); *(amigo)* disloyal (a, to).

**infiernillo** *nm* portable stove.

**infierno** *nm* hell. [LOC] **¡vete al infierno!** go to hell!, get lost!

**infiltrar** *vt* to infiltrate.
▶ *vpr* **infiltrarse** to infiltrate (en, -).

**ínfimo,-a** *adj* *(en calidad)* lowest, poorest; *(precio)* ridiculous.

**infinidad** *nf* **1** *(infinito)* infinity. **2** *(gran cantidad)* infinite number.

**infinitivo** *nm* infinitive.

**infinito,-a** *adj* infinite.
▶ *nm* **el infinito** the infinite, infinity.

**inflamable** *adj* inflammable.

**inflamación** *nf* MED inflammation.

**inflamar** *vt* MED to inflame.
▶ *vpr* **inflamarse** MED to become inflamed.

**inflar** *vt* **1** *(balón)* to blow up, inflate. **2** *fig (hechos, noticias)* to exaggerate. **3** *(precios)* to inflate.
▶ *vpr* **inflarse 1** to inflate one's opinion of os. **2** *fam (hartarse de comer)* to stuff os (de, with).

**inflexible** *adj* inflexible.

**influencia** *nf* influence.

**influir** *vt* to influence.
▶ *vi* to have influence.

**influyente** *adj* influential.

**información** *nf* **1** *(conocimiento)* information. **2** *(noticia)* piece of news; *(conjunto de noticias)* news. **3** *(en telefónica)* directory enquiries *pl*.

**informal** *adj* **1** *(desenfadado)* informal. **2** *(persona)* unreliable.

**informar** *vt* *(dar noticia)* to inform (de, about).
▶ *vi* to inform (de, about), tell (de, about).
▶ *vpr* **informarse** to find out (de, about).

**informática** *nf* computing.

**informático,-a** *adj* computer.
▶ *nm & nf* computer expert.

**informativo,-a** *adj* *(ilustrativo)* informative: *una campaña con carácter informativo* a public awareness campaign.
▶ *nm* **informativo** news programme.

**informatizar** *vt* to computerize.

**informe** *nm* report.
▶ *nm pl* **informes** references.

**infracción** *nf* infringement.

**infractor,-ra** *adj* offending.
▶ *nm & nf* offender.

**infraestructura** *nf* infrastructure.

**infranqueable** *adj* **1** impassable. **2** *fig* insurmountable.

**infrarrojo,-a** *adj* infrared.

**infravalorar** *vt* to underestimate.

**infrecuente** *adj* infrequent.

**infringir** *vt (gen)* to infringe; *(ley)* to break.

**infructuoso,-a** *adj* fruitless, unsuccessful.

**infundado,-a** *adj* unfounded.

**infundir** *vt (respeto)* to command; *(miedo)* to fill with; *(valor)* to instil.

**infusión** *nf* infusion.

**ingeniar** *vt* to devise.
▸ *vpr* **ingeniárselas** to manage, find a way, contrive.

**ingeniería** *nf* engineering.

**ingeniero,-a** *nm & nf* engineer.

**ingenio** *nm* **1** *(talento)* talent; *(chispa)* wit. **2** *(habilidad)* ingenuity.

**ingenioso,-a** *adj (inteligente)* ingenious, clever; *(con chispa)* witty.

**ingenuo,-a** *adj* naive, ingenuous.
▸ *nm & nf* naive person.

**ingerir** *vt (alimentos)* to eat; *(bebida)* to drink.

**Inglaterra** *nf* England.

**ingle** *nf* groin.

**inglés,-esa** *adj* English.
▸ *nm & nf (persona)* English person; *(hombre)* Englishman; *(mujer)* Englishwoman.
▸ *nm* **inglés** *(idioma)* English.

**ingratitud** *nf* ingratitude, ungratefulness.

**ingrato,-a** *adj* **1** *(persona)* ungrateful. **2** *(trabajo, tarea)* thankless.

**ingrediente** *nm* ingredient.

**ingresar** *vt (dinero)* to pay in, deposit.
▸ *vi* **ingresar en 1** *(entrar)* to join. **2** *(hospital)* to be admitted to.

**ingreso** *nm* **1** *(en club, ejército)* joining; *(en hospital)* admission; *(en universidad)* entrance. **2** *(entrada)* entry.
▸ *nm pl* **ingresos** *(sueldo, renta)* income *sing*; *(beneficios)* revenue *sing*.

**inhabitable** *adj* uninhabitable.

**inhalar** *vt* to inhale, breathe in.

**inherente** *adj* inherent (a, in).

**inhibir** *vt (reprimir)* to inhibit.

▸ *vpr* **inhibirse 1** *(reprimirse)* to be inhibited. **2** *(abstenerse)* to refrain (de, from); *(negarse)* to refuse (de, to).

**inhóspito,-a** *adj* inhospitable.

**inhumano,-a** *adj* **1** *(persona)* inhuman, cruel. **2** *(dolor, sufrimiento)* inhuman.

**iniciación** *nf* **1** *(comienzo)* start, beginning. **2** *(de una persona)* initiation.

**inicial** *adj* initial.
▸ *nf* initial.

**iniciar** *vt* **1** *(empezar)* to start, begin. **2** *(introducir)* to initiate (en, in).
▸ *vpr* **iniciarse** *(empezar)* to start, begin.

**iniciativa** *nf* initiative.

**inicio** *nm* beginning, start.

**inimitable** *adj* inimitable.

**injertar** *vt* to graft.

**injerto** *nm* graft.

**injuria** *nf* insult, affront.

**injuriar** *vt (insultar)* to insult.

**injusticia** *nf* injustice, unfairness.

**injusto,-a** *adj* unfair, unjust.

**inmadurez** *nf* immaturity.

**inmaduro,-a** *adj* immature.

**inmediaciones** *nf pl (de una zona)* surrounding area *sing*; *(de una casa)* vicinity *sing*.

**inmediato,-a** *adj* **1** *(poco después)* immediate. **2** *(contiguo)* next (a, to), adjoining (a, -).

**inmejorable** *adj (gen)* unbeatable.

**inmensidad** *nf* **1** immensity. **2** *(gran cantidad)* great number.

**inmenso,-a** *adj* immense, vast.

**inmersión** *nf (gen)* immersion; *(de un buceador, submarino)* dive.

**inmerso,-a** *adj* immersed (en, in).

**inmigración** *nf* immigration.

**inmigrante** *adj* immigrant.
▸ *nm o nf* immigrant.

**inmigrar** *vi* to immigrate.

**inminente** *adj* imminent.

**inmobiliario,-a** *adj* property, US real estate.
▸ *nf* **(agencia) inmobiliaria** estate agency, US real estate company.

**inmolar** *vt* to immolate, sacrifice.

**inmoral** *adj* immoral.

**inmoralidad** *nf* immorality.

**inmortal** *adj* immortal.

**inmortalidad** *nf* immortality.

**inmortalizar** *vt* to immortalize.

**inmóvil** *adj* still, motionless.

**inmovilizar** *vt* to immobilize.

**inmueble** *nm* building.

**inmundo,-a** *adj* (*sucio*) dirty, filthy.

**inmune** *adj* MED immune (a, to).

**inmunidad** *nf* immunity.

**inmutar** *vt* to affect.
  ▶ *vpr* **inmutarse** to react.

**innato,-a** *adj* innate, inborn.

**innecesario,-a** *adj* unnecessary.

**innegable** *adj* undeniable.

**innovación** *nf* innovation.

**innovador,-ra** *adj* innovatory.
  ▶ *nm & nf* innovator.

**innovar** *vi* to innovate.

**innumerable** *adj* innumerable, countless.

**inocencia** *nf* innocence.

**inocentada** *nf* practical joke.

**inocente** *adj* **1** innocent. **2** (*ingenuo*) naive, innocent.
  ▶ *nm o nf* naive person, innocent person.

**inocuo,-a** *adj* innocuous, harmless.

**inodoro,-a** *adj* odourless.
  ▶ *nm* **inodoro** toilet.

**inofensivo,-a** *adj* harmless, inoffensive.

**inolvidable** *adj* unforgettable.

**inoperante** *adj* ineffective, inoperative.

**inopia** LOC **estar en la inopia 1** *fam* (*distraído*) to have one's head in the clouds. **2** (*ignorante*) to be in the dark.

**inoportuno,-a** *adj* inopportune.

**inorgánico,-a** *adj* inorganic.

**inoxidable** *adj* rustproof.

**input** *nm* input.

**inquebrantable** *adj* (*promesa*) unbreakable; (*fe*) unshakeable.

**inquietante** *adj* disturbing.

**inquietar** *vt* to worry.
  ▶ *vpr* **inquietarse** to worry (por, about).

**inquieto,-a** *adj* **1** (*agitado*) restless. **2** (*preocupado*) worried, anxious.

**inquietud** *nf* **1** (*agitación*) restlessness. **2** (*preocupación*) worry, anxiety.

**inquilino,-a** *nm & nf* tenant.

**inquina** *nf* animosity, antipathy. LOC **tener inquina a** ALGN to feel animosity towards SB.

**insaciable** *adj* insatiable.

**insalubre** *adj* unhealthy.

**insano,-a** *adj* **1** (*no sano*) unhealthy. **2** (*loco*) insane.

**insatisfecho,-a** *adj* dissatisfied, unsatisfied.

**inscribir** *vt* **1** (*grabar*) to inscribe. **2** (*apuntar*) to register; (*en un curso*) to enrol.
  ▶ *vpr* **inscribirse** (*gen*) to register; (*para un curso*) to enrol.

**inscripción** *nf* **1** (*grabado*) inscription. **2** (*registro*) registration; (*en un curso*) enrolment.

**insecticida** *adj* insecticidal.
  ▶ *nm* insecticide.

**insecto** *nm* insect.

**inseguridad** *nf* **1** (*falta de confianza*) insecurity. **2** (*duda*) uncertainty. **3** (*peligro*) lack of safety.

**inseguro,-a** *adj* **1** (*sin confianza*) insecure. **2** (*que duda*) uncertain. **3** (*peligroso*) unsafe.

**insensato,-a** *adj* foolish.
  ▶ *nm & nf* fool.

**insensible** *adj* **1** insensitive, unfeeling, thoughtless. **2** MED insensible.

**inseparable** *adj* inseparable.

**insertar** *vt* to insert (en, into).

**inservible** *adj* useless.

**insigne** *adj* distinguished, eminent.

**insignia** *nf* (*distintivo*) badge.

**insignificante** *adj* insignificant.

**insinuación** *nf* **1** (*indicación*) insinuation, hint. **2** *fam* (*amorosa*) overture. LOC **hacerle insinuaciones a** ALGN (*insinuarse*) to make a pass at SB.

**insinuar** *vt* to insinuate, hint.

**insípido,-a** *adj* insipid.

**insistencia** *nf* insistence.

**insistente** *adj* insistent.

**insistir** *vi* **1** to insist (en, on). **2** *(enfatizar)* to stress (en, -).

**insobornable** *adj* incorruptible.

**insolación** *nf* MED sunstroke.

**insolencia** *nf* **1** *(atrevimiento)* insolence. **2** *(palabra)* cheeky remark.

**insolente** *adj* **1** *(descarado)* insolent. **2** *(soberbio)* haughty.

**insolidario,-a** *adj* unsupportive.

**insólito,-a** *adj* extremely unusual.

**insolvente** *adj* insolvent.

**insomne** *adj* sleepless.
▶ *nm o nf* insomniac.

**insomnio** *nm* insomnia.

**insondable** *adj* unfathomable.

**insonorizado,-a** *adj* soundproof.

**insonorizar** *vt* to soundproof.

**insoportable** *adj* unbearable.

**insospechado,-a** *adj* unexpected.

**insostenible** *adj* untenable.

**inspección** *nf* *(gen)* examination, inspection; *(policial)* search.

**inspeccionar** *vt* *(gen)* to inspect; *(zona, lugar del crimen)* to search.

**inspector,-ra** *nm & nf* inspector.

**inspiración** *nf* **1** inspiration. **2** *(inhalación)* inhalation.

**inspirado,-a** *adj* inspired.

**inspirar** *vt* **1** *(aspirar)* to inhale, breathe in. **2** *(infundir)* to inspire.
▶ *vpr* **inspirarse** to be inspired (en, by).

**instalación** *nf* installation.
▶ *nf pl* **instalaciones** *(de un servicio)* facilities *pl*.

**instalador,-ra** *nm & nf* installer, fitter.

**instalar** *vt* **1** *(colocar)* to install. **2** *(equipar)* to fit out.
▶ *vpr* **instalarse** *(persona)* to settle; *(empresa)* to set up.

**instancia** *nf* *(petición)* request; *(solicitud)* form.

**instantánea** *nf* *(foto)* snapshot, snap.

**instantáneo,-a** *adj* **1** *(inmediato)* instantaneous, immediate. **2** *(momentáneo)* brief, fleeting.

**instante** *nm* moment, instant.

**instar** *vi* *(insistir)* to press, urge.

**instauración** *nf* establishment.

**instaurar** *vt* to establish.

**instigar** *vt* to instigate.

**instintivo,-a** *adj* instinctive.

**instinto** *nm* instinct.

**institución** *nf* **1** *(organismo)* institution. **2** *(creación)* establishment, institution; *(introducción)* introduction.

**institucional** *adj* institutional.

**instituir** *vt* **1** *(crear)* to institute, establish. **2** *(nombrar)* to appoint.

**instituto** *nm* **1** *(asociación)* institute. **2** EDUC state secondary school, US high school. COMP **instituto de bachillerato** state secondary school, US high school.

**institutriz** *nf* governess.

**instrucción** *nf* **1** *(enseñanza)* instruction; *(cultura)* education. **2** MIL military training.
▶ *nf pl* **instrucciones** *(indicaciones)* instructions.

**instructivo,-a** *adj* *(conferencia)* instructive; *(juguete)* educational.

**instructor,-ra** *adj* *(gen)* instructing.
▶ *nm & nf* instructor.

**instruido,-a** *adj* well-educated.

**instruir** *vt* **1** *(enseñar)* to instruct. **2** MIL to train. **3** JUR to investigate.

**instrumental** *adj* *(música)* instrumental.
▶ *nm* instruments *pl*.

**instrumentar** *vt* *(gen)* to arrange; *(para orquesta)* to orchestrate.

**instrumentista** *nm o nf* *(músico)* instrumentalist.

**instrumento** *nm* instrument.

**insubordinado,-a** *adj* insubordinate.
▶ *nm & nf* insubordinate person.

**insubordinar** *vt* to stir up.
▶ *vpr* **insubordinarse** to rebel.

**insuficiente** *adj* insufficient.
▶ *nm* EDUC fail.

**insufrible** *adj* insufferable.

**insular** *adj* insular.
▶ *nm o nf* islander.

**insulina** *nf* insulin.

**insulso,-a** *adj* insipid, tasteless.

**insultante** *adj* insulting.
**insultar** *vt* to insult.
**insulto** *nm* insult.
**insumisión** *nf (gen)* rebelliousness.
**insumiso,-a** *adj* rebellious.
▸ *nm & nf* MIL *person who refuses to do military service or community service in lieu.*
**insuperable** *adj (calidad, capacidad)* unbeatable; *(obstáculo, miedo, complejo)* unsurmountable, insuperable.
**insurgente** *adj* insurgent.
**insurrección** *nf* insurrection.
**intachable** *adj* irreproachable.
**intacto,-a** *adj* intact.
**integración** *nf* integration.
**integral** *adj* **1** *(completo)* full. **2** *(pan, pasta)* wholemeal; *(arroz)* brown.
**integrante** *adj* integral.
▸ *nm o nf* member.
**integrar** *vt (formar)* to make up.
▸ *vpr* **integrarse** to integrate.
**integridad** *nf* integrity.
**integrismo** *nm (gen)* reaction; *(religioso)* fundamentalism.
**integrista** *adj (gen)* reactionary; *(religioso)* fundamentalist.
▸ *nm o nf (gen)* reactionary; *(en religión)* fundamentalist.
**íntegro,-a** *adj* **1** *(completo)* whole, entire; *(versión)* unabridged. **2** *(honrado)* honest, upright.
**intelecto** *nm* intellect.
**intelectual** *adj* intellectual.
▸ *nm o nf* intellectual.
**inteligencia** *nf* intelligence. COMP **inteligencia artificial** artificial intelligence.
**inteligente** *adj* intelligent.
**intemperie** *nf* bad weather. LOC **a la intemperie** in the open (air).
**intempestivo,-a** *adj* inopportune.
**intemporal** *adj* timeless.
**intención** *nf (propósito)* intention.
**intencionado,-a** *adj* deliberate!.
**intendencia** *nf* MIL *(cuerpo)* ≈ service corps, US quartermaster corps.
**intendente** *nm* **1** supervisor. **2** MIL quartermaster general.

**intensidad** *nf* **1** *(gen)* intensity. **2** *(de una enfermedad)* severity; *(del dolor)* acuteness. **3** *(de la luz, del color)* brightness, intensity; *(del amor, de la fe)* strength.
**intensificar** *vt* to intensify.
**intensivo,-a** *adj* intensive.
**intenso,-a** *adj* **1** *(gen)* intense. **2** *(dolor)* acute. **3** *(luz, color)* bright, intense. **4** *(amor)* passionate.
**intentar** *vt* to try.
**intento** *nm* attempt, try.
**interactivo,-a** *adj* interactive.
**intercalar** *vt* to insert.
**intercambiar** *vt* to exchange.
**intercambio** *nm* exchange.
**interceder** *vi* to intercede.
**interceptar** *vt* **1** *(mensaje, correspondencia)* to intercept. **2** *(obstruir)* to block.
**interceptor** *adj* intercepting.
▸ *nm* interceptor.
**intercesión** *nf* intercession.
**intercesor,-ra** *adj* interceding.
▸ *nm & nf* intercessor.
**interconexión** *nf* interconnection.
**interés** *nm* **1** *(gen)* interest; *(propio)* self-interest. **2** FIN interest.
**interesado,-a** *adj* **1** *(gen)* interested. **2** *(egoísta)* selfish, self-interested.
▸ *nm & nf* **1** *(gen)* interested party. **2** *(egoísta)* selfish person.
**interesante** *adj* interesting.
**interesar** *vt* **1** to interest. **2** *(afectar)* to concern.
▸ *vpr* **interesarse** to take an interest (por, in).
**interfaz** *nf* interface.
**interferencia** *nf* **1** *(gen)* interference; *(intencionada)* jamming. **2** *fig* interference.
**interferir** *vt* **1** *(transmisión, programa)* to jam. **2** *(obstaculizar)* to interfere in.
▸ *vi* to meddle, interfere.
**interfono** *nm* intercom.
**interino,-a** *adj* **1** temporary, provisional. **2** *(director, presidente)* acting.
▸ *nm & nf (sustituto)* stand-in.
**interior** *adj* **1** *(bolsillo)* inside; *(habitación)* without a view, interior; *(jardín)* in-

terior. **2** *(del país)* domestic, internal. **3** GEOG inland.

▸ *nm* **1** *(en una vivienda)* inside: *pasemos al interior* let's go inside. **2** *(conciencia)* inside. **3** GEOG interior.

**interiorismo** *nm* interior design.

**interiorista** *n o nf* interior designer.

**interiorizar** *vt (creencia, principio)* to internalize.

**interjección** *nf* interjection.

**interlocutor,-ra** *nm & nf* speaker, interlocutor.

**intermediario,-a** *nm & nf (gen)* intermediary; *(en disputas)* mediator.

**intermedio,-a** *adj (gen)* intermediate; *(tamaño)* medium; *(calidad)* average; *(tiempo)* intervening; *(espacio)* between.

▸ *nm* **intermedio** *(de un espectáculo)* interval, intermission.

**interminable** *adj* endless, interminable.

**intermitencia** *nf* intermittence.

**intermitente** *adj (gen)* intermittent.

▸ *nm* AUTO indicator, US blinker.

**internacional** *adj* international.

**internado** *nm* boarding school.

**internar** *vt (en un colegio)* to send to boarding school; *(en un hospital)* to confine (en, to).

▸ *vpr* **internarse** *(penetrar)* to penetrate.

**internauta** *nm o nf* internaut, netsurfer.

**interno,-a** *adj* **1** *(órgano)* internal. **2** *(alumno)* boarding.

▸ *nm & nf* **1** *(alumno)* boarder. **2** *(médico)* intern. **3** *(preso)* prisoner.

**interpelar** *vt* POL to interpellate.

**interponer** *vt* to interpose.

▸ *vpr* **interponerse 1** *(físicamente)* to interpose os. **2** *fig* to intervene.

**interpretación** *nf* **1** *(gen)* interpretation. **2** *(de pieza, obra)* performance.

**interpretar** *vt* **1** to interpret. **2** *(obra, pieza)* to perform; *(papel)* to play.

**intérprete** *nm o nf* **1** *(traductor)* interpreter. **2** *(actor, músico)* performer.

**interrelación** *nf* interrelation.

**interrelacionar** *vt* to interrelate.

**interrogación** *nf* **1** *(acción)* interrogation, questioning. **2** *(signo)* question mark. **3** *(pregunta)* question.

**interrogador,-a** *nm & nf* interrogator.

**interrogante** *nm (incógnita)* question mark.

**interrogar** *vt* **1** to question. **2** *(a testigo, etc)* to interrogate.

**interrogativo,-a** *adj* interrogative.

**interrogatorio** *nm* interrogation.

**interrumpir** *vt* **1** *(gen)* to interrupt. **2** *(tráfico)* to block.

**interrupción** *nf* interruption.

**interruptor** *nm* switch.

**intersección** *nf* intersection.

**interurbano,-a** *adj (gen)* inter-city; *(llamada)* trunk, long-distance.

**intervalo** *nm* **1** *(de tiempo)* interval. **2** *(de espacio)* gap.

**intervención** *nf* **1** *(gen)* intervention. **2** *(discurso)* speech. **3** MED operation.

**intervenir** *vi* **1** *(tomar parte)* to take part (en, in). **2** *(hablar)* to speak (en, at).

▸ *vt* **1** MED to operate on. **2** *(alijo, mercancía)* to seize.

**interventor,-ra** *nm & nf (gen)* inspector, auditor.

**intestinal** *adj* intestinal.

**intestino** *nm* intestine.

**intimar** *vi* to become close (con, to).

**intimidación** *nf* intimidation.

**intimidad** *nf* **1** *(amistad)* intimacy. **2** *(vida privada)* privacy, private life.

**intimidar** *vt* to intimidate.

**íntimo,-a** *adj* **1** *(vida)* private. **2** *(amigo, relación)* close. **3** *(sentimiento, emoción)* most intimate. **4** *(higiene)* personal.

▸ *nm & nf (amigo)* close friend.

**intocable** *adj* untouchable.

**intolerable** *adj* intolerable.

**intolerancia** *nf* intolerance: *intolerancia a la lactosa* intolerance of lactose.

**intolerante** *adj* intolerant.

**intoxicación** *nf* poisoning.

**intoxicar** *vt* to poison.

▸ *vpr* **intoxicarse** to poison os.

**intraducible** *adj* untranslatable.

**intranquilidad** *nf* worry, uneasiness.

**intranquilizar** *vt* to worry.
▶ *vpr* **intranquilizarse** to get worried.
**intranquilo,-a** *adj* worried, uneasy.
**intransferible** *adj* nontransferable.
**intransigencia** *nf* intransigence.
**intransigente** *adj* intransigent.
**intransitable** *adj* impassable.
**intransitivo,-a** *adj* intransitive.
**intrascendente** *adj* unimportant, insignificant.
**intratable** *adj (persona)* unsociable.
**intrépido,-a** *adj* intrepid.
**intriga** *nf* 1 *(maquinación secreta)* intrigue. 2 *(curiosidad)* curiosity. 3 *(de una narración, película)* intrigue.
**intrigado,-a** *adj* intrigued.
**intrigante** *adj* intriguing.
**intrigar** *vt (interesar)* to intrigue.
**intrínseco,-a** *adj* intrinsic.
**introducción** *nf* introduction.
**introducir** *vt* 1 *(gen)* to introduce; *(legislación)* to introduce, bring in. 2 *(meter)* to put, place; *(insertar)* insert. 3 *(importar)* to bring in, import.
▶ *vpr* **introducirse** *(entrar)* to get in.
**intromisión** *nf* interference, meddling.
**introspectivo,-a** *adj* introspective.
**introvertido,-a** *adj* introverted.
▶ *nm & nf* introvert.
**intruso,-a** *adj* intrusive.
▶ *nm & nf* intruder.
**intuición** *nf* intuition.
**intuir** *vt* to sense, feel.
**intuitivo,-a** *adj* intuitive.
**inundación** *nf* flood, flooding.
**inundar** *vt* 1 to flood. 2 *fig* to inundate.
**inusitado,-a** *adj* uncommon, rare.
**inusual** *adj* unusual.
**inútil** *adj* 1 *(gen)* useless. 2 *(intento)* vain.
▶ *nm o nf fam (persona)* hopeless case.
**inutilizar** *vt* 1 to render useless. 2 *(máquina)* to put out of action.
**invadir** *vt* to invade.
**inválido,-a** *adj* disabled, handicapped.
▶ *nm & nf* disabled person.
**invariable** *adj* invariable.
**invasión** *nf* invasion.

**invasor,-ra** *adj* invading.
▶ *nm & nf* invader.
**invencible** *adj (ejército)* invincible; *(obstáculo)* unsurmountable.
**invención** *nf* invention.
**invendible** *adj* unsaleable.
**inventar** *vt* 1 *(crear)* to invent. 2 *(mentir)* to make up, fabricate.
**inventario** *nm* inventory.
**inventiva** *nf* inventiveness.
**invento** *nm* invention.
**inventor,-ra** *nm & nf* inventor.
**invernadero** *nm* greenhouse.
**invernal** *adj* winter, wintry.
**invernar** *vi (animales)* to hibernate.
**inverosímil** *adj* unlikely.
**inversión** *nf* 1 *(gen)* inversion. 2 FIN investment.
**inverso,-a** *adj* inverse, opposite.
**invertebrado,-a** *adj* invertebrate.
▶ *nm* **invertebrado** invertebrate.
**invertido,-a** *adj* reversed, inverted.
**invertir** *vt* 1 *(orden)* to invert, reverse. 2 *(dirección)* to reverse. 3 *(tiempo)* to spend (en, on). 4 FIN to invest (en, in).
**investidura** *nf* investiture.
**investigación** *nf* 1 *(indagación)* investigation, enquiry. 2 *(estudio)* research.
**investigador,-ra** *adj* 1 *(que indaga)* investigating. 2 *(que estudia)* research.
▶ *nm & nf* 1 *(científico)* researcher. 2 *(detective)* investigator.
**investigar** *vt* 1 *(indagar)* to investigate. 2 *(campo)* to do research on.
**investir** *vt* to invest.
**inviable** *adj* non-viable, unfeasible.
**invidente** *adj* blind.
▶ *nm o nf* blind person.
**invierno** *nm* winter.
**invisible** *adj* invisible.
**invitación** *nf* invitation.
**invitado,-a** *adj* invited.
▶ *nm & nf* guest.
**invitar** *vt* to invite.
▶ *vi (incitar)* to encourage.
**invocar** *vt* to invoke.
**involucrar** *vt* to involve (en, in).

**involuntario,-a** *adj (reflejo, movimiento)* involuntary; *(error)* unintentional.

**invulnerable** *adj* invulnerable.

**inyección** *nf* injection.

**inyectable** *adj* injectable.
▶ *nm* injection.

**inyectar** *vt* to inject (en, into).

**iodo** *nm* iodine.

**ir** *vi* **1** *(gen)* to go; *(acudir)* to come. **2** *(camino, etc)* to lead. **3** *(funcionar)* to work, go. **4** *(sentar bien)* to suit; *(agradar)* to like. **5** *(tratar)* to be about.
▶ *aux* **ir + a +** **1** going to: *voy a venderlo* I'm going to sell it. **2** **ir +** : *fuimos andando* we walked, we went on foot. **3** **ir +** to be: *ir cansado,-a* to be tired.
▶ *vpr* **irse** **1** *(marcharse)* to go away, leave. **2** *(deslizarse)* to slip. **3** *(gastarse)* to go, disappear.

**ira** *nf* wrath, rage.

**iracundo,-a** *adj* irritable, irate.

**Irak** *nm* Iraq.

**Irán** *nm* Iran.

**iraní** *adj* Iranian.
▶ *nm o nf* Iranian.

**iranio,-a** *adj* Iranian.
▶ *nm & nf (persona)* Iranian.
▶ *nm* **iranio** *(idioma)* Iranian.

**iraquí** *adj* Iraqi.
▶ *nm o nf (persona)* Iraqi.
▶ *nm (idioma)* Iraqi.

**irascible** *adj* irascible, irritable.

**iris** *nm inv* iris.

**Irlanda** *nf* Ireland. COMP **Irlanda del Norte** Northern Ireland.

**irlandés,-esa** *adj* Irish.
▶ *nm & nf (persona - hombre)* Irishman; *(- mujer)* Irish woman.
▶ *nm* **irlandés** *(idioma)* Irish.

**ironía** *nf* irony.

**irónico,-a** *adj* **1** ironic. **2** *(burlón)* mocking.

**irracional** *adj* irrational.

**irradiar** *vt* to irradiate, radiate.

**irreal** *adj* unreal.

**irreconocible** *adj* unrecognizable.

**irreflexivo,-a** *adj (acto)* rash; *(persona)* impetuous.

**irregular** *adj* irregular.

**irregularidad** *nf* irregularity.

**irrelevante** *adj* irrelevant.

**irremediable** *adj (daño)* irremediable.

**irrepetible** *adj* unrepeatable.

**irreprochable** *adj* irreproachable.

**irresistible** *adj* **1** irresistible. **2** *pey (insoportable)* unbearable.

**irrespetuoso,-a** *adj* disrespectful.

**irresponsable** *adj* irresponsible.
▶ *nm o nf* irresponsible person.

**irreversible** *adj* irreversible.

**irrigar** *vt* to irrigate.

**irrisorio,-a** *adj* derisory, ridiculous.

**irritable** *adj* irritable.

**irritación** *nf* irritation.

**irritante** *adj* irritating, annoying.

**irritar** *vt* to irritate.
▶ *vpr* **irritarse** to get annoyed.

**irrumpir** *vi* to burst (en, into).

**irrupción** *nf* irruption.

**isla** *nf* island.

**islam** *nm* Islam.

**islámico,-a** *adj* Islamic.

**islandés,-esa** *adj* Icelandic.
▶ *nm & nf (persona)* Icelander.
▶ *nm* **islandés** *(idioma)* Icelandic.

**Islandia** *nf* Iceland.

**isleño,-a** *adj* island.
▶ *nm & nf* islander.

**islote** *nm* small unhinhabited island.

**isósceles** *adj* isosceles.

**Israel** *nm* Israel.

**israelí** *adj* Israeli.
▶ *nm o nf* Israeli.

**istmo** *nm* isthmus.

**Italia** *nf* Italy.

**italiano,-a** *adj* Italian.
▶ *nm & nf (persona)* Italian.
▶ *nm* **italiano** *(idioma)* Italian.

**itinerante** *adj* itinerant.

**itinerario** *nm* itinerary.

**izar** *vt* to hoist.

**izquierda** *nf* **1** *(mano)* left hand; *(pierna)* left leg. **2** POL the left.

**izquierdista** *adj* left-wing.

**izquierdo,-a** *adj* left.

# J

**J, j** *nf* (*la letra*) J, j.

**jabalí** *nm* wild boar.

**jabalina** *nf* DEP javelin.

**jabato** *nm* ZOOL young wild boar.

**jabón** *nm* soap. COMP **jabón de tocador** toilet soap.

**jabonera** *nf* soap dish.

**jabonoso,-a** *adj* soapy.

**jaca** *nf* cob, small horse.

**jacinto** *nm* hyacinth.

**jactarse** *vpr* to boast, brag (de, about).

**jacuzzi®** *nm* jacuzzi®.

**jade** *nm* jade.

**jadear** *vi* to pant.

**jadeo** *nm* panting.

**jaguar** *nm* jaguar.

**jalea** *nf* jelly. COMP **jalea real** royal jelly.

**jalear** *vt* **1** (*animar*) to cheer (on), clap and shout at. **2** (*caza*) to urge on.

**jaleo** *nm* **1** (*alboroto*) din, racket: *no se oye nada con este jaleo* I can't hear a thing with all this racket. **2** (*escándalo*) fuss, commotion.

**jalón** *nm* **1** (*estaca*) stake, post. **2** *fig* milestone, landmark.

**jalonar** *vt* (*con estacas*) to stake out.

**Jamaica** *nf* Jamaica.

**jamaicano,-a** *adj* Jamaican.
▶ *nm & nf* Jamaican.

**jamás** *adv* (+ *indic*) never; (+ *subj*) ever: *jamás volveré* I shall never return. LOC **jamás de los jamases** never ever. ▌ **por siempre jamás** for ever (and ever).

**jamba** *nf* jamb.

**jamón** *nm* (*curado*) cured ham; (*pata del cerdo*) leg of ham. COMP **jamón de York/ jamón en dulce** boiled ham. ▌ **jamón serrano** cured ham.

**Japón** *nm* Japan.

**japonés,-esa** *adj* Japanese.
▶ *nm & nf* (*persona*) Japanese.
▶ *nm* **japonés** (*idioma*) Japanese.

**jaque** *nm* check. COMP **jaque mate** checkmate.

**jaqueca** *nf* migraine, headache.

**jarabe** *nm* MED syrup, mixture. COMP **jarabe para la tos** cough syrup.

**jardín** *nm* garden. COMP **jardín botánico** botanical garden. ▌ **jardín de infancia** nursery school.

**jardinera** *nf* **1** (*mujer*) gardener. **2** (*mueble para tiestos*) plant stand; (*en ventana*) window box.

**jardinería** *nf* gardening.

**jardinero,-a** *nm & nf* gardener.

**jarra** *nf* **1** (*para servir*) jug, US pitcher. **2** (*para beber*) tankard, beer mug.

**jarro** *nm* **1** (*recipiente*) jug. **2** (*contenido*) jugful.

**jarrón** *nm* **1** vase. **2** ARTE urn.

**jaspeado,-a** *adj* mottled, speckled.

**jaula** *nf* cage.

**jauría** *nf* pack of hounds.

**Java** *nf* Java.

**javanés,-esa** *adj* Javanese.
▶ *nm & nf* Javanese.

**jazmín** *nm* jasmine.

**jazz** *nm* jazz.

**jeep®** *nm* jeep.

**jefatura** *nf* (*sede*) central office; (*militar*) headquarters.

**jefe,-a** *nm & nf* **1** boss, head, chief. **2** COM (*hombre*) manager; (*mujer*) manageress. **3** POL leader. **4** (*de una tribu*) chief. COMP **jefe de cocina** chef. ▌ **jefe de estación** station master. ▌ **jefe de Estado** Head of State.

**jengibre** *nm* ginger.

**jeque** *nm* sheik, sheikh.

**jerarquía** *nf* **1** hierarchy. **2** *(grado)* scale. **3** *(categoría)* rank.

**jerárquico,-a** *adj* hierarchical.

**jerez** *nm* sherry.

**jerga** *nf (lenguaje)* jargon.

**jergón** *nm (colchón)* pallet.

**jeringuilla** *nf* syringe.

**jeroglífico,-a** *adj* hieroglyphic.
▶ *nm* jeroglífico **1** hieroglyph, hieroglyphic. **2** *(juego)* rebus.

**jersey** *nm* sweater, pullover, jumper.

**jesuita** *nm o nf* Jesuit.

**jet** *nm* jet.

**jilguero** *nm* goldfinch.

**jinete** *nm* rider, horseman.

**jirafa** *nf* giraffe.

**jirón** *nm* shred: *una camisa hecha jirones* a tattered shirt.

**jocoso,-a** *adj (persona)* jocular; *(tono)* humorous, jokey.

**jofaina** *nf* washbasin.

**jogging** *nm* jogging: *practican el jogging* they go jogging.

**jolgorio** *nm* **1** *(juerga)* binge. **2** *(algazara)* party.

**Jordania** *nf* Jordan.

**jordano,-a** *adj* Jordanian.
▶ *nm & nf* Jordanian.

**jornada** *nf* **1** *(día de trabajo)* working day: *una jornada de ocho horas* an eight-hour day. **2** *(camino recorrido)* day's journey. **3** *(en periodismo)* day: *las noticias de la jornada* today's news. COMP **media jornada** half-day.

**jornal** *nm* day's wage.

**jornalero,-a** *nm & nf* day labourer.

**joroba** *nf (deformidad)* hump.

**jorobado,-a** *adj* hunchbacked.
▶ *nm & nf* hunchback.

**jorobar** *vt* **1** *fam (fastidiar)* to bother, annoy. **2** *fam (romper)* to smash up, break. **3** *fam (estropear)* to ruin, wreck.

**jota** *nf popular Spanish dance and music.*

**joven** *adj* young.
▶ *nm o nf (hombre)* youth, young man; *(mujer)* young lady, girl.

**jovial** *adj* jovial, cheerful.

**jovialidad** *nf* joviality, cheerfulness.

**joya** *nf* jewel, piece of jewellery.

**joyería** *nf (tienda)* jewellery shop, jeweller's shop.

**joyero,-a** *nm & nf* jeweller.
▶ *nm* joyero jewellery case.

**juanete** *nm (en el pie)* bunion.

**jubilación** *nf* **1** *(acción)* retirement. **2** *(dinero)* pension.

**jubilado,-a** *adj* retired.
▶ *nm o nf* pensioner, retired person.

**jubilar** *vt* **1** *(retirar)* to retire. **2** *(persona)* to pension off; *(objeto)* to get rid of.
▶ *vpr* jubilarse *(retirarse)* to retire.

**júbilo** *nm* jubilation, joy.

**jubiloso,-a** *adj* jubilant, joyful.

**jubón** *nm arc* doublet.

**judaico,-a** *adj* Judaic.

**judaísmo** *nm* Judaism.

**judería** *nf* Jewish quarter.

**judía** *nf (planta)* bean. COMP **judía verde** French bean, green bean.

**judicatura** *nf* **1** *(profesión)* judgeship. **2** *(cuerpo)* judiciary, judicature.

**judicial** *adj* judicial.

**judío,-a** *adj (gen)* Jewish.
▶ *nm & nf (persona)* Jew.

**judo** *nm* judo.

**judoca** *nm o nf* judoka.

**juego** *nm* **1** *(gen)* game; *(actividad deportiva)* sport. **2** *(con dinero)* gambling. **3** *(acción de jugar)* playing. **4** *(conjunto de piezas)* set: *un juego de llaves* a set of keys. COMP **juego de azar** game of chance. **juego de café/té** coffee/tea service.

**juerga** *nf fam* rave-up, bash.

**juerguista** *adj* fun-loving.
▶ *nm o nf* raver.

**jueves** *nm inv* Thursday: *todos los jueves* every Thursday; *el jueves que viene* next Thursday; *el jueves pasado* last Thursday; *el jueves por la mañana/tarde/noche* Thursday morning/afternoon/night.

**juez,-za** *nm & nf* judge. COMP **juez de línea** linesman. **juez de paz** justice of the peace.

**jugada** *nf* **1** *(en ajedrez)* move; *(en billar)* shot; *(en dardos)* throw. **2** *(momento del juego)* move, piece of play. **3** *fam* dirty trick.

**jugador,-ra** *nm & nf* **1** player. **2** *(apostador)* gambler.

**jugar** *vi* to play.
▶ *vt (intervenir)* to play, go: *¿quién juega?* whose go is it?
▶ *vpr* **jugarse 1** *(arriesgar)* to risk. **2** *(apostarse)* to bet: *¿cuánto te juegas a que no viene?* what's the betting he won't come?

**jugarreta** *nf fam* dirty trick.

**juglar** *nm* minstrel.

**jugo** *nm* **1** *(gen)* juice. **2** *(interés)* substance.

**jugoso,-a** *adj (fruta, carne)* juicy.

**juguete** *nm* **1** toy. **2** *fig* plaything.

**juguetear** *vi* to play (con, with).

**juguetería** *nf (tienda)* toy shop.

**juguetón,-ona** *adj* playful.

**juicio** *nm* **1** *(gen)* judgement: *a mi juicio* in my opinion. **2** *(sensatez)* reason, common sense. **3** JUR trial. LOC **en su sano juicio** in one's right mind. ‖ **llevar a ALGN a juicio** to take legal action against SB. ‖ **perder el juicio** to go mad.

**juicioso,-a** *adj (persona)* sensible, wise.

**juliana** *nf* damewort.

**julio**¹ *nm* July.

✎ Para ejemplos de uso, consulta marzo.

**julio**² *nm* FÍS joule.

**jumbo** *nm* jumbo jet.

**juncal** *nm* BOT reedbed.

**junco** *nm* BOT rush, reed.

**jungla** *nf* jungle.

**junio** *nm* June.

✎ Para ejemplos de uso, consulta marzo.

**júnior** *adj* DEP junior.

**junta** *nf (reunión)* meeting, assembly.

**juntar** *vt* **1** *(unir)* to put together; *(piezas)* to assemble. **2** *(reunir - dinero)* to raise; *(- gente)* to gather together.
▶ *vpr* **juntarse 1** *(unirse)* to join, get together; *(ríos, caminos)* to meet. **2** *(acercarse)* to squeeze up: *juntaos un poco que no quepo* squeeze up, I can't get in.

**junto,-a** *adj* together. LOC **junto a** next to. ‖ **junto con** along with, together with.

**jura** *nf (acción)* oath; *(ceremonia)* swearing-in, pledge.

**jurado,-a** *adj* sworn.
▶ *nm* **jurado** JUR *(tribunal)* jury; *(miembro del tribunal)* juror, member of the jury.

**juramentar** *vt* to swear in.

**juramento** *nm* **1** JUR oath. **2** *(blasfemia)* swearword.

**jurar** *vt* to swear, take an oath.
▶ *vi (blasfemar)* to curse, swear.

**jurásico,-a** *adj* Jurassic.

**jurel** *nm* scad, horse mackerel.

**jurídico,-a** *adj* legal, juridical.

**jurisdicción** *nf* jurisdiction.

**jurisprudencia** *nf* jurisprudence.

**jurista** *nm o nf* jurist, lawyer.

**justicia** *nf* **1** *(equidad, derecho)* justice, fairness. **2** **la justicia** *(organismo)* the law.

**justiciero,-a** *adj* avenging.

**justificable** *adj* justifiable.

**justificación** *nf* justification.

**justificante** *adj* justifying.
▶ *nm (prueba)* written proof.

**justificar** *vt* **1** *(acción)* to justify. **2** *(persona)* to excuse.
▶ *vpr* **justificarse** *(persona)* to justify os; *(acción)* to be justified.

**justo,-a** *adj* **1** *(persona, decisión)* just, fair. **2** *(ropa)* tight. **3** *(exacto)* exact: *tengo el dinero justo para el autobús* I have the exact money for the bus. **4** *(escaso)* just enough: *me queda lo justo para llegar a fin de mes* I have just enough money to get by.
▶ *adv* **justo** *(en el preciso momento)* just; *(en el preciso lugar)* right: *vivo justo en el centro de la ciudad* I live right in the centre of town.

**juvenil** *adj* **1** young, youthful. **2** DEP junior, youth.

**juventud** *nf* **1** *(período)* youth. **2** *(los jóvenes)* young people *pl*, youth *pl*.

**juzgado** *nm (local)* court. COMP **juzgado de guardia** court, police court.

**juzgar** *vt* **1** *(formar juicio)* to judge. **2** *(considerar)* to consider, think.

# K

**K, k** *nf (la letra)* K, k.

**kaki** *nm* **1** *(árbol)* persimmon tree. **2** *(fruta)* persimmon.

**Kampuchea** *nf* Kampuchea.

**kampucheo,-a** *adj* Kampuchean.
▶ *nm & nf* Kampuchean.

**karst** *nm* karst.

**kárstico,-a** *adj* karstic.

**kart®** *nm* go-kart, kart.

**karting** *nm* go-kart racing, karting.

**Kathmandu** *nm* Katmandu, Kathmandu.

**kayac** *nm* kayak.

**kazajio,-a** *adj* Kazakh.
▶ *nm & nf (persona)* Kazakh.
▶ *nm* **kazajio** *(idioma)* Kazakh.

**Kazajstán** *nm* Kazakhstan.

**Kenia** *nf* Kenya.

**keniano,-a** *adj* Kenyan.
▶ *nm & nf* Kenyan.

**keroseno** *nm* kerosene.

**Khartum** *nm* Khartoum.

**kilo** *nm* **1** kilogram. **2** *argot (antiguamente)* million pesetas.

**kilobyte** *nm* kilobyte.

**kilocaloría** *nf* kilocalorie.

**kilogramo** *nm* kilogram.

**kilohertz** *nm inv* kilohertz.

**kilolitro** *nm* kilolitre, US kiloliter.

**kilometraje** *nm* ≈ mileage.

**kilómetro** *nm* kilometre, US kilometer.

**kilowatt** *nm* kilowatt.

**kirguís** *adj* Kirghiz.
▶ *nm o nf (persona)* Kirghiz.
▶ *nm (idioma)* Kirghiz.

**Kirguizistán** *nm* Kirghizstan, Kirghizia.

**Kiribati** *nm* Kiribati.

**kiwi** *nm* **1** *(ave)* kiwi. **2** *(fruta)* kiwi, kiwi fruit.

**km/h** *abrev* (kilómetros hora) kilometres (US kilometers) per hour; *(abreviatura)* kph.

**knock-out** *nm* knockout.

**koala** *nm* koala.

**kurdo,-a** *adj* Kurdish.
▶ *nm & nf (persona)* Kurd.
▶ *nm* **kurdo** *(idioma)* Kurdish.

**Kuwait** *nm* Kuwait.

**kuwaití** *adj* Kuwaiti.
▶ *nm & nf* Kuwaiti.

**kW/h** *abrev* (kilovatios hora) kilowatts per hour; *(abreviatura)* kWh.

**L, l** *nf (la letra)* L, l.
**la¹** *art def* the: *la casa* the house.
**la²** *pron (persona)* her; *(cosa)* it: *la invité a cenar* I invited her to supper; *no la he leído* I haven't read it.

    ✎ Consulta también las.

**la³** *nm* MÚS la, lah, A.
**laberíntico,-a** *adj* labyrinthic.
**laberinto** *nm* labyrinth, maze.
**labial** *adj (gen)* labial.
   ▶ *nf* LING labial.
**labio** *nm* lip.
**labor** *nf* **1** *(gen)* work: *las labores del campo* farm work.

    ✎ Consulta también las.

**laborable** *adj (de trabajo)* working.
**laboral** *adj* labour.
**laboratorio** *nm* laboratory.
**laborioso,-a** *adj (trabajoso)* laborious.
**labrador,-ra** *nm & nf* farmer.
**labranza** *nf* farming.
**labrar** *vt* AGR *(campo)* to work; *(con arado)* to plough (US plow).
**labriego,-a** *nm & nf* farm worker.
**lacio,-a** *adj (cabello)* straight.
**lacón** *nm* ham.
**lacónico,-a** *adj* laconic.
**lacra** *nf* **1** *(señal)* mark, scar. **2** *(defecto)* fault.
**lacrado,-a** *adj (sobre)* sealed with wax.
**lacrar** *vt* to seal (with sealing wax).
**lacre** *nm* sealing wax.
**lacrimal** *adj* tear, lacrimal, lachrymal.
**lacrimoso,-a** *adj* tearful.
**lactancia** *nf* lactation.
**lactante** *nm o nf* unweaned baby.

**lácteo,-a** *adj* milk, milky. COMP **productos lácteos** dairy products.
**láctico,-a** *adj* lactic.
**lactosa** *nf* lactose.
**lacustre** *adj* lake.
**ladear** *vt* to tilt.
**ladeo** *nm* tilt.
**ladera** *nf* hillside.
**lado** *nm (gen)* side. LOC **al lado de** ALGN next to SB: *me puse a su lado* I sat next to her. ▪ **estar al lado** *(muy cerca)* to be very near. ▪ **por un lado... por otro...** on the one hand… on the other hand…
**ladrador,-ra** *adj* barking.
**ladrar** *vi* to bark.
**ladrido** *nm* bark.
**ladrillo** *nm* brick.
**ladrón,-ona** *nm & nf (persona - que roba)* thief; *(- que tima, engaña)* crook.
**lagartija** *nf* small lizard.
**lagarto,-a** *nm & nf (animal)* lizard.
**lago** *nm* lake.
**lágrima** *nf* tear. LOC **llorar a lágrima viva** *fam* to cry one's eyes out.
**lagrimal** *adj* tear, lachrymal.
   ▶ *nm* corner of the eye.
**lagrimear** *vi* to run, water.
**lagrimeo** *nm* watering.
**lagrimón** *nm* large teardrop, large tear.
**laguna** *nf* small lake, lagoon.
**laico,-a** *adj* lay, secular.
**laja** *nf* slab.
**lama¹** *nm* REL lama.
**lama²** *nf* **1** *(lámina)* slat. **2** *(barro)* slime.
**lamentable** *adj (injusticia)* regrettable, deplorable; *(estado)* sorry, pitiful.
**lamentar** *vt* to regret.
   ▶ *vpr* **lamentarse** to complain.

**lamento** *nm* moan, cry.

**lamer** *vt* to lick.

**lametazo** *nm* lick.

**lametón** *nm* lick.

**lámina** *nf* **1** *(gen)* sheet, plate. **2** *(ilustración)* illustration; *(grabado)* engraving.

**laminado,-a** *adj* laminated.

**laminar** *vt* to laminate.

**lámpara** *nf* lamp.

**lamparón** *nm fam* stain.

**lamprea** *nf* lamprey.

**lana** *nf* wool. LOC **de lana** woollen (US woolen).

**lanar** *adj* wool-bearing.

**lance** *nm* **1** *(suceso)* event. **2** *(pelea)* quarrel.

**lanceolado,-a** *adj* lanceolate.

**lancero** *nm* lancer.

**lanceta** *nf* lancet, lance.

**lancha** *nf (bote)* launch, boat. COMP **lancha salvavidas** lifeboat.

**landa** *nf* moor.

**lanero,-a** *adj* wool.

**langosta** *nf* **1** *(crustáceo)* crawfish, spiny lobster. **2** *(insecto)* locust.

**langostino** *nm type of* prawn.

**languidecer** *vi* to languish.

**languidez** *nf (falta de vigor)* languor.

**lánguido,-a** *adj (falto de vigor)* languid, languorous.

**lanilla** *nf (tejido)* flannel.

**lanza** *nf* lance, spear.

**lanzadera** *nf* shuttle.

**lanzado,-a** *adj (impetuoso)* impetuous; *(decidido)* determined.

**lanzador,-ra** *nm & nf (de jabalina)* thrower; *(de béisbol)* pitcher; *(de cricket)* bowler.

**lanzamiento** *nm* **1** *(acción de lanzar)* throwing. **2** *(de cohete)* launching. COMP **lanzamiento de peso** shot put.

**lanzar** *vt* **1** *(gen)* to throw. **2** *(cohete)* to launch. **3** *fig (grito)* to let out.
▶ *vpr* **lanzarse** *(actuar decididamente)* to throw os, launch os into.

**Laos** *nm* Laos.

**laosiano,-a** *adj* Laotian.
▶ *nm & nf (persona)* Laotian.
▶ *nm* **laosiano** *(idioma)* Laotian.

**lapa** *nf (molusco)* limpet.

**laparoscopia** *nf* laparoscopy.

**lapicero** *nm* pencil.

**lápida** *nf* tombstone, slab.

**lápiz** *nm* pencil. COMP **lápiz de ojos** eyeliner. ▌**lápiz óptico** light pen.

**lapso** *nm (de tiempo)* period of time.

**lapsus** *nm inv (error)* slip; *(de memoria)* memory lapse, lapse of memory.

**laquear** *vt* to lacquer.

**largar** *vt* **1** *fam (dar)* to give: *le largó un discurso de media hora* he gave him a half-hour speech. **2** *fam (contar)* to tell: *esa lo larga todo* she can't keep anything to herself.
▶ *vpr* **largarse** *fam (irse)* to go, leave: *me largo* I'm off, US I'm out of here.

**largo,-a** *adj (en longitud)* long. LOC **a lo largo de** along, throughout: *a lo largo del año* throughout the year. ▌**dar largas a** ALGN to put SB off. ▌**pasar de largo** to pass by.
▶ *nm* **largo 1** length: *¿qué mide de largo?* how long is it?, what length is it? **2** *(de piscina)* length, US lap.

**largometraje** *nm* feature film.

**larguero** *nm (en fútbol)* crossbar.

**larguirucho,-a** *adj fam* lanky.

**largura** *nf* length.

**laringe** *nf* larynx.

**laríngeo,-a** *adj* laryngeal.

**laringitis** *nf inv* laryngitis.

**laringología** *nf* laryngology.

**laringólogo,-a** *nm & nf* laryngologist.

**larva** *nf* larva.

**larvario,-a** *adj* larval.

**las** *art def* the: *las casas* the houses.
▶ *pron (objeto directo)* them: *las vi* I saw them.

🖎 Consulta también **la**.

**lasca** *nf* chip.

**láser** *nm inv* laser.

**lasitud** *nf* lassitude, weariness.

**lástima** *nf* pity.

**lastimar** *vt (herir)* to hurt, injure.
▶ *vpr* **lastimarse** to hurt os.

**lastimero,-a** *adj* pitiful.

**lastimoso,-a** *adj* pitiful, sorry.

**lastrar** vt MAR to ballast.

**lastre** nm MAR ballast.

**lata** nf **1** (hojalata) tin plate. **2** (envase) tin, can. **3** (fastidio) bore, drag, pain: *es una lata tener que estudiar los fines de semana* it's a pain having to study at weekends.

**latente** adj latent.

**lateral** adj (gen) side.

**látex** nm inv latex.

**latido** nm beat.

**latifundio** nm (finca) latifundium.

**latigazo** nm lash.

**látigo** nm whip.

**latín** nm Latin.

**latino,-a** adj Latin.
 ► nm & nf Latin.

**Latinoamérica** nf Latin America.

**latinoamericano,-a** adj Latin American.
 ► nm & nf Latin American.

**latir** vi to beat.

**latitud** nf latitude.

**latitudinal** adj latitudinal.

**latón** nm brass.

**latoso,-a** adj fam annoying, boring.

**laúd** nm lute.

**laudatorio,-a** adj laudatory.

**laureada** nf MIL (insignia) decoration.

**laureado,-a** adj prizewinning.

**laurear** vt **1** to award a prize to. **2** (militar) to decorate.

**laurel** nm (árbol) bay.

**lava** nf lava.

**lavable** adj washable.

**lavabo** nm **1** (pila) washbasin. **2** (cuarto de baño) washroom. **3** (público) toilet.

**lavada** nf big wash.

**lavadero** nm **1** (en casa) laundry room. **2** (público) public washing place.

**lavado** nm wash.

**lavadora** nf washing machine.

**lavafrutas** nm inv finger bowl.

**lavamanos** nm inv washbasin.

**lavanda** nf lavender.

**lavandería** nf (automática) launderette, US laundromat; (con servicio) laundry.

**lavaplatos** nm inv dishwasher.

**lavar** vt **1** (ropa, cuerpo, etc) to wash. **2** (platos) to wash up.
 ► vpr **lavarse** to wash os.

**lavativa** nf enema.

**lavavajillas** nm inv dishwasher.

**laxante** nm laxative.

**laxitud** nf laxity, laxness.

**laxo,-a** adj (sin tensión) slack.

**lazada** nf **1** (nudo) knot. **2** (lazo) bow.

**lazar** vt to lasso.

**lazarillo** nm guide. COMP **perro lazarillo** guide dog.

**lazo** nm **1** (cinta) ribbon; (de adorno) bow. **2** fig (vínculo) tie, bond.

**le** pron **1** (objeto directo) him; (usted) you: *¿quién le sirvió?* who served you? **2** (objeto indirecto - a él) him; (- a ella) her; (- a usted) you: *le regalaron un perrito* they gave him a puppy; *le repito la pregunta* I'll repeat the question for you.

✎ Consulta también les y leísmo.

**leal** adj **1** loyal, faithful. **2** (justo) fair.

**lealtad** nf loyalty, faithfulness.

**lebrel** nm greyhound.

**lebrillo** nm bowl.

**lección** nf lesson. LOC **dar una lección a** ALGN fig to teach SB a lesson.

**lechada** nf whitewash.

**lechal** adj sucking.

**lechazo** nm (cordero) sucking lamb.

**leche** nf milk. COMP **leche desnatada** skimmed milk.

**lechera** nf (recipiente) milk churn.

**lechería** nf dairy.

**lechero,-a** nm milkman, dairyman.

**lecho** nm (gen) bed; (de un río) river bed.

**lechón** nm (animal) piglet.

**lechuga** nf lettuce.

**lechuza** nf owl.

**lectivo,-a** adj school.

**lector,-ra** nm & nf reader. COMP **lector óptico** optical scanner.

**leer** vt (gen) to read.
 ► vi to read.

**legado,-a** nm **1** (herencia) legacy, bequest. **2** (persona) legate.

**legajo** nm dossier.

**legal** *adj (gen)* legal.

**legalidad** *nf (de una acción, etc)* legality.

**legalista** *adj* legalistic.

**legalización** *nf* **1** *(de una situación)* legalization. **2** *(de documento)* to authenticate.

**legalizar** *vt* **1** *(situación)* to legalize. **2** *(documento)* to authenticate.

**legaña** *nf* sleep.

**legar** *vt* to bequeath.

**legendario,-a** *adj* legendary.

**legibilidad** *nf* legibility.

**legible** *adj* legible.

**legión** *nf* MIL legion.

**legionario,-a** *nm* legionary.

**legislación** *nf* legislation.

**legislador,-ra** *adj* legislative.

**legislar** *vi* to legislate.

**legislativo,-a** *adj* legislative.

**legislatura** *nf (período)* term of office.

**legitimación** *nf* legitimization.

**legitimar** *vt* to legitimate.

**legitimidad** *nf* legitimacy.

**legítimo,-a** *adj (genuino)* real, authentic.

**legua** *nf (medida)* league.

**legumbre** *nf* **1** *(planta)* legume. **2** *(fruto)* pulse.

**leguminoso,-a** *nf pl* leguminous plants.

**leído,-a** *adj* well-read.

**leísmo** *nm incorrect use of* le *and* les *as direct object instead of* lo *and* los.

**leísta** *adj given to* leísmo.
▶ *nm o nf person who is given to* leísmo.

**lejanía** *nf* distance.

**lejano,-a** *adj (tierra, país)* distant.

**lejía** *nf* bleach.

**lejos** *adv* far, far away, far off. [LOC] **a lo lejos** in the distance, far away. ‖ **de lejos** from a distance.

**lelo,-a** *adj fam* gormless, stupid.

**lema** *nm (gen)* motto; *(en publicidad)* slogan.

**lencería** *nf (ropa interior)* lingerie.

**lengua** *nf* **1** ANAT tongue. **2** *(idioma)* language. [LOC] **irse de la lengua** *fam* to let the cat out of the bag. ‖ **tener** ALGO **en la punta de la lengua** *fig* to have STH on the tip of one's tongue. ‖ [COMP] **lengua materna** mother tongue.

**lenguado** *nm* sole.

**lenguaje** *nm* **1** *(gen)* language. **2** *(habla)* speech.

**lenguaraz** *adj (hablador)* garrulous.

**lengüeta** *nf (de zapato)* tongue.

**lente** *nm & nf* lens.
▶ *nm pl* **lentes** lenses. [COMP] **lentes de contacto** contact lenses.

**lenteja** *nf* lentil.

**lentejuela** *nf* sequin.

**lentilla** *nf* contact lens.

**lentitud** *nf* slowness.

**lento,-a** *adj* slow.
▶ *adv* **lento** slowly.

**leña** *nf* wood, firewood.

**leñador,-ra** *nm & nf* woodcutter.

**leñera** *nf* woodshed.

**leño** *nm* log.

**leñoso,-a** *adj* ligneous, woody.

**león,-ona** *nm & nf (animal - macho)* lion; *(- hembra)* lioness. [COMP] **león marino** sea lion.

**leonera** *nf* lion's den.

**leonino,-a** *adj* **1** *(de león)* lion-like.

**leopardo** *nm* leopard.

**leotardos** *nm pl* thick woollen tights.

**lepra** *nf* leprosy.

**leproso,-a** *adj* leprous.

**lerdo,-a** *adj fam* slow-witted.

**les** *pron* **1** *(objeto directo)* them; *(ustedes)* you: *dice que les vio ayer* she says she saw them yesterday; *no les entiendo* I don't understand you. **2** *(objeto indirecto)* them; *(a ustedes)* you: *entraron en casa ladrones y les robaron* burglars broke in and robbed them; *les doy una oportunidad más* I'll give you one more chance.

✎ Consulta también le.

**lesión** *nf (daño físico)* wound, injury.

**lesionado,-a** *adj* injured.

**lesionar** *vt (herir)* to injure.
▶ *vpr* **lesionarse** to get injured.

**lesivo,-a** *adj* damaging, injurious.

**Lesotho** *nm* Lesotho.

**letal** *adj* lethal, deadly.

L

**letanía** *nf fam (lista)* long list.
**letargo** *nm* lethargy.
**letón,-ona** *adj* Latvian.
 ▶ *nm & nf (persona)* Latvian.
 ▶ *nm* letón *(idioma)* Latvian.
**Letonia** *nf* Latvia.
**letra** *nf* **1** *(del alfabeto)* letter. **2** *(de imprenta)* character. **3** *(escritura)* handwriting. **4** *(de canción)* lyrics *pl*, words *pl*. COMP **letra de imprenta** block capitals *pl*. ‖ **letra mayúscula** capital letter.
**letrado,-a** *nm & nf* lawyer.
**letrero** *nm* sign, notice.
**letrina** *nf* latrine.
**leucemia** *nf* leukaemia, US leukemia.
**leucocito** *nm* white blood cell.
**leva** *nf* MIL levy.
**levadizo,-a** *adj* which can be raised.
**levadura** *nf* yeast.
**levantamiento** *nm (de objeto, etc)* lifting.
**levantar** *vt (alzar)* to raise, lift: *no lo puedo levantar, pesa mucho* I can't lift it, it's heavy. LOC **levantar la vista** to look up.
 ▶ *vpr* **levantarse 1** *(alzarse)* to rise. **2** *(ponerse de pie)* to stand up. **3** *(dejar la cama)* get out of bed. **4** *(viento)* to get up.
**levante** *nm (este)* East.
**levar** *vt (ancla)* to weigh.
**leve** *adj* **1** slight, light.
**levedad** *nf* lightness, insignificance.
**levitar** *vi* to levitate.
**léxico,-a** *adj* lexical.
**lexicón** *nm (diccionario)* lexicon.
**ley** *nf* law.
**leyenda** *nf (narración)* legend.
**lezna** *nf* awl.
**liado,-a** *adj (ocupado)* busy.
**liana** *nf* liana.
**liar** *vt* **1** *(atar)* to tie up, bind; *(envolver)* to wrap up. **2** *fam (complicar)* to mix up, make a mess of; *(confundir)* to confuse: *cuéntale la verdad y no lo líes más* tell him the truth and stop messing him about.
 ▶ *vpr* **liarse a + *sustantivo*** to start + *ger*: *se liaron a discutir* they started arguing.
**libanés,-esa** *adj* Lebanese.
 ▶ *nm & nf* Lebanese.
**Líbano** *nm* el Líbano the Lebanon.

**libar** *vt (néctar)* to suck.
**libélula** *nf* dragonfly.
**liberación** *nf (de una persona)* release.
**liberado,-a** *adj* liberated.
**liberador,-ra** *adj* liberating.
**liberal** *adj* liberal.
 ▶ *nm o nf* liberal.
**liberalismo** *nm* liberalism.
**liberalización** *nf* liberalization.
**liberar** *vt* to free.
**Liberia** *nf* Liberia.
**liberiano,-a** *adj* Liberian.
 ▶ *nm & nf* Liberian.
**libertad** *nf (gen)* freedom, liberty. LOC **poner en libertad** to free, release. COMP **libertad de expresión** freedom of expression.
**libertar** *vt* to liberate.
**libertario,-a** *adj* libertarian.
**Libia** *nf* Libya.
**libio,-a** *adj* Libyan.
 ▶ *nm & nf* Libyan.
**libra** *nf (moneda, medida)* pound. COMP **libra esterlina** pound sterling.
**librar** *vt* to save (de, from): *me libraron de toda responsabilidad* they absolved me of all responsibility.
 ▶ *vi fam (tener libre)* to be off: *libro todos los lunes* I've got Mondays off.
 ▶ *vpr* **librarse** to escape (de, from).
**libre** *adj (gen)* free. COMP **entrada libre** free admittance.
**librecambio** *nm* free trade.
**librería** *nf (tienda)* bookshop.
**librero,-a** *nm & nf* bookseller.
**libreta** *nf (para anotar)* notebook.
**libreto** *nm* libretto.
**libro** *nm (gen)* book. COMP **libro de bolsillo** paperback. ‖ **libro de consulta** reference book. ‖ **libro de texto** textbook.
**licencia** *nf (permiso)* licence.
**licenciado,-a** *nm & nf* EDUC graduate.
**licenciar** *vt* EDUC to award a degree to.
 ▶ *vpr* **licenciarse** to graduate.
**licenciatura** *nf* university degree.
**liceo** *nm (colegio)* secondary school.
**lícito,-a** *adj* **1** *(legal)* licit. **2** *(justo)* fair.

**licor** *nm (dulce)* liqueur; *(bebida alcohólica)* liquor, spirits *pl*.

**licuadora** *nf* juice extractor.

**licuar** *vt* to liquefy.

**lid** *nf fig (controversia)* dispute.

**líder** *nm o nf* leader.

**liderar** *vt* to lead.

**liderazgo** *nm* leadership.

**lidia** *nf (de toros)* bullfight.

**liebre** *nf (animal)* hare.

**Liechtenstein** *nm* Liechtenstein.

**lienzo** *nm* ARTE *(tela)* canvas.

**liga** *nf* 1 *(asociación)* league, alliance. 2 DEP league.

**ligadura** *nf (atadura)* tie, bond.

**ligamento** *nm* ligament.

**ligar** *vt* 1 *(atar)* to tie, bind. 2 *(unir)* to link, connect.

**ligero,-a** *adj* 1 *(liviano)* light. 2 *(sin importancia)* minor, light.

**lignito** *nm* lignite.

**lija** *nf (papel)* sandpaper.

**lijar** *vt* to sand.

**lila** *adj (color)* lilac.
▶ *nf (flor)* lilac.

**lima** *nf* 1 *(herramienta)* file; *(para uñas)* nail file. 2 *(fruta)* lime; *(árbol)* lime tree.

**limar** *vt (pulir)* to file.

**limitación** *nf* limitation.

**limitado,-a** *adj* limited.

**limitar** *vt (gen)* to limit.
▶ *vi* **limitar con** to border with. LOC **limitarse a + *inf*** to restrict os to + *ger*, do no more than + *inf*: *una persona inteligente no se limita a ver la televisión* an intelligent person does not restrict himself to watching television.

**límite** *nm* 1 *(extremo)* limit. 2 *(frontera)* boundary. COMP **límite de velocidad** speed limit.

**limítrofe** *adj* bordering.

**limo** *nm* slime.

**limón** *nm* lemon.

**limonada** *nf* lemonade.

**limonero** *nm* lemon tree.

**limonita** *nf* limonite.

**limosna** *nf* alms *pl*, charity. LOC **pedir limosna** to beg.

**limpiabotas** *nm inv* bootblack.

**limpiacristales** *nm inv (producto)* window cleaning fluid.

**limpiador,-ra** *adj* cleaning.
▶ *nm & nf (persona)* cleaner.

**limpiamente** *adv* cleanly.

**limpiaparabrisas** *nm inv* windscreen wiper, US windshield wiper.

**limpiar** *vt (gen)* to clean, cleanse.

**limpieza** *nf (acción de limpiar)* cleaning.

**limpio,-a** *adj (sin suciedad)* clean.
▶ *adv* fairly: *no juegan limpio, hacen trampa* they don't play fair, they cheat.

**linaje** *nm (ascendencia)* lineage.

**linaza** *nf* linseed.

**lince** *nm* ZOOL lynx.

**linchar** *vt* to lynch.

**lindar** *vi* to border (**con**, on), adjoin (**con**, -).

**linde** *nm & nf* boundary.

**lindo,-a** *adj* pretty, nice, lovely.

**línea** *nf (gen)* line. COMP **línea aérea** airline. ‖ **línea recta** straight line.

**lineal** *adj* linear.

**linfático,-a** *adj* lymphatic.

**lingote** *nm* ingot.

**lingüística** *nf* linguistics.

**lino** *nm* 1 *(tela)* linen. 2 BOT flax.

**linterna** *nf (de pilas)* torch.

**lío** *nm (embrollo)* mess. LOC **hacerse un lío** 1 *(uso literal)* to get tangled up. 2 *(uso figurado)* to get muddled up.

**lípido** *nm* lipid.

**lipotimia** *nf* blackout.

**liquen** *nm* lichen.

**liquidación** *nf (venta)* sale.

**liquidar** *vt* 1 *(deuda)* to settle, liquidate. 2 *(mercancías)* to sell off.

**líquido,-a** *adj* liquid.

**lira** *nf* 1 MÚS lyre. 2 *(moneda)* lira.

**lírica** *nf* poetry, lyric poetry.

**lirio** *nm* lily.

**lirón** *nm* dormouse. LOC **dormir como un lirón** to sleep like a log.

**lis** *nf (planta)* lily.

**liso,-a** *adj* 1 smooth. 2 *(pelo)* straight.

**lista** *nf (relación)* list.

**listo,-a** *adj* **1** *(inteligente)* clever, smart. **2** *(preparado)* ready: *¿estás lista?* are you ready?

**litera** *nf* bunk bed; *(tren)* couchette.

**literal** *adj* literal.

**literario,-a** *adj* literary.

**literatura** *nf* literature.

**litigar** *vi* *(disputar)* to argue, dispute.

**litigio** *nm* *(disputa)* dispute.

**litio** *nm* lithium.

**litoral** *nm* coast.

**litosfera** *nf* lithosphere.

**litro** *nm* litre, US liter.

**Lituania** *nf* Lithuania.

**lituano,-a** *adj* Lithuanian.
  ▶ *nm & nf (persona)* Lithuanian.
  ▶ *nm* lituano *(idioma)* Lithuanian.

**liviano,-a** *adj (ligero)* light.

**lívido,-a** *adj* livid.

**llaga** *nf (gen)* sore; *(en la boca)* ulcer.

**llagar** *vt* to cover with ulcers.

**llama** *nf* **1** *(de fuego)* flame. **2** ZOOL llama.

**llamada** *nf (gen)* call.

**llamamiento** *nm (convocatoria)* call.

**llamar** *vt* **1** *(gen)* to call. **2** *(dar nombre)* to name. **3** *(atraer)* to appeal to. LOC llamar por teléfono to call, phone, GB ring, ring up.
  ▶ *vi (a la puerta)* to knock; *(al timbre)* to ring; *(al teléfono)* to ring, call, phone.
  ▶ *vpr* llamarse *(tener nombre)* to be called.

**llamativo,-a** *adj* showy, flashy.

**llamear** *vi* to blaze.

**llano,-a** *adj* **1** *(plano)* flat. **2** *(sencillo)* simple.
  ▶ *nm* llano *(llanura)* plain.

**llanta** *nf* wheel rim, rim.

**llanto** *nm* crying, weeping.

**llanura** *nf (llano)* plain.

**llave** *nf (de puerta, etc)* key.

**llavero** *nm* key ring.

**llegada** *nf* **1** arrival. **2** DEP finishing line.

**llegar** *vi* **1** to arrive (a, at/in), get (a, at), reach (a, -): *llegó el primero* he arrived first. **3** *(alcanzar)* to reach: *¿llegas a ese estante?* can you reach that shelf? **4** *(ser suficiente)* to be enough, suffice:

*¿te llega con diez euros?* is ten euros enough? **5** *(cantidad)* to amount (a, to). **6** llegar a + *inf (uso enfático)*: *llegó a llamarme tonto* he even called me a silly.

**llenar** *vt* **1** *(espacio, recipiente)* to fill. **2** *(formulario)* to fill in. **3** *(tiempo)* to fill, occupy. **4** llenar de *(alegría)* to fill with.
  ▶ *vpr* llenarse **1** *(gen)* to fill. **2** *(de gente)* to fill up.

**lleno,-a** *adj* **1** full (de, of): *está lleno de gente* it's full of people. **2** *(cubierto)* covered (de, with).

**llevadero,-a** *adj* bearable.

**llevar** *vt* **1** *(gen)* to take: *llévale esto a tu abuela* take this to your granny. **2** *(tener)* to have; *(tener encima)* to have, carry: *¿qué llevas ahí?* what's that you've got there? **3** *(prenda)* to wear, have on: *no me gusta llevar sombrero* I don't like wearing a hat. **4** *(aguantar)* to cope with. **5** *(dirigir)* to be in charge of: *¿quién lleva los pedidos?* who's in charge of orders? **6** *(conducir - coche)* to drive: *lleva un Seat azul* he drives a blue Seat. **7** *(años)* to be older: *te llevo tres años* I'm three years older than you.
  ▶ *vi* **1** llevar a *(conducir)* to take, lead: *esta senda lleva a la cima* this path takes you to the summit. **2** llevar a + *inf (inducir)* to lead to, make: *esto me lleva a pensar que...* this leads me to think that...
  ▶ *vpr* llevarse **1** *(obtener)* to get; *(ganar)* to win: *los rusos se llevaron todas las medallas* the Russians won all the medals. **2** *(recibir)* to get: *se llevó un buen susto* he got quite a shock. **3** *(estar de moda)* to be fashionable: *este color ya no se lleva* this colour is not fashionable any more. **4** *(entenderse)* to get on (con, with), get along (con, with): *se lleva bien con sus padres* he gets on well with his parents. **5** MAT to carry over.

**llorar** *vi* to cry, weep.
  ▶ *vt* to mourn.

**llorón,-ona** *nm & nf fam* crybaby.

**lloroso,-a** *adj* tearful, weeping.

**llover** *vi* [se usa sólo en tercera persona; no lleva sujeto] to rain: *llueve* it's raining.

**lloviznar** *vi* [se usa sólo en tercera persona; no lleva sujeto] to drizzle.

**lluvia** *nf* **1** rain. **2** *fig* shower, barrage.

**lo** *art neut* the: *dime lo que quieres* tell me what you want. LOC **lo que** what.
▶ *pron* **1** *(objeto directo - él)* him; *(- usted)* you: *no lo conozco de nada* I don't know him from Adam. **2** *(objeto directo - cosa, animal)* it: *¿lo has probado?* have you tried it?

**loar** *vt* to praise, extol.

**lobezno,-a** *nm & nf* ZOOL wolf cub.

**lobo,-a** *nm & nf (macho)* wolf; *(hembra)* she-wolf.

**lóbulo** *nm* lobe.

**local** *adj* local.
▶ *nm (para negocio)* premises *pl*.

**localidad** *nf* **1** *(ciudad)* town. **2** TEAT *(asiento)* seat; *(billete)* ticket.

**localizar** *vt* **1** *(encontrar)* to locate, find. **2** *(infección, incendio)* to localize.

**locativo,-a** *adj* locative.

**loción** *nf* lotion.

**loco,-a** *adj (gen)* mad, crazy, insane.
▶ *nm & nf* lunatic.

**locomoción** *nf* locomotion.

**locomotor,-ra** *adj* locomotive.

**locomotora** *nf* locomotive.

**locución** *nf* phrase, locution.

**locura** *nf (perturbación)* madness.

**locutor,-ra** *nm & nf* announcer.

**locutorio** *nm* telephone booth.

**lodo** *nm* mud.

**logarítmico,-a** *adj* logarithmic.

**logaritmo** *nm* logarithm.

**lógica** *nf* logic.

**lógico,-a** *adj* **1** *(de la lógica)* logical. **2** *(natural)* normal, to be expected.

**logística** *nf* logistics.

**logopeda** *nm o nf* speech therapist.

**logotipo** *nm* logo, logotype.

**logrado,-a** *adj (conseguido)* successful.

**lograr** *vt (conseguir)* to get, achieve.

**logro** *nm (éxito)* achievement.

**loísmo** *nm incorrect use of* lo *and* los *as indirect objects instead of* le *and* les.

**loma** *nf* hill.

**lombriz** *nf (intestinal)* worm.

**lomo** *nm* **1** CULIN *(de cerdo)* loin; *(de ternera)* sirloin. **2** ANAT back.

**lona** *nf* canvas.

**loncha** *nf (de jamón, queso, etc)* slice.

**londinense** *adj* of London.
▶ *nm o nf* Londoner.

**Londres** *nm* London.

**longaniza** *nf* cured pork sausage.

**longitud** *nf* **1** length. **2** GEOG longitude.

**lonja** *nf (mercado)* exchange, market.

**lontananza** *nf (fondo)* background.

**loor** *nm lit* praise.

**lord** *nm* lord.

**loriga** *nf* HIST cuirass.

**loro** *nm (pájaro)* parrot.

**los** *art def* the: *los niños* the boys.
▶ *pron (objeto directo)* them; *(ustedes)* you: *los vi* I saw them; *a ustedes dos no los quiero volver a ver* I don't want to see you two again.

✎ Consulta también **lo, el.**

**losa** *nf* flagstone, slab.

**loseta** *nf* floor tile.

**lotería** *nf* lottery.

**loto** *nm (flor)* lotus.

**loza** *nf (cerámica)* china.

**lozanía** *nf (de persona)* healthiness.

**lozano,-a** *adj* **1** *(persona)* healthy, lusty. **2** *(planta)* fresh.

**lubina** *nf* bass.

**lubricante** *nm* lubricant.

**lubricar** *vt* to lubricate.

**lucerna** *nf* skylight.

**lucero** *nm* bright star.

**lucha** *nf* **1** *(gen)* fight, struggle. **2** DEP wrestling. COMP **lucha libre** free-style wrestling.

**luchador,-ra** *nm & nf* **1** *(gen)* fighter. **2** DEP wrestler.

**luchar** *vi* **1** to fight. **2** DEP to wrestle.

**lucidez** *nf* lucidity.

**lucido,-a** *adj* beautiful.

**lúcido,-a** *adj* lucid, clear-headed.

**luciérnaga** *nf* glow-worm.

**lucífero,-a** *adj lit* resplendent.

**lucimiento** *nm* showing off.

**lucio** *nm* pike.

**lución** *nm* slowworm.

**lucir** *vt (mostrar)* to show, display; *(ropa)* to wear, sport.
▶ *vpr* **lucirse** *(sobresalir)* to be brilliant.

**lucrarse** *vpr* to make a profit.

**lucrativo,-a** *adj* lucrative, profitable.

**lucro** *nm* gain, profit.

**luctuoso,-a** *adj lit* mournful, sorrowful.

**lúdico,-a** *adj* recreational.

**ludópata** *nm o nf* compulsive gambler.

**ludopatía** *nf* compulsive gambling.

**luego** *adv* **1** *(después)* then, afterwards, next. **2** *(más tarde)* later.
▶ *conj* so, therefore.

**lugar** *nm* **1** *(sitio, ciudad)* place. **2** *(posición, situación)* place, position: *llegó en quinto lugar* he finished in fifth place. **3** *(espacio)* room, space: *ya no hay lugar para más muebles* there's no room for any more furniture. LOC **en lugar de** instead of.

**lugareño,-a** *adj* local.
▶ *nm & nf* local.

**lugarteniente** *nm* deputy.

**lúgubre** *adj (triste)* bleak, lugubrious.

**lujo** *nm* luxury.

**lujosamente** *adv* luxuriously.

**lujoso,-a** *adj* luxurious.

**lumbago** *nm* lumbago.

**lumbar** *adj* lumbar.

**lumbre** *nf (fuego)* fire.

**lumbrera** *nf (persona)* genius, luminary.

**luminaria** *nf (en fiestas)* light.

**lumínico,-a** *adj* light.

**luminiscencia** *nf* luminiscence.

**luminiscente** *adj* luminiscent.

**luminosidad** *nf* luminosity.

**luminoso,-a** *adj* bright, luminous.

**luminotecnia** *nf* lighting.

**luminotécnico,-a** *adj* lighting.

**luna** *nf* **1** *(satélite)* moon. **2** *(cristal)* window pane; *(de ventana)* glass. **3** *(espejo)* mirror. COMP **luna llena** full moon. ❙ **luna de miel** honey moon.

**lunación** *nf* lunation.

**lunar** *adj* lunar, moon: *las fases lunares* the phases of the moon.
▶ *nm (en la piel)* beauty spot. LOC **de lunares** spotted.

**lunático,-a** *nm & nf* lunatic.

**lunes** *nm inv* Monday.

✎ Consulta también **jueves**.

**luneta** *nf car* window. COMP **luneta térmica** heated rear windscreen.

**lúnula** *nf* half-moon, lunule.

**lupa** *nf* magnifying glass. LOC **con lupa** meticulously.

**lúpulo** *nm* hop.

**lustrabotas** *nm o nf* bootblack.

**lustrar** *vt* to polish.

**lustre** *nm (brillo)* polish, shine, lustre, US luster.

**lustro** *nm* five years *pl*.

**lustroso,-a** *adj* shiny.

**luto** *nm* **1** mourning. **2** *fig* grief.

**luxación** *nf* dislocation.

**Luxemburgo** *nm* Luxembourg.

**luxemburgués,-esa** *adj* of Luxembourg, from Luxembourg.
▶ *nm & nf* Luxembourger.

**luz** *nf* **1** *(gen)* light. **2** *fam (electricidad)* electricity. **3** *(iluminación)* lighting. LOC **dar a luz** to give birth. ❙ **salir a la luz** to come out. COMP **luces de posición** sidelights. ❙ **luz del sol** sunlight.

**M, m** *nf (la letra)* M, m.

**m¹** *sím* (metro) metre (US meter); *(símbolo)* m.

**m²** *sím* (milla) mile; *(símbolo)* m.

**m³** *abrev* (minuto) minute; *(abreviatura)* min.

**maca** *nf (en fruta)* bruise.

**macabro,-a** *adj* macabre.

**macaco,-a** *nm & nf* ZOOL macaque.

**macarrón** *nm (pasta italiana)* piece of macaroni.
▶ *nm pl* **macarrones** macaroni.

**macedonia** *nf* fruit salad. ⬚COMP⬚ **macedonia de frutas** fruit salad.

**maceración** *nf (remojo - de fruta)* maceration, soaking; *(- de carne, pescado)* marinading.

**macerar** *vt (poner en remojo - fruta)* to macerate, soak; *(- carne, pescado)* to marinade.

**maceta** *nf* flowerpot.

**macetero** *nm* flowerpot holder.

**macha** *adj (almeja)* type of clam.

**machacar** *vt* **1** *(triturar)* to crush. **2** *fam (vencer)* to hammer, thrash. **3** *fam (insistir en)* to harp on about, go on about.
▶ *vi* **1** *(estudiar)* to swot up, cram, US grind. **2** *(insistir en)* to go on (con, about), harp on (con, about).

**machacón,-ona** *adj fam* insistent, repetitive.

**machaque** *nm* beating.

**machetazo** *nm* blow with a machete.

**machete** *nm* machete.

**machihembrado,-a** *nm* tongue and groove joint.

**machismo** *nm* male chauvinism.

**machista** *adj* male chauvinist.

**macho** *adj* **1** *(animal, planta)* male. **2** *(persona)* macho, tough.
▶ *nm* **1** *(animal, planta)* male. **2** *fam (hombre)* macho man, tough guy.

**macilento,-a** *adj* wan, pallid.

**macizo,-a** *adj* solid.
▶ *nm* **macizo** *(montañoso)* massif, mountain mass.

**macro** *nf* INFORM macro.

**macrocefalia** *nf* macrocephaly..

**macrocosmos** *nm inv* macrocosm.

**macroeconomía** *nf* macroeconomics.

**macroeconómico,-a** *adj* macroeconomic.

**macroscópico,-a** *adj* macroscopic.

**mácula** *nf lit* blemish.

**macuto** *nm* knapsack, rucksack.

**Madagascar** *nm* Madagascar.

**madeja** *nf (de lana)* skein, hank.

**madera** *nf (en el árbol)* wood; *(cortada)* timber, US lumber: *es de madera* it's made of wood, it's wooden.

**maderero,-a** *adj (industria)* timber.

**madero** *nm* piece of timber.

**madona** *nf* Madonna.

**madrastra** *nf* stepmother.

**madraza** *nf fam* doting mother.

**madre** *nf* mother. ⬚COMP⬚ **madre soltera** single mother.

**madreselva** *nf* honeysuckle.

**madrigal** *nm* madrigal.

**madriguera** *nf (de conejo)* burrow, warren; *(de zorro)* den, lair.

**madrina** *nf* godmother.

**madroño** *nm* strawberry tree.

**madrugada** *nf (después de medianoche)* early morning: *a las cinco de la madrugada* at five o'clock in the morning.

**madrugador,-ra** *nm & nf* early riser.
**madrugar** *vi (levantarse pronto)* to get up early.
**madrugón** LOC pegarse un madrugón *fam* to get up at the crack of dawn.
**madurar** *vi* 1 *(fruto)* to ripen. 2 *(persona)* to mature.
▶ *vt* 1 *(fruto)* to ripen. 2 *(plan, proyecto)* to think about carefully.
**madurez** *nf (de la persona)* maturity.
**maduro,-a** *adj* 1 *(persona)* mature. 2 *(fruta)* ripe.
**maestre** *nm* HIST master.
**maestría** *nf (destreza)* mastery, skill.
**maestro,-a** *adj (principal)* master; *(pared, viga)* main, supporting.
▶ *nm & nf* 1 *(de primaria - hombre)* schoolmaster; *(- mujer)* schoolmistress. 2 *(instructor)* teacher. COMP **maestro de escuela** schoolteacher.
**magacín** *nm (revista)* magazine.
**magdalena** *nf* small sponge cake.
**magenta** *nf* magenta.
**magia** *nf* magic.
**mágico,-a** *adj (pócima, palabra)* magic.
**magisterio** *nm (profesión)* teaching profession.
**magistrado,-a** *nm & nf (juez)* judge.
**magistral** *adj* masterly, masterful.
**magistratura** *nf (cuerpo)* judges *pl.*
**magma** *nf* magma.
**magnanimidad** *nf* magnanimity.
**magnánimo,-a** *adj* magnanimous.
**magnate** *nm* tycoon, magnate.
**magnesio** *nm* magnesium.
**magnético,-a** *adj* magnetic.
**magnetismo** *nm* magnetism.
**magnetización** *nf* magnetization.
**magnetizar** *vt* to magnetize.
**magnetofónico,-a** *adj* sound recording.
**magnetófono** *nm* tape recorder.
**magnicidio** *nm* assassination.
**magnificar** *vt (ensalzar)* to praise.
**magnificencia** *nf* magnificence, splendour.
**magnífico,-a** *adj* splendid.
**magnitud** *nf* FÍS magnitude.

**magno,-a** *adj* great.
**magnolia** *nf (árbol, flor)* magnolia.
**magnolio** *nm* magnolia.
**mago,-a** *nm & nf (gen)* magician, conjurer; *(de los cuentos)* wizard.
**magro,-a** *adj* lean.
**magulladura** *nf* bruise, contusion.
**magullar** *vt* to bruise.
**maicena** *nf* cornflour.
**mailing** *nm* mailshot.
**maitre** *nm o nf* head waiter, maître.
**maíz** *nm* 1 *(planta)* maize, US corn. 2 *(grano)* sweet corn, US corn.
**maizal** *nm* maize field, US corn field.
**majada** *nf* sheepfold.
**majadería** *nf* nonsense, balderdash.
**majadero,-a** *adj* stupid, dim-witted.
**majar** *vt* to crush.
**majestad** *nf (distinción)* majesty.
**majestuoso,-a** *adj* majestic.
**majo,-a** *adj (simpático)* nice.
**majuelo** *nm (viña)* young vine.
**mal** *nm* 1 evil. 2 *(daño)* harm. 3 *(enfermedad)* sickness.
▶ *adj (forma apocopada de malo)* bad.
▶ *adv* 1 *(no adecuadamente)* badly: *se portó mal con nosotros* he treated us badly. 2 *(enfermo)* ill, sick: *me encuentro mal* I feel ill, I don't feel well. 3 *(incorrectamente)* wrong: *lo has hecho mal* you've done it wrong. 4 *(en frases negativas)* bad, badly: *la película no está mal* the film's not bad.
**malabarismo** *nm* juggling. LOC **hacer malabarismos** to juggle.
**malabarista** *nm o nf* juggler.
**malacostumbrado,-a** *adj* spoilt.
**malacostumbrar** *vt* to spoil.
**malaria** *nf* malaria.
**malasio,-a** *adj* Malaysian.
▶ *nm & nf* Malaysian.
**malaventura** *nf* misfortune.
**malaventurado,-a** *adj* unfortunate.
**Malawi** *nm* Malawi.
**malawiano,-a** *adj* Malawian.
▶ *nm & nf* Malawian.
**malayo,-a** *adj* Malay.
▶ *nm & nf (persona)* Malay.
▶ *nm* **malayo** *(idioma)* Malay.

**Malaysia** *nf* Malaysia.
**malcarado,-a** *adj* grim-faced.
**malcomer** *vi* not to eat enough.
**malcriado,-a** *adj (mimado)* spoilt.
**malcriar** *vt* to spoil.
**maldad** *nf* **1** *(cualidad)* evil, wickedness. **2** *(acto)* evil thing, wicked thing.
**maldecir** *vt* to curse, damn.
▶ *vi* to curse.
**maldiciente** *adj* slanderous.
**maldición** *nf* curse.
**maldito,-a** *adj* damned.
**Maldivas** *nm* Maldives.
**maldivo,-a** *adj* Maldivian.
▶ *nm & nf* Maldivian.
**maleabilidad** *nf* malleability.
**maleable** *adj* malleable.
**maleante** *nm o nf* delinquent.
**malear** *vt (dañar)* to spoil, damage.
**malecón** *nm* mole, jetty.
**maledicencia** *nf* evil talk, gossip.
**maleducado,-a** *adj* rude.
▶ *nm & nf* rude person: *es una maleducada* she's really rude.
**maleducar** *vt (niño)* to spoil.
**maleficio** *nm* curse, evil spell.
**maléfico,-a** *adj* evil, harmful.
**malentendido** *nm* misunderstanding.
**malestar** *nm fig* unrest.
**maleta** *nf* suitcase, case. [LOC] **hacer la maleta 1** *(empacar)* to pack. **2** *(irse)* to pack up.
**maletero** *nm* AUTO boot, US trunk.
**maletín** *nm* briefcase.
**malévolo,-a** *adj* malevolent.
**maleza** *nf (malas hierbas)* weeds *pl*.
**malformación** *nf* malformation.
**malgache** *adj* Madagascan, Malagsy.
▶ *nm o nf* Madagascan.
**malgastador,-ra** *nm & nf* squanderer.
**malgastar** *vt* to waste, squander.
**malhablado,-a** *adj* foul-mouthed.
**malhecho,-a** *adj* deformed.
**malhechor,-ra** *nm & nf* criminal.
**malherir** *vt* to wound badly.
**malhumor** *nm* bad temper.

**malhumorado,-a** *adj* bad-tempered.
[LOC] **estar malhumorado,-a** to be in a bad mood.
**Malí** *nm* Mali.
**malicia** *nf (mala intención)* malice.
**maliciosamente** *adv* maliciously.
**malicioso,-a** *adj* malicious, spiteful.
**maliense** *adj* Malian.
▶ *nm o nf* Malian.
**maligno,-a** *adj* malignant.
**malintencionado,-a** *adj* malicious.
▶ *nm & nf* malicious person.
**malinterpretar** *vt* to misinterpret.
**malísimo,-a** *adj* terrible.
**malla** *nf (red)* mesh.
▶ *nf pl* **mallas** *(medias sin pie)* leggings.
**malnacido,-a** *nm & nf* despicable person.
**malnutrición** *nf* malnutrition.
**malnutrido,-a** *adj* malnourished.
**malo,-a** *adj* **1** bad: *¡qué día tan malo hace!* what dreadful weather! **2** *(malvado)* wicked, evil: *es muy mala persona* he's a nasty piece of work. **3** *(travieso)* naughty: *¡qué niño más malo!* what a naughty child! **4** *(nocivo)* harmful: *el tabaco es malo para la salud* smoking is bad for you. **5** *(enfermo)* ill, sick: *no ha venido a trabajar porque está malo con gripe* he's off sick with flu. **6** *(estropeado)* off: *este pescado ya está malo* this fish has gone off already.
▶ *nm & nf (en la ficción)* baddy, villain: *¿quién es el malo?* who's the baddy?
**malogrado,-a** *adj* wasted.
**malograr** *vt (desaprovechar)* to waste.
**maloliente** *adj* foul-smelling.
**malparado,-a** [LOC] **salir malparado,-a** to come off badly.
**malpensado,-a** *adj* nasty-minded.
**malsano,-a** *adj (ambiente, vida)* unhealthy; *(curiosidad)* morbid, unhealthy; *(mente)* sick.
**malsonante** *adj* offensive, rude.
**malta** *nf* malt.
**Malta** *nf* Malta.
**maltear** *vt* to malt.
**maltés** *adj* Maltese.
▶ *nm & nf (persona)* Maltese.
▶ *nm* **maltés** *(idioma)* Maltese.

M

**maltratar** vt (tratar mal) to ill-treat, mistreat; (pegar) to batter.

**maltrato** nm mistreatment.

**maltrecho,-a** adj 1 (persona) battered. 2 (cosa) damaged, destroyed.

**malva** adj (color) mauve.
▶ nf mallow.

**malvado,-a** adj wicked, evil.

**malvarrosa** nf hollyhock.

**malvasía** nf (uva) malvasia.

**malvavisco** nm marshmallow.

**malvender** vt to sell at a loss.

**malversar** vt to embezzle.

**Malvinas** nf pl **Islas Malvinas** Falkland Islands, Falklands.

**malvinense** adj of the Falklands.
▶ nm o nf Falklander, Falkland islander.

**malvivir** vi to live very badly.

**mama** nf (pecho) breast.

**mamá** nf fam mummy, US mom.

**mamar** vt (succionar) to suck.
▶ vi (bebé) to feed. LOC **dar de mamar** to breast-feed.

**mamario,-a** adj mammary.

**mambo** nm mambo.

**mamífero,-a** adj mammalian.

**mamografía** nf mammography.

**mamotreto** nm (armatoste) monstrosity.

**mampara** nf screen.

**mampostería** nf masonry.

**mamut** nm mammoth.

**maná** nm manna.

**manada** nf (vacas, elefantes) herd; (ovejas) flock; (lobos, perros) pack. LOC **en manada** en masse.

**mánager** nm o nf manager.

**manantial** nm spring.

**manar** vi (salir) to flow (de, from), pour (de, from), well (de, from).

**manatí** nm manatee.

**manazas** adj inv clumsy.

**mancha** nf stain, spot.

**manchado,-a** adj stained.

**manchar** vt to stain, dirty.
▶ vpr **mancharse** to get dirty.

**mancillar** vt arc to sully.

**manco,-a** adj (sin un brazo) one-armed; (sin una mano) one-handed.

**mancomunidad** nf association.

**mandamiento** nm REL commandment.

**mandar** vt 1 (ordenar) to order, tell. 2 (enviar) to send.
▶ vi (dirigir - un grupo) to be in charge.

**mandarina** nf mandarin, tangerine.

**mandatario,-a** nm & nf POL leader.

**mandato** nm (orden) order.

**mandíbula** nf jaw.

**mandil** nm apron.

**mandioca** nf manioc, cassava.

**mando** nm 1 (autoridad) command: le han relevado en el mando he's been dismissed. 2 (dispositivo) control. COMP **mando a distancia** (sistema) remote control.

**mandolina** nf mandolin.

**mandón,-ona** adj fam bossy.
▶ nm & nf fam bossy boots.

**mandrágora** nf mandrake.

**mandril** nm ZOOL mandril.

**manecilla** nf (de reloj) hand.

**manejable** adj easy-to-handle.

**manejar** vt to handle, operate, use.

**manejo** nm (uso) handling, use.

**manera** nf way, manner. LOC **de cualquier manera** 1 (en cualquier caso) in any case. 2 (sin cuidado, consideración, interés) carelessly. ▌ **de ninguna manera** certainly not. ▌ **de todas maneras** in any case.

**manga** nf sleeve: en mangas de camisa in shirt sleeves.

**manganeso** nm manganese.

**mangar** vt fam to pinch, nick, swipe.

**manglar** nm mangrove swamp.

**mango¹** nm handle.

**mango²** nm BOT mango.

**mangonear** vt fam to boss about.

**mangoneo** nm fam meddling.

**mangosta** nf mongoose.

**manguera** nf (de riego) hose.

**manguito** nm (de manos) muff.

**maní** nm peanut.

**manía** nf 1 MED mania. 2 (ojeriza) dislike, grudge. 3 (costumbre) habit; (obsesión) obsession, mania: tiene la manía de morderse las uñas she has a habit of biting her nails.

**maníaco,-a** *adj* MED manic.
▶ *nm & nf fam* maniac.

**maniatar** *vt* to tie up.

**maniático,-a** *adj (raro)* cranky.
▶ *nm & nf (quisquilloso)* fusspot.

**manicomio** *nm* mental hospital.

**manicura** *nf* manicure.

**manido,-a** *adj (tema)* stale.

**manifestación** *nf* demonstration.

**manifestante** *nm o nf* demonstrator.

**manifestar** *vt (expresar)* to express.
▶ *vpr* **manifestarse** to demonstrate: *se manifestaron a favor del desarme nuclear* they demonstrated in favour of nuclear disarmament.

**manifiesto,-a** *adj* obvious, evident.
▶ *nm* **manifiesto** manifesto.

**manija** *nf* handle.

**manilla** *nf (de reloj)* hand.

**manillar** *nm* handlebars *pl*.

**maniobra** *nf* manoeuvre.

**maniobrar** *vi* to manoeuvre.

**manipulación** *nf* manipulation.

**manipulador,-ra** *adj* manipulative.
▶ *nm & nf* manipulator.

**manipular** *vt* to manipulate.

**maniqueísmo** *nm (doctrina)* Manichaeism.

**maniquí** *nm (muñeco)* dummy.

**manirroto,-a** *adj fam* spendthrift.
▶ *nm & nf fam* spendthrift.

**manitas** *nm o nf* handyman.

**manivela** *nf* crank, handle.

**manjar** *nm* delicious dish, delicacy.

**mano** *nf* **1** ANAT hand. **2** *(de pintura)* coat. LOC **a mano 1** *(escrito)* handwritten, by hand. **2** *(hecho)* handmade, by hand. **3** *(cerca)* to hand, handy, near. **ǀ echar una mano** to give a hand, lend a hand.

**manojo** *nm* bunch.

**manómetro** *nm* pressure gauge.

**manopla** *nf (guante)* mitten.

**manotazo** *nm* slap, smack, swipe.

**mansarda** *nf* attic.

**mansedumbre** *nf* meekness, docility.

**mansión** *nf* mansion.

**manso,-a** *adj (animal)* tame.

**manta** *nf (gen)* blanket.

**mantear** *vt* to toss in a blanket.

**manteca** *nf (elaborado)* lard. COMP **manteca de cacao** cocoa butter. **ǀ manteca de cerdo** lard.

**mantecado** *nm (helado)* dairy ice cream.

**mantecoso,-a** *adj* greasy.

**mantel** *nm* tablecloth.

**mantelería** *nf* table linen.

**mantener** *vt* **1** *(conservar)* to keep. **2** *(sustentar)* to support, maintain: *ella sola mantiene a toda la familia* she supports the whole family by herself. **3** *(conversación, relaciones)* to have; *(correspondencia)* to keep up.
▶ *vpr* **mantenerse 1** *(sostenerse)* to remain, stand. **2** *(continuar en un estado, una posición)* to keep: *se mantuvo a distancia* she kept her distance. **3** *(sostenerse)* to manage, maintain os, ssupport os.

**mantenimiento** *nm* maintenance.

**mantequera** *nf* butter dish.

**mantequería** *nf (tienda)* delicatessen.

**mantequilla** *nf* butter.

**mantilla** *nf* **1** *(de mujer)* mantilla. **2** *(de niño)* shawl.

**mantillo** *nm (abono del suelo)* humus.

**mantis** *nf* mantis. COMP **mantis religiosa** praying mantis.

**manto** *nm (capa)* cloak.

**mantón** *nm* large shawl.

**manual** *adj* manual.
▶ *nm* manual, handbook.

**manualidad** *nf* handicraft.
▶ *nf pl* **manualidades** arts and crafts.

**manubrio** *nm* crank, crankhandle.

**manufacturar** *vt* to manufacture.

**manuscrito,-a** *adj* handwritten.
▶ *nm* **manuscrito** manuscript.

**manutención** *nf (gen)* maintenance.

**manzana** *nf* BOT apple.

**manzanilla** *nf (planta)* camomile.

**manzano** *nm* apple tree.

**maña** *nf (habilidad)* skill, knack.

**mañana** *nf* morning: *hace una mañana preciosa* it's a beautiful morning. LOC **por la mañana** in the morning.
▶ *adv* tomorrow: *mañana no tengo que ir al cole* I don't have to go to school to-

**M**

morrow. LOC **¡hasta mañana!** see you tomorrow!

**mañoso,-a** *adj (habilidoso)* skilful.

**maorí** *adj* Maori.
▶ *nm & nf (persona)* Maori.
▶ *nm (idioma)* Maori.

**mapa** *nm* map.

**mapache** *nm* racoon.

**mapamundi** *nm* map of the world.

**maqueta** *nf (de edificio, monumento, etc)* scale model.

**maquetar** *vt* to do the page layout of.

**maquetista** *nm o nf* **1** *(de maquetas)* model maker. **2** *(de libros)* page designer.

**maquiavélico,-a** *adj* Machiavellian.

**maquillador,-ra** *nm & nf* make-up assistant.

**maquillaje** *nm* make-up.

**maquillar** *vt* to make up.
▶ *vpr* **maquillarse** *(ponerse maquillaje)* to make os up.

**máquina** *nf* **1** *(gen)* machine. **2** *(de un tren)* engine. COMP **máquina de afeitar** shaver, electric razor. ▮ **máquina de coser** sewing machine. ▮ **máquina de escribir** typewriter. ▮ **máquina de fotos** camera. ▮ **máquina de lavar** washing machine.

**maquinar** *vt* to scheme, plot.

**maquinaria** *nf* **1** machinery. **2** mechanism.

**maquinilla** *nf* razor.

**maquinista** *nm o nf (de tren)* engine driver, US engineer.

**mar** *nm & nf (gen)* sea. LOC **en alta mar** on the high sea, on the open sea. ▮ **la mar de...** *(muy)* very, really.

**marabunta** *nf* **1** swarm of ants. **2** *fam fig* mob, crowd.

**maraca** *nf* maraca.

**maracuyá** *nf* passion fruit.

**marajá** *nm* maharajah.

**maraña** *nf (espesura)* thicket.

**maratón** *nm* marathon.

**maratoniano,-a** *adj* marathon.

**maravilla** *nf* wonder, marvel. LOC **de maravilla** wonderfully.

**maravillar** *vt* to astonish, amaze.
▶ *vpr* **maravillarse** to marvel (de, at).

**maravilloso,-a** *adj* wonderful.

**marca** *nf* **1** *(señal)* mark, sign. **2** *(en comestibles, productos del hogar)* brand; *(en otros productos)* make. **3** DEP record. COMP **marca registrada** registered trademark.

**marcado,-a** *adj* **1** *(señalado)* marked. **2** *(acento)* marked, pronounced.

**marcador** *nm* **1** DEP scoreboard. **2** INFORM bookmark.

**marcapasos** *nm inv* pacemaker.

**marcar** *vt* **1** *(señalar)* to mark; *(ganado)* to brand. **2** DEP *(gol, canasta)* to score. **3** *(en teléfono)* to dial.

**marcha** *nf* **1** *(de protesta, soldados)* march. **2** *(progreso)* course, progress. **3** *(abandono)* leaving. **4** AUTO gear. **5** DEP walk. **6** *fam (de persona)* go, energy; *(de lugar, ambiente)* life. LOC **dar marcha atrás 1** *(coche)* to reverse. **2** *(proyecto)* to fall through. ▮ **ir de marcha** *(por la noche)* go out on the town. ▮ **poner en marcha 1** *(coche)* to start. **2** *(proyecto)* to start up.

**marchar** *vi* **1** *(ir)* to go, walk. **2** *(funcionar)* to work, run. **3** MIL to march.
▶ *vpr* **marcharse** to leave.

**marchitar** *vt* to wither.
▶ *vpr* **marchitarse** to wither.

**marchito,-a** *adj (planta)* withered; *(belleza)* faded.

**marchoso,-a** *adj fam (persona)* fun-loving, wild; *(música, sitio)* lively.
▶ *nm & nf* raver, fun-lover.

**marcial** *adj* martial.

**marciano,-a** *adj* Martian.
▶ *nm & nf* Martian.

**marco** *nm* **1** *(de cuadro, ventana)* frame. **2** *(moneda)* mark.

**marea** *nf* tide. COMP **marea alta** high tide. ▮ **marea baja** low tide. ▮ **marea negra** oil slick.

**mareado,-a** *adj (en general)* sick: *estoy mareado* I feel sick.

**mareante** *adj (que marea)* sickening.

**marear** *vt* to make sick.
▶ *vpr* **marearse 1** to get sick. **2** *(sentir vértigo)* to get dizzy.

**marejada** *nf* swell.

**marejadilla** *nf* slight swell.

**maremoto** *nm* tidal wave.

**mareo** *nm* sickness.

**marfil** *nm* ivory.

**marfileño,-a** *adj (de Costa de Marfil)* of the Ivory Coast.
▶ *nm & nf* native of the Ivory Coast.

**marga** *nf* marl.

**margarina** *nf* margarine.

**margarita** *nf* **1** BOT daisy. **2** *(de máquina)* daisywheel.

**margen** *nm (del papel)* margin.

**marginación** *nf* exclusion.

**marginado,-a** *adj* marginalized.
▶ *nm & nf* social outcast.

**marginal** *adj* **1** *(asunto)* marginal, minor. **2** *(persona)* marginalized.

**marginar** *vt (persona)* exclude; *(grupo social)* marginalize.

**marido** *nm* husband.

**marimandón,-ona** *nm & nf fam* bossy boots.

**marina** *nf (flota)* navy.

**marinar** *vt* to marinate.

**marine** *nm* marine.

**marinero,-a** *nm* sailor.

**marino,-a** *adj (corriente, animal)* marine.

**marioneta** *nf* puppet. COMP (teatro de) marionetas puppet show.

**mariposa** *nf (insecto)* butterfly.

**mariposear** *vi (andar alrededor)* to buzz around.

**mariquita** *nf* ZOOL ladybird, US ladybug.

**marisabidilla** *nf fam* know-all.

**mariscada** *nf (comida)* seafood dish.

**mariscal** *nm* marshal.

**mariscar** *vi* to fish for shellfish.

**marisco** *nm* seafood, shellfish.

**marisma** *nf* salt marsh.

**marismeño,-a** *adj (cultivo)* marshy.

**marisquería** *nf* seafood restaurant.

**marital** *adj* marital.

**marítimo,-a** *adj* maritime, sea.

**marketing** *nm* marketing.

**marmita** *nf* casserole, cooking pot.

**mármol** *nm* marble.

**marmolería** *nf (taller)* marble cutter's workshop.

**marmóreo,-a** *adj* marmoreal.

**marmota** *nf* ZOOL marmot.

**maroma** *nf* thick rope.

**marqués,-esa** *nm & nf (hombre)* marquis, marquess; *(mujer)* marchioness.

**marquesina** *nf* bus shelter.

**marquetería** *nf* marquetry.

**marrano,-a** *adj fam* filthy, dirty.
▶ *nm & nf fam (sucio)* filthy pig, dirty pig.
▶ *nm* **marrano** ZOOL pig.

**marrón** *adj* brown.
▶ *nm (color)* brown.

**marroquí,-ina** *adj* Moroccan.
▶ *nm & nf* Moroccan.

**marroquinería** *nf (artículos)* leather goods *pl*.

**Marruecos** *nm* Morocco.

**marrullero,-a** *adj fam* crafty.

**marsupial** *nm* marsupial.

**marsupio** *nm* marsupium.

**marta** *nf* marten.

**Marte** *nm* Mars.

**martes** *nm* Tuesday.

✎ Consulta también **jueves**.

**martillazo** *nm* blow with a hammer.

**martillear** *vt* to hammer.

**martilleo** *nm* hammering.

**martillo** *nm* hammer.

**martinete** *nm (ave)* heron.

**martingala** *nf fam (artimaña)* ruse.

**Martinica** *nf* Martinique.

**martín pescador** *nm* kingfisher.

**mártir** *nm o nf* martyr.

**martirio** *nm* **1** martyrdom. **2** *fig* torture, torment.

**martirizar** *vt* **1** to martyr. **2** *fig* to torment, torture.

**marzo** *nm* March: *el día 16 de marzo* March the sixteenth, the sixteenth of March; *nací el 6 de marzo de 1993* I was born on March 6th 1993; *durante el mes de marzo* in March; *en marzo del año pasado* last March; *en marzo del año que viene* next March; *a principios de marzo* at the beginning of March; *a mediados de marzo* in mid-March; *a finales de marzo* at the end of March.

**mas** *conj* but.

M

**más** *adv* **1** *(comparativo)* more: *este año ha llovido más* it has rained more this year. **2** *(con números o cantidades)* more: *más de tres* more than three. **3** *(superlativo)* most: *es la más guapa* she's the prettiest. **4** *(después de pron interrog e indef)* else: *¿algo más?* anything else? **5** *(exclamativo)* so: *¡qué película más buena!* what a wonderful film! ▎ LOC **de más** spare, extra. ▎ **más bien** rather. ▎ **más o menos** more or less.
▸ *prep* MAT plus: *dos más dos igual a cuatro* two plus two is four.
▸ *nm (signo)* plus sign.

**masa** *nf* **1** *(en general)* mass. **2** FÍS mass: *unidad de masa* unit of mass. **3** CULIN *(para pan)* dough; *(para tartas)* pastry. **4** *(de gente)* mass, crowd.

**masacre** *nf* massacre.

**masaje** *nm* massage.

**masajear** *vt* to massage.

**masajista** *nm o nf (hombre)* masseur; *(mujer)* masseuse.
▸ *nm & nf* DEP *(en fútbol)* physiotherapist, physio.

**mascar** *vt* to chew.

**máscara** *nf (careta)* mask.

**mascarilla** *nf (de belleza)* face mask.

**mascota** *nf* **1** *(figura)* mascot. **2** *(animal doméstico)* pet.

**masculinidad** *nf* masculinity.

**masculino,-a** *adj* **1** male: *la población masculina* the male population. **2** *(propio de hombres)* masculine. **3** GRAM masculine.

**mascullar** *vt* to mumble, mutter.

**masificado,-a** *adj* overcrowded.

**masilla** *nf* putty.

**masivo,-a** *adj* mass, massive.

**master** *nm* EDUC Master's degree.

**máster** *nm (estudios)* master's degree.

**masticar** *vt* to chew, masticate.

**mástil** *nm* **1** *(asta)* mast. **2** MAR mast.

**mastodóntico,-a** *adj fam* enormous.

**mastoides** *nf inv* mastoid.

**mata** *nf (arbusto)* shrub, bush.

**matadero** *nm* slaughterhouse.

**matador,-ra** *adj fam (agotador)* killing.

**matalahúva** *nf (planta)* anise.

**matamoscas** *nm* **1** *(insecticida)* fly spray. **2** *(pala)* fly swat.

**matanza** *nf (gen)* slaughter.

**matar** *vt (persona - gen)* to kill.
▸ *vpr* **matarse** *(involuntariamente)* to die; *(voluntariamente)* to kill os.

**matasellos** *nm inv (marca)* postmark.

**mate¹** *adj (sin brillo)* matt.

**mate²** *nm (ajedrez)* mate.

**mate³** *nm (hierba)* maté.

**matemática** *nf (ciencia)* mathematics.

**matemáticas** *nf pl* mathematics *sing*.

**matemático,-a** *adj* mathematical.
▸ *nm & nf* mathematician.

**materia** *nf* **1** *(sustancia)* matter. **2** *(asignatura)* subject. COMP **materia prima** raw material.

**material** *adj (en general)* material.
▸ *nm (conjunto de cosas)* equipment.

**materialismo** *nm* materialism.

**materialista** *adj* materialistic.

**materializar** *vt* to put into practice.

**maternal** *adj* maternal, motherly.

**maternidad** *nf* maternity.

**materno,-a** *adj (abuelo, etc)* maternal.

**matinal** *adj* morning.

**matiz** *nm* **1** *(color)* shade, tint. **2** *(variación)* nuance.

**matizar** *vt* **1** ARTE *(colores)* to blend. **2** *(sonido)* to modulate. **3** *(añadir un matiz)* to tinge (de, with).

**matojo** *nm* small shrub, bush.

**matón,-ona** *nm & nf fam* bully, thug.

**matorral** *nm (maleza)* bushes *pl*.

**matraca** *nf* wooden rattle.

**matraz** *nm* flask.

**matriarca** *nf* matriarch.

**matriarcado** *nm* matriarchy.

**matriarcal** *adj* matriarchal.

**matrícula** *nf* **1** *(registro - de personas)* registration, enrollment: *plazo de matrícula* registration period. **2** *(tasa)* registration fee(s), tuition fee(s). **3** AUTO *(placa)* number plate, US license plate. COMP **matrícula de honor** distinction.

**matricular** *vt (persona)* to register.

▶ *vpr* **matricularse** to register, enroll: *me he matriculado en Informática* I've enrolled for computer science.

**matrimonial** *adj (derecho)* matrimonial.

**matrimonio** *nm* **1** *(estado)* marriage. **2** *(pareja)* married couple.

**matriz** *nf* **1** ANAT womb. **2** MAT matrix.

**matrona** *nf (comadrona)* midwife.

**matutino,-a** *adj* morning.
▶ *nm* **matutino** *(periódico)* morning paper.

**maullar** *vi* miaow, US meow.

**Mauritania** *nf* Mauritania.

**mauritano,-a** *adj* Mauritanian.
▶ *nm & nf* Mauritanian.

**mausoleo** *nm* mausoleum.

**maxilar** *nm* jaw, jawbone.

**máxima** *nf (temperatura)* maximum temperature.

**máxime** *adv fml* especially.

**maximizar** *vt* to maximize.

**máximo,-a** *adj (velocidad)* maximum; *(puntuación, condecoración)* highest.
▶ *nm* **máximo** maximum: *tenéis una hora como máximo para acabar* you must be finished in an hour.

**maya** *adj* Mayan.
▶ *nm o nf (persona)* Mayan.
▶ *nm* **maya** *(idioma)* Mayan.

**mayestático,-a** *adj* majestic.

**mayo** *nm* May.

✎ Para ejemplos de uso, consulta marzo.

**mayólica** *nf* majolica.

**mayonesa** *nf* mayonnaise.

**mayor** *adj* **1** *(comparativo)* bigger, greater, larger; *(persona)* older; *(hermanos, hijos)* elder, older. **2** *(superlativo)* biggest, greatest, largest; *(persona)* oldest; *(hermanos, hijos)* eldest, oldest. **3** *(de edad)* mature, elderly: *la gente mayor* elderly people. **4** *(adulto)* grown-up. **5** *(principal)* main. **6** MÚS major.
▶ *nm pl* **los mayores** *(adultos)* grown-ups, adults.
▶ *nm & nf* **el/la mayor** *(entre varios)* the oldest.

**mayoral** *nm (capataz)* foreman.

**mayordomo** *nm* butler.

**mayoría** *nf* majority: *la mayoría de los hombres...* most men...

**mayorista** *nm o nf* wholesaler.

**mayoritario,-a** *adj* majority.

**mayúscula** *nf* capital, capital letter.

**mayúsculo,-a** *adj (enorme)* enormous, gigantic

**maza** *nf* HIST *(arma)* mace.

**mazapán** *nm* marzipan.

**mazmorra** *nf* dungeon.

**mazo** *nm (martillo)* mallet.

**mazorca** *nf* cob. COMP **mazorca de maíz** corncob.

**me** *pron* **1** me: *no me lo dijo* she didn't tell me; *dámelo* give it to me. **2** *(reflexivo)* myself: *me veo en el espejo* I can see myself in the mirror.

**meandro** *nm* meander.

**meca** *nf* mecca, Mecca.

**mecánica** *nf (ciencia)* mechanics.

**mecánico,-a** *adj* mechanical.
▶ *nm & nf* mechanic.

**mecanismo** *nm* mechanism.

**mecanización** *nf* mechanization.

**mecanizado,-a** *adj* mechanized.

**mecanizar** *vt* to mechanize.

**mecano®** *nm* Meccano.

**mecanografía** *nf* typing.

**mecanografiar** *vt* to type.

**mecedora** *nf* rocking chair.

**mecenas** *nm o nf* patron.

**mecer** *vt* to rock.
▶ *vpr* **mecerse** *(en una silla)* to rock; *(en un columpio)* to swing.

**mecha** *nf* **1** *(de vela)* wick. **2** MIL fuse.

**mechado,-a** *adj* larded.

**mechar** *vt (carne)* to lard.

**mechero** *nm* (cigarette) lighter.

**mechón** *nm (de pelo)* lock, strand.

**medalla** *nf* medal.

**medallero** *nm* DEP medals table.

**medallista** *nm o nf* DEP medal winner.

**medallón** *nm (joya)* medallion.

**media** *nf* **1** *(calcetín)* sock. **2** *(promedio)* average. **3** MAT mean. **4** **la media** *(hora)* half past, half past the hour. COMP **media aritmética** arithmetic mean.

► *nf pl* **medias** *(enteras)* tights, pantihose; *(no enteras)* stockings.

**mediación** *nf* mediation.

**mediado,-a** *adj (recipiente)* half-empty; LOC **a mediados de** halfway through.

**mediador,-ra** *adj* mediating.
► *nm & nf* mediator.

**mediana** *nf* MAT median.

**medianero,-a** *adj* dividing.

**mediano,-a** *adj (de calidad)* average; *(de tamaño)* medium, medium-sized.

**medianoche** *nf* midnight.

**mediante** *adj* by means of.

**mediar** *vi* **1** *(interceder)* to intercede (en favor de, on behalf of). **2** *(interponerse)* to mediate (en, in), intervene (en, in). **3** *(estar en medio)* to be. **4** *(llegar a la mitad)*.

**medicación** *nf* medicines *pl*.

**medicamento** *nm* medicine, drug.

**medicar** *vt (recetar)* to prescribe.
► *vpr* **medicarse** to take medicine.

**medicina** *nf* medicine.

**medicinal** *adj* medicinal.

**medición** *nf (acción)* measuring.

**médico,-a** *adj* medical.
► *nm & nf* doctor. COMP **médico,-a de cabecera** general practitioner, GP. ‖ **médico,-a de familia** family doctor.

**medida** *nf* **1** *(acción)* measuring; *(dato, número)* measurement. **2** *(disposición)* measure. LOC **a medida que** as.

**medidor,-ra** *nm* AM *(contador)* meter.

**medieval** *adj* medieval.

**medievalista** *nm o nf* medievalist.

**medievo** *nm* Middle Ages *pl*.

**medio,-a** *adj* **1** *(mitad)* half: *las dos y media* half past two; *un año y medio* a year and a half. **2** *(intermedio)* middle: *a media tarde* in the middle of the afternoon. **3** *(de promedio)* average.
► *adv* half: *medio terminado,-a* half-finished.
► *nm* **medio** **1** *(mitad)* half. **2** *(centro)* middle. **3** *(contexto - físico)* environment. COMP **medio ambiente** environment.
► *nm pl* **medios** *(recursos)* means.

**medioambiental** *adj* environmental.

**mediocampista** *nm o nf* midfield player.

**mediocre** *adj* mediocre.

**mediocridad** *nf* mediocrity.

**mediodía** *nm (las doce)* midday.

**mediopensionista** *nm o nf* day student.

**medir** *vt* to measure.
► *vpr* **medirse** to measure os.

**meditación** *nf* meditation.

**meditar** *vt* to meditate, think.
► *vi* to meditate (sobre, over).

**mediterráneo,-a** *adj* Mediterranean.
► *nm & nf* Mediterranean. COMP **el (mar) Mediterráneo** the Mediterranean (Sea).

**médium** *nm o nf* medium.

**medrar** *vi (mejorar socialmente)* to get rich.

**médula** *nf* **1** ANAT marrow. **2** BOT pith. COMP **médula espinal** spinal cord.

**medular** *adj* ANAT marrow.

**medusa** *nf* jellyfish.

**megabyte** *nm* megabyte.

**megafonía** *nf* sound amplification.

**megáfono** *nm* megaphone.

**megahercio** *nm* megahertz.

**megalítico,-a** *adj* megalithic.

**megalito** *nm* megalith.

**megalómano,-a** *nm & nf* megalomaniac.

**megatón** *nm* megaton.

**megavatio** *nm* megawatt.

**megavoltio** *nm* megavolt.

**mejicano,-a** *adj* Mexican.
► *nm & nf* Mexican.

**Méjico** *nm* Mexico.

**mejilla** *nf* cheek.

**mejillón** *nm* mussel.

**mejor** *adj* **1** *(comparativo)* better: *este libro es mejor que aquél* this book is better than that one. **2** *(superlativo)* best: *mi mejor amigo,-a* my best friend. LOC **a lo mejor** perhaps, maybe.
► *adv* **1** *(comparativo)* better: *cada vez mejor* better and better every day. **2** *(superlativo)* best.
► *nm & nf* **el/la mejor** the best (one).

**mejora** *nf (progreso)* improvement.

**mejorable** *adj* which could be improved.

**mejorar** *vt* to improve.

► *vi* to improve, get better.

► *vpr* **mejorarse** to get better: *¡que te mejores!* I hope you get better.

**mejoría** *nf* improvement.

**melancolía** *nf* melancholy, sadness.

**melancólico,-a** *adj* melancholic.

**melanina** *nf* melanin.

**melaza** *nf* molasses.

**melena** *nf* **1** *(de persona)* hair. **2** *(de león)* mane.

**melisa** *nf* lemon balm.

**mella** *nf* *(hendedura)* nick, notch.

**mellar** *vt* **1** *(objeto)* to chip, nick. **2** *fig* to dent, damage.

**mellizo,-a** *adj* twin.

► *nm & nf* twin.

**melocotón** *nm* peach.

**melocotonero** *nm* peach tree.

**melodía** *nf* melody.

**melódico,-a** *adj* melodic.

**melodrama** *nm* melodrama.

**melodramático,-a** *adj* melodramatic.

**melómano,-a** *adj* music lover.

**melón** *nm* *(fruto)* melon.

**meloso,-a** *adj* *(dulce)* sweet, honeyed.

**membrana** *nf* membrane.

**membrillo** *nm* *(fruta)* quince.

**memo,-a** *adj fam* stupid, dim.

**memorable** *adj* memorable.

**memorándum** *nm* *(cuaderno)* notebook.

**memoria** *nf* **1** *(gen)* memory. **2** *(informe)* report. **3** *(inventario)* inventory.

► *nf pl* **memorias** *(biografía)* memoirs. LOC **de memoria** (off) by heart, by memory. I **hacer memoria** to try to remember. COMP **memoria RAM** RAM memory.

**memorial** *nm* *(acto)* conmemoration.

**memorizar** *vt* to memorize.

**mena** *nf* ore.

**menaje** *nm* household goods. COMP **menaje de cocina** kitchen equipment.

**mención** *nf* mention.

**mencionar** *vt* to mention, cite.

**mendelismo** *nm* Mendelism.

**mendicante** *adj* mendicant.

**mendicidad** *nf* begging.

**mendigar** *vi* to beg.

**mendigo,-a** *nm & nf* beggar.

**mendrugo** *nm* hard crust (of bread).

**menear** *vt* *(cabeza)* to shake; *(cola)* to wag; *(cuerpo, caderas)* to wiggle.

**menestra** *nf* vegetable stew.

**mengua** *nf* *(disminución)* decrease.

**menguado,-a** *adj* diminished.

**menguante** *adj* *(luna)* waning.

**menguar** *vi* **1** *(cantidad)* to decrease. **2** *(luna)* to wane.

**menhir** *nm* menhir.

**meninge** *nm* meninx.

**meningitis** *nm inv* meningitis.

**menisco** *nm* meniscus.

**menopausia** *nf* menopause.

**menopáusico,-a** *adj* menopausal.

**menor** *adj* **1** *(comparativo - en tamaño)* smaller; *(- en calidad, importancia)* lesser; *(- en edad)* younger. **2** *(superlativo - en tamaño)* smallest; *(- en calidad, importancia)* least; *(- en edad)* youngest. **3** *(inferior)* minor. **4** MÚS minor.

► *nm o nf* JUR minor. COMP **menor de edad** minor.

**menos** *adj* **1** *(comparativo - en cantidad)* less; *(- en número)* fewer: *yo tengo menos años que tú* I'm younger than you. **2** *(superlativo - de cantidad)* least; *(- de número)* fewest: *yo soy la que menos culpa tiene* I'm the least guilty.

► *adv* **1** *(comparativo - de cantidad)* less; *(- de número)* fewer: *voy al gimnasio menos que antes* I go to the gym less than before. **2** *(superlativo)* least: *es el menos guapo* he's the least good-looking. **3** *(con horas)* to: *las tres menos cuarto* a quarter to three. **4** MAT minus. LOC **a menos que** unless. I **al menos** at least. I **por lo menos** at least.

► *prep* but, except: *todo menos eso* anything but that.

► *pron* *(cantidad)* less; *(número)* fewer: *me pagó menos* he paid me less.

► *nm* MAT minus sign.

**menospreciar** *vt* **1** *(despreciar)* to despise, scorn. **2** *(no valorar)* to undervalue, underrate.

**menosprecio** *nm* *(poco aprecio)* under-estimation, lack of appreciation.

**mensaje** *nm* **1** *(en general)* message. **2** *(envío electrónico)* posting.

**mensajería** *nf* courier service.

**mensajero,-a** *nm & nf* courier.

**menstruación** *nf* menstruation.

**menstrual** *adj* menstrual.

**menstruar** *vi* to menstruate.

**mensual** *adj* monthly.

**mensualidad** *nf* *(que se cobra)* monthly salary; *(que se paga)* monthly instalment.

**mensurable** *adj* measurable.

**menta** *nf* *(hierba)* mint.

**mental** *adj* mental.

**mentalidad** *nf* mentality.

**mentalizar** *vt* to make aware.
▶ *vpr* **mentalizarse** *(hacerse a la idea)* to get used to the idea.

**mente** *nf* **1** *(pensamiento)* mind. **2** *(facultades)* mind, intelligence, intellect.

**mentir** *vi* to lie.

**mentira** *nf* lie.

**mentiroso,-a** *nm & nf* liar.

**mentón** *nm* chin.

**mentor** *nm* mentor.

**menú** *nm* **1** CULIN menu. **2** INFORM menu. COMP **menú del día** set menu.

**menudo,-a** *adj* **1** *(pequeño)* small, tiny. **2** *(enfático)* what a…: ¡menudo lío! what a mess! LOC **a menudo** often.

**meñique** *adj* little. COMP **(dedo) meñique** little finger.

**meollo** *nm* *(lo esencial)* core, heart, crux.

**mercader** *nm arc* merchant.

**mercadería** *nf* merchandise.

**mercadillo** *nm* flea market, bazaar.

**mercado** *nm* market. COMP **Mercado Común** Common Market. ‖ **mercado de abastos** wholesale food market.

**mercancía** *nf* *(gen)* goods.

**mercante** *adj* merchant.

**mercantil** *adj* commercial.

**mercantilismo** *nm* mercantilism.

**mercenario,-a** *nm & nf* mercenary.

**mercería** *nf* *(tienda)* haberdasher's shop, US notions store.

**mercurio** *nm* QUÍM mercury.

**merecedor,-ra** *adj* worthy.

**merecer** *vt* to deserve, be worth: *merece la pena verlo* it's worth a visit.

**merecido,-a** *nm* (just) come-uppance. LOC **llevar su merecido** to get one's come-uppance.

**merendar** *vi* to have tea.
▶ *vt* to have something for tea.

**merendero** *nm* open-air snack bar.

**merengue** *nm* CULIN meringue.

**meridiano,-a** *nm* meridian.

**meridional** *adj* southern.

**merienda** *nf* afternoon snack, tea.

**merina** *nf* merino sheep.

**mérito** *nm* *(de alguien)* merit.

**merluza** *nf* hake.

**mermar** *vt* to reduce.
▶ *vi* to decrease, diminish.

**mermelada** *nf* jam; *(de cítricos)* marmalade.

**mero** *nm* *(pez)* grouper.

**merodear** *vi* *(curiosear)* to prowl about.

**mes** *nm* month.

**mesa** *nf* *(gen)* table; *(de oficina)* desk. LOC **poner la mesa** to set the table, lay the table. ‖ **quitar/recoger la mesa** to clear the table.

**meseta** *nf* GEOG plateau.

**mesianismo** *nm* Messianism.

**mesías** *nm inv* Messiah.

**mesilla** *nf* small table. COMP **mesilla de noche** bedside table.

**mesocarpio** *nm* mesocarp.

**mesolítico,-a** *nm* the Mesolithic.

**mesón** *nm* old-style restaurant.

**mestizaje** *nm* crossbreeding.

**mestizo,-a** *adj* of mixed race.
▶ *nm & nf* person of mixed race.

**mesura** *nf* restraint, moderation.

**meta** *nf* **1** *(en una carrera)* finishing line. **2** *(portería)* goal. **3** *fig* purpose.

**metabolismo** *nm* metabolism.

**metabolizar** *vt* to metabolize.

**metafísica** *nf* metaphysics.

**metáfora** *nf* metaphor.
**metafórico,-a** *adj* metaphorical.
**metal** *nm* metal.
**metálico,-a** *adj* metallic.
▶ *nm* **metálico** cash.
**metalista** *nm o nf* metal worker.
**metalistería** *nf* metal work.
**metalizado,-a** *adj* metallic.
**metalizar** *vt* to metallize (US metallize).
**metalurgia** *nf* metallurgy.
**metalúrgico,-a** *adj* metallurgical.
▶ *nm & nf* metallurgist.
**metamórfico,-a** *adj* metamorphic.
**metamorfosis** *nf inv* metamorphosis.
**metano** *nm* methane.
**metanol** *nm* methanol.
**metástasis** *nf inv* metastasis.
**metatarso** *nm* metatarsus.
**meteórico,-a** *adj* meteoric.
**meteorito** *nm* meteorite.
**meteoro** *nm* meteor.
**meteorología** *nf* meteorology.
**meteorológico,-a** *adj* meteorological.
**meteorólogo,-a** *nm & nf* meteorologist.
**metepatas** *nm o nf fam* bigmouth.
**meter** *vt* **1** *(introducir)* to put. **2** *(implicar)* to put into (en, -), get into (en, -), involve in (en, -).
▶ *vpr* **meterse 1** *(introducirse en)* to get in: *se metió en la cama* he got into bed. **2** *(tomar parte - negocio)* to go into (en, -); *(involucrarse en)* to get involved (en, in/with), get mixed up (en, in/with). **3** *(introducirse)* to get involved (en, in): *me metí totalmente en el papel* I got completely into in the role. **4** *(ir)* to go: *¿dónde se habrá metido?* where can he have got to?
**meticuloso,-a** *adj (cuidadoso)* meticulous.
**metido,-a** *adj (envuelto, implicado)* involved (en, in).
**metileno** *nm* methylene.
**metílico,-a** *adj* methylic.
**metódico,-a** *adj* methodical.
**método** *nm* method.

**metodología** *nf* methodology.
**metodológico,-a** *adj* methodological.
**metonimia** *nf* metonymy.
**metraje** *nm (película rodada)* footage. COMP **largo metraje** (full-length) feature film.
**metralla** *nf* shrapnel.
**metralleta** *nf* sub-machine-gun.
**métrica** *nf* metrics *pl*.
**métrico,-a** *adj* **1** *(sistema, unidad)* metric. **2** *(del verso)* metrical, metric. COMP **sistema métrico** metric system.
**metro** *nm* **1** metre (US meter). **2** *(cinta)* tape measure. **3** *(transporte)* underground, tube, US subway. COMP **metro cuadrado** square metre.
**metrónomo** *nm* metronome.
**metrópoli** *nf* metropolis.
**metropolitano,-a** *adj* metropolitan.
▶ *nm* **metropolitano** *fml* underground, tube, US subway.
**mexicano,-a** *adj* Mexican.
▶ *nm & nf* Mexican.
**México** *nm* Mexico.
**mezcla** *nf* **1** *(acción)* mixing, blending. **2** *(producto)* mixture, blend.
**mezclar** *vt* **1** *(incorporar, unir)* to mix, blend. **2** *(desordenar)* to mix up.
▶ *vpr* **mezclarse 1** *(personas)* to mix (con, with). **2** *(cosas)* to get mixed up.
**mezquindad** *nf* **1** meanness, stinginess. **2** *(acción)* mean thing.
**mezquino,-a** *adj* low, base.
**mezquita** *nf* mosque.
**mi** *nm* MÚS E.
**mí** *pron* me: *éste es para mí* this one is for me.
**miau** *nm* miaow, meow, mew.
**mica** *nf* GEOL mica.
**michelín** *nm fam* spare tyre.
**mico** *nm (animal)* monkey.
**micología** *nf* mycology.
**micosis** *nf inv* mycosis.
**micra** *nf* micron.
**micro** *nm fam* mike, microphone.
**microbio** *nm* microbe.
**microbiología** *nf* microbiology.

**M**

**microchip** *nm* microchip.
**microclima** *nm* microclimate.
**microcomputador** *nm* microcomputer.
**microcosmos** *nm inv* microcosm.
**microeconomía** *nf* microeconomics.
**microelectrónica** *nf* microelectronics.
**microfilme** *nm* microfilm.
**micrófono** *nm* microphone.
**microondas** *nm* microwave. COMP horno microondas microwave oven.
**microordenador** *nm* microcomputer.
**microprocesador** *nm* microprocessor.
**microscópico,-a** *adj* microscopic.
**microscopio** *nm* microscope.
**miedo** *nm* fear. LOC tener miedo to be scared, be frightened, be afraid: *tiene miedo a la oscuridad* he's afraid of the dark.
**miedoso,-a** *adj* easily frightened.
**miel** *nf* honey.
**miembro** *nm* **1** *(extremidad)* limb. **2** *(socio)* member. **3** MAT member.
**mientras** *adv* meanwhile.
▶ *conj* **1** *(temporal)* while, whilst: *mientras estés de vacaciones no pienses en el trabajo* while you're on holiday, don't think about work. **2** *(adversativa)* whereas: *yo al menos he estudiado, mientras que tú no* at least I have studied, whereas you haven't.
**miércoles** *nm* Wednesday.

✎ Consulta también jueves.

**mies** *nf* corn, grain.
**miga** *nf (parte blanda del pan)* crumb.
**migración** *nf* migration.
**migraña** *nf* migraine.
**migrar** *vi* to migrate.
**migratorio,-a** *adj* migratory.
**mijo** *nm* millet.
**mil** *adj* **1** thousand. **2** *(milésimo)* thousandth.
▶ *nm* a thousand, one thousand.

✎ Consulta también seis y sexto,-a.

**milagro** *nm* miracle.
**milagroso,-a** *adj* miraculous.
**milanesa** LOC a la milanesa done in breadcrumbs.
**milano** *nm* kite.

**milenario,-a** *adj* millennial.
▶ *nm* milenario millennium.
**milenio** *nm* millennium.
**milésimo,-a** *adj* thousandth.
▶ *nm & nf* thousandth.

✎ Consulta también sexto,-a.

**milhojas** *nm inv* CULIN millefeuille.
**mili** *nf fam* military service. LOC hacer la mili *fam* to do one's military service.
**milicia** *nf (gente armada)* militia.
**miliciano,-a** *adj* of the militia.
▶ *nm & nf (hombre)* militiaman; *(mujer)* militiawoman.
**miligramo** *nm* milligram.
**mililitro** *nm* millilitre (US milliliter).
**milimétrico,-a** *adj* pinpoint.
**milímetro** *nm* millimetre (US millimeter).
**militante** *adj* militant.
**militar** *adj* military.
▶ *nm* military man, soldier.
**milla** *nf* mile. COMP milla náutica nautical mile.
**millar** *nm* thousand.
**millón** *nm* million.
**millonario,-a** *nm & nf (hombre)* millionaire; *(mujer)* millionairess.
**mimar** *vt (consentir)* to spoil.
**mimbre** *nm* wicker.
**mimetismo** *nm* mimicry.
**mímico,-a** *adj* mimic.
**mimo** *nm* **1** *(actor)* mime artist. **2** *(cariño)* pampering. **3** *(cuidado)* care. LOC hacerle mimos a ALGN to pamper SB.
**mimosa** *nf* BOT mimosa.
**mimoso,-a** *adj (cariñoso)* loving.
**mina** *nf* **1** mine. **2** *(explosivo)* mine. **3** *(de lápiz)* lead. COMP mina de carbón coal mine.
**minar** *vt (terreno)* to mine.
**minarete** *nm* minaret.
**mineral** *adj* mineral. COMP agua mineral mineral water.
▶ *nm* mineral.
**minería** *nf (técnica)* mining.
**minero,-a** *adj* mining.
▶ *nm & nf* miner.

**miniatura** *nf* miniature.

**minifalda** *nf* mini skirt.

**minifundio** *nm* smallholding.

**minigolf** *nm* crazy golf.

**mínima** *nf (temperatura)* minimum temperature.

**minimizar** *vt* to minimize.

**mínimo,-a** *adj* minimum, lowest.
▶ *nm* **mínimo** minimum: *pon el gas en el mínimo* turn the gas right down. LOC **como mínimo** at least. COMP **mínimo común múltiplo** lowest common multiple.

**minino** *nm fam* pussy, kitty.

**minio** *nm* red lead, minium.

**ministerio** *nm* POL ministry, US department.

**ministro,-a** *nm & nf* POL minister, US secretary. COMP **primer,-ra ministro,-a** prime minister.

**minoría** *nf* minority.

**minorista** *adj* retail.

**minoritario,-a** *adj* minority.

**minucia** *nf* trifle.

**minucioso,-a** *adj* meticulous.

**minúscula** *nf (letra)* small letter.

**minúsculo,-a** *adj (letra)* small; *(detalle)* insignificant.

**minusvalía** *nf* handicap, disability.

**minusválido,-a** *adj* disabled, handicapped.
▶ *nm & nf* disabled person.

**minuta** *nf (factura)* bill.

**minutero** *nm* minute hand.

**minuto** *nm* minute.

**mío,-a** *adj* my, of mine: *es muy amiga mía* she's a good friend of mine.
▶ *pron* mine: *este abrigo es mío* this coat is mine.

**miocardio** *nm* myocardium.

**miope** *adj* short-sighted, myopic.
▶ *nm o nf* short-sighted person.

**miopía** *nf* short-sightedness.

**mira** *nf* **1** *(dispositivo)* sight. **2** *fig* intention.

**mirada** *nf (gen)* look; *(vistazo)* glance. LOC **echar una mirada a** ALGO/ALGN to take a look at STH/SB.

**mirador** *nm* **1** *(balcón)* glassed-in balcony. **2** *(lugar)* viewing point.

**miramiento** *nm* consideration.

**mirar** *vt* **1** *(observar)* to look at; *(con atención)* to watch. **2** *(buscar)* to look; *(registrar)* to search: *me miraron todo al pasar por la aduana* they went through everything at customs. **3** *(tener cuidado con)* to watch: *mira bien lo que haces* watch what you do.
▶ *vi* **1** *(gen)* to look. **2** *(buscar)* to look: *mira debajo de la cama* look under the bed. **3** *(tener cuidado)* to mind, watch, be careful: *mira que no te engañen* mind they don't cheat you. LOC **¡mira!** look!

**miríada** *nf* myriad.

**mirilla** *nf* peephole, spyhole.

**miriópodo** *nm* myriapod.

**mirlo** *nm* blackbird.

**mirón,-ona** *nm & nf fam pey (curioso)* nosy parker.

**mirra** *nf* myrrh.

**mirto** *nm* myrtle.

**misa** *nf* mass.

**misal** *nm* missal.

**misántropo,-a** *nm & nf* misanthrope, misanthropist.

**miscelánea** *nf* miscellany.

**miserable** *adj* **1** *(tacaño)* mean. **2** *(malvado)* wretched.
▶ *nm o nf* **1** *(malvado)* wretch. **2** *(tacaño)* miser.

**miseria** *nf (pobreza)* extreme poverty.

**misericordia** *nf* mercy.

**mísero,-a** *adj* miserable.

**misil** *nm* missile.

**misión** *nf (tarea)* mission, task.

**misionero,-a** *nm & nf* missionary.

**mismo,-a** *adj* **1** *(idéntico)* same: *el mismo color* the same colour. **2** *(enfático)* very: *en esta misma casa nací yo* I was born in this very house.
▶ *pron* same: *es el mismo del año pasado* it's the same one as last year.
▶ *adv* **mismo** same: *piensa lo mismo que tu* he thinks the same as you. LOC **es lo mismo 1** *(la misma cosa)* it amounts to the same thing. **2** *(no importa)* it doesn't matter.

**misógino,-a** *adj* misogynous.

**míster** *nm (en fútbol)* manager, coach.

**misterio** *nm* mystery.

**misterioso,-a** *adj* mysterious.

**mística** *nf* **1** *(misticismo)* mysticism. **2** *(teología)* mystic theology.

**misticismo** *nm* mysticism.

**místico,-a** *adj* mystic, mystical.
▶ *nm & nf (persona)* mystic.

**mitad** *nf* **1** half: *me llevo la mitad* I'll take half. **2** *(medio)* middle: *en mitad de la plaza* in the middle of the square.

**mítico,-a** *adj* mythical.

**mitificar** *vt (convertir en mito)* to mythicize.

**mitin** *nm* meeting, rally.

**mito** *nm* myth.

**mitología** *nf* mythology.

**mitológico,-a** *adj* mythological.

**mitosis** *nf inv* mitosis.

**mixto,-a** *adj* mixed.

**mobiliario** *nm* furniture.

**moca** *nf (café)* mocha.

**mocasín** *nm* moccasin.

**mochila** *nf* rucksack, backpack.

**mochuelo** *nm* ZOOL little owl.

**moción** *nf* motion.

**moco** *nm* **1** *(mucosidad)* mucus; *(familiarmente)* snot. LOC **limpiarse los mocos** *fam* to blow one's nose.

**mocoso,-a** *nm & nf fam* brat.

**moda** *nf* fashion.

**modales** *nm pl* manners.

**modalidad** *nf* form, means, way.

**modelado** *nm* modelling (US modeling).

**modelar** *vt* to model, shape.

**modélico,-a** *adj* model.

**modelismo** *nm (de arcilla, etc)* modelling.

**modelo** *adj* model.
▶ *nm o nf (persona)* (fashion) model.

**módem** *nm* modem.

**moderación** *nf* moderation.

**moderado,-a** *adj* moderate.

**moderador,-ra** *nm & nf (de reunión)* chairperson.

**moderar** *vt* to moderate.

**modernismo** *nm (arte, literatura)* Modernism.

**modernista** *adj* Modernist.
▶ *nm o nf* Modernist.

**modernizar** *vt* to modernize.

**moderno,-a** *adj* modern.

**modestia** *nf* modesty.

**modesto,-a** *adj* modest.

**modificar** *vt* to alter, modify.

**modista** *nm o nf (de ropa para mujer)* dressmaker.

**modisto** *nm* **1** *(diseñador)* fashion designer. **2** *(sastre)* tailor.

**modo** *nm* **1** way, manner. **2** LING mood: *el modo subjuntivo* the subjunctive mood. LOC **de modo que** so: *de modo que ya lo sabes* so now you know. ▌ **en cierto modo** in a way.
▶ *nm pl* **modos** manners. LOC **de todos modos** anyhow, at any rate.

**modorra** *nf fam* drowsiness.

**modular** *vt* to modulate.
▶ *adj* modular.

**módulo** *nm* **1** *(gen)* module. **2** *(mueble)* unit.

**mofa** *nf* mockery, derision.

**mofarse** *vpr* to scoff, mock.

**mofeta** *nf* skunk.

**moflete** *nm fam* chubby cheek.

**mogollón** *nm fam* loads *pl.*
▶ *adv fam* a lot: *nos gustó mogollón* it was dead brilliant.

**mohair** *nm* mohair.

**moho** *nm* mould, (US mold).

**mohoso,-a** *adj* mouldy (US moldy).

**mojado,-a** *adj (húmedo)* wet, moist.

**mojama** *nf* dried salted tuna.

**mojar** *vt* **1** *(gen)* to wet. **2** *(alimento)* to dip
▶ *vpr* **mojarse 1** to get wet. **2** *fam (comprometerse)* to commit os.

**mojigato,-a** *adj (gazmoño)* prudish.

**mojón** *nm (poste - de distancia)* milepost.

**molar** *nm (diente)* molar.

**molde** *nm* mould (US mold).

**moldeable** *adj* mouldable.

**moldeado,-a** *adj* moulded (US molded).

**moldear** *vt* ARTE *(dar forma)* to mould (US mold).

**moldura** *nf* moulding (US molding).

**mole** *nf* mass, bulk, hulk.

**molécula** *nf* molecule.

**molecular** *adj* molecular.

**moler** *vt* **1** *(gen)* to grind. **2** *(cansar)* to wear out.

**molestar** *vt* **1** *(interrumpir)* to disturb. **2** *(perturbar)* to bother, upset: *me molestan los ruidos* noise bothers me. **3** *(importunar)* to pester: *¡deja de molestarme ya!* stop pestering me! **4** *(hacer daño - apretar)* to hurt: *estos zapatos me molestan* these shoes hurt my feet.
▶ *vpr* **molestarse** to bother: *perdone que le moleste* I'm sorry to bother you.

**molestia** *nf* **1** *(incomodidad)* bother, trouble; *(fastidio)* nuisance. **2** MED trouble.

**molesto,-a** *adj* **1** annoying. **2** *(enfadado)* annoyed.

**molido,-a** *adj* **1** *(café)* ground. **2** *fam (cansado)* worn-out. LOC **estar molido,-a** *fam* to be worn-out.

**molienda** *nf* *(de café)* grinding.

**moliente** LOC **corriente y moliente** run of the mill, common or garden.

**molinero,-a** *nm & nf* miller.

**molinillo** *nm* grinder, mill.

**molino** *nm* mill. COMP **molino de viento** windmill.

**molla** *nf* *(pulpa)* flesh.

**molleja** *nf* *(de ave)* gizzard.

**mollera** *nf* *fam (inteligencia)* brains *pl.*

**molón,-na** *adj* argot cool, brill, fab.

**molusco** *nm* mollusc (US mollusk).

**momentáneo,-a** *adj* momentary.

**momento** *nm* **1** moment. **2** *(período)* time.

**momia** *nf* mummy.

**momificación** *nf* mummification.

**momificar** *vt* to mummify.

**monacal** *adj* monastic.

**monacato** *nm* *(institución)* monastic community.

**Mónaco** *nm* Monaco.

**monada** *nf* *(cosa bonita)* beauty, lovely thing; *(persona)* gorgeous person.

**monaguillo** *nm* altar boy.

**monarca** *nm* monarch.

**monarquía** *nf* monarchy.

**monárquico,-a** *adj* monarchic.

**monasterio** *nm* monastery.

**monástico,-a** *adj* monastic.

**monda** *nf* *(piel)* peel, skin.

**mondadientes** *nm inv* toothpick.

**mondadura** *nf* *(piel - de fruta)* peel.

**mondar** *vt* *(pelar)* to peel.

**mondo,-a** *adj* *(limpio)* bare.

**mondongo** *nm* innards *pl.*

**moneda** *nf* *(pieza)* coin.

**monedero** *nm* purse.

**monegasco,-a** *adj* Monegasque.
▶ *nm & nf* Monegasque.

**monetario,-a** *adj* monetary.

**monetarismo** *nm* monetarism.

**monetarista** *adj* monetarist.

**mongólico,-a** *adj* affected by Down's syndrome.
▶ *nm & nf* person affected by Down's syndrome.

**mongolismo** *nm* Down's syndrome, mongolism.

**monicaco** *nm* *fam* dodgy geezer.

**monigote** *nm* **1** *(figura)* rag doll, paper doll. **2** *(dibujo)* matchstick man.

**monismo** *nm* monism.

**monista** *adj* monistic.

**monitor,-ra** *nm & nf (profesor)* instructor.
▶ *nm* **monitor** *(pantalla)* screen.

**monja** *nf* nun.

**monje** *nm* monk.

**mono,-a** *adj (bonito)* nice, lovely, cute.
▶ *nm & nf* ZOOL monkey.
▶ *nm* **mono** *(prenda de trabajo)* overalls *pl.*

**monocarril** *nm* monorail.

**monocolor** *adj* monochrome.

**monocorde** *adj fig (monótono)* dull.

**monocotiledónea** *nf* monocotyledon.

**monocotiledóneo,-a** *adj* monocotyledonous.

**monocromático,-a** *adj* monochromatic.

**monocromía** *nf* monochrome.

**monocromo,-a** *adj* monochrome.

**monocular** *adj* monocular.

**monóculo** *nm* monocle.

**M**

**monocultivo** *nm* monoculture.
**monódico,-a** *adj* monodic.
**monofásico,-a** *adj* single-phase.
**monofonía** *nm* mono.
**monofónico,-a** *adj* mono.
**monogamia** *nf* monogamy.
**monógamo,-a** *adj* monogamous.
**monografía** *nf* monograph.
**monográfico,-a** *adj* monographic.
**monograma** *nm* monogram.
**monolingüe** *adj* monolingual.
**monolítico,-a** *adj* monolithic.
**monolito** *nm* monolith.
**monologar** *vi* to soliloquize.
**monólogo** *nm (reflexión)* monologue.
**monomanía** *nf* 2 *fam* obsession.
**monomaníaco,-a** *adj* MED monomaniac.
**monomio** *n* MAT monomial.
**monoparental** *adj* one-parent.
**monopatín** *nm* skateboard.
**monoplano** *nm* monoplane.
**monoplaza** *adj* single-seat.
**monopolio** *nm* monopoly.
**monopolista** *adj* monopolistic.
**monopolización** *nf* monopolization.
**monopolizador,-ra** *adj* monopolizing.
**monopolizar** *vt* to monopolize.
**monorraíl** *nm* monorail.
**monosilábico,-a** *adj* monosyllabic.
**monosílabo,-a** *adj* monosyllabic.
▶ *nm* **monosílabo** monosyllable.
**monoteísmo** *nm* monotheism.
**monoteísta** *adj* monotheistic.
▶ *nm o nf* monotheist.
**monotonía** *nf* monotony.
**monótono,-a** *adj* monotonous.
**monovolumen** *nm* people carrier.
**monóxido** *nm* monoxide. COMP **monóxido de carbono** carbon monoxide.
**monseñor** *nm* Monsignor.
**monserga** *nf fam (lección)* nagging.
**monstruo** *adj fam* fantastic, terrific.
▶ *nm* **1** monster. **2** *fam (genio)* genius.
**monstruosidad** *nf (cosa)* monstrosity.
**monstruoso,-a** *adj* monstrous.

**monta** *nf* **1** *(importancia)* value, account, importance. **2** *(de un caballo)* riding.
**montacargas** *nm* service lift.
**montador,-ra** *nm & nf (operario)* fitter.
**montadora** *nf* splicing machine.

✎ Consulta también montador,-a.

**montaje** *nm* **1** *(de piezas)* assembly. **2** *(en foto)* montage. **3** *fam (farsa)* setup.
**montante** *nm* **1** *(total)* total, total amount. **2** *(pieza vertical)* upright. **3** *(ventana)* skylight.
**montaña** *nf* mountain.
**montañero,-a** *nm & nf* mountaineer.
**montañés,-esa** *nm & nf* highlander.
**montañismo** *nm* mountaineering.
**montañoso,-a** *adj* mountainous.
**montaplatos** *nm inv* dumb waiter.
**montar** *vi* **1** *(subir - caballo, bicicleta)* to mount, get on; *(- coche)* to get in; *(- avión)* to get on, board. **2** *(ir en bicicleta)* to ride: *¿sabes montar en bicicleta?* can you ride bicycle?
▶ *vt* **1** *(subir - caballo)* to mount, get on. **2** *(subir - persona)* to put on: *monté al niño en la bicicleta* I lifted the kid onto his bike. **3** *(ensamblar)* to assemble, put together; *(tienda de campaña)* to put up. **4** *(nata)* to whip; *(claras)* to whisk.
▶ *vpr* **montarse 1** *(subirse)* to get on; *(- en un coche)* to get in; *(- en un caballo)* to mount, get on. **2** *fam (armarse)* to break out: *se montó un buen jaleo* there was a real to-do.
**montaraz** *adj (de montaña)* mountain.
**monte** *nm* **1** mountain, mount. **2** *(bosque)* wild, woodland.
**montenegrino,-a** *adj* Montenegrin.
▶ *nm & nf* Montenegrin.
**Montenegro** *nm* Montenegro.
**montepío** *nm* friendly society.
**montera** *nf* bullfighter's hat.
**montería** *nf (caza)* hunt.
**montero,-a** *nm & nf* hunter.
**montés** *adj* wild.
**montículo** *nm* mound, hillock.
**monto** *nm* total, total amount.
**montón** *nm* **1** heap, pile. **2** *fam (gran cantidad)* stacks *pl*, loads *pl*, heaps *pl*:

*vino un montón de gente* loads of people came.

**montura** *nf* **2** *(silla)* saddle. **3** *(armazón - de gafas)* frame.

**monumental** *adj* monumental.

**monumento** *nm* ARTE monument.

**monzón** *nm* monsoon.

**monzónico,-a** *adj* monsoon.

**moña** *nf fam (borrachera)* bender.

**moño** *nm* bun.

**moquear** *vi* to have a runny nose.

**moqueta** *nf* fitted carpet.

**moquillo** *nm (de perro)* distemper.

**mora** *nf* **1** *(de moral)* mulberry. **2** *(zarzamora)* blackberry.

**morada** *nf* adobe, dwelling.

**morado,-a** *adj (color)* purple.
▶ *nm* **morado** *(color)* purple.

**morador,-ra** *nm & nf* dweller.

**moral¹** *adj* moral.
▶ *nf* **1** *(reglas)* morals *pl*. **2** *(ánimo)* morale, spirits *pl*.

**moral²** *nm* BOT mulberry tree.

**moraleja** *nf* moral.

**moralidad** *nf* morality.

**moralina** *nf* false morals *pl*.

**moralista** *adj* moralistic.

**moralizador,-ra** *adj* moralizing.

**moralizar** *vi* to moralize.
▶ *vt* to moralize.

**morar** *vi* to reside, dwell.

**moratón** *nm fam* bruise.

**moratoria** *nf* moratorium.

**morbidez** *nf* softness, tenderness.

**morbo** *nm fam* thrill.

**morbosidad** *nf (interés)* morbid curiosity.

**morboso,-a** *adj fam* kinky.

**morcilla** *nf* black pudding.

**mordaz** *adj* mordant, sarcastic.

**mordaza** *nf* gag.

**mordedura** *nf* bite.

**morder** *vt* to bite: *le ha mordido mi perro* my dog's bitten him.
▶ *vi* to bite: *ten cuidado que muerde* be careful, it bites.
▶ *vpr* **morderse** to bite. LOC **morderse la lengua** *(callarse)* to hold one's tongue.

**mordida** *nf fam (soborno)* bribe.

**mordiente** *nm* mordant.

**mordisco** *nm* bite.

**mordisquear** *vt* to nibble.

**morena** *nf (pez)* moray eel.

**moreno,-a** *adj* **1** *(pelo)* dark. **2** *(pan, azúcar)* brown.
▶ *nm* **moreno** suntan.

**morera** *nf* white mulberry.

**moretón** *nm* bruise.

**morfema** *nm* morpheme.

**morfina** *nf* morphine.

**morfinómano,-a** *nm & nf* morphine addict.

**morfología** *nf* morphology.

**morfológico,-a** *adj* morphological.

**morganático,-a** *adj* morganatic.

**morgue** *nf* morgue.

**moribundo,-a** *adj* moribund.

**morir** *vi (ser vivo)* to die.
▶ *vpr* **morirse** to die.

**mormón,-ona** *adj* Mormon.
▶ *nm & nf* Mormon.

**mormónico,-a** *adj* Mormon.

**moro,-a** *adj* Moorish.
▶ *nm & nf* Moor.

**morosidad** *nf* **1** *(tardanza)* delay; *(- en un pago)* arrears *pl*.

**moroso,-a** *adj* FIN *(cliente)* in arrears.
▶ *nm & nf* defaulter.

**morral** *nm* haversack.

**morralla** *nf* **1** *(pescado)* small fish. **2** *pey (gente)* riffraff.

**morrazo** LOC **pegarse un morrazo** *fam* to give os a bash.

**morrena** *nf* moraine.

**morriña** *nf* homesickness.

**morrión** *nm* helmet.

**morro** *nm* **1** *fam (de persona - boca)* lips *pl*, mouth; *(cara)* face. **2** *fam (cara dura)* cheek. **3** *(de animal)* snout, nose.

**morrocotudo,-a** *adj fam* terrific.

**morrón** *adj* COMP **pimiento morrón** sweet red pepper.

**morrudo,-a** *adj fam* thick-lipped.

**morsa** *nf* walrus.

**Morse** *nm* Morse code.

**mortadela** *nf* mortadella.

**M**

**mortaja** *nf* shroud.
**mortal** *adj* **1** *(criatura, ser)* mortal. **2** *(peligro, herida)* fatal. **3** *(aburrimiento, susto)* deadly.
  ▶ *nm o nf* mortal.
**mortalidad** *nf* mortality.
**mortandad** *nf* death toll.
**mortecino,-a** *adj* **1** *(luz)* faint, dull. **2** *(color)* lifeless, dull.
**mortero** *nm* mortar.
**mortífero,-a** *adj* deadly, lethal.
**mortificación** *nf* mortification.
**mortificante** *adj* mortifying.
**mortificar** *vt* to mortify.
**mortuorio,-a** *adj* mortuary.
**moruno,-a** *adj* Moorish.
**mosaico** *nm* mosaic.
**mosca** *nf* fly.
**moscada** COMP **nuez moscada** nutmeg.
**moscardón** *nm* **1** blowfly. **2** *(persona)* pest.
**moscatel** *nm* muscatel.
**mosconear** *vt fam* to pester.
  ▶ *vi fam* to be a pest, be a pain.
**mosquear** *vt fam* to annoy.
  ▶ *vpr* **mosquearse** *fam (enfadarse)* to get cross.
**mosquete** *nm* musket.
**mosquetero** *nm* musketeer.
**mosquetón** *nm* **1** *(arma)* short carbine. **2** *(cierre)* snap link.
**mosquitera** *nf* mosquito net.
**mosquitero** *nm* mosquito net.
**mosquito** *nm* mosquito.
**mostacera** *nf* mustard pot.
**mostacho** *nm* moustache.
**mostaza** *nf* mustard.
**mosto** *nm* *(zumo)* grape juice.
**mostrador** *nm* *(de tienda)* counter.
**mostrar** *vt* to show.
  ▶ *vpr* **mostrarse** to appear.
**mostrenco,-a** *adj (grande)* mammoth.
**mota** *nf (partícula)* speck.
**mote** *nm* nickname.
**moteado,-a** *adj* dotted, speckled.
**motear** *vt* to fleck, speck.

**motejar** *vt* to nickname.
**motel** *nm* motel.
**motilidad** *nf* motility.
**motín** *nm (levantamiento)* riot, uprising.
**motivación** *nf* motivation, motive.
**motivar** *vt* **1** *(causar)* to cause, give rise to. **2** *(estimular)* to motivate.
**motivo** *nm* motive, reason, cause.
**moto** *nf fam (motocicleta)* motorbike.
**motocarro** *nm* three-wheeled van.
**motocicleta** *nf* motorcycle.
**motociclismo** *nm* motorcycling.
**motociclista** *nm o nf* motorcyclist.
**motocross** *nm* motocross.
**motocultivo** *nm* mechanised agriculture.
**motonáutica** *nf* speedboat racing.
**motonáutico,-a** *adj* speedboat.
**motor,-ra** *adj* **1** motive. **2** BIOL motor: *función motora* motor function.
  ▶ *nm* **motor** TÉC engine.
**motora** *nf* small motorboat.
**motorismo** *nm* motorcycling.
**motorista** *nm o nf* motorcyclist.
**motorizado,-a** *adj* motorized.
**motorizar** *vt* to motorize.
**motosierra** *nf* power saw.
**motriz** *adj* [sólo se usa con monbres en femenino] motive.
**mousse** *nf* CULIN mousse.
**mouton** *nm (piel)* sheepskin.
**movedizo,-a** *adj (inestable)* unstable.
**mover** *vt* to move.
  ▶ *vpr* **moverse** **1** *(gen)* to move. **2** *fam (darse prisa)* to get a move on.
**movible** *adj* movable.
**movida** *nf fam (animación)* action.
**movido,-a** *adj* **1** *(día, temporada)* busy. **2** *(fiesta, concurso)* lively. **3** *(foto)* blurred.
**móvil** *adj* movable, mobile.
  ▶ *nm* **1** FÍS moving body. **2** *(motivo)* motive. **3** *(decoración, juguete)* mobile. **4** *(teléfono)* mobile (phone), cell phone.
**movilidad** *nf* mobility.
**movilización** *nf* mobilization.
**movilizar** *vt* to mobilize.
**movimiento** *nm* **1** *(gen)* movement; *(técnicamente)* motion. **2** *(de gente, ideas)*

activity. **3** *(artístico, político)* movement.

**moviola®** *nf (máquina)* Moviola.

**moza** *nf (chica)* lass.

**Mozambique** *nm* Mozambique.

**mozambiqueño,-a** *adj* Mozambiquean.
▶ *nm & nf* Mozambiquean.

**mozárabe** *adj* Mozarab.
▶ *nm o nf* Mozarab.

**mozo,-a** *adj* young.
▶ *nm* **mozo 1** *(joven)* young man, lad. **2** *(camarero)* waiter. **3** *(de estación)* porter.

**MP3** *abrev* (Moving Pictures Experts Group Audio Layer 3) MP3.

**mu** *interj (mugido)* moo.

**muaré** *nm* moiré.

**muchacho,-a** *nm & nf (chico)* boy; *(chica)* girl.

**muchedumbre** *nf (de personas)* crowd.

**mucho,-a** *adj* **1** *(singular - en afirmativas)* a lot of; *(- en negativas, interrogativas)* a lot of, much: *hicieron mucho ruido* they made a lot of noise; *no tiene mucho dinero* he hasn't got a lot of/much money. **2** *(plural - en afirmativas)* a lot of, lots of; *(- en negativas, interrogativas)* a lot of, many: *¿tienes muchos libros?* have you got a lot of/many books? **3** *(demasiado - singular)* too much; *(- plural)* too many.
▶ *pron (singular)* a lot, much; *(plural)* a lot, many: *muchos de sus amigos acudieron* many of his friends came.
▶ *adv* **1** *(de cantidad)* a lot, much: *mucho mejor/peor* much better/worse. **2** *(de tiempo)*: *mucho antes/después* much earlier/later. **3** *(de frecuencia)* often: *no vienen mucho por aquí* they don't come here often. [LOC] **como mucho** at the most: *te pagarán como mucho treinta euros* they'll pay you thirty euros at the most.

**mucosa** *nf* mucous membrane.

**mucosidad** *nf* mucus.

**mucoso,-a** *adj* mucous.

**muda** *nf (de ropa)* change of clothes.

**mudable** *adj* **1** changeable. **2** *(carácter)* fickle.

**mudanza** *nf (de residencia)* moving.

**mudar** *vt* **1** to change, alter. **2** *(plumas)* to moult (US molt). **3** *(voz)* to break: *le está mudando la voz* his voice is breaking. **4** *(piel)* to shed.
▶ *vpr* **mudarse 1** to change. **2** *(de residencia)* to move.

**mudez** *nf* dumbness, muteness.

**mudo,-a** *adj* **1** *(por defecto)* dumb; *(por voluntad)* silent, quiet. **2** *(vocal, consonante)* mute.

**mueble** *nm* piece of furniture.
▶ *nm pl* **muebles** furniture *sing*.

**mueca** *nf* **1** *(de burla)* mocking gesture, face. **2** *(de dolor)* grimace.

**muela** *nf (diente)* tooth, molar.

**muelle** *nm* **1** *(elástico)* spring. **2** MAR dock, wharf; *(malecón)* pier, jetty.

**muérdago** *nm* mistletoe.

**muerdo** *nm fam* bite.

**muermo** *nm fam* drag, pain, bore.

**muerte** *nf* **1** death. **2** *(asesinato)* murder.

**muerto,-a** *adj* **1** *(sin vida)* dead; *(sin actividad)* lifeless. **2** *fam (cansado)* tired.
▶ *nm & nf* dead person.

**muesca** *nf (corte)* nick, notch.

**muesli** *nm* muesli.

**muestra** *nf* **1** *(ejemplar)* sample. **2** *(modelo)* pattern. **3** *(señal)* proof, sign: *daba muestras de alegría* she looked happy. **4** *(exposición)* show, display.

**muestrario** *nm* collection of samples.

**muestreo** *nm (gen)* sampling.

**mugido** *nm (de vaca - uno)* moo.

**mugir** *vi (vaca)* to moo.

**mugre** *nf* grime, filth.

**mugriento,-a** *adj* grimy, filthy.

**muguete** *nm* lily of the valley.

**mujer** *nf* **1** woman. **2** *(esposa)* wife.

**mujeriego,-a** *adj pey* fond of the ladies.

**mujerona** *nf fam* big woman.

**mújol** *nm* grey mullet.

**muladar** *nm* dump.

**mulato,-a** *adj* mulatto.
▶ *nm & nf* mulatto.

**mulero** *nm* muleteer.

**muleta** *nf (para andar)* crutch.

**muletilla** *nf* **1** *(bastón)* cross-handled cane. **2** *(frase repetida)* pet phrase.

**muletón** *nm* flannelette.

**mullido,-a** *adj* soft, springy.

**mullir** *vt (lana)* to soften; *(almohada, colchón)* to fluff up.

**mulo,-a** *nm & nf (macho)* mule; *(hembra)* she-mule. LOC **ser más terco,-a que una mula** to be as stubborn as a mule.

**multa** *nf (gen)* fine; *(de tráfico)* ticket.

**multar** *vt* to fine: *¿cuánto te multaron?* how much did they fine you?

**multiacceso** *nm* multiaccess.

**multicines** *nm pl* multiplex *sing.*

**multicolor** *adj* multicoloured.

**multicopiar** *vt* to duplicate.

**multicopista** *nf* duplicator.

**multicultural** *adj* multicultural.

**multidimensional** *adj* multidimensional.

**multidireccional** *adj* multidirectional.

**multidisciplinar** *adj* multidisciplinary.

**multifacético,-a** *adj* multifaceted.

**multiforme** *adj* multiform.

**multigrado** *adj* multigrade.

**multilateral** *adj* multilateral.

**multimedia** *adj* multimedia.

**multimillonario,-a** *adj (de libras)* multimillion-pound; *(de dólares)* multimillion-dollar: *un contrato multimillonario* a multimillion-dollar contract.
▶ *nm & nf* multimillionaire.

**multinacional** *adj* multinational.
▶ *nf* multinational.

**multípara** *nf* multiparous.

**múltiple** *adj* **1** multiple. **2** *(muchos)* many, a number of, numerous: *opiniones múltiples* a number of opinions.

**multiplicable** *adj* multipliable.

**multiplicación** *nf* multiplication.

**multiplicador,-ra** *adj* multiplying.
▶ *nm* **multiplicador** multiplier.

**multiplicar** *vt* to multiply (por, by).

**multiplicidad** *nf* multiplicity.

**múltiplo** *adj* multiple.
▶ *nm* multiple.

**multipropiedad** *nf* time-share.

**multirracial** *adj* multiracial.

**multirriesgo** *adj* fully comprehensive.

**multitud** *nf* **1** *(de personas)* crowd. **2** *(de cosas, ideas)* multitude.

**multitudinario,-a** *adj* multitudinous.

**multiuso** *adj* multipurpose.

**mundanal** *adj* of the world, mundane. LOC **huir del mundanal ruido** to get away from it all.

**mundano,-a** *adj* of the world.

**mundial** *adj* worldwide, world.
▶ *nm* world championship. LOC **de fama mundial** world-famous. COMP **mundial de fútbol** World Cup.

**mundialmente** *adv* worldwide. LOC **mundialmente conocido,-a** world-famous.

**mundillo** *nm* world, circles *pl*: *el mundillo teatral* theatrical circles.

**mundo** *nm* world: *ha dado la vuelta al mundo dos veces* he's been around the world twice; *vive aislado en su propio mundo* he's isolated himself in his own little world; *el mundo del cine* the cinema, the world of cinema. LOC **no ser nada del otro mundo** to be nothing to write home about. ▌**por nada del mundo** not for all the world. ▌**tener mundo** to know the ways of the world. ▌**venir al mundo** to come into the world. ▌**el fin del mundo** the end of the world. COMP **el Nuevo Mundo** the New World. ▌**el Tercer Mundo** the Third World.

**mundología** *nf fam* worldliness.

**munición** *nf* ammunition.

**municipal** *adj (gobierno)* town, municipal; *(instalaciones)* council.
▶ *nm o nf (hombre)* policeman; *(mujer)* policewoman.
▶ *nf pl* **las municipales** local elections.

**municipio** *nm* **1** municipality. **2** *(ayuntamiento)* town council.

**muñeca** *nf* **1** ANAT wrist. **2** *(juguete)* doll. COMP **muñeca de trapo** rag doll.

**muñeco** *nm (juguete)* doll. COMP **muñeco de nieve** snowman.

**muñequera** *nf* wristband.

**muñir** *vt (amañar)* to fix.

**muñón** *nm* ANAT stump.

**mural** *adj* mural.
▶ *nm* mural.

**muralla** *nf* city wall.

**murciélago** *nm* bat.

**murga** *nf fam* nuisance. LOC **dar la murga** *fam* to be a pain in the neck.

**murmullante** *adj* babbling.

**murmullo** *nm (susurro)* whisper, whispering; *(voz baja)* murmur, murmuring.

**murmuración** *nf* gossip, backbiting.

**murmurador,-ra** *adj* gossipy.
▶ *nm & nf* gossip.

**murmurar** *vt (susurrar)* to murmur, whisper.
▶ *vi* **1** *(criticar)* to gossip. **2** *(decir en voz baja)* to murmur.

**muro** *nm* wall.

**murria** *nf* sadness, melancholy.

**mus** *nm card game in which players use signs to communicate.*

**musa** *nf* muse.
▶ *nf pl* **las musas** the Arts.

**musaraña** *nf* ZOOL shrew. LOC **estar pensando en las musarañas** to day-dream.

**musculación** *nf* body-building.

**muscular** *adj* muscular.

**musculatura** *nf* muscles *pl*.

**músculo** *nm* muscle.

**musculoso,-a** *adj* muscular.

**muselina** *nf* muslin.

**museo** *nm* museum. COMP **museo de arte** art museum.

**musgo** *nm* moss. LOC **cubierto,-a de musgo** mossy, moss-covered.

**musgoso,-a** *adj* mossy.

**música** *nf* music. COMP **música de fondo** background music. ‖ **música clásica** classical music.

**musical** *adj* musical.
▶ *nm* musical.

**musicalidad** *nf* musicality.

**musicar** *vt* to write the music for, set to music.

**músico,-a** *nm & nf* musician.

**musicología** *nf* musicology.

**musicólogo,-a** *nm & nf* musicologist.

**musiquilla** *nf fam pey* tacky music.

**musitar** *vi (susurrar)* to whisper.

**muslo** *nm* **1** thigh. **2** CULIN *(de ave)* drumstick.

**mustiarse** *vi* to wilt, wither.

**mustio,-a** *adj* **1** *(plantas)* withered, faded. **2** *(persona)* down, downcast.

**musulmán,-ana** *adj* Muslim.
▶ *nm & nf* Muslim.

**mutabilidad** *nf* changeability.

**mutable** *adj* mutable.

**mutación** *nf* **1** change. **2** BIOL mutation.

**mutante** *adj* mutant.
▶ *nm o nf* mutant.

**mutilación** *nf* mutilation.

**mutilado,-a** *adj (persona)* disabled.
▶ *nm & nf* cripple.

**mutilar** *vt* to cripple

**mutis** *nm* TEAT exit.

**mutismo** *nm* silence.

**mutua** *nf* mutual benefit society. COMP **mutua de seguros** mutual insurance company.

**mutualidad** *nf (asociación)* mutual benefit society.

**mutualista** *nm o nf* member of a mutual benefit society.

**mutuamente** *adv* mutually: *se quieren mutuamente* they love each other.

**mutuo,-a** *adj* mutual, reciprocal: *por mutuo acuerdo* by mutual agreement.

**muy** *adv* very: *es muy difícil* it's very difficult; *se levantó muy temprano* he got up very early; *lo has hecho muy bien* you've done it very well. LOC **muy de mañana** very early in the morning. ‖ **por muy que...** however…: *por muy tarde que sea* however late it is.

**N, n** *nf (la letra)* N, n.
**N** *sím* **(norte)** north; *(símbolo)* N.
**nabo** *nm (planta)* turnip.
**nácar** *nm* mother-of-pearl.
**nacarado,-a** *adj* nacred.
**nacer** *vi* **1** *(persona)* to be born; *(ave)* to hatch out; *(semilla, planta)* to sprout. **2** *(río)* to rise; *(agua)* to spring; *(camino)* to start, begin. **3** *(sol)* to rise. LOC **al nacer** at birth.
**nacido,-a** *adj* born. LOC **bien nacido,-a** *(de buen corazón)* kind-hearted. ▌ **mal nacido,-a** despicable.
**naciente** *adj* **1** *(nuevo)* new. **2** *(creciente)* growing.
▶ *nm (este)* East.
**nacimiento** *nm* **1** birth. **2** *fig* origin, beginning. LOC **de nacimiento** from birth.
**nación** *nf* nation. COMP **Naciones Unidas** United Nations.
**nacional** *adj* national.
**nacionalidad** *nf* nationality.
**nacionalismo** *nm* nationalism.
**nacionalista** *adj* nationalist.
▶ *nm o nf* nationalist.
**nacionalización** *nf* naturalization.
**nacionalizar** *vt* **1** *(persona)* to naturalize. **2** *(empresa)* to nationalize.
▶ *vpr* **nacionalizarse** *(persona)* to become naturalized: *nacionalizarse español/británico/etc* to take up Spanish/British/etc citizenship.
**nada** *pron* nothing: *no quiero nada* I don't want anything.
▶ *adv* (not) at all: *no me gusta nada* I don't like it at all.
▶ *nf* nothingness. LOC **de nada 1** *(no hay de qué)* don't mention it, think nothing of it, (US you're welcome). **2** *(insignificante)* insignificant: *gracias, –de nada* thanks, – don't mention it. ▌ **nada más...** as soon as…, no sooner…
**nadador,-ra** *nm & nf* swimmer.
**nadar** *vi* to swim.
**nadería** *nf* trifle.
**nadie** *pron* nobody, not… anybody: *aquí no hay nadie* there's nobody here.
**nado** LOC **a nado** swimming: *cruzaron el río a nado* they swam across the river.
**nafta** *nf* naphtha.
**naftalina** *nf* naphthalene. COMP **bola de naftalina** mothball.
**naif** *adj* naïf, naive.
▶ *nm* naïf art.
**nailon®** *nm* nylon®.
**naipe** *nm* playing card.
**nalga** *nf* buttock.
**Namibia** *nf* Namibia.
**namibio,-a** *adj* Namibian.
▶ *nm & nf* Namibian.
**nana** *nf* lullaby.
**naranja** *nf (fruto)* orange.
▶ *adj (color)* orange.
**naranjada** *nf* orangeade, orange drink.
**naranjal** *nm* orange grove.
**naranjo** *nm* orange tree.
**narcisismo** *nm* narcissism.
**narcisista** *adj* narcissistic.
▶ *nm o nf* narcissist.
**narciso** *nm* **1** *(flor)* daffodil, narcissus. **2** *(hombre)* narcissist.
**narcótico,-a** *adj* narcotic.
▶ *nm* **narcótico** *(medicamento)* narcotic; *(droga)* drug.
**narcotraficante** *adj* drug trafficking.
▶ *nm o nf* drug trafficker.

**narcotráfico** *nm* drug trafficking.

**nardo** *nm* nard, spikenard.

**narigón,-ona** *adj fam* big-nosed.

**nariz** *nf* **1** ANAT nose. **2** *fig (sentido)* sense of smell. LOC **meter las narices en** ALGO to poke one's nose into STH.
▶ *interj* **¡narices!** *fam* not on your life!

**narración** *nf (historia)* story.

**narrador,-ra** *nm & nf* storyteller.

**narrar** *vt (gen)* to tell, relate, narrate.

**narrativa** *nf (género)* fiction.

**narval** *nm* narwhal.

**nasa** *nf (aparejo)* keepnet; *(cesta)* creel.

**nasal** *adj* nasal.
▶ *nf (letra)* nasal.

**nata** *nf* **1** cream. **2** *(de leche hervida)* skin. COMP **nata montada** whipped cream.

**natación** *nf* swimming.

**natal** *adj* native. COMP **ciudad natal** home town: **l país natal** native country.

**natalicio** *nm* birthday.

**natalidad** *nf* birth rate.

**natillas** *nf pl* custard *sing*.

**natividad** *nf* nativity.

**nativo,-a** *adj* native.

**nato,-a** *adj* born.

**natural** *adj* **1** *(no artificial)* natural. **2** *(fruta, flor)* fresh. LOC **al natural** CULIN in its own juice.
▶ *nm (nativo)* native, inhabitant. LOC **ser natural de** to be a native of, come from.

**naturaleza** *nf* **1** nature. **2** *(complexión)* physical constitution.

**naturalidad** *nf* **1** *(sencillez)* naturalness. **2** *(espontaneidad)* ease, spontaneity.

**naturalismo** *nm* naturalism.

**naturalista** *adj* naturalist.
▶ *nm o nf* naturalist.

**naturalizar** *vt* to naturalize.
▶ *vpr* **naturalizarse** to become naturalized: *se ha naturalizado español* he has taken up Spanish citizenship.

**naturista** *adj* naturist.
▶ *nm o nf* naturist.

**naturopatía** *nf* naturopathy.

**naufragar** *vi* **1** *(barco)* to sink, be wrecked; *(persona)* to be shipwrecked. **2** *fig* to fail.

**naufragio** *nm* shipwreck.

**náufrago,-a** *adj* shipwrecked.
▶ *nm & nf* shipwrecked person.

**Nauru** *nm* Nauru.

**nauruano,-a** *adj* Nauruan.
▶ *nm & nf* Nauruan.

**náusea** [también se usa en plural con el mismo significado] *nf* nausea, sickness.

**nauseabundo,-a** *adj* nauseating.

**náutica** *nf* navigation, seamanship.

**náutico,-a** *adj* nautical. COMP **deportes náuticos** water sports.

**navaja** *nf (cuchillo)* penknife.

**naval** *adj* naval.

**nave** *nf* **1** *(náutica)* ship, vessel. **2** *(espacial)* spaceship, spacecraft. **3** *(almacén)* industrial warehouse.

**navegable** *adj (río)* navigable.

**navegación** *nf (arte)* navigation.

**navegador** *nm (de internet)* browser.

**navegante** *nm o nf* navigator.

**navegar** *vi* **1** *(barco)* to sail. **2** *(avión)* to fly.

**Navidad** *nf* Christmas. LOC **felicitar las Navidades a** ALGN to wish SB a merry Christmas.

**navideño,-a** *adj* Christmas.

**naviera** *nf (empresa)* shipping company.

**navío** *nm* vessel, ship.

**Neanderthal** *adj* Neanderthal.

**neblina** *nf* mist.

**neblinoso,-a** *adj* misty.

**nebulizador** *nm* nebulizer.

**nebulosa** *nf* nebula.

**nebulosidad** *nf* nebulosity.

**nebuloso,-a** *adj* cloudy, hazy.

**necedad** *nf (ignorancia)* stupidity.

**necesario,-a** *adj* necessary.

**neceser** *nm (bolsa de aseo)* toilet bag.

**necesidad** *nf* **1** necessity, need. **2** *(pobreza)* poverty, want. LOC **pasar necesidades** to be in need.

**necesitado,-a** *adj* needy, poor.

**necesitar** *vt* to need.

**necio,-a** *adj* stupid.

**nécora** *nf* fiddler crab.

**necrología** *nf (biografía)* obituary.
**necrológico,-a** *adj* obituary.
▶ *nf pl* **necrológicas** *(sección prensa)* obituaries *pl*.
**necrópolis** *nf inv* necropolis.
**necrosis** *nf inv* necrosis.
**néctar** *nm* nectar.
**nectarina** *nf* nectarine.
**neerlandés,-esa** *adj* Dutch.
▶ *nm & nf* **1** *(persona - hombre)* Dutchman; *(- mujer)* Dutch woman. **2** *(idioma)* Dutch.
**nefasto,-a** *adj* unlucky, ill-fated.
**nefrítico,-a** *adj* nephritic. COMP **cólico nefrítico** nephrocolic.
**negación** *nf* **1** *(de un derecho)* negation. **2** refusal. **3** *(en gramática)* negative.
**negado,-a** *adj (inepto)* hopeless.
**negar** *vt* **1** *(rechazar)* to deny. **2** *(no conceder)* to refuse.
▶ *vpr* **negarse** to refuse (a, to): *se negó a devolverme el dinero* he refused to give me my money back.
**negativa** *nf (rechazo)* refusal.
**negativo,-a** *adj* negative.
▶ *nm* **negativo** *(en fotografía)* negative.
**negligencia** *nf* negligence.
**negligente** *adj* negligent.
▶ *nm o nf* negligent person.
**negociable** *adj* negotiable.
**negociación** *nf* negotiation.
**negociado** *nm (sección)* department.
**negociador,-ra** *adj* negotiating.
▶ *nm & nf* negotiator.
**negociante** *nm o nf* dealer, merchant.
**negociar** *vi (comerciar)* to do business, deal (con, in).
▶ *vt* POL to negotiate.
**negocio** *nm* **1** *(actividad)* business. **2** *(gestión)* deal, transaction.
**negra** *nf* MÚS crotchet, US quarter note.
**negro,-a** *adj* **1** *(gen)* black. **2** *(cine, novela)* detective.
▶ *nm & nf (hombre)* black (man); *(mujer)* black (woman).
▶ *nm* **negro** *(color)* black.
**negrura** *nf* blackness.
**negruzco,-a** *adj* blackish.

**nene,-a** *nm & nf* baby.
**nenúfar** *nm* water lily.
**neoclasicismo** *nm* neoclassicism.
**neoclásico,-a** *adj* neoclassical.
**neocolonialismo** *nm* neocolonialism.
**neófito,-a** *nm & nf* neophyte.
**neolítico,-a** *adj* neolithic.
▶ *nm* **neolítico** Neolithic.
**neologismo** *nm* neologism.
**neón** *nm* neon.
**neonatal** *adj* neonatal.
**neorrealismo** *nm* neorealism.
**neozelandés,-esa** *adj* of New Zealand, from New Zealand.
▶ *nm & nf* New Zealander.
**Nepal** *nm* Nepal.
**nepalés,-esa** *adj* Nepalese, Nepali.
▶ *nm & nf (persona)* Nepalese, Nepali.
▶ *nm* **nepalés** *(idioma)* Nepalese, Nepali.
**nepotismo** *nm* nepotism.
**nereida** *nf* nereid.
**nervadura** *nf* BOT nervures *pl*.
**nervio** *nm* ANAT nerve.
▶ *nm pl* **nervios** nerves. LOC **tener los nervios de punta** to be on edge.
**nerviosismo** *nm* nervousness.
**nervioso,-a** *adj (gen)* nervous. LOC **ponerse nervioso,-a** to get nervous.
**neto,-a** *adj (peso, cantidad)* net.
**neumático,-a** *nm* tyre (US tire).
**neumonía** *nf* pneumonia.
**neura** *nf fam* obsession.
**neurálgico,-a** *adj fig (fundamental)* key.
**neurocirujano,-a** *nm & nf* neurosurgeon.
**neurología** *nf* neurology.
**neurólogo,-a** *nm & nf* neurologist.
**neurona** *nf* neuron, neurone.
**neurosis** *nf inv* neurosis.
**neurótico,-a** *adj* neurotic.
▶ *nm & nf* neurotic.
**neutral** *adj* neutral.
**neutralidad** *nf* neutrality.
**neutralizar** *vt* to neutralize.
**neutro,-a** *adj* **1** neutral. **2** LING neuter.
▶ *nm* **neutro** neuter.
**neutrón** *nm* neutron.
**nevada** *nf* snowfall.

**nevado,-a** *adj* covered with snow.

**nevar** *vi* [se usa sólo en tercera persona; no lleva sujeto] to snow.

**nevera** *nf (eléctrica)* fridge, refrigerator.

**nevero** *nm* ice field.

**newton** *nm* newton.

**nexo** *nm* **1** link. **2** LING connective.

**ni** *conj* **1** neither, nor. **2** not even.

**Nicaragua** *nf* Nicaragua.

**nicaragüense** *adj* Nicaraguan.
▶ *nm o nf* Nicaraguan.

**nicho** *nm* niche.

**nicotina** *nf* nicotine.

**nidada** *nf (polluelos)* brood.

**nidificar** *vi* to nest.

**nido** *nm* nest.

**niebla** *nf* **1** *(nubes)* fog. **2** *fig* mist.

**nieto,-a** *nm & nf* grandchild; *(niño)* grandson; *(niña)* granddaughter.

**nieve** *nf* snow.

**Nigeria** *nf* Nigeria.

**nigeriano,-a** *adj* Nigerian.
▶ *nm & nf* Nigerian.

**nigromancia** *nf* necromancy.

**nihilismo** *nm* nihilism.

**nihilista** *adj* nihilistic.

**nilón®** *nm* nylon®.

**nimbo** *nm* nimbus.

**nimiedad** *nf (cosa nimia)* trifle.

**nimio,-a** *adj* insignificant, trivial.

**ninfa** *nf* nymph.

**ningún** *adj* [se usa ante un nombre masculino en singular] → **ninguno,-a.**

**ninguno,-a** *adj* no, not any.
▶ *pron* **1** *(persona)* nobody, no one. **2** *(objeto)* not any, none: *ninguno me gusta* I don't like any of them.

✎ Consulta también **ningún.**

**niñato,-a** *nm & nf fam* brat.

**niñera** *nf* nanny.

**niñería** *nf (chiquillada)* childishness.

**niñez** *nf (de una persona)* childhood.

**niño,-a** *nm & nf* **1** *(gen)* child; *(chico)* boy, little boy; *(chica)* girl, little girl.
▶ *nm pl* **niños** children, kids.

**nipón,-ona** *adj* Nipponese.
▶ *nm & nf* Nipponese.

**níquel** *nm* nickel.

**niquelado,-a** *adj* nickel-plated.

**niquelar** *vt* to nickel.

**niqui** *nm* T-shirt.

**nirvana** *nm* nirvana.

**níscalo** *nm* milk cap.

**níspero** *nm (fruto)* medlar.

**nitidez** *nf (transparencia)* clearness.

**nítido,-a** *adj (claro)* accurate.

**nitrato** *nm* nitrate.

**nítrico,-a** *adj* nitric.

**nitrito** *nm* nitrite.

**nitrógeno** *nm* nitrogen.

**nitroglicerina** *nf* nitroglycerine.

**nitroso,-a** *adj* nitrous.

**nivel** *nm* **1** *(altura)* level. **2** *(categoría)* standard. COMP **nivel del mar** sea level.

**nivelación** *nf (de un terreno)* levelling.

**nivelado,-a** *adj* level.

**nivelar** *vt (gen)* to level out, level off.

**níveo,-a** *adj lit* snow-white.

**no** *adv* no, not.
▶ *nm* no: *un no rotundo* a definite no.

**nobel** *nm* Nobel prize.

**nobiliario,-a** *adj* noble.

**noble** *adj (gen)* noble; *(madera)* fine.
▶ *nm o nf* noble.

**nobleza** *nf* **1** honesty. **2** nobility.

**noche** *nf* night. LOC **buenas noches 1** *(saludo)* good evening. **2** *(despedida)* good night. **| por la noche** at night, after dark.

**Nochebuena** *nf* Christmas Eve.

**Nochevieja** *nf* New Year's Eve.

**noción** *nf* notion, idea.

**nocividad** *nf* noxiousness.

**nocivo,-a** *adj* noxious, harmful.

**noctámbulo,-a** *adj* nocturnal.
▶ *nm & nf fam (trasnochador)* night owl.

**nocturno,-a** *adj (gen)* nocturnal; *(vida)* night; *(clase)* evening.

**nodo** *nm* node.

**nodriza** *nf* wet nurse.

**nodular** *adj* nodular, nodulated.

**nódulo** *nm* nodule.

**nogal** *nm* walnut tree.

**nogalina** *nf* walnut dye.

**N**

**nómada** *adj* nomadic.
▶ *nm o nf* nomad.
**nomadismo** *nm* nomadism.
**nombrado,-a** *adj* well-known.
**nombramiento** *nm* appointment.
**nombrar** *vt* to name.
**nombre** *nm* **1** name. **2** LING noun.
**nomenclatura** *nf* nomenclature.
**nomeolvides** *nm inv (flor)* forget-me-not.
**nómina** *nf* pay cheque (US check).
**nominación** *nf* nomination.
**nominal** *adj* nominal.
**nominalismo** *nm* nominalism.
**nominalista** *adj* nominalist.
**nominalizar** *vt* to substantivize.
**nominalmente** *adv* nominally.
**nominar** *vt* to nominate.
**nominativo,-a** *adj* **1** *(cheque)* personal.
  **2** LING nominative.
**non** *nm* odd number.
**nonagenario,-a** *nm & nf* nonagenarian.
**nonagésimo,-a** *nm & nf* ninetieth.
▶ *adj* ninetieth.
**nones** *interj* no way!
**noquear** *vt* to knock out.
**norcoreano,-a** *adj* North Korean.
▶ *nm & nf* North Korean.
**nordeste** *nm* northeast.
**nórdico,-a** *adj* **1** *(del norte)* northern. **2**
*(de los países del norte)* Nordic.
▶ *nm & nf (persona)* Scandinavian.
**noreste** *nm* → nordeste.
**noria** *nf* **1** *(para agua)* water wheel.
  **2** *(de feria)* big wheel.
**norma** *nf* norm, rule.
**normal** *adj (habitual)* normal, usualy.
▶ *nf (gasolina)* two-star petrol.
**normalidad** *nf* normality.
**normalización** *nf* normalization.
**normalizar** *vt* to normalize.
**normativa** *nf* rules *pl*, regulations *pl*.
**normativo,-a** *adj* normative.
**noroeste** *nm* northwest.
**norte** *nm* north.
**Norteamérica** *nf* North America.
**norteamericano,-a** *adj* North American.
▶ *nm & nf* North American.

**Noruega** *nf* Norway.
**noruego,-a** *adj* Norwegian.
▶ *nm & nf (persona)* Norwegian.
▶ *nm* **noruego** *(idioma)* Norwegian.
**nos** *pron* **1** *(complemento)* us: *nos dijo que
no nos moviéramos* he told us not to
move. **2** *(uso reflexivo)* ourselves: *nos la-
vamos* we wash ourselves. **3** *(uso recíproco)* each other: *nos vemos mucho* we see
each other often.
**nosotros,-as** *pron* **1** *(sujeto)* we: *nosotros
no fuimos* we didn't go. **2** *(complemento)*
us: *con nosotros,-as* with us.
**nostalgia** *nf* homesickness.
**nostálgico,-a** *adj* nostalgic.
**nota** *nf* **1** *(anotación)* note. **2** *(calificación)*
mark, grade. **3** MÚS note.
**notable** *adj* considerable, remarkable.
**notación** *nf* notation.
**notar** *vt* **1** *(percibir)* to notice. **2** *(sentir)* to
feel: *noto un poco de calor* I feel a bit hot.
▶ *vpr* **notarse 1** *(percibirse)* to show:
*apenas se le nota la cicatriz* you can hardly
see his scar. **2** *(sentirse)* to feel.
**notario,-a** *nm & nf* notary public.
**noticia** *nf (información)* news *pl*.
▶ *nf pl* **las noticias** the news.
**noticiario** *nm* news.
**notición** *nm fam* bombshell.
**notificación** *nf* notification.
**notificar** *vt* to notify, inform.
**notoriedad** *nf (fama)* fame, prestige.
**notorio,-a** *adj* well-known.
**novatada** *nf (broma)* practical joke.
**novato,-a** *nm & nf (principiante)* beginner.
**novecientos,-as** *adj* nine hundred;
*(ordinal)* nine-hundredth.

✎ Consulta también seis.

**novedad** *nf* **1** *(cualidad)* newness. **2**
*(cambio)* change, innovation.
**novedoso,-a** *adj* novel.
**novel** *adj (escritor, escultor)* novice.
**novela** *nf* novel.
**novelar** *vt* to novelize.
**novelesco,-a** *adj (de novela)* fiction-like.
**novelista** *nm o nf* novelist.
**novena** *nf* REL novena.

**noveno,-a** *adj* ninth.
▶ *nm & nf* ninth.

✎ Consulta también **sexto**.

**noventa** *adj* ninety.
▶ *nm* ninety.

✎ Consulta también **sesenta**.

**novia** *nf (amiga)* girlfriend.
**noviazgo** *nm* engagement.
**novicio,-a** *nm & nf* REL novice.
**noviembre** *nm* November.

✎ Para ejemplos de uso, consulta **marzo**.

**novillada** *nf* bullfight with young bulls.
**novillero,-a** *nm & nf* novice bullfighter.
**novillo** *nm* young bull.
**novio** *nm* boyfriend.
**nubarrón** *nm* storm cloud.
**nube** *nf* cloud.
**núbil** *adj* nubile.
**nublado,-a** *adj* cloudy, overcast.
▶ *nm* **nublado** storm cloud.
**nubosidad** *nf* cloudiness.
**nuboso,-a** *adj* cloudy.
**nuca** *nf* nape (of the neck).
**nuclear** *adj* nuclear.
**núcleo** *nm* nucleus.
**nudillo** *nm* knuckle.
**nudismo** *nm* nudism.
**nudo** *nm* knot.
**nudoso,-a** *adj (madera)* knotty.
**nuera** *nf* daughter-in-law.
**nuestro,-a** *adj* our, of ours.
▶ *pron* ours.
**nueva** *nf* tidings *pl*, news *sing*.
**nueve** *adj* nine; *(noveno)* ninth.
▶ *nm* nine.

✎ Consulta también **seis**.

**nuevo,-a** *adj* new. LOC **de nuevo** again.
**nuez** *nf* BOT walnut.
**nulidad** *nf* **1** *(ineptitud)* incompetence. **2** JUR nullity.
**nulo,-a** *adj (sin valor)* invalid.

**numeración** *nf* **1** *(proceso)* numbering. **2** *(conjunto)* numbers *pl*. **3** *(sistema)* numbers *pl*, numerals *pl*.
**numerador** *nm* numerator.
**numeral** *adj* numeral.
▶ *nm* numeral.
**numerar** *vt* to number.
**numérico,-a** *adj* numerical.
**número** *nm* **1** *(gen)* number. **2** *(de una publicación)* number, issue. **3** *(de zapatos)* size: *¿qué número calzas?* what's your shoe size?, what size shoe do you take? **4** *(de un espectáculo)* act. **5** *(de lotería)* lottery ticket number. **7** LING number. COMP **número impar** odd number. **I número ordinal** ordinal number. **I número par** even number. **I número primo** prime number. **I número quebrado** fraction. **I número romano** Roman numeral.
**numeroso,-a** *adj* numerous: *son familia numerosa* they're a large family.
**numismática** *nf* numismatics.
**numismático,-a** *adj* numismatic.
**nunca** *adv* **1** never. **2** *(en interrogativa)* ever. LOC **más que nunca** more than ever. **I nunca más** never again. **I**
**nupcial** *adj (marcha, tarta)* wedding; *(misa)* nuptial; *(lecho)* marriage.
**nupcias** *nf pl fml* wedding *sing*, nuptials.
**nurse** *nf* nanny.
**nutria** *nf* otter.
**nutrición** *nf* nutrition.
**nutrido,-a** *adj (alimentado)* nourished.
**nutriente** *adj* nutrient.
▶ *nm* nutrient.
**nutrir** *vt* **1** *(alimentar)* to feed, nourish. **2** *fig* to encourage. **3** *(abastecer)* to supply (de, with).
▶ *vpr* **nutrirse 1** *(alimentarse)* to receive nourishment (de, from). **2** *fig (abastecerse)* to draw (de, on).
**nutritivo,-a** *adj* nutritious, nourishing. COMP **sustancia nutritiva** nutrient. **I valor nutritivo** nutritional value.

N

# Ñ

**Ñ, ñ** *nf the fifteenth letter of the Spanish alphabet.*

**ñandú** *nm* AM rhea.

**ñoñería** *nf (tontería)* inanity, nonsense.

**ñoño ,-a** *adj* **1** *(soso)* insipid, dull. **2** *(tímido)* shy. **3** *(remilgado)* fussy. **4** *(poco seguro)* wet, drippy, wimpish: *no seas ñoño, no es más que un rasguño* don't be such a wimp, it's no more than a scratch. **5** AM old.

**ñoqui** *nm* gnocchi *pl.*

**ñora** *nf type of* red pepper.

**ñu** *nm* gnu.

**O, o** *nf (la letra)* O, o.

**o** *conj* **1** or: *¿té o café?* tea or coffee? **2** *(concesiva)* whether… or: *estudie o no, tiene que aprobar* whether he studies or not, he has to pass.

**O** *sím (oeste)* west; *(símbolo)* W.

**oasis** *nm inv* oasis.

**obcecado,-a** *adj* blind.

**obcecar** *vt* to blind.
► *vpr* **obcecarse** to be obstinate.

**obedecer** *vt (regla, ley)* to obey.
► *vi (persona)* to obey.

**obediencia** *nf* obedience.

**obediente** *adj* obedient.

**obertura** *nf* MÚS overture.

**obesidad** *nf* obesity.

**obeso,-a** *adj* obese.

**obispo** *nm* bishop.

**objeción** *nf* objection.

**objetar** *vt* to object.

**objetividad** *nf* objectivity.

**objetivo,-a** *adj* objective.
► *nm* **objetivo 1** *(fin)* aim, objective. **2** *(lente)* lens.

**objeto** *nm* **1** *(cosa)* object. **2** *(fin)* aim, purpose, object.

**objetor,-ra** *adj* objecting, dissenting.
► *nm & nf* objector.

**oblea** *nf* wafer.

**oblicuo,-a** *adj* oblique.

**obligación** *nf (deber)* duty, obligation.

**obligado,-a** *adj (forzoso)* required.

**obligar** *vt* to force, make.
► *vpr* **obligarse** to undertake, promise.

**obligatorio,-a** *adj* compulsory.

**obnubilar** *vt (fascinar)* to fascinate.

**oboe** *nm* oboe.

**obra** *nf* **1** *(trabajo)* work. **2** *(construcción)* building site. COMP **obra de teatro** play.
► *nf pl* **obras** *(en casa)* repairs.

**obrar** *vi (proceder)* to act, behave.

**obrero,-a** *adj* working.
► *nm & nf* worker, labourer.

**obscenidad** *nf* obscenity.

**obsceno,-a** *adj* obscene.

**obscurantismo** *nm* obscurantism.

**obscurantista** *adj* obscurantist.

**obscurecer** *vt* to darken.
► *vpr* **obscurecerse** *(día)* to get cloudy.

**obscuridad** *nf* darkness.

**obscuro,-a** *adj* **1** *(cielo, color)* dark. **2** *(idea, razonamiento)* obscure.

**obsequiar** *vt (regalar)* to give, offer.

**obsequio** *nm* gift, present.

**observación** *nf (acción)* observation.

**observador,-ra** *adj* observant.
► *nm & nf* observer.

**observar** *vt* **1** *(mirar)* to observe, watch. **2** *(notar)* to notice.

**observatorio** *nm* observatory.

**obsesión** *nf* obsession.

**obsesionar** *vt* to obsess.
► *vpr* **obsesionarse** to get obsessed.

**obseso,-a** *nm & nf* maniac.
► *adj* obsessed.

**obsidiana** *nf* obsidian.

**obsoleto,-a** *adj* obsolete.

**obstáculo** *nm (inconveniente)* objection.

**obstante** *adv* **no obstante** nevertheless, however.

**obstetricia** *nf* obstetrics.

**obstinado,-a** *adj* obstinate.

**obstinarse** *vpr* to persist (en, in), insist (en, on).

**obstrucción** *nf* obstruction.

**obstruir** *vt* to obstruct, block.
▸ *vpr* **obstruirse** to get blocked up.
**obtener** *vt (beca, resultados)* to get, obtain; *(premio)* to win.
**obturador** *nm* shutter.
**obtuso,-a** *adj* obtuse.
**obviar** *vt fml* to obviate, remove.
**obvio,-a** *adj* obvious.
**oca** *nf* goose.
**ocasión** *nf (oportunidad)* opportunity.
**ocasional** *adj (gen)* occasional.
**ocasionar** *vt (causar)* to cause.
**ocaso** *nm (anochecer)* sunset.
**occidental** *adj* western, occidental.
**occidente** *nm* the West.
**Oceanía** *nf* Oceania.
**océano** *nm* ocean.

✎ En poesía también se escribe oceano.

**oceanografía** *nf* oceanography.
**ochenta** *adj* eighty; *(octagésimo)* eightieth.
▸ *nm* eighty.

✎ Consulta también sesenta.

**ocho** *adj* eight; *(octavo)* eighth.
▸ *nm* eight.

✎ Consulta también seis.

**ochocientos,-as** *adj* eight hundred; *(ordinal)* eight hundredth.
▸ *nm & nf* eight hundred.
**ocio** *nm (tiempo libre)* leisure.
**ocioso,-a** *adj (desocupado)* idle.
**ocre** *adj* ochre.
**octagonal** *adj* octagonal.
**octágono,-a** *nm* octagon.
**octano** *nm* octane.
**octava** *nf (en música)* octave.
**octavilla** *nf (impreso)* pamphlet.
**octavo,-a** *adj* eighth: *llegó en octavo lugar* he came eighth.
▸ *nm & nf* eighth: *era la octava en la lista* she was the eighth on the list.
▸ *nm* **octavo** *(parte)* eighth.

✎ Consulta también sexto.

**octeto** *nm* octet.
**octogésimo,-a** *adj* eightieth.

**octogonal** *adj* octagonal.
**octógono** *nm* octagon.
**octosílabo,-a** *adj* octosyllabic.
▸ *nm* **octosílabo** octosyllable.
**octubre** *nm* October.

✎ Para ejemplos de uso, consulta marzo.

**ocular** *adj* eye, ocular.
**oculista** *nm o nf* eye specialist.
**ocultar** *vt (gen)* to hide, conceal.
**oculto,-a** *adj (escondido)* hidden.
**ocupación** *nf (empleo)* occupation, employment.
**ocupado,-a** *adj* 1 *(persona)* busy. 2 *(asiento)* taken; *(teléfono)* engaged.
**ocupante** *nm o nf* occupant.
**ocupar** *vt* 1 to occupy, take. 2 *(llenar)* to take up. 3 *(habitar)* occupy. 4 *(estar - en un cargo)* to hold, fill.
▸ *vpr* **ocuparse de** to take care of.
**ocurrencia** *nf* idea.
**ocurrir** *vi* to happen: *¿qué fue lo que ocurrió?* what happened?
▸ *vpr* **ocurrirse** to occur to: *no se me ocurre nada* nothing occurs to me.
**odiar** *vt* to hate, loathe.
**odio** *nm* hatred, loathing.
**odioso,-a** *adj* hateful, despicable.
**odontólogo,-a** *nm & nf* odontologist.
**odorífico,-a** *adj* odoriferous.
**odre** *nm* wineskin.
**oeste** *nm* west.
**ofender** *vt (herir)* to offend: *no quisiera ofenderte, pero...* no offence, but...
▸ *vpr* **ofenderse** to get offended.
**ofendido,-a** *adj* offended.
**ofensa** *nf* offence.
**ofensivo,-a** *adj* offensive.
**oferta** *nf* 1 offer. 2 *(suministro)* supply.
**ofertar** *vt (ofrecer)* to offer.
**oficial** *adj* official.
▸ *nm o nf* office worker, officer.
**oficiala** *nf (operaria)* assistant.
**oficialmente** *adv* officially.
**oficiante** *nm o nf* officiant.
**oficiar** *vi (ejercer)* to act (de, as).
**oficina** *nf* office.
**oficinista** *nm o nf* office worker, clerk.

**oficio** *nm (ocupación)* job.

**oficioso,-a** *adj (noticia)* unofficial.

**ofidio** *nm* snake.

**ofimática** *nf* office automation.

**ofrecer** *vt (dar)* to offer.
▶ *vpr* **ofrecerse** *(prestarse)* to offer.

**ofrecimiento** *nm* offer, offering.

**ofrenda** *nf* offering.

**ofrendar** *vt* to make an offering of.

**oftalmología** *nf* ophthalmology.

**oftalmólogo,-a** *nm & nf* eye specialist.

**ofuscar** *vt (confundir)* to muddle.
▶ *vpr* **ofuscarse** to get muddled.

**ogro** *nm* ogre.

**oh** *interj* oh!

**ohm** *nm* ohm.

**ohmio** *nm* ohm.

**oídas** LOC de oídas by hearsay.

**oído** *nm* **1** *(sentido)* hearing. **2** *(órgano)* ear.

**oiga** *interj (para llamar la atención)* excuse me!; *(por teléfono)* hello?

**oír** *vt* **1** *(percibir)* to hear: *no oí nada* I didn't hear anything. **2** *(atender)* to answer.

**ojal** *nm* buttonhole.

**ojalá** *interj* I hope so: *¡ojalá sea verdad!* I hope it's true!

**ojeada** *nf* glance, quick look.

**ojear** *vt (mirar)* to have a quick look at.

**ojeras** *nf pl* dark rings under the eyes.

**ojeriza** *nf fam* dislike.

**ojeroso,-a** *adj* haggard.

**ojival** *adj (arte)* ogival.

**ojo** *nm* **1** eye. **2** *(agujero)* hole; *(de aguja)* eye. COMP

**okupa** *nm o nf argot* squatter.

**ola** *nf* wave. COMP **ola de frío** cold spell.

**oleáceo,-a** *adj* oleaceous.

**oleada** *nf* **1** big wave. **2** *fig* wave.

**oleaginoso,-a** *adj* oleaginous.

**oleaje** *nm* swell.

**oleicultura** *nf (cultivo)* olive-growing.

**óleo** *nm (material)* oil; *(obra)* oil painting.

**oleoducto** *nm* pipeline.

**oleoso,-a** *adj* oily.

**oler** *vt* to smell.
▶ *vi* to smell: *huele a gas* it smells of gas in here.

▶ *vpr* **olerse** to sense: *se ha olido que nos vamos* she has sensed that we are leaving.

**olfatear** *vt (oler)* to sniff, smell.

**olfateo** *nm* sniffing.

**olfativo,-a** *adj* olfactory.

**olfato** *nm* sense of smell.

**olfatorio,-a** *adj* olfactory.

**oligarca** *nm o nf* oligarch.

**oligarquía** *nf* oligarchy.

**oligárquico,-a** *adj* oligarchic.

**oligoelemento** *nm* trace element.

**oligofrenia** *nf* **1** *(enfermedad)* mental handicap. **2** *pey* mental deficiency.

**oligofrénico,-a** *adj* mentally retarded.
▶ *nm & nf* mentally retarded person.

**olimpiada** *nf* HIST Olympiad.

✎ También se escribe **olimpíada**.

**olisquear** *vt (olfatear)* to sniff.

**oliva** *nf* olive.

**olivar** *nm* olive grove.

**olivarero,-a** *adj (industria)* olive.
▶ *nm & nf* olive grower.

**olivo** *nm* olive tree.

**olla** *nf (utensilio)* pan.

**olmo** *nm* elm tree.

**olor** *nm* smell.

**oloroso,-a** *adj* fragrant.

**olvidadizo,-a** *adj* forgetful.

**olvidar** *vt* to forget.
▶ *vpr* **olvidarse** to forget (de, -).

**olvido** *nm* **1** *(desmemoria)* oblivion. **2** *(lapsus)* oversight, lapse.

**Omán** *nm* Oman.

**omaní** *adj* Omani.
▶ *nm o nf* Omani.

**ombligo** *nm* navel.

**omega** *nf (letra)* omega.

**omisión** *nf* omission.

**omitir** *vt (no decir)* to omit, leave out.

**ómnibus** *nm inv* bus.

**omnipotente** *adj* omnipotent.

**omnipresente** *adj* omnipresent.

**omnívoro,-a** *adj* omnivorous.

**omoplato** *nm* shoulder blade.

✎ También se escribe **omóplato**.

O

**once** *adj* eleven; *(undécimo)* eleventh.
▶ *nm* eleven.

✎ Consulta también seis.

**onceavo,-a** *adj (parte)* eleventh: *la onceava parte de...* an eleventh of...
▶ *nm* eleventh: *tres onceavos* three elevenths.

✎ Consulta también sexto.

**oncología** *nf* oncology.
**oncólogo,-a** *nm & nf* oncologist.
**onda** *nf* wave.
**ondear** *vi (bandera)* to fly, flutter.
**ondina** *nf* water nymph, undine.
**ondulación** *nf* undulation, wave.
**ondulado,-a** *adj (pelo)* wavy.
**ondulante** *adj (movimiento)* rolling.
**ondular** *vt (pelo)* to wave.
**ondulatorio,-a** *adj* undulatory.
**oneroso,-a** *adj* onerous.
**ónice** *nm* onyx.
**onírico,-a** *adj* dream, of dreams.
**ónix** *nm* onyx.
**onomástica** *nf* saint's day.
**onomástico,-a** *adj* onomastic.
**onomatopeya** *nf* onomatopoeia.
**onomatopéyico,-a** *adj* onomatopoeic.
**ontología** *nf* ontology.
**ontológico,-a** *adj* ontological.
**ONU** *abrev* (Organización de las Naciones Unidas) United Nations Organization; *(abreviatura)* UNO.
**onza** *nf (peso)* ounce.
**opacidad** *nf* opaqueness, opacity.
**opaco,-a** *adj* opaque.
**opalino,-a** *adj (de ópalo)* opal.
**ópalo** *nm* opal.
**opción** *nf (en general)* option.
**opcional** *adj* optional.
**open** *nm inv* DEP open.
**ópera** *nf* opera.
**operación** *nf (gen)* operation.
**operador,-ra** *nm & nf* operator.
**operando** *nm* operand.
**operante** *adj* operative.
**operar** *vt* MED to operate (a, on).

▶ *vpr* **operarse** MED to have an operation.
**operario,-a** *nm & nf* operator, worker.
**operativo,-a** *adj* operative.
**opereta** *nf* operetta.
**operístico,-a** *adj* operatic.
**opinable** *adj* debatable.
**opinar** *vi* to think (de, about).
**opinión** *nf (juicio)* opinion.
**opio** *nm* opium.
**opíparo,-a** *adj fml* lavish.
**oponente** *nm o nf* opponent.
**oponer** *vt* to reply with.
▶ *vpr* **oponerse** *(estar en contra)* to oppose (a, -), be against (a, -).
**oporto** *nm* port.
**oportunidad** *nf* opportunity, chance.
**oportunismo** *nm* opportunism.
**oportunista** *nm o nf* opportunist.
**oportuno,-a** *adj (a tiempo)* opportune.
**oposición** *nf (antagonismo)* opposition.
**opresión** *nf* oppression.
**opresivo,-a** *adj* oppressive.
**opresor,-ra** *nm & nf* oppressor.
**oprimido,-a** *nm & nf* oppressed person.
**oprimir** *vt* **1** *(botón)* to press: *oprima el botón* press the button. **2** *fig* to oppress.
**oprobio** *nm* opprobrium.
**optar** *vi (elegir)* to choose (entre, from).
**optativa** *nf* EDUC *(asignatura)* optional subject.
**optativo,-a** *adj* **1** optional. **2** LING *(oración, modo)* optative.
**óptica** *nf* **1** *(tienda)* optician's. **2** FÍS optics.
**óptico,-a** *nm & nf* optician.
**optimismo** *nm* optimism.
**optimista** *adj* optimistic.
**optimizar** *vt* to optimize.
**óptimo,-a** *adj* very best, optimum.
**opuesto,-a** *adj* **1** *(contrario)* contrary, opposed. **2** *(de enfrente)* opposite.
**opulencia** *nf* opulence.
**opulento,-a** *adj* opulent.
**oquedad** *nf (hueco)* cavity.
**oración** *nf* **1** REL *(plegaria)* prayer. **2** LING clause, sentence. COMP
**oráculo** *nm* oracle.

**orador,-ra** *nm & nf* speaker, orator.

**oral** *adj* oral.

**orangután** *nm* ZOOL orang-utan.

**orar** *vi* to pray.

**oratoria** *nf* oratory.

**oratorio,-a** *adj (estilo, arte)* oratorical.

**orbe** *nm (esfera)* orb; *(mundo)* world.

**órbita** *nf (de un astro)* orbit.

**orbital** *adj* orbital.

**orca** *nf* killer whale, orc.

**orden** *nm (ordenación)* order.
▶ *nf (mandato)* order.

**ordenación** *nf* arrangement.

**ordenada** *nf* MAT ordinate.

**ordenado,-a** *adj* tidy.

**ordenador,-ra** *nm* INFORM computer.

**ordenamiento** *nm* ordering.

**ordenanza** *nf (norma)* ordinance.

**ordenar** *vt* **1** *(arreglar)* to put in order; *(habitación)* to tidy up. **2** *(mandar)* to order.

**ordeñar** *vt* to milk.

**ordinal** *adj* ordinal.
▶ *nm* ordinal.

**ordinariez** *nf (defecto)* vulgarity.

**ordinario,-a** *adj* **1** *(corriente)* ordinary, common. **2** *(grosero)* vulgar, common.

**orégano** *nm* oregano.

**oreja** *nf* ear.

**orejera** *nf* earflap.

**orejero** *nm (sillón)* wing chair.

**orfanato** *nm* orphanage.

**orfandad** *nf* orphanage.

**orfebre** *nm* goldsmith, silversmith.

**orfebrería** *nf (en oro)* gold work.

**orfeón** *nm* choral society.

**órfico,-a** *adj lit* orphic.

**organdí** *nm* organdie.

**orgánico,-a** *adj* organic.

**organigrama** *nm* organization chart.

**organillero,-a** *nm & nf* organ-grinder.

**organillo** *nm* barrel organ.

**organismo** *nm* **1** *(humano)* organism. **2** *(institucional)* organization, body.

**organista** *nm o nf* organist.

**organización** *nf* organization.

**organizar** *vt* to organize.

**organizativo,-a** *adj* organizational.

**órgano** *nm* organ.

**orgullo** *nm (propia estima)* pride.

**orgulloso,-a** *adj* proud.

**orientación** *nf* aspect.

**oriental** *adj* eastern, oriental.
▶ *nm o nf* Oriental.

**orientar** *vt* **1** *(antena)* to point. **2** *(esfuerzos)* to direct. **3** *(aconsejar)* to advise.
▶ *vpr* **orientarse** to find one's bearings.

**oriente** *nm* East.

**orificio** *nm (agujero)* hole.

**origen** *nm (causa)* cause, origin.

**original** *adj (gen)* original.
▶ *nm* original.

**originalidad** *nf* originality.

**originar** *vt* to cause, give rise to.

**originario,-a** *adj* original.

**orilla** *nf* **1** *(borde)* edge. **2** *(del río)* bank; *(del mar)* shore.

**orillar** *vt (sortear)* to get round.

**orina** *nf* urine.

**orinar** *vi* to urinate.

**oriundo,-a** *adj* native of.

**orla** *nf (adorno)* edging.

**ornamentación** *nf* ornamentation.

**ornamental** *adj* ornamental.

**ornamentar** *vt* to adorn, decorate.

**ornamento** *nm* ornament.

**ornitología** *nf* ornithology.

**ornitológico,-a** *adj* ornithological.

**ornitólogo,-a** *nm & nf* ornithologist.

**ornitorrinco** *nm* platypus.

**oro** *nm* gold.

**orografía** *nf* orography.

**orográfico,-a** *adj* orographic.

**orondo,-a** *adj* hearty, plump.

**orquesta** *nf* orchestra, dance band.

**orquestal** *adj* orchestral.

**orquestar** *vt* to orchestrate.

**orquídea** *nf* orchid.

**ortiga** *nf* nettle.

**ortodoncia** *nf* orthodontics.

**ortodoxia** *nf* orthodoxy.

**ortodoxo,-a** *adj* orthodox.
▶ *nm & nf* orthodox.

**ortografía** *nf* spelling.

**ortográfico,-a** *adj* spelling.

O

**ortopedia** *nf* orthopaedics.

**ortopédico,-a** *adj* orthopaedic.

**ortopedista** *nm o nf* orthopaedist.

**oruga** *nf* caterpillar.

**orzuelo** *nm* sty.

**os** *pron* **1** *(complemento directo)* you: *os escucho* I am listening to you. **2** *(complemento indirecto)* you: *os traje un libro* I brought you a book. **3** *(reflexivo)* yourselves: *¿ya os estáis vistiendo?* are you getting dressed already? **4** *(recíproco)* each other: *os parecéis mucho* you look very much alike.

**osadía** *nf* *(audacia)* audacity, daring.

**osado,-a** *adj* *(audaz)* audacious.

**osamenta** *nf* *(esqueleto)* skeleton.

**osar** *vi lit* to dare, have the audacity to.

**oscilación** *nf* *(de precios)* fluctuation.

**oscilar** *vi* *(variar)* to vary, fluctuate.

**oscilatorio,-a** *adj* oscillating.

**oscurantismo** *nm* obscurantism.

**oscuras** LOC a oscuras in the dark.

**óseo,-a** *adj* *(tejido, estructura)* bone.

**osera** *nf* bear's den.

**osezno** *nm* bear cub.

**osificación** *nf* ossification.

**osificar** *vt* to ossify.

**osmio** *nm* osmium.

**ósmosis** *nf inv* osmosis.

**oso** *nm* bear.

**ostentación** *nf* ostentation.

**ostentar** *vt* *(poseer)* to hold.

**ostentoso,-a** *adj* ostentatious.

**osteópata** *nm o nf* osteopath.

**osteopatía** *nf* osteopathy.

**osteopático,-a** *adj* osteopathic.

**ostra** *nf* oyster.

**ostracismo** *nm* ostracism.

**ostrero,-a** *adj* oyster.

**ostrícola** *adj* oyster.

**OTAN** *abrev* (Organización del Tratado del Atlántico Norte) North Atlantic Treaty Organization; *(abreviatura)* NATO.

**otear** *vt* *(horizonte)* to scan.

**otero** *nm* hillock.

**otitis** *nf inv* ear infection, otitis.

**otomano,-a** *adj* Ottoman.
  ▶ *nm & nf* *(persona)* Ottoman.

**otoñal** *adj* autumnal, autumn, US fall.

**otoño** *nm* autumn, US fall.

**otorgante** *adj* *(de un premio)* awarding.

**otorgar** *vt* *(conceder)* to grant, give (a, to); *(premio)* to award (a, to).

**otorrinolaringólogo,-a** *nm & nf* ear, nose and throat specialist.

**otorrinolaringología** *nf* ear, nose and throat, ENT.

**otro,-a** *adj* other, another.
  ▶ *pron* other, another: *otros* others.

**ovación** *nf* ovation, applause.

**ovacionar** *vt* to give an ovation (a, to).

**oval** *adj* oval.

**ovalado,-a** *adj* oval.

**óvalo** *nm* oval.

**ovario** *nm* ovary.

**oveja** *nf* sheep, ewe.

**overtura** *nf* MÚS overture.

**ovillar** *vt* to roll into a ball.

**ovillo** *nm* ball of wool.

**ovino,-a** *adj* ovine, sheep.

**ovíparo,-a** *adj* oviparous.

**ovulación** *nf* ovulation.

**ovular** *adj* ovular.
  ▶ *vi* to ovulate.

**óvulo** *nm* ovule.

**oxiacetilénico,-a** *adj* oxyacetylene.

**oxiacetileno** *nm* oxyacetylene.

**oxidable** *adj* oxidizable.

**oxidación** *nf* **1** QUÍM oxidation. **2** *(proceso)* rusting.

**oxidado,-a** *adj* rusty.

**oxidar** *vt* to rust.
  ▶ *vpr* **oxidarse** to rust, go rusty.

**óxido** *nm* *(herrumbre)* rust.

**oxigenado,-a** *adj* QUÍM oxygenated.

**oxigenar** *vt* to get some fresh air in.
  ▶ *vpr* **oxigenarse** to get some fresh air.

**oxígeno** *nm* oxygen.

**oye** *interj fam* *(para llamar la atención)* hey!

**oyente** *nm o nf* RAD listener.

**ozono** *nm* ozone. COMP capa de ozono ozone layer.

# P

**P, p** *nf (la letra)* P, p.
**pabellón** *nm (en una feria)* stand.
**pabilo** *nm* wick.
**pábulo** *nm* fuel.
**pacana** *nf* pecan nut.
**pacer** *vi* to graze.
**pachón,-ona** *adj (perro)* pointer.
**paciencia** *nf* patience.
**paciente** *nm o nf* patient.
**pacificación** *nf* pacification.
**pacíficamente** *adv* peacefully.
**pacificar** *vt* to pacify.
**pacífico,-a** *adj* peaceful.
**pacifismo** *nm* pacifism.
**pacifista** *adj* pacifist.
  ▶ *nm o nf* pacifist.
**pactar** *vt* to agree (to).
  ▶ *vi* to come to an agreement.
**pacto** *nm* pact, agreement.
**padecer** *vt* to suffer.
  ▶ *vi (sufrir)* to suffer (de, from).
**padecimiento** *nm* suffering.
**padrastro** *nm (padre)* stepfather.
**padrazo** *nm fam* loving father.
**padre** *nm* father.
  ▶ *nm pl* **padres** parents.
**padrino** *nm (de bautizo)* godfather.
  ▶ *nm pl* **padrinos** godparents.
**padrón** *nm (censo)* census.
**paella** *nf (comida)* paella.
**paellera** *nf* paella pan.
**paga** *nf* **1** *(sueldo)* pay. **2** *(de los niños)* pocket money.
**pagadero,-a** *adj* payable.
**pagador,-ra** *adj* paying.
  ▶ *nm & nf (gen)* payer.
**paganismo** *nm* paganism.
**pagano,-a** *nm & nf* REL pagan.

**pagar** *vt* to pay: *ya he pagado lo que debía* I've already paid what I owed.
  ▶ *vi* to pay: *en esta empresa pagan muy bien* this company pays very well.
**página** *nf* page.
**paginación** *nf* pagination.
**pago** *nm* payment.
**paguro** *nm (ermitaño)* hermit crab.
**país** *nm* country.
**paisaje** *nm* landscape.
**paisajista** *nm o nf (pintor)* landscape artist.
**paisajístico,-a** *adj* landscape.
**paisano,-a** *nm & nf* **1** *(compatriota)* fellow countryman. **2** *(campesino)* countryman.
**paja** *nf* **1** straw. **2** *fig (relleno)* waffle.
**pajar** *nm (lugar)* hayloft.
**pajarera** *nf* aviary.
**pajarería** *nf (tienda)* caged-bird shop.
**pajarero,-a** *adj* of birds.
**pajarita** *nf (de cuello)* bow tie.
**pájaro** *nm (animal)* bird.
**paje** *nm* page.
**pajita** *nf (para beber)* straw.
**pajizo,-a** *adj* straw-coloured (US straw-colored).
**Pakistán** *nm* Pakistan.
**pakistaní** *adj* Pakistani.
  ▶ *nm o nf* Pakistani.
**pala** *nf* **1** shovel. **2** DEP *(de ping-pong)* bat.
**palabra** *nf* word.
**palacete** *nm* mansion.
**palaciego,-a** *adj* palatial.
**palacio** *nm* palace.
**palada** *nf (gen)* shovelful.
**paladar** *nm* **1** palate. **2** *fig* taste.
**paladear** *vt* to savour, relish.
**paladín** *nm fig* champion.

**palafito** *nm* house on stilts.

**palanca** *nf (gen)* lever. LOC **hacer palanca** to lever.

**palangana** *nf* bowl.

**palangre** *nm (arte de pesca)* boulter.

**palatal** *adj* palatal.
▶ *nf* palatal.

**palco** *nm (en el teatro)* box.

**paleografía** *nf* palaeography.

**paleógrafo,-a** *nm & nf* palaeographer.

**paleolítico,-a** *adj* Palaeolithic.
▶ *nm* **el paleolítico** the Palaeolithic.

**paleontología** *nf* palaeontology.

**paleontólogo,-a** *nm & nf* palaeontologist.

**Palestina** *nf* Palestine.

**palestino,-a** *adj* Palestinian.
▶ *nm & nf* Palestinian.

**palestra** *nf* arena, forum.

**paleta** *nf* 1 *(de pintor)* palette. 2 *(de albañil)* trowel.

**paletada** *nf (de albañil)* going over with a trowel.

**paletilla** *nf* 1 ANAT shoulder blade. 2 CULIN shoulder.

**paliar** *vt* to palliate, alleviate.

**paliativo,-a** *adj* palliative.
▶ *nm* **paliativo** palliative.

**palidecer** *vi* 1 to turn pale. 2 *fig* to fade.

**palidez** *nf* paleness, pallor.

**pálido,-a** *adj* pale.

**palillero** *nm* toothpick holder.

**palillo** *nm (mondadientes)* toothpick.

**palio** *nm* canopy.

**palisandro** *nm* rosewood.

**paliza** *nf* beating, thrashing.

**palma** *nf* 1 BOT palm (tree). 2 *(de la mano)* palm.
▶ *nf pl* **palmas** *(aplausos)* clapping *sing*.

**palmada** *nf (golpe)* slap, pat.

**palmar** *nm* palm grove.

**palmarés** *nm (lista)* list of winners.

**palmatoria** *nf* candlestick.

**palmeado,-a** *adj* 1 BOT palmate. 2 ZOOL *(dedos)* webbed.

**palmear** *vi* to clap.

**palmera** *nf* BOT palm tree, palm.

**palmeral** *nm* palm grove.

**palmetazo** *nm* stroke of the cane.

**palmípedo,-a** *adj* web-footed.
▶ *nf pl* **palmípedas** ZOOL *(género)* web-footed birds.

**palmito** *nm* 1 CULIN palm heart. 2 BOT palmetto.

**palmo** *nm (medida)* span.

**palmotear** *vi* to clap.

**palmoteo** *nm* clapping.

**palo** *nm* 1 *(estaca)* stick; *(de valla)* post; *(de telégrafos)* pole. 2 *(golpe)* blow.

**paloma** *nf (gen)* pigeon; *(blanca)* dove.

**palomar** *nm* dovecote.

**palometa** *nf* Ray's bream.

**palomilla** *nf (tuerca)* wing nut.

**palomino** *nm* young pigeon.

**palomitas** COMP **palomitas de maíz** popcorn *sing*.

**palomo** *nm* cock pigeon.

**palote** *nm (dibujo)* stroke.

**palpable** *adj* palpable.

**palpar** *vt* MED to palpate.

**palpitación** *nf* palpitation.

**palpitante** *adj (tema, cuestión)* burning.

**palpitar** *vi* to palpitate, throb.

**pálpito** *nm* hunch, feeling.

**paludismo** *nm* malaria.

**palurdo,-a** *nm & nf* country bumpkin.

**palustre** *adj (de las lagunas)* lake.

**pamela** *nf* wide-brimmed straw hat.

**pampa** *nf* pampas *pl*.

**pámpano** *nm* vine shoot.

**pamplina** *nf (tontería)* daft thing.

**pamplinero,-a** *adj* sweet-talking.

**pan** *nm* 1 *(masa)* bread; *(hogaza)* loaf of bread. 2 *(alimento)* food, bread. COMP **barra de pan** loaf of bread. ‖ **pan integral** wholemeal bread.

**pana** *nf* corduroy.

**panacea** *nf* panacea.

**panadería** *nf* bakery, baker's.

**panadero,-a** *nm & nf* baker.

**panal** *nm* honeycomb.

**Panamá** *nm* Panama.

**panameño,-a** *adj* Panamanian.
▶ *nm & nf* Panamanian.

**panamericano,-a** *adj* Pan-American.

**pancarta** *nf* **1** placard. **2** INFORM banner.
**panceta** *nf* bacon.
**páncreas** *nm inv* pancreas.
**pancreático,-a** *adj* pancreatic.
**panda** *nm* ZOOL panda.
**pandemónium** *nm* pandemonium.
**pandeo** *nm (torcedura)* warp.
**pandereta** *nf* small tambourine.
**pandero** *nm* tambourine.
**pandilla** *nf* group of friends.
**panecillo** *nm* bread roll.
**panel** *nm (gen)* panel.
**panera** *nf* breadbasket.
**panfleto** *nm fig* propaganda.
**pánico** *nm* panic.
**panificadora** *nf* industrial bakery.
**panocha** *nf (de maíz)* corncob.
**panorama** *nm* panorama, view.
**panorámica** *nf* panorama.
**panorámico,-a** *adj* panoramic.
**pantalla** *nf* screen.
**pantalón** [también se usa en plural con el mismo significado] *nm* trousers *pl*, US pants. COMP **pantalón vaquero** jeans *pl*.
**pantano** *nm* **1** *(artificial)* reservoir. **2** *(natural)* marsh.
**pantanoso,-a** *adj* marshy.
**panteísmo** *nm* pantheism.
**panteón** *nm* pantheon.
**pantera** *nf* panther.
**panties** *nm pl* tights.
**pantomima** *nf* **1** *(representación)* pantomime, mime. **2** *fig* farce, pretence.
**pantorrilla** *nf* calf.
**pantufla** *nf* slipper.
**panza** *nf* belly.
**panzada** *nf (en el agua)* belly flop.
**pañal** *nm* nappy, US diaper.
**pañería** *nf* draper's, draper's shop.
**paño** *nm* cloth.
**pañoleta** *nf* shawl.
**pañuelo** *nm* handkerchief.
**papa¹** *nm* **1** *fam* dad. **2 el Papa** the Pope.
**papa²** *nf (patata)* potato. COMP **papas fritas** chips, US French fries.

**papá** *nm fam* dad, daddy. COMP **Papá Noel** Santa Claus.
**papada** *nf* double chin.
**papagayo** *nm* parrot.
**papaya** *nf* papaya.
**papayo** *nm* papaya tree.
**papel** *nm* **1** *(gen)* paper. **2** *(en película)* role, part. COMP **papel higiénico** toilet paper. ‖ **papel pintado** wallpaper.
▶ *nm pl* **papeles** *fam (documentación)* papers.
**papeleo** *nm fam* paperwork.
**papelera** *nf* **1** wastepaper basket. **2** *(en la calle)* litter bin.
**papelería** *nf* stationer's.
**papelero,-a** *adj (del papel)* paper: *la industria papelera* the paper industry.
**papeleta** *nf* **1** *(de voto)* ballot paper. **2** *(de examen)* results slip.
**paperas** *nf pl* mumps.
**papi** *nm fam* dad, daddy.
**papila** *nf* papilla.
**papilla** *nf (infantil)* baby food.
**papiro** *nm* papyrus.
**papú** *adj* Papuan.
▶ *nm o nf* Papuan.
**Papúa** *nf* Papua. COMP **Papúa Nueva Guinea** Papua New Guinea.
**paquete** *nm* **1** *(cajita)* packet, pack. **2** *(conjunto)* set, packet: *un paquete de galletas* a package of biscuits. COMP **paquete postal** parcel.
**paquidermo** *nm* pachyderm.
**Paquistán** *nm* Pakistan.
**paquistaní** *adj* Pakistani.
▶ *nm o nf* Pakistani.
**par** *adj* **1** equal. **2** MAT even.
▶ *nm (dos)* couple; *(pareja)* pair.
**para** *prep* **1** *(finalidad)* for: *es para su cumpleaños* it's for her birthday. **2** *(uso, utilidad)* for: *¿tienes algo para el dolor de cabeza?* have you got anything for a headache? **3** *(destino, dirección)* for, to: *¿para dónde vas?* where are you going? **4** *(tiempo, fechas límites)* by, before: *lo necesito para el viernes* I need it by Friday.
▶ *conj (finalidad)* to, in order to: *lo hice para ahorrar tiempo* I did it to save time.
**parábola** *nf* MAT parabola.

**parabólica** *nf* satellite dish.

**parabólico,-a** *adj* parabolic. COMP antena parabólica satellite dish.

**parabrisas** *nm inv* windscreen.

**paracaídas** *nm inv* parachute.

**paracaidismo** *nm* parachuting.

**paracaidista** *nm o nf* DEP parachutist.

**parachoques** *nm inv* AUTO bumper.

**parada** *nf* **1** (*gen*) stop, halt. **2** (*de autobús, etc*) stop. **3** (*pausa*) pause. COMP parada de autobús bus stop.

**paradero** *nm* whereabouts *pl.*

**paradigmático,-a** *adj* paradigmatic.

**paradisíaco,-a** *adj* heavenly.

**parado,-a** *adj* **1** (*quieto*) still. **2** (*sin trabajo*) unemployed.
  ▶ *nm & nf* unemployed person.

**paradójico,-a** *adj* paradoxical.

**parador** *nm* (*hotel*) state-run hotel.

**parafina** *nf* paraffin.

**paraguas** *nm inv* umbrella.

**Paraguay** *nm* Paraguay.

**paraguaya** *nf type of* peach.

**paraguayo,-a** *adj* Paraguayan.
  ▶ *nm & nf* Paraguayan.

**paraíso** *nm* paradise.

**paraje** *nm* spot.

**paralela** *nf* (*línea*) parallel line.
  ▶ *nf pl* paralelas DEP parallel bars.

**paralelo,-a** *adj* parallel.
  ▶ *nm* paralelo parallel.

**paralelogramo** *nm* parallelogram.

**parálisis** *nf inv* paralysis.

**paralítico,-a** *adj* paralytic.
  ▶ *nm & nf* paralytic.

**paralización** *nf* paralysis.

**paralizar** *vt* **1** MED to paralyse. **2** (*circulación*) to bring to a standstill.

**parámetro** *nm* parameter.

**páramo** *nm* moor.

**paranoia** *nf* paranoia.

**paranoico,-a** *nm & nf* paranoic.

**parapente** *nm* paragliding.

**parapeto** *nm* parapet.

**parapléjico,-a** *nm & nf* paraplegic.

**parapsicología** *nf* parapsychology.

**parapsicológico,-a** *adj* parapsychological.

**parar** *vt* **1** to stop. **2** DEP to save: *ha parado tres disparos* he's made three saves.
  ▶ *vi* to stop: *aquí no para el tren* the train doesn't stop here.
  ▶ *vpr* pararse to stop.

**pararrayos** *nm inv* lightning conductor.

**parasitario,-a** *adj* parasitic.

**parásito,-a** *nm* BIOL parasite.

**parasol** *nm* parasol, sunshade.

**parcela** *nf* (*de tierra*) plot (of land).

**parcelar** *vt* (*finca*) to divide into plots.

**parche** *nm* patch.

**parchís** *nm inv* ludo.

**parcial** *adj* (*gen*) partial.
  ▶ *nm* (*examen*) *examination covering part of the course and counting towards the final mark.*

**parcialidad** *nf* (*injusticia*) bias, partiality.

**parco,-a** *adj* (*escaso*) frugal, sparing.

**pardo,-a** *adj* (*color tierra*) brown.

**pareado,-a** *adj* (*casa*) semidetached.

**parecer** *nm* (*opinión*) opinion, mind.
  ▶ *vi* **1** (*opinar*) to seem, look (like): *parece un oso* it looks like a bear. **2** (*opinar*) to think: *¿qué te parece?* what do you think?
  ▶ *vpr* parecerse to be alike, look like: *se parecen mucho* they're very much alike.

**parecido,-a** *adj* similar.
  ▶ *nm* parecido resemblance, likeness.

**pared** *nf* **1** wall. **2** (*de una montaña*) side.

**paredón** *nm* execution wall.

**pareja** *nf* **1** (*gen*) pair: *he perdido la pareja de este calcetín* I've lost the other sock. **2** (*de personas*) couple; (*de baile*) partner.

**parejo,-a** *adj* (*sin diferencia*) the same; (*por igual*) even.

**parentela** *nf* relatives *pl*, relations *pl.*

**parentesco** *nm* kinship, relationship.

**paréntesis** *nm inv* **1** (*gen*) parenthesis. **2** *fig* (*interrupción*) break, interruption.

**paria** *nm o nf* pariah.

**paridad** *nf* (*gen*) parity, equality.

**pariente,-a** *nm & nf* relative.

**parir** *vt fam* to give birth to.
  ▶ *vi* to give birth.

**parlamentario,-a** *adj* parliamentary.
  ▶ *nm & nf* member of parliament.

**parlamento** *nm* parliament.
**parlante** *adj* talking.
**parlotear** *vi fam* to chatter, prattle on.
**parmesan** *nm (queso)* Parmesan cheese.
**paro** *nm* **1** stop. **2** *(desempleo)* unemployment.
**parodia** *nf* parody.
**parodiar** *vt* to parody.
**paroxismo** *nm* paroxysm.
**parpadear** *vi (ojos)* to blink, wink.
**párpado** *nm* eyelid.
**parque** *nm (jardines)* park. COMP **parque de atracciones** amusement park.
**parqué** *nm* parquet.
**parquímetro** *nm* parking meter.
**parra** *nf* grapevine.
**parrafada** *nf fam (conversación)* chat.
**párrafo** *nm* paragraph.
**parranda** *nf fam* spree.
**parrilla** *nf* **1** grill, US broiler, barbecue. LOC **a la parrilla** CULIN grilled.
**parrillada** *nf* mixed grill *(of meat or fish)*.
**párroco** *nm* parish priest.
**parroquia** *nf (iglesia)* parish church.
**parsimonia** *nf (lentitud)* slowness.
**parsimonioso,-a** *adj (tranquilo)* slow.
**parte** *nf* **1** *(gen)* part; *(en una partición)* portion: *divide el pastel en tres partes* cut the cake into three (slices). **2** *(en negocio)* share. **3** *(lugar)* place: *no lo venden en ninguna parte* they don't sell it anywhere. **4** *(en un conflicto)* side: *las dos partes quieren llevar la razón* both sides believe they are right.
▶ *nm (comunicado)* official report.
▶ *nf pl* **partes** *fam* privates, private parts. LOC **en parte** partly. ▌ **por una parte,... por otra...** on the one hand…, on the other hand…
**partera** *nf* midwife.
**parterre** *nm* flowerbed.
**partición** *nf (de una herencia)* partition.
**participación** *nf* involvement.
**participante** *nm o nf* participant.
**participar** *vi* to participate, take part.
▶ *vt (notificar)* to notify, inform.
**partícipe** *adj* participating.
▶ *nm o nf* participant.

**participio** *nm* participle.
**partícula** *nf* particle.
**particular** *adj (concreto)* particular.
▶ *nm* **1** private individual. **2** *(asunto)* matter, subject.
**particularidad** *nf (gen)* peculiarity.
**particularizar** *vt* to distinguish.
**partida** *nf* **1** *(remesa)* consignment, lot. **2** *(documento)* certificate. **3** *(juego)* game. LOC **jugar una partida** to play a game. COMP **partida de nacimiento** birth certificate.
**partidario,-a** *adj* supporting.
▶ *nm & nf* supporter.
**partidista** *adj* biased, partisan.
**partido,-a** *adj* **1** divided. **2** *(roto)* broken.
▶ *nm* **partido** **1** *(grupo político)* party, group. **2** DEP *(equipo)* team; *(juego)* game, match. COMP **partido amistoso** friendly game.
**partir** *vt* **1** *(dividir)* to divide, cut: *voy a partir pan* I'll cut some bread. **2** *(romper)* to break; *(nueces, almendras)* to crack.
▶ *vi (irse)* to leave, set out, set off.
▶ *vpr* **partirse** to break: *se ha partido la pierna* he's broken his leg.
**partitivo,-a** *adj* partitive.
▶ *nm* **partitivo** partitive.
**partitura** *nf* score.
**parto** *nm* childbirth: *fue un parto difícil* it was a difficult birth. LOC **estar de parto** to be in labour (US labor).
**parvulario** *nm* nursery school.
**párvulo,-a** *nm & nf* infant.
**pasa** *nf* raisin.
**pasable** *adj* passable.
**pasadizo** *nm* passage.
**pasado,-a** *adj* **1** past. **2** *(año, semana, etc)* last. **3** *(después)* after: *pasadas las once* after eleven. **4** *(estropeado)* bad. COMP **pasado mañana** the day after tomorrow.
▶ *nm* **pasado** **1** *(tiempo)* past. **2** LING past, past tense.
**pasador** *nm* slide.
**pasaje** *nf* **1** *(tarifa)* fare, ticket. **2** *(pasajeros)* passengers *pl*. **3** *(fragmento)* passage.
**pasajero,-a** *adj & nf* passenger.
**pasamanos** *nm inv* handrail.

P

**pasamontañas** *nm inv* balaclava.

**pasaporte** *nm* passport.

**pasapurés** *nm inv* vegetable mill.

**pasar** *vi* **1** *(ir)* to pass, pass by, go: *pasa de un idioma a otro sin darse cuenta* he goes from one language to another without realizing. **2** *(tiempo)* to pass, go by: *¡cómo pasa el tiempo!* doesn't time fly! **3** *(entrar)* to come in, go in: *pasa, está abierto* come in, it's not locked. **4** *(cesar)* to pass, cease: *en cuanto pase la tormenta salimos* we'll go out when the storm has passed. **5** *(límite)* to exceed (de, -). **6** *(ocurrir)* to happen. **7** *(sufrir)* to suffer.

▸ *vt* **1** *(trasladar)* to move, transfer: *pasa este documento al otro CD* move this file to the other CD. **2** *(comunicar, dar)* to give: *pásale el informe al jefe* give this report to the boss. **3** *(cruzar)* to cross: *pasamos la frontera ayer* we crossed the border yesterday. **4** *(alcanzar)* to pass, reach: *pásame la sal, por favor* pass me the salt, please. **5** *(aventajar)* to surpass, be better than: *tu hermano ya te pasa en matemáticas* your brother is better than you at maths. **6** *(adelantar)* to overtake: *me pasó un deportivo rojo en una curva* a red sports car overtook me on a bend. **7** *(deslizar)* to run: *pasó el dedo por el estante* he ran his finger along the shelf. **8** *(tolerar)* to overlook: *esta vez te la paso, pero que no se repita* I'll overlook it this time, but don't let it happen again. **9** *(aprobar)* to pass: *pasé el examen a la primera* I passed my test first time. **10** *(proyectar)* to show: *pasaron unas diapositivas* they showed some slides. **11** *(tiempo - estar)* to spend; *(- disfrutar, padecer)* to have: *pasamos unas vacaciones estupendas* we had a wonderful holiday.

▸ *vpr* **pasarse 1** *(cambiar)* to pass over (a, to): *se ha pasado al otro bando* she's gone over to the other side. **2** *(pudrirse)* to go off. **3** *(olvidarse)* to forget: *se me pasó la fecha de entrega* I forgot about the deadline. **4** *(ir)* to go by (por, -), call in (por, at): *pásate por casa cuando quieras* pop in any time.

**pasarela** *nf (puente)* footbridge.

**pasatiempos** *nm pl* puzzles.

**pascua** *nf* Easter.

▸ *nf pl* **pascuas** Christmas *sing*.

**pase** *nm (permiso)* pass.

**pasear** *vi* to stroll, go for a walk.

▸ *vt* to take for a walk.

**paseo** *nm* **1** *(a pie)* walk; *(a caballo)* ride. **2** *(en coche)* drive; *(en bicicleta, moto)* ride. LOC **dar un paseo** to go for a walk.

**pasillo** *nm* corridor.

**pasión** *nf* passion.

**pasividad** *nf* passiveness, passivity.

**pasmado,-a** *adj* flabbergasted.

**pasmar** *vt* to astonish, amaze.

▸ *vpr* **pasmarse** *fam (asombrarse)* to be astonished, be amazed.

**pasmo** *nm (asombro)* amazement.

**pasmoso,-a** *adj* astonishing.

**paso** *nm* **1** *(movimiento)* step, footstep. **2** *(camino)* passage. LOC **abrirse paso** to force one's way through. ‖ **estar de paso** to be passing through. COMP **paso de peatones** pedestrian crossing.

**pasta** *nf* **1** *(masa)* paste. **2** CULIN *(italiana)* pasta. **3** *(croissant, etc)* pastry; *(de té)* biscuit.

**pastar** *vt* to pasture, graze.

▸ *vi* to pasture, graze.

**pastel** *nm* CULIN *(dulce)* cake; *(salado)* pie.

**pastelería** *nf (tienda)* cake shop.

**pastelero,-a** *nm & nf* pastrycook.

**pasteurizado,-a** *adj* pasteurized.

**pasteurizar** *vt* to pasteurize.

**pastilla** *nf* **1** *(medicina)* tablet, pill. **2** *(de chocolate, jabón)* bar.

**pasto** *nm (pastizal)* pasture.

**pastor,-ra** *nm & nf* shepherd.

**pastoso,-a** *adj (sustancia)* pasty.

**pata** *nf* **1** *(gen)* leg. **2** *(garra)* paw. **3** *(pezuña)* hoof. LOC **a cuatro patas** on all fours. ‖ **meter la pata** *fam* to put one's foot in it. ‖ **patas arriba** upside down.

**patada** *nf* kick.

**patalear** *vi* **1** *(con enfado)* to stamp one's feet. **2** *(protestar)* to kick up a fuss.

**pataleo** *nm* **1** *(con los pies)* stamping. **2** *(protesta)* complaining.

**pataleta** *nf fam* tantrum.

**patata** *nf* potato. COMP **patatas fritas 1** *(de bolsa)* crisps. **2** *(de sartén)* chips.

**paté** *nm* pâté.

**patear** *vt* **1** to kick. **2** *(andar)* to walk.
**patentado,-a** *adj* patented.
**patentar** *vt* to patent.
**patente** *adj (evidente)* obvious, patent.
**patera** *nf* boat.
**paternal** *adj* paternal.
**paternalista** *adj* paternalistic.
**paternidad** *nf* paternity.
**paterno,-a** *adj* paternal.
**patético,-a** *adj* pathetic.
**patíbulo** *nm* gallows *sing*.
**patilla** *nf* **1** *(pata)* leg. **2** *(de las gafas)* arm.
▶ *nf pl* sideboards, US sideburns.
**patín** *nm* **1** *(de ruedas)* roller skate, skate; *(de hielo)* ice skate. **2** *(tabla)* skateboard. **3** *(patinete)* scooter. **4** *(en el mar)* pedalo.
**pátina** *nf* patina.
**patinador,-ra** *nm & nf* skater.
**patinaje** *nm* skating. COMP **patinaje artístico** figure skating. ‖ **patinaje sobre hielo** ice-skating. ‖ **patinaje sobre ruedas** roller skating.
**patinar** *vi* **1** *(como diversión)* to skate. **2** *(vehículo)* to skid.
**patinazo** *nm* **1** skid. **2** *fam (error)* boob.
**patinete** *nm* scooter.
**patio** *nm* **1** *(de una casa)* courtyard; *(de un colegio)* playground. **2** TEAT pit.
**pato,-a** *nm & nf (ave)* duck.
▶ *nm* **pato** *fam (persona)* clumsy person.
**patológico,-a** *adj* pathological.
**patria** *nf* homeland.
**patriarca** *nm* patriarch.
**patriarcado** *nm* patriarchy.
**patrimonio** *nm* patrimony.
**patrio,-a** *adj* of one's homeland.
**patriota** *nm o nf* patriot.
**patriótico,-a** *adj* patriotic.
**patriotismo** *nm* patriotism.
**patrocinador,-ra** *nm & nf* sponsor.
**patrocinar** *vt* to sponsor.
**patrocinio** *nm* sponsorship.
**patrón,-ona** *nm & nf* **1** *(dueño de una casa)* landlord. **2** *(jefe)* employer. **3** REL patron saint.
▶ *nm* **patrón 1** *(en costura)* pattern. **2** *(de barco)* skipper. **3** *(modelo)* standard.

**patronal** *adj (fiesta)* of one's patron saint.
▶ *nf (institución)* employers' association.
**patronato** *nm (patronal)* employers' association.
**patrulla** *nf (de vigilancia)* patrol.
**patrullar** *vt* to patrol.
**paulatino,-a** *adj* gradual.
**pausa** *nf* **1** pause. **2** MÚS rest.
**pausado,-a** *adj* unhurried, slow.
**pauta** *nf (norma)* rule, guideline.
**pavimentar** *vt (con losas)* to pave.
**pavimento** *nm (de losas)* pavement.
**pavo,-a** *nm & nf (ave - macho)* turkey; *(- hembra)* turkey hen. COMP **pavo real** peacock.
▶ *nm* **pavo** *fam (timidez)* shyness.
**pavonearse** *vpr* to brag, swagger.
**pavoneo** *nm* strutting.
**pavor** *nm* terror.
**pavoroso,-a** *adj* frightful.
**payasada** *nf* **1** buffoonery. **2** *fam* silly thing.
**payaso,-a** *nm & nf* **1** *(artista de circo)* clown. **2** *fam* joker.
**paz** *nf* peace. LOC **dejar en paz** to leave alone. ‖ **hacer las paces** to make up.
**peaje** *nm* **1** *(dinero)* toll. **2** *(lugar)* tollbooth.
**peana** *nf* pedestal, stand.
**peatón** *nm* pedestrian.
**peatonal** *adj (calle, zona)* pedestrian.
**peca** *nf* freckle.
**pecado** *nm* sin.
**pecador,-ra** *nm & nf* sinner.
**pecaminoso,-a** *adj* sinful, wicked.
**pecar** *vi* to sin.
**pecera** *nf* fishbowl, fish tank.
**pechera** *nf (de camisa)* shirt front.
**pechina** *nf* scallop.
**pecho** *nm* **1** *(gen)* chest. **2** *(seno)* breast. LOC **dar el pecho** to breast-feed.
**pechuga** *nf (de un ave)* breast.
**pecíolo** *nm* petiole.
**pecoso,-a** *adj (persona)* freckly.
**pectina** *nf* pectin.
**pectoral** *nm (músculo)* pectoral muscle.

**pecuario,-a** *adj* cattle.
**peculiar** *adj (característico)* particular.
**peculiaridad** *nf* peculiarity.
**pecuniario,-a** *adj* pecuniary.
**pedagogía** *nf* pedagogy.
**pedagógico,-a** *adj* pedagogic(al).
**pedagogo,-a** *nm & nf* educator.
**pedal** *nm* **1** pedal. **2** *fam* bender.
**pedalear** *vi* to pedal.
**pedaleo** *nm* pedalling.
**pedanía** *nf* hamlet.
**pedante** *adj* pedantic, pompous.
**pedantería** *nf* pedantry, pomposity.
**pedazo** *nm* piece, bit.
**pedernal** *nm* **1** *(sílex)* flint. **2** *fig* rock.
**pedestal** *nm* pedestal.
**pedestre** *adj (a pie)* on foot.
**pediatra** *nm o nf* paediatrician.
**pediatría** *nf* paediatrics.
**pedicuro,-a** *nm & nf* chiropodist.
**pedido** *nm (de mercancías)* order. LOC hacer un pedido to place an order.
**pedigrí** *nm* pedigree.
**pedigüeño,-a** *nm & nf* pest.
**pedir** *vt* **1** *(gen)* to ask for: *me pidió que la acompañara* she asked me to go with her. **2** *(mercancías, en restaurante)* to order: *¿qué has pedido de postre?* what did you order for dessert?
▶ *vi (por la calle)* to beg.
**pedrada** *nf* blow with a stone.
**pedregal** *nm* rocky ground.
**pedregoso,-a** *adj* stony, rocky.
**pedrera** *nf* stone quarry.
**pedrería** *nf* precious stones *pl*.
**pedrisco** *nm (granizo)* hail.
**pedrusco** *nm* rough stone.
**pedúnculo** *nm (de planta)* stem.
**pega** *nf fam (dificultad)* snag: *me pusieron muchas pegas* they made it difficult for me.
**pegadizo,-a** *adj* **1** *(canción, música)* catchy. **2** *(sustancia)* sticky, adhesive.
**pegajoso,-a** *adj* **1** *(mano)* sticky. **2** *pey (persona)* clingy.
**pegamento** *nm* glue.
**pegar¹** *vt* **1** *(gen)* to stick. **2** *(contagiar)* to give: *me has pegado la gripe* you've given

me your flu. **3** *(acercar)* to move close to: *pega la estantería a la pared* move the bookcase against the wall. **4** INFORM to paste.
▶ *vi (combinar)* to match: *esta blusa no pega con la falda* this blouse doesn't go with the skirt.
▶ *vpr* **pegarse 1** *(quemarse)* to stick: *se me ha vuelto a pegar el arroz* the rice has stuck again. **2** *(persona)* to latch onto.
**pegar²** *vt* **1** *(golpear)* to hit: *mamá, Pablo me ha pegado* mum, Pablo hit me. **2** *(dar)* to give: *¡vaya susto me has pegado!* you didn't half scare me!
**pegatina** *nf* sticker.
**pego** LOC dar el pego *fam* to look like the real thing.
**pegote** *nm fam (masa)* sticky dollop.
**peinado** *nm* combing.
**peinado,-a** *adj* combed.
**peinar** *vt* **1** *(gen)* to comb; *(con cepillo)* to brush. **2** *(registrar)* to comb, search.
**peine** *nm* comb.
**peineta** *nf* ornamental comb.
**peladilla** *nf* sugared almond.
**pelado,-a** *adj* **1** bald, bare. **2** *(cabeza)* hairless, bald.
**peladuras** *nf pl* peelings.
**pelaje** *nm (de animal)* coat, fur.
**pelambrera** *nf fam* hair.
**pelapatatas** *nm inv* potato peeler.
**pelar** *vt* **1** *(persona)* to cut sb's hair. **2** *(fruta, patata, etc)* to peel.
▶ *vpr* **pelarse 1** *(cortarse el pelo)* to get one's hair cut. **2** *(piel)* to be peeling.
**peldaño** *nm* step.
**pelea** *nf (física)* fight; *(verbal)* quarrel.
**peleador,-ra** *adj* argumentative.
**pelear** *vi* to fight, to quarrel, argue.
▶ *vpr* **pelearse** to fight, to quarrel.
**peleón,-ona** *nm & nf* quarrelsome.
**peletería** *nf (establecimiento)* fur shop.
**peletero,-a** *adj (industria)* fur.
▶ *nm & nf* furrier.
**peliagudo,-a** *adj* tricky.
**pelícano** *nm* pelican.
**película** *nf* film. COMP película de suspense thriller. ‖ película muda silent movie.

**peligrar** *vi* to be in danger.

**peligro** *nm* danger. LOC **correr peligro de** to be in danger of. ▍ **estar fuera de peligro** to be out of danger.

**peligroso,-a** *adj* dangerous.

**pelín** *nm fam* teeny bit.

**pelirrojo,-a** *adj* red-haired.

**pellejo** *nm (piel)* skin.

**pelliza** *nf (forrada de piel)* fur-lined coat.

**pellizcar** *vt* to pinch, nip.

**pellizco** *nm* pinch, nip.

**pelo** *nm* **1** hair. **2** *(de animal)* coat, fur. **3** *fam* bit: *perdí el tren por un pelo* I missed the train by seconds. LOC **no tener un pelo de tonto,-a** *fam* to be nobody's fool. ▍ **poner los pelos de punta** to make one's hair stand on end. ▍ **tomar el pelo a** ALGN to pull sb's leg.

**pelota** *nf* ball. COMP **pelota de fútbol** football.
 ► *nm o nf fam* creep.

**pelotazo** *nm* blow with a ball.

**pelotilla** *nf* small ball.

**pelotón** *nm* **1** *fig (grupo)* bunch. **2** *(de ciclistas)* pack, peloton.

**peltre** *nm* pewter.

**peluca** *nf* wig.

**peluche** *nm (muñeco)* teddy bear.

**peludo,-a** *adj* hairy.

**peluquería** *nf* hairdresser's.

**peluquero,-a** *nm & nf* hairdresser.

**peluquín** *nm* hairpiece.

**pelusa** *nf (pelo)* fluff.

**pélvico,-a** *adj* pelvic.

**pelvis** *nf inv* pelvis.

**pena** *nf* **1** *(castigo)* sentence, punishment. **2** *(tristeza)* grief, sorrow. **3** *(lástima)* pity: *¡qué pena que no podáis venir!* it's a shame you can't make it! **4** *(dificultad)* hardship, trouble.

**penado,-a** *nm & nf* convict.

**penal** *adj (derecho)* criminal.
 ► *nm (prisión)* prison, US penitentiary.

**penalidad** *nf* trouble, hardship.

**penalización** *nf (acción)* penalization.

**penalizar** *vt* to penalize.

**penalti** *nm* penalty.

**penar** *vt (castigar)* to punish, penalize.
 ► *vi (padecer)* to suffer, grieve.

**pender** *vi* to hang (de, from).

**pendiente** *adj* **1** hanging. **2** *(asunto)* pending, outstanding. LOC **estar pendiente de** ALGO *(a la espera)* to be waiting for STH.
 ► *nf (cuesta)* slope; *(inclinación)* gradient.
 ► *nm (joya)* earring.

**pendular** *adj* pendular.

**péndulo** *nm* pendulum.

**penetración** *nf* penetration.

**penetrante** *adj* penetrating.

**penetrar** *vi* **1** *(introducirse - en un territorio)* to penetrate (en, -); *(- en propiedad)* to enter. **2** *(atravesar)* to penetrate, seep through: *la humedad ha penetrado por el suelo* damp has seeped through the floor.
 ► *vt (atravesar)* to penetrate; *(ruido)* to pierce.

**penicilina** *nf* penicillin.

**península** *nf* peninsula. COMP **la Península Ibérica** the Iberian Peninsula.

**penique** *nm* penny.

**penitencia** *nf* REL *(virtud)* penitence; *(castigo, sacramento)* penance.

**penitenciaría** *nf* penitentiary.

**penitenciario,-a** *adj (institución, sistema)* prison.

**penoso,-a** *adj (doloroso)* painful.

**pensador,-ra** *nm & nf* thinker.

**pensamiento** *nm (idea)* thought.

**pensante** *adj* thinking.

**pensar** *vi* **1** *(gen)* to think (en, of/about): *estuvo pensando en sus amigos* he was thinking about his friends. **2** *(considerar)* to consider, think (en, about). **3** *(creer)* to think, think about. **4** *(opinar)* to think (de, about). **5** *(decidir)* to decide. **6** *(tener la intención)* to intend to, plan, think of.

**pensativo,-a** *adj* pensive.

**pensión** *nf* **1** *(para jubilados)* pension. **2** *(casa de huéspedes)* boarding house. COMP **pensión completa** full board.

**pensionista** *nm o nf (jubilado)* pensioner.

**pentagonal** *adj* pentagonal.

**pentágono** *nm* pentagon.

**pentagrama** *nm* MÚS stave, staff.

**pentatlón** *nm* pentathlon.

**penúltimo,-a** *adj* penultimate.
 ► *nm & nf* last but one, next to last.

P

**penumbra** *nf (gen)* semidarkness.

**penuria** *nf (escasez)* shortage.

**peña¹** *nf (piedra)* rock; *(monte)* crag.

**peña²** *nf (grupo)* group of friends; *(asociación)* club.

**peñasco** *nm* crag.

**peñón** *nm* craggy rock. LOC **el Peñón de Gibraltar** the Rock of Gibraltar.

**peón** *nm* **1** *(trabajador)* unskilled labourer (US laborer). **2** *(en el ajedrez)* pawn.

**peonía** *nf* BOT peony.

**peonza** *nf* top, spinning top.

**peor** *adj* **1** *(comparativo)* worse: *tu coche es peor que el mío* your car is worse than mine. **2** *(superlativo)* worst.

**pepinillo** *nm* gherkin.

**pepino** *nm* cucumber.

**pepita** *nf (de fruta)* → seed, pip.

**peque** *nm* kid.

**pequeñez** *nf* **1** *(de tamaño)* smallness. **2** *(insignificancia)* trifle.

**pequeñito,-a** *adj fam* teeny, wee.

**pequeño,-a** *adj* **1** *(de tamaño)* little, small: *este jersey me está pequeño* this jumper is too small for me. **2** *(de edad)* young. **3** *(en tiempo)* short: *nos hemos tomado unas pequeñas vacaciones* we've taken a short holiday.
► *nm & nf (niño)* little one: *a esta hora los pequeños tienen que estar en la cama* kids should be in bed by now. LOC **de pequeño,-a** as a child.

**pequinés,-esa** *adj* Pekinese.
► *nm* **pekinés** *(perro)* Pekinese.

**pera** *nf (fruta)* pear.

**peral** *nm* pear tree.

**perca** *nf* perch.

**percance** *nm* mishap.

**percatarse** *vpr* to notice (de, -).

**percebe** *nm* goose barnacle.

**percepción** *nf* perception.

**perceptible** *adj* perceptible.

**perceptivo,-a** *adj* perceptive.

**percha** *nf* **1** *(de ropa)* hanger. **2** *(perchero de pared)* rack; *(gancho)* hook.

**perchero** *nm (de pie)* coat stand.

**percherón,-ona** *adj (caballo)* Percheron.

**percibir** *vt (notar)* to perceive, notice.

**percusión** *nf* percussion.

**percusionista** *nm o nf* percussionist.

**percutir** *vt (golpear)* to strike.

**perdedor,-ra** *adj & nf* loser.

**perder** *vt* **1** *(gen)* to lose. **2** *(malgastar, desperdiciar)* to waste: *se pasa el día perdiendo el tiempo* he's always wasting time. **3** *(tren, etc)* to miss.
► *vi* **1** *(gen)* to lose; *(salir perdiendo)* to lose out. **2** *(empeorar)* to get worse.
► *vpr* **perderse** **1** *(extraviarse - persona)* to get lost; *(- cosa, etc)* to go missing: *se me ha perdido un pendiente* I've lost an earring. **2** *(dejar escapar)* to miss: *¡no te lo pierdas!* don't miss it!

**perdición** *nf (moral)* undoing, ruin.

**pérdida** *nf* **1** *(daño)* loss: *las tormentas han originado muchas pérdidas materiales* the storms have caused serious damage. **2** *(desperdicio)* waste. **3** *(escape)* leak.

**perdido,-a** *adj* **1** *(extraviado)* lost. **2** *(desperdiciado)* wasted. **3** *(bala)* stray.

**perdigón** *nm* pellet.

**perdiguero** *nm* gun dog.

**perdiz** *nf* partridge.

**perdón** *nm* pardon, forgiveness. LOC **pedir perdón** to apologize, say sorry.

**perdonable** *adj* excusable, forgivable.

**perdonar** *vt* **1** *(gen)* to forgive. **2** *(excusar)* to excuse: *perdona que te interrumpa* excuse me for interrupting. **3** *(deuda)* to write off.

**perdurar** *vi* to last, continue to exist.

**perecedero,-a** *adj* perishable.

**perecer** *vi* to perish, die.

**peregrinación** *nf* pilgrimage.

**peregrinar** *vi* to go on a pilgrimage.

**peregrino,-a** *nm & nf* REL pilgrim.

**perejil** *nm* parsley.

**perenne** *adj* perennial.

**pereza** *nf* laziness. LOC **tener pereza** to feel lazy.

**perezoso,-a** *adj* lazy.
► *nm* **perezoso** ZOOL sloth.

**perfección** *nf* perfection. LOC **a la perfección** perfectly: *habla inglés a la perfección* he speaks perfect English.

**perfeccionar** *vt* **1** *(mejorar)* to improve. **2** *(hacer perfecto)* to perfect.

**perfeccionista** *adj* perfectionist.
▶ *nm o nf* perfectionist.

**perfecto,-a** *adj* perfect.

**perfidia** *nf* perfidy.

**pérfido,-a** *adj* perfidious.

**perfil** *nm* **1** *(gen)* profile. **2** *(silueta)* outline.

**perfilar** *vt* *(dar forma)* to outline.

**perforación** *nf* *(gen)* perforation.

**perforadora** *nf* **1** *(en una mina)* drill. **2** *(de papeles)* punch.

**perforar** *vt* **1** *(gen)* to perforate. **2** *(terreno)* to drill, bore. **3** *(papel)* to punch.

**perfumar** *vt* to perfume, scent.

**perfume** *nm* perfume.

**perfumería** *nf* *(tienda)* perfumery.

**pergamino** *nm* parchment.

**pérgola** *nf* pergola.

**pericardio** *nm* pericardium.

**pericarpio** *nm* pericarp.

**pericia** *nf* skill.

**periferia** *nf* *(de una ciudad)* outskirts *pl*.

**periférico,-a** *adj* **1** *(gen)* peripheral. **2** *(barrio, zona)* outlying.
▶ *nm* periférico INFORM peripheral unit.

**perifollo** *nm* BOT common chervil.

**perífrasis** *nf* periphrasis.

**perifrástico,-a** *adj* periphrastic.

**perilla** *nf* goatee.

**perímetro** *nm* perimeter.

**periodicidad** *nf* periodicity.

**periódico,-a** *adj* periodical.
▶ *nm* periódico newspaper.

**periodismo** *nm* journalism.

**periodista** *nm o nf* journalist.

**período** *nm* period.

**peripecia** *nf* incident.

**peripuesto,-a** *adj* fam all dressed up.

**periquito,-a** *nm o nf* parakeet.

**periscopio** *nm* periscope.

**peristilo** *nm* peristyle.

**peritaje** *nm* *(informe)* expert's report.

**perito,-a** *nm & nf* *(experto)* expert.

**perjudicado,-a** *nm & nf* person who loses out, person affected: *los más perjudicados han sido los campesinos* farmers have been worst affected.

**perjudicar** *vt* to adversely affect.

**perjudicial** *adj* harmful.

**perjuicio** *nm* *(material)* damage; *(económico)* loss.

**perjurio** *nm* perjury.

**perla** *nf* **1** pearl. **2** fig gem.

**permanecer** *vi* to stay, remain.

**permanencia** *nf* *(estancia)* stay.

**permanente** *adj* permanent, lasting.

**permanganato** *nm* permanganate.

**permeabilidad** *nf* permeability.

**permeable** *adj* permeable.

**permisividad** *nf* permissiveness.

**permisivo,-a** *adj* permissive.

**permiso** *nm* **1** permission. **2** *(documento)* permit. **3** leave. COMP **permiso de conducir** driving licence, US driver's licence.

**permitir** *vt* to allow, let: *permitió que sus hijas fueran al concierto* he let his daughters go to the concert.
▶ *vpr* permitirse to allow os, afford.
LOC **¿me permite?** may I?

**permuta** *nf* exchange.

**permutación** *nf* permutation.

**permutar** *vt* **1** to exchange. **2** MAT to permute.

**pernicioso,-a** *adj* pernicious, harmful.

**pernoctar** *vi* to spend the night.

**pero** *conj* but.

**perol** *nm* cooking pot.

**peroné** *nm* fibula.

**perorata** *nf* spiel.

**peróxido** *nm* peroxide. COMP **peróxido de hidrógeno** hydrogen peroxide.

**perpendicular** *adj* perpendicular.

**perpetrar** *vt* to perpetrate, commit.

**perpetuación** *nf* perpetuation.

**perpetuar** *vt* to perpetuate.
▶ *vpr* perpetuarse to be perpetuated.

**perpetuidad** *nf* perpetuity.

**perpetuo,-a** *adj* *(gen)* perpetual; *(cargo)* permanent. COMP **nieves perpetuas** perpetual snows.

**perplejidad** *nf* perplexity.

**perplejo,-a** *adj* perplexed.

**perrera** *nf (lugar)* dog pound.

**perro,-a** *nm* perro ZOOL dog. COMP **perro caliente** hot dog. | **perro pastor** sheepdog.

**persecución** *nf* **1** pursuit. **2** *(represión)* persecution.

**perseguidor,-ora** *nm & nf* pursuer.

**perseguir** *vt* **1** to pursue, chase. **2** *fig (seguir)* to follow: *este perro me persigue* this dog follows me everywhere.

**perseverante** *adj* persevering.

**perseverar** *vi* to persevere.

**persiana** *nf* blind.

**persignarse** *vpr* to cross OS.

**persistente** *adj* persistent.

**persistir** *vi (mantenerse firme)* to persist, persevere.

**persona** *nf* person. LOC **en persona** in person.

**personaje** *nm* **1** *(famoso)* celebrity. **2** *(en obra, película)* character.

**personal** *nm (de una empresa)* staff.

**personalidad** *nf (carácter)* personality.

**personalizar** *vt* to personalize.
▶ *vi* to get personal.

**personarse** *vpr* to appear in person.

**personificación** *nf* personification.

**personificar** *vt* to personify.

**perspectiva** *nf* **1** ARTE perspective. **2** *(posibilidad)* prospect: *este negocio presenta muy buenas perspectivas* this business has good prospects. **3** *(vista)* view, perspective. **4** *(punto de vista)* point of view.

**perspicacia** *nf* sharpness.

**perspicaz** *adj* sharp, perspicacious.

**persuadir** *vt* to persuade, convince.
▶ *vpr* **persuadirse** to be convinced.

**persuasión** *nf* persuasion.

**persuasivo,-a** *adj* persuasive.

**pertenecer** *vi* to belong (a, to).

**perteneciente** *adj* belonging (a, to).

**pertenencia** *nf* **1** *(propiedad)* property: *esto es de mi pertenencia* this belongs to me. **2** *(afiliación)* membership.
▶ *nf pl* **pertenencias** *(bienes)* belongings.

**pértiga** *nf* pole. COMP **salto de pértiga** pole vault.

**pertinaz** *adj* **1** *(sequía, frío)* prolonged, persistent. **2** *(persona)* obstinate.

**pertinente** *adj* **1** *(oportuno)* appropriate. **2** *(relevante)* pertinent, relevant.

**pertrechar** *vt* to supply (de, with).
▶ *vpr* **pertrecharse** to equip OS.

**pertrechos** *nm pl* equipment *sing*.

**perturbación** *nf* disruption.

**perturbado,-a** *adj* **1** *(trastornado)* mentally disturbed. **2** *(intranquilo)* perturbed.

**perturbar** *vt* **1** *(alterar)* to disturb, perturb. **2** *(inquietar)* to perturb.

**Perú** *nm* Peru.

**peruano,-a** *adj* Peruvian.
▶ *nm & nf* Peruvian.

**perversidad** *nf (maldad)* wickedness.

**perversión** *nf (maldad)* wickedness.

**perverso,-a** *adj (malvado)* evil, wicked.
▶ *nm & nf* evil person.

**pervertir** *vt (gen)* to corrupt.

**pervivencia** *nf* survival.

**pervivir** *vi* to live on, persist.

**pesa** *nf* weight.

**pesadez** *nf* **1** *(lentitud)* sluggishness. **2** *(molestia)* bore.

**pesadilla** *nf* nightmare.

**pesado,-a** *adj* **1** *(gen)* heavy. **2** *(molesto)* tiresome; *(aburrido)* boring.
▶ *nm & nf (persona)* bore, pain. LOC **ponerse pesado,-a** to get boring.

**pesadumbre** *nf* sorrow, grief.

**pésame** *nm* condolences *pl*. LOC **dar el pésame** to offer your condolences.

**pesar** *vi* **1** to weigh: *¿cuánto pesas?* how much do you weigh? **2** *(tener mucho peso)* to be heavy. **3** *(sentir)* to be sorry, regret: *me pesa mucho no haberle invitado* I really regret not having invited him.
▶ *vt* to weigh.
▶ *nm (pena)* sorrow, grief. LOC **a pesar de** despite, in spite of.

**pesca** *nf (actividad)* fishing.

**pescadería** *nf* fishmonger's.

**pescadero,-a** *nm & nf* fishmonger.

**pescadilla** *nf* young hake.

**pescado** *nm* fish. COMP **pescado azul** blue fish. | **pescado blanco** white fish.

**pescador** *nm & nf* fisherman.

**pescar** *vi (ir a pescar)* to fish, go fishing. LOC **ir a pescar** to go fishing.
▶ *vt* **1** *(sacar del agua)* to get, catch. **2** *fam (agarrar)* catch: *he pescado un buen resfriado* I've caught a really nasty cold.

**pescuezo** *nm* neck.

**pesebre** *nm* manger, stall.

**pesimismo** *nm* pessimism.

**pesimista** *adj* pessimistic.
▶ *nm o nf* pessimist.

**pésimo,-a** *adj* dreadful, awful.

**peso** *nm* **1** *(gen)* weight. **2** *(balanza)* scales *pl*. **3** *(carga)* load, burden. LOC **de peso 1** *(pesado)* heavy. **2** *(importante)* important. **3** *(convincente)* strong, powerful.

**pespunte** *nm* backstitch.

**pesquero,-a** *nm* fishing boat.

**pesquisa** *nf* inquiry.

**pestaña** *nf (del ojo)* eyelash.

**pestañear** *vi* to blink.

**peste** *nf (mal olor)* stink, stench.

**pesticida** *nm* pesticide.

**pestilente** *adj (apestoso)* stinking.

**pestillo** *nm* bolt. LOC **cerrar con pestillo** to bolt.

**pétalo** *nm* petal.

**petanca** *nf* petanque, boules.

**petardo** *nm (de verbena)* firecracker.

**petate** *nm (de soldado, marinero)* kit bag.

**petición** *nf* **1** *(gen)* request. **2** plea.

**petirrojo** *nm* robin.

**peto** *nm (pantalón)* pair of dungarees.

**pétreo,-a** *adj* stony.

**petrificar** *vt (fosilizar)* to petrify.

**petróleo** *nm* oil.

**petrolero,-a** *adj* oil.
▶ *nm* **petrolero** oil tanker.

**petrolífero,-a** *adj* oil-bearing.

**petroquímica** *nf* petrochemistry.

**petroquímico,-a** *adj* petrochemical.

**petulancia** *nf* vanity.

**petulante** *adj* vain.

**petunia** *nf* petunia.

**peyorativo,-a** *adj* pejorative.

**pez** *nm* fish.

**pezón** *nm* nipple.

**pezuña** *nf* hoof.

**piadoso,-a** *adj* pious, devout.

**pianista** *nm o nf* pianist.

**piano** *nm* piano.

**pianola®** *nf* Pianola.

**piar** *vi* to chirp, tweet.

**piara** *nf* herd of pigs.

**pica** *nf* **1** *(lanza)* pike. **2** *(de la baraja)* spade.

**picada** *nf (picadura - de avispa)* sting; *(- de mosquito)* bite.

**picadero** *nm (escuela)* riding school.

**picadillo** *nm (de carne)* minced meat; *(de verduras)* chopped vegetables.

**picado,-a** *adj* **1** CULIN *(cortado - verdura)* finely chopped; *(- carne)* minced. **2** *(diente)* decayed. **3** *fam (ofendido)* offended.

**picador** *nm (minero)* face worker.

**picadora** *nf* mincer.

**picadura** *nf (de insecto, serpiente)* bite; *(de abeja, avispa)* sting.

**picante** *adj* **1** *(comida)* hot. **2** *fig (chiste)* spicy.

**picapedrero** *nm* stonecutter.

**picaporte** *nm* **1** *(para llamar)* door knocker. **2** *(para abrir)* door handle.

**picar** *vt* **1** *(morder - insecto)* to bite; *(- abeja, avispa)* to sting. **2** *(perforar - papel, tarjeta)* to punch. **3** *(dar con un pico)* to jab, goad. **4** CULIN *(cortar)* to chop finely; *(carne)* to mince. **5** *(comida)* to nibble: *vamos a salir a picar algo* we're going to get a bite to eat.
▶ *vi* **1** *(sentir escozor)* to itch: *me pica todo el cuerpo* I'm itching all over. **2** *(estar picante)* to be hot. **3** *(pez)* to bite; *(persona)* to fall for it. **4** *(comer)* to have a nibble.
▶ *vpr* **picarse 1** *(muela)* to decay, go bad. **2** *(mar)* to get choppy. **3** *(ofenderse)* to take offence.

**picardía** *nf (astucia)* craftiness.

**picaresco,-a** *nf* picaresque genre.

**pícaro,-a** *adj (astuto)* crafty, sly.
▶ *nm & nf (persona astuta)* slyboots.

**picazón** *nf (picor)* itch.

**pichichi** *nm (goleador)* top goal scorer.

P

**pichón,-ona** *nm & nf* pigeon.

**pico** *nm* **1** *(de ave)* beak. **2** *(herramienta)* pickaxe, pick. **3** *(de montaña)* peak. **4** *(punta)* corner. LOC **y pico** *(cantidad)*: llegaremos sobre las seis y pico we'll be there just after six.

**picor** *nm* itch.

**picotazo** *nm* **1** *(de ave)* peck. **2** *(de insecto, reptil)* bite; *(de abeja, avispa)* sting.

**picotear** *vt* to peck, peck at.

**picoteo** *nm* **1** *(de ave)* pecking. **2** *(acción de comer)* nibbling, snacking.

**pictórico,-a** *adj* pictorial.

**picudo,-a** *adj* pointed.

**pie** *nm* **1** ANAT foot. **2** *(base - de una lámpara)* base; *(- de una escultura)* plinth. **3** *(medida de longitud)* foot. LOC **a pie** on foot. ▌ **ponerse de pie** to get to one's feet, stand up.

**piedad** *nf* *(misericordia)* pity, mercy.

**piedra** *nf* stone. COMP **piedra preciosa** gem, precious stone.

**piel** *nf* **1** *(de persona)* skin. **2** *(de la fruta, patatas)* peel.

**pienso** *nm* fodder.

**pierna** *nf* leg.

**pieza** *nf* **1** *(gen)* piece; *(de un aparato)* part. **2** MÚS piece, piece of music. **3** TEAT play. **4** *(de un juego de tablero)* piece.

**pigmentación** *nf* pigmentation.

**pigmento** *nm* pigment.

**pigmeo,-a** *adj (raza)* Pygmy.
▶ *nm & nf (raza)* Pygmy.

**pijama** *nm* pyjamas (US pajamas) *pl*.

**pila** *nf* **1** ELEC battery. **2** *(de fregar)* sink. **3** *fam (montón)* pile, heap: tengo una pila de cosas que hacer I've got piles of work to do. LOC **ponerse las pilas** *fam* to get one's act together.

**pilar** *nm* pillar.

**pilastra** *nf* pilaster.

**píldora** *nf* pill, tablet.

**pileta** *nf* AM swimming pool.

**pillaje** *nm* looting.

**pillar** *vt* **1** *(coger)* to catch. **2** *fam (robar)* to nick. **3** *fam (atropellar)* to run over. **4** *fam (entender)* to catch, get, grasp.
▶ *vi fam (encontrarse)* to be: me pilla muy cerca de casa it's very near home.

**pillo,-a** *nm & nf (niño)* little monkey, little devil.

**pilón** *nm* *(de una fuente)* basin.

**píloro** *nm* pylorus.

**pilotar** *vt (avión)* to pilot, fly; *(coche)* to drive; *(barco)* to sail.

**pilote** *nm* pile.

**piloto** *nm* *(conductor - de avión)* pilot; *(- de coche)* driver; *(- de barco)* pilot.

**pimentero** *nm* **1** *(recipiente)* pepper pot. **2** *(planta)* pepper plant.

**pimentón** *nm* paprika. COMP **pimentón picante** cayenne pepper.

**pimienta** *nf (especia)* pepper.

**pimiento** *nm* *(gen)* pepper; *(rojo)* red pepper; *(verde)* green pepper.

**pinacoteca** *nf* art gallery.

**pináculo** *nm* pinnacle.

**pinar** *nm* pine grove.

**pincel** *nm* paintbrush.

**pincelada** *nf* brush stroke.

**pinchadiscos** *nm o nf* disc jockey, DJ.

**pinchar** *vt* **1** *(punzar)* to prick. **2** MED *(poner inyección)* to give an injection. **3** *(sujetar)* to spear, jab. **4** *(enfadar)* to needle.

**pinchazo** *nm* **1** *(de neumático)* puncture. **2** *(inyección)* injection, jab, US shot.

**pinche** *nm & nf (de cocina)* kitchen assistant.

**pincho** *nm* **1** *(de una planta)* thorn. **2** *(de un erizo)* spine, prickle. **3** *(de aperitivo)* snack. **4** *(brocheta)* skewer. COMP **pincho moruno** shish kebab.

**pineda** *nf* pine grove.

**pingo** *nm fam (de ropa)* rag.

**ping-pong** *nm* table tennis, ping-pong.

**pingüe** *adj* substantial.

**pingüino** *nm* penguin.

**pino** *nm (árbol)* pine tree; *(madera)* pine.

**pinta** *nf* **1** *(mancha)* dot. **2** *(medida)* pint. **3** *fam (aspecto)* look.

**pintada** *nf* graffiti.

**pintado,-a** *adj (maquillado)* made-up.

**pintalabios** *nm inv* lipstick.

**pintar** *vt* **1** *(gen)* to paint; *(dibujar)* to draw. **2** *(maquillar)* to make up.
▶ *vi* **1** *(gen)* to paint. **2** *(marcar)* to write.

▶ *vpr* **pintarse** *(maquillarse)* to put one's make up on.

**pintarrajear** *vt fam* to daub.

**pintarrajo** *nm fam* daub.

**pintaúñas** *nm inv* nail varnish.

**pinto,-a** *adj* spotted.

**pintor,-ra** *nm & nf* artist, painter.

**pintoresco,-a** *adj* **1** *(lugar)* picturesque. **2** *(persona)* bizarre.

**pintura** *nf* **1** *(arte)* painting. **2** *(producto)* paint: *un bote de pintura* a tin of paint.

**pinza** *nf* **1** *(de cangrejo)* pincer. **2** *(de la ropa)* clothes peg.

▶ *nf pl* **pinzas 1** *(de depilar)* tweezers. **2** *(de servir hielo)* tongs.

**pinzamiento** *nm* trapped nerve.

**pinzón** *nm* finch.

**piña** *nf* **1** *(fruta)* pineapple. **2** *(del pino)* pine cone.

**piñata** *nf* hollow figure filled with sweets (which children try to break open at parties).

**piñón** *nm (comestible)* pine nut kernel.

**pío** *nm* chirp.

**pío,-a** *adj* pious.

**piojo** *nm* louse.

**piolet** *nm* ice axe (US ax).

**pionero,-a** *nm & nf* pioneer.

**pipa¹** *nf (de tabaco)* pipe.

**pipa²** *nf (de girasol)* sunflower seed.

**pipeta** *nf* pipette.

**pique** *nm (rivalidad)* rivalry, needle.

**piqueta** *nf* pickaxe.

**piquete** *nm (de huelga)* picket.

**pira** *nf* pyre.

**pirado,-a** *adj fam (loco)* loony, wacky.

**piragua** *nf* canoe.

**piragüismo** *nm* canoeing.

**piragüista** *nm o nf* canoeist.

**piramidal** *adj* pyramidal.

**pirámide** *nf* pyramid.

**piraña** *nf* piranha.

**pirata** *adj* pirate.

▶ *nm o nf (de la informática)* hacker.

**piratear** *vt* **1** *(gen)* to pirate. **2** *(informática)* to hack.

**piratería** *nf (gen)* piracy.

**pirita** *nf* pyrite.

**pirómano,-a** *nm & nf* pyromaniac.

**piropear** *vt* to make flirtatious comments to.

**piropo** *nm* compliment.

**pirotecnia** *nf* fireworks *pl*.

**pirotécnico,-a** *adj* pyrotechnic.

▶ *nm & nf* fireworks expert.

**pirueta** *nf* pirouette.

**piruleta** *nf* lollipop.

**pirulí** *nm fam (de caramelo)* lollipop.

**pisada** *nf (huella)* footprint.

**pisapapeles** *nm inv* paperweight.

**pisar** *vt* **1** *(gen)* to tread on. **2** *(acelerador, embrague)* to put one's foot on. **3** *fig (entrar)* to set foot in.

▶ *vi* to tread, walk, step: *no pises muy fuerte que nos oyen los vecinos* tread more quietly, the neighbours will hear us.

**piscifactoría** *nf* fish farm.

**piscina** *nf* swimming pool.

**piso** *nm* **1** *(para vivir)* flat. **2** *(planta)* floor.

**pisotear** *vt (pisar)* to trample.

**pisotón** *nm* stamp.

**pista** *nf* **1** *(rastro)* trail, track. **2** *(indicio)* clue. **3** *(de baile)* dance floor. **4** *(camino)* track. **5** *(de tenis)* court. **6** *(de circo)* ring. **7** *(de aterrizaje)* runway. COMP **pista de esquí** ski slope.

**pistachero** *nm* pistachio tree.

**pistacho** *nm* pistachio (nut).

**pistilo** *nm* pistil.

**pistola** *nf* gun.

**pistolera** *nf* holster.

**pistolero** *nm* gunman.

**pistoletazo** *nm* gunshot.

**pistón** *nm (de un motor)* piston.

**pita** *nf* BOT pita.

**pitada** *nf* **1** *(bocinazo)* hoot. **2** *(pitido)* whistle.

**pitar** *vi* **1** *(silbar)* to blow a whistle. **2** *(tocar la bocina)* to hoot. **3** *(abuchear)* to boo and hiss. LOC **ir/irse pitando** *fam* to rush out, dash off.

▶ *vt* DEP *(falta)* to whistle.

**pitido** *nm* **1** *(silbido)* whistle. **2** *(bocinazo)* hoot, honk.

**pitillera** *nf* cigarette case.

**pitillo** *nm* cigarette.

P

**pito** *nm (silbato)* whistle.
**pitón¹** *nf* ZOOL python.
**pitón²** *nm (del toro)* horn.
**pitonisa** *nf* fortune teller.
**pitorro** *nm* spout.
**pituitaria** *nf* pituitary (gland).
**pívot** *nm o nf* centre.
**pivotar** *vi* to pivot.
**pivote** *nm* pivot.
**pizarra** *nf* 1 *(mineral)* slate. 2 *(para escribir)* blackboard.
**pizca** *nf fam (gen)* bit; *(de sal)* pinch.
**pizza** *nf* pizza.
**pizzería** *nf* pizzeria, pizza parlour.
**placa** *nf* 1 *(de metal)* sheet. 2 *(con el nombre)* plaque. 3 *(de matrícula)* number plate. 4 *(de hielo)* sheet.
**placaje** *nm* tackle.
**placar** *vt (en rugby)* to tackle.
**placebo** *nm* placebo.
**placenta** *nf* placenta.
**placentero,-a** *adj* pleasant.
**placer** *nm* pleasure.
 ▶ *vi* to please: *haz lo que te plazca* do as you please.
**placidez** *nf* placidity.
**plácido,-a** *adj* placid, calm.
**plafón** *nm (lámpara de techo)* ceiling light.
**plaga** *nf* 1 *(epidemia)* plague. 2 *(de insectos)* plague, pest. 3 *fig* invasion.
**plagar** *vt* to plague, infest.
**plagiar** *vt* to plagiarize.
**plagio** *nm* plagiarism.
**plaguicida** *nm* pesticide.
**plan** *nm* 1 *(intención)* plan. 2 *(programa)* project.
**plana** *nf (página)* page: *la noticia viene en primera plana* the news is on the front page.
**plancha** *nf* 1 *(de metal)* plate. 2 *(electrodoméstico)* iron. LOC **a la plancha** grilled.
**planchado,-a** *nm (acción)* ironing.
**planchar** *vt* to iron, press.
**planchista** *nm o nf* panel beater.
**plancton** *nm* plankton.
**planeador** *nm* glider.
**planear** *vt (futuro, idea)* to plan.
 ▶ *vi (en el aire)* to glide.

**planeo** *nm* gliding, glide.
**planeta** *nm* planet.
**planetario,-a** *adj* planetary.
 ▶ *nm* planetario planetarium.
**planicie** *nf* plain.
**planificación** *nf* planning.
**planificador,-ra** *adj* planning.
 ▶ *nm & nf* planner.
**planificar** *vt* to plan.
**plano,-a** *adj (superficie)* flat.
 ▶ *nm* plano 1 *(de una ciudad)* street plan, map. 2 *(de una casa)* plan. 3 *(nivel)* level. 4 MAT plane.
**planta** *nf* 1 BOT plant. 2 *(del pie)* sole. 3 *(de un edificio)* floor. COMP **planta baja** ground floor, US first floor.
**plantación** *nf* 1 *(terreno)* plantation. 2 *(acción)* planting.
**plantar** *vt* 1 AGR to plant. 2 *(colocar - gen)* to put, place; *(- tienda de campaña)* to pitch, put up.
 ▶ *vpr* **plantarse** *fam (colocarse)* to place os, position os: *se plantó en la esquina* she positioned herself on the corner.
**plante** *nm (laboral)* protest action.
**planteamiento** *nm* 1 MAT *(formulación - de un problema)* formulation.
**plantear** *vt* 1 *(pregunta)* to pose, raise. 2 *(problema)* to cause. 3 MAT *(problema)* to formulate.
 ▶ *vpr* **plantearse** to consider.
**plantel** *nm* cadre.
**plantilla** *nf* 1 *(patrón)* model, pattern. 2 *(personal)* staff.
**plantón** LOC **darle plantón a** ALGN *fam (no presentarse)* to stand SB up.
**plañidero,-a** *adj* plaintive, mournful.
**plañir** *vi* to mourn.
**plaqueta** *nf (de sangre)* platelet.
**plasma** *nm* plasma.
**plasmar** *vt fig* to give expression to.
**plastelina** *nf* Plasticine.
**plástica** *nf* plastic arts *pl*.
**plasticidad** *nf* plasticity.
**plástico,-a** *adj* plastic.
 ▶ *nm* plástico *(material)* plastic.
**plastificado,-a** *adj* laminated.
**plastificar** *vt* to laminate.

**plastilina®** *nf* Plasticine®.

**plata** *nf* silver.

**plataforma** *nf* platform. COMP plataforma petrolífera oil rig.

**platanal** *nm* banana plantation.

**platanero,-a** *nm* banana tree.

**plátano** *nm* banana.

**platea** *nf* stalls *pl*.

**plateado,-a** *adj (color)* silvery.

**platear** *vt* to silver-plate.

**plateresco,-a** *adj* plateresque.

**platería** *nf (taller)* silversmith's.

**platero,-a** *nm & nf* silversmith.

**plática** *nf* talk.

**platicar** *vi* to chat, talk.

**platillo** *nm* **1** *(de postre)* dessert plate; *(de café)* saucer. COMP platillo volante flying saucer.

**platina** *nf* MÚS → pletina.

**platino** *nm* platinum.

**plato** *nm* **1** *(recipiente)* plate, dish. **2** CULIN dish. **3** *(en comida)* course: *de primer plato hay sopa* we've got soup for starters.

**plató** *nm (de cine)* set, film set; *(de televisión)* floor.

**platónico,-a** *adj* platonic.

**plausible** *adj (probable)* plausible.

**playa** *nf* **1** *(superficie de arena)* beach. **2** *(costa)* seaside.

**playeras** *nf pl* canvas shoes.

**plaza** *nf* **1** *(de una población)* square. **2** *(mercado)* marketplace. **3** *(puesto de trabajo)* position. COMP plaza de parking parking space.

**plazo** *nm* **1** *(período de tiempo)* time. **2** *(de compra)* instalment, US installment. LOC comprar ALGO a plazos to buy STH on hire purchase, US buy STH on an installment plan.

**plazoleta** *nf* small square.

**pleamar** *nf* high tide.

**plebe** *nf (gen)* common people.

**plebeyo,-a** *nm & nf* plebeian.

**plebiscito** *nm* plebiscite.

**plegable** *adj* folding, collapsible.

**plegamiento** *nm* folding.

**plegar** *vt* to fold.
► *vpr* **plegarse** to yield, give in.

**plegaria** *nf* prayer.

**pleitear** *vi* to sue.

**pleito** *nm* litigation, lawsuit.

**plenamente** *adv* fully.

**plenario,-a** *adj* plenary.

**plenilunio** *nm* full moon.

**plenitud** *nf (sensación física)* fullness.

**pleno,-a** *adj (gen)* full, complete: *en pleno centro de la ciudad* right in the centre of the city.

**pleonasmo** *nm* pleonasm.

**pletina** *nf* deck, cassette deck.

**pletórico,-a** *adj* full. LOC pletórico de alegría jubilant, euphoric.

**pleura** *nf* pleura.

**plexiglás®** *nm* Perspex®.

**plexo** *nm* plexus.

**pliego** *nm (papel)* sheet of paper.

**pliegue** *nm* **1** fold. **2** *(en la ropa)* pleat.

**plinto** *nm (en gimnasia)* vaulting horse.

**plisado,-a** *adj* pleated.

**plomada** *nf* **1** *(de albañil)* plumb line. **2** *(sonda)* lead. **3** *(para pescar)* weights *pl*.

**plomazo** *nm o nf fam* bore.

**plomizo,-a** *adj (color)* lead-coloured.

**plomo** *nm* **1** lead. **2** *(pesa)* lead weight. **3** ELEC fuse. **4** *fam fig* bore. LOC sin plomo *(gasolina)* unleaded, lead-free.

**pluma** *nf* **1** *(de ave)* feather. **2** *(de escribir)* fountain pen.

**plumaje** *nm (de ave)* plumage.

**plumero** *nm (para el polvo)* feather duster.

**plumilla** *nf* nib.

**plumón** *nm* **1** *(de un ave)* down. **2** *(anorak)* down-filled anorak.

**plural** *adj* plural.
► *nm* plural.

**pluralidad** *nf (gen)* multiplicity; *(diversidad)* diversity.

**pluralismo** *nm* pluralism.

**pluralista** *adj* pluralist.

**pluralizar** *vt* LING to pluralize.
► *vi (generalizar)* to generalize.

**pluriempleo** *nm having more than one job*.

**plurilingüe** *adj* multilingual.

**pluscuamperfecto** *nm* pluperfect.

**plusmarca** *nf* record.

P

**plusmarquista** *nm o nf* record holder.
**plusvalía** *nf* **1** *(aumento)* appreciation. **2** *(impuesto)* capital gains tax.
**plutocracia** *nf* plutocracy.
**Plutón** *nm* Pluto.
**plutonio** *nm* plutonium.
**pluvial** *adj* rain, pluvial.
**pluviómetro** *nm* rain gauge.
**pluviosidad** *nf* rainfall.
**población** *nf* **1** *(número de habitantes)* population. **2** *(lugar - ciudad)* town; *(- pueblo)* village.
**poblado,-a** *adj (zona)* populated.
**poblamiento** *nm* settlement.
**poblar** *vt* **1** *(ocupar territorio)* to settle. **2** *(habitar)* to inhabit. **3** *(llenar)* to fill: *han poblado de árboles el campo* they've planted the field with trees.
**pobre** *adj* **1** *(gen)* poor. **2** *(infeliz)* poor.
  ▶ *nm o nf* **1** *(con poco dinero)* poor person; *(mendigo)* beggar. **2** *(infeliz)*: *la pobre se cree que le van a devolver el dinero* the poor thing thinks she is going to get her money back.
**pobreza** *nf (escasez de dinero)* poverty.
**pocilga** *nf* pigsty.
**pócima** *nf (preparado)* potion.
**poción** *nf* potion.
**poco,-a** *adj* little; *(plural)* few, not many: *hago muy poco ejercicio últimamente* I do very little exercise these days. LOC **hace poco** not long ago. ▌ **poco antes** shortly before. ▌ **poco después** shortly afterwards. ▌ **por poco** nearly.
  ▶ *pron* **poco** little; *(en plural)* not many: *lo poco que aprendí se me ha olvidado* what little I learned I've forgotten.
  ▶ *adv* little, not much: *voy poco por allí* I rarely go there.
  ▶ *nm* **un poco** a little, a bit: *¿me das un poco?* could you give me a little?
**poda** *nf* pruning.
**podadera** *nf* pruning shears *pl*.
**podar** *vt* to prune.
**podenco** *nm* hound.
**poder** *vt* **1** *(de facultad)* can, be able to: *¿puedes echarme una mano?* can you lend me a hand?; *no pude abrirlo* I couldn't open it, I was unable to open it. **2** *(de per-*

*miso)* may, can: *pueden pagar en efectivo o con tarjeta* you can pay in cash or by credit card; *puede retirarse* you may leave. **3** *(conjetura)* may, might: *podría haberlo dejado sobre la mesa* I may have left it on the table. **4** *(sugerencias)* can: *podríamos ir a esquiar* we could go skiing. LOC **puede que** maybe, perhaps: *puede que venga más tarde* she may come later.
  ▶ *vi (superar)* to be stronger than: *tú puedes a todos* you can beat all of them.
  ▶ *nm* **1** *(gen)* power. **2** *(posesión)* possession, hands *pl*: *la pelota está ahora en mi poder* the ball is now in my hands.
**poderío** *nm (autoridad)* power.
**poderoso,-a** *adj* powerful.
**podio** *nm* podium.
**podólogo,-a** *nm & nf* chiropodist.
**podredumbre** *nf* rottenness.
**podrido,-a** *adj* **1** rotten. **2** *fig* corrupt.
**poema** *nm* poem.
**poesía** *nf* **1** poetry. **2** *(poema)* poem.
**poeta** *nm o nf* poet.
**poético,-a** *adj* poetic.
**poetisa** *nf* poetess.
**polaco,-a** *adj* Polish.
  ▶ *nm & nf (persona)* Pole.
  ▶ *nm* **polaco** *(idioma)* Polish.
**polar** *adj* polar. COMP **estrella polar** Pole Star, Polaris.
**polaridad** *nf* polarity.
**polarizar** *vt* **1** FÍS to polarize. **2** *(atención)* to focus.
**polaroid®** *nf* Polaroid.
**polea** *nf* pulley.
**polémica** *nf* controversy.
**polémico,-a** *adj* controversial.
**polemizar** *vi* to debate.
**polen** *nm* pollen.
**poleo** *nm* **1** *(planta)* pennyroyal. **2** *(infusión)* mint tea.
**policía** *nf* police, police force.
  ▶ *nm o nf (gen)* police officer; *(hombre)* policeman; *(mujer)* policewoman.
**policíaco,-a** *adj* detective.
**policial** *adj* police.
**policromía** *nf* polychromy.
**policromo,-a** *adj* polychrome.

**polideportivo** *nm* sports centre.

**poliedro** *nm* polyhedron.

**poliéster** *nm* polyester.

**poliestireno** *nm* polystyrene.

**polietileno** *nm* polythene.

**polifacético,-a** *adj* versatile.

**polifónico,-a** *adj* polyphonic.

**poligamia** *nf* polygamy.

**polígamo,-a** *adj* polygamous.
  ▶ *nm & nf* polygamist.

**polígloto,-a** *adj* polyglot.
  ▶ *nm & nf* polyglot.

**poligonal** *adj* polygonal.

**polígono** *nm* 1 *(figura)* polygon. 2 *(gen)* area. COMP **polígono industrial** industrial estate.

**polígrafo,-a** *nm & nf* polygraph.

**poliinsaturado,-a** *adj* polyunsaturated.

**polilla** *nf* moth.

**polímero** *nm* polymer.

**polimorfo,-a** *adj* polymorphic.

**polinización** *nf* pollination.

**polinizar** *vt* to pollinate.

**polinomio** *nm* polynomial.

**poliomielitis** *nf inv* poliomyelitis.

**polisemia** *nf* polysemy.

**polisémico,-a** *adj* polysemous.

**polisílabo,-a** *adj* polysyllabic.

**politécnico,-a** *adj (gen)* polytechnic.
  ▶ *nm* **politécnico** *(instituto)* technical college.

**politeísmo** *nm* polytheism.

**politeísta** *adj* polytheistic.
  ▶ *nm o nf* polytheist.

**política** *nf* politics.

**político,-a** *adj* 1 political. 2 *(por matrimonio)* -in-law: *madre política* mother-in-law; *padre político* father-in-law.
  ▶ *nm & nf* politician.

**politizar** *vt* to politicize.

**poliuretano** *nm* polyurethane.

**polivalente** *adj fig (versátil)* versatile.

**polivinilo** *nm* polyvinyl.

**póliza** *nf* 1 *(de seguros)* policy. 2 *(sello)* official tax stamp.

**polizón** *nm* stowaway.

**pollera** *nf* AM skirt.

**pollería** *nf (tienda)* poultry shop; *(sección de supermercado)* poultry section.

**pollino,-a** *nm & nf* ZOOL donkey.

**pollo** *nm* chicken.

**polluelo** *nm* chick.

**polo** *nm* 1 TÉC pole. 2 *(caramelo)* ice lolly. 3 DEP polo. COMP **Polo Norte** North Pole. ‖ **Polo Sur** South Pole.

**Polonia** *nf* Poland.

**poltrona** *nf* easy chair.

**poltrón,-ona** *adj* lazy.

**polución** *nf (atmosférica)* pollution.

**polucionar** *vt* to pollute.

**polvareda** *nf (de polvo)* cloud of dust.

**polvera** *nf* (powder) compact.

**polvo** *nm* 1 *(suciedad)* dust. 2 *(medicamento, etc)* powder. LOC **en polvo** 1 *(leche, cacao)* powdered. 2 *(nieve)* powdery. COMP **polvos de talco** talcum powder *sing*.

**pólvora** *nf* gunpowder.

**polvoriento,-a** *adj* dusty.

**pomada** *nf* cream.

**pomelo** *nm (fruto)* grapefruit; *(árbol)* grapefruit tree.

**pómez** *nf* pumice stone.

**pomo** *nm (de puerta)* knob.

**pompa** *nf* 1 *(de jabón, chicle)* bubble. 2 *(ostentación)* pomp. COMP **pompas de jabón** soap bubbles.

**pomposo,-a** *adj* pompous.

**pómulo** *nm* 1 *(hueso)* cheekbone. 2 *(mejilla)* cheek.

**ponche** *nm* punch.

**ponderado,-a** *adj (prudente)* measured.

**ponderar** *vt* 1 *(sopesar)* to ponder, consider, think over, weigh up. 2 *(alabar)* to praise highly.

**ponedero** *nm* nest box.

**ponedora** *adj (gallina)* laying.

**ponencia** *nf (académica)* paper; *(parlamentaria)* address, speech.

**ponente** *nm o nf* speaker.

**poner** *vt* 1 *(gen)* to place, put, set. 2 *(prenda)* to put on: *me pondré el pantalón negro* I'll put my black trousers on, I'll wear my black trousers. 3 *(encender)* to turn on, put on: *puso la radio* she put the radio on. 4 *(programar)* to set: *he* *puesto el despertador a las siete* I've set the alarm clock for seven. **5** *(escribir)* to put, write: *pon tu nombre aquí* put your name here. **6** *(decir)* to say: *¿qué pone ese letrero?* what does that sign say? **7** *(en cine, televisión)* to show: *lo ponen mañana a las tres* it's on tomorrow at three o'clock. **8** *(dar nombre)* to name, call: *le pusieron Laura* they called her Laura. **9** *(dinero)* to put in: *pusimos veinte euros cada uno* we put in twenty euros each. **10** *(telegrama, fax)* to send; *(nota)* to leave. **11** *(deber, multa)* to give: *nos han puesto deberes para las vacaciones* they've given us homework for the holidays. **12** poner + *adj* to make, turn: *la has puesto triste* you've made her sad.

▶ *vpr* **ponerse 1** *(sol)* to set. **2** *(volverse)* to become, get, turn: *se puso muy contenta con la noticia* the news made her very happy. **3** *(contestar al teléfono)* to answer the phone; *(hablar por teléfono)* to come to the phone: *en este momento no se puede poner* he can't come to the phone right now. **4** ponerse a + *inf* to start + *to* + *inf/-ing*: *se puso a cantar* he started to sing, he started singing.

**poniente** *nm (dirección)* west.

**pontificar** *vi* to pontificate.

**pontífice** *nm* pope, pontiff.

**pontón** *nm* pontoon.

**ponzoña** *nf* venom.

**ponzoñoso,-a** *adj* venomous.

**popa** *nf* stern.

**populacho** *nm* mob, masses *pl*.

**popular** *adj* **1** *(del pueblo)* traditional. **2** *(muy conocido)* popular.

**popularizar** *vt* to popularize.

**populista** *adj* populist.

**populoso,-a** *adj* populous.

**popurrí** *nm* potpourri.

**póquer** *nm* poker.

**por** *prep* **1** *(gen)* for: *lo hice por ti* I did it for you. **2** *(a través de)* through, by: *iremos por la autopista* we'll go on the motorway. **3** *(calle, carretera)* along, down, up: *íbamos por la calle cuando…* we were walking along the street when… **4** *(lugar aproximado)* in, near, round: *está por aquí* it's somewhere round here. **5** *(cau-*

*sa)* because of: *suspendieron el concierto por la lluvia* they cancelled the concert because of the rain. **6** *(tiempo)* at, for: *nos veremos por vacaciones* I'll see you during the holidays. **7** *(medio)* by: *llegó por correo* it arrived by post. **8** *(autoría)* by: *fue escrito por Azorín* it was written by Azorín. **9** *(distribución)* per: *cinco por ciento* five per cent. **10** *(tras)* by: *les interrogó uno por uno* he interrogated each one in turn. **11** *(con pasiva)* by: *fue comprado por la reina* it was bought by the queen. **12** *(en calidad de)* as: *la tomó por esposa* he took her as his wife. **13** *(en lugar de)* instead of, in the place of: *vas tú por mí* you go in my place. **14** *(multiplicado por)* times, multiplied by: *tres por cuatro, doce* three fours are twelve, three times four is twelve. LOC **estar por** + *inf* *(a punto de)* to be on the point of + *-ing*. ▌**por más que** + *subj* however much, no matter how much. ▌**por mucho que** + *subj* however much, no matter how much.

**porcelana** *nf* china, porcelain: *una porcelana* a piece of china.

**porcentaje** *nm* percentage.

**porcentual** *adj* percentage.

**porche** *nm* veranda(h), US porch.

**porcino,-a** *adj* porcine. COMP **ganado porcino** pigs *pl*, US hogs *pl*.

**porción** *nf (gen)* portion, part.

**pordiosero,-a** *nm & nf* beggar.

**porfiar** *vi (insistir)* to insist (en, on).

**pormenor** *nm* detail. LOC **al pormenor** retail.

**pormenorizar** *vt* to detail.

**poro** *nm* pore.

**poroso,-a** *adj* porous.

**porque** *conj* **1** *(de causa)* because: *no voy porque no quiero* I'm not going because I don't want to. **2** *(de finalidad)* in order that, so that.

**porqué** *nm* cause, reason: *nunca sabremos el porqué* we'll never know why.

**porquería** *nf (suciedad)* dirt, filth.

**porqueriza** *nf* pigsty.

**porra** *nf* (*de policía*) truncheon. LOC **mandar a la porra a** ALGN *fam* to tell SB to get lost, send SB packing.

**porrazo** *nm* (*con bastón*) blow; (*al caer*) bump, knock.

**porrón** *nm* typical glass drinking vessel with a thin spout used for pouring wine into the mouth.

**portaaviones** *nm inv* aircraft carrier.

**portada** *nf* (*de revista, periódico*) front page; (*de libro*) title page.

**portador,-ra** *adj* carrying.
▶ *nm & nf* (*de un virus*) carrier.

**portaequipajes** *nm inv* 1 (*de un coche - maletero*) boot, US trunk; (*- en el techo*) roof rack. 2 (*de un tren*) luggage rack.

**portafolios** *nm inv* 1 portfolio, folder. 2 (*maletín*) briefcase.

**portal** *nm* (*entrada de edificio*) hallway.

**portalámparas** *nm inv* bulbholder.

**portaminas** *nm inv* propelling pencil.

**portamonedas** *nm inv* purse.

**portar** *vt* to carry.
▶ *vpr* **portarse** to behave. LOC **portarse bien** to be good, behave OS.

**portátil** *adj* portable.

**portavoz** *nm o nf* (*gen*) spokesperson.

**portazo** *nm* bang, slam (*of a door*).

**porte** *nm* (*transporte*) carriage, freight. COMP **portes debidos** carriage due.

**porteador,-ra** *nm & nf* porter.

**portentoso,-a** *adj* prodigious.

**portería** *nf* 1 (*de un edificio*) porter's lodge. 2 DEP goal.

**portero,-a** *nm & nf* 1 (*de un edificio*) porter. 2 DEP goalkeeper. COMP **portero automático** entryphone.

**pórtico** *nm* portico.

**portillo** *nm* breach.

**portón** *nm* large door.

**Portugal** *nm* Portugal.

**portugués,-esa** *adj* Portuguese.
▶ *nm & nf* (*persona*) Portuguese.
▶ *nm* **portugués** (*idioma*) Portuguese.

**porvenir** *nm* future.

**pos** LOC **en pos de** after, in pursuit of.

**posada** *nf* inn.

**posar** *vi* (*para foto, etc*) to pose.
▶ *vt* (*colocar*) to rest.

▶ *vpr* **posarse** 1 (*pájaro*) to alight, perch, sit. 2 (*sedimento*) to settle.

**posavasos** *nm inv* coaster.

**posdata** *nf* postscript.

**pose** *nf* (*postura*) pose.

**poseedor,-ra** *nm & nf* owner.

**poseer** *vt* 1 (*propiedad*) to own. 2 (*conocimientos, talento, etc*) to have.

**posesión** *nf* possession. LOC **tomar posesión** (*de un cargo*) to take up.

**posesivo,-a** *adj* possessive.

**poseso,-a** *nm & nf* possessed person.

**posguerra** *nf* postwar period.

**posibilidad** *nf* possibility.

**posible** *adj* possible. LOC **hacer todo lo posible** to do one's best.

**posición** *nf* (*postura, situación*) position.

**positivo,-a** *adj* positive.

**poso** *nm* 1 (*del café*) dregs *pl*. 2 *fig* trace.

**posología** *nf* dosage.

**posparto** *nm* postpartum.

**posponer** *vt* (*en el tiempo*) to postpone.

**posta** *nf* (*de caballos*) change of horses. LOC **a posta** on purpose.

**postal** *nf* postcard.

**poste** *nm* post.

**póster** *nm* poster.

**postergar** *vt* (*retrasar*) to postpone.

**posteridad** *nf* posterity.

**posterior** *adj* 1 (*en el espacio*) back, rear: *en la parte posterior del edificio* at the back of the building. 2 (*en el tiempo*) later.

**posteriori** LOC **a posteriori** a posteriori.

**postgrado** *nm* postgraduate course.

**postgraduado,-a** *nm & nf* postgraduate student.

**postigo** *nm* (*de ventana*) shutter.

**postilla** *nf* scab.

**postizo,-a** *adj* false.

**postor,-ra** *nm & nf* bidder.

**postrar** *vt* to prostrate.
▶ *vpr* **postrarse** to prostrate OS.

**postre** *nm* dessert.

**postular** *vt* (*defender*) to postulate.

**póstumo,-a** *adj* posthumous.

**postura** *nf* 1 (*de un cuerpo*) posture, position. 2 (*actitud*) attitude.

P

**potable** *adj* drinkable.

**potaje** *nm* CULIN hotpot.

**potasio** *nm* potassium.

**pote** *nm (vasija)* pot.

**potencia** *nf* **1** *(capacidad)* power: *este coche tiene mucha potencia* this car is very powerful. **2** *(país)* power. **3** *(en matemática)* power: *elevamos seis a la tercera potencia* we raise six to the power of three.

**potencial** *adj* potential.
  ▶ *nm* **1** potential. **2** LING conditional tense.

**potenciar** *vt* to strengthen.

**potentado,-a** *nm* tycoon, potentate.

**potente** *adj* powerful.

**potestad** *nf* power.

**potestativo,-a** *adj* optional.

**potingue** *nm fam (crema)* face cream.

**potrero** *nm (lugar)* paddock.

**potro,-a** *nm & nf* ZOOL *(macho)* colt.

**poza** *nf (en un río)* pool.

**pozo** *nm (de agua, petróleo)* well.

**práctica** *nf* practice.
  ▶ *nf pl* **prácticas** practical *sing*. LOC en la práctica in practice.

**practicable** *adj (realizable)* feasible.

**practicante** *nm o nf (persona)* nurse.

**practicar** *vt* **1** *(gen)* to practise (US practice). **2** *(hacer)* to make; *(deporte)* to play.
  ▶ *vi* to practise (US practice).

**práctico,-a** *adj* **1** *(gen)* practical. **2** *(hábil)* skilful (US skillful).

**pradera** *nf* prairie, grassland.

**prado** *nf* meadow.

**pragmático,-a** *adj* pragmatic.

**pragmatismo** *nm* pragmatism.

**preámbulo** *nm* preamble.

**preaviso** *nm* notice.

**precalentamiento** *nm* DEP warming up.

**precalentar** *vt* to pre-heat.

**precariedad** *nf* precariousness.

**precario,-a** *adj* precarious.

**precaución** *nf* precaution.

**precavido,-a** *adj* cautious.

**precedente** *adj* preceding.
  ▶ *nm* precedent.

**preceder** *vt* to precede.

**preceptiva** *nf* precepts *pl*.

**preceptivo,-a** *adj* compulsory.

**precepto** *nm* precept.

**preceptor,-ra** *nm & nf* EDUC tutor.

**preciado,-a** *adj* precious.

**preciarse** *vpr* to be proud (de, of).

**precintar** *vt* to seal.

**precinto** *nm* seal.

**precio** *nm* **1** *(coste)* price. **2** *fig (valor)* value.

**preciosidad** *nf (belleza)* loveliness.

**precioso,-a** *adj (bello)* beautiful.

**precipicio** *nm* cliff, precipice.

**precipitación** *nf* **1** *(prisa)* rush, haste. **2** METEOR precipitation, rainfall.

**precipitado,-a** *adj (apresurado)* hasty.

**precipitar** *vt* **1** *(apresurar)* to rush. **2** QUÍM to precipitate.
  ▶ *vpr* **precipitarse** **1** *(apresurarse)* to rush, be hasty. **2** *(caer)* to fall.

**precisar** *vt* **1** to say exactly. **2** *(necesitar)* to need.

**precisión** *nf* precision, accuracy.

**preciso,-a** *adj* **1** precise. **2** *(necesario)* necessary.

**precocinado,-a** *adj* precooked.

**preconcebido,-a** *adj* preconceived.

**preconizar** *vt* to advocate.

**precoz** *adj* **1** *(persona)* precocious. **2** *(cosecha)* early. **3** *(diagnóstico)* early.

**precursor,-ra** *nm & nf* precursor.

**predador,-ra** *adj* predatory.

**predecesor,-ra** *nm & nf* predecessor.

**predecir** *vt* to predict.

**predestinado,-a** *adj* predestined.

**predestinar** *vt* to predestine.

**predeterminar** *vt* to predetermine.

**prédica** *nf* sermon.

**predicación** *nf* preaching.

**predicado** *nm* predicate.

**predicador,-ra** *nm & nf* preacher.

**predicar** *vt* to preach.

**predicativo,-a** *adj* predicative.

**predicción** *nf* prediction.

**predilección** *nf* predilection.

**predilecto,-a** *adj* favourite.

**predisponer** *vt* to predispose.

**predisposición** *nf* predisposition.

**predominante** *adj* predominant.

**predominar** *vt* to predominate.
**predominio** *nm* predominance.
**preeminente** *adj* pre-eminent.
**preescolar** *adj (enseñanza, edad, etapa)* preschool, nursery-school.
**preestablecer** *vt* to pre-establish.
**preestablecido,-a** *adj* pre-established.
**preestreno** *nm* preview.
**prefabricado,-a** *adj* prefabricated.
**prefacio** *nm* preface.
**preferencia** *nf* preference.
**preferente** *adj* preferential.
**preferible** *adj* preferable.
**preferido,-a** *adj* favourite (US favorite).
**preferir** *vt* to prefer.
**prefijo** *nm* **1** LING prefix. **2** *(telefónico)* dialling code, US area code.
**pregón** *nm (discurso de fiestas)* opening address.
**pregonar** *vt (noticia)* to announce, make public.
**pregonero** *nm* town crier.
**pregunta** *nf* question. LOC **hacer una pregunta a ALGN** to ask SB a question.
**preguntar** *vt* to ask.
▶ *vpr* **preguntarse** to wonder: *me pregunto si vendrá* I wonder if he'll come.
**preguntón,-ona** *adj fam* inquisitive.
**prehistoria** *nf* prehistory.
**prehistórico,-a** *adj* prehistoric.
**prejuicio** *nm* prejudice.
**prejuzgar** *vt* to prejudge.
**preliminar** *adj* preliminary.
**preludio** *nm* prelude.
**prematrimonial** *adj* premarital.
**prematuro,-a** *adj* premature.
**premeditación** *nf* premeditation.
**premeditado,-a** *adj* premeditated.
**premeditar** *vt* to premeditate.
**premiado,-a** *adj* prizewinning.
▶ *nm & nf* prizewinner.
**premiar** *vt* to award a prize to.
**premio** *nm* prize.
**premisa** *nf* premise.
**premonición** *nf* premonition.
**premonitorio,-a** *adj* premonitory.

**premura** *nf (prisa)* urgency.
**prenatal** *adj* antenatal.
**prenda** *nf* **1** *(de vestir)* garment. **2** *(en juego)* forfeit.
**prendarse** *vpr* to fall in love (de, with).
**prendedor** *nm (broche)* brooch; *(alfiler)* pin.
**prender** *vt* **1** *(sujetar)* to attach; *(con agujas)* to pin. **2** *(encender - fuego)* to light; *(- luz)* to turn on.
▶ *vi* **1** *(arraigar - planta, costumbre)* to take root. **2** *(fuego, madera, etc)* to catch light, catch fire.
**prensa** *nf* **1** *(máquina)* press. **2** *(periódicos)* papers *pl*.
**prensar** *vt* to press.
**preñado,-a** *adj* pregnant.
**preñar** *vt (mujer)* to make pregnant; *(animal)* to impregnate.
**preocupación** *nf* worry.
**preocupado,-a** *adj* worried.
**preocupar** *vt* to worry.
▶ *vpr* **preocuparse 1** *(sentir preocupación)* to worry (por, about).
**preparación** *nf* **1** *(gen)* preparation. **2** *(física, deportiva)* training.
**preparado,-a** *adj* ready, prepared.
**preparador,-ra** *nm & nf* DEP coach.
**preparar** *vt* **1** to prepare, get ready: *voy a preparar el desayuno* I'll get breakfast ready. **2** DEP *(entrenar)* to train, coach: *se está preparando para el maratón* she's training for the marathon. **3** *(estudiar)* to revise for, work for.
**preparativos** *nm pl* arrangements.
**preposición** *nf* preposition.
**prepotencia** *nf (arrogancia)* arrogance.
**prepotente** *adj* arrogant.
**prerrogativa** *nf* prerogative.
**presa** *nf* **1** *(embalse)* dam. **2** *(acción)* capture. COMP **ave de presa** bird of prey.
**presagiar** *vt* to be a warning of.
**presagio** *nm (señal)* omen.
**presbítero** *nm* priest.
**prescindir** *vi* **prescindir de** *(pasar sin)* to do without.
**prescribir** *vt (recetar)* to prescribe.
**prescripción** *nf* prescription.

P

**presencia** *nf (gen)* presence.

**presenciar** *vt (acontecimiento)* to be present at.

**presentación** *nf* **1** *(de un objeto, documento, etc)* presentation, showing: *la presentación del carné es imprescindible para entrar* passes must be shown to allow access. **2** *(de personas)* introduction.

**presentador,-ra** *nm & nf* presenter.

**presentar** *vt* **1** *(gen)* to present; *(mostrar)* to show. **2** *(entregar)* to hand in. **3** *(sacar al mercado)* to launch. **4** *(personas)* to introduce: *¿te han presentado ya?* have you been introduced yet? **5** TV to present.
▶ *vpr* **presentarse 1** *(comparecer)* to turn up. **2** *(para elección)* to stand.

**presente** *adj* present.
▶ *nm* **1** *(tiempo)* present. **2** LING present tense. **3** *(obsequio)* gift.
▶ *nm pl* **presentes** those present.

**presentimiento** *nm* premonition.

**presentir** *vt* to have a feeling (que, that).

**preservar** *vt* to preserve.

**preservativo** *nm* condom.

**presidencia** *nf* **1** POL presidency. **2** *(de una empresa)* chairmanship.

**presidente,-ta** *nm & nf* POL president. **2** chairman, US president.

**presidiario,-a** *nm & nf* convict.

**presidio** *nm* prison, penitentiary.

**presidir** *vt (reunión)* to chair.

**presilla** *nf* fastener.

**presión** *nf* pressure.

**presionar** *vt* **1** *(objeto)* to press. **2** *(persona)* to pressure, put pressure on.

**preso,-a** *nm & nf* prisoner.

**prestación** *nf* **1** *(servicio)* service. **2** *(de la Seguridad Social)* benefit, allowance. COMP **prestación por desempleo** unemployment benefit.

**prestado,-a** *adj* lent, on loan.

**prestamista** *nm o nf* moneylender.

**préstamo** *nm (crédito)* loan. LOC **pedir un préstamo** to ask for a loan.

**prestar** *vt (dejar prestado)* to lend, loan.

**prestidigitador,-ra** *nm & nf* conjuror.

**prestigio** *nm* prestige.

**prestigioso,-a** *adj* prestigious.

**presto,-a** *adj* **1** *(preparado)* ready. **2** *(rápido)* quick.

**presumible** *adj* probable, likely.

**presumido,-a** *adj (en el vestir)* vain.

**presumir** *vi* **1** *(vanagloriarse)* to boast (de, about), show off (de, about). **2** *(ser presumido)* to be vain.
▶ *vt (suponer)* to suppose, assume.

**presunto,-a** *adj* presumed, alleged.

**presuntuoso,-a** *adj (presumido)* vain.

**presuponer** *vt* to presuppose.

**presupuestar** *vt (proyecto)* to budget for; *(construcción, obra, etc)* to estimate.

**presupuesto** *nm (en finanzas)* budget; *(de una obra)* estimate.

**pretencioso,-a** *adj* pretentious.
▶ *nm & nf* pretentious person.

**pretender** *vt* **1** *(querer)* to want to: *pretende ganar el concurso* he wants to win the contest. **2** *(intentar)* to try to: *no sé qué pretende hacer* I don't know what he's trying to do. **3** *(cortejar)* to court.

**pretendido,-a** *adj* supposed.

**pretendiente** *nm (enamorado)* suitor.

**pretensión** *nf* **1** *(intención)* aim; *(ambición)* ambition. **2** *(derecho)* claim.

**pretérito,-a** *adj* past: *en tiempos pretéritos* in the past.
▶ *nm* **pretérito** simple past, preterite.

**pretexto** *nm* pretext.

**prevalecer** *vi* to prevail.

**prevención** *nf (precaución)* prevention.

**prevenido,-a** *adj* forewarned.

**prevenir** *vt (evitar)* to avoid, prevent.

**preventivo,-a** *adj (medicina)* preventive.

**prever** *vt (anticipar)* to foresee.

**previo,-a** *adj* previous.

**previsible** *adj* foreseeable.

**previsión** *nf* forecast. COMP **previsión meteorológica** weather forecast.

**previsor,-ra** *adj* farsighted.

**prieto,-a** *adj* tight.

**prima** *nf (gratificación)* bonus.

**primacía** *nf* primacy.

**primar** *vi (predominar)* to be important.

**primaria** *nf* primary education.

**primario,-a** *adj* primary.

**primate** *nm* primate.

**primavera** *nf* **1** spring. **2** *lit (año)* year.

**primaveral** *adj* spring, spring-like.

**primera** *nf* **1** AUTO first gear. **2** *(en transportes)* first class.

**primerizo,-a** *nm & nf* beginner.

**primero,-a** *adj* first: *el primer día del año* the first day of the year.
► *nm & nf* first: *es la primera de la clase* she's top of the class.
► *adv* **primero** *(en primer lugar)* first: *primero vamos a mirarlo en el diccionario* let's look it up in the dictionary first.

✎ Antes de los nombres masculinos en singular se usa **primer.**

**primicia** *nf (noticia)* scoop.

**primigenio,-a** *adj* original.

**primitiva** *nf* ≈ National Lottery.

**primitivo,-a** *adj* HIST primitive.

**primo,-a** *nm & nf (familiar)* cousin.

**primogénito,-a** *adj* first-born, eldest.
► *nm & nf* first-born, eldest.

**primor** *nm (delicadeza)* delicateness.

**primordial** *adj* essential.

**primoroso,-a** *adj* delicate.

**princesa** *nf* princess.

**principado** *nm* principality.

**principal** *adj* main: *lo principal es que duerma* the main thing is that he sleeps.
► *nm (piso)* first floor, US second floor.

**príncipe** *nm* prince.

**principiante,-a** *nm & nf* beginner.

**principio** *nm* **1** *(inicio)* beginning, start: *me voy de vacaciones a principios de mes* I'm going on holiday at the beginning of the month. **2** *(moral)* principle.

**pringar** *vt (ensuciar)* to make greasy: *me he puesto las manos pringando de grasa* I've got my hands covered in grease.

**pringoso,-a** *adj* greasy.

**prior,-ra** *nm & nf (hombre)* prior; *(mujer)* prioress.

**prioridad** *nf* priority.

**prioritario,-a** *adj* priority.

**prisa** *nf* hurry: *¡date prisa que no llegamos!* hurry up or we'll never make it! LOC correr prisa to be urgent. ‖ **tener prisa** to be in a hurry.

**prisión** *nf* prison.

**prisionero,-a** *nm & nf* prisoner.

**prisma** *nm* prism.

**prismáticos** *nm pl* binoculars.

**privacidad** *nf* privacy.

**privación** *nf* deprivation, privation.

**privado,-a** *adj* private.

**privar** *vt (despojar)* to deprive (de, of).

**privativo,-a** *adj (exclusivo)* exclusive.

**privatizar** *vt* to privatize.

**privilegiado,-a** *adj* privileged.

**privilegiar** *vt* to privilege.

**privilegio** *nm* privilege.

**pro** *nm* advantage. COMP **los pros y los contras** the pros and cons.

**proa** *nf* bow, prow.

**probabilidad** *nf* probability.

**probable** *adj (posible)* probable, likely.

**probado,-a** *adj* proven.

**probador** *nm* changing room.

**probar** *vt* **1** *(demostrar)* to prove. **2** *(comprobar)* to test, check: *prueba el coche a ver cómo responde* check the car to see how it performs. **3** *(vino, comida, etc)* to taste, try. **4** *(prenda, zapato)* to try on.
► *vi* to try: *prueba a cambiarle la pila* try changing the battery.

**probeta** *nf* test tube.

**problema** *nm* problem. LOC **tener problemas con** to have trouble with.

**problemático,-a** *adj* problematic.

**procedencia** *nf* **1** origin.

**procedente** *adj* coming (de, from): *el tren procedente de Sevilla* the train arriving from Seville.

**proceder** LOC **proceder de** to come: *el queso procede de la leche* cheese comes from milk.

**procedimiento** *nm (método)* procedure.

**procesado,-a** *adj* **1** INFORM processed. **2** JUR tried.
► *nm & nf* **el/la procesado,-a** the accused.

**procesador** *nm* processor. COMP **procesador de textos** INFORM word processor.

**procesar** *vt* **1** *(gen)* to process. **2** JUR to try.

**procesión** *nf* procession.

**proceso** *nm (gen)* process. COMP **proceso de datos** data processing.

**proclamar** *vt* to proclaim.
▸ *vpr* **proclamarse** to proclaim os.

**proclive** *adj* prone.

**procreación** *nf* procreation.

**procrear** *vi* to procreate.

**procurador,-ra** *nm & nf* JUR procurator.

**procurar** *vt* **1** to try. **2** *(proporcionar)* to get.

**prodigar** *vt* to be lavish with.

**prodigio** *nm* prodigy, miracle.

**prodigioso,-a** *adj* prodigious.

**pródigo,-a** *adj (generoso)* lavish.

**producción** *nf* production.

**producir** *vt* **1** *(gen)* to produce. **2** *(causar)* to cause.
▸ *vpr* **producirse** to happen.

**productividad** *nf* productivity.

**productivo,-a** *adj* productive.

**producto** *nm (gen)* product.

**productor,-ra** *adj* producing.
▸ *nm & nf* producer.

**productora** *nf* CINE production company.

**proeza** *nf* feat, heroic deed.

**profanar** *vt* to desecrate, profane.

**profano,-a** *adj (no sagrado)* profane.

**profecía** *nf* prophecy.

**proferir** *vt (palabra, sonido, etc)* to utter.

**profesión** *nf* profession.

**profesional** *adj* professional: *es futbolista profesional* he's a professional footballer.
▸ *nm o nf* professional: *es todo un profesional* he's a real professional.

**profesionalidad** *nf* professionalism.

**profesor,-ra** *nm & nf* teacher. COMP **profesor,-ra particular** private tutor.

**profesorado** *nm* teaching staff.

**profeta** *nm* prophet.

**profético,-a** *adj* prophetic.

**profetizar** *vt* to prophesy.

**prófugo,-a** *nm & nf* fugitive.

**profundidad** *nf* depth: *tiene cuatro metros de profundidad* it's four metres deep.

**profundizar** *vt* **profundizar en** *(tema, cuestión)* to look deeply into.

**profundo,-a** *adj (gen)* deep.

**profuso,-a** *adj* profuse.

**progenitor,-ra** *nm & nf (padre)* father; *(madre)* mother.
▸ *nm pl* **progenitores** parents.

**programa** *nm* **1** *(gen)* programme (us program). **2** INFORM program. **3** EDUC *(de un curso)* syllabus.

**programación** *nf* **1** *(de televisión, radi, etco)* programming (us programing). **2** *(de teatro)* billing. **3** INFORM programming.

**programador,-ra** *nm & nf* INFORM programmer.

**programar** *vt* **1** *(gen)* to programme (us program). **2** INFORM to program. **3** *(organizar, planear, etc)* to plan.

**progresar** *vi* to progress.

**progresión** *nf* progression. COMP **progresión aritmética** arithmetic progression.

**progresista** *adj* progressive.
▸ *nm o nf* progressive.

**progresivo,-a** *adj* progressive.

**progreso** *nm* progress.

**prohibición** *nf* prohibition, ban.

**prohibido,-a** *adj* forbidden.

**prohibir** *vt* to forbid.

**prohibitivo,-a** *adj* prohibitive.

**prójimo** *nm* fellow man, neighbour (us neighbor).

**prole** *nf* offspring.

**proletariado** *nm* proletariat.

**proletario,-a** *nm & nf* proletarian.

**proliferar** *vi* to proliferate.

**prolijo,-a** *adj (meticuloso)* meticulous.

**prólogo** *nm* prologue, us prolog.

**prolongación** *nf (gen)* prolongation.

**prolongado,-a** *adj (largo)* prolonged.

**prolongar** *vt* **1** *(en el tiempo, etc)* to prolong. **2** *(en el espacio)* to extend.
▸ *vpr* **prolongarse** to go on.

**promedio** *nm* average.

**promesa** *nf* promise.

**prometedor,-ra** *adj* promising.

**prometer** *vt* to promise: *¿lo prometes?* promise?
▶ *vi* to be promising: *esta chica es una pintora que promete* this girl is a promising artist.

**prometido,-a** *nm & nf (hombre)* fiancé; *(mujer)* fiancée.

**prominente** *adj* prominent.

**promiscuo,-a** *adj* promiscuous.

**promoción** *nf* promotion.

**promocionar** *vt* (to promote.

**promontorio** *nm* promontory.

**promotor,-ra** *nm & nf (inmobiliario)* developer.

**promover** *vt* to promote.

**promulgar** *vt* to enact, promulgate.

**pronombre** *nm* pronoun.

**pronosticar** *vt* to predict.

**pronóstico** *nm (del tiempo)* forecast. [COMP] **pronóstico meteorológico** weather forecast.

**pronto,-a** *adv* **1** *(rápido)* soon: *no llores que pronto vendrá tu mamá* don't cry, your mummy will be here soon. **2** *(temprano)* early: *has llegado demasiado pronto* you've arrived too early. [LOC] **de pronto** suddenly.

**pronunciación** *nf* pronunciation.

**pronunciado,-a** *adj (marcado)* marked.

**pronunciar** *vt* **1** *(gen)* to pronounce. **2** *(discurso)* to make.

**propagación** *nf* propagation.

**propaganda** *nf* **1** *(publicidad)* advertising. **2** *(electoral)* propaganda.

**propagar** *vt* to propagate, spread.

**propano** *nm* propane.

**propasarse** *vpr* to go too far.

**propensión** *nf* inclination, tendency.

**propenso,-a** *adj* inclined. [LOC] **ser propenso,-a a** ALGO to be prone to sth.

**propiciar** *vt (favorecer)* contribute to.

**propiciatorio,-a** *adj* propitiatory.

**propicio,-a** *adj (gen)* suitable.

**propiedad** *nf (bien inmueble)* property. [COMP] **propiedad privada** private property.

**propietario,-a** *nm & nf* owner.

**propina** *nf* tip.

**propinar** *vt* to give.

**propio,-a** *adj* **1** *(de nuestra propiedad)* own. **2** *(indicado)* appropriate. **3** *(mismo - él)* himself; *(- ella)* herself; *(- cosa, animal)* itself; *(- en plural)* themselves.

**proponer** *vt (persona, plan, etc)* to propose.
▶ *vpr* **proponerse** to intend.

**proporción** *nf* proportion.

**proporcionado,-a** *adj* in proportion.

**proporcional** *adj* proportionate.

**proporcionar** *vt (ayuda, etc)* to supply.

**proposición** *nf (idea)* proposal.

**propósito** *nm* **1** *(intención)* intention. **2** *(objetivo)* aim.

**propuesta** *nf* proposal.

**propugnar** *vt* to advocate.

**propulsar** *vt (medida, idea, etc)* to promote.

**propulsión** *nf* propulsion.

**propulsor,-ra** *nm (motor)* motor.

**prórroga** *nf (de un plazo)* extension.

**prorrogable** *adj* renewable.

**prorrogar** *vt (alargar)* to extend.

**prosa** *nf* prose.

**prosaico,-a** *adj* prosaic.

**proscribir** *vt (prohibir)* to proscribe.

**proscrito,-a** *nm & nf (criminal)* outlaw.

**proseguir** *vt* to continue, carry on.

**proselitismo** *nm* proselytism.

**proselitista** *adj* proselytic.
▶ *nm o nf* proselytizer.

**prosodia** *nf* prosody.

**prosopopeya** *nf (figura retórica)* prosopopoeia.

**prospección** *nf (del suelo)* surveying; *(para minerales)* prospecting.

**prospecto** *nm* leaflet, prospectus.

**prosperar** *vi* to prosper, thrive.

**prosperidad** *nf* prosperity.

**próspero,-a** *adj* prosperous.

**próstata** *nf* prostate, prostate gland.

**prostitución** *nf* prostitution.

**prostituir** *vt* to prostitute.
▶ *vpr* **prostituirse** to prostitute OS.

**prostituta** *nf* prostitute.

**protagonismo** *nm* leading role.

**protagonista** *adj* main, leading.
▶ *nm o nf (de película - actor)* leading man; *(- actriz)* leading lady.
**protagonizar** *vt (película, etc)* to star in.
**protección** *nf* protection.
**proteccionismo** *nm* protectionism.
**proteccionista** *adj* protectionist.
**protector,-ra** *nm & nf (persona)* protector.
**proteger** *vt* to protect.
**protegido,-a** *nm & nf (hombre)* protégé; *(mujer)* protégée.
**proteína** *nf* protein.
**proteínico,-a** *adj* proteinic.
**prótesis** *nf* MED *(uso formal)* prosthesis. COMP **prótesis dental** denture.
**protesta** *nf* protest.
**protestante** *adj* Protestant.
▶ *nm o nf* Protestant.
**protestar** *vi (mostrar disconformidad)* to protest (contra, against).
**protocolo** *nm (gen)* protocol.
**protón** *nm* proton.
**protoplasma** *nm* protoplasm.
**prototipo** *nm* prototype.
**protozoo** *nm* protozoan.
**protuberancia** *nf* protuberance.
**provecho** *nm (beneficio)* benefit. LOC ¡buen provecho! enjoy your meal!
**provechoso,-a** *adj (beneficioso)* beneficial.
**proveedor,-ra** *nm & nf* supplier.
**proveer** *vt (suministrar)* to provide (de, with).
**provenir** *vi* to come (de, from).
**proverbial** *adj* proverbial.
**proverbio** *nm* proverb, saying.
**providencia** *nf* JUR ruling.
**providencial** *adj* providential.
**provincia** *nf* province. LOC **de provincias** provincial.
**provinciano,-a** *adj pey* provincial.
**provisión** *nf (suministro)* provision.
**provisional** *adj* provisional.
**provisto,-a** *adj* provided (de, with), equipped (de, with).
**provocación** *nf (gen)* provocation.
**provocar** *vt* to incite, to provoke.

**provocativo,-a** *adj* provocative.
**próximamente** *adv* shortly, soon.
**proximidad** *nf* proximity.
**próximo,-a** *adj* **1** *(cerca)* near. **2** *(siguiente)* next: *el mes próximo* next month.
**proyección** *nf* **1** *(gen)* projection. **2** CINE screening, showing.
**proyectar** *vt (película)* to show.
**proyectil** *nm* projectile, missile.
**proyecto** *nm* **1** *(propósito)* plan. **2** *(plan)* project.
**proyector** *nm (de cine)* film projector.
**prudencia** *nf (cuidado)* care, caution; *(moderación)* moderation.
**prudente** *adj* sensible, prudent.
**prueba** *nf* **1** *(demostración)* proof. **2** *(experimento)* experiment, trial: *haz la prueba* try it. **3** *(examen)* test. **4** MED test. **5** DEP event. LOC **poner a prueba** to put to the test. COMP **prueba de acceso** entrance examination.
**psicoanálisis** *nm inv* psychoanalysis.
**psicología** *nf* psychology.
**psicopatía** *nf* psychopathy.
**psicosis** *nf inv* psychosis.
**psique** *nf* psyche.
**psiquiatría** *nf* psychiatry.
**psiquiátrico,-a** *adj* psychiatric.
**psíquico,-a** *adj* psychic, psychical.
**pterodáctilo** *nm* pterodactyl.
**púa** *nf* **1** *(de peine, cepillo)* tooth. **2** *(de erizo)* quill. **3** MÚS plectrum.
**pubertad** *nf* puberty.
**pubis** *nm inv* **1** pubes *pl.* **2** *(hueso)* pubis.
**publicable** *adj* publishable.
**publicación** *nf* publication.
**publicar** *vt (libro, etc)* to publish.
**publicidad** *nf (comercial)* advertising.
**publicista** *nm o nf* advertising executive.
**publicitario,-a** *adj* advertising.
**público,-a** *adj* public.
▶ *nm* **público** *(de un espectáculo)* audience; *(de televisión)* audience, viewers *pl*: *el público aplaudió entusiasmado* the audience applauded warmly. LOC **en público** in public.

**publirreportaje** *nm (documentary style)* television advertisement.

**puchero** *nm (olla)* cooking pot.

**púdico,-a** *adj* chaste, decent.

**pudiente** *adj* wealthy, rich.

**pudor** *nm (decencia)* decency.

**pudoroso,-a** *adj* decent, chaste.

**pudrir** *vt* to rot.
▶ *vpr* **pudrirse** to rot.

**pueblerino,-a** *adj (de pueblo)* village.

**pueblo** *nm* **1** *(población)* village. **2** *(gente)* people.

**puente** *nm (sobre un río, etc)* bridge.

**puerco,-a** *nm & nf* pig. [COMP] **puerco espín** porcupine.

**puericultor,-ora** *nm & nf* child care specialist.

**puericultura** *nf* child care.

**pueril** *adj (infantil)* puerile, childish.

**puerro** *nm* leek.

**puerta** *nf* **1** door. **2** *(verja)* gate. **3** DEP *(portería)* goal. [COMP] **puerta de embarque** gate.

**puerto** *nm* **1** MAR port, harbour. **2** *(de montaña)* (mountain) pass. [COMP] **puerto deportivo** marina.

**Puerto Rico** *nm* Puerto Rico.

**puertorriqueño,-a** *adj* Puerto Rican.
▶ *nm & nf* Puerto Rican.

**pues** *conj* **1** *(ya que)* since, as. **2** *(por lo tanto)* therefore, so. **3** *(repetitivo)* then. **4** *(enfático)* well: *pues bien* well then; *¡pues claro!* of course!; *pues no* well no.

**puesta** *nf* **1** *(colocación)* setting. **2** *(de huevos)* laying. [COMP] **puesta de sol** sunset.

**puesto,-a** *nm* **1** *(sitio)* place: *ya han llegado al primer puesto* they've made it to the top. **2** *(de mercado)* stall; *(de feria, etc)* stand. **3** *(empleo)* position, post. [LOC] **puesto que** since, as.

**púgil** *nm* boxer.

**pugnar** *vi* to fight, struggle.

**puja** *nf (acción)* bidding.

**pujante** *adj* thriving.

**pujar** *vt (en subasta)* to bid higher.

**pulcritud** *nf* neatness.

**pulcro,-a** *adj* neat.

**pulga** *nf* flea.

**pulgada** *nf* inch.

**pulgar** *nm* thumb.

**pulgón** *nm* aphid.

**pulimentar** *vt* to polish.

**pulir** *vt (superficie)* to polish.

**pullover** *nm* pullover.

**pulmón** *nm* lung.

**pulmonar** *adj* lung, pulmonary.

**pulmonía** *nf* pneumonia.

**pulpa** *nf* pulp.

**púlpito** *nm* pulpit.

**pulpo** *nm* ZOOL octopus.

**pulsación** *nf* **1** pulsation. **2** *(de corazón)* beat. **3** *(en mecanografía)* stroke.

**pulsador** *nm (gen)* push button.

**pulsar** *vt* **1** *(botón, timbre, etc)* to press. **2** *(tecla - de máquina de escribir)* to tap; *(- de piano)* to play.

**pulsera** *nf* **1** bracelet. **2** *(de reloj)* watch strap.

**pulso** *nm* **1** *(presión sanguínea)* pulse: *déjame que te tome el pulso* let me take your pulse. **2** *(firmeza en la mano)* steady hand: *para dibujar hay que tener buen pulso* to be able to draw you need a steady hand.

**pulular** *vi* to swarm.

**pulverizador** *nm* spray, atomizer.

**pulverizar** *vt* **1** *(líquido)* to atomize, spray. **2** *(sólido)* to pulverize. **3** *(enemigo)* to crush, wipe out.

**puma** *nm* puma, mountain lion.

**punción** *nf* puncture.

**punitivo,-a** *adj* punitive.

**punta** *nf (extremo)* tip; *(extremo afilado)* point. [LOC] **sacar punta a** *(lápiz)* to sharpen.

**puntada** *nf* stitch.

**puntal** *nm* **1** prop. **2** *fig* support.

**puntapié** *nm* kick.

**puntear** *vt* **1** *(dibujar)* to dot. **2** MÚS to pluck.

**punteo** *nm* MÚS plucking, US picking.

**puntera** *nf (de zapato, calcetín, etc)* toe.

**puntería** *nf* aim: *¡qué buena puntería!* what a good shot!

**puntero,-a** *adj* leading.
▶ *nm* **puntero** *(para señalar)* pointer.

**puntiagudo,-a** *adj* pointed.

**P**

**puntilla** *nf* COST lace. LOC **de puntillas** on tiptoe.

**puntilloso,-a** *adj* (exigente) punctilious.

**punto** *nm* **1** (gen) point. **2** (tanto) point: *nos llevan cinco puntos de ventaja* they're five points ahead of us. **3** (detrás de abreviatura) dot; (al final de la oración) full stop, US period. **4** (lugar) spot: *¿en qué punto de la carretera se encuentran?* exactly where on the road are they? **5** (tejido) knitwear: *me he comprado una falda de punto* I bought a knitted skirt. **6** (en costura, sutura, etc) stitch: *me caí y me dieron tres puntos en la barbilla* I fell and needed three stitches on my chin. LOC **en punto** sharp, on the dot: *son las tres en punto* it's exactly three o'clock. COMP **dos puntos** colon. ‖ **punto cardinal** cardinal point. ‖ **punto de vista** point of view. ‖ **punto débil** weak point. ‖ **punto y coma** semicolon. ‖ **punto y seguido** full stop, new sentence, US period, new sentence.

**puntuable** *adj* valid.

**puntuación** *nf* **1** (en ortografía) punctuation. **2** (acción de puntuar) scoring; (total de puntos) score. **3** EDUC (acción) marking; (nota) mark: *obtuvo una puntuación muy alta* she got a very high mark.

**puntual** *adj* (que llega a su hora) punctual: *han llegado muy puntuales* they've arrived right on time.

**puntualidad** *nf* punctuality.

**puntualización** *nf* remark.

**puntualizar** *vt* (especificar) to point out.

**puntuar** *vt* **1** LING to punctuate. **2** EDUC to mark.
▶ *vi* DEP to score.

**punzada** *nf* sharp pain, stab of pain.

**punzante** *adj* stabbing.

**punzar** *vt* to prick.

**punzón** *nm* punch.

**puñado** *nm* handful.

**puñal** *nm* dagger.

**puñalada** *nf* (herida) stab wound.

**puñetazo** *nm* punch.

**puño** *nm* **1** (mano) fist. **2** (de arma) handle. **3** (de camisa, abrigo, etc) cuff.

**pupila** *nf* pupil.

**pupilaje** *nm* (de persona) board and lodging; (de coche) garaging.

**pupilo,-a** *nm & nf* (de un tutor) pupil.

**pupitre** *nm* school desk.

**purasangre** *adj* thoroughbred.
▶ *nm* (caballo) thoroughbred.

**puré** *nm* (espeso) purée; (sopa) thick soup: *hoy tenemos puré de zanahoria* today we've got thick carrot soup. COMP **puré de patatas** mashed potatoes.

**pureza** *nf* purity.

**purga** *nf* purge.

**purgación** *nf* (acción) purging.

**purgante** *nm* purgative, laxative.

**purgar** *vt* to purge (de, of).

**purgatorio** *nm* purgatory.

**purificación** *nf* purification.

**purificador,-ra** *adj* purifying.
▶ *nm* purificador purifier.

**purificante** *adj* purifying.

**purificar** *vt* to purify.

**purismo** *nm* purism.

**purista** *adj* purist.
▶ *nm o nf* purist.

**puritano,-a** *adj* puritan, puritanic.
▶ *nm & nf* puritan.

**puro,-a** *adj* **1** (sin mezcla) pure: *tiene un perro de pura raza* he has a purebred dog. **2** (mero) sheer, mere, pure: *me enteré por pura casualidad* I found out by pure chance.
▶ *nm* puro cigar.

**púrpura** *adj* purple.
▶ *nm* purple.

**purulento,-a** *adj* purulent.

**pus** *nm* pus.

**pusilánime** *adj* faint-hearted.

**pusilanimidad** *nf* faint-heartedness.

**pústula** *nf* pustule.

**putrefacción** *nf* putrefaction.

**putrefacto,-a** *adj* putrefied, rotten.

**pútrido,-a** *adj* putrefied, rotten.

**puya** *nf* (comentario) gibe.

**puyazo** *nm* (comentario) gibe.

**puzzle** *nm* jigsaw, puzzle.

**Q, q** *nf (la letra)* Q, q.
**Qatar** *nm* Qatar.
**quásar** *nm* quasar.
**que¹** *pron* **1** *(sujeto, persona)* who, that; *(cosa)* that, which: *la chica que vino ayer está enferma* the girl who came yesterday is ill. **2** *(complemento, persona)* whom, who; *(cosa)* that, which: *el coche que me prestaste está ahí* the car (that) you lent me is there. **3** *prep +* que *(complemento circunstancial)* which; *(lugar)* where; *(tiempo)* when: *la casa en que vivía estaba lejos* the house where he lived was far away. **4** *art def +* que the one which, the one that: *ese libro es el que me gusta* that's the book I like.
**que²** *conj* **1** that: *dice que no vendrá* he says (that) he won't come. **2** *(en comparaciones)* than: *es más alto que su padre* he is taller than his father. **3** *(deseo, mandato)*: *¡que te diviertas!* enjoy yourself! **4** *(duda, extrañeza)*: *¿que no te hicieron pagar nada?* (you say) they didn't make you pay anything? **5** *(causal, consecutiva)*: *¡arriba, que ya son las ocho!* get up, it's eight o'clock! **6** *(tanto si... como si...)* whether... or not...: *que llueva que no llueva, iremos de excursión* whether it rains or not, we're going on a trip. **7** *(reiterativo)* and: *charla que charla se nos pasó la hora* we were so busy talking that the hour just flew by. **8** *(final)* so that: *ven aquí que te vea bien* come here so that I can see you properly. **9** *fam (condicional)* if: *que te gusta, te lo quedas; que no te gusta, lo cambias* if you like it, keep it; if you don't, you can change it. **10** *que no (adversativa)* not: *justicia pido, que no perdón* I want justice, not mercy.

**qué** *pron* what: *no sé qué hacer* I don't know what to do; *¿qué querías?* what did you want?
▶ *adj* **1** *(cuál)* which: *no sé qué libro quiere* I don't know which book he wants. **2** *(en frases interrogativas)* how, what: *¿qué años tienes?* how old are you?; *¿qué has dicho?* what did you say? **3** *(en frases exclamativas)* how, what: *¡qué bonito!* how nice!; *¡qué flor más bonita!* what a lovely flower! **4** *(cantidad)* what: *¡qué de gente!* what a crowd!
**quebrada** *nf* GEOL *(paso)* gorge, ravine.
**quebradizo,-a** *adj* **1** *(frágil)* fragile, brittle; *(pastel)* short. **2** *fig (débil moralmente)* weak, frail.
**quebrado,-a** *adj* **1** *(terreno)* rugged, rough, uneven; *(camino)* tortuous. **2** *(número)* fractional.
**quebrantar** *vt* **1** *(cascar)* to crack. **2** *(romper)* to break, shatter; *(machacar)* to grind. **3** *(debilitar)* to weaken. **4** *fig (salud, posición, fortuna)* to undermine, shatter. **5** *fig (incumplir)* to break, violate. **6** *fig (suavizar)* to take the edge off, temper; *(ablandar)* to soften. **7** *fig (causar lástima)* to wound, shatter.
▶ *vpr* **quebrantarse 1** *(cascarse)* to crack. **2** *(romperse)* to break. **3** *(la salud)* to be shattered.
**quebrar** *vt (romper, incumplir)* to break.
▶ *vi* **1** FIN to go bankrupt. **2** *fig (flaquear)* to weaken.
▶ *vpr* **quebrarse 1** *(romperse)* to break. **2** *(herniarse)* to rupture os. **3** *(interrumpirse)* to be broken, open up. **4** *fig (ánimo)* to break, crack.
**quedar** *vi* **1** *(permanecer)* to remain, stay. **2** *fig (terminar)* to end. **3** *(cita)* to arrange to meet. **4** *(resultado de algo)* to

be. **5** *(favorecer)* to look, fit. **6** *(estar situado)* to be. **7** *(restar)* to be left, remain. **8** *(faltar)* to be still. **9 quedar en** *(convenir)* to agree to. **10 quedar por** + *inf* not to have been + *pp*: *la cama quedó por hacer* the bed had not been made, the bed was left unmade. **11 quedar** + *ger* to be, remain: *cuando me fui el niño quedaba durmiendo* when I left the child was sleeping.
▶ *vpr* **quedarse 1** *(permanecer)* to remain, stay, be. **2** *(resultado de algo)* to be, remain. **3** *euf (morirse)* to die. **4** *(mar, viento)* to become calm; *(viento)* to drop. **5 quedarse con** *(retener algo)* to keep.

**quehacer** *nm* task, chore, job.

**queja** *nf* **1** *(descontento)* complaint. **2** *(de dolor)* moan, groan.

**quejarse** *vpr* **1** *(de descontento)* to complain (de, about). **2** *(de dolor)* to moan, groan.

**quejido** *nm* groan, moan.

**quejumbroso,-a** *adj* **1** *(persona)* whining, plaintive. **2** *(tono)* querulous.

**quemado,-a** *adj* **1** burnt; *(por el sol)* sunburnt. **2** *fig (resentido)* embittered. **3** *fam (acabado)* spent, burnt-out.

**quemador,-ra** *nm* burner.

**quemadura** *nf* **1** *(acción)* burning. **2** *(herida)* burn; *(de sol)* sunburn; *(escaldadura)* scald.

**quemar** *vt* **1** *(gen)* to burn; *(plantas)* to scorch. **2** *(incendiar)* to set on fire. **3** *fam (acabar)* to burn out.
▶ *vi (estar muy caliente)* to be burning hot.
▶ *vpr* **quemarse** *(persona)* to burn os; *(cosa)* to be burnt.

**querella** *nf* **1** JUR action, lawsuit. **2** *(queja)* complaint. **3** *(enfrentamiento)* dispute, quarrel.

**querencia** *nf* **1** *(acción)* love. **2** *(inclinación del animal)* homing instinct; *(inclinación del hombre)* homesickness.

**querer** *vt* **1** *(amar)* to love. **2** *(desear)* to want. **3** *(buscar)* to be asking for, be looking for. **4** *(petición)* would. **5** *(verificarse)* may, might.
▶ *nm* love, affection.

**querido,-a** *adj (amado)* dear, beloved; *(en carta)* dear.
▶ *nm & nf* **1** *(amante)* lover; *(mujer)* mistress. **2** *fam (apelativo)* darling.

**quesera** *nf* **1** *(fábrica)* cheese factory. **2** *(para servirlo)* cheese dish.

**queso** *nm* cheese.

**quicio** *nm* pivot hole.

**quid** *nm* crux.

**quiebra** *nf* **1** *(rotura)* break, crack. **2** *(bancarrota)* failure, bankruptcy; *(crack)* crash, collapse. **3** *(pérdida)* loss. **4** GEOG gorge. **5** *fig (fracaso)* failure.

**quien** *pron* **1** *(sujeto)* who: *me encontré a Toni, quien me dijo que estabas enfermo* I met Toni, who told me you were ill. **2** *(complemento)* who, whom: *las personas a quienes me encontré ayer están aquí* the people (whom) I met yesterday are here. **3** *(indefinido)* whoever, anyone who: *quien sepa la respuesta que me lo diga* anyone who knows the answer tell me.

**quién** *pron* **1** *(sujeto)* who: *¿quién te lo dijo?* who told you? **2** *(complemento)* who, whom: *¿con quién hablas?* who are you talking to? **3 de quién** *(posesivo)* whose: *¿de quién es esto?* whose is this?

**quienquiera** *pron* whoever: *entre, quienquiera que sea* come in, whoever you may be.

**quieto,-a** *adj* **1** *(sin movimiento)* still, motionless. **2** *fig (sosegado)* quiet, calm.

**quilate** *nm* **1** *(unidad de peso)* carat. **2** *(unidad del oro)* carat (US karat).

**quilogramo** *nm* → kilogramo.

**quilométrico,-a** *adj* → kilométrico,-a.

**quilómetro** *adj* → kilómetro.

**quimera** *nf* **1** *(mitología)* chimera. **2** *fig (ilusión)* wild fancy, fantasy. **3** *fig (preocupación)* worry; *(sospecha infundada)* unfounded suspicion.

**quimérico,-a** *adj* unrealistic, fantastic.

**química** *nf* chemistry.

**químicamente** *adv* chemically.

**químico,-a** *adj* chemical.
▶ *nm & nf* chemist.

**quincalla** *nf (objetos de metal)* cheap metalware; *(baratija)* trinket.

**quincallero,-a** *nm & nf (de objetos de metal)* seller of cheap metalware; *(de baratijas)* trinket seller.

**quince** *adj (cardinal)* fifteen; *(ordinal)* fifteenth.
▶ *nm* fifteen.

✎ Consulta también seis.

**quinceañero,-a** *adj* **1** *(de quince años)* fifteen-year-old. **2** *(adolescente)* teenage.
▶ *nm & nf* **1** *(de quince años)* fifteen-year-old. **2** *(adolescente)* teenager.

**quinceavo,-a** *adj* fifth.
▶ *nm & nf* fifth.

✎ Consulta también sexto,-a.

**quincena** *nf* **1** *(tiempo)* fortnight. **2** *(paga)* fortnightly pay.

**quincenal** *adj* fortnightly.

**quincuagenario,-a** *adj* quinquagenarian.
▶ *nm & nf* quinquagenarian.

**quincuagésimo,-a** *adj* fiftieth.
▶ *nm & nf* fiftieth.

✎ Consulta también sexto,-a.

**quingentésimo,-a** *adj* five hundredth.
▶ *nm & nf* five hundredth.

✎ Consulta también sexto,-a.

**quiniela** *nf* football pools *pl*.

**quinientos,-as** *adj (cardinal)* five hundred; *(ordinal)* five-hundredth.
▶ *nm* **quinientos** *(número)* five hundred.

✎ Consulta también seis.

**quinina** *nf* quinine.

**quinqué** *nm* oil lamp.

**quinquenal** *adj* quinquennial, five-year.

**quinquenio** *nm* quinquennium, five-year period.

**quinta** *nf* **1** *(casa)* country house. **2** *(reemplazo militar)* call-up, conscript, US draft. **3** MÚS fifth.

**quintal** *nm* quintal *(46 kilograms)*.

**quinteto** *nm* quintet.

**quintilla** *nf* five-line stanza.

**quintillizo,-a** *nm & nf* quintuplet, quin.

**quinto,-a** *adj* fifth.
▶ *nm & nf* fifth.
▶ *nm* **quinto 1** MIL. conscript, recruit. **2** *fam (de cerveza)* small bottle of beer *(= 20 cl)*.

✎ Consulta también sexto,-a.

**quintuplicación** *nf* quintupling.

**quintuplicar** *vt* to quintuple.

**quíntuplo,-a** *adj* quintuple.
▶ *nm* **quíntuplo** quintuple.

**quinzavo,-a** *adj-nm & nf* → quinceavo,-a.

**quiosco** *nm* kiosk; *(de periódicos)* newsstand; *(de música)* bandstand.

**quiosquero,-a** *nm & nf* newsagent.

**quirófano** *nm* operating theatre (US theater).

**quirúrgico,-a** *adj* surgical.

**quitaesmaltes** *nm inv* nail polish remover.

**quitamanchas** *nm inv* stain remover.

**quitamiedos** *nm inv* handrail.

**quitanieves** *nm inv* snowplough (US snowplow).

**quitapinturas** *nm inv* paint stripper.

**quitar** *vt* **1** *(separar)* to remove, take off. **2** *(sacar)* to take off, take out; *(prendas)* to take off; *(tiempo)* to take up. **3** *(apartar)* to take away, take off. **4** *(hacer desaparecer)* to remove; *(dolor)* to relieve; *(sed)* to quench. **5** *(despojar)* to take; *(robar)* to steal. **6** *(restar)* to subtract; *(descontar)* to take off. **7** *(prohibir)* to forbid, rule out. **8** *(impedir)* to prevent. **9** *(disminuir)* to take away. **10** *fam (radio, agua, etc)* to turn off.
▶ *vpr* **quitarse 1** *(desaparecer)* to go away, come out. **2 quitarse de** *(del juego, bebida, etc)* to give up.

**quizá** *adv* → quizás.

**quizás** *adv* perhaps, maybe.

# R

**R, r** *nf (la letra)* R, r.

**rábano** *nm* radish. LOC ¡me importa un rábano! I don't give a toss!, I couldn't care less!

**rabí** *nm* rabbi.

**rabia** *nf* 1 MED rabies. 2 *fig (enfado)* rage, fury, anger. LOC dar rabia to make furious.

**rabiar** *vi* 1 *(enfadarse)* to rage, be furious: *Elena está que rabia* Elena is furious. 2 *fig (padecer)* to suffer (de, from): *rabiar de dolor* to writhe in pain. LOC hacer rabiar a ALGN to make SB see red.

**rabieta** *nf fam* tantrum. LOC coger una rabieta *fam* to throw a tantrum.

**rabillo** *nm (pecíolo)* stalk, stem. LOC mirar por el rabillo del ojo to look out of the corner of one's eye.

**rabino** *nm* rabbi.

**rabioso,-a** *adj fig (airado)* furious, angry. LOC ponerse rabioso,-a to fly into a rage.

**rabo** *nm (gen)* tail.

**rácano,-a** *adj fam (tacaño)* mean, stingy.

**racha** *nf* 1 *(ráfaga)* gust, squall. 2 *fig (período)* spell, patch. 3 *fig (serie)* string, run, series *sing*: *hubo una racha de incendios* there was a series of fires. LOC a rachas in fits and starts, on and off. ‖ tener una buena racha to have a run of good luck.

**racimo** *nm* bunch, cluster.

**ración** *nf* 1 *(parte)* portion, share. 2 *(de comida)* portion, serving, helping: *«Cuatro raciones»* «Serves four».

**racional** *adj* rational.

**racionar** *vt (limitar)* to ration.

**racismo** *nm* racism, racialism.

**radiación** *nf* radiation.

**radiactivo,-a** *adj* radioactive.

**radiador** *nm* radiator.

**radiante** *adj fig* radiant: *radiante de alegría* radiant with joy.

**radiar** *vt* 1 *(irradiar)* to radiate, irradiate. 2 *(retransmitir)* to broadcast, transmit.

**radical** *adj* radical.

**radicalizar** *vt* 1 to radicalize. 2 *(postura)* to harden.
▶ *vpr* radicalizarse 1 *(conflicto)* to intensify. 2 *(postura)* to harden.

**radio¹** *nm* 1 *(de círculo)* radius: *en un radio de 10 metros* within a radius of 10 metres. 2 *(de rueda)* spoke. 3 *(campo)* scope. COMP radio de acción *fig* field of action, scope.

**radio²** *nf* 1 *(radiodifusión)* radio: *lo oí por la radio* I heard it on the radio. 2 *(aparato)* radio, wireless.

**radioactivo,-a** *adj* radioactive.

**radioaficionado,-a** *nm & nf* radio ham.

**radiocasete** *nm* radio cassette.

**radiodifusión** *nf* broadcasting.

**radiofónico,-a** *adj* radio: *concurso radiofónico* radio quiz programme.

**radiografía** *nf* 1 *(técnica)* radiography. 2 *(imagen)* X-ray, radiograph. LOC hacerse una radiografía to have an X-ray taken.

**radionovela** *nf* serial.

**radiorreceptor** *nm* radio, radio set.

**radioterapia** *nf* radiotherapy.

**radiotransmisión** *nf* broadcasting.

**radiotransmitir** *vt* to broadcast.

**radioyente** *nm o nf* listener.

**raer** *vt* to scrape (off).

**ráfaga** *nf* **1** *(de viento)* gust, squall. **2** *(de disparos)* burst. **3** *(de luz)* flash.

**rafia** *nf* raffia.

**raid** *nm* *(incursión)* raid.

**raigambre** *nf* **1** *(raíces)* roots *pl*, root system. **2** *fig* tradition, history.

**raíl** *nm* rail.

**raíz** *nf* root. LOC **de raíz** entirely. ▌ **echar raíces 1** *(planta)* to take root. **2** *(persona)* to settle, put down roots. COMP **raíz cuadrada** square root.

**raja** *nf* **1** *(corte)* cut, slit. **2** *(hendidura)* crack, split. **3** *(tajada)* slice.

**rajá** *nm* rajah.

**rajar** *vt* **1** *(hender)* to split, crack. **2** *(hacer tajadas)* to slice.
▶ *vpr* **rajarse 1** *(partirse)* to split, crack. **2** *fam* *(desistir)* to back out, quit.

**rajatabla** LOC **a rajatabla** strictly.

**ralentí** *nm* CINE slow motion. LOC **al ralentí** *(motor)* ticking over.

**ralentizar** *vt* to slow down.

**rallado,-a** *adj* *(queso, etc)* grated.

**rallador** *nm* grater.

**ralladura** *nf* grated rind: *ralladura de limón* grated lemon rind.

**rallar** *vt* to grate.

**rally** *nm* rally.

**rama** *nf* branch. LOC **andarse por las ramas** *fam* to beat about the bush. ▌ **en rama** raw: *canela en rama* cinnamon stick.

**ramaje** *nm* foliage, branches *pl*.

**ramal** *nm* *(de camino, etc)* branch.

**ramalazo** *nm* *fam* *(ataque)* fit.

**rambla** *nf* *(paseo)* boulevard, avenue.

**ramificación** *nf* ramification.

**ramificarse** *vpr* to ramify, branch (out).

**ramillete** *nm* **1** posy. **2** *fig* *(conjunto)* bunch, group, collection.

**ramo** *nm* **1** *(de flores)* bunch, bouquet. **2** *fig* *(sector)* field: *el ramo de la alimentación* the food sector, the food industry.

**rampa** *nf* *(pendiente)* ramp. COMP **rampa de lanzamiento** launching pad.

**rana** *nf* frog.

**rancho** *nm* AM *(granja)* ranch, farm.

**rancio,-a** *adj* **1** *(comestibles)* stale. **2** *fig* *(antiguo)* old, ancient: *de rancio abolengo* of ancient lineage.

**rand** *nm* rand.

**rango** *nm* rank.

**ranking** *nm* ranking.

**ranura** *nf* *(para monedas, fichas)* slot.

**rapapolvo** *nm* *fam* dressing-down, ticking off, talking-to.

**rapar** *vt* *(pelo)* to crop.

**rapaz** *adj* ZOOL predatory, of prey: *ave rapaz* bird of prey.

**rape**¹ *nm* *(pez)* angler fish.

**rape**² *nm* *fam* *(rasura)* quick shave. LOC **al rape** close-cropped, short.

**rapero,-a** *nm* & *nf* rapper.

**rapidez** *nf* speed, rapidity: *con rapidez* quickly.

**rápido,-a** *adj* quick, fast.
▶ *adv* quickly: *¡rápido!* hurry up!
▶ *nm* **rápido** *(tren)* fast train.
▶ *nm pl* **rápidos** *(del río)* rapids.

**rapiñar** *vt* *fam* to pinch, steal.

**rappel** *nm* abseiling. LOC **hacer rappel** to abseil.

**raptar** *vt* to kidnap, abduct.

**rapto** *nm* *(secuestro)* kidnapping.

**raqueta** *nf* *(de tenis)* racket; *(de ping-pong)* bat, US paddle.

**raquítico,-a** *adj* **1** *fig* *(exiguo)* meagre (US meager), small. **2** *fig* *(débil)* weak.

**rareza** *nf* **1** *(poco común)* rarity, rareness. **2** *(extravagancia)* eccentricity.

**raro,-a** *adj* **1** *(escaso)* scarce, rare: *los gorilas albinos son animales raros* albino gorilas are rare animals. **2** *(peculiar)* odd, strange, weird: *últimamente la encuentro rara* I think she's been acting a little strange recently. LOC **¡qué raro!** how odd!, that's strange!

**ras** LOC **a ras de** (on a) level with. ▌ **a ras de tierra** at ground level.

**rasante** *adj* *(vuelo)* low, skimming.
▶ *nf* *(inclinación)* slope. COMP **cambio de rasante** brow of a hill.

**rascacielos** *nm inv* skyscraper.

**rascador** *nm* *(para rascar)* scraper.

**rascar** *vt* **1** *(la piel)* to scratch. **2** *(con rascador)* to scrape, rasp.

**rasero** *nm* strickle. LOC **por el mismo rasero** *fig* equally.

**rasgado,-a** *adj (roto)* torn, ripped.

**rasgar** *vt* to tear, rip.

**rasgo** *nm* 1 *(facción del rostro)* feature. 2 *(peculiaridad)* characteristic, feature. LOC **explicar a grandes rasgos** to outline.

**rasguear** *vt (instrumento)* to strum.

**rasguñar** *vt* to scratch, scrape.

**rasguño** *nm (arañazo)* scratch, scrape.

**raso,-a** *adj* 1 *(plano)* flat, level; *(liso)* smooth: *una cucharada rasa* a level spoonful. 2 *(atmósfera)* clear.
▶ *nm* **raso** *(tejido)* satin.

**raspa** *nf (de pescado)* bone, backbone.

**raspar** *vt* 1 *(rascar)* to scrape (off); *(dañar)* to scratch, graze. 2 *(rasar)* to graze, skim.

**rasposo,-a** *adj* rough, sharp.

**rasqueta** *nf* scraper.

**rastra** *nf (rastro)* trail, track. LOC **a rastras** 1 *(arrastrando)* dragging. 2 *(sin querer)* unwillingly, grudgingly: *llevar a rastras* to drag along.

**rastrear** *vt (seguir el rastro)* to trail, track.

**rastrillar** *vt (hojas, etc)* to rake.

**rastrillo** *nm* 1 *(rastro)* rake. 2 *fam (mercadillo)* flea market.

**rastro** *nm* 1 *(señal)* trace, track: *ni rastro de sangre* not a trace of blood. 2 *(vestigio)* vestige. 3 *(mercado)* flea market. LOC **seguir el rastro de** ALGN to follow SB's trail.

**rastrojo** *nm (paja)* stubble.

**rasurar** *vt* to shave.

**rata** *nf* ZOOL rat.

**ratero,-a** *nm & nf* pickpocket.

**ratificar** *vt* to ratify.
▶ *vpr* **ratificarse** to be confirmed.

**rato** *nm* 1 *(tiempo)* time, while, moment: *charlamos un rato* we chatted for a while. 2 *(espacio)* way: *hay un buen rato hasta Vigo* it's a long way to Vigo. 3 *fam (mucho)* very, a lot: *sabe un rato de deportes* she's a mine of information about sports. LOC **a ratos** at times. ▌ **pasar un buen rato** to have a good time. COMP **ratos libres** free time *sing.*

**ratón** *nm* mouse.

**ratonera** *nf (trampa)* mousetrap.

**raudal** *nm* 1 *(agua)* torrent, flood. 2 *fig (abundancia)* flood, wave. LOC **a raudales** in torrents.

**raudo,-a** *adj lit* swift, rapid.

**raviolis** *nm pl* ravioli.

**raya¹** *nf* 1 *(línea)* line. 2 *(de color)* stripe: *pantalón a rayas* striped trousers.

**raya²** *nf (pez)* skate.

**rayado,-a** *adj* 1 *(tejido)* striped. 2 *(papel)* ruled.
▶ *nm* **rayado** stripes *pl.*

**rayar** *vt* 1 *(líneas)* to draw lines on, line, rule. 2 *(superficie)* to scratch.

**rayo** *nm* 1 ray, beam: *rayo de sol* sunbeam; *rayo de luz* ray of light. 2 *(relámpago)* lightning. COMP **rayo de luna** moonbeam. ▌ **rayos ultravioletas/UVA** ultraviolet rays. ▌ **rayos X** X-rays.

**rayuela** *nf* hopscotch.

**raza** *nf* 1 race. 2 *(animal)* breed. LOC **de raza** 1 *(perro)* pedigree. 2 *(caballo)* thoroughbred. COMP **raza humana** human race.

**razón** *nf* 1 *(facultad)* reason. 2 *(motivo)* reason, cause. 3 *(mensaje)* message. 4 *(justicia)* justice. 5 MAT ratio, rate. LOC **dar la razón a** ALGN to agree with SB, say that SB is right. ▌ **perder la razón** to lose one's reason. ▌ **tener razón** to be right.

**razonable** *adj* reasonable.

**razonamiento** *nm* reasoning.

**razonar** *vi* 1 *(discurrir)* to reason. 2 *(hablar)* to talk.
▶ *vt (explicar)* to reason out.

**re** *nm* re, ray, D.

**reacción** *nf* reaction. LOC **reacción en cadena** chain reaction.

**reaccionar** *vi* to react.

**reacio,-a** *adj* reluctant, unwilling.

**reactivar** *vt* to reactivate.

**reactor** *nm* 1 reactor. 2 AV jet, jet plane.

**readmitir** *vt (gen)* to readmit; *(un trabajador)* to reinstate.

**reafirmar** *vt* to reaffirm, reassert.

**reagrupar** *vt* to regroup.
▶ *vpr* **reagruparse** to regroup.

**reajustar** *vt* to readjust.

**real¹** *adj (verdadero)* real: *en la vida real* in real life.

**real²** *adj (regio)* royal.

**realce** *nm (adorno)* relief.

**realeza** *nf* royalty.

**realidad** *nf* reality. ⊡⊙⊙ **en realidad** actually, in fact.

**realista** *adj (de la realidad)* realistic.
► *nm o nf (de la realidad)* realist.

**realización** *nf* **1** *(de un deseo)* fulfilment (us fulfillment). **2** *(ejecución)* execution, carrying out.

**realizador,-ra** *nm & nf* producer.

**realizar** *vt* **1** *(ambición)* to realize, fulfil, achieve; *(deseo, esperanza)* to fulfil. **2** *(llevar a cabo)* to accomplish, carry out, do, fulfil. **3** *(un viaje)* to make.
► *vpr* **realizarse 1** *(ambición, deseo)* to be fulfilled, be achieved; *(sueño)* to come true. **2** *(llevarse a cabo)* to be executed, be carried out.

**realmente** *adv* **1** *(de verdad)* really, truly. **2** *(en realidad)* actually, in fact: *realmente no hacía tanto frío* in fact it wasn't too cold.

**realzar** *vt* **1** *(elevar)* to raise, lift. **2** *fig (engrandecer)* to enhance, heighten.

**reanimar** *vt* **1** *(persona)* to revive. **2** *(fiesta, conversación)* to liven up.
► *vpr* **reanimarse** *(persona)* to revive.

**reanudar** *vt (gen)* to renew, resume.

**reaparecer** *vi* **1** *(gen)* to reappear. **2** *(un artista, etc)* to make a comeback. **3** *(un fenómeno)* to recur.

**reavivar** *vt* **1** *(fuego)* to stoke. **2** *(dolor)* to intensify; *(interés)* to revive.

**rebaba** *nf* rough edge.

**rebaja** *nf (descuento)* discount, reduction.
► *nf pl* **rebajas** sales.

**rebajado,-a** *adj* **1** *(precio)* reduced. **2** *(humillado)* humbled.

**rebajar** *vt* **1** *(nivel)* to lower. **2** *(precio)* to reduce. **3** *(color)* to soften. **4** *fig (humillar)* to humiliate.
► *vpr* **rebajarse** *fig (humillarse)* to humble os.

**rebanada** *nf* slice.

**rebañar** *vt (comida)* to finish off.

**rebaño** *nm (gen)* herd; *(de ovejas)* flock.

**rebeca** *nf* cardigan.

**rebelarse** *vpr* to rebel, revolt.

**rebelde** *adj* **1** rebellious. **2** *fig (tos, etc)* persistent.
► *nm o nf* rebel.

**rebelión** *nf* rebellion, revolt.

**reblandecer** *vt* to soften.
► *vpr* **reblandecerse** to soften.

**rebobinar** *vt* to rewind.

**reborde** *nm (de mesa)* edge; *(de taza, de tela)* edging.

**rebosar** *vi* **1** *(derramarse)* to overflow, brim over. **2** *fig* to brim (de, with), burst (de, with): *rebosar de alegría* to be brimming with joy.
► *vt fig (sentimiento)* to brim with; *(salud)* to exude.

**rebotar** *vi (pelota)* to bounce, rebound.

**rebote** *nm (de balón)* bounce, rebound. ⊡⊙⊙ **de rebote** *fig* on the rebound.

**rebozado,-a** *adj* coated in batter.

**rebozar** *vt* CULIN to coat in batter.

**rebrotar** *vi* to shoot, sprout.

**rebuscado,-a** *adj* affected, recherché.

**rebuscar** *vt* to search carefully for.

**rebuznar** *vi* to bray.

**rebuzno** *nm* bray, braying.

**recabar** *vt* **1** *(solicitar)* to ask for, entreat. **2** *(obtener)* to manage to get.

**recadero,-a** *nm & nf (gen)* messenger.

**recado** *nm* **1** *(mensaje)* message. **2** *(encargo)* errand: *me hizo un recado* she ran the errand for me.
► *nm pl* **recados** *(compras)* shopping sing.

**recaer** *vi (enfermedad)* to relapse, have a relapse.

**recaída** *nf (enfermedad)* relapse. ⊡⊙⊙ **sufrir una recaída** to have a relapse.

**recalcar** *vt fig* to emphasize, stress.

**recalentar** *vt* **1** *(volver a calentar)* to warm up. **2** *(calentar demasiado)* to overheat.

**recámara** *nf* **1** *(cuarto)* dressing room. **2** *(de arma)* chamber.

**recambio** *nm* spare, spare part; *(de pluma, bolígrafo)* refill.

**recapacitar** *vi* to think (sobre, over).

**R**

**recapitular** *vt* to recapitulate, sum up.

**recargado,-a** *adj fig (exagerado)* overe-laborate, exaggerated, contrived.

**recargar** *vt* **1** *(volver a cargar)* to reload; *(pilas)* to recharge; *(mechero)* to refill. **2** *(sobrecargar)* to overload. **3** *fig (exagerar)* to overelaborate, exaggerate.

**recargo** *nm* extra charge, surcharge.

**recatado,-a** *adj* **1** *(prudente)* cautious, prudent. **2** *(decente)* decent.

**recauchutar** *vt* to retread, remould.

**recaudar** *vt* to collect.

**recelar** *vt* **1** *(sospechar)* to suspect, dis-trust. **2** *(temer)* to fear.
  ▶ *vi (desconfiar)* to be suspicious (de, of): *recela de todos* he is suspicious of everybody.

**recelo** *nm* suspicion.

**recepción** *nf* **1** *(gen)* reception. **2** *(de documento, carta, etc)* receipt.

**recepcionista** *nm o nf* receptionist.

**receptivo,-a** *adj* receptive (a, to).

**receptor,-ra** *nm & nf* receiver, recipi-ent.
  ▶ *nm* **receptor** *(de radio, etc)* receiver.

**receta** *nf* **1** MED prescription. **2** CULIN recipe.

**recetar** *vt* to prescribe.

**rechazar** *vt* **1** *(gen)* to reject, turn down. **2** *(ataque)* to repel, drive back.

**rechazo** *nm* **1** rejection, refusal. **2** *(negativa)* denial, rejection.

**rechinar** *vi (madera)* to creak; *(metal)* to squeak, screech; *(dientes)* to grind.

**rechistar** *vi* to say, reply.

**rechoncho,-a** *adj fam* chubby, tubby.

**rechupete** LOC **de rechupete** *fam (muy bien)* super, brill, fantastic. *(comida)* delicious, scrumptious.

**recibidor** *nm (de casa)* entrance hall.

**recibimiento** *nm* reception, wel-come.

**recibir** *vt* **1** *(gen)* to receive. **2** *(salir al encuentro)* to meet: *nos recibió en la puerta* he met us at the door.

**recibo** *nm* **1** *(resguardo)* receipt. **2** *(factura)* invoice, bill.

**reciclar** *vt (materiales)* to recycle.

**recién** *adv* [se usa sólo ante un participio pasado] recently, newly; *(café, pan)* freshly: *un pastel recién hecho* a freshly baked cake. LOC **«Recién pintado»** "Wet paint".

**reciente** *adj* recent.

**recinto** *nm* grounds *pl*, precincts *pl*.

**recio,-a** *adj (fuerte)* strong, robust.

**recipiente** *nm* container, receptacle.

**recíproco,-a** *adj* reciprocal, mutual: *un sentimiento recíproco* a mutual feeling.

**recital** *nm* **1** MÚS recital, concert. **2** LIT reading: *recital de poesía* poetry reading.

**recitar** *vt* to recite.

**reclamación** *nf* **1** *(demanda)* claim, de-mand. **2** *(queja)* complaint. LOC **presentar una reclamación** to lodge a complaint.

**reclamar** *vt (pedir)* to demand, claim.
  ▶ *vi (protestar)* to protest (contra, against): *reclamaron contra aquella medida* they protested against the measure.

**reclamo** *nm* **1** *(para cazar)* decoy bird, lure. **2** *(anuncio)* advertisement; *(eslogan)* advertising slogan.

**reclinar** *vt* to lean.
  ▶ *vpr* **reclinarse** to lean back, recline: *se reclinó sobre la almohada* he lent back on the pillow.

**recluir** *vt (encerrar)* to shut in.

**recluso,-a** *nm & nf* prisoner.

**recluta** *nm o nf* recruit.

**reclutar** *vt* to recruit.

**recobrar** *vt* **1** *(gen)* to recover. **2** *(aliento)* to get back. **3** *(tiempo)* to make up.
  ▶ *vpr* **recobrarse** *(recuperarse)* to recover (de, from).

**recodo** *nm* twist.

**recogedor** *nm* dustpan.

**recoger** *vt* **1** *(volver a coger)* to take again, take back. **2** *(coger)* to pick up, take back. **3** *(ir a buscar)* to pick up, collect: *me recogerá a las cuatro* he'll pick me up at four o'clock. **4** *(cosecha)* to har-vest, gather; *(fruta)* to pick. **5** *(juntar)* to gather, collect. **6** *(velas)* to take in; *(cortinas)* to draw. **7** *(dar asilo)* to take in, shelter: *lo recogieron sus abuelos* he

was taken in by his grandparents. **8** *(ordenar)* to clear up, tidy up.
► *vpr* **recogerse 1** *(irse a casa)* to go home. **2** *(irse a dormir)* to go to bed.

**recolectar** *vt* **1** *(reunir)* to gather, collect. **2** *(cosechar)* to harvest.

**recomendar** *vt* to recommend, advise: *te recomiendo que estudies más* I recommend that you study harder.

**recompensa** *nf* reward, recompense. LOC **en recompensa** in return.

**recompensar** *vt* **1** *(compensar)* to compensate. **2** *(remunerar)* to reward.

**recomponer** *vt* to repair, mend.

**reconcentrar** *vt* **1** *(concentrar)* to concentrate (en, to). **2** *(reunir)* to bring together.
► *vpr* **reconcentrarse** *(ensimismarse)* to become absorbed in thought, concentrate.

**reconciliar** *vt* to reconcile.
► *vpr* **reconciliarse** *(uso recíproco)* to be reconciled.

**recóndito,-a** *adj* hidden, secret.

**reconfortar** *vt* **1** *(confortar)* to comfort. **2** *(animar)* to cheer up.

**reconocer** *vt* **1** *(gen)* to recognize. **2** *(admitir)* to recognize, admit: *reconoció su error* she admitted her mistake. **3** *(afrontar)* to face: *reconozcámoslo* let's face it. **4** MIL *(terreno)* to reconnoitre (US reconnoiter). **5** MED *(paciente)* to examine.
► *vpr* **reconocerse 1** to recognize each other. **2** *(admitirse)* to admit: *se reconoció culpable* he admitted his guilt.

**reconocimiento** *nm* **1** *(gen)* recognition. **2** *(admisión)* admission. **3** MIL reconnaissance. **4** MED checkup.

**reconstituyente** *nm* tonic.

**reconstruir** *vt* to reconstruct.

**reconvertir** *vt* to restructure.

**recopilar** *vt* to compile, collect.

**récord** *adj* record: *en un tiempo récord* in record time.
► *nm* record.

**recordar** *vt* **1** *(rememorar)* to remember: *¿recuerdas?* do you remember? **2** *(traer a la memoria)* to remind (a, of): *me recuer-*

*da a mi hermano* he reminds me of my brother.

**recorrer** *vt* **1** *(distancia)* to cover, travel. **2** *(país)* to tour, travel over, travel round. **3** *(ciudad)* to visit, walk round.

**recorrido** *nm* **1** *(trayecto)* journey, trip. **2** *(distancia)* distance travelled: *un tren de largo recorrido* a long-distance train. **3** *(itinerario)* itinerary, route.

**recortar** *vt* **1** *(muñecos, telas, etc)* to cut out. **2** *(lo que sobra)* to cut off. **3** *(el pelo)* to trim. **4** *fig* to cut, restrict: *han recortado los gastos* expenses have been cut.

**recorte** *nm* **1** *(acción)* cutting. **2** *(trozo)* cutting, clipping. **3** *(de periódico)* press clipping, newspaper cutting. **4** *(de pelo)* trim, cut. **5** *fig (reducción)* cut, reduction: *recorte del presupuesto* budget cut.

**recostar** *vt* to lean.
► *vpr* **recostarse 1** *(apoyarse)* to lean. **2** *(tumbarse)* to lie down.

**recoveco** *nm* turn, bend.

**recrear** *vt* *(divertir)* to amuse, entertain.
► *vpr* **recrearse** to amuse OS, enjoy OS.

**recreo** *nm* *(en la escuela)* playtime, break.

**recriminar** *vt* **1** *(reprender)* to recriminate. **2** *(reprochar)* to reproach.

**recrudecer** *vi* *(empeorar)* to worsen, aggravate.
► *vpr* **recrudecerse 1** *(empeorar)* to worsen. **2** *(aumentar)* to be increasing.

**recta** *nf* **1** *(línea)* straight line. **2** *(en carretera)* straight.

**rectangular** *adj* rectangular.

**rectángulo,-a** *adj* rectangular: *triángulo rectángulo* right-angled triangle.
► *nm* **rectángulo** rectangle.

**rectificar** *vt* **1** to rectify. **2** *(corregir)* to correct.

**recto,-a** *adj* **1** *(derecho)* straight. **3** *(ángulo)* right.
► *adv* straight, straight on: *vaya todo recto* go straight on.

**recuadro** *nm* box.

**recubrir** *vt* to cover (con/de, with).

**recuento** *nm* recount, count.

**recuerdo** *nm* **1** *(imagen)* memory. **2** *(regalo)* souvenir, keepsake.
LOC **en recuerdo de** in memory of.

**R**

▶ *nm pl* **recuerdos** *(saludos)* regards: *me dio recuerdos para ti* he sends you his regards.

**recular** *vi (retroceder)* to go back.

**recuperación** *nf* recovery.

**recuperar** *vt* 1 *(gen)* to recover. 2 *(afecto)* to win back; *(conocimiento)* to regain; *(tiempo, clases)* to make up.
▶ *vpr* **recuperarse** to recover (de, from).

**recurrir** *vi (acogerse - a algo)* to resort (a, to); *(- a algn)* to turn (a, to): *recurrió a sus padres* she turned to her parents.

**recurso** *nm (medio)* resort.
▶ *nm pl* **recursos** resources, means.

**red** *nf* 1 *(gen)* net. 2 *(sistema)* network, system. 3 ELEC mains *pl*. 4 INFORM network. 5 *fig (trampa)* trap. COMP **red de carreteras** road network.

**redacción** *nf* 1 *(escritura)* writing. 2 *(escrito)* composition, essay. 3 *(estilo)* wording. 4 *(oficina)* editorial office. 5 *(redactores)* editorial staff.

**redactar** *vt (escribir)* to write.

**redactor,-ra** *nm & nf* editor. COMP **redactor jefe** editor in chief.

**redada** *nf fig* raid.

**redención** *nf* redemption.

**redescubrir** *vt* to rediscover.

**redil** *nm* fold, sheepfold.

**redimir** *vt* to redeem.
▶ *vpr* **redimirse** to redeem OS.

**redoblar** *vt (aumentar)* to redouble: *redoblar esfuerzos* to redouble one's efforts.
▶ *vi (tambores)* to roll.

**redoble** *nm* roll.

**redonda** LOC **a la redonda** around.

**redondear** *vt* 1 *(poner redondo)* to round, make round. 2 *(cantidad)* to round up.

**redondo,-a** *adj* 1 *(circular)* round. 2 *fig (perfecto)* perfect, excellent: *un beneficio redondo* an excellent profit. 3 *fig (cantidad)* round: *en números redondos* in round figures.

**reducción** *nf* reduction.

**reducir** *vt* 1 *(gen)* to reduce: *reducir a cenizas* to reduce to ashes. 2 *(disminuir)* to reduce, cut, cut down on: *reducir gastos* to cut down on expenses.

▶ *vpr* **reducirse** 1 *(gen)* to be reduced. 2 *(resultar)* to come down (a, to): *todo se redujo a una equivocación* it all came down to a mistake.

**redundante** *adj* redundant.

**redundar** *vi* 1 *(abundar)* to abound. 2 *(resultar)* to redound (en, to): *redundó en nuestro beneficio* it was to our advantage.

**reembolsar** *vt* 1 *(pagar)* to reimburse. 2 *(devolver)* to refund.

**reembolso** *nm* 1 *(pago)* reimbursement. 2 *(devolución)* refund. COMP **contra reembolso** cash on delivery.

**reemplazar** *vt* to replace.

**reemplazo** *nm* 1 replacement. 2 MIL call-up.

**reencarnación** *nf* reincarnation.

**reencuentro** *nm* reunion.

**reestreno** *nm (teatro)* revival; *(cine)* rerelease, rerun.

**reestructurar** *vt* to restructure.

**referencia** *nf (relación)* reference. LOC **hacer referencia a** ALGO to refer to STH.
▶ *nf pl* **referencias** *(informes)* references.

**referéndum** *nm inv* referendum.

**referente** *adj* concerning (a, -), regarding (a, -).

**referir** *vt* 1 *(expresar)* to tell, relate. 2 *(remitir)* to refer.
▶ *vpr* **referirse** to refer (a, to).

**refilón** LOC **mirar** ALGO **de refilón** to look at STH out of the corner of one's eye.

**refinado,-a** *adj (gen)* refined.

**refinamiento** *nm* refinement.

**refinar** *vt (azúcar, etc)* to refine.

**refinería** *nf* refinery.

**reflector,-ra** *adj* reflecting.
▶ *nm* **reflector** 1 *(cuerpo)* reflector. 2 ELEC searchlight, spotlight.

**reflejar** *vt* 1 *(gen)* to reflect. 2 *(mostrar)* to show: *su rostro refleja sus sentimientos* her face shows her feelings.
▶ *vpr* **reflejarse** to be reflected.

**reflejo,-a** *adj (movimiento)* reflex.
▶ *nm* **reflejo** 1 *(imagen)* reflection. 2 *(destello)* gleam, glint.

**reflexión** *nf* reflection.

**reflexionar** *vi* to reflect (**sobre**, on), think (**sobre**, about): *reflexionamos sobre el tema* we reflected on the subject.

**reflexivo,-a** *adj* reflective, thoughtful.

**reforma** *nf* **1** *(gen)* reform. **2** *(mejora)* improvement.

▶ *nf pl* **reformas** *(en construcción)* alterations, repairs, improvements. COMP **reforma agraria** agrarian reform.

**reformar** *vt* **1** *(gen)* to reform. **2** ARQUIT to renovate, do up.

▶ *vpr* **reformarse** *(corregirse)* to reform OS.

**reformatear** *vt* INFORM to reformat.

**reformatorio** *nm* reformatory, reform school. COMP **reformatorio de menores** remand home.

**reforzar** *vt* to reinforce, strengthen.

**refracción** *nf* refraction. COMP **ángulo de refracción** angle of refraction.

**refrán** *nm* proverb, saying.

**refregar** *vt* **1** to rub hard. **2** *fam fig* to rub in: *me refregó mi error* he kept on about my mistake.

**refrenar** *vt* to restrain, curb, control.

**refrescante** *adj* refreshing.

**refrescar** *vt* **1** *(poner fresco)* to cool, refresh. **2** *fig (la memoria)* to refresh; *(idiomas)* to brush up on.

▶ *vi* **1** *(el tiempo)* to get cooler, cool down, turn cooler. **2** *(comida, bebida)* to be refreshing.

▶ *vpr* **refrescarse 1** *(gen)* to cool down, cool off; *(lavarse)* to freshen up; *(tomar el fresco)* to get a breath of fresh air. **2** *(beber)* to have a cold drink.

**refresco** *nm* *(bebida)* soft drink.

**refriega** *nf* *(lucha)* scuffle, brawl.

**refrigeración** *nf* **1** refrigeration. **2** *(aire acondicionado)* air conditioning. **3** *(sistema)* cooling system.

**refrigerador** *nm* fridge, refrigerator.

**refrigerar** *vt* **1** *(enfriar)* to refrigerate. **2** *(con aire acondicionado)* to air-condition.

**refrigerio** *nm* refreshments *pl*, snack.

**refuerzo** *nm* *(fortalecimiento)* reinforcement, strengthening.

**refugiado,-a** *nm & nf* refugee. COMP **refugiado político** political refugee.

**refugiar** *vt* to shelter, give refuge to.

▶ *vpr* **refugiarse** *(gen)* to take refuge; *(de la lluvia)* to shelter.

**refugio** *nm* *(gen)* shelter, refuge.

**refunfuñar** *vi fam* to grumble, moan.

**refutar** *vt* to refute, disprove.

**regadera** *nf* watering can.

**regadío,-a** *adj* irrigable.

▶ *nm* **regadío 1** *(acción)* irrigation, watering. **2** *(tierras)* irrigated land. COMP **cultivo de regadío** irrigation farming.

**regalar** *vt* *(dar un regalo)* to give as a present: *le podemos regalar un libro para su cumpleaños* we can get him a book for his birthday.

**regaliz** *nm* liquorice (US licorice).

**regalo** *nm* **1** *(obsequio)* gift, present. **2** *(ganga)* bargain, steal.

**regañadientes** LOC **a regañadientes** reluctantly, grudgingly, unwillingly.

**regañar** *vt* to scold, tell off.

▶ *vi (reñir)* to argue, quarrel, fall out: *no hacen más que regañar* they're always quarrelling.

**regar** *vt* **1** *(plantas, tierra, río)* to water. **2** *(calle)* to wash down, hose down.

**regata** *nf* MAR regatta, boat race.

**regatear** *vt* **1** *(un precio)* to haggle over, barter for. **2** *(escatimar)* to be sparing with. LOC **no regatear esfuerzos** to spare no effort.

▶ *vi* **1** *(comerciar)* to haggle, bargain. **2** DEP to dribble. **3** MAR to race.

**regateo** *nm* **1** *(precios)* haggling, bargaining. **2** DEP dribbling.

**regazo** *nm* lap.

**regenerar** *vt* to regenerate.

**regentar** *vt* **1** POL to govern, rule. **2** *(cargo)* to hold. **3** *(dirigir)* to manage.

**regente,-a** *adj* ruling, governing.

▶ *nm o nf* POL regent.

**reggae** *nm* reggae.

**régimen** *nm* **1** POL regime. **2** MED diet. **3** *(condiciones)* system, regime, rules *pl*. LOC **estar a régimen** to be on a diet.

**regimiento** *nm* regiment.

**regio,-a** *adj (real)* royal, regal.

**región** *nf* region.

**regir** *vt* **1** *(gobernar)* to govern, rule. **2** *(dirigir)* to manage, direct, run.

**R**

▶ *vi (ley, etc)* to be in force, apply: *esta ley aún rige* this law is still in force.

▶ *vpr* **regirse** *(guiarse)* to follow, abide (por, by), go (por, by): *se rige por la opinión de su padre* he goes by his father's opinion.

**registrador,-ra** *adj* registering, recording: *caja registradora* cash register.

▶ *nm & nf* registrar.

**registrar** *vt* **1** *(inspeccionar)* to search. **2** *(cachear)* to frisk. **3** *(inscribir)* to register, record, note.

▶ *vpr* **registrarse 1** *(matricularse)* to register, enrol (US enroll). **2** *(detectarse)* to be recorded. **3** *(ocurrir)* to happen: *se ha registrado un terremoto* there has been an earthquake.

**registro** *nm* **1** *(inspección)* search, inspection. **2** *(inscripción)* registration, recording. **3** JUR *(oficina)* registry. COMP **registro civil** *(oficina)* registry office.

**regla** *nf* **1** *(norma)* rule. **2** *(pauta)* pattern, rule. **3** *(instrumento)* ruler. **4** *(menstruación)* period. LOC **en regla** in order.

**reglamentar** *vt* to regulate.

**reglamentario,-a** *adj* statutory, prescribed, required; *(arma)* regulation.

**reglamento** *nm* regulations *pl*, rules *pl*.

**reglar** *vt (regular)* to regulate.

**regocijarse** *vpr* **1** *(alegrarse)* to be delighted (con, by). **2** *(regodearse)* to delight (de, in), take pleasure (de, in).

**regocijo** *nm (placer)* delight, joy.

**regresar** *vi* to return, come back, go back.

**regreso** *nm* return. LOC **estar de regreso** to be back.

**reguero** *nm* **1** *(corriente)* trickle of water. **2** *(señal)* trail, trickle.

**regular** *adj* **1** *(gen)* regular. **2** *fam (pasable)* so-so, average, not bad.

▶ *vt* **1** *(gen)* to regulate. **2** *(ajustar)* to adjust.

**regularizar** *vt* to regularize; *(normalizar)* to standardize; *(arreglar)* to sort out.

**rehabilitar** *vt* to rehabilitate.

▶ *nf (en rango)* to reinstate.

**rehacer** *vt (volver a hacer)* to do again.

▶ *vpr* **rehacerse** *(recuperarse)* to recover, recuperate.

**rehén** *nm o nf* hostage.

**rehogar** *vt* to fry lightly.

**rehuir** *vt* to avoid, shun.

**rehusar** *vt* to refuse, decline: *rehusé la invitación* I declined the invitation.

**reimprimir** *vt* to reprint.

**reina** *nf (gen)* queen.

**reinado** *nm* reign.

**reinar** *vi* **1** to reign. **2** *fig (prevalecer)* to reign, prevail: *reina el desconcierto* disorder reigns.

**reincidente** *adj* **1** relapsing. **2** JUR reoffending, recidivist.

▶ *nm o nf* JUR reoffender, recidivist.

**reincidir** *vi* **1** to relapse (en, into), fall back (en, into). **2** JUR to reoffend.

**reincorporar** *vt* to reincorporate.

▶ *vpr* **reincorporarse** to rejoin (a, -): *se reincorporará al trabajo el lunes* she will go back to work on Monday.

**reiniciar** *vt* to restart.

**reino** *nm* kingdom, reign.

**reinserción** *nf* reintegration, rehabilitation: *la reinserción social* social rehabilitation.

**reinsertar** *vt* to reintegrate.

▶ *vpr* **reinsertarse** to reintegrate.

**reintegrar** *vt* **1** *(reincorporar)* to reinstate, restore. **2** *(pagar)* to refund, reimburse.

▶ *vpr* **reintegrarse** *(volver a ejercer)* to return (a, to): *se reintegró a su puesto* he returned to his job.

**reintegro** *nm* **1** FIN reimbursement, repayment, refund. **2** *(de lotería)* refund of the price of the ticket.

**reír** *vt* to laugh at: *reír las gracias* to laugh at jokes.

▶ *vi* to laugh.

▶ *vpr* **reírse** to laugh (de, at): *¿de qué te ríes?* what are you laughing at?

**reiterar** *vt* to reiterate, repeat.

**reiterativo,-a** *adj* repetitive.

**reivindicación** *nf* claim, demand.

**reivindicar** *vt* to claim, demand.

**reivindicativo,-a** *adj* protest.

**reja** *nf (de ventana)* grill, grille, bar.

**rejilla** *nf* **1** *(celosía)* grill, grille. **2** *(de chimenea)* grate. **3** *(de silla)* wickerwork. **4** *(de horno)* grid iron. **5** *(de ventilador)* grill. **6** *(para equipaje)* luggage rack.

**rejuvenecer** *vt* to rejuvenate.
▶ *vpr* **rejuvenecerse** to become rejuvenated.

**relación** *nf* **1** *(correspondencia)* relation, relationship. **2** *(conexión)* link, connection. **3** *(lista)* list, record. **4** *(relato)* account, telling. **5** *(en matemática)* ratio.
▶ *nf pl* **relaciones** *(conocidos)* acquaintances; *(contactos)* contacts, connections. [LOC] **con relación a / en relación a** with regard to, regarding.

**relacionar** *vt* **1** *(poner en relación)* to relate, connect, associate. **2** *(relatar)* to tell, list.
▶ *vpr* **relacionarse 1** *(estar conectado)* to be related (con, to), be connected (con, with). **2** *(alternar)* to get acquainted (con, with), mix (con, with), meet (con, -).

**relajante** *adj* relaxing.

**relajar** *vt* *(gen)* to relax.
▶ *vpr* **relajarse** *(descansar)* to relax.

**relamer** *vt* to lick.
▶ *vpr* **relamerse** to lick one's lips repeatedly.

**relamido,-a** *adj* *(pulcro)* prim and proper.

**relámpago** *nm* flash of lightning.

**relampaguear** *vi* [se usa sólo en tercera persona; no lleva sujeto] to flash.

**relatar** *vt* **1** *(una historia)* to narrate, tell. **2** *(un suceso)* to report, tell.

**relativizar** *vt* to lessen the importance of, play down.

**relativo,-a** *adj* relative.

**relato** *nm* **1** *(narración)* story, tale. **2** *(informe)* report, account.

**relegar** *vt* to relegate (a, to).

**relente** *nm* dew.

**relevante** *adj* **1** *(significativo)* relevant. **2** *(importante)* excellent, outstanding.

**relevar** *vt* **1** *(sustituir)* to relieve, take over from. **2** *(eximir)* to exempt (de, from). **3** *(destituir)* to dismiss, relieve.

**relevo** *nm* **1** MIL relief, change of the guard. **2** DEP relay.

**relieve** *nm* **1** relief. **2** *fig (renombre)* renown, fame. [LOC] **en relieve** in relief. **| poner de relieve** *fig* to emphasize, highlight, underline.

**religión** *nf* religion.

**religioso,-a** *adj* religious.
▶ *nm & nf (hombre)* monk; *(mujer)* nun.

**relinchar** *vi* to neigh, whinny.

**reliquia** *nf* relic.

**rellano** *nm* landing.

**rellenar** *vt* **1** *(volver a llenar)* to refill, fill again. **2** *(cuestionario)* to fill in, fill out. **3** CULIN *(ave)* to stuff; *(pastel)* to fill.

**relleno,-a** *adj* **1** *(totalmente lleno)* stuffed. **2** CULIN stuffed; *(pasteles)* filled.
▶ *nm* **relleno** CULIN *(aves)* stuffing; *(pasteles)* filling.

**reloj** *nm* clock; *(de pulsera)* watch. [LOC] **contra reloj** against the clock. [COMP] **reloj de arena** hourglass. **| reloj de pulsera** wristwatch.

**relojería** *nf* **1** *(arte)* watchmaking. **2** *(tienda)* watchmaker's, jeweller's.

**relojero,-a** *nm & nf* watchmaker.

**reluciente** *adj* shining, gleaming.

**relucir** *vi* *(brillar)* to shine, gleam. [LOC] **sacar a relucir** ALGO to bring up STH.

**relumbrar** *vi* to shine, dazzle, gleam.

**remachar** *vt* *(clavo, etc)* to clinch; *(metal)* to rivet.

**remangar** *vt* *(mangas, pantalones)* to roll up; *(faldas, vestidos)* to pull up, hitch up.
▶ *vpr* **remangarse** *fig* to decide quickly, make a snap decision.

**remanso** *nm* **1** *(estanque)* pool. **2** *(lugar tranquilo)* quiet place.

**remar** *vi* to row.

**remarcar** *vt* to stress, underline.

**rematado,-a** *adj* **1** absolute, utter, out-and-out. **2** convicted.

**rematar** *vt* **1** *(acabar)* to finish off, round off. **2** *(precios)* to knock down. **3** DEP to shoot.
▶ *vi* DEP to take a shot at goal, shoot.

**remate** *nm* **1** *(final)* end, finish. **2** DEP shot. [LOC] **de remate** *fam* utter, out-and-out, total.

**R**

**remediar** vt 1 *(poner remedio)* to reme-dy. 2 *(reparar)* to repair, make good. 3 *(resolver)* to solve.

**remedio** nm 1 *(cura)* remedy, cure. 2 fig *(solución)* solution. LOC **como último remedio** as a last resort. ∥ **no tener más remedio que** to have no choice but to.

**rememorar** vt to remember, recall.

**remendar** vt COST to mend; *(ropas)* to patch; *(calcetines)* to darn.

**remero,-a** nm & nf DEP rower; *(hombre)* oarsman; *(mujer)* oarswoman.

**remesa** nf 1 *(de dinero)* remittance. 2 *(de mercancías)* consignment, shipment.

**remeter** vt *(meter adentro)* to tuck in.

**remiendo** nm mend, darn.

**remilgado,-a** adj 1 *(afectado)* affected. 2 *(con la comida)* fussy, finicky.

**remite** nm sender's name and address.

**remitente** nm o nf sender.

**remitir** vt 1 *(enviar)* to remit, send. 2 *(referir)* to refer.
▶ vi *(ceder)* to subside: *la fiebre ha remiti-do* the fever has subsided.
▶ vpr **remitirse** *(atenerse)* to refer (a, to): *se remitió a su propio acuerdo* he referred to his own agreement.

**remo** nm 1 *(pala)* oar, paddle. 2 DEP rowing.

**remodelar** vt *(modificar)* to reshape.

**remojar** vt *(empapar)* to soak (en, in).

**remojo** nm soaking. LOC **poner en re-mojo** to soak, leave to soak.

**remolacha** nf beetroot. COMP **remola-cha azucarera** sugar beet.

**remolcador** nm 1 MAR tug, tugboat. 2 AUTO breakdown truck.

**remolcar** vt to tow.

**remolino** nm 1 *(de polvo)* whirl, cloud; *(de agua)* whirlpool, eddy; *(de aire)* whirlwind. 2 *(de pelo)* tuft.

**remolón,-ona** adj lazy, slack.

**remolonear** vi to shirk, slack.

**remolque** nm 1 *(acción)* towing. 2 *(vehí-culo)* trailer.

**remontar** vt 1 *(elevar)* to raise. 2 *(subir)* to go up. 3 *(río)* to sail up; *(vuelo)* to soar.

▶ vpr **remontarse** 1 *(al volar)* to soar. 2 *(datar)* to go back (a, to).

**remorder** vt fig *(desasosegar)* to trouble, worry.

**remordimiento** nm remorse.

**remoto,-a** adj remote, far-off.

**remover** vt 1 *(trasladar)* to move. 2 *(tie-rra)* to turn over, dig up. 3 *(líquido)* to stir. 4 *(comida)* to stir; *(ensalada)* to toss. 5 fig *(agitar)* to get moving, stir up.
▶ vpr **removerse** to stir, shift.

**remunerar** vt to remunerate, reward.

**renacimiento** nm 1 *(vuelta a nacer)* re-birth. 2 fig revival, renaissance. 3 **el Renacimiento** HIST the Renaissance.

**renacuajo** nm 1 ZOOL tadpole. 2 fam *(niño)* shrimp.

**rencor** nm 1 *(odio)* rancour (US rancor). 2 *(resentimiento)* resentment.

**rencoroso,-a** adj 1 *(hostil)* rancorous. 2 *(resentido)* resentful.

**rendido,-a** adj 1 *(sumiso)* humble, sub-missive. 2 *(muy cansado)* worn out, exhausted.

**rendija** nf crack, split.

**rendimiento** nm 1 *(producción - de terreno)* yield; *(- de máquina)* output; *(- de perso-na)* progress, performance; *(- de inver-sión)* yield, return. 2 *(trabajo - de motor, máquina)* performance.

**rendir** vt 1 *(vencer)* to defeat, conquer. 2 *(cansar)* to exhaust, wear out. 3 *(producir)* to yield, produce; *(progresar)* to progress.
▶ vi *(dar fruto)* to pay.
▶ vpr **rendirse** 1 *(entregarse al enemigo)* to surrender, give in. 2 *(darse por vencido)* to give up: *¡me rindo!* I give up!

**renegar** vt *(negar)* to deny vigorously.
▶ vi 1 *(gen)* to renounce (de, -). 2 *(pro-testar)* to grumble, complain.

**renglón** nm *(línea)* line.

**reno** nm reindeer.

**renombre** nm renown, fame.

**renovación** nf 1 *(de contrato, etc)* renew-al. 2 *(de casa)* renovation.

**renovar** vt 1 *(gen)* to renew. 2 *(casa)* to renovate; *(de decoración)* to redecorate.

**renta** *nf* **1** *(ingresos)* income. **2** *(declaración de renta)* tax return. **3** *(beneficio)* interest, return. **4** *(alquiler)* rent. `COMP` **renta per cápita** per capita income.

**rentable** *adj* profitable.

**rentar** *vt* to produce, yield.

**renuncia** *nf* **1** renunciation. **2** *(dimisión)* resignation.

**renunciar** *vi* **1** *(abandonar)* to give up (a, -), abandon (a, -). **2** *(dimitir)* to resign. **3** to renounce (a, -).

**reñido,-a** *adj* **1** *(enemistado)* on bad terms, at odds. **2** *(de rivalidad)* bitter, tough, hard-fought.

**reñir** *vi* **1** *(discutir)* to quarrel, argue. **2** *(desavenirse)* to fall out.
▶ *vt (reprender)* to scold, tell off.

**reojo** `LOC` **de reojo** out of the corner of one's eye.

**repantigarse** *vpr fam* to lounge, loll.

**reparación** *nf* **1** *(arreglo)* repair. **2** *fig (desagravio)* reparation, redress *pl*.

**reparar** *vt* **1** *(arreglar)* to repair, mend, fix. **2** *(remediar - daño)* to make good; *(- perjuicio, insulto)* to make up for.

**reparo** *nm* objection. `LOC` **no tener reparos en** not to hesitate to.

**repartición** *nf* distribution.

**repartidor,-ra** *nm & nf (hombre)* delivery man; *(mujer)* delivery woman; *(chico)* delivery boy; *(chica)* delivery girl.

**repartir** *vt* **1** *(dividir)* to distribute, divide, share out. **2** *(entregar)* to give out, hand out; *(correo, leche)* to deliver; *(premios)* to give out. **3** *(comida)* to hand out. **4** *(distribuir)* to spread out.

**reparto** *nm* **1** *(división)* sharing out, division; *(distribución)* distribution. **2** *(de un terreno)* parcelling out; *(de un país)* partition. **3** *(entrega)* handing out; *(de mercancías)* delivery. **4** *(de obra, película)* cast.

**repasar** *vt (volver a examinar)* to revise, go over.

**repaso** *nm* check; *(lección)* review. `COMP` **curso de repaso** refresher course.

**repatriar** *vt* to repatriate.

**repecho** *nm* short steep slope.

**repelente** *adj* repellent, repulsive.

**repeler** *vt* **1** *(rechazar)* to repel, repulse. **2** *(repugnar)* to disgust, repel.

**repente** *nm* **1** *fam (movimiento)* sudden movement. **2** *fam (ataque)* fit. `LOC` **de repente** suddenly, all of a sudden.

**repentino,-a** *adj* sudden.

**repercusión** *nf* repercussion.

**repercutir** *vi fig (trascender)* to have repercussions (en, on), affect.

**repertorio** *nm* **1** *(resumen)* list, index. **2** TEAT repertoire, repertory.

**repesca** *nf fam* second chance; *(examen)* resit. `LOC` **hacer un examen de repesca** to resit an exam.

**repetición** *nf (gen)* repetition.

**repetido,-a** *adj* repeated.

**repetidor,-ra** *nm & nf* EDUC repeat student.
▶ *nm* **repetidor** TÉC relay, booster station.

**repetir** *vt* **1** *(gen)* to repeat: *se lo repetí dos veces* I told him twice. **2** *(volver a hacer)* to do again, do over again.
▶ *vi* **1** *(volver a servirse)* to have a second helping. **2** EDUC to repeat a year.
▶ *vpr* **repetirse** **1** *(persona)* to repeat OS. **2** *(hecho)* to recur.

**repetitivo,-a** *adj* repetitive.

**repicar** *vt (campanas)* to peal, ring out.

**repique** *nm* peal, ringing.

**repisa** *nf* ledge, shelf.

**replantear** *vt (asunto, problema)* to reconsider, rethink.

**replegarse** *vpr* to withdraw, retreat.

**repleto,-a** *adj* jam-packed (de, with).

**réplica** *nf* **1** *(respuesta)* answer, reply.

**replicar** *vt (contestar)* to answer, reply.
▶ *vi* to argue, answer back.

**repliegue** *nm (pliegue)* fold, crease.

**repoblar** *vt* to repopulate; *(bosque)* to reafforest, reforest.

**repollo** *nm* cabbage.

**reponer** *vt* **1** *(reemplazar)* to replace. **2** *(en el cine)* to rerun.
▶ *vpr* **reponerse** *(salud, susto)* to recover.

**reportaje** *nm* **1** *(prensa, radio)* report. **2** *(noticias)* article, news item.

**reportero,-a** *nm & nf* reporter.

**R**

**reposar** *vi* **1** *(descansar)* to rest, take a rest. **2** *(yacer)* to rest, lie, be buried. **3** *(un líquido)* to settle. LOC **dejar reposar** CULIN to leave to stand.

**reposo** *nm* **1** *(descanso)* rest. **2** *(tranquilidad)* peace.

**repostar** *vt* **1** *(provisiones)* to stock up with. **2** *(coche)* to fill up.

**repostería** *nf* *(pastas)* cakes *pl*; *(chocolate, bombones)* confectionery.

**reprender** *vt* to reprimand, scold.

**represa** *nf* dam.

**represalia** *nf* reprisal, retaliation.

**representación** *nf* **1** *(gen)* representation. **2** TEAT performance. LOC **en representación de** as a representative of.

**representante** *adj* representative.
  ▶ *nm o nf* representative.

**representar** *vt* **1** *(gen)* to represent. **2** *(símbolo)* to represent, stand for: *una paloma representa la paz* a dove stands for peace. **3** TEAT *(obra)* to perform; *(papel)* to play (the part of).

**representativo,-a** *adj* representative.

**represión** *nf* repression.

**represivo,-a** *adj* repressive.

**reprimenda** *nf* reprimand.

**reprimido,-a** *adj* repressed.
  ▶ *nm & nf* repressed person.

**reprimir** *vt* *(gen)* to repress, suppress.
  ▶ *vpr* **reprimirse** to control OS.

**reprochar** *vt* to reproach, censure.

**reproche** *nm* reproach, criticism.

**reproducción** *nf* reproduction.

**reproducir** *vt* to reproduce, repeat.
  ▶ *vpr* **reproducirse 1** *(gen)* to reproduce. **2** *(volver a ocurrir)* to recur.

**reproductor,-ra** *adj* **1** *(gen)* reproducing. **2** ANAT reproductive.

**reptar** *vi* *(arrastrarse)* to crawl, slither.

**reptil** *nm* reptile.

**república** *nf* republic.

**republicano,-a** *adj* republican.
  ▶ *nm & nf* republican.

**repudiar** *vt* to repudiate.

**repuesto,-a** *nm* **1** *(prevención)* store, supply, stock. **2** *(recambio)* spare, spare part. LOC **de repuesto** spare, in reserve.

**repugnante** *adj* repugnant, disgusting.

**repugnar** *vt* **1** *(negar)* to deny. **2** *(contradecir)* to contradict.

**repujado,-a** *adj* embossed, repoussé.

**repujar** *vt* to emboss.

**repulsión** *nf* repulsion, repugnance.

**repulsivo,-a** *adj* repulsive, revolting.

**repuntar** *vi* **1** *(la marea)* to turn. **2** *(economía)* to recover, pick up.

**reputación** *nf* reputation.

**requemado,-a** *adj* scorched, burnt.

**requemar** *vt* **1** *(gen)* to scorch, burn.

**requerimiento** *nm* **1** *(súplica)* request. **2** JUR *(aviso)* summons *pl*; *(intimación)* injunction.

**requerir** *vt* **1** *(necesitar)* to require, need: *esto requiere gran paciencia* this requires a lot of patience. **2** *(decir con autoridad)* to demand, call for. **3** *(solicitar)* to request.

**requesón** *nm* cottage cheese.

**réquiem** *nm* requiem.

**requisar** *vt* **1** MIL to requisition. **2** *fam (apropiarse)* to grab, swipe.

**requisito** *nm* requisite, requirement.

**res** *nf* *(gen)* beast, animal; *(cabeza de ganado)* head.

**resaca** *nf* **1** *(de las olas)* undertow, undercurrent. **2** *(de borrachera)* hangover.

**resaltar** *vi* fig *(distinguirse)* to stand out (de, from).
  ▶ *vt* to highlight, stress, emphasize.

**resbaladizo,-a** *adj* slippery.

**resbalar** *vi* **1** *(deslizarse)* to slide. **2** *(sin querer - persona)* to slip.

**resbalón** *nm* slip.

**rescatar** *vt* **1** *(rehén, náufrago, persona atrapada, etc)* to rescue; *(cadáver)* to recover. **2** *(ciudad)* to recapture. **2** *(recuperar)* to recover.

**rescate** *nm* **1** *(salvamento)* rescue; *(de ciudad)* recapture. **2** *(dinero)* ransom. **3** *(recuperación)* recovery, recapture.

**resecar** *vt* to dry up.
  ▶ *vpr* **resecarse** to dry up.

**reseco,-a** *adj (seco)* very dry, parched.

**resentido,-a** *adj* resentful. LOC **estar resentido,-a con** ALGN to bear resentment towards SB.

**resentimiento** *nm* resentment.

**reseña** *nf* **1** *(crítica)* review; *(en prensa)* write-up. **2** *(descripción)* description.

**reseñar** *vt* **1** *(crítica)* to review. **2** *(describir)* to describe.

**reserva** *nf* **1** *(de plazas, entradas)* booking, reservation. **2** *(provisión)* reserve; *(existencias)* stock. **3** *(cautela)* reservation. **4** *(discreción)* discretion, reserve. **5** *(vino)* vintage. **6** *(de animales)* reserve; *(de personas)* reservation. **7** MIL reserve, reserves *pl*.
▶ *nf pl* **reservas** COM reserves, stock *sing*.

**reservado,-a** *adj* **1** *(persona)* reserved. **2** *(asunto)* confidential.
▶ *nm* **reservado** *(en local)* private room; *(en tren)* reserved compartment.

**reservar** *vt* **1** *(plazas, etc)* to book, reserve. **2** *(guardar)* to keep, save. **3** *(ocultar)* to withhold, keep to OS.
▶ *vpr* **reservarse 1** *(conservarse)* to save OS *(para,* for). **2** to withhold, keep to OS: *se reservó su opinión* she kept her opinion to herself.

**resfriado,-a** *adj* with a cold.
▶ *nm* **resfriado** cold.

**resfriar** *vt (enfriar)* to cool.
▶ *vpr* **resfriarse** MED to catch a cold.

**resguardar** *vt* **1** *(proteger)* to protect (de, from), shelter (de, from). **2** *(salvaguardar)* to safeguard (de, against).
▶ *vpr* **resguardarse** *(protegerse)* to protect OS.

**resguardo** *nm* **1** *(protección)* protection, shelter. **2** *(garantía)* safeguard, guarantee. **3** *(recibo)* receipt, ticket.

**residencia** *nf (gen)* residence. COMP **residencia de ancianos** old people's home.

**residir** *vi* **1** to reside (en, in), live (en, in). **2** *fig* to lie (en, in).

**residuo** *nm* residue.
▶ *nm pl* **residuos** waste *sing*, refuse *sing*.

**resignación** *nf* resignation.

**resignado,-a** *adj* resigned.

**resignar** *vt* to resign, relinquish.
▶ *vpr* **resignarse** to resign OS (a, to).

**resina** *nf* resin.

**resistencia** *nf* **1** *(gen)* resistance. **2** *(aguante)* endurance, stamina. **3** *(oposición)* resistance, opposition. **4** ELEC resistance. **5** *(de materiales)* strength.

**resistente** *adj* **1** *(que resiste)* resistant (a, to). **2** *(fuerte)* tough, strong.

**resistir** *vi* **1** *(aguantar - algo)* to hold (out); *(- alguien)* to hold out, take (it), have endurance. **2** *(durar)* to endure, last. **3** *(ejército)* to hold out, resist.
▶ *vt* **1** *(soportar)* to stand, tolerate. **2** *(peso, etc)* to bear, withstand, take. **3** *(tentación, etc)* to resist.
▶ *vpr* **resistirse 1** *(rechazar)* to resist. **2** *fam (costar)* to be difficult, be hard: *la física se le resiste* he's struggling with physics. **3** *(negarse)* to refuse: *me resisto a creerlo* I find it hard to believe.

**resolución** *nf* **1** *(decisión)* resolution, decision; *(determinación)* determination, resolve. **2** *(solución)* solution; *(de un conflicto)* settlement; *(en técnica)* resolution.

**resolver** *vt* **1** *(solucionar - gen)* to resolve, solve; *(- asunto, conflicto)* to resolve, settle; *(- dificultad)* to overcome. **2** *(decidir)* to resolve, decide (-, to). **3** *(deshacer)* to resolve. **4** QUÍM to dissolve.
▶ *vpr* **resolverse 1** *(solucionarse)* to be solved; *(resultar)* to work out. **2** *(reducirse)* to end up (en, in), turn out.

**resonancia** *nf* **1** resonance. **2** *(eco)* echo. **3** *fig (importancia)* importance; *(consecuencias)* repercussions *pl*.

**resorte** *nm* **1** spring. **2** *fig* means *pl*.

**respaldar** *vt* to support, back (up).
▶ *vpr* **respaldarse 1** to lean back (en, on). **2** *(apoyarse)* to lean (en, on).

**respaldo** *nm* **1** back. **2** *fig* support, backing.

**respectivamente** *adv* respectively.

**respectivo,-a** *adj* respective. LOC **en lo respectivo a** with regard to, regarding.

**respetar** *vt* to respect.

**respeto** nm **1** (gen) respect. **2** fam (miedo) fear.
▶ nm pl **respetos** respects. COMP **falta de respeto** lack of respect.

**respetuoso,-a** adj respectful.

**respiración** nf **1** (acción) breathing, respiration. **2** (aliento) breath more easily, breathe.

**respirar** vi **1** to breathe. **2** (estar vivo) to be breathing. **3** fig (relajarse) to breathe more easily, breathe a sigh of relief: al oír al doctor, respiramos when we heard what the doctor had to say we breathed a sigh of relief. LOC **sin respirar 1** (sin descanso) nonstop. **2** (con atención) attentively.
▶ vt (absorber) to breathe, breathe in, inhale.

**respiratorio,-a** adj respiratory.

**respiro** nm **1** (resuello) breathing. **2** fig (descanso) breather, break. **3** fig (alivio) relief, respite.

**resplandor** nm (de luz) brightness, brilliance; (de metales, cristales) gleam, glitter; (del fuego) glow, blaze.

**responder** vt (contestar) to answer.
▶ vi **1** (contestar) to answer, reply. **2** (replicar) to answer back. **3** (corresponder) to answer, respond to: tengo que responder a su amabilidad I have to respond to his kindness. **4** (tener el efecto deseado) to respond: el motor respondió bien the engine responded well. **5** (ser responsable) to answer (de, for), accept responsibility (de, for).

**responsabilidad** nf responsibility.

**responsable** adj responsible.
▶ nm o nf **1** (encargado) person in charge. **2** (de un crimen) perpetrator, culprit, person responsible. LOC **hacerse responsable de** ALGO to assume responsibility for STH.

**respuesta** nf **1** (gen) answer, reply. **2** (reacción) response. LOC **en respuesta a** in response to.

**resquebrajar** vt to crack.
▶ vpr **resquebrajarse** to crack.

**resta** nf subtraction.

**restablecer** vt (gen) to reestablish; (orden, monarquía) to restore.

▶ vpr **restablecerse 1** (gen) to be reestablished; (orden, etc) to be restored. **2** MED to recover, get better.

**restablecimiento** nm **1** (gen) reestablishment; (orden, etc) restoration. **2** MED recovery.

**restante** adj remaining.
▶ nm **lo restante** the rest, the remainder, what is left over.

**restar** vt **1** MAT to subtract, take (away). **2** fig (quitar) to reduce, deduct. **3** DEP to return.
▶ vi (quedar) to be left, remain. LOC **restar importancia a** ALGO to play STH down, play down the importance of STH.

**restauración** nf (restablecimiento) restoration.

**restaurante** nm restaurant.

**restaurar** vt (obra, etc) to restore.

**resto** nm **1** remainder, rest. **2** MAT remainder.
▶ nm pl **restos 1** (gen) remains; (ruinas) ruins. **2** (de comida) leftovers.

**restricción** nf restriction.

**restringir** vt **1** (limitar) to restrict, limit. **2** (astringir) to contract.

**resucitar** vt **1** to resuscitate. **2** fig to revive.
▶ vi to resuscitate.

**resuelto,-a** adj (decidido) resolute, determined.

**resultado** nm result.

**resultar** vi **1** (gen) to result, be the result of. **2** (ser) to be: resultó vencedor he won. **3** (acabar siendo) to turn out to be: resultó ser muy agradable he turned out to be very nice. **4** (salir) to come out, turn out, work out: todo resultó como esperábamos it all worked out as we expected. **5** (ocurrir) to turn out: resulta que está enfermo y no puede venir it turns out that he's ill and can't come. **6** (ser conveniente) to be advisable. **7** (tener éxito) to be a success, come off: el negocio resultó the business was a success. LOC **resulta que** it turns out that.

**resumen** nm summary.

**resumir** vt **1** (reducir) to summarize. **2** (concluir) to sum up: resumiendo, es una *novela excelente* in short, it's an excellent novel.

▶ *vpr* **resumirse 1** to be summarized, be summed up. **2** *(venir a ser)* to be reduced (en, to), boil down (en, to).

**resurgir** *vi* **1** *(volver a aparecer)* to reappear. **2** *(revivir)* to revive.

**retablo** *nm* altarpiece, reredos.

**retaguarda** *nf* rearguard. LOC **ir a la retaguarda** to bring up the rear.

**retal** *nm* *(de tela)* offcut, remnant.

**retama** *nf* broom.

**retar** *vt* **1** *(desafiar)* to challenge. **2** *fam* *(reprender)* to scold.

**retazo** *nm* remnant, fragment.

**retención** *nf* **1** *(gen)* retention. **2** FIN withholding, deduction. **3** *(de tráfico)* traffic jam, (traffic) hold-up.

**retener** *vt* **1** *(contener)* to restrain, hold back. **2** *(no dejar marchar)* to keep, keep back: *no quiero retenerte* I don't want to keep you. **3** *(no devolver)* to keep. **4** *(en la memoria)* to retain, remember. **5** *(detener)* to detain; *(arrestar)* to arrest. **6** FIN to deduct, withhold. **7** *(absorber)* to retain, hold: *el algodón retiene el agua* cotton holds water.

▶ *vpr* **retenerse** to restrain os, hold os back.

**retina** *nf* retina.

**retirada** *nf* MIL retreat, withdrawal.

**retirado,-a** *adj* **1** *(apartado)* remote. **2** *(tranquilo)* secluded, quiet. **3** *(jubilado)* retired.

▶ *nm & nf* retired person, US retiree.

**retirar** *vt* **1** *(apartar - gen)* to take away, remove; *(- un mueble)* to move away. **2** *(un carnet)* to take away. **3** *(algo dicho)* to take back. **4** *(dinero, ley, moneda)* to withdraw. **5** *(jubilar)* to retire.

▶ *vpr* **retirarse 1** MIL to retreat, withdraw. **2** *(apartarse del mundo)* to go into seclusion. **3** *(apartarse)* to withdraw, draw back, move back: *retírate, no veo* move back, I can't see. **4** *(alejarse)* to move away: *retírate de la ventana* move away from the window. **5** *(irse a descansar)* to retire: *se retiró a su habitación* she retired to her bedroom. **7** *(jubilarse)* to

retire. LOC **no se retire** *(al teléfono)* hold on, don't hang up.

**retiro** *nm* **1** *(jubilación)* retirement. **2** *(pensión)* pension.

**reto** *nm* challenge.

**retocar** *vt* *(dibujo, fotografía)* to touch up, retouch.

**retoque** *nm* finishing touch.

**retorcer** *vt* **1** *(gen)* to twist. **2** *(ropa)* to wring (out).

▶ *vpr* **retorcerse 1** *(gen)* to become twisted, twist. **2** *(doblarse)* to bend. LOC **retorcerse de risa** *fig* to double up with laughter.

**retorcido,-a** *adj fig* twisted: *mente retorcida* warped mind.

**retornable** *adj* returnable. LOC «**Envase no retornable**» "Non-returnable".

**retorno** *nm* **1** return. **2** *(recompensa)* reward.

**retortijón** *nm* *(de tripas)* stomach cramp.

**retozar** *vi* to frolic, gambol.

**retraído,-a** *adj* **1** *(tímido)* shy, reserved. **2** *(poco comunicativo)* unsociable, withdrawn.

**retraimiento** *nm* *(timidez)* shyness, reserve, retiring nature.

**retransmisión** *nf* broadcast, transmission.

**retransmitir** *vt* RAD TV to broadcast. LOC **retransmitir** ALGO **en directo** to broadcast STH live.

**retrasado,-a** *adj* **1** *(en conocimientos, trabajo)* behind. **2** *(pagos)* late. **3** *(reloj)* slow. **4** *(tren, avión, etc)* delayed. **5** *(país)* backward, underdeveloped.

▶ *nm & nf* mentally retarded person.

**retrasar** *vt* **1** *(atrasar)* to delay, put off, postpone. **2** *(reloj)* to put back. **3** DEP to pass back.

▶ *vpr* **retrasarse 1** *(atrasarse)* to be late, arrive late, be delayed. **2** *(reloj)* to be slow. **3** *(trabajo, conocimientos, pagos)* to fall behind.

**retraso** *nm* **1** *(demora)* delay. **2** *(subdesarrollo)* backwardness, underdevelopment.

**R**

**retratar** vt 1 *(pintura)* to portray, paint a portrait of. 2 *(foto)* to photograph, take a photograph of. 3 *fig* to describe, portray, depict.
▶ *vpr* **retratarse** *(darse a conocer)* to be described, be portrayed.

**retrato** nm 1 *(pintura)* portrait. 2 *(foto)* photograph. 3 *fig (descripción)* description, depiction, portrayal. [LOC] **ser el vivo retrato de** ALGN to be the spitting image of SB.

**retrete** nm toilet, lavatory.

**retribución** nf 1 *(pago)* pay, payment. 2 *(recompensa)* recompense, reward.

**retribuir** vt 1 *(pagar)* to pay. 2 *(recompensar)* to remunerate, reward.

**retroceder** vi 1 *(recular)* to go back, move back. 2 *(bajar de nivel)* to go down.

**retroceso** nm 1 *(movimiento)* backward movement. 2 *(económico)* recession.

**retrógrado,-a** adj 1 *(que retrocede)* retrograde. 2 *fig (reaccionario)* reactionary.
▶ nm & nf *(reaccionario)* reactionary.

**retrospectivo,-a** adj retrospective.

**retumbar** vi 1 *(resonar)* to resound, echo. 2 *(tronar)* to thunder, boom.

**reuma** nm rheumatism.

**reúma** nm rheumatism.

**reumático,-a** adj rheumatic.
▶ nm & nf rheumatic.

**reumatismo** nm rheumatism.

**reunificar** vt to reunify.

**reunión** nf *(gen)* meeting, gathering.

**reunir** vt 1 *(congregar)* get together. 2 *(juntar algo)* to put together: *reunimos todos nuestros libros* we put all our books together. 3 *(recoger)* to gather (together); *(dinero)* to raise. 4 *(coleccionar)* to collect. 5 *(tener)* to have, possess. 6 *(requisitos)* to satisfy, meet, fulfil (US fulfill).
▶ *vpr* **reunirse** to meet (con, -), get together, have a meeting with.

**reutilizar** vt to reuse.

**reválida** nf final examination.

**revalidar** vt to confirm, ratify, validate.

**revalorización** nf *(de moneda)* revaluation; *(de precio)* appreciation, increase in value.

**revalorizar** vt *(moneda)* to revalue; *(precio)* to increase the value of.
▶ *vpr* **revalorizarse** *(moneda)* to revalue; *(precio)* to appreciate, go up in value.

**revancha** nf 1 revenge. 2 *(en naipes)* return game. 3 DEP return match.

**revelación** nf revelation.

**revelado** nm developing.

**revelador,-ra** adj revealing.
▶ nm **revelador** developer.

**revelar** vt 1 to reveal, disclose. 2 *(fotos)* to develop.

**revender** vt 1 *(gen)* to resell. 2 *(al por menor)* to retail. 3 *(entradas)* to tout.

**reventa** nf 1 *(gen)* resale. 2 *(al por menor)* retail. 3 *(de entradas)* touting.

**reventar** vt 1 *(gen)* to burst. 2 *(neumático)* to puncture, burst. 3 *(romper)* to break, smash. 4 *(estropear)* to ruin, spoil. 5 *fig (agotar)* to exhaust, tire out.
▶ vi 1 *fam (fastidiar)* to annoy: *me revientan sus preguntas* her questions get on my nerves. 2 *(estallar)* to burst: *la cañería reventó* the pipe burst.
▶ *vpr* **reventarse** 1 *(estallar)* to burst. 2 *fam (cansarse)* to tire OS out.

**reventón,-ona** nm 1 *(de cañería)* burst. 2 *(de neumático)* blowout.

**reverendo,-a** adj 1 reverend. 2 *fam (enorme)* enormous, great.
▶ nm & nf reverend.

**reversible** adj reversible.

**reverso** nm reverse, back.

**revés** nm 1 *(reverso)* back, reverse, wrong side; *(de tela)* wrong side. 2 *(bofetada)* slap; *(golpe)* backhander. 3 *(en tenis)* backhand (stroke). 4 *fig (contrariedad)* misfortune, setback, reverse. [LOC] **al revés** *(al contrario)* the other way round.

**revestimiento** nm covering, coating.

**revestir** vt 1 *(recubrir)* to cover (de, with), coat (de, with), line (de, with). 3 *fig (presentar)* to take on: *la*

*ceremonia revistió gran solemnidad* the ceremony took on great solemnity.
▶ *vpr* **revestirse** to arm OS: *revestirse de pacienca* to arm OS with patience.

**revisar** *vt* **1** *(gen)* to revise, go through, check. **2** *(examen, etc)* to check, look over. **3** *(cuentas)* to check, audit.

**revisión** *nf* **1** *(gen)* revision, checking. **2** *(de billetes)* inspection. **3** *(de coche)* service, overhaul. COMP **revisión médica** checkup.

**revisor,-ra** *nm & nf* ticket inspector.

**revista** *nf* **1** *(publicación)* magazine, review, journal. **2** *(inspección)* inspection. **3** MIL review. **4** TEAT revue: *chica de revista* chorus girl.

**revistero** *nm* magazine rack.

**revitalizar** *vt* to revitalize.

**revivir** *vi* to revive.
▶ *vt* to revive, bring back to life.

**revocar** *vt* *(ley)* to revoke, repeal; *(orden)* to cancel, rescind.

**revolcar** *vt* *(derribar al suelo)* to knock down, knock over.
▶ *vpr* **revolcarse** *(echarse)* to roll about.

**revolotear** *vi* to fly about, flutter about, hover.

**revoloteo** *nm* fluttering, hovering.

**revoltijo** *nm* *(mezcla)* mess, clutter, jumble.

**revoltoso,-a** *adj* **1** *(rebelde)* rebellious.
▶ *nm & nf* rebel, troublemaker.

**revolución** *nf* revolution.

**revolucionario,-a** *adj* revolutionary.
▶ *nm & nf* revolutionary.

**revolver** *vt* **1** *(agitar)* to stir. **2** *(mezclar)* to mix. **3** *(ensalada)* to toss. **4** *(habitación, casa, etc)* to turn upside down. **5** *(papeles)* to rummage through; *(bolso, bolsillo, etc)* to rummage in. **6** *(producir náuseas)* to upset, turn: *le revolvió el estómago* it turned his stomach.
▶ *vpr* **revolverse 1** *(moverse)* to fidget; *(en la cama)* to toss and turn. **2** *(volverse con rapidez)* to turn around, spin round. **3** *(tiempo)* to turn stormy; *(mar)* to become rough.

**revólver** *nm* revolver.

**revoque** *nm* *(enlucido)* plastering.

**revuelta** *nf* *(revolución)* revolt, riot.

**revuelto,-a** *adj* **1** *(desordenado)* confused, mixed up, in a mess. **2** *(gente)* agitated, restless, up in arms. **3** *(tiempo)* stormy, unsettled; *(mar)* rough. **4** *(época)* turbulent: *tiempos revueltos* turbulent times.

**rey** *nm* king.

**rezar** *vi* **1** *(orar)* to pray. **2** *(decir)* to say, read.

**ría** *nf* *(gen)* estuary, river mouth; *(técnicamente)* ria.

**riachuelo** *nm* brook, stream.

**riada** *nf* **1** flood, flooding. **2** *fig* flood.

**ribera** *nf* **1** *(de río)* bank. **2** *(del mar)* shore, seashore. **3** *(tierra cercana a un río)* riverside, waterfront.

**ribete** *nm* *(cinta)* border, trimming, edging.

**ribetear** *vt* to edge, border.

**ribonucleico,-a** *adj* ribonucleic.

**rico,-a** *adj* **1** *(acaudalado)* rich, wealthy. **2** *(abundante)* rich: *rico en potasio* rich in potassium. **3** *(sabroso)* tasty, delicious. **4** *(tierra)* rich, fertile. **5** *(excelente)* rich, excellent. **6** *fam* *(bonito)* lovely, adorable: *tiene un niño muy rico* she's got a lovely boy.
▶ *nm & nf* rich person.

**ridiculizar** *vt* to ridicule, deride.

**ridículo,-a** *adj* ridiculous, absurd.
▶ *nm* **ridículo** ridicule. LOC **hacer el ridículo** to make a fool of OS.

**riego** *nm* irrigation, watering. COMP **riego sanguíneo** blood circulation.

**riel** *nm* rail.

**rienda** *nf* **1** rein. **2** *fig* *(control)* restraint. LOC **llevar las riendas** *fig* to hold the reins, be in control.

**riesgo** *nm* risk, danger. LOC **a todo riesgo** *(seguro)* fully-comprehensive.

**rifa** *nf* raffle.

**rifar** *vt* to raffle (off).
▶ *vpr* **rifarse 1** MAR to split. **2** *(solicitar, desear)* to fight over.

**rifle** *nm* rifle.

**rigidez** *nf* **1** *(dureza)* stiffness, rigidity. **2** *fig* *(rectitud)* strictness, firmness, inflexibility.

R

**rígido,-a** *adj* **1** *(duro)* rigid, stiff. **2** *fig (severo)* strict, firm, inflexible.

**rigor** *nm* **1** *(severidad)* rigour (US rigor), strictness, severity. **2** *(dureza)* rigour (US rigor), harshness. **3** *(exactitud)* precision, exactness.

**rigurosamente** *adv* **1** *(con severidad)* rigorously, severely, strictly. **2** *(con exactitud)* accurately. **3** *(minuciosamente)* meticulously. **4** *(totalmente)* absolutely.

**rigurosidad** *nf* rigorousness, strictness.

**riguroso,-a** *adj* **1** *(severo)* rigorous, severe, strict. **2** *(clima)* rigorous, severe, harsh. **3** *(exacto)* exact. **4** *(minucioso)* meticulous.

**rima** *nf* rhyme.
   ▶ *nf pl* **rimas** poem *sing*.

**rimar** *vt* to rhyme.
   ▶ *vi* to rhyme.

**rincón** *nm* corner.

**rinconera** *nf* corner unit.

**ring** *nm* ring.

**rinoceronte** *nm* rhinoceros.

**riña** *nf* **1** *(pelea)* fight. **2** *(discusión)* quarrel.

**riñón** *nm* **1** kidney.

**río** *nm* **1** river. **2** *fig* stream, river: *un río de sangre* a river of blood.

**riqueza** *nf* *(cualidad)* richness, wealthiness.

**risa** *nf* **1** laugh. **2** *(risas)* laughter. LOC **darle risa a ALGN** to make SB laugh. **entrar la risa** to begin to laugh. ▌**ser cosa de risa** to be laughable. COMP **ataque de risa** fit of laughter.

**risco** *nm* crag, cliff.

**ristra** *nf* string.

**risueño,-a** *adj* **1** *(sonriente)* smiling. **2** *(animado)* cheerful.

**rítmico,-a** *adj* rhythmic, rhythmical.

**ritmo** *nm* **1** rhythm. **2** *fig* pace, speed.

**rito** *nm* **1** REL rite. **2** *fig (costumbre)* ritual.

**ritual** *adj* ritual.
   ▶ *nm* ritual.

**rival** *adj* rival.
   ▶ *nm o nf* rival.

**rivalidad** *nf* rivalry.

**rivalizar** *vi* to rival.

**rivera** *nf* brook, stream.

**rizado,-a** *adj* **1** *(pelo)* curly. **2** MAR choppy.
   ▶ *nm* **rizado** *(de pelo)* curling.

**rizar** *vt* *(pelo)* to curl.
   ▶ *vpr* **rizarse 1** *(pelo)* to curl, go curly. **2** *(el mar)* to ripple.

**rizo** *nm* **1** *(de pelo)* curl. **2** *(en el agua)* ripple. **3** *(tejido)* towelling (US toweling), terry towelling. **4** AV loop.

**rizoma** *nm* rhizome.

**robar** *vt* **1** *(banco, persona)* to rob; *(objeto)* to steal; *(casa)* to break into, burgle. **2** *(raptar)* to kidnap. **3** *(en naipes)* to draw. **4** *fig (cobrar muy caro)* to rip off. **5** *fig (corazón, alma)* to steal.

**robinia** *nf* robinia, false acacia.

**roble** *nm* oak, oak tree.

**robledal** *nm* oak grove, oak wood.

**robo** *nm* **1** *(gen)* theft, robbery; *(en casa)* burglary; *(en banco)* robbery. **2** *(en naipes)* draw. **3** *fig (estafa)* robbery.

**robot** *nm* robot.

**robótica** *nf* robotics.

**robótico,-a** *adj* robotic, robot-like.

**robotizar** *vt* to automate.

**robustecer** *vt* to strengthen.
   ▶ *vpr* **robustecerse** to grow stronger, gain strength.

**robusto,-a** *adj* robust, strong, sturdy.

**roca** *nf* rock.

**roce** *nm* **1** *(fricción)* rubbing; *(en piel)* chafing. **2** *(señal - en zapatos)* scuff mark; *(- en piel)* graze; *(- en coche, etc)* mark. **3** *(contacto físico)* light touch, brush. **4** *fam (trato)* contact. **5** *fam (disensión)* friction, brush.

**rociar** *vt* **1** *(salpicar)* to spray, sprinkle. **2** *fig (esparcir)* to scatter, strew.

**rocín** *nm* *(caballo)* nag, hack.

**rocío** *nm* dew.

**rock** *nm* rock.

**rockero,-a** *nm & nf (músico)* rock musician; *(fan)* rock fan.

**rococó** *adj* rococo.

**rocoso,-a** *adj* rocky, stony.

**rodaballo** *nm* turbot.

**rodaja** *nf* slice. LOC **en rodajas** sliced.

**rodaje** *nm* **1** CINE filming, shooting. **2** AUTO running-in.

**rodamiento** *nm* bearing.

**rodapié** *nm* skirting board, US baseboard.

**rodar** *vi* **1** *(dar vueltas)* to roll; *(rueda)* to turn. **2** *(caer rodando)* to roll down. **3** *fig (ir de un lado a otro)* to roam. **4** *(vehículos)* to run; *(velocidad)* to do.
▶ *vt* **1** *(hacer que dé vueltas)* to roll. **2** CINE to film, shoot. **3** AUTO to run in. **4** *(recorrer)* to travel.

**rodear** *vt (cercar)* to surround, encircle.
▶ *vpr* **rodearse** to surround OS *(de,* with).

**rodela** *nf* round shield.

**rodeno,-a** *adj* red.

**rodeo** *nm* **1** *(desviación)* detour. **2** *fig (elusión)* evasiveness.

**rodera** *nf* tyre (US tire) mark, track.

**rodilla** *nf* **1** ANAT knee. **2** *(paño)* cloth, floorcloth.

**rodillazo** *nm* blow with the knee, blow to the knee.

**rodillera** *nf* **1** DEP knee pad. **2** COST knee patch.

**rodillo** *nm* **1** roller. **2** CULIN rolling pin.

**rododendro** *nm* rhododendron.

**rodomiel** *nm* rose honey.

**roedor,-ra** *adj* rodent.
▶ *nm* **roedor** rodent.

**roer** *vt* **1** *(hueso)* to gnaw. **2** *fig (desgastar)* to wear away.

**rogar** *vt (pedir)* to request, ask; *(implorar)* to beg, implore, plead.

**rogativa** *nf* rogation.

**roído,-a** *adj* gnawed, eaten away.

**rojear** *vi* to redden, turn red.

**rojez** *nf* redness.

**rojizo,-a** *adj* reddish.

**rojo,-a** *adj (color)* red.
▶ *nm & nf* POL *(gen)* red, Communist.
▶ *nm* **rojo** red.

**rol** *nm (papel)* role.

**rollista** *nm o nf fam (cuentista)* over-dramatic person.

**rollizo,-a** *adj* plump, chubby.

**rollo** *nm* **1** *(gen)* roll. **2** *fam (aburrimiento)* drag, bore, pain: *esta peli es un rollo* this film is a drag. **3** *fam (discurso, explicación, etc)* long drawn-out speech, boring lecture. **4** *fam (amorío)* affair. **5** *fam (asunto)* business.

**romance** *adj* LING Romance.
▶ *nm* **1** LING *(gen)* Romance language; *(castellano)* Spanish. **2** *(amorío)* romance.

**romancero** *nm* collection of romances.

**románico,-a** *adj* **1** *(arquitectura, arte - gen)* Romanesque. **2** *(lengua)* Romance.

**romanizar** *vt* to Romanize.

**romanticismo** *nm* romanticism.

**romántico,-a** *adj* romantic.
▶ *nm & nf* romantic.

**rómbico,-a** *adj* rhombic.

**rombo** *nm* **1** rhombus. **2** *(naipes)* diamond.

**romboedro** *nm* rhombohedron.

**romboide** *nm* rhomboid.

**romería** *nf* pilgrimage.

**romero** *nm* BOT rosemary.

**romo,-a** *adj (sin punta)* blunt, dull.

**rompecabezas** *nm inv* **1** *(juego)* (jigsaw) puzzle. **2** *fig (problema)* riddle, puzzle, conundrum.

**rompecocos** *nm inv* brain-teaser.

**rompecorazones** *nm o nf inv fam* heart-throb, heartbreaker.

**rompehielos** *nm inv* icebreaker.

**rompeolas** *nm inv* breakwater, jetty.

**romper** *vt* **1** *(gen)* to break; *(papel, tela)* to tear. **2** *(rajar, reventar)* to split. **3** *(gastar)* to wear out. **4** *fig (relaciones)* to break off. **5** *fig (ley)* to break. **6** *fig (cerca, límite)* to break through, break down.
▶ *vi* **1** *fig (acabar - con algo)* to break; *(- con alguien)* to split up, US break up. **2** *(olas, día)* to break. **3** **romper a +** *inf fig (empezar)* to burst out: *romper a reír* to burst out laughing. **4** **romper en +** *sust fig (prorrumpir)* to burst into: *romper en llanto* to burst into tears.
▶ *vpr* **romperse** **1** *(gen)* to break: *se me ha roto esta uña* I've broken this nail. **2** *(papel, tela)* to tear, rip. **3** *(rajarse, reven-*

**R**

*tarse*) to split. **4** (*desgastarse*) to wear out: *se me han roto los zapatos* my shoes are worn out. **5** (*coche*) to break down.

**ron** *nm* rum.

**roncar** *vi* to snore.

**roncha** *nf* (*en la piel*) swelling, lump, spot.

**ronco,-a** *adj* hoarse.

**ronda** *nf* **1** (*patrulla*) patrol, watch. **2** (*de policía*) beat. **3** (*vuelta*) round. **4** (*de bebidas, cartas*) round. **5** (*negociaciones*) round. LOC **hacer la ronda** to do one's rounds.

**rondar** *vt* **1** (*vigilar*) to patrol, do the rounds of. **2** (*merodear*) to prowl around, hang about, haunt: *siempre ronda la casa* he's always prowling around the house. **3** *fig* (*años*) to be about: *ronda los cincuenta* she's about fifty.
▶ *vi* **1** (*vigilar*) to patrol. **2** (*merodear*) to prowl around, roam around.

**ronquera** *nf* hoarseness.

**ronquido** *nm* snore, snoring.

**ronronear** *vi* to purr.

**ronroneo** *nm* purring.

**roña** *nf* (*suciedad*) filth, dirt.

**roñería** *nf fam* meanness, stinginess.

**roñica** *nm o nf fam* scrooge, miser.

**roñoso,-a** *adj* **1** (*sucio*) filthy, dirty. **2** *fam* (*tacaño*) mean, stingy.
▶ *nm & nf fam* scrooge, miser.

**ropa** *nf* clothing, clothes *pl*: *ropa de invierno* winter clothes; *ropa de esquí* ski wear. COMP **ropa blanca** linen, household linen. ‖ **ropa interior** underwear.

**ropero** *nm* wardrobe, US closet.

**roquefort** *nm* (*específicamente*) Roquefort; (*en general*) blue cheese.

**roquero,-a** *adj-nm & nf* → rockero,-a.

**rosa** *nf* (*flor*) rose.
▶ *nm* (*color*) pink.
▶ *adj* **1** (*color*) pink. **2** *fig* (*novela*) romantic. LOC **fresco,-a como una rosa** *fig* as fresh as a daisy.

**rosado,-a** *adj* **1** (*color*) rosy, pink. **2** (*vino*) rosé.
▶ *nm* **rosado** (*vino*) rosé.

**rosal** *nm* rosebush.

**rosaleda** *nf* rose garden.

**rosario** *nm* **1** REL rosary, beads *pl*. **2** *fig* string, series: *rosario de mentiras* string of lies. LOC **rezar el rosario** to say the rosary.

**rosbif** *nm* roast beef.

**rosca** *nf* **1** (*de tornillo*) thread. **2** CULIN doughnut. **3** (*carnosidad*) roll of fat. **4** (*anilla*) ring.

**rosco** *nm* ring-shaped bread roll.

**roscón** *nm* ring-shaped pastry; (*de Pascua*) Easter ring.

**rosetón** *nm* rose window.

**rosquilla** *nf* doughnut, ring-shaped pastry.

**rostro** *nm fml* (*cara*) face.

**rotación** *nf* rotation.

**rotativo,-a** *adj* rotary, revolving.
▶ *nm* **rotativo** newspaper.

**roto,-a** *adj* **1** (*gen*) broken. **2** (*tela, papel*) torn. **3** (*gastado*) worn out. **4** (*cansado*) tired.
▶ *nm* **roto** (*agujero*) hole, tear.

**rotonda** *nf* (*plaza*) roundabout, US traffic circle.

**rótula** *nf* ANAT kneecap.

**rotulación** *nf* lettering, labelling.

**rotulador** *nm* felt-tip pen.

**rotular** *vt* to label.

**rotulista** *nm o nf* signwriter.

**rótulo** *nm* **1** (*letrero*) sign; (*luminoso*) neon sign. **2** (*titular*) heading, title.

**rotundo,-a** *adj* **1** (*redondo*) round. **2** *fig* (*éxito*) resounding. **3** (*negativa*) flat, categorical; (*afirmación*) categorical, emphatic: *un no rotundo* a flat refusal.

**rotura** *nf* **1** (*gen*) break, breaking, crack. **2** (*en tela, papel*) tear, rip. **3** MED fracture.

**roturar** *vt* to plough (US plow).

**roulotte** *nf* caravan.

**rozadura** *nf* scratch, abrasion.

**rozamiento** *nm* (*roce*) rubbing, friction.

**rozar** *vt* **1** (*tocar ligeramente*) to touch lightly, brush. **2** (*raspar*) to rub against,

brush against; *(herir)* to graze: *el zapato me roza el pie* my shoe's rubbing my foot.
▶ *vi* **1** *(raspar)* to rub. **2** *fig (tener relación)* to border (con, on), verge (con, on).
▶ *vpr* **rozarse 1** *(rasparse)* to rub (con, against), brush (con, against). **2** *(desgastarse)* to wear (out). **3** *fig (tratarse)* to come into contact (con, with), rub shoulders (con, with).

**Ruanda** *nf* Rwanda.

**ruandés,-esa** *adj* Rwandan.
▶ *nm & nf* Rwandan.

**rubeola** *nf* German measles, rubella.

**rubí** *nm* ruby.

**rubia** *nf* blonde.

**rubio,-a** *adj* **1** *(cabello)* fair; *(persona)* fair-haired; *(hombre)* blond; *(mujer)* blonde. **2** *(tabaco)* Virginia.
▶ *nm & nf (hombre)* blond; *(mujer)* blonde.

**rublo** *nm* rouble.

**rubor** *nm* blush, flush.

**ruborizarse** *vpr* to blush, go red, redden.

**rúbrica** *nf* **1** *(de firma)* flourish (in signature). **2** *(título)* title, heading.

**ruda** *nf* rue.

**rudeza** *nf* roughness, coarseness.

**rudimentario,-a** *adj* rudimentary.

**rudo,-a** *adj* rough, coarse.

**rueca** *nf* distaff.

**rueda** *nf* **1** *(gen)* wheel: *de cuatro ruedas* four-wheeled. **2** *(círculo)* circle, ring. COMP **rueda de la fortuna** wheel of fortune. **I rueda de molino** millstone. **I rueda de prensa** press conference. **I rueda de recambio** spare wheel. **I rueda delantera** front wheel.

**ruedo** *nm (en las plazas de toros)* bullring, arena.

**ruego** *nm* request, petition. COMP **ruegos y preguntas** any other business.

**rufián** *nm (canalla)* scoundrel, villain, ruffian.

**rugby** *nm* rugby.

**rugido** *nm* roar, bellow.

**rugir** *vi* to roar, bellow; *(viento)* to howl; *(tripas)* to rumble.

**rugosidad** *nf* rugosity.

**rugoso,-a** *adj* rough, wrinkled.

**ruibarbo** *nm* rhubarb.

**ruido** *nm* **1** *(gen)* noise. **2** *(sonido)* sound. **3** *(jaleo)* din, row. **4** *fig* stir, commotion. LOC **hacer ruido 1** to make a noise. **2** *fig* to cause a stir. **I mucho ruido y pocas nueces** *fam* much ado about nothing.

**ruidoso,-a** *adj* **1** noisy, loud. **2** *fig* sensational.

**ruin** *adj* **1** *pey (vil)* mean, base, despicable, vile. **2** *(pequeño)* petty, insignificant. **3** *(tacaño)* stingy, mean.

**ruina** *nf* **1** ruin, collapse. **2** *fig* fall, end, downfall.
▶ *nf pl* **ruinas** ruins. LOC **estar hecho,-a una ruina** *fig* to be a wreck.

**ruindad** *nf* **1** *(maldad)* meanness, vileness. **2** *(acto)* mean act, low trick.

**ruinoso,-a** *adj* **1** ruinous, disastrous. **2** *fig* tumbledown, dilapidated.

**ruiseñor** *nm* nightingale.

**rular** *vt (funcionar)* to work.

**ruleta** *nf* roulette.

**rulot** *nf* caravan.

**Rumanía** *nf* Romania.

**rumano,-a** *adj* Romanian, Rumanian.
▶ *nm & nf (persona)* Romanian, Rumanian.
▶ *nm* **rumano** *(idioma)* Romanian, Rumanian.

**rumba** *nf* rumba, rhumba.

**rumbo** *nm* **1** *(dirección)* course, direction. **2** *fam fig (pompa)* pomp, show. **3** *fam fig (generosidad)* lavishness, generosity. LOC **perder el rumbo 1** to go off course. **2** *fig* to lose one's bearings.

**rumiante** *adj* ruminant.
▶ *nm* ruminant.

**rumiar** *vi (animal)* to ruminate, chew the cud.
▶ *vt* **1** *(mascar)* to chew. **2** *fig (pensar)* to ruminate, chew over, reflect on.

**rumor** *nm* **1** *(murmullo)* murmur. **2** *(noticia, voz)* rumour (US rumor).

**rumorearse** *vpr* [se usa sólo en tercera persona; no lleva sujeto] to be rumoured (US rumored): *se rumorea que está enfer-*

R

*mo* it is rumoured that he's ill, he's rumoured to be ill.

**rupestre** *adj* rock. [COMP] **pintura rupestre** cave painting.

**rupia** *nf* rupee.

**ruptura** *nf* 1 *(rotura)* breaking, breakage, break. 2 *fig* breaking-off, breakup.

**rural** *adj* rural, country: *médico rural* country doctor.

**Rusia** *nf* Russia.

**ruso,-a** *adj* Russian.
▶ *nm & nf (persona)* Russian.
▶ *nm* **ruso** *(idioma)* Russian.

**rústico,-a** *adj* rustic, rural.
▶ *nm* **rústico** peasant. [LOC] **en rústica** in paperback.

**ruta** *nf* route, way, road. [COMP] **ruta aérea** air route, airway.

**rutina** *nf* routine: *la rutina diaria* the daily routine.

**rutinario,-a** *adj* 1 *(gen)* routine. 2 *(persona)* unimaginative, dull.

# S

**S, s** *nf (la letra)* S, s.
**S** *sím* (sur) south; *(símbolo)* S.
**sábado** *nm* Saturday.

✎ Para ejemplos de uso, consulta jueves.

**sábana** *nf* sheet.
**sabelotodo** *nm o nf inv pey* know-all, know-it-all.
**saber** *nm* knowledge.
▸ *vt* **1** *(gen)* to know. **2** *(tener habilidad)* to be able to, know how to. **3** *(enterarse)* to learn, find out.
▸ *vi (tener sabor)* to taste (a, of).
▸ *vpr* **saberse** to know.
**sabido,-a** *adj* known.
**sabiduría** *nf* **1** *(conocimientos)* knowledge. **2** *(prudencia)* wisdom.
**sabio,-a** *adj* **1** *(con conocimientos)* learned, knowledgeable. **2** *(con prudencia)* wise, sensible.
▸ *nm & nf* **1** *(instruido)* learned person. **2** *(prudente)* sage, wise person.
**sable** *nm* sabre (us saber).
**sabor** *nm* **1** taste, flavour (us flavor). **2** *fig* feeling.
**saborear** *vt* **1** to taste. **2** *fig* to savour (us savor), relish.
**sabroso,-a** *adj* **1** *(con mucho sabor)* tasty, delicious. **2** *(agradable)* pleasant, delightful.
**sabueso** *nm* **1** *(perro)* bloodhound. **2** *fig (persona)* sleuth.
**sacacorchos** *nm inv* corkscrew.
**sacapuntas** *nm inv* pencil sharpener.
**sacar** *vt* **1** *(poner en el exterior)* to take out, pull out, get out. **2** *(obtener - gen)* to get; *(- premio)* to win; *(- dinero)* to get, make, earn; *(- billete)* to get, buy. **3** *(dinero del banco)* to draw, withdraw, take

out. **4** *(resolver)* to work out, solve. **5** *(encontrar)* to get, find. **6** *(enseñar)* to show. **7** *(quitar)* to remove. **8** *(extraer de algo)* to extract, obtain. **9** *(agua)* to draw. **10** *(llevar fuera)* to take out. **11** *(fotografía)* to take; *(fotocopia, copia)* to make. **12** *(producir)* to produce. **13** *(moda)* to introduce, set; *(nuevo producto)* to bring out. **14** *(publicar)* to publish, bring out. **15** *fam (ir por delante)* to be ahead. **16** *fam (ser más alto)* to be taller. **17** DEP *(tenis)* to serve; *(fútbol)* to kick off. **18** MAT *(restar)* to subtract; *(raíz)* to extract, find out. **19** *(mineral)* to extract. **20** QUÍM to extract.
▸ *vpr* **sacarse 1** *(desvestirse)* to take off. **2** *(fotografía)* to have taken.
**saciar** *vt* **1** *(hambre)* to satiate; *(sed)* to quench. **2** *fig (deseos)* to satisfy; *(ambiciones)* to fulfil (us fulfill).
▸ *vpr* **saciarse** to satiate os, be satiated.
**saco** *nm* **1** *(bolsa)* sack, bag. **2** AM *(americana)* jacket.
**sacrificar** *vt* **1** *(gen)* to sacrifice. **2** *fig (reses)* to slaughter; *(animal doméstico)* to destroy, put down.
▸ *vpr* **sacrificarse** to sacrifice os (por, for).
**sacrificio** *nm* sacrifice.
**sacro,-a** *adj* **1** *(sagrado)* sacred. **2** ANAT sacrum.
▸ *nm* **sacro** *(hueso)* sacrum.
**sacudida** *nf* **1** *(gen)* shake. **2** *(movimiento violento)* jolt, jerk. **3** *(terremoto)* earthquake.
**sacudir** *vt* **1** *(gen)* to shake. **2** *(alfombra, etc)* to shake out; *(polvo, arena)* to shake off. **3** *(golpear algo)* to beat. **4** *(cabeza)* to shake. **5** *(dar una paliza)* to

beat up. **6** *fig (emocionar, alterar)* to shake.

**sagacidad** *nf* **1** sagacity, cleverness. **2** *(astucia)* shrewdness, astuteness.

**sagaz** *adj* **1** clever, sagacious. **2** *(astuto)* shrewd, astute.

**sagrado,-a** *adj* sacred, holy.

**Sáhara** *nm* Sahara.

**saharaui** *adj* Saharaui, Sahrawi.
▶ *nm o nf* Saharaui, Sahrawi.

**sahariana** *nf* safari shirt, safari jacket.

**sahariano,-a** *adj* Saharan.

**sal** *nf* salt. COMP **sal fina** table salt.
▶ *nf pl* **sales** smelling salts.

**sala** *nf* **1** *(aposento)* room; *(grande)* hall. **2** *(sala de estar)* lounge, living room. **3** *(de hospital)* ward; *(de cine)* cinema; *(de teatro)* theatre. **4** JUR *(lugar)* courtroom; *(tribunal)* court.

**salado,-a** *adj* **1** *(con sal)* salted; *(con demasiada sal)* salty. **2** *fam fig (agudo)* witty; *(gracioso)* funny; *(encantador)* charming, attractive.

**salamandra** *nf* salamander.

**salamanquesa** *nf* ZOOL gecko.

**salar** *vt* **1** *(curar)* to salt. **2** *(sazonar)* to salt, add salt to.

**salarial** *adj* salary, wage.

**salario** *nm* salary, wages *pl*, wage.

**salazón** *nf* **1** *(acción)* salting. **2** *(carne)* salted meat; *(pescado)* salted fish.

**salchicha** *nf* sausage.

**salchichón** *nm* salami-type sausage.

**saldo** *nm* **1** *(de una cuenta)* balance. **2** *(pago)* liquidation, settlement. **3** *(resto de mercancía)* remnant, leftover, remainder. **4** *(venta a bajo precio)* sale.

**salero** *nm* **1** *(recipiente)* saltcellar, US salt shaker. **2** *fig (gracia)* charm, wit.

**salida** *nf* **1** *(partida)* departure. **2** *(puerta, etc)* exit, way out. **3** *(momento de salir)*. **4** *(viaje corto)* trip. **5** *(de un astro)* rising. **6** DEP start. **7** COM outlet, market. **8** FIN outlay, expenditure. **9** *fig (ocurrencia)* witty remark, witticism. **10** *fig (escapatoria)* solution, way out. **11** *fig (perspectiva)* opening. **12** TÉC outlet. **13** INFORM output.

**saliente** *adj* **1** *(que sobresale)* projecting. **2** *(cesante)* outgoing.
▶ *nm* projection, overhang, ledge.

**salina** *nf* **1** *(mina)* salt mine. **2** *(establecimiento)* salt works.

**salir** *vi* **1** *(ir hacia afuera)* to go out *(de, of)*. **2** *(venir de dentro)* to come out. **3** *(partir)* to leave. **4** *(no estar)* to be out. **5** *(amigos, novios)* to go out. **6** *(aparecer)* to appear, be. **7** *(revista, novela, etc)* to come out; *(moda)* to come in. **8** *(proceder)* to come *(de, from)*. **9** *(resultar)* to turn out, turn out to be. **10** *(examen, prueba)* to go, turn out. **11** *(venir a costar)* to come to, cost, work out. **12** *(sobresalir)* to project, stick out. **13** *(sol, etc)* to rise, come out; *(vegetales)* to come up; *(flores)* to come out. **14** *(granos)* to get, break out in, come out in; *(pelo)* to grow; *(diente)* to cut. **15** *(mancha)* to come out, come off. **16** *(parecerse)* to take after *(a, -)*. **17** *(al azar)* to be drawn. **18** *(nombre, palabra)* to be able to think of. **19** *(solucionar)* to work out. **20** *(librarse)* to get out *(de, of)*. **21** *(trabajo, oportunidad)* to come up. **22** *(dar a)* to open *(a, onto)*, come out *(a, at)*.
▶ *vpr* **salirse 1** *(líquido, gas)* to leak, leak out; *(río)* to overflow. **2** *(al hervir)* to boil over. **3** *(tornillo, etc)* to come off, come out. **4** *(de la carretera)* to go off *(de, -)*.

**salitre** *nm* saltpetre (US saltpeter).

**saliva** *nf* saliva.

**salmón** *nm* *(pez)* salmon.
▶ *adj (color)* salmon, salmon pink.

**salmonete** *nm* red mullet.

**Salomón** *nm* Solomon. COMP **Islas Salomón** Solomon Islands.

**salón** *nm* **1** *(en casa)* sitting room, drawing room, lounge. **2** *(en edificio público)* hall. **3** *(exposición)* show, exhibition.

**salpicar** *vt* **1** *(rociar)* to sprinkle. **2** *(caer gotas)* to splash.

**salpullido** *nm* rash.

**salsa** *nf* **1** sauce. **2** *fam fig (gracia)* zest, spice. **3** MÚS salsa.

**saltamontes** *nm inv* grasshopper.

**saltar** *vi* **1** *(gen)* to jump, leap. **2** *(en paracaídas)* to parachute. **3** *(romperse)* to break; *(estallar)* to burst. **4** *(desprenderse)* to come off. **5** *(tapón, corcho)* to pop out, pop off. **6** *fig (enfadarse)* to blow up, explode. **7** *fig (de una cosa a otra)* to jump, skip. **8** *fig (decir)* to come out (con, with); *(contestar)* to answer (con, with).
▶ *vt* **1** *fig (salvar de un salto)* to jump (over), leap (over). **2** *(arrancar)* to pull off. **3** *(ajedrez, etc)* to jump. **4** *fig (omitir)* to skip, miss out.
▶ *vpr* **saltarse 1** *(ley, etc)* to ignore. **2** *(omitir)* to skip, miss out. **3** *(desprenderse)* to come off; *(- lentilla)* to fall out.

**salto** *nm* **1** *(gen)* jump, leap. **2** DEP jump; *(natación)* dive. **3** *(de agua)* waterfall. **4** *(despeñadero)* precipice. **5** *fig (omisión)* gap.

**salubridad** *nf (estado de salud)* healthiness; *(de lugar, clima)* salubriousness, salubrity.

**salud** *nf* health.

**saludable** *adj* **1** *(sano)* healthy, wholesome. **2** *fig (beneficioso)* good, beneficial.

**saludar** *vt* **1** *(demostrar cortesía)* to greet. **2** *(decir hola)* to say hello to. **3** MIL to salute.

**saludo** *nm* **1** greeting. **2** MIL salute.

**salvación** *nf* **1** *(gen)* salvation, rescue. **2** REL salvation.

**salvado** *nm* bran.

**Salvador** *nm* **El Salvador 1** El Salvador. **2** REL the Saviour (US Savior).

**salvadoreño,-a** *adj* Salvadorian, Salvadoran.
▶ *nm & nf* Salvadorian, Salvadoran.

**salvaguardar** *vt* to safeguard (de, from).

**salvaje** *adj* **1** *(planta)* wild. **2** *(animal)* wild. **3** *(pueblo, tribu)* savage, uncivilized. **4** *fam fig (violento)* savage, wild. **5** *(bruto)* uncouth, boorish.
▶ *nm o nf (no civilizado)* savage. **2** *(bruto)* brute, boor.

**salvamento** *nm* rescue.

**salvar** *vt* **1** *(librar de peligro)* to save, rescue. **2** *(barco)* to salvage. **3** *(honor, ruina)* to save. **4** *(obstáculo)* to clear. **5** *(dificultad)* to overcome, get round. **6** *(distancia)* to cover.
▶ *vpr* **salvarse 1** *(sobrevivir)* to survive, come out alive. **2** *(escaparse)* to escape (de, from). **3** REL to be saved, save one's soul.

**salvapantallas** *nm inv* INFORM screensaver.

**salvavidas** *nm inv* life belt.

**salvedad** *nf (excepción)* exception.

**salvia** *nf* sage.

**salvo,-a** *adj (ileso)* unharmed, safe.
▶ *adv* **salvo** except, except for.

**salvoconducto** *nm* safe-conduct.

**Samoa** *nf* Samoa.

**samoano,-a** *adj* Samoan.
▶ *nm & nf (persona)* Samoan.
▶ *nm* **samoano** *(idioma)* Samoan.

**san** *adj* saint.

✎ Se usa delante de nombres de santos masculinos, excepto Tomás, Tomé, Toribio y Domingo. Consulta también **santo,-a**.

**sanar** *vt* to heal, cure.
▶ *vi* **1** *(enfermo)* to recover, get better. **2** *(herida)* to heal.

**sanatorio** *nm* clinic, nursing home; *(hospital)* hospital.

**sanción** *nf* **1** *(aprobación)* sanction, approval. **2** *(pena)* sanction, penalty.

**sandalia** *nf* sandal.

**sándalo** *nm* sandalwood.

**sandía** *nf* watermelon.

**sándwich** *nm* sandwich.

**sanear** *vt* **1** *(limpiar)* to clean; *(desinfectar)* to disinfect. **2** *(económicamente)* to make financially viable.

**sangrado** *nm* indention, indentation, indent.

**sangrar** *vt* **1** *(abrir una vena)* to bleed. **2** *(dar salida a un líquido)* to drain. **3** *fam fig (dejar sin dinero)* to bleed dry. **4** *(en impresión)* to indent.

**sangre** *nf* blood.

**sangría** *nf* **1** *(bebida)* sangria. **2** MED bleeding, bloodletting. **3** *fig (de dinero, etc)* drain.

**sangriento,-a** adj 1 *(que echa sangre)* bleeding. 2 *(con sangre)* bloody.

**sanguijuela** nf leech, bloodsucker.

**sanidad** nf 1 *(calidad de sano)* health, healthiness. 2 *(servicios)* health: *sanidad pública* public health.

**sanitario,-a** adj sanitary, health.
▶ nm & nf health officer.
▶ nm pl **sanitarios** bathroom fittings.

**sano,-a** adj 1 *(con salud)* healthy, fit. 2 *(saludable)* healthy, wholesome. 3 *fig (sin corrupción)* sound.

**santo,-a** adj 1 *(gen)* holy, sacred. 2 *(persona)* holy, saintly. 3 *fam (para enfatizar)* hell of a, real, right. 4 *(como título)* saint: *Santa Elena* Saint Helen.
▶ nm & nf saint.
▶ nm **santo** 1 *(imagen)* image of a saint. 2 *fam (dibujo)* picture. 3 *(onomástica)* saint's day.

✎ Consulta también **san**.

**santuario** nm sanctuary, shrine.

**saña** nf 1 *(enojo)* rage, fury. 2 *(crueldad)* cruelty, viciousness.

**sapiencia** nf 1 *fml (sabiduría)* wisdom. 2 *(conocimiento)* knowledge.

**saque** nm 1 *(tenis)* service. 2 *(fútbol)* kick-off. [COMP] **saque de banda** *(fútbol)* throw-in.

**saquear** vt *(casas)* to plunder, pillage; *(casas, comercios)* to loot.

**sarampión** nm measles pl.

**sarcasmo** nm sarcasm.

**sarcástico,-a** adj sarcastic.

**sarcófago** nm sarcophagus.

**sardina** nf sardine.

**sarga** nf serge, twill.

**sargento** nm 1 MIL sergeant. 2 *fig* tyrant.

**sarmiento** nm vine shoot.

**sarna** nf MED *(en personas)* scabies; *(en animales)* mange.

**sarpullido** nm rash.

**sarro** nm 1 *(en los dientes)* tartar. 2 *(sedimento)* deposit.

**sarta** nf string.

**sartén** nf frying pan, US fry pan.

**sastre,-a** nm & nf tailor.

**satélite** nm satellite.

**satén** nm satin.

**satisfacción** nf *(gen)* satisfaction.

**satisfacer** vt 1 *(gen)* to satisfy. 2 *(deuda)* to pay. 3 *(requisitos, exigencias)* to meet, fulfil satisfy. 4 *(agravio, ofensa)* to make amends for.

**satisfactorio,-a** adj satisfactory.

**satisfecho,-a** adj 1 *(contento)* satisfied, pleased. 2 *(pagado de sí mismo)* self-satisfied.

**saturación** nf saturation.

**saturado,-a** adj 1 saturated. 2 *fig* sick, tired.

**saturnismo** nm lead poisoning.

**Saturno** nm Saturn.

**sauce** nm willow.

**saúco** nm elder.

**saudí** adj Saudi.
▶ nm o nf Saudi.

**saudita** adj-nm o nf → **saudí**.

**sauna** nf sauna.

**saurio,-a** adj saurian.
▶ nm & nf saurian.

**savia** nf 1 BOT sap. 2 *fig* sap, vitality.

**saxofón** nm *(instrumento)* saxophone, sax.
▶ nm o nf *(músico)* saxophonist, sax player.

**saya** nf 1 *(falda)* skirt. 2 *(enagua)* petticoat.

**sazón** nf 1 *(madurez)* ripeness. 2 *(sabor)* taste, flavour (US flavor). 3 *(aderezo)* seasoning.

**sazonar** vt 1 *(madurar)* to ripen, mature. 2 *(comida)* to season, flavour (US flavor).

**se¹** pron 1 *(reflexivo - él)* himself; *(- ella)* herself; *(- usted, ustedes)* yourself, yourselves; *(- ellos, ellas)* themselves; *(- esto)* itself. 2 *(recíproco)* each other, one another: *se quieren* they love each other. 3 *(pasiva)*: *se han abierto las puertas* the doors have been opened. 4 *(impersonal)*: *se ve que no* apparently not.

**se²** pron *(objeto indirecto - a él)* him, to him; *(- a ella)* her, to her; *(- a ellos, ellas)* them, to them; *(- a esto)* it, to it; *(- a* *usted, ustedes)* you, to you: *se lo dije* I told her.

✎ Se usa delante de los pronombres **la, las, lo** y **los** en vez de **le** o **las**.

**sé¹** *pres indic* → **saber**.

**sé²** *imperat* → **ser**.

**sebo** *nm* **1** *(grasa)* fat. **2** CULIN suet. **3** *(para velas)* tallow.

**seca** *nf (sequía)* drought.

**secado** *nm* drying.

**secador** *nm* **1** dryer, drier. **2** *(de pelo)* hairdryer.

**secadora** *nf* tumble dryer, dryer.

**secano** *nm* dry land.

**secante** *adj (geometría)* secant.
▶ *nf* secant.

**secar** *vt* **1** *(gen)* to dry. **2** *(lágrimas, vajilla)* to wipe; *(líquido)* to wipe up, mop up. **3** *(planta)* to wither, dry up; *(río, fuente, etc)* to dry up.
▶ *vpr* **secarse** **1** *(gen)* to dry. **2** *(líquido, río, etc)* to dry up; *(planta)* to wither, dry up.

**sección** *nf* **1** *(corte)* section, cut. **2** *(geometría)* section. **3** *(departamento)* section, department. **4** *(en periódico, revista)* page, section.

**seco,-a** *adj* **1** *(gen)* dry. **2** *(frutos, flores)* dried. **3** *(marchito)* withered, dried up. **4** *fig (carácter)* dry; *(tono, respuesta)* curt, sharp. **5** *fig (golpe, ruido)* sharp.

**secreción** *nf* secretion.

**secretaría** *nf* **1** *(cargo)* secretaryship, office of secretary. **2** *(oficina)* secretary's office; *(en la administración)* secretariat.

**secretario,-a** *nm & nf* secretary.

**secreteo** *nm* whispering.

**secreto,-a** *adj* secret.
▶ *nm* **secreto** **1** *(lo reservado)* secret. **2** *(reserva)* secrecy.

**secta** *nf* sect.

**sector** *nm* **1** *(gen)* sector. **2** *fig (zona)* area. **3** *fig (parte)* section.

**secuela** *nf* consequence, result.

**secuencia** *nf* sequence.

**secuenciar** *vt* to arrange in sequence, put in sequence.

**secuestrar** *vt* **1** *(personas)* to kidnap; *(avión)* to hijack. **2** JUR to sequester, seize, confiscate.

**secuestro** *nm* **1** *(personas)* kidnapping; *(de avión)* hijacking. **2** JUR sequestration, seizure, confiscation.

**secundar** *vt* to support, second.

**secundaria** *nf* EDUC secondary education.

**secundario,-a** *adj* secondary.
▶ *nm* **secundario** GEOL secondary.

**secuoya** *nf* sequoia, redwood.

**sed** *nf* thirst.

**seda** *nf* silk.

**sede** *nf* **1** *(oficina central)* headquarters, central office. **2** *(del gobierno)* seat.

**sedentario,-a** *adj* sedentary.

**sediento,-a** *adj* **1** thirsty. **2** *fig (poder, etc)* hungry (de, for), thirsty (de, for).

**sedimentar** *vt* to settle, deposit.
▶ *vpr* **sedimentarse** to settle.

**sedimento** *nm* sediment, deposit.

**seductor,-ra** *adj* **1** seductive. **2** *(atractivo)* captivating. **3** *(persuasivo)* tempting.
▶ *nm & nf* seducer.

**segador,-ra** *nm & nf* harvester, reaper.

**segadora** *nf* harvester, reaper; *(de césped)* lawnmower.

**segar** *vt* **1** *(gen)* to reap, cut; *(césped)* to mow. **2** *fig (matar)* to mow down, cut down. **3** *fig (truncar)* to cut off.

**segmento** *nm* **1** *(gen)* segment. **2** INFORM overlay.

**segregar** *vt* **1** *(separar)* to segregate. **2** *(secretar)* to secrete.

**segueta** *nf* fret saw.

**seguido,-a** *adj* **1** *(continuo)* continuous. **2** *(consecutivo)* consecutive, successive. **3** *(en línea recta)* straight, direct.
▶ *adv* **seguido** straight.

**seguidor,-ra** *nm & nf* **1** follower. **2** DEP follower, supporter, fan.

**seguir** *vt* **1** *(gen)* to follow. **2** *(perseguir)* to pursue, chase. **3** *(continuar)* to continue, carry on. **4** *(un camino)* to continue

**S**

on. **5** *(curso, etc)* to do; *(explicaciones)* to follow.

▶ *vi* **1** *(proseguir)* to go on, carry on. **2** *(continuar)* to follow on, continue. **3** *(permanecer, mantenerse)* to continue to be, be still.

▶ *vpr* **seguirse 1** *(inferirse)* to deduce. **2** *(suceder a continuación)* to follow.

**según** *prep* **1** *(conforme)* according to. **2** *(dependiendo)* depending on. **3** *(como)* just as. **4** *(a medida que)* as. **5** *(tal vez)* it depends.

**segunda** *nf* **1** *(tren, etc)* second class. **2** *(marcha del auto)* second, second gear. **3** *fig (intención)* ulterior motive.

**segundero** *nm* second hand.

**segundo,-a** *adj* second.
▶ *nm & nf* second.
▶ *nm* **segundo** *(tiempo)* second.

✎ Para ejemplos de uso, consulta **seis**.

**seguridad** *nf* **1** *(gen)* security. **2** *(física)* safety. **3** *(certeza)* certainty, sureness. **4** *(confianza)* confidence.

**seguro,-a** *adj* **1** *(asegurado)* secure. **2** *(a salvo)* safe. **3** *(firme)* firm, steady. **4** *(cierto)* certain, sure. **5** *(de fiar)* reliable. **6** *(confiado)* confident.
▶ *nm* **seguro 1** *(contrato, póliza)* insurance. **2** *(mecanismo)* safety device, safety catch.
▶ *adv* for sure, definitely.

**seis** *adj* **1** six: *pesa seis kilos* it weighs six kilos; *son las seis en punto* it's exactly six o'clock; *el seis de junio* the six of june; *tienen un hijo de seis años* they have a boy of six; *somos seis* there are six of us. **2** *(sexto)* sixth: *soy el seis de la lista* I'm sixth on the list.
▶ *nm* six: *el seis* number six; *seis por seis treinta y seis* six times six is thirty-six, six sixes are thirty-six.

**seisavo,-a** *adj-nm & nf →* **sexto,-a.**

**seiscientos,-as** *adj (cardinal)* six hundred; *(ordinal)* six hundredth.
▶ *nm* **seiscientos** *(número)* six hundred.

**seísmo** *nm (terremoto)* earthquake.

**selección** *nf* **1** *(gen)* selection. **2** DEP *(gen)* team; *(fútbol)* squad.

**seleccionar** *vt* to select.

**selectividad** *nf* EDUC university entrance examination.

**selenio** *nm* selenium.

**sellar** *vt* **1** *(timbrar)* to stamp; *(oficial)* to seal. **2** *(monedas, etc)* to hallmark, stamp. **3** *fig (habitación, etc)* to close (up), seal up. **4** *fig (dejar señal)* to stamp, brand. **5** *fig (concluir)* to seal, settle, conclude.
▶ *vi* to sign on.

**sello** *nm* **1** *(de correos)* stamp. **2** *(de estampar, precinto)* seal.

**selva** *nf* **1** *(bosque)* forest. **2** *(jungla)* jungle.

**selvicultura** *nf* forestry.

**semáforo** *nm* traffic lights *pl*.

**semana** *nf* **1** *(tiempo)* week. **2** *fig (salario)* weekly wage.

**semanal** *adj* weekly.

**semanario,-a** *adj* weekly.
▶ *nm* weekly magazine.

**semántica** *nf* semantics.

**sembrado,-a** *adj fig (cubierto)* covered (de, with), full (de, of).
▶ *nm* **sembrado** sown field.

**sembrador,-ra** *nm & nf* sower.

**sembradora** *nf* seed drill.

**sembrar** *vt* **1** AGR to sow. **2** *fig (esparcir)* to scatter, spread.

**semejante** *adj* **1** *(parecido)* similar. **2** *pey (tal)* such, like that. **3** *(geometría)* similar.
▶ *nm* fellow being.

**semejanza** *nf* similarity, likeness.

**semen** *nm* semen.

**semental** *nm* stud.

**semestral** *adj* half-yearly, semestral.

**semestre** *nm* **1** six-month period, semester. **2** EDUC semester.

**semicírculo** *nm* semicircle.

**semicircunferencia** *nf* semicircumference.

**semiconductor** *nm* semiconductor.

**semicorchea** *nf* semiquaver, sixteenth note.

**semiesférico,-a** *adj* hemispheroidal.

**semifinal** *nf* semifinal.

**semifusa** *nf* hemidemisemiquaver, sixty-fourth note.

**semilla** *nf* **1** seed. **2** *fig* seed, seeds.

**semillero** *nm* **1** seedbed. **2** *fig* hotbed, breeding ground.

**seminal** *adj* seminal.

**semiología** *nf* semiology.

**semiótica** *nf* semiotics.

**semiseco,-a** *adj* medium dry.

**semitono** *nm* semitone, half-step.

**semivocal** *adj* semivocal.
 ► *nf* semivowel.

**sémola** *nf* semolina.

**senado** *nm* **1** senate. **2** *fig (reunión)* assembly.

**senador,-ra** *nm & nf* senator.

**sencillez** *nf* **1** *(gen)* simplicity. **2** *(naturalidad)* simplicity, lack of affectation, unpretentiousness. **3** *(ingenuidad)* gullibility, naivety.

**sencillo,-a** *adj* **1** *(sin adornos)* simple, plain. **2** *(fácil)* simple, easy. **3** *(no compuesto)* single. **4** *fig (persona - natural)* natural, unaffected, unpretentious; *(- ingenua)* naive, gullible.

**senderismo** *nm* trekking.

**sendero** *nm* path.

**sendos,-as** *adj* each, either.

**Senegal** *nm* Senegal.

**senegalés,-esa** *adj* Senegalese.
 ► *nm & nf* Senegalese.

**seno** *nm* **1** *(pecho)* breast, bosom. **2** *(hueco entre el pecho y la ropa)* bosom. **3** *(matriz)* womb. **4** *(cavidad)* cavity, hollow, hole. **5** MAT sine. **6** ANAT sinus.

**sensación** *nf* **1** *(impresión)* sensation, feeling: *sensación de calor* feeling of warmth. **2** *(emoción)* sensation.

**sensacional** *adj* sensational.

**sensatez** *nf* good sense.

**sensato,-a** *adj* sensible.

**sensibilidad** *nf* **1** *(percepción, sentido artístico)* sensitivity, feeling. **2** *(emotividad)* sensibility. **3** *(precisión)* sensitivity.

**sensible** *adj* **1** *(capaz de sentir)* sentient. **2** *(impresionable)* sensitive. **3** *(piel, oído)* sensitive. **4** *(perceptible)* perceptible, appreciable, noticeable. **5** *(considerable)* significant, considerable, sizeable. **6** *(que causa pena)* terrible, sad. **7** TÉC *(preciso)* sensitive.

**sensorial** *adj* sensory.

**sentado,-a** *adj* **1** seated, sitting. **2** *(establecido)* established, settled.

**sentar** *vt* **1** *(en silla, etc)* to sit, seat. **2** *fig (establecer)* to establish.
 ► *vi* **1** *(color, ropa, etc)* to suit. **2** *(comida, etc)* to do; *(comentario, etc)* to take.
 ► *vpr* **sentarse 1** *(en silla, etc)* to sit, sit down. **2** *(líquido)* to settle. **3** *(tiempo)* to settle, settle down.

**sentencia** *nf* **1** JUR *(decisión)* judgement; *(condena)* sentence. **2** *(aforismo)* proverb, maxim, saying, motto.

**sentenciar** *vt* to sentence (a, to).

**sentido,-a** *adj* **1** *(muerte, etc)* deeply felt. **2** *(sensible)* touchy, sensitive.
 ► *nm* **sentido 1** *(gen)* sense. **2** *(significado)* sense, meaning. **3** *(conocimiento)* consciousness. **4** *(dirección)* direction.

**sentimental** *adj* sentimental.
 ► *nm o nf* sentimental person.

**sentimiento** *nm* **1** *(gen)* feeling. **2** *(pena)* sorrow, grief.

**sentir** *nm* **1** *(sentimiento)* feeling. **2** *(opinión)* opinion, view.
 ► *vt* **1** *(gen)* to feel. **2** *(lamentar)* to regret, be sorry about, feel sorry. **3** *(oír)* to hear. **4** *(presentir)* to feel, think, have a feeling that.
 ► *vpr* **sentirse** to feel.

**seña** *nf* **1** *(indicio, gesto)* sign. **2** *(señal)* mark.
 ► *nf pl* **señas** address *sing*.

**señal** *nf* **1** *(signo)* sign, indication. **2** *(marca)* mark; *(en libro)* bookmark. **3** *(aviso, comunicación)* signal. **4** *(placa, letrero)* sign. **5** *(vestigio)* trace. **6** *(cicatriz)* scar. **7** *(de teléfono)* tone. **8** *(de pago)* deposit.

**señalado,-a** *adj* **1** *(famoso)* distinguished, famous. **2** *(fijado)* appointed, fixed. **3** *(significativo)* noticeable. **4** *(marcado)* marked, scarred.

**señalar** *vt* **1** *(marcar)* to mark. **2** *(hacer notar)* to point out. **3** *(apuntar hacia)* to point to, show. **4** *(con el dedo)* to point at. **5** *(fijar - cita)* to arrange, make; *(fecha, lugar, precio)* to set, fix.

**S**

**señalización** *nf* **1** *(señales)* road signs *pl*; *(de aeropuerto, estación)* signposting, signs *pl*. **2** *(colocación)* signposting.

**señalizar** *vt* to signpost.

**señor,-ra** *adj* **1** *(noble)* distinguished, noble. **2** *fam* fine.
▶ *nm & nf* **1** *(hombre)* man, gentleman; *(mujer)* woman, lady. **2** *(amo - hombre)* master; *(- mujer)* mistress. **3** *(tratamiento - hombre)* sir; *(- mujer)* madam, US ma'am. **4** *(ante apellido - hombre)* Mr; *(- mujer)* Mrs.

**señora** *nf (esposa)* wife.

**señorita** *nf* **1** *(mujer joven)* young woman; *(con más formalidad)* young lady. **2** *(tratamiento)* Miss. **3** *fam (puro)* small cigar. **4** **la señorita** EDUC the teacher, Miss.

**señuelo** *nm* **1** decoy. **2** *fig* bait.

**sépalo** *nm* sepal.

**separación** *nf* **1** separation. **2** *(espacio)* space, gap.

**separado,-a** *adj* **1** separate. **2** *(divorciado)* separated. [LOC] **por separado** separately, individually.

**separar** *vt* **1** *(gen)* to separate. **2** *(hacer grupos)* to separate, sort out. **3** *(guardar aparte)* to set aside, put aside. **4** *(apartar)* to move away (de, from). **5** *(de empleo, cargo)* to remove (de, from), dismiss (de, from). **6** *fig (mantener alejado)* to keep away (de, from).
▶ *vpr* **separarse 1** *(tomar diferente camino)* to separate, part company. **2** *(matrimonio)* to separate. **3** *(apartarse)* to move away (de, from). **4** *(desprenderse)* to separate (de, from), come off (de, -). **5** *(de amigo, etc)* to part company (de, with). **6** **separarse de** *(dejar algo)* to part with.

**sepia** *nf (pez)* cuttlefish.

**septenario,-a** *adj* septenary.
▶ *nm* **septenario** septenary.

**septenio** *nm* septennium.

**septentrional** *adj* northern.

**septeto** *nm* septet.

**septicemia** *nf* septicaemia (US septicemia).

**séptico,-a** *adj* septic.

**septiembre** *nm* September.

✎ Para ejemplos de uso, consulta marzo.

**séptimo,-a** *adj* seventh.

✎ Para ejemplos de uso, consulta sexto,-a.

**septuagenario,-a** *nm & nf* septuagenarian.

**septuagésimo,-a** *adj* seventieth.

✎ Para ejemplos de uso, consulta sexto,-a.

**sepulcro** *nm* tomb.

**sepultar** *vt* to bury.

**sepultura** *nf* **1** *(lugar)* grave. **2** *(acto)* burial.

**sequía** *nf* drought.

**ser** *vi* **1** *(gen)* to be: *Sócrates era filósofo* Socrates was a philosopher. **2** *(pertenecer)* to be, belong (de, to): *estas sillas son nuestras* these chairs are ours. **3** *(ser propio)* to be like (de, -): *es muy de Pilar* it's just like Pilar. **4** *(costar)* to be, cost: *¿cuánto es?* how much is it? **5** *(causar)* to cause, be. **6** *(consistir en)* to lie in, consist of. **7** *(suceder)* to happen (de, to): *¿qué fue de Iván?* what happened to Iván? **8** *(ocurrir, tener lugar)* to take place, be held: *la reunión será en el salón de actos* the meeting will be held in the assembly hall. **9** *ser de (proceder)* to be from, come from: *Santi es de Cáceres* Santi is from Cáceres. **10** *(indica material)* to be made of: *la puerta es de madera* the door is made of wood. **11** *(devenir)* to become of: *¡qué sería de nosotros sin ti!* what would become of us without you! **12** *(estar escrito)* to be by, be written by: *es de García Márquez* it's by García Márquez. **13** *ser de + inf (ser digno)* to be worth: *es de ver* it's worth seeing; *es de admirar* she's to be admired.
▶ *aux (pasiva)* to be: *fue encontrado por Raúl* it was found by Raúl.
▶ *nm* **1** *(ente)* being. **2** *(esencia)* essence, substance. **3** *(valor)* core, heart. **4** *(vida)* life, existence. [COMP] **ser humano** human being.

**serbal** *nm* service tree.

**serbio,-a** *adj* Serb, Serbian.
▶ *nm & nf* Serb, Serbian.
▶ *nm* **serbio** *(idioma)* Serbian.

**serenar** *vt* **1** *(gen)* to calm. **2** *fig (a alguien)* to calm down.

▶ *vpr* **serenarse 1** METEOR to clear up. **2** *(mar)* to grow calm. **3** *fig (persona)* to calm down.

**serenidad** *nf* serenity, calm. LOC **conservar la serenidad** to keep calm.

**sereno,-a** *adj* **1** METEOR *(cielo)* clear; *(tiempo)* fine, good. **2** *fig (persona - tranquila)* calm. **3** *fig (ambiente, etc)* calm, peaceful, quiet.
▶ *nm* **sereno 1** *(vigilante)* night watchman. **2** *(ambiente de la noche)* night air, night dew.

**serie** *nf* **1** *(gen)* series. **2** *(conjunto)* series, string, succession.

**seriedad** *nf* **1** *(gravedad)* seriousness, gravity. **2** *(formalidad)* reliability, dependability. LOC **con seriedad** seriously.

**serio,-a** *adj* **1** *(importante)* serious, grave. **2** *(severo)* serious. **3** *(formal)* reliable, responsible, dependable. **4** *(color)* sober; *(traje, etc)* formal. LOC **tomar en serio** to take seriously.

**sermón** *nm* **1** REL sermon. **2** *fam* sermon, ticking-off, lecture.

**seropositivo,-a** *adj* **1** seropositive. **2** *(con el VIH)* HIV positive.

**serpentear** *vi* **1** *(gen)* to crawl, wriggle. **2** *(camino)* to wind, twist; *(río)* to wind, meander.

**serpentín** *nm*

**serpentina** *nf (de papel)* streamer.

**serpiente** *nf* snake.

**serpol** *nm* wild thyme.

**serranía** *nf* mountain range, mountains *pl*.

**serrar** *vt* to saw.

**serrería** *nf* sawmill.

**serrín** *nm* sawdust.

**serrucho** *nm* handsaw.

**servicial** *adj* obliging, helpful, accommodating.

**servicio** *nm* **1** *(gen)* service. **2** *(criados)* servants *pl*; *(asistente)* domestic help. **3** *(juego, conjunto)* set. **4** *(favor)* service, favour (US favor). **5** DEP service, serve. **6** [también **servicios**.] *(retrete)* toilet, US rest room.

**servidor,-ra** *nm & nf* **1** servant. **2** *euf* myself.
▶ *nm* **servidor 1** MIL gunner. **2** INFORM server.

**servilleta** *nf* napkin, serviette.

**servio,-a** *adj* Serb, Serbian.
▶ *nm & nf* Serb, Serbian.
▶ *nm* **servio** *(idioma)* Serbian.

**servir** *vt* **1** *(gen)* to serve. **2** *(comida, bebida)* to serve, wait on. **3** *(ayudar)* to help. **4** COM *(suministrar)* to serve, supply with; *(entregar)* to deliver.
▶ *vi* **1** *(gen)* to serve. **2** *(ser útil)* to be useful, be helpful, be a help. **3** *(objeto)* to be no good: *esto no sirve* this is no good. **4** *(estar al servicio de otro)* to be a servant, be in service. **5** *(asistir a la mesa)* to serve (en, at), wait (en, at): *servir en la mesa* to wait at table.
▶ *vpr* **servirse 1** *(comida, etc)* to serve os, help os. **2** *(usar)* to use (de, -), make use of (de, -).

**sésamo** *nm* sesame.

**sesenta** *adj (cardinal)* sixty; *(ordinal)* sixtieth.
▶ *nm (número)* sixty.

✎ Para ejemplos de uso, consulta **seis**.

**sesentavo,-a** *adj* sixtieth.

✎ Para ejemplos de uso, consulta **sexto,-a**.

**sesión** *nf* **1** *(reunión)* session, meeting. **2** CINE showing. COMP **sesión continua** continuous session. ❙ **sesión plenaria** plenary session.

**seso** *nm* **1** brain. **2** *fam fig* brains *pl*, grey matter, sense.
▶ *nm pl* **sesos** CULIN brains.

**seta** *nf (comestible)* mushroom; *(no comestible)* toadstool.

**setecientos,-as** *adj (cardinal)* seven hundred; *(ordinal)* seven-hundredth.
▶ *nm* **setecientos** *(número)* seven hundred.

✎ Para ejemplos de uso, consulta **seis**.

**setenta** *adj (cardinal)* seventy; *(ordinal)* seventieth.
▶ *nm (número)* seventy.

✎ Para ejemplos de uso, consulta **seis**.

**setentavo,-a** *adj* seventieth.
▶ *nm & nf* seventieth.

✎ Para ejemplos de uso, consulta **sexto,-a**.

**setiembre** *nm* September.

✎ Para ejemplos de uso, consulta **marzo**.

**seto** *nm* hedge.
**severidad** *nf* **1** *(gravedad)* severity, harshness. **2** *(rigurosidad)* strictness.
**severo,-a** *adj* **1** *(grave)* severe, harsh. **2** *(riguroso)* strict.
**sexagenario,-a** *adj* sexagenarian.
▶ *nm & nf* sexagenarian.
**sexagesimal** *adj* sexagesimal.
**sexagésimo,-a** *adj* sixtieth.
▶ *nm & nf* sixtieth.

✎ Para ejemplos de uso, consulta **sexto,-a**.

**sexenio** *nm* six-year period.
**sexismo** *nm* sexism.
**sexista** *adj* **1** sexist. **2** *(machista)* chauvinistic.
▶ *nm* **1** sexist. **2** *(machista)* male chauvinist.
**sexo** *nm* **1** sex. **2** *(órganos)* sexual organs *pl*, genitals *pl*.
**sextante** *nm* sextant.
**sexteto** *nm* sextet.
**sexto,-a** *adj* sixth: *una sexta parte* a sixth; *el siglo sexto* the sixth century; *Alfonso sexto* Alfonso the sixth; *vive en un sexto piso* he lives in a sixth-floor flat; *acabó en sexto lugar* he finished in sixth palce. **2** *(sexto)* sixth: *soy el seis de la lista* I'm sixth on the list.
▶ *nm & nf* sixth: *le correspondió un sexto del pastel* he got a sixth of the cake.
**sextuplicar** *vt* to multiply by six, sextuplicate.
**séxtuplo,-a** *adj* sextuple.
▶ *nm* **séxtuplo** six times as much, six times as many.
**sexual** *adj (gen)* sex; *(relaciones)* sexual: *vida sexual* sex life.
**sexualidad** *nf* sexuality.
**Seychelles** *nm pl* las (islas) Seychelles the Seychelles.
**sha** *nm* shah.
**shérif** *nm* sheriff.

**si¹** *conj* **1** *(condicional)* if: *si quieres puedes venir con nosotros* you can come with us if you want to. **2** *(disyuntiva, duda)* if, whether: *no sé si decírselo (o no)* I don't know whether to tell her (or not). **3** *(énfasis)* but: *¡pero si es facilísimo!* ¡but it's really easy! |LOC| **como si** as if. ▮ **por si acaso** just in case: *llévatelo por si acaso* take it with you just in case.
**si²** *nm* MÚS ti, si, B.
**sí¹** *pron* **1** *(él)* himself; *(ella)* herself; *(cosa)* itself; *(ellos, ellas)* themselves; *(usted)* yourself; *(ustedes)* yourselves: *lo hizo por sí misma* she did it by herself; *hablaban para sí* they were talking to themselves. **2** *(uno mismo)* oneself. **3** *(recíproco)* each other: *hablaban entre sí* they were talking to each other.
**sí²** *adv* **1** yes: *dijo que sí* she said yes. **2** *(enfático)* of course: *sí que me gusta* of course I like it. |LOC| **creo que sí** I think so. ▮ **porque sí 1** *(sin razón)* just because I *(you, etc)* say so. **2** *(por naturaleza)* that's the way it is: *no puedes marcharte porque sí* you can't leave just because you feel like it.
**siberiano,-a** *adj* Siberian.
▶ *nm & nf* Siberian.
**sicoanálisis** *nm inv* psychoanalysis.
**sicodélico,-a** *adj* psychedelic.
**sicología** *nf* psychology.
**sida** *abrev* MED (síndrome de inmunodeficiencia adquirida) acquired immune deficiency syndrome; *(abreviatura)* AIDS.
**siderurgia** *nf* iron and steel industry.
**sidra** *nf* cider, US hard cider.
**siega** *nf* **1** *(acción)* harvesting, reaping. **2** *(época)* harvest, harvest time. **3** *(mieses)* harvest.
**siembra** *nf* **1** *(acción)* sowing. **2** *(época)* sowing time. **3** *(sembrado)* sown field.
**siempre** *adv* always: *siempre recordaré sus palabras* I'll always remember her words.
**siempreviva** *nf* everlasting flower, immortelle.
**sien** *nf* temple.
**sierra** *nf* **1** TÉC saw. **2** GEOG mountain range.

**Sierra Leona** *nf* Sierra Leone.
**sierraleonés,-esa** *adj* Sierra Leonean.
▶ *nm & nf* Sierra Leonean.
**siesta** *nf* siesta, afternoon nap.
**siete** *adj* (*cardinal*) seven; (*séptimo*) seventh.
▶ *nm* 1 (*número*) seven. 2 *fam* (*rasgón*) tear.

✎ Para ejemplos de uso, consulta **seis**.

**sigilo** *nm* 1 (*secreto*) secrecy. 2 (*discreción*) discretion.
**sigla** *nf* acronym, abbreviation.
**siglo** *nm* 1 century. 2 *fig* (*vida mundana*) world. COMP **el Siglo de Oro** the Golden Age.
**significación** *nf* 1 (*sentido*) meaning. 2 (*trascendencia*) significance.
**significado,-a** *adj* well-known, important.
▶ *nm* **significado** 1 meaning. 2 LING signifier.
**significar** *vt* 1 to mean: *no sé lo que significa* I don't know what it means. 2 (*hacer saber*) to make known, express.
**significativo,-a** *adj* 1 (*que da a entender*) meaningful. 2 (*importante*) significant.
**signo** *nm* 1 (*gen*) sign. 2 GRAM mark. 3 (*destino*) fate, destiny. 4 (*tendencia*) tendency.
**siguiente** *adj* following, next: *vamos a leer el capítulo siguiente* we're going to read the next chapter. LOC **¡el siguiente!** next, please!
**sílaba** *nf* syllable.
**silbar** *vi* 1 to whistle. 2 (*abuchear*) to hiss, boo.
**silbato** *nm* whistle.
**silbido** *nm* 1 (*acción*) whistle, whistling. 2 (*abucheo*) hissing.
**silenciar** *vt* 1 (*ocultar*) to hush up. 2 (*pasar por alto*) not to mention.
**silencio** *nm* silence. LOC **guardar silencio** to keep quiet.
**silencioso,-a** *adj* (*persona*) quiet; (*objeto*) silent.
**silepsis** *nf inv* syllepsis.
**sílex** *nm inv* flint.

**silicato** *nm* silicate.
**sílice** *nf* silica.
**silíceo,-a** *adj* flinty.
**silícico,-a** *adj* silicic.
**silicio** *nm* silicon.
**silla** *nf* 1 chair. 2 (*de montar*) saddle.
**sillar** *nm* (*piedra*) ashlar.
**sillín** *nm* saddle.
**sillón** *nm* armchair.
**silueta** *nf* 1 (*contorno*) silhouette. 2 (*figura*) figure, shape.
**silvestre** *adj* wild.
**silvicultura** *nf* forestry.
**sima** *nf* abyss, chasm.
**simbiosis** *nf inv* symbiosis.
**simbólico,-a** *adj* symbolic, symbolical.
**simbolizar** *vt* to symbolize.
**símbolo** *nm* symbol.
**simetría** *nf* symmetry.
**simétrico,-a** *adj* symmetric.
**simiente** *nf* seed.
**simiesco,-a** *adj* simian, apelike.
**símil** *nm* 1 (*comparación*) comparison. 2 (*semejanza*) resemblance. 3 LIT simile.
**similar** *adj* similar.
**simio** *nm* simian, monkey.
**simpatía** *nf* 1 (*cordialidad*) affection (por, for), liking (por, for). 2 (*amabilidad*) warmth, pleasantness. 3 (*afinidad*) affinity (por, with). 4 (*solidaridad*) sympathy (por, towards), solidarity (con, with). 5 MED sympathy.
**simpático,-a** *adj* 1 (*amable*) nice, likeable; (*agradable*) kind, friendly; (*encantador*) charming. 2 MED sympathetic.
**simpatizante** *nm o nf* supporter.
**simpatizar** *vi* 1 (*con persona*) to get on (con, with). 2 (*con idea, etc*) to sympathize (con, with).
**simple** *adj* 1 (*gen*) simple. 2 (*único*) single, just one. 3 (*mero*) mere. 4 (*persona*) simple, simple-minded.
**simplicidad** *nf* 1 simplicity. 2 (*ingenuidad*) naivety, ingenuousness.
**simplificar** *vt* to simplify.
**simposio** *nm* symposium.
**simulación** *nf* simulation.

**S**

**simulacro** *nm* sham, pretence (US pretense): *simulacro de incendio* fire drill.

**simulado,-a** *adj* simulated.

**simulador,-ra** *adj* simulative.
▶ *nm & nf* pretender.
▶ *nm* **simulador** TÉC simulator.

**simular** *vt* **1** to simulate. **2** (*fingir*) to pretend.

**simultanear** *vt* **1** (*hacer dos cosas*) to do simultaneously, do at the same time. **2** (*combinar*) to combine.

**simultaneidad** *nf* simultaneity.

**simultáneo,-a** *adj* simultaneous.

**sin** *prep* **1** (*carencia*) without. **2** (*además de*) not counting. LOC **estar sin +** *inf* not to have been + *pp*: *está sin planchar* it hasn't been ironed. ∎ **sin querer** accidentally, by mistake: *lo hizo sin querer* he didn't mean to do it.

**sinagoga** *nf* synagogue.

**sinalefa** *nf* synalepha, synaloepha, elision.

**sincerarse** *vpr* (*abrirse*) to open one's heart (con, to).

**sinceridad** *nf* sincerity.

**sincero,-a** *adj* sincere.

**sinclinal** *nm* syncline.

**síncopa** *nf* **1** MÚS syncopation. **2** LING syncope.

**sincopado,-a** *adj* MÚS syncopated.

**sincopar** *vt* **1** (*notas, palabras*) to syncopate. **2** *fig* (*abreviar*) to abridge.

**síncope** *nm* syncope.

**sincretismo** *nm* syncretism.

**sincronía** *nf* synchrony.

**sincrónico,-a** *adj* synchronic.

**sincronismo** *nm* synchronism.

**sincronización** *nf* synchronization.

**sincronizar** *vt* to synchronize.

**sindicado,-a** *adj* who belongs to a trade union.

**sindical** *adj* trade union, union.

**sindicalismo** *nm* trade unionism, unionism.

**sindicalista** *nm o nf* trade unionist, unionist.

**sindicar** *vt* to unionize.

▶ *vpr* **sindicarse** (*unirse a un sindicato*) to join a trade union.

**sindicato** *nm* trade union, union.

**síndico** *nm* **1** POL elected representative. **2** (*depositario*) trustee.

**síndrome** *nm* syndrome.

**sinéresis** *nf inv* syneresis, synaeresis.

**sinergia** *nf* synergy.

**sinfín** *nm* endless number.

**sinfonía** *nf* symphony.

**sinfónico,-a** *adj* symphonic.

**Singapur** *nm* Singapore.

**singular** *adj* **1** (*único*) singular, single. **2** (*excepcional*) extraordinary, exceptional.
▶ *nm* GRAM singular. LOC **en singular** GRAM in the singular.

**singularidad** *nf* **1** (*unicidad*) singularity. **2** (*excepcionalidad*) strangeness, uniqueness.

**singularizar** *vt* **1** (*distinguir*) to distinguish, single out. **2** GRAM to use in the singular.
▶ *vpr* **singularizarse** to distinguish os (por, by/with), stand out ((por, for).

**siniestra** *nf* (*izquierda*) left hand.

**siniestrado,-a** *adj* lit damaged.

**siniestro,-a** *adj* **1** lit (*izquierdo*) left, lefthand. **2** (*malo*) sinister, ominous.
▶ *nm* **siniestro** disaster, catastrophe; (*accidente*) accident; (*incendio*) fire.

**sinnúmero** *nm* endless number.

**sino¹** *conj* **1** (*contraposición*) but: *no es blanco sino negro* it isn't white but black. **2** (*excepción*) but, except for: *nadie lo sabe sino Antonio* nobody knows except for Antonio.

**sino²** *nm* (*destino*) fate, destiny.

**sinonimia** *nf* synonymy.

**sinónimo,-a** *adj* synonymous.
▶ *nm* **sinónimo** synonym.

**sinopsis** *nf inv* synopsis.

**sinóptico,-a** *adj* synoptic, synoptical.

**sinrazón** *nf* wrong, injustice.

**sinsabor** *nm* *fig* worry, trouble, heartache.

**sintáctico,-a** *adj* syntactic, syntactical.

**sintagma** *nm* phrase. COMP **sintagma nominal** noun phrase.

**sintaxis** *nf inv* syntax.

**síntesis** *nf inv* synthesis.

**sintético,-a** *adj* synthetic.

**sintetizador** *nm* synthesizer.

**sintetizar** *vt* **1** to synthesize. **2** *(resumir)* to summarize: *sintetizando diría que…* to sum up, I'd like to say that…

**síntoma** *nm* symptom.

**sintomático,-a** *adj* **1** symptomatic. **2** *fig* significant.

**sintomatología** *nf* symptomatology.

**sintonía** *nf* **1** *(de radio)* tuning. **2** *(música)* signature tune. **3** *fig (armonía)* harmony. LOC **estar en sintonía con** ALGN *fig* to be in tune with SB, be on SB's wavelength.

**sintonizador** *nm* **1** *(botón)* tuning knob. **2** *(de cadena de sonido)* tuner.

**sintonizar** *vt (radio)* to tune in to: *sintonizó una emisora local* he tuned in to a local radio station.
▶ *vi fig (llevarse bien)* to get on well, be on the same wavelength.

**sinuosidad** *nf* **1** *(cualidad)* sinuosity. **2** *(curva)* bend, curve. **3** *fig (de argumento, etc)* tortuousness; *(de persona)* deviousness.

**sinuoso,-a** *adj* **1** *(camino)* winding. **2** *fig (argumento)* tortuous; *(persona)* devious.

**sinvergüenza** *nm o nf (pícaro)* rotter, swine, louse. **2** *(descarado)* cheeky devil.

**siquiatra** *nm o nf* psychiatrist.

**siquiatría** *nf* psychiatry.

**síquico,-a** *adj* → psíquico,-a.

**siquiera** *conj* **1** *(adversativa)* even though, even if: *quisiera hablar contigo, siquiera fuera un momento* I would like to speak to you, even if it's only for a moment. **2** *(distributiva)* whether.
▶ *adv (por lo menos)* at least: *dame siquiera la mitad* give me at least half of it.

**sirena** *nf* **1** *(ninfa)* siren, mermaid. **2** *(alarma)* siren.

**Siria** *nf* Syria.

**sirio,-a** *adj* Syrian.
▶ *nm & nf* Syrian.

**sirviente,-a** *nm & nf* servant.

**sisa** *nf* COST armhole.

**sisal** *nm* sisal.

**sisar** *vt* **1** COST to dart, take in. **2** *(hurtar)* to pilfer, pinch, nick; *(estafar)* to cheat.

**sisear** *vi* to hiss.
▶ *vt* to hiss.

**siseo** *nm* hiss, hissing.

**sísmico,-a** *adj* seismic.

**sismo** *nm* earthquake, tremor.

**sismógrafo** *nm* seismograph.

**sismología** *nf* seismology.

**sismólogo,-a** *nm & nf* seismologist.

**sistema** *nm* system. COMP **sistema de ecuaciones** simultaneous equations *pl*. ▌**sistema métrico decimal** decimal metric system. ▌**sistema nervioso** nervous system. ▌**sistema operativo** operative system.

**sistemático,-a** *adj* systematic.

**sistematizar** *vt* to systematize.

**sístole** *nf* systole.

**sistólico,-a** *adj* systolic.

**sitiado,-a** *adj* besieged.
▶ *nm & nf* besieged.

**sitial** *nm* seat of honour (US honor).

**sitiar** *vt* to besiege, lay siege to.

**sitio** *nm* **1** *(lugar)* place. **2** *(espacio)* space, room. **3** *(asiento)* seat. **4** MIL siege. COMP **sitio web** website.

**sito,-a** *adj fml* located, situated.

**situación** *nf* **1** *(circunstancia)* situation. **2** *(posición)* position. **3** *(emplazamiento)* situation, location.

**situado,-a** *adj* situated, located.

**situar** *vt* to place, locate, situate, put.
▶ *vpr* **situarse 1** *(colocarse)* to be placed, be located, be situated. **2** *(lograr una posición)* to get on, do well, be successful.

**soasar** *vt* to roast lightly.

**sobaco** *nm* armpit.

**sobado,-a** *adj* **1** *(desgastado)* worn, shabby. **2** *(manoseado)* well-thumbed, dog-eared. **3** *fig (manido)* well-worn.

S

**sobar** *vt* **1** *(ablandar)* to knead. **2** *fig* *(manosear - objeto)* to finger; *(- persona)* to grope, paw, touch up.

**soberanía** *nf* sovereignty.

**soberano,-a** *adj* **1** sovereign. **2** *fig* extreme, supreme. **3** *fam* huge, great.
▸ *nm & nf* sovereign.

**soberbia** *nf* **1** *(orgullo)* pride; *(arrogancia)* arrogance, haughtiness. **2** *(cólera)* rage, anger.

**soberbio,-a** *adj* **1** *(orgulloso)* proud; *(arrogante)* arrogant, haughty. **2** *(suntuoso)* sumptuous, magnificent. **3** *(magnífico)* superb, splendid, magnificent.

**sobornable** *adj* bribable, venal.

**sobornar** *vt* to bribe, suborn.

**soborno** *nm* **1** *(acción)* bribery. **2** *(regalo, etc)* bribe.

**sobra** *nf* *(exceso)* excess, surplus. LOC **saber** ALGO **de sobra** to know STH only too well.
▸ *nf pl* **sobras** *(desperdicios)* leftovers.

**sobrado,-a** *adj* *(que sobra)* ample, more than enough, plenty of.

**sobrante** *adj* leftover, remaining, spare.

**sobrar** *vi* **1** *(haber más de lo necesario)* to be more than enough, be too much. **2** *(estar de más)* to be superfluous, be unnecessary. **3** *(quedar)* to have left over, be left over.

**sobre** *prep* **1** *(encima)* on, upon, on top of. **2** *(por encima)* over, above. **3** *(acerca de)* about, on. **4** *(alrededor de)* about, around.
▸ *nm* **1** *(de correo)* envelope. **2** *(de sopa, etc)* packet. LOC **sobre todo** above all, especially.

**sobre-** *pref* super-, over-.

**sobreabundancia** *nf* superabundance, overabundance.

**sobrealimentar** *vt* to overfeed.

**sobreático** *nm* penthouse.

**sobrecarga** *nf* **1** overload. **2** *fig* additional burden, further worry.

**sobrecargar** *vt* **1** to overload. **2** *fig* to overburden.

**sobrecogedor,-ra** *adj* **1** *(conmovedor)* dramatic, awesome. **2** *(que da miedo)* frightening.

**sobrecoger** *vt* **1** *(coger de repente)* to startle, take by surprise. **2** *(asustar)* to frighten, scare.

**sobrecubierta** *nf* jacket, dust cover.

**sobredosis** *nf inv* overdose.

**sobreentender** *vt* **1** *(comprender)* to understand. **2** *(deducir)* to deduce.
▸ *vpr* **sobreentenderse** to be implied, be inferred: *se sobreentiende que su respuesta será afirmativa* one assumes that she will say yes.

**sobreexcitación** *nf* overexcitement.

**sobreexcitar** *vt* to overexcite.
▸ *vpr* **sobreexcitarse** to get overexcited.

**sobreexponer** *vt* to overexpose.

**sobreexposición** *nf* overexposure.

**sobrehilar** *vt* COST to whipstitch.

**sobrehumano,-a** *adj* superhuman.

**sobreimpresión** *nf* overprint.

**sobrellevar** *vt* to bear, endure.

**sobremanera** *adv* exceedingly.

**sobremesa** *nf* **1** *(período)* afternoon: *la programación de la sobremesa* the afternoon's television programmes. **2** *(charla)* table talk.

**sobrenadar** *vi* to float.

**sobrenatural** *adj* supernatural.

**sobrenombre** *nm* nickname.

**sobrentender** *vt-vpr* → sobreentender.

**sobrepaga** *nf* bonus.

**sobrepasar** *vt* **1** to exceed, surpass, be in excess of. **2** *(competición)* to beat.

**sobrepeso** *nm* **1** overload, excess weight. **2** *(de persona)* excess weight.

**sobreponer** *vt* to put on top (en, of), superimpose (en, on).
▸ *vpr* **sobreponerse 1** *fig (al dolor, etc)* to overcome (a, -). **2** *fig (animarse)* to pull os together.

**sobreproducción** *nf* excess production, overproduction.

**sobresaliente** *adj* **1** sticking out, protruding. **2** *fig* outstanding, excellent.
▸ *nm (calificación - colegio)* A; *(- universidad)* first, US A.

**sobresalir** *vi* **1** to stick out, protrude. **2** *fig* to stand out, excel.

**sobresaltar** *vt* to startle.
▶ *vpr* **sobresaltarse** to be startled.

**sobresalto** *nm* start; *(de temor)* fright, shock.

**sobresdrújulo,-a** *adj* accented on the antepenultimate syllable.

**sobrestimar** *vt* to overestimate.

**sobretodo** *nm (abrigo)* overcoat.

**sobrevalorar** *vt* to overestimate.

**sobrevenir** *vi* to happen to, befall: *no sabremos nunca lo que le sobrevino* we'll never know what happened to her.

**sobreviviente** *nm o nf* survivor.

**sobrevivir** *vi* **1** *(gen)* to survive. **2** *(a alguien)* to outlive.

**sobrevolar** *vt* to fly over.

**sobrexcitación** *nf* overexcitement.

**sobrexcitar** *vt-vpr* → **sobreexcitar**.

**sobrexponer** *vt* → **sobreexponer**.

**sobriedad** *nf* sobriety, moderation, restraint.

**sobrino,-a** *nm & nf (hombre)* nephew; *(mujer)* niece.

**sobrio,-a** *adj* **1** *(estilo, color, etc)* sober, plain. **2** *(persona)* sober, moderate.

**socavar** *vt* **1** *(excavar)* to dig under. **2** *fig* to undermine.

**socavón** *nm* **1** *(cueva excavada)* excavation. **2** *(bache)* hollow, hole. **3** *(de una mina)* gallery, tunnel.

**sociabilidad** *nf* sociability.

**sociable** *adj* sociable, friendly.

**social** *adj* social.

**socialdemocracia** *nf* social democracy.

**socialdemócrata** *adj* social democratic.
▶ *nm o nf* social democrat.

**socialismo** *nm* socialism.

**socialista** *adj* socialist.
▶ *nm o nf* socialist.

**socializar** *vt* **1** *(gen)* to socialize. **2** *(nacionalizar)* to nationalize.

**sociedad** *nf* **1** *(gen)* society. **2** COM company. **3** *(asociación)* society, association.

**socio,-a** *nm & nf* **1** *(miembro)* member. **2** COM partner, associate. **3** *(accionista)* shareholder, member.

**socioeconómico,-a** *adj* socioeconomic.

**sociología** *nf* sociology.

**sociólogo,-a** *nm & nf* sociologist.

**socorrer** *vt* to help, assist, come to the aid of, go to the aid of.

**socorrista** *nm o nf* life-saver, lifeguard.

**socorro** *nm* **1** *(ayuda)* help, aid, assistance. **2** *(provisiones)* supplies *pl*, provisions *pl*.
▶ *interj* help!

**soda** *nf* **1** *(bebida)* soda water. **2** QUÍM soda.

**sódico,-a** *adj* sodium.

**sodio** *nm* sodium.

**sofá** *nm* sofa, settee.

**sofá-cama** *nm* sofa bed, studio couch.

**sofisticación** *nf* sophistication.

**sofisticado,-a** *adj* sophisticated.

**sofocante** *adj* suffocating, stifling.

**sofocar** *vt* **1** *(ahogar)* to suffocate, stifle, smother. **2** *fig (incendio)* to put out, extinguish; *(rebelión)* to suppress, put down.
▶ *vpr* **sofocarse 1** *(de calor, etc)* to suffocate. **2** *fig (ruborizarse)* to blush.

**sofoco** *nm* **1** *(ahogo)* suffocation, stifling sensation. **2** *fig (vergüenza)* embarrassment; *(rubor)* blushing. **3** *fam (disgusto)* shock.

**sofocón** *nm fam* shock. [LOC] **llevarse un sofocón** *fam* to get into a state.

**sofreír** *vt* to fry lightly, brown.

**sofrito** *nm* fried tomato and onion sauce.

**software** *nm* software.

**soga** *nf* rope, cord.

**soja** *nf* soya bean, US soybean. [COMP] **salsa de soja** soy sauce.

**sojuzgar** *vt* to subjugate.

**sol¹** *nm* **1** *(estrella)* sun. **2** *(luz)* sun, sunlight, sunshine. **3** *fam (persona)* darling. **4** *(moneda de Perú)* sol, standard monetary unit of Peru. [LOC] **hace sol** it's sunny, the sun's shining. ▌**tomar**

**S**

**el sol 1** *(tendido)* to sunbathe. **2** *(al caminar)* to get some sun.

**sol²** *nm* MÚS sol, G.

**solapa** *nf* **1** *(de prenda)* lapel. **2** *(de sobre, libro)* flap.

**solapado,-a** *adj fig* sly, evasive.

**solapar** *vt* **1** COST to put lapels on. **2** *fig (ocultar)* to conceal, cover up.
▶ *vi (cubrir)* to overlap.

**solar¹** *adj (del sol)* solar.

**solar²** *nm* **1** *(terreno)* plot, lot; *(en obras)* building site. **2** *(casa solariega)* ancestral home.

**solar³** *vt (suelo)* to floor.

**solaz** *nm* **1** *(esparcimiento)* recreation, entertainment. **2** *(descanso)* rest, relaxation.

**solazar** *vt* **1** *(entretener)* to amuse, entertain. **2** *(descansar)* to rest, relax.
▶ *vpr* **solazarse 1** *(divertirse)* to enjoy os. **2** *(relajarse)* to relax.

**soldado** *nm* soldier. COMP **soldado raso** private.

**soldador,-ra** *nm & nf* welder.
▶ *nm* **soldador** soldering iron.

**soldadura** *nf* **1** *(acción)* welding, soldering. **2** *(unión)* weld, soldered joint.

**soldar** *vt* **1** *(metal)* to weld, solder. **2** *fig (enmendar)* to mend.
▶ *vpr* **soldarse** *(huesos)* to knit.

**soleado,-a** *adj* sunny.

**solear** *vt* to expose to the sun, put in the sun.

**soledad** *nf* **1** *(estado)* solitude. **2** *(sentimiento)* loneliness. **3** *(lugar)* lonely place.

**solemne** *adj* **1** solemn, majestic. **2** *pey* downright: *es una solemne tontería* it's downright stupidity.

**solemnidad** *nf* **1** *(pompa)* solemnity, pomp, formality. **2** *(acto, ceremonia)* solemn ceremony, ceremonial occasion.

**solemnizar** *vt (celebrar)* to solemnize, celebrate; *(conmemorar)* to commemorate.

**soler** *vi (acostumbrar - presente)* to be in the habit of + *-ing*; *(- pasado)* used to:

*solía venir cada martes* she used to come every Tuesday.

**solicitante** *nm o nf* applicant.

**solicitar** *vt* **1** *(pedir)* to request. **2** *(trabajo)* to apply for; *(permiso, etc)* to ask for; *(votos)* to canvass for. **3** *(persona)* to chase after. **4** *(cortejar)* to woo, court.

**solícito,-a** *adj* obliging, attentive.

**solicitud** *nf* **1** *(petición)* request; *(de trabajo)* application; *(- impreso)* application form. **2** *(instancia)* petition. **3** *(diligencia)* solicitude, care. COMP **solicitud de empleo** job application.

**solidaridad** *nf* solidarity.

**solidario,-a** *adj* **1** *(ligado)* united. **2** *(responsabilidad, causa)* common.

**solidarizarse** *vpr* **1** *(gen)* to show one's solidarity (con, with). **2** *(apoyar)* to support (con, -).

**solidez** *nf (resistencia)* solidity, strength; *(firmeza)* firmness.

**solidificación** *nf* solidification.

**solidificar** *vt* **1** *(líquido)* to solidify. **2** *(pasta)* to harden, set.
▶ *vpr* **solidificarse 1** *(líquido)* to solidify. **2** *(pasta)* to harden, set.

**sólido,-a** *adj* **1** *(fuerte)* solid, strong; *(firme)* firm. **2** *fig (color)* fast. **3** *fig (principios, etc)* sound.
▶ *nm* **sólido** solid.

**solista** *nm o nf* soloist.

**solitaria** *nf* MED tapeworm.

**solitario,-a** *adj* **1** *(que está solo)* solitary, lone. **2** *(que se siente solo)* lonely. **3** *(lugar)* deserted, lonely.
▶ *nm & nf (persona)* solitary person.
▶ *nm* **solitario** *(diamante, naipes)* solitaire.

**sólito,-a** *adj* usual, customary.

**soliviantar** *vt* **1** *(inducir)* to rouse, stir up. **2** *(irritar)* to irritate.

**sollozar** *vi* to sob.

**sólo** *adv* → **solo¹**.

**solo¹** *adv* [sólo se usa si se puede producir confusión con el adjetivo o con el nombre] only, just: *solo quiero café* I just want a coffee.

**solo,-a** *adj* **1** *(sin compañía)* alone, on one's own, by os; *(sin ayuda)* (by) os, (for) os. **2** *(solitario)* lonely. **3** *(único)* only, sole, single. **4** *(café)* black.

▶ *nm* **solo 1** *(naipes)* solitaire. **2** *fam (café)* black coffee. **3** MÚS solo. [LOC] **a solas** alone, by os.

**solomillo** *nm* sirloin.

**soltar** *vt* **1** *(desasir)* to let go of, release, drop. **2** *(desatar)* to untie, unfasten, undo; *(aflojar)* to loosen. **3** *(preso)* to release, free, set free. **4** *(animal)* to let out; *(perro)* to unleash. **5** *(humo, olor)* to give off. **6** *(puntos)* to drop. **7** *(de vientre)* to loosen. **8** *fam (arrear)* to give, deal. **9** *fam (decir)* to come out with, blurt out.

▶ *vpr* **soltarse 1** *(desatarse)* to come untied, come unfastened. **2** *(desprenderse)* to come off. **3** *(tornillo, etc)* to come loose. **4** *(animal)* to get loose, break loose. **5** *(puntos)* to come undone. **6** *(vientre)* to loosen. **7** *fig (adquirir habilidad)* to become proficient, get the knack. **8** *fig (desenvolverse)* to become self-confident, loosen up.

**soltero,-a** *adj* single, unmarried.

▶ *nm & nf (hombre)* bachelor, single man; *(mujer)* single woman.

**soluble** *adj* soluble.

**solución** *nf* solution.

**solucionar** *vt* **1** *(problema)* to solve. **2** *(huelga, asunto)* to settle.

**solventar** *vt* **1** *(dificultad, problema)* to solve, resolve. **2** *(deuda, asunto)* to settle.

**solvente** *adj* **1** FIN solvent. **2** *(fiable)* reliable.

▶ *nm* QUÍM solvent.

**somalí** *adj* Somali.

▶ *nm o nf* Somali.

**Somalia** *nf* Somalia.

**sombra** *nf* **1** *(falta de sol)* shade. **2** *(silueta)* shadow. **3** *(espectro)* ghost, shade. **4** *fig (persona que sigue a otra)* shadow. **5** *fam fig (gracia)* wit. **6** *fig (parte pequeña)* trace, shadow, bit. **7** *fig (clandestinidad)* secrecy.

**sombreado** *nm* shading.

**sombrero** *nm* **1** *(prenda)* hat.

**sombrilla** *nf* parasol, sunshade.

**sombrío,-a** *adj* **1** *(lugar)* dark. **2** *fig (tenebroso)* gloomy, sombre (US somber). **3** *fig (persona)* gloomy, sullen.

**someter** *vt* **1** *(rebeldes)* to subdue, put down; *(rebelión)* to quell. **2** *(hacer recibir)* to subject (a, to). **3** *(pasiones)* to subdue. **4** *(proponer, presentar)* to submit.

▶ *vpr* **someterse 1** *(rendirse)* to surrender (a, to). **2** *(tratamiento, etc)* to undergo (a, -). [LOC] **someter a prueba** to test, put to the test. ▮ **someter** ALGO **a votación** to put STH to the vote.

**somnolencia** *nf* sleepiness, drowsiness, somnolence.

**somnoliento,-a** *adj* sleepy, drowsy.

**son** *nm* **1** *(sonido)* sound. **2** *fig (modo)* manner, way: *a mi son* my way. [LOC] **en son de paz** in peace.

**sonado,-a** *adj* **1** *(conocido)* famous. **2** *(escándalo, etc)* much talked-about. **3** *fam fig (loco)* mad, crazy.

**sonámbulo,-a** *nm & nf* sleepwalker, somnambulist.

**sonar¹** *vi* **1** *(hacer ruido)* to sound. **2** *(timbre, teléfono, etc)* to ring. **3** *(alarma, reloj)* to go off. **4** *(instrumento)* to play. **5** *(letra)* to be pronounced.

▶ *vt* **1** *(conocer vagamente)* to sound familiar, ring a bell. **2** *(timbre, etc)* to ring; *(bocina)* to blow, sound; *(instrumento)* to play.

▶ *vpr* **sonarse** *(nariz)* to blow.

**sonar²** *nm* MAR sonar.

**sonda** *nf* **1** MED *(para intervenciones quirúrgicas)* probe; *(para evacuar líquidos)* catheter. **2** MAR sounding line. **3** *(barreno)* drill, bore. **4** *(atmosférica)* sonde; *(espacio)* probe.

**sondear** *vt* **1** MED to sound, probe. **2** MAR to sound. **3** *(subsuelo)* to drill, bore. **4** *fig (encuestar)* to sound out.

**sondeo** *nm* **1** MED sounding, probing. **2** MAR sounding. **3** *(del subsuelo)* drilling, boring. **4** *fig (encuesta)* poll.

**soneto** *nm* sonnet.

**sónico,-a** *adj* sonic.

**sonido** *nm* sound.

**sonoridad** *nf* sonority.

**S**

**sonoro,-a** *adj* **1** *(resonante)* loud, resounding. **2** LING sound.

**sonreír** *vi* to smile.
► *vt* **1** to smile at. **2** *fig (favorecer)* to smile on, smile upon.
► *vpr* **sonreírse** to smile.

**sonriente** *adj* smiling.

**sonrisa** *nf* smile.

**sonrojar** *vt* to make blush.
► *vpr* **sonrojarse** to blush.

**sonsacar** *vt* **1** *(gen)* to wheedle. **2** *fig (secreto)* to get out of, worm out.

**soñador,-ra** *nm & nf* dreamer.

**soñar** *vt* **1** *(al dormir)* to dream. **2** *fig (fantasear)* to daydream, dream.
► *vi* **1** *(al dormir)* to dream (**con**, about/of). **2** *fig (fantasear)* to daydream (**con**, about), dream (**con**, about/of).

**soñolencia** *nf* sleepiness.

**soñoliento,-a** *adj* drowsy, sleepy.

**sopa** *nf (plato)* soup.

**sopesar** *vt* **1** to try the weight of. **2** *fig* to weigh up.

**soplar** *vi* **1** *(viento, etc)* to blow. **2** *fam (denunciar)* to squeal.
► *vi* **1** *(polvo, etc)* to blow away, blow off; *(vela)* to blow out; *(sopa)* to blow on; *(globo)* to blow up. **2** *(vidrio)* to blow. **3** *fam fig (delatar)* to split on, grass on. **4** *fam fig (en un examen, etc)* to whisper the answer, tell the answer.

**soplete** *nm* blowtorch, blowlamp.

**soplido** *nm* blow, puff.

**soplo** *nm* **1** *(con la boca)* blow, puff. **2** *(de viento)* puff. **3** *fig (momento)* moment, minute. **4** MED murmur. **5** *fam (de secreto, etc)* tip-off.

**soportar** *vt* **1** *(aguantar)* to support, bear. **2** *fig (sufrir)* to stand, bear, endure. **3** *fig (lluvia, tormenta, etc)* to weather.

**soporte** *nm* support. COMP **soporte de datos** INFORM data carrier.

**sorbo** *nm* **1** *(acción)* sip. **2** *(trago)* gulp.

**sordera** *nf* deafness.

**sordidez** *nf* **1** *(suciedad)* squalor. **2** *(mezquindad)* meanness.

**sórdido,-a** *adj* **1** *(sucio)* squalid, sordid. **2** *(mezquino)* mean.

**sordo,-a** *adj* **1** *(persona)* deaf. **2** *(sonido, dolor, golpe)* dull. **3** LING voiceless.
► *nm & nf (persona)* deaf person.

**sordomudez** *nf* deaf-mutism.

**sordomudo,-a** *adj* deaf and dumb.
► *nm & nf* deaf mute.

**sorgo** *nm* sorghum.

**sorprendente** *adj* surprising, amazing, astonishing.

**sorprender** *vt* **1** *(coger desprevenido)* to catch unawares, take by surprise. **2** *fig (descubrir)* to discover; *(conversación)* to overhear. **3** *fig (maravillar)* to surprise, astonish, amaze.
► *vpr* **sorprenderse** *fig* to be surprised.

**sorpresa** *nf* surprise.

**sortear** *vt* **1** *(echar a suertes)* to draw lots for, cast lots for. **2** *(rifar)* to raffle. **3** MIL to draft. **4** *fig (obstáculos, dificultad)* to get round, overcome; *(preguntas)* to dodge, evade, get round.

**sorteo** *nm* draw; *(rifa)* raffle.

**sortija** *nf (anillo)* ring.

**sortilegio** *nm* **1** *(hechicería)* sorcery, witchcraft. **2** *(hechizo)* spell.

**sosa** *nf* **1** QUÍM soda. **2** BOT saltwort.

**sosegado,-a** *adj* calm, quiet.

**sosegar** *vt (aplacar)* to calm, quieten.
► *vpr* **sosegarse** *(calmarse)* to calm down.

**sosiego** *nm* calmness, peace.

**soso,-a** *adj* **1** *(insípido)* tasteless; *(sin sal)* unsalted. **2** *fig* dull, insipid.

**sospecha** *nf* suspicion.

**sospechar** *vt (imaginar)* to suspect, think, suppose.
► *vi (desconfiar)* to suspect (**de**, -).

**sospechoso,-a** *adj* suspicious.
► *nm & nf* suspect.

**sostén** *nm* **1** *(apoyo)* support. **2** *(sustento)* sustenance. **3** [también se usa en plural con el mismo significado] *(prenda)* bra.

**sostener** *vt* **1** *(mantener firme)* to support, hold up. **2** *(sujetar)* to hold. **3** *fig (apoyar)* to support, back. **4** *fig (afirmar)* to maintain, affirm. **5** *fig (alimentar)* to support, keep. **6** *fig (velocidad, correspondencia, relación, etc)* to keep up.
► *vpr* **sostenerse** **1** *(mantenerse)* to support os; *(de pie)* to stand up. **2** *(permanecer)* to stay, remain.

**sostenibilidad** *nf* sustainability.

**sostenible** *adj (gen)* sustainable; *(argumento)* tenable.

**sostenido,-a** *adj* **1** *(continuado)* sustained; *(constante)* steady. **2** MÚS sharp: *fa sostenido* F sharp.
▸ *nm* **sostenido** MÚS sharp.

**sota** *nf (cartas)* jack, knave.

**sótano** *nm (gen)* basement; *(de casa)* cellar, basement.

**sotavento** *nm* lee, leeward.

**soterrar** *vt* **1** to bury. **2** *fig* to hide.

**soto** *nm* **1** *(arboleda)* grove, copse.

**Sri Lanka** *nf* Sri Lanka.

**stop** *nm* **1** *(señal)* stop sign. **2** *(parada)* stop.

**su** *adj (de él)* his; *(de ella)* her; *(de usted, de ustedes)* your; *(de ellos, de ellas)* their; *(de animales, cosas)* its; *(de uno)* one's.

**suave** *adj* **1** *(agradable al tacto)* soft, smooth. **2** *(liso, llano)* smooth, even. **3** *fig (apacible)* gentle, mild. **4** *fig (tranquilo)* easy. **5** *fig (música, palabras, voz, luz, movimiento, viento)* soft, gentle. **6** *fig (clima)* mild, clement.

**suavizante** *nm* **1** *(de pelo)* hair conditioner. **2** *(de ropa)* fabric softener.

**suavizar** *vt* **1** *(hacer agradable)* to soften. **2** *(alisar)* to smooth (out). **3** *fig* to soften.

**subacuático,-a** *adj* underwater.

**subafluente** *nm* tributary.

**subalimentación** *nf* undernourishment.

**subalimentar** *vt* to underfeed.

**subalterno,-a** *nm & nf* subordinate.

**subasta** *nf* **1** *(venta)* auction. **2** *(adjudicación de obra)* invitation to tender.

**subastador,-ra** *nm & nf* auctioneer.

**subastar** *vt* to auction (off).

**subatómico,-a** *adj* subatomic.

**subcampeón,-ona** *nm & nf (en competición)* runner-up; *(en ránking)* number two.

**subdesarrollo** *nm* underdevelopment.

**subdirector,-ra** *nm & nf* assistant director, assistant manager.

**súbdito,-a** *nm & nf* **1** *(de un rey)* subject. **2** *(ciudadano)* citizen.

**subida** *nf* **1** *(ascenso)* ascent, climb. **2** *(pendiente)* slope, hill. **3** *fig (aumento - gen)* increase; *(- de temperatura)* rise; *(- de precios, salario)* rise, increase.

**subíndice** *nm* subscript, subindex.

**subir** *vi* **1** *(ir hacia arriba - gen)* to go up, come up; *(- avión)* to climb. **2** *(en un vehículo - coche)* to get in; *(autobús, avión, barco, tren)* to get on, get onto. **3** *(montar - bicicleta)* to get on; *(- caballo)* to get on, mount. **4** *(a un árbol)* to climb up. **5** *fig (elevarse, aumentar)* to rise. **6** *fig (categoría, puesto)* to be promoted.
▸ *vt* **1** *(escaleras, calle)* to go up, climb; *(montaña)* to climb. **2** *(mover arriba)* to carry up, take up, bring up; *(poner arriba)* to put upstairs. **3** *(cabeza, etc)* to lift, raise. **4** *(pared)* to raise. **5** *fig (precio, salario, etc)* to raise, put up. **6** *fig (subir el volumen - voz)* to raise; *(- aparato)* to turn up. **8** *fig (color)* to strengthen.
▸ *vpr* **subirse 1** *(piso, escalera)* to go up. **2** *(árbol, muro, etc)* to climb up (a, -). **3** *(en un vehículo - coche)* to get in (a, -); *(autobús)* to get on (a, -); *(avión, barco, tren)* to get on (a, -), get onto (a,-): *¡súbete, súbete al coche!* get in, get into the car! **4** *(en animales, bicicleta)* to get on (a, -), mount. **5** *(ropa, calcetines)* to pull up; *(cremallera)* to do up, zip up; *(mangas)* to roll up.

**súbito,-a** *adj* sudden.

**subjetivo,-a** *adj* subjective.

**subjuntivo,-a** *adj* subjunctive.
▸ *nm* **subjuntivo** subjunctive.

**sublevación** *nf* uprising, revolt.

**submarinismo** *nm* skin diving.

**submarinista** *nm o nf* skin-diver.

**submarino,-a** *adj* underwater.
▸ *nm* **submarino** submarine.

**submúltiplo,-a** *adj* submultiple.
▸ *nm* **submúltiplo** submultiple.

**suboficial** *nm* **1** MIL noncommissioned officer. **2** MAR petty officer.

**subordinación** *nf* subordination.

**subordinado,-a** *adj* subordinate.
▸ *nm & nf* subordinate.

**subordinar** *vt* to subordinate.
▸ *vpr* **subordinarse** to subordinate os.

S

**subproducto** *nm* by-product.

**subrayar** *vt* **1** to underline. **2** *fig* to emphasize, underline, stress.

**subreino** *nm* subkingdom.

**subrepticio,-a** *adj* surreptitious.

**subrogar** *vt* to subrogate, substitute.

**subsanar** *vt* **1** *(remediar)* to rectify, correct. **2** *(dificultad, etc)* to overcome.

**subscribir** *vt-vpr* → suscribir.

**subscriptor,-ra** *adj & nf* subscriber.

**subscrito,-a** *adj-nm & nf* → suscrito,-a.

**subsecretaría** *nf* **1** *(cargo)* under-secretaryship. **2** *(oficina)* under-secretary's office.

**subsecretario,-a** *nm & nf* under-secretary.

**subsidiario,-a** *adj* subsidiary.

**subsidio** *nm* allowance, benefit.

**subsistencia** *nf* **1** *(hecho)* subsistence. **2** *(lo necesario para vivir)* sustenance.
 ▸ *nf pl* **subsistencias** *(provisiones)* food *sing*, provisions, supplies.

**subsistir** *vi* **1** *(conservarse)* to subsist, last. **2** *(vivir)* live on, survive.

**substancia** *nf* → sustancia.

**substancial** *adj* → sustancial.

**substanciar** *vt* to condense, abridge.

**substancioso,-a** *adj* → sustancioso,-a.

**substantivar** *vt* to use as a noun.

**substantivo,-a** *adj-nm* → sustantivo.

**substitución** *nf* substitution.

**substituible** *adj* replaceable.

**substituir** *vt* → sustituir.

**substituto,-a** *nm & nf* → sustituto,-a.

**substracción** *nf* → sustracción.

**substraendo** *nm* subtrahend.

**substraer** *vt-vpr* → sustraer.

**substrato** *nm* substratum.

**subsuelo** *nm* subsoil.

**subterfugio** *nm* *(escapatoria)* subterfuge; *(pretexto)* pretext.

**subterráneo,-a** *adj* underground.
 ▸ *nm* **subterráneo** underground passage, tunnel, subway.

**subtítulo** *nm* **1** subtitle. **2** LIT subhead.

**subtotal** *nm* subtotal.

**subtropical** *adj* subtropical.

**suburbano,-a** *adj* suburban.
 ▸ *nm* suburbano suburban train.

**suburbio** *nm* *(periferia)* suburb.

**subvención** *nf* subsidy, grant.

**subvencionar** *vt* to subsidize.

**subversión** *nf* subversion.

**subversivo,-a** *adj* subversive.

**subyacente** *adj* underlying.

**subyacer** *vi* to underlie (en, -).

**subyugar** *vt* **1** to subjugate. **2** *fig* to captivate.

**succionar** *vt* to suck up.

**suceder** *vi* **1** [sólo se usa en tercera persona; no lleva sujeto] *(acontecer)* to happen, occur: ¿qué sucede? what's the matter? **2** *(seguir)* to follow (a, -), succeed (a, -). **3** *(heredar)* to succeed.
 ▸ *vpr* **sucederse** to follow one another.

**sucesión** *nf* **1** *(herencia)* succession, inheritance. **2** *(descendencia)* issue, heirs *pl*. **3** *(al trono)* succession. **4** *(serie)* series, succession.

**sucesivo,-a** *adj* **1** *(siguiente)* following, successive. **2** *(consecutivo)* consecutive, running.

**suceso** *nm* **1** *(hecho)* event, happening, occurrence. **2** *(incidente)* incident. **3** *(delito)* crime.

**sucesor,-ra** *nm & nf* successor.

**suciedad** *nf* **1** *(inmundicia)* dirt, filth. **2** *(calidad)* dirtiness, filthiness.

**sucio,-a** *adj* **1** *(con manchas)* dirty, filthy. **2** *(que se ensucia fácilmente)* which dirties easily. **3** *fig (deshonesto)* shady, underhand. **4** DEP *fig* foul, dirty, unfair. **5** *fig (trabajo, lenguaje)* dirty, filthy.
 ▸ *adv* **sucio** *fig* in an underhand way, dirty. LOC **en sucio** in rough.

**sucumbir** *vi* **1** *(rendirse)* to succumb (a, to), yield (a, to). **2** *(morir)* to perish. **3** *fig (tentación, etc)* to give in (a, to), yield (a, to).

**sucursal** *nf* **1** *(oficina)* branch, branch office. **2** *(delegación)* subsidiary.

**sudadera** *nf* **1** *(prenda)* sweatshirt. **2** *fam (acción)* sweat.

**Sudáfrica** *nf* South Africa.

**sudafricano,-a** *adj* South African.

**Sudamérica** *nf* South America.

**sudamericano,-a** *adj* South American.

**Sudán** *nm* Sudan.

**sudanés,-esa** *adj* Sudanese.
▶ *nm & nf* Sudanese.

**sudar** *vi (transpirar)* to sweat, perspire.

**sudario** *nm* shroud.

**sudeste** *adj* **1** *(del sudeste)* southeast, southeastern; *(hacia el sudeste)* southeasterly. **2** *(viento)* southeast.
▶ *nm* **1** *(punto cardinal)* southeast. **2** *(viento)* southeast wind.

**sudoeste** *adj* **1** *(del sudoeste)* southwest, southwestern; *(hacia el sudoeste)* southwesterly. **2** *(viento)* southwest.
▶ *nm* **1** *(punto cardinal)* southwest. **2** *(viento)* southwest wind.

**sudor** *nm* **1** sweat. **2** *fig* effort.

**sudoríparo,-a** *adj* sweat. COMP glándulas **sudoríparas** sweat glands.

**sudoroso,-a** *adj* sweaty.

**Suecia** *nf* Sweden.

**sueco,-a** *adj* Swedish.
▶ *nm & nf (persona)* Swede.
▶ *nm* **sueco** *(idioma)* Swedish.

**suegro,-a** *nm & nf (hombre)* father-in-law; *(mujer)* mother-in-law.

**suela** *nf (del calzado)* sole.

**sueldo** *nm* salary, pay, wages *pl*.

**suelo** *nm* **1** *(superficie)* ground; *(de interior)* floor. **2** *fig (tierra)* soil, land; *(mundo)* earth. **3** *(territorio)* soil, land. **4** *(terreno)* land. **5** *(pavimento)* surface. **6** *fig (de vasija, etc)* bottom.

**suelto,-a** *adj* **1** *(no sujeto)* loose. **2** *(desatado)* undone, untied. **3** *(no envasado o empaquetado)* loose. **4** *(desaparejado)* odd. **5** *(dinero)* in change. **6** *(en libertad)* free; *(huido)* at large. **7** *(disgregado)* scattered. **8** *(con diarrea)* loose. **9** *(prenda)* loose, loose-fitting. **10** *fig (ligero)* agile, nimble; *(veloz)* swift.
▶ *nm* **suelto** *(cambio)* change, small change, loose change.

**sueño** *nm* **1** *(acto)* sleep. **2** *(ganas de dormir)* sleepiness. **3** *(lo soñado)* dream. **4** *fig (ilusión)* dream, illusion.

**suero** *nm* **1** MED serum. **2** *(de la leche)* whey.

**suerte** *nf* **1** *(fortuna)* luck, fortune. **2** *(azar)* chance. **3** *(destino)* destiny, fate. **4** *(estado, condición)* lot, situation. **5** *fml (tipo)* sort, kind, type. LOC **¡buena suerte!** good luck!

**suéter** *nm* sweater.

**suficiente** *adj* **1** *(bastante)* sufficient, enough. **2** *(apto)* suitable. **3** *fig (engreído)* smug, complacent.

**sufijo,-a** *adj* suffixal.
▶ *nm* **sufijo** suffix.

**sufragar** *vt (costear - gastos)* to defray, pay; *(- empresa)* to finance.

**sufragio** *nm* **1** suffrage. **2** *(voto)* vote.

**sufrido,-a** *adj* **1** *(persona)* patient, long-suffering. **2** *(color)* practical; *(tejido)* hardwearing.

**sufrimiento** *nm* suffering.

**sufrir** *vt* **1** *(padecer)* to suffer. **2** *(accidente, ataque)* to have; *(operación)* to undergo. **3** *(dificultades, cambios)* to experience; *(derrota, consecuencias)* to suffer. **4** *(aguantar)* to bear put up with.
▶ *vi (padecer)* to suffer.

**sugerencia** *nf* suggestion.

**sugerente** *adj* suggestive.

**sugerir** *vt* **1** to suggest. **2** *(insinuar)* to hint. **3** *(suscitar)* to suggest.

**sugestión** *nf* suggestion.

**sugestionar** *vt* to influence.

**sugestivo,-a** *adj (que atrae)* fascinating, attractive.

**suicidarse** *vpr* to commit suicide.

**suicidio** *nm* suicide.

**Suiza** *nf* Switzerland.

**suizo,-a** *adj* Swiss.
▶ *nm & nf* Swiss.

**sujeción** *nf (acción)* subjection.

**sujetador,-ra** *adj* fastening.
▶ *nm* **sujetador** bra.

**sujetar** *vt* **1** *(fijar)* to fix, secure, hold. **2** *(agarrar, sostener)* hold on to. **3** *(papeles)* to fasten; *(pelo)* to hold in place. **4** *fig (dominar, someter)* to control.
▶ *vpr* **sujetarse** **1** *(agarrarse)* to hold on, hold tight. **2** *fig (someterse)* to subject os (a, to).

S

**sujeto,-a** *adj* **1** *(sometido)* subject (a, to), liable (a, to). **2** *(agarrado, atado)* fastened, secure.
  ▶ *nm* **sujeto 1** LING subject. **2** *(individuo)* fellow, individual, character.

**sulfato** *nm* sulphate (US sulfate).

**sulfhídrico,-a** *adj* sulphuretted (US sulfureted).

**sulfito** *nm* sulphite (US sulfite).

**sulfurar** *vt* **1** QUÍM to sulphurate (US sulfurate). **2** *fam fig (irritar)* to infuriate.
  ▶ *vpr* **sulfurarse** *fam fig* to blow one's top, lose one's rag.

**sulfúrico,-a** *adj* sulphuric (US sulfuric).

**sulfuro** *nm* sulphide (US sulfide).

**sulfuroso,-a** *adj* sulphurous (US sulfurous).

**sultán,-ana** *nm & nf (hombre)* sultan; *(mujer)* sultana.

**suma** *nf* **1** *(cantidad)* sum, amount. **2** MAT sum, addition. **3** *(resumen)* summary.

**sumando** *nm* addend.

**sumar** *vt* **1** MAT to add, add up. **2** *(componer una cantidad)* to total, amount to, come to. **3** *(compendiar)* to sum up.
  ▶ *vpr* **sumarse** *(unirse)* to join (a, in).

**sumario,-a** *adj* **1** summary, brief. **2** JUR summary.
  ▶ *nm* **sumario 1** *(resumen)* summary. **2** JUR legal proceedings *pl*, indictment.

**sumergible** *adj* submersible.
  ▶ *nm* submarine.

**sumergir** *vt* **1** *(meter bajo líquido)* to submerge, submerse, immerse. **2** *fig (hundir)* to plunge, sink.
  ▶ *vpr* **sumergirse 1** *(meterse bajo líquido)* to submerge (en, in), go underwater. **2** *fig* to become immersed (en, in).

**sumidero** *nm* drain, sewer.

**suministrador,-ra** *nm & nf* supplier.

**suministrar** *vt* to provide, supply.

**suministro** *nm* supply, supplying.

**sumisión** *nf* **1** *(acto)* submission. **2** *(carácter)* submissiveness.

**sumiso,-a** *adj* submissive, obedient.

**sumo,-a** *adj* **1** *(supremo)* supreme, highest. **2** *fig (muy grande)* greatest.

**suntuario,-a** *adj* sumptuary.

**suntuoso,-a** *adj* sumptuous.

**supeditar** *vt* **1** *(subordinar)* to subordinate (a, to). **2** *(condicionar)* to subject (a, to).
  ▶ *vpr* **supeditarse** *(someterse)* to subject os (a, to), bow (a, to).

**súper** *nm fam (supermercado)* supermarket.
  ▶ *nf fam (gasolina)* four-star.

**superable** *adj* surmountable.

**superabundante** *adj* superabundant.

**superar** *vt* **1** *(exceder)* to surpass, exceed, excel. **2** *(obstáculo, etc)* to overcome, surmount.
  ▶ *vpr* **superarse 1** *(sobrepasarse)* to excel os. **2** *(mejorarse)* to improve os, better os.

**superconductividad** *nf* superconductivity.

**superconductor** *nm* superconductor.

**superdotado,-a** *nm & nf* genius.

**superestrato** *nm* superstratum.

**superestructura** *nf* superstructure.

**superficial** *adj* superficial.

**superficialidad** *nf* superficiality.

**superficie** *nf* **1** *(parte externa)* surface. **2** *(área)* area.

**superfluo,-a** *adj* superfluous.

**superhombre** *nm* superman.

**superíndice** *nm* superscript.

**superintendente** *nm o nf* superintendent.

**superior** *adj* **1** *(encima de)* upper, top: *labio superior* upper lip. **2** *(por encima de)* greater (a, than), higher (a, than), above (a, -). **3** *fig (persona - que supera)* superior; *(- mejor)* better. **4** *fig (calidad, etc)* superior, high, excellent. **5** EDUC higher.
  ▶ *nm* **1** *(jefe)* superior. **2** REL superior.

**superioridad** *nf (persona)* superiority.

**superlativo,-a** *adj* superlative.
  ▶ *nm* **superlativo** superlative.

**supermercado** *nm* supermarket.

**supernova** *nf* supernova.

**superpoblación** *nf* overpopulation.

**superpoblado,-a** *adj* overpopulated.

**superponer** *vt* **1** to superimpose, lay on top. **2** *fig* to put before.

**superposición** *nf* superimposition.

**superpotencia** *nf* superpower.

**superpuesto,-a** *pp* → superponer.

**supersónico,-a** *adj* supersonic.

**superstición** *nf* superstition.

**supersticioso,-a** *adj* superstitious.

**supervisar** *vt* to supervise.

**supervisión** *nf* supervision, control.

**supervisor,-ra** *nm & nf* supervisor.

**supervivencia** *nf* survival.

**superviviente** *adj* surviving.
  ▶ *nm o nf* survivor.

**suplemento** *nm* **1** *(de revista, etc)* supplement. **2** *(de dinero)* extra charge. **3** *(geometría)* supplement.

**suplencia** *nf* substitution.

**suplente** *nm o nf* **1** *(gen)* substitute. **2** DEP reserve player. **3** TEAT understudy.

**súplica** *nf* **1** request, entreaty, plea. **2** JUR petition.

**suplicar** *vt* **1** to beseech, beg, implore. **2** JUR to appeal to.

**suplicio** *nm* *(castigo)* torture.

**suplir** *vt* **1** *(reemplazar)* to replace, substitute. **2** *(compensar)* to make up for.

**suponer** *vt* **1** *(gen)* to suppose, assume. **2** *(significar)* to mean. **3** *(conllevar)* to mean, entail, require. **4** *(adivinar)* to guess; *(imaginar)* to imagine, think. **5** *(creer)* to think.
  ▶ *nm fam* supposition.

**suposición** *nf* supposition, assumption.

**suprarrenal** *adj* suprarenal.

**supremo,-a** *adj* **1** *(gen)* supreme. **2** *(decisivo)* decisive. **3** *(último)* last, final.

**suprimir** *vt* **1** *(libertad, etc)* to suppress; *(ley, impuestos)* to abolish; *(dificultades)* to eliminate, remove; *(restricciones)* to lift. **2** *(tabaco, alcohol)* to cut out. **3** *(palabra)* to delete, take out, leave out. **4** *(omitir)* to omit.

**supuesto,-a** *adj* **1** *(que se supone)* supposed, assumed. **2** *(pretendido)* so-called, self-styled.

  ▶ *nm* **supuesto 1** *(suposición)* supposition, assumption. **2** *(hipótesis)* hypothesis.

**supurar** *vi* to suppurate.

**sur** *nm* **1** south. **2** *(viento)* south wind.

**Suramérica** *nf* South America.

**suramericano,-a** *adj-nm & nf* → sudamericano,-a.

**surcar** *vt* **1** AGR to plough (US plow). **2** *(agua)* to cut through, cross; *(aire)* to fly through.

**surco** *nm* **1** *(en tierra)* furrow. **2** *(arruga)* wrinkle. **3** *(de disco)* groove.

**surcoreano,-a** *adj* South Korean.
  ▶ *nm & nf* South Korean.

**sureste** *adj-nm* → sudeste.

**surfista** *nm o nf* surfer.

**surgir** *vi* **1** *(agua)* to spring forth, spurt up. **2** *fig* *(aparecer - gen)* to appear, emerge; *(- dificultades)* to crop up, arise, come up. **3** MAR to anchor.

**Surinam** *nm* Surinam.

**suroeste** *adj-nm* → sudoeste.

**surtido,-a** *adj* **1** *(variado)* assorted. **2** *(bien provisto)* well stocked.
  ▶ *nm* **surtido** assortment, selection.

**surtidor** *nm* **1** *(fuente)* fountain. **2** *(chorro)* jet, spout.

**surtir** *vt* *(proveer)* to supply (de, with), provide (de, with).
  ▶ *vi* *(brotar)* to spout, spurt.
  ▶ *vpr* **surtirse** to supply os, provide os.

**susceptibilidad** *nf* **1** *(gen)* susceptibility. **2** *(sensibilidad)* sensitivity.

**susceptible** *adj* **1** *(gen)* susceptible. **2** *(sensible)* oversensitive.

**suscitar** *vt* **1** *(gen)* to cause, provoke. **2** *(rebelión)* to stir up, arouse; *(discusión)* to start; *(problemas)* to cause, raise; *(interés)* to arouse.

**suscribir** *vt* **1** FIN to subscribe. **2** *fig* *(convenir con alguien)* to subscribe to, endorse. **3** *(a una revista, etc)* to take out a subscription for. **4** *fml* *(firmar)* to subscribe.
  ▶ *vpr* **suscribirse** *(abonarse)* to subscribe.

**suscripción** *nf* subscription.

**suscriptor,-ra** *nm & nf* subscriber.

S

**suscrito,-a** *adj* **1** *(abonado)* subscribed. **2** *(firmado)* undersigned.
▸ *nm & nf* undersigned.

**suspender** *vt* **1** *(levantar)* to hang, hang up, suspend. **2** *(aplazar - gen)* to postpone, put off, delay; *(- reunión)* to adjourn. **3** EDUC *fig* to fail. **4** *fig (pagos)* to suspend; *(servicio)* to discontinue.

**suspensión** *nf* **1** *(acto de levantar)* hanging, hanging up, suspension. **2** AUTO suspension. **3** *(aplazamiento - gen)* delay, postponement; *(- de reunión)* adjournment. **4** *(supresión)* suspension, discontinuation.

**suspenso,-a** *adj* **1** *(colgado)* hanging, suspended. **2** REL *fig (alumno)* failed. **3** *fig (asombrado)* bewildered, amazed.
▸ *nm* **suspenso** EDUC fail.

**suspicacia** *nf (sospecha)* suspicion.

**suspicaz** *adj* **1** *(desconfiado)* mistrustful, distrustful. **2** *(que sospecha)* suspicious.

**suspirar** *vi* to sigh.

**suspiro** *nm* sigh.

**sustancia** *nf* **1** *(gen)* substance. **2** *(esencia)* substance, essence.

**sustancial** *adj* **1** *(gen)* substantial. **2** *(fundamental)* essential, fundamental. **3** *(importante)* important, substantial.

**sustanciar** *vt* to condense, abridge.

**sustancioso,-a** *adj* **1** *(nutritivo)* wholesome. **2** *fig (libro, etc)* meaty.

**sustantivar** *vt* to use as a noun.

**sustantivo,-a** *nm* noun, substantive.

**sustentable** *adj* tenable.

**sustentación** *nf* **1** *(soporte)* support. **2** *(mantenimiento)* sustenance, maintenance.

**sustentar** *vt* **1** *(familia, etc)* to maintain, support, sustain. **2** *(sostener)* to hold up, support. **3** *(teoría, opinión)* to support, defend.

**sustento** *nm* **1** *(alimento)* sustenance, food. **2** *(apoyo)* support.

**sustitución** *nf* substitution, replacement.

**sustituible** *adj* replaceable, expendable.

**sustituir** *vt (reemplazar)* to substitute (por, with), replace (por, with).

**sustitutivo,-a** *adj* substitutive.
▸ *nm* **sustitutivo** substitute.

**sustituto,-a** *nm & nf* substitute, stand-in, replacement.

**susto** *nm* fright, scare, shock.

**sustracción** *nf* **1** *(robo)* theft. **2** MAT subtraction.

**sustraendo** *nm* subtrahend.

**sustraer** *vt* **1** *(robar)* to steal. **2** MAT to subtract.
▸ *vpr* **sustraerse** *(faltar al cumplimiento)* to evade (a, -), elude (a, -); *(tentaciones)* to resist (a, -).

**sustrato** *nm* substratum.

**susurrar** *vi* to whisper.

**susurro** *nm* **1** whisper. **2** *fig (agua)* murmur; *(hojas)* rustle.

**sutil** *adj* **1** *(delgado)* thin, fine. **2** *(aroma)* delicate; *(color)* soft. **3** *(brisa)* gentle. **4** *fig* subtle.

**suturar** *vt* to stitch.

**suyo,-a** *adj (de él)* his, of his; *(de ella)* her, of hers; *(de animales, cosas)* its; *(de usted, de ustedes)* yours, of yours; *(de ellos, de ellas)* theirs, of theirs: *este libro es suyo* this book is hers; *aquel amigo suyo* that friend of yours.
▸ *pron (de él)* his; *(de ella)* hers; *(de usted, de ustedes)* yours; *(de ellos, de ellas)* theirs: *éstos son los míos, los suyos están sobre la mesa* there are mine, hers are on the table.
▸ *nf* **la suya** *(ocasión, oportunidad)* one's chance, one's opportunity.
▸ *nm* **lo suyo** **1** *(lo que toca)* what one deserves. **2** *(habilidad)* forte, one's thing: *lo suyo es el tenis* tennis is his thing. **3** *fam (mucho)* a lot: *comió lo suyo* he ate a lot.
▸ *nm pl* **los suyos** *(familiares)* his *(her, your, etc)* family *sing*; *(amigos)* his *(her, your, etc)* friends, his *(her, your, etc)* people.

**Swazilandia** *nf* Swaziland.

**T, t** *nf (la letra)* T, t.

**tabaco** *nm* **1** *(gen)* tobacco. **2** *(cigarrillos)* cigarettes *pl; (cigarro)* cigar. **3** *(enfermedad)* black rot. COMP **tabaco rubio** Virginia tobacco.

**tábano** *nm* horsefly.

**taberna** *nf* pub, bar.

**tabique** *nm* partition, partition wall.

**tabla** *nf* **1** *(de madera)* board, plank. **2** *(de piedra)* slab; *(de metal)* sheet. **3** *(estante)* shelf. **4** ARTE panel. **5** COST pleat. **6** *(índice)* index. **7** *(lista)* list; *(catálogo)* catalogue (US catalog). **8** MAT table. COMP **tabla de multiplicar** multiplication table.
   ▶ *nf pl* **tablas 1** TEAT stage *sing*, boards. **2** *(ajedrez)* stalemate *sing*, draw *sing*.

**tablado** *nm* **1** *(suelo)* wooden floor. **2** *(entarimado)* wooden platform. **3** *(del escenario)* stage.

**tablero** *nm* **1** *(tablón)* panel, board. **2** *(en juegos)* board. **3** *(encerado)* blackboard. **4** AUTO dashboard. **5** INFORM display board. COMP **tablero de ajedrez** chessboard.

**tableta** *nf* **1** *(pastilla)* tablet. **2** *(de chocolate)* bar.

**tablón** *nm* **1** plank. **2** *(en construcción)* board. COMP **tablón de anuncios** notice board, US bulletin board.

**tabulación** *nf* tabulation.

**tacaño,-a** *adj* mean, stingy.

**tacha** *nf* **1** *(defecto)* flaw, blemish, defect. **2** *(descrédito)* blemish.

**tachadura** *nf* crossing out.

**tachar** *vt* **1** *(borrar)* to cross out. **2** *(culpar)* to accuse (de, of): *lo tachan de fascista* they accuse him of being a fascist.

**tachuela** *nf* tack, stud.

**tacita** *nf* little cup.

**tácito,-a** *adj* tacit.

**taco** *nm* **1** *(tarugo)* plug, stopper. **2** *(para pared)* plug, Rawlplug. **3** *(bloc de notas)* notepad, writing pad; *(calendario)* tear-off calendar. **4** *(de entradas)* book; *(de billetes)* wad. **5** *(de billar)* cue. **6** CULIN *(de queso, etc)* cube, piece; *(en Méjico)* taco, rolled-up tortilla. **7** *fam (palabrota)* swearword.

**tacón** *nm* heel.

**táctica** *nf* tactic, tactics *pl*, strategy.

**tacto** *nm* **1** *(sentido)* touch. **2** *(acción)* touch, touching. **3** *fig (delicadeza)* tact. LOC **tener tacto** to be tactful.

**Tadjikistán** *nm* Tadzhikistan.

**tadjiko,-a** *adj* Tadzhiki.
   ▶ *nm o nf (persona)* Tadzhik.
   ▶ *nm* **tadjiko** *(idioma)* Tadzhiki.

**Tahití** *nm* Tahiti.

**tahitiano,-a** *adj* Tahitian.
   ▶ *nm & nf (persona)* Tahitian.
   ▶ *nm* **tahitiano** *(idioma)* Tahitian.

**tailandés,-esa** *adj* Thai.
   ▶ *nm & nf (persona)* Thai.
   ▶ *nm* **tailandés** *(idioma)* Thai.

**Tailandia** *nf* Thailand.

**Taiwan** *nm* Taiwan.

**taiwanés,-esa** *adj* Taiwanese.
   ▶ *nm & nf* Taiwanese.

**tajada** *nf* **1** *(rodaja)* slice. **2** *(corte)* cut; *(cuchillada)* stab.

**tajo** *nm* **1** *(corte)* cut, slash. **2** *(filo)* cutting edge. **3** *(escarpa)* steep cliff.

**tal** *adj* **1** *(semejante)* such: *en tales condiciones* in such conditions. **2** *(tan grande)* such, so: *tal es su ignorancia que...* he is so ignorant that... **3** *(cosa sin especificar)* such and such: *tal día* such and such a day. **4** *(persona sin especificar)* someone called, a certain: *vino un tal Alberto* someone called Alberto came.

► *pron (alguno - cosa)* such a thing, something; *(- persona)* someone, somebody: *yo no dije tal cosa* I didn't say such a thing.

► *adv (así)* in such a way, so: *tal me contestó que no supe cómo reaccionar* he answered in such a way that I didn't know how to react. LOC **tal como 1** *(ejemplos)* such as. **2** *(de la misma manera)* just as. ‖ **tal cual** just as it is.

**tala** *nf* tree felling.

**taladrar** *vt* **1** *(gen)* to drill; *(pared)* to bore through. **2** *fig (los oídos)* to pierce.

**taladro** *nm* **1** *(herramienta)* drill, bore. **2** *(agujero)* hole.

**talar** *vt* **1** *(cortar)* to fell, cut down. **2** *(destruir)* to devastate.

**talento** *nm* **1** *(entendimiento)* talent, intelligence. **2** *(aptitud)* gift, talent: *tiene talento para las matemáticas* she has a gift for mathematics.

**talla** *nf* **1** *(estatura)* height. **2** *fig (moral, intelectual)* stature. **3** *(de prenda)* size: *¿qué talla usa?* what size is he? **4** *(escultura)* carving, sculpture. **5** *(tallado - piedras)* cutting; *(- metal)* engraving.

**tallar** *vt* **1** *(madera, piedra)* to carve, shape; *(piedras preciosas)* to cut; *(metales)* to engrave. **2** *(medir)* to measure the height of.

**talle** *nm* **1** *(cintura)* waist. **2** *(figura - de hombre)* build, physique; *(- de mujer)* figure, shape.

**taller** *nm* **1** *(obrador)* workshop. **2** *(de artista)* studio. **3** *(en fábrica)* shop, workshop. **4** AUTO garage, repair shop.

**tallo** *nm* BOT stem, stalk; *(renuevo)* sprout, shoot.

**talón** *nm* **1** *(de pie, zapato, etc)* heel. **2** *(cheque)* cheque (US check). COMP **talón bancario** counter cheque (US check). ‖ **talón de Aquiles** Achilles' heel.

**talonario** *nm (de cheques)* cheque book (US check book); *(de recibos)* stub book.

**tamaño,-a** *adj (semejante)* such a, so big a: *no pude aguantar tamaña imperti-*

nencia I couldn't tolerate such an impertinent remark.

► *nm tamaño (medida)* size: *¿de qué tamaño es?* what size is it?

**tamarindo** *nm* tamarind.

**tambalearse** *vpr* **1** *(persona)* to stagger; *(mueble)* to wobble. **2** *fig* to be shaky.

**también** *adv* **1** *(igualmente)* also, too, as well, so: *Pedro también estaba* Pedro was also there, Pedro was there too, Pedro was there as well. **2** *(además)* besides, in addition.

**tambor** *nm* **1** *(instrumento)* drum. **2** *(maquinaria)* drum. **3** *(de arma)* cylinder, barrel. **4** *(de lavadora)* drum. **5** *(de freno)* brake drum.

**tamiz** *nm* sieve.

**tamizar** *vt* **1** *(harina, tierra)* to sieve. **2** *(luz)* to filter. **3** *fig (seleccionar)* to screen.

**tampoco** *adv* neither, nor, not… either: *no quiere estudiar y tampoco quiere ir al cine* he doesn't want to study and he doesn't want to go to the cinema either.

**tan** *adv* **1** *(tanto)* such, such a, so: *no seas tan cruel* don't be so cruel. **2** *(comparativo - como)* as… as, so… (that); *(- que)* so…, so… (that): *está tan gordo como tú* he's as fat as you (are). LOC **tan solo** only, just: *tan solo quiero uno* I only want one.

**tanda** *nf* **1** *(conjunto)* batch, lot; *(serie)* series, course. **2** *(turno)* shift. **3** *(en billar)* game.

**tangente** *adj* tangent.

► *nf* tangent.

**tanque** *nm* **1** *(depósito)* tank, reservoir. **2** MIL tank. **3** *(vehículo cisterna)* tanker.

**tantear** *vt* **1** *(calcular)* to estimate, guess. **2** *(probar medidas)* to size up. **3** *fig (ensayar)* to try out, put to the test. **4** *fig (persona)* to sound out. **5** *(dibujo)* to sketch.

► *vi* **1** DEP to score, keep score. **2** *(andar a tientas)* to feel one's way.

**tanto,-a** *adj* **1** *(incontables)* so much; *(contables)* so many: *no comas tantos caramelos* don't eat so many sweets. **2** *(comparación - incontable)* as much; *(- contables)* as many: *tengo tantos libros como tú* I've got as many books as you.

▸ *pron (incontable)* so much; *(contable)* so many: *no había tantos* there weren't so many.

▸ *adv* **1** *(cantidad)* so much: *¡te quiero tanto!* I love you so much! **2** *(tiempo)* so long: *esperamos tanto* we waited for so long. **3** *(frecuencia)* so often: *no los telefonees tanto* don't phone them so often.

▸ *nm* **tanto 1** *(punto)* point; *(fútbol)* goal. **2** *(cantidad imprecisa)* so much, a certain amount: *percibes un tanto al mes* you get so much a month. **3** *(poco)* bit: *es un tanto estrecho* it's a bit narrow. LOC **a las tantas** *fam* very late, at an unearthly hour. ▮ **por lo tanto** therefore.

**Tanzania** *nf* Tanzania.

**tanzano,-a** *adj* Tanzanian.
▸ *nm & nf* Tanzanian.

**tapa** *nf* **1** *(cubierta)* lid, top; *(de botella)* cap, top, stopper. **2** *(de libro)* cover. **3** *(de zapato)* heel-plate. **4** CULIN *(comida)* appetizer, savoury (US savory), tapa.

**tapadera** *nf* **1** cover, lid. **2** *fig* cover.

**tapar** *vt* **1** *(cubrir)* to cover; *(con tapa)* to put the lid on. **2** *(con ropas, etc)* to wrap up. **3** *(obstruir)* to obstruct; *(tubería)* to block. **4** *(ocultar)* to hide; *(a la vista)* to block. **5** *fig (encubrir)* to cover up.
▸ *vpr* **taparse 1** *(abrigarse)* to wrap up. **2** *(la nariz)* to be blocked up.

**tapia** *nf* *(cerca)* garden wall; *(de adobe)* mud wall, adobe wall.

**tapiar** *vt* **1** *(área)* to wall in, wall off. **2** *fig (puerta, ventana)* to wall up, close up.

**tapicería** *nf* **1** ARTE tapestry making. **2** *(tapices)* tapestries *pl*. **3** *(de muebles, etc)* upholstery. **4** *(tienda)* upholsterer's, upholsterer's workshop.

**tapiz** *nm* **1** *(de pared)* tapestry. **2** *(alfombra)* rug, carpet.

**tapón** *nm* **1** stopper, plug; *(de botella)* cap. **2** *(del oído)* wax in the ear. **3** *(baloncesto)* block. **4** *(embotellamiento)* traffic jam.

**taponar** *vt* **1** *(orificio, etc)* to plug, stop. **2** *(atascar)* to block. **3** *(poner el tapón)* to put the plug in. **4** MED to tampon, plug.

**taquilla** *nf* **1** *(de tren, etc)* ticket office; *(de cine, teatro)* box office. **2** *(recaudación)* takings *pl*, returns *pl*. **3** *(casillero)* pigeonholes *pl*. **4** *(armario)* locker.

**tara** *nf* **1** *(peso)* tare. **2** *(defecto)* defect, blemish, fault.

**tardar** *vt* *(emplear tiempo)* to take: *tardé cuatro horas* it took me four hours.
▸ *vi (demorar)* to take a long time: *se tarda más a pie* it takes longer on foot.

**tarde** *nf* **1** *(hasta las cinco aprox.)* afternoon. **2** *(después de las cinco aprox.)* evening.
▸ *adv* **1** *(hora avanzada)* late: *se está haciendo tarde* it's getting late. **2** *(demasiado tarde)* too late: *es tarde para salir* it's too late to go out.

**tarea** *nf* task, job.

**tarifa** *nf* **1** *(precio)* tariff, rate; *(de transporte)* fare. **2** *(lista de precios)* price list.

**tarima** *nf* platform, dais.

**tarjeta** *nf* card. COMP **tarjeta de crédito** credit card. ▮ **tarjeta de memoria** memory card, chip card. ▮ **tarjeta postal** postcard.

**tarro** *nm* **1** *(vasija)* jar, pot, tub. **2** *fam (cabeza)* bonce.

**tarta** *nf* flan, tart, pie: *tarta de manzana* apple pie.

**tartamudear** *vi* to stammer, stutter.

**tartamudez** *nf* stammering.

**tartamudo,-a** *nm & nf* stutterer.

**tasa** *nf* **1** *(valoración)* valuation. **2** *(precio)* fee, charge. **3** *(impuesto)* tax, levy. **4** *(límite)* limit; *(medida)* measure. **5** *(índice)* rate. COMP **tasa de natalidad** birth rate.

**tasar** *vt* **1** *(valorar)* to value. **2** *(poner precio)* to set the price of, fix the price of.

**Tasmania** *nf* Tasmania.

**tasmano,-a** *adj* Tasmanian.
▸ *nm & nf* Tasmanian.

**tata** *nf fam* nanny.

**tatarabuelo,-a** *nm & nf (hombre)* great-great-grandfather; *(mujer)* great-great-grandmother.

**tataranieto,-a** *nm & nf (hombre)* great-great-grandson; *(mujer)* great-great-granddaughter.

**tatuaje** *nm* **1** *(dibujo)* tattoo. **2** *(técnica)* tattooing.

**tatuar** *vt* to tattoo.

**tauromaquia** *nf* bullfighting, art of bullfighting, tauromachy.

**taxi** *nm* taxi, cab.

T

**taxista** *nm o nf* taxi driver.

**taza** *nf* **1** *(recipiente)* cup. **2** *(contenido)* cupful. **3** *(de retrete)* bowl.

**te¹** *nf* **1** *name of the letter* t. **2** *(regla)* T-square.

**te²** *pron* **1** you, to you, for you: *te mandaré una carta* I'll send you a letter. **2** *(uso reflexivo)* yourself: *ponte el abrigo* put your coat on. **3** *(uso pronominal) no se traduce: vete a casa* go home.

**té** *nm* tea. COMP **la hora del té** teatime.

**teatral** *adj* **1** *(del teatro)* theatrical, dramatic. **2** *fig (exagerado)* stagy, stagey, theatrical.

**teatro** *nm* **1** theatre (US theater). **2** ARTE theatre (US theater), acting, stage. **3** *fig (exageración)* show, play-acting.

**tebeo** *nm* children's comic.

**teca** *nf (árbol, madera)* teak.

**techo** *nm* **1** *(interior)* ceiling; *(de coche, tejado)* roof. **2** *fig (límite superior)* ceiling.

**tecla** *nf* key.

**teclado** *nm* keyboard.

**teclear** *vi (piano)* to press the keys; *(máquina de escribir, ordenador)* to type, tap the keys.

**técnica** *nf* **1** *(tecnología)* technique, technology. **2** *(habilidad)* technique, method. **3** *(ingeniería)* engineering.

**técnico,-a** *adj* technical.
▶ *nm & nf* technician, technical expert.

**tecnología** *nf* technology.

**tectónica** *nf* tectonics.

**tedio** *nm* tedium, boredom.

**teja** *nf (de barro)* tile.

**tejado** *nm* roof.

**tejano,-a** *adj* Texan.
▶ *nm & nf* Texan.
▶ *nm pl* **tejanos** *(pantalón)* jeans.

**tejar** *vt* to tile.

**tejer** *vt* **1** *(en telar)* to weave. **2** *(hacer punto)* to knit. **3** *(araña)* to spin. **4** *fig (plan)* to weave, plot, scheme.

**tejido** *nm* **1** *(tela)* textile. **2** ANAT tissue.

**tejo** *nm (árbol)* yew tree.

**tejón** *nm* badger.

**tela** *nf* **1** *(textil)* material, fabric, cloth. **2** *(de araña)* cobweb. **3** ARTE *(lienzo)* canvas; *(cuadro)* painting. **4** *fam (dinero)* dough. **5** *fam (asunto, tema)* subject, matter. COMP **tela metálica** wire gauze.

**telar** *nm* **1** *(para tejer)* loom. **2** *(para encuadernar)* sewing press.

**telaraña** *nf* cobweb, spider's web.

**tele** *nf fam* telly, TV.

**telecomunicación** *nf* telecommunication.

**telediario** *nm* television news bulletin, TV news.

**teleférico** *nm* cable car.

**telefilm** *nm* TV film.

**telefonear** *vi* to phone.

**teléfono** *nm* telephone, phone. COMP **teléfono móvil** mobile phone.

**telegrafiar** *vt* to telegraph, wire.

**telégrafo** *nm* telegraph.

**telegrama** *nm* telegram, cable.

**telemando** *nm* remote control.

**telenovela** *nf* soap opera.

**teleobjetivo** *nm* telephoto lens.

**telepatía** *nf* telepathy.

**telescopio** *nm* telescope.

**telesilla** *nm* chair lift.

**telespectador,-ra** *nm & nf* TV viewer.

**telesquí** *nm* ski lift, drag lift.

**teletexto** *nm* teletext.

**televisar** *vt* to televise.

**televisión** *nf* **1** *(sistema)* television. **2** *fam (aparato)* television set.

**televisor** *nm* television set.

**télex®** *nm* telex.

**telón** *nm* curtain. COMP **telón de acero** POL iron curtain. ‖ **telón de fondo** TEAT backdrop.

**tema** *nm* **1** *(de discurso, escrito, etc)* topic, subject, theme. **2** MÚS theme.

**temario** *nm (de examen)* programme (US program); *(de conferencia)* agenda.

**temática** *nf* subject matter.

**temático,-a** *adj* **1** thematic. **2** LING stem.

**temblar** *vi* **1** *(de frío)* to shiver (de, with); *(de miedo)* to tremble (de, with). **2** *(voz)* to quiver.

**temblor** *nm* **1** *(gen)* tremor; *(de frío)* shivering, shivers *pl*. **2** *fig* shiver.

**temer** vt 1 *(tener miedo)* to fear, be afraid of. 2 *(sospechar)* to fear, be afraid.
▶ vi 1 *(tener miedo)* to be afraid. 2 *(preocuparse)* to worry.
▶ vpr **temerse** to be afraid: *me temo que sí* I'm afraid so.

**temerario,-a** adj reckless, rash.

**temible** adj dreadful, fearful.

**temor** nm fear.

**temperamento** nm temperament.

**temperatura** nf temperature.

**tempestad** nf 1 storm. 2 fig turmoil.

**templado,-a** adj 1 *(agua)* warm, lukewarm; *(clima, temperatura)* mild, temperate. 2 *(moderado)* moderate; *(sereno)* composed, unruffled. 3 *(valiente)* brave. 4 MÚS tuned. 5 *(metal)* tempered.

**templar** vt 1 *(moderar)* to moderate, temper. 2 *(algo frío)* to warm up; *(algo caliente)* to cool down. 3 *(fig cólera)* to appease; *(apaciguar)* to calm down. 4 *(cuerda, tornillo)* to tighten (up). 5 MÚS to tune. 6 TÉC to temper. 7 *(colores)* to match.
▶ vpr **templarse** *(contenerse)* to control os.

**templo** nm temple.

**temporada** nf 1 *(en artes, deportes, moda)* season. 2 *(período)* period, time. [COMP] **temporada alta** high season. ∎ **temporada baja** low season.

**temporal¹** adj 1 *(transitorio)* temporary.
▶ nm METEOR storm.

**temporal²** adj ANAT temporal.
▶ nm ANAT temporal bone.

**temprano,-a** adj early.
▶ adv early: *nunca se levanta temprano* he never gets up early.

**tenaza** nf [también se usa en plural con el mismo sigificado] *(herramienta)* pliers pl, pincers pl; *(para el fuego)* tongs pl.

**tendedero** nm *(cuerda)* clothesline; *(lugar)* drying place.

**tendencia** nf *(inclinación)* tendency, inclination, leaning; *(movimiento)* trend.

**tender** vt 1 *(extender - mantel, etc)* to spread; *(- red)* to cast. 2 *(puente)* to throw; *(vía, cable)* to lay; *(cuerda)* to stretch. 3 *(ropa, colada)* to hang out. 4 *(mano)* to stretch out. 5 *(emboscada, trampa)* to lay, set.

▶ vi *(tener tendencia)* to tend (a, to), have a tendency (a, to): *tiende al aburrimiento* it tends to be boring.
▶ vpr **tenderse** *(tumbarse)* to lie down.

**tendero,-a** nm & nf shopkeeper.

**tendón** nm tendon, sinew.

**tenedor,-ra** nm *(utensilio)* fork.

**tener** vt 1 *(gen)* to have, have got: *tuvimos un día estupendo* we had a wonderful day. 2 *(poseer)* to own. 3 *(sostener)* to hold: *¿qué tienes en la mano?* what are you holding? 4 *(coger)* to take: *ten tu copa* take your glass. 5 *(sensación, sentimiento)* to be, feel: *tengo hambre* I'm hungry. 6 *(mantener)* to keep: *la lluvia me ha tenido despierta toda la noche* the rain has kept me up all night. 7 *(medir)* to measure. 8 *(contener)* to hold, contain. 9 *(edad)* to be. 10 *(un hijo)* to have. 11 *(celebrar)* to hold: *tener una reunión* to hold a meeting. 12 *(considerar)* to consider, think: *lo tienen por muy listo* they think he's very smart. [LOC] **¡ahí tienes!** so, there you are! ∎ **tener cariño a** to be fond of. ∎ **tener compasión** to take pity (de, on). ∎ **tener ilusión** to be enthusiastic.
▶ aux **tener que** *(obligación)* to have to, have got to, must: *tengo que quedarme* I must stay.
▶ vpr **tenerse** *(sostenerse)* to stand up. [LOC] **tenerse por** to consider os: *se tiene por guapo* he thinks he's handsome.

**tenia** nf tapeworm.

**teniente** nm lieutenant.

**tenis** nm *(deporte)* tenis. [COMP] **tenis de mesa** table tennis, ping-pong.

**tenista** nm o nf tennis player.

**tensar** vt 1 *(cable, cuerda)* to tauten. 2 *(arco)* to draw.

**tensión** nf 1 ELEC tension, voltage. 2 *(de materiales)* stress; *(de gases)* pressure. 3 MED pressure. 4 fig *(de una situación)* tension; *(de una persona)* stress, strain. [COMP] **alta tensión** ELEC high tension. ∎ **tensión arterial** blood pressure.

**tenso,-a** adj 1 *(cuerda)* tense. 2 fig *(relaciones)* strained. 3 fig *(persona)* tense.

**tentación** nf temptation.

**tentáculo** nm tentacle.

**tentador,-ra** adj tempting, enticing.

**T**

**tentar** vt **1** *(palpar)* to feel, touch. **2** *(incitar)* to tempt, entice.

**tentempié** nm fam *(refrigerio)* snack.

**teñir** vt **1** *(dar un color)* to dye. **2** *(rebajar un color)* to tone down.
▶ vpr **teñirse** *(el pelo)* to dye one's hair.

**teoría** nf theory. LOC **en teoría** theoretically.

**teórica** nf theory, theoretics.

**teórico,-a** adj theoretic, theoretical.
▶ nm & nf theoretician, theorist.

**terapeuta** nm o nf therapist.

**terapia** nf therapy.

**tercer** adj [se usa ante nombres en masculino singular] third: *el tercer mundo* the third world.

✎ Consulta también **tercero,-a**.

**tercera** nf **1** *(clase)* third class. **2** *(marcha de auto)* third gear, third. **3** MÚS third.

**tercermundista** adj third-world.

**tercero,-a** adj *(ordinal)* third.
▶ nm & nf *(parte)* third.
▶ nm **tercero 1** *(mediador)* mediator. **2** *(persona ajena)* outsider.

✎ Consulta también **sexto,-a**.

**tercio,-a** adj third.
▶ nm **tercio 1** *(parte)* third. **2** *(en tauromaquia)* stage, part.

**terciopelo** nm velvet.

**terco,-a** adj obstinate, stubborn.

**termal** adj thermal.

**termas** nf pl *(baños)* spa *sing*, hot baths.

**térmico,-a** adj thermal.

**terminación** nf **1** *(acción)* ending, termination. **2** *(conclusión)* completion. **3** *(parte final)* end. **4** GRAM ending.

**terminal** adj *(último)* final, terminal.
▶ nf **1** *(estación)* terminus. **2** *(en aeropuerto)* terminal.
▶ nm *(de ordenador)* terminal.

**terminar** vt **1** *(acabar)* to finish, complete. **2** *(dar fin)* to end.
▶ vi **1** *(acabar)* to finish, end: *terminó a las cuatro* it finished at four. **2** *(acabar de)* to have just (de, -): *termina de marchar* he has just left. **3** *(final de una acción, de un estado)* to end up: *terminó por marcharse* he ended up leaving. **4** *(eliminar)* to put an

end (con, to). **5** *(estropear)* to damage (con, -), ruin (con, -): *la lluvia terminó con la cosecha* the rain damaged the crops. **6** *(reñir)* to break up (con, with). **7** *(enfermedad)* to come to the final stage.
▶ vpr **terminarse 1** *(acabarse)* to finish. **2** *(agotarse)* to run out: *se ha terminado el azúcar* the sugar has run out.

**término** nm **1** *(fin)* end, finish. **2** *(estación)* terminus, terminal. **3** *(límite)* limit, boundary; *(hito)* boundary marker. **4** *(plazo)* term, time, period. **5** *(palabra)* term, word: *término técnico* technical term. **6** *(estado)* condition, state. **7** *(lugar, posición)* place. **8** *(en matemáticas, gramática)* term. LOC **dar término a** ALGO to conclude STH.
▶ nm pl **términos** *(condiciones)* conditions, terms.

**terminología** nf terminology.

**termita** nf termite.

**termitero** nm termite's nest.

**termo** nm *(recipiente)* flask, thermos flask.

**termómetro** nm thermometer.

**termostato** nm thermostat.

**ternera** nf CULIN veal, beef.

**ternero,-a** nm & nf *(animal)* calf.

**ternura** nf tenderness, gentleness.

**terraplén** nm embankment.

**terráqueo,-a** adj earth.

**terrateniente** nm o nf landowner.

**terraza** nf **1** *(balcón)* terrace. **2** *(azotea)* roof terrace. **3** *(de un café)* terrace.

**terremoto** nm earthquake.

**terrenal** adj earthly, worldly.

**terreno,-a** adj worldly, earthly.
▶ nm **terreno 1** *(tierra)* land, piece of land, ground; *(solar)* plot, site. **2** GEOG terrain. **3** AGR *(de cultivo)* soil; *(campo)* field. **4** DEP field, ground.

**terrestre** adj **1** *(de la tierra)* terrestrial, earthly. **2** *(por tierra)* by land.

**terrible** adj terrible, awful.

**terrícola** nm o nf *(habitante)* earth dweller; *(en ciencia ficción)* earthling.

**territorial** adj territorial.

**territorio** nm territory.

**terrón** *nm* **1** *(de tierra)* clod. **2** *(de azúcar, etc)* lump.

**terror** *nm* **1** *(gen)* terror. **2** CINE horror.

**terrorismo** *nm* terrorism.

**terrorista** *adj* terrorist.
▶ *nm o nf* terrorist.

**tesoro** *nm* **1** *(gen)* treasure. **2** *fig* treasure.

**testamento** *nm* **1** JUR will, testament. **2** REL Testament. LOC **hacer testamento** to make one's will.

**testarudo,-a** *adj* obstinate, stubborn.

**testigo** *nm o nf* witness.
▶ *nm* **1** *(prueba)* proof. **2** DEP baton.

**testimonio** *nm* **1** JUR testimony, evidence. **2** *(prueba)* evidence, proof.

**tétanos** *nm inv* tetanus.

**tetera** *nf* teapot.

**tetraedro** *nm* tetrahedron.

**textil** *adj* textile.
▶ *nm* textile.

**texto** *nm* text.

**textura** *nf* **1** *(textil)* texture. **2** *(minerales)* structure.

**tez** *nf* complexion.

**ti** *pron* [se usa sólo después de una preposición] you: *te lo doy a ti* I'll give it to you.

**tía** *nf (pariente)* aunt.

**tibio,-a** *adj* **1** tepid. **2** *fig* cool.

**tiburón** *nm* shark.

**tic** *nm* **1** tic, twitch. **2** *fig (manía)* habit.

**ticket** *nm* → tique.

**tiempo** *nm* **1** *(gen)* time. **2** *(época)* time, period, age, days *pl*: *en tiempo de los romanos* in Roman times. **3** METEOR weather: *¿qué tiempo hace?* what's the weather like? **4** *(edad)* age: *¿qué tiempo tiene el niño?* how old is your baby? **5** *(temporada)* season: *fruta del tiempo* fruit in season. **6** *(momento)* moment, time: *no es tiempo de preguntarle eso* it's not the time to ask him that. **7** MÚS tempo, movement. **8** DEP half. **9** GRAM tense. **10** TÉC stroke. LOC **hacer buen tiempo** the weather is good. COMP **tiempo libre** free time.

**tienda** *nf* **1** *(establecimiento)* shop, US store. **2** *(de campaña)* tent. **3** *(de carro)* cover. LOC **ir de tiendas** to go shopping. COMP **tienda de campaña** tent.

**tierno,-a** *adj* **1** *(blando)* tender, soft. **2** *fig (reciente)* fresh: *pan tierno* fresh bread. **3** *fig (cariñoso)* affectionate.

**tierra** *nf* **1** *(planeta)* earth. **2** *(superficie sólida)* land. **3** *(terreno cultivado)* soil, land. **4** *(país)* country, land. **5** *(suelo)* ground. **6** ELEC earth, US ground.
▶ *nf pl* **tierras** land *sing*. LOC **tierra adentro** inland. COMP **tierra de nadie** no-man's-land. ‖ **tierra firme** terra firma.

**tieso,-a** *adj* **1** *(rígido)* stiff, rigid. **2** *(erguido)* upright, erect. **3** *(tenso)* taut, tight.

**tiesto** *nm* flowerpot.

**tifón** *nm* typhoon.

**tigre** *nm* tiger.

**tijera** *nf* [se suele usar en plural] *(instrumento)* scissors *pl*, pair of scissors.

**tila** *nf* **1** *(tilo)* lime. **2** *(flor)* lime blossom. **3** *(infusión)* lime-blossom tea.

**tilde** *nf* **1** *(gen)* written accent; *(de la ñ)* tilde. **2** *fig (tacha)* fault, flaw.

**tilo** *nm* lime tree.

**timar** *vt* to swindle, cheat, trick.

**timbre** *nm* **1** *(de la puerta)* bell. **2** *(sello)* stamp, seal. **3** MÚS timbre.

**timidez** *nf* shyness, timidity.

**tímido,-a** *adj* shy, timid.

**timo¹** *nm (estafa)* swindle.

**timo²** *nm (glándula)* thymus.

**timón** *nm* **1** *(barco, avión)* rudder. **2** *(del arado)* beam. **3** *fig (negocio, etc)* helm.

**Timor Oriental** *nm* East Timor.

**tímpano** *nm (del oído)* eardrum.

**tiniebla** *nf* [también se usa en plural con el mismo significado] *(oscuridad)* darkness.
▶ *nf pl* **tinieblas** *fig (ignorancia)* ignorance *sing*, confusion *sing*.

**tinta** *nf* **1** *(gen)* ink. **2** *(tinte)* dyeing.
▶ *nf pl* **tintas** colours (US colors). COMP **tinta china** Indian ink.

**tinte** *nm* **1** *(colorante)* dye. **2** *(proceso)* dyeing. **3** *(tintorería)* dry-cleaner's. **4** *fig (aspecto)* shade.

**tintero** *nm* inkwell.

**tintinear** *vi* → tintinar.

**tinto,-a** *adj* **1** *(teñido)* dyed. **2** *(vino)* red.
▶ *nm* **tinto** *(vino)* red wine.

**tintorería** *nf* dry-cleaner's.

**tío** *nm* **1** *(pariente)* uncle. **2** *fam (hombre)* guy.
▶ *nm pl* **tíos** aunt and uncle.

**tiovivo** *nm* merry-go-round.

**típico,-a** *adj* **1** *(característico)* typical, characteristic. **2** *(pintoresco)* picturesque; *(tradicional)* traditional: *un plato típico* a traditional dish, a local dish.

**tipo** *nm* **1** *(clase)* type, kind. **2** FIN rate. **3** ANAT *(de hombre)* build, physique; *(de mujer)* figure. **4** *fam (persona)* guy, fellow, bloke. **5** *(en impresión)* type. COMP **tipo de interés** FIN rate of interest.

**tíquet** *nm* → tique.

**tira** *nf* **1** *(cinta, banda)* strip. **2** *(de dibujos)* comic strip. LOC **la tira** *(cantidad)* a lot, loads; *(mucho tiempo)* for yonks, for ages: *comimos la tira* we ate loads.

**tirada** *nf* **1** *(acción)* throw: *en la segunda tirada le salieron dos seises* he got two sixes on the second throw. **2** *(impresión)* print run: *una tirada de cinco mil ejemplares* a print run of five thousand. **3** *(distancia)* stretch: *hay una buena tirada hasta allí* it's a good few miles away. **4** *(serie)* series.

**tirado,-a** *adj* **1** *fam (precio)* dirt cheap. **2** *fam (problema, asunto)* dead easy. **3** *fam (abandonado)* let down.

**tirador,-ra** *nm & nf (persona)* shooter.
▶ *nm (de puerta, cajón)* knob, handle.

**tirano,-a** *nm & nf* tyrant.

**tirante** *adj* **1** taut. **2** *fig (situación)* tense.
▶ *nm* **1** *(de ropa en general)* strap. **2** TÉC brace, stay. **3** ARQUIT beam.
▶ *nm pl* **tirantes** *(de pantalón)* braces, US suspenders.

**tirar** *vt* **1** *(echar)* to throw, fling. **2** *(dejar caer)* to drop. **3** *(desechar)* to throw away. **4** *(derribar)* to knock down; *(casa, árbol)* to pull down. **5** *(derramar)* to spill. **6** *(vaso, botella)* to knock over. **7** *(estirar)* to pull. **8** *(imprimir)* to print. **9** *(un tiro)* to fire; *(una bomba)* to drop; *(cohete)* to launch. **10** DEP to take. **11** *fig (malgastar)* to waste, squander.
▶ *vi* **1** *(cuerda, puerta)* to pull *(de, -)*. **2** *(estufa, chimenea)* to draw. **3** *(en juegos)* to be a player's move, be a player's turn: *tira él* it's his turn. **4** *fam (funcionar)* to work, run: *esto ya no tira* this doesn't

work any more. **5** *fam (durar)* to last: *con esta reparación tirará un par de meses* after these repairs it'll last for a couple of months. **6** *fam fig (atraer)* to attract, appeal: *no le tira la mecánica* mechanics doesn't appeal to him. **7** *fig (inclinarse)* to be attracted *(a/hacia, to)*, be drawn *(a/hacia, to)*: *esta chica tira hacia las artes* this girl is drawn to the arts. **8** *fig (parecerse)* to take after *(a, -)*: *tira a su padre* she takes after her father. **9** *fig (mantenerse)* to get by, get along: *ella tira con poco dinero* she gets by with little money. **10** *(disparar)* to shoot, fire. **11** DEP *(fútbol)* to shoot; *(ciclismo)* to set the pace.
▶ *vpr* **tirarse 1** *(lanzarse)* to throw os. **2** *(abalanzarse)* to rush *(sobre, at)*, jump *(sobre, on)*. **3** *(tumbarse)* to lie down. **4** *fam (tiempo)* to spend: *se tiró una hora en la ducha* he spent an hour in the shower.

**tirita®** *nf* sticking plaster, plaster.

**tiritar** *vi (gen)* to shiver, shake.

**tiro** *nm* **1** *(lanzamiento)* throw. **2** *(disparo, ruido)* shot. **3** *(galería de tiro)* shooting gallery. **4** DEP shooting. **5** *(caballerías)* team. **6** COST *(de pantalón)* distance between waist and crotch. **7** *(de chimenea)* draught (US draft). **8** *(fútbol, etc)* shot. COMP **tiro al blanco** target shooting.

**tirón** *nm* pull, tug. LOC **de un tirón** *fam* in one go.

**tiroteo** *nm* shooting.

**títere** *nm* **1** *(marioneta)* puppet, marionette. **2** *fig (persona)* puppet, dupe.
▶ *nm pl* **títeres** puppet show *sing*. LOC **no dejar títere con cabeza 1** *fam (destruir)* to break everything in sight. **2** *(criticar)* to spare nobody.

**titulado,-a** *adj* **1** *(llamado)* called. **2** EDUC *(diplomado)* qualified.

**titular** *vt* to entitle, title, call.
▶ *adj* regular.
▶ *nm o nf* **1** *(poseedor)* holder. **2** *(de un puesto)* office holder.
▶ *nm (prensa)* headline.
▶ *vpr* **titularse 1** *(llamarse)* to be called, be titled. **2** EDUC to graduate *(en, in)*.

**título** *nm* **1** *(de obra)* title. **2** *(de texto legal)* heading. **3** *(dignidad)* title. **4** *(persona noble)* noble (person). **5** EDUC *(licenciatura)* degree; *(diploma)* certificate. **6** *(documento)* title. **7** *(titular de prensa)* headline.

▶ *nm pl* **títulos** *(titulación)* qualifications; *(méritos)* qualities. COMP **título de propiedad** deeds *pl*.

**tiza** *nf* chalk.

**toalla** *nf* towel. COMP **toalla de baño** bath towel.

**toallero** *nm* towel rail, towel rack.

**tobillera** *nf* ankle sock.

**tobillo** *nm* ankle.

**tobogán** *nm* **1** *(rampa)* slide, chute. **2** *(trineo)* toboggan, sledge.

**tocadiscos** *nm inv* record player.

**tocado** *nm* **1** *(peinado)* coiffure, hairdo. **2** *(prenda)* headdress, hat.

**tocado,-a** *adj* **1** *(fruta)* bad, rotten. **2** *fam (perturbado)* crazy, touched.

**tocador** *nm* **1** *(mueble)* dressing-table. **2** *(habitación)* dressing-room, boudoir.

**tocar** *vt* **1** *(gen)* to touch: *no tocar la mercancía* do not handle the goods. **2** *(sentir por el tacto)* to feel: *tócalo, está frío* feel it, it's cold. **3** *(revolver)* to rummage amongst, root around: *no toques mis papeles* leave my papers alone. **4** *(hacer sonar - instrumento, canción)* to play; *(timbre)* to ring; *(bocina)* to blow, honk; *(campanas)* to strike. **5** *(la hora)* to strike. **6** DEP *(diana)* to hit; *(esgrima)* to touch. **7** *fig (mencionar)* to touch on. **8** *fig (impresionar)* to touch, reach: *me tocó el corazón* he touched my heart.

▶ *vi* **1** *(ser el turno)* to be one's turn: *le toca a él* it's his turn. **2** *(corresponder)* to be up to: *le toca a él explicarse* it's up to him to explain himself. **3** *(ganar)* to win. **4** *(en un reparto, etc)* to fall. **5** *(un destino)* to be posted: *le tocó en Cartagena* he was posted to Cartagena. **6** *(tener que)* to have to: *nos tocó llevarla* we had to take her. **7** *(afectar)* to concern, affect: *le toca directamente* it directly concerns you. **8** *(entrar en contacto)* to touch.

▶ *vpr* **tocarse** *(uso reflexivo)* to touch os; *(uso recíproco)* to touch each other.

**tocino** *nm* **1** *(carne)* bacon. **2** *(grasa)* fat.

**todavía** *adv* **1** *(a pesar de ello)* still. **2** *(tiempo)* still, yet: *todavía están allí*

they're still there. **3** *(para reforzar)* even: *esto todavía está mejor* this is even better.

**todo,-a** *adj* **1** *(sin excluir nada)* all: *todos los vecinos lo vieron* all the neighbours saw it. **2** *(verdadero)* real: *era todo un reto* it was a real challenge. **3** *(cada)* every: *todos los días* every day.

▶ *pron* **1** *(sin excluir nada)* all, everything: *llamaron todos* they all phoned. **2** *(cualquiera)* anybody: *todo el que yo diga* anybody I say.

▶ *nm* **todo** *(totalidad)* whole.

▶ *adv* completely, totally, all: *está todo mojado* it's all wet.

**todoterreno** *adj* four-wheel-drive.

▶ *nm* four-wheel-drive vehicle.

**Togo** *nm* Togo.

**togolés,-esa** *adj* Togolese.

▶ *nm & nf* Togolese.

**toldo** *nm* **1** *(cubierta)* awning. **2** *(de playa)* sunshade.

**tolerancia** *nf* tolerance.

**tolerante** *adj* tolerant, lenient.

**tolerar** *vt* **1** *(permitir, soportar)* to tolerate, put up with: *no te toleraré esa actitud* I won't put up with that attitude. **2** *(inconvenientes)* to stand.

**toma** *nf* **1** *(acción)* taking. **2** MED dose. **3** MIL capture. **4** *(de aire)* intake, inlet; *(de agua)* outlet, tap; *(de electricidad)* plug, socket. **5** *(grabación)* recording. **6** CINE take, shot. COMP **toma de posesión** takeover.

**tomar** *vt* **1** *(gen)* to take: *lo tomó en broma* she took it as a joke. **2** *(baño, ducha)* to have, take; *(foto)* to take. **3** *(comer, beber)* to have; *(beber)* to drink; *(comer)* to eat: *tómate la leche* drink your milk. **4** *(el autobús, el tren)* to catch. **5** *(aceptar)* to accept, take. **6** *(comprar)* to buy, get, have: *tomaré manzanas* I'll get some apples. **7** *(adquirir)* to acquire, get into: *tomar una costumbre* to acquire a habit. **8** MIL to capture, take.

▶ *vi* *(encaminarse)* to go, turn.

▶ *vpr* **tomarse 1** *(gen)* to take: *me tomé una aspirina* I took an aspirin. **2** *(beber)* to drink; *(comer)* to eat. LOC **tomarse las cosas con calma** to take it easy.

**tomate** *nm* *(fruto)* tomato.

**tómbola** *nf* tombola.

T

**tomillo** *nm* thyme.

**tomo** *nm (volumen)* volume.

**tonel** *nm* barrel, cask.

**tonelada** *nf* ton. COMP **tonelada métrica** metric ton, tonne.

**Tonga** *nf* Tonga.

**tongano,-a** *adj* Tongan.
► *nm & nf (persona)* Tongan.
► *nm* **tongano** *(idioma)* Tongan.

**tónica** *nf* 1 *(tendencia)* tendency, trend. 2 *(bebida)* tonic, tonic water.

**tónico,-a** *adj* 1 *(sílaba)* tonic, stressed. 2 *(nota musical)* tonic.
► *nm* **tónico** MED tonic.

**tono** *nm* 1 *(gen)* tone: *el tono de su discurso* the tone of her speech. 2 *(energía)* energy. LOC **fuera de tono** *fig* inappropriate, out of place.

**tontear** *vi (decir tonterías)* to act the clown, fool about.

**tontería** *nf* 1 *(calidad de tonto)* stupidity, silliness. 2 *(dicho, hecho)* silly thing, stupid thing. 3 *(insignificancia)* trifle. LOC **hacer tonterías** to mess about, fool around.

**tonto,-a** *adj* silly, stupid, US dumb: *¡qué idea más tonta!* what a stupid idea!
► *nm & nf* fool, idiot. LOC **hacerse el tonto** to play dumb.

**topacio** *nm* topaz.

**topar** *vi* 1 *(chocar)* to bump into: *el coche topó contra un poste* the car bumped into a pole. 2 *(encontrar - algo)* to come across, find; *(- alguien)* to bump into, run into. 3 *fig (dificultades, etc)* to come up against, run into.

**tope** *nm* 1 *(límite)* limit, end. 2 TÉC stop, check. 3 *(de ferrocarril)* buffer, bumping post, bumper. 4 MAR masthead.
► *adj fig* top, maximum.
► *adv argot* really, absolutely: *la fiesta fue tope divertida* the party was absolutely brilliant. LOC **a tope 1** *argot (al límite)* flat out. **2** *(lleno)* jam-packed, chock-a-block.

**tópico,-a** *adj* MED external: *uso tópico* external use.
► *nm* **tópico** commonplace, cliché.

**topo** *nm* mole.

**toque** *nm* 1 *(acto)* touch. 2 *(de campana)* ringing, peal, pealing; *(de trompeta)* blare, sounding; *(de claxon)* honk; *(de sirena)* hoot; *(de tambor)* beat, beating. 3 *(pincelada)* touch. 4 *fig (advertencia)* warning. LOC **dar un toque a ALGN 1** *(llamar)* to take SB to task. **2** *(llamar la atención)* to call sb's attention.

**tórax** *nm inv* thorax.

**torcer** *vt* 1 *(gen)* to twist. 2 *(doblar)* to bend; *(madera)* to warp.
► *vi (girar)* to turn: *torció a la derecha* he turned right.
► *vpr* **torcerse 1** *(gen)* to twist. **2** *(doblarse)* to bend; *(madera)* to warp. **3** *(ladearse)* to become slanted. **4** MED to sprain, twist. **5** *fig (plan)* to fall through.

**torcido,-a** *adj* 1 *(que no es recto)* twisted. 2 *(madera)* warped; *(metal)* bent. 3 *(ladeado)* slanted, crooked, lopsided: *el cuadro está torcido* the painting is crooked.

**torear** *vt* 1 *(lidiar)* to fight. 2 *fig (entretener)* to put off. 3 *fig (burlar)* to tease, confuse. 4 *fig (asunto, etc)* to tackle skilfully. 5 *fig (evitar)* to avoid.
► *vi (lidiar)* to fight.

**torero,-a** *nm & nf* bullfighter.

**tormenta** *nf* storm.

**tornado** *nm* tornado.

**torneo** *nm* 1 *(justa)* tourney, joust. 2 DEP tournament, competition.

**tornillo** *nm* screw, bolt.

**toro** *nm (animal)* bull.
► *nm pl* **los toros** *(corrida)* bullfight *sing*; *(arte)* bullfighting *sing*.

**torpe** *adj* 1 *(poco hábil)* clumsy. 2 *(de movimiento)* slow, awkward. 3 *(poco inteligente)* dim, thick.

**torpedo** *nm* MIL torpedo.

**torpeza** *nf* 1 *(falta de habilidad)* clumsiness, awkwardness. 2 *(mental)* dimness, stupidity. 3 *(de movimiento)* slowness, heaviness. 4 *(error)* blunder.

**torre** *nf* 1 *(gen)* tower. 2 *(campanario)* bell tower. 3 *(chalé)* country house, house, villa. 4 *(ajedrez)* rook, castle.

**torrencial** *adj* torrential.

**torrente** *nm* **1** *(de agua)* mountain stream. **2** *fig (abundancia)* flood, stream.

**torta** *nf* **1** CULIN cake. **2** *fam (golpe)* blow, crack; *(bofetada)* slap, wallop. LOC **ni torta** *fam* not a thing: *no ve ni torta* he can't see a thing.

**tortazo** *nm* **1** *fam (golpe)* whack, thump. **2** *fam (bofetada)* slap, punch.

**tortícolis** *nf inv* stiff neck.

**tortilla** *nf* **1** omelette (US omelet). **2** AM tortilla, pancake. COMP **tortilla de patatas** potato omelette.

**tórtola** *nf* → tórtolo,-a.

**tortuga** *nf* **1** *(de tierra)* tortoise. **2** *(marina)* turtle.

**torturar** *vt* to torture.

**tos** *nf* cough, coughing. LOC **tener tos** to have a cough.

**toser** *vi* to cough.

**tostada** *nf* toast, slice of toast.

**tostador,-ra** *nm & nf (de pan)* toaster; *(de café)* roaster.

**tostar** *vt* **1** *(pan)* to toast; *(café)* to roast; *(carnes)* to brown. **2** *fig (piel)* to tan.
▶ *vpr* **tostarse** *fig (la piel)* to get brown, turn brown, tan.

**total** *adj* total, complete, overall: *anestesia total* general anaesthetic.
▶ *nm* **1** *(totalidad)* whole: *el total de la población* the whole population. **2** *(suma)* total, sum.
▶ *adv* **1** *(en conclusión)* in short, so: *total, que se fueron porque quisieron* they left because they wanted to. **2** *(al fin y al cabo)* after all.

**totalitario,-a** *adj* totalitarian.

**totalitarismo** *nm* totalitarianism.

**tótem** *nm* totem; *(efigie)* totem pole.

**tóxico,-a** *adj* toxic, poisonous.
▶ *nm* **tóxico** toxicant, poison.

**toxicómano,-a** *nm & nf* drug addict.

**tozudo,-a** *adj* stubborn, obstinate.

**trabajador,-ra** *adj* **1** *(que trabaja)* working. **2** *(laborioso)* hard-working.
▶ *nm & nf* worker (US laborer).

**trabajar** *vi* **1** *(gen)* to work: *trabaja mucho* she works hard. **2** *(en obra, película)* to act, perform: *¿quién trabaja en la obra?* who's in the play?

▶ *vt* **1** *(materiales)* to work (on). **2** *(idea, idioma, etc)* to work on. **3** *(la tierra)* to till. **4** CULIN *(pasta)* to knead.

**trabajo** *nm* **1** *(ocupación)* work. **2** *(tarea)* task, job. **3** *(empleo)* job. **4** *(esfuerzo)* effort. **5** EDUC report.
▶ *nm pl* **trabajos** *fig (penalidades)* hardships. COMP **trabajos manuales** arts and crafts, handicrafts.

**trabalenguas** *nm inv* tongue twister.

**trabar** *vt* **1** *(unir)* to join, link. **2** *(sujetar)* to lock, fasten. **3** *(mecanismo)* to jam. **4** *(prender a alguien)* to shackle. **5** *(caballería)* to hobble. **6** *fig (empezar)* to start. **7** *fig (conversación, amistad)* to strike up. **8** *fig (impedir)* to impede.
▶ *vpr* **trabarse** *(enredarse)* to get tangled up. LOC **trabársele la lengua a ALGN** to get tongue-tied.

**tractor** *nm* tractor.

**tradición** *nf* tradition.

**tradicional** *adj* traditional.

**traducción** *nf* translation.

**traducir** *vt* **1** *(gen)* to translate. **2** *(expresar)* to express, show.
▶ *vpr* **traducirse** *(resulta)* to result in.

**traductor,-ra** *adj* translating.
▶ *nm & nf* translator.

**traer** *vt* **1** *(gen)* to bring. **2** *(llevar consigo)* to carry: *traía un bolso* she was carrying a bag. **3** *(vestir)* to wear: *traía una falda verde* she was wearing a green skirt. **4** *(causar)* to cause, bring: *esto le trajo muchos problemas* it caused him a lot of problems. **5** *(contener)* to contain: *el paquete trae un regalo* the package contains a gift.
▶ *vpr* **traerse** *(llevar consigo)* to bring along: *tráete al bebé* bring your baby along.

**traficante** *nm o nf* **1** trader, dealer. **2** *(ilegal)* trafficker.

**traficar** *vi* **1** to deal. **2** *(de forma ilegal)* to traffic (en, in), deal (en, in): *trafica en/con drogas* he traffics in drugs.

**tráfico** *nm* **1** AUTO traffic. **2** COM traffic.

**tragaperras** COMP **máquina tragaperras** slot machine.

**tragar** *vt* **1** *(ingerir)* to swallow. **2** *(absorber)* to soak up. **3** *fig (hacer desaparecer)* to swallow up. **4** *fig (gastar, consumir)*

T

to eat up, guzzle: *este coche traga mucha gasolina* this car guzzles petrol. **5** *fig (creer)* to swallow, believe. **6** *fig (aguantar)* to put up with; *(disimular)* to hide: *tuvo que tragar sus exigencias* she had to put up with his demands. **7** *fig (soportar a alguien)* to stand, stomach: *no trago a Pedro* I can't stand Pedro.
▶ *vi* to swallow, swallow up.
▶ *vpr* **tragarse** *(ingerir)* to swallow: *se tragó un botón* he swallowed a button.

**tragedia** *nf* tragedy.

**trágico,-a** *adj* tragic.

**trago** *nm* **1** *(sorbo)* swig, drop. **2** *fam (bebida)* drink. **3** *fam fig (adversidad)* rough time.

**traición** *nf* treason, betrayal. [LOC] **a traición** treacherously.

**traicionar** *vt* **1** *(gen)* to betray. **2** *fig (delatar)* to give away, betray: *su expresión traicionó sus pensamientos* his expression gave away his thoughts.

**traidor,-ra** *adj* treacherous.
▶ *nm & nf* traitor.

**traje** *nm* **1** *(de hombre)* suit. **2** *(de mujer)* dress. [COMP] **traje de chaqueta** tailored suit. ‖ **traje de noche** evening dress.

**trama** *nf* **1** *(textil)* weft, woof. **2** *(argumento)* plot.

**tramar** *vt* **1** *(tejidos)* to weave. **2** *fig (maquinar)* to plot, cook up.

**tramitación** *nf* JUR procedure.

**tramitar** *vt* **1** *(gestionar)* to deal with, process: *tramitaremos su pasaporte* we'll get your passport sorted out. **2** *(solicitar, negociar)* to arrange, negotiate: *tramitar un préstamo* to negotiate a loan.

**trámite** *nm* **1** *(paso)* step. **2** *(formalidad)* formality, requirement.

**tramo** *nm* **1** *(camino, etc)* stretch. **2** *(de escalera)* flight. **3** *(de terreno)* lot.

**trampa** *nf* **1** *(abertura)* trapdoor, hatch. **2** *(para cazar)* trap. **3** *fig (engaño)* fiddle; *(truco)* trick. **4** *fig (deuda)* debt. [LOC] **tender una trampa** to set a trap.

**trampolín** *nm* **1** *(de piscina)* springboard. **2** *(de esquí)* ski jump.

**tramposo,-a** *adj* deceitful, tricky.

▶ *nm & nf* trickster, cheat; *(en las cartas)* cardsharp.

**trancazo** *nm* **1** *(golpe)* blow with a cudgel. **2** *fam fig (resfriado)* cold; *(gripe)* flu.

**trance** *nm* **1** *(momento crítico)* critical moment. **2** *(dificultad)* fix, tight spot. **3** *(éxtasis)* trance.

**tranquilidad** *nf* *(quietud)* calmness; *(sosiego)* peace and quiet. [COMP] **paz y tranquilidad** peace and quiet.

**tranquilizante** *nm* tranquillizer (US tranquilizer).

**tranquilizar** *vt* **1** *(calmar)* to calm down, tranquillize (US tranquilize). **2** *(dar confianza)* to reassure, set one's mind at rest.
▶ *vpr* **tranquilizarse 1** *(calmarse)* to calm down. **2** to set one's mind at rest.

**tranquilo,-a** *adj* **1** *(sin inquietud)* calm, relaxed, tranquil. **2** *(sin preocupación)* reassured. **3** *(sin movimiento)* calm, still, quiet. **4** *(sin ruidos)* quiet, still, peaceful. **5** *(persona)* calm, easy-going, placid. **6** *(agua)* still; *(conciencia)* clear.

**transacción** *nf* transaction, deal.

**transatlántico,-a** *adj* transatlantic.
▶ *nm* **transatlántico** liner, ocean liner.

**transbordar** *vt* to transfer.
▶ *vi* change *(de tren, etc)*.

**transbordador** *nm* ferry. [COMP] **transbordador espacial** space shuttle.

**transbordo** *nm* **1** *(de vehículo)* change, US transfer. **2** *(de barco)* transshipment.

**transcribir** *vt* to transcribe.

**transcripción** *nf* transcription.

**transcurrir** *vi* **1** *(tiempo)* to pass, elapse. **2** *(acontecer)* to take place, go off.

**transcurso** *nm* **1** *(paso)* course. **2** *(duración)* space, period: *en el transcurso de dos años* in the space of two years.

**transeúnte** *nm & nf (peatón)* pedestrian.

**transferencia** *nf* FIN transfer.

**transferible** *adj* transferable.

**transferir** *vt* FIN to transfer, convey.

**transformación** *nf* transformation.

**transformador,-ra** *adj* transforming.
▶ *nm* **transformador** transformer.

**transformar** *vt* to transform, change.

▶ *vpr* **transformarse** to change, be transformed: *se transformó completamente* he was completely transformed. ⎣LOC⎦ **transformarse en 1** *(persona)* to become. **2** *(objeto)* to convert into.

**transfusión** *nf* transfusion. ⎣COMP⎦ **transfusión de sangre** blood transfusion.

**transgénico,-a** *adj* genetically modified.

**transgresión** *nf* transgression.

**transgresor,-ra** *nm & nf* transgressor, law-breaker.

**transición** *nf* transition.

**transigencia** *nf* **1** *(actitud)* tolerance, lenience. **2** *(concesión)* compromise.

**transigente** *adj* accommodating, tolerant, lenient.

**transigir** *vi* **1** *(ceder)* to compromise, give in, yield. **2** *(tolerar)* to tolerate.

**transistor** *nm* transistor.

**transitable** *adj* passable.

**transitado,-a** *adj* busy.

**transitar** *vi* **1** *(viajar)* to travel, travel about. **2** *(pasar)* to pass, go, walk.

**transitivo,-a** *adj* transitive.

**tránsito** *nm* **1** *(acción)* passage, transit, movement. **2** AUTO traffic. **3** *euf (muerte)* death, passing. **4** *(lugar de parada)* stopping place.

**transitoriedad** *nf* transience.

**transitorio,-a** *adj (pasajero)* transitory; *(de transición)* transitional, interim.

**transmediterráneo,-a** *adj* trans-Mediterranean.

**transmisible** *adj* transmissible.

**transmisión** *nf* **1** *(propagación)* transmission. **2** JUR transfer, transference. **3** RAD TV broadcast. **4** TÉC drive.
▶ *nf pl* **transmisiones** MIL signals. ⎣COMP⎦ **derechos de transmisión 1** JUR *(de herencia)* succession duty. **2** *(de televisión, etc)* broadcasting rights. ❙ **transmisión en directo** RAD TV live broadcast.

**transmisor,-ra** *adj* transmitting.
▶ *nm & nf* transmitter.

**transmitir** *vt* **1** *(gen)* to transmit. **2** RAD TV to broadcast. **3** *(enfermedad)* to transmit, pass on. **4** JUR to transfer, hand down.

**transmutar** *vt* to transmute.
▶ *vpr* **transmutarse** to change, transform.

**transoceánico,-a** *adj* transoceanic.

**transparencia** *nf* **1** transparency. **2** *(diapositiva)* transparency.

**transparentar** *vt fig (emociones, etc)* to reveal.
▶ *vpr* **transparentarse 1** *(ser transparente)* to be transparent, show through. **2** *fig (emociones, etc)* to show.

**transparente** *adj* **1** *(gen)* transparent. **2** *(tela, vestido)* transparent. **3** *fig* straight, plain.

**transpiración** *nf* perspiration.

**transpirar** *vi* to perspire, transpire.

**transplantar** *vt* **1** *(gen)* to transplant. **2** *(trasladar)* to transfer.

**transplante** *nm* transplant.

**transportable** *adj* transportable.

**transportar** *vt* **1** *(gen)* to transport. **2** *(pasajeros)* to carry; *(mercancías en barco)* to ship. **3** MAT to transfer. **4** MÚS to transpose. **5** *fig (hacer perder la razón)* to carry away, send into raptures.
▶ *vpr* **transportarse** *fig* to be transported, be enraptured.

**transporte** *nm* **1** *(medio)* transport. **2** *(acción)* transport, US transportation. **3** COM freight, freightage. **4** MÚS transposition. **5** *fig* transport, ecstasy, bliss. ⎣COMP⎦ **transporte público** public transport.

**transportista** *nm o nf* carrier.

**transvasar** *vt* **1** *(líquidos)* to decant. **2** *(entre ríos)* to transfer.

**transvase** *nm* **1** *(de líquidos)* decanting. **2** *(de ríos)* transfer.

**transversal** *adj* transverse.

**transverso,-a** *adj* transverse.

**tranvía** *nm* **1** *(sistema)* tramway. **2** *(vehículo)* tram, tramcar, US streetcar.

**trapecio** *nm* **1** DEP trapeze. **2** *(geometría)* trapezium, US trapezoid. **3** ANAT *(hueso)* trapezium; *(músculo)* trapezius.

**trapecista** *nm o nf* trapeze artist.

**trapería** *nf* secondhand clothes shop.

**trapero,-a** *nm & nf (hombre)* rag-and-bone man, US junkman; *(mujer)* rag-and-bone woman.

**trapezoide** *nm* trapezoid, US trapezium.

**trapo** *nm* 1 *(tela vieja)* rag. 2 *(paño, bayeta)* cloth. 3 MAR sails *pl*. 4 *(telón)* curtain. 5 *(del torero)* red cape.
▸ *nm pl* **trapos** clothes, rags. LOC **poner a ALGN como un trapo (sucio)** *fam* to tear SB apart. COMP **trapo del polvo** duster.

**tráquea** *nf* trachea, windpipe.

**traqueal** *adj* tracheal.

**traqueotomía** *nf* tracheotomy.

**tras** *prep* 1 *(después de)* after: *tras la salida del avión* after the departure of the plane. 2 *(detrás)* behind: *tras el muro* behind the wall. 3 *(en pos de)* after, in pursuit of: *iba siempre tras el éxito* he was always in pursuit of success. LOC **día tras día** day after day.

**trasbordador** *nm* ferry, car ferry.

**trascendencia** *nf* 1 *(importancia)* significance, importance. 2 *(filosofía)* transcendence, transcendency.

**trascendental** *adj* 1 *(importante)* significant, very important, consequential; *(de gran alcance)* far-reaching. 2 *(filosofía)* transcendent, transcendental.

**trascendente** *adj* → **trascendental**.

**trascender** *vi* 1 *(olor - despedir)* to smell; *(- llegar hasta)* to reach. 2 *(darse a conocer)* to become known, leak out: *el resultado trascendió* the result leaked out. 3 *(extenderse)* to spread, have a wide effect.

**trascribir** *vt* to transcribe.

**trascripción** *nf* transcription.

**trasegar** *vt* 1 *(mudar)* to move about, shuffle. 2 *(líquidos)* to decant.

**trasero,-a** *adj* back, rear.
▸ *nm* **trasero** *fam euf* bottom, bum.

**trasferencia** *nf* → **transferencia**.

**trasferible** *adj* transferable.

**trasferir** *vt* → **transferir**.

**trasfondo** *nm* 1 background. 2 *fig* undertone.

**trasformación** *nf* transformation.

**trasformador,-ra** *adj-nm* → **transformador,-ra**.

**trasgresión** *nf* transgression.

**trasgresor,-ra** *nm & nf* transgressor, law-breaker.

**trashumancia** *nf* transhumance, seasonal migration.

**trashumante** *adj* transhumant.

**trasiego** *nm* comings and goings *pl*, hustle and bustle.

**traslación** *nf* 1 *(de la Tierra)* passage, movement. 2 *(en matemáticas)* translation.

**trasladar** *vt* 1 *(cambiar de sitio)* to move. 2 *(de cargo, etc)* to transfer. 3 *(aplazar)* to postpone, put off.
▸ *vpr* **trasladarse** 1 *(ir)* to go. 2 *(cambiar de residencia)* to move.

**traslado** *nm* 1 *(cambio de lugar)* move, moving; *(de residencia)* removal. 2 *(de cargo, etc)* transfer. 3 *(copia)* copy. 4 JUR notification.

**traslúcido,-a** *adj* translucent, semi-transparent.

**traslucir** *vt* *fig* to show, reveal, betray.
▸ *vpr* **traslucirse** 1 *(material)* to be translucent. 2 *fig (dejar ver)* to show, show through.

**trasluz** *nm* diffused light, reflected light. LOC **mirar ALGO al trasluz** to look at STH against the light.

**trasmano** *nm o nf* second hand.

**trasnochado,-a** *adj* 1 *fig (viejo)* old, hackneyed. 2 *fig (desmejorado)* haggard, bleary-eyed.

**trasnochador,-ra** *nm & nf* night bird, nighthawk.

**trasnochar** *vi* to stay up late, stay up until the early hours.

**traspapelado,-a** *adj* mislaid, misplaced.

**traspapelar** *vt* to mislay, misplace.
▸ *vpr* **traspapelarse** to get mislaid, get misplaced.

**traspasar** *vt* 1 *(atravesar)* to go through, cross. 2 *(cambiar de lugar)* to move. 3 *(perforar)* to go through, pierce. 4 *(dar,*

**pasar)** to transfer; *(vender)* to sell. **5** *fig (exceder)* to exceed, go beyond.

**traspaso** *nm* **1** *(de negocio, etc)* transfer, sale. **2** *(precio)* transfer fee.

**traspié** *nm* **1** *(tropezón)* stumble, trip. **2** *fig (equivocación)* blunder.

**trasponer** *vt-vpr* → transponer.

**trasportista** *nm o nf* carrier.

**trasposición** *nf* transposition.

**traspuesto,-a** LOC quedarse traspuesto,-a to nod off, doze off.

**traspunte** *nm* callboy.

**trasquilado,-a** *adj* **1** *(oveja)* sheared; *(pelo)* hacked, unevenly cut. **2** *fam fig* curtailed, cut down.

**trasquilar** *vt* **1** *(animales)* to shear. **2** *(pelo)* to hack, cut unevenly. **3** *fig* to curtail.

**trastabillar** *vi* **1** *(dar traspiés)* to stumble, trip. **2** *(tambalearse)* to stagger, totter.

**trastada** *nf fam (mala pasada)* dirty trick.

**trastazo** *nm fam* whack, wallop, thump. LOC **darse un trastazo** *fam* to come a cropper.

**traste** *nm* MÚS fret. LOC **irse al traste** *fig* to fall through.

**trastear** *vi* **1** MÚS to play. **2** *(revolver)* to rummage in. **3** *fig (manejar)* to twist around one's little finger.
▸ *vi (revolver)* to rummage.

**trastero,-a** *nm* junk room.

**trastienda** *nf* **1** *(de tienda)* back room. **2** *fig (astucia)* cunning.

**trasto** *nm* **1** *(algo inútil)* piece of junk. **2** *fam (niño)* little devil. **3** *fam (persona)* useless person, good-for-nothing, dead loss.
▸ *nm pl* **trastos 1** *(utensilios)* tackle *sing*, gear *sing*. **2** *fam (pertenencias)* belongings, things. LOC **tirarse los trastos a la cabeza** *fig* to have a blazing row.

**trastocar** *vt (cambiar)* to change.
▸ *vpr* **trastocarse** *(trastornarse)* to go mad.

**trastornado,-a** *adj* **1** *(preocupado)* upset. **2** *(loco)* mad. **3** *(mente)* unbalanced.

**trastornar** *vt* **1** *(revolver)* to turn round, turn upside down. **2** *(alterar - planes)* to disrupt; *(- paz, orden)* to disturb. **3** *(estómago)* to upset. **4** *fig (enloquecer)* to drive crazy.
▸ *vpr* **trastornarse** *(perturbarse)* to go mad, go out of one's mind.

**trastorno** *nm* **1** *(desorden)* confusion. **2** *(molestia)* trouble, inconvenience. **3** *(perturbación)* disruption, upheaval, upset. **4** MED upset.

**trastrocar** *vt* **1** *(gen)* to switch around, change around. **2** *(orden)* to invert, reverse; *(significado)* to change.

**trasunto** *nm* **1** *(copia)* copy. **2** *(representación)* representation.

**trata** *nf* slave trade.

**tratable** *adj* friendly, congenial, easy to get along with.

**tratadista** *nm o nf* treatise writer.

**tratado** *nm* **1** *(pacto)* treaty. **2** *(estudio)* treatise.

**tratamiento** *nm* **1** *(gen)* treatment. **2** *(de datos, materiales)* processing. **3** *(título)* title, form of address. COMP **tratamiento de textos** word processing.

**tratar** *vt* **1** *(gen - objeto)* to treat, handle; *(- persona)* to treat: *nos trató bien* he treated us well. **2** *(asunto, tema)* to discuss, deal with. **3** *(gestionar)* to handle, run. **4** *(dar tratamiento)* to address as. **5** *(calificar, considerar)* to consider, call: *lo trató de idiota* she called him an idiot. **6** MED to treat. **7** *(datos, texto)* to process. **8** QUÍM to treat.
▸ *vi* **1** *(relacionarse)* to be acquainted (con, with), know (con, -). **2** *(tener tratos)* to deal (con, with). **3** *(negociar)* to negotiate (con, with). **4** *(intentar)* to try (de, to): *trata de hacerlo* try to do it. **5** *(versar)* to be about: *trata de/sobre espías* it's about spies.
▸ *vpr* **tratarse 1** *(relacionarse)* to talk to each other, be on speaking terms: *no se tratan* they're not on speaking terms. **2** *(llamarse)* to address each other as, call each other. **3** *(referirse)* to be about: *se trataba de un atraco* it was about a robbery.

**trato** *nm* **1** *(acción)* treatment. **2** *(modales)* manner. **3** *(contacto)* contact. **4** *(acuerdo)* agreement. **5** COM deal. **6** *(tratamiento)* title. LOC **cerrar un trato** to close a deal. ‖ **¡trato hecho!** it's a deal!

**trauma** *nm* trauma.

**traumático,-a** *adj* traumatic.

**traumatismo** *nm* traumatism.

**traumatizar** *vt* **1** MED to traumatize. **2** *fam* to shock.

**través** *nm* **1** *(inclinación)* slant. **2** *(pieza de madera)* crosspiece, crossbeam. **3** MAR beam. **4** *fig (desgracia)* misfortune. LOC **a través de 1** *(de un lado a otro)* across, over. **2** *(por dentro)* through. **3** *(mediante)* through, from.

**travesaño** *nm* **1** ARQUIT crosspiece. **2** DEP crossbar.

**travesía** *nf* **1** *(viaje)* crossing; *(por mar)* voyage, crossing. **2** *(calle)* cross-street, passage. **3** *(distancia)* distance.

**travesura** *nf* piece of mischief, childish prank. LOC **hacer travesuras** to get into mischief.

**traviesa** *nf* **1** *(de ferrocarril)* sleeper, US tie. **2** *(en construcción)* trimmer.

**travieso,-a** *adj* mischievous, naughty.

**trayecto** *nm* **1** *(distancia)* distance, way. **2** *(recorrido)* route, itinerary.

**trayectoria** *nf* **1** trajectory. **2** *fig* line, course, path.

**traza** *nf fig (apariencia)* looks *pl*, appearance.

**trazado** *nm* **1** *(plano)* layout, plan. **2** *(dibujo)* drawing, sketch. **3** *(de carretera, ferrocarril)* route, course.

**trazar** *vt* **1** *(línea, plano, dibujo)* to draw, draw up. **2** *(parque)* to lay out; *(edificio)* to design. **3** *(itinerario)* to trace. **4** *fig (plan, etc)* to outline, draft.

**trazo** *nm* **1** *(línea)* line. **2** *(de una letra)* stroke. **3** *fig (rasgo facial)* feature.

**trébol** *nm* **1** *(planta)* clover, trefoil. **2** *(naipes)* club.

**trece** *adj (cardinal)* thirteen; *(ordinal)* thirteenth.

► *nm (número)* thirteen; *(fecha)* thirteenth.

✎ Consulta también seis.

**treceavo,-a** *adj* thirteenth.

► *nm & nf* thirteenth.

✎ Consulta también sexto,-a.

**trecho** *nm* **1** *(espacio)* distance, way; *(tiempo)* while, time. **2** *(de camino, ruta)* stretch. **3** AGR plot, patch. **4** *fam (parte)* piece, bit.

**tregua** *nf* **1** truce. **2** *fig* respite, rest.

**treinta** *adj (cardinal)* thirty; *(ordinal)* thirtieth.

► *nm (número)* thirty; *(fecha)* thirtieth.

✎ Consulta también seis.

**treintañero,-a** *adj* thirty-year-old.

► *nm & nf* thirty-year-old person.

**treintavo,-a** *adj* thirtieth.

► *nm & nf* thirtieth.

✎ Consulta también sexto,-a.

**treintena** *nf (exacto)* thirty; *(aproximado)* about thirty.

**tremendo,-a** *adj* **1** *(terrible)* terrible, dreadful, frightful. **2** *(muy grande)* huge, enormous, tremendous. **3** *(travieso)* terrible. LOC **tomarse** ALGO **por la tremenda** *fig* to make a great fuss about STH.

**trementina** *nf* turpentine.

**tremolar** *vt* to wave.

► *vi* to wave, flutter.

**trémulo,-a** *adj* **1** *(tembloroso)* tremulous, quivering. **2** *(luz, llama)* flickering.

**tren** *nm* **1** *(ferrocarril)* train. **2** *(conjunto de máquinas)* convoy, line. **3** *fig (ritmo, modo)* speed, pace. LOC **coger el tren / tomar el tren** to catch a train. COMP **tren de alta velocidad** high-speed train.

**trenca** *nf (abrigo)* duffel coat, duffle coat.

**trenza** *nf* **1** *(peluquería)* plait, US braid. **2** COST braid.

**trenzado** *nm* **1** *(trenza - de pelo)* plait, US braid; *(- de costura)* braid. **2** *(en danza)* entrechat. **3** *(de caballo)* crossover step.

**trenzar** *vt* **1** to plait, braid. **2** *(peluquería)* to plait, US braid.

**trepador,-ra** *adj (planta)* climbing.
▶ *nm & nf fam pey* go-getter, social climber.

**trepanación** *nf* trepanation, trephination.

**trepanar** *vi* to trepan, trephine.

**trépano** *nm* **1** MED trephine. **2** TÉC bit.

**trepar¹** *vt (escalar)* to climb.
▶ *vi (escalar)* to climb.

**trepar²** *vt* **1** *(taladrar)* to drill. **2** *(un bordado)* to trim.

**trepidante** *adj* **1** vibrating, shaking. **2** *fig (vida, etc)* hectic, frantic.

**trepidar** *vi* to vibrate, shake.

**tres** *adj (cardinal)* three; *(ordinal)* third.
▶ *nm (número)* three; *(fecha)* third. COMP **tres en raya** noughts and crosses, US tick-tack-toe.

✎ Consulta también seis.

**trescientos,-as** *adj (cardinal)* three hundred; *(ordinal)* three hundredth.
▶ *nm (número)* three hundred.

✎ Consulta también seis.

**tresillo** *nm (mueble)* suite, three-piece suite.

**treta** *nf* trick, ruse.

**tríada** *nf* triad.

**triangular** *adj* triangular.

**triángulo,-a** *adj* triangular.
▶ *nm* **triángulo** triangle. COMP **triángulo equilátero** equilateral triangle. ▎ **triángulo isósceles** isosceles triangle. ▎ **triángulo rectángulo** right-angled triangle.

**triatlón** *nm* triathlon.

**tribal** *adj* tribal, tribe.

**tribu** *nf* tribe.

**tribuna** *nf* **1** *(plataforma)* rostrum, dais. **2** DEP grandstand.

**tribunal** *nm* **1** JUR court. **2** *(de examen)* board of examiners. LOC **llevar a los tribunales** to take to court. COMP **Tribunal Supremo** High Court, US Supreme Court.

**tributación** *nf* taxation, levy.

**tributar** *vt* to pay.

**tributario,-a** *adj* tributary, tax.
▶ *nm & nf* taxpayer.

**tributo** *nm* **1** *(impuesto)* tax. **2** *(a cambio de algo)* tribute. **3** *fig (carga)* price. **4** *fig (de sentimiento)* token.

**tricéfalo,-a** *adj* tricephalous.

**tríceps** *nm inv* triceps.

**triciclo** *nm* tricycle.

**tricornio** *nm (sombrero)* three-cornered hat.

**tricotar** *vt* to knit.

**tridente** *nm* trident.

**tridimensional** *adj* three-dimensional.

**triedro** *nm* trihedron.

**trienal** *adj* triennial.

**trienio** *nm* triennium.

**trifásico,-a** *adj* ELEC three-phase.

**trigal** *nm* wheat field.

**trigésimo,-a** *adj* thirtieth.
▶ *nm & nf* thirtieth.

✎ Consulta también sexto,-a.

**triglifo** *nm* triglyph.

**trigo** *nm (cereal)* wheat.

**trigonometría** *nf* trigonometry.

**trigonométrico,-a** *adj* trigonometric, trigonometrical.

**trigueño,-a** *adj* **1** *(pelo)* corn-coloured (US corn-colored), dark blonde. **2** *(piel)* dark, swarthy. **3** *(persona)* olive-skinned.

**triguero,-a** *adj* wheat.

**trilateral** *adj* three-sided, trilateral.

**trilingüe** *adj* trilingual.

**trilita** *nf* TNT, trinitrotoluene.

**trilla** *nf* threshing.

**trillado,-a** *adj* **1** *(camino)* beaten, well-trodden. **2** *fig (expresión, etc)* overworked, well-worn.

**trilladora** *nf* threshing machine.

**trillar** *vt* **1** to thresh. **2** *fig* to wear out.

**trillizo,-a** *nm & nf* triplet.

**trilogía** *nf* trilogy.

**trimestral** *adj* quarterly, three-monthly, trimestral.

**T**

**trimestre** *nm* 1 quarter, trimester. 2 EDUC term.

**trimotor** *nm* three-engined aircraft.

**trinar** *vi* 1 *(ave)* to warble, trill. 2 MÚS to trill. 3 *fam (enfadarse)* to rage, fume: *Pedro está que trina* Pedro is fuming.

**trinchar** *vt* to carve, slice (up).

**trinchera** *nf* trench.

**trineo** *nm* sleigh, sled, sledge.

**Trinidad** *nf* Trinidad. COMP **Trinidad y Tobago** Trinidad and Tobago.

**trinitrotolueno** *nm* trinitrotoluene.

**trino** *nm* 1 *(ave)* warble, trill. 2 MÚS trill.

**trino,-a** *adj* trine.

**trinomio** *nm* trinomial.

**trinquete¹** *nm (lengüeta)* pawl; *(mecanismo)* ratchet.

**trinquete²** *nm* 1 *(frontón)* pelota court. 2 MAR *(palo)* foremast; *(vela)* foresail.

**trío** *nm* trio.

**tripa** *nf* 1 *(intestino)* gut, intestine. 2 *(barriga)* gut, stomach. 3 *(de vasija)* belly. 4 *fam (embarazo)* belly.
▶ *nf pl* **tripas** *fam (interior)* innards.

**tripartito,-a** *adj* tripartite.

**triple** *adj* 1 triple. 2 *(tres veces)* three times: *pagamos el triple del precio real* we paid three times the real price.
▶ *nm* triple. COMP **triple salto** triple jump.

**triplicado** *nm* triplicate.

**triplicar** *vt* to triple, treble.

**trípode** *nm* tripod.

**tríptico** *nm* triptych.

**triptongo** *nm* triphthong.

**tripulación** *nf* crew.

**tripulante** *nm* crew member.

**tripular** *vt* to man.

**tris** *nm fam fig* bit; *(sonido)* crack. LOC **en un tris** *fam* in a jiffy: *lo hizo en un tris* he did it in a jiffy.

**trisílabo,-a** *adj* trisyllabic.
▶ *nm* **trisílabo** trisyllable.

**triste** *adj* 1 *(infeliz)* sad, unhappy; *(futuro)* bleak. 2 *(oscuro, sombrío)* gloomy, dismal. 3 *(único)* single, only: *ni un triste libro* not a single book. 4 *(insignificante)*

poor, humble. LOC **es triste que...** it's a pity…: *es triste que no los podamos ayudar* it's a pity we can't help them.

**tristeza** *nf* sadness.
▶ *nf pl* **tristezas** problems, sufferings.

**tristón,-ona** *adj fam* gloomy, sad, melancholy.

**tritón** *nm* 1 *(anfibio)* newt. 2 Tritón *(mitología)* Triton.

**triturado,-a** *adj* 1 ground, crushed. 2 *fig* crumpled up.

**triturador,-ra** *adj* grinding, crushing, triturating.
▶ *nm* **triturador** waste disposal unit, US garbage disposal unit.

**trituradora** *nf* grinder, crushing machine. COMP **trituradora de papel** paper shredder.

**triturar** *vt* 1 to grind (up), crush; *(papel)* to shred. 2 *fig (físicamente)* to beat (up); *(moralmente)* to tear apart.

**triunfador,-ra** *adj* winning.
▶ *nm & nf* winner.

**triunfal** *adj* triumphant.

**triunfalismo** *nm* 1 triumphalism. 2 POL jingoism.

**triunfalista** *adj* 1 triumphalist. 2 POL jingoistic.
▶ *nm o nf* 1 triumphalist. 2 POL jingoist.

**triunfar** *vi* to triumph. LOC **triunfar en la vida** to succeed in life.

**triunfo** *nm* 1 *(victoria)* triumph, victory. 2 DEP win. 3 *(éxito)* success. 4 *(naipes)* trump.

**trivial** *adj* trivial, petty.

**trivialidad** *nf* triviality, pettiness.

**trivializar** *vt* to trivialize, minimize.

**triza** *nf* bit, fragment. LOC **estar hecho, -a trizas** *fam* to feel washed out.

**trocar** *vt* 1 *(permutar)* to exchange, swap: *trocar un lápiz por un bolígrafo* to exchange a pencil for a biro. 2 *(transformar)* to turn (en, into), convert (en, into).

**trocear** *vt* to cut up.

**trofeo** *nm* trophy.

**trófico,-a** *adj* food.

**troglodita** *nm o nf* troglodyte.

**trolebús** *nm* trolley bus.

**tromba** *nf* waterspout. COMP **tromba de agua** downpour.

**trombo** *nm* thrombus.

**trombón** *nm* MÚS trombone.
▶ *nm o nf* trombonist. COMP **trombón de varas** slide trombone.

**trombosis** *nf inv* thrombosis.

**trompa** *nf* 1 MÚS horn. 2 *(de elefante)* trunk. 3 *(de insecto)* proboscis. 4 ANAT tube. 5 *fam fig (nariz)* hooter, snout. LOC **estar trompa** *fam* to be plastered. COMP **trompa de Eustaquio** Eustachian tube. | **trompa de Falopio** Fallopian tube.
▶ *nm o nf* MÚS horn player.

**trompazo** *nm* bump. LOC **darse un trompazo** to have a bump, have a crash.

**trompeta** *nf* MÚS trumpet.
▶ *nm o nf* trumpet player.

**trompetista** *nm o nf* trumpet player, trumpeter.

**trompicón** *nm* 1 *(tropezón)* trip, stumble. 2 *(golpe)* blow, hit. LOC **a trompicones** in fits and starts.

**trompo** *nm* top, spinning top.

**tronar** *vi* 1 *[se usa sólo en tercera persona; no lleva sujeto] (trueno)* to thunder. 2 *(cañón, etc)* to thunder.

**tronchar** *vt* 1 *(árboles)* to cut down, fell. 2 *fig* to destroy. LOC **troncharse de risa** *fam* to split one's sides with laughter.

**troncho** *adj* stem, stalk.

**tronco** *nm* 1 ANAT trunk, torso. 2 BOT *(tallo de árbol)* trunk; *(leño)* log. 3 *fig (linaje)* family stock. 4 *fig (persona inútil)* blockhead. 5 *(geometría)* frustum. 6 *argot (compañero)* mate, pal, chum. LOC **dormir como un tronco** *fam* to sleep like a log. COMP **tronco de cono** truncated cone.

**tronera** *nf* 1 *(de fortificación)* loophole, embrasure. 2 *(de barco)* porthole. 3 *(de billar)* pocket.

**trono** *nm* throne.

**tropa** *nf* 1 MIL troops *pl*, soldiers *pl*. 2 *(muchedumbre)* crowd.

▶ *nf pl* **tropas** MIL troops, fighting soldiers.

**tropel** *nm* throng, mob. LOC **en tropel** in a mad rush.

**tropelía** *nf* 1 *(atropello)* outrage. 2 *(tropel)* throng, mob. 3 *(delito)* crime.

**tropezar** *vi* 1 *(trompicar)* to trip, stumble: *tropezó con mi pie* he tripped over my foot. 2 *fig (encontrar a alguien)* to come (con, across), bump (con, into). 3 *fig (encontrar dificultades, etc)* to come up (con, against), run (con, into).

**tropezón** *nm* 1 *(traspié)* trip, stumble. 2 *fig (error)* slip-up, faux pas. 3 *fam (de comida)* chunk of food. LOC **dar un tropezón** to trip.

**tropical** *adj* tropical.

**trópico** *nm* tropic.
▶ *nm pl* **trópicos** tropics.

**tropiezo** *nm* 1 *(obstáculo)* trip. 2 *fig (error)* blunder; *(revés)* setback, mishap. 3 *(riña)* quarrel.

**tropismo** *nm* tropism.

**tropo** *nm* trope.

**troposfera** *nf* troposphere.

**troquel** *nm* die.

**troqueladora** *nf* stamping machine.

**troquelar** *vt* (gen) to stamp; *(monedas)* to strike; *(cuero)* to emboss.

**trotamundos** *nm o nf inv* globe-trotter; *(mochilero)* backpacker.

**trotar** *vi* 1 to trot. 2 *fig (andar)* to bustle, run, run about.

**trote** *nm* 1 *(de caballo)* trot. 2 *fam fig (actividad)* chasing about, hustle and bustle, bustle. LOC **al trote** at a trot.

**trovador,-ra** *nm & nf* troubadour, minstrel.

**trozo** *nm* piece, chunk.

**trucaje** *nm* trick photography.

**trucar** *vt* 1 *(foto, etc)* to doctor, alter, tamper with. 2 AUTO to soup up.

**trucha** *nf* trout.

**truco** *nm* 1 *(ardid)* trick. 2 *(fotográfico)* trick effect, trick camera shot. 3 *(tranquillo)* knack. LOC **coger el truco a** ALGO *fam* to get the knack of STH, get the hang of STH.

**T**

**truculencia** *nf* 1 cruelty. 2 *fig* sensationalism.

**truculento,-a** *adj* 1 *(cruel)* cruel. 2 *fig* *(excesivo)* sensationalistic.

**trueno** *nm* 1 thunder, thunderclap. 2 *fam (joven)* hare brain.

**trueque** *nm* exchange, swap.

**trufa** *nf* 1 *(hongo)* truffle. 2 *(de chocolate)* chocolate truffle.

**trufar** *vt* to stuff with truffles.
▶ *vi fig* to tell lies.*f*

**truhan,-ana** *nm & nf* rogue, crook.

**truncado,-a** *adj (geometría)* truncated.

**truncar** *vt* 1 *(cortar)* to truncate. 2 *fig (ilusiones, esperanzas)* to shatter, cut short. 3 *fig (escrito)* to leave unfinished; *(sentido)* to upset.
▶ *vpr* **truncarse** *fig (ilusiones, etc)* to cut short.

**trust** *nm* trust, cartel.

**tu** *adj* your: *tu coche* your car; *tus coches* your cars.

**tú** *pron* 1 you. 2 REL Thou. [LOC] **tratar de tú** to address as *tú*.

**tuareg** *adj* Tuareg.
▶ *nm* Tuareg.

**tuba** *nf* tuba.

**tubérculo** *nm* 1 BOT tuber. 2 MED tubercle.

**tuberculosis** *nf inv* tuberculosis.

**tuberculoso,-a** *adj* 1 BOT tuberous. 2 MED tubercular, tuberculous.

**tubería** *nf* 1 *(de agua)* piping, pipes *pl*, plumbing. 2 *(de gas, petróleo)* pipeline.

**tuberoso,-a** *adj* tuberous.

**tubo** *nm* 1 *(de ensayo, etc)* tube. 2 *(tubería)* pipe. 3 ANAT tube. [COMP] **tubo de ensayo** test tube. ‖ **tubo de escape** exhaust pipe, exhaust. ‖ **tubo digestivo** alimentary canal.

**tubular** *adj* tubular.
▶ *nm* bicycle tyre.

**tucán** *nm* toucan.

**tuerca** *nf* nut.

**tuerto,-a** *adj* one-eyed, blind in one eye.
▶ *nm & nf* one-eyed person.

**tuétano** *nm* 1 marrow. 2 *fig* essence, core.

**tufo** *nm* 1 *(mal olor)* pong, foul smell, stink. 2 *(emanación)* fume, vapour (US vapor).

**tugurio** *nm* 1 *(choza)* shepherd's hut. 2 *(casucha)* hovel, shack. 3 *fig* hole, dive.

**tul** *nm* tulle.

**tulipa** *nf* 1 *(bot)* small tulip. 2 *(lámpara)* tulip-shaped lampshade.

**tulipán** *nm* tulip.

**tullido,-a** *adj* crippled, disabled.
▶ *nm & nf* cripple.

**tumbado,-a** *adj (estirado)* lying, stretched out: *tumbado al sol* lying in the sun.

**tumbar** *vt* 1 *(derribar)* to knock out, knock over. 2 EDUC *fam* to fail.
▶ *vpr* **tumbarse** *(acostarse)* to lie down, stretch out.

**tumbo** *nm* jolt, bump. [LOC] **dar tumbos** to jolt, bump along.

**tumbona** *nf* 1 *(hamaca)* deck-chair. 2 *(silla extensible)* lounger.

**tumor** *nm* tumour (US tumor).

**túmulo** *nm* 1 *(montecillo)* tumulus, burial mound, barrow. 2 *(catafalco)* catafalque.

**tumulto** *nm* tumult, commotion.

**tumultuoso,-a** *adj* tumultuous, riotous.

**tuna** *nf* student minstrel group.

**tunda** *nf* 1 *fam* thrashing, beating. 2 *fig (trabajo agotador)* exhausting job, drag.

**tundra** *nf* tundra.

**tunecino,-a** *adj* Tunisian.
▶ *nm & nf* Tunisian.

**túnel** *nm* tunnel.

**Túnez** *nm* 1 *(ciudad)* Tunis. 2 *(país)* Tunisia.

**tungsteno** *nm* tungsten.

**túnica** *nf* tunic.

**tuno** *nm* BOT prickly pear.

**tupí** *adj* Tupi.
▶ *nm & nf* Tupi.
▶ *nm (idioma)* Tupi.

**tupido,-a** *adj* 1 dense, thick. 2 *fig (torpe)* clumsy, dense.

**tupir** *vi (apretar)* to pack tight, press down.
▶ *vpr* **tupirse 1** *(comiendo)* to stuff os. **2** *(ofuscarse)* to get muddled up, get in a muddle.

**turba¹** *nf* **1** *(combustible)* peat, turf. **2** *(abono)* peat, peat moss.

**turba²** *nf (muchedumbre)* mob, crowd.

**turbación** *nf* **1** *(alteración)* disturbance. **2** *(preocupación)* anxiety, worry. **3** *(desconcierto)* confusion, uneasiness.

**turbado,-a** *adj* **1** *(alterado)* disturbed, unsettled. **2** *(preocupado)* worried, upset. **3** *(desconcertado)* confused.

**turbador,-ra** *adj* **1** *(que altera)* disturbing, unsettling. **2** *(preocupante)* worrying, upsetting. **3** *(desconcertante)* confusing, disconcerting.

**turbante** *nm* turban.

**turbar** *vt* **1** *(alterar)* to unsettle, disturb. **2** *(enturbiar)* to stir up. **3** *(preocupar)* to upset, worry. **4** *(desconcertar)* to baffle, put off.
▶ *vpr* **turbarse 1** *(preocuparse)* to be upset, become upset. **2** *(desconcertarse)* to be confused, be baffled.

**turbera** *nf* peat bog.

**turbina** *nf* turbine.

**turbio,-a** *adj* **1** *(oscurecido)* cloudy, muddy, turbid. **2** *fig (dudoso)* shady, dubious. **3** *fig (turbulento)* turbulent. **4** *fig (confuso)* confused. **5** *fig (vista)* blurred.

**turbo** *nm* turbo.

**turbogenerador** *nm* turbogenerator.

**turbohélice** *nm* turboprop.

**turborreactor** *nm* turbojet, turbojet engine.

**turbulencia** *nf* turbulence.

**turbulento,-a** *adj* turbulent, troubled.

**turco,-a** *adj* Turkish.
▶ *nm & nf (persona)* Turk.
▶ *nm* **turco** *(idioma)* Turkish.

**turgencia** *nf* turgidity, turgidness.

**turgente** *adj* turgid.

**turismo** *nm* **1** *(gen)* tourism. **2** *(industria)* tourist trade, tourist industry. **3** AUTO private car, saloon. LOC **hacer**

**turismo 1** *(país)* to go touring. **2** *(ciudad, pueblo)* to go sightseeing.

**turista** *nm o nf* tourist.

**turístico,-a** *adj* tourist. LOC **de interés turístico** of interest to tourists.

**Turkmenistán** *nm* Turkmenistan.

**túrmix®** *nm inv* liquidizer, blender.

**turnar** *vi* to alternate.
▶ *vpr* **turnarse** to take turns.

**turno** *nm* **1** *(tanda)* turn, go: *es mi turno* it's my turn; *¿a quién le toca el turno?* who's next? **2** *(período de trabajo)* shift. LOC **estar de turno** to be on duty. COMP **turno de día / turno de noche** day shift / night shift.

**turquesa** *adj* turquoise.
▶ *nf (piedra)* turquoise.
▶ *nm (color)* turquoise.

**Turquía** *nf* Turkey.

**turrón** *nm type of* nougat.

**turronería** *nf* shop selling nougat.

**tute** *nm* **1** *(naipes)* card game. **2** *fig (esfuerzo)* beating, thrashing.

**tutear** *vt* **1** to address as *tú*. **2** *fig* to be on familiar terms with.
▶ *vpr* **tutearse** *(uso recíproco)* to address each other as *tú*.

**tutela** *nf* **1** JUR guardianship, tutelage. **2** *fig* protection, guidance. LOC **bajo la tutela de** under the protection of.

**tutelar** *adj* tutelary.

**tuteo** *nm* use of the *tú* form of address.

**tutor,-ra** *nm & nf* **1** JUR guardian. **2** *fig* protector, guide. **3** EDUC tutor.
▶ *nm* **tutor** AGR stake, prop.

**tutoría** *nf* **1** JUR guardianship, tutelage. **2** EDUC post of tutor.

**Tuvalu** *nm* Tuvalu.

**tuyo,-a** *adj* of yours, one of your: *¿es primo tuyo?* is he a cousin of yours?, is he your cousin?
▶ *pron* yours, your own: *el tuyo está allí* yours is there.
▶ *nm* **lo tuyo** *(lo que es tuyo)* what is yours; *(lo que te concierne)* your business, your own business.
▶ *nm pl* **los tuyos** *(familiares)* your family *sing*; *(amigos)* your friends.

**T**

# U

**U, u** *nf (la letra)* U, u.
**u** *[se usa ante palabras que empiezan por o u ho] conj* or: *diez u once* ten or eleven.

✎ Consulta también **o**.

**ubre** *nf* udder.
**ucraniano,-a** *adj* Ukranian.
▶ *nm & nf (persona)* Ukranian.
**Uganda** *nf* Uganda.
**ugandés,-esa** *adj* Ugandan.
▶ *nm & nf* Ugandan.
**úlcera** *nf* ulcer. [COMP] **úlcera de estómago** stomach ulcer.
**ulceración** *nf* ulceration.
**ultimar** *vt* to finish, complete.
**ultimátum** *nm inv* **1** ultimatum. **2** *fam* final word.
**último,-a** *adj* **1** last. **2** *(más reciente)* latest; *(de dos)* latter. **3** *(más alejado)* furthest; *(más abajo)* bottom, lowest; *(más arriba)* top; *(más atrás)* back. **4** *(definitivo)* final. [LOC] **por último** finally.
**ultraje** *nm* outrage, insult.
**ultraligero** *adj* ultralight.
▶ *nm* **ultraligero** *(avión)* microlight.
**ultramar** *nm* overseas: *viene de ultramar* it comes from overseas, it's imported.
**ultramarino,-a** *adj* overseas.
▶ *nm pl* **ultramarinos** groceries.
**ultrasonido** *nm* ultrasound.
**ultravioleta** *adj inv* ultraviolet.
**ulular** *vi* **1** *(animal)* to howl; *(búho)* to hoot. **2** *fig* to howl.
**umbilical** *adj* umbilical.
**umbral** *nm* **1** threshold. **2** *fig* threshold, outset.
**un,-na** *art indef* a, an: *un libro* a book; *un ojo* an eye.

▶ *adj* **1** *(numeral)* one: *tiene un año* he's one year old. **2** *(indef)* some: *un día volverá* he'll come some day.

✎ Consulta también **uno,-a**.

**unánime** *adj* unanimous.
**unanimidad** *nf* unanimity.
**undécimo,-a** *adj* eleventh.
▶ *nm & nf (ordinal, partitivo)* eleventh.

✎ Consulta también **sexto,-a**.

**ungüento** *nm* ointment.
**ungulado,-a** *adj* ungulate, hoofed.
▶ *nm* **ungulado** ungulate.
**unicelular** *adj* unicellular, single-cell.
**único,-a** *adj* **1** *(solo)* only, sole: *la única persona* the only person. **2** *(extraordinario)* unique.
**unicornio** *nm* unicorn.
**unidad** *nf* **1** unit. **2** *(barco)* vessel; *(avión)* aircraft; *(de tren)* carriage, coach. **3** *(cohesión)* unity.
**unido,-a** *adj* **1** *(junto)* united. **2** *(avenido)* attached: *estar muy unidos* to be very close.
**unifamiliar** [COMP] **vivienda unifamiliar** detached house.
**unificación** *nf* unification.
**unificador,-ra** *adj* unifying.
▶ *nm & nf* unifier.
**unificar** *vt* to unify.
**uniformado,-a** *adj* in uniform.
**uniformar** *vt* **1** *(igualar)* to make uniform, standardize. **2** *(poner un uniforme)* to put into uniform, give a uniform.
**uniforme** *adj* **1** uniform. **2** *(superficie)* even.
▶ *nm (prenda)* uniform.
**uniformidad** *nf* **1** *(igualdad)* uniformity. **2** *(de superficie)* evenness.
**uniformizar** *vt* to standardize.
**unilateral** *adj* unilateral.

**unión** *nf* **1** union. **2** TÉC *(acoplamiento)* joining; *(junta)* joint.

**unir** *vt* **1** *(juntar)* to unite, join. **2** *(combinar)* to combine (a, with).

**unitario,-a** *adj* unitary.

**univalvo,-a** *adj* univalve.

**universal** *adj* universal.

**universidad** *nf* university.

**universitario,-a** *adj* university.
▶ *nm & nf (que está estudiando)* university student; *(licenciado)* university graduate.

**universo** *nm* universe.

**unívoco,-a** *adj* univocal.

**uno,-a** *adj (numeral)* one: *el número uno* number one.
▶ *pron* **1** one: *uno (de ellos)* one of them. **2** *(impersonal)* one, you: *uno tiene que velar por sus intereses* one has to look after one's own interests. **3** *fam (persona)* someone, somebody: *estaba hablando con una* he was talking to some woman.
▶ *nm* **uno** *(número)* one.
▶ *nf* **la una** *(hora)* one o'clock.
▶ *adj vpr* **unos,-as** *(indefinido)* some; *(aproximado)* about, around: *unas cajas* some boxes; *habrá unos treinta* there must be around thirty. LOC **a (la) una** together. **de uno,-a en uno,-a** one by one.

**untar** *vt* **1** to grease, smear: *untar pan con mantequilla* to spread butter on bread. **2** *fam (sobornar)* to bribe.

**uña** *nf* **1** nail; *(del dedo)* fingernail; *(del dedo del pie)* toenail. **2** *(garra)* claw; *(pezuña)* hoof.

**uralita®** *nf* uralite.

**uranio** *nm* uranium.

**Urano** *nm* Uranus.

**urbanismo** *nm* town planning.

**urbanización** *nf* **1** *(proceso)* urbanization. **2** *(conjunto residencial)* housing development, housing estate.

**urbanizar** *vt* to urbanize, develop.

**urbano,-a** *adj* urban, city.

**urbe** *nf* large city, metropolis.

**uréter** *nm* ureter.

**uretra** *nf* urethra.

**urgencia** *nf* urgency, emergency.
▶ *nf pl* **urgencias** *(servicio)* casualty department *sing*, casualty *sing*, US emer-

gency room. LOC **en (un) caso de urgencia** in an emergency.

**urgente** *adj* **1** urgent. **2** *(correo)* express (post, US mail), first-class (post, US mail).

**urgir** *vi* to be urgent, be pressing.

**urinario,-a** *adj* urinary.
▶ *nm* **urinario** *(retrete)* urinal.

**urna** *nf* **1** POL ballot box. **2** *(vasija)* urn. **3** *(caja)* glass case.

**urraca** *nf* **1** magpie. **2** *fig (cotorra)* chatterbox.

**urticaria** *nf* hives *pl*, urticaria.

**Uruguay** *nm* Uruguay.

**uruguayo,-a** *adj* Uruguayan.
▶ *nm & nf* Uruguayan.

**usado,-a** *adj* **1** *(gastado)* worn out, old. **2** *(de segunda mano)* second-hand, used.

**usar** *vt* **1** to use. **2** *(prenda)* to wear.
▶ *vi* to use (de, -).
▶ *vpr* **usarse** *(estar de moda)* to be used, be in fashion.

**uso** *nm* **1** use. **2** *(ejercicio)* exercise. **3** *(de prenda)* wearing. **4** *(costumbre)* usage, custom. **5** GRAM usage.

**usted** *pron fml* you.

**usual** *adj* usual, common.

**usuario,-a** *nm & nf* user.

**usurero,-a** *nm & nf* usurer.

**usurpar** *vt* to usurp.

**utensilio** *nm* **1** *(herramienta)* tool, utensil. **2** *(aparato)* device, implement.

**uterino,-a** *adj* uterine.

**útero** *nm* uterus, womb.

**útil¹** *adj* useful.

**útil²** *nm (herramienta)* tool, instrument.

**utilidad** *nf* **1** utility, usefulness. **2** *(beneficio)* profit.

**utilitario,-a** *adj* utilitarian.
▶ *nm* **utilitario** *(coche)* utility vehicle.

**utilizar** *vt* to use, make use of.

**utopía** *nf* utopia.

**utópico,-a** *adj* utopian.

**uva** *nf* grape.

**uve** *nf name of the letter* v.

**uzbeco,-a** *adj* Uzbek.
▶ *nm & nf (persona)* Uzbek.
▶ *nm* **uzbeco** *(idioma)* Uzbek.

**Uzbekistán** *nm* Uzbekistan.

**U**

**V, v** *nf (la letra)* V, v.

**V** *sím* **(voltio)** volt; *(símbolo)* V.

**vaca** *nf* **1** cow. **2** *(carne)* beef. **3** *(cuero)* cowhide.

**vacaciones** *nf pl* holiday, holidays *pl*, US vacation: *se fueron de vacaciones a Mallorca* they went to Majorca for their holidays. LOC **irse de vacaciones** to go on holiday.

**vacante** *adj* vacant.

▶ *nf* vacancy.

**vaciar** *vt* **1** *(recipiente)* to empty; *(local)* to empty, clear. **2** *(contenido)* to pour away. **3** *(dejar hueco)* to hollow out. **4** *(moldear)* to cast, mould (US mold).

**vacilación** *nf* **1** *(duda)* hesitation. **2** *(oscilación)* swaying, vacillation.

**vacilar** *vi* **1** *(oscilar)* to sway, vacillate. **2** *(estar poco firme)* to wobble. **3** *(al andar)* to sway, stagger; *(al hablar)* to falter. **4** *(luz)* to flicker. **5** *fig (dudar)* to hesitate, waver. **6** *fam (tomar el pelo)* to joke, tease: *¡no me vaciles!* don't tease me! **7** *fam (presumir)* to show off.

**vacío,-a** *adj* **1** *(gen)* empty: *el cine está vacío* the cinema is empty. **2** *(no ocupado)* vacant, unoccupied; *(sin muebles)* unfurnished. **3** *(hueco)* hollow.

▶ *nm* **vacío 1** *(gen)* emptiness, void. **2** *(hueco)* gap; *(espacio)* space, empty space; *(espacio en blanco)* blank space. **3** *(vacante)* vacancy. **4** FÍS vacuum. **5** *fig (falta)* emptiness, void.

**vacuna** *nf* MED vaccine.

**vacunación** *nf* MED vaccination.

**vado** *nm* **1** *(de río)* ford. **2** *(de acera)* dropped kerb. COMP **«Vado permanente»** "Keep clear".

**vagabundo,-a** *adj* **1** wandering, roving. **2** *pey* vagrant.

▶ *nm & nf* **1** *(trotamundos)* wanderer, rover. **2** *pey* vagrant, tramp, US hobo. **3** *(sin casa)* tramp, US hobo.

**vagar¹** *vi (estar ocioso)* to idle about.

**vagar²** *vi (errar)* to wander (por, about), roam (por, about): *pasa su tiempo vagando por el pueblo* he spends his time wandering about town.

**vago,-a¹** *adj* **1** *(vacío)* empty; *(desocupado)* vacant. **2** *(holgazán)* lazy, idle.

**vago,-a²** *adj (impreciso)* vague: *idea vaga* vague idea.

**vagón** *nm* **1** *(para pasajeros)* carriage, coach, US car. **2** *(para mercancías)* wagon, goods van, truck, US boxcar.

**vaho** *nm* **1** *(vapor)* vapour (US vapor), steam. **2** *(aliento)* breath.

**vaina** *nf* **1** *(de espada, etc)* sheath. **2** *(de instrumento, etc)* case. **3** BOT pod.

**vainilla** *nf* vanilla.

**vajilla** *nf* tableware, dishes *pl*, crockery. COMP **una vajilla** a dinner service.

**vale** *nm* **1** *(comprobante)* voucher; *(recibo)* receipt. **2** *(pagaré)* promissory note.

▶ *interj fam* OK!

**valedor,-ra** *nm & nf* protector.

**valentía** *nf (valor)* bravery, courage.

**valer** *vt* **1** *(tener un valor de)* to be worth: *no vale nada* it is worthless. **2** *(costar)* to cost, be: *vale siete euros el kilo* it costs seven euros a kilo **3** *(hacer merecedor)* to win, earn, get: *el suspenso le valió un rapapolvo* failing the exam earned him a good ticking-off. **4** *(ocasionar)* to cause: *me ha valido muchos problemas* he's caused me a lot of problems. **5** MAT to equal.

▶ *vi* **1** *(tener un valor de)* to be worth. **2** *(ser útil, adecuado)* to be useful, be of use, be good for: *¿te vale este libro?* is this book any use (to you)? **3** *(costar)* to cost,

be worth. **4** *(ser válido, contar)* to count. **5** *(tener validez)* to be valid; *(monedas)* to be legal tender: *ese billete aún vale* that ticket is still valid. **6** *(ser suficiente, bastar)* to do, be enough: *con esto ya me vale* this will be enough for me. **7** *(estar permitido)* to be allowed, be permitted.
▶ *nm (valía)* value.
▶ *vpr* **valerse 1** *(utilizar)* to use (de, of), make use (de, of): *se valió de un bastón* he used a stick. **2** *(espabilarse)* to manage, cope. LOC **valerse por sí mismo** to be able to manage on one's own.

**valeroso,-a** *adj* courageous, brave.

**validez** *nf* validity.

**válido,-a** *adj* valid.

**valiente** *adj* **1** *(valeroso)* brave, courageous, bold. **2** *(fuerte)* strong.

**valioso,-a** *adj* valuable, precious.

**valla** *nf* **1** *(cerca)* fence; *(construcción)* wall. **2** MIL stockade. **3** DEP hurdle. **4** *(para publicidad)* hoarding, US billboard. **5** *fig* obstacle. COMP **valla publicitaria** hoarding, US billboard.

**vallado** *nm* **1** *(cerca)* fence. **2** MIL stockade.

**vallar** *vt* to fence (in).

**valle** *nm* valley.

**valor** *nm* **1** *(valía)* value, worth, merit: *una persona de gran valor* a person of great merit. **2** *(precio)* price. **3** *(validez)* value: *estas monedas dejarán de tener valor muy pronto* these coins will soon be of no value. **4** *(importancia)* importance. **5** *(coraje)* courage. **6** MAT value.
▶ *nm pl* **valores 1** FIN securities, bonds. **2** *(principios)* values.

**valorar** *vt* **1** *(tasar)* to value, calculate the value of. **2** *(aumentar el valor)* to raise the value of.

**vals** *nm* waltz.

**válvula** *nf* valve. COMP **válvula de seguridad** safety valve.

**vampiro** *nm* **1** *(espectro)* vampire. **2** *(mamífero)* vampire bat. **3** *fig* parasite.

**vandalismo** *nm* vandalism.

**vándalo,-a** *adj* Vandal.
▶ *nm & nf* **1** Vandal. **2** *fig* vandal.

**vanidad** *nf* vanity, conceit.

**vanidoso,-a** *adj* vain, conceited.

**Vanuatu** *nm* Vanuatu.

**vapor** *nm* **1** *(gas)* vapour (US vapor), steam. **2** *(barco)* steamship, steamer. LOC **al vapor** CULIN steamed. COMP **vapor de agua** water vapour (US vapor).

**vaquero,-a** *adj* cow, cattle.
▶ *nm & nf (pastor)* cowherd, US cowboy; *(pastora)* cowherd, US cowgirl.
▶ *nm pl* **vaqueros** *(pantalones)* jeans, pair of jeans.

**vara** *nf* **1** *(palo)* staff, rod, pole. **2** *(de mando)* staff, mace. **3** *(medida de longitud)* unit of length equal to approximately 33 inches. **4** *(tauromaquia)* lance, pike.

**variable** *adj* variable, changeable.
▶ *nf* MAT variable.

**variación** *nf* variation, change.

**variado,-a** *adj* **1** varied, mixed. **2** *(galletas, helados)* assorted.

**variante** *adj* variable.
▶ *nf (versión)* variant. **2** *(diferencia)* difference.

**variar** *vt* **1** *(cambiar)* to change. **2** *(dar variedad)* to vary, give some variety to.
▶ *vi* **1** *(cambiar)* to change: *han variado de planes* they have changed their plans. **2** *(diferir)* to be different (de, to), differ (de, from): *lo que dices varía de tus primeras declaraciones* what you're saying differs from your first statement. **3** MAT to vary. LOC **para variar** *irón* as usual, just for a change.

**varicela** *nf* MED chickenpox, varicella.

**variedad** *nf* **1** *(diversidad)* variety, diversity: *una gran variedad de productos* a wide variety of products. **2** *(clase, tipo)* variety.
▶ *nf pl* **variedades** *(espectáculo)* variety show *sing*.

**varilla** *nf* **1** *(vara)* stick, rod. **2** *(de paraguas, abanico)* rib; *(de corsé)* stay.

**vario,-a** *adj* **1** *(diverso)* different, diverse. **2** *(variado)* varied, assorted. **3** *(mudable)* changeable, variable.
▶ *nm pl* **varios** *(algunos)* some, several.

**varita** *nf* small stick. COMP **varita mágica** magic wand.

**varón** *nm* **1** *(hombre)* man; *(chico)* boy. **2** *(sexo)* male.

**vasco,-a** *adj* Basque.
▶ *nm & nf (persona)* Basque.
▶ *nm* **vasco** *(idioma)* Basque. COMP **País Vasco** Basque Country.

**vasija** *nf* vessel, pot, jar.

**vaso** *nm* **1** *(para beber)* glass. **2** *(para flores)* vase. **3** ANAT vessel. COMP **vaso capilar** capillary. ‖ **vasos sanguíneos** blood vessels.

**vasto,-a** *adj* vast, immense, huge.

**váter** *nm fam* toilet.

**vatio** *nm* watt.

**vaya** *interj* what a: *¡vaya idea!* what an idea!

**vecindario** *nm* **1** *(lugar)* neighbourhood (US neighborhood). **2** *(vecinos)* neighbours *pl* (US neighbors *pl*), community, residents *pl*.

**vecino,-a** *adj* nearby, next, neighbouring (US neighboring).
▶ *nm & nf* **1** *(del barrio)* neighbour (US neighbor). **2** *(residente)* resident. **3** *(habitante)* inhabitant.

**vegetación** *nf* vegetation.
▶ *nf pl* **vegetaciones** MED adenoids.

**vegetal** *adj* vegetable.
▶ *nm* **1** vegetable, plant. **2** *(persona)* vegetable.

**vegetariano,-a** *adj* vegetarian.
▶ *nm & nf* vegetarian.

**vehículo** *nm* **1** *(gen)* vehicle. **2** *(coche)* car. **3** *fig* vehicle. **4** *fig (enfermedades)* transmitter, carrier.

**veinte** *adj (cardinal)* twenty; *(vigésimo)* twentieth.
▶ *nm (número)* twenty; *(fecha)* twentieth.
COMP **los años veinte** the twenties.

✎ Consulta también seis.

**veinteavo,-a** *adj* twentieth.
▶ *nm & nf* twentieth.

✎ Consulta también sexto.

**veintena** *nf (exacto)* twenty; *(aproximado)* about twenty.

**veinticinco** *adj (cardinal)* twenty-five; *(ordinal)* twenty-fifth.
▶ *nm (número)* twenty-five; *(fecha)* twenty-fifth.

**veinticuatro** *adj (cardinal)* twenty-four; *(ordinal)* twenty-fourth.

▶ *nm (número)* twenty-four; *(fecha)* twenty-fourth.

**veintidós** *adj (cardinal)* twenty-two; *(ordinal)* twenty-second.
▶ *nm (número)* twenty-two; *(fecha)* twenty-second.

**veintinueve** *adj (cardinal)* twenty-nine; *(ordinal)* twenty-ninth.
▶ *nm (número)* twenty-nine; *(fecha)* twenty-ninth.

**veintiocho** *adj (cardinal)* twenty-eight; *(ordinal)* twenty-eighth.
▶ *nm (número)* twenty-eight; *(fecha)* twenty-eighth.

**veintiséis** *adj (cardinal)* twenty-six; *(ordinal)* twenty-sixth.
▶ *nm (número)* twenty-six; *(fecha)* twenty-sixth.

**veintisiete** *adj (cardinal)* twenty-seven; *(ordinal)* twenty-seventh.
▶ *nm (número)* twenty-seven; *(fecha)* twenty-seventh.

**veintitrés** *adj (cardinal)* twenty-three; *(ordinal)* twenty-third.
▶ *nm (número)* twenty-three; *(fecha)* twenty-third.

**veintiún** *adj* [se usa sólo ante nombres en masculino] twenty-one.

**veintiuna** *nf* pontoon, blackjack.

**veintiuno,-a** *adj (cardinal)* twenty-one; *(ordinal)* twenty-first.
▶ *nm (número)* twenty-one; *(fecha)* twenty-first.

**vejar** *vt* **1** *(molestar)* to vex, annoy. **2** *(humillar)* to humiliate.

**vejez** *nf* old age.

**vejiga** *nf* bladder.

**vela¹** *nf* **1** *(vigilia)* watch, vigil; *(de muerto)* wake. **2** *(desvelo)* wakefulness. **3** *(candela)* candle. LOC **pasar la noche en vela** to have a sleepless night.

**vela²** *nf* **1** *(de barco)* sail. **2** DEP sailing. **3** *fig (barco de vela)* sailing ship.

**velamen** *nm* sails *pl*.

**velar¹** *vi* **1** *(no dormir)* to stay awake; *(no acostarse)* to stay up. **2** *fig (cuidar)* to watch (por, over), look (por, after): *velaron por él* they looked after him.

▸ *vt (enfermo)* to sit up with, watch over; *(muerto)* to keep vigil over.

**velar²** *adj* LING velar.

▸ *vt* **1** *fig (cubrir)* to hide, cover, veil. **2** *(fotografía)* to fog. **3** *(pintura)* to glaze.

▸ *vpr* **velarse** *(fotografía)* to become fogged, get exposed.

**velero,-a** *nm & nf (fabricante de velas)* sailmaker.

▸ *nm* **velero** sailing ship, sailing boat.

**veleta** *nf (para el viento)* weathercock, weather vane.

▸ *nm o nf fam fig (persona)* fickle person.

**vello** *nm* **1** *(de persona - pelusa)* down; *(-en las piernas, etc)* hair. **2** *(de fruta, planta)* down, bloom.

**velo** *nm* **1** *(gen)* veil. **2** ANAT velum.

**velocidad** *nf* **1** *(rapidez)* speed, velocity. **2** AUTO *(marcha)* gear. COMP **velocidad de la luz** speed of light. ‖ **velocidad de transmisión** INFORM bit rate.

**velocímetro** *nm* speedometer.

**velódromo** *nm* cycle track, US velodrome.

**veloz** *adj* fast, quick, swift, rapid.

**vena** *nf* **1** ANAT vein. **2** *(yacimiento)* vein, seam. **3** BOT vein. **4** *(en mármol, etc)* vein, streak. **5** *fig (disposición)* mood. LOC **tener vena de...** to have a gift for...: *tiene vena de cantante* he has a gift for singing.

**venado** *nm* **1** ZOOL stag, deer. **2** CULIN venison.

**vencedor,-ra** *adj* winning.

▸ *nm & nf* **1** *(equipo, etc)* winner, victor.

**vencejo** *nm (ave)* swift.

**vencer** *vt* **1** DEP to beat. **2** *(exceder)* to outdo, surpass: *la vence en belleza* she surpasses her in beauty. **3** *(problema, etc)* to overcome, surmount. **4** *(ser dominado)* to overcome: *la venció el cansancio* she was overcome by tiredness.

▸ *vi* **1** *(ganar)* to win. **2** *(deuda, etc)* to fall due, be payable. **3** *(plazo)* to expire.

▸ *vpr* **vencerse** **1** *(romperse)* to break; *(doblarse)* to bend, incline. **2** *fig (reprimir)* to control OS.

**venda** *nf* bandage.

**vendaje** *nm* dressing.

**vendar** *vt* to bandage.

**vendaval** *nm* strong wind, gale.

**vendedor,-ra** *adj* selling.

▸ *nm & nf* **1** *(gen)* seller; *(hombre)* salesman; *(mujer)* saleswoman. **2** *(dependiente)* shop assistant.

**vender** *vt* **1** *(gen)* to sell. **2** *fig (traicionar)* to betray.

▸ *vpr* **venderse** **1** *(uso impersonal)* to be on sale, be sold: *se vende en farmacias* on sale at your chemist's. **2** *(dejarse sobornar)* to sell OS. LOC **«Se vende»** "For sale".

**vendimia** *nf (cosecha)* grape harvest.

**veneno** *nm (química, vegetal)* poison; *(animal)* venom.

**venenoso,-a** *adj* **1** poisonous, venomous. **2** *fig* spiteful, venomous.

**venezolano,-a** *adj* Venezuelan.

▸ *nm & nf* Venezuelan.

**Venezuela** *nf* Venezuela.

**venganza** *nf* revenge, vengeance.

**vengar** *vt* to avenge.

▸ *vpr* **vengarse** to take revenge (de, on).

**venir** *vi* **1** *(gen)* to come: *el mes que viene* next month. **2** *(llegar)* to arrive: *vino tarde* he arrived late. **3** *(proceder)* to come *(de, from)*: *viene de París* it comes from Paris. **4** *(estar, aparecer)* to be, come: *las explicaciones vienen en español* the instructions are in Spanish. **5** *(ser)* to be: *eso te viene grande* that's too big for you.

▸ *aux* **1** venir a + *inf (aproximación)* to be about; *(alcanzar, llegar a)* to arrive at; *(terminar por)* to end up. **2** venir + *ger (acción durativa)*: *lo venía avisando desde hace tiempo* he has been warning us about it for a long time. **3** venir + *pp (ser, estar)* to be: *eso viene motivado por la inflación* it's caused by inflation.

▸ *vpr* **venirse** to come back, go back.

**venoso,-a** *adj* **1** *(sangre)* venous. **2** *(manos, etc)* veined, veiny.

**venta** *nf* **1** *(acción)* sale, selling. **2** *(hostal)* country inn; *(restaurante)* restaurant.

**ventaja** *nf* **1** *(gen)* advantage. **2** *(provecho)* profit LOC **llevar ventaja a** ALGN to have the advantage over SB.

**ventajoso,-a** *adj* **1** advantageous. **2** *(beneficioso)* profitable.

**ventana** *nf* **1** ARQUIT window. **2** *(de la nariz)* nostril.

**V**

**ventanilla** *nf* **1** *(banco, coche, sobre, etc)* window. **2** *(barco)* porthole. **3** *(de taquilla)* window, ticket window.

**ventilación** *nf* ventilation.

**ventilador** *nm* ventilator, fan.

**ventilar** *vt* **1** *(lugar)* to air, ventilate. **2** *(agitar al viento)* to air. **3** *fig (dar a conocer)* to air. **4** *fig (discutir)* to discuss, clear up.
▶ *vpr* **ventilarse 1** *(lugar)* to be ventilated. **2** *(objeto)* to be aired. **3** *fam (terminar)* to finish off: *se ventiló el pastel en un minuto* he finished off the cake in a minute.

**ventisca** *nf* snowstorm, blizzard.

**ventoso,-a** *adj* windy.

**ver** *vt* **1** *(gen)* to see: *no te veo* I can't see you. **2** *(mirar)* to look (at). **3** *(televisión)* to watch. **4** *fig (entender)* understand: *no veo por qué lo hizo* I can't understand why she did it. **5** *(visitar)* to visit, see: *ven a verme* come and see me. **6** JUR to try, hear. **7** *(parecer)* to look: *te veo triste* you look sad. ⌐LOC⌐ **a ver** let's see, let me see.
▶ *nm* **1** *(vista)* sight, vision. **2** *(apariencia)* looks *pl*, appearance.
▶ *vpr* **verse 1** *(ser visto)* to be seen: *aquí dentro no se ve nada* you can't see a thing in here. **2** *(con algn)* to meet, see each other. **3** *(en una situación, etc)* to find os, be: *se vio en un apuro* he was in a fix. **4** *(imaginarse)* to imagine os.

**veranear** *vi* to spend the summer (holiday) (en, in/at).

**veraneo** *nm* summer holiday. ⌐LOC⌐ **ir de veraneo** to go on holiday.

**veraniego,-a** *adj* summer, summery.

**verano** *nm* summer.

**veras** ⌐LOC⌐ **de veras** really, seriously.

**veraz** *adj* truthful, veracious.

**verbal** *adj* verbal, oral.

**verbena** *nf* **1** BOT verbena. **2** *(fiesta)* night party.

**verbo** *nm* verb.

**verdad** *nf* **1** truth, truthfulness: *es verdad* it's true. **2** *(confirmación)*: *es bonita, ¿verdad?* she's pretty, isn't she?

**verdadero,-a** *adj* true, real.

**verde** *adj* **1** *(color)* green. **2** *(fruta)* unripe, green; *(madera)* unseasoned. **3** *fig (persona)* green, immature. **4** *fam (chiste)* blue, dirty.
▶ *nm* **1** *(color)* green. **2** *(hierba)* grass. **3** POL green: *los verdes* the Greens.

**verdugo** *nm* **1** *(persona)* executioner. **2** *(prenda)* balaclava, balaclava helmet.

**verdulera** *nf fig* coarse woman, foul-mouthed woman.

**verdulería** *nf* greengrocer's (shop).

**verdulero,-a** *nm & nf* greengrocer.

**verdura** *nf* **1** *(hortaliza)* vegetables *pl*, greens *pl*. **2** *(color)* greenness, greenery.

**vereda** *nf* footpath, path.

**veredicto** *nm* verdict.

**vergonzoso,-a** *adj* **1** *(acto)* shameful, shocking: *un asunto vergonzoso* a shocking business. **2** *(persona)* bashful, shy.

**vergüenza** *nf* **1** *(deshonor, etc)* shame, sense of shame: *sus palabras me dan vergüenza* her words make me feel ashamed. **2** *(timidez)* bashfulness, shyness; *(turbación)* embarrassment: *me da vergüenza bailar* I'm too shy to dance. **3** *(escándalo)* disgrace, shame: *lo que han hecho es una vergüenza* what they did is a disgrace. ⌐LOC⌐ **¡qué vergüenza!** it's a disgrace!, how disgraceful!

**verídico,-a** *adj* truthful, true.

**verificar** *vt* **1** *(comprobar)* to verify, check. **2** *(probar)* to prove. **3** *(efectuar)* to carry out, perform.
▶ *vpr* **verificarse 1** *(comprobarse)* to come true. **2** *(efectuarse)* to take place.

**verja** *nf* **1** *(reja)* grating, grille. **2** *(cerca)* railing, railings *pl*. **3** *(puerta)* iron gate.

**verruga** *nf* wart.

**versión** *nf* **1** *(gen)* version, account. **2** *(traducción)* translation. **3** *(adaptación)* adaptation. ⌐LOC⌐ **en versión original** in the original language.

**verso** *nm* **1** LIT verse. **2** *fam (poema)* poem.

**vértebra** *nf* vertebra.

**vertebrado,-a** *adj* vertebrate.
▶ *nm pl* **los vertebrados** the vertebrates.

**vertebral** *adj* vertebral, spinal.

**vertedero** *nm* rubbish dump, rubbish tip.

**verter** vt **1** *(líquido - voluntariamente)* to pour, pour out. **2** *(derramar)* to spill. **3** *(vaciar)* to empty, empty out. **4** *(basura)* to dump. **5** *fig (conceptos, ideas, etc)* to express, voice.

**vertical** adj vertical: *lo puso vertical* she put it upright.
▶ nf vertical, vertical line.
▶ nm vertical.

**vértice** nm vertex.

**vertiente** nf **1** *(gen)* slope. **2** *fig (aspecto)* angle.

**vértigo** nm **1** MED vertigo. **2** *(mareo)* dizziness, giddiness: *me da vértigo* it makes me feel dizzy. **3** *fig* frenzy.

**vesícula** nf vesicle. COMP **vesícula biliar** gall bladder.

**vestíbulo** nm **1** *(de casa)* hall, entrance. **2** *(de hotel, etc)* hall, lobby, vestibule, foyer.

**vestido,-a** adj dressed: *vestida de blanco* dressed in white.
▶ nm **vestido 1** *(indumentaria)* clothes pl, dress, costume. **2** *(de mujer)* dress; *(de hombre)* suit.

**vestigio** nm vestige, trace, remains pl.

**vestimenta** nf clothes pl, garments pl.

**vestir** vt **1** *(llevar)* to wear, be dressed in: *vestía un vestido rojo* she was wearing a red dress. **2** *(ayudar a vestirse)* to dress; *(hacer vestidos)* to make clothes for: *la vistió su madre* her mother dressed her. **3** *(cubrir)* to cover (de, with).
▶ vi **1** to dress: *vestir de negro* to dress in black. **2** *(ser elegante, lucir)* to be classy, look smart: *esa falda viste mucho* that skirt is very classy.
▶ vpr **vestirse 1** *(uso reflexivo)* to dress OS, get dressed. **2** *(comprarse la ropa)* to buy one's clothes: *se viste en Milán* she buys her clothes in Milan.

**vestuario** nm **1** *(ropas)* wardrobe, clothes pl. **2** TEAT *(ropa)* wardrobe, costumes pl; *(camerino)* dressing room. **3** DEP changing room.

**veta** nf **1** *(de mármol, roca)* seam, vein; *(de madera)* streak. **2** *fig* streak.

**vetar** vt to veto, put a veto on.

**veterinario,-a** adj veterinary.

▶ nm & nf veterinary surgeon, vet, US veterinarian.

**veto** nm veto. LOC **poner el veto a** to put a veto on, veto.

**vez** nf **1** time: *fue la única vez que la vi* it was the only time I saw her; *una vez* once; *dos veces* twice; *cuatro veces* four times. **2** *(turno)* turn; *(ocasión)* occasion. LOC **a veces** sometimes. ▌**otra vez** again.

**vía** nf **1** *(camino)* road, way; *(calle)* street; *(carril)* lane. **2** *(de tren)* track, line; *(en la estación)* platform: *el tren de la vía uno* the train at platform one. **3** ANAT passage, canal, track. **4** *fig (modo)* way, manner, means. **5** JUR procedure. **6** *(rumbo, dirección)* via, through: *Barcelona-Singapur vía Frankfurt* Barcelona-Singapore via Frankfurt. LOC **dar vía libre a** to leave the way open for. ▌**por vía aérea 1** *(gen)* by air. **2** *(correo)* airmail. COMP **transmisión vía satélite** satellite transmission.

**viajante** nm commercial traveller (US traveler), travelling (US traveling) salesman.

**viajar** vi to travel: *ha viajado por el mundo entero* she's travelled all over the world.

**viaje** nm **1** *(gen)* journey, trip. **2** *(en coche)* drive, journey. **3** *(travesía por mar)* voyage. **4** [se suele usar en plural] *(concepto de viajar)* travel. **5** *(carga)* load. LOC **¡buen viaje!** bon voyage!, have a good trip! ▌**estar de viaje** to be away, be away on a trip. COMP **viaje de ida y vuelta** return trip, US round trip.

**viajero,-a** adj travelling (US traveling).
▶ nm & nf **1** traveller (US traveler). **2** *(en transporte público)* passenger.

**víbora** nf viper.

**vibración** nf **1** vibration. **2** LING rolling, trilling.

**vibrar** vi **1** *(gen)* to vibrate; *(pulsar)* to throb, pulsate: *toda la ciudad vibraba de actividad* the whole city throbbed with activity. **2** *fig (conmoverse)* to be moved, be overcome with emotion: *el cantante hizo vibrar al público* the singer thrilled the audience. **3** LING to roll, trill.

**vibratorio,-a** adj vibratory.

**V**

**viciar** vt 1 *(corromper)* to corrupt, lead astray. 2 *(aire)* to pollute.
▶ vpr **viciarse** 1 *(enviciarse)* to take to vice, become corrupted. 2 *(objeto)* to go out of shape.

**vicio** nm 1 *(corrupción)* vice, corruption. 2 *(mala costumbre)* bad habit; *(inmoralidad)* vice. 3 *(del lenguaje)* incorrect usage. 4 *(defecto)* defect.

**vicioso,-a** adj 1 *(cosa)* faulty, defective. 2 *(persona)* depraved, perverted.
▶ nm & nf depraved person.

**víctima** nf victim, casualty.

**victoria** nf victory, triumph. LOC cantar victoria to proclaim a victory.

**victorioso,-a** adj victorious, triumphant.

**vid** nf grapevine, vine.

**vida** nf 1 *(gen)* life. 2 *(viveza)* liveliness. 3 *(tiempo)* lifetime, life. 4 *(modo de vivir)* life, way of life. 5 *(medios)* living, livelihood. LOC darse la gran vida / pegarse la gran vida / darse la vida padre *fam* to live it up. ‖ de por vida for life. ‖ de toda la vida lifelong: *un amigo de toda la vida* a lifelong friend. ‖ estar con vida / estar sin vida to be alive / be dead. ‖ ganarse la vida to earn one's living. ‖ quitarle la vida a ALGN to take SB's life. COMP vida familiar family life.

**vídeo** nm *(aparato)* video, video recorder; *(cinta)* video, video tape.

**videoconferencia** nf videoconference.

**videoclip** nm video, pop video.

**videoclub** nm video club.

**videojuego** nm video game.

**vidriera** nf 1 *(ventana)* picture window. 2 *(puerta)* glass door. 3 *(de balcón, galería)* French window. 4 *(vitral)* stained-glass window. 5 *(escaparate)* shop window.

**vidriero,-a** nm & nf 1 *(fabricante)* glassmaker. 2 *(colocador)* glazier.

**vidrio** nm *(material)* glass.

**viejo,-a** adj 1 *(gen)* old: *un coche viejo* an old car. 2 *(desgastado)* old, worn-out. 3 *(antiguo)* old, ancient.
▶ nm & nf *(hombre)* old man; *(mujer)* old woman. LOC hacerse viejo,-a to grow old.

**viento** nm 1 *(gen)* wind. 2 *(rumbo)* direction. 3 *(de caza)* scent. 4 *(cuerda)* rope, guy. 5 *fam (flatulencia)* wind, flatulence. LOC contra viento y marea *fig* come hell or high water. ‖ hacer viento / soplar viento to be windy. ‖ ir viento en popa 1 MAR to sail before the wind. 2 *fig* to do very well.

**vientre** nm 1 ANAT belly, abdomen. 2 *(vísceras)* bowels pl. 3 *(de embarazada)* womb.

**viernes** nm inv Friday. COMP Viernes Santo Good Friday.

✎ Consulta también jueves.

**Vietnam** nm Vietnam.

**vietnamita** adj Vietnamese.
▶ nm & nf *(persona)* Vietnamese.
▶ nm *(idioma)* Vietnamese.

**viga** nf 1 *(de madera)* beam, rafter. 2 *(de acero, etc)* girder.

**vigésimo,-a** adj twentieth: *vigésimo primero* twenty-first.
▶ nm & nf twentieth.

✎ Consulta también sexto,-a.

**vigía** nm o nf lookout.

**vigilante** adj 1 *(que vigila)* vigilant, watchful. 2 *(alerta)* alert.
▶ nm o nf *(hombre)* guard, watchman; *(mujer)* guard. COMP vigilante nocturno night watchman.

**vigilar** vt 1 *(cuidar)* to watch (over), look after: *vigila al niño* look after the baby. 2 *(con armas, etc)* to guard. 3 *(supervisar)* to oversee. 4 *(estar atento)* to keep an eye on, take care of: *vigila la puerta, que no entre nadie* keep an eye on the door and see nobody gets in.
▶ vi *(gen)* to keep watch.

**vigor** nm 1 *(fuerza)* vigour (US vigor), strength. 2 *(validez)* force, effect. LOC en vigor in force.

**vigoroso,-a** adj vigorous, strong.

**VIH** abrev MED (virus de inmunodeficiencia humana) Human Immune Deficiency Virus; *(abreviatura)* HIV.

**vil** *adj* vile, base, despicable.

**vileza** *nf* **1** *(cualidad)* vileness, baseness. **2** *(acto)* vile act, despicable deed.

**villa** *nf* **1** *(casa)* villa, country house. **2** *(pueblo)* small town; *(ciudad)* town.

**villancico** *nm* carol, Christmas carol.

**villano,-a** *nm & nf* HIST villein, serf. **2** *fig (persona ruin)* villain.

**vinagre** *nm* **1** vinegar. **2** *fig* sourpuss.

**vinculación** *nf* **1** *(acción)* linking, binding. **2** *(vínculo)* link, bond.

**vincular** *vt* **1** *(unir)* to link (a, to), bind (a, to). **2** *(relacionar)* to relate (con, to), connect (con, with), link (con, with). **3** JUR to entail.
▶ *vpr* **vincularse** to link OS (a, to).

**vínculo** *nm* **1** tie, bond, link. **2** *fig* link.

**vinícola** *adj* wine-producing.

**vinicultor,-ra** *nm & nf* wine producer.

**vinicultura** *nf* wine production, wine growing.

**vino** *nm* wine. COMP **vino blanco** white wine. ▌**vino tinto** red wine.

**viña** *nf* vineyard.

**viñedo** *nm* vineyard.

**viñeta** *nf* **1** *(en impresión)* vignette. **2** *(dibujo humorístico)* cartoon.

**viola** *nf* viola.

**violáceo,-a** *adj* violaceous, violet.

**violencia** *nf* **1** *(fuerza)* violence. **2** *(embarazo)* embarrassment. **3** *(situación embarazosa)* embarrassing situation. **4** *(violación)* rape.

**violentar** *vt* **1** *(forzar algo)* to force, break open. **2** *(obligar a alguien)* to force, use force on. **3** *fig (entrar)* to break into, enter by force.
▶ *vpr* **violentarse 1** *fig (molestarse)* to get annoyed. **2** *fig (avergonzarse)* to feel ashamed.

**violento,-a** *adj* **1** *(gen)* violent. **2** *(molesto)* embarrassed, awkward, ill at ease.

**violeta** *adj (color)* violet.
▶ *nm (color)* violet.
▶ *nf* BOT violet.

**violín** *nm* violin.

**violinista** *nm o nf* violinist.

**violón** *nm* double bass.

**violoncelista** *nm o nf* cellist.

**violoncelo** *nm* cello.

**violonchelista** *nm o nf* cellist.

**violonchelo** *nm* cello.

**viraje** *nm* **1** *(curva)* turn, bend. **2** *(en coche)* turn. **3** MAR tack. **4** *(fotografía)* toning.

**viral** *adj* viral.

**virar** *vi* **1** MAR to tack, put about. **2** AUTO to turn round.

**virgen** *adj* **1** *(persona)* virgin. **2** *(puro)* virgin, pure.
▶ *nm o nf* virgin. COMP **la Santísima Virgen** the Blessed Virgin.

**vírico,-a** *adj* viral.

**virtual** *adj* virtual.

**virtud** *nf* **1** *(cualidad)* virtue. **2** *(propiedad, eficacia)* property, quality: *con virtudes curativas* with medicinal properties. LOC **en virtud de** by virtue of.

**virtuosismo** *nm* virtuosity.

**virtuoso,-a** *adj* virtuous.
▶ *nm & nf* virtuous person.

**viruela** *nf* **1** MED smallpox. **2** *(marca)* pockmark. LOC **picado,-a de viruelas** pockmarked.

**virulencia** *nf* virulence.

**virulento,-a** *adj* virulent.

**virus** *nm inv* virus.

**viruta** *nf* shaving.

**visado,-a** *adj* endorsed with a visa.
▶ *nm* **visado** visa.

**visar** *vt* **1** *(pasaporte)* to endorse with a visa. **2** *(documento)* to endorse, approve.

**víscera** *nf* internal organ.
▶ *nf pl* **vísceras** viscera, entrails.

**visceral** *adj* **1** visceral. **2** *fig* profound, deep-rooted.

**viscosa** *nf* viscose.

**viscoso,-a** *adj* viscous.

**visera** *nf* **1** *(de gorra)* peak; *(de casco)* visor. **2** *(suelta)* eyeshade. **3** AUTO sun visor.

**visibilidad** *nf* visibility.

**visigodo,-a** *nm & nf* Visigoth.

**visillo** *nm* small lace curtain.

**visión** *nf* **1** *(acción)* vision. **2** *(vista)* sight. **3** *(ilusión)* vision. **4** *fig (persona fea)*

fright, sight. LOC **ver visiones** to dream, see things.

**visita** *nf* **1** *(acción)* visit. **2** *(invitado)* visitor, guest; *(invitados)* visitors *pl*, guests *pl*. LOC **estar de visita en** to be visiting. COMP **horas de visita** MED surgery hours.

**visitante** *nm o nf* visitor.

**visitar** *vt* **1** *(ir a ver a alguien)* to visit, pay a visit to, call on, go and see: *vamos a ver a la abuela* let's go and visit grandma. **2** *(lugar)* to visit, see. **3** *(inspeccionar)* to inspect, visit, examine.

**vislumbrar** *vt* **1** *(ver)* to glimpse, catch a glimpse of, make out. **2** *fig (conjeturar)* to begin to see: *vislumbraron una solución al problema* they began to see a solution to the problem.

**viso** *nm* **1** *(reflejo)* sheen, shimmer. **2** *(ropa interior)* underskirt. **3** *fig (apariencia)* appearance. LOC **tener visos de** to seem, appear.

**visón** *nm* mink.

**visor** *nm* **1** *(de arma)* sight. **2** *(de máquina fotográfica)* viewfinder.

**víspera** *nf* **1** *(día anterior)* day before. **2** *(de fiesta)* eve.
▶ *nf pl* **vísperas** REL vespers.

**vista** *nf* **1** *(visión)* sight, vision. **2** *(ojo)* eye, eyes *pl*. **3** *(panorama)* view. **4** *(aspecto)* appearance, aspect, look. **5** *(dibujo, cuadro, foto)* view. **6** *(intención)* intention. **7** *(propósito)* outlook, prospect. **8** JUR trial, hearing.
▶ *nf pl* **vistas** view *sing*: *la habitación tiene vistas al mar* the room has a view of the sea. LOC **a primera vista / a simple vista** at first sight: *a primera vista parecía más complicado* at first sight it looked more complicated. ▌**con vistas a 1** *(hacia)* overlooking. **2** *(pensando en)* with a view to, in anticipation of. ▌**en vista de** in view of, considering. ▌**hacer la vista gorda** *fam* to turn a blind eye. ▌**ser corto,-a de vista** to be short-sighted. ▌**tener vista de lince** *fig* to be eagle-eyed, have eyes like a hawk.

**vistazo** *nm* glance. LOC **dar un vistazo a** ALGO / **echar un vistazo a** ALGO **1** *(mirar)* to

have a look at STH. **2** *(vigilar)* to keep an eye on.

**visto,-a** *adj* **1** *(anticuado)* old-fashioned. **2** *(dado)* in view of, considering. **3** *(corriente)* common. **4** *(ladrillo, viga, obra)* exposed. **5** JUR *(dictaminado)*: *el caso está visto para sentencia* the case has been heard and a verdict may be decided upon.
▶ *nm* **visto** approval. LOC **dar el visto bueno a** ALGO to approve STH, O.K. STH. ▌**estar bien visto,-a** to be well looked upon, be considered acceptable. ▌**por lo visto** apparently. ▌**visto que...** in view of the fact that..., given that..., seeing that...

**vistoso,-a** *adj* **1** *(llamativo)* showy, flashy. **2** *(colorido)* bright, colourful (US colorful).

**visual** *adj* visual.
▶ *nf* *(línea)* line of vision, line of sight.

**visualización** *nf* display.

**visualizar** *vt* **1** to visualize. **2** INFORM to display.

**vital** *adj* **1** *(de la vida)* vital. **2** *fig (esencial)* essential, vital.

**vitalicio,-a** *adj* life, for life: *un cargo vitalicio* a post held for life.

**vitalidad** *nf* vitality.

**vitalizar** *vt* to vitalize.

**vitamina** *nf* vitamin.

**vitícola** *adj* wine-growing, wine-producing, viticultural.

**viticultor,-ra** *nm & nf* wine grower, viticulturist.

**viticultura** *nf* wine-growing, viticulture.

**vitorear** *vt* *(aclamar)* to cheer, acclaim.

**vitral** *nm* stained-glass window.

**vítreo,-a** *adj* vitreous.

**vitrina** *nf* **1** *(armario)* glass cabinet, display cabinet. **2** *(de exposición)* glass case, showcase. **3** *(escaparate)* shop window.

**vitro** *loc* in vitro in vitro. COMP **fecundación in vitro** in vitro fertilization.

**vitrocerámica** COMP **encimera vitrocerámica** ceramic hob.

**vitualla** *nf* [generalmente se usa en plural] provisions *pl*, food.

**viudedad** *nf* **1** *(estado)* widowhood. **2** *(pensión - hombre)* widower's pension; *(- mujer)* widow's pension.

**viudez** *nf* widowhood.

**viudo,-a** *adj* widowed.
▶ *nm & nf (hombre)* widower; *(mujer)* widow.

**viva** *nm* cheer, shout.

**vivaz** *adj* **1** *(vivo)* vivacious, lively. **2** *(perspicaz)* sharp, quick-witted.

**víveres** *nm pl* food *sing*, provisions, supplies.

**vivero** *nm* **1** *(de plantas)* nursery. **2** *(de peces)* fish farm, fish hatchery; *(de moluscos)* bed.

**viveza** *nf* **1** *(persona)* liveliness, vivacity. **2** *(color, relato)* vividness. **3** *(al hablar)* vehemence. **4** *(agudeza)* sharpness, quick-wittedness.

**vivienda** *nf* **1** *(gen)* housing, accommodation. **2** *(morada)* dwelling. **3** *(casa)* house. **4** *(piso)* flat.

**vivir** *vi* **1** *(tener vida)* to live; *(estar vivo)* to be alive: *vivió hasta los ochenta años* he lived to the age of eighty. **2** *(habitar)* to live: *vive en Barcelona* she lives in Barcelona. **3** *(mantenerse)* to live, live on, make a living: *ese trabajo no le da para vivir* he can't live on what that job pays. **4** *fig (durar)* to last, live on.
▶ *vt (pasar por, experimentar)* to live through, go through, experience: *mi abuelo vivió la guerra* my grandfather lived through the war.

**vivo,-a** *adj* **1** *(que tiene vida)* living; *(que está)* alive: *materia viva* living matter; *Pepe está vivo* Pepe is alive. **2** *(fuego, llama)* live, burning. **3** *(lengua)* living. **4** *fig (color, etc)* bright, vivid. **5** *fig (animado)* lively, vivacious. **6** *fig (dolor, emoción, etc)* acute, deep, intense. **7** *fig (descripción, etc)* lively, graphic. **8** *fig (carácter)* quick, irritable. **9** *fig (listo)* quick-witted. **10** *fig (astuto)* shrewd, sly. **11** *fig (llaga, herida)* open. LOC **en vivo** TV live.
▶ *nm & nf* **1** living person: *los vivos* the living. **2** *fam fig (astuto)* quick-witted person.

**vocablo** *nm* word, term.

**vocabulario** *nm* vocabulary.

**vocación** *nf* vocation, calling.

**vocacional** *adj* vocational.

**vocal** *adj* vocal.
▶ *nf* vowel.
▶ *nm o nf (de junta, etc)* member.

**vocativo** *nm* vocative.

**vocear** *vi (dar voces)* to shout, cry out.
▶ *vt* **1** *(divulgar)* to publish. **2** *(gritar)* to shout, cry out. **3** *(divulgar)* to publish, proclaim. **4** *(aclamar)* to cheer, acclaim.

**vocero,-a** *nm & nf (gen)* spokesperson; *(hombre)* spokesman; *(mujer)* spokeswoman.

**voladizo,-a** *adj* projecting, jutting out.
▶ *nm* **voladizo** projection.

**volador,-ra** *adj* flying.

**volante** *adj (que vuela)* flying.
▶ *nm* **1** COST flounce; *(adorno)* frill, ruffle. **2** AUTO steering wheel. **3** TÉC flywheel.

**volar** *vi* **1** *(ir por el aire)* to fly. **2** *fig (papeles, etc)* to be blown away. **3** *fig (ir deprisa)* to fly: *el tiempo vuela* time flies. **4** *fam fig (desaparecer)* to disappear, vanish. **5** *fig (sobresalir de un edificio)* to jut out, project. **6** *fig (noticia, etc)* to spread rapidly.
▶ *vt* **1** *fig (hacer explotar - edificio)* to blow up, demolish; *(- caja fuerte)* to blow open; *(- en minería)* to blast. **2** *fig (en impresión)* to raise. **3** *(en caza)* to flush.
▶ *vpr* **volarse** *(papeles, etc)* to be blown away. LOC **echarse a volar** to fly away, fly off.

**volcán** *nm* volcano.

**volcánico,-a** *adj* volcanic.

**volcar** *vi* **1** *(coche, etc)* to turn over, overturn. **2** MAR to capsize.
▶ *vt* **1** *(gen)* to turn over, knock over, upset. **2** *(vaciar)* to empty out, pour out. **3** *fig (hacer cambiar de parecer)* to make change one's mind.
▶ *vpr* **volcarse** *fig (entregarse)* to do one's utmost.

**volear** *vt* to volley.

**V**

**voleibol** *nm* volleyball.

**voleo** *nm* DEP volley. LOC **a voleo / al voleo** *fig* at random, haphazardly.

**volquete** *nm* dumper-truck.

**voltaje** *nm* voltage.

**voltear** *vt* **1** *(dar vueltas)* to whirl, twirl. **2** *(poner al revés)* to turn over, toss. **3** *(campanas)* to peal, ring out. **4** *(a una persona)* to toss up in the air.

**voltereta** *nf* somersault. LOC **dar volteretas** to do somersaults.

**voltímetro** *nm* voltmeter.

**voltio** *nm* volt.

**voluble** *adj* changeable, fickle.

**volumen** *nm* **1** *(gen)* volume. **2** *(tamaño)* size. COMP **volumen de negocios** turnover.

**voluminoso,-a** *adj* **1** voluminous. **2** *(enorme)* bulky, massive.

**voluntad** *nf* **1** *(cualidad)* will. **2** *(fuerza de voluntad)* willpower: *tiene mucha voluntad* she's very strong-willed. **3** *(deseo)* wish. **4** *(propósito)* intention, purpose: *tiene buena voluntad* her intentions are good. **5** *(afecto)* affection. LOC **a voluntad** at will. ‖ **buena voluntad** goodwill. COMP **voluntad de hierro / voluntad férrea** will of iron, iron will.

**voluntariado** *nm* **1** MIL voluntary enlistment. **2** *(civil)* group of volunteers.

**voluntario,-a** *adj* voluntary.
▶ *nm & nf* volunteer.

**voluntarioso,-a** *adj* *(con voluntad)* willing.

**voluta** *nf* **1** ARQUIT volute, scroll. **2** *(espiral)* spiral, column. **3** *(de humo)* ring.

**volver** *vt* **1** *(dar vuelta a)* to turn, turn over; *(hacia abajo)* to turn upside down; *(de dentro afuera)* to turn inside out; *(lo de atrás hacia delante)* to turn back to front: *volver la tortilla* to turn the omelette. **2** *(convertir)* to turn, make, change: *el dinero ha vuelto tonto a Paco* money has made Paco foolish. **3** *(devolver)* to give back; *(a su lugar)* to put back.
▶ *vi* **1** *(regresar)* to return; *(ir)* to go back; *(venir)* to come back: *vuelve*

*cuando quieras* come back whenever you want. **2** *(a un tema, etc)* to return, revert. **3** **volver a** *(hacer otra vez)* to do again: *volver a leer* to read again. LOC **volver a las andadas** to fall back into one's old habits. ‖ **volver del revés** to turn inside out. ‖ **volver en sí** to regain consciousness, come round. ‖
▶ *vpr* **volverse** **1** *(regresar - ir)* to go back; *(- venir)* to come back. **2** *(darse la vuelta)* to turn. **3** *(convertirse)* to turn, become. LOC **volverse atrás** *fig* to go back on one's word, back out. ‖ **volverse en contra de** ALGN to turn against SB.

**vomitar** *vt* **1** to vomit, bring up. **2** *fig* to belch, spew out.
▶ *vi* to be sick, vomit: *tengo ganas de vomitar* I feel sick.

**vómito** *nm* **1** *(resultado)* vomit. **2** *(acción)* vomiting.

**voracidad** *nf* voracity, voraciousness.

**vorágine** *nf* vortex, whirlpool.

**voraz** *adj* **1** voracious. **2** *fig* fierce, raging.

**vórtice** *nf* **1** vortex, whirlpool. **2** *(de ciclón)* centre (US center) of a cyclone.

**vos** *pron* **1** *arc (usted)* thou, you. **2** AM *(tú)* you.

**vosotros,-as** *pron (sujeto)* you; *(objeto)* you, yourselves: *con vosotros* with you; *entre vosotras* among yourselves; *¿cómo lo sabéis vosotros?* how do you know?

**votación** *nf* **1** *(voto)* vote, ballot. **2** *(acto)* vote, voting. LOC **someter** ALGO **a votación** to put STH to the vote, take a ballot on STH. COMP **votación a mano alzada** voting by a show of hands.

**votante** *nm o nf* voter.

**votar** *vi (dar el voto)* to vote.
▶ *vt (proponer para aprobar)* to pass.

**voto** *nm* **1** *(gen)* vote: *tres votos a favor* three votes for. **2** REL vow. **3** *(deseo)* wish. **4** *(blasfemia)* curse, oath. COMP **derecho al voto** the right to vote. ‖ **voto de censura** vote of no confidence. ‖ **voto de confianza** vote of confidence.

**voz** *nf* **1** *(sonido)* voice. **2** *(grito)* shout. **3** *(vocablo, palabra)* word. **4** GRAM voice: *voz activa* active voice. **5** MÚS *(de instrumento)* tone; *(cantante)* voice: *canción a tres voces* three-part song. **6** *fig (rumor)* rumour (US rumor). **7** *fig (en asamblea - facultad de hablar)* voice, say; *(- voto)* vote. LOC **alzar la voz / levantar la voz** to raise one's voice. **| dar voces** to shout. **| en voz alta** aloud. **| en voz baja** in a low voice. **| tener voz y voto 1** *fam* to have a say. **2** *fml* to be a voting member.

**vuelco** *nm* **1** *(gen)* tumble, upset. **2** *(barco)* capsizing. **3** *fig* change. LOC **dar un vuelco 1** *(coche)* to overturn. **2** *(empresa)* to go to ruin. **| me dio un vuelco el corazón** my heart missed a beat.

**vuelo** *nm* **1** *(acto, espacio, etc)* flight. **2** *(acción)* flying. **3** ARQUIT *(voladizo)* projection. LOC **al vuelo** in flight. **| alzar el vuelo / emprender el vuelo / levantar el vuelo** to take flight. **| cazarlas al vuelo / cogerlas al vuelo** *fig* to be quick on the uptake. COMP **vuelo chárter / vuelo regular** charter flight / scheduled flight.

**vuelta** *nf* **1** *(giro)* turn. **2** *(en un circuito)* lap, circuit. **3** *(paseo)* walk, stroll: *vamos a dar una vuelta* let's go for a walk. **4** *(regreso, retorno)* return; *(viaje de regreso)* return journey, journey back: *a la vuelta de las vacaciones* after the holidays. **5** *(dinero de cambio)* change: *quédese con la vuelta* keep the change. **6** *(curva)* bend, curve. **7** *(reverso)* back, reverse. **8** *(de torneo, etc)* round. **9** *(cambio)* change, alteration. **10** COST *(de pantalón)* turn-up; *(forro)* lining. **11** *(al hacer punto)* row. LOC **a vuelta de correo** by return of post. **| dar la vuelta a 1** *(alrededor)* to go round. **2** *(girar)* to turn (round). **3** *(de arriba abajo)* to turn upside down. **4** *(de dentro a fuera)* to turn inside out. **5** *(cambiar de lado)* to turn over. **| dar la vuelta al mundo** to go round the world. **| dar vueltas a** ALGO *fig* to worry about STH: *¡no lo des más vueltas!* don't worry about it! **| dar media vuelta** to turn round. **| estar de vuelta de todo** to have seen it all before. **| ¡hasta la vuelta!** see you when I get back! COMP **la vuelta al colegio 1** *(en publicidad)* "Back to school". **2** *(primer día)* first day back at school.

**vuelto,-a** *adj (cuello)* roll: *jersey de cuello vuelto* roll-neck sweater.

**vuestro,-a** *adj* your, of yours: *vuestra casa* your house; *un amigo vuestro* a friend of yours.

▶ *pron* yours: *éstas son las vuestras* these are yours.

▶ *nm* **lo vuestro** what is yours, what belongs to you.

**vulgar** *adj* **1** *(grosero)* vulgar, coarse, common: *lenguaje vulgar* coarse language. **2** *(general)* common, general. **3** *(banal)* banal, ordinary; *(idea)* commonplace. **4** *(no técnico)* lay: *término vulgar* lay term.

**vulgaridad** *nf* **1** *(grosería)* vulgarity, coarseness. **2** *(banalidad)* banality, triviality.

**vulgarismo** *nm* vulgarism.

**vulgarización** *nf* vulgarization, popularization.

**vulgarizar** *vt* **1** *(popularizar)* to popularize, vulgarize. **2** *(hacer vulgar)* to make common.

▶ *vpr* **vulgarizarse** *(popular)* to become popular, become common; *(grosero)* to become vulgar, become common.

**vulgo** *nm* *pey* common people *pl*, masses *pl*.

**vulnerable** *adj* vulnerable.

**vulneración** *nf* **1** *(gen)* violation. **2** *fig (reputación)* damaging, harming.

**vulnerar** *vt* **1** *(ley, etc)* to violate. **2** *fig (honor, etc)* to damage, harm.

V

**W, w** *nf (la letra)* W, w.

**W** *sím* (vatio) watt; *(símbolo)* W.

**wáter** *nm fam* toilet.

**waterpolo** *nm* water polo.

**watt** *nm* watt.

✎ Consulta también **vatio**.

**web** *nf* website.

**whisky** *nm* whisky; *(irlandés)* whiskey.
COMP **whisky escocés** Scotch, Scotch whisky.

**windsurfing** *nm* windsurfing.

**wolframio** *nm* wolfram.

**X, x** *nf (la letra)* X, x.
**xenofobia** *nf* xenophobia.
**xenófobo,-a** *adj* xenophobic.
  ▶ *nm & nf* xenophobe.

**xerocopia** *nf* Xerox, photocopy.
**xerografía** *nf* xerography.
**xilófono** *nm* xylophone.
**xilografía** *nf* xylography.

**Y, y** *nf (la letra)* Y, y.

**y** *conj* **1** and: *Alberto y María* Alberto and María. **2** *(hora)* past: *son las tres y cuarto* it's a quarter past three. **3** *(en pregunta)* what about: *¿y Pepe, se viene?* what about Pepe, is he coming? **4** *(repetición)* after: *veces y veces* time after time, time and time again. `LOC` **y eso que** even though. ∎ **¿y (qué)?** so (what)? ∎ **¿y si... ?** what if... ? ∎ **¡y tanto!** you bet!, and how!

✎ Consulta también e.

**ya** *adv* **1** already: *esa película ya la he visto* I've already seen that film. **2** *(más tarde)* later: *ya lo haré* I'll do it later. **3** *(ahora mismo)* at once, right now, straightaway: *tienes que mandarlo ya* you must send it at once. **4** *(ahora)* now: *ya viven en el piso nuevo* they're living in the new flat now. **5** *(uso enfático)*: *ya lo sé* I know that; *es facilísimo, ya verás* it's dead easy, you'll see. **6** *(denota satisfacción)*: *¡ya tenemos coche nuevo!* we've got the new car! **7** *(con tono amenazante)*: *¡ya verás ya!* just you wait! **8** *(con indignación)*: *¡ya está bien!* enough is enough! **9** *(para tranquilizar)*: *ya encontrarás trabajo, ya verás como sí* you'll find a job, you'll see. **10** *(para afirmar)* I know, yes: *tienes que estudiar –ya, pero...* you have to study – I know, but... `LOC` **¡ya está!** there we are!, all done! ∎ **ya que** since, seeing that: *ya que estás aquí, quédate a cenar* seeing that you're here, why don't you stay for supper?
▶ *interj irón* oh yes!

**yacer** [92] *vi* **1** *(estar enterrado)* to lie. **2** *fml (hallarse)* to lie. **3** *lit (dormir)* to be lying; *(acostarse)* to lie (con, with): *Aquí yace...* Here lies...

**yacimiento** *nm* bed, deposit. `COMP` **yacimiento petrolífero** oilfield.

**yarda** *nf* yard.

**yate** *nm* yacht.

**yedra** *nf* ivy.

**yegua** *nf* mare.

**yeísmo** *nm* pronunciation of ll as y.

**yema** *nf* **1** *(de huevo)* yolk. **2** BOT bud. **3** *(del dedo)* fingertip. `COMP` **yema de huevo** egg yolk.

**Yemen** *nm* Yemen.

**yemení** *adj* Yemeni.
▶ *nm o nf* Yemeni.

**yerba** *nf* → hierba.

**yermo ,-a** *adj* **1** *(estéril)* barren. **2** *(despoblado)* deserted, uninhabited.

**yerno** *nm* son-in-law.

**yesca** *nf* tinder.

**yeso** *nm* **1** *(mineral)* gypsum. **2** *(para la construcción)* plaster. **3** *(tiza)* chalk. **4** *(escultura)* plaster cast.

**yeyuno** *nm* jejunum.

**yihad** *nf* jihad.

**yo** *pron* I: *el jefe soy yo* I'm the boss; *soy yo* it's me; *entre tú y yo* between you and me; *yo en tu lugar...* if I were you...; *yo que tú...* if I were you...
▶ *nm* **el yo** the ego, the self.

**yodo** *nm* iodine.

**yogur** *nm* yoghurt.
▶ *pl* **yogures**.

**yogurt** *nm* yoghurt.
▶ *pl* **yogurts**.

**yóquey** *nm* jockey.

**yugo** *nm* yoke.

**yugular** *adj* jugular.
▶ *nf* jugular vein.

**yunque** *nm* anvil.

**yunta** *nf* team of oxen, yoke.

**yuxtaposición** *nf* juxtaposition.

**Z, z** *nf (la letra)* Z, z.

**zafarrancho** *nm* **1** MIL clearing for action. **2** *(jaleo)* commotion. **3** *(desorden)* mess.

**zafarse** *vpr* to get away (de, from), free OS (de, from), escape (de, from): *logró zafarse de la policía* he managed to get away from the police.

**zafiro** *nm* sapphire.

**zaga** *nf* **1** rear. **2** *(en deporte)* defence (US defense). LOC **a la zaga** behind. ▌**no irle a la zaga a** ALGN not to lag behind SB: *es muy travieso, pero su hermano no le va a la zaga* he's really naughty, but his brother's every bit as bad.

**zagal,-la** *nm & nf* **1** *(muchacho)* lad; *(muchacha)* lass. **2** *(pastor)* shepherd; *(pastora)* shepherdess.

**zaguán** *nm* hall, hallway.

**zaherir** *vt* **1** to wound, hurt. **2** *(sentimientos)* to hurt.

**Zaire** *nm* Zaire.

**zaireño,-a** *adj* Zairean.
▶ *nm & nf* Zairean.

**zalamero,-a** *adj* charming, winning.
▶ *nm & nf* charmer. LOC **ponerse zalamero,-a** to turn on the charm.

**zamarra** *nf* sheepskin jacket.

**Zambia** *nf* Zambia.

**zambiano,-a** *adj* Zambian.
▶ *nm & nf* Zambian.

**zambo,-a** *adj* knock-kneed.
▶ *nm (mono)* spider monkey.

**zambullida** *nf* plunge, dive. LOC **darse una zambullida** to take a dip.

**zambullir** *vt* to plunge.

**zampar** *vi fam* to stuff oneself.

**zampoña** *nf* panpipes.

**zanahoria** *nf* carrot.

**zanca** *nf (de pájaro)* leg; *(de persona)* long leg.

**zancada** *nf* stride. LOC **en dos zancadas** in two shakes.

**zancadilla** *nf* **1** trip. **2** *fam (engaño)* ruse, trick. LOC **ponerle la zancadilla a** ALGN to trip SB up.

**zanco** *nm* stilt.

**zancudo,-a** *adj* **1** long-legged. **2** *(ave)* wading. COMP **aves zancudas** waders, wading birds.
▶ *nm* **zancudo** AM mosquito.

**zángano,-a** *nm & nf fam (persona)* loafer.
▶ *nm (insecto)* drone.

**zanja** *nf* trench. LOC **abrir una zanja** to dig a trench.

**zanjar** *vt fig (asunto)* to settle.

**zapata** *nf* **1** *(arandela)* washer. **2** TÉC shoe. **3** *(de cámara fotográfica)* hot shoe. COMP **zapata de freno** brake shoe.

**zapatear** *vi (bailar)* to stamp one's feet rhythmically.

**zapateo** *nm* rhythmic stamping.

**zapatería** *nf* **1** *(tienda)* shoe shop. **2** *(taller de reparación)* shoe repairer's, cobbler's; *(taller de fabricación)* shoemaker's. **3** *(oficio)* shoemaking.

**zapatero,-a** *nm & nf* **1** *(que arregla)* shoe repairer, cobbler. **2** *(que fabrica)* shoemaker. **3** *(que vende)* shoe seller. COMP **zapatero remendón** cobbler.

**zapatilla** *nf* **1** *(de estar en casa)* slipper. **2** *(de loneta)* plimsoll. COMP **zapatilla de ballet** ballet shoe. ▌**zapatilla de deporte** trainer, running shoe.

**zapato** *nm* shoe. COMP **zapatos de tacón** high-heeled shoes.

**zar** *nm* tsar, czar.

**zarabanda** *nf* **1** MÚS saraband. **2** *fam (jaleo)* bustle, confusion.

**zarandear** *vt* **1** *(sacudir)* to shake; *(empujar)* to jostle, knock about. **2** *(cribar)* to sieve.

**zarandeo** *nm* **1** *(sacudida)* shaking; *(empujones)* jostling about. **2** *(criba)* sieving. **3** *(contoneo)* swaggering, strutting.

**zarcillo** *nm* **1** *(pendiente)* earring. **2** BOT tendril.

**zarigüeya** *nf* opossum.

**zarina** *nf* tsarina, czarina.

**zarpa** *nf* claw, paw. LOC **echarle la zarpa a** ALGO **1** *(animal)* to pounce on STH. **2** *(persona)* to grab STH.

**zarpar** *vi* to weigh anchor, set sail.

**zarza** *nf* bramble, blackberry bush.

**zarzal** *nm* bramble patch.

**zarzamora** *nf (zarza)* blackberry bush; *(fruto)* blackberry.

**zarzuela** *nf* **1** MÚS zarzuela, *Spanish operetta.* **2** CULIN fish stew.

**zenit** *nm* zenith.

**zeta** *nf (letra)* zed, US zee.
▶ *nm argot* police car.

**Zimbabwe** *nm* Zimbabwe.

**zimbabwense** *adj* Zimbabwean.
▶ *nm o nf* Zimbabwean.

**zinc** *nm* zinc.

**zócalo** *nm* **1** *(de habitación)* skirting board; *(de edificio)* plinth course, plinth. **2** *(pedestal)* plinth, socle.

**zodiaco** *nm* zodiac.

**zona** *nf* **1** area. **2** *(fronteriza, militar)* zone.
▶ *nm* MED *(herpes)* shingles. COMP **zona azul** parking meter zone. ∎ **zona edificada** built-up area. ∎ **zona fronteriza** border zone. ∎ **zona glacial** frigid zone. ∎ **zona templada** temperate zone. ∎ **zona tórrida** torrid zone. ∎ **zona verde** green zone.

**zoología** *nf* zoology.

**zoológico,-a** *adj* zoological.
▶ *nm* zoo.

**zoólogo,-a** *nm & nf* zoologist.

**zorra** *nf* **1** *(animal)* vixen. **2** *tabú (mujer)* bitch.

**zorro,-a** *adj (astuto)* cunning, sly.
▶ *nm* **zorro 1** *(animal)* fox; *(macho)* dog fox, fox. **2** *(piel)* fox-fur, fox-skin. **3** *(persona)* old fox. COMP **zorro viejo** sly old fox.
▶ *nm pl* **zorros** *(para el polvo)* duster *sing.*

**zorzal** *nm (ave)* thrush.

**zozobrar** *vi* **1** *(barco)* to sink, capsize. **2** *(persona)* to worry, be anxious. **3** *(proyecto)* to fail, be ruined.

**zueco** *nm* clog.

**zulo** *nm* hide-out.

**zumbar** *vi (abejorro, oídos)* to buzz: *me zumban los oídos* my ears are buzzing.
▶ *vt fam (pegar)* to thrash.

**zumo** *nm* juice: *zumo de naranja* orange juice.

**zurcir** *vt* to darn, mend.

**zurdo,-a** *adj (persona)* left-handed; *(mano)* left.
▶ *nm & nf* left-hander, left-handed person.
▶ *nf (mano)* left hand: *un golpe con la zurda* a left-handed blow.

**zurra** *nf fam* thrashing.

**zurrar** *vt* **1** *fam* to thrash. **2** *fam (cuero)* to tan.

**zurrón** *nm* shepherd's pouch, shepherd's bag.